HARVARD POLITICAL CLASSICS

PUBLISHED UNDER THE DIRECTION OF
THE DEPARTMENT OF GOVERNMENT

Jean BODIN

THE SIX BOOKES OF A COMMONWEALE

A Facsimile reprint of the English translation of 1606
Corrected and supplemented in the light of a new
comparison with the French and Latin texts

Edited with an Introduction by
KENNETH DOUGLAS McRAE
Associate Professor of Political Science
Carleton University, Ottawa, Canada

CAMBRIDGE

Harvard University Press

1962

© Copyright, 1962, by the President and Fellows of Harvard College

All rights reserved

Distributed in Great Britain by Oxford University Press, London

Publication of this volume has been
aided by a grant from the American
Academy of Arts and Sciences

Library of Congress Catalog Card Number 60-10039

Printed in the United States of America

To
Carl J. Friedrich

PREFACE

"The needs of a thorough student of the history of political thought can never be adequately met by mere fragments torn out of the classical writings of the past, useful though such fragments may be. For the student needs to know not alone *what* the masters thought, but also *how* they thought; and this he can never learn solely from modern histories, or even from detached bits of contemporary writings without the nexus of continuous argument by which the writers originally wove these *disjecta membra* into one whole. For such a student the thing most necessary—particularly if the ideas are of an age far removed from his own—is not the bare outline, the mere anatomy of the political thought of that age. He needs above all somehow to gain an appreciation of the whole political mind of the period, the very breath and movement that once galvanized these elements into a thing of life capable of inspiring the thoughts and guiding the actions of generations of men."

It is just forty years since these words were written by Professor C. H. McIlwain. They constitute the opening sentences of his preface to *The Political Works of James I*, the first volume of this Political Classics series. But if they are applicable to the all-but-forgotten writings of King James, with far greater force do they apply to the work of Jean Bodin. For Bodin is a thinker whose cardinal doctrines have strikingly outlasted their original context. His concept of sovereignty, his theory of climate, and his advocacy of religious toleration have today become commonplaces in practically all the histories of political thought.

The very frequency of these references and citations is a testimony to the continued vitality of his ideas, but inherent in it is the danger that what he actually thought and said will be lost to view. It is fairly obvious that many recent textbook treatments of his work are based on secondary sources only, or at best upon a fragmentary reading of the originals. This neglect of the primary sources may be due in part to their scarcity. There has been no complete edition in any language of Bodin's most important work, his epoch-making *République*, since the Latin edition of 1641, none in French since 1629,

Preface

none in English since the Knolles translation of 1606. This translation was printed only once and is now virtually unobtainable.

The aim of this book is to present Bodin's political thought *in extenso*. If we are to understand Bodin properly, we must, for example, study his doctrine of sovereignty in its full intellectual and historical setting. We must look beyond its surface contradictions, so prominently displayed in the textbooks, to the deeper consistency of the concept when viewed as a whole. We must set his theory of climate against a background of Renaissance Platonism, with its firm conviction of the continuous relationship of all things in the world of nature. To understand Bodin's attitude towards religious toleration we must know both the circumstances in which he advised toleration and those in which he did not, as well as his views on the nature of religious belief. In short, if we do not understand the man and his modes of thought, we can attain only the shallowest appreciation of his specific ideas.

Admittedly, the *République* does not embody the whole of Bodin's thought. A student interested in the wider aspects of his intellectual system cannot ignore the *Methodus*, now available in a good edition in English,[1] nor even the *Démonomanie*, the *Theatrum*, and the *Heptaplomeres*. Nevertheless to understand Bodin's place in the development of political and legal theory the one absolutely essential book is the *République*.

However it is far easier to demonstrate the importance of the *République* than to produce a satisfactory edition. To the editor the work presents two special difficulties. The first is its substantial length, for abridgment cannot be employed to any appreciable extent if the aim outlined above is to be properly served. The second and more serious problem stems from the existence of two entirely distinct versions of the text, one in French and one in Latin, both written by Bodin himself. The Latin, which appeared some ten years later than the French, sometimes enlarges upon the earlier version, sometimes merely summarizes it, occasionally contradicts it openly, more often runs roughly parallel to it, but seldom indeed mirrors it exactly. It is obvious in these circumstances that any serious edition must take both versions into account. Yet a full translation of both was not only impossible for financial reasons, but also too cumbersome to be justified on scholarly grounds. What was needed was to isolate and emphasize, by means of notes, the significant *differences* between the French and

[1] *Method for the Easy Comprehension of History*, ed. B. Reynolds (New York, 1945).

Preface

the Latin as the argument develops in the text. But the crux of the problem remains: *which text?*

As I have shown at some length in the Introduction, each of Bodin's versions has its own distinctive advantages over the other, and each has its particular shortcomings. However there exists a third possibility in the English version of 1606, which claims to be based on both the French and the Latin. When this text is examined more closely it reveals that the translator has carefully worked the multiple strands of Bodin's twin versions into a single, closely textured argument. After a thorough comparison of the three texts, Knolles's translation was selected as the basis of the present edition, chiefly because the comparison showed it to be a fuller and more comprehensive version of the *République* than either the French or the Latin taken in isolation. Further, in contrast with any other English version that might be produced, it has the characteristic advantages of a translation that is almost contemporary with its original.

Of course the Knolles version also has its weaknesses, but these can be largely overcome in the critical apparatus. Thus the notes and page corrections serve not only to record the variations between the French and Latin versions but also to amend the misprints, translation errors, and omissions—whether deliberate or accidental—in the English one. However there is no need to discuss these in detail here, since I have dealt with them at some length in the Introduction.[2] Perhaps it is sufficient to observe that the actual critical examination of Knolles's text in relation to the French and Latin versions, together with the editing and summarizing of the vast mass of notes taken in the process, have constituted by far the largest portion of the work involved in preparing this edition.

The obligations which I have incurred are many, but it is a pleasure to acknowledge here the assistance of many kinds that I have received from individuals and institutions. First of all, I wish to express my thanks to the Warden and Fellows of Nuffield College, Oxford, for the research studentship at the college which was extended to me in 1953–1954, and to the Rockefeller Foundation for a grant under its Legal and Political Philosophy program in 1954–1955. These two years, spent within the hospitable walls of Nuffield College, saw the virtual completion of the textual work. A travel grant from Carleton University permitted me a final summer of research in England in 1957.

[2] See especially section IV and Appendix D.

Preface

I am similarly indebted to two bodies which at an early stage agreed to provide subsidies in the form of loans sufficient to enable Harvard University Press to undertake publication. They are the Harvard University Department of Government and the American Academy of Arts and Sciences, and I thank them now for the financial support which made this edition possible.

I have sought—and have almost invariably received in generous measure—assistance on many unfamiliar topics, ranging from numismatics to Renaissance astronomy, from mathematics to Carolingian French. My indebtedness in this respect to friends, colleagues, and mere strangers is such that space will hardly permit a detailed recital here. Perhaps the others will forgive me if I single out four Oxford scholars who have helped me very substantially. Robert Shackleton, of Brasenose College, spent many hours in clarifying ambiguities and obscure passages in the French texts. Similarly Dr. Lotte Labowsky, then research fellow of Somerville College, elucidated many unusual words and constructions in Bodin's Latin style and supplemented wherever necessary my rudimentary knowledge of Greek. Canon C. A. Simpson, of Christ Church, was kind enough to check the Hebrew and to suggest corrections where necessary. Finally Dr. E. J. Dobson applied his extensive knowledge of sixteenth-century English to the solution of a number of perplexing problems in the Knolles text.

I am under an obligation of much greater duration to Alastair D. McCann. Throughout the wearisome task of collating the English, French, and Latin versions he acted with exemplary patience as reader, in order to facilitate the simultaneous threefold comparison. He also compiled the entries for the index of proper names. In editing this index I have had further help from one of my students, Carl M. Wolff.

My obligations extend to Cambridge University as well. In particular I want to thank a fellow laborer in the same rich vineyard, J. H. M. Salmon, now returned to New Zealand but at the time a research student at St. John's, not only for sharing generously the fruits of his research but also for long and animated discussions in which sixteenth-century issues and ideas came graphically alive. More than any other person, Peter Laslett, of Trinity College, taught me the responsibilities and potentialities of editing a text. I hope that some of his insight and skill will be reflected in this volume.

In tracing the career of Knolles, I became indebted to Brian Kennett, history master at Sir Roger Manwood's Grammar School in

PREFACE

Sandwich, and to the Reverend John K. Cavell, of Cheltenham. Their wide knowledge of manuscript sources helped me to form a clearer picture of the Manwood family, of the early years of the school, and of the history of Sandwich in the sixteenth century. They also read section v of the Introduction and offered helpful criticisms. For material on Knolles's career in Oxford, I am indebted to the former Rector of Lincoln, Sir Keith Murray, who allowed me access to the manuscript registers of the college.

The detailed comparison of texts would have been highly inconvenient, if not impossible, had the major French and Latin editions not been assembled in one place. Several colleges permitted me to keep rare sixteenth-century editions in my Nuffield College study on long-term loan while this important work proceeded. For this concession I am grateful to the governing bodies and librarians of Balliol, Brasenose, Corpus Christi, Oriel, and Queen's Colleges in Oxford, and of King's and St. John's Colleges in Cambridge. Nor would this paragraph be complete without a mention of the rich sixteenth-century holdings in the Bodleian Library and of the many kindnesses of its staff.

Several years ago the late Judge H. C. Dowdall very generously lent me his copy of the English translation. It was his intention to donate it, when the present edition was complete, to some library which did not possess an English version. In accordance with his wish, therefore, his copy, which bears in several places the signatures, in seventeenth-century hands, of Francis Drake and Dorothea Drake, has been given by his daughter, Mrs. Patrick Campbell, to the National Library of Canada.

In compiling the bibliography of the *République* in Appendix C I have had the willing cooperation of officials in more than three hundred libraries in Europe and North America who answered my requests for information about their holdings. Their vigilance brought to light about a dozen editions and adaptations not recorded in any previous bibliography. It might be added that the so-called Iron Curtain proved no barrier to these inquiries.

My wife typed most of the notes, working from a much revised and barely legible manuscript. She also worked with great care and precision to transform my personal copy of the English edition, which when purchased had been heavily underscored throughout in red pencil, into a volume eminently suitable for photography. The introductory

Preface

material was typed by Mrs. Frances Templeton, of Oxford, and Mrs. Eileen Cox, of Ottawa. Several officials of the Clarendon Press helped a good deal in shaping the present edition by introducing me to the technical problems and possibilities of the photographic offset process before the manuscript had taken its final form.

For a general willingness to take quite unusual pains in bringing a complex project to fruition, I am very much indebted to Harvard University Press, to its printers, and perhaps most of all to its chief editor, Mrs. Eleanor D. Kewer, and her assistants, Miss Nora Brown and Miss Blair McElroy.

Despite this assistance from so many sources, the responsibility for any errors or omissions which remain must rest with me.

This book had its origins in Professor Carl J. Friedrich's seminar in political thought given at Harvard in the spring of 1948. It was he who brought home to me the importance of reading the *République* at first hand and who made me aware of the English translation of 1606. From the first moment that I undertook the preparation of the present edition he has warmly supported the project in every way, attacking the financial obstacles with characteristic vigor, prodding me when necessary, and offering encouragement at all times. The dedication is offered to him in simple recognition of a debt that extends far beyond the confines of this volume.

My final obligation, which is appreciated in retrospect more than it was at the time, is to a number of Canadian and American universities that could find no opening in their teaching ranks for the session 1953–1954. For it is certain that without that year of involuntary unemployment this project would never have been properly begun.

K. D. McRae

Ottawa, Canada
June, 1958

CONTENTS

INTRODUCTION

I.	Bodin's Career	A 3
II.	Bodin's Contributions to Political Science	A 13
III.	The French and Latin Versions of the République	A 28
IV.	The English Edition of 1606	A 38
V.	The Life and Background of Richard Knolles	A 52
VI.	The République in English Political Thought	A 62

Appendix A. Bodin's Prefaces	A 69
Appendix B. The Principal Definitions and Distinctions	A 74
Appendix C. A Bibliography of the République	A 78
Appendix D. A Note on the Present Edition	A 87

THE ARGUMENT of the *République*   A 91

THE SIX BOOKES OF A COMMONWEALE

Dedication	iii
To the Reader	iv
Table of Contents	vii
BOOK I	1
BOOK II	183
BOOK III	253
BOOK IV	406
BOOK V	545
BOOK VI	637

NOTES	A 105
INDEX NOMINUM	A 173
INDEX RERUM	A 209

INTRODUCTION

INTRODUCTION

1. BODIN'S CAREER

There is much that remains obscure in the life of Jean Bodin, including some questions of the highest importance. Any attempt at a detailed biography must still contend with evidence that is often tantalizingly inconclusive, and occasionally contradictory. Thanks to several important discoveries of documents in recent years, however, we now possess a far clearer picture of Bodin the man than would have seemed possible a generation ago. In spite of the very considerable gaps which remain, one can construct from the known outlines of his life a portrait which is reasonably clear and consistent.

Jean Bodin was born, in all probability, between June 1529 and June 1530. His father, Guillaume Bodin, was a master tailor of Angers, a man sufficiently well off to provide each of his four daughters with a substantial dowry, and to own vineyards in the surrounding countryside. A brother or near relation of his wife became *procureur* of the Carmelite monastery in Angers; one of his daughters married the organist of the Cathedral of Angers. Clearly the family belonged both economically and socially to the bourgeoisie. But Jean, the author, a younger son in a family of seven children, could expect little in the way of an inheritance. It was probably at a very early age that he was admitted to the Carmelite order at Angers to obtain an education and to train for the priesthood.

From Angers he was sent by the Carmelites to their house in Paris. Precise dates are lacking here, but probably he witnessed from Paris the close of the reign of Francis I, so beneficial to French humanism, and the accession of Henry II to the throne in 1547. For at least two years he lived as a brother in the monastery and engaged in the study of philosophy. This formal training was to leave a permanent impression upon his thought. The University of Paris during this period was deeply divided by the attempts of Peter Ramus to revolutionize the traditional Aristotelian logic and to apply the simplified procedures of Ramus' own logical methods to the rearrangement of the other academic disciplines. There is evidence to show that the young Bodin was profoundly influenced by Ramus and his disciples, and I shall have occasion later to show just how this intellectual ferment in philosophy helped to shape his own approach to history and politics.

Paris contributed in another way to his intellectual development, for there he was brought into contact with leading humanist scholars, whose lectures at the Collège Royal—the future Collège de France—had elevated the city to the first rank in the world of letters. There he acquired fluency in Greek and a working knowledge of Hebrew. There he expanded his already considerable knowledge of classical authors. The most direct result of this phase of his education was an edition, published in 1555, of Oppian's *Cynegetica*, a didactic poem on hunting. Bodin translated the Greek text into Latin verse and added an erudite commentary—partly philological and textual, partly a logical analysis of Oppian's argument—which illustrates the blending of humanist scholarship and Ramist logical method. It is a testimony to the range of interests of the youthful scholar that this commentary refers to more than two hundred different authors and sources. He was accused, however, of plagiarizing some of his textual emendations from Adrian Turnebus, professor of Greek at the Collège Royal.[1]

At this point the picture darkens. We have it from good authority that Bodin returned to Angers and left his religious order, being released from his vows on the ground that he had been professed at an early age. The underlying reason for his leaving the Carmelites, however, may well have been a growing unorthodoxy in his religious beliefs. We know that a Carmelite named "Jehan Baudin" was brought to trial at Paris in August 1548 on charges of heresy. He may well have recanted, for the outcome is unknown. A few years later, between August 1552 and July 1553, the registers of Geneva bear witness to the presence of a Jean Bodin in the stronghold of Calvinism. This Bodin, styled a doctor of theology, contracted a marriage with the widow of a converted priest who had been martyred at Paris in 1549, and shortly afterwards was admitted formally to the status of resident (*habitant*) of Geneva.

Do these episodes belong to the career of Jean Bodin the author or not? In the last decade this question has been warmly disputed, and the full evidence is too complex to be summarized here. The biography of our Jean Bodin is obscure during these years, and nothing that we know of his early life from other sources is sufficient to rule out the possibility that he himself underwent these experiences. On the other hand, an argument based on the identity of names is weakened by the fact that his surname was a common one in sixteenth-century France. Until more conclusive documentary evidence is at hand, therefore, it seems best to treat this period as an unsolved problem in Bodin's career.[2]

The next phase of his development is clearer. From 1556 to 1559, and perhaps for a considerably longer period, Bodin studied civil law at the University of Toulouse, the foremost center of legal studies in France. Probably he began the study of law while still in the North, perhaps at the University of Angers. In any case after leaving the Carmelites he must have looked rather anxiously for a new career, and next to the Church the legal profession offered the best prospects for a man of ample talent but modest means. The years in Toulouse were divided between study, writing, and teaching. To this period undoubtedly belong several legal treatises which have been lost, for Bodin requested in his will that

[1] Whether Bodin was guilty of this charge is extremely difficult to decide, particularly since another edition of the *Cynegetica*, a bare Greek text without any editor's name, had appeared in 1549. Both editions were produced by the same printer, Vascosanus.

[2] Personally I do not believe that the Bodin who dwelt in Geneva in 1552–1553 was the future author, chiefly because the Geneva Bodin is specifically described as having been born at St. Amand in the diocese of Bourges, whereas our Bodin, as I hope to prove below, was born in Angers. But if we reject as irrelevant the Geneva evidence, there is no need to rule out the heresy trial of 1548, or even to assume that our Bodin never visited Geneva himself.

the manuscripts be destroyed. Though they may have been inferior to the later works, it is clear from the nature of his references to them in his later writings that their loss has prevented us from tracing the early development of some of the most important concepts of his political system, concepts such as citizenship, magistracy, and sovereignty. During these years at Toulouse he also taught law, probably in a junior capacity. Perhaps he cherished expectations of a permanent academic post; if so, his hopes were disappointed. A few years later he was to pour scorn upon academic jurists on account of their preoccupation with theoretical aspects of the law. There may have been an element of personal bitterness in this, but both temperament and inclination made him more at home in the realm of public affairs and diplomacy than in the academic cloister.

He is next to be found in Paris, practicing as an advocate. Just when he left Toulouse is uncertain, but by June 1562 the move had been effected. At that time all members of the Parlement of Paris, advocates included, were required to make public profession of the Catholic faith. On June 10 the required oath was taken by 367 advocates, and among these were two named Jean Bodin.[3] There can be no doubt that one of the two was the Angevin law student recently arrived from Toulouse. But was this a sincere profession of religious conviction, or was it, on the contrary, a necessary gesture of conformity for a struggling young advocate faced with the sort of dilemma which, in these days of loyalty oaths and official secrets acts, has become so depressingly familiar to our own generation? As evidence of Bodin's real religious inclinations, the oath clearly should be viewed with caution.

That his practice during the early years in Paris was not onerous is indicated by the composition of three books in his leisure time. The first and most substantial of these was the *Methodus ad facilem historiarum cognitionem*,[4] published in 1566, a work which gave its author an immediate European reputation. The *Methodus* is a treatise on the use of historical materials. Its purpose was to formulate principles according to which the complex data of history—and the vast range of Bodin's reading may be seen again by a cursory glance at his bibliography—may be organized for more effective utilization. I have suggested elsewhere that this project owes its conception to the teachings of Peter Ramus and that the *Methodus* shows many instances of Ramist precepts in its opening chapters.[5] Its chief importance for our purposes is that it lays down a pattern for man's intellectual development. History—Bodin uses the term as a synonym for factual knowledge generally—has three main divisions: human, natural, and divine. Over the course of their lives men should study these three branches of knowledge in that order, starting with matters within their social and political experience, progressing to the more complex world of natural phenomena, and finally, following an ascending order of difficulty, developing an intellectual capacity to meditate on the mysteries

---

[3] R. Delachenal, *Histoire des avocats au Parlement de Paris* (Paris, 1885), pp. 28–30, 399–406.

[4] Translated by Miss B. Reynolds under the title *Method for the Easy Comprehension of History* (New York, 1945). All references below are to this edition except where another is specified.

[5] See "Ramist Tendencies in the Thought of Jean Bodin," *Journal of the History of Ideas*, XVI (1955), 306–323.

of religion.⁶ It was a pattern to which Bodin himself was to adhere with remarkable tenacity throughout the vicissitudes of his own life. The *Methodus* itself is almost entirely concerned with the organization and handling of the data of human history, the first of the three levels. Several of its themes reappear in the *République* ten years later in an expanded and more systematic form.

But the systematic arrangement of historical materials outlined in the *Methodus* was intended only as a means to a more general end, the formulation of a comprehensive science of society. For Bodin, history was only raw data, not a discipline in itself. Trained as he was in civil law, he saw his task primarily as a problem in jurisprudence. By 1566 he had conceived the plan for a comprehensive system of universal law. His intentions are carefully described in the dedication of the *Methodus*, and the outline of the system is given in another work which belongs to this period even though it was not published until 1578, the brief *Juris universi distributio*.⁷ To implement the project on the scale planned would have required first a vast comparative inquest into the laws and institutions of all peoples, both past and present, conducted according to the principles of gathering data laid down in the *Methodus*. Then the materials so obtained would be fitted into the institutional framework outlined in the *Distributio*. By means of this twofold process Bodin confidently expected to discover certain normative standards of political and social organization which would be common to all well-conducted societies.

Two points in this project deserve emphasis. First, several schemes for the systematic reorganization of law were in the air at the time, put forward both by academic jurists and by practicing lawyers whose aim was to rationalize the complex customary law of France; but Bodin deliberately sets himself apart from all his contemporaries in insisting that the civil law, derived from Rome alone, is inadequate as a starting point, and that the new law must be founded upon the common practice of all nations, a true *jus gentium*. Second, the universal law which he envisages clearly has boundaries far wider than we would nowadays assign to jurisprudence; for Bodin the term implied a social framework for the entire complex of human relationships, political, social, economic, and legal. In the end his project was never completed, and perhaps it was inevitable that any project so ambitious should fail of execution. The plan is significant, however, because much of the material intended for it was to be incorporated in the *République*, and from one point of view the latter work is simply a substantial segment of the much larger scheme originally projected.

The third product of these early years in Paris was a brief tract on an economic issue of some importance—inflation. One of the gentlemen of the court, Malestroit, who had been commissioned to investigate the monetary situation, had concluded that the relentless rise in prices which was visibly ruining those with fixed incomes was due only to the debasement of the currency, and that in terms of the actual gold and silver content of the coinage, prices had remained substantially unchanged for three hundred years. Bodin wrote a

⁶ *Methodus*, pp. 15–16, 24–25.
⁷ Reprinted in Bodin's *Oeuvres philosophiques*, ed. P. Mesnard (Paris, 1951), I, 71–80.

reply contesting this view.⁸ He maintained not only that gold and silver would buy less than formerly, but that the primary reason for this phenomenon lay in the increased quantities of precious metals imported into Europe from the Spanish colonies in the New World. His tract has gained a secure place in the history of economic thought as the first clear statement of the quantity theory of money and of the causes of the persistent inflation that plagued the sixteenth century.

Bodin's growing reputation now brought him a series of minor public charges. In 1567 he had been sent to Poitiers as deputy for the *procureur-général*. Before advancing to more important posts, however, his career was brusquely interrupted. In September 1568 a royal edict prescribed stringent measures against those of the reformed religion, dismissing all Protestants holding offices under the Crown and enjoining a new oath of Catholicity upon the Parlements and Universities. At Paris the strict application of this edict in the early months of 1569 led to the imprisonment of considerable numbers of suspected Huguenots on charges of heresy. Many of their names have been preserved in the register of imprisonments in the Conciergerie, which still survives. In this register there is an entry for Sunday, March 6, 1569, which records the detention of "Mᵉ Jehan Baudin soy disant advocat en la cour de parlemᵗ natif d'Angers" on the ground that he was an adherent of the new religion. Beside each entry there is a record of the disposition of the case; in this instance the register reveals that the prisoner was released as a result of the amnesty contained in the Edict of Pacification of August 11, 1570, and that the *arrêt* for his actual release was obtained on August 23.⁹ One might be tempted to attribute this episode to Bodin's colleague at the bar and homonym, Jean Bodin de Montguichet. But this soon proves impossible, for on May 21, 1569, during the very period in question, Bodin de Montguichet was named Master of Requests to the Queen.¹⁰ In these circumstances we can scarcely avoid the conclusion that Bodin the author spent almost a year and a half in detention at the time of the third war of religion, a fact which he would understandably hesitate to mention in his own writings.

If I have gone into details concerning the imprisonment, it is because no other biographer has ever mentioned it. Yet its importance for an understanding of Bodin's life scarcely needs emphasizing. First and foremost, it testifies to his continuing unorthodoxy in religion during middle life, and in doing so it offers strong support to some later testimony by a young Englishman which might otherwise have been discounted as biased. From Blois, where the Estates General were in session, William Wade wrote home to Lord Burghley in February 1577: "I have good and famylyar acquaintance with Bodinus, his profession is the Cyvill law though he is constrayned to retyr him selfe from the practise for his safety beinge of the Religion and

---

⁸ *La Response à M. de Malestroit*, first published in 1568, and edited recently by H. Hauser (Paris, 1932). There is an English translation by G. A. Moore (Chevy Chase, Md., 1946) of the revised French edition of 1578. On the revisions, see the note below at 687 A2.

⁹ For a partial transcription of this register, see N. Weiss, "Huguenots emprisonnés à la Conciergerie du Palais à Paris en mars 1569," *Bulletin de la Société de l'histoire du protestantisme français*, 5th series, XXI (1923), 86–97.

¹⁰ P. Cornu, "Jean Bodin de Montguichet," *Revue de l'Anjou*, new series, LIV (1907), 110.

therfore his estate is poore."[11] Taken together, these two pieces of evidence seem adequate to justify the conclusion that Bodin's "protestantism," whatever its precise form, was no mere youthful aberration but a basic characteristic of his mature years, of the very years which saw the composition of the *République*. But the brief entry in the register of the Conciergerie tells us more than this. First, it casts a very serious doubt upon the earlier evidence for a stay in Geneva, for the Geneva Bodin was born, as noted above, at St. Amand in the diocese of Bourges. Secondly, it confirms what Angevin writers have been telling us—without written evidence—for generations: that Bodin the author was actually *born* in the city of Angers.

After the Edict of Pacification, he was free to resume his interrupted career. By the end of the same year he was given a commission from the King for the reformation of forest tenures in Normandy. One may well ask whether so rapid a reinstatement does not cast some doubt upon the evidence of his imprisonment. The answer here would seem to lie in the edict itself, which, though wrested from the King by sheer force, was in itself a thoroughly generous and tolerant settlement. The memory of the late troubles was to be buried forever, and among other specific concessions Protestants were declared capable of holding all public offices. Against this background Bodin's rather obscure appointment in Normandy is fully compatible with his previous imprisonment. More important tasks lay ahead. In 1573 King Charles IX's brother, Henry of Anjou, was elected King of Poland, and Bodin appears in a delegation sent to Metz to welcome the Polish ambassadors to France. Meanwhile he had been appointed in 1571 to the household of the King's youngest brother, Francis, Duke of Alençon, in the capacity of Master of Requests and counselor.

This new post gave him a regular status and a more direct access to those concerned with national administration and diplomacy, but it also appears to have placed him in a very dangerous situation a few years later. By the spring of 1574 it was clear that Charles IX was dying of tuberculosis, and the Duke of Alençon, with substantial support from the Huguenots and the Politiques, aspired to seize the throne at his death and thereby supplant the lawful heir, Henry, by this time far away in Poland. Alençon's plan was a rather vague one, but a conspiracy to bring it to fruition developed under the leadership of two gentlemen attached to his household, La Molle and Coconat. Suddenly the principal conspirators were arrested, and under interrogation Coconat revealed that a "secretary named Bodin" had gone to the English ambassador, Dr. Valentine Dale, to seek aid for the enterprise from Queen Elizabeth. Was Jean Bodin the author the secretary in question? Again the evidence is not quite conclusive, but there is a strong presumption that he was. In any case, he now disappears from public life for more than two years, to reappear towards the end of 1576 as representative of the third estate for Vermandois at the Estates General of Blois. When we remember that much of the *République* was undoubtedly written during these years, their importance needs no

[11] The abstract of this letter is printed in the *Calendars of State Papers Foreign, 1575–1577*, No. 1244.

further emphasis. Yet the most that we can say about them from present evidence is that in all likelihood he wrote this best-known of all his works while living in seclusion at Laon, the residence of his later years, awaiting the opportune moment to return to public life.

It is important to realize the complexity of the situation in which the *République* was written. In the first place, Bodin was suspect as an adviser to Alençon, and the book afforded him an opportunity to demonstrate his loyalty to the Crown and to win the favor of the new King, now securely established on the throne. This helps to explain the dedication of the French editions to Gui du Faur, Sieur de Pibrac,[12] a friend of Bodin's who was at this time one of Henry's closest advisers. Secondly, the *République* directly reflects the gathering crisis in national politics. Since the appearance of the *Methodus* in 1566 there had been four separate outbreaks of civil war over the religious issue; and this somber fact, brought home to Bodin, perhaps, by the daily prospect of a wasted countryside and by bitter memories of the Conciergerie in Paris, is sufficient to explain why the buoyant optimism of the *Methodus* gives way to a sense of grave urgency in the *République*. During these critical years the point of view of the Politiques, the moderate party which asserted the claims of peace, order, and national unity against religious extremists whether Catholic or Protestant, was heard with increasing insistence. Though Henry III was eventually to prove a failure as a ruler, in 1576 it was not yet too late for moderates to look hopefully to the new King for a bold solution to the religious problem which was tearing France asunder.

Bodin found himself wholly in accord with the aims of the Politiques, and from this standpoint the *République* is a direct and comprehensive statement of their program for the regeneration of royal authority in France. Finally, one must remember Bodin's wider theoretical interests. The *République* comes the nearest of all his writings to fulfilling the earlier plan for a system of universal law. It is, in a very real sense, an attempt at a general system of politics, and contemporaries were not far wrong in likening it to the *Politics* of Aristotle. As soon as one appreciates its fundamental duality, its endeavor to combine a prescription for the needs of the moment with universal principles —and to justify the specific program by presenting it as an integral part of the general theory—the significance of the *République* becomes much clearer.

Within a few months of the publication of the *République*, Bodin attended the Estates General of Blois, where he distinguished himself as a stubborn defender of constitutional tradition against new financial proposals devised by the Crown to increase its revenues. His financial conservatism on this occasion seems to have been dictated to a large degree by the reflection that without greater revenues the Crown was powerless to accede to the wishes of religious extremists who sought a renewal of the civil wars. During the early weeks of the Estates, Bodin had dined frequently with the King and had won popularity on account of his encyclopedic knowledge. But as the session drew to a close, his unyielding constitutionalism drove Henry to exasperation and cost Bodin whatever chances he had of an appointment at

[12] See below, Appendix A, section 1.

Introduction

court. When the session ended he withdrew to Laon to practice law and to write. In 1578 he published the *Juris universi distributio*, as noted above. Shortly after, he was at work upon his surprisingly credulous study of witchcraft, *De la Démonomanie des sorciers*, first printed in 1580. He then wrote, under a pseudonym, a defense of his *République* against certain of his most important critics, under the title *Apologie de René Herpin pour la Republique de I. Bodin*. The first edition bears the date 1581, but before it appeared Bodin had returned once more to the public stage.

The Duke of Alençon, having failed to seize the French throne, sought by other means to gain a position commensurate with his birth and ambition. He lent his rather ineffective aid to the Low Countries in their revolt against Spain, and he aspired to a marriage with Queen Elizabeth. The two projects were closely related, for English support was necessary to the success of the venture in the Netherlands. On Alençon's second visit to England in 1581, Bodin was among the advance party, and for several months he observed English affairs at first hand. He met leading statesmen and scholars, saw the English Parliament in session, heard the fate of Edmund Campion and his fellow Catholics discussed in the Privy Council, and questioned his hosts on the succession issue with more curiosity than tact. In short the visit afforded him a fine opportunity to test, modify, and supplement many of the views on English politics already expressed in the *République*.

Alençon left England for Flanders in February 1582, and Bodin appears in Antwerp by the end of that month. As a military effort the campaign to drive out the Spaniards was a dismal failure. Alençon lost whatever chances of success he might have had by an abortive *coup d'état* in January 1583. Bodin himself witnessed one phase of this plan, the attempt to seize Antwerp by treachery, and wrote a vivid account of it to his brother-in-law. After this episode cooperation between French and Flemings was impossible, and to remain was a waste of time. Bodin returned to France early in 1583, traveling via England to avoid the dangers of an overland journey through hostile territory.

In June 1584 Alençon died, and once again Bodin settled down at Laon. This time his retirement from national politics was permanent. One of his first actions was to make a Latin translation of the *République*. Possibly it had been begun even before the visit to England; the dedication shows that it was completed by November 1584, though not published until 1586. The Latin version is not merely a translation of the original French, but a completely revised and rewritten text which reflects Bodin's intellectual development over almost a decade. The differences between the two versions are important enough to be examined in some detail in a later section of this Introduction.[13]

Bodin now had a family, a fact which was to influence his conduct during the critical years that lay ahead. Early in 1576 he had married the widow of a Laon official, and she bore him a daughter and two sons. When he returned from abroad his sons were three and four years old, and he himself undertook their education. He devised a curriculum

[13] See below, section III.

which included natural history, cosmology, Latin, mathematics, and the memorization of moral maxims compiled and collected by himself. There was also the problem of earning a living through his legal practice. In 1587 his brother-in-law died, and Bodin succeeded to the dead man's office of *procureur du roi* for Laon.

He was too prominent a figure, however, to be left in peace for very long. As early as September 1585 he was forecasting in his correspondence the overthrow of Queen Elizabeth. In the following year his predictions of her death coincided so closely with the unfolding of the Babington plot—with which he may have been acquainted—that in August the English authorities sought his arrest, though apparently without success. Again, in May 1587 complaints were made at the French court that offices were being granted to men whose orthodox Catholicism was in doubt, and Bodin's name was mentioned specifically as an example. Five days later he underwent an investigation at Laon, presumably to determine his religious beliefs, and was cleared by the testimony of ten leading citizens, two of whom were priests.

Far worse was still to come. When Alençon died the Catholic party, alarmed at the prospect of a Protestant heir to the throne in the person of Henry of Navarre, revived the Catholic League. So rapidly did their power grow that King Henry III, in desperation, ordered the assassination of their leaders, the Duke and the Cardinal of Guise, in December 1588. With this deed the whole country erupted violently in open rebellion. To officials in the provinces came direct orders from the Parlement of Paris to join in the revolt against the King. Bodin, as a known supporter of the monarchy and as *procureur du roi* for Laon, was placed in the extremely difficult position of having to explain and justify the rebellion before an assembly of his fellow citizens. His only alternatives were flight or imprisonment; either course would have imperiled his family and lost him his office, his livelihood, and his modest property. He chose instead a precarious policy of collaboration with the insurgents which left him despised by the few Royalists that remained in Laon and mistrusted by the Leaguers. But he retained his office throughout the five troubled years of League supremacy at Laon, surviving a second inquisition and search of his house in January 1590, as a result of which certain books from his library were publicly burned. In April 1594, with the tide visibly turning, Bodin and other Royalists slipped away to join Henry IV as he approached. By doing so they escaped the siege of the town but were placed under temporary detention. When Laon capitulated in August, Bodin could return home in safety, still *procureur du roi*.

His adherence to the League has been censured by some, excused by others. Whichever judgment be adopted, it is clear that force and fear were major factors in his decision. Yet though he could not approve the aims of the Leaguers, his policy of collaboration with them was based, paradoxically, upon sincere convictions. The proof can be found in his private correspondence during these years. He had come to believe that the days of Henry III were numbered on account of the cold-blooded murder of his subjects, the Guises; that God would intervene directly to strike down the House of Valois and establish a new line of kings in

Introduction

France; that the League, though evil in itself, was God's chosen instrument for the execution of His purpose; and that the ultimate result of this divine action was far beyond human understanding. In the circumstances resistance to the League would be not only futile but impious; the devout man—and Bodin was devout—could only wait in patient resignation for the divine plan to reach its inscrutable fulfillment.

In keeping with this growing concern for the supernatural element in human history, the writings of his later years are primarily philosophical and religious. The period of League supremacy, with all its difficulties and dangers, saw him at work upon two of his most ambitious books, both of which are to some extent foreshadowed by the plan outlined in the *Methodus*. One of these was a dialogue on the principles of natural science, the *Universae naturae theatrum*. He had already begun it as early as 1590, though the date of the dedication, February 25, 1596, suggests that its completion may have been delayed. The other was the more controversial *Heptaplomeres*, a dialogue between seven friends of seven different religious beliefs, a work which shocked Protestants and Catholics alike by its boldly critical examination of the fundamental doctrines of Christianity. Though widely circulated in manuscripts, it was not published until the nineteenth century.[14] Similar religious tendencies are discernible in a Latin poem of seventy-four verses, now lost, which was written the day before his death. Apparently it was some sort of religious testament, for contemporaries were quick to note that it was conspicuous for its failure to mention Jesus Christ. Yet this evidence should not go unqualified, for by his will, written in all probability as he lay on his deathbed, and dated June 7, 1596, he expressed the wish to be given a Catholic burial in the Church of the Franciscans at Laon.

What conclusions, then, are we to draw concerning Bodin's religion? At first glance the question seems a baffling enigma, but after examination the area of uncertainty can be narrowed considerably. What are really in question are his formal religious affiliations, and these have assumed for some biographers an importance which they scarcely deserve. There can be no serious doubt of Bodin's early training as a Carmelite, but afterwards he seems to have been suspected by his contemporaries of religious unorthodoxy at almost every stage of his career. For his sympathy with the new opinions there is substantial evidence, of which only the high lights could be mentioned in this brief sketch. But we should note that his was a "protestantism" singularly free from fanaticism and dogma. He could discuss religious differences with his Catholic friends, as he did in an undated letter to Jan Bautru des Matras. He could conform, outwardly at least, to the religion established in France by law, as he did in 1562, in 1587, throughout the years of League supremacy at Laon, and in his will in 1596. Most important of all, he could place the welfare of the body politic and the desirability of social order above the claims of any religious group, as did the other Politiques. The later years brought not a return to the Catholic fold but a still bolder line of speculation, an attempt to come closer to the source and archetype of all Western

[14] The only complete edition to date is that edited by L. Noack (Schwerin, 1857).

religious teaching. From a Protestantism grounded firmly on the Old Testament it was but another step to Judaism, the faith presented most sympathetically in the *Heptaplomeres*. But the importance of this later work lies not so much in its apparent preference for any one religion as in its adoption of the same comparative method of inquiry which had previously been applied to social and political institutions. At the time of writing the *Heptaplomeres* Bodin may have been a nominal Catholic, but it is doubtful whether he can be considered in any real sense an adherent of any formal religious faith.

His personal religious convictions are quite another matter, and these he states clearly enough in his writings. True religion, he proclaims several times, is strictly a personal affair, the turning of an individual mind towards God. It is best practiced in solitude, requires no outward church, and by its very nature cannot be interfered with by the state. The point is stressed more often in the later writings, but it is also stated clearly in the early years when he was closer to Protestantism. This continuing belief in the primacy of a personal religion divorced from any church must be considered as the fundamental tenet of Bodin's religious thought. Such an attitude enabled him to conform the more easily to ceremonies and doctrines in which he did not personally believe. More important, it made possible his distinctive approach to religious toleration.[15] Individual religious beliefs are by their very nature beyond the reach of the state; but the outward manifestations of religious worship are primarily a question of social order, a problem in politics, to be handled as expediency dictates. Thus he advocated toleration not because it is invariably right and just, but because toleration is the only sensible policy when a state is as deeply divided on religious matters as France was in his lifetime.[16]

---

[15] See below, pp. 535–540.

[16] This brief biographical outline is based on a wide variety of sources, and to document it adequately would require considerably more space than to state the original facts. I have given the sources fully and have discussed the controversial points at some length, however, in a more comprehensive biography which forms part of a dissertation on Bodin submitted to Harvard University in 1953. A revised version of this study, publication of which is planned for the near future, will present a more complete picture of his political thought as a whole than is possible within the limits of this Introduction.

II. BODIN'S CONTRIBUTIONS TO POLITICAL SCIENCE

When the political scientist of today hears the name of Jean Bodin, he thinks, almost automatically, of sovereignty. And this association is justified, for Bodin's most important contribution to the history of political ideas was an analysis of political authority that went far beyond the work of his predecessors. But what was new and distinctive in his analysis? To the medieval mind the question of political supremacy was one of great difficulty. Under the system of feudal tenure political and property rights had become so thoroughly confused that the notion of undisputed political supremacy within a definite territory could hardly be stated with any clarity. The consolidation of national monarchies in Western Europe paved the way for a clearer understanding of the issue, but even in the sixteenth century men were still groping for a theoretical analysis which would fit the changed political structure. Bodin's work represents the culmination of a long development. It was he who first defined the state (or commonweal, to use his own term) in a way that is unmistakably modern. It was he who stressed that the state must by definition possess a supreme political authority; otherwise it is not a state but some lesser type of association. Unlike previous theorists, Bodin made authority the central feature of his entire system of politics, and it is easy to see why he did so. He was writing at a time when religious warfare had brought the royal authority in France perilously close to total destruction. To express the concept of supremacy in the state, he adopted the special term sovereignty and worked out its precise meaning with great theoretical precision. On this point he did his work well, for the concept of sovereignty, though criticized, modified, and even repudiated altogether by some theorists, has survived as a central feature of Western political thought from his day to ours.

But it was in discussing the characteristics of sovereignty that Bodin made his greatest innovation. Analysis of political supremacy was a common topic of sixteenth-century French lawyers. Almost invariably they described it in terms of the traditional prerogatives of the Crown, a collection of rights of various kinds which might vary not only from state to state but even from one French province to another. Bodin was the first to emphasize—and only in the *République*, for the *Methodus* still approaches the question of authority in traditional fashion—that the most fundamental of these various rights was the power to make laws. All others were subordinate and incidental. To say this was to take a long stride towards modern political thought and to break sharply with the past in yet another respect. In medieval thought the ruler's judicial and administrative functions were more important than his role as a legislator. His lawmaking function was hampered and restricted by the widespread view that all man-made law is supplementary to and consonant with the higher laws of God and nature. Further, the concept of social change was virtually absent from medieval thought, but in the sixteenth century, when society was changing visibly and rapidly, it was vitally important for the ruler to be able to devise new laws to meet rapidly changing situations. The political thought of Bodin and others recognizes and attempts to meet this need.

The concept of sovereignty itself is developed with great care and close attention to detail. In two key chapters Bodin defines sovereignty, discusses its characteristics and its limits, and then enumerates the functions generally vested in the sovereign authority.[17] These two chapters constitute the core of his theoretical argument concerning supreme authority. At the definition stage two characteristics are particularly stressed: sovereignty must be perpetual, and it must be absolute. By the first, Bodin means simply that supreme authority held for a specified time, or held indefinitely during another's pleasure, is not supremacy in the sense that he means it. Sovereignty must be unlimited in duration, or else the true sovereign is the person or persons to whom supreme authority eventually reverts. But no man lives forever, and

[17] See below, Book I, chapters 8 and 10.

this introduces a difficulty concerning monarchies. Because of his preference for the monarchical form of government, Bodin adopts the position that an unconditional grant of power for life is near enough to a perpetuity. A monarch may, therefore, have no right to choose his successor and yet still be a sovereign ruler. In an elective kingdom authority reverts, on the death of the king, to the body which elects the new king. Even a hereditary kingdom may have a law of succession which the sovereign himself cannot change. But in neither case is the sovereignty of the king diminished by this restriction. The reasoning behind this apparent paradox will be seen shortly.

Probably no point in Bodin's writings has led to greater misunderstanding than his insistence that the sovereign authority must be "absolute." Behind the term itself there are several distinct implications. First, there must be no human superior, in the form either of an individual or of a corporate body. Neither pope nor emperor, estates nor feudal overlord, ought to have any authority whatever over the true sovereign. The regent, the agent for another man, the holder of absolute authority upon sufferance of a greater prince—all of these are not sovereigns. Further, if authority is conferred by an electoral college or by the estates, to create a true sovereign requires that the grant be made freely and without condition. Finally, absolute authority means that the sovereign is not bound by the laws of his country, whether enacted by himself or by his predecessors. It will easily be seen that this freedom from existing law was logically necessary in order to safeguard the main characteristic of sovereignty, the unlimited power of the sovereign to make new laws, or to make exceptions to old ones, as he alone saw fit. It is this particular sense of absolute authority that is stated more clearly in the Latin version of the *République*, for there the rather vague term *puissance absolue* of the French version becomes the more specific *potestas legibus soluta*.[18]

It is when this concept of "absolute" authority must be reconciled with restraints upon it that the apparent contradictions begin. In Bodin's political system the sovereign is not at the ultimate apex of the authority structure; above all earthly rulers there is the still higher authority of God. The highest human authority must therefore function in a world governed by divine and natural law, and this type of law (properly, but not invariably, designated as *jus* or *droit* in the original versions) has a far different relationship to the sovereign than does the statutory law (*lex* or *loi*), over which he has the fullest control. Writing in the sixteenth century, Bodin could not treat the laws of God and nature as merely moral obligations, as might the jurist of today. Like most of his contemporaries, he firmly believed that the sovereign is directly responsible to God, and he had an unquestioning faith in divine retribution for actions which contravened the higher law. Political sovereignty operated within the wider framework of an ordered universe governed by God.

But this view could serve, it should be noted, as a powerful support for the doctrine of nonresistance to authority. If the sovereign's responsibility is to God alone, then obviously the subjects are not to pass judgment on the actions of their rulers. The

[18] Cf. the definitions of sovereignty given below in Appendix B, no. 4.

Introduction

duty of a subject is to obey the sovereign without question in whatever he commands and to leave punishment, when it is merited, to the Almighty. The only exception of any significance that Bodin allows is one which few in his day would have dared to deny: that subjects need not obey when they are commanded to do something clearly and unmistakably contrary to divine or natural law. But in no circumstances may they use such an unjust command as a pretext for active resistance or rebellion.

The concept of natural law had by this time developed a fairly precise meaning in European jurisprudence. The basic precepts had been formulated in Roman law, and judicial precedents had added concrete meaning to these philosophical injunctions in a wide variety of specific situations. As a lawyer Bodin was thoroughly familiar with this development, and he used natural law as a foundation for two specific limitations upon the sovereign. First, a ruler is bound, at least as strictly as private men are, to keep his promises, and with certain exceptions this obligation extends to promises made by his predecessors. This limitation upon the sovereign is founded upon the belief that the keeping of faith and the performance of covenants are absolutely essential to the preservation of social order. Second, natural law asserts that every man shall have his due, and upon this precept Bodin builds a defense of private property so sweeping that even taxation of property requires the consent of the owners, except when necessity is so pressing that to wait for consent would endanger the very existence of the state. Many later writers have treated this insistence upon consent to taxation as a logical impasse in Bodin's theory, but his position may be understood fairly easily when it is remembered that property rights are protected by natural law and that natural law is superior to the sovereign. The real difficulty lies in the machinery to implement the consent. Bodin felt this should be done by the Estates General and by the regional estates, the only existing representative bodies; but he also emphasized that these assemblies had no authority independent of the king, and to insist on this point would logically deprive them of the right to veto taxation. On the whole, then, it would seem that his main safeguard against arbitrary taxation lies not in constitutional machinery but in natural law. In relying upon natural law rather than upon the constitutional tradition of the country concerned he was undoubtedly attempting to secure for the doctrine of consent to taxation the widest possible application, but in this very search for universality he was setting a dangerous precedent for the time when sovereigns should no longer feel bound so rigidly by the dictates of natural law.

In addition to these restraints founded on a higher law Bodin also mentions certain specific limitations upon the sovereign which have proved a stiff exercise in logic for all later commentators on his theory. He calls them by the special term *leges imperii*, or—in the French version—"laws which concern the form of government (*l'estat*) of the realm."[19] In the final analysis he finds only two of these in France. The first is that governing the succession to the throne; the Salic law, barring female succession, constitutes one provision of this law. The second forbids the king to alienate any part of the public

[19] See below, 95 A6-10.

domain. Bodin sees both of these rules as essential to the continued existence of the particular form of sovereignty which existed in France: the first assures the peaceful transmission of sovereignty when the king dies, and the second guarantees, theoretically at least, sources of revenue adequate to the performance of the kingly duties. Clearly if the king's authority enabled him to infringe either of these basic safeguards, the position of his successors would be impaired.

To understand why Bodin incorporated these particular limitations into his theory, one must look first not to logic but to the constitutional history of France. French writers of every description, including some far more absolutist in temperament than Bodin, accepted various fundamental laws as binding upon the monarch. Some writers drew up considerable lists of fundamental laws; others held that new ones could be created at need, even against the wishes of the Crown. Bodin, while striving for a logically consistent theory, was even more interested in having one that was consonant with the actual constitutional structure. Since the fundamental laws were so generally accepted, he could not ignore them altogether, but he could—and did—restrict them as much as a firmly established constitutional tradition would permit. His theoretical justification was that the *leges imperii* are only those laws which are integrally related to the sovereignty itself, laws upon which the sovereignty itself depends. Though his primary concern was with France, it is clear that he considered the concept applicable to other states. He himself noted that an aristocratic state might have a "law concerning sovereignty" according to which decisions were to be made by a two-thirds majority rather than by simple majority.[20] This example suggests further possibilities. Indeed if we accept Bodin's conception of the *leges imperii*, it seems possible from a logical standpoint to extend them much further than he did in the *République*. He himself had a somewhat wider interpretation of them in the *Methodus*, but by 1576 his concern was to minimize them as far as possible.

The philosopher, preoccupied with the notion of power, may object to the logical difficulties here. But Bodin, less concerned with logic than with the practical effects of his theory, was approaching his problem as a jurist. He was looking for a supreme authority and a supreme will which could normally be manifested by means of regular, orderly procedures. We must not allow the occasional exceptions that he cites to deceive us as to his main purpose. To attribute sovereignty to whoever could obtain physical mastery in competition against all comers was clearly no solution to the problem of social order. The late Roman Empire afforded ample proof of this point, if examples were needed. In the circumstances, then, any theory of political supremacy which could bring about the results desired of it required a minimum framework of law or custom to determine such questions as the location of sovereignty, the nature of the sovereign, and perhaps even the procedure by which its will would be expressed. But Bodin carefully avoids the vexing question of who, in turn, is to control or alter this framework. He is scrupulously noncommittal, for example, as to the origins of the Salic law, a question of

[20] See below, 231 E7–8.

warm controversy at the time. Other writers quickly recognized his dilemma and sought to solve it. Althusius attributed to Bodin a distinction between two kinds of sovereignty, that of the ruler and that of the realm.[21] Then by asserting the superiority of the latter he developed a careful theoretical justification for current Calvinist doctrines of popular sovereignty. But this solution, while more logical than Bodin's, bore little relation to constitutional realities in France.

Bodin's sovereign, then, is the supreme lawmaking authority in the state, but it is also limited by some few fundamental rules which relate to the sovereignty itself. It is perhaps worth a short digression to note that after almost four centuries this question of limitations remains with us. Today we are no longer concerned with the rules of succession in monarchies, but the development of the modern legislature brought forth new rules to take their place. Consider, for example, the Parliament of Great Britain. As a result of the constitutional struggles of the seventeenth century the initiative passed from the Crown to the House of Commons, but the formal expression of the will of Parliament remained an Act of Parliament, passed by both Houses and then given royal assent. This procedure may be considered as a fundamental rule, a *lex imperii* in Bodin's sense, and the Parliament Act of 1911 introduced an important change in this rule by providing an alternative procedure for securing a valid Act of Parliament in cases where the consent of the Lords could not be had.

The constitutional issue of the past few years in South Africa furnishes another and indeed a better example, for it has caused many a constitutional lawyer to re-examine his thinking about sovereignty. In its decision in *Harris* v. *Minister of the Interior*,[22] the South African Supreme Court upheld the entrenched clauses of the South Africa Act, 1909, which protected the Cape Province colored franchise and the equality of the English and Dutch languages by a special legislative procedure. More explicitly, the entrenched clauses required that any statute affecting these areas be passed at a joint sitting of the Senate and House of Assembly by a two-thirds majority of the combined membership. The significance of the Harris case lay in the Court's view that despite the sovereign status of the Union Parliament conferred by the Statute of Westminster, 1931, there could still be two different methods of passing a valid statute of that Parliament, a bicameral procedure for ordinary matters and a unicameral one with special majority for matters protected by the entrenched clauses.[23]

All this suggests that an uncritical belief in the supremacy of Parliament is no longer a sufficient basis for a theory of sovereignty. There still remains the question: what constitutes a valid Act of Parliament? The

[21] See his *Politica methodice digesta*, edited by C. J. Friedrich as Vol. II of the Harvard Political Classics (Cambridge, Mass., 1932), p. 93. In my opinion Althusius misrepresents Bodin's position, which is admittedly an awkward one. Though he speaks of *leges imperii*, Bodin would scarcely admit the existence of a corresponding *legislator*.

[22] [1952] 2 S.A.L.R. 428 (A.D.). The literature upon the constitutional issue is already vast and is still growing rapidly.

[23] Since then the Nationalist government has achieved its original intention of altering the Cape colored franchise, but only after enlarging and reconstructing the Senate in 1955 so as to give itself the two-thirds majority of the combined membership needed for the special procedure. Constitutionally speaking, the important point is that the entrenched clauses successfully withstood a frontal assault by the government as long as it lacked the special majority to change them.

examples cited above have shown that the answer to this question may be neither clear nor uniform for all occasions. Yet unless and until Parliament observes the appropriate procedures for lawmaking, its actions will not be recognized in the courts as acts of the sovereign. What does emerge clearly is that even today, even in those countries where legislative sovereignty is restricted the least, we are not yet free of the notion of a few basic restraints upon sovereignty which arise out of the very nature of the sovereign authority itself.[24] And this, it seems to me, was the way in which Bodin viewed the few undeniable constitutional restraints surrounding the French monarchy, in order to fit them into his theory of sovereignty. But his conception of a few basic *leges imperii* was progressively obscured, first by the theories of popular sovereignty developed primarily by Calvinist writers, later by Hobbes's and Spinoza's concentration upon the philosophical problem of power, later still—and most effectively—by Austin's restatement of sovereignty in terms reflecting the unquestioned legislative supremacy of nineteenth-century British parliaments. The influence of Hobbes and Austin held sway for a long time, but in recent years theorists have been re-examining the concept of legislative sovereignty, particularly in the English-speaking world. Their writings suggest that Bodin's pioneer theory should be reconsidered with some care, for we are undoubtedly closer today to his original conception of *leges imperii* than at any time in the past three hundred years. In placing the sovereign under the laws of God and nature Bodin was following medieval tradition. But in defining and restricting the sovereign by means of certain basic "laws concerning sovereignty" he was being more sophisticated than Hobbes, more modern than John Austin. He was, in fact, developing a theory of sovereignty strikingly similar to those of the present time.

In his own day the theory of sovereignty constituted a great analytical advance over the work of his predecessors. But he was not content to stop there. The first step in making use of it was to reconcile it with traditional thinking about the types of state.[25] Accordingly he redefines the three classic forms of monarchy, aristocracy, and democracy in the most rigid fashion by making the number of persons holding sovereignty the sole distinction among the three forms.[26] More important, he insists that these are the only possible forms of state and that the mixed state discussed by many writers is nothing but a vain chimera. If sovereignty is to be exercised by two persons or more, the group holding it must act with a degree of organic unity. Otherwise an inevitable struggle for power would soon give undisputed mastery to one side or the other. But no such unity is possible when authority is shared between king and estates. Sovereignty, then, can neither be exercised jointly by entities with diverse interests nor parceled out between them, and this suggests another of its basic characteristics: it is indivisible.

One important consequence of this rigidly simplified classification of states is to free sovereignty from

[24] This idea has interesting possibilities. If the South African example suggests that legislative sovereignty may be reconciled with a rigid constitution, it seems equally possible to reconcile it with a federal constitution.
[25] This is the general purpose of Book II. See below, pp. 183ff.
[26] See Appendix B, no. 6.

ethical overtones. The tyrant, whatever his misdeeds, is just as much a sovereign in Bodin's analysis as is the most upright of kings. Whether sovereignty is exercised justly or unjustly does become the basis for a distinction between *types of rule*, but it has no bearing whatever upon *types of state*. Both the just and the unjust ruler, it should be noted, are in one sense "bound" by the higher laws of God and nature. Even though a tyrannical monarch is by definition one who flouts the higher law,[27] he does not really escape its operation, for Bodin has a firm faith in eventual divine retribution. But the essential point is that within his definitions neither a tyrannical king nor an outright usurper forfeits sovereignty by his actions so long as he has an undoubted mastery over his subjects. There can be no question that this moral neutrality of the concept of sovereignty is developed quite deliberately, for while ethical qualifications still appear in the definition of the state, or commonweal, they are conspicuously absent from the definition of sovereignty.[28] The aim was not, of course, to advocate tyranny, but to facilitate clear thinking about authority.

There is one implication of this position which gives rise to a serious ambiguity in the theory. Although Bodin first develops the notion of sovereignty as a concept in legal theory, he is intensely interested in applying it to the contemporary European scene. He had acquired— probably from his early contact with Ramus, who shared the same outlook —a thorough distrust of theoretical concepts and a passion for getting at the realities of the everyday world. He realized that in some instances a constitutional structure may be no more than an empty shell masking the true location of power. In the case of Germany he attacked the pretensions of the Emperor with typical Gallic enthusiasm and attributed actual sovereignty to the Estates of the Empire. But in the case of Poland and the Scandinavian countries his awareness of the strong influence of the nobility in these countries made him waver uneasily in his quest for sovereignty. The basic difficulty was that he never made a sufficiently clear decision as to whether sovereignty is the highest legally defined authority in the state or the entity exercising actual supremacy. Sometimes he upheld constitutional tradition, treating facts to the contrary as mere abuses; at other times he preferred obvious facts before constitutional shadows.[29] Consequently, while asserting that sovereignty is perpetual and inalienable as a legal right, he was quite ready to recognize that in actual fact it is overthrown whenever a usurper establishes his power. There is a basic conflict here which Bodin, torn between respect for constitutional tradition and fascination with power politics, could never resolve.

It might be concluded from the fact that both the usurper and the legitimate ruler are fully sovereign that Bodin is placing them on the same footing. This is not the case, for he allows an unlimited right of resistance to usurped authority. But he does show a curious lack of concern for the basis of a ruler's claim to legitimacy. Some kind of title to

---

[27] See below, Appendix B, no. 7, and 210 G3-5.
[28] Cf. the respective definitions given below in Appendix B, nos. 1 and 4.
[29] For examples of these opposing tendencies, cf. his statements about Rome (below, 160 I1-4 and 168 K7-8) with those about Poland and the Scandinavian countries (below, 165 E8-166 F4 and *Methodus*, p. 264).

authority there must be, but whether it be acquired by descent, election, donation, legacy, or casting of lots is a matter of small moment to Bodin. Even the harshest tyranny, founded upon conquest alone, can become a legitimate monarchy through prescription. The reason for this indifference concerning the kind of title deed to authority may be found in his general purpose: he wished to justify not merely particular governments, nor even particular forms of government, but rather government in general, including even governments of unjust origin. His concern was the general problem of social order. Accordingly he wished to show that all sovereignty, regardless of its origin—with the one exception of outright and recent usurpation—had by its very existence a claim to the subjects' obedience.

The nature of this claim is nowhere developed systematically, perhaps because Bodin felt it to be obvious to contemporary readers. It rests on the double assumption, which was taken for granted by the sixteenth-century mind, of an ordered, divinely governed universe and of a close correspondence between the social order and the cosmic order. Beyond this philosophical foundation there were the obvious practical advantages of strong government, all of which suggested that if the ultimate choice had to be made, tyranny was preferable to anarchy. It was a choice to which not everyone today would assent, but in the France of Henry III it found many willing adherents.

This is not the place for a general critique of Bodin's theory, and still less is it appropriate to discuss here the later development of the concept of sovereignty. Yet it ought to be noted that in several respects later thought has not always followed Bodin's doctrine. In the first place, the theory of the mixed state has persisted tenaciously in the face of his rigid insistence that sovereignty is indivisible, and indeed it still constitutes the formal basis of parliamentary sovereignty in many countries. Secondly, there is nothing in Bodin's theory to enable him to explain a federal state, and his difficulties in analysing the Swiss Confederation serve to underline this weakness in his system. Finally, the whole notion of constitutionalism and limited government in the modern sense has developed as a direct challenge to the theory of absolute sovereignty. Bodin had encountered the problem of constitutional limitations in discussing the Polish constitution, and although he considered them most unwise, he was able to reconcile them juristically with sovereignty by considering them as a treaty or contract made binding upon the monarch at his election, a somewhat artificial solution at best. There is no doubt that a logical solution to these difficulties can be found, but to ask merely whether these later developments *can* be reconciled with the theory of sovereignty in its classic form is not enough. The main question that ought to be asked today is whether the theory of sovereignty, and the legal positivism that it entails, afford the most suitable basis for a theory of political authority. An answer to this question, which is one of the more difficult problems of modern legal theory, may well be postponed for another occasion. For the present it is sufficient to note that the problem itself was first posed clearly by Bodin's formulation of the theory of sovereignty, and that most discussion of political authority has revolved ever since about this framework that he propounded.

Almost as widely known as his concept of sovereignty is Bodin's theory of climate. The term itself is a misleading one, in that it suggests to us something far more limited than what he had in mind. For the theory of climate in his system is but one part of a wider theory of environmental influences which includes not only climate and geography but also astrology. The sixteenth-century mind believed firmly in a close interrelationship of the whole order of nature, and it never occurred to Bodin to doubt this widely received assumption. The philosophic basis of the theory was the Platonic notion of the "great chain of Being," a chain of causation running from God through the angels and heavenly bodies down to living beings and the smallest material objects, and affecting man in consequence of his corporeality.[30]

Such a doctrine prompted Bodin to look to both celestial and geographical forces as significant factors in the study of politics. In astrology, however, he is cautious. Though he never doubted the influence of the heavenly bodies upon the material world, and particularly their influence during planetary conjunctions, he was deeply impressed with the contradictions he found among other writers and with the difficulty of making significant generalizations on such matters. The influence of climate and geography on human physique and temperament was far easier to trace, and here he was able to find many parallels between national characteristics and the physical environments in which they were found. But while Bodin's theory of climate is now remembered as an important contribution to political thought, his astrological observations, which were as highly esteemed by many of his contemporaries, and also the cosmological assumptions upon which both were founded, have been discarded today as mere picturesque beliefs of a bygone age.

The theory of climate, then, is built upon intellectual foundations which were very generally held at the time, and indeed the notion that climate affects temperament has roots in both classical and medieval thought. But Bodin was an innovator in two main respects. In the first place, he had far more sources to draw upon, and he used them more perceptively than did his predecessors. The voyages of discovery, the accounts of the new lands, and the multiplication of topographical and travel literature which accompanied the popularization of printing, all provided new materials with which to verify, modify, or reject the more restricted generalizations of earlier writers. Bodin used this new literature extensively, and he was not afraid to go against time-honored beliefs when his evidence warranted a modified theoretical framework. In the second place, he approached his subject as a social theorist, frankly concerned with the political implications of man's environment. Essentially his interest lay in group characteristics rather than individual differences. In considering the heavens he ignored individual nativities and sought to determine which planets predominated over entire zones of the earth; likewise in examining human temperament he disregarded individual variations and concentrated upon those general regional

[30] Note the reference to this concept at 436 K7.

characteristics which might be traced directly to the physical environment. It was essential, in Bodin's view, for men to be thoroughly conversant with these elements of national character, for it was axiomatic that successful human laws had to be framed in close harmony with the laws of the physical universe. The theory of climate, as elaborated in the *République*, was intended to teach a ruler what was appropriate to the particular nation that he governed and what was plainly unachievable; clearly ignorance of such fundamental knowledge would lead straight to disaster.

There was one apparent consequence of the climate theory which Bodin tried to avoid: that human actions were in any sense necessarily determined by environmental factors. The problem had been a familiar one to medieval theologians. Bodin followed orthodox opinion in asserting, vigorously and rather dogmatically, the doctrine of free will, possibly as an echo of his youthful philosophical and theological studies with the Carmelites. But it must be pointed out that he did not attempt seriously to reconcile this blunt assertion with his belief in the influence of climate, of geography, of planetary movements, and even of numbers, upon the course of human history. The traditional solution to the problem lay in maintaining a clear distinction between body and soul. The body, because of its corporeal nature, was subject to these natural influences, whereas the soul was incorporeal and therefore free. Provided that reason predominates over the appetites, man can overcome his natural physical inclinations. But Bodin appears to have felt that in the long run, and for large groups of men, this freedom was far from complete. Though he insisted, for the sake of consistency, that climate produces only tendencies and inclinations of various kinds, and that nature could be overcome by discipline and training, it is clear that by the time he wrote the *République* he was thoroughly convinced that the natural tendencies of a people are strong forces to be reckoned with— stronger, under most circumstances, than the uncertain vacillations of the human will. And hence a knowledge of these forces is of particular advantage to the political scientist, because the human will is variable and unpredictable, while the natural forces which help to shape man's history are constant and intelligible.

Bodin did not systematically relate the theory of climate to his theory of sovereignty and his classification of states, but its impact on this part of his thought may be clearly seen. The theory of climate served as a strong conservative force, depriving his political theory of its otherwise revolutionary implications. Bodin had a strong preference for the monarchical form of government, but he did not advocate its indiscriminate export. The best form absolutely is not necessarily the best form for particular situations, and some peoples were plainly unfitted for a constitution on the French model. The whole tenor of the theory of climate was to justify existing forms of government, to promote broad tolerance for the world as it is, and to cast doubt upon the wisdom of deliberate political change. Bodin is very close to Burke in his attitude towards social innovation, and this accounts for his tendency to disguise what is revolutionary in his interpretation of the French monarchy under the venerable robes of constitutional tradition.

INTRODUCTION

If the concept of sovereignty and the theory of climate are the two contributions for which Bodin is chiefly remembered today, the *République* contains in addition a veritable treasury of materials on other topics, the wealth of which can barely be indicated here. Its chapters on the family and the concept of paternal authority, on slavery, on associations, on the orders or classes of citizens, and on censorship are sufficient to give a thorough treatment of social structure. Its several chapters on magistrates, officers, and commissioners examine in detail the organization of administrative power. The chapter on the problem of factions in the state is deservedly remembered for its forthright plea for religious toleration as a remedy for the ills of France. Its analysis of revolutions and political change does not stop at speculation concerning the stars and the force of numbers but treats with a sure hand the more immediate and practical causes of revolutions. The two chapters on alliances and protection reveal a close familiarity with contemporary diplomacy and diplomatic correspondence, while the chapters on finance and coinage show that Bodin also had free access to strategically placed financial officials. The chapter on military training and fortification, almost an essential item in any sixteenth-century treatise on politics, is by contrast somewhat perfunctory, though not entirely negligible. Yet all these topics, as well as a number of other questions of a rather ephemeral nature, are treated generously and even profusely, for it was Bodin's intention to write nothing less than a complete textbook of politics, to explore every possible aspect of the science of governing men. And in the scope of his inquiry at least he came very near to achieving his aim.

Yet the *République* is much more than a mere agglomeration of political data. In attempting this massive work Bodin appears to have had a clear appreciation of the general problem of sixteenth-century thought. The great medieval efforts at a synthesis of all knowledge had suddenly been rendered inadequate by the unfolding of Renaissance civilization. Both the geographical discoveries and the findings of classical scholarship revealed a world far more complex and variegated than that known to medieval man. When the religious question added a further element of disunity, the strain proved too great, and the resultant breakdown of traditional values was acutely felt by a generation accustomed to thinking in comfortable terms of unity, order, and harmony. Bodin took up this problem and set out to fashion new intellectual foundations to replace the older and narrower ones which men now found insufficient to explain the world they knew.

I have shown how the first part of his answer—that dealing with social and political questions—was embodied in his scheme for a system of universal law. For some years after the completion of the *Methodus*, this project appears to have been shelved, and when Bodin returned to his literary labors it was to write the *République*. Now this work, as noted above, was very closely affected by the current political situation and by Bodin's own precarious position at the time of writing it, but despite its intense topicality it attempts to carry out the earlier scheme, at least insofar as public law is concerned. What mattered above all was to develop a theory of politics general enough to assimilate and explain all the data which the new discoveries had revealed. Behind the *République*, therefore, lies an attempt at a new and a wider synthesis, comparable in its aim with the earlier systems of Aristotle and St. Thomas Aquinas. The project was an ambitious one, and it is not difficult to find conflicts within the framework which Bodin constructed. But it is the design itself rather than his failure to achieve it that should be noted, for without some understanding of Bodin's general aim the reader can hardly appreciate the structure and organization of the *République*.

Closely linked with this general aim is his method of executing his design. Few major writers have been more severely criticized in modern times for their organization of material and their literary style. In the eighteenth century Bodin's doctrines were still highly esteemed, but the *République* was considered virtually unreadable, and adaptations were made to suit the changing fashion in literary taste.[31] In the twentieth century, references to Bodin's ideas remain surprisingly numerous in several different academic fields, but the scholar who has actually read the *République* is rare indeed. This failure to read the original text explains why there have grown up around the work certain stock criticisms, which portray it as a vast and formless chaos of undigested material, as a display of erudition and pedantry that all but submerges its positive contributions, as a dull and ponderous volume unrelieved by any ornaments of style or sprightliness. Admittedly the *République* is by no means light reading, but much of this criticism is simply ill-informed, in that it ignores completely the canons of style and organization that Bodin sought to follow. No doubt we are entitled, if we wish, to judge an author by any standards of literary taste that we may choose, but a balanced judgment of his achievement demands some understanding of the intellectual milieu in which he lived and wrote.

Bodin's youthful contacts with the revolutionary movement in philosophy initiated by Peter Ramus in the 1540's have already been mentioned. Closer study of Bodin's work will reveal many points of contact with Ramist doctrines. In particular the new techniques of logic left their imprint on the *République* and on several of his other works. What were these techniques? Very briefly, Ramus aimed at a simplification of teaching methods to enable students to digest the traditional academic disciplines at an earlier age. In place of the rather complex Aristotelian logic he set up an alternative technique, known as invention, that was alleged to be applicable to any subject whatsoever. The order of treatment was standardized: first, a general definition of the subject as a whole; then a division of the subject into parts, wherever possible by a dichotomy which neatly split the subject into two logically distinct parts. With the parts so obtained the process was repeated until it could go no further. The sequence ran always from the most general concept down to the smallest and least important details. Another part of the logic, known as *methodus*, indicated the best arrangement of the unorganized data of a subject when

---

[31] These adaptations are listed below in Appendix C.

these were to be treated systematically.³²

Now the *République*, it will be noticed, conforms to this pattern. It begins with a definition of the subject to be discussed, the Commonweal, and the remainder of the first book is an elaborate discussion of the terms of this definition. The second book divides Commonweals into three types and then defines, analyses, and subdivides each of these types. The third book examines what Bodin considered to be the component parts of the state: deliberative bodies, magistracies of all kinds, associations, and orders of citizenry. In the remaining three books the Ramist pattern is less visible and the topics discussed are more heterogeneous, perhaps because the troubled circumstances of composition intruded upon an orderly execution of the design. Still it is not easy to suggest how the extremely diverse topics included in these last three books could have been organized more coherently within the framework developed by Ramus.

The Ramist logic was not without its weaknesses. In particular the process for formulating the first general definitions was never clearly explained. Once they were formulated one proceeded by deduction from general concepts to details and to concrete examples. The test of a good conceptual framework was whether all the examples and concrete data would fall naturally and easily into their appropriate place in the scheme, like the pieces of a jigsaw puzzle. For this reason Ramists had an intense, practical interest in the everyday world; there, they felt, was the only place where logical concepts could be verified or proved false. Nevertheless their method was not based on genuine induction from the raw data.³³ In practice there was always a tendency for the framework, once established, to distort the presentation of the supporting data. This point can be illustrated by Bodin's concept of sovereignty, which is developed so rigidly that the data for certain countries are simply forced into the pattern. But elsewhere, as a comparison of the French and Latin versions will show, he occasionally recognizes the virtues of flexibility and modifies his conceptual framework to accommodate new examples. It is probably the Ramist concern for the everyday world that explains his willingness to sacrifice logical consistency in order to arrive at a political system closely in touch with constitutional realities.

It is against this background of Ramist method that we ought to judge the criticisms that have been advanced against the organization and style of the *République*. I have shown that the general plan of the work follows a Ramist pattern, and that its defects are to a considerable extent those of the Ramist system generally. It follows that Bodin's almost overwhelming proliferation of examples is not simply vain pedantry; rather it is an essential part of the development of his theory—the verification, according to Ramist principles, of his conceptual framework. This preoccupation with examples

---

³² There is a more detailed description of these operations in my article cited above, which gives further readings on Ramism and traces its considerably stronger influence on Bodin's earlier writings. To the references on Ramism given there should now be added Father W. J. Ong's two masterly volumes, *Ramus, Method, and the Decay of Dialogue* and *Ramus and Talon Inventory* (Cambridge, Mass., 1958).

³³ In fairness it should be noted that Ramus developed his logic as a teaching device, for the specific purpose of imparting knowledge rather than discovering it.

explains his rather peculiar use of sources. Because his main interest is in concrete data, in actual examples of the laws and customs of all peoples and all ages, he depends heavily upon the historians, for history is the storehouse of such examples. Even when he draws upon previous writers on politics, such as Plato, Aristotle, or Cicero, it is more often to cite facts reported by them than to support his argument with their authority. There is a similar reason for Bodin's rather pedestrian style. Ramists valued simplicity and plain exposition and had a deep distrust of ornament and complexity. As they emphasized repeatedly, they were less interested in "words" than in "things," the objective entities for which words were mere symbols. To those who are irritated by Bodin's didactic and straightforward exposition one can only point out that in all likelihood he was trained to cultivate just such a style during his early years in Paris.[34]

Bodin's indebtedness to Ramism does not stop here. Undoubtedly it was from the Ramists that Bodin acquired his dislike of Utopian theorizing in politics, a prejudice which comes out strongly in his criticisms of Plato's *Republic* and More's *Utopia*. Doubtless too it was they who fostered his distaste for academic subtleties and for the philological minutiae of humanist scholarship, as being too remote from the practical questions of the day. Even more obviously his rather carping criticism of Aristotle suggests their influence. Ramus himself had begun his career by sustaining the audacious thesis that "whatever had been said by Aristotle was false." In maturity he continued, but in a more moderate tone, his attacks upon the Aristotelian tradition as the focal point of all that he despised; yet he himself remained close to this tradition, and his own system was little more than a reformulation of it. Bodin shares this same ambivalent position. Frequently he cites Aristotle's definitions only to emphasize his disagreement with them, but in many other respects the *République* borrows heavily from the *Politics*, often without acknowledgment. All in all, it owes more to the *Politics* than to any other source, with the possible exception of the *Corpus juris civilis*, and Bodin's ingratitude towards Aristotle is one of the clearest indications of his Ramist outlook.[35]

Though Ramism was later to degenerate into a narrower and more rigid formalism than that of the Aristotelianism which it was intended to replace, in its earlier stages at least it had one outstanding merit. Its stress upon simplicity, directness, and practicality; its insistence that knowledge is for use rather than for the scholar's study; its emphasis on the experience of the everyday world as the only test of the value of a system—all these factors enabled it to break away sharply from a deep-rooted but decadent academic tradition. In intellectual history the demolition of the old and outworn is often far more difficult than its replacement with something new. Generally a sharp shock is needed to topple the old structure. Ramism provided this

[34] Cf. his remarks on style in the Preface to the Latin version (Appendix A, section III), his criticism of eloquence and rhetoric (271 B5–C8 and 543 D1–544 H9), and his jibe at those who pursue mere words (450 K5–6).

[35] Yet it would be incorrect, I believe, to classify him as a disciple or follower of Ramus. Rather he was profoundly and perhaps even unconsciously influenced by the Ramist movement, as were many of his generation, because it provided a basis and stimulus for his own intellectual development.

shock, and in doing so it helped Bodin enormously. It taught him—though in practice he was occasionally forgetful of the lesson—to mistrust even the most respected authorities and to seek for the truth in the data of man's experience. It provided new techniques to simplify the handling of these data. It may even have suggested to his perceptive mind the original plan for his system of universal law, a scheme which has some striking resemblances to Ramist efforts to systematize other disciplines. And finally its very brashness and audacity helped to give him the confidence that a man of the sixteenth century, in a country still deeply conscious of the medieval intellectual tradition, could deliberately turn his back upon the past in order to produce something better.

It is only when we understand the *République* in this context of intellectual revolution that we can appreciate the extraordinary impact it had upon the first generation of readers. To many of them Bodin appeared first and foremost as the author of a magistral treatise on systematic politics, worthy to be compared with Aristotle, and even superior to Aristotle in that he had gathered the fruits of a further two thousand years of political experience and had reached conclusions more in keeping with the structure of sixteenth-century society.[36] Similar treatises on systematic politics followed soon after the *République*, notably those of Peter Gregorius of Toulouse and Joannes Althusius, but none attained either the reputation or the number of editions of Bodin's great work. What seems to have appealed to readers was that it had just the requisite qualities for a great synthesis: comprehensiveness, balance, erudition, brilliant insight, and the practical good sense that comes only from experience in public life. Even today, if we read the *République* with sufficient care and due reflection, we can appreciate the exceptional breadth of mind which so commended Bodin to his contemporaries. We can even share their feeling, if we make the effort to think in their terms, that it is the grandeur of the synthesis itself even more than the treatment of its component parts, which is his greatest intellectual achievement. Today, of course, we feel differently. But if Bodin is now remembered primarily for certain basic ideas on sovereignty, climate, and a few other topics, this is largely because political systems seldom outlive the generation that gives them birth, whereas some individual political concepts exhibit an astonishing vitality.

[36] Cf. Knolles's own estimate in his prefatory remarks.

III. THE FRENCH AND LATIN VERSIONS OF THE *RÉPUBLIQUE*

Serious study of the *République* is complicated by the existence of two versions of the text, both written by Bodin, published ten years apart, and differing substantially one from the other. As already noted, the Latin version of 1586 is not a direct translation from any one of the French editions. From time to time the arrangement of a topic is changed, sometimes quite drastically. Frequently new material is added, as we might well expect, but then other passages disappear altogether. Some topics are greatly expanded, but others are just as obviously condensed. The process of revision had been going on from the start in the successive French editions, but there the changes were confined to straightforward additions, substitutions of a word or a phrase, and occasional deletions—changes which could be written upon the printed page of the preceding edition. Translation into Latin necessitated a complete rewriting of the text and enabled subtle changes in emphasis which piecemeal alteration of the French text could never have achieved. Bodin availed himself fully of the opportunity, and there are few sentences in the entire work which do not show at least some nuance of difference from the corresponding part of the earlier version. Rather than a translation, the Latin version represents a complete redrafting and a rewriting of the French text. It is obvious, therefore, that comparison of the two versions will throw a great deal of light upon the development of Bodin's thought during the most active period of his public life. Even where his ideas remain basically unchanged the Latin version helps to clarify his original meaning by offering an alternative reading. Hence it is important—and doubly so in this present edition, which by combining the French and Latin versions necessarily obscures the variations between them—to describe these differences clearly and to indicate wherever possible the reasons underlying them.

Much had happened to Bodin between the writing of the two versions. He had married and fathered a family. He had written the *Démonomanie des sorciers*. He had visited England. He had participated in Alençon's ill-starred venture in Flanders, right down to the miserable debacle at Antwerp. He had become embittered at the policy of Queen Elizabeth and disillusioned with King Henry III. Above all there was the change in his own career. When he wrote the French version he was a rising advocate, with a considerable reputation and a ready access to the highest circles of royal administration, acutely sensitive to the delicate interplay of factions within the court, and probably closely implicated in them himself. When he touches on these areas he writes cautiously, discreetly, guardedly, so as not to jeopardize his own career. A decade later his own career had been shattered by the premature death of Alençon, and he was too old to begin anew. His unsought retirement to Laon gave him a freedom and detachment from contemporary events which he had not possessed earlier, and he used it to speak out more forcefully against abuses and malpractices at court, and against certain episodes in French history which showed the Crown in a less than favorable light. Retirement also brought leisure, with time to reflect upon his earlier conclusions, to revise and rephrase, to seek a better balance and proportion, to add to the Latin version what the French had omitted through haste or carelessness. The Latin version was Bodin's final treatise on political and social questions, and when viewed against the vicissitudes of his career and the events he had witnessed since 1576, what is surprising is the relative constancy of his doctrines. We ought to marvel that the differences between the two versions are no greater than they actually are.

Many of the differences fall into sharply defined categories. In the first place, there are certain changes in the order and arrangement of material. Bodin himself mentions these structural changes in his preface to the Latin version, and it is clear from his description of them that his main concern is with improving the scheme of divisions and classifications along Ramist lines.[37] Examples of these attempts at better classification may be seen in his discussions of the various types of slaves[38] and of the feudal hierarchy,[39] and perhaps best of all in the summary of the various kinds of public authority, which is very obviously grouped in Ramist dichotomies.[40] Similarly there are some transfers of illustrative material from one chapter to another in the interests of a more orderly presentation.

More important are his efforts in the Latin version to broaden and generalize his conclusions. For example where the French version will often discuss a topic with reference to monarchy only, the Latin will examine its implications for aristocracies and democracies as well; where the French will discuss a topic in terms of French practice alone, the Latin will frequently suggest a rule applicable to all countries. The horizons of the inquiry are perceptibly widened, and it is Bodin the political theorist who tends to replace Bodin the defender of the French monarchy. But these revisions concern minor matters only, and they do not significantly alter the general balance of the work.

On the other hand the Latin is not in all respects superior to the French in its organization. Bodin had much to add to his previous version, and the additions do not always fit into his previously established patterns. However he was too honest to distort or suppress the evidence to suit the framework, and in consequence the easy symmetry of the earlier version is occasionally broken beyond repair by the rugged intractability of new data. Moreover, the Latin reveals a tendency to anticipate and summarize topics that clearly belong later in the discussion and so is more repetitious than the French. The tendency is less evident in the English version because Knolles omits quite a few of the repetitions. Accordingly when these defects are balanced against the rather limited improvements of the Latin version, there is little to choose, from the standpoint of organization, between the earlier and the later text.

Some of the differences between the two versions arise from differences between the French and Latin languages as media of expression. Bodin wrote both with equal fluency, but they were not equally suitable to all the topics that he wished to discuss. His French is simple, direct, unpretentious, and remarkably flexible, though his sentences are rather too loosely constructed for real clarity of expression or precise translation. His Latin is classical, and the vocabulary and syntax, if not the style, are generally Ciceronian. He shunned barbarisms himself and condemned them in others. His own lapses are very few indeed, and when he is forced to use a medieval term, he generally does so somewhat apologetically.[41] For most purposes classical Latin was flexible enough, but in discussing special topics, such as feudal rights, or legal procedure before the Parlement of Paris, he

[37] See below, Appendix A, section III.
[38] See note at 32 H1.
[39] See note at 115 A9.
[40] See note at 309 A8.
[41] See, for example, the note at 278 G8.

carefully avoided even widely accepted terms like *homagium* or *arrestum* in favor of a purer but less meaningful classical vocabulary. Sometimes he even resorts to awkward circumlocutions to preserve purity of language. On specialized topics of this sort the French version is more natural and more intelligible. On the other hand Latin, as the established language of the academic disciplines, was more adaptable than French to the treatment of philosophical questions. The greater incidence of the terminology of formal logic in the Latin version is undoubtedly due at least in part to differences between the two languages themselves.

Translation into Latin also created a problem concerning the handling of sources, particularly classical sources. In the French version Bodin had often been content to summarize or paraphrase his authorities, but to retranslate these approximations back to the original language was clearly unsatisfactory. Accordingly he went back to his original sources—or possibly to notes taken verbatim from them—for a great many of the classical quotations which appear in the Latin version. While doing so he often uncovered and incorporated further illustrations drawn from the same authorities. Thus in general his use of Latin and Greek sources is both more accurate and more copious in the later version. However he occasionally neglects this precaution, forgets the context of his original illustration, and errs in his translation.[42]

Other changes in the Latin version may be ascribed to the nature of the audience to which it was addressed. In the French version Bodin was writing expressly for his own compatriots, and particularly for the French nobility, at a time of acute national crisis. Ten years later, with the crisis apparently receding, he was addressing a European audience, more cosmopolitan in its outlook and more scholarly in its interests than the relatively broad section of French society that he had hoped to reach with the French version. It was, by any standards, a learned audience, and if Bodin took special pains to improve his scholarship and precision, it was to win a favorable reception from this more critical circle of readers. His stubborn nationalism remained sufficiently in evidence to irritate the English, the Germans, and others, but in the Latin version it is a less strident nationalism, more moderate in its claims, more urbane in its expression.

He made a genuine attempt to accommodate the new version to the foreigner's point of view. I have already noted that in the later version he attempted to generalize, to reach universal rules of political behavior, at points where formerly he had been concerned only with constitutional practice in France. Correspondingly, numerous passages dealing with specific French institutions, whether judicial, financial, or military, were either greatly condensed or omitted altogether in the Latin, as being of slight interest for the foreign reader. Even the units of coinage, weights, and measures were converted in translation from current French standards to the most appropriate international standards known to the sixteenth century, those of classical Rome. But this experiment was an unfortunate one, for there are so many serious discrepancies between

---

[42] Most of these slips are avoided in the English translation, but for a typical one see the note at 422 F10.

the French and Latin figures that it is often quite impossible to say which is to be taken as the more authoritative. All these changes, however, were undertaken in order to produce a general study of politics which would be applicable to all countries, and the faults in execution should not blind us to the merits of Bodin's plan.

Perhaps the most important change in the Latin edition is the direct addition of extra material, ranging all the way from short phrases and individual items in lists to sentences, extensive passages, and even an entire chapter.[43] These additions are very numerous, and the point needs special emphasis here because Knolles automatically incorporated the vast majority of them in his translation without any special indication of the fact. Hence only those which Knolles omitted are to be found in the notes to the present text. To what sources may these additions be attributed? Some of them were clearly suggested by Bodin's experiences in England and the Low Countries in the interval between publication of the two versions. Rather more were the product of his intellectual development over the same period, of his further reading, and perhaps of his more mature reflection on what he had read earlier. A number of others are simply a restatement of matters discussed in his other writings of this period, in the *Juris universi distributio* (1578), in the *Démonomanie* (1580), and in the *Apologie de René Herpin* (1581). All these additions together are the measure of his development after 1576. But even the *Methodus*, written almost twenty years earlier, was not forgotten as he rewrote his greatest treatise. Some of the most extensive additions are taken with very little change directly from the *Methodus*, even though they had been omitted—either accidentally or deliberately—during the first writing of the *République*. The Latin version, then, represents a careful and deliberate assembly of all the material on politics that Bodin had used in his previous works, and as such it has an authority and a completeness that we cannot afford to ignore.

But what is the subject matter of these additions in the Latin version? Generalization is difficult because the additions touch on a wide range of topics, but in some areas they are particularly conspicuous. First, the theory of climate is overhauled and very appreciably expanded. New examples are added, and new environmental influences are suggested.[44] Secondly, there are philological and critical digressions which give Bodin's views on some of the disputed questions of contemporary humanist scholarship, passages of scant importance for the study of his political ideas. Finally, the appearance in the Latin version of certain passages concerning God, providence, divine vengeance, and freedom of the will clearly indicates the growing interest in philosophical and religious questions that was characteristic of his later years. On the other hand, some areas of his thought reveal no appreciable additions, no major changes, and no significant development from the French to the Latin version. A comparison of these respective areas of change and continuity in the *République* suggests that Bodin's political doctrines in the narrow, orthodox sense—his conceptions of state and sovereignty, of types of states and governments, of magis-

[43] Chapter 8 of Book III appears for the first time in the Latin version.
[44] Some idea of the extent of these additions may be seen from the notes to Book V, chapter 1.

tracies, and his attitudes towards most questions of public policy—were relatively stable between 1576 and 1586. It is what we might now consider the fringe areas of political studies—his theory of climate, his cosmology, his philosophy of history, and his religious views—that were changing and developing during these years. Nor should this surprise us, for these are the subjects towards which his thoughts increasingly turned during the final decade of his life.

If the addition of new materials is important, one must not overlook certain outright changes in political doctrines that occur in the Latin version. I have stated that a very high proportion of the text was recast as it was translated, but it is well to remember that not all these revisions represent a changed point of view. Often the result is merely a clarification, or a neater and happier phrasing, of the original idea. Occasionally, however, there is a clear and significant change of doctrine. Not many of these changes directly affect Bodin's political thought, but a few are important enough to merit specific mention. For example, in explaining the concept of citizenship, the French text insists that the obligation of subject and sovereign is a reciprocal one, analogous to that between a vassal and his lord. In the Latin this idea of mutual obligation all but disappears.[45] There is also a change concerning the right to resist tyrannical authority. When a king plays the tyrant the French version allows intervention by a foreign prince to check his course; the Latin goes significantly further and allows active resistance by any foreigner, whether prince or private man—by anyone, that is, except the subjects themselves, for whom the person of the sovereign must remain inviolable.[46] The Latin version takes a harsher view of the sharing of sovereignty between prince and people, probably because of Bodin's unhappy experiences in the Netherlands. While the French version is prepared to classify this shared power as a democratic form of government, the Latin views it as mere anarchy.[47] The Latin version modifies somewhat Bodin's earlier insistence that only the Estates could authorize special grants to the Crown in time of need, a position logically inconsistent with his view that the Estates were a purely advisory body. What had been alleged in the French version as a constitutional necessity becomes no more than a precept of wise policy.[48] Finally, the Latin version states more clearly than the French his developing belief that divine retribution will be the inevitable penalty of any ruler who flouts divine and natural law.[49] Clearly these are matters of political significance upon which Bodin had simply changed his mind as he grew older.

Among the more specific changes should be mentioned another group made in response to criticisms of the French version. These changes begin early. In 1577 there appeared at Geneva an unauthorized edition of the *République* which amended some of Bodin's statements concerning the constitution and foreign relations of that city by the simple expedient of altering his text. He criticized this action vigorously—and with justification—in a prefatory letter added to the 1578 and later editions, but

[45] To be precise, some vestiges of the idea remain, but it is emphasized far less than in the French version. See the notes at 58 H7 and 64 H5.
[46] See the note at 220 K1.
[47] See the notes at 185 D8 and 717 A7.
[48] See the note at 384 G7.
[49] See the note at 92 G3.

despite his condemnation of the practice he incorporated without acknowledgment some of the anonymous corrections into his own revised French text.[50] A similar situation arose before the Latin version was written. This time the critic was Auger Ferrier, a physician, mathematician, and astrologer, who had known Bodin personally during the latter's residence in Toulouse. Ferrier wrote a tract entitled *Advertissemens à M. Jean Bodin sur le quatriesme livre de sa Republique* (1580), in which he pointed out a number of errors in the work, chiefly on astronomical and mathematical calculations. His tone was friendly but patronizing, and Bodin, piqued by the criticism, devoted three quarters of his *Apologie de René Herpin pour la Republique de I. Bodin*, written the same year and published in 1581, to a spirited and sarcastic attack upon Ferrier. When he translated the *République* into Latin, however, he quietly accepted and incorporated in the text a surprising number of Ferrier's suggested emendations, including some that were clearly erroneous.[51] Study of the changes introduced into chapters 1 and 2 of Book IV suggests that Bodin respected Ferrier's judgment far more than he was prepared to admit, and that the effect of Ferrier's tract was to undermine seriously his confidence in his own earlier astronomical and chronological calculations. The Geneva edition and the Ferrier tract show that despite his ingratitude towards his critics Bodin was particularly sensitive to what he felt to be informed criticism of his work; we may therefore suppose that oral discussion and oral criticism played a similar role in bringing about other changes in the Latin version, even though we lack the evidence to prove it.

If there are changes on points of doctrine, there are some equally obvious changes in Bodin's attitude towards leading personalities. Perhaps the most interesting examples are his changed estimates of Queen Elizabeth and of Mary Queen of Scots. One can detect his altered feelings at several different points in the text. In the French version England's improvement in civility and courtesy is attributed to the rule of "a mild and peacefull princesse";[52] the Latin pointedly omits this flattering reference to the Queen. In the Latin, on the other hand, it is the Queen of Scots who is designated "most noble" (*clarissima*) and "most illustrious" (*illustrissima*), while the French omits any such compliment.[53] The French version merely notes without comment the fact of Elizabeth's imprisonment of her cousin; the Latin boldly expresses a wish for Mary's early release and restoration.[54] Shortly afterwards Bodin was forecasting Elizabeth's early overthrow in his private correspondence.[55] Clearly he had become embittered towards Elizabeth, and the reason is not far to seek. He held the Queen directly responsible for Alençon's failure in the Low Countries and thus indirectly for his own ruined career. Similarly he revised his opinion of Henry III, though he expressed his disappointment more guardedly. The French version salutes the new King as the restorer of peace and the

---

[50] See the notes at 50 F6 and 233 B3, and textual corrections at 265 A3 and 713 C5. For a change in the Latin version which is probably prompted by the Geneva edition, see the note at 225 B7.
[51] Such as his date for the fall of Constantinople. See the note at 443 C7.
[52] See below, 565 C4–5.
[53] See 454 I3 and the note at 751 C5.
[54] See the note at 229 D10.
[55] Letter to Castelnau, September 30, 1585, printed in R. Chauviré, *Jean Bodin, auteur de la République* (Paris, 1914), pp. 529–530.

savior of France;⁵⁶ the Latin quietly drops the entire sentence which contains this compliment. Disappointed in the King, disillusioned with Queen Elizabeth, and left unemployed by the death of Alençon, Bodin apparently looked to the Queen of Scots for his own and his family's advancement. This was his sole prospect for a further public career as he wrote the Latin version. But hardly a year after its publication even this distant hope was abruptly terminated by the executioner's axe.

I have postponed until the end the examination of certain rather abstract changes in Bodin's general outlook which are of the highest importance for his development as a political thinker. On turning from the French to the Latin version one becomes gradually aware of a greater concern for justice and a greater readiness to criticize injustice. The notion of a sharp distinction between just and unjust war recurs several times in the Latin, though it is barely mentioned in the French. The Latin reveals a stronger emphasis on humanitarian considerations, a sharper condemnation of acts of cruelty, and a distinct reluctance to judge issues solely from the standpoint of state policy. In short, Bodin's values were changing, slightly but perceptibly. He was moving from a Machiavellian realism which sometimes verges upon an insensitive brutality to a position in which he reacts vigorously against injustice wherever he finds it, even in the history of the French monarchy.

Examples of this enlarged concern for justice are numerous, for the tendency is a general one in the Latin version. However a few of the more striking instances will serve best to illustrate the change. The French version refers to the confiscation of the Templars' possessions by Philip IV without adverse comment; the Latin is sharply critical of the action.⁵⁷ The French discusses the sovereign's rights over wreckage cast on the seashore in the most detached, matter-of-fact terms; the Latin, departing from this objectivity, substitutes one of the strongest attacks upon injustice embodied in the law that Bodin ever wrote.⁵⁸ The French version states flatly that the sovereign has none of the responsibilities towards foreigners that he has towards his own subjects;⁵⁹ the Latin version qualifies this harsh conclusion and suggests that a sovereign may, if he is asked to act, have some responsibility even towards foreigners by virtue of the community of all mankind.⁶⁰ Similarly the Latin version recalls that the coronation oath of the German emperors specifically enjoins upon them the care and protection of foreigners, a point which the French version does not mention at all.⁶¹ Finally, the question of slavery is raised again. Even though slavery had already been criticized severely in the French version as unjust, cruel, and a constant source of danger to the state, the extra chapter which is added to the Latin version makes a further plea for compassionate treatment of slaves and for their inclusion, as human beings, within the body politic.⁶²

Along with this increased concern for justice we find the first, barely perceptible evidence of Bodin's disillusionment with the political system which he had so labored to construct. Apparently he was beginning to

⁵⁶ See below, 654 I9-10.
⁵⁷ See the note at 575 C9.
⁵⁸ See the note at 179 C8.
⁵⁹ See below, 58 H10-I1.
⁶⁰ See the note at 64 H5.
⁶¹ See the second note at 93 E1.
⁶² See below, 387 C1-388 F5.

doubt the basis of his system of universal law, the theoretical framework upon which the *Methodus* and the *République* are founded. The difficulty lay in his growing appreciation of the complexity of human affairs, of the endless variety and variability of political and social institutions. It is the added chapter in the Latin editions that provides the clearest illustrations. There are several matters, it points out, about which we cannot generalize because practice will vary significantly from one country to another. For example, no definition of nobility is common to every nation.[63] Similarly there is disagreement as to which occupations are to be accounted base.[64] Even the law of what is honest and what is dishonest, of what is useful and what is unprofitable is not everywhere the same.[65] Now the system of universal law assumed—and indeed required— at least certain basic uniformities in human behavior, for otherwise no results were possible. Yet it would seem that as Bodin wrote the Latin version he was beginning to entertain doubts on this very point. He was embarking here upon the road which marks the final stage of his intellectual development, the desertion of political studies for scientific and religious speculation. Already he was turning to disciplines whose principles could be universally valid, whose generalizations need not suffer from the unpredictable vagaries of human nature. His final view as to the possibility of a true social science is deeply pessimistic.

Yet more is involved here than mere negation and despair. The French version attempts basically to develop the principles of universal law through a study of the *legal rules* of all the countries for which Bodin could find information. In the Latin version his greater maturity enabled him to appreciate more clearly that bare legal regulations do not necessarily correspond to everyday realities. Between the French and the Latin, then, occurs a slight but discernible change in emphasis; the latter places less stress upon legal rules and rather more upon actual practice. There is a further point of some importance. Bodin's early belief had been that empirical formulation of his system of universal law would eventually reveal the best state,[66] that the laws of mankind, whatever their multiplicity, were interrelated by a common thread of justice, that comparative study of mere *leges* would ultimately uncover a true *jus*. But by the time that he wrote the Latin version of the *République* this hope was fading, and he saw more clearly the stark contrast between the ideal and the actual. Probably too he saw by now that the chasm between them was too wide to be bridged by any system of universal law. Both public and private laws, he admits rather despairingly in the added chapter in the Latin edition, rest mainly upon popular errors.[67] Later he adds a passage in the Latin which points out that certain moral precepts of the natural law are nowhere set down in human law and that many human laws, on the other hand, are unjust and pernicious.[68] The demise of his youthful optimism could hardly be more clearly expressed. It is no wonder that the Latin version, while probing more deeply into the political and social realities underlying the

[63] See below, 389 B5–10.
[64] See below, 397 B1–3.
[65] See below, 400 H1–2.
[66] Cf. *Methodus*, p. 2.
[67] See below, 396 H7–8.
[68] See the note at 644 H5.

legal façade, is also far more critical of what it finds.

In the final analysis one can distinguish three stages in Bodin's development as a social theorist. The first, represented by the *Methodus*, is dominated by the philosophical and constitutional ideals of his early years, acquired from his early education, from extensive reading, and from his colleagues at the Paris bar. Already he knew a great deal about the world around him, but this factual knowledge seems to have had relatively little immediate impact upon his social and political ideals, which somehow stand apart and which clearly had been formulated at an earlier date. The second stage is best represented by the French editions of the *République*. His primary concern now is with comparative law, and he remains optimistic regarding his projected political system. He is still working chiefly in the area of the normative, but the norms are now legal rather than ethical in character. At the same time his own experience in public affairs had given him a tough, Machiavellian realism which temporarily dulled his concern for absolute ethical standards. Political necessity is, as he well knew, a demanding master. With the Latin version of the *République* he embarked upon the third phase. In it he attempts to go behind even the legal norms and to study the bare political actualities underlying them. At the same time his reawakened concern for morality leads him to react more sharply against injustice and to draw a clearer line between the actual and the ideal. Once again he has become a moral philosopher. But in doing so he is now undermining the foundations of his system of universal law and thus opening the way for his eventual desertion of political inquiry altogether. We should remember, of course, that these three stages all belong to the thought of one man. For this reason they are far less distinct and separate than I have suggested here; much of Bodin's thought remained constant throughout his lifetime. But insofar as change did occur, these three stages mark out the general directions of his intellectual development.

Which of the two versions of the *République*, then, is the better, or the more authoritative? The question is bound to be asked, but it is fairly obvious from what has been said already that no simple answer can be given. The better French editions are clearly superior to all the Latin editions, which were never revised by Bodin personally, in their accuracy on points of detail, such as dates, figures, and even proper names; on the other hand, the Latin, being a later version, is generally better in its balance and sense of proportion. The French gives the impression of a simpler and more direct style; but the Latin is usually more meticulous in quoting authorities. The French draws a clearer and a more detailed picture of the contemporary problems of France; but the Latin gives evidence of a broader knowledge of comparative politics. The French is more directly inspired by Bodin's optimistic plan for a system of universal law; but the Latin brings a wider experience and a more mature judgment to bear upon a wide range of specific political problems. The French version exemplifies the hard realism of a rising man of affairs; the Latin displays a sympathetic humanitarianism and a lively sense of justice which testify eloquently to Bodin's changed outlook after his return from England

and Flanders. There are, finally, the passages added in the Latin and the passages deleted or condensed. What emerges clearly from any serious comparison between the two versions is that both are essential to the detailed study of Bodin's political thought. Most emphatically, neither can be ignored. But what is equally clear is that this situation poses a problem of formidable dimensions for any conscientious translator of the *République*, and it is to the question of translation that we shall now turn.

IV. THE ENGLISH EDITION OF 1606

It is the differences between Bodin's French and Latin versions that give to the English edition of 1606 its special value and that justify its reproduction here. For Richard Knolles, in making his translation—the only complete translation of the *République* into English ever to be made—worked from both of Bodin's versions, carefully fashioning from the French and the Latin together the best text that he could achieve.[69] In short, his translation stands as a work of independent judgment. No translator today could properly adopt this procedure, but it seems amply justified for a translation completed within a decade of Bodin's death. When we read the 1606 translation we read Bodin through the eyes of one of his younger contemporaries, and where variations arise, which of the two texts Knolles chose to follow is a matter of some significance. Knolles expresses his general aim clearly enough in his preface: he states that he "followed neither the one nor other copie alone, but the true sence of both together." But the matter is not quite so simple as this. In view of the differences between the French and Latin versions which I have already discussed, it is worth examining with some care just how he carried out his intentions, what special problems he encountered in doing so, and how far he succeeded in his aim.

As far as possible Knolles aimed at a genuine combination of the two versions, an interweaving of the two texts which would incorporate whatever appeared in the French only, or in the Latin only, into a continuous narrative. The most obvious result of this policy is that the English text is noticeably longer than either the French or the Latin. Where the two originals differed, Knolles attempted to strike a judicious balance between them. Where they could not be reconciled, he tried to follow the sounder and more appropriate version. In carrying out this policy he made some errors and sometimes deliberately omitted portions of the text, but the great bulk of his translation is faithfully and even meticulously executed. It is necessary to emphasize this point at once because some writers, misunderstanding his method, have criticized his translation as being too free.[70] Nothing could be farther from the truth. Knolles's translation is surprisingly literal, far more so than his own prefatory statement would suggest, but it follows both of Bodin's versions rather than one, and any fair assessment of it can be based only upon a triple comparison of the English, French,

[69] The German translation is also a combined one, but the Italian and Spanish editions are based on the French text alone. Cf. Appendix C below.

[70] See, for example, the misleading remarks of F. J. C. Hearnshaw, who apparently compared it with the Latin version only, in *Tudor Studies*, ed. R. W. Seton-Watson (London, 1924), p. 129.

and Latin. Admittedly the English version has its weaknesses, but these are largely confined within specific areas and even specific passages. Against these weaknesses may be set one important source of strength: in the substantial sections of the *République* which deal with sixteenth-century politics, Knolles moves with an ease and assurance which few present-day translators could match.

What Knolles has given us, then, is a text which is generally sound, perceptive, and solidly grounded upon both of Bodin's versions, but which is defective, for a variety of reasons which I shall examine, at certain specific points. Accordingly wherever his text does not meet modern standards of scholarly accuracy, it must be supplemented by notes. However once it is amended by means of notes and corrections based upon a new comparison of the English, French, and Latin versions, it can serve three distinct purposes. First, it can provide a more comprehensive and in many ways a better text of the *République* than any translation based either on the French or on the Latin text alone. Second, it can serve as a useful guide to the differences between the French and the Latin and consequently to the evolution of Bodin's thought during a critical decade. Finally it can show us how an Englishman of the late sixteenth century interpreted Bodin, and how the *République* was seen by those seventeenth-century Englishmen who read it in their native tongue. Of course it may be objected that any combined version is necessarily inferior to separate translations of the French and of the Latin. This can hardly be denied, but in answer it must be said that few scholars nowadays have either the leisure or the patience to make a full-scale comparison for themselves. Nor would it be worth their while. Even if separate English translations were presently available, a combined version would still serve a useful end.

But what are the weaknesses in Knolles's translation, and why do they arise? These are questions which deserve careful consideration. Most readers of a translation will never see the original, and they are entitled to be fully informed of the limitations of the version that they read.

The most serious defect of any translation lies in what it omits, if only because omissions can be effectively concealed. There are a fair number of omissions in the English edition, and they occur for a wide variety of reasons. In the first place, and most important by far, are a number of Bodin's opinions with which Knolles vigorously disagreed, opinions which aroused Knolles's sensitivities as an Englishman and as a son of Oxford. In a few of these cases where Bodin is particularly outspoken, any other course but deletion would have been imprudent. Secondly, there are a few remarks of Bodin's which are probably omitted because Knolles considered them sheer nonsense.[71] Thirdly, Knolles omitted many of Bodin's rather pedantic digressions into philology, etymology, mathematics, and scholarly controversy in general, which became more numerous with each revision of the *République*, presumably on the quite sensible ground that they detracted from the interest and forcefulness of the main argument. Fourthly, some omissions had to be made for technical reasons. At many

---

[71] See, for example, the note on the regeneration of mineral resources at 662 H3, and perhaps also the note at 7 B2 on the effects of lunar behavior.

points it was quite impossible to incorporate all the material from the French and the Latin in a single version. Some material is lost in the process of synthesis, especially where the Latin differs considerably from the French. Sometimes also misprints in the French or Latin editions obscured Bodin's meaning, and Knolles simply left out what he could not understand. Finally, some of the briefer omissions appear to be simple oversights on the part of the translator. To miss the occasional sentence or part of a sentence was all too easy when working from two texts simultaneously. Practically all of these omissions have been recorded in the notes to the present edition.[72] The vast majority have been translated in full. For the very few passages, mostly on philology or mathematics, where translation seemed a waste of space, there is in each instance a note to indicate the omission and its subject matter.

It is the first category of these omissions, those arising from outright disagreement, which we should examine more closely. The most important examples in this group are comments upon English affairs which either impinged too closely upon governmental policies or wounded English national pride. In a number of places Knolles felt compelled to omit Bodin's references to certain actions of the Crown and the government during the Tudor period, such as Henry VIII's condemnation of the Howards, the trial of Sir Thomas More, Elizabeth's imprisonment of Mary Queen of Scots, the condemnation of Edmund Campion and his fellow Catholics, and also his references to the problem of Elizabeth's successor.[73] There is again a whole sequence of omissions and modifications which Knolles introduced into Bodin's very forthright discussion of female rule.[74] The issue was a delicate one, and it is not difficult to understand Knolles's caution. Rather less dangerous, but still galling enough to provoke their exclusion, were a few of Bodin's remarks on English national character. In all probability it was outraged patriotism that led Knolles to delete rather unflattering references to the quarrelsomeness and inconstancy of the English.[75] There are a number of other remarks which Knolles probably omitted because he found them either dangerous or distasteful, but in some instances it is difficult to be sure of his motives.[76] It is only fair to add that these deletions constitute only a small fraction of Bodin's remarks on English life. Knolles resorted to this hidden form of censorship only when he considered that Bodin had clearly gone too far, and he translated a good many other comments on English history and English life, whether flattering or not, exactly as Bodin had written them.

A second area of flat disagreement concerns the broad philosophical outlook of the two men. Bodin, as I have indicated, was profoundly influenced by the Ramist movement, which shook the medieval university tradition to its foundations. Knolles, on the other hand, had been educated in Oxford, and was a product of the older tradition in its most conservative form. This background made him react vigorously against Bodin's

[72] For the minor exceptions, see Appendix D below.
[73] For the passages omitted, see the notes at 97 B10, 513 B8, 229 D10, 537 B2, 728 K6 and K9.
[74] These may be studied in the notes to pp. 746–751.
[75] See the notes at 565 C3 and 567 C7.
[76] See, for example, the remarks on Henry VIII's testament (note at 205 D1) and on testamentary rules in Britain (note at 784 H1).

constant animadversions upon Aristotle and Aristotelianism. Thus we find him omitting one of Bodin's specific criticisms of Aristotle altogether, switching from the French to the Latin version to avoid another, and suppressing in still another instance the illustration by which Bodin explains the basis of his disagreement.[77] Similarly he ignores some slighting remarks on scholastic arguments and scholastic methods which are in characteristic Ramist vein.[78] Part of the attack upon tradition is expressed obliquely, but Knolles is not deceived for a moment. Bodin's comment that the best and surest teacher is experience and his rather extreme praise for Plato—both typical of the new Ramist outlook—are quietly but deliberately dropped.[79] It is true that only a few incidental remarks are lost in this way, for where Bodin's disagreement with Aristotle is the focal point of his argument Knolles could hardly avoid expressing it. Yet even these minor omissions clearly demonstrate that Knolles's loyalty to the Aristotelian tradition was strong enough to interfere with his otherwise very fair presentation of Bodin's views.

Outside of these two general areas —English affairs and Aristotelianism —omissions which may clearly be ascribed to Knolles's personal outlook are extremely rare. One might cite his omission of a remark concerning papal attempts to stir up religious strife in Switzerland[80] and link this with his own desire, which I shall describe shortly, to work for the restoration of Christian unity. But examples of this sort are few, and in most cases we cannot be sure of Knolles's motives. The great majority of the omissions in the English text were apparently prompted by technical and literary considerations rather than by disagreements over doctrine. The bulk of the material lost in translation consisted of extra examples, references to authorities, short digressions, and the repetition of points made elsewhere in the work. Much of it is of secondary importance at best. Knolles's basic reason for omitting this type of material was his desire to make a straightforward, readable translation out of his divergent originals.

There might well have been more substantial omissions owing to differences of opinion and outlook had Knolles not possessed other means of reconciling Bodin's views with his own. In the first place, the existence of the two originals gave him some latitude in fashioning his own version. He could sometimes avoid an embarrassing point and find an unexceptionable way of stating Bodin's views by simply switching from one version to the other. Secondly, he could tone down the most extreme of Bodin's statements when a full-flavored translation would have invited trouble. He seldom resorted to this practice, but he did use it freely when Bodin discussed female rule in highly uncomplimentary fashion.[81] We may condemn a translator for taking liberties with his text, but we must remember the conditions under which he worked. In this case the only practical alternative was to delete the offending remarks altogether.

A third device lay in the marginal notes, which for the most part are of Knolles's own composition. The vast

[77] See the notes at 409 E5, 552 K5, and 782 F10.
[78] For an example, see the note at 450 K6.
[79] See the notes at 460 I5 and 484 K9.
[80] See the note at 77 E1.
[81] See the notes at 746 K9, 747 A10, 747 D6, 751 C2, and 754 G5.

majority of them merely summarize the argument of the text, but Knolles also used them on occasion to dissociate himself personally from Bodin's views even while translating and presenting them accurately. These marginal comments provided a useful element of flexibility. They enabled him to amend Bodin's errors without formally altering the text and to express freely his disapproval—and also to emphasize his approval—of specific points in the text.[82] The main areas of his dissent are those that I have already mentioned, feminine rule, English matters, and the authority of Aristotle, but a few new ones appear. Knolles criticizes Bodin's antipathy towards the Emperor Charles V, becomes exasperated by his nationalistic fervor, and seems irritated also by his bold criticism of authors other than Aristotle. In these marginalia we begin to sense the differences in the personalities of the two men. Bodin had little respect for authorities, but Knolles was a thoroughgoing traditionalist.

A second possible weakness in a translation lies in its mistakes. In one sense errors are less pardonable than omissions, for generally omissions are the result of deliberate policy, while errors are due to ignorance or carelessness. When we examine Knolles's work in detail we soon discover that many of his faults in translation relate to his special problem of combining the French and Latin versions. Structural and grammatical weaknesses seem to be far more numerous than mistranslations of the more conventional kind. Sometimes these are hardly the fault of Knolles, for the gulf between the French and the Latin is often wide enough to make a smoothly integrated narrative almost impossible. Sometimes, on the other hand, they appear to be the direct result of carelessness or haste. Knolles was a schoolmaster when he translated the *République*, and we may legitimately suppose that he was often pressed for time and that interruptions were frequent. Occasionally he slips so far as to translate the same point twice, first from one version and then from the other, as though two separate statements were involved. Not infrequently the structure of a sentence becomes hopelessly confused long before the end. Close study of his work suggests that Knolles did not reread his manuscript with care, that his revisions and additions to it were not always reconciled grammatically with the original draft, and that the printer was occasionally compelled to round out a sentence or supply his own punctuation, often with unfortunate results.

There are, of course, some errors in the actual translation of words and phrases, but they are not particularly numerous, and some of these errors are corrected in the later portions of the work.[83] Knolles scores quite well on this point, and one reason is fairly obvious. If the two separate French and Latin texts were a source of difficulty in other respects, they enabled him to reduce to a minimum his direct errors in translation because a great many of the unfamiliar terms appeared in both languages. It is no coincidence that a disproportionate number of his slips in translation occur

---

[82] Occasionally too he uses them to explain a concept or reference which he considers obscure or difficult for English readers.

[83] These do not need to be discussed here since they have been individually corrected in the notes to the text. For characteristic examples, see the remarks on *militia ex casu* (notes at 114 G7 and 395 B3), on *ressort* (note at 77 C1), on *remède* as a technical term in coining money (note at 688 I9), and on *le fonds* (note at 672 I3).

on matters which are dealt with in one of the original versions only. When we set the actual mistranslations against the vast bulk of the work itself, we must concede that Knolles achieves a high standard of accuracy in this aspect of his work.

However such a conclusion could hardly be suggested by a casual comparison of the 1606 edition with the French and Latin. At first reading the English text appears to be honeycombed with errors, but closer study will soon show quite conclusively that many of these apparent errors in translation were in fact mistakes made by the compositors in reading Knolles's manuscript.[84] It becomes quite evident that the text suffered many corruptions at the printers' hands, and it is equally clear that the proofs of the work were never read with any care by Knolles, nor, for that matter, by anyone else.

But this problem is to a large extent capable of solution. Although we do not have Knolles's manuscript of the text, there exists in the Bodleian Library a comparable sample of his handwriting in a translation which he made of William Camden's *Britannia*.[85] By experimenting a little with his handwriting and spelling as revealed in the *Britannia* manuscript, it is possible to restore, with the aid of Bodin's original texts and a little reflection, most of the original words and phrases which the typesetters misread.[86] Sometimes the reconstruction is so similar in appearance as to leave no doubt whatever of its accuracy. Sometimes it may be fully convincing to an editor familiar with Knolles's style, but not, perhaps, to his readers. Sometimes it must remain a conjecture.

Similarly, many minor slips by the compositors may be corrected with some confidence by a comparison of the English version with the originals. We can resolve the frequent confusion of singular and plural nouns, which in most cases must be the result of Knolles's tendency to write a small and rather indistinct final "s." We can rectify mistakes in numerals, which are frequent in all editions. We can amend faulty quotations and eliminate the more conventional typographical errors. Provided the French and Latin texts agree, minor corrections of this sort offer no difficulties. But where the English printed version omits something more substantial which was evidently in the manuscript, we can only guess at what Knolles actually wrote, guided by the French, the Latin, and Knolles's general style. There are several points where the compositors clearly missed as much as a whole line in the manuscript, and the reconstruction of these passages can be only an approximation.

Our general verdict on the compositors must be a harsh one. Their work was slipshod, and they took no great pains to detect their errors. Their rendering of French and Latin quotations, which—to judge again from the *Britannia* manuscript—must have been written in a fine, legible italic script quite different from Knolles's normal hand, is often

---

[84] In the notes below these misreadings of the manuscript have been grouped along with typographical errors under the general heading of "misprints."

[85] Ashmole MS. 849. A note by Sir Peter Manwood at the end of the section on England corroborates the handwriting: "Thus far Mr Knolles hys owne hand ..." The script in question, though small and at some points crowded, is fairly regular and relatively easy to read. I have found no trace of a manuscript of the *Six Bookes*; presumably it was destroyed when the printed version appeared.

[86] It would seem from some of the mistakes made that parts of the manuscript at least were read aloud by one compositor to another. For examples which rather suggest this, see the textual corrections at 110 G10 and 458 G7.

faulty in the extreme.[87] Even the printing is not of a very high standard. One is almost forced to the conclusion that the London printers of this period were inferior to their French and German counterparts in both technical proficiency and general knowledge.

But the French and Latin editions, in spite of their superiority, are themselves not wholly free from typographical faults, and these constitute a further source of errors in Knolles's translation. Far too frequently he was led astray by the corrupt text of one or another of the editions which he had before him.[88] Now a careful comparison of these errors with the variations in the various French and Latin editions will reveal which editions Knolles used in making his translation. Some of the evidence on this point, probably enough for the reader to reach his own conclusions, is presented below in the textual corrections and notes. But it should be remembered that there is far more evidence available than could be profitably retained in the critical apparatus. The bulk of it concerns points of little importance, such as marginal references, the spelling of names, and punctuation, and to include all of it would needlessly complicate the text.

When we examine the French text from this point of view, we find that very nearly the whole of Knolles's version is based upon the Lyon edition of 1593 printed by Barthélemy Vincent.[89] This edition has quite a few misprints which occur in no other edition, so that we may be quite sure of its identification. Misprints apart, however, it was a fortunate choice, for unlike several other editions of the same period it follows the text of earlier editions without deletions. Among other things its use shows that Knolles did not begin his translation before 1593. But here one must add a slight qualification. For a few pages—or perhaps even less—during the discussion of the rights of sovereignty Knolles quite definitely departs from this French text and reverts to one of the first four French editions, dating from 1576 or 1577. There is one short passage of four lines which could not possibly have been translated from any later edition, French or Latin.[90] Further traces of this (or possibly another) early edition can be detected at the very end of the work.[91] They are not very conclusive, but they do rule out one of the two folio editions of 1577, the one cited below as Fr 2. What had happened? Probably Knolles translated a few brief sections from another edition while away from home, perhaps on a visit to his patron, Sir Peter Manwood, or to Oxford, where the Bodleian Library had a copy of the 1576 French edition.[92] Whatever the explanation, his use of any French text other than the 1593 Vincent edition is confined to a few isolated pages.

The Latin version presents a more difficult problem. Unlike the French version, there are no substantial variations in the text of successive editions, and to all appearances it was never revised by Bodin himself. The

---

[87] Though sometimes Knolles himself fails to transcribe word for word.

[88] And perhaps also by paper faults or other defects found only in the copies from which he worked.

[89] Referred to in the textual corrections and notes as Fr 7. For a bibliography of editions and an explanation of their numbering, see Appendix C below.

[90] See the note at 180 H3.

[91] See the notes at 792 I3 and I4.

[92] The Bodleian copies of the first French and the first Latin editions are both listed in the Library's printed catalogue of 1605, and they still contain the shelf marks given in this catalogue.

evidence as to which edition Knolles used consists entirely of typographical differences and minor editorial changes by other hands. At first glance these variations are inconclusive, and even somewhat contradictory, but eventually a definite pattern does emerge. The evidence suggests that Knolles began to work from the first folio Latin edition of 1586 and that he used this edition continuously down to the end of the third book. One can see clear evidence of this particular edition in his translation of Book III, chapter 8, where the absence of any French text makes the comparison easier. Yet soon after the beginning of Book IV it becomes apparent that Knolles has switched to one of the later editions published in Germany, in which there are numerous minor revisions, by another editor, in spelling, in punctuation, and even in some marginal references. Closer study shows that the actual edition used was that of 1601, published at Ober Ursel (Ursellae) near Frankfurt.[93] Knolles appears to have worked from this edition for the whole of the remaining three books. It is just possible that the 1586 edition remained available to him for consultation on difficult points, but if so, he clearly preferred the German edition, perhaps for its careful editing, perhaps for its convenience and ease of handling. However no single French edition and no Latin edition could give Knolles the accurate text that he wanted. Even the best editions have textual errors which can only be eliminated by studying Bodin's intentions as expressed in the complicated sequence of editions from 1576 to 1586.[94] Because Knolles could not conveniently do this, his translation suffers accordingly.

So far we have been considering Knolles's translation in rather general terms. Now we may turn to a few of the special problems that he encountered in the *République*. For it is the degree of his success or failure in solving these problems that will determine to a very considerable extent not only our estimate of him as a translator, but also what sort of critical apparatus is appropriate to a new edition of his translation.

Perhaps the foremost of these problems was that of expressing in English the rather technical political and juridical concepts which Bodin was striving so hard to clarify. The task was complicated by divergences in phraseology between the French and the Latin and by Knolles's preference for a combined translation whenever he could find one. Thus Bodin's central concept of sovereignty, which usually appears simply as *souveraineté* in the French and *majestas* in the Latin, gives rise on occasion to such complicated and inexact phrases as "the majestie of absolute soveraigntie" in the English edition.[95] Again, Knolles applies the word "parliament" ambiguously to the *parlements* of France and to the meetings of the Estates General, so that only the context discloses which of these very different institutions is intended. For Bodin's term *république* or *respublica*, Knolles regularly uses the term "Commonweale" (or occasionally "Commonwealth"), but even here he is not wholly consistent. On a very few occasions he substitutes the word

---

[93] The first definite sign of his use of the 1601 edition appears in the textual correction at 430 H6. Probably the most conclusive evidence is in the correction at 529 D8.

[94] For the various stages in the evolution of the text, see Appendix C below.

[95] See the note at 101 A6. Many similar examples could be cited.

"state," thus using this word in its modern sense.[96]

Significantly, Knolles shows little aptitude for theoretical reasoning. He stands out primarily as an historian and a man of letters, concerned less with terminological precision than with literary effect. In general this creates no serious difficulties, for the bulk of the *République* is descriptive rather than closely analytical. But precision becomes important wherever Bodin attempts to define his basic political concepts, and at these points even the slightest variations between the French and Latin versions may be important. The English edition, combining as it does the French and Latin texts, is imprecise in its definition of concepts, but in its defense it should be urged that when a high degree of precision is required, no translation will ever suffice. Accordingly the present edition attempts to meet this problem by restating Bodin's principal definitions separately in their original form.[97] For only in the original languages can the reader get at the exact meaning of the basic concepts upon which the whole structure of the *République* is built.

Knolles shows a similar lack of precision in legal terminology. In part this springs from certain characteristic limitations of the English language. Because, for example, we cannot properly express in English the usual Continental distinction between *jus* and *lex*, between *droit* and *loi*, a translation cannot sufficiently emphasize Bodin's important point that *lex* or *loi* means purely and simply the command of the sovereign, stripped of all moral implications, while *jus* connotes something altogether different, a purely normative concept. In part, too, Knolles's imprecision springs from his unfamiliarity with Roman law, and especially with the procedural differences of French jurisprudence. On legal matters he remains a layman interpreting the work of a specialist, and even though he does so intelligently, his language and thought are not those of a lawyer. Finally, a part of Knolles's inexactitude may be attributed to his lack of interest. He has a tendency to omit or condense legal details pertaining solely to France and to disregard Bodin's references to his legal sources. Even the eulogy of the English common law in his dedication to Sir Peter Manwood serves mainly to emphasize his indifference to Roman-law jurisprudence in general.

Weights, measures, and monetary standards created further difficulties for Knolles. I have already mentioned Bodin's adoption of classical Roman units of measurement and coinage in his Latin version and the serious discrepancies that resulted from the conversion of his original figures. In a few instances Knolles followed the units given in the Latin, and with unhappy results.[98] Generally, however, he preferred to follow the French, which used units familiar to him and to his readers. But even here he was inconsistent, particularly on fiscal matters. Sometimes he gave a figure in the French unit, either *livres tournois* or crowns; elsewhere he converted to sterling equivalents at the rate of ten livres to the pound sterling, and often a reference back to

---

[96] For example, at 713 D8 and E6, 714 F1, 252 G2, 363 C10, and 376 G3. But generally he employs the term "state" in its more usual contemporary senses. The word itself has a complex history. See H. C. Dowdall, "The Word 'State,'" *Law Quarterly Review*, XXXIX (1923), 98–125.

[97] See below, Appendix B.

[98] Cf. the notes at 2 G10 and 217 D6, and the text at 37 E7.

the original is necessary to determine whether Knolles's unqualified term "pounds" means livres or sterling. If he took no special pains to clarify the bewildering variations in contemporary standards of coinage, weights, and measures, it was because his chief interest in the text lay in other directions.

Proper names are another problem. Knolles presents the major historical developments with a hand that seldom errs, but this grasp of general history does not save him from occasional slips in identifying personages and places, particularly the more obscure ones. This is especially true where misprints occur in the texts from which he worked.[99] Frequently too the spelling of names in seventeenth-century English differs widely from modern practice. The more puzzling of these variations are of course explained in the textual corrections, but where a footnote seemed unnecessary it is hoped that the index of proper names will dispel any lingering ambiguities.

Knolles faced yet another problem in translating Greek and Hebrew quotations. Since Bodin gave French or Latin equivalents for virtually all of them, it was not translation so much as accurate transcription that they required. Accuracy, however, was not attained; the English edition contains numerous errors in both Greek and Hebrew. It might be tempting to blame the printers for these, were it not that in at least one instance several elementary errors in Greek in the English edition are carried over directly from the 1586 Latin edition, the one which Knolles was using at the time.[100] Clearly Knolles simply copied the line, misprints and all. But the French gives a substantially correct version of the same line, and the only possible explanation is that Knolles's knowledge of Greek was so limited that he did not recognize the correct version of the two that were before him. Undoubtedly the printers were no better informed, or else they would have corrected some of the elementary errors in the manuscript. Similarly many of the Hebrew words and phrases are mistranscribed, but here it is not so easy to determine whether the fault lies with Knolles or with the printer. Lacking evidence to the contrary, we may fairly assume that Knolles's knowledge of Hebrew was no better than his manifestly negligible acquaintance with Greek.

Bodin's other quotations, particularly the Latin ones, create further difficulties. Frequently there are minor discrepancies between the French and Latin versions as to the wording of a quotation. Some of the Latin editions even differ among themselves as to where certain quotations end. Sometimes what is printed in italics as a quotation is in fact only a close paraphrase, and even the passages from classical authors that are quoted accurately frequently follow textual readings which have since been rejected or amended by modern scholarship. But Knolles virtually never went beyond Bodin's text to check the source of the quotation.[101] Probably not very many of these sources were available to him as he worked, and in any case to verify all or most of the quotations would have involved a prodigious amount of labor. In these circumstances it would

---

[99] For examples, see the note at 214 I10 and the textual correction at 346 I2.

[100] See below, 100 F1 and note.

[101] For an exception, see the biblical quotation at 455 A6–9, where Knolles substitutes an English prose translation for a French metrical one.

be quite unrealistic to expect Knolles to satisfy modern standards of scholarly accuracy in his handling of Bodin's quotations. All that we can reasonably expect of him is a faithful and accurate transcription of what he saw. The aim of the textual apparatus in the present edition, therefore, is to record the errors and omissions made by Knolles and the printers in reproducing the quotations as they appear in the *République*.[102] To do this properly requires attention to the significant discrepancies between the various French and Latin editions, but no systematic attempt is made to show the extent of Bodin's own departures from his sources when these are common to all editions of the *République*.

Closely allied to the preceding question is that of marginal references. On some pages of the French and Latin versions the margins are literally filled with closely printed notes which give the sources of Bodin's argument. Knolles omits a very large proportion of these in his edition, and he does so on a rather selective basis. He is most reliable on biblical references, though these are not invariably included. His weakest area—and Bodin's strongest—is that of Roman law and the medieval glosses upon it, but again not all of these juristic references are omitted.[103] The number retained in other areas falls somewhere between these extremes. To complicate matters further, many of those that are retained are erroneous, sometimes as a result of error by Knolles or his printers, more often as a result of misprints in the particular French and Latin editions from which they are copied.

What should be done concerning these marginal references? An early plan to incorporate them all in the present edition had to be abandoned. A great many of Bodin's references to sources are very general. Exact quotations, which can be verified fairly easily, are relatively few. The reference itself is usually phrased in the broadest terms, such as "Plut. in Lycurgo," or "Livius lib. 8," or "Fran. Alvarez en l'hist. d'Ethiopie." It would be of no great value to print these as they stand, and to trace them all would be a labor of many years. Besides, very few readers would have either the desire or the patience to unravel the complex web of influences which lies beneath Bodin's intellectual system. Finally, there are some sources and influences—particularly contemporary ones—which Bodin does not explicitly acknowledge, and merely to restore the omitted marginal references would give an incomplete picture. After careful consideration, therefore, it was decided that while faulty marginal references should be corrected, those which Knolles saw fit to exclude should not be inserted in the present edition.[104]

One more characteristic of the Knolles translation deserves special mention. This is the change in the quality of the translation itself that occurs at the beginning of Book V. Up to this point Knolles works

[102] At the very beginning Knolles adopted the policy of merely translating the quotations. From Book I, chapter 6, onwards, however, he usually gives both the original version and a translation.

[103] Possibly the printers are partly to blame once again. Only four marginal references to the Roman law itself are retained, and all of them are to be found in gatherings *Iii* to *Mmm* (pp. 637–684) which are printed in slightly larger type and presumably by another printer. This suggests that the manuscript may have contained more of these references, which were then deliberately omitted by the printers.

[104] I have in progress, however, a study of the sources of Bodin's thought as a whole, and I hope eventually to be able to list all the sources of the *République* when presenting the results of this study.

faithfully from both the French and the Latin texts, but the nine chapters which comprise Book V and the first half of Book VI are based very substantially upon the French version alone, and the corresponding Latin is virtually ignored. Where additions in the Latin text are noted at all, they are often summarized or condensed rather than translated fully.[105] Knolles's standard of accuracy slips perceptibly in these chapters. Instances of careless or abbreviated translation occur more frequently. The changed character of the translation calls for a considerable expansion of the textual notes upon these chapters, partly to give an accurate rendering of Bodin's thought, but chiefly to present the very substantial additions which occur in the Latin text of some of these chapters, additions which elsewhere in the work would have been incorporated in the English text.

What were the reasons underlying this abrupt change in Knolles's policy? Possibly he considered the subject matter of these later chapters less interesting and less worthy of the painstaking work of combination. Perhaps he was deterred by special difficulties. It is to be noted that the new policy begins with the famous chapter on the theory of climate, in which the wide gap between the French and Latin versions would make a combined version particularly difficult. More probably, however, the explanation lay in Knolles himself. He was already old, and he knew that his powers were declining. Probably failing eyesight contributed somewhat to the list of errors. Doubtless, too, after completing four books he was wearied by the sheer magnitude of his task. Other projects were awaiting completion, and time was short. The biographical evidence suggests that the principal reason for his changed technique was simply a desire to complete the project before he died. Better an imperfect book than none at all. Whatever the reason may have been, the quality of the translation changes once more in the final three chapters. In them Bodin returns once more to the major theme of the earlier books, and once again the English version is firmly grounded upon both the French and the Latin. The more exalted becomes Bodin's argument in his majestic final comparison of human and cosmic justice, the more meticulously and judiciously does Knolles weave together the two strands of the original text, sentence by sentence, word by word, so as to achieve in carefully selected English prose the fullest effect that his author's thought could be made to produce. One can sense that he was consciously striving here for an ending worthy of his vast undertaking, for it is in this final chapter that he shows to best advantage the fine literary craftsmanship of which he was capable.

This sketch of the English translation would be incomplete if it failed to consider the questions of language and style. It is evident that we must expect very considerable changes in these matters, particularly in the use of language, over the course of three and a half centuries. Many words in common use during Knolles's lifetime have become mere archaisms today. More important, many words current then and now have lost, or

[105] The change may be illustrated statistically. Book V constitutes 16.2 per cent of the total text in the French version, 16.7 per cent in the Latin version, but only 12.9 per cent in the English version. In general the more faithfully Knolles draws from both versions, the longer is the resulting translation.

have almost lost, their sixteenth-century meanings and have acquired entirely different significance in modern English. Of course the barrier of language is not insurmountable, nor even particularly formidable; we still read Shakespeare or Hobbes without serious hesitation as to their meaning. But it is well to remember that the barrier is there. If we read Hobbes easily today, it is partly because we are not constantly comparing his usage with ours through the measuring rod of another language. What really brings home the extent of the change in written English is to watch the conversion of the French and Latin texts into an unexpected and unfamiliar idiom.[106]

To compare Knolles's own usage with the standard English idiom of the period is obviously the task of a trained philologist. Yet certain tendencies are visible even to the non-specialist. The *Six Bookes* reveals certain Gallicisms and Latinisms which obviously spring from Knolles's habit of following the originals very closely. There are besides a few special usages, perhaps peculiar to Knolles alone, for which no adequate precedents can be found in the *Oxford English Dictionary*. Most of these peculiarities of language, however, remain concealed during a casual reading of the translation, and they emerge clearly only when the English usages are set against a background of the French and Latin equivalents. Some of the more interesting and unusual of these equivalents have been noted in the present edition, but limitations of space have made it impossible to do so on a very wide scale.

Of the broader question of style it is easier to speak. Bodin's own prose, while occasionally capable of a striking effect, is generally unemotional and unadorned. Undoubtedly it was deliberately so, for he clearly shared the Ramists' concern for "things" rather than mere "words." Knolles, however, brought to his writing a sense of craftsmanship, and he possessed a touch of artistry, a flair for the telling phrase, which is normally absent in Bodin. To some extent he could find expression for these stylistic aspirations without departing from the translator's function in the strictest sense, for his unusual task of combining the French and Latin originals gave him considerable latitude in the actual translation of a given idea. But where this degree of freedom proved inadequate he did not hesitate to fall back on pure literary invention to produce the touch of color that he wanted.

A few examples will illustrate these added touches. Sometimes Knolles will substitute a more vivid phrase for a conventional one, such as "fall together by the eares" (423 A4) where the originals have simply *faire la guerre* and *bellum inferre*, or "everie mothers son" (37 A3) for the Latin version's *omnes ad unum*, or "a man well strucken in yeares" (255 E5) for the simple *vieillard* and *senio*. Occasionally he will add something entirely new for the sake of vividness or emphasis. In the following examples the words italicized have no equivalents in either the French or the Latin:

... executed by the *bloudie* executioners hands (229 C5).
... which the judge may at his pleasure every way turne like *a nose of* waxe ... (760 G6–7).

[106] Bodin's French, of course, is similarly archaic, but the English-speaking reader tends to be less sensitive to development in a language other than his own.

> ... againe appease the *turbulent* motions of *headstrong and giddie* common people (530 K6-7).
>
> And so to doe [i.e., to crown the son while the father is still alive], unto mee seemeth a thing verie daungerous ... except the king have many kingdomes, with great fluds, most high mountaines, or the deepest seas, one from an other divided, *not easily with the wings of aspiring ambition to be passed* (209 C4-9).

In a few instances the added material is explanatory or corrective rather than ornamental, as:

> ... and the scite thereof [i.e., the site of Byzantium] given to the Perinthians, who reedified it, being afterwards called Constantinople, and now *corruptly* Stamboll, *the choyce seat of the Turkish emperours* (410 I6-8).

For Knolles himself was a well-informed man, competent to explain or clarify many of Bodin's more casual references, not only to English matters, but also, as I shall indicate shortly, to Turkish affairs and Eastern European history in general.

It will of course be objected that all these embellishments, whether stylistic or otherwise, are inimical to faithful translation. In Knolles's defense it might be replied that the ornamentation is seldom so obvious and so easily illustrated as in the examples cited above. Much of it is achieved by the subtle choice of a word or by a touch of artistry in rephrasing a sentence. Moreover, the tone of the originals is not altered; with rare exceptions Knolles's ornaments merely highlight ideas already latent in the text. Further, the stylistic touches tend to appear most obviously in the narration of the historical episodes which serve Bodin as illustrations.[107] The fact that they add a touch of color to a rather drab narrative suggests that when Knolles chose to depart from a strictly literal translation, it was chiefly because he wished to tell a good story.

It is important here to remember the literary environment. The *Six Bookes* is one of a very considerable number of works translated into English during this period. The translators sought to bring the best in both classical and modern literature and history within the reach of a middle class that was visibly growing in numbers, in wealth, in political influence, in the range of its intellectual interests, and in its demand for books. Their aim was to entertain as well as to instruct the reader, and accordingly they placed a high value upon a fresh and vigorous prose style. In this respect at least Knolles's work resembles that of many of the others, and we ought to appreciate the nature and aims of the translation movement in general before passing judgment upon a single example of it. In its subject matter, of course, the *Six Bookes* is hardly typical of the remainder of the movement. The work abounds in difficult legal problems, and in any case men did not yet consider it the prerogative of the general reader to meddle with the art of government. As a study of the titles translated will show, middle-class taste ran primarily to lighter and more entertaining fare.

To conclude, then, Knolles has given us an English text that is reasonably accurate, vigorous in its expression, and meticulously patient in its attempt to blend the French and Latin originals into a single, harmonious narrative. He does resort to a few deliberate alterations, but most of these were virtually forced upon

---

[107] Such as the rebellion of Ghent against the Count of Flanders (376 G7-I2) or the choice of a hermit to be King of Tunis (411 A4-B1).

him by the political circumstances under which he wrote. Here and there we can detect a few prejudices too—patriotism, bias against the French, loyalty to Aristotle—but these are the feelings that we might expect of any Oxford-educated Englishman of Knolles's generation, feelings that most of his readers undoubtedly shared to the full. What is striking is that the work reveals to us so little of the man himself. From the whole of the translation one can glean very little of his own personality and virtually nothing about the events of his life.[108] Yet these things are important, for a knowledge of Knolles's career can give us a clear understanding of many different aspects of his translation and may even explain why he chose the *République*, rather than some other work, as his subject. For answers to these questions, however, we must look beyond the covers of the English edition.

[108] One possible exception is his corroboration of the debate on elective versus hereditary monarchy which took place during Queen Elizabeth's visit to Oxford in 1566. Probably Knolles was present, although characteristically he does not say so. See his marginal comment at 722 F4.

V. THE LIFE AND BACKGROUND OF RICHARD KNOLLES

What sort of man was Knolles? We must begin with the actual records and then, since these are rather sketchy, examine the particular environment he lived in with some care, for only in this way can we understand some important facets of his retiring personality. The Register of Oxford University records that on January 26, 1564/5, Knolles was admitted Bachelor of Arts as a member of Lincoln College.[109] From this we may assume that he came up to Oxford about 1560 or 1561 and that he was born—if his matriculation took place at the usual age—in the later 1540's. Anthony à Wood asserts that he came from a family "living at Cold-Ashby in Northamptonshire,"[110] but without further documentary evidence this statement should be treated with caution.

After taking the bachelor's degree Knolles continued his studies in Oxford, and was soon elected to a fellowship in his own college which he held for several years. The manuscript *Register Vetus* of Lincoln still preserves his signature on a number of decrees promulgated by the Rector and Fellows between 1566 and 1572. His studies continued during these years, and the University Register shows that he was granted the Master of Arts degree on July 4, 1570.[111]

The college of which Knolles had become a member in the early years of Elizabeth's reign was passing through a period of the deepest disruption and despair. Lincoln had always been a small and unimportant college, relatively poor in its endowments. But from its beginnings it had been a training ground for young theologians devoted to the traditions of the medieval Church. The founder, Bishop Fleming, himself a prince of the Church, had played an active part in counteracting the heresies of Wycliffe, and a strict religious orthodoxy had become part of the conservative tradition of his foundation. The college had submitted to the changes in Church government under Henry VIII and Edward VI in the knowl-

[109] *Register of the University of Oxford*, ed. C. W. Boase (Oxford, 1885), I, 256.
[110] *Athenae Oxonienses*, ed. P. Bliss (London, 1813–1820), II, 79.
[111] *Register of the University of Oxford*, I, 256.

edge that they would be followed by a Catholic restoration under Mary. But her death and the accession of Elizabeth in 1558 initiated a period of trouble which lasted until well after Knolles had left Oxford.

The extent of the disruption and the tenacity of Lincoln's Catholic tradition are seen best in the careers of the members of the college. Weston, the chairman of the commission that tried Cranmer, Ridley, and Latimer in 1554, was Rector of Lincoln from 1539 to 1556. Three of his successors were deprived of office on religious grounds. Henshaw was ejected by Queen Elizabeth's visitors in 1560, and several of the fellows, according to Wood, departed with him. His successor, Babington, thrust upon the college from outside to break down resistance to reform, was himself forced to resign in 1563 under suspicion of Romanist opinions. Again an outsider was imposed on the college, and again tradition proved the stronger. John Bridgewater, who held the Rectorship during the whole period of Knolles's fellowship, was forced to resign it in 1574. He then took refuge on the Continent and became active in the Jesuit cause.[112]

The careers of the fellows and undergraduates are equally revealing. Though I cannot outline them individually here, practically all of Knolles's contemporaries at Lincoln went almost directly from Oxford to the English Roman Catholic College at Douay. Their names may be found, sometimes singly, sometimes in groups, in the Douay Diaries,[113] which give the names of those who studied and were ordained at the English College and of those who were sent on the English missions. Indeed, of the ten men whom the Lincoln *Register* shows to have been fellows of the college between 1566 and 1570, no fewer than eight—Bridgewater, Thomas Marshall, Thomas Smyth, Robert Parkinson, William Harris, Thomas Stampe, William Morris, and John Michell—went abroad in the Catholic cause in the 1570's.[114] The ninth I have been unable to trace,[115] and the tenth was Knolles himself. Nor is this all. Several undergraduates who were at Lincoln while Knolles was fellow also went abroad to be ordained as priests, a further testimony to the pervasiveness of Lincoln's Catholic tradition. Wood portrays the atmosphere well in his sketch of William Hart, who was elected to a Traps Scholarship in the College in May 1571:

> In his time were several young scholars of Lincoln coll. educated, and afterwards professed themselves openly to be R. Catholics, having received instructions from some of the fellows that were inclined that way, but chiefly from the rector thereof Joh. Bridgwater beforementioned, who always was in his heart a R. Catholic, and resign'd at last his rectory to prevent expulsion.[116]

Hart, whom Knolles must certainly have known, returned to England as a missionary, and was hanged at York in 1583.

---

[112] See A. Clark, *Lincoln* (University of Oxford College Histories series, London, 1898), pp. 39–40, 44–46; A. à Wood, *History and Antiquities of the University of Oxford*, ed. J. Gutch (Oxford, 1792–1796), II, 146.

[113] *The First and Second Diaries of the English College, Douay*, ed. by fathers of the Congregation of the London Oratory (London, 1878).

[114] See the index entries for these names in the *Diaries*. There is some possibility of identical names and mistaken identities here, but the nature of the evidence makes it a very slight one, applicable to one or two of the names at the most.

[115] Henry Hull, a somewhat older man, already a fellow in Mary's reign, who does not appear in the *Register* after 1568.

[116] *Athenae Oxonienses*, I, 490.

INTRODUCTION

It is clear that virtually all of Knolles's contemporaries at Lincoln remained faithful adherents of the old religion. In the daily life of a small Oxford college these men were his constant companions. Even though he apparently did not follow them into exile, their influence may nevertheless be clearly discerned in his later writings, for these were impressionable, formative years. In a university noted for its loyalty to the old faith, Lincoln was one of the most steadfast of colleges in remaining constant to the purposes of its founder. Yet college life was badly disrupted. Degrees were refused to those whose religious opinions were suspect, and Knolles was one of the very few Lincoln men to be given the Bachelor of Arts degree during the first two decades of the new reign. As early as 1555 the college, after obtaining special permission from the Bishop of Lincoln to depart from its statutes, elected four undergraduates to fellowships "on account of the scarcity of graduates in the University."[117] Clearly standards of scholarship were at a low level, and they could scarcely have improved very much during the turbulent years that followed.

The gradualness of change in the university as a whole is reflected in the Edwardian and Elizabethan statutes defining the curriculum. The Edwardian code of 1549, the first association of the university with the reformed Church of England, had left the traditional program of studies in arts largely unchanged. The youngster just up from school was to begin with mathematics, which included arithmetic, geometry, and what he could absorb of astronomy and cosmography. The second year was devoted to dialectic; in the third and fourth years philosophy was added. Four years led to the Bachelor of Arts degree and three more, spent upon philosophy, astronomy, perspective, and Greek, led to the degree of Master of Arts.[118] When the Marian restoration came it was not deemed necessary to alter this program of study, and this was the curriculum that Knolles would have followed during his first years in Oxford.

After taking the bachelor's degree he probably came under the Elizabethan statutes, adopted in 1565, and if so, the studies for the master's degree included geometry, astronomy, and three branches of philosophy. The texts prescribed in philosophy are revealing: in natural philosophy students were to read Aristotle's *Physics*, or *De coelo et mundo*, or the *Meteorologica*, or the *Parva Naturalia*, or *De anima*; in moral philosophy the texts were Aristotle's *Politics* or *Ethics* or Plato's *Republic*; in metaphysics only Aristotle's *Metaphysics* is mentioned.[119] Other subjects reflect just as strongly the continuing influence of the medieval curriculum. Geography and astronomy were to be taught from classical authorities, Pliny, Strabo, and Ptolemy, for the Renaissance interest in exploration and the Copernican astronomy had as yet found little foothold in the university.

On the whole the Reformation brought about less change in Oxford life than might be supposed. If medieval manuscripts from the libraries were dispersed and destroyed, traditional ideas proved far more difficult to root out. The revolution in Church government brought a ban

[117] Clark, *Lincoln*, pp. 39–40.
[118] *Statuta Antiqua Universitatis Oxoniensis*, ed. S. Gibson (Oxford, 1931) p. 344.
[119] *Ibid.*, p. 390.

upon the study of canon law and certain texts in scholastic philosophy but had little effect on the curriculum in arts. The 1549 statutes provided in detail for the study of Greek and Hebrew in the university. When the first wave of Renaissance enthusiasm had subsided, however, these languages lost ground, and the 1565 statutes fail to mention Greek in the curriculum for the master's degree. The official retreat from Greek and Hebrew, together with the general disruption of studies occasioned by the religious issue, seem sufficient to explain Knolles's extreme weakness in handling Bodin's quotations in these languages. But the core of the medieval curriculum, the study of Aristotle, was scarcely altered. Oxford produced no Ramus to raise a revolt against the Philosopher, and his doctrines found a secure defense in the general conservatism of the university. Knolles's protests against Bodin's unfavorable estimate of Aristotle in the *République* reflect not so much a difference in the temperaments of the two men as a difference in the respective intellectual climates of the Universities of Paris and Oxford.

In this university environment, which had become an oasis of the past in a changing world, Knolles spent some dozen years. From 1566 onwards his name appears in the college records as a fellow, at first near the bottom of the list, but gradually approaching the top as resignations and new elections gave him greater seniority. In August 1572 two decrees appear in his own handwriting, with his signature heading the list in the absence of the Rector.[120] Knolles may by this time have become Subrector of the College, for the second of these decrees, dated August 17, begins "The Subrector and fellows . . ." After this date he disappears from sight, and in all likelihood he left the college before March 1574, at which date the next decree which survives in the Registers does not bear his name. The next twenty years of his career are a blank. The only thing we know about him in this period is that he returned to Lincoln as a visitor to dine in 1576.[121] Evidently the break was not a complete one. When he next reappears it is as master of Sir Roger Manwood's Grammar School at Sandwich, in Kent.

The date of his appointment remains uncertain. Since it was made by Sir Roger himself, it must have taken place before the latter's death in 1592. In all probability, though we cannot be sure, it dates from 1572 or soon after. It is also probable that Manwood first met Knolles while the latter was still at Lincoln, for in 1568 Manwood, as executor of the Traps estate, had been instrumental in founding four scholarships in Lincoln College. Two of these Traps scholarships were reserved for pupils of Manwood's school. Nor was this the only connection, for Manwood provided that after his death the master of the school should be nominated by the college.[122] In all likelihood, then, Knolles went to Sandwich directly from Oxford, obtaining the mastership through his seniority at Lincoln. If so he passed these two silent decades under Sir Roger's watchful eye, attending diligently, we may be sure, to his duties at the school, but quietly preparing to embark upon more ambitious projects when the occasion should arise.

[120] *Register Vetus*, fol. 24.
[121] S. A. Warner, *Lincoln College, Oxford* (London, 1908), p. 9.
[122] W. Boys, *Collections for an History of Sandwich in Kent* (Canterbury, 1892 [1792]), pp. 200–201.

Introduction

Why had Knolles exchanged Oxford for Sandwich? There appears to have been one simple and direct reason: by doing so he was improving his financial position very considerably. The value of a Lincoln fellowship in Henry VIII's reign was under five pounds a year, and it was probably not much higher under Elizabeth. Even in 1610, when an extra fellowship was added, the value was only ten pounds a year. The mastership of the school, on the other hand, carried an annual salary of twenty pounds, together with an apartment in the new school building, which still stands today beside the Canterbury Road at the outskirts of the old town. Academic careers, however, are seldom motivated by monetary considerations alone, and the confining atmosphere of the university itself may have been an even more telling reason for Knolles's departure. The religious issue was assuming greater and greater proportions. Practically all of Knolles's close friends and colleagues were going into exile for their religious opinions. Younger men—his own students, perhaps—were being refused their degrees on suspicion of holding papist views. Even for a man willing to accept the reformed Church of England university life must have appeared increasingly futile as suspicion mounted. There was the additional consideration that by the college statutes of 1479 fellows of Lincoln were required to proceed to holy orders within a given period. The college records contain a number of short-term dispensations from this rule, but they also show that one of Knolles's contemporaries was expelled in 1574 for not having complied with it.[123] The post at Sandwich may therefore have provided a welcome escape from a long course of theological studies for which he felt little inclination.

We can reconstruct a detailed picture of Knolles's life at Sandwich from the meticulous rules which Sir Roger set down for his school in 1580.[124] The master was to have an usher, or assistant master, to teach the lower forms under his supervision. By the time that the master took over instruction, a good grounding was to have been laid in Latin grammar and translation. The master was to continue with Terence, Sallust, Virgil, Horace, Livy, and large quantities of Cicero. The main emphasis was upon translation, both from Latin and into Latin. Only a vague reference is made to Greek.

Even more important than the curriculum in these regulations is the founder's emphasis upon building character and a proper respect for religion. Regular church attendance "in the nexte parishe churche in Sandwich wherin Englishe service is used"—that is, in St. Mary's—was strictly enjoined. On Saturday afternoons the master, usher, and scholars were to say together "one prescribed fourme of praier, wherin shalbe made mencion of the church, the realme, the prince, the estate of the towne, and the fownder and his posteritie." All in all, the circumstances of Knolles's appointment afford the best proof of his adherence to the reformed religion. The rules of 1580 required that the master be suitable, among other things, for his "righte understandinge of Godes trewe religeon nowe sett fourth by publique awcthoritie." We may be sure that Manwood, a zealous servant

[123] *Register Vetus*, fol. 133.
[124] Printed in full in Boys, *Collections for an History*, pp. 222–232.

of the Crown, would examine Knolles rigorously on the point, and that Knolles must have proved his orthodoxy to the founder's satisfaction. Beyond this, the master and usher were to set the pupils "an example of honest, contynente and godlie behavior." They were to shun gaming, taverns, and "any extraordinarie or unnecessarie expences in apparell." They were to be absent from the school no more than twenty days per year, and never simultaneously. If either the master or the usher neglected his duties, the governing body of the school, the mayor and jurats of Sandwich, had the power of expelling the offender, but only after twice admonishing him to mend his ways. As long as the founder lived, however, this rule remained a dead letter. Manwood himself was a strict disciplinarian, respected and feared by his contemporaries, and the school which he had established in his native town was a project close to his heart. We may be sure that even Manwood's high position as Lord Chief Baron of the Exchequer did not prevent him from exercising the closest personal supervision over Knolles.

But whatever his commitments to the school and to his employer, Knolles could not have remained unacquainted with certain important developments in the town. Sandwich had a long and proud history as one of the Cinque Ports, and in medieval times it could boast of the finest harbor on the East Kentish coast. In the fifteenth century, however, the shrinking of the channel between the mainland and the Isle of Thanet diminished the action of the tide along the coast, so that silt brought down by the River Stour began to block the harbor. By the time Knolles came to Sandwich it was useless for all but the smallest vessels and was visibly deteriorating year by year. The ancient seaport, now being strangled by the action of the sea, was in acute economic decline, for the loss of the harbor made itself felt in unemployment, deserted houses, and a dwindling population. Probably it was this economic crisis that had prompted the mayor and jurats to arrange in 1561 for the resettlement in the town of some twenty-five households of Dutch Protestant refugees then living in London. The number of refugees grew rapidly, so rapidly indeed that the Privy Council initiated action to remove some of the foreign population from the invasion coast. In 1574 some hundred households of the French-speaking Walloon congregation were moved from Sandwich to Canterbury. Despite this loss the numbers remained significant. In 1565 the foreigners are reported to have comprised 129 households out of a total of 420, and even in 1582 the Dutch settlers still totaled 351.[125] The newcomers were mainly skilled textile workers, and they quickly established Sandwich as a center for the manufacture of flannel, bays, and says. Those in other trades, especially tailoring, were subjected to numerous petty restrictions on their work, instigated by English tradesmen fearful of their competition. However friction with the townspeople seems never to have reached serious proportions, and the general result of the migration was a very considerable increase in the town's prosperity at a time when new industries were desperately needed. It was a lesson on

[125] E. Hasted, *The History and Topographical Survey of the County of Kent* (Canterbury, 1778–1799), IV, 252–253. On their activities in Sandwich, see also D. Gardiner, *Historic Haven, the Story of Sandwich* (Derby, 1954), ch. 18.

the practical benefits of religious toleration that could hardly escape the notice of anyone living in the town.

The death of Sir Roger Manwood in 1592 brought a very considerable change in Knolles's life. Sir Peter Manwood, who succeeded his father, had little interest in the school, control of which was now formally vested in the mayor and jurats of Sandwich. But he did have a substantial and growing reputation as a patron of learning and a friend of men of letters. He it was who awakened Knolles's nascent literary aspirations, and gave him every encouragement to write. Self-confidence was not one of Knolles's strong points, and we may imagine that a good deal of encouragement was necessary to break the ingrained routine of years of teaching.

The results, however, were impressive. Foremost among them was the writing of Knolles's massive *Generall Historie of the Turkes*, first published in 1603. Its dimensions alone are sufficient to command respect: the first—and shortest—edition fills a folio volume of some twelve hundred pages. But beyond mere size it is worthwhile history, broadly conceived, judicious in its handling of sources, and executed in a polished style. The Ottoman Empire loomed large and ominous on the sixteenth-century horizon, but of all the many Elizabethan writings on the subject, Knolles's volume is undoubtedly the most thorough and scholarly attempt to study the relentless westerly advance of Turkish power and to probe for the reasons underlying its successes.[126] The work was not only well written, but topical too. It found a ready public and ran through five further editions, each of which contained additions bringing the narrative down to the date of publication.[127] It gave to Knolles a very considerable literary reputation which lasted into the nineteenth century.[128] But the *Generall Historie* does not stand alone. Beside it must be placed his two substantial translations of Camden's *Britannia* and Bodin's *République*. While working on the latter he also translated for Sir Peter Manwood the treaty with Spain of August 1604,[129] and it is fair to assume that he translated other documents concerning current political developments for his patron's use. His final literary effort was a far-from-negligible continuation of 150 pages to the *Generall Historie*, which carried the narrative down to 1610, the year of Knolles's death.

If we wish to date accurately the translation of the *République*, this can be done with some confidence when all the available evidence is pieced together. In the first place it seems most unlikely that Knolles would have begun to work seriously on the *République* while writing the *Generall Historie*, and the latter is obviously a labor of several years. Knolles himself tells us that he had been reading about the Turks for many years before he ever contemplated writing anything on the subject, and he speaks with obvious sincerity of the encouragement given him by Sir

---

[126] Hence Knolles, as an authority on Turkish and Eastern European affairs, is able to amend several errors of fact in the *République* as he translates.

[127] These editions were published in 1610, 1621, 1631, 1638, and 1687–1700 (3 vols.). There is a two-volume abridgment of 1701.

[128] See, for example, Dr. Johnson's highly favorable estimate of it in *The Rambler*, No. 122, May 18, 1751.

[129] British Museum Addl. MS. 38139, fols. 84–88. This document is bound in a volume of Manwood's papers, and contains an explicit notation by Sir Peter: "Translated by Mr. Knolles for mee."

Peter Manwood, "the first moover of me to take this great Worke in hand, and my continuall and onely comfort and helper therein."[130] But Sir Peter, born about 1565 or 1566, could hardly have assumed this role of patron before about 1585 at the very earliest. In all likelihood, therefore, the project of writing a history of the Turks was conceived some considerable time after Knolles's arrival in Sandwich, and little progress had been made towards its execution before Sir Roger Manwood's death in December 1592. Its completion must have occupied most of Knolles's free time in the decade that followed. Moreover, as we know already from textual evidence, the translation of the *République* cannot possibly have been begun earlier than 1593 because it is based upon a French edition of that year, and indeed the latter half at least of the translation was made after the arrival in England of the Latin edition of 1601. Finally, Knolles mentions in the dedication of the translation that when he turned to it he was already gathering materials to continue the *Historie*; the *Historie* itself had presumably gone to the printer. Now the Introduction to the first edition of the *Historie* is dated "From Sandwich the last of September 1603," and probably the manuscript had been completed sometime within the preceding year. That Knolles set to work on the *République* without delay is suggested by another date that we know: the work had been licensed in the Stationers' Register to the printer Adam Islip on January 8, 1603. It is further to be noted that the entry in the Stationers' Register describes it as "a booke to be translated into English and so printed," as though the translation were not yet begun. But Islip was also the printer of the first five editions of the *Generall Historie*, and only a few weeks before this date, on December 5, 1602, the first edition of the *Historie* had been licensed to him in partnership with George Bishop and John Norton.[131] It seems quite probable, therefore, that Knolles discussed the project of translating the *République* with Islip or with Bishop at the same time that he was arranging for publication of the *Generall Historie*. Then with publication arranged in advance he could set to work in earnest early in 1603. That he was already into the translation by the following September is suggested by the Preface to the *Historie*: by not condemning too hastily its discrepancies from other writers, he remarks to the reader, "thou maiest hereafter encourage me to performe some other worke to thy no lesse contentment." By the end of 1605, as the dedication shows, the translation was complete, having been in progress for a period, it would seem, of just under three years.

We might safely conclude from the evidence of Knolles's writing alone that his work at the school must have suffered considerably during this later period. It is hardly surprising to find corroboration of this point in an extract from the town records:

Oct. 19th. 1602. Whereas motion was formerly made by the lord warden for reformation of the freeschool, and as mr Richard Knolles now master is found not to have intended the same with that diligence as was meet he should, it was by his honor thought convenient, for the better education of the youth of this town,

[130] See the dedication and Introduction (1603 edition).
[131] See *A Transcript of the Registers of the Company of Stationers of London, 1554-1640*, ed. E. Arber (London and Birmingham, 1875-1894), III, 223-224.

that a more industrious master should be appointed for the said school, and that m^r Knolles being dismissed, in respect he was placed there by the late lord chief baron, founder of the same school, should be allowed a yearly stipend of twelve pounds during his life, upon his quitting the school and school house at michaelmas next, to be paid quarterly by the treasurer of the town.[132]

The date is significant. Though the governors of the school apparently did not know it, Knolles was now completing his *Generall Historie*. Far from being guilty of lack of industry, he was merely diverting it to other channels. He paid scant attention to the proceedings against him. When the *Historie* was completed, he set to work upon his translation of Bodin. And yet—as we learn in a later extract from the town records—he did not leave the school until after the translation was complete:

> 1606. The annuity granted in 1602 not having been paid, m^r Knolles consents to accept the same, and to depart at michaelmas; it is therefore agreed, that, for employing a more industrious schoolmaster hereafter, the said Richard Knolles in respect of his departure, being first placed there by the founder, shall have an annuity of twelve pounds during his natural life out of the treasury of this town, he leaving the school at michaelmas, and putting in surety to that effect.[133]

We may well wonder how Knolles could defy so successfully the school's governing body.

The answer is simple. The governors soon found that their control over the schoolmaster was illusory, for they did not control the purse strings. Sir Peter Manwood continued his father's practice of taking the rents from the lands originally set aside to support the school and paying the master's salary personally.[134] To retain his post Knolles had only to retain Manwood's favor, and as we have seen it was Manwood who had first encouraged him to write. In this instance the role of literary patron cost Manwood nothing, for he was responsible for the schoolmaster's salary in any case. The real losers were the school authorities and probably the usher or assistant master, on whose unfortunate shoulders the burden of teaching undoubtedly fell. The relationship between Knolles and Manwood seems to have grown into a genuine friendship, and the appearance of Knolles's signature as a witness on several documents concerning the Manwood family suggests that he was a frequent guest in Sir Peter's household at St. Stephens, near Canterbury.[135] Whether he left the school in 1606 is not clear. He may have continued as nominal master until his death, for a salary of twenty pounds a year with free living accommodation in the school building was clearly more attractive than the pension offered by the town. He died in Sandwich, and was buried in St. Mary's Church on July 2, 1610, "leaving behind him," as Wood reports, "the character of an industrious, learned, and religious person."[136]

It is Knolles's sense of religious dedication that provides the key to the burst of literary activity late in his

---

[132] Printed in Boys, *Collections for an History*, p. 271.
[133] *Ibid.*, p. 272.
[134] *Ibid.*, pp. 203, 217–218.
[135] The dates of these signatures are: May 1, 1594; December 15, 1600; July 2, 1602; and July 27, 1607. See British Museum Addl. MS. 29759, fols. 82^v, 154, 162, 165. It may also be indicative of Knolles's influence that three of Sir Peter's sons took B.A. degrees from Lincoln College, Oxford.
[136] *Athenae Oxonienses*, II, 81.

life. While still at Lincoln College some thirty years before, he writes in the Introduction to the *Generall Historie*, he had formed the intention to perform something "profitable to the Christian commonweale." The same motivation had carried most of his colleagues of Oxford days into exile on the Continent, yet when Knolles found the occasion to carry out his intention, he chose the very different course of writing a history of the Ottoman Empire. This project was not so unrelated to his professed end as it might appear at first glance. Turkish expansion in the fifteenth and sixteenth centuries had been so rapid and so extensive as to threaten the very survival of the Christian world. Knolles saw in his *Historie* the means of impressing upon the European nations the magnitude of the danger facing them in the East. Indeed he seems to have felt that the mere realization of their peril would alone be sufficient to stimulate the Christian sovereigns to more unified action against the Turks. Indirectly, therefore, the *Generall Historie* is an impassioned plea for Christian unity and religious pacification in the light of the external threat. It is no accident that the closing pages of the 1610 edition examine at some length the growth of religious toleration in the Imperial lands bordering on the Turkish dominions, particularly in Bohemia, Austria, Moravia, and Silesia, a policy which Knolles explicitly commends because it heals the existing division over religion, "the incurable maladie of the Christian estates and Common weales,"[137] and so strengthens Christendom against the infidel invaders. In his own way, therefore, Knolles was working just as directly for the cause of Christendom as were his Oxford colleagues who chose exile and even martyrdom to demonstrate their adherence to the once universal Church.

This same desire for religious pacification provides the main link between the *Generall Historie* and the *Six Bookes*. The original suggestion to translate Bodin may have come from Manwood, or even from Adam Islip, for Bodin's reputation was already great enough in England to justify translation of the *République* on several different grounds. But Bodin's insistence that the religious strife which had torn Europe asunder had to be ended found the fullest response in Knolles's heart. It was a belief interwoven through the whole fabric of his life, from the earliest years in Oxford down to the closing pages of the 1610 continuation of the *Generall Historie*. It mattered little that Bodin's basic loyalty was directed towards the secular national state, while Knolles looked beyond the national state to the older and more spiritual ideal of a Christian commonweal. What did matter was that author and translator were at one in their belief that the solution to this fundamental political issue of the sixteenth century lay along the path of conciliation and toleration.

In most other respects, however, the careers of Bodin and Knolles offer a strange contrast. Bodin knew periods of defeat and even personal danger, but he also had brilliant successes in the realms of thought and action. Knolles passed his entire life in relative obscurity, amid a succession of lost and losing causes. In Oxford he saw virtually all his colleagues driven into exile and his college thwarted on every side by the victorious reformers. Removed to

[137] *Generall Historie* (1610 edition), p. 1295.

Sandwich, he watched the doomed seaport fighting the last stages of its hopeless battle to save the harbor, its main source of livelihood. When he entered the world of letters, it was to portray the crumbling of a divided Christendom before the infidel onslaught from the East. Perhaps the last and keenest disappointment was personal. Probably he lived just long enough to discover that Philemon Holland's translation of Camden's *Britannia*, which was published in 1610,[138] would supersede his own. When we remember also that Knolles's writing was hampered, as he tells us himself, by frequent illnesses, by the uncomfortable and unhealthy situation of the school, and by his relative isolation from books and men of learning, it is no wonder that we find in the *Generall Historie* a recurring note of weary resignation and gentle melancholy which stands out in sharp contrast to Bodin's boundless self-confidence. To some slight degree these same qualities may be detected in his translation of the *République* as well. Thus when Bodin speaks through Knolles the stridency of his tone and the forcefulness of his manner are slightly but unavoidably muted, for although Knolles had little difficulty in expressing the meaning of Bodin's texts, he was by temperament unable to convey to the English reader the full force of Bodin's ebullient personality.

[138] It was licensed on June 4, 1610, with George Bishop and John Norton sharing in the publication *A Transcript of the Registers*, III, 435.

VI. THE *RÉPUBLIQUE* IN ENGLISH POLITICAL THOUGHT

It seems appropriate to conclude this Introduction with a glance at the importance of Bodin's and Knolles's work for the history of English political thought. The *République* became known in England immediately after publication of the first French edition. A few years later, when he visited England in 1581, Bodin found it being expounded, but with some difficulty and obscurity, in London and Cambridge. The same year saw the publication in London of a short tract that is clearly inspired by it, Charles Merbury's *A Briefe Discourse of Royall Monarchie*. From this time onwards further references to it occur frequently in a wide range of political and legal literature, particularly in the writings on the succession question during the last ten years of the reign.[139]

Yet Elizabethan Englishmen were hardly in a position to understand the real significance of Bodin's central doctrines. It was the prolonged constitutional crisis of the seventeenth century, the painful probing for the ultimate seat of political authority in the pamphlet literature of the Civil War years, the soul-searching quest for means to justify a chosen allegiance—whether to the King or to Parliament or to the Army—which drove the lesson home. These developments gave to the *République* a topicality it would never have had in more settled times. But Bodin's doctrines did not become the monopoly of any one faction in the struggle. We must remember the distinction

[139] The issue was precipitated chiefly by the Jesuit Robert Parsons' *Conference about the next Succession to the Crowne of Ingland* (n.p., 1594). On the wider impact of the *République* in this period, see G. L. Mosse, "The Influence of Jean Bodin's *République* on English Political Thought," *Medievalia et Humanistica*, V (1948), 73–83, and also his *Struggle for Sovereignty in England* (East Lansing, Mich., 1950), *passim*.

drawn earlier between Bodin the scientific analyst of forms of government and Bodin the proponent of a specific program of royal absolutism, for both aspects of his thought were utilized extensively by English writers. While his specific program was most readily adaptable to Royalist use, at the other extreme his rigorous analysis of sovereignty proved almost equally useful to those who placed the highest political authority ultimately in the people. Even the more moderate proponents of a mixed constitution or limited monarchy did not hesitate to draw upon Bodin as far as it suited their purpose. It is no exaggeration to say that the *République* was used and cited by writers of every shade of the political spectrum, indeed frequently to support views from which Bodin himself would have recoiled in horror. With the rarest exceptions his name is mentioned with great respect, and it is clear from the number and tone of these references that to cite Bodin was to appeal to an authority of the greatest weight. "In the period from 1600 to the outbreak of civil war," Professor C. H. McIlwain has asserted in a recent article, "there was no political writer cited in England more often or more favorably than Jean Bodin."[140]

Now if we examine these numerous references to Bodin, we find that in many instances it is relatively simple to discover which version of the *République* the various authors followed. Where a quotation remains in French or Latin, it is usually only a formality to verify it against the original text. Where it is in English one can usually tell whether the author followed the Knolles version or made his own translation by comparing the quotation in question with the wording of the *Six Bookes*.

Occasionally it is possible to prove conclusively that the Knolles version was used by the fact that a single quotation will include materials drawn from both the French and the Latin versions. Some of the references give page numbers, and where this is so it is possible to state the actual edition, or family of editions, which the author used, even when there are no direct quotations. A few authors state the edition used, but in this period they are a very small minority. By following up these references, then, one should naturally expect to discover some interesting examples of the use of the Knolles edition by other writers, and this is in fact the case.

One writer definitely to use the Knolles edition was William Prynne, whose *Soveraigne Power of Parliaments and Kingdomes* was published in London in 1643. He wrote this ponderous tract of over six hundred pages in defense of the parliamentary proceedings of the previous year against the King. To strengthen his argument concerning England he concludes with a long appendix showing the supremacy of the estates over the monarch in many other countries as well. Prynne cites many authorities and refers to Bodin extensively. His work contains several long verbatim quotations in which both wording and page references correspond exactly to those of the Knolles edition.[141]

A second instance is found in a pamphlet entitled *The Armies Vindication*, which appeared in London in 1649 under the pseudonym "Eleutherius Philodemius." This tract is a

[140] "Sovereignty in the World Today," *Measure*, I (1950), 110.
[141] For examples, see *Soveraigne Power*, Pt. I, p. 46; Pt. II, pp. 9–10, 45; Pt. III, pp. 21–22; Appendix, pp. 10–11, 17–18.

good example of the contemporary theory of popular sovereignty. Written in order to refute the charge that the Army had unlawfully and wrongfully trodden underfoot both King and Parliament, it asserts the right of the people, as represented in this instance by the Army, to depose and punish an erring king and to change the form of government as they see fit. Yet even this author found arguments in the *République* to support his position, and he refers to Bodin several times. "I mention him the oftner," he explains at one point, "because he is a great kingsman." In his case also it can be shown very easily that his direct quotations are taken word for word from the English edition.[142]

Undoubtedly the most striking instance of Bodin's influence on English thought is the use made of the *République* by Sir Robert Filmer. He too knew the Knolles edition, as we learn at once from the fact that he explicitly commends "our translator of *Bodin de Republica* into English" for his discrimination in using the term "Commonweal" rather than the more ambiguous "Commonwealth."[143] Quite probably Filmer knew the Manwoods, and as a young man he might even have met Knolles in Sir Peter Manwood's household. In any case his thought owes much more to the English edition of the *République* than might appear at first glance. Among his political tracts written in defense of the Royalist cause was one which appeared in 1648 under the outspoken title, *The Necessity of the Absolute Power of All Kings: And in particular, of the King of England*. Though it appeared anonymously in 1648 and in Filmer's own name when it was reprinted later in the century, there is a variant title page for the 1648 edition which attributes it to "John Bodin a Protestant according to the Church of Geneva."[144] Closer analysis reveals that apart from one or two isolated sentences the whole of the pamphlet is made up of extracts from the *République*, and also that these extracts correspond word for word with the Knolles translation. What is more, many of these passages recur in Filmer's other writings, together with still other extracts from the English version, and here they are very often presented, without acknowledgment, as Filmer's own arguments. The extent of Filmer's debt to Bodin is nothing short of astonishing: the Knolles edition must have been constantly at his side for reference as he wrote.

The connection between Bodin, Knolles, and Filmer assumes more than just a passing interest when we remember that the *Patriarcha* became, a full generation after its author's death, the main bastion of Restoration Toryism and the chief target of Sydney and Locke. The underlying issue at the time of the struggle over the Exclusion Bill, though it was often lost to view in the heat of the controversy, was whether, as the Whigs contended, the right to govern was conventional, contractual, and revocable at the will of the governed, or whether, as the Royalists believed, it was something fixed, immutable, inherent in the nature of human society. Of the two positions Bodin inclined more closely to the latter, and when we look at the *République*

[142] See in particular pp. 49 and 63, and cf. below, 174 G7–H6, 713 E6–714 F1.
[143] *Patriarcha and Other Political Works*, ed. P. Laslett (Oxford, 1949), p. 240. In fact the *Six Bookes* employs both forms, though the former predominates.
[144] Reprinted *ibid.*, pp. 317–326. For the various editions, see Appendix C below.

we can discern the seeds of Filmer's patriarchal justification of monarchical supremacy in Bodin's analysis of paternal authority over the family. The *Six Bookes*, therefore, provided raw materials for Filmer to build with, and his work in turn forced the Whig opposition to rethink its premises and organize a counterattack. Thus the Knolles translation of the *République* contributed, indirectly but nevertheless substantially and unmistakably, to the production of the most influential of all English works on political philosophy, John Locke's *Two Treatises of Government*.[145]

From a purely quantitative standpoint, however, the contribution of Knolles's edition to later developments is disappointing. Out of a very considerable number of writers whose references to the *République* have been examined, the three that I have just mentioned, Prynne, "Eleutherius Philodemius," and Sir Robert Filmer, are the only ones who can definitely be shown to have used the Knolles translation.[146] Significantly, these three men represent the views of the three main groups in the constitutional struggle of the 1640's, the Parliamentarians, the Army, and the Royalists. A more extended survey might well add a few further names to this lonely trio, but the sample of references examined has been large enough and representative enough to show conclusively that the great majority of writers who can be identified with a specific version of the *République* worked either from the French or from the Latin version, with the latter predominating heavily.

What can explain this apparent neglect of the English edition? In the first place, the original versions presented no special barrier—and the English translation no special advantage—for most of these writers. Drawn into political controversy by unhappy circumstances rather than by inclination, they were, by and large, well-educated men, the heirs of the European intellectual tradition, lawyers, divines, academics, historians, and antiquaries. They read Latin as easily as English, and many had a good acquaintance with French as well. It is only to be expected that most of them would work from Continental editions. The French and Latin versions had been reprinted a great many times and as late as 1641,[147] so that copies were undoubtedly far more easily available. Further, the majority of these editions were octavos, and so would be both cheaper and more convenient to handle than the rather bulky folio English translation.

Probably the Knolles edition fared rather better among the groups for whom it was chiefly intended, the landed gentry and the urban middle classes. These were the men whose knowledge of languages frequently left something to be desired, and the English translation may well have played a more important part in shaping the political outlook of these increasingly powerful groups than the paucity of references to it suggests. But we lack the written evidence to support this hypothesis because in general squires and merchants were not the sort of men to set down their

---

[145] Yet it would be wrong to suppose that Locke's opposition to Filmerism implied a corresponding antipathy towards Bodin's ideas, for we find that in the 1660's Locke was recommending the *Methodus* to his pupils at Christ Church. Cf. Locke's *Essays on the Law of Nature*, ed. W. von Leyden (Oxford, 1954), p. 20.

[146] Most of the references for this survey were very generously made available to me by Mr. J. H. M. Salmon, of St. John's College, Cambridge, who gathered them while writing a thesis, now published as *The French Religious Wars in English Political Thought* (Oxford, 1959).

[147] See Appendix C below.

political convictions in print. Filmer did so, of course, but he is an exception. Even if the hypothesis is correct, however, it must not be exaggerated. The *Six Bookes* was a relatively rare book in the seventeenth century, and it has remained so down to the present day. So little is it known, indeed, that an authority as eminent as the late J. W. Allen could remark of the *République* that "no English translation seems to have been made."[148] Why, then, was the English edition never reprinted? This is a complex question, but the answer probably lies in the fact that by the 1640's, when a second edition might well have been appropriate, the *République* was too remote from the immediate issues, too Olympian in its detachment, and—it must be added —too thorough and ponderous, to be of much immediate use to either the Royalist or the Parliamentary cause. Public taste ran more and more to short partisan tracts which were usually stronger in invective than in logic and which often lost sight of broader constitutional issues altogether. The *République*, therefore, remained a highly respected authority, but as the struggle intensified it seems to have become increasingly a repository of arguments for other writers rather than a work to be read by the public at first hand.

When, towards the end of the century, the lengthy constitutional crisis was at last resolved, Bodin's influence on English political thought dwindled rapidly, not because of a parting of the ways, but rather because the settlement of 1689 in effect conceded to the Lords and Commons a legislative supremacy so sweeping that Bodin himself would have found no fault with it. The Glorious Revolution banished royal absolutism and opened the door to parliamentary absolutism. With its triumph the *République* quickly became a forgotten book,[149] forgotten, that is, until modern times, until the apotheosis of the national state had gone so far as to provoke a strong reaction. This reaction has taken various forms; it is exemplified in the pluralist movement, in guild socialism and syndicalism, in the formation of associations to defend civil liberties, in the Imperial Federation movement, in recent progress towards European integration, and in plans for world federation and world government. As will be noted, it attacks widely different aspects of the problem of modern nationalism, from the question of international anarchy at the one extreme to that of freedom of association and individual liberty within the state at the other. The net effect of this broad challenge to the national state has been a serious, but as yet inconclusive, re-examination of the foundations of political authority, as a result of which Bodin, as one of the principal architects of the modern state, has become a figure of interest once more to students of politics.

Can we discover in the *République* any lessons for our present situation? It is tempting to compare the threat to social order posed by religious differences in the sixteenth century with that posed by ideological differences in the twentieth. But we soon realize that the internal disorders of the sixteenth century and the international anarchy of the

---

[148] *A History of Political Thought in the Sixteenth Century* (London, 1928), p. 396. Nor is the English edition recorded in Chauviré's bibliography, *Jean Bodin*, pp. 517–518.

[149] Though not so quickly in America, where the constitutional struggle still lay ahead. Thomas Jefferson possessed a copy of the French octavo edition of 1580, which is now in the Library of Congress, Washington.

twentieth, though similar in some respects, are by no means an exact parallel. Indeed we may look to the *République* in vain for specific precepts directly applicable today. The lesson that we can learn from Bodin is of a different order and far more complicated. It is that by understanding the problems of his age and the solutions he devised we can acquire a measure of political wisdom, a deeper understanding of the nature of political organization, and so become capable of devising better solutions to the quite different problems of our own time. The nature of the historical process being what it is, the real lesson that we derive from the great thinkers of the past is that we must meet new situations with a degree of knowledge, intelligence, and inventiveness comparable to theirs. Perhaps it is not a very helpful one, since it still leaves a heavy burden on our own shoulders, but it is nevertheless a lesson of the highest importance. For once again in our generation the penalty for failure to solve the perennial yet ever-changing problems of political authority and human liberty might easily prove to be as drastic as it threatened to be for the men of the sixteenth century, who faced a problem of similar magnitude: the complete collapse of civilized society as we know it.

APPENDIX A

BODIN'S PREFACES

THE Preface to the 1606 edition is of Knolles's own composition, though he borrowed several of the ideas in it from Bodin's prefaces and from the *Apologie de René Herpin*. Apart from this indirect use of them, however, Knolles passed over Bodin's own prefaces. There are three in all, an introduction which appears with minor variations in all French editions, a prefatory letter in Latin which appears in the revised French editions from 1578 onwards, and another introduction to the Latin editions. They are well worth study because they tell us a great deal about Bodin's personal outlook at the respective times that they were written. However, they are too long for full reproduction here and are, moreover, somewhat repetitious and uneven in value. I have therefore translated what I feel to be the more significant passages, and these are reproduced below, together with a brief summary of the remainder. The parts translated amount to a little more than a third of the total length of the three prefaces. It will be noticed that while the first French preface brings its heaviest guns to bear upon the advocates of tyranny—doubtless Bodin is attacking the Italian elements at court—the second French preface comes down much more sharply upon the Calvinist advocates of popular sovereignty. The Latin preface hardly mentions this issue but dwells instead upon the reasons for undertaking a Latin translation, upon problems of organization and method, and upon the general difficulties inherent in the study of political science.

I

[The Preface to the first French edition is addressed to Bodin's friend Gui du Faur, Sieur de Pibrac. It opens by emphasizing strongly the extent of the crisis confronting France. The ship of state, rocked by a violent tempest, is in imminent danger of foundering altogether. To meet this danger Bodin has undertaken this treatise on the Commonweal. He proceeds to outline a brief plan of his work:]

I begin with the family, and proceed in logical order to sovereignty, discussing each constituent part of the Commonweal: the sovereign prince and all the types of Commonweal; then the senate, officers and magistrates; then corporations and colleges, estates and communities, and the authority and duties of each. After this I have distinguished the origin, growth, zenith, alteration, decline and fall of Commonweals, continuing with several political questions that I feel must be thoroughly understood. And for the conclusion of the work I have touched upon justice, distributive, commutative, and harmonic, showing which of the three is suitable to the well-ordered state.

[When one considers that the study of politics is "la Princesse de toutes sciences," very little has been written about the state, and what there is, is defective. The political writings of Plato and Aristotle are too brief, and in their time much of the subject was still veiled in obscurity. Later writers have had no knowledge of laws and of public right:]

These men, I say, have profaned the sacred mysteries of political philosophy, a matter which has been the occasion for troubling and overturning good governments. We have a Machiavelli, for example, who has been fashionable among the agents of tyrants. Paulus Jovius places him in the ranks of remarkable men, yet calls him an atheist, and ignorant of good literature. As for atheism, he glorifies it in his writings. As

A 69

Appendix A

for knowledge, I believe that those who are accustomed to discuss learnedly, to assess wisely and to resolve subtly important matters of state will agree that he never explored the terrain of political science. The latter is not a matter of tyrannical ruses, such as he sought out from all the nooks and crannies of Italy and poured like a slow poison into his book The Prince. *In it he uplifts to the skies, and sets out as a model for all kings, the most perfidious son of a priest that ever lived. Yet this man, for all his trickery, was ignominiously cast down from the high and slippery rock of tyranny on which he was ensconced, and in the end exposed like a beggar to the mercy and derision of his enemies. The same has since befallen other princes who have followed in his footsteps, and practiced those goodly precepts of Machiavelli, who laid down as the twin foundations of Commonweals impiety and injustice, and condemned religion as hostile to the state.*

However Polybius,[1] tutor and lieutenant of Scipio Africanus, and deemed the wisest statesman of his time, even though he was an outright atheist nevertheless recommends religion above everything else as the principal ground, in all Commonweals, for the execution of the laws, for the subjects' obedience to the magistrates, for their awe towards princes, for mutual amity among themselves, and for justice to all. He states that the Romans never had anything of greater force than religion for extending the frontiers of their Empire and spreading the fame of their great deeds throughout the world. As for justice, if Machiavelli had cast his eye ever so lightly over good authors, he would have found that Plato calls his Republic *the books of justice, this being one of the firmest supports of all Commonweals. And inasmuch as it occurred to Carneades, the Athenian ambassador to the Romans, in order to try his eloquence, to praise injustice one day and justice the day following, Cato the Censor, who had heard him declaim, said in full Senate that they must dismiss and send away such ambassadors, who might soon undermine and corrupt the good morals of a people, and eventually overthrow a good constitution.*

Moreover, this attitude is an unworthy betrayal of the sacred laws of nature, which requires not only that scepters be wrested from the hands of the wicked, to be given to good and virtuous princes, as the Hebrew Sage says, but also that the good in the world at large be stronger and mightier than the evil. For just as the great Lord of nature, strong in wisdom and righteousness, rules over the angels, so the angels rule over men, men over beasts, the soul over the body, Heaven over the earth, and reason over the appetites; so that whatever is less fitted to rule may be directed and guided by that which can protect and preserve it, in return for its obedience. But if it happen, on the other hand, that the appetites are disobedient to reason, private men to magistrates, magistrates to princes, and princes to God, then we see that God moves to avenge these wrongs, and to secure execution of the eternal law by Him established. He gives kingdoms and empires to the wisest and most virtuous princes, or to speak more accurately, to the least unjust and most proficient in managing affairs and governing peoples. Sometimes He brings them from one end of the earth to the other, to the astonishment of conquerors and conquered alike. When I speak of justice here, I understand the practical wisdom of ruling in rectitude and integrity. It is, therefore, the grossest incongruity in matters of state, and of dangerous consequence, to teach princes the rules of injustice in order through tyranny to consolidate their power, which has no foundation more disastrous than that . . . This is the most likely means that may be imagined for the ruin of princes and their estate.

There are other men who take the directly opposite view to those just mentioned. They are no less dangerous, and perhaps more so, for under the pretext of an exemption from charges, and popular liberty, they induce the subjects to rebel against their natural princes, opening the door to a licentious anarchy, which is worse than the harshest tyranny in the world. These are two sorts of men who, while writing from completely contrary points of view, conspire together for the ruin of Commonweals, not so much from malice as from ignorance of affairs of state. . . .

[1] *Histories,* VI, 56.

II

[The second preface to the French version is a congratulatory letter, dated September 29 (1577 or 1578), to Gui du Faur upon his appointment as *président à mortier* in the Parlement of Paris, which occurred in 1577. After some personal compliments Bodin digresses to explain how he has answered certain critics of the *République* in the revised (1578) edition, a copy of which is being sent to du Faur. Two kinds of criticism have been advanced. The first type is from "those who begin disputes in schoolboy fashion over words and trivial matters," particularly the great Cujas, who has not only vehemently attacked Bodin personally but also extended his indictment to include all practicing advocates. Bodin springs to the defense of the legal profession:]

Indeed the most illustrious men in the Commonweal not only are, and always have been, in the order of advocates, but from this position they also progress further, that is to say, as orators, ambassadors, privy councilors and judges. And it has been the practice to seek out, wholly from their ranks, as though from a nursery of knowledge and virtue, the jurists who have learned to establish Commonweals, to mark out the boundaries of states, to decide the causes of kings, to build up the morality of a people, to ratify the treaties of princes, to settle the suits and controversies of the citizens, and to adjust divine and human laws to the needs of men living in society.

[However the error of Cujas is understandable. Bodin himself had once been equally ignorant of the value of practical experience:]

That was when I was lecturing publicly in Roman law at Toulouse, and amid the throng of young men I seemed very wise. I thought that those princes of legal science—that is, Bartolus, Baldus, Alexander, Faber, Paulus, and Molinaeus, all outstanding figures— and virtually the whole order of judges and advocates knew nothing, or very little. But after I had been initiated into the mysteries of jurisprudence in the law courts, and had found corroboration through long experience in public affairs, then at last I understood that a real and solid knowledge of the law is found not in the dust of the schools, but in the battleground of the forum; not in the quantities of syllables, but in the scales of justice and equity. Those who know nothing of public affairs remain in the greatest ignorance of Roman law. . . . Thus I declare that of all those disciplines whose end relates to action, the one that least of all can do without practical experience is jurisprudence; and most of all at the present time, when the endless variety of laws and customs would overburden the tender minds of the young before they have learned to know what is useful.

[The second type of criticism is from those who brought out the Geneva edition of the *République* of 1577. Their criticisms have been fully answered at the appropriate points in the revised text:]

Nevertheless I am amazed that there are people who think that I concede somewhat more to the power of one man than befits a worthy citizen of a Commonweal. For specifically in Book I chapter 8 of my République, *and frequently elsewhere, I have been the very first, even in the most perilous times, to refute unhesitatingly the opinions of those who write of enlarging the rights of the treasury and the royal prerogative, on the ground that these men grant to kings an unlimited power, superior to divine and natural law. But what could be more in the interest of the people than what I have had the courage to write: that not even to kings is it lawful to levy taxes without the fullest consent of the citizens? Or of what importance is my other statement: that princes are more stringently bound by divine and natural law than those subject to their rule? Or that princes are bound by their covenants exactly as other citizens are? Yet nearly all the masters of legal science have taught the contrary. But when I perceived on every side that subjects were arming themselves against their princes; that books were being brought out openly, like firebrands to set Commonweals ablaze, in which we are taught that the princes sent by providence to the human race must be thrust out of their kingdoms under a pretense of tyranny, and that kings must be chosen not by their*

Appendix A

lineage, but by the will of the people; and finally that these doctrines were weakening the foundations not of this realm only but of all states; then I denied that it was the function of a good man or of a good citizen to offer violence to his prince for any reason, however great a tyrant he might be; and contended that it was necessary to leave this punishment to God, and to other princes. And I have supported this by divine and human laws and authorities, and most of all by reasons which compel assent.

[However, Bodin continues, his integrity has been clearly demonstrated by his actions in public life, which will vindicate him from the charges of his critics. For at the Estates General of Blois he (1) opposed renewal of the civil wars, (2) resisted the plausible but dangerous proposal for a small committee chosen from the Estates to participate at the judgment of the *cahiers*, and (3) prevented alienation of the public lands. All these policies were in the interest of the people, so much so indeed that they cost Bodin the royal favor and the office, promised earlier, of Master of Requests to the King.]

III

[The Preface to the Latin editions, dated November 29, 1584, from Laon, takes the form of a dedication to Jacques du Val, Seigneur de Mondreville, Comte de Dampierre. Like the first French preface it opens with a reference to the political crisis "of recent years." Bodin had noticed that the confusion of this period arose in large part from widespread ignorance of the art of government:]

This impelled me to place whatever I had learned about the Commonweal before my fellow citizens for their consideration, after they had had a very brief respite from the wars. I did so either that they might preserve, as far as possible, this royal form of government from destruction; or else if this realm, which seems almost to have withered away through its own antiquity, is threatened with such certain destruction that no efforts nor plans of men can ward it off, that I, as though seeing it from a watchtower, may so warn those who have survived the earlier disasters, lest they be entirely ruined by the unforeseen destruction of the state. For sometimes such a host of calamities breaks out through the onset of divine vengeance that God suffers those ruling princes whom His almighty hand has marked out for destruction, deprived of all counsel and emptied of wisdom, to plunge headlong into the greatest ignominy. The proof of this is seen in that they believe themselves to be at their sanest when they are governing the Commonweal with incurable folly. But since the divine plans have always been concealed from mortal minds, we have investigated with the greatest care, and reported afresh from the very beginning, those matters which could be discerned and understood by human effort and wisdom.

[Bodin wrote the first version in French to reach the greatest possible number of his countrymen, particularly among the nobility. However at the persuasion of du Val he reluctantly agreed to prepare a Latin version. It was delayed by his voyage to England and the Low Countries, but after Alençon's death he set to work:]

In these circumstances, not being bound by the obligations of a translator, we have taken some things out, amended many others, and added still others. We have illustrated with clearer reasons and examples whatever seemed inaccurately or obscurely written on sovereignty, on the authority and duties of magistrates, and on the law of treaties. We have also added to the discussion of corporations and colleges a whole chapter on the classes of citizens, because the subject matter calls for it at this point. To this end, indeed, we have striven to bring it about that the later matters shall correspond to the earlier, the middle to both, and all to each other; and that things logically connected one with another, and related and linked among themselves, shall remain together in the same sequence; for in this way I thought it was easier to understand not only what follows what, but also what agrees with what.

We have used an ordinary and quiet kind of exposition, caring very little whether a melodious discourse flows gently to the ears and sweetly soothes the minds of readers, as long as the work commends itself by its ease and clarity. For the illnesses of sick men, as Celsus the physician fitly wrote, are not cured by ornamental words, nor are the diseases of Commonweals. I am very far from thinking that difficult and sublime matters, in the presentation of which the things themselves carry along the words, become more splendid by means of an excessively elevated and sumptuous style, as though served on plates of gold; nor do I think that the dignity and importance of things themselves is enhanced by this kind of allurement. I am content to eat choice delicacies from earthenware dishes, if only the latter are bright and clear.

Nevertheless two conflicting kinds of criticism have arisen. Some think that every question concerning the Commonweal could have been brought to a conclusion more briefly. Others consider it an outrage that anything was passed over. But when we contemplated individual instances, which are infinite, there were many things to be omitted in order that we might arrive at general rules, which is the proper method of expounding sciences. For long ago in my youth I learned from the philosophers that common saying: that there is no science of individual things. On the other hand those who wish to have less written on the Commonweal, and who lay down limits for someone else's labor, demand a moderation that is really difficult in a subject which up to now has not been assigned any boundaries or confined within a specific area by earlier writers. Indeed not even in sciences whose precepts are more definite do we see any boundaries being drawn. Certainly there is no way of finding out the truth except by searching, and fatigue in reading is shameful in a matter which is that much better the more it is unfolded, and sought out from more sources. Now if so many writers escape just criticism in other sciences which suffer from no graver defect than the volume of literature concerning them, why should we not permit ourselves to write a little more fully on a subject which is itself without limits? And especially since the advantages of this science are so many and so great that all kingdoms and all assemblies of men associated by law seem to endure by its aid alone, and since only this, of all the disciplines, seems fitting for princes, great men, and kings?

[However, scarcely any writers have covered the subject seriously, for various reasons (which are discussed in Knolles's Preface). Among the ancients those who understood it were considered supremely wise:]

But these wise men do not agree with us, nor even among themselves, as to the best type of Commonweal, not only because there is conflicting factual evidence on the question, but also because reason very often seems to contend against itself, although by nature this is impossible. But of the endless variety of opinions which arise from human error it must be either that none of them is true or else that no more than one of them is true. Accordingly we have felt that we must seek out, by the most exact balancing of reasons, not what each man has said or thought, and how great is his authority, but to what extent his opinion conforms to reason.

[To judge these matters a man needs a wide knowledge of constitutional law, of political philosophy, of the careers of good princes and the machinations of tyrants, of the institutions and environment of every nation, of the history of every Commonweal, and finally he needs also that practical wisdom which is gained not from precepts alone but from experience in public affairs.]

APPENDIX B

THE PRINCIPAL DEFINITIONS AND DISTINCTIONS

Certain concepts in the *République* are so central to Bodin's entire political system that it is desirable to reproduce his definitions of them in the most exact form possible, that is, in the original terminology of the French and Latin versions. I have selected the passages which follow to illustrate, as comprehensively as space will permit, the most important of these fundamental concepts. Where significant parallels are available in the *Methodus* or in the *Juris universi distributio*, these have been included to show the development of Bodin's thought. The question of definitions is not always a simple one, for often the repetition of a definition gives rise to considerable departures from the original wording. I have tried to reduce repetitions to a minimum, but all too often the variations which they contain are too important to be ignored. The passages from the *République* are based primarily upon the 1593 Vincent French edition and the 1591 du Puys Latin edition, but I have not hesitated to correct misprints and improve punctuation on the authority of other editions. The references following these quotations refer to the corresponding page and line of the present edition. The passages from the *Methodus* and the *Distributio* are from the first volume of Bodin's *Oeuvres philosophiques*, ed. P. Mesnard (Paris, 1951), hereafter cited as *O.P.*, I.

1. THE COMMONWEAL OR STATE

République: Republique est un droit gouvernement de plusieurs mesnages, & de ce qui leur est commun, avec puissance souveraine. (1 B8–10).

(Repeated at 9 A3–4. Also at 12 F6–7 and 84 I5–7 with *familles* in place of *mesnages*.)

De Republica: Respublica est familiarum rerumque inter ipsas communium summa potestate ac ratione moderata multitudo. (1 B8–10).

Diximus Rempublicam esse legitimam plurium familiarum & earum rerum, quae illis communes sunt, cum summa potestate gubernationem. (9 A3–4).

Quemadmodum igitur Respublica est legitima plurium familiarum & rerum inter se communium cum summa potestate gubernatio . . . (12 F6–7).

Et quoniam superius Rempublicam definivimus rectam plurium familiarum, ac rerum inter ipsas communium cum summa perpetuaque potestate, gubernationem . . . (84 I5–7).

(Among other variations here it will be noted that the last three of these definitions revert to a more literal translation of the original French definition.)

Methodus: Ex quo illud efficitur, ut Respublica nihil aliud sit, quam familiarum, aut collegiorum sub unum & idem imperium subjecta multitudo. (*O.P.*, I, 169).

Tres ergo pluresve familiae, aut quinque plurave collegia Rempublicam constituunt, si legitima imperii potestate simul conjungantur. (*Ibid.*, p. 168).

2. THE FAMILY

République: Mesnage est un droit gouvernement de plusieurs subjects, sous l'obeissance d'un chef de famille, & de ce qui luy est propre. (8 G6–8).

Repeated at 12 F7–10 with *famille* in place of *mesnage*).

De Republica: Familia est plurium sub unius ac ejusdem patrisfamilias imperium subditorum, earumque rerum, quae ipsius propriae sunt, recta moderatio. (8 G6–8).

... sic familia est plurium sub unius ac ejusdem patrisfamiliae imperio subditorum, & earum rerum, quae ipsius propriae sunt, recta gubernatio ... (12 F7–10).

Methodus: ... si plures, puta vir, uxor, liberi, servi; aut plures collegae ejusdem imperio privato, ac domestica potestate retineantur, familiam aut collegium efficiunt. (*O.P.*, I, 168).

3. THE CITIZEN

République: ... citoyen: qui n'est autre chose en propres termes, que le franc subject tenant de la souveraineté d'autruy. (47 A4–5).

(Repeated at 48 F3–4 and 57 B10–C1.)

De Republica: Est autem civis nihil aliud quam liber homo, qui summae alterius potestati obligatur. (47 A4–5).

Ex quo intelligitur veram esse civis, quam posuimus, definitionem, id est, liberum hominem, qui summae potestatis imperio teneatur. (48 F2–4).

Methodus: ... civis autem qui communi libertate fruitur, ac imperii tutela. (*O.P.*, I, 169).

4. SOVEREIGNTY

République: La souveraineté est la puissance absolue & perpetuelle d'une Republique ... (84 H6–7).

De Republica: Majestas est summa in cives ac subditos legibusque soluta potestas ... (84 H6–7).

The *Methodus* does not precisely define sovereignty but lists its characteristics as follows: Imperium multiplex est, sunt tamen omnino quatuor partes, ac totidem actionum genera, in quibus elucet imperii majestas. Prima in creandis magistratibus & imperio cuique tribuendo: altera in legibus jubendis aut abrogandis: tertia in bello indicendo ac finiendo: postrema in praemiis ac paenis decernendis, summaque vitae ac necis potestate. (*O.P.*, I, 120).

... video summam Reipublicae in quinque partibus versari. Una est ac praecipua, in summis magistratibus creandis, & officio cujusque definiendo: altera in legibus jubendis aut abrogandis: tertia in bello indicendo ac finiendo: quarta in extrema provocatione ab omnibus magistratibus: postrema in potestate vitae & necis, cum lex ipsa nec facilitatis ullum, nec clementiae locum relinquit. (*ibid.*, pp. 174–175).

(For a third but rather similar version, see *ibid.*, p. 168.)

5. LAW: THE DISTINCTION BETWEEN *JUS* AND *LEX*

République: ... mais il y a bien différence entre le droit & la loy: l'un n'emporte rien que l'equité, la loy emporte commandement: car la loy n'est autre chose que le commandement du souverain, usant de sa puissance. (108 I8–K1).

... veu que loy ne signifie autre chose que le commandement du souverain, ainsi que nous avons dit. (325 E7–8).

De Republica: ... sed plurimum distat lex a jure: jus enim sine jussu, ad id quod aequum, bonum est: lex autem, ad imperantis majestatem pertinet. Est enim lex nihil aliud, quam summae potestatis jussum. (108 I8–K1).

... ac verbum legis aliud nihil est, quam summae potestatis jussum. (325 E7–8).

Distributio: Jus est bonitatis & prudentiae divinae lux hominibus tributa, & ab iis ad utilitatem humanae societatis traducta ... Cum lex nihil aliud sit quam summae potestatis jussum sive sanctio. Est enim sancire & sciscere, jubere. (*O.P.*, I, 72).

(This clear separation between *jus* and *lex*, which recurs several times, seems to represent Bodin's predominant view, but on one occasion at least he introduces a normative element into his definition of *lex*:)

République: ... le mot de loy sans dire autre chose, signifie le droit commandement de celuy ou ceux qui ont toute puissance par dessus les autres sans exception de personne. (156 H8–10).

Appendix B

De Republica: ... leges propria sui acceptione definiemus recta summae potestatis jussa, sive unius, sive omnium, sive paucorum sit potestas. (156 H8–10).

6. THREE TYPES OF STATE: MONARCHY, ARISTOCRACY, AND DEMOCRACY

République: La Monarchie s'appelle quand un seul a la souveraineté, comme nous avons dit, & que le reste du peuple n'y a que voir: la Democratie ou l'estat populaire, quand tout le peuple, ou la plus part d'iceluy en corps a la puissance souveraine: l'Aristocratie, quand la moindre partie du peuple a la souveraineté en corps, & donne loy au reste du peuple, soit en general, soit en particulier. (184 F4–10).

Nous avons dit que la Monarchie est une sorte de Republique, en laquelle la souveraineté absolue gist en un seul Prince. (197 D6–8).

L'Aristocratie est une forme de Republique, où la moindre partie des citoyens commande au surplus en general par puissance souveraine, & sur chacun de tous les citoyens en particulier. (230 G7–9).

L'Estat populaire est la forme de Republique, où la pluspart du peuple ensemble commande en souveraineté au surplus en nom collectif, & à chacun de tout le peuple en particulier. (244 I9–K1).

De Republica: Monarchiam definiemus cum in unius dominatu versatur Reipublicae majestas, ad eum quem diximus modum. Democratiam cum omnes, aut major pars omnium civium simul collecta, summum Reipublicae imperium habet. Aristocratiam cum paucis quibusdam civibus in reliquos summum jus est. (184 F4–10).

Monarchiam Reipublicae genus esse diximus, in qua penes unum summa totius Reipublicae potestas est. (197 D6–8).

Aristocratia Reipublicae forma quaedam est in qua minor pars civium in universos, & singulos cives summae potestatis jus habet. (230 G7–9).

Respublica popularis est, in qua cives universi, aut maxima pars civium caeteris omnibus, non tantum singulatim, sed etiam simul coacervatis & collectis imperandi jus habent. (244 I9–K1).

7. THREE TYPES OF RULE: ROYAL, LORDLY, AND TYRANNICAL

République: Donc la Monarchie Royale, ou legitime, est celle où les subjects obeissent aux loix du Monarque, & le Monarque aux loix de nature, demeurant la liberté naturelle & proprieté des biens aux subjects. La Monarchie Seigneuriale est celle où le Prince est faict seigneur des biens & des personnes par le droit des armes, & de bonne guerre, gouvernant ses subjects comme le pere de famille ses esclaves. La Monarchie Tyrannique est où le Monarque mesprisant les loix de nature, abuse des personnes libres comme d'esclaves, & des biens des subjects comme des siens. La mesme difference se trouve en l'estat Aristocratique & populaire: car l'un & l'autre peut estre legitime, Seigneurial, ou Tyrannique en la sorte que j'ay dit. (200 F7–G5).

(The substance of this extract is repeated at 204 I1–8 and 210 G3–5.)

De Republica: Est igitur monarchia regalis, in qua subditi libertate ac dominio rerum fruentes, sui principis legibus obsequuntur: perinde ut Princeps ipse divinis ac naturae imperiis, obtemperandum judicat. Dominatus vero dicitur, cum Princeps unus, libertatis ac fortunarum omnium dominus, jure belli factus, aut foedere, subditos, quasi pater familias servos, moderatur. Tyrannis denique si Princeps imperiose, spretis gentium ac naturae legibus, subditorum bonis ac libertate ad libidinem abutatur. Eadem distinctio ad Aristocratiam & Democratiam adhiberi potest. (200 F7–G5).

(As in the French version, the substance is repeated at 204 I1–8 and 210 G3–5.)

Methodus: Monarchiam appello, quum summa potestas est in uno, qui jure imperat aut injuria. Hic tyrannus; ille rex appellatur ... Regum autem qui jure imperant, duo sunt genera: alteri quidem nulla tenentur lege: alteri legibus obligantur. (*O.P.*, I, 186).

(The discussion which follows reveals that these latter restraints include not only natural but also positive laws.)

8. THE SENATE

République: Le Senat est l'assemblee legitime des Conseillers d'estat, pour donner advis à ceux qui ont la puissance souveraine en toute Republique. (253 B10–C2).

De Republica: Senatus est legitimus eorum coetus qui de Republica, deque iis qui summam Reipublicae potestatem habent consilium capit. (253 B10–C2).

9. OFFICER, COMMISSIONER, AND MAGISTRATE

République: L'Officier est la personne publique qui a charge ordinaire limitee par edict. Commissaire, est la personne publique qui a charge extraordinaire, limitee par simple commission. Il y a deux sortes d'Officiers & de Commissaires: les uns qui ont puissance de commander, qui sont appellés magistrats: les autres de congnoistre ou d'executer les mandemens: & tous sont personnes publiques. (278 G6–H5).

Magistrat est l'officier qui a puissance en la Republique de commander. (293 B4–5).

De Republica: Officialis est publica persona quae munus habet lege definitum. Curator qui munus publicum extra ordinem sine lege, imperantis arbitrio gerit... Personas publicas appello, quae publicis muneribus incumbunt: harum autem duo sunt genera, alterum sine imperio, alterum cum imperio conjunctum. (278 G6–9, H1–5).

(The distinction between *officialis* and *curator* is repeated in substance at 293 B5–9.)

Magistratus est officialis qui publicum imperium habet. (293 B4–5).

Methodus: Sit ergo magistratus, is qui imperii publici partem habet. Publicum adjeci, ut ab imperio patrio & herili distinguatur. (*O.P.*, I, 173).

10. COLLEGE, CORPORATION, AND UNIVERSITY

De Republica: Collegium est legitima trium pluriumve personarum ejusdem conditionis consociatio: corpus vero plurium collegiorum conjunctio. Universitas est omnium familiarum, collegiorum, & corporum ejusdem oppidi juris communione sociata multitudo. (See the note at 361 B4.)

(The French version, which Knolles follows closely at this point, does not attempt precise definitions of these concepts. Cf. 361 C7–D3 and the note at 361 B4.)

11. JUSTICE

République: J'appelle justice le droit partage des loyers, & des peines, & de ce qui appartient à chacun en termes de droit ... (755 C9–10).

De Republica: Justitiam appello poenarum ac praemiorum, & earum rerum quae cujusque propriae sunt, aequabilem distributionem ... (755 C9–10).

APPENDIX C

A BIBLIOGRAPHY OF THE *RÉPUBLIQUE*

It may be helpful to begin with a word of explanation concerning the development of the text. It should be noted that a comparison of the early French editions yields many interesting insights into the evolution of Bodin's thought. From 1576 to 1580 there are no fewer than six separate stages in the development of the French text towards its ultimate form. The final stage of the French version was reached with the Paris octavo edition of 1580 (and possibly with the Lyon folio edition of 1579, which was not continuously available to me for comparison). Many of the more important variations between the French editions have been noted below, but since the text of the present edition already represents a combination of the French and Latin versions, it would have been far too cumbersome to document these variations in detail. It is greatly to be hoped that when a new edition of the French text is undertaken, the successive additions, deletions, and variant readings will be recorded in full. After 1580 the principal change in the French text is a gradual deterioration due to the cumulation of misprints. This slow corruption of the text, which particularly affects dates, numerals, and source references, is noticeable as early as the 1578 edition, but as long as Bodin was revising his text between editions, the corrections and additions were more significant than the extra misprints.

The Latin editions reveal no such process of textual evolution. Indeed it is doubtful whether Bodin himself had a part in revising any of the Latin editions. The first edition, like the first French edition, contains many misprints and apparent misreadings of the manuscript. On points of detail it is generally less reliable than the best French editions. The du Puys edition of 1591 does contain a few corrections, mainly of source references, that go further than the mere elimination of misprints, but they are so few and so conservative as to suggest that Bodin had no hand in them. The Frankfurt edition of 1591 was carefully revised on points of detail by someone who was obviously more familiar with German affairs. This anonymous editor improved the spelling and punctuation and clarified many of the proper names. In doing so, however, he sometimes misunderstood Bodin's meaning and corrupted the text. This edition became the first of a numbered series of editions of similar format and pagination, all printed in Germany. Like the later French editions, however, the later Latin editions tended to become less accurate from one edition to the next, sometimes as a result of smudged or defective print in the preceding edition, sometimes as a result of mere carelessness on the part of the printers.

The bibliography which follows was compiled through personal visits and inquiries by letter to more than three hundred major libraries and several union catalogues in Europe and North America. It contains at least seven editions and several adaptations which are not listed in any of the earlier bibliographies of Bodin's writings. I have been able to examine copies of most of the items listed at first hand, and in every case where this was impractical I have obtained microfilms or photostats of the title pages and of crucial passages in the text.

Although an inquiry of this sort does not permit a full bibliographical description of each item, I have tried to obtain for each entry enough data to eliminate any errors in identifying editions (e.g., as when two editions appeared in the same year and with the same place of publication), and also to make clear wherever possible the pedigree of the text itself of each edition or adaptation. In gathering these data quite a number of variant title pages have come to light, as the descriptions below will indicate. For each of the full-scale editions and for certain of the adaptations I have indicated the number of copies revealed by my survey, omitting a number reported as destroyed or doubtful as a result of the war. Since the survey undertaken was far from exhaustive, these figures should be taken merely as a very rough guide to the relative frequency of the various items. Probably the returns under Part II are less complete than those under Part I. As the results show, however, several of the items are extremely rare, and in these cases libraries reporting copies are listed by name.

The thirteen editions used in editing the present English text are indicated at the end of their respective entries by the symbols at the right-hand margin (Fr 1, Fr 2, L 1, L 2, etc.), and these same symbols are retained as standard abbreviations for these editions throughout the textual corrections and notes to the present edition. For each entry the number of pages refers to the text only, excluding the index, if any.

PART I: FULL-SCALE EDITIONS

French editions, under the title *Les six Livres de la Republique*

(1). 1576, Paris, folio, Jacques du Puys, 759 pp. The date of the privilege is August 12, 1576. Contains many misprints. Copies recorded: 19. —Fr 1

(2). 1577, Paris, folio, Jacques du Puys, 759 pp. The arrangement of chapters is that of Fr 1. Misprints noted at the end of the first edition remain listed and uncorrected, and the typesetting appears to be identical throughout with that of Fr 1. Copies recorded: 18.

(3). 1577, n.p. [Geneva], octavo, no printer [le Juge], 1102 pp. (as numbered, but actually 1086 pp). The printer and place of publication are known from a note by Jacques du Puys at the beginning of Fr 3–6. The arrangement of chapters is that of Fr 1. This edition was unauthorized, and the editor not only added a preface criticizing certain of Bodin's doctrines, but also amended the text in several places. Bodin made a vigorous reply in the Letter to Gui du Faur which is printed in Fr 3 and later French editions, but he also quietly incorporated some of the textual amendments of the Geneva editor in Fr 3 and later editions. For details of this edition, see M. Reulos, "L'Édition de 1577 de *La République*," *Bibliothèque d'humanisme et renaissance*, XIII (1951), 342–354. Copies recorded: 18.

(4). 1577, Paris, folio, Jacques du Puys, 797 pp. (as numbered). The text actually has 765 pages, and there is a gap in pagination between pp. 519 and 552. Contains corrections and additions to Fr 1 which constitute Bodin's first revision of the text. Among other changes, chapter 8 of Book I of Fr 1 becomes chapter 6 of Book V in this and all later editions. Copies recorded: 29.
—Fr 2

(5). 1578, Paris, folio, Jacques du Puys, 773 pp. "Reveue, corrigee & augmentee de nouveau. Troisieme edition." There are some fairly extensive additions which constitute a major revision of the text. Copies recorded: 25.
—Fr 3

(6). 1579, Paris, octavo, Jacques du Puys, 1058 pp. "Quatrieme edition." The text is largely that of Fr 3, but there are a few passages added which are to be found in no other edition (cf. below, notes at 92 G2, 95 E6, 99 B4, 99 C3, and 275 B1). Copies recorded: 20.
—Fr 4

(7). 1579, Lyon, folio, Jacques du Puys, 739 pp. The colophon reads: "A Lyon, de l'imprimerie de Jean de Tournes, M.D.LXXIX." The Preface occurs in two different typesettings, exemplified by copies in the British Museum and the Harvard Law School Library. There is a variant title page on which the imprint reads: "A Lyon, de

Appendix C

l'imprimerie [*or* l'inprimerie] de Jean de Tournes, M.D.LXXIX." At least some of the copies with this variant lack the Preface, the Letter to Pibrac, and the table of contents. Copies recorded: 27 (of which seven have the Jean de Tournes title page).

(8). 1580, Lyon, folio, Jacques du Puys, 739 pp. The colophon is the same as that of the 1579 folio edition, and the text appears to be from the same typesetting. The Preface of copies examined follows the typesetting of the Harvard Law School copy—rather than that of the British Museum copy—of the 1579 edition. Copies recorded: 23.

(9). 1580, Paris, octavo, Jacques du Puys, 1060 pp. The first and most accurate of a long series of octavo editions with identical or almost identical pagination. The text, which is apparently the same as that of (7) and (8), is thoroughly revised and enlarged in comparison with Fr 4. Copies recorded: 17.   —Fr 5

(10). 1583, Paris, octavo, Jacques du Puys [*or* du Puis], 1060 pp. The text is that of Fr 5, except for a few errors in typesetting. Copies recorded: 29 (at least five of which read "du Puis" instead of "du Puys" in the imprint).   —Fr 6

(11). 1587, Paris, octavo, Jaques (*sic*) du Puys, 1060 pp. This edition, though exceedingly rare, differs in its typesetting from all of the previous du Puys editions. Further, the characteristic printer's mark depicting Christ and the Samaritan woman, which is found in all previous du Puys editions, is replaced in this one by another simpler design. The only copy recorded is in the Bibliothèque Municipale at Rouen.

(12). 1587, Lyon, octavo, Gabriel Cartier, 1060 pp. The text is apparently based on Fr 6, but in contrast with all the du Puys editions there is at least one major deletion, that at p. 788 of a passage on the relationship of Geneva to Berne which had been altered in the Geneva edition of 1577 (cf. below, 618 110–619 B8). This deletion affects the pagination, but only to the end of the chapter in question. Copies recorded: 3 (London, Library of London School of Economics; Cambridge, Mass., Harvard Law School Library; Lausanne, Faculty of Theology of the Evangelical Church of the Canton of Vaud). But see remarks under (13).

(13). 1588, Lyon, octavo, Gabriel Cartier, 1060 pp. The typesetting is apparently identical with that of the Cartier edition of the previous year, and the same deletion occurs at p. 788. Copies recorded: 3 (Toulouse, University Library; Austin, University of Texas Library; and a private copy in the library of the Marquis de Villoutreys at Chaudron-en-Mauges, Maine-et-Loire). However there is some doubt about the dating of copies of (12) and (13). The 1587 London and Cambridge copies have an extra "I" added separately (making 1588), while the 1588 Texas copy appears to have the final "I" printed but not properly aligned, as if it too were added later. All six copies have ink alterations in varying degree to the "V," so that for M.D.LXXXVII(I) one might read M.D.LXXXXII(I). Further, the Cambridge, Lausanne, Toulouse, and Texas copies are bound with a 1594 edition of the *Apologie de René Herpin*, also printed at Lyon by Cartier.

(14). 1591, Lyon, octavo, Librairie des Jontes, 1060 pp. The text is apparently based on Fr 6. This edition retains the note by du Puys criticizing the 1577 Geneva edition, and unlike the Cartier editions it has no deletion at p. 788. Copies recorded: 2 (Toulouse, Bibliothèque Municipale; Avignon, Bibliothèque Calvet).

(15). 1593, Lyon, octavo, Barthelemy Vincent, 1060 pp. The text is based on Fr 6, but there are numerous additional misprints. This is the edition used by Knolles for almost all of his translation. Copies recorded: 34. Probably a few of these should have been reported under (16). —Fr 7

(16). 1593, Lyon, octavo, Gabriel Cartier, 1060 pp. The typesetting is apparently the same as that of (12) and (13), and the same deletion occurs on p. 788. Unlike (12) and (13), however, the date is printed in the form M.D.XCIII. Copies recorded: 9.

(17). 1594, Lyon, octavo, Gabriel Cartier, 1060 pp. The typesetting appears to be identical with that of (16), and the same deletion is of course found at p. 788. Copies recorded: 6.

(18). 1599, n.p., octavo, Gabriel Cartier, 1060 pp. The text appears to be based on that of (16) and (17), though the type has been reset. The same deletion occurs at p. 788. Most copies have no place of publication, but a few do have one as part of the imprint. Copies recorded: 23 (including two with a Cologne imprint at Lyon, Bibliothèque Municipale, and Vienna, Austrian National Library). —Fr 8

(19). 1608, n.p., octavo, Gabriel Cartier, 1060 pp. The text is based on Fr 8, but the typesetting is not identical. The usual deletion is found at p. 788. Most copies show no place of publication, but there are a few exceptions, as in the case of (18). Copies recorded: 19 (including one with a Cologne imprint at New York, Public Library, and two with a Geneva imprint at Reading, University Library, and Oxford, All Souls' Library).

(20). 1610, Lyon, folio, Gabriel Cartier, 739 pp. The text seems to be identical with that of (7) and (8), and this very scarce edition would appear to be a reissue of the earlier ones. The only copy reported, one which lacks the Preface, the Letter to du Faur, and the colophon leaf of (7) and (8), is in the Biblioteca Governativa at Lucca.

(21). 1612, Paris, octavo, Jacques du Puis, 1060 pp. The typesetting appears to be the same as that of the rare du Puys edition of 1587, (11) above, but unlike it this edition reverts on its title page to the usual printer's mark of Christ and the Samaritan woman. The only copy reported is in the Bibliotheek der Rijksuniversiteit at Ghent.

(22). 1629, Geneva, octavo, Estienne Gamonet, 1060 pp. The text is based upon one of the octavo Cartier editions, and the same deletion concerning Geneva occurs on p. 788. Copies recorded: 25 (including one with Lyon overprinted in place of Geneva, at Madrid, Biblioteca Nacional).

Latin editions, under the title *De Republica libri sex*

(23). 1586, "Lugduni, et venundantur Parisiis," folio, "apud Jacobum Du-puys," 779 pp. "Latine ab authore redditi, multo quam antea locupletiores." The colophon on p. 779 reads: "Lugduni, Impensis Jacobi du Puys." A note at the end of the privileges reads: "Achevé d'Imprimer le 25. Mars 1586," but the Preface is dated November 29, 1584. A few copies have a variant title page with a smaller version of the printer's mark (Christ and the Samaritan woman) and with the place of publication given simply as "Parisiis." Copies recorded: 93 (including five with the "Parisiis" variant at Dublin, Trinity College Library; Aarau, Aargauische Kantonsbibliothek; Cologne, Universitäts- und Stadtbibliothek; Cracow, Biblioteka Jagiellońska; Rome, Vatican Library). —L 1

(24). 1591, n.p., octavo, "apud Jacobum Du-puys," 1132 pp. (as numbered). "Et nunc hac secunda editione ex authoris autographo recogniti, multisque mendis quae partim in contextum, partim in legum adnotationes ad marginem appositas, in priore editione irrepserant, repurgati." These emendations are of a minor nature only. There are actually 1032 pages of text, and p. 662 follows immediately after p. 561. Copies recorded: 30. —L 2

Appendix C

(25). 1591, Frankfurt, octavo, "apud Joannem Wechelum & Petrum Fischerum consortes," 1221 pp. "Editio altera, priore multo emendatior." The text is based on that of L 1, but as noted above it has been carefully revised by another editor. Copies recorded: 40.
—L 3

(26). 1594, Frankfurt, octavo, "apud Joan. Wecheli viduam, sumtib[us] Petri Fischeri," 1221 pp. "Editio Tertia." The text is based closely on that of L 3, but there are additional misprints. Copies recorded: 37. —L 4

(27). 1601, "Ursellis" (i.e., Ober Ursel), octavo, "ex officina Cornelii Sutorii: sumtibus Jonae Rhodii Bibliopolae," 1221 pp. "Editio Quarta." The text is based closely on that of L 4, but there are quite a few additional misprints. Copies recorded: 32. —L 5

(28). 1609, Frankfurt, octavo, "e Typographeo Nicolai Hoffmanni, Impensa Haeredum Petri Fischeri," 1221 pp. "Editio Quinta." The text is based on that of L 5. Copies recorded: 41.

(29). 1619, "Lutetiae Parisiorum, et venundantur Francofurti in Officina Elzeviriana," folio, 779 pp. The colophon on p. 779 reads: "Lugduni, Impensis Jacobi du Puys," and the typesetting of the text appears to be identical with that of L 1. Apparently a reissue of (23). Copies recorded: 3 (Dublin, Trinity College Library; Lund, University Library; Naples, Biblioteca Nazionale Vittorio Emanuele III).

(30). 1622, Frankfurt, octavo, "sumptibus Viduae Jonae Rosae Bibl[iopolae] typis vero Hartmanni Palthenii," 1221 pp. "Editio Sexta." The text is probably based on that of the 1609 edition. Copies recorded: 30.

(31). 1641, Frankfurt, octavo, "sumptibus Jonae Rosae viduae, typis Anthoni Hummi," 1221 pp. "Editio Septima." The text is probably based on that of the 1622 edition. Copies recorded: 38.

Italian edition, under the title *I sei libri della republica*

(32). 1588, Genoa, small folio, Girolamo Bartoli, 691 pp. (as numbered). "Tradotti di lingua Francese nell' Italiana da Lorenzo Conti gentil' huomo Genovese." Actually the text has 703 pages, the first twelve leaves being numbered on the recto side only. There are some substantial omissions in the text, notably on papal questions, but these omissions are indicated by asterisks. The translation is made from (7) or (8) or (9). Copies recorded: 23.

Spanish edition, under the title *Los seis libros de la republica*

(33). 1590, Turin, folio, "por les herederos de Bevilaqua," 638 pp. "Traducidos de lengua Francesa, y enmendados Catholicamente por Gaspar de Añastro Ysunza, Thesorero General de la Serenissima Infanta de España Doña Catalina, Duquesa de Savoya... Con licencia de los Inquisidores." There are omissions in the text similar to those of the Italian edition but not identical with them, and there are also a few passages added to Bodin's text, which are in italics. The translation is made from (7) or (8) or (9). Copies recorded: 8.

German editions

(34). 1592, Mumpelgart (i.e., Montbéliard), small folio, "Gedruckt... durch Jacob Foillet Fuerstlichen Buchdrucker in verlegung Nicolai Bassaei," 775 pp. A translation made from the French and the Latin versions by Johann Oswaldt, pastor of Mömpelgard. There is a long title which begins: *Respublica Das ist: Gruendtliche und rechte Underweysung, oder eigentlicher Bericht, in welchem ausfuehrlich vermeldet wirdt, wie nicht allein das Regiment wol zubestellen, sonder auch in allerley Zustandt, so wol in Krieg unnd Widerwertigkeit, als Frieden und Wolstand zu erhalten sey*... Copies recorded: 15.

(35). 1611, Frankfurt, small folio, "Gedruckt... bey Johann Saurn, in verlegung Petri Kopffen," 775 pp. The title differs somewhat from that of the earlier German edition, beginning: *Von Gemeinem Regiment der Welt. Ein Politische, gruendtliche und rechte Underweisung, auch herrlicher Bericht, in welchem ausfuehrlich vermeldet wirdt, wie nicht allein das Regiment wol zubestellen, sonder auch in allerley Zustandt, so wol in Krieg und Widerwertigkeit, als Frieden und Wollstandt, zu erhalten sey...* The text is the same as that of the 1592 edition, and the University of Basel, which has both editions, reports that the later one is a reissue under a new title. Copies recorded: 3 (Basel, University Library; Hamburg, Staats- und Universitäts-Bibliothek; Munich, Bayerische Staatsbibliothek).

English edition, under the title *The Six Bookes of a Commonweale*

(36). 1606, London, small folio, "Impensis G. Bishop," 794 pp. (as numbered, but actually 806 pp). The text forms the basis of the present edition. The colophon shows that Adam Islip was the printer. The leaves from 625 to 636 inclusive are numbered on the recto side only. There is a variant title page, lacking the engraving, which bears the title: *Of the Lawes and Customes of a Common-wealth. Learnedly discoursing of the power of Soveraignety and Majestracy, and of the Orders and degrees of Citizens, with the priviledges of Corporations and Colledges: and other things pertinent to Estates and Societies.* Copies recorded: 49 (including seven with the "Lawes and Customes" title page at Ann Arbor, University of Michigan Law Library and Clements Library; Dublin, National Library of Ireland; London, Library of London School of Economics; Ottawa, National Library of Canada; Oxford, Christ Church Library; Washington, Library of Congress Law Library).

PART II: ADAPTATIONS AND ABRIDGEMENTS

Note: This list is deliberately selective. I have excluded, for example, reprints of the financial and monetary chapters of the *République* which were closely associated with later editions of the *Response à M. de Malestroit*, such as those by Renerus Budelius (*De monetis et re numaria*, Cologne, 1591), by Hermann Conring (Helmstadt, 1671, and reprinted in his *Opera*, IV, Braunschweig, 1730), and by Henri Hauser (Paris, 1932). Items like these are narrowly specialized and belong more properly to the study of Bodin's economic doctrines. The works listed below reflect the influence of his political ideas.

(37). *De speciebus rerumpublicarum.* 1581, Magdeburg, octavo, "apud Johannem Francum," 190 pp. (pages not numbered). A Latin translation of Book II by Johann Schröder, together with a table of contents of the entire work. This is the earliest appearance of the *République* in Latin. The translation is a faithful one and is made from either (5) or (6). Copies recorded: 3 (Wolfenbüttel, Herzog August Bibliothek; Budapest, National Széchényi Library; Cambridge, Mass., Harvard Law School Library).

(38). *Synopsis: sive medulla in sex libr. Johan. Bodini Andegavensis, De Republica.* 1635, Amsterdam, duodecimo, "apud Joannem Janssonium," 883 pp. Questions and answers based upon a Latin edition, by Johann Angelius von Werdenhagen. There is much extraneous material, particularly of a theological nature, and the work is of little use for the study of Bodin. Copies recorded: 8.

(39). *De republica librorum breviarium.* 1645, Amsterdam, duodecimo, "ex officina Joanni Janssonii," 883 pp. New edition, under another title, of Werdenhagen's *Synopsis* of 1635. Copies recorded: 28.

(40). *The Necessity of the Absolute Power of all Kings: And in particular, of*

Appendix C

the Kings of England. 1648, London, quarto, no printer or publisher [Richard Royston], 12 pp. A tract prepared by Sir Robert Filmer and later republished as his own. Apart from one or two brief sentences it consists entirely of extracts from the English edition of 1606. In most copies of the 1648 edition no author is named, but there is a variant title page (at King's College, Cambridge, and at the London School of Economics) which accurately ascribes it to "John Bodin a Protestant according to the Church of Geneva."

(41). *The Power of Kings: And in Particular, of the Kings of England.* 1680, London, folio, "Printed for W. H. & T. F. and are to be sold by Walter Davis," 12 pp. Second edition of the *Necessity*, which is now attributed specifically to Sir Robert Filmer.

(42). *The Free-holders Grand Inquest* ... 1684, London, octavo, Richard Royston, 346+141 pp. A collection of Sir Robert Filmer's tracts which includes *The Power of Kings* (pp. 293–308).

(43). *Observations concerning the Original and Various Forms of Government.* 1696, London, octavo, "Printed for R. R. C. and are to be sold by Samuel Keble ... and Daniel Brown ..." 346+141 pp. Another issue, with a cancel title leaf, of the Filmer collection of 1684. It retains *The Power of Kings* (pp. 293–308).

(44). *Abrégé de la République de Bodin.* 1755, London, duodecimo, Jean Nourse, 2 vols, 466, 417 pp. A very free adaptation of the *République* by Jean-Charles de Lavie, a president of the Parlement of Bordeaux and a colleague of Montesquieu's. The work is heavily influenced by the *Esprit des Lois*. Lavie revises Bodin's order and style, omitting a good deal of detail and adding reflections of his own, some of which are quite contrary to Bodin's own views. Copies recorded: 19.

(45). *De la République, traité de Jean Bodin, ou traité du gouvernement.* 1756, "A Londres, et se trouve à Paris," duodecimo, la Veuve Quillau, 480 pp. An adaptation, into the eighteenth-century setting, of the contents of Book I only. A note on the title page indicates that the text is checked against the Latin edition of 1591 (L 3), but the chapter arrangement follows the order of Fr 1. The editing is attributed to Charles-Armand L'Escalopier de Nourar (1709–1779). Copies recorded: 4 (Paris, Bibliothèque Nationale and Bibliothèque de l'Institut de France; Amsterdam, University Library; Aarau, Aargauische Kantonsbibliothek).

(46). *Des Corps politiques et de leurs gouvernements.* 1764, Lyon, duodecimo, Pierre Duplain, l'aîné, 2 vols., 453, 559 pp. A free adaptation by J.-C. de Lavie of his own earlier *Abrégé* (44). The arrangement of materials is altered once again, the chapters being divided into nine books instead of six, and several new topics are discussed. "Ce n'est point un Abrégé de la République de Bodin: on y trouvera plus d'ordre, de méthode, de raisonnements que dans cet Auteur, & plus de matieres qu'il n'en a traité. On ne prétend pas cependant disconvenir que c'est lui qui a donné l'idée de cet Ouvrage, & même fourni le canevas. On a cru se rendre utile en remettant au jour la plupart des maximes de ce savant homme; & par l'aveu que l'on en fait, éviter le titre de plagiaire." Copies recorded: 5.

(47). *Des Corps politiques et de leurs gouvernements.* 1766, Lyon, quarto, Pierre Duplain, l'aîné, 2 vols., 420, 332 pp. "Seconde édition revue & très-augmentée." Copies recorded: 2 (Leipzig, Karl Marx University Library, and a private copy owned by Robert Shackleton, Oxford).

(48). *Des Corps politiques et de leurs gouvernements.* 1766, Lyon, duodecimo, Pierre Duplain, l'aîné, 3 vols., 492, 483, 362 pp. "Seconde édition revue & très-augmentée." Copies recorded: 8.

(49). *Des Corps politiques et de leurs gouvernements.* 1767, Lyon, duodecimo,

Pierre Duplain, l'Aîné, 3 vols., 492, 483, 362 pp. "Quatrieme Edition revue & corrigée." Copies recorded: 3 (Limoges, Bibliothèque Municipale; Marburg, Westdeutsche Bibliothek; New Haven, Yale University Library, which lacks Vol. III).

(50). *De la Législation; ou du gouvernement politique des Empires: extrait de Bodin.* 1768, "A Londres, et se trouve à Paris," duodecimo, Cailleau, 2 vols., 466, 417 pp. Second edition (or a reissue) of Lavie's *first* adaptation, (44) above. The only copy recorded is in the Harvard College Library, Cambridge, Mass.

(51). *Des États Généraux, et autres assemblées nationales.* 1788–1789, "A La Haye, & se trouve à Paris," octavo, Buisson, 18 vols. A collection of sources and documents concerning the Estates General, edited by Charles-Joseph Mayer, which appeared on the eve of the critical meeting of the Estates in 1789. Pages 305–401 of Vol. VI are devoted to extracts from the *République* consisting of passages on sovereignty (Book I, ch. 8), on the limited powers of the Estates General (Book I, ch. 8), on hereditary versus elective monarchy (Book VI, ch. 5), on popular consent to taxation (Book VI, ch. 2), on voting procedure in the Estates (Book III, ch. 7), and on the advantages of regional estates (Book III, ch. 7).

(52). *Abrégé de la République de Bodin.* 1793, Paris, duodecimo, Cailleau, 2 vols., 466, 417 pp. Third edition of Lavie's *first* adaptation, (44) above. The only copy recorded is that in the Bibliothèque Nationale, Paris.

(53). *La Repubblica e suo governo.* 1808, "Italia," octavo, "presso i principali Librai," 83 pp. A rather free summary in Italian of the argument of the *République*, based on the French version. At the end of the summary there are a number of anecdotes drawn from the text (pp. 60–83). The work is anonymous. Copies recorded: 2 (Pavia, Biblioteca Universitaria; Bergamo, Biblioteca Civica).

(54). *Patriarcha and Other Political Works of Sir Robert Filmer.* Edited by P. Laslett. 1949, Oxford, Basil Blackwell, 326 pp. A scholarly edition with an excellent introduction to Filmer's thought. The *Necessity* pamphlet (40) is reprinted at pp. 317–326.

(55). *De la République: Extraits.* 1949, Paris, Librairie de Médicis, 111 pp. Selected passages from the French version, based on the 1580 folio edition, (8) above. The inner title page bears the subtitle "Fragments."

(56). *Six Books of the Commonwealth.* n.d. [1955], Oxford, Basil Blackwell, and New York, Macmillan, 212 pp. An abridged translation by Miss M. J. Tooley comprising about one fifth of the French text. It is based on (7) or (8).

DOUBTFUL EDITIONS

The following editions are also mentioned by various bibliographical authorities which are listed beside each entry, but I have found no trace of them in my own survey. A few seem fairly obviously to be mistakes, but in view of the extreme rarity of some editions that unquestionably do exist, it would be rash to suppose them non-existent, and still more so to assume that they never did exist.

1577, Lausanne (J.-P. Nicéron, *Mémoires pour servir à l'histoire des hommes illustres* [Paris, 1729–1745]). Doubtless an error for the 1577 Geneva edition, which carries no place of publication, but repeated in J.-C. Brunet, *Manuel du Libraire*, 5th ed. (Paris, 1860–1864), and in J. G. T. Graesse, *Trésor de livres rares et précieux* (Dresden, 1859 1865).

1582, Paris, folio (A. du Verdier, *La Bibliothèque* [Lyon, 1585]).

1597, Paris, octavo, G. Cartier, 2 vols. (Graesse, *Trésor de livres rares et précieux*).

Appendix C

1598, Lyon, octavo, Librairie des Jontes (H. Baudrier, *Bibliographie Lyonnaise*, 13 vols. [Lyon, 1895–1950]).

1600, Geneva, octavo (Nicéron, *Mémoires*, and Moreri, *Le grand Dictionnaire historique*, new ed. [Paris, 1759]). Since Moreri states that Bodin's "monetary treatises" are appended to this edition, he is apparently referring to a French edition.

1588, Genevae, octavo (Nicéron, *Mémoires*). Though Nicéron does not specify, this is listed as though it were a Latin edition.

1598, Argentorati (i.e., Strasbourg), octavo (Nicéron, *Mémoires*). Also listed as though it were a Latin edition.

1614, Francofurti, octavo (Nicéron, *Mémoires*). Misprint for 1641 edition?

1645, Coloniae, duodecimo (Nicéron, *Mémoires*). Error for (39) above?

APPENDIX D

A NOTE ON THE PRESENT EDITION

In the preparation of the present edition Knolles's text has been subjected to a thorough comparison, line by line, and sometimes even word by word, with the French and Latin versions. Wherever discrepancies exist I have sought to trace their cause and to establish the reading that Bodin intended. For this textual work some thirteen French and Latin editions have been used regularly, and further French editions where they are helpful. The five Latin editions represent all that had been published when Knolles's translation was made. The eight French editions were carefully selected so as to represent not only the various stages in the evolution of the French text, but also its gradual corruption by misprints as one edition succeeded another to the end of the sixteenth century. To facilitate references and to show the pattern of textual development more clearly these editions were given symbols in chronological sequence from Fr 1 to Fr 8 and from L 1 to L 5. The editions to which these symbols correspond are fully identified in Appendix C. In the case of the French editions two further textual collations were made. Bodin's final revision of the text (represented by Fr 5) was compared with that of the stage immediately preceding (Fr 4) and—at a somewhat earlier point in the project—with his first revision of the text (Fr 2), in order to throw further light upon the growth of the text. The results of these extra comparisons have been useful both directly and indirectly in preparing the present edition.

Because of the rigidity of a text that is photographically reproduced, the critical apparatus takes two forms, textual corrections at the bottom of the individual page and notes following the end of the text. For both I have indicated the location on any page by counting the lines from the block letters found in the margins of the 1606 edition (e.g., A7, B4, G10, K3, etc.). The textual corrections themselves need little explanation. At points where the printers have obviously missed a word or two—or occasionally even a whole line—in the manuscript, or where the manuscript itself may have contained an accidental omission, I have employed small capitals to indicate my reconstruction of the missing part. These additions are generally confined to changes which *must* be made in order to read the English text as a sensible translation of what Bodin wrote. Misprints have been corrected wherever found, even the more obvious ones, on the supposition that this will make for easier recognition of spelling variations then current. On the other hand, punctuation changes have been suggested very sparingly, indeed only where their absence might lead to confusion. Even though textual evidence suggests that the printers decided much of the punctuation on their own authority, there are so many faults and so many variations in the French and Latin editions that a fully authoritative English version would be extremely difficult to achieve, if not impossible. Minor variations in the French and Latin editions, especially those which have corrupted Knolles's text, have also been noted in the corrections rather than in the notes wherever this is feasible. Beyond this, a few English words which either have become obsolete or have lost their sixteenth-century meanings have been explained, particularly where they might mislead a modern reader as to the reading in the original versions. Finally the textual corrections indicate in every case the lines concerning which notes will be found at the end of the text.

The notes have three main purposes.

APPENDIX D

They amend Knolles's errors in translation, they record the more significant variations between the French and Latin, and they translate additional passages not included in Knolles's version. As explained in the Introduction, virtually all passages omitted in the Knolles version have been indicated in the notes, and almost all of these have been translated in full. The only exceptions are (1) source references mentioned in the text rather than in the margin, which Knolles occasionally omits just as he omits many of the marginal source references, (2) a few dates, which generally occur either in the French text only or in the Latin only, (3) minor additions and embellishments that add nothing of substance to the text, and (4) a few additions, usually in the Latin version, which simply repeat points made elsewhere in the book. I have used the symbol ‖ to indicate the point in Knolles's text at which an addition occurs in one or both of the original versions, although in a few instances this point is difficult to determine exactly, owing to major variations between the French and Latin. Occasionally too the notes will seem disjointed when Knolles's translation errs in such a way that it cannot easily be patched up. In these cases one must simply make the best possible reconstruction of an awkward and intractable passage.

In general I have tried as far as possible to adopt a consistent boundary line between textual corrections and notes. Errors which appear to be printer's faults or perhaps inadvertent slips in the manuscript are corrected at the foot of the page. Genuine translation errors, deliberate departures from Bodin's text, and outright omissions are treated in the notes. It is almost needless to add that in some instances this line is exceedingly difficult to draw, and in others the limited space for corrections has prevented its full application.

Further conventions which I have adopted deserve to be mentioned here. Since sixteenth-century typography interchanged the letters "u" and "v," and also "i" and "j," without any rigid rule, I have written these letters in accordance with modern spelling, except in the relatively few instances where the actual form used helps to explain a misprint. Again, I have written diphthongs as separate letters except where there is a misprint involving the diphthong itself. In quoting from the French version I have followed carefully the orthography of the printed editions, using accents only in the relatively few places where sixteenth-century usage has them. Knolles's own quotations differ in many details of punctuation and spelling from Bodin's, but only the outright misprints and the more barbarous spelling variations in the English edition have been corrected. A fair number of variations sanctioned by contemporary usage have been allowed to stand. In all likelihood the corrected English text differs no more from the originals than the various French and Latin editions differ among themselves. Finally, the lettering on the inner margins of the text is frequently out of alignment. To make the numbering of corrections and notes more consistent I have tried to read the letters where they *ought* to be (i.e., reckoning four sections of ten lines and a fifth of nine lines), and I have capitulated to the inaccuracy of the spacing only when the misplacement is as much as the full depth of a line, or more.

It may be appropriate to add a few notes on the physical reproduction of the text. The great bulk of the present edition has been photographed from a copy of the 1606 edition in my own possession. When purchased this copy was heavily defaced and underlined in red pencil on most of its pages, but careful work with a soft eraser reduced these markings enough to make them disappear in photography. Fortunately this copy had very few pen-and-ink markings on its pages, and it has been relatively simple to remove practically all of these on the photographic negatives. Similarly, the negatives have been retouched wherever feasible to remove or diminish black spots caused by stains and defects in the copy photographed.

It is quite probable that no two copies of the 1606 edition are completely identical. One finds misprints in some copies that do not occur in others, and no obvious printing

A Note on the Present Edition

sequence stands out from the copies that I have examined. Even grammatical changes occur from one copy to another. Thus in the sixth line from the end of Knolles's Dedication to Manwood the verb "excell" reads more correctly "excelleth" in some copies.

Although by far the greatest part of the present edition is founded upon my own copy of the 1606 edition, some readers may wish to know which pages are not. Two pages only, seriously defective in my copy, were photographed wholly from other copies: page 159 is reproduced from the copy in the Harvard Law School Library, page 536 from a copy owned by the late Judge H. C. Dowdall and now donated to the National Library of Canada. Some thirteen other pages were partially defective in my copy owing to bad printing, stains, or holes in the paper. For these pages a photographic negative was made from the McRae copy, and the missing or faulty portions were then repaired by stripping in small portions of the text or marginal notes photographed from the corresponding page of the Dowdall or Harvard Law School copy, or from other pages of the McRae copy where the needed words recur. The pages put together in this way are: 54, 210, 303, 317, 333, 397, 398, 441, 442, 443, 444, 630, 727. On most of these pages the inserted portions can barely be detected.

Beyond this the offset printers have carried out minor retouching of the negatives in some instances where individual letters have wholly or partially vanished owing to faint print or minor paper defects in the photographed copy. The aim has been to keep these changes at a minimum and to present a text as close to the original as is consistent with reasonable legibility. Unlike the blending of photographic negatives, retouching by hand is generally discernible on close examination.

Page numbering presents something of a problem. Rather more than a dozen pages were misnumbered in the original English edition—though the count varies slightly from copy to copy—and a few other page numbers are faint to the point of illegibility. Moreover, twelve leaves at the end of Book V are numbered on the recto side only. For this new edition correct page numbers have been set beside the old ones wherever the latter are erroneous or illegible. But the twelve verso pages that have no numeration at all have been given a simple verso designation in order to preserve the original pagination throughout the remainder of the text. Thus on these twelve leaves the sequence runs 625, 625^v, 626, 626^v, etc.

During the photographic process the original type size has been reduced very slightly to enable the volume to conform to the format of the series.

The following abbreviations have been adopted:

Methodus   J. Bodin, *Method for the Easy Comprehension of History*, tr. B. Reynolds, New York, 1945 (except for instances where another edition is specifically cited).

Response (ed. Hauser)   J. Bodin, *La Response de Jean Bodin à M. de Malestroit*, ed. H. Hauser, Paris, 1932.

Response (ed. Moore)   J. Bodin, *The Response of Jean Bodin to the Paradoxes of Malestroit*, tr. G. A. Moore, Chevy Chase, Md., 1946. Translation of the considerably revised second edition.

O.P., I   J. Bodin, *Oeuvres philosophiques*, I, ed. P. Mesnard, Paris, 1951.

Apologie   [J. Bodin], *Apologie de René Herpin pour la Republique de I. Bodin*, Lyon, 1593. This edition is appended to the 1593 Vincent edition of the *République*.

Ferrier   A. Ferrier, *Advertissemens à M. Jean Bodin sur le quatriesme livre de sa Republique*, Paris, 1580.

Reulos   M. Reulos, "L'Édition de 1577 de La République," *Bibliothèque d'humanisme et renaissance*, XIII(1951), 342–354.

Cotgrave   R. Cotgrave, *A Dictionarie of the French and English Tongues*, London, 1611.

O.E.D.   *The Oxford English Dictionary*, ed. J. A. H. Murray, H. Bradley, W. A. Craigie, and C. T. Onions,

Appendix D

12 vols. and supplement, Oxford, 1933.

In citing Greek and Latin authors I have attempted in all cases to give references in a form common to most modern editions, either by book and chapter (e.g., Livy, XXXIV, 9) or by a generally recognized and standardized pagination (e.g., Aristotle, *Politics*, 1303a). References to the *Digest* and *Code* are based on the stereotype editions of the *Corpus Juris Civilis* edited by Mommsen and Krueger.

THE ARGUMENT OF THE *RÉPUBLIQUE*

Book I

CHAPTER 1 (PAGES 1–8)

Definition of the state, 1. The state, as a lawful association, differs from associations of robbers and pirates, 1. Status of robbers and pirates, 2–3. The state defined by some as an association for living well, 3. Defects of this definition, 3. The *summum bonum* for state and individual: the contemplative versus the active life, 4–7.

CHAPTER 2 (PAGES 8–14)

The family defined, 8. Family and state compared, 8. Minimum and maximum size, 9. The essential feature is the authority relationship, 10. Property, public and private, 11. Necessity of private property, 11–13. Certain families bound by family or private laws, 13. Relation of family laws to public law, 13–14.

CHAPTER 3 (PAGES 14–20)

All associations, public or private, bound by the relationship of command and obedience, 14. Four kinds of domestic authority, 14. Even the state of natural liberty involves the rule of reason, 14–15. Domestic authority I: husband and wife, 15. Authority of the husband based on lawful marriage, 15. Wives generally under the authority of their husbands, 15–18. Divorce, 18–19. Wives usually take the social status of their husbands, 19–20.

CHAPTER 4 (PAGES 20–31)

Domestic authority II: father and children, 20. Children obliged to obey their fathers, 20–21. Examples of disobedience, 21–22. Parents should have the power of life and death, 22–25. Emancipation of children, 25–26. Sons should not resist or kill their fathers for any reason whatever, 26–27. Objection: that some fathers may abuse their power, 27–28. Second objection: that inheritances may be divided unjustly, 28–29. Questions concerning adoptive children, 29–31.

CHAPTER 5 (PAGES 32–46)

Domestic authority III and IV: masters over slaves and wage servants, 32. Types of slavery, 32. Servants cannot prejudice their liberty, but do have special obligations to their masters, 33. Whether slavery is natural and in the public interest, 33. Arguments for slavery, 33–34. Arguments against slavery, 34–39. Decline and revival of slavery, 39–44. Resolution of the question, 44–46.

CHAPTER 6 (PAGES 46–69)

The transition from the family to civil society, 46–47. Definition of citizen and subject, 48. Different classes of subjects, 48–49. Distinctions among commonweal, city, and town, 49–53. Criticism of Aristotle's definition of the citizen, 53. Types of citizenship at Rome, 54–57. Honorary citizenship, 58–59. Citizenship doubtful in certain border territories, 59–60. Subjects require the sovereign's permission to leave the country, 60–62. How citizenship is acquired or lost, 62–64. Differences between citizens and aliens: (1) subjection to the sovereign, 64; (2) holding of offices and benefices, 64; (3) freedom from impositions and tributes, 64–65; (4) right to make testaments and to inherit, 65; (5) right to own land, 65–66. Other differences, 66–67. Subjects remain bound to their sovereign, 67–68. Citizens everywhere divided into social classes, 68–69.

CHAPTER 7 (PAGES 69–84)

The concept of protection, and its different forms, 69–70. Protection differs from

Argument: Book I

vassalage, 70–71. Protection applied to sovereign princes, 71–72. Protection does not involve loss of sovereignty, 72. Types of treaties, 73–74. Position of co-allies, 74. Commercial treaties, 74. Enemies defined, 75. Treaties do not affect sovereignty, 75. Whether close confederacies constitute a unified state, 75. Consideration of Switzerland and other examples that retained divided sovereignty, 75–79. The Achaean League and other examples of unified sovereignty, 79–81. All confederacies require a unified military command, 81–82. Special position of the German Empire in Swiss treaties, 82–83. Whether subjects may enter into treaties without the sovereign's consent, 83–84.

Chapter 8 (pages 84–113)

Sovereignty defined, 84. Sovereign authority must be perpetual, 84–86. It must not be accountable to any person or group, 86. Regencies, 86–87. Grants of authority for life, 87–88. Perfect and imperfect donations of authority, 88. Examples of investiture of authority, 89–90. A subject may be exempted from the laws without becoming sovereign, 90–91. A sovereign is not bound by the laws of his predecessors, 91. Nor by his own laws, 91–92. But he is bound by the laws of God and nature, 92. If he promises to observe the laws, he is bound by his promise, as far as it is equitable, 92–93. Examples of coronation oaths, 94–95. The sovereign is bound by *leges imperii*, 95. Subordinate role of estates or parliaments in legislation, 95–98. The sovereign may legislate alone, and he cannot logically be bound to observe the laws, 98–100. Promises to observe the laws derogate from sovereignty, 100–101. Alleged examples of irrevocable laws, 101–102. These examples refuted, 102–103. The sovereign is bound by divine and natural law, 104–106. He is bound by his contracts and promises, 106–107. But he is not bound by Roman law, 107–108. Even popes and emperors are bound by divine and natural law, 108–109. Corollary: the inviolability of private property rights, 109–111. To what extent a sovereign is bound to the promises and contracts of his predecessors, 111–113.

Chapter 9 (pages 114–153)

Whether sovereignty is compatible with feudal obligations, 114–115. Nine degrees of inferiority and superiority, 115. Difference between vassal and subject, 115–116. Consideration of examples: England, 116; Scotland, 116–117; Denmark, 117; Brittany, 117–119. Feudal service is incompatible with sovereignty, 119. Manner of doing homage, 119–121. Feudal obligations of the Emperor Charles V, 121–123. Digression on liege fealty, 123–125. Other territories of Charles V also held in fealty, 125–127. The French claim to Castile, 127. Sovereignty in the German Empire is in the estates, 128. Italian cities not sovereign, 128–131. German cities not sovereign, 131. Switzerland, 131. Lorraine and other border territories, 132–133. Savoy, 133. Relationship between France and the Empire, 134–135. Lithuania and Poland, 136. Rise of the papacy, 136–140. Hungary, 140. The Kingdom of Jerusalem, 140. Navarre, 141. Other papal claims, 141. The popes are vassals of the Empire, 141–142. Relationship between the Pope and the Emperor, 142–145. Between the Pope and the King of France, 145–147. Superior and inferior princes in other countries, 147–149. Prerogative of honor among princes and states, 149–153.

Chapter 10 (pages 153–182)

The marks of sovereign authority: consideration of earlier views, 153–154. The marks of sovereignty must be only those rights which are not exercised by vassals, magistrates, or subjects, 154–155. Criticism of Aristotle's definition, 155–156. Law (*lex*) as the command of the sovereign authority, 156. Definition of edict, 156–157. Consideration of objections: other bodies make laws by sufferance of the sovereign, 157–159. The first and highest mark of sovereignty is a general power to make laws, 159–160. Laws differ from privileges, 160. And from customs, 160–

Argument: Book I

161. Abrogation and interpretation of laws, 161. Second mark: the power of war and peace, 162. Consideration of examples and objections, 162–166. Third mark: appointment of higher magistrates, 166. Examples and exceptions, 166–168. Fourth mark: power to hear last appeals, 168. Examples and exceptions, 168–171. Fifth mark: power of pardon, 171. Examples and exceptions, 171–174. Offenses against the law of God not to be pardoned, 174–175. Sixth mark: liege fealty and homage, 175. Seventh mark: coining of money, 175–176. Examples and exceptions, 176–177. Eighth mark: regulation of weights and measures, 177. Ninth mark: exclusive rights of taxation, 177. Examples and exceptions, 177–179. Imposts on salt, 179. Various minor rights of sovereignty, 179–182.

Book II

CHAPTER 1 (PAGES 183–197)

Three types of state: monarchy, aristocracy, and democracy, 183–184. Whether the mixed state is possible, 184–185. Consideration of alleged examples of the mixed state: Lacedemon, 186–188; Rome, 188–190; Venice, 190–191; France, 191–192. Consideration of authorities: Aristotle, 192–193; Plato, 193. Only three forms of state are possible, 193. A division of the rights of sovereignty is unstable, and soon reverts to one of the three pure forms, 193–195. Variations in the size of the sovereign body in aristocracies, 196. Concept of the principate, 196–197.

CHAPTER 2 (PAGES 197–204)

The term monarchy restricted to the rule of a single individual, 197–199. Three types of rule or government: royal (or lawful), lordly, and tyrannical, 199–200. Origin and spread of lordly monarchy, 200–201. Its traces seen in Europe in feudal tenures, 201–203. Differences between lordly monarchy and tyranny, 203–204.

CHAPTER 3 (PAGES 204–210)

Characteristics of royal monarchy, 204–205. The manner of attaining the sovereignty is incidental, 205–206. Criticism of Aristotle's classification of monarchies, 206–207. Commissioners and magistrates not kings, 207–208. Importance of royal insignia, 208. To accept insignia from another ruler impairs sovereignty, 208–209. Dangers of crowning a successor prematurely, 209–210.

CHAPTER 4 (PAGES 210–218)

Original meaning of the term tyrant, 210. Need to balance virtues and vices carefully in judging princes, 211. Comparison of the good king and the tyrant, 211–213. Tyrants live miserable and precarious lives, 213–215. Virtues of the good king, 215. Severity not a sign of tyranny, but often the mark of a good and wise king, 216–218.

CHAPTER 5 (PAGES 218–230)

Whether tyrants may be resisted: (1) the tyrant by usurpation may be either brought to justice or removed by force, 218–220; (2) the legitimate but tyrannical monarch may be chastised by foreign intervention, 220–221; but not by the subjects, if he is an absolute sovereign, 221–222. Consideration of examples and authorities, 222–224. Exception: direct authorization from God, 224. Further arguments against resistance, 224–225. Miserable lives of tyrants, 226. Tyrants' agents, 226. Whether tyrants' enactments should be ratified or annulled after their death, 227–228. Whether conspirators against the sovereignty are to be treated with severity or lenity, 228–230.

CHAPTER 6 (PAGES 230–244)

Aristocracy defined, 230. The criterion of aristocracy is not virtue, courage, nobility, or wealth, but the number holding sovereignty, 230–232. Examples, 232. The constitution of Genoa, 232–233. Of Geneva, 233. Of the Swiss cantons, 233–235. Of Ragusa, 235. Of Lucca, 236. Of the German Empire, 236–240. Of the Imperial cities, 240–241. Magistracies and councils in an aristocracy, 241–242. Criticism of Aristotle's classification of aristocracies, 242–243. Equity and justice more important than the rule of law, 243–244.

CHAPTER 7 (PAGES 244–252)

Democracy defined, 244. Methods of voting in democracies, 244–248. Criticism of Aristotle's treatment of democracy, 248–249. Importance of distinguishing between type of state and type of rule, 249–250. Democratic states strive after liberty and equality, 250–252.

Book III

CHAPTER 1 (PAGES 253–278)

Definition of a senate, 253. Advantages of a senate, 253–255. Qualities requisite in a senator: age, 255–256; public reputation, 256; wisdom and sense of justice, 256–257; flexibility, 257–258; impartiality and patriotism, 258. Other qualities required in some countries: nobility, wealth, experience in public office, 258–259. The number of senators: disadvantages of a large senate, 259–261. Establishment of small privy councils, 261–263. Separation of large and small councils in various countries, 263–265. Councils in monarchies function differently from those in aristocracies and democracies, 265–267. Further problems of large senates, 267–268. Procedural questions: who should introduce matters for deliberation, 268–269; order of speaking, 269; time of meeting, 269–270; matters for discussion and manner of speaking, 270–272. A senate ought not to have power to command, 272–273. Consideration of the functions of the senate at Rome, 273–276. A senate with power to command endangers sovereignty, 277. Senatorial appointments should be permanent, 277–278.

CHAPTER 2 (PAGES 278–293)

Definitions of officer and commissioner, 278. Criticism of other writers' definitions, 278–280. Differences between offices and commissions, 280–284. Different types of commissions, 284–285. Examples at Rome, 285–286. Commissions terminate either by revocation or by the death of the grantor, 286–288. Officers retain authority despite the death of the king, 288. Offices created or suppressed by specific edicts, 288–289. Officers have wider discretionary power than commissioners, 289–291. Consideration of Roman examples, 291–292. Tendency of commissions to develop into offices, 292–293.

CHAPTER 3 (PAGES 293–309)

The magistrate defined, 293. Public charges originally held by commission only, 293. Difference between officer and magistrate, 294. Criticism of other authorities, 294–295. Whether the *duumviri* at Rome should be accounted magistrates, 295–296. Power to impose fines, 296. Digression on the value of fines, 297–298. Relationship between ecclesiastical and secular jurisdiction, 298–300. Whether all magistrates have jurisdiction and *imperium*, 300–301. The Roman tribunes, 301–303. Aediles, 303. Quaestors, 304. Censors, 304–306. *Triumviri capitales*, 306. The term magistracy, properly defined, implies *imperium*, 306. Other types of public charge, 306–307. Questions concerning the selection of magistrates: (1) who may choose, (2) who may be chosen, (3) methods of choice, 307–308. Classification of offices and public charges, 308–309.

CHAPTER 4 (PAGES 309–325)

Relationship of the magistrate to the sovereign: complexity of the magistrate's position, 309–310. Variety of commands issuing from the sovereign, 310. *Lettres de justice*, 311–312. *Lettres de commandement*, 312. Whether the magistrate should execute unjust commands, 312–313. Derogations from general edicts, 314. Enforcement of obsolete edicts, 314. Cases of apparent injustice, 314–315. Remonstrances in the *parlements* of France, 315–316. Whether magistrates should be permitted to resign on

Argument: Book III

conscientious grounds, 316–317. Injustices arising from special circumstances, 317–318. Distinction between edicts already published and those not yet published, 318. Distinction between wrongs already committed and proposed acts of injustice, 318–319. Commands countermanded during execution, 319–320. Magistrates should examine the facts before execution, 320–321. Dangers of excessive privileges extorted from princes, 321–322. Magistrates should not examine the facts if expressly forbidden to do so, 322–323. Disobedience of magistrates sets a dangerous example to the subjects, 323–324. But the highest obligation is to God, 324–325.

CHAPTER 5 (PAGES 325–342)

Relationship between the magistrate and the law, 325–326. The different degrees of public power, 326–327. The controversy between Lothair and Azo concerning the power of the sword, or *merum imperium*, 327–330. The question generalized: (1) the office of the magistrate is the property of the state, but (2) the power and authority of the magistrate is vested either in the sovereign when the magistrate merely executes the law, or in the magistrate's office when he has discretionary power, 330–333. Law and equity in the administration of justice, 333–335. The praetorship at Rome, 335–336. Magistrates' commands are binding, 336–337. Whether magistrates may be resisted by force, 337–338. Punishment of injuries done to magistrates, 338–340. Respect and honor owed to magistrates, 340. Qualities of a good magistrate, 341–342. Military authority stricter than civil, 342.

CHAPTER 6 (PAGES 343–361)

Three degrees of authority among magistrates, 343. Dangers of instituting sovereign magistrates, 343–344. In the presence of the sovereign the magistrates' power is suspended, 344–345. But their office continues, 345. A greater magistrate or a sovereign may voluntarily submit his case to a lesser, 345–346. Whether magistrates may prevent appeals by banishing the offender, 346. A magistrate has authority over inferior magistrates, but not over his equals, colleagues, or superiors, 346–348. But he may veto or oppose the proceedings of an equal or colleague, 348. Except in colleges, where majority rule is the practice, 349. Special case of the tribunes at Rome: the individual veto, exercised even against superior magistrates, 349–351. Appeals after actions are completed must be from inferior to superior, 351–352. Whether the superior magistrate's deputy may command the inferior magistrate, 352–353. Magistrates equal in power may differ in prerogatives of honor, 353–354. Relationship between *coseigneurs* of the same territory, 354–355. Relations between different jurisdictions, 355–357. Whether commands may be executed after an appeal to a superior magistrate has lapsed, 357. Digression on the term *fatales dies*, 357. The question resolved, 358. Execution of judgments between different states, 358–359. Extradition, 359–360. The structure of magistracies is similar in various countries, 360–361.

CHAPTER 7 (PAGES 361–386)

Definitions of college, corporation, and university, 361. The origins of civil society, 361–362. Need for amity and association among men, 362–364. Feasts to promote amity, 364. Classification of colleges and corporations, 364–365. Elaboration of the definition of a college, 365–366. Legacies and donations to colleges, 366–367. The power of colleges: authority over their own members, 367–369. How the corporate will of the college may be expressed, 370–372. How the college may be assembled, 372. Conclusions as to the power of colleges, 372–373. The punishment of rebellious corporations and colleges, 373–376. Importance of the mean between severity and lenity, 377–379. Conclusions as to the punishment of colleges, 379. Whether colleges are advantageous or necessary to the state, 379–380. Dangerous associations arise under the veil of religion, 380. Religious sects a source of civil discord, 381. Policy to be adopted towards strong religious sects, 382. Examples of religious persecution, 382–383. Advantages of corporations and colleges in democracies, 383–384. Advantages of meetings of the estates in a royal monarchy, 384–385. However in aristocracies and royal monarchies a policy of the mean is indicated, 385–386.

CHAPTER 8 (PAGES 386–405)

Importance of order and orderly arrangement, 386–387. The ordering of citizens, 387. Even slaves ought to be accounted members of society, 387–388. Position of slaves, 388. *Statu liberi* and *libertini*, 388–389. An order of nobles found almost everywhere, but the criteria of nobility vary widely, 389. How nobility is acquired: (1) by bearing arms, 389–390; (2) by holding office, 390–392; (3) by descent from kings and heroes, 392; (4) by membership in the priesthood, 392–393; (5) by virtue, 394; (6) by knowledge, 394; (7) by civil ennoblement, 394–395. Whether fees ennoble their holders, 395. Relation between nobility and riches, 395–396. Inheritance of nobility, 396–397. Nobility lost by the exercise of base trades, but nations disagree as to which occupations are base, 397. Whether manual trades are base, 397–398. Conflicting views of the merchant, 398–400. Of artists and physicians, 400. Of husbandmen, 400–401. Of executioners, 401. The problem of idlers, 401. *Rentiers*, 402. The hierarchy of social classes in a monarchy, 402–403. Danger of civil seditions in dividing orders of citizens, 403. Three orders less dangerous than two, 403–404. Segregation of orders in the theater at Rome, 404–405.

Book IV

CHAPTER 1 (PAGES 406–436)

All states grow, flourish, and decline, 406–407. Various classifications of changes in states: (1) conversions and alterations, 407; (2) amalgamation and disintegration, 407–408; (3) natural and violent changes, 408; (4) necessary and voluntary changes, 408–409. Six perfect conversions and six alterations, 409. Anarchy, 410. Extinction of states, 410. Dynastic overthrows in monarchies, 410–411. The "flourishing estate" to be judged in terms of virtue rather than wealth or power, 411–412. Causes of changes in states, 412. Origin and widespread adoption of monarchy, 412–413. The corrupting influence of power, 414. Scarcity of virtuous princes, 414–415. The principle of succession makes for durable monarchies, 415. Vulnerability of new monarchies, 415–416. Causes of the downfall of tyrants, 416–418. Tyrants need strong guards, 418–420. How democracies and aristocracies are changed into monarchies, 420–421. How democracies are changed into aristocracies, and vice versa, 421–423. Democracies are maintained by war, 422–423. Tyrannies change into democracies and vice versa, 423–424. Distinction between internal and external sources of change, 424. Fickleness of the people, and instability of democracies, 424–426. Weaknesses of aristocracies, 426–427. Imperceptible change of democracies into aristocracies, 427–428. Further weaknesses of aristocracies, 428–430. Great men dangerous to democracies, 430–431. And are to be befriended or destroyed, but not banished, 431–432. Danger of two opposing factions in states, 432. Civil discord leaves a state vulnerable to overthrow from outside, 433. But monarchies are less vulnerable to external overthrow, 433–434. Since change is inevitable, gradual change is the best, 434. Examples of gradual change, 434–435. Danger of great men in monarchies when the royal stock fails, 435–436.

CHAPTER 2 (PAGES 436–467)

Three sources of changes in states: human, natural, and divine, 436–438. All things are transitory, and must perish, 438. The influence of the stars is difficult to discover because of wide discrepancies among earlier authorities, 439. The creation of the world and the problem of the beginning of the year: evidence for the autumn, 439–441.

Argument: Book IV

Error of judging changes in states by the date of foundation of towns, 441. Digression on the valuation of houses in Roman law, 441. Faults in the horoscopes of Rome and Constantinople, 441–444. The conjunction theory: errors of Pierre d'Ailly, 444–445. Towards a valid conjunction theory, 445–446. The triplicities theory of the ancients, 446. Advocated by vain and ignorant men, 446–447. Faults in the triplicities theory, 447–448. Evidence to corroborate the conjunction theory, 448–449. Prophecies as to the end of the world, 449–450. The possibility of a valid science of astrology, 450. Significance of the month of September in world history, 451–453. Errors of Leowitz, 453. Further evidence of celestial influence on world history, 454. Refutation of Copernicus, 454–455. The influence of numbers on changes in states: Plato's theory of harmonic proportion, 455–456. Influence of music on character, 456–457. Plato's theory of the perfect number, 457–458. Criticism of Plato's theory, 458–460. Significance of certain numbers in human affairs, 460–462. Significance of numbers in world history, 462–465. Reply to critics of the *Methodus* concerning the prophecies of Daniel, 465–467.

CHAPTER 3 (PAGES 467–475)

Since the wise are not bound by necessity, they should study and avoid the causes of changes in states, 467–468. Wise government, discipline, and constancy can often overcome adverse circumstances, 468–469. The different types of state are preserved by different laws, 469. Old laws should not be changed without good cause, 469–471. When laws must be changed, the change should be effected gradually, 471–472. Magistracies also should be reformed gradually, 472–474. Examples of gradual reformation of religious orders, 474–475. Time also remedies tyranny, unless the tyrant has children, 475. Conclusion, 475.

CHAPTER 4 (PAGES 476–493)

Whether magistracies ought to be annual or perpetual, 476. Arguments for annual magistracies: to reward virtuous men, 476; to promote amity and equality, and to avoid sedition, 476–477; to enable punishment of corrupt magistrates, 477–479; to avoid nepotism, 479; to promote a concern for the public welfare, 479–480; to avoid plural officeholding, 480; to moderate men's appetite for power, 480–482; to avoid the evils of inheritance of offices, 482. Arguments for perpetual magistracies: to avoid the inconveniences of the one-year term, 482–483; to satiate corrupt magistrates, 483–484; to enhance the magistrate's dignity and status, 484; to avoid dangerous innovations, 484. Perpetual magistracies supported by authorities and by experience, 484–485. Resolution of the question: the doctrine of the mean, 485. Different structures of magistracies appropriate to the different types of state, 485–488. General considerations, 488–489. Whether offices should be held by law during good behavior, or at the pleasure of the sovereign, 489–492. Conclusion: the doctrine of the mean applied to the different types of state, 492–493.

CHAPTER 5 (PAGES 493–499)

Whether concord or discord among the magistrates better serves the public interest, 493. Arguments for concord among the magistrates, 493–494. Arguments for discord among the magistrates, 494–496. The question related to the different types of state and resolved, 497–499.

CHAPTER 6 (PAGES 500–518)

Whether the sovereign should personally judge his subjects, 500. Arguments for personal administration of justice by the sovereign, 500–501. Notable examples, 501–502. The principle extended: argument for personal exercise of sovereignty, 502. The case against personal administration of justice: subjects perceive and imitate their prince's vices, 502–504; familiarity breeds contempt, even of a virtuous prince, 504–505. Examples, 505–506. The prince should always preserve his majesty when appearing before his subjects,

ARGUMENT: BOOK IV

506–507. How to avoid the danger of a mayor of the palace, 507. The case for administration of justice by magistrates: complexities and burdens of the judicial process, 507–509; growth of the rule of law, 509; true justice should be stern and inflexible, whereas princes should incline towards clemency and pity, 509–510; in democracies the populace is too easily swayed, 510–511; if the prince is not too lenient, he risks falling into the other extreme of cruelty, 511–512; even if he holds the mean in punishing offenders, he will forfeit the love of the subjects, 512–513; even nobles and peers of the realm ought not to be judged by the prince in person, 513–515; the argument of speedier justice considered and rejected, 515; the question concluded, 515–516. Princes must preserve their majesty even more carefully in the presence of foreigners, 516–517. Sovereignty is best assured when there is appropriate delegation of subordinate functions, 517–518.

CHAPTER 7 (PAGES 519–544)

Factions are dangerous in every type of state, 519–520. Methods for their suppression, 520–521. Conspiracies against the state: the prince himself must act, 521; but punishment of the guilty should be applied with moderation, 521–522; the discovery of conspiracies, 522–523; individual assassins, 523–524. Factions among the subjects not directed against the state: they are dangerous and must be pacified, 524–525; but the good prince, unlike tyrants who foster discord, must show no favoritism, nor judge the matter himself, 525–527; settlement of individual differences by combat, 527–529; differences between families or corporations to be settled by legal means, backed by force, 529–530. Civil strife coincides with external peace, 530. Civil strife more easily prevented than cured, especially in democracies, 530. An enraged populace must be pacified gently and gradually, 531–533. Civil strife may be appeased: (1) by the influence of a virtuous man, 534; (2) by the fear of religion, 534; (3) by the mediation of outsiders, 534–535. The religious question: subjects should never be permitted to debate a religion generally received and established, 535–537; but if the subjects are already divided, a good example is more effective than force, 537; examples of tolerance and intolerance, 537–539; the private exercise of a minority religion is preferable to atheism, 539–540. Two factions more dangerous than many, 540. Whether citizens should be compelled to take sides in civil strife, 540–541. Specific remedies for civil strife: (1) banning the use of bells, 541–542; (2) forbidding the wearing of arms, 542. Causes of civil sedition: summary of causes treated in earlier chapters, 542–543; a further cause is excessive freedom of speech granted to orators, 543–544.

Book V

CHAPTER I (PAGES 545–568)

The theory of climate: human temperament varies profoundly from region to region, 545–547. An understanding of these differences is essential to the science of government, 547. Three climatic zones from the equator to the poles, 547. Characteristics of peoples of the North, the middle zone, and the South: color of hair and eyes, 548; the differences arise from internal heat and cold, 548; climatic variations between North and South, 548–549; effects on armies and travelers moving from one region to another, 549; each region excels in different disciplines, 550; the military prowess of the North, 550–551; northerners are internally hot and moist, southerners cold and dry, 551–552; the middle peoples hold the mean between North and South, 552; southerners excel in subtlety of mind, 552–553; southerners have a disadvantage in war, but an advantage in diplomacy, 553–554; the climatic zones related to the four humors, 554; trustworthiness of northerners, 554–555; different types of cruelty, 555–556; different types of madness, 556; northerners are chaste, southerners lustful, 557; jealousy of the southerners, 557–558; abundant

Argument: Book V

population of the North, *note at* 558 F6; monogamy and polygamy, 558; diseases and length of life, 558; southerners run to extremes of virtue and vice, 558–559; northerners governed by force, the middle nations by reason and the rule of law, southerners by religion, 559–561. Comparison of soul, state, and world, 561. The influence of the planets related to the three climatic zones, 561. Comparison of the human body and the world, 562. Other sources of differences between peoples: (1) the East has affinities with the South, the West with the North, 562; (2) valleys sloping to the South and those sloping to the North, 562–563; (3) mountain peoples have northerly characteristics, 563–564; (4) influence of the sea and of commerce, 564; (5) of strong winds, 564–565; (6) of marshlands, 565; (7) of fertility of the soil, 565; (8) political frontiers make for war and barbarism, 565. How far education and civil discipline can alter the nature of a people, 565–566. Some accuse the French of lightness, but this is liveliness and alacrity rather than inconstancy or perfidy, which is characteristic of the North, 566–567. Constancy and inconstancy in religion: the doctrine of the mean, *note at* 567 C10. Conclusion: the relation between civil institutions and environment, 567–568. The influence of environment on pronunciation, 568.

Chapter 2 (pages 569–579)

Extremes of wealth and poverty as a problem of government, 569. Artificial redistribution of wealth is pernicious and dangerous, 569–570. Limitation of population considered and rejected, 571. Property institutions and the law of inheritance should be modeled on the law of God, 571–572. The remedy for oppression by the rich is not abolition of debts, but prohibition of usury, 572–574. Excessive wealth of the clergy a source of civil discord, 574–575. Agrarian laws at Rome, 575–576. The regulation of inheritances and dowries, 576–579. Measures against loss of wealth to aliens and idlers, 579.

Chapter 3 (pages 580–584)

Whether the property of those condemned should be confiscated: arguments on both sides, 580–581. Resolution of the question: the problems of debts, trial costs, informers' rewards, and entailed lands, 581–582; the dangers of confiscation of property in monarchies, 582–583. Assignment of forfeited property to religious or charitable uses, 583–584.

Chapter 4 (pages 584–596)

Importance of rewards and punishments for maintaining the state, 584. Rewards explained, 585. Their distribution varies according to the type of state, 585–586. The well-governed democracy is best for giving virtue its due rewards, 586–587. Rewards are scorned when the unworthy obtain them, 587–588. Rewards are to be distributed in fitting proportion, 588. The orders of knighthood, 588–589. Honors should be few in number, 589–590. Prevention of corruption and favor in the distribution of rewards, 590–591. Pernicious effects of the sale of offices, 591–592. Severity wiser than prodigality in giving rewards, 592–593. The prince should give rewards in person, but leave punishment to the magistrates, 593. The ends of punishment, *note at* 593 C5. Laws for recording gifts in France, 593. General precepts and policies for the distribution of rewards, 594–596.

Chapter 5 (pages 596–614)

Importance and difficulty of military questions: warlike citizens and fortifications mutually contradictory, 596. Arguments against fortifications, 596–598. The argument against military training: the end of the state is peace, 598–599. Arguments for fortifications, 599–601. Arguments for military training, 601–604. The two questions resolved differently in the different types of state, 604–605. The problem of military training in aristocracies: the Venetian solution, 605–606. Weak nations may properly ask for peace where warlike

Argument: Book V

ones could not do so without loss of honor, 606–607. Virtuous actions weaken the enemy's morale, 607–608. Wars should be fought on foreign soil, 608. The presence of the prince on the battlefield strengthens morale, 608–609. But rashness is to be avoided in military affairs, 609. Many of the ancients excelled in both military and civil pursuits, but the general practice is to separate the art of war from other vocations, 610. Standing armies, 611. Military aid from allies, 611–612. Dangers of military aid from strangers without alliance, 612–613. Summary and conclusion, 613–614.

CHAPTER 6 (PAGES 614–636^v)

Treaties founded upon good faith, *note at* 614 I3. Classification of treaties, *note at* 614 I3. To be kept, the treaty must first be a fair one, 614–615. Treaties of protection: the dependents or clients should be left in full liberty, or subjugated completely if unfaithful, 615–616; distinction between pensions and tributes, 616–617; examples and illustrations of protection, 617–618; the chief problem is to assure the liberty of the weaker party, 618–619. Even treaties of equality often lead to subjection, 619–621. Protection involves risks, and should be undertaken only for just cause, 621. Neutrality: arguments for and against neutrality, 622; distinction between neutrality with and without friendship of the other parties, 623; the neutral may arbitrate in quarrels, 623; example of the papacy, 623; the neutrality of strong states preserves the balance of power, 624; it is dangerous for neutrals to foster hostilities, and honorable for them to mediate peace, 624–625. Examples of leagues to preserve the balance of power, 625–625^v. Of secret leagues directed against certain states, 625^v. On keeping and breaking faith: faith the foundation of state and society, 625^v–626; but unjust promises are excluded, 626; treaties founded on force are nevertheless binding, 626–626^v; hostages are an alternative to a promise, 626^v–627; vindication of King John and King Francis I, 627; excuses commonly alleged for breaking faith, 627–627^v; examples of double dealing, 627^v; faith is to be kept with infidels and heretics, 628–628^v; whether faith is to be kept with those who break their faith, 628^v; examples of perjury and broken faith, 628^v–629^v; whether faith should be pledged to exiles, robbers, and pirates, 630; violation of pledges for the safety of rebellious subjects, 630–630^v. Treaties should name arbitrators for future differences, 630^v–631. Negotiation and ratification of treaties, 631. Examples of deceit and broken faith, 631–631^v. Various ways of sanctifying treaties, 631^v–632. Agreements between a prince and his subjects can be assured only by the aid of other princes, 632–632^v. Digression on the release of subjects from their obedience, and the Strasbourg Oaths, 633. Whether, in a case of unjust oppression, a prince may assist (a) a stranger not allied, or (b) an ally, against (a) an ally, or (b) a stranger not allied, 633–633^v. Further distinctions, 633^v–634. Arbitration of disputes, 634. Whether treaties extend to the fathers or brothers of the parties allied, 634. Treaties should be made for a specified period, 634–634^v. The Romans granted truce instead of peace to faithless peoples, 635. And punished broken faith severely, 635. And dealt openly and honorably with enemies, 635–635^v. Treacherous treatment of ambassadors, 635^v–636. Proper conduct of ambassadors, 636–636^v. Miscellaneous remarks, 636^v.

Book VI

CHAPTER I (PAGES 637–649)

Census explained, 637. History of the censorship at Rome, 637–638. Its adoption in other countries, 638–639. Population figures for the Israelites and for Rome, 639–640. Advantages of a census of population and property, 640–642. The objection of loss of privacy considered and rejected, 642–643. Importance and high reputation of the censorship at Rome, 643–644. The gulf between law and morality: magistrates punish crimes, but censors correct vices, 644. And maintain respect

Argument: Book VI

for religion, 644–645. And oversee education, 645. The censorship of plays, 645–646. Of music, 646. Of dress, 646. Whether censors ought to have jurisdiction or *imperium*, 646. Distinction between ignominy and infamy, 647. Ecclesiastical censure and the power of excommunication, 647–648. Adoption of ecclesiastical censure in Protestant countries, 648–649. Relation between temporal and ecclesiastical censure, 649.

CHAPTER 2 (PAGES 649–686)

Treasure is to be discussed in a context of honor and honesty, 649. Lacedemonian attitude towards treasure, 650. Seven sources of public revenue: (1) the *domaine*, or revenues of the Crown, which is inalienable, and belongs to the state rather than to the prince, 650–655; (2) conquest from enemies, 655–656; (3) gifts and legacies, 656–658; (4) pensions from allies, 658–660; (5) profits from trade in merchandise, 660–661; (6) customs duties, 661–663; (7) taxation of the subjects, which is to be used as a last resort in urgent necessities, 663–664. Various types of impost, 664–666. New taxes a source of civil discord, 666. But abolition of all taxes also endangers the state, 666. Nor can taxes remain at traditional levels, because of higher prices following the influx of gold and silver from the New World, 666–668. Countries vary in tax potential, 668. New princes should tax lightly, 668. Imposts in kind, 668. The incidence of taxation: the privileged orders, 668–669; remedies for unequal incidence, 669–670; taxes on luxuries, 670; on bachelors, 670; on lawsuits, 670–671; other desirable and undesirable taxes, 671. New schemes of taxation are to be shunned, 671–672. The Italian mount of piety explained, 672. The Romans profited by lending out the public treasure, but modern princes must borrow at high rates of interest, 673. Evil consequences of public borrowing for France and other countries, 673–676. But borrowing may save a prince in desperate circumstances, 676. The uses of treasure: (1) charity for the poor, 676–677; (2) payment of the army, 677; (3) public works, which relieve both poverty and idleness, 677–679. The control of public expenditures: importance of written records, 679–680; verification of the prince's gifts, 680–682. Reserves of treasure: needed for emergencies, 682; methods of storage, 682; size of reserves of various princes, 683. Shortage of reserves in France: financial resources of the Crown, 683–684; multiplication of offices and corruption of officials, 684–686.

CHAPTER 3 (PAGES 687–700)

Debasement of the coinage is harmful to the state, 687. And is beyond the sovereign's authority, 687. All coins and articles of gold or silver should be of uniform standard, 687–689. Gold and silver coins should be of the same weight, 689. Denominations of silver coinage, 689–690. The diversity of weights from city to city can be reconciled with a universal, invariable coinage, 690. Need for coins of small denominations, 690–691. But copper coinage is inconvenient because the price of copper fluctuates, 691. Ratio between prices of gold and silver, 691–692. This ratio destroyed by debasement, 692. Debasement of the silver coinage in France and elsewhere, 692–693. Variations in monetary units and weights, 693. Difficulties of understanding exchange rates, 693. Standards of weight and fineness of various gold and silver coins, 694–695. Difficulties of preventing debasement: losses to foreigners and to goldsmiths, 695–696. The remedy is to set a uniform standard for all gold and silver, 696. Reform of abuses in the mints, 696–697. Counterfeiting cannot be abolished, but it can be reduced by a pure coinage, 697–698. A profit from the mints is another man's loss, 698. Need for international agreement to stop debasement of coinage, 698. Techniques of coining, and relative weights of various metals, 698–700. Advantage of standard denominations, 700. The issue of currency reform at the Estates of Blois, 700.

CHAPTER 4 (PAGES 700–721)

Comparison of the three forms of state, 700–701. Arguments for democracy, 701.

Argument: Book VI

Arguments against democracy, 701–709. Arguments for aristocracy, 709. Arguments against aristocracy, 709–713. Arguments against monarchy, 713–714. Arguments for monarchy, 715–718. Monarchy upheld by experience, 718–719. And by the authority of great thinkers and of God himself, 719–720. The Jewish *sanhedrim* not an aristocracy, 720. Conclusion: the best state is a royal monarchy, 720. But the statesman must proceed cautiously in seeking changes, and fit the form of state to the situation of the people, 720–721.

Chapter 5 (pages 721–754)

The issue of elective versus hereditary monarchy, 721. Specious arguments for election, 722. Aristotle's view refuted by the experience of many peoples, 722–723. The case against election: perils of the interregnum, 723–724; spoliation of the public domain, 724–725; corrupting influence of newly acquired power, 725; problems of electing (a) a subject, and (b) a foreign prince, 725–726; elective kings strive to make their power hereditary, 726–727; an uncertain succession endangers the life of the candidate elected, 727–728. The succession question in England, 728 *and note at* 728 K9. Hereditary kingdoms may resort to election when the royal house fails, 728–729. Whether the principle of election has any historical basis in France, 729–730. The coronation procedure, 730–732. The French monarchy purely hereditary, 732–733. Election promotes faction and strife among those who elect, 733–734. Conclusions concerning election, 734. If the hereditary line fails, it is better to draw lots than to elect, 734. Primogeniture: common to almost all nations, 734–735; its violation causes civil wars, 735–736; it should be observed even if the eldest is deformed, 736–737; or if he is born before his father succeeds, 737; whether the son of the deceased eldest son should be preferred before his uncles, 738–740. Monarchies should descend without division, 740–742. And appanages should revert to the Crown when male heirs fail, 742–743. Princes cannot limit their ambition, nor share their power, 743–744. Princes of the blood should be kept from positions of power, 744–745. And even base men should not be raised too high, 745–746. Female succession: the rule of women is against divine, natural, and human law, 746; a married queen retains the sovereignty and upsets the pattern of domestic authority, while an unmarried queen is an object of scorn and a source of civil discord, 746–747; evil examples of female rule, 747; origin and spread of female succession in modern Europe, 747–749; problems of marriage with a subject, 749 *and note at* 749 C9; problems of marriage with a foreign prince, *note at* 749 C9 *and* 749–752; female rule conflicts with the position of the husband established by the law of nations, 752; in France these difficulties are avoided by the Salic law, 753–754. Conclusion, 754.

Chapter 6 (pages 755–794)

The principle of justice in the government of the state, 755. The views of Plato, Xenophon, and Aristotle, 755–756. Explanation of geometric, arithmetic, and harmonic justice, 757–759. Democracies incline towards arithmetic justice, aristocracies towards geometric justice, 759–760. Harmonic justice illustrated in the relation between law and equity: comparison with number ratios, 760–761; origin and growth of the rule of law, 761–763; the equitable function of the magistrate is circumscribed by the law, and is narrower than that of the sovereign, 763–764; the magistrate's discretion is also limited by conscience and good faith, 764–765; laws cannot provide for every circumstance, 765–766; multiplicity of laws increases the number of suits, 766–767; equitable jurisdiction varies in degree, but is always bound by conscience, 767–768; no man should be both judge and witness, 768; examples of equitable jurisdiction established to expound doubtful laws, 769. Harmonic justice illustrated in public punishments: in fines scaled according to wealth and social status, 769–771; in lighter punishments for noble offenders,

Argument: Book VI

heavier punishments for offenses against nobles, and in different methods of inflicting the death penalty, 771–774; punishments should be heavier when a special vocation or trust is violated, 774–775; pecuniary penalties lose their force as wealth increases, 775–776; punishments should be adjusted to age and sex, 776; comparison of laws concerning forgery, 777; questions of intent and effect, 778; variety of punishments required in cases of robbery and homicide, 778–780; how the principle of retribution is to be understood, 780–781; punishment should take into account the offender's previous record, 781–782; the concept of multiple restitution, 782. Harmonic justice illustrated in civil matters: in the laws concerning usury, 782–783; in wages of laborers and fees of surgeons and judges, 783–784; in the laws concerning inheritance, 784. Further illustration from the law of God concerning whipping, 784–785. Democracies and aristocracies are more stable when their government is tempered harmonically, 785–786. A royal monarchy governed harmonically is the best of all, 786–787. The class struggle at Rome due to a government based on geometric rather than harmonic proportion, 787–788. Harmonic proportion in the distribution of offices, 789–790. Analogies of harmony in the state, in music, in geometry, in man's body, and in the soul, 790–791. Harmony involves a mingling of discord and concord, light and dark, virtue and vice, 791–792. Refutation of Plato's theory of geometric proportion, 792. Harmonic proportion illustrated in the relation between matter and form, 792. Harmonic proportion in the universe and in nature, 792–793. Just as the world, compounded of good and evil, is united and ruled by the power of God, so should the monarch of a well-governed state combine and direct its contrasting elements, 793–794.

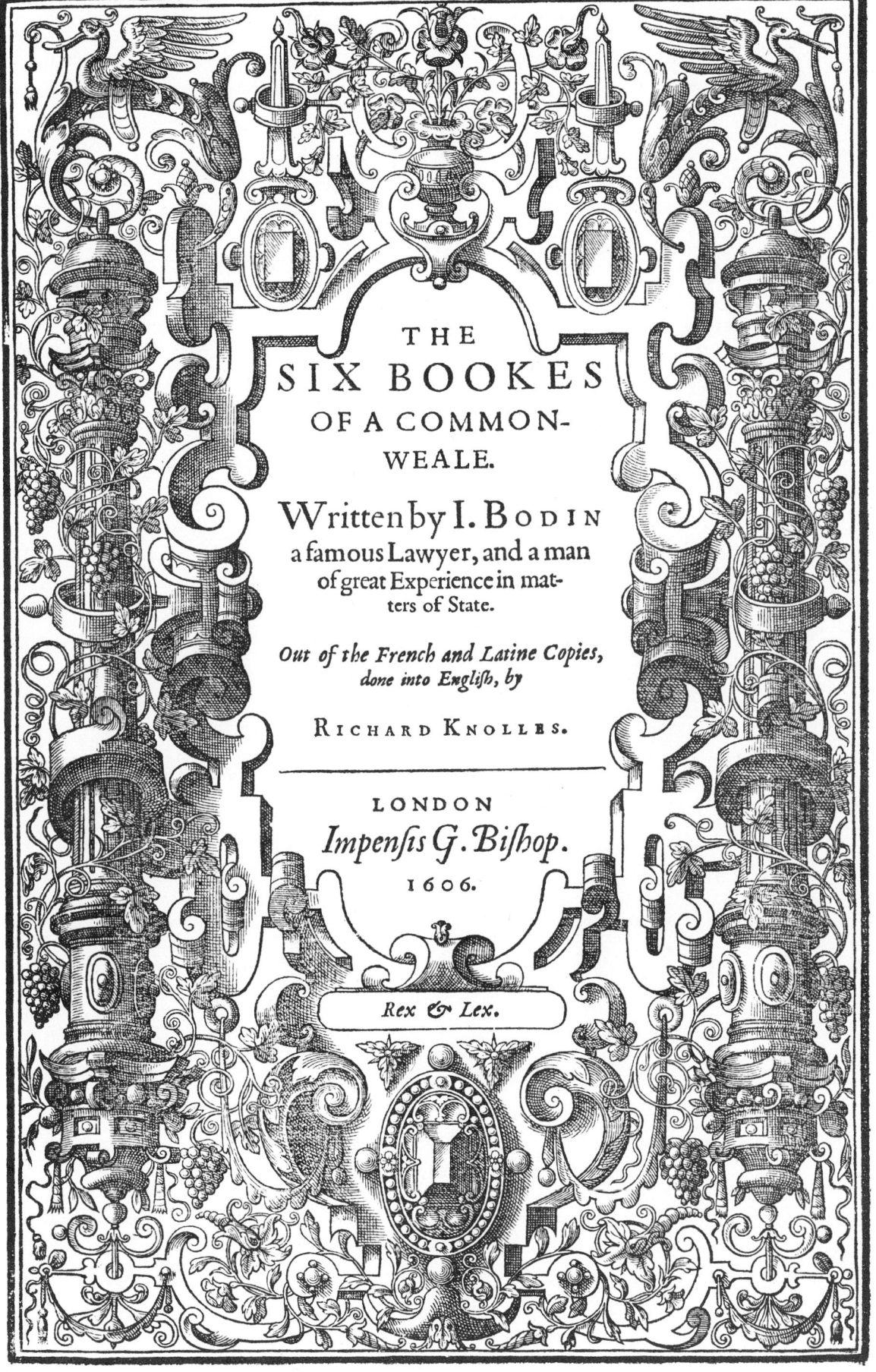

THE SIX BOOKES OF A COMMON-WEALE.

Written by I. BODIN a famous Lawyer, and a man of great Experience in matters of State.

Out of the French and Latine Copies, done into English, by

RICHARD KNOLLES.

LONDON
Impensis G. Bishop.
1606.

Rex & Lex.

TO MY MOST ESPECIALL
good Friend, Sir *Peter Manwood*, Knight
of the Honourable order of the Bath.

SIR, gathering matter to continue the liues of the Turkish Emperours, but finding nothing hetherto worthy the writing, more than matters common: such hauing been the policies of latter times, as to keepe secret the reasons and certaine knowledge of the doings of great Estates, that if some of the most wise, mightie, and Honorable, sitting at the helmes of Commonweales, doe not shew the way, posteritie will be defrauded of the most excellent things that many ages haue before brought forth: and yet succeeding times shall bring to light so much as God in his good time seeth best for the good of the Christian Commonwealth. The Sarasin Historie also not to be performed without the light of their owne Chronicles, and the stories of many other countries by them conquered and possessed; a more famous and mightie people, and of longer continuance than the Turkes, and the first planters, spreaders, and maintainers of the Mahometane religion. Besides the difficulty of the labour to so weake a body, apace declining, wanting all comfort and helpe but your owne, by the experience of so many yeares spent in the former (and the beginning of this, which you haue long since seene) I doubt (if it please God I liue to performe it) I must write it shortly, as I did the generall Historie to my Liues. In the meane time hauing had some leisure, and loath to bestow good houres euill, I thought good to translate these six bookes of *Bodin* his Commonwealth, vvhich I here commend vnto you. But Sir (my most worthy and onely friend) if beside the diuers formes of Commonweales, and such other worthie matter, as is here by the Author set downe, you wish also to see by what lawes and customes they haue been also gouerned, a thing infinite; I in stead of all referre you vnto the reading of the common law of this Realme, which without all doubt in the auntient puritie thereof, for religious sinceritie, wisdome, power, and equall vpright iustice, excell all the laws of men that euer yet were, and a knowledge best beseeming the noble gentrie of this land. To make an end, the vvhole labours of my life haue been and euer shall be comfortable to me, when they may please you, to whom I haue vvholly dedicated my selfe. The Lord in his great mercy euer keepe you and all yours. From Sandwich this 18 day of December, 1605.

Yours euer to be commaunded,
Rich. Knolles.

To the Reader.

Mongst many the great and deepe deuices of worldly wisedome, for the maintenance and preseruing of humane societie (the ground and stay of mans earthly blisse) the fairest, firmest, and the best, was the framing and forming of Commonweales; wherein people of all estates, sort, and callings, being comprehended, are by many orderly degrees so vnited and combined together, as that the great are therein onely honoured, and yet the meanest not neglected, and they in the middest betwixt both, of both according to their places duly respected and regarded: whereof proceedeth the mutuall exchange of all kind and friendly offices, the surest bond of all good and well ordered Commonweales: euery man so finding that which vnto him in priuate belongeth, well vnto himselfe assured, together with the common good, wherein euery priuate mans estate is also comprehended and included. But to find out a good and reasonable meane, whereby such multitudes of people, so farre differing in qualitie, estate, and condition, and so hardly to be gouerned, might yet into one bodie politicke be in such sort vnited, as that euery one of them should in their degree, together with the common good (as members of one and the selfe-same naturall bodie) haue a present feeling of others good and harmes, was so hard and difficult a matter, as that the first deuisers thereof were accounted more than men, or at leastwise (as indeed they were) of farre more wisedome and discretion than others; the common sort as then and yet also not knowing rightly how to gouerne either themselues or others. Such was Solon amongst the Athenians, Lycurgus amongst the Lacedemonians, Pitacus, and many moe in other places; who although by diuers and almost quite contrarie meanes, ayming at one and the selfe-same marke, (viz. the quiet common good) to attaine thereunto, framed diuers and farre different formes and fashions of Commonweales: some of them giuing the Soueraignetie vnto the people in generall, some vnto the Nobilitie alone, and some others (better aduised than the rest) vnto one most royall Monarch; which both by reason and experience being found the best, is not onely of the more ciuile nations, but euen of the most barbarous people of the world (taught as should seeme by the onely and mightie gouernour thereof) in their gouernments receiued. And now whereas of all other arts and professions, and of whatsoeuer thing els belonging vnto the necessitie, vse, or ornament of the ciuile man in particular, so much is by the great and learned wits of all ages set downe, and by writing to all posteritie commended, as may well content euen curiositie it selfe: yet of this so great, so worthie, and so profitable an argument as is the nature, forme, and essence of all sorts of Estates and Commonweales (wherein the strength and power not onely of all the most mightie and glorious kingdomes and monarchies that euer yet were, are, or shall bee, but euen the good and welfare of all lawfull humane societie euer also rested, and a knowledge onely proper vnto kings and princes, and such other heroicall minds) so few haue written, as that it may seeme right strange in so many worlds of yeares, scarce one to haue beene found, which seriously and substantially tooke vpon him the handling (I againe say) of this

so

TO THE READER.

so great, so stately, necessarie, and profitable an argument; whether it were, for that they, whose wealth gaue them leisure to write, did of their owne accord in such sort withdraw themselues from learning, as did the more learned sort themselues from the affaires of State; or els that they which excelled both in the one and the other, viz. wealth and learning both, suffered themselues to be so ouerwhelmed with the weight of their other businesse, as that they had no spare time left them for to meditate, or write any thing at all of this so high and maiesticall an obiect, or els that for the difficultie of the matter it selfe they abstained to meddle therewith. Which vnto the auntient writers seemed so great, as that they which had gained the same, were still accounted the only wise men of the world. Long and many yeares agoe Plato, Xenophon, and Aristotle, and in the memorie of our fathers, Sir Thomas Moore (sometimes Lord Chauncellour of this land) all men of great fame and learning (and besides them not many moe, whose works in the space of 2000 years euer came to light) tooke this so noble and weightie an argument in hand; which they yet so passed through (Aristotle onely excepted) as that in their most graue and learned discourses is to be seene a certaine imaginarie forme of a perfect Commonweale, by themselues diuersly fantasied (such as indeed neuer was, either yet euer shall be) rather than any true shape or fashion of such a perfect Estate and Commonweale, as hath indeed been, or yet reasonably may be set downe for an example for others to imitate and conforme themselues vnto. So that according to these great and learned mens high and stately conceits, was neuer yet any Commonweale framed, neither yet any great matter from their so absolute imaginations drawn, for the behoofe and profit of such Estates and Commonweales as haue indeed since been, and wherein we now liue. Which I say not in any thing to impaire or deminish the fame and credite of these so renowned and excellent men (whose memoriall liue for euer) but onely that the strong opinion conceiued of the great knowledge of them, so graue and learned auncients, and especially in matters of state, wherein they as schoolemen had but little or no experience, might not be altogether preiudiciall vnto the honourable and reasonable endeuors of some others of our times, no lesse, yea and happily better acquainted with the studies and affaires of Estates and Commonweales than were they. For if the true value of things bee to be deemed by the necessarie and profitable vse thereof, I see not what should let, but that the six bookes of Io. Bodin de Repub. wherein hee (being himselfe a most famous Ciuilian, and a man much employed in the publicke affaires both of his Prince and Countrey) so orderly and exactly prosecuteth all formes and fashions of Commonweales, with the good and euill, the perfections and imperfections incident into the same, and many other matters and questions most necessarie to be knowne for the maintenance and preseruation of them, may well be compared, yea and happily not without cause also preferred before any of them, which haue as yet taken that so great an Argument vpon them. Which bookes by him for the common good of his natiue countrey onely, first written in French, (and seuen times printed in three yeares space, a thing not common) at such time as that mightie kingdome began now after the long and bloodie ciuile warres againe to take breath, were by him afterwards for the publicke benefit of the rest of the Christian Kingdomes and Commonweales turned into Latine also: which to doe he was the rather mooued, for that (as hee himselfe sayth) at the time of his employment here in England, he certainely vnderstood one Olybius a Frenchman, priuatly in noble mens houses in London, and another likewise in the Vniuersitie at Cambridge, with great obscuritie and difficultie there to interprete those his bookes of a Commonweale, then written but in French onely: which was as much as in him lay to make the same common vnto all men, the chiefe scope and drift of him in the whole Worke being to make the subiects obedient vnto the magistrates, the magistrates vnto the Princes, and the Princes vnto the lawes of God and Nature. Which his so good and Chri-
stian

TO THE READER.

than an intent and purpose in some part to further, I out of those his French and Latine copies haue into our owne vulgar translated that thou here seest: seeking therein the true sence and meaning of the Author, rather than precisely following the strict rules of a nice Translator, in obseruing the very words of the Author; a thing by me which followed neither the one nor other copie alone, but the true sence of both together, was not possibly to bee performed. And albeit that this the Authors so worthie a worke, euen at the first publishing thereof (and since also) was by some more maliciously than deseruedly impugned, as namely by Serre *and* Ferrier, *both Frenchmen, by one* Frankberger *a Germane,* Albergat *an Italian, and by* Possouinus *his pamphlets censured; yea, and that some few points thereof were by some Preachers also in Fraunce with greater zeale than iudgement found fault with: Sufficeth it that* Serre *after he had with good leaue both written and said what he could, was by the French king his expresse and iust commaund therefore imprisoned, and both the words and scholler-like writings of the rest little or rather nothing at all regarded, the Authors fame euen vnto this day more and more still encreasing, and their writings scarce hearkened after So that in defence of him, as also of this my Translation, I will vse no other Apologie than that which he yet liuing in few words most mildly vsed, in an Epistle to a friend of his, perswading him not so to put vp the matter:* Satis opinor, mea me scripta, & vitæ ante-actæ rationes, ab improborum contumelia vindicabunt: *I suppose (said he) my writings, with the course of my fore-passed life, shall sufficiently defend me from the reproch and slander of enuious and malitious men. And so wishing such as of themselues doe nothing, were no lesse courteous in the amending, than they are curious in the finding out of faults in other mens well meant labors; commending my selfe with these mine endeuours to thine vpright and fauourable censure, and thee vnto the Almighties protection, I in briefe bid thee most heartely farewell.*

A SVMMARIE TABLE OF ALL THE CHAPTERS CONTAINED IN THE SIX BOOKES OF I. BODIN.

The Contents of the first Booke.

What the principall end is of a well ordered Commonweale.   *Chap.* 1

Of a Familie, and what difference there is betweene a Familie and a Commonweale.   *Chap.* 2.

Of the power of an Husband ouer his Wife, as also of the mutuall duties betwixt them: and whether it be expedient to renew the law of Diuorcement or not.   *Chap.* 3.

Of the power of a Father, and whether it be meet for the Father to haue power of life and death ouer his children, as had the auntient Romans.   *Chap.* 4.

Of the power of a Lord or Maister ouer his Slaues, and whether Slaues are to bee suffered in a well ordered Commonweale.   *Chap.* 5.

What a Citisen is, and how much Citisens differ from Citisens, and how much from Straungers: what also is to be vnderstood by the name of a Towne, a Citie, and of a Commonweale.   *Chap.* 6.

Of them that are vnder protection, and the difference betwixt Allies, Straungers, and Subiects.   *Chap.* 7.

Of Soueraigntie.   *Chap.* 8.

Of a Prince tributarie or feudatarie: and whether hee bee a Soueraigne Prince: and of the prerogatiue of honour amongst Soueraigne Princes.   *Chap.* 9.

Of the markes of Soueraigntie.   *Chap.* 10

The

A Table of the Contents.

The Contents of the second Booke.

Of all sorts of Commonweales in generall, and whether there bee any mo than three. Chap. 1.
Of a Lordly Monarchy, or of the sole gouernment of one. Chap. 2.
Of a Royall Monarchy. Chap. 3.
Of a Tyrannicall Monarchy. Chap. 4.
Whether it bee lawfull to lay violent hand vppon a Tyrant; and after his death to disanull all his acts, decrees, and lawes. Chap. 5.
Of an Aristocratie. Chap. 6.
Of a Popular Estate. Chap. 7.

The Contents of the third Booke.

Of a Senat, or Councell of Estate, and also of the power thereof. Chap. 1.
Of the Officers and Commissioners in a Commonweale. Chap. 2.
Of Magistrats. Chap. 3.
Of the obedience that the Magistrat oweth vnto the Lawes and Soueraigne Prince. Chap. 4
Of the power and authoritie of a Magistrat ouer particular and priuat men, and of his office and duetie. Chap. 5.
Of the mutuall duties of Magistrats among themselues, and of the power that one of them hath ouer another. Chap. 6.
Of Corporations, and Colledges, Estates and Communities, and what profits or inconueniences ensue thereof vnto the Commonweale. Chap. 7.
Of the orders and degrees of Citisens. chap. 8.

The Contents of the fourth Booke.

Of the rising, encreasing, flourishing estate, declining, and ruine of commonweales. chap. 1.
Whether there be any meane to know the chaunges and ruines, which are to chaunce vnto commonweales. Chap. 2.

That

A Table of the Contents.

That it is a most daungerous thing at one and the selfe same time to chaunge the Forme, Lawes, and Customes of a Commonweale. Chap. 3.

Whether it be better in a Commonweale to haue the Magistrats changeable, or else perpetuall. Chap. 4.

Whether the vnitie and concord of Magistrats amongst themselues bee good and wholesome for the Commonweale, or not. Chap. 5.

Whether it be conuenient or expedient for the Maiestie of a Soueraigne Prince to iudge his subiects himselfe, or to be much conuersant with them. Chap. 6.

Whether a Prince in ciuill factions ought to ioyne himselfe to one of the parties, and whether a good subiect ought to bee constrained to take part with the one or the other faction: with the meanes to remedie seditions. Chap. 7.

The Contents of the fift Booke.

What order and course is to be taken, to apply the forme of a Commonweale to the diuersitie of mens humors, and the meanes how to discouer the nature and disposition of the people. Chap. 1.

The meanes to preuent the changes of Commonweales, which happen through the great riches of some, and exceeding pouertie of of others Chap. 2.

Whether the goods of men condemned should bee applied vnto the common treasure, or to the church, or els left vnto the heires. Chap. 3.

Of reward and punishment. Chap. 4.

Whether it be more conuenient to trayne vp the subiects in armes, and to fortifie their townes or not. Chap. 5.

Of the suretie of alliances and treaties betwixt Princes and Commonweales, and of the lawes of armes. Chap. 6.

The Contents of the Sixt Booke.

OF *Censuring or Reformation, and whether it be expedient to inroll and number the subiects, and to force them to make a declaration, or giue a certificat of their priuat estates.* Chap. 1.

Of

A Table of the Contents.

Of Treasure.   *Chap.* 2

Of Coynes, and the meanes how to preuent that they bee not altered.   *Chap.* 3.

A Comparison of the three lawfull Commonweales, that is, a Popular Estate, an Aristocraticall, and a Royall, and that a Royall Monarchy is the best.   *Chap.* 4.

That a well ordered Commonweale dependeth not either of lot, either of choyce, and much lesse of women; but by discent to be deriued from a most honourable stocke: and that it ought to bee giuen but to one alone, without partition.   *Chap.* 5.

Of the three kinds of Justice, Distributiue, Commutatiue, and Harmonicall and what proportion they haue vnto an Estate Royall, Aristocratique, and Popular.   *Chap.* 6.

FINIS.

THE FIRST BOOKE OF A COMMONWEALE.

Chap. I

¶ *What the principall end is of a well ordered Commonweale.*

Commonweale is a lawfull gouernment of many families, and of that which vnto them in common belongeth, with a puissant soueraigntie. This definition omitted by them which haue written of a Commonweale, wee haue placed in the first place: for that in all arts and actions, it behoueth vs first to behold the end, and afterward the meanes to attaine therunto. For a definition is nothing else than the very end and scope of the matter propounded, which if it be not well and surely grounded, whatsoeuer you build thereupon must together and in a moment fall. And yet oftentimes it falleth out with many, that hauing propounded vnto themselues certaine ends, yet can they not attaine vnto the end by them desired; no more than the vnskilfull archer who shooteth farre and wide from the marke he aimed at, whereas he which shooteth markeman-like, although he misse somewhat the marke, yet shall he shoot neerer than he, neither shall he want the commendation of a good archer, hauing performed what a skilfull archer should haue done. But he which knoweth not the end of the matter he hath in hand, is as farre from the hope of attaining thereunto, as he is from hitting the marke, which shooteth at randon, not knowing whereat. Wherefore let vs well examine the end, and euery part of the definition by vs before propounded. First we said that a Commonweale ought to be a lawfull or rightfull gouernment: for that the name of a Commonweale is holy, as also to put a difference betwixt the same, and the great assemblies of robbers and pirats, with whome we ought not to haue any part, commercement, societie, or alliance, but vtter enmitie. And therefore in all wise and well ordered Commonweales, whether question be of the publike faith for the more safetie to bee giuen; of leagues offensiue or defensiue to bee made; of warre to bee denounced, or vndertaken, either for the defending of the frontiers of the kingdom, or for the composing of the controuersies and differences of Princes amongst themselues; robbers and pirats are still excluded from all the benefit of the law of Armes. For why? Princes which gouerne their States by their owne lawes, and the lawes of nations, haue alwayes diuided their iust and lawfull enemies, from these disordered, which seeke for nothing but the vtter ruine and subuertion of Commonweales, and of all ciuill societie. For which cause, if ransome promised vnto robbers for a mans redemption, bee not vnto them accor-

The definition of a Commonweale.

That a commonweale ought to be a lawfull gouernmens.

Note at E 5.

accordingly payed, there is no wrong done: for that the lawes of Armes ought neither to be communicated vnto them, neither are they to enioy the benefit of those lawes, which lawfull enemies being taken prisoners, or free men enioy. Yea the lawes do permit him that is taken of robbers, not therby to loose his libertie; but that he may neuerthelesse make his will, and do all other lawfull actes: which for all that was not in former time lawfull for them to doe, which were taken by their iust enemies. For that he which was fallen into the hands of his lawfull enemies, by the law of nations did together with his libertie loose also all such power as he had ouer his owne things. Now if a man should say, that the law commaundeth to restore vnto the robber his pawne, his things committed vnto thee vpon trust, or what thou hast of him borrowed; or to repossesse him, beeing by force thrust out of a possession, neuer so vniustly by him obtained; there is thereof a double reason: the one, for that the robber in submitting himselfe vnto the Magistrat, and shewing his obedience vnto the lawes, in demaunding justice, deserueth to be therein regarded: the other, for that this is not so much done in fauour of the theefe or robber, as in hatred of him which would vnconscionably detaine the sacred thing left to his trust, or by way of force proceed to the gaining of that which he might by course of justice haue otherwise obtained. Of the first whereof we haue examples enow, but none more memorable than that of *Augustus* the Emperour, who caused it to be proclaimed by the sound of the Trumpet, that he would giue ten *Sestertiees* vnto him which should bring vnto him *Coracotas*, the ring leader of the theeues and outlawes in Spaine: which thing *Coracotas* vnderstanding, of his owne accord presented himselfe vnto the Emperour, and demaunded of him the promised reward: which *Augustus* caused to be paid vnto him, and so receiued him into his fauour, to the intent that men should not thinke, that hee would take from him his life, to deceiue him of the reward promised; or yet violate the publike faith and securitie with him, who of himselfe offered himselfe vnto the triall of justice: albeit hee might haue justly proceeded against the fellon, and so haue executed him. But he that should vse such common right towards pirats & robbers, as is to be vsed against just enemies, should open a dangerous gap to all vagabonds, to ioyne themselues vnto robbers and theeues; and assure their capitall actions and confederacie, vnder the vaile of justice. Not for that it is impossible to make a good Prince of a robber, or a good King of a rouer: yea, such a pirat there hath beene, who hath better deserued to be called a King, than many of them which haue carried the regall scepters and diadems, who haue no true or probable excuse of the robberies and cruelties which they cause their subiects to endure. As *Demetrius* the pirat by way of reproach said to *Alexander* the great, That he had learned of his father no other occupation than piracie, neither from him receiued any other inheritance than two small frigots: whereas he which blamed him of piracie, roamed about neuerthelesse, and with two great armies robbed the world without controlment, albeit that he had left him by his father the great and flourishing kingdome of Macedon. Which frank speech so moued *Alexander*, not to the reuenge of the iust reproach giuen him, but vnto commiseration, with a certaine remorse of conscience: in so much that he pardoned *Demetrius*, & made him general ouer one of his legions. And not to go further for examples, in our age *Solyman* the great Sultan of the Turks, with great rewards allured vnto him *Hariadenus Ænobarbus*, *Dragut Reis*, & *Occhial*, three of the most famous pirats of our memory; whom he made his Admirals, and great commaunders at Sea; by their strength to confirme his owne power, and to keepe vnder the other pirats, then roaming all about the seas, and so to assure his traffique. Truly by such allurements to draw arch pirats into good order, is, and shal be alwaies commendable: not onely to the end, not to make such people through dispaire

to

Note at G 10.

A to inuade the State of other princes, but also by their meanes to ruinate and bring to naught other pirats, as enemies to mankind: who although they seeme to liue in neuer so much amitie and friendship together, and with great equalitie to diuide the spoile, (as it is reported of *Bargulus* and *Vitriatus*, the arch pirats) yet for al that they ought not to be of right called societies and amities, or partnerships; but conspiracies, robberies, & pillages: neither is that their equal parting of the spoile, to be tearmed a lawful diuision, but a meere robberie: for that the principall point wherein consisteth the true marke and cognisance of amitie in them wanteth, that is to wit, right gouernment, according to the lawes of nature. And that is it, for which the auncient writers haue called Common weals, Societies of men assembled to liue well and happily together.

B Which as it may serue for a description of a Citie, so can it not stand for a true definition of a Commonweale, as hauing in the one part thereof too much, and in the other too little: three principall things especially to bee required in euery Commonwealth, wanting in this description, that is to say, the family, the soueraigntie, and those things which are common to a Citie, or commonweale: joyning hereunto also, that this word, Happily, as they vnderstand it, is not necessarie: for otherwise vertue should haue no prize, if the fauourable wind of prosperitie still blew not in the poope thereof, which a good man will neuer consent vnto. For a Commonweale may be right well gouerned, and yet neuerthelesse afflicted with pouertie, forsaken of friends, besieged by enemies, and ouerwhelmed with many calamities: vnto which estate *Cicero* himselfe

The auncient definition of a Commonweale defectiue.

C confesseth him to haue seene the Commonweale of *Marseils* in Prouince to haue fallen, at such time as it was by *Caius Cæsar* triumphed vpon: which he saith to haue bene the best ordered and most accomplished that euer was in the world, without exception. And so contrariwise it should come to passe, that a Citie, or Commonweale, fruitfull by situation, abounding in riches, flourishing, and well stored with people, reuerenced of friends, feared of enemies, inuincible in arms, strong in fortification, prowd in buildings, triumphant in glorie, should therefore be rightly gouerned, albeit, that it were surcharged with all villanies, and grounded in all maner of vices. And yet neuerthelesse most certaine it is, that vertue hath not a more capitall enemie, than such a perpetual successe as they cal most happy; which to ioine together with honesty, is no lesse

D difficultie, than to combine things by nature most contrarie. Wherfore sith that we may without reproach want other things; as also without praise abound therein: but that vertues we cannot without great imputation want; or be with vices polluted without infamie: it must needs follow, that those things which are thought to make the life of man more blessed, that is to say, riches, wealth, large territories and possessions, not to be of necessitie required vnto well ordered Cities, and commonweals: so that he which will looke further into the matter, must as little as hee may decline from the best or most perfect state of a Commonweale. For as much as by the goodnes of the end we measure the worth and excellencie, as well of Cities and Commonweals, as of all other things: so that by how much the end of euery Citie or Commonweale is

E better or more heauen-like, so much is it to be deemed worthily to excell the rest. Yet is it not our intent or purpose to figure out the onely imaginary forme and Idea of a Commonweale, without effect, or substance, as haue *Plato*, and Sir *Thomas More* Chauncelor of England, vainely imagined: but so neere as we possibly can precisely to follow the best lawes and rules of the most flourishing cities and Commonweals. In which doing, a man is not bee iustly blamed, although hee fully attaine not vnto the end hee aimeth at, no more than the good Pilot, by force of tempest driuen out of his course; or the skilfull Physitian ouercome with the force of the maladie, are the lesse esteemed: prouided, that the one hath yet in the cure well

gouerned

gouerned his sicke patient; and the other in his course, his ship.

The chief felicitie of one citizē, and of a Citie or common weale all one; and wherein it consisteth.

Now if the greatest felicitie and happinesse of one citisen, and of a whole Citie, be all one and the selfe same, and the chiefe good of both consisteth in those vertues which are proper vnto the mind, and are onely conuersant in contemplation (as they which in wisedome are said to haue farre excelled the rest, haue with great agreement affirmed) it must needs follow also, those citisens and people to enioy true felicitie, which exercising themselues in the sweet knowledge of things naturall, humane, and diuine, referre all the fruits of their contemplation vnto the almightie God, and great Prince of nature. If we then confesse this to be the principall end of the most blessed and happy life of euery one in particular, we conclude, that this is the felicitie and end also of a Commonweale. But for as much as men of affaires, and Princes, are not in this point agreed, euery man measuring his good by the foot of his pleasures and contentments; and that those which haue had the same opinion of the chiefe felicitie of a man in particular, haue not alwayes agreed, That a good man and a good citisen are not all one; neither that the felicitie of one man, and of a whole Common weale are both alike: this hath made that we haue alwaies had varietie of lawes, customs, and decrees, according to the diuers humors and passions of Princes and gouernours. Most men thinking the life of man to be but base, if his endeuours should bee onely directed vnto necessitie, and not also vnto pleasure, and ornament: they would (I say) account it a miserable thing to dwell in poore cottages couered with turfe, or in strait cabins and lodges to shrowd themselues from the iniury of the weather. But for as much as the wise man is in a sort the measure of right and wrong, of truth and falshood; or as it were an inflexible rule: and they which are thought to excell all others in iustice and wisdom, with one consent affirme the chiefe good of euery one in particular, and of all in common, to be but one, and the same, we also putting no difference betwixt a good man, and a good citisen, measure the chiefe felicitie and happinesse of euery particular man, and of all men in general, by that most beautifull and and sweet contemplation of high matters, which we before spoke of.

Aristotle blamed

Albeit that *Aristotle* sometimes following the vulgar opinion, seemeth doubtfull in setting downe the chiefe good thing, and not well to agree in opinion with himselfe; as thinking it necessarie vnto vertuous actions to ioyne also wealth and power: yet when he reasoneth more subtilly thereof, placing the chiefe good and felicitie of man, in Contemplation. Which seemeth to haue giuen occasion vnto *Marcus Varro* to say, That the felicitie of man consisteth in a mixture of action and contemplation together: whereof this may seeme to haue bene the reason, For that as of one simple thing, the felicitie is simple; so of things double or compound, the felicitie is also double and compound. For the goodnesse of the bodie consisteth in the health, strength, agilitie, comlinesse, and beautie thereof: but the goodnesse of the mind, that is to say, of that facultie or power which is the true bond of the bodie and vnderstanding together, consisteth in the due obedience of our desires vnto reason, that is to say, in the action of morall vertues: whereas the chiefe goodnes and felicitie of the vnderstanding and mind it selfe, consisteth in the intellectuall vertues, that is to say, Wisedom, Knowledge, and true Religion: Wisedome, concerning worldly affairs; Knowledge, concerning the searching out of the secrets of nature; and Religion, the knowledge of things diuine. Of which three vertues, the first seeth the difference betwixt good and euill, the second betwixt truth and falshood, and the third betwixt true holinesse and impietie: and so altogether containe what is to be desired, or to be fled from. In which three vertues, true wisedome consisteth, better than which God hath not giuen any thing vnto man: For that it cannot be taken from vs by theft, consumed by fire, or lost by shipwrack; but is of it selfe sufficient to make men, otherwise

G4–5 are not all one *i.e.* are all one (Cf. Fr and L. For the construction, cf. 553 C 9 and note.)
Notes at I8, K2.

Of A Commonvveale. 5

A wise destitute and bare of all other things, happie; and that not euery one in particular onely, but euen altogether also. Yet for all that shall a citie be much more blessed and fortunate, which encreased by these vertues, shal haue also sufficient territorie, and place capable for the inhabitants; a fertill soyle to plant in, with beasts and cattell sufficient to feed and cloath the people with; and for the maintenance of their health, the sweet disposition of the heauens, temperate and fresh ayre, plentifull and wholsome water, also matter fit for building and fortification, if the countrey of it selfe bee not safe and strong enough against the iniuries both of the weather and the enemy. These are the first beginnings of a growing commonweale, *viz*. That those things be first prouided for, without which people can in no wise liue; and then after that, such other things as
B wherewith men liue the more commodiously and better, as medicines to cure diseases, mettals wherwith conuenient tools may be made for workmen, & armes for souldiers, not onely to repulse, but also to take reuenge vpon the enemie and robber. And for as much as the desires of men are insatiable, after that those things are prouided for which are necessarie, as also those which are profitable; it lusteth vs also to seeke after, and to abound with vaine delights and pleasures, that so we may more sweetly & pleasantly liue. And as we haue no care of nurturing our children, before that they by conuenient education being growne, become capable both of speech and reason; no more regard haue cities also for the conforming of manners, or searching after the knowledge of naturall and diuine things, before they haue gotten such things as must needs
C be had to feed and defend their citisens; but are with meane wisedome content to repulse their enemies, and defend their people from iniurie. But the man that hath got all things needfull for him to lead a safe and happy life withall, if he be well by nature, and better by education instructed, abhorreth the companie of loose and wicked men, sorteth himselfe with the good, and seeketh after their friendship: and afterwards when he feeleth himself cleane & free frō those perturbations and passions which trouble and molest the mind; and hath not set his whole hope vpon his vaine pelfe, hee at great ease beholdeth the chaunges and chances of the world, the vnstaidnesse and diuersitie of mens maners, their diuers ages, and conditions; some in the height of power and soueraigntie; others in the bottome of calamitie and woe: he then studiously beholdeth
D the mutations, risings, and downfals of Commonweals; and wisely ioyneth things forepast, vnto those that are to come. After that, turning himselfe from mens affaires vnto the beautie of nature, he delighteth himselfe in beholding the varietie of natures worke in plants, liuing creatures, and minerals, hee considereth of euery one of them, their forme, their strength, and excellencie: yea he seeth the successiue transmutations of the elements themselues one into another, the singular Antipathie and contagiousnesse of things, the wonderfull order and consent of causes; whereby the things lowest, are ioyned vnto the highest, they in the middle vnto both, and so in briefe all to all: as also whereof euery thing tooke beginning, whether it returneth againe, when and how it shall take end; what in things is mortall and transitory, what immortall and e-
E ternall: and so by little and little, as it were with the swift wings of contemplation carried vp into heauen, wondreth at the brightnesse of the notable starres; the power, placing, distance, and vnequall course of the heauenly bodies; and so the good agreement and as it were most sweet harmonie of the whole world, and of euery part thereof: so rauished with a wonderfull pleasure, accompanied with a perpetuall desire to see the causes of all things, he is still caried on, vntill hee bee brought vnto God, the first cause, and gouernour of all this most faire and beautifull worke: whither when hee is once come, he staieth to search further, seeing that he is of an infinite and incomprehensible essence, greatnesse, power, wisedome, and beautie, such as cannot either by

B iij   tongue

Things requisit for the first beginning of a growing commonweale.

A notable discourse of the course that men hold for the attaining of felicitie.

D9 whether *i.e.* whither (L)   E9 *For* beautie *probably read* bountie (*bonté* in Fr).   Notes at B2, B7.

tongue be expressed, or by any mind of man conceiued: yet so much as in him is hee prayseth, extolleth, and with great deuotion honoureth, that so great brightnes of the diuine Maiestie, which by such heauenly contemplation draweth him vnto the true glorie, and chiefe end of all goodnesse. For by these meanes men seeme in a manner to haue obtained the most goodly knowledge of things naturall, ciuill, and diuine, and the very summe of humane felicitie and blisse.

A small commō-weale may yet be happie.

If therefore we iudge such a man wise and happie, as hath not gotten store of common wealth and pelfe, but the knowledge and vnderstanding of most excellent things, and remote from the rude capacitie of the vulgar people: how much more happie ought we to iudge a commonweale, abounding with a multitude of such ciuisens, although it contented with strait bounds, contemne the proud wealth and pleasures of the greatest cities, which measure their greatest felicitie, by their greatest delights, or by their aboundant wealth and store, or by the vanitie of their glory? Neither yet for all that doe we make that chiefe good of a man, or of a common weale, to be a thing confused, or mixt: For albeit that man be composed of a bodie which is fraile and mortall, and of a soule which is eternall and immortall; yet must it needs be confessed the cheifse goodnesse of man to rest and be in that part which is more excellent than the rest, that is to say, the Mind. For if it be true (as true it is) that this our bodie is compact and framed of flesh and bones, to serue the soule; and our desires to obey reason: who can doubt the chiefe felicitie of man wholy to depend of the most excellent vertue thereof, which men call the action of the mind? For although *Aristotle*, according to the opinion of the Stoiks, had placed the chiefe goodnes of man in the action of vertue; yet he the same man was of opinion, that the same action was still to bee referred vnto the end of contemplation: otherwise (saith hee) the life of man should bee more blessed than that of the Gods, who not troubled with any actions or businesse, enioy the sweet fruit of eternall contemplation, with a most assured repose and rest.

Aristotle blamed.

And yet not willing to follow the doctrine of his maister *Plato*, and also accounting it a shame to depart from the opinion by himselfe once receiued and set downe; for as much as he at the first had put the blessed life in action; he afterward with great ambiguitie of words, hath placed the chiefe felicitie of man, in the action of the mind, which is nothing else but contemplation: to the intent he might not seeme to haue put the chief good, both of men and commonweals, in things most contrary vnto themselues; motion (I say) and rest, action and contemplation. And yet hee neuerthelesse seeing men and commonweals to be still subiect vnto motion, and troubled with their necessary affaires, would not plainly put that chiefe good or happinesse which we seeke after, in contemplation onely; which for all that he must of necessitie confesse. For albeit that the actions whereby mans life is maintained, as to eat, to drinke, to sleepe, and such like, are so necessarie, as that a man cannot long want them: yet is no man so simple, as in them to put mans chiefe good or felicitie. The moral vertues also are of much more worth and dignitie than they: for that the mind by them (or by the vertue diuine) purged from all perturbations, and affections, may bee filled with the most sweet fruit and cleare light of contemplation. Whereby it is to be vnderstood, the morall vertues to be referred vnto the intellectuall, as vnto their end. Now that can in no wise be called the chiefe good or happinesse, which is referred vnto a farther thing, better and more excellent than it selfe: as the bodie vnto the soule, appetite vnto reason, motion vnto quiet rest, action vnto contemplation. And therefore I suppose that *Marcus Varro*, who deemed man his chiefe good to bee mixt, of action and contemplation; might (in mine opinion) haue more aptly and better said mans life to haue need of both; yet the chiefe good and felicitie thereof to consist in contemplation:

which

Note at H1.

A which the Academicks called the sweet, and the Hebrews the pretious death; for that it doth in a sort rauish the mind of man from out of this fraile and vile bodie, and carrieth the same vp into heauen. Yet neuertheles true it is, that a commonweale cannot long stand if it be quite or long time destitute of those ordinary actions which concerne the preseruation of the peoples welfare, as the administration and execution of iustice, the prouiding of victuals, and such other things necessary for the life of man; no more than can a man long liue whose mind is so strongly rauished with the contemplation of high things, that he forgetteth to eate or drinke, and so suffereth the bodie with hunger and thirst to perish, or for lacke of rest to die.

B But as in this fabrick of the world (which we may cal the true image of a perfect and most absolute commonweale) the Moone, as the soule of the world, comming neerer vnto the Sunne, seemeth to forsake this perspirall and elementarie region; and yet afterwards by the coniunction of the Sunne, filled with a diuine vertue, wonderfully imparteth the same vnto these inferiour bodies: so also the soule of this little world, by the force of contemplation rauished out of the bodie, and in some sort as it were vnited vnto the great * Sun of vnderstanding, the life of the whole world, wonderfully lightned with diuine vertue, with that celestiall force marueloufly strengtheneth the bodie, with all the naturall powers thereof. Yet if the same become too carefull of the bodie, or too much drowned in the sensuall pleasures thereof, shall forsake this diuine Sunne; it shall befall it euen as it doth vnto the Moone, which shunning the sight of the Sun,
C and masked with the the shadow of the earth, looseth her brightnesse and light, by which defect many fowle monsters are engendred, and the whole course of nature troubled: and yet if the Moone should neuer be seperated from the coniunction of the Sunne, it is most certaine that the whole frame of this elementarie world should in right short time be dissolued and perish. The same iudgement we are to haue of a well ordered commonweale; the chiefe end and felicitie wherof consisteth in the contemplatiue vertues: albeit that publick and politicall actions of lesse worth, be first and the fore-runners of the same, as the prouision of things necessarie for the maintenance and preseruation of the state and people; all which for all that we account farre inferiour vnto the morall vertues, as are also they vnto the vertues intellectuall; the end of
D which, is the diuine contemplation of the fairest and most excellent obiect that can possibly be thought of or imagined. And therefore we see that Almightie God who with great wisdome disposed all things, but that especially, for that he appointed only six dayes for vs to trauell and to do our businesse in, but the seuenth day he consecrated vnto contemplation and most holy rest, which onely day of all others hee blessed as the holy day of repose and rest, to the intent we should imploy the same in contemplation of his works, in meditation of his law, and giuing of him praises. And thus much concerning the principall end and chiefe good of euery man in particular, as also of all men in generall, and of euery well ordered commonweale: the neerer vnto which end they approach, by so much they are the more happie. For as we see in par-
E ticuler men, many degrees of worldly calamitie or blisse, according to the diuers ends of good or bad that they haue vnto themselues propounded; so haue also commonweals in a sort their degrees of felicitie and miserie, some more, some lesse, according to the diuers ends they haue in their gouernment aimed at.

The Lacedemonians are reported to haue alwayes bene valiant and couragious men; but in the rest of their actions iniust and perfidious, if question once were of the common good: for that their education, their lawes, customs, and manners, had no other scope or end than to make their people couragious to vndertake all dangers, and painfull to endure all manner of labour and toyle; contemning all such pleasures and delights

Marginal notes: A notable comparison. A man is called the little world. * GOD. Gen. cap. 2. Deut. Exod. cap. 20. A fit comparisõ. Plato, Plutarch in the liues of Lysander, Agesilaus, and Lycurgus.

B2 perspirall *i.e. spirabilis*, breathable, capable of supporting life   E8 their people   Note at B2.

8 THE FIRST BOOKE

delights, as commonly effeminate the minds of men, and weaken their strength, referring all their thoughts & deeds, to the encreasing of their state. But the Romane commonweale hauing flourished in iustice, farre passed the Lacedemonians; for that the Romans, besides that they were passing couragious, had propounded also vnto themselues true iustice, whereunto, as to a marke they addressed all their actions. Wherefore we must so much as in vs lyeth endeuour our selues to find the meanes to attaine or at least wise to come so neere as we possibly can, vnto that felicitie wee haue before spoken of, and to that definition of a Commonweale by vs before set downe. Wherfore prosecuting euery part of the said definition, let vs first speake of a Familie.

Dionis. Halicar. li. pri.

CHAP. II.

¶ Of a Familie, and what difference there is betweene a Familie and a Commonweale.

The definition of a familie.

A Familie is the right gouernment of many subiects or persons vnder the obedience of one and the same head of the family; and of such things as are vnto them proper. The second part of the definition of a Commonweale by vs set downe, concerneth a Familie, which is the true seminarie and beginning of euery Commonweale, as also a principall member thereof. So that *Aristotle* following *Xenophon*, seemeth to me without any probable cause, to haue diuided the Oeconomicall gouernment from the Politicall, and a Citie from a Familie: which can no other wise be done, than if wee should pull the members from the bodie; or go about to build a Citie without houses. Or by the same reason he should haue set downe by it selfe a treatise of Colleges, and Corporations; which being neither families nor cities, are yet parts of a Commonweal. Wheras we see the Lawyers, and law makers (whome we ought as guides to follow in reasoning of a Commonweale) to haue in the same treatise comprehended the lawes and ordinances of a commonweale, corporations, colleges, and families; howbeit that they haue otherwise taken the Oeconomicall gouernment than did *Aristotle*; who defineth it to be a knowledge for the getting of goods: a thing common vnto corporations and Colleges, as vnto Cities also. Whereas we vnder the name of a Familie, do comprehend the right gouernment of an house or familie; as also the power and authoritie the maister of the house hath ouer his people, and the obedience to him due: things not touched in the treatise of *Aristotle* and *Xenophon*. Wherefore as a familie well and wisely ordered, is the true image of a Citie, and the domesticall gouernment, in sort like vnto the soueraigntie in a Commonweale: so also is the manner of the gouernment of an house or familie, the true modell for the gouernment of a Commonweale. And as whilest euery particular member of the bodie doth his dutie, wee liue in good and perfect health; so also where euery family is kept in order, the whole citie shall be well and peaceably gouerned. But if a man shall be crosse and froward vnto his wife, if the wife shall be about to take vpon her the office of her husband, and not shew her selfe obedient vnto him; if both of them shall account of their children as of seruants, and of their seruants as of beasts, and so tyrannise ouer them; if children shall refuse the commands of their parents, and the seruants of their maisters; who seeth not no concord to be in that house, no agreement of minds and wils, but all full of strife, brawling and contention? Seeing therfore the way to order wel a citie, leaneth & resteth in the good gouernment of families, as it were vpon certain proper foundations:

The good gouernment of a familie the true modell for the gouernment of a Common weale.

tions: it behoueth vs first to haue an especiall regard and care for the good ordering and gouernment of families.

Wee said a Commonweale to bee a lawfull gouernment of many families, and of such things as vnto them in common belongeth, with a puissant soueraigntie. By the word, Many, you may not in this case vnderstand two, as for most part we do; for seeing that the law requireth at the least three persons to make a College, we according to the Lawyers opinion account three persons also, besides the maister of the house, necessary to make a familie; be they children, or slaues, or men enfranchised, or free borne men which haue voluntarily submitted themselues vnto the maister of the house or family, who maketh vp the fourth, and is yet neuerthelesse a member of the family. But for as much as Families, Colleges, Companies, Cities, and Commonweals, yea, and mankind it selfe would perish and come to end, were it not by marriages (as by certaine Seminaries, or nurseries) preserued and continued, it followeth well that a family cannot be in all points perfect and accomplished without a wife. So that by this account it commeth to passe, there must be fiue persons at least to make vp an whole and entire familie. If therefore there must needs bee three persons, and no fewer, to make a College, and as many to make a familie, beside the maister of the houshold and his wife; wee for the same reason say three families and no fewer to bee necessarie for the making of a Citie, or Commonweale, which should be three times fiue, for three perfect families. Whereupon (in mine opinion) the auncient writers haue called fifteene a people, as saith *Appuleius*, referring the number of fifteene vnto three entire families. For albeit that the maister of the family haue three hundred wiues, as had *Salomon* King of the Hebrews; and sixe hundred children, as had *Hermotimus* king of the Parthians by his multitude of wiues; or fiue hundred slaues, as had *Crassus*; if they bee all vnder the commaund of one and the same head of the familie, they are neither to be called a people nor a citie, but by the name of a family onely: Yea although hee haue many children, or seruants maried, hauing themselues children also; prouided alwaies, that they be vnder the authoritie of one head, whome the law calleth father of the family, although he yet crie in his cradle. And for this cause the Hebrews, who alwayes show the proprietie of things by their names, haue called a family אלף, not for that a family containeth a thousand persons, as saith one *Rabbin*, but of the word אלוף, which signifieth an head, a Prince, or Lord, naming the familie by the chief therof: better as I suppose than did the Greeks, of οἶκω, or the Latines of *Famulis*. But what should let (may some man say) three Colleges, or many other particular assemblies without a familie to make a Citie, or Cōmon weale, if they be gouerned by one soueraigne commaund? Truly it maketh a good show, and yet for all that is it no Commonweale: for that no Colledge, nor bodie politique can long stand without a familie, but must of it selfe perish and come to nought.

Now the law saith, that the people neuer dieth, but a thousand yeare hence to be the same that it was before: although the vse and profit of any thing granted vnto a common weale be after an hundred yeare extinguished, and againe reunited vnto the proprietie, which proprietie should otherwise be vnto the Lord thereof vaine and vnprofitable: for it is to be presumed, that all they which now liue wil in the course of an hundred yeares be dead, albeit that by successiue propagation they be immortal; no otherwise than *Theseus* his ship, which although it were an hundred times changed, by putting in of new plancks, yet still retained the old name. But as a ship, if the keele (which strongly beareth vp the prow, the poup, the ribs, and tacklings) be taken away, is no longer a ship, but an euil fauoured houp of wood: euen so a Commonweale without a soueraintie of power, which vniteth in one body all the members and families of the same

No perfect familie without a wife.

How many persons be requisite to make vp an whole and entire familie, and how many families make a Citie.

Iustin. lib. 4.

C2 three hundred wives (Fr) 700 wives (L). Cf. 1 Kings 11:3.   C3 Hermotimus (Fr) *preferably* Hierotimus (L). Cf. 557 B5.   Notes at D4, E9.

It is not the greatnes of the number that maketh the Commō weale, but the vnion of the people vnder one soueraigne commaund.

same is no more a common weale, neither can by any meanes long endure. And not to depart from our similitude : as a ship may be quite broken vp, or altogether consumed with fire ; so may also the people be into diuers places dispersed, or els be vtterly destroyed, the Citie or state yet standing whole ; for it is neither the wals, neither the persons, that maketh the citie, but the vnion of the people vnder the same soueraigntie of gouernment, albeit that there be in all but three families. For as an Emot is as well to be called a liuing creature, as an Elephant : so the lawfull gouernment of three families, with a soueraigntie of power maketh as well a common weale, as a great signiorie. So Rhaguse one of the least signeuries in all Europe, is no lesse a common weale, than are those of the Turkes, the Tartars, or Spanyards, whose Empires are bounded with the same bounds that the course of the Sun is. And as a little familie shut vp in a small cottage, is no lesse to be accounted a familie, than that which dwelleth in the greatest and richest house in the citie : so a little king is as well a Soueraigne as the greatest Monarch in the world. So *Vlisses*, whose kingdome was contained within the rock of *Ithaca*, is of *Homer* as well called a King, as *Agamemnon*: for a great kingdome (as saith *Cassiodorus*) is no other thing than a great Commonweale, vnder the gouernment of one chiefe soueraigne : wherefore if of three families, one of the chiefe of the families hath soueraigne power ouer the other two, or two of them together ouer the third, or all three ioyntly and at once exercise power and authoritie ouer the people of the three families ; it shall as well be called a Commonweale, as if it in it selfe comprehended an infinite multitude of citisens. And by this meanes it may chaunce, that one familie may sometimes be greater and better peopled then a common weale : as was wel said of the familie of *Æmilius Tubero*, who was head of a family of sixteene of his owne children, all maried, whome he had all vnder his power, together with their children and seruants, dwelling in the same house with him. And on the contrary part, the greatest Citie or Monarchie, and the best peopled that is vpon the face of the earth, is no more a common weale or citie, than the least. Albeit that *Aristotle* saith, the citie of Babylon (whose circuit in a square forme was so great, that it could scarce on foot bee gone about in three dayes) was to bee called rather a nation, than a common weale, which ought not, as he saith, to haue more than ten thousand citisens in it at the most : as if it were any absurditie to call an infinite number of nations, and dwelling in diuers places, gouerned by one soueraigne commaund, by the name of a Commonweale. By which meanes the citie of Rome (more famous than which was neuer any) should not deserue the name of a Commonweale, which at the foundation thereof had not aboue 3000 citisens ; but in the time of *Tiberius* the Emperor, had cessed in it fifteene millions, besides an hundred and ten thousand others dispersed almost throughout the world : not accounting the slaues, the number of whom was ten times greater : and yet in this number were not comprised they of the Prouinces subiect vnto the Empire of Rome, neither the confederat cities, or free nations, who had their Commonweals in soueraigntie diuided from the Roman Empire. Which soueraigntie of gouernment is the true foundation and hinge whereupon the state of a citie turneth : whereof all the magistrats, lawes, and ordinances dependeth ; and by whose force and power, all colleges, corporations, families, and citisens are brought as it were into one perfect bodie of a Commonweale : albeit that all the subiects thereof be enclosed in one little towne, or in some strait territorie, as the commonweale of Schwitz, one of the least of the confederat Cantons of Suisers ; not so large as many farms of this * kingdom, nor of greater reuenue : or els that the Commonweale hath many large prouinces and countries, as had the Persians, which * is reported to haue had an hundred twentie seuen prouinces from the vttermost part of India, vnto the sea of *Hellespontus* : or as is now also the Common-

Sometimes one familie may be greater than some Common weale. Plut. in Emili. The greatest & best peopled citie no more a cōmon weale than the least.

The multitude of people no hinderance to the vnitie of a common weale, so that they be vnder one soueraigne commād.

* *Fraunce.*
* Ester. cap. 1
* *Herodotus, Plutar. in Artax.*

OF A COMMONWEALE. 11

A commonweale of the Æthiopians, wherein are fiftie prouinces, which *Pau. Iouius* without reason calleth kingdomes; albeit that they haue not but one king, one kingdome, one Monarch, one Commonweale, vnder the puissant soueraigntie of one and the same Prince whome they call *Negus*.

But beside that soueraigntie of gouernment thus by vs set downe, as the strong foundation of the whole Commonweale; many other things besides are of citisens to be had in common among themselues, as their markets, their churches, their walks, wayes, lawes, decrees, iudgements, voyces, customs, theaters, wals, publick buildings, common pastures, lands, and treasure; and in briefe, rewards, punishments, sutes, and contracts: all which I say are common vnto all the citisens together, or by vse and profit: or publick for euery man to vse, or both together. That is also a great communitie which ariseth of colleges and corporations of companies, as also of benefits both giuen and receiued. For otherwise a Commonweale cannot be so much as imagined, which hath in it nothing at all publick or common. Although it may so be, that the greatest part of their lands be common vnto the citisens in generall, and the least part vnto euery one of them in particular: as by the law of *Romulus*, called *Agraria*, all the lands of Rome, at that time containing eighteene thousand acres, was diuided * into three equall parts, whereof the first part was assigned for the maintaining of the sacrifices; the second for the defraying of the necessarie charges of the commonweale; and the third was equally diuided among the citisens; who being in number but three thousand, had to euerie one of them allotted two acres: which equal partage long time after continued with great indifferencie, for *Cincinnatus* the Dictator himself 260 yeres after had no more but two acres of land, which hee with his owne hands husbanded. But howsoeuer lands may be diuided, it cannot possibly bee, that all things should bee common amongst citisens; which vnto *Plato* seemed so notable a thing, and so much to be wished for, as that in his Commonweale he would haue all mens wiues and children common also: for so he deemed it would come to passe that these two words, Mine and Thine, should neuer more be heard amongst his citisens, being in his opinion the cause of all the discord and euils in a Commonweale. But he vnderstood not that by making all things thus common, a Commonweale must needs perish: for nothing can be publike, where nothing is priuat: neither can it be imagined there to bee any thing had in common, if there be nothing to be kept in particular; no more than if al the citisens were kings, they should at al haue no king; neither any harmonie, if the diuersitie and dissimilitude of voyces cunningly mixed together, which maketh the sweet harmony, were al brought vnto one and the same tune. Albeit that such a Commonweale should be also against the law of God and nature, which detest not onely incests, adulteries, and ineuitable murders, if all women should bee common; but also expresly forbids vs to steale, or so much as to desire any thing that another mans is. Whereby it euidently appeareth this opinion for the communitie of all things to bee erroneous, seeing Commonweals to haue bene to that end founded and appointed by God, to giue vnto them that which is common; and vnto euery man in priuat, that which vnto him in priuat belongeth. Besides that also such a communitie of al things is impossible, and incompassible with the right of families: for if in the familie and the citie, that which is proper, and that which is common, that which is publick, and that which is priuat, be confounded; we shall haue neither familie nor yet Commonweale. In so much that *Plato* himselfe (in all other things most excellent) after he had seene the notable inconueniences & absurdities which such a confused communitie of all things drew after it, wisely of himselfe departed from that so absurd an opinion, and easily suffered that Commonweale which he had attributed vnto *Socrates* to be abolished; that

Many things common vnto citisens among themselues.

No commonweale where nothing is common.

Dionisius Halycarnasseus lib. 2.

Plato his opinion for the communitie of all things in a commonweale, refuted.

so

Note at A 10.

so he might more moderatly defend his owne. But some will say, that the Massagets had all things in common: yet they which so say, confesse also euery one of them to haue had his pot, his sword vnto himselfe, as also must they needs haue their priuat apparell and garments also; for otherwise the weaker should bee still spoiled of the stronger, hauing his garments still taken from him.

Wherefore as a Commonweale is a lawfull gouernment of many families, and of those things which vnto them in common belongeth, with a puissant soueraigntie: so is a Familie the right gouernment of many subiects or persons, and of such things as are vnto them proper, vnder the rule and commaund of one and the same head of the familie. *The chief difference betwixt a Familie and a Commonweale.* For in that especially consisteth the difference betwixt a Commonweale and a Familie: for that the maister of a familie hath the gouernment of domesticall things, and so of his whole familie with that which is vnto it proper; albeit that euery house or family be bound to giue something vnto the Commonweale, whether it be by the name of a subsidie, taxe, tribute, or other extraordinarie imposition. And it may bee that all the subiects of a Commonweale may liue together in common, in manner of Colleges, or companies, as did in auncient time the Lacedemonians, where the men apart from their wiues and families, vsed to eat and sleep together by fifteene and twentie in a company: As also in auntient time in Creet, all the citisens of all sorts men and women, young and old, rich and poore, alwaies eat and dranke together; and yet for all that, euerie man had his owne proper goods apart, euery one of them still contributing what was thought expedient for the defraying of the common charge. Which thing the Anabaptists in our time began to practise in the towne of Munster, hauing commaunded all things to be * common, excepting their wiues (of whom they might haue many) and their apparell, thinking thereby the better to mainteine mutuall loue and concord among them: in which their account they found themselues farre deceiued. For they which admit this communitie of all things, are so farre from this good agreement of citisens among themselues, which they hope thus to maintaine, as that thereby the mutuall loue betwixt man and wife, the tender care of parents towards their children, and their dutifulnesse againe towards them, and in briefe the mutuall loue of neighbours and kinsmen among themselues, is quite extinquished; all the kind bond of bloud and kindred (than which none stronger can be imagined for the friendship and good agreement of citisens) being by this meanes taken away. For that which thou shouldest dearely loue must be thine owne, and that also all thine: whereas communitie is of the Lawyers iustly called of it selfe, the mother of contention and discord. Neither are they lesse deceiued, which think greater care to bee had of things that bee common, than of things that be priuat; for wee ordinarily see things in common and *Things common smally regarded* publick to be of euery man smally regarded and neglected, except it be to draw some priuat and particular profit thereout of. Besides that, the nature of loue and friendship is such, that the more common it is, or vnto moe diuided, the lesse force it is of: not vnlike to great riuers, which carry great vessels, but being diuided into small branches, serueth neither so keep back the enemie, neither for burthen: in which maner loue also diuided vnto many persons or things, looseth his force and vertue. So the lawfull and certaine gouernment of a familie, diuideth euery priuat mans wiues and children, seruants and goods, from all other mens families; as also that which is vnto euery particular man proper, from that which is to them all common in generall, that is to say, from a Commonweale. And withall in euery well gouerned Commonweale we see the publick magistrat to haue a certaine especiall care and regard of the priuat goods of orphans, of mad men, and of the prodigall: for that it concerneth the Commonweale to haue their goods preserued vnto them to whome they belong, and that they be not embeseled.

* *Sleidan.*

Of A Commonweale. 13

embeseled. As in like case the lawes oftentimes forbiddeth a man to procure, to alienat, or to pawne his own goods or things, except vpon certain conditions, as also vnto certaine persons; for that the preseruation of euery priuat mans goods in particular, is the preseruation of the Commonweale in generall. And yet neuerthelesse although lawes be common to al, it is not inconuenient, but that families may haue their certaine particular statutes for themselues and their successors, made by the auntient heads of their families, and confirmed vnto them by their soueraigne Princes. As we haue example in the most honourable nation of the Saxons, amongst whome are many families, which vse certaine their owne priuat lawes, quite differing both from the lawes of the Empire, and from the common lawes and customs of Saxonie. And betwixt the dukes of Bauaria, and the Counties Palatines there are also their particular lawes, as well for the lawfull succession in the inheritance of their houses, as in the right of the Electorship, which is in these two honourable houses, alternatiue, by the auntient decrees of their predecessors: which laws & customs the duke of Bauaria, with great instance required to haue renewed at the diet of the Empire at Auspurge, in the yere 1555 which is not so in the other families of the Electors. Betwixt the houses also of Saxonie and Hess, are their domesticall and proper laws * confirmed vnto them by the Emperour *Charles* the fourth, and *Sigismund*. In like maner it was decreed betwixt the houses of Austria, and Bohemia, that for lack of heirs male, the one of them should succeed into the inheritance of the other, as we see it is now come to passe. And not to go further than this * Realme, I haue seene a charter of the house of Laual granted by the King, and confirmed by the Parliament of Paris, directly contrarie to the customes of Aniou, Britagne, and Mayne, wherein the most part of their inheritance lie: by which Charter the first inheritor (able to succeed) is to enioy all, being not bound to giue any thing vnto his coheirs, more than the moueables; with charge, that the heire male shall beare the name of *Guy de Laual*; or of *Guionne*, if she bee an inheritrix, and the armes plaine. In like manner in the houses of Baume, Albret, and Rhodez, the daughters by the auntient lawes of their aunceftors, were excluded both in direct and collaterall line from inheriting, so long as there were any males in what degree soeuer; deriuing as it were into their families, the law Salique, vsual vnto the Princes of Sauoy. Such lawes of families, which the Latines had also, and called them *Ius familiare*, were made by their aunceftors and chiefe of their families, for the mutuall preseruation of their inheritance, name, and auntient armes; which may in some sort well be suffered in some great and honourable families: which priuat lawes and customs by vs thus spoken of, haue oftentimes preserued from destruction, not onely families, but whole common weals; which was the cause that in the diet at Auspurge in the yeare 1555, the Princes of the Empire after long ciuill warre, wisely renewed the auntient lawes of great houses and families, as hauing well perceiued that by that meane the Empire was to be preserued from ruine, and the state of Almaigne from a generall destruction. Which for all that, is not to take place in other obscure and particular base families, to the intent that the publick lawes, so much as is possible, should be vnto all men common and the selfe same. For it is not without great cause to bee suffered, that the lawes of priuat families should derogat from the customes of the countrey, and so, much lesse from the generall lawes and ordinances. Neither are they which come after, by this law of families by their grand-fathers, & great grand-fathers made, contrarie to the common customs and lawes, further bound than they themselues shall thereunto giue their consent. For which cause the successors of the house of Albret, of Laual, and of Montmorency obtained decrees from the Parliament of Paris, contrarie to the auntient charters of their predecessors; for that they were contrary vnto the customes of those places, when

Particular families may haue also their particular lawes: and how.

* Anno 1370. and 1431.

* Fraunce.

The great benefit which oftentimes commeth vnto a Commonweale, by certain priuat lawes and customs granted vnto some great and honourable houses & families.

C question

A8 nation of the Saxons *i.e.* the *gens*, or house, of Saxony (cf. Fr)   B1 Counties *i.e.* Counts (frequently used in this sense)   E3 customes of the countrey *i.e.* regional customs

question was of the successions of Laual, of the Countie of Dreux, and of Montmorency, which they would make indiuisible, contrarie to the custom of the Viscomptie of Paris: For it beseemeth that the customes of families should bee subiect vnto the lawes, in like maner as the heads of families are subiect vnto their soueraigne Princes. Much lesse are the lawes of families and kindreds, allowed by the decrees of the Romans, to be be suffered least for the priuat the publick should be neglected: as *Camillus* complained with *Liuie*, * What (saith he) if the sacred rites of families may not in time of warre be intermitted, pleaseth it you that the publick sacrifices and Roman gods should euen in time of peace be forsaken? For it was a law of the twelue tables conceiued in these words, *Sacred priuat Rites, firme be they for euer*: which M. *Tullius* translated into his lawes. And thus much in generall, concerning the similitude and difference of a Common weale and Familie: now let vs discourse also of the singular parts of a Familie.

marginalia: Liuius lib. 5

Chap. III.

¶ *Of the power of an Husband ouer his Wife, as also of the mutuall duties betwixt them: and whether it be expedient to renew the law of diuorcement or not.*

ALL assemblies of men lawfully ioyned together, whether they be Families, Colledges, Vniuersities, or Commonweals, are kept together and preserued by the mutuall duties of commanding and obeying: for as much as that libertie which nature hath giuen vnto euery one to liue at his owne pleasure, bound within no lawes, is yet subiect vnto the rule and power of some other. All which power to commaund ouer others, is either publick or priuat: The power publick, is either free from law, as is theirs which hold the chiefest place of soueraigntie; or els restrained by law, as is the power of the Magistrats, who although they commaund ouer priuat men, are yet themselues subiect vnto the commaunds and laws of others their superiours. The power priuat, consisteth either in the heads of families, or in corporations, or colledges, where all by a generall consent, or the greater part, commaundeth ouer the rest. But the domesticall power is of foure sorts: *viz.* The power of the Husband ouer his Wife, the power of the Father ouer his children, the power of the Lord ouer his slaues, and the power of the head of a Familie ouer his mercenarie seruants. And for as much as the right and lawfull gouernment of euerie Commonweale, Corporation, Colledge, Societie, and Familie dependeth of the due knowledge of commaunding and obeying; let vs now speake of euery part of commaunding in such order as is by vs before set downe. For naturall libertie is such, as for a man next vnto God not to be subiect to any man liuing, neither to suffer the commaund of any other than of himselfe; that is to say, of Reason, which is alwaies conformable vnto the will of God. This naturall commaundement of Reason ouer our affections and desires, is the first, the greatest and most antient that is: for before that one can well commaund ouer others, hee must first learne to commaund himselfe, giuing vnto Reason the soueraigntie of commaund; and vnto his affections obedience: so shall it come to passe that euerie one shall haue that which of right vnto him belongeth, which is the first and fairest iustice that is; and that whereof the common Hebrew prouerb grew, That euery mans charitie should first begin of himselfe: which is no other thing than to keepe our affections obedient vnto Reason. This is the first law of naturall commaund, which God by his expresse commaundement * established, as we see in the speech which God had both vnto her that was the
first

marginalia: The diuision of power and commaund.

marginalia: Domesticall power of foure sorts.

marginalia: The first & greatest commaund is the commaund of Reason ouer our affections, & so ouer our selues.

marginalia: Gen. cap. 2.

F6 to be suffered   G10 Colledges, Universities *i.e.* corporate bodies (cf. Book III, ch. 7)

Note at H2.

OF A COMMONWEALE. 15

A first *mother of vs all; as also against him who first defiled himself with his brothers *Gen cap.3
bloud*. For that commaund which he had before giuen the Husband and his Wife, *Gen.cap.4
is two wayes to be vnderstood; first literally for the power the Husband hath ouer his
Wife, and then morally for the commaund the soule hath ouer the bodie, and reason
ouer affection. For that reasonable part of vnderstanding, is in man as the Husband;
and Affection, as the Woman: For before God had created *Eua*, it was said of *A-
dam*, Male and female created he them *. Wherefore the woman in holy writ is of- *Gen.cap.1.
tentimes taken for affection: but neuer more than with *Salomon*, who so liued as a
man vnto women most kind; but so writ, as if he had bene vnto them a sworne enemie, whereas he thought nothing lesse, all that his speech being to bee vnderstood of
B mans vnreasonable desires, as well declareth the wise and graue *Rabbin Maymon**. *Rabbi May-
But leaue we the morall discourse vnto Philosophers and Diuines to dispute of, and let mon.lib.1. ne-
vs take that which belongeth vnto ciuill policie, and speake of the power the Husband more.
hath ouer the Wife, as proper vnto this our question By the name of a Wife I vnderstand a iust and lawfull Wife, and not concubine, which is not in the power of him
that keepeth her; albeit that the Roman lawes call it mariage, and not concubinage, *A man hath no
if the concubine be franke and free: which all nations haue of good right reiected, and power ouer his
as it were by secret consent abrogated, as a thing dishonest and of euill example. Nei- *Concubine, or
ther doth this power that the Husband hath ouer his Wife extend vnto her that is her that is but
but betrothed, vpon whome the betrothed man may not lay his hand; which hath *thed*.
C euer bene lawful vnto the Husband, both by the Ciuil and Canon law: yea if the betrothed man shall lay violent hand, or force her that is to him affianced or betrothed,
he shall therefore by right suffer capitall punishment. But what if by consent of the
man and of the woman, contract of mariage be made by words of the present time, before they know one another; for that, the law calleth iust marriage: I am for all that of
opinion the power of an Husband not to be yet gotten by such a contract, except the
Wife haue followed her Husband: for as much as by the decrees of the Diuines and
Canonists (whose authoritie is in this matter the greatest) as often as question is made
of the right of mariages, scarce any regard is had of such mariages betwixt man and
wife, except it be of fact consumat, by the mutuall coniunction of their bodies; which
D by the consent of many nations is expresly receiued, as often as question is made of enioying of such commodities as are to be gained by mariage. But after that lawful con- *How the Husk-
iunction of man and wife (which we haue spoken of) the Wife is in the power of her band sometimes
Husband, except he be a slaue, or the sonne of the maister of the Familie, who haue *power ouer his
no authoritie ouer their wiues, & much lesse ouer their children; which although their *Wife, and why*.
married father were manumised, should yet fall into the power of their grandfather.
The reason whereof is, for that a Familie should haue but one head, one maister, and
one Lord: whereas otherwise if it should haue many heads, their commaunds would
be contrarie, one forbidding what another commandeth, to the continuall disturbance
of the whole familie. And therefore the woman by condition free, marrying her selfe
E vnto the maister of the families sonne, is in the power of her father in law, as is also the
free man marrying himselfe vnto the maister of the families daughter, in the power of
another man if he go to dwell in the house of his Father in law: albeit that in all other
things he enioy his right and libertie. Neither seemeth it a thing reasonable, that is by
the Roman laws ordained, That the married daughter, except she be before by her Father set at libertie, although she haue forsaken his house and dwell with her Husband,
shall not yet for all that be in the power of her Husband, but of her father: A thing
contrary vnto the law of nature, which willeth, That euery man shuld be maister of his
owne house, (as saith *Homer*) to the end that he may be a law vnto his familie: and re-

C ij pugnant

C10 conjunction

pugnant also vnto the law of God, which commaundeth the Wife to forsake father and mother to follow her Husband; and also giueth power vnto the Husband to confirme or breake the vowes of his Wife. Wherefore that law of the Romans is worthily abrogated, and especially with vs: for that the custome generally exempteth the married woman out of the power of her father; as was likewise in the Lacedemonian Commonweale, as *Plutarch* writeth, where the married woman saith thus; When I was a daughter I did the commaund of my father, but since that I am married, it is my Husband to whome I owe mine obeysance: for otherwise the wife might tread vnder foot the commaundement of her Husband, and acquit her selfe when shee saw good vnder the guard of her father. Now the interpreters of this Roman law haue vsed many cautions to auoid the absurdities and inconueniences following, if the wife should not be subiect to her husband, vntill shee were set at libertie by her father. Yet in that point the lawes of all people agree with the lawes of God and nature, That the wife ought to be obedient vnto her husband, and not to refuse his commaunds not repugnant vnto honestie. One Italian Doctor there is of opinion, That the wife is not in the power of her husband: but for that of his assertion so singuler and absurd, hee hath brought neither reason nor authoritie, there hath bene none so fond to follow the same. For it is certaine by the law of *Romulus*, that the husband had not onely the commaund of his wife, but also power of life and death ouer her, in foure cases, without any forme of judiciall processe against her: that is to wit, for Adulterie, for suborning of a child, for counterfeiting of false keyes, and for drinking of wine. Howbeit the rigor of those lawes were by the kindnesse of husbands by little and little moderated, and the punishment of adulterie committed to the discretion of the parents of the wife: which began to be renewed & again put in practise in the time of *Tiberius* the Emperour; for that the husband putting away his wife for adulterie, or himselfe attainted with the same crime, the offence remained vnpunished, not without the great reproach of their kindred, who in auncient time (after the manner of the Romans) punished the adulterous women with death, or with exile. And albeit that the power of the husband ouer his wife was much diminished, yet neuerthelesse by the oration *which *Marcus Cato* the Censor made vnto the people in defence of the law *Oppia* (which tooke from women their habilliments of collours, and forbad them to weare aboue one ounce of gold) it appeareth that the women were al their liues in the gouernment of their fathers, their brethren, their husbands, & next kinsmen, in such sort, as that without their leaue or authoritie, they could make no contract, or yet doe any lawfull act. This *Cato* the Censor flourished about 550 yeates after the lawes of *Romulus*: and 200 years after, *Vlpian* the Lawyer writeth, That Tutors and Gouerners were wont to be giuen to women and orphans; but when they were married, that then they were in the hand of the man, that is to say in the power of the husband. And if any should say That he diuided the title of persons that are in the power of others, from them that are in the power of others; it followeth not thereof that wiues were in the power of their husbands, but was by him so done, to show the difference of power the husband hath ouer his wife, the father ouer his children, and the lord ouer his slaues. And what doubt is there but that this word *Hand*, signifieth oftentimes power and authoritie? the Hebrews, Greeks, & Latines, hauing alwaies so vsed it, as when they say, The hand of the King; and, To come into the *hand* of the enemie. And *Festus Pompeius*, speaking of the husband bringing home his wife, vseth the word *Mancipare*, a word proper vnto slaues: which word we yet vse in many our customes and lawes, where question is of the emancipating of women. But to make it plaine, this power of husbands ouer their wiues to haue bene common vnto all people, we will by two or three examples declare

Margin notes:
- *Numeri. 3.
- *The wife by all the lawes of God and man bound to obey her husband.*
- *Foure cases wherein a man by Romulus his law had power of life and death ouer his wife.*
- *Tacitus lib. 2
- *Liui lib. 33.

OF A COMMONWEALE. 17

clare the same. *Olorus* King of Thracia compelled the Dacians ouercome by their enemies, to serue their wiues, in token of extreame seruitude, & of the greatest reproach that he could deuise to doe them. We read also that by the lawes of the Lombards the woman was in the same subiection that the auntient Romans were, and that the husbands had all power of life and death ouer their wiues, which they yet vsed in the time of *Baldus*, not yet 260. yeares ago. And not to seeke farther, what people had euer so great power ouer their wiues as had our aunceſtors? The French men (saith *Cæsar) haue power of life and death ouer their wiues and children, in like manner as ouer their slaues: and beeing neuer so little suspected to haue wrought their husbands death, are to be tortured by their owne kinsmen, and being found guiltie are by them to be cruelly executed, without any further authoritie from the Magistrat. But for drinking of wine it was much more manifest that it was cause sufficient by the Roman lawes for the husband to put his wife to death; wherein all the * auntient writers agree; which was not only the custome of the Romans, but also (as *Theophrastus* writeth) of the auntient inhabitants of Marseiles in Prouince, and the Milesians, who vsed the same law against their wiues that had drunke wine, iudging that the disordered desires of the woman subiect to wine, would also make her drunke, and so afterwards an adultresse. We also find that the power giuen vnto the husband by the law of *Romulus*, To put his wife to death for adulterie, without the authoritie of the Magistrat, was common to all Greece, as well as to the Romans. For the law of *Iulia* which gaue leaue onely vnto the father to kill his daughter together with the adulterer, being taken in the deed doing, and not otherwise, was made by *Augustus* the Emperour aboue seuen hundred yeares after the law of *Romulus*: And yet by the same law it was permitted vnto certaine persons to do the same that the father might, against their adulterous wiues: a right small punishment being appointed for the husband, who besides the persons in the law excepted, had killed the adulterours taken in the fact. But the publick punishment of adulterie derogateth nothing from the power of the husband, in other sorts of corrections ouer his wife, not extending vnto death, which is vnto husbands forbidden. After that *Theodora* the Empresse hauing got the maisterie ouer *Iustinian* the Emperour her husband, a blockish and vnlearned Prince, when she had made al the lawes she could for the aduantage of women against their husbands; she amongst others also changed the paine of death for adulterie, into the note of infamie: as did also in auntient time the Athenians, excommunicating the adulterors, with the note also of infamie, as we read in the Pleas of *Demosthenes*: which seemeth but a thing ridiculous, considering that the note of infamie cannot take any honour from her which hath already lost the same, and is altogether defamed: so that vpon the matter shee remaineth altogether vnpunished, & that for such a crime as the law of God * punisheth with the most rigorous death that then was, (that is to say with stoning) and which the auntient Ægyptians punished at the least with cutting off the nose of the woman, and the mans priuities. But in other crimes which more concerned the husband than the publicke state, and deserued not death, power is by the consent of all men giuen vnto the husband to chastice his wife, so that it be sparingly done, and within measure. And to the end that husbands should not abuse the power the law gaue them ouer their wiues, they had an action against their husbands, in case of euill entreatment, or froward vsage; which was afterward by the law of *Iustinian* taken away, and a penaltie decreed against them that had giuen the cause of the seperation: which were especially grounded vpon adulterie; and poisoning attempted, but not hauing taken effect. Yet notwithstanding the decree of *Iustinian*, it is by our custome permitted vnto the wife wronged or euill entreated by her husband, to require seperation. And yet for all

Iustin. lib. 32.

* *Lib. 6. Belli Gallici.*

That it was lawfull for a man to kill his wife for drinking of wine
* *Dion Halic. lib. 2. Plin. li. 4 cap. 13. Valer. de instit. antiq. Cicero de nat. lib. 3. & de Repub. lib. 1. Plu. in Problem. Rom. cap. 6. Arnob. lib. 2. aduersus gentes. Tertul in Apolog. cap 6. Gellius lib. 10 cap. 23. & Alcimus Siculus apud Athenæum.*

The punishment of wiues for adulterie.

* *Leuit. 20. Daniel 12. Deu. 24*

C iij   that

18   THE FIRST BOOKE

No action of iniurie to be admitted betwixt a man & his wife, and why.

The hatred betwixt man and wife of all others most deadly.

that is no action of iniurie to be suffered betwixt the husband and the wife (as some would haue it) and that for the honour and dignitie of marriage; which the law hath had in so great regard, that it permitteth not the husband, or any third man to haue an action of felonie against the wife, although she haue embeseled or purloyned all her husbands moueables. But as no loue is greater than that of marriage, (as saith *Artemidorus*) so is the hatred of all others most deadly, if it once take root betwixt man and wife; as was well declared by *Leo* Embassadour from them of Bizance vnto the Athenians, whome when they in a great assembly had laughed to scorne for his small stature, Why (said he) do you laugh at me a dwarfe, seeing my wife is much lesse than my selfe, and scarce so high as my knee; who pleased, although wee lie in a verie little bed, yet falling out the one with the other, the great Citie of Constantinople is too little for vs two? Which his pleasant speech serued wel to the matter he had in hand, which was to persuade the Athenians vnto peace; which is not easie to doe betwixt the husband and the wife, especially if one of them hath once sought after the life of the other. And for that cause the law of God concerning diuorcement (which was afterwards common to all people, and yet at this present is vsed in Affrick, and in all the east) gaue leaue to the husband to put away his wife, if she pleased him not, with charge that he might neuer take her againe, and yet might well marrie another: which was a meane to keepe the insolent wiues in subiection, as also to represse the anger of the wayward husbands; for what woman (except she were an arrant whore) would bee so desirous of a man, as to marry an husband that without any iust or probable cause had put away his wife. Now if it shall seeme to any an vnreasonable thing, to bee lawfull for a man to put away his wife, for no other cause but for that hee liketh her not, I will not greatly striue, either therefore depart from the law now with vs in vse. Yet nothing seemeth vnto me more pernitious, than to constraine the parties so in dislike to liue together (except they will) to declare the cause of the diuorcement they desire, & also wel proue the same before the Iudge: For in so doing, the honor of the one or of both the parties is hazarded, which should not so be if neither of them were enforced to proue the cause of the diuorce vnto the Iudge. As did in aunctent time the Hebrews, and yet do at this present also, as we see in their Pandects, where is described the lawful act of diuorcement, & the bil of diuorcement which *Rabi Ieïel* of Paris gaue vnto his wife the xxix. of Octob. in the yere from the creation of the world * 5018. Another example thereof is also extant in the Epitome of the Hebrew Pandects, collected by the Lawyer *Moyses de Maymon* in Chaldea, where the Iudge of the place hauing seene the special procuratiõ, & the act of him that had put away his wife in the presence of three witnesses, adioyneth thereunto these words, That he did purely and simply diuorce her, and without any cause showing, giuing them both leaue to marry whome they should see good. In which doing the woman was not dishonoured, but might with safe reputation marrie with another sortable to her owne qualitie. And albeit that the Athenians admitted no diuorcement, except the cause were first proued before the Iudges, yet seemed it to all good men to be a thing of great daunger: insomuch that * *Alcibiades* fearing the publick scandall tooke his wife openly complaining before the Iudges, and carried her away home vpon his shoulders. More indifferently delt the auncient Romans, in ioyning no cause at all vnto the bill of diuorcement: as is to be seene when *Paulus Æmilius* put away his wife, whome he confessed to be very wise, honest, and nobly descended, and by whom he had also many faire children: but when his wiues friends complaining vnto him, would needs know of him the cause of the diuorce, he showed them his shoo, which was very handsomly and well made; and yet said he, none of you but my selfe feeleth where this shoo wringeth mee. But what if the

Diuorcements by the law of God allowed.

Whether in diuorcement it be better to expresse the cause thereof, or els to haue the same concealed.

* *In the yeare of Christ 1240.*

* Plut. in Alci.

* Plut. in Æmi.

H6 together, except they will to declare   I9 sortable *i.e.* suitable, appropriate

the cause seeme not sufficient vnto the Iudge? or be not well proued? is it therefore meet to enforce the parties to liue together, in that societie which is of all other the straitest, hauing alwaies the one the other the obiect of their griefs stil before their eies. Truly I am not of that opinion: for seeing themselues brought into extreame seruitude, feare, and perpetuall discord, hereof ensue adulteries, and oftentimes murthers and poysonings, for the most part to men vnknowne; as it was discouered in Rome, before the law of diuorcement (first made by *Spurius Caruilius*, about 500. yeares after the foundation of the citie) a woman being apprehended and conuicted for poysoning her husband, accused other her companions in the fact, who afterward by mutuall accusations appeached seuentie others of the same crime for poysoning their husbands, who were all therefore executed: which how much the more is it to bee feared where diuorcements are altogether forbidden? For both the Greek and the Roman Emperours, willing to take away the often vse and easinesse of diuorcements, and to amend the auncient custome, ordained no other penaltie than the losse of the dowry, or of the other matrimonial conuentions, vnto the partie that shuld be the cause of the diuorce. *Anastasius* also suffered diuorcement, by consent of both parties, to bee made without any penaltie or punishment: which was by *Iustinian* the Emperour, or rather *Theodora* his wife forbidden. Now of that which we haue alreadie said, euery man as I suppose, may of himselfe iudge which is most expedient for a Commonweale.

Diuorcement necessarie.

But what change or varietie of lawes soeuer in such diuersitie of Commonweals, there was neuer law or custome that exempted the wife from the obeysance, and not onely from the obeysance, but also from the reuerence that shee oweth vnto her husband; in such sort that the law permitteth not the wife to sue her husband without the leaue of the Magistrat. But as nothing is greater, better, or more necessarie for the preseruation not of Families only, but of Commonweals also, than the honest obedience of wiues towards their husbands, as saith *Euripides*: so beseemeth it not the husband vnder the shadow of this power, to make a slaue of his wife. And wheras *Marcus Varro* is of opinion that slaues ought rather to be corrected with words than with stripes; much more ought the wife to be, whom both God and mans law doth call his housefellow. So *Homer* bringing in *Iupiter* reprouing his wife *Iuno*, and seeing her rebellions, vseth great threats, but proceedeth vnto no further extremities. And *Cato* commonly reputed to be a sworne enemie vnto women, did neuer beat his wife, reputing that to be as it were a sacrilege; but vsed so to maintaine the power and dignitie of a husband, as that he had his wife alwaies at commaund: which he shal neuer do which of a maister is become her companion, & afterward her seruant, & of a seruant her very slaue. As was of old obiected vnto the Lacedemonians, who called their wiues their Ladies and Mistresses: which the Romans did also, not the priuat men only, but euen their Emperors themselues, in the declination of their Empire; who at length together with their domesticall gouernment lost also their publick soueraigntie. Albeit that such women as take pleasure in commaunding their effeminat husbands, are like vnto them that had rather to guide the blind, than to follow the wise and cleere sighted.

Wiues to be corrected rather with words than with stripes.

Plut. in Laconicis.
Arist. lib. 2. Politic.
Tranquillus in Claudio.

Now the law of God, and the holy tongue, which hath named all things according to the true nature and proprietie thereof, calleth the husband *Bahal*, that is to say, Lord and maister; to show that vnto him belongeth the soueraigntie to commaund. The lawes also of all nations, to abate the pride of women, and to make men know that they ought to excell their wiues in wisedome and vertue, haue ordained that the honor and glorie of the wife should depend of her husband, as of the Sunne: in such sort that if the husband be noble, he enobleth his base wife; but if the wife beeing nobly borne marry a man of base degree, shee looseth her nobilitie, albeit that of auncient time

The authoritie and power of the husband ouer his wife.

C iiij there

C10—D1 rebellious   Note at C9.

there haue bene many and yet are, which take their nobilitie and gentrie from their mothers, and not from their fathers; as the Lycians, the Delphiens, the Xanthiques, the Iliensēs, and the Capadocians: whether it were for the vncertaintie of their fathers, or for that they had lost all their nobilitie in the warres; as in Campagne, where the wiues (for the cause aforesaid) ennoble their base husbands and their children; as also among the Indians in Calecut, the kings euen yet, and the Nobilitie which they call *Naires* haue scarce at any time their owne children inheritors of their kingdome or goods, but the children of noble women although they be bastards: yet for all that the interpretors of the law hold, that it ought not so to be done either by custome or decrees; for the generall agreement of almost all people to the contrarie, as *Herodotus* hath long ago written. And therefore it is most right that the wife should follow the Condition, Countrie, Familie, Dwelling, and beginning of her husband: and in case that her husband be an exiled or banished man, yet is the wife bound to follow him, wherein all the interpretors both of the Canon and Ciuill law agree. All lawes and customes also haue made the husband maister of his wiues actions, and to take the profit of all the lands and goods that to her befall: and suffer not the wife to stand in iudgement either as plaintiue or defendant, without the authoritie of her husband; or at least without the authoritie of the Iudge who may giue her authoritie so to do in the absence of her husband, or he refusing so to doe. All vndoubtfull arguments to shew the authoritie, power, and commaund that the husband hath ouer his wife, by the lawes both of God and man: as also of the subiection, reuerence, and obedience which the woman oweth vnto her husband, in all honour and things lawfull. Yet I doubt not, but that women in their matrimoniall contracts haue sometimes vsed to couenant not to be in any thing subiect vnto their husbands: but for as much as such couenants and agreements are contrarie to the lawes both of God and man, as also vnto publick honestie, they are not to bee obserued and kept, in such sort, as that no man can thereunto to be bound by oath.

Chap. IIII.

¶ *Of the power of a Father, and whether it be meet for the Father to haue power of life and death ouer his children, as had the auntient Romans.*

He right gouernment of the Father and the children, consisteth in the good vse of the power which God (himselfe, the Father of nature) hath giuen to the Father ouer his owne children: or the law ouer them whom any man adopteth for children vnto himselfe: and in the obedience, loue, and reuerence of the children towards their Fathers. This word Power, is common vnto all such as haue power to commaund ouer others, either publickly or priuatly. So the Prince (saith *Seneca*) hath power ouer his subiects, the Magistrat ouer priuat men, the Father ouer his children, the Maister ouer his schollers, the Captaine ouer his souldiers, and the Lord ouer his slaues. But of all these the right and power to commaund, is not by nature giuen to any beside the Father, who is the true Image of the great and Almightie God the Father of all things, as saith *Proclus* the Academick. *Plato* also hauing first in certaine chapters set downe lawes concerning the honour of God, saith them to bee as a Preface to the reuerence which the child oweth vnto the Father, vnto whome next vnto God he is beholden for his life, and for whatsoeuer thing els he hath in this world. And as the Father is by nature bound to nourish his children according to his abilitie, and to instruct them in all ciuilitie and vertue: so the children also when they are once growne

The power of the Father ouer his children is the onely naturall power.

vp are bound, but with a much more straiter bond, to loue, reuerence, serue, and nourish their Father, and in all things to shew themselues dutifull and obedient vnto them, and by all meanes to hide and couer their infirmities and imperfections, if they see any in them, and neuer to spare their liues and goods to saue the life of them by whome they themselues tooke breath. The which bond, albeit it bee sealed with the seale of nature, and engrafted in euery one of our minds, and carrieth with it a readie execution: yet so it is neuerthelesse, that to show the greatnes thereof there can be no greater argument, than the first commaundement of the second table, which alone of all the ten Commaundements propoundeth a reward vnto children which honour their parents: although no reward be vnto him due that doth but his dutie: and so much the lesse, for that there is no more religious a decree in all the lawes both of God and man; neither any curse greater in holy writ, than against him who wickedly laughed at the naked priuities of his Father. Neither is it maruell if wee in holy Scripture read * of the contentions and strife of the sonnes among themselues, for the getting and foregaining their Fathers blessing; as they which feared more their curse than death: As young *Torquatus* who cast off by his Father, slew himselfe for sorrow. And that is it why *Plato* saith, that aboue all things we must haue care of the cursings and blessings that the Fathers giue vnto their children: for that there is no prayer that God doth more readily heare, than that of the Father towards his children. If children then bee so straitly bound to obey and reuerence their parents? what punishment then deserue they that are vnto them disobedient, irreuerent, or iniurious? what punishment can be great enough for him which shall presume to lay violent hand vpon his Father or Mother? for against him that shal murder either of them, there was neuer yet Iudge or law maker that could deuise torment sufficient for a fact so execrable: although that by the law *Pompeia*, a punishment be appointed rather new and strange, than fit for such a crime. And albeit that we haue seene one in our memorie (who had caused his Father to be slaine) torne with hot yron tongs, afterwards broken vpon the wheele, and so at last (being yet aliue) burnt: yet was there no man which did not more abhorre the wickednesse of his villanie, than the horror of his punishment, and which said not that he had deserued more than he had yet suffered. Also the wise *Solon*, when hee had made lawes for the Athenians, being asked why he had appointed no punishment against him which had killed his Father; answered, That he thought there was no man so wicked as to commit so horrible a fact: which was grauely answered: for the wise law maker should neuer make mention of an offence which is not at all, or but very little knowne, for feare he should not seeme so much to forbid the fact, as to put the wicked in remembrance thereof. But if the crime be great and execrable, he must neither colour it by sufferance, as forgotten, neither point it out vnto the eye with his finger; but by circumstances and propounding of the punishments of like facts, deterre the wicked from such hainous offences. As we see the law of God hath not appointed any punishment against him that murdereth his Father or his Mother, neither against him that beateth either the one or the other (as doth the law *Seruia*, which condemneth them to death for such a crime) yet giueth it full power and authoritie vnto the Father and Mother to stone the disobedient child, so that it be done in the presence of the magistrat, to whome for all that it belongeth not to enquire of the truth thereof, or to examine the matter: which was so decreed least the Father should in his anger secretly kill his sonne. As was one in hunting slaine by his Father, whose wife he had defiled: which thing when *Adrian* the Emperour had vnderstood, said, That so to kill was not the part of a Father, but of a theefe or murtherer: for that the greatest profit of punishment is, that it be exemplarie vnto all. Another part of the law of God * willeth

The dutie of parents towards their children: and their great dutie againe towards them.

Exod. 22.
Deut. 5.

Gen 27. 28.

* Valer. Max. lib. 2.

* Leui 20.
Deu. 17. Exo. 21.

leth, That the child which reuileth his Father or mother should die the death: the examination whereof is not left vnto the parents, but to the Iudges themselues, to the intent that the offence should not remaine vnpunished. For so great is the loue of the father and of the mother towards their children, that they would neuer (if they might) permit the Iudges to determine of the life of their children, although they had bene of them mortally wounded. As not long agoe it happened with vs, that a Father hauing receiued a deadly wound of his sonne, whome he would haue lightly corrected; and fearing least his sonne apprehended by the magistrat should die for it, ceased not euen to his last gaspe to crie out vnto his son, by speedie flight to saue his life: whom for all that being afterward taken, and confessing the fact, the Iudges condemned to be hanged from an high beame for a time by the feet, with a great stone about his neck, and so afterwards to be burnt quicke. We haue also another example of our time, of a Mother who would rather endure to be reuiled, wronged, beaten, and troden vnder foot by her owne sonne, than to complaine of him vnto the Iudge; vntill that at length he in most beastly manner discharged his bellie into her pottage: with which fowle fact the Iudge moued, condemned him to make her an honorable amends, and to aske her forgiuenesse: from which sentence hee appealed vnto the parlement of Toulouze, where the former sentence was reuersed as not iust, and the sonne condemned to be burnt quick; the most wretched mother in vaine complaining and crying out against the rigor of the lawes and seueritie of the Iudges, protesting that she did pardon him, and that she had not of him receiued any iniurie at all. And *Seneca* speaking of a Father who but thrust his sonne out of his house; O with what griefe (saith hee) doth the Father cut off his owne limmes! what sighes doth he fetch in the cutting! how often doth he mourne for those limmes cut off! and how often doth hee wish to haue them againe!

All this that I haue said, and the examples of fresh memorie by me produced, serue to show that it is needful in a well ordered Commonweale, to restore vnto parents the power of life and death ouer their children, which by the law of God and nature is giuen them, the most auntient law that euer was common vnto the Persians, vnto the people of the vpper Asia, as also vnto the Romans, the Hebrews, the Celtes, and in vse in all the West Indies, vntill they were conquered by the Spaniards: otherwise wee must neuer hope to see the good orders, honour, vertue, or antient glorie of Commonweals reestablished. For *Iustinian* the Emperour deceiueth vs in saying that no people had such power ouer their children as had the Romans: For we haue the law of God, which ought to be holy and inuiolat among all people; wee haue the testimonies of the Histories both Greeke and Latine, whereby it is sufficiently to be vnderstood, the Hebrews, Celtes, and Persians to haue had the same power ouer their children that the Romans had. The French men (saith *C.esar*)* haue power of life and death ouer their wiues and children, as well as ouer their slaues. And although that by the law of *Romulus* power was giuen vnto the husband, for foure causes onely to kill his wife: yet neuerthelesse by the same law, full power was giuen vnto the Father to dispose of the life and death of his children, without condition or exception thereunto adioyned; and that whatsoeuer they got, was not theirs, but their Fathers: Which power the Romans had not only ouer their owne children, but also ouer the children of other men by them adopted. Which power was about 260 yeares after ratified and amplified by the lawes of the xij Tables, which gaue power also vnto the Father to sell his children: and in case they had afterward redeemed themselues, or were set at libertie by such as had bought them, they might yet sell them againe, and so the third time. The like whereof in all points is to be found in the Westerne islands, as we read in the Historie

of

Of A Commonvveale. 23

A of the Indies. And yet at this present amongst the Moscouits and Tartars (whom the auncient Historiographers called the Asian Scythians) it is lawfull for the Father to sell his sonne foure times, after which if he shall redeeme himselfe he is for euer free. By meanes of this fatherly power the Romans long flourished in all honour and vertue; and oftentimes was their Commonwealth therby deliuered from most imminent destruction, when the fathers drew out of the Consistories their owne sonnes being Tribunes, publishing laws tending to sedition. As amongst others *Cassius* threw his sonne headlong out of the Consistorie, publishing the law *Agraria* (for the diuision of lands) in the behoofe of the people, and afterward by his owne priuat iudgement put him to death, the magistrats, Sergeants, & people standing thereat astonied, & not daring to

B withstand his fatherly authoritie, althogh they wold with al their power haue had that law for the diuision of lands. Which is sufficient proofe, this power of the father not onely to haue bene sacred and inuiolable, but also to haue bene lawfull for him either by right or wrong to dispose of the life and death of his children, euen contrarie to the will of the magistrats and people. Also when * *Pomponius* the Tribune of the people, had for diuers causes accused *Torquatus* vnto the people, and amongst other things had charged him that he too much oppressed his sonne with countrey labour: so it fell out that the sonne himselfe going vnto the Tribune, and finding him in bed, setting his dagger vnto his throat, caused him to sweare to desist from further prosecuting of the accusation against his father. So the Tribune comming againe into the Con-

C sistorie least he might seeme to vse collusion with *Torquatus*, whome he had before accused, now excused himselfe vnto the people for not presenting his accusation, by the oath extorted from him: which the people vnderstanding, would not suffer him to proceed therein any further. By which two examples a man may iudge that the Romans in their estate, made greater reckoning of the power of the father, than of the lawes themselues, which they called Sacred: by which the head of him was vowed to *Iupiter*, who had onely attempted in offensiue manner, but to touch the * most holy Tribunes bodie. For they were of opinion that domesticall iustice and power of fathers, were the most sure and firme foundation of lawes, honour, vertue, pietie, wherewith a Commonweale ought to flourish. Neither was it maruell if in the Roman

D Commonwealth we see such rare examples of reuerend dutie of children towards their parents, as are not els where to be read of: one I haue amongst a thousand alreadie spoken of; and another such there is, as that Painters euen vnto these times vse therewith to embellish their Tables: that is to wit, of the daughter which secretly gaue sucke vnto her father condemned to be pined to death (which neuer suffereth the healthfull man to liue past the seuenth day) which act of piety the Gaoler hauing perceiued, gaue the magistrats to vnderstand thereof; which by them reported vnto the people, not onely obtained her fathers pardon, but also found such grace as that in the selfe same place in perpetuall remembrance of the fact, they built a Temple dedicated vnto *Pietie*. Yea the very vnreasonable beasts haue a naturall feeling of this kind dutie, and are

E seene to feed their parents now growne weake with age: but especially the Storke, which the holy tongue * (which nameth things according to their secret proprieties) calleth *Chasida*, that is to say, dutifull and charitable; for so much as shee nourisheth her father and mother in their age. And albeit that the father be in dutie bound to instruct his children in all vertues, but especially in the feare of God: yet if hee shall forget his dutie, are not the children therefore excused of theirs: albeit that *Solon* the lawmaker contrarie vnto reason, hath by his lawes acquited the sonne from the nourishing of his father, if he haue taught him no trade or occupation whereby to get his liuing. But the right instruction of children (than which nothing can be deuised more profitable

or

A notable example of a fathers seueritie against his sonne, being a great officer.

* Valer. Maxi. lib. 4.

* Dion. Halycr lib. 7. & Liuius lib. 3.

The rare pietie of a daughter toward her father.

* Leuit. 11. Iob. 38.

D5 pined *i.e.* starved   E3 (margin) Job. 38 (L) Job. 36 (Fr 3–8) *properly* Job. 39 (Fr 1–2)

Note at A6.

or better in a Commonweale) dependeth of that fatherly power which I haue before spoken of. For publick iustice taketh no knowledge of the disobedientnesse & vnreuerentnesse of children toward their parents, neither of their other vices, which disordered libertie bringeth their young years vnto, as dicing, drunkennesse, whoredome: and albeit that punishment be appointed against such offences, yet neuerthelesse the poore parents carefull of their reputation and credit, neuer are to complaine of their children vnto the Magistrat, neither accuse them; and yet the power to punish them is taken from them: so that children now standing in no feare of their parents, and much lesse of God doe for most part escape the iudgement of the magistrat, who commonly punisheth but slaues and such others of base condition.

The power of fathers ouer their children much profitable to the Commonweale: and the want thereof much hurtfull.

But impossible it is that the foundation of a Commonweale being euill laid, (that is to say, the bringing vp of children and families) any thing that is firme and sure should be thereupon built. Besides that, the contention, strife, and discord, which we daily see amongst brethren and sisters, were easily appeased and extinguished whilest the father yet liued, their marriages not taking from him this power ouer them: and albeit that he had set at libertie them that were maried, & departed out of his house, to keep house by themselues, (which they easily did not) yet neuerthelesse the remembrance of the reuerend duty they ought vnto their parents for euer remained fast imprinted in the harts and minds of the children. Wherefore should wee then maruell the magistrat to be troubled with so many sutes, and those for most part betwixt the husband and the wife, betwixt brethren and sisters; yea and that more, is betwixt parents and their children? but that the wife, the children, and seruants, are all loased from the domesticall power of their ancestors. So the fatherly power being by little & little diminished vpon the declination of the Roman Empire; so also shortly after vanished away their antient vertue, & al the glorie of their Commonweal: and so in place of pietie & ciuilitie, ensued a million of vices and villanies. The first staine, and beginning of taking away the power of life and death from parents, proceed from the ambition of the Magistrats, who seeking to encrease their iurisdiction, & by little and little drawing vnto them the deciding of all matters, extinguished all domesticall powers: which happened especially after the death of *Augustus Cæsar*; at which time wee read the magistrats to haue bene almost alwayes occupied in punishing of such as had murthered their parents. As we read in *Seneca*, who directing his speech vnto *Nero*, saith, We haue seene more murtherers of their parents executed in fiue yeares of thy father, than were euer in all ages accused since the foundation of Rome. Now to him that will looke neerer into the matter, it is no doubt, but that if one or two that haue murthered their fathers haue bene executed, ten others haue escaped mans punishment; the health and life of parents being subiect to a thousand daungers, except their children either by the feare of God, or the goodnesse of their owne nature, be kept within the bounds of their dutie; neither ought it seeme straunge vnto any man, that *Nero* made no conscience to kill his mother, neither repented him to haue killed her, for that it was a thing common: the cause whereof *Seneca* giueth not, which was, for that the father to chastice his son must then go to the magistrat to accuse him, which the auntient Romans could neuer endure. For *Quintus Fuluius* the Senator in the time of *Cicero*, of his owne authority put to death his sonne, for taking part in the conspiracie of *Cateline*. And in the time of *Augustus*, *Tatius* the Senator being about to proceed against his sonne in a capitall crime, requested *Augustus* home to his house, who being come thither, tooke not vpon him the place of a Iudge (as saith *Seneca*) but of a priuat man, as come onely to giue counsell. We see also that by the law *Pompeia*, made against parricides, all they which are next of kinne are bound to the penaltie of the law, except the father. Yet it sufficiently

How the power of life and death ouer their children was in Rome first taken from their parents.

ently

G2 children and   H1 more is, betwixt   H2 loased *i.e.* loosed, released   K5 Tarius

OF A COMMONWEALE. 25

ently appeareth, that in the time of *Vlpian* and *Paul* the Lawyers, the power that fathers had of life and death ouer their children lay then in a sort buried and forgotten: for that one of them saith, The father must accuse his sonne before the Iudge: and the other, That the children are not of right to complaine, if they be by their fathers disinherited, considering that in auncient time (saith he) they might put them to death. Both of them flourished in the time of *Alexander Seuerus*. And yet is there no expresse law to be found which hath taken from parents the power of life and death, before the time of *Constantine* the great: neither did that law of *Constantine* directly in expresse tearmes abrogat the old lawes: *Dioclesian* the Emperour but a little before *Constantine* hauing decreed that the Iudge ought to giue such sentence against the sonne as the father was willing vnto. Now it is manifest by the law, that a positiue law cannot bee abrogated by any custome, be it neuer so old; except it be repealed by a contrary law, carrying expresse derogation with it: otherwise being in force and readie to be againe put in vse: insomuch that it was necessarie that certaine lawes of the xij. tables by long custome out of vse, yet for all that should by a new law bee abrogated: which was done at the motion of *Æbutius*, in whose time the fathers power of life and death, yet kept their children with in the compasse of their dutie. But when the children in the time of *Constantine* had by the sufferance of their fathers by little and little shaken off that power and authoritie of their fathers, they obtained also of the same Emperour, That of their mothers inheritance their fathers should haue but the vse and profit, and they themselues the proprietie, which their fathers might not alienate. And afterwards they likewise obtained of *Theodosius* the yonger, That the proprietie of all manner of goods in generall howsoeuer they came by them, should belong vnto the sonnes, the vse and profit thereof onely being left vnto the fathers; so that they could not alienat the proprietie, neither in any sort dispose thereof: yea and with vs not onely the vse and profit of such goods, but not so much as the bare vse is left vnto the father, which hath so puffed vp the hearts of the children, as that they oftentimes commaund their parents, by necessitie constrained to obey them, or to die for hunger.

Note.

Iustinian also would not that children should be set at libertie by their parents without their owne consent, that is to say, without some bountie which the father ought to giue vnto his sonne: when as yet for all that in old time emancipation or setting at libertie, was the reward of the childs kindnesse and dutifulnes towards his parents. Hereof proceeded that filthie buying and selling of emancipation betwixt fathers and their children: insomuch that such things as the father had giuen vnto the sonne in reward of his emancipation, remained vnto him for gaine; neither was he bound to communicat the same with his brethren, or to haue any whit the lesse therefore of his fathers inheritance, except the same were expressely comprehended in the lawfull act of emancipation: which they also yet vse amongst vs, which haue the Roman decrees for lawes. But if the sonne hath learned any gainefull trade, or is by trafficke in marchandise become rich, and giueth something vnto his father that setteth him at libertie, it is counted vnto the father for the right he should haue in the goods of his son dying before him, so that he can claime no part therein, although it be not at all expressed in the act of the sonnes emancipation; or yet be expressed that such gift vnto the father yet liuing, should be no let wherefore he should the lesse haue the whole right of the lawfull inheritance, his sonne dying before him. For why? that whatsoeuer it is that is giuen to the father, is accounted as giuen him for his lawfull part: so that by this means the father is in worse state than the sonne; who for all that both by the lawes of God and man is bound to nourish his parents so long as they liue, the father not being bound by the law of *Romulus* to nourish his sonne, but vntill he be seuen yeares old. And although

How parents were woonts to emancipat their children.

D

though

though Lawyers goe farther, neuerthelesse to make it plaine that parents are not bound to feed their children, it was neuer by any law permitted for children to sue their parents for their food, but by the leaue of the magistrat by humble request before obtained. Besides all these indignities, *Iustinian* hath exempted all Senators, Bishops, & Consuls from the power of their fathers: as in like case them also which enter into houses of Religion. And in countries also where we vse Statute laws, besides those we haue spoken of, they haue also exempted out of their fathers powers them that are married, or haue beene out of their fathers houses by the space of ten yeares: which hath caused the Italian Lawyers to write that the French men are not in the power of their fathers: as in truth there remaineth nothing thereof, but the imaginarie shadow, when as the father authoriseth his children vnto lawfull acts, as to redeeme lands of inheritance, which the father himselfe hath sold, or to take a possession doubtfull, or for the trade or traffique of marchandise: in which case the Iudge without the kings letters royall at the request of the father may set at libertie his sonne. And albeit that *Philip* of Valois set at libertie his sonne *Iohn*, to giue vnto him the dutchie of Normandie: yet such his emancipation serued to no purpose, no more than those which were ordinarily made; seeing that neither the giuer, neither he to whome the thing was giuen, neither the thing it selfe giuen, were subiect vnto the Roman ciuill law: nor that the fathers (in countries gouerned by customs) had any thing to do with the goods of their children.

Whether parents be bound to nourish their children: and how long.

But the fathers thus dispoiled of their power, and of the goods got by their children, it is yet by many demanded, If the sonne may of right defend himselfe, or withstand his father, offering him violence? Neither haue there wanted some which were of opinion, That the sonne might of right so do: as if in that there were no difference whether the father or any other should offer him violence. But if it be so that the souldior which had onely broken the vine trunchion of his Captaine, beating him by right or wrong, was by the law of armes to be put to death: then what punishment deserueth the sonne which layeth hand vpon his father? Yea some haue passed further, and written that the sonne might kill his father, if he were an enemie vnto the Commonweale. But in mine opinion that is not vnlawfull onely for any man to doe, but impietie also for any man so to write: for these men in so doing propound not onely pardon vnto parricides, but giue leaue also vnto others to presume to do the like, secretly encouraging them to commit so detestable a fact, vnder the color of the publick profit: whereas an antient author saith, That no fault so great can by the father be committed, as that the same should with his murther be reuenged. O what a number of fathers should be found enemies vnto the Commonwealth, if these resolutions should take place? And what father is there which in the time of ciuill warre could escape the hands of his murtherous child? For men know well that in such warres the weakest goeth to the wals, and they that get the vpper hand make all traitors whom they list. And in other wars not onely they are iudged traitors which haue giuen vnto their enemies help and counsell, but also they which haue sold them armour, corne, or other victuals. As by the laws of England, to aid the enemie in any sort whatsoeuer, is accounted high treason. Which points of treason I see not to be distinguished by these interpretos of the Roman law. But by these resolutions, that is come to passe which posteritie will not beleeue: as that a banished man of Venice, hauing brought to Venice his owne fathers head, who was banished as well as himselfe, demaunded and obtained also in reward of his so execrable a murther, the honours and rewards by the Venetian lawes due; *viz*. His returne into his countrey, his goods, his children, and the liberties of the citie, before taken from him. But happily it had beene better that the citie of Venice had

Whether the sonne may resist his father offering him violence; or for any cause kill his father. Souldiors in antient times were beaten with vines. Plin. lib. 12.

A strange example of a most vnnaturall sonne.

F6 in countries also where we use Statute laws *i.e.* in the *pays coutumier*   F8 space   K3 ii terpretors
Note at K2.

had bene swallowed vp with the sea, than to haue giuen a reward vnto so great and detestable a villanie. *Henrie* the second the French king, tooke in good part the excuse of *Maximilian* king of Bohemia in the yere 1557, in that he had refused to giue safe conduct vnto the duke of Wittemberg, ambassadour for the French; confessing that it was indeed against the law of nations, but that yet neuerthelesse he durst do no other for disobeying of his father. Now if it be lawfull to violat the lawes of nations rather than to disobey our father in so small a matter; what iust excuse can there bee, or reason giuen for the killing of ones father? Wherfore I thus resolue, That there can be no iust cause for which a man may lawfully lay violent hand vpon his father. And albeit that such killing of ones father be in it selfe a fowle fact, yet fowler is the reward thereof; but of all other things most fowle and pernitious it is to allow reward for the same, for that by prouiding such rewards for killing of a mans father, neither brethren can be in safetie from being murthered by their brethren; neither the nighest kinsmen for being slaine one by another. As indeed it chaunced in the yeare 1567 that *Sampetre Corse* was slaine by his owne cosin germaine; for which he had giuen him in reward ten thousand crownes, which the Senat and people of Genua had caused to be leuied for him. But how much better were it to follow the example of *Cicero*, who thought it better as it were in silence to passe ouer the selfe same questions moued by the two auncient Philosophers *Antiochus* and *Antipater*, as a place too slipperie and daungerous. Ioyning hereunto also, that the law of the Romans it selfe forbiddeth any reward to be propounded vnto banished men for the killing of theeues: howbeit that *Adrian* the Emperour would haue him pardoned that had killed a theefe. Wherefore I thus conclude, That princes and law makers should measure the power and authoritie of parents, according to the law of God; whether they be their lawful, or naturall children, or both together; so that they be not conceiued in incest, for such the lawes both of God and man haue alwaies had in detestation.

Now if some shall obiect it to be a thing dangerous, least some furious or prodigall fathers should abuse the goods or liues of their children, vnder colour of their fatherly power: to him I aunswere, that the lawes haue for such men prouided guardians, and taken from them that power ouer another man, considering that they haue not power ouer themselues. And if the father be not sencelesse or mad, hee will neuer without cause kill his sonne, seeing that he willingly chastiseth him not though he deserue the same. For so great is the loue and affection of parents towards their children, that the law neuer presumed that they would do any thing to their disgrace, but all to their honour and profit. Wherefore the parents are euer thought to be free from all fraud in their childrens affaires, whome to encrease with riches and honor, they doubt not oftentimes to forget the lawes both of God and man. And for this cause the Father hauing slaine his sonne, is not by the law *Pompeia* subiect to the paine of patricides: for why? the law presumeth that he would not without good and iust cause so doe; and hath priuatly giuen power vnto him to kill the adulterer and his daughter found in the fact together. All most certaine and vndoubted arguments, whereby it is to be vnderstood, that parents cannot abuse the power of life and death ouer their children; neither that if they could, yet would they. But haply some man will say, there haue bene many which haue abused the same to the vnworthy death of their children; yet bring no example therof: Let vs grant some such to haue bene: should therfore a good law giuer leaue a good law vnmade for the inconueniences which some few times ensue thereof? It being a common saying in the law, That of such things as seldome happen the lawmaker ought to take no care. And where euer was there a law so iust, so natural, or so necessarie, that was not subiect vnto many inconueniences? So that he which would

Obiections against the power of fathers ouer their children.

B2 by propounding D10 privately *i.e.* to the exclusion of all others Note at A4.

would abrogat al laws for some few absurdities ensuing of them, should not leaue one of them, as *Cato* the greater wisely reasoned. In briefe (I say) that the natural loue of fathers and mothers toward their children, is impossible and incompatible with so great crueltie, as is the vniust killing of their children: and that the greatest torment that a father can endure, is, to haue either by right or wrong killed his sonne. As in fact it chaunced in our memorie, in the countrey of Aniou, that a father desiring to chastice his sonne, whome running from him he could not ouertake, hauing by chaunce without any such purpose slaine him with a blow vpon the head, with an hard clod of earth which he threw after him, forthwith for griefe hung himselfe, although no man knew any thing therof. Which things the antient Ægyptian law giuers wel vnderstanding, appointed no other punishment against him that had wrongfully or without cause slaine his sonne, but for the space of three daies after to bee shut vp together with the dead bodie of his sonne so by him slaine: For they thought it a thing detestable, for the death of the sonne to take away the life of the father, from whome he had receiued his. Yet might one say, that if fathers had the power of life and death ouer their children, they might constraine them to do something hurtfull vnto the Commonweale: Whereunto I aunswere first, that that is not to be presumed; and then that although it were so, yet that the lawes had therefore wisely prouided, hauing at all times exempted the children out of the power of their fathers, in that which concerned the publick State. As also *Fabius Gurges* gaue vs well to vnderstand, who being Consull, and seeing his father a priuat man mounted on horseback comming towards him, commaunded him by one of his sergeants to alight, which he did, doing honour vnto his sonne, and bidding him in such sort to proceed to defend the Consuls dignitie. And so farre hath it bene from wise fathers to commaund their children any thing that might be hurtfull to the Commonweale, as that there haue bene some of them found to haue put them to death for transgressing the publick lawes: as first did *Brutus* his two sonnes, and after him *L. Torquatus* the Consul, who hauing caused his sonne to triumph in his campe for vanquishing his enemie in combat, presently after caused his head to be struck off, for that he had fought with him contrarie to his commandement and contrarie to the law of armes. There is yet one obiection concerning the childrens goods, which if they should be in the full disposition of the fathers, they might without cause disinherit some, and enrich others: whereunto mine aunswere is, That the lawes haue therefore also prouided, by offering iustice vnto children disinherited; and propounding the causes of lawfull disinheriting. Howbeit that the auntient law of the Romans is more commendable, which neuer permitted the child by way of action to impugne his fathers will and testament; but onely by the way of request, and speaking of his dead father in all humilitie all honour and reuerence, leauing all the matter vnto the discretion and conscience of the Iudge. But after that the Pretors, who could not make any man heire vnto his father, yet by their decrees gaue possession of the goods (the force of which possession, was almost the same that it was to be appointed heire,) & that the magistrats had bound certain definit portions vnto the children; then forthwith began the parents by little and little to be contemned of their children, & their death by them longed for. Which thing was the cause that one of the Ephori of the Lacedemonians made a law * concerning the making of Testaments, whereby it was lawfull for euery man to bequeath his goods as he pleased (when as before, the libertie of making of Wils was by long custome taken away) alledging that the pride and insolencie of children against their parents was so by the feare of disinheriting to be restrayned. But if any man shall account it better for inheritances to be conferred by the appointment of the lawes than by Testament, I will not striue with him

Plu. in Lycurg.

him therefore, seeing it is by the law of God * set downe that children should not by *Numer.23.
assentation and flatterie rather than by their kind duties preuenting their fathers inheritances, spoyle themselues of their mutuall and brotherly loue: but yet why vse we not
the same diuine law * which giueth vnto the father the power of life and death ouer his *Deut.21.
children.

We haue before said, fathers to haue had that power of life and death ouer them *Adoptiue children as well in the power of their adoptiue fathers, as were the children begot in lawfull matrimonie.*
also whome they had adopted: in like manner as they had ouer them whom they had
in lawfull matrimonie begotten: and although the lawes of adoption were by the new
lawes of *Iustinian* almost abrogated; yet I thinke no man doubteth but that the law of
adoption was of so auntient right, & so common also almost vnto all people, as that it
deserueth to be againe called into vse. Wee see the most auntient people to haue had
it in singuler estimation: as we read *Iacob* himselfe to haue adopted *Ephraim* and *Manasses* * his nephewes, (albeit he had twelue children yet liuing, who had diuers others *Gen.cap.vlt.
also) and gaue them part of the land which hee had by force of armes conquered.
Which to haue bene before also in vse with the Ægyptians, is manifest by *Moyses*,
whome the kings daughter * adopted for her owne. Wee see also *Theseus* to haue *Exod.1.
bene solemnly adopted by *Ægeus* king of Athens, who made him his successor in the
State, albeit that he was but his base sonne: After which time all the Athenians which
had base children by Athenian women, were constrained to adopt them, and to cause
them to be registred as their lawfull children, and to leaue them their part and portion of their goods as they did vnto the rest of their children. For why? they accounted none a bastard but him that was begotten of a father or a mother, being a straunger;
albeit she were a woman of neuer so great honour. As also all the people of the East
made little or no difference betwixt the children that they had by their wiues and their
handmaids. For *Iacob* the Patriarch made like reckoning of those which hee had by
his wiues, and of those which he had by his handmaids: although that *Sara* had driuen out of his fathers house the child begotten by the handmaid, * least he should haue
had part in the lawfull inheritance. And *Diodorus* * also writeth, The children of the *Lib.2.cap.3
Ægyptians begotten of their bondwomen, to haue had as great prerogatiue as the rest
that were begot in lawfull marriage. For why? it was lawfull for them to haue as many wiues as they would; as it was also vnto the Persians & all the people of Asia: and
almost onely the Germans of all the barbarous nations (as saith *Tacitus*) had euery one Tacit.lib.de
of them but one wife. Thus hauing confirmed the matter by course of historie, it fol- moribus Germanorum.
loweth by consequence all the children of one and the same father to haue bene in his
power, were they adoptiue or not. But the Romans of auntient time made no more
account of their base children than of meere straungers: neither were they compelled
to adopt them, as were the Athenians, neither to bequeath them any thing by their
will, neither had they any power ouer them. Which seueritie of the lawes was yet
moderated in the raigne of *Theodosius* and *Arcadius*. And afterward it was ordained
by the Emperor *Zeno*, that such base children should be accounted for legitimat, by the
marriage of their father afterwards ensuing with their mother. And that more is, *Anastasius* decreed that all bastards should by adoption be reputed legitimat: but first *Iustinus*, and after him *Iustinian* abrogated that decree, and shut the gate against bastards,
to the end that euerie man should desire to haue lawfull wiues and children; and that
auntient houses, and the rights of successions and inheritances should not bee altered
and troubled by the adoption of bastards: the rights of adoption neuerthelesse yet
still remaining, which had bene receiued to supplie the defect of nature; and whereof
the auntient Romans had had so great esteeme, as that the adoptiue fathers had the
same power of life and death ouer their adoptiue children, that they had ouer their

D iij   owne:

A2 preuenting *i.e.* obtaining prematurely   B5 haue bene   Notes at B6, C3, D1, D3.

owne: which was the true cause that women could not adopt children before the edict published by *Dioclesian*, considering that they themselues were in the perpetuall power of their parents, husbands, or neere kinsmen: as also in Greece it was not lawful for them to adopt, as writeth the Orator *Isæus*. So then the right of adoptions, ennobled by the Romans (and especially after that they had extended the frontiers of their Empire more than euer before) other people also had it so much the more in regard: the Gothes, (I say) the Germans, the French, the Saliens; as we see in the lawes of the Ripuaires, where they vse the word *Adfatinir* for adopter: holding their adoptiue children in the same degree that they did their owne naturall and lawfull children, in the right of their succession into their inheritance: For by the auntient custome of the Romans they were both indifferently called vnto their fathers inheritances as his heirs. For so we read in *Cassiodorus*, that *Theodoric* king of the Gothes, adopted the king of the Herules: and that *Luitprand* king of the Lombards adopted the sonne of *Charles* prince of Fraunce, by cutting his haire, although he had sonnes of his owne in lawfull marriage begotten: as did in auntient time *Micipsa* king of the Numidians, adopting *Iugurtha* his base sonne, albeit he had two lawfull children of his owne, and leauing his kingdome equally diuided amongst them three: when as yet the first and chiefe cause of adoptions was to supplie the defect of nature; that he to whome nature had altogether denied children, or at leastwise male children, might by the authoritie of the law haue that defect supplied. As *Scipio Africanus* hauing no more children but *Cornelia* the mother of the Gracchi, adopted the sonne of *Paulus Æmilius*, afterwards called *Africanus* the younger, whome he left the inheritor not of his name only, but of his goods also. And so also *Cæsar* the Dictator, hauing no children of his foure wiues, more than *Iulia*, which was married to *Pompeius*, adopted *Octauius* his sisters sonne, whom by his will he made heire of three parts, with charge that he should beare his name; whereby his owne fathers name was taken away, and hee knowne by the name of his adoptiue father. And he againe hauing no children but *Iulia* (whome he called the Impostume of his house) adopted *Caius* and *Lucius* his sisters sonnes bought at home of their father *Agrippa*, according to the auntient manner: who afterward dead also without issue, he adopted *Tiberius*, who adopted *Caligula*: so did *Claudius* adopt *Nero*, vnto whome *Galba* succeeding without children, * adopted *Piso* before his armie, which custome was afterwards kept in the adoption of * *Aurelianus* the Emperour; as would *Iustinian* the Emperour haue adopted *Cosroe* king of Persia, which he refused; supposing (though yet falsly) the way vnto the Empire to bee by that meane shut vp. * We read also that the Emperour *Nerua* for lacke of children adopted *Traian*; & he *Adrian*; who afterward adopted *Antoninus Pius*; and not contented to haue adopted so good a man, charged him also whilest he yet liued, to adopt *Ælius Verus*, and *Marcus Aurelius*, surnamed the Philosopher, to the intent the Empire should not want the most vertuous Emperours that euer were. But this last hauing begot *Commodus* heire apparant to the Empire, (but the most vicious man that might be) was about to haue adopted another more worthie of the Empire, had hee not bene otherwise persuaded by his friends. For that almost no man vsed to adopt others, if he had legitimat children of his owne. For which cause *Claudius* the Emperour was euil spoken of, for being persuaded by the inticement of *Agrippina* his second wife, he had adopted *Nero* her sonne, hauing sonnes and one daughter by his former bed, who were afterwards slaine by *Nero*. But to leaue straungers which are infinite, and to come to our owne domesticall examples: *Lewes* duke of Aniou and brother to king *Charles*, was for want of heire adopted by *Ioane* (who of her incontinencie was in reproach called *Lupa*) who in the right of that adoption left vnto him the kingdome of Naples,

Tranquil in Galba. Vopiscus in Aureliano.

Procopius.

F8 Adfatinir (Fr) *preferably* Adfatinire (L) of his estate   F8 for adopt   H5 of three parts *i.e.* of three quarters of his estate   Notes at F3, H6.

A Naples, hauing reiected her nephew *Alphonsus* king of Aragon, whom she had before by consent of, the * Pope adopted. Afterwards also *Rene* of Aniou, *Lewes* his nephew, was adopted by *Ioane* the yonger queene of Naples for want of children. And at the same time as it were, that is to say, in the yere 1408, *Henry* duke of Pomeran was adopted by *Margaret D'wolmar* queen of Denmark, Sweden, & Norway, to succeed her in the same kingdoms. And not long after, *Henry* the fift king of England was adopted, not by *Charles* the sixt then distracted of his wits, but by his wife: who by her new son in law, caused *Charles* her owne sonne to be denounced incapable of the Crowne, albeit that he were a right wise and vertuous Prince. But *Iustinian* the Emperour willing to remedie such abuses, ordained that adoptiue children should neuerthelesse not faile B to enioy the inheritance of their owne naturall or lawfull fathers; for that their adoptiue fathers would oftentimes vpon small occasion cast them off againe, whereby it came to passe that they went without the inheritance of both their fathers: yet did he wrongfully take away the right of the fathers power, which was the onely marke of adoption, which taken away, nothing more remained. Now it were much better to prohibit adoptions to them, which had sonnes either naturall or legitimat: & in case they had none, that the adoptiue children should succeed in all the right of their owne naturall and lawfull children. Truely by our custome it is lawfull for euerie man to adopt: yet no preiudice is thereby made vnto the next of kin, or them which should lawfully inherite: for that more cannot be giuen or bequeathed vnto the adoptiue C sonne, than to him that is a meere straunger: and yet that the father might for all that receiue the profit of the adoption; whereof *Scipio Africanus* the Great, in his time complained in the Oration which he had vnto the people of his Censureship: as also after the publication of the law *Iulia Pappia*, which gaue great priueledges vnto them which had children: they which had none adopted some (to haue the benefit of the lawas, to be capable of some Magistracie or office) and in short time after they had once gained that they sought for, cast off those their adoptiue children againe, so abusing the law. As contratiwise *Clodius* beeing a noble man borne, caused himselfe to be adopted by a man of base condition, that so discharged of his Nobilitie, hee might bee made Tribune of the * people; but hauing got that office, caused himselfe presently to D be set at libertie by his adoptiue father: Which the Senat vnderstanding, decreed that from thenceforth they which were adopted should not enioy the priuiledge of any publick office: neither that any man should vnder the colour of such children as hee had adopted obtaine any magistracie or honour vnto himselfe; neither hinder substitution made for want of children; neither to haue the benefit of any conditionall legacies, or couenants made or conceiued in hope of children; nor that for such adoptiue children, such donations should be void, as were by the law it selfe to be reuoked when the donatour had any children, either naturall or legitimat; nor that by the adoption of male children, women should be kept from their lawfull inheritance, from which they by the law are wont by the male children to bee excluded; neither that the word E *Sonne* added vnto the lawes, testaments, or other lawfull acts was to be extended vnto them whome we adopt: all which deceits it is good to cut off, and yet not to extinguish the right of adoptions; and at the least to leaue vnto the adoptiue father his fatherly power, to keepe in obedience his adoptiue sonne. And thus much of the second part of a Familie, concerning the power of a father ouer his children, and of their mutuall duties. Now let vs likewise speake of the third part also.

Martinus. V.

Cicero pro dotio.

Chap. V.

Of the power of a Lord or Maister ouer his Slaues, and whether Slaues are to be suffred in a well ordered Commonweale.

Whereof a Familie tooke name.

HE third part of the gouernment of a Familie dependeth of the power of the Lord oues his Slaues, and of the Maister ouer his seruants; and in their mutuall duties one toward another. For the very name of a Familie, came of *Famulus* and *Famulatio*, for that it had in it a great number of Slaues: and so of the greatest part of them that are in subiection in the Familie, men call all the whole houshold a Familie; or els for that there was no greater meanes to gather wealth than by slaues and seruants, which the Latines call *Famuli*, the auntients not without cause haue called this multitude of Slaues and seruants a Familie. And *Seneca* willing to show of what moderation a Maister ought to be toward his Slaues, saith our ancestors to haue called the head of a Familie, Father of the Familie, and not Lord. And for that the whole world is full of Slaues, excepting certaine countries in Europe (which since also by little and little receiue them) it is needfull here to reason of the power of Lords and Maisters ouer their Slaues, and of the profits and disprofits which may redound vnto a Commonweale, if slauery should againe be called into vse: a question of great moment not for Families and societies onely, but for all Commonweals also in generall.

The diuision of Slaues.

Now euery Slaue is either naturall, that is to wit, begotten of a woman Slaue, or made a Slaue by law of armes; or by some crime committed (whome men call a slaue to punishment) or one which hath for money departed with his libertie, or hath plaid away his libertie, as did in auntient time the Almans · or else such an one as hath voluntarily vowed himselfe to be a perpetuall Slaue vnto another man; as was the manner of the Hebrewes. The prisoner in warre was Slaue vnto the vanquisher, who was not bound to put him to his ransome, if it were not otherwise agreed vpon; as it was in auntient time in Greece, that the Barbarian prisoner taken in warre, might bee put to the chayne, and kept as a Slaue; but as for the Greeke, that he should be set at libertie in paying for himselfe a pound of gold. The like law almost was made amongst the Polonians, * where it was decreed by the States, That all enemies taken prisoners in iust wars, should remaine Slaues vnto the vanquishers, except the king would pay two Florins for euery head. But he that had paid the ransome of any prisoner, was bound to set him at libertie, hauing againe receiued his money: otherwise he might keepe him, not as his Slaue, but as his prisoner; according to the most auntient law of the Greeks, which from them deriued vnto the Romans, was afterward in vse with all nations. As for debtors, prisoners vnto their creditors, although it were lawfull by the law of the twelue Tables, to diuide them in peeces amongst their creditors, giuing to some more, some lesse, according to the proportion of euery mans debt, if they were not able to pay: yet for all that so it was, that if he had one creditour, he could not take from him his life, and much lesse his libertie, a thing much dearer than life. For the father might well sell, chop, and chaunge his children, yea and take away their liues also, but yet could not take away their libertie: for the good and noble hart would alwaies rather chuse to dye honestly, than vnworthily to serue as a base Slaue. And that is it wherfore the law of the twelue Tables (which adiudged the debtor not able to pay, vnto the creditor) was shortly after at the request of *Petilian* Tribune of the people, taken away, and a decree made, That from that time forward the debtor should no more bee adiudged vnto his creditor, or diuided in peeces among his creditours, neither by them for his debt be detained; yet reseruing vnto the creditor power to ceise vpon his goods,

* Cromer in hist. Polon. & in statutis Pol.

A cruell law against debtors.

or

F6 Lord over Fr 1-6, 8). F8 *For* Famulatio *read* Famulitium (*a...famulatio* in Fr 7, *a...famulitio* in Note at H1.

or by other way of iustice to come by his debt, so as he saw he might by reason: which law continued firme and inuiolat 700 yeares, vnto the time of *Dioclesian*, who caused the same law afterward to be published vpon paine of death.

And thus much concerning all sorts of slaues: for as for them which are taken by theeues or pirats, or by false titles are sold for slaues, they continue neuerthelesse free, and in tearms of right may do all lawfull acts. As for other domestical seruants, which for wages or without wages do their seruice, they cannot by contract or agreement whatsoeuer, doe any thing preiudiciall to their libertie: neither in receiuing any legacie vpon condition be it neuer so little seruile: neither can the slaue himselfe when hee is manumised, promise vnto his lord that hath set him at libertie, any thing preiudiciall vnto his libertie, other than the seruices ordinarie & agreeable vnto all such as are enfranchised. And this is it for which the Arrests of the Parlement of Paris haue oftentimes disanulled the contracts of seruants free borne, which haue bound themselues vpon a paine to serue certaine yeres: which neuertheles they yet do in England & Scotland, where the maisters after the terme of seruice expired, comming before the Iudges of the places, enfranchise their seruants, & giue them power to weare their caps; which was the auntient marke of a slaue newly enfranchised, to couer his shauen head vntill his haire were growne: which gaue occasion vnto *Brutus* after that *Cæsar* was slaine, to cause certaine money to be coined * with the impression of a cap vpon it; as hauing set at libertie the people of Rome. And after the death of *Nero*, the common people went vp and downe the streets with caps vpon their heads, in signe of their libertie. And king *Eumenes* after the death of *Mithridates*, comming to Rome, and with his cap on his head entring the Senat, acknowledged himselfe to hold his libertie by the people of Rome. Now albeit that domesticall seruants be not slaues, and that they may do such acts of libertie as free men may, bee it in iudgement or out of iudgement; yet are they not as simple mercinarie men which labour for their daies wages, ouer whome he that hath hired them hath neither power nor commaund, nor any manner of correction, as the maister hath ouer his domesticall seruants, who owe seruice, honor, and obedience vnto their maisters, so long as they are in his house, and may with moderat discretion chastice and correct them. For domesticall seruants ought to reuerence their maister, and do them all honest seruice and duties: wherof, for that they haue a mutuall comportment one of them towards the other, and belong vnto morall discipline, we will not in this place reason.

But as concerning Slaues, there are two great difficulties, not yet resolued vpon: the one, Whether slauerie be naturall & profitable to a Commonweale, or contrarie vnto nature, and vnprofitable? the other, What power the lord of right ought to haue ouer his slaue. Concerning the first point, *Aristotle* is of opinion that the seruitude of slaues is of right naturall: and to proue the same, We see (saith he) some naturally made to serue and obey, and others to commaund and gouerne. But Lawyers, who measure the law not by the discourses or decrees of Philosophers, but according to the common sense and capacitie of the people, hold seruitude to be directly contrarie vnto nature; and do what they can to maintaine libertie, still interpreting such things as are obscure and doubtfull (whether it be in the lawes, or in testaments, in couenants, or iudgements) so in fauour of libertie, as that they giue no way either to lawes or to testaments: And if so be that the force of the lawes be so great and so plaine as that they may not swarue from them; yet do they protest that bitternesse of the lawes to displease them, calling it hard and cruell. But of these two opinions wee must chuse the better. Now many reasons there bee to proue that seruitude is profitable vnto the Commonweale, and also agreeable vnto nature: For euery thing that is contrarie vn-

Domestical seruants cannot make themselues slaues by any contract that they make with their maisters.

Prentises of England by couenant, for some slaues.

Plutar in vita Cæsaris.

Mercinarie labourers no slaues

Two notable questions concerning slauerie.

Slauerie is the opinion of Aristotle, a thing naturall, but not so in the iudgement of the Lawyers.

34   THE FIRST BOOKE

Reasons to proue that seruitude or slauery is profitable vnto a Commonweale: as also agreeable vnto nature.

to nature, is of no long continuance: and if you would force it against nature, yet will it of it selfe againe returne vnto the naturall course thereof; as is plainly seene in all naturall things. But seruitude seemeth to haue taken the beginning thereof immediatly after the generall deluge; and euen so soone as any forme of a Commonweale was to be seene, and so hath alwaies euer since continued: and although seruitude in these latter times was left off, for about three or foure hundred yeares, yet is it now againe approued, by the great agreement and consent of almost all nations; yea the people of the West Indies, which are three times greater than all Europe, who neuer heard speech of the lawes of God or man, haue alwaies bene full of slaues; neither hath there bene any Commonweale in the world, which hath not had slaues in it: yea the holiest men that euer liued haue vsed them: yea and that more is, in euery Commonweale the lord had power ouer the goods, the life and death of his slaue, except some few, where the Princes and lawmakers haue something moderated this power. Now like it is not, that all people and nations in euerie place, so many kings and princes, so many lawmakers (men for their vertue and experience most famous) would with so great consent, and so many worlds of yeares, haue receiued slaues, if it had bene a thing repugnant vnto reason and nature. And what can be more agreeing vnto curtesie and naturall reason, than after victorie obtained, to saue them whome thou hast taken prisoners in iust warre, to giue them meat, drinke, and cloathing, & with great charitie to releeue them? & for so great benefits to exact of them only their seruice & labor? is it not much better than in cold bloud to kill them? And this was the first beginning of slaues. Now whereas it agreeth also with the lawes of God and man, that he that hath not wherewith to pay for the fault by him committed, should be punished in his bodie; is it not better and more curtesie to haue him kept to labour in the publicke works? whereof such were also called seruants to paine, another kind of seruitude. In like sort, he that shall vniustly lie in wait for another mans goods, life, or state; what doubt is there but that he is a verie theefe and robber, and deserueth death? Then is it not contrarie vnto nature, to saue him for labour, in stead of putting him to death: for the word Seruant, commeth of sauing, albeit that some vnskilfull Grammarians reprehend *Iustinian* in so saying. Now if it were contrarie vnto nature, that one man should haue power of life and death ouer another, there should be neither kingdoms nor seignories, which were not contrarie vnto nature, seeing that kings and monarches haue the same power ouer their subiects, be they lords or slaues, if they once fall into any capitall crime.

How seruitude is agreeable vnto nature: and how not.

These arguments haue some good show to proue that seruitude is naturall, profitable, and honest, but it may well be answered. I confesse that seruitude is well agreeing vnto nature, when a strong man, rich and ignorant, yeeldeth his obedience and seruice vnto a wise, discreet and feeble poore man: but for wise men to serue fools, men of vnderstanding to serue the ignorant, and the good to serue the bad; what can bee more contrarie vnto nature? except a man should thinke it reasonable for a wise counsellour to be ouerruled by his foolish Prince; or a sober and temperat seruant to bee gouerned by his bedlem and riotous Maister. As for them that thinke it a charitable courtesie, in vniust warres to haue saued the liues of their prisoners whome they might haue killed, it is the charitie of theeues and pirats, who brag themselues to haue giuen life vnto them whome they haue not depriued of life. For oftentimes it commeth to passe in vniust warres, (as are for most part those that are made by the mightie) that good men are most miserably and shamefully enforced to serue the wicked. And if the vanquished haue wrongfully and without cause (as theeues) made warre, why then put they them not to death? why take they not of them exemplarie punishment? why take they them

The former reasons answered: and slauerie proued not to bee a thing agreeable vnto nature:

H9 Servant, commeth of saving *i.e. servus a servando*   Notes at H5, H10.

Of a Commonweale.   35

them then vnto mercie, seeing that they are theeues. As for that which is said, That seruitude could not haue continued so long if it had bene contrarie vnto nature: true it is in things meerely naturall, which according to their naturall proprietie follow the immutable ordinance of God: but hauing giuen vnto man the choice of good & euill, it chaunceth oftentimes to the contrarie; him to chuse the worse, contrarie to the law both of God and nature: in whom his corrupt opinion hath so great power, that it passeth in force of a law, of greater power than nature it selfe; in such sort, that there was neuer so great impietie or wickednesse, which hath not bene esteemed for vertue and godlinesse. Let one example serue for many. We know right well that there can be no more cruell or detestable a thing than to sacrifice men, and yet there are almost no people which haue not vsed so to doe, who all for many ages couered the same with the vaile of pietie and religion: as yet vnto this our age they of Peru and Brasiles doe, and certaine other people vpon the riuer of Plat; vnto which so prophane sacrifices our auncestors for all that with great deuotion resorted. With like pietie and deuotion the Thracians also vsed to kill their fathers and mothers, growne weake with age, and so afterwards did eat them, to the end they should not languish with sicknes, nor being dead become meat for wormes; as they aunswered the Persian king. Neither must we say that there were none but the auntient Gauls that sacrificed men; which indeed they did vnto the time of *Tiberius* the Emperour: for long time before, the Amorits and Ammonits vsed to sacrifice their children: neither was it a solemnitie among the Barbarians onely, as generally among the Scythes (as *Plutarch* writeth) but also among the Greeks (in whome ciuilitie not onely rested, but euen from whome it was vnto all other nations deriued): for *Achilles* (as *Homer* reporteth) sacrificed vnto his dead friend *Patroclus* with the slaughtar of men. * *Themistocles* also in the Persian watre, sacrificed three men; as did the Persian king at the same time twelue: neither could *Iupiter Licius* (as is reported) be otherwise appeased but by the slaughter of man, led by the ambiguitie of an old Oracle, and of the Greeke word φως, which without accent signifieth either Light, or a Man. *M. Tullius* detesteth our auncestors, for that they sacrificed with mans blood: but that he spoke as an Orator, and as best serued his cause: for *M. Varro* attributeth it to all the people of Italie: *as also the manner of vowing in the sacred spring time to haue bene, that whatsoeuer man or beast was that yere first borne should be sacrificed.* A man might also bring for example * *Iephte* general of the armie of the Israelites, who is reported to haue sacrificed his daughter vnto almightie God, much about the same time that *Agamemnon* king of the Greeks sacrificed his daughter *Iphigenia* * (whereof some well learned men haue made Tragedies) although that he sacrificed nothing vnto God but the virginitie of his daughter; as the Hebrew text plainly declareth; and as *Rabbi Leui*, and the other Hebrew interpetors all agree. Howbeit other people did the like with great pietie and deuotion: which proueth well that we must not measure the law of nature by mens actions, bee they neuer so old and inueterat: neither thereof conclude, that the seruile estate of slaues is of right naturall: as also much lesse to attribute it to charitie, or to courtesie, that the people in auntient time saued their prisoners, taken in warres, whome they might haue slaine; to draw a greater gaine and profit from them as from beasts. For who is hee that would spare the life of his vanquished enemie, if he could get a greater profit by his death than by sparing his life? Of a thousand examples I will produce but one. At the siege of Ierusalem vnder the conduct of *Vespasian*, a Roman souldier hauing found gold in the entrails of a Iew that was slain, made his companions therwith acquainted, who forthwith cut the throats of their prisoners, to see if they had also swallowed any of their crownes; so that in a moment there were slaine * aboue twentie thousand of those

* Cæs. lib. 6. Belli Gallici.

* Plut. in Themist. & Artax.

* Iud. 11.
* Euripides.

* Ioseph in bello Iudaico.

D7 interpretors   E9 (margin) Ioseph.   Note at D5.

those Iewes. O faire example of charitie towards captiues! But say some, they are nourished, they are well entreated for their seruice: but how I pray you are they nourished? and for what seruice doing? *Cato* the Censor (reputed the best and wisest man of his time) after that he had drawne all the seruice and profit he could from his slaues, euen vntill they were growne crooked with age, so that he could wring nothing more from them, set them then to sale to such as would giue most for them, to draw yet from them the verie price of their blood which yet remained in them, least he should be enforced to nourish them for nought, now growne impotent with age, or else bee faine to kill them, or to set them at libertie; in such sort that the poore slaues in recompence of all their seruice made, were drawne to the gallows by their new masters: not yet so happie as *Pallas* her mule in Athens, which growne old went about whither she list vnhaltred, no man daring in her old age to load or charge her. And whereas there is nothing more holy or more naturall giuen by God vnto mankind, than mariage; yet so it is, that it was not permitted vnto slaues: yea in case that a free man taken captiue had a child lawfully begot by his wife; if the father died in the hands of the enemie, although the mother returned into her libertie, yet neuerthelesse was the child reputed illegitimat.

The miserable estate and condition of slaues.

What should I rehearse the execrable and profuse filthinesse of both sexes, which the poore slaues heretofore were and yet are enforced to endure and suffer? But as for crueltie showed vpon them, it is incredible that we read, and that a man might speake of, if but the thousand part thereof were written: for Authors would thereof say nothing, if good occasion were not giuen; and we haue not but the histories of the most ciuill people that euer were in the world. For they were enforced to till the ground in *chaines (as yet they do in Barbarie,) and to lie in dungeons, the ladders being drawn vp from them, as they yet do in all the East, for feare they should be lost, or that they should set fire on the house, or otherwise kill their maisters. Now as for euerie light offence of the slaue, except he were of great price, it was so rigorously punished, as that to haue broken a glasse was vnto him death: as for example, the Emperour *Augustus* being at supper in the house of *Vedius Pollio*, it chaunced one of the slaues to breake a glasse; who hauing done no other fault but that (as saith *Seneca) was forthwith drawn vnto a pond of Lampreis, which were fed with mans flesh: whereat the poore slaue crying out, fled vnto the feet of *Agustus*, entreating him, not for his life, but that hee might not after he was put to death be eaten vp of those fishes, for hee found himselfe worthie of death for the glasse he had broken: but the common opinion was, that the soule of the drowned neuer passed ouer into the *Elysian fields; or els that it died together with the body: as *Synesius* writ of his companions sailing to Alexandria, who in a tempest sodainly risen, seeing the outragious violence of the Sea, drew their swords to cut their owne throats, so to giue way vnto the soule, which they thought otherwise to be in daunger to be drowned together with the bodie: so much the poore slaue feared to be eaten vp of the fishes. But *Augustus* moued with compassion (as saith *Seneca*) pardoned the slaue, causing all the rest of the glasses to be broken, and the pond to bee filled vp. Yet *Dion* the Historiographer, reporting the same historie, saith that *Augustus* could not obtaine pardon of *Pollio* for his slaue, neither to haue commaunded the pond of Lampries to haue bene filled vp, than which nothing was more pretious amongst the Remans: which for all that seemeth to haue bene more probable, seeing that *Seneca* confesseth *Augustus* to haue bene therwith contented, neither to haue bene therefore angrie with his friend *Pollio*. And to shew that this was no new matter more than two hundred yeares before, *Quintus Flaminius a Senator of Rome, caused one of his slaues to be slaine, for no other cause but to gratifie and please his *Bardache*, which

*Colum. lib. 1

*Lib. tertio de Ira.

*Vir. 6. Æneid

*Plot. in vita Titi Flaminii.

I1 (margin) de Ira   I2 Augustus   K5 Romans   K9 Bardache *i.e.* bardash, catamite

which said that he had neuer seene a man slaine. Now if it chaunced the maister to be slaine in his house, by whomsoeuer that it was, all the slaues that at the same time were vnder the same roofe, were put to death euerie mothers son. As chanced at the murther of *Pedanius* great Pretor of Rome; when question was made of putting to death al his slaues, following (as saith *Tacitus*) the auntient custome, the common people being for the most part men enfranchised, fell in mutinie, for that they knew well the murtherer was but one, & yet neuerthelesse there must be put to death 400 of his slaues, all innocent of the fact: neuerthelesse the matter being debated in the Senat, it was there resolued, That the antient custome shuld be kept, & so accordingly al the slaues were put to death. I let passe the murthering of slaues, enforced to kill one another in the lists, or to be torne with wild beasts, so to giue pleasure vnto the people, and to breed in them a contempt of death. And although the law *Petronia* had forbidden slaues without cause to be cast vnto the wild beasts: yet was it neuer obserued, no more than the edict of the emperour *Nero*, who was the first that appointed commissioners to heare the complaints of slaues: and after him the emperour *Adrian* ordained that inquisition should be made against such as had maliciously without cause slaine their slaues: howbeit that long time before they were culpable as murtherers, by the law *Cornelia*: but that was holden in no regard, and all that the poore slaues could do to saue themselues from the fury of their maisters, was to flie vnto the images of the gods, or of the emperours. For neither the temple of *Diana* in Rome, which king *Seruius* (himselfe the sonne of a slaue) had appointed as a sanctuarie for slaues; neither the image of *Romulus*, which the Senat had of long time appointed for the selfe same purpose; neither the Sepulcher of *Theseus* at Athens; neither the image of *Ptolemee* at Cyrene; neither the temple of *Diana* at Ephesus, could defend the slaues from the furie of their angrie lords and masters. Howbeit that by the law of the Ephesians the slaue which without iust cause had fled vnto the temple of *Diana*, was againe restored vnto his master, being before sworne not therefore to entreat him euill: but if the cause of his flight were iust, then was he taken from his master and made seruant to *Diana*: except women, who might not enter into her temple. But *Tiberius* of all other tyrants that euer were, the most craftie in his old age, appointed his image for a sanctuarie, propounding capitall punishment vnto all such as should by violence draw any slaue from the same; to the intent that by that meane the slaues might for the least occasion come to accuse their masters, yea euen of high treason. Insomuch that as *Seneca* writeth, a certaine Senator fearing to bee bewraied of his slaue, craued pardon of *Tiberius* for that he had but bene about to touch his chamber pot with a ring vpon his finger, wherein the image of *Tiberius* was engrauen. In such sort, that the images of the emperours, but especially of tyrants were as snares to entangle the magistrats in, who oftentimes secretly murthered their slaues, for hauing recourse vnto the images, so soone as they were returned thence. But the law of God had therefore much better prouided, appointing euerie mans house for a sanctuarie vnto the slaue flying from his master, forbidding to restore him againe vnto his maister whilest he was yet in choller. For all masters are not of like discretion to *Plato*, which said to his slaue, That he would sharply haue corrected him, but that hee was angrie: whereas the Germans (as *Tacitus* saith) neuer punish their seruants or children but in their rage, and that as if they were their enemies. Thus we see the liues of masters not well assured against their slaues; and the liues of slaues much lesse against their masters. For who could assure himselfe of his life, or of his goods in the time of the tyrannie of *Sylla*, who had proposed thirtie Sesterties vnto free men, and vnto bond men liberty, as a reward if they should discouer their masters, or bring in the head of any one of them that were by him proscribed? In which feare the citisens were, vntill

*Lib 14.

*Sene. lib. 3. de Benefic.

*Plu. in Thes.

D7 *For* magistrats *read* masters (Fr).   E7 thirtie Sesterties *i.e.* 30 sestertia or 30,000 sesterces

till that threescore thousand of them being slaine, and so the state in a manner againe appeased, a certaine slaue yet presented vnto *Sylla* the head of his lord & master, whom *Sylla* for so doing according to his promise set at liberty, but by and by after caused him to be cast headlong from the rocke Tarpeia. At such time also as persecution grew hot against the Christians, there was no Christian master but was in daunger of his life, or els glad to set at libertie his slaues. But the feare of persecution once ceasing, the lords and masters themselues became tyrants ouer their slaues.

To great a multitude of slaues daungerous in a Commonweale.

So the state of Families and Commonweals is alwaies in daunger of trouble and ruine, by the conspiracie of slaues combining themselues together: all Histories being full of seruile rebellions and warres. And albeit that the Romans were right great and mightie, yet so it was that they could not let the slaues to rise against the state in al the townes of Italie except Messana: and afterwards for all the lawes they could make, they could not preuent but that threescore thousand slaues rise in rebellion vnder the conduct of *Spartacus*, who in set battaile ouerthrew three armies of the Romans. For it is most certaine, that in euerie country whatsoeuer, there was at least ten slaues for one free man: as it is easie to iudge by the musters taken in Athens, where for twentie thousand citisens were found ten thousand strangers, and foure hundred thousand slaues. And Italie (victorious ouer all nations) had many moe, as a man may perceiue by the Oration of *Cassius* the Senator, whereby he persuaded the Senat for the confirming of *Sylla* his decree: We haue at home (said he) whole nations of slaues much differing among themselues in manners, fashions, language, and religion. And namely *M. Crassus* alone had fiue hundred slaues, who daily brought in vnto him the profit of their gainfull arts and trades; besides them whome he imployed in his ordinarie and domesticall seruice. *Milo* also in one day set at libertie 300 slaues, least they should haue bene put to torture to depose concerning the death of *Clodius* Tribune of the people. And that multitude of slaues was it for which the Roman Senate, desirous to put a difference in the habit of slaues, to the intent to haue them knowne from free men: one of the grauest Senators dissuaded the same, showing the daunger like to ensue thereof, if the slaues should begin to enter into the number of themselues; for that so they might easily dispatch themselues of their maisters, for the easinesse of their rising into rebellion, and the difference of their habits. Vnto which daunger Africke & some part of Spaine should be subiect, if there were such a multitude of slaue as in times past: for that they marked their slaues in the face, which they did not in auntient time, except such of them as were villanous and sturdie knaues, who were thereof called *Stigmatici*; who at any time beeing manumised, could for all that neuer enioy the full fruit of their libertie or the priuelege of citisens: marking the rest vpon their armes. And this was it for which the Lacedemonians seeing their slaues to multiply exceedingly aboue the citisens (for the hope their masters gaue them of libertie which could get most children, and for the profit euery man drew out of them in particuler) made a decree that three thousand of them such as had the most able bodies should bee taken vp for the warres: whome so pressed out, they forthwith caused to be all in one night slaine, and that so sodainly and secretly, as that no man knew what was become of them, more than they which had the doing of the matter.

Why slaues were not suffred to beare armes.

Now this feare that Cities and Commonweals had of their slaues, was the cause that they neuer durst suffer them to beare armes, or to be enrolled in their musters, and that vpon paine of death: and if by necessitie they were constrained to take their slaues, they at the same time freely set them at libertie. As did *Scipio Africanus* the Greater, who after the great ouerthrow of Cannas manumised 300 of his slaues, al able bodies. Howbeit that *Florus* writeth, That arms were giuen to 8000 slaues; which we also read

to

G 10 For Sylla *read* Silanus (Syllanianum Senatusconsultum in L).   I 2 of slaves as

Of A Commonweale. 39

A to haue bene done in the confederat warre. But *Cleomenes* king of Lacedemonia finding himselfe vnable to withstand the multitude of his enemies, as also of his slaues, his citisens being for the most part slaine; in his so great necessitie proclaimed libertie to al such slaues as were able to pay fiftie crownes for their heads: in which doing he prouided himselfe both of souldiors and money. Yea not so much as the effeminat people of Asia vsed their slaues in warres, except the Parthians, who might not by their lawes manumise their slaues, whom they made almost as much of as of their children: wherby they grew into such a multitude, that in their armie wherwith they put to flight the power of *M. Antonius*, consisting of fiftie thousand men, there was but 4500 free men, as we read in *Iustin*: yet had they no cause to rebell, being of their masters so well entreated.

B But as for other people, they were so mistrustfull of their slaues, as that sometimes they would not haue them to serue in their gallies before they were enfranchised: as did *Augustus*, who at one time set at libertie twenty thousand to serue him in his gallies. And for feare they had least they should conspire together against the state, to keepe them alwaies busied in other mechanicall arts, *Lycurgus* amongst the Lacedemonians, and *Numa Pompilius* in Rome, forbad their owne citisens to vse any manuall occupation. And yet they could not so well prouide, but that euer there was some one or other desperat man, who propounding libertie vnto slaues, still robbed the State. As *Viriatus* the Pirat, who made himselfe king of Portugall: *Cinna, Spartacus, Tacfarinas,* and *Simon* the son of *Gerson*, captaine of the Iewes, who all of base companions made

C themselues great lords, by giuing libertie vnto the slaues that followed them. And the ciuill warres yet continuing betwixt *Augustus* and *M. Antonius*, was not to be seene but fugitiue slaues stil on the one side or the other: in such sort, as that after the discomfiture of *Sex. Pompeius*, there were found thirtie thousand slaues which had taken part with him, whome *Augustus* caused to be apprehended through his dominions, and by a prefixed day to be againe restored vnto their masters, commaunding the rest to bee hanged that had no masters to lay claime vnto them; as we read in *Appian*. And in truth the power of the Arabians grew by no other meanes. For as soone as *Homar* one of *Mahomets* lieutenants, had begun to raise warre in Arabia, and promised libertie vnto the slaues that should follow him, he drew such a number after him, that in few

D yeares they made themselues lords of all the East. The fame of which libertie, and the conquests made by those slaues, so encouraged the slaues of Europe, that they began to take vp armes, first in Spaine in the yeare 781, and afterward in Fraunce in the time of *Charlemaigne*, and of *Lewes* the godly; as is to bee seene by their Edicts then made against the conspiracie of slaues. And after that also *Lothaire* the sonne of *Lewes*, hauing lost two battels against his brethren, called the slaues vnto his aid with promise of libertie: who afterwards gaue the ouerthrow vnto their masters in the yere 852. When sodainly this fire took such hold in Germanie, where the slaues hauing taken vp armes, so troubled the state of the German princes and cities, that *Lewes* king of Almans was constrained to raise all his forces to subdue them.

E And this was the cause that the Christian princes by little and little released their seruitude, and enfranchised their slaues, reseruing onely vnto themselues certaine seruices, and the auntient right of succession, if their enfranchised slaues should chance to die without issue: a custome yet in vse in all the lower Germanie; as in many places in Fraunce, and England also. For as yet many remembrances of bondage remaine in the Christian Commonweale: as is to be seene in the lawes of the Lombards & Ripuaires whereby slaues could not haue their iust libertie, or alienat their goods, vntill they had bene twice manumised: and oftentimes the lord or master ioyned vnto the act of infranchisment, That it was done for the health of his soule. For they which first laid the

margin notes:
* Appian in bellis ciuilib.
* Ios. in bello Iudaico.
The cause why Christian princes by little and little released their slaues.

E ij   foundati-

A9 *For* 4500 *read* 450 (Fr) *or* 500 (L).   B8 *For* robbed *probably read* trobled *i.e.* troubled (cf. Fr).
B10 Simon the son of Gerson *i.e.* Simon of Gerasa, son of Giora (cf. Josephus, B.J., IV, 9)

foundation of the Christian Commonweale, had nothing in more regard, than to
find the means how Christian slaues might be set at liberty: so that in hope therof many of them oftentimes became Christians; & their masters for the health of their souls were content so to enfranchise them. Wee also read in the Histories of Africk, how that *Paulinus* bishop of Nolo, after hee had sold all his goods to redeeme Christian slaues, at last (which a man would wonder at) sold himselfe also vnto the Vandales for his brethren. And hereof came the manumission of slaues made in churches before the bishops. Whereof, in the raigne of *Constantine* the Great, ensued such a multitude of poore and needie men, who had nothing but their libertie to liue vpon (of whome the most part would do nothing, and the rest could do nothing) as that cities were with nothing more charged than with them. Hereof, began the almes-houses, and hospitals, for the reliefe of little children, of the aged, of the sicke, and of them that could not labour, to be erected and endowed by the Christian princes, at the requests of the bishops. Hereof S. *Basil* in his sermons complaineth, that the cries and gronings of the poore and weake were in the Churches confounded and mingled with the songs and prayers of the Priests. Much about which time *Iulian* the Apostata in despite of the Christians * exhorted the Pagan bishops by the example of the Christians to the building and endowing of almes-houses and hospitals for the reliefe of their poore. And for that poore men set at libertie, did oftentimes lay forth their children to bee brought vp of the charitie and liberalitie of the Christians: *Gratian* made a law, That the children so exposed and left vnto the world, should be slaues vnto them that had so nourished and brought them vp. And not long after, *Valens* the Emperour by an Edict gaue power to euerie man to take vp the vagrant and idle persons, and to cause them to serue them as slaues; forbidding also and that vpon paine of death, any to goe into the woods or deserts there to liue as Hermits; of whome he caused a great number which had contrarie to his Edict so gone out, to be executed; to the intent to cut off idlenesse, and to draw euerie man vnto labour. But after that Idolatrie began to decay, and the Christian religion to encrease, the multitude of slaues began also to diminish; and yet much more after the publishing of the law of *Mahomet*, who set at libertie all them of his religion. To the imitation of whome, the Christians also so frankly set at libertie their slaues, as that all seruitude and slauerie seemed in that age to haue bene shut vp with the West Indians, wherein the Christians had shaken off from their necks all bondage, about the yere 1250: yet for all that, that there were slaues in Italie in the yeare 1212, it is euident, as well by the lawes of *William* king of Sicilie, and *Frederick* the second Emperour; as also by the decrees of the bishops of Rome, *Alexander* (I say) the third, *Vrban* the third, and *Innocentius* the third, concerning the marriages of slaues, which the Lawyers call *Contabernia*, or keeping of companie together: which *Alexander* was chosen Pope in the yeare 1158, *Vrban* in the yeare 1185, and *Innocentius* in the yeare 1188. Whereby it is euident, the Christian Commonweale to haue bene cleere of slaues since the yeare 1250, or there about. For *Bartholus* who flourished in the yeare 1300, writeth that there were no slaues in his time; and that by Christian lawes men might no more sell themselues, vnderstanding the Edicts made by the Christian princes: which when *Nicholas* the Sicilian, otherwise called the Abbot of Panormo had learned of *Bartholus*, he thought it a thing well worth the noting. Neuerthelesse we read in the Historie of Polonia, that euerie prisoner taken in good warre, was then and long time after slaue vnto him that had taken him, if the king would not pay two Florins for his head, as I haue before said: and yet at this present the subiects bound vnto the soyle whereon they were borne, which they call *Kmetos*, are in the power of their lords, who may at their pleasure kill them, and not bee called

The beginning of almes houses and hospitals.

* *Nicephorus.*

A time wherein there were no slaues in the Christian Commonweale.

in

F5 Nola   F9 needie men   I7 Contubernia   I9 *For* 1188 (L) *read* 1198 (Fr).

Notes at H7, H10.

Of A Commonwealth. 41

into question therefore: and if so be that they kill another mans subiect, then are they acquited by paying ten crownes; the one moitie to the lord, and the other moitie vnto the heires: so as we read in the lawes of Polonia; which are the like in the kingdoms of Denmarke, Sweden, and Norway. But it is more than 400 yeares agoe, since that Fraunce suffered in it any true slaues. For as for that which we read in our histories, that *Lewes Hutin*, who came to the crowne in the yeare 1313 (the selfe same time that *Bartholus* liued) set at libertie all slaues for money, to defray the charges of his warres; that is, as I take it, to be vnderstood of manumised men, which we call Mort-maines, whome we euen yet at this present see to be set at libertie by the kings royall letters patents, from that bond of seruitude wherby they are prohibited to marrie a wife, or to alienat their goods out of the territories of their Patron. So also we are to vnderstand the edict of *Charls* the fift the French king, wherin in cities euery 70 families, in country villages euerie hundred families, and euery 200 heads of slaues, were be charged with a man at armes; which they should not haue done if they had bene in the possession of another man, & accounted as another mans goods. So it is also to be vnderstood that is written of *Humbert Dauphin*, who at the same time by one edict enfranchised all the slaues of Dauphine, and commaunded the same to be enrolled in the publick acts and lawes of the countrey. The same curtesie vsed *Theobald* countie *d'Blois* towards his slaues, in the yeare 1245. To this also belongeth that which wee read of *Sugerius* abbot of the couent of S. *Dionyse*, who set at libertie his manumised slaues, so that they chaunged their dwelling. And also the auntient decree of the Parliament of Paris, whereby it was permitted to the bishop of Chalons, by the consent of his Chapiter, to enfranchise his slaues. *Charles* the seuenth also comming to the crowne in the yeare 1430 enfranchised diuers persons of seruile condition. And in our memorie king *Henry* the second by his letters pattents enfranchised them of *Burbonnois*, in the yere 1549. By whose example also the duke of Sauoy did the like in all his countries, in the yeare 1561. All which we see done in the great fauour of libertie. Whereas otherwise the Prince, of his owne lawfull power could not enfranchise another mans slaue, and much lesse the magistrat, what intercession soeuer the people should make: neither could he so much as giue vnto him that was by another man enfranchised, so much as leaue to weare a ring of gold, without the consent of his patron. For *Commodus* the Emperour by his edict tooke from all them their rings of gold, who had obtained that priueledge of the prince without leaue of their Patron: neither would he haue it any thing preiudiciall vnto the Patron, that his enfranchised slaue had obtained of the prince this priueledge, albeit that the prince had restored him to the state of a free borne man: which was a far greater matter than to haue obtained the priueledge to weare a ring of gold: which albeit that it belonged vnto the prince onely to grant, yet so it was neuerthelesse in the time of *Tertullian*, that the patrons had in a manner got that power vnto themselues, giuing vnto their enfranchised slaues a ring of gold and a white gowne, in stead of yron giues and whips, causing them so attired to sit downe at the table with them, and to beare their name. And at last *Iustinian* himselfe by a generall edict restored all them that had bene slaues enfranchised vnto the state of free borne men; so that for the confirmation thereof they needed not afterwards any the princes charter. Which law for all that we vse not: for in * this realme he must of necessitie obtaine the prince his letters patents, which haue alwaies vsed to restore vnto manumised men and of seruile condition, the state of free borne men, and to blot out all the staine of their old slauerie; which letters were woont to be both requested and obtained without the leaue of the patron: who for all that may lay hands vpon such goods of his enfranchised slaue as were got before he was set at libertie wheresoeuer they be; as not long since

When slaues ceased in France

* Tertul. in de resurrection.

* viz. France.

E iij

was adiudged by the court of Paris: as for such things as they get afterwards they may hold them to themselues; and hauing no children, by their testaments bestow them vpon whome they please. I haue seene the lord of the White Rocke in Gascongue claime to haue not onely a right ouer his manumised subiects, and also that they were bound to trimme his vines, to till his grounds, to mow his meddows, to reape and thresh his corne, to carrie & recarrie whatsoeuer he should command them, to repaire his decayed house, to pay his ransome, and also the foure accustomed payments vsed in this realme; but also that if without his leaue they should chaunge their dwelling places wherein they were borne, or depart out of his land, hee might lead them home againe in an halter: vnto all which the aforesaid seruices his manumised people yeelded, sauing vnto the last, which by a decree of the Parlement of Tholouze was cut off, as preiudiciall vnto the right of libertie. Truly they whome the Polonians call Kmetons, are not compelled to do their patrons so great seruice; but yet suffer things much grieuous: for that any man may kill them for the small paiment of ten crownes, and their lord may so doe for nothing. And in former time it was lawfull amongst the Indians by all meanes to tyrannise vpon their seruants, which were in number infinit, yea and to kill them also; vntill that *Charles* the fift by a law which he made commanded then all to be free. But in Fraunce, although there be some remembrance of old seruitude, yet is it not lawfull there to make any slaue, or to buy any of others: Insomuch that the slaues of strangers so soone as they set their foot within Fraunce become franke & free; as was by an old decree of the court of Paris determined against an ambassador of Spain, who had broght a slaue with him into France. And I remember that of late a Genua marchant hauing brought with him vnto Tholouze a slaue whome he had bought in Spaine, the hoast of the house vnderstanding the matter, persuaded the slaue to appeale vnto his libertie. The matter being brought before the magistrats, the marchant was called for; the Atturney general out of the records showed certaine auntient priueledges giuen (as is said) vnto them of Tholouze by *Theodosius* the Great, wherein he had granted, That slaues so soone as they came into Tholouze should be free. The marchant alledging for himselfe that he had truly bought his slaue in Spaine, and so was afterward come to Tholouze, from thence to goe home to Genua, and so not to be bound to the lawes of Fraunce. In the end hee requested that if they would needs deale so hardly with him, as to set at libertie another mans slaue, yet they should at least restore vnto him the money hee cost him: whereunto the Iudges aunswered, That it was a matter to be considered of. In the meane time the marchant fearing least he shoutd loose both his dutifull slaue and his money also, of himselfe set him at libertie, yet couenanting with him that he should serue him so long as he liued. Yet for all that, those priueledges which they of Tholouze boast to haue bene granted them by *Theodosius*, seeme not to haue bene so, seeing that Narbona a true Colonie of the Romans, and the most auntient that was in Fraunce, Lectore, Nysmes, Vienne, Lyons, Arles, Romans, and many others, which were also Roman Collonies, no nor Rome it selfe the verie seat of the Empire, had not any such priueledge. And thus much concerning the enfranchising of slaues.

Slaues by comming into France become free.

But now here might a man say, If it be so that the Mahometans haue enfranchised all the slaues of their religion, which hath course in all Asia, and almost in all Africke, with a good part of Europe also; and the Christians haue semblably done the like (as we haue before showed:) how commeth it to passe that yet the world is so full of slaues and slauerie? For the Iewes may not by their lawes haue any slaue of their own nation, neither by the lawes of the Christians may they haue any Christian. Truely all in that swerue from the law of God: For the law of God forbiddeth any slaue to be

How is it commeth to passe that yet there be so many slaues in the world.

F3 the White Rocke *i.e.* La Roche-blanche   F3 Gascongne   G3-4 *For* much grievous *read* more grievous (L).   G8 them all   I5 should   Note at I8.

be made by the order of the Israelites amongst themselues, except that any of them shall of his owne accord giue himselfe in bondage to another, and suffer his eare to be bored through to a post with an aule: truely it adiudgeth the debtors vnto *the creditors, and suffereth the Iewes to bee sold for pouertie: yet the same law commaundeth them at the seuenth yeare to be set at libertie. And although a man haue enthraled himselfe, and suffered himselfe to be thrust through the eare with an aule, insomuch that he be bound to perpetuall seruitude: yet neuerthelesse all the interpretors of the law affirme, That in the yeare of Iubiley he shall againe recouer his libertie, except he had rather againe serue than become free. But such bondslaues as were borne of those kind of slaues which had of their owne accord giuen themselues into bondage, they were in the fistith yeare to be set free: at which time the law by * the sound of trumpet denounceth libertie vnto all manner of slaues. Yet doth the law permit them to haue straungers, of another nation and religion than their owne, in perpetuall bondage; and that their posteritie and nephews might vse the same right against straungers, that straungers might against the Israelites: than which kind of slaues *Iulian* the Emperour writeth none to haue bene better. You see (saith he) how willingly the Syrians serue other nations: and contrariwise what a loue of libertie is in the people of the Celtes. But the Iewes when they had bought any straunge bond-slaues of the Christians, or of the Pagans, they instructed them in their owne religion, and so circumcised them: which thing *Traian* by a speciall law forbad: and albeit that they had yeelded vnto their lords or maisters religion, yet neuerthelesse they enforced them still to serue: Whereas by * the law it was prouided, that such straungers as being circumcised had receiued the law of God, should enioy the same priuiledges and benefits that the natural citisés did. The same law (saith it) shal be vnto the stranger & the citisen. That is it that God by the Prophet *Ieremie* * complaineth of, Slaues not to be set at libertie according to the law: and therefore a most heauie bondage to hang ouer the maisters heads from their enemies. Hereupon also *Philip* the French king draue the Iewes out of his kingdome, confiscating their goods, for that contrarie vnto the law they circumcised Christians, and tooke them vnto themselues into bondage for slaues. The like deceit we see the Mahometans to vse, whose manner is to circumcise and to instruct in their religion such Christians as they haue taken in warre, or bought of pirats, or at leastwise their children, whome neuerthelesse they compell to serue with all their children and posteritie. Whose example the Portingals following, compell the bondmen whome they haue bought out of Africke, to abiure the Mahometan religion, and instructing them in the Christian religion, cause them neuerthelesse with their children and ofspring to serue them in perpetuall slauerie: so that now whole droues of slaues are sold and that openly in all parts of Portugall, as if they were beasts. In like manner the Spaniards hauing brought the Neigros vnto the Christian religion, keepe them neuerthelesse and all their posteritie for slaues. And albeit that *Charles* the fift had by a generall edict made in the yeare 1540 set at libertie all the slaues of the West Indies, neuerthelesse a sedition there rising through the couetousnesse and insolencie of them that were in greatest power, *Gonsales Pizzare* gouernor of that prouince reuolted from *Charles*: whose power when *Lagasca* had discomfited, and for publike example had caused him to be beheaded together with the chiefe men of that rebellion, hee according to the edict, set at libertie all the slaues; yet with condition, that they should still serue their patrons. And yet for all that it could not be brought to passe, but that *Lagasca* returning into Spaine, these late enfranchised men fell againe into their slauerie: and especially for the profit which their lords and masters were in hope to haue by the selling of them: to the imitation of the Portugals, who first called in againe Serui-

* Exod. 21.
* Deut. 15.

* Leuit. 25.
Hierom. 32.
Num. 13.

* Exod. 12.
Numer. 49.

* Hier. 34.

E iiij   tude,

44   The First Booke

The Portugals the first that called in slauery againe into Europe.

tude, now for many worlds of yeares buried in forgetfulnesse in Europe; and are in short time like enough to disperse the same ouer all Europe, as it is now alreadie begun in Italie. For now a good while ago Africa and Asia, and the Easterne part of Europ also haue accustomed to nourish and bring vp in euery citie, stocks of slaues, in like maner as if they were beasts, and of them to make a great marchandise and gaine. For within this hundred yere the Tartars (a kind of Scythian people) in great number with fire and sword entring into the borders of Moscouia, Lituania, and Polonia, carried away with them three hundred thousand Christians into captiuitie. And not long ago euen in our memorie, *Sinan Bassa* hauing taken the Isle of Gozo neere vnto Malta, led away with him 6300 Christians, and all the inhabitants of Tripolis in Barbarie, which he sold in Græcia. So that it is not to be marueiled that the captaine of the Turkes Ianizaries, and either of his Chauncellors (whome they call Cadelesquiers) vse euerie one of them at their entrance into their office to receiue of the prince three hundred slaues. For as concerning the Turkes Pretorian souldiors, and those youths which are taken from the Christians as tribute, and are called tribute children, I neuer accounted them for slaues; seeing that they are enrolled in the princes familie, and that they alone enioy the great offices, honours, priesthoods, authoritie and honour; which nobilitie extendeth also vnto their nephewes in the fourth degree, and all their posteritie afterward beeing accounted base, except by their vertue and noble acts they maintaine the honour of their grandfathers: For the Turkes almost alone of all other people measure true nobilitie by vertue, and not by difcent or the antiquitie of their stocke; so that the farther a man is from vertue, so much the farther hee is (with them) from nobilitie.

No man noble among the Turkes but for his valor or his vertue.

Wherefore seeing it is proued by the examples of so many worlds of years, so many inconueniences of rebellions, seruile warres, conspiracies euersions and chaunges to haue happened vnto Commonweals by slaues; so many murthers, cruelties, and detestable villanies to haue bene committed vpon the persons of slaues by their lords and masters: who can doubt to affirme it to be a thing most pernitious and daungerous to haue brought them into a Commonweale; or hauing cast them off, to receiue them againe? Now if any man shall say, That the rigour of the lawes may by forbidding, and seuere punishment moderat the cruelty of maisters ouer their slaues: What law can there be more iust, more strong, and indifferent, or better than the laws of God, which hath so wisely prouided as to forbid to chastise slaues with whips (which the Roman lawes permitted) and willeth the slaue to be enfranchised, if his maister shal breake any lim of him? which law *Constantine* the Emperour afterward approued. But who shall prosecute the suite against the lord for the death of the slaue? who shall heare the complaint? who shall exact due punishment therefore? shall hee that hath nothing to do therwith? considering that tyrants hold it for a rule in policie, That one cannot be too seuere vnto his subiects, so to keepe them low and obedient. But the Spaniards (some will say) entreat their slaues courteously, teach them, and bring them vp, yea and that much more kindly than they do their hired seruans: and they againe on their part serue their lords and masters with all chearefulnes and loue incredible. But concerning the Spaniards it is a common saying, That there are no maisters more courtious than they at the first; as generally all beginnings are pleasing: so also it is most certaine, That there is no greater loue, than the loue of a good slaue towards his lord: prouided that it meet with an humor agreeing with it selfe. For which cause the law of God (in mine opinion) hath so wisely prouided that no man should serue a perpetuall seruitude, but he which hauing serued seuen yeres, and so well tasted the humor and disposition of his master or creditor, had consented to bee his slaue for euer. But

Reasons for the bringing in againe of slauery answered.

sith

Notes at G8, K3.

sith there are so few men one like vnto another; and contrariwise the varietie and naturall disposition of them infinit, what law giuer can vnto them all prescribe one generall edict, law, or rule. The auntient prouerb, which saith, *So many slaues, so many enemies in a mans house*, showeth right well what friendship, faith and loyaltie a man may looke for of his slaues. Of a thousand examples of antiquitie I will recite but one, which happened in the time of *Iulius Pontanus*, who reporteth, That a slaue seeing his lord absent, barred the gates, and hauing shamefully abused his mistresse, bound her, tooke his maisters three children, and so going vp to the highest place of the house, seeing his maister comming home, first cast downe vnto him vpon the pauement one of his children, and after that another: the wofull father all dismaid, and fearing least hee should throw downe the third likewise, with prayers and teares besought the slaue to spare him that was yet left, promising him forgiuenesse for that hee had alreadie done, and libertie also if he would but saue that third. Which his request the slaue yeelded vnto, vpon condition that he should cut off his owne nose: which he chose rather to doe, than to loose his child. But this done, the slaue neuerthelesse cast downe the third child also; and so at last to take that reuenge of himself, which his lord thought to haue done, cast headlong downe himselfe also. And not to be tedious, I omit poysonings, murders, burnings, and many other mischiefes oftentimes euerie where done by slaues. But these inconueniences, you will say, are counteruailed and recompensed with other mutuall profits; for that by receiuing in of slaues we cut off the infinit number of vagabonds and bankrupts, who after they haue deuoured al, would pay their creditors with bils: & that by that means might be driuen away such a multitude of rogues & naughtie doers, which eat vp whole townes, and as drones sucke the hony from the bees: ioyne also vnto this, that of such idle mates, theeues and pirats furnish themselues; besides that, famine and euil prouision for the poore, draw into townes all populer diseases; for the poore we must nourish and not kill, although it be in a sort to kill them, to refuse to nourish them (as saith S. *Ambrose*.) These reasons beare some show of truth. For as concerning debtors, if they be not able to pay, God his law commaundeth them to be adiudged to their creditors for seuen yeares, but yet not into perpetuall bondage: howbeit that the law of the twelue tables, practised in all the West Indies, and in the greatest part of Africke, will that they remaine still prisoners vnto the creditors, vntill they be fully satisfied. For they which haue taken away from debtors in ciuil cases the benefit, to leaue vnto their creditors all such goods as they had, and command them to be committed not to their creditors, but to prisons, as the Turkes do; seeme to mee to take away not onely from the creditors, but also from the debtors, all power to keepe themselues, yea and their liues also, as taking from them the meane for them to trauell, and to gaine to acquit themselues. But as for theeues and pirats, there was neuer in any time moe than when the multitude of slaues was encreased: For that the slaue not able to endure slauerie, and at length breaking from his maister, was alwaies constrained to be a theefe or a pirat, not being able to endure his maister, neither to show himself being marked, nor to liue hauing nothing to liue vpon. A better example whereof cannot be than that of *Spartacus* the fensor, who at one time assembled out of the verie bowels of Italie three score thousand slaues; when as at the same time aboue fourescore thousand pirats with nine hundred saile of ships were rouing ouer all the Mediterannean, and had with so great forces taken 400 cities vpon the sea coast; as that the Roman Empire was both by land and sea as it were beset with theeues and robbers. But the wise law giuer is not hee that driueth robbers out of the Commonwealth, but he that suffereth them not therein to enter: which may easily bee done without that direfull slauerie, so dreadfull vnto states and cities; by erecting in euery towne and citie

An horrible example of the crueltie of a faithlesse slaue.

Reasons for the maintaining of slauerie in a Commonweale.

The same reasons answered.

A6 Julius Pontanus: Jovius Pontanus (Fr) Junius Pontanus (L 1-2) *preferably* Jovianus Pontanus (L 3-5)   C2-3 naughtie doers *i.e. faitneants*, idlers   D6 to trauell *i.e.* to travail, labor   E5 *For* 400 cities *read* 500 cities (L).

tie publick houses for poore chidlren, where they may learne diuers trades and occupations, as they do in Paris, Lions, and Venice, and other well gouerned towns, where Seminaries of Artizans are brought vp to the great benefit of the Commonweale. But in such places as wherein slaues are now alreadie receiued, I am not of opinion to haue them altogether and at one time set at libertie, as *Charles* the Emperour did at Peru: for that so they hauing nothing to liue vpon, nor occupation to gaine by, and delighted with the sweetnesse of idlenesse and libertie, would take no paines: in such sort that the most part of them died for hunger: but the best way is, by little and little to enfranchise them, hauing before their enfranchisement taught them some occupation whereby to releeue themselues. Now if some shall say, That no man is a good master, but he that hath before bene a good seruant: I say that to be an opinion euill grounded, although it be right auntient: for there is nothing that doth more discourage and ouerthrow, (and if I may so say) a bastardise a good and noble mind, than seruitude; or that doth more abate the naturall maiestie of good natures to commaund ouer others, than to haue bene once a slaue. *Salomon* also the maister of wisedom saith in his Prouerbs, That there is nothing more intollerable, than when a slaue is become a maister, or a handmaid a mistresse: which he referreth not only vnto a more misticall sence; as when our intemperat desires beare rule ouer our reason: but vnto him also which sodainly passeth from one extremitie to another; as from seruitude to commaund. But if it be true that reason and the law of God is alwaies and euerie where to take place, and that it was not shut vp only within the bounds of Palestine: why should not that law so profitably & so wisely made by God himselfe, concerning slauerie & libertie, stand in force, rather than that which was by mans wisedom deuised? Howbeit that the Tartars (which are by many thought to bee descended from the ten tribes of Israel) haue alwaies enfranchised their slaues at the end of seuen yeres: yet with condition that they should depart out of their country: which condition was first by *Papinian* (the great lawyer) reiected, but afterwards by him againe receiued; but beeing ioyned vnto enfranchisments, is accounted as if it were not written at all. And thus much concerning the power of a maister ouer his slaue, and whether slaues are to be suffered in a well ordered Commonweal. But now that we haue sufficiently, & yet also as briefly as was vnto vs possible, entreated of a Familie, & of all the parts therof, which is the foundation of the whole cōmonweale: let vs now likewise also speak of a Citisen & a City.

The old saying, That no man can be a good maister, but he which hath before bene a good seruant, refuted.

Chap. VI.

¶ *What a Citisen is, and how much Citisens differ from Citisens, and how much from strangers: what also is to be vnderstood by the name of a Towne, a Citie, and of a Commonweale.*

What we haue before said concerning a whole Familie, and euery part thereof, containeth in it the beginning of all Commonweals. And as foundations can of themselues stand without the forme of an house, before the walles be built higher, or any roofe laid vpon them: so also a Familie can of it selfe be without a Citie or a Commonweale: and so can also the maister of a Familie vse his power and command ouer his houshold without depending of the power of any other man: as they say there are many such families in the frontiers of the kingdomes of Fes and of Marocco, and in the West Indies: but a Commonweale can no more be without a Familie, than a Citie without houses, or an house without a foundation. Now when the maister of the Familie goeth out of his owne house where he commaundeth, to entreat and trafficke with other heads of

OF A COMMONWEALE.   47

A of Families, or that concerneth them all in generall, he then looseth the title of maister, head, and lord, to be a companion, equall and fellowlike with others, leauing his familie to enter into a Citie, and his domesticall affaires to entreat of publick; and in stead of a lord calleth himselfe a Citisen, which is no other in proper tearmes than *A free subiect holding of the soueraigntie of another man*. For before there was either Citie or citisen, or any forme of a Commonweale amongst men, euerie master of a familie was a maister in his owne house, hauing power of life and death ouer his wife and children: but after that force, violence, ambition, couetousnesse, and desire of reuenge had armed one against another, the issues of warres and combats giuing victorie vnto the one side, made the other to become vnto them slaues: and amongst them that ouer-

B came, he that was chosen cheefe and captaine, vnder whose conduct and leading they had obtained the victorie, kept them also in his power and commaund as his faithfull and obedient subiects, and the other as his slaues. Then that full and entire libertie by nature giuen to euery man, to liue as himselfe best pleased, was altogether taken from the vanquished, and in the vanquishers themselues in some measure also diminished, in regard of the conquerour; for that now it concerned euerie man in priuat to yeeld his obedience vnto his chiefe soueraigne; and he that would not abate any thing of his libertie, to liue vnder the lawes and commaundement of another, lost all. So the word of *Lord* and *Seruant*, of *Prince* and *Subiect*, before vnknowne vnto the world, were first brought into vse. Yea Reason, and the verie light of nature, leadeth vs to beleeue very

C force and violence to haue giuen course and beginning vnto Commonweals. And albeit that there were no reason therefore, it shal be hereafter declared by the vndoubted testimonies of the most credible historiographers, that is to say, of *Thucydides, Plutarch, Cæsar*, & also by the laws of *Solon*, That the first men that bare rule, had no greater honour and vertue, than to kill, massacre and rob men, or to bring them in slauerie. These be the words of *Plutarch*. Yet haue we more also the witnesse of the sacred history, where it is said, that *Nimroth* the nephew of *Cham*, was the first that by force and violence brought men into his subiection, establishing his kingdome in the countrey of *Assyria*: and for this cause they called him the *Mightie hunter*, which the Hebrews interpret to be a theefe and robber. Which thing also *Philo* the Iew, and *Iosephus* by

D their testimonies confirme, *viz. Nimroth* by his wealth and power to haue first exercised tyrannie. Wherein it appeareth *Demosthenes, Aristotle*, and *Cicero*, to haue mistaken themselues, in following the errour of *Herodotus*, who saith, That the first kings were chosen for their iustice and vertue; and haue hereof faigned vnto vs I wot not what heroicall and golden worlds: an opinion by me by most certaine arguments and testimonies elswhere refelled; seeing that the first Cities and Commonweals, long before the time of *Abraham* were full of slaues: as also not long agoe the Westerne islands did swarme with them at such time as the Spaniards subdued them: a thing that could not possibly be, but by extreame violent forcing the free lawes of nature. And it is not yet past seuentie yeares that the people of Gaoga in Africke had neuer

E felt or heard of any king or lord whatsoeuer, vntill that one amongst them a trauellor had in his trauell seene and noted the maiestie of the king of Tombut: and thereupon conceiuing a desire to make himselfe a king also in his owne countrie, hee at first to begin withall, killed a rich marchant; and so possessed of his horses armes and marchandise, diuided them amongst his nie kinsfolks and friends, acquainted with his purpose; by whose aid he by force and violence subdued now some, and after others, killing the richest, and ceasing vpon their goods: in such sort that his sonne became rich with the robberies of his father, made himselfe king, whose successor hath so continued after him in great power, as we read in *Leo* of Africke. This was the beginning of

the

The definition of a Citisen.

That violence and oppression gaue the beginning vnto Commonweals.

That kings were not first chosen for their iustice and vertue.

A 5 another   C 7 nephew *i.e.* grandson (cf. Genesis 10:6–9)   Notes at C 10, D 5, E 7.

the kings of Gaoga, which in short time greatly encreased.

And thus much concerning the beginning of Commonweals, which may serue to manifest the definition of a Citisen, by vs before set down, to be true, which is no other thing to say, but *A free subiect holding of the soueraigntie of another man*. A free subiect I say, for albeit that a slaue be much more subiect vnto the commaund of the highest authoritie than a free man; yet so it is, that al people haue alwayes with their common consent agreed, That a slaue is no Citisen, and in questions of right is accounted no bodie; which cannot truely be said of mens wiues and children, who are free from all seruitude and bondage; albeit that their rights and liberties, and the power to dispose of their owne goods, be from them in some sort cut off by the domesticall power: in sort that a man may say, that euerie Citisen is a subiect, some small part of his libertie being diminished by the maiestie of him to whome he oweth obeysance. But euerie subiect is not a Citisen, as we haue said of a slaue; and may also so say of a stranger, who comming into an other mans segniorie, is not receiued for a Citisen, hauing not any part in the rights and priueledges of the Citie; neither is to bee accounted in the number of friends, allies, or coallies, who are not altogether straungers, (as the Lawyer saith) neither enemies also. Howbeit that the Greeks of old called straungers enemies, as also did the Latines, which *Cicero* hath noted out of the law of the twelue tables; The mildnesse of the word (saith he) mitigating the hardnesse of the thing: and they were called enemies which had conspired against the state. And it may well bee also that those whom we yet by a common word cal *Hotes*, or *Hostes*, were in antient time nothing els but straungers. But men haue since corrected the proprietie of words, the forme of speech still remaining: for the Greeks haue called their enemies πολεμιους, as men making warre vpon them; and straungers ξενους, which signifieth not pilgrims (as saith *Acursius*) but straungers, be they another mans subiects, or themselues soueraignes in their owne countrey.

Now amongst them whome we said to be subiects vnto publick empires and soueraigne power; some are naturall, some are naturallised; and of them which are naturall some are free borne, some are slaues, and these slaues being set at libertie, in an instant become Citisens, whereas straunger slaues be not so. Yet true it is that the enfranchised slaues in Greece were not admitted to be Citisens, although that they were of the same countrie, and naturall subiects. For the request of *Demosthenes* the Orator, which he made vnto the people after the great ouerthrow at Cherronæa, That all the inhabitants of Athens, as well the enfranchised as others, might be accounted Citisens; was reiected and denied, for feare least the enfranchised men (of whom there was a great multitude) should become lords of their estate, and with the number of voyces exclude the naturall Citisens from all honours and promotions; which the greatest number still carried away: which thing the Romans at the first not regarding, had almost before they were aware fallen into the power of the enfranchised men, had not *Fabius Maximus* in good time foreseene the matter, and thrust the multitude of the enfranchised men, before dispersed amongst all the tribes, into foure tribes apart by themselues; to the intent that one and thirtie tribes of the free borne men and auntient Citisens, might stil with the number of voices preuaile: for they counted not in Rome their voices by the poll, as in auntient time they did at Athens, and now doe also at Venice; but by degrees and centuries, in the assemblies of their great estates; and by lines or tribes, in their lesse estates. And for that it so great a matter was without sedition done by the onely wisedome of *Fabius* the Censor, he tooke the surname of *Maximus* (or of the Greatest:) in which doing he amended the errors of *Appius* the Censor, who had dispersed the enfranchised and naturallised Citisens (the issue of slaues and strangers)

Marginalia:
- A Citisen must be a free subiect.
- Slaues not to bee accounted Citisens.
- * Cice. officiorum lib. 1.
- The diuision of subiects.
- Why Fabius was called Maximus.

H4 ξενους, WHOM THE LATINS HAVE NAMED PEREGRINOS, which signifieth Note at H10.

OF A COMMONWEALE.   49

A straungers) amongst all the tribes of the free borne men: yet afterwards (notwithstanding the order taken by *Fabius*) it was granted vnto the Citisens enfranchised, that they might enroll one of their sonnes beeing fiue yeares olde or more in the tribe or line of their patron: But when those foure tribes of the enfranchised Citisens seemed yet too puissant and strong, it was decreed, That there should by lot one tribe bee drawne out, wherein all the enfranchised Citisens should giue their voyces. And this was the state of the enfranchised Citisens, vntill the ciuill warre betwixt *Marius* and *Sylla*, at which time the people at the motion of *Pub. Sulpitius* made a law, That the enfranchised Citisens should from that time forward be againe diuided amongst all the tribes, which was the first and principall cause of the ruine of that Commonweale. Wherefore as

B of slaues some are borne, some are made; so also of Citisens some are made, some are borne: the naturall Citisen, is he that is free of that wherein he is borne; whether he be borne but of one of his parents a Citisen, or of both of them Citisens. True it is that of auntient time (and yet at this present also in diuers Commonwealsʒ) to bee a Citisen it was needfull to haue both father and mother Citisens, as in Greece, otherwise they called them Bastards, or Mungrels, which were but Citisens on the one side, and could not themselues neither their children be partakers of the greatest benefits or offices in the Commonweale, which they called Archontes, as saith *Demosthenes* in his Oration against *Næara*, albeit that many (as *Themistocles* himselfe) were thereinto secretly entered. But in the time of *Pericles* fiue thousand of them were sold slaues, who had born

C the countenance of Citisens. And *Pericles* himselfe hauing lost his children that were right Citisens, made request vnto the people, That his sonne might be enrolled among the Citisens, which sonne he had begot at Athens of his wife being a straunger. Wee also read that the Romans made a Collonie of foure thousand Spaniards, whome the Romans had begot of Spanish women, for that they were not true Citisens. But afterward it tooke place that he should be a Citisen whose father was a citisen: and in many places it is sufficient for the making of a citisen, that his mother was a citisen. For the place maketh not the child of a straunger (man or woman) to be a citisen: and hee that was borne in Africk of two Roman citisens is no lesse a citisen, than if hee had bene borne in Rome. Now the made or naturallised citisen is he who hath submitted him-

D selfe vnto the soueraigntie of another, and is so receiued into the number of citisens. For the citisen of honour onely, who for his merits towards the Commonweale, or of speciall fauour hath obtained the right and priueledge of a citisen, cannot of right bee called a citisen, for that hee hath not put himselfe vnder the power of of anothers commaund.

Wherfore of many citisens, be they naturals, or naturallised, or els slaues enfranchised (which are the three meanes that the law giueth to become a citisen by) is made a Commonweale, when they are gouerned by the puissant soueraigntie of one or many rulers: albeit that they differ among themselues in lawes, language, customes, religions, and diuersitie of nations. But if all the citisens be gouerned by the selfesame lawes

E and customes, it is not onely one Commonweale, but also one very citie, albeit that the citisens be diuided in many villages, townes, or prouinces. For the enclosure of wals make not a citie, (as many haue written) no more than the wals of an house make a familie, which may consist of many slaues or children, although they bee farre distant one from another, or in diuers countries, prouided that they bee all subiect vnto the commaund of one head of the familie: So say we of a Citie, which may haue many townes and villages, which vse the same customes and fashions, as are the Bailiwicks, or Stewardships of this realme: And so the Commonweale may haue many cities and prouinces which may haue diuers customes, and yet are neuerthelesse subiect vnto the

The naturall citisen.

* Plut. in Peri.

The naturalised citisen.
The citisen of honour properly no citisen.

The enclosure of wals make not a citie, but the gouernment of the citisens vnder the selfsame lawes: although they dwell in diuers townes or prouinces dispersed.
* viz. France.

F   command

D4 power of anothers   D8 puissant soveraigntie *i.e. puissance souveraine*   Note at B2.

command of their soueraigne lords, and vnto their edicts and ordinances. And it may also be that euery towne and citie may haue certaine priuileges in particuler, which are not common vnto them of the suburbes; and the suburbs also may haue certaine prerogatiues which are not common vnto the villages, nor to the inhabitants of the open countrie; who are yet neuerthelesse subiects of the same Commonweale, and citisens of their citie; yet are they not for all that burgesses: for the word citisen hath I know not how a more speciall signification with vs, than hath the word Burgesse: and is properly the naturall subiect, who hath the right of a corporation, or colledge, or certaine other prieuledges, which are not common also vnto the burgesses. I haue said the naturall subiect, for that the subiect naturallised although hee dwell in the towne, and enioy the right of a burgesse, is yet called in many places a burgesse: & the other is called a citisen, who enioyeth a certaine particular priueledge proper vnto free borne citisens. As in Paris there is none but naturall citisens, and borne in Paris, that can be Prouost of the marchants. And in Geneua a burgesse cannot be Syndic, or Senator of the priuie counsell of xxv, which a citisen may well be: which is also vsed amongst the Swissers, and all the townes of Germanie.

The difference betwixt a citisen and a burgesse.

And thus much briefly concerning the difference of subiects, citisens, burgesses, and straungers; as also concerning a Commonweale, a Citie, and a Towne. But for as much as there is neither Greeke nor Latine, nor any other writer that I haue seene, which haue vsed these definitions, it is needfull by lawes and by examples to make plaine that which I haue before said, being otherwise of it selfe obscure. For we oftentimes see great quarrels and controuersies to arise as well betwixt princes, as citisens of the same towne or citie amongst themselues. For not vnderstanding the difference of these words, yea they from whome wee ought to expect the true resolutions of these things, are themselues oftentimes farre wide, mistaking a citie for a towne, a Commonweale for a citie, and straungers for citisens. But they which write of a Commonweale without knowledge of the law, and of the common right, are like vnto them which go about to build faire high houses, without any foundations at all. *Aristotle* hath defined vnto vs, A citie to be a multitude of citisens, hauing all things needfull for them to liue well and happily withall: making no difference betweene a Commonweale and a citie: saying also, That it is not a citie if all the citisens dwell not in one and the selfe same place: which is absurditie in matter of a Commonweale; as *Iulius Cæsar* in his Commentaries well declareth, saying, That euerie citie of the Heluetians had foure villages, or cantons. Where it appeareth that the word Citie, is a word of right or iurisdiction, which signifieth not one place or region, as the word Towne, or Citie; which the Latines call *Vrbem* of *Vrbo*, that is to say of *aratio*, or plowing: for that as *Varro* saith, the compasse and circuit of cities was marked out with the plough. It is also certaine in question of right, That he which hath caried out of the citie, that which was by the law forbidden to be caried out, and hath carried the same into another citie or towne of the same prouince; is neither to be said to haue caried the thing out of the citie, neither to haue offended against the law. Yea the doctors go farther, saying, That hee hath not done contrarie vnto the law, that hath transported the thing forbidden into any other citie or towne subiect vnto the same prince. And albeit that writers oftentimes confound both, taking sometimes the one for the other, as the greeks oftentimes vse the word πόλις ἀντὶ τοῦ ἄστεως, and the Latines the word *Ciuitas* for a towne, a citie, or the right of citisens, for that the generall which is the citie, comprehendeth in it the particular, which is the town: yet so it is, that they abused not the word ἄσυ ἀντὶ τῆς πόλεως, as we see that *Cicero* hath well kept the proprietie both of the one and of the other: for the word ἄσυ signifieth properly a towne, whereof came the word *astuti*, which with the Greeks signifi-

Arist. Politic. lib. 3. cap. 6.

Cice. ad Atticum. lib. 4.

OF A COMMONWEALE. 51

signifieth as much as doth with the Latines *Vrbani*, for that the inhabitants of townes are commonly in their behauiour more ciuill and gratious, than are the pesants or rude countrey men: for the word *Ciuilis*, which we call ciuill, was not of the auntient Latines receiued for *Vrbanus*, that is to say courteous, or after the manner of the citie. And least any man should thinke them to be rashly confounded, and to be but a question of words, and not of matter: it may be that a towne may be well built and walled, and that more is well stored also with people, and furnished with plentie of all things necessarie to liue withal, & yet for all that be no citie, if it haue not laws and magistrats for to establish therin a right gouernment (as we haue said in the first chapter) but is more truely to be called an Anarchie than a citie. And so contrariwise it may be, that a towne may be in all points accomplished and haue the right of a citie, and of an vniuersitie, and well ruled also with lawes and magistrats; and yet neuerthelesse shall it not bee a Commonwealth: as we see the townes and cities subiect vnto the seignorie of Venice, which are no Commonweals no more than the townes in the prouinces subiect and tributarie vnto the citie of Rome were of auntient time no Commonweals, neither enioyed the right or priuiledge of Commonweals; but the citie of Rome it selfe onely, which had great priueledges and prerogatiues against them all in generall, and against euery one of them in particuler: albeit that the lawes speaking, of the other townes, doe oftentimes vse this word (Citie) but that also vnproperly, for *Traian* the emperour writing to *Plinie* the yonger, Proconsul of Asia, denieth the citie of the Bithynians to haue the right of a Commonweale, in being preferred before other priuat creditos in the right of a pledge, and that truely. For why? that was proper vnto the citie of Rome, and to them to whome they had especially giuen this prerogatiue, as was onely the citie of Antioch in all the Roman Empire. So wee see that a towne may be without a citie, and a citie without a towne, and neither the one nor the other of necessitie a Commonweale: and that more is, one and the same citie may still bee kept in the whole and entire state of a citie, the wals thereof being laid flat with the ground, or it quite abandoned by the citisens; as did the Athenians at the comming of the Persian king, vnto whome they left their towne, putting all themselues vpon the sea, after they had put their wiues and children in safetie amongst the Trezenians; following therein the counsell of the Oracle, which had aunswered them, That their citie could not be saued but by woodden wals: which *Themistocles* interpreted, That the citie (which consisteth in the lawfull bodie of citisens) could not be saued but by ships. In like manner it happened also vnto the inhabitants of Megalopolis, who vnderstanding of the comming of *Cleomenes* king of Lacedemonia, all voyded their towne, which for all that was no lesse a towne than before; yet was it then neither citie nor Commonweale: in sort that a man might say, That the citie was gone out of the towne. So spake *Pompey* the Great, after he had drawne out of Rome two hundred Senators, and the better part of the citisens, and so leauing the towne vnto *Cæsar*, said thus, *Non est in parietibus respublica*, The Commonweale is not in the wals. But forasmuch as it had in it two sorts of partakers, and that the citisens diuided into two parts had put themselues vnder the protection of two diuers heads, they now seeme of one Commonweale to haue made two. Wherfore by these words Citie, Towne, Commonweale, Colledge, Court, Parish, Familie, are signified the right of these things. And as oftentimes it hath bene iudged that the church being without the wals of the citie, and the parishioners within the citie, that they should enioy the right of citisens, as if the parish were within the compasse of the wals: so also is it to bee iudged of a citie. Neither let it seeme vnto any man straunge, that I stand something the longer vppon this matter; if he but remember what importance the lacke of knowledge of these

That the citisens, and not the wals or buildings of a citie, make a citie.

things was long ago vnto the Carthaginensians. For at such time as question was made in the Senat of Rome, for the rasing of Carthage: the report thereof being bruited abroad, the Carthaginensians sent their ambassadors to Rome, to yeeld themselues vnto the mercie of the Romans, and to request the Senat not vnworthily to rase that their citie one of the fairest of the world, famous for the noble acts therof, an ornament of Rome it selfe, and a monument of their most glorious victories. Neuerthelesse the matter being long and throughly debated in the Senat, it was at last resolued vpon, That for the safetie of the Roman empire Carthage should bee destroied, as well for the oportunitie of the place, as for the naturall perfidiousnesse of the Carthaginensians themselues, who had now alreadie made warre vpon the allies of the Romans, rigged vp a number of ships contrarie to the agreement of peace, and secretly stirred vp their neighbour people vnto rebellion. The matter thus resolued vpon, the Carthaginensian ambassadors were sent for into the Senat, vnto whome aunswere was giuen by the Consull, That they should continue in their faith and fidelitie vnto the Senat and the people of Rome, and in pawne thereof to deliuer vnto the people of Rome three hundred hostages and their ships: in which doing they should haue their citie safe, with all their rights, priueledges and liberties, that euer before they had enioyed. With this answere the ambassadors returned merily home. But by and by after commission was giuen vnto *Scipio Africanus* the yonger, To go in all hast with a fleet to Carthage, and with fire and sword to destroy the towne, sauing the citisens and all other things else that they could carrie out of the towne. *Scipio* ariuing in Africke with his armie, sent *Censorinus* his lieutenant to Carthage, who after he had receiued the promised hostages together with the Carthaginensian ships, commaunded all the people of Carthage to depart out of the towne, yet with free leaue to carrie out with them what they would, and to build them a citie further off from the sea, or elswhere to their best liking. With this strait commaund of the lieutenant the Carthaginensians astonished, appealed vnto the faith of the Senat, & of the people of Rome, saying, That they had promised them that their citie should not be rased: to whome it was aunswered, That the faith giuen vnto them by the Senat should in all points be kept; but yet that the citie was not tied vnto the place, neither vnto the wals of Carthage. So the poore inhabitants were constrained to depart and abandon the towne vnto the fire, which was set vpon it by the Romans, who had not had it so good cheape, had the ambassadors before vnderstood the difference betweene a towne and a citie. As oftentimes it chanceth that many embassadors ignorant of the law of armes, and of that which right is, do euen in matters of state commit many grosse faults. Although that *Modestinus* writeth, That Carthage was no more a citie after it was rased, and that the vse and profit left vnto the citie, was in this case extinct aboue an hundred yeares before: but hee was in the same errour wherein the ambassadours of the Carthaginensians were, vnto whome all their rights, prerogatiues, and priueledges were reserued. The like errour was committed in the agreement made betwixt the Cantons of Berne and Friburg, in the yeare 1505, wherein it was agreed, That the amitie and alliance betwixt those two Commonweals should be for euer, and so long to endure as the wals of both the cities should stand. Neither are we to stay vpon the abuse which is ordinarily committed, or vpon the acts of greatest importance of them, which call one and the same thing a towne, a citie, and an vniuersitie: as some say of Paris, and certaine other places, calling that the citie which is contained in the Isle, and the vniuersitie the place wherein the colledges stand, and all the rest the towne, when as the towne it selfe is contained within the compasse of the wals and suburbs: howbeit that wee herein follow not the proprietie of the law, calling it the towne and suburbs, for the diuers priuiledges graunted vnto

The Carthaginensian ambassadors deceiued for not well vnderstanding what a citie in truth is.

Note at I7.

A vnto them by diuers kings; and the vniuersitie the bodie of all the burgesses of Paris together: but the citie the coniunction or ioyning together of the towne it selfe and the liberties, as also of the men vsing the same lawes and customes, that is to say the coniunction of the prouostship and of the countie of Paris together: which abuse is growne, for that of auntient time all the towne was not but the isle inuironed with wals, and the riuer about the wals, so as we read in the Epistle of *Iulian*, gouernour of the West empire, who made his ordinarie residence in Paris; the rest of the citie that now is being then in gardens and arable land.

But the fault is much more, to say, That he is not a citisen, which is not partaker of the offices of gouernment, of giuing of voices in the consultations of the people, whe- *Aristotle his de-*
B ther it be in matters of iudgement, or affaires of the state. This is the definition of a ci- *finition of a Ci-*
tisen, which *Aristotle* hath left vnto vs by writing, which he afterward correcting him- *tisen impugned.*
selfe, sayeth it not to haue place put in the popular state only. Now he in another place *& cap.4. Polit.*
himselfe confesseth that definition not to be good which is not generall. Small appa- ** Topi.lib.6.*
rance also is there in that he saith in another place, The noble to be more a citisen than ** Pol.li.3.ca.5*
the base, and the inhabitant of the towne rather than the plaine country peasant; and that as for the yong citisens, they as yet but grow as nouices, whilest the elder citisens decay; and that they of the middle age are the entire citisens, and the other but in part. Now the nature of a definition neuer receiueth diuision; neitheir containeth in it any thing more or lesse than is in the thing defined. And yet neuerthelesse that description
C of a citisen that *Aristotle* hath giuen vnto vs, is defectiue and lame, not being aptly to be applied euen vnto the popular estate, seeing that in the Athenian estate it selfe which had no peere for the libertie and authoritie of the people, the fourth ranke or degree of citisens being more than three times as great as all the rest of the people, had no part in the offices of gouernment, or in iudgements. So that if we will receiue the definition of *Aristotle*, we must needs confesse, that the greater part of the naturall bur- gesses of Athens, were in their owne Commonweales strangers, vntill the time of *Pericles*. And as for that which he saith, The noble to be alwaies more citisens than the base and vnnoble, is vntrue, not onely in the popular estate of the Athenians, but also in the popular Commonweals of the Swissers, and namely in Strasbourg, where
D the nobles (in the qualitie of nobles) haue no part in the offices of state and go- uernment.

Wherefore it is better and more truly said of *Plutarch*, That they are to bee called *Who indeed be*
citisens that enioy the rights and priueledges of a citie. Which is to be vnderstood ac- *citisens.*
cording to the condition and qualitie of euerie one; the nobles as nobles, the commo- ners as commoners; the women and children in like case, according vnto the age, sex, condition, and deserts of euery one of them. For should the members of mans bodie complaine of their estate? Should the foot say to the eye, Why am not I set aloft in the highest place of the bodie? or is the foot therefore not to be accounted amongst the members of the bodie? Now if *Aristotles* definition of a citisen should take place,
E how many seditions, how many ciuill warres, what slaughters of citisens would arise euen in the middest of cities? Truly the people of Rome, for no other cause departed from the Senators, than for that they enioyed not the same authoritie and priueledges that the nobilitie did; neither could it otherwise be appeased than by the meane of the fable of the members of mans bodie, whereby the graue and wise Senator *Agrippa* reconciled the people vnto the Senators. For *Romulus* the founder of the citie of Rome, excluded the people from the great offices of commaund, from the offices of priesthood, and from the auguresbips; commaunding the same to be bestowed vpon such onely as were descended from them whome he himselfe had chosen into the Se- nat,

F iiij

A10 (margin) Aristotle   B3 place but in   C7 Commonweale strangers   C10 namely *i.e.* particularly, especially (frequently used in this sense)

nat, or els from them whome he had afterwards ioyned vnto them. And this new people hauing vanquished their neighbours, enforced many of them to abandon their owne countrey and customes, to become inhabitants and citisens of Rome, as they did the Sabines. Afterwards hauing vanquished the Tusculans, the Volscians, and Herniques, they agreed together that the vanquished should haue part in their offices, and voices also in the assemblies of their estates, without any other chaunge either in their law or customes; who for that cause were not called citisens, but municipes (as who should say, Men made partakers of their immunities) yet indeed lesse esteemed and honoured than the Romans themselues, albeit that their estate were vnited vnto that of the Romans. As we see that *Cateline* descended of the auntient familie of the *Sergians* in Rome, and so a naturall Roman, by way of disgrace obiected to *M. Tullius Cicero*, That he was but a new vpstart of Arpinas. And that was the cause that many municipiall townes chose rather to vse the Roman lawes than their owne, to become true citisens of Rome, vntil the time of *Tiberius* the emperor, who vtterly took away the verie shadow of the popular libertie which *Augustus* the emperour had yet left; hauing remoued the popular assemblies from the people vnto the Senat: at which time the municipiall townes of Italie refused the priueledges of the citie of Rome, whereat the emperour *Adrian* maruelled (as saith *Aul. Gellius*) but without cause, for that they seeing the popular honours and offices to be all in one mans bestowing, they thought it now better to vse their owne lawes than others.

The diuers sorts of citisens in Rome.

Thus we see two sorts of citisens differing in priueledges, that is to wit, the Roman citisen, and the municipiall or countrey citisen. Now the third sort were the Latines, who had at the beginning threescore townes, but were afterward augmented with twelue Latine Colonies, who after long warres made peace with the Romans vppon condition, That they should liue after their own maners and customes, and yet should be made citisens of Rome, whosoeuer of them should remoue his dwelling into the citie, hauing yet left behind him some lawfull issue at home in the countrey. Yet when many of them fraudulently abused this agreement, and gaue their children vnto the citisens of Rome in adoption, or vnder the color of seruitude, to the intent that by them forthwith againe set at libertie, they might in a moment enioy the liberties and priueleges of the citie; order was taken by the law *Claudia*, confirmed by a decree of the Senat, and edict of the Consuls, That all the Latines which had so by craft obtained the freedome of the citie, should be constrained againe to returne into the Latine cities: which thing was done at the request of the Latine cities themselues. And so is that to be vnderstood that *Boetius* writeth, The Romans sent into the Latin Colonies, to haue lost the liberties of the citie: as also that which *Titus Liuius* saith, The Roman Colonies sent to Puteoli and Salerne by the decree of the Senat, to haue bene no more citisens: which is not further to be vnderstood or extended, but to their right for giuing of voices, by that meanes now taken from them. So were they of Reims, of Langres, of Saintonges, of Bourges, of Meaux, and of Autun, free people of Fraunce, allies of the Romans, and citisens also, but without voice (as saith *Tacitus*) before that it was permitted vnto them to haue states and honourable offices in Rome. And those of Autun were the first that had the priueledge to bee Senators of Rome, and therefore called themselues Brethren vnto the Romans: howbeit that the Auuergnats tooke vnto them the same priueledge & title, as descended from the Troians (as saith *Lucan*.) Now it is not to be doubted, but that that the Roman Colonies were true and natural citisens of Rome, drawne out of the Roman blood, vsing the same lawes, magistrats, and customes; the true markes of a true citisen. But the further that these Colonies were distant from the citie of Rome, the lesse they felt of the glorie and brightnesse of the

Notes at F7, H1, K1.

the sunne, and of the honours and offices which were diuided among the citisens and inhabitants of Rome: insomuch that the inhabitants of the Roman Colonies at Lyon, Vienne, and Narbone, thought themselues verie happie to haue gained but the prieuledges of the Italians, who were of auntient time the allies and confederats of the Romans, enioying the honourable freedome of citisens, and yet without chaunging either of their owne lawes or customes, or loosing any point of their liberties. And forasmuch as the Romans, holpen by the strength & power of their friends and allies, had subdued diuers other nations, and yet suffered not those their friends and companions to be admitted to sue for the honours and honourable offices in the citie; there of rise the confederats warre in all Italie against the Romans, which neuer tooke end vntill that after much harme on both sides both done and receiued, the libertie of the citie of Rome was by the law *Iulia* graunted vnto * all Italians, some few onely excepted. For the cities of Italie were called some Colonies, some Allies, some of them of the Latines, and some of the Italian iurisdiction, and all of them different. And that is it for which *Titus Liuius* saith, *Iam inde morem Romanis Colendi socios, ex quibus alios in ciuitatem, atque æquum ius accepissent: alios in ea fortuna haberent, vt locii esse quam ciues mallent.* viz. Now since that time the manner of the Romans was to honour their fellowes, of whome some they tooke into the citie, and into like freedome with themselues: othersome they had in that estate, as that they had rather to haue them their fellowes, than citisens with them. And hereof proceeded that speech of *Tiberius* the emperour, in the Oration which he had in the Senat, which is yet seene engrauen in brasse in Lyon. *Quid ergo? Num Italicus Senator prouinciali potior est?* What then? Is an Italian Senator better than the prouinciall Senator. As if he would haue said them both to haue bene Senators alike. And yet the same emperour excluded the Frenchmen which had obtained the freedome of the citie of Rome, from suing for the honours or offices thereof. Whereby is better to be vnderstood that which *Plinie* writeth, Spaine to haue in it 470 townes; that is to wit, 12 Colonies: 3 of citisens of Rome, 47 of them which had the freedome of the Latines: 4 of Allies, 6 of them that were enfranchised, and 260 tributaries. And albeit that the Latines were so straitly allied vnto the Romans, as that they seemed to be verie citisens; yet neuerthelesse that they were not so, it is to be well gathered by that saying of *Cicero: Nihil acerbius Latinos ferre solitos esse, quam id, quod perraro accidit, a Consulibus iuberi ex vrbe exire.* viz. The Latines vsed to take nothing more heauily, than that which but verie seldome times happened, To be commaunded by the Consuls to void the citie: for as for other straungers we read, them to haue oftentimes bene driuen out of the citie. In briefe, such was the varietie of prieuledges and prerogatiues amongst them which were contained within the Roman empire, besides their confederat and free people, as that almost no one thing was so proper vnto the Roman citisens in generall, as that the magistrats and gouernours might not proceed in iudgement against them in matters concerning their life and libertie, without the peoples leaue. Which prerogatiue was by the tribunitiall law *Iunia* graunted to all the citisens of Rome, after that the people had expulsed their kings, and was called The holy Law, being oftentimes after reuiued and confirmed by the *Valerian* Consull laws, at diuers times made by the Consull *Publius, Marcus,* and *Lucius,* of the honourable familie of the *Valerians*: and last of all by the Tribunitiall law *Sempronia,* and *Portia*, where to meet with the proceedings of the magistrats and gouernours, who encroached vpon the iurisdiction of the people, and proceeded oftentimes against the people, without yeelding thereunto, there was the penaltie of treason annexed vnto the law; for that those lawes were oftentimes broken by the magistrats. And at such time as *Cicero* was about to haue commaunded the

The cause of the confederat warre in Italie against the Romans.

* Plu. in Sylla.

* Liui. lib. 26.

No one prieuledge more common vnto the Roman citisens in generall, than that the magistrats might not proceed against them in cases concerning life or libertie, without the peoples leaue.

the Roman citisens priuie to the conspiracie of *Cateline* to be strangled in prison: *Cæsar* desiring to dissuade the matter in the Senat, said, Our auncestors imitating the maner of the Grecians, did punish and correct their citisens with stripes; and of men condemned tooke the extreamest punishment: but after that the Commonwealth was growne strong, the law *Portia* and other lawes were prouided, whereby for men condemned banishment was appointed. Which law *Cicero* hauing transgressed, was therefore not onely driuen into exile, but also proscribed, his goods confiscated, his house (esteemed to be worth fiftie thousand crownes) burnt, and a temple built in the plot thereof, which the people at the motion of *Clodius* their Tribune, commaunded to be consecrated to Libertie: wherewith the magistrats terrified, durst not but from that time forward with lesse seueritie proceed against the Roman citisens, yea euen after that the popular state was chaunged. And that is it for which *Plinie* the younger, Proconsull of Asia, writing to *Traian* the emperour, concerning the assemblies made by the Christians in the night, to the disquiet of his iurisdiction: I haue (saith he) many in prison, amongst whome there are certaine citisens of Rome, whom I haue put apart for to send them vnto Rome. And S. *Paul* at such time as he was drawne into question, as a seditious person, and a troubler of the common quiet; so soone as he perceiued that *Felix* the gouernor would proceed to the triall of his cause, he required to bee sent vnto the emperour; saying, That he was a citisen of Rome, for that his father being of the tribe of *Beniamin*, and borne at Tharsis in Catamania, had obtained the right of a Roman citisen: Which so soone as the gouernour vnderstood, hee surceased to proceed any further in the matter; and sent him to Rome, saying, This man might haue bene set at libertie, if he had not appealed vnto *Cæsar*. Whereas otherwise if hee had not bene a citisen of Rome, the gouernour would haue proceeded in the matter, seeing the countrey of Palestine was before brought into the forme of a prouince. As in like case *Pontius Pilat*, gouernour of the same countrey, was constrained to condemne Christ Iesus as a tributarie subiect of his prouince, whome for all that hee seemed to haue bene willing to haue deliuered out of the hands of his enemies, and from all punishment, if he could well in so doing haue auoided high treason, which the people threatned him with: Which the gouernour fearing least he should seeme to haue any thing therein offended, sent the whole processe of the matter vnto *Tiberius* the emperour (as saith *Tertullian*.) For if the municipiall magistrats of the Iewes had had soueraigne power and iurisdiction, they would not haue sent him back againe vnto the gouernour, crying That he had deserued the death, but that they had not the power to proceed thereunto against him. For the municipiall magistrats of prouinces had not any iurisdiction, more than to commit the offendors into safe keeping, for feare of the present daunger, and to receiue cautions, or to giue possession, and sometimes to appoint tutors vnto poore orphans: but in criminall causes, had no power or authoritie, neither ouer the citisen of Rome, neither ouer the straunger or prouinciall subiect, or ouer others that were enfranchised; but onely ouer their slaues, whome they might at the vttermost but with stripes correct. For as for the iurisdiction giuen to them that had the defence of townes, they were established by *Valentinian* three hundred and fiftie yeares after. Whereby it is to be gathered, all power and authoritie for the execution of iustice to haue bene giuen to the Roman gouernours, and their lieutenants in their prouinces, and taken from the rest. For they but deceiue vs, which thinke the Iewes priests, for the qualitie of their priesthood to haue made conscience to condemne to death our Saviour Christ Iesus, as if by their religion they had bene hindred so to do; and hereupon haue concluded, That churchmen ought not to giue iudgement that carried with it the execution of blood: which proceeded of the ignorance

Notes at G6, I2, I10, K7.

rance of antiquitie: For it is euident that before the land of Palestine was brought into the forme of a prouince, it had but the Senat of the Iewes, consisting of 71 persons, composed in part of priests and Leuites, who had the power of condemning offendors to death, as the Chaldean interpretor plainly sheweth, and the Hebrew Pandects more plainely than he.

Wherefore this was the greatest and chiefest priueledge proper to the citisens of Rome, That they could not by the magistrats be punished either with death or exile, but that they might still from them appeale; which libertie all the citisens of Rome enioyed. The other Roman subiects which had not this priueledge, were not called citisens: yet thereof it followeth not, that to speake properly they were not indeed citisens, and according to the true signification of a citisen: for they must needes be citisens, or straungers, allies, or enemies, seeing that they were not slaues; for so much as they were contained within the bounds of the Roman empire. But we cannot say that they were allies, for that onely free people which defended the maiestie of their estate, were called the fellowes or allies of the Romans: neither could it bee said that they were enemies or straungers, seeing that they were obedient subiects, and that more is, paid tribute vnto the Roman empire: wee must then conclude that they were citisens; for it were a verie absurd thing to say, That the naturall subiect in his owne countrey, and vnder the obeysance of his soueraigne prince, were a straunger. And that is it for which we haue said, That the citisen is a franke subiect, holding of the soueraigntie of another man. But the prerogatiues and priueledges that some haue more than others, maketh vs to call some of them citisens, and others tributaries. Yet we read that the emperour *Augustus* was so iealous of these priueledges, that hee would neuer giue the right of a Roman citisen vnto French men, for any request that his wife *Liuia* could make vnto him; yet for all that, not refusing to ease them from paying of tributes: neither liked he well of it, that his vncle *Cæsar* had together & at once giuen the freedome of the citie, vnto that legion which he had raised of Frenchmen, and in generall to all the inhabitants of Nouocome: and blamed also *M. Antonius*, for that he had for money sold the freedome of the citie vnto the Sicilians. Neuerthelesse the succeeding princes kept not with so great deuotion the rights and priueledges of the Roman citisens. *Antonius Pius* by a generall edict gaue the freedome of the citie of Rome vnto all the citisens of the Roman empire (slaues alwaies excepted) that so the citie of Rome might be the common countrey of all nations. Wherein hee seemed in a sort to imitat the example of * *Alexander* the Great, who called the whole world but one citie, and his campe the chiefe fortresse thereof. But *Antoninus* contented himselfe with the Roman world. And albeit that the citie, or rather the grant of the immunities of the citie seemed so to be communicated vnto all, yet were the priueledges of citisens diuers, some alwaies enioying more than others; as is to bee seene not onely in the Commentaries and answeres of the great lawyers, which flourished after *Antoninus Pius*, but also in the edicts of other princes. For *Seuerus* more than fiftie yeres after *Antoninus* was the first that gaue the priueledge to them of Alexandria, that they might be made Senators of Rome: but the other Ægyptians could not be made citisens of Rome, except they had before obtained the freedome of the citie of Alexandria. Which well sheweth, that the greatnesse of the priueledges make not the subiect therefore the more or lesse a citisen. For there is no Commonwealth where the citisen hath so great freedome, but that he is also subiect vnto some charge: as also the nobilitie, although with vs exempted from taxes and tallages, are yet bound to take vp armes for the defence of the Commonweale and others: and that vpon paine of their goods, their blood, and life. For otherwise if the largenesse of prerogatiues and priuileges

The greatest & chiefest priuelege proper vnto the citisens of Rome.

* Plut. in Alexandro.

The greatnes of the priueleges and immunities which a man enioyeth, maketh him neuer a whit the more therefore a citisen.

ges should make a citisen, then verely straungers and allies were to bee called citisens, seeing that oftentimes greater and larger priueledges are giuen vnto strangers or allies, than to citisens themselues: For why? the freedome of the citie is oftentimes for an honour giuen vnto straungers, who yet for all that are bound vnto no commaund or necessarie duties. As the Swissars gaue the freedome of their citie first to *Lewes* the eleuenth, and so afterwards vnto the rest of the French kings. So *Artaxerxes* king of Persia, gaue the freedome of the citie vnto *Pelopidas* (and all his posteritie) entreating of alliance with him. So the Athenians made free of their citie *Euagoras* king of Cyprus, *Dionysius* the tyrant of Sicilie, and *Antigonus* and *Demetrius* kings of Asia. Yea that more is, the Athenians gaue vnto all them of the Rhodes the freedome of their citie: and the Rhodians with like courtesie vpon the agreement of the league, made all the Athenians citisens of their citie, as we read in *Liuie*: which league was called, The treatise of *Comburgeosie*. What manner of league that was made betwixt the Valesians, and the fiue little Cantons in the yeare 1528; and betwixt the Cantons of Berne and them of Friburg, in the yeare 1505; and againe betwixt them of Geneua & them of Berne in the yeare 1558: the force of which leagues was such, as that there should be a mutuall communication betwixt them both of their citie and amitie: and in case that any of the confederats forsaking his owne citie, had rather to goe vnto the citie of his fellowes and confederats, he should presently become a citisen and subiect of the other citie, without any new choyce or speciall letters of his naturalisation or enfranchising. But the freedome of any citie giuen for honour sake vnto any, bindeth no man vnto the commaund thereof; but him which forsaketh the dwelling place of his natiuitie or citie, that so he may come into the power of another prince: For neither were those kings whom we haue spoken of; neither *Hercules*, or *Alexander* the Great, when they were made honourable citisens of the Corinthians, subiect or bound vnto their commaunds; in such sort as that the right of a free citisen was vnto them but as a title of honour. Wherefore seeing it impossible for one and the same person to bee a citisen, a stranger, and an allie; it may well be said that the priueleges make not a citisen, but the mutuall obligation of the soueraigne to the subiect, to whome for the faith and obeisance he receiueth, he oweth iustice, counsell, aid, and protection, which is not due vnto strangers.

But some may say, How can it then bee, that the allies of the Romans, and other people gouerning their estate, were citisens of Rome (as those of Marseilles and of Austun?) Or what is that which *M. Tullius* crieth out: O the notable lawes, and of our auncestors by diuine inspiration made and set downe, euen from the beginning of the Roman name, That none of vs can be the citisen of more than one citie: (for dissimilitude of cities must also needs haue diuersities of lawes) nor that any citisen can against his will be thrust out, or against his will be detained in the citie. For these are the surest foundations of our libertie, Euery man to bee master both of keeping and of leauing of his right and libertie in the citie. And yet he the same man, before had said it to be a thing granted vnto all other people, that euerie man might be a citisen of many cities: with which errour (saith he) I my selfe haue seene many of our citisens, ignorant men, led; to haue at Athens bene in the number of the judges, and of the Areopagi, in certaine tribe, and certaine number, when as they were yet ignorant whether they had obtained the libertie of that citie; and to haue lost this, except they had by the law made for the recouerie of things lost, againe recouered the same. Thus much hee.

But first to that which he writeth concerning the Athenians, that law of *Solons* was long before abolished, which admitted not a straunger to the freedome of a citisen of

Honourable citisens.

of Athens, except he were banished out of his owne countrey: at which law *Plutarch* wondreth aboue measure; not foreseeing that to haue bene done of *Solon*, to the end (as it is like) That no man should enioy the immunitie and priueleges of a citisen of Athens, and that popular prerogatiue which the people had, except he were bound vnto the commaund and lawes of the Athenians. But he which is against his will detained vnder the commaund of a straunge citie, hath without doubt lost the right of his owne citie: which can in no wise be applied vnto those kings whome wee haue before spoken of, or yet to the Rhodians which had ordained the freedome of the Athenians. Wherefore this is it, as I suppose, that *M. Tullius* meant (for why, hee well agreeth not with himselfe) That he which was indeed a true citisen of Rome, that is to say, which was bound vnto the Senat and the lawes of the people of Rome, could not be bound vnto the commaund of another citie. As *Pomponius Atticus* borne in the citie of Rome, being a Roman citisen, and of the honourable order of the knights, who for his loue towards the Athenians, was thereof called *Atticus* (and vnto whome three of the Roman emperours referred the beginning of their discent) refused the freedome of the citie of Athens offered him by the Athenians; least (as saith *Cornelius Nepos*) he should haue lost the freedome of the citie of Rome: which is true in regard of the true subiects and citisens; but not in the citisens of honour, which are not indeed subiects: neither in respect of them which are citisens of diuers cities, vnder the power of one and the same prince, a thing lawfull vnto all euen by the Roman law. For although one may be the slaue or vassall of many maisters or lords, yet can no man be the subiect of diuers soueraigne princes, but by the mutuall consent of the princes; because that these are vnder no mans commaund, as are they vnto whome seruice is by turne done by slaues, who may by the magistrats be enforced to sell their slaue, except the seruile labours, which cannot at once be done to them all, be by turnes done by the slaue. And this is the point for which we oftentimes see warres betwixt neighbour princes, for the subiects of their frontiers, who not well knowing whome to obey, submit themselues sometimes to the one and sometimes to the other: and oftentimes exempting themselues from the obeisance of both two, are ordinarily inuaded and preyed vpon by both the one and the other. As the countrey of Walachie hauing exempted it self from the obeisance of the Polonians, hath become subiect vnto the Turks; and afterwards submitting it selfe vnto the kings of Polonia, paied tribute neuerthelesse vnto the Turke, as I haue learned by the letters of *Stanislaus Rasdrazetoski* sent to the cunstable of France, bearing date the 17 of August 1553. Neuerthelesse there are many people vpon the frontiers, which haue set themselues at libertie, during the quarrels of princes, as it is come to passe in the low countrey of Leige, of Lorraine, & of Burgundie: where there are more than twelue subiects of the French king, or of the empire, or of Spaine, who haue taken vpon them the soueraigntie. Amongst whome *Charles* the fift reckoned the duke of Bouillon, whome he called his vassall: and for that he was his prisoner in the yeare 1556, at the treatie made for the deliuerance of prisoners, hee demaunded an hundred thousand pound for ransome; for that he called himselfe a soueraigne prince. But there are well also others beside the duke of Bouillon: & to go no further than the marchesse of Burgundie (which is called, The forbidden countrey) six princes haue soueraigne power ouer their subiects, which the mutual wars betwixt the French and the Burgundians haue by long prescription of time brought forth. And in the borders of Lorraine, the counties of Lume & of Aspremont haue taken vpon them the right and authoritie of soueraigntie. Which hath also happened vpon the borders of England and Scotland, where some particular men haue made themselues great commaunders within this twenty or thirty yeres, against the antient agreements. For, for to meet with such

---

D3 Rasdrazetoski: Rasdrazeroski (Fr 7) Rosdrazeroski (Fr 1–6, 8) *i.e.* Rozdrazewski   D3 constable
D6 Leige *i.e.* Liège   E3 marchesse *i.e.* marches, borderlands   Notes at B1, E1.

such enterprises, the English and the Scots had of auntient time agreed, That the Batable ground, (that is to say a certaine part of the countrey so called, vpon the frontiers of both realmes, being fiue miles long, and two miles broad) should neither be tilled, built, or dwelt vpon; howbeit that it was lawfull for both people there to feed their cattell: with charge that if after the sunne setting, or before the sunne rising, any of their beasts were there found, they should be his that so found them: which was one of the articles agreed vpon by the states of Scotland, in the yere 1550, and sent to Henrie the second the French king, as was by him prouided. But where the soueraigne lords are good friends, as the Swissers of the countrey of Lugan, and the other territories which belong in common to all the lords of the league, whither they send their officers euerie Canton by turne: there the subiects are not reputed to bee the subiects of diuers soueraignes, but of one onely, which commaundeth in his order; in such sort as that one of them seeke not to encroach vpon the others. Whereof rise a sedition betweene the seuen Cantons Catholick, and the foure Protestants, in the yeare 1554, the Catholicks desiring to chastice the inhabitants of Lugan and Louerts, who had seperated them from the church Catholike: and the Protestants hindring them so to do, and were now vpon the point to haue taken vp armes the one against the other, if the Cantons of Glaris, and Appenzell, who allow of both religions, had not together with the ambassadour of the French king, interposed themselues, and so pacified the matter. Now therefore the full and entire citisen or subiect of a soueraigne prince, can bee no more but a citisen of honour of another seignorie. For so when as we read that king Edward the first gaue the freedome of citisens vnto all the inhabitants of base Britaine; that is to be vnderstood for them to enioy the liberties, exemptions and freedoms, that they of the countrey enioyed. So say we also of the Bernois, and the inhabitants of Geneua, who call themselues by their treaties of alliance, Equall, and by their letters Combourgeses. For as for that which *Cicero* saith, That the citisens of Rome might at their pleasure leaue their freedome of citisens, to become citisens of another citie: nothing was vnto them therein more lawfull, than that was in like case vnto all other people lawfull also: and that especiallie in a popular estate, where euerie citisen is in a manner partaker of the maiestie of the state, and doe not easily admit strangers vnto the freedome of citisens. As in Athens where to make a straunger free of their citie there must of necessitie 6000 citisens, by their voices in secret giuen consent therunto. But in such places and countries as wherein tyrants rule, or which for the barrennesse of the soile, or intemperature of the ayre are forsaken by the inhabitants; not onely the citisens, but euen the strangers also are oftentimes by the princes of such places prohibited to depart, as in Moscouia, Tartaria, and Æthiopia; and that so much the more, if they perceiue the[ir] anger to be ingenious and of a good spirit, whome they detaine by good deserts, or els by force, if he would depart: in stead whereof hee must buy it deare, or right well deserue of the Commonweale, that shall get his freedome of a citisen amongst the Venetians or Ragusians, or such other free states. And although that by the Roman law euerie man might giue vp his freedome; and that in Spaine it is free for euery man to remoue elswhere, and to be enrolled into another citie, so that it be done by protestation to the prince: yet hath it and shall bee alwayes lawfull to all princes and cities, by the right of their maiestie and power to keepe their citisens at home. And therefore princes in making of their leagues, protest that they will not receiue any the subiects or vassals of their confederats into their protection, freedome, or prieueleges, without their expresse consent. Which is conformable vnto the auntient clause of the Gaditane confederation reported by * *Cicero*: *Ne quis fœderatorum a populo Romano ciuis reciperetur, nisi is populus fundus factus esset; id est auctor. viz.* That

none

marginalia:
A citisen of Rome might at his pleasure giue vp his freedome.

Not citisens onely but euen strangers also in some places prohibited to depart.

* Cic. in orat. pro Corn. Bal.

G5 Louerts *i.e.* Louverts, variant of Luwertz, Germanic form of Lugano (cf. Fr)   H2 base Britaine *i.e.* Lower Brittany   K8 fœderatorum   Notes at F8, F9, G2.

OF A COMMONWEALE. 61

none of the confederats, should of the people of Rome be receiued for a citisen, except that people so confederat had bene the ground, (that is to say, the author thereof.) For therein lieth the state of that cause: for that *Cornelius Balbus* was a citisen of a confederat citie, & therfore could not contrarie to the league, by *Pompeius* be made a citisen of Rome without the consent of the confederats. The same *Cicero* writeth also in the leagues of the French with the Romans to haue bene excepted, That none of them should of the Romans be receiued for a citisen. The same laws we yet at this present vse. For althogh that the Swissers are with vs ioined in a most strait bond of amity & frendship: yet neuerthelesse is the same clause conceiued in that league, which was with them made in the yeare 1520. And againe at such time as the fiue lesser Cantons of the Swissers made a league of alliance and amitie amongst themselues, it was excepted that no citisens of the confederats should be receiued; or if they should desire the freedome of another citie, they should not otherwise obtaine it, except they would dwell in the countrey, their land and goods remaining as before. And besides these leagues, there is no prince which hath not taken the like order. So that oftentimes the subiect dare not so much as to depart out of the countrey without leaue, as in England, Scotland, Denmarke, and Sweden, the noble men dare not to goe out of their countrey without leaue of the prince, except they would therefore loose their goods: which is also obserued in the realme of Naples, by the custome of the countrey. As also it was forbidden by the emperour *Augustus* to all Senators to goe out of Italie without his leaue, which was alwaies right straitly looked vnto. And by the ordinances of Spaine it is forbidden the Spaniards to passe ouer into the West Indies, without the leaue of the king of Spaine: which was also of auntient time forbidden in Carthage, when *Hanno* their great captaine had first discouered the islands of the Hesperides. And by the decrees of Milan, it is not lawfull for any subiect to receiue the freedome of any other citie; or to enter into alliance or league with any other princes or Commonweales, without the expresse leaue of the Senat of Milan. And that more is, we see oftentimes that it is not permitted vnto the subiect, so much as to change his dwelling place, albeit that he depart not out of the seignorie and obeysance of his soueraigne prince: as in the dutchie of Milan, the subiect comming to dwell in the citie of Milan, or within a certaine circuit of Milan, must first haue leaue so to doe; and also pay vnto his prince three duckets. We also find that it was in auntient time forbidden the Bithynians (subiects vnto the Romans) to receiue any other subiects into their towne, or to giue vnto them the freedome of a citisen, as they oft times did, to decline the iurisdiction of others, or to ease them of paying of customes and tributes due: in which case the law commaundeth, That he which hath so chaunged his dwelling should beare the charges of both places; which was also decreed by the kings, *Philip* the faire, *Iohn*, *Charles* the fift, and *Charles* the seuenth. Howbeit that the decree of *Philip* the long would, That the Prouost or bailiefe of the place, asisted with three burgesses, should receiue into the freedome of their citie, whosoeuer of the kings subiects as would, prouided, That within a yeare and a day he should in the same citie into which hee remoued, buy an house of the price of 60 soulz Paris at the least; and to signifie the same by a sergeant, vnto the lord vnto whome the iurisdiction of the place wherein he dwelled belonged: and after that, that he should dwell in the same citie whereinto he was receiued for a citisen, from the first of Nouember, vnto the 24 of Iune; and yet paying the like tax or tribute that he did before he remoued, so long as hee dwelleth in that new freedome; and without declining the iurisdiction for any suit commenced against him three months before.

And albeit that it be lawfull for euerie subiect to chaunge the place of his dwelling,

The subiect may not depart out of his countrey without the leaue of his prince.

The Canaries.

G yet

Not lawfull for any man to forsake his natiue countrey.

yet is it lawfull for no man to forsake his natiue countrie; and much lesse for them which are enrolled and tied to the soyle, whome we call Mort-maines, who of auntient time might not chaunge their dwelling place without speciall leaue. And so generally a man may say in tearmes of right, That the freedome of a citisen is not lost, neither the power of a prince ouer his subiect, for chaunging of the place or countrey; no more than the vassall can exempt himselfe from the faith and obedience hee oweth vnto his lord; or the lord without iust cause refuse to protect and defend his vassall, without the consent of one to the other, the bond betwixt them being mutuall & reciprocall. But if the one or the other haue giuen their expresse or secret consent; or that the subiect forsaking his prince, hath yeelded himselfe vnto the protection of another prince, by the sufferance of the first, without contradiction, he is no more bound vnto the obeisance that he oweth him: neither can otherwise than as a stranger afterwards returne into the former citie.

Why princes oftentimes by large gifts and priueleges draw into their countries ingenious straungers.

For princes oftentimes by large gifts or priueleges draw into their countries ingenious straungers; whether it be so to weaken their neighbour princes, or for the better instruction of their owne people, or so to encrease their wealth and power, or els for their immortall fame and glorie which they hope to get in making the towns and cities by them built, more renowned with the multitude of citisens and plentie of all things. So *Theseus* by proposing the libertie of the citie to all strangers, made the citie of Athens most famous of all the cities of Greece. So *Alexander* the Great by granting of great priueleges, least the city by him built at the mouth of the riuer Nilus (which he after his owne name called Alexandria) the greatest, and best traded of all the cities of Ægypt. So king *Lewes* the eleuenth gaue the priueleges of the citie of Burdeaux to all straungers whether they were friends or enemies (except the English) so that they dwelt within the towne. So *Frauncis* the Great, founder of the citie by him built at the mouth of the riuer Sequana, which they call The Port of Grace, proponing immunitie from all tributes, to all them that should dwell therein, in short time made it a most populos citie. Neither should the citie of London abound with so great wealth, nor such a multitude of citisens, had not *Richard* king of England proposed vnto straungers all the immunities graunted vnto the citisens: so that they had dwelt ten yeares in the citie: which space of time for the obtaining of the libertie of the citie, most part of the Swissers and Germans, indifferently propounded to al strangers: a thing well agreeing with the Roman lawes. True it is that more or lesse time is required in one place then in another, according to the commodiousnesse of the place, or the greatnesse of the priueleges. As in Venice to obtaine the grant and priueledges of a simple citisen (without hauing any other interest in the state, except in certain meane offices) a man must haue dwelt foureteene yeares within the citie. They of Ferrara were content with ten yeares, so that the inhabitants had all the meane while borne the same burthen with the citisens.

To haue dwelt long in another princes countrey maketh him neuer a whit the more the strange princes subiect.

And yet it sufficeth not to haue dwelt in another mans countrey the time presined in the customes, to obtaine the freedome of a citisen; if the straunger do not demaund the citisens right and freedome, and be thereinto also receiued: for it may bee that the straunger would not for any thing chaunge his prince, howbeit that his affaires hold him out of his owne countrey. For howbeit that many be of opinion, that a man hauing staid the prefixed time in another mans countrey, without hauing obtained letters of naturalising, is yet capable of testamentary legacies: they in that agree in fauour of testaments, and especially of charitable legacies giuen vnto poore straungers, who are alwaies as much to be fauoured as the widdowes and orphans. But to obtaine the full right and priueledge of a citisen, it sufficeth not to haue dwelt the time appointed by the decrees and ordinances of the place, if a man haue not both demaunded and obtained the same. For as a gift is to no purpose, except that

---

F4 That the G10 *For* least *read* left. H5 The Port of Grace *i.e.* Le Havre de Grace or Le Havre

that both he which giueth, and he to whome it is giuen agree, the one in giuing and the other in receiuing: so neither is he made a citisen that would not; neither if he would could he so be, either of the princes interposing themselues. For which cause those Consuls, of whome the one was by an herald at armes yeelded vnto the Numantines; and the other to the Samnites, for that they had without the commaundement of the people made peace with the enemies; left not therefore to bee citisens of Rome: because they were not receiued by the enemies. Which question for all that could not yet be fully decided, for the different opinions of *Brutus* & *Scæuola* betwixt themselues. For when the Consull yeelded to the Samnites, returning to Rome was come into the Senat, the Tribune of the people compelled him to go out of the Senat: howbeit in fine the Senat by decree declared, That hee had not lost the right of a citisen of Rome, being refused by the enemie: howbeit that in truth he was not onely depriued of the right of a citisen, but also made a slaue of the enemies, by the decree of the people, for hauing without their leaue capitulated and treated of peace with the enemies: and ought to haue bene againe restored by the people. Neuerthelesse the milder opinion of the Senat interpreted that the depriuing of him of his freedome was conditionall, as in case that he were of the enemie receiued. But if so be that a straunger doth euen against his will retaine the rights of his owne citie, when as hee yeelded himselfe vnto the power of another prince, by whom he is refused: much more doth he retaine the same when he requireth not the right of a straunge citie: and then when it hath bene offered him, hath refused the same: and much lesse if he haue not bene presented vnto the strange prince, neither hath of him required letters of his naturalising, but onely to stay in his countrey as a straunger the time prefixed by the decrees. Whereby is decided the difficultie and doubt which the Senat of Naples made, and therin resolued nothing; that is to wit, If he that had dwelt all his life in a strange countrey should enioy the right and freedome of a citisen in his owne countrey. And many there be, that thinke he ought not to enioy the same; saying, That regard is to be had to the place of his long dwelling: but I am of opinion (if mine opinion may take place) That hee ought neuerthelesse to enioy the priueledge of a free citisen, if he haue not by consent of his prince expresly renounced it, or els done some fact contrarie to the dutie of a naturall subiect. Neither am I alone of this opinion. For the the court of parliament of Paris, by decree made the xiiij of Iune, in the yeare 1554 adiudged that a French man hauing dwelt fiftie yeares in Venice, continued yet still subiect to the French king, and was receiued vnto the succession of his next kinsmen: hee hauing in the meane time done no harme against his countrey, neither committed any crime for which he ought to loose his libertie, neither hauing refused to come being called home by his prince; nor yet requested the freedome of the citie of Venice to haue bene giuen him. For as for secret consent it ought to hurt no man, being esteemed as no consent in things preiudiciall, except it be by word or deed plainly expressed: especially when wee may otherwise interpret the mind of him that hath not declared the same. Whereby it is to be vnderstood what is to be iudged of the question propounded: which the court of Burdeaux all the judges being assembled together could not determine. As whether a Spaniard borne and brought vp in Spaine, and yet the sonne of a French man (which French man had alwaies dwelt in Spaine, & expresly renounced the place of his birth) being come into Fraunce there to make his perpetuall residence, ought to enioy the priueleges of a citisen, without letters of his naturalizing? Neuerthelesse I am of opinion that he is a straunger, for the reasons before alleged, and that he ought not to enioy the priuelege of a citisen; sauing vnto the prince to reforme it if it shall so seeme good vnto him. And if a straunger which hath obtained letters of his naturalising out of his owne countrey, and yet will not there dwell, he looseth the right he there pretendeth: for that the lawes suffer not a double fiction. And for this cause *Lewes* the xij the French king thrust out from the right of free citisens all straungers, who had obtained of him letters of their naturalising, and were retired out of his realme home. For by our customes he that will get the freedome of a citisen, must obtaine the princes letters to that purpose, and hauing obtained them, pay his fine vnto maisters of the receipt.

These reasons show not onely the difference that is betwixt a citisen and him that is none, but also of citisens amongst themselues; and that if we follow the varietie of priueleges to iudge of the definition of a citisen, there shall bee fiue hundred thousand of definitions of citisens, for the infinit diuersitie of the prerogatiues that citisens haue one against another, and also ouer straungers: seeing that it is oft times better in the same citie to be a straunger, then a citisen, especially in such cities as are oppressed with the crueltie and insolencie of Tyrants. As in Florence many citisens requested *Cosmus* the new duke to be reputed and esteemed as straungers, by reason of the libertie of straungers, and thraldome of the citisens, which they obtained not: and yet hee allured fiftie straungers to sue for the freedome of the citie, putting them in hope of the great offices and commaunds: whereby it was brought to passe, that from those fiftie citisens so made, he extorted fiftie thousand crownes, confirmed the authoritie of the new citisens gotten by deceit, and thereby brake the power of the conspirators against him. So in auntient time the Venetians empouerished and brought low by the warres against the Genowayes, and fearing the rebellion of many subiects, with a few of the great states, sold the right and priueledge of a gentleman of Venice vnto three hundred citisens, so to strengthen themselues with their goods, their force, and counsell, against the power of the people. It is then the acknowledgement and obedience of the free subiect towards his soueraigne prince, and the tuition, iustice, and defence of the prince towards the subiect, which maketh the citisen: which is the essentiall difference of a citisen from a straunger, as for other differences they are casuall and accidentarie; as to haue part in all or certaine offices or benefices; from which the straunger is debarred as it were in euerie Commonweale. As for offices it is cleere. And although the Bishops of Rome haue of long time attempted to giue all benefices to all men as of right: yet haue princes oftentimes reiected those ambitious decrees of the Popes. I except the kings of Spaine, of all others the most obedient seruants of the Bishops of Rome, who not without great reward obtained by the decree of *Sixtus* Bishop of Rome, That benefices should not be bestowed vpon straungers. And so in Boulongne la Grace, where the Pope is soueraigne lord, the offices and benefices are not giuen but to the naturall inhabitants and subiects. The like whereof is done also in all the seignorie of Venice. But the Swissers haue farre otherwise proceeded than by way of agreement, who by a law made in the yeare 1520, decreed the Popes Buls and Mandats, whereby he had not doubted to giue benefices vnto straungers, to bee publickly torne, and they that vsed them to be cast in prison. And by the lawes of the Polonians also euen from the time of *Casimire* the Great, vnto the raigne of *Sigismundus Augustus*, straungers were kept farre from all benefices; which thing also the Germans by couenants, of late wrested from the Popes: in which couenants they of Mets were also comprised, and so iustly by their letters complained vnto *Charles* the ix the French king, those couenants to bee broken by the craft of the Bishops of Rome.

Another priueledge there is also graunted more vnto citisens than to straungers, in that they are exempted from many charges and payments, which the straunger is constrained to beare: as in auntient time in Athens the straungers payed a certaine speciall tribute

Better sometimes to be a straunger than a naturall citisen.

The true difference betwixt a citisen and a stranger.

---

15 benefices 16 Boulongne la Grace *i.e.* Bologna   Notes at F10, H2, H5.

tribute for the right of their dwelling place, which they called μετοίκιον: whereas the citisens were free from all impositions. But the most notable priueledge that the citisen had aboue the straunger, is, that he had power to make his will, and to dispose of his goods, according to the customes; or leaue his neerest kinsmen his heires; whereas the straunger could do neither the one nor the other, but his goods fell vnto the lord of the place where he died. Which is no new law in Fraunce, as the Italians complaine, but a thing common also vnto the kingdome of Naples, of Sicilie, and all the East, where the Grand Signior is not onely heire vnto the straungers, but also to his Timariots, for their immouables; and to his other subjects for the tenth. As in auntient time in Athens, the common treasure receiued the sixt part of the inheritance of straungers, and al their slaues borne in the citie: wheras in Rome the rigour was much greater (the common treasure swallowing vp all the inheritance of straungers.) And albeit that where *Diodorus* saith, The Ægyptians and Romans to haue suffered the heires of straungers to succeed them: he spoke therein like a straunger himselfe without regard; for it is most certaine, that it was no way permitted for a straunger to dispose of his goods, neither to receiue any thing by the testament of a citisen of Rome, the common treasure carrying away the succession: whereof our laws are ful. Which we may also iudge by the oration of *Cicero*, who to show that *Archias* was a citisen of Rome, saith amongst other things, That he had by his testament disposed of his goods. And himself in his own cause to giue men to vnderstand that the decree of banishment made against him at the sute of *Clodius* the Tribune, was of none effect: What Roman citisen is there (saith he) that hath made any doubt to leaue me what hee pleased by his testament, without regard to the decree of my banishment. The selfe same argument vsed also *Demosthenes*, to proue that *Euxithenes* was a citisen of Athens: Haue not his next of kinne (saith he) recouered the inheritance of their father that suruiued? And like as in Fraunce, and in England, particular lords take vnto them the inheritance of straungers which die within their iurisdiction: so the Romans also after the manner of their auncestors, tooke vnto them the heredetarie goods of straungers, whome they had receiued into their protection, being left at Rome, which they called, The right of application. And that is it for which they said in Rome, That the right to make a will and testament was onely granted to a citisen of Rome. Whereby it is plaine that right of application, or of Albinage (as some call it) to haue beene most auntient, and common as well to the Greeks and Romans, as to other people also, vntill that *Frederick* the second had derogated from the same by his edict, which was but euill kept: For he gaue leaue to all straungers dying within the compasse of his empire, by their testament to dispose of their goods; or if they dyed intestat, to leaue their next of kin their heires. But the force of that law is euen in Germanie it selfe nothing, and much lesse in Italie, where straungers are much worse dealt withall than in Fraunce. For by our customes it is permitted vnto the straunger to get in this * realme all the goods mouable and immouable that he can, and them whilest he yet liueth, to sell, giue, exchaunge, or dispose of by contracts made with men yet liuing, according to his owne pleasure; and for a small sum of money, as for some twentie or thirtie crownes paid into the common treasure, to obtaine letters of naturalisation, and the right of a citisen; so that he may by his will giue legacies, or appoint such an heire as himselfe pleaseth. But in many countries of Germanie, and by the generall custome of Bohemia, it is not suffered straungers to haue one foot of land. As in like case in Italie it is forbidden all straungers to get any immouables in proprietie, as in the duchie of Ferrara it is a formall custome. And that more is, by the custome of Perouze, it is forbidden to transfer vnto a straunger not onely the proprietie, but euen the possesion of any immouable.

The greatest priueledge that a naturall citisen had in auntient time aboue a straunger.

viz. Fraunce.

Straingers in many places hardly delt withall.

G iij

Note at C 5.

uable. And by the custome of Milan it is not permitted vnto the straunger, so much as to haue the vse and profit of any thing immouable, and that vpon paine of confiscating the reuenew with the inheritance; forbidding inheritours also to marrie with straungers, vpon like paine of confiscating their goods. And that which more vniust is, it is not lawfull for the creditor being a straunger, to take his debtors immouables or land, for default of paiment afsigned vnto him, but that he must within the yere againe cleere his hands thereof; which causeth the creditor oftentimes to sell his land vnderfoot, or for little, especially if the naturall inhabitants feare or loue the debtour. And not long since, by the ordinance of the emperour *Charles* the fift, all straungers are embarred from the succefsion of the subiects of Milan. By the custome of Venice also it is lawfull to bind a citisen to a stranger, yet by that bond are not the heirs bound, more than for so much profit as came vnto them thereby; quite contrarie vnto the Roman ciuill law. And by the custome of Brixia in Italie, a woman married vnto a straunger cannot transferre her immouables vnto straungers, neither the value thereof, neither directly, or indirectly. See now the good entertainment that straungers haue in Italie; whereof they haue no occasion to complaine of Fraunce, seeing that in England the subiects cannot pawne their lands vnto their creditors being straungers: whereof the ambafsadors of forraine nations haue oftentimes complained to haue reason of their debtors: yet suffer they the next of kinne to enioy the goods and money of the straunger. The contrarie whereof is done in Lituania, Moscouia, Tartaria, and all the Turkish empire: in which place the goods of straungers dying there, are confiscat in like manner as in Fraunce: where neuerthelefse it is permitted to straungers if they die out of Fraunce, to make a will, and to appoint his children borne in Fraunce his heires, so that their mother be not a stranger. And as for the clause commonly ioyned vnto the letters of their naturalisation: *Modo hæredes sint Regnicolæ*, the judges haue so interpreted it of straungers dwelling in Fraunce, who are preferred before them that are neerer of kinne dwelling out of the realme, in the succefsion of the naturalised straunger: for otherwise it is requisit to make the straungers children to succeed, for that they were borne in France, and of a free citisen, or naturall subiect. But the children of straungers borne in Frannce, enioy their fathers inheritance, not by will (which is not lawfull for strangers to make) but as from him dying intestat, if their mother be a free woman when the inheritance descendeth. And more than this, it is graunted by our kings of an extraordinarie bountie vnto such marchant strangers as frequent the fairs of Champagne and Lyon, That none of their goods, if they die in the meane time shall be confiscated: which right the English marchants enioy also in Guienne. But as for them of the low country of Henault & Artois, of the townes of Amiens, Cambray, & Turnay, they are in the same state that citisens be, for so much as concerneth the right of succefsion: and that the edicts of our princes, and iudgements giuen, haue oft times proued yet so as that the same should also be lawfull for vs, that was for them. The companies also of marchants of those cities which stand vpon the Baltique sea, haue obtained the same, or greater priueledges, now euer since the time of *Lewes* the younger, and more solemnly confirmed by king *Charles* the eight: which a few yeares agoe were sent to king *Charles* the ninth (by *Danezay* the French ambafsadour, vnto the king of Denmarke) to be by him renewed. And yet this priueledge granted vnto those marchants, extendeth not vnto other strange marchants, which haue obtained the right of citisens, as hath bene adiudged by the priuie counsell. Of which so many and so great priueleges, by our kings graunted vnto straungers, our marchants could obtaine none in all Græcia, Asia, or Africa. For in our time when as *Crozile* a rich marchant of Tours, diing, had left behind him almost two hundred thousand crownes, nothing thereof came

vnto

F7–8 underfoot *i.e.* below its actual value   F10 subjects   H1 *For* place *read* places (L).
H1 straungers   H10 Fraunce   18–9 proved; yet   Notes at F10, G8, H8.

vnto his neerest kindred, all the same being by the Turkish emperor giuen vnto *Abraham* the chiefe of the Visier Bassaes.

There is yet another difference (besides those we haue alreadie spoke of) betwixt citisens and straungers; for that citisens by the auntient law *Pætilia* and *Iulia*, may forsake their goods, leauing them in satisfaction vnto their creditors, which the straunger may not doe: for otherwise it should bee lawfull for straungers, for their aduantage to sucke the blood and iuice of the subiects, and afterward to pay them with papers, although there be not fewer of these bankrups than of them that forsake their goods. This also a citisen differeth from a straunger, that the straunger in euerie place before he can plead in action, either reall or personall, must put in caution for the paiment of that which shall bee adiudged. Which caution our citisens, except they haue before plaid bankrupt, or forsaken their goods, are not bound to performe. But in a personall action, whether the defendant be a citisen or a straunger, he is not bound to put in caution to pay the thing that is adiudged, as was in auntient time determined, as well in the court of Rome, as in the court of Paris. But the same court hath departed from the opinion of our aunceftors, and adiudged it to be a thing reasonable, that the straunger whether he be plaintife or defendant, should put in caution to pay the thing that is adiudged. But there is one difference which is and hath alwaies bene common to al people, that is to wit, the right of marque against straungers, which hath no place against the subiects: for which cause the emperour *Frederick* the second, sent backe vnto the states of the empire, those which demaunded the right of reprisall against the subiects of the empire. And in briefe the straunger might be driuen out of the countrey, not onely in time of warre (for then we dismisse the ambassadours themselues) but also in time of peace; least the naturall subiects manners should by the euill companie of straungers be corrupted: for which onely cause *Lycurgus* seemeth to haue forbidden the Lacedemonians his subiects without leaue to depart out of his kingdome, or to haue the vse of gold or siluer; as the East Indians of China forbid their subiects vpon paine of death from receiuing of straungers: so to meet with the enterprises that the straunger might make against another mans estate. Wherefore *Cicero* well foresaw not what harmes hang (as it were) ouer our heads from straungers, when as he writ, They do euil which forbid straungers their cities, and cast them out, as with our auncestors *Penuus*, and of late *Papius*: For by such straungers, who for the most part are banished men, the good manners of the naturall subiects are corrupted. But if warre be proclaimed against the prince, the straunger may be detained as an enemie, according to the law of armes: whereas otherwise he might not be staied, if he had not otherwise bound himselfe by contract, or by some offence by him committed.

Now if the straunger shall against the will, or without the consent of his owne prince, submit himselfe vnto the power of another prince, and be of him also receiued for his subiect; yet hath his owne prince still for euer power ouer him, and authoritie to lay hands vpon him as vpon his fugitiue seruant; yea although he come as an ambassadour sent from his new prince. For so the emperour *Theodosius* the Great pronounced *Danus* the tyrant to be a rebell vnto his maiestie, and cast in prison his ambassadours, being subiect to his power. So the emperour *Charles* the fift did the like against the ambassadours of the duke of Millan his subiect, whom he detained prisoner, at such time as he vnderstood the duke his maister to haue entred into league with the other princes, and to haue proclaimed warre against him. And howbeit that the news thereof being come into Fraunce, *Granuellan*, *Charles* his ambassador, was by the kings commaundement there likewise imprisoned, yet was hee forthwith againe deliuered, so soone as it was vnderstood that the ambassadors and heralds of Fraunce, England, and Venice

Other differences betwixt a citisen and a straunger.

Plu. in Lycurg.

A straunger submitting himselfe vnto the power of another prince, is yet the subiect of his naturall prince.

Venice, were with safe conduct sent out of Spaine. Neither seemeth *Charles* in so doing to haue violated the law of nations, or to haue done any thing against the law: seethat the Romans did with greater seueritie punish the fugitiue subiect, than they did the verie enemie. And the best excuse that the Imperials could find to excuse the murther done vpon the persons of *Rincon* and *Fregosius* the French ambassadors toward the Turke, was, That the one of them was a Spaniard, a naturall subiect of the emperours, and the other a Genoway vnder his protection, both sent in the seruice of his enemie; the bruit being giuen out, that they went to raise new warres against him: howbeit that the emperour would not auouch the murther, but promised to do iustice vpon them that had done the same, if they should fall into his power. But doe the subiect what he can, yet can he not exempt himselfe from the power of his naturall soueraigne, albeit that he become a soueraigne prince in another mans countrey: no more than *Philip Barbarius* a slaue, who being for his vertue become Pretor of Rome, being pursued and chalenged by his maister, was yet glad to agree with him for his libertie. For in that the lawyers all agree, That the subiect in what place soeuer he bee become soueraigne, may by his prince be called home. As not long since *Elizabeth* queene of England called home againe vnto her the earle of Lineux, together with his son, who but a little before had maried the queene of Scots; for not obeying of which her command, she confiscated their goods, for that contrarie to the custome of that realme, they had without leaue departed out of England, and maried contrarie to the queenes commaundement. For the subiect wheresoeuer he be, is bound to the lawes of his prince conceiued, concerning his person; in such sort, as that if the subiect be forbidden to contract or to alienat, the alienations are void, albeit that he make them in a forren country, and of such goods as he hath without the territorie of his owne prince: and if the husband being out of his owne countrie, giue any thing vnto his wife, contrarie to the commaundement of his prince, or the customes of his country, such a donation is nothing worth: for that the power to tie and bind a subiect, is not tied vnto places. And for this cause princes haue accustomed to vse mutuall requests one towards another, either to call home their subiects, or to enforce them to obey, in such places as wherein they haue not power to commaund: or els by mutuall denouncing of their griefes themselues to lay hand vpon straungers, vntill that they doe obey them. For when the marquesse of Rotelin, who had the tuition of the duke of Longueuille, was sued vnto to suffer the controuersie of Neufchastel to be decided before the judges of the court of Requests at Paris: the lords of Berne reuoked the cause, for that iudgement was to be giuen by them, of lands contained within the precinct of their country. See here the principal differences of subiects and citisens, from strangers; leauing the particular differences of euerie countrey, which are in number infinit. As for the differences of subiects amongst themselues, there are in many places no fewer, or happely moe than betwixt the subiects and the straungers (whereof we haue much spoken before) as not onely of the difference of the nobilitie among themselues, but of the difference betwixt the nobilitie and the vulgar people also. But particularly to prosecute how much the vulgar people differ among themselues, with such other things as appertaine vnto the sex, age or state of euerie man, were a thing almost infinit.

Now to make the matter short, it may be that of right among citisens, some be exempted from all charges, taxes, and imposts, whereunto others are subiect: whereof wee haue infinit examples in our lawes. As also the societie is good and auailable, where some of the associats haue part in the profit, and yet beare no part of the losse. And that is it for which we see the diuision of citisens or subiects into three estates, that is to say, the Spiritualtie, the Nobilitie, and Commonaltie, which is obserued almost

No subiect can exempt himselfe from the power of his naturall prince.

New Castell.

The diuision of citisens or subiects into three estates, a thing obserued in all Commonweals.

G7 Lineux *i.e.* Lennox   K6 available *i.e.* valid, admissible in law

most in all Europe. And beside this so generall a diuision, there bee other more speciall in many Commonweales, as in Venice the gentlemen, the citisens, and the common people: in Florence before it was brought vnder one prince, they had the great ones, the common people, and the rascall menie. And our auntient Gauls had their Druides, their Chiualrie, and the vulgar people. In Ægypt the priests, the souldiers, and the artizans; as we read in *Diodorus*. Also the auntient law giuer *Hippodamus*, diuided the citisens into souldiors, handie-crafts men, and labourers; & hath without cause bene blamed by *Aristotle*; as we read in the Fragments of his ordinances. And albeit that *Plato* enforced himselfe to make all the citisens of his Commonwealth equall in all rights and prerogatiues; yet so it is, that he diuided them into three states; that is to wit, into Gouernours, Souldiors, and Laborers: which is to show that there was neuer Commonweale, were it true, or but imaginarie, or the most popular that a man could thinke of; where the the citisens were equall in all rights and prerogatiues; but that alwaies some of them haue had more or lesse than others.

* Lib. 2. Polit.

Chap. VII.

¶ *Of them that are vnder protection, and the difference betwixt Allies, Strangers, and Subiects.*

WE haue now alreadie told what difference there is betwixt Subiects, Citisens, and Straungers: let vs now also speake of Allies, and first of them which are in protection; for that there is not one of them which haue written of a Commonweale, which haue touched this string; which for all that is the most necessary for the vnderstanding of the states of Commonweales. The word of protection in generall extendeth vnto all subiects which are vnder the obeysance of one soueraigne prince or seignorie; as we haue said, That the prince is bound by force of armes, and of his lawes, to maintaine his subiects in suretie of their persons, their goods, and families: for which the Subiects by a reciprocall obligation owe vnto their prince, faith, subiection, obeysance, aid, and succour. This is the first and the strongest protection that is. For the protection of maisters towards their slaues, of patrons towards their enfranchised, of lords towards their vassals, is much lesse than that of princes towards their Subiects: insomuch that the slaue, the enfranchised, the vassall, oweth faith, homage, and succour, vnto his lord; but yet that is after his owne soueraigne prince, to whome he is a bound Subiect: the souldior also oweth obeysance and succour vnto his captaine; and by the law deserueth death, if hee defend him not at his need. Yet in all treaties and actions of peace betwixt princes & people in amitie and friendship ioyned together: the word of Protection is speciall, importing not any subiection of him that is in protection, neither commaund of the protecture towards his adherents, but onely an honourable and reuerent respect of the adherents towards their protector, who hath taken vpon him their defence and protection, without any other impeachment of the maiestie of the adherents ouer whome the Protector hath no power at all. So that the right of protection is well deemed to bee the greatest, fairest, and most honourable of all others that are amongst princes. For the soueraigne prince, the maister, the lord, the patron, draw vnto themselues great profit and obedience, for the defence of their subiects, their slaues, their enfranchised, and vassals: but the Protector is to content himselfe with the honour and acknowledgement of his adherent, seeing that of all duties of courtesie, none is greater, than as euerie man standeth in most need of helpe, so to giue him the greatest reliefe; neither of so great kindnesse to accept any other reward than thanks: for if hee couenant for any thing

Protection.

How in treaties of peace princes are said to be one of them in the protection of another.

To protect others is a thing most honourable.

D8 *For* protecture *read* protector.

thing farther, he looseth the name of a Protector. For as he which lendeth vnto another man part of his goods or trauell, if he receiue any gaine or profit thereby, he is no more to be called a lender, or that his doing to be tearmed a lending or pleasuring, but a meere mercinarie gaining: so he which hath liberally promised to doe any thing for another man, is without any hire by the law bound to accomplish his promise: and the reason is, for that vnto dutie no hire is due. Neither is there any band of promise stronger, or more effectuall, than that which is made to defend the goods, the life, the honor of the weake against the stronger, of the poore against the rich, of the good distressed against the violence of the wicked. And that is it for which *Romulus*, founder of the citie of Rome, setting in order the state of his subiects, to keepe them all at peace and vnitie among themselues, asigned vnto euery one of the hundred gentlemen, or Senators that he had chosen to be of his priuie counsell, a certaine number of his other meaner subiects, to be by them maintained vnder their protection and safegard; holding him accursed and execrable, who should leaue the defence of any his adherents. And the Censors marked them with the note of infamie, that had forsaken their adherents. The law also of the xij tables in that case carrieth with it the paine of excommunication, as in these words: *If the Patron deceiue his Client let him be accursed*. Yet *Plutarch* writeth, The clients to haue giuen money to the bestowing of their patrons daughters: which I remember not to haue bene elswhere written; for in so doing they should haue cosened their clients: but it may bee that he mistooke clients, for men enfranchised; who albeit that they be both called clients or adherents, yet is the bond of the enfranchised greater towards their patrons that set them at libertie; than is that of the free borne clients, who had no patrons but aduocats, who defended the causes of their clients. Howbeit with vs the patrons exact money of their enfranchised clients, the better to bestow their daughters, which is like enough to haue come from the Romans vnto vs. Now when that forren people saw the Roman clients or adherents to be safe from the iniurie and oppression of the more mightie, not onely euery particular man, but men euen generally, yea whole cities and prouinces yeelded themselues into the protection of the Senators. For so the house of the *Marcelles* had in their protection the citie of Syracusa, the *Antonies* had likewise the citie of Boulongne la Grasse: and so others afterwards tooke vpon them the protection and defence of others also. Yea the straungers in like case, that frequented the citie of Rome, had also their protectors, who by the law of application or patronage, tooke vnto them whatsoeuer the straunger dying in the citie possessed. And of these same Romans that filled Fraunce with the multitude of their Colonies, it is like this law of protection, which of the aduocats and not of the clients, they cal the law of *Auoison*, or *Auouerie* to haue taken beginning. But the enfranchised clients differ much from the free borne clients, albeit that they be both called clients, for the likenesse that is betwixt the one and the other) but especially in this, that the enfranchised clients may from their libertie be againe reduced into slauerie, if they shall be proued to haue bene vngratefull vnto their patrons whereas the free borne clients cannot so be. The enfranchised clients are constrained also to helpe their patrons with their labours: wheras the free borne clients are bound to reuerence their protectors or aduocats, and to do them mutuall kindnesse, but not seruile seruice or labour: neither if they haue done any thing to deceiue their patrons do they therefore loose their libertie: beside that the patrons suruiuing may by the law take part of the goods of their enfranchised clients: whereas the aduocats, or protectors can take nothing of the goods or inheritance of their free borne clients or adherents.

And although there be so many things common to the free borne clients, with the vassals or adherents, as that they are almost accounted for one, yet is there great difference

How whole cities sometimes put themselues into the protection of some one honourable house of the Roman Senators.

Great difference betwixt the free borne clients and the clients enfranchised.

F 1–2 unto another man   F 6 band *i.e.* bond   I 3 unto them   I 7 clients (albeit
Notes at F 5, G 5, K 8.

OF A COMMONWEALE. 71

rence betwixt them. For the vassall is bound with all fidelitie to honour and reuerence his lord, to helpe him being in daunger, and to do him all the kindnesse possible: and if so be that he shall deceiue his lord, disgrace him, perfidiously abiure him, or giue him the lye: hee by and by looseth therefore his fee, which escheateth vnto his lord by the right which the lord hath against his vassall in such case: whereas from the vndutifull or vnkind client, or adherent, nothing can at all be taken. Moreouer if the vassall hath without any exception giuen his faith vnto his lord, or acknowledge no man greater than him; whether he be sworne or not, he is bound vnto the subiection & command of him the same his lord and prince: whereof he cannot be said to be discharged, albeit that he neuer so much renounce his fee: whereas the client or adherent standeth not in these tearmes, being in nothing subiect to his aduocat or protectour. The vassall also whether he be a king or pope, or whatsoeuer els oweth faith and seruice vnto the lord of whome he holdeth his fee, except he renounce the fee: whereas the free borne client or adherent, whether he be prince or priuat man, is free from all seruice and commaund of his more mightie aduocat or protectour. In briefe the right of a vassallage seemeth in a manner to be but new, and before the comming of the Lombards into Italie vnknowne: whereas the law of protection is most auntient and before the time of *Romulus*, who borrowed it of the Greeks: for it was long before vsed in Thessalie, Ægypt, Asia, and Sclauonia, as we read in auntient writers: that so the weaker might be the safer from the violence or iniurie of the more mightie. The vassall also receiueth inheritance and fees of his lord, from whose fealtie and obesance which he oweth vnto him, he cannot bee exempted, albeit that the soueraigne prince should raise the fee of his vassall depending of him into a countie, dutchie, or principalitie, as hath beene adiudged by the decree of the parliament of Paris. Whereby it is to be vnderstood them to erre and be deceiued, who out of *Cæsars* Commentaries interpret them whome he calleth *Soldurios et deuotos*, to be vassals, seeing that hee hath made no mention of their fee, without which they cannot so be, ioyning thereunto also, that they were indeed true and naturall subiects: for that their liues, their goods, and their persons, were consecrated vnto their lord: which is the true marke of subiection, which the vassals owe onely vnto their soueraigne prince, not in the qualitie of vassals, but in the qualitie of naturall subiects, who ought to runne the same fortune with their prince, and to liue and die for him if need bee, albeit that the vassall bee more specially bound, than the other subiects.

The difference betwixt the free borne client and the vassall. This right is of the Latins called Ius commissi: & of the French Droit de commise.

Vassalage but new: protection most auntient.

All which things tend to this purpose, that it may plainely be perceiued, what and how much difference there is betwixt the rights of patronage, vassallage, and protection, which we see to bee of many for the likenesse among themselues confounded. For the vassall and the adherent owe their fidelitie vnto their lord and protector; and the one of them are reciprocally bound vnto the other, albeit that the lord be not bound by expresse word to giue his oath of fidelitie to his vassall, as the protector ought to his client or adherent, and so solemnly to keepe all the treaties of protection. The lord and the vassell also ought to deliuer solemne letters of their mutuall obliging of themselues the one to the other: like as the protectour and the adherent, are bound to giue letters of protection the one of them to the other: but especially if one soueraigne prince vpon a league made, receiue another soueraigne prince into his protection, which are to be renewed either of the princes dying. For the right of protection belongeth not vnto the heires, except the same be in the league so comprised: and bee it neuer so prouided for yet neuerthelesse either of the princes being dead, it is needful for his successor by lawfull acts to professe his protection, & to haue the league renewed. But to make more manifest the matter of protection betwixt soueraigne princes, whereof

The difference betwixt patronage, vassallage, and protection.

A7 (margin) commise   B2 els, oweth   C3 of his vassall depending of him *i.e.* of the undervassal (Fr)
E6 comprised

whereof we are to entreat: it seemeth that the soueraigne prince or people, which hath put it selfe into the protection of another, is become his subiect. And if he be a subiect, then is he no more a soueraigne, and his subiects shall also be the subiects of the protector. And what subiection would a man haue greater, than to put himselfe into the protection of another man, and to acknowledge him for his superiour? For protection betwixt great princes, is nothing else but the confederation and alliance of two princes, or soueraigne lords, wherein the one acknowledgeth the other for superiour; whome he bindeth himselfe to obserue and reuerence, and into whose protection hee is receiued, so to be the safer from the iniurie of some other more mightie: also when the subiect of a prince retireth himselfe into the territorie of another prince, hee is likewise in his protection; in such sort, as that if he be pursued after by the enemie, & taken prisoner in the territorie of another soueraigne prince, hee is not prisoner of him that pursueth him, but of him into whose territorie he hath fled: as was iudged by the law of armes at the interparle of peace, which was betwixt the French king & the emperor *Charls* the fift, in the yere 1555, when question was made of the imperial prisoners that the French had taken in the countie of Guynes, which was then in the subiection of the English; it was maintained by the Chancellor of England, That they could not be detained as prisoners, being taken in the territorie and protection of the English: howbeit that the contrarie might be said: for albeit it was not permitted to pursue or take prey in another mans territorie, yet it is lawfull hauing raised it in his owne territorie, to pursue it into another mans ground: which yet suffereth this exception, If the lord of the ground forbid him not so to do: as did the lord *Grey*, gouernour of Calais and Guines, who comming in the time of the pursute, was said to haue taken the flying Spaniards into his protection, although that they were carried away by the French. Now in this case the word Protection, is not taken in proper signification; for there is no protection, if there be no conuention: and the strange prince cannot take another princes subiect into his protection without the consent of his owne prince, as wee shall hereafter declare.

What protection betwixt great princes is.

But yet before let vs determine the propounded question, Whether a soueraigne prince submitting himself vnto another soueraigne prince, looseth the right of his own soueraigntie; and whether he become subiect to the other? For it seemeth that he is no soueraigne, acknowledging a greater than himselfe. Neuerthelesse I am of opinion that he continueth still a soueraigne, and not a subiect. And this point is decided by a law, whereof there is not the like, and hath in diuers readings bene altered: but we follow the originall of the Pandects of Florence, which hold, That soueraigne princes who in treatie of alliance acknowledge the protectour to bee greater than themselues, are not yet for al that their subiects. I doubt not (saith the law) but that allies, and other people vsing their libertie are not straungers vnto vs, &c. And albeit that in the treatie of confederats and allies, by vnequall alliance, it be expresly said, That one of them shall respectiuely regard the maiestie of the other; that maketh not that hee should bee therefore his subiect, no more than our adherents and clients are lesse free than our selues, although they be not equall with vs, neither in goods, power, nor honour. And the ordinarie clause inserted into the treaties of vnequall alliance in these words, *Comiter maiestatem conseruare* (that is to say, curteously to preserue the maiestie of the greater) importeth no other thing, but that betwixt the princes allied the one is greater and more honourable than the other; and that the lesser allies should in al modestie respect the greater. So that it euidently appeareth, that protection importeth not subiection, but the superioritie and prerogatiue of honour. And the more cleerely to vnderstand this point, and the nature of treaties and alliances, we may say that all treaties amongst princes

Whether a soueraigne prince submitting himselfe vnto the protection of another prince, looseth thereby his own soueraignty, and so becommeth the other princes subiect.

Protection importeth not subiection.

princes are made either with friends, enemies, or newters. The treaties betwixt enemies, are made to haue peace and amitie, or truce, or to compose warres begun for seignories or for persons, or to redresse the iniuries and displeasures of one of them against the other, or for traffick and hospitalitie that might bee betwixt enemies during the time of truce. As for the others which are not enemies, the treaties which are made with them, are either by alliance equall, or vnequall: in this the one acknowledgeth the other to be superiour in the treatie of alliance; which is in two sorts, that is to wit, when the one acknowledgeth the other to be his superiour for honour, and yet is not in his protection: or els the one receiueth the other into protection, and both the one and the other is bound to pay a certaine pention, or to giue certaine succours; or els owe neither pention nor succours. As for allies by alliance equall, which the Latines call *Æquo fœdere*, the qualitie is vnderstood, when the one is in nothing superiour vnto the other in the treatie: and that the one hath nothing aboue the other for their prerogatiue of honour, albeit that the one must do or giue more or lesse than the other for the aid that the one oweth vnto the other. And in this sort of treatie, they haue alwaies entreated of amitie, traffique, and hospitalitie, to harbour the one with the other, and to traffique together with all kind of marchandise, or some certaine kindes onely, and at the charge of certaine imposts agreed vpon by the treaties. And both the one and the other alliance is of two sorts, that is to wit, defensiue onely, or defensiue and offensiue; and yet may be both the one & the other, without exception of person, or with the exception of certaine princes: and the most strait alliance is that which is both defensiue and offensiue, towards all, and against all; as to be a friend to friends, and an enemie to enemies; and so most commonly order is taken, and treaties of mariages one of them had with the other. But yet the alliance is more strong, when as one king is allied with another king, realme with realme, and one man with another man; as were in auntient times the kings of Fraunce and Spaine, and the kings of Scotland and Fraunce. And that was it for which the ambassadours of Fraunce aunswered *Edward* the fourth, being driuen out of the realme of England, That the king could not giue him aid, for that the alliances of Fraunce and England were made with the kings, and the realmes, in such sort that king *Edward* chased out of his realme, the league continued with the realme and the king that therein raigned: the effect of which words was this, *With such a king, his countries, territories, and seignories*: which words are as it were in all treaties expressed. But these treaties ought also to bee published in soueraigne courts or parliaments, and ratified by the estates, by the consent of the Atturney generall, as was decreed in the treatie made betwixt king *Lewes* the eleuenth, and *Maximilian* the arch duke, in the yeare 1482. The third sort of alliance is that of neutralitie, which is neither defensiue nor offensiue, which may be betwixt the subiects of two princes being enemies; as those of the Franche-countie haue alliance of neutralitie with the house of Fraunce, and are assured in time of warre: in which alliance was also comprised the countrie of Bassigny, by the decree of Bade in the yeare 1555, in confirming with the king the renouation of the neutralitie for the Franch-countie. And all these aforesaid alliances are perpetuall, or limited to a certaine time, or for the life of princes, and some yeares more, as is alwaies in treaties of alliance agreed vpon betwixt the kings of Fraunce, and the lords of the leagues.

And thus much for the generall diuision of all the treaties which are made betwixt princes, vnder the which are comprehended all the particular alliances. For as for the diuision of the Roman ambassadors, at the enterparle of peace betwixt them and *Antiochus* the great, it is verie short. *Liuie* saith, *Tria sunt Genera fœderum, vnum cum bello victis dicerentur leges: alterum cum pares bello æquo fœdere in pacem & amicitiam venirent:*

Alliance equall, or vnequall. Vnequall of two sorts.

Alliance equall.

Alliance defensiue only, or both defensiue and offensiue.

Alliance of neutralitie.

B2 *For* the qualitie *read* the equalitie (cf. 770 H5, 776 H8, 784 I10).

rent: tertium cum qui hostes nunquam fuerunt in amicitiam fœdere coeunt, qui neque dicunt neque accipiunt leges. There are (saith he) three kinds of leagues or confederations; one, when as lawes and conditions are appointed to them that be in battell ouercome: another when men in warre equall come together in like league into peace & friendship: the third, when as they which neuer were enemies, by league ioyne in amitie, who neither giue nor take lawes. All the others, which are neither subiects nor allies, are either coallies, or enemies, or newters without alliance or hostilitie, who all generally, if they be not subiects (bee they allies, coallies, enemies, or newters) are straungers. The coallies are the allies of our allies, which are not for all that our allies, no more than the companion of our associat is our companion; who yet neuerthelesse either in generall or speciall tearmes, are alwaies in all leagues comprised. As the lords of the three confederats of the Grises, the antient allies of the Swissers, were in expresse tearmes comprised in the treatie of alliance made in the yere 1531, betwixt king *Frances* the first of that name, and the Swissers, in qualitie of coallies. But in the yeare 1550 they were allies vnto the house of France, and comprised in the treatie of alliance renewed betwixt king *Henrie* and the Swissers, in qualitie of allies by alliance equall, in like degree and pension with the Swissers, that is to wit 5000 pound, for euerie league or confederacie, to take away the partialitie that was betwixt the one and the others. For although the Swissers were allied with the league of the Grises, by alliance equall by the treatie made betwixt the Grisons and the seuen little Cantons, in the yeare 1498: so it was yet neuerthelesse that they constrained the lords of the leagues of the Grises to obey the decrees made in their diets, if it should be there otherwise determined; which was like to haue broken the alliance betwixt the Grisons and the Swissers, in the yeare 1565, for no other cause, (as said the Grisons) than to make the Swissers to know that they were their equals in alliance: but the truth is, that the emperour practised vnder hand, and gaue eleuen thousand crownes vnto certaine of the most factious of the Grisons, to make head, as they confessed afterwards being put to torture, and were condemned in a fine of ten thousand crownes; as I haue learned out of the Commentaries and letters of the French ambassadours, which then was sent vnto the Grisons. Wee haue also example of them of Geneua, who were comprised in the treaties of alliance made betwixt the house of Fraunce and the Bernois, in whose protection they then were; and so were since the yeare 1527, vnto the yere 1558, that they exempted themselues out of protection, and entreated in alliance equall, and haue alwaies in alliance bene comprised in the qualitie of coallies.

Coallies who they be.
Coallies alwaies comprised in the league of their allies.

But as those alliances which are defensiue and offensiue towards and against all persons without exception, are of all others the straitest and strongest: so also there is no alliance more vnsure or weaker, than the simple alliance of commerce and traffique which may be euen betwixt enemies: which although it may seeme to bee grounded vpon the law of nations, yet we see it oftentimes to bee forbidden by princes in their own countries, least their subiects should riotously abuse the store of things broght in, or be pinched with the want of things carried out. And for this cause princes haue in this respect vsed particular treaties, & granted certaine special priueleges & liberties: as in the treaty of commerce or traffick betwixt the house of France & the port towns of the Easterlings, & the Milanois with the Swissers; wherein they are by the treaties of commerce bound to deliuer a certain quantitie of graine, at a certain price expressed in the said treaties, which the French ambassadors would oftentimes haue broken, for the doubt that the Swissers made to enter vpon the Milanois, enemies vnto the French, for feare the transportation of corne shuld haue bene forbidden: which when the gouernor of Millan had done, in the yeare 1550, the Swissers were vpon the point to haue made alliance

No alliance more vnsure or weake, than the simple alliance of commerce and traffick.

F7 are either   G3 *For* 1531 (Fr 7) *read* 1521 (Fr 1-6, 8 and L). Cf. 633 K2.   K3-4 port towns of the Easterlings *i.e.* the Baltic or Hanseatic towns

alliance defensiue with the Millanois, or at leastwise to haue had them excepted amongst the confederats as newters. The force of which league was, that such as were in the same league excepted, could not become prisoners to any the confederats; when as yet for all that straungers, although they were no enemies, were by the law prisoners to them that tooke them: For so *Pomponius* writeth vnto *Quintus Mutius*: For (saith he) if we haue neither friendship nor hospitalitie, nor league of amitie with any nation, these truely are not enemies: yet what thing soeuer of ours falleth into their hands becommeth theirs; insomuch that a free man borne of ours, by them taken, becommeth their slaue; and so likewise it is, if any thing come from them to vs: thus much he. But this law we now vse not, for regard of that curtesie which ought to bee betwixt man and man. But by the name of enemies we vnderstand them vnto whome we, or they vnto vs, haue publickly denounced warre; or els without any denuntiation haue of fact made warre vpon vs: as for the rest they are to be deemed of, as of theeues or pirats, with whome we ought to haue no societie or communitie. In auntient time also there was a treatie of alliance to haue iustice done them in a straunge citie, as we read in the books of the Grecians; but at length by the great consent and agreement of all nations, the port of iustice hath by little and little bene still opened, as well to strangers as to citisens.

Who indeed are to be accounted enemies.

But in euerie alliance, league, confederation, or conuention whatsoeuer, it behoueth that the lawes of maiestie be vnto euerie prince or people reserued safe and vntouched: for otherwise the one should fall into the power and mercie of the other; as the weaker oftentimes are by the power & might of the stronger enforced to receiue lawes; which is not so in the treaties of alliance equall: wherein euen little cities are in the indifferent lawes of leagues equall vnto most mightie kings and people, being not bound either to obserue the maiestie of their more mightie confederats, or to giue them place. As a man may see in that treatie of alliance made betwixt the kings of Persia, & the seignorie of Thebes: For albeit that the Persian empire was bounded almost with the same bounds that the course of the sunne was, *viz.* from the riuage of Hellespontus vnto the remotest parts of India; and that the citie of Thebes was enclosed but in strait wals, and the countrey of Beotia; yet for all that were they both in the league of their alliance equall. Now where we said, that in alliance of protection, the protector hath a prerogatiue of honour; that is not to be vnderstood onely, that hee ought to be the chiefe allie, as was *Lewes* the eleuenth the French king with the Swissers, who did him that honour aboue the duke of Sauoy, who was before the chiefe: For alwayes the soueraigne prince be he neuer so little, in alliance equall, is maister in his owne house, and holdeth the first place aboue all other princes comming into his countrie: but if the protector himselfe come, he is the first both in sitting and all other honours.

In all alliances the soueraigntie is still vnto all Princes, & people to bee reserued safe and vntouched.

But here might one say, Why should allies in league defensiue & offensiue against all without exception, vsing the same customes, the same lawes, the same state, the same diets, be reputed straungers one to another? Wee haue hereof example of the Swissers, who are allied amongst themselues, with such alliance as I haue said, since the yeare 1315; yet say I neuerthelesse that such alliance letteth not, but that they are still straungers one vnto the other, and maketh not that they are one citisens to the other. We haue also hereof example of the Latines, and the Romans, who were allies in league defensiue and offensiue, vsed the same customes, the same armes, the same language, and had the same friends and enemies: Whereupon the Latines maintained, that it was and ought to be one and the selfe same Commonweale; and therfore by their ambassadours demaunded to haue their part in the estate & offices of Rome, as had the Romans themselues. *Si societas* (said they) *equatio iuris est, si socialis exercitus*

Alliance maketh not but that men may still bee one of them strangers vnto another, & not of the same Cittie or Commonweale.

H ij

tus illis est quo duplicent vires suas; cur non omnia æquantur? cur non alter ab Latinis Consul datur? Vbi pars virium, ibi & imperij pars est. And immediatly after, *Vnum populum, vnam rempublicam fieri æquum est. Tum Consul Romanus. Audi Iupiter hæc scelera: peregrinos Consules, & peregrinum Senatum in tuo templo, &c.* If societie (said they) be an equalitie of right, if they haue their allies armie, whereby they double their strength: why then are not all things made equall? why is not one of the Consuls chosen of the Latines? where part of the strength is, there should also part of the gouernment be. And immediatly after, It is but right that there should bee but one people and one Commonweale. Then said the Roman Consull, Heare ô *Iupiter* these villanies, straunge Consuls, and a straunge Senat in thy temple, &c. So hee calleth them straungers which were allied vnto the Romans with the strongest alliance that was possible to deuise, insomuch that they seemed to be all of one and the selfe same citie. Yea *Festus* teacheth vs the Municipes (or enfranchised men) not to haue bene citisens: whose words we haue thought good here to set downe: *Municipium id genus hominum dicitur, qui cum Romam venissent, neque ciues Romani essent, participes tamen fuerunt omnium rerum ad munus fungendum vnà cum Romanis ciuibus, præterquam de suffragio ferendo aut magistratu capiendo: sicut fuerunt Fundani, Formiani, Cumani, Acerrani, Lanuuini, Tusculani, qui post aliquot annos ciues Romani effecti sunt. Alio modo id genus hominum dicitur, quorum ciuitas vniuersa in ciuitatem Romanam venit, vt Aricini, Cerites, Anagnini. Tertio definiuntur ij qui ad ciuitatem Romanam ita venerunt, vt Municipia essent suæ cuiusque ciuitatis coloniæ, vt Tiburtes, Prænestini, Pisani, Arpinates, Nolani, Bononienses, Placentini, Sutrini, Lucenses.* That kind of men (saith hee) is called Municipials, who comming to Rome and being no citisens, were yet partakers of all things together with the Roman citisens, except in giuing of voyces, and bearing of offices; as were the *Fundani*, the *Formiani*, the *Cumani*, the *Acerrani*, the *Lanuuini*, and the *Tusculani*, who after certaine yeares were made citisens of Rome. And otherwise that sort of men is so called also, whose whole citie came into the citie of Rome; as the *Aricini*, the *Cerites*, and the *Anagnini*. And thirdly they who so came vnto the citie of Rome, as that the Colonies of euerie citie were accounted Municipials; as were the *Tiburts*, the *Prænestini*, the *Pisani*, the *Arpinates*, the *Nolani*, the *Bononienses*, the *Placentini*, *Sutrini*, and *Lucenses*.

That the Cantons of the Swissers are not one but diuers Commonweales.

Now many I see to be in the same errour, as that the Swissers for like reason are all but one Commonweale: and yet it is most certaine that they be thirteene Commonweals, holding nothing one of another, but euerie one of them hauing the soueraignty thereof diuided from the rest. In former time their countrey was but one member of the German empire, gouerned by the emperours deputie. The first that rebelled were the inhabitants of Schwits, Vri, and Vnderuald, who treated of alliance both defensiue and offensiue, in the month of December, in the yeare 1315: whereof the first article was, That none of them should more admit the commaund of any prince, or endure any soueraigne prince ouer him. And afterwards in the yeare 1332 alliance was made of foure Cantons, which were called the foure townes of the wood, *viz.* Vri, Schwits, and Lucerne. And in the yeare 1351, Zurith entred into alliance with these foure. And in the yeare 1352 Zug was also receiued with these fiue; and the yeare following Berne. And afterwards in the yeare 1393, was made the treatie of Sempach (after that the nobilitie of the Swissers was by the commonaltie discomfited and ouerthrowne) wherein they of Zurich, Lucerne, Berne, Soleure, Zug, Vri, Schwits, Vnderuald, and Glaris, entred into alliance defensiue and offensiue; which they renewed in the yeare 1481. Basill was also receiued in the yeare 1501: Schaffuse also and Apenzel in the yeare 1513, Mulhouse in the yeare 1520, Rotwill in the yeare 1519. The Valesians also

The beginning of the Swissers revolt from the Empire, and the first establishing of their Commonweales.

in

K1–2 Schwits, UNDERUALD, and Lucerne   K2 *For* Zurith (Fr 7) *read* Zurich (Fr 3–6, 8; but Suric in Fr 1–2).   K8 1501, and Schaffuse also;   K9 *For* 1520 (Fr 7) *read* 1515 (Fr 1–6, 8 and L).
Note at K9.

OF A COMMONWEALE. 77

A in the yeare 1528, with whom beside the auntient treatie, a particular treatie was made betwixt them and the Bernoies for league defensiue. Bienne also entred into league offensiue and defensiue with the Bernoies, in the yere 1352, after that they had exempted themselues out of the power of the bishop of Basill their soueraigne prince. All which treaties of alliance, the abbat of Orbez, ambassadour for the French king vnto the Swissers, hath let me see. Whereby a man may not onely note the pluralitie of Commonweals, but the diuersitie of alliances also. For they of Berne may summon the three little Cantons of Vri, Schwits, and Vnderuald, vnto their succour, by vertue of their first league: and they of Zurich and Berne, may reciprocally summon the one the other: they of Lucerne may of eight Cantons summon fiue: And the three little
B Cantons of Schwits, Vri, and Vnderuald, may summon all the rest of the Cantons vnto their aid, if they chaunce to be inuaded, and that for diuers causes. The assemblies of al the Swissers, except the Rhætians, them of Geneua, and the Valesians, are holden euerie yeare: and whatsoeuer is decreed by the greater part of the ambassadours of the cities, bindeth them all in particular, and the lesser part of the whole in common. The last that entred into the league vnder the protection of the Bernois, were they of Geneua. All these allies, confederats, and coallies, made two and twentie Commonweales, with the abbat of St. Gal a soueraigne prince; all seperated in soueraigntie, and euerie one of them hauing their magistrats apart, their state apart, their bursse, their demaine and territorie apart. In briefe, their armies, their crie, their name, their money,
C their seale, their assemblies, their iurisdiction, their ordinances in euerie estate diuided. And if one of the Cantons of themselues get any thing, the rest haue no part therein: as the Bernoies haue well giuen to vnderstand: For since they entred into the league, they haue ioined vnto their own domesticall gouernment little lesse than fortie towns, vpon whome they leuie men and money, and giue vnto them lawes: ouer which the other Cantons haue no power at all: as was iudged by *Frauncis* the first, the French king, by them chosen arbitrator in this matter. They of Basil also, when in the yeare 1560 they had lent fiftie thousand crownes vnto the French king, they tooke the Canton of Soleure to themselues in caution: but hauing by the common aid of al the Cantons taken in the bailiwike of Lugan, with certaine other lands beyond the moun-
D taines; euerie Canton by turne one after another, sent thither their magistrats and gouernours, for the administration of iustice; that so vnto euery Canton of the Swissers might be reserued their right and due. The towne also of Bade, where they commonly hold their yearely assemblies or diets, is common vnto eight Cantons, which after the victorie of Sempech ioyned in league together. It is also (as I suppose) wel known vnto all men, how that they are not all of one and the same religion, but to bee therein diuided, and had therfore oftentimes taken vp arms one of them against another, if the French king had not wisely prouided therfore; as well for the sincere loue and affection hee bare vnto them, as for the notable interest hee had to maintaine them in peace: for that of their health and welfare the securitie of Fraunce seemeth almost wholy
E to depend.

But vnto manie it may seeme, that they altogether make but one estate, considering that, that which is decreed in their diets in common, bindeth euerie one of the Cantons, and the lesser part of them all: as the seuen Cantons Catholike gaue well to vnderstand vnto the foure Cantons Protestants, at the diet holden in September, in the yeare 1554, insomuch that the common countrie situat beyond the mountaines, diuided in religion, and gouerned by the magistrats that euerie Canton sendeth thither by turne; it chaunced that the seuen Cantons Catholike caused them of the common countrey to bind themselues not to chaunge the religion Catholike: and so following

Geneua the last that entred into league with the Swissers, vnder the protection of the Bernois.

The Cantons of the Swissers diuided among themselues for religion.

H iij the

B9 bursse *i.e.* treasury   B10 *For* armies *read* armes.   Notes at C1, E1.

the same obligation would afterwards haue proceeded against them of the religion there, against whome the cantons protestants opposed themselues, and were now readie to haue entred into armes, had not the ambassadour of Fraunce stept in betwixt them, and wisely pacified the matter: yet for all that with this prouiso, That the common subiects of the religion should be punished (for chaunging their religion, contrary vnto the league) if the greater part of the cantons should be of that opinion, and that the cantons catholike should neuerthelesse redeliuer the letters obligatorie of the common subiects. By which meane their differences were againe well appeased. Wherunto the cantons of Glaris and Apenzel serued in good stead; who indifferently receiued both the one and the other religion, and made as it were an equall counterpoise betwixt the one of them and the other. So that it appeareth that the greater part of the cantons bindeth the lesse, and euerie one of them in particular. Yea and that more is, *None of the cantons may make alliance with any prince, without the whole consent of the rest of the cantons* none of the cantons may haue alliance with any prince whatsoeuer without the whole consent of the rest. As the cantons protestants hauing made alliance with *Philip* the Landgraue of Hessen, and the seignorie of Strasburg, in the yeare 1532, were by the rest of their allies enforced againe to depart from the same. As in like case the cantons catholike were compelled to renounce their new alliance made with the house of Austria. And albeit that the fiue cantons catholike Lucerne, Vri, Schwits, Vnderuald, and Zug, had made alliance with Pope *Pius* the fourth, for the defence of their religion; yet could they not with any rewards (were they neuer so great) be enduced to renew the same with his successours. But when treatie was had, for alliance to bee made betwixt *Frauncis* the first, the French king, and the Swissers, nothing more letted the same, than the opposition of the cantons protestants; who before instructed in the new religion, and persuaded by the earnest sermons of *Zuinglius* their preacher, who affirmed it to be vnlawfull for them to serue straunge princes in their warres, preuailed so much, that his followers and countrie men would no other wise make alliance with the king, but by the way of peace and friendship onely. But the leagues renewed with *Henry* the second, they of Basil and Schaffuse, with the catholike cities, ioyned themselues vnto the French, not in league of friendship onely, but in giuing of their aid also: when as for al that, they of Zuric and Berne, in the yeare 1554, forbad their subiects vpon paine of death to serue the French king in his warres. And the same yere the gouernors of the canton of Vnderuald, requested by the cardinall of Trent, That by their leaue hee might leuie certaine men in their countrey; forbad their subiects in generall, vppon paine of death, and confiscation of their goods, to go to serue any other prince than the French king: which are all vndoubted arguments to shew, that among the Swissers there are as many Commonweals as there are cities or cantons. In like case the three confederat cities of the Grisons, which consist of fiftie companies or fellowships, haue their gouernments diuers one from another; and yet as oft as they haue their assemblies, the greatest citie of the Grisons vseth to send thereunto eight and twentie deputies, the second twentie foure, and the last fourteene: with power, that whatsoeuer the greatest part of these their deputies shall agree vpon, in matters concerning their common societie, shall bind euery one of them in particular: and sometimes also in matters of greater importance all the people assemble themselues. Wherefore they are deceiued, which of those three cities would make one Commonweale. For common assemblies and meetings, common demaines, common enemies and friends, make not the same Commonweale; no not although they haue the same bourse, or certaine common treasure: but the soueraigntie of power that euerie one hath to commaund or restraine their subiects: as in like case, if many heads of families should become partners of all their goods, yet should they not therefore make one and the selfe same familie.

lie. The same opinion we may haue of the alliance contracted betwixt the Romans and the rest of the townes of Italie, combined in league both offensiue and defensiue, against all men without exception: who yet neuerthelesse were diuers Commonweales, diuided both in their assemblies and soueraigntie. The like we may say of the league of the seuen townes of the Amphictioniques, who had their meetings and soueraigntie diuided: to whose example most of the townes and seignories of Greece afterwards entred into the same league and confederation, for the deciding of their controuersies: and euerie yeare euery seignorie sent their ambassadours and deputies vnto the common estates, where the greatest affaires, proceedings, and differences, betwixt the princes and seignories, were determined by their deputies, whom they called *Myrios*: by whom the Lacedemonians were condemned to the seignorie of Thebes, in the summe of thirtie thousand crownes: and for not obaying the decree, were condemned in double thereof: for that contrarie to the treatie of peace, they had surprised the castle of Cadmee. The Phocences also afterwards when they had robbed the holy treasure at Delphos, were by the decree of the Amphictioniques, enioyned to restore the money by them so euill taken out of the temple: for default of which doing, all their country was adiudged vnto the treasurie of the temple: so that if there were any person which shewed himselfe disobedient vnto the decrees of the Amphictioniques, he therefore incurred the indignation of all Greece.

Here might one say, That all Greece was but one Commonweale, considering the power of the Amphictioniques: and yet neuerthelesse there were almost as many diuers Commonweales, as cities, holding nothing one of them of another, neither of the states of the Amphictioniques; but that they had so promised one to another, as princes haue accustomed to promise among themselues, and to chuse their allies for their arbitrators: which neither the Lacedemonians, nor the Phocenses had done, neither could against their wils be of right thereunto enforced. Yea the Phocenses to giue the Amphictioniques to vnderstand that they had no power ouer them, pluckt downe and tore in peeces the decrees of the Amphictioniques, fastened vnto the pillers of the temple of Delphos. Yet true it is, that *Philip* king of Macedon (beeing himselfe none of the league) tooke hereupon occasion to denounce the sacred warre vnto the Phocenses, and to ruinat their state: and in recompence therof obtained the place and priueleges of the Phocenses: the Lacedemonians being also excluded out of the league of the Amphictioniques, for hauing giuen vnto them succours. The like league almost we also find to haue bene amongst the auntient Gaules, as is to bee seene in the Commentaries of *Cæsar*, where he saith, That *Vercingentorix* chosen their generall, caused all the states of Gaule to be assembled. And albeit that the lords of Autun, of Chartres, of Gergoye in Auuergne, and of Beauuois, held nothing one of them of another; and that the seignorie of Bourges was in the protection of Autun, and those of Viarron in the protection of Bruges, and so consequently the other townes in like sort: yet so it was, that all the princes and seignories passed their differences by the decrees and iudgements of the Druydes; vnto whose censure if they refused to obey, they were by them excommunicated, and so of euerie man shunned, as men of all others most detestable. And yet is it most manifest that these Commonweales which I haue spoken of, had their soueraignties diuided one of them from another, the territories of their cities certainely bounded out, and euery one of them their owne proper state and maiestie.

The alliance of the auntient Commonweals of Gaule.

But it may also happen, that to become but one estate, one Commonweale, & one seignorie, when the partners of one league doe agree in the same soueraigntie: a thing not easie to be iudged, if a man looke not neere into it. As the league of the Achæans was

The league of the Achæans.

was not at the first but of three cities, diuided in estate, assemblies, and soueraigntie; allies by alliance equal, both defensiue & offensiue: who hauing the same enemies & the same friends, yet at the beginning kept euery one of them vnto themselues the maiesty of their owne citie. But being troubled with continuall warres, and enforced to hold their often assemblies, they by little and little became so straitly vnited together, that in fine they became but one Commonwealth composed of many: and in tract of time drew vnto their estate all the townes and cities of Achaia and Morea, they all retaining still the first name of the Achæans. As it happened vnto them of the league, whome they call Swissers; for that the canton of Schwits, the least of all the rest, was the first that reuolted, after that they had slaine their gouernor. And as the Achaians were called the correctors of tirants, so also the Swissers (to their great praise) carried this title of honour. The townes also of the kingdome of Naples, after the massacre of the Pithagorians, being much troubled, and not knowing vnto whome to haue recourse, cast themselues into the protection of the Achaians. But the author and meane of all these cities, to make one and the same Commonweale, was *Aratus*, who procured it to be decreed by the estates, That euerie yere one chiefe generall should bee chosen to commaund in their warres, and to gouerne their estates: and hee was prince of the Achaians, that is to say, the first that called together their assemblies. And whereas before euerie citie sent their ambassadours and deputies with instructions vnto the assemblie of the Achaians (as the Swissers vse to doe) there to giue their voyces deliberatiue: *Aratus* brought to passe, that the assemblie of the ambassadours and deputies so sent, should make choyce of ten principall men, whome they called Demiurges, who alone had voices deliberatiue, and power to resolue, to determine, and decide matters of state: the rest of the ambassadours and deputies hauing onely voyces consultatiue. These two points gained, there by little and little grew vp an Aristocraticall Commonweale, in stead of diuers particular Monarchies, Aristocraties, and popular Seignories: many tyrants partly for loue, partly for feare, being drawne thereunto. Now all the spoyle of the enemies, and conquests made by the generals, were not any one cities, but belonged to them all. So that at length such was the vnion and consent of the confederats, that all the townes of Achaia and Morea being made subiect, vnited, and incorporat vnto the state of the Achaians, vsed the same lawes, the same right, the same customes, the same religion, the same tongue, the same language, the same discipline, the same manners, the same money, the same weights and measures, as saith *Polybius*. The kings of Macedon entred also into this league; yea the two *Philips*, *Antigonus*, and *Demetrius*, were chosen chiefe captaines of the Achaians, holding neuerthelesse their realme seperated apart from the seignorie of the Achaians. And the Romans knowing well that they could not possibly conquer Greece, the league of the Achæans standing whole, gaue commaundement vnto *Gallus* their Proconsull, by all meanes possible to doe what he might to breake the same; which hee not in vaine attempted. For diuers cities complaining vnto the states, that vnder colour of a league and alliance equall, they had taken from them the managing of their estate and soueraigntie; and assuring themselues of the aid of the Romans, reuolted from the communitie of the Achaians: to meet wherewith, and to stay the other cities from doing the like, *Aratus* obtained commission from the states to enforme against these rebels: after which the cities before reuolted, put themselues into the protection of the Romans; yet with prouiso, that their estate and soueraigntie should remaine vnto them still. But when the power of the Romans seemed vnto the rest of the Achæans inuincible, they for the safegard of their libertie, entred into amitie with the Romans also; yet with condition, That the Lacedemonians, whome the Romans had in a manner

drawne

H5 little and little   K4 to enforme *i.e. informer*, to conduct a criminal inquiry, prepare charges

A drawne from the state of the Achæans, should from thenceforth be vnder the protection and power of the Achæans, except in case concerning the life or goods of a Lacedemonian citisen, wherewith the Achæans might not meddle. Which was by the Romans most subtilly done: that so there might still be matter of perpetuall discord and ciuill warre betwixt the Lacedemonians and the Achæans. For if the Lacedemonians had bene altogether in power of the Achæans, they had with their wealth greatly augmented the strength of the associats: and on the other side if the Romans should haue left them altogether free, it was to be feared least they should together with their wonted valour, haue recouered their auntient Commonweale also. The like deceit they vsed also against the Ætolians, which was another estate and league diuided from the Achæans, composed of three cities, who had also their estate, assemblies, & soueraigntie diuided; but in fine, following the example of the Achæans, they of three Commonweals allied with alliance equall, both defensiue and offensiue, established one Aristocratical Commonweale, mannaged by the states of the three confederats, & by one common Senat, wherein was president one chiefe captaine euery yeare chosen. The like we may say of the three and twentie cities of Lycia, which established one Aristocraticall Commonweale, like vnto that of the Achæans; sauing that the deputies of the greater cities had in their generall assemblies three deliberatiue voices, the meaner citisens two, and the rest but one; as saith *Strabo*: and moreouer out of the estates they chose a captaine generall, whome they called the Lyciarque, and so the other magistats and judges of all the cities also. Other alliances also and leagues there were of the thirteene cities of Ionia, of the twelue cities of Tuscanie, and of the fortie seuen cities of the Latines, strongly made by alliance equall, both defensiue and offensiue, holding their assemblies of their states euerie yeare, and chusing also sometimes (but not euer) a chiefe captaine or generall, especially in time of warre: and yet neuerthelesse the soueraigntie of euerie citie continued in the estate of it selfe, as doth the Swissers. For albeit that the citie of Rome was entred into league with the Latines, and that *Seruius Tullius*, and *Tarquin* the proud king of Rome, had bene chosen chiefe captaines of the league of the Latines; yet so it is neuerthelesse, that euerie citie kept still the assemblies and soueraigntie thereof: and yet the kings of Rome lost nothing thereby of their maiestie. Now it seemeth at the first show, that such leagues of cities were like vnto those of the Achæans: but the like thereof there is not one, except those of the Ætolians: and at this present the estate of the empire of the Germans, which we will in due place show to bee no monarchie, but a pure Aristocratie, composed of the princes of the empire, of the seuen electors, and the imperiall cities. Yet this is a thing common to all confederat cities, that in time of warre they haue vsed to make one generall captaine, euery yeare to be chosen, or els once for all. For as the seignorie of the Achæans chose for their captaines the kings of Macedon, *Antigonus*, and *Philip* the second; and the league of the Ætolians made choice of *Attalus* king of Asia, as saith * *Liuie*; and likewise the Latines, of the kings of Rome, and other their neighbour princes: so also the electors haue oftentimes chosen straunge princes, as *Henrie* of Lutzemburg, *Alphonsus* the tenth, and *Charles* the fift, kings of Castile; who although they were soueraignes in their owne realmes, were yet neuerthelesse subiects to the empires, as captaines in chiefe. For as a captaine in chief, being not soueraigne to them that haue chosen him, maketh not them of the league to be one Commonweale: so also he chaungeth in nothing the estate and vnion of the Commonweale whereunto hee is called. So *Philip Valois* the French king, was chosen generall of the ecclesiasticall forces, as we see in that league which was made betwixt *Philip Valois*, & *Henry* count Palatine, who was afterwards of the Germans chosen emperour. And not long since *Adolphus* vncle

The league of the Ætolians.

The league of the Lycians.

The league of the 13. Cities of Ionia. The 12. Cities of Tuscanie: and the 47. Cities of the Latines.

* Lib. 27.

A General chosen by many Cities or States in League together, maketh not them that haue so chosen him euer a whit the more one Commonweale.

to

B8–9 meaner citisens *i.e.* deputies of medium-sized (*mediocres*) cities B10 magistrats C8 the proud, kings of Rome,
Notes at B5, D1, E1.

to the king of Denmarke, was chosen chiefe captaine of the league of the Hauns cities. The Venetians also as oft as they are to make warre, haue vsed to make choyce of any straunge generall, rather than of a citisen of their owne. But the German emperours take vpon them a stile of much higher qualitie than of Captains in chief, or Generall; auoching themselues not onely to bee cheife captaines and magistrats, but euen monarchs also: which whether it be so or no, we will in due place declare. They pretend also to haue power to commaund not onely the princes of the empire, but euen them also who hold of them nothing. For it is not long since that the emperour *Ferdinand* sent his ambassadours vnto the Swissers, to the end they should not receiue *Grombach*, nor the conspiratours his adherents, banished out of the empire: which thing, when the emperour seemed by his letters rather to commaund than to request; the Swissers (a free people) were therewith not a little moued. And before that also, *Morlet Musa* ambassadour for the French king vnto the Swissers, certified the king, How that the gouernour of Milan (as hauing such charge from the emperour) had forbidden the cardinall of Syon to enter into league with the French king, for that hee was a prince of the empire: of which his commaund the cardinall made no great account, but without regard of his prohibition made alliance with the French king; from whome he receiued twelue hundred pounds pention yearly. True it is, that in all the leagues of the Swissers with forren princes, the empire is alwayes excepted, if there be not thereof expresse mention made. And for that cause *Guiche* the kings ambassadour to the Swissers had thereof expresse charge (as I haue seene by the instructions that were giuen him) to make mention of the emperour in the treatie of alliance, of the yere 1521. For the Germans grounded themselues vpon a maxime, in vertie whereof the emperour *Sigismund* caused the Swissers to take vp armes against *Frederick* of Austria, to the preiudice of the alliance made with the house of Austria: presupposing that the empire was superiour vnto the Swissers, and that in all treaties of alliance, the right of the superiour is still to be excepted, although there be thereof no expresse mention made. Which is certaine, for as much as concerneth the lawes of maiestie; but the Swissers confesse not that the emperor hath any superioritie ouer them, and much lesse the emperour, subiect to the states of the empire. It is also true, that by the treatie made betwixt the eight auntient cantons, there is an expresse clause, whereby the cantons of Zurich, Berne, Schwits, and Vnderualden (as hauing sometime bene part of the German empire) declared, That for their part they entended to comprehend in that treatie the maiestie of the sacred empire, the right whereof they purposed not to preiudice by that treatie of alliance. And within a few yeares after, the cantons of Zurich, Berne, Lucerne, Vri, and Glaris, in the name of all the cantons of the Swissers, sent their ambassadours to obtaine the confirmation of their auntient priueledges, of *Ferdinand*, then holding a diet of the states of the empire, at Ausburg. And by the treaties of alliance made betwixt the sacred empire and the cities of the cantons, it is expresly articulated, That they should not giue any aid vnto any straunge prince, to make warre vpon the territorie of the empire; as I haue learned by a copie of the letters of the emperour *Charles* the fist, written to the lords of the cantons; whereby hee complaineth, That their subiects ioyned with the forces of the French king, had entred vpon the territories of the empire, contrarie to the expresse tenour of the alliance that they had with the empire. And not long after, he by other letters demandeth of the lords of the cantons to punish their subiects, who had inuaded the territories belonging to the house of *Austria*, contrarie to the hereditarie alliance made betwixt the princes of the house of *Austria* and the Swissers, in the yeare of Grace 1467, and renewed in the yere 1501, in which league, the See of Rome, the Pope, and the empire, are excepted: and a yerely

The Swissers in all their leagues with forren Princes still except the Empire

---

G8 twelve hundred pounds *i.e.* 1200 livres   H3 in vertue   H5 made with   H9 *For* emperor hath *read* empire hath.   I5 *Delete* Berne (not in Fr or L).   K8 1467 (Fr 3–8 and L) 1477 (Fr 1–2) Notes at G8, H8, K9.

A ly pention set downe, of two hundred florins to be yearely paid vnto euery canton. Which alliance was againe renewed by the xiij cantons, at the diet of Bade holden the xx day of Iuly 1554. As for the league betwixt the said lords of the cantons, and the French king, it was onely a league defensiue, for the preseruation of the states of the allies, and not for the inuading of forreners: which are the true reasons for which the Swissers are withholden to inuade the territories of the empire, and of the house of *Austria*; and not for the right of any preheminence, or superioritie that the empire hath ouer them. Which is also yet more expresly verified by the treatie of alliance, renewed betwixt the French king and the lords of the cantons, in Iune 1549 out of which are excluded all such as are not subiect to the Swissers, nor vse not the German tongue.

B And that is it for which *Charles* the fift, the emperour, laboured by all meanes to make agreement with the Swissers, that the dukedome of Millan, with the kingdoms of Naples and Sicilie, might be comprised in the hereditarie treaties of alliance, made with them for the house *Austria*: which the Swissers flatly refused to grant in the yere 1555. The same we may iudge of the cities of the Grisons, rent from the German empire, who sufficiently declared themselues to bee in nothing bound vnto the edicts of the empire, or of the emperor; in that they would not accept euen of a German prince by the emperor appointed to be their bishop: but the 3 cities of the Grisons, being at variance among themselues, about the choice of their bishop the Swissers by the authority of the league, taking vpon them to be arbitrators of all controuersies arising betwixt

C the confederat cities, without any regard had to the prouision of the pope, or confirmation of the emperour appointed him to be bishop which was chosen by the Chapiter, subiect to the Grisons; and decreed, that from that time forward hee should be bishop whome the league of the Cadde should make choyce of.

Now seeing that our reasoning is of leagues, and of lawes of armes, question might be made, Whether it be lawfull for subiects to entreat of any particular league or alliance among themselues, or with other forren princes, without the leaue or consent of their owne soueraignes? Such alliances, and especially with strangers, princes haue vsed to embarre, for the euill consequences that might ensue thereon: and namely the king Catholike by expresse edicts hath forbidden all his subiects so to do. And at such time

D as *Lewes* of Fraunce, duke of Orleance (he which was slaine at Paris) was charge with many matters, nothing was more grieuously obiected against him beeing slaine, than that he had secretly entred into league with *Henrie* duke of Lancaster. Yet for all that the princes of the empire thinke it lawfull for them so to doe: and for their owne safetie to enter into league of alliance, both among themselues, and with other forren princes, so that it be done without the preiudice of the German empire. For whatsoeuer leagues are by them otherwise made, are void and of none effect. But when the empire is excepted, the emperour himselfe is not therefore excepted, as hath oftentimes but neuer more plainely bene vnderstood, than in the league which many of the German princes made with *Henrie* the second, the French king, at Chambort, for the de-

E fence of the German empire, against the emperour *Charles* the fift, in the yeare 1552. In which league they acknowledged king *Henry* for their superiour, promising curteously to reuerence his maiestie; and so by their common consent made him generall of their warres, calling him The Protectour of Princes, and of the libertie of the empire. And in the yeare 1559 the like alliance both defensiue and offensiue was made betwixt the king of Sweden, the marques Assemberg, the duke of Brunsuich, the duke of Cleue, the prince of Orange, the countie Aiguemont, and diuers other imperiall townes on the one part, and the king of Denmarke, the duke of Saxonie, the Landgraue of Hesse, the duke of Holste, the duke of Bauyere, the towne of Nuremberg, the bishops

Not lawfull for subiects to entreat of any particular league or alliance among themselues, or with forren princes, without the leaue or consent of their own soueraignes.

B4 house OF Austria C4 league of the Cadde *i.e.* the League of God's House D1 was charged Note at A10.

bishops of Wirciburg, and Bamberg, the towne of Lubec, and diuers other, with *Sigismund Augustus* king of Polonia, on the other part. Yea the emperour *Charles* the fift himselfe made particular alliance with the duke of Bauaria, and other the catholike princes, to chuse his brother *Ferdinand* king of Romans. And a little after also the league of Franconia was made betwixt the house of *Austria*, the duke of Bauaria, the three bishops of Franconia, the archbishop of Salisburg, and the cities of Nuremberg and Ausberg. And *Ferdinand* also king of the Romans, for the catholike religion sake made a particular league with the bishop of Salisburg against the protestants, in the yeare 1556. Wee haue seene also the league which was called The league of Sueuia, to haue made alliance offensiue and defensiue for 40 yeares, without excepting any thing saue the empire. And the like league also betwixt the Sea townes, which they cal the Vandales, that is to wit, Lubech, Hambourg, Vimare, Rostoc, Bresme, Suid, imperiall townes, chusing for their chiefe captaine *Adolph* vncle to the king of Denmarke, who was not any way subiect to the empire. Yet in all these leagues was euer excepted the maiestie of the German empire. Yea that more is, the nobilitie of Denmarke entred into a league defensiue with *Sigismund Augustus* king of Polonia, & the towne of Lubec, against the king of Denmarke himselfe: greater treason than which none could haue bene deuised, if the king of Denmarke had the highest power ouer his people, and were an absolute soueraigne: of which matter, and of all the law of armes wee will in due place reason: but first it behoueth vs to speake of maiestie, or Soueraigntie.

A foule and rebellious league of subiects against their prince.

Chap. VIII.
¶ Of Soueraigntie.

The definition of Maiesty or Soueraigntie.

Aiestie or Soueraigntie is the most high, absolute, and perpetuall power ouer the citisens and subiects in a Commonweale: which the Latines cal *Maiestatem*, the Greeks ἄκραν ἐξουσίαν, & κυρίαν ἀρχὴν, and κύριον πολίτευμα; the Italians *Segnoria*, and the Hebrewes תדמר שבט, that is to say, The greatest power to commaund. For maiestie (as *Festus* saith) is so called of mightinesse. For so here it behoueth first to define what maiestie or Soueraigntie is, which neither lawyer nor politicall philosopher hath yet defined: although it be the principall and most necessarie point for the vnderstanding of the nature of a Commonweale. And forasmuch as wee haue before defined a Commonweale to be the right gouernment of many families, and of things common amongst them, with a most high & perpetuall power: it resteth to be declared, what is to be vnderstood by the name of a most high and perpetuall power. We haue said that this power ought to be perpetuall, for that it may bee, that that absolute power ouer the subiects may be giuen to one or many, for a short or certaine time, which expired, they are no more than subiects themselues: so that whilest they are in their puissant authoritie, they cannot call themselues Soueraigne princes, seeing that they are but men put in trust, and keepers of this soueraigne power, vntill it shall please the people or the prince that gaue it them to recall it; who alwaies remained seased thereof. For as they which lend or pawne vnto another man their goods, remaine still the lords and owners thereof: so it is also with them, who giue vnto others power and authoritie to iudge and commaund, be it for a certaine time limitted, or so great and long time as shall please them; they themselues neuerthelesse continuing still seased of the power and iurisdiction, which the other exercise but by way of loane or borrowing.

That Soueraigntie consisteth in a perpetuall power.

G4 these leagues   H9 For πολέτευμα (L 1) read πολίτευμα (L 2–5 and Fr).   H10 שבט תומך (cf. Amos 1:5, 8)   K4 seased *i.e.* seised, in legal possession   Note at H9.

Of a Commonweale.   85

A ing. And that is it for which the law saith, That the gouernour of a countrey, or lieutenant of a prince, his time once expired, giueth vp his power, as but one put in trust, and therein defended by the power of another. And in that respect there is no difference betwixt the great officer and the lesser: for otherwise if the high and absolute power graunted by a prince to his lieutenant, should of right be called Soueraigntie, he might vse the same against his prince, to whome nothing was left but the bare name of a prince, standing but for a cipher: so should the subiect commaund his Soueraigne, the seruant his maister, than which nothing could be more absurd: considering that in all power graunted vnto magistrats, or priuat men, the person of the prince is alwaies to be excepted; who neuer giueth so much power vnto another, but that hee alwayes kee-

B peth more vnto himselfe; neither is euer to be thought so depriued of his soueraigne power, but that he may take vnto himself the examination and deciding of such things as he hath committed vnto his magistrats or officers, whether it be by the way of preuention, concurrence, or euocation: from whome he may also take the power giuen them by vertue of their commission or institution, or suffer them to hold it so long as shall please him. These grounds thus laid, as the foundations of Soueraigntie, wee conclude, that neither the Roman Dictator, nor the Harmoste of Lacedemonia, nor the Esmynæt of Salonick, nor he whom they cal the Archus of Malta, nor the antient Baily of Florence, (when it was gouerned by a popular state) neither the Regents or Viceroyes of kingdoms, nor any other officers or magistrats whatsoeuer, vnto whom

C the highest, but yet not the perpetual power, is by the princes or peoples grant committed, can be accounted to haue the same in Soueraignty And albeit that the antient Dictators had all power giuen them in best sort that might be (which the antient Latines called *Optima Lege*) so that from them it was not lawfull to appeale, and vpon whose creation all offices were suspended; vntill such time as that the Tribunes were ordayned as keepers of the peoples libertie, who continued in their charge notwithstanding the creation of the Dictator, who had free power to oppose themselues against him; so that if appeale were made from the Dictatour, the Tribunes might assemble the people, appointing the parties to bring forth the causes of their appeale, & the Dictator to stay his iudgement; as when *Papirius Cursor* the Dictator, condemned *Fabius Max.*

D the first, to death; and *Fabius Max.* the second had in like manner condemned *Minutius*, both Colonels of the horsemen, for that they had fought with the enemie contrarie to the commaund of the Dictator; they were yet both by appeale and iudgement of the people acquited. For so saith *Liuie*, *Then the father of* Fabius *said, I call vpon the Tribunes, and appeale vnto the people, which can do more than thy Dictatorship: whereunto king* Tullus Hostilius *gaue place*. Wherby it appeareth that the Dictator was neither soueraigne prince, nor magistrat, as many haue supposed; neither had any thing more than a simple commission for the making of warre, the repressing of sedition, the reforming of the state, or instituting of new officers. So that Soueraigntie is not limited either in power, charge, or time certaine. And namely the ten commissio-

E ners established for the reforming of customes and lawes; albeit that they had absolute power, from which there was no appeale to be made, and that all offices were suspended, during the time of their commission; yet had they not for all that any Soueraigntie; for their commission being fulfilled, their power also expired; as did that of the Dictators. So *Cincinnatus* hauing vanquished the enemie, forthwith discharged him selfe of the Dictatorship, which he had not had but fifteene dayes, *Seruilius* in eight dayes, *Mamercus* in one day. And the Dictator was also named, not by the Senat, or the people, neither by the magistrats, or request made vnto the people, nor by any laws which were alwayes necessarie to the creating of officers; but by an interrex, or a king

                                                                I   crea-

* Liui. lib 7. *The dictator of Rome, neither soueraign prince nor magistrate.*

B8 Esymnæt (*more properly* Aesymnetes)   C9-10 to stay *i.e.* support, sustain (cf. Fr)
                                                              Notes at A2, B3, B5, D9.

created for a time, borne of honourable blood: for why, it was not enough for him to be a noble Senator onely, that should name the Dictator. Now if one should say, that *Sylla* was by the law Valeria made Dictator for threescore yeares: I will aunswere as *Cicero* did, That it was neither Dictatorship nor law, but a most cruell tyrannie; whereof for all that he discharged himselfe the fourth yere after he was made Dictator, when as he with the blood of the citisens had quenched the flames of the ciuill warres; hauing yet still in the meane time reserued vnto the Tribunes their free power to oppose themselues against his authoritie. And although *Cæsar* fortie yeares after had inuaded the perpetuall Dictatorship together with the libertie of the people, yet left hee vnto the Tribunes of the people, their power to oppose themselues against his proceedings: but when as before, *Pompeius* being Consull, the verie name of the Dictatorship was taken out of the Commonweale, and *Cæsar*, contrarie to the law of *Pompeius*, had procured himselfe by the law Seruia, to be created Dictator, hee was by the conspiracie of the Senators slaine in the middest of the Senat. But let vs graunt an absolute power without appeale or controlement to be graunted by the people to one or many to mannage their estate and entire gouernment: shall wee therefore say him or them to haue the state of Soueraigntie, when as hee onely is to bee called absolute soueraigne, who next vnto God acknowledgeth none greater than himself? wherefore I say no soueraigntie to be in them, but in the people, of whom they haue a borrowed power, or power for a certaine time, which once expired, they are bound to yeeld vp their authoritie. Neither is the people to be thought to haue depriued it selfe of the power thereof, although it haue giuen an absolute power to one or moe for a certaine time: and much more if the power (be it giuen) be reuocable at the pleasure of the people, without any limitation of time: For both the one and the other hold nothing of themselues, but are to giue account of their doings vnto the prince, or the people of whome they had the power so to commaund: whereas the prince or people themselues, in whome the Soueraigntie resteth, are to giue account vnto none, but to the immortall God alone.

Who is to be called an absolute soueraigne.

But what if such absolute power as we haue spoken of, be giuen to one or moe for nine or ten yeares? as in auntient time in Athens the people made one of the citisens their soueraigne, whome they called Atchon. I say neuerthelesse that hee was no prince, neither that the Soueraigntie of the state rested in him: albeit that hee was a soueraigne magistrat, but yet countable of his actions, vnto the people, his time beeing expired. Yet might one say, What if that high & absolute power which we haue spoken of, were giuen to one or moe, for a yere, with condition not to giue any account at all for their doings: For so the Cnidiens euery yeare chose 60 of their citisens, whome they called Amymones, that is to say, Men without imputation, with such soueraignty of power, as that they might not be called to account for any thing that they had done, neither during the time of their charge, nor after that the same was expired: I say yet for al that, that the soueraigntie of the state was not in them seeing that they were bound at the yeares end to restore againe vnto the people, the authoritie they were put in trust withall, the Soueraigntie still remaining with the people, and the execution thereof with the Amymones, whome a man might well call soueraigne magistrats, but not simple Soueraignes. For the one was the prince, the other the subiect; the one the lord, the other the seruant; the one the proprietarie and seised of the Soueraigntie, the other neither proprietarie nor possessed thereof, neither holding any thing thereof, but as a feoffer or keeper in trust.

The great Archon of Athens no soueraigne.

The Amymones soueraigne magistrats, and yet not simple soueraignes.

The Regents of Fraunce.

The same we may say of the Regents of Fraunce, created for the infancie, furie, or absence of the king, whether the edicts, mandats, and letters pattents, be signed and sealed

F3 *For* threescore *read* fourscore (Fr and L, and cf. 219 E8). G6 their Notes at F1, H3.

OF A COMMONVVEALE. 87

led with the signe and seale of the Regents, and in their name (as they did before the law of *Charles* the fift the French king) or els that it be done in the name of the king, and the mandats sealed with his seale: for in that there is little or no difference at all: seeing that whatsoeuer is done by the atturney, the lord allowing the same, may well be thought to be done by the lord himselfe. Now the Regent is the true protectour of the king and of his kingdome: for so the good countie *Theobald* called himselt *Procuratorem regni Francorum*, that is to say, Protectour of the kingdome of Fraunce. So when a prince giueth absolute power to a Regent, or to a Senat, in his presence, or in his absence, to gouerne in his name; albeit that the edicts or letters of commaund go in his or their name, yet is it alwaies the king that speaketh or commaundeth. So we see that the Senat of Milan or Naples, in the absence of the king of Spaine hath absolute power to dispatch all mandates in his name: As a man may see by the decree of the emperour *Charles* the fift in these words. *Senatus Mediolanensis potestatem habeat constitutiones principis confirmandi, infirmandi, tollendi, dispensandi, contra statuta, habilitationes, prerogationes, restitutiones faciendi, &c. A Senatu ne prouocari possit, &c. Et quicquid faciet, parem vim habeat vt si à principe factum ac decretum esset: Non tamen possit delictorum veniam tribuere, aut literas salui conductus reis criminum dare*. That is to say, The Senat of Milan hath power to confirme the constitutions of the prince, as also to infirme the same, to disanull them, to dispense with them contrarie to the statutes, to make enablements, prerogatiues, and restitutions, &c. No appeale shall be made from the Senat, &c. And whatsoeuer it shall doe, shall haue like force as if it were done or decreed by the prince: yet may it not graunt pardon for offences committed, or giue letters of safe conduct vnto parties conuicted. This power almost infinit, is not giuen vnto the Senat of Milan and Naples, in any thing to diminish the maiestie of the king of Spaine, but altogether to the contrarie, to ease him of his care and paines: ioyne hereunto also, that this power how great soeuer it be, is to be reuoked at the pleasure of him that gaue it.

The Senat of Millan, or Naples, what power it hath in the absence of the king of Spaine.

But suppose that such great power be giuen to a kings lieutenant, or the gouernour of a countrey for tearme of his life, is not that a soueraigne and perpetuall power? For otherwise if we should interpret that onely to be a perpetuall power which shall neuer haue end, there should be at all no soueraigntie, but in the Aristocraticall and popular state, which neuer dieth except it be vtterly rooted out. Or if we vnderstand the word, Perpetuall, in a monarch for him and his heires, there should be few perpetuall soueraigne monarches, seeing there bee but few that be hereditarie; so that they which come to the crowne by way of election, should not be soueraignes: wherefore we must vnderstand the word Perpetuall, for the tearme of the life of him that hath the power. Now if the soueraigne and annuall onely, or which hath a certaine prefixed and limited time to rule, chance to continue his gouernment so giuen him, beyond the appointed time; that must either be by the good liking of him that gaue the power, or els by force: if by force, it is called tyrannie; and yet neuerthelesse the tyrant is a soueraigne: as the violent possession of an intruder is in nature a possesion, although it be contrarie to the law, and they which had the possesion before are so thereof dissei sed: but if such a magistrat continue his soueraigne power by the good liking of the superiour that gaue it him, wee will not therefore say that hee is a soueraigne prince, seeing that he holdeth nothing but by sufferance; and that a great deale the lesse, if the time be not limited, for in that he hath nothing but by commission during pleasure: and he that so holdeth his power, is neither lord nor possessor therof. Men know right well, that there was neuer greater power giuen to magistrat next vnto his prince, than that which was of late yeares graunted to *Henrie* of Fraunce, duke of Aniou, by king

Princes, lieutenants or gouernours of countries for tearme of life, yet no soueraignes.

Henrie duke of Aniou.

I ij   Charles

B4 dispensandi contra   D7 Now if the MAGISTRATE WHO IS soueraigne

Charles the ninth his brother, for it was most great and perpetuall, without any exception of the regall power: yet for all that one cannot say that it was soueraigne, inasmuch as he was called Lieutenant General for the king, *So long as it shall stand with our good pleasure*, ioyned vnto it in his letters patents: which wel declareth a power but during pleasure. Which power of lieutenancie (as of all other magistracies) ceaseth in the presence of the prince.

How the people may create a soueraigne Monarch.

But what shall we then say of him to whom the people haue giuen absolute power so long as he liueth? in this case we must distinguish: If such absolute power bee giuen him purely and simply without the name of a magistrat, gouernour, or lieutenant, or other forme of deputation; it is certaine that such an one is, and may call himselfe a Soueraigne Monarch: for so the people hath voluntarily disseised and dispoyled it selfe of the soueraigne power, to sease and inuest another therein; hauing on him, and vppon him transported all the power, authoritie, prerogatiues, and soueraignties thereof: as if a man should by pure gift deliuer vnto another man the proprietie and possession that vnto him belongeth: in which case such a perfect donation admitteth no conditions.

The regall, or royall law.

In which sort the regall law is by the lawyer said to haue bene made in these words, *Cum populus ei & in eum omnem potestatem contulit*: when as the people conferred vnto him, and on him all their power. But if the people shall giue all their power vnto any one so long as he liueth, by the name of a magistrat, lieutenant, or gouernour, or onely to discharge themselues of the exercise of their power: in this case he is not to be accounted any soueraigne, but a plaine officer, or lieutenant, regent, gouernour, or guerdon and keeper of another mans power. For as the magistrat, although hee make a perpetuall lieutenant, and hath no care of his own iurisdiction, leauing the entire exercise thereof vnto his lieutenant, yet for all that, it is not in the person of the lieutenant that the power lyeth to commaund, or iudge, neither the exercise and force of the law: but if he passe beyond the power vnto him giuen, it is to none effect; if his doings bee not ratified, liked, and approued by him that hath giuen the power. And for this cause king *Iohn* of Fraunce, led prisoner into England, after his returne thence, solemnly ratified all the acts of *Charles* the Dolphin, his eldest sonne, made regent in his absence, to strengthen and confirme the same, so farre as should be conuenient and needfull. Be it then that a man either by commission, or institution, or by delegation, for a certaine time, or for euer, exercise the power of another man: he that so exerciseth this power, is not therefore a soueraigne, although that by his letters of commission or deputation he be not called a protector, lieutenant, regent, or gouernour: no not, albeit that such power be giuen him by the customs and lawes of the countrey, which should be much stronger than election.

Hector Boet. in hist. Scot.

As by an auntient law amongst the Scots, the entire gouernment of the kingdome was committed vnto him that was neerest of blood vnto the king in his minoritie, or vnder the age of xxv yeares, yet with charge that all things should be done in the kings name: which law was long ago abrogated, for the danger might grow vnto the young king, by his nigh kinsmen affecting the kingdome: for which, *Cæsar* thought it lawfull for a man to become villanous.

Vnto soueraigntie belongeth absolute power, and what that absolute power is.

Now let vs prosecute the other part of our propounded definition, and show what these words, *Absolute power*, signifie. For we said that vnto Maiestie, or Soueraigntie belongeth an absolute power, not subiect to any law. For the people or the lords of a Commonweale, may purely & simply giue the soueraigne and perpetuall power to any one, to dispose of the goods and liues, and of all the state at his pleasure: and so afterward to leaue it to whome he list: like as the proprietarie or owner may purely and simply giue his owne goods, without any other cause to be expressed, than of his owne meere bountie; which is indeed the true donation, which no more receiueth condition, being

H2 *For* guerdon *read* guardian.   Notes at F9, H7.

OF A COMMONWEALE. 89

A being once accomplished and perfected: as for the other donations, which carrie with them charge and condition, are not indeed true donations. So also the chiefe power giuen vnto a prince with charge and condition, is not properly soueraignitie, nor power absolute; except that such charge or condition annexed vnto the soueraigntie at the creation of a prince, be directly comprehended within the lawes of God and nature. As it is at the intiesting of the Tartar king. For the great king of Tartarie beeing dead, the prince and the people to whome the right of the election belongeth, make choice of one of the kinsmen of the dead king, which they thinke best of (prouided that he be either his sonne or his nephew) and hauing placed him in a throne of gold, the bishop (after a solemne song sung according to the manner of their aunceftours) turning his speech vnto the king, in the name of the people, saith thus, Wee pray thee, and charge thee to raigne ouer vs: to whom the king aunswereth, If you will haue me so to doe, you must be readie to performe whatsoeuer I commaund; whomsoeuer I appoint to be slaine, you shall slay him presently, and into my hand you shall commit the whole estate of the kingdome: whereunto the people aunswere, Bee it so: after which the king continuing his speech, saith, My word shall be my sword: whereunto the people giueth a great applause. This done, he is taken out of his high throne, and set vpon the ground vpon a bare boord, vnto whome the bishop againe turning his speech, saith, *Looke vp vnto heauen and acknowledge almightie God, the king of the whole world: and behold also this table whereon thou sittest below: if thou rule well, thou shalt haue al things according to thy harts desire; but if thou forget thy dutie and calling, thou shalt be cast headlong downe from thy high seat, and dispoiled of thy regall power and wealth, bee brought so low, as that thou shalt not haue so much as this boord left thee to sit vpon.* This said, hee is lifted vp on high, and by all the people proclaimed king of the Tartars. This so great a power giuen by the people vnto the king, may wel be called absolute and soueraigne, for that it hath no condition annexed thereunto, other than is by the law of God and nature commaunded

The forme of chusing the great king of Tartarie.

The same or like forme of inuesting we may also see to haue bene sometimes vsed in realmes and principalities, descending by succession. But the like is not to that of Carinthia, where yet at this present neere vnto the citie of St. *Vitus*, in a meddow is to be seene a marble stone, whereunto a countrey pesant vnto whom that office of right belonged, stept vp, hauing vpon his right hand a blacke cow, and on his left a leane euill fauoured mare, and all the people about him; towards whome he that is to be created duke commeth marching, with a great number of lords, all apparelled in red, and his ensignes displayed before him; all in good and seemely order, except the new duke himselfe, who is apparelled like a poore shepheard, with a sheephooke in his hand: whome the clowne vpon the stone seeing comming, crieth alowd in the Sclauonian tongue, *Who is that* (saith he) *that commeth marching so proudly?* whereunto the people aunswere, That it is their prince: then demaundeth he, *Is he a iust iudge? seeketh hee the good of his countrey? is he free borne? is he worthie of that honour? and withall religious?* Hee is, saith the people, and so shall hereafter be. Then the peasant giuing the duke a little blow on the eare, goeth downe from the stone, and is for euer after free from all publique charges: so the duke mounting the stone, and brandishing his sword, promiseth vnto the people, To be a good and a iust man: and in that habit goeth to heare masse; which in solemne manner done, he putting off his shepheards apparrell, and attired like a prince, goeth vp to the stone againe, and there receiueth the homage and oath of fidelitie of his vassals and subiects. True it is, that in auntient * time the duke of Carinthia was the emperours greatest Huntsman: but since that the empire fell into the house of Austria, wherunto that dukedome belonged, both the name of the Great Huntsman,

The forme of inuesting the duke of Carinthia.

* Anno. 1331

I iij

Huntsman, and the old maner of inuesting the duke grew out of vse, and the duchies of Carinthia, Stiria, and Croatia, with the counties of Cilia, and Tirol, remaine annexed vnto the dukedome of Austria.

The manner of crowning of the kings of Arragon.

As for those things which are reported concerning the inuesting of the king of Arragon, they are long since growne out of vse; but this wee haue heard them to haue wont to bee done. The great magistrat of Arragon, whome they call the Chief Iusticoi, thus said vnto the king: *We which are vnto thee in vertue nothing inferiour, and in power greater than thy selfe, create thee our king; yet with this condition that one amongst vs shall still haue more power and commaund than thy selfe.* Wherein he is deceiued that so writeth, the king to haue bene then chosen of the people; a thing that neuer was there done. For *Sanctius* the Great by force of armes draue the Moores out of the kingdome of Arragon, after they had seuen hundred yeares possessed the same: after which time his posteritie of both Sexes, held that kingdome by inheritance. And also *Peter Belluga*, who most exactly writ of the kingdome of Arragon, denieth the people to haue any right in chusing the king; but when the line of the king vtterly faileth. That were also a new and more absurd thing, that the king of Arragon should haue lesse power than the states of Arragon, seeing that the same author *Belluga* saith, That the states might not assemble themselues without the kings expresse commaundement; neither being assembled, might depart without leaue giuen them from the king. That were also more absurd and ridiculous, that such speech should bee vsed by the magistrat, vnto him that was now crowned, sacred, and receiued a king by right of succession, who also placed and displaced the same great magistrat whensoeuer hee list. For the same author writeth, *Martin Didato* the greatest magistrat, to haue beene placed in that office by the queen of Aragon, in the absence of *Alphonsus* her husband, king of Arragon and Sicilia; and also by her againe discharged of the same office. And albeit that by sufferance of the king, that great magistrat or justice of Arragon, determineth of the processe and controuersies betwixt the king and his people: as it is also in England sometime by the high court of Parliament, and sometime by the magistrat, whome they call the *Lord Chiefe Iustice of England*, and by all the judges of this * realme, and in all places: yet neuerthelesse so it is, that the great justice of Arragon, and all the estates remaine in full subiection to the king, who is no wayes bound to follow their aduice, neither to consent to their requests, (as saith the same doctor) which is generall to all estates of a monarchie, as saith *Oldard*, speaking of the kings of Fraunce and Spaine, Who haue (saith he) absolute power. Yet true it is, that none of these doctours tell vs, what absolute power is. For if wee shall say, that hee onely hath absolute power, which is subiect vnto no law; there should then bee no soueraigne prince in the world, seeing that all princes of the earth are subiect vnto the lawes of God, of nature, and of nations.

* *viz. Fraunce.*

That a subiect may be dispensed withall from all the lawes and customes of his Commonweale, yet be neither prince nor soueraigne.

So to the contrarie it may be, that some one subiect may be dispensed withall, and absolued from all the laws, ordinances, and customes of his Commonweale, and commaundement of the magistrat; and yet be neither prince, nor soueraigne. Example we haue of *Pompey* the great, who was dispensed withall from the lawes for fiue yeres, by expresse decree of the people, published at the request of *Gabinius* the Tribune, at such time as extraordinarie power was giuen him to make warre against the pirats: neither is it any new thing or straunge thing to dispence with a subiect for his obedience to the lawes, seeing that the Senat sometimes so dispenced without the consent of the people: vntill the law Cornelia published at the request of a Tribune, whereby it was ordained, That no person should be exempted out of the power of the laws, nor dispenced withall by the Senat, if he had not at the least the consent of two hundred

Sena-

I3 Oldrad   K3 request of Gabinius   Notes at F5, H8, I8.

OF A COMMONWEALE. 73 [91]

A Senators. For by the law of the twelue tables, it was forbidden vpon paine of death to graunt any priueledge but by the great assemblies of the people; but that law was euill executed, being still infringed by the Senat. Yet he that is so exempted from one law, or moe, or all lawes, is for all that alwaies in the subiection and obeysance of them which haue the soueraigntie: yea although he bee for euer absolued from all the lawes of his countrey. As *Augustus*, who although he was the prince of the people of Rome, that is to say, the chiefe in that Commonweale, yet faigning himselfe to be inferiour to the people in generall, he oftentimes propounded questions vnto the people, as if the people, and not *Augustus*, should make the lawes: and at the chusing of magistrats, would shake the citisens by the hands, that so hee might commend them that

B stood for the offices vnto the people. But it behoueth him that is a soueraigne not to be in any sort subiect to the commaund of another: which thing *Tiberius* wisely meaning in these words, reasoned in the Senat concerning the right of soueraigntie, saying that *The reason of his doings were no otherwise to be manifested, than in that it was to be giuen to none*: whose office it is to giue laws vnto his subiects, to abrogat laws vnprofitable, and in their stead to establish other: which hee cannot do that is himselfe subiect vnto lawes, or to others which haue commaund ouer him. And that is it for which the law saith, That the prince is acquitted from the power of the lawes: and this word the Law, in the Latine importeth the commaundement of him which hath the soueraigntie. Wee also see that vnto all edicts and decrees there is annexed this clause,

C *Notwithstanding all edicts and ordinances whereunto we haue derogated, and do derogat by these presents*: a clause which hath alwaies bene ioyned vnto the antient lawes, were the law published by the present prince or by his predecessours. For it is certaine, that the lawes, ordinances, letters pattents, priueleges, and grants of princes, haue no force, but during their life, if they be not ratified by the expresse consent, or at least by sufferance of the prince following, who had knowledge thereof, and especially of the priueleges. As when *Bartolus* was sent ambassadour vnto *Charles* the fourth, the German emperour, for the confirmation of the priueleges of the citie of Perouze, hee obtained the same, yet with condition, That they should so long haue force, vntill they were reuoked by the succeeding emperours: vnto whom for all that, no preiudice could haue bene done, although that clause had not bene put to: which was the cause that *Mi-*

D *chael Del Hospital* chauncelour of Fraunce, constantly refused, yea euen at the request of the queene, to seale the priuileges by *Charles* the ix. graunted vnto S^t. Maur des Fossez, for that they carried with them a perpetuall enfranchisment and immunitie from taxes, which is contrarie to the nature of personall priueledges, and tended to the diminishing of the power of his successours, and could not be giuen vnto corporations or colleges, which liue for euer, but for the life of the prince that graunted them onely, although the word (perpetuall) were thereunto adioyned. Which for all that if they were graunted vnto corporations or colleges, by a popular or Aristocraticall state, must needs bee for euer, or at leastwise so long as that popular or Aristocraticall state

E should continue. And for this cause *Tiberius* the emperour, successour to *Augustus*, would not that the priueledges graunted by the dead emperours, should bee of any effect, if their successors had not confirmed them: when as before the priueleges granted by princes, if they were not limited vnto a time certaine, were accounted as giuen for euer. Wee also see in this * realme, that at the comming of new kings, colleges and corporations require to haue their priueleges, power, and iurisdiction confirmed; yea the verie parliaments and soueraigne courts, as well as other particular officers.

If then the soueraigne prince be exempted from the lawes of his predecessors, much lesse should he be bound vnto the lawes and ordinances he maketh himselfe: for a

margin notes:
A soueraigne prince is not bound to giue a reason of his doings.

That the lawes, letters pattents, priueleges, grants of princes haue no force, but during the life of the princes that granted them.

* *viz. Fraunce.*

I iiij   man

E6 require *i.e.* ask, request   Notes at B4, E1.

THE FIRST BOOKE

A soueraigne prince is not subiect vnto the lawes and ordinances that he himselfe maketh

man may well receiue a law from another man, but impossible it is in nature for to giue a law vnto himselfe, no more than it is to commaund a mans selfe in a matter depending of his owne will: For as the law saith, *Nulla obligatio consistere potest, quæ a voluntate promittentis statum capit*, There can be no obligation, which taketh state from the meere will of him that promiseth the same: which is a necessarie reason to proue euidently that a king or soueraigne prince cannot be subiect to his owne lawes. And as the Pope can neuer bind his owne hands (as the Canonists say;) so neither can a soueraigne prince bind his owne hands, albeit that he would. Wee see also in the end of all edicts and lawes, these words, *Quia sic nobis placuit*, Because it hath so pleased vs: to giue vs to vnderstand, that the lawes of a soueraigne prince, although they be grounded vpon good and liuely reasons, depend neuerthelesse vpon nothing but his meere and franke good will.

All princes and people are subiect vnto the lawes of God and nature.

But as for the lawes of God and nature, all princes and people of the world are vnto them subiect: neither is it in their power to impugne them, if will not be guiltie of high treason to the diuine maiestie, making warre against God; vnder the greatnesse of whome all monarches of the world ought to beare the yoke, and to bow their heads in all feare and reuerence. Wherefore in that wee said the soueraigne power in a Commonweale to be free from all lawes, concerneth nothing the lawes of God and nature.

* *Innocentius Quartus.*

For amongst the Popes, * hee that of all others best knew the lawes of maiestie or soueraigntie, and had almost brought vnder him the power of all the Christian emperours and princes, said him to be indeed a soueraigne that was able to derogat from the ordinary right (which is as I vnderstand it, from the laws of his countrey) but not from the lawes of God or nature.

Whether a prince be subiect vnto the lawes of his countrey that he hath sworne to keepe, or not.

But further question may be, Whether a prince bee a subiect to the lawes of his countrey, that he hath sworne to keepe, or not? wherein wee must distinguish. If the prince sweare vnto himselfe, That he will keepe his law: hee is no more bound to his law, than by the oath made vnto himselfe: For the subiects themselues are not any way bound by oath, which they make in their mutuall conuentions, if the couenants be such as from which they may by law shrinke, although they be both honest and reasonable. But if a soueraigne prince promise by oath to keep the lawes which he or his predecessours haue made, he is bound to keepe them, if the prince vnto whome hee hath so giuen his word haue therein any intrest; yea although he haue not sworne at al: But if the prince to whom the promise was made haue therin no intrest, neither the promise nor the oath can bind him that made the promise. The like we say, if promise be made by a soueraigne prince vnto his subiects, or before hee bee chosen; for in that case there is no difference, as many thinke: not for that the prince is bound to his laws, or by his predecessours; but to the iust conuentions and promises that hee hath made, be it by oath, or without any oath at all; as should a priuat man bee: and for the same causes that a priuat man may be releeued from his vniust and vnreasonable promise, as for that it was too grieuous, or for that he was by deceit or fraud circumuented; or induced thereinto by errour, or force, or iust feare; or by some great hurt: euen for the same causes the prince may be restored in that which toucheth the diminishing of his maiesty, if he be a soueraigne prince. And so our maxime resteth, That the prince is not subiect to his lawes, nor to the lawes of his predecessours: but well to his owne iust and reasonable conuentions, and in the obseruation whereof the subiects in generall or particular haue intrest. Wherein we see many to be deceiued, which make a confusion of lawes, and of a princes contracts, which they call also lawes: as well as he which calleth a princes contracts pactionarie lawes; as they tearme them in the state of Arragon, when the king maketh any law at the request of the people, and receiueth therefore any money or subsidie; then the Arragonians say that the king is vnto that law bound,

---

G3–4 if THEY will not G4 warre H9 soueraigne prince promise TO ANOTHER PRINCE by oath
(cf. Fr and L) Notes at F7, G2, G3, H4, I3, K1.

A bound, but not so vnto other lawes: and yet neuerthelesse they confesse that the prince may derogat from the same, the cause of the law ceasing: which to bee true, as it may by reason and authoritie be confirmed, so was there no need of money, or of oath, to bind the soueraigne prince, if it concerned his subiects (to whome he had promised) to haue the law kept. For the word of a prince ought to bee as an Oracle; which looseth his dignitie, if his subiects haue so euill an opinion of him, as not to beleeue him except he sweare; or else to be so couetous, as not to regard his promise except therefore he receiue money. And yet neuerthelesse the maxime of right still standeth in force, That the soueraigne prince may derogat vnto the lawes that hee hath promised and sworne to keepe, if the equitie thereof ceased, and that of himself without consent
B of his subiects: yet true it is, that a generall obscure or doubtfull derogation, in this case sufficeth not, but that there must bee a derogation in words speciall. But if there bee no probable cause of abrogating the law he hath promised to keepe, he shall do against the dutie of a good prince, if he shall go about to abrogat such a law: and yet for al that is he not bound vnto the couenants and oathes of his predecessours, further than standeth with his profit, except he be their heire. And for this cause the states of Arragon complained to king *Alphonsus*, for that he for gaine had altered and chaunged the money of Arragon, to the great preiudice of the subiects, and marchants straungers, contrarie to the promise made by *Iames* the first, king of Arragon, in the yeare 1265, in the moneth of August, and confirmed by king *Peter*, in the yeare 1336, who swore
C vnto the estates neuer to chaunge the money; in recompence wherof the people had promised euery one of them euery seuen yeares to pay vnto him a maruedie, if they were in goods worth fifteene maruadies. Now the kingdome of Arragon discendeth by inheritance vnto the heires, both males and females; but the effect of the contract betwixt the prince and the people ceasing, as the subsidie for which the kings of Arragon had made that order which I haue said, the king was no more bound to keepe his promise: then were the people to pay the subsidie vpon them imposed.

We must not then confound the lawes and the contracts of soueraigne princes, for that the law dependeth of the will and pleasure of him that hath the soueraigntie, who may bind all his subiects, but cannot bind himselfe: but the contract betwixt the prince
D and his subiects is mutual, which reciprocally bindeth both parties, so that the one partie may not start therefrom, to the preiudice, or without the consent of the other. In which case the prince hath nothing aboue the subiect, but that the equitie of the law which he hath sworne to keepe, ceasing, he is no more bound to the keeping thereof, by his oath or promise, as we haue before said: which the subiects cannot do among themselues, if they bee not by the prince releeued. The soueraigne princes also wel aduised, will neuer take oath to keepe the lawes of their predecessours; for otherwise they are not soueraignes. But then might some man say, Why doth the German emperour, who hath a preheminence aboue all other Christian kings, before he be crowned sweare betwixt the hands of the archbishop of Cullen, to keepe the laws of the empire,
E the golden Bul, to establish iustice, to reuenge the pope, to keepe the catholike faith, to defend the widdowes, the fatherlesse, and poore? Which forme of oath, wherewith the emperour *Charles* the fift bound himselfe when he was crowned, cardinall *Caietan* is said to haue sent vnto the pope, whose legat he then was in Germanie. Whereunto I aunswere, that the emperour is subiect vnto the states of the empire; neither taketh vpon him the soueraigntie ouer the princes electours, nor ouer the estates; as we shall in due place declare. And if a man say, That the kings of the Epirots in auntient time swore, that they should raigne well and orderly according to the lawes and customs of the countrey, and the subiects also on their part swore to defend and maintaine their

king

The word of a prince ought to be as an Oracle.

The reason of the law ceasing, the law it selfe ought also to cease.

Soueraigne princes not bound vnto their lawes, may yet by their contracts bind themselues vnto their subiects.

Whether Soueraigne princes well aduised, ought to bind themselues by oath to keepe the lawes of their predecessors.

B10 *For* August *read* April.   C7 promise, then (*i.e.* than)   D10 Cullen *i.e.* Cologne
Notes at A2, B5, E1.

king, according to the lawes and customes of their countrey : I say yet notwithstanding all these oathes, that the soueraigne prince might derogat from the lawes, or frustrat and disanull the same, the reason and equitie of them ceasing. The oath also of our kings, which is the fairest and shortest that can be, containeth nothing in it concerning the keeping of the lawes and customes of the countrey or predecessours. The words I will set downe, as they be taken word for word out of the librarie of Rheims, out of an auntient booke, which thus beginneth *Iuliani ad Erigium Regem Anno* 1058 *Henrico Regnante* 32. *iiij. Calend. Iunij. Ego Philippus Deo propiciante mox futurus Rex Francorum, in die ordinationis meæ promitto coram Deo & sanctis eius, quod vnicuique de nobis commissis canonicum priuilegium, & debitam legem atque iustitiam conservabo, & defensionem adiuuante Domino quantum potero exhibebo: sicut Rex in suo regno vnicuique Episcopo & Ecclesiæ sibi commisse per rectum exhibere debet : populo quoque nobis credito, me dispensationem legum in suo iure consistentem, nostra auctoritate concessurum. viz.*

The oath of Philip the first, son to Henry the first, king of Fraunce, at the time of his Coronation.

The booke of *Iulian Erigius,* Anno 1058, in the xxxij. yeare of the raigne of *Henrie* the first, the fourth of the calends of Iune. I *Philip*, by the grace of God forthwith to become king of Fraunce, on the day of my inuesting, doe promise before God and his Saints, that I will keepe canonicall prieueledge, with due administration of law and iustice, to euerie one committed to our charge : and by the help of God to the vttermost of my power defend them, in such manner as a king in his kingdome ought of right to giue vnto euerie bishop & church committed vnto him : & by our authoritie to grant vnto the people committed vnto vs, the execution of the lawes remaining in force. I know that which is found in the librarie of the Beauuais is like vnto this, and the oath of the same *Philip* the first : but I haue seene another in a little auntient booke in the Abbay of S. Allier in Auergne, in these words ; *Ie iure au nom de Deiu tout puissant, & promets de gouuerner bien et deuement les subiects commis en ma garde, & faire de tout mon pouuoir iudgement, iustice, et misericorde:* I sweare by the name of the Almighty God, and promise well and duly to gouerne my subiects committed to my charge : and with all my power to doe them iudgement, iustice, and mercie. Which seemeth to haue bene taken from the prophet *Hieremie*, where he saith, *I am the great eternall God, which do iudgement, iustice, and mercie ; and in which things I take singular pleasure.* Which formes of oathes shew plainely vnto the eye, that the oathes contained in the booke lately printed and published by the title of *Sacre Du Roy*, are much changed and altred from the auntient forme. But both in the one and the other oath, a man may see that there is not any bond for the soueraigne prince to keepe the lawes, more than so farre as right and iustice requireth. Neither is it to be found that the auntient kings of the Hebrewes tooke any oath : no not they which were anointed by *Samuel, Helias* and others. But some take a more precise oath, such as is the oath of *Henry* the 3 king of Fraunce, and of Polonia. *Ego Henricus Rex Poloniæ, &c. Iuro Deo omnipotenti, quòd omnia iura, libertates, priuilegia publica & priuata iuri communi non contraria, Ecclesijs, principibus, Baronibus, nobilibus, ciuibus, incolis, per meos prædecessores Reges, & quoscumque principes Dominos, Regni Poloniæ iustè concessa, & quæ in interregno decreta sunt seruabo, iusque omnibus incolis more maiorum reddam. Ac si quidem (quod absit) Sacramentum meum violauero nullam nobis incolæ Regni obedientiam præstare tenebuntur, &c. sic Deus adiuuet. viz.* I *Henrie* king of Polonia, &c. Sweare vnto almightie God, that I will keepe all the lawes, liberties, publick and priuat prieueleges, not contrarie to the common law, iustly graunted vnto churches, princes, barrons, noble men, citisens, or inhabitants, by the kings my predecessours, or whatsoeuer other princes, lords of the kingdome of Polonia: as also all such things as were decreed in the time of the vacancie of the kingdome : and that I will administer iustice vnto all the inhabitants

Chap. 9.

The auntient Hebrew kings not sworne when they were annointed by the Prophets.

of

OF A COMMONWEALE.

A of this kingdome, after the manner of our auncestours: And if I shall violat this mine oath (which God forbid) then the inhabitants of this kingdom shall be bound to yeeld vnto vs no obedience, &c. And so God helpe vs. But this forme of oath sauoureth not of royall maiestie, but the condition of a meaner prince, such an one as (amongst others) is chiefe in a Commonweale.

But touching the lawes which concerne the state of the realme, and the establishing thereof; forasmuch as they are annexed & vnited to the crowne, the prince cannot derogat from them, such as is the law Salique: & albeit that he so do, the successor may alwaies disanull that which hath bene done vnto the preiudice of the laws royall, vpon which the soueraigne maiestie is stayed & grounded. Yet might one say, That *Henry* B the 5, king of England & France, marying *Katherine* of France, sister to *Charles* the 7, took an oath to keep the high court of parliament in the liberties & soueraigntie thereof; and to cause iustice to be administred in the realme, according vnto the customes and lawes thereof. See the words of the decree agreed vpon for to make him successour vnto the crowne of Fraunce, the xxj of May, in the yeare 1420. I say they caused him to take such an oath, for that he was a straunger come to a new kingdome; from which the lawfull inheritour was excluded by a decree of the Parliament of Paris, giuen for default and contumacie; for the murther committed vppon the person of *Iohn* duke of Burgoigne, which was by sound of trumpet pronounced at the marble table in the presence of the princes. But as for generall and particular lawes and customs, C which cancerne not the establishing of the state of the realme, but the right of men in priuat, they haue not vsed to haue bene with vs otherwise chaunged, but after generall assemblie of the three estates of Fraunce well and duly made; or of euery bailiwike in particular: not for that it is necessarie for the king to rest on their aduice, or that hee may not do the contrarie to that they demaund, if naturall reason and iustice so require. And in that the greatnesse and maiestie of a true soueraigne prince, is to bee knowne; when the estates of all the people assembled together, in all humilitie present their requests and supplications to their prince, without hauing any power in any thing to commaund or determine, or to giue voice, but that that which it pleaseth the king to like or dislike of, to commaund or forbid, is holden for law, for an edict and ordinance. D Wherein they which haue written of the dutie of magistrats, & other such like books, haue deceiued themselues, in maintaining that the power of the people is greater than the prince; a thing which oft times causeth the true subiects to reuolt from the obedience which they owe vnto their soueraigne prince, & ministreth matter of great troubles in Commonweals. Of which their opinion, there is neither reason nor ground, except the king be captiue, furious, or in his infancie, and so needeth to haue a protector or lieutenant appointed him by the suffrages of the people. For otherwise if the king should be subiect vnto the assemblies and decrees of the people, hee should neither bee king nor soueraigne; and the Commonwealth neither realme nor monarchie, but a meere Aristocratie of many lords in power equall, where the greater part commaun- E deth the lesse in generall, and euery one in particular: and wherein the edicts and lawes are not to be published in the name of him that ruleth, but in the name and authoritie of the states, as in an Aristocraticall Seignorie, where hee that is chiefe hath no power, but oweth obeysance vnto the commaundements of the seignorie: vnto whome yet they all and euerie one of them faigne themselues to owe their faith and obedience: which are al things so absurd, as hard it is to say which is furthest from reason. So when *Charles* the eight, the French king, being then but about xiiij. yeres old, held a parliament at Tours, although the power of the parliament was neuer before nor after so great as in those times, yet *Rell*, then speaker for the people, turning himselfe

Marginal notes:
- *Lawes royall which concerne the state of the realme not to bee infringed by a soueraign prince.*
- *Parliaments impaire not, but most of all show the maiestie and greatnesse of a soueraign prince.*
- *The parlements of Fraunce.*

A1 auncestours C1 concerne   Notes at A4, A8, E6.

himselfe vnto the king, thus beginneth his oration, which is yet in print extant. *Most high, most mightie, and most Christian king, our naturall and onely lord, we your humble and obedient subiects, &c. Which are come hither by your commaund, in all humilitie reuerence and subiection, present our selues before you, &c. And haue giuen mee in charge from all this noble assemblie, to declare vnto you the good will and hartie desire they haue with a most firme resolution and purpose to serue, obey, and aid you in all your affaires, commaundements and pleasures*. In briefe, all that his oration and speech is nothing els but a declaration of all their good wils towards the king, and of their humble obedience and loialtie. The like speech almost we see was also vsed in the parliament at Orleans, vnto king *Charles* the ninth, when he was yet but scarce eleuen yeares old. Neither are the parliaments of Spaine otherwise holden, but that euen a greater obedience & a greater loialtie of all the people in generall, is giuen vnto the king, as is to bee seene in the acts of the parliament holden at Toledo by king *Philip*, in the yeare 1552, when he was yet scarce full xxv yeares old. The aunswers also of the king of Spaine vnto the requests and humble supplications of his people, are giuen in these words, *We will*; or else, *We decree and ordaine*; and such other like aunsweres, importing the refusall or consent of the prince: yea the subsidie that the subiects pay vnto the king of Spaine, they call seruice. Wherby it appeareth them to be deceiued, which say that the kings of Arragon cannot derogat from the priueledges of the states, by reason of the priueleges giuen them by king *Iames*, in the yeare 1260, and confirmed in the yeare 1320. For as the priueleges was of no force after the death of the king, without the confirmation of his successours: so also the same confirmation of the rest of the kings following was necessarie, for that by the law no man can raigne ouer his equals. And albeit that in the parliaments of England, which haue commonly bene holden euerie third yeare, there the states seeme to haue a verie great libertie (as the Northerne people almost all breath thereafter) yet so it is, that in effect they proceed not, but by way of supplications and requests vnto the king. As in the parliament of England, holden in October, 1566, when the estates by a common consent had resolued (as they gaue the queene to vnderstand) not to entreat of any thing, vntill she had first appointed who should succeed her in the crowne: She gaue them no other aunswere, But that they were not to make her graue before she were dead. All whose resolutions were to no purpose without her good liking: neither did she in that any thing that they required. Now also the estates of England are neuer otherwise assembled (no more than they are in this realme of Fraunce, or Spaine) than by parliament writs, and expresse commandements proceeding from the king. Which showeth verie well that the estates haue no power of themselues to determine, commaund, or decree any thing; seeing that they cannot so much as assemble themselues; neither beeing assembled, depart, without expresse commaundement from the king. Yet this may seeme one speciall thing, that the lawes made by the king of England, at the request of the states, cannot bee againe repealed, but by calling a parliament of the estates: Which is much vsed and ordinarily done, as I haue vnderstood by M. *Dale*, the English ambassadour, an honourable gentleman and a man of good vnderstanding, who yet assured me, that the king receiued or reiected the law as seemed best vnto himself: and stucke not to dispose therof at his pleasure, and contrarie to the will of the estates: as wee see *Henry* the eight to haue alwaies vsed his soueraigne power, and with his onely word to haue disanulled the decrees of parliament: albeit that the kings of England are not otherwise crowned, but that they must sweare inuiolatly to keepe the lawes and customes of the land: which how that oath is to be vnderstood, I referre you to that which wee haue before reported. But here might some obiect and say, That the estates of England suffer not any extraordinary

The parliament of Spaine.

The parliaments of England.

D. Dale.

F 5 *For* noble (Fr 7) *read* notable (Fr 1–6, 8). Note at K 9.

rie charges and subsidies to be laid vpon them, if it be not first agreed vpon and consented vnto in the high court of parliament: for so it is prouided by an auntient law of *Edward* the first, king of England, wherewith the people as with a buckler hath bene oftentimes seene to defend it selfe against the prince. Whereunto mine aunswere is, That other kings haue in this point no more power than the kings of England: for that it is not in the power of any prince in the world, at his pleasure to rayse taxes vpon the people, no more than to take another mans goods from him; as *Philip Commines* wisely shewed in the parliament holden at Tours, as we read in his Comentaries: and yet neuerthelesse if the necessitie of the Commonweale be such as cannot stay for the calling of a parliament, in that case the prince ought not to expect the assemblie of the states, neither the consent of the people; of whose good foresight and wisedome, next vnto God, the health & welfare of the whole state dependeth: but concerning all sorts of taxes and tributes, more shall be said in place conuenient. True it is, that the kings of England, since the time of *Henrie* the first (as we read in *Polidore*) haue as it were alwaies accustomed euery third yeare to demaund of the people an extraordinarie subsidie, which is for the most part graunted. As in the parliament holden in Aprill, in the yeare 1570, the queene of England by the consent of the estates, drew from them fiue hundred thousand crownes (as the like whereof is sometime also vsed to bee done in Spaine) from which manner of tribute she had now many yeares before abstained. Now here might some obiect also, That the estates of England haue power to condemne, as king *Henrie* the sixt was condemned by the estates, to be kept prisoner in the Towre of London. I say that that was done by the ordinarie judges of England, the lords spirituall and temporall of the vpper house, at the request of them of the neather house; who presented also a bill of request to the vpper house, in the yeare 1571, tending to the end, that the earles of Northumberland, and Westmerland, & other conspiratours, might be declared to haue incurred the paines contained in the lawes of the land, made against them that were guiltie of treason. Which showeth well that the estates in bodie together haue neither power nor iurisdiction, but that the power is with the judges of the vpper house, as should be, if the parliament of Paris assisted by the prince and peers, should be from the estates in bodie together seperated, to iudge of themselues of great matters.

Polydor. in hist. Anglorū.

But yet there remaineth another difficultie to resolue vpon, concerning the aforesaid estates of England, who seemed to haue power to commaund, resolue, and decide of the affaires of state. For queene *Marie* hauing assembled them for the passing of the articles of agreement concerning the marriage with king *Philip*: after many disputes and difficulties proposed, in fine, the conclusion of the treatie was made the second day of Aprill in the yeare 1554, in forme of a decree conceiued in the name of the estates, in these words: The articles aforesaid, and that which dependeth thereof, seene and considered of, by the estates assembled in parliament, holden at the palace of Westminster, it hath bene said, That concerning the disposition and collation of all benefices and offices, they are reserued vnto the queene; as also of all the fruits, profits, rents, reuenews of her countries, lands, and seignories, the queene, as sole and alone shall enioy the royaltie and soueraignetie of her said realmes, countries, lands, and subiects, absolute, after the consummation of the mariage; so that the said prince shall not pretend by the way of the courtesie of England, any claime to the crowne or soueraigntie of the realme, nor to any other rights, preheminences, or authorities: That all mandats and letters pattents shal passe vnder the name of the said prince and queene iointly: which letters signed with the hand of the queene alone, and sealed with the great seale, shall be auailable: but being not signed by the said queene, shall be void and

K to

B1 foresight   C10 the princes (Fr)   E9 available *i.e.* valid   Notes at A5, B10, C10, D6, E5.

to none effect. I haue willingly set downe the ratification at large, to show that the soueraigntie wholly without diuision belonged vnto the kings of England, and that the estates had but the view thereof: For the ratification of the estates, no more than of a court, a parliament, a corporation, or colledge, sufficeth not to show the power to commaund, but rather their consent to strengthen the acts, which otherwise might haue bene called into some doubt, after the death of the queene: or in her life time by the magistrats and officers of the realme, opposing themselues against her. Wherfore we conclude the maiestie of a prince to be in nothing altered or diminished by the calling together or presence of the states but to the contrarie his maiestie thereby to bee much the greater, & the more honorable, seeing all his people to acknowledge him for their soueraigne: albeit that in such assemblies, princes not willing to reiect their subiects, graunt, and passe many things, whereunto they would not otherwise yeeld their consent, if they were not ouercome by the requests, prayers, and iust grieuances of the people, afflicted and vexed oftentimes without the knowledge of the prince, who yeeldeth many things vnto them all, which he would deny vnto them in particular; or at leastwise not so easily graunt them: either for that the voyces of euerie one in particular, are lesse heard, than of al together: or for that the prince at other times commonly vseth to see but by other mens eyes, and to heare but by other mens eares and reports: whereas in parliament hee seeth and heareth his people himselfe, and so enforced with shame, the feare of religion, or his owne good disposition, admitteth their iust requests.

The principall point of soueraigntie. Laws in Fraunce altered by the prince, without the assembling or consent of the states.

So wee see the principall point of soueraigne maiestie, and absolute power, to consist principally in giuing laws vnto the subiects in generall, without their consent And not to speake of straunge countries, we haue oftentimes seene in this realme of Fraunce certaine generall customs abolished by the edicts of our kings, without the assembling or consent of the estates: when the iniustice of the same is plainely to be seene; as the custome of this realme, commonly vsed in euery place, concerning the succession of mothers vnto the goods of their children, hath bene chaunged without assembling of the estates, either in generall or particular. Which chaunging of customes is no new thing, for since the time of *Philip* the faire, the custome generall in this realme, which suffered not him that was ouerthrowne in sute, to be condemned in charges also, was disanulled by edict, without assembling the estates. And the generall custome which forbad to receiue the testimonie of women in ciuill causes; was abolished by the edict of *Charles* the sixt, without calling together of the estates. For it behoueth that the soueraigne prince should haue the lawes in his power, to chaunge and amend them, according as the case shall require; as saith the lawyer *Sextus Cecilius*: euen as the master pilot ought to haue the helme alwaies in his hand, at discretion to turne it as the wether or occsion requireth: for otherwise the ship might oftentimes perish before hee could take aduice of them whome he did carrie. Which is a thing necessarie, not onely vnto a soueraigne prince, but sometimes vnto a magistrat also, the necessitie of the Commonweale so requiring, as we haue said of *Pompee*, and of the Decemuiri. And for that cause *Augustus* after he had ouerthrowne *Marcus Antonius* at Actium, was by the Senat absolued from the power of the lawes, albeit that he as then was but chiefe of the Commonweale, and no soueraigne prince, as we shall in due place declare. And after that *Vespatian* the emperour was also exempted from the power of the lawes, not by the Senat onely, but onely by the expresse law of the people as many thinke, and as yet it is to be found engrauen in marble in Rome: which the lawyer calleth the law Royall, howbeit that it hath no great probabilitie, that the people which long time before had lost al their power, should giue it to him that was stronger than themselues.

Now

F5 otherwise   G4 afflicted   G8 eyes, and   I6 Cecilius (Fr 7) Cæcilius (Fr 1–6, 8 and L)
I8 occasion   K6 *For* but onely *read* but also.   Note at H7.

Of A Commonweale. 99

Now if it be profitable that the soueraigne prince, for the good gouernment of an estate, should haue the power of the laws vnder him; then it is more expedient for the gouernour in an Aristocraticall estate; and necessarie for the people in their popular estate: for the monarch is diuided from the people; and in the Aristocraticall state, the lords or gouernours are diuided from the commonaltie and vulgar people; in such sort as that in both the one & other Commonweal, there are two parties, that is to wit, he or they that hold the soueraigntie on the one part, and the people on the other; which causeth the difficulties which are betwixt them for the rights of soueraigntie, which cease in the popular estate. For if the prince or lords which hold the estate be bound to obserue the laws, as many think they are, and that they cannot make any law without the consent of the people, or of the Senat; it cannot also bee againe by law repealed, without the consent of the one or of the other: which can take no place in a popular estate, seeing that the people make but one bodie, and cannot bind it selfe vnto it selfe. But, Why then (will some say) did the people of Rome sweare to keepe the lawes? That was first begun by *Saturnius* the Tribune of the people, that so hee might the more straitly bind the Senators to the lawes by him made: which *Dio Nicæus* writeth to haue bene afterward done in all lawes. But it is one thing to bind all together, and to bind euerie one in particular: for so al the citisens particularly swore to the obseruation of the lawes, but not all together; for that euery one of them in particular was bound vnto the power of them all in generall But an oath could not be giuen by them all: for why, the people in generall is a certaine vniuersall bodie, in power and nature diuided from euery man in particular. Then againe to say truly, an oath cannot bee made but by the lesser to the greater, but in a popular estate nothing can bee greater than the whole body of the people themselues. But in a monarchie it is otherwise, where euerie one in particular, and all the people in generall, and (as it were) in one bodie, must sweare to the obseruation of the lawes, and their faithfull alleageance to one soueraigne monarch; who next vnto God (of whome he holdeth his scepter & power) is bound to no man. For an oath carrieth alwaies with it reuerence vnto whom, or in whose name it is made, as still giuen vnto a superiour: and therefore the vassall giueth his oath vnto his lord, but receiueth none from him againe, although that they be mutually bound the one of them vnto the other.

An oath cannot be made but by the lesser to the greater.

But if it be so, that a soueraigne prince next vnder God, is not by oath bound vnto any, why did *Traian* the emperor standing vpright, before the Consul sitting, solemnly sweare to the keeping of the lawes? That seemeth to haue beene so done by him for two causes, the one, for that hauing gotten the Consulship, together with his principalitie, he swore as the Consuls did at their entrance into their Consulship; as also al the new magistrats did the first of Ianuarie, after they had sacrificed in the Capitoll: The other reason was, for that the Roman emperours at the first had not any soueraigne power, but were onely called princes, that is to say, the chiefe men in the Commonweale; which forme of a Commonweale, is called a principalitie, and not a monarchy: but a principalitie is called a certaine forme of an Aristocratie, wherein one is in honor dignitie and place, aboue the rest: as amongst the Venetians: For the Roman emperour or prince, at the first was in honour aboue the rest, but not in power: howbeit that in truth the greatest part of the Roman emperors were indeed tyrants. Which is well to be vnderstood, for that which happened in the raigne of *Caligula* the cruell tyrant, who hauing bid certaine forren kings and allies of the people of Rome to supper, and question there at the table arising about their honour and greatnesse; hee to stay their strife, rapt out this verse, taken out of *Homers Iliades*;

A principalitie no Monarch.

The Roman emperours for most part tyrants.

K ij 'Our

A3 For governour (Fr 5-8) *read* governours (Fr 1-4).   B5 Saturninus   B7-8 and ANOTHER to bind
Notes at B4, B7, C3, D7, D10.

Ὀυκ ἀγαθὸν ἡ πολυκοιρανίη, ἒς κοίρανος ἔςω, ἒς βασιλεύς.
Good it is not to be ruled by many,
One king, one lord, if there be any.

<small>Sueton. in Caligula.</small>

And it missed but a little (as saith *Suetonius*) but that hee had euen then chaunged his principalitie into a monarchie, and set a crowne vpon his owne head. For in a principalitie the prince or chiefe magistrat, who is aboue the rest, is yet no soueraigne; as we shall hereafter show in the Commonweals of the Venetians, and of the Germans. And albeit that many of the Roman emperors, had taken vpon them the soueraigntie, and by diuers sleights wrested from the people their libertie; yet neuerthelesse it was no maruell if *Traian*, one of the best princes that euer liued in the world, swore (as is aforesaid) to keep the laws, although he in the name of a soueraigne prince were exempted; to the end by his own example to moue his subiects to the more carefull obseruing of them: but neuer one of the emperours before him so swore to the obseruing of the lawes. And therefore *Plinie* the younger, who in a pannegiricall oration, set forth the praises of that most worthy prince, speaking of the oath of *Traian*, crieth out in this sort, *A great noueltie* (saith he) *and neuer before heard of, hee sweareth by whome wee sweare*. And after that in the declination of the empire, *Theodoric* desirous to gaine the fauour of the Senat and people of Rome, followed the example of *Traian*, as wee read in *Cassiodore*, *Ecce Traiani nostri clarum seculis reparamus exemplum*; *iurat vobis per quem iuratis*, Behold (saith he) we renew the example of our *Traian*, famous through all ages; he sweareth vnto you, by whome you your selues sweare. And like it is, that other princes haue vsed the same custome, of taking the like oath at their coronation, although they haue the soueraigntie by the right of succession. True it is, that the kings of the Northerne people take such oathes as derogat from their soueraigntie: As for example, the nobilitie of Denmarke withstood the coronation of *Frederick*, in the moneth of August, in the yeare 1559, vntil that he had solemnly sworne that he should not put any noble man to death, or confiscat his goods, vntill he were iudged by the Senat; and that all noble men should haue iurisdiction & power of life & death ouer their subiects, without appeale; and that the king should haue no part in their fines or confiscation of their goods; and also that the king should not giue any office without consent of the counsell: which are all arguments, that the king of Denmarke is no absolute soueraigne. But this oath was first drawne out of the mouth of *Frederick* this mans grandfather, at such time as he made warre against *Christierne* king of Denmark (who was driuen out of his kingdome, and after long banishment returning, at length died in prison, wherein he had liued twentie fiue yeares) and was afterward confirmed by *Christierne* father of *Frederick*, who tooke the same oath. And to the end hee should not violat, or breake the same, the nobility to that purpose treated a league with the towne of Lubec, and *Sigismundus Augustus* king of Polonia, who also himselfe seemes not to haue much more power ouer his owne subiects than hath the king of Denmarke ouer his.

<small>Why Traian & some other good princes haue sworne to obserue and keepe the lawes.</small>

<small>Two great inconueniences ensuing vnto soueraigne princes by swearing to obserue the lawes.</small>

But of two things the one must be: that is to wit, the prince that sweareth to keepe the lawes of his countrey, must either not haue the soueraigntie; or els become a periured man, if he shall abrogat but one law, contrarie vnto his oath: whereas it is not only profitable that a soueraigne prince should sometimes abrogat some such lawes, but also necessarie for him to alter or correct them, as the infinit varietie of places, times, and persons shall require. Or if wee shall say the prince to be still a soueraigne, and yet neuerthelesse with such condition, as that he can make no law without the aduice of his counsell or people; he must also be dispensed with by his subiects, for the oath that hee he hath made for the inuiolat obseruation of the laws; & the subiects againe which are obliged & bound vnto the lawes, be it in particular, or in generall, haue also need to be dispensed withall by their prince, for feare they should bee periured: so shall it come to passe that the maiestie of the Commonweale, enclining now to this side, now to that side, sometimes the prince, sometimes the people bearing sway, shall haue no certaintie to rest vpon: which are notable absurdities, & altogether incompatible with the maiestie of absolute soueraigntie, & contrarie both to law & reason. And yet we see many, euen them that thinke themselues to see more in the matter than others, which maintaine it to be most necessarie, that princes should be bound by oath to keep the laws & customs of their country. In which doing they weaken & ouerthrow all the rights of soueraign maiesty, which ought to be most sacred & holy, & confound the soueraigntie of one soueraigne monarch, with an Aristocratie, or Democratie: whereby it commeth to passe, that many princes, seeing that power to be taken from them, which properly belongeth vnto them, & that men would make them subiect to the laws of their country, dispense in the end, not only with those their country laws, but euen with the laws of God & nature, making account of them all alike, as if they were bound to neither, but of both discharged. But to make all this matter more plaine to be vnderstood, we will by examples make manifest that before said. Wee read it thrice repeated in *Dan.* that by the customs of the Medes & Persians, the laws by their kings made, were immutable & irreuocable; & albeit that the king of the Medes would haue exempted the Prophet *Daniel*, from the punishment of death, which by the edict which hee had broken was to haue bene inflicted vpon him; yet was he by the princes forbidden so to doe, who shewed him, that the edict by him made could not by the law of their countrey be reuoked: wherunto when the king euen against his will (as should seeme) had assented, *Daniel* was accordingly condemned vnto the beasts, and so cast vnto the hungrie lions. If then the greatest monarch vpon earth could not derogat from the lawes by himselfe made; the grounds of maiestie and soueraigntie by vs before laid, must needs faile: and that not onely in a monarchie, but in a popular state also: as was that of Athens, whereof *Thucydides* speaking, showeth that the warre of *Peloponesus* began for a law made by the Athenians, whereby the Megariens were forbidden to come into the port of Athens; wherein the Megariens complained vnto their allies and friends themselues to be wronged and the lawes of nations violated: whereupon the Lacedemonians sent their ambassadours to Athens, to request the Athenians, that that law might be againe repealed. Wherunto *Pericles* then in greatest grace & authoritie with the people, aunswered the ambassodours, That by the expresse lawes of their aunceftours, the lawes once made and confirmed by the people, and so hanged vp vpon the common pillar, might neuer be taken away. Which if it were so, the people was bound not to their owne lawes onely, but euen to the lawes of their predecessours also. And that more is, *Theodosius* the emperour would not that the lawes by himself made, should be of any force, except they were confirmed by the generall decree of the whole Senat. In like maner also by the decree of *Lewes* the eleuenth, the French king, concerning the institution of knights of the order, in the eight article, it is expresly said, That the king shall vndertake no warre, nor other thing whatsoeuer of great importance, concerning the high estate of the Common weale, without knowledge thereof giuen vnto the knights of the order, so to haue and vse their aduice and counsell. And for that cause, as I suppose, the edicts of our kings are of none effect, vntill they be read, published, verified, and registred in parliament, with the consent of the great Atturney generall, and the approbation of the court. And in England it is by auntient custome receiued, that lawes concerning the state of the Commonweale

Examples to proue that lawes once made and established, may not by them that haue the soueraigntie be againe chaunged.

The lawes of the Athenians to be chaunged.

Polydore.

should

Note at A6.

102 THE FIRST BOOKE

should take no place, except they were authorised by the Estates assembled in the high court of Parliament.

The former reasons aunswered.

These reasons, although they seeme probable, yet are they not sufficient to proue the rule concerning Soueraignetie before by vs set downe, not to be true: For, as for that which was obiected concerning the law of the Medes, and authoritie of the king in abrogating of the lawes; it is manifest that it was false, and by the courtiers his enemies deuised against the life of *Daniel*: who grieuing to see a man for his wisdome and royall discent honourable, and yet a stranger, to be in greater grace and fauour with the king than themselues, and exalted in their countrey in degree next vnto the king, made that false allegation of the strength of their lawes against him, with whose accusation the king deceiued, or els to proue if *Daniels* God could saue him from death, caused him to be cast vnto the hungrie lyons. But hauing in him seene the wonderfull power and mercie of God towards his seruants, he gaue *Daniels* enemies to bee deuoured of the same lyons: wherein the end well shewed, the king to haue beene aboue the lawes of his countrey.

Ahashuerosh Hester.

In like sort *Darius Memnon* at the request of a young Iewish ladie reuoked the decree whereby he had appointed all the nation of the Iewes to be vtterly rooted out. As for that which *Pericles* answered vnto the ambassadours of the Lacedemonians, he therein respected not so much the truth, as the shew thereof, that so taking occasion of warre, which he sought after, he might frustrate the accusations of his aduersaries, and danger of the law, as *Timæus* and *Theopompus* haue truly written, and *Plutarch* hath not denied. And that was it for which hee said to the Lacedemonian ambassadours, That the edicts once hanged vpon the pillars, might not be taken away: which his sophistication the ambassadours returned vnto him againe, with a Lacedemonian quip, saying, That they desired not to haue the edict taken away from the pillar, but onely the table turned. For if the lawes of the Athenians had bene immutable, why had they such varietie, and infinit multitude of lawes, which they were wont to establish at the continuall motion of their magistrats, & to abrogat the old, that so the new might take place? But that *Pericles* therin abused the Lacedemonian ambassadors, it is manifest by the oration of *Demosthenes* against *Leptines*, who had preferred a request vnto the people, to the end that by a perpetuall and irreuocable edict it might from that time forward bee forbidden vpon paine of death, to present any request vnto the people for the obtaining of any priueledge or exemption, and the like paine to bee inflicted vpon him that should so much as speake for repealing that edict. Wherein *Demosthenes* hardly withstood *Leptines*, & so wrought the matter, that his request was receiued, hauing manifestly showed the people by consenting to this law, to be dispoiled not onely of the prerogatiue that it had to graunt exemptions and priueledges to such as should well deserue of them, but also of the power to abrogat lawes by them made, if the necessitie of the Commonweale should so require. They had also a popular action, concerning the breaking of lawes, which was commenced against them that would haue the people to passe any edict contrarie to the lawes before receiued; as one may see in all the orations of *Demosthenes*: but yet that neuer letted, but that the new and profitable lawes were still preferred before the old vniust lawes. And in like case the generall edict, wherein it was decred, That the offendors fine once adiudged and set downe by the people, might not in any wise bee forgiuen or abated; was yet many times reuoked, and that once in fauour of *Pericles* himselfe, and another time in fauour of *Cleomides* and *Demosthenes*, who by diuers iudgements of the people, had bene euerie one of them condemned in a fine of *thirtie thousand crownes. They say also in this realme of Fraunce, the fine once being paid, be it right or be it wrong, is neuer againe to be restored: and yet we see oftentimes the contrarie, and the same to bee againe

*Plut in Peri. Demetri. Demost.

G5 Darius Mnemon (cf. 466 I1)   I4 hardly *i.e.* vigorously   I5 *For* received *read* reiected (cf. L).
K6 Cleomides: Cleomedes (L) *properly* Cleomedon (Fr)   Note at G10.

A againe recouered. It is then a formalitie which is and hath alwaies beene in euerie Commonweale, that the law makers to giue vnto their lawes the greater weight and authoritie, ioyne thereunto these words of course, *Edicto perpetuo & irreuocabili sancimus, &c.* By a perpetuall and irreuocable decree we ordaine. And with vs in the beginning of euery law, *Vniuersis præsentibus & futuris:* which words are added to the eternall memorie of posteritie, least the law should by any be infringed. And the more to shew the difference of the lawes, such as be made for perpetuitie, are with vs sealed with greene waxe, and strings of greene and purple silke: whereas vnto the temporary Edicts are put neither strings of silke, nor greene waxe, but yellow onely. And yet for all this, there is no law which is perpetuall, no more than were those of the Greekes
B and Romanes, who in making their lawes, commonly vsed to ioyne thereunto this clause, *Vt nec per Senatum, nec per populum, lex infirmari possit:* That the law might not either by the Senate or the people bee weakened: which wordes if they imported a perpetuitie, why did the people almost in the same moment that it had established a law, againe abrogate the same. Concerning which matter, *Cicero* writing vnto his friend *Atticus: Thou knowest* (sayth he) *the Tribune Claudius to haue decreed that his law should hardly, or not at all, by the Senate or the people be infringed. But it is sufficiently knowne that regard was neuer had vnto this clause: Vt nec per Senatum nec per populum lex infirmari possit: for otherwise* (sayth he) *one should neuer see law repealed, seeing that there is no law which carieth not this clause with it: from which men yet doe ordinarily de-*
C *rogate.* Thus much he. Which is yet more plainely to be vnderstood out of the Oration of *Fabius Ambustus* against the intercession of the Tribunes of the people, who maintained, that the people could not chuse both the Consuls of the nobilitie, for that by a law before made it was ordained, That one of the Consuls should be still chosen out of the people: *Fabius* alledged the law of the twelue Tables in these words, *Quod postremum iussit populus id ratum esto,* What the people shall last decree, let that stand for good.

So we see the Medes, the Persians, the Greeks, the Latines, to haue vsed the same forme and cautions, for the establishing of their edicts and lawes, that our kings doe: who vnto the lawes by them made, oftentimes ioyne this clause: *Without that there-*
D *from can by vs, or our successors be derogated.* Or els, *without regard hauing vnto any derogation, which from this present we haue declared to be of none effect.* And yet no man can so make a law vnto himselfe, but that he may depart therefrom, as we haue before said. Wherefore the repeales and derogations of the former edicts and lawes, are almost alwaie subiect vnto the latter edicts and derogations. And therefore *Solon* did wisely, who would not bind the Athenians to keep his lawes for euer, but contented himselfe to haue them kept for an hundred yeares: and yet neuerthelesse hee yet liuing, and present, suffered (though against his will) the greatest part of them to bee chaunged.

But that publication or approbation of lawes in the assembly of the Estates or par-
E liament, is with vs of great power and importance for the keeping of the lawes; not that the Soueraigne prince is bound to any such approbation, or cannot of himselfe make a law without the authoritie or consent of the States or the people: but yet it is a courteous part to do it by the good liking of the Senat, as saith *Theodosius,* which *Baldus* enterpreted not to be a thing so much of necessitie, as of courtesie: as that is also a speech well beseeming soueraigne maiestie, for a prince to professe himself bound vnto the lawes of himselfe that raigneth. And certainely there is nothing better, or more beseeming a prince, than by his deeds and life to confirme those lawes which hee himselfe hath made: for that is of greatest force, for the honour and obedience of the subiects

The clause of perpetuitie why annexed vnto lawes, and yet no lawes perpetuall.

* *Plut. in Sol.*

The soueraigne prince more of curtesie than of necessitie bound to obserue the lawes.

K iiij

Note at D5.

subiects towards their prince: as contrariwise nothing is more daungerous for the contempt both of the prince and of the lawes, than without iust cause to breake or infringe that which thou hast commaunded: as an auntient Roman Senatour said, *Leuius est, & vanius, sua decreta tollere quam aliorum,* It is more lightnesse and vanitie to take away a mans owne decrees, than the decrees of other men. But it is one thing for a man so to doe willingly and of his owne accord, and another thing to bee bound by bond or oath so to do it.

Liuius lib.3.

But what if a prince by law forbid to kill or to steale, is hee not bound to obay his owne lawes? I say that this law is not his, but the law of God and nature, whereunto all princes are more straitly bound than their subiects: in such sort as that they cannot be from the same exempted, either by the Senat, or the people, but that they must bee enforced to make their appearance before the tribunall seat of almightie God: For God taketh a straiter account of princes than of others, as the maister of wisdome *Salomon* himselfe a king, hath most truly written. Whereunto well agreeth that saying of *Marcus Aurelius,* who for his desire of knowledge, was called the Philosopher: *The magistrats are iudges ouer priuat men, princes iudge the magistrats, and God the princes.* This is the opinion of 2 great princes, esteemed of all other the wisest; vnto whom we wil ioine the third, *Antigonus* king of Asia, who hearing a flatterer say, that al things were lawfull for kings: Yea, said he, for barbarous kings and tyrants. The first that vsed this kind of flatterie, was *Anaxarchus* towards *Alexander* the Great, whome hee made to beleeue, That the goddesse *Iustice,* was still at the right hand of *Iupiter,* to shew that princes could do nothing but that was right and iust: Of which their iustice he shortly after made proofe, for being fallen into the hands of the king of Cyprus, he was by his commaundement with hammers beaten to death vppon an anuill. But how much more truely did *Seneca* say to the contrarie, *Cæsari cum omnia licent, propter hoc minus licet,* When all things are vnto *Cæsar* lawfull, euen for that are they lesse lawfull. And therefore they that generally say, that princes are not subiect vnto lawes, nor to their owne conuentions, if they except not the lawes of God and nature, and the iust contracts and conuentions made with them, they do great wrong both vnto God and nature, in that they make not the speciall exemption to appeare; as men say in matters of priueleges. So *Dionisius* the tyrant of Sicilie, said to his mother, That he could dispence with the lawes and customes of Syracusa, but not with the lawes of nature. For as the contracts and testaments of priuat men, cannot derogat from the decrees of the magistrats, nor the decrees of the magistrats from the auntient customes, nor the auntient customes from the generall lawes of a soueraigne prince: no more also can the lawes of soueraigne princes alter or chaunge the lawes of God and nature. Wherefore the Roman magistrats did notably, who vnto the end of all their requests & laws which they propounded vnto the good liking of the people, commonly annexed this clause, *Si quid ius non esset E. E. L. N. R. eius ea lege nihilem rogaretur,* that is to say, That if any thing were therein contained that was not iust and reasonable, they by that law requested nothing. But of all others they are most absurd, which say, That a soueraigne prince can decree nothing against the lawes of God and nature, without most apparant reason. For what apparant reason can there be diuised, for which wee ought to breake the lawes of God? And hereof proceed such paradoxes as this, That he whome the Pope hath dispensed withall for the lawes of God, is sufficiently assured before God: which how true it is let others iudge.

All princes bound and subiect vnto the lawes of God and nature, and to their owne iust conuentions.

There resteth yet another obiection, by them obiected which with more reason examine matters. If princes (say they) be bound vnto the lawss of nature, that is to say, of vpright reason: and that ciuill lawes be (in all things) agreeable vnto right and reason,

An obiection that princes are bound to the ciuill lawes.

G9 for barbarous   G10 flatterie   I3 cannot   I9 nihilum   K8 lawes   Notes at F6, H9.

OF A COMMONWEALE. 105

A son, it must needs thereof follow, that the prince is also bound vnto the ciuil laws. And to that end they alleage that saying of *Pacutius* vnto *Theodosius* the emperour, *Tantum tibi licet quantum per leges licebit*, So much is lawfull for thee to do, as thou maiest by law doe. For the plainer aunswering of which doubt, we must thus distinguish: That the lawes of a soueraigne prince, whereof question is made, concerne either that which is publick, or priuat, or common to both: and generally when question is, it is either of that which is profitable and not honest, or of that which is honest and not profitable, or is both profitable and honest; or els of that which is neither of both. And that I call honest, which is agreeing vnto the equitie of nature; vnto which naturall equitie it is manifest all princes to be bound, seeing that which nature teacheth, is altogether

The answere, declaring to what lawes a prince is bound, and to what lawes not.

B comprehended in the law of nature, whereunto euery prince is bound to obey: neither is such a law to bee called a ciuile law, albeit that the prince cause it to bee published, but rather the law of nature. And with so much the more reason, when the law is both honest and profitable. But if that which is by law commaunded, bee neither honest nor profitable, although of such things there ought to be no law; yet may the prince bind his subiects vnto those lawes, whereunto he is not himselfe bound, if they haue no dishonour or dishonestie ioyned with them. For there bee some things honest, some things dishonest, and some in a meane betwixt both. But if profit repugne against honestie, it is good reason that honestie should take place. As *Aristides* the iust, to whom *Themistocles* was commanded to communicat his deuice, aunswered, That

C the counsell of *Themistocles* was profitable to the Commonweale; but yet in his iudgement dishonest: the Athenians hearing so much, enquired no farther after the matter, but decreed that his profitable counsell to be reiected. But here when we reason of a Commonweale, we must speake according to the common manner; which our speech is not to be examined according to the subtiltie of Philosophers: for they set downe, nothing to be profitable which is not honest, neither any thing to bee honest which is not iust: but that old custome is growne out of vse, so that of necessitie we must make a difference betwixt things honest, and things profitable. But if that which the prince by his law commaundeth, be not honourable, but profitable, he himselfe is not by that law bound, although his subiects be, so that nothing bee therein

D contained contrarie to the lawes of God and nature: and such lawes the prince may at his pleasure abrogat, or from them derogat, and in stead of them make others, either more or lesse profitable: for things honest, iust, and profitable, haue their degrees of more and lesse. If then it be lawfull for a prince amongst lawes profitable, to make choice of them that be more profitable; so also amongst lawes iust and honest, he may chuse out them that be most vpright and honest, albeit that some therby receiue profit, and some others losse; prouided that the profit be publicke, and the losse particular: and yet if the prince shall otherwise decree, it is not lawfull for the subiect to breake the laws of his prince, vnder the colour of honestie, or iustice: as if the prince in time of famine, forbid the carrying out of victuals (a thing not only profitable to the Common-

E weale, but oft times also iust and reasonable) he ought not to giue leaue to some few to carry thē out, to the preiudice of the common state, & of other marchants in particular; for vnder the colour of profit that these flatterers and scrapers carrie things, many good marchants suffer losse, and all the subiects in generall are famished: and yet neuerthelesse the famine and dearth ceasing, it is not yet lawfull for the subiect to transgresse the edicts of his prince, and to carrie out victuals, vntill the law forbidding the same, be by the prince abrogated, no not though there seeme neuer so great occasions for the transgressing of the law: as that now the citie is full of victuall, and all other things necessarie; and that the law of nature persuadeth vs to giue reliefe vnto distressed

A2 Pacatius (*but properly* Pacatus)   C10 although   Notes at D2, D5, E3.

sed strangers, in letting them haue part of such good things as it hath pleased God to send encrease of more in one countrey than in another: for as much as the power of the law that forbiddeth, is greater than the apparant equitie, the show whereof euerie man might pretend to his desires, except the prohibition in the law be directly against the lawes of God and nature.

A law may be good, iust, and reasonable, and yet the prince no way subiect or bound thereunto.

But so sometimes things fall out, as that the law may be good, iust, and reasonable, and yet the prince to be no way subiect or bound thereunto: as if he should forbid all his subiects, except his guard and garrison souldiors, vpon paine of death to carrie weapon, so to take away the feares of murders and seditions; he in this case ought not to be subiect to his owne law, but to the contrarie, to be well armed for the defence of the good, and punishment of the euill. The same we may say of other edicts and lawes also, which concerne but some part of the subiects; which edicts and lawes are called priueleges, and are iust in respect of certaine persons, or for a certaine time, or place; or for the varietie of punishments which depend alwaies of the lawes; albeit that the forbidding of offences is proceeding from the lawes of God and nature. Vnto which edicts and lawes the princes are not any way bound, further than the naturall iustice of the same hath place; which ceasing, the prince is no more thereunto bound, vntill the prince haue abrogated the same. For it is not onely a law of nature, but also oftentimes repeated amongst the lawes of God, That we should be obedient vnto the lawes and ordinances of such princes as it hath pleased God to set to rule and raigne ouer vs, if their lawes and decrees be not directly repugnant vnto the lawes of God and nature, whereunto all princes are as well bound as their subiects. For as the vassall oweth his oath of fidelitie vnto his lord towards & against al men, except his soueraigne prince; so the subiect oweth his obedience to his soueraigne prince, towards and against all, the maiestie of God excepted, who is the absolute soueraigne of all the princes in the world.

That a soue-prince is bound to his owne contracts, aswell as other men be.

Out of this resolution we may draw another rule of estate, that is to wit, that the soueraigne prince is bound vnto the contracts by him made, bee it with his subiect, or with a straunger: for seeing he is the warrant to his subiects of the mutuall conuentions and obligations that they haue one of them against another: of how much more reason is he the debter of iustice in his owne fact, and so bound to keepe the faith and promises by himselfe giuen and made to others? As the court of parliament at Paris writ backe vnto king *Charles* the ix, in the moneth of March, in the yeare 1563, That his maiestie alone could not breake the contract made betwixt him and the clergie, without the consent of the clergie; and that for this reason, For that he was himselfe the debtor of iustice, and so bound to giue euerie man his right. Which putteth mee in remembrance of a resolution concerning the vpright dealing of princes, worthy to be engrauen in letters of gold, in their lodgings and pallaces; which is, *That it ought to bee accounted amongst things which by chaunce seldome happen, if a prince fayle of his promise; and that it is not otherwise to be presumed*.

A notable saying.

For that of his promise there is a double bond; the one for the naturall equitie thereof: for what can be more agreeing vnto naturall equitie, than to haue iust promise kept? The other, for the honour of the prince himselfe, who is bound to keepe his promise, although it be vnto his losse; for that he is the formall warrant to all his subiects, of the faith that they haue amongst them; as also for that there is no more detestable crime in a prince, than to bee false of his oath and promise. And that is it for which the soueraigne prince ought alwaies in iustice to bee lesse respected or releeued than his subiects, when question is of his promise. For if a prince haue once bestowed an honour or an office vpon a man, it is deemed, that he may not without iust cause take it againe away from him; but a particu-

A soueraigne prince lesse in iustice to be respected or releeued, than his subiects, when question is of his promise.

lar

Of A Commonweale. 107

lar subiect may: and so it is ordinarily iudged. And wheras by the law the patron might without cause take his fee from his vassall; yet was it not lawfull for the prince so to doe. Whereby it is well to be perceiued, the doctors of the Canon law to erre, and to be deceiued, who deny a prince to be bound to his owne conuentions or agreements, otherwise than with a naturall bond: for that say they, euery bond is proper vnto the ciuill law; which their errour is to be remoued: For who can doubt, but that the bond is of the same nature with the couenant? Wherefore if the couenant be naturall, and common to all nations, the bonds and actions arising thereof must needs consequently be of the same nature also. But no couenant almost, neither any obligation or bond can be deuised, which is not common both vnto the law of nature and nations. But let vs graunt some couenants to proceed from the meere ciuill law; yet who dare to deny a prince to be more straitly bound euen vnto such ciuill couenants, and promises, than are the priuat subiects themselues? yea and that in so strait a maner as that he cannot with all the absolute power he hath derogat from the same? For so almost all the learned lawyers are of opinion and accord. And what maruell? seeing God himselfe is bound vnto his promises. For so he plainly protesteth with the prophet *Hieremie*, *Call together vnto me* (saith he) *all the people of the earth, that they may iudge betwixt me and my people, if there be any thing that I ought to haue done, which I haue not done*. Let vs noth therefore call into question those things wherof many doctors haue doubted. As whether a prince be bound vnto the couenants which he hath made with his subiects? whereat we need not to maruell, seeing that out of the same fountaine is sprung, that no lesse straunge position: that a prince may of right, without any iust cause enrich himselfe with another mans losse: an opinion repugnant vnto the lawes both of God and nature. But how much more vprightly was it of late iudged in the court of Paris, that the prince might giue his intrest vnto the partie condemned; but not the intrest of another man. And that in confiscations creditours are by right first to be preferred. The same court also by another decree determined, That the prince might derogat from the ciuill lawes, so that it were done without preiudice to any particular mens right: which is to confirme the resolutions which wee before haue set downe, concerning the absolute soueraignetie. And *Philip* of Valois, by two testaments which he made in the yeare 1347, and 1350, (which are in the treasurie of France in a coffer, intituled The testaments of kings, number 289) ioyneth a clause derogatorie vnto the lawes of his countrey, from which he protested himselfe to be discharged, as not vnto them bound. The like protestations he also vsed, when hee gaue vnto the queene his wife certaine treasure, and priuat lands, contrarie vnto the lawes: with aswel his prodigall gift, as also that his derogation from the lawes of his countrey, are yet extant in the publick records. Howbeit that *Augustus* the emperor thought it not good for himselfe in like case to vse the like libertie in his Commonweale, but being willing to giue vnto his wife *Liuia*, that which he could not by reason of the law Voconia, hee requested to be dispensed with all from that law by the Senat (although that it was not needfull for him so to haue done, considering that he was long time before in all other things dispensed with from the lawes) to the intent the better to assure his gift, for that he was not a soueraigne prince, as we haue before showed. For otherwise hee had not bene any way bound so to doe; as it was in most strong tearmes iudged by a decree in the court of Paris, in the case of *Philip* the second, the French king, That he was not bound vnto the customes of the ciuil law, at such time as they which were next of kindred would haue redeemed of him the countie of Guynes: howbeit that many both thinke and write, the prince to be bound to that law: for that they thinke that law to be common to all nations, and not proper to any citie: and yet then the which law the

That a soueraigne prince is bound to his own ciuil couenants.

Romans

108　　　　　　　　　　　　　　　The First Booke

What account was made of the Roman ciuill lawes in France.

Romans themselues (in some cases) thought nothing more vnreasonable. But our ancestours would not haue euen their subiects bound vnto the Roman lawes; as we see in the auntient records, that *Philip* the faire, erecting the parliament of Paris and Monpellier declared, That they should not be bound vnto the Roman laws. And in the erection of Vniuersities, the kings haue alwaies declared, That their purpose was to haue the ciuill and canon laws in them publickly professed and taught, to make vse therof at their discretion, but not that the subiects should be any way bound therunto, least they should seeme to derogat from the lawes of their owne country by aduancing the laws of straungers. And for the same cause *Alaricus* king of the Gothes, forbad vpon pain of death, any man to allege the Roman lawes contrarie to his decrees and ordinances. Which *M. Charles du Moulin* (my companion, and ornament of all lawyers) mistaking, is therefore with him verie angrie, and in reproach calleth him therefore barbarous: howbeit that nothing was therein by *Alaricus* decreed or done, but that which euerie wise prince would of good right haue decreed and done: for subiects will so long both remember, and hope for the gouernment of strangers, as they are gouerned by their lawes. The like edict there is of king *Charles* the faire, and an old decree of the court of Paris, whereby we are expresly forbidden to alleage the laws of the Romans, against the lawes and customes of our auncestours. Yea the kings of Spaine also haue vpon capitall paine forbidden any man to alleage the Roman laws, in confirmation of their owne laws, (as *Oldrad* writeth.) And albeit that there were nothing in the lawes and customes of their countrey which differed from the Roman lawes, yet such is the force of that edict, that all men may vnderstand that the iudges in deciding of the subiects causes, were not bound vnto the Roman lawes: & therfore much lesse the prince himselfe, who thought it a thing daungerous to haue his iudges bound vnto straunge lawes. And worthy he is to be accounted a traitor, that dare to oppose straunge lawes and straunge decrees against the lawes of his owne prince. In which doings when the Spaniards did too much offend, *Stephen* king of Spaine forbad the Roman lawes to be at all taught in Spaine, as *Polycrates* writeth: which was more straitly prouided for by king *Alphonsus* the tenth, who commaunded the magistrats and iudges to come vnto the prince himselfe, as often as there was nothing written in the lawes of their countrey concerning the matter in question. Wherein *Baldus* is mistaken, when hee writeth the Italians to bee bound to the Roman lawes; but the French no otherwise than so farre as they should seeme vnto them to agree with equitie and reason. For the one are as little bound as the other; howbeit that Italie, Spaine, the countries of Prouince, Sauoy, Languedoc, and Lyonnois, vse the Roman lawes more than other people: and that *Frederike Barbarussa* the emperour, caused the books of the Roman laws to be published and taught: the greatest part whereof haue yet no place in Italie, and much lesse in Germanie. But there is much difference betwixt a right, and a law: for a right still without commaund respecteth nothing but that which is good and vpright; but a law importeth a commaundement. For the law is nothing els but the commaundement of a soueraigne, vsing of his soueraigne power. Wherefore then as a soueraigne is not bound vnto the laws of the Greeks, nor of any other stranger whatsoeuer he be, no more is he bound vnto the Roman laws, more than that they are conformable vnto the law of nature; which is the law whereunto (saith *Pindarus*) all kings and princes are subiect. From which we are not to except either the pope or the emperour (as some pernitious flatterers do) saying, That those two *viz.* the pope and the emperour, may of right without cause take vnto themselues the goods of their subiects. Which opinion the Canonists themselues, the interpretors of the popes law detest, as contrarie to the law of God: whereunto for all that they ioine this euill limitation, in saying,

The Roman lawes forbidden to be taught in Spaine.

Neither pope nor emperour exempted from the law of nature. A dangerous opinion, and not to be taught to princes.

H8 Polycrates *i.e.* the *Policraticus* of John of Salisbury, which in fact refers (VIII, 22) to Stephen, King of England
Notes at F1, K3.

OF A COMMONWEALE. 109

saying, That they may yet do it of their most high and absolute power and authority, as they tearme it: which is as much as if they should say it to bee lawfull for them to rob and spoyle their subiects, oppressed by force of armes: which law, the more mightie vse against them that be weaker than themselues, which the Germans most rightly call, The law of theeues and robbers. But pope *Innocent* the iiij himself, most skilfull in both the lawes, saith that most high and absolute power, to bee able but to derogat from the ordinarie law: whereas they would haue such absolute and soueraigne power to extend to the abrogating of the lawes of God and nature. For what is more religiously by Gods lawes forbidden, than to rob and spoyle other men of their goods? what thing do we read more often repeated, than to keepe our hands from other mens things? yea we are by the most holy Decalogue commaunded, not so much as to desire that which is another mans. Now certainly it is a greater offence to infect princes with this doctrine, than it is to rob and steale. For pouertie commonly causeth theeues to seeke after other mens goods: but they that maintaine such opinions, show the lion his clawes, and arme the prince so instructed, to pretend vnto his outrages, this goodly show of Law and Iustice: who by nature naught, & made worse by instruction: so prouing to be a tyrant, maketh no question most shamefully to confound and breake all the lawes both of God and man: and afterward enflamed with corrupt desires and affections, which altogether weaken the more noble parts of the mind, hee quickly breaketh out from couetousnesse to vniust confiscations, from lust to adulterie, from wrath to murder. So that as thunder is indeed before the lightning, although it be latter heard so also an euill prince, corrupted with these pernitious & pestilent opinions, peruerting iustice, causeth the fine to runne before the accusation, and the condemnation before the iudgement. Howbeit it is an incongruitie in law, to say that a prince can do any thing which is not agreeing with honestie; seeing that his power ought alwaies to be measured with the foot of iustice. For so said *Plinie* the younger vnto *Traian* the emperour, *Vt enim fœlicitatis est posse quantum velis: sic magnitudinis velle quantum possis*, As it is (saith he) in thy happinesse to be able to doe what thou wilt; so beseemeth it thy greatnesse, to will what thou maist. Whereof may be gathered, that a prince can do nothing that is fowle or vniust. It is also euill done, to say, that a soueraigne prince hath power by violence to take away another mans goods, to rob, to commit adulterie, or to do euill, seeing that so to doe, is rather an impotencie, or feeblenes, proceeding from a weake mind ouercome with impotent lust and desire, rather than any soueraignty. Now then if a soueraigne prince may not remoue the bounds which almightie God (of whom he is the liuing & breathing image) hath prefined vnto the euerlasting lawes of nature: neither may he take from another man that which is his, without iust cause, whether it be by buying, by exchaunge, by confiscation, by league with friends, or peace made with enemies, if it cannot otherwise bee concluded than by priuat mens losse; whose goods princes oftentimes permit the enemies to enioy, for the generall welfare of the subiects and of the Commonweale: howbeit that many be not of this opinion, but would that euerie man should keepe his owne; and that no publick diminution should be made of any priuat mans goods, or that if publicke necessitie so required, it were againe to bee made good by the whole state: which opinion I like well of, if conueniently it might so be done. But forasmuch as the welfare of priuat men, and all the goods of the subiects are contained in the health of our country, it beseemeth priuat men without grudging to forgiue vnto the Commonwealth, not onely their priuat displeasures, and iniuries receiued from their enemies, but to yeeld also for the health of the Commonweale, their goods. For peace hath for the most part some hard measure in it, which is againe recompenced with the

That a princes power ought alwaies to be measured with the foot of iustice.

Priuat mens losses by princes sometimes to bee sufferd, for the greater benefit of the Commonweale.

L publick

B6 naught *i.e.* bad, wicked   Note at D7.

publique profit: and this law doth all people vse, that in conclusions of peace, not onely publick things are recompensed with publike, and priuat things with priuat; but both with the mutuall profits and detriments of both. And yet I see many great maisters of both lawes, both to be, & to haue bene of opinion, that in those leagues wherein it is excepted, that no question should be made of the losse on both sides receiued, such exception should be void, neither to be any thing preiudiciall vnto priuat men: howbeit that we vse it otherwise; for in the peace of Peronne, made for the deliuerance of *Lewes* the xj the French king, prisoner vnto *Charles* earle of Burgundie, it was in one article prouided, That Seigneur *de Torci* should not execute the sentence of the court of Paris against the lord of Saneuses. And therefore is *Thrasibulus* (and that not vnworthily) commended, that hauing ouerthrowne and driuen thirtie tyrants out of the citie of Athens, he caused the law of forgetfulnesse to be proclaimed. Wherein was contained the forgetting of all priuat iniuries and losses receiued in the late ciuill warre: which was also afterwards proclaimed in Rome, after that *Cæsar* was slaine in the Senat, at the treatie made betwixt the conspirators on the one side, and *Cæsars* partakers on the other. Yet is it by all meanes to be enduoured, that mens harmes receiued, should be recompensed with other mens profits, and so as neere as may bee euery man to haue his owne, which if it cannot be done without tumult and ciuill warres, we must defend the possessors of other mens things, although they hold them wrongfully, vntill the right honours may be satisfied out of the common treasure: or if the common treasure be exhausted, to borrow money to content them. As did *Aratus*, who hauing restored his countrey to libertie, after it had for the space of fiftie yeares bene oppressed with tyranny, restored also sixe hundred banished men, whose lands & goods had bene by the tyrant confiscated. Yet would hee not the possessors of those lands, which the tyrants had vniustly taken from those citisens, to be spoyled therof: for that much thereof was lawfully bought and sold, and much of it holden in dowrie, so that it could not be done without a most daungerous turmoile in the state. Wherefore he bound all the citisens by oath, That they should keep peace and amitie vntill such time as he returning out of Ægypt, should then take order for all things. For hauing there borrowed threescore thousand crownes of K. *Ptolemæus Philadelphus*, he returned into his countrey, and prising the land, so wrought the matter, that some made choice to take money and leaue the land; and other some thought it better to take mony themselues, than to recouer againe that which had beene before their owne. Wherefore these causes that I haue said ceasing, the prince cannot take nor giue another mans goods, without the consent of the owner. And in all gifts, grants, immunities, and priueledges, this clause is still annexed, *Sauing alwaies our owne right: and the right of other men*: Which clause added vnto the inuestiture of the dutchie of Milan, which *Maximilian* the emperour made to king *Lewes* the xij, was the occasion of new warres, for the right which the *Sforces* pretended to the dutchie, which the emperour could not nor would not giue away. And this clause although it be left out, is yet supposed to be still put in: for that euen the emperour would he neuer so faine, can no otherwise giue or graunt any other thing to any bodie. For that which the common people commonly saith, *All to be the princes*, is to be vnderstood concerning power and soueraigntie, the proprietie and possession of euerie mans things yet reserued to himselfe. For so saith *Seneca*, *Ad reges potestas omnium pertinet, ad singulos proprietas*, Vnto kings belongeth the power of all things, and vnto particular men the proprietie. And a little after, *Omnia rex imperio possidet singuli dominio*, The king in power possesseth all things: and priuat men as owners. And for this cause our kings by the lawes and decrees of Court, are bound to void their hands of such lands as are fallen vnto them by

way

The law of forgetfulnes necessarie for the ending of ciuile warres, and composing of controuersies betwixt princes.

How is it to bie vnderstood, All to be the princes.

The king in some cases lesse priuiledged than the subiect.

F10 Saneuses: Sanusius (L) Sanenses (Fr 1) properly Saveuses (Fr 2–8)   G6 endeauoured
G10 untill *i.e.* as far as, to the same extent that (cf. L)   G10 For honours *read* owners.   H2 libertie
H10 threescore   K2 any other thing *i.e.* anything belonging to another man

Of A Commonweale. 111

A way of confiscation (if they be not simplie and without meane holden of the crowne) to the end that the patrons of them that were proscribed, should loose nothing of their right in the lands confiscated. And if the king be debtor to any priuat man his subiect, he is therefore oft times sued, condemned, and enforced to pay the debt. But that straungers aswell as subiects, and all posteritie may know of what integritie our kings haue bene, and with what moderation they haue borne themselues towards their subiects, let this be for example, That the king himselfe in the yere 1266, was by the iudgement of the court of Paris, condemned to pay vnto the curat, the tyth of the fruits euen of his garden of pleasure. So when another of our kings had by the negligence of his aduocat, made default of appearence at his day; hee by ordinarie course requested to

B haue that negligent ouersight pardoned: which the kings request the court of Paris denied, as appeareth by the decree of the court, in the yeare 1419. But no such strict proceeding is vsed against priuat men, who alwaies in such case are againe restored into the state they before were. And albeit that subiects vnder xxv yeares old, almost in all priuat iudgements vse to be againe restored into the state they were, by the priuelege of their age; yet our kings although but children, are neuer so restored by the benefit of their age, but in all iudgements are deemed to bee of full age. And yet the Commonweale neuerthelesse is alwaies reputed to be in minoritie: which is to aunswere them which are of opinion, That the Commonweale ought not to be restored; in that they confound the patrimonie of the prince, with the Commonweale, which is

C alwaies in a monarchie diuided: but all one in a popular or an Aristocraticall state. With this stoutnesse of courage the magistrats bare themselues towards our kings, & with this moderation also did our kings reuerence iustice, preferring still in all sutes the Commonweale before priuat men, and priuat men before princes. There is also extant in the records of the court of Paris, a iudgement giuen against king *Charls* the seuenth, wherein he was condemned to suffer a wood of his to bee cut downe which hee had neere vnto the citie of Paris, for the publike vse in generall, and the vse of euerie one of the citisens in particular: and that more was, the price thereof was set downe for him in the decree, whereunto a priuat subiect could hardly haue bene driuen. Then was it plainely to be seene how much a king differed from a tyrant: for when this *Charls* the

D vij had driuen the English forces out of the hart of Fraunce, and easily taken the citie of Paris (which confederated with the English, had wrested the scepter out of this kings hand) he was so farre from reuenging of his receiued iniuries, that hee vsed the citisens most curteously, and showed himselfe more obedient vnto the judges than priuat men haue vsed to be. When at the same time *Philip Maria*, duke of Milan, hauing oppressed the Commonweale with taxes and tributes, embarred also his ports and riuers, in such sort as that none of the citisens without his leaue could passe or trauell thereby, but that first they must therefore pay money.

Thus we haue hitherto showed in what sort a soueraigne is subiect vnto the lawes and conuentions by him made with his subiects: Now it resteth for vs to see whether

E he be subiect vnto the contracts and promises of the kings his predecessours; and whether such his obliging be compatible with soueraigne maiestie or not. Which in few words to discusse, passing ouer a multitude of nice questions which might bee made in this matter: I say that a prince is bound vnto the couenants of his aunceftors as well as other priuat heirs, if his kingdome come vnto him by inheritance, or bee giuen him by testament being not next of kinne: as *Ptolemee* king of Cyrene, *Nicomedes* king of Bithynia, *Attalus* king of Asia, and *Eumenes* king of Pergame, by their wils appointed the people of Rome to inherit their kingdomes. But what if a kingdome be by will giuen vnto the next of kinne? as *Henry* the eight by his will left the kingdome of England

Whether a soueraigne prince be bound to the promises or conuentions of the kings his predecessours or not.

L ij

land to his son *Edward* the sixt: and substituted vnto him his sister *Mary*, and vnto her *Elizabeth* her sister, who all successiuely enioyed the kingdome. In this case wee must distinguish, whether the appointed heire will accept the state in the qualitie of an heire by testament appointed; or renouncing the succession of the testator, demaundeth the crowne by vertue of the custome and law of his countrey. For in the former case the successour is bound vnto all the hereditary obligations and actions of his predecessors, as if he were a priuat inheritour: but in the second case, he is not bound vnto the dome of his predecessour, albeit that his predecessour were thereto sworne. For neither the oath nor the obligation of the dead predecessour, bindeth the successour in the law, more than so farre as the obligation made by the testatour tendeth to the good of the Commonweale, and so farre he is bound. And therefore king *Lewes* the xij, when he was demaunded the artillerie lent vnto *Charles* the eight, answered, That he was none of *Charles* his heire. So of late king *Francis* the second, to like effect writ his letters vnto the lords of the Swissers, demaunding of him his fathers debts, the copie whereof taken out of the records, bearing date the xix of Ianuarie 1559, I haue here set downe as followeth, *viz. Although that we be not bound to pay the debts of our most honourable Lord, and dead father: for that we haue not taken vpon vs this crowne by right of inheritance as his heire, but by the royall law and custome generally obserued euen from the first institution thereof, which bindeth vs not, but onely to the obseruing of such confederations and treaties, passed and made by the kings our predecessors, with other forren princes and Commonweales, for the good and profit of this crowne. Neuerthelesse desiring to discharge the credit and conscience of the said our dead lord and father, wee are resolued to discharge his lawfull debts, &c. Onely this requesting you, to moderat the interest, in such sort as you haue vsed, according to the lawes and customes of your countrey, and that no greater be of vs exacted.* Which his request the Swissers by their common decree approued, so that whereas before they had taken of our people so deepe intrest, as euery sixt yeare came almost to as much as the principall, (which is twice so much as they doe in Fraunce) they brought it downe to a third part, which commeth to so much as the principal but in twentie yeares. But that our kings were not bound vnto the bonds of their predecessours, the court of Paris determined, *viz*. In the yeare 1256. Wherefore they are greatly deceiued, which receiue as from an oracle the formall and conceiued words of the oath which the bishops of Rheims haue at their pleasure not long since deuised, which our kings at their coronation now vse. For after that the archbishop of Rheims hath set the crowne vpon the kings head, the twelue peers of Fraunce putting to their hands, he saith vnto him these words, *Stay you here* (saith he) *and the kingdome which you haue before vntill now holden by succession from your father, now from henceforth hold as the true heyre thereof, put into your hands by the power of almightie God, and by the iust deliuerie thereof, which we the bishops and other the seruants of God here presently make vnto you*. An honest speech if it were true. But I thinke no man doubteth, but that the king euen before his consecration enioyeth both the possession and proprietie of the kingdome, not by inheritance or his fathers right, and much lesse by the bountie of the bishops or peers, but by the royall law and custome of the realme, as was long since decreed by *a decree of the French men, That no man should thinke the power of the king to depend of the pleasure of the bishops: not for that the Senat euer doubted of the power of the king before his coronation; but that those vaine quirkes of the bishops might be vtterly refelled. For it is an old prouerbe with vs, That the king doth neuer die, but that so soone as he is dead, the next male of his stocke is seised of the kingdome, and in possession thereof before he be crowned, which is not conferred vnto him by succession of his father, but by vertue of the law of the land; least the succession

The letters of the French king vnto the Swissers

Anno. 1463

The king neuer dieth.

F1 Edward the sixt (Fr 6–8) *erroneously* Edward V (Fr 1–5 and L)   F7 dome *i.e.* enactment, decree (But Bodin writes *faicts*, deeds, actions.)   G8 observed IN THIS KINGDOM even from

Of A Commonweale. 113

A sion of the kingdome should be vncertaine, then which nothing can be more daungerous in a Commonweale. Wherefore let vs this hold, that the king which is by lawfull right called vnto his kingdome, is so farre bound vnto the couenants and promises of the kings his predecessours, as is for the good of the Commonweale: and so much the more if the contracts were made by the consent and good liking of the people in generall, or of the states, or high court of parliament: which it is not onely seemely for a king to keepe, but also necessarie, although it be hurtfull vnto the Commonweale, considering that it concerneth the faith and obligation of his subiects. But if the soueraigne prince hath contracted either with strangers, or with his subiects, for such things as concerne the Commonweale, without the consent of them wee haue before said, if

B any great harme redound vnto the Commonweale by such contract, it is not reason the lawfull successour to be thereunto bound: and much lesse if hee haue obtained the kingdome by election: For that he holdeth nothing from his predecessor, as he should doe if he held his state by resignation, for then he should be bound vnto the contracts and promises of his predecessours, except it were expresly otherwise excepted. But by what right soeuer the prince shal haue receiued his kingdome, whether it be by law, by testament, by election, or by lot, it is reason that the successours should performe all such contracts of his predecessor, as redounded to the profit of the Commonweale: for otherwise it should be lawfull for him contrarie to the law of nature, by fraud and indirect meanes to draw his owne profit out of others harmes: but it much concerneth

C a Commonweale, so much as in it lieth, to preserue and keepe the publike faith, least in the extreame daungers thereof, all the meanes for the reliefe thereof should be shut vp. And thus are to bee vnderstood, those things which the court of Paris decreed in the yeares 1256, and 1294, viz. The king not to be bound vnto the couenants and agreements of the former kings his predecessours: their opinion being reiected, which say, That a soueraigne prince is to be thrust out of his kingdome, if he performe not the testament of the former prince his predecessor: without putting the difference of princely successions, by vs before put, but vtterly confounding the succession of princes.

But what needeth (might some man say) this distinction in succession of princes? seeing that all princes are bound and subiect vnto the lawes of nations, whereof contracts

D and testaments do depend. Which is not so if wee speake of all contracts and testaments in generall: but admit that to be true, yet thereof it followeth not, that a prince is more bound vnto the laws of nations, than vnto his owne: and that so far as they agree with the laws of God and nature: wherunto all that we haue said concerning the obliging of princes, is to be referred. For as for the laws of nations, if they be any of them vniust, the prince may abrogat them by the law of his realme, & forbid his subiects to vse the same: as we said before of seruitude and slaues: which by a daungerous example, by the law almost of all nations brought into Commonweales, were againe by the wholsome decrees of many princes well agreeing with the lawes of nature taken away: which being said of one thing, may also be extended vnto other things of like

E condition: prouided alwaies, that nothing be done contrarie to the lawes of God and nature. For if iustice be the end of the law, and the law is the worke of the prince, and the prince is the liuely image of almightie God; it must needes follow, that the law of the prince should be framed vnto the modell of the law of God.

L iij CHAP

A 5-6 in generall   B 7 successour should

Chap. IX.

¶ *Of a Prince tributarie or feudatarie: and whether he be a soueraigne Prince: and of the prerogatiue of honour amongst Soueraigne Princes.*

THis question deserueth a speciall Chapter by it selfe, for that it hath no communitie with the auntient markes of Soueraigntie, which were before the right of Fees, vsed in all Europe and Asia, and yet more in Turkie than in any place of the world: where the Timariots hold not the Fees they haue to serue in the warres, but so long as pleaseth the king of the Turkes, who giueth them no longer but for tearme of their liues: which haue them with condition, that in time of warre the Timariots shall of their owne charge without any pay bring such a number of horsemen and horses, as is appointed in the subsidie bookes, according to the proportion of the rent of the fees, which they cal *Timar*, which is to say in their language, the *Vse and profit* deriued as I suppose of the Greeke word τιμᾶν; and the word *Timar* signifying with them the honourable vse and profit, which is the true nature of Fee, to bee free from all tribute or base charges. And for this cause the vassall in the auntient law of the Lombards, is called *Leude*, which is to say, franke and free: *Aldius* and *Alda*, affranchised, from whence the words *Alaudium* and *Laudimia* are deriued, signifying the honourable rewards woont to be giuen to the lord of the fee, taking the oath of fealty of his vassall. But hauing thus much said for the explanation of these words, let vs proceed vnto our purpose.

We haue said here before, him to be an absolute soueraigne, who next vnto almightie God, is subiect vnto none: neither holdeth any thing next vnto God, but of his owne sword: For if he be enforced to serue any man, or to obey any mans commaund (be it by his owne good liking, or against his will) or if he hold of another man, he looseth the title of maiestie, and is no more a soueraigne, as saith a certaine Poet:

* *These Vicarij were slaues commannded.*

Esse sat est seruum, iam nolo vicarius esse:
Qui Rex est, Regem Maxime non habeat.

To be a slaue it is enough, I will not serue a slaue:
Who is a king, friend *Maximus*, no other king must haue.

If they then which hold in fealtie and homage haue no maiestie or soueraigntie, there should be but few soueraigne princes to be found. And if wee graunt that they which hold in fealtie and homage, or that are tributaries, be soueraignes, wee must by the same reason confesse, the vassall and his lord, the master and the seruant, to be equal in greatnes, power, and authoritie. And yet the doctors of the law hold that the dukes of Milan, Mantua, Ferrara, and Sauoy, yea euen and some Counties also are soueraignes: which altogether differ from those things which wee haue before said of the right of maiestie and soueraigntie. Wherefore it is requisit for vs more exquisitly to entreat of these matters, whereof dependeth the principall point of soueraigntie, and the prerogatiue of honour amongst princes, which they esteeme as a thing vnto them most deare of all things in the world.

The county of Asti.

Wee said before in the Chapter of Patronage (which we otherwise call Protection) that princes which are in protection, if they haue no other subiection, hold yet their maiestie and soueraigntie, although they haue enred into inequal alliance, whereby they are bound to acknowledge their protectors in all honour. But there is great difference betwixt them which are in simple protection onely, and them which hold

in

G8 *For* Alda *read* Aldia.   H7 a certaine Poet *i.e.* Martial (*Epigrams*, II, 18)
H9-10 (margin) slaves commaunded BY OTHER SLAVES.   K7 entred (*i.e.* entered) Notes at F5, G7.

Of A Commonweale. 115

in fealtie and homage. For the client, or he which is the simple protection of another prince onely, acknowledgeth his patron his superiour, in the league of their confederation, but no further than the dignitie of the person and place requireth: but the vassall, or he which holdeth in fealtie and homage, is glad not onely to acknowledge his lord for his superiour, but is enforced also in humble wise to giue vnto him his faith and dutie, or els to forgo his fee. When I say fealtie & homage, I meane the oath of fidelity, the submission, the seruice, and dutie of the vassall, which he is by the tenour of his fee bound to giue vnto his lord.

The difference betwixt him which is onely in the simple protection of another prince, and him that oweth vnto him fealtie and homage.

Which that it may be the better vnderstood, we will make nine degrees of inferiours, in respect of their superiours: beside him who next vnto almightie God, acknowledgeth none superiour vnto himselfe. The first sort, is of such princes as are in the protection of him whose maiestie they obserue and reuerence, and commonly giue themselues into his protection, so to bee the safer against their most mightie enemies. The second, is of such princes as acknowledge a superiour in their confederation, vnto whome they vse to pay a tribute or pension, so by his helpe and aid to bee the safer: which deserueth not to be called patronage, because it is mercenarie, whereas vnto kind dutie no reward is due. The third is, of such princes as being overcome by the more mightie, haue of him receiued peace, who yet keepe their maiestie and soueraigntie, with condition, courteously to reuerence the maiestie of the victor, and to pay vnto him a yearely tribute, for which they are from him to receiue neither protection nor aide. And albeit that these seeme to be more charged than they which are but in protection; yet is it so, that in effect they are greater, for in paying the tribute they haue promised for their peace, they are acquited, and haue nothing to doe with any other for the defence of their estate. The fourth sort is of them which are themselues kings, and freely exercise their soueraigntie ouer their owne subiects; but yet are vassales or feudataries to some other prince for some fee, bee it greater or bee it lesse, which they from him receiue. The fift sort, is of them which are not kings, neither haue any soueraigntie, but are become vassals for their fee, and are simply called meere vassals, who are bound to defend the honour of their lord, and to take vp arms for him, but not at all times, nor against all men. The sixt sort are they whom wee call liege vassals, who are not naturall subiects vnto the prince, but hauing giuen him their faith, are bound to defend his dignitie and honour, and for his defence to take vp armes without exception; yet not alwaies, nor in all places, but so farre forth as the profit of the fee, or the contract of their vassallage extendeth. The seuenth sort are they whom we call subiects, whether they be vassals or tenants, or such as hold no land at all, who are bound to fight for the honour and defence of their prince as well as for themselues, and to haue the same enemies and the same friends that he hath. The eight sort is of them, which in former time deliuered from slauerie, yet retaine a certaine kind of seruitude, as doe they which are tied vnto the soyle, and are of vs called Mort-maines. The last sort are the right slaues. This distinction of the degrees of subiection, I haue made to take away the confusion that many make of the subiect with the vassall; and of the simple vassall with the liege man; and hold, that the liege man oweth all obedience vnto his lord towards and against all men; and that the simple vassall reserueth his superior: and yet neuerthelesse there is but the subiect onely which oweth his obeysance. For the vassall, be he liege or simple, if he be not a subiect, oweth but the seruice and homage expressed in his inuestiture, from which hee may without fraud exempt himself, by yeelding vp his fee: but the naturall subiect, which holds in fee, in farme, or fee simple, or be it that he hold nothing at all that he can call his owne, yet can hee not by any meanes without the consent of his prince exempt himselfe from the personall obliga-

Nine degrees of subiection of inferiors towards their superiors.

The difference of a vassall, or a liege man from a naturall subiect.

L iiij

obligation wherewith he is vnto him bound, as we have before declared. The simple vassall is bound but once in his life to giue his oath of fidelitie vnto his lord: and such a vassall it may be as is neuer bound to giue his oath: for that the fee may bee without any such obligation of giuing his faith, as is to be seene in the old lawes of fees, (contrarie to that which *M. Charles du Molin* hath both thought and writ) but the subiect whatsoeuer is alwaies and in all places bound to give his oath, and so oft as it shal please his soueraigne prince to require it: yea although he were a bishop without any temporalitie at all. As for the liege man, it is not requisite that he should bee subiect vnto the lord of whom he holdeth: for it may be, that he may be a soueraigne prince, holding some seignorie of another prince in liege, fealtie and homage: it may also be, that he may be the naturall subiect of one prince, and liege man to another, by reason of his fee: or well the simple vassall of one Lord, without being subiect or liegeman to another: and naturall subiect to another, to whome he is iusticiable, and yet holdeth of him neither fee nor reuenew. For the vassall of a vassall is not for that, either vassall or subiect of the same lord, if it bee not in regard of the same fee. But it is needfull to explaine that we haue said by examples.

We find that the kings of England haue giuen their liege faith and homage vnto the kings of Fraunce for all the countries which they hold on this side the sea, except the counties of Oye and Guynes: And yet neuerthelesse they held the kingdomes of England and Ireland in soueraigntie without acknowledgement of any other prince whatsoeuer. But after in the yeare 1212 they made themselues vassals vnto the Pope and the church of Rome, and not onely vassals, but also tributaries: beside the annuall gift of smoke money, of auntient time graunted by *Ine* king of England, in the yeare 740, & augmented by *Etelpe*, which they called *S. Peters pence*. For it is found, that *Iohn* king of England, by the consent of all the counties, barrons and lords of the land, made himselfe vassall vnto the pope and church of Rome, and vowed to hold the realmes of England and Ireland of him in fealtie and homage, with the charge to pay the yearely rent and reuenew of a thousand markes for euer, vpon *Michaelmas* day, beside the *Peter* pence, which I haue spoken of: & gaue his faith and homage vnto the legat of pope *Innocent* the third, in the yeare 1213, in the presence of his chauncelor, the archbishop of Canterburie, foure bishops, sixe counties, and many other great lords. The Bull was made in autentique forme, whereof I haue seene the copie in a register of the Vatican, taken out by the commaundement of chauncelour du Prat, when he was Legat. And albeit that *Sir Thomas More*, chauncelour of England, was the first that maintained the contrarie: yet so it is, that in the same time, and vntill that king *Henrie* the eight reuolted from the pope, in the yeare 1534, the yearely reuenew and tribute was alwaies paied. But that is worth the noting, that the act of fealtie and homage, giuen vnto pope *Innocent* the the third, importeth that *Iohn* then king of England, humbly requested forgiuenesse of his sinnes of the popes legat. Whereby it is plaine, that patronage of the bishop of Rome to haue bene by him sought for, to extenuat the horrible murder which he had cruelly committed vpon the person of young *Arthure* his brothers sonne, duke of Britaine, and lawfull successour to the crowne of England; least otherwise he should haue bene therfore excommunicated by the pope. Whereas *Philip Augustus*, king of Fraunce, for the same cause had confiscated the duchies of Normandie, Guyenne, Aniou, Touraine, le Maine, & all the countries wherevnto he pretended any right, on this side the sea: which the kings of England held by fealtie and liege homage of the king of Fraunce; and yet had the chiefe soueraigntie ouer the realmes of England, Ireland, and Scotland. For first *Constantine* king of the Scots, with the rest of the nobilitie of that country, did fealtie and homage to *Adelstan* king

The kings of Scots vassals to the English.

OF A COMMONWEALE. 117

A king of England; and after that *Baliol* king of Scots did fealtie and homage also to the king of England, declaring himselfe to hold the kingdome of Scotland vnder the protection of the English, excepting the xxxij Islands of the Orcades, which then & afterwards also were holden in fealtie and homage of the kings of Norway; and owe vnto the new king comming to the crowne ten markes of gold, as was agreed betwixt the kings of Scotland and Denmark, to end the warres, which were renewed for the same isles, in the yeare 1564; as I haue learned by the letters of *M. DanZai*, ambassador for the king in Denmarke. Howbeit the kings of Scotland which raigned after *Baliol*, renounced their homage vnto the English, neither acknowledging them for their superiours, or yet to be vnto them vassals. And albeit that *Dauid* king of Scots did what

B he could with his subiects to consent that the kingdome of Scotland might bee holden of England in fealtie and homage: yet so it was, that he remained nine yeares in prison, and by the treatie made betwixt *Edward* the third his brother in law, and him, it was agreed, that he should be set at libertie, without any more obtained from his estates but that he should liue in amitie and friendship with him. As for the realme of Ireland, it is not long since it receiued the English gouernment, excepting yet the earle of Argueil, who seemed alwayes to keepe the state of soueraigntie.

So might we say also of the king of Denmarke, who is a soueraigne prince in part of the kingdome of Norway, without acknowledging any prince for his superiour whatsoeuer; and yet holdeth part of the duchie of Holsatia of the emperour in fealty

C and homage: in which sort he in auntient time held the countrey of Denmarke, which was but a plaine dukedome, when *Canutus* duke of Denmarke yeelded fealtie and homage vnto the emperour *Lothaire*, and afterward to the emperour *Frederike* the fift: who first of all sent vnto *Peter* duke of Denmarke the sword and the crowne, and honoured him with royall dignitie; yet with condition, That hee should for euer yeeld vnto the emperour fealtie and homage: howbeit that his posteritie afterwards reuolted from the empire. And yet neuerthelesse these whome I haue named, beeing no subiects, neither acknowledging the greatnes of any prince, but in respect of the fees that they hold of other princes, are acquitted of their fealtie homage and seruice, by giuing vp their fee without fraud. I say without fraud, for that it is not lawfull for the vas-

D sall to forsake his lord and patron at his need, although he would renounce his fee: albeit that there be no other penaltie but the losse of fee appointed for him who in time of warre forsaketh his lord; for that he doth an irreparable preiudice vnto his honour, which for euer remaineth engaged for so foule a fact, as to haue forsaken his lord in time of daunger: seeing that by the oath of fidelitie the vassall, but especially the liege vassall ought to aide him, were it against his owne brethren and children. Yea some lawyers are of opinion, that he ought to aid his lord and patron, euen against his owne father: wherein I can in no wise agree with them, for that the first and chiefe fidelitie is due vnto our parents. But if the vassall be also a subiect, hee looseth not onely his fee and honour, if he forsake his soueraigne prince at his need, but euen his life thereon

E dependeth: seeing that it is death euen for a common souldior, not to defend his captaine in battell. Wherefore we are not to maruell, if *Iohn de Montfort*, and *Peter*, dukes of Britaigne would neuer yeeld their fealtie vnto the French kings without exception, as their liege men for the dukedome of Britaigne: about which matter the chauncelors of Fraunce and Britaigne were twice at debate before the kings, *Charles* the fift, and *Charles* the sixt. And albeit that these two kings caused two acts to be produced, concerning the fealtie and homage done by the dukes of Britaigne, to *Philip* the victorious and *Lewes* the eight: yet for all that, the dukes would not doe their homage as liege men, but were receiued doing their simple homage onely. True it is, that the liege

homage

The kings of Denmarke in antient time vassals vnto the German empire.

A fee is not to be giuen vp but simply and without fraud.

B10 *For* the emperour *Bodin writes* the empire (Fr and L).   C3 *For* Frederike the fift *read* Frederike the first.   C6 *For* the emperour *Bodin writes* the empire (Fr and L).   Note at B7.

homage yeelded to *Lewes* the eight, was not but for the life of him that did it, as appeared by the act, without binding of his successours. And the other act which is of yong *Arthure*, was not pure and simple, but onely conditionall; as to be restored by *Philip* the victorious, vnto the territories and segnories from which he was embarred; which he did not. Now such is the force and nature of true and lawfull acts, as not to admit any time or condition, and the act of sealtie and homage of all other acts the least. But the end of the controuersie was, that the simple oath of *Iohn* and *Peter* should bee taken, least they should seeme to bee the liege vassals of the French: although both those dukes ought of right to haue bene depriued of the fee of the dukedome of Britaigne, for that they had renounced the French king their lawfull patron. Neither is there any doubt, but that in truth the auntient counties of Britaigne were true subiects and liege men vnto the kings of Fraunce (as is to be seene in the histories of *Gregorie* bishop of Tours) and being reuolted, were subdued by *Charlemaigne*, and afterwards by *Lewes* the deuout, to whome they did homage, and yeelded all obeysance with hostages; as a man may see in the histories of *Floard* and *Gerald*, whome some call *Vitald*, the nephew of *Charlemaigne*. And againe for another rebellion against *Charles* the Bauld, in the yeare 1359, they were accused vnto the estates, of treason, & so condemned and executed: which could not haue taken place but against the naturall subiect, for treason against his soueraigne prince. And after that *Herisso* countie of Britaigne, doing his fealtie, and with a great summe of money giuen appeased *Charles* the Bauld: as had also before him duke *Iudicael* pleased *Dagobert*. Neither is it true, or like to be true, that *Clodoueus*, who had bounded the kingdome of Fraunce with the Pyrenei Mountaines, both the seas, and the riuer of Rheine; or *Charlemaigne* that had in many places vanquished infinit numbers of the barbarous nations, and had subdued Spaine, Italie, Hungarie, Germanie, the Saxons, them of Pomerland, the Polonians, and Russians, and had extended his empire euen as faire as Scithia, would haue receiued the dukes of Britaigne, euen in the bowels of Fraunce, as companions of the French empire. And admit that by the sauour of any the French kings, they obtained respite of homage, that could not be preiudicial vnto the kings their successors, and much lesse vnto the crowne of Fraunce. And that more is, in the treaties betwixt the kings of Fraunce, and the first dukes of Normandie, it is expresly set downe, That the counties of Britaigne, should be vassals vnto the dukes of Normandie, vnto whome they had oftentimes giuen their fealtie and homage: which could not possibly haue bene, if they had not bene vassals and liege men vnto the crowne, seeing that the dukes of Normandie had giuen their fealtie and liege homage vnto the kings of Fraunce, & the counties of Britaigne vnto the dukes. And if true it be, that the vassall can neuer prescribe for his fealtie and homage against his lord; how then can the subiect prescribe for his subiection against his prince? So the Seneschall of Renes (a man verie well learned) cannot abide that *Peter de Dreux* prince of the blood, surnamed *Maucler*, had acquited the soueraigntie of Britaigne vnto the kings of Fraunce, seeing that hee was vassall and naturall subiect vnto the king: and yet neuertheleffe, in yeelding the homage, had reseruation to make lawes, to graunt pardons, to call parliaments, to take the benefit of confiscations euen in cases of high treason, the regall rights in churches, and seofments of trust. By which arguments not onely probable, but also necessarie, I am persuaded to write the dukedome of Britaigne, now euen from the times of the first kings of Fraunce, to haue bene a prouince of the kingdome of France, although *Argentraeus* otherwise thinke. Yet is it worth the noting that *Iohn Montfort* and his successors, although they went about to haue rent the dukedome of Britaigne from the kingdome of Fraunce, yet as counties of Montfort and Virtus to haue alwaies yeelded

The auntient counties of Britaigne, vassals to the kings of France.

Roialties reserued vnto the dukes of Britaigne, notwithstanding their homage due vnto the French king.

F10 French G6 nephew *i.e.* grandson (cf. Fr) G7 For 1359 (Fr) *read* 859 (L). H6 as farre as
I3 could not I7 prescribe for *i.e.* cease to be liable for, owing to lapse of time
Notes at F3, G5, I9, K6.

ded their fealtie vnto the French kings, without exception, as we read in the records, although that they still exercised in the countries of Britaigne certaine roialties granted them by the king.

There is then great difference betwixt him which holdeth simply in fealtie and homage (being himselfe no soueraigne, nor subiect vnto him which is lord of the fee) and him which is soueraigne of a countrey, and yet vassall to some other lord for some fee; as of him which is in protection onely, or which is tributarie vnto a prince, hauing soueraigntie ouer his subiects, or which is himselfe a naturall subiect. Wherfore we conclude, that there is none but he an absolute soueraigne, which holdeth nothing of another man; considering that the vassall for any fee whatsoeuer it be, be hee Pope or Emperor, oweth personall seruice by reason of the fee which he holdeth. For albeit that this word *Seruice*, in all matter of fees, and customes, is not preiudiciall vnto the naturall libertie of the vassall; yet so it is, that it importeth a certaine right, dutie, honor and reuerence that the vassall oweth vnto the lord of the fee: which is not indeed a seruitude reall, but is annexed and inseperable from the person of the vassall, who cannot be therefrom freed, but by quitting his fee: prouided yet, that hee bee no naturall subiect of the lords of the fee, from whome he cannot discharge himselfe by renouncing his fee.

The prince that holdeth of another, is himselfe no absolute Soueraigne.

Now when I say, that homage and personall seruice is inseperable from the vassall; that is so true, as that the vassall cannot acquit himselfe thereof by his deputie or atturney, as was permitted by the auntient lawes of fees; which in this point is abrogated in Europe, and Asia; yea and in Italie it selfe from whence the lawes of fees (as many thinke) first tooke their beginning. For *Lewes Sfortia*, gouernour of Lombardie, sent his Agent into Fraunce, to king *Charles* the eight, to haue obtained of him that his nephew the duke of Milan might by him be receiued to do his homage by his deputie for the duchie of Genes: whereunto the king would not condescend. And when question was made of taking of fealtie and homage of the marques of Salusse, the court of Paris decreed, That his deputie shuld be admitted in his name, if the king so thought it good; for that the marques pretended himselfe to be sicke: yet with that condition, that so soone as he was able he should come and doe it himselfe in person. The same hath also bene oft times iudged in such like cases. But contrariwise the lord of the fee may constraine his vassall to yeeld his fealtie and homage vnto his deputie, as is commonly vsed. But if the vassall be yet vnder age, or so young as that he yet wanteth vnderstanding, he is to be borne with for doing of his fealtie and homage, vntill he be of age to do it, except it pleaseth the lord of the fee to receiue it by his deputie: As did king *Lewes* the xj, who by *Philip Commines* his ambassador receiued fealtie & homage of the mother of young *Galeas* duke of Milan, for the duchie of Genes, the duke her sonne being vnder age, and paying fiftie thousand ducats for reliefe. And for the same cause in the treatie made betwixt *Lewes* the eleuenth, and *Maximilian* archduke of Austria, in the yeare 1482, in the 56 article it was expresly set downe, That the subiects on both parts should be receiued to do their homage by their atturneies, which otherwise they should haue bene constrained themselues in person to haue done, if they had not bene sicke, or had some other iust and reasonable let; or that it was some bodie collegiat. For it much concerneth the honour of the lord and patron, whether homage be done vnto him in the person of a king his vassall, or by some other base atturney or deputie. And for this cause it was agreed in the treatie of Amiens, made betwixt *Philip the faire* the French king, and *Henrie* king of England, in the yeare 1303, That the king of England should himselfe in person come to do his fealtie and homage without exception, if he were not otherwise letted by sicknesse without deceit: in which case he

Homage a personall seruice, and not to be performed by a deputie.

he should send his eldest sonne to doe the fealtie in his stead. And by another treatie made in the yeare 1330, betwixt *Philip Valois*, and king *Edward* the third, it was also said, That the king of England should in person come to doe his fealtie and homage, if he were not without fraud by sicknesse letted; which ceasing, hee should then also come. And by the treatie of peace, made in the yeare 1259, betwixt *Lewes* the ninth the French king, and *Henrie* the second, king of England, it is expresly declared, That the king of England should in person himself yeeld his fealtie & liege homage vnto the French king. Which liege homage (as they tearme it) is of that force, as that the person of no prince, pope, or emperour, is therein excepted. Now the forme of the homage declared by the treatie, in the yeare 1331, betwixt *Philip Valois* the French king, and *Edward* the third, is this: The king of England hauing his hands ioyned, and put betwixt the hands of the French king, the Chauncelor of Fraunce for the French king, shall thus say vnto the king of England, *Thou shalt become a liege man to the king of Fraunce, who here is, as duke of Guyenne, and peere of Fraunce, countie of Poitou, and Monstrueil, and shalt promise to beare vnto him faith and loyaltie*: Whereunto the king of England shall say, *I consent thereunto*: Then the king of Fraunce shall receiue the king of England into his fealtie with a kisse. But the oath of *Charles* the king of Nauarre was more religious, when he yeelded his fealtie vnto *Charls* the fift, the French king, in the yeare 1370: for that he was not onely the French kings vassall, but his subiect also, vnto whome hee promised his faith and loialtie towardes and against all men, which could liue or die: albeit that he was then soueraigne king of Nauarre, and pretended a right vnto the soueraigntie of Berne, which yet resteth vndecided. The forme of the simple homage done by *Iohn de Montfort, Arthure* the second, and *Peter* the second, dukes of Britaigne, is like, excepting the word *Liege man*. But for vasals which be also subiects, the forme of fealtie is more religious & precise, for that they are bound with a double bond, whereas the forren vassals are not so. For the king of England, *Edward* the third being come to Amiens to doe his homage vnto the king of Fraunce, refused to ioyne his hands betwixt the hands of the king, and so returned into his kingdome, where it was sixe moneths debated betwixt the French kings commissioners, and the assembly of the estates, about the resolution for the forme of the homage: in fine, king *Edward* thought it better to follow the prescript forme, than to loose so many benefits as he then enioyed in Fraunce. But if the vassall be also a naturall subiect vnto his lord and patron, he is bound to lay by his sword, his gloues, his hat, his cloke, his spurres, and vpon his knees to put his hands ioyned together, into the hands of his prince, or of his deputie, and so to take his oath: and by the custome of this realme, if it pleaseth not the lord, he is not bound to be present, or to kisse his vassall; but may (if he so please) being present, see him in forme, as we haue aforesaid, giue his fealtie and homage to some small officer, or before his house, by kissing the hammer of his doore. But by the customs of Vermandois, the vassall is bound to do his fealtie vnto his lord being present; but if he be absent, it is sufficient for the vassall being present, to cause it to be done by his atturney, least the honour of the vassall should bee impaired by the basenesse of the person of his lords atturney. But if the vassall haue thirtie heires, euery one of them is constrained to yeeld his fealtie vnto his patron requiring the same: as was long since prouided by the decree of *Philip* the Victorious, the French king, in the yeare 1209. Yet some vse another custome.

Shall we then say, a Vassall (that is to say another mans man) although he at home enioy a kingdome, to haue a soueraigne maiestie and power? Shall we call him that is bound to doe most vile seruices, (and to vse the words of fealtie) him that serueth another man, shall we call him, I say, a soueraigne prince? And that is it for which manie honoura-

The forme of the homage made by the kings of England vnto the kings of Fraunce.

Homage a base & seruile thing, and therefore detested of honorable princes.

H2 *For* Berne *read* Béarn.

honourable princes had rather to loose and forgoe right great seignories, and their most rich fees, than to serue such a slauerie. And othersome againe, to the contrarie, would not sell their soueraigntie for any thing in the world. As the prince of Orange refused of king *Lewis* the eleuenth, ten times so much as his principalitie was worth, which stood him in more than hee receiued profit thereby: And for the same cause *Edward* the third, king of England, in the first article of the treatie of Bretigni expresly excepted, that all royalties should be giuen vnto himselfe in those countries which he had by inheritance in Fraunce; least he should for them haue beene enforced to haue yeelded fealtie and homage vnto the French kings. Neither for any other cause did *Stephen*, Vayuod of Valachia, reuolt from the kings of Polonia, but for that the king of Polonia had caused his tent to be cast wide open at the same very instant that the Vayuod was therein doing vnto him his homage, that so he might be seene of all men in doing of it. Which slie disgrace the Vayuod tooke in very euill part: which is not to be maruelled at in so great a lord as he, if wee doe but consider, that *Calisthenes* the nephew of *Aristotle* chose rather to loose his life, than after the Persian guise, in humble and deuout manner vpon his knees to honour *Alexander* the Great: albeit that *Alexander* courteously tooke them vp with a kisse that so honoured him. Which was also an vsuall thing with the Romane emperours, when they gaue vnto the kings that were in their protection, their scepters and diademes. For so *Tiridates* king of Armenia being come to Rome, humbled himselfe vpon his knee before the emperour *Nero*, whom *Nero* taking by the hand, lift him vp, kissed him, and taking his turbant from off his head, set thereon a royall crowne, and caused him to sit on his right hand. For albeit that the kingdomes were giuen by the Romane emperours without reseruation of fealtie or homage, yet so it was, that the kings laying aside their scepters and crownes, of their owne accord serued the Romane emperours, some as seruitors in their chambers, othersome called themselues but the Romane stewards, as *Adherball* king of Numidia tearmed himselfe nothing but the steward of the people of Rome. And *Eumenes* king of Pergame after the discomfiture and death of *Mithridates* king of Pontus came to Rome, and with a cap vpon his head (in token of his late recouered libertie) thanked the people of Rome for the same. But *Prusias* king of Bithynia as oft as he went into the Senate, commonly kissed the threshold of the gate, calling himselfe the Senates slaue: albeit that he was neither subiect nor tributarie, nor so much as in the Romanes protection, but ioyned vnto them in equall confederation. All these honours, were they neuer so great, proceeding from their owne voluntarie will, did little or nothing at all diminish the maiestie of a soueraigne prince, as doth that forme of homage which is seruile and constrained, and which the Tartars, Persians, and Turkes esteeme to bee the true seruice of a very slaue. And truly *Solyman* the Turkish king was about to haue restored *Iohn* king of Hungarie into his kingdome in the yeare 1555, with condition to haue holden the same of him in fealtie and homage, without other subiection (as he by a Chiaus his embassadour, certified *Sigismundus Augustus* king of Polonia) if king *Ferdinand*, who pretended the kingdome of Hungarie to belong vnto himselfe by inheritance, had not letted him so to doe; as I haue seene by the letters of *Sanislaus Rosdrazeroski*, a Polonian, written to *Anne Mommorancie* constable of Fraunce the same yeare 1555. And for this cause *Francis* the French king to hinder that *Charlet* of Austria should not bee chosen emperour, declared vnto the princes, Electors of the Empire, that the maiestie of the Empire should be much debased, if they should of his vassall make their head and Emperour: wherewith the emperour not a little moued, and afterwards at the battell of Pauie hauing taken him prisoner, would neuer consent vnto his deliuerance, vntill hee had quite

The wearing of a cap was in ausient time the marke of them that were but lately made free, to couer their heads that were shauen when they were slaues.

discharged the Low countries from the fealtie and homage wherein they were before bound vnto the French.

But it seemeth that it is not enough to say, that *Charles* of Austria was vassall vnto the crowne of Fraunce, but that he was thereunto a liegeman also; and not onely a liegeman, but euen the French kings naturall subiect; as borne & brought vp in Flanders, then a prouince of the French kingdom: although many think the citie of Gaunt the natiue place of *Charles*, and the cities vpon the sea coast to haue bene excepted. For the earles of Flaunders were alwaies accounted peers of Fraunce, euen from the first beginning of that kingdome: and the soueraigne roialties thereof, alwaies before reserued vnto the same, but especiallie at the solemne treatie of Arras betwixt *Charles* the seuenth and *Philip* the second duke of Burgundie. Also *Charles* the fift beeing chosen emperour, asked leaue of *Francis* the French king, that hee might leuie of his subiects the subsidie graunted him at Arras, in the yeare 1520; whereunto the kings aunswere was, That he would therein do what he might, without diminishing in any thing the right of his crowne: as I haue seene by the instructions giuen to *M. De la Roche-Gaucourt* at such time as hee was sent ambassadour into Spaine. Although that greater causes might haue beene alleaged, which might haue stayed German princes from the election of *Charles* the fift. For *Charles* of Austria was as then not onely the vassall, liegeman, and naturall subiect to the king of Fraunce, but also a liegeman vnto the pope and the church of Rome, for all the countries, lands, and seignories that he then held, except that which he held of the crowne of Fraunce, or of the empire; howbeit that he as then held nothing of the empire, but the lands neere vnto the Rhene, and Cambray: For *Arnold* the last of that name, countie of Burgundie, gaue it with the other countries to the emperor *Conrade* the second, in the yeare 1205, and after that, the emperour *Charles* the fourth gaue it to *Charles* the sixt, the Dolphin, by fealtie and homage, as appeareth by the inuestiture thereof in the treasure of Fraunce, the copie whereof we haue out of the records. But at such time as he professed himselfe to be the liegeman of the bishop of Rome, in his fealtie giuen for the kingdome of Naples, he then promised by his oath, not to take vpon him either the charge of the German empire, if he were chosen emperour by the German princes; either of the dukedome of Milan; and with these conditions gaue his fealtie and homage vnto the pope: which is not to be thought any new clause, but an auntient condition, ioyned vnto all the acts of fealtie and homage giuen vnto the pope by the kings of Naples and Sicilie, since the time that pope *Vrban* the fift, therin inuested *Charles* of France brother vnto king *Lewes*. And in the inuestiture of that kingdome, made by *Innocent* the fourth, vnto *Edmond* the sonne of *Henrie* king of England, in the yeare 1255, the copie whereof we haue written out of the Vatican records, are these words, *Ego Henricus, Dei gratia Rex Angliæ, nomine Edmundi fily nostri Regis Siciliæ, plenum & ligeum vassallagium facio ecclesiæ Romanæ.* viz. I *Henrie*, by the grace of God king of England, in the name of *Edmund* our sonne, king of Sicilie, yeeld full and liege homage vnto the church of Rome, &c. And in the act of fealtie and liege homage giuen by *Robert* king of Sicilie, in the 1338, he by oath promised neuer to receiue the imperiall crowne, neither the dukedome of Milan, nor any seignorie whatsoeuer in Tuscanie, vpon paine of the losse of all such right as he might pretend vnto the kingdomes of Naples and Sicilie. The like is also found giuen by *Charles* king of Naples, in the yeare 1295: and by queene *Ione* in the yeare 1348, as I haue read in the register of the Vatican. And for this onely cause pope *Julius* the second refused to inuest *Ferdinand* king of Arragon, *Charles* the fift the emperours grandfather by the mothers side, in the kingdome of Naples, but vpon the conditions I haue aforesaid: and a yearely rent

Charles the fift a naturall subiect of these French Kings.

Charls the fift vassall and liegeman vnto the pope and the Church of Rome.

The kingdoms of Naples and Sicilie holden of the pope.

F4 but that   G8 princes   I8–9 ligium   I9 ecclesiæ Romanæ   I10 Edmund   K2 in the YEAR 1338

A rent of eight thousand ounces of gold, or of foure score thousand crownes, which the kings of Naples were bound to pay euerie yeare, and a white ambling gelding, beside the aid expressed in the inuesture, with reseruation of the countie of Beneuent. Which their obligation was of such consequence vnto the popes, that so soone as they denounced warre vnto any, the kings of Naples were straight wayes in armes for the defence of the Church of Rome. So *Alphonsus* king of Naples, at the denuntiation of pope *Sextus*, made warre vpon the state of Florence, for that they had hanged the Cardinall of Pisa, the popes Legat *a latere* in his pontificalibus. And in our time pope *Paulus* the third by his Ambassadour *Alexander Farnesius*, summoned the emperour *Charles* the fift, being then with a great armie in France, to make peace with the French

B king, so with their vnited forces to make warre vpon the Protestant princes, as was agreed vpon in the first article of the treatie of Soissons, made in September in the yere 1544: which haply the emperour would not haue done (hauing had his armie but a little before by the French men ouerthrowne in Italie, and now with doubtfull euent making warre in Fraunce) if he had not bene liege vassall vnto the pope, & by him threatned to loose the kingdoms of Naples and Sicilie, as he was well giuen to vnderstand. Which the pope did, not so much moued with the publike calamitie or troubled estate of the Church, as with the power of *Charles*, wherewith he was like to haue subdued most part of Europe, had hee not bene letted by the armes and power of the French. And albeit that in the yeare 1528, by the treatie made betwixt pope *Clement*

C the vij and his Cardinals, besieged in the castle S. Angelo on the one side, and the emperour *Charles* the fift on the other, it was set downe, That the kings of Naples should for euer be acquited of the yerely rent of 8000 ounces of gold, and of all the arearages, which amounted vnto great summes: yet so it was, that all the rest of the pointes of the auntient inuestiture, still stood in their former force and vertue. But euer since, the German emperours haue well knowne, and the pope better, (seeing Rome sacked, and himselfe put to ransome of 400000 duckets, after he had released the fairest rights of S. *Peters* demaine) what daunger it was to make choice of the vassall of a soueraigne prince, and the natural subiect of another, to be head of the Empire: For with the forces of Germanie he brought downe the pope, and with the popes power hee ruinated

D the princes of Germanie. And albeit that by the imperiall title hee held the duchies of Milan, of Gelders, and other seignories of the empire, yet so it is, that hee was the popes antient vassall & liege man, and so consequently to him first bound, & that more straitly vnto the Church than to the empire. Ioine hereunto also, that the popes haue since this 300 yeres pretended that the emperor may not take vpon him the empire, but hauing before of them receiued the imperiall crowne; as pope *Pius* the fift by his Legats sharply rebuked the emperour *Ferdinand*, for that he had not of him receiued the imperiall crowne, which his brother *Charles* had not before doubted so to receiue; and had by excommunication compelled him so to doe, had hee not by the intreatie of king *Philip* his kinsman, and of the French king, otherwise appeased.

Pius Quintus the pope angrie with Ferdinand the emperour for not receiuing of him the imperiall crowne.

E But here some man will say, How could it be that the emperor *Charls* the fift, should be liege man vnto the pope, the French king, and the empire? seeing that no man can be liege man vnto many lords, although he haue many fees holden of them all separatly: For his faith and aid is due to one alone, and him the first and chiefest, without exception of any man liuing. And in case he be the vassall of many coheires for one and the same fee, he is liegeman vnto them all together, but not to any of them separatly, considering that his fealtie cannot be diuided; neither can he do his liege homage vnto one of them without exception, for the concurrence of the rest: yet truer it is, his fealtie to be due vnto one onely of his patrons, whome he shall make choice of, if that

The same man cannot be liegeman to diuers princes.

M ij his

A8 pontificalibus *i.e.* pontifical attire   D10 For otherwise appeased *probably read* otherwise BEEN appeased.   E8 concurrence *i.e.* rivalry, conflict

his patrons cannot agree, or els to them altogether; and that law we now vse. For the condition of the vassall ought not to be made more hard, than if there were vnto one man, but one heire; but it should be much harder if he should bee enforced to doe many duties, many seruices, and many times to giue his faith: and that much more the liege vassall, who cannot giue vnto manie his faith seuerally, without exception.

I here vnderstand the liege homage properly as it is to bee vnderstood in the lawes of Fees; for that our auncestors haue abused this word *Liege*, in all their auntient treaties of alliance and oathes that they made: I remember that I haue seene 48 treaties of alliance, which our kings *Philip* the v, and *Charles* the v. vj. vij. and *Lewes* the xj, made with the three electors on this side the Rhine, and diuers other the princes of the empire, wherein they by oath sworne betwixt the hands of the kings deputies, solemnly promised to serue them in their warres against all men, except the emperour, and the king of the Romans; vowing to be their vassals and liege men, more or lesse; some calling themselues councellours, some other pentioners, all liege vassals: except the Archbishop of Treuers, Elector of the empire, who no otherwise called himselfe, but the kings confederat, and not his vassall, although he receiued his pention from the king, as did the other princes; who for all this held nothing of the crowne of France, but were nothing but pentioners vnto the French kings, to whome they gaue their oath to aid them, at their charge, vpon the conditions expressed in their oathes. Onely the oath of the duke of Guelders, and countie of Iuliers, I will for example set downe, that thereby men may iudge of the rest, in Latine conceiued in these words, *Ego deuenio vassallus ligius Caroli Regis Francorum, pro ratione quinquaginta millium scutorum auri, ante festum D. Rhemigij mihi soluendorum, &c. viz.* I become liege vassall of *Charles* the French king, for the summe of fiftie thousand crownes of gold, to be paid vnto mee before the feast of S. *Rhemigius*, &c. This oath bore date in Iune, in the yeare 1401. Yea, euen betwixt kings themselues leagues were oftentimes conceiued in such words, as that the one of them professed himselfe to be the others vassall. As in the league made betwixt *Philip* of Valois the French king, and *Alphonsus* king of Castile, in the yeare 1336, it is said, *That they should giue and receiue fealtie and homage the one of the other*: which proceeding but of the ignorance of their ambassadours, is now better vnderstood, as but an abuse of the words *Vassall* and *Liege*: the oathes also of the kings pentioners, and their treaties, carrie no more such words.

The vassall ought first to serue his most auntient Lord

Wherefore againe to returne from whence we haue a little digressed. I say then, that the emperour *Charls* the fift could not yeeld his liege fealtie and homage vnto the pope without exception, considering that he was liege man, peere, and naturall subiect vnto the French king, and that the seruice and homage is inseparable from the person. And admit he were not the kings subiect, but his liege man, or not his liege man but his vassall onely; yet so it is, that in tearmes of right the liege homage is due vnto the most auntient, and that the vassall ought to serue his most auntient Lord. But if the lords be equall, and yet at variance amongst themselues for the seruice, hee oweth aid neither to the one nor to the other: For that in matter of seruices or seruitude, the seruice (for the indiuisible nature therof) is letted by the concurrence of them to whom it is to be done. For amongst equals the condition of him which forbiddeth (the seruice) is better: howbeit that in question of simple alliance, the aid is due vnto him that is wronged and inuaded in his countrey against the other common allie which maketh warre vpon him, as it commonly falleth out if the assailant haue no iust cause, and that after denuntiation to him giuen by the common allies to come to some reasonable agreement, he refuse so to doe.

But most certaine it is, that the naturall subiect ought alwayes to preferre his naturall

rall lord aboue all, if he bee present, as him to whome he is first bound, & from whom he cannot exempt himselfe. And therefore in the decrees of king *Lewes* the eleuenth, and of *Philip* the second, duke of Burgundie, made for the order of Fraunce, the xiij article, and for the order of the golden Fleece, the ix article, it is set downe, That the knights of what prince soeuer it be, ought to aid their naturall lord, whose liege men they are, and the countrey wherein they were borne, against him that shall make war vpon them, without any blemish to their honour; prouided that their naturall lord be there in person, and not otherwise, and that they signifie so much vnto the chiefe of the order whereof they are knights. Whereby it appeareth that the emperour *Charles* the fift could not giue his faith vnto the electors of the empire, but with reseruation of his fealtie vnto the French king, and afterward vnto the Pope. For beside the kingdome of Naples and Sicilie, holding of the pope immediatly and without meane, hee was also his vassall and liege man for the kingdome of Arragon, as I haue red in the records taken out of the Vatican. where the graunt giuen by *Peter* king of Arragon is set downe in these words, *Ego Petrus Dei gratia Rex Arragonum, Comes Barcinonæ, Dominus Montispessulani, cupiens præter Deum, principali beati Petri, & Apostolicæ sedis protectione muniri, tibi reuerendissime pater, & Domine summe Pontifex Innocenti, & pro te, sacrosanctæ Romanæ Ecclesiæ, & Apostolicæ sedi, offero regnum meum: illudque tibi pro remedio animæ meæ primogenitorum meorum constituo censuale, vt annuatim de Camera Regis ducenta quinquaginta Massimitinæ Apostolicæ sedi reddantur: & ego at successores mei, specialiter & fideles & obnoxi teneamur: hac autem lege perpetua seruandum forum decerno, quia spero & confido, quod tu & successores tui, quasi beati, Petri manibus in regem duxeris solemniter coronandum. Actum Romæ anno Christi* 1204. In English thus: I *Peter* by the grace of God king of Arragon, Countie of Barcelona, Lord of Moutpelier, desiring next vnto God to be strengthened with the principall protection of blessed S. *Peter* and the Apostolicall See; do offer vnto thee most reuerent father and high Lord, Pope *Innocent*, and for thee vnto the most holy Church of Rome, and to the Apostolicall See, my kingdome; and the same for the health of my soule and of my predecessours, I make vnto thee tributarie, so that out of the kings chamber shall bee yerely paied vnto the Apostolical See, two hundred & fifty Massimitines, & that I and my successors shall be especially bound to be (vnto you) faithfull and subiect; and by this perpetuall law decree a court to be kept: for that my hope and trust is, that thou & thy successors shalt lead vs as it were with the hands of blessed *Peter*, to be solemnly crowned king. Enacted at Rome in the yeare of Christ 1204. So that kingdome of Arragon was by the Arragonian kings offered vnto the Bishops of Rome, least they should for their enormities and murders haue bene well beaten. But the kingdomes of Sardinia and Corsica, was by the popes giuen vnto the kings of Arragon (as the popes guise is bountifull to giue that is none of their owne) for which kingdome the Emperour was also liege man vnto the Pope, as I haue seene by the inuestiture thereof made vnto *Peter* the third, king of Arragon, in this sort, *Pontifex M ix. de fratrum suorum assensu, dat in feudum regnum Sardiniæ & Corsicæ, proprietatē ecclesiæ Romanæ &c. Per capam Auream te præsentialiter inuestimus, &c. Ita tamen quod tu & successores tui, præstabitis homagium ligium, vassallagium plenum, & fidelitatis iuramentum, &c. Et centū equites armatos, & vno equo ad arma, & duobus equitaturis ad minus per quēlibet, & quinta gentis peditibus terræ vestræ de Arragonia, cum gagijs per trimestre, a die quo intrabūt terrā Ecclesiæ, &. Et in super censum duoru milliū marcarū argenti bonorum, & legaliū strelingoru: vbicunq̄, fuerit Romanus Pontifex in festo beatorus Petri & Pauli, annis singulis, sub pœna excommunicationis post quatuor menses, &c. & post tertium terminum non solueris, tu hæredesq̄, tui, a dicto regno Sardiniæ & Corsicæ cadetis ex toto, & regnum ad Ro-*

The act of the oath of the king of Arragon giuē to the pope.

The inuestiture of the kingdomes of Sardinia and Corsica granted by the pope.

B8 illudque tibi, & SUCCESSORIBUS TUIS IN PERPETUUM, pro meae, & (L 3–5)   B9 primogenitorum (L) progenitorum (Fr)   C1 obnoxii   C2 *For* quali *read* quasi.   C2 beati Petri   D6 *For* kingdomes *read* kingdome.   D8 bountifull *i.e.* bountifully   D10–E1 assensu   E4 duabus   E4–5 quingentis   E7 beatorum   E8 terminum si non   E9 haeredesve tui   B9 animae, & (Fr and L 1–2) animae

manam ecklesiam reuertetur . viz. The great bishop by the assent of his bretheren, doth giue in fee the kingdome of Sardinia and Corsica, the inheritance of the church of Rome, &c. And we personally therein, inuest thee by a cape of gold, &c. yet so as that thou and thy successours shall therefore giue liege homage, full vassalage, and oath of fidelitie, &c. And an hundred armed horse-men, and one horse for seruice, and two furnitures at the least for euery one, and fiue hundred foote-men of your country of Aragon, with pay for three moneths from the day that they shall enter into the territorie of the church, &c. And moreouer the rent of two thousand markes of good and lawfull sterling money, wheresoeuer the pope shall be in the feast of the blessed Apostles, *Peter and Paul*, euerie yeare, vpon paine of excommunication after foure moneths, &c. and if after the third time thou shalt not pay it, thou and thy heires from the said kingdome of Sardinia and Corsica, shall altogether fall; and the same kingdome shall againe returne vnto the church of Rome. And after that, *Iames* king of Aragon, did also like homage at Valence, betwixt the hands of the popes legate, in the yeare 1353, with reseruation vnto the pope of appeales, put in by the clergie, and abolishing of the lawes and customes brought in by the kings of that country. I finde also that *Ferdinand*, and after him *Alphonsus*, kings of Aragon, did the like fealtie and homage in the yeare 1455. And in the publike records of the court of Rome, are to be seene the names of the vassall kings set downe in this order: the kings of Naples, Sicilia, Aragon, Sardinia, Hierusalem, England, Ireland, and Hungary. And this is the old description of such princes as 380 yeres ago, yeelded their

The kingdom of Portugall holden of the pope.

fealtie & homage vnto the bishops of Rome. And since the kingdome of Portugall, was by the valour of *Henry* of *Benonia*, taken from the Moores, the kings thereof made themselues vassalls vnto the bishop of Rome, and payd the yearely tribute of two thousand duckats into the bishop of Rome his treasure. And therefore *Innocent* the fourth, bishop of Rome, by his letters admonished the princes of the kingdome of Portugall, to appoint ouerseers to their prodigall king, who should also take vpon them the gouernement of the kingdome. And as for the Islands of the *Canaries*, *Nigaries*,

The islands of the Canaries, holden of the pope.

and the *Gorgonides*; the emperour holdeth them also of the pope. We also reade, that *Lewes* king of Spaine, did fealtie and homage vnto the pope, in the yeare 1343, with charge to pay yearely into the chamber of Rome, foure hundred florines of the weight and coine of Florence. And as for the remainder of the westerne Isles, and of Peru, it is certaine that pope *Alexander* the sixt, diuiding the new world betwixt the kinges of Castile and Portugall, expresly kept vnto himselfe the inheritance, the iurisdiction and soueraignetie thereof, by consent of the two kings; who from that time made themselues his vassalls, of all the purchases and conquests by them already gained, and that they should from that time forward, gaine or make, as the Spaniards themselues haue written. In like manner pope *Iulius* the second, gaue vnto *Ferdinand* king of Spaine, *Charles* the fift, his grandfather by the mothers side, the kingdomes of *Granado* and *Nauarre*; when he had driuen the Moores out of the one, and *Peter D'Albret* out of the other, vpon condition to hold them by fealty and homage of the church of Rome. For albeit that *Charles* the fift, the emperor pretended right vnto the kingdome of *Nauarre*, by reason of the donation to him made by *Germaine D'Foix*, second wife vnto king *Ferdinande*: yet so it was, that his ambassadours and deputies, when they came to the conference, seeing that their donation to want sure foundation, doubted not to pretend the popes interdictions, as the surest stay of their most vniust rapines. And the cause of the interdiction was, for that *Peter Albret*, king of *Nauarre*, would not at the command of pope *Iulius* the second, breake faith and friendship with *Lewes* the xij, the French king, who was first called father of his country, when as hee was

---

F1 ecclesiam   G5 1353 (Fr) 1453 (L)   G8 *For* 1455 *read* 1445 (Fr and L).   H3 Henry of Bononia   H10 *For* Lewes king of Spaine (L) *read* Lewis of Spain (Fr) *i.e.* Luis de la Cerda.
Notes at H9, H10.

was king *Lewes* his liege vassall, and no way bound vnto the pope. So that there remained no kingdome, no not any little territorie or peece of ground, which *Charles* the emperour held not by fealtie aud homage, or whereof he could call himselfe a soueraigne. For as for the Islands of Maiorca and Minorca, they were long time before reunited vnto the kingdome of Aragon, after that they were taken from the heires of *Iames* the Fortunate. And in the Low-countries, he had nothing which was not of necessitie holden of the crowne of France, or of the empire. And albeit that our princes haue by diuers leagues, granted the principalitie of Flanders and Artoise vnto *Charles* the emperour, yet remaineth there a country in Burgundie, which they call the countie of Charrolois, the proprietie whereof belongeth vnto the king of Spaine, but the soueraignetie thereof vnto the French king, and is by the king of Spaine holden in fealty: so that euen for that, he is to ackdowledge himselfe to be our kings vassall. As for the kingdome of Castile, no man doubteth (which hath but looked into the Spanish affaires) but that the kingdome of Castile by inheritance, descended vnto king *Lewes* the ix. of France, in the right of *Blanch* his mother: yea, and the nobilitie of Castile by solemne acts, which are yet extant in the records of France, inuited king *Lewes* to haue taken vpon him his mothers kingdome. Howbeit I doubt not, but that the Spaniards will reply, that *Blanch*, the daughter of *Lewes* the ix. married the king of Castile, vpon condition that all such right vnto the kingdome, as might haue fallen vnto her father, should now be giuen vnto his sonne in law: which thing *Lewes* could not doe vnto the preiudice of his successours, without the consent of the states: ioyning therevnto also that the French kings daughters or sisters, when they are bestowed and married, can receiue nothing but money of the royall possessions of the crowne of France. And albeit that some may thinke that the French king might giue those lands vnto his daughter, as not yet vnited or incorporate into the crowne of France; yet neuerthelesse there is yet extant in the records of France, a league made in the yeare 1369, betwixt king *Charles* the fift and *Henry* king of Castile, then driuen out of his kingdome, whereby I haue seene, that *Henry* promised as well for himselfe, as for his successours, to become vassall, and to hold his kingdome of Castile, of the kings of Fraunce: for that by the meanes of the king of France, he was againe restored into his kingdome. Seeing then that the kingdome of Castile is hereditarie descending vnto the heires both males and females, the successours of *Henry* are bound vnto his deedes and promises. True it is, that the promise of *Henry* had not power to preiudice his successours, neither the estates of Castile, without the consent of whom, the treatie was made, if the realme of Castile had not beene hereditarie. But of the kingdome of Fraunce, it is otherwise to be thought and determined. And therefore it was by the wise resolued, that *Phillip* the Faire, the French king, could not make *Arthur* duke of Britaine, vassall vnto the king of England, without the dukes consent; except he would by the same right, giue vp his kingdome of France vnto the king of England, which he could by no soueraigne power doe, without the consent of the estates of France. For otherwise, his yeelding of it vp, should be to none effect or purpose, no more then that of king *Iohn* of Fraunce, made vnto the king of England in the treatie at Calais, wherein he without consent of the states, yeelded vnto the king of England, all the right and title he had in the kingdome of France: which was againe disanulled by the treatie of *Chartres*, whereby the king of England refused that right giuen vnto him by such yeelding vp. The same is to be thought of the league of Tricasse, wherein *Charles* the sixt, without the consent of the states, yeelded the kingdome of France vnto *Henry* the fift, king of England. And therefore pope *Martine* could by no request of the English, be perswaded to ratifie that league, but called *Charles* the seauenth, sonne to *Charles* the sixt,

The maiestie of Charles the fift impugned by this French author.

Title pretended by the French vnto the kingdom of Castile.

The author haply is in this partiall, or els mistaken.

B2 acknowledge   E6 Tricasse *i.e.* Troyes

by the name of the French king: for that the kingdome of Fraunce is neither deuolued by right of succession, (which they tearme from one intestate,) neither by testament, neither by resignation, but by vertue of the law royall, from which the kings themselues cannot derogat without the consent of the estates; which is not so in the kingdomes of Spaine, England, Scotland, Naples, and Nauarre.

But cannot the imperiall title (may some man haply say) make him a soueraigne which is another mans vassall? As the prince or the people making a slaue a magistrat seemeth thereby to haue also enfranchised him; whereof there is no doubt, if he be the princes or the peoples slaue, for otherwise it is not lawfull either for the prince, or for the people, to dispose of another mans seruant: so neither haue the German princes any power ouer other mens citisens or subiects, such as was *Charles* the fift. Ioyne hereunto also, that the imperiall title of the emperour carrieth with it no soueraigntie: albeit that the emperour writing vnto the princes of the empire, vse these wordes, *Wee command you, &c. You shall do this, &c.* which other princes do not toward their own subiects: yea and that more is, that the princes electors carrie the titles of Butlers, Esquiers, and Tasters to the emperour, yet the soueraigntie of the empire resteth not in the person of the emperour, but in the assemblie of the states of the empire, who are able to giue law vnto the emperour, and to euerie prince of the empire in particular, in such sort as that the emperour hath not power to make any particular edict, neither peace nor warre, neither to charge the subiects of the empire so much as with one impost, nor to call or dismisse the diets of the empire, without the consent of the princes. And that is it for which the emperour *Maximilian* the first, at the diet of Constance, holden in the yeare 1507, said vnto the estates (the popes legat then vrging that the imperiall crowne was both to be requested and receiued of the pope,) That to take the imperiall crowne of the pope was but a needlesse ceremonie, seruing to no purpose; considering that the imperiall authoritie and power depended of the estates of the empire: which in due place we will more particularly declare.

The emperour no absolute soueraigne.

Whereby a man may easily iudge, that there are few or none absolute soueraigne princes. For the Venetian Commonweale excepted, there are no princes or Commonweals in Italie, which hold not of the empire, the pope, or the crowne of Fraunce: which concerning the kingdome of Sicilie and Naples, we haue alreadie declared. As for the duke of Milan he is a naturall vassall of the empire, from which hee taketh his inuesture, and thereto payeth reliefe: for which the emperour *Maximilian* the first, in lesse than xv, or xvj yeares space, drue thence vnto himselfe, aboue three hundred thousand pounds: For king *Lewes* the twelfth at one time paid therfore an hundred thousand pounds: and the Storces had it no better cheape. For they which are now called dukes of Milan, in the remembrance of our auncestors, that is to say about an hundred and fiftie yeares agoe, were called but lieutenants, and the citie it selfe but the ordinarie chamber of the empire. And so namely *Iohn Galeace* the second, and *Barnabas* his brother, in the inuestiture which they had from the emperour *Charles* the fourth, are simply called lieutenants of the empire. And *Galeace* the first being accused for charging the subiects with subsidies, without the emperours leaue, was by a decree from the emperour sent prisoner vnto the castle of Modene; where after he had of long time liued, he at length died; whose sonne *Actius* being by the emperour *Lewes* of Bauyere put into his fathers place, for the summe of an hundred thousand crownes, obtained of him the first title of a prince, in the yeare 1338. And after that, *Galeace* the third, father in law to *Lewes* duke of Orleans, payed vnto the emperour *Fredericke* the third, an hundred thousand florines, for the honour and title of a duke, in the yeare one thousand three hundred ninetie seuen.

No prince in Italie which holdeth not of the pope, or of the empire. The duke of Milan.

So

I5,16 pounds *i.e.* livres (Fr)   K6 1338 (L) 1328 (Fr)   K8–9 one thousand three hundred ninetie seuen (Fr) 1398 (L) *properly* 1395

OF A COMMONWEALE.

So say we also of the duke of Mantua, who acknowledgeth himselfe to hold of the Germaine empire, and to be also a prince thereof. *The duke of Mantua.*

As for the duke of Ferrara he confesseth euen at this present to hold part of his seignorie, euen Ferrara it selfe, of the pope, and therefore payeth a yearely rent or fee into the popes coffers. For not long ago, *viz.* in the yeare 1372, the marques of Este was by pope *Gregory* first established his lieutenant in the city of Ferrara, reseruing vnto the church fealtie and homage, iurisdiction and soueraigntie; with condition also, that he should yearely pay ten thousand florens of gold into the chamber of S. *Peter*, and to find an hundred men at armes paied for three monethes, for the defence of the Church of Rome, so often as need should require, as I haue learned out of the Vatican records. *The duke of Ferrara.*

And as for Rhegium and Modene, he acknowledgeth him to hold them of the empire: albeit that pope *Iulius* the second maintained them to be the Church fees, and in that quarrell made warres vpon the Ferrariens and the French king, who gaue them aide: as also to haue the entire reuenue of the fee, beeing before diminished by pope *Alexander* the sixt, in marrying his base daughter *Lucrece* vnto the duke *Alphonsus*. And true it is, that the French kings long since tooke vpon them the defence and patronage of the prince of Ferrara, since the time that *Borsus*, first duke of Ferrara, acknowledged himselfe liege vassall vnto *Charles* the sixt, and therfore it was vnto him permitted, that those dukes of Ferrara might beare the armes of Fraunce, the publike acts whereof yet remaine in the records of Fraunce.

As concerning the Florentines, they of long time haue pretended libertie against the empire, for the payment of sixe thousand Florines vnto the emperour *Rodolphe*. As also do the Genowayes, who as they say, were by the same emperour enfranchised. How be it that afterwards they hauing receiued great harme from the Venetians, gaue themselues into protection vnto king *Charles* the sixt, the French king: and not long after vnto the duke of Milan, who receiued them vpon condition that they should therefore do fealtie and homage vnto the French kings. *The Florentines. The Genowayes.*

In like case they of Luca paied vnto the emperour *Henrie* the fift, twelue thousand Florines to be enfranchised; Sienna ten thousand; And *Peter Gambecourt* payed twelue thousand vnto the emperour *Charles* the fourth for the seignorie of Pisa.

But these were not true alienations, nor exemptions from subiection; but rather simple graunts and gifts, with certaine priueleges to gouerne their estate, vnder the obeisance of the empire. It was not also in the power of the emperours, neither of any prince whatsoeuer, to alienat any thing of the publike demaine, and much lesse of the rights of the soueraigne maiestie, but that it was alwayes in the power of the successour to lay hand thereon againe, as it is lawfull for the lord to lay hold vppon his fugitiue slaue. As the emperour *Maximilian*, hauing thrust his armie into Italie, with the power of king *Lewes* the xij, and hauing brought a great feare vpon all the cities of Italie, gaue them well to vnderstand: At which time the Florentines sent their ambassadors vnto him, to yeeld vnto him fealtie and homage for their estate, and to obtaine of him the confirmation of their priueleges, which cost them fortie thousand ducats. And albeit that *Cosmus* duke of Florence, by force of armes made himselfe lord of Sienna: yet so it was, that he tooke the inuestiture therof, & yeelded therfore fealtie & homage vnto the king of Spaine, as perpetuall lieutenant of the empire. Which is sufficient reason to show, that they of Sienna were not before enfranchised or exempted from the empire; or if they were, why did then pope *Iulius* the second pay thirtie thousand ducats to *Maximilian* the emperour, to redeeme of him the libertie of Sienna, to the intent to inuest therein * the duke of Vrbin. And yet neuerthelesse all that letted not, but that the duke of Florence, which had conquered it by force of armes, was constrai- *That a prince cannot alienat any thing of the publike demaine but that his successors may again resume the same.*

* *Guichardin.*

constrained to take the inuestiture thereof of the king of Spaine, and to pay therefore sixe hundred thousand crownes, which afterwards the king of Spaine would haue againe repayed vnto the duke of Florence, to haue restored Sienna into the former estate; which he would not do, being enformed that the king of Spayne would haue giuen it to the duke of Parma, to reunite Placence and Parma vnto the duchie of Milan, from whence they had bene before distracted. And how then could the German emperours, which are subiects vnto the estates of the empire, alienat the demaine and rights of soueraigntie, in giuing the rights of soueraigntie vnto the cities of Italie, or libertie vnto the tributarie people; seeing that the absolute soueraigne prince cannot so do? no not so much as to distract one clod of the publike land, much lesse to giue away the proprietie. For kings and other great princes (to say truely) haue not the proprietie of the publike demaines, nay not so much as the whole vse and profit: for that contenting themselues with the bare vse, the rest belongeth vnto the common-weale. And for that cause the Emperour *Charles* the fourth, granting the confirmation of the priuileges to them of Perouze, ioyned thereunto this clause, *Quoad viueret*: So long as he should liue. And yet for all that pope *Iulius* the second tooke that towne from the Baillions, and put it vnder the obeysance of the Church, from whence it was said to haue bene taken. And how could the cities of Italie, or duke of Florence, haue any absolute soueraigntie, seeing that for all differences and controuersies concerning their estates, frontiers, demaines, and tenures, they plead the same before the emperour, or at least wise in the imperiall chamber, where their causes are decided, and they enforced to doe as is there adiudged. And albeit that they of Genes, who seemed to hold lesse of the empire than any one of the other townes of Italie, where by the marques of Finall (whome they had driuen out of his estate) summoned before the emperour *Maximilian* the second, in the yeare 1559: and that they would receiue the emperour as an arbitratour, and not as a judge or a superiour: yet so it was, that the emperour taking vpon him the authoritie of a judge, caused them before warned, to be summoned, and when that after many peremptorie edicts they made not their appearance, he pronounced sentence against them, and by an herault at armes threatned to proscribe the territorie of Genes if they obeyed not his censure. Now most certaine it is, that there is none but the cities and townes which hold of the empire, that can be proscribed by the imperiall proscription, whether it be by sentence of the emperour, or by decree of the imperiall chamber. For the imperiall chamber could not haue proscribed Minde, Munster, Magdeburg, and others, had they not bene contained within the bounds and power of the German empire: much lesse could the emperour haue proscribed Genes, if it had not bene within the power of the Germans. And therfore when they of Genes had appealed from the interlocutorie sentence of *Maximilian* vnto the pope, they afterwards renouncing their appeale, yeelded to the sentence, acknowledging the iurisdiction and soueraigntie of the empire. And so at length the emperour gaue sentence for the marques, acknowledging himselfe to be a vassal vnto the German empire, whome they of Genes would haue had to haue bene theirs. And since that the marques hath by that definitiue sentence bene maintained in possession of his marquisat, as I haue seene by the letters of Signior *D'la Forest*, embassadour for the king, dated at Vienna the xviij of Iuly, in the yeare 1560: which iudgement the emperour gaue after he had seene the opinions of the lawyers of foure vniuersities. And not long after they were by another sentence of the same emperours, giuen in the moneth of Iuly, in the yeare one thousand fiue hundred sixtie foure, condemned in a processe which they had against *Anthonie Flisque*, by them banished, who ouerthrew them by an appeale made vnto the emperour.

That princes haue not the proprietie of the publike demaine but onely the bare vse.

Genes threatned by Maximilian the Emperor.

Which

G7 the Baillions *i.e.* the Baglioni   H3 *For* where *read* were.

OF A COMMONWEALE. 131

Which things although they bee so plaine as that there ought thereof to bee no doubt, but that the cities of Italie on this side the riuers Rubicon and Tiber, excepting some few, are contained within the bounds of the German empire, & so haue of themselues no soueraigntie; yet is the same made more euident by the generall consent of all the lawyers of Italie, who deny it to be lawfull for any cities of Italie to make any lawes or customes, contrarie or derogatorie to the Roman laws, published by the commaundement of the emperour *Frederick*. And that the cities of Italie either had no right of soueraintie at al, or else renounced the same, it is manifest by that league which was made in the citie of Constance; for in that league among such priuileges as are confirmed vnto the cities of Italie, the rights of soueraignty are expresly excepted. And therfore *Alexander Imolensis* of all the lawyers of his time the most skilful, saith, A certaine iurisdiction to be thereby giuen vnto the cities of Italie; but not the rights of maiestie or soueraigntie to be therefore vnto them graunted, and that euen for that reason, for that the cities doubting or disagreeing about their right, the emperours were wont to appoint them judges and commissioners for the deciding of their controuersies.

Much lesse therefore may the imperiall townes and cities contained within the bounds of the German empire, pretend themselues to haue any soueraigntie, albeit that we see certaine of them to boast of a certaine show of libertie, which they of old receiued from the emperors; as Nuremberg from the emperour *Fredericke* the first; Isne from *Otho* the third; Egre from *Lewes* of Bauyere: yea and some of them there were, which not able longer to endure the hard bondage of their lords, princes of the empire, set themselues at libertie, as did the cities of Vlme, Brunswic, Lubec, and others: but that which they call libertie, is but an old vacation from certaine seruices, and an immunitie from customes and tributes graunted by the emperours, without any impeachment to their maiestie. And therefore those cities which I haue spoken of, honour the maiestie of the German empire, receiue from it lawes, obey the magistrats thereof, accept of the decrees of the imperiall chamber, and of the assemblies of the empire: and not onely publique and priuat iudgements of princes and cities among themselues, but also the priuat iudgements of particular men are decided by the imperiall chamber, if appellation be made from the sentence which exceedeth the summe of fiftie crowns. Seeing therefore that the imperiall chamber may of the power of it selfe confirme or disanull the iudgements of princes or cities, it must needs follow, that neither those princes nor cities haue the power of soueraigne maiestie: For as a certaine Poet (I know not who) saith,

The imperial townes and cities subiect vnto appeales made vnto the imperiall chamber

> *Rescindere nunquam Dijs licet acta Deûm.*
> It is not lawfull for the Gods the acts of Gods t'vndoe.

As for the Swissers Commonweals, we said before, them to haue bene rent from the German empire, as oppressed with the tirannnie of their gouernours: and yet they so honour and reuerence the maiestie of the German empire, as that they in generall requested of the emperour *Ferdinand*, to haue the libertie of their priuileges vnto them confirmed: which is a certaine forme of auntient fealtie, and acknowledgement that they hold their libertie of the empire. And albeit that some there be on this side the Rhene, which vaunt themselues to haue soueraigne power ouer their subiects, yet must they needs be the subiects and vassals either of our kings, or of the German empire. For there is no man which knoweth not (if he remember the antiquitie of the French) that all the countrey of Loraine, and the realme of Arles, after the death of the three children of *Lothaire* were diuided betwixt the emperour *Charles* the Bauld of Fraunce,
and

The Swissers Commonweals to be subiect either to the Empire or the king of France.

D3 those princes   D3-4 a certaine Poet *i.e.* Ovid (*Metamorphoses*, XIV, 784-785)   D10 tirannie

and *Lewes* king of Germanie his brother. As Vitald, Floard, and Lambert the best antiquaries do in their histories at large declare. Now so it is that the vassall can neuer prescribe for his homage towards his lord, nor the subiect against the iurisdiction of his prince; and that the graunts and sufferances of the emperour, and the kings of France could not preiudice either the crowne or the empire: wherfore we must conclude these possessours of this maiestie by sufferance, to bee subiects and vassals either vnto our kings, or to the German empire.

The Duke of Loraine no absolute Soueraigne, but vassall of the German empire.

And albeit that many thinke the duke of Loraine to be an absolute soueraigne, by reason of the Armes that he beareth, being an armed arme, saying, as it should seeme, That he holdeth nothing but of the sword: yet neuerthelesse so it is, that in his title he calleth himselfe a prince of the empire; which is indeed to acknowledge the imperiall maiestie. Ioyne thereunto also, that he hath vsually receiued iudges from the imperial chamber, and submitted himselfe to the iurisdiction thereof. For as for that that hee is the last among the German princes, nor in their ceremonies holdeth not the place of the auntient dukes of Loraine; that is, for that he holdeth but a little, *viz.* scarce the sixt part of the auntient duchie of Loraine (a prouince of the German empire) which containeth all that countrey which lyeth betwixt the riuer of the Maze and the Rhene. And therefore the dukes of Brabant, and the German emperours, called themselues dukes of Loraine. So the emperour *Charles* the fourth, in the league which he made with *Iohn* the French king, calleth himselfe duke of Loraine. But this countrey which now is called Loraine, is a part of the German empire and the duke himselfe a vassall of the empire. For *Stephen* countie of Boulongne, was in that dukedome inuested by the emperour *Henrie* the first, and for that cause acknowledged himselfe a vassall of the empire, in the yeare 1019. And *Frederick* of Loraine countie of Vaudemont, duke *Charles* being dead without heire male, before *Sigismund* the emperour and the fathers assembled at Constance, claimed that dukedome of right to belong vnto him, as next of kin; for that it was an imperiall fee, whereof *Isabel* duke *Charles* his heire, who had married *Renat* duke of Aniou, was not (as he said) capable: which *Renat* denyed it not to be an imperiall fee, but shewed many such imperiall fees to haue descended vnto the daughters. And afterward the title comming to be tryed by the sword, *Renat* being ouerthrowne and taken prisoner by *Frederick*, could not be before deliuered, vntill that he had married his daughter *Yoland* vnto *Anthonie* the sonne of *Frederick*, with condition, that if *Renat* died without heires male, the duchie of Loraine should descend vnto the heires of *Frederick*, & so vnto the house of Vaudemont, as it is come to passe.

The duchie of Loraine deuolued vnto the counties of Vaudemont.

Now if so it be that the dukedome of Loraine be an imperiall fee, comprehended within the bounds of the German empire: neither the lord of Lumes nor the countie of Aspremont, who are contained within the precinct of Loraine, can chalenge vnto themselues any right of soueraigntie, as they haue done, seeing that it is plaine by the law, that he which hath a limited territorie, hath but the same right ouer euerie one of his subiects which are within the compasse of his territorie, that hee hath ouer them all in generall; except it appeare, him by some speciall priuiledge to be free and from the generall expresly exempted. By which reason all such as pretend a soueraigntie, being enclosed within the bounds and territorie of another man, may bee thereof debarred: which a man cannot so easily iudge of them, which in the frontiers of kingdomes, take vpon them a kinde of soueraigne power; as do the fiue lords or princes in the confines of Burgundie, whome both the free counties, and the dukes haue oftentimes chalenged for their vassals: and for the soueraigntie of whome, at such times as they had taken vp armes, they obtained of the generals of both parts, that in the meane time they beeing free might be as newters, vntill the euent of the warre had decided the cause: and so at length

G7 the Maze *i.e.* the Maas, or Meuse   G10 French

length abusing the long possession of soueraigntie, made of that their right, which they had but by sufferance, a perpetuitie: but as we haue oftentimes before said, so wee must hereafter oftentimes say, That neither the right of soueraigne maiestie, nor the right of libertie, can by the client or vassall be prescribed against: and much lesse if it be withholden by concealement or by sufferance. In like sort the countrey of Bearne, betwixt the confines of Fraunce and Nauarre, which the kings atturney generall in the court of Paris maintained to be a prouince holden of the crowne of Fraunce, and disallowed of the plea of the kings atturney of the parliament of Thoulouze, who had confessed it not to hold of the crowne, in the yeare 1505; which although it remaine vndecided, yet the king of Nauarre for all that by sufferance holdeth it in soueraigntie.

The right soueraigntie and libertie not to be prescribed against.

In like case the principalitie of Dombes was maintained by *Lizet* the kings atturney, to hold in fee of the crowne of Fraunce, and that the duke of Sauoy had no power to giue it to the empire, vnder the colour of being the emperours lieutenant, which hee showed to be done in the most wofull times of the ciuill warre, when as the dukes of Orleans and Burgundie had drawne all the whole kingdome into parts, in the yeare 1398: in like manner the princes of East Frizeland, and they which hold the territory betwixt England and Scotland, which they call the Batable ground: as also the abbot of Gosen, betwixt Metz and Pont a Mousson, who holdeth the abbey and twenty fiue villages, in title of soueraigntie, without acknowledging any superior lord whatsoeuer: as also the lords of Beauieu, willing to exempt themselues from the crowne of Fraunce, yeelded themselues vnto the empire, and so by the duke of Sauoy, the emperours lieutenant, were receiued into the protection of the empire, from which they also by little and little exempted themselues, without acknowledging either duke, king, or emperour for their soueraigne.

As for the dukes of Sauoy, the Italian doctors with one common errour haue holden them to haue absolute power and soueraigntie, and to haue so beene iudged by the decree of the parliament of Sauoy: a thing altogether contrarie vnto the office of a lieutenant and vassall. And also *Osazque* the first president of Piemont writeth, That the dukes of Sauoy haue obtained this power of the emperors, which they could not haue as lieutenants of the empire; as *Felinus* the best interpretor of the law hath most truly written. For what can be more contrarie vnto soueraigne maiestie, than to professe ones selfe to be another mans deputie or officer, (for so the name of a lieutenant doth signifie) or from whom shouldest thou think thy selfe to haue the power of soueraigntie in that prouince wherein thou thy selfe bearest rule? But euen the dukes of Sauoy themselues confesse, and all their histories declare, this prouince of the German empire which is now called Sauoy, to haue bene a fee of the same empire, erected into a countie (holden of the empire in fealtie) by *Henry* the fift; and afterwards into a duchie by the emperour *Sigismund*. And euident it is the dukes alwayes heretofore, and not long since duke *Charles* restored vnto his countrey, to haue yeelded fealtie and homage vnto the emperour: and two yeares after, *viz.* in the yeare 1561, to haue sent speciall letters of atturney vnto the countie *D'Arques* chiefe chamberlaine to the emperour, to obtaine for him of the emperour another inuestiture: for because that that which hee had before taken at *Ausburg*, seemed not vnto him in sufficient good forme, as I haue seene by the letters of *M. D'la Forest*, ambassadour for the king vnto the emperour. But an hard matter it was to make such a forme as should be vnto him good; for that it seemeth that the title or qualitie of a perpetuall lieutenant, doth preiudice not only vnto soueraigntie, but also vnto the qualitie of a feudatarie & proprietarie in those lands which he holdeth of another man, if it bee not by a doubtfull or improper kind of speech.

The Duchie of Sauoie to hold of the empire.

The dukes of Saxonie and the county Palatine lieutenants of the empire.

The dukes of Saxonie and the counties Palatine are also perpetuall lieutenants of the empire; but that is in the emperours absence, to doe iustice vnto the princes and imperiall townes, yea euen against the emperour himselfe, (as shall in due place bee declared) and to all them which are of their gouernment: which is a personall office, and not belonging vnto lands; neither can he that taketh vpon him the qualitie of a deputie, lieutenant, or gouernour, be feudatarie or proprietarie of those seignories that he holdeth of him whose lieutenant he is. And so the title of perpetuall lieutenantship ought to haue relation vnto other countries, without the terrritorie and demaines of his countrey of Sauoy: which neither the Swissers, nor other princes of Italie & Germanie could endure, and much lesse the French king, who holdeth nothing of the empire, whereby he might be iusticiable to the lieutenants of the empire. Ioyne hereunto also, that the Emperour *Charles* the fourth made *Charles* the sixt Dauphin of Viennois, his perpetuall lieutenant, the xiiij day of Ianuarie, in the yeare 1378. And for that he was but nine yeares old, he gaue him the priuelege of his age, by a most ample and gracious charter, whereunto hang seales of gold, which I haue read in the records of our kings. But withall made him perpetuall lieutenant of the kingdome of Arles, (excepting onely the countie of Sauoy) and that more is, gaue him power of life and death ouer the subiects of the empire; with power also to conferre honors, to impose and raise taxes, and from the same to exempt whome he saw good, to receiue appeales made vnto the emperour, to make peace and warre, to giue laws vnto the subiects, and to disanull and abrogat the same, and such other like. This lieutenancie was for all the kingdome of Arles, which extended from the mountaine Iura (commonly called saint *Claudius* mount) and the riuers Araris and Rhodanus, vnto the Alpes, and the sea of Genes; all which the imperials haue alwaies pretended to be holden of the empire. But the earles of Prouince haue long since exempted themselues from the German empire, amongst whome was *Raymund* the last, one of whose daughters was married vnto *Lewes* the ninth, the French king, and the other vnto *Charles* duke of Aniou, by which meanes the countie of Prouence is come to the house of Aniou, & from thence by the bountie of countie *Renat*, vnto the crowne of Fraunce. Albeit that *Philip Valois* the French king, had bought of the emperour *Henrie* the fift, the soueraigntie of all the realme of Arles, without excepting either the countie of Sauoy, or the principality of Oreng, or Beiauieu, which was afterwards giuen to *Lewes* duke of Burbon; either of the countie of Prouence, which was then in the house of Aniou; either of the franke countie, which was giuen to *Philip* the hardie, by the emperour *Charles* the fourth, in the yeare 1362, being deuolued to the empire for want of heires male. And the sale of soueraigntie of the said kingdome of Arles, was made for the summe of three hundred thousand markes of siluer, with promise to cause it to be ratified by the princes of the empire, who afterwards consented thereunto: of which their confirmation the emperour gaue *Iohn* king of Bohemia suretie, who sold also the towne of Luques vnto the same king, for an hundred and fourescore thousand florines of gold, in the yeare 1330. The contracts, ratifications, and quittances, are yet in the treasurie of Fraunce to bee seene; from whence I haue the exemplifications conferred with the originals, wel worthy to haue bene seene of them who were deputed for the affaires of Sauoy, in the yeare 1562. But that me thinke well worth the marking, that in the deedes of bargaine and sale, are comprised all the lawes of soueraigne maiestie, which the German emperours giue vnto themselues in all the prouinces of the kingdome of Arles: wherein are contained the Sauoians, they of Belloioci, they of Prouence, they of free Burgundie, which the emperour *Charles* the fourth gaue to *Philip* duke of Burgundie to bee possessed in the imperiall right, the issues male of the counties fayling. Whereby it is manifest

Charles the sixt of Fraunce by the emperour made perpetual lieutenant of the empire.

The soueraignty of the kingdome of Arles bought of the emperour by the French king.

F8 territorie   G3 xiiii (Fr 7) xiii (Fr 1–6, 8)   H3 Araris and Rhodanus *i.e.* the Saône and the Rhône   I2 Beauieu   I3–4 the franke countie *i.e.* Franche-Comté

nifest the French kings to haue the right of soueraigne maiestie ouer all the people of the kingdome of Arles, and not therefore to owe any fealtie or homage vnto the German empire.

And at the same time as it were the emperour *Lewes* of Bauaria made *Edward* the third, king of England his perpetuall lieutenant; and by his letters pattents gaue him power to make lawes, and to administer iustice to all the subiects of the empire: and that all the subiects of the empire should obey him, and in his name to yeeld vnto him fealtie and homage: which was an occasion rather sought for, than offered, for him to make warre vpon the French king, who then held *Cambray* and the castles of Creueceur, and Payerne, members of the empire: for that by the auntient leagues made betwixt the French kings and the emperours, it was prouided, That they should not one of them take any thing from the other, or molest one the others subiects; as was declared vnto king *Edward* by the imperiall princes allied with him, and then assembled in the towne of Hale: which is a most certaine argument that the kings of Fraunce hold nothing of the empire; neither that the emperours haue any right in that kingdome. Which is also expresly set downe in the contract of purchase of *Philip Valois*, which I haue here before rehearsed, which beareth this clause: *And the kings and realmes of Fraunce shall continue in their priueleges, enfranchisments, and liberties, that they haue alwayes holden against the German empire, whereunto they are in nothing subiect.* Which was well giuen the emperour *Sigismund* to vnderstand, at such time as he of his imperiall power would haue made the countie of Sauoy duke, in the towne of Lyons: against whome the kings officers there so opposed themselues, as that hee was glad to get him out of the kingdome, at libertie to vse his owne power, which he did in great choller and displeasure. And this was done by the expresse commaundement of the king, *Charles* the sixt, to couer two notable errors that had bene before committed: the one passing by sufferance, in that the emperour *Sigismund* being magnifically receiued at Paris, and as beseemed the kings vncle, had place in a royall seat in full parliament; and the other, that afterwards he was suffered to make *Seneschal D'Beaucaire* knight; although the court had in this last point admonished the king, that vnto him onely it belonged to make knights in his owne kingdome; as it had twice before bene solemnely iudged by two decrees against the counties of Flaunders and Neuers. Which I haue the more willingly noted, to show the errour of *Alciat*, who hath maintained, that the French king is subiect to the empire; which is a wilfull errour or ingratitude, considering the entertainment he had in Fraunce to teach and write the truth: which I thinke not to haue proceeded from him of ignorance, but in fauour of the emperour *Charles* the fift, who drew him to Pauie, and there doubled his salarie: or els to the imitation of *Bartholus*, author of that errour, who writ the same things of the French kings that *Alciat* did: at such time forsooth as he was by the emperour *Charles* the fourth of a bastard not onely made legitimat, and by him ennobled, but power also giuen him to take the benefit of age to him and his, which should professe to teach the lawes, with armes also answerable vnto his dignitie and honour: *viz.* a Lyon Azure in a field Argent. For which so many and so great benefits he writ all them to be heretikes, which should deny the German emperour to be lord of all the world: which hee seemeth to haue gathered of the words of *Antoninus Augustus*, vnto the law Rhodia; *I am* (saith he) *the lord of the world, and law of the sea*: which words seeing they were spoken but for ostentation sake, and for the augmenting of his honour, lesse need to bee refuted; seeing that the Roman empire when it was at the greatest, (which was in the time of *Traian* the emperour) contained scarce the thirtieth part of the world, and that the German empire is not now the tenth part of the Roman empire. And yet the empe-

---

C8 *For* Seneschal D'Beaucaire *read* the Seneschal of Beaucaire.   D4 entertainment *i.e.* wages
E1 *For* Azure *Bodin writes* Gules.   Note at C2.

rout *Sigismund* sick of that incurable disease of ambition, sought to haue brought euery mans gouernment vnder his, although he was in that his hope much deceiued. For intruding himselfe to haue made the duke of Lituania a king (whose countrey lieth aboue two hundred leagues from the frontiers of the empire of Germany) hee sent him a crowne and a sword, which for all that the duke refused, neither thought it good to chaunge the name of the *Great Duke* (whereby he was called) although he had of himselfe shaken off the seruile yoke of the Tartars, least in so doing hee might seeme to haue attributed his power and soueraigntie vnto the Germans.

<small>The kings of Polonia hold nothing of the empire.</small>

We see also that the Germaine Emperors haue sent the royall Crownes vnto the Dukes of Polonia, before they were by the Pope suffered to beare the Royall title; which they refused: and yet certaine it is, that the Kings of Polonia neuer held any thing of the Empire. Oftentimes indeed the Germaines haue attempted to haue subdued the Polonians, whose vaine attempts the Polonians haue not onely repulsed, but also ioyned vnto their kingdom the countries of Silesia and Prussia, both rent from the body of the Germaine Empire. Which when the Prutenian knights had taken in euil part, and thereof oftentimes complained to the states of the empire, yet the emperors thought it not good for to attempt any thing against the Polonians, by whom they had knowne the imperiall armies to haue been many times repulsed and ouerthrown. And yet for all this, the Polonians refused not to take their royall scepters from the bishops of Rome.

<small>The fruit that came of the strife betwixt the German emperor and the pope for the soueraigntie of the Christian Commonweale.</small>

True it is that the bishops of Rome of long time striue with the Germaine emperours for the soueraigntie and chiefe gouernment of the Christian Commonweale, and as chiefetaines of the faction, drew all the Christian princes and cities into armes; so that many cities and Commonweales, especially in Italie, were at such mortall hatred amongst themselues, as that they receiued not greater harme from the enemies of the Christian religion and name, than they did from one another. Neither wanted there some which writ in earnest, al Christian kings to be the bishop of Romes clyents and vassals; and in case that they were foolish, furious, or prodigall, that they might haue ouerseers appointed ouer them by the pope: which we haue before said, to haue been done by pope *Innocent* the fourth, against the king of Portugall. And albe it that pope *Innocent* said, That his meaning therein was not in any thing to preiudice the regall power, in appointing such an ouerseer; yet did not his sayings at all agree with his dooings. Pope *Vrban* the fift also made no doubt, to make legitimate *Henry* the bastard king of Castile, so to thrust out of his kingdom his brother *Peter*, borne in lawfull wedlocke: who thereupon, by the power of the French, was not onely thrust out of his kingdom, but slaine also by his bastard brother.

<small>The immoderat and absurd power which some attribute vnto the pope.</small>

Some there haue been also which haue passed further, saying that the pope hath in power iurisdiction ouer the emperour; but ouer all other kings and princes really and indeed: excepting ouer the French king, whom the canonists themselues confesse, indeed, and of right to acknowledge none greater than himselfe vnder God. Which *Belluga* a Spanish doctor, and *Oldrade* the beautie of his time do also better declare, saying that the French king neither in fact nor of right acknowledgeth any prince of the world superiour vnto himselfe. But these great clearks which thus giue the popes power ouer other princes, haue no better reason for that they say, than the authoritie of pope *Gelasius*, who hath written, That the pope hath power to dispoyle all kings and princes of their soueraigntie and power. And some others there be which haue maintained, That appeales may be made from all people and princes vnto the pope, That there is none but the emperour and the pope which can reuoke their owne decrees, and depriue other kings and princes of their soueraigntie and rule; That there is no prince but hee, vnto whom the pope hath confirmed his principalitie: And that which of all other is most absurd,

That

Notes at H6, I6.

that hee of himselfe may giue prileleges, exemptions, and immunities vnto another princes subiects contrarie to the decrees and lawes of all princes; and that he is the only and supreme vmpiere and judge of all mans lawes. And what maruell if he rule ouer princes, which commaundeth ouer angels? For so truely *Clement V. P. M.* doubted not to commaund the angels. Yea some there be that haue written, That so often as the pope shall put this clause to his rescripts, *De plenitudine potestatis*, Of the fulnesse of our power: so oft doth he therein derogat from the lawes of all princes. And albeit that some haue holden also, That we must rest vpon that that the pope saith, without farther enquire of the veritie therof; yet so it is neuertheleffe, that *Baldus* hath written, That a man may say vnto him, *Salua reuerentia vestra*, By your reuerences leaue. And vpon the maxime set downe by the canonists, *That the pope can do all*: the diuines graunting it to be so, do yet more subtilly, and as it were in two words moderat the same, *Claue non errante*, The key not erring. And forasmuch as it is euery good subiects part to maintaine the greatnesse and maiestie of their owne princes, I will not enter into the disputes of *Iaques de Terranne* the popes chamberlaine, nor of *Capito*, nor of *M. Charles du Moulin*, and others, who haue oftentimes ouershot themselues either of set purpose, or els pressed with violent passions, haue vnawares entred into matter of religion, and so carried away either with loue or hatred of the pope, haue filled their writings with raylings. Whereas I here speake not but of temporall soueraigntie, which is the subiect that I entreat of, (whereof they speake not) to the end it may be vnderstood, who be absolute soueraigne princes; and whether the other princes be subiect vnto the emperour, or the pope, or not.

For at the beginning, after that pope *Gregorie* (he which first called himselfe the seruant of the seruants of God) had obtained of *Phocas* emperour of Constantinople, the prerogatiue ouer all the bishops; his successours after turning the spirituall power into the temporall, by little and little still encreased their power, in so much that the princes as wel for the fear they then had towards God, as for the dignitie of the prelacie, began to reuerence them much more than in former times; but much more after that the empire of the East began to decline, which was after that the popes had by their interdictions forbidden the people of Italie their obedience vnto the Constantinopolitan emperours, or to pay them any tribute; vpon occasion taken, that *Leo* the emperour, surnamed *Monomachus*, or the *Image breaker*, and also *Thomas* the emperor, had caused the images of Saints to be cast downe and broken: wherewith the people moued, and enraged with the authoritie of the bishop of Rome, slew *Thomas* in the temple of Saint *Sophia*. Wherefore the power of the Greeke empire being weakened in the East, by the incursions of the Barbarians; and the Greeke emperors out of hope againe to recouer Italie; the kings of Lombardie then also doing what they might to make themselues lords of all Italie, and the popes also on their parts no lesse desirous to haue therein a share, and finding themselues too weake to make their partie good against the Lombard kings, vppon this difference cast themselues into the protection of the kings of Fraunce, who then were the greatest Monarches of Christendome; wherein they were not of their hope deceiued. For hereupon, *Pipin* Grande M. of Fraunce (a man of great wealth and power, who then disposed of all the affaires of the realme) with a great army passing ouer the Alpes, ouerthrew and discomfited the power of the Lombards, and afterward going to Rome, was the first that gaue vnto pope *Zacharie*, part of the seignorie of Italie, who had before crowned him king of Fraunce, forbidding the peeres and people of Fraunce to make choyce of any other for their kings but of the house of *Pipin*, hauing publikely pronounced king *Childerike* for his sottishnesse to bee vnable for the gouernment. Whereunto the people of

The beginning of the popes greatnes.

The popes put themselues into the protection of the French Kings, Pipin and Charlemaigne his sonne, the popes great champion.

Da *For* Monomachus *read* Iconomachus.

Fraunce made so much the lesse resistance, for that *Pipin* then had the nobilitie and the armie of Fraunce at commaund: and for that the pope (who as then was esteemed as a God vpon earth) was the author thereof, vnto whome *Pipin* had before solemnly promised, and giuen him letters pattents thereof, That if hee should become victorious ouer the Lombards, he should giue vnto the Church of Rome the Exarchat of Rauenna, which contained thirtie cities, and the prouince of Pentapole, which contained sixteene cities moe: which he after the victorie performed, laying the keyes of the said cities vpon Saint *Peters* altar: yet reseruing vnto himselfe and his successours in the crowne of Fraunce, the soueraigntie of both the prouinces; and that more is, power also to chuse the popes. Whereunto the pope not onely willingly graunted, but almost persuaded *Pipin* to take vppon him the name of an emperour: which title none then vsed, but the emperours of Constantinople. But *Pipin* being dead, the Lombards againe tooke vp armes, to the great disquiet of the popes, who againe had recourse vnto the French kings, as vnto a most sure sanctuarie. Whereupon *Charles, Pipin* his sonne (for his many and worthy victories surnamed the *Great*) with a strong army passing the Alpes, not onely ouerthrew the king of the Lombards, but euen their kingdome also: and hauing surely established the power of the Roman bishops, was by them called Emperour: and they againe by *Charles* so long as he liued, all chosen bishops of Rome. But after the death of this *Charlemaigne*, they which were of great credit in Rome, caused themselues to be chosen pope by the clergie, whether it were for the distrust they had to obtaine that dignitie of the kings of Fraunce, hauing no fauour in the court; or through the negligence of the French kings, who had thereof no great care; or that it was by reason of the great ciuill warres which arose betwixt the children of *Lewes* the Gentle, wherewith the French kings busied, lost the prerogatiue they had in chusing of the chiefe Bishop. Yet *Guitard*, a good antiquarie, who liued in the same time writeth, 3 popes successiuely to haue come into France to excuse themselues to *Lewes* the Gentle, That they had beene by the clergie of Rome constrained to accept of the papal dignitie, beseeching him to confirme the same: which he either as a man not desirous of glorie, or els fearing to prouoke the clergie (being then in great authoritie) did: of which his error he afterwards though to late full sore repented him; being by the colledge of cardinals constrained to yeeld vp his crowne, & to make himself a monke, and the queene his wife a nunne, shut vp apart from her husband in a cloister with other nunnes, who yet were againe afterwards deliuered by the princes and nobilitie of Fraunce, (disdaining to see the pride of the clergie) and so againe restored vnto their former honours.

How the French Kinges lost the prerogatiue they had in the chusing of the Pope.

But after the death of this *Lewes* the Gentle (who was emperour of Fraunce, of Germanie, and of the greater part of Italie, and Spaine) the empire was diuided into three kingdomes, which the brethren *Charles* the Bauld, *Lothaire*, and *Lewes*, euerie one of them held in title of soueraigntie, without acknowledging any superioritie of one another; and againe, the kingdom of *Lothaire* was diuided amongst his children into three parts: vnto one fell the kingdome of Loraine, vnto another the kingdome of Arles, and to the third the kingdome of Italie: *Lewes* holding Germanie, and *Charls* the emperour, Fraunce. So their diuided power began to decay, and the wealth of the bishops of Rome greatly to encrease: they now succeeding one another by way of election, and in nothing acknowledging the maiestie of the French kings, as they ought to haue done: which came to passe especially in the time of pope *Nicholas* the first, who better vnderstood to mannage matters of state than had his predecessours, and was the first that vsed the rigour of excommunication against princes, hauing excommunicated *Lothaire* the younger brother of *Lewes* king of Italie. But the children of

When the pope began first to excommunicat Princes.

Lothaire

Lothaire being afterwards dead without issue, those three kingdomes which I spoke of, viz. of Loraine, Arles, and Italie, were diuided betwixt their vncles, Charles and Lewes. Wherefore Lewes king of Germanie gouerned Italie, which fell vnto his part, by his lieutenants and deputies; whose power was not such as to withstand the popes, but that they still by little and little extended their power and gouernment: which especially hapned at such time as Guiscard the Norman had subdued the kingdome of Sicilie and Naples, taken from the Greekes and Moores; who to weaken the power of the Germans, and to raigne himselfe the more safely in Italie, ioyned hands against them with the Bishops of Rome. But the posteritie of Guiscard being dead without heires male, left the kingdome of Naples and Sicilie vnto a woman their heire; married vnto the German emperor Frederick the second, who going into Italy, there to confirme his power, made choice of another pope (one of his own fauorites) than was he whom the colledge of cardinals had before chosen: which was pope Innocent the fourth, a man both for his birth and learning famous; who driuen out of Italie, and comming into Fraunce (the popes surest sanctuarie) and strengthened with the wealth and power of Lewes the ix, the French king (whether it were for reuerence of him the pope so solemnly by the cardinals chosen, or to weaken the power of the Germans) excommunicated the emperour Frederick the second: who seeing himselfe thereby become odious vnto all men, & himselfe like to be forsaken euen of his own subiects, & great troubles arising also against him in Italy, fearefully returned into Germany, hauing obtained absolution of pope Innocent, by yeelding vp his authoritie and power for any more creating of the bishops of Rome, leauing the kingdomes of Naples and Sicilie vnto his base sonne Manfred, who was also excommunicated by pope Vrban the fift: who not yet so contented, called in Charles of France, duke of Aniou, brother to king Lewes the ix, whome he inuested in the aforesaid two realmes of Naples and Sicilie, reseruing vnto the See of Rome the countie of Beneuent; fealtie, homage, iurisdiction, and soueraigntie for the rest; with a yearely and perpetual fee of eight thousand ounces of gold, as we haue before said. After which time the house of Arragon, which by right of kindred succeeded the posteritie of Manfred, being alwaies at oddes with the house of Aniou, and so in continuall warres for these kingdomes of Naples and Sicilie; and seeing it not possible for them to recouer them so long as the pope was their enemie, they found meanes to gaine the popes fauour, and so made themselues the popes vassals, not onely for the kingdomes of Naples and Sicilie, but also for the kingdomes of Arragon, Sardinia, Corsica, Maiorque, and Minorque: which they partly did also for to obtaine the popes pardon for their offences, as we haue before said. The bishops of Rome in the meane time out of the troubles of these two great houses, encreasing their owne power and profit, peaceably enioyed the territorie about Rome, Spolet, and Beneuent, with a good part of Tuscanie, by vertue of the donation which wee haue before spoken of.

The increasing of the popes power.

Why the kings of Arragon made themselues the popes vassals for the kingdomes of Naples and Sicilie, and submitted also vnto him the rest of their kingdomes.

As for the citie of Rome, sometimes mistresse of the world, they brought it vnder their obeysance, hauing by little and little oppressed the libertie thereof, no man gainsaying them. Albeit that Charlemaigne hauing conquered Italie, expresly commaunded that it should remaine in full libertie, with power left vnto the inhabitants to gouerne their estate, which the Roman bishops had also by their oathes confirmed; as Augustine Onuphre the popes chamberlaine writeth, and as it well appeareth by the Vatican records.

How the citie of Rome was brought vnder the popes obeysance.

Now if there were any soueraigne prince that were a tyrant, or an heretike, or that had done any notorious crime, or not obeyed the popes commaund; hee was by the pope forthwith excommunicated: which was occasion enough to cause his subiects

The great danger princes were sometimes in by reason of the popes excommunication.

to reuolt from him, and to arme other princes against him which was so excommunicated; who then had no other meane left to be againe receiued into fauour, but to make himselfe feudatarie to the Church of Rome, and the popes vassall. As I haue before said of *Iohn* king of England, who made himselfe vassall to *Innocent* the third, for the murther committed in the person of young *Arthur* duke of Britaine. And augmented also the feodall rent of England, for the murder committed by the commaundement of the king of England, in the person of *Thomas* Archbishop of Canterburie. As in like case it chaunced for the murther committed in the person of *Stanislaus* archbishop of Guesne, by the commaundement of the king: for which the pope excommunicated the king, and tooke the roiall title from the kings of Polonia; enioyning also their subiects therefore (as some haue written) to shaue their heads behind, in such sort as we yet see them to doe: which whether it be true or no, I dare not to affirme, neither could the Polonians tell me the cause thereof when I asked it of them: but manifest it is by auntient records, that after the murther of that bishop, the kings of Polonia all thought they had the power of soueraigne maiestie, yet were they called but by the name of dukes, vntill the time of *Lucold* duke of Polonia, who receiued the royall crowne and title, of pope *Iohn* the xxij, vpon condition to pay into the popes coffers a certaine yearely tribute, which is yet at this day paid for the lampe of Saint *Peter*, as we read in their histories. And beside those kingdomes which wee haue spoke of, viz. England, Arragon, Naples, Sicilie, Hierusalem, Polonia, Sardinia, Corsica, and the Canaries, all feudataries or tributaries vnto the popes, or els both together; they haue also pretended the soueraigntie of the kingdome of Hungarie, to belong vnto them, and so it is comprised in the Catalogue of the Chauncerie of Rome. And I haue seene in the Vatican Register, an act dated in the yeare 1229, whereby *Ladislaus* the first, king of Hungarie, promiseth his obedience vnto pope *Benedict* the xij, and acknowledgeth that he ought to receiue the crowne at his hands. And by another act of *Ladislaus* the second, king of Hungarie, excommunicated for the disobedience by him committed against the popes Legat; for to haue his absolution, he bound himselfe to pay yearely into the popes chamber an hundred markes of siluer; which obligation beareth date the yeare 1280. Yet in the same Vatican register, dated in the yeare 1308, whereby it appeareth also, the barons of Hungarie to haue sharply opposed themselues against the popes Legat, alleaging Saint *Stephen* the first king of Hungarie, to haue receiued his crowne of the pope, and that they would not endure the pope to haue any such prerogatiue ouer them: and yet neuerthelesse they letted not, but that the king by themselues chosen, might if so pleased him cause himselfe to bee crowned by the pope. And in the end of that act are many decrees of the popes legat, concerning the state of that kingdome, with prohibitions to the kings of Hungarie for alienating any the demaines of the crowne: which may seeme to haue bene the cause that *Andrew* king of Hungarie, was by *Honorius* the pope cited to Rome, to show why he had alienated part of the publike demaines. *Innocentius* also the third expresly enioyned the king of Hungarie to fulfill his dead fathers vow; threatning if he should refuse so to doe, to depriue him of his kingdome, and to giue it to him that was next of kin. Which a man need not to thinke strange in those times, seeing that at the same time wee see the prohibitions made by the pope vnto the counties of Tholouze, (and inserted into the Decretals) that they should not raise any new charges vpon their owne subiects. As for the kingdome of Hierusalem and Syria, wonne by *Godfrey* of Buillon and his allies, it is manifest that he therefore professed himselfe to be the popes vassall, and to hold it of him by fealtie and homage: besides that we find it comprised in the Catalogue of the feudatarie kings of the church of Rome. And as concerning the Grand Masters of the ho-

Thomas Cromerus. Soueraigntie by the pope pretended vnto the Kingdome of Hungarie.

F8–9 archbishop of Gnesne (*but properly* bishop of Cracow) G5 For *all thought* read although.
G6 Lucold: Lacolde (Fr) Lacoldus (L) *i.e.* Ladislas Lokietek H6 receive

OF A COMMONWEALE.

A honourable order of S. *Iohn Hierusalem*, which was composed of eight sundrie people of diuers language, they were alwayes inuested by the pope, and yet do fealtie and homage vnto the popes for the soueraigne power which they haue ouer the knights of their order: albeit that they did homage also vnto the emperour *Charles* the fift, for Tripolis in Barbarie, before it fell into the hands of the Turke: as now also they doe at this present vnto the king Catholike, for the isle of Malta, which was vpon that condition giuen them. *The Grand Master of S. Iohn Hierusalem feudatarie both to the king of Spaine and the pope.*

And as for the kingdome of Nauarre, vnder the colour of excommunication taken from *Peter Albret*, we said before, that it is by the kings of Spaine holden of the popes of Rome by fealtie and homage. And not many yeares ago pope *Pius* the fift would B vnder the same colour of religion, haue taken also the rest that was yet left, from *Ione* queene of Nauarre, hauing caused her to be cited to Rome; and afterward for default and contumacie, causing her by his commissioners to bee condemned: had not king *Charles* the ix taken vpon him to protect her, as being his subiect, vassall, and neere kinswoman: which he gaue all Christian princes to vnderstand, vnto whose maiestie the proscription of that most honourable queene might well haue seemed preiudiciall. *The kingdome of Nauarre holden of the pope.*

For many were of opinion that the pope was absolute soueraigne lord of all the kingdoms of Christendome. And in our age, at such time as *Henry* the eight, king of England, was reuolted from the pope, the earle of Aisimund, an Irish man, sent letters vnto *Henry* the second the French king, (the copie whereof I haue taken out of the reC cords) whereby he offered himselfe to become his subiect, if he should of the pope obtaine the soueraigntie of the kingdome of Ireland, which we said to haue bene vnder the fealtie of the bishop of Rome, since the time of *Innocent* the third. They haue also pretended themselues to haue the soueraigntie of Mirandula, and of the counties of Concorde, Rege, Modene, Parma, & Placence, for which the popes *Iulius* the second and third, both of them made great warres against the French king, when as yet it was most manifest those cities to depend of the German empire. Of Parma, and Placence there is no doubt; and the rest they confesse *Maud* the countesse to haue had by inheritance, holden by fealtie of the emperours, which she gaue to the church of Rome.

Now if we graunt the aforesaid cities might haue beene giuen vnto the bishop of D Rome, and to haue bene indeed giuen, as the bishops themselues vaunt; they must also confesse themselues to haue bene vassals vnto the German empire. But for that it seemed a dishonour to the bishop of Rome, which said himselfe to haue power ouer all princes, to be accounted a vassall and client of the emperours; they said (but falsly) the soueraigntie of all the cities of Italie, which were within the dominions of the Church of Rome, to haue bene by the emperours graunted vnto the bishop of Rome. And to exempt themselues, they produce a donation which I haue read in the Vatican register without date or name of bishop, whereby *Otho* the emperour (but which *Otho* it is not said, when as there haue bene foure of that name) doth giue vnto the church of Rome Pisaurum, Ancona, Fossabrum, and Ausun. Other letters pattents also there is of the E emperour *Otho* the fourth, vnto pope *Innocent* the third, conceiued in these words, *Ego Otho quartus rex Romanorum semper Augustus, tibi domino meo papæ Innocentio tertio, tuisque successoribus ecclesiæ Romanæ, spondeo, polliceor, & iuro, quod omnes possessiones Ecclesiæ, &c.* I *Otho* the fourth, king of the Romans, alwayes victorious, do auow, promise, and sweare, to thee my lord pope *Innocent* the third, and to thy successours of the church of Rome, that all the possessions of the Church, &c. And that which followeth after, conteineth a most copious confirmation of all the lands and cities which then were in the dominion or patrimonie of the church of Rome, whether they were giuen by the emperours themselues, or by any other lords or princes whatsoeuer: in the *The pope of right vassall vnto the German empire for the cities he holdeth thereof in fee.*

num-

A1 *For* people *read* peoples.   A2 (margin) Hierusalem   B9 Aisimund *i.e.* Desmond

Note at B6.

number of which cities are these contained: *Comitatus Perusiæ, Reatæ, Saluiæ, Interamnæ, Campaniæ, nec non Romam, Ferrariam, &c. Marchiam, Anconitanam, terram Comitissæ Matildis & quæcunque sunt circa Rodicosanum vsque Ceperanum, exerchatum Rauennæ, Pentapolim cum alij terris, &c.* The same forme of confirmation is in the Vatican records to be seene, both of *Rodolph* the emperour, and *Charles* the fourth, bearing date the yeare 1289, and 1368, importing that they also out of their aboundance gaue vnto the pope and to the church of Rome so much as should be needfull, and all that which *Henrie* the fift his grandfather had before giuen and confirmed vnto the church, that so all the occasions of discord which had before bene betwixt the emperors & the popes, might be altogether taken away. So that if these donations be good, the popes are exempted from their fealtie and homage due vnto the emperours, by reason of the fees that they hold, and which are members of the German empire. But if the emperours could not without the consent of the princes and cities of the empire, giue away the publike territories and rights of soueraigntie; and that the imperiall and publike territories cannot be encroached vpon; and much lesse the right of soueraigntie and patronage, whose authoritie for euer ouer the subiects and vassals cannot bee prescribed against; it must needes follow, the popes to bee the vassals of the German empire.

Right pretended by the German Emperours to the election of the pope.

The same we may say of the election of the bishops of Rome, which the German emperours pretend of right to belong vnto them. For the emperour *Frederick* the second to haue absolution from pope *Innocent* the fourth, caused to be deliuered vnto him his letters pattents, sealed with a seale of gold, dated the yere 1229: whereof I haue seene the extract, and of his empire the seuenth, and of his raigne in the kingdome of Sicilie the xxij. Whereby he entirely renounceth the right of election which he had in the creating of bishops, vsing these words, *Illum abusum abolere volentes, quem quidam prædecessorum vt electiones libere fiant & canonice,* Wee willing to abolish that abuse which some of our predecessours were knowne to haue exercised in the elections of prelats, graunt that those elections may be freely and canonically made. By which words he seemeth to renounce not onely the creation of the bishop of Rome, but all other bishops also. Howbeit that in truth that right of chusing of the popes belonged to the kings of Fraunce, and not vnto the German princes, who haue but vsurped the name and title of emperours, got by the prowesse and force of *Charlemaigne* king of Fraunce, and by him left vnto his successors the kings of Fraunce, and not vnto the kings of Germany: for so they were called in all the auntient treaties and histories of Germanie and Fraunce, and not emperours, except those which were crowned by the popes. But after that the power of the German kings was farre spred in Italie, they then sought to vsurpe vnto themselues that right of chusing of the bishops of Rome: whether it were for the encreasing of their owne wealth and power, or for to take away the ambition and foule corruption then vsed in voyces giuing, and in their elections. For the emperour *Henrie* the third thrust out of his papacie *Gregorie* the sixt, chosen pope by the clergie, and set *Clement* the second in his place; and afterwards compelled the clergie to sweare, not from thenceforth to admit any into the papacie, without the consent of the German emperours; as we haue learned out of the Vatican records. But *Clement* the second being dead, the colledge of Cardinals sent ambassadours vnto the emperour to appoint whome hee thought good to bee pope, who appointed *Pepon,* afterwards called *Damasus* the second; who dead, the clergie againe sent ambassadours vnto the emperour, for the creating of a new pope: who sent vnto them *Brunon,* otherwise called *Leo* the ix: and after him *Victor* the second. After whose death the clergie made choyce of *Frederick,* and after him of *Alexander* the

Popes chosen and placed by the Germane emperour.

F1 Salviae (L 1-3, 5) Salivae (Fr 1-6, 8) Salvae (Fr 7, L 4) F2 Marchiam, Anconitanam (Fr 1-4, L 1-2) *properly* Marchiam Anconitanam (Fr 5-8, L 3-5) F2 Comitissæ F3 quæcunque
F3 circa (L) citra (Fr) F3 exarchatum Ravennæ F4 aliis H2 1219 H6 praedecessorum
NOSTRORUM EXERCUISSE DIGNOSCUNTUR IN ELECTIONIBUS PRAELATORUM, CONCEDIMUS ut
Notes at F1, H1.

OF A COMMONWEALE.   143

A second: which when the emperour *Henry* the fourth vnderstood, he sent them *Cadol* bishop of Parma for pope, who although he were so receiued in all Lombardie, yet was he thrust out by pope *Alexander*. After *Alexander* succeeded *Hildebrand*, otherwise called *Gregorie* the seuenth, chosen also by the clergie, who vpon the grieuous paine of excommunication, forbad all lay men to bestow any Ecclesiasticall liuings or benefices vpon any whomsoeuer: And also excommunicated the emperour *Henrie* the fourth, for disobeying his commaundement in creating of bishops in Germanie. Wherewith the emperour moued, and with his armie passing ouer the Alpes, chased this *Gregorie* the seuenth out of the citie, who had holden the papacie eleuen yeares, and placed in his stead *Clement* the third, who held that dignitie seauenteene yeares,
B against foure popes successiuely chosen by the clergie. After whose death *Henrie* the 5 the emperour made *Bourden* pope; without regard of whom, the clergie neuerthelesse made choice of *Calistus* the second a Burgundion, who draue out *Bourdin*, before nominated by the emperour: and by a decree made at Wormes, enforced *Henrie* to sweare neuer more to take vpon him to bestow any spirituall liuings vpon anie: yet with condition, that he might be in the assemblies of the Bishops assistant, if he thought it so good. Which decree of the emperour *Henry* the fift is yet extant in the Vatican records, in these words, *Pro salute animæ meæ dimitto Deo & sanctis Apostolis Petro & Paulo, sanctæque Ecclesiæ Catholicæ, omnem inuestituram per annulum & baculum, & concedo in omnibus ecclesijs quæ in imperio meo sunt, Canonicam fieri electionem*. For
C the health of my soule I remit vnto God and the holy Apostles *Peter* and *Paule*, and to the holy Catholique Church, all inuestiture to bee made by Ring and pastorall staffe, and do graunt Canonicall election to be made in all the Churches which are in mine Empire. Neuerthelesse 229 yeares after, the Emperour *Lewes* of Bauaria created *Nicholas* the fift bishop of Rome: *Iohn* the two and twentith, a Frenchman, then sitting as pope at Auignion, who peremptorily citied the emperor to appeare before him and for default & contumacie, pronounced sentence of excommunication against him: The emperour likewise on the contrarie side summoned the same pope *Iohn* to come before him, saying the bishops of Rome to be subiect vnto his edicts and commaunds, as emperour: and by sentence giuen at Rome, where *Nicholas* the Antipape
D held his seat, depriued *Iohn* of his papacie. Which *Nicholas* afterwards retiring himselfe vnto Pisa, was by the citizens there betraied into the hands of pope *Iohn* his mortall enemie at Auignion, where he shut vp in prison, for sorrow languished to death: and the emperour excommunicated, and therefore detested of all men, was forsaken of his subiects. And this was the eight emperour whome the bishop of Rome excommunicated: after whose fall the German emperours thought it not good afterwards to attempt any thing against the bishops of Rome. But to the contrarie the emperour *Charles* the fourth gaue out his letters pattents, in the yeare 1355, whereby he acknowledgeth vnto pope *Innocent* the fift, That although hee were chosen emperour by the princes, yet that he ought to take the confirmation of his election, and the imperiall
E crowne of him the pope; beginning in these words, *Post pedum oscula beatorum, &c.* After the kissing of your blessed feet, &c. Which words we see still repeated in all the emperours letters vnto the bishop of Rome, euen from the time of *Lewes* of Bauaria, vntill now.

The eight emperours excommunicated by the pope were these, Fredericke the first, Frederick the second, Philip, Conrade, Otho the fourth, Lewes of Bauaria, Henrie the fourth, and Henry the fift.

There is also extant in the Vatican, the forme of the coronation of the emperors, and by the emperour *Charles* the fourth approued; but no where more seruile seruices: where amongst other ceremonies, the emperour is as a subdeacon to minister vnto the pope whilest he is saying masse; and after diuine seruice done, to hold his stirrop whilest he mounteth to horse, and for a certaine time to lead his horse by the bridle: with diuers

Base seruices to be done by the emperour to the pope.

uers other ceremonies at large set downe in the Vatican records, which it is needlesse here to rehearse. And yet one thing more is worth the marking which is not in the record expressed, which is, that the emperour to receiue the imperiall crowne, must goe to seeke the pope wheresoeuer he be, and to follow him if hee chaunce to remoue; as did the emperour *Charles* the fift, who being come into Italie, with hope to haue gone vnto the * pope at Rome, being aduertised of his departure thence to Bononia, was glad thither to follow him: that so the dutie of an inferiour prince towards the maiesty of his superiour might the more plainely be perceiued. But after the death of *Charles* the fift, *Ferdinand* the emperour could not obtaine, that the pope should in his absence ratifie his election; but was oftentimes by the pope threatned, That hee would take such order for him, as that he should haue nothing to doe with the affaires of the German empire: neither would he admit the emperours lawfull excuse, vntill hee was by the requests and meditation of the French king, and of the king of Spaine appeased: which the German princes tooke in euill part, seeing they had promised vnto *Ferdinand* to imploy their whole power for the defence of the maiestie of the empire, against that the popes enterprises; as I haue learned by the letters of the kings ambassadour, dated at Vienna, in Iuly 1559. And to show a greater submission of the emperours vnto the popes, the subscription of the emperours letters vnto the pope, is this, *Ego manus ac pedes vestræ sanctitatis deosculor, viz.* I kisse the hands and feet of your Holinesse. So vsed alwayes the emperour *Charles* the fift to subscribe to his letters, when he writ vnto pope *Clement* the seuenth. Which he did not vpon a faigned courtesie, but indeed in most humble and seruile manner kissed the popes feet, in the open sight of the people, and the greatest assemblies of many noble princes, at Bononia, Rome, and last of al at Marsielles in Prouence, where were met together the pope, the emperour, the kings of Fraunce and Nauarre, the dukes of Sauoy, of Buillon, Florence, Ferrara, Vitemberg the Grand Master of Malta, with many other princes and great lords, who all kissed the popes feet, except the dukes of Buillon and Vitemberg, Protestant princes, who had forsaken the rites and ceremonies of the church of Rome. In farre more base sort did that duke of Venice humble himselfe (who of the Venetians themselues is called a dog) for that he with a rope about his necke, and creeping vpon all foure like a beast, so craued pardon of pope *Clement* the 5. But nothing was more base, than that which almost al historiographers which writ of the popes affairs, report of the emperor *Fredericke* the second; who to redeeme his sonne out of prison, lying prostrat vpon the ground at the feet of pope *Alexander* the fourth, suffered him to tread vppon his head, if the histories be true. VVhereby it is well to be perceiued, the maiestie of the Emperours, by the power (should I say) or by the outragiousnesse of the Bishops of Rome, to haue bene so diminished, as that scarce the shadow of their antient maiestie seemeth now to remaine. They also say themselues to be greater than the emperours, and that so much greater, as is the Sunne greater than the Moone: that is to say, six thousand six hundred fortie and fiue times, if we will beleeue *Ptolomee* and the Arabians. And that more is, they haue alwaies pretended a right vnto the empire; for the imperiall seat being vacant, they haue giuen the inuestitures vnto them which held of the empire, and receiued of them their fealtie: as they did of *Iohn* and *Luchin*, vicounts of Milan, the imperiall seat being emptie in the yeare 1341, who are in the records called vassals of the church of Rome, and not of the empire; and are forbidden their odedience vnto *Lewes* of Bauaria the emperour, who was then excommunicated, as we haue before said. For which cause the Canonists haue maintained, that the emperour cannot giue vp his imperiall dignitie vnto any, but vnto the pope: for which they yeeld this reason, That the emperours haue their soueraigntie of men, and the popes of God: howbeit

Clement the seuenth.

The humble subscription Charls the fift vsed in his letters to the pope.

The base submission of the Duke of Venice and of Fredericke the second vnto the pope.

The maiestie of the emperours greatly diminished by the pope

G3 *For* meditation *read* mediation (cf. 624 K7 and note; 625 C8, D2; 632 D9). H5 Vitemberg *i.e.* Württemberg K5 obedience Note at I6.

Of a Commonweale. 145

howbeit that both of them, as all others also in general, are of right to attribute all their power vnto almightie God. Neuerthelesse the emperour *Charles* the fift worne with yeares and sicknesse, resigned his imperiall dignitie into the hands of the princes electors, and sent vnto them his resignation by the prince of Orenge. But howsoeuer the Bishop of Rome pretended to haue a soueraigntie ouer all Christian princes, not only in spirituall, but also in temporall affaires; whether they got it by force of armes, or by the deuotion and graunt of princes; or by long possession and prescription: yet could not our kings euen for any most short time endure the seruitude of the bishop of Rome, nor be moued with any their excommunications, which the popes vsed as firebrands to the firing of the Christian Commonweales. For these the popes interdictions, or excommunications, were wont with other nations, to draw the subiects from the obedience and reuerence of their prince: but such hath alwaies bene the loue of our kings towards their people (and so I hope shall be for euer) and the loyaltie of the people towards their kings: that when pope *Boniface* the eight saw himselfe nothing to preuaile by his excommunication, nor that the people were to be drawne from the obedience of their king, after he had publikely excommunicated *Philip* the Faire, he in like maner excommunicated all the French nation, with all them which tooke *Philip* for a king. But *Philip* hauing called together an assemblie of his princes, and other his nobilitie, and perceiuing in his subiects in generall a wonderfull consent for the defence of his state and soueraigntie: he thereupon writ letters vnto *Boniface* (which are common in euerie mans hand) to reproue him of his folly: and shortly after sent *Nogaret* with his armie into the popes territorie, who tooke the pope prisoner, (giuing him well to vnderstand that the king was not his subiect, as he had by his Bull published) but seeing him through impatiencie to become furious and mad, he set him againe at libertie. Yet from that the popes interdiction, the king by the aduice of his nobilitie and Senat, appealed vnto a generall councell, which had power ouer the pope, abusing the holy cities. For the king next vnto almightie God had none his superiour, vnto whom he might appeale: but the pope is bound vnto the decrees and commaunds of the councell. And long tims before *Philip* the Victorious, and his realme being interdicted by pope *Alexander* the third, who would haue brought him into his subiection: answered him by letters, That he held nothing of the pope, nor yet of any prince in the world. *Benedict* the third, and *Iulius* the second, had vsed the like excommunication against *Charles* the seuenth, and *Lewes* the twelfth (who was called the *Father of his countrey*) that so as with firebrands they might inflame the people to rebellion: yet failed they both of their hope; the obedience of the subiects being in nothing diminished, but rather increased: the Bull of excommunication which the popes legat brought into Fraunce, being by the decree of the parliament of Paris openly torne in peeces, and the legat for his presumptuousnesse cast in prison. And not long after *Iohn* of Nauarre, who called himselfe countie Palatine, when he had made certaine publike notaries in Fraunce, and made legitimat certaine of his bastards, by vertue of the authoritie which he had (as he said) from the pope, he was therfore by a decree of the parliament of Tholouze condemned of treason. True it is, that they which haue thought better to assure the maiestie of the kings of Fraunce against the power of the pope, haue obtained the popes buls whilest they yet sate in the citie of Auignion, to bee exempted from their power. And namely there is in the records of Fraunce a Bull of pope *Clements* the fift, whereby he not onely absolueth *Philip* the Faire and his subiects from the interdiction of *Boniface* the eight, but also declareth the king and the realme to be exempted from the popes power. Pope *Alexander* the fourth also gaue this priuilege vnto the realme of Fraunce, That it could not for any cause bee interdicted.

The French kings not afraid of the pops excommunication.

O

C7 *For* cities *read* rites.   C9 long time   D2 *For* Benedict the third *read* Benedict the thirteenth.
Notes at D1, D10.

dicted: which was afterward by seuen popes successiuely confirmed, *viz.* by *Gregory* the viij. ix. x. xj, *Clement* the fourth, *Vrban* the fift, and *Benedict* the twelft; whose buls yet remaine in the records of Fraunce: which yet seeme vnto me not to encrease, but rather to diminish the maiestie of our kings, who were neuer in any thing beholden vnto the popes. And that more is, the court of parliament of Paris, hath by many decrees declared that clause, *Auctoritate Apostolica*, By the authoritie Apostolicall: vsually inserted into the popes rescripts sent into France, to be void, meere abusiue, and to no purpose: and therefore it behoueth him, that would helpe himselfe by any such the popes rescript, to protest in iudgement, That he would not any way take benefit of that clause. By all which things it is plainely to be vnderstood, not onely the kings, but the kingdome of Fraunce also, to haue bene alwayes free from all the popes power and commaund. For as for that which *Iohn Durand* himselfe a French writer, saith, That the French kings are subiect vnto the pope, so farre as concerneth their oath, it needeth no refuting; as by him written being bishop of Mende, and at such time as vnder the color of oathe ioined vnto contracts, the ecclesiastical iudges drew vnto themselues the hearing and determining of all matters: which their iugling craft was both by the kings edicts, and the decrees of the high courts of parliament, long since met withall, and taken away. But if the French king shall in his owne priuat name contract with the pope, he may voluntarily and of his owne accord bind himselfe vnto the popes iurisdiction, which we read to haue bene done by *Philip Valois*, at such time as he borrowed the summe of three hundred and thirtie thousand florines of gold, of pope *Clement* the sixt, which is an ordinarie clause in all obligations, in which sort the pope himselfe might aswell as a priuat man be bound also. But this money the pope may seeme also not to haue lent without reward; but beeing himselfe of the house of *Turene*, it may be thought that he for this summe so lent, procured of the king the great priueleges which the counties of Turene yet at this day enioy. Yea but I know some to pretend, that the French kings ought to receiue their royall crowne at the hands of the pope: for that king *Pipin* so receiued it at Saint *Denise* in Fraunce, of pope *Zacharie*: as though one act in discontinued solemnities, and of so great consequence, could giue a right, or establish a perpetuall law: which it cannot do in the getting of the least discontinued seruice; but by the prescription of 100 yeres: albeit that in truth the king leaueth not to bee king, without any coronation or consecration, which are not things of the soueraignty. And that no man can deny, but that if the donation of the exarchat of Rauenna & Pentapolis, one of the fairest countries of al Italie, be made by the kings of Fraunce vnto the popes, and the church of Rome; it is also holden of that crowne of Fraunce: seeing that the confirmation of the seignories so giuen, was requested of *Lewes* the Gentle, successour to *Charlemaigne*: which confirmation *Carolus Sigonius*, a most skilfull man in the antiquities of Italie, writeth himselfe to haue seene and read. Wherefrom a man may draw two most certaine arguments; The one, That the donation was made by the predecessours of *Lewes* the Gentle: And the other that the soueraigntie of the seignories so giuen, was yet reserued: For otherwise there should not haue needed any of king *Lewes* his confirmation; considering that king *Pipin* had by law of armes wonne those territories from the emperours of Constantinople, & therfore might of right both giue them by himselfe so wonne, and also appoint lawes vnto them so by him giuen. Albeit that the Constantinopolitan emperour sent ambassadors into France vnto *Pepin*, to haue had him to haue infringed & reuoked the said donatiō: which they could not of him obtaine, but returned as they came; as is to be seene in the histories of *Floardus* and *Sigonius*. And that more is, *Augustinus Onuphrius* the popes chamberlaine, who had diligently searched all the Vatican records (speaking of the popes)

The clause, Auctoritate Apostolica, vsually put into the popes buls or decrees, reiected in France.

OF A COMMONWEALE. 147

popes) confesseth, that the exarchat of Rauenna, Romandiola, the duchie of Vrbin, and part of Tuscanie, were giuen to the Church of Rome. But hee speaketh not of that which I haue read in the extract of the Vatican register, *viz. Iohn*, surnamed *Digitorum*, to haue written in letters of gold, the donation pretended to haue bene made by *Constantine*: in the end whereof are these words, *Quam fabulam longi temporis mendacia finxit*; which words I thought not good in any thing chaunge: as being much stronger arguments than those of *Lau. Valla*, to conuince the lies of *Augustin Egubin*, who of purpose to deceiue, hath forged in Greeke the donation of *Constantine*, to giue it the more credit; whose deceit is easie to be refuted both by the manner of the stile, and the knowledge of antiquitie: and is sufficiently refelled by *Sigonius* and *Onuphrius* both Italians. Which is also well iustified by the epistle of pope *Iohn*, written in the yeare 876, who therein confesseth the great largeses and donations bestowed vpon the church of Rome by *Pipin, Charlemaigne*, and his successours: and by the auntient marble table, which is yet to be seene at Rauenna, wherein are these words contained, *Pipinus Pius primus amplificandæ ecclesiæ viam aperuit, & exarchatum Rauennæ cum ampliss.* The rest of the inscription time hath defaced. And thus much concerning the greatnesse and soueraigntie of our kings.

I will not here touch the greatnesse and soueraigntie of the *Negus* of Æthiopia commonly called *Prester Iohn*, whome *Pau. Iouius* writeth to haue fiftie tributarie kings vnder him, or (to say better) gouernours of Prouinces, which yeeld vnto him not onely their ordinarie tributes, but also their fealtie and homage, and that in greater humilitie, than verie slaues do vnto their lords: as a man may see in the historie of *Francis Aluares* a Portugall, who dwelt sixe yeres in Æthiopia, and yet neuerthelesse they are called kings without cause, because they be no absolute soueraignes, seeing that they be but tributaries, yeelding fealtie and homage vnto another man.

The princes seruing the great Negus of Æthiopia no kings nor soueraigns.

As for those princes which are no Christians, I haue nothing to say, for the small assurance we haue by the writings and reports of others, much differing among themselues. Yet neuerthelesse so it is, that in one chapter of the Alcoron, it is expresly forbidden all the *Musulman* (that is to say the right beleeuing) princes, to call themselues lords, except their Caliph or great bishop their great prophet *Muhamed* his vicar. By meanes of which prohibition the Mahometan bishops haue vsurped absolute soueraigntie aboue all their princes, giuing kingdomes and principalities, to whome they thought good, in name and title of gouernments: which may be also the cause that no Musulman prince weareth a crowne vpon his head: albeit that before the most auntient kings of Asia and Afrike did weare crownes. And namely *Ioiada* the high priest, hauing consecrated *Ioas* king of Iuda, set a crowne vpon his head. But the Musulman princes think that chapter not to haue bene made by *Muhamed* their law giuer, but by their Caliphes, (who of many diuers corrupt Alcorans made but one, long time after the death of *Muhamed*, defacing the rest, and for the augmenting of their maiestie, to haue bene into their Alcoran by them inserted. But at such time as three of their great bishops had for the desire of soueraignty, at one time taken vpon them the name of the great Caliph, the princes of Persia, the Curdes, the Turkes, the Tartars, the Sultans of Ægypt, the kings of Marocco, of Fez, of Telensin, of Tanes, of Bugia, and the people of Zenetes, and of Luntune, exempted themselues from the obeysance of the Caliphs, to hold their kingdomes in soueraigntie: as also the kings of Tombut, of Guynee, of Gaoga, and other kings, which dwell more into the hart of Afrike, who know not the Caliphes commaund, neither acknowledge any greater than themselues: except they which hold in fealtie and homage of the king of Portugall, as the kings of Calecut, of Malachie, of Cambar, and of Canor, whome they haue compelled so to do, and to pay

The Mahomitaine princes by their lawe forbidden to cal themselus lords or soueraigns.

Diuers Mahomitaine kings tributaries vnto the king of portugal

O ij them

A5-6 Quam fabulam, etc. *i.e.* "Which tale he supposed to be lies of long standing"   A6 chaunge *i.e.* to change   A7 convince *i.e.* confute   B2 876 (Fr 6-8) 1276 (L 1-5) 1726 (Fr 5) omitted (Fr 1-4)
D8 Caliphes, who   E3 For Tanes *read* Tunes.

them tribute; hauing also subdued all the sea coast of Afrike, and of the East Indies, and almost in infinit number of places built fortresses; yea and in the island of Ormus euen vnder the nose of the Persian king, hauing built a most strong castle, and straitly exacting tribute and custome of such as passe that way, or chaunce to arriue in the Persian gulfe; and had done the like in the red sea, had not *Barnagas* gouernour of that coast, and the king of Æthiopia his subiect, cut the Portugals in peeces, and rased the fortresses which they had begun to build, vnder the colour of alliance and amitie contracted by *Lopes* ambassadour for the king of Portugall, with the king of Æthiopia, in the yere 1519. And yet for all that certaine it is, that the king of Portugall was of auntient time feudatarie or vassall vnto the king of Castile, and the kingdome of Portugall a member of the kingdome of Castile: which for the greater part holden by force by the Moores, was giuen to *Henrie*, brother to *Godfrey* of Buillon, in marriage with the base daughter of *Alphonsus* king of Castile: from whome are descended all the kings of Portugall, since this foure hundred and fiftie yeares, vnto *Henrie* the Cardinall, who last raigned: hauing (of long) exempted themselues from the soueraigntie of Castile, and holding diuers kings their tributaries and feudataries, of whome *Emanuel* was the greatest, and for his martiall prowesse amongst the rest most famous; who vanquished the aforesaid kings, and caused them to pay him tribute. For there are now no feudatarie kings in Asia, or Africa, which are not also tributarie; howbeit in auntient time the kings of Persia, and the Romans, hauing subdued kings vnto their empire, for most part made them to become their tributaries: as for such fealtie and homage as is of vassals exacted, they knew not what it ment. For *Philip* the second, king of Macedon, being by the Romans ouercome, they graunted him peace vppon condition, that he should pay them into their common treasure, a certaine yearly tribute; which *Perseus*, *Philip* his sonne, afterwards refusing to pay, drew vpon himselfe a great and heauy warre, to his owne vtter destruction. And yet oftentimes such tributarie kings had others tributarie vnto themselues, who had also power of life and death, and other roiall soueraignties ouer their owne subiects. So the kingdome of *Dauid* was contained within the bounds of Palestine, and yet he enforced the neighbour kings to pay vnto him tribute, his posteritie neuerthelesse not long after yeelding tribute vnto the Ægyptians, and the Assirians. So the kings of Slauonia, and the Commonweale of Carthage vsed the like authoritie and right ouer the princes vnder their dominion, that the Romans exercised ouer them, enforcing them to bring their yearely tributes into their treasuries.

Yet is there difference betwixt a tribute and a pention: for a pention is paid in respect of fealtie, or in time of warres to receiue aid against our enemies: but a tribut is giuen, thereby to haue peace; howbeit that he which receiueth such a pention, commonly boasteth of it, as of a tribute: as the kings of England called the pention of fiftie thousand crownes, which *Lewes* the xj paid vnto them by the treatie of Piqueni, by the name of a tribute; vntill that *Elizabeth* the daughter of *Edward* king of England was married vnto *Charles* the eight, king *Lewes* his sonne. Howbeit that *Philip Comines* denyeth it to haue bene either pention or tribute; yet needes it must bee either the one or the other. So the Grand Signior calleth the German emperour his tributarie, for the pention which he payeth euerie yeare for the peaceable enioying of a part of Hungarie. The Venetians also, the Genowayes, the Ragusians, the kings of Algiers and of Tunes, in his letters and in the conuentions of peace, he calleth by the name of his great friends and allies, but accounteth them indeed his tributaries. But the great Precop Tartar, who in auntient time was soueraigne of all the realmes from Volga to Boristhenes, held all the princes and lords of those countries as his vassals and tributa-

ries

G6 of whome *i.e.* of which Kings of Portugal (cf. L) H7–8 roiall soveraignties *i.e.* "rights of sovereignty" K9 Boristhenes *i.e.* the Dnieper

Marginalia:
- Portugall of auntient time a member of the kingdom of Castile.
- Difference betwixt a pention and a tribute.

ries, who not onely kneeled before himselfe, but stood before his ambassadours sitting: For so the Knez of Moscouie behaued himselfe before the ambassadours of this Tartar prince, and was therefore of other princes commonly called but by the name of a duke: howbeit that the dukes of Moscouie, for this and diuers other such indignities cast off the seruile Tartars yoke, in the yeare 1524. And the first that reuolted from them was *Basilius* the first, who called himselfe *The Great Chamberlaine of God, and King of Moscouie*: and so he which at this present raigneth, in despight that other princes tearme him but a duke, stileth himselfe *The Great Emperour*: as in truth he in power either excelleth, or is equall vnto the greatest kings his neighbours, excepting the kings of the Turkes: albeit that the right of soueraigne maiestie be not defined by the spatiousnesse of places, or the greatnesse of countries, as if that might make a prince either more or lesse soueraigne: as *Eumenes* being ouerthrowne, and hauing nothing left him of his owne more than the castle wherein he was besieged, yet when as he was to treat of peace with *Antigonus* king of Asia (who as he was in power, would also in honor haue seemed to haue bene his superiour) answered, That he * acknowledged no man greater than himselfe, so long as he had his sword in his hand.

The Moscouite an absolute soueraigne prince.

The notable saying of Eumenes to king Antigonus.

* Plutar. in Eumene.

And yet among soueraigne princes there is a certaine prerogatiue of honour due vnto the more auntient Monarches and Commonweals, although they bee in wealth & power inferior vnto them that be more new or of later time: as we see amongst the xiij Cantons of the Swissers, who are all soueraignes, acknowledging nether prince nor monarch in the world for their soueraigne: the Canton of Zurich in all their assemblies hath the prerogatiue of honour: For their deputie as a prince in the name of all the rest of the Cantons, receiueth and dismisseth the ambassadours of other kings and Commonweals; and vnto him onely it belongeth to call a generall assemblie of all the states of the Cantons, and againe to dismisse the same; albeit that the Canton of Berne be much greater and stronger: Next vnto them of Berne, are Lucerne, and Vri, albeit that they are defended neither with wals nor ditches, no more than are the Schwits, and Vnderuald, which follow in order vnto them of Vri: then follow after them Zug, Glaris, Basill, Friburg, and Soleurre. Now haply a man may say, That this is done according to the time that euerie Canton entred into their alliance: which is not so; for by their treaties it appeareth, that the first that entred in that confederation and alliance were they of Vri, Schwits, Zug, and Vnderuald.

Degrees of honour among soueraigne princes being equall.

The order of the Cantons of the Swissars.

Sometimes also the more auntient Monarches and Commonweals lose their prerogatiue of honour; as when they put themselues into the protection of latter princes, or yeeld themselues tributaries: in which case it is most certaine, that they are alwaies lesse than the other into whose protection they put themselues, or vnto whome they pay tribute. As it chaunced almost to all kings and princes which sought the protection of the Romans: whereas others which were come into equall alliance with them, as the Hedui, were in their leagues called their confederats, their equals and brethren: and yet for all that, they in truth and effect were inferiour vnto them in honour. And verily *Augustus* the emperour showed himselfe wonderfull ceremonious and difficult in the honours which he bestowed on kings and princes, allies and vnder the protection of the empire of Rome; making Tetrarques, inferiour vnto Ethnarques, and these inferiours vnto kings; and the more auntient allies of the Romans, superiours vnto the rest that came into their alliance after them. And albeit that the Romans in the flourishing time of their popular estate, seemed not much carefull of such ceremonies of dignitie and honour which is of kings and princes more regarded, yet did *Q. Martius Philippus* their ambassadour show himselfe therein curious: Who contending with *Perseus* king of Macedon, which of them shuld come ouer the riuer vpon the frontiers

Degrees of honour betwixt soueraign princes being in alliance together.

of Macedon, vnto the other: and *Perseus* for that he was a king, refusing to come ouer vnto the Roman ambassadour, the ambassadour yet by sweet speech drew him ouer: Which he did (as he said vnto the ambassadors of the allies and confederats there present with him) to show that the honour of the Romans was greater than that of the Macedonian kings; who for all that would in nothing giue place vnto the Romans. Yet was there a greater cause than that, which *Martius*, or els *Liuie* omitted, which was for that *Philip* the father of *Perseus* had vpon conditions, receiued peace of the Romans and also paid vnto them tribute; which his father *Philips* act, if he had disliked, he should not haue medled with the kingdome: although that he was otherwise vnworthy therof, who his father yet liuing, had aspired vnto his inheritance: and being but borne of a concubine, had slaine his brother borne in lawfull marriage. But after that hee ouerthrowne and vanquished by *Paulus Æmilius*, had lost the hope of his kingdome, he writ letters vnto *Æmilius*, generall of the Roman army, yet stiling himselfe a king: which his letters the Roman generall reiected, and would not vouchsafe to open them, except he first renounced his roiall dignitie, which can onely agree vnto him which hath a soueraigne power, subiect to no other princes commaund.

And for the same cause *Francis* the first the French king declared vnto Cardinall *Bibiene* the popes legat, that the pope his master ought not to suffer the emperour *Charles* the fift to call himselfe king of Naples and of Sicilie, seeing that he was but the Popes vassall. Whereof the legat gaue aduertisement vnto *Iulian Cardinall de Medices*, who was afterwards pope; to the end that that title might haue beene rased, which as he certified him by his letters, was by the charters of fealtie, forbidden the kings of Naples to take: whereas for all that, in all the records which wee haue got out of the Vatican, that is not onely not forbidden, but the name and dignitie of the king of Naples and Sicilie expressely set downe, as namely in the inuestitures of *Charles* of France, of *Carobert*, and of *Iohn*. So many times ambassadours euill instructed in their masters affaires, through ignorance commit therein many notable defaults. And by the same reason we should take the royall title of a king from the king of Bohemia, who holdeth his kingdome in fealtie and homage of the empire; and not for that it is so little, as many haue written, that it is for that cause no kingdome, which were to measure kings by the elne: but it is, for that the countrey of Bohemia was by the emperour *Fredericke* the first, for title of honour onely erected a kingdome, without preiudice vnto the right or soueraignetie of the empire. But to say truth, this title agreeth vnto none that is another mans vassall, nor hath nothing of his owne in title of soueraigntie. And it may be, that for this cause pope *Pius* the fourth gaue not the royall title to *Cosmus* duke of Florence, albeit that he would very gladly haue so done: whereof the emperour *Maximilian* the second, being by the French embassadour aduertised, not vnfitly replied, *Italia non habet regem nisi Cæsarem*: Italy hath no king but the emperor. Although that be to be vnderstood of the maiestie of the German empire (whereof the Florentine state dependeth) & not of the emperour, who is himselfe subiect vnto the estate of the empire: albeit that all christian princes giue him the prerogatiue of honor, next vnto the pope, whether it be for that he is chiefe of the German empire, or els hath got it by long prescription of time. So also next vnto the emperour, all other princes haue vsed to giue this prerogatiue of honour vnto the French kings; not only for the long possession thereof, but also for that in all the world (whether you looke among the Christians, or the Tartars, the Turkes, the Ethyopians, the Indians, or Barbarians) is not to be found so auntient a kingdome, or such a continuall discent of kings of the same stocke and line as is among the French kings. And therefore *Balaus* (being himselfe an Italian Lawyer and a subiect of the empire) sayth well, That the French king car-

The title of a king belongeth not vnto another mans vassal neither to him which holdeth nothing of his owne in soueraigntie.

The maiestie of the empeour still impugned by this French author, and the French kings too much exalted.

H6 *For* John *read* Joanne.   I1 by the elne *i.e.* by the ell, "by the yard"   K1 *For* estate of the empire *read* estates of the empire. Note at F2.

Of A Commonweale. 151

carieth the crowne of glorie aboue all the kings, who haue alwaies giuen him that preheminence of honour. And there is also yet extant an epistle of pope *Gregories* vnto king *Childebert*, the beginning whereof is this: *Quanto cæteros homines regia maiestas antecellit, tanto cæterarum gentium regna, regni vestri culmen excellit*: by how much the royall Maiestie excelleth other men, by so much doth the Maiestie of your kingdome excell the kingdomes of other nations. As in truth this prerogatiue is vnto him due: for the Germane emperours themselues cannot denie, but that the German empire was sometime a prouince and member of the auntient kingdome of Fraunce, conquered by the prowesse of *Charlemaigne* king of France, and power of the French nation: but afterwards rent againe from the same, being giuen in partition to *Lewes* of France, yongest son to *Lewes* the Gentle, at such time as *Charles* the Bauld the French emperour held the imperiall seat of the empire: Howbeit that yet neuerthelesse the Germane princes the *Othons*, by the graunt of the Roman bishops hauing got the imperial title, haue by little & little through the ignorance of our embassadors vsurped & taken vnto themselues this prerogatiue of honour aboue the French kings. As in like case the king of Spaine not many yeares agoe would haue preuented our kings ambassadours: but was at the request of *M. Nouuaille*, ambassadour for the French king, by a decree of the Venetian Senat embarred so to doe, in the yeare 1558: and so likewise afterwards by a decree of the pope, giuen by the consent of all the colledge of Cardinals: where the pope said with a lowd and cleare voyce, That the French kings had beene alwayes the auntient protectours of the church of Rome, and that the fairest and fruitfullest prouinces of the kingdome of Spaine, had bene dismembred and rent from the kingdome of Fraunce: than which nothing could in that kind haue beene more truely spoken; for by our kings, the authoritie of the bishops of Rome hath bene deliuered from contempt, their wealth encreased, and their power confirmed. Wherein the pope also in some sort amended the errour committed in the councell of Trent; where *Mendoza* the Spanish ambassadour, preferring himselfe and taking place before the French ambassadour (which then was *M. Lansac*, assisted with the M.M. of Ferrier & Faut) was to haue bin compelled to haue departed from the councell, or els to haue kept the auntient order of ambassadours, and so to haue followed the French ambassadours: who withstanding the Spanish ambassadors presumption, requested that he might not so inuert the order of the ambassadours: saying, that otherwise he would himselfe forsake the Councell, and cause the French bishops to depart thence also. Whereunto the Spanish ambassadour craftily answered, That as he would not go before the French ambassadour, so would he not be enforced to follow him; and so tooke his place by himselfe apart from all the rest of the ambassadors. Yet notwithstanding these two former decrees which I haue spoken of, the Spanish ambassadour not long after at Vienna in Austria, earnestly requested of the emperor, That he might goe in the same degree and order with the French ambassadour; or that they might at leastwise go formost by turnes (as did the Roman Consuls, who had the preheminence, the twelue sergeants, and power to commaund, successiuely, each of them his day) which *Henrie* the second the French king hearing of, writ againe to his ambassador, That prerogatiue of dignitie to be of so great moment and consequence, as that nothing therein was by him to be said or done more than he had commission for. And *Ferdinand* the emperour not willing to offend either the one or the other, thought it good to forbid them both from comming together, either vnto sermons or other publike assemblies. The Senat of Polonia troubled with the same difficultie, thought it not good to preferre one ambassadour before another, neither to preferre them by turnes, or yet to make them equall: but decreed of all ambassadours in generall, that

Contention at the counsel of Trent betwixt the Spanish and French embassadours about their places.

A good order for the auoiding of contention betwixt the ambassadors of great princes, for their places.

O iiij as

B6 prevented *i.e.* preceded   C9 Faur   Note at C9.

as euery of them first came into the frontiers of the kingdome of Polonia, so should they be first in order heard. And so accordingly *M. De Monluc* bishop of Valence (who for his wisedome and dexteritie for mannaging of matters of estate, had beene fifteene times ambassadour) hauing by great celeritie preuented the Spanish ambassador, had also first audience; wherewith the Spanish ambassadour offended, would as then say nothing: as I haue vnderstood by *M. de Nouuaille* abbot of Belle-isle, a man of great honour and vertue; who then was also ambassadour into Polonia, as he now is at Constantinople. But before the yeare 1558, neuer Christian prince made question of the preheminence of the French ambassadours before them of Spaine: and namely the English men alwayes preferred them before the Spaniard; albeit that they had bene auntient allies and friends vnto the one, and enemies vnto the other. As after the death of queene *Marie*, in the chapter holden by the knights of the most honourable order of the Garter, vpon Saint *Georges* eue, in the yeare 1555, concerning the conferring of honours, it was decreed, That the French kings place should be aboue the rest, next vnto the prince on the right hand; where before was the place for Spaine, while king *Philip* was married vnto the queene. And the next day after being Saint *Georges* day, a day of great solemnitie vnto the knights of that order, a seat was accordingly reserued for the French king, on the right hand next vnto the prince: and another on the left hand for the king of Spaine, next vnto the emperours seat on the same side, being then emptie. And afterward in the time of *Charles* the ix, the queene of England caused to be sent vnto him the banner of Fraunce, of the same stuffe and greatnes that her owne was, as the king was aduertised by *M. de Foix* then his ambassador there; and in the roll or Catalogue of these knights, which is signed euerie yeare by the queene, the French kings name is euer the first, next vnto her owne.

The French preferred before the Spanish.

But to take away these difficulties and ielousies betwixt princes, about their honors, which are otherwise ineuitable and daungerous: it is declared in the xiij article of the ordinances of king *Lewes* the xj, touching the order of knights, that they should bee placed according to the time of their receiuing into the order, without prerogatiue of king or emperour. For euerie soueraigne prince who is neither tributarie, vassall, nor in the protection of another, may as seemeth vnto him best in his owne countrey bestow the prerogatiues of honour vpon whomsoeuer hee pleaseth, and to reserue the chiefe place vnto himselfe. We know right well that the Venetians, the Rhagusians, the Genowayes, the Moscouites, and the Polonians, are in league with the great Turk, and yet hath he alwaies giuen the prerogatiue of honour vnto the French king, calling him in his letters the Greatest, and the *Greatest among the most Great Princes of the Christians*: & stileth himselfe *The greatest of all Princes, and the chiefe Serrach or Prince of the Musulmans*; that is to say, *Chiefe Prince of the right beleeuing or faithfull*, which last prerogatiue of honour the Christian princes themselues haue giuen him by their letters: and as for the first title it seemeth himselfe to haue taken it from the auntient emperours of Constantinople, who bare in their armes foure B. which we call *Fusils*, wherby these words are signified; ΒΑΣΙΛΕΥΣ ΒΑΣΙΛΕΩΝ, ΒΑΣΙΛΕΤΩΝ ΒΑΣΙΛΕΥΣΙ, that is to say *King of kings, raigning ouer kings*. Which was the title that the kings of Babilon in auntient time tooke vpon them also, as we may see in *Ezechiel*, who calleth the great king *Nabucodonosor* מלך מלכים that is to say, King of kings; for that all the kings of Asia were vnto him tributaries: after which the kings of Persia hauing ouercome the kings of Asiria, as *Esdras* writeth, vsed the same title: & after them the Parthian kings also, as *Dion* writeth, that *Phraates* the king of Parthia called himselfe King of kings. But neither feudatarie kings which hold all their territories of others; neither dukes, marquesses, counties, or other like princes can of right vse the title of soueraigne Maiestie,

The armes of the antient emperors of Constantinople.

Notes at G3, G5

maiestie, but only of *his Highneße, his Serenitie*, or his *Excellencie*, as wee haue before said. Wherfore seeing that princes Tributaries, and Feudadaries, are not to be accounted absolute soueraignes; neither they which are in the protection of others: let vs now speake of the true markes of Soueraigntie, thereby the better to know them who they be that be such.

Chap. X.

¶ Of the true markes of Soueraigntie.

Seeing that nothing vpon earth is greater or higher, next vnto God, than the maiestie of kings and soueraigne princes; for that they are in a sort created his lieutenants for the welfare of other men: it is meet diligently to consider of their maiestie and power, as also who and of what sort they be; that so we may in all obedience respect and reuerence their maiestie, and not to thinke or speake of them otherwise than of the lieutenants of the most mightie and immortall God: for that he which speaketh euill of his prince vnto whome he oweth all dutie, doth iniurie vnto the maiestie of God himselfe, whose liuely image he is vpon earth. As God speaking vnto *Samuel*, of whome the people of Israel had vnaduisedly asked a king, *It is not thee* (saith God) *but me whome they haue despised*. Soueraigne princes God his lieutenants vpon earth.

Now to the end that one may know him that is such an one (that is to say a Soueraigne prince) we must know the markes, which are not common vnto other subiects also: for if they were common vnto others, than should there be no soueraigne prince. And yet they which haue writ best of or concerning a Commonweale, haue not sufficiently and as it ought, manifested this point, than which none is more plentifull or more profitable in the discourse of a Commonweale: whether it were by them for flatterie, for feare, for hatred, or by forgetfulnesse omitted. For when *Samuel* had denounced him king whome God had before chosen, and consecrated him before the people, as if he had but come by chaunce; he is reported to haue writ a booke of the power and Soueraigntie of a king, which the Hebrew priests haue written to haue bene by their kings suppressed and rent, that so they might more freely tyrannise ouer their subiects. Wherein *Phi. Malancthon* in mine opinion is deceiued, who hath thought those things which *Samuel* spoke vnto the people, concerning the crueltie or insolencie of tyrants, to belong vnto the right of soueraigne maiestie: Whereas hee in that his Oration vnto the people, would haue reclaimed them from the alteration and innouation of the state, and to haue beene better aduised. *Will you* (saith he) *know the custome of tyrants? It is to take away the goods of their subiects, and to dispose of them at their pleasure; to take the tenth of their labours, to rauish other mens wiues, to take from them their children to abuse them, or to make of them their slaues*: For the word משפטים which hee vseth, signifieth not lawfull rights in that place, but mens customes and manner of doing. For otherwise the good prince *Samuel* should in all his speech be contrarie vnto himselfe: for in giuing of an account before the people, of the charge that God had giuen him ouer them; *Which of you* (saith he) *is it amongst you that can accuse me of euill, or say that I haue taken of him either gold or siluer, or other present whatsoeuer?* Whereunto all the people with great applause and acclamation gaue him this prayse, *That he had neuer done them wrong, nor taken any thing of any person whomsoeuer*. Should then this good prince being of so great integritie, godlinesse, and iustice, as he is reported to haue bene of, haue pronounced the crueties, insolencies, and adulteries of Tyrants, as lawes of Soueraigntie for princes to imitate? And amongst the Greeks How Samuel his speech vnto the people concerning the power of a king, by them demaunded, is to be vnderstood.

A2 Feudataries D10 משפטים Note at D7.

Greekes there are none, who haue any thing written concerning the lawes of Soueraigntie, except *Aristotle*, *Polybius*, and *Dionysius Halicarnasseus*, who haue writ with so great breuitie and obscuritie, as that they seeme rather to haue propounded the question, than to haue declared what was to be thought thereof, as not therein well resolued themselues. For there are (saith *Aristotle*) three parts of a Commonweale, the one to take aduice and councell, the other to establish magistrats and officers, and euerie man in his charge, and the third to administer and execute iustice. Here (in mine opinion) or else no where he seemeth to speake of the right of Soueraigntie; for that a Commonweale can by no meanes receiue that diuision, as it were of the whole into parts, except the soueraigne gouernment were also spoken of. Nether hath *Polybius* also determinatly defined or set downe the rights and marks of Soueraigntie: but in speaking of the Roman Commonwealth, he saith, That their estate was mixt of the *Power royall*, of the *Aristocraticall gouernment*, and the *Popular libertie*: seeing (saith he) that the people made lawes and officers; the Senat disposed of the prouinces and common treasure, receiued and dismissed ambassadours, and had the mannaging of the greatest affaires; the Consuls held the prerogatiue of honour, in royall forme and qualitie, but especially in warres, wherein they were all in all. Wherein it appeareth, that he hath touched the principall points of Soueraigntie, seeing that they vnto whom he attributeth the same, had the chiefe gouernment of the Commonwealth. But *Dionysius Halycarnasseus* seemeth thereof to haue written better, and more plainly than the other. For he saith, That king *Seruius*, to take away power from the Senat, gaue power to the people, to make and abolish lawes, to determine of peace and warre, to place and displace officers, to heare the appeales of all the magistrats. And in another place speaking of the third trouble which happened in Rome, betwixt the nobilitie and the people, he saith, That *Marcus Valerius* the Consul showed vnto the people, that it ought to content it selfe, to haue the power to make lawes, to chuse officers, to receiue appeales from all the magistrats, and so to leaue the rest vnto the Senat. Since which time the lawyers haue amplified these rights, and they of later time, much more than they before them, in the treaties which the call *The rights of Regaltie*, which they haue filled with an infinit number of particularities, such as are common vnto dukes, counties, barons, bishops, officers, and other subiects of soueraigne princes: in such sort that they call dukes soueraigne princes, as the dukes of Milan, Mantua, Ferrara, and Sauoy: yea euen some counties also dukes subiects, being all or most part blinded with this errour, which hath in it a great appearance of truth. For who is there that would not deeme him to be a soueraigne, which giueth lawes vnto his subiects, which maketh peace and warre, which appointeth all the officers and magistrats of his countrey, which imposeth tributes, and at his pleasure easeth whome he seeth good: which hath power of life and death, and in briefe to dispose of the whole Commonweale. All which they before rehearsed, haue power to doe; and what more can a man desire in a Soueraigne prince? For all these are the markes of Soueraigntie. And yet neuerthelesse we haue before shewed that the dukes of Milan, of Sauoy, of Ferrara, of Florence, and of Mantua, hold all of the empire: and that the most honourable title that they haue, is to be princes and deputies of the empire: we haue also said that they haue their inuestiture from the empire: and that they yeeld their fealtie and homage vnto the empire: in briefe that they are naturall subiects of the empire, and borne in the territories subiect vnto the empire. Then how can they be absolute soueraignes? For how should hee be a soueraigne, which acknowledgeth the iurisdiction of another greater then himselfe? of one which reuerseth his iudgements, which correcteth his lawes, which chastiseth himselfe, if he commit abuse? We haue before shewed that *Galeace* the first, vi-

count

count of Milan, was accused, attainted, conuinced, and condemned of treason by the emperour, for hauing without leaue raysed taxes vpon his subiects, and that hee therefore died in prison. And if any of them shall contrarie vnto the lawes, by force, sufferance, or by vsurpation take vpon them the soueraigntie; are they therefore soueraigns? or shall they prescribe against the fealtie and obedience which they owe vnto their prince? Seeing that they confesse themselues but princes and deputies of the empire. They must then renouce the titles of princes and dukes, of *Highnesse* and *Excellencie*, & stile themselues kings, to vse the title of soueraigne maiestie, which they cannot doe, without reuolting from the empire; as did *Galuagno* vicount of Milan, who therefore endured the grieuous punishment of his rashnesse. We haue also shewed that the cities of Lombardie were subiect vnto the empire. In briefe we had declared also the intollerable absurdities that should ensue, if the vassals should be soueraignes, especially when they haue nothing but what they hold of another: and that this were nothing else but to make the subiect equall with his lord, the seruant with his maister: he that receiueth the law, with him that giueth the law, him that oweth his obedience vnto him that is to commmaund, which seeing they are things impossible, wee may well conclude that dukes, counties, and all they which hold of another man; or that receiue law or commaundement from another, be it by force, or otherwise by contract, are in no wise soueraignes.

The same opinion we haue of the greatest magistrats, of kings Lieutenants general, Gouernours, Regents, and Dictators; what power soeuer they haue, if they be bound vnto the lawes appeales, and commaund of an other man, they are not to be accounted soueraigns. For it behoueth that the markes and recognisances of soueraigntie be such, as that they cannot agree to any other, but to a soueraigne prince: for otherwise if they be to be communicated with subiects, a man cannot say them to be the true markes of soueraigntie. For as a crowne if it be broken in peeces or opened, looseth the name of a crowne; so soueraigne maiestie looseth the greatnesse thereof, if any way bee opened to tread vnder foot any right thereof; as by communicating the same with subiects. And for this cause in the exchange made betwixt king *Charles* the fift, and the king of Nauarre, for the territories of Mante and Meullan, with Montpellier, wherin the royall rights are articulated, they are said all wholly and alone to belong vnto the king. It is also by the common opinion of the lawyers manifest, that those royall rights cannot by the soueraigne be yeelded vp, distracted, or any otherwise alienated; or by any tract of time be prescribed against: and therefore *Baldus* calleth them *Sacra Sacrorum*, of Sacred things the most Sacred: and *Cynus Indiuidua*, things inseparable, or not to bee diuided. And if it chance a soueraigne prince to communicat them with his subiect, he shall make him of his seruant, his companion in the empire: in which doing he shall loose his soueraigntie, and be no more a soueraigne: for that he onely is a soueraigne, which hath none his superiour or companion with himselfe in the same kingdome. For as the great soueraigne God, cannot make another God equall vnto himselfe, considering that he is of infinit power and greatnes, and that there cannot bee two infinit things, as is by naturall demonstrations manifest: so also may wee say, that the prince whom we haue set down as the image of God, cannot make a subiect equall vnto himselfe, but that his owne soueraigntie must thereby be abased; which if it be so, it followeth that the administration of iustice, which *Aristotle* maketh the third part of a Commonweale, is not the true marke of soueraigntie; for that it indifferently agreeth almost to all magistrats aswell as to the prince: neither in like sort to make or displace officers; for that the prince and the subiect haue both this power; not only in appointing the officers seruants at home, and in time of warre, but euen of the officers,

and

The greatest magistrats or lieutenants no soueraigns.

A fit comparison.

Soueraigntie admitteth no companion or pertaker therin.

A1 convinced *i.e.* convicted   A7 renounce   B6 commaund   C2 lawes, appeales,
E9 officers servants *i.e.* inferior officers

and magistrats themselues, which commaund in peace or in warre. For we read that the Consuls, in auntient time created the militarie Tribunes, who were as marshals in the armie, and he whome they called the Interrex created the dictator, and the dictator appointed the collonel of the horsemen: & in euery Commonweale where iustice is giuen with fees, the lord of the fee may at his pleasure appoint officers, and without cause displace them againe, if they haue not their offices in recompence of some their deserts. The same opinion we haue of punishments and rewards, which magistrats or captaines inflict or giue vnto them that haue deserued the same, aswell as the soueraigne prince. Wherefore it is no true marke of Soueraigntie to giue reward, or to inflict punishment vnto such as haue so deserued, sith it is common both to the prince and the magistrat: albeit that the magistrat haue this power of the prince. It is also no marke of Soueraigntie to haue power to consult of the affaires of the state, which is the the proper charge of the priuie Councell, or Senat of a Commonweale; which is alwayes diuided from him which is therein soueraigne; but especially in a popular estate where the soueraigntie lieth in the assemblie of the people, which is alwaies an enemy vnto wisedome and good councell. Whereby it is to be perceiued, not any one thing of those three wherein *Aristotle* said a Commonweale to consist, to be the true marke of Soueraigntie.

As for that which *Dionysius Halycarnasseus* saith of *Marcus Valerius* the Consull, in the Oration which he made vnto the people of Rome, for the appeasing of the troubles then risen betwixt the Senat and them; That the people ought to content themselues to haue the power to make lawes and magistrats; that is not sufficient to declare a Soueraigntie of power in them, as I haue before declared concerning the magistrats. Yea the power to make lawes is not the proper marke of Soueraigntie, except we vnderstand thereby the soueraigne princes lawes; for that the magistrat may also giue lawes vnto them that are within the compasse of his iurisdiction, so that nothing be by him decreed contrarie to the edicts and lawes of his soueraigne prince. And to manifest this point, we must presuppose that this word *Law*, without any other addition, signifieth *The right commaund of him or them, which haue soueraigne power aboue others, without exception of person*: be it that such commaundement concerne the subiects in generall, or in particular: except him or them which haue giuen the law. Howbeit to speake more properly, *A law is the commaund of a Soueraigne concerning all his subiects in generall*: or els concerning generall things, as saith *Festus Pompeius*, as a priuilege concerneth some one, or some few: which law if it bee made by the priuie councel, or Senat of a Commonweale, it is called *Senatus consultum*, as the priuie councell: or decree of the senat. But if the vulgar people made any such commaund, it was called *Plebiscitum*, that is to say, The commaund of the meniall people: which after many seditions and sturs, betwixt the Nobilitie and the common people, was in the end called a law. For the appeasing whereof all the people in the assemblie of the great estates, at the request of *M. Horatius* the Consull made a law, that the Nobilitie and the Senat in generall, and euerie one of the people in particular, should bee bound to keepe the decrees and lawes which the common people should make, without appealing therefrom; or that the Nobilitie should haue any voyce therein. But forasmuch as the nobilitie and the Senat made small account of such the peoples decrees and ordinances; the aforesaid law was afterward renewed, and againe published, at the instance of *Q. Hortentius* and *Pub. Philo* Dictators: From which time forward such the peoples decrees were no more called *Plebiscita*, but simply laws, whether they concerned euery man in particular, or all men in generall. As for the commaundements of the magistrates, they were not called lawes, but onely edicts. For an Edict (as
M. Varro

What lawe properly is.

The difference betwixt Senatus consultum, and Plebiscitum, a decree of the Senate and of the people.

F2 created   H10 exception   I 5–6 as the ADVICE OF THE priuie councell (cf. Fr)
Notes at F7, I2, I7

M. *Varro* defineth it) *is the commaund of a Magistrat;* which his commaund bound none, but them which were of his owne iurisdiction; prouided alwaies that such his comands were not contrary vnto the ordinances of the great magistrats, or to the laws and commaundements of his soueraigne prince, and were no longer in force than the magistrat pleased, or had charge. And for that all the magistrats were annuall in the Roman Commonweale, there edicts had not force but for one yeare at the most. And therefore they which succeeded in the same office, were either to allow or reuoke the edicts, by their predecessors before made: & if so be that they were against the laws, or for longer time than the magistratie of him that made them, then were they to none effect: which when *C. Verres* did, he was in these words accused by *Cicero, Qui plurimum (inquit) edicto tribuũt, legem annuam appellãt, tu plus edicto complecteris, quàm lege,* They that attribute most (saith he) vnto an edict, cal it but an annual law; but thou comprehendest more in an edict, than in a law. And for that the emperour *Augustus,* hauing oppressed the liberty of the cõmonweal, called himself but *Imperator* (that is to say chief captain & Tribune of the people) he called also his own decrees by the name of edicts: but such as the people made at his request, he called them *Leges Iuliæ;* which maner of speech the other emperors after him vsed also; in such sort, that this word Edict, is by litle & litle taken for a law, especially when it commeth out of the mouth of him which hath a soueraigne power; be it for one, or for al, be it an edict perpetual or onely prouisionall. Wherefore they abuse the words, which call edicts which are proper vnto magistrats by the name of laws: but in what sort soeuer that it be, there are none but soueraigne princes, which can giue laws vnto their subiects, without exception, be it in generall or in particular. But here might some man obiect, That the Senat of Rome had power to make laws, & that the more part of the greatest affaires of estate, in peace or war, were in the power of the Roman Senat to determine of. But what the authority of a Senat is, or ought to be in euery Commonweale, we shal in due place declare. But by the way to answere that that is obiected, I say, that the Senat of Rome, from the expulsion of the kings, vntill the time of the emperours, had neuer power to make law, but onely certaine decrees and ordinances: which were not in force past a yeare, wherewith for all that the common people were not bound, and so much lesse the whole body and estate of the people. Wherein many are deceiued and especially *Conan,* who saith, That the Senat had power to make a perpetuall law: for *Dionysius Halycarnasseus,* who had diligently read the Commentaries of *Marcus Varro,* writeth, That the decrees of the Senat had not any force, if they were not by the people confirmed: and albeit that they were so confirmed, yet if they were not published in forme of a law, they then had force but for one yeare. No more than the citie of Athens, where the decrees of the Senat were but annuall, as saith *Demosthenes* in the Oration which hee made against *Aristocrates:* and if it were a matter of importance, it was referred vnto the people to dispose thereof as they thought good: which *Anacharsis* the philosopher seeing merily said, *The wise and graue propound matters at Athens, and fooles and mad men resolue thereof.* And so the Senat in Rome did but consult, and the people commaund: For so *Liuie* oft times saith, *Senatus decreuit, populus iussit,* The Senat hath decreed, and the people commaunded. Yet true it is, that the magistrats, and namely the Tribunes, oft times suffered the decrees of the Senat, in a maner to haue the force of lawes, if the matter seemed not to impare the power of the people, or to be preiudiciall vnto the maiestie of the estates in generall. For so properly the auntient Romans said * *Imperium in magistratibus, auctoritatem in Senatu, potestatem in plebe, maiestatem in populo inesse dicebant,* Commaund to be in the magistrats, authoritie in the senat, power in the meniall people, and maiestie in the people in generall. For the word

What an edict is.

That the senate of Rome had no power to make lawes, but annuall decrees only.

A pretie quip of Anacharsis.

* *Cicero pro Rabirio Perduellionis reo.*

P Maiestie,

158   THE FIRST BOOKE

Maiestie proper only vnto a soueraigne prince.

Maiestie, is proper vnto him which stirreth the helme of the soueraigntie of a Commonweale. And albeit that the law Iulia concerning maiestie made by the people at the request of *Augustus*, hold him guilty (*Læsæ maiestatis*, or as we say) of treason, which striketh a magistrat in the execution of his office: and that sometime the Latine historiographers, yea and the lawyers themselues also giue the title of maiestie vnto the Consull and Pretor; as in saying, *Maiestatem consulis, maiestatem prætoris*, The maiestie of the Consull, the maiestie of the Pretor: yet is it but improperly spoken, neither by our lawes is he guiltie *læsæ maiestatis*, that hath hurt a prince, a duke, a countie, or a magistrat: but he onely that hath violated the person of a soueraigne prince. And so by the lawes of *Sigismundus Augustus* king of Polonia, made in the yeare 1588, it is set downe that the crime *Læsæ maiestatis*, should take no place further than his owne person; which is according to the true signification of *læsa maiestas*. And for this cause it seemeth that the dukes of Saxonie, of Bauaria, of Sauoy, of Loraine, Ferrara, Florence, and Mantua, put not into their stiles of honour, this word *Maiestie*, contenting themselues with the title of *Highnesse*: and the duke of Venice with the addition of his *Serenitie*, who (to speake properly) is but a verie prince, that is to say, the first, for hee is nothing else but the first of the gentlemen of Venice: and hath no more aboue the rest of the Senators, than the chiefe place and dignitie of the Commonweale in all their assemblies, wherein he sitteth as chiefe; and the concluding voyce into what corporation or colledge he come, if there be any question of voyces. And as in Rome the edicts of the magistrats bound euery man in particular (so that they were not contrary to the decrees of the Senat) and the decrees of the Senat in some sort bound the magistrats (if they were not contrarie to the ordinances of the common people) and the ordinances of the common people were aboue the decrees of the Senat; and the law of the whole bodie and estates of the people, was aboue all the rest: euen so in the Venetian Commonweale, the decrees of the magistrats bind euerie man in particular, according to the precinct and iurisdiction of euerie magistrat: but the corporation and colledge of the Decemuiri is aboue particular magistrats: the Senat is aboue the Decemuiri, and the great Councell (which is the assemblie of all the gentlemen of Venice) hath the power of soueraigntie, containing the Senat, and all the rest of the magistrats, within the power of the commaund thereof, in such sort, that if the Decemuiri bee diuided with euen voyces, they appeale vnto the councell of the Sages, consisting of xxij, who if they cannot agree, the Senat is assembled, and if the matter concerne the high points of soueraigntie, as is the maiestie of the Commonweale, then it is referred vnto the great Councell. And therefore when any thing is decreed by the Decemuiri these words are ioyned vnto the decree, *In consiglio Di Dieci*: whereunto if the colledge of Sages be ioyned, there is also commonly added, *Con la Giunta*, but if it be a decree of the Senat, it is declared in these words, *In Pregaidi*: but if it be in the great assemblie of the gentlemen of Venice, these words are commonly adioyned thereunto, *In Consiglio Magiore*. For in these three corporations or colleges, are almost all things dispatched which belong vnto their lawes, their customes, and Commonweale, except such matters which the Septemuiri (the most secret councell of the State) vse by themselues to determine. It is therefore but by sufferance that the Decemuiri or the Senat make decrees and ordinances, which for that they are found iust and reasonable, they passe sometime into the force of law, as did the edicts of the auntient Roman Pretors, which if they were equall and iust, their successours kept them: and so by tract of time were receiued as lawes; yet for all that was it alwayes in the power of the new Pretors to make others: neither were they bound to obserue or keepe them of their predecessors. But *Iulian* the lawyer gathered a great number of such of these edicts of the former

The duke of Venice no soueraigne prince.

The order of the Venetian Commonweale.

Pretors

F10 *For* 1588 *read* 1538 (Fr and L).   I2 *For* xxii (Fr 7) *read* xxxii (Fr 1-6, 8).   I8 Pregaidi: Pregaedi (Fr 7) *properly* Pregadi (Fr 1-6, 8 and L)   K6 equall *i.e.* equitable   Note at I3.

OF A COMMONWEALE. 159

Pretors, as he thought best, and after that he had interpreted them, and brought them into ninetie bookes, he gaue the same vnto the emperour *Adrian* for a present; who in recompence of so great a worke, made him great Prouost of the citie of Rome, and thereby made way for his nephew *Didius Iulianus*, afterwards to aspire vnto the Roman empire. *Adrian* himselfe also perswaded the Senat, that not onely the edicts which *Iulian* had gathered, but other his owne writings should bee taken for lawes, which he confirmed also by his authoritie, and yet neuerthelesse still held the name of edicts, which hath deceiued many, who haue accounted those lawes as Pretors edicts. So also *Iustinian* the emperour, to the example of *Adrian*, by decree commaunded many things which the lawyers had after *Iulian* written vnto the Pretors decrees (after they had bene by him as he thought good corrected) to be receiued for laws, the name of edicts still remaining, being yet indeed nothing lesse than edicts, but lawes aswell as those which euery soueraigne prince in his owne Commonweale by the decrees of his lawyers and courts, hath commaunded to be receiued for lawes; as it oft commeth to passe in this realme, that the kings seeing diuers ordinances and decrees of parliament most equall and iust, haue confirmed the same, and caused them to be published, and to passe in force of lawes; to show that the power of the law lyeth in him that hath the soueraigntie: and which giueth force vnto the law by these words, *Sancimus Iubemus*, We ordaine and commaund; which are words proper vnto soueraigne maiestie, as saith the Consull *Posthumius*, in the oration which he made vnto the people, *Nego iniussu populi quicquam sanciri posse, quod populum teneat*, I deny that any thing can bee ordayned without the peoples commaund, that can bind the people. The magistrat also presenting his request vnto the people, for the enacting of a law, commonly began with these words, *Quod bonum, faustum, foelixque sit vobis ac Reipub. velitis, Iubeatis*, Will you, and commaund you, that which may be good, happie, and fortunat, to you, and the Commonweale. And in the end of the law are still these words, *Si quis aduersus ea fecerit, &c*. If any man shall do against these things, &c. Which they called *Sanctio*, that is to say an ordaining or enacting, declaring the punishments or rewards due vnto them that should keepe or breake the law: which are speciall formalities and proper vnto the maiestie of them which had the power to make the law; but neuer vsed by the Senat in their decrees, nor by the magistrats in their edicts. Ioyne hereunto also, that the penaltie annexed vnto the lawes of a soueraigne prince, is farre different from that which is ioyned vnto the decrees or ordinances of magistrates, or of corporations and colledges, which haue certaine limited penalties and fines, for the most part concluded by a mercement or forfeit of money, or with whipping chere: For there is none but the soueraigne prince, which can vnto his edicts ioyne the paine of death, as it hath bene also forbidden by an auntient act of parliament, and the clause of arbitrarie punishment ioyned vnto the ordinances and decrees of magistrats and gouernours, which euer inclusiuely extended vnto death.

Wherefore let this be the first and chiefe marke of a soueraigne prince, to bee of power to giue lawes to all his subiects in generall, and to euerie one of them in particular, (yet is not that enough, but that we must ioyne thereunto) without consent of any other greater, equall, or lesser than himselfe. For if a prince be bound not to make any law without consent of a greater than himselfe, he is then a verie subiect: if not without his equall, he then hath a companion: if not without the consent of his inferiours, whether it be of his subiects, of the Senat, or of the people, hee is then no soueraigne. And as for the names of Lords and Senators, which wee oftentimes see ioyned vnto lawes, they are not thereunto set as of necessitie to giue thereunto force or strength, but to giue vnto them testimonie and weight, as made by the wisedome and discretion of

Magistrats edicts confirmed by him or them that haue the soueraigntie become lawes.

The first and chiefe marke of soueraigntie.

P ij the

D5 *whipping chere i.e.* flogging   D9 *For ever read* never (cf. Fr).   Note at A4.

the chiefe men, so to giue them the better grace, and to make them to bee the better receiued; and not for any necessitie at all. For we find the most auntient edicts of Saint *Denys* in Fraunce, of *Philip* the first, and of *Lewes* the Grosse; whereunto the names and seales of the Queenes *Anne* and *Adella*, as also of *Robert* and *Hugh* are annexed: And namely in the twelft yeare of the raigne of *Lewes* the Grosse, and of *Adella* the sixt.

<small>It belongeth onely vnto soueraigne princes to grant priuileges, and what a priuilege is.</small>

Now when I say that the first and chiefe marke of Soueraigntie is for the prince to be of power to giue lawes vnto all his subiects in generall, and to euerie one of them in particular: these last words concerne priuileges, which only belong vnto soueraigne princes to graunt, and particularly to others, to whome they be graunted. A priuilege I call a law made for one, or some few particular men: whether it bee for the profit or disprofit of him or them for whome it is graunted. For so speaketh *Cicero*, *Priuilegium de meo capite latum est*, A priuilege was made concerning my life, he meaneth the law made against him by the common people at the motion and instigation of *Clodius* the Tribune, (to haue him called to account for certaine citisens put to death contrarie to their appeale, about the conspiracie of *Cateline*) which he in many places calleth *Lex Clodia*, or a Law made by *Clodius*, whereof he oftentimes most grieuously complained, both in the Senat and before the people, saying, That by the law of the xij Tables it was forbidden any priuileges to be graunted, but *Comitijs Centuriatis*, that is to say, in the generall assembly of the whole bodie of the people. For so be the words of the law, *Priuilegia nisi comitijs centuriatis ne irroganto; qui secus faxit capital esto*, Priuileges let them not be graunted but in the greatest assemblies of the people; and hee that shall otherwise do, let it be vnto him death. As for such priuileges as bring profit and commoditie to them to whome they be graunted, they are more truely called benefits. And in this all that haue written of Royalties agree, that it belongeth not to any, but vnto a Soueraigne, to graunt priuileges, exemptions, immunities, and to dispence with the edicts and ordinances of other former princes: howbeit that priuileges in monarchies haue not bene vsed, but onely for the tearme of the life of the monarch himselfe that graunted them: as *Tiberius* the emperour made them all to know which had obtained any priuileges from the emperour *Augustus*, as *Suetonius* writeth. But now if any shall obiect vnto me, the magistrats themselues to discharge men oftentimes of the lawes: and the Senat of Rome to haue so oftentimes done. I will aunswere him as did *Papinian* the lawyer, *That we are not to consider what is done at Rome, but what ought indeed to be there done*. For by the tribunitiall law Cornelia, the Senat is forbidden to discharge any Roman of the lawes, except there were two hundred of the Senators present: which exemption from the laws seemeth also to haue bene granted vnto the Senat, by reason of the difficult assembling of the whole people.

<small>* *Cicero pro domo sua et post reditum in Senatu.*</small>

<small>The difference betwixt the beginning of customes and lawes: and that both of them depend of the power of the soueraign prince.</small>

But some man may say, that not onely the magistrats haue power to make edicts and lawes, euerie one according to his authoritie and iurisdiction, but also that particular men make customes, both generall and particular. Which customes haue almost the force of lawes, and yet depend not of the iudgement or power of the soueraigne prince, who as he is maister of the law, so are particular men maisters of the customes. Whereunto I answere, that custome by little and little take force; and in many yeres by the common consent of all or most part; but the law commeth forth in a moment and taketh strength of him which hath power to commaund all: custome creepeth in sweetly and without force, whereas the law is commaunded and published with power, yea and oftentimes contrarie to the good liking of the subiects. For which cause *Dion Chrisostome* compareth the law to a tyrant, and custome to a king. Moreouer the power of the law is much greater than the power of custome: for customes

are

F2–3 of Saint Denys *i.e.* at Saint Denys (cf. Fr)   Notes at F10, H7.

are by lawes abolished, but not lawes by customes; it beeing alwayes in the authoritie and power of the magistrat againe to put in execution such lawes as are by custome almost out of vse. Custome also propoundeth neither reward nor punishment, whereas the law alwayes carrieth with it either the one or the other, if it be not a law permissiue, which easeth the penaltie of another law: and in briefe custome hath no force but by sufferance, and so long as it pleaseth the soueraigne prince, who may make thereof a law, by putting thereunto his owne confirmation: whereby it is to be seene, that all the force of lawes and customes lieth in the power of him that hath the soueraigntie in a Commonweale.

This then is the first and chiefest marke of Soueraignty, to be of power to giue laws and commaund to all in generall, and to euerie one in particular; which cannot bee communicated vnto subiects. For albeit that a soueraigne prince giue power to any one to make lawes, of such strength and vertue as if he himselfe had made them: as did the people of Athens to *Solon*, and the Lacedemonians to *Lycurgus*: yet were these lawes neither the lawes of *Solon* nor *Lycurgus*, who were but as commissioners and procurators for them which had giuen them that charge; but they were the lawes of the Athenians, and Lacedemonians: neither had these lawes had any force, had not the people by their consent authorised the same. They indeed wrot those lawes, but the people commaunded them; they composed them, but the people enacted them. And almost alwayes in a Popular or Aristocraticall state, the lawes tooke name of him which propounded or engrossed the same, who was nothing els but the simple procurer thereof: the confirmation of the same being from him which had the soueraigntie. So when the Decemuiri by the people created at Rome for the making of lawes without appeale, had sent ambassadours into Greece, to amplifie their lawes, and in xij tables comprehended the best of them, they commaunded all the people to bee called together, to behold and consider of those lawes publikely set vp: and so at length after three Faire dayes (the vsuall time appointed for the establishing of laws) the people in their greatest and generall assembly, commaunded, or rather enacted them to stand for laws. But vnto what power it belongeth to make a law, vnto the same also it appertaineth to abrogat or derogat from the same. Vnder this power of making & of abrogating of the law, is also comprised the declaration & correction of the same, when it is so obscure, that the magistrats vpon the cases propounded find contrarietie or intollerable absurdities, yet may the magistrat according vnto right and reason also interpret the laws, & encline them either vnto lenitie or seueritie: so that he beware that in bending them too much, he breake them not; yea although that they seeme vnto him hard or vniust: but let him heare what *Vlpian* saith, *Dura lex, sic tamen scripta est*, An hard law (saith he) but so it is written: which if the judge shall presume vnder the colour of equitie to breake, he is by the law condemned of infamie. So ought the law called *Lætoria*, (or rather *Prætoria*) to be vnderstood, which *Papinian* reciteth, without naming of the author. Wherby it is permitted vnto the Great Prætor of the citie of Rome, to supply, to correct or amend the laws: which must (as we said) be moderatly & in a measure done: for if a man should otherwise vnderstand it, it should thereof follow, that a simple magistrat should be aboue the lawes, if hee might at his will and pleasure alter and infringe the same: and also that he might bind both the people and the prince vnto his edicts; which we haue before showed to be a thing impossible.

Vnder this same soueraigntie of power for the giuing and abrogating of the law, are comprised al the other rights & marks of soueraignty: so that (to speak properly) a man may say, that there is but this only mark of soueraigne power considering that all other the rights thereof are contained in this, *viz.* to haue power to giue lawes vnto all and euery

That the power to make lawes cannot be vnto subiects communicated.

What power the magistrate hath to interpret the lawe.

All the other markes of soueraigntie contained vnder the first.

C6–7 after three Faire dayes *i.e. post trinundinum*, a period of seventeen days supplement, to complete   D10 to supply *i.e.* to Notes at C4, D8.

Other the marks of Soueraigntie

euerie one of the subiects, & to receiue none from them. For to denounce warre vnto the enemie, or to make peace with him, although it seeme to be a thing different from the name of the law, yet is it manifest these things to bee done by the law, that is to say by the commaundement of the soueraigne power. So also is it proper vnto soueraigne maiestie, to receiue the subiects appeales from other, and the greatest magistrats, to place and displace the greatest officers, charge or exempt the subiects from taxes and subsidies, to graunt pardons and dispensations against the rigour of the law, to haue power of life and death, to encrease or diminish the valour and weight of the coyne, to giue it title, name, and figure: to cause all subiects and liegemen to sweare for the keeping of their fidelitie without exception, vnto him to whome such oath is due: which are the true markes of soueraigntie, comprised vnder the power of being able to giue a law to al in generall, and to euery one in particular, and not to receiue any law or commaund from any other, but from almightie God onely. For a prince or duke who hath power to giue lawes vnto all his subiects in general, & to euery one of them in particular, is yet no soueraigne, if he receiue his power from the emperour, the pope, or the king, or any other greater than himselfe: or yet haue a companion in his gouernment, a companion I say, for that he seemeth in a manner to haue a superiour or maister, which hath a companion, without whose helpe and consent hee can commaund and doe nothing: much lesse is he a soueraigne, if hee bee another mans lieutenant or deputie.

The second marke of Soueraigntie.

But forasmuch as the word *Law*, is too general a marke, it is the more expedient particularly to specifie the rights of Soueraigntie, comprised (as I haue said) vnder that soueraigne law; as to denounce warre, or treat of peace, one of the greatest points of soueraigne maiestie: for that oftentimes it draweth after it the ruine, or assurance of a Commonweale; which is to be verified not onely by the law of the Romans, but of al other nations. And for that there was more daunger to be feared from warre, than from peace, it was lawfull for the common people of Rome, to commaund peace, but if question were for making of warre, it might not be decreed, but in the greatest assembly of all the states together, vntill such time as that the meniall people had also full power to make lawes. And therefore was it that warre was decreed against Mithridates by the law Manilia, against the pirats, by the law Gabinia, against *Philip* the second, king of Macedon, by the law Sulpitia: peace was also made with the Carthaginensians, by the law *Martia*. And for because *Cæsar* had without commaund of the people made warres in Fraunce, *Cato Vticensis* was of opinion in the Senat, that the armie was to be called home, and *Cæsar* for his presumption deliuered vnto the enemie. In like case the estates of the people of Athens determined of warre and peace. As a man may see by the war by them decreed against the Megarians, against the Syracusians, and against the kings of Macedon. I here but briefly set downe certaine examples of two of the greatest and most famous popular Commonweales that euer yet were: For in a regall state there is none (as I suppose) which doubt all the power of peace and warre to be in the king: insomuch as that for any man to attempt euen the least thing therein without the kings commaund, is vnto the dooer thereof dangerous, if the king might thereof haue before bene aduertised: and what charge soeuer that they giue vnto their deputies or commissioners, to entreat of peace or of alliance, yet consent they vnto nothing, without the aduertising of the king; as was to be seene in the last treaty of Cambray, betwixt the French king & the king of Spain; the cōmissioners on the kings behalfe writ to him from howre to howre, the whole proceedings both of the one part and of the other. But in popular or Aristocraticall estate, we oft times see that after the warre is once denounced, it is then managed by the aduise of the Senat, or priuie

Note at H2.

priuie counsell onely: yea and sometimes by the aduice of one onely captaine also: for that nothing is more dangerous in warre, than to haue the secret pollicies thereof reuealed: which must needes be, if the people haue therein to doe. And therefore we read in the Greeke and Latine histories the designes and enterprises of warre to haue beene still managed by the wisdome and direction of some one or other captaine, or in case that the matter were of greater importance and consequence, by the counsell of the Senate, without any more speaking thereof vnto the people, after it was once by the peoples commaund denounced and proclaimed against this or that enemie. But if one should say, warre to haue beene oftentimes denounced by the advice of the Senate, without the consent or commaund of the people: I confesse it to haue sometimes indeed so happened and fallen out, but yet very seldome: and that the Senate in so doing did vsurpe the maiestie of the people: which was the cause, that the Tribunes of the people, and faithfull keepers of their libertie, oftentimes interposed themselues to crosse the matter, as we see in *Liuie*, where he sayth: *Controuersia fuit vtrum populi iussu indiceretur bellum, an satis esset S. C. peruicere Tribuni, vt Q. Consul de bello ad populum ferret, omnes Centuriæ iussere.* Controuersie was (sayth he) whether war should be denounced by the commaundement of the people: or els that the decree of the Senate was sufficient, but the Tribunes preuailed; so that *Quintus* the Consull propounded the matter vnto the people, which all the assembly of the people commaunded. Howbeit, that the Senat it selfe would not ordinarily denounce war, except the people had before so decreed, As *T. Liuius* speaking of the second Carthaginensian war, sayth, *Latum inde ad populum vellent iuberent, populo Carthaginensi bellum indici*: It was afterward propounded vnto the people, whether they willed and commaunded war to be denounced vnto the people of Carthage. And in another place, *Ex S.C. populi iussu bellum prænestinis indictū*. By a decree of the Senat, by commandement of the people war was proclaimed against them of Præneste. And againe, *Ex authoritate patrum populus Palæpolitanis bellum fieri iussit*, The people following the authoritie of the Senat, commaunded warre to be made against them of Palæpolis. And afterward, *Populus bellum fieri Æquis iussit*, The people commaunded warre to be made against the Æqui. And at such time as warre was to be vndertaken against the Samnites, *Patres solemni more indicto decreuerunt, vt ea de re ad populum ferretur*, The fathers after the solemne manner decreed, that concerning that matter it should bee referred vnto the people: Where *Liuie* in calling it the solemne manner, declareth it to haue bene a thing so vsed to be done. And so against the Herniques, *Populus hoc bellum frequens iussit*, The people in great number commaunded this warre. And against the Vestines, *Bellum ex authoritate patrum populus aduersus vestinos iussit*, The people following the authoritie of the Senators commaunded warre to be made against the Vestines. The like manner of denouncing warre was also amongst the Tarentines, so long as their popular state endured. For so saith *Plutarch*, *Ex authoritate Senatus populum Tarentinum Romanis inferri bellum iussisse*, The people of Tarentum following the authoritie of the Senat, to haue commaunded warre to bee made against the Romans. And *Liuie* speaking of the Ætolians, which were gouerned by a popular gouernment, saith it to haue bene by their lawes forbidden, that any thing should bee determined concerning peace and warre, but in the Panætolian and Pylaican counsell. And for that the nobilitie of Polonia, Denmarke, and Sweden, pretend the right of Soueraigntie to belong vnto them, it is not lawfull for their kings without their authoritie and consent either to denounce warre, or to vndertake it being denounced against them, except in case of urgent necessitie, according to the order of *Casimire* the great. True it is that in Rome concerning peace the Senate oftentimes determined thereof without the consent of the

The greatest daunger in war.

The Senate in Rome had no power to denounce warre without the consent of the people.

Lib. 1. Dec. 3.
Lib. 1. Dec. 2.
Lib. 8. Dec. 1.
Lib. 9. Dec. 1.
Lib. 8. Dec. 1.
Lib. 5. Dec. 1.

the people; as we may see in all the treaties of peace betwixt the Romane and the Latines: and in the confederats warre the Senate passed all the treaties of peace and alliance without the people, *viz.* in the tumult and vprore of Italie: least the hard assembly of the people, and danger of delay, might haue brought some detriment vnto the Commonweale. Yea sometimes the generals and great commaunders in the warres, of themselues determined of peace and warre, without the commaundement of the people or Senate, especially if the warres were in some countrey a farre off: as wee see in the second warre of Carthage, the three *Scipioes* made all the treaties of peace and alliance with the people and princes of Spaine and Affricke, without the aduise of the Senat. Yet true it is, that the Senate, yea and oft times the people authorised their actions, and ratified their treaties, after that they were made: and it they were in anie thing preiudiciall vnto the estate, had of them no regard. In which case the hostages and captaines yeelded vnto the enemie, were at their owne perill to answer the matter. As the Consull *Mancinus*, who for that the peace he had made with the Numantines, was reiected and not ratified by the Senate and the people, was himselfe deliuered vnto the enemie. And that is it which a certaine Senatour of Carthage, as *Liuie* reporteth by way of exprobration obiected vnto the Romane embassadours, saying, *Vos cum Luctatius Consul primò nobiscum fedus icit, quia neque authoritate Patrum, nec populi iussu ictum erat, negastis vos eo teneri. Itaque aliud foedus publico consilio ictum est.* You at such time as *Luctatius* the Consull first made peace with vs; for that it was made without the authoritie of the Senat, or commaundement of the people, said you were not therunto bound: and therefore another peace was by your common councell made. And the same author speaking of *Manlius* the Proconsull of Asia saith, *Gallogræcis bellum illatum, non ex Senatus authoritate, non populi iussu: quod quis vnquam de sua sententia facere ausus est?* Warre was made vpon the Gallogrekes, neither by the authority of the Senat, nor the commaund of the people, which what man durst of himselfe euer do? But this was Orator like spoken by the aduersarie against *Manlius* being absent; for that it was sometime so done, we haue by examples declared. *Spurius Posthumius* the Consull, also being himselfe with his armie shut vp in the Straits and rockes of the Appennin mountaines, in daunger with hunger to perish, before hee could haue heard from the Senat or the people, what they would haue had him to haue done; to deliuer himselfe and the Roman armie out of those straites, of himselfe made peace with the enemie, though vpon verie hard and dishonourable conditions. But when he with his armie disarmed, was returned to Rome; the Senat and the people reiected the peace with the conditions by him accepted. Yea *Posthumius* the Consull himselfe, in the assembly of the people said, *Cùm me seu turpi, seu necessaria sponsione obstrinxi, qua tamen, quando iniussu populi facta est, non tenetur populus Romanus, nec quicquam ex ea præter Corpora nostra debentur Samnitibus, dedamur per fæciales nudi vinctique*, Seeing that I haue bound my selfe, whether it be with a shamefull or a necessarie promise and agreement, wherewith for all that the people of Rome is not bound, forasmuch as it was without their commaundement made, neither is there any thing thereby vnto the Samnites due, more than our bodies; let vs naked and bound be so yeelded vnto them. So the Consull called it not a treatie of peace, but a simple or necessarie promise. And in truth the enemies had caused the Consull and all the captaines and lieuetenants of the army to sweare, and further taken sixe hundred hostages, al which they might haue put to death, if the people would not confirme the agreement taken; in which making they yet committed one grosse ouersight, in that they bound not all the souldiers in the armie by oath to returne into those straits and enclosures of the mountaines, and euen into the same state they were before, or els to yeeld themselues all prisoners, in case the

people

F1 Romans   G8 foedus icit   G8 patrum

Of A Commonweale.

people would not confirme the agreement by them made; which had they done, no doubt but that the Senat and the people would haue sent them againe into the same state they were, as they did the Consull, with the sixe hundred sworne hostages, whom for all that, the Samnites refused to receiue of the herauld. For in like case after the great ouerthrow by the Romans receiued at Cannas, when *Hanniball* had sent eight thousand souldiers, there taken prisoners, to Rome, to redeeme their libertie with the ransome of a pound of gold for euery head; and that the Senat would not agree thereunto, but decreed, that they should either become the enemies slaues, or die: the Consuls charged those souldiers, before the appointed day to returne vnto the enemie; who all obeyed their commaund, but one, who by a craftie wile sought to delude the oath, before by him giuen vnto the enemie for his returne; whome the Senat for all that sent bound hand and foot vnto *Hannibal*. Or if it had seemed too hard a thing vnto the Senat, to haue yeelded the whole army being sworne vnto the Samnites, they would vndoubtedly yet haue confirmed those hard conditions of peace by them agreed vpon. As did *Lewes* the xij, the French king, in the treatie made at *Dijon* by the lord *Trimouille* with the Swissers, giuing them hostages of the chiefest men of his army, with condition that the Swissers might put them to death, if the king should not ratifie the agreement with them made. As did the duke of Aniou vnto the hostages which those which were besieged in the castle of Etuall had giuen him: when he saw that *Robert Knolles*, captaine of the castle, being arriued within the castle, after the agreement, would by no meanes suffer the castle to be surrendred, saying, That the besieged without him could couenant nothing: and so also caused the prisoners that he had taken to be beheaded. For otherwise, if it were lawful for captains to entreat or conclude of peace at their pleasure, without expresse commaundement or ratification, they might bind both people and soueraigne princes, vnto the pleasure and appetite of their enemies, and such hard conditions as they pleased: a thing most absurd and vnreasonable, seeing that a common aduocat may not in the least matter of another mans, come to agreement, without expresse charge from him whome it concerneth.

But some may say, that these rules take no place in Venice, where the Senat doth wholly discerne and determine of peace and warre, neither amongst the customes of the Swissers and Grisons, which are popular estates. And in the conuersion of the Florentine Commonweale, from the nobilitie vnto the popular estate, it is in one article especially prouided, that the people shall haue to do with nothing, but with making of lawes, creating of magistrats, and the common treasure; as for peace and warre, and other things concerning the soueraigntie of the state, should be wholly in the power of the Senat. Whereunto we haue before said, that Popular and Aristocraticall estates cannot if they would, well mannage martiall affaires, for the hard assembling together of the people: and in case that the people might be at all times assembled, yet were it a thing of great perill and daunger, to haue those things which ought of all others to bee most secret in a Commonweale, the councels (I say) of peace and warre, reuealed and made knowne vnto the Vulgar people: which therfore were of necessitie to be left vnto the Senat, yet the power of peace and warre cannot be taken from the nobilitie or people in either state, the soueraigne maiestie thereof saued. And albeit that the people giue the charge thereof vnto the Senat, yet a man knoweth right well, that the commissions and mandats which are giuen out for such purpose, depend of the authority of the people, and vnder the peoples name are put in execution by the Senat, which is but the peoples procurator and agent, taking authoritie from the people, as all other their magistrats doe. As for monarchies, it is without any question that the resolution of peace and warre dependeth of the soueraigne prince, if the estate bee a pure monarchie.

Hard for the popular or Aristocraticall estats by the multitude well to mannage martiall affaires; and why.

A 10 delude *i.e.* elude, evade

narchie, For the kingdome of Polonia, Denmarke, Sweden, and Norway, as they are states changeable and vncertaine, as the nobilitie is stronger than the prince, or the prince than the nobilitie: the resolution of peace and warre so dependeth of the nobilitie, as that the state seemeth to be rather Aristocraticall than regall. And therefore the names of their dukes, marquesses, counties, gouernours, and councellors, commonly to be in their leagues expressed, and their seales thereto annexed: as the peace betwixt the Polonians and the Prussians, made by king *Sigismundus Augustus* was sealed with an hundred and three seales of the nobilitie of his countrey: neither was there fewer in the act of the lawfull creation of king *Henry* to be king of Polonia.

<small>The third mark of soueraigntie.</small>

The third marke of Soueraigne maiestie is to be of power to create and appoint magistrats, than which no more certaine signe can be, especially the principall officers, which are not vnder the commaund of other magistrats. This was the first law that *Publius Valerius* made after the expulsion of the kings out of Rome: that the magistrats should be chosen and appointed by the people. Which selfe same law was published also by the Venetians, at such time as they first assembled into the Gulfe, for the establishing of their state, as *Contarenus* writeth: than which law there is none more religiously kept by the Senat and the Venetian people. Yet much better is it kept in monarchies, where all is gouerned by one, and where the greatest, the meaner, yea and the least offices of all, as of *Porters, Sergeants, Clarkes, Trumpeters, Criers*, which in the Roman state were placed and displaced by the Roman magistrats are prouided for by order from the prince, euen vnto the meanest offices. I haue said the appointing of princes officers, that is to say, of the chiefe magistrats, for there is no Commonweale, where it is not permitted vnto greater magistrats, as also to many corporations and colledges, to make certaine meniall officers vnder them: as I haue before showed of the Romans. But yet that they doe by vertue of the office, which they hold, and as proctours created with power, to substitute other their deputies vnder them. We see also that clients and vassals, albeit that they hold their iurisdiction of some soueraigne prince in fealtie and homage, haue neuerthelesse power to establish judges and officers in their iurisdiction: but yet this power is giuen them by some soueraigne prince. For no doubt dukes, marquesses, counties, barons, and lieutenants of countries, were no other of their first institution but judges and officers; as we shall in due place declare. But sometimes in a popular estate power is giuen vnto the greater magistrats to create

<small>The lesser magistrates in a popular estate somtime created by the greater, but not without power from them which had the soueraigntie</small>

the lesser; as we read that the people of Carthage had a custome to make fiue magistrats, for to make choyce of the hundred and foure magistrats of the Commonweale; as they do also at Nuremberg, where the Censors which are chosen of the great Councell, chose the new Senators, and that done, giue vp their charge. The Senate which is of xxvj, making choyce of the eight Auntients: and afterward of the xiij of the seuen Burgamasters, and of the xij Iudges for ciuill causes, and fiue for criminall. Neither is this any new matter; but an old and auntient fashion. For *Aristotle* writeth, the people of Carthage to haue vsed to chuse fiue men, who according to their discretion still made of the hundred and foure magistrates: which was also a thing ordinarie vnto the Roman Censors, who by their discretion supplied the number of the Senators, which the Consuls did before by the sufferance of the people, who from the beginning made them, as *Festus Pompeius* saith. And sometime the dictators were for that purpose onely made to supply the number of the Senators. As *Fabius Buteo* named Dictator by the Consull *Terentius*, following the decree of the Senat, made choyce at one time of an hundred seuentie seuen Senators, in stead of them that were dead. Howbeit that to speake properly, a Senator is no magistrat, as we will show in the discourse concerning the Senat. But howsoeuer that it was, whether it were the

Consuls,

<small>H2 *For* princes officers *read* principal officers (cf Fr).   I7 of the xiii, of   Note at H1.</small>

Consuls, the Dictators, or Censors, that made choice of the Senators, & so supplied the Senat, they did it not but by the power of the people, which was also to be reuoked at the peoples pleasure. So may we also say of the Turkes Cadelesquires, which are as the kings two great Chauncelours, who haue power to place and displace all the Cadies and Paracadies, that is to say, the judges and their deputies. And in Ægypt, in the time of the Sultans gouernment, before it was by *Selymus* the first conquered, the great Edegnare, which was a Cunstable to the Sultan, had power to place all the other officers: as had in auntient time the Grand M. of the Pallace in Fraunce. And it is not long ago but that the chauncelour of Fraunce had power at his pleasure to bestow all offices which had none, or but some little fees, *viz.* of some three or foure crownes at the most: which was reuoked by king *Francis* the first. And albeit that alwaies the chauncelor, the great Edegnare, and the Grand M. of the pallace, had all their power from the kings and Sultans, as by them placed: yet was so great power verie daungerous vnto the former kings and Sultans, which by little and little haue since beene cut so short, as that in the raigne of *Charles* the seuenth, the verie baylieffes and seneschals were placed by the prince, who before were wont to be placed by the maiors, whose lieutenants they were. Sometime also it may be that magistrats, corporations, or colleges, haue power to nominat and chuse the principall magistrats: as we read in the records of the court of Paris, that by a law made in the yeare 1408, it was decreed that the officers of the high court of parliament should be made by election; and so thereupon commaundement was giuen vnto the chauncelour to go into parliament for the election for the offices vacant. Which law was againe reuiued by king *Lewes* the xj, in the yeare 1465. And after him in the time of *Charles* the eight, not only the presidents, the kings councellors, and aduocats, were made by election, but euen the kings atturney generall (who is the onely man of all the body of the court, which oweth not oath but to the king alone: albeit that the atturneyes of other parliaments, which he calleth substitutes, take their oath in the court) was chosen also by the suffrages of the court: In the yeare 1496. But yet all their letters of prouision & confirmation of their elections into their offices, then were, and yet are, always graunted by the king: without whose confirmation their election was to no purpose. Which may serue for aunswere to that which one might say, that *Arthure* duke of Bretaigne, was chosen Cunstable of Fraunce, by the voyces of all the princes, of the great Councell, and of the parliament in the yeare 1324. For albeit that the king *Charles* the sixt, was then distraught of his wits, & that the seales of France had in them not the image of the king, but of the queene onely: yet neuerthelesse the said new constable taking vpon him the gouernment of the kings sword, and of the French armie, being sworne to the keeping of the lawes, at the same instant acknowledged himselfe to hold his office and power in fealtie and homage of the king: so that all authoritie and power to commaund, may well seeme to flow and be deriued from the fountaine of the prince onely.

Yet may some say that the Great Palatine of Hungarie, who is the greatest magistrat of that kingdome, and the kings lieutenant generall, is chosen by the estates of the countrey: it is true; but yet his prouision, institution, and confirmation, belongeth vnto the king, who is the chiefe head and author of his power. Howbeit that the estates of the kingdome of Hungarie, yet pretend to haue the right to make choyce of their kings; the house of Austria maintaining the contrarie. And it seemeth that the kings haue by sufferance passed it ouer, that the estates should still haue the chusing of the great Palatine, so to cause them to forget the election of the king. Whereunto for all that they haue beene so obstinatly wedded, as that they haue chosen vnder the colour of protection, to put themselues vnder the Turkes slauerie, rather than to haue this

Great magistrats somtime chosen by the estats of the countrey, or otherwise: but still approued and confirmed by the king.

power

C 7–8 *of the court, in the yeare* 1496.   D 3 *For* 1324 (Fr) *read* 1424 (L).

power for the choyce of their kings (by the house of Austria) wrested from them. It is not therefore the election of great officers which declareth the right of soueraigntie; but the princes approbation, ratification, and confirmation, without which the magistrat is of no power at all. Yet if such creation of magistrats were by the founders of Commonweales, and law makers, so giuen vnto the people, or colleges, as that they could not from the people or colleges be taken, then truly the prince should not haue the right of soueraigne maiestie or power: for that the magistrats power were not to be attributed vnto the prince, but to the people; as by little and little it happened vnto the kings of Polonia. For when as by a law made by *Sigismundus Augustus*, all the magistrats of euerie countrey, were to be chosen by the particular states of euery gouernment; the maiestie of the kings, who also raigned by the good liking of the people, was therby much impaired. Which confirmation of magistrats so chosen, is no new thing; for euen from the time of the Gothes we read in *Cassiodorus*, that *Theodoricus* king of the Gothes, gaue his letters of confirmation vnto the officers whome the Senat had chosen; vsing these words in his letters directed vnto the Senat, for one whom they had made a Senator, *Iudicium vestrum P. C. noster Comitatur assensus*, Our consent, Reuerent fathers, doth accompany your iudgement. Now seeing that power to commaund ouer all the subiects of a Commonweale belongeth vnto him that holdeth therein the soueraigntie; it is good reason also that all magistrats should acknowledge their authoritie to proceed from him.

* Cassiodorus.lib. 1.Epist.6.

The fourth marke of soueraigntie.

But now let vs speake of the fourth marke of Soueraigntie, that is to wit, of the *Last Appeal*, which is and alwayes hath beene one of the most principall rights of soueraigntie. As a man may see after that the Romaines had driuen out their kinges: not onely the last Appeal, but euen all Appeales from the Magistrates, were by the Law Valeria reserued vnto the people. And for that the Consuls and other Magistrates oftentimes gaue small eare vnto them that did appeal vnto them, the same Law was often times * renewed: and by the Tribunitiall law Duillia the paine of death adioyned there vnto, for him that should oppose himselfe against the same; which Law *Liuie* calleth the foundation of the popular libertie: albeit that it were euill executed. The same Law was yet more straitly kept in Athens, where the last Appeal was reserued vnto the people, not onely from the Magistrates of the citie, but euen from the Magistrates of their allies and fellowes also: as the writings of *Zenophon* and *Demosthenes* do right well declare. The same Law *Contarenus* writeth to haue been the first that was by the Venetians made for the establishing of their Commonweale: viz. That all men might freely appeal from the Magistrates, vnto the Graund counsell of the people. Nether was *Francis Valori* Duke of Florence for any other cause slaine, then for not hauing giuen way vnto the Appeal, made from him vnto the Great counsell of the people, by three Florentines by him condemned to die, and so notwithstanding their appeal by him executed. But some may say, that not onely this Duke at Florence, but at Rome the *Dictators*, and other Magistrates also oftentimes put to death condemned citisens, notwithstanding their appeal made vnto the people, as is in many histories to be seene. Whereof there was an heauie example made by the Senate of Rome, which caused the remainder of the Legion sent to *Rhegium* being taken and brought to Rome, to be whipped and afterward beheaded without regard of the appeales by them made vnto the people: or to the intercessions of the Tribunes exclaiming, the sacred Lawes concerning Appeales to be violated, and troden vnder foote. Whereunto in briefe I aunswere, as did *Papinian*, That we ought not to rest our selues vpon that they doe at Rome, but on that which ought to bee there done. For it is most certaine, that a man might appeale from the Senat vnto the people: and that ordinatily

Liuius lib. 1. & 7 & 10.

F 10 countrey *i.e.* province   I 2 Xenophon

dinarily the opposition or intercession of one of the Tribunes, stayed the proceedings of the whole Senat; as we haue before touched. And the first that gaue the power vnto the Roman Senat to iudge without appeale, was *Adrian* the emperour, for the edict of *Caligula*, whereby he gaue power to all magistrats to iudge without appeale, tooke no place. And albeit that *Nero* decreed, that they which without cause had appealed vnto the Senat, should be punished with like punishment, as if they had appealed vnto his owne person: yet forbad he not men to appeale from the Senat vnto himselfe, although he had referred the appeales from all the magistrats vnto the Senat. But this aunswere seemeth directly contrary vnto that we haue before said. For if no appeale were to be made from the Senat vnto the emperour, but that the last appeale was vnto the Senat, then was not the last appeale the true marke of soueraigntie. I ioine also hereunto, that the Great master of the Pallace, whome they called *Præfectum Prætorio*, gaue iudgement without appeale, receiuing also the appeales of all the magistrats and gouernours of the empire, as sayth *Flauius Vopiscus*: as in euery Commonweale we see certaine courts and parliaments which gaue iudgement without appeale; as the eight parliaments in Fraunce, the foure courts in Spaine, the imperiall chamber in Germanie, the councell at Naples; the sortie at Venice, the Rota at Rome, the Senat at Milan; and so the greater courts of other cities, who heare and decide either all or most part of causes, both publike and priuat, without appeale: and in all the imperiall townes, duchies, and counties, depending of the empire, no appeale is to be made vnto the imperiall chamber, in criminall causes once iudged by the magistrats of the prince, or of the imperiall cities: whereby it appeareth the last appeale not to belong onely vnto the right of soueraigne maiestie. Whereunto I aunswere, vnder the name of Appeale, to be also contained requests made vnto the prince, which the law call Ciuill Supplications: so that when we may not appeale from the sentence of the greater magistrats, yet may we by way of request put vp our supplications vnto the prince; which hath moued many of our late lawyers to say, Ciuill supplications to belong vnto the right of soueraigne maiestie: and albeit that almost alwaies the decrees are againe iudged by the same judges as oft as request is made vnto the prince concerning a iudgement giuen: yet is it in his wil & power either to receiue or reiect the request: and oftentimes hee calleth the cause vnto himselfe therof to determine, or to reuerse that which hath bene done; or else remitteth it vnto other judges, which is the true marke of soueraigntie and last appeale, wherein the maiestie of the prince or people doth most appeare: forasmuch as it is not lawfull for any magistrat or judge to chaunge or amend their iudgement once giuen or recorded, without leaue of their soueraigne prince, and that vpon paine of false iudgement. And if so bee that the soueraigne prince would make an edict, that none of his subiects should appeale from any of his magistrats, or preferre any request vnto himselfe against their iudgements, as the emperour *Caligula* was about to haue done: yet neuerthelesse should it alwaies be lawfull for the subiects to appeale, or to exhibit their requests vnto the prince: For that the prince cannot so bind his owne hands, or make such a law vnto himselfe; either prohibit his grieued subiects from comming vnto him with their humble supplications and requests: For that such edicts concerning appeales and iudgements, are but ciuill decrees and lawes wherewith the prince cannot be bound, as we haue before said. For which cause it seemed a new and absurd thing vnto the Senat of France, and especially vnto *Michael de l' Hospital*, that the commissioners appointed to proceed against the president of Allemand, forbid him by a decree made against him, to come within twentie leagues of the court, so to cut him off from the meanes to preferre his petitions; which the king himself could not of right take from his subiect, althogh it were in his power to grant or

*Flauius Volpiscus in Floriano.

A soueraigne prince cannot by any edict prohibit his subiects to appeale from his magistrates or to prefer their humble requests vnto himselfe.

Q   reiect

E6–7 *For* of Allemand *read* l'Allemand (cf. Fr) *i.e.* François Alamant.   Notes at C2, D6.

reiect his request being once made vnto him knowne. We see also, that in all graunts of publike lands by way of pention, with power and iurisdiction vnto the children or neere kinsmen of the house of Fraunce, and generally in the erection of duchies, marquisats, counties, and principalities, fealtie and homage, appeale and soueraigntie, are still reserued: that sometime there is onely reseruation made of appeale and soueraigntie: as in the declaration made by king *Charles* the fift, to *Iohn* duke of Berrie, bearing date the third of March, in the yeare 1374: wherein is also fealtie and homage comprised. For it is certaine that the duchie of Berrie was then the portion giuen vnto the duke of Berry with the charge of rights royall, and reuersion to the crowne for want of heires male: as I haue learned by the letters of graunt, which are yet in the treasurie of Fraunce. We see also the like declaration of *Philip* Archduke of Austria, (*Charles* the fifts father) made to king *Lewes* the twelft, and another of him the same, in the yeare 1505: wherein he acknowledgeth and professeth himselfe readie to obey the decrees of the parliament of Paris, in regard of the countries of *Artois* and *Flaunders*, and of other lands which he held of the king; and not to forbid them of those countries to appeale vnto the court at Paris. And in the treatie of Arras, made betwixt king *Charles* the seuenth, and *Philip the* second, duke of Burgondy, there is expresse reseruation made of fealtie and homage, appeale and soueraigntie, for those lands which he and his aunceftors held in fee of the crowne of Fraunce. Neither did *Charles* the fift the French king take any other occasion to make warre against the English men, than for that their English magistrats and gouernors which had the gouernment of Aquitaine, vnder the fealtie of the French, would not heare the subiects appeales. At which time the court of Paris commaunded the king of England to be summoned, and for default of appearance pronounced sentence against him: whereby the duchie of Aquitaine was for that cause confiscated vnto the king, as is to bee seene by the decree of the parliament of Paris, giuen the xiiij of May, in the yeare 1370. For otherwise if a soueraigne prince shall remit vnto his vassall the right of appeale and soueraigntie; which is vnto himselfe due, he maketh him of a subiect a soueraigne prince; as did king *Francis* the first, discharging the duke of Loraine of all fealtie and homage, appeale and soueraigntie, for the castle of Chastelet vpon the Maze in the yeare 1517. But when hee suffered the same duke in soueraigne manner without appeale to gouern in the duchie of Bar; and that the dukes, officers, and magistrats afterward abused their permissiue authoritie, as in absolute soueraigntie, the kings atturney generall thereof complained vnto the king, aduising him not to suffer the rights of his soueraigne maiestie to be so impaired. Which thing *Anthonie* then duke of Loraine vnderstanding, and after him *Francis* his sonne, by recognisance in autentique manner declared, that their purpose was not in any thing to derogat from the fealtie and homage, appeale and soueraigntie that they ought vnto the crowne of Fraunce, by reason of the said duchie; and that they had not therein vsed soueraigne iustice but by sufferance: which letters of recognisance are in the publique records to be seene, and were afterward exhibited vnto the priuie councell, in the yeare 1564, in the raigne of *Charles* the ninth, who by all means sought by a most gratious and large charter to haue giuen vnto *Charles* then duke of Loraine, the soueraigntie of the duchie of Bar: but all in vaine, forasmuch as the king can by no meanes alienat from himselfe, the rights belonging vnto his soueraigntie, no not the high court of Paris assenting thereunto, although the power and authoritie of that court may where the king is, seeme to be nothing; in the presence of whom all the power and authoritie of all magistrats cease.

Wherfore the best & most expedient way, for the preseruation of a state is, neuer to giue any marke or right of soueraigntie vnto a subiect, and much lesse vnto a straunger:
for

F2 by way of pention *i.e.* in apanage (Fr)   H5 confiscated   H10 *For* Maze *read* Moselle.
Note at F7.

OF A COMMONWEALE. 171

for that is one step and degree to mount vnto his soueraigne maiestie. And therefore it was long doubted in the councell, whether power and authoritie without appeale, should be graunted vnto *Francis* duke of Alencon (who had made mee master of the requests and one of his councell) in that his dukedome; as had before bene graunted vnto the auntient dukes there. And although he were the kings best and most louing brother, yet one of the atturneyes generall was so bold as to say in full councell, That it were better to bring in twelue courts of parliament, than to suffer that, albeit that that iurisdiction was for a short time granted, and extraordinarie judges by the king appointed; with reseruation of appeales, in many cases and causes, as also with exception of fealtie and homage. Wherein our auncestors much offended, who with too much facilitie (should I say, or necessitie) graunted the same iurisdiction vnto the dukes of Normandie. For by this meanes the dukes of Britaigne and Burgundie reuolted from our kings vnto the kings of England; for that such judges were denied them, as had bene graunted vnto the dukes of Alencon: taking it grieuously themselues, in the name of their magistrats to be summoned vnto the court at Paris, there to haue those things reuersed which their magistrats had vniustly determined; althogh sometime they were things of right small weight and importance; whereof the dukes of Britaigne complained both vnto king *Philip* the Faire, and *Philip* the Long, who by their letters patents sent vnto the court of parliament in February 1306, and in October 1316, declared that their meaning was not, that the duke of Britaigne or his officers, should bee called before them into the court; but in question of soueraigntie, or in case they should deny to doe iustice, or els had giuen false iudgement.

No marke or right of soue-raigntie is by the prince to be bestowed vpon his subiect, or a stranger.

The same we are to thinke of all the princes and cities of Germanie, from whome euen in priuat iudgements men may iustly appeale vnto the imperiall chamber, if the matter exceed the summe of 50 crowns, or if any controuersie be betwixt the cities and princes themselues. Whereby it is to be vnderstood, neither the German princes, nor cities to haue in them the right of soueraigntie: For that it is a capitall crime, euen treason it selfe, to appeale from a soueraigne prince, except he appeale as did that Greeke (whosoeuer he was) who appealed from *Philip* king of Macedon euill aduised, vnto himselfe being better aduised. Which manner of appeale *Lewes* of Burbon, prince of Conde vsed also from the interlocutorie sentence of *Francis* the second, the French king, which he hauing vnderstood the cause, is said to haue giuen against him in the priuie councel: Which manner of appeale *Baldus* the great lawyer alloweth as good, and to be receiued. And well it would beseeme the maiestie of soueraigne princes to behold and follow the example of that Macedonian king, who receiued the appeale; or if they would needs that their decrees whatsoeuer should stand fast and irremouable, because they would not seeme vnconstant or variable, that then they should do as did the same king to *Machetas*, who of his owne goods recompensed him, for that hee had vniustly condemned him in, without chaunging of his former decree and iudgement.

From this marke of Maiestie, and benefit of supreame Appeale, dependeth also the power to grant grace and pardon vnto the condemned, contrarie to iudgement giuen, and to the rigour of the lawes; be it for life, be it for goods, be it for honour, or recalling from banishment: for it is not in the power of the magistrats or judges, how great soeuer that they be, to graunt the least of these things vnto the condemned person, or of themselues, to alter any thing of the iudgements by them once giuen. And albeit that the Proconsuls and gouernours of prouinces, had as much power in their iurisdiction, as had all the magistrats of Rome together: yet so it was, that it was not lawfull for them so much as to restore him whome they had but for a time banished (as wee

The sixt marke of soueraigntie.

Q ij read

read in the letters of *Plinie* the younger, gouernor of Asia vnto *Traian* the emperor) and much lesse giue pardon vnto men condemned to die: which is most straitly forbidden all magistrats in euery Commonweale, be it well or euill ordered or gouerned. And albeit that *Papirius Cursor*, the dictator, may seeme at the request of the people to haue giuen pardon to *Fabius Max*. collonell of the horsemen, for hauing giuen battle contrarie to his commaund, although he had slaine xxv thousand of the enemies: yet neuerthelesse in effect it was the people which gaue the pardon: albeit that they most instantly besought the dictator to pardon the fault: Which they themselues might at the same time haue done, but yet had rather to request it of *Papirius*, than to take the guiltie person from him against his will. For *Fabius* vnderstanding himselfe in his absence to be by the dictator condemned, appealed vnto the people: before whom *Papirius* defended his iudgement, as iustly giuen against *Fabius*: which a man of his vertue and seueritie would not haue done, if an appeale might not haue bene made from the dictator, vnto the people: and that in it was the power of life and death. *Sergius Galba* the Orator also, in like iudgement by *Cato* the Censor, attainted of treason, tooke his refuge vnto the people, who moued with his teares, and embracing of his children, pardoned him. Whereupon *Cato* said, That *Galba* had beene well whipped, had hee not taken himselfe vnto his teares and his children. The same power of life and death had also the people of Athens, as appeareth by *Demosthenes*, and *Alcibiades*, who both condemned, were afterward by the people pardoned, and againe restored both vnto their goods and honour. And amongst the Venetians it is not lawfull for any their magistrats, no not for the duke himselfe, the Senat, or the Decemuiri, to graunt pardon vnto the condemned: for that is left vnto the discretion of the great councel of the Venetian gentlemen onely. The Decemuiri before abusing their power by sufferance, graunted pardons, and neuerthelesse was order taken in the yeare 1523, that the counsell of the Sages, which are in number xxij, should therein be assisting vnto them: and that the pardon should take no place, without the generall consent of them all: but at length in the yeare 1562, the councell was forbidden at all to meddle, or to haue to doe in that matter. And albeit that the emperour *Charles* the fift, in the erection of the Senat at Milan, graunted thereunto all the markes of soueraigntie, as vnto his lieutenant and deputie in his absence, comming verie neere vnto absolute soueraigntie: yet so it is, that hee still reserued vnto himselfe the power to graunt pardon and mercie vnto the condemned; as I haue learned by the letters patents by him graunted: which hath bene a thing right straitly obserued and kept in all Monarchies. And although that in Florence during the popular state, the eight men without all right had vsurped the power to graunt pardons: yet was that power againe restored vnto the people by *Sodorin*, after the chaunge of the state. As for other kings they haue still thought nothing more royall, than to deliuer the condemned from death: neither do they suffer the judges or magistrats of other dukes and princes, to examine the letters graunted by the king for the restoring of the condemned: although that they examine the pardon graunted. And albeit that king *Francis* the first had giuen vnto his mother power to graunt pardon vnto the condemned: yet for all that the court of Paris, hauing taken order to haue it showed vnto the king, that it was one of the fairest markes of soueraigntie, which could not be communicated vnto a subiect without impairing of his maiestie: the Queene mother thereof aduertised, renounced this priuilege, and restored the letters patents vnto the king, before they were of her requested. For indeede that prerogatiue could not of right bee graunted vnto the French Queene, neither any other the proper markes of Soueraigntie.

And albeit that the Roman lawes say that the empresse is dispensed with from all edicts

Things properly belonging vnto the soueraigntie of a prince can in no wise be imparted vnto a subiect.

H5 1523 (Fr) 1524 (L)   H6 For xxii *read* xxxii (Fr, and cf. 158 I2).   I7 *For* other kings *read* our kings. Note at I10.

OF A COMMONWEALE. 173

A edicts and lawes: yet that taketh no place in this realme of Fraunce; yea there is found a decree in the records of the court, in the yeare 1365, in Iuly: whereby the queene was condemned to lay downe in the court the money of her demaunded, whilest the matter was in tryall; that the creditor might demaund it so laid downe vppon good caution giuen: which by the Roman law is a meere iniurie, so to begin sute of execution. I find also that king *Charles* the sixt, gaue power to *M. Arnald de Corbie*, chauncelour of Fraunce, by letters pattents, the xiij of March, in the yeare 1401, to grant pardons vnto the condemned, some of the great Councell being present with him: but that was at such time as the chauncelours were almightie, hauing all in their owne hands: and that king *Charles* the sixt was then not in the power of himselfe but of
B others, by reason of his maladie.

Now if any man shall obiect and say, That in auntient times the gouernours of prouinces gaue pardons, as we yet may see by the custome of Henault, and of Daulphinie: as also that the bishop of Ambrun, by autentique charters pretended this power. Hereunto I aunswere, that such customes and priuileges, wrongfully wrested and extorted from our kings, were of good right abrogated by an edict of king *Lewes* the twelft. And if such priuileges be of no force: so may we also say their confirmations to bee of no more strength. For the confirmation is neuer any thing worth, if the priuilege bee of it selfe naught. Now must it needes be naught, for that it cannot bee seperated from the crowne. For as wee haue before said, that the priuileges by princes
C euen lawfully graunted, cannot stand good for euer: so the rightes of Soueraigntie, which cannot by the kings themselues bee graunted vnto any, without giuing away of ther Scepter and kingdome, can much lesse being granted, bee by them confirmed.

Priuileges wrongfully wrested from kings cannot by any new confirmation be made good.

As for Gouernours, Deputies, Lieutenants generall of Soueraigne princes, it is another reason; for that they haue not that power by priuilege, or by office, but by commission, as the deputies or lieutenants of their princes. But in the state of a well ordered Commonweale, this power of Soueraigntie ought not to bee giuen to any, neither by commission, neither by title of office, except it bee for the establishing of a Regent in his gouernment, for the great distance of places; or for the cap-
D tiuitie of Soueraigne princes: or for that they are furious; or else in their infancie. As it was done by *Lewes* the ninth, who for his tender yeares, was by the estates of Fraunce committed to the tuition of his mother *Blanche* of Castile; after that she had giuen certaine princes for assurance that shee should not giue the tuition of him to any other person. So the gouernment of the kingdome was committed vnto *Charles* the fift, as Regent during the captiuitie of his father king *Iohn*. And in the captiuitie of *Francis* the first, *Louise* of Sauoy his mother, tooke vppon her the protection of the kingdome committed vnto her by the king her sonne; with all the royalties thereof, in the title of Regent. And the duke of Bedford Regent in Fraunce, king *Charles* the sixt being there distraught of his wits.

E But heer may one say vnto mee, that notwithstanding the decree of *Lewes* the xij. the chapiter of the church of Roan pretendeth alwaies to haue priuiledge to graunt pardon in the fauour of S. Romane: the day before whose feast, it forbiddeth all the judges, yea and the parlament of Roan it selfe, to execute or put to death any one of such as then be condemned; (as I haue seene it put in practise being in commission for the Prince, for the generall reformation of Normandie) and for that the court notwithstanding the chapiters pardon, had after the feast caused to bee put to death one, which it had before the feast condemned: the chapiter thereof greeuously complayned vnto the king; hauing to friend one of the princes of the blood; the parlament

The great priuilege of the chapiter of the church of Roan in granting pardon vnto the condemned.

Q iij sent

E2 Roan *i.e.* Rouen   Notes at A5, C5, C7, E9.

sent also their deputies, amongst whom *Bigot* the kings attourney was verie earnest in his oration in the Senat for the abuse, and encroaching vpon the kings maiestie: but the fauour of the great bishops more preuailing then reason, that priuilege was for all that he could say or do with the publike shame and losse continued: but was since taken away by king *Henry* the third. This priuilege had great affinitie with that which was giuen vnto the Vestall virgins at Rome, which was to giue pardon vnto him that was going to execution, if any one of the Vestal virgins by chaunce happened to meete him, as saith *Plutarke* in the lyfe of *Numa*. The like custome whereof is yet kept in Rome, for if a condemned man there meet a Cardinall, he is thereby deliuered from punishment. But I deeme that to bee most pernitious in the priuilege of S. Romane, that no man could enioy the benefit thereof which had but lightly offended: but he onely that had done the most execrable villanies that were possible to be found, such as the king vsed not to pardon, that such offences as could nether by the lawes of God nor man, nor by the fauour of Princes be pardoned, might yet vnder the colour of S. Romanes priuilege be remitted and forgiuen. But that is ioyned with the greatest impietie to thinke the pardon to be so much the more acceptable to God, by how much the fact committed is the more haynous or detestable. But I am of opinion (sauing alwaies the better iudgement) that no soueraigne Prince, nether yet any man a liue can pardon the punishment due vnto the offence which is by the law of God death, no more then he can dispence with the law of God, wherevnto he is himselfe subiect. And if it be so, that the magistrat deserue capitall punishment, which dispenseth with the law of his king; how shall it be lawfull for a soueraigne prince, to dispence with his subiect from the law of God? And further if the Prince him selfe cannot giue away the least ciuill interest of his subiect, or pardon the wrong done vnto an other man: how can he than pardon the wrong done vnto almightie God? or the murther wilfully committed; which by the law of God is death, for all the pardon he can giue. But then wherein (might a man say) should the princes mercie show it selfe or appeare? if it could not show grace vnto the punishment appointed by the law of God? Wherunto I aunswere, that there are meanes plentie, as in pardoning bloodshed committed by chaunce, or in defence of a mans selfe, or in mitigating the rigour of the positiue ciuill lawes: as if the prince should vpon paine of death forbid a man to beare armes, or to carrie victuals vnto the enemie; pardon shall yet well be bestowed vpon him that hath borne armes for the defence of himselfe onely; or on him which constrained by pouertie, hath sold victuals deere vnto the enemie, to releeue his owne great necessitie. Or whereas by the law the punishment for theft is death, the good prince may conuert that punishment into the restitution of foure fold, which is the punishment by the law * of God appointed. But the wilfull murderer *You shall take him* (saith the law) *from my sacred altar, neither shalt thou haue pitie on him, but cause him to dye the death: and afterwards I will stretch forth my great mercies vpon you*. Neuerthelesse the Christian kings on that day which they commaund to bee most holy kept, as on *Good Friday*, vse for most part to pardon some one man or other, condemned of most horrible and notorious crime. Now pardons graunted to such villaines drawe after them plagues, famine, warres, and ruines of Commonweales; and that is it for which the law of God saith, That in punishing them that haue deserued to dye, they shall take away the cause from among the people: for of an hundred villaines there commeth scarce two of them into the triall of iustice: and of those that come, the one halfe of them for want of proofe and of witnesses escape vnpunished: and then if when they are proued princes graunt vnto them pardon, what exemplarie punishment shall there be for offences and villanies committed in the Commonweale? And many offendors fenders, when they cannot of their owne prince obtaine grace and pardon, interpose the fauour of some other forren prince, who becommeth an intercessour for them. Whereof the States of Spaine complained vnto king *Philip*, presenting vnto him a request, to the end he should aduertise his ambassador in Fraunce, no more in the behalfe of the French king, to request pardon of the king of Spaine, for the condemned men which had retired themselues out of Spayne into Fraunce: for that hauing obtained pardon, they many times slew the judges, who had before condemned them. But of all the graces and pardons that a prince can giue, there is none more commendable, than when he pardoneth the iniurie done against his owne person: and of all capitall punishments none is more acceptable vnto God, than that which with most seueritie is executed, for the wrong done vnto the maiestie of himselfe. But what then are we for to hope for of the prince, which most cruelly reuengeth his owne iniuries, and pardoneth the wrong done to others; and especially those which are directly done to the dishonour of almightie God. *The most gratious and commendable pardon that a prince can giue.*

Now that which we haue said concerning the grace and pardon graunted by a soueraigne prince vnto men condemned, is to the vttermost to be extended, euen vnto the preiudice of the great lords, vnto whome the confiscation of the offendours lands or goods by law or custome belong, who are not to be receiued to debate or impugne the pardon graunted by the prince; as by decree of parliament hath bene adiudged. Now many there be, which draw the grace of the princes gracious restitutions vnto priuat iudgements: as when a man is for want of councell deceiued or cosoned; or requesteth the benefit of his minoritie, which in many cities and Commonweals are proper vnto soueraigne princes: but yet are not the markes of soueraigne maiestie, except onely the legitimating of bastards, of fees, and such like: for why the rest were partly by the magistrats hauing vnderstood the cause, and partly by the lawes and customes vsually graunted. For in the lawes of *Charles* the vij and *Charles* the viij, it is expresly commaunded vnto the judges, in deciding of causes, not to haue any regard of the decrees of forraine courts, further than they should with equitie agree: which by this common clause vnto all decrees in this realme commonly annexed (*Si satis superque apparet*, If it shall sufficiently, and more than sufficiently appeare) is declared. Which clause if it be not ioyned vnto the decree, the magistrat hath but to vnderstand of the fact; the punishment thereof being reserued vnto the law, and the pardon vnto the soueraigne prince. And that is it for which *Cicero* crauing pardon of *Caesar* for *Ligarius* saith, *I haue oftentimes pleaded with thee before the iudges, but I neuer said, for him whom I defended, Pardon him my lords, he was deceiued, he thought it not, if euer hee do so againe, &c.* So children vse to say vnto their parents, of whome they craue pardon: *But before the iudges we say, That the crime is for euill will forged, the accusor is a slanderer, the witnesses false and subborned.* In which words he plainely shewed, that *Caesar* hauing soueraigne power, had also the power of life and death, (and so to graunt pardon) which the judges had not.

Now as for liege fealtie and homage, it appeareth, that it is one of the greatest rights of soueraigntie; as we haue before declared: in respect of him to whom it is due, without exception. *The sixt marke of soueraigntie.*

As for the right and power to coyne money, it is of the same nature with the law, and there is none but he which hath power to make a law, which can appoint the valew, weight, and stampe of the coyne: which is well to be vnderstood by the Greeke and Latine worde; for the Latine word *Nummus*, seemeth well to haue beene deriued of the Greek word νόμος. For nothing is in a Commonweale of greater consequence next vnto the law, than the value, weight, and stampe of the coyne; as we haue in a spe- *The seuenth marke of soueraigntie.*

Q iiij ciall

E9–176 F1 in a speciall treatise *i.e.* in his *Response de Jean Bodin à M. de Malestroit*

ciall treatise declared: and in euerie well ordered Commonweale, none but the soueraigne prince hath power to appoint the same. As we read they did in Rome, when the value of the Victoriat was appointed and set downe, it was done by an expresse law of the people. And albeit that the Senat by decree to ease the publike necessitie, made the halfe pound of copper as much worth as the pound; and a while after the quarter, as much worth as the pound, vntill that the ounce was valued as much worth as the pound: yet all this was done by the consent of the Tribunes, without which nothing that the Senat had therein decreed was of any force. And after that, *Constantine* the emperour made a law, That they which had coyned false money should be punished as men guiltie of high treason: which law all princes haue most straitly kept, taking vnto themselues the confiscations of false coynes, excluding all others, which haue any claime thereto. With like punishment also are they to be pnnished, which without the princes leaue coyne good money. And albeit that many particular men in this realme, had in auntient time priuilege to coyne money, as the countie of Touraine, the bishops of Meaux, Cahors, Agde, and Ambrun, the counties of S. Paule, of Marche, Neuers, Blois, and others: yet for all that king *Francis* the first, by a generall edict took away all those priuileges: which could not indeed be graunted: but beeing graunted, were by the law made void: ioyning hereunto also, that they were not to endure, but for the life of them that graunted them, as we haue before showed in the nature of priuileges: howbeit that this marke and right of soueraigntie ought not in any sort to be at all communicated vnto a subiect. As it was well declared to *Sigismundus Augustus*, king of Polonia, who in the yeare 1543, hauing giuen priuilege vnto the duke of Prusse, to coyne money: the estates of the countrey made a decree, wherein it was comprised, that the king had no power to giue away that right, as beeing inseparable from the crowne. For which selfe same reason the Archbishop of Gnesne in Polonia, and the Archbishop of Canterburie in England, both chauncelours, hauing obtained the same right and priuilege from their kings, were thereof againe depriued. And for this cause all the cities of Italie holden of the empire, which had of the former emperours obtained this priuilege of coyning of money; in the treatie at Constance gaue vp the same vnto the emperour, excepting them of Luca, vnto whom in fauor of pope *Lucius* the third, their countrey man, the emperour at his request graunted that priuilege. We read also, that the principall occasion that *Peter* king of Arragon tooke hold of, to driue *Iames* king of Maiorque out of his kingdome was, for hauing coined money; pretending that he had no right nor power so to doe. Which was also one of the occasions that *Lewes* the xj tooke hold of, to make warre vpon *Francis* duke of Britaigne, for that hee had stamped a coyne of gold, contrarie to the treatie made in the yeare 1465. And the Romans when as they suffered money of Brasse, and siluer to be coyned in all their prouinces, yet did they forbid any to be there coyned of gold, reseruing that still vnto themselues. Howbeit that *Iohn* duke of Berry had priuilege of *Charles* the fift, the French king, to coyne money of both mettals; who because hee would not any thing therein offend, caused peeces of gold to bee coyned with the figure of a sheepe vpon them, of the finest and purest gold that euer was either before or since coyned in this realme.

Yet is it not to be omitted, that though the prince contrarie vnto the law, shall giue to any man power to stampe money, that the worth and valour thereof stil dependeth of the soueraigne prince; in such sort, that they which so coyne the same, haue no other profit thereby but the stampe onely; whereof princes do wonderfully vaunt and glorie. But of auntient time in the Roman Commonweale, whilest it was a popular state, the *Triumuiri Monetales*, or masters of the mint, coyned the money with such a stamp

or

The right and power to coine monie the inseperable marke of soueraigntie: to be granted vnto subiects.

G1 *For* confiscations of false coynes *read* confiscations of false coyners (cf. Fr) *i.e.* of their property. G2 punished   G4 *For* countie *i.e.* count *read* viscount (Fr and L).   G4 Touraine (Fr 3–8) Turaine (Fr 1–2) *properly* Turenne (L).

OF A COMMONWEALE.

or marke as they themselues thought good, with their names & these letters thereupon, *III Viri, A.A.A. FF.* which *Caulis* bailieffe of the mountaines interpreteth, *Ære, Argento, Auro, Flauo, Ferunto*: but more truely thus, *Trium viri, Auro, Argento, Ære, Flando, Feriundo*. And truely *Seruius* king of the Romans was the first that there stamped an heauy coyne of brasse, with the figure or impression of an Oxe vpon it, to the imitation of *Theseus* king of Athens, who had coyned money with the same figure or marke, and the figure of an Owle. Whereby it appeareth the Greeke and Latine princes of old, not to haue bene touched with that vaine desire of glorie, wherewith other princes were tormented: and wherafter the kings of Asia and Affrike most greedily longed. The first that coyned money in Greece with his owne image thereon, was *Philip* king of Macedon: which peeces of money were therof called *Philippæi*; therein imitating the Persean kings, who called their peeces of gold first stamped with the image of *Darius*, by the name of *Dariques*. Whereof king *Darius* was so ielous (as *Herodotus* writeth) as that he caused *Ariander* gouernour of Ægypt to bee beheaded, for hauing stamped the money with his owne image. As for the same cause also the emperour *Commodus* beheaded his minion *Pecenninus*. And also king *Lewes* the xij hauing left all the power and right of Soueraignty vnto the Genowayes, whom he had ouercome, forbad them neuerthelesse to stampe their money with any other marke or figure, than with his owne image, in stead of the forme of a Gibbet, which they before gaue, and yet giue vpon their money, as the marke of iustice.

King Seruius the first that coined monie in Rome.

Plutarch in Theseo.

Philip of Macedon the first that coined monie in Grece with his owne image thereon.

Now if the power of coyning money be one of the rights and markes of Soueraigntie; then so is also the power to appoint measures and weights; although that by the customes receiued there is none so pettie a lord, which pretendeth not to haue this right. Whereby it commeth to passe, that by the infinit varietie of weights and measures, the Commonweale taketh no small harme. Which was the cause that the kings *Philip* the Faire, *Philip* the Long, and *Lewes* the xj had resolued, that there should be in this kingdome but one manner of weight and measure: and now the commissioners appointed for that purpose, by comparing them together, had made euen all the measures and weights of this realme, and brought the matter to good effect, had not king *Lewes* by death bene taken away, before it was fully perfected: yet the booke whereby the same might more easily be brought to passe, is yet extant in the court of accounts howbeit that the execution thereof proued more difficult than was thought it would haue done, by reason of the great contention, and sutes that thereof arise. Neuerthelesse we read in *Polybius*, that the same was wel executed in all the cities of Achaia, and Morea, where they had not but like money, like weights, like measures, customes, lawes, religion, officers, and gouernment.

The eight marke of soueraigntie.

The great varietie of waights and measures hurtfull to a commonweale.

Lib. 3.

As for the right to impose taxes, or imposts vpon the subiects, is as proper vnto soueraigne maiestie, as is the law it self: not for that a Commonweale cannot stand without taxes and tallages, as the President the M. hath well noted, that taxes were not leuied in this realme, but since the time of Saint *Lewes* the king. But if it must needs be that they must for the publike necessitie be leuied or taken away; it cannot bee done but by him that hath the soueraigne power; as it hath bene iudged by a decree of parliament, against the duke of Burgundie; and many times since, aswell in the high court of parliament, as also in the priuie Councell. And for that diuers particular lords, cities, and corporations, vnder show of the common good, haue imposed diuers taxes and payments vpon their people: king *Charles* the ninth, by a generall edict by him made in the parliament at Orleans, expresly forbiddeth them so to doe without leaue: albeit that for the common necessitie they be borne withall in so doing without commission, so that they exceed not the summe of twentie fiue pounds. And afterward

The ninth marke of soueraigntie.

A2 *Caulis i.e.* Guillaume du Choul   B6 *Pecenninus*: Pecennius (L 1) Perennius (L 2 and Fr) properly Perennis (L 3–5)   D9 *For* the M. *read* le Maistre *i.e.* Gilles le Maistre.   Note at E7.

ward the same edict was more straitly againe renewed at *Moulins*, well agreeing both with law and equitie. And although that the Roman Senat in time of warres, yea and the Censors themselues imposed certaine taxes and payments, which could hardly haue bene extorted from the bodie of the whole commonaltie: yet so it was, that that still passed by the sufferance of the Tribunes of the people, who oft times also opposed themselues against the same. Yea and that in such sort, that they presented a request vnto the people, that from that time forward no man vpon paine of his head should bee so hardie, as to cause any law to be passed in the campe: for that the Senat by subtill meanes had there in the campe at Sutrium, caused to be published that notable imposition, which they called *Vicesima Manumissorū*, that is to say, the twentith part of the goods of them that were manumised; vnder colour that it was to pay the armie withall: which thereunto right willingly agreed: and so suffered the law to passe. And in the second Carthaginensian warre, at such time as there was great want of coyne in the common treasurie; there was by a law made a taxe generally imposed vppon euery man, which was by another contrarie law againe repealed, after the returne of *Paulus Æmylius*, who with the spoyles of *Perseus* king of Macedon, so filled the citie, and euerie priuat man also with wealth, as that the people was from that time discharged of all taxes and payments, vntill the Triumuirat ciuill warre, about an hundred yeares after, vntill that such new taxes and tributes as by the power or couetousnes of former tyrants had bene imposed vpon the people, were by the good * emperour *Pertinax* againe eased and taken away.

marginal note: The Romaine commonweale greatly relieued by the great riches by Paulus Emilius brought to Rome, after the ouerthrowe of king Perseus

marginal note: *Herodianus*.

But here might some say, diuers particular lords here and there, to exact not onely customes, but tributes also, not onely in Fraunce, where (*as Cæsar* hath most truly written) nothing is more contemptible than the vulgar people: but in England and Germanie, and much more straitly in Denmarke, Polonia, and Norway: which impositions and tributes, are confirmed and growne strong, both by long prescription of time, and vse of iudgements: yea and that to be lawfull, euen vnto such as haue neither soueraigntie, nor any iurisdiction at all, the court of Paris hath adiudged. Whereunto I aunswere, that the thing hauing begun by abuse, and by long continuance of time inueterat, hath well some colour of prescription: but yet an abuse can neuer be so ouergrowne, but that the law shall euer be of greater force than it; whereby the abuse is to be reformed: and for that cause it was forbidden by an edict of Moulins, that any tribute should be exacted of the subiects, vnder the colour of prescription: for that many lawyers and judges haue exposed all the strength and force of iudgements onely in prescription alone: not regarding whether that which is in question can of right bee prescribed or not.

Now if *Pompeius* hath denied, that the common high way can by any continuance of time be prescribed vpon: why then should these men thinke the rights of customes and tributes, or of soueraigne maiestie to be prescribed against; and yet the common high way belongeth not vnto the right of Soueraigntie. Wherefore it were better to confesse (which yet without deadly wrong cannot bee done) those aforesaid things which we haue spoke of, not at all to belong vnto the right of soueraigne maiestie: or else to say that the kingdome it selfe, and in briefe the royall crowne and scepter might be prescribed vpon. The same we are to thinke also of the exemptions from the payment of taxes and tributes, which no man can graunt vnto another man, but hee which hath the soueraigne power in a Commonweale: which is also prouided for in an article of the edict at Moulins: neither is that enough, but that the charters of such immunities graunted, must be also enrolled in the records of the court of accounts, and be allowed of by the judges of the court of Aydes. But what kind of taxes and tributes there

---

G8–9 hundred yeares after, WHEN TRIBUTE WAS AGAIN DEMANDED OF THE PEOPLE; AND MUCH INCREASED, untill that such (cf. L) (cf. *Digest*, 43, 11, 2).   I7 For Pompeius *read* Pomponius (L only) *but properly* Javolenus
Notes at G7, H10.

there be, and how farre they are to be exacted, shall in due place be declared: let it now for the present suffice, it to appeare, that right and power to belong only vnto Soueraigne maiestie.

Now many there be that thinke also, that to haue power to lay an imposition vpon salt, is a more proper marke of Soueraigntie than the rest: and yet therof giue no good reason. For almost in euery Commonweale we see salt pits and mines both to be, & alwayes to haue bene in priuat mens possession, not onely vpon the sea coasts towardes the South (for toward the north it hardeneth not with the Sunne) but also in the mediterranean regions, wherein mines of salt, and wels of salt water are found. As in Spaine, in Italie, Fraunce, and the countrey of Cracouia, is found salt in great aboundance. Yea euen at Rome we read, some priuat men to haue had salt mines. Yet true it is, that manie soueraigne princes haue of auntient time imposed tribute vpon salt; as did *Lysimachus* king of Thrace, *Ancus Martius* king of Rome, *Philip Valois* king of France, who were the first that exacted tribute vpon salt, euery one in his owne kingdome. And albeit that by the law Valeria the people of Rome were freed from such customes & tributes, as had by their kings bene brought in and imposed vpon them: yet *Liuius* the Censor thought no imposition in the Commonweale lighter or fitter, than that which was laid vpon salt; who thereof surnamed *Liuius Salinator*, (or *Liuius* the Salter.) For why that imposition little or nothing impaireth the right of priuat men: but that they still remaine lords and owners of their salt pits, aswell as of their other mines, sauing vnto the Soueraigne prince his rights and customs.

But forasmuch as the sea it selfe cannot be proper vnto any priuat man, the rights thereof belonging vnto such soueraigne princes as dwell thereby, who may lay impositions thereupon thirtie leagues off from their owne coast, if there bee no other soueraigne prince neerer to let them, as it was adiudged for the duke of Sauoy. Neither can any but a soueraigne prince giue them letters of safe conduct; which the Italians call *Guidage*; nor yet of right take any wracke: as is expresly prouided for by the decree of the emperour *Fredericke* the second. A thing truely most barbarous, and not in auntient time of soueraigne princes vsed, shamefully to suffer the reliques of the goods and fortunes of such as haue by shipwracke miserably perished, and whome we ought with some part of our owne to releeue, being cast vpon our coast, and which ought with good faith to be againe restored, to be most shamefully I say spoyled. Yet such is the manner of all that haue ports vpon the sea, in this case to show such extremitie aswell vnto their owne people, as to straungers. But by what right doe you aske? The common errour maketh the right: or if the wrong be done not by errour, but by knowledge, then it is meere wickednesse, masked with the vaile of errour. For I haue heard that at such time as the emperours ambassadours complayned vnto *Henry* the second, the French king, in the yeare 1556, that two gallies which had suffered wracke vpon the coast of Corcyca, were taken by *Iordan Vrsin*, requesting to haue the same gallie againe restored: he was aunswered by *Anne Mommerance* then constable of Fraunce, that wracks by the law of all nations belonged vnto such princes as ruled vpon the coasts whereon they were cast. Which law was so strong, as that *Andrew Doria* neuer so much as complained of the losse of two of his gallies, confiscated by the prior of Capona the French Admyrall, for casting anchor onely vppon the land without leaue, which of antient time men by the law of nations might right lawfully do. And whereas by the Roman law it was lawfull for any man to seise vppon things lost, or vppon goods or lands vacant and forbidden: now it is onely lawfull vnto them which haue the soueraigne power, or some other iurisdiction by law or custome confirmed vnto them, to take vnto themselues things lost or forsaken, and that after a certaine determi-

Sidenotes: To lay an imposition vpon salt, no marke of soueraigntie. — The kings which layed the first imposition vpon salt. — How farre off a soueraign prince may lay impositions vpon the sea, from his owne coast. — Wrackes by what small right they belong to soueraigne princes.

A9 salt water   B8 thereof WAS surnamed   C3 *For* belonging *read* belong.   E3–4 Capoua
Notes at C8, E2.

nat time: which in a thing moueable is defined to be fortie dayes after the publication of the thing lost or forsaken: except it be in the meane time by the right owner chalenged. And as for vacant possessions, the Roman emperours haue decreed, That they may at any time within foure yeares be againe recouered by the prince: but that after foure yeares once expired, a man may prescribe euen against the common receipt. But forasmuch as these things are also graunted vnto priuat men, they no more belong vnto the right of Soueraigntie, than it doth to haue a receipt of his owne: which is not a thing common vnto priuat men onely, but euen the prince himselfe hath his owne receipt diuided from the publike receipt; and his owne possessions seperat apart from the possessions of the Commonweale: and so diuers officers were by the Roman emperours appoynted vnto both. So *Lewes* the xij the French king, hauing obtained the crowne, erected the chamber at Blois, for his particular demaines of Blois, Montfort, and Cousi, which he commaunded to be diuided from the dukedome of Orleans, and the other publike possessions; and the accounts thereof to be kept apart by themselues. But amongst the rights of receipt, there be some that belong not, but vnto the soueraigne prince onely: as the confiscation of goods or lands in cases of high treason, vnder which are comprehended also such as be conuicted of impietie against God, which we call Heresie; or of offence against the Commonweale, as in coyning false money. Howbeit if our late lawyers haue with two much learned and curious subtiltie in an hundred and fiftie chapters found out the lawes and rights of the receipt: but yet so as that of one they make ten, that so they may seeme the moe: so confounding and mingling the rights of soueraigntie with the rights of receipt (which are also common vnto priuat men) and publike things with things priuat. The other rights of receipt are almost all common vnto the soueraigne prince, with other lords iusticiaries, as to haue right vnto treasure found: and the power to graunt Faires, which was in auntient time a marke of Soueraigntie; as now it is at this present comprised vnder the case of priuileges.

To grant letters of Marque, or of reprisall now to belong only vnto the soueraign prince.

As for the right of Marque, or of Reprisall, which soueraigne princes haue proper vnto themselues from all others, it was not of auntient time proper vnto a soueraigne prince; but permitted vnto euery man without leaue, either of magistrat or of prince to take reprisall, which the Latines called *Clarigatio*: howbeit that the princes by little and little gaue this power vnto magistrats and gouernours; and in the end reserued this right vnto their owne soueraigntie, for the better assurances of their peaces and truces, which were oftentimes broken by the rashnesse of some particular men, abusing this right of Marque or Reprisal. In this realme the parliament graunted letters of Marque, as we find by the decree of the xij of Februarie 1392, vntill that *Charles* the eight by an especiall edict, reserued that power vnto himselfe, in the yeare 1485. It is also of our men properly called a royaltie or right of soueraigntie, whereby the prince, a bishop being dead, taketh vnto himselfe the profits of the bishopricke, in the meane time whilest another bishop is chosen by the chapter, or by the prince himselfe appointed: and so being sworne, is put into possession thereof: but forasmuch as that in all places is not obserued: and few there be that haue that right, it is not to bee accounted among the markes of soueraigntie.

Small things and yet proper only vnto soueraign princes.

There be many other right small things, which are accounted proper vnto princes, as things concerning their greater reputation and dignitie, as in their edicts, mandats, and commissions to vse these words, *Dei Gratia*, by the grace of God; which wordes *Lewes* the xj, the French king, forbad the duke of Britaigne to vse in his life; although we read them to haue bene vsed almost in all auntient leagues; and attributed not vnto great princes and commaunders onely, but euen to the least magistrates and deputies

---

F1 publication *i.e.* a making public, confiscation   F2-3 challenged *i.e.* claimed   F5 receipt *i.e.* treasury   G9 *For* Howbeit if our *read* Howbeit our.   G9 too much   H6 Soveraigntie, as now it is at this present, comprised   Notes at H3, I1, K7.

OF A COMMONWEALE. 181

A ties also. The kings of Fraunce haue also reserued vnto themselues the right to seale with yellow waxe, a thing forbidden their nobilitie and other their iusticiaries; which *Lewes* the xj by speciall priuilege and letters patents graunted as a great fauour vnto *Renate* of Aniou, king of Naples and Sicilie, that in sealing he might vse yellow waxe: with like priuilege vnto his heires also, confirmed in parliament the 28 of Iune 1465. He which copied the Comentaries of *Tillet*, calleth it white waxe, which I find our kings neuer to haue vsed.

To seale with yealowe wax graunted vnto a great prince as a fauour.

But much more it belongeth vnto the royaltie of soueraigne maiestie, to be able to compell the subiects to vse the language and speech of him that ruleth ouer them: which the Romans so commaunded their subiects, that euen yet at this day they seeme

To be able to chang the subiects language a marke of soueraigntie.

B farre and wide to raigne ouer a great part of Europe. But the king of the Hetruscians, who last was by the Romans ouercome in all other things yeelded vnto them, but in that he could in no wise be perswaded to yeeld, to chaunge his countrey language, and to receiue the Latine tongue, as *Cato Censorius* writeth. But France for that it swarmed as it were with citisens of Rome, did so confound the Latine tongue, with the naturall countrey speech, as that the auntient writers called our countrey men Romans; yea the iudgements and decrees of the higher court of parliament, *viz.* of Paris were set downe in Latine (which the presidents and gouernours were commaunded to doe) vntill that *Francis* the first had giuen order that they should vse their owne countrey language: as by like edict *Edward* the third commaunded the judges and magistrats of

The cause whie the French toungeis so much confounded with latine.

C England, to giue iudgements in their owne countrey language, when as before they vsed the French. And at such time as the Sarasins had subdued the greatest part of Asia, and Afrike: they withall most farre spred their language and religion euen into the farther part of Spaine: which when *Philip* king of Spaine would gladly haue suppressed, yet could he by no meanes effect it.

Some amongst the markes of Soueraigntie, haue put also the power to iudge and decide matters, according to their conscience; a thing common to all iudges, if they be not by expresse law or custome prohibited so to doe. And that is it for which wee oftentimes see in the edicts vpon the articles committed to the arbitratarie iudgement of the judges, this clause added, *wherewith we haue charged our conscience*. For if there

A soueraigne prince may according to his cōscience decide matters beyond either lawe, or custome.

D be either custome or law to the contrarie, it then is not in the power of the judge, to passe beyond the law, or to dispute against the receiued law. For that was a thing forbidden by the most politike lawes of *Lycurgus*: and also by the most auntient lawes of Florence, whereas a soueraigne prince may do both, if he be not by the law of God forbidden; whereunto we haue before showed him to be still subiect.

As for the title of Maiestie it selfe, it sufficiently appeareth, that it onely belongeth to him that is a soueraigne prince: so that for him that hath no soueraigntie to vsurpe the same, were a verie absurd thing: but to arrogat vnto himselfe the addition of most excellent and sacred maiestie, is much more absurd; the one being a point of lightnes, and the other of impietie: for what more can we giue vnto the most mightie and immor-

The title of maiestie proper to soueraigne princes.

Titles dewe to God beseeme not princes.

E tall God, if we take from him that which is proper vnto himselfe? And albeit that in auntient time neither emperours nor kings vsed these so great addition or titles: yet the German princes neuerthelesse haue oft times giuen the title of Sacred Maiestie vnto the kings of Fraunce; aswell as vnto their emperour. As I remember my selfe to haue seene the letters of the princes of the empire, written vnto the king, for the deliuerance of countie *Mansfeld*, then prisoner in Fraunce. wherein there was sixe times *V. S. M.* that is to say, *Vestra, Sacra, Maiestas*, or Your Sacred Maiestie; an addition proper vnto God, apart from all worldly princes. As for other princes which are not soueraignes some vse the addition of *His Highnesse*, as the dukes of Loraine, Sauoy, Mantua, Ferra-

R   1a,

A5 28 (Fr 1-6, 8 and L) 18 (Fr 7)   A5 *For* June 1465 *read* July 1468 (Fr and L).   B2 overcome, in all   C9 arbitrarie   E6 sixe times (Fr) ten times (L)   Notes at A5, C3, C10, D8.

ra, and Florence: some of *Excellencie*, as the princes of the confines; or else of *Serenitie*, as the duke of Venice.

I omit here many other meaner rights which Soueraigne princes euery one of them pretend in their own countries, in number infinit, which yet are no marks of soueraignty, such as ought to be proper to all soueraigne princes in generall, apart from all other lords, iusticiaries, magistrats, and subiects, and which are of their owne nature incessible and not to be alienated from the soueraigntie: nor by any course of time to be prescribed. And if the soueraigne prince shall giue or grant any lands or lordship of the publique possessions, vnto any, with iurisdiction and power to vse the same, in such sort as he himselfe might: albeit that the royall rights properly belonging vnto soueraigntie, be not in the charter or writings expresly excepted: yet are they always by the verie law it selfe thought to be excepted, which by an old decree of the counsell of France was decreed not only for graunts made vnto priuat men, but also for such gifts or grants as were made vnto the princes themselues descended of the royall blood and familie: which royall rights can by no tract of time whatsoeuer, be prescribed against or vsurped vpon. For if publique place, or the publique possessions of the Commonweale cannot be got by any prescription: how much lesse then can the royalties proper vnto soueraigne maiestie be prescribed vpon. But it is certaine by the edicts and lawes concerning the publike demaine, that it is not to bee alienated, neither by any tract of time to be gained. Which is no new thing: For it is two thousand yeares agoe since that *Themistocles*, making seisure of certaine lands belonging vnto the publike demaine, vsurped by some priuat men; said in the oration which hee made vnto the people of Athens, *That mortall men could nothing prescribe against the immortall God: neither could priuat men in any thing prescribe against the Commonweale*. The selfe same speech *Cato* the Censor vsed also in the Oration which he made vnto the people of Rome, for the reuniting of some part of the publike demain, vsurped vpon by certaine priuat men. How then can a man prescribe vpon the rights and markes of Soueraigntie? And that is it, for which in law he is guiltie of death, that in any sort vseth the markes properly reserued vnto the maiestie of a Soueraigne prince. And thus much concerning the principall points of Soueraigne maiestie, in as briefe manner as I possibly could, hauing handled this matter more at large in my booke *De Imperio*. And forasmuch as the forme and estate of a Commonweale dependeth of them that haue the Soueraigntie therein: Let vs now see how many sorts of Commonweales there be.

Finis Lib. Primi.

THE SECOND BOOKE OF OR CONCERNING A COMMONWEALE.

Chap. I.

¶ *Of all sortes of Commonweales in generall, and whether there bee any moe then three.*

Orasmuch as we haue before sufficiently spoken of Soueraigntie, and of the rights and markes thereof; now it behoueth vs to consider who they bee which in euery Commonweale hold that Soueraigntie; thereby to iudge what the estate is: as if the Soueraigntie consist in one onely prince, wee call it a Monarchie: but if all the people bee therein interressed, we call it a Democracie, or Popular estate: So if but some part of the people haue the Soueraigne commaund, we account that state to be an Aristocracie. Which words we will vse, to auoide the obscuritie and confusion which might otherwise arise, by the varietie of gouernours good or bad: which hath giuen occasion vnto many, to make moe sorts of Commonweales than three. But if that opinion should take place, and that we should by the foot of vertues & vices, measure the estate of Commonweales; we should find a world of them, and them in number infinit. Now it is most certaine, that to attaine vnto the true definitions and resolutions of all things, wee must not rest vppon the externall accidents which are innumerable, but rather vpon the essentiall and formall differences: for otherwise a man might fall into an infinit and inextricable labyrinth, whereof no knowledge is to bee had, or certaine precept to be giuen. For so a man should forge and fashion infinit numbers of Commonweales, not onely according to the diuersitie of vertues and vices; but euen according to the varietie of things indifferent also. As if a Monarch were to bee chosen for his strength, or for his beautie, for his stature, or for his nobilitie, or riches, which are all things indifferent; or for his martial disposition, or for that he is more giuen to peace, for his grauitie, or for his iustice, for his beautie, or for his wisdom, for his sobrietie, or his humilitie, for his simplicitie, or his chastitie; and so for all other qualities, a man should so make an infinitie of Monarchies: and in like sort in the Aristocratique state, if some few of many should haue the soueraigntie aboue the rest, such as excelled others in riches, nobilitie, wisedome, iustice, martiall prowesse, or other like vertues, or vices, or things indifferent, there should thereof arise infinit formes of Commonweales: a thing

R ij

most

Note at C8.

most absurd, and so by consequent the opinion whereof such an absurditie ariseth, is to be reiected. Seeing therefore that the accidentall qualitie chaungeth not the nature of things: let vs say that there are but three estates or sorts of Commonweales; namely a Monarchie, an Aristocratie, and a Democratie. We call it a Monarchie, when one man alone hath the soueraigntie in a Commonweale, in such sort as wee haue aforesaid. And a Democratie, or Popular estate, when all the people, or the greater part thereof hath in it the soueraigne power and commaund, as in one bodie. The Aristocratie is, when the lesser part of the people hath the Soueraigntie, as in one bodie, and giueth lawes vnto the rest of the people, whether it be in generall, or in particular: all which things are of themselues more cleerer than the day. And true it is, that the writers of auntient time do therein well agree, that there can be no lesse then three kindes or sortes of Commonweales: Whereunto some others haue ioyned a fourth, composed of all three: and some other a fift, diuers from all the rest.

Plato hath vnto these three well adioyned a fourth kind, that is to wit, where some few of the better sort excelling the rest in vertue, haue the soueraignetie: which for all that in proper tearmes, is nothing else but a pure *Aristocratie*: how be it, he hath not receiued the mixture of the aforesaid three states, for an other diuers forme of a Commonweale. *Aristotle* beside these three kinds of Commonweales which we haue spoken of: and the fourth also named by *Plato*, setteth downe a fift kind of Common weale, by confounding together the three former states, and so maketh fiue sorts of states or Commonweales. But *Polybius* reckneth vp seauen sorts; three commendable: three faultie: and the seauenth compounded of the mixture of the three first. *Dionysius Halycarnasseus, Marcus Tullius, Thomas More, Gaspar Contarenus, Francis Machiauell*, and many other following *Polybius*, haue as it were with one consent approoued his opinion, which in deed is most auntient, and tooke not beginning from *Polybius*, although he would seeme to be the authour thereof, neither from *Aristotle*, but aboue foure hundred yeares before *Aristotle*. *Herodotus* (the father of antiquitie) writeth, that fourth kind of a Commonweale, confused of the three other, to haue ben commended of many, and yet for all that contenting himselfe with the three former kinds, reiecteth the rest as imperfect: And were it not that I were not onely by probable arguments, but euen by forcible reasons drawne from that opinion of *Polybius, Tullie*, and the rest, I could easilie haue suffered my selfe to haue been ouercome by the authoritie of so great and graue men. It behoueth vs therefore by liuely reasons to shew them to haue erred and been deceiued, which haue brought in that fourth kind of Commonweale composed of the mixture of the other three: which I trust the more plainly to bring to passe, if I shall vse the same examples in refelling of them, that they them selues haue before vsed. For they them selues haue set downe the Lacedemonian, Roman, and Venetian Commonweales to haue been compounded and sweetely mingled with the three kind of states, that is to say, with the Monarchie, Aristocratie, and Democratie. But when *Plato* said, the best kind of a Commonweale to be composed of the mixture of a Monarchie and Democratie, he was therefore forthwith reprehended by his scholler *Aristotle*, saying, that of these two could no commendable state be made, and that therefore it was better of all three estates to make a fourth: wherein *Aristotle* reasoneth also against himselfe; for if he confesse no good thing possiblie to be made of two extreames; what shall then bee made of three confounded amongst them selues? And for that this opinion for the making of a fourth estate of the confusion of the rest, may moue great troubles in Commonweales, and therein worke maruelous effects, it is requisite for vs well to examine the same: For when states of Commonweales are in them selues contrarie, as a Monarchie and a Demo-

That there are but three sorts of commonweales viz: a Monarchie, a Democratie: and an Aristocratie.

The diuers opinions of the auntient writers concerning diuers sorts of commonweals.

No fourth estate of a commonweale to be made of a confusion of a Monarchie, a Democratie and an Aristocratie.

Note at K1.

A Democratie, they are by contrarie lawes and ordinances to be gouerned. The Florentins throughly perswaded of that opinion of the auntients for the mingling of the three estates together, as the best forme of a Commonweale; when they moued with the seditious sermons of *P. Soderin*, and *Hierome Sauanirola*, had translated the soueraignetie or chiefe power of the Commonweale vnto the people: thought it best to keepe the rout of the vulgar and common people from bearing of offices and rule, and altogether from the affaires of state: that so the chiefe managing of matters might be reserued vnto the more auntient sort of the citizins, and such as were of greater wealth and abilitie then the rest: who yet had not power to dispose of all matters, but onely of such things as were the chiefest, viz. the making of lawes, the creating of magistrats, B and disposing of the common treasure: reseruing the rest vnto the Senat and magistrats, that so they might inioy that moderat state of a Commonweale, whereof they had so strongly dreamed. And certes if of the three estates moderately mixed might a fourth state arise, it should haue a certein power by nature diuers from the rest: as we see in Harmonicall consent, composed of Arithmeticall and Geometricall proportion artificially confused; yet quite differing from them both: so as if the mixture of things of diuers and contrarie natures, ariseth a third all together differing from the things so together mixed. But that state which is made of the mixture of the three kinds of Commonweales, differeth in deede nothing from a meane popular state; For if three cities, whereof one of them is gouerned by a king, and so a Monarchie; the second C by the nobilitie, and so an Aristocratie; the third by the people, and so a Democratie; should be confounded, and so thrust together into one and the same forme of a Commonweale, and so the chiefe power and soueraignetie communicated vnto all: who is there that can doubt but that that state shall be all together a state popular? except the soueraignetie should by turnes be giuen; first to the king, then to the nobilitie, and afterwards to the people; As in the vacancie of the Roman kingdome, the king being dead, the Senators ruled by turnes: yet must they needes againe fall vnto one of these three kinds of a Commonweale which we haue spoken of: nether could this alternatiue manner of gouernement be of any long continuance, either yet more profitable to the Commonweale, then as if in an euill gouerned familie, the wife should first D commaund the husband; then the children them both; and the seruants after them to dominier ouer all.

But to confound the state of a monarkie, with the Populat or Aristocratical estate, is a thing impossible, and in effect imcompatible, and such as cannot be imagined. For if soueraignetie be of it selfe a thing indivisible, (as wee haue before showed) how can it then at one and the same time be diuided betwixt one prince, the nobilitie, and the people in common? The first marke of soueraigne maiestie is, to be of power to giue lawes, and to commaund ouer them vnto the subiects, and who should those subiects bee that should yeelde their obedience vnto that law, if they should also haue the power to make the lawes? who should he be that could giue the law? being himselfe E constrained to receiue it of them vnto whom he him selfe gaue it? So that of necessitie we must conclude, that as no one in particular hath the power to make the law in such a state, that then the state must needs be a state popular. Now if we shall giue power vnto the people to make lawes, and to creat magistrats, and not to meddle in the rest; we must yet needs confesse that such power giuen vnto the magistrats belonged vnto the people, and that it is not giuen but as in trust vnto the magistrats: whom the people may againe displace, euen aswell as they placed them, in such sort as that the state should alwaies be popular.

And to proue that which wee haue said to be true, let vs take the same examples that

Polybius

B6 so as of   D4 incompatible   D7-8 to give lawes unto the subjects, and to commaund over them; and who   Note at D8.

186 THE FIRST BOOKE

Polybius, Contarenus, and the rest haue left vs; They say that the state of the Lacedemonians was composed of all the three kinds of states which we spoke of: For that in that Commonweale they had two kings representing a Monarchie; eight and twentie Senators representing an Aristocratie; and fiue Ephori figuring and patronizing the popular estate. But what will these men then say to *Herodotus*, who bringeth the Lacedemonian estate for an example of a most pure Aristocratie? what will they also aunswere vnto *Theucidides, Xenophon, Aristotle*, and *Plutarche*? who speaking of the warres of Peloponnesus (which continued twentie yeres betwixt the Popular and the Aristocratique Commonweals) say, that the whole drift of the Athenians and their allies was to chaunge the Aristocraties into Democraties, as they did in Samos, Corfu, and all the other cities by them subdued. Whereas contrariewise the Lacedemonians purpose and intention was to chaunge the Popular states into Aristocraties, as in deede they did in all the cities of Greece after the victorie of *Lysander*; yea euen in the citie of Athens it selfe, where after he had layed the wals euen with the ground, he tooke the soueraignetie from the people, and gaue the same vnto thirtie citizens, (who are therefore of the Athenians called the thirtie Tyrants) to rule and gouerne in such sort and manner as they did amongst the Lacedemonians, where so many, and no moe had the gouernement of the state. But among the citizens of Samos, the Siæyons, the Æginits, the Mylesians, and other cities of Ionia and the lesser Asia, they gaue the soueraignetie vnto Tenne principal men, with one chiefe Captaine ouer them, for the managing of the warres; calling hoame againe such as had bene banished for holding with the Aristocratie, and driuing into exile them that were chiefe of the popular factions.

What will they also say to *Maximus Tyrius*, who reckning vp the States which held the pure Aristrocratie first of all nameth the Lacedemonians, and after them the Thessalians, the Pellenians, the Cretentians, and the Mantineans. We must first conuince these so many and so famous authours of vntruth, before we can thrust the Lacedemonians from their Aristocratie: which writers liuing almost in the same time wherein the Athenian and Lacedemonian Commonweales flourished, and beeing themselues Grecians, were like more certainly and truely to know these things, than a Venetian Senator, a Florentine, or an English man.

What was it then that deceiued *Polybius*, who was himself a Megalopolitan, borne neere vnto the Lacedemonians? Truely it was euen the name of the Lacedemonian kings. For *Lycurgus* hauing altered the state of the Commonweale, and by the good will and consent of the kings themselues (who deriued their pedegree from *Hercules*) hauing translated the soueraigntie vnto the people, left vnto the kings, but the bare name and title onely, and to be the generals in warres. For why the regall power was now before alreadie sore shaken and weakned: after that *Aristodemus* king of Lacedemonia, had at once left his two sonnes to raigne together ouer the Lacedemonians (to the imitation of the Messenians, ouer whome *Amphareus* and *Leucippus* together raigned) who whilest they would both be kings and commaund ouer all, could neither of them so be, but by their ielous conceits and contentions, drawing the state into factions, gaue occasion to *Lycurgus*, being descended also of the same stocke with them, to ouerthrow their royall power, leauing vnto them and their house nothing els but the name and show of kings, giuing the rest vnto the Senat and the people. But as in Athens and Rome, after the kings were thence driuen out, they yet left the name of a king vnto a certaine priest, whome they called King of the Sacrifices, to doe a certaine sacrifice, which the king himselfe onely had in former time done: Which priest for all that was himselfe subiect vnto the great bishop, and could not (as *Plutarch* saith) haue

any

Marginal notes:
- That the Lacedemonian commonweale was meare aristocraticall, and not composed of the confusion or mixture of the three sorts of commonweals.
- Gasper Contarenus, Nicholas Machiauel, Sir Thomas Moore. The cause that induced Polybius and others to say that the Lacedemonian estat was a state composed of the mixture of the three states and forms of a commonweale. The historie of a Lacœdemonian commonweale.

F4 figuring *i.e.* representing (Fr)   F4 patronizing *i.e.* protecting, defending (L)   G9 Sicyons
G9 Mylesians *i.e.* people of Miletus (L) *but* Melians *i.e.* people of Melos (Fr)   H5 Aristocratie
Note at F8.

any estate, or beare any office as the other priests might: euen so did *Lycurgus* vnto the two kings of Lacedemonia, who vpon the matter were nothing but Senators, hauing but their voyces with the rest, without any power at all to commaund; but to the contrarie were themselues constrayned to obey the commaundements of the Ephori, who oftentimes put them to their fines, yea and condemned them to death also, as they did the kings *Agis* and *Pausanias*, the soueraigntie still resting with the people, in whose power it was to confirme or infirme the acts and decrees of the Senat. *Thucidides* also himselfe reiecteth the opinion of them which thought the kings each of them to haue had two voyces. But about an hundred yeares after the popular state, ordayned, was againe chaunged by the kings *Polydorus and Theopompus*; seeing it to bee an hard matter to call the people together, and a great deale harder to rule them by reason, being assembled; oftentimes at their pleasure reuersing the most wholesome and religious decrees of the Senat. Wherefore they chaunged that popular gouernment into an Aristocratie, subtilly wresting an Oracle of *Apollo* to that purpose: whereby the God (as they said) commaunded that from thenceforth the gouernment of the Commonweale should be in the power of the Senat: and yet to please the people so grieued to haue left their power, they gaue them leaue to draw out of themselues fiue judges, called Ephori, as Tribunes or patrons of the people, who should examine the sayings, doings, and deuises of the kings, and by all meanes let them from the exercising of tyranny. And these Ephorie, euerie ninth yeare once, vpon some cleere night gazing vpon the firmament (as *Plutarch* saith) if they then saw any starre, as it were, sparkle or shoot, they thereupon committed their kings to prison, who might not thence be deliuered, vntill the Oracle of *Apollo* had so declared. In like manner the Phylactes or Gailor, euerie yeare had the king of Cumes in prison, vntill the Senat had determined what should be done with him. Now this state of the Lacedemonian Commonweale endured about fiue hundred yeares, vntill the time of *Cleomenes*, who hauing slaine the Ephori and the Senatours, and so oppressed the Commonweale, tooke vppon himselfe the soueraigntie, and so held it vntill such time as he was ouercome by *Antigonus* king of Macedon; who hauing vanquished him, restored that Commonweale into the state it was before: howbeit that twentie yeares after, being fallen againe into the power of *Nabis* the tyrant, who was afterward slaine by *Philopomenes*, that Commonweale was vnited vnto the state of the Achæans, whereof it was a prouince, vntill that about thirty yeares after, it was by *Gallus* the Roman Proconsull taken from the Achæans, and by Roman emperours set at libertie. Thus in few words you may see the true historie of the the Lacedemonian Commonweale, for most part taken from *Xenophon*, *Thucidides*, *Liuy*, & *Polybius*, whereof yet no man hath more curiously written than *Plutarch*, who out of the Lacedemonian acts and publike records, hath corrected such things as of others haue bene but slightly or falsly set downe and reported: which hath giuen occasion to many to be deceiued, and to thinke that state to haue bene mingled of the three diuers kindes of Commonweales. Which is plainly to be gathered out of *Liuie*, where he bringeth in *Nabis* the first tyrant of Lacedemonia, thus speaking to *Titus Flaminius*, *Noster legulator Lycurgus, non in paucorum manu Rempub. esse voluit, quem vos Senatum appellatis, nec eminere vnum aut alterum ordinem in ciuitate, sed per æquationem fortunæ & dignitatis fore credidit, vt multi essent qui pro patria arma ferrent*, Our lawgiuer *Lycurgus* (saith he) would not the state of our Commonweale to bee in few mens hands, which you call the Senat, neither would haue any one or other order to excell the rest in our citie; but by the making equall of mens fortune and dignitie, thought it would come to passe, that there should be many which would beare armes for their countrey. Thus he couereth his tyrranny with the show of a popular state, when

R iiij

A9–10 ordayned BY LYCURGUS, was againe (cf. Fr)   D6 curiously *i.e.* carefully   E2 legumlator

188   THE SECOND BOOKE

when as then there was no popular estate at all; yet in that he said most truely, that Lycurgus at the beginning gaue the soueraigntie vnto the people.

But let vs see the rest. They also haue put for example the Roman Commonweale, which they said to haue bene mingled of the three kinds of Commonweales: For so saith *Polybius* (who was maister to *Africanus* the Great) Wee see (saith hee) the regall power in the Consuls, the Aristocratie in the Senat, and the Democratie in the people. Vnto whome do plainely assent *Dionysius Halycarnasseus, Cicero, Contarenus, Sir Thomas More*, and many others: which opinion for all that is neither grounded vppon truth nor reason. For where is this Monarchie, that is to say, the soueraigne gouernment of one man? which in the two Consuls cannot bee imagined. But soueraigne maiestie, if it were in the consuls could not possibly be diuided betwixt two, for the indiuisible nature thereof, which it seemeth more probable and reasonable to attribute the same vnto the dukes of Genua or Venice. But what regall power could there bee in the two Roman Consuls? who could neither make law, nor peace, nor warre, neither any great officer, neither graunt pardon, neither take a peny out of the common treasure, neither so much as to whip a citisen, if it were not in time of warre, without leaue of the people: which hath bene a power alwaies giuen to all gouernours of armies, whome we also may so call kings, and with greater appearance than the Consuls, who had not power but the one of them after the other, and that but for the space of one yeare onely. The constable of Fraunce, the chiefe Bassa of the Turkes, the Bethudere in Æthiopia, the Edegnare in the kingdome of Afrike, haue ten times more power than had the two Consuls together, & yet for all that they are but subiects & slaues to other princes, as were the Consuls subiects and seruants vnto the people. And to what purpose say they, that the Consuls had such royall authoritie, seeing that the least of the Tribunes of the people might imprison them. As did *Drusus* the Tribune, who by a sergeant tooke *Philip* the Consull by the coller, and cast him in prison, for that hee had interrupted him, as he was speaking vnto the people: and that he might lawfully so doe, shall hereafter be declared. The power of the Consuls was to lead the armies, war being before denounced, to assemble the Senat, to present the letters of the captaines and allies vnto the Senat, to giue audience vnto ambassadours before the people or the Senat, to call together the great estate, and to demaund the aduise of the people, about the election of officers, or promulgation of lawes; who yet standing, spake vnto the people sitting, and their mases downe, in token of their subiection vnto the people. The same authoritie with the Consuls had the chiefe gouernour of the citie in their absence. Ioyne hereunto also, that the Consuls had power but for one yeare: wherefore I leaue this opinion as scarce worthy the refuting.

Now as concerning the Senat, which they say to haue had the forme and power of an Aristocratie, it was so farre there from, as that there was neuer priuie councell, which had not more authoritie: for it had no power to commaund either particular men, or magistrats: yea the Senators might not assemble themselues, except it so pleased the Consuls, or the Prætor in the absence of the Consuls: insomuch that *Cæsar* a popular man, perceiuing himselfe not gratious with the Senat, oftentimes called the people together in the yeare of his Consulship: but the Senat in all that yeare he assembled but once or twice, still presenting his request vnto the people when he would obtaine any thing: which was no great noueltie, for the Consull for his pleasure to doe, contrarie to the good liking and mind of the Senat. For we read (that the Senat at such time as it was in greatest authoritie that euer it was) in the daungerous time of the Commonwealth, hauing requested the Consuls to name a dictatour, the Consuls would therein doe nothing: insomuch that the Senat hauing no power to commaund them, neither

any

Margin notes: The Romaine commonweale a meare popular state and not composed of the three formes of commoweals. — No soueraigntie in the Romaine Consulls — The smal power of the Romaine Senate: and that therein was no resemblance of an Aristocratie

F10(margin) commonweals   I1 For *the great estate* read *the great estates i.e.* the assembly of the people.   K6 we read that the Senat (at such   Note at G10.

A any sergeant or like officer, which are the true markes of them which haue the power to commaund, sent *Seruilius Priscus* with their request vnto the Tribunes in this sort, * *Vos (inquit) Tribuni plebis Senatus appellat, vt in tanto discrimine Reipublicæ dictatorem dicere, Consules pro vestra potestate cogatis: Tribuni pro collegio pronunciant, placere Consules Senatui dicto audientes esse, aut in vincula se duci iussuros*, The Senat (saith he) appealeth vnto you the Tribunes of the people, that in so great daunger of the Commonweale, you for the great authoritie you haue, would compell the Consuls to nominat a Dictator: whereupon the Tribunes pronounced for their whole societie, that their pleasure was, that the Consuls should be obedient vnto the Senat, or els that they would commaund them to prison. And in another * place the same author saith, That B the Senat was of aduise, that the Consull should present the request vnto the people, for the commaunding of him whom they would haue Dictator: which if the Consull should refuse to doe, that then the Prætor of the citie should do it: who if he should refuse also, that then the Tribunes of the people should propound the matter. *Consul negauit se populum rogaturum, Prætoremque rogare vetuit: Tribuni plebis rogarunt*, The Consull denied to request the people, and forbad the Prætor also to request them, the Tribunes made the request. Wherby it euidently appeareth that the Senat could not so much as commaund the lesser magistrats, the greater magistrats forbidding them. And as for that which *Polybius* saith, That the Senat had power to iudge of cities and prouinces, and to take punishment of conspirators against the state: * *Liuie* C sheweth it to haue bene otherwise, as when question was made for the chastising of the traitors of Campania, who after the battell at Cannas had ioyned themselues vnto *Hannibal*, an auntient Senator said in full Senat, *Per Senatum agi de Campanis iniussu populi non video posse*, I see not that any thing can by the Senat bee done concerning the Campanians without the commaundement of the people. And a little after, *Rogatio feratur ad populum, qua Senatui potestas fiat statuendi de Campanis*, Let request bee made vnto the people, wherby power may be giuen vnto the Senat, to determine concerning the Campanians. And vpon the request to that purpose presented vnto the people, the people gaue them commission, and commaunded the Senat to proceed against them in this sort, *Quod Senatus maxima pars censeat, qui assident id volumus iu-* D *bemusque*, What the greatest part of the Senat shall agree vppon, wee that here sit will and commaund the same. Neither is *Polybius* lesse deceiued, in saying, That the Senat at pleasure disposed of the prouinces and gouernments: whereas *Liuie* the best author of the Roman antiquities, is of contrarie opinion, writing thus, *Quintus Fuluius postulauit a Consule vt palam in Senatu diceret, permitteret ne Senatui vt de prouincijs decerneret: staturusque eo esset quod censuisset, an ad populum laturus: Scipio respondit se quod e Republica esset facturum. Tum Fuluius a vobis peto Tribuni plebis vt mihi auxilio sitis*. *Quintus Fuluius* requested of the Consul, that hee should openly say in the Senate whether hee gaue leaue or not vnto the Senat, to determine of the prouinces, and whether he would stand to that it should decree, or els would referre the matter E vnto the people: Whereunto *Scipio* answered, That hee would do that which should be for the good of the Commonweale. Then said *Fuluius*, I request you the Tribunes of the people to aid and helpe me. So that it plainely appeareth, the Senat to haue had no power at all, neither the decrees thereof to haue bene of any force, without the consent of the Tribunes of the people: and that the rest they had by the sufferance of the same people. Now he that hath nothing but by sufferance, hath indeed nothing of his owne, as we haue before said Yea such decrees of the Senat, as were confirmed by the consent of the Tribunes of the people, vnto whome they were to be communicated, could not yet be put in execution, except that either the Consuls did so command;

or

Liuius lib. 4.

Liuius lib. 27.

Liuius lib. 26.

The people of Rome in their assemblies did sit in token of their soueraigntie.

C5–6 *For* Rogatio feratur *Bodin writes* Ut rogatio feratur (Fr and L).   D4 Quintus
D5 permitteretne   D7 Tum Fulvius, a vobis   E7 said. Yea

190　THE FIRST BOOKE

or that the Consuls refusing so to do, the Tribunes themselues propounded the same vnto the people. So that in briefe all matters of estate, and namely all the councels and decrees of the Senat were of no force or vertue, if the people did not so command: or if the Tribunes of the people consented not thereunto, as wee haue before touched, and shall more at large declare in speaking of a Senat. Wherefore in the Roman state, the gouernment was in the magistrats, the authoritie and councell in the Senat, but the soueraigne power and maiestie of the Commonweale was in the people. Excepting that time wherein the Decemuiri contrarie to the law, kept in their hands longer than a yeare, the soueraigne power to make lawes committed vnto them; from which they were shortly after by force of armes remoued: for then it might of right haue bene called an Aristocracie, or more properly to say an Oligarchie. Now as we haue before said, that the power of magistrats (how great soeuer it be) is not of themselues, neither theirs, but as committed vnto them in trust: so at the first, after the driuing out of the kings, the Senators were chosen by the people; who to discharge themselues of that labour, committed that charge to the Censors, who were also chosen by the people, so that vpon the matter all the authoritie of the Senat depended of the people, who at their pleasure vsed to confirme or infirme, to ratifie or disanull the decrees of the Senat.

The Venetian estate a pure Aristocratie and not composed of the three formes of commonweals

　　The same opinion hath *Contarenus* of the Venetian Commonweale, saying it to be also mixt of the three formes of Commonweales, as were those of Rome and Lacedemonia: For, saith he, the royall power is in a sort in the duke of Venice, the Aristocracie in the Senat, and the popular estate in the Grand Councell. But *Ianot* after him hath most curiously brought to light the true estate of the Venetian Commonweale; wherein he sheweth by most euident testimonies, drawne out of the most auntient and true Venetian records. That *Contarenus* in so saying was much deceiued. He sheweth plainely, that not past three hundred yeares ago, before the time of *Sebastian Cyanee* duke of Venice, the Venetian estate was a pure monarchie. Howbeit that *Contarenus* writeth it to haue bene established in the state it now is eight hundred yeares: and *Pau. Manutius*, saith it to haue so stood twelue hundred yeares: all which *Ianot* proueth out of the publike records, and certaine historie to be vntrue. But howsoeuer that be, plaine it is, at this day to be a pure Aristocracie: For by the view of the citie and the citisens, which was taken about thirtie yeares ago, were reckoned nine and fiftie thousand three hundred fortie nine citizens, beside children vnder seuen yeares old, but of Gentlemen, in whome resteth the soueraigne power of that state, betwixt foure and fiue thousand yong and old: yet had the church men and gentlemen vnder fiue and twentie yeares old, nothing to do with the state, more than to looke on, neither had they accesse into the Grand Councell, but by way of request: the young gentlemen beeing so vpon request recciued at the age of thirtie yeares, according as discretion was to be seene more in some one, than in some others: and yet hath it not bene found this hundred yeare, that the Grand Councell assembled, to decide the great affaires of that state, hath exceeded the number of fifteene hundred, as is to be seene in the histories of *Sabellicus*, and of cardinall *Bembus*, the rest being absent. It is therefore the least part of the Venetians that haue the soueraigntie, and they also of certaine noble families, for all the gentlemen borne in Venice, are not receiued into the Grand Councell; but there are of one and the same stocke, of the same race, of the same name, whereof some are citisens, and come not into the councell, and the others come. I do not here set downe the reason why, which euery man may see in *Sabellicus*. This great councel as *Contarenus* saith, hath soueraigne power to make and repeale lawes, to place or displace all officers, to receiue the last appeales, to determine of peace and warre, and to

A viewe taken of the Citizens and gentlemen of Venice.

The soueraigntie of the Venetian estate to be in the grand counsel.

giue

I2 thirtie yeares ago (L) twenty years ago (Fr) *i.e.* in 1555. Cf. 427 B4 (margin).　　18 For age of thirtie *read* age of twentie.

give pardon vnto the condemned. Wherein *Contarenus* condemneth himselfe: for seeing it is (as he saith) it cannot be denied, but that the state of this Commonweale is Aristocratique. For were it that the Great Councell had no other power than to make lawes and magistrats, it were enough to proue it to be an Aristocraticall state, as we haue before said: for if those officers haue any power, they hold it of the Seigneurie: which sufficeth to show, that neither the Decemuiri, neither the Senat, neither the Sages, nor yet the duke with his sixe councellors, haue any power but by sufferance, and so farre as it shall please the Great Councell. As for the duke himselfe he alone of all other magistrats hath no command at all, as not hauing power to condemne any man before him, neither to stay or examine any man; which is the first marke of command, giuen euen vnto the least magistrats, neither may he decide any cause whether it be in matters of state, or administration of iustice; either in the assembly of the sixe councellors, or of the Decemuiri, or of the Sages, or of the Senat, or of the fortie judges in ciuill or criminall causes, or of the Grand Councell. For albeit that he may enter into all their corporations and colleges, yet so it is, that he hath but his voice, as any one of them; but that he vseth to giue it to the last: neither dare he to open any letter directed vnto the Seigneurie, or admit or discharge any ambassadours, but in the presence of his sixe councellors, or of the Decemuiri, or to go out of the citie without leaue. Yea *Falerius* the duke, for that he had without the consent of the councell married a straunger, was by the Decemuiri hanged. And beside him *Sabellicus* reckoneth vp twelue dukes moe, either by the tumultuous people slaine, or otherwise put to death for abusing their authoritie. But he weareth a most pretious cap, a robe of gold, he is followed, honoured, and respected as a prince: and the coyne carrieth his name, albeit that the stampe of the Seigneurie be vpon it, which are all tokens of a prince: all which royall magnificence we graunt him to haue, but yet all without power or commaund. Now if it were so that we should not according vnto truth, but after showes and appearances iudge of the estate of Commonweales, there should be found none simple and pure, but all mixt and confused in such sort as they say. Yea the empire of Germanie should be much more mixt, than the Venetian state. For the emperour hath other markes and more royall than hath the duke of Venice: then the seuen princes electors, with the other princes, haue the show of an Aristocracie, or of an Oligarchie: and the ambassadours of the imperiall townes resemble a Democracie. And yet for all that most certaine it is, that the imperiall state of Germanie is a pure Aristocracie, composed of three or foure hundred persons at most, ouer whome one prince beareth rule, to put in execution the decrees of the councell, or els is to be forced to giue vp his office, as wee shall in due place declare. In like manner they say also the states of the Swissers to be mixed of the three diuers formes of a Commonweale: Amongst whome the Burgamaister representeth the king, the Senat an Aristocracie, and the assemblies generall and particular, the state popular: and yet for all that men know right well, that all their states and Commonweales are either popular, as are they which inhabit the mountaines, or els Aristocratike, as are almost all the rest.

And this opinion of the mixed state hath so possessed the mindes of men, that many haue both thought and writ this monarchie of Fraunce (than which none can bee imagined more royall) to be mixt and composed of the three kinds of Commonweals, and that the parliament of Paris hath the forme of an Aristocracie, the three estates of a Democratie, and the king to represent the state of a monarchie: which is an opinion not onely absurd, but also capitall. For it is high treason to make the subiect equall to the king in authoritie and power, or to ioyne them as companions in the soueraigntie with him. And what popular power appeareth, when the three states are assembled?

The small authoritie and power the Duke of Venice hath.

The state of the Germaine empire and of the Swissars, Aristocraticall and not mixt.

The estate of France a pure Monarchie and not mixed.

A 2 seeing it is as he saith, it cannot   B 2 *For* either in the assembly *read* except in the assembly (cf. Fr). Note at E 2.

assembled? or the parliament called? or wherein is the soueraigne maiestie of a prince so much manifested, as when euery man in particular, and all men in generall, aswel the noble as the meniall, with bended knee, and bare head, adore their king? offer vnto him their requests, which he at his pleasure admitteth or reiecteth. What counterpoise of a popular power against the maiestie of a monarch can there be in the assembly of the three estates? yea of the whole people, if it could be gathered into one place, which humbleth it selfe, requesteth and reuerenceth their king. So farre is it from that such an assembly in any thing diminisheth the power of a soueraigne prince, as that thereby his maiestie is the more encreased and augmented. For it cannot bee exalted into a more high degree of honour, of power, and of glorie, than to see an infinit number of great lords and princes, and people innumerable, of men of all sorts and qualitie, to cast themselues downe at his feet, and to doe homage vnto his maiestie; seeing that the honour, glorie, and power of princes, consisteth not but in the obeysance, homage, and seruice of their subiects. If then no forme or fashion of a popular power can bee imagined in the assembly of the three estates, which they make in this realme, no more or haply lesse than in England and Spaine: much lesse shall there be an Aristocracie in the Court of Peeres, (who are so called, for that they bee equall one with another among themselues, but not with the prince, as some haue too rustically deemed) or in the assembly of all the officers of the realme, considering that the presence of the king doth make all power and authoritie of all corporations and colleges, and of all officers aswell in generall as in particular to cease: in such sort, as that no magistrat hath power to commaund any thing in his presence, as we will in due place declare. And albeit that the king sitting in his seat of iustice, the chauncelour first addresseth himselfe vnto him, to know his pleasure, by commaundement from whome he goeth, gathering the aduise and opinions of the princes of the blood, and other great lords, the peeres and magistrats, which he reporteth againe vnto him: yet is not that so done, to the intent to number the voyces, as in the consistorie among the judges, but that the king vnderstanding their opinions, may as seemeth vnto him good, receiue or reiect the same. And albeit that most times he follow the opinion of the greater part, yet to make it knowne, that it is not the judges or magistrats decree, but the decree of the prince onely, and that the rest of the magistrats haue therein no power, the chauncelor pronounceth not this or that to be thought good vnto the judges of the court, but with a lowd voice vseth these words, *The king sayeth vnto you*. Wee see also that the court of parliament, writing vnto the king, keepeth euen yet the auntient stile, which is this in the superscription of their letters, *To our Soueraigne Lord the King*. The beginning of which letters is on this sort, *Our Soueraigne Lord in most humble wise, and so much as in vs is we recommend vs to your good grace*, And the subscription placed as low as may be: *Your most humble and obedient subiects and seruants, the men holding your court of Parliament*. Which is not the manner of the lords of an Aristocracies speech: neither of such as are companions in Squeraigntie with the king, but of true and humble subiects. And for that I haue touched this point before, I will now lightly passe it ouer. The state of Fraunce therefore is a pure Monarchie, not mingled with the popular power, and so lesse with the Aristocratique Seigneurie: which mixture of states is altogether impossible, and incompatible. And *Aristotle* most subtilly examining this opinion, for the mixture of states, truly calleth the state composed of an Aristocratie and a Democratie πολιτείαν, that is to say a Commonweale: but showeth not how that may be done, neither giueth thereof example, as he vsually doth in others: but to the contrarie confesseth, that he knew none such in his time; or yet had found any such before, albeit that he is reported to haue gathered an hundred Commonweales into one

The power of a soueraign prince in nothing diminished by his parliament, but rather much the more therby manifested.

The forme the courtes of parliament in Fraunce hold in writing to the king.

OF A COMMONWEALE. 193

A one booke, which booke is now lost. And forasmuch as *Aristotle* seldome or neuer reporteth the true opinions of *Plato*, but to the contrarie alwaies disguiseth and obscureth them as the antient Academiques haue right well noted; and namely where hee reiecteth his Commonweale; vpon whose sayings many resting themselues haue oftentimes deceiued both themselues and others. We not addicted to either, will in few words set downe the true opinion of *Plato* concerning his Commonweale, deseruing well to be knowne for the better vnderstanding of the question we haue in hand, which some which neuer read the same, call a diuine opinion: some others in the meane time treading the same vnder foot, and rayling thereat as fast.

Plato faigned vnto himselfe onely two Commonweales, whereof the first hee attributed to *Socrates*, who neuer thought (as saith *Xenophon*) of that which *Plato* maketh him to say: and in his Commonwealth he taketh away these words, *Mine*, and *Thine*, as the source and fountaine of all euil, and would haue al goods, yea wiues and children to be common. But seeing euerie man to find fault therewith, he quietly left it, as if he had so writ more for argument sake, than for that he so thought, or to haue the same put in effect. The second is his owne, wherein hee taketh away the communitie of goods, of women and children: as for the rest those Commonweales are both in all things alike. For both in the one and the other, he would not haue aboue fiue thousand and fortie citisens, a number by him chosen to haue 59 entire parts: in which Commonweales he also maketh three estates or degrees of men: *viz.* the Guardes, C Souldiors, and Labourers: and after that diuideth the citisens into three degrees, according to the vnequall rate of their substance. As for the soueraigntie hee giueth it vnto the whole multitude of the people; as to make and abrogat lawes, cause sufficient enough to iudge that he ment to make it a popular estate, if there were nothing else. But he passeth on farther, and giueth vnto the whole assembly of the people power to place and displace all the officers: and not content with that, willeth also that the people should haue all the power to iudge in criminall causes; for that they are (as he saith) all therein interessed. In briefe he giueth vnto the people power of life and death, to condemne, and to graunt pardon; which are all euident arguments of a popular state. For he appointeth no soueraigne magistrat, which might represent the state royall, and D but a little of the forme Aristocratique: for he willeth, that the Senat, or the counsel for the affaires of the state, which he calleth Guards or keepers should consist of foure hundred citisens, to be chosen of the people. Whereby it is most euidently to bee vnderstood, that *Plato* his Commonwealth is the most popular that euer was, yea then that of his owne countrey of Athens, which *Xenophon* thought to haue bene the most popular state in the world. I omit the 726 lawes set downe by *Plato*, in the twelue books for the gouernment of his Commonweale: sufficeth it mee to haue showed *Plato* his imagined Commonweale not to haue bene made of a mixture of an Aristocracie, and Democracie, as *Aristotle* said, whose errour *Cicero*, *Contarenus*, and others, one after another following, led the rest that followed them into errour also.

E Let vs therefore conclude, neuer any Commonwealth to haue beene made of an Aristocracie and popular estate; and so much lesse of the three states of Commonweales, and that there are not indeed but three estates of Commonweales, as *Herodotus* first most truely said amongst the Greekes, whome *Tacitus* amongst the Latins imitating, saith, *Cunctas nationes & vrbes, populus, aut primores, aut singuli regunt*, The people, the nobilitie, or one alone, do rule all nations and cities.

But some man will say, May there not be a Commonweale, wherin the people hath the power to create the magistrats, to dispose of the common reuenew, and power of life and death; which are three markes of soueraigntie, & the nobilitie to haue power

S to

Plato his commonweale a pure popular estate and not mixt.

Notes at A1, B2, B9.

to make lawes, to dispose of peace and warre, and of the impositions and taxes; which are also markes of soueraigntie: and besides all these to haue one royall magistrat aboue all, vnto whome all the people in generall, and euerie one in particular should yeeld their faith and liege loyaltie, and from whose iudgement none might appeale or present any ciuill request. For so the rights and markes of soueraigntie should seeme to be diuided in three parts: the people chalenging one part thereof, the nobilitie another, and the king the third: whereby in that state a mixture might seeme to bee made of the royall Aristocratique and popular state together. Whereunto I aunswere, that such a state was neuer found, neither that such a state can bee made, or yet well imagined, considering that the markes of soueraigntie are indiuisible. For the nobilitie which should haue the power to make the lawes for all: (which is as much as to say to command and forbid what them pleased, without power to appeale from them, or for a man to oppose himselfe against their commaunds) would by their lawes at their pleasure forbid others to make peace or warre, or to leuie taxes, or to yeeld fealtie and homage without their leaue: and he againe to whome fealtie and homage is due, would bind the nobilitie and people not to yeeld their obedience vnto any other, but vnto himselfe. And admit that euerie one would seeke to defend his owne right, and not suffer any thing to be taken from him that he thought belonged to himselfe: yet that doth most differ from the nature of a Monarchie, that he which hath the soueraigntie, should himselfe bee enforced to obey any other but especially his subiect. Whereby it commeth to passe, that where the rights of soueraigntie are diuided betwixt the prince and his subiects: in that confusion of the state, there is still endlesse sturres and quarrels, for the superioritie, vntill that some one, some few, or all together haue got the soueraigntie. Whereof as there be many examples of old, so is there none fitter in our time, than the example of the kings of Denmarke, whome the nobilitie euer since *Christiern* the great grandfather of *Frederike* which now raigneth, hath almost made subiect vnto the lawes. *Christiern* they thrust out of his kingdome, and set vp his cosen in his place, with condition that he should neither make peace nor warre, without the leaue of the senat: nor that he should haue any power to condemne any gentleman to death; with many other like articles, which I will in their place set downe: which the kings since that time haue sworne to keepe: which that they should not go against, but that they might be the more firmly kept, the nobilitie will in no case that the king should of himselfe make any peace; and yet haue themselues made a league with the king of Polonia, and them of Lubec, against the king, for the defence of their libertie. So indeed are the rights of Soueraigntie diuided betwixt the king and the nobilitie, but so as that they both liuing in perpetuall feare and distrust; do seeke for the alliance and fellowship of their neighbour princes and people, so to receiue the lesse harme one of them from another. With like surges and tempests is the kingdome of Sweden also tossed, the king whereof liued in such distrust with his nobilitie, as that king *Henry* was glad to take a German for his Chauncelour, and one *Varennes* a Norman for his high Constable: and yet at length was by his nobilitie thrust out of his royall seat, and by them cast in prison, wherein hee liued seuenteene yeare. Wherefore such states as wherein the rights of soueraigntie are diuided, are not rightly to bee called Commonweales, but rather the corruption of Commonweales, as *Herodotus* hath most briefly, but most truely written. For as bodies by nature well framed, if they begin to change, with wonderfull stinke and contagion annoy all that come neere them, vntill they bee quite altered, and become new things; as when egges are set vpon, which before they were set, and after they be hatched also haue a good smell and taste, though in the verie alteration of them not so: so also Commonweales which chaunge their state, the soueraigne

---

G9 of a Monarchie *i.e.* of an absolute authority (*imperium*) in a general sense

Of A Commonweale. 195

uetaigne right and power of them being diuided, find no rest from ciuill warres and broiles, vntill they againe recouer some one of the three formes, and that the soueraigntie be wholie in one of the states or other.

Yet might one say, that in the estate of the Romans the lesse part of the people chosen out of the richer sort made the lawes, and greatest officers; namely the Consuls, the Prætors, the Censors, had both soueraigne power of life and death: and disposed of warre, and that the greater sort of the people made the lesser officers and magistrats, to wit, the Tribuns of the people; the foure and twentie militarie Tribunes; the two Ædiles or Sherifes; the Treasourers; the Scout, and mynt masters, and gaue also all benefices vacant, and more then that the greater part of the people iudged of the great criminall processes before Sylla, if it tended not to the naturall or ciuill death of any. And by this meane it seemeth that that Commonweal was composed of an Aristocracie, and of a popular estate: Whereunto I answere, that it had well some appearance, but yet neuerthelesse was in effect a true popular estate: for albeit that the great estate of the people was diuided into sixe degrees, or companies, according to euery ones abilitie, and that the knights, and the greatest part of the Senators, and of the nobilitie, and richer sort of the people were of the first companie: who agreeing among them selues, the lawes by them made were published, and the great magistrats by them chosen receiued to take their oath: yet neuerthelesse true it is that the fiue companies that remayned, had tenne times as many citizens in them: and in case that all the Centuries of the first companie agreed not vpon the matter, they then came to the second companie, and so by order euen to the sixt and last, which in deede seldom times or neuer happen. Matters being still so agreed vpon, as that they came not alwayes vnto the second companie, but seldom to the third, and most seldom to the fourth, scarcely at all vnto the fift, and neuer vnto the sixt: wherein was all the rabble of the poore and base people, in number farre exceeding all the rest: yet sufficeth it for our purpose, that all the people had thein part, to shew it to haue beene a popular state: albeit that the most noble and richer sort were first called. And yet for all that the meniall people, (that is to say, the greater sort of the people) without the nobilitie, seeing them selues sometime deceiued of their voices (after that the kings were driuen out) and little or no regard to be had of them, began tumultuously to arise: whereof grew the three departures of the people into the mount Auentine, whither the people in armes had retired them selues for the defence of their libertie and power against the nobilitie: which could not bee appeased vntill it was lawfull for them to chuse vnto them selues their owne sacred magistrats, and that in their owne assemblies, from which the nobilitie was excluded: and then the Commonweal seemed in a maner to haue beene mixt of the nobilitie and the people. But if a man will consider the shortnes of the time, and the turmoyles where with the Commonweal was in the meane time afflicted, he shall confesse that it could scarce haue stood in that state, although most miserable twentie or thirtie yeares: neither yet so long, had it not on euery side beene beset with enemies. For shortly after the people tooke vnto them selues the power to make lawes, wherein the maiestie of the Commonweal is contained; and so by little and little wrested from the nobilitie (much against their will & long strugling therefore) the other soueraigne rights also: insomuch that the nobilitie scarce made twelue lawes in the space of foure or fiue hundred; And yet at the same time that the people chose the greater magistrats by their greatest assemblies, the vulgar people was there present, and enrolled in the sixt companie, which although it most seldom gaue suffrage or voice, yet might it so do, if the other companies should haue disagreed among them selues: a reason sufficient to showe the state even at that time also to haue

S ij

beene

A5 officers, namely   A6 Censors; had   A7 *For* greater sort *read* greater part (cf. A10). A9 the Scout *i.e.* the watch   B6 abilitie *i.e.* wealth, means   C7 had therin   C9 *For* greater sort *read* greater part.   D10 miserable, twentie   E5 hundred YEARS; And   Notes at B3, D6.

beene a popular state.

Yet for all that a man may say that it followeth not hereof that there are not but three sorts of Commonweals, although they cannot be amongst them selues mixed: for it may be that of threescore thousand citizens in a citie, fortie thousand may haue the soueraigntie, and twentie thousand be excluded: where, for that the greater part beareth the sway, it shal be a popular state: and contrariewise if but an hundred of that multitude shall haue the soueraigntie, it shall be an Aristocracie; for that the lesse part of the citizens gathered together hath the soueraigne power: what then, if of the same number of citizens fiue and twentie thousand shall hold the chiefe power? Truely, it may be doubted whether such a state be an Aristocracie, although the lesse part of the citizens enioy the soueraigntie, the rest being reiected: for why, it differeth much whether an hundred citizens, or fiue and twentie thousand beare rule, and much more if of an hundred thousand citizens fiue and fortie thousand haue the soueraigntie: or of so great a multitude thirtie onely should beare the sway, the rest excluded, as among the Lacedemonians: yet I alwaies deeme it to be an Aristocracie, if the lesser part of the citizens beare rule ouer the rest: for otherwise if the diuersitie of the number should make the diuersitie of Commonweals, there should be of them a million, yea an infinite of diuers kinds of Commonweals: for the number of them which should haue part in the state encreasing or diminishing, should make an infinite diuersitie, whereof no knowledge is to be had; suffiseth it the soueraigne power to be with the greater or lesser part of the people, for the making of an Aristocracie or Democracie. The rest of the difficulties which might be moued concerning the nature of euery Common weal shall hereafter be in due place declared.

In what state soeuer the lesser number beareth rule ouer the greater it is to be accounted an Aristocratie.
What a principalitie is.

Yet one thing remayneth in the question we haue in hand to be discussed, which is that the Roman Commonweal vnder the emperour *Augustus*, and the other emperours after him, vnto the time of *Flauius Vespatianus*, was called a principalitie, of which sort of Commonweal, neither *Herodotus*, neither any of the Greek or Latine writers, except *Tranquillus*, seemeth to make any mention: for he writeth that the emperour *Caligula*, seeing diuers kings at his table to enter into the teatmes of honour, and the antiquitie of their houses among themselues; with a loude voice brought forth that verse of *Homer* which *Agamemnon* vseth against *Achilles*, who would needs make himselfe equall and companion with him.

Οὐκ ἀγαθὸν πολυκοιρανίη, εἷς κοίρανος ἔστω, εἷς βασιλεύς.

An euill thing it is to be ruled by many:
one prince, and one king, where there is any.

And much it missed not but that hee had euen than taken vpon him the imperiall crowne, and chaunged the forme of the Roman principalitie into a kingdome; and thus much he. where by it is to be vnderstood the Roman state vnder *Augustus* after the battell at Actium, to haue beene neither a Popular state, an Aristocracie, nor a Monarchie. Now a principalitie is nothing else then an Aristocracie, or a Democratie, in which one chiefe commaunded euery man in particular, and it is but the first in generall: for this word (*Prince*) to speake properly signifieth no other thing but him that is first. So the Iewes complained *Aristobulus* the first of the house of the Amoneans, to haue chaunged the principalitie which was Aristocratique, into two kingdomes, at such time as he tooke one crowne to himselfe, and sent an other to his brother. The like wee find, that the auncient cities of Tuscanie made alliance with *Tarquinius Priscus* king of the Romans; vpon condition that hee should not haue power

What a Principalitie is.

K3 *For* and it is but *read* and is but.   K6 Asmoneans   Note at G9.

A power ouer them of life and death: neither to put garrisons into their townes, nor to impose vpon them any taxes or tallages; or to chaunge any of their customes or laws, *Sed vt ciuitatum principatus penes regem Romanum esset*, but that the principalitie of their cities onely should be with the Roman king: for so saith *Florus*. Now all those cities were of a popular state. Wherefore *Tarquinius* was but the first and chiefe in the assemblies of those cities, who might gouerne the multitude no otherwise than doth the emperour in the German empire, or the duke in Venice, or Genua, who may most rightly be called princes, as in the same sence in antient time the chiefe magistrat among the Athenians, was called ἄρχων, or prince: yet was that Commonweale of all other most popular.

B But if there be two chiefe magistrats of like power, as in Rome; or three, as in many cities of the Swissers; or foure, as amongst them of Geneua; it cannot there be called a principalitie, for that none is there chiefe or principall. But in the Roman Commonweale, *Augustus* by a crafty deuise hauing made himselfe but great Generall of the armie (by the name of Imperator) and Tribune of the people for defence of their profit, (from whome for all that he had taken their libertie) and as it seemed almost enforced by the Senat, had taken vpon him the charge of the Commonweale for ten yeares, made that state in show and false semblant but a principalitie, when as before hee had placed in all the prouinces fortie legions, and taken three for the safetie of his person, and put sure garrisons into all the castles and strong fortresses of the empire: so inua-
C ding the royal power without a Scepter, without a Diadem, or a Crowne; whose successors (excepting some few) some more, some lesse, exercised most cruell tyranny. For *Tiberius* in the beginning of his raigne, rise vpon the Consuls, and meeting them gaue them way, (as sayth *Tranquillus*) but afterwards oppressed the Commonweale with most filthy seruitude and slauerie. But here is to be considered what was in deed done, and was not made show of: for he that beareth greatest sway in the Commonweale, him men thinke to haue the soueraigntie: but if question be made of the right, then are we to looke not what is indeed done, but what ought to be done. Wherfore it appeareth a principalitie to be nothing els, but an Aristocratie, or a Democratie, hauing some one for chiefe or principall aboue the rest, the soueraigntie yet still remaining
D with the nobilitie or the people.

In matter of state he that is maister of the forces, is master of the men, of the lawes, and of all the commonweale.

Chap. II.

¶ *Of a Lordly Monarchie, or of the sole gouernment of one.*

E Wee haue before said, that a Monarchie is a kind of Commonweale, wherein the absolute soueraigntie lyeth in the power of one onely prince: which definition we are now to explaine. When we say of one, so the word Monarchie of it selfe importeth: For if we shall in the gouernment ioyne two or moe, no one of them shall haue the soueraigntie: for that a soueraigne is hee which commaundeth all others, and can himselfe by none be commanded. If then there be two princes equall in power, one of them hath not the power to commaund the other, neither can hee suffer the commaund of the other his companion, if it stand not with his owne pleasure, otherwise they should not be equals. Wee may then conclude, that of two princes equall in power in the same Commonweale, and both of them in al things lords of the same people, and of the same countrey indiuisibly, neither the one nor the other hath therein the soueraigntie: but it may well be said them both together to haue the soueraignty of the state comprised vnder the name of an *Oligarchie*, but is more properly

A true soueraign commaundeth all others his subiects, but is himselfe by none commaunded.

called

C3 rise upon *i.e.* arose out of respect   Note at C10.

called a *Duarchie*, a kind of Aristocracie, which may be of continuance and durable, so long as the two princes shall well agree together. As *Romulus* and *Tatius*, one of them king of the Romans, and the other of the Sabines, after certaine conflicts, making peace entred into societie together, vpon condition, that both their people vnited together, should dwell within the same walles, and by the name of Quirites by common soueraigntie be gouerned by both kings. But *Romulus*, who before by the slaughter of his brother *Remus* had rid himselfe of his fellow in the kingdome, could not long endure the straunger to raigne with him, but caused him to be slaine, or at leastwise held the murtherer excused, being for the fact apprehended. Long time after the Roman empire was conuerted from a Monarchy into a Binarchie: at such time as *Antoninus Pius* left *M. Aurelius*, and *Ælius Verus*, emperours, and both fellowes in the same empire: of which two *Ælius* in short time after died, and not without the suspition of poison. For it is, and alwayes hath bene a thing most hard to maintaine the equall soueraigntie of both together. And that which *Lucan* writeth,

A very hard matter for two princes in one and the same commonweale long to hold the soueraigntie togeather.

> *Nulla fides regni socijs, omnisque potestas,*
> *Impatiens consortis erit.*

No sincere loue is to be found in partners of the soueraigne state,
And fellowship in power great, is alwaies mixt with mortall hate.

Is especially to be vnderstood of a Diumuirat, or soueraigne gouernment of two together. For that the gouernment of three or moe together in the soueraigntie, may bee firme, but of two not so; seeing that by nature one thing is but contrarie to one, and not to many: the third as a meane still ioyning the extreames together. And therefore the Roman emperours, when as they at the same time tooke vpon them the same soueraigntie of gouernment, least by the mutuall concurse of their power, they should violat their faith and friendship, diuided the empire, the one being emperor of the East, and the other of the West; the one residing at Constantinople, and the other at Rome, in manner as if they had bene two Monarches, although sometimes the same edicts and lawes were in both empires by the common consent of both princes published. Yet so soone as they began to quarrell, the two empires were indeed diuided in power lawes and estate. So might a man say of the Lacedemonian Commonweale well gouerned by one king. But when *Aristodemus* left the kingdome to be gouerned wholly, and diuided by his two sonnes *Proclus* and *Euristhenes* both at once, they quickly fell at oddes, and had their state taken from them, by *Lycurgus* (beeing himselfe a prince descended of the blood of *Hercules*) and the soueraigntie by him giuen vnto the people. The like happened vnto *Amphareus* and *Leucippus*, kings of the Messians. But the Argiues least they should fal into the same troubles, to auoid the plurality of kings, at such time as *Atreus* and *Thyestes* at once seised vpon their fathers kingdome, the people (I say) made choyce of the wiser, or as *Lucian* saith of the more learned. And the princes of the blood of *Meronee* and *Charlemaigne*, diuided the kingdome amongst them. So the children of *Clodoueus*, of their fathers one kingdom made foure of equall power. And the three children of *Lewes* the Debonaire diuided so many kingdomes amongst them. Neither do we read many at once long to haue holden a kingdome together vndiuided: for the indiuisible nature of soueraigntie, and the fellowship of gouernment, is always full of dangers, where no one hath the soueraigntie, except when a straunge prince marrieth a queene, among such as are acquainted with womens gouernment: where commonly the pictures of the man and his wife, their names and armes are ioined together; as if the soueraigntie belonged vnto them both: as it chanced

---

H1 Diumvirat *i.e.* Duumvirate   I1–2 power, lawes   I4 *For* divided *read* undivided.   I7 *For* Messians *read* Messenians.   K1 Merouee

ced when king *Ferdinand* married *Isabel* queene of Castile, *Anthonie* of Burbon, *Ioane* queene of Nauarre, and *Philip* king of Spaine *Marie* the daughter of *Henrie* king of England. Howbeit the English men would not suffer him to haue any part with her in the soueraigntie, or of the fruites or profis thereto belonging, but that the same should remaine wholly vnto her selfe; albeit that they were contented that they should both (for fashion sake) beare the name, and both the one and the other signe charters, and commissions, but yet so, as that the signe of the queene might of it selfe bee sufficient, but that without hers the signe of king *Philip* should be to no purpose. Which was also agreed vpon with *Ferdinand* king of Arragon, hauing married *Isabel* of Castile, where all the commaunds were signed, *Yo el Roy*, and *Yo la Reyna*; and by the secretarie of the state, with sixe doctors: but as for the soueraigntie it was wholly in the queene. Than which no more effectuall reason can be giuen against the Manichies, who erroneously appointed two gods of equall power; one good, & the other euill: for if it were so they being contrarie the one to the other, should either ruinat the one the other, or els being at continuall variance, should without ceasing trouble the sweet harmonie and concord that we see in this great world. And how could the world endure those two lords of equall power, and contrarie in will the one to the other, seeing that the least citie or Commonweale cannot suffer two, albeit that they were brethren, if they should fall neuer so little at variance: much more easily could it endure three such princes than two; for that the third might vnite the two, or els ioyning himselfe with the one, constraine them both to liue in peace. As it happened so long as *Pompee, Cæsar*, and *Crassus* liued, whome the people called the monster with three heads: for so long they peaceably gouerned the Roman empire, which then depended of their power. But so soone as *Crassus* was slaine in Caldea, straight way the other two fell in sunder, and so egerly made warre the one of them vpon the other, as that to reconcile them was impossible, vntill that one of them had quite ouerthrowne the other, and made himselfe maister of all. The like happened after the death of *Cæsar*, in the Triumuirat of *Augustus, M. Antoninus*, and *Lepidus*, who hauing of one popular Commonweale, made three Monarchies; and *Lepidus* vnfit for gouernment, had submitted his authoritie vnto *Augustus*, although *Antoninus* had married *Augustus* his sister, and that they two had equally diuided the empire betwixt them, and liued in countries farre distant one from another; yet rested they not long, but that the one of them was shaken out of all, by the authoritie and power of the other. Whereafter ensued the sure state of the empire, established vnder one mans gouernment. Wherefore let vs hold it as resolued vpon, that it cannot be called a Monarchie, where the soueraigntie is in two mens power; neither that any gouernment can consist in that state, if they shall fall at variance betwixt themselues.

Now Monarchie is diuided into three formes: for he that hath the soueraigntie, is either lord of all: or else a king, or a tyrant, which maketh no diuersitie of Common weals, but proceedeth of the diuersitie of the gouernour in the Monarchie. For there is great difference betwixt the state, and the gouerment of the state: a rule in pollicie (to my knowledge) not before touched by any man: for the state may be in a Monarchie, and yet the gouernment neuerthelesse popular; if the king do distribute all places of commaund, magistracie, offices, and preferments indifferently vnto all men, without regard of their nobilitie, wealth, or vertue. But if the prince shall giue all commaund, honours, and offices, vnto the nobilitie onely, or to the rich, or to the valiant, or to the vertuous onely, it shall be a royall Monarchie, and that simple and pure, but yet tempered in maner of an Aristocracie. So also an Aristocratique seigneurie, may gouerne their estate popularly; diuiding the honours and preferments therein vnto all

S iiij the

Marginal notes: I the king, and I the queene. — A commonweale better gouerned by three great soueraigns then by two. — Three sortes of monarchies. Great difference betwixt the state, and the gouernment of the state of a commonweale.

the subiects indifferently: or else Aristocratically, bestowing them vpon the nobilitie or richer sort onely; which varietie of gouernment hath deceiued them which haue made a mixture of Commonweals, and so made more sorts thereof then three, without hauing regard that the state of a Commonweal is different from the administration and gouernment of the same: But this point we will farther touch in place conuenient.

The three sorts of Monarchies aptly described.

Wherefore a lawfull or royall Monarchie is that where the subiects obey the lawes of a Monarque, and the Monarque the lawes of nature, the subiects inioying their naturall libertie, and proprietie of their goods. The lordly Monarchie is that where the prince is become lord of the goods and persons of his subiects, by law of armes and lawfull warre; gouerning them as the master of a familie doth his slaues. The tyrannicall Monarchie, is where the prince contemning the lawes of nature and nations, imperiously abuseth the persons of his free borne subiects, and their goods as his owne. The same difference is also found in the Aristocratique and popular estate: for both the one and the other may be lawful, lordly, and tirannicall, in such sort as I haue said: for the greatest tyrannie of all other is of *Tully* called the rage of the furious and turbulent people.

The lordly Monarchie the first that was amongst men.

Now as concerning the lordly Monarchie, it is conuenient for vs first to intreat thereof, as of that which was first amongst men: for they are deciued which following the opinion of *Aristotle*, suppose that golden kind of men (more famous for the poets fables, then for that there were any such in deed) to haue made first choice of their heroicall kings: seeing we find, and all men are perswaded that the first Monarchie was established in *Assiria*, vnder the power of *Nemrod*, whom the holie scripture calleth the great hunter; which is a common phrase of speach amongst the *Hebrewes*, by which word they signifie a theefe, or robber. For the auntient writers, viz. *Plato*, *Aristotle*, and *Xenophon*, haue put robberie among the kinds of hunting, as wee haue elswhere noted. For before the time of *Nemrod* no man is found to haue had power

Nemrod the first Monarkie.

and rule one ouer an other, all men liuing in like libertie; he being the first that tooke vpon him the soueraigntie, and that caused free borne men to serue: whose name seemeth to haue beene giuen him according vnto his qualitie, for asmuch as *Nemrod* signifieth a terrible lord. Soone after the world was seene full of slaues, *Sem* one of the sonnes of *Noe* yet liuing. And in the whole course of the Bible, the scripture speaking of the subiects of the kings of Assiria and Ægipt, calleth them alwaies slaues: and not the holie scripture onely, but the Greekes also, who alwayes in their writings tearme them selues free, and the Barbarians slaues; meaning by the Barbarians the people of Asia and Ægipt. And therefore the kings of Persia denouncing warre, demaunded the earth and the waters, (as *Plutache* writeth) to showe that they were absolute Lords of all that was in the land and sea conteined. And that is it for which *Xenophon* in his *Cyropædia* writeth, that it is a thing good and commendable among the Medes, that the prince should be lord and owner of all things: And thereof came the adoration which not onely the subiects, but straungers also, yea and the embassadors of forren nations vsed towards the kings of Persia, to showe that all was in his power. For when *Themistocles*, whose name euen then and long before was most famous, would after the manner of the Greeks haue spoken vnto the Persian king, *Atabanus* captaine of the kings gard, kept him from comming vnto him, neither would suffer him to preferre any request vnto him, vntill such time as he had after the Persian manner adored him: but afterwards when he was gon out of the kings presence, hee courteously spake vnto him, and in these words excused that he had done; It is seemely O *Themistocles*, to follow the fashion of the countrey wherein a man is: you Grecians

---

H7 elswhere noted *i.e.* in his commentary on Oppian, *De venatione libri IIII* (Paris, 1555), fol. 45
I7 Plutarche   K4 Artabanus

Of A Commonvveale. 201

ans make great reckning of your libertie and equalitie of commaund; but we esteeme it for the best thing in the world to reverence, serue, and honour our king, as the image of the living God. Wherevnto agreeth that which *Liuie* writeth, *Barbaris pro legibus semper dominorum imperia fuerunt*. The commaund of their lords haue beene alwaies vnto the Barbarians for lawes. Neither ought this lordly monarchie to be accounted a tyrannie: for it is not inconuenient, that a soueraigne prince hauing in good and lawfull warre vanquished his enemies, should make himselfe lord of their goods and persons by the law of armes, governing them now his subiects, as doth the good housholder his seruants or slaues: as wee see it a thing receiued by the manner and custome of almost all nations. But the prince which shall by vniust warre, or other vnlawfull meanes make of freemen his slaues, and possesse himselfe of their goods, is not a lordlike Monarche, but a verie tyrant: from which *Adrian* the emperour was so farre, as that he would not that a slaue a player, should enioy his libertie, which his master at the request of the people of Rome had giuen him in the Theater, but left it to the discretion of his master, to be as he thought good disposed of: As had *Tiberius* before, and after that *Marcus Aurelius Adrian* his sonne in like case forbid the same: whatsoeuer consent the master had giuen at the clamour of the people; reputing it rather forced than done of good will: to the end that the full disposition should be in euery mans power, of that which vnto him belonged. And now although at this present there be few princes which haue in their absolute power the bodies and goods of their subiects, although we see many tyrants; yet are there many in Asia and Africa: but in Europe I know none which take so much vpon them, beside the Princes of the Turkes, and of the Moscouits. True it is that the Moscouits call themselues Chlopes, that is to say, seruants, which wee corruptly call slaues. But the Emperour of the Turkes styleth himselfe *Sultan*, that is to say Lord: not so much for the largenes of his possession, (seeing that the king of Spaine hath vnder his dominion and rule, people for their crueltie barbarous, for their multitude innumerable, in places infinite: which his kingdome is bounded with the same countries, wherewith the course of the sunne is bounded, being ten times greater then the Turkes empire) but is therefore called Lord of the Turkes, for that he is lord of their persons and goods; whom for all that he gouerneth much more courteously and freely, then doth a good housholder his seruants: for those whom wee call the princes slaues, or seruants, the Turkes call them Zamoglans, that is to say tribute children; whom the prince vseth no otherwise to instruct, then if they were his children: and to bestow on them noble preferments, which are of others desirously sought after. As for his Timariot horsmen, they hold all their possessions in fealtie of the Prince, as it were during pleasure, renewing their letters patents from ten yeares to ten yeares: neither when they dye can they leaue their children heires of their possessions, but of their moueables onely; except by the gift of the prince they keepe the possession of their fathers lands, as they doe of his goods. Other princes there are none in Europe which call themselues lords of the bodies and goods of their subiects, and fewer in auncient time then at this present: for *Augustus* the emperour himselfe, although he were in effect the greatest monarch in the world, yet so it was that he so abhorred to be called Lord: neither had any that held of him in fealtie and homage.

Now if one say that there is no Monarque in Europe which pretendeth not all the goods and lands of his subiects to belong vnto him in right of direct soueraigntie, neither any man which confesseth not to hold his goods of his soueraigne prince: yet I say that that sufficeth not that any man should therefore of right be called lord of all, or a lordly Monarche: seeing that euery subiect hath the true proprietie of his owne things,

A lordly Monarchie, not to be accounted a tirannie and whie.

The great Turk and the Moscouite the only lordly Monarqus in Europe

How the goods and landes of subiects belong vnto the soueraigne prince.

A9 received   C4 slaves *i.e. sclavi*, a term originally applied to Slavic captives   C4 Emperour

things, and may thereof dispose at his pleasure: although the prince for pompe and show challenge vnto himselfe the soueraigntie thereof. And yet there are diuers lands which are called Allodial, wherein the prince hath neither proprietie, nor soueraigne right, as not holden of him. The Hunns a Tartar-like nation come from the farthest parts of Scythia, at such times as they with fire and sword destroied almost all Europe, first showed the example vnto the Lombards and Almans, Germaine nations, and to the Frankes, the auncient inhabitants of Fraunce, calling themselues Lords of all, and so accustomed these nations to lord it ouer all: as that no man could hold a turfe of ground but by their leaue. True it is that the Romans hauing vanquished their enemies, most commonly solde them for slaues, or else condemned them to lose the seauenth part of their lands: which lands they straight waies gaue vnto their Colonies in pure proprietie. But princes and people instructed in ciuilitie, for feare of rebellion, or distrust of their owne power, reiected such lordlike soueraigntie as had the kings of Persia and Asia ouer their subiects: contenting themselues with the shadow of such lordly Monarchie. And albeit that the Persian kings before the time of *Artaxerxes*, had vsed to cause their great lords and magistrats to be stript starke naked before them and whipped as slaues: yet king *Artaxerxes* was the first that ordained that they should in deed be stript, but should not haue but their cloathes and garments onely beaten: and wheras their haire was wont in dispite to be pulled off, he commaunded the wooll of their cappes onely to be so pulled. True it is that *Francis Aluarez* writeth, that he hath seene in Æthiopia the great Chauncelour, and other great lords and gouernours of prouinces stript starke naked, and cast vpon the ground whipped as slaues before their prince: who held the same as a great honour vnto them; by the discourse of whose hystorie, a man may easilie gather the great Negus of Æthiopia to be a Lordly Monarque. But the people of Europe more couragious, and better souldiers then the people of Africke or Asia, could neuer endure the lordly Monarques, neither had euer vsed them before the incursions of the Hunnes into Europe, as I haue before said. And first of all *Odonacre* king of the Herules, who almost at the same time invaded Italie, that *Attila* did Germanie; hauing brought Italie vnder his subiection, tooke the third part of the territorie from the subiects (the punishment of all people by him vanquished,) but left their persons free, and themselues lords of their goods, without any tenure, or yeelding vnto him of any fealtie or homage. But after that the Almans, Lombards, Frenchmen, Saxons, Burgundians, Gothes, Ostrogothes, Englishmen, and other Northren people had tasted the maners and customes of the Hunnes, they began to make themselues Lords, not of the persons, but of all the lands of them whom they had vanquished: and yet afterward reseruing vnto themselues the most fruitfull part thereof, left the rest vnto the auncient inhabitants, to be by them inioyed, yet as holden of them in fealtie, with paying of some small tribute if they should change the possession thereof: which for this cause are called Seigneuries, or Lordships; to show that the shadow of the auncient lordly Monarchie as yet remayneth, although greatly diminished. For these fees and lordships were in auncient time nothing else but benefits and rewards giuen to souldiors for terme of their liues, and afterward by fauour continued from the father to the sonne: except dukedomes, marquisats, earledomes, and other like honours and dignities, giuen vnto dukes, marqueses, earles, and such like honorable personages, and not vnto the lands: a custome not yet chaunged in England and Scotland for regard of the dignities, where the dukes and counties being dead, their children and successours haue their lands; but not still the dignities, prerogatiues, and titles of their predecessours: for when fees or lands were giuen to souldiours for terme of their liues, they afterward obtained, that they might either by their wills,

The Hunnes the first that brough the lordly soueraignmēt of Monarks into Europ.

*Plutar in Rosmalo.

The great Negus of Æthiopia a lordly Monarque.

The beginning of tenants and fees, and what in auntient time they were.

F 5 (margin) brought   H 8 Odouacre   Note at F 4.

A wills, or else dying intestate, leaue them vnto their children; and that if there were no heires males left, they should by law descend vnto the women: excepting in Germany, where the women are excluded from the inheritance of lands in fee: which was the strongest argument which *Fredericke* countie of Vaudemont vsed against *Renat* of Aniou king of Sicilie at the counsell of Constance, demaunding of the Emperour that he might be invested in the dukedome of Loraine, considering that it was an imperial fee, and by consequent that *Isabel* wife to *Renate* was not thereof capable: although she were the duke of Lorains daughter. Howbeit that *Renate* the king of Sicilie, might by an other reason haue defended himselfe; that is to say, that in question of fees, and

B seruices, we are to follow the lawes and customes of the land that oweth the seruice, and not of that wherevnto the seruice is due: now by the custome of Loraine the daughters succeede in fees. But howsoeuer it be, most certein it is that the marks of Lordly Monarchies, haue continued in Germanie, and towards the North more than in the other parts of Europe. For albeit that *William* the Conquerour, hauing conquered the realme of England, by force of armes, called himselfe not onely lord of that realme, but also caused it to be proclaimed, that the soueraigntie and proprietie of al his subiects goods, mouable, and immouable vnto him belonged: yet neuerthelesse so it was, that he contented himselfe with the direct soueraigntie, fealtie and homage: the subiects still enioying their libertie, and full propertie of their goods. But the emperour *Charles* the fift, after he had subdued the great counttey of Peru, made himselfe

C Lordly Monarch thereof, causing all things to be holden of him, excepting the slaues, whome for that they were innumerable he caused to be set at libertie. As for the lands he left them to be enioyed by them that possessed them at his pleasure: and not to descend vnto their children by inheritance. A craftie and subtill deuice, whereby *Lagasca* the lawyer, the emperours lieutenant in Peru (*Gonsulo Pizarra*, and the rest of the authors of rebellion vanquished and ouerthrowne) by a perpetuall bond to keepe the inhabitants of that country, within the compasse of their duety, compelled them for euer to aske of the king of Spaine, the possession of their goods, their kinsmen beeing dead: except the parents themselues yet liuing, had before procured the same to be graunted for their children in time to come: which was not to be obtained without a great sum of money to be paid into the kings coffers: they of greater power in the meane time

D being thereby kept from raising of any new sturres. For like cause whereof in one chapter of *Mahomets*, it is forbiden all persons of what degree or qualitie soeuer to call themselues in any sort lords, except the Caliph, or great bishop the successour of *Mahomet*, who at the first was the onely Lordly Monarch or lord of all, giuing vnto kings and princes their principalities and kingdomes, during his pleasure, vntill that the Othoman princes, the Curdes, and the kings of the higher part of Asia and Afrike, by little and little exempted themselues out of their power (by reason of the diuision betwixt them and the Anticaliphes) and so tooke vnto themselues the kingdomes of those countries.

E But yet here might some man doubt whether the lordly Monarchie be not a Tyranny, considering that it seemeth to be directly against the law of nature; which reserueth vnto euerie man his libertie, and the soueraigntie ouer his owne goods. Wherunto I aunswere, that of auntient time it was indeed against the law of nature to make free men slaues, and to possesse himselfe of other mens goods: but if the consent of all nations will, that that which is gotten by iust warre should bee the conquerours owne, and that the vanquished should be slaues vnto the victorious, as a man cannot well say that a Monarchie so established is tyrannicall: seeing also wee read that *Iacob* the Patriarch, by his testament leauing vnto his children certaine lands that hee had

gotten

The markes of lordly Monarchies more to be seene in the Northren countries then in any other parts of Europ.

Charls the fift made himselfe the lordly Monarque of Peru.

All persons of what degree soeuer forbidden by the Mahometain lawes, the great Caliph only excepted.

A lordly monarkie no tiranny.

D3 Mahomets LAW, it is forbiden   E7 *For* as a man cannot *read* a man cannot (cf. Fr).

Notes at A8, B2, E4, E5.

gotten, said that it was his owne, for that he had got it by force of armes. And that more is, the rule that willeth that the law of armes should take no place where there be superiours to do iustice (which is put in practise against the greatest princes, and imperiall cities of Germany, who be proscribed by the empire, for not making restitution of that which belonged to others) sheweth right well, that where there is no superiour to commaund, their force is reputed iust. For otherwise, if we will mingle and confound the Lordly Monarchie, with the tyrannicall estate, we must confesse that there is no difference in warres, betwixt the iust enemie and the robber; betwixt a lawfull prince and a theefe; betwixt warres iustly denounced, and vniust and violent force; which the antient Romans called plaine robberie and theft. We also see tyrannicall states and gouernments, soone to fall, and many tyrants in short time slaine: whereas the seigneure-like states, and namely the Lordly Monarchies haue bene both great and of long continuance, as the auntient Monarchies of the Assyrians, the Medes, Persians, & Ægyptians; and at this present that of Æthiopia (the most auntient Monarch of all Asia and Afrike) whereunto are subiect fiftie kings as slaues, if we may beleeue *Pau. Iouius*, who all are, and tearme themselues the slaues of the Grand Negus of Æthiopia. And the reason why the Lordly Monarchie is more durable than the royall, is for that it is more maiesticall, and that the subiects hold not their liues, goods, and libertie, but of the soueraigne prince, who hath by iust warre conquered them; which plucketh downe the courage of subiects, so that the slaue acknowledging his condition, becommeth humble, abiect, and hauing as they say a base and seruile hart. Where to the contrarie, men free borne, and lords of their owne goods in a royall Monarchie, if one would make them slaues, or take from them that theirs is, they would not take it, but easily rebell, bearing noble harts, nourished in libertie, and not abastardised with seruitude. And thus much concerning a Lordly Monarchie: Now let vs speake of the Monarchie Royall.

Whie the lordly monarchie is more durable then the royall monarchie.

Chap. III.

Of a Royall Monarchie.

A Royal Monarch or king, is he which placed in soueraignty yeeldeth himselfe as obedient vnto the lawes of nature as he desireth his subiects to be towards himselfe, leauing vnto euery man his naturall libertie, and the proprietie of his owne goods. I haue put to these last words for the difference of a Lordly Monarch, who may be a iust and vertuous prince, and equally gouerne his subiects, being himselfe yet neuerthelesse lord both of their persons and goods. And if it so chaunce the Lordly Monarch hauing iustly conquered his enemies countrey, to set them againe at libertie, with the proprietie of their goods; of a lord he becommeth a king, and chaungeth the Lordly Monarchie, into a Monarchie Royall. And that is it for which *Plinie* the younger saith vnto *Traian* the emperour, *Principis sedem obtines, ne sit Domino locus*, Thou holdest the seate of a prince, Lord it not. This difference (betwixt a Royall Monarch and a Lordly) was well noted by the auntient Persians, calling *Cyrus* the elder (which ouerthrew the Monarchie of the Medes) by the name of a king: but tearming *Cambyses* a lord, and *Darius* a marchant; for that *Cyrus* was a gentle and courteous prince towards his subiects, but *Cambyses* his sonne was haughtie and proud, and *Darius* too great an exactor and couetous. So it is also reported *Alexander* the Great to haue bene advised by *Aristotle*, to beare himselfe towards the Greekes as a father; but towards the Barbarians as a Lord:

A royall Monarque.

The difference betwixt a royall and a lordly Monarque.

F6 their *i.e.* there (cf. Fr and L)   G 3–4 Ægyptians (Fr) Parthians (L)

lord: which his councell *Alexander* neuerthelesse reiected, willing that the Greekes should be reckoned of according to their vertue, and the Barbarians according to their vices; saying, that the whole earth was but one citie, and his campe the Castle thereof.

We haue moreouer said in our definition, that the subiects ought to be obedient vnto the Royall Monarch, to show that in him alone lyeth the soueraigne maiestie; & that the king ought to obey the lawes of nature: that is to say, to gouerne his subiects, and to guide his actions according vnto naturall iustice, whose luster was brighter than the light of the sunne it selfe. It is then the true marke of a Royall Monarchie, when the prince sheweth himselfe as obedient vnto the lawes of nature, as he wisheth his subiects to be vnto himselfe. Which it is not hard for him looking into the dutie of a good prince to obtaine; as fearing God aboue all; if he be also pitifull vnto the afflicted, wise in his enterprises, hardie in his exploits, modest in prosperitie, constant in aduersitie, aduised in his speech, wise in his councell, careful of his subiects, comfortable to his friends, terrible to his enemies, courteous to the good, dreadfull towards the euill, and iust towards all. Which royall soueraigntie so set downe, as that the subiects stand obedient vnto the lawes of their prince, and the prince likewise vnto the lawes of nature: the law being on both sides a mistresse, or as saith *Pindarus*, a queene raigning ouer both, it shall in the same bonds vnite the subiects among themselues, and together with their prince: whereof shall grow a most sweet harmony, which may with wonderfull pleasure and felicitie blesse them both. This is that regall and lawfull Monarchie of one, which we seeke after, whether the kingdome descend by succession, as it most commonly doth; or by the law, as this of ours, or by election, as in many kingdomes towards the North; or by gift, as the kingdome of Numidia (which by *Cæsar* brought into the forme of a prouince, was by *Augustus* the emperour giuen to young *Iuba*, who so of a slaue became a king) or as the kingdome of Naples, and Sicilie, giuen to *Charles* of Fraunce, and after to *Lewes*, first duke of Aniou, or left by testament, as in former times the kingdomes of Tunes, Fez, and Marocco, and was also of late put in practise by *Henrie* the eight king of England, who by his will left that kingdome vnto his son *Edward* the sixt, to whom hee substituted his sister *Marie*, and vnto her *Elizabeth*, who was afterward queene: or that the kingdome bee got by fraud and deceit, so that he raigne iustly, as *Cecrops, Hieron, Gelon*, and *Pisistratus*, who right wisely vsed their power, as saith *Plutarch*: and in our time *Cosmus de Medices*: or by chaunce, as the kingdome of Persia, by the neying of an horse fel to *Darius Histaspis* one of the seuen Persian lords, it being so before agreed, after they had slaine the Mages, who had vsurped the kingdome, that he whose horse first neyed, should haue the kingdome: or be it that the prince by force of armes, by right or wrong conquer his kingdome, prouided that he vprightly gouerne the same so by him conquered; as *Titus Liuius* saith of king *Seruius, Neque enim præter vim quicquam ad ius regni habebat*. Neither had he any thing but force vnto the right of the kingdome; and yet he was a good king, as it oftentimes hath bene seene of a robber and a theefe, to haue proued a vertuous prince; and of a violent tyranny, to haue growne a iust royaltie. Or be it that the king bee chosen for his nobilitie, as was *Campson* chosen Sultan of Ægypt by the Mamalukes: or for his iustice and deuotion, as *Numa* in Rome: or for his age, as the antient Arabians made choice of the eldest amongst them for their king, as saith *Diodorus*, and they of Taprobana, as saith *Pliny*: or for his strength and force, as *Maximinus* the Roman emperor, being of such stature and strength, as that he seemed to haue come of the race of Giants: or for his feature and beautie, as was *Heliogabalus*, therefore chosen emperour of the same Roman empire: or for his height and stature, as in Æthiopia the kingdomes were

The true markes of a royall Monarque.

were still giuen to the tallest: or for that he could drinke most, as in Scythia, as *Aristotle* saith; who defineth a king to be him, who chosen by the people, raigneth according to the desire of them his subiects: from whose will (as hee in another place saith) if he neuer so little depart, he becommeth a tyrant. Which his description is not only without reason, but also daungerous: for that soueraigne power which he said to bee most proper vnto a king, must so needs fall, if the king could nothing command against the liking and good will of his subiects; but must to the contrarie be constrained to receiue lawes of them. In briefe it should be lawfull for the people to do all things; and the most iust and best kings should so be accounted for tyrants: neither were a king to be reputed of any thing else, than as of a meane magistrat, vnto whome power were to bee giuen, and againe taken away at the peoples pleasure. Which are all things impossible, and no lesse absurd also, than is that which the same *Aristotle* saith, That they are barbarous people, where their kings come by succession. When as yet his owne king and scholler *Alexander* the Great, was one of them which descended in right line from the blood of *Hercules*, and by right of succession came to the kingdom of Macedon. The Lacedemonians should be also barbarous, who from the same stocke of the Heraclides, had had their kings about a thousand yeares. The people of Asia also, the Persians, and Ægyptians, should so all bee barbarous: in whome not onely rested, but from whome all humanitie, courtesie, learning, knowledge, and the whole source and fountaine of good lawes and Commonweales haue sprung: and so at last none but *Aristotle* with some handfull of Greekes should bee free from barbarisme. Whereas indeed nothing can be deuised more daungerous vnto the state of a Commonweale, than to commit the election of kings vnto the suffrages of the people; as shall in due place be hereafter declared. Although *Aristotle* be in that also deceiued, where he saith, That there be three sorts of kings; & yet hauing in his discourse reckoned vp foure, in casting vp of the account he findeth out a fift. The first hee calleth Voluntarie kings, as raigning by the will and good liking of the people, such as were the kings of Heroique times, whome he supposeth to haue bene Captains, Iudges, and Priests. The second he saith, are proper vnto the barbarous nations, where kings come by succession. The third are made by election. The fourth was proper to the Lacedemonians, whome he saith to haue bene perpetuall generals in their warres; the sonne still succeeding his father. The fift and last kind, is of them which hauing themselues got the Lordly soueraigntie, vse their subiects, as doth the maister of the house his slaues. As for the first sort of kings, we find, that they indeed executed the offices of judges, captaines, and priests, yet none of them are found to haue ruled at the will and pleasure of the people, either to haue receiued their authoritie from the people, before *Pitacus* king of Corinth, and *Timondas* king of Nigropont: but to the contrarie * *Plutarch* writeth, That the first princes had no other honour before their eyes, than to force men, and to keepe them in subiection as slaues: whereof the holy scripture also certifieth vs of the first Lordly Monarch *Nemrod*; leauing the soueraigntie to their children, in right of succession; as saith *Thucidides*. Which hath also beene well confirmed by the succession of a great number of kings of the Asirians, Medes, Persians, Indians, Ægyptians, Hebrewes, Lacedemonians, Macedonians, Sicyonians, Epirots, Athenians: and their lines failing, the people in part proceeded to make choice of their kings by way of election, some others inuaded the state by force, other some maintained themselues in Aristocratike and popular seigneurie; as witnesseth *Herodotus, Thucidides, Iosephus, Berosus, Plutarch, Xenophon*, and other most auntient historiographers of the Hebrewes, Greeks, and Latines, sufficient to conuince the opinion of *Aristotle* of vntruth in those things that he hath writ concerning kings. Whereas also he

Polit lib.3.
Aristotle blamed.

The opinion of Aristotle concerning kings impugned.
Arist. Polit.3

Plutar in Thesé.

OF A COMMONWEALE. 207

he comprehendeth the Lacedemonian generals, vnder the name of kings: he is therein deceiued, seeing it is before declared, that he cannot be a king, which hath not the rights of soueraigntie. And that the Lacedemonian kings, after the conuersion of that Commonweale, were nothing but Senators, and subiect to the magistrats commaund, wee haue also before shewed. Yea the generals power was not alwaies giuen vnto them, as *Aristotle* supposeth, who calleth them the perpetuall generals of the warres: forasmuch as that power and authoritie was communicated to their citisens also, as to *Lysander, Leonidas, Callicratides, Gilippus*, whome the Lacedemonians oppressed with warres preferred before their kings. And albeit that *Agesilaus* was one of their kings, yet so it was, that he durst not take vpon him the charge of a generall, vntill the Seigneurie had so commanded; as *Plutarch* in his liues reporteth. And when they were chiefe captaines and generals, they gaue them yet no royall power, no more than had the generals of the Acheans, which were made by election, considering that they were subiect vnto the state of the Acheans, who if they so deserued punished them, as they did *Democritus* their generall, whome they fined at thirtie thousand crownes, as wee read in *Pausanias*. So the Ephori punished their kings with banishment, imprisonment, and fines, yea and sometime with death, as we haue before said. We must not therefore put these in the ranke of kings, no more than him which is a Lordly Monarch, lord of the persons and goods of his subiects, who hath his proper difference seperated from a Monarch Royall.

As for the third sort of kings, which he said was made by election, that can make no difference of kings, no more than can the second, which he said was by succession, for otherwise he should by the same meanes make also a sixt kind of kings, made by chaunce; as was *Darius* the first: and so a seuenth by donation, an eight by testament, and a ninth by finnes and deceit, and a tenth by force: which were nought else, but to make an infinit sort of kings, who all neuerthelesse are comprehended vnder one kind. For the difference of Monarches is not to be gathered by the meanes of the comming to the state, but by the meanes of gouerning of the estate. Which as we said is comprised in three kinds or sorts, viz. the Lordly Monarchie, the Royall Monarchie, and the Tirannicall Monarchie. But whereas *Aristotle* vnder the name of kings comprehendeth them also which were woont for a short time to be chosen, to establish or reforme the Commonweale, and that done, to giue vp their charge, are quite different from the regall power. Neither hath it any apparance to call them kings, which are nothing els but simple commissioners, such as were the dictators in the Roman Commonweale, whome *Dionysius Halicarnasseus* writeth, to haue bene in power and office like vnto them whom the Thessalians called *Archos*, the Lacedemonians *Cosmos*, the Mitylenians *Æsymnetes*, hauing like charge that the baily of Florence had at such time as that Commonweale was gouerned by a popular gouernment; that is to wit, the Grand Councell of the people made choyce of eight or ten persons, best seene in their affaires, to reestablish the state, and to put againe in order that which by processe of time was fallen into disorder, either in their lawes, or in their customes, in their reuenewes, or in creating of their officers: which done they discharged themselues of their offices: like as the Decemuiri, or ten commissioners, which were chosen in Rome, to reforme that was amisse in the state, whome wee should by this meanes, according to the opinion of *Aristotle* call also kings; which should be a thing verie absurd; forasmuch as the qualitie of a magistrat, and much lesse of a commissioner hath nothing agreeing or common with the soueraigne maiestie of a king. And albeit that *Cæsar* in his Commentaries saith, the inhabitants of Autun to haue euerie yeare chosen them a magistrat with royall power; that is of him but improperly spoken: for why, it is manifest,

T ij

The difference of Monarques how it is to be gathered.

nifest, that he which was a magistrat could be no king. And that more is, the gouernours of the countries and prouinces conquered by *Alexander* the Great, although that after his death euerie one of them tooke vpon him the soueraigntie in the country or prouince that he gouerned; yet it was a long time before they durst stile themselues by the name of kings. The first that began was *Antigonus*, after the victorie by him obtained against *Ptolomeus Lagus*: after which he set a crowne vpon his head, and vsed in his titles the name of Βασιλεὺς, or king. And immediatly after, the Ægyptians called *Ptolomee* king; as to their imitation did the Assyrians *Seleucus*, and the Thracians *Lysimachus* also. And not to go further, the auntient kings of Loraine and Burgundie, after that they had yeelded fealtie and homage vnto the German emperour, lost the name and soueraigntie of kings, and called themselues but dukes: for that now they were no more kings, according to that fit saying of *Martial, Qui rex est, regem Maxime non habeat*. For why, the name of a king is alwaies maiesticall, and the most honourable that a soueraigne prince can haue: and for that cause the habit, the markes, the signes of kings, haue bene alwaies particular, and proper vnto themselues; as the royal armes, the golden robes, the crowne and scepter, not to be communicated vnto other men. And there was nothing that made the maiestie of the Roman kings so venerable, as the royall ornaments which *Tarquinius Priscus* brought from the antient kings of Hetruria, as we read in the histories. And the Romans themselues, after they had driuen out the proud *Tarquin* their king, although they abhorred the verie name of a king, and much more the gouernment, hauing chaunged the royall state into a popular: yet so it was, that the Roman Senat vsed to send vnto kings, their allies and confederats, the royall marks of kings; namely a diadem or crowne of gold, a cup of gold, the iuorie scepter; and sometime the popular robe embroidered with gold, & a chaire of iuorie, as the histories declare. And in the Commentaries of pope *Gregory* the seuenth, we read that *Demetrius* was by the scepter, crowne, and ensigne established king of Croatia and Sclauonia: of which things the bishops of Rome haue oftentimes bene liberall (should I say) or prodigall? aswell as the emperours: yet had they no more so to do, then had the Greeke emperour *Anastasius*, who sent the Consularie ornament and titles of *Augustus* vnto *Clodoueus* king of Fraunce, who (as *Aymon* saith) receiued them in the citie of Tours: or than *Iustinian*, who gaue vnto king *Childebert* the title of a Senator: by which things it is certaine, to be derogated from the soueraignty of anothers maiestie, which is it selfe the chiefest, except they bee receiued from them that are in their confederation their superiours. But as for the Frenchmen they had not made any league with the Greeke emperours, but by their valour had thrust the Romans out of the possession of their kingdome. True it is, that betwixt confederats of equall power, ornaments of honour, as girdles, rings, and such like, may both bee giuen and receiued, without any emparement to their maiestie: but to receiue the honor of a Consull, or of a Senator, is as much as to acknowledge the maiestie of a superiour. *Frederike* the emperour (first of that name) sent vnto *Peter* prince of Denmarke, a sword and a crowne, with the title of a king, which was a title contrarie to the effect, considering that he yeelded himselfe vassall vnto the empire, and did fealtie and homage vnto the emperour, for the realme of Denmarke, promising and binding aswell himselfe as his successours, to hold that kingdome of the empire, in this forme, * *Rex Danorum Magnus se in potestatem Imperatoris tradidit, obsides dedit, iuramentum fecit, se successoresque suos, non nisi imperatoris & successorum eius permissu regnum adepturos*, The great king of the Danes hath deliuered himselfe into the power of the emperour, hath giuen hostages, taken his oath, that he and his successours shall not but by the sufferance of the emperour and his successours, take vpon them that kingdome. Wherein

Marginalia:
Antigonus the first of the successours of Alexander that stiled himselfe king.

* Tacitus lib 2. Appianus, Liuius Val. Max.

* Tritemius cap. 17.

H4 *For* popular robe *read* purple robe.   H8–9 no more POWER so to do (cf. Fr and L)   H9–10 *For* ornament and titles *read* ornaments and title.   I7 power   Notes at I2, I9.

in he two wayes offended, first, for that allured with the ornaments sent him by the emperour, hee diminished his owne maiestie: and then for that he bound vnto perpetuall seruitude, not himselfe onely, but his posteritie also: who perceiuing the errour, reuolted from the empire. for seeing that the kingdome of Denmarke depended of the voices and suffragies of the Senat and the people, hee could not bind, not onely his posteritie, but not so much as himselfe vnto that law. The duke of *Austria* also was by the same emperour, and almost at the same time, honored with the same ornaments and title, yet with condition that hee should still remaine in the perpetuall obeisance of the German Empire, wherein he then was, and euer had beene: but when he breaking his faith, had reuoulted from the empire, he was within twelue yeares after spoyled both of his royall dignitie and title. By like errour *Henry* the first king of England, sonne to *William* the Conquerour, whilest he yet liued caused *Henry* his eldest sonne to bee crowned king. for he straight way after, would needs be equall with his father, and take vpon him to mannage the greatest affaires of state; in such sort that great quarrels and contentions arise betwixt the father and the sonne, euen vnto parts taking, which had without doubt ruinated the state, had not the sonne beene before by death preuented. So also in this realme, when the familie of the *Capets* had vsurped the kingdom, the better to confirme their wealth and power, not as yet well grounded; lest the kingdom after the death of their kings should fall into an Anarchie, they still caused their sonnes (whilest they themselues yet liued) to be crowned and proclaimed kings. So *Hugh* to assure this succesidy, caused his sonne *Robert* to be crowned king: *Robert, Henry*: and he afterwards *Philip*; which manner of crowning of the sonnes, the fathers yet liuing, after their estate and power better confirmed and established, was againe left. And so to doe, vnto mee seemeth a thing verie daungerous, especially if the new crowned king be sicke with the ambitious desire of rule: for that the subiects more willingly behold the sunne rising then setting: except the king haue many kingdomes, with great fluds, most high mountaines, or the deepest seas, one from an other diuided, not easily with the wings of aspiring ambition to be passed. So *Seleucus* king of both Asiaes, graced his sonne *Antiochus* not onely with the royall dignitie, but also placed him in the gouernment of the kingdome of the higher Asia; which is a thing may well be suffered where kings haue vsed to be created by the voices of the Senat, and the people: as are the kings of Denmarke, Sueuia, Polonia, Tartaria, Bohemia, Hungarie, and Tunes: who commonly cause him whom they desire to raigne, to be before hand elected by the suffragies of the people, and to bind the princes by oath vnto him. So *Changuus* first of all the Tartar kings, chosen king by his subiects, caused *Hoccata* his eldest sonne to be crowned king, himselfe yet liuing. And *Gostanus* king of Sweden hauing vsurped vpon that state against the king of Denmarke, caused his sonne *Henry* to be also chosen king. And *Frederik* now king of Denmarke, was chosen king in the yeare 1556, two yeares before the death of his father: who not yet so secured, but doubting least his vncles *Iohn* and *Adolphe* after his death should practize a new election, and so raise new stirres, requested the French king by *M. Danzai* the French embassadour, and afterward by an embassadour of his owne, (sent directly for that purpose) to stand his friend, and to receiue him into his protection. So haue done, and yet also doe the kings of Marocco, Fez, and Tunes. And in our memorie *Ferdinand* of Austria yet liuing, caused *Maximilian* his sonne to be chosen and crowned king of Hungarie and Bohemia: as shortly after *Maximilian* did the like for his sonne *Ernestus*; and so peoples voices by little and little taken away are at length quite buried in obliuion. The like was also attempted for the nominating of his successour by *Sigismundus Augustus* king of Polonia, but was letted so to

doo

Daungerous for soueraign princes to cause their sonnes whilst they themselues yet liue to be crowned kings with them.

D2 Suevia *i.e.* Sweden   D5 Changuis *i.e.* Genghis Khan   D6 Hoccata *i.e.* Ogodai or Oktai
D7 Gostanus (L 2) Costanus (L 1) Gostauus (L 3–5) Gostave (Fr) *i.e.* Gustavus Vasa   Note at C8.

210 THE SECOND BOOKE

doe by the states of that kingdom, although it seemed for the good of that Common weal, for the auoyding of sedition, which might rise about the election: yet would not the states of that kingdom thereto agree; for feare least the right of their election, should so passe into the force of succession. As we see the Germain Empire to haue taken so deepe roote in the most honorable familie of the house of *Austria*, as that there is but little hope for the pulling of it out thence againe. And thus much concerning a royall Monarchie: now let vs likewise speake of the third kind, which is a Tyrannicall Monarchie.

Chap. IIII.

¶ Of a Tirannicall Monarchie.

A tirannicall Monarchie.

A Tirannicall Monarchie is that where one man treading vnder foot the lawes of God and nature, abuseth his free borne subiects as his slaues: and other mens goods as his owne. This word *Tyrant* deriued from the Grekes was of the proprietie thereof honorable, and in aunceint time signified no other thing then a Prince, which without the consent of the people, had by force or fraud possessed himselfe of the state; and of a companion made himselfe their master: whom they called a Tyrant, although he were

The name of a tirant in auntient time taken in good part; and how the same became odious.

a right wise and iust prince. So *Plato* writing to *Dionysius* the Tyrant of Syracusa by way of honour giueth him this title; *Plato to Dionysius the Tyrant greeting*, and the answere was; *Dionysius the Tyrant to Plato health*. And so the rest aswell philosophers as friends, honestly called them Tyrants which had by force or finenesse got the soueraigntie of their cities and states: in which name the Tyrants themselues also gloried. And to show that the name of a Tyrant was aswell giuen vnto a good and iust prince, as to an euill and wicked, it appeareth euidently in that, that *Pittacus* and *Periander* reckened among the seauen Sages of Græce, were called Tyrants, hauing taken vnto themselues the state and gouernment of their countries. But for the mercie of their enemies, were constrained for the safetie of their liues and goods to haue gardes of straungers about their persons, and great garisons in their fortresses and strong holds: and for the maintenance of their souldiours and retinue were enforced to lay vpon their subiects great impositions and tributes: and seeing their liues not yet so assured, hauing but poore friends, and puisant enemies, put to death, or banished the one, to enrich the other; and hauing taken their goods, rauished also their wiues and children: they with these outragious enormities raised a wonderful hatred of themselues through out the whole world. For we read that *Dionysius* the elder which had oppressed Syracusa had alwaies about him for the garding of his person and the citie ten thousand footmen, and as many horsemen; beside a fleete of foure hundred gallies still readie furnished with all things necessarie: and yet thought it not a sttrength sufficient to keepe vnder those fewe citizens that were left, whom he had vtterly disarmed, and in most seruile manner oppressed: although hee had before taken away not onely their societies and companies; but forbidden also neighbours and friends to eate together, and oft times commaunded them returning home from supper or making merie, to be robbed and spoiled by his garde; to the intent there might bee the lesse friendship amongst them, and so they more hardly conspire against him. And yet for all that *Plutarque* hath giuen him the praise of a good prince, as one who in iustice and vertue exceeded many, who abusing the most honorable names of Kings, are themselues polluted and defiled with all maner of vices. For we are not much to rest vpon the vaine show of

words

H9 BUT THOSE WHO HAD INVADED THE SOVEREIGNTY BY FORCE OR FINESSE, SEEING THAT THEIR LIVES WERE EXPOSED TO the mercie (cf. Fr) Note at F6.

OF A COMMONWEALE. 211

A words and glorious titles; when as often times the worst men arrogate vnto themselues the most commendable names, showes, and recognancies of vertue; against which sort of Princes, the subiects for all that vse to cast forth most reproachfull taunts: as the three *Ptolemeis* kings of Ægypt; of whom the one had put to death his brother; the other his mother; and the third his father: the subiects in derision called them * *Philadelphe*, * *Philometor*, and * *Philopator*. Also the most reuerend and holy names haue become abhominable, for the wickednesse of them that haue most filthyly abused the same. The name truely of a king is holy, yet was it for the pride of *Tarquinius*, and the rauishment of *Lucretia* by his sonne, made hatefull vnto the Romans. And the crueltie of *Scylla* in his Dictatorship made the Dictators odious. So the im-
B moderat ambition of *Francis Valori* made the Confalonniers of Florence hatefull vnto the Florentines. And so also it is euident, the name of Tyrant to haue bene hateful to all nations for oppressing of the people.

* A louer of his brother.
* A louer of his mother.
* A louer of his father.

But it may be, that one and the same prince, whose dominion is large and wide, may beare himselfe as a king vnto his naturall subiects: and as a lordly monarch towards them, whome he hath by iust warre subdued, and as a tyrant toward the rest: or that in the same citie he may tyrannise ouer the rich and better sort of the citisens; and yet show himselfe courteous and gentle vnto the poore and baser sort. And amongst tyrants there are diuers sorts and degrees of more or lesse: and as there is not so good a prince, which hath not some notable vice; so wee see that there is none so cruell a
C tyrant, which is not endued with some good vertue, or hath not in him some thing to be commended. Wherefore it is a thing of most euill example, and thereto daungerous withall, rashly and foolishly to censure a prince, whose actions and comportments we throughly know not; whereas we ought first wisely to weigh his vertues and vices, his heroicall or base and euill disposition: after the manner of the Persians, who condemned no man to death (although conuicted of the crime whereof he was accused) except it first appeared by his former life, whether his vices exceeded his vertues or not. For so *Liuie* did well, who hauing diligently reckoned vp *Hannibal* his vertues, and comming afterward vnto his vices, saith, *Has tot ac tantas virtutes ingentia vitia æquabant*, These his so many and great vertues, were counteruailed with great vices.
D Wherefore least the good should be confused and so confounded with the bad; or that we should vnder the name of a tyrant comprehend them also which were right worthy and famous men: let vs compare the worst tyrant with the best king; that by such comparison of the two extreames, those may bee the better perceiued which are in the middest betwixt both. Now when I say the best king, my meaning is after the common manner: neither doe I seeke after such an one as is accomplished with all heroicall vertues; or the rare paragon of iustice, wisedome, and religion, a man without all imputation: which in the fables of auntient worthies, were propounded with more magnificence than truth, for princes to looke vpon and to imitat; such as neuer was, nor euer shall be: but rather such an example of a good and iust king, as is indeed in the
E ranke of princes to be found; and such an one as is alwayes readie to bestow his goods, his blood, and life, for the good of his people: What manner of prince is of *Homer* in two words called ἤπιος πατήρ, whose whole endeuour is to bee indeed such an one as *Codrus* and *Decius* are reported to haue bene, who aduertised by the Oracle, that the victorie ouer their enemies depended of their death, without farther delay sodenly sacrificed their liues: and *Moyses* aboue all, whome *Philo* calleth the most wise law-giuer; a most iust prince, who besought God, That he might rather die the euerlasting death of the wicked, and haue his name blotted out of the booke of life, than that the people committed to his charge, should endure so great and grieuous punishment as it

A soueraign princes actions are not by his subiects to be rashly censured.

The best king.

T iiij   had

C4 throughly *i.e.* thoroughly   E3 πατήρ   Note at E7.

had deserued: by which prayers hee appeased the wrath of God, like a most good king, & true father of his people: than which name *Augustus* the great emperor is reported neuer to haue heard any title or addition, vnto him more pleasing, at such time as *M. Valerius Messala*, was by a decree of the Senat, and of the people of Rome called *Father of his countrey*. For why, the best prince nothing differeth from the best father, as *Xenophon* was woont most excellently to say.

<small>The greatest difference betwixt a king and a tyrant.</small>

Now the greatest difference betwixt a king and a tyrant is, for that a king conformeth himselfe vnto the lawes of nature, which the tyrant at his pleasure treadeth vnder foot: the one of them respecteth religion, iustice, and faith; whereas the other regardeth neither God, faith, nor law: the one of them referreth all his actions to the good of the Commonweale, and safetie of his subiects; whereas the other respecteth nothing more than his owne particular profit, reuenge, or pleasure: the one doth all his endeuour for the enriching of his subiects; whereas the other seeketh after nothing more, than by the impouerishment of them, to encrease his owne wealth: the one of them accounteth his owne goods to be the goods of his people; the other reckoneth not onely the goods, but euen the bodies of his subiects also to be his owne: the one of them seuerely reuengeth the publique iniuries done against the state, and easily pardoneth the wrongs done vnto himselfe; the other most cruelly reuengeth his owne, and pardoneth that which is done against others: the one easily forgiueth the offences of other men, but is of his owne misdeeds a seuere iudge; whereas the other most sharply reuengeth euen the least offences of others, but is vnto himselfe most fauourable: the one of them fauoureth the honour of modest matrons, and other mens wiues; the other triumpheth in their shame and dishonour: the one refuseth not to bee freely and discreetly reproued for that he hath done amisse; the other hateth nothing more than the graue free spoken man: the one enforceth himselfe to maintaine and keepe his subiects in peace and vnitie; whereas the other seeketh still to set them at ods, so to ruinat them one by another; and with the confiscation of their lands and goods to enrich himselfe: the one taketh pleasure to see his subiects, and to be of them oftentimes seene and heard; whereas the other feareth their presence, and hideth himselfe from them, as from his enemies: the one reposeth his estate and fealtie in their loue towards him; the other in their feare: the one taketh no care but for his subiects; the other feareth nothing more than them: the one chargeth his subiects as little as he can, neither exacteth any thing of them, but when the publike necessitie so requireth; whereas the other drinketh his subiects blood, gnaweth their bones, and out of them also sucketh euen the marrow, so by all meanes seeking to weaken them: the one aduanceth vnto the highest degrees of honour the best and most vertuous men; whereas the other stil promoteth the greatest theeues and villaines, whome he may vse as spunges, to sucke vp the wealth of his subiects: the one frankly bestoweth the greatest and most gainful offices of the state vpon men of best deserts, who free from briberie & corruption, may defend the people from all iniurie and oppression; whereas the other setteth the same to sale to such as will giue most for them, so by their robberies and vnreasonable exactions, to keepe the people vnder, and then afterward when they are well fatted, to cut such caterpillers throates also, so to be accounted great iusticiars: the one measureth his manners, according vnto his lawes; the other measureth his lawes, according to his owne disposition and pleasure: the one is readie to expose his life for the good of his countrey and people; the other wisheth it and them all to perish for himselfe: the one is beloued and honoured of his subiects; the other hateth them all, and is likewise of them hated: the one in time of warre hath no recourse but vnto his owne subiects; whereas the other hath no greater warre than against them: the one hath neither

guard

<small>Note at F3.</small>

Of A Commonwealth. 213

A guard, nor garrison, but of his owne people; whereas the other for the defence of his person, and keeping of his subiects in awe, hath alwayes a garrison of armed straungers to go before him: the one liueth secure in all quiet and tranquilitie of mind; the other troubled with carefull and contrarie thoughts, still languishing in perpetuall feare: the one expecteth a most blessed and eternall life in heauen; the other still fearing euerlasting paines of hell: the one hath the immortall good author of all his actions; the other followeth the aduise of wicked men and damned spirits: in briefe the one is praised and honoured of all men whilest he liueth, and much missed after his death; whereas the other is defamed yet liuing, and most shamefully reuiled both by word and writing when he is dead. And albeit that a tyrant abound in wealth, haue honour, soue-
B raigntie, health, and surpasing Champion like strength of bodie, with the deepe and profound knowledge of many and great matters, and flowing eloquence most of tyrants to be in others feared; yet shal he therefore be neuer the better, but wel the worse; abusing his wealth to fulfill his lust; his soueraigntie, to the oppressing of other mens libertie; his strength for the performing of his villanie; and his knowledge for the circumuenting of the plaine and simple, and shamefull confusion of all things. Which so many and notable gifts, if they chaunce by the grace and goodnesse of God to bee giuen to any good prince: we then esteeme of him, as of a God, sent euen down from heauen into the earth here amongst vs.

But what need we to vse many examples to proue this to be true, being of it selfe so *Tirants slaine by*
C manifest in euerie mans eye. And seeing that we find in histories tyrannie to haue bene *effeminate and weake persons.*
of all men so much feared, hated and detested, that euen schollers and weake women haue not doubted to aduenture with daunger of their liues, to gaine vnto themselues the honour of the killing of tyrants. As did *Aristotle* (not hee of Stagira, but hee that was surnamed the Logitian) who slew a tyrant of Sicione. And *Thebe*, who slew her *Tirants neuer in safetie.*
husband *Alexander*, tyrant of the Pheræans. And to thinke that tyrants might by force warrant themselues, is but meere and vaine errour. For who were of greater force than were the Roman emperors, who ordinarily had fortie legions at their command in their prouinces, and three moe in Italie, beside their Prætorian bands, for the defence of their persons: and yet in no place in the world were there so many princes
D slaine; yea sometimes the captaines of their guards slew them euen in their pallaces, whome they guarded. As *Cherea* the tyrant, and the Mamalukes eight Sultans of Ægypt.

But he that would see the miserable ends of tyrants, let him but read the liues of
* *Timoleon*, and of *Aratus*, where hee shall see the tyrants drawne out of the *Plutar in A-*
nest of their tyranny, stripped starke naked, theeues beaten to death with clubbes in the *rato et Timoleone*
presence of Children, and the rest of the common people: and after that their wiues and children, their kinsfolkes and familiar friendes most cruelly murthered and slaine: and that more is the verie image & statues of them that were dead in their tyranny, accused, and publikely condemned, deliuered vnto the common hangman to bee as it
E were executed; their bones also taken out of their graues, and cast into most lothsom iakesses, and the raking officers of these tyrants dismembred, and most miserably tormented with al the cruelty that a people enraged could deuise: their edicts & laws torn, their castles and proud houses rased and laid euen with the ground, and the verie memorie of their name, by publike iudgements and written bookes, condemned to perpetuall infamie, as an example to all future princes, to the end they might haue in detestation such plagues, so pernitious and dangerous vnto mankind.

And albeit that tyrants whilest they liued, haue not wanted their flattering claw- *Tyrants alwayes*
backs, whome they with rewards enduced to write their vnworthie prayses; yet wee *infamous and detested.*
read,

A6 *For* good *read* God.   D2 Cherea [slew] the tyrant CALIGULA, and   D6 naked, AND LIKE
theeues (cf. L)   Notes at B2, E2.

read, that after their death, such their histories, and panegiricall orations, before written in their prayses, were burnt, torne and suppressed, and the truth (yea sometime with more too) brought to light, & in stead of them other most reprochfull and contumelious writings published, in such sort, as that not so much as one small fragment of any booke written in the prayse of any tyrant, were he neuer so great, is now extant or to be found. Which thing maketh tyrants, whilest they yet liue to fret and fume as if they were mad: for that they see they must in time become a laughing stocke vnto the people and their verie enemies. And albeit that they euill perswaded of the immortalitie of the soule, thinke the same to perish together with the bodie, or haply before the body, which embaulmed with sweet odours may be long preserued, yet so long as they liue they still feele the torment of the infamie to come, which they yet liuing see shall befall them after their death. Whereof *Tiberius* the emperour grieuously complained, but *Nero* much more, who wished that when he died, yea that whilest hee yet breathed, all the world might with fire be consumed. And for this cause *Demetrius*, surnamed *Poliorcetes*, to gratifie the Athenians vndertooke the warre for the defence of their rights and libertie, to the intent to be honoured by their learned writings; knowing well that the citie of Athens was as it were the watch of the whole world, which might in like sort make the glorie of his noble acts to shine throughout the world, as doth a beacon set on fire vpon the top of an high tower: neither was he therein deceiued: but so soone as he gaue himselfe ouer vnto vices and villanies, there was neuer tyrant better (than he was by them) washed; hauing his name most shamefully by them defamed, by whome he had bene before commended. And albeit that some may think tyrants, for that they haue no taste of true praise, to care the lesse what posteritie either thinke or say of them, yet in truth liue they most miserably, if their life be so to be called, which liue in continuall feare, still feele the most sharpe sting of greefe; seeing themselues, their lawes, their wiues and children, their kinsfolks and friends, euer in daunger. For it is impossible for him that hateth and feareth his subiects; and is againe of them all himselfe also hated and feared, to be able long to continue or stand. Whereby it commeth to passe, that in stead of being assailed by his enemies, hee is oft times vppon the sodaine assailed by his owne subiects. Neither may hee repose any trust or confidence in his friends, vnto whom he is himselfe oftentimes a traytour and disloyall, causing them for the least suspition to be slaine: as we read it reported of *Nero, Commodus, Caracalla*, and such other tyrants. And sometime the whole people with one rage and furie runneth headlong vpon the tyrant, as it did vpon *Phalaris, Heliogabalus, Alcetes* tyrant of the Epirots, and vpon *Andronicus* emperour of Constantinople, whom stript and set vpon a bare asses backe, the people of Constantinople caused to endure all the indignities and reproaches that were possible, before they would giue him leaue to die. Yea and sometimes it chanceth, that euen they themselues are the occasion of the hastening of their owne death, as it is reported of *Caracalla* the emperour, who would needs know of *Iulius*, his mothers Mathematician, whom he thought should succeed him in the empire (for that is a common course amongst tyrants in their affairs and doings, to aske the councell and aduise of wisards and diuels) vnto whome the Astronomer by his letters aunswered, That *Macrinus* was the man that should succeed him; which letters by chaunce falling into the hands of *Macrinus*: he thereupon forthwith caused *Caracalla* to be slaine, for feare of the danger prepared for him by *Caracalla*. So *Commodus* also, hauing hardly escaped the stabbe which a murtherous villaine was about with a dagger to haue giuen him, (who in giuing of the blow said, That the Senat had sent him that) straight waies after made a roll of al them whom he purposed to put to death: which roll by good hap comming into the hands of *Martia* his concubine,

---

marginalia: Tyrants still tormented with the feare of future infamy.

marginalia: Tyrants oftentimes to hasten their owne deathes in seeking to eschue the same.

G7 watch *i.e.* watchtower, lookout point (cf. Fr and L)   H1 washed *i.e. lavé*, mocked, derided
I6 set upon a bare asses backe *i.e.* set naked upon an ass (Fr and L)   Note at I10.

A bine and she therein finding her owne name enrolled amongst the rest, to auoid the daunger prepared for her and the rest, caused the tyrant to be forthwith slaine. Of like examples all the auntient histories are full, which show plainly the liues of tyrants to bee alwayes beset with a thousand ineuitable mischiefs, death still hanging ouer their heads.

Now the state of a royall Monarchie is quite contrarie vnto a tyrannie: for the king is so vnited with his subiects, that they are still willing to spend their goods, their blood, and liues, for the defence of his estate, honour, and life; and cease not after his death to write, sing, and publish his prayses, amplifying them also in what they can. As we see in *Xenophon* the liuely purtract of a great and vertuous prince, drawne vnder the per- B son of *Cyrus*, whose praises he hath with wonderfull eloquence set forth, to giue eaxmple to other princes for to imitat and conforme themselues vnto; as did *Scipio Africanus*, who hauing alwaies before his eyes and in his hands *Xenophon* his *Cyropædia*, and framing himselfe to the imitation thereof, profited so much, as that he in vertue, honor, and prowesse, surmounted all the kings and princes, not of his owne age onely, but of former times also; in such sort, that certaine pirats enflamed with the report of his fame, and knowing that he was in his house in the countrey farre from any towne, came and beset the same: against whom as he was about to put himselfe with his people in readinesse, and so to haue stood vpon his guard: they perceiuing the same, forthwith threw downe their armes, assuring him that they were not come thither, but one- C ly to see him, and to do him honour, which they most humbly requested, that they might be admitted to do him. Now if the lustre and brightnesse of vertue in such a prince, hath drawne euen theeues and pirats into the admiration thereof; than of how much greater force ought it to be in good and loyall subiects? And what prince is there so foolish or void of sence, which would not wonderfully reioyce to heare it reported, how that *Menander* king of the Bactrians, was for his vertue & iustice so well beloued of his subiects, as that after his death the cities were at great strife & debate amongst themselues, which of them shuld haue the honor of his sepulchre: neither could the matter be appeased, vntill that at length it was agreed, that euerie one of them should in the honour and memoriall of him build a seuerall tombe or sepulchre.

D What tyrants malice also or dissimulation is so great, whome *Plinie* his Panegyricall oration would not driue into a phrensie? who when he had therein with all worthie prayses so adorned *Traian* the emperour, as that it seemed nothing more could thereunto be added: he so concludeth the period, That nothing greater or better could bee wished for vnto the Commonweale, but that the immortall gods would imitat the life of *Traian*. Which excessiue amplification, although it sauour of impietie, yet who doubteth but that it proceeded from the zeale of a most famous man, towards his most excellent prince? for whose daunger at his going out, and welfare at his comming home, all the temples were filled; and who himselfe in his solemne prayers, was thus woont to couenant with the gods, That they should keep and preserue him, if they saw E it to be for the good of the Commonweale. What tyrant is so cruell, what show soeuer he make, which most hartily wisheth not for the honour which king *Agesilaus* receiued, at such time as he was fined by the Ephori, for hauing alone robbed the hearts and gained the loue of all the citisens vnto him? What king is there, which wisheth not to haue the surname of *Aristides* the Iust? a title more diuine and royall than euer prince yet knew how to get: albeit that in stead thereof many haue caused themselues to be called Conquerors, Besiegers, Lightnings. Now on the contrarie part, when as we read of the most horrible cruelties of *Phalaris, Busiris, Nero,* and *Caligula*, who is he which is not moued to a iust indignation against them? or hearing of their miserable

and

The happie estate of a good Royal prince, in comparison of a Tyrant.

The worthie praise of Scipio Africanus.

and wretched ends, can containe himselfe from reioycing thereat?

Thus haue we seene the most remarquable differences betwixt a king and a Tyrant, which are not hard to be perceiued betwixt the two extremes of a most good king, and a most detestable Tyrant: but is not so easilie to be deemed, when the prince taketh part of a good king, and some other part of a tyrant: so as it were tempering the good with the bad. For so things oft times fall out, that for the varietie of times, places, persons, and other occasions presenting themselues, princes are constrained to doe such things, as may seeme vnto them tyrannicall, and vnto others commendable. Wherefore let no man measure Tyrannie by Seueritie, which is oft times in a prince most necessarie: neither for his castles, gardes, and garisons: neither by the soueraigntie of his commaunds, which are in deed more to be wished for, then the sweet requests of tyrants: which draw after them an ineuitable violence. And that is it for which in law, he which hath bound himselfe at the request of a Tirant, is alwaies againe to be restored into his former estate, wherein he was: whereas if he that shall so doe at the commaundement of a good prince shall not by the law be relieued: neither are those murthers, proscriptions, banishments, incests, rauishments, and other such villanies which happen in ciuill warres, in the chaunging or destruction of the states of Common weales, or the establishment of the same, to be called tyranies: for that in such violent conuersion and chaunge of state, it cannot otherwise be. As it fell out in the Roman Triumuirat, in the election of diuers Emperours, and in our time *Cosmus de Medices*, first taking vpon him the dukedome of Florence. For he after the death of his kinsman *Alexander Medices*, slaine by the conspiracie of his enemies, tooke vnto himselfe a strong garde of straungers for the defence and safetie of his owne person: built castles and strong holds: fortified the citie with strong garrisons: imposed new tributes and customes vpon the subiects; which vnto the common people, and men abusing the popular libertie, seemed violent oppressions and tiranies: but vnto the wise men necessarie and wholsome remedies: especially in such a sicke citie and Commonweal, as with most desperate diseases and incurable vlcers was like otherwise to haue perished: as also against such vnruly citizens, and inured to all licentious libertie; who had a thousand times conspired against this new Duke, reputed for one of the most wise and vertuous princes of his time: but of them accounted a tyrant.

Now to the contrarie it hapneth often that the state of a citie or Commonweal ruinated by the too much lenitie and facilitie of one prince, is againe relieued and vpholden by the austeare seueritie of an other. It is sufficiently knowne how terrible the tyranie of *Domitian* was vnto the Senat, the nobilitie, and other the great lords and gouernours of the Roman Empire; in somuch that all his lawes and edicts were by their procurement after his death repealed: and yet for all that was he euen after his death also most highly by the generall consent of all the prouinces commended: for that the Proconsuls with the other magistrats and officers of the Commonweal, were neuer before more vpright or freer from corruption then they were in his time, for feare they had of his seueritie, & him. But when *Nerua* who succeeded him in the Empire, abhorring seuerity, enclined altogether to lenitie, & things began to fall into a most miserable estate; the lawes being prostituted, iustice peruerted, and the poore by the mightie oppressed: then *Fronto* the Consul with many moe with most earnest desire, wished for that crueltie and tyranie which they before had condemned in *Domitian*. Also when a prince with most sharpe seueritie as with a bridle, keepeth in the mindes and licentious desires of a furious and headstrong people, as if it were an vntamed beast: such wholsom seueritie ought in no wise to be accounted or called tiranie; but to the contrarie *Cicero* calleth such licentious libertie of the vnrulie people meere tiranie.

It may be also that a prince may exercise tiranie against the great ones in the state, as it

Necessarie seueritie not to be accounted tirannie but to be in a soueraigne prince much commended.

Seueritie in a prince more wholsome for the Commonweale then lenitie.

F8 *For* unto them *read* unto some.   G4 *For* whereas if he *read* whereas he.   Notes at F8, K7.

it alwaies hapneth in the violent chaunge of an Aristocratie into a Monarchie, when as the new prince being in necessitie and poore, and not knowing where to haue money, oft times falleth vpon the rich, without regard of right or wrong: or else infranchiseth the common people from the seruitude of the nobilitie, and the rich by that one and selfe same act to gaine the goods and wealth of the rich, and the fauour of the poore. But of all tirants there is none lesse to be detested than he which preieth vpon the rich to ease the necessitie of the poore. Now they that praise the goodnes, bountie, and courtesie of a prince, without wisedom; are themselues vnwise and ignorant in matters of state, abusing therein both their praises and leasure: for asmuch as such simplicitie without wisedome is most dangerous and pernitious vnto a king, and much more to be feared than is the great seueritie of a cruell, couetous, and inaccessible prince. So that it seemeth our auntient fathers not without cause to haue vsed this Prouerbe, *That of a craftie and subtill man is made a good king*: which saying vnto the delicate eares of such as measure all things by false opinions rather than by sound reasons, may seeme right strange: for by the too much sufferance and simplicitie of too good a king, it commeth to passe that flatterers, extorcioners, and men of most wicked disposition, without respect, inioy the principall honors, offices, charges, benefits, and preferments of the Commonwealth, spoyling the reuenues of the state: wherby the poore people are gnawne vnto the verie bones, and cruelly made slaues vnto the great: in somuch as that in stead of one tirant, there is ten thousand. Out of which corruption also of the magistrats, and too much curtesie of the king, proceed many mischiefes and euils; as impunitie of offenders, of murderers, and oppressours: for that the king so good and so gratious cannot refuse to graunt them pardon. In briefe, vnder such a prince the publique good is turned into particuler, and all the charge falleth vpon the poore people: as wee see in cathares and fluxes in sicke and rheumatique bodies, the maladie still falleth vnto the weakest parts; which to be so, we might proue by many examples aswell of the Grekes as of the Latins: but we will go no farther than to this our owne * realme, which was in the most miserable case that euer it was, vnder the raigne of *Charles* surnamed the simple, and of some called *Charles do nothing*. It was seene also, great, rich, and florishing, in armes, lawes, and learning of all sorts in the time of *Francis* the first: but especially some few yeares before his death, when as he waxing old, became so wayward and inaccessible, as that no man durst come vnto him to craue any thing of him; hauing driuen the courtly doggs, and shameles persons far from him, bestowing rewards, offices, honours, and benefits vpon none but such as were vertuous, and had well deserued of the Commonweal: and withall so gouerning his bountie, as that at the time of his death were found in the common treasurie almost a thousand *Sestertioes*, that is to say, seauentie hundred thousand french crownes, besides three moneths tribute which was now due: neither was the Commonweale vnto any then indebted, more than vnto the Swissers, and the Banque of Lyons, whom he would not pay, so to keepe them in awe: at which time he had firme amitie and peace also with all princes and people: and the bounds of his kingdom extended euen vnto the gates of Millan: his realme full of great captaines, and of the wisest men of the world.

But within twelue yeares after that *Henry* the second his sonne raigned (whose bountie was so great, as that the like was neuer in any prince of his time,) we saw the state almost quite chaunged: for as he was sweet, gratious, and courteous, so could he not denie any thing to any person; so that his fathers treasures were in few moneths scattered, the great offices and places of commaund were set to sale more than euer, the greatest spirituall preferments without respect bestowed vpon vnworthy men, magistracies

Marginalia: Diuers causes ducing princes vnto Tyrannie. — A true Paradox. — The happie estate of France vnder king Francis the first, a wayward and hard Prince. — The lenitie and immoderat bountie of king Henry the second, most hurtfull vnto the kingdome of Fraunce.

A4 nobilitie and the rich, by   A8 without wisedom *i.e.* exercised without wisdom (cf. L)
B7 without respect *i.e.* indiscriminately   D7 For seauentie *read* seventeen (cf. 593 A4-5, 681 D9).
D10 in awe *i.e.* in subjection, under obligation   Notes at B3, C9, D6.

stracies sold to them that would giue most, and so consequently to the most vnworthie greater customes and payments exacted than euer were before: and yet when he died, the estate of the receipt of Fraunce was found charged with two and fortie millions, after it had lost Piemont, Sauoy, the isle of Corsica, and the frontiers of the Low countrey: Howbeit that all these losses were but little, in comparison of the losse of his reputation and honour. Whereas had the facilitie of this great king bene tempered with seueritie, his lenitie with some rigour: his bountie, with a certaine sparing, and that for a weake and soft spirit, he had borne a stout and couragious mind: we had no doubt liued both well and happily, neither had the Commonweale fallen into such miserable calamities as now we haue endured.

But to hold this golden meane (some man will say) as it is hard for euerie man to do: so for princes whom diuers strong perturbations call out of the middle course vnto the one or other of the the extreames, it is of all others most hard. True it is, that vertue consisting in the meane, is enuironed with many vices, much like vnto a straight line, which is hard to be found among a million of crooked: which graunted, yet so it is neuerthelesse, that it is better and more expedient for the people and the preseruation of an estate to haue a rigorous and seuere prince, than too gentle and courteous. The bountie of the emperour *Pertinax*, and the enraged youthfulnesse of *Heliogabalus* had brought the Roman empire euen vnto the verie point of vtter ruine: when as the emperours *Seuerus* of Afrike, and *Alexander Seuerus* of Syria, by a rude kind of seueritie and imperiall austeritie reestablished the same, in the former brightnes and maiestie, to the great and wonderfull contentment of all good men. Thus therefore is the prouerbe that we receiued from our aunceƒtors (*That of an euill and subtill man is made a good king*) to be vnderstood: for otherwise the word *euill*, of the proprietie of it selfe signifieth not so much seueritie, as the vttermost point, or the extremitie of impietie, which our aunceƒtors called *euill*: so *Charles* king of Nauarre was called an euil king, than whom none was more wicked of his time. Wee must not therefore iudge a prince to be a tyrant for his seueritie and rigour, so that he do nothing contrarie to the lawes of God and nature. But forasmuch as this discourse hath brought vs on so far, let vs see also whether it be lawfull for a good man to lay violent hand vpon the person of a tyrant.

How the paradoxe, That of an euill and craftie man is made a good king, is to be vnderstood.

Chap. V.

¶ *Whether it be lawfull to lay violent hand vpon a tyrant; and after his death to disanull all his acts, decrees, and lawes.*

Who is properly a Tyrant and that hee may lawfully be of any man slaine.

He proprietie of the word *Tyrant*, being not well knowne, hath deceiued many, and armed the subiects vnto the destruction of their princes. We haue before said him properly to be called a Tyrant, who of his owne authoritie taketh vpon him the soueraigntie, against the will of the people, without election, or right of succession, neither by lot, by will, nor iust warre, nor speciall calling of God: and this is he, whome poth the lawes and the writings of auntient fathers commaund to bee slaine; propounding also most ample rewards vnto such as should kill him: viz. the honourable titles of nobilitie and prowesse, armes, statues, crownes, and in briefe the goods of the Tyrant also; as vnto the true deliuerer of his countrey, or as the Cretensians vse to say of his mother. Neither in this case make they any difference betwixt a good and a vertuous prince; or a wicked man and a villaine. For it is not lawfull for any man liuing, of himselfe to inuade the soueraigntie, and to make himselfe maister of

of his fellowes, what colour of vertue or iustice soeuer they pretend: and that more is, in law he is guiltie of death, that wrongfully taketh vppon him any the markes proper vnto soueraigne maiestie. If then the subiect will inuade or take vppon him the state of his king by any meanes whatsoeuer; or in a popular or Aristocraticall state, doth of a companion make himselfe a soueraigne, hee deserueth death: So that our question in this respect hath in it no difficultie, but that such aspirers may of all the people, or any of them, be lawfully slaine. Yet true it is, that the Greekes haue in this point differed from the Latins; as whether a man in this case ought by way of fact to preuent the course of iustice? For why, the law Valeria published at the request of *Pub. Valerius Publicola* giueth leaue to euery man to kill a Tyrant, and afterward to trie the cause of him so slaine. Which law seemeth also not to want good ground of reason: for that to proceed by way of iustice, the Commonweale should bee consumed with the firebrands of tyranny, before the fire once kindled could bee quenched: Besides that, who should cal into question of iustice the Tyrant, armed with his guard and garrisons? who should take him being possessed of the castles and strong holds? were it not better by times to oppresse him by force, than by too religious standing vpon the proceeding of the law, to loose the law together with the state? Howbeit the law of *Solon* is quite contrarie vnto this, expresly forbidding to proceed by way of fact, or to kil him that seeketh to possesse himselfe of the soueraigntie, but first to bring him vnto his triall; which seemeth more reasonable than the law Valeria: For that otherwise good & innocent men might oftentimes be taken out of the way and slaine by their enemies, vnder the color of aspiring, before the truth could be tried: who so once dead, are in that regard alwayes accounted as men iustly slaine. But these two lawes so repugnant and contrarie, may in mine opinion thus be well reconciled; if the meaning of *Solons* law be referred vnto him, who suspected of aspiring, hath not as yet possessed the castles or strong places, seduced the people, nor armed himselfe with strong garrison: and the law Valeria vnto him who hath openly declared himselfe a Tyrant, seised vppon the castles and citadels, and strengthned himselfe with garrisons. In the first case wee find that *Furius Camillus* the dictator, by way of iustice proceeded against *Marcus Manlius Torquatus*: and in the second case *Brutus* and *Cassius* euen in the Senat and most open assembly of the people, flew *Cæsar*, thinking of nothing lesse. But *Solon*, when as he too religiously (should I say) or superstitiously, had ordained that Tyrants should be lawfully tryed before they were put to death, whilest he yet liued saw *Pisistratus* of a subiect to aspire vnto the soueraigntie of the Athenian state, against whome for all that they which slew the Tyrants at Athens proceeded not by way of iustice; whose children neuerthelesse *Harmodius* and *Aristogiton* slew, contrarie vnto the law, by the priuat authoritie of *Solon* onely.

But here might many questions be made, as, Whether a Tyrant who by force or fraud hauing oppressed the libertie of the people, and so aspired vnto the soueraigntie, may be iustly slaine; hauing after his aspiring caused himselfe to be so chosen or confirmed by the voyces of the people in generall? For why, it seemeth that such a solemn act of election, is a true ratification of him in his tyrannie, the people consenting thereunto. Yet am I neuerthelesse of opinion, that he may lawfully be slaine, and that without any lawfull processe or triall, except he shall first renounce his authoritie, quit his forces, and so put himselfe into the power of the people: for why, that cannot bee thought to be done by the free consent of the people, which they do by constraint, being by the Tyrants dispoyled of their authoritie and power. As when *Sylla* caused himselfe to be confirmed dictator for fourescore yeares, by the law Valeria, which hee caused to be published, hauing at the same time a strong and puissant armie of his own

marginalia: Whether a Tyrant may be lawfully slayne before he be lawfully tried and conuicted.

marginalia: Whether a Tyrant hauing aspired vnto the soueraigntie, and afterwards confirmed therin by the consent of the people in generall, may yet lawfully be slayn.

A8 to prevent *i.e.* to anticipate   B6 by times *i.e.* betimes, early   Note at D4.

within the citie: *Cicero said, That it was no law at all. And in like case *Cæsar*, who about thirtie sixe yeares after, caused himselfe by the law Seruia, to bee made dictatour perpetuall. And also *Cosmus Medices*, who after the death of his kinsman *Alexander* hauing an armie in the citie of Florens, caused the Senators to chuse him duke of that citie for euer: about which election whilest they made some doubt, hee so thundered with his artillerie before the pallace, as that the Senat doubting otherwise of the safetie of themselues, and of the rest of the citisens, hasted the rather to make choyce of him. Howbeit if the children or posteritie of a tyrant, shall for long time, as by the space of an hundrd yeares, in continual possession hold the soueraigntie, possessed by their great grandfathers or auncestours, and so by their iust commaunds, gouern the Commonweale; such a gouernment ought not now to be called a tyrannie, for that in this case, as in all other things, a prescription of so many yeares serueth in stead of a iust title. And whereas it is said, that the rights of soueraigntie cannot be prescribed: that is to say, in lesse then an hundred yeares, and concerneth priuat men, who the Commonweale yet standing vpright, seeke to vsurpe the soueraigntie, but concerneth not the generall conuersion or chaunge of the whole state of a Commonweale. Wee said that the possession of the posteritie of a tyrant ought to be of long continued without interuption or interpellation: that is to say, that the subiects haue not with any conspiracie rebellion, or intercession, troubled the gouernment of the tyrant, or of his posteritie: for thereby it is in a sort euident, and to bee gathered, the subiects of their owne accord to haue yeelded vnto his commaunds, and to haue taken him for their iust prince. But interpellation or gain-saying, and resistance, may aswell be showed & declared by deeds as by words: of which sort was that which *Aquila* the Tribune of the people did, who in sight of all the people tooke off the crowne that was set vpon the head of *Cæsars* statue, *Cæsar* himselfe in vaine fretting thereat; who afterwards vnto such grants of honours and preferments as he gaue vnto his friends, would still adde that, *If by Aquila his leaue we may do it*. And thus much concerning a Tyrant, whether hee bee a good man or an euill, who without all right hath aspired vnto the soueraigntie of the Commonweale wherein he liueth.

But the chiefe question of this our discourse, is to know, whether a soueraigne prince come vnto that high estate by election, or by lot, by rightfull succession, or by iust warre, or by the especiall vocation of all-mightie God; forgetting his dutie, and become without measure cruell, couetous, and wicked, so peruerting the lawes of God and man, and such an one as we commonly call a Tirant, may be lawfully slaine or not. And true it is that many interpretours, both of Gods and mans lawes, haue said it to be lawfull: many of them without distinction ioyning these two incompatible words together, *a King a Tyrant*: which so daungerous a doctrine hath bene the cause of the vtter ruine and ouerthrow of many most mightie empires, and kingdomes. But to discide this question wel, it behoueth vs to distinguish an absolute soueraigne prince, from him which is not so: and also subiects from straungers, according as wee haue before declared. For it is great difference to say that a Tirant may lawfully be slaine by a prince a straunger; or by his owne subiect. For as of all noble acts, none is more honorable or glorious then by way of fact, to defend the honour, goods, and liues of such as are vniustly oppressed by the power of the more mightie, especially the gate of iustice being shut against them: as did *Moyses* seeing his brother the Israelite beaten and wronged by the Ægyptian, and no meanes to haue redresse of his wrongs; so is it a most faire and magnificall thing for a prince to take vp armes to relieue a whole nation and people, vniustly oppressed by the crueltie of a tirant: As did the great *Hercules*, who traueling ouer a great part of the world with wonderfull prowes and valour destroyed

destroyed many most horrible monsters, that is to say Tirants: and so deliuered people without number among the gods: his posteritie for many worlds of yeares after, holding most great kingdomes, and other the imitatours of his vertues: as *Dio, Timoleon, Aratus, Harmodius, Aristogiton*, with other such like honorable princes bearing the titles of chastisers and correctors of Tyrants. And for that onely cause *Temir-Cutla*, whom our writers commonly call *Tamerlan* emperour of the Tartars, denounced warre vnto *Baiazet* king of the Turkes, who then besieged Constantinople; saying that he was come to chastice his tiranie, and to deliuer the afflicted people; whom indeed he in a set battell vanquished in the plaines neare vnto *Mount Stella*: and hauing slaine and put to flight three hundred thousand Turkes, kept the tirant (taken prisoner) in chaines in an yron Cage vntill he dyed. Neither in this case is it materiall whether such a vertuous prince being a straunger proceed against a Tirant by open force, or finenes, or else by way of iustice. True it is that a valiant and worthy prince hauing the tirant in his power, shall gaine more honour by bringing him vnto his triall, to chastice him as a murtherer, a manqueller, and a robber: rather then to vse the law of armes against him. Wherefore let vs resolue vpon that, that it is lawfull for any straunger to kill a Tirant; that is to say a man of all men infamed, and notorious for the oppression, murder, and slaughter of his subiects and people. But as for subiects to do the same, it is to be knowne whether the prince that beareth rule be an absolute soueraigne; or not: for if he be no absolute soueraigne, then must the Soueraigntie of necessitie be either in the people, or in the nobilitie: in which case there is no doubt, but that it is lawfull to proceed against a Tirant by way of iustice, if so men may preuaile against him: or else by way of fact, and open force, if they may not otherwise haue reason. As the Senat did in the first case against *Nero*: and in the other against *Maximinus*: for that the Roman Emperours were at the first nothing else but princes of the Common weal, that is to say the chiefe and principall men, the soueraigntie neuerthelesse still resting in the People and the Senat: as I haue before showed, that this Commonweal was then to haue bene called a principalitie: although that *Seneca* speaking in the person of *Nero* his scholler sayeth: *I am the onely man amongst liuing men, elect and chosen to be the Lieutenant of God on earth: I am the Arbitratour of lyfe and death: I am able at my pleasure to dispose of the state and qualitie of euery man*. True it is that he tooke vpon him this soueraigne authoritie by force wrested from the Senat and people of Rome: but in right he had it not, the state being but a verie principalitie, wherein the people had the soueraigntie. As is also that of the Venetians, who condemned to death their Duke *Falier*, and also executed many others, without forme or fashion of any lawfull processe: forasmuch as Venice is an Aristocraticall principalitie, wherein the Duke is but the first or chiefe man, soueraigntie still remayning in the state of the Venetian Gentlemen. As is likewise the Germain Empire, which is also nothing else but an Aristocraticall principalitie, wherein the the Emperour is head and chiefe, the power and maiestie of the Empire belonging vnto the States thereof: who thrust out of the gouernment *Adolphus* the emperour in the yeare 1296: and also after him *Wenceslaus* in the yeare 1400, and that by way of iustice, as hauing iurisdiction and power ouer them. So also might we say of the state of the Lacedemonians, which was a pure Aristocratie, wherein were two kings, without any soueraigntie at all, being indeed nothing but Captaines and Generals for the managing of their warres: and for that cause were by the other magistrats of the state, sometime for their faults condemned to pay their fine; as was king *Agesilaus*: and sometime to death also as were *Agis* and *Pausanias*. Which hath also in our time hapned vnto the kings of Denmarke and Sweden, whereof some haue beene banished, and the others died in prison

prison: for that the nobilitie pretendeth them to be nothing but princes, and not Soueraignes, as we haue before showed: so also are they subiects vnto those states which haue the right of their election. And such were in auntient times the kings of the cities of the Gauls, whom *Cæsar* for this cause oftentimes calleth *Regulos*, that is to say little kings: being themselues subiects, and iusticiable vnto the Nobilitie, who had all the soueraigntie: causing them euen to be put to death, if they had so deserued. And that is it for which *Amphiorix* the captaine generall, whom they called the king of the Liegeois said; *Our commaundes (saith he) are such, as that the people hath no lesse power ouer vs, then we ouer the people*: wherein he showed euidently that he was no soueraigne prince: howbeit that it was not possible for him to haue equall power with the people, as we haue before showed. Wherefore these sorts of princes, hauing no soueraigntie, if they polluted with wickednes and villanie, cannot be chastised by the authoritie and seueritie of the magistrat, but shall abuse their wealth and power vnto the hurt and destruction of good men; it alwayes hath and shall be lawfull not for strangers onely, but euen for the subiects themselues also, to take them out of the way.

That it is not lawfull for the subiects either by the way of fact, or iustice to attempt any thing against the honour, life, or dignitie of their soueraigne prince, be he neuer so euill or wicked.

But if the prince be an absolute Soueraigne, as are the true Monarques of Fraunce, of Spain, of England, Scotland, Turkie, Moschouie, Tartarie, Persia, Æthiopia, India, and of almost all the kingdomes of Affricke, and Asia, where the kings themselues haue the soueraigntie without all doubt or question; not diuided with their subiects: in this case it is not lawfull for any one of the subiects in particular, or all of them in generall, to attempt any thing either by way of fact, or of iustice against the honour, life, or dignitie of the soueraigne: albeit that he had committed all the wickednes, impietie, and crueltie that could be spoken; For as to proceed against him by way of iustice, the subiect hath no such iurisdiction ouer his Soueraigne prince: of whom dependeth all power and authoritie to commaund: and who may not onely reuoke all the power of his Magistrats; but euen in whose presence the power of all Magistrats, Corporations, Colleges, Estates, and Communities cease, as we haue said, and shall yet more fully in due place say. Now if it be not lawfull for the subiect by way of iustice to proceed against his prince; the vassall against his lord; nor the slaue against his master; and in breife, if it be not lawfull, by way and course of iustice to proceed against a king, how should it then be lawfull to proceed against him by way of fact, or force. For question is not here, what men are able to doe by strength and force, but what they ought of right to do: as not whether the subiects haue power and strength, but whether they haue lawfull power to condemne their soueraigne prince. Now the subiect is not onely guiltie of treason in the highest degree, who hath slaine his soueraigne prince, but euen he also which hath attempted the same; who hath giuen councell or consent thereunto; yea if he haue conccaled the same, or but so much as thought it: which fact the lawes haue in such detestation, as that when a man guiltie of any offence or crime, dieth before he be thereof condemned, he is deemed to haue died in whole and perfect state, except he haue conspired against the life and dignitie of his soueraigne prince: this onely thing they haue thought to bee such, as that for which hee may worthily seeme to haue bene now alreadie iudged and condemned; yea euen before he was thereof accused. And albeit that the lawes inflict no punishment vpon the euill thoughts of men; but on those onely which by word or deed breake out into some enormitie: yet if any man shall so much as conceit a thought for the violating of the person of his soueraigne prince, although he haue attempted nothing, they haue yet iudged this same thought worthie of death, notwithstanding what repentance soeuer he haue had thereof.

Treason but thought of punished with death.

As in proofe it fell out with a gentleman of Normandie, who confessed himselfe vnto a Franciscan Frier, to haue had a purpose in himself to haue slaine *Francis* the first,

---

F2 *For* those states *probably read* the estates (cf. Fr).   F7 *For* Amphiorix *read* Ambiorix (Fr and L).
I6 even   I7 concealed

A firſt, the French king: of which euill purpoſe and intent he repenting himſelfe, receiued of the frier abſolution, who yet afterward told the king thereof; who ſending for the gentleman, and he confeſsing the fact, turned him ouer to the parliament of Paris for his triall, where he was by the decree of that high court condemned to death, and ſo afterwards executed. Which wee cannot ſay, that the judges did for feare, ſeeing that they had oftentimes refuſed to ratifie the edicts and letters patents by that gratious king granted, notwithſtanding whatſoeuer commaundement hee did giue for them to confirme the ſame. And ſo in Paris, although a fooliſh man and altogether out of his wit, called *Caboche*, drew his ſword vpon *Henrie* the ſecond, *Francis* his ſon, as with a purpoſe to haue ſlaine him; but without effect or hurt done, yet was he neuertheleſſe condemned, and ſo put to death, without any regard had vnto his luneſie or frenſie; although the lawes euerie where excuſe the madde and lunitike man, from all puniſhment, what murther or villanie ſoeuer he doe; ſeeing that hee is more than enough tormented with the frantike furious paſsion it ſelfe. And leaſt any man ſhould thinke themſelues to haue bene the authors of theſe lawes and decrees, ſo the more ſtraitly to prouide for their owne ſafetie and honour, let vs ſee the lawes and examples of holy Scripture. *Nabugodonozor* king of Aſsyria, with fire and ſword deſtroyed all the countrey of Paleſtine, beſieged the citie of Hieruſalem, tooke it, robbed and raſed it downe to the ground, burnt the temple, and defiled the ſanctuarie of God, ſlew the king, with the greateſt part of the people, carrying away the reſt that remained into captiuitie into Babilon; and yet not ſo contented, cauſed * the image of himſelfe made in gold, to be ſet vp in publike place, commaunding all men without exception to adore and worſhip the ſame, vpon paine of being burnt aliue: and cauſed them that refuſed ſo to doe, to be caſt into a burning furnace: and yet for all that the holy * Prophets directing their letters vnto their brethren the Iewes, then in captiuitie at Babilon, will them to pray vnto God, for the good and happie life of *Nabuchodonoſor* and his children, and that they might ſo long rule and raigne ouer them as the heauens ſhould endure. Yea euen God himſelfe doubted not to call *Nabuchodonoſor* his ſeruant; ſaying, That he would make him the moſt mightie prince of the world. And yet was there euer a more deteſtable tyrant than he? who not contented to be himſelfe worſhipped, but cauſed his image to be alſo adored, and that vpon paine of being burnt quick. And yet for all that we ſee the prophet *Ezechiel*, enſpired with the ſpirit of God, angrie with *Sedechia* king of Hieruſalem, greatly to deteſt his perfidious dealing, diſloyaltie, and rebellion againſt king *Nabuchodonoſor*, whoſe vaſſall hee was, and as it were reioyceth him to haue bene moſt iuſtly ſlaine. We haue alſo another more rare example of *Saul*, who poſſeſſed with an euill ſpirit, cauſed the prieſts of the lord to be without iuſt cauſe ſlain, for that one of them had receiued *Dauid* flying from him, and did ofttimes what in his power was, to kill, or cauſe to haue bene killed the ſame *Dauid*, a moſt innocent prince, by whome he had got ſo manie victories ouer his enemies: at which time he fell twice himſelfe into *Dauid* his hands; who blamed of his moſt valiant ſouldiers (ouer whom he then commaunded) for that he would not ſuffer his ſo mortal an enemie then in his power, to be ſlaine, being in moſt aſſured hope to haue enioyed the kingdome after his death, he deteſted their counſel, ſaying, God forbid that I ſhould ſuffer the perſon of a king, the Lords annointed to be violated. Yea moreouer hee himſelfe defended the ſame king perſecuting of him, when as hee commaunded the ſouldiers of his guard ouercome by wine and ſleepe to be wakened. And at ſuch time as *Saul* was ſlaine, and that a ſouldiour thinking to do *Dauid* a pleaſure, preſented him with *Saul* his head: *Dauid* forthwith cauſed the ſame ſouldier to be ſlain, which had brought him the head, ſaiing, Go thou wicked, how durſt thou lay thine impure hands vpon the Lords annointed?

That ſoueraigne princes whatſoeuer ought to bee vnto their ſubiects ſacred and inuiolat.

Dan. cap. 5.

Baruc. 1. Hier. 29

Hier. 25; Ezec. 29

ted? thou shalt surely die therefore: and afterwards without all dissimulation mourned himselfe for the dead king. All which is worth our good consideration. For *Dauid* was by *Saul* persecuted to death, and yet wanted not power to haue reuenged himselfe, being become stronger than the king by the aid of his enemies, vnto whome hee fled euen against his will: besides that he was the chosen of God, and annointed by the hands of *Samuel*, to be king of the people, and had also married the kings daughter: and yet for all that he abhorred to take vpon him the title of a king, and much more to attempt any thing against the life or honour of *Saul*, or to rebell against him, but chose rather to banish himselfe out of the realme, than in any sort to seeke the kings destruction. So we also read, that the most holy and best learned men that euer were amongst the Iewes. whome they called the *Essei* (that is to say, the true executors of the law of God) held, that soueraigne princes whatsoeuer they were, ought to bee vnto their subiects inuiolable, as persons sacred, and sent vnto them from God. And wee doubt not, but that *Dauid* a king and prophet, led by the spirit of God, had alwaies before his eies the law of God, which saith, *Thou shalt not speake euill of thy prince, nor detract the Magistrat*. Neither is there any thing more common in all the holy Scripture, than the forbidding not onely to kill or attempt the life or honour of a prince, but euen for the verie magistrats also, although (saith the Scripture) they be wicked and naught. If therfore he be guiltie of treason against God and man, which doth but detract the magistracie; what punishment then can be sufficient for him that shall attempt his life? For the law of God is in this case yet more precise than are the lawes of men: For the law *Iulia* holdeth but him guiltie of treason, which shall giue councell to kill the magistrat, whereas the law of God expresly forbiddeth in any sort to speake of the magistrat euil, or in any wise to detract him. Wherefore to aunswere vnto the vaine and friuolous obiections & arguments of them which maintain the contrarie, were but idly to abuse both our time and learning. But as he which doubteth whether there bee a God or not, is not with arguments to be refuted, but with seuere punishments to bee chastised: so are they also which call into question a thing so cleere, and that by bookes publikely imprinted; that the subiects may take vp armes against their prince beeing a Tyrant, and take him out of the way howsoeuer: howbeit that the most learned diuines, and of best vnderstanding, are cleere of opinion, that it is not lawfull for a man not only to kill his soueraigne prince, but euen to rebell against him, without an especiall and vndoubtfull commaundement from God; as we read of *Iehu*, who was chosen of God, and by the prophet annointed king of Israel, with expresse commandement vtterly to root out all the house of king *Achab*. He before as a subiect had right patiently borne all his wickednesse and outrages. Yea the most cruell murthers and torturing of the most holy prophets, and religious men, the vnworthy murthers, banishments, and proscriptions of the subiects; as also the most detestable witchcraft of queene *Iesabel*: yet for all that durst he attempt nothing against his soueraigne prince, vntill he had expresse commaundement from God, by the mouth of his prophet, whome God indeed so assisted, as that with a small power he slew two kings, caused seuentie of king *Achab* his children to be put to death, with many other princes of the kings of Israel and of Iuda, and all the idolatrous priests of *Bahal*, that is to say of the Sunne, after that hee had caused *Iesabel* the queene, to be cast headlong downe from an high tower, and left her bodie to be torne in peeces and eaten vp of dogges. But we are not to apply this especiall commaundement of God, vnto the conspiracies and rebellions of mutinous subiects against their soueraigne princes. And as for that which *Caluin* saith, if there were at this time magistrats appointed for the defence of the people, and to restraine the insolencie of kings, as were the Ephori in Lacedemonia, the Tribunes in Rome, and the

*Exod. 22.28.

the Demarches in Athens, that they ought to resist and impeach their licentiousnesse and crueltie: he sheweth sufficiently, that it was neuer lawfull in a right Monarchie, to assault the prince, neither to attempt the life or honour of their soueraigne king: for he speaketh not but of the popular and Aristocratique states of Commonweales. And we haue before shewed, that the kings of Lacedemonia were no more but plaine Senators and captaines: and when he speaketh of states, he saith, Possibly, not daring to assure any thing. Howbeit that there is a notable difference betwixt the attempting of the honour of his prince, and the withstanding of his tyranny; betwizt killing his king, and the opposing of ones selfe against his crueltie. We read also, that the Protestant princes of Germanie, before they entred into armes against *Charles* the emperor, demaunded of *Martin Luther* if it were lawfull for them so to doe or not; who frankly told them, That it was not lawfull, whatsoeuer tyrannie or impietie were pretended; yet was he not therein of them beleeued: so thereof ensued a deadly and most lamentable warre, the end whereof was most miserable, drawing with it the ruine and destruction of many great and noble houses of Germanie, with exceeding slaughter of the subiects: whereas *No cause (as saith Cicero) can be thought iust or sufficient for vs to take vp armes against our countrey.* And yet it is most certaine, that the soueraigntie of the empire resteth not in the person of the emperour (as we will in due place declare) but being chiefe of the state, they could not lawfully take vp armes against him, but by a generall consent of the state, or of the greater part of them, which was not done: then much lesse is it lawfull to take vp armes against a soueraigne prince. I cannot vse a better example, than of the dutie of a sonne towards his father: the law of God saith, That he which speaketh euill of his father or mother, shall be put to death. Now if the father shall be a theefe, a murtherer, a traytor to his countrey, as an incestuous person, a manqueller, a blasphemer, an atheist, or what so you will else; I confesse that all the punishments that can bee deuised are not sufficient to punish him: yet I say, it is not for the sonne to put his hand thereunto, *Quia nulla tanta impietas, nullum tantum scelus est, quod sit parricidio vindicandum.* For that (as saith an auntient Orator) no impietie can be so great, no offence so hainous, as to be reuenged with the killing of ones father. And yet *Cicero* reasoning vpon the same question, saith, our country to bee deerer vnto vs than our parents. Wherfore the prince whom you may iustly call the father of the country ought to be vnto euery man dearer & more reuerend than any father, as one ordained & sent vnto vs by God. I say therfore that the subiect is neuer to be suffered to attempt any thing against his soueraign prince, how naughty & cruel soeuer he be: lawful it is, not to obey him in things contrarie vnto the laws of God & nature: to flie and hide our selues from him; but yet to suffer stripes, yea and death also rather than to attempt any thing against his life or honour. O how many Tirants should there be; if it should be lawfull for subiects to kill Tirants? how many good and innocent princes should as Tirants perish, by the conspiracie of their subiects against them? He that should of his subiects exact subsidies, should be then (as the vulgar people accompt him) a Tirant: he that should rule and commaund contrarie to the good liking of the people, should be a Tirant: (as *Aristotle* in his Politiques sayeth him to be) he that should keepe strong gardes and garrisons for the safetie of his person, should be a Tirant: he that should put to death traitors and conspirators against his state should be also counted a Tirant. And indeed how should good princes be assured of their liues, if vnder the colour of tirannie they might bee slaine of their subiects, by whom they ought to be defended? Not for that I would say it not to be lawfull for other Princes by force of armes to prosecute tiranie (as I haue before said) but for that it is not lawful for subiects so to doe. Howbeit that I am rather of *Diogenes* the Cinique his opinion, who

The warrs of the Germaine princes against Charles the fift in Germanie in Luthers iudgment not lawful. Sledan. lib. 4.

What great inconueniencies should ensue if it were lawful for subiects vnder the colour of tyrants to kil their soueraign princes

who one day meeting with *Dionysius* the yonger, then liuing in exile at Corinth, and seeing him merily sporting himselfe in the streats with iesters and minstrels; verie soberlie said vnto him, Truely thou art now in an estate vnworthie of thee. I hartilie thank thee (said *Dionysius*) for hauing compassion on me. And thinkest thou said *Diogenes* that I thus say for any compassion I haue of thee? mistake me not, for I speake it rather in dispite of the life thou now leadest, to see such a vile slaue as thee, worthy to grow old, and die in the accursed state of tirannie, as did thy father, thus to sport thy selfe in securitie, and quietly to passe thy time among vs. For can any hangman more cruelly torment a man condemned to torture, than feare? Feare I say of death, of infamie, and of torture: these bee the reuenging furies which continually vex Tirants, and with eternall terrours torment them both night and day: Then enuie, suspition, feare, desire of reuenge, with a thousand contrarie passions at variance among themselues, do so disquiet their minds, and more cruelly tiranize ouer them, than they themselues can ouer their slaues, with all the torments they can deuise. And what greater wretchednesse can happen vnto a man, than that which presseth and forceth the tirant? to haue a desire to make his subiects beasts and fooles, by cutting from them all the waies to vertue and learning? To bee a slaue and subiect vnto a thousand spyes and pryers into other mens liues? to heare, see, and vnderstand, what is done, saied, or thought of all and euery man? and in stead of ioyning and vniting of his subiects in loue and amitie together; to sow amongst them a thousand quarrels and dissentions: to the end they should alwaies be at defiance among themselues, and in distrust one of an other? And who can doubt but that a Tirant still languishing in such torment, is of all men most miserable, and more afflicted and tormented, than if he should die a thousand deaths? Death (as sayeth *Theophrastus*) is the end of all miseries; and the repose of the vnfortunate, as sayeth *Cæsar*: neither the one nor the other being in that point superstitious, as not persuaded of the immortalitie of the soule, or that it longer liued than the bodie, or that there remayned any farther paines for the wicked after this life: so that to wish a Tirant slaine as a punishment for his deserts, is but to wish his good and rest.

The miserable state and condition of a Tyrant whilst he liueth.

But most Tirants haue ordinarilie neare vnto their owne persons certeine Mynnions, of whom they make great account and reckning: whom they vse as spunges to suck vp their subiects blood, vpon whom when occasion serueth, they discharge themselues; to the end that the people entering into furie, should seise vpon them, and spare themselues: So had *Tiberius*, *Seian*; *Nero*, *Tigillin*; *Dionyse* the younger, *Phyliste*; and of late *Henry* king of Sweden, *George Preschon*, whom we read to haue beene giuen as a prey vnto the furious people, and by them to haue beene rent and torne in peeces. So the Emperour *Anthonius Caracalla* to please the people, put to death all the flatterers who had before induced him to kill his brother. Neither did *Caligula* in better sort intreat his claw-backs. And by these sleights haue Tyrants oftentimes wel escaped the rage and furie of the people. But if the conspiratours began their furie at the person of the Tyrant himselfe, then were not onely his friends and fauourites, but euen his wiues, children, and neerest kinsmen, most cruelly slaine. Which they did not onely all Greece ouer, but in Sicilie also: as after the death of *Hiero* the Tyrant, ensued the slaughter of all his friends and kinsfolks, the rage of the people with vnspeakable crueltie bursting out, euen to the dismembring of his sisters and cosens: his statues were cast downe, all his edicts reuoked, not only those which were vniust and vnreasonable, but euen those also which were right commendable and necessarie; to the intent that no memoriall of Tyrants might remaine: yet true it is, that oftentimes their good decrees were still kept. And that is it for which *Cicero* said, That there was nothing

The policie of some Tyrants to auert from themselues the peoples rage.

I 7 *For* Anthonius *read* Antoninus.   K 3 *For* Hiero *read* Hieronymus.

thing more common, than to approue the acts of a Tyrant, and yet to place in heauen them that had slaine them. And yet he in another saith it be a doubt, not yet resolued vpon, *viz. Whether a good man ought to come vnto the counsell of a Tyrant consulting euen of good and profitable matters?* And yet this question dependeth of the other: for if a man make conscience to be assistant vnto a Tyrant, consulting of good things, for feare least in so doing he should seeme to approue his tyrannie: wherefore should he then approue the good lawes and decrees by him made? for that is also no lesse to ratifie his tyranny, and to giue example to others, aswell as to giue councell vnto a Tyrant, in good and commendable things. Except one should say, that tyrannie which yet is in the force and strength of it selfe, is shored and countenanced by the councell of good and honest men, vnder the couert of some one or other good and commendable act, which would otherwise of it selfe fall, by the onely euill opinion conceiued of tyrannie; whereas he which is alreadie dead, cannot be againe reuiued to ratifie his other euill acts. Yea it oftentimes falleth out, that not onely the good & profitable acts of Tyrants, but euen their euill and vniust acts and orders are of necessitie to be retained also, if we will haue the Commonwealth in safetie to stand. Wherefore *Thrasibulus* after he had put to flight the thirtie Tyrants of Athens: and *Aratus* hauing slaine *Nicholas* the Tyrant of Sicyone: and to the imitation of them *Cicero* after the death of *Cæsar* the dictator, perswaded the publication of the lawes of forgetfulnesse, to extinguish the desire of reuenge: yet for the most part ratifying the acts of those Tyrants, which they could not vtterly disanull, without the ruine of the whole Commonweale. As for that we read the acts of *Nero* and *Demetrian*, to haue beene reuoked, and disanulled by the Senat, that concerneth certaine perpetuall edicts of theirs, which for that they had a perpetuall inconuenience annexed vnto them, would if they had not bene abrogated, haue in time vtterly ruinated all that was now againe set in order: as for their good & comendable lawes, they were not at all altred. For what time was more glorious than *Nero* his first fiue yeares raigne? what more fit or better for the well ordering of a Commonweale? Insomuch that *Traian* himselfe a most excellent prince, deemed no man to haue bene like vnto *Nero*, for the well gouerning of a Commonweale. Vnto this the opinions of the lawyers agree, who hold the successours of Tyrants to be bound vnto all such things as the Tyrants their predecessours haue iustly promised or done, but not vnto the rest. So the emperour *Constantine* the Great, by a law abrogated such things, as *Licinius* the Tyrant had before vniustly decreed, but confirmed the rest. The like we read to haue bene done by *Theodosius* the younger, and *Arcadius* the emperours, after the death of the Tyrant *Maximus*, by this law, *Quæ Tyrannus contra ius rescripsit non valere præcipimus: legitimis eius rescriptis non impugnandis*, What the Tyrant hath against right decreed, we commaund to be of none effect; not impugning his lawfull decrees. And albeit that these two yong emperours, to be reuenged of the Tyrant *Maximus*, had by a generall edict reuoked all the prodigall gifts and preferments, which he lauishly had bestowed vppon wicked men, and of no desert in the Commonweale: and also disanulled his iudgements and decrees: yet would they not repeale any thing that had bene by him decreed or graunted, without fraud and deceit, and the hurt of the Commonweale. Those last wordes without *fraud and deceit*, which we read in *Theodosius*, his law, are added against Tyrants Agents, & Brokers, who are especially to be laid hold vpon, to the end that others take not example by them, to build their houses, or enrich themselues by the ruine or hurt of others, during the time that tyranie beareth sway; or that the Commonwealth is with ciuill warres diuided. As it happened in the state of Milan, rent in sunder by the Venetians, the French, the Swissers, and the Spaniards, euerie one of them taking

vnto

That not only the good acts and decrees of Tyrants, but euen their euill acts and decrees also are oftentimes of necessitie after their death to be retained in a commonweal.

The successours of Tyrants how farre they are bound to that which the Tyrants their predecessours haue promised.

A2 *another* PLACE *saith*   B8 *For* Nicholas *read* Nicocles.   C2 *For* Demetrian *read* Domitian.
D7 *For* non impugnandis *read* minime impugnandis (Fr and L).   Note at B3.

vnto themselues so much thereof, as they could by force and strength, as if it had bene by good right, and the *Sforces* the rest: where amongst others it fortuned *Iason* the famous lawyer, a fauourit of the Spaniards, by fraudulent meanes to obtaine the goods of *Triuultius*, a worthie captaine of the French part: but the Spaniards afterwards driuen out, and the French returned, *Iason* was right well beaten with his owne lawes and decisions, being by the captaine *Triuultius* againe thrust out of his vniust possession, and that by his owne doctrine. In which case yet the force of lawes and decrees ought not to be of so great force and power, as naturall and vpright equitie it selfe, which cannot be fully comprised in any lawes, but is to be left vnto the religious arbitrement of them who know how to mannage the affaires of state, and wisely to ballance the particular profit, with the counterpoise of the publique, according to the infinit varietie of times, places, and persons; alwaies remembring the profit of euerie man in particular, and of all together in generall, not to be one and the same: and that the publike is alwaies to be preferred before the priuat, except the priuat be grounded vpon the greatest equitie and reason. As if the Receiuers in the heat of the ciuill warres, or in the raigne of a Tyrant, or in such time as lawfull enemies make inuasion, shall be enforced to pay the publike money: it is good reason it should be allowed them, as paid vnto the Commonwealth. For so it was iudged by decree of the parliament of Naples, for them that had paid vnto the receiuers of *Charles* the eight, when as after the returne of the Spaniards, they would haue enforced the receiuers to haue paid the money twice, naturall reason (in this case) preferring the priuat profit before the publike. For the receiuers could not otherwise doe, the Frenchmen then fully possessed of the kingdom of Naples. But if the Receiuers or debtors of the Commonweale, shall without any summons or constraint, or for some colourable suit, pay vnto the enemie, or a Tyrant, part of that which is due, to accept in stead of the whole, they shall yet still remaine not onely debtors for the whole, but be in daunger also of treason. Wherefore to conclude this question, It is not meet that the good decrees or laws of a slaine tyrant should be repealed or disanulled.

Naturall equitie in all cases cannot in any lawe be comprised, but is oft times to be left vnto the religious arbitremēt of men expert in matters of state.

And in this, the princes much deceiue themselues, which ouerthrow and make void all the acts of Tyrants, their predecessours; and namely they which giue reward to them that haue slaine Tyrants, to make them a way vnto the soueraigntie. For they shall neuer assure themselues of their owne liues, if they seuerely punish not the conspiratours against their owne prince and murtherers of him, although hee were neuer so great a Tyrant. As most wisely did *Seuerus* the emperour, who put to death all them which had any part in the murther of the emperour *Pertinax*: which was the cause (as saith *Herodian*) that there was no man which durst attempt his life. So also *Vitellius* the emperour put to death all the murtherers and conspirators against *Galba*, who had presented requests signed with their owne hands vnto the emperour *Otho*, to haue had of him reward for their disloialtie. And *Theophilus* emperour of Constantinople caused them all to be called together, who had made his father emperour, after they had slaine *Leo* the Armenian, as if he would haue well recompensed them for so great a good turne: who being come together with many other, who though not partakers of the murther, were yet desirous to be partakers of the reward; hee caused them altogether to be slaine. And that more is, the emperour *Domitian* put to death *Epaphroditus*, *Nero* his manumised seruant, and secretarie to the state, for hauing holpen *Nero* to kill himselfe, who most instantly requested him so to doe, being thereby deliuered from the executioners hands, and cruell exemplarie death. And these things wee read not onely Tyrants, but euen good kings also to haue done, not so much in regard of their owne safetie, as of the dignitie of them that were slaine. As *Dauid* did vnto him who

Murthers euen of euill and tyrannicall princes, not to be rewarded, but seuerely punished.

Note at H5.

who in hope of reward brought him his father in lawes head cut off, but slaine by his enemies. And *Alexander* the Great caused cruelly to bee put to death him that had murthered king *Darius*, abhorring the subiect which durst to lay hand vpon his king: although *Alexander* himselfe by lawfull warre sought after his life and state, as beeing his lawfull enemie. And yet in mine opinion the thing that hath most preserued the kings of Fraunce and their persons inuiolated, is for that they haue not vsed crueltie towards them which were neere vnto them in blood, albeit that they were attainted, conuicted, yea and condemned as enemies to their prince, and guiltie of treason. As *Iohn* the second, duke of Alencon, although he was twice for the same cause condemned, as for that he had with the enemies conspired against king *Charles* the seuenth and the Commonweale, and the sentence of death pronounced against him by the Chancelour, yet for all that would not the king, that he should bee executed. Many haue blamed this the kings too much clemencie, as daungerous: but they see not, that kings in so doing, do not so much deliuer their kinsmen from punishment, as themselues; neither so much to prouide for other mens safetie, as for their own; nor that in forbidding the blood of their kinsmen to be shed, they spare their owne; nor that hee which putteth a prince of his owne blood into the executioners hands, or causeth him to be murthered, forgeth a knife to cut his owne throat. For wee haue seene the emperours of Constantinople both of auntient and latter time, and many kings of Spaine and England, who fouling their hands in the blood of their princes, suffered themselues afterward in their persons that which they had done to others. For not to speake of those things which are reported to haue of late bene done in the house of Castile: one king in that nation cruelly murthered six of his brethren: and in lesse than thirtie six yeares fourescore princes of royall blood, were (as *Philip Comines* in his Commentaries reporteth) in England either slaine or executed by the bloudie executioners hands Now the greatest safetie of a soueraigne prince, is to haue their subiects persuaded, that they ought to be holy and inuiolat; although it much concerne the Commonweale also, the kings stocke to be most sacred, least the princes of the blood being taken out of the way, the Commonweale fall also; or else troubled with endlesse sedition, bee rent in peeces, as we shall in due place declare. I know well that some haue blamed *Seleucus*, for not hauing put to death *Demetrius*, surnamed the Besieger, one of the most valiant princes that euer was; but hauing onely kept him in prison: And *Hugh Capet*, for hauing kept in prison in the castle at Orleans, *Charles* the last of the blood of king *Charlemaigne*: And *Henrie* the first, king of England, for hauing kept in prison vntill his death, his elder brother *Robert*, hauing before caused his eyes to bee put out: As also *Christiern* father to *Frederike* king of Denmarke, for hauing kept his cosen the king of Denmarke thrust out of his kingdome, fiue and twentie yeares prisoner, who as a priuat man there died in prison, in the castle of Calemboug, being 77 yeares old: And *Iohn* king of Sweden, who keepeth his elder brother *Henrie* (reiected by the people) prisoner euer since the yeare 1567, least he should trouble both him and the Commonweale. But they haue bene, and yet are by this meanes more reuerenced and honoured of their subiects, than if they had put these their so honourable prisoners to death.

But here some men wil obiect, The keeping of such princes prisones, to be a thing full of perill and daunger: which I confesse, and was the onely reason that moued the pope to counsell *Charles* of Fraunce, to put to death *Conradin* his prisoner, the sonne of *Manfroy* king of Naples. As with like crueltie had *Ptolomie*, last king of Ægypt caused *Pompey* the Great, after his flight vnto him from the battaile of Pharsalia, to be slaine; his councellors saying vnto him, *That dead men bit not*. And yet neuerthelesse

margin notes: Lenitie of soueraign princes towards them of their owne blood offending them, and so in their daunger, or otherwise their honorable prisoners, vnto themselues both commendable and profitable

The keeping of great princes prisoners, daungerous.

230 THE SECOND BOOKE

neither could this *Ptolomee* escape destruction: neither wanted there heires enow of the house of Aragon, who ceased not to driue out them of the house of Aniou, and to recouer againe the kingdome: and albeit that he which put him to death, beeing himselfe afterward also condemned to die, escaped: yet so it was, that the infamie of so detestable a murther, without cause committed vppon the person of a young innocent prince, hath yet rested vpon them which did the execution to their owne destruction. And truely our auncestours seeing *Iohn* duke of Burgundie, rashly in the verie time of iudgement, confessing the murther of *Lewes* his kinsman, duke of Orleans; and yet to haue easily escaped the daunger, said, That surely from thence foreward a man might haue the blood of princes good cheape, and in so saying said well. For the same *Iohn* comming afterward vnder safe conduct, was himselfe likewise serued, and in cold blood slaine, they that were the authors of his death escaping vnpunished.

CHAP. VI.
¶ Of an Aristocratie.

What an Aristocratie is.

AN Aristocratie is a forme of Commonweale, wherein the lesse part of the citisens with soueraigne power commaundeth ouer all the rest; and euerie citisen in particular. And in that it is contrarie vnto the estate Popular, for that in the Aristocraticall state the lesser part of the citisens command, and in the Popular state the greater: and yet in that they both agree, that they which haue the soueraignty, haue power to commaund ouer euery one in particular, but not ouer all in generall. Wherefore a Monarchie is in that better and more honourable than the other two; for that in it the power of one extendeth it selfe ouer all in generall, and in particular also: a thing in mine opinion well worthy the noting. And like as a Monarchie is either Royall, Lordlike, or Tyrannicall: so also an Aristocratie may be Lordly, lawfull, or factious; which in auntient time the called an Oligarchie; that is to say, a Seignorie of a verie small number of Lords. As were the thirtie lords of Athens, ouerthrowne by *Thrasibulus*, whom they called the thirtie Tyrants. Or the ten commissioners, commonly called the Decemuiri, appointed to reforme the lawes and customes of Rome: and long after the Triumuiri, who by force oppressing the libertie of the people, inuaded the soueraigntie. And that is it for which the auntients haue alwaies taken this word Oligarchie, in the euill part, and Aristocratie in the good; defining it to be *A gouernment of good men*. But we haue before declared, that in matters of state (to vnderstand of what forme euerie Commonweale is) we must not haue regard whether the gouernours thereof bee vertuous, or otherwise; but to the gouernment thereof. It is also a difficult matter, and almost impossible, to establish an Aristocratie composed onely of good men; for that cannot bee done by lot, neither by election, the two vsuall meanes: whereunto we may ioyne the third, by lot and election together, as impossible as the other; vertue with fortune hauing no agreement. Neither is lot and fortune to be admitted vnto the consultations of honest causes: and if the same should be committed vnto the choyce of the promiscuous and vulgar people, they would not make choyce of men altogether vnlike themselus; that is of fools, of wicked and most impudent men, good and wise men (if there be any) euerie where being the least part of the people: and what more shamefull thing could there be, than the honour and reputation of wise men, to depend of the iudgement (should I say, or of the rashnesse) of the head strong people. Yet let vs grant some few good and wise men to bee in the citie, truely they will shun euen the verie sight of the wicked,

Three sorts of Aristocraties.

Impossible to establish an Aristocratie onely of good men.

OF A COMMONWEALE.

wicked and of the bedlem multitude: neither if they come vnto their common assemblies, be so shamelesse and impudent, as to name and make their choice of themselues as of wise men. For so *Lactantius Firmianus* meerely iesteth at the seuen Sages of Greece: If they were but wise (saith he) in their owne iudgements, then were they not wise: but in the iudgement of others, much lesse, who were not wise in iudging no mo wise but seuen, and all the rest fooles.

But some may say it should do well herein to imitate the auncient Romans, and other Latins, in the choice that they by solemne oath made of the most valiant and warlike man of all other for their Generall: who so chosen, should make choice of a second for his Lieutenant most like himselfe: and he likewise of the third: and the third of the fourth; and so in order one valiant man of an other, vntill the number of their Legions were filled. This truely might seeme a good way for the forming of a Commonweal of good and worthie men, at the first beginning thereof: But who should presine the measure and number of those good men? and who should be suertie vnto the Commonweal, that euery one of those good men, should still make choice of an other good man like himselfe; rather then of his sonne, his brother, his kinsman, or his friend? and admit it were so done, sith euery where there are so few good men, who should defend them from the multitude, and violence of them that were left, as fooles and wicked men? But admit that a Commonweal may at the first be made of such a select number of good men; how long shall we think it can so stand? And that is it for which there neither is, nor euer was any pure Aristocratie; wherein the most vertuous onely had the soueraigntie. For albeit that the Pythagorians hauing drawne vnto their line the most noble and honorable princes of Italie: in the time of king *Seruius Tullius* had chaunged certeine Tyrants, into iust Regalities, and were in hope also by little and little to haue brought the Oligarchies, and Democraties, into Aristocraties, as in some places they had alreadie done: yet neuerthelesse it so fell out, that the popular men, and ringleaders of the people, seeing all power and authoritie, vnder the coulour of vertue, to be taken out of their hands, entered into great conspiracies, and so arming the people against the Pythagoreans, and the desperate rout, against the better sort: (as easie it was for the stronger to oppresse the weaker) burnt them in their diet, and massacred almost all the rest that escaped from the daunger of the fire: which shamefull murther of the Pythagorians raised great sturres in Italie.

Wherefore whether they be of the better sort, or of the worse; of the richer sort, or of the poorer; of the nobler, or of the baser; of the more warlike, or otherwise which hold the soueraigntie, so that it be the lesser part of the citizens or people, we call it by the name of an Aristocratie. This lesser part of citizens or people we need not to define by any certein number: for that the varietie of numbers is infinite, and can by no man be comprehended. As admit there be ten thousand citizens, of whom an hundred haue the soueraigntie; if in their common assemblie three score of them shall be of one opinion for the making of a law: that law shall in generall bind the other fortie which haue part also in the soueraigntie, but are the fewer in number, together with the other nine thousand nine hundred excluded from the gouernment, and the same three score being of one mind together, shall rule the whole ten thousand in particular: Neither yet for all that is the soueraigne right drawne vnto those three score; But as in euery lawfull Colledge and Corporation, the greater part is euery where the better: so it followeth that three score being of one accord, shall ouer rule the other fortie both altogether and apart: except by law concerning soueraigntie it be prouided, that two thirds of the citizens agreeing among themselues, should preuaile against the rest; as we see it set downe in almost all the lawes and statutes of Colledges: by which

Wheresoeuer the lesser part of the people hath the soueraigntie; there is one kind or other of an Aristocratie.

The lesser part of the people in an Aristocratie not to be defined by any certaine number.

X ij meanes

meanes threescore foure citizens, shall in the aforesaid number of an hundred, be superiour vnto the other thirtie six. Wherefore in an Aristocratie we are not to haue regard how little, or how great the number of the citizens is; prouided that they which haue the soueraigntie ouer the rest, be fewer in number than the one half of the whole. For admit there be an hundred thousand citizens in a Commonweale, of whom ten thousand haue the soueraigntie ouer the rest, it shall as well be called an Aristocratie; as if of ten thousand citizens, one thousand onely should hold the estate: considering that both in the one and other Commonweal, the tenth part hath the soueraigntie: so we may say where the hundred, or the thousand part of the citizens beare the sway; and the fewer that they be, the more assured and durable is the state; so that they be not at variance amongst themselues. As the estate of the Pharsalians was the most durable of Græce, and yet it had but twentie Gouernours. And the Lacedemonian Commonweal, which caried away the prize of honour from all the others of the East: albeit that it was most populous, yet for all that it had in it but thirtie Gouernours, chosen out of the better sort, to continue in the gouernment so long as they liued. The Epidaurians saith *Plutarche* had but an hundred and foure score of the noblest and welthiest of the citizens which had part in the soueraigntie: out of which number they chose the counsellours of the state. The auntient Commonweale of Marseilles in Prouence (which in the iudgement of *Cicero* was the best ordered Commonweal that euer was in the world) had in it six hundred citizens which held the soueraigntie: out of which number of six hundred were taken the Senators, and fifteene magistrats, and of these fifteene magistrats were three Presidents set ouer them in maner of the Roman Prætors. The like we may deeme of the Rhodians and Theban Common-weales, after that their popular estates were chaunged into Aristocraties, the richer sort possessing themselues of the soueraigntie: than which nothing can bee more commodious for the Commonweal, especially if good citizens cannot be had. For which cause *Titus Flaminius* the Consul established the townes and cities of the Thessalians in forme of an Aristocratie, making Senatours and Iudges of the richer sort, and giuing to them the soueraigne power, whom it concerned most, that their Commonweal should continue in rest and peace. Which order *Andrew Doria* seemeth to haue followed in reforming the Commonweal of Genua, by him drawne from the obeysance of the French, in the yeare 1528, at which time he by the consent of the citizens there established an Aristocratie of eight and twentie families, chosen as well out of the base commonaltie, as out of the nobilitie, so that they had six houses within Genua, all whom by a law he made noble, & partakers of the soueraigntie of the state: leauing vnto their discretion, euery yere to chuse vnto them ten other citizens, such as they should think fittest for their vertue, for their nobilitie or riches. Out of these eight and twentie families, he established a Counsell of fower hundred men, euery yeare to be chosen for the gouernment of the state: who also made choice of the Duke, and eight gouernours for two yeares to continue, whom together they call the Seignorie; for that vnto them it belongeth to manage the waightie affaires of the Common wealth: except some such great matter happen, as may require the aduise of the Senate, which consisting of an hundred persons, is vsually euery yeare chosen by the nobilitie, by secret voices, by lot giuen, as they do in Venice. And euery one of these eight Gouernours after his office expired, continueth for two yeares Procurour of the Common wealth: and from that time forward, remayneth one of the priuie councell, together with them which are and haue beene Dukes, who are Procurours of the Common weal so long as they liue. Besides that there are fortie Captaines euery yeare chosen, and an hundred men deputed to euery one of those captaines, which is a legion of foure

The Aristocratical estate of the Pharsalians.

The estate of the Lacedemonians.

The auntient estate of them of Marseilles.

The Aristocraticall estate of Genua framed by Andrew Doria.

H2 Praetors (L) Consuls (Fr) 51. H7 *For* Consul *Bodin writes* Proconsul (Fr and L). Cf. Livy, XXXIV, Note at K4.

foure thousand men, appointed for the strength and defence of the citie: Ouer which legion there is one Colonell, or chiefe Captaine, whom they call the Generall; who are all chosen by the voices of the nobilitie: As for their iurisdiction or administration of justice, they vse strangers, *viz.* a Prætor, who is alwaies a stranger; with two Lieutenants his assistants, the one for the receit, the other for criminall causes: and fiue other Ciuilians, judges for all priuat causes for two yeares, all strangers also; whom they call the *Rota*. Yet besides them, there are seauen extraordinarie Iudges chosen out of the Citizens, for the extraordinarie deciding of causes. Besides whom were also fiue Syndicques, to receiue informations against the Duke, and the eight Gouernours, after that their charge was expired, causing proclamation to be openly made, That if any man had any complaint against them, for any wrong or iniurie receiued from them, he should come in and be heard: at which time if none complained, they had letters testimoniall giuen them, in witnesse of their vpright dealing in their office. The same yeare that *Doria* established an Aristocratie at Genua, they of Geneua also changed their Pontificall monarchie into a Popular state, gouerned in maner of an Aristocratie. And albeit that the Towne long time before pretended it selfe not to bee subiect vnto the laws either of the Duke of Sauoy or of the Pope, but to be free from them both; yet the citizens thought it not best for them to attempt any thing, vntill that discord about the Soueraigntie was risen not only betwixt the Duke & the bishop, but euen betwixt the bishop and the people also: at which time they tooke hold vpon the occasion then presented vnto their desires for the changing both of their Religion & state. Wherefore their Commonweale now set at libertie, they established a Counsell of two hundred citizens, with soueraigne and perpetuall power; but that the people still reserued vnto themselues the confirmation of lawes, the election of their Syndicques and other the great magistrats, and the treaties of peace and warre; all which belong vnto the right of Soueraigntie, as we haue before declared. Now out of this great Counsell of two hundred, they made choice of a perpetuall Senat of threescore persons: and out of that Senat, they take fiue and twentie to be of the priuie Counsell for euer, chosen all by the great Counsell, and the foure Syndicques chosen euery yeare for soueraigne Magistrats, beside the other Iudges and magistrats ordinarie. But the difference betwixt this Commonweal and that of Genua is notable, but especially in this, that the Genowaies vse euery yeare to change their great Counsell of fower hundred, and Senat of three score, with other their Magistrats, except some few which continue for two yeares. Whereas the great Counsell of Geneua, the Senat, and priuie counsell are once chosen for euer: yet so, as that the censuring of euery one of them euery yere is still reserued vnto the Citizens: which is most straitly looked vnto; whereby it commeth to passe, that the Commonweal of Geneua is more firme, and lesse subiect vnto alteration or seditious innouation than is that of Genua. Moreouer the choice of the great Counsell, the Senat, and of the priuie Counsell at Geneua is not made all at once, as at Genes and Venice; but a roome being become void by the death or attainder of a councelour of the priuie Counsell of fiue and twentie, they proceed to the choice of another out of the great counsell, to put in his place into the priuie Councell: and after that of a citizen, or at least wise of a Burgeois, to put into the great counsell, a man not any way spotted or defamed: not hauing any regard in the choice of them, vnto their wealth, or nobilitie, but in what they may vnto their vertue and integritie only: a thing (as we read) vsed amongst the Lacedemonians, who after the death of their Senators, made choice of others in respect of their honour and vertue onely.

The Swissers except the Grisons, and the other fiue little cantons, haue almost the same forme of a Commonweale; as we see at Zurich the great Councell of two hun-

The estate of Geneua

The state of the Swissers.

B7 *For* the Pope *read* the bishop (cf. B9–10). Note at B3.

dred, the Senat, and the priuie Councell, established after the maner of Geneua: or to say better, that of Geneua after the forme of Zurich; which is almost like vnto that of Berne. Which neuerthelesse differ in this, that with these the great Councel & the Senat chaunge euerie yeare: which they do not at Geneua: for with these the fraternities, which they call *Zunfft*, euerie one of them composed of one, two or three occupations: which are eleuen at Schaffouse, twelue at Zurich, fifteene at Basil; and in other places more or lesse, chuse twelue persons of euerie fraternitie, for the great Councell: and for the Senat they chuse two, as at Zurich; or three, as at Basil; of whome one is the chiefe of the fraternitie. So that the great Councell at Zurich, consisteth of two hundreth, of 244 at Basil, of 86 at Schaffuse. And of Senators at Zurich the number is fiftie, at Schaffuse twentie sixe, and at Basil sixtie three. But they which are so chosen by the voyces of the fraternitie, are confirmed also by the great Councell, and by the Senators or magistrat, or by the old Senat, as at Basil. For the one halfe of the Senat is that which was before, which had the charge alreadie sixe monethes. And the other moytie of the Senat, is of those which are but newly chosen, to the intent that the Senat should not be wholy chaunged all at once. True it is, that the auntient Senat of Basil, chose alwaies the Senat for the yeare following: and the Burgamasters who had for their companions three Tribunes at Zurich, and two at Basil, who with the Bourgamasters being foure, haue nine other persons, as assistants ioyned vnto them, and so together make the colledge of the thirteene men (as they call it) vnto whome all the mannaging of the secret affaires of the Commonwealth are committed: and without whose authoritie nothing vsually is propounded vnto the Senat or great Councell to resolue of. There are also at Zurich eight men, which haue charge of the common receit, ouer whome one Bourgomaster is gouernour. And at Zurich and Shaffuse the new Senators determine all causes criminall: whereas in all the other townes the Prouost of the empire, with three Senators in the name of the whole Senat decide the same: which prouost is also chosen of the Senat, and generally none may bee chosen into the Senat which is defamed or base borne. By all which it is manifest, that their estate is gouerned Aristocratically; and yet more at Berne, Lucerne, Friburg, and *Soleure*, where the fraternities and companies haue no voyces in the state, neither power or authoritie to meet together, more then for matters concerning their occupations and trades: but euerie yeare foure captaines or chiefe men of euerie citie, chose out sixteen other citisens, men of greatest integritie, and without all imputation: who three daies before Easter make choice of the great Councell, consisting of an hundred of the better sort of the citisens at Lucerne, and of more than two hundred at Berne: which great Councell afterwards chuseth the Auoyer, which they call *Schuldthessen*, and the other magistrats. And particularly the Auoyer, with the aforesaid sixteene, and the foure captaines chose the Senat, which is of xxvj at Berne, and xviij at Lucerne: who haue the power of the state at Berne for a yeare. The foure captaines are also annuall chosen by the great Councell; by which captaines and the treasurors, all the judges are elected and confirmed by the Senat: which Senat hath also the deciding of the first appeales. The second appeales are decided by the same Senat of xxvj, and xxvj others whome the Senat shall make choice of. But the last appeale of all is vnto the great Councell, the chiefe whereof is the Auoyer: where if question be of the life, fame, or fortune of any the citisens: it is by the decree there made decided, without further appeale. The same order almost is vsed in the state of Friburg, in making choyce of the great Councell, consisting of two hundred of the better sort of the citisens: by whome afterwards is chosen the Senat of twentie foure persons, and the Auoyer with the foure captaines.

Whereby

I3 other   I9—10 annuall, chosen   Notes at F3, G2, I9, K2.

OF A COMMONWEALE.   235

A   Whereby it is well to be vnderstood those estates of the Swissers to bee Aristocratique, yet popularly tempered: for that the way is open for all the citisens of what degree soeuer vnto all the officers and places of commaund, benefits and charge in the Commonweale, if they be not men infamed, distracted of their wits, or otherwise vtterly ignorant of gouernment. That is also belonging vnto popularitie, that almost all their magistrats are annuall: which temperature of the better or richer sort with the meaner or poorer, in being capable of the honours of the Commonweale, maketh the same much more firme and stable, than if the honours and preferments were communicated but vnto the Senators or richer sort onely; with whome the vulgar people is most commonly at oddes: and that so much the more amongst the Swissers, where

B   the nobilitie (except some few) long sithence destroyed and almost rooted out, the people tooke vpon them the soueraigntie: which by little and little falling againe vnto the nobilitie (excepting in the fiue mountaine cities) haue with a popular moderation tempered their states with better lawes and orders than the rest. For commonly the Aristocraticall state admitteth none but the Senators, the nobilitie, or richer sort, vnto the honours and offices of the state, the rest being quite excluded. Howbeit there haue bene moe Aristocraties, consisting of the more auntient and noble families, than of the richer or more vertuous. As the Commonweales of the Samians, the Corcyreans, the Rhodians, and Cnidians, and almost all the Commonweales of Greece, after the victorie of *Lysander*, were by him chaunged into Aristocraties of the most auntient

C   families, in chusing out ten or twentie, or at the most thirtie, vnto whome hee committed the soueraigntie for the gouernment of their estates. Wee see also the state of Venice, to be as we haue before shewed meere Aristocratike: And them also of Rhaguse, of Luca, of Ausbourg, of Nuremberg, to be composed in forme of Aristocraties, of the most auntient families, although they be but few in number. For as for the Rhagusians (in auntient time called Epidaurians) hauing new built the citie of Rhaguse, neere vnto the auntient citie of *Epidaurus*, vtterly rased by the furie of the Gothes, and exempting themselus from the gouernment of the Alhanois, established among themselues an Aristocratike forme of a Commonwealth, gouerned by the most noble and auntient families; following therein almost the example of the Venetians: yet still much more respectiue and carefull of their nobilitie, than are the Venetians. For a Ve-

D   netian gentleman may marrie a base woman, or a common citisens daughter: whereas the Rhagusian gentleman may not marrie a common citisen, neither a straunger, how noble soeuer, if she be not a gentlewoman of Zarafi, or Catharo, and bee farther worth at the least a thousand ducats. There are also but twentie foure houses, which haue part in the state: out of whom are drawne diuers families, out of which the great Councell of about three hundred gentlemen is drawne; prouided alwaies that they bee twentie yeares old, when they are so chosen. These make choyce of threescore gentlemen Senators, for the mannaging of the affaires of the state, and in cases of appeale, so that they be aboue the value of three hundred ducats: who haue also the hearing of criminall causes of importance, as if question be of the life, honour, or state of any gentle-

E   man. Beside this Senat there is a priuie councell of twelue persons, with a yearely prince or gouernour of the citie; and fiue masters of requests (whome they call Prouisors) men appointed to receiue the requests of the people presented vnto them in what court soeuer. There are also six Consuls to decide ciuill causes, and fiue other judges for criminall matters, and thirtie others for the deciding of such suits and controuersies as exceed not the summe of three hundred ducats. Many other meaner officers they haue also, of whome we will in due place speake. Truely this Commonweale of Rhaguse hath of all others that we haue heard, the purest Aristocratie, and farthest from all

X iiij   popu-

The estate of the Swissers Aristocraticall, yet temperated with a certaine mixture of popularitie.

The estate of the Rhagusians.

A3 all the offices   A3 *For* charge *read* charges *i.e.* commissions (cf. L).   C8 Albanois

The estate of them of Luca.

popular mixture. The citie of Luca also gouerned after the same fashion, admitteth onely the auntient families to bee partakers of the soueraigntie of their gouernment, who are but few, albeit that about the yeare 1555 there were numbred two and fiftie thousand citisens, besides women. Out of the nobilitie are created an hundred & twentie yearely Senators: out of whome are chosen the ten Councellors of the priuie Councell, with the prince whome they call the Gonfalonnier. And in these consisteth the soueraigne state of this Commonweale. Other officers there be also, as Censors, Pretors, and Receiuers, of whome we will in due place speake. Suffiseth it now for the present to haue shewed diuers Aristocraticall estates, in respect of soueraigntie, to the end by diuers examples both of the auntient and new Commonweales, we may the better vnderstand the true nature of an Aristocratie.

Whether the Germaine empire be a Monarchie, or a meere Aristocratie.

And forasmuch as diuers men beleeue, and some of them of greatest knowledge of the Germans haue by writing also published, the German empire to be a true Monarchie: we will also speake of that estate, whereof although we haue in briefe somewhat spoken before, yet here we will more at large thereof discourse, and show the same to be an Aristocraticall estate. True it is, that from the time of *Charlemaigne* vnto the raigne of *Henrie* surnamed the Falconer, it was a pure Monarchie by right of succession, continued in the royall blood of the said *Charlemaigne*. But the descent of *Charlemaigne*, taking end in this *Henrie* the Falconer, the Monarchie by the voyces of the princes being translated from this *Henrie*, hath of long time continued by the right of election: insomuch that the seuen princes Electours, hauing by little and little withdrawne the soueraigntie, haue left nothing vnto the emperour, but the bare marks therof in show; the soueraigntie it selfe in effect remaining vnto the state of the seuen electors, of three hundred German princes or thereabouts, and the ambassadours deputed for the imperial cities. Which when it first happened, I see no man to haue yet written: For that such things as by little and little and little creepe into a Commonweale, are scarcely at all perceiued, neither well felt, vntill the change bee quite made. Now wee haue before shewed that it is an Aristocratike state, wheresoeuer the lesser part of the citisens or people commaund ouer the rest together, and ouer euerie one in particular.

In whom the soueraigntie of the Germaine empire consisteth.

And so it is, that the estates of the empire, composed of three or foure hundred men (as I haue said) haue the soueraigne power priuatly ouer the emperour himselfe, and ouer all the other princes, and townes of the empire in particular: as also to giue lawes to all the subiects of the empire, to determine of peace and warre, to lay taxes and impositions vpon the people, to appoint judges both ordinarie and extraordinarie, to iudge of the goods, honour, and liues of the emperour, the princes and imperiall townes: which all are the true markes of soueraigntie. Which if it be so, as most certaine it is, who can denie but that the state of the German empire is a true Aristocratie? And that to bee true which I haue said, is most euident; sith it is so, that the power of soueraigne commaund dependeth of the acts and decrees of the estates. But the decrees are made by the seuen princes electors, accounted for one third part of the voyces: and by the other princes of the empire, in number not aboue three hundred, who haue also another third part of the voyces: and by the deputies of the free cities or imperiall townes, in number seuentie, or thereabouts, which haue the other third part of the deliberatiue voyces: by whome all the lawes and decrees of the empire, or whatsoeuer els is propounded, haue vsed to be made, established, disanulled, or confirmed. And hath nothing particular in respect of the state, different from other Aristocraties, but that the seuen princes electors haue (as we said) one third part of the voyces; the princes another, and the imperiall townes the rest: in such sort, as that if the seuen electors and the deputies, or the deputies and the princes, or the electors and the other princes, be

---

H1 and little   H3 unto the state *i.e.* unto the estates   I2 (margin) consisteth   Notes at H1, I1.

be of accord and agree in one, the decree whatsoeuer passeth. And for that the ecclesiasticall princes are the greater number, they oftentimes carrie away the matter against the lay princes: which was the cause that the same lay princes, who had before renounced the Romish religion, tooke in euill part the diet which *Charles* the fift held at Ratisbon; neither being thither sent for, would come. And like as the gentlemen of Venice, Luca, and Rhaguse, vntil they be twentie yeares old enter not into the great councell, neither haue any part in the soueraigntie: euen so likewise the children or neere kinsmen of the German princes, be they young, or be they old, haue no voyces in the diet, if they be not qualified princes of the empire: which are a certaine number of Dukes, Marquesses, Counties, Lantgraues, Burgraues, Margraues, Barons, Archbishops, Bishops, and Abbats. And albeit that the duke of Loraine be a prince of the empire, and hath a voyce with the rest of the princes, yet so it is, that his vncle the countie *Vaudemont*, of the same stocke and house with him, as other like princes of the same ranke and order, haue neither voyces nor places in the assembly of the states and princes of the empire, but are reckoned amongst the children of those princes. Howbeit yet many are of opinion, the princes and imperial cities to haue their soueraigne states apart, neither to be bound vnto any other mens commaunds or lawes, otherwise than as friends and confederats; in such sort and manner, as the Swissers haue their cities and iurisdictions among themselues, one diuided from another. But the difference is to him that looketh neerer thereinto, right great, euerie Canton being soueraigne in it self, and not subiect vnto the lawes and commaundements of others; neither otherwise bound among themseues, than in aliance offensiue or defensiue, as we haue in due place declared: whereas the German empire is vnited by the estates generall in soueraigntie, who not onely haue power to bridle the princes and cities, with fines, exile, proscription, and other seuere punishments, but also to depose and thrust out of the empire euen the emperours themselues, as they did the emperours *Adolphus* and *Veneslaus*, with many others. Beside that, the estates make ordinarie decrees and lawes, which bind all the subiects of the empire, as well in generall, as in particular. And that more is, the ten circles or circuits of the empire, hold their particular estates, and yet bring their requests, complaints, and grieuances, vnto the estates generall, to receiue their commandements and resolutions, as lawes. Moreouer the princes electours, the day after the coronation of the emperour, protest themselues to hold their states of the empire, and not of the emperour, albeit that they doe their homage betwixt the emperours hands. In briefe, all iurisdiction and soueraigntie of all appeales in ciuill causes, aboue twentie crownes by the auntient lawes, and fortie by the new, appertaine vnto the imperiall chamber, as to all the appeales of the subiects of the empire: which chamber is composed of twentie foure judges, and one prince of the empire, chosen euerie yeare, according to the order of the ten prouinces or circuits. And if so be that any controuersie arise betwixt any of the princes, or the imperiall cities themselues; whether it bee for their bounds, their liues, their honour or states, the deciding thereof belongeth vnto the judges of the imperial court: except it please the whole states of the empire to take vnto themselues the hearing and determining of the matter, in such their generall assemblies as we haue before spoken of. As in the yeare 1555, it is set downe in a decree of the empire, That if from that time forward any prouince, prince, towne, or subiect of the empire should beare armes against the German nation, hee should bee iudged by the states of the empire; who to that end were appointed to hold a diet at Wormes. And in the same diet holden at Ausburg, it was forbidden all the princes of the empire, to raise any armie, or to take vp armes in the aid of any straunge prince, and that vppon a great penaltie. And that more is, it is expresly and most straitly forbidden by the laws

* of

The princes Electors hold their states of the empire and not of the emperour.

*Lib.2.cap.23.

*of the empire, any prince, towne, or corporation, to be so hardie, as to prohibit or let the appeales of the subiects vnto the imperiall chamber, and that vpon great paine also. And in fine, the emperour himselfe, as head of the assemblie of the states, more straitly bindeth them as it were into one bodie and Commonweale, than if they were but of themselues onely: and yet in him resteth not the maiestie of the empire, but in the whole assemblie of the states. For other which hold the soueraigne power in Commonweales, doe themselues creat princes, dukes, and earles, whereas the emperour is himselfe by the other dukes and princes of the empire created. How therefore can hee being the selfe same man be both the soueraigne and subiect of the empire, lord, and vassall, maister, and yet constrained to be obedient vnto the estates? And not vnto the estates onely, but euen vnto the deputies and lieutenants of the empire? Which vnto some may seeme right straunge, and yet is indeed most true. I truely my selfe haue read the letters of a great lord, pentionarie vnto the king, directed vnto *Mommorancie* the Connestable, bearing date the twelft of May, in the yeare 1552: whereby hee aduertiseth, that *Henrie* the second (then the French king) had iust cause to complaine vnto the duke of Saxonie, and the countie Palatine, lieutenant for the empire, to haue iustice against the emperour *Charles* the fift and his brother *Ferdinand* king of the Romans, according to the golden bull, and decrees of the states: for that they contrarie vnto the lawes of the empire and customes of their auncestors, hauing intercepted the kings letters directed vnto the estates of the empire, had not suffered the same to bee vnto them deliuered, but also forbidden the archbishop of Mets, chauncelour of the empire to receiue or present the same vnto the states, as his office was. And by the assemblie of the imperiall diet holden at Heidelberg, in the yere 1553, it was decreed that none of the emperours court should mannage any the affaires of the empire; as I haue seene by letters from the French ambassadour. And as for monies extraordinarily raysed by the decree of the estates, for the affaires of the empire, they are not brought into the emperours coffers, but are laid safely vp in store in certaine cities therefore appointed: *viz.* Strausbourg, Lubec, and Ausbourg: Neither is it lawfull for the emperour to take so much as one peny out of the common treasure, without the consent of the state. Al which most plainly show them to be in an errour, and much deceiued, which call the German emperour a Monarch; or which deeme that Aristocraticall estate to bee a right Monarchie. Whereas all to the contrarie the emperour *Maximilian* the first, great grandfather to him which now raigneth (albeit that hee was ambitious enough) yet in a discourse which hee had with the states of the empire concerning such matter, told them, That hee thought it not needfull to take the imperiall crowne at the hands of the Bishop of Rome, neither to stand vpon such ceremonies, seeing that the soueraigne power, as they knew, rested in the states themselues. Neither is it lawfull for the emperour of himselfe, or at his pleasure to call together a diet of the empire, without some especiall and extraordinarie vrgent cause, neither to dissolue the same: but at the breaking vp of euerie diet, order is there taken for the diet to bee holden the yeare next following. So that it is not lawfull for the emperour to rall an assemblie of the states, which it was lawfull for the Roman magistrats to do, as also for other magistrats in euerie popular and Aristocraticall Commonweale, so that it were done by commaunding of euerie one, as in particular, but not of altogether, as in common: After the auntient manner of the Romans, whereby the Consull might by his edict call together all the Senators, one by one into the Senat, vpon paine of proceeding against them, by seising vpo their bodies or goods, by way of imprisonment, taking of pledges or rasing of their houses. And yet for all that the German princes are not bound to come vnto the diet of the empire, if they be by none commaunded, but by the emperour,

The maiestie of the empire not to rest in the emperour but in the whole assemblie of the estates of the empire.

F6 other *i.e.* others   G6 *For* lieutenant *read* lieutenants.   H1 *For* Mets *probably read* Ments *i.e.* Mainz (cf. 629v H9).   H9 the state *i.e.* the estates   K1 to call   Note at F4.

rour, as they gaue *Charles* the fift the emperour well to vnderstand, in the yeare 1554: and also *Maximilian* the second, refusing in the yeare 1566, to haue any diet then according to his request holden. And if it fortune the emperour, or king of the Romans, to come vnto the frontiers of their territories, the princes euerie one of them in their degree goe to meet them, but yet in such sort, as if it were but to meet a straunge prince.

Now if one should say that the Emperour beareth himselfe as a Iudge, and determiner of all quarrels and controuersies betwixt the Princes, or the imperiall Townes; True it is at the first motion, and when the parties are content to accept thereof, and that also but as Lieutenant for the Empire: as in like case the Duke of Saxonie, and the Countie Palantine might also iudge as the Imperiall Lieutenants: and yet for all this, appeal made vnto the Estates of the Empire suspendeth the power of the Emperour, aswell as of the imperiall Lieutenants. Yet might some say, that the Princes of the Empire by their letters, and in the assemblies of the States, vse these magnificall titles towards the Emperour, *Your sacred Maiestie*, and such like, which cannot be applied but vnto him which is himselfe a Soueraigne: such as slaues would scarce vse towards the greatest kings on earth: titles for fashion sake, foolishly or wickedly (should I say) giuen by flatterers vnto men, which are onely fitting the most mightie and immortall God. And yet do in deed no more increase the power of the Germaine Emperour, then of the King of the Romains: whom by such like prodigall pompe and words, a man might also think to haue the power of soueraigne Maiestie; so that in that Empire there should be two Soueraignes: and yet for all that one of them subiect vnto the other. For so *George Helfustein* Baron of Gondelphsingen, pronouncing the speach of *Ferdinand* king of the Romans in the generall assemblie of the States of the Empire in the yeare 1556, calleth him their Soueraigne Lord.

How the emperour determineth the quarels and controuersies betwixt the princes, or the imperial townes of the empire.

Glorious flattering titles giuen to princes neuer awhit encrease their soueraigntie.

But the greatest argument of Soueraigntie is, that the Emperour giueth the fees of the Empire being void, vnto whom he pleaseth, and inuesteth in them whom he seeth good: and that without the consent of the States. Whereunto I againe answere, that the expresse consent of the Estates is not necessarie, and yet is it not altogether done without their good liking, who neuerthelesse permit the same; when as they might aswell cut of this point, as they haue done the other marks of Soueraigntie. And howbeit that the embasadour *Marillac* was of opinion, that the Emperour had not this power: and therefore aduertised king *Henry*, how that the Emperour *Charles* the fift had at Bruxels in the yeare 1551, inuested *Philip of Spaine* in the Duchie of Millan without the consent of the States of the empire: yet can he not find so much as any one inuestiture of any Imperiall fee, in the conferring whereof the expresse consent of the Estates was had. But certein it is, that the Emperour bestoweth not these fees or inuestitures, but as in qualitie of the Lieutenant of the empire: in such sort as he receiueth the fealtie and homage of the princes, for, and in the name of the empire. As in like case *Ferdinand* the emperour without the consent of the estates of the empire, receiued *Granuellan* sent vnto him with speciall charge and deputation from *Philip* king of Spayne in the yeare 1565, to do for him the fealtie and homage due vnto the Empire, for the Duchie of Millan, and the perpetuall Lieutenancie of the principalitie of Sienna: granting vnto him as a vassall of the Empire charters of his fealtie done: and for the confirmation of his possession therein. The same is to be thought concerning the confirmations of benefices, and other royall rights, which giuen by the princes or cities of the empire, or by the Chapters and Colleges of priests themselues, are yet neuerthelesse to be confirmed by the Imperial authoritie: according to the agreement made betwixt the Bishop of Rome, and the estates of the Empire. As for letters of conduct

How the emperour bestoweth the fees of the empire.

240   The Second Booke

The maiestie of the Germaine emperour by this French author still empaired

safe conduct which he giueth vnto embassadors, heralts at armes, and other strangers, whereunto the ordinarie clause is adioyned in these words, *Forasmuch as wee for our Imperiall power may do all things*: they show right well that the Emperour was in auncient time a soueraigne Monarchie; which he now is not: For why then should the Electors and other princes of the Empire refuse to grant vnto the emperour, the diet which he requested of them in the yeare 1566? or why then should both hee and his officers be by them forbidden so much as to touch the monies by them raised for the maintenance of the warres. And to cut it short, we need not but to look into the articles of the oath made by the Emperours (by vs before declared) to know yet more euidently, that the soueraigntie of the Empire is not any wise in the emperour, albeit that he carrie the crowne, the scepter, and weare the other most precious and imperial habits, and in all solemnities and ceremonies hath the precedence before other the Christian kings, yea and that men attribute vnto him the title of *Most sacred Maiestie*, all in deed hauing the show of soueraigne and royall maiestie, but yet not the thing it selfe. And yet to say the trueth, a man knoweth not how to do him so great honour as the maiestie of the sacred empire, whereof he is the head, deserueth. But the maner

A great pollicy in Aristocratical estates to giue vnto him least power to whom they giue most honour.

of well gouerned Aristocratike states, is to graunt vnto him the least power to whom they giue the greatest honour: and sometimes also least honour vnto them that be of most power: as of all others the Venetians in the ordering and gouernment of their Commonweal best know how to vse that matter. Seeing therefore wee haue thus showed the Empire to bee but an Aristocraticall estate, we may well conclude, That there is neither prince nor imperiall citie which hath therein the soueraigntie, being nothing else but members of the empire, euery one of them gouerning their estate vnder the power, and without any thing derogating from the lawes and ordinances of the empire. Wherein many are deceiued, which make so many Commonweals as there are princes and imperiall townes; the contrarie wherof we haue before showed. But as in this realme euery citie and seigniorie haue their Iudges, Consuls, Sheriffes, and other their particular officers which gouerne their estate; so is it in the Imperiall townes and cities: but that here are moe roiall judges; whereas in the empire there is none but the Imperiall chamber onely which receiueth the Appeales from the other judges and lieutenants of the empire. And yet neuerthelesse when it chanceth the empire to be diuided into factions, and part takings; or that the princes bandie themselues one of them against an other (which hath beene too often seene) then euery towne and prince for the most part beare them selues as diuers Aristocraticall estates, and particular Monarchies; making of euery member a particular bodie of a soueraigne Commonweale.

Now as the state of the Empire it selfe is entirely Aristocratique, so also the great imperiall townes and cities hold their estates in Aristocraticall forme: as Ausburg, Nuremberg, Wormes, and others, which are almost all Aristocraties; albeit that in trueth some of them are more popular than others, as is the citie of Strasbourg. But

The estate of Nuremberg Aristocraticall.

for breuitie sake I will for example onely set downe the state of the citie of Nuremberg, the greatest, most famous, and best ordered of all the imperial cities, established in forme of an Aristocratie; wherein of an infinite number of citisens there are but xxviij. auntient families which haue power ouer all the rest of the subiects, which are within the iurisdiction of Nuremberg. Out of these xxviij. families, they euery yeare first make choice of two Censors, men without any imputation; which done, all the rest of the magistrats are euery one of them displaced: then these Censors according to their owne discretion make choice of xxvj. Senators: who out of themselues chuse xiij. persons, for the managing of the secret affaires of that Commonweal: and out of the

F4 *For* Monarchie *read* Monarche (Fr).   H8 their estate   Notes at G6, I8, K6.

OF A COMMONWEALE. 241

A the same Senat also make choice of other xiij. Sheriffes also: beside the vij. Bourgmasters, which are an other particular counsell, whose authoritie and power is much like vnto that of the Decemuiri in Venice. And these Magistrats which we haue spoke of, are they which mannage all the greatest affaires of that Commonwealth. I speak not of the fiue criminall judges: nor of the twelue appointed for the deciding of ciuill causes; neither of the Prouiditor for victuals, the two treasurers: nor of the three maisters of the wards: almost of like authoritie with the procurators of Saint *Marke* at Venice, to the imitation of whome they of Nuremberg seeme in some sort to haue bene desirous to fashion their Commonweale. And albeit that of the imperiall townes some of them be freer than other; as are those which be neither in subiection nor protection

B of other princes, namely Nuremberg, Strasbourg, Lubec, Hambourg, Breme, Wormes, and Spires. Yet so it is, that they all as subiects haue a reuerent regard vnto the maiestie of the German empire. True it is, that there are many which haue exempted themselues from the power of their princes, to maintaine themselues in libertie: and now of late to hold of the empire, as the towne of Brunswich, which hath withdrawne it selfe from the obeysance of the princes of Brunswich, Wormes and others, which haue exempted themselues from the power of their auntient lords. As in like case the Swissers and Grisons, now diuided Commonweals, but sometimes subiects of the empire. And namely, the lords of the Canton of Fribourg, in the treatie of Combourgeoisie, betwixt them and the lords of Berne, call the towne of Fribourg a member of

C the empire, albeit that they haue their state therefrom diuided vnto themselues in full souueraigntie. Some others acknowledge and confesse themselues to hold their liberties and priuileges, for the gouernment of their estate from the emperour; as they of Vri, vnderuald, and Schwits, hauing their letters patents therefore from *Lewes* of Bauaria the emperour, bearing date the yeare 1316. They also of Tietmarsh for the confidence they had reposed in the strength and situation of their countrey, (placed in the frontiers of the kingdome of Denmarke) withdrew themselues from the German empire, and established their Commonweale in forme of an Aristocratie, of eight and fortie of the better sort of them, who so long as they liue haue the souueraigntie, and when one of them is dead, still chusing another in his place. True it is, that in the yeare

D 1559, *Adolph* duke of Holst did what he could to haue subdued them, pretending that *Christiern* his great grandfather had of the emperour *Frederike* the third obtained the souueraigntie ouer them of Tietmarsh, for hauing dismembred themselues from the empire; as I haue seene by the letters of Maister *Danzai*, ambassadour for the king into Denmarke.

Wherefore it is manifest not onely the whole estate of the Germaine empire, but euen the imperiall citties, themselues also to be gouerned in manner and forme of pure Aristocraties. But heere we must haue regarde in considering of the Aristocratique estate that wee confound not the princes and chiefe magistrates of a Commonweale with kings: nor a counsell of the nobilitie with a Senate: wherein Historiographers

E often times erre and goe astray, and that specially when as in a Commonweale there are so few of the nobilitie or better sort to mannage the state, as that they are both Senatours and magistrats: which gouernment of few, the Greekes call an Oligarchie. So the Pharsalian estate was gouerned by twentie of the nobilitie: the Lacedemonians by thirtie, neither were there moe in all the cities of the Greeks after the victorie of Lysander. They of Thetmarsh were gouerned by eight and fortie; and had no other Senatours then the Seignorie it selfe: the Cnidians by threescore (whome of their integritie of life they called Amymones) but these were but annuall magistrates: whereas the other were perpetuall. And all be it that the Cnidians neuer gaue any account

Y   of

Most of the Imperiall cities of Germanie gouerned in forme of Aristocraties.

C4 Vnderuald   E4 Lacedemonians   Note at B4.

of that they had done in time of their gouernment, yet were they not therefore foueraigne lords, but foueraigne magiftrats; who their magiftracie once expired, were again to reftore vnto the nobilitie, the foueraigne gouernments by them committed to their charge. In like cafe they of Zurich chofe euerie yeare thirtie fix magiftrats, of whom twelue by courfe gouerned foure moneths: which forme of gouernment continued vnto the yeare 1330, that the common people enraged and rifing vp in mutinie caft them out, creating in their ftead a Senat of two hundred of the nobility, with a Confull chiefe amongft them: and all thofe eftates had the counfell of their nobilitie and Senat all one. Yet doe they better and much more furely, which in an Ariftocratie (how little foeuer) be it deuide the counfell of the nobilitie from the Senat: as amongft the Rhagufians, where although the number be but fmall of them that gouerne that Commonweale, being it felfe fhut vp into a fmall roome: yet of them is made a Senat of threefcore men, out of whom are felected twelue to mannage the fecret affaires of their ftate. Heretofore alfo the Commonweale of Chio eftablifhed in forme of an Ariftocratie by certaine Genua gentlemen of the houfe *Auftinian*, hauing won it from the emperours of Conftantinople; euery yeare made choice of twelue counfellors of eftate for the Senat: out of whome they chofe foure, who with one foueraigne prince or magiftrat gouerned all the affaires of ftate: the authoritie of which foure for all that, was but for fix months, the foueraign magiftrat yet ftil holding his place for two yeres: in which manner of gouernment they honorably maintained their eftate, vntill that of late yeares it was by the Grand Signior taken from the Genowayes, and fo vnited vnto the Turkifh empire.

And thus much concerning the definition of an Ariftocratie. Now as concerning the profits and dangers incident vnto an Ariftocratique eftate: & the manner of the gouernment thereof, we will in due place declare. It refteth now to anfwere vnto that which Ariftotle faith concerning an Ariftocratie, being altogether contrarie vnto that which is by vs before fet downe. There are (* faith hee) foure forts of Ariftocraties: The firft, where none but the richer fort, and that to a certaine reuenue, haue part in the gouernment of the Seignorie: The fecond, where the eftates and offices are giuen by lot vnto them which hold moft wealth: The third, where the children fucceed their fathers, in the gouernment of the Seignory: And the fourth, when they which take vpon them the ftate, vfe a lordlike power and commaund without lawe. And yet neuertheles in the fame booke, and a little after, hee maketh fiue forts of Commonweales, viz. the Regall, the Popular, the gouerment of a few, the gouernment of the nobilitie; and after thefe a fift kind, compofed of the other foure: which (as hee faith afterwards) is no where to be found. But fuch a medley of Commonweales wee haue before not onely by probable but euen by neceffarie reafons alfo, prooued to bee impofsible, and by nature altogether imcompatible: wherefore letting that paffe, let vs now alfo fhow the diuers formes of Ariftocraties by *Ariftotle* fet downe, to bee no way confiderable. Firft hee no where defineth what an Ariftocratie is: the verie caufe of his errour. For what can bee more vaine, than to fay it to be an Ariftocratie where the ritcher or the better fort haue onely part in the gouernment? For it may bee that of ten thoufand citifens, fix thoufand of them hauing two hundred crownes of yerely reuenue, haue all part in the Seignorie; and yet neuertheleffe the ftate fhall be a popular ftate, confidering that the greater part of the citifens haue the foueraignitie: for otherwife there fhall be no popular Commonweale at all. The like might be faid for the gouernment of the better fort alfo, who might chaunce to be the greater number of the citifens, which fhould haue part in the Seignorie: and yet according to the opinion of *Ariftotle*, it fhould alfo be an Ariftocraticall eftate, albeit

---

F10 soever be it) devide G5 For Austinian *read* Justinian. I5 nobilitie *i.e. gents de bien*, men of virtue, "the better sort" (cf. K2, K7, and also Aristotle, *Politics*, 1293a–b) I8 incompatible Note at K3.

*[marginalia: Four fortes of Ariftocraties by Ariftotle fet downe. * Polit.lib.4. Cap.5.]*
*[marginalia: * Lib.4.Cap.7.]*
[marginalia: Ariftot. by the author impugned.]

be it that the greater part of the people beare therein the sway. As for the gouernment of good men, if we shall measure them according to the highest degree and perfection of vertue, we shall not finde one such: but if after the common manner, and opinion of the people, so euerie man will call himselfe a good man. But to iudge of an other mans integritie and vertue, as it is an hard matter for any man to do, so hath it it also vnto wisemen alwaies seemed a thing most dangerous: Insomuch that the wise and graue *Cato* being chosen out for the purpose, durst not giue sentence whether *O. Luctacius* was a good man or not. But admit that in euerie Commonweale the good are in number fewer than the bad; & yet haue the gouernment of the common state: why for the same reason hath not *Aristotle* made one sort of Aristocraty, wherin the nobilitie hold the soueraignitie? seeing that they are euer fewer in nuber then the base & vulgar sort: why also maketh he not an other sort of Aristocratie, wherein the most antient families although but of base degree bore rule? As it chanced in Florence after that the nobilitie were driuen out. For it is right certain that there are many base families, who although they be not famous or much spoken of for any great thing by them or their aunceftours done, are yet more auncient and honest then a number of vpstart gentlemen, who happily scarce knowe their owne fathers. He might also make an other sort of Aristocratie, wherein the tallest and greatest should haue the soueraignitie as he himselfe * saith they do in Ethiopia: and so consequently also an Aristocratie of the fairest, of the strongest, of the valiantest, of the wisest, of the learnedst, and of others with such like qualities of the bodie, or of the minde: as wee see to bee incident but into the fewer sort: whereof should ensue an infinite multitude and varietie of Aristocratique Commonweales. But that seemeth also vnto mee most strange that hee should say the second sort of an Aristocraty, to be where the richer sort by lot haue the gouernment and mannaging of the state, whereas alwaies, elsewhere, hee had said lots properly to appertaine vnto the popular state. Thus the Athenian Commonweale was of all other most popular, he with *Xenophon* agreeth: and yet for all that the greatest honours, offices, and preferments were not their giuen, but vnto the richest before the time of Pericles. And in Rome which was also a popular state, before the law Canuleia the greatest honours, priesthood, and preferments, were not bestowed vpon any of the common vulgar sort of people, but vpon the most auntient gentlemen whome they called Patricii: a most certain argument that the Commweale may bee in state popular, and yet gouerned Aristocratically: and that there is a notable difference betwixt the state of a Commweale, and the gouernment of the same, as we haue before said. As for the fourth sort of Aristocraties, wherin (as *Aristotle* saith) some few which take vpon them the mannaging of the state, vse a Lordlike power and command ouer all without law, in manner of a tiranie: we haue before showed the difference betwixt a Monarchie royall, Lordlike, and tirannical: the like difference whereof is also in the Aristocraticall gouernment: wherein the Lords may gouerne their subiects as slaues, and dispose of their goods, as may the Lordly Monarke, without law and yet without tiranising also: not vnlike the good maister of the familie, who is alwaies more carful of his slaues, than of his hired Seruants: and so also loueth them better. For why it is not the law which maketh the iust and rightfull gouernment, but the true administration of iustice, and equall distribution thereof. And the fairest thing in the world that can be desired in matter of state, (in the iudgement of *Aristotle* himselfe) is to haue a wise and vertuous king, knowing how to gouerne his people without lawe: considering that the lawe oftentimes serueth many but as a snare to deceiue and snarle men in: and is also of it selfe dumb and inexorable: as the nobilitie of Rome complained at such time as the people would needes haue lawes, and be gouerned by them.

Marginalia:
- Hard to iudge who is a good man.
- * *Polit. lib. 3. cap. 5.*
- A wise and vertuous king the greatest ornament and stay of a Commonweal.

A5 so hath it also   A10–B1 nobilitie *i.e.* civil nobility (cf. Fr and L)   B2–3 antient   C8 their *i.e.* there   C10 priesthoods (Fr and L)   D2, D4 Commonweale   Note at C4.

them, after that the kings were driuen out, who gouerned without law & gaue iudgement according to the diuersitie of the facts or causes presented before them: which manner of iustice the consulls and nobilitie, who in some measure held the Commonweale in an Aristocratique state continued, vntil that the people desirous to bring it vnto a popularitie, requested to bee gouerned by the equalitie of lawes, and not to haue their liues, fame, and fortune, to depend of the iudgement of the nobilitie & choice magistrats only: which their request after that it had bin, with much a do 6 yeres debated, against the Lordlike Aristocraticall gouernment of the nobilitie: they at length at the instance of their Tribune *Terentius Arsa* caused it to passe in force of a law, that from that time forward the nobilitie, consulls, and magistrates, should themselues as well as the people, be bound to all such lawes, as the *Decemviri* to that purpose appointed by the people should set downe and make. It is not therfore the law which maketh good Princes, or magistrats in a Commonweale, be it a Monarchie or Aristocratie; but vpright reason and iustice, engrauen in the mindes and soules of iust princes and Magistrats; and that much better then in tables of stone. Neither euer were there more cruell tirants then were they, which bound their subiects with greatest multitude of edicts and lawes, which the tyrant Caligula of purpose, and to no purpose, caused to bee set downe in so small letter, as that they could hardly be of any man red, but with *Linceus* eyes, to the intent thereby to entangle the moe through ignorance transgressing the same: whose successour and vncle *Claudius* in one day made twentie edicts: and yet for all that there was neuer greater tiranie then then: neither worse or more vilanous men. But as an Aristocratie well ordered is of it selfe a maruelous faire and goodly state: so can there be none worse if it be once corrupted: when as for one tirant there shal be many: and that especially when the nobilitie shal bandie it selfe against the people: as it often times chaunceth; and as we reade it to haue in aunciert time fallen out, when as in many Aristocratique estates none was by the nobilitie admitted into their number for the gouerment of the state; but that they must first sweare, to be for euer enemies vnto the people, and all popular men: a course not so much tending to the destruction of the cominaltie and people, as of the nobilitie and mightie men themselues: and so to the vtter subuersion of all Aristocraties, as we shall in due place declare And thus concerning the Aristocraticall estate: now let vs likewise see what a popular estate is.

Neuer worse gouernment then where the greatest multitude of lawes were.

No forme of a commonweale worse then a corrupt Aristocratie

Chap. VII.

¶ Of a Popular Estate.

What a popular estate is.

A Popular estate is a forme of Commonweale, wherin all or most part of the people togeather commaundeth in soueraignetie ouer the rest altogether, and ouer euerie one in particular. The principall point of a popular estate is seene in this, that the greater part of the people hath the Soueraigne commaund and power not onely ouer euerie one in particular, but also ouer the lesser parte of all the people together. As for example in Rome, where there were but fiue and thirtie tribes or companies of the people: eighteene of these companies together, had soueraigne power ouer the other seauenteene: and authoritie to establish lawes, whereunto both they and euerie one of the Citisens in particular were subiect and bound, wherfore *Tiberius Gracchus* the factious *Tribune* of the people requested *Marcus Octauius* his companion and fellow of himself to giue

vp

OF A COMMONWEALE. 245

A vp his office, before that the eighteene tribes had giuen their voices for the deposing of him: for withstanding of *Tiberius* propounding and vrging the lawes for the diuision of lands: and for opposing himselfe against the profit of the people. Also at such time as *Lucius Rullus*, the busie Tribune by request which hee presented vnto the people, concerning the diuision of lands, desired that the commissioners which had that charge, might bee chosen by the greater part of the seauenteene tribes of the people onely: *Cicero*, then *Consull* tooke thereupon occasion amongst the other things to crosse the entertainement of his request, and publication of the law, saying: that the Tribune in so doing went about to deceiue the other eightteene Tribes, that is to say the greater part of the people of their voices, which the Consuls obiection was the lesse

B to haue bene regarded, and the more easily to haue by the Tribune bene answered, for that his request was, but if it pleased the people (that is to say: the greater part of the 35 Tribes) that the lesse part of the people (that is to say the seauenteene tribes) might appoint the commissioners; so that the maiestie of the people notwithstanding his request remained still whole and vntouched: considering that the lesser part of the people was thereunto to be deputed, but at the will and pleasure of the greater part: to the end that the greater part of the people should not still for euerie trifling matter be called together. So by the law *Domitia* it was prouided that if by the death of any of the Augures, Preests or Bishops any benefice fell voide, they should assemble but 17 tribes of the people for the nominating of him, whom they would haue chosen Bi-

C shop: so that he which was by nine of the tribes of the people nominated and allowed, was by the chapiter or Colledge of Augures or Bishopps to be admitted and receiued.

When I say the greater part of the people to haue the souueraignitie in the popular estate; that is so to be vnderstood, when the voices are to bee taken by Pole as in Venice, in Rhaguse, in Genua, in Luca, and almost al Aristocratique Commonweales: but if the voices be taken by tribes, parrishes, or companies sufficeth it, of them to haue the greater part, also albeit that there be in them far the lesser part of citisens, as it hath commonly chanced in auncient popular Commonweales. In Athens the people was diuided into ten principall tribes, whereunto in fauour of *Demetrius*, and *Antigonus* they ioyned two others, of them called *Antigonia* and *Demetria*: and againe the peo-

D ple was diuided into thirtie sixe classes or companies. But such diuisions according to the diuers encreasings of the people, and more easie and commodious giuing of voices are often time changed. So *Romulus* at first deuided all the people in Rome which then was about 3000 into three tribes or parts: and after that euerie part into ten companies, appointing ouer euerie one of them an head: how be it the voices (as *Liuy* saith) were then al giuen by poll. But by the ordinance of king *Seruius* the people was againe diuided into sixe companies, according vnto euery mans wealth and reuenue: in such sort: as that the first companie wherein the richest were enrolled, had asmuch power as all the rest: if the centuries of this first companie were al of one accord and mind in giuing of their voices, that is to say fourescore centuries, which were but

E eight thousand persons; for in that case the voices of the other fiue companies were neuer asked. But if two or three centuries of the first companie were not of the same opinion with the rest: so many centuries of the second company were drawne out as might supply that defect, and that so often in euerie companie, vntill the number of fourescore companies were filled vp. So that in taking voices they seldom came vnto the third & fourth company: but most seldom vnto the first, and vnto the sixt neuer: in which sixt companie was the refuse of the people, and poorest citisens, which according to the view then taken, were in number aboue threescore thousand: beside the bourgesses and citisens of the fiue first companies in number sixteene thousand.

Y iij   And

Great difference whether voyces betaken by Poll or by Tribes & companies, in a popular Commonweale.

The small number of the people of Rome, and how they were diuided in the time of Romulus, and how they were againe diuided in the time of King Seruius, with the manner of their giuing of voyces.

C7 *For* also albeit that *read* albeit that.   E6 *For* first *read* fifth.   E8 number above
Notes at D10.

How the people of Rome wrested vnto it selfe the soueraigntie, and how that state of an Aristocratie became a Democratie, or a meere popular state.

And had this ordinance of king *Seruius* still remained in force after kings were driuen out, it had not bene a popular state but an Aristocraticall, for that the lesser part of the people had then therein the soueraigntie. But shortly after the expulsion of the kings the common people seeing themselues oppressed by the wealth & power of the greater, reuolted thrice from the nobilitie, and held their state apart: to the intent they might euery one of them, as wel the poore as the rich, the base as the noble, haue their voices alike; neither could they be before quieted, vntill they had obtained power out of the bodie of themselues to chuse their Tribunes, the maintainers of their liberties: whereof their Tribunitial assemblies began first to be holden. But for asmuch as the nobility & richer sort dispersed among the tribes, caused the poorer & meaner sort (for the most part their followers) to giue their voices at their appointment & pleasure; there was a decree made, That from thenceforth the nobilitie should no more be present at the assemblies of the common people: which was then diuided into eighteene tribes, which by little and little in continuance of time tooke such increase, that they grew to the number of fiue and thirtie tribes: who at length by meanes of their factious Tribunes got vnto themselues the soueraigntie of the Commonweal, with power to make all the lawes, and chuse all the magistrates, except the Consuls, the Prætor, and Censors, which for that they were the greatest magistrates, they were still chosen by the greatest assemblies, that is to say of the nobilitie and people together, the whole bodie of the people beeing (as wee said before) diuided into tribes or companies. But forasmuch as the enfranchised men, and such as by desert had obtained the libertie of the cittie, mingled through all the tribes of the people of Rome, in number far exceeded the naturall and antient citisens, and so by multitude of voices, carried all things away from them: which (as we haue before said) was by *Appius* the Censor done, thereby to gratifie the vulgar people, and by that meanes to obtaine of them what so he would: *Fabius Maximus* the Censor by great wisdom ouerthrew all the grace that *Appius* had by cunning got, by thrusting all the enfranchised men, and such as were of them discended, into foure tribes by themselues: so to preserue the antient and freeborn citisens in the right of their voices. For which onely fact by him brought to passe without tumult or sedition, hee obtained the name of *Maximus*, or as we say, the Greatest. Which his order still continued, vntill that about 300 yeares after, *Seruius Sulpitius* Tribune of the people, would needes haue the enfranchised men againe enrolled into the Tribes of their maisters by whome they were before manumised or set at libertie: but before this his motion was brought to effect, he was himselfe slaine: which for all that in the time of the ciuill warres betwixt *Marius* and *Silla*, was by *Marius* (hauing ceised vpon the citie) effected: so to make the estate of the Commonweale more popular, and to weaken the authoritie of the nobilitie and richer sort. *Demosthenes* after the victorie of *Philip* king of Macedon at Chæronea attempted the like at Athens; by presenting a request vnto the people, That the enfranchised, and other the inhabitants of Athens, might be enrolled in the number of citisens: which his request was then euen openly reiected, albeit that there then were not aboue 20000 citisens: which was seuen thousand moe than was in the time of *Pericles*, when as were found but thirteene thousand citisens enroled, out of whom also 5000 strangers, who had slyly crept in for citisens, were sold for slaues: and yet the multitude of the slaues was than ten times more than the number of the citisens.

How Fabius by great wisedome ouerthrew the popular deuise of Appius, and so obtained the name of Maximus.

Marius popular.

No Commonweal so popular as that all the people gaue therein voice, it being sufficient that the greater part of the tribes still caried away the matter.

This which I haue said, may well serue to aunswere that which might bee alleaged, That there is not, neither haply euer was any so popular a Commonweale, as wherein the subiects had all voyces alike; or if they had, that they could all meet together to make lawes, create magistrats, and vse the other markes of soueraigntie: a good part of them

---

F 5 state *i.e.* estates (Fr)   G 7 *For* Praetor *Bodin writes* Praetors (L).   Notes at F 8, G 3.

them to the contrarie being ordinarily still abfent, and fo the leffe part making the law. But it fufficeth, that the greater part of the tribes carried away the matter, albeit that haply in fome one tribe a thoufand citifens were in voyces equall vnto another, wherein there were ten thoufand; confidering that the prerogatiue of euerie mans voyce was in this tribe referued vnto him. Yet hereby it came to paffe, that the more ambitious fort of men oftentimes by bribes or fauour corrupted the chiefe men, and as it were the ringleaders of the tribes, efpecially at fuch time as the leffer part of the people was prefent at the affemblies: Which to meet withall, it was therefore oftentimes prouided, that when any law of importance was made, it fhould in no wife bee againe repealed, except there were fix thoufand citifens at the leaft prefent at the affemblie, who gaue their confent to the reuoking thereof; as is oftentimes to bee feene in *Demofthenes*. And the Oftracifme (as *Plutarch* writeth) tooke no place vpon any man, except fix thoufand citifens at the leaft agreed in one therein: which yet was the leffer part of the people. The like whereof is alfo obferued in the lawes of the Venetians, being of any great weight or importance; and namely in laws concerning the execution of iuftice, wherunto this claufe is adioyned, That the great Councel fhal not in any thing derogat from the law eftablifhed, except there be at the leaft a thoufand Venetian gentlemen there prefent; and that of them, eight hundred all agree in one and the fame opinion, for the repealing of the law. Whereunto the Roman lawes, concerning corporations and colleges, feeme alfo to haue had regard; where two third parts of the Collegiats, and of them alfo the moft voyces muft agree, to giue any law or order vnto the reft. And in all the affemblies of the Venetians, which haue bene called together for the gouernment of the feignorie in our daies, there haue fcarcely at once met together fifteene hundred gentlemen: fo that when the law willeth a thoufand of them at the leaft to be prefent, the meaning of the law is, that there fhould two third parts of thofe which haue voyces in the ftate be ftill prefent, and of them eight hundred to be all of one opinion for the pafsing of any matter: which I thinke to bee therefore done, for that eight hundred of them make the greater part of fiftene hundred: a thing requifit, where voices are taken by the Poll, as in Venice, and not by tribes or companies, as they did in Rome and other popular eftates, by reafon of the infinit multitude of them which had part in the feignorie. And in Rome, vntill the law Fufia, (made 693 yeares after the building of the citie) they confounded the voices of the tribes, to the intent it might leffe be vnderftood which way euery tribe had gone, fo to auoid the difpleafure of the citifens among themfelues, about the giuing of their voices. So at Strasbourg the moft popular of the German cities, and at Mets, although it came into the power of the French, yet they giue their voices by tribes; as the three popular Commonweals alfo of the Grifons, call the tribes and companies vnto their affemblies, for the creating of their magiftrats, and making of lawes: yet fo, as that the greater tribes haue the greeter part of the fuffrages or voyces. True it is, that the cantons of Vri, Schwits, Vnderuald, Zug, Glatis, and Apenzel, which are true Democraties, and hold the more popular libertie, for that they are mountainers, make their affemblies for moft part in open places, and there euerie one of them (being fourteene yeares old) giue their voices for the chufing of the Senat, the Aman, and their other magiftrats, which they doe by lifting vp their hand, after the auntient forme of the Athenian χειροτονια, and manner of other fuch popular Commonweales, fometimes conftraining their neighbours with drie blowes to hold vp their hand, as they did of old. In like manner the tribes of the Grifons, which are of others moft popular, and moft popularly gouerned of any Commonweale that is, make their common affemblies for the choice of their Aman: (which is the foueraigne magiftrat in euerie one of their little cantons:)

C1 of the Collegiats MUST BE PRESENT, and of them (Fr and L)

where he which hath bene Aman the three yeares before, standing vpright, and excusing himselfe vnto the people, craueth of them pardon for whatsoeuer hee hath done amisse in his office before: then after that hee appointeth out three citisens, out of whome the people chose one for their Aman or chiefe magistrat for the yeare following: after whome they chose also his lieutenant, who is as it were the chauncellour, and thirteene other councellors, of whom foure are of the councell for the more secret affaires of the state, and after them the Camarlign, or Chamberlaine treasurer for the common treasurie. But in this there is a notable difference, betwixt the gouernment of the Grisons, and of the other Cantons of the Swissers: for that hee which can giue vnto his side, two or three of the principal officers, of any one canton of the Swissers, who are ruled by certaine great men bearing sway amongst them, may assure himselfe to haue gained the whole canton: whereas the people of the Grisons hold themselues in nothing subiect or pliant vnto their officers, if the good liking of the whole commons be not gained; as I haue seene by the letters of the bishop of Bayonne, ambassadour for the French king: and afterward by Maister *Bellieure* ambassadour also, and a man of good vnderstanding in matters of state, hauing the same charge, gaue the king to vnderstand, in the moneth of May 1555, how that the ambassadour of Spaine had almost caused all the companies of the Grisons to reuolt, insomuch that in assemblie of the Cade, there were moe voyces for Spaine, than for Fraunce. And after that how that they of the Comminaltie of Linguedine, hauing not receiued the money promised them by the Spaniards, laid hand vppon the Spanish pentioners amongst them, and putting them to torture, afterward condemned them in a fine of ten thousand crownes to be by them paid into the common treasure. Wherein the French ambassadour so well bare himselfe, that notwithstanding the Spanish practise, they within two moneths after, together with the rest of the cantons of the Swissers sent 27 ambassadours into Fraunce, to renue and confirme their former alliances.

The cantons of the Swissers much ruled by their great men, but the Grisons not so.

These examples of popular cities we haue set downe, that thereby the force and nature of popular states and Commonweales might the better be vnderstood: Wherefore let vs then conclude; That to be a popular State or Commonweale wherein the greater part of the people haue the soueraigntie; whether their voices be giuen by poll, by tribes, companies, parishes, or communities. And yet *Aristotle* writeth vnto the contrarie: We must not saith he, according to the common opinion iudge the estate popular, where the greater part of the people haue the soueraigntie: And afterward for example bringeth forth xiij. hundred citisens in a citie, of whom a thousand of the better & richer sort haue the soueraigntie, excluding the rest: we ought not saith he to deeme this a popular state; no more than that to be an Aristocratie, wherin the lesser part of the citisens haue the soueraigntie, being men of the poorer sort. And after that he concludeth thus: The popular estate is wherein the poorer sort of the citisens haue the soueraigntie; and an Aristocratie where the richer sort beare the rule, whether they be moe or fewer in the one or in the other much concerneth not. And by this meanes *Aristotle* to establish his owne, reiecteth the common opinion of all people: yea euen of the Philosophers and law-giuers themselues: which common receiued opinion hath alwaies beene, is, and shall be mistris in matters of state. And yet he had neither true nor probable reason to depart from the common opinion: whereas thereof ensueth a thousand intollerable and ineuitable absurdities. For so we might say that the faction of the Decemuiri or ten commissioners, appointed for the correcting and amending of the euill lawes and customes of Rome, taking vpon them the soueraigntie, was a popular estate; albeit that all histories call it an Oligarchie, although they in that barenes of the Commonwealth were not chosen for their wealth, but for their

Aristotle his opinion concerning an Aristocratical or popular Commonweale.

F7 *For* Camarlign *Bodin writes* Camarling (Fr).   F10 *For* give unto his side *read* gain unto his side (Fr).   G7 *For* 1555 (Fr 7) *read* 1565 (Fr 1–6, 8 and L).   G10 Linguedine *i.e.* the Engadine

Of A Commonweale. 249

their wisedome onely. And to the contrarie, when the people for the maintenance of their popular estate had driuen them out, a man might say that the state was then chaunged into an Aristocratie. So should we also say, if twelue thousand of the richer sort had the soueraigntie, and but fiue hundred of the poorer sort were excluded, that that state were an Aristocratie. And againe to the contrarie, if there were but fiue hundred poore gentlemen, which had the gouernment ouer the rest of the richer sort, one should call such a Commonweal a popular state. For so saith *Aristotle*, calling the Commonweales of Appollonia, Thera, and Colophon popular states, wherein a few auntient verie poore families had the soueraigntie ouer the rich. Yea he passeth on further and saith, that if the greater part of the people hauing the soueraigntie, giue the great offices and honours of their state vnto the fairest or tallest of their citisens, it shall no more be a popular, but an Aristocratique estate: which is an other foule errour in matter of state, considering that to iudge of an estate, the question is not to know who haue the magistracies or offices: but onely who they bee which haue the soueraigntie and power to place and displace the magistrats and officers, and to giue lawes vnto euery man.

To iudge of an estate we are not to consider who haue the magistracies or offices but who they be in whom the soueraigntie resteth.

And these absurdities, and others also much greater then they, ensue hereof, in that *Aristotle* hath mistaken the manner and forme of the gouernment of a Commonweale, for the soueraigne state thereof. For as we haue before said, the state may be a pure royall Monarchie, and yet the gouernment thereof popular: as namely if the prince giue honours, offices, and preferments therein to the poore, aswell as to the rich: to the base aswell as to the noble, and so indifferently to all without respect or accepting of person. As also it may be that the state be royall, and yet the gouernment aristocraticall: as if the prince giue the honours and offices to a few of the nobilitie, or to a few of the richer sort onelie, or some few of his fauorits. And to the contrarie, if the people hauing the soueraigntie, giue the most honorable offices, rewards, and preferments vnto the nobilitie onely, as they did in Rome, vntill the law Canuleia, the estate should be in deed popular, and yet the gouerment Aristocratique. So if the nobilitie, or a few of the better sort should haue the soueraigntie, and yet bestow the most honorable charges and preferments vpon the poorer and baser sort, aswell as vpon the rich, without fauour or respect of persons: the state should be Aristocratique, and yet popularly gouerned. But if all or the greatest part of the people hauing the soueraigntie, shall giue the honorable offices and preferments indifferently to all, without respect of person, or by lot bestow the same vpon all the citisens: a man might wel iudge that estate not onely popular, but also to be most popularly gouerned. As was done at Athens at the request and motion of *Aristides* the iust, whereby all the citisens were receiued into all the offices of the Commonweale, without respect of their wealth, contrarie to the law of *Solon*, whereby it was prouided, that in bestowing of honours and places of authoritie and commaund, regard also bee had vnto mens abilitie and wealth. So likewise if the nobilitie onely, or some few of the richer sort should haue the soueraigntie in the state, and so exclude all the rest of the people from the honorable places and preferments in the Commonweal, so to keepe them to themselues alone: one might say that estate not to be aristocratike only, but also aristocratically gouerned; as wee may see in the state of Venice. But here happily some man will say, that none but my selfe is of this opinion, and that not one of the auntient, and much lesse of the moderne writers which intreat of matters of state or Commonweales, haue once touched this point. True it is that I cannot denie the same; yet this distinction neuerthelesse seemeth vnto me more then necessarie, for the good vnderstanding of the state of euery common weal; if a man will not cast himselfe headlong into an infinite

That the state of a commonweale may be of one sort, and yet the gouernment therof of another and that quite contrarie.

A3 *For* twelue thousand *read* twentie thousand (Fr and L).   D9 abilitie *i.e.* wealth, means (cf. L)
Notes at C8, C10.

nite labyrinth of errours, where into we see *Aristotle* himselfe to haue fallen: mistaking the popular Commonweal for the Aristocratique: and so contrarie wise, contrarie to the common receiued opinion, yea and contrarie to common sence also: For these principles euill grounded, nothing that is firme and sure can possiblie be thereon built. From this errour likewise is sprung the opinion of them which haue forged a forme of a Commonweale mingled of all three, which we haue for good reasons before reiected.

That the state of a Commonweal may be of one sort and the gouernment of an other, without confusion of the states.

Wherefore let vs firmely set downe and resolue that there are but three formes of Commonweales, and no moe, and those simple also, and without any confused mixture one of them with an other; albeit that the gouernment be sometimes contrarie to the state: As a Monarchie is contrarie to a Democratie or popular estate; and yet neuerthelesse the soueraigntie may be in one onely prince, who may popularly gouerne his estate, as I haue before said: and yet it shall not be for that a confusion of the popular estate with a Monarchie, which are states of themselues incompatible, but is well (as it were) a combyning of a Monarchie with a popular gouernment, the most assured Monarchie that is. The like we may deeme of the Aristocratique estate, and of the popular gouernment: which is by farre more firme and sure, then if the estate and gouernment were both Aristocratique: the state standing almost inuiolable, when as the subiects by such a moderat kind of gouerment are amongst themselues combyned, as also vnto the Commonweale. And albeit that the gouernment of a Commonweale may be more or lesse popular, aristocratique, or royall, (as of tyrannies, some may be more cruell than others,) yet so it is that the state in it selfe receiueth no comparison of more or lesse.

Soueraigntie allwaies by nature of itselfe indiuisible.

For the soueraigntie is alwaies indiuisible and incommunicable in one alone, or in the lesse part of all the people, or in the greater part thereof; which are the three sorts of Commonweales by vs set downe. And as for that which we haue said, that the gouernment may be more or lesse popular, may be deemed so to be, by the Commonweales of the Swissers, where the mountaine Cantons of Vri, Schwits, Vnderuald, Zug, Glaris, and Apensel are so popular, as that the soueraigntie of the Commonweal resteth onely in them all, so that they be fourteene yeares old, in somuch that their chiefe magistracies & places of greatest commaund are sometime giuen euen to verie Sadlers, and such other mechanicall men: neither of the aforesaid Cantons is any one of them walled except Zug. The other new Cantons and Geneua, are lesse popular, gouerning themselues by certein lords, which they call the Councell, as I haue learned by Master Basse-fountaine Bishop of Limoges, who long and discreetly without blame, as any one embassadour, hath to his great honour mannaged this charge. And albeit that the Bernoies and they of Zurich compose their Senat of diuers handy crafts men, yet they vse commonly to creat their Auoyers (or chiefe magistrats) of their most noble and auntient families: whereby they are lesse subiect vnto seditions and tumults: whereas the lords of the three Cantons of the Grisons being more popular, are also more subiect vnto seditions and sturres, the people in their assemblies being hard to be gouerned; and once moued, hard to be pleased; as the ambassadours of princes haue alwaies by experience found.

The popularitie of the mountain Cantons.

The true nature of the people.

For the true nature of the people is, to desire libertie without restraint of bit or bridle whatsoeuer: and to haue all men equall in wealth, in honour, in paines, and rewards; without regard of nobilitie, wisedome, or vertue: and as *Plutarch* saith wisely to haue all cast into lot, and euen ballance, without respect or fauour of any man, then if any valiant or honourable minded of the nobilitie or richer sort shall by any meanes attempt to restraine the people so intemperatly abusing their libertie; them straight waies they do what they can to kill or to banish, and confiscating their goods, diuided the same among the poorer sort, and that

---

I2 For new *read* nine (Fr only).   I3 themselues   K6 any man; then   Note at K2.

OF A COMMONWEALE.

A that the rather, if they be rich, or seeme to aspire: Yea oft times it happeneth, that the common people puft vp with the punishment or slaughter of some one mightie man, violently breaketh out vpon the rest, and that especially if it be once come to armes, and that the nobilitie be by the force of the people ouerthrowne. As it happened at the establishing of the popular estate of the Swissars, after the battell of Sempach, where almost all the nobilitie was slaine, and the rest which were left constrained to renounce their nobilitie; and yet neuerthelesse were excluded from all honours and offices of charge in the Commonweale, except at Zurich and Berne (which is in them the lesse to be maruelled at, for that the nobilitie there, with great safetie and without force of armes, made their peace with the victorious common people, now before quite spent with ciuill warres.)

The beginning of the popular estate of the Swissars.

B Yet for all this insolencie, did the Swissers more moderatly vse their popular libertie, than did in antient time the Grecians or Italians, who oftentimes would needs haue all bonds and obligations burnt or canceled: yea sometime the common people set on by such as were farre endebted, ranne vppon the creditours and rich men, robbed their houses, and enforced them to make an equall diuision of their possessions and lands, forbidding them the hauing or possessing of cattell or lands, aboue a certaine number or rate by them set downe: from which kind of dealing the Swissers haue alwaies abhorred. And albeit that the publike pensions of princes, and gifts of straungers, in some of the Swissers cities, are not laid vp in the common treasure, but diuided among the people in particular; in the diuision whereof hee that hath

The auntient Gretians and Italians in their popular libertie more insolent than were the Swissars.

C most male children hath also a greater part than the rest: yet for all that, when as they of the canton of Glaris requested of *Morlet*, the French kings ambassadour, in the yere 1550, That the priuat and extraordinarie pensions, which the greater men yearely receiued of the king, might together with the publike pension bee equally diuided amongst them all: King *Henrie* denied so to doe, and said, He would rather restraine his bountie, than suffer his priuat liberalitie to be so at their pleasure confounded with the common. Yea that worse is, the insolent libertie of the auntient Greeke popular Commonweales, proceeded to that libertie (should I say) or rather lewd madnesse, as to banish them that were more wise and discreet than the rest for the mannaging of their affaires, as they did *Damon*, maister to *Pericles*: and not onely wise and discreet,

D but euen the most iust and vertuous also; as was *Aristides* in Athens, & *Hermodorus* at Ephesus: which what thing is it else, than to go about to pluck vp vertue it selfe by the root? But they were afraid least so great brightnesse of vertue in one great citisen or subiect, should so dazle the eyes and minds of the rest of the common people, that forgetting their libertie, they should chuse rather to liue in subiection vnto so wise and vertuous a man, than to rule theselues. Which thing they the more feared, if vnto his vertues and good parts were ioyned nobilitie, or power, or experience in great matters; who with force ioyned thereunto, might from the citisens either with their will, or against their will, extort their libertie. Whereas the nobilitie and better sort, to the contrarie make no account or reckoning of the popular state: but thinke it good rea-

Why in popular commonweales they oftentimes bannished the most wise and vertuous men.

E son, that he which hath the most nobilitie, wealth, vertue, or knowledge, should be also the more esteemed, respected and honoured; and that the honourable charges in the Commonweale, should of right be due vnto such men: and therefore alwaies desire and seeke to haue themselues alwaies diuided and seperated from the dregges and rascal sort of the common people. Sith therefore the princes and nobilitie so much differ from the common and base people, it is a thing impossible by any meanes to make them together equall: or being made in honors and commaund, euen to reconcile the among themselues, together with the Commonweale: and so (as they say) with one and the same brewing to moderat two so contrarie humors. Albeit that *Solon* vaunted, that

The inequalitie of the nobilitie and of the vulgar or common people, not possible to be brought to any good conformity in one and the same state.

E7 and commaund even [*i.e.* equal], to reconcile (cf. L)   Note at E8.

that if he had power to make lawes, he would make them such as should be most indifferent, both for the rich and the poore, the nobilitie and the base: which the nobilitie thought *Solon* to meane of the equalitie in Geometricall proportion; and the people of the proportion Arithmeticall: whereby it came to passe, that both the states yeelding vnto him, gaue him power for the making of them lawes, and establishing of their Commonweale. But these things, as also what commodities or inconueniences attempted vpon euerie Commonweale, shall in their due places bee more at large declared: sufficeth it now with what breuitie well might be, to haue set downe the descriptions and kinds of all Commonweales, as also what is to euerie one of them proper, straunge, or common with others: and also who in euerie Commonweale hath the power of Soueraigne maiestie. Now let vs prosecute euerie part and limme, as it were, of a Commonweale, which are tied vnto the soueraigntie of the state, as members vnto the head; *viz* the Senat, the magistrats, the officers, colleges, and corporation, and that in such order as wee haue here rehearsed them.

Finis Lib. Secundi.

THE

F5 of their lawes   F7 *For* attempted upon *probably read* attend upon (cf. L).   Note at G4.

THE THIRD BOOKE OF OR CONCERNING A COMMONWEALE.

Chap. I.

¶ *Of a Senat, or Councell of Estate, and the power thereof.*

Senat is a lawfull assemblie of Councellors of Estate, to giue aduise to them which haue the soueraigntie in euerie Commonweale. For so order requireth, that hauing before spoken of them which haue the power of soueraigne maiestie, and of the markes thereof, and also touched the diuersitie of Commonweales: We should now also speake of the Senat, as of the chiefe and principal part of a Commonweal, next vnto the prince. Not for that a Commonweale cannot altogether be without a Senat or Councell: for a prince may be so wise and discreet, as that he cannot find better councell than his owne: or els hauing not whome to trust, taketh aduice neither of his owne people nor of strangers; but of himselfe alone, as we read of *Antigonus* king of Asia, and of *Lewes* the eleuenth the French king; whome the emperour *Charles* the fift doubted not in that to imitat: as also of *Caius Iulius Cæsar* among the Romans; who neuer spoke any thing vnto others, of the enterprises he had in hand: nor of his iourneies, no not so much as of the day of battell; and yet performed great matters, albeit that he were beset with many great and right puissant enemies: and was therefore the more redoubted, for that his designes were so close and couert, as that they were still executed before they enemy could perceiue them: who still was by that meane ouertaken, and ere hee were aware surprised. Besides that, the captaines and souldiors reposing themselues in the wisedome of such a prince or generall, were alwaies in expectation, prest, and readie euen in a moment, to performe whatsoeuer he should command, but with the holding vp of his hand. No otherwise than the members of a bodie well composed are alwaies readie to receiue & put into execution whatsoeuer reason shal commaund them, although they be no whit partakers of the concell thereof.

The definition of a Senat.

That a wise prince needeth not allwaies to be aduised by his counsell. The wonderfull secresie of Iulius Cæsar in all his affaires.

Now many haue (and that in mine opinion) without cause doubted, Whether it were better for the Commonweale to haue a most wise and vertuous prince to gouern the same without councell; or a dull and vnfit man of himselfe for gouernment, but well prouided of a graue and wise councell? And truely vnto the wise neither the one nor the other seemeth any thing worth. But if the prince be so wise as they suppose, as

Z that

Secrecie in a prince most needfull.

that he greatly needeth not of councell: yet the greatest point for his aduantage in matters of any consequence is, to keep his designes and resolutions secret, which once laid open and so made knowne, serue no more but as mines discouered; causing oft-times the ruine and decay of most famous cities and states. And therefore the wisest princes haue still vsed to speake and talke most of such things as they meant least. And as for an heauie headed and foolish prince, how should he be well prouided of a graue and wise councell, sith that the choice thereof dependeth of his owne will? and that in a prince there is no greater signe of wisdome, than to know well how to make choice of wise men, whose councell he may vse and follow.

Whether it be lesse daungerous vnto a Commonweale to haue a good prince assisted with euil counsel, or an euill prince directed by good counsell.

But forasmuch as the brightnesse and beautie of wisedome is so rare amongst men, and that we must with all obedience reuerence such princes as it shall please God to send vs; the fairest wish that they can make is, That they may haue a graue and wise councell. For it is not by much so dangerous to haue an euill prince and a good councell, as it is to haue a good prince misleled by euill councellours; as said the emperor *Alexander*. Wherefore we say, that a prince ought to follow the good aduise and councell of his graue and wise councellors, not onely in his more great and weightie affaires, but euen in his meane and least matters also (albeit that in truth nothing can be meane or little, which concerneth the Commonweale) For there is nothing that giueth greater credit and authoritie vnto the lawes and commandements of a prince, a people, or state, or in any manner of Commonweale, than to cause them to passe by the aduise of a graue and wise Senat or Councell: and the rather, if it be doubtfull whether it be profitable or no, which the prince or state would haue done. And that of all others, *Charles* the fift the French king, was woont best to doe: For hauing a purpose to driue out of his kingdome the Englishmen, who in fealtie held all the castles and townes in Aquitaine; and now prouided of all things, which he thought needfull for the doing thereof, he receiued the complaints of the Frenchmen of Aquitaine (the king of England his subiects) against the English gouernours, directly contrarie vnto the treatie of Bretignie: who for such appeales and complaints vnto the king, had vsed them euill. Vpon which occasion, whether of purpose sought for, or by chaunce offered, the king tooke hold: but yet would not vndertake the warre, without the councel and good liking of the nobilitie and people, whose helpe he was to vse therin. Wherfore he commanded them all to be assembled vnto the parliament of Paris, pretending that he had sent for them to haue their aduise, and by their wisedome to amend what had by himselfe not altogether so wisely bene done or considered of. Which warre by that councell decreed, prospered in his hand, and tooke good successe. But when the subiects see things done either without councell, or contrarie to the will and decrees of the Senat or councell, then they contemne them and set them at naught; or els fearfully and negligently do the commaunds of their princes and magistrats: of which contempt of lawes and magistrats, ensue the seditious and slaunderous speeches of the people; and so at length most daungerous rebellion, or els open conspiracie against the prince, drawing after it the vtter subuersion of all estates. And so *Hiero* king of Sicilie was together with all his kindred and friends most cruelly slaine, for that hee so proudly and insolently contemned the Senat, nor in any thing asked the aduise therof, by the aduise whereof (his grandfather hauing inuaded the soueraigntie) had before gouerned the state fiftie yeares and more. The same errour committed *Cæsar*, not onely in the time that he was Consull, but in his dictatorship also, neuer vsing the aduise or councell of the Senat: The principall occasion that was taken for the killing of him, being for that he vouchsafed not to rise vnto the whole bodie of the Senat (consisting of about a thousand Senators) comming at once vnto him; too arrogantly and indeed

The great benefit that a prince hath by following the good aduise of his wise counsel, and the daungers to him ensuing by the reiecting therof:

K2 *For* Hiero *read* Hieronymus.   K5 whereof his grandfather (having

indeede too foolishly done; not that *Cæsar* was by nature or disposition so prowd, but for that when he would haue risen vp vnto the Senate, he was by *Cornelius Balbus* (his flattering claw-backe, and a man of all other most inward with him) persuaded not so to doe. For which selfesame cause, also the Romans had long before slaine their first king and founder of their cittie, and driuen out their last king the prowd *Tarquin*: for that both of them contemning the Senate, did all things on their owne heads; and the latter of them seeking also quite to suppresse the Senate, by putting of the Senatours to death: which thing was not dangerous onely vnto those princes which wee haue now spoken of, but also vnto *Lewes* the eleuenth the French king, who in nothing asked the aduice of his Counsell, but had thereby (as hee afterward confessed) brought himselfe within an inch of his vtter ruine: for which cause, hee would not that his sonne *Charles* the eight, should vnderstand any more but three words of Latine (and those, such as are razed out of the historie of *Philip Comines*,) to the end that mistrusting of his owne wisedome, he should rest himselfe vpon the graue counsell of others, and so by their aduice to mannage his affaires rather than by his owne. For it is right certaine, that great learning in princes is often times a thing no lesse dangerous than a knife in a mad mans hand, except he be by nature well giuen, and more vertuously instructed and brought vp. Neither is there any thing more to be feared, than great learning accompanied with iniustice, and armed with power. There was neuer yet prince lesse learned (except in deedes of armes) than *Traian*, neither any of greater knowledge than *Nero*, and yet for all that, this man had neuer his peere for crueltie, nor the other for bountie: the one of them deadly hating the Senat, and the other in all things following the aduice thereof. Seeing therefore that a Senat is a thing so profitable in a Monarchy, and so necessarie in all Popular and Aristocraticall estates, as is in man wit and reason, without which his body cannot long gouerne it selfe, or haue at all any being: let vs first speake of the qualities requisite in Senatours or Counsellors; then what number they ought to be, and whether there ought in a Commonweale to bee moe Counsells than one, and of what things they are to counsell of: and last of all, what power is to be giuen vnto the Senat or Counsell in a Commonweale.

margin: Great learning in a prince sometime daungerous.

First we said the Senat to be a lawfull assemblie: which is to be vnderstood of the power which is giuen them by the prince, or soueraigntie in other states, to assemble themselues in time and place to them appointed. As for the time and place when and where they are to meet, it is not much materiall, sith that the diuers occasions and opportunities of occurrents doe oft times of themselues require, and as it were point out the same. Yet is the decree of *Lycurgus* in the mean time to be commended, forbidding any pourtraitures or pictures to be in the place where the Senat shuld consult, for that the obiect of such things as wee behold, often times distract the phantasie, and transport reason else where, which ought wholy to be intentiue vnto that which then is to be consulted of. We said moreouer in the definition of a Senat, That they should be Counsellors for the estate: to put a difference betwixt them and other counsellours and magistrats of the Commonweale, who are oftentimes called to giue their aduise vnto the counsellours of estate, yea and vnto the prince himselfe, euery one according to his qualitie and vocation; and yet are not for all that counsellours for the estate, but onely vpon occasion men extraordinarilie called. And as for the name and title of Senatour, it signifieth a man well strucken in yeares: as also the Greeks call the Senat γερουσίαν, which showeth well that the Greeks and Latins composed their Senats of seniors or aged men, whom our countrie men call Seigneurs, for the authoritie, reuerence, and dignitie, which hath alwaies beene giuen vnto the auntients, as vnto the wiser sort, and men of greatest experience: vpon that hope and opinion that they

margin: Senators from whom they haue their lawfull power.

margin: Whereof a Senator tooke name; and that a Senate ought to consist of men wel strucken in yeares.

which

Note at C3.

256   THE THIRD BOOKE

which were elder than the rest, should also in wisedome exceed the rest. For so it is prouided for, in the lawes of *Charles* the great; *Nulli per sacramentum fidelitas permittatur, nisi nobis & vnicuiq́; proprio seniori*: Let credit be giuen to no man vpon his oath, but vnto vs and euery proper elder: whereby he meant the manumised mens patrons, rather than the Senators; as if honour and reuerence were due rather vnto the elder, than the yonger. Also by the custome of the Athenians, when the people were assembled to giue their aduice, the huisher with a loud voice called all them that were fiftie yeares old together, to consult of that which should be good and profitable for the Commonweale. And not only the Greeks and Latins haue giuen this prerogatiue vnto the aged, to giue counsell vnto the Commonweale, but also the Ægiptians, Persians, and Hæbrewes, who taught other people well and wisely to gouerne their estates. And what more diuine order would we haue than that of God? who when he would establish a counsell vnto the Israelits his people,* *Assemble vnto me* (saith he) *seauentie of the most auntient of the people, wise men, and fearing God*. For albeit that a man might find a number of discreet, wise, and vertuous yong men, experimented also in the affaires of the Commonweale (a thing for all that right difficult,) yet so it is that it should yet be a thing right perilous to compose of them a Senat (which were rather to be called an assemblie of yong men) for that their counsell should not be receiued, either of the yong or of the old: for that they of like age would esteeme themselues as wise as they, and the other themselues much wiser than such yong counsellours. And in matters of state (if in any thing in the world) opinion hath no lesse, yea and oftentimes more force than the trueth it selfe. The common people thinketh, and that right well, yong men neuer, or else right seldome to excell in wisedome: but they which are such, can neither gouerne the people, nor chastice the offendours, or in the open assemblies of the people persuade them vnto that which is good and profitable. Neither is there any thing in a Commonweale more dangerous, than the subiects to haue an euill opinion of the Counsell or magistrats which commaund ouer them: for then how shall they obey them? and if they obey them not, what issue is thereof to be expected. And therefore *Solon* forbad any yong man to be admitted into the Senat seemed he neuer so wise; which the Græcians in their owne language haue better set downe than the Latins: εἰ καὶ ἄρισα δοκοίε γνώμες ἔχειν. And *Licurgus* before him, had composed his Senat of the elder sort. And not without cause haue the lawes giuen the prerogatiue of honour, priuileges, and dignities vnto the Elders; for the presumption we ought to haue that they are wiser, of better vnderstanding, of more experience, and fitter to giue counsell than the yonger sort. Yet for all that, is not that graunted to all old men: no not to them which hauing before excelled in vertue and wisedome, are now growne so old and decrepit, as that their naturall forces faile them, and their braines weakned, can no longer do their dutie, but are now as men destitute of wit and iudgement, vnable longer to vse the instruments by nature giuen them to reason with, so that in them their verie mind seemeth to be with age both weak and sicke; whom *Plato* himselfe, who appointed the Elders to be keepers of his Commonweal, hath excused from any longer bearing of charges in the Commonweal, or for any more giuing of counsell. It is also said in the holie Scripture, That God hauing chosen seauentie Elders, powred vpon them aboundance of wisedome: for which cause the Hebrewes call their Senators, the Sages, or wise men. And *Cicero* elegantly (as he doth all things) calleth the Senat the soule, the reason, and vnderstanding, of a Commonweale; meaning thereby to conclude, that a Commonweale can no more maintaine it selfe without a Senat, than the bodie can it selfe without a soule, or a man himselfe without reason: and that Senators should by long experience and practise be able

Marginalia:
*Deut. Cap. 1.
Youngmen by Solon forbidden to be admitted into the Senat, seemed they neuer so wise.
The Senat the soule of the commonweale.*

F2–3 permittatur (L) promittatur (Fr 5–8) omitted (Fr 1–4)   F7 huisher *i.e.* usher, sergeant
I1 δοκοίε: δοκοίη (Fr 1–4, L 3–5) δοκοία (Fr 5–7) δοκοίοι (L 1–2) δοκοίει (Fr 8)   I1 γνώμης
Notes at F3, G4

able and readie, to heare, consider, and resolue of the greatest affaires of the Common weale. For whatsoeuer things are notably done in warre, or peace, in making of lawes, in appointing the orders and degrees of the subiects, in reforming the manners and conditions of the people; and in briefe in the whole disposing of the Common weal, are all nothing else but the execution of such things as are by a wise counsell deuised and resolued vpon: which the Greeks for that cause called τὸ ἱερόν τὴν βουλὴν, as if nothing could be more sacred than good counsell, and the Hebrewes יסוד, as who should say, the most sure foundation of all things whereupon all faire and commendable actions are built, and without which all things fall, and are turned vpside downe. When I say a wise counsell, my meaning is that politique wisdome should bee euer ioyned with faith and iustice: for it is no lesse, and I know not whether more dangerous, to haue a Senat or Counsell consisting of euill and wicked men, how wise and expert soeuer they be; than of the ignorant and foolish: for that these as they cannot much profit, so can they not much hurt the Commonweal; whereas the other by their mischieuous counsell to reuenge themselues, make no question or doubt to endanger or ouerthrow the whole state of the Commonweal, so that they onely may stand safe in the middest of the ruines thereof, yea and many times contrarie to their own conscience, stick not most earnestly to crosse their aduersaries opinions, although most profitable to the Commonweal, turning their priuat hatred vnto the common destruction? albeit that they reap no other profit thereby, then the triumph which they account themselues to haue gotten of the shame of them, whom they haue in counsell vanquished, drawing them of their owne faction as it were in a string after them.

Politique wisdome euer to be ioyned with faith and iustice.

An other sort of Senators there are also which are led neither with enuie, hatred, nor loue of any man, but with an obstinate conceit and loue of their owne opinions, from which they will not by any reason or perswasion suffer themselues to be remoued, and therefore come into the Senat armed with such a force and multitude of arguments, as if they were euen there to combat with their enemies; least that they should seeme to haue erred in their discourses, or lightly to haue changed their opinions. And that worse is, such strong conceited men, account it a great shame to them, to agree with any other man in opinion; but thinke themselues to haue most brauely acquited themselues, if as when men driue but one naile with another, they also shall obtrude one opinion to another: than which I cannot tell whether any thing can bee worse, being a thing no lesse to be shunned, than a rocke in the deepe sea. But as a wise maister in a wrought sea, if he cannot by reason of the tempest in safetie put his ship into the desired port, yeeldeth then vnto the wind, and taketh in all his sailes, lest otherwise carried away by force of tempest he suffer shipwracke: and so trieth it out, vntill the sea be againe calmed, and more fauourable winds arise: Euen so the irremouable resolution of a Councellor, in consultations of matters of state, was neuer of wise men commended; but alwaies deemed as a thing ioyned not onely with a certaine obstinacie, but also arrogancie of mind: Whereas to the contrarie, sometimes to change a mans opinion, is not onely commendable, but also wholsome and profitable vnto the Commonweale: and according to the new occurrents of time, to apply also the deuises of new councels: sometime with the agreeing voices, approuing the opinion euen of the more ignorant and simple sort. And therefore Sir *Thomas Moore* in the Vtopian Commonweale by him deuised, wisely set downe, That nothing should bee disputed or reasoned vpon, the same day it was propounded, but to be still reserued vnto the next assembly of the Senat; to the end, that he which had rashly and vnaduisedly deliuered his opinion, should not afterward enforce himselfe to maintaine the same, rather

A Senatour to be too much conceited of his owne opinion, a thing vnto the Commonweale dangerous.

Z iij

ther

A7 the Hebrewes יסוד (faulty in L 1-2)   B10 destruction; albeit   E4 with the agreeing voices
i.e. by voting in agreement   Note at E5.

ther than to yeeld to reason.

The dutie of a wise Senator.

Wherefore it beseemeth a wise Senator, euen in the entrance of the Senat, to lay downe all fauour towards his friends, all hatred towards his enemies, and all high conceite of himselfe; ayming at no other end, but to the aduancement of the glorie of God, and the welfare of the Commonweale. Wherein the manner of the Lacedemonians was to be commended, who were so readie to defend whatsoeuer was once decreed for the good of the Commonweale, as that they which had before impugned the same, would now so conforme themselues for the establishing thereof, as that they would themselues refell what they had before to the contrarie commended: and all because it was not lawfull for them to dispute of the lawes once established by the Senat: which manner of custome the Achæans and Florentine Commonweales, afterwards borrowed from the Lacedemonians. And albeit that learning be alwaies necessarie for a Senat or Councellor, especially the knowledge of antiquitie, and of the estates of Commonweals: as also to be seene in the lawes of his owne country, which he ought not to be altogether ignorant of, yet is a sound iudgement ioyned with faith iustice, and integritie more necessarie: by meanes whereof he may easily persuade any thing without much eloquence. But aboue all things a Senator must beware that hee suffer not himselfe to be corrupted with the bountie of forren princes: neither bee beholden to any forren lord or prince, for any thing that he holdeth of him, whether it be by fealtie and homage, by mutuall obligation, or by pention, which hee receiueth: which although it be a thing most daungerous in a Commonweale, and ought therefore to be capitall: yet for all that there is nothing than that more common in the Councell of princes. Except in the citie of Venice, which hath a Senat so free from this kind of base corruption, as that euen for that cause their priests (bee they neuer so free or nobly borne) out from comming into the Councell of state; for that they are thought to be sworne to doe nothing against the commoditie or profit of the bishop of Rome. Whereupon it is, that commonly the citisens before the giuing of their voyces, crie out alowd *Fora i Preti. And namely they banished *Hermolaus Barbarus* their ambasadour vnto the pope; as they did not long ago cardinall *Mule*, their ambasadour vnto him also, for that they had of him receiued the cardinals hat, without leaue from the Seigneurie. But I find, that in this realme there haue bene thirtie fiue chauncellors, which haue bene cardinals or bishop at least: and so in England the like. And in Polonia, where the archbishop of Gnesne is by inheritance alwaies chancellour of the realme: the kings of that country haue bene glad to make a lay man their vicechauncellor, by no oath bound vnto the bishop of Rome. As for pentions giuen by straungers vnto the minions or ambassadors of other princes, it is a thing so ordinarie, as that it is growne into a verie custome. Yea Mounsier *Cotignac* the French ambassadour into Turkie, was so bold as to presume to marrie a Greeke gentlewoman, without making of the king at all acquainted therewith. And not long after, another also at the instigation of *Mhemet Bassa*, and the duke of Naxo, would likewise haue married the prince of Valachia his sister: which poore prince for refusing to giue his consent thereunto, which he for feare had before graunted, was by the Bassa thrust out of his estate, and *Stephen Bathor* (who now gouerneth the kingdome of Polonia) placed in his stead. All which, with other such like enterprises, are dangerous in an estate, and therefore in a well ordered Commonweale, in no wise to be suffered. And these vnto me seeme to be the chiefe qualities and ornaments of a good Councellour of Estate.

Learning necessarie for a Senator, but vpright integritie more.

That a Councellor of estate ought not to be pensionar to another prince.

* Out of doores with the priests.

But beside these, in many Commonweales nobilitie of birth is alwaies in a Senator required; as at Venice, Rhaguse, and Nuremberg: and amongst the Polonians it was

by

G3 Senator or (cf. note at 135 C2)   H5 borne) ARE SHUT out (cf. Fr and L)   I4 glad to make *i.e.* constrained to make
I10 Mehemet   Note at K3

OF A COMMONWEALE. 259

by *Sigismundus Augustus*, in the yeare 1550 by law prouided, That no man should be chosen a Senator, except he were nobly descended, by the fathers side at least, & had also borne armes. In other places choyce was made of them by their wealth, as at Genes, and in auntient time in Athens by the lawes of *Solon*: and so almost in all other auntient Commonweales. And namely *Augustus* the emperour, would not that a Roman Senator of his time should be lesse worth than thirtie thousand crownes, supplying of his owne bountie what the wis Senators being poorer wanted: not that it was so necessarie vnto their Councell, but that so they might haue wherewith to maintaine their estate, aunswerable vnto their calling: as also least the rest proud of their wealth, should contemne the other which were poorer, as commonly it falleth out in the Aristocratique estate, where the Senator is chosen by his wealth. And by the auntient order of the Romans also, no man could be made a Senator, except he had before borne some honourable place or charge in the Commonweale. And therefore the Censors from fiue yeares to fiue yeares, registred in the roll of the Senat, all them which had borne any great or honourable office or place in the Commonweale; *viz.* such as had bene Consuls, Prætors, Ædiles, or at least Quæstors. And for that in the ouerthrow of *Marius* 90 Senators were slaine; *Sylla* created Dictator, to supply the order of the Senators, which he fauoured, created twentie Quæstors, and *Cæsar* fortie, who at the same time should be made Senators, with power also to giue voyces, which before was not lawfull, vntill they had by the Censors bene nominated and registred. Which indeed is a laudable custome, and in many well ordered Commonweals at this present obserued. As in Polonia none is receiued to be a Senator, which is not a Palatine, a Bishop, a Castellan, or Captaine; or else before hath beene imployed in some honourable ambassage, or bene generall of an armie. Neither hath any man place in the Great Turkes Diuano or Councell, but the foure Visier Bassaes, the two Cadilisquiers or Chauncellors, and the twelue Beglerbegs, gouernours of great prouinces.

But whereas we haue before said, that Senators are to be chosen out of such as haue before borne some honourable place or office in the Commonweale: that concerneth not them which shamefully buy their offices, neither the Commonweale wherein honours and offices are bought for money: for those vertues which we said to bee required in a Senator; namely iustice, faith, integritie, wisedome, experience, and knowledge in the lawes both of God and man, are things so sacred and diuine, as that they cannot for any reward or money be bought. Now that a Senator should by the Senat be examined or tried, is a new and vnwonted thing: as men whome either the Censors, or the other offices and honours by them before obtained, had sufficiently alreadie tried. Yet in the time of the Gothes, the Commonweale being by them chaunged, we read it to haue bene done: For so saith *Theodoricus*, with *Cassiodore*, *Admittendos in Senatum examinare cogit solicitus honor Senatus*, The carefull care we haue of the honour of the Senat, causeth vs to examine such as are to be admitted into the Senat.

As for the number of Senators it cannot be great, considering the perfection requisit in a Counselour of estate. True it is, that in popular and aristocratique Commonweales, to auoid seditions, and to feede the enraged famine of the ambitious, which haue part in the soueraignetie: they are oft times enforced to augment the number of the Senatours; as in Athens by *Solons* law, they by lot euery yeare made choice of foure hundred Senatours; whereunto it pleased them afterwardes to adde another hundred, that so fifty might by lot yearely bee drawne out of euery one of the ten tribes: vnto whom they ioyned also another hundred, to make vp the full number of 600. After that they had vnto the ten tribes ioyned two others, namely the tribes of

Antigonus

Nobility of birth and also wealth to be in a Senator required.

The number of Senators commonly moe is an Aristocratique or popular Commonweale, than in a Monarchie.

Antigonus and *Demetrius*, albeit that in the time of *Pericles*, there were not in the citie aboue 13 thousand citisens, and 20 thousand in the time of *Demosthenes*. For which cause (as I haue said) *Plato* in his popular Commonweale: by him set downe, appointeth the Senate to consist of an hundred threescore and eight of the better and wiser sort, which was the thirtith part of 5040 citisens the full number of them, of whom he would haue his Commonweale to stand. And in like case, *Romulus* tooke the thirtith part of his subiects to make the first Roman Senate of, choosing out of 3000, (the whole number that then was of the citisens) an hundred, and them also by him chosen not by lot, but by discretion, euen of the nobler sort of his people : viz. such as whose auncestours had neuer serued as slaues. But afterward, the Sabins being according to the league receiued into the citie, hee added vnto the former number another hundred; vnto whom, after the kings driuen out, *Brutus* also put to an hundred moe, which number of three hundred Senatours, so continued by the space of almost foure hundred yeares, without increasing or diminishing. But in the time of *Cicero*, it is manifest that there were about fiue hundred, by that he writeth foure hundred and fifteene Senatours, to haue giuen voices when *Pub. Claudius*, who was afterwards tribune, was brought in question for hauing polluted the sacrifices of *Bona Dea*, by committing of adultery with *Pompeia*: at which time, when the Senatours were not constrained to be present in the Senate, no man can doubt, but that many of them then dispersed into all the prouinces of the Roman empire, or otherwise busied with their owne affaires, or letted with age and sicknesse, were then also absent. And after that, *Cæsar* to haue moe beholden vnto him, and for the better establishing of his owne gouernement, augmented the number of the Senatours vnto a thousand, chusing into that honourable order, not onely citisens of all sorts, but euen Frenchmen and other strangers also, namely *Lu. Licinius* the Barber, as saieth *Acron*. But *Augustus* (after the Commonweale againe pacified) seeing the danger of so great a number of Senatours, brought them to the number of sixe hundred, with purpose to haue brought them also to the antient number of three hundred, which was not much more then the ten thousand part of the whole number of the citisens, being then almost infinite.

<small>Of whom it is fittest to make choice for Senators in an Aristocratique or popular Commonweale.</small>

Wherefore the number of Senatours is not to bee appointed, according to the multitude of the people, neither to serue the ambitious desire of the ignorant; and much lesse for the drawing of money from them, but onely for the respect of the vertue and wisdome of them which haue deserued the place; or if it be not possible otherwise to satisfie the ambition of them, which haue part and interest in the estate of popular and aristocratique Commonweales, but that of necessitie the gate of the Senate must bee opened vnto the multitude, that it be yet so ordered, that none should therein haue deliberatiue voices, but such as had borne the greatest offices and charges in the state: as in the Cretensian popular Commonweale, all the citisens had free accesse and enterance into the Senate, and there might franke and freely deliuer their opinions, but not with authoritie to determine any thing, that power being still reserued vnto them onely which then were, or had before beene the great magistrates. And in the Senate of the *Achaans*, none but the generall and the ten Dimiurgi, had power to determine

<small>The daunger of hauing many Senators.</small>

of such things as were in counsell propounded. Howbeit a wise lawegiuer will neuer goe so farre, if hee may otherwise auoid the popular sedition : for beside the manifest daunger, which is for reuealing of counsell communicated to so many persons : it giueth also occasion vnto the factious for troubling of the state, if they which haue the power to determine and resolue vpon matters, shall in opinion differ from them which haue but voices consultatiue; which indeede are accounted as nothing : for preuenting of which dangers, both the one and the other, the antient Greekes in their Commonweales

F3 Commonweale by   G5 about fiue hundred (Fr) about six hundred (L)

OF A COMMONWEALE. 261

weales, still created a counsell apart, of the grauest and wisest of their Senators (whom they called πρόβουλοι and πρόσκλητοι) to consult of the more secret and vrgent matters of state; as also by themselues to dispose of the greatest affaires of the Commonweale, and to consider what thing were to be consulted of in the open Senat, or publikely to be propounded vnto the people. Besides that, what an hard matter it was of such a multitude of Senatours, to assemble so many as were requisite, and to make them to agree when they were assembled; the estate in the meane time standing in danger & the opportunitie for the well mannaging of matters passing. The Senators office amongst the Romans was most glorious and full of honour; and yet could *Augustus* the emperour neuer bring to passe, that the Senators should be present at the ordinarie Senat, which was holden the calends or ides of euerie moneth at the farthest; albeit that he set great fines vpon them that were absent, and gaue not their assistance: which grew so heauie vpon the offendors, as that he was glad to take of them so offending euerie fift man by lot. And *Ruscius Cæpio* the rather to inuite them to that their dutie, by his last will and testament left a certaine summe of money to them that came into the Senat. For it was requisit that there should be fiftie Senators at the least for the making of any decree, and oftentimes an hundred, or two hundred, yea and sometimes foure hundred, which was two third parts of sixtie Senators; as in corporations and colledges the manner is. Howbeit *Augustus* the emperour at length taking away the necessitie of so great a number, appointed two hundred to be sufficient, beeing two thirds of three hundred; which was the lawfull number of the Senators appointed by *Brutus*. Moreouer the Senat was not ordinarily assembled but three times a moneth; and if it pleased not the Consull (without whose commandement the Senat might not assemble it selfe) or the greatest magistrat in the absence of the Consull, sometime an whole yeare passed without calling together of the Senat: as *Cæsar* did in his first Consulship, hauing the Senat bent against him; and yet in the meane time by prodigall bountie caused euen what he would to be decreed by the people. Whereas *Solon* had much better prouided for the matter among the Athenians, hauing beside the ordinarie Senat of 400, euerie yeare to be changed, appointed also a priuie and perpetuall Councell of the Areopagi, consisting of threescore of the wisest and grauest sort of the citisens, men without reproach, who by all the degrees of honour were risen to haue the mannaging of all the most secret affaires of the state, and to foresee that in time of daunger the Commonwealth should take no harme. Of which councell how great the need was, was then well vnderstood, when as *Pericles* to gaine the fauour of the common sort, had taken away the authoritie from the Areopagits, and translated the same vnto the people: for shortly after, the state of that Commonweale sore shaken both with forren and domesticall warres, began forthwith to decline and decay. Wee find also, that the Ætolians, beside their great Councell, which they called *Panætolium*, had also their priuie Councell chosen of the grauest and wisest men amongst them; of whome *Liuie* speaking, saith, *Sanctius est apud Ætolos consilium eorum quos apocloets appellant*, There is among the Ætolians a more sacred (or priuie) Councel, of them whom they call *apocletos*: and immediatly after, *Arcanum hoc gentis Consilium*, This is the secret Councell of the nation: Whereas before he had said, *Legibus Ætolorum cauebatur, ne de pace belloue, nisi in Panætolio & Pilaico Consilio ageretur*, It was prouided by the lawes of the Ætolians, that nothing should be entreated of concerning peace or warre, but in their Panætolio, or Pilaican Councell. Wee read also, that the popular Commonweale of the Carthaginensians, beside their Senat of foure hundred Senators, had also a particular or priuie Councell of thirtie Senators, men of greatest experience in their publike affaires and matters of state: Of whome *Liuie* thus saith,

The counsel of the Areopagi in Athens.

*Select counsellours.

The counsel of the Carthaginensians.

Cartha-

A2 πρόσκλητοι (L) ἀπόκλητοι (Fr)   B3 glad to take *i.e.* constrained to take (cf. note at 135 C2)
B8 *For* sixtie *read* six hundred.   D10 apocletos

Carthaginenses xxx legatos seniorum principes ad pacem petendam mittunt: id erat sanctius apud eos Consilium, maximaque ad Senatum regendum vis, The Carthaginensians (saith he) send thirtie ambassadors, the princes of their elders to sue for peace: and that was the more sacred Councell with them, and the greater power for the ruling of the Senat: which manner of Councell the Romans wanted. And therefore *Liuie* wondereth (as at a right strange thing) that the ambassadors of Greece and Asia, which came to Rome, could of so great a number of Senators vnderstand nothing of that which king *Eumenes* then plotted in the full Senat, against *Perseus* king of Macedon, *Eo silentio curia clausa erat*, The court (saith he) was with such silence shut vp: Whereby he sufficiently sheweth, that in his time, as also long before that, nothing was done or agreed vpon in the Senat, which still was not by one or other of so great a number reuealed. For which cause the Senators themselues sometimes were constrained to become clarkes and secretaries in the secret affaires of the state, and to take of euerie man an oath, not to reueale any such thing as was in the Senat decreed, vntill such time as it was put in execution: For as yet no capitall punishment was appointed for such as shuld reueale or bewray the secret councel of princes. And indeed how could any thing there be kept secret, where fiue or 600 Senators were priuie to all that was done in the Senat, beside the clarks and secretaries for the state? When as also the yong Senators children, before the time of *Papyrius Prætextatus* might come into the Senat, & carrie the news of such things as were there done, vnto their mothers. *Augustus* was the first, who out of the Senat made choice of some few of the wiser sort to be of his priuy councel, without giuing the rest of the senat to vnderstand, that he would with them resolue of the most important and secret affaires of state, but onely to haue their aduise concerning such things as were to be afterward propounded in the open assemblie of the Senat. Immediatly after whose death, *Tiberius* the emperour requested of the Senat, to haue twentie Senators appointed him, with whome he might (as he would haue them to beleeue) consult of such things as the Senat was further to bee moued of. Whose example the wiser sort of the emperours afterwards followed; namely *Galba*, *Traian*, *Adrian*, *Marcus Aurelius*, and *Alexander Seuerus*: of whome *Lampridius* speaking, He neuer (saith he) made decree without the aduise of twentie lawyers, and diuers other of the Senators, (men of great euidently and vnderstanding in matters of state) euen to the number of fiftie to the end there might be no fewer than were necessarie for the making of a decree of the Senat. Whereby it euidently appeareth, that in that priuat Councell of fiftie Senators, with the prince, were the greatest matters dispatched; and that it was not onely to consult of that which was to be in the Senat propounded, but euen to resolue and determine of the most secret and important affaires of the state, and so by little and little to draw them from the Senat, vnto the more priuat councel of the prince. By which meanes was also prouided for another difficultie (otherwise in a Monarchie ineuitable) which is the multitude of Senators, which could not still follow the prince; vnto whome for all that his councell ought to bee alwaies assistant, especially in a Monarchie, where the prince is to visit diuers his prouinces: or is himselfe in person busied in his warres. For which cause and no other, the auntient diuines and poets, haue faigned *Pallas* alwaies to sit on the right hand of *Iupiter*, but not *Iupiter* on the right hand of *Pallas*: to giue vs thereby to vnderstand, That the Councell ought alwaies to be present with the prince, but not the prince to bee tied to the place where the Councell is resident: which were a thing not onely not agreeable with the maiestie of a soueraigne prince, but also impossible. And albeit that there bee many things in euerie Commonweale dispatched by the priuie Councell, wherewith it is not needfull either the people or the rest of the nobilitie to be made acquainted: yet so

Augustus the first in Rome who out of the whol body of the Senate made choice of some fewe of the wiser sort, to be of his priuie counsels

it

I1 *For* great evidently *possibly read* great eminency (*gents signalés* in Fr).

it is, that in a Monarchie it is expedient and requisit that the prince should himselfe vnderstand them: or at leastwise that euerie man should thinke that he so doth, so to giue the greater authoritie and credit vnto such things as are by the Councell decreed, and that the subiects should not complaine and say, *The king vnderstandeth not hereof.* And for this cause the Grand Signior of the Turkes hath alwaies a lattise or grate, opening into the Diuano, or chamber wherein his Councell sitteth, to the intent to keepe his Bassaes and them of his councell in awe; whilest they thinke him their prince alwaies to see them, and to obserue their proceedings and doings.

But it may be (may some man say) that a Commonweale may be so little, and men of experience in it so few in number, as that not a Senat, but euen such a priuie Councell as we spake of, cannot therein be made. In which case of so strait a Commonweale, it is not needfull to diuide the Senat apart from the priuie Councell. As in the Commonweale of the Pharsalians (which was within most narrow bounds shut vp) there were but twentie persons which had the soueraigntie, who in that state serued for the nobilitie, the Senat, and priuie Councell. And yet neuerthelesse in the Lacedemonian Commonweale alwaies both before and after the conquest of Greece, there were but thirtie lords, both for the state and the Senat: and yet out of this number of thirtie, they made choice but of twelue for the mannaging of the secret affaires of their state, as we read in *Xenophon*: establishing the same forme of gouernment in Athens also, where they deputed thirtie lords for the gouernment of that state, as they did in all the rest of the cities of Greece, except some little ones, ouer whome *Lysander* placed ten chiefe men, without any other Senat or priuie Councell. And the reason was, for that they had resolued to chaunge all the popular states of Greece, into Aristocraties; which they could not haue done in the lesser townes, if they should in them haue erected a seignorie, a Senat, and a priuie Councell. But for the present there is almost no Commonweale, be it Popular or Aristocratique, which hath not a Senat and particular or priuat Councell: yea and oftentimes beside both them, a Triumuirat of some few, for the mannaging of the more secret affaires of state, and that especially in a Monarchy. For so *Augustus* the emperour (albeit that he surpassed all the rest that came after him, both in wisdome, and happinesse) beside the Senat, which he had filled with 600 Senators, and the priuat councell of twentie select men, had also another neerer and more inward councell of *Mæcenas* and *Agrippa*, with whome he resolued of his highest affaires, calling vnto him none but them two after the victorie of Actium, to resolue with, Whether he should still hold, or discharge himself of the empire. So *Iulius Cæsar*, had none but *Q. Pedius*, and *Cornelius Balbus* of his most inward councell, vnto whom also he gaue his manner of writing in secret caracter, for them the better to vnderstand his secrets thereby. So *Cassiodorus* speaking of the secrets of princes, saith, *Arduum nimis est principis meruisse secretum,* Too high a thing it is (saith he) to haue deserued to be of the princes priuitie. We see in like case, that the court of the parliament of Paris, was the auntient Senat of the realme of Fraunce: but when it tooke pleasure in deciding of ciuill controuersies, nor could not well bee remoued from the citie; the kings appointed another councell, which for that it handled matters of greatest importance, in the time of *Charles* the seuenth, was called the Great Councell: which when it was also entangled with deciding of extraordinarie suits and controuersies, by the lawes of *Charles* the eight, and much more by the lawes of king *Lewes* the xij, who appointed a court of twentie judges; king *Francis* the elder remoued that Great Councell from medling with the secret affaires of state, hauing got vnto himselfe another councell of certaine select princes his friends: which of the Latines is called; The Familiar Councell, and of our countrey men, The princes priuat Councell. But *Francis*

cis being dead, *Henrie* his sonne got another councell also: which for that it consisted of few, was called the narrow or strait Councell. But at last, when that Familiar or priuat Councell, was thought to exceed also with the multitude of Councellors, *Henrie* the third, the sonne of *Henrie* ordained another Councell, which for that it was only to consult of matters concerning the state of the Commonweale, and not of suits and controuersies, was called the Councell for the State. Beside these, it was thought meet that there should also be a more secret or chamber Councell, wherein the king rising from his bed, should confirme or reiect such things as were by the Councell decreed: there are princes letters opened, ambassadors reported, and messages deliuered. There is also apart another Councell of the Finances instituted by *Henrie* the second, and by little and little taken from the auditors, wherein are assistant the intendants and secretaries of estate of the Finances, and the treasuror for the common treasure. Beside all which princes haue alwaies had a more strait Councel, of two or three of their most inward and faithfull friends; who so highly stand in the princes fauour, not so much for their youth or person, as for their wisedome and vertue. As for the chamber Councell whereof we spoke, it consisteth but of a few, and albeit that by the decree of *Charles* the ninth, made in Nouember, in the yere 1563, it is in the first article expressed, that so soone as the king was vp, all the princes and the councell might come into the chamber, yet was not that his decree therein obserued or kept.

<small>Seauen counsels in Spaine.</small>

Which pluralitie and diuersitie of Councels in the kingdome of Fraunce, ought not to seeme straunge, seeing that in Spaine there be seuen, beside the strict and inward Councell, which are alwaies in diuers chambers neere vnto the king, and yet within the compasse of the same house or lodging, to the intent, that the king going from one of them to the other, may the better be enformed of his affaires: as namely the councell of Spaine, the councell of the Indies, the councell of Italie, and the councell of the Low countries, the councell for the warres, the councell for the order of Saint *Iohn*, and the Inquisition. Now if any man there be, that thinke the greatnesse of that kingdome (than which neuer yet was any greater) to require so many councels: I denie it not, but yet so he may see also in Venice, which hath no verie great territory, foure councels, beside the Senat and Great Councell: *viz*. the councell of the Sages for matters at sea,

<small>Diuers counsels in Venice.</small>

the councell of the Sages for matters at land, the councel of the Decemuiri, or ten men, and the councell of the Septemuiri, or seuen men; where the duke maketh the seuenth man, which they cal the Seignorie, when it is ioyned with the councell of the ten men, and the three presidents of the fortie, beside the Senat of sixtie; which with the magistrats may come to the number of six score. And what then should let, but that where there be but few men worthy to be of councell for the state, but that the Senat may be made right little, and the priuie councell lesse, and yet diuided from the Senat also. The state of the Rhagusians is but strait, & comprised almost within the same bounds, wherewith the wals of the citie are enclosed, and yet the Senat consisteth of threescore. In the citie of Nuremberg is a Senat of twentie six Senators, and a priuie councell of thirteene, beside another councell of the seuen Bourgomasters. The Canton of

<small>The counsels of the Cantons of the Swissars.</small>

Schwits is the least of all the Cantons, and yet for all that beside the Senat of fortie fiue persons, it hath a priuie councell of seuen, of whome the Aman is chiefe. Which selfe same forme of councell is also kept in the canton of Vri. As for the cantons of Zurich, Berne, Schaffuse, Basill, Soleurre, Friburg, and Lucerne, they haue alwaies beside the Great Councell, a little councell also. The Great Councell of Berne consisteth of two hundred Senators; and the little of twentie six: At Lucerne of an hundred, and the little of twentie eight: At Saint Gal also the Great Councell is of sixtie six, and the little of twentie foure: At Coire the Senat is of thirtie, and the priuie councell

---

I9–10 threescore, THE PRIVY COUNCIL OF TWELVE. In 'K5 Schaffuse, Basill, K8 *For* twentie eight *read* eighteen (Fr and L).

councell of fifteene. And without going so farre, it is well knowne, that the state of Geneua is enclosed within the compasse and circuit of a mile, yet for all that beside the councell of two hundred, it hath a Senat of sixtie; and after that a priuie councell of twentie fiue. Neither is there any canton so little, (except the three cantons of the Grisons, gouerned by the common popularitie) which hath not a priuie councell beside the Senat, wherein some haue three, and some haue foure. As in the canton of Basill, where the secret affaires of state are mannaged by two Bourgomasters, and two other chiefe men of their colleges, whom they call Zunfft maisters. And in like case at Berne the two Auoyers, and foure ensigne bearers, haue the ordering of all the secret businesse of their state; as hath the priuie councell in a Monarchie. And namely in the diets and assemblies of the thirteene cantons, there is none but the priuie councell of the ambassadours, which make their decrees, and direct their commissions, concerning their common affaires: I say then that it is a thing most profitable in euerie Common weale, to haue at the least one priuie councell beside the Senat, sith that the auntient rulers of both the Greekes and Latines haue so taught vs, reason so shewed vs, and experience therein confirmed vs.

The counsel of Geneua.

A priuie counsell besids the Senat necessarie in euerie Commonweale.

But there is a notable difference betwixt the Senat of a popular or Aristocratique Commonweal, and the Senat of a Monarchie: for in them the diuises and consultations are had in the secret or priuie counsell; but the resolutions and decrees are all made in the great Counsell, or in the assemblie of the States, or of the people, if the matter be such as is to be vnto them published: whereas in a Monarchie the manner of proceeding is quite contrarie, wherein nothing is communicated or imparted to the people, or the nobilitie, but such things as seeme vnto the Senat doubtfull, or being of greater importance, are still referred vnto the priuie Counsell; and if the matter concerne the soueraigntie, it is reserued vnto the iudgement of the soueraigne prince onely. And albeit that the Senat or Counsell in a Monarchie seeme to do all the rest of it selfe, yet still we see all to depend of the princes commaund. And this which we haue said concerning the manner of consultation, is almost no where better put in practise then in Venice: where if any difficultie arise in the counsell of the sages, it is commonly discided by ioining of the Decemuiri vnto them, (and therefore vnto such decrees as are by them made are ioined *Con la Giunta*) and if they cannot so agree, but still rest among themselues in opinion diuided, they call vnto them the Septemuiri or counsell of seauen: but if so nothing can be decreed for the diuersitie of opinions, the matter is then propounded in open Senat: And sometimes also (although but seldome) if the matter be of such consequence, or so much concerne the maiestie of the State, as that the authoritie of the Senat seemeth not to be thereunto sufficient, or that the Senat be thereupon diuided, it is propounded in the great counsell of all the gentlement of Venice, where it taketh the last and finall resolution; which as *Aristotle* writeth, was also the auncient custome of the Carthaginensians, where if the Senat could not agree, the difference was disputed, debated, and discided by the people.

The manner of consultation in the Senat of a popular or Aristocratique estate, and in the Senat of a Monarchie much different.

The manner of the proceding in their consultations in matters of state, in Venice.

Now all this differing of resoluing and determining, proceedeth from the diuersitie of the soueraigntie, and of them which haue the mannaging of the gouernment: for what the Senat decreeth in an Aristocratique, or popular Commonweal, that the nobilitie, or people ratifieth and commaundeth if the matter so require: contrarie to that we see to be done in a Monarchie, where the wiser the prince thinketh himselfe, the lesse he vseth the counsell of the Senat: (albeit that he oft times aske the aduise thereof, to make his doings the more acceptable, or for the easing of himselfe, committeth vnto them commissions for extraordinarie iustice, or the iudgement of inextricable matters and causes of appeales) especially if the Senat be so great as that the prince by publi-

Aa shing

A3 sixtie (Fr 3–8 and L) seventy-five (Fr 1–2). Cf. note at 233 B3.   C3 nobilitie; but
D7 gentlemen   Notes at A2, B7.

shing of his secrets to so many persons, shall not come to the point of his designes. By this meane *Tiberius* the Emperour sought to kepe the Senat busied in disciding of great and extraordinarie causes, to make it by little and little to forget the vnderstanding of matters of state. And after him *Nero* likewise ordeyned that the Senat should haue the hearing of Appeales which before were made vnto himselfe, and that the fine for the offence set downe by the Senat should be as great, as if he had heard the cause himselfe; By this meane making of a Senat an ordinarie court and iurisdiction of Iudges: who in the time of freedome of that popular Commonweal neuer vsed to judge, except ordinarilie in conspiracies, and other such like great offences against the state: or that the people which had the hearing of many causes, had committed the vnderstanding thereof vnto the Senat. For which cause *Cicero* accusing *Verres* saith in this sort, *Quo confugient socij? quem implorabunt? ad Senatum deuenient, qui de Verre supplicium sumat? non est vsitatum, non est Senatorium*: Whither shall our friends and allies flie? whom shall they aske help of? shall they come vnto the Senat, to take punishment of Verres? it is no thing in vse, it appertaineth not vnto the Senat. Wherein many deceiue themselues, which think that the Senat judged, when they saw that the Senatours were drawne by lot to judge of publike and criminall causes, sometimes by themselues, sometime with the knights, by the law Liuia, and afterwards with the knights and the Treasurours, by the law Aurelia: for there is great difference betwixt the bodie of the Senat, and the Senatours taken in the qualitie of judges, and betwixt the priuie Counsell, and the counsellours thereof, comming into the soueraigne courts to judge. For before *Nero* the Senat neuer had so much as ordinarie iurisdiction or power to judge of any matter; And namely *Augustus* would not that the Senat should trouble it selfe, with the judging of the honour, or of the life of Senatours, albeit that he were thereunto importuned by his friend *Mæcenas*. And albeit that *Tyberius* the emperour often times sent vnto them such causes, yet was it but extraordinarie and by way of commission; which *Adrian* the emperour afterward caused to passe into the forme of an ordinarie iurisdiction. We see in like case that *Philip* the faire, or as some others say *Philip* the long, to discharge himselfe of the Court of parlament, and easilie to take from it the dealing with the affaires of state, made it an ordinarie Court, giuing it iurisdiction, and a fitting place in Paris: which Court was in auntient time the Senate of Fraunce, and yet at this day calleth it selfe the Court of Peeres, erected by *Lewes* the yong, (according to the truer opinion) to giue counsell vnto the king; as we may see by the creation of Countie D'*Mascon* for a Peer, by king *Charles* the fift, in the yeare 1359, where it is said that the king of Fraunce ordained the twelue Peers, to giue them their counsell and aide, and tearmed it selfe, as yet it doth at this present, (by way of prerogatiue of honour) the Court of parlament (without any other addition) as it is to be seene in the letters which it wrote vnto the king: whereas the other Courts of later time established, vse their particular additions; As, *The Parlament of Tholouse, of Roan, of Burdeaux, of Dion, of Gratianople, and Aquasexia*. But in the raigne of *Charles* the ix, at such time time as the Court of Paris liked not of the decree of the Senat, whereby the king in the Court of Roan was by the voices of the princes declared sufficient for the gouernment of the kingdome without a Regent, according to the law of king *Charles* the first: the king yet vnder age, aduised the court, to meddle only with the desciding of controuersies, and the equall administration of justice: for that the king his predecessours had for that onely purpose appointed that Court, and there placed them, and not to become his tutors, or protectors of the realme, or keepers of his towne of Paris: and therefore commaunded such lawes and edicts as hee had appointed to be proclaimed in the court of Paris, to be published: wherein if any thing

---

Marginalia:

The policie of the Romain emperours to drawe the Senat from matters of state by busying it with other extraordinarie causes.

The Senators of Rome as Senators no iudges, but when they were thereunto extraordinarilie by commission appoynted.

The court of Paris sometime the auntient Senat of Fraunce by the king forbidden to deale with matters of state.

F9 *For* ordinarilie *read* extraordinarilie.   I1 sitting place (*seance* in Fr)   I5 kings of Fraunce
I10 of Dion, of Gratianople, and Aquasexia *i.e.* of Dijon, Grenoble, and Aix   K4 *For* Charles the first *read* Charles the fifth.   Note at I10.

OF A COMMONWEALE. 267

A thing should be contained that seemed not to stand with right and reason, he could (as he said) be content to be thereof tould; but yet so as that after he had vnderstood the matter, if it were his pleasure to haue the law proclaimed, they should forthwith without farther reply do that they were commaunded: with which the kings edict the court was wonderfully troubled; and for that the judges were equally diuided into two opinions: the one being willing to haue the kings edict published, and the other denying the same. The Court thought good againe to aduise the king, that the court might not be enforced to allow or publish such things as should thereunto seeme vnreasonable or vniust. Wherewith the king displeased, caused his priuie Counsell to be called, and by the authoritie thereof a decree to bee made the xxiiij. of September,

B whereby the parlament of Paris was forbidden once to call in question the lawes or decrees proceeding from the king concerning matters of state: which was also before by king *Francis* decreed in the yeare 1528. In like case the great Counsell which was not almost employed but in affaires of state, in the raigne of *Charles* the seauenth, and *Charles* the eight, was by little and little so filled with sutes, that *Charles* the viij. made it an ordinarie court of seauenteene counsellours; whom *Lewes* the xij. made vp xx. beside the Chauncelour, who was President thereof, (in such sort, that vnder king *Francis* there was but a President in steed of a Chauncelour) who were not imploied but in hearing of extraordinarie causes by way of commission, or remitting of the priuie counsell, and ordinarily the appeales of the Prouost of the houshold. We se also

C the priuie Counsell it selfe to be as it were brought into the forme of an ordinary court, by hearing the differences betwixt the Townes and the Parlaments, and oft times betwixt particular men, euen for small matters: to the end that such a great companie of the nobilitie, and men of marke, should be busied with some thing, hauing as it were lost the vnderstanding of the affaires of state, which can neuer sort to good end, if they be communicated to so many persons: where the wiser sort are commonly ouer ruled by the greater part, ioining hereunto also, that it is impossible, to keepe the counsell of the state secret: or to know in such a multitude who it is that discouereth the same, nor to cast them out who are holden for suspect: Except by vsing the custome of the auntient Athenians, by vertue whereof the Senatours by a secret iudgement which

D they called τῆς ἐκφυλλοφορίας might with all libertie, and without displeasure condemne the blabbing Senator, or him that had defiled the honour of his estate. As in like case the Roman Censors without forme or fashion of processe, had accustomed to remoue the vnworthie Senators, and by that meanes to exclude them out of the Senat; except they would put themselues vpon their triall before the judges which were aboue the Censors, or that the people had giuen some new office, or honorable charge to him that was so remoued by the Censors, or condemned by the judges. But the Romans were much to blame, both for too easie receiuing and remouing of the Senatours, and that in too great number: For *Fabius Buteo* made Dictator to supply the defect of the Senat, at one time receiued in an 177 Senatours. Whereas *Lentulus* and *Gellius* Censors at one dash remoued 64. Howbeit, it were more seemly and agreeing

E with the dignitie and honour of a Senat to receiue into it few, and them also chosen and culled out as pearles; than to exalt vnto so high degree of honour men worthie and vnworthie, and afterwards to cast them downe againe with eternall infamie and dishonour, vnto whom they had before giuen their helping hands: Besides that it cannot alwaies be done without danger and sedition, or the dishonour of him that ruleth. It is foure hundred yeare since that the Priuie Counsell of England, at the instance and sute of the Archbishop of Canterburie (then Chauncelour) established, there were there into but fifteene persons then chosen; neither hath it euer since passed the number

Aa ij ber

The priuie counsel of Fraunce almost brought into the forme of an ordinarie court by hearing of priuat and particular causes

Matters of state not without daunger to be communicated vnto many.

Senators or counsellours of estate not easily to be admitted nor without greate cause to be againe displaced. The auntient counsel of England in number fewe.

ber of twentie; and yet by meanes of that little Counsell they haue retained their state most faire and florishing in times both of peace and warre, as is by their histories to be seene; and by the treatie of peace made betwixt *Lewes* the ix, and *Henry* the first, king of England; which for the more assurance thereof was sworne by the Prince and the xvij priuie Counsellors: viz. one Archbishop, one Chauncelor, one Bishop, six Earls, and six other Lords, with the great Treasurour, and a magistrat whom they call chiefe Iustice of England. Now I doubt not but that in euery Commonweale, many by vaine ambition, fauour, impudency, or corrupt briberie, in sort euen against the Prince and peoples will find meanes to enter into the sacred Senat; against which inconuenience remedie might be well prouided, if we would but vse *Solons* law. For he would haue none to bee admitted into the Senat of the Areopagits, but such as had without touch, by all the degrees of honour ascended vnto the highest places and preferments of the Commonweale: for so he deemed him to be well able to hold a place in the Senat without staggering or falling, that could hold himselfe vpright in such dangerous and slipperie wayes. And that is it for which all the auntients both Greeks and Latins, haue so highly commended the Senat of the Areopagits, composed of sixtie persons, as we read in Athens. The same manner is yet vsed among the fiue lesser cantons of the mountaine Swissers, that they which haue passed through all the honourabre estates should continue Senators for euer: but this is not the way to haue good resolution, and yet lesse to keepe the affaires of state in secret, in that the Senators of the little cantons, which are fortie fiue in Zug, and an hundred sixtie foure in Appenzel, and more or lesse in the others, when question is of matters of importance, may euerie one of them bring with him into the councell two or three of the citisens, such as he liketh best of. Whereby it commeth to passe, that sometime there are foure or fiue hundred, part Senators, part others, assembled together into the Senat, and yet all haue deliberatiue voices therein. Whereas multitude is euer an enemie, vnto wise resolutions.

Who they be that ought to propound matters in the Senat or counsel.

And thus much concerning the number of Councellors of estate: let vs now also breefly speake of them that are to propound matters in the Senat; and then of such things as are there also to bee propounded. As touching the first, men of auntient time haue alwaies had great regard vnto the qualitie of them which were to propound any thing in the Senat. For we see that to haue bene the proper charge of the greatest magistrats in Rome, whome for that cause they called Consuls: or in their absence the greatest magistrat that was in Rome (to wit, the Prætor of the citie) supplied the place of the Consull: receiuing the particular requests both of the citisens and straungers, of ambassadours from forren princes, and allies letters from the gouernours of their prouinces: which letters he read in the Senat, asked euerie mans opinion, commaunded the decrees of the Senat to be written, & also dismissed the Senat. Amongst the Grecians the greatest Prætor executed the same office, who among the Athenians was called ἄρχων ἐπώνυμος; & the rest as they were created in some places πρόληπτοι & πρόβουλοι, who bare almost the same office that do the prouiditors in the cōmonwealth of Rhaguse, & the sages in the state of Venice: howbeit that there the three Auogadors ordinarily propounded vnto the senat, that wherof it is to consult. In the councel of the Greeks the president caused to be cried aloud by a sergeant, That if there were any person that had any thing to say concerning the good of the state, he should speake: which *Titus Liuius* speaking of the Achæans affirmeth generally of all the Greeks. But as for the Ætolians, their custome was most notable, worthy to be of all men regarded, being highly commended and approued by *Philipemen* generall of the Achæan league; which was, that the president, or hee which in full councell propounded any thing which

A notable custome of the Aetolians in propounding of matters in their Senat.

G2 without touch *i.e.* without stain, blemish   G7 *For* Athens *read* Athenaeus.   G9 honourable
I6 princes and allies, letters   I10 ἄρχων   K8 *For* Philipemen *read* Philopemen (Fr) *or* Philopœmen
(L).   K9 president   Note at F1.

which seemed vnto himselfe good, should therein haue no voice himselfe. A great meanes to take away the practises and couert traines, which are commonly made in Popular and Aristocratique estates, where the busiest heads easily draw others to their opinions. Howbeit I cannot commend the fashion and custome of them of Genes, where none but the duke alone hath power to propound in the Senat that which pleaseth himselfe. For beside the difficultie of speaking with the duke on euerie side beset, and troubled with infinit affaires, and to lay before his eyes a thousand diuers reasons for the debating of the matter in the councell: it is also daungerous to giue so great authoritie to one person, that he may open or keepe secret to or from the Senat, whatsoeuer himselfe pleaseth; it being not lawfull for any man to propound any matter but himselfe. It is also much perilous one citisen, who first deliuereth his opinion to be of such authoritie and power, as that the rest which are to speake after him, dare not freely say what indeed they thinke. And that is it for which it is wisely prouided in the realm of Fraunce, that it is permitted to all them which haue accesse into the councell (although they therin haue neither deliberatiue voice nor place) euerie man to propound his owne requests, & to aduertise the councell of that which is profitable for the Commonweale; to the end it may be the better prouided for. And oftentimes their opinion is also thereof demanded, and then afterward the aduise of the councellors of the estate, which in councell haue place and deliberatiue voice, in such sort and order, as that the great lords deliuer their opinions last; to the end, that the libertie of the lesser should not be impaired by the authoritie of the greater princes or magistrats, and especially by the power of ambitious and factious men, who cannot in any case abide to be contradicted. In which course they which haue onely voyces consultatiue, make way for them which haue voyces deliberatiue: and oftentimes broach vnto the councell good and liuely reasons: and where they in any thing erre, they are without ielousie againe by the others brought into the right. Which is a custome much more commendable than that of the Romans, where the Consull first demaunded the opinion of the chiefe man in the Senat, or els of him that was appointed Consull for the yeare following. And yet neuerthelesse the contrarie was vsed before the people: for first the particular men deliuered their opinions, and after them the lesser magistrats, and last of all the greatest, to the intent that the libertie of the lesser should not be preuented by the authoritie of the greater. Ioyne hereunto also, that the ambition to speake first doth oftentimes draw after it the enuie of some, and the ielousie of others. So wee see the cruell emperours to discharge vpon the Senat, the discontentment that the people had of their cruelties, caused such things as they would haue done to bee propounded or red in the Senat: which to gainesay or seeme to dislike of was death. Which was not to demaund the aduise of the Senat, but indeed most imperiously to command the same. Whereof an auntient Senator complaining saith, *Vidimus curiam elinguem, in qua dicere quod velles periculosum: quod nolles miserum esset*, We haue seene (saith hee) the court dombe, wherin to speake that thou wouldest was daungerous; and to say that thou wouldest not, was a thing right miserable: For that the emperor *Dometian*, (*vnus solus censebat quod omnes sequerentur*) alone decreed what all men should follow: and commendeth *Traian* (*quod eo rogante, sententias libere dicere liceret, vinceretque sententia non prima, sed melior*) for that he propounding of matters, euerie man might freely speake his mind: and that opinion preuailed not which was first, but best. By the custome of the auntient Hebrewes, the king refrained from comming into the Senat, least any should bee contrarie vnto him, or hee to any; for so they writ in their Commentaries.

It were also to be wished, that the Councell should sit in the morning yet fasting,

The custome of Genes discommended.

The laudable custome for the propounding of matters vsed in Fraunce.

* *Plinius iunior in panegirico.*

for that is not to be holden for a councell well disgested, which is done after dinner, as saith *Philip de Commines*, and especially in countries where the people are subiect vnto wine. *Salomon* detesteth those princes, who when they ought in the morning to feed their mind with religious contemplation of high and diuine matters, doe with full feeding pamper the inordinat desire of their languishing & broken lust, & with new nourishment kindle the fire of new desires: Which he in three words declareth, *Wo* (saith he) *vnto princes which eate early*. Which is a thing so much the more to be detested, by how much many thinke it to be the greatest brauerie, to bee well whitled with wine. For what can be more beastly than was the old maner of the Germans, who neuer vsed to consult of their greatest affaires but in middest of their cups persuaded so that euery one of them warme with wine, should discouer the verie secret of his hart, and to be the more eloquent to persuade what they thought to bee most expedient. Which custome they haue now well changed, insomuch that euen their priuat and domesticall contracts made when they are in drink, are to none effect or purpose, it being alone a sufficient cause for the iudge to reuoke them being so made. Now as concerning such things as are to be consulted of in the Senat, they depend of such occasions & affairs, as in course of time present themselues. The antient Romans first consulted of matters concerning their religion, as the marke and end wherat all humane actions ought both to begin and end. There was neuer also, saith *Polybius* (he himselfe being an Atheist) a people more deuout than this: adioining therunto moreouer, That by meanes of religion they had established vnto themselues the greatest monarchy in the world. Then after matters of religion, and worship of the immortall gods, are to be entreated of the greatest and most vrgent affaires of state, and most concerning the Commonweale, as the making of peace or war: in both which, long delay is no lesse dangerous, than is too hastie resolution. In which case, as in all things doubtful, the antients had a rule which suffered no great exception, which was, That we ought not to do, neither to councell any thing to be done, wherof we doubt whether it be iust or iniust, profitable or hurtfull; or if the harme that may ensue bee greater than the profit that may come of the enterprise that is to be taken in hand: but if the harme be euident, & the profit doubtful, or contrariwise, there is then no deliberation to be had or doubt made which to chuse. But the doubt is greater, when as that which we are to consult of, hath in show moe & greater profits, if we can bring it to good effect, than it hath hurt if wee faile therein. Howbeit the more wholsome opinion of the antients is to bee preferred, *viz*. That when question is of matters of estate, things doubtfull, or subiect to the change of fortune, are not at al to be embraced. And therfore the subtiller sort, cause the that be more simple, to propound and persuade in councell such things as seeme vnto themselues doubtfull; to the intent that so the blame may rest vpon them, if things fall out euill: & yet the honor redound vnto themselues if it fall out wel. Howbeit nothing ought to be thought commendable and well done, which dependeth of the euent. For it behoueth vs by most certaine arguments and reasons to show wherfore this or that is to be done, and not by the euent: yea it behoueth a wise man rather to feare vnfortunat euents, than to presume of happie successe. And therfore a wise councellor neuer resteth himselfe vpon the chances of fawning fortune, or vpon aduentures, but still forceth himselfe by good and wise discourse to gather the true effects of precedent causes: albeit that hee oft times see, the most aduenturous and rash, to be the most happie & fortunat in their attempts. And therefore the antient diuines (who couered wisedome in fables) doubted not to exclude that goddesse whom they called Fortune, out of the coucell of the gods; least that which should be sought for by wisedome, should seeme to haue bene obtained by the rashnesse of fickle fortune. And yet for all that wee see nothing

OF A COMMONWEALE. 271

thing to be comended or blamed, than the good or euil end of mens actions: and so wisdome measured by the foot of fortune. But if the law condemne the souldior that fighteth with the enemie without the commaundement of his captaine, although hee carrie away the victorie; how much more dangerous ought it to be, to put the hope of councels, & state of the Commonweal in the vncertaine hope of fortune? Besides that, such continuall aduentures do oftentimes draw after them the ruine of aduenturous princes. And therefore to auoid that nothing should be rashly or vnaduisedly decreed in the councel, I like well the aduise of sir *Thomas Moore*, To propound the day before what was in the Senat to be resolued on the day following; to the end that such deliberations might the better be disgested: prouided for al that, That question be not of the particular interest of any of them which haue voice in the councell: for in that case it is much better to resolue vpon the matter the same day, & without delay, than to attend vntil the sound iudgement of some be preuented by the subtilties of others, & that men come prepared with long traines of reasons, to reuerse that which ought of right to be concluded. For as the truth, the more naked and simple it is produced, the fairer it is; so is it most certaine, that they which disguise it by figures or colours of Rethorique, take from it the lustre and naturall beautie thereof: a thing which a man ought aboue all things in matters of councell to shun. True it is, that to vse oloquence, in the assemblies of the people, and with the sweetnes of speech to delight the ears of the ignorant multitude, or with faire words to blind their eies, or with pleasing reasons to turne their minds from rage and furie to peace and quietnes, is a thing not onely commendable, but necessary also. But al these things are far to be remoued from a Senat or councell, if aduise be to be sought for or required of such Senators as we haue spoken of, that is to say of wise men. And the Lacedemonian breuitie full of good reasons, is to be vsed, that they all may haue time to speake: & that no orator hauing got the possession of speaking, shold with long discourse or speech exclude the best & wisest of the senators. And therefore by an old decree of the Areopagits, it was not lawfull in that graue councell, to vse either any induction or after-speech. As for the deliuering of their opinions by secret suffrages, as amongst the Venetians; or by changing of places, as amongst the Romans, I cannot greatly commend of either, but especially if the matter in consultation consist of many points, of which some are to be liked of, and othersome to be reiected: so that it is necessarie to propound euerie article or point apart, which the Latins terme *diuidere sententiam*, and so to cause the Senators to passe & repasse from one side to another. Into which difficulties the Venetians falling, are oftentimes constrained to leaue their secret voices giuen by lots, and to giue the same by word of mouth; which they vse to do, when question is of the life, fame, or fortune of any man, according to the maner of the antient Greeks & Romans; a thing which cannot by secret voices, by lot, without iniustice be done, for the infinit varietie of cases which may present themselues to be iudged vpon. Now as the Senat of a Commonweale is not bound to the certaine hearing and deciding of causes, so ought it not to trouble it selfe with intermedling with the iurisdiction of the magistrats, except it be in the controuersies of the greatest magistrats, or soueraigne courts among themselues. And for this cause *Tiberius* the emperour, in the beginning of his raigne protested in the Senat, That he would not alter any thing in the course of iustice, neither haue to do with the iurisdiction of the ordinarie magistrats. And they which make a confusion of a Senat & priuie councel, do greatly diminish the dignitie & honor therof, for that it ought to be regarded as to confirme the princes actions, & wholly to attend the publike affairs: worke enough to busie a senat, except it be when question is of the life or honour of the greatest lords and princes, or of the punishment of cities, or other such causes of like consequence and importance,

That the Senat ought not to intermedle with the iurisdiction of the magistrats.

Aa iiij

B8 eloquence C8 induction *i.e.* introduction, preamble D10 (margin) intermedle

Note at D4.

tance, as may well deserue the assemblie of the Senat; as in auntient time the Roman Senat, by commission from the people, had the hearing of the treasons and conspiracies of their allies, against the state, as we see in *Liuie*.

Liuius lib. 26

What power a Senat or counsel of state is of right to haue in a well ordered Commonweale.

Yet resteth the last point of our definition, that is to say, that the Senat is established to giue aduise and councell to them which haue the soueraigntie in euerie Commonweale. To giue aduise (I say) and councell; for that the Senat in a well ordered Commonweale, ought not to haue power to commaund, nor to direct out their mandats, neither to put into execution their aduises and consultations, but onely to make report thereof vnto them which haue the soueraigntie. Now if a man should aske, Whether there be any Commonweale wherein the Senat hath such power? It is a question but of fact: but if demaund were made, whether of right it ought so to haue or not? our opinion is, that in a well ordered Commonweale it is in no wise to be suffered: for that it cannot be without impeaching of the soueraigntie, and that much lesse in a Monarchie, than in an Aristocratie, or a Popular estate. And in that the maiestie of a soueraigne prince is knowne, in that he can, and his wisedome, in that he knoweth to weigh and iudge the aduise of his councell, and so conclude according to the resolution of the wiser part, and not of the greater.

Why magistrates and soueraigne courts haue a greater commaunding power then hath a Senat or counsel of state.

Now if any man thinke it straunge or inconuenient for all other magistrats and soueraigne courts, to haue power to commaund, in their owne names to direct out their commissions, and the Senat that iudgeth of their authoritie and controuersies, to be depriued of this power: let him consider that vnto such magistrats and courts, power is giuen them euen by their institution, election, and creation, and by the charters and grants vnto them made for the limiting of their charge and power, without which neither martiall nor ciuill or domesticall affaires can well be gouerned: whereas there was neuer Senat in any auntient well ordered Commmonweale, which had any power to commaund by vertue of the institution thereof. So we see, that in the kingdoms of Fraunce, Spaine, and England, the priuie councell is not erected or instituted in forme of a bodie politique or colledge; neither to haue power by the election or ordaining thereof, to order or commaund any thing, so as is necessarie for all magistrats, as we shall hereafter declare. And as for that that some will say, That the priuie councell may disanull and reuerse the iudgements and decrees of the magistrats and soueraigne courts: and so conclude, that it is not without great authoritie and power: mine answere is, that the decrees of the councell depend not in any thing of the councell it selfe; but of the royall power, and by commission onely, in qualitie of extraordinarie iudges for the execution of iustice, besides that the commission and authoritie of the priuie councell is alwayes ioyned with the person of the king. And therefore we see in a Monarchie all the decrees of the priuie councell to carrie these words with them, *By the king in his priuie councell*: which can do nothing if the king bee not present or at leastwise confirme the acts of his councell. But wee haue before shewed the power of all magistrats and corporations to cease, and bee suspended in the presence of the prince. Now if the power of the Senat be nothing in the absence of the prince, and much lesse in his presence, where then is the Senats power? And if the Senat cannot of it selfe decide and determine a controuersie; how can it then dispose of such things as belong vnto the state of the Commonweale? and that is it wherfore we see such things as are decreed vpon by the Senat, to be still referred vnto the prince: or if they bee of lesse importance, yet to be still confirmed with the princes authoritie, hand, and seale. Which is no new matter, but of auntient time done. For we see an old charter making mention of one *Endobalde*, countie of the Pallace of king *Clotoire*, who sitting in councell with the Senat, was to report the decrees thereof vnto the king, to the end to haue

Of A Commonweale. 273

haue them by him either approued or reiected.

But the doubt is greater, whether the Senat in a Popular or Aristocratique estate ought to haue more power than in a Monarchie, or not? considering the great difference there is betwixt one lord and many, or betwixt one prince the soueraigne commaunder of his people; and an infinit number of men; as in a Popular estate. Besides that, we read also, that in the Roman Commonweale (which is holden to haue beene one of the most flourishing and best ordered that euer was) the Senat had power to dispose of the common treasure, and publike reuenue (one of the greatest points of soueraigntie) to appoint lieutenants and gouernours of princes, to grant triumphs, and to dispose of religion. And for this cause *Tertullian* saith, That neuer any God was receiued in Rome, without the decree of the Senat. And as for ambassadours of kings and people, none but the Senat receiued and dismissed them. And that which more is, it was forbidden vpon paine of treason, to present any request vnto the people, without the aduise of the Senat before had, as we haue before declared. Which was not onely in Rome obserued, but also in all the Græcian Commonweales. For offending wherin *Thrasibulus* was in Athens accused of treason, as was afterwards also *Androtian* by *Demosthenes*. Which order is euen at this time better obserued and kept at Venice, than euer it was in Rome or Greece. And yet notwithstanding all this I say, that the Senat of the Popular or Aristocratique estates ought not to haue but the aduise and consultation of matters of state onely, the power still depending of them, which had the soueraigntie. And as for that which is said of the power of the Roman Senat, that which it had, was nothing else but dignitie, authoritie, councel, and not power: for that the people of Rome might when it saw good confirme or repeale the decrees of the Senat, which had no power to commaund, and much lesse to execute the decrees therof; *Dionysius Halycarnassæus* hath well noted, and *Liuie* himselfe oft times vsing this forme of speech, *Senatus decreuit, populus iussit*, The Senat decreed, and the people commanded. Wherein *Festus Pompeius* is deceiued, interpreting the word *iussit*, commaunded, for *decreuit*, or decreed. So that it belonged to the Senat to decree, and to the people to commaund. As when *Liuie* speaking of the authoritie of *Scipio Africanus*, saith, *Nutus eius pro decretis patrum, pro populi iussis esse*, His beck was in stead of the Senators decrees, and the peoples commaunds. And that the least Tribune of the people, opposing himselfe against the Senat, might stay all the decrees thereof. I haue here before noted certaine places out of *Titus Liuius*: whereby it euidently appeareth, that the Senat could in nothing commaund: and especiall by the decree where it is said, That the Consull if he should thinke it so good, should present the request vnto the people, for the making of a dictator: and if it pleased not the Consull, then the Prætor of the citie should take that charge vpon him: who if he would therin do nothing, that then one of the Tribunes should do it. The Consuls (saith *Liuie*) would therein doe nothing, and forbad the Prætor also to obey the Senat: Now had the Senat had so much power to commaund, as had the Consull, or one of the Tribunes of the people, it would neuer haue vsed such kind of speech; neither would the Consul haue forbidden the Prætor to obey the Senat. For indeed the Senat could not commaund the Prætors, but vsed these or like words, *If it should so seeme vnto them good; or if so it were their pleasure*. So the same man in another place saith, *Decreuerunt patres vt Marcus Iunius Prætor vrbanus si ei videretur, Decemuiros agro Samniti, Appuloque, quoad eius publicum erat metiendo, deuidendoque crearet*, The Senators decreed, that *Marcus Iunius*, Prætor of the citie, if he should thinke it so good, should appoint ten men for the measuring and diuiding of so much of the Samnite and Appulian land, as belonged to the Commonweale.

Now

margin notes:
Whether the Senat in a popular or Aristocratique estate ought to haue more power then in a Monarchie.

What power the Senat or counsel ought to haue in a popular or Aristocratique estate.

That the Senat of Rome had no power to commaund in matters of state.

A9 *For* appoint lieutenants and gouernours of princes *read* appoint lieutenants to gouernours of prouinces.   B1–2 kings and peoples   B6 Androtion   D8 *For* The Consuls *read* The Consull (cf. Fr and L).   E6 erat, metiendo devidendoque

Now if any man should say that these words, *Si ei videretur* (if it should so seeme vnto him good) imported a commaund: the contrarie is proued in that, that *Liuie* speaking of the punishment of the Campanians, saith, That the Consull *Fuluius* hauing red the decree of the Senat which caried these words: *Integram rem ad Senatum reijceret si ei videretur: interpretatum esse, quid magis è Republica duceret, æstimationem sibi permissam*: That he should, if he thought it so good, referre the whole matter vnto the Senat: to haue so interpreted the decree, as if the matter had beene committed to his discretion, to deeme what he should think best and most expedient therein to doe for the Commonweale: at which time question was of the liues and goods of all the Campanians, part of whom the Consull of himselfe without farther authoritie from the Senat caused to be put to death, and the rest to be sold by the drume. But that the dignitie of the Magistrats was in the Roman Commonweale greater than the Senats, it appeareth by that, that such as writ letters vnto the Senat and people of Rome, if they therein comprehended the Magistrats also, they still placed them in order before the Senat; as is manifest by the inscription of their letters, in this sort; *Cn. Plancus Imp. Cos. desig. S. P. D. Coss. Pret. Tribb. pleb. Senatui, Populo, plebique Romano*: Cn. Plancus Generall, Consull elect, vnto the Consuls, Pretors, Tribunes of the people, the Senat, People, and Comminaltie of Rome sendeth greeting. Wherefore *Cicero* doth but orator like taunt *Vatinius*, when he saith, Art not thou a most certein murtherer of thy countrey? thou leftest not vnto the Senat, that which neuer man tooke from it; that Legates should be appointed by the authoritie of that order. And he in *Liuie* when as he speaketh of Triumphes, saying, It was neuer before by the people determined of triumphes, the estimation and bestowing of that honour hauing alwayes beene with the Senat: no not the kings themselues to haue impaired the maiestie of that order: he speaketh (I say) but like an orator: for that there was nothing which might not be taken from the Senat, the magistrat propounding a request to the contrarie vnto the people: as we haue by examples before declared. But how soeuer the Senat for the maintenance of the authoritie thereof made decrees, yet could it not commaund or put in execution any of those things that were by it decreed: neither had it so much as any Lictors or Sergeants, the true markes of them which haue power to commaund. But the Magistrats hauing the decrees of the Senat in their hand, directed their owne mandats and commissions for the execution thereof, if they thought it so good: assuring themselues to be out of blame in doing that the Senat had before decreed, it being alwaies readie to maintaine them in so doing: So the Senat being no way able to restraine *Cæsar*, tooke their refuge to that auntient decree of the Senat, which was commonly made but in the dangerous times of the Commonweale, *viz. Videant Consules ac cæteri Magistratus ne quid detrimenti capiat Respublica*: Let the Consuls and other magistrats foresee that the Commonweale take no harme: with which decree of the Senat (saith *Cæsar*) the Consuls armed, sodenly raised their power and took vp armes against *Cæsar*: by which words it appeareth, authoritie to haue beene in the Senat, but the chiefe commaund in the Magistrats. But if any Tribune of the people once opposed himselfe against the decree of the Senat, not onely the authoritie of the Senat, but of the Consuls and other magistrats also ceased. And for that cause there were ordinarily some of the Tribunes at the gate of the Senat, (before that the law Atinia gaue them entrance into the Senat house) vnto whom the decrees of the Senat were brought and showed, for them to confirme by writing ouer them this letter *T*, or reiect by putting thereunto this word *Veto*, that is to say, *I forbid it*. So that the Senat did nothing but by sufferance of the people, or of the Tribunes, who were as it were espials of the Senat, and keepers of the libertie of the people, hauing alwaies

---

G1 by the drume *i.e.* publicly

alwaies free power to take exception to whatsoeuer was decreed, if the people by expresse law tooke it not from them, permitting the whole disciding of the matter propounded, vnto the Senat, without the interruption of the Tribunes. As it did at the request of *Tiberius Graccus* Tribune of the people, giuing leaue vnto the Senat for that yeare to dispose of the Consularie prouinces, with expresse prohibition vnto the Tribunes for the opposing of themselues, for that time onely. For after that time the people oft times gaue the prouinces and gouernments, without the aduise or authoritie of the Senat. Now to say that the Senat had the disposing of the common treasure, true it is, but that was but vpon sufferance, and so long as it pleased the people; as we may see by the law Sempronia, whereby the people decreed that the souldiours should be apparelled of the charge of the common treasure. And he that hath no power but by sufferance, and by way of intreatie hath no power at all, as we haue before said. So in like case we see the Auogadours or Triumuiri in the Venetian state often times to oppose themselues, not onely against the proceedings of the Sages and Decemuiri, but euen of the Senat also, and so cause the matter to be brought vnto the hearing of the graund Counsell.

But here againe a man may say, that if the Senat in bodie or lawfull assemblie had no power to command, there was then no difference betwixt the decrees of the Senat, and that which they call *The authoritie*: for so it was that if there were lesse then foure hundred Senatours, by the decree of *Augustus*, (who were afterward brought to the number of fiftie) that they agreed vpon, was called an Authoritie, but not a Decree of the Senat. As also we may see by the law Cornelia, published at the request of a Tribune of the people: whereby it was forbidden the Senat any more to graunt priuileges or dispensations, except there were two hundred Senatours at the least present. Whereby it is to be gathered, that the Senat in such number had power to commaund: whereunto I say that a decree in the nature of it selfe carrieth with it no commaund, no more then the sentence of the judge, if the commission be not on foot. Now the Senat neuer iudged or determined, neither could giue out any commission or mandate; and therefore neuer had the power to commaund their decrees to be put in execution, without the power and authoritie of the magistrats still being of none effect. And yet whatsoeuer decree the Senat had made, and were it neuer so well by the power of the magistrat confirmed; was but annuall as *Dionysius Halicarnasseus* hath well written; and not perpetuall as *Conan* supposeth. *What authoritie was among the Romans.*

But how then (might some man say) did the Senat cause three hundred souldiours citisens of Rome, which remayned of the Legion that had sacked Rhegium in Sicilie where they were left in garrison, to be led away, and being stript and beaten, to be all afterward beheaded before the people, without any regard had vnto the opposition of the Tribunes, or appeales of the condemned, most miserably crying out, the sacred lawes to be therein broken and troden vnder foot. But herein question was of militarie discipline, which in that respect hath nothing common with domesticall lawes and customes. Beside that it was done but by the aduise of the Senat, the execution thereof being performed by the magistrats, who were not bound to obey the Senat, if they had not beene thereunto willing. Yea moreouer such was the crueltie and horriblenes of the villanie by the garrison souldiours committed at Rhegium, who themselues most cruelly rifled the citie, which they ought with their blood to haue defended against the assaults of the enemie: as that it caused all the ordinarie power of the lawes to cease: no punishment being thought sufficient to reuenge the same. Which cases when they chaunced, the tittles and querks of lawes were little at all regarded, especially in the midest of such a noise of weapons. But as oft as the Senat or Consuls attemp- *Martiall discipline respecteth not the common or domesticall lawes.*

A4 *For* Tiberius Graccus *read* Caius Graccus (Fr and L). Notes at B1, B9, C7.

attempted to infringe the soueraigntie of the people, or to breake the laws, as oft times they did the Tribunes, were straight waies readie to oppose themselues against them. For in that *Caius Cornelius* Tribune of the people, made a request vnto the people, that the Senat from that time forward, should not decree any thing against the libertie of the people, and the maiestie thereof: it sufficiently declareth the Senat oft times before contrarie vnto the law, to haue vsurped the rights of soueraigntie: howbeit therein is not to be respected what was done, but what of right ought to haue bene done. Howbeit it is manifest, that the Senat in the latter times thereof had power to make lawes: but then it had left off to be a Senat, and was then become rather an ordinarie court of judges. And yet the magistrats themselues, as the Prætors, the Ædiles, yea and the famous lawyers also made a great part of the Roman law, albeit that they had no power to commaund at all: but all this dependeth of the good liking of the prince or people, without whose authoritie and commaund, the force of the law, edict, or decree made, was nothing. Seeing then that the Senat in a Popular estate hath no ordinarie power to commaund, nor to do any thing but by sufferance; much lesse power shall it haue in an Aristocratique estate, or in a Monarchie: and so much the lesse in a Monarchie by how much kings are more ielouse of their estates, than are the people, and better know than they, how to defend their owne soueraigntie.

But whereas we said, It was not lawfull without the priuitie of the Senat, to propound any request vnto people, that indeed was so prouided by the law Popilia and Hortensia: yet was it lawfull alwaies without the priuitie of the Senat, to propound requests vnto the Comminaltie: and although that by the Consularie law Cornelia, it was also forbidden without the priuitie of the Senat, to propuund any request vnto the Comminaltie, yet was that law shortly after againe by the law Pompeia repealed and abrogated. Wherein many with great libertie abuse the words *Populi ac Plebis Romanæ*, (the People and Comminaltie of Rome) and especially the Greekes, and such as ignorant of the Roman antiquitie, interpret the Greeke writers.

That is also worth the noting, that albeit that the request which the magistrats were about to propound vnto the people, were disliked of the Senat, yet might they neuerthelesse lawfully moue the same vnto the people, after they had once made the Senat acquainted therewith. The same may serue also for an aunswere to that which *Iosephus* the histotiographer saith, That *Moyses* forbad the king to denie any thing concerning the publike, without the aduise of the Senat, and the high priest (howbeit that this article is not to be found in all the law) yet thereof it followeth not, that the king was thereby of necessitie bound to follow their aduise. For albeit that the Roman emperours terme themselues the principall Senators, or chiefe of their councell; yet such additions in nothing diminished their maiestie. Yea albeit that they called the Senators their companions, or good lords and maisters; as did *Tiberius*, who in the beginning of his raigne called the Senators, *Indulgentissimos dominos*, His most louing Lords, as we read in *Tacitus*. But how much princes gaue vnto the Senat, and the Senat vnto princes, *Plinie* the younger doth in two words (as it were) declare; where hee thus speaketh of a certaine decree of the Senat, *Voluntati tamen principis sui, cui in nulla re fas putaret repugnare, in hac quoque re obsequi*, but to obey the will of their prince, whereunto they thought it not lawfull in any thing to resist, euen so in this this thing also to show themselues obedient.

And further also, the Senators or Councellors of the estate, to speake properly are no where accounted either as officers or commissioners: neither in *this realme are they by any law, or edict, or charter of the kings made councellors, but only by a short briefe without any seale, signed with the kings hand, expressing in few words, that the king

Why the Romain emperours somtime called the Senators their companions, or good lords.

**Viz Fraunce.* *Senators neither officers nor commissioners.*

F2 they did, the Tribunes were decree *or* decide (*statueret* in L). G10 unto THE people H3 propound I2 *For* denie *read* K4 in this thing

king during his pleasure giueth them place and deliberatiue voice in his councell. But the king being dead, they must haue another such briefe for the holding of their places; except such as for their calling, or the charge they haue in the Commonweale, haue accesse and entrance into the councell.

Now if any man aske, Why a Senat in a well ordered Commonweale, should not haue also power to commaund? The principall reason is, for that if it should haue power to commaund also what it had in councell decreed, the soueraigntie should rest only in the councell: and so the councellors of the estate, in stead of councellors should therof become maisters, hauing the mannaging of the affaires, and power to dispose of all at their pleasure; a thing impossible to be done, without the impairing, or to say better the vtter subuersion of all soueraigntie and maiestie: which is so high and so sacred, as that it belongeth not vnto subiects, of what estate or condition soeuer, once to touch it either nie, or a farre off. Whereby it is to be vnderstood, them that giue commaund vnto a Senat, to go about the destruction of the Commonweale, and vtter ruine of the state. And for this cause the Great Councell of Venice (wherein the maiestie of their state consisteth) seeing the Decemuiri to take vpon them aboue that which was committed to their charge, forbad them vpon pain of high treason to commaund or determine of any thing concerning the state, nor so much as to write their definitiue letters; but to haue therein recourse vnto the Seignorie, vntill the Grand Councel were assembled. For which selfe same reason, and that moe of the citisens also might be partakers of that honour, hey haue decred, That the six councellors of estate, assistants vnto the duke, shall not be but two moneths in that so honourable a charge: to the end that the custome to commaund should not breed in them a desire still to continue the same, as also to aspire higher. Howbeit I am not of opinion so to haue the councellours of estate changed and rechanged; but rather to haue them perpetuall, as they were of antient time at Rome, Lacedemonia, and Pharsalia, and yet are in Polonia and Geneua. For the yearely chaunging which they made in Athens, and yet make in Venice, Rhagusium, Luques, Genes, Nuremberg, and diuers other townes of Germanie, doth not onely greatly obscure the glorie of the Senat, which ought to shine as the sunne, but also draweth after it the ineuitable daunger of disclosing and publishing of the secrets of the estate: ioining hereunto also, That the Senat, all new, cannot bee enformed of affaires passed, neither yet well continue the entertainment of the affaires present. Which for that it seemed vnto the Florentines a thing verie daungerous, they at the request of *Peter Soderin* their Gonfalonier (and a chiefe man in the reforming of their estate) decreed, That all the Senat of fourescore, should from six moneths to six moneths bee remoued; excepting such as had before bene Gonfaloniers or chiefe officers in the Commonweale, whome they appointed perpetuall Senators, of purpose to instruct the other new Senators in the affaires of state. The same order they of Genes are faine also to take in their mutable common Senat, wherein such as haue bene dukes and Syndics are perpetuall Senators. Wherein the Rhagusians are better prouided of their Senat than are the Venetians, whose example they seeme to haue followed in the forming of their Commonweale: For in Venice the Senat changeth euery yeare all at once: but in Rhaguse the Senators which are also but one yeare in charge, change still one after another, and not all in one yeare. But if the desire of honour bee so great, as that the citisens cannot otherwise be satisfied, except they all by turnes may haue place in the Senat, we must then imitat that which *Solon* did; who in the Popular estate of the Athenians by him framed, appointed a mutable Senat of foure hundred citisens euery yeare to be changed: but withall hee made a perpetuall priuie Councell of the Areopagits, to the intent, that that mutable Senat, and yearely change of all the other magistrats

278 THE THIRD BOOKE

magistrats might thereupon rest, as vpon a most fit me and sure stay. And thus hauing spoken of a Senat, order requireth that we should also speake of the Officers and Commissioners in a Commonweale.

CHAP. II.

¶ Of the Officers and Commissioners in a Commonweale.

AS in the whole bodie of the law concerning Commonweales, are contained many things right fruitfull and commodious: so also amongst the rest, the reasoning and discourse concerning publike persons, hath alwayes bene thought most profitable: and albeit that many things concerning magistrats are thought common and vsuall, yet lie the same for most part almost wrapped vp in obscuritie: For that they which haue thereof reasoned, do therein define nothing plainely. Wherefore I haue thought it best to begin this our discourse of their definitions. An Officer therefore is a publike person, who hath an ordinarie charge by law limitted vnto him. A Commissioner is a publike person, but with an extraordinarie charge limited vnto him, without law, by vertue of commissionely. Which definitions so by vs set downe, that they may become more plaine, it shall not be amisse to make a diuision of publike persons, euen from the first beginning of them. And first I call them publike persons, who are to attend vpon the publike affaires: of whome there are two sorts, one which hath power to commaund, whome they call Magistrats: and another sort which hath no such commaunding power, but is onely to vnderstand or to put in execution the commaundements of the others; and are yet all publike persons also. Howbeit for all that, all publike persons are not Officers, or Commissioners; as Archbishops, Bishops, and Ministers, are publike persons, and beneficed men rather than Officers: which we must not mingle together, considering that the one sort is established for matters diuine, and the other for worldly affaires, which ought not to be confounded. Ioyning hereunto also, that the establishing of them which are employed in diuine matters, dependeth not of the politike edicts or lawes, as the Officers do. Let vs then see the definitions by vs set downe, whether they be good or no, before we enter into the deuision of Officers, for that no man, either lawyer, or of them which haue before entreated of the state of Commonweales, hath truely told what an Officer, a Commissioner, or a Magistrat is: which for all that is a thing most necessarie to be vnderstood, seeing that the Officer is one of the most principall parts of a Commonweale, which cannot stand without Officers and Commissioners. But forasmuch as Commonweales were first serued by Commissioners, before they were serued by Magistrats or Officers (as wee will hereafter show) it is fit that we should first speake of Commissioners, and of the difference betwixt them and the Magistrats or Officers.

Aristotle saith, That a Magistrat is he that hath a deliberatiue voice in the Senat, and in iudgement, with power also to commaund. He also calleth the magistrat ἀρχὴν which is not proper but to them which are of power to commaund, and agreeth not vnto officers that serue, as Vshers, Sergeants, Trumpetors, Scribes and Notaries, whom he putteth into the ranke of Magistrats, and yet haue no power to commaund: so that this definition is in that respect too short. Besides that, it is a thing more absurd, that he should not be a Magistrat, which hath no entrance into the priuie councell, neither yet deliberatiue voyce, nor power to iudge: for if it were so, there should be but few magistrats in all Commonweales, considering that there are so few conncellors of the priuie

What an Officer is? what a Commissioner is?

A publique person who? Two sorts of publique persons.

Aristotle his definition of a Magistrat impugned.

G8–9 commission onely.   K3 ἀρχὴν   Notes at F8, G8.

A nie councell in well ordered Commonweales, and among them not one which hath deliberatiue voice, but by commission: and albeit that they had such voice, yet had they no commaund, as we haue before declared.

And as for the lawyers, there be but few of them which haue touched this string: and namely doctor *Iouean* confesseth, That it alwaies seemed vnto him an hard thing, rightly to define a Magistrat. And indeed in the definition of a Magistrat by him made he is deceiued: For he saith, That a Magistrat is he to whome the prince hath giuen any charge; in which sence and sort all Commissioners should be magistrats. But *D. Cuiacius*, beside the definition of *Aristotle*, promiseth to bring three others: A Magi-B strat (saith he) is a publike person, who hath preheminence in doing of iustice; or hee which sitteth in seate of iustice; or else he which hath iurisdiction and publike iudgement: so that by his account he appointeth foure definitions, with that of *Aristotle*. Which is directly against the Maximes of all Philosophie, and contrarie to the principles of Logike, that one should giue more than one definition to one thing: and is also impossible by nature. But if any say, That many descriptions may be giuen of one and the same thing, for that the accidents are manie which are in one thing: true it is, but an hundred descriptions cannot declare and make manifest the substance or nature of a thing: Which in the Art of reasoning is a great fault: but in the knowledge of the law much greater, and especially in the matter of Magistrats and officers, which is the entrance of the law, where the lawyers begin. For the principall marke C whereby a Magistrat is knowne, which is, To haue power to commaund; is in these three definitions wanting: and the magistrats lieutenants haue the hearing of causes, are presidents in iudgement, and sit in the seat of iustice, and yet for all that are no magistrats at all. The bishops also sit in publike iudgement, and seat of iustice, and haue the hearing of causes: For when *Lentulus* the Great Bishop, made relation vnto the Senat, of the decrees of the colledge of Bishops, and the law Clodia, concerning the consecration of *Ciceroes* house, thus he began his speech, *Pontifices religionis sunt iudices, legis Senatus*, The Bishops (said he) are judges of religion, and the Senat of law. So doe the Cadies, or Mahometane Bishops in the East; and yet for all that they are no magistrats, considering that they had or haue no power to commaund, nor to call men be-D fore them, to imprison them, or to put their owne iudgements in execution: neither haue they any sergeant or officer whome they can commaund, no more than haue the Cadies, or Paracadies in Turkie, or the auntient bishops of Rome; which is a thing worth the marking. And sometimes cleane contrarie, some haue authoritie and power to commaund, which haue no iurisdiction or hearing of the cause at all, as wee will hereafter shortly show. And that more is, the Commissioners of publike extraordinarie causes, in antient time deputed by the people of Rome, whom the law calleth *quæstores parricidij*, had (as at this present Commissioners appointed by the prince haue) power to heare the cause, to sit in iustice, to iudge, to commaund, to compell, and yet for all that were no magistrats. Which being so, none of the aforesaid definitions can bee good.
E Besides that there is another fault in them, for not hauing distinguished the magistrats from the other officers, nor made any difference betwixt an officer, & a commissioner; whereof a great confusion and medley of commissioners and officers must needs ensue. *Carolus Sigonius*, who seemeth more curiously to haue searched into the definition of a Magistrat, is yet therein many waies also deceiued: For he calleth all them magistrats which haue any publike charge of worldly affaires, without making of any difference betweene officers and commissioners, or betwixt the magistrats and other officers, which haue also publike charge; besides that he giueth power to al magistrats, to iudge, to commaund, and to put in execution, euen vnto the Aruspises. Howbeit as a defini-

Bb ij tion

Notes at A7, C5, E9.

tion ought not to extend farther, or lesse way, than doth the thing that is defined: so ought also the description of a magistrat in this our treatise of a Commonweale, to agree to all magistrats of all Commonweales indifferently.

Now in the definition by our selues proposed, we first said, all officers (whither they were magistrats, or magistrats seruants) to be publique persons: who in that differ from priuat men: for that priuat men haue nothing to doe with the affaires of the Common weale. We said also the Magistrats to haue an ordinarie charge, whereby to differ from Commissioners, who haue also publique charge, but yet extraordinarie, according to the occasions in the occurents of time presented: such as were in auntient time the Dictators, criminall Quæstors, and other judges extraordinarily by the people of Rome appointed, at the motion and request of the Magistrats. And last of all we said, their ordinarie charge to be to them by law limitted and bounded: for the erection of their publique ordinarie charges, erected by the name of offices, which otherwise should be no offices, if there were not for them an expresse edict or law. A thing alwaies obserued in the auntient Commonweales both of the Greeks and Latins; and now also better than euer: and to this end Princes cause their edicts to be published, in their soueraigne and inferiour courts: and in this realme of Fraunce, the charters of offices newly erected are sealed with greene wax, with labels of greene and red silke, and this style, *viz. To all men present and to come*, with a continuance perpetuall: whereas the letters pattents of commissions, are sealed with yellow wax, with a labell of plaine parchment, without any perpetuitie. And albeit that all Corporations and Colleges be graunted by the prince with a charge by law limitted for euer, as I haue said; yet so it is, that if the king will augment or increase the number of the corporation or colleges of judges, or other magistrats, yea or of the most base or vile officers: as of Sergeants, criers, trumpetours, land measurers, broakers, and such like, it must be done by publique edict, verified and inrolled: of examples whereof all the records of the courts of justice are full. But whereas we said the lawes concerning officers to be perpetuall, that is to be vnderstood of the perpetuitie of the offices, which continue for euer after they be once by edict erected, (what time soeuer it be that is prescribed vnto the officers themselues,) vntill that by contrarie edicts or lawes the same offices be againe put downe. Although the officer hold his place but for the space of eighteene moneths, as did of long the Censors their censorship, (which for al, that was at length prorogued for fiue yeares, for that so great an office could not in lesse time well be discharged,) or for a yeare: as did all the other offices in Rome, by the law Villia: or for six moneths, as did the Senators of Florence, after it was a popular estate: or for two moneths, as did the six Counsellours of the seignorie which are assistant vnto the duke of Venice: or for one day onely, as the Captaines of the two fortresses of the castle of Rhaguse, whose office is perpetuall, albeit that their commaund last but for one day. But howsoeuer it be that offices be erected with ordinarie and publique charge, it must still be done by law: not for that it is needfull to haue parchment to write it in, or greene waxe to seale it with, or yet magistrats to publish the edicts concerning the erection of such offices: for the writing, the seale, the verification, albeit that they giue credit vnto the lawes which are made, yet make they no lawes; no more than they doe other acts and contracts. But to the contrarie there were neuer lawes more strong or better kept, than those of the Lacedemonians, which *Lycurgus* forbad to be written, and were for that cause called Rhetes: for so he was persuaded that they should the rather remaine inuiolat and of long continuance, if they were once writ in the hearts of his citisens, and not in tables, in their mindes, and not in bookes. The Athenians in like case had a certeine forme of presenting their requests vnto the people, which if the people receiued

OF A COMMONWEALE.

A ceiued, it then passed into the force of a law: which they vsed to ingraue in brasse, and to fasten it vnto a pillar, lest any man should vnder the colour of ignorance excuse him selfe in transgressing the same. So when question was for the erecting of an hundred new Senators in Athens out of the two new Tribes of *Antigonus* and *Demetrius*, the law for the erection of them was published vnto the people: which was also done in the erection of all other offices as is to be seene in *Thucydides, Plutarch*, and *Demosthenes*. The like is to be said of the Roman magistrats: for the Consuls were created by the law Iunia: and the Tribunes of the people by the law Duillia: and when question was for the creating of one of the Consuls out of the people, it was done by the law Licinia. And afterward the Prætor for the administration of iustice in the citie was
B made by the law Sextia. And the foure Prætors for publique criminall causes, (beside the other before erected) by the lawes Cornelia and Bæbia. So may we also see of all the other Magistrats erected by the Emperours: that it was alwaies done by expresse Edict, wherein the time, the place, and their ordinarie charge are limited. As in all the first & twelft bookes of the Code, and in the Edicts of *Iustinian* it appeareth where euery magistrat hath his particular Edict.

Al offices in Rome erected by one or other expresse lawes

We haue put also into our definition of an Officer, that he must haue an ordinarie charge, for that the commaunds of the people of Rome granted by commissions and extraordinarie charges were aswell called by the name of Lawes, as were those that were made for ordinarie offices: the charge, the time, and place being still limited
C by commission: as a man may see by the commissions granted vnto the Dictators, which were sometime made by the decree of the people, as I haue before shewed. And also by the commission granted to *Pompee* for fiue yeares, therein to end the Pirats warre: with commaund ouer all the coasts and hauen townes of the Mediterranean Sea, all granted vnto him by the law Gabinia. As also by commission giuen him for the warre against king *Mithridates*, granted by the law Manilia. But forasmuch as these were not but extraordinarie charges, a man could not call them offices, which are still ordinarie and perpetuall. And for because those warres were in short time to be ended, it was not meete therfore to create a new magistrat, whose office and charge
D should be perpetuall, but onely extraordinarily to commit the care of that warre vnto a most sufficient Captaine and Generall: vnto whom fiue yeares time was limited at the request of *Catulus*: to the intent that *Pompee* in that time might end the warre, and not longer to protract it to be so alwaies in imployment: Or if the warre were sooner ended, that then his commission should end also. And all such extraordinary charges we call by the name of Commission. The Dictatorship was also a charge giuen by commission, and not an ordinarie power: for why, the Dictator was not but extraordinarily and without law nominated by the Interrex or Consul, some great matter so requiring: and for that all offices ceased the Dictator being created, his commission was limited but vnto six moneths at the most, and if he had soner dispatched the businesse for which he was appointed Dictator, his commission then also expired, and
E his authoritie ceased; as we haue by many examples before declared. And as a man may see by * *Æmilius Mamercus*, who chosen Dictator, and the same day hauing dispatched the businesse for which he was chosen, the verie next day following gaue vp his charge: showing therein how little he liked of long rule or authoritie. Howbeit such is the nature and power of all Commissions, as that according to the pleasure of him that hath the soueraigntie, they may be either reuoked or protoged. And albeit that commissions in Popular and Aristocratique Commonweales are almost still limited vnto a certaine time: yet in a Monarchie that extraordinarie and permissiue charge is tyed to no time at all: for why, in Popular and Aristocratique estates and gouern-

An officer alwaies hath an ordinary charge, and in that he differeth from a commissioner whose charge is alwaies extraordinarie.

* *Liuius lib. 9.*

Commissions to depend of the pleasure of him or them that haue the soueraigntie in the state.

Bb iij

D9 soner *i.e.* sooner   E2 (margin) lib. 9 (Fr 7) lib. 6 (F1 1–6, 8)

gouernments, the greater the charge is giuen by commission, the more need it is to haue it in short time expired; least longer power might giue occasion to ambitious minds to take vnto themselues the gouernment, and so to oppresse the libertie of the state. And therefore the dictatorship was but for six moneths, neither was that power euer longer proroged to any man in that free Commonweale, except to *Furius Camillus*. For at such time as the people of Rome had extraordinarily created the Decemuiri with a yearely and soueraigne power, for the reforming of their old lawes and customes, and the making of new and more commodious for the state: their commission which should not haue passed, a yeare being expired, was againe by the people for another yere proroged, with absolute and soueraigne power: and all other magistrats suspended during the time of their commission; vntill that out of the best lawes of other cities they had gathered the lawes of the twelue tables. Vpon which continuance of bearing rule, these Decemuiri tooke occasion to oppresse the libertie of the state, and to take vpon themselues the soueraigntie, had it not by force againe bene wrong out of their hands, and that not without the great trouble and turmoile of the citie. For which cause the people from thenceforth erected the offices of the Tribunes of the people, as defendors and keepers of their libertie; who alone of all the magistrats held their places after the creation of the dictator, all other magistrats and officers being for that time suspended. The Florentines did otherwise, who almost euerie sixt yeare extraordinarily created eight or ten Commissioners, with soueraigne power, and without limitation of time, for the ordering of their Commonweale, and the reforming of the abuses therein: who being once created, all other their magistrats ceased. By which meane these ambitious in effect tooke vpon themselues the gouernment, albeit that in outward appearance they made faire show of the giuing vp of their charge. For the suspending of all magistrats in generall, is a thing right dangerous, not onely in Popular and Aristocratike estates, but euen in a Monarchie also: which yet I neuer knew to haue happened in this kingdome of Fraunce, but at such time as king *Iohn* was taken prisoner by the Englishmen: For then *Charles* the fift hauing gotten of his father the gouernment of the kingdome, appointed fiftie commissioners for the reforming of the Commonweale, with power to examine the doings and abuses of all the other magistrats, from whome as then all power was taken. At which time the Commonweale destitute of gouernours, was by the seditious wonderfully disturbed: but more of these things in their place.

But the better and the more easily to vnderstand the difference betwixt an office and a commission, a man may in some sort say, that an office is a thing borrowed, which the owner cannot demaund againe before the time it was lent for bee expired: but a commission is a thing which one hath but by sufferance, end as it were by leaue, which the owner may againe demaund when he seeth good. And that is it for which *Tacitus* merily speaking of the raigne of *Galba*, which continued but three moneths, saith, *Precarium seni imperium, & breui transiturum*, The old mans empire was but by sufferance and in short time to passe away: not for that he had indeed his empire by sufferance, but for that he was now growne extreame old, and being vnfit for the gouernment of the empire, foresaw that in short time it must againe by naturall death bee taken from him, although he had not (as indeed he was) bene before slaine. Howbeit a Commission is of such nature, as that it expireth so soone as the charge thereof is executed, although it be not reuoked, or that the time was graunted longer for the execution therof, and yet neuerthelesse may be alwaies reuoked, whensoeuer it shall please him that graunted it, whether the matter for which it was graunted be yet entire or not, as wee haue before showed by the example of the Dictators. And to this purpose there is an
old

The greater the charge is that is giuen by commission the shorter time it ought to endure.

Large and long commissions daungerous to the state.

The difference betwixt an office and a commission.

F9 passed a yeare, being I7 and as it were I9-10 Precarium Note at H4.

A old decree of parliament yet extant in the records of the court of Paris, against the purseuants sent to Troy with the judges for the publike extraordinary causes, being indeed none of the bodie of the court, who (the commission expired) neuerthelesse yet bearing themselues as purseuants, were by the court commaunded to resigne vp their office, and a decree made them to be no officers at all.

I stand longer vpon this point, which although it may seeme easie vnto men of experience, yet vnto others it may seeme strange: yea two of the greatest orators of their time, namely *Demosthenes* and *Æschines* grounded the state of their orations and pleas vpon this point. For when *Ctesiphon* had presented a request vnto the people, That it would please them, that *Demosthenes* for his good deserts towards the Commonweale B (and namely for hauing most strongly fortified the walles and castles of the citie of Athens) might in the open theater be rewarded with a crowne of gold. *Æschines Demosthenes* his greatest enemie, opposed himselfe against the entertainment of the request, alleaging for the cause thereof, That by the law no man was to be rewarded, except he had first giuen an account vnto the people of his office well discharged, as all magistrats were bound to do. *Demosthenes* for that it concerned his owne honour and reputation, taking the matter in hand, made of all others a most excellent oration for *Ctesiphon*, or more truely to say, for the crowne he would haue had, alleaging, That the law spake not but of Magistrats; and that charge of repairing and fortifying of the wals and other fortresses, was no magistracie or office, but onely a simple commission; and C therefore in his vulgar tongue saith, τειχοποιόν, οὐκ ἄρχην εἶναι, ἀλλ᾽ ἐπιμέλειαν τινὰ καὶ διακονίαν. Which the Latines properly called *Curatio*, which is to say a Commission. Wherby it appeareth, that publike charge, for repairing of the walles, not to haue bene an ordinarie matter, but extraordinarie, for that there is not still need for to repaire them. Neither ought it to seeme strange, if *Demosthenes* well knew to distinguish and put a difference betwixt a commission and an office (as hauing bene of long time exercised in the publike affaires, and as it were in the middest of the Commonweale) both which *Aristotle* altogether confounded. The one of them also hauing alwaies mannaged the affaires of state; and the other as saith *Laertius*, neuer intermedling therein. And that is it for which *Nicholaus Grouchius*, and *Carolus Sigonius*, for not hauing vnD derstood the difference betwixt an office and a commission, haue so much troubled themselues with replies and reioynders, without any resolution at all, as men ignorant in the knowledge of matters of law and of state. All which shall I hope be well manifested, by that which shall be set downe in this booke.

To fortifie is no magistracie but a certaine charge and ministrie.

In the laws of *Charlemaigne* Commissioners were called *missi, a mittendo*; which signifieth sent; which the Germans call by an old word *Skaken*: whereof they called the court of judges, which were extraordinarily sent into the prouinces (& were indeed nothing else but Commissioners) *Scacarium*. But here perhaps may some man say, That the Commissioners of the castle of Paris, and judges of the court of Requests of the Pallace, are also officers: which being so, how could it then be, that an office and E a commission should not be also all one? Whereunto I answere, That of antient time those judges were but simple commissioners, with authoritie and power during pleasure who yet afterwards for the common good and profit were made perpetuall officers, with an ordinarie and perpetuall charge and power committed vnto them: their old and former name of commissioners, yet by abuse or for the honor of that court still remaining: whereby those judges of the court of Requests, are yet called the Commissioners of the Parliament; as judges appointed, and againe to be reuoked at the pleasure of the prince. Which judges of the court of Requests (for all that) cannot now be reuoked by the king himselfe, except they first bee by capitall iudgement condem-

Commissioners turned into iudges, and yet still knowne by the name of commissioners

---

A1-2 pursevants *i.e.* attendants, sergeants (cf. Fr)   A2 publike extraordinary causes *i.e.* the *Grands-Jours*   Notes at A7, C2, C7.

284　　　　　　　　The Third Booke

condemned, or willingly of themselues resigne their places: for so it was by the law of *Lewes* the eleuenth prouided. Not for that commission is incompatible with an office, most part of compassions being not directed but vnto magistrats or officers: but for that an officer in the qualitie of an officer, cannot be also a commissioner, for the self same charge limited vnto him by his office. For such commissions as they call Excitatiues, extraordinarily directed vnto officers for matters concerning the reuiuing the iurisdiction, or authoritie of their offices, are not properly commissions, if the time or the place be not by the commission altred; as to iudge according to the latter proceedings, and to leaue the former: for after that the time and order appointed by the law, is altered by the authoritie of the prince or magistrat, it is to be now determined by commission. Now the difference herein which the lawyers hold, is notahle, as, That if any officer haue iudged of a fact contained in his commission, in the qualitie of an officer, that his iudgement is naught: but yet that is to be vnderstood in a thing which concerneth not his office: For if there bee a concurrence of the commission Excitatiue, with the charge contained in the erection of his office, the ordinarie hearing of the cause is to be preferred before the commission, euen as the qualitie of the officer is to be preferred before the qualitie of the Commissioner; and the acts of the officers more assured than the acts of the Commissioners. And so in such concurrence of authoritie, if the officer commissionat also in a matter belonging to his owne charge, haue not declared in what qualitie he had the hearing of the cause: the act by him done shall be taken, as the act of an officer, to the intent it may be the more firme and sure. It is also manifest, extraordinarie commissions extenuating the power and authoritie of magistrats or officers to be odious, or at leastwise lesse gratious, if they bee not for the reforming and amending of the abuses and corruption of the officers. As they do in Venice, from fiue yeares to fiue yeares: And euerie yeare in Genes, where the Sindies are afterwards Commissioners, to heare the abuses committed by the magistrats & officers (which in auntient time in Athens was giuen to certaine ordinarie magistrats) as also at Rome by the law Bebia; when as before Quæstors or judges were by commission appointed by the people. That extraordinarie hearing of causes of the judges by commission, was also gratious; which *Vespasian* the emperour appointed for the hearing and determining of suits and controuersies, which in the time of the ciuill warres were growne infinitly, and for the deciding whereof the whole liues of all the magistrats would haue scarce sufficed. Commissions may also bee graunted for things concerning the greater part of officers, or a whole corporation or colledge, in which and like cases commissions are necessarie. And I remember that king *Charles* the ninth, hauing directed his letters patents, in the yeare 1570, for the generall reformation of the waters and forrests of Normandie, which drew after it question of the fairest of his demaine; from the hearing whereof the precedent and councellors of the parliament of Roan were forbidden: Which interiection although they left nothing vnattempted to haue letted, yet so it was, that in fine they agreed thereunto, after that I had againe and againe presented vnto them the kings commaunds, to that effect and purpose, and commenced suit not onely against the principall men of that prouinciall court, about matters concerning my commission, but also against the whole bodie and corporation of the citie of Roan, for the rights which they pretended against the king; and that, that was the cause for which I had obtained the interdiction.

But briefly, and yet more plainely and plentifully to make plaine all sorts of Commissioners, whether they be for the gouernment of prouinces, or for the warres; or for the administration of iustice, or for the kings receits and treasure, or other things concerning the state. We say, that the commissions come still from the soueraigne princes

Extraordinarie commissions extenuating the authoritie of the magistrate odious.

Diuers sortes of commissioners, and from whom they haue their commissions.

F3 *For* compassions *read* commissions.　　G1 notable　　H5 Sindics　　I9 *For* precedent *i.e.* president *read* presidents.　　I10 *For* interjection *probably read* interdiction (cf. K6).

Notes at F8, H5.

OF A COMMONWEALE.

prince, or from the magistrats, or from commissioners deputed by the soueraigne prince; for a fourth there is not. Againe Commissioners deputed, are either taken out of the number of magistrats and officers, or out of other priuat men. And if the commission be directed vnto the magistrats or officers, it is either for matter belonging vnto them by their office, or otherwise not belonging vnto them. And in what sort soeuer it be that commission be directed, whether it be to an officer, or a particular person, it is directed with power and authoritie to heare and proceed in the cause; either without appeale, or else with appeale reserued vnto the soueraigne prince, (if the commission came from him) or vnto the magistrats named in the commission; or els a commissioner is appointed by him whome the soueraigne hath deputed: as sometime commission is giuen out for the instruction of the affaires, or proceedings vnto the definitiue sentence exclusiuely to inclusiuely, sauing the execution thereof, if appeale bee made. Sometime also Commissioners are appointed by the magistrats to examine a fact, or the right of a matter, or both the one and the other together; sometimes without any power or commaund, and sometime with both.

This diuision extendeth to all Commissioners, in what forme of Commonweale soeuer it be. As is to be seene in the state of the Romans, where the mannaging of the warres, and gouernment of the countries and prouinces newly conquered, at the first belonged vnto the ordinarie magistrats and officers, viz. the Consuls, Prætors, and Quæstors, yea euen a good way from the citie, whilest that the Roman empire was yet contained within the bounds of Italie: But after that the bounds thereof were extended further, they then began to appoint Commissioners to gouerne their prouinces, in stead of their ordinarie magistrats, who although they were all by one name called *Potestates*, yet for all that they gouerned the prouinces in stead of Consuls, Prætors, and Quæstors: they were also called Proconsuls, Proprætors, Proquæstors, that is to say, Commissioners, or Lieutenant sent in stead of Consuls, Prætors, or Quæstors: As is in *Liuie* to be seene, who speaking of *Philo* the first Proconsull saith, *Actum cum Tribunis Plebis est, ad populum ferrent vt cum Philo Consulatu abijsset, pro consule rem gereret*, The tribunes of the people were dealt with, that they would moue it vnto the people, that when *Philo* was out of his consulship he might rule as proconsul. But after that the empire was growne great, and also extended farre, such commissions were by the sufferance of the people graunted by the Senat, to such as were lately gone out of their offices in the citie, who agreed among themselues for the gouernment of the prouinces; or if they could not so fall to agreement, cast lots for them, which they called *Comparare inter se, & sortiri*: Except the charge and commission were of such consequence and importance (by reason of some great warre alreadie risen, or like to arise in the prouince) as deserued to haue some valiant and great captaine without lot thereunto by the Senat appointed: Where if any partaking or factions chanced to arise about the matter, the people at the request of the Tribunes appointed one thereunto by commission. As it did *Scipio Africanus*, to whome the people gaue commission for the mannaging of the warres in Spaine and Affrike, and by that meanes drew *Hannibal* out of Italy, and discharged that country of a long and most dangerous war. The like commission was without lot extraordinarilie by the people also granted to *Paulus Æmylius*, to make warre against *Perseus* king of Macedon. And so also to the great captaine *Pompey* against the pirats, by the law Gabinia, and against king *Mithridates*, by the law Manilia: all they which the yeare before had borne office, beeing reiected, the people naming whome they pleased and best liked. Howbeit that this was no vsuall matter, but right seldome times done: For ordinarily the Consuls, Prætors, and Quæstors discharged, and so going out of their offices in the cities, cast lots for the prouin-

The gouernours of the prouinces in the Romaine empire nothing but commissioners

---

B2 or inclusiuely   B3 magistrats   C6 Lieutenants sent   D5 Comparare   E9 going out
E9 *For* cities *read* citie.

286 THE THIRD BOOKE

The cause of the ciuil war betwixt Silla and Marius.

prouinces, if they could not otherwise agree for the gouernment of them among themselues: and for that the charge of the warre against *Mithridates* by lot fell vnto *Cor. Sylla*, *Marius* by the working of *Pub. Sulpitius*, one of the Tribunes by him suborned, caused it to be by the people taken from him; and by extraordinarie commission giuen vnto himselfe: which was the cause of the most cruell and bloodie ciuill warre that euer was in Rome. So also was the prouince extraordinarily appointed vnto *Cato Vticensis*, against *Ptolomee* king of Cyprus; which by him vndertaken, *Clodius* boasted, That he had pluckt out *Catoes* tongue, which had alwaies before beene at libertie to speake against extraordinarie powers and commissions. Sometime also if the horriblenesse of some enormious fact required a more seuere triall, the matter was propounded vnto the people, who put it ouer by commission vnto the Senat; which out of the bodie of it selfe appointed some one or moe, not onely for instructions, but euen to heare and end the matter. As when *Lucius Tubullus* the Pretor, had with grieuous extortion most filthily polluted the Tribunall seat, and peruerted iustice; so that the people leauing the ordinarie course, and the magistrats to whom the hearing of the matter belonged, referred it wholly vnto the Senat by extraordinarie commission: the Senat forthwith deputed *Cn. Scipio* to iudge and end the cause. So also when *Tiberius* the emperor by comission appointed the Senate to enquire of the murthers committed betwixt the Nucerians & Neapolitans: the Senat deputed the Consuls to enquire thereof. Yea sometime the senat without commission from the people, but as it were by meere soueraignty appointed commissioners, if the case in question were committed in Italy, out of the territorie of the citie of Rome, as a thing belonging to the Senat, apart from all others; as saith *Polybius*: as it happened in a straunge robberie and murther, wherof *Cicero* speaketh in his booke *De Claris Oratoribus*; to the hearing whereof (hee saith) the Senat deputed the Consuls. By which examples here before produced, it appeareth

Whether commissioners appointed by the prince, or people hauing the soueraigntie, may appoint their Deputies and so commit the matter to others.

that Commissioners appointed by the prince, or people hauing the soueraigntie, whether they be magistrats or priuat men, may appoint their deputies, and so commit the matter to others, if it be not expresly forbidden them by their commission so to doe; or that question be of the estate it selfe in the commission: as the ambassadours or Commissioners which are to entreat of peace, or alliance, or other such like things cannot commit the same to others. As is also to be said if question be of the life, fame, or state of any man: wherein the manner and examination for better instructions may be deputed to others, but not the iudgement it selfe, except the judge before appointed by commission excuse his absence by sicknesse or some other lawfull cause. But *Iustinian* the emperour afterwards ordained better by forme of a perpetuall edict, That Commissioners appointed by the prince, should depute nothing of their commission to others more than the instructions of the suit: neither thought he that sufficient, but decreed also, that the Commissioners appointed by the prince should themselues heare the appeale, and instructions of the suit. But to meet with all that is to be met with, the most sure rule is to haue al that is commited, particularly in the commission, expressed, and so the commissioners to be ruled by the commission, as is the manner in all well established Commonweals.

Diuers waies whereby commissioners cease.

And albeit that a man might make many questions concerning commissions graunted, as well by the soueraigne prince, as by the magistrates, in time both of peace and warre: yet will I thereof touch but two or three, and those most necessarie to bee vnderstood of them which haue the managing of the affaires of state, whether it be in peace or warre. Wherefore leauing the rest, and to bee briefe: wee say that the commission ceaseth by the death of him that graunted the same, or by his reuoking of the commission: or in case that the commissioner during the time of the commission

OF A COMMONWEALE. 287

sion, obtaine some office or preferment equall to him that graunted the commission: for then one of them cannot commaund the other. But as for the expresse reuocation declared by the princes letters or edicts, concerneth as well them which are ignorant of such reuocation of their authoritie and commission, as them which know it. And albeit that the acts of a commissioner so reuoked, done after the reuocation of the commission, and yet before the knowledge of such a reuocation to him giuen, hold for good but in regard of particular men, towards whom the commissioner hath executed his commission; and especially, if they haue voluntarily yeelded vnto the commissioner, knowing the commission to be alreadie reuoked: and that towards others the acts of the commission after the reuocation of the commission, are of none effect by the rigour of the law, yet equitie and reason bindeth them thereunto, vntill that the commissioners or appointed iudges doe know that their commission is reuoked. For as a commissioner hath no power vntill he haue receiued his commission: so likewise the commission dureth, vntill the reuocation thereof be signified; or at leastwise vntill the commissioner know that it is reuoked. And therefore *Celsus* sayth, that the acts of the gouernour of a prouince are good and auaileable, if the commissioner know not that his commission is called in. And although Pope *Innocent* were of opinion, that it was otherwise to be iudged, if question were of life or honour, and was therein of many followed, yet he continued not in that opinion. And albeit that he was a pope & soueraigne prince, and a man most skilfull in both the lawes, yet willed he no greater authoritie to be giuen vnto his writings than to other mens, neither to rest thereon further than there were good and strong reason therefore. But to take away these antient difficulties, the secretaries to the state haue vsed to ioyne vnto commissions, and almost to all mandats and letters pattents this clause, *A die qua rescriptum significabitur*, From the day that the rescript shall be notified: which clause if it be omitted, yet is it alwayes necessarily to be vnderstood. And thus much concerning the expresse reuocation of a commission.

Whether the acts of a commissioner done after his commission reuoked, and yet before he had knowledg of the reuocation thereof, be good or not?

A good decree of Pope Innocent the fourth.

So also a Commission taketh end by the death of him that graunted it, bee hee prince or magistrat; prouided alwaies, that the thing committed bee yet whole and entire: for otherwise the commissioner may continue that which hee hath begun, so that it be done without fraud. But it is fraud in law, when a Commissioner not aduertised by a pursuant or expresse rescript (but by some other certaine meanes) of the death of the prince, the matter being yet whole, neuerthelesse proceedeth therein. Now the matter is not whole and entire, which cannot by the Commissioner bee left off without proiudice to the publike state, or to the right of priuat men: as in matter of iustice, if the parties haue contested, the thing is no more entire, but the Commissioners may and ought to go through with that they haue begun, whether it bee the prince or the magistrat that hath giuen them commission. And so in warre the matter is said not to be entire, if the battell stand ranged before the enemie, and that the retreat cannot without euident perill be made: in which case the generall is not to forbeare the giuing of battaile, although he be certainly enformed of the death of the prince; or that it be forbid him to ioyne battaile. So if rebellion arise, which cannot otherwise be appeased but by the execution of the authors thereof; that is first to bee done, and afterward knowledge thereof to be giuen, (as saith the lawyer) although the death or countermaund of the prince happen or come in the meane time. Yet the commissions comming from the prince, or letters mandatorie, are in that different from the other letters royall, which they call letters of iustice: for that these continue in their force and vertue, whereas the letters of commaund expire after the death of the prince. Yet neuerthelesse the new prince oftentimes ratifieth that which was done by the commaundement

Whether a commission alwaies taketh end by the death of him that graunted it?

D5 prejudice   E7 continue

dement of his predecessour, although he died, the matter yet whole and entire, and the rather if it be well and for his profit done; which the magistrats cannot do to the commissioners by them appointed, for that their ratifications in tearmes of iustice are neuer to be receiued. And thus much concerning all the sorts of Commissioners.

Whether the power of officers end together with the death of the prince?

Now, that we haue alreadie said of Commissioners, hath no place in officers, for that their power endeth not together with the death of the prince, although it bee in some sort holden in sufferance, and as it were suspended vntill they haue letters from the new prince, or confirmation from him for the continuance of their offices. And for this cause the parliament of Paris after the death of king *Lewes* the eleuenth, decreed that the officers should continue in their charge, as they had before done, vntil that they receiued commaund to the contrarie from the new king; following therein an auntient decree giuen in like case in the moneth of October, in the yeare 1380. Howbeit the court of Toulouse after the death of *Charles* the seuenth, otherwise decreed than had the parliament of Paris, viz. That all their iurisdiction should cease, vntill they had receiued new commaundement from the new king; and yet that if any occurrents should chance wherein the authoritie of the court should bee requisit, that then the court should proceed by letters and commissions, intituled *The people holding the Parliament royall of Toulouse*, firmed with the seale of the court, without any mention making of the king. But forasmuch as the king comming vnto his kingdome by right of succession, vseth his maiestie before he be consecrated; as it was iudged by a decree of the parliament of Paris, the nineteenth of Aprill, in the yeare 1398 (contrarie to the opinion of many) it belongeth not vnto any officers, parliament, or Senat, to doubt of the power or maiestie of the prince: which if it were not, neither were they to haue any authoritie or power: neither are in any other sort to proceed, but as officers vnto the king, and vnder his obeysance. But if it were lawfull for the people to make choice of their king, as it is in Polonia, Denmarke, and Hungarie; (where the kings beeing dead, the maiestie of the kingdome is to returne vnto the people) another thing were to bee said: For then the magistrats vse not the princes name in the vacancie of the kingdom (for that then there is no king) but euery one of them do their lawfull acts and duties, as if they had such power from the Senat and the people) by force of the law, and power proper vnto the magistrats: whereas Commissioners and judges extraordinarily appointed, can by no meanes (the prince being dead) hold their authoritie and power; for that they do nothing by the vertue of the law or of ordinarie power: and not for that commissions be odious, and offices gratious (as some haue thought) for oftentimes a commission is more gratious, yea and more profitable also vnto the Commonweal, than any officers ordinarie power. And as for the decree of the parliament of Paris (bearing date the sixteenth of October 1381) whereby it was ordained, that the kings edicts and commands should haue like power the king being dead, that they had whilest he yet liued; that is so to be vnderstood, if the charge committed bee then begun to be put in execution. And therefore if the power of the magistrats be annuall, and the king die before the magistrats yeare be expired, yet may the magistrat neuerthelesse hold his office for his yeare: or if it be perpetuall, continue the same in such sort and so long as the law giueth him leaue, for that his office dependeth not of a simple commaund which may still be reuoked, or of a charge which cannot be recommaunded, but is grounded vpon a law, receiued, published, verified, and registred: in such sort as that his office cannot be suppressed but by a contrarie edict or law. As when question was for the suppressing of the militarie Tribunes, (for the discord betwixt the Senat and the people, before created with the power of the Consuls) and in their steads to restore again the Consuls, it could not be done vntill that by the law Licinia, that power

Offices by lawe established, are not but by contrarie edicts or lawes to be put downe.

of

F4 much   G2 1380 (L) 1381 (Fr)   H1 *For* 1398 (Fr 7) *read* 1498 (Fr 1–6, 8 and L).   I1 people,
by   I8 *For* sixteenth *read* sixth.   Notes at G1, I4.

of the Tribunes was againe taken away. And in our time when as the fift and sixt president of the parliament of Paris were to be suppressed, they were not yet therefore displaced (for that against their wils they could not, except that for some capital crime they had bene before condemned) but an expresse edict was made, that after their death none should be more placed in their roomes, but so their offices to bee suppressed. So by a generall edict made by *Charles* the ninth, at the request of the estates of Orleans, in the yeare 1560, all offices erected after the death of king *Francis* his grandfather, were againe suppressed. And oft times it happeneth, that one officer is by one law made; but more often, that many are made at once: as when threescore sergeants were at once created by one edict of king *Francis* the first; and the criminall judges at once erected throughout the realme by an edict in the yeare 1527, when as before the same man was judge both of criminall and ciuill causes. Which course was so straitly obserued and kept in the kingdome of Fraunce, as that the verie clarkes of the clarke of the parliament, were by expresse edict made an office, though afterwards by another edict againe suppressed, at the instance of the chiefe clarke, in the yeare 1544: as were other small charges, which the Roman Commonweale were by the magistrats themselues commonly giuen vnto their seruants, without any law at all. Neither is it sufficient for the magistrats and other officers to be by the law created, but that their successours also haue a particular declaration, to testifie that they haue obtained their offices, and yet no need of any new edict or law. And for this cause the princes commissions directed vnto the officers in the quality of officers, continue in force to their successors: for that the prince therein maketh choice of the magistrat or officer, and not of the person: but if choice be made of any mans person, whose name is expressed in the commission, he being dead, his successour in the same office cannot execute the commission, for that the prince made choyce not of the magistrat but of the person.

Yet there are other differences also betwixt an officer and a commissioner: for that the power of an officer besides that it is ordinarie, it is also better authorised, and larger than is a commissioners, & that is it for which the Edicts and lawes leaue many things to the consciences and discretions of the Magistrats: who indifferently applie and interpret the lawes according to the occurrents & exigence of the causes presented: Whereas Commissioners are otherwise bound, and as it were tyed vnto the verie words of their commission, and especially where question is of the affaires of state: as in the charges and commissions of Embassadours or Commissioners deputed to negotiate betwixt princes, where the Commissioners may not without danger of their liues passe one point beyond the lesson they haue in writing, if this clause (which is oft times put vnto the charges and instructions of Embassadours and Commissioners to treat with princes) be not thereunto annexed, *viz.* That if any thing else be to be done, the Embassadour shall at his wisedome and discretion, according to the chaunge of places, times, and persons, haue care thereof: much like vnto that clause whereof *Æschines* the Orator speaketh in the oration which hee made for the defence of his legation; where he saith, that this clause put into the the commission of Embassadours, *viz.* That they should do whatsoeuer they saw to be for the common good; extended not vnto that they had in their expresse and particular charge: so that the aforesaid clause extendeth not vnto the principall obligations and resolutions of treaties, as to the making or breaking of peace, but onely vnto the accessories and matters of lesse importance. As if question be of any thing to be graunted vnto the enemies or friends, for the inlarging of their power to the hurt of the Commonweale, it is not lawfull for the Embassadours without speciall commaund to intreat thereof: For seeing that in the lesse affaires of priuat men, an Attourney or Proctor hauing a generall authoritie with

The power of an officer or magistrat larger, than the power of a commissioner.

full and entier power, may not yet for all that giue, acquite, or alienate any thing, or giue or take an oath of any person without a speciall charge; much lesse ought he so to doe in things touching the publique, and namely in things concerning the state: well may things done without commission, be confirmed, yet could they not of right without commission be so done. For albeit that in priuat matters he may say himselfe to haue well and duely executed his charge, which hath done it better than was to him inioyned, yet in publique affaires of the estate it is not alwaies so: for the Souldiour which hath assailed the enemie, or the Captaine which hath giuen battell contrarie to the Generals commaund, are both worthie of death, although they obtaine the victorie. For what could euer haue more honorablie beene done, or more worthie eternall praise, than was that which was done by *Fabius*, collonell of the horsemen vnder *Papyrius Cursor* the Dictator? who with the losse but of an hundred men onely, slew twentie thousand of the enemies; and yet for that he contrarie to the Dictators commaund had ioyned battell with the enemie, he was brought in question of his head, neither had so escaped, had not the Dictator (ouercome by the earnest intreating of the people) so rested contented. And therefore *Cæsar* in like case speaking of one of his captaines called *Syllanus*, said him to haue done well and wisely in not giuing of battell, although he were sure to haue caried away the victorie: for that said he it is not the dutie of a captaine, to do any thing that is by his Generall forbidden him. Yea so much it concerneth not to doe any thing that is forbidden in matters of warre, as that the Lieutenant generall to an other man, ought not to giue the enemie battell, except it be so expresly giuen him in charge: which was the cause that the Countie of *Aiguemond* was shrewdly shent of the Spaniards, for giuing battell vnto the Mareshall *de Termes* (although he therein tooke him prisoner and discomfited the French armie) for that he had hasarded the whole state of the low Countries, if he had lost the battell. But this latter point is to be vnderstood of such as be Lieutenants, or subiect to the commaund of others, who by vertue of their office haue not power to command. For an officer, as the Consull, or in his absence his Lieutenant; or with vs the Constable, the Marshall, or other Generall of the armie, placed as in title of office, to haue full and absolute commaund ouer the armie, and to mannage the warre, may by vertue of his office, and without attending any other speciall commaund, make warre vpon the denounced enemies, pursue them and giue them battell, besiege them, and take their fortresses and strong holdes, and dispose of the armie according to his discretion, if he haue not expresse commaundement to the contrarie from his soueraigne, and so his power suspended: yet hauing taken any strong places, or the enemies Generall, he may not without speciall commaund deliuer them, or yet make peace with the enemie. True it is that in popular estates these points are not, neither can bee so straitly kept, the generals thereof themselues doing almost all; which in a Monarchie depend of the will and pleasure of one onely prince: For why it is more easie to know the pleasure of the prince, than of the people; of one man, than of many thousands. As we may still see in *Liuie* large commissions by the people giuen vnto the generals of their warres; as in the warres against the Hetrusceans, all power was giuen vnto *Fabius*, *Omnium rerum arbitrium & a Senatu, & a populo, & a collega, Fabio Consuli Commissum*, The disposing of all things (saith he) was both of the Senat, and the people, and his fellow in office committed to *Fabius*. And in another place, *Initio liberum pacis ac belli arbitrium permissum*, At the beginning the free disposing of peace and warre was committed vnto him. And yet neuerthelesse they kept this difference betwixt them which had the mannaging of their warres by vertue of their office, and them which did the same by commission; as that the Consuls, Prætors, and others, hauing power

to

In matters of state he that goeth beyond his commission is worthely blamed, although that things fall out neuer so wel.

Larger commissions to be giuen to generals for the wars in popular commonweals than in Monarchies, and why?

H3 *shrewdly shent i.e.* severely reprimanded   K3-4 *For* Commissum *read* permissum (Fr and L).

to make warre by vertue of their office, might auow and iustifie their owne actions, without any other ratification, except they had taken vpon them some thing that concerned the soueraigntie of the people; whereas the Commissioners, if they therein passed their comission, must of necessitie haue their actions by the Senat or by the people ratified. As *Pompey* hauing had commission for the mannaging of the warre against king *Mithridate*, passing farther made warre also against diuers other nations and people, at his pleasure bestowing the kingdomes, estates, and towns by him conquered and wonne: and albeit that the people would infringe or reuoke nothing of that hee had done, yet neuerthelesse after his triumph, he oftentimes requested the Senat, that those his doings might by it be ratified: and finding the Senat to make thereof difficultie, and to vse therein long delayes; he to strengthen and backe himselfe against his enemies, and such as were about to looke into his doings, ioined himselfe in friendship and alliance with *Cæsar*, so to make themselues both of them the stronger. For albeit that hee had a generall commission, and that in that case all was at his discretion: and therefore (as some thinke) needed no ratification: yet is it not so, the generall clauses of commissions being alwaies to be interpreted and ruled to the best good and profit of the Commonweale, not in any thing giuing power to doe that is hurtfull vnto the publike state; which is not a thing lawful or permitted euen vnto a priuat man to do, hauing a charge in generall teatmes committed vnto him. Wherefore these words expressed in commissions, be they Gouernors, Captaines, Iudges, or ambassadors (for things to be done) *At their discretion according to their wisedome*; or at *their will and pleasure*: and others such like, are still to be so interpreted and vnderstood, as euerie good and wise man would interpret and vnderstand them, still respecting the good and profit of the Commonweale: wherein if any fault be committed, account thereof is to be giuen; the least fault that can be, being still in matters of state, and publike interest to be enquired after: no excuse of errour, or ignorance, being therein to be admitted or accepted. And much the lesse, if he which hath taken vppon him such publike charge had it not laid vpon him, but was by him sought for: neither offered vnto him, but by force by him extorted. For if priuat mens faults, when they haue taken vpon them the charge to do any thing one of them for another (although it bee of their owne accord) be not excusable; how should they then be excused in matters concerning the state and Commonweale.

Generall clauses in commissions for things to be done according to the descriptiō of the commissioners how they are to be vnderstood?

But to the intent that the force of Commissions and offices may the better bee vnderstood, it shall not be amisse to produce the examples of the auntient Romans, and to compare their manner of speech in the making of them, with that of ours. As in that which *Festus Pompeius* saith, *Cum imperio esse dicebatur apud antiquos, cui nominatim a populo dabatur imperium*, He was said of the auntients to haue power, to whome by name power was by the people giuen: which is asmuch as to say, by expresse commission, without appeale vnto any other magistrat, vnto whome so authorised the law gaue power to command: For that a magistracie or office cannot be wishout power to commaund. So we see in *Liuie*, at such time as *Hannibal* besieged Rome, *Placuit omnes qui Dictatores, Consules, Censoresue fuissent cum imperio esse, donec recessisset hostis a muris*, that is to say, A decree was made (or commission giuen) that all such as had bene Dictators, Consuls, or Censors, should haue power and authoritie to command, vntill the enemie were departed from the walles. So *Cicero* speaking of *Augustus Cæsar* saith, *Demus imperium Cæsari, sine quo res militaris geri nō potest*, Let vs giue (saith he) power and authoritie vnto *Cæsar*, without which militarie affaires cannot be mannaged. For why, *Octauianus* yet but yong, could by the law neither beare office, nor lead the armie, much lesse without power and authoritie take vpon him a generals charge:

How the auntient Romaines gaue extraordinarie power vnto their generals by commission.

charge: and therefore *Cicero* perswaded, That the charge for the mannaging of the warre should with power by commission be giuen vnto him: which place of *Cicero* hath much troubled both *Sigonius* and *Grachius*. For had *Octauianus* bene either Consul or Prætor, *Cicero* would not haue vsed these words, for that he should then by law haue had the power and commaund of a magistrat.

<small>The manner of propounding of requests vnto the people for the creating of magistrates and commissioners in auntient time diuers.</small>

Beside this, there was also a notable difference betwixt the manner of propounding the request for the creating of a magistrat, and of a Commissioner: For the magistrat was vsually created by vertue of the lawes before made; the magistrat thus asking the people, *Quos vellent Consules fieri*, Whome they would to be made Consuls? and so of the other magistracies and offices being vacant. But for commissions of command, they vsed these words, *Vellent iuberent vt huic vel illi imperium esset in hac vel illa prouincia*, If they willed and commaunded that this or that man should haue the gouernment in this or that prouince. As is reported of *Scipio Africanus*, who had commission with power to commaund, although he were not yet of age to beare office, or to be a magistrat. And *Cicero* speaking of all sorts of commissions saith, *Omnes Potestates, Imperia, curationes, ab vniuerso populo proficisci conuenit*, It beseemeth al potestats, commaunds, and commissions, to come from the bodie of the whole people. Where by the word *Potestates*, he vnderstandeth the gouernours of princes, who were properly so called. And by the word *Imperia*, Captains, who had particular commission to mannage the warres (howbeit that the word *Imperia*, is vnderstood also of the ciuill magistrats) with power to commaund. By the word *Curationes*, is meant all other charges, without power to commaund. The word *Imperator*, signifieth properly a generall or chiefe captaine, as *Plinie* speaking of *Pompey*, *Toties Imperator antequam miles*, So often a generall before he was a souldior. But generally the word *Curatio*, importeth all sorts of commissions; as is easily to be gathered by this place of *Cicero*, *Idem transfero in magistratus, Curationes, Sacerdotia*: The same I transferre into magistracies, Commissions, and Priesthoods; which are the three sorts of publike charges. *Vlpian* the lawyer also well distinguisheth a magistrat from him whome he calleth *Curator republicæ*, of whome he hath made an expresse booke: whome the law calleth by a Greeke word λογιϛὴν; who had no power to condemne, nor to appoint any fine, which was lawfull for all magistrats to do as we haue before showed.

<small>How commissions passe into the nature of offices.</small>

But it is to be noted, that al commissions passe into the nature of offices, as oft as that is by law made an ordinarie charge, which was before done by commission, as we haue by the examples of our owne Commonweale before declared. And that which was before giuen at the pleasure of the magistrats, becommeth also an office, if he that hath the soueraigntie doth by law establish the same. As in auntient time the Consuls, as it were by commission made choice of the six Colonels, whome they called *Tribunos militum*, vntill that about 642 yeares after the foundation of the citie of Rome, it was by an expresse law (made at the request of the Tribunes of the people) set downe and decreed, That from that time forward it should bee an ordinarie office, and the people to haue the choice of them: which was euer after obserued, except some such great warre were in hand, as that it was thought needfull, that extraordinarie choice should be made of those Colonels by commission: As in the Macedonian warre against king *Perseus, Licinius* and *Cassius* the Consuls, made a motion vnto the people, That the Tribunes, or Collonels of the souldiors, might for that yeare bee chosen by the Consuls, as indeed they were. So likewise in auntient time also, the Consuls, Prætors, and other great magistrats made choice of their slaues and seruants for their vshers, secretaries, sargeants, Trumpetors, and such like; as they did also in this realme, vntill the time of *Philip* the Faire, who was the first that tooke this power from the bailiefs and seneschals

---

G8 *For* governours of princes *read* governours of provinces.   H8 also   I8 *For* six Colonels *Bodin writes* sixteen Colonels (Fr only).   I9 *For* 642 (Fr 7) *read* 442 (Fr 1-6, 8 and L 1, 3-5; but 441 in L 2).
Notes at F3, H2.

schals, and yet leauing vnto the lords justices, power to establish sergeants and notaries in the prouinces of their iurisdiction and territorie. And in like case the kings atturney generall, in the time of our fathers, made choice of such aduocats as hee thought best for the pleading of the kings causes; who are now as ordinarie officers created by the prince himselfe, the particular commission before giuen vnto the atturney generall, being conuerted into the forme of a most honourable office. And thus much in generall concerning Commissioners and officers: it followeth now that wee should also speake of Magistrats, and of such other things as are vnto euerie one of them properly belonging.

Chap. III.

¶ Of Magistrats.

Magistrat is a publike officer, which hath power to commaund in a Commonweale. And an Officer we said to bee a kind of publike person, who hath an ordinarie charge by law appointed vnto him. But a Commissioner wee said to bee a publike person also, with a publike, but an extraordinary charge, at the pleasure of the prince. Now orderly proceeding required that wee should before speake of Commissioners, then of officers; for that they were before any lawyers or Officers established. For right certaine it is, the first Commonweales were by soueraigne power gouerned without law, the princes word, becke, and will, seruing in stead of all lawes, who both in time of peace and war, by commissions gaue out charge to whome they pleased; and againe at their pleasure reuoked the same, all depending of their full and absolute power, being themselues not bound to any lawes or customes at all. And that is it for which *Pomponius* writeth, the Roman Commonweale to haue bene at the first gouerned by regall power, without vse of any law. And *Iosephus* the historiographer, in his second booke against *Appian*, desirous to show the most honourable antiquitie of the Hebrewes, and of their lawes, saith, That *Moyses* of all others was the first that euer writ lawes. And that in fiue hundred yeares after, the word Law was neuer heard of. Alleaging in proofe thereof, That *Homer* in so many books as were by him written, neuer vseth this word νόμος or Law: a good argument that the first Commonweals vsed not but Commissioners, considering that an officer cannot be established without an expresse law (as we haue said) to giue him his ordinarie charge, and limited to a certaine time: a thing seeming to diminish from the power of soueraigntie. For which cause kings and princes (ielous of their state and greatnesse) haue vsually annexed vnto all their letters pattents of office, an auntient clause retaining the marke of lordly Monarchy, *viz. That the officer should enioy his office so long as it stood with the princes pleasure.* Whereby it appeareth the officers power to depend of the princes power, rather than of order. And albeit that this clause be to no purpose in the kingdome of Fraunce, for that by a law by *Lewes* the eleuenth established, ordinary offices and charges by the prince once lawfully bestowed, cannot from them on whom they are so bestowed be againe taken, except they haue committed some criminall cause worthy of death; and that in Spayne, England, Denmarke, Sweden, Germanie, Polonia, and all Italie the like order be obserued: yet for all that, the Secretaries of estate neuer forget the same: a great argument that all charges and offices were of auntient time in the nature of commissions; which whither it bee profitable vnto Commonweales or not, shall in due place be hereafter declared. But let vs before speake of the Magistrat which whaue before defined

What a magistrate is.

The first commonweales gouerned without lawes.

Moses the first that euer writ lawes.

Cc iij

fined to be a common or publique officer with power to commaund.

Al magistrates to be officers but not al officers to be magistrats.

Al magistrates to haue power to commaund.

Now there is no lesse difference amongst writers betwixt the officer and magistrate, then there is betwixt the officer and commissioner. For albeit that euery Magistrat be an officer, yet euery officer is not a magistrat; but onely they bee Magistrats which haue power to commaund, which their greeke names ἄρχαι, and ἄρχοντες well declare; as who should say Commaunders, and the latine word *Magistratus*, which is asmuch as to say masters and commaunders. And for that the Dictator was he which had the greatest power to commaund, the auntient writers called him *Magister populi*, the word Dictator signifying a Commaunder; as who should say, saying the word, and it was done: for that *edicere* is as much as to commaund, which is proper vnto Magistrats: for that edicts are the Magistrats commaunds. Howbeit that many herein deceiue themselues, who supposing the bookes written in latin in the name of *Mar Varro* to be his, say that the Dictator is so called, *quasi dictus ab interrege*, as so called of the *Interrex*: But by the same reason the Collonell of the horsemen might be also called a Dictator; for that he was then also so appointed by the Dictator, as is to be seene through all the historie of *Liuie*, and should rather be called *Dictatus*, as a man appointed; in the signification passiue, than *Dictator* in the actiue. Wherefore *Dionysius Halycarnasseus Varro* his domesticall friend better saith, the Dictator to haue beene so called as an *Edictator*, that is to say, a soueraigne commaunder, and was therefore called *Populi magister*, or the Master of the people.

Aristotle by the author impugned.

Now we haue before declared the definition of a Magistrat by the yonger lawiers, and by *Aristotle* himselfe set downe, to be in no wise to be allowed or maintained: who call none but him a Magistrat which hath a deliberatiue voice in iudgement, and in the priuie counsell, with power to commaund; and principally saith hee to commaund: for in his sixt booke *de Republica*, seeing the number of officers to be infinite, whom he calleth all ἀρχάς, a name proper vnto Magistrats hauing commaund in the Common weale: he findeth himselfe therein much entangled, for that he seeth others also besides them necessarie for the ornament and glorie of the Commonweale: and then after them all the Magistrats ministers, as Sargeants, Vshers, Secretaries, Notaries, all whom he calleth by the common name of Magistrats: euen as he doth them which haue power to commaund: and so passing on further, saith, such ministers to haue also power to commaund, τῆς ἀρχῆς μετέχοντας. And yet for all that in an other place* he maketh question, whether that the Iudges and Orators are to be called Magistrats: whereunto he aunswereth, that a man may say them tô be no magistrats, hauing no part of the commaund of the Commonweale; And therefore *Cato Vticensis* chastising the Registers, Comptrollers, and Receiuers, you ought (saith he) to remember your vocation, and that you are but ministers, and not Magistrats, as *Plutarke* reporteth. As for Preachers and Orators whom he calleth ἐγκλησιαστάς, if so it be that they haue no commaund or ordinarie power, it is right certein that they are no magistrats at all: but yet often times they are also Magistrats, I meane such as in Popular and Aristocratique estates and Commonweales haue power to perswade or disswade the people, to or from such things as they thought to be for them vnprofitable or disprofitable, whom they called Rhetoras. Howbeit that in Athens euery particular man, (so that he were fiftie yeres old) had of himselfe power to speake; and the rest by the magistrats leaue: whereas in Rome it was not lawfull for any man to deliuer any speech vnto the people, but by the leaue of the chiefe Magistrat in the assemblie. And as for the doubt that he maketh of Iudges, as whether they be Magistrats or not, the resolution is easie, if we will graunt the diuision of judges set downe by *Iustinian* the emperour to be good: which is, that some of them be Magistrats, and some of them

* Initio lib. 3. Politic.

be

G3 *For* quasi *Bodin writes* quia (Fr).   Notes at G1, I7.

be not. We must therefore now confesse, that amongst them which haue publique and ordinarie charge; that is to say, of Officers, some of them are Magistrats, (*viz.* such as haue power to commaund) and some of them not, (as hauing no such commaunding power) but seruing onely as the magistrats ministers: which diuision seemeth vnto vs necessarie for the auoyding of such businesse as might arise of a diuision of it selfe imperfect. Wherefore we haue said that such publique persons as haue an ordinarie charge limited vnto them by lawes, or by edicts, without any commaund at all, to be simple officers, whom the Emperours of latter times often times in their lawes call *officiales*, being indeed but ministers vnto the magistrats. The auntient Doctors of the law haue for most part followed the opinion of *Accursius*, who set downe neither any definition nor distinction of Officers; nor of Commissioners, nor of Magistrats; but simply saith, That there are foure sorts of Magistrats, *viz.* them whom they called *Illustres*, the *Spectabiles*, the *Clarissimos*, and the *Perfectissimos*, to whom he giueth all commaund. All which are rather honorable qualities and titles attributed vnto the magistrats and Officers, according to the conditions of their persons. Howbeit that in this diuision of them also according to their titles and qualities, he hath left out the *Patricij*, who were of greater reputation and dignitie than the rest: as also the *Augustales*, who were superiours vnto the *Clarissimos*: for why *Iustinian* the emperour appointeth these degrees of honour, the *Patricij*, *Illustres*, *Spectabiles*, *Clarissimi, siue Speciosi*, and the *Perfectissimi*, all which honors and titles were giuen aswell vnto priuate men as vnto magistrats. But as for that which *Bartholus* saith, That there are some which haue honour without charge; as Counties and Marquises, vnto whom for all that he attributeth power to commaund, and the administration of iustice, it deserueth not aunswer; for that he therein is most manifestly contrarie vnto himselfe. So also is there small probabilitie in that he saith, Scholmasters as magistrats to haue iurisdiction ouer their schollers, and power to establish lawes and ordinances: for so domesticall power and the discipline of families should be also altogether confounded with the publique iurisdiction, which we haue before shewed to be a thing impossible. *Alexander Imolensis* the greatest lawier of his time, hath touched much neerer the true definition of a Magistrate: in that he saith, None to be Magistrats but they which are ordinarie judges; And yet is not this enough: for why they are such magistrats as haue power to commaund, and yet haue not any ordinarie iurisdiction: as the Censors, and the Tribunes of the people. And so to the contrarie some there be (which being no magistrats) haue an ordinarie iurisdiction, but without any commaunding power, without Pursiuant or Sargeant, as had in auncient time, and now also in euery place the Bishops, who haue the hearing and determining of all sacred and religious things, and yet were neuerthelesse no magistrats. The Bishops saith *Lentulus* are judges of Religion, and the Senat are judges of the law. So one may see neither the auntient nor late writers to haue handled this point, or yet so much as touched the difficulties or differences of Officers, Magistrats, and Commissioners, as the matter well deserued. And albeit that the true definitions of Magistrats, officers, and commissioners be not to be found in the papers and writings of Lawyers, yet are the same to be gathered from them, and from the discourse of good histories. For *Vlpian* writeth it to be lawfull for all magistrats, excepting the Duumuiri, by inflicting of iudiciall pains to defend their iurisdiction: which extendeth not onely vnto the imposing of fines vpon the offendors, but euen to the attaching of their goods and bodies, and casting of them into prison. And yet it appeareth (may some say) that *Vlpian* hauing excepted these Duumuiri (who were in like power that the Sherifes were in townes without any iurisdiction at all) yet neuerthelesse accounteth them in the number of Magistrats,

Which officers be also magistrats.

Acursius and Bartholus censured.

and seemeth also to say, these Duumuiri to haue also had iurisdiction: For otherwise in vaine were they excepted, if they had not such authoritie and power. And yet the same lawyer in another place saith, these Duumuiri to haue had no iurisdiction nor the hearing of any causes whatsoeuer, but were onely to receiue needfull cautions, and to deliuer possession: which sauoured more (as saith he) of power than of iurisdiction. And yet in this case (saith he) they were but simply the Prætors deputies, who in their absence gaue them this commission, for preuenting of the daunger which might in the meane time happen, if men of necessitie must be driuen to runne still vnto the Prætors: who in like case also afterwards gaue them power to appoint tutors vnto the poorer sort of orphanes for the preseruation of their goods. Whereby it is euident them to haue had no iurisdiction or power by vertue of their owne magistracie, but onely part of the Prætors iurisdiction, and that also by leaue and sufferance. But they which haue nothing but such deputed or precarie iurisdiction, can of right call nothing thereof their owne: Wherefore whether the power of the Duumuiri consisted onely in hauing power to commaund, or in iurisdiction, it was vndoubtedly but by leaue and sufferance: whereby it is to be vnderstood, these Duumuiri not properly to haue bene at all magistrats. But they which haue power to commaund, together with iurisdiction, may call men before them, attache them, and with penall iudgement defend their iurisdiction, & also put their iudgements in execution: wheras they which haue power onely to command without any iurisdiction, may well cause a man to be apprehended, but not proceed further. And in that some are deceiued, who for that by the old law Alteria Tarpeia power was giuen to all magistrats, to impose fines vnto the summe of threescore six shillings, therefore suppose all magistrats to haue had iudiciall power also. For if the fine were by the magistrat imposed for publike iudgement sake (as by a Tribune of the people,) it was lawfull for the partie that was so fined either to pay the fine, without further examination of the matter, or to appeale vnto the people, and so to trie the cause of his fine, as is in *Liuie* oft times to bee seene: which was done by the law Icilia. For why the fine of it selfe inflicted not any infamie vpon the partie so fined, but for the publike crimes sake: as the punishment of beating with staues impaired not any mans reputation, but the cause wherefore he was so beaten. But if a fine were set vpon him that had not obeyed the magistrat sending for him, or for not aunswering being asked, or for any other cause, not impairing his credit; it was lawfull for the magistrat by taking of distresse to exact the fine, without appeale: For that by the law Tarpeia, there was a certaine stint and measure for fines appointed and set downe vnto the magistrat, that so the disobedient citisens might without any trouble of the state be kept in order, and their insolencie restrained.

<small>The auntient fynes that the Romaine magistrats were to impose vpon offenders.</small>

Now the least fine vpon any man to be imposed, was one sheepe; and the greatest two oxen, or thirtie sheepe: which for that according to the diuersitie of the cattell it made the penaltie either lighter or heauier, and for that they could hardly be brought and looked vnto in the citie, a sheepe was valued at ten asses, and an oxe at an hundred, that is to say, at so many pound of brasse. But afterward the riches and territorie of the Romans encreasing, extraordinatie and greater fines were imposed, if greater cause so required. As *Liuie* writeth of *Fuluius*, who for that hee being Prætor and generall against the enemie, the Roman armie was put to flight, and he the Prætor reported to be the first that fled; the Tribunes of the people fined him at thirtie thousand peeces of brasse, when as before the greatest fine was but two oxen, or thirtie sheepe: howbeit that the fine was oftentimes forgiuen, for that the sentence of the people condemning a man vnto a fine, carried alwaies with it the note of infamie.

And for that we are by way of discourse drawne thus farre, wee will here amend an

errour

F7 preventing of   H1–2 Ateria Tarpeia (cf. 298 F1)   Notes at H1, H9.

Of A Commonweale. 297

errour in *Aulus Gellius* (about this matter) not as yet corrected. For hee in his *Noctes* — Aulus Gellius a-
Atticae, speaking hereof, writeth, The greatest fine to haue bene of thirtie oxen, or two mended.
sheepe; in stead of thirtie sheepe, or two oxen: and thereof gathereth, that as then there
were moe oxen than sheepe in Italie, and that it was thereof called Italie: the word
ἰταλὸς with the Greekes, and with *Varro* signifying an oxe. But *Dionysius Halicarnasseus*, *Varro* his domesticall friend, writeth, That by the law Tarpeia, it was permitted to
all magistrats, to impose fines: and yet a measure thereof to haue bene by the law appointed, viz. That the fine should not exceed two oxen, or thirtie sheepe at the most.
In like errour offendeth *Festus Pompeius*, and in the same words with *A. Gellius*; so that
the one of them seemeth to haue bene deceiued by the leading and authoritie of the
other. Both of them also writ, a sheepe in auntient time to haue bene called *Ouis*, in
the masculine gender, which yet you shall no where find; although wee see *Boues* for
oxen, to be oft times vsed in the feminine gender: But it may bee that they mistooke
Duos Oues, that is, Two Sheepe, for *Duos Boues*, which is, Two Oxen. And least any
man should thinke me to attribute more to *Dionysius Halycarnasseus* a Grecian, than to
Au. Gellius, or to *Festus*, both citisens of Rome, they themselues are of themselues refuted: For both of them confesse, the least fine to be imposed, to haue bene a fine of
one sheepe; and the greatest, of thirtie oxen, or two sheepe: whereas (if they would
haue agreed with themselues) they should haue said, the least fine to haue beene of one
oxe. Neither do we as yet see whome we may preferre in the searching out of the Roman antiquities, before this *Dionysius Halicarnasseus*, excepting *Varro*, whose domesticall
and familiar friend this man was, out of whome he had many good things: For as for
the books which are in his name carried about in the Latine tongue, as wel the foolish-
nesse thereof declare them to be none of *Varroes*, as for that in them it is read, many
things to be in them spoken by contraries. But *Au. Gellius* writeth, *Varro* in his one &
twentieth booke *Rerum Humanarum*, to call *Mulctam* a Sabine word: but the latter
Grammarians to take it to be so called by the contrarie: whereby it is cleere those
bookes not to haue bene *Varroes*. Yet these things which we haue written concerning
the estimation of the cattell exacted for a fine, are confirmed by the authoritie of *Demetrius Phalerius*: For he writeth, a dramme of siluer to haue bene appointed by *Solons* laws, for a reward to him that had killed a shee wolfe; but fiue drammes vnto him
that had killed an hee wolfe: for that a shee wolfe easily killeth a sheepe; but that the
he wolfe being stronger, killeth an oxe. Whereby it is manifest, oxen to haue beene
thrice as cheape in the countrey about Athens, as in Italie. For ten Asses, or the Roman Denarius ouer-weigheth the Greeke dramme. And in the same place in *Au.
Gellius* there is another more notable fault, where he saith, *Mulctam, quae suprema dicitur, in singulos dies institutam fuisse*, The fine which is called the greatest, to haue
bene imposed euerie day: where the word *dies*, or daies, is to bee put out; for the
meaning of the law was, that the greater fine might be exacted of euerie citisen in particular, if so be that many of them had in the same fault offended: for otherwise it had
not bene lawfull for the magistrat the same day to impose diuers fines, if many had offended: whereof the impunitie of offences, and contempt of the magistrat should ensue. For proofe hereof let that example of *Au. Gellius* serue, *Marco Terentio quando
neque citatus respondit, neq; excusatus est, ego ei ouem mulctam dico*, Forasmuch as *Mar.
Terentius*, being summoned, aunswered not, neither made his excuse, I set the fine of a
sheepe vpon him. Another errour also there is in *Festus*, where he writeth *T. Menenius Lanatus*, & *Sestius Capitolinus* the Consuls, to haue made the law concerning fines:
for it is a thing not heard of, lawes to haue bene made by the Consuls: and as for that
law it was made in the yeare 297, after the building of the citie: in which yeare *Sp. Tarpeius*,

C10 dramme *i.e.* drachma   D9 exacted   E2 offences   Notes at C3, C4.

The auntient manner of fynes imposed vpon offenders in Rome in Cattel, conuerted into fynes in money.

peius, and *Au. Aterius* were chosen Consuls: but true it is, that about six yeares after *T. Menenius*, and *Pub. Sestius Capitolinus*, being Consuls, made a request vnto the people, That the fine before imposed in cattell, might be conuerted into money, valuing euerie sheepe at ten Asses, and euerie oxe at an hundred. But whereas *Dionysius* writeth it to haue bene lawfull onely for the Consuls to impose a fine, ought not to seeme strange; for that at such time as the law was made, there was neither Prætor nor Ædile in Rome, the first Prætor being there made 386 yeares after the foundation of the citie. And *Cicero* hauing as he thought best, made lawes for his Commonweale, which he to the imitation of *Plato* had conceited, amongst the rest made one, whereby he giueth vnto all magistrats iurisdiction and diuination. But they which thinke the same to haue bene the verie Roman lawes which we see in *Cicero*, are much deceiued; as we will hereafter show, all magistrats not to haue had also iurisdiction, which yet seemed vnto *Cicero* both good and profitable. And yet the magistrat that hath iurisdiction (to

Power to commaund still annexed to iurisdiction.

speake properly) whether it be that he haue it in his owne right, or from others, hath also (saith a certaine lawyer) all such things as without which he cannot exercise that his iurisdiction; that is to say, power to commaund: which is still said to be annexed vnto iurisdiction, and without which iurisdiction is but vaine and to no purpose. Whereof it followeth, that the iurisdiction of the auntient bishops, and of our bishops also, without power to commaund, was not properly a iurisdiction, but onely a simple hearing and vnderstanding of matters. For that which *Lucullus* the bishop said in the Senat, The bishops to haue bene the judges of religion, and the Senat of the law, tendeth to that end, and is so to be vnderstood, as that when question is of religion, credit is to bee giuen vnto them, as is vnto other men skilfull in their professions and trades; or as vnto judges appointed either for the bare examination of the fact, who are properly called *Recuperatores* (or as we terme them Delegates:) or for the vnderstanding of that is iust and right, who more truely are arbitrators by law appointed, and not by the agreement of the parties, and yet are often called judges. And therefore wee see the Vestall Virgins (in *Liuie*) which had polluted their virginitie, to haue beene alwaies chastised and punished by the Prætors of the citie, but neuer by the bishops. And so when *Publius Clodius* was about to haue committed adulterie with *Pompeia Cæsars* wife, in the temple of the goddesse *Bona Dea*, the full Senat had the determining of the matter, concerning the religion and sacrifices by him polluted. So in the beginning of the Christian religion, the Christian bishops (as *Augustine*, *Nicephorus*, and *Iustinian* do witnes) had not so much as the least iurisdiction of any matter, or the examination of the priestes themselues: howbeit that *Iustinian* graunted to them the examination of them that were of their owne order and calling. Neither would our auncestors haue any part of commaunding power to be giuen vnto bishops, and that the court of the parliament of Paris, hath oftentimes by the decrees and ordinances thereof witnessed. But why then (might some man say) do we see consistories, prisons, examinations, and fines to be permitted vnto bishops? What other thing else do all these things declare, but a meere commaunding power? Yea *Philip* the Faire, and king *Lewes* his sonne, granted vnto the bishop of Paris power to apprehend and arrest men offending in his Diocesse. Howbeit I suppose those former things to belong rather to their vocation, than to their power to commaund; for that the execution thereof belongeth vnto magistrats: and yet such power of staying and apprehending graunted to the bishop of Paris was by a decree of the Senat forthwith againe from him taken. And although that not long since *Henrie* the second had graunted vnto all bishops the power to stay and apprehend men for heresie and impietie: yet neuerthelesse was that law shortly after againe abrogated. Yea the bishops themselues do in their owne decrees professe

them-

K3 vocation *i.e.* power to summon

Notes at F9, G10.

OF A COMMONWEALE.

themselues to haue no power for the execution of any thing: yet is it with vs permitted vnto them, to stay and apprehend offendours, within the boundes of their consistories and courts; so that they go no farther.

And when as fines contrarie vnto the lawes were by the Bishops vpon men imposed, the Parliament of Paris receiued euery mans free appeal from them: yea and afterwards power was taken from them also, for calling of men before them; which they call, A liuely summoning or Citation. For there is an old decree yet extant, whereby the Bishop of Paris was grieuously fined, for that he had vsed such calling of men before him. But when as the Bishops vnder the colour of ministring of oathes, and of the contempt of Religion, had with vs drawne vnto themselues the hearing almost of all matters, (for *Alexander Immolensis* was of opinion, the power of administring an oath to be sufficient to giue vnto the Bishops iurisdiction also) the greater Courts forbad them vnder the colour of ministring an oath, to take vnto them the hearing of any matter. And at length it was forbid them also to haue the hearing of the causes concerning the possession of benefices: and so after much, long, and hard sute, prouided for by the decree of *Martin* the fift Bishop of Rome; which decree is yet extant in the publique records. Yea the Spaniards truely, the most earnest defendours of the See of Rome, would not that their Bishops should haue to doe with any publique or priuat iudgements: except it were for Religion and Church matters, of which opinion I see *Felinus* (a man skilfull in both the lawes, and a most subtill interpretor of the Popes decrees) to haue beene. And albeit that certain ambitious decrees do giue vnto the Bishop of Rome more authoritie and power than to all other princes and people: yet pope *Innocentius* the fourth, and euery other good expounder of the law, haue long since reiected these decrees: with all such others as haue preferred the bishop of Rome before the Councell of other Bishops and Princes. And *Bartholus* himselfe when he had fearfully written, The subiects not to be guilty of treason, which for the honor and welfare of the Bishop of Rome had taken vp armes against their prince; craued pardon for that his errour. Trulie in mine opinion it were better and more profitable also for the Commonweal, commaunding power to be giuen vnto Bishops together with so great iurisdiction as they haue: or else that their iurisdiction, to be restrained vnto the hearing of matters of religion onely; as we see the auntient Romans, the Swissers, them of Geneua, and the Germans to haue done. And yet the censuring of manners is of necessitie to be giuen vnto the Bishops: which beeing once taken away, I see not what course would be taken for the punishment of secret wickednes & villanie, whereof we will in place conuenient hereafter speake. Howbeit for all that, the imposing of fines is not to be permitted vnto bishops, or yet commaunding power to bee giuen them: For why should the magistrat be enforced to put into execution the vniust sentence of the bishop? for it is vtterly forbidden magistrats to enter into examination of the bishops proceedings: except appeale be made as from the bishop abusing his power, vnto the more higher courts; which with vs is seldome done, for the heauines of the penaltie, if it shall be found the appeal to haue bene made without iust cause: for so the interpretors of both the lawes determine the acts of magistrats which haue taken vpon them the determining of things belonging vnto the bishops, to be of none effect: as also if such things chaunce to be discided in the bishops consistorie as belong vnto the magistrat, they confesse them to be to no purpose. So that if a Priest be conuicted of incest, or of forgerie, before the magistrat, and confesse the same, in the bishops consistorie no regard is had of such his confession made: for so it is in the Popes decree expressed. But when this case had happened, wherein the Popes Legat called before himselfe the acts and things done before the magistrat, & disannulled the same: appeal

The authoritie of the bishop of Rome not to be preferred before the authoritie of other princes.

was made vnto the parliament of Paris, where I remember it was long time doubted, whether the euident proofes wherupon the priest was before the magistrat conuicted, ought to be void or not; for of the rest of the acts it was lesse doubted: wherein the court at last iudged, That it was in the Councell to be discided. And againe when the like case was in question before the criminall iudges, I my selfe being present, the same court delayed againe the cause, and referred it vnto the Councell: least it should haue seemed either to abrogate the ambitious decrees of the Pope, or to giue vnto the wicked licence to offend. For what could be more absurd, than to suffer a priest by the law Cornelia conuicted of forgerie, and by witnesses published, by retracting the cause, to reiect the witnesses; and so when as no moe could iustifie the matter, freely and without punishment to commit villanie euen in the middest of the Commonweale? Our auncestours neuer handled the publique iudgements of priests, with diuided examinations: But the Court of Paris, although it often times by iust decrees either quite abrogated, or with equitie tempered the Popes decrees and ordinances, yet neuer more iustly than in this case: which when it had often times beene delayed, at length by a law made at Molines, that decree of the Popes law was with vs taken away. So by little and little are the Popse lawes to be cut short and abolished. For at first in the beginning of the Christian Church, the authoritie of Bishops was shut vp within verie strait bounds, which *Iustinian* would haue to extend farther by this law by him made. *Si quis aduersus Clericos, Monachos, Diaconos, Asceterias, actionem habeat Episcopus iudex esto: sententiam vero episcoporum magistratus exequitor*: If any man haue any sute against Clarkes, Monkes, Deacons, or other the religious persons, let the Bishop be the judge, but let the Magistrats haue the execution of the bishops sentence: but the words of the law following, do giue leaue vnto the magistrat to examine the bishops sentence, except there bee an other judge by the prince appointed.

Whether the ciuill magistrat be to put the Bishops sentence into execution, before he vnderstand of the equitie therof or not?

Which words haue troubled many, doubting whether they ought to put in execution the bishops commaund or not, before they haue vnderstood of the equitie of the sentence. Now if no appeal be made from the sentence, most are of opinion, That it is without farther examination of the magistrat, to bee put in execution: but if appeal be made, that then enquirie is to be made of the equitie of the appeal, which yet some denie to be lawfull. Yet in mine opinion, if question be of the thing it selfe, or of the matter of the iudgement, and that the iudgement be not giuen contrarie to the Popes decrees, that then the magistrat ought not farther to enquire of the cause. But if the bishop shall by his sentence go about manifestly to infringe the popes lawes, whether the errour be in the matter it selfe, or in the forme of the iudgement; that then the magistrat may farther enquire of the sentence; that is, in case he abuse the popes authoritie and decrees. The magistrat may also farther examine the sentence, if the bishop shall in iudgement giue sentence contrarie to the lawes of the kingdome, although he seeme to haue grounded the same vpon the popes decrees: as indeed many of their decrees are quite contrarie vnto the positiue lawes of Commonweales: in which case, the magistrat shall not suffer the lawes of the kingdome to be infringed by the Popes authoritie. In all other cases it is ment that the magistrat should faithfully put the bishops sentence in execution: and so with vs we vse. The same law, and like maner of proceeding the Easterne people vse also: with whom their Bishops haue the bare hearing of matters, and the magistrats the execution: for which cause the bishops haue neither sargeants nor pursiuants, the chiefe tokens and marks of authoritie and magistracie.

The positiue laws of a kingdome not to be infringed by the Popes authoritie.

But yet question might be made whether all magistrates haue iurisdiction and power to commaund or not? for that *M. Messala* the lawier, and *M. Varro* haue left in writing, That some magistrats had power to call men before them, and also to lay hands

---

F9 witnesses published *i.e.* public attestations, testimony (*testificari* in L).   G6 Molines *i.e.* Moulins   G7 Popes   F10 For iustifie *probably read* testifie   K3 it is meet that (cf. L)

Note at F9.

hands vpon them: othersome had power also onely to lay hands vpon men: and other which had power to doe neither the one nor the other: and that they which had power onely to lay hands vpon men, had also onely a Sargean, and nothing else: and that they which had power to doe both, had both Sargeants and mase-bearers: whereas they which had neither power to call men before them, neither to lay hands vpon them, had neither sargeants nor mase bearers. When I say power to lay hands vpon men, my meaning is to haue power to seise vpon the bodie or goods of men; for by our customes many hauing prædiall iurisdiction, (or as we tearme them mannours) may lay hand vpon mens lands, but not vpon their bodies: which was not by the auntient Roman lawes permitted; of whom it is needfull here to speake, and in briefe to declare their power, the more manifestly to show the power of all sorts of Magistrats, in euery kind of Commonweale. For the great magistrats, that is to say, the Consuls, Prætors, and Censors; and amongst the commissioners, the Dictator, and he whom they called the Interrex; then also the Proconsuls, the Proprætors, and in generall all the Lieutenants & Gouernours of countries, had power to call before them not onely the priuat citisens particularly, but euen the lesser magistrats also: excepting the Tribunes of the people, whose bodies (for that they were most sacred) it was not lawfull to violate. Neither might these aforesaid magistrats onely summon and apprehend men, but it was lawfull for them also to punish and imprison them, and in briefe to pluck downe and raze their houses and pallaces, who refused to obey these magistrats commaunding them. But the Tribunes of the people had no power to call men before them, yet had they authoritie to commaund any citisen to prison, yea euen the Consuls themselues. So *L. Drusus* Tribune of the people cast in prison *Philip* the Consull, for that he had interrupted him as he was speaking vnto the people: which then by the law was death. Beside that it was also lawfull for them to oppose theselues not only against all the magistrats, and the whole bodie of the Senat, but the opposition euen of one of the Tribunes was of power to stay all the proceeding of the rest of the Tribunes his fellowes in office: On which great power they presuming and bearing themselues, doubted not contrarie vnto the law to call men before them, and to take vpon them authoritie and iurisdiction. Which thing *Labeo* the lawier gaue them well to vnderstand, who being by one of them summoned, refused to make his apparance before him, openly protesting for defence of himself, That the Tribunes were not ordained or appointed for the administration of justice, or to haue iurisdiction, but onely to oppose themselues against the violence and abuse of other magistrats, and to giue ayde and succour vnto such as appealed being vniustly oppressed, and to imprison them which would not yeeld and giue place to their opposition. So the Tribune *Sempronius*, seeing that the Censor *Appius* would not giue vp his office, after that he had bene eighteene moneths Censor, (according to the law Æmylia, which had brought the tearme of fiue yeares before prefixed to the Censor, vnto the tearme of eighteene moneths) told him that he would thrust him into prison, if he obeyed not that law (which he did by consent of six others of the Tribunes his fellowes in office) but *Appius* hauing practised with three other of the tribunes to oppose themselues against the commaundement of the other seauen, by that meanes held still his office: for why, the opposition of one onely of the Tribunes suffised to stay the proceedings of all the rest, if order were not otherwise taken by the people, by taking from him his power and office; as by the request of *Tiberius Gracchus*, it was taken from *Marcus Octauius* the Tribune, opposing himselfe against the law Agraria, that it might not take place. And this is it for which a Tribune of the people, speaking to the nobilitie said, *Faxo ne iuuet vox ista* VETO, *qua Collegas nostros concinnentes tam læti auditis*, I will make

(say

The power of the Consuls and other the great magistrats in Rome.

The power of the Tribunes of the people in Rome.

(said he) that this word VETO shall not helpe, wherewith you so merrie heare our fellowes in office singing in accord together. And but a little after, *Contemni iam Tribunos Plebis, quippe quæ potestas iam suam ipsa vim frangit intercedendo, non posse æquo iure agi, vbi imperium penes illos, penes se auxilium tantum sit, nisi imperio communicato, nunquam Plebem in parte pari Reipublicæ esse*, The Tribunes of the people (he said) now to be contemned, as whose power did now of it selfe breake the strength of it selfe, by opposing of it self against it self, that things could not be there indifferently ordered, where the commaunding power was with the nobilitie: and onely the power of giuing help with the Tribunes. And that the people could neuer haue like part in the Commonweale, except the power to command were made common vnto both. The Tribunes complained the people to haue no magistrats which had power to commaund: the Tribunes (they said) to haue power to oppose themselues, and to yeeld the people releese, but yet to haue no power to commaund; neither that the comminaltie could be made equall with the nobilitie, except the offices and power to commaund were made common vnto both: and therfore they made request, That the Consuls might be chosen as well out of the comminaltie, as out of the nobilitie: which when it could not be obtained of the nobilitie, it was agreed, certaine Tribunes of the souldiours with the power of Consuls, to be indifferently chosen out of both sorts: which manner of gouernment continued fortie fiue yeares, without any Consull, vntill such time as that it was agreed, That one of the Consuls should be still chosen out of the people. Howbeit a man might say, That the Tribunes in so saying made their power lesse than indeed it was, they hauing power to oppose themselues, and to commaund men to prison; which is a part of power. For so *Vlpian* speaking properly and as a lawyer, saith, That it is not lawfull without leaue and commission from the magistrat, to call into iudgement the Consuls, Pretors, or Proconsuls, or generally any of them saith hee, *Qui imperium habent, & iubere possunt in carcerem duci*, which haue power and can commaund men to be laid in prison. And so wee conclude, that they which haue power to commit men to prison, although they haue no iurisdiction, are in right magistrats, as the Tribunes in Rome, the kings atturneyes in Fraunce, and the three Auogadours at Venice. Neither do I in that agree with *Plutarch*, who saith in his Problems, That the Tribunes were no magistrats, for that they had neither mase-bearer nor seat of Iuorie, the true markes (as he saith) of magistracie: for why, they had sergeants, the token of their commaund; as *M. Messala* affirmeth. And lesse is it to the purpose, that hee alleageth of *Appius* the Consull: of whom, contending with one of the Tribunes in the assemblie of the people, *Liuie* thus writeth, *Tribunus viatorem mittit ad Consulem, Consul Lictorem ad Tribunum, priuatum esse clamitans, sine imperio, sine magistratu*, The Tribune sent a sergeant vnto the Consull, and the Consull sent a Lictor vnto him again, crying out, That he was but a priuat man, without power, without magistracie: For so the Consull said but to impaire the power of the Tribunes. Which for all that was so great, as that *Licinius Stolo* one of the Tribunes, was so bold, as by force to constrain *Manlius* the Dictator to depose himselfe of his Dictatorship. Another of them also committed both the Consuls to prison, for that they would not at the request of the Tribunes discharge ten souldiours from going to the warres. Yet true it is, that the power of the ten Tribunes of the people was shut vp and contained within the walles of Rome. And therefore *Mar. Fabius*, and *Luc. Valerius* the Consuls, seeing that they could not leuie their souldiours, for that the Tribunes opposed themselues against them, commaunded their chaires to be carried out of the citie, and so did there what they saw good. Yet oftentimes the Tribunes tooke vpon them more than belonged to their place, or than was by law permitted them, oftentimes propounding their edicts

The power of the tribunes shut vp within the wals of Rome.

Note at I 4.

A edicts and prohibitions. Whereof *Liuie* speaking saith, *Communiter edicunt Tribuni ne quis Consulem faceret: si quis fecisset se id suffragium non obseruaturos*, The Tribunes generally forbad any man to giue his voyce to the making of a Consul, but if any man so did, that they would haue no regard of any such voice giuen. Which was but an abuse, and presumption vpon the power of the people, to forbid them the free and entire choice of their magistrats: ouer whome in generall, albeit that no man could commaund, yet did the Tribunes so do ouer euerie one of them in particular, although they could by no right so doe. Moreouer they tooke vpon them the administration of iustice, to all such as came vnto them, as is if they had had power to call men before them: as it is to be seene in *Plutarch*, where hee saith, That the Tribunes

B administred iustice in the place which was called *Basilica Porta*. And *Æsconius Padianus* saith, *Tribunos, Quæstores, Triumuiros, Capitales non in sellis Curulibus sed in subsellijs iura dixisse*, The Tribunes, the Questors, and Triumuiri, iudges of criminall causes, to haue administred iustice not in Iuorie chaires, (as the manner of the great Roman magistrats was) but vpon their benches. And *Appian* also saith, *Liuius Drusus* the Tribune, to haue bene most diligent in the administration of iustice, and doing of right to euerie man. *Pomponius* also reckoneth the Tribunes of the people amongst the Consuls, Pretors, and other magistrats which administred iustice vnto the citisens and strangers in Rome. Wherefore *Cicero* saith them to haue bene called Tribunes of the people, for that they might examine the wrong done by the Pretors: which what man-

C ner of examination should it haue bene, if they had wanted iurisdiction? Yea they had not onely taken vpon themselues iurisdiction, but appointed also commissioners: and in many causes made them whome they called *Ædiles ædituos*, their deputies or Lieutenants; which they could not haue done, had they not had authoritie and iurisdiction: For why, that authoritie thou thy selfe hast not, thou canst not giue vnto another. Howbeit yet all this their presumption was but vsurpation and abuse; as *Labeo* the lawyer well shewed them, who being sent for by them, would neuer (as we said) come before them.

The same opinion we are to haue of those officers or magistrats whome they called *Ædules Curules*, who had neither power to call men before them, neither to attache

D any mans bodie; and therefore neither had mase-bearer nor sergeant, (as *Marcus Varro* and *Messalla* haue noted) and yet by the sufferance of the Pretors vsurped a great part of their authoritie and iurisdiction. Which the Pretors of the citie oppressed with the multitude of causes easily suffered, at the first committing vnto them causes concerning the sale or alienating of things mouable: who afterward tooke vpon them to haue to do with lands and things immouable also: and after that drew vnto them also the hearing of courtisans and common harlots causes, who might by no meanes set vp that base and filthie trade of life, but that they must first openly professe the same before the Ædiles, and that they would prostitute themselues. Which the auntients did, to the intent that such women as reason could not keepe within the bounds of modestie,

E should yet for shame of such publike profession (of so lewd a life before the magistrat) be restrained. But after that in latter times many euen of the most noble dames in Rome (hauing together with their chastitie also lost their modestie) ashamed not right impudently to make such open profession before the Ædiles, That they would prostitute themselues. The emperour *Tiberius* tooke order, that from thenceforth the magistrats should proceed against them by way of iustice: & at the same time also to represse the presumption and encroaching of the Ædiles and others, by decree appointed vnto what summe, and what causes, their authoritie was to extend: which yet they had not by their auntient institution, and much lesse to call particular men before them, or to

The power of the Ædiles.

com-

commit them, although they had power to call a generall assembly of the common people.

The power of the Questors.

As for the Questors, I see not that they euer had, or yet tooke vpon them to haue had any iurisdiction or power to commit men: for so *Varro* saith, that they had not: albeit that the yeare after their office expired, they had sometime the gouernment of some prouince bestowed vpon them: as *Gracchus* the younger after his Questorship had the gouernment of Sardinia giuen vnto him. From which time they had as much and more power in the gouernment of the prouinces committed vnto them, than had all the magistrats in Rome: but that was not by way of commission, as had all the rest of the gouernours of prouinces.

The power of the Censors.

As concerning Censors, *Fr. Ottoman*, and *Carolus Sigonius* (both of them most skilfull antiquaries) say, That they had well as they writ, *Potestatem, sed non Imperium*, (that is to say) power, but not commaund a thing altogether impossible: for that the word *Potestas* (or power) in termes of law, or in the person of a magistrat, importeth alwayes with it power to commaund. And namely *Vlpian*, where he saith, That the gouernour of a prouince had almost ample iurisdiction and power of life and death, calleth it properly by the name of *Potestas*. And wee oftentimes in antiquities read, the Censors Edicts, that is to say, their commaundements and lawes. *Varro* also and *Messala* call the Consuls, Censors, and Pretors, *Maiores Magistratus* (that is to say) greater Officers; and the rest, *Minores*, or lesser. And saith moreouer, That it was not in the power of the Pretors (who yet had both iurisdiction and commaund) to assemble the armie of the citie, which the Censors might, *Praetori exercitum vrbanum conuocare non licere: Consuli, Censori, Interregi, Dictatori licere*, He said it not to be lawfull for the Pretor to call together the armie of the citie; but yet to be lawful for the Consull, the Censor, the Interrex and the Dictator so to do. And at such time as *Hannibal* besieged Rome, there was an edict made, That all such as had bene Dictators, Consuls, or Censors, should haue a commaunding power, vntill such time as that the enemie had raised his siege. *Placuit* (saith *Liuie*) *omnes qui antea Dictatores, Consules, Censoresue fuissent, cum imperio esse donec hostis a muris discessisset*. Which they would not haue done if the Censors had not had a commaunding power, whilest they yet were in their office; especially seeing that they which had bene Pretors, had no such power giuen them. Besides that, if the Tribunes (whom *Varro* putteth in the number of the lesser magistrats) had power to command, why should not then the Censors so haue, whome he calleth the Greater Magistrats? Yea that more is, *Plutarch* giueth more authoritie and power vnto the Censors, than to any other of the Roman magistrats: yet attribute I not so much vnto his writings, but that I see him being a Grecian, to be oftentimes deceiued in the antiquities of the Romans. Wherefore that is it which hath deceiued many, that the Censors although they had power, yet had they no iurisdiction: albeit that *Onophrius* writ, That the Censors in some cases, and for some crimes had power to condemne men: but what those cases or crimes were, hee sheweth not. For either they must haue bene publike crimes, or priuat crimes: of priuat crimes the Pretor of the citie iudged, but of publike crimes the Pretor of the publike iudgements, and Triumuiri of criminall and capital causes determined. True it is, that the Censors were controllers of the peoples manners: but there is great difference betwixt the iudging of criminall causes, and the reprehending of mens manners and behauiours. And therefore *Cicero* said, The Censors iudgement, no farther to touch the partie by them condemned, than to make him blush. And that therefore, as all that the Censors iudgement concerned onely a mans name and credit, so it was called an ignominie or discredit, but not an infamie. For why, he saith not, That the Censors touched any mans honour, to the intent

Plutarch noted.

OF A COMMONWEALE.

tent to note it with infamie, but rather with a certaine ignominie, or kind of disgrace, which many haue rashly abused for infamie; howbeit that there is great difference betwixt infamie & ignominie. *Carolus Sigonius* hath therein erred defining ignominie to be an infamie: and in the same place saith, That there are certaine capital causes, which draw infamie with them, and yet without crime, contrarie to the principles of the law: Whereby we are taught, that he which is by publike iudgement for any crime condemned, is thereby become infamous: And that the souldiour for his fault worthily by his captaine cassired, was thereby become ignominious, but not infamous, vntill that by the Pretors expresse edict he were so declared. The auntient doctors of the law haue called Ignominie, the infamie of a fact done: Whereof *Cassius* the lawyer saith, That he thinketh that a Senator put out of the Senat, can neither bee judge, nor beare witnesse, vntill he be againe restored: howbeit he doth say, That hee doth but thinke so. Which phrase of speech *Vlpian* also vseth, when as he saith, *Se putare ei quæ in adulterio deprehensa est & absoluta: notam obesse*, That he did thinke, that vnto her that was taken in adulterie and acquited, yet the note thereof was a blemish. For certaine it is, that he which is by iudgement acquited, is safe from the infamie of the law, but yet not from the ignominie of the fact. And *Calistratus* saith, That hee did also thinke the honour and reputation of a man to be impaired, *Quando quis ordine mouetur*, when a man is put out of his place. *Festus Pompeius* also setteth downe three sorts of militarie punishments, *viz. Deprehensa, castigatio, ignominia, Deprehensa*, saith he, is greater than *castigatio*, and lesser than *ignominia*; and aboue all these the law addeth infamie. For otherwise if infamie, and the Censors note of ignominie were all one, the threescore and foure Senators by *Lentulus* and *Gellius* the Censors at once displaced and thrust out of the Senat, as also the foure hundred knights, who by *Valerius* and *Sempronius* the Censors were cassired, and their horses and publike wages taken from them, had bene also infamous. Yea that more is, all the people of Rome had beene noted with infamie, by the censure of *Liuius Salinator*, who rased and noted all the tribes, and as *Valerius Maximus* saith, *Inter ærarios retulit*, put them all from their freedome, and made them to pay all duties as straungers; For that they had by publike sentence first condemned him, and afterward made him Consull and Censor: only the tribe Metia he excepted, which had neither condemned nor acquited him, neither thought him worthie of those so honourable offices in the Commonweale. Hee also afterward noted *Claudius Nero* his companion in the Censorship, who also requited him againe with the like. Wherefore *Cicero* speaking of the Censorship, thus saith, * *Illud commune proponam, nunquam animaduersionibus Censorijs hanc ciuitatem ita contentam, vt rebus iudicatis fuisse*, I will (saith he) set before you that common matter, this citie neuer to haue bene so contented with the Censors animaduersions, as with iudgements. And bringeth for example *C. Geta* a Senator, who by the Censors thrust out of the Senat, was afterwards himselfe made Censor. And after that he addeth, *Quod si illud quoque iudicium putaretur, vt cæteri turpi iudicio damnati in perpetuum omni honore ac dignitate priuarentur, sic hominibus ignominia notatis, neque ad honorem, neque in curiam reditus esset: timoris enim causam non vitæ pœnam in illa potestate esse voluerunt. Quare qui vobis in mentem venit hæc apppellare iudicia, quæ a populo Romano rescindi, ab iuratis iudicibus repudiari, a magistratibus negligi, ab ijs qui eandem potestatem adepti sunt solent commutari?* If that (saith he) should also be thought a iudgement, as others with infamous iudgement condemned, they should for euer be depriued of all honour and dignitie: so vnto men (by the Censors) noted with ignominie, should bee no meanes for them againe to returne vnto their honour, or into the court: For why, our auncestors would cause of feare, but not danger of life to be in the Censors power. Wherefore

Ignominie is a kind of disgrace, but not the same that infamie is.

That men may be noated with ignominie and so disgraced, and yet not thereby become infamous.

* *pro Cluentio.*

fore how came it into your mind, to call these iudgements, which may by the people of Rome be reuoked, by the sworne judges be reiected, by the magistrats bee neglected; and of them which haue obtained the same power be vsually changed. Wherby it euidently appeareth the Censors to haue bene without all manner of iurisdiction. For the Pretors had the hearing and examination of the suits of the farmars of the publike reuenewes of all such things as concerned tributes, rents, writings, repairations, and farming out of publike things, made or done by the Censors: for that the power of the Censors was quite different from the iurisdiction of the Pretors. And so with vs (here in Fraunce) power is giuen vnto the gouernours of prouinces, but yet without iurisdiction: except it be, that they by consent of both the parties, take vpon them to decide or determine any matter. And so we may in like sort say, That the Censors had power to commaund, but without any iurisdiction.

The power of the Triumuiri Capitais in Rome.

There were also other magistrats in Rome, which had power to command, and iurisdiction also in criminall causes, as those whome they called *Triumuiri Capitales*, whose power and authoritie extended yet onely vnto straungers or slaues: except perhaps such were the vnworthinesse of the magistrats, and their corruption, or offence so great, as that the other magistrats did willingly winke at the proceeding of these Capital Triumuiri, & at the publike punishment by them taken vpon such notorious offendors. These Triumuiri beside this had also the putting in execution of all the capitall iudgements of the people, or of the other magistrats.

Now by this discourse of the Roman magistrats and their power, it appeareth, that in Rome there were some magistrats, who at the beginning of their first institution had no power or commaund, or els power yet without iurisdiction; and yet to haue at length vsurped both. Howbeit I deeme not them to be called Magistrats, which haue no power; well they may enioy some publike honour or charge, but no magistracie. For the true proprietie of the word Magistrat, importeth and draweth with it a power to commaund. And he that will haue regard vnto the phrase and manner of speech of the auntient Latines, and especially of the lawyers, shall find them to haue called the offices with honest charges in the Commonweale, by the word *Honores*, Honor (saith *Calistratus*) *est administratio Reipublicæ cum dignitate*, Honour is a gouernment of the Commonweale with dignitie or reputation: and those which beside their honor had power also to commaund, them they noted by the word *Imperia*. As in *Liuie* we see the nobilitie to complaine in this sort, *Salios, ac Flamines sine Imperijs ac potestatibus relinqui*, The Salij and Flamines to be left without command, without power: vnderstanding by the word *Imperia*, the great estates of the citie, whether it were by commission, or by office, such as had Mase bearers and power to commaund allowed them. And by the word *Potestates*, meaning the gouernours of prouinces, whome *Vlpian* the lawyer in proper tearmes calleth also *Potestates*. VVhich also *Alexander Seuerus* the emperour meant, when he with a loud voyce saith, *Non patiar mercatores potestatum*, I will not suffer the buiers of the gouernments of prouinces.

No magistrat without power

Now as a man may haue a publike charge without honour, as Criers, Sargeants, Trumpetors, (which in auntient time were slaues, & of the magistrats familie without title of office) and especially the towne clarkes and notaries vnto the magistrats, or Commonweale, vntill the time of *Valentinian*, who forbad slaues any longer to haue that charge. So a man may say also, That there are publike charges with honour, without power to commaund; as ambassadours and priuie councellors, secretaries of estate, and treasorours; the auntient Ediles and Questors, and our Receiuers. So also some other there be which haue honorable charge, hauing also the hearing of many causes, and yet without commaund: as the auntient Roman Bishops, and our

great

F6 revenewes, AND of all   F6 writings *i.e. scripturae*, which also means taxes paid on public pastures
G4(margin) Capitales   K4 Valentinian

A great Prelats. Others haue honorable charge, with power also to commaund, and yet without iurisdiction: as the Tribunes of the people, the Censors, and our Gouernours of countries, together with the kings Attourney. Some others there bee also which haue ordinarie, and honorable publique charge, and power to commaund with iurisdiction: and those are they, whom properly we call Magistrats: such as were the two Consuls and Prætors; who were encreased euen to the number of sixteene. As for the Dictators, Gouernours of prouinces, and those whom the Romans called *Interreges*: and *Præfectos vrbi Latinarum feriarum causâ*: they had more power and authoritie, then all the other magistrats we haue spoken of: yet were they not magistrats, but commissioners onely, as we haue before showed: albeit that some called B them by the common name of Magistrats; but yet not they which knew how properly to speake. And so oftentimes it happeneth: that they which haue the greatest honors, are yet destitute of all power and commaund: as amongst the Venetians the Chauncelour is created out of the people, which is with them the greatest honour; and yet without any power. So the Procurators of S. Marke, are also (with them) highly honored, and in all Commonweales the counsellors of estate, Embassadours, Bishops, and prelates, who haue no commaund, and yet are more respected, than the other little Prouosts, and diuers other judges, which haue power to commaund, and iurisdiction to discide controuersies, with administration of justice both high and low.

The great diuersitie of magistrats in their honor, power, and authoritie.

C There are also publique charges, who haue neither honour nor commaund, but rather to the contrarie draw after them a certain kind of dishonour: as the Hangmans office; who after the charge committed vnto him for the execution to death, was by the Prætors edicts commaunded still to lodge out of the citie: a custome yet obserued in Tholouse, and in diuers other cities also. Other publique charges also there be, not much more honest, and yet neuerthelesse necessarie vnto the Commonweale, and profitable vnto them that haue execution of the same: to the end that the profit arising thereby, might in some sort couer the dishonour thereof. And vnder this diuision are generally comprehended all publique persons placed in title of office, or in commissions, or in simple dignitie without power to commaund.

Certaine publike charges dishonorable.

D And in like maner we might diuide all publique officers & magistrats, according to the diuersitie of the publike charges, which euerie one of them hath: some *in* matters of religion, other some in the affaires of state; these haue the administration of iustice: others haue the charge of the publike reuenewes, some of the fortification and repairation of publike places, and others the prouision of victuals, and other things needfull: these haue the mannaging of the warres, for the defence of the subiects against their enemies: these the care of the publique health and welfare of the people, and these the ouersight and charge of the high waies, riuers, forrests, ports and passages: all which publicke charges may bee giuen either in title of office, or in commission, or simple dignitie without commaund: or els with a commanding power also, or only by way E of the execution of the commaunds of others, such as are the magistrates ministers, towne clarkes, notaries, vshers, surueyers, sergeants, criers. Which so great a multitude of honours, offices, and publicke charges, to comprehend under the simple name of magistrates, or as the Greekes call it ἀρχόντων, were but to confound the whole discourse of publicke honours and offices, of all magistrates and commissioners together.

Wherefore in euerie Commonweale for the creating of magistrats and officers, and such as are to be imploied in common charge, three things are chiefly to bee respected: First them that haue the choyce and creation of them: then of what manner of persons

Three things especially to be respected in the creating of Magistrats & officers in euerie Commonweale.

C4 *For* Prætors edicts *read* Censors' edicts (Fr and L). Cf. Cicero, *Pro Rab. Perd.*, 5. D9 office
E2–3 multitude   Note at C1.

persons choice is to be made: and thirdly in what maner and forme they are to be created or chosen. As for the first, it is a thing belonging onely vnto the soueraigntie, as we haue in due place declared. And the second, although it most properly belong also vnto soueraigntie, yet for the most part it ordinarily followeth the lawes to that end and purpose established, and especially in the Popular and Aristocratike estates: wherin (as generally in all sorts of Commonweales) offices, and publike charges are giuen vnto men, either for their vertue and wisedome, or else for their wealth, or for their nobilitie; or indifferently for all these things together; for why there is no Commonweale so barbarous, which hath not some regard of these things in bestowing of the offices and publike charges of the state: but which of these considerations were most to be respected, belongeth not to this place to discusse. And as concerning the third point, which is the manner and forme for the choice and creation of magistrats and officers, it is of three sorts: For either it is done by election, or lot; or by a mixture of both together. Election is made either by liuely voyce, or by holding vp of hands, (which the auntient Greekes called χειροτονεια) a thing yet vsed amongst the Swissers: or else by tables or billets, by beanes or stones; and that in two sorts, viz. by open, or by secret suffrages. By lot choice is made of one, or mo of the citisens to be magistrats, or out of all sorts and degrees of the people, at a certaine age, by the laws appointed. Now as for choice to be made by election and lot mingled together, although it be a thing not much vsed in auntient time, yet is it now at this present a a thing most common in Aristocraticall estates, and especially in Genes and Venice. As the Romans alwaies also did in making choice of the judges of capitall causes, concerning life and death; who were by lot drawne onely out of the order of the Senators, before the law Sempronia, or out of the orders of the Senators and the knights by the law Sempronia also; or out of both those orders, and the Tribunes of the common treasure, by the law Aurelia, the people being still excluded. But in a Popular estate, either must all the citisens together iudge of euerie one in particular, or of the lesser part together, and that without lot or election. (For where the whole multitude of citisens haue authoritie and power, there is no place left for election or lot:) or else must some citisens by lot, or choice, or both drawne out, iudge of euery man in particular: or some, of some chosen by lot or election onely, or by both together; or else some partly by lot, partly by election taken out of all the estates of the Commonweale, to iudge of some of the other citisens; or else some by lot drawne out of all, with some other taken out of one or many estates of the Commonweale: or part by lot and election drawn out of all, and other part out of a certaine order of the citisens. And thus much concerning all the meanes that can be imagined concerning the varietie of them which haue any publike charge: and for the estate, qualitie, and condition of euerie one of them, with the forme of their calling and imploiment.

Æschines the orator, diuiding the offices and publike charges of the Athenians, hath cut them much shorter, and more obscurely reckoned them vp, than was fit for so great a citie, considering that therein were moe magistrats and officers, than in any other Commonweale that then was, for the greatnesse thereof. Hee said, That there were therein three sorts of officers: one sort of them which were taken by lot or choice; another of them which had publike charge aboue the space of 30 dayes, such as were they which had the ouersight of publike repairations and buildings; and the third sort, of such as were by the auntient lawes appointed; as commissioners chosen for the warres, or for the administration of iustice, such as were the magistrats. But by this diuision cannot the diuersitie of magistrats and officers be iudged, no more than by that of *Demosthenes*, (altogether different from that of Æschines his aduersarie.) For hee saith

them

K4 three sorts   Notes at G7, K8.

Of a Commonweale.

them onely to be magistrats, which were by lot drawne in the temple of *Theseus*: or they to whome the people had giuen extraordinarie power to commaund, or made choice of for captaines. The diuision also of *Varro*, and *Messala*, is also too short, who make but two sorts of magistrats in Rome, *viz.* the great and the little. The great magistrats they called the Consuls, the Pretors, and Censors, as chosen by the great estates: and the other they called the little, as chosen by the common people; the ceremonie of their soothsayers diuination being more solemne in the choice of the greater, than in the choice of the lesser. But better it were to search and find out the essentiall diuisions of magistrats, and such as might serue in euerie Commonweale; as are those by vs alreadie set downe, concerning the charge of magistrats. VVee may also otherwise diuide magistrats into three sorts, in respect of their power. The first may bee called Soueraigne Magistrats, as owing obedièce vnto none, but vnto the soueraigne maiestie onely. The second are lesser Magistrats, who owe obedience vnto the soueraign Magistrats, and yet haue commaund ouer other magistrats also. The last sort are they which owe obedience vnto other superiour Magistrats, and yet haue no commaund but ouer particular persons onely. Let vs then in order speake of these three sorts of Magistrats, and first of the obedience of Magistrats towards their Soueraigne Prince.

Chap. IIII.
¶ Of the obedience that the Magistrat oweth vnto the Lawes and Soueraigne Prince.

Seeing that the Magistrat next vnto the Soueraigne Prince, is the principall person in the Commonweale, & vpon whom they which haue the soueraigntie discharge themselues, communicating vnto him the authoritie, force, and power to commaund: it is good reason before we passe further, briefly to touch what obedience he oweth vnto his Soueraigne Prince; which is the chiefe part of his dutie. Now in this the Prince and Magistrat, and both of them do most differ from a priuat man: for that the Prince seeth no man in the state or Commonweal, whome he may compare or preferre before himselfe; but as one placed in a most high degree, and next vnto the immortall God, beholdeth all his subiects set a great way beneath him: whereas the priuat man cannot by any publike right commaund ouer any other subiect, although that he by priuat and domesticall commaunds rule and gouerne his owne familie. As for the Magistrat, for that he is to regard many persons, hee must oftentimes change his port, his gesture, his speech and countenance, for the good performance of his dutie towards all: which no man can well discharge, except he first know his duty towards his Soueraigne prince, as also how to submit himselfe vnto the other Magistrats his superiours, how to respect his equals, and how to commaund his inferiours, how to defend the weake, to withstand the great, and to doe iustice to all. And that is it, for which the auntients commonly said, *Magistracie or authoritie to declare what was in a man*, hauing as it were vpon the stage in the Theatre, and in the sight of all men, to performe the parts of many persons. And so also may we say, A man to show what his office is: For if he be such an one as he ought to be, hee graceth his place: whereas if he bee otherwise, hee debaseth not only the authoritie of his place and office; but euen of the maiestie of the state and Commonweale. So *Liuie* speaking of *Quintus Flaminius*, a man vnworthy his high place, saith of him, *Non qui sibi honorem adiecisset, sed indignitate sua vim ac ius Magistratui quem gerebat dempsisset*, That hee had not (by his

Marginalia: How much a prince differeth from a magistrat, and both of them from a priuat man.

Note at A8.

his office) encreased his honour; but by the vnworthinesse of himselfe, impaired the force and power of the office which he bare.

Now the better to know what obedience the Magistrat oweth vnto his Soueraign, it is needfull first to vnderstand, what it is that a Soueraigne Prince may of right commaund euery Magistrat to doe. For why, the lawfull commands of Soueraigne Princes are right diuers, and vnlike themselues. Some of them seruing for perpetuall edicts or lawes concerning all persons, of what condition or qualitie soeuer they bee; or but for certaine persons, and for a certaine time, by way of prouision: othersome containe some priuilege or exemption contrarie to the edicts or lawes, for some one onely, or for some few of the subiects: or some graunt not contrarie vnto the law, or some reward for the good, or punishment for the euill, or some office or commission; or else serue for the expounding of some edict or priuilege, or for the denouncing of warre, or the making of peace, or for raising of souldiours, or for the erecting of Faires or Markets, or for the leuying of taxes, subsidies, fifteenes, new impositions, or loanes: or for the sending of ambassadours to congratulat the good haps of other princes; or to mone their misfortunes, or to entreat of marriages, and alliances, or other such like things; or for the building or fortifying of places to be fortified, for the repairing of bridges, hie wayes, ports or passages, or for to iudge of certaine suits and proceedings in the law, or for the execution of some commaunds, or for the maintenance of letters of iustice, or for the restoring of such as be vnder age, or of full age, or of such as be condemned, or for some particularitie, or for some remission, or pardon, which may bee of diuers sorts. Of which commaunds so before declared, some containe diuers kinds, as do priuileges and graunts, whether it be for some gift giuen, or for exemption and immunitie from all charges, or from some one: or letters of discharge, or of estate, or to haue the freedome of a citisen, or for to be made legitimat, or for nobilitie, or knighthood, or for the erecting of corporations or colleges, or other such like things. All which letters may be diuided into two sorts, that is to say, into letters of iurisdiction or commaund, or letters of iustice or state. Albeit that the word *Iubemus*, or we commaund, be as well in the letters of iustice, as in the letters of grace and fauour, as is to bee seene in the lawes and letters pattents of the Greeke emperours. Yet the letters of grace, or which proceed from the onely power and authoritie of the prince, are properly in Fraunce called Mandements, or Commands; and the secretaries which dispatch them are also called the Secretaries of the Commaunds: whereas the letters of iustice are most commonly dispatched by the other secretaries; beside the difference of the great and little seale, and for the most part the diuersitie of the waxe: or the single or double labell, or the seale hanging in silke of diuers colours, making the difference of the letters to be knowne. The auntient Latines called such instructions as were by princes giuen to their ambassadours, or gouernours of countries, or generals of their armies, *Mandata Principum*, or Princes Commands, which we do call by the name of of instructions: For so the word *Mandata* is taken in the law, where *Iustinian* the emperour saith, That hee had made a booke of Mandats or Commaundements for the gouernours of prouinces.

But leauing the subtilitie of words, let vs go vnto the matter, and examine the force of the clauses commonly set downe in the letters patents and mandates of princes. And first these wordes, *Vniuersis præsentibus & futuris* (To all men present and to come) are ioyned onely vnto such letters patents as are to endure for euer: (howbeit that no worldly thing can so for euer continue) but not vnto temporarie edicts made by way of prouision, nor to commissions, nor to any other letters of prouision. But this clause, *Quantum satis est &c.* (so much as shall suffice) is of much greater importance

The lawful commaunds of soueraigne princes right diuers.

The power and force of certaine clauses commonly set down in the letters patents, and princes Mandats expounded.

tance, & ordinarily ioyned vnto letters which they call letters of iurisdiction or iustice, whereby the prince leaueth vnto the discretion of him to whom such his letters are addressed, to allow of them, or to refuse them, as his conscience, and the equitie of the cause shall require: which is not in letters of commaundement which leaue nothing vnto him to whom they are directed, except happily sometimes the examination of the fact onely: as in these words, *Si paret &c.* (If it shall appeare vnto you &c.) In such sort that one may say of all sorts of charters or letters of iustice, albeit that they be granted by the prince, that they import not any commaund or constraint whatsoeuer vnto the magistrat to whom they are directed: But to the contrarie, that by our lawes and customes it is most religiously prouided, that the magistrats or judges should vnto such charters or letters haue no further respect, than in that they were agreeable with equitie and trueth. And although that the same forme of letters of justice, be graunted in England, as also in Spayne, and other kingdomes; yet so it is neuerthelesse, that it is done rather for the particular profit of some one, than for the greatnes or increasing of the maiestie of the king, (who graunted them by way of benefit vnto the partie) or for any necessitie there is thereof: seeing that the whole is remitted vnto the power of the magistrat, after the graunting of such letters, which was not before the graunt thereof. Which was the cause that the people in the assemblie of the Estates in parliament at Orleans, presented a request vnto the king for the cutting off of this formalitie of letters: as seruing not but to the oppressing of the people, without any profit therout of to be drawne vnto the king or Commonweale. The auntient Greeks and Latins also neuer knew this forme of letters of iustice: but the magistrats vpon the request of the parties did as much as do our judges vpon the graunt of such letters of iustice. And the clause, *Quantum satis erit quod liqueat* (so much as may suffice for the manifesting of the matter) is the same which was conteined in the Prætors edicts, in this forme, *Si qua mihi iusta causa videbitur,* (if any iust cause shall seeme vnto me.) True it is that the power to correct, supply, and expound the lawes, concerning the ciuill iurisdiction, together with the restitution & relieuing of them which had beene circumuented, or deceiued by the formalities of the lawes, (a power before giuen vnto the Prætors by the vertue of their office) resteth now (I know not how) amongst the marks of soueraigne maiestie; and for this cause the Prætors authoritie and lawes were called honorable; which the interpretors of the law call *Nobile officium*. Wherefore as offices are confounded, when as the prince conuerteth vnto himselfe such things as belong vnto the magistrat; euen so also are the rights of soueraigntie impaired, when as they are by the magistrats vsurped. Now as for the declaration, and correcting of the edicts and lawes, we haue before said that it appertaineth and belongeth vnto them which haue the soueraigntie: But as for restitutions against the extremitie of the law, and all that concerneth letters of iustice, it greatly appeareth not that the soueraigne princes haue much troubled themselues therewith, but haue left them to the magistrats to be in their name decided. I except only certain letters of iustice, which passe vnder the great Seale, and whereunto the aforesaid clause, *If it shall be iust, If it shall be agreeable vnto equitie and truth,* is inserted: which clause so much displeased a certaine great personage, holding one of the highest places of honour in this Realme, (who vnderstood not the force thereof) as that he would haue raced out the same; saying the maiestie of the king to be thereby impaired: howbeit that he was therein to be excused, as being a straunger, and not well seene in the lawes and customes of a straunge countrey. But how could the maiestie of kings be in this respect empaired or diminished? seeing that the auntient kings of Ægipt caused their magistrats solemnely to sweare, neuer to obey their commaundements, in case they commaunded them any thing that

The princes charters or letters of iustice, no commaundes vnto the magistrat to whom they are directed

A notable order

312　　　　　　　　　　　The Third Booke

that was vniust: as we read in the sayings of the Ægiptian kings reported by *Plutarch*. Seeing therefore that the allowance or reiecting of letters of iustice directed in the kings name vnto the magistrats, dependeth of the equitie and discretion of the magistrats themselues, it needeth not vs to speake any more thereof. Wherefore let vs now proceed to those rescripts or letters of commaund, which for that they concerne the state of the Commonweale, and publique and not priuat causes, are called rescripts of State; or letters of commaund or state. Concerning which, a double question may be made: One whether such Rescripts or letters of the prince, containing onely the simple examination of the fact, without giuing any further hearing of the matter vnto the magistrat, according to the desert thereof; whether (I say) the magistrat fully informed of the truth of the fact according to the tenour of his letters, ought to proceed to the further execution thereof being vniust, or to hearken vnto the vniust commaunds of his prince? The other, whether the magistrat hauing neither power to examine the equitie nor truth of a matter, may refuse the vniust commaunds of his prince: the doubt therein being the greater, if they shall be thereunto by the prince more straitly vrged, or expresly commaunded: For sometime princes by their particular and secret letters, vse to request the magistrats; so with couert requests accompanying their vniust commaunds: yea oftentimes in their letters patents their requests are ioyned with their commaunds, because they would not seeme to wrest all things from them against their wils; but to request many things of them: as when they say, *We pray and commaund you*, wherein the prince seemeth as in nothing more to derogate from his soueraigne maiestie: for if the thing be iust and honest which hee commaundeth, what needeth requests? if vniust or dishonest, why doth he commaund it? Now the magistrat is neuer to be requested to doe his dutie, or intreated not to doe wrong, or that which is vniust or dishonest, as *Cato* the Censor saith. Besides that, to commaund is a thing incompatible with request. It is wisely said, τῶν τυράννων δεήσεις παραγγέλματα εἶναι, Tyrants requestes to bee commaunds: wherefore let vs suppose nothing to be more straitly commaunded, than that which the prince seemeth by fyled speech or intreatie to persuade. Wherefore to resolue this point, if the princes letters giue vnto the magistrat neither the examination nor the hearing or disciding of the fact, or of the right and truth of the cause, but that onely the execution of the princes commaund be vnto him committed: the magistrat in this case may not in any sort take vpon him the examination or hearing of the matter; except the letters of commaund be notoriously false, faultie, or absurd, and contrarie to the lawes of God and nature (as we read of the commaunds of *Pharao* and *Agrippa*:) or else to robbe and spoile the poore people; as in our time *Albert* Marques of Brandeburg, who amongst other his notable cruelties, set vp sundrie gibbets in all such townes and cities as he had taken in, threatning his souldiours to hang them thereupon, if that contrarie to his commaund they should spare to robbe and spoile the poore inhabitants: albeit that he had neither true, nor yet any colourable cause, for his taking vp of armes against his countrey. Now if a man subiect vnto a particular Lord or Iustice, be not in law or right bound to obey him passing the bounds of his territorie, or the power to him giuen, (albeit that the thing which hee commaundeth be both iust and honest) but may well refuse his commaund: how should the magistrat then be bound to obey or to put into execution the princes commaunds in things vniust and dishonest, the prince in this case transgressing and breaking the sacred bounds of the lawes both of God and nature? But some will say, no prince to be found so euill aduised, nor that it is to be supposed that he would commaund any thing contrarie vnto the lawes of God and nature: and true it is; for why he worthily loseth the title and honour of a Prince, which

depar-

Whether the magistrat be bound to obey his princes vniust commaunds or not?

Princes requests to haue the power of the most strait cōmaund.

H8 fyled *i.e.* polished, smooth　　　　　　　　　　　　　　　　　　Note at I5.

departing from reason, and forgetting the dutie of a prince, breaketh the lawes of God and nature.

We haue before (as we suppose) sufficiently enough declared, what and how much a prince may doe by the right of his soueraigntie, from whence many things may be deriued pertinent vnto this question here in hand: for why it is not well to be vnderstood what obedience is by the magistrat due vnto the soueraigne maiestie, except the rights of Soueraigntie be before well vnderstood and fully knowne. But here the question is, what commaunds of the prince, and how farre the magistrat ought to execute the same? for sometime dishonest and vniust thinges are by princes commaunded, which the ciuill magistrats themselues do more willingly, and shamefully put in execution, than they were by the princes commaunded. As not long agoe in the time of the ciuill warres, (wherewith all Fraunce was on a light fyer) the president of the court of Normandie (whose name deserueth to be buried in perpetuall obliuion) beeing commaunded extraordinarily to leuie thirtie thousand crownes of them which professed the reformed religion, extorted from them three hundred thousand; and for so doing (the calamitie of the time considered) receiued a great reward. Howbeit that *Tiberius* the emperour (a man of incredible crueltie) sharply reproued the gouernour of Ægypt for exacting more of the subiects than he was commaunded: saying, *Tonderi oues meas non cutem detrahi volo*, I would haue my sheepe shorne, but not flaine. If therefore the commaundement of the prince be not contrarie vnto the lawes of God and nature, the magistrat is to put it in execution, although it seeme to differ from the lawes of other nations: which lawes it is not against nature for the princes to chaunge, for the profit or disprofit of their Commonweales. For albeit that the princes (as wee haue said) ought to keepe the oath by him made vnto his people, if hee haue so bound himselfe by oath; and although hee were not by oath so bound, yet neuerthelesse of duetie ought to keepe the lawes and customes of the estate and Commonweal whereof hee is soueraigne: yet for all that wee must not thereof conclude or gather, That if the prince doe in that case commaund any thing contrarie vnto his oath or the duetie of a Prince, that the Magistrat is therefore to refuse to obey his commaund. Forasmuch as it belongeth not vnto the Magistrat to examine or censure the doings of his prince, or to crosse his proceedings concerning mans lawes, from which the prince may as he seeth cause derogat. Yet if the Magistrat bee commaunded by the Prince to abrogat an auntient law, being more vpright and profitable to giue way vnto another lesse iust, and lesse profitable for the Commonweale; he may stay the execution of such a law or commaundement in suspense, vntill he haue shewed his reasons therefore vnto the prince, which he is in dutie bound to do, not once, but euen twice or thrice: and then if the prince notwithstanding his remonstrances, will not by him be aduised, but refuse his wholsome and profitable admonition, and will needes haue the law to passe further; then the Magistrat (as hauing alreadie done his dutie) shall put it in execution: which he may also at the first commaund of his prince doe, if the delaying thereof be daungerous. And to that end and purpose tendeth that which is by *Innocentius* the fourth written, before he was Pope, That Magistrats ought to put in execution the princes commaunds, albeit that they be vniust: which is to bee vnderstood of ciuill iustice and vtilitie: but not if such commaunds bee contrarie to the lawes of nature. Which interpretation may serue also for the right vnderstanding of that which the lawyers say, *That the prince may derogat euen from the law of nature.* Wherein their meaning is, from the law of nations, and common constitutions of other people: least any deceiued by the obscuritie of the words, or equiuocation of the law of nature, should thereby rashly presume to breake the sacred lawes of God and nature.

Marginalia: What commands of the prince, and how far the magistrat ought to execute the same.

Marginalia: The magistrat is not to censure his princes commaund, beeing not contrarie vnto the lawes of God & nature.

Marginalia: How it is to be vnderstood that a prince may derogate from the law of nature.

C3 *For* that the princes *read* that the prince (Fr and L).

Now if any man shall obiect and say, That the emperour *Anastasius* expresly commaunded, That the judges and Magistrats should not so much as suffer men to produce the princes rescripts or letters graunted vnto particular persons, contrarie to the generall edicts or lawes: Mine aunswere is, that that is to be vnderstood, if in such the princes rescripts or letters no speciall clause be comprehended, derogating from the generall lawes: notwithstanding which derogation, yet the Magistrat ought neuerthelesse to aduertise the prince thereof, and to put him in mind of his dutie: who if he be not by the Magistrats reasons to be remoued from his former opinion, but command the same the second time, the Magistrat is then to obey his commaund, although the thing so commaunded be not agreeing with the common profit, and contrarie vnto the lawes. For why, the Magistrat hauing so done his dutie, is not to expect but the second commaund; as is by the law prouided. To the example whereof the edict of *Charles* the ninth was made, concerning the magistrats admonitions vnto their prince. So long before this *Theodosius* the Great, at the request of Saint *Ambrose* the good bishop of Milan, made a law, whereby he willed, That the execution of his letters patents and commaunds, should be holden in suspense thirtie dayes after the signification thereof, when he had commaunded any to be more rigorously punished than the vsual manner and custome was. The occasion of the making of which law was, the execution of seuen thousand Thessalians, put to death by the commaundement of this *Theodosius*, for that they had murthered and slaine certaine of his Receiuers and Magistrats. For which cause Saint *Ambrose* excommunicated the emperour, neither would suffer him to be reconciled, vntill he had made the aforesaid law. And hereof (as I suppose) proceed those rescripts, which are yet vsed by the bishops of Rome: the first called *Monitorie*, the second *Iussorie*, and the third *Executorie*; or as we say in English, Edicts of admonition, of Commaund, and of Execution.

How the Magistrat commaunded by his prince to put in execution old penall lawes, now of themselues or through the negligence of the magistrats forgotten, is to proceed in the execution thereof.

The same opinion we are to haue, if the prince by his letters patents command the Magistrat to proceed to the execution of the penaltie vppon them that haue offended against such his edicts and lawes, as by the antiquitie of themselues, or by the negligence of the Magistrats seeme to haue bene quite forgotten and abrogated. For why, the long sufferance of the prince, and conniuence of the magistrats, in the sight and knowledge of whome the lawes are so broken, remitteth the penaltie due by the law: which could not otherwise haue bene infringed, by the abuse of them which transgressed the same, had it by the prince or magistrat bene still looked vnto. And therefore the magistrat ought not rashly to proceed to the execution of the penaltie of such forgotten or neglected lawes, before he haue caused the same to be againe republished, being by his default before neglected. Yea the prince ought rather to proceed against his magistrats, who through their remisse negligence haue suffered his edicts and lawes to be contemned. For otherwise it should be a thing verie vniust and sauouring of tyrannie, to make edicts and lawes, and after long neglecting of them, vpon a sodaine to proceed against them, who by the example of others, had transgressed against them, seeing others before them to haue escaped vnpunished. Which was one of the tyrannicall slights of the most cruell emperour *Nero*, as of other auntient tyrants also. Wheras the good emperour *Traian* to the contrarie commaunded *Plinie* gouernour of the lesser Asia, of new to publish such edicts and lawes as were any wise before buried in obliuion, by the disobedience or errour of his subiects, or the sufferance of the magistrats: for that a common errour is reputed for a law, if the errour bee not against the law of nature, against which no errour can probably be pretended.

But some man may aske, Whether the magistrat owe obedience vnto such his princes commaunds, as shall vnto him seeme contrarie vnto the law of nature, albeit
that

F 1 emperour K 3 slights *i.e.* tricks, ruses

OF A COMMONWEALE. 315

A that indeed they be not contrarie thereunto? For the equitie and reason which we call naturall, is not alwaies so cleere and manifest, but that it findeth impugners. Yea oftentimes the greatest lawyers and philosophers are therein intangled, and of quite contrarie opinions, and the lawes of people are therein sometime so repugnant, as that some of them appoint reward, and some others punishment for the selfe same fact, whereof bookes, lawes, and histories are ful, all which to prosecute were a matter infinit. Wherunto I aunswere, that if that which the auntients say may take place, a man neuer ought to doe that whereof he doubteth, whether it be iust or not; and much lesse ought hee so to doe, if he be thereof certainly persuaded that the thing which the prince commaundeth, is of it selfe by nature vniust. But if question be of ciuill iustice onely, the
B magistrat ought in such case to verifie and put in execution his princes commaunds, although he thinke them to be in ciuill equitie or law vniust. And therfore the magstrats in euerie Commonweale were compelled to sweare to obserue the lawes and ordinances; to the end they should not call into dispute or question, that which they ought to hold, as before resolued vpon. And this was the manner and custome of the Romans when the old magistrats receiued the oath of the new, before they entred into their charge: which was commonly done vpon the calends of Ianuarie, in the capitoll, after solemne sacrifices there made: for otherwise the magistrat lost his place of estate, if hee tooke not his oath within fiue daies after. Yea sometimes the Tribunes which held the estate of the people, constrained them in particular which had withstood the pub-
C lishing of a law, to sweare to obserue the same, after that it was once published, and that vpon the paine of banishment. So L. *Metellus Numidicus* was by a decree of the people banished, for refusing to sweare vnto the lawes published at the instance of the factious Tribune *Saturninus*. So also after that the lawes of *Lewes* the twelfth were published in the high court of the parliament of Paris: for that many disliked of the same, the kings atturney generall there made a request, That they might be duely obserued, and prohibition giuen for any man to call them in doubt, and that vpon paine of high treason; as is to be seene in the records of the court. For why, it is lawfull for euerie man before the publishing of the law, to despute and reason of the equitie thereof:
D which to doe after the publication thereof, is not lawfull. And so, before that, when as king *Lewes* the eleuenth had commaunded certaine vniust decrees of his to be published in the court of the parliament at Paris: the court refused to yeeld thereunto, for that they seemed vnto euerie man vniust: but the king neuerthelesse still vrging his former requests, ioyned thereunto grieuous threats also; as that they should loose their heads that would not yeeld thereunto. Which thing *Lauacrie*, president of the parliament vnderstanding, accompanied with the rest of the judges of that honourable court in their red robes, came vnto the king, not to excuse the fault by him and the rest committed, in refusing the kings vniust decrees, but to show the reasons of their such refusall, and to request, That he with the rest might rather bee put to death, than enforced to giue their consent to the publishing of the propounded lawes. The king beholding
E the grauitie, the port, and dignitie of these persons, and almost abashed with the so constant resolution of such his great magistrats, and withall doubting the power and authoritie of the parliament, caused those his decrees so much misliked, to bee abrogated, and in their presence torne in peeces requesting them to continue so still to maintaine iustice; solemnly protesting neuer more to send vnto them any edict which should not be both iust and reasonable. It is a wonderfull thing to say of what power and moment this thing was to keepe the king within the bounds of reason, who otherwise had alwayes vsed his absolute power and commaund. As before hee came vnto the kingdome, being as yet Dauphin, he caused the presidents of the court of Paris to bee

Ee ij cal-

The law of nature not alwaies cleare and manifest.

The magistrate bound in ciuil causes to put his princes commaunds in execution, although they seeme vnto himselfe vniust or contrarie vnto lawe.

Lawes once established ought not by priuat persons to be againe called into dispute or question.

A notable example.

A4 lawes of peoples (Fr and L) B9 *For* Tribunes *Bodin writes* Magistrates (cf. Fr and L). B10 the estate *i.e.* the estates (cf. Fr)

called before him, to rase out the clause, *De expresso mandato* (by expresse commaundement) which the court had caused to be put vnto the confirmation of the priuileges graunted vnto the countie of Maine, protesting, That he would neuer goe out of the citie, vntill it were done, or yet take vppon him the charge by the king committed vnto him. Whereupon the court indeed commaunded those words to bee cancelled: but yet that the cancelling might appeare, commaunded the acts to be kept, which are yet preserued vndefaced. Now these words, *De expresso mandato*, and *De expressissimo mandato*, whereunto these words are also sometimes annexed, *Multis vicibus iterato* (or oftentimes repeated) which are many times to be found in the records of soueraign courts ioyned vnto the publication of the princes edicts and decrees, haue this illation or meaning, that such edicts and priuileges (graunted by the princes expresse commandement) should not be so precisely kept, but that shortly after they might by the sufferance of the magistrats be againe forgotten and neglected, as not much regarded. And by this secret of the courts, hath the state of this kingdome bene preserued in the greatnesse thereof: which otherwise would haue bene ruinated by the flatterers of princes, who by such extorted priuileges scrape vnto themselues whatsoeuer they desire: and the good kings not stil able to satisfie the hungry courtiers, sometimes wel eased, which haue vsed these restrictions, being so of their subiects well beloued, the confirmation of such edicts and priuileges not carrying with them any effect vnto the subiect, or disobedience vnto the king to giue good words, or charge of conscience vnto the magistrat in not performing it.

How the wordes de expresso or expresissimo mandato are in princes graunts, edicts or decrees to be vnderstood.

But yet farther question might be made, Whether a magistrat may bee suffered to giue vp his place, rather than he will allow an edict, a commission, or commandement from his prince, which he for certaine thinketh to be vniust and contrarie vnto naturall reason, when as the equitie of it is called in question, & especially if the other magistrats and multitude of the people shall hold it to be iust, contrarie to the others. For the force of iustice, and power of vpright reason, is not perceiued but of the fewer and wiser sort: and a wise man being as it were the rule of reason, is of all others the greatest enemie vnto the multitude. Which if it be so, why should a wise man bee enforced to giue his consent vnto the multitude of mad magistrats. In which case I say, that the magistrat is not to be suffered to giue vp his place, if it please not his soueraign prince he should so do, but ought rather to bee constrained to obey his princes commaunds, if the equitie thereof being called in doubt, be approued by the greater part of the magistrats, which haue charge to confirme such edicts: For otherwise if they should be permitted to giue vp their places, rather than to passe an edict approued by others, it would open a perilous gap to all the subiects, by their example to refuse and reiect the edicts and commaunds of their prince: and so euerie one in his charge might leaue the Commonweale vnto danger, and expose it vnto the tempest, as a ship without a Rudder, and that vnder the shadow of an opinion of iustice: which may haply be but a deuise of a subtill braine, to no other purpose than to contradict the more common opinion. And therefore among the most lawdable laws made by *Lewes* the xij, there is one which importeth, That if the judges be of three or moe opinions, those which were the fewer in number should be constrained to conforme and ioyne themselues vnto one of the greater parties, for the concluding of the decrees. Whereupon the court of Paris of long time doubted, whether this law should be published or not: for that it seemed a very hard and a most strange thing vnto many, to force the conscience of the judges contrarie to their owne opinions, and so enforce them to iudge contrarie to that they ought, and that especially in such things as were committed vnto the wisedome and deuotion of the judges, as are almost all both publike and priuat iudgements.

Whether a magistrate be to be suffered to giue vp his place, rather than to allow an edict or commaund of his prince which he for certaine thinketh to be vniust, and contrarie vnto reason

---

G10 to give good words *i.e.* to speak properly (cf. Fr, but Fr 7 defective here)   Note at G7.

A iudgements. Yet neuerthelesse after the court had considered of inconueniences which it saw ordinarily to arise vpon the varietie of opinions, and that the course of iustice, and the concluding of many good decrees, was thereby also often letted, the court confirmed the aforesaid law, which by processe of time hath bin found to be most iust & profitable. Hereunto also agreeth the maner and custome of the antient Romans: for their judges oftentimes to change their opinions, and to ioine themselues vnto the greater part, albeit that they were not thereunto constrained. As is to bee seene in *Plinie*, of a iudgement wherin one part of the iudges had condened the guiltie person vnto death, another part had cleerely and fully acquited him, and the third part had for a time banished him: in this diuersitie of opinions, as well they which had before acquited him, as

B they which had condemned him to death, consented both to them which would haue him banished. But our law is in that point better, which compelleth the fewer to ioyne themselues vnto the more. For in all corporations & colledges reason would, that that which pleaseth the greater part should take place and preuaile, as strengthened with the most voices. Howbeit that in all such consultations and actions the rule of the auntient wise neuer faileth; which willeth, That of many honest and profitable things propounded vnto vs, we should chuse those which be most honest, and most profitable: and so of many inconueniences and daungers, to make choice of the least: for otherwise mens actions should neuer sort to good end. And a man may also say, That the equitie of a law is not properly naturall, if it bee obscure or doubtfull; for that true na-

C turall iustice is more cleere and resplendent than the brightnesse of the sunne, as not wrapped vp in obscuritie, nor depending of the erroneous opinions of men, but of the most cleere and immutable wisedome of the euerlasting.

And yet neuerthelesse since the law of *Lewes* the xij. I find not that any magistrat hath giuen vp his place, as fearing to be inforced to maintaine or yeeld to any opinion contrarie vnto his conscience: and especially since the places of iustice were giuen vnto men for vertue, and not for reward and fauour. Neither hath the law of *Lewes* the xij. at any time constrayned the judges to iudge contrarie vnto their conscience, but hath rather silently giuen them leaue to giue vp their places; howbeit that it were more equitie so to constraine them, than to leaue it vnto their will and pleasure. For which

D cause the kings Attourneyes general haue oftentimes constrained the Iudges to iudge according vnto Lawes and customes of the land, albeit that all the Iudges were of contrarie opinion. As I remember that whilest I was at Tholouse, one *Bartholomew* President of one of the Chambers of Inquirie, seeing all the counsellours of his court of one and the same opinion in a suit, and directly against the law: after he had assembled all the rest of the courts vpon the matter, he constrayned them to change their opinions, and to iudge according to the law; And that iustly also: for who enforced thee to seeke for thine office? or to accept of it being offered thee? and hauing taken it vpon thee, (being happily got either by suspending of voices, or by sute, or briberie,) and being sworne, wilt thou now forsweare the lawes, which thou mightest before haue red,

E or at least wise oughtest to haue red? wilt thou by thy false opinion of the law and iustice, wrong the place thou bearest? delude the lawes? or forsake thy prince and Commonweale.

Yet sometime it happeneth that such lawes as of themselues seeme vnto euery man most iust, may vpon some suddein occurent appeare and proue to be most vniust. In which case, whereas the wrong is in the fact presented plaine and euident, wise magistrats vse to certifie the king thereof, (as I remember it to haue most oftentimes bene done in the parliament at Paris,) who imparting the matter vnto his Counsell, doth as he seeth cause derogate from the positiue law; or adde some thing vnto the same:

What the magistrate is to do in case the lawe otherwise iust, now vpon some soden occurrents seeme to be hard and vniust.

Ec iij (which

Note at B9.

(which our men call the exposition or declaration of the law) a thing properly belonging vnto the soueraigntie of a Prince, as we haue before declared. So that in this case, it is not lawfull for the magistrat to iudge against the law, although he may suspend his sentence vntill that the Princes pleasure be further knowne. But otherwise the law being cleare and without difficultie, the magistrat is to iudge according thereunto without disputing of the equitie thereof: for otherwise if the judge shall wittingly and wilfully iudge contrarie vnto the law, he is by the lawes themselues noted of infamie: but if he shall so iudge of ignorance, or supposing himselfe to iudge according vnto the law; he is not therefore to be accounted infamous: howbeit that such his iudgement is of it selfe void, as if it had not beene giuen at all, in such sort as that a man by the auntient Roman law need not at all to appeale therefrom.

Now there is great difference whether question be of the lawes alreadie established, or of those which yet are by the magistrat to be published. For why, such as be alreadie established, euery man is bound to keepe, and especially the magistrats, who if they wittingly swarue therefrom, (beside the penaltie appointed by the law) are subiect also vnto the note of infamie, as periurours and forsworne men. But as for such Edicts and lawes as are not yet published, but are but as yet presented vnto the magistrats to be confirmed and published, of them it behoueth the greater magistrats (to whom the publication of lawes especially appertaineth) well to consider, and to show the reasons if they shall dislike of them vnto the prince, albeit that it concerne but the particular interest of some one priuat person; but much more, in case it concerne the great harme or good of the Commonweale: which good if it be verie great, may in some sort couer the iniustice of the law; (as the auntient states-men say.) Yet must we not proceed so farre in respecting of the publike profit be it neuer so great, as therefore to forget reason, and to be caried headlong with wrong and iniustice: as were in auntient time the Lacedemonians, who measured all iustice by the common profit, whereunto they directed all their lawes, all their iudgements, and counsels; so that if that were once in question, neither oath, nor reason, nor iustice, nor yet the law of nature was by them once respected. But much better it were for the Commonweale, and more beseeming the dignitie of the magistrat, of himselfe to giue vp his office (as did the Chauncelour of *Philip* the second, duke of Burgundie) than to giue way vnto a law that is contrarie vnto the lawes of God and nature, or that in euery mans iudgement seemeth to be dishonest or vniust; howbeit the Duke seeing the irremoueable constancie of his Chauncelour, readie to giue vp his office, thought it better to reuoke such his commaunds, than to want so stout & wise a man. Which so constant resolutions of the magistrats, hath oftentimes preserued Princes from infamie, lawes from decay, and Commonweales from destruction. But when such constancie cannot heale the diseases of the Commonweale, or faults of soueraigne princes; and that the prince commaundeth the magistrats, to haue his actions excused vnto his subiects; it is much better for the magistrat to obey his commaund, and in so doing to couer and burie the memorie of a wicked fact alreadie done, than in refusing so to do, to irritate the prince to the doing of worse; and so (as they say) to cast the helue after the hatchet. As did *Papinian* the great Gouernour of the empire, (and by *Seuerus* the Emperour in his will appointed Tutor vnto the yong emperours *Anthonius Caracalla*, and *Geta* his sonnes) who by *Caracalla* commaunded to excuse vnto the Senat the murder by him committed vpon the person of his brother *Geta*, would therein do nothing, but cut him off with this sharpe and short answere, saying, *That murthers were more hardlie excused, than committed*: which was of him more stoutly then wisely said. For *Caracalla* with this aunswere enraged, and yet not satisfied with his brothers blood, in his rage commaunded

Papinian

Great care to be had by the greater magistrats in the publication of lawes.

Better it is for the magistrat of himselfe to giue way vnto the law contrarie vnto the lawes of God and nature.

That a princes faults which cannot be amended ought by all meanes to be of the magistrate couered.

A *Papinian* also to be slaine: and after the death of him so great a man, (as who alone might haue gouerned the furious yong prince, and repressed his rage) neuer ceased without any contradiction or controulment to kill, murther, and tyrannize, vntill such time as he had brought himselfe together with the Empire vnto destruction. Which I would not haue to bee so vnderstood, as spoken of vs in any respect to impaire the worthie praises of so notable a man, (for that can in no wise be done) but that magistrats may hereby vnderstand, how farre they are to beare with the faults of princes, which once done, cannot by them be amended. For had *Papinian* couered that he could not now amend, he had saued his owne life, and counterpeased the tyrannies and cruelties of the Emperour, who alwaies before had him in greatest honour and regard. **B** Which fault in *Papinian* I haue thought good to note, for that many haue right highly commended him for the same; without respecting, that such his resistance auailed nothing, but brought an irrepairable losse vnto the affaires of the empire, being so depriued of so great a personage, as might therein doe more than any other; for that he was a prince of the blood, and the greatest magistrat in the state. But had the matter then stood whole and entier, and that the Emperour had commaunded him to put his brother *Geta* to death, he had then done both stoutly and wisely in refusing so to doe, and had had iust cause rather to die than to consent to that vnnaturall fact, for one brother to murther another. But *Seneca* and his companion *Burra* (the gouernors of *Nero*) shall be for euer blamed, as hauing no excuse to pretend for their most wicked **C** counsell, persuading *Nero* to kill his mother, who by chaunce had escaped drowning: which most cruell counsell, commaund, or fact, shall together with the authors thereof be for euer crowned with eternall infamie and shame.

But what if the prince shall command any thing to be done, and that the same thing being begun to be put in execution, he changing his mind shall reuoke his former commaund; shall the magistrat in this case stay from proceeding any further, or go on with that he hath begun? Whereunto a man at the first sight would say, That he ought to stay and to proceed no farther: following therein the maximes of the law. Howbeit to aunswere rightly thereunto, the matter is by distinction to be opened; that is to wit, **D** that if the thing so begun may be left off without the publike harme, it is then so to bee left off according to the last commaund: but if it be so begun, as that it cannot bee left off, whithout the manifest hurt of the state and Commonweale; the magistrat in this case is to proceed on with that he hath so begun, notwithstanding the latter countermaund, and that especially in matters of warre; as wee haue before said. And to this purpose *Marcellus* the Consull saith, *Multa magnis ducibus sicut non aggredienda, ita semel aggressis non dimittenda*. As many things are not of great captaines to be at all taken in hand: so being once by them vndertaken, are not by them to bee againe giuen ouer. And this in time of warre. But if at home the magistrat following the commandement to him giuen, hath begun to execute the condemned, or them that the prince hath commaunded to be put to death, he ought forthwith to surcease from any further **E** execution, if the commaundement be reuoked: and not to do, as did the Consull *Fuluius*, who hauing taken the citie of Capua, as he was punishing the authors of the rebellion, and had now caused the greater part of the Senators of that citie to bee beheaded, receiuing letters from the Senat of Rome, willing him to stay and cease the execution, put those letters in his bosome, without reading of them, & doubting of the contents thereof, proceeded to the execution of the rest, vntill he had put to death fourescore of them. True it is, that the Senat had no power in any thing to commaund the Consuls (as we haue before said) yet for all that, the gouernours of prouinces, and the generals of the Roman armies, yea and the Consuls also, vsed most commonly to be obedient

A princes commaund being begun to bee put in execution, whether it be by the princes contrary commaund to be giuen ouer.

Great things by great men vndertaken, ought also to be by them performed, or else neuer taken in hand.

Ee iiij

D2 without   E5 doubting of *i.e.* suspecting, surmising (cf. Fr and L)

ent vnto the Senate, and to yeelde vnto the decrees thereof, as vnto lawes. And truely the principall cause why they of Gaunt put to death sixe and thirty of their lawyers, after the death of *Charles* Duke of Burgundy, was for nothing else, but for that they had condemned a citisen to death, after the death of the Duke; before they were againe confirmed in their authoritie and office, although it was not a thing altogether necessarie; as with like examples wee haue declared. Yea it is almost a perpetuall thing, for them which are in authoritie and haue power to commaund, to bee able of their owne right to execute that was commanded them, yea after that the time of their authoritie is expired, if he that gaue them the authoritie and charge knowing and wittingly shall dissemble the fact, or not forbid it when he might.

Now all that we haue hitherto said, is to be vnderstood onely of such letters or rescripts of commaund, as yet carrie with them no power for the magistrat to examine the fact or matter they concerne. But then what shall wee say, if such rescripts or commaunds report such things as certainely knowne and true, which yet are neither publikely, nor vnto the magistrat so knowne to be. Heere we must againe consider, whether the examination of the matter, be by speciall commaund expresly taken from the magistrat, or else left vnto him: if it be left vnto him, there is then no doubt, but that the magistrat may and ought to enquire of the truth of such things, as are reported in the princes rescripts or letters: but if al examination of the matter be taken from the magistrat, then some doubt, whether he may inquire of the truth thereof or not; and especially if it be expressed in the rescript or mandate, that the prince being well enformed of the truth, commaundeth the magistrat to proceede to the execution of his letters or commaunds: howbeit the best opinion is, that the magistrat both in the one case and the other, ought to examine the truth of the matter. For when to inquire of the truth of the cause, is neither forbidden nor commaunded, although it bee expressed in the princes rescripts or letters, to proceede to execution, yet ought the magistrat neuerthelesse to examine the truth of the mater. And to the intent, that the magistrats should not pretend to excuse themselues by ignorance, the emperour *Constantine*, prouided by an expresse law, that the magistrats should inquire, whether these things were true or not, which were set downe in his rescripts or letters of commaund, whether it were so in them expressed, or left out. And as for the other point, if in the rescripts or letters, it be expresly set downe to proceede to execution, for that the prince is well enformed of the truth of the matter; yet neuerthelesse ought the magistrat to examine the truth thereof: notwithstanding the clause which I haue said, which ought not to hinder the examination of the matter, nor to be preiudiciall to any other mans right; and so much lesse vnto the publike, and least of all vnto the truth: and so generally, all such narratiue clauses as are but reported in rescripts, mandates, commissions, lawes, priviledges, testaments, and sentences, cannot be any thing preiudiciall vnto the truth. And albeit, that during the tyranny of the *Sforces*, they made a law, that all faith and credence should be giuen vnto the princes commaunds and letters; yet was the same law againe disanulled, after that they were by the French, driuen out of the estate of Milan. And if the faith and credite must needes bee giuen vnto the narratiue clauses of princes rescripts and letters of commaund, that is to bee vnderstood, onely of such clauses, as whereby the obscure places of their edicts, and lawes, commissions, mandates, or iudgements are expounded, which none can better declare, then they themselues that made them; howbeit, that such their declarations ought rather to be called decrees, then expositions or declarations. But if the prince shall in the bestowing of offices, places of charge, or other his grants in his rescripts or letters, testifie for the fidelity, integrity, wisedome, or religion of any man, it is so farre from, that the magistrat should rest contented

margin: Whether the magistrate be to examine the trueth of that he is by the prince commaunded, before he proceede to the examination thereof?

G10 (margin) *For* examination *read* execution.

tented with that testification, as that hee ought therefore with greater diligence to inquire of him, for that the prince supposed him to be indeede such, and would not haue such benefits or preferments bestowed vpon an ignorant or vnwise man. But contrary wise, if the prince shall simply giue vnto any man an office or place of commaund, he is no farther by the magistrat to bee inquired of, for that the prince in his wisedome hath thought him worthy such honour and place; if the prince first giue him not leaue so to doe, or that the custome of the countrey so require: as in the latter times they did in Rome; but afterwards, almost euery where: but especially in the appointing of iudges. So also in antient time, in the raigne of the Gothes, triall was made of the Senators, before they were to bee admitted into the Senate. For *Theodoric*, king of the Gothes, writing vnto the Roman Senate, for the receiuing of a new Senator, saieth, *Admittendos in Senatum examinare cogit sollicitus honor Senatus*: the care (we haue) of the honour of the Senate, causeth vs to examine such as are to be admitted into the Senate.

Whether the magistrate ought to enquire of the sufficiensie of him of whose wisdom and integritie the prince shal himselfe by his rescripts or letters testifie, in the bestowing of any office or other charge vpon him

But if any man vnder a false pretensed colour shall encroach vppon the prince the profits and commodities vnto him graunted, being in the princes rescript expressed, yet is he thereof by the magistrat to be embarred; and the rather, if the common treasure be with immoderat gifts exhausted: vnto which disease euerie where spreading, remedie might be giuen, if the law of *Valois* concerning gifts might take place. For *Philip Valois* the French king, commaunded those gifts and graunts to bee reuoked from them, who in the letters of such gifts or graunts, had not expressed what they or any other for them, had for the same cause in the letters of their graunts, before obtained; which yet also is in vse in Millan. For seeing that it much concerneth the Commonweale what money and profit, what rewards, and priuileges, euery man obtaineth, the magistrats must thereunto haue a most vigilant eye, and especially in popular estates, wherin as all publike things lie open vnto the spoyle of all men; so for the same cause occasion is ministred vnto the seditious, to the trouble and oftentimes to the ruine of the Commonweale. And for this cause it was most straitly prouided by a law in the twelue tables, that no priuilege or dispensation might in any wise be graunted, and that vpon paine of death, but onely in the great assembly of the whole estate of the people: the words of the law being these, *Priuilegia nisi Commitys Centuriatis ne irroganto, qui secus faxit Capital esto*, Let no priuilege be graunted, but in the great and general assembly of the people: and he that shall otherwise doe, let him die the death. And after that *Constantine* the emperour writing vnto the people, saith, *Nec damnosa fisco, nec legibus contraria impetrari oportet*, It is not fit, things hurtfull vnto the common treasure, or contrarie vnto the laws, to be obtained: howbeit that all priuileges are directly contrarie vnto the law; for otherwise they should not be priuileges. And if it bee so, that they must needs passe after the second commaund (as we haue before said) yet beseemeth it the magistrat to cut them short, and to interpret them in strictest maner that he can, and to the least hurt of the Commonweale, as things odious, and contrarie vnto the law; and not by fauourable interpretations to encrease their strength, or to draw them into consequence, as heretofore haue the judges and the clergie, which by their faire gloses, haue drawne the profit and priuileges graunted onely vnto souldiors, vnto themselues also; vsing these faire gloasing words, of worldly Souldiours and heauenly Souldiours: so laying all the burthen vpon the poore countrey man, vnto whom the same priuileges ought of better right to be communicated than to them.

It much concerneth the Commonweale what gifts or priuileges be graunted vnto particular men.

Priuileges as things odious and contrarie vnto the lawes, how they are to be interpreted.

But for that our purpose is not here to enter into the disputing of priuileges, which were a thing infinit, sufficeth it, in passing by, in generall to aduertise the magistrat to haue speciall regard vnto the priuileges by princes graunted, and most straitly to examine

Priuileges to be most straitly examined.

D1 comitiis centuriatis   D5 treasure   Notes at B5, C5, E4.

mine them, what good report soeuer the prince therin make of him that hath obtained such priuilege: For that euery man well knoweth, that the prince oftentimes knoweth not them to whome such priuileges are graunted; vnworthy men still not so much obtaining them, as indeed wresting them from princes, euen as it were against their wils: no craft or subtiltie in this case left vnsought out, to defraud the lawes, and abuse the prince and magistrats, and that with so many shifts and quirkes of words, and so much deceit, as that they seeme hardly to be by the magistrat to be met withal, but by plaine force. Such is that clause, *De motu proprio* (of our owne meere motion) which inuented at Rome, hath from thence crept abroad into all Europe. For why, there is almost neither king nor kesar, which when question is for the breaking of a law, or repealing an edict, or for giuing way vnto dispensations and priuileges, ioyneth not thereunto this clause, *De motu nostro proprio* (Of our owne proper motion) howbeit that the same princes haue bene importuned, and as it were enforced to graunt that euen vnto vnknowne and most vnworthy men, for whome they haue bene so importunatly requested. There is at Rome a field called Flory, or Flourishing, not so much for the plentie of flowers, as of witnesses that are therein; out of which euerie man may take testimonies, for the bestowing of benefices vpon them which dwell euen in the remotest places of Asia and Affrica, and that with these words, *De motu proprio*. By which onely clause, all the fraud and deceit of them that sued for preferment, be they neuer so bad or vniust, are easily excused: and by vertue of which words the examination of all slye incommings or craftie intrusions, cease, if wee will receiue the opinion of some most pernitious and daungerous vnto the state: but such sleights and deceits wee haue long since bid farewell out of our Commonweale. And for that princes and magistrats circumuented with the wiles of deceitfull men, could hardly, or not at all escape the same, it was wisely decreed, That the princes rescripts, nor letters pattents, should be of none effect, except they were presented vnto the magistrat the same yere that they were obtained; neither should be of any force, before they were by the magistrat approued. And yet it seemeth vnto me, that the law of Milan is better, that is to wit, that the princes mandats and letters pattents directed vnto the Senat, were not to be receiued after the yeare expired: neither those that were directed vnto the magistrat after a moneth were past: and that not onely the yeare and day, but euen the verie howre also, should be therein set downe, as the manner is almost throughout all Germanie; following therein the opinion of many great lawyers, to stop the suits and controuersies which oft times arise for gifts, offices, and benefices graunted vnto diuers in one day, as it was decreed by the parliament at Blois, at the request there made by *Bodin* deputie of Vermandois.

Whether the magistrat expressely forbidden to examin the trueth of things contained in the princes grants or letters, may yet passe beyond such his soueraignes prohibition.

But what if the prince by his rescript or letters pattents, shall expresly forbid the magistrat to examine the truth of such things as are contained in them, albeit that they be false or doubtfull; ought the magistrat in this case to examine the matter? And it seemeth that he ought so to doe: For we haue before said, that hee may, and ought to examine the cause, and enquire of the truth of things expressed in the princes rescripts and letters, albeit that the prince therein declare himselfe to know the truth thereof. Yet for all that, I say, that it belongeth not vnto the magistrat in this case to passe beyond the prohibition of his soueraigne prince: For there is great difference when the prince declareth, That he knoweth the truth; and when he forbiddeth to enquire thereof: For in him it is to be presumed, that he hath bene circumuented, and so mistaking things false for true, and things vnknowne for knowne, to haue commaunded them so to be put into his rescript, which he would not haue done, had hee beene truely thereof enformed: As if hee should giue a judges place vnto a souldior, or a captaines place

vnto

F10 kesar *i.e.* emperor G5 Flory (Fr 7) Fiori (Fr 1–6, 8) G5 Flourishing *i.e.* flowering, flowery
I10 (margin) forbidden   Notes at H1, I6, K7.

vnto a lawyer, neither the one nor the other ought by the magistrat to be admitted or receiued, although the souldiour were commonly called a lawier, and the lawier a souldiour, such pretended qualitie hauing happely giuen occasion vnto the prince to be so in his graunt deceiued. But when the prince shall expresly forbid the magistrat to examine the fact or matter, it is to be presumed, that he well knoweth that which he doth, and that he would not that the magistrat should farther enquire thereof. Yet may the magistrat well vse the remedie by vs before spoken of, and show the prince the truth, and the importance of his commaund, with the inconueniences and harmes ensuing thereof, and so in what he may to draw him from his former purpose: and hauing so discharged his duetie, yet neuerthelesse then to yeeld his obedience, if he shall be againe so commaunded: for otherwise the maiestie of a prince or Commonweal should be but a mockerie, as still subiect vnto the controlement of the magistrates. Besides that, it is much more also to be feared, least that the other magistrates, by the example of one or two, and after them other priuat men also, should presume to contemne the princes commaund, to the great endangering and ruine of the Commonweale.

Now if a man should say that a Prince ought not to commaund any thing that is dishonest or vniust, he therein sayth well: neither ought the prince (if it were possible) to commaund any thing not beseeming his honour, or that were so much as subiect vnto reprehension or slaunder, or knowing the magistrates to be of contrarie opinion vnto his, to constraine them thereunto: for that the ignorant and common people is no way more moued vnto disloyaltie, and contempt of their princes edicts and lawes, then to see the magistrates hardly delt withall, and the lawes by them contrarie to their good liking published and forced. But now here the question is, what the magistrat ought to doe, in case the prince forgetting his duetie, commaund any thing contrarie to the common profit and ciuill iustice; yet prouided still that it be not against the law of God and nature: whether the magistrat ought to obey such his princes commaund, or to giue vp his place? And if so it be, that the worldly magistrat ought to be obeyed, albeit that he commaund such things as are vniust: *Ne Prætoris maiestas contempta videatur*, Lest the maiestie of the Prætor should seeme to be contemned (as saith the law) how much more then ought men to obey their soueraigne Prince, of the maiestie of whom all magistrates depend? Now it is in many lawes repeated that we must obey the magistrat, whether the thing that he commaundeth be iust or not, following the counsell of all the wise which haue hereof written. And to this purpose saith *Cicero* (albeit that he was a mortall enemie vnto the Tribunes of the people) that men were to obey euen the vniust oppositions of the Tribunes, in these words: *Parere iubet lex intercessori, quo nihil præstantius: impediri enim bonam rem melius est, quàm concedi malè*, The law (saith he) commaundeth vs to obey the magistrat that opposeth himselfe, then which nothing is better: for better it is a good thing to be crossed then euill graunted. And before he had said: *Nihil exitiosius ciuitatibus, nihil tam contrarium iuri ac legibus, nihil minùs ciuile & humanum, quàm composita & constituta republica quicquam agi per vim*, Nothing is more dangerous vnto cities, nothing more contrarie vnto right and law, nothing more vnciuill or inhumaine, then in a well ordered and setled Commonweale to haue any thing done by force. We oft times see the subiects to take vp armes against their prince, the lawes violated, and iustice go to wracke, and all for the false opinion that the people haue of the equitie and integritie of the judges, refusing to verifie and put in execution the Edicts and commaunds of their prince. O but say they it is an vniust Edict or law, neither can we, nor ought we, to obey the same: an honest speech, if indeed thou canst not; but where learnedst thou that thou oughtest not? from whence haddest thou that doctrine? wilt thou (being a magi-

Whether the magistrat commaunded by his prince any thing contrarie to the common profit, or course of ciuill iustice, ought to obey such his princes commaund, or to giue vp his place.

Dangerous vnto Commonweales for the the magistrates to refuse to put in execution their princes Edicts or commaunds.

A2 although   C7 *For* worldly magistrat *read* least magistrat (*monde* in Fr 7, *moindre* in Fr 1-6, 8).
E4(margin) for the magistrates   Notes at E5, E8.

magistrat) with stripes, imprisoment, fines, yea, and with death it selfe enforce priuat men to obey, yea euen thine vniust commaunds, and yet thy selfe not obey the commaundement of thy Prince? But thou wilt denie thine owne commaunds to be vniust: so doth the prince also denie that which he commaundeth to be so: shalt thou now be iudge herein, or he? or if thou wilt needs be iudge, why shouldst thou not thinke to suffer the same in thine owne decrees concerning priuat men. Besides that, as no man enforced thee to take vpon thee thine office, so no man forbiddeth thee to giue vp the same, if the law thou likest not seeme to thee so vniust: it is therefore the desire of bearing rule, that maketh thee that thou wouldest beare rule ouer priuat men, and yet not obey thy prince thy selfe. Wherefore let vs vpon this conclude it to be much better in all obedience to stoupe vnto the soueraigne maiestie, than in refusing of his soueraigne commaunds to giue example and occasion of rebellion vnto the subiects; yet still keeping the respects that we haue before set downe, and especially when it concerneth the honour of God, which is and ought to bee vnto all subiects greater, and more precious than the wealth, the life, the honour of all the princes of the world. And to know how a man should beare himselfe herein, amongst many examples we will vse but one or two. *Saul* commaunded all the priests of God without iust cause in his presence to be slaine, yet was there no man which refused not his vngodly commaund, except *Doeg*, who himselfe alone performed that so cruell an execution. Another notable example there is of one *Petronius* gouernour of Syria, who receiued commaundement to place the image of *Caligula* the emperour, in the fairest place of the Temple of Hierusalem, as it had beene in all other Temples of the empire: howbeit that the Iewes had neuer suffered those images to stand in their Temples, but had still cast them downe, and broken and beaten them all to peeces, euen to the verie shieldes of the emperours, which they had there placed. Whereof *Petronius* aduertised the Emperour, and that it could not be done without great trouble and slaughter of the people: wherewith *Caligula* more incensed, sent more expresse and strait commaund vnto *Petronius*, to assemble all the old bands of his garison souldiours in those quarters, and so with a puissant armie to put his commission in execution. Of whose comming the Iewes hearing, left their Townes, and the tillage of their grounds, and so in great companies all vnarmed, went to meet him, if happily they so might by their humble prayers intreat him; telling him withall, that they ought not so much to feare any mortall man, as to commit so abhominable a sinne against the maiestie of the immortall God: and therfore most humbly requested him to take in good part such their constant resolution, which was rather to die, than to see so great an abhomination, as the most sacred Temple of God to be so polluted with the images of men. Neuerthelesse *Petronius* told them that it concerned his life, to performe his commission: and so to terrifie them the more, marched with his armie vnto Tiberias, (as supposing himselfe to doe nothing contrarie to his owne religion, or to the lawes of God or man) but there the people came running vnto him from all parts, disarmed, and resolued all to die, rather than to see the image set vp in the Temple, humbling themselues, and bowing their heads before the armie wherewith *Petronius* had beset them round: who seeing the great constancie of the people, and their exceeding zeale towards the honour of their God, as to chuse rather to die, than so much as to see the image of a man in the Temple of God; wonderfully moued therewith, and with their pitifull complaint and teares, (and being himselfe also a man of a courteous and milde nature, and farre from that crueltie, which the Iewes feared not whatsoeuer it had beene) he commaunded them all to returne home; promising againe to write in their behalfe vnto the Emperour, and rather himselfe to die than to execute his commission, accounting

A notable example of a wise gouernour or magistrat.

ting his life a worthie ransome for the sauing of the guiltles blood of so many innocent people. Neuerthelesse *Caligula* therewith the more enraged, sent vnto him a new commaund, with grieuous threats to put him vnto the most grieuous torture that he could possibly deuise, if he forthwith put not his commission in execution, according to his commaund. But the ship, together with them that brought the commission, was by force of tempest caried an other way, and newes brought into Iurie of the death of the tyrant, before that the cruell commission could come thither. And so *Petronius* hauing discharged his conscience towards God, his duetie towards his prince, and well showed his great loue toward the subiects, and discharged all the parts of a most wise Gouernour: was himselfe by the diuine prouidence wonderfully preserued from the cruelties vnto him by the tyrant threatned. But yet this is especially to be considered, that we pretend not the vaine show of religion, or rather of superstition, against our princes commaunds, and so vpon a conscience euill grounded open a way vnto rebellion: for when the magistrat maketh conscience, and a matter of religion, about the executing of his princes commaunds, he seemeth himselfe (and giueth occasion vnto others also) to suspect euill both of the religion and conscience of his prince. Wherefore he ought to be well assured of the true knowledge of the eternall God, and of the true worship and seruice vnto him due: which consisteth not in vaine and counterfeit showes of religion or conscience. Diuers other examples I could to the same purpose produce, were I not afraid lest those whom we call Pagans should therein ashame vs, with whom the feruent zeale vnto the honour of God is so abated, and by processe of time cooled, as that it is to be feared lest at length it be altogether frosen. And thus much for the obedience of the Magistrat vnto his Soueraigne Prince. Let vs now also speake of his power and authoritie ouer particular and priuat men, and what a manner of man we wish him for to to be towards them.

That the Magistrat ought not vpõ a vaine show of religion, or a conscience euill grounded, to refuse to execute his princes commaunds.

Chap. V.

¶ *Of the power and authoritie of a Magistrat ouer particular and priuat men, and of his office and duetie.*

WE haue before said, That a Magistrat is an officer which hath publike power to commaund, or to forbid: Now he hath power so to command or forbid, which hath publike power to enforce or constraine them which will not obey that which he enioyneth them, or which do contrarie to his prohibition, and may also ease the prohibitions by himselfe made. For albeit that the law saith, That the force of the lawes consisteth in commaunding, and forbidding; in suffering, and punishing: yet is this power more proper vnto the Magistrat, then vnto the law, which is of it selfe dombe: wheras the Magistrat is a liuing and breathing law, which putteth all this in execution, seeing that the law in it selfe carrieth or containeth nothing but commaunds or prohibitions, which are but mockeries and to no purpose, if the Magistrat and the punishment were not attendant at the foot of the law, readie for him which transgresseth the same. Howbeit that to speake properly, the law containeth nothing but the verie prohibition, and the threats for not obeying the same; considering that he which commaundeth (inclusiuely) forbiddeth to transgresse his command: and as for sufferance, that is no law: for sufferance taketh away prohibition, and carrieth with it neither penaltie nor threat, without which the law cannot be, considering that the law is no other thing, then the commandement of the soueraigne, as we haue before declared: and whatsoeuer threat or penaltie is propounded by the law, yet the punishment neuertheless neuer ensueth the breach thereof, vn-

The Magistrat a liuing law.

Ff till

till it be pronounced by the mouth of the Magistrat. Whereby it euidently appeareth all the force of the law to consist in them which haue the commaund, whether it bee prince, people, or magistrat, vnto whome so commaunding, except the subiects yeeld their obedience, they haue power to enforce or punish them, which *Demosthenes* calleth the verie sinewes of the Commonweale.

The force of the law to consist in the Magistrate, or him that hath the power to commaund and constraine.

We haue said, that the Magistrat ought to haue publike power, to put a difference betwixt this power and the domesticall power. We said also, that the Magistrat should haue power to constraine such as would not obey: for the difference from them which haue the hearing of matters, who may also iudge and pronounce sentence, & call men before them, but yet haue no power to compell or constraine men, or to put their sentences or commaundements in execution; such as were in auntient time the bishops, and now our bishops also: such were also the auntient commissioners, delegats vnto the Magistrats, hauing power to heare the causes vnto them committed; as also to condemne the parties, but yet had no power to constraine them, but sent their sentences vnto the Magistrats, to be ratified or reuersed, and by them to be put in execution as they saw good: So might these delegates call men before them, but yet so, as that no man, except he listed, needed to obey them, except the Magistrats themselues had by vertue of their authoritie so commaunded. And therefore he was not in danger of the law, who had by force rescued a priuat man, as he was to be brought before these priuat judges or delegates appointed by the Magistrats, which he should haue incurred, had the delegates had of themselues any power to commaund. Howbeit that now by our lawes and customes the delegates haue with vs power to command, and to cause their sentences to be put in execution by sargeants and other publike persons, by vertue of their decrees which they giue out, signed and sealed with their owne hands and seales: whereas the bishops with vs haue no such power to constraine men, but send their sentences to be executed by the Magistrats. As the Cadies, and Paracadies do in all the East, who haue the hearing of all matters, but yet haue no power to constraine men, but send their iudgements vnto the Sabbassaes, which haue the commaund and power in their hand.

What power the Magistrat ought to haue?

The first constraining power that the magistrat hath.

We haue before said, that the first constraint of all them which had power to commaund, is the ceising or attaching both of mens goods and persons; which the auntients called *prehensio*, or as we say an apprehending or laying on of hands: for it were to no purpose, for the Magistrat to call a man before him, to iudge him, or to fine him; and when all is done not to haue power to seise vpon their goods nor person of him that shall disobey him. Now we haue before said, that some there be, which haue such power to apprehend and attache men; which yet haue no authoritie or power to call a man before them, neither to examine a matter, neither to rescue a man, neither to enlarge them whome they haue committed; as we haue showed of the Tribunes of the people, of the eleuen Magistrats in Athens, of the Capitall Triumuiri in Rome, of the Auogadours in Venice, of the kings Attourneies, and the deputies of them which haue power of the common treasure in other realmes and Commonweales: and of the Commissioners of the Chastelet of Paris, who may all imprison men, and seise vppon them, and yet for all that cannot releeue or enlarge them, which belongeth onely vnto the publike Magistrats, which haue power to condemne and acquite, and to iudge, some of them of mens goods onely, other some of mens goods and honour also, aud other some of mens goods and honour, with power to inflict corporall punishment also, but not death: and some hauing power to put to death also, and that some of them such power, as from whome men may appeale; and some others, such as from whom men may not appeale. But the last and highest degree, is of such as haue the absolute power

The diuers power of Magistrats.

K6 and other   Notes at F4, H4, K10.

Of A Commonweale. 327

A er of life and death; that is to say, power to condemne to death, and againe to giue life vnto him which hath deserued to die; which is the highest marke of soueraigntie, aboue all lawes, and aboue the power and authoritie of all Magistrats, as proper onely vnto soueraigntie, as we haue before declared. Whereby it appeareth, that there are two kinds of commaunding by publike power: the one in soueraigntie, which is absolute, infinit and aboue the lawes, the Magistrats, and all other priuat persons: the other is a lawfull commaund, as subiect vnto the lawes and soueraigntie, and is proper vnto the Magistrats, and them which haue extraordinarie power to commaund, vntill it be againe reuoked, or the time of their commission expired. The soueraigne prince next vnder God knoweth none greater than himselfe; the Magistrat vnder God holdeth

The highest marque of soueraign maiestie is to haue power of life and death.

Two sorts of commmaunding by publique power: the one in soueraigntie, and the other by lawe

B his power of his soueraigne prince, and remaineth alwaies subiect vnto him and his lawes: the particular man next after God (whome wee must alwayes put in the first place) acknowledgeth the soueraigne prince, his lawes, and his Magistrats, euerie one of them in his place. Vnder the name of Magistrats I vnderstand also them which haue iurisdiction annexed vnto their fees, considering that they hold them also as well of the soueraigne prince, as do the Magistrats, in such sort, as that it seemeth that there are none in the Commonweale but the soueraigne princes, which may properly vse these words, *Impero & iubeo,* I charge and commaund: which in auntient time signified, I will and commaund, seeing that the will of euerie Magistrat, and of all others also, which haue power to command, is bound and dependeth wholly of the soueraigne,

C which may alter, chaunge, and reuoke it at his pleasure. For which cause there is neither any one Magistrat, nor yet all together, which can put in their commissions, *Such is our pleasure*: or this clause, *Vpon paine of death,* for that none but a soueraigne prince or state, can vse the same in their edicts or lawes.

And hereof riseth a notable question, which is not yet well decided, *viz.* Whether the power of the sword (which the law calleth *Merum imperium,* or meere power) be proper vnto the soueraigne prince, and inseparable from the soueraigntie; and that the Magistrats haue not this *merum imperium* (or meere power) but onely the execution thereof: or that such power is also common vnto the Magistrat, to whome the prince hath communicated the same. Which question was disputed betwixt *Lothaire* and

Whether the power of the sword be proper onely vnto the soueraign prince or common also vnto the magistrat to whom the prince hath communicated the same?

D *Azon,* two of the greatest lawyers of their time: and the emperour *Henrie* the seuenth chosen thereof judge, at such time as he was at Bononia, vpon the wager of an horse, which he should pay, which was by the iudgement of the emperour vppon the aforesaid question condemned. Wherein *Lothaire* indeed carried away the honour, howbeit that the greater part, & almost all the rest of the famous lawyers then held the opinion of *Azon*; saying, That *Lothaire equum tulerat, sed Azo æquum* (*Lothaire* had carried away the horse, but *Azon* the right) neuertheles many since haue holden the opinion of *Lothaire*: so that the question remaineth yet (as we said) vndecided, which for all that deserueth to be well vnderstood, for the consequence it draweth after it, for the better vnderstanding of the force and nature of commaunding, and the rights of soueraign

E maiestie. But the difficultie thereof is growne, for that *Lothaire* and *Azon* neither of them well knew the estate of the Romans, whose lawes and ordinances they expounded; neither tooke regard vnto the chaunge in that estate made by the comming in of the emperours. Certaine it is, that at the first, after that the kings were driuen out of the citie, none of the Roman Magistrats had power of the sword ouer the citisens: yea that which much lesse is, they had not so much power, as to condemne any citisen to be whipped or beaten, after the law Portia. published at the request of *Cato* Tribune of the people, 454 yeares after the foundation of the citie. By which law the people tooke this power, not from the Magistrats onely, but dispoyled euen it selfe thereof also so

No magistrate in Rome after the kings once driuen out, had power of the sword.

much

Ff ij

A8(margin) commaunding   D1 Henrie the seventh (Fr) Henry V (L) *properly* Henry VI

Note at C5.

much as it could, giuing the condemned leaue for what fault or offence soeuer it were, to void the countrey, and to go into exile: and that which more is, there was not any one magistrat, which had power to judge a citisen, if once question were but of his honour, or good name, or of any publike crime by him committed; for then the hearing thereof was reserued vnto the comminaltie, or common people: but if it concerned the losse of life, or of the freedome of a citisen, none might then iudge thereof, but the whole estate of the people in their greatest assemblies, as was ordained by those lawes, which they called Sacred. Which although that they were not alwaies so precisely kept, but that they were sometime broken; yet *Cicero* for transgressing the same escaped not, but being Consull, and hauing caused certaine of the conspirators with *Cateline* to be executed, was therefore himselfe afterwards banished, and his goods all confiscated. Long after the lawes Valeria, Sempronia, and Portia, which had now remoued the Consuls hatchets and rods from the heads and backs of the citisens of Rome: *Cornelius Sylla* the dictator published his lawes concerning publike iudgements, wherby were appointed a certaine number of Prætors, as ordinarie officers, which were to iudge of all such causes as whereof the comminaltie before iudged, or at leastwise appointed commissioners for to iudge of such crimes, as of murders, of robbing of the common treasure, of treason, or of extortion; but yet so, as that these Pretors had their lesson by writing, beyond which they might not passe a iot. For they by lot drew a certaine number of particular judges out of them, which by the lawes might in such causes be iudiciarie judges, who before all the people hauing heard the accusations and defenses both of the one part and the other, had brought vnto euerie one of them the judges, three little tables of diuers colours, vpon one of which was written an A. vppon another a C. and vpon the third N. L. the A. signifying acquited, C. condemned, and N. L. as much as to say, *Non Liquet*, or it is not manifest, or the matter is farther to bee inquired of (which they called *Ampliare*, and *Amplius quærere*.) With these tables was also brought vnto the judges a vessell whereinto euerie one of them did cast one of the three aforesaid tables, without any word speaking: Which done they counted the tables so cast in, and if there were moe marked with C. cast in, then the Pretor in his purple robe mounting into an high seat, in open place, and in the sight of all the people pronounced these words, *Reus parum cauisse videtur*, which is to say, It seemeth that the partie accused, hath not kept himselfe from doing amisse; or else *Non iure fecisse videtur*, He seemeth not to haue done right; or *Videtur prouinciam spoliasse*, He seemeth to haue spoyled the prouince. This was the Roman grauitie in iudgement mixt with modestie, least they should seeme therein to lie, or rashly to affirme any thing which was not altogether most manifestly tried. Of which sort are these words also, *Si quid mei iudicij est*, If my iudgement be any thing. So presently after the Pretor had pronounced the aforesaid words, the penaltie of the law was put in execution, the partie condemned voided the countrie and went into exile, and the receiuers seised vpon his goods. If such penaltie were for the offence of the law appointed, vnto which law except the partie so condemned yeelded himselfe obedient, he was forthwith by the Triumuirie of causes capitall, apprehended and cast in prison. Wherefore, might some man say, that these capitall Triumuiri had power ouer the citisens: But wee said before them to haue had power onely ouer straungers, and that truely: and so men condemned to exile, are but to be accounted straungers, for that they haue lost the libertie of the citie. To like purpose is that which *Martian* the lawyer writeth, concerning the decree of the Senat, at the motion of *Turpilian*, *Si iudex pronunciauit hæc verba, calumniatus es, condemnauit eum*, If the judge (saith he) hath pronounced these words, Thou hast slaundered, he hath therein condemned him: and albeit that he say no more concerning

The great modestie of the Romaines in their judgments.

G10–H1 *For which by the lawes might in such causes be judiciarie judges* read which by the judiciarie lawes might in such causes be judges (cf. Fr). I10 goods, if such I10 of the law *i.e.* by the law

A cerning the punishment of the offendor, yet shall the penaltie of the law neuerthelesse be executed vpon him. Not to speake in the meane time of the inscriptions of their libels, with the examination of witnesses and writings. This was the manner of the publike iudgements vsed by the auntient Romans: VVherby it is easily to be vnderstood, that the Pretors or judges were but onely the simple executioners of the law, without power to adde or diminish one iot thereof, hauing not onely no power of the sword, but not so much as to whip, or yet lightly to punish a citisen.

Now if question were for the fine of any publike crime, which was not prouided for by the law, the lesser assembly of the common people or comminaltie, was called together therefore: But if question were of the life, good name, or the whole estate of
B any citisen, the people then in their greatest and most solemne assemblies gaue iudgement thereof: and that in both cases extraordinarily, as commonly they vse to doe which haue the soueraigntie in all Commonweals: neither were voyces in these cases giuen by tables or markes: for that the law it selfe, and not the people, was made iudge of the punishment to be inflicted. The sentence of which law was almost this, or such like, *Si M. Posthumius ante Calendas Maias non prodisset, neque excusatus esset, videri eum in exilio esse: ipsi aqua & igni placere interdici*, If *M. Posthumius* made not his appearance before the first of May, neither made his excuse, it should seeme good that hee should be banished, and decreed, That he should be forbid the vse of fire and water: all which things are more plentifully and at large set downe by *Liuie Asconius*, and
C *Cicero*. But if the state of the Commonweale being chaunged, and the power of iudgement and of giuing of voices, being taken from the people, yet for a certaine time continued this manner and forme of iudiciall proceedings, euen after that the forme of the Commonweale was chaunged from a Popular estate into a Monarchie, as a man may see in the time of *Papinian* the great lawyer, who gaue occasion vnto *Lothaire* & *Azon* to make question of the matter, in these words by him set downe as a maxime, *Whatsoeuer it is that is giuen vnto Magistrats by decree of the Senat, by speciall law, or by the constitution of princes, that is not in their power to commit vnto other persons: and therefore* (saith he) *the Magistrats do not well in committing that their charge vnto others, if it bee not in their absence: which is not so* (saith he) *in them that haue power, without the limita-*
D *tion of speciall laws, but onely in vertue of their office, which they may commit vnto others, albeit that they themselues be present*. And thus much for that which *Papinian* doth say, vsing the words, *Exercitionem publici iudicij*: as if he should say, That they which haue the soueraigne maiestie haue recciued vnto themselues the power of the sword, and by speciall law giuen, but the execution thereof vnto the Magistrats. And this is the opinion of *Lothaire*. By which words yet *Azon* vnderstandeth the right and power of the sword it selfe to haue bene translated and giuen vnto the Magistrats. Now there is no doubt, but that the opinion of *Lothaire* was true, if hee had spoken but of the auntient Pretors of Rome, and so kept himselfe within the tearmes and compasse of *Papinian* his rule: but in that he was deceiued, that he supposed that maxime or rule of *Papinians*,
E to extend to all Magistrats which haue bene since or yet are in all Commonweals, who yet for the most part haue the hearing of murders, robberies, riots, and other such like offences, and so the power of the sword giuen vnto them euen by vertue of their offices. For the emperours and law giuers hauing in the processe of time seene the inconuenience and iniustice that arise by condemning all murtherers, vnto one and the selfe same punishment, or els quite to absolue them: and so the like in other publike crimes also, thought it much better to ordaine and appoint certaine Magistrats, who according to their conscience and deuotion, might encrease or diminish the punishment, as they saw equitie and reason to require. And first of all *Augustus* vnto the three little tables

Great magistrats in commonweals to haue now oftentimes the power of the sword committed vnto them euen by vertue of their offices.

Ff iij

A2-3 libels *i.e. libelli*, written documents   B10 Livie, Asconius   D4 *For* received *read* reserved.
D5 given but   Notes at A1, B4, C6.

tables noted with A. C. and N. L. added a fourth, whereby it was lawfull for the judges to pardon them, who by other mens fraud or deceit had offended the law, as wee read in *Suetonius*. And by little and little the auntient order and manner in the iudicial or penall laws set downe, was chaunged; the penaltie by euery one of them appointed yet neuerthelesse still remaining, not by any to be encreased or diminished, but by them which we haue before said, what diuersitie of causes soeuer happened. And oftentimes the emperours committed it vnto the Senat, or some other the great and most worthy magistrats extraordinarily to iudge of great personages, or of some notable crimes, and to punish them as they saw cause, or thought best, without binding them vnto the ordinarie penall lawes. But in the time of *Papinian*, *Seuerus* the emperour gaue power vnto the great Prouost of Rome, extraordinarily to iudge of all offences and crimes, whatsoeuer they were, committed within the citie or within fortie leagues round about it. Yea the other Pretors of the citie, who but by the ordinarie course of law were to iudge of ciuill causes and priuat crimes, dealt also with certaine publike iudgements referred vnto them, not by vertue of their office, but by the law it selfe: whereof *Papinian* sheweth example. And sometime the Pretor preuenting the great Prouost, so by way of preuention extraordinarily iudged of extraordinarie crimes, together with the great Prouost. As for the presidents and gouernours of prouinces, in that they had power and authoritie of all the Magistrats of the citie, and extraordinarily iudged of all offences, and according to their owne discretion appointed both penall and capitall punishment vnto all men, except the citisens of Rome; no man can reasonably doubt, but that they had the power of the sword, and were therefore called *Potestates*: for that before the creating of the great Prouost, there was none but the gouernours of the prouinces which had the power of the sword; whom they yet call euen to this present in Italie, by the name of Potestats. Now it is plaine by the maximes of the law, that the Magistrats which had power extraordinarily to iudge, might condemne the guiltie parties to such punishments as they would, yet so, as that they exceeded not measure: For so *Vlpian* the lawyer writeth, him to exceed measure, who for a small or light offence inflicteth capitall punishment; or for a cruell murther imposeth a fine. VVhereof wee may then conclude, that the great Prouost, and the gouernours of prouinces, and generally all such Magistrats as haue extraordinarie authority to iudge of capitall crimes (whether it bee by commission, or by vertue of their office) haue the power of the sword, that is to say, to iudge, to condemne, or acquit; and not the bare execution of the law onely, whereunto they are not in this respect bound as are the other Magistrats, vnto whome the law hath prescribed what and how they are to iudge, leauing vnto them the naked execution of the law, without the power of the sword.

Al magistrats hauing athoritie to iudge of capital crimes, to haue the power of the sword.

And thus much briefly, concerning the question betwixt *Lothaire* and *Azon*: for the fuller and more plentifull declaration whereof, it is needfull for vs yet to search farther: where it is first to be enquired, Whether the Magistrats office be proper vnto the Commonweale, or vnto the prince, or vnto the magistrat himself that beareth office, or else be common vnto the Magistrat himselfe together with the Commonweale? Then whether the power graunted vnto the Magistrats be proper vnto the Magistrats, in that they are magistrats, or els be proper vnto the prince, the execution therof only belonging vnto the magistrats; or else be common vnto them both together? Now concerning the first question, there is no doubt, but that all estates, magistrats, & offices, do in proprietie belong vnto the Commonweale (excepting in a lordly Monarchie) the bestowing of them, resting with them which haue the soueraigntie (as we haue before said) and cannot by inheritance be appropriat vnto any particular persons, but by the graunt

To whom the proprietie of estats, magistracie, and offices doe properly belong.

G7 by way of prevention *i.e.* by being the first to exercise jurisdiction   K9 of them   K9 them
which have   Note at I9.

OF A COMMONWEALE. 331

A graunt of the soueraigne; and long and secret consent of the estates, confirmed by a long lawfull and iust possession. As in this kingdome, the Dukes, Marquesses, Counties, and such others as haue from the prince the gouernment of the castles in sundrie prouinces, and so the commaund of them, had the same in auntient time but by commission onely, to be againe reuoked at the pleasure of the soueraigne prince, but were afterward by little and little graunted vnto particular men for tearme of their liues, and after that vnto their heires males, and in processe of time vnto the females also: insomuch as that in fine, through the negligence of princes, soueraigne commaunds, iurisdictions, and powers, may lawfully be set to sale, as well as may the lands themselues, by way of lawfull buing and selling, almost in all the empires and kingdoms of the West; and so are accounted of, as other hereditarie goods, which may lawfully bee bought and sold. Wherefore this iurisdiction or authoritie which for that it seemeth to bee annexed vnto the territorie or land (and yet in truth is not) and is thereof called Prædiatorie, is proper vnto them which are possessed of such lands, whether it bee by inheritance, or by other lawfull right, and that as vnto right and lawfull owners thereof, in giuing fealtie and homage vnto the soueraigne prince, or state, from whome all great commaunds and iurisdictions flow, and in sauing also the soueraigne rights of the kingdome, and the right of the last appeale.

Dukedomes, earledomes, marquisats, and such like in auntient time but simple commissions, now for most part are become hereditarie.

Other publique officers there bee also which haue neither iurisdiction nor commaund, but onely a certeine publique and seruile charge: as the foure offices of the Waxe-chafers in this realme, by right of inheritance belonging vnto certein men, by the graunt of king *Lewes.* Diuers also haue attempted by processe of time to prescribe the offices of the Constables both of Normandie and Champagne; as also the offices of the great Chamberlaines, by right of inheritance to belong vnto them: howbeit that in that their sute they haue beene often times by diuers decrees reiected, and amongst others by one solemne one, in the records of the court made in the yeare 1272. True it is that the word (Constable) was in auntient time no other thing than the captaine of a companie, which they called a Constableship, as we oftentimes read in *Frosard.* And in the records of the Chamber of accounts I remember I haue red, three hundred Constables to haue beene at once in the armie. We read also that by the decree of the yeare 1274. *Simon* Countie of Montfort was excluded from the successiue right which he pretended to the honor of the Mareshalship *D'la foy*, which the lords of Mirepoix challenge vnto themselues in their styles. And forasmuch as certeine Mareshals of Fraunce would haue continued their estates in their posteritie and successors, they were embarred so to doe by a decree made in Parliament the xxij of Ianuarie, in the yeare 1361, as is to be found in the records of the court: wherein it is expresly set downe, That the estates of the Marshalships of Fraunce should bee as part of the demaine of the Crowne, and the execution thereof to remaine vnto the Marshals so long as they liued. And albeit that the power of the Mareshals was not of force but in time of warre, (as was iudged by a decree of the xv of August in the yeare 1459,) yet neuerthelesse the militarie discipline carried with it the power of the sword, albeit that it were not giuen vnto it by expresse Edict or law; as in nothing communicating with the decrees and lawes of ciuill pollicie, or of other the ciuill magistrats; which seemeth from the auntient manners and customes of the Romans to haue beene vnto vs translated. For albeit that the power of the sword, yea and of punishing with rods also was by the law Portia taken from all the Roman magistrats (so that it was not lawfull for any of them, or for all of them in the citie to beate or scourge a Roman citisen, as we haue before noted,) yet neuerthelesse the Consull had still full power of life and death ouer the souldiours and men of warre, (without which their militarie discipline

Some publique offices to be without any iurisdiction or commaund at al.

The states of the marshalships of Fraunce part of the demaine of the crowne.

Ff iiij   could

Notes at C2, C9.

Marshal magistrats and Generals must of necessitie haue the power of the sword giuen them.

could neuer haue bene kept and preserued) from whom there was no mean to appeal as saith *Polybius*, and for that cause saith he, the Consuls had royall power: howbeit he marked not, that the Prætors, Dictators, Quæstors, and other Generals of their armies, had euen the selfe same power. In like manner the Constable of Fraunce by his letters of commission hath not the power of the sword, or of life and death graunted vnto him: but hauing the managing of the warres, and conducting of the armyes, as in his absence the Mareshals of Fraunce haue: the power of the sword is also left vnto them, as without which militarie discipline cannot possibly be maintained: which martiall power the simple captaines abused also, putting their souldiours to death, without any forme or fashion of iust triall. Vnto that *Henry* the second the French king, at the request of *Francis Colineus* the Dandelot, then Colonell of the footmen, by expresse edict forbid them any more so to do.

If then the martiall Magistrats and Generals haue in euery Commonweal the power of the sword without any limitation or restriction vnto the forme of proceeding or of the punishment to be by them inflicted, according to the varietie of crimes and offences, all being as it were left vnto their owne discretion and iudgement, a man then cannot truely say them to be but the simple executioners of the law, considering that they haue no law whereunto they are in this regard subiect: and so consequently we may conclude, that the power of the sword is transferred into their persons, that power now not remayning in the prince alone. Whereby it also followeth, that they being present, may commit vnto others, so much of that power and authoritie which they haue by vertue of their place and office, as they please, and retaine thereof vnto themselues what shall seeme vnto them good, which they could in no wise doe, if by speciall law they were constrained and bound, to heare & determine of matters themselues, and from word to word to follow the solemnitie and paines set downe in the lawes. And this is it for which the law saith, That the Prætor of the citie, being himselfe present, might commit his authoritie and power to whom soeuer hee saw good, which the Prætors for publike causes could not do: for the Prætor of the citie had the hearing and disciding of all ciuill and criminall causes, (except such as they called publique, as belonging to the common state) which fell out betwixt the citisens of Rome: as had also the Prætor, established for the hearing of causes betwixt straungers and citisens, who according to their discretion condemned, or acquited such as were conuented before them, moderating, correcting, or supplying the rigour or lenitie of the law as they saw cause, which their power was limitted by the will and discretion of the Pretor so iudging, and not by the necessitie of the law. And yet when as by the law or decree of the Senat, any particular cause otherwise out of their iurisdiction was committed vnto them, albeit that it were referred vnto their conscience to iudge thereof, yet neuerthelesse could they not in this case commit the same vnto others, as is to be seene by many examples noted by the lawyers. Which point so manifested leadeth vs vnto the disciding of an other question by vs before propounded: *viz*. That the power and authoritie graunted vnto Magistrats by vertue of their office, is proper vnto the office, albeit that the honour and dignitie of the office be not proper vnto the person: for *Papinian* saying, That Commissioners and Lieutenants haue nothing proper vnto themselues, but that they vse the power and authoritie of them, which haue commissionate and deputed them, sufficiently showeth, that the power is proper vnto them which so commissionate and deputed them, whether they be Soueraigne Princes, or Magistrats hauing power so to doe. And so in like case the law sayth, That the Gouernour of a countrey or prouince, hath within his gouernment all power and authoritie next vnto his Prince: wherefore it is not then onely in the prince. But the difficultie

The power and authoritie graunted vnto magistrats by vertue of their office, proper vnto the office and not to the person of the magistrats.

I 10 an other question *i.e.* the second question (cf. 330 K4-6)   K6 Soueraigne   K8 the Gouernour Note at K2.

A difficultie of this question dependeth principally on this distinction, (whereunto the interpretours of the law haue had no regard,) as namely, that it is great difference to say that the power or authoritie is proper vnto the Magistrat in the qualitie of a magistrat, or in the qualitie of a particular person: for it followeth not, that if the authoritie or iurisdiction be proper vnto the Prætorship, that therefore the Prætorship should be proper vnto the person: but to the contrarie the law saith, That he hath it in trust, and that he is but the keeper thereof. So we call the Prouost of Paris the keeper of the Prouostship of that citie; which is to speake properly, and to show, that the estates and offices rest and remaine in the possession and propertie of the Commonweale, as a thing put in trust vnto the magistrat. And for that cause the Bailiffes of cities and
B townes are so called of the word (Bail,) that is to say Gardiens or keepers. So also the Florentines called the Ten men deputed to the keeping of their state and soueraigntie by the name of Bailifes. And that is it for which the Court of parliament in the decree concerning the Mareschals of Fraunce (before noted) saith, That their estate was of the proper demaine of the Crowne, as thereunto properly appertaining, and the exercise thereof belonging vnto them so long as they liued. And so we may discide the generall question, and discusse the controuersie betwixt *Lothaire*, and *Azon*, who spake but of the power of the sword onely: and conclude, that as oft and whensoeuer the Magistrats and Commissioners are bound by the lawes and decrees, to vse the power and authoritie which is giuen them, in such prescript forme and manner as is therein
C set downe, whether it be in the forme of proceeding, or concerning the punishment; without power for the magistrats to adde or diminish any thing thereunto, or from: in this case they are but meere executors and ministers of the lawes and of the princes, from whom they haue their authoritie: yet not hauing any power in this point or respect in themselues, whether it be concerning ciuill pollicie, or the administration of iustice, or the mannaging of warre, or treaties to be had betwixt princes, or the charges of Embassadours: but in that which is left or committed to the magistrates integritie and discretion, in that case the power and authoritie lyeth in themselues.

Now as in euery Commonweale there are two principall points which the magistrats ought alwaies to haue before their eyes: that is to say, the Law, and Equitie: so
D say we, that there is also the execution of the law, and the dutie of the magistrat, which the auntients called *Legis actionem*, and *Iudicis officium*: or as we say, the action or execution of the law, and duetie of the judge; which is to commaund, to decree, or to put in execution. And as the word *Iudicium*, or judgement, is properly vnderstood of that which is ordained by the magistrat following the strict teatmes and tenour of the law: so the word *Decretum*, is likewise properly vnderstood of that which the magistrat ordaineth or decreeth, following equitie without the prescript law; the law it selfe being still referred to the strict execution thereof, and equitie vnto the duetie of the magistrat. And for this cause all the decrees of the Prince are properly called *Decreta*, and not *Iudicia*, Decrees I say not judgements: for why the soueraigne prince is not
E subiect vnto the law; wherein they deceiue themselues, which take a decree to be any thing else then the resolute sentence of the Senat in their consultations: or the decree of a soueraigne prince, or the voluntarie ordinance of a magistrat, without being bound to law or custome in the making thereof. Now such proportion as there is of the law vnto the execution thereof, the like there is of equitie vnto the office of the judge. And so likewise of magistrats, who in case wherein they are not subiect to the law, resemble arbitrators: but being strictly and wholly bound vnto the law, are but as judges appointed to vnderstand of the fact onely, without any power of themselues to determine of the merit or iustice of the cause, otherwise than the verie strictnesse of the law appoin-

B2 the Ten men (Fr) the eight men (L)   Notes at A9, E4.

appointeth. Now of these the one is is seruile, the other is noble; the one is bound vnto the law, the other is not so; the one vnderstandeth but of the fact, the other of the right; the one is proper vnto the magistrat, the other is reserued vnto the law; the one is precisely written in the law, the other is without the lawes: the one is in the magistrats power, and the other quite without the same. And the better to note and perceiue this difference, the law saith, That it is not lawfull for a man to appeale from the punishment set downe by the law, being pronounced by the magistrat, but onely from that the judge hath declared and denounced the partie accused to be guiltie: whereas it is right lawfull for a man to appeale from the punishment which the judge by his owne discretion appointeth: For he which appealeth from the law, appealeth from the prince, from whome no appeale is to be made. And thus much concerning the distinction of the power of magistrats, whereby not onely the question of *Lothaire* and *Azon* is decided, but many others also concerning the charge and duetie of magistrats, wherewith diuers haue sore entangled themselues, some mistaking the practise, and some the theorique, but most part, for not hauing vnderstood the Roman estate, albeit that they were well exercised and seene in all the parts of their lawes, and yet neuerthelesse in the state of magistrats, concerning their power and authoritie they found themselues greatly troubled. For *Moulin* himselfe (the honour of lawyers) not vsing the distinctions by vs before set downe, hath without reason followed the opinion of *Alciat* and *Lothaire*: Whereunto he addeth the Pretors of cities, whome wee call Bailifes, and Seneshals, by the lawes of this realme, to haue had the power taken from them for the appointing of their deputies: for that they are but as simple vsagers or occupiers, and that he which hath a thing but onely to vse and occupie, cannot make any other vsager or occupier but himselfe; which is a reason without apparance, as we haue before shewed. VVhereunto ioyne also, that it is not past an hundred or six score yeares at the most, since that *Charles* the seuenth, and the eight, were the first which made an office of the Lieutenants, or deputies of Bailifes and Seneschals. For if *Moulin* his opinion were grounded vpon reason, why should *Papinian* expresly say, That magistrats may depute and commit in their presence so much and so long, and with such limitation as they themselues please, of such things as they haue by vertue of their office, and which are proper to their estate? Now their magistrats estates and offices in auntient time were much lesse proper, and lesse appropriat vnto the persons, than they be at this present. For with vs they are perpetuall, and in Rome they continued but for one yeare; and therefore might with much better reason than they appoint their lieutenants or deputies. Besides that, the lawyers themselues haue made and written diuers expresse bookes concerning lieutenants and deputies, which were all to no purpose, if the comparison of him, which hath but the vse onely vnto the magistrat, were to be admitted and receiued. And as for others, the auntient doctors and interpretors of the law; they haue in such sort entangled themselues, as that it euidently appeareth them to haue had no insight into the estate or gouernment of the Roman Commonweale: without which it is impossible to determine any thing concerning these questions. For whereas the Romans had properly separated the office of the Proconsuls Lieutenant, whome they called *Legatum*, from the office of the Proconsull himselfe: and so of the deputie tearmed a particular Commissioner, whome they called *Iudicem datum*, from the Commissioner himselfe, and of him vnto whome power was giuen by the magistrat to commaund, whome they called *Eum cui mandata iurisdictio est*, the doctors haue confounded all together vnder the name of Delegats, which were a thing too long, and too superfluous to refute, hauing proposed vnto our selues no other end, but to entreat of that which concerneth the estate and duetie of magistrats in generall.

It

No appealing from the lawe: and why?

It is also worth the noting, that in Popular and Aristocratique estates, such as were those of the Greekes, and of the Italians, their chiefe drift was so much as they could, so to bind their magistrats, gouernours, ambassadours, captaines, lieutenants, and other their great officers & ministers vnto their lawes, as that they should not one iot swarue or stray therefrom: which the auntients did much more than they of our time: whereas in a regall monarchie it is quite otherwise, where in publike iudgements all paines and penalties, and in priuat iudgements that which concerneth euerie priuat mans right, is left to be iudged and determined according to the discretion of the magistrat. And albeit that *Iustinian* the emperour made a law, That euerie mans right should be tried by the law, so to haue kept the magistrats within the power of the lawes: yet was that his law to no purpose, but much troubled all the judges and lawyers, willing to obserue the same his law, being impossible to be kept, and incompatible with the other auntient former lawes. For why, that which concerneth euerie mans right, consisteth in fact, and not in the law: by which words *Paulus* (the great lawyer) seemeth euen by the root to haue cut vp all the opinions of all the interpretors of the law, being not only in number almost infinit, but also altogether inexplicable, thereby giuing men to vnderstand that that which concerneth euerie mans right, ought not only in priuat, but euen in publike iudgements also to be left vnto the fidelitie, integritie, conscience, and wisedome of the magistrat. VVhich with vs is by a royall constitution prouided for, and by the vse of iudiciall proceedings, in respect of the infinit varietie of causes, places, times, and persons: which for that they are infinit, can in no lawes, writings, or tables, be comprised, and much lesse vnder any certaine rule be comprehended.

The Magistrates in Popular and Aristocratique estats much more bound vnto the prescript lawes then in a regall Monarchie.

Why in triall of priuat mens right, as also in publique iudgements, many things are to be left vnto the wisedome and conscience of the magistrat?

Now I haue before said, that there was a new officer erected in Rome, who was the Prouost or Pretor of the citie, with power giuen him, to correct, supply, and amend, the lawes and customes, in that which concerned his iurisdiction, so farre as hee saw good in priuat iudgements: and euerie yeare the new chosen Pretor in the Tribunall seat appointed for the making of orations, after he had thanked the people for the honour he had of them receiued, gaue them there to vnderstand of his edicts, and in what sort his purpose was to administer the law. VVhich his edicts he caused afterwards to bee painted, and set vp in some publike place: which for al that were not lawes, neither had the force of lawes, but were only edicts (that is to say, the magistrats commands) wherunto neither the people, nor the Senat, nor the Consuls, nor the other Pretors, nor the Tribunes, nor yet the successors in the selfe same office, were not in any wise bound, but onely particular men, and they also but in that which was within the Pretors power and authoritie, as concerning their priuat suits, and businesse betwixt man and man. And therefore *Cicero* taunting *Verres*, intemperatly abusing the power and authoritie of his Pretorship, saith, *Qui plurimum edicto tribuunt legem annu amappellant, tu plus edicto complecteris quàm lege*, They which attribute most vnto an edict, call it but an annuall law, but thou comprehendest more in an edict, than in a law. For the magistrat how great soeuer he be, cannot of himselfe derogat from the law, and much lesse abrogat the same: for these things we haue shewed properly to belong vnto soueraigntie. Neither must we vnderstand, that the * lawyer when he saith, That the Pretor might correct, amend, or supply the laws, that he had therefore power to derogat from them, or to disanull them, which is the highest point of soueraigntie: but that hee might by the authoritie of his office expound the obscure lawes, and in what they might with equitie be extended, yet without breaking or impugning the same. And that is it, for which the law generally saith, That the Pretor neuer could giue possession of the goods vnto them, who by the lawes and ordinances could not be the heires. Neither was it also in the power of the Pretors, nor yet of all the magistrats together, to make

The power of the Prouost or Prætor in the citie of Rome.

Papinian.

an

D7 annuam appellant   Note at C2.

an heire of him which by the lawes could be none; for why, that was to be done onely by vertue of the law, whereby the magistrat by his definitiue sentence declared, the succession to belong to such, or such a man, whome the law or the testator had appoinred heire. And albeit that diuers of the Pretors edicts were more reasonable and indifferent then the lawes themselues; yet so it was, that the first Pretor that would, might (without regard vnto all the edicts of his predecessors) make all new, or againe reuiue such lawes, which by reason of their antiquitie, were before buried in obliuion. And this was the cause that the Tribune *Æbutius* presented a request vnto the people, which passed in force of a law; which was that the lawes of the twelue tables, which by long tract of time were then growne out of vse, might by an expresse law bee repealed and abolished: which law needed not, if the Pretors by vertue of their edicts had had power to derogat from the positiue lawes. Yea the Pretors themselues did not alwaies in the administration of iustice follow their owne edicts, but spared not sometime to giue iudgement quite contrarie vnto them, especially if the equitie of the causes vpon some straunge occurrents so required; sometimes also chaunging them for the grudge or fauour that they bare vnto certaine priuat men: which thing *Cicero* by way of reproach obiected to *Verres*, saying, *Ille nulla religione motus, contrà quàm edixerat, decernebat,* That he moued with no religion, iudged quite contrarie vnto that which hee himselfe had before decreed. Howbeit that this reproach was but a flourish of the Orators, and not of any great importance: For as no man was subiect vnto the law which hee himselfe made; so also might he vpon good and iust cause derogat from the same. Yet certaine yeares before it was enacted by the people at the motion of *Cornelius* the Tribune, That the Pretors, and so euerie other magistrat also should bee constrained in giuing of iudgement, to obserue their owne edicts by themselues published and set vp at their first entrance into their office, and not to depart therefrom; which cut off many courtesies and fauours which the magistrats before shewed vnto such as they thought good. Neuerthelesse this law being published without the good liking and consent of many: and also contrarie vnto the nature of lawes (which can neuer bind them that made them) was shortly after abolished. Howbeit that the magistrats for their owne particular, and in their owne causes, were constrained to endure the same edicts, iudgements, and decrees, which they themselues had made, and caused to be executed vppon others: yet that notwithstanding the magistrats were alwaies at libertie, to derogat from their owne edicts, or to alter the same, whether they were published for the whole yeare that they were Pretors, or for a moneth, or for some few dayes or howres. For generally the law saith, That the magistrat may reuoke that which he hath decreed, and forbid that which he hath commaunded, although that he cannot reuoke that which he hath once iudged and pronounced sentence of. For that iudgements and decrees giuen or made vpon the hearing of a cause, cannot without iniurie be reuersed or changed, as also for that nothing ought to be more firme and sure then iudgements once giuen, as whereby all ciuill societie is especially maintained: wherein many interpretors of the law haue deceiued themselues, calling the magistrats simple commaunds, precepts, and not edicts: whereas an edict (as saith *Varro*) is nothing els but *Magistratus iussum* (that is to say) the magistrats commaund, and whereof another errour hath risen also, *viz.* That such the magistrats simple commaunds should bind no man: For so the auntient doctors affirme. Which their opinion, if it were true, wherefore then should the law commaund vs to obey the magistrats bare commaund, without regard whether it be iust or vniust? Or why should the lawyer *Mætian* say, *Reipublicæ interesse, vt iniustis & ambitiosis decretis pareatur,* It behoueth the Commonweale, that euen vniust and proud decrees (of the magistrats) should be obeyed. Yea and all the auntient

The Magistrat may reuoke his owne decree or commaunds, but not his iudgement once giuen.

The Magistrates simple cōmands of right ought to be obeyed.

H9–10 their owne particular *i.e.* their private matters

auntient Philosophers and law makers, haue more religiously recommended nothing vnto vs, not onely than the lawes, but euen than the writings and decrees of the wise. Now it is more reasonable to obey a simple verball commaund, which is but for a day or an howre (if we doubt or mislike of the equitie thereof) than to the commaundements which were for a yeare, as were all the edicts of the magistrats: besides that it was more easie to performe the one than the other. And that more is, the lawes, the ordinances, the decrees, and sentences, of themselues bind no man, if the commission (that is to say, the magistrats commaund) be not on foot. And therefore the Roman Pretors, and other their great magistrats, seldome times troubled themselues with giuing of iudgements, but were still occupied in appointing of judges, in commannding and the putting in execution of the sentences and iudgements of such iudges as had by them bene appointed. Whose verball commands (as these men tearme them) had they bene of no force to bind men, the decrees and iudgements of such as were by them appointed, should haue bene to no end or purpose, neither should they haue bene obeied. And therefore the law permitteth all magistrats by punishment or penaltie to cause their commaunds to be obeyed, without distinction whether they bee commaundements verball, or by way of commission, or by decrees by them made, or by iudgements by them giuen.

Of this errour (for not obeying the magistrats command) is risen also a farre greater, some defending that it is lawfull for men in fact, and by force to resist the magistrates, offering them violence, (for that is the word which they vse) whether it be in the administration of iustice, or otherwise out of the same. Howbeit that the difference is great betwixt the one and the other: for that the magistrat out of iudgement, and out of the qualitie of a magistrat, is no more but as a particular man, and so if he by word or deed wrong any man, he may be resisted, in such sort as the law permitteth: but in the execution of his charge within his power, not exceeding the bounds of his iurisdiction, there is no doubt but that he ought to be obeyed, whether it bee right or wrong, as saith the law. But if he shall exceed his authoritie or power, a man is not bound to obey him, especially if the excesse be in it selfe notorious, but may defend himselfe by oppositions and appeales: but if he may not appeale, or that the magistrat will not admit his appeale, but proceed against him; in this case it is to be considered, whether the griefe be to be recouered, or otherwise irrecouerable: which if it be to be recouered, no resistance is then to be made against the magistrat; but if the case be irrecouerable, as in question of life, or of corporall punishment, and that the magistrat will needs proceed without regard of any appeale, in this case it is lawful for euery man to make resistance, not of purpose to crosse or offend the magistrat, but onely to defend the life of the innocent man in danger, yet so farre as that it be done without fraud or seditious tumult: not for the violating of the magistrat, as we said, but for the deliuerance of him which is with iniurie by the magistrat oppressed. As when *Appius Claudius* enflamed with the desire and lust of the faire maiden *Virginia*, (wresting the lawes) was about to giue sentence against her libertie, *Virginius* her father to preserue the honour of his house, and wishing rather the death of his so faire a daughter, than that she should so loose her virginitie, slew her openly with his owne hand, and so set all the citie on an vproare. Which desperat boldnes of the man was not indeed to haue beene suffered, neither ought the quiet estate of the Commonweale to be with such outragious facts troubled, what violence soeuer be done by the magistrat. Howbeit that it belongeth not vnto priuat men to iudge whether the magistrat offer to doe wrong, or not: which to determine, if it apperteine but vnto the greater magistrats, or the Prince onely, in vaine then it is to aske whether priuat men may by force resist the

Whether priuat men may by force resist the Magistrat offering them violence or wrong.

Priuat men are not to iudge whether the Magistrat do them wrong or not.

magistrates, offering them violence? but onely this, whether Magistrats which go about to put in execution their sentences of life and death, or for the inflicting of some corporall punishment, contrarie vnto appeales from them made, may of right bee withstood? which that they lawfully may be, I doubt not, so that it be done without fraud or tumult, in cases of life and death: but if iudgement be of goodes, or fines, or imprisonment, I thinke it not to be lawfull, for that all these things may be amended, either by intercessions, or by appeales, or by actions of trespasse, or iniurie, or by way of petition. But in other causes lawfull it is not by the law either of God or man to withstand the magistrat offering vs violence: as many euill taught, and worse instructed in ciuill pollicie and gouernement most daungerously affirme: by whose positions (if they will be like themselues) the estates of all cities and Empires must needs be troubled and confounded. For if it were lawfull for the subiects by force to defend themselues against the magistrats, they might vpon the same reasons and grounds resist their soueraigne Princes also, and tread the lawes vnderfoot. Wherefore we see the lawmakers and lawyers to haue respected nothing more, than to keepe all force, and violence, not from the magistrats onely, but euen from priuat men themselues, hauing violence in so great detestation, as that they haue restored euen theeues and robbers into places, vniustly by them possessed, if they were from thence by force cast out, and excluded the true owners thereof from their rights for proceeding by way of force. And albeit that some particular men hauing territoriall iurisdiction, may (in the opinion of many) in a sort in their owne right of themselues lay violent hand, vpon the land holding of them: when as the vassall neglecteth his duetie vnto his Lord, yet the truer opinion is that he cannot in his owne cause so doe, for that it is a thing iniurious and vnreasonable, that any man should be a judge in his owne cause, or giue sentence for himselfe. Now the law which forbiddeth priuat men to doe that, which ought to be done by the magistrat, hath this reason ioyned with it, lest occasion should be giuen of greater sturre and tumult. The law also of the xij Tables, which saith: *Vis in populo abesto*, Let violence be from among the people, is not to be vnderstood onely of violence to be done by force of armes, whether it be publiquely or priuately done: but also when men would haue things otherwise done then by the ordinarie way of iustice: as when things are done by priuat mens authoritie, which should haue beene done by the Magistrat or judge. And if it bee not lawfull for the true lord or owner to put his seale vnto his owne things being in the possession of an other man; how then should it be lawfull vnto the territoriall lord of himselfe to enter or seize vpon lands, the propertie whereof belongeth vnto an other man? Wherefore the opinion of *Plato* is to be of vs reiected, who in his bookes of lawes hath left the shamefull violence and abuse offered vnto maydens or boyes, to be reuenged by their kinsfolke, and not by the Magistrat.

Now of this question dependeth an other; as whether the Magistrat may reuenge the wrong and iniurie offered him, as he sitteth in place of iustice: whereof what to say the lawiers haue not yet determined. Neuerthelesse without entering into farther dispute, it is and alwaies hath beene lawfull for all Magistrats exercising their estate or commission, to condemne or chastice them, which giue vnto them rash or contumelious speech, and to proceed against them by way of fine, or by seizing vpon their bodies or goods, according to the power and authoritie vnto them giuen; if the wrong or iniurie offered be not such as may deserue corporall punishment: for then the magistrat ought to lay aside his publique person, and to receiue iustice at an other mans hand. But yet if the iniurie be done vnto the whole companie or bench of Iudges, or Magistrats, in this case they may enquire and iudge of the crime or offence, and so

altogether

altogether lawfully do that which they could not do apart: and the reason seemeth to be, for that in so doing they punish not the wrong done vnto themselues, but vnto the Commonweale, which is therein farre more wronged than are they which beare the persons of magistrates. And albeit that the law saith, That the action of iniurie is easely to be forgiuen, and that it is soonest by sufferance buried; that is to be vnderstood of particular men, & not of publique persons, and especially of Magistrats vnto whom whosoeuer shall offer violence, is by the law in danger of treason. And for this cause an outrage committed against the person of a Magistrate, the indignitie of the fact is together with the heauinesse of the punishment therby encreased: and that not onely when he exerciseth his estate, but also in what place soeuer it be wherein he carrieth with him the marks and tokens of his office, or is knowen to be such a man, he ought to be inuiolable, and as the auntient Latins say, *Sacrosanctus*, or most holy: for that word the law, Horatia (published for the safetie of Magistrats) vseth, conceiued in these words: *Qui Tribunis plebis, Ædilibus, Iudicibus nocuerit eius caput Ioui sacrum esto; familia ad ædem Cereris, liberi, liberæque vænum ito*, He that shall hurt the Tribunes of the people, the Ædils, or Iudges, let his head be sacrificed to Iupiter, and his familie and children, male and female, sold at the Temple of Ceres. Wherein some are of opinion that the word *Iudicibus* (or judges) is meant or to be vnderstood of the consuls, who were afterwards the onely judges amongst all the magistrats: whereof they haue some probabilitie, for they were first called Pretors, and after that Iudges; and after that their iurisdiction for the citie was giuen to one speciall Pretor, they were called Consuls. Howbeit neuerthelesse it seemeth that the law Horatia hauing put the judges after the Tribunes, and the Ædiles whome they called *Ædituos* (for why, the great and honourable Aediles, whome they called *Curules*, were not yet erected) was meant to comprehend all judges; considering withall, that the law it selfe was not published at the request or motion of any of the Tribunes, or in disgrace of the Consuls, but at the motion of *Horatius* the Consull himselfe. And this law Horatia was made fortie foure yeares after the sacred law Iunia, made for the safetie of the Tribunes of the people: whereby they were as by a speciall law, more religiously prouided for than were the rest of the magistrats. VVhereby it appeareth this law to appertaine to all magistrats, but especially vnto judges, whose liues and persons are the more subiect to all daungers, in that they are to iudge of the liues, honour, and goods of all the subiects. And therefore the law saith not, That he that killeth the judges (shall die therefore) but if hee shall offer them neuer so little violence; that is to say, *Si nocuerit*, which is, if hee but hurt them. And well it is to be noted, that it is not said, as they are exercising their authoritie and iurisdiction onely, but euen in what other place soeuer they bee: which otherwise were but to open a gap to haue them slaine in euerie other place where they sat not in iudgement. So when as with vs a certaine noble gentleman beeing called into question, had with his sword wounded one of the judges of the court of Paris, not as then sitting in iudgement: the court condemned him to haue his right hand cut off, his bodie afterward to be quartered, his goods confiscated, and a most great fine to bee paid vnto the judge. But if the magistrat disguised, or walking the streets by night to do any man harme, shall himselfe chance to be by any man hurt, hee cannot redresse such his wrong as done vnto a magistrat, but as vnto a priuat man. So *Aulus Hostilius* the Aedile, when as by night hee had attempted to haue broken open a Courtisans doores, was there grieuously hurt: whereof he complaining vnto the people, in hope to haue found some good remedie, was sent away with shame enough; for that the outrage vnto him done, was not to be punished as done vnto a magistrat. VVhich ought not to seeme strange, seeing that one of the Tribunes, who had ynlawfully abu-

Priuat iniurie soonest by sufferance buried.

That the person of the magistrat ought to be alwaies sacred and inuiolate.

An heauie censure vpon a man for striking of a magistrat.

sed a boy, and taken by the Capitall Triumuiri, was by him punished as a slaue or stranger (the rest of the Tribunes his fellowes forsaking him, as abhorring his most filthy lust) albeit that the sacred lawes forbid vpon paine of death to offend the Tribune, or to commaund him to be punished for what thing soeuer. In like case if the magistrats went roaming vp and downe masked, and priuat men went masked also, carrying with them the markes of magistrats, as in Rome they did during the feast of Cybele: if any iniurie happened to be so done vnto the magistrat, it was not punished as done vnto a magistrat, but vnto a priuat person: howbeit that out of these cases the magistrat is to be holden for such as he is, in what place soeuer he be.

Magistrats to be alwaies religeously respected.

Neither is it not onely vnlawfull to offend or abuse the magistrats by word or deed, but necessarie it is, that we should duetifully respect and honour them, as them vnto whome God hath giuen this power: which thing we see the auntient Romans (from whom the fountaines of law and iustice flowed into all the world) to haue much more religiously obserued, than did the other nations. For the Censors disgraced and degraded from his order a bourgeous of the citie, by taking away from him his horse, for that he had but coughed and spauled a little too lowd in their presence. And *Vectius* a citisen of Rome, for not rising vnto the Tribune of the people, but passing by him, was by the people slaine. Yea the law it selfe calleth it sacrilege, not to reuerence the magistrat. VVe vnderstand also not the same, but yet great reuerence to haue beene giuen vnto the magistrats euen amongst the Greekes also, in that it was not lawfull for a man to laugh in the councell of the Areopagits. VVe read also, that *Fabius Maximus* his sonne seeing his father a farre off comming towards him, and that the Lictors or officers for his fatherly reuerence durst not cause him to alight from his horse, commaunded him himselfe to alight: which his commaund the father obeying, alighted and embraced his sonne, making much more of him, than if he had done otherwise. For domesticall power (as saith the law) ought to stoope vnto publike authoritie. True it is, that in those times and in those places offices were giuen to vertue, and not to them that offered most: for then verily was the time wherein rewards were set vp for vertue: Howbeit that the lawes against ambition, and the auntient histories sufficiently declare honours and offices to haue bene oftentimes in Rome, *de lapide emptos*, as saith *Cicero*. But howsoeuer power and authoritie be got, whether it be by fauour, by wealth, or force of armes, we must not therefore contemne the magistrat, which cannot bee done without the contempt of God, from whome he hath his authoritie, in whatsoeuer sort it be. As witnesseth that speech of God vnto *Samuel* judge of Israel, now growne weake with age: whose commaunds when as the people did refuse, It is not thee (saith he) but me, whome they haue despised.

The dutie of the magistrat for the maintenance of his reputation.

Now if these deriders of authoritie and power, be not to be moued either with the feare of God, or the touch of religion, yet can they not denie, but that it is more than necessarie for priuat men to obey, respect and honour the magistrats, for the defence of Commonweales, and of the ciuill societie of men. Which the auntient Poets haue vnto vs well set forth in their deuised fables, making the goddesse *Pitharchie* (which signifieth the obedience of subiects vnto their princes and magistrats) wife vnto *Iupiter Sauiour*: and of that marriage *Eutuchia* (that is to say Felicitie) to haue bene engendred and borne. Wherefore the magistrat on his part also ought to giue a good opinion of himselfe, for his iustice, wisedome, and sufficiencie, that so the subiects may haue occasion to honour and reuerence him: and not by his vnworthinesse to suffer the honour of the Commonweale to be troden vnderfoot or despised: for the fault which in a priuat man is but light, is in the person of the magistrat doubled. And therefore *Solon* in his lawes gaue leaue to kill the drunken magistrat, without any daunger of punishment

---

F1 a boy (L) a girl (Fr). Fr is incorrect. Cf. Valerius Maximus, *Facta et dicta memorabilia*, VI, 1, 7.
H10 de lapide emptos *i.e.* "bought like marketed slaves" (but cf. Cicero's use of the phrase, *In Pisonem*, 15) Note at G6.

OF A COMMONWEALE. 341

A ment therefore. Truely an vnreasonable law, for that it was thereby to be feared, least vnder the pretence of drunkennesse the magistrats life should be oftentimes endaungered. VVhereby yet we may gather, how much vice was then detested, as also with what integritie, seueritie, and wisdome, magistrats ought to excell other men. And yet ought we not to imitat them, who by the rigour of punishment seeke to bee accounted seuere; or by their too much lenitie, desire to be accounted gentle, both the one and the other being therefore worthily reproued by the law. VVherein many haue mistaken themselues, who hauing extraordinarie power to punish without law, haue thought equitie to consist in lenitie and mercie, repugnant to the rigour of the lawes: howbeit that equitie is of such a nature, as that it in nothing communicateth either

Lenitie or rigor neither of them commendable in a magistrat.

B with rigour, or with mercie; but declining from both the extreames, crueltie (I say) and mercie, keepeth clemencie, the preseruer of them both: not vnlike the Lesbian rule, which being of lead, yeelded as well vnto the one side as to the other. Now if the offence be greater than the punishment appointed in the ordinarie lawes, the magistrat hauing extraordinarie iurisdiction and power may as an vpright iudge augment the punishment: So if the fault be lesse, he may with like equitie mitigat the punishment by the rigour of the law appointed. And truely the magistrat in seeking to be accounted pitifull offendeth more, than if he should seeme to be cruell: For crueltie, although it be indeed to be blamed, yet keepeth it the subiects in obedience vnto the laws, for feare of punishment; whereas too much lenitie giueth libertie vnto offence, and causeth the

Lenitie more hurtful in a magistrat than seueritie.

C magistrat himselfe, the lawes, yea and the prince which established the lawes, to bee altogether contemned. And this is it for which the law of God expresly forbiddeth to haue any pitie of the poore in iudgement. Some others there bee, which iudge well and vprightly, enclining neither vnto crueltie nor mercie, but yet cannot keepe that grauitie and seueritie which best beseemeth a magistrat: as in our time one of the chiefe magistrats of this realme, who in the highest seat of iustice, and euen then when he pronounced the sentence of death vpon the condemned, would with one merrie conceit or other, minister vnto the hearers occasion of laughter. VVhereas *Augustus Cæsar* did farre otherwise, who albeit that he was accounted a sincere and vpright iusticiar, yet for all that he neuer pronounced sentence of death vpon any, but with deepe sighes

Grauitie best beseemeth a magistrat.

D set euen from the bottome of his heart. Some other to the contrarie, all enraged, threaten and reuile them whom they giue iudgement of: as did ordinarily the emperour *Claudius*, who one day with a countenance more like a beast than an emperour, strucke him in the face with a pen knife, whom he was to pronounce sentence of death of. Yet blame I not the graue exhortations, and bitter reproofes of the magistrat vnto the offendors, and then especially, when as hee meaneth to vse more lenitie than the rigour and extremitie of the law requireth. For why, it is one of the things most requisit in a magistrat to cause the offendors to haue the better vnderstanding and feeling of the greatnesse of their offences: that so they may the better also perceiue and see what they haue therefore deserued, and so to be the rather induced to repentance. But

E it were a kind of iniurie, and not beseeming the authoritie and wisedome of a magistrat to charge him whome he hath condemned to death, with opprobrious words also. *Papirius Cursor* was of all that liued in his time (than which none is said to haue bene more plentifull of vertues) a man most famous both at home and abroad in the wars, but so terrible with the maiestie of his commaund, as that hee caused euen the stoutest of his followers to tremble and quake at the force of his commaunding speech: which his roughnesse of speech he for all that wisely tempered with great lenitie in the executing of punishment. As when the generall of the Prenestines was come vnto him with his promised aid after the battaile fought & the victorie obtained, *Papirius* with sterne

Papirius Cursor a notable man.

Gg iij counte-

D1 set *i.e.* fetched   Note at C4.

countenance, and such speech as caused all there present to tremble thereat, hauing first reproued him, forthwith commaunded one of the Lictors to vnbind his bundle of rods, and to make readie his axe: the fearefull captaine in the meane time expecting nothing but present death, when sodenly *Papirius* commaunded the same Lictor standing readie with the axe in his hand, to haue done execution (as all men thought) but to cut vp a stub of a tree which stood in his walke, and condemned the negligent captaine in a great fine, which he right willingly paid, with great thankes that hee had so spared him his life. Whome if he had put to death, it was in daunger least that those his followers the Romans allies would haue thereupon reuolted: which so great a fault no doubt *Papirius* would not haue pardoned a Roman. But as there is great difference betwixt faults which are committed in warre, and elsewhere (for that as an antient captaine said, In martial matters men scarcely offend twice) so must the militarie magistrats vse another manner of fashion of commaunding, of punishing, and execution of penalties, than must the magistrats in time of peace. For that the discipline of warre ought to be much more seuere than the domesticall or ciuill gouernment. And yet for all that ought not this martiall rigour to passe into crueltie, nor the generall to exceed the bounds of seueritie, as many commaunders do, who in nothing show themselues valiant, but in killing their souldiors without hearing. As *Seneca* propoundeth one act of *Piso* the Proconsull, for an example of his notorious crueltie towards his souldiours. For seeing a souldiour returning alone out of the field into the campe, from forraging, in a rage condemned him to death, for that he was returned out of the field without his companion, charging him, That hee had slayne him: the souldiour still alleaging, That his fellow was comming after him: which his excuse for all that *Piso* would not admit, but sent him presently to be executed. But lo, whilest that the execution was about to be done, he sodenly returned who was supposed to haue bene slaine. Wherupon the captaine which had the charge to see the execution done, returned to the Proconsull with both the souldiours, who embrasing one the other, were with great applause and reioycing of their fellow souldiours brought before him: Wherewith the Proconsull enraged, caused them all three to bee put to death: The first, for that hee was before condemned: The second, for that he was the cause of his fellowes condemnation: And the captaine, for that hee had not done what hee was by him his generall commanded. So that for the appearing of one innocent mant, he put three to death: which was not iustly to vse, but most cruelly to abuse his authoritie. VVhich his crueltie was so much the more to be detested, for that there was there no meanes to appeale, nor prince to flye vnto, nor ciuill exception to bee taken, by reason of the rigour of the militarie discipline. And thus much concerning the power and authoritie of Magistrats ouer particular and priuat men: It remaineth now to speake also of the power and duetie of one of them towards another.

CHAP.

G 10 a souldiour I 3 innocent man Note at I 7.

Marginalia:
- More seueritie to be required in a Martial magistrat then in a ciuil which seueritie ought not yet to passe into cruelty.
- The notorious crueltie of Piso the Proconsull.

Chap. VI.

¶ *Of the mutuall duties of Magistrates among themselues, and of the power that one of them hath ouer an other.*

N euery well ordered Commonweale there be three degrees of Magistrates: The highest, which is of them which may be called soueraigne magistrats, and know none greater then themselues, but the soueraigne Maiestie onely: The middle sort which obey their superiours, and yet commaund others: And the lowest degree of all, which is of them which haue no commaund at all ouer any other magistrats, but onely ouer particular men subiect to their iurisdiction. Now of soueraigne magistrats, some haue power to commaund all magistrats without exception, and other some acknowledge no superiour but the soueraigne Maiestie, and yet haue no power ouer all the rest of the magistrats which are placed in the middle & lowest degrees, but ouer such onely as are subiect vnto their iurisdiction. Of the first sort of soueraigne magistrates which haue power ouer all others, and that know none their superiours, but the soueraigne power, there are but verie few, and fewer at this present then in auntient time: for that it is by daily experience found, nothing to be more dangerous in a Commonweale, then for some one magistrat to be aboue the rest, who may lawfully commaund all the rest, aswell priuate persons as magistrats, wanting himselfe but one step or degree to mount vnto the soueraigntie, and that especially if his soueraigne magistrate which hath such power bee alone, and without a companion, hauing all in his owne hand: as had sometime the Grand Prouost of the Empire, whom they called *Præfectum Prætorio*, who had commaund ouer all the Magistrates throughout the whole Empire, and might receiue the appeales from all the other magistrates and gouernours; but might not be appealed from himselfe, no not although the appeal were made euen vnto the Emperour himselfe, albeit that the first which were promoted to this dignitie and honour, were but captaines of the prætorian legions: as *Seius Strabo* the first that was preferred vnto this office vnder *Augustus*: and after that *Seianus* vnder *Tiberius*. Which honour the other succeeding Emperours thought good to bestow vpon such as of whose integritie, fidelitie, and deuotion towards them they had had good experience and proofe: such as they would in some sort to be their imperiall Lieutenants, vpon whom they for the most part discharged the mannaging of their greatest affaires, such as were by the Emperours themselues to haue beene discharged: as the hearing of imperiall causes: the receiuing and dismissing of Embassadours: the hearing of appeales from the Magistrats of all prouinces, which great charge for that no man could well execute, except he were skilfull in the Lawes, the Emperours in steed of captaines of their legions, preferred lawyers to that honour. So did *Otho* the emperour promote *Martian*: *Seuerus*, *Papinian*: and *Alexander*, *Vlpian*. And at length vnder the Greek emperours, two great Prouosts of the empire were by the Emperours created, and at last three also, that the greatnes of their power so diuided might be lessened; and yet the honour thereof imparted to moe. Such soueraigne Magistrats were with our aunceestours: the Master of the Pallace: and he whom they called the Prince of Fraunce: and of late *Henry* duke of Aniou, king *Charles* his great Lieutenant: and the chiefe *Bassa* in the Turkes empire: and the great *Edegnare* or *Diadare* in Ægypt vnder the principalitie of the Mamaluke Sultans. Yet in this they differ, that in the Turkish empire the Great Sultans children in the absence of their father commaund aboue all the Bas-

Marginalia:
Three degrees of Magistrats in euery well ordered Commonweale.

Daungerous in a Commonweale to giue power to one Magistrat to commaund ouer all the rest.

C3 *For* if his soueraigne magistrate *read* if this soueraigne magistrate (cf. L).

saes, and had the preheminence and precedence before them: and in Ægypt the great Edegnare commaunded ouer all the rest of the Magistrates, excepting such onely as had the keeping of the castles & fortresses of the kingdom committed to their charge, ouer whom he had no commaund. Which manner and custome whether the Princes of the East tooke it from ours, or our Princes from them, we still keepe together with the Italians, Germaines, Spaniards, and most of other Nations also. Wherefore the soueraigne power to commaund ouer all Magistrats and officers without exception, ought not to be giuen to one alone, but in case of necessity; as when the Commonweale cannot otherwise be preserued: and yet then not with the authoritie and countenance of a standing office, but by way of commission onely, such as were in auntient time graunted vnto the Roman Dictators, the Archo of the Thessalians, and Azymnets of the Lacedemonians; and now with vs are giuen vnto Protectors and Regents, in the absence, furie, or minoritie of soueraigne Princes. In the absence I say of the soueraigne prince, for that in his presence all the power & commaund of magistrates and commissioners cease: For as the force and strength of all riuers and flouds is together with their names lost and swallowed vp when they once fall into the Sea; and as the other heauenly lights, as well the planets as other starres, lose their light in the presence of the Sunne, or as soone as he approcheth the Horizon, in so much as that they seeme againe to render vnto him the whole light that they had before borowed of him: euen so likewise all the authoritie of the Senat, and all the commaund and power of Magistrats cease in the presence of the prince. So we see that he which deliuereth the soueraigne princes mind, whether it be in counsell, or in soueraigne court, before the states, or vnto the people, still vseth these wordes, *So and so the king commaundeth, or saieth*. But to the contrarie, if the prince be absent, the Chauncelour or President keeping the kings place aboue the other princes, pronounceth sentence or iudgement according to the opinion and mind of the Senat or Court wherein he sitteth, hauing ordinarie iurisdiction and power, and not in the name of the king. And for asmuch as *William Poyet* Chauncelour of Fraunce, and President of the great Counsell, in the absence of the king, oftentimes in iudgement vsed this forme of speech, *The king saith so and so vnto you*; he was therefore charged with treason, besides the other points of his accusation. Wherefore many are deceiued which thinke those lawes or Edicts which are published or ratified in the councell or court, in the presence of the prince, to be so published or confirmed by the Court or Councell: seeing that the Court hath then the hands bound, and that it is none but the king that so commaundeth, the motion or consent of his Attourney, the prince himselfe being then present, seruing to no purpose at all. And in Popular estates, the greatest magistrats as well as the least, in token of their humilitie, laid downe their maces and other tokens of honour before the people, and so standing, spake vnto the people sitting: showing, that in their presence they had no power at all to commaund. So all the motions made by the magistrates of Rome, were by way of humble request, as in this forme, *Velitis, Iubeatis*, May it please you, or commaund: Whereunto the people there present, giuing their consent with a lowd voice, before the law *Cassia Tabellaria*, vsed these words, *Omnes qui hic assident volumus, iubemusque*, All we that here sit will and commaund. And after the lawes called Tabellarias, the letters A. and V. R. written in the tables, signified *Antiquo*, (or, I repeale the law) and *Vti Rogas* (or, as you request). And in like manner the people of Athens gaue their voyces sitting, the magistrat in the meane time speaking vnto them standing, so long as they had any thing to say vnto them.

But then might some man say, If it be so, that the magistrats had no power to commaund particular men, nor yet one another, in the presence of the people which had

the

the soueraigntie. VVhy did the Tribune of the people send his vsher vnto *Appius Claudius* the Consull, to commaund him to silence? And why did the Consull to requite him with like, send his sergeant vnto him likewise, crying with a lowd voice, That the Tribune was no magistrat? VVhereunto I aunswere, that such contention and debate oftentimes fell out amongst the magistrats, and especially betwixt the Consuls and the Tribunes: yet may we not thereof conclude, that either of them had any power to commaund the one the other, in the presence of the people, both their authorities then ceasing. So a controuersie arising betwixt the high court of Paris, and the court of Aids, for wearing of their purple robes, and accompanying the king, not farre from *Henrie* the second the French king, the president of the greater court of Paris sent a sergeant vnto the judges of the court of Aides, to forbid them to go any further: (and albeit that the king was not so nie as that he could heare such the presidents commaund) yet receiued he such aunswere from the judges, That hee had no such power to commaund ouer the court of Aids, and if he had, that yet he could not rightly there vse the same in the presence of the king.

But yet some man might obiect and say, That if the magistrats had no power to commaund in the presence of the prince, they were no more magistrats, neither should so great regard be had of their honours and dignities the prince being present, so as we see there is. VVhereunto mine aunswere is, That the magistrats by the presence of the prince loose nothing, but still continue in their offices, and so consequently in their dignities and honours, their power to commaund being but suspended. As in like case the Dictator being created, all the magistrats continued in their estates and offices, howbeit that all their commaunding power was then holden in suspence: but so soone as the Dictators commission was expired, and he once out of his office, the magistrats againe commaunded by the same right they had before: which they could not haue done, if their magistracies and offices had so, & indeed bene from them taken. Which may serue for aunswere to that which might be alleaged of these words, which are oftentimes to be read in the writings of the auntient Romans, *viz. Creato Dictatore magistratus abdicant*, VVhereby it might seeme that the Dictator being created, the magistrats were out of office: which is not to be vnderstood of their offices, but of their power, as we haue before said, which was so for a while suspended. For otherwise the Dictator yeelding vp his office, the magistrats must haue sought for new power and authoritie from the people, their former power being before together with their office expired. And the reason is generall, that the power of the inferiour should bee holden in suspence, in the presence of the superiour: for otherwise the subiect might command contrarie to the will of his lord, the seruant contrarie to the good liking of his master, and the magistrat contrarie to the will and pleasure of his soueraigne prince: or might at leastwise oppose himselfe against him, and by the vertue of his office forbid the inferiour persons to performe the commaunds of their superiours: which can in no wise be done, without ineuitable preiudice vnto the soueraigntie; except it be that the prince laying aside the soueraigntie of his person, goeth to see how his magistrats commaund; as the emperour *Claudius* ofttimes went openly to see the doings of his magistrats, and without disguising himselfe sat beneath them, foolishly giuing to them the more honourable place: or else in case that the prince, his maiestie in a sort set aside, giue leaue to the magistrat to iudge of his cause. For the maxime of the law, which saith, That the magistrat of equall or greater power may bee iudged by his companion or fellow in office, or by his inferiour also, when he submitteth himselfe vnto his power, hath place not onely in priuat persons and magistrats, but euen in soueraigne princes also; whether it please them to submit themselues or their causes to the iudgement of

other

Why the power of the inferior magistrat is in the presence of the superior to be suspended.

Much more honorable for soueraign princes to referr the hearing of their own causes vnto the magistrats, than to iudge thereof themselues.

other princes, or of their owne subiects. And albeit that they may bee judges in their owne causes, vnto whome power is by God giuen to iudge, without beeing bound to the law, as *Xenophon* saith; yet neuerthelesse it is much better beseeming their maiestie, and more indifferent also for them in their owne causes to abide the iudgement of their magistrats, than to become judges thereof themselues. But to the intent that the soueraigne maiestie of princes should not in any thing be impaired of the greatnesse thereof, and yet that the brightnesse and glorie of the royall name should not dazle the eies of the judges, it was wisely in this realme ordained by our auncestors, That the king should not plead but by his atturney; and that in all publike causes wherein the king or Commonweale were priuatly interessed, the kings name should be still cancelled, and the matter pleaded but in the name of his attourney. Which thing the rest of the princes and others hauing territorial iurisdiction, haue afterwards imitated and followed. So *Augustus* the emperour writ vnto the lieutenants of his prouinces, That they should not suffer his name to be debased with being too common in their commissions, as *Tranquillus* reporteth. Yet is it by a certaine speciall custome by our auncestors receiued, that if the king will in priuat iudgements against priuat men, be restored, the kings attourney shall not in demaunding thereof hold his seat and place, but chaunge the same, least he should seeme to plead a publike and not a priuat cause. But whereas we haue said, the power of the magistrats to be suspended in the presence of the prince, belongeth vnto the whole princes familie, so long as they waite vppon the prince: for ouer them the ciuil magistrats haue no power, except such magistrats as the prince hath appointed for the executing of the iurisdiction of the court.

Whether a magistrat may forbid a subiect to come vnto the court being as then within the iurisdiction of his territorie?

Yet a man might demaund, Whether the magistrat might forbid a subiect or priuat man to come vnto the court, being within the iurisdiction of his territorie? Which is not without some difficultie: howbeit without entring into farther dispute, I say, that the magistrat banishing the guiltie subiect out of the territorie of his iurisdiction, where the prince may then be, secretly also forbiddeth him to approach the court, albeit that he cannot expresly forbid him to come vnto the princes court. Wherein the rule of *Vlpian* the lawyer taketh place, which saith, *Expressa nocent, non expressa non nocent*, Things expressed hurt, but things not expressed hurt not. And I remember how that it seemed a thing right strange vnto the court, and especially vnto the chauncellours of the houshold, that the Commissioners deputed by the prince, for the triall of the president *Allemand* (who familiarly vsed my councell) hauing by their sentence condemned him, forbad him also to come within ten leagues of the court. Which thing the councell vnderstanding, decreed, That it was lawfull for no man but the prince only to make any such prohibition. And haply was the chiefe cause that the president (of whose councell I was) obtained of the king, to haue the iudgement reuersed. For it were not onely an hard and inhumane thing, to keepe the subiects from hauing accesse vnto the prince, to deliuer vnto him their petitions (as well agreeing with the lawes both of God and nature) but it should also be a thing much preiudiciall vnto the maiestie of a soueraigne prince, as I haue before said. And albeit that the superiour courts of this kingdome haue vsed to banish men out of the realme, and so out of the bounds of their iurisdiction, yet should such their iudgement take none effect, if the king in whose name the courts of Parliament giue iudgement, gaue them not commission so to do, and that his royall commaunds were not vnto such their sentences subscribed: So their decrees also in forme begin in the kings name.

The power of the lesser magistrates to cease in the presence of the greater.

Now as the presence of the Prince holdeth the power of all Magistrats in suspence, so is it also to be deemed of the power of the superiour magistrates or commissioners ouer the inferior. As a man may see in Fraunce, where the Presidents & Councelours, euery

---

G10 the whole princes familie *i.e.* the royal household, the court   H9 Ulpian (Fr 5–8) Papinian (Fr 1–4) *properly* Modestinus (*Digest*, 50, 17, 195)   I2–3 *For* chauncellours of the houshold *read* Chancellor de l'Hôpital (*hospitali* in L 1, *Hospitali* in L 2–5).

OF A COMMONWEALE. 347

A euery one in his iurisdiction, and the Masters of Requestes in all seates of iustice, (except the soueraigne courts) haue power to commaund the Seneschals, Bailiffes, Prouosts, and other inferior magistrates, when they come into their prouinces, and sit in their places of iustice, and there may iudge, ordaine, and commaund as superiours vnto their inferiours, and prohibit them to proceed any further, which is generall to all superiour magistrats towards their inferiours, as saith the law: *Iudicium soluitur, vetante eo qui iudicare iusserat, vel qui maius imperium in ea iurisdictione habet*, The iudgement is stayed, he forbidding it which commaunded it, or he which hath greater power in the same iurisdiction. Where the word, *Imperium*, or power, signifieth not onely the power to commaund, or forbid, but euen the magistrat himselfe: As when *Cicero* saith:

B *Maius imperium à minori rogari ius non est*, Lawfull it is not, for the greater power to be examined by the lesse; he would say, that the magistrat or commissioner equall or superiour in power, is not bound to answere before his companion, or one lesse then himselfe, which is a Maxime of the auntients, which *Messala* the Lawyer declareth by example, as thus: *A minore imperio, maius, aut a maiore collega rogari iure non potest: quare neque Consules aut Prætores, Censoribus, neque Censores, Consulibus aut Prætoribus turbant aut retinent auspicia, at Censores inter se; rursus Prætores Consulesq́; inter se, & vitiant et obtinent*, The greater power cannot by right be examined by the lesse, or a fellow in office, by an other his fellow officer though greater then him selfe: wherefore neither the Consuls or Pretors trouble, or keepe the south-sayings

C from the Censors, neither the Censors from the Consuls or Pretors, but the Censors amongst themselues; and so againe the Pretors and Consuls among themselues, do one hinder an other, and so preuaile. And these be the words of *Messala*, which hee saith himselfe to haue writ out of the xiiij booke of *C. Tuditanus*, but hath failed in that which he saith after: *Prætor etsi Collega Consulis est, neque Prætorem, neque Consulem iure rogare potest*, The Pretor although he be the Consuls companion, can by right examine neither the Pretor nor the Consul, which was happely done by the errour of him that write it: For he should haue said: *Prætor etsi Collega Prætoris est*, The Pretor although he be the Prætors companion, and not, *Consuls*, or the Consuls: except we should salue the matter, in saying that the Consuls, Pretors, and Censors were all

D fellowes and companions: *Quia soli ijsdem auspicijs, ijsdem comitijs, id est maioribus creabantur, cæteri magistratus minoribus auspicijs & comitijs*, for that they alone were created and chosen, by the same diuinations and assemblies, that is to say the greater: whereas the other magistrats were chosen by the lesser, for otherwise the Latins neuer abused the word (*Collega*) in that sence; Besides that the Prætor was neuer the Consuls companion or fellow: but well to the contrarie, appeal might lawfully be made from the Pretor to the Consul. As we read that *Æmylius Lepidus* the Consul receiued a man appealing from the Pretor *Orestes*; and by a contrarie decree reuersed the Pretors decree. So we read also that *Luctatius* the Consull tooke the triumph from *Valerius* the Pretor, for that he being Consull was the generall of the armie, although he

E were that day from the armie wherein the victorie was got. That showeth also the power of the Consull to haue beene greater then the Pretors, for that the Consull had twelue Lictors, and the Pretors but two in the citie, and sixe at the most if they were sent into the prouinces, whom the Greekes therefore called ἑξαπελέκεις, for so it is by the law Lectoria prouided, which was made concerning the power of the Pretor of the citie; who was of all other Pretors the greatest: *Prætor Vrbanus duos Lictores apud se habeto, isque ad supremum solis occasum ius inter ciues dicito*, The Pretor (or Prouost) of the citie, let him haue with him two Lictors, and let him administer iustice amongst the citizens vnto the going downe of the sunne. Wherefore let this stand for good,

not

B1 minore   E5 For Lectoria (L) *read* Lætoria (Fr) *or* Plaetoria (cf. Censorinus, *De die natali*, 24).

not onely fellowes and companions in the same power, but also magistrats of like and equall power, not to haue power to examine one another, and therefore much lesse them which haue greater power than themselues.

Whether a companion or fellow in office may stay the proceedings of his equall or superiour in authoritie.

But yet question may be, whether a companion or fellow in office, or one of lesser power, or he which is no fellow in office at all, yet hauing power in his owne iurisdiction, may therein stay the acts or proceedings of his equall or superiour in authoritie? For oftentimes great cōtrouersies haue fallen amongst magistrats about such prerogatiues. And the difference is right great betwixt commaundement, and empeachment or opposition: for companions or fellowes in office haue no commaunding power one of them ouer an other, and yet neuerthelesse they may in publique actions one of them oppose themselues against an other, and so hinder one an others procee-

Fellowes in office although they haue no power one of them ouer another, yet may they well hinder one an others proceedings, and why?

dings. As *Piso* the Pretor or judge betwixt straungers and the citisens of Rome, oft times troubled *Verres* the Pretor of the citie, sitting in iudgement of causes betwixt citisen and citisen: causing his tribunall seat to be brought neere vnto the tribunall seat of the Pretor of the citie, so to hinder the vniust and iniurious decrees of *Verres*; and so administred iustice vnto the citisens flying from the tribunall seat of the citie, vnto him, as by the law they might. And therefore *Cicero* in one of his lawes sayth: *Magistratus nec obedientem, & nociuum ciuem, mulcta, verberibus, vinculis coerceto, nisi par maiorue potestas prohibessit*, Let the magistrat restraine the disobedient and hurtfull citisen, with fine, stripes, and bondes, except an equall or greater power forbid it to be done:

The Magistrat can do nothing in the presence of his companion equall in power with himselfe without his expresse consent.

neither sufficeth it to say *prohibessit*, or forbid it, for that the magistrat can do nothing in the presence of his companion equall in power with himselfe, without his expresse consent, or else that he submit himselfe vnto his power. As it appeareth in that which *Paulus* the lawyer saith: *Apud eum cui par imperium est manumitti non posse, & Pratorem apud Pratorem manumittere non posse*, Before him which hath equall power (with himselfe) a man cannot manumize, and a Pretor before another Pretor cannot manumize. Neither doth that saying of *Vlpian* contradict or impugne the same: *Consulem apud Consulem manumittere posse*, which is, That one of the Consuls may manumize before the other Consul: seeing that that is to be vnderstood that he might not doe it vpon the same day that hee which did manumize or enfranchise had the bundels of rods and power to commaund; for that they both neuer had power vpon the same day, as saith *Festus Pompeius*, as is in many places to be seene, whether they were at vnitie betwixt themselues or not. And therefore *Liuie* surnamed the Salter, carried away the triumph from *Claudius Nero* his fellow and companion in the Consulship, for that he commaunded that day wherein the victorie was obtained (as saith *Liuie*) albeit that the battell were giuen against *Hasdruball* by consent of them both; For *Lucius Cæsar* (as *Festus Pompeius* writeth) deemeth him to be called the greater Consul, which had the bundels of rods or maces; or him which was first made Consul; which *Paulus* himselfe confirmeth. And all this wisely, for if both of them should at once haue had the power, nothing could haue beene peaceable, nothing firme or sure in the great affaires of the Commonweale. Wherefore the Decemuiri beeing created at Rome for the reforming of the Commonweale, and making of the lawes of the xij Tables; it was added vnto the law, That they should by turnes haue the maces with the power to commaund. Now if any man aske the reason why a fellow in office may impeach or stay his fellow officer in his proceeding, if they both haue authoritie and power at the same time: it is grounded vpon the reason generall, of all them which haue any thing in common, wherein he which forbiddeth hath most force, and his condition in that case is better than his which would proceed on further. Which reason preuaileth also, when question is of the force & power of laws, wherein the

Notes at H9, K4, K8.

the force of the law which forbiddeth, is greater then of that which commaundeth.

But whereas we haue said Magistrats of like power or fellowes in office not to be bound to the power or commaund of their companions or fellowes, that is so true if that they both be in number equall: for in all Corporations and Colleges, they which are in number most, are also superiour in power: and therefore the lesse part of magistrats fellowes in office, cannot forbid the greater. But if all the Magistrats were of one mind and opinion, these words were wont to be written vpon their decrees and edicts, *Pro Collegio*, for the Colledge, (which shall in their place be expounded.) But if it be true that we haue said, why did then *Messala* say? *Consulem ab omnibus magistratibus concione auocare posse, ab eo neminem: deinde Prætorem ab alijs preterquàm a Consulibus: minores magistratus nusquam nec concionem nec comitatum auocasse*, That the Consull might call the assemble of the people from al the Magistrats, but none might call them from him, and so next after him that the Pretors might call them from all others, excepting from the Consuls: but that the lesser magistrats could no where call away, neither the assemblie nor sessions of the people. Wherof it followeth, that the impeachment & opposition of the lesser magistrats could not in any sort let or hinder the actions or commaunds of the greater. Whereunto I aunswere, that to call away belongeth to power and commaund, which opposition doth not. Now there is great difference, whether you commaund, or otherwise hinder any thing to be done, as we will hereafter more plainely declare. But first it is to be noted, that that which *Messala* saith is true in other magistrats, but not in the Tribunes of the people: whome wee haue showed to haue had the title of magistrats, with power to assemble and call together the common people, and to constraine the Consuls to giue place vnto their opposition, not so much by the power they had to commaund; as by imprisoning of their persons, and seising of their goods: for if they commaunded any thing, and the magistrat refused or reiected their commands, they forthwith for such their contempt, commanded them to be cast in prison: For so *Seruilius* the Senator directing his speech vnto the Tribunes, saith, *Vos Tribuni plebis Senatus appellat, vt in tanto discrimine Reipublicæ Dictatorem dicere Consules pro vestra potestate cogatis, Tribuni pro collegio pronuntiant, placere, Consules Senatus dicto audientes esse, aut in vincula se duci iussuros*, The Senat calleth vpon you the Tribunes of the people, that in so great a daunger of the Commonweale, you for the power you haue, would compell the Consuls to nominat a Dictator. The Tribunes in the name of the colledge of Tribunes pronounced that their pleasure was, that the Consuls should be obedient vnto the commaund of the Senat: threatning otherwise to commaund them to bee cast into bonds. And it was so farre from being lawfull for the Consuls to haue power to hinder the assemblies of the common people called together by the Tribunes, as that it was not in their power so much as to interpret them in speaking vnto the people, and that vppon paine of death by the law Icilia, if he that had so interpreted the Tribune in his oration or speech, paied not the fine or amercement imposed vpon him by the Tribune. As the Tribune *Drusus* well caused *Philip* the Consull to vnderstand, whome he made to be cast in prison for interrupting him in his speech vnto the people.

That also which we haue said, the greater part of a companie, or colledge of magistrats to preuaile against the lesser, taketh not place amongst the Tribunes of the people, one of the Tribunes voices being able of it selfe to stay all the proceedings, not of the Senat onely, but of all other the magistrats, yea & of the rest of his fellow Tribunes also: whereas to the contrarie, the acts of one Tribune alone, were of force, except some of his fellowes and companions openly opposed himselfe against the same. As is in *Liuie* to be seene, where he saith, The farmers of the publike demaine to haue beene

Magistrats of like power, or fellows in office, bound to the power or commaund of their fellowes, being in number more.

The opposition of one of the Tribunes of the people, sufficient to hinder the proceedings of all the magistrats in Rome, as also the proceedings of the rest of his fellow Tribunes.

Hh   discharged

B1 *For* comitatum *read* comitiatum (Fr and L).   B2 assemblie   D8 *For* interpret *read* interrupt.
D9 *For* interpreted *read* interrupted.

discharged by a decree published vnder the name but of one of the Tribunes only. And that the power of the greater part of the Tribunes might bee withstood by the fewer opposing themselues against them, it is manifest by that, that at such time as *Appius* the Censor by force held his power and Censorship longer than he should haue done, and the time thereof being now expired, contrarie to the law Aemilia, *Sempronius* the Tribune of the people in the open assemblie of the people, said vnto him, *Ego te Appi in vincula duci iubebo nisi Aemiliæ legi parueris, approbantibus sex Tribunis actionem collegæ, tres auxilio fuerunt summaque inuidia omnium ordinum solus Censuram gessit*, I will commannd thee, O *Appius* (saith he) to be cast into bonds, except thou obey the law Aemilia; and six so of the Tribunes allowing & approuing the doing of their companion and fellow Tribunes, three others of them tooke part with *Appius*, and so hee alone held his Censorship, with the great enuie and hart-burning of all sorts of men. So likewise at such time as *Cicero* then Consull (the armie of *Cateline* beeing discomfited and ouerthrowne, by the conduct of *C. Antonius* the other Consull) bare all the sway in the citie, and had turned all the fauour of the people vnto himselfe alone, nine of the Tribunes of the people to restraine such his immoderat power, were all of opinion to send for *Pompey* with his armie; and had so done, had not *Cato* one of the Tribunes of the people alone opposed himselfe in *Ciceroes* behalfe, and so hindered the ptoceeding of his fellow Tribunes. So when *Scipio Africanus* accused of extortion, was to haue bene cast in prison, he was saued onely by *Sempronius* one of the Tribunes, and father of the Gracchies, opposing himselfe against his fellowes.

But how (might some man say) could one Tribune alone let the actions and proceedings of the Senat, of the Consuls, yea and of all his companions and fellowes in office also? Yet most certaine it is that he might so do, if the other Tribunes preferred not a request against him vnto the people, to haue him put out of his office and authoritie. And therefore at the request of *Tiberius Gracchus* the Tribune, *Marcus Octauius* another of the Tribunes, withstanding the profit of the people, and the enacting of the lawes for the diuision of lands, was of necessitie to be thrust out of his office of the Tribuneship, before the law Sempronia for the diuision of lands could bee established. And to that end tendeth that speech of the Tribune vnto the Senators, in *Liuie*, *Faxo ne iuuet vox ista veto, qua collegas nostros tam læti concinentes auditis, contemni iam Tribunos plebis, quippe potestas Tribunitia suam ipsa vim frangat intercedendo*, I shall make (saith he) that this word *Veto*, (or, I forbid) which you now so merrie heare our fellowes together singing, shall helpe you nothing, the Tribunes of the people must now needs be contemned, for that the Tribunitial power doth weaken the power of it selfe, by opposing it selfe against it selfe. But this power and opposition of the Tribune, was ordained and prouided for the libertie of the people, and against force offered them, and not for the priuat profit of the Tribunes themselues: who if question were of any particular of theirs, whether it were in ciuill or criminall causes, were not in any thing respected, but suffered iudgement, as other men did, if some one or other of their fellowes in office enterposed not themselues, and so letted the proceeding. As when *Lucius Cotta* one of the Tribunes of the people, being sued, would neither answere nor pay his creditors, *Fiducia sacrosanctæ potestatis*, as bearing himselfe vpon the reputation and credit of the most sacred power of the Tribuneship; his companions in office openly denounced vnto him, That they would aid the creditors against him, except hee made them payment. Yet at length by little and little it was agreed, That the colledge or companie of Tribunes, should be also bound vnto the same lawes and customes that other colledges and companies were, *viz*. That decrees made by the consent of the greater part should bind the rest. As is easily to be gathered of that which *Liuie* saith,

Ex

F9 commaund   G8 proceeding   G9 *For* Scipio Africanus *read* Scipio Asiaticus (Fr and L).
H4 he might

A *Ex auctoritate Senatus latum est ad populum, ne quis templum arcemue iniussu Senatus, aut Tribunorum plebis maioris partis dedicaret*, It was by the authoritie of the Senat propounded to the people, That no man without the commaund of the Senat, or of the greater part of the Tribunes of the people, should dedicat a temple or a castle. And afterwards by the law Attilia it was ordained, That the Pretor of the citie, and the greater part of the Tribunes of the people, might appoint tutors vnto women and fatherlesse children. Which custome grew into such force, as that the Senat commaunded *Quintus Pompeius Rufus* a Tribune of the people to be cast into prison, for that he being but one, went about to forbid an assemblie of the states to bee called. Whereas otherwise the wilfull rage of one furious Tribune might haue troubled the whole state

B of the Commonweale. And this was the cause why the Consull being about to assemble the great estates of the people, by sound of trumpet caused an edict to bee proclaimed, forbidding all magistrats lesser than himselfe, to haue regard vnto the *Auspicia*; that is to say, vnto the disposition of the ayre, or the flight of birds, for the coniecturing thereby, whether the thing which was then taken in hand, were agreeable with the wil and pleasure of their gods or not. For if it thundered or lightned neuer so little, or if the birds were seene to flie on the right hand, or if any of them there present fell of the falling sicknes, (which was therefore called *Morbus comitialis*) or if any other monster were borne, the assembly was accounted thereby polluted, and so the people presently broke vp and departed without any thing doing: the sooth-sayers thereby denouncing

C vnto them, That the gods were then angrie, and not well pleased with their doings. Which was the charge of the Augures or soothsayers so to denounce vnto them, but yet might not lawfully oppose themselus against that was to be done, as might the magistrats of equall power, or greater: but if the magistrats were inferiour vnto him that held the assembly of the estates, their opposing of themselues could not let the further proceeding of the superior magistrat, howbeit that such acts or proceedings were thereby defectiue, and so subiect to reuocation. In such sort, as that *Caius Figulus* the Consull with his companion, after he had bene chosen, taken his oath, and transported his armie euen into Spaine; yet was he neuerthelesse with his fellow Consull, by a decree of the Senat, called backe againe home and enforced to giue vp their power and

D authoritie: For that the soothsayers had before declared vnto *Tiberius Gracchus* the Consull (then holding the great assemblies for the choyce of the Consuls) That the signes and tokens whereby they tooke their predictions were vnfortunat and contrary. Wherefore the lesser magistrats could not trouble the assemblies of the greater, or cal the people alreadie assembled from them, but such magistrats onely as were equall and of like power with them. But the Tribunes of the people although they might not interrupt the assemblies of the greater magistrats, or cal the assembled people from them, yet might they by opposing of themselues hinder their other actions and proceedings: and in case that the magistrats would yet needs proceed contrarie to their oppositions, the Tribunes would then vse plaine force against them; so that oftentimes murthers

E were thereabouts committed. For so *Asellius* the Pretor, or Prouost of the citie, for fauouring the debtors against their creditors, was as he was doing sacrifice slain by a tumultuous company of the creditors, hauing for their leader one of the Tribunes of the people. In like sort *Appius Saturninus* Tribune of the people, slew *Munius* the Consul, in the verie assemblie of the people.

And as publike actions are troubled or letted by magistrats equal or greater in power than they by whome they are done, opposing themselues against them: so beeing once done, appeale is to be made from the lesser magistrats vnto the greater, sauing vnto euerie man his iurisdiction and power. Now if it bee not in the lesser magistrats

Appeales to be still made from the lesser magistrats to the greater; and not from the greater to the lesser, or to any other, but equal in authoritie with them.

A1 *For* arcemve (L) *read* aramve (Fr) *i.e.* "or an altar" (cf. Livy, IX, 46). Munius (L 1-2) *read* Memmius (L 3-5).   C9 yet was   E4 *For* Notes at B8, C7, D3.

power to commaund the greater, or to stay his proceedings, much lesse can he vndoe what he hath alreadie done, reuerse his iudgements, or receiue appeales made from him, which are not lawfully to be admitted from the greater magistrats vnto their fellowes or men equall in authoritie with themselues. But euen to the contrarie, if a magistrats deputie or lieutenant be preferred to like estate or degree with the magistrat whose deputie or lieutenant he is, his commission of deputation or lieutenancie ceaseth, and the acts by him begun are interrupted and broken off. Wherefore if the equall or lesser magistrat, shall receiue one appealing from the equall or greater magistrat, an action of iniurie may be commenced against such a magistrat, as also against him who hath so appealed vnto the lesser magistrat, or fellow in office with him from whom he hath appealed. For so *Cæsar* as then but Pretor, beeing accused before one of the Questors, as hauing an hand in the conspiracie of *Cateline*, caused both the accuser and the Questor being both grieuously fined to bee cast in prison, and especially the Questor, for that he had suffered a greater magistrat than himselfe to be accused before him, as saith *Suetonius*. So the court of Paris by a seuere decree forbad the judges or magistrats of them which haue territoriall iurisdiction, to bind the kings magistrats or judges with their edicts or prohibitions: and that if they did otherwise, the kings magistrats or judges might by way of iustice proceed against them for so doing.

Whether the inferiour magistrat which may be commaunded by the superior, may also be commaunded by the superiour magistrates Lieutenant or deputie.

But here a man might doubt, Whether the inferiour or lesser magistrat, who may be commaunded by the superiour, may also be commaunded by the superiour magistrats lieutenant, or deputie? Which most haue thought to be a thing without doubt, considering that the lieutenants, or deputies, command nothing in their owne names, neither can do any thing but in the name of the magistrat whose place they hold, and vnto whome the inferiour magistrat oweth obedience. For otherwise if it were lawfull for the inferiour magistrats to disobey the lieutenants or deputies of their superiours, other particular men by the same reason might likewise withstand them, which were the way to ruinat & ouerthrow the whole estate of the Commonweal. Howbeit that it might also be said, that magistrats lieutenants erected in title of office haue power and authoritie by the law, and so also power to commaund in their owne names, and in that qualitie to constraine the inferiour magistrats to obey them. Yet neuerthelesse I say, that in that they are lieutenants or deputies vnto other the superiour magistrats, they cannot commaund or giue out commission in their owne names; which if they do, the inferiour magistrats are not bound to obey them: As was adiudged by a decree of the parliament of Paris, at the suit of the Seneschal of Touraine against his lieutenant, who published edicts and decrees in his owne name, which should haue bene set forth in the name of the Seneschall himselfe. Which was a thing without all doubt before the edict of king *Charles* the seuenth, that the lieutenants should bee placed and displaced by the Seneschals: but the doubt arose after that they were by him erected in title of office, as hauing then their power from the king, and not from the Seneschals. But we must not thereupon presume, that the purpose and intent of the king therein, was to take away the power from the Seneschals or Bailifes (which could not be done but by an expresse edict for the suppressing of those offices) but contrariwise the erection of their lieutenants in the title of lieutenants, was much more to establish the honour of the Seneschals and Bailifes, and yet so to diminish their power. As first the Senators at Rome, and after that the emperours themselues, were woont to appoint lieutenants vnto the Proconsuls (or gouernours of their prouinces) who yet for all that had not their power to commaund from the Senat or the emperour, but from the Proconsuls or gouernours themselues. Wherefore the law saith, *Apud legatum Proconsulis non est legis actio*, that is to say, that he might do no exploit or act of iustice, but

Note at F7.

OF A COMMONWEALE. 353

A but in the name of another man: not for that it was not lawfull for the Proconsuls lieutenants, as it was for the lieutenants of al other magistrats to manumise or enfranchise within the precinct and territorie of the prouince of those magistrats whose lieutenants they were. Which the doctor *Cuias* hath denied, and in the auntient reading corrected these words, *Ex quo prouinciam ingressus est*: Which his correction if it were to be admitted, thereof should follow diuers ineuitable absurdities, these words (as hee would haue them) being left out: for so the lieutenants could not in the territorie of their magistrats, ordaine, decree, commaund, or do any thing; which is all that the law properly calleth *Legis actiones*, or the actions of the law; all which we read lieutenants to haue still done in their owne prouinces: and yet neuerthelesse the Maires, and Du-
B umuirs, or Consuls of villages & townes, had power to manumise or enfranchise, and to appoint tutors by commission within their owne iurisdiction. Wherfore the execution or action of the law, is not in the magistrats lieutenāts or deputies, but in the which so appointed the lieutenants or deputies. Yea the magistrat himselfe, who doth but exercise another mans iurisdiction, can in his owne name commaund nothing. Wherof it commeth, that a man cannot appeale from a lieutenant or deputie, vnto him whose lieutenant or deputie he is: for so appeale should be made from the same man to himselfe. Howbeit that the magistrat may examine the iniurie and wrong done to priuat men by his lieutenant or deputie; and that because the lieutenant or deputy hath not all the iurisdiction and power of the magistrat, whose lieutenant or deputie hee is:
C and yet lesse in auntient time, than at this present, when as the lieutenants of the Proconsuls or gouernours of countries, had no power to inflict corporall punishment vpon any. The princes lieutenants generall also in the wars, albeit that they haue a most high commaund and power ouer all souldiors, of what degree or condition soeuer, yet if any of the princes of the blood offend against the lawes militarie, the hearing and triall thereof belongeth not vnto the lieutenants generall, but vnto the soueraigne prince himselfe; or at leastwise vnto the chapiter of the knights of the order, especially in case it concerne either honour, or life. And in much more strong tearmes, if question be of ecclesiasticall discipline, onely the bishops are not bound to aunswere before the archbishops officials, or vicars generall; as it was by a decree of the parliament of
D Paris, adiudged for the bishops of Troy, and Neuers: Whereby it was said, that they were not bound to obey, but onely vnto the archbishops in person themselues. But that which I haue said of the power of the superiour magistrats ouer the inferiour, is to bee vnderstood in their owne territorie, seat, and iurisdiction, out of which they are but as other priuat and particular men, without power or commaund.

But now the question might be asked, Whether that magistrats equall and fellows in authoritie and power, be also equall in honour and dignitie? Whereunto I aunswere, that honor and dignitie doth in nothing communicat with authoritie and power: yea oftentimes it chaunceth and commeth to passe, that hee which hath most honour, hath so much the lesse power: than which secret none is almost greater, or more
E profitable for the maintenance & preseruation of the Aristocraticall or Popular Commonweales, or that is in any place of the world better kept than in Venice. Of the Consuls he that was first chosen Consull, was also first named in all their publike acts and fastes, and so had the honour of precedence: but if they were both at once chosen, he that was the elder was in honour also aboue his fellow, vntill the law Pappia Poppeia, which gaue the prerogatiue of honour vnto the married Consull: or if they were both married, then vnto him that had most children, which supplied the number of yeares. So amongst the Pretors, who were all of one colledge or companie, and their power all one; he which was called *Vrbanus* (or the Pretor of the citie) was in dignitie

Hh iiij and

The power of the superior magistrats ouer the inferior, extendeth not farther than their owne territory seat and iurisdiction.

Honour and dignitie in nothing to communicate with authoritie and power.

C2 corporall punishment (Fr) capital punishment (L). Cf. *Digest*, 1, 16, 11.   E7 supplied *i.e.* took the place of   Note at A5.

and honour aboue the rest, and so called the Greatest Pretor, for that he was first of all chosen, and in the absence of the Consuls held their places, assembled the Senat, and called together the greatest estates, with such other like things belonging to the office of the Consuls. And amongst the ten Archontes of equall power in Athens, there was one, who yet in honour exceeding the rest, had the publike acts authorised in his name, and gaue himselfe names also vnto the Annales and publike acts and decrees, and was thereof called ἀρχων ἐπώνυμος. So amongst all the parliaments of Fraunce (beeing almost all of like power) the parliament of Paris hath the prerogatiue of honour aboue the rest, as more auntient; and by a certaine singular right is yet called the Court of the peeres of Fraunce, as hauing the triall and iudgement of the peeres, which none of the rest of the courts of parliament haue. And albeit that in the time of *Charles* the viij, the great Councell mannaged the affaires of state, yet so it is, that the king by expresse edict ordained and appointed, That in all edicts and mandats, wherein mention should bee made of the court of parliament, and of the great Councell, the Court of parliament of Paris should alwayes be set formost. So whereas the kings Attourneies are almost in number infinit, he of the parliament of Paris hath alwaies the prerogatiue of honour aboue all the rest of the kings Attourneies, who all are sworne vnto the judges of the soueraigne courts (wherein they are Attourneies) except the Attourney generall of the Parliament of Paris, who is not to bee sworne but vnto the king onely. So wee see that the Constable of Fraunce, and the Chauncelor, albeit that they haue not power or commaund one of them aboue the other, but are equall in sitting, and in going side by side, yet neuerthelesse the more honourable place is reserued vnto the Constable, which is on the right hand of the king, and the Chauncellor on the left: except some haply may say him to haue that place for to beare the kings sword vpon the kings right hand: yet besides that, at the consecration and coronation of the king, and other ceremonies wherein place of precedence is, the Constable goeth before the Chauncellour, and next vnto the Chauncellour followeth the Grand Maister of Fraunce. Which I would haue vnderstood to be of me so spoken, not as if my purpose were to determine any thing of honours, but as an example by the way whereby to perceiue how much honour differeth from authoritie or power.

Whether equall lords or cōpeeres of the same territorie and iurisdiction, may chastice or reforme one another.

But forasmuch as we haue said, that magistrats equall in power, or which hold nothing one of them another, cannot be commaunded one of them by another; a man may doubt whether if amongst many princes or coequall lords, one offend, hee may be restrayned or corrected by the other princes or lords his equels? For why, iurisdiction is of it selfe by nature indiuisible: and lords of one and the same iurisdiction haue one of them as much power as the other; and euerie one of them hath entire power for all: which is not so amongst princes or magistrats which haue their charges or territories diuided, and which haue not any thing to commaund one of them the other; and much lesse when many magistrats in one bodie or colledge haue one and the same charge together; where no one of them hath of himselfe any power or commaund, except it be by commission from the whole colledge giuen him. Yet many there be which hold, that one of these lords may be restrained and corrected by the other lords his compeers and coequals, as hauing by his fault lost his iurisdiction and right, as it hath bene iudged in the court at Rome. Which iudgement may well be borne with, howbeit that the reason thereof is not good; for to say that hee offending hath thereby forthwith lost his power and iurisdiction, were to do execution before iudgement, and to spoile the lord or magistrat of his estate or place before he were heard. And albeit that the threats, penalties, edicts, and decrees, expressed and set down in the lawes, had the force of a thing alreadie iudged, as some haue thought them to haue;

I3 *For* one of them another *read* one of them OF another.   Note at G1.

haue: yet so it is, that the fact in question is alwaies in iudgement to be tried, whether it were done or no; and in case it be confessed, yet before the execution, must the sentence be pronounced by the mouth of the iudge, who can haue no power ouer his compeere, who hath equall power and authoritie in the same territorie with himselfe, as we haue before declared, following therein the sounder opinion of the greater part of lawyers, not much regarding that others say, That euerie man is there to be iudged where he hath offended: which is so true, if there be no lawfull cause which may hinder iudgement to be in the same place giuen. In a colledge or companie of magistrats, or judges, if the greater part of them agree in one, there is no doubt but that they may iudge or chastice any one, or the lesser part of their fellowes: as they did in the Senat of Rome, after the law which *Adrian* the emperour made for the iudging of Senators; and as they doe in all the courts of this realme. But betweene many equall lords or compeers of the same territorie, the reason is farre otherwise; for that euerie one of them hath himselfe the whole iurisdiction and power, nor cannot iudge but by turnes, one of them after another, neither haue more than one seat of iustice, in one and the same iurisdiction, but by the new grant of their patron or predominant lord. And in this, seruice differeth from iurisdiction; for that seruice suffereth it selfe to be at once & together enioyed of euerie one that hath right thereunto: but iurisdiction not so, as many haue thought, hauing excepted dutchies, marquisats, and counties; which by the auntient lawes of fees are of an indiuisible nature. But it is neither for vs needfull, neither doth this place require vs by reasons to refute the opinion of them which affirme iurisdictions so to cleaue vnto the territories, as if they were indeed seruices; least in so doing we should passe without the bounds of our purpose. Sufficeth it in passing by, to say, Iurisdiction to hold so little of fee, as that the soueraigne prince selling or giuing a fee, of what nature soeuer it be, is not therefore to be reputed to haue giuen or sold the iurisdiction thereto belonging; as it hath ofttimes bene iudged, & at length because it should no more be doubted of, was by an edict of *Philip* the faire more straitly prouided for: yea although the donation were by the soueraigne prince made to religious or deuout vses; which many (but without cause) haue excepted, the law being made generall. Seeing therefore that magistrats in power equall, or which hold not any thing one of them of another, cannot be commaunded or corrected one of them by another; much lesse can the equall lords or compeers of the same territorie and iurisdiction commaund or reforme one another, but the superiour magistrat or predominant lord is to haue the hearing and determining of the matter. By our customes the superiour courts haue reserued vnto themselues, the controuersies of the kings magistrats and officers amongst themselues, concerning their power and iurisdiction. But if question be for the executing of the decrees or iudgements of one of them in the territorie of another, it is to be done by honest request and leaue before obtained: howbeit that by a new law, that custome is taken away out of this our Commonweale, and power giuen vnto pursiuants to put in execution all the magistrats commaunds, almost throughout all the kingdome. As for soueraigne princes, not subiect to the power or commaund of others, they must in such case, of necessitie vse requests one to another, for that they cannot be compelled by the command of any greater power, as magistrats may, who without any leaue asked, suffer the iudgements of other magistrats to be put into execution in their prouinces: or in case they refuse so to doe, are to be constrained by the superior powers. Which asking of leaue of the greater or equall power to execute or suffer iudgement giuen out of their territories, to bee executed therein, offering to do or suffer the like to be done in theirs, as occasion shall require, hath of all antiquitie beene obserued and kept. Howbeit it seemeth the Roman empire

In a colledge or companie of magistrats or judges the greater part agreeing in one, may iudge or chastice any one or the lesser part of their fellowes. A difference betwixt seruice and iurisdiction.

yet florishing, that to put in execution a mandat or iudgement out of ones owne territorie, it was needfull first to obtaine the Emperours letters of commaund, seeing that the law saith, *Sententiam Romæ dictam, possunt Præsides in prouincys, si hoc iussi fuerint exequi*, The Presidents in their prouinces may put in execution a sentence (or iudgement) giuen at Rome, if they be thereunto commaunded: yet much more seemely it were by the good leaue of the magistrat to obtaine the same, than by force to extort it against his will. As in like cause the Emperour said vnto him which complayned of his companion, without hauing before spoken vnto him, *Alloquere illum, ne rem iniustam faciat*, Speake vnto him, that he do thee no wrong: forasmuch as the princes commaund, or constraint of the superiours in such case, giueth occasions of quarrels and iealousies amongst Magistrats, seeing the decrees of their equals, or of their inferiours, against their wils to be put in execution in their owne territories: which oft times turne to the great hurt of the subiects, and dishonour of the Commonweale, one of the magistrats, or of such as are in authoritie, in dispite of the other discharging their cholerique passions vpon the poore innocents: As did the Consul *Marcellus*, who in despite of *Cæsar* caused certeine of the citisens of Nouocome to be whipped, to make them to know (as he said) that *Cæsar* had no power to giue vnto them the right and freedome of the citisens of Rome. But much greater is the poore subiects harmes if such contention and difference for power and authoritie, fall out amongst the greatest magistrats, or highest Courts. As I remember such a difference fell out betwixt the parliament of Paris, and of Burdeaux, about the execution of an arrest giuen in the parliament of Paris; which the parliament of Burdeaux vpon the princes commaund suffered to be executed within the iurisdiction thereof, but with condition, that if any opposition or appeale were in the doing thereof made, the parliament of Burdeaux should haue the hearing and disciding thereof. He which had the execution of the matter, willing to proceed farther, notwithstanding the opposition of the defendant, appeal was by the partie made vnto the parliament of Bourdeaux, whom the plaintife preuented in the parliament of Paris. This contention betwixt the two parliaments was by the king referred vnto the great Counsel; where it was decreed, That to receiue and heare the appeale belonged vnto the parliament of Paris; for that euery man ought of right to be the interpreter and expounder of his owne meaning: and as none but the prince may declare his lawes and commaundements, so it belongeth to the magistrat to declare the meaning of his owne sentence. Now here question was of the right meaning of a thing alreadie iudged, at such time as the partie guiltie offered his opposition vnto the officer, putting into execution the decrees of the higher Court, from which a man may not by the lawes appeale: vnto which opposition of the partie guiltie, if the officer giue not way, then it is vsuall to appeale, not so much from the sentence of the higher Court, as from the iniurie of the officer which would not heare the opposition, which he must needes, except the Court haue commaunded the iudgement thereof to be put in execution, notwithstanding any opposition.

Contention betwixt great magistrats or courts, about their power and iurisdiction, alwaies vnto the poore subiect hurtfull.

But what if the Magistrat shall haue no respect or regard vnto the requestes or detrees of his equall, or of the inferiour magistrat, nor suffer their commaundements to be put in execution within his iurisdiction. Truely in this case he is to be thereunto by the superiour magistrats compelled: or if they be of the higher sort of magistrats which are at controuersie among themselues about their iurisdiction and power, they are by the princes authoritie to be enforced: for so these wordes of *Vlpian* the Lawier are to be vnderstood, *Si hoc iussi fuerint*, If they shall be so commaunded: viz. by the prince, (but not by the magistrats) at such time as the Presidents or gouernours of countries, euery one of them in his own prouince had the chiefest power and authoritie next vnto the

Wilful magistrats by the prince or their superiors to be enforced to suffer iustice to bee done within their iurisdiction.

OF A COMMONWEALE. 357

the Prince, by whom onely they were to be commaunded. And whereas in the Edicts or lawes any thing is commaunded to be done, it is thus to be vnderstood, that euery Magistrat in his owne prouince is to be obeyed, for that the magistrat hath no power to commaund out of his owne territorie or iurisdiction. In auntient time the kings Pursuiuants or officers, if they were to put in execution the commaunds of the royall magistrats in the territorie of such lords as had therein territoriall iurisdiction, were first to aske them leaue; vntill that afterwards it was by the most strait decrees of the highest courts forbidden them so to doe, for that therein the soueraigne maiestie of the king seemed to be something empaired.

But yet it might be demaunded, whether the inferiour Magistrats might cause their commaunds to be put in execution, without the leaue of the superiour magistrat, vnto whom appeale was made? and that after the same appeale let fall, and the time past, appointed for the prosecuting thereof; which the Lawiers to no purpose call *Fatalia*, enduced thereunto by an old errour and inueterat fault of them which haue translated the Code, and authentiques out of Greeke into Latin, wherein for κυρίας ἡμέρας, they haue red κυρίας ἡμέρας, which is to say, fatall daies, for daies prefixed and of assignation: which the law of the twelue Tables called *Statos dies*, daies appointed; as in this law, *Si status dies cum hoste*, that is to say, If the day appointed with a straunger Neither euer did lawier or man that could speak Latin, vse this forme of speaking, neither hath any of the Latins or Greeks called them for κυρίας ἡμέρας κυρίας or *Fatales*. The Lawiers haue oftentimes diuided *Dies sessionum*, *a diebus continuis*, Daies of Session, from daies of Continuation. And if any thing were by the magistrat commaunded to be done within a certaine time, the Lawiers called it *Statutum tempus*, and *edictum peremptorium*, a time appointed, or edict peremptorie: but when the time wherein the sute ought to be determined is expired and past, or that the sute is let fall, we say, *Litem mori*, the sute to die; or *instantiam perimi*, the instance to be lost: as before, we say, *Litem viuere*, or, the suit to liue: but none of the Lawiers hath vsurped *Fatalem diem*, or *Fatalia tempora*, a fatall day, or fatall times. But all this errour is deriued of the chaunging of this one Greeke letter *v.* into *η*, for seeing that by the word κὴρ, or קיר, the Greeks aswell as the Hebrewes signifie *Fatum*, or destinie, they must needes translate κυρίαν ἡμέραν, *fatalem diem*, that is to say, a fatall day. *Demosthenes* oft times calleth it κυρίαν ἡμέραν, which the Latins call *statum diem*; and we in our practise, *præfixam*, that is to say, an appointed, or prefixed day: for so *Demosthenes* saith against *Media*, ἐπειδὴ ἧκεν ἡ κυρία τοῦ νόμου, & against *Stephanus*, κυρίαν ἐγγράψαι: and sometimes also he saith, ἡμέραν διαμεμετρημένην, as to *Nicostratus*: and the later Greeks haue called it ἡμέραν ἐμπρόθεσμον, & ὡρισμένην, but neuer called it κυρίαν. And so pope *Synesius* metaphorically calleth the last day of a mans life κυρίαν, because he would not call it κυρίαν, or Fatall; a word vnto Christian men and true religion straunge. Wherefore for Fatall daies of appeales, we shall more truely and better vse the tearmes of Appointed times, for so the lawyer calleth them. But that *Iustinians* lawes were written in Greeke before they were written in Latin, I suppose no man to doubt. And that the *Theodosian* and *Hermogenian* Codes, out of whome *Iustinians* Code was almost all compiled, were as well written in Greek as in Latin, it is plaine: and so the law *Properandum* to haue beene translated rather by a Greeke than by a Latinist, being altogether writ in the Greeke phrase, as namely calling the defendant *fugientem*, or the partie flying away; which is the proper Greeke word φεύγοντα. Neither ought it to seeme straunge, that the Greekes translated the Roman lawes, and euen *Iustinians* Institutions into Greeke; seeing them to haue translated most of the writings of *Thomas Aquinas*, as also the latter bookes of *Aristotles* Metaphysikes out of Arabike

Whether the inferiour Magistrat be to haue leaue from the superiour, vnto whom appeale was made, to put his owne sentence in execution, the appeale being now let fall.

The errour of the word Fatalia.

bike into Greeke, the Greeke copie being before lost. But to returne againe from whence we haue digressed, and to resolue the propounded question; I say, that it is not needfull for the inferiour magistrat, the appeale being let fall, to haue leaue of the superiour magistrat (vnto whome the appeale was made) for the putting in execution of their owne iudgements: as in the time of our auncestors, the manner was, by letters of iustice (as they tearmed them) which by a decree of *Charles* the seuenth, were vtterly abolished and taken away: sufficeth it the appeale being once giuen ouer before the iudge that gaue the sentence, to request, that the same may now be put in execution, except the superiour magistrat vnto whome the partie condemned hath appealed, hath expresly before forbid the executionto be done. In which case it is needfull, that such prohibitio be taken away, before the inferior magistrat proceed further. For otherwise it is not requisit, that the appeale should by the superiour magistrat be declared to be let fall or giuen ouer, that the sentence may be put in execution; for that the benefit of the appeale let fall, is obtained by the law, & not by vertue of the magistrats sentence. Neither is the honour or reputation of the superiour magistrats impaired by the inferiours, not hauing from them expresse prohibition: in reuerence & respect of whom, the inferiour magistrats ought to stay the execution, if the stay thereof bee not perilous vnto the Commonweale. In which case they may proceed, although it were in question of life, and afterwards write back their aunswere; whereas otherwise, in causes concerning life and death, if the magistrat giue not way vnto the appeale, he himselfe is in danger of capitall punishment. Yea and in this case, the magistrat for not yeelding vnto the appeale, is guiltie of treason, albeit that question were but concerning the whipping of a citisen.

Now all that which we haue hitherto said concerning magistrats, and of the obedience that one of them oweth vnto another, is to be vnderstood of magistrats that be of the selfe same Commonweale. But what shal we then say of magistrats of diuers Commonweales? As if a man by the magistrats condemned in this kingdome shall flie into Greece, whether shall the Grand Signior of the Turkes, at the request of the French king, or of some other priuat man whome the matter doth concerne, cause the iudgement to be put in execution, without further enquirie of the equitie of the cause? The like question whereunto I remember to haue hapned in the parliament of Paris, concerning a French marchant condemned by default and contumacie at Venice, at the suit of a Venetian marchant; who came into Fraunce to demaund execution of the iudgement giuen in Venice, hauing before obtained letters of request frō the seigneurie to that purpose, as the vsuall manner & custome of soueraigne princes & lords in such cases is: For a mutuall respect and care which all princes haue vnto iustice, wherof they hold their Sceptets and Crownes. The French marchant excepteth against the Venetian, and no regard being had to his exception, appealeth vnto the court of parliament. Where most were of opinion, that the sentence so giuen was to bee put in execution, without any farther examination, whether it were rightfully iudged or not: which otherwise might seeme a wrong offered vnto the Seigneurie of Venice, which might vse the like circumstāce, & examine the iudgements of the magistrats of France, and also reuerse them, rather in reuenge of their wronged maiestie, than for the iniquitie of the same. Yet for that the marchant was condemned by default, it was thought meet to haue it enquired, whether he had by couenant in this point submitted himselfe vnto the Venetian Seigneurie and iurisdiction or not? And then, whether the iudgement were duely giuen, after certaine peremptorie edicts and appointed times, according to the laws and customs of the Venetians? Which being found to be so, the court adiudged the sentence to be put in executiō. And this is the course in priuat iudgements.

How-

OF A COMMONWEALE. 359

A Howbeit if question were of the honour, or life, not of one of our owne subiects only, but euen of a straunger flying vnto vs, the iudgement of a straunge magistrat is not to be put in execution, before the truth of the matter be againe of fresh and throughly examined and tried. Yea *Adrian* the emperour commaunded the gouernours of his prouinces, to vse ἀνάκρισιν (for that word the law vseth) that is to say, to iudge againe of them which had beene condemned, by the iustices of peace euen of the same Roman empire. And that which I haue said, is right straitly obserued and kept in the Commonweales of the Swissers, of Geueue, of Venice, Lucque, and Genes, who cause the condemned straungers flying vnto them, to be againe of new tried, before they restore them vnto forrein princes, demaunding from them such their condemned
B subiects againe. For so all lawiers almost with one consent say; Soueraigne Princes not to be bound to restore Straungers flying vnto them, vnto their owne Princes demaunding them againe. Which is true that they are not bound in any ciuill obligation, from which all soueraigne princes are exempted: but they without any distinction of the Law of nations or nature, altogether denie that a forrein subiect is to be restored vnto his prince requiring him againe. Onely *Baldus* addeth this condition therunto, Not to restore him to be right, so that the prince vnto whom the condemned or guiltie person is so fled, do vpon him iustice. But if they will confesse euery Prince by the lawes both of God and nature to be bound to doe iustice; they must also confesse that he is bound to restore another mans subiect vnto his owne natural prince, deman-
C ding him: not onely for the more manifest trying out of the truth, and discouering of the conspirators their partakers, for which their personall presence and confrontation is most necessarie; but also for exemplarie punishment to be done, in the same places where the offences were committed: which of all other things seemeth most to belong vnto the profit to arise vnto the Commonweale by punishments, as examples of common reuenge, the death of the offender, being one of the least thing that in matter of iustice is to be sought after. And if Magistrats in the same Commonweale are by mutuall obligation bound to helpe one an other, and so the Commonwealth, (whereunto next vnto God we owe all our endeuours) for the prosecuting and punishing of malefactors and offenders; why then should Princes be exempted from the
D like bond, so well agreeing with the lawes both of God and nature? Wherein the notable act of *Mahomet* (the second of that name) emperour of Constantinople, euen he which was surnamed the Great, is right worthily commended; in that he caused the murtherer, who had most cruelly slaine *Iulian de Medices* in the Church before the Aultar, to be apprehended at Constantinople whether he was fled, and so bound hand and foote, to be restored to *Laurence de Medices* and the state of Florence, requesting of him: which he did not as respecting the power of the Florentines, being then but small, but as fearing the hand and power of the immortall and almightie God. And in this Realme the custome hath alwaies beene to restore the guiltie fugitiues vnto their owne Lords and Princes demaunding of them, except therein question be made of
E the maiestie, boundes, or state of the kingdome, which hath beene by their decrees determined. One of the parliament of Paris: Another of the court of Rome against the king of England, who demaunding his fugitiue subiect, was denyed him: And the third of the parliament of Tholouse: that of Rome being then grounded vpon the soueraigntie of the See of Rome ouer the realme of England. But out of teatmes of estate, and where question is but of publique punishment, there is no Prince which is not bound to restore another mans subiect vnto his Prince demaunding him, as hath beene solemnly iudged by the parliament of Bourdeaux: howbeit that the same hath beene also expresly articulated in diuers treaties of peace. As in the treatie which
the

Whether soueraign princes be bound to restore straungers flying vnto them, vnto their owne princes demaunding them againe.

A notable acte of Mahomet the Great, first emperour of the Turkes.

A6 condemned by   A8 Geneve   D3 right worthily   D5 whether *i.e.* whither   E1 *For* their decrees *read* three decrees.

the Swissers made with the emperour *Charles* the fift, as Duke of Millan, the vij article caried an expresse clause, for the restoring of guiltie fugitiues. And for this cause king *Henry* the second, after he had by his Embassadour requested the Lords and people of Geneua, to restore vnto him *Baptista Didato* an Italian, his Receiuer generall of Roan, who was thither fled with all the money of the receipt: which they being thereto oftentimes requested, refused to doe: At length the king protested vnto the Lords of Berne, in whose protection the Seignorie of Geneua then was, that he would vse the law of Reprisall against them of Geneua; who before had resolued in their grand Councell of two hundred, in no wise to restore him: but afterwards being by an Herault sent from them of Berne, willed to deliuer him vnto the king, they chaunged that their former opinion for the detaining of him; So at length the robber of the comon treasure was forsaken by them of Geneua, lest they in doing otherwise should haue stirred vp the displeasure of a most mighty king, or of the Swissers against them, as also seeme to haue opened a sanctuarie or place of refuge for theeues, and other such like wicked men. And this we haue gathered out of the letters of the French embassador to *Anne Mommorancie* Constable of Fraunce, so that they are to be blamed which otherwise either thinke or write. Wherefore I hold it to be an iniurie vnto the estate of another man, to detaine a guiltie fugitiue after he is demaunded to be againe vnto his owne prince restored; and much more if he should be so detained by the subiects among themselues. For which cause all the Tribes of Israel combined themselues against the Tribe of Beniamin, which was so vtterly destroyed, except sixe hundred persons, for refusing to restore the guiltie persons demaunded of them. And for the same cause we find that the Hippotæ were all destroyed, and their citie vtterlie razed by the Thebans; for that they chose rather to defend the murtherers of *Phox* the Bæotian, and for them to take vp armes, then to restore them vnto the Thebans, demaunding them. But if the Prince vnto whom the fugitiue is retired certeinly know him whom he hath so receiued, to be an innocent and guiltles man, and to be vniustly pursued and sought after, as hauing but escaped the crueltie of a tyrant, it is not onely a shamefull and iniurious thing to betray the poore innocent and straunge man vnto the cruell tyrant: but he should rather for the miserable mans defence, and safegard of his life take vp armes, seeing that by the law of God, we ought not to restore a fugitiue seruant vnto his angry master, from whose furie he is fled into anothers mans house.

And thus much concerning Magistrats; and the obedience that they owe vnto Princes, and of the power that they haue ouer particular men, and of the respect that they ought to haue one of them towards an other. But to compare the Magistrats of auntient time, with ours now, belongeth not to this our purpose, considering that they are still in chaunge, howbeit that wee see them to be like in effect, although that they differ in names. As we read in the booke of the kings, where it is said, That *Azarias* the sonne of the high priest *Tsadoc* was neere vnto the person of *Salomon* to instruct him in matters concerning Religion; that *Iosophat* was chiefe of his councell, or his Chauncellour; that *Eliphore*, and *Aiah* were his Secretaries for the estate; that *Banaia* was his Constable; and *Azarias* the sonne of *Natan* his Lieutenant generall ouer the gouernments of the twelue Tribes, which are and haue beene as it were like in all Monarchies. So in like maner we see in the Turkish Empire, that the first and principall *Bassa* is Generall of the armie, as Constable or chiefe Mareschall; and Beglerbegs are gouernours generall of Prouinces; the Zanzacks are as more particular and inferiour gouernours, the two Cadilesquires are the Chauncelours, attendinding vnto the administration of justice, the one in Asia, the other in Europe; the Sabbassaes and Cadies are the ordinarie magistrats and judges; the Mophti is the great Bishop. So in the kingdomes

OF A COMMONWEALE. 361

A kingdomes of Thunes, of Fes, and of Maroch, the Munafide is as Chauncelour, the Admirall is Generall of the armie at Sea, a word or name which we haue borowed from the Arabians. So we see the charges and offices to be as it were like, although their names be diuers, as the Great Master of Ethiopia is called Bethudere, which is an Hebrew word, signifying Master of the houshold. But forasmuch as Magistrats in euery Commonweale are diuided into Corporations and Colledges, and that there are more Corporations and Colledges of priuat men than of Magistrats, let vs also say somewhat of such Corporations and Colledges.

CAAP. VII.

B ¶ *Of Corporations, and Colledges, Estates, and Communities, and what profits or inconueniences ensue thereof vnto the Commonweale.*

Ow after that we haue spoken of a Familie, and of the parts thereof, of Soueraigntie, and of Magistrats; we must speake of Corporations and Colledges also: wherefore let vs then first speake of the cause of Corporations and Colledges, and after of their power and priuileges in generall, and of the maner of punishing of them, if they offend: and last of all whether the Commonweale can be without them. The difference of a Familie, from Corporations and Colledges, and so of them from

C a Commonweale, is such as is the difference of the parts from the whole: for the communitie of many heads of a familie, or of a village, or of a towne, or of a countrie, may be without a Commonweale, aswell as a familie without a colledge. And, as many families by amitie alyed, are members of one corporation and communitie; so many corporations and communities allyed by a soueraigne power, make one Commonweale. Now a familie is a communitie naturall; a colledge is a communitie ciuill; and a Commonweale hath that moreouer, That it is a communitie gouerned by a soueraigne power, and may be so strait, as that it may haue neither corporation nor colledges, but onely many families in it. And so the word Communitie is common

D vnto a familie, a colledge, and a commonweale. And properly a Corporation is vnderstood to consist of diuers families, or colledges, or of many families and colledges together. But the beginnings of all ciuill societies are deriued from a familie, which is (as we say) it selfe a naturall societie, and by the father of nature it selfe first founded in the beginning together with mankind. But when reason, by God himselfe ingrafted in vs, had made man desirous of the companie and societie of man, and to participate together both in speech and conuersation; the same so wrought, as that proceeding farther from the loue of them that were domesticall & their owne, it extended farther, to take pleasure in the propagation and encrease of families. So also families by little and little departing from their first beginning, learned by ciuill societie to imitate the

E naturall societie of a familie. For why, a Commonweale is a ciuill societie, which can of it selfe stand without corporations or colleges; but not without a familie: besides that, Commonweales may be dissolued, for that they are deriued from the Lawes and institutions of men: whereas families cannot altogether perish, but that all mankind must before perish also. Whereby it is to be vnderstood, From the roote of one familie, by the euerliuing God himselfe planted, at the first to haue sprung vp as it were certeine plants, who by necessitie constrained, built for themselues houses and dwelling places, so to be the safer from the iniurie of the weather, and the rage of wilde beasts: and after that Hamlets and villages, which in processe of time became Boroughes and

I i   Townes.

The difference betwixt a familie, a colledge, and a Commonweale.

A Familie the beginning of all ciuill societies.

A4 *For* Bethudere *Bodin writes* Bethudete (Fr) *and* Bethudeta (L). Cf. 188 G10 and note.
A10 Chap. VII   D7 conversation *i.e.* association, society (*usus* in L)   Note at B4.

Townes. But being growne to such a multitude, as that they could not longer be contained within the compasse and precinct of the same countrie, they were driuen to depart thence also, and to seeke out new dwelling places. So that now thus diuided in places, in regions, and kinred, being bound vnto no law or commaund, as euery one of them exceeded the other in strength and power, so he forced himself to thrust them that were neere vnto him, and weaker than himselfe, out of their houses and dwelling places; or to take from them their springs, their fountaines, or pleasant places; or to driue them from their pastures or feedings: which violence so offered by the stronger, enforced the weaker either to seeke out places by nature defencible and strong, or else by art or wisedome to fortifie themselues, their children, wiues, and families, with ditches, trenches, and walles, whereof strong townes and cities arise. For so *Dionysius* long since writeth king *Seruius* to haue placed certeine places of refuge in the mountaines & strongest hilles, whether the poore countrie men might retire themselues out of the fields, so to saue themselues from the incursions of their enemies. And yet could not the enemies force be so kept off with walles and other fortifications, but that they which had so shut vp themselues therein, were yet neuerthelesse besieged by the stronger. For why, the first sort of men was most giuen to rapine, murther, and theft, delighting in nothing more, nor accounting any honour greater than to robbe and kill, and to oppresse the weaker sort as slaues: as *Plutarch* well agreeing with the sacred historie most truely writeth. And long before *Plutarch*, *Thucidides* the most famous historiographer of them that florished among the Greekes reporteth, all Greece but a little before his time to haue beene troubled with the robberies and outrages committed by the mightier sort; and then robberie & theft to haue bene no disgrace or shame. Yea such as traueiled by Sea or land (as the same authour reporteth) when they met, before they came neere together, vsed commonly (and that without any reproach or imputation) to aske whether they were Robbers or Pyrates or not. And not onely *Plato*, and his disciple *Aristotle*, haue put robberie among the kinds of hunting, but the Hebrewes also, who call Theeues and Robbers, mightie hunters, as they did *Nimroth*. And by the lawes of *Solon* it is plaine, that men might lawfully ioine in fellowship to robbe and steale, (prouided alwaies that it were not from the subiects of their owne estate) as appeareth by these words, ἐπὶ λείαν οἰχόμενοι, which the Latin interpretour thinking to be absurd and false, hath wrested them another way: For what other thing is ἐπὶ λείαν οἴχεσθαι, than to robbe? And what other thing is λεία, but ἐκ τῶν πολεμίων λάφυρα? Neither were robberies lesse allowed of the auntient Latines than they were of the Greeks and Hebrewes, as it is to be perceiued by the first league made betwixt the Romans and the Carthaginensians: wherein it was thus expresly set downe: **Vltra Promontorium pulchri prædæ aut mercaturæ gratia Romani ne nauiganto*, Beyond the faire Promontorie, the Romans shall not saile either for bootie, or in trade of marchandize. From which kind of robberies long it was before other people also abstained: for so *Cæsar* speaking of the Germaines in his time saith, *Latrocinia nullam habent infamiam, quæ extra fines cuiuscunque ciuitatis fiunt, atque ea iuuentutis exercendæ, ac desidiæ minuendæ causa fieri prædicant*, Robberies done without the boundes of euery citie, haue with them no infamie; and those they say to be done for the exercise of the youth, and auoiding of slouth. This licence and impunitie of robbing and reauing, constrained men which as yet had no Princes nor Magistrats, to ioyne themselues in societie and amitie for the defence of one an other, and to make Communities and Fraternities, which the Greekes called φρατρίας, and φράτορες, as brethren which drew water of the same well, which they called φρέαρ, as also παγανος, which are rurall and countrie people vsing the faire fountaine, which the

---

I2 ἐπὶ λείαν οἰχόμενοι   I5 πολεμίων   K2 cuiusque (Fr and L)   K10 For παγανος *read* paganos (Fr, and cf. Festus, ed. Müller, p. 221).   K10 For faire fountaine *read* same fountaine.

Side notes:
- The beginning of strong townes and cities.
- The first sort of men, most delighted in theft and murther, and oppressing of others weaker than themselues.
- Theft and robberie in auntient time no disgrace nor shame.
- Theft in auntient time lawfull both amongst the Greekes and Latins.
- *Polyb. Lib.3.*

OF A COMMONWEALE.   363

A the Dorians called πάγοι, and whereof such countrie villages were called *Pagi*, as the Latines also said them *Commeßari*, who in the same countrey villages, which the Greekes called κώμας, did ordinarily eate and drinke together: as * *Festus* writeth. Whereby it is plainely to be seene, the societies of men among themselues, to haue bene at the first sought out for the leading of their liues in more safetie and quiet: and them first of all to haue sprung from the loue which was betwixt man and wife: From them to haue flowed the mutuall loue betwixt parents and their children: then the loue of brethren and sisters one towards another: and after them the friendship betwixt cosens and other nie kinsmen: and last of all, the loue and good will which is betwixt men ioyned in alliance: which had all at length growne cold, and bene vtterly exstin-
B guished, had it not bene nourished, maintained, and kept, by societies, communities, corporations, and colledges: the vnion of whome hath for long time in safetie maintained many people, without any forme of a Commonweale, or soueraigne power ouer them. So the people of Israel for a long time florished in great tranquilitie without kings, and without any Popular or Aristocraticall estate, euerie man liuing at his pleasure in all libertie, euerie Tribe being in it selfe vnited by the bond of bloud and kindred, and all of them together by the communitie of their law and sacrifices. Who when they were by any enemie to be assailed or inuaded, the estates of their Tribes and communities assembling together, made choyce of a chieftaine, vnto whom they gaue soueraigne power; and namely of such an one as God had with his spirit enspired and
C stirred vp amongst them. So of many Tribes and families together vnited, was made a Commonweale, by meane of a soueraigne power set ouer them. And for this cause the princes and lawgiuers which first founded Commonweals, who had not yet discouered the difficulties they were to proue, to keep & maintaine their subiects by way of iustice, ordained and maintained fraternities, communities, and colledges; to the end, that the parts and members of the self same body of a Commonweale, being at accord among themselues, it might be for them the more easie to rule the whole Commonweale together. So we see that *Numa Pompilius*, king and lawgiuer vnto the Romans (after he had abolished the name of the Sabines, which some thing diuided the Roman state) established certaine fraternities, and colledges, or companies of men, of all maner
D of occupations; appointing vnto euerie fraternitie certaine pattons, priests, and solemne sacrifices, which were kept on certaine appointed dayes of the yeare. And afterwards also ordained a fraternitie of marchants, to whome he gaue *Mercurie* for their patron: which he seemed to haue done to the imitation of *Solon*, who by a positiue law permitted all manner of fraternities and communities whatsoeuer, with power for them to make such lawes and statutes among themselues as they should see good, so that they were not contrarie vnto the publike positiue lawes of the state. *Lycurgus* also did not onely permit, but straitly commaund also to maintaine and cherish such societies and communities, as well generall as particular; and that all his subiects should take their refection and diet in companies of fifteene and fifteene together: which for that
E they were kept for friendship sake, were called φιλίτια, of the friendship that they had one of them with another. As also in almost all the other townes of Greece, there were the like fraternities and companies, whome they called ἑταιρίας, as in Italie the same colledges and companies were called *Sodalitia*; for the vnitie, companie, and friendship they had among themselues, eating and drinking together for the most part: and hauing no judges but themselues, if any difference or strife chaunced to fall out amongst them, being such companions and fellowes; as knowing that amitie and friendship was the onely foundation of all humane and ciuill societie, and much more requisit for the keeping and maintaining thereof, than iustice it selfe: For that iustice

Ii ij   neuer

* *Festus in verbo pagi.*
The societies of men, why they were first sought out.

The happy estate of the people of Israel before they had any king, or other forme of Aristocratique or popular commonweale.

Fraternities, communities, and colleges, why they were first instituted and ordained.

Amitie and friendship the foundation of all humane and ciuill societie: and more requisite for the keeping and maintaining thereof than iustice it selfe.

Note at E2.

neuer flexible, but alwayes keeping the vprightnesse of it selfe, by iust iudgement well endeth suits; but not hatred, making oft times of friends foes: wheras amitie and friendship, which is by company nourished, yeelding of the right of it selfe, best establisheth the true naturall iustice, and plucketh vp all controuersies by the root, with great quietnesse and loue reconciling subiects among themselues, together with the Commonweale. Now the principall end & scope of all laws, both diuine and humane, is to keep and maintaine the loue of men one towards another amongst themselues, and them altogether in their dutie towards God; which cannot better be done, than by ordinarie and orderly conuersing and combining of men themselues together.

Wherefore the Cretentians in auntient time did all eat and drinke together, young and old, men and women; for to maintaine the loue and amitie which we haue before spoke of amongst them: Howbeit that afterwards to auoid confusion, the ages and sexes were into certaine orders diuided So we see in the law of God, the feasts of Passeouer, to haue bene commaunded to be holden by companies of ten and ten persons together: beside the feasts of Tabernacles, and the ordinarie banquets of sacrifice, which God commaunded to be solemnised with all ioy and gladnesse: and that for no other cause, but that so men might be together vnited in religion towards God, and mutuall loue and friendship one to another among themselues. The same was also well obserued & kept in the Christian primitiue church, who oftentimes made such feasts, which they called ἀγαπὰς, for the deuout kissings, and charitable embracements one of them (in the feruensie of their zeale) gaue to another, in the ending of them, besides their ordinarie behauiour and communication. And albeit that many things are long since by tract of time growne out of vse, yet neuerthelesse a resemblance of those old feastes is yet shadowed in our holy feasts and banquets: which not faigned but true feasts the Venetians do with most great care and solemnitie keepe: but the Swissers better than in any place of the world, where the fraternities and companies in euerie towne haue their common houses or halles, wherein they oftentimes make their feasts and bankets, neither is there any village so little, which hath not a common house in it for that purpose. Where if any strife or contention shall arise amongst them that be of the fellowship or companie, it is by the common consent there ended, and the definitiue sentence there written, not in paper, but vpon the verie table whereon they haue banqueted, and that not with inke, but with chalke. And as in auntient time artisans, marchants, priests, bishops, and all sorts of men had their fraternities, and companies: so had also the philosophers, and especially the *Pythagorians*, who ordinarily met together, and liued for most part of their time in common. And thus much concerning the cause, the beginning, and progresse of corporations, and colledges, communities, and companies: which afterwards by succession of time haue in all Commonweales beene better ruled by lawes, statutes, and customes.

Orderly feasts and meetings of old time instituted to maintaine loue and amitie amongst men.

But that all things which are to be said of corporations and colledges, may in order be declared: Let vs first orderly set downe and show, what power euery corporation or colledge is of, and what priuilege is to euerie one of them giuen; then how they are to be gouerned, and kept within the bounds of their dutie; and last of all, whether a Commonweale can be without colledges or companies, and what colledges are most necessarie and best fitting a Commonweale. Which the better to vnderstand, we may say, that all colledges and companies are ordained either for religion, or for policie, and so concerne but worldly things. If they be instituted but for policie, either they haue iurisdiction, or are without all iurisdiction. Colledges without iurisdiction, are such as are ordained for the bringing vp of youth, or for fellowship of physitians, or of other schollers, or of marchants, or of handie craft and trades men, or of companies of husbandmen

The diuision of colleges and companions.

H8 for that   K4(margin) *For* companions *read* companies.

bandmen: but such as haue iurisdiction, are colledges of magistrats, and judges, such as of whome we haue before spoken. Colledges ordained and made for religion, or for publike deuotion, are growne into number almost infinit, differing as wee see, in lawes, manners, life, attire, orders, fashions, and apparell. And it may be, that a colledge may be particular to one occupation, or to one science, or to one companie of marchants, or to one iurisdiction: and it may also be, that two or moe colledges, may bee vnited into one bodie, as all manner of occupations together, all sorts of marchants, or all maisters of sciences, or all the magistrats; which ought not of right to bee called a colledge, but a bodie politique, or corporation: albeit that by the ambiguitie of words they be oftentimes together confounded. For there was one colledge of the Tribunes, another of the Pretors, and another of the Questors: but when these three colledges meet together into one and the selfe same bodie, it is foolishly called a colledge: and yet can it not rightly be tearmed an Vniuersitie, which consisteth of the companie and assemblie of all the citisens, colledges, and corporations, yea and sometimes also of the villages of the same countrey. Wherefore we shall rather call it a bodie politique than a colledge: which so together groweth of many colledges, or persons of vnlike condition. And it may be also, that all the particular colledges may haue the right of a generall communitie, or of an vniuersitie. And that not onely all the colledges and communities, but that also all the inhabitants ioyned together with the corporation & colledges of a towne, or of a countrey, or of a prouince, may haue the right of a communitie for to hold their estates. Moreouer the right of a colledge or companie may be giuen to euerie mysterie or occupation in particular, and yet forbidden them in generall. And euerie one of them may haue diuers rules, statutes, and particular priuileges. So that we may say, that euerie corporation or colledge, is a lawfull communitie or consociation vnder a soueraigne power. Where the word Lawfull importeth the authoritie of the soueraigne, without whose permission there can be no colledge: and is referred not onely vnto the power of meeting together: but vnto the place also where it ought to meet, vnto the time and manner of meeting, and to what things ought to bee entreated of, in their assembly. And the word communitie, or consociation, signifieth that there ought some thing to be common to all that be fellowes of the colledge or societie: For where there is nothing common, there is no colledge: sufficient it is for them to haue their meeting common, their attourney or agent common, and the priuileges giuen vnto the colledge common vnto all the fellowes thereof: albeit that they haue neither common treasure, neither ordinarily liue or conuerse together. So that they haue not well defined a colledge, which haue said it to bee a fellowship of three persons dwelling together, hauing their goods and substances in common. Wherein they are two wayes deceiued, for it may be, that three persons or moe may haue their goods in common, and liue together, and yet be all no colledge, but a societie of themselues, contracted for the getting of goods, and liuing together: as also to the contrarie, fellowes of the same colledge may dwell separat in houses, not hauing their goods in common, nor any common treasure; neither yet commonly liuing together: and yet enioy indeed the right of a colledge or companie, as hauing by law and the princes graunt, power to assemble themselues and meet together at certaine places, and times: and to intreat of certaine their affaires, such as are the fraternities or companies of artificers and trades men, whome the law calleth *Collegia*, or colledges. Yet some colledges there be, which haue almost all those things among themselues common, as wee see those to haue, which are together ioyned for studie, religion or deuotion sake.

As for the number of fellowes in a colledge or societie, it is no matter what it bee, so that they be not fewer than three: for that otherwise it cannot be a colledge. Where-

What a corporation or colledge is.

No corporation or colledge to be suffered without the leaue of the soueraign.

Euery college or societie must haue somthing common to al the fellowes thereof, being otherwise no college.

What number of fellowes ought to be in a college or societie.

C2 *mysterie i.e.* trade, profession   Note at D3.

366   THE THIRD BOOKE

What number of fellowes ought to be in a colledge or societie.

fore the Romans called it not a colledge of their Censors, or Consuls, as they did of their Pretors, Tribunes, and Questors. And as for the fellowes themselues, my meaning is, that they should be equall of power, in respect of their communitie or fellowship, hauing euerie one of them a deliberatiue voice in their affayres: howbeit that it may be, that the colledge, or prince, may make choyce of one of the fellowes to commaund, reforme, and chastice euerie one of the fellows in particular, but not all of them in generall: such as are our bishops and abbats, hauing power to chastice their religious and chanons. But if this head or chiefe haue power ouer the whole body of the societie or colledge in grosse, it is not then rightly a colledge, but rather a forme of familie, such as are colledges or schooles ordained for the bringing vp of youth: wherein there bee no bursors or fellowes, which haue therein any deliberatiue voice: For if it haue in it any such bursors or fellowes, hauing the right of the societie or colledge, and deliberatiue voice in their assemblies, it is then a colledge, albeit that the rest of the yonger sort be vnder the power and correction of the principall.

Whether the head or principal of a college be to be also accounted a fellowe thereof

And hereof ariseth a question, Whether a bishop in the companie of his priests, or an abbat amongst his religious, be to be accounted fellowes, hauing the verie title and right of a fellow, and himselfe making a part of the colledge, without the qualitie or title of a bishop or abbat? Which question being by the learned on both parts disputed, yet remaineth vndecided. But to leaue the disputation apart, it seemeth, that he which is chosen by the colledge or prince to commaund all the fellowes in particular, hath a double qualitie; one in respect of euerie one of the fellowes, and another in respect of the whole colledge or societie: where in regard of the fellowes he is called Principall, Bishop, Abbat, Prior, President, or such like, hauing power and authoritie to commaund euerie one of them in particular: howbeit that in the bodie of the colledge or corporation, he is no more than a fellow, although he haue the place of precedence: and that is it for which they put their titles diuided, as, the Bishop, Chanons, and Chpiter; the Abbat, Religious, & Couent; the Principall, Bursors, & Colledge. Wherein one of the chiefest lawyers hath bene deceiued, saying, That the Philosophers haue called the persons of a colledge, the colledge: showing indeed no Philosophie in so saying, considering that a colledge is a name of right, and that all the reuenew and right of a colledge may remaine in one person, the rest of the fellowes being all dead. And in case that all the fellowes of a colledge were dead, yet doth the right of a colledge remaine: neither can the lands or goods thereof be confiscated, except the right of a colledge be before by the supreme authoritie suppressed. For one of the principall priuileges of corporations and colleges is, that legacies may be vnto them giuen by testament: wheras societie by the law forbidden, are not colleges, but vnlawfull assemblies, vnto whom it is not by the law permitted, to leaue any thing by testament, albeit that legacies may be giuen vnto euerie one of the colledges. But to the intent such vnlawfull companies and assemblies might be repressed, I thinke it needfull, that it should by law bee forbidden, any lands or legacies to be vnto al or any of them left by testament, as vnto fellows of such corporations or colledges.

That a college is a name of right: and consisteth not in the persons of the fellows, but may stil remaine, all the fellowes thereof being dead.

Antoninus first that gaue leaue for legacies to be giuen to colleges

And whereas we haue said, that a colledge or societie may be without any common stocke or treasure: that is also to be vnderstood, that a colledge or societie may bee ordained with such prouiso, that nothing shall be left vnto it by gift or legacie. *Antoninus* the emperour was the first which gaue leaue for legacies & donations to be giuen to al colledges, except to the colledges of the Iewes, vnto whome it was yet lawfull to meet together for religion sake, and to haue their Synagogues: as is to be seene in the oration of the ambassadour *Philo*, vnto the emperour *Caligula*. And *Augustus* himselfe by letters pattens directed vnto the gouernours of the prouinces of the empire, commanded,

---

H6 and Chapter   I7 societies by   I9 For the colledges read the fellows (*collegues* in Fr 1–2, 5–8; *collegis* in L 1–3; but *colleges* in Fr 3–4; *collegiis* in L 4–5). Cf. *Digest*, 34, 5, 20 (21).

Notes at F2, F8, H9.

ded, That they should permit and suffer the Iewes to enioy their colledges. Whereupon *Narbanus* Proconsull of Asia, forbad the magistrats of Ephesus in any sort to let or disturbe them. Yea that more is, *Augustus* himselfe commaunded a dailie and perpetuall sacrifice of a calfe, a goat, and a ram, to be made at Hierusalem for the welfare of himselfe, and of the Commonweale: and willed an ordinarie almes or doale to bee giuen vnto the Iewes, of his owne proper costs and charges, for the reliefe of their necessitie. There be also corporations and colledges of judges and magistrats, which yet are not capable of testamentarie legacies, if they haue not expresse leaue by their erection and institution so to doe. As was iudged against the Senat of Rome: whereunto *Russius Cæpio* one of the Senators, had giuen by legacie a certaine summe of money, which he willed to be still distributed to them onely which came vnto the councell: which legacie the Senat demaunding, *Cæpio* his heires denied it to bee vnto the Senat due: in which controuersie *Domitian* the emperour gaue sentence for the heire, and excluded the Senat, although it were the most auntient, and most necessarie corporation of all the Roman Commonweale.

Augustus a great fauorour of the Iewes.

And thus hauing set downe and declared the beginning and definition of colledges, and communities: let vs now also speake of their power in generall; which is not determined by their particular foundations, statutes, and priuileges, which are diuers and almost infinit, according to the diuersitie of the particular colledges and communities themselues. Now the chiefe corporations or colledges, and which haue most power in a Commonweale, are the colledges of judges and magistrats: who not onely haue power ouer euerie one of their fellowes, and the lesser part of their owne colledge, but ouer other particular colledges also; and so ouer others subiect to their iurisdiction, and yet without their colledge. And in this the colledges of judges and magistrats notably differ from other colledges: for that other colledges are established euerie one of them for the good gouernment of that onely which is vnto themselues common; whereas the colledges of judges and magistrats, are principally erected for the good of other subiects, and to rule the other colledges, as also to chastice them if they shall transgresse their lawes and statutes. But as a wise man ought first to be wise for himselfe, and then for others; as also to looke first into himselfe, before he can rightly iudge of others; or as the Hebrewes in their prouerbes say, That charitie ought first to begin of it selfe, if it be well ruled: So ought the colledges of judges and magistrats, first to establish iustice amongst themselues, euerie one of them in particular, and to themselues all in generall, the better to distribute the same to the other subiects.

The colledges of judges and the cheif colleges in a Commonweal.

But question might be made, Whether it were more expedient that the colledges of magistrats and judges, should be iudged by their fellowes, or by others? for some particular reasons, which in due place we shall hereafter set downe. But here to make the matter short, If the colledge for the most part be composed of euill and naughtie men, it is not to be left vnto themselues, to iudge of their owne misdemainers; but they are to be iudged by the superiour magistrats, if they haue power ouer them; or by the prince, in case they be not by any other superiour magistrat to be reformed. But if the greater part of them be good and honest men, there is then no doubt but that it is better and more expedient both for the colledge and the Commonweale, that the fellows should be iudged by their fellowes, rather than by other iudges: For that euerie colledge I know not how hath in it some particularitie which cannot so well bee vnderstood or iudged, as by the fellowes of the same corporation themselues. Ioyning hereunto also, that by this meane the loue and vnitie of the fellowes among themselues, is in their colledge and societie the better maintained. And for this cause chiefly the emperour *Adrian* decreed, That the Roman Senators should be iudged by the Senat onely.

Whether it were more expedient the colledges of magistrats and judges to be iudged and reformed by their fellowes of the same societie, or by others.

Ii iiij

A2 Norbanus   B2 *For* his heires (L) *read* his heire (Fr). Cf. Suetonius, *Domitian*, 9.   Note at D2.

ly. And for the selfe same reason the ciuill iurisdiction of marchants, and for the trade of marchandise hath bene wisely in all Italie, and since that in Fraunce committed and giuen to certaine magistrats and Consuls of the corporation and companie of marchants, summarily to decide the differences arising about the contracts of marchandise, which haue in them I know not how certaine secrets, not to others well knowne.

<small>Colleges not hauing any iurisdiction but only a restraining power, how they are to vse the same.</small>

As for other corporations and colledges, as of physitians, and tradesmen, albeit that by their foundation they haue not any iurisdiction or commaunding power; yet neuerthelesse so it is, that they alwayes haue a certaine restrayning authoritie and power by their statutes and priuileges, limited and allowed them; and sometime without any limitation at all left vnto the wisdome and discretion of the corporation or colledge, or of the head thereof: which ought to be vsed with such moderation, as the father is to vse towards his children: which ought not to be with crueltie or rigour. For if the law condemne him to pay the price of the slaue, slaine by him that hath taken vppon him to teach him, albeit that it were in correcting of him: of much greater reason were he to be condemned, which hauing but the moderat correction of men of free condition, should vse such rigour as that death should thereof ensue? As it sometimes happened in Lacedemonia, where yong children were by the Great Maister of the youth so rigorously whipt, at that sometimes they gaue vp the ghost vpon the altar of *Diana* whilest they were yet in whipping; most part of them not daring so much as to sigh or grone, for feare they had to be accounted faint harted cowards. And albeit that the emperour *Frederike* the second gaue power and authoritie vnto the rectours of Vniuersities, and that the principals of schooles and colledges haue alwayes had the correction of their disciples and schollers: yet that is to bee vnderstood but of light matters, and not of such chastisement and correction as the magistrat hath by the princes graunt ouer priuat offendors; as many haue beene of opinion. For why, neither the German emperour, nor the pope can giue any such power vnto the principalles of colledges, or to the colledges themselues: but in such countries as are vnto themselues subiect. For albeit that pope *Gregorie* the eleuenth in a Bull graunted for the confirmation of the priuileges of the Vniuersitie of Paris, before graunted by the popes *Vrban* the fift, and *Innocent* the sixt, in one article prouided, That if a scholler committed any thing deseruing punishment, the hearing thereof should belong vnto the bishop of Paris onely: and in another article also, That no scholler should from thenceforth bee imprisoned for whatsoeuer debt. Yet the French kings and magistrats haue oftentimes well declared themselues not to bee bound to any such the popes Bulles. Yet true it is, that colledges instituted for religion, haue ordinarily the correcting of them that are therein professed; and that so much the more, as their rule and order is the straiter: For which cause such as haue therein taken vppon them such profession, are exempted from the power and correction of their owne fathers: albeit that many hold the contrarie: whose opinion for all that is not in that point followed. And yet neuerthelesse certaine it is, that the naturall dutie and reuerence of children towards their parents, remaineth alwaies in force and power, notwithstanding whatsoeuer bond and vow they haue made to any corporation or colledge. For why, neither mans lawes, nor the statutes or priuileges of princes can derogat from the lawes of God and nature, which hath expresly bound children vnto the obedience of their fathers and mothers; from which they can by no otherwise free, or yet deliuer tthemselues, than by lawfull emancipation: or their fathers silence who in saying nothing, seeme to haue consented vnto their childrens vowes, which by speaking they might haue letted: which consent for all that excuseth not children from doing the

<small>Whether children hauing taken vpon them any vowe of religion, be yet neuerthelesse bound to honor and obey their parents.</small>

G7 ensue. As   G9 as that   I5 oftentimes   K7 themselves the honour and reuerence due vnto their parents, although that they being so professed, be from thenceforth accounted children of the colledge; vnto whome also their colledges in right of inheritance succeed, they themselues beeing accounted of seruile estate & condition. For which cause the canonists giue vnto the abbies power and authoritie ouer their owne religious, exempt from the bishops, which hath oftentimes by the decrees of the parliament of Paris bene confirmed. In such sort, as that they which are once entred into such religious orders, may not from that time be called to account or into questiõ for any thing by them committed before they entred into the monastery: which yet is to be vnderstood but of light & youthful faults; which otherwise were but to open a way to theeues and murtherers, to retire themselues into such colledges, as into forrests, for the auoiding of due punishment; as indeed it ofttimes happeneth: wherewith the wise magistrats ought to meet, & according to the law of God to draw the murtherers from the altar to doe vpon them iustice. As the court of parliament of Thoulouse (not long agoe) condemned two religious monks of the order *D'aurade*, to be in their habits shamefully drawne vpon a hurdle to the place of execution, and there to be quartered, without disgrading of them, for hauing most cruelly murthered the head of their monasterie, whose seueritie they could by no meanes endure. Yea the abbat himselfe may by his monkes be conuented before the ordinarie judge, and that as well in criminall as ciuill matters: who may also freely appeale from the sentence of their abbat vnto his superiour, as it hath oftentimes beene iudged by the decrees of the parliament of Paris; & that without leaue, as witnesseth * the abbat of Palermo; and hath also bene iudged by the parliament of Bourdeaux. And for the same reason if the colledge would without cause thrust out or depriue one of the fellowes of his right, priuilege, and libertie in the colledge, the hearing of the cause belongeth to the ordinarie judge of the colledge. Howbeit that in auntient time the corporations and colledges of Artisans, Marchants, and other such like, had this power (for the remouing of their fellowes) as we read in *Cicero* of the Roman marchants, *Mercuriales & Capitolini, M. Furium hominem nequam, equitem Romanum de collegio deiecerunt*, The *Mercuriales* and *Capitolini* (saith he) thrust *M. Furius* a naughtie man, and yet a gentleman of Rome, out of their colledge or companie. And in Lacedemonia (as *Plutarch* writeth) it was lawfull for to thrust out of their colledges or companies, him that had discouered or reuealed the secrets of their companie. As in like case *Panormitan* the abbat writeth, That in abbies or colledges erected for deuotion, the chapiters haue power to thrust out any of the fellowes, or to depriue him of his ordinarie diuidents, but not to beat him, or to vse seuere correction vpon him, or yet to imprison him; as hath bene iudeged by a decree of the parliament of Paris.

But yet here a man might aske, Whether a colledge may make a decree, That none of the fellowes shal conuent or sue another of his fellowes, before any other judges but the colledge? And in case it be so decreed, whether hee that shall breake the decree so made and sue his fellow before another judge, shall bee bound vnto the ciuill penaltie in the decree set downe? Wherein *Sceuola* the lawyer is of opinion, the decree to bee good; and that the fellow of a colledge or societie cannot haue recourse vnto other magistrats, contrarie vnto the decree of the colledge, but in paying the penaltie in the decree of the colledge expressed. Howbeit (in mine opinion) this decree is not general, neither can take place in causes criminall, no more than the conditionall penalties set downe in arbitrements, which haue no place if they concerne matters of crime. Secondarily mine opinion is, That the decree of a colledge or companie, euen in ciuill causes hath no place, if all the fellowes of the colledge or societie giue not thereunto their consents, as they do in arbitrements, whereunto no man is bound that
would

That Monks may conuent their Abbot before the ordinarie iudge: and also appeale from the iniust sentence of their Abbot.
* Panormitan the Abbot.

A4 *For* abbies *Bodin writes* abbots (Fr).   C8 de collegio eiecerunt (Fr and L)   D5 severe
D6 bene judged   D9 colledge

How decrees are in colledges and societies to be made, to bind euery one of them to that is common to euery one of them in particular, as also to that which is common to them all iointly and indiuisibly together.

would not. For in all communities, corporations and colledges, and so generally in euerie societie and companie, if question be of any thing which is common to them al in particular & apart from the community, the expresse consent of euery one of them is therin requisit, if any thing be therin to be done. But if question be of that which is commo to them all iointly & indiuisibly, it sufficeth that the greater part be of one opinion, for the binding of the rest: Prouided alwaies, that nothing be ordained or decreed, contrarie to the statutes of the colledge, established by the soueraigne prince, or by the founder of such corporation or colledge, authorised by the prince. Wherfore the laws of the Commonweale, and the statutes of the colledge standing whole and entire, the colledge may make decrees which may bind the lesser part all together, and all the fellowes in particular: yet still prouided, that two third parts of the fellowes consent vnto the making of the decree: albeit that they be not all of one aduise or opinion, in matters concerning their common societie, although that such decrees so made cannot bind the greater part of the fellows collectiuely, and much lesse the whole corporation and college: no more than the prince is bound to his owne law, or the testator to his owne will, or particular men vnto their owne agreements, from which they may by their common consent reuolt, nothing beeing more agreeing with reason and nature, than euerie thing to be dissolued, by the same meanes that it was made.

Whether decrees made by the consent of an whole colledge or societie, may by the greater part thereof againe be abrogated or repealed.

But yet it might be doubted, Whether decrees made by the consent and good liking of an whole colledge or societie, might bee againe repealed and abrogated by the greater part, or two third parts of the same societie or colledge? Which I doubt not but that they may in al common estates, corporations, and colledges, if question be but of things common to them al in generall (as they are one vnited body:) but if question be of euerie mans right by himselfe particular and apart from others, then euerie man is to giue his consent thereunto. Wherefore if the assemblies of the estates in a Commonweale consist and be of diuers bodies, as in the diets of the empire, and in all other Commonweales are composed of three orders and degrees of men, *viz.* of the Clergie, the Nobilitie, and Comminaltie, nothing can be done or decreed by any two of the orders, to the hurt or preiudice of the third, especially if the matter concerne euery one of the orders by themselues apart. By which reason I caused two of the orders of Fraunce, to chaunge their opinions in matter concerning the third. For at such time as I was sent deputie for the prouince of Vermandois to Blois (whither king *Henry* the iiij had called an assemblie or parliament of al the kingdome of France) a great and weightie question was moued amongst the three estates, Whether it were more indifferent, and better also, the requests of the people to bee before the prince iudged and determined by 36, men which euerie one of the three orders should by voice chuse, than by the prince himselfe with his councel? And now the Clergie and Nobilitie had not onely so decreed, but had drawne a great part of our sort vnto their side also, hauing with hope of great rewards gained their voices. At which time I perceiuing the drift and purpose of certaine ambitious persons that were dealers in the matter, aunswered, That the matter was further to bee considered of. For why, it was laboured, that such things as could not bee obtained of the people in generall, might so be from a few in the name of the whole extorted. Wherefore the question being more throughly debated, I denied that the matter could so by vs bee passed, without a more speciall commission from the people. Neither that if wee had any such speciall commission from the people, could it yet by vs bee done, without the great daunger of the whole Commonweale; and that for many reasons, by me then discouered: whereby I drew the rest of my fellowes backe againe to mine opinion, who laied this charge vppon mee to remoue also the other two orders of estate

from

H2 *For* common estates, corporations *read* communities, estates, corporations (Fr, but Fr 7 corrupt).
I7 36 men, which   Note at G1.

OF A COMMONWEALE. 371

A from their former receiued and setled opinion. But when the Archbishop of Lyons (President of the Ecclesiasticall estate) earnestly withstood me, seriously alleaging that the Clergie and Nobilitie had before so resolued; I shewed him, that such a Prerogatiue had from all antiquitie beene kept to euery of the three Estates, as that no two of them could decree any thing to the preiudice of the third: as it had before without any difficultie passed in the parliament at Orleance; and as it is also vsed in the diets of the Empire, and the Parliaments of England, and of Spayne. For which cause, and other reasons then alleaged, I requested the other two orders of Estate, to take it in good part, in that they were by me hindered, as hauing the charge of the third estate. Which was the cause, that the thing beeing againe called into consultation, both the estates

B chaunged their opinions. Which the king hearing, and dissembling his griefe, said in the presence of Ruze Bishop of Angiers, and other Lords, That Bodin at his pleasure had ouer ruled the Estates.

But if question be of a thing common to all a corporation or colledge, and which concerneth not any the particular members apart from the whole bodie, but the whole and entire bodie onely; the greater part of the societie, may at their discretion thereof determine: albeit that the whole communitie haue determined that their Statutes and orders should not be infringed, but by the consent of all the fellowes. For why, The greater part of a Communitie is alwaies reputed for the whole. Yea the law willeth, that he which is chosen of a communitie or colledge to entreat and discide of their

C common affaires, may bind euery one of the colledge. Wherefore they are deceiued which write the greater part, or two third parts of a Colledge, to be able to do nothing, if the colledge haue made a statute, That they must all thereto consent: for if that might take place, then any one of the fellowes himselfe alone might empeach and stay the aduise, decrees, and resolutions of the whole societie; which is contrarie to the formall disposition of the law, which willeth, That in all acts concerning a communie or corporation, the greater part should be the stronger; and that the more part of two third parts, may giue lawe to all the fellowes in particular, whether the rest of the fellowes be there present or absent. For why, it is not needfull that they should all be present, that the decrees should stand good, and that especially in light matters; prouided yet

D that they be all thereunto summoned or called. Howbeit that in matters of waight & consequence, it is needfull that two third parts be there present, albeit that they all giue not their consents, except it be by a speciall law prouided that the two third parts must of necessitie agree in one. As by the iudiciall lawes of Lewes the xij the French king, it is ordained, That two parts of the Iudges, and no fewer, may in the higher Courts end any ciuill cause: whereas in criminall causes, equall voices acquite the partie accused; who yet otherwise is to be condemned, if the greater part do but by one voice exceed the lesser. So also by a decree of Gregorie the x, concerning the election of the Pope, he must haue two third parts of the colledge of Cardinals that is to be chosen Pope. As also in many elections of the heads of Colledges, it is necessarie that two third

E parts of the colledge should agree in one. Yea sometime it is necessarie that all the fellowes should be of one and the selfe same accord. As in Rome it was by the Tribunitiall law requisite that all the ten Tribunes should be of one opinion and mind, or at least wise not openly to discent, for that otherwise one Tribune alone might empeach and stay the proceedings of the whole Colledge. Now if they all agreed in one, then vnto the decree were ioyned these words, Pro Collegio, for the Colledge: otherwise if there be no speciall statutes or law to the contrarie, the greater part of two third parts sufficeth in all acts concerning the communitie of corporations and colledges.

It is also necessarie, that the consent whereof we speake, bee giuen in the common assem-

The greater part of a Colledge or Communitie al waies reputed for the whole, and therefore may as it seemeth good, determine of any thing which concerneth the whole corporation or colledge.

A1 received   C6 communitie   C7–8 the more part of two third parts *i.e.* a bare majority when two thirds are present (cf. note at 370 G1)   Note at B1.

For the making of a decree in a colledge, or corporation, the consent is to be giuen in the common assembly of the same, & that in time & place by the Statutes thereof appointed.

assembly of the corporation or colledge: for albeit that all the fellowes had seperately and apart consented vnto any thing concerning that which is common to all the Colledge, yet so it is that such act is not to any effect or purpose, neither for nor against them which haue so giuen their consents, although it were done euen before publique notaries: for that it is not done by the Colledge, which is done by all the fellowes apart. Neither sufficeth it that all they of the Corporation or Colledge were called together, if it were not in time and place, by the Statutes appointed. Wherefore two parts of the fellowes gathered together, can do more, than all the fellowes consenting apart.

To whom it belougeth to call the fellowes together in a colledge or societie.

But here some man may aske, who shall call the fellowes together? Wherein many are of opinion, that the most auntient fellow of the Colledge or Societie, hath power to call the rest together; as also to condemne them of contumacie for not comming: and yet for all that not to haue power to fine them, which is but a ridiculous thing, if such contumacie cannot be punished, neither by him, nor yet by the colledge; as certein it is that it cannot: wherfore such calling of the fellows together, by the most auntient fellow, is but vaine, except that the fellowes of their owne accord be content to obey the same. And therefore the Senat during the Consulship of *Cæsar* could not be assembled or called together, *Cæsar* the greatest magistrat forbidding the same, as is afore said. Othersome are of an other opinion, and hold, That two third parts of a Colledge may of right call together the rest: but yet who shall then call together those two third parts they say not. Howbeit if two third parts suffice to do and determine the affaires of a corporation or communitie, we need not to trouble our selues with the rest, all the fellowes being called. Howbeit the custome kept almost in all corporations and colledges is, for the elders by their seruants or other ministers to call together the rest; or else for them of them selues to come together at the tolling of a bell, or the sound of a Trumpet; as in auntient time they did in Græce and Rome, when as the magistrats which had power to assemble the people, or the Senat, caused their commaunds by the sound of a Trumpet to be published to the people in particular, but not to all in generall, for that they could not be so in that sort commaunded. And who so obeyed not but refused to come, him the magistrat had power to fine, or seize vpon his goods. As we see how that *Marcus Antonius* being Consull, threatned *Cicero* to pull downe his house, if he came not to the Senat being called. So that there is no question where he that calleth together the fellowes, hath power to commaund. But if the Colledge or societie be destitute of an head or magistrat which hath power to commaund, or hauing power, yet is not willing to constraine them which will not obey him; then he whom it concerneth to haue the societie assembled, is to obtaine commission from the magistrat to constraine them to come together, and so we vse to doe. Yet may the greater part of the fellowes together, depriue euery particular fellow of part of the profit and commoditie he is to haue of his Colledge, if being orderly called he shall refuse to come, it being so decreed; yet so that it be moderately done.

That it is lawful for all colleges & corporations to make such orders as they shall thinke best for themselues, not derogating from such orders as were giuen them from their soueraigne prince, or from the lawes and ordinances of the Common weale.

Wherefore to conclude this question of the power of Communities, Corporations, and Colledges, we may say *Solons* law to haue generally place in euery Commonweale, and to be approued by the Interpretors of both the lawes: that is to say, that it is free for all lawfull communities, corporations, and colledges, to make such orders as they shall think for themselues best; so that therby they do not derogate from the statutes of the Colledge, made or established by the Soueraigne Prince, or that they be not repugnant or contrarie to the lawes and ordinances of the Commonweale. And in auntient time it was not forbidden corporations and colledges to make decrees and ordinances within themselues, without derogating from the publique
lawes;

OF A COMMONWEALE.

A lawes; as also to put thereunto such and so great a penaltie and punishment, as pleased the Colledge. But since that time by the statutes and ordinances of euery Colledge & Commonweale, that power hath beene ordinarily cut short, and brought vnto some small fine. Neither am I of their opinion, which hold that a Colledge may make ordinances and decrees without any penaltie annexed vnto them; for that such an ordinance, degree, or statute, should be but vnprofitable and ridiculous, if no punishment were thereunto apposed against them that should disobey the same, especially if he that maketh the orders or decrees haue not power by arbitrarie punishment to cause them to be obserued and kept. We see also in many places the Corporations of artificers and such like, which haue the right of a communitie, to haue also a certeine
B forme of restraining, and visiting of the workes and wares of their occupations or trades, with power to seise vpon them, or to breake or confiscate them, if any thing be done contrarie to their decrees and orders: sauing yet alwaies the Magistrats authoritie for the hearing of the matter, if it be so reserued vnto him. But whereas we said that a lawfull Corporation or colledge may make ordinances and decrees, not derogating from the lawes of the Commonweale: that is so yet to be vnderstood, as that they in their assemblies and meetings entreat onely of that which is vnto themselues common, and not of such things as whereof they are by the law prohibited not onely to determine, but euen to consult also: lest in so doing they incurre the penaltie appointed against vnlawfull Colledges and Companies.

What things Corporations and colleges are in their assemblies & meetings to entreat and consult of?

C And thus much concerning the power, rights, and priuileges of Corporations and Colledges in generall. Let vs now see also how and in what sort they are to be corrected and punished when they shall offend. Howbeit that one might say that where no offence is committed, there no punishment is to be inflicted. Now so it is that a colledge or corporation cannot offend, nor so much as consent, or doe any thing by fraud or deceit (as the law saith;) and therefore there lyeth no action of fraud or deceit against a colledge or corporation, although all the fellowes of the same colledge, or all the inhabitants of a citie, or all the estates of a countrie, had particularly and euery one of them apart consented thereunto: a thing yet altogether impossible in corporations and communities of Townes, Countries, Prouinces, & Commonweales, considering
D that the children and furious persons which therein are, cannot yeeld their consent thereto. But forasmuch as things done by the greater part of the fellowes of a colledge collegiatly assembled, or by the greater part of the inhabitants of a towne or citie in a lawfull assemblie, are supposed to be done by them all, therefore the whole colledge or corporation is punished: as in rebellions of Townes, and seditions of communities, which are punished in their Corporations by losse of their priuileges, or of the right of their communitie, by fines, charges, seruices, and other punishments, according to the qualitie of the offence: which punishment yet ought not to take place, if the rebellion or other crime be not committed by the consent of the communitie or corporation, and decree for the doing thereof made in their common assemblie: as it was iudged by
E a decree of the parliament of Paris, for the communitie of the citie of Corbeil. And yet neuerthelesse, if the corporall punishment be for the offence committed, to be inflicted, as whipping, torture, or death, none of the societie or corporation are so to be punished, but they which were therein partakers, or at least thereunto priuie, although the whole bodie of the communitie or colledge be therefore condemned. As in priuat offences done by many being of no colledge or communitie, there lyeth not an action but against euery one of the offendours in particular, and for the whole, in such sort, as that one of them hauing made satisfaction, the others are thereby acquited. But if such fact or offence be done by any one, following therein the aduise, counsell, and

How Corporations & colleges are to be corrected and punished when they shall offend.

How Corporations and Colleges are said to offend.

K k delibe-

Note at B4.

deliberation of all, they may be all therefore conuented, and euery one of them apart for the whole, neither one of them making satisfaction, are the others thereby discharged. But happely it may seeme a thing verie vnreasonable and absurd, that many, yea the greater part of the same colledge or corporation, should be found innocent, and yet to be altogether punished in the whole bodie, as in the cases by vs before rehearsed. Whereunto I answere, That it is yet more straunge, that the innocents should by lot be drawne together with the offendours, and that these should be punished, vpon whom the lot should fall; as the maner was in the Decimation (or as it were tything) of the armie, for hauing borne it selfe cowardly against the enemie, where the most hardie & valiant, were oftentimes by lot drawne out, and for cowards executed. Which example the Senator *Cassius* vsed, at such time as he in full Senat, perswaded the Senators to put foure hundred Slaues to death, although that there was one (and he vnknowne) amongst them guiltie of the murther committed in the person of their master, ioyning thereunto these wordes: *Omne magnum exemplum habet aliquid ex iniquo, quod publica vtilitate compensatur*, Euery great example fauoreth something of iniustice, which (yet for all that) is with the common profit againe recompensed or required. But this is not (may some say) to pay the debt, to alleage one inconuenience in defence of an other, and of one absurditie to conclude an other. Whereunto I say, that the best iustice that a man can doe is, of diuers inconueniences at once propounded, to shunne the greatest, especially when question is of such offences as may in no wise be left vnpunished. For we see that the wisest, & most aduised Lawiers haue descided, That if there be any one slaine, or beaten, or robbed by many, they are all bound for the whole, albeit that happely it was but one of them which gaue to him the mortall wound: but if it shall appeare, which of them killed him, and that it was done without the conspiracie of the rest, onely he is bound that so slew him: But if it appeare not at all by whom he was slaine, neither that they had conspired against him, they are all acquited from corporall punishment; but yet are to be therefore fined: For nothing is more effectuall for the finding out of that which is true and iust, then that in doubtfull things it is admitted, still to shunne those things which are more absurd and vniust. As if a felonie bee done which cannot by one man be performed; as if many haue caried away an other mans timber log, and amongst those many it appeareth not who it was that did it, none of them is guiltie of the theft, if we will sticke vnto the subtillitie of the words of the law; and yet are they all indeed guiltie: whereof the Lawiers haue no other reason, but that the inconuenience falleth greater on the one side, when they would shunne it on the other, which is (as we said) the greatest reason that a man can haue, to find out the truth of all things, when all other reasons faile. We speake not here of that which enemies do to townes besieged, and by force taken, pilling, killing, sacking aswell the good as the bad; and where the better that a man is, the worse commonly he fareth: but what a prince ought to do against his rebellious subiects. Howbeit that the Romans, although accounted the most iust people of the world, haue not alwaies followed that rule of equitie and iustice which we before spoke of, but sometimes punished not onely in generall, but euen in particular, all the inhabitants of their rebellious Townes after that they had taken them: and yet alwayes obserued this point, to punish the heads more seuerely than the rest, and to preserue them that had resisted the seditious; hauing still a speciall regard whether the rebellion were consulted of and decreed in the Corporation and communitie or not. So *Linie* saith: *Valerius Leuinus Agrigento capto qui capita rerum erant, virgis cæsos securi percussit, cæteros prædamque vendidit*, Valerius Leuinus hauing taken Agrigentum beheaded them that were the chiefe authours (of the rebellion) being

before

before whipped, the rest and the prey he sold. And in an other place: *Quoniam defectionis authores meritas pœnas a dijs immortalibus, & a vobis habent P. C. quid placet de innoxia multitudine fieri? tandem ignotum est illis, & ciuitas data,* For that the authours of the rebellion (saith he) haue from the immortall Gods, and you the appointed fathers, receiued their deserued punishment, what is it your pleasure to be done with the rest of the guiltlesse multitude? at length they were pardoned, and the freedome of the citie giuen them. The Consull *Fuluius,* hauing after a long siege taken the citie of Capua, beeing reuolted from the Romans, beheaded fourescore of the Senatours, beside xxvij others which had before poysoned themselues, and caused three hundred moe of their chiefe gentlemen to be in prison starued, the rest of the inhabitants he sold for slaues. As for the other Townes which were vnder the obedience of them of Capua, there were none but the chiefe men punished. *Atella, Calatiaq̃, in deditionem acceptæ, ibi quoque in eos qui capita rerum erant animaduersum,* Atella and Calatia (saith *Liuie*) were taken in by composition, and there also execution was done vpon such as were chiefe doers in the rebellion. The other Consull *Appius* more seuere than his fellow *Fuluius,* would haue enquirie made also of their allyes, who had had secret part in the same conspiracie: Whereunto *Fuluius* would not agree, saying, That so to do, were but to prouoke their faithfull and loyall allyes to rebell, in giuing credit vnto the traiterous Campanians. Whereby it is manifest with what seueritie the Romans thought it good to punish their rebellious conspirators, during the time of their popular gouernment. And as for the Roman Emperours, some of them vsed towards such offendours gratious fauour, and other some extreame crueltie. The emperour *Aurelianus* for his clemencie deserueth to be for euer commended, who laying siege vnto the citie Thyane, swore that there should not a dog escape aliue, if he should take the citie: but hauing by force wonne it, chaunging his mind, as with compassion moued, he straitly forbid any man to be therein slaine; and when some to prouoke him vnto wrath, put him in remembrance of the oath he had made: he said it concerned but dogs, which hee commaunded to be all forthwith killed. The like clemencie *Henry* the fift the Germaine Emperour, hauing condemned the citie of Brixia to bee vtterly rased, and laid euen with the earth; yet when he had wonne the same, pardoned the citisens neuerthelesse, least the innocent people should so haue perished together with the offendors; following therein the mercie of God, who would not onely the good not to perish together with the euill and wicked, but promised to be mercifull vnto certeine cities, and a multitude of wicked persons, for some few good men to bee found amongst them. Some others of the Emperours haue contrariwise vsed most barbarous cruelties, without discretion killing the good and bad together, and that for the fault of some few. As the emperour *Antonius Caracalla,* who in reuenge of certeine rymes and songes made and sung against him at Alexandria, caused certeine of his garrison souldiours and Prætorian bandes to bee entermingled with the people as they were there beholding playes: who vpon a signall giuen, slewe an infinite number of the poore Citisens one with an other without respect, as they came to hand. The like whereof hee had also before commaunded to bee put in execution at Hierusalem. And afterward at Thessalonica, where the Emperour *Theodosius* the great caused seauen thousand of the inhabitants to bee slaine one with another pell mell in reuenge of certeine of his Receiuours and other his magistrates and officers there slaine, without any deliberation or decree for the doing thereof, before made in their Communitie or Corporation. *Xerxes* king of Persia vsed an other manner of reuenge, not in deede so cruell as the other, but yet farre more ignominious and despitefull, causing

The notable clemencie of the emperour Aurelianus.

The great crueltie of Antonius Caracalla, Theodosius the great, Xerxes, and Sylla.

the noses of all the people of a citie in Syria to bee cut off (which citie after that was of that euent called *Rhinocura*) for the like fault done by some few of them. But of all cruelties that of *Syllaes* passed, who beside three score thousand citisens of Rome by him slaine, caused also all the inhabitants of Preneste to bee put to death, pardoning none but his hoast, who would also needs die with the rest, saying, That he would not be beholden for his life, vnto the murtherer of his countrey. Which cruelty may yet be borne with, when the vanquished shal chuse rather to die than to become subiects; as in all ages there haue bene such: but not if they shall bee content to serue and obey them, by whome they are ouercome and vanquished. So the Pisans (in the memorie of our fathers) not able to endure the iust gouernment of the Florentines their lords, by the fauour of *Charles* the eight the French king, yeelded themselues to Countie *Valentine Borgia*, who beeing not able to protect them, they in vaine offered themselues first to the Genowayes, and then to the Venetians: By both which states they being reiected, after that they had for a long time beene most straitly besieged, they yeelded themselues subiects vnto the Florentines their old lords, of whome they easily obtained pardon, and so afterwards continued their good and faithfull subiects.

The great mischeife which befel Lewes earle of Flaunders, in seeking to take too sharp reueng vppon the Gantoies his rebellious subiects.

But *Lewes* earle of Flaunders, and the last of his house (for after his death that earledom fell into the house of Burgundie) hauing brought the Gantois rebelling against him to such extremitie, as that they were glad to craue of him grace and pardon, would not so receiue them, but propounded vnto them most hard conditions, and not beseeming a free people to accept of: as that they should all come vnto him out of the citie to craue pardon with halters about their neckes; and that then he would consider what he were to do with them. Which put the poore distressed people into such a desperat feare, as that they went out being in number but fiue thousand (but all armed with dispaire) against the earle, who then was fortie thousand strong, whome they in a great battell ouerthrew; and so brought vnder their obeysance all the townes of Flaunders, except Audenard. The earle flying out of the ouerthow hid himselfe vnder a poore womans bed; who afterwards found meanes for his escape, by couering him in an heape of apples: but being so escaped, for euer lost his power, together with his honour. With which so great an ouerthrow giuen, the Gantois became much more arrogant than before, & neuer afterwards willingly endured their princes commands. Whereby it was then perceiued, No more cruell enemies to be found against the prince, than his desperat subiects, Nor any war to be more iust, than that which is by necessitie imposed; as said an auntient Roman Senator.

No more cruel enemie against the prince, than are his desperate subiects.
Some princes vnto crueltie to haue also added contumelie, in reuenge of their rebellious subiects.

But that the aforesaid warre was such, it is euident & plaine, seeing that together with their most shamefull yeelding, most cruell death did hang ouer all their heads, and a reproach heauier than death it selfe; reproach and disgrace being alwayes more dreadfull vnto men of honourable minds, than most cruell death. But in that time it should seeme, that princes tooke pleasure to encrease their crueltie with reproach and despight against their disobedient and disloyall subiects. For

* This Frederike hauing sharply chastised the rebellious Millanoies his subiects, afterwards in dispite caused such of them as would haue their liues spared with their teeth to drawe a figue out of a mules taile: whereof grewe the dispitefull mocke yet vsed by the Italians, by showing the thombe betwixt two fingars, with these words; Ecco, la fico.

so * *Frederike* the second, the German emperour, to reuenge the iniurie done vnto his wife, with great disgrace at Milan, hauing besieged and taken the citie, after he had put to death the chiefest of the citisens, and rifled and rased the citie, vsed a contumelie and despight towards the rest that had escaped the souldiours furie, as was vnto them more despightful than cruel; & yet worse than death. So *Dagobert* king of France, not cótented to haue slaine the inhabitants of Poitiers, for ayding his enemie against him, caused also the towne to be rased, and the ground to be plowed with an eternall curse, and salt to be sowne vpon it to make it barren: whereof they are yet called Salted men of Poitiers. But as princes which with sufferance passe ouer the seditions & rebellions of the corporation or communitie of any towne or prouince, giue example to others to doe the

the like: so those princes also which without measure exercise crueltie vpon their vanquished subiects, get vnto themselues not onely the title of most barbarous and cruell tyrants, but in so doing sometimes also hazard their whole estates. But hee shall deserue the prayse and commendation of a iust prince, and preserue also his estate, which shall keepe the meane in punishing the authors and ringleaders of rebellions, tempering seueritie with lenitie. As did *Charles* of Fraunce king *Lewes* the ninth his brother: (afterwards king of Naples) who hauing commission from the king, to chastice the inhabitants of Mont Pelier, who had slaine certaine of the kings receiuers & officers: tooke from them all their liberties and priuileges, appointed the walles of their citie to be rased, their steeples pulled downe, and a fine of six score thousand crownes to be set vpon them: or as some write, caused halfe the goods of the citisens to bee confiscated, and of six hundred of them one part to be drowned, another part to bee hanged, and the third part burnt. And so indeed the iudgement was to the terrour of them giuen, and the decree set downe: howbeit that it was afterwards by the good prince moderated, in such sort, as that none but the offendors themselues were executed: for that the kings officers and magistrats had bene so murthered by no publike councel, or assembly of the citisens orderly called, but by the insolencie of the rash tumultuous people onely. With like lenitie *Charles* the sixt the French king disarmed the Parisians risen vp in rebellion against him, and executing the authors thereof, restrayned the rest of the whole bodie of the citisens, by imposing vpon them a great fine. And admit all the citisens of a citie, by their common consent, and the matter being before well debated, to haue all together with one mind rebelled, and chosen vnto themselues a new prince: Yea and to haue augmented their wickednesse with contumelie and despight against their soueraigne: yet were it not the part (I will not say) of a good prince, but euen of a wise prince, to take reuenge of all of them of whome he might, for blemishing thereby for euer of his fame and reputation; than which nothing ought to bee vnto a prince more deere: albeit that he might so doe (which yet were a most hard thing) the state of the Commonweale reserued whole. Wherefore *T. Quintius* the Consul did wisely, who when he could not with the safetie of the Commonweale chastice the armie which he then had vnder his conduct and leading, for their rebellious mutinie, after he had appeased all matters, and yet thought it not safe for the souldiours so in danger of the law to returne into the citie, he himselfe came first to Rome, and there by consent of the Senat presented a request vnto the people, *Ne cui militum fraudi esset secessio*, That the mutinous reuolt might not be daungerous to any of the souldiours: which he with the great good liking both of the Senat and of the people obtained. With like wisdome *Scipio Affricanus* the father, repressed the mutinie of his army at Seuerone, with the execution of thirtie fiue of the souldiours onely: *Certabatur vtrum in authores tantum seditionis xxxv animaduerteretur, an plurium supplicio vindicanda defectio magis esset quam seditio: vicit sententia lenior, vt vnde culpa orta esset, ibi pœna consisteret, ad multitudinis castigationem satis esse*, Question was (saith *Liuie*) whether execution were to be done onely vpon thirtie fiue, the authors of the sedition: or that so great a reuolt rather than a sedition, were to be reuenged with the execution of moe: wherein the milder opinion preuailed, That from whence the offence was begun, there should the punishment rest: and that to suffice for the chastising of the whole multitude. And shortly after in the oration which *Scipio* made vnto the armie, he vseth these words, *Se non secus quàm viscera secantem sua cum gemitu & lachrimis xxx hominum capitibus, expiasse octo millium noxam*, Him no otherwise but as a man cutting his owne entrels, with sighes and teares to haue made satisfaction for the offence of eight thousand men, with the heads of thirtie. So when *Appius* the Consull (with great rashnesse should

Seueritie in punishing of rebellion ought stil to be tempered with lenitie.

The wisdom of T. Quintus and Scipio Affricanus in chastising of their mutinous souldiours.

A6 Charles   A6 Lewes   C3 with contumelie   D7 *For* Seuerone *read* Sucrone (Fr) *i.e.* Sucro. D7 thirtie five (L) thirty (Fr). The figures at D8 and E6 are quoted correctly (cf. Fr and Livy, XXVIII, 26 and 32), but L is faulty here.

should I say, or pride) would by strong hand haue restrained and corrected his armie, then all in a mutinie, he was by the Colonels and captaines staied from so doing: who all with one voice told him, Nothing to be more daungerous, than to seeke by force to chastice them, in whose loialtie and fidelitie the whole force of the empire consisted. And albeit that nothing were to bee feared in the punishing of an whole armie, or of a citie, yet such generall and popular punishments are not to be vsed: but in chastising of such offences, an especiall regard is to be had, *Vt pœna ad paucos, metus ad omnes perueniat*, That the punishment it selfe should touch but few, but that the feare thereof should come vnto all; * as an auntient orator no lesse eloquently than wisely said.

marginal notes: A notable regard to be had in al general and popular punishments. * Tullie. That it beseemeth not a soueraign prince to be the executor or to behold the general execution of his rebellious subiects. The wise moderation of some great princes in chastising of their rebellious subiects.

Yea moreouer it beseemeth not a soueraigne prince to be the executor or beholder of the execution of such generall punishments; (if otherwise it may bee in his absence done) to the intent his subiects minds should not so be alienated from him: but to the contrarie it is needfull for him with a conuenient lenitie to moderat euen the iust and necessarie seueritie of his deputies and magistrats, to the imitation of *Antiochus* the great king of Asia, who hauing giuen commission to *Hermeas* his constable, to punish the rebellion of them of Seleucia: and he condemning the corporation of the citie in a fine of six hundred thousand crownes, and banishing also a great number of the citisens, and taking away the liberties and priuileges of the citie: *Antiochus* called home againe the banished; and contenting himselfe almost with the tenth part of the fine, restored againe vnto the citie the auntient liberties and priuilegs thereof. But not to goe further, *Henrie* the second the French king, hauing giuen commission to the duke *Mont-morencie* constable of Fraunce, to chastise the rebellion of the countrey of Guyenne, and especially of the inhabitants of Bourdeaux, graunted them afterward a generall pardon, and forgaue them the rasing of their towne hall, wherein they had made their assemblies, with the fine of two hundred thousand pound, and the charges of the armie brought against him: in all which the inhabitants of Bourdeaux were by the duke condemned; restoring vnto them also the right and freedome of the corporation of the towne, excepting them only who had laid hands vpon his officers, and some few priuileges and demaines of the towne, which were then abridged and cut off. But the emperour *Charles* the fift, not so cruelly as wisely, by one and the selfe same iudgement, reuenged the often rebellions and iniuries which they of Gaunt had of old vsed to doe against his aunccestors, and which till then remained vnpunished: partly by the sufferance, and partly through the weakenesse of the earles of Flaunders. For when the citisens of Gaunt had now compelled the Bourgamaster openly to teare in peeces the emperours edicts, and had sent ambassadours vnto *Fraunces* the French king to receiue them with their citie into his protection: and he refusing them, had solicited his other subiects, their neighbours to rebellion: the councell of Spaine decreed, That the citie should be rased and laid euen with the ground, and all the goods of the citisens confiscated. Howbeit the emperour hauing it in his power, spared the countrey and citie wherein he was borne and brought vp: but executed thirtie of the chiefe authors of the rebellion, tooke away all their corporations and colledges, depriued the citie of part of the publike lands thereunto belonging, as also of all the priuileges; and caused a most strong castle to be there built, and a garrison therein to be kept and maintained, and all at the citisens charge. This the emperours sentence I receiued of them of Gaunt, at such time as I was of councell to *Fraunces* duke of Aniou, and of the Low countries. And not long after king *Fraunces*, who had refused to protect the Gantoies going in person himselfe to represse the rebellion at Rochell, raised for the custome of salt, with the maiestie of his speech terrified them of Rochell, and fined them, but yet put no man to death: yea he left vnto the citie the liberties and societies thereof whole, yet

marginal note: The wisdome of Charls the fift in the seueritie by him vsed in chastising the rebellious Gaunties: and in the lenitie to the contrarie by him vsed towards the Spaniards rebelling against him in Spaine.

H5 two hundred thousand pound *i.e.* 200,000 livres   K2 part of the

yet protesting himselfe to haue had no lesse occasion to reuenge himselfe than had *Charles* the fift, but that he had rather to encrease his commendation, by sauing, than by spilling of his subiects, and by gentlenesse rather than by crueltie. By these examples before set downe it is well to be vnderstood, what is to bee determined for the punishment of Communities, Corporations, and Colledges: wherein they which affect lenitie, do giue occasion vnto the same citisens oftentimes to rebell: which in a Commonweale is of a prince especially to be taken heed of. In which thing no man seemeth to haue behaued himselfe more wisely than *Charles* the fift. Yet he that seemed to haue bene so seuere against the Gauntois, vsed the greatest lenitie that might bee towards the Spaniards of all sorts, at such time as they had not only rebelled against him, (when he went to take possession of the empire) but also chosen the duke of Calabria for their king, who refused that so daungerous a preferment. Of which so great a multitude *Charles* thought it not good to punish one, and that right wisely: for that in so doing he should haue launced all the members of the Commonweale. For albeit that it is an wholesome thing to cauterise or cut off a mortified member for the preseruation of the whole bodie; must we therefore if all the members of the bodie bee in a consumption, or taken with a Gangrena vse sections or cauterisations? *Hypocrates* the great physitian saith no, forbidding vs to apply remedies to desperat diseases, and so much the lesse, if a consumption shall take hold of the chiefe and principall members of the bodie. Wherefore to conclude this question, if the offence be committed by the councell or deceit of a communitie or corporation, that which belongeth vnto such a communitie or corporation so offending, is therefore to be confiscated or forfeited: but if there be no such thing thereto belonging that may so be forfeited, then a fine in money is to be set thereupon, but yet to be exacted onely of them which gaue counsell or aid to the committing of the offence: for as much as it could not bee committed by the whole communitie or corporation it selfe: but if the guiltie parties be not to be known from the guiltles, then are they altogether to be fined: but as for any corporall punishment, it is not to be inflicted, except that euerie one of them, and all of them together, haue most grieuously offended. Neither yet are they to be thought all to offend, although they follow the ensignes displaied, except that they altogether and euerie one of them apart gaue their councell or consent thereunto before: but the communitie or corporation being punished, doth not therefore exempt them that are guiltie of the offence committed, from their due deserued punishment.

How a communitie or corporation offending is to be punished.

But these things being thus declared, concerning the punishments of Communities and corporations: it remaineth for vs to see, whether that a Commonweale can bee without such Communities, Corporations, and Colledges. Wee said at first, men euery where to be, and alwaies to haue bene desirous of the societie and companie of men: and so out of a familiar and naturall societie by little and little to haue growne into a colledge, into a corporation, into a communitie, and so at length into a citie: and so to haue made these empires and kingdomes, which we here in the world see, hauing no surer foundation wherupon to rest (next vnto God) than the loue and amitie of one of them towards another: which can in no wise be maintained, but by alliances, societies, estates, communities, fraternities, corporations, and colledges. So that to demand, whether communities and colledges be necessarie in a Commonweale? is as much, as to demaund, Whether that a Commonweale can be maintained and vpholden without loue and amitie? without which the world it selfe cannot long stand. Which I haue said, for that there haue bene, and yet are some of opinion, That all corporations and colleges are out of a Commonweale to bee excluded and banished; not considering that a familie, and the verie Commonweale it selfe, are nothing else but communities.

Whether a commonweale can be without communities, corporations, or colledges.

A 3 spilling *i.e.* destroying, killing   A 10 of all sorts *i.e.* of all orders or estates   Note at A 3.

nities. Which is an errour whereat the greatest spirits haue oft times stumbled; for one absurditie or incommoditie which ensueth of one good custome or ordinance, willing to haue the same custome or ordinance abolished and quite taken away, without regard of the great good which otherwise ensueth thereof vnto the Commonweale. I confesse that colledges and communities euill gouerned, draw after them many factions, seditions, part-takings, monopolies, yea and sometime the ruine of the whole Commonweale also: and that in stead of sacred loue and amitie, there ariseth of them coniurations, and conspiracies of one of them against another. And that more is, it hath bene seene, that vnder the shadow of religion diuers colledges haue couered some most detestable and execrable impietie. Whereof no better example can bee giuen, than of the fraternitie of the Bacchanals in Rome, which deuised vnder the colour of religion, so long couered the most execrable and detestabble filthinesse of both sexes, vntill that the secrets thereof opened, polluted the citie then mirrour of the world, and all Italie with the loathsome sauour thereof, aboue seuen thousand persons beeing partly accused, attainted, conuinced, and many of them executed and banished, for the abhominable villanies by them committed vnder the colour of that religion, which hath alwaies the fairest and most glorious show that can bee deuised, to bee set vppon a fowle matter; as said *Flaminius* the Consull speaking vnto the people of Rome, concerning the impieties by him found out, *Nihil in speciem fallacius praua religione; vbi Deorum numen prætenditur sceleribus, subit animum timor*, Nothing is in show more deceitfull than corrupt religion: For where the maiestie of the gods is pretended for the cloaking of villanies, there feare pierceth the mind. Which was the cause that the fraternities of the Bacchanals was by a decree of the Senat put downe through all Italie: VVhich decree of the Senat confirmed by the people, passed into the force of a law, That from that time forward no moe sacrifices should bee made by night, but alwayes done in publike. VVhich thing *Damonax* a wise Grecian had long time before attempted to persuade the Athenians of, saying, Those night-sacrifices to haue alwaies seemed vnto him verie suspitious. And better it is in euerie Commonweale openly to suffer whatsoeuer assemblies or sacrifices to bee done by day, in the sight of all the people, then nightly assemblies to bee made vnder the colour of religion. VVhereof *Cato* the Censor most grieuously said, *Ab nullo genere non summum periculum est, si cœtus, & consilia, & secretas consultationes esse sinas*, There is no sort of men from whom the greatest daunger is not to bee feared, if you shall suffer conuenticles, and secret councels and consultations to be kept amongst them: VVhich can so much the lesse be auoided, when as the false opinion of religion is pretended for to colour villanies. For that there is no conspiracie, which may not be contriued and made in such secret assemblies: which growing by little and little, and not perceiued vntill they bee growne great, at length bursting like to a rotten impostume, infecteth the whole bodie of the Commonweale. As for proofe thereof in our remembrance, whereas there haue alwaies beene many conuenticles and meetings of seditious persons, vnder the pretensed show of religion, so a more daungerous companie of filthie fellowes neuer more sodenly in any place brake out, than did that of the Anabaptists in Munster, the chiefe citie of VVestphalia, who there secretly multiplying, vppon the sodaine tooke vp armes, and by the leading of a Taylour draue out the bishop and magistrats, and so possessed the citie wholly to themselues, which could not bee againe recouered from them, nor those phantasticall seditions repressed, but by a strong armie of the whole German empire. The Colledges and Fraternities of the Pythagorians dealt more moderatly in Italie, who professing the studie of wisedome, and hauing drawne vnto them

so

Great harms ensuing of corporations or communities euill gouerned.

Religion the fairest colour for a foule matter.

Nightly conuenticles vnder the colour of religion suspitious and in euerie Commonweale daungerous.

G5 convinced *i.e.* convicted   G5 executed   I3 concilia (Fr and L)   Notes at G3, I2.

OF A COMMONWEALE. 381

A so many disciples, as that many the greatest lords & princes, both of Italie and Greece, moued with the admiration of their doctrine, were now become both their auditors and followers: they bearing themselues thereupon, went about to haue euerie where ouerthrowne the popular estates, and tyrannicall gouernments, and for them to haue established Aristocraties, and the gouernments of wise men. But that their so good a purpose was ouerthrowne by certaine ambitious and popular men, who setting the people in an vprore with fire and sword, destroyed all the Pythagorians. Which (as saith *Polibius*) troubled almost all the estates both of Italie and of Greece. And for this cause the emperours, and almost all other princes, popes, and councels, giuing the Iews leaue to haue their meetings & synagogues (which *Tyberius, Claudius,* & *Domitian*) the
B emperours, had of antient time taken from them) commaunded yet, That they should alwaies do their sacrifices, and haue their prayers openly, and in publike. Which libertie *Pharao* king of Ægypt (terrified with the iudgements of God) would haue also graunted them, but was by *Moyses* refused, alleaging, That it was to be feared least the Ægyptians should ouerwhelme with stones the Iewes, vsing a strange religion, and by the lawes of the countrey forbidden. And to say the truth, it is a thing most hard and difficult to maintaine colledges or corporations in a Commonweale of what religion soeuer, either publikely or priuately, being contrarie to the religion of the people, or of the greater part of them: For that the people euery where most iealous of their religion, cannot but most hardly endure any rites and ceremonies, differing from the religion
C by themselues generally receiued: neither are by the lawes, or by the magistrats commaund, or bands of men so to be restrained and kept in, but that their rage will ofttimes most furiously breake out, not against the weaker sort onely, but euen against the most mightie ones also. For so *Thomas* emperour of Constantinople, pulling downe the altars and images of the saints, was by the angrie people most cruelly slaine in the verie temple of saint *Sophia*. We haue also seene in the citie of Franckford foure corporations and colledges of diuers religions, to haue bene publikely allowed and exercised, namely those of the Iewes, of the Catholikes, of the Protestants, and of the Confession of Geneua: But it so fell out in the yeare 1562, in the moneth of May, that the Protestants assuring themselues of the strength of their partakers, fell vpon them of the
D Confession of Geneua, (who in their profession came neerest vnto them) and bearing with the other which more differed from them, caused that of the Confession to bee there vtterly forbidden. Which is lesse to be feared in such religions and sects as haue bene of auntient time receiued, and which as it were in their owne right defend their profession: such as is the religion of the Iewes, from which all other religions, except Διαβολολατρείαν, seeme to haue taken their beginning: which *Chrysostome* therefore calleth The mother of the Gentiles: the princes of Europe and of Barbarie hauing alwaies granted vnto the Iews, their antient priuileges, corporations, & colledges, for the exercising of their religion, in paying vnto them certaine tribute, as they did vnto the Roman emperors, which was called *Aurum Coronarium*; which the German empe-
E rours ordinarily giue vnto the emprises, for the confirmation of the Iewes priuileges, which are yet greater in Polonia and Lituania, than in any other place of the world, since they were by *Cazimir* the great king of Polonia graunted vnto them, at the request of a Iewish ladie, called *Hester*; such as had of antient time by a Persian king bene vnto this nation giuen, at the instance of another Iewish ladie of the same name. Where they so mightily encreased, as that there was no prince in the greater Asia, which had not in it one or other Collonie of the Iewes; as we read in *Iosephus*, and *Philo*. Wherefore the most auntient antiquitie of that the Iewish religion, together with the great pouertie of the Iewes themselues, who in no place of the world may possesse

any

The common people hardly to endure any religion contrarie or repugnant to their owne.

The Iewes, and Catholiques by the protestants borne within Franckford; and they of the confession of Geneua forbidden.

A7 uprore, with fire and sword destroyed   A10 Domitian the   C8 (margin) borne   E6 For prince *read* province.

382　　　THE THIRD BOOKE

any lands, maketh that they need the lesse, and are indeed the lesse able to fight for their religion and libertie.

That a sect or religion grown so strong, as that it cannot without the extreame perill of the state and commonweale be altered, is of a wise prince to be suffered.

But it may be, that the consent and agreement of the nobilitie and people in a new religion or sect, may be so puissant & strong, as that to represse or alter the same, should be a thing impossible, or at leastwise maruelous difficult, without the extreame perill and daunger of the whole estate. In which case the best aduised princes and gouernours of Commonweales do imitat the wise pilots, who when they cannot attaine vnto the port by them desired, direct their course to such port as they may: Yea and oft times quite chaunging their course, giue way vnto the stormes and tempests, least in seeking too much to put into the desired hauen, they suffer shipwracke. Wherefore that religion or sect is to be suffered, which without the hazard and destruction of the state cannot be taken away: The health and welfare of the Commonweale being the chiefe thing the law respecteth. Wherefore *Constans* the emperour suffered the companies and colledges of the Arrians, not so much for the loue and affection he bare towards them, as diuers haue written but so in quiet to preserue his subiects, and estate. And *Theodosius* the Great being himselfe a Catholike, and alwaies contrarie to the Arrians opinion, yet bare with their religion, which hee could by no meanes suppresse, maintaining both the one sort and the other in peace and obedience. And after him *Zeno* the emperour, to reconcile the companies of all sorts of religions among themselues, and together with the Commonweale, commaunded an edict, which they called ἑνωτικον, which is to say, of vnion and tranquilitie or quietnesse to be published. After whose example *Anastasius* caused the law of forgetfulnesse to bee set forth, cherishing the graue and modest preachers, and remouing such as were of vehement and turbulent spirits.

How a prince fauouring one sect or religion and disciding another, may without force or stur suppresse that religion he disliketh, and aduaunce the other which hee better liketh of.

And yet, no doubt, but that a prince fauouring one sect or religion, and disliking another, may if he will without force or constraint, or any violence at all, suppresse that which he liketh not (except it be by the hand and power of the almightie supported) & that by keeping the maintainers thereof from all preferments and places of command; and by shewing himselfe in deeds rather than in words, to abhorre that religion which he desireth to haue extinguished. For the maner of men is, to loue such things as their princes embrace: and minds resolued, the more they are crossed, the stiffer they are, which otherwise of themselues grow weake and feeble, if they be not at all resisted. Besides that, there can be nothing more daungerous vnto a prince, than to make proofe of his forces against his subiects, except he be wel assured to preuaile against them: which otherwise were but to arme a lion, and to show him his clawes wherewith to teare his master. But if the wiser sort of princes do in the varietie of religions right, hardly keepe the concord and vnitie of their subiects: what then is to be hoped for of such princes, as haue no experience of gouerning of the state, on euerie side beset with their flatterers? pressed by their false enformers, thrust forward by their furious followers: aiming only at this, how to fill themselues with other mens wealth and blood. So in the beginning of the Primitiue Church, vnder the first emperours, so many grosse and impudent calumnies, and slaunderous reports, were deuised and put in writing against the Christians, for the taking away of their assemblies and meetings, as the like whereof were neuer before deuised, and would indeed seeme incredible, were they not yet in writing extant. As witnesseth *Anaxagoras* the orator, in his apologie to *Antoninus*: *Tertullian* in his apologie for the Christians: and *Origen* against *Celsus*, certaine of whose writings are yet extant. Whereby it is to be vnderstood, that it was commonly obiected vnto the Christians, that they were Atheists, irreligious contemners of all gods, incestuous murtherers: and such as in their secret assemblies and meetings vsed

A daungerous practise of such as are neere vnto great princes: to deuise false calumnies against the professors of any religion, so to bring them into hatred, and to enrich themselues with their wealth.

to

G5 *written, but*   H6(margin) *favouring*   H7(margin) *For* disciding *read* disliking.   I6 right hardly   K5 *For* Anaxagoras *read* Athenagoras.   Note at G8.

to kill yong infants conceiued of their mutuall incests, and after that they had so killed them, to eate them. Which thing indeed *Epiphanius* reporteth of the heretiques called *Gnostici*: as that they should in their meetings beat in a morter their new borne children, begotten in incest,, with the yeolkes of egges, flower, honie, and certeine spices mingled together, and so to make cakes of them, and to bake them, and eate them: and that to haue beene with them accounted a sacrament of the bodie and blood. Which slaunders so falsely obiected against the Christians, might seeme altogether incredible, if in the time of our auncestours the like accusation had not beene commenced against the Templers, viz. vnder the raigne of *Philip* the faire; for which the Colledges in Fraunce before graunted vnto the Templers, at last by a decree of pope *Boniface* the viij were taken from them, the maister with a great number of his fellowes most cruelly burnt, and the order quite suppressed. All which for all that, the Germans by their writings haue since showed to haue beene but a malitious false accusation, inuented for the taking away of their great lands and wealth from them. The like practise was also vsed against the Corporations and societies of the Iewes, aswell in Fraunce vnder *Dagobert*, *Philip Augustus*, and *Philip* the long: as afterward in Spaine vnder *Ferdinand* king of Aragon and Castile, who of a mercilesse deuotion driue them quite out of their countries, and enriched themselues with their goods, it being giuen out, that they had crucified boyes, and poysoned wels with the blood of their leprous persons.

The Templers falsely accused, and for their great wealth wrongfully suppressed.

The Iewes in like manner wronged.

Wherefore, to discide the question before propounded, as whether Communities, Corporations, Societies, and Colledges be good in a Commonweale, or no? or that the Commonweale may well be without them? Truely in mine opinion nothing could euer haue beene deuised more effectuall or better for the keeping & mainteining of popular estates, or for the ouerthrow of tyrannicall gouernements, than corporations and societies: For why, the Commonweales and estates being one vnto an other contrarie, doe by quite contrarie meanes both mainteine and ruinate themselues. And therefore the people and popular estates, accept and embrace all manner of communities, corporations, and colledges; as we said that *Solon* did, in establishing the popular estate of Athens. All which tyrants in their tyrannicall gouernments seeke vtterlie to ouerthrow, as well knowing, the vnitie and amitie of subiects among themselues, to be the tyrants ineuitable ruine and destruction: the iust royall, and Aristocraticall estates, euen for the same reasons still holding the meane betwixt both, neither accepting nor reiecting of all communities and colledges, but admitting onely such as they see needfull for the state and Commonweale; which with good lawes and orders they still keepe within the compasse of duetie and obedience. The good king *Numa* was the first that ordained Societies and Fraternities of artificers and men of occupation; and so *Tarquin* the proud was the first that tooke them away, and that forbid the assemblies of the people, and that had in himselfe a purpose also to haue suppressed the bodie of the Senat, by the death of the Senatours, not suffering any new to be chosen in the roomes of them that died. But he was no sooner by his subiects driuen out, but that the popular estate was established, the number of the three hundred Senatours supplied, and the colledges and companies before abolished againe restored. But when the people by the helpe of their Tribunes began more insolently to rule, and that in the bodie of the Senat were almost six hundred of the nobilitie and chiefe men of the citie, who had almost drawne vnto themselues the soueraigntie, the colleges, and companies of the citisens, were by a decree of the Senate, for the most part suppressed and put downe: Howbeit shortly after *Clodius* the Tribune to be the more gracious with the people, and to maintaine them in iarre and discord with the nobilitie

(which

Communities, Corporations, and Colledges, necessarie in euery Commonweale, but especially in a popular estate.

D1 utterlie   D5 with   Notes at A9, E2.

(which he had renounced, causing himselfe to be adopted by a base fellow, so to become Tribune) not onely restored all the Colleges and companies by the Senat before suppressed, but ordained and erected a great number moe: which *Cæsar* being got to be Dictator, to maintaine his owne power and weaken the peoples, put downe; but were afterwards by *Augustus* hauing assured his estate, by an expresse edict againe restored. All which *Nero* the the tyrant againe suppressed. Whereby it appeareth, Tyrants alwaies to haue hated the corporations and communities of the people, and by all meanes endeuored to haue them vtterly extinguished: Insomuch that *Dionysius* the tyrant of Sicilie would not that euen neere kinsfolks should so much as visit one an other, but as they came late from supper from their friends, caused them to be robbed and spoiled. As in like manner did *Nero*, who oft times by night walking the streats, spoiled and slew such as he met, which returned late from supper with their friends; so much he feared the assemblies of his subiects, for the conspiracies they might so make against the tyrannie of him so wicked a prince. And yet for all that the iust Monarchie, hath not any more assured foundation or stay, than the Estates of the people, Communities, Corporations, and Colleges: For if need be for the king to leuie money, to raise forces, to maintaine the Estate against the enemie, it cannot be better done, than by the estates of the people, and of euery Prouince, Towne, and Commutie. Yea we see that they themselues which would haue these estates of the communities and societies of the people suppressed and abolished, haue in time of their necessitie no other refuge or stay to flie vnto, but euen to these estates and communities of the people: which being together vnited, strengthen themselues for the defence and protection, not of their Prince onely, but euen of themselues also, and of the whole estate and subiects in generall, especially the Prince himselfe there being in person present. For where can things for the curing of the diseases of the sicke Commonweale, or for the amendment of the people, or for the establishing of lawes, or for the reforming of the Estate, be better debated or handled, than before the prince in his Senat before the people? There they conferre of the affaires concerning the whole bodie of the Commonweale, and of the members thereof; there are heard and vnderstood the iust complaints & greeuances of the poore subiects, which neuer otherwise come vnto the princes eares; there are discouered and laid open the robberies and extortions committed in the princes name; whereof he knoweth nothing, there the requests of all degrees of men are heard. Besides that, it is almost a thing incredible to say, how much the subiects are eased, and how well they are also pleased, to see their king to sit as chiefe in the assemblie of the estates, and to heare him discoursing; how euery man desireth to be seene of him, and if it please him to heare their complaints, and to receiue their requests, albeit that they be often times denied the same; yet O how it pleaseth them to haue had accesse vnto their Prince, yea sometime they goe away better pleased with such a deniall, than if they had had that they requested, being by their prince altogether contemned. All which is better obserued and kept in Spayne, than in any place of the world, where the assemblies of the estates heretofore haue beene holden euery two or three yeares one. And in England also, for that the people graunt no payments, if the Estates be not assembled: as I remember was done, when as I passed ouer into England embassadour from *Frauncis* duke of Aniou. Our kings do not so often call together the assemblies of their estates, as doe the kings of England. But whereas there are accounted sixteene Prouinces in this kingdome, whereof six haue their particular assemblies among themselues, (namely Bretagne, Normandie, Bourgundie, Languedoc, Dauphine, and Prouence) some there were, who for feare their villanies and extortions should in those assemblies haue beene found out, laboured to the vttermost

of

of their power to haue had the same assemblies and meetings of the Estates of the aforesaid prouinces, in any wise taken away and changed into elections. As also in the beginning of the raigne of *Charles* the eight, at such time as it was with one generall voice called vpon, that a generall assemblie of all the Prouinces might be had; there wanted not some who threatned it to be Treason to such as in the counsell should consent with the people for the calling of such an assembly: whose opinion *Philip de Commines* (a most worthy counsellour and a man of great experience) most earnestly withstood. But how necessarie the assemblies & meeting of the whole people for to consult of matters, are, is hereby perceiued; in that the people which may so call together such their counsels, with them all things go well: wheras others which may not so do, are oppressed with tributes & seruitude. For as the shot of many pieces of artillerie deliuered one after another, is not of so great force and power for the battering of a fort, as when the whole tyre of the great ordinance is together discharged, so the particular requests of men often times vanish but into smoake. But when whole Colleges or Communities, or the estates of a prouince, or of a people, or of a realme, shall make their requests vnto their king; the voice is so loude, and the requests so effectuall, as that it is hard for him to refuse it. Howbeit that there is a thousand other commodities & vses of the generall assemblies of the Estates in euery prouince and countrie, for the common good therof. As if question be for the leuying of forces, or of money to withstand the enemie, or for the building of fortresses, for the mending of high waies, repairing of bridges, or for the scouring of the countrie of theeues, or withstanding of the great; all these things which can in no wise be done by particular men, are best of all performed by them all in their generall assemblies. As to passe ouer the rest, all these things haue beene better done in the prouince of Languedoc by their assembled Estates, than in any other prouince of this Realme. They within a few yeares erected a Schole, and appointed twelue hundred pounds yearely pension for the instruction of all the youth of the countrie. In the Towne of Nismes, beside the other particular Colleges, they built the fairest fortresses of this realme; and caused *Buzac* to be executed, the most notable robber that euer was in our remembrance, of whom neither judge, nor magistrate, no nor yet the parliament of Thoulouse it selfe, could take punishment, he being growne so strong as to doe his robberies in forme of iustice, and yet no man so hardie as to dare to lay hands vpon him: of whose execution I was a beholder, & saw the people wonderfully reioycing to see themselues deliuered of a theefe and robber, of all others the greatest: albeit that I remember ten thousand crownes to haue bene before laide out about the same matter. And to keepe that prouince the safer from theeues & robbers, they appointed farre greater rewards for the Prouost Marshal, than did any other prouince, as twelue hundred pound for his maintenance, and xxv pound for euery processe he should bring of the execution by him done. I haue bene willing in passing by, thus the rather to note these particularities, to show the great good which ariseth vnto Comonweals by the assemblies of their Estats: which are yet better ordered in the Commonweals of the Swissers, & the Germaine empire than in other the Commonweals of Europe. For the Swissers beside the assemblies of Estate, in euery Towne and Canton, haue their generall assemblies of their Estates also; and the ten Circles or Circuits of the Empire haue their assemblies of their Estates separate, vnto whom the particular estates of the Imperiall Townes & Countries referre themselues: and so likewise the estates of the circuits refer themselues and their decrees vnto the assemblie of the estates of the Empire, which without this pollicie had long ago bene ruinated & fallen.

We said that the meane and measure which is in all things commendable, ought also to be kept in all iust Monarchies and Aristrocraties, in regard of the number of

The generall assemblies & meetings of the people to consult of matters, necessarie for the good of the Common weale.

Buzac a notable theefe and robber.

A measure to be had for the number of Corporations and Colleges in a Commonweale.

Corporations and Colleges to be had in their kingdomes and Commonweales: For as quite to take away all Corporations and Communities were to weaken or ruinate the estate, and to establish a barbarous tyrannie, or tirannicall gouernment; so likewise to permit and suffer all assemblies, and all fraternities, is not also without danger, as not easely to be ruled by the princes power, or nobilities commaund. In them also oft times are couered conspiracies, and secret Monopolies, whereof we haue many examples, which hath bene the cause often times by expresse Edict in this Realme to take away these fraternities; which for all that could neuer yet be put into execution. Howbeit much better it were to take away the abuse, than the thing it selfe that is abused, and to pluck vp the weeds alone, rather then both the good and bad together. And to auoid Monopolies amongst artificers and trades men, it is good to diuide them into diuers streets and quarters of the citie, and not to seat them in one street or quarter together, (as they do in Affricke, and also in many townes and cities of Europe) except the place for the hauing of water, or some other such common respect so require: For besides the incomoditie that it is in great cities not to haue artificers which are ordinarily required in euery quarter thereof, there must needs either be secret monopolies amongst them so to sell their marchandize and wares the dearer, or else iealousies and quarels, if one of them shall sell better cheap than another, before his face that hath refused to take the money. I said artificers ordinarily required for that it is not fit in their dwellings to mingle men giuen vnto their studie and quiet, together with Fishmongers, or Armorers, or Curriors with Schollers. for as for such as are lesse requisite as hammermen, they may well enough be raunged in the same street or quarter of a citie together, and that better than to trouble the quiet of others. But as there is nothing better for the maintenance of the strength and vnitie of the subiects, than Corporations & Communities: so is there nothing which can so much weaken & keepe vnderfoot a Commonweale, as by the vtter taking away of Communities, Corporations, and Colleges, or Societies: Which the Romans well knowing, wisely put in practise, who after they had vanquished the kings of Macedonia, and conquered the countrie, vtterly forbid all assemblies and meetings together of the people there to consult of matters. And so afterwards also the Achæans being ouercome, the consul *Mummius* as saith *Liuie*: *Concilia omnia singularū Achaiæ nationum, & Phocensium, & Bæotorum, aut in alia parte Græciæ deleuit*, Suppressed all the councels of all the particular nations of Achaia, and of the Phocensians, and of the Bæotians, or in what soeuer other part of Græcia else: But after that they were once become good and obedient subiects vnto the Romans: *Antiqua concilia genti cuique restituta*, The auntient councels were vnto euery nation againe restored, as saith *Strabo*.

Chap. VIII.

¶ *Of the orders and degrees of Citisens.*

Ow forasmuch as we haue alreadie spoken of Corporations and Colledges, it remaineth for vs also to speake of the orders and degrees of Citisens. For if so be that in all things wee desire and seeke after a conuenient and decent order, and deeme nothing to be more ougly or foule to looke vpon, than confusion and broyle: then how much more is it to be sought for in a Commonweale, so to place the Citisens or subiects in such apt and comely order, as that the first may be ioyned with the last, and they of the middle sort with both; and so all with all, in a most true knot and bond among themselues together with the Commonweale? For why, it is a most antient

tient and receiued opinion of the wise, Almightie God himselfe the great and supreme workemaster and creator of this great and wonderfull Fabrick of all things, in the creating thereof, to haue performed nothing either greater or better, than that hee diuided the mingled and confused parts of the rude *Chaos*, and so setled euerie thing in his due place and order. Neither can there be any thing fairer to behold, more delightfull to the mind, or more commodious for vse, than is order it selfe. But they which goe about so to make all subiects or Citisens equall one vnto another in dignitie, order, and place, as that there shall be nothing in a Citie or Commonweale first, or in the middest, but will haue all degrees so mingled together and confounded, without respect of sexe, age, or condition; they seeme to mee to do as they doe which thrust barly, wheat, rise, mill, and all other kind of pulse into one heape together; whereby they loose the vse both of euerie kind of graine in particular, as also of the whole heape together. Wherefore there was neuer any law-giuer so vnskilfull, but that he thought that there ought still to bee some diuision, ordering, and sorting of the Citisens or subiects in a citie, or Commonweale. Here by ordering and sorting of the Citisens or subiects, my meaning is, that there should be a part of the citisens diuided from the rest in condition, state, or sexe: in condition, as the nobilitie from them that were but from the Senators descended; the knights and gentlemen, from the common people: in sexe, as women from men; in state, as free borne men from them which are but of manumised slaues made free; and they which are by state free, are diuided from them both.

As for slaues we haue before said, them by the generall consent of almost all people, to haue bene still exempted out of the number of Citisens. Yea *Aristotle* hath tearmed slaues, but instruments for other mens vses; whereas some others haue accounted of them, but as of beasts, or rather worse: and yet the question resteth vndecided, Whether that slaues are to be accoūted in a mans goods or substance, or not. But if the determining hereof might be vnto me referred, surely I should wish the right and libertie of the citie to be set open, as well vnto the slaues as vnto the free borne men. For what is this so arrogant temeritie (should I say) or impietie of men, that forgetting mens condition and state, they should enforce this so diuine a creature, hauing his libertie shamefully taken from him, not onely to serue their lust, but also to make no more account of him, yea and peraduenture lesse too, than of a verie beast? But bee it that slaues be indeed of the basest sort of men, do they therefore not deserue to be tearmed by the name of citisens? There be in mans bodie some members, I may not call them filthie (for that nothing can so be which is naturall) but yet so shamefull, as that no man except he be past all shame, can without blushing reueale or discouer the same: and doe they for that cease to be members of the whole bodie? The feet themselues, with perpetuall labour hold vp and carrie about the whole bulke of the bodie, and are oft times foule with durt, filth, and dust; but yet who is so mad, as to thinke them therefore worthy to be cut off from the bodie? Now if these baser members indeed bee and are still called parts of the whole bodie, why shall wee not by the same reason suffer slaues, who are still pressed and kept vnder with the most heauie burthens and commaunds of the other citisens, to bee called and accounted members of the same citie with them? But if we thinke this to be an absurd thing, then are they to bee driuen out of the citie, and as rotten limmes to be cut off: but if we will still retaine them in a citie, in a familie, and so in our obedience and seruice, we must also make them partakers of the citie with vs. For seeing they be subiects and not straungers, they must needes make vp a part of the citisens, and bee accounted in the number of them. Which I would haue vnderstood to be of me so spoken, not for that I should desire slauerie long since taken away out of our Commonweale, to be thereinto againe restored: but

Slaues accounted no citisens and yet indeed worthie to be so reckoned of, though in the lowest and basest degree of citisens

that forasmuch as the force and boldnesse of men is so farre broken out, as that wee see seruitude and slauerie by little and little to creepe in, and to returne againe: it might be forseene and prouided for, that such slaues might not hereafter bee more hardly vsed, than the state and condition of man requireth, and might also haue their certaine place and order in the citie. Wherefore let the order of slaues bee of all others the lowest in degree in a citie; and of them wee will begin first to speake. For as for that which *Cicero* obiecteth vnto *Antonius*, That he had so contracted affinitie, as that hee might thereby the better commend himselfe vnto them that were of the meanest degree: hee ment it by them which had bene mannumised men, and not by the slaues indeed: for that in the citie Rome, slaues indeed had neither place nor degree. Neither did *Metellus* his speech concerning marriages to bee made in degrees together belong vnto slaues, to whome the rites and rights of marriage were altogether forbidden, hauing onely their mutuall conuersing and companie one of them of another; as *Paulus* the lawyer writeth in the second booke of Sentences, albeit not altogether aduisedly, for that they held the right of blood, as did other citisens, and were forbidden incestuous marriages as well as others; although that they had not the other rights of marriages. And for that slaues were oftentimes borne of vncertaine fathers, their children were also accounted vncertaine: and therefore slaues and manumised men were not said to be of any familie, stocke, or house; onely they which were of the nobilitie descended, boasted themselues to haue stocke, or house from whence they came. Hereof came that speech of *Decius* against them that were descended from the nobilitie, *Semper ista audita sunt, vos solos gentem habere: an hoc, si Claudiæ familiæ non sim, nec ex Patricio sanguine ortus, sed vnus Quiritium quilibet, qui modò me duobus ingenuis ortum sciam, reticere possim?* These things haue alwaies bene heard, you alone to haue a stock & house, But if I were not of the house and familie of the Claudians, neither borne of noble blood, but some one of the common people, which but knew my selfe to bee borne of two free borne persons, could I in this hold my peace? Whereby he sufficiently insinuateth neither slaues nor mannumised men to haue had any stocke or house from which they might account themselues descended: and them onely to haue beene accounted so to haue, which had their beginning from them that were free borne: and hereof it commeth that we call such as be nobly borne by the name of Gentlemen, as hauing an house or familie from which they are descended. Howbeit that they which were so nobly borne, went yet further, vaunting them onely to haue an house and familie, from which they might produce their discent, none of whose aunccestors had at any time serued as slaues: For why, the multitude of the vulgar and common sort of the people, was thought almost all to haue taken their beginning from such as hauing bene slaues, were by mannumission become free.

Why we call such as be noble borne by the name of gentlemen?

Next vnto slaues are they whome they call State-free men, and after them the Libertines, or as we may tearme them the manumised men, who were euery where of diuers sorts and condition, as there were also diuers sorts of slaues. And to let other cities passe, wee see in Rome to haue bene foure sorts or kinds of these Libertines, or enfranchised men; viz. those whome they called *Romani, Latini, Iuniani*, and *Dediticij*: whome for that they be vsuall and common, I let them passe: sufficeth it as it were with the finger to point out the fountaines of them, least in a citie these diuers orders of enfranchised or manumised men might bee together confounded. Now the order or degree of state free men, was in a meane betwixt slaues and the Libertines or manumised men, for in that their libertie was yet holden in suspence, they were in better case and condition than were the slaues, and yet withall in worse than were the libertines, or men alreadie enfranchised. And these orders euerie one of them according

Foure kind of libertines or of manumised men in Rome.

State free men better then slaues and worse then libertines.

ding to the qualitie of their condition and state, were also likewise in their degrees placed.

The rest of the citisens are diuided according to the varietie of their conditions and estates, and diuersitie of their manners and customes. Yet that is common almost to all people, that noble men should in order and dignitie be diuided from the vulgar and common people, since first *Nimrod* the great robber, most notably attended vppon with a great power of wicked companions, and such as himselfe was, with cruell seruitude oppressed them that were too weake for him, and so first tooke vpon him the gouernment of the Assyrians, as we haue before said. So left his nobilitie got by villanie, for his posteritie to imitat: which opinion further spreading, tooke such deep root, as that euerie man as he was the mightier in violence and murthering of others, hee was thought to be so much more the nobler: vntill such time as that the people by good lawes and ciuilitie better instructed, deemed, that the true nobilitie, was by vertue and not so by villanie to be sought for.

The nobilitie alwaies diuided from the vulgar and common people.

The first nobilitie grounded vpon violence and oppression.

True nobilitie grounded vpon vertue.

But forasmuch as one man excelleth another in some one or other vertue: and for that such vertues as are in one citie or place most highly commended, are in some other no lesse contemned. Hereof it commeth, that no one definition of nobilitie could euer yet be made agreeable vnto the nobilitie of all the people: honour and infamie being still deemed and reputed of, according to the manner and custome of euerie countrey. For by the customes of the Perusines and Florentines, he which but now began to beare arms and serue in warre, was of one before vnnoble, now thereby become noble: whereas with vs he is not so by and by: but if his posteritie shall follow the wars, they are reputed to haue gotten nobilitie as it were by the continuance of time. But not so at Venice, who still measure the nobilitie of their gentlemen, by the honourable antiquitie of such houses and families as haue alwaies attended their publike councels and affaires. And albeit that the Decurions or pettie captaines by the Roman law, bee reputed of by the name of gentlemen: which law is also receiued with them of Poitiers by the consent of all the three estates, yet is it no where els with vs so found. But that the bearing of armes should of it selfe make a gentleman, I see it to haue so pleased not onely the Florentines and Perusines, but diuers interpretors of the law also, and especially *Alciat*, who hath not doubted to cite *Triuultius* the great captaine as author therof. Truely amongst the Ægyptians it was not lawfull but for the *Calasyres*· and many worlds of yeres after, for the Mammalukes in the raigne of the Sultans, to serue and beare armes: who therefore enioyed most great priuileges. Yet other people haue diuided genterīe from warre, neither haue therefore reputed any one to be a gentleman, for that he was a souldiour: vnto which opinion all the greatest lawyers together with *Plato* haue almost with one voice consented. And albeit that the Romans farre exceeded all other people in martiall honour, and bestowed the greatest priuileges vppon souldiours: yet for all that they bound not gentrie vnto martiall seruice: seeing that it was lawfull for the Libertines or manumised men to serue in the warres, and that men for the filthinesse of their liues, and iudgements, therefore vpon them passed, infamous, who were therefore embarred from all honours, had yet no exemption from the warres.

Nobilitie in diuers places diuersly accounted of, and neither in al places alike.

Whether the bearing of armes in the warres make a man therfore a gentleman or not?

But forasmuch as all citisens after they had taken vpon them the manlike attire, were bound to beare arms, so by that reason al the citisens should haue bin therby ennobled, which were a thing absurd: for were all the citisens noble, none of them were indeed in that vulgaritie of nobilitie to be accounted at all noble. Wherefore *Lucius Siccius Dentatus* is of *Dionysius Halicarnasseus*, called a common and ordinarie man, whose speech against them of the nobilitie and gentrie is yet at this present extant:

Where-

A7 power *i.e.* fighting force, army   B8 *For* of all the people *read* of all peoples.   Note at A6.

Lucius Siccius Dentatus, a most worthie and famous souldiour, and yet not therefore accounted any gentleman.

Wherein he boasteth himselfe to haue bene in pay fortie yeares in the seruice of his countrey, to haue fought in an hundred and twentie set battels, to haue receiued 45 wounds, and twelue of them in one day, all of them in the fore part of his bodie: and in token of his good seruice, to haue receiued fourteene Ciuic or oken crowns (the honourable rewards due vnto him that had saued so many citisens) three others the rewards of his good seruice done in the besieging of townes, fourescore and three gold chaynes, an hundred and threescore bracelets of gold, ten faire launces, and thirtie fiue faire furnitures for horses. And yet this so worthy & valiant a man, adorned with so many trophies in reward of his valour, was by the Roman lawes no more but as a common person. For they accounted him first a gentleman, that was the sonne of a new raised man: and him they called a new man, who was the first in his familie that had borne some honourable charge or office, and so had power to erect vnto himselfe his statue or image; such as were *Caius Marius*, and *M. Tullius Cicero* of Arpine, both of them beeing but new men. Of whome the one beeing first made Quæstor, and then Ædilis, and afterwards Pretor, at last came to bee Consul; who in the time of his Consulship, in an oration which hee made vnto the people, boasting therein of his newnesse, thus said, *Ego nouus homo primus omnium claustra nobilitatis refregi, &c.* I beeing but a new man, was of all others the first which brake open the barres of nobilitie. The other hauing beene seuen times Consull, in an oration which he made against the nobilitie, said, *Contemnunt nouitatem meam, ego illorum ignauiam: mihi fortuna, illis probra obiectantur. Quod si me iure despiciunt, faciant idem maioribus suis, quibus vti mihi nobilitas ex virtute cæpit. Nunc videte quàm iniqui sunt: quod ex aliena virtute sibi arrogant, id mihi ex mea non concedunt: scilicet quia imagines non habeo, & noua nobilitas est, quam perperisse melius est, quam acceptam corrupisse*, They contemne (saith he) my newnesse, I their cowardise: my fortune is to mee obiected, but vnto them their vices. But if they therefore of right contemne and despise me, let them so also doe their owne auncestours, whose nobilitie begun of their owne vertues, as doth mine. Now but see how partiall they are in their owne cause; that honour which they arrogat vnto themselues by other mens vertues, that they will not graunt vnto me for mine owne: and all forsooth, because I haue no images of mine auncestours to show, and for that my nobilitie is but new, which yet is better for me to haue of my selfe raised, than hauing receiued it from mine auncestors, to haue my self stained the same. For *Cicero* had six competitors in his Consulship, wherof two were noble men, two other of them were the first of their familie which had borne office, onely *Cicero* himselfe was a gentleman borne: whose father, as also the father of *Marius*, of *Cato* the Censor, of *Q. Pompeius*, of *Curius*, of *Philo*, and of *Genutius*, were all base persons of the comminaltie, but yet their sonnes were accounted of as new men and gentlemen. But such as were descended from the Senators, by *Romulus* in the beginning of his raigne appointed, or from them which were afterwards by the Consull *Publius Valerius* ioyned vnto them, were called *Patricij* (as hauing their beginning from the Senators, whome they called *Patres*) all the rest were common men, or else men of some better note, whome they called *Equites*, or Gentlemen; who were in the middest betwixt the Senators & the cōmon people, being partly dissended from the Senators, and part of them risen out of the communaltie: who if any of them were chosen into the Senat, they were no more to be accounted amongst those *Equites* or gentlemen: as is to be seene by *Lucius* & *Nero* the Censors, who yet seruing vpon publike horses, were one of them by the other commaunded to sell them: for after the ouerthrow by the Romans receiued from the Veians, the gentlemen began to serue vpon horses prouided for them of the publike charge. Now I find that there were of the Patrician Families,

Whom the Romaines first accounted a gentleman.

The Patritij who they were in Rome.

The Equites or gentlemen in Rome what place they held.

F7 *For* thirtie five *read* twentie five. H2 cœpit H4 peperisse K6 *For* Lucius *read* Livius.
Notes at F8, I3.

A milies in Rome, about fortie: but of such as by their valour left nobilitie to their posteritie in *Ciceroes* time scarcely thirtie: of which families, or houses, seuen were of the same name with the *Patricij*, viz. *Pompilia, Martia, Tullia, Iunia, Mutia, Claudia*, and *Sempronia*. And for that the entrance and way vnto the honourable preferments in the state, before the law Canuleia, was kept shut vp and stopped by the *Pratricij* (or them that were of the Senators descended) against the common and vulgar sort of the people; and yet for all that none of these *Patricij* was accounted noble, except some of their auncestors had borne the honourable offices of the state: many of the *Patricij*, who were descended from the Senators, and yet could not cite such their auncestors as had borne such honourable charge in the estate, (which was well to be vnderstood by

B their statues or images) were accounted of as of men of base & low degree. So it came to passe, after the law Canuleia was made, that some euen of the common sort of the people became noble, and some of the *Patricij* vnnoble, that is to say, obscure and vnknowne. As *Marcus Æmylius Scaurus*, a man descended of the Senators race, had his auncestours base and obscure men: whereas he himselfe being but a new man, came to be Pretor, Consull, and Censor, and at last being made chiefe of the Senat, raised nobilitie to all his posteritie. Wherfore the Roman nobilitie lay in the voyces and iudgement of the people, which as they thought best, bestowed the honourable preferments in the estate and Commonweale. Yet was it an absurd and most vnreasonable thing, that any most wicked murtherer and manquellar, were he neuer so basely borne, might

C by the benefit of bearing of some great place or office in the estate, leaue nobilitie vnto his posteritie: whereas he which excelled in wisedome, iustice, fortitude, and temperance, and so in all other vertues, godlinesse, and learning, yea and was descended also of the Senators race, if he could not show his auncestors statues, was euen therefore accounted but as base and obscure. For such is the force of this word *Ignobilis* with the Latines, which in the selfe same sense is of the Greekes called γνωριμός, and ἀπιφανὴς; that is to say, such as either by some foule or notable fact or deed done, came into the knowledge of men: which is yet oftentimes taken in the better part, for they which are called ἐυγενεῖς, refer it vnto the honor of their house & stock: which amongst the Romans did especially appeare amongst the *Patricij* or posteritie of the antient Senators:

D which for that they were almost dead and worne out, *Caius Cæsar* by the law Cassia, and after that *Augustus* by the law Seruia, chose many of the more noble families into the order of the *Patricij*. For before the law Canuleia it was lawfull onely for the *Patricij* to be bishops and priests, and for them alone to make sacrifices, and to keep the Auspicia or diuine obseruations. But after that *Genutius* (first Consull that was made of the people) was in battell with the great slaughter of his armie vnder his conduct ouerthrowne, *Patres non tam publica calamitate mæsti, quàm feroces infælicis Consulis plebei ductu, fremunt, omnibus locis, irent, crearent Consulem ex plebe, transferrent auspicia quo nefas esset*, The fathers (as saith *Liuie*) not so heauie for the publike calamitie, as become insolent with the euil conduct of the vnfortunat Consull chosen from amongst

E the people, murmured and fretted in all places, that they should go and againe create a Consull of the people; and thither to translate the Auspicia or diuinations, whither it was not lawfull for them so to doe. And *Appius Claudius* the Consull, before that answered one of the Tribunes, asking him in an assembly of the people, Why one of the Consuls might not be chosen out of the people? Because (said he) none of the vulgar and common sort of the people can hold the Auspicia or diuinations; and that therefore the Decemuiri had appointed a certaine order of mariage, least the sacred diuinations should haue bene polluted with persons vncertainly descended. At which answere, the people was with indignation exceedingly enraged, to heare it denied them

The Patritian families in Rome: Syluia, Pompilia, Potitia, Martia, Hostilia, Tullia, Tarquinia, Fabia, Antonia, Iunia, Sergia, Iulia, Gegania, Nautia, Æmylia, Chloelia, Valeria, Horatia, Posthumia, Menenia, Virginia, Sulpitia, Furia, Lucretia, Quinctia, Papiria, Claudia, Seruilia, Cornelia, Marilia, Cassia, Aebutia, Pinaria, Veturia, Sempronia, Mutia, Aquila, Quintilia, Hortensia.

The noble Families in Rome. Licinia, Aurelia, Decia, Cæcilia, Ælia, Domitia, Clandia, Mutia, Portia, Curia, Fabritia, Cornelia, Acilia, Mæria, Pompeia, Liuia, Iunia, Tullia, Fuluia, Sempronia, Atilia, Calpurnia, Marcia, Pompilia, Lutatia, Platia.

A5 Patricii   A7(margin) Chloelia: Clælia (L 1-2) Choelia (L 4-5) *properly* Cloelia (L 3)
B4(margin) Aquilia   C5(margin) Plautia   C6 ἐπιφανὴς   D8 fremunt omnibus

to hold the diuinations, as if they were vnto the immortall gods, more hatefull than others. And albeit that the people at length had all things common with the Senators, *viz.* honours, commaunds, iudgements, diuinations, cures, priesthoods, councels, powers, statues, triumphs, and all other the greatest preferments in the Commonweale; yet could it neuer be obtained, that any one of the common sort of the people, should nominat the Interrex, or pronounce who should be the Archpriest, the Priest of *Mars*, or of *Romulus*: or yet be chosen into the colledge of the Salij. But as a statue or image was among the Romans the signe of nobilitie obtained: so in antiét time with vs arms, with Cognisances set ouer them, were the tokens of nobilitie. Lawfull it hath alwaies bene, and so still will be, for euerie man to deuise vnto himselfe his Cognisance to bee known by, but yet not to vsurpe the Cognisances, or beare the armes of other noble families. But the antient Grecians deemed not of nobility by the obtaining & bearing of great offices; which euerie man among the Athenians (after the law of *Aristides*, and the seditious declamations of *Ephialtis*) might by lot, and few by voyces obtaine: but nobilitie with them was still to be deriued from the stock of their kings, or race of their great worthies, as from the *Heraclidæ*, the *Æacidæ*, or *Cecropidæ*, or from such other like: or else from such, as who for the worthie acts, either by themselues, or by their auncestours done, had by the generall good liking, and publike decree of the people, and of the nobilitie, with commendation obtained a crowne of gold, extraordinarie priuileges, statues, to sit in the highest places, or to haue their diet allowed them in the *Prytanæo*, or other like publike places: Such as is that decree of the Athenians (whereof *Plutarch* writeth) concerning *Lycurgus* the sonne of *Lycophron*, It pleased the people of Athens (saith he) that requitall should bee made vnto such as had well deserued of the state, as to praise *Lycurgus* the sonne of *Lycophron* for his vertue and iustice sake: and in the honor of him to erect a brasen Statue for him in the market place, except in such place as where the law forbiddeth any statue to be erected, and diet in the Prytanæo to be for euer allowed vnto the eldest of the posteritie of *Lycurgus*. So in like maner *Isæus* the orator writeth publique diet, the first places, and priuileges, to haue bene graunted vnto the posteritie of *Harmodius* the tyrant queller. Which thing *Aristotle* reporteth to haue bene a thing common vnto all the cities of Græce, to allow diet of the publique charge vnto the children of such as had valiantly dyed for their countrie. Howbeit that the Grecians with too much lenitie (should I say) or rather leuitie erected statues for such as had of them well deserued, which they vppon the least displeasure againe cast downe, and that with greater despite than they had with honor before set them vp. So when the Athenians had appointed 365 statues to be set vp in euerie place of the citie in honor of *Demetrius Phalereus*, they againe in a moment caused them all to bee cast downe: & not yet so contented brake them also with such furie, as that no fragment of them was left, except that onely which was kept fast shut vp in the tower of *Pallas*.

Amongst the Hebrewes were two sorts of noble men; the one descended from the stock of *Aaron*, who only were priests: the other from the stock of the kings. For why, that nation wisely reposing their chief felicitie in the sinceritie of their religion, and the true worshipping of God, so likewise deemed their priests, which came neerest vnto the power of the immortall God, to be of all others most noble. Yea God himselfe had an especiall regard in making choice of *Aaron*, & in establishing of him after the most grieuous reuolts & miserie of his people. And therfore as often as he cōmandeth extreame destruction to be denounced & threatned vnto his people, he oftentimes doubleth that כעם ככהן, which is to say, That the state of the priest and of the common person, should bee all one. And therefore when the Iewes had cast off from the seruile yoke of *Antiochus* the Noble: the Familie of the *Æsmonæans* being of the stocke of *Aaron*, held the high priesthood, together with the kingdome about two hundred yeres,

that

F3 cures *i.e. curationes*, commissions   H10 to have   K9 Asmonæans

Of A Commonweale. 393

that is to say, euen vnto the raigne of *Herod* the Great. Wherein the Hebrewes did well: for if great offices in Rome, got oft times by corruption and briberie, left nobilitie vnto their posteritie which had so got them: what let is there why the priesthood of the eternall God, should not much more also ennoble men, especially if we measure nobilitie by the places men hold, and not by their persons. Truely all the best learned lawyers are of opinion, That the priestly dignitie is to be preferred before all other honours and vocations: and that the ministers of diuine things, & moderators of the most sacred rites, are not to be accounted among the nuber of the vulgar & common people: which is no new or strange opinion, but drawn & deriued euen from the most antient antiquitie. For the most antiēt kings, to make their roial power the more reuerend and stately, exercised also the priestly dignitie Neither did the Greeks only, but the Roman kings also, yea and the greatest emperors themselues, stile themselues high Priests or Bishops, whome the chiefe Arabian princes being also bishops, seeme therein to haue followed. And so the Christian kings beeing by their religion forbidden to mingle prophane things with sacred, or armes with religions; yet tooke that which was next; that is to say, in preferring a sacred, order of the Clergie, not only before the common and vulgar sort of the people, but before the Senators, yea and not before them alone, but euen before dukes, earles, and other magistrats whatsoeuer: giuing vnto them the highest roomes, and first places next vnto the kings themselues, in all assemblies, councels, enacting of lawes, and graunting of liberties and priuileges. And why not? when as the most antient people of the Celtes, accounted their Druides, who were the princes of their religion and iudgements, superiours not vnto the common sort of the people onely, but euen vnto their captaines and rulers also. For which cause *Cæsar* in recounting of their degrees, first reckoneth vp the Druides, then their knights or horsmen, and after them the common people. For the order of knights in the time of their auncestors, with a most strong power of horsemen excelled all people; as witnesseth *Cæsar* himselfe, as also *Marcus Antonius*: so that therefore I suppose them to haue bene called κελτοὺς; for the Greeks call him κελὰς ἵππος ἀζὺξ, whome the Latines called *Sellarium*, and we an horseman. We said before the Turkish and Arabian princes yet in all their kingdomes and empires, to honour and obserue their Mufties, or high Bishops, with the greatest honour and respect possibly to bee giuen vnto them, still referring vnto them the greatest and most doubtful questions of their law, to be by them decided. Yet the Venetians vse to exclude their priests from their councels, from all places of commaund, and from all offices, least haply they should bewray the secrets of the citie vnto the pope, to whome they are by dutie & oath bound. Wherfore among the Venetians, the order of the Senators is first and chiefe of all others, for that in it is the soueraigne power of that state: next vnto the Senators follow the gentlemen, who are not accounted of the number of the Senators; and last of all the commoners, who yet are both by one name called *Citadinia*, or Citisens. But the Florentines before that all was swayed by one mans commaund, diuided not onely the nobilitie from the clergie, but euen from the common people also; and the common people they diuided againe into three sorts, of whome such as exceeded in wealth were called the Great ones, others of meaner wealth were called Popular Commoners, and they of the third sort, the refuce of the whole people. The auntient Ægyptians much better diuided their whole multitude of citisens, into Priests, Souldiours, and Labourers: setting the Priests and Souldiours, whome they called *Calasyri*, free from all taxes and payments. *Hyppodamus*, who gaue lawes vnto the Melesians, did a little otherwise diuide the people into Souldiours, Artificers, and Husbandmen: whose writings *Aristotle* seemeth either not to haue well vnderstood, or else not so wisely reproued, as is euidently to be

gathered

Priesthood honorable.

The most auntient kings to haue bene also preists.

The great honor the Turkish and Arabian princes do vnto their Mufties or high preists.

The order of the Venetian Commonweale.

The Florentine how they diuided their citisens

The auntients, Egiptians how they diuided their citisens.

B1 dignitie. Neither B6 sacred order C6 *For* their auncestors *Bodin writes* our auncestors.
D8 commoners D9 *For* Citadinia *read* Cittadini (citadini in L). Note at C8.

gathered of those fragments which are yet to be seene extant in *Stobæus*. I know not also how it came into *Plato* his mind, that hauing made a diuision of his citiſens into Keepers, Souldiors, and Husbandmen, he ſeparateth the Souldiors (vnder whoſe bucklers and defence the citiſens ought to reſt) I know not how, from keepers. But in briefe, he would haue the keepers of his Commonweale to excell all others in wiſedome and experience: and ſo to rule ouer them, without any reſpect to bee had either to the honour of their diſſent, or to the greatneſſe of their wealth or ſubſtance. Truely it was wiſely ſo ſet downe by that moſt wiſe man: who although he were himſelfe deſcended of the moſt auntient ſtocke of the Senators, and deriued his pedegree by the mothers ſide euen from *Solon* himſelfe, the Athenian law-giuer, yet thought the true glorie of nobilitie and ſoueraigntie to conſiſt in vertue onely: Which thing *Euripides* had before alſo wittily ſaid, ὁ μὲν γὰρ ἐσθλὸς εὐγενὴς ἐμοί γ' ἀνήρ: ὁ δ' ἄδικος, κἢν ἀμείνονος πατρὸς Ζηνὸς πέφυκε, δυσγενὴς εἶναι δοκεῖ. Wherefore let vs meaſure true nobilitie by vertue, for that therein not onely Philoſophers and Diuines, but alſo Poets, Hiſtoriographers, and almoſt all Lawyers, do with one conſent in mine opinion agree, denying any place to bee left for nobilitie without honeſtie. And two things propounded, to wit, Noble diſcent, & Vertue, they haue decreed, That the more higher & more honorable place is to bee giuen vnto vertue, whether queſtion be of bearing of rule, or of honour, or concerning the grauitie and weight of their teſtimonies and witneſſe. The next cauſe of nobilitie vnto vertue, many haue appointed to be the knowledge of hidden and moſt excellent things, whome they which haue attained therunto, the law it ſelf expreſly calleth moſt noble: whom (ſaith the law) *Knowledge maketh moſt noble*: or els as *Caſſiodorus* ſaith, *ex obſcuro nobilem efficit doctrina*, Learning maketh of an obſcure man a gentleman. But then how much more noble is he than both of them, whome morall vertue concurring with the vertues of the mind and knowledge, hath together ennobled? But yet if integritie be diuided from ſuch knowledge of moſt ſecret and moſt excellent things, the prioritie in this caſe is of right to be giuen vnto integritie and vertue: except in ſuch vocations and callings, as wherein ſuch excellent knowledge is of neceſsitie required: For why, it is better and more agreeing with reaſon, to haue a Generall skilfull in martiall affaires, although he be otherwiſe a naughtie man to gouerne an armie, than a good man which is no ſouldiour at all: but of theſe things more ſhall in due place be ſaid.

But yet that which *Plato* ſetteth downe, That they which are but obſcurely borne, excelling in vertues, are to be preferred before them which are nobly deſcended, excelling alſo in the ſame vertues with them; ſeemeth to me a thing verie abſurd and vnreaſonable. And truely theſe two things thus propounded, it is right that ſome regard ſhould be had of the vertue and nobilitie of a mans aunceſtours: and on that opinion the Lawiers haue alwaies been, whether queſtion be for the obtaining of honours, or for the taking of places in ſolemne aſſemblies & meetings. That they are ſtil to be preferred, which both for their owne vertues and the nobilitie of their aunceſtours together, are to be cōmended. But he whom the prince hath made noble, althogh he be not of any account or worth, either for his own vertue, or for the vertues of his auncestors, or for his learning & knowledge: yet by the conſent of all the Lawyers he is to be accounted in the ranke and order of the Nobilitie. And therfore *Plinie* writing to *Traian* ſaid: *Cæſaris eſſe vt nobiles efficeret ac tueretur*, That it was the Emperors part to make noble men, & alſo to defend thē. But this nobilitie *Bartholus*, not vnfitly hath called Ciuil nobilitie; declaring therby them to haue ſo gotten a certein counterfeit kind of nobilitie in the opinion of men, but yet indeed to haue no part of the honor of true nobilitie, without vertue. Wherfore let vs graunt them to inioy the fruits of ſuch their ciuill nobilitie, vnto whō they are ſo by the princes gift & grant conferred: whether that ſuch their

Marginalia:
- True nobilitie to be meaſured by vertue.
- The knowledge of ſecret and moſt excellent things, the ſecond cauſe of nobilitie.
- Integritie to be preferred before knowledge.
- Vertue ioyned with noble diſcent to be preferred before nobilitie for vertue only.
- Ciuil nobilitie by the prince vnworthily beſtowed, no true nobilitie.

F7 diſſent *i.e.* deſcent   Note at G2.

OF A COMMONVVEALE.   395

A their nobilitie be for money or reward, or for the pryme of their youth, or for some other their most foule and filthy seruices, by the princes bestowed vpon them. But to bestow such nobility belongeth onely to them which haue the power in soueraigntie: and to them also whome *Bartholus* writeth to haue but the principalitie, especially if they be subiect vnto the commaund of superiour princes, or haue fellowes or companions in their gouernment: who cannot so much as make a man base borne to bee legitimate. Much lesse true it is, that some haue written, the minions and domesticall attendants of princes to be therefore become noble: for albeit that they thereby enioy certaine priuileges and exemptions from other seruices, yet are they not therefore to be accounted noble, except they haue borne the greater and more honorable offices and
B places of commaund.

Yet question is, and I see it to haue often times beene before demaunded, whether he which by some chaunce or casualtie hath obtained some great place of seruice, or other fee, be thereby made noble? which I see to haue so pleased many, so that an honorable power and commaund be knit and ioined to such fee; such as are those of Dukes, Counties, and Marquesses, or that the title of nobilitie be by the soueraigne Prince expresly set downe in the charters and graunts of homage and fealtie, and so giuen vnto the things themselues, and the professors thereof. And hereof rise that beginning of noble and vnnoble fees. But by the custome of our countrie, wherein fees are deemed by of the same right and nature that other lands and possessions be: as con-
C cerning the right of the persons that had them, the Artificer which by inheritance, or by purchace possesseth a Dukedome, is nothing therefore the more noble, then if he possessed other tributarie lands: For why it seemed vnto our auncestours an absurd thing, out of the right of the land to fish out that honour which they otherwise had not, and the persons themselues to giue place vnto the things as a picture vnto the table where on it is painted, and much more indignitie that the right of nobilitie should be so bought and sold. For of two of the greatest things, namely, of Vertue, and of Nobilitie, as *Euripides* plainly witnesseth no trafique is to be made, μόνον δ' ἂν αὐτὰ χρημάτων οὐκ ἂν λάβοις γενναιότητα καὶ ἀρετήν.

Wherefore seeing that by our customes, aswell as by the customes of the Ger-
D mans, the Spanyards, the Brittons, and Italians, all these fees, whether it please you to tearme them priuileges or seruices by chaunce obtained are to be bought and sold, who can of right thinke himselfe any whit the more noble for the hauing of such mercenarie things? And yet it is lawfull for euery most base Cobler hauing got such fee, to create his vassals to hold of him; as it is also for euery most honorable person to receiue his owne base vassall. Whereby it appeareth, that wealth and riches be they neuer so great, can neither get nor bring forth any true nobilitie at all. Howbeit that *Euripides* bringeth in a person according to the opinion of the common people thus speaking: τὴν δ' εὐγένειαν ἐν χρήμασιν, Nobilitie is in riches. And in *Aulide*: εὐδαίμονες ἐν πᾶσι κλεινοὶ καὶ περίβλεπτοι βροτοῖς.

E And yet we read not onely the vulgar add common sort of men, but euen *Aristotle* also himselfe to haue placed the first degree of nobilitie in wealth; the second in honorable discent; and the third in vertue, placing that last which should haue beene in order first. *Solon* also in like maner made choice of the Citisens of Athens by their wealth and riches, vnto honors and places of commaund: the cause whereof we will in due place declare. Which opinion hath taken so deepe roote, that many thinke wealth, riches, and great substance, not onely to beget nobilitie, but that all the glorie of nobilitie is by pouertie & want of wealth quite extinguished and blotted out: howbeit that they which so say are themselues but men of small authoritie and credite.

Truely

Side notes:
- Whether an honorable fee, make a man noble or not.
- Nobilitie not to depend of lands or fees.
- Of vertue and nobilitie no trafique is to be made.
- Wealth & riches be they neuer so great to bring forth no true nobilitie.
- Lib.4. polit.

A4 and NOT to them also   B8 *For* professors *read* possessors.   D10 εὐδαίμονες, etc. *i.e.* "the prosperous are renowned and conspicuous in all men's eyes" (*Iph. at Aulis*, 428–429)   E1 vulgar and common   Note at B3.

396   THE THIRD BOOKE

Truely *Augustus* the emperour supplied the wants of the poorer sort of the Senators, lest that most honorable order should haue beene with pouertie oppressed. But *Bartholus* hath expresly written, True nobilitie to be neither got by wealth, nor lost by pouertie. Neither did *M. Æmylius Scaurus* deeme the honour of his house to be taken from him by his pouertie: yea the nobilitie and glorie of his familie deliuered him from the power of his most gratious and mightie accusors. Now then if there be a most shamefull villaine, and thereto rich withall; shall he therefore be in degree superiour vnto the honest poorer sort? men I thinke will not so say: then how much lesse ought we to iudge murtherers and men polluted with all kind of villanies, because they abound with wealth to be therefore the more noble? For why the Romans alwaies diuided wealth from nobilitie, for so *Tacitus* reporteth of *Cassius* and *Syllanus*, the one of whom saith he excelled in auntient wealth, & the other in the honour of his auncestours. And so *Cicero* called *Rossius* for nobility and wealth the chiefe man of the towne wherein he dwelt. Wherefore our kings at such time as they, troubled with warres and pressed with want of coyne, had set nobilitie to sale, and that many men for their bad liues infamous, were yet for their money become noble: the Prince by a law made, declared none of them to be therefore so to be deemed noble, but that he might still be accounted amongst the number of the meaner sort, and beare offices amongst them. For what can be more absurd or pernitious, than to measure reputation by gaine, degree by money, and nobilitie by wealth? whereas these things often times by theft and robberie, or immoderat lauash prodigalitie of tyrants are bestowed vpon euery bad fellow, or by some other chaunce, (although in truth nothing be by chaunce done) or fortunes frailtie (whereof they be called the goodes of fortune) giuen vnto men, and so also againe from them taken. Whereas honestie doth in nothing participate with fortune, nor the true possession of vertue and nobilitie can by theft be taken away, nor by fire be consumed, nor by the inundation of waters drowned, nor by any other force extinguished. But for asmuch as we are for the most part led by the vaine opinion and popular errours of men, whereof both all publike and priuat lawes consist; it hath also preuailed, that hee which hath either by the Princes graunt, or by his owne vertue, or wealth, or learning, or seruice in warres obtained nobilitie, may of right transferre the same not onely vnto his posteritie, but euen vnto them also whom he hath adopted. And that contrarie to the decrees as well of the Diuines, as of the Philosophers: Whereby it is sufficiently vnderstood all sorts of men to haue had their beginning from the rotten earth, as it is said, τὸ πηλὸν πάντων προπάτορα γένος ἔχειν. But it is one thing to reason of degrees and dignities in the assemblie of wise men; and another thing to doe it in the presence of the vulgar sort, and scumme of the people. And yet neuerthelesse it not onely is, but alwaies also hath beene a thing both honest and necessarie, for euery man to yeeld and consent vnto the Lawes and customes of his owne citie and countrie. And yet for all that some would not that the vertues, deserts, and honour of the Grandfathers should be extended farther then vnto their Nephues sonnes, and that also vnto such as were of themselues lawfully descended, and not vnto their bastards or base borne. True it is, that by the customes of the Turkes, euery mans degree & reputation is esteemed by his owne worth and vertue; neither doth the grandfathers valour or nobilitie reach farther then their nephues: wherein they doe also wisely, to the intent that euery one of them should endeuour themselues by their owne vertues to renew the declyning honour of their stocke and kinred; being otherwise, to be accounted in the number of the base and common sort of people. Howbeit that by our depraued and corrupt manners, the farther that a man is in discent or degree from the vertue of his auncestors, from whom he tooke the beginning of his honour, the more

Marginal notes:
- True nobilitie to be neither got by wealth, nor lost by pouertie.
- How farre the honor of the aunceftours should extend vnto their posteritie.
- A good custome of the Turkes, whose reputation still dependeth of their owne worth and vertue, and not of their auncestours.

F5(margin) to be neither   F6 gratious *i.e.* popular, enjoying favor   G3 Roscius   I5 τὸ πηλὸν πάντων (L 1–2) preferably τὸν πηλὸν πάντας (L 3–5)   I5 ἔχειν   K1 Nephues sonnes *i.e.* great-grandsons

more noble he is therefore reputed: neither if he shall by all manner of villanies, or loosenes of life dishonest himselfe, doth he therefore loose his degree or honour, except hee be in publique iudgement noted with infamie: in which case although hee leaue his lewde life and the companie of wicked men, and ioine himselfe with the good, yet shall he not againe recouer his nobilitie, so by iudgement once lost, but by the Princes restoring of him, and by speciall rescript. And as hee himselfe from his auncestours receiued nobilitie, so doth he also vnto his posteritie deriue the note of infamie, whether he were by right or wrong condemned: for that a thing by iudgement passed, is still accounted to be indeede a thing true. And what maruell? seing that he which exerciseth base trades, and not beseeming a noble man, is euen without any such publique iudgement to be thrust into the order of common persons. But which be such base trades is an high question, by reason of the diuers Lawes of diuers nations, in that point one of them most vnlike another. *Herodotus* writeth, That in his time they were by the customes of all people accounted base, which vsed handycraftes: of which opinion we read *Xenophon* also to haue beene, who yet yeeldeth a reason thereof not beseeming a philosopher; as forsooth that men of such occupations were still busied, and led a close and sedentarie life: for what can bee more painfull or troublesome than the Generalls life? or more close and sedentarie than the judges calling? And yet what can bee more glorious or more noble than they both are in euery Citie and Commonweale? But *Aristotle* said better, who writ all Mechanicall or handiecraftes men in the cities of Græce to haue beene still kept from councell, from all commaund, and honours: for that they beeing mercenarie men, and to be hired for wages, had quite lost the strength and power of a noble and heroicall minde. And truely the *Master of wisedome it selfe repelleth husbandmen, Smithes, Potters, Image makers, and such other handycrafts men from bearing of authoritie and rule, from honors, and from taking places with the judges. *Lycurgus* also and *Romulus* seperated their citisens farre from all handycrafts; yet *Romulus* permitted his citisens to vse husbandrie, and to beare armes: whereas *Lycurgus* gaue his leaue onely to exercise armes. And to the end it may be the lesse doubted of, *Dionysius Halycarnasseus* repeating the same thing saith: *Hoc lustro, qui puberes essent supra centum millia censa: mulierum autem, seruorum, mercatorum, artesque sordidas exercentium (siquidem Romanorum nemini cauponariam artem, aut vlla opificia tractare licet) triplo plus quàm turbæ ciuilis*, In this view were mustered of them that were fourteene yeare old, aboue an hundred thousand: but of women, seruants, marchants, & such as vsed base occupations and trades, (for why it is not lawfull for any Roman to keepe a Tauerne, or to exercise any other handicraft) were reckned three times moe than there were of the ciuiler sort or citisens. Yet some there be which think *Numa Pompilius* to haue derogated from the law of *Romulus*, seeing that he appointed Colleges or Companies of artificers, as if they might not haue beene made of straungers, or of slaues. Which seemeth to be also confirmed by that which *Cicero* said, Many to haue beene in *Catilins* conspiracie, which flockt together about the Tauernes, in hope that the minds of the needie might for money be moued to take his part. And by that also, that the Tribunes of the people had by the companie and rout of the Artificers, wonted to guard themselues against the insolencie of the Consuls. But against these repugneth that which *Dionysius Halycarnasseus* writeth, *viz.* that in the seauenth view were mustered an hundred thousand citisens, beside artificers: By which words it is manifest, that *Numa* derogated not from *Romulus* his law, for asmuch as king *Seruius*, the third from *Numa*, was the first that so viewed or mustered the people. Neither doth that which is alleaged conuince them to haue bene citisens whom the Tribunes or seditious

Noble men by exercising of base trades, to loose their nobilitie thereby.

Handycrafts accounted base trades.

Handycrafts men why they commonly are basely minded.

Eccles. cap. 38.

The Lacedemonian and Roman citisens by Lycurgus and Romulus their lawgiuers forbidden to exercise mechanicall or handycrafts.

Mm citisens

B2 high *i.e.* arduous, difficult

citisens stirred vp to rebellion, seeing that very slaues in like case were often times called vnto libertie: as we read they sometimes were by *C. Cinna*. *Cicero* also thus speaketh of the Artificers, whom the conspirators with *Catiline* stirred vp to rebellion: *Etenim omne eorum instrumentum, omnis opera, ac quæstus, frequentia ciuium sustinetur, alitur otio*, For (saith he) all their instruments and tooles, all their worke and gaine, is maintained by the multitude of Citisens, and with quietnesse nourished. Now it were verie improperlie said, artificers to be maintained by the multitude of citisens, if they themselues had bene also citisens. But by the Martiall law of the Romans, the citisens after they had begun once to weare the *mans gowne, were compelled to serue in the wars vntill they were fiue and fiftie yeates old. Neither was there any way for a citisen of Rome to attaine vnto any honor, except he had serued in the warres ten yeares: For which cause it is by *Liuie* reported, two thousand of the citisens to haue beene openly sold, for that they had not for foure yeares space serued in the warres; which could by no meanes haue bene done vnto artificers: whom *Liuie* also in one place writeth, to haue beene men altogether vnfit for the warres. That testimonie of *Cicero* is in this point also of more waight: *Illiberales sunt & sordidi quæstus mercinariorum omnium, quorum opera non quorum artes emuntur, est enim in illis ipsa merces autoramentum seruitutis*, The gaines (saith he) of all mercinarie men are seruile and base, whose works and not whose skill are of men bought, for in them their verie wares is the earnest penie of their slauerie. But where he speaketh of the Roman citisens indeed, he neither thinketh nor writeth any thing of them which is contemptible or base, or that soundeth not vnto their reputation and honour. Whereby it is to bee vnderstood Artificers and men of occupation in Rome, to haue beene either slaues, or straungers, and men of most base and lowe estate and condition: or if that by manumission they were become citisens of Rome, yet they were therefore but in the number of Libertines, hauing as it were in some sort lost the right of the citisens of Rome, no otherwise then Noble men with vs, which haue giuen themselues to base and gainfull occupations or trades, who as they haue thereby left their nobilitie: so haue they also lost their degrees and places: except they haue therefore obtayned pardon of our Prince, as that enforced with necessitie, they haue so intermedled in such base trades.

Howbeit concerning the trade of marchandize, it is not well agreed vpon betwixt the Lawiers and the auntient writers amongst themselues, whether it be repugnant vnto a mans credit and reputation or not. We read that by the Tribunall law *Claudia*, it was forbidden the Senatours to haue any greater ship at Sea, then of the burthen of three hundred Amphoras, and that also for the carrying of the fruits of their landes: *Quæstus omnis* (saith *Liuie*) *patribus indecorus visus*, All gayning by trade (saith he) seemed vnto the Senatours vnseemely. Which law *Hortensius* said to be in his time dead: as in *Cicero* we read: Whereby it is yet to bee gathered, that not onely to haue beene lawfull for the rest of the citisens to doe, euery mans credit and reputation saued whole: But also euen the Senators themselues, not to haue altogether abstained from the trade of marchandize, or at least wise to haue had their factors; as wee see the manner is for the Venetian, Spanish, and English gentlemen to haue. And that it was lawfull for the Romaine knights or gentlemen to vse the trade of marchandize, or at least wise that it was not altogether forbidden them, is to be proued by that which *Cicero* saith against *Verres*: *Lucius Prætius splendidissimus Eques Romanus qui Panormi negotiatur*, Lucius Prætius a most worthie Romaine knight, which doth trade at Panormo. And in another place: *Q. Mutius Eques Romanus qui Syracusis*, Q. Mutius a Romaine knight who tradeth at Syracusa. Much lesse there-

---

G6 mercenariorum   G7 *For* opera *read* operæ *i.e.* manual labour (cf. Cicero, *Offices*, I, 42).
G9 *For* wares *read* wages (cf. 401 B4).

OF A COMMONWEALE. 399 [399]

A therefore was the trade of marchandise forbidden the common sort of men. And yet although by the old custome of the Romans, it was no shame for the citisens to trade marchandise; (yet I say) it seemeth not for all that to haue bene altogether lawful for them so to doe: as is to be proued out of *Dionysius Halycarnasseus*, who writeth aboue an hundred thousand citisens to haue bene cessed: but of women and marchants, and others of base trades, three times as many as of the citisens: whereby hee seemeth to haue exempted marchants out of the number of the Roman citisens.

Neither do we see that to haue bene the manner and fashion of the Romans only, but of the Lacedemonians and Thebans also. Howbeit that the vse of gold and siluer, being taken from the Lacedemonians, there was no place left for marchandise: yet
B was it *Lycurgus* his pleasure, by an especiall law more solemnly to prouide therefore. As for the Theban citisens, it was not otherwise lawfull for them either to sue for the magistracies, or honourable offices of the Commonweale, or to accept thereof beeing offered them, except they had full ten yeares before abstained from the trade of marchandise. And at length by the imperiall lawes all entrance vnto honors, and places of commaund were shut vp vnto the order of marchants: and not that onely, but euen to deale in the trade of marchandise was aswell forbidden the nobilitie, as to intermeddle with martiall affaires was forbidden marchants. By which lawes the trade of marchandise seemeth vnto many either base, or not verie honest or commendable. Truely *Plato, Aristotle, Apollonius, Thyaneus*, say, The trade of marchandise to bee an
C enemie vnto vertue. Yea the law of God seemeth also to haue restrained the holy people from the trade of marchandise, in these words, *Non erit mercator in populo tuo*, There shall be no marchant in thy people: that is to say, רכול, which word improperly signifieth a deceiuer, but more properly a marchant: for רכל, is properly to buy & sell; and in that sence it is almost alwaies vsed. For that diuine law which forbad the people, but not straungers, to commit vsurie, seemeth also to haue forbidden to buy any thing, to sell the same thing the deerer vnto a naturall Israelite. Whervnto agreeth that which he the * *Prince of wisdome* writeth, *Mercatorem manus a scelere puras vix habitūrum*, A marchant hardly to haue his hands cleane from wickednesse. Where-
D fore the * Prophets most often, and the interpretours of holy scripture, more often doe so detest the trade of marchants, as that * *Chrysostome* not obscurely or doubtfully, but euen plainely denieth, That marchants can please God, by reason of their lies, periuries, and deceits, and for that they are still prone vnto vnhonest gaine, as *Vlpian* the lawyer writeth.

Yet of that we are to be warned, that whereas the immortall God forbid his people (whome he by a singular right and choice had consecrated vnto himselfe) to trade in marchandise: belongeth not to other people in like manner also; for that he would haue this his people to excell all others in puritie and integritie of life. For why, marchandise is not onely vnto cities profitable, but honest also; and not onely honest, but also necessarie. For what if a citie be built in such a barren soile, or situat in such a place,
E as that men cannot therin not commodiously, but euen not at all otherwise liue? Such as we haue heard the citie of Athens to haue bene, and as our Limoge, and the German Nuremberg is: and Venice also the beautie of the Mediterranean sea. Which foure cities without traffique and the trade of marchandise had neuer bene such and so great as they were and are. Wherefore *M. Tullius* out of the number of marchants, or at leastwise of base men, exempteth them which exercise a plentifull and gainfull, and not a base and bare trade of marchandise, *Mercatura si tenuis est, sordida putanda est, si magna & copiosa, multa vndique apportans, multisque sine vanitate impertiens, non est admodum vituperanda*, The trade of marchandise (saith he) if it be small and bare, is to be accounted

Mm ij

The better sorte of citisens in diuers commonweales forbidden to deale in the trade of marchandize.

The people of God forbid to be marchants

Ecclef. 2 &.
Ezech chap. 8.

Chrysost. Homil. 2 1. in Matheum.

The trade of marchandize both honest and necessarie.

B10 Apollonius, Thyaneus: Apollonius, Thyanæus (L 1-2) *properly* Apollonius Tyaneus (L 3-5)
C3 רכול   C4 רכל   C9(margin) Ezech chap. 82 (L 1-2) *properly* Ezech. chap. 28 (L 3-5)
D5 are to be warned   Notes at C5, D7.

ted also base, but if it be great and plentifull, bringing in on euerie side many commodities, and without vanitie communicating the same vnto many, it is not much to be discommended. Whereunto I would add that of *Platoes*, if it bring in but such things as are necessarie, or at leastwise profitable for the citisens, and carrie out but such things as are vnprofitable, and to be spared. And therefore many lawyers say, The trade of marcandise abounding in plentie of all things, in nothing to derogat from the honour of a mans birth, his degree, or nobilitie. Which haply may be so in Italie, in England, and in Portugall, but not with vs in France, nor yet in Germany. Yet that is euery where true which *Cicero* writeth, *Sordidos iudicari qui mercantur a mercatoribus quod eodem loco ac momento vendant*, Them to be deemed but base, which buy of marchants that which they hold euen in the same place, and selfe same moment againe sell: for why, they should gaine nothing, except they should lye loudly: whereas nothing is more foule than vanitie and lying. Wherfore they do wisely which forbid not only the nobility, but euen the magistrats & souldiors also to deale in the trade of marchandise, least vnder the colour of such traffique, a way be opened and giuen to basenesse and rapine: neither is it to be suffered, that he which cannot by himselfe, should by the help and ministerie of his seruants in that point defraud the law.

The marchants trade in diuers countries diuersly reputed of.

But baser than these are the buyers and sellers of things dishonest, bee they neuer so precious, and to be placed beneath handie crafts-men and laborers, or rather so much as is possible to be quite driuen out of all cities: which cannot yet altogether bee done, for that the law for things honest and dishonest, for things profitable and disprofitable, is not euerie where one and the same. We haue heard painting and engrauing to haue bene much commended and respected, by the estimation that the Greekes and Latines had of them. For who was more famous than *Protogenes*? or more glorious than *Apelles*? one of whose tables, which for that it was most curiously wrought, preserued the Rhodes from distruction, *Demetrius* besieging of it: Which table is reported to haue bene esteemed at more than three hundred talents. And as *Tully* saith, It was giuen as a praise & commendation to *Fabius*, a most noble gentleman, That he was seene in painting: which yet the Hebrews account of all other occupations the basest. And by the lawes and customes of the Turkes, as of all them of the East, and of Affrike also, it is not onely a base thing, but capitall also, with the needle, pencill, or moulding, with any pictures or lineaments to shadow or draw the purtrature of any plant, or liuing creature, or of whatsoeuer thing else that nature hath created. Wee read also the profession of Physike to haue bene amongst the Romans a seruile and abiect thing, and Physike it selfe to haue bene excluded from the other liberall sciences; which yet for all that the Hebrewes and Greekes euer had in great estimation: and begun then to be of our countreymen regarded, when as the Arabians had first diuided Surgions and Apothecaries from Physitians, vsing them but as their instruments and ministers. And albeit that Physitians be in cities to be reuerenced, yet is it not to be suffered them to be equall with orators and lawyers. For why, the most famous Philosophers haue defined the ciuill and lawfull knoledge of the law, to bee the moderatour and chiefe gouernour, not of arts onely, but euen of all liberall sciences also. And Rome (as *Marcus Cato* witnesseth) flourished aboue six hundred yeares without Physitians: whereas no citie can without lawes, and the lawfull knowledge of the law, any small while endure or stand.

The same thing that in one place is accounted honest or profitable in some other to be reputed dishonest or vnprofitable.

Ecclef. cap. 38

The vocation of husbandmen and grasiers in auntient time right commendable, and which now lesse respected.

The order and vocation of Husbandmen and Grasiers, is also right commendable: as they which by those two most auntient trades, haue taught cities, townes, villages, and families, to releeue and maintaine themselues with things of all others most necessarie. And truly *Cyrus* the Greater, of nothing vaunteth so much, as of the fields set and

planted

F2 communicating   G10 cannot   H2 engrauing *i.e.* sculpture   I2 moulding *i.e. fusio*, casting

OF A COMMONWEALE. 401

A planted by his owne industrie and labour. *Serranus*, also *Curius, Concinnatus, Torquatus*, and *Cato*, men no lesse famous for their ciuill than their domesticall prayses, were yet for that most commended, *Quod attritis opere rustico manibus salutem publicam stabilirent: quaeque modo arantium boum iuga rexerant, triumphalis currus habenas retinerent,* That with their hands worne with countrey labour, they established the welfare of the Commonweale: and that those hands which of late ruled the yokes of oxen at plow, now held the raines of the triumphall chariots in the citie of Rome. But these things were chiefly done in that age when as such men as had before-bene Consuls were now from the plow called vnto the Dictatorship. Truly of all things whereby any thing is gotten, nothing is better than husbandrie & grasing, nothing more plentiful, nothing

B more pleasant, and I might say also with *Theophrastus*, nothing better beseeming a free borne man, οὐδ'ἐν μᾶλλον ἀνδρὸς τοῦ ἐλευθέρου ἄξιον: were not these most notable arts, in seruile manner contumeliously let out vnto base men, for wages hired. Now wee haue said those arts to be accounted base, whose wages is the earnest penie of their slauerie: so that it ought not to seeme straunge, if that husbandmen in the fall of the Roman Commonweale were put backe from the warres. Whereof it followeth, both the orders and degrees of husbandmen (I say) and shepheards to be placed in the rank and number of labouring men. For necessitie it selfe (yea oft times against reason) enforceth the dignitie of degrees and vocations of men to be disposed of according to the lawes and customes of euerie citie and countrey.

C The Hangmans office almost euerie where is deemed of all other the basest: neither by the Censors lawes was it for him lawfull to haue a dwelling place within the citie: as in this our age it is not lawfull for him at Tholouse. Whereas by the lawes of the Hebrewes it was not onely honest, but necessarie also, euen the noblest of them if they had bene witnesses of capitall crimes, to be also the executioners therein. Yea and in England the neerest kin to them that be hanged, be it their fathers, their brethren, or neerest kinsmen, the last kindnesse they can doe them, is to play the part of the hangman, and to strangle them hanging vpon a low paire of gallowes. But by our customs we see gainfull rewards propounded vnto this so base an office, least wee should bee at any time destitute of an office so necessarie for the cities: as we haue heard say it to haue

D long since happened in Gaunt, where the iudge for lacke of an hangman commaunded the father and the sonne, both convicted and condemned for the same offence, to cast lots which of them should be the others hangman; wherein the lot fell vnto the father, who now growne verie aged, with much entreatie obtained that his sonne, as by age the stronger, and so fitter to liue, might become the executioner; who without feare hanged his father: the eternall monument of which impietie and villanie (which I against my will haue beholden) the Gantois suffer yet to stand in statues of brasse, and that in a publike and open place euen in the middest of the citie.

The hangmans office in some places respected.
Deut. 17. and 19.

The author in this custome by him reported much mistaken and deceiued.

There is also in cities a great multitude of idle lazie fellowes, who neither in time of peace, nor warre, haue any occupations to set themselues to worke, or other trade to

E busie themselues withall: whome it is needfull either to banish out of the citie, or to keepe them in publike workes: for why, they can in no degree be placed, and so much the more, if they haue nothing of their owne wherewith to maintaine that their idle life. And these kind of men *Amasis* king of Aegypt put to death, in like manner as if they had bene theeues and robbers. Wherein they of Paris doe much better, who thrust the strong and lustie of these idle mates into their publike workes; courteously feeding and curing the sicke and aged, and diligently instructing the fatherlesse and poore boyes and maids, some in learning, some in occupations, in foure diuers colleges, besides a great hospitall endowed with most faire reuenewes.

Idle people to be thrust out of the citie, or else set to worke.

Mm iij   But

A1 Cincinnatus   B2 τοῦ ἐλευθέρου   B6 put backe *i.e.* kept away, removed (cf. L)   D10 or other

But if citisens liue idle vpon such goods as they haue themselues before got, or were of old left them, albeit that they lead a foule and sluggish kind of life, yet are they to be therein suffered, if it were but that they might with their wealth helpe the poore Commonweales wherein they liue. But if these men feed also their mind with the contemplation of high and heauenly things, I deeme them then of all sorts of citisens the happiest, and to be placed in the highest rankes and degrees of them. But if they had rather lead an actiue than a quiet kind of life, it is much better to call them than poorer men vnto honours and magistracies, if no dishonestie of life let: for that they are like to bee cleerer from briberie and corruption, than they which are pressed with pouertie and want. Wherefore in obtaining of magistracies and honours, the law commaundeth the richer sort to be oftentimes placed together with the nobler; yea and some times also to bee preferred before them, if no staine of their fore passed life let: and that is well agreeing vnto the lawes and customes of the Indians, whom *Plinie* writeth to preferre still the best and richest man vnto honours and places of commaund.

How citisens are in a Monarchy to be ordered and placed.

Wherefore in what order citisens are to be placed, is to be referred vnto the iudgement and discretion of the masters of the ceremonies of euerie citie, for the vnliknesse of their lawes and customes almost infinit. Yet I suppose, that citisens in a monarchie might in this order not vnaptly be placed. That next vnto the king himselfe, who out of the number of the citisens, going farre before the rest should follow the holy order of the clergie: next vnto the sacred order of the clergie, the Senat: after the Senat should follow the martiall men, and amongst them, first the generall of the armie, or great constable, & then the dukes, counties, marquesses, gouernors of prouinces, landgraues, burgraues, captaines of castles, vassals, and other souldiours, with such others, as vppon whome the charge of the warres, by the custome of our auncestours lieth. After them should follow the order of gowne men, which should containe the colledges of magistrats, and companies of judges, partly diuided into their places, with oratours, lawyers, pleaders, aduocats, attourneies, proctors, scribes, registers, notaries, sergeants, apparitors, garders, tryers, trumpeters, gailors, and all the companie belonging to the law. Next vnto whome should follow the order of physitians, surgeons, and apothecaries. And after them schoole men, such as professed to instruct the youth, or are themselues instructed; the professors (I say) of diuinitie, law, and physike, natural philosophers, mathematitians, logitians, rhetoritians, historiographers, poets, and grammarians. After the order of gowne men, I suppose are to be placed marchants, agents, farmers of the common custome, bankers, money chaungers, brokers, and especially they which haue the charge for the bringing in of corne into the citie, and of such other things as are most necessarie for the feeding of the citisens, such as are the cornmungers, butchers, fishmungers, fishers, bakers, puddingmakers, cookes, vnto whome we will ioyne husbandmen and grasiers; and vnto these all kind and sort of handycrafts men: which for that they seeme almost innumerable, of them, they which are the most profitable, ought to haue the first place, carpenters (I say) armourers, masons, metall men, coyners, gold beaters, goldsmiths, metall melters, glasse makers, smiths, bakers, potters, horners, chaundlers, weauers also, and such as deale in spinning of silke, wool, beasts, haire, flaxe, hempe, cotten wool, and such other like, whereof we see cloath, ropes, garments, hangings, sayles, and paper to be made. Next vnto whome follow curriers, skinners, fullers, diers, taylors, shoomakers: vnto which occupations, although printing be not for antiquitie to be compared, yet seemeth it for the excellencie thereof, before al the rest worthily to be preferred. For as for painters, image makers, caruers, makers and sellers of womens paintings, minstrels, players, dauncers, fencers, tumblers, iesters, and bauds, are in mine opinion either to be quite driuen out of cities, or else to be placed in the lowest place of all:

Printers to be amongst men of occupations especially to be regarded.

G9 rest, *should*   H3 burgraues, BARONS, captaines   H6 *For* partly divided *probably read* aptly divided *or* properly divided (*apte distinctas*).   H8 *For* tryers *read* cryers.   K2 beasts haire, Note at K3

all: so that euen bath keepers, barbers, sailers, hucksters, ostlers, coach men, carters, graue makers, sargeants, and hangmen, are to be placed before them: For that these are indeed necessarie for the carrying out of filth, and the clensing of the citisens and cities: whereas the other with their most base trades, the ministers of foule and vaine pleasures, not onely corrupt the citisens maners, but vtterly ouerthrow euen the cities themselues. But we haue so described the orders of citisens, not so much that the dignitie, as the condition of euerie one of them might so the better be vnderstood.

Neither are citisens but most seldome, and that also in time of great necessitie, to bee in orders from other citisens diuided: for that so doing may giue occasion and minister matter vnto ciuill sedition: when as some of them diuided from other some, shall perceiue themselues to be noted also with a difference of their order and degree. Yea we said, that the citisens of one and the same trade or occupation were not in one street or quarter of the citie to be together placed: except they were by the straitnesse of the places or opportunitie of the waters they were to vse, thereto enforced; as butchers, curriers, felmungers, bath keepers: who for that they are to haue the continuall vse of water for their oft washings, must haue their dwellings also neere vnto the riuers sides: so are also armourers, and smithes, to be placed apart by themselues from schollers and students, as for other handicrafts men, marchants, and trades men, it is good to haue them separated one from another, and to be diuided into euerie part of the citie, that the citisens may more commodiously vse their helpe in generall, and not in time of daunger be enforced oftentimes to runne from the furthest place of the citie to the furthest. Whereunto is to be ioyned, that citisens of the same occupation or trade, diuided into diuers parts of the citie, cannot so easily conspire against the common good, or delude the lawes, as if they dwell together. But if assembly of all the orders and degrees of citisens, must of necessitie be made (for that degrees must needes in some sort bee distinguished from degrees, that a certaine dignitie of degrees may be kept) especiall care is to be had, that the citisens be not diuided into two parts onely, and yet that in such assemblies there be not more than three degrees or places: for that contention arising betwixt two, they easily breake out into force; or else vpon equall voyces breake off, and leaue the matter vndecided: when as one thing is contrarie but onely vnto one, and that by nature many things cannot vnto one be contrarie, but that the third must of necessitie ioyne it selfe vnto the one of the two, so to reconcile them together: whereas if there be more than three parts, and in number equall, the same inconueniences doe follow (that doe of two) the euen number being easily to bee diuided into two parts: but if in number vnequall the number of opinions diuers will hardly end the controuersies once moued.

Citisens but seldome and that also vpon great necessitie to be into orders diuided.

Citisens better to be diuided into three parts, than into two.

It shall also be more commodious and profitable to haue one oratour or speaker, for all the degrees of citisens together, then for diuers orders and degrees, diuers: so that it be agreed vpon amongst all the degrees and orders what is to be requested, determined of, or done: as heretofore at *Thurin* and *Orleance*, when they called their assemblies. But if the orders and decrees of citisens shall therein differ among themselues, it is then needfull for euery order and degree of the citisens, to haue their owne speaker. As of late in the parliament of *Bloyse*, when as the Bishops grieuously complained of the Nobilitie; and againe the Nobilitie of the Bishops; and the Comminaltie of them both, it was then needfull to haue three Speakers appointed: and yet so could not the good of the people bee sufficiently prouided for; but that the Speakers were blamed of falshood and collusion, and that diuers great and grieuous complaints of the people were thereof giuen out. But these things are especially to be taken heed of in a Monarchie, wherein one man is judge of all controuersies: Wheras in other kinds of states, albeit

Whether it bee good for to haue one speaker for all the degrees of citisens, or diuers.

B8 students: as for   D10 *For* Thurin *read* Tours.   E1 *For* decrees *read* degrees.

albeit that there be many speakers, yet the matter is still in the end put to voyces.

Better three parts taking in a commonweale than two.

But that diuision of the citisens (which we haue spoken of) into three degrees or parts, as it is vnto all kinds of cities profitable, so is it in an Aristocratie most necessarie, that two of them disagreeing, the third may end the strife, or taking part with one, may draw the other whether it wil or no from the former receiued opinion. For if two factions shall arise, they which are wise, & wish the good & welfare of the Commonweale, should set vp an head of a third faction, and ioyne themselues vnto him: For three leaders of diuers factions, or part takers, are right easily reconciled; whereas two are most hardly brought to agreement: whereof oftentimes arise seditions and ciuill warres, and that especially in the Aristocratike estate: For that in that estate, betwixt the nobilitie and common people, can be no third degree, all the right of soueraigntie being in the nobilitie, and nothing thereof in the people; all the same right in a Popular citie, or estate, being common to the nobilitie and Senat together with the people. Wherefore it is an easie matter to create a third degree or order: as at Rome the order of knights or gentlemen, was in a sort an arbitratour or vmpier betwixt the *Patricij* and the people, as made of both degrees.

Not good in great assemblies to diuide the people into three degrees and orders.

But for that both the *Patricij* and the knights made scarcely the fifth part of the whole people, the people did therefore the more imperiously raigne & rule: which was then especially vnderstood, when as by a law concerning the Theatres, place for the beholding of playes, was first giuen to the Senat, & next after them vnto the knights or gentlemen, all apart by themselus from the people: whereof *Liuie* thus writeth, *C. Attilij Serrani, L. Scribonij Libonis Ædilium Curulium Ludis Romanis primum Senatus a populo secretus spectauit, præbuitque sermones sicut omnis nouitas solet alijs tandem, quòd mentò antè debuerit tributum censentibus amplissimo ordini, alijs demptum ex dignitate populi quicquid maiestati patrum adiectum esset interpretantibus: & omnia discrimina talia quibus ordines discernerentur, & concordiæ, & libertatis æquè minuende esse: ad quingentissimum quinquagissimum Sextum annum in promiscuo spectatum esse, quid repente factum? Cur non immisceri sibi in cauea Patres plebem vellent? Cur diues pauperem confessorem fastidierit? Nonam & superbam libidinem ab nullius ante gentis Senatu neque desideratam, neque institutam Postremo Africanum quoque ipsum, quod Consul auctor eius rei fuisset, pænituisse ferunt,* At the Roman plaies of *C. Atilius Serranus,* and *L. Scribonius Libo,* the honourable Ædiles, the Senat apart and diuided from the people, first beheld the same: which thing (as euerie nouelty vseth to doe) gaue occasion of speech, some deeming it now at length to be giuen vnto that most honourable order, which should long time before haue of right beene giuen it; other some interpreting it to be taken from the dignitie of the people, whatsoeuer was added vnto the honour of the Senat: and all such differences as whereby degrees were discerned asunder to tend alike to the diminishing both of concord and of libertie: that the people indifferently together had beholden the plaies, now fiue hundred fiftie six yeares. What was that now so sodenly done? Why should not the Senators be contented to haue the people mingled with them in the Theatre? Why should the rich scorne the poore man to sit by him? A new and proud insolencie, neuer before of the Senat of any nation either desired or ordained. Last of all it is reported, *Africanus* also himselfe to haue repented him, That being Consull, hee had beene author of that matter. Thus much he. Whereby it is to be vnderstood, that for the preseruing of the popular libertie, and concord, degrees ought so to be placed with degrees, as that al of them may more easily bee ioyned vnto all in societie and communion together. Wherefore this fact of *Africanus* was blamed, not onely of the common people, but euen of the Senators themselues, whose fauour he was thought to haue gotten: For so *Tullie* writeth him to haue bene blamed, not onely of the wiser sort, but euen of himselfe,

---

G7 *For* fifth part *read* fiftieth part.   H3 quod multo ante   H5 concordiæ   H6 minuendæ
H6 quingentesimum quinquagesimum sextum   H8 Novam   H9 institutam. Postremo

selfe also; for that, that was by force from the people extorted, which had before vntill then bene willingly graunted vnto the Senators: for that albeit that the seats were indifferent vnto all, yet neuer any of the people would presume to sit to behold the playes before the Senators. About an hundred yeares after was a law made by *L. Roscius Otho*, Tribune of the people, That the knights or gentlemen should sit and take their places vpon the fourteene steps or degrees next vnto the stage: For when the magistrats and the rest of the Senators. by the Censors law, did more commodiously see and heare from the first and neerest places vnto the stage, the higher degrees and farther off, were accounted of lesse credit: & albeit that the places of the Theater were of right great receit (as which contained oftentimes threescore thousand of the citisens) yet could they not containe them all: & therfore by the law Roscia concerning the Theater, it was needfull that place should be kept for the knights, in the fourteene steps and degrees neere vnto the stage: and for that thereby the peoples voyces seemed secretly in some sort to be taken from them by *Roscius* the Tribune, whom it beseemed to haue bene a keeper & preseruer of the popular libertie and dignitie; at such time as he came to behold the playes, he was by the knights (whose fauour he had won) with great acclamation and applause receiued, but of the people with greater tumult and sturre, in so much that *Cicero* the Consull was glad to call all the assembly of the people out of the Theater. And so as a man of great wisedome and eloquence, with a graue oration repressed the peoples insolencie, and with a reproofe and chiding, well beseeming the dignitie of a Consull, so appeased the tumult, as that the people returned againe into the Theatre well pleased. Hereof came that speech of *Plinie* in commendation of *Cicero*, *Te suadente tribus Roscio Theatralis legis auctori ignouerunt, notatasque se discrimine sedis æquo animo tulerunt*, The tribes (saith he) at thy persuasion pardoned *Roscius*, author of the law of the Theatre, and tooke it patiently themselues to bee noted with the difference of their seats and sittings. Now a punishment was set downe by the law of the Theatre, *Ne quis nisi censum equestrem haberet in xiiij spectaret*, That no man except he had a knights wealth, should stand in the xiiij steps or degrees to behold the playes. But when many, their patrimonie being by the ciuill warres wasted, durst not for feare of this Theatrall law behold the playes from the fourteene steps or seats, *Augustus* the emperour decreed, That they should not be therewith bound, who themselues or their parents had euer had a knights wealth or abilitie. Now as for the order and degree of women, I meddle not with it; onely I thinke it meet them to be kept far off from all magistracies, places of commaund, iudgements, publike assemblies, and councels: so to be intentiue onely vnto their womanly and domesticall businesse. And thus much concerning the order and degrees of Citisens. But by what meanes prouision is to bee made against the reuolt and tumultuous stormes of the common people, wee will in due place more at large declare.

Finis Lib. Terty.

THE FOVRTH BOOKE OF OR CONCERNING A COMMONWEALE.

Chap. I.

¶ *Of the rising, encreasing, flourishing estate, declining, and ruine of Commonweales.*

The beginning of Commonweals.

ALl Commonweales take their beginning either from a Familie, by little and little encreasing; or els arise at once, as when a multitude of people as a Colony drawne out of another Citie or Commonweale, doe as a young swarme of bees fly abroad vnto another place: or as a slip or science pluckt off from a tree, and planted in a straunge soyle, which taking root, bringeth forth much more plentifull and pleasant fruit, than doe those trees which grow vp of small kernels, or of their owne accord. Yet both the one and the other of these Commonweales, are established either by the strength of some stronger than themselues, or by the power of some others, who voluntarily had subiected themselues together with their libertie, vnto the power and pleasure of others, to be by them disposed of, as by a soueraigne power without any law at all, or else vpon certaine laws and conditions betwixt them agreed vpon. So the Commonweale hauing taken beginning if it be well rooted and grounded, first assureth it selfe against al externall force, and then against the inward diseases of it self, and so by little & little gathering strength, groweth vp vntill it be come to the full perfection of it selfe: which wee may call the

The florishing estate of commonweales endure not long.

Flourishing estate thereof; which cannot be of any long continuance, by reason of the chaunges of worldly things, which are so mutable and vncertaine, as that the greatest Commonweales oftentimes fall euen all at once with the weight of themselues, some others by ciuill warres, some by popular diseases, but most by the enemies violence, being as then ruinated, when as they thought themselues most assured: other some by the wrath of God, being vpon the sudden, and in a moment ouerthrowne: some few by age growing old, and by their inward sicknesse taking end. But yet no Commonweales, finding or feeling greater chaunges or falles than the fairest of them: which for all that, are not in that to be blamed, especially if the change or alteration come by any externall force, as most commonly it chaunceth, the fairest things being still the most enuied at. And as *Demetrius* (he which was called the Besieger) deemed no man more happy, than him who had longest quietly liued in the greatest abundance of al things,

neuer

H5 science *i.e.* scion   K9–10 *For* more happy *read* more unhappy.   Notes at I1, I3.

neuer hauing tasted of aduersitie, as a man by fortune deemed most abiect and vnworthie, with whom shee should contend or striue: so we see some Commonweales so shamefully buried in pleasures and idlenes, or else so to be corrupted, as that they might well moue any man rather to pitie then to enuie at their state. Wherefore the risings and ruines of the Commonweales are well of vs to be considered, and what the causes be of euery such their conuersion and change before that we giue iudgement of them, or propound them as examples to be imitated and followed. Now I call that a Conuersion of a Commonweale, when as the state thereof is altogether chaunged: as when a Popular estate is changed into a Monarchie; or an Aristocratie into a Democratie; or contrarywise: For as for the change of customes, lawes, religion, or place, it is but a certaine kind of alteration, the state and soueraigntie continuing still: which may also to the contrarie it selfe be changed, without any change of religion, or lawes, or any other things else, besides them which belong vnto soueraigntie. As when in our time the Florentine popular estate was changed into a Monarchie. Neither is the age or continuance of a Commonweale to be measured by the long standing of a citie, or of the walles thereof, as *Paulus Manutius* seemeth to haue done: who writeth the Venetian Commonweale that now is, to haue stood twelue hundred yeares; which hath yet suffered three changes, as we shall forthwith declare. Sometime it happeneth also no change either of the citie, or of the citisens, of the customes, or religion to be made, or any other force offered, or wrong done to any man; and yet that the state may perish: as when any soueraigne prince willingly subiecteth himselfe, his kingdome, and people vnto the power and obeysance of some other Prince, or else by his testament appointeth some popular Commonweale inheritour of his State and kingdome: As is reported of *Attalus* king of Asia; of *Cottius* king of Alpes; of *Ptolemee* king of Cyrenæ; of *Eumenes* king of Pergamus; of *Nicomedes* king of Bithynia; of *Polemon* king of Pontus, who left the people of Rome heires of those so many their kingdomes: for then those kingdomes were quite taken away, and those Commonweales brought into the forme of Prouinces, and no change made of their Monarchies into a popular Estate. And so contrariwise, if of one or many cities or prouinces be made one or manie Monarchies or popular estates diuided in soueraigntie, that is not to be accounted any conuersion or change, but euen a verie beginning of diuers new Commonweales: As when the countrie of the Swissers and the Grisons reuolted from the Germaine Empire, they became eighteene Commonweals, euery one of them holding their estates (diuided from the other) in soueraigntie. Sometime also of two is made one and the same Commonweale: as were the Romans and the Sabines, their two kings and people being in the same power and league ioyned and combyned together, neither of them subiect vnto the Lawes or commaund of the other; but with equall power both of them growing together into the same citie. And lest the Sabines so ioyned vnto the Romans should haue seemed to haue accrewed vnto another mans kingdome, it pleased them that the names of both the people being taken away or suppressed, they should be called *Quirites*, which name the Magistrates in their orations vnto the people euer after vsed: Albeit that Romulus (who because he would not seeme to endure a fellow in the kingdome with him, had not spared his owne brother) caused *Tatius* king of the Sabines not long after to bee also slaine: wherefore the Sabines Commonweale so perished not, either accrewed vnto the Romaines (as some haue beene of opinion) albeit that other people called them neither Sabines, nor Quirites, but Romans: For that that name once giuen vnto the Citie and the people, could neuer more be changed; or for that the name of the Romans was more stately; or else for that those two people so grew together within the wals

of

of Rome, yet so as that the one became not subiect vnto the other: as it chanceth when the one being vanquished, yeeldeth it selfe vnto the other, and so suffereth the lawes of the vanquisher. Which may serue for the disciding of the question of *Cuneus* the lawier, who doubteth, Whither the subiects of the one Commonweale, if they be ioyned into one and the selfe same bodie with the subiects of another Commonwealth, be thereby the subiects of them with whom they are so ioyned: which thing *Bartholus* denieth, and for example thereof alleageth *Raimond* Countie of Toulouse, not erring indeed in his resolution of the question, but in the example by him produced, not hauing good regard vnto the treatie made betwixt the Countie and the estates of Languedoc of the one part, and *Lewes* the ix the French king on the other part, wherin it was comprised, That the only daughter of the countie *Raymond* should be espoused to *Alphonsus* countie of Poitiers, the kings brother, with condition, that if they died without heires of their bodies lawfully begotten, the countrey of Languedoc should in full right returne vnto the crowne; yet for all that so, as that the customes of the countrey should not be chaunged, neither any taxe imposed without the consent of the estates of the countrey: which hath alwaies beene obserued, the soueraigntie ouer the country and the inhabitants of Languedoc remaining vnto the kings, as it had before that the countie was therefrom exempted. But most certaine it is, that an estate subiect vnto another, maketh not another Commonweale, but onely a part of the subiects.

But that these things may the better be perceiued, it is to be vnderstood, that al conuersions and chaunges of Commonweales, are either voluntarie or necessarie, or else mingled of both: and as for necessitie, it is also either naturall or violent: For albeit that the birth of things be more faire and pleasing than their death, yet for all that so it is, that the source and course of flowing nature rauishing all things, giueth vs also to vnderstand, that the one cannot be without the other: so that all things which had beginning, although they haue stood many hundred yeares, yet must at length in time take end and perish also. But, as we deeme that death more tollerable which by little and little creepeth on through the weakenesse of age, or the course of some long lingering disease, and that almost without any sensible feeling thereof: so also may wee say the chaunge or fall of a Commonweale, which proceeding as it were of age, and after hauing endured a long tract of worlds, to be necessarie, and yet not violent: for that nothing can well be called violent, which is agreeing vnto nature: seeing also that the course of euerie things age is certaine, and a certaine ripenesse vnto euerie age appointed: so that in due time to take end seemeth to bee a thing of euerie thing to bee wished for.

The naturall change or fall of a Commonweale.

Now Commonweales be also chaunged some times to the better, and sometimes to the worse, whether such chaunge bee naturall or violent: yet the violent change still hauing violent motions, and so quickely done; and the naturall chaunging still be little and little, and so the lesse felt. But of all chaunges of Commonweales, no voluntarie chaunges is more pleasing or easie than that which is made by the consent and good will of him which hath the soueraigntie, and of his subiects: when as hee which hath the soueraigntie, chooseth rather to yeelde the same vnto the nobility, or the people, than to hold it himselfe: as we haue heard *Sylla*, with incredible violence to haue taken vpon him the Dictatorship, and that not without the most cruell slaughter of the people, and so to haue turned the soueraignty of the Commonweale from a popular estate, into a Monarchie; and yet him the same man within foure yeares after, voluntarily and of his owne accord, dispoiling himselfe of the Monarchy, which he had coueted vnder the colour of his Dictatorship, to haue againe restored the soueraignty vnto

The most pleasing and easie change of a Commonweale.

Of A Commonweale. 409

to the people, to the great contentment of them all in generall, and the good liking of euery one of them in particular. So also the nobilite of the state of Sienna, by their common consent, yeelded the soueraignty of that state vnto the people, and abandoned the city themselues, which *Pandulphus* the tyrant, violently afterwards inuaded. And as in mens bodies diuers changes happen from the qualities of the elements, the disposition of the body or the minde, the temperature of the humours, as also from the manner of the education thereof, and diuersity of diet: so also the Commonweale may suffer an vniuersall change or ruine, from friends or enemies externall or internall, or from both, whether it be from good to euill, or euill to good, and that oft times contrary to the good liking of the subiects, who must sometimes as children and mad folkes, be cured euen against their wills, as *Lycurgus*, who changed the lawes and royall state of his country, into a popular gouernment, contrary to the good liking of the subiects, or of the greater part of them; howbeit that in so doing, hee was well beaten of them, and lost one of his eyes (the reward of his vertue) although hee had before renounced the claime and right that he and his successours had vnto the kingdome, as princes of the blood, and nearest vnto the crowne.

But forasmuch as there are but three sorts of Commonweales, as wee haue before declared: there are also but six perfect conuersions or chaunges thereof, viz. of a Monarchie into a Popular estate, or of a Popular estate into a Monarchie: and so likewise of a Monarchie into an Aristocratie, and of an Aristocraty into a Monarchie: and of an Aristocratie into a Popular estate, and of a Popular estate into an Aristocratie. So also of euerie estate there be six other imperfect chaunges, or rather alterations; that is to wit, from the Royall estate vnto the Lordlike: from the Lordlike estate vnto the Tyrannicall: from the Tyrannycall vnto the Royall, or from the Royall into the Tyrannicall: from the Tyrannicall into the Lordlike, and from the Lordlike into the Royall. So might one also say of an Aristocratie, lawfull, lordlike or factious: And of a Popular estate, lawfull, lordlike, and turbulent. I call it an vnperfect chaunge, as the change of a lawfull Aristocratie into a faction; or of a Royall estate into a tyranny: for that therein is nothing but the chaunging of the qualities of good gouernors into euil, the Monarchie yet still remaining in the one, and the Aristocratie in the other. I speake not here of the chaunging of a Monarchie into a Duarchie (or soueraigne gouernment of two) for that we haue before declared such a Duarchie to bee comprehended vnder an Oligarchie (or gouernment of few) otherwise a man might make also a Truarchie of three princes, ruling together in one Commonweale (as it chaunced in the Triumuirat of *Marcus Antonius, Augustus*, and *Lepidus*) as also a Tetrarchie (or gouernment of foure) and so other chaunges of Commonweals in number infinit: whereof there is not onely no rule or precept to be giuen, but are also of themselues most absurd: For when wee once passe the soueraigne gouernment of one, wee forthwith enter into the popularitie of moe: which as the lawyers say, is still contained in the number of two.

Six perfect conuersions or changes of Commonweales.

Vnperfect changes of Commonweale.

But besides these conuersions and chaunges of estates, which wee haue alreadie spoke of, it happeneth some time that the estate of a Commonweale is holden in suspence and sufferance: as after the death of *Romulus*, the people of Rome was a yeare without a Monarchie, a Popular estate, or Aristocratie: For the hundred Senatours which commaunded one of them after another, had no soueraigne power, neither commaunded but onely by commission: true it is, that one might say, That the soueraigntie was againe returned vnto the people, and the charge of commaund vnto the Senators, vntill that by common consent they had chosen them a king.

A Commonweale sometime holden in suspence.

And sometimes againe it chaunceth, that the Royall, Aristocratike, or Popular Common-

An Anarchie.

D7 For Truarchie *read* Triarchie (cf. Fr and L).   E5 the popularitie of moe *i.e.* plurality
                                                                                                                       Notes at E5, E8.

Commonweale being quite extinguished, there ensueth a meere Anarchie: when as there is neither soueraigntie, nor magistrats, nor commissioners, which haue power to commaund; as it chaunced the people of Israel after the death of *Iephte*, when as their estate was brought to a meere Anarchie, and vpholden onely by the prouidence and power of God alone, the best and greatest king: for so it is in holy writ reported. So likewise at Syracusa, after the death of *Dion*, and in Florence after that the nobilitie was thence driuen out by the people: which so continued a certaine time without gouernment, as a ship without a pilot or gouernour. And so after the death of *Abusahit* king of Fez, that kingdome was in most miserable case eight yeares without a king. As also after diuers murthers of many the Ægyptian Sultans, the Mammalukes made choyce of *Campson Gaurus*, hauing liued a certaine time in a pure Anarchie. And in like manner the Russians, being wearie and spent with ciuill warres, for lacke of a soueraigne, of themselues made choice of three of the German princes to rule ouer them.

Iud. 27.

Wherefore when an estate is come vnto a meere Anarchie, that is to say, when no man either commaundeth or obeyeth, it is to bee accounted the verie ruine and destruction, and not the chaunging of a Commonweale: although that the families and colledges therein continue friends together. But if the nobilitie or people haue power to create the prince, and he being dead the magistrats shall themselues retaine the soueraigne power and commaund: yet is it not therefore to be deemed an Anarchyie, for that the soueraigntie is still like againe to fall either vnto the nobilitie, or to the people.

A meere Anarchie the verie ruine of a Commonweale.

The last point is, when as an Estate or Commonweale is together with all the peopled quite extinguished: as it hapned vnto the people and seigneurie of Thebes, which *Alexander* the Great vtterly rooted out, together with their city, sauing only the house of *Pindarus* the Poet: vpon the entrance whereof was written, μὴ καίετε ςεγὰν τȣ̃ Πινδάρȣ, Burne you not *Pindarus* his house. So also the Madianites, the Amorites, the Iebusites, and Phærezites, were by the people of Israel vtterly destroyed: which was not the chaunging of one estate into another, but a meere ruine of the estate with the people together. But yet it may well be, that some one member of a Commonweale, or that some one prouince thereof may be destroyed, or a towne rased, and all the people therein slaine, and yet the Commonweale stand: as it chaunced to the towne of Arzille, in the kingdome of Fez, which the Englishmen rased, and put all the people therein to the sword: and to *Sebastia*, in the kingdome of Amasia, which *Tamarlan* the Tartar king vsed in like sort: and to the towne of Bizance, a member of the Roman empire, which after it had bene three yeares besieged by the emperour *Seuerus*, was in the end taken, sacked, rased, and all the people slaine, and the site thereof giuen to the Perinthians, who reedified it, being afterwards called Constantinople, and now corruptly Stamboll, the choyce seat of the Turkish emperours.

Commonweales sometime together with the people vtterly extinguished.

But this is in Monarchies speciall and proper, that the Monarches one of them oftentimes by force driuen out by another, do not yet therefore chaunge their estate: as in a few moneths in our remembrance it happened in the kingdome of Telesin, where the king *Abuchemo* was by the people driuen out of his kingdome, and *Abyamein* chosen king in his stead: who forthwith after was also cast out by *Hariadenus Barbarussa*, who long time raigned not there, but that *Abuchemo* returning with the forces of the emperour *Charles* the fift chased away *Barbarussa*, and tooke sharpe reuenge vpon his disloiall subiects, making himselfe the emperours tributarie and vassall: but was againe not long after driuen out againe by *Barbarussa*: the state of a Monarchie yet neuer chaunging, no more than did the Roman empire, for hauing had foure emperours in one yeare; one of them slaine by another: the estate of the Monarchie neuerthelesse still remaining,

A thing vnto Monarchies speciall.

H2–3 people quite   I6 scite *i.e.* site   Notes at H2, I7.

maining as the prise and reward of the victor.

Sometime also rule and soueraigntie is euen thrust vpon men by force and against their will: as first *Claudius*, and then *Gordianus* the elder were euen drawne and enforced to take vpon them the Roman empire. And in our remembrance the inhabitants of Tripolis in Barbarie, after they were reuolted from *Iachia* king of Tunes, chose *Mucamen* for their king: who being shortly after poysoned, they vpon the sudden enforced a religious Hermit to take vpon him the crowne and the kingdome; wherein he raigned against his will, vntil that *Peter* of Nauarre, by force tooke the citie of Tripolis, together with the king, whome he sent prisoner into Sicilie: but was afterwards by the emperour *Charles* the fift (to his great contentment) sent backe againe to liue in his solitarie cell in Affricke. *An Heremite against his will chosen and crowned king of Tripolis.*

But as of men some perish and die in the most flourishing time of their age, some others in their youth, some in their childhood, and some before they could bee well borne; so wee also see some kingdomes and cities to bee cut vp and destroyed before they could strengthen themselues with lawes and armes, othersome as abortiues to be dead and extinguished before they were borne: as in our time the kingdome of the Anabaptists at Munster (the metropoliticall citie of Westphalia) was taken away and subuerted before it was well thought to haue bene borne. *Iohn* of Leiden, a Sadler, and their ringleader, who had there by the space of three yeares borne himselfe for a king, and taken vpon him the soueraigntie (though still by the imperiall hoast besieged) being at last together with the citie taken and publikely executed. *Some commonweales euen in their beginning destroyed.*

Now when I speake of the flourishing estate of a Commonweale, my meaning is not, that it should be come to the height of most absolute perfection: for that in these transitorie things there is nothing so perfect, and in mans actions lesse than in any thing in the world: but I call that the flourishing estate of a Commonweale, when it hath attained vnto the highest degree of the perfection and beautie thereof; or to say better, then when it is least imperfect, and farthest from all kind of vice: which cannot be wel knowne, but after the declination, chaunge, or ruine of euerie Commonweale: As the Romans hauing made proofe of the Royall, Tyrannicall, Aristocratike, and Popular estates and Commonweales, yet neuer flourished more than in the Popular estate: neither did that their Popular estate euer flourish more in armes and lawes, than in the time of *Papirius Cursor*: *Illa ætate, qua nulla virtutum feracior fuit, nemo erat, quo magis innixa res Romana, quàm in Papirio Cursore staret*, In that time (saith *Liuie*) than which none was more plentifull of vertues, there was no man on whome the Roman Commonweale resting staied, than vpon *Papirius Cursor*. This was the iudgement of the Romans, of the most flourishing time of their Commonweale: for neuer after was the militarie and domesticall discipline, the lawes and ordinances better executed, faith better kept, religion more sincerely embraced, nor vices more seuerely punished: So that it ought not to seeme straunge, if there was neuer than then greater store of most valiant and worthy men. *When the flourishing estate of a commonweale is.* *The florishing estate of the Romaine commonweale to haue bene in the time of Papirius Cursor*

Now if any man shal obiect and say, That the Romans were then but poore, as not yet got out of Italie, neither hauing as yet extended their armes into Grecia, Asia, and Afrike, no not hauing as then so much as subdued Italie, neither that the Capitoll did as then glister with guilded vaults, but was couered with shards: I say againe, That vertue is not to be measured by the foot of wealth and riches; neither the excellencie and perfection of a Commonweale, by the largenesse of the bounds thereof, but by the bounds of vertue it selfe. So that I deeme those their vntrimmed and rough shades and groues, to haue had in them more maiestie and honor, than had afterwards their plea- *The excellencie and perfection of a commonweale how it is to be deemed.*

412　　　　　　　　THE FOVRTH BOOKE

sant greene woods, with the trees most artificially planted in order of the curious Quincunx, and reckon Rome homely and vntrimmed, more stately and replenished with maiestie, than when it was neuer so well deckt, and with precious ointments perfumed. For neuer was the power of the Romans greater than in the time of *Traian* the emperour, who ioyned vnto the Roman empire, not onely Arabia Felix, but many other great prouinces also beyond the riuer Euphrates, and with incredible workmanship hauing built a bridge ouer the Danubie, (the remainders whereof are yet to bee seene) subdued *Decebald*, with the kingdom of Dacia, & with the Roman legions danted the most cruell and barbarous nations that then liued; when as the citie of Rome it selfe, being head of the whole empire, did so abound and flow with ambition, couetousnesse, pleasures and delights, as that it seemed to retaine no more but the shadow of the auntient vertue thereof. Neither was the Lacedemonian Commonweale then most flourishing, when as it had by force of armes subdued all Grecia, with some parts of Asia also: for now they contrarie vnto the lawes, had giuen way for gold and siluer to enter into the citie, now the discipline of *Lycurgus* seemed to haue beene almost extinct, and so indeed not long after that same Commonweale came headlong tumbling downe. And thus much concerning the differences of the changes of Commonweales, which it is needfull for vs to note, the better to conceiue such conuersions and changes of estates, which none haue touched heretofore.

The Romaine commonweale at the highest in the time of Traian the emperor, and yet not then in the greatest perfection.

Now as for the causes of the chaunges of Commonweales, although they bee right many, and hard to be all reckoned, yet so it is that they may bee brought into some certaine number, which may suffice for our instruction. The most common cause of the chaunge of Commonweales is, that when the posteritie of princes failing, the great men fall out among themselues, and so take vp armes for the gouernment of the state: or for the too great pouertie of the greater part of the subiects, and the excessiue riches of some few: or for the vnequall diuision of estates and honours, or for ambition and the great desire some haue to commaund, or for the reuenge of iniuries, or for the crueltie and oppression of Tyrants, or for the feare that some haue to bee punished for their deserts, or for the chaunging of lawes or of religion, or for the desire of some at full to enioy their pleasures, or for the casting out of them which with their excessiue and beastly pleasures pollute and defile the place of maiestie and honour. All which causes wee will particularly entreate of, and as need shall bee, manifest the same with examples.

The causes of the changes of commonweales.

Wee haue now here before declared, That Commonweales had their beginning by violent tyrannies: whereof some haue afterwards continued in the state of Lordlike Monarchies, and othersome in Royall Monarchies by right of succession: vnto whome diuers chaunges haue also happened for the causes by vs before touched. And that it is so, all the Histories, both sacred and prophane agree, That the first soueraigntie and forme of a Commonweale had beginning by the Monarchie of the Assyrians, and that the first prince called *Nimroth* (which is to say a *Bitter Ruler*) whome the Histories for the most part call *Ninus*, by force and tyranny made himselfe a soueraigne prince; and that after him his successours continued that Lordlike Monarchie, taking vnto themselues the whole and entire disposition of their subiects and their goods, vntill that *Arbaces* gouernour of the Medes, draue out *Sardanapalus*, which was the last king of the Assyrians, and made himselfe king, without any forme of fashion of election at all. The cause why, being for that *Sardanapalus* drowned in vaine pleasures and delights, was more amongst women than hee was amongst men: a thing which men of courage and valour take most impatiently, to see them-

The first monarchies to haue taken their beginnings from oppression and tyrannie.

F8–9 danted *i.e.* daunted, vanquished　　K6 forme or fashion　　Note at K1.

OF A COMMONWEALE.   413

A themselues subiect to such an one, as hath nothing of a man more than the figure onely. We see also, that the princes of the Medes descended from *Artabazus*, the kings of Persia, of Aegypt, of the Hebrews, the Macedonians, the Corinthians, the Sicionians, the Athenians, the Celtes, and Lacedemonians, are all come by right of succession vnto their kingdomes and principalities, for most part founded by force and violence; but afterward by iustice and good lawes polished, vntill that their posteritie failed (which oftentimes drew after it the chaunging of the estate) or that the princes abusing their power, and euill entreating their subiects, were themselues driuen out or slaine: and the subiects fearing againe to fall into a Tyrannicall gouernment, if they should giue the soueraigntie to one alone, or not willing to endure the commaund of one of their owne companions, founded amongst them the Aristocraticall estates, lit-
B tle regarding the common people: at which time if there were any of the poorer or popular sort, which would also haue had part in the seigneurie or gouernment, they sung vnto them the fables of the Hares, which would commaund together with the Lions: Or if it were that the Monarchie chaunged into a Popular estate, yet so it was neuerthelesse, that the nobilitie or richer sort still carried away all the great offices and places of state: as for example, *Solon* hauing founded the Popular estate in Athens, yet would not that the poore and common sort of the people should haue part in the estates. Neither the Romans hauing chased out their kings (albeit that they had established a Popular estate) yet so it was, that the honorable offices and preferments were
C still reserued vnto the nobilitie onely. Wee also read, that the first tyrants beeing driuen out, the men at armes and gentlemen were indeed alwaies chosen vnto the honourable places of estate, and the vulgar people still excluded: vntill that *Aristides* and *Pe-
ricles* in Athens, and *Canuleius* and the other Tribunes in Rome, first opened the gate of honourable offices and preferments vnto all the people in generall. But afterwards when as it was by long experience found out, That Monarchies were more sure, more profitable, and more durable also, than were the Popular estates, or Aristocraties; and amongst the Monarchies, them also which were founded in the succession of the next heires male: these successiue Monarchies were generally receiued almost throughout all the world, and the Popular and Aristocratike estates driuen out. Yea the people
D sometime fearing the death of their princes, without heires male, persuaded them whi-
lest they yet liue, to make choice of their successours: as diuers of the emperours of Rome did, and as they yet at this present time doe in many places of Affrike: or else the right of the election of the prince remaineth in the people, the prince beeing dead without heires: yea and in some places the people hauing power for the election of their prince, albeit that their princes haue heires male also: as in the kingdomes of Polonia, Bohemia, Hungarie, Denmarke, Sweden, and Norway, where they haue oft times thrust their kings out of their kingdomes, for staining the maiestie of their go-
uernment with tyrannie, licentious liuing, or cowardise. So sometimes also the peo-
ple hauing had a cruell tyrant, chose for him a iust and courteous prince: or hauing had
E an idle, an effeminat, or contemplatiue prince, make choyce of some valiant captaine: as did the Romans, who after the death of *Numa Pompilius* (to rule their religion to-
gether with their policie) made choice of *Tullus Hostilius*, a good captaine. Yea most commonly it chaunceth, that vnto the greatest and most cruell tyrants succeeded the most iust and vpright princes, as men ashamed to follow or imitat the doings of them whose ends they abhorre; or els vpon certaine conditions, hauing taken the soueraigntie vppon them, and so hauing their lesson by writing, haue also their power therein somewhat diminished. So after the vnfortunat end of *Marcus Antonius*, a man altoge-
ther giuen to riot and voluptuous pleasure, succeeded the great *Augustus*, a most wise &
Nn iij   sober

marginalia:
The beginning of Aristocraties.
The greatest honors and offices euen in Popular estates still bestowed vpon the nobilitie and richer sort of the people.
A monarchie of all estates most sure and durable.
Vnto most cruell tirants oftentimes succede most iust and vpright princes.

E2 Numa Pompilius (WHO DID NO OTHER THING BUT to rule (cf. Fr) administration, government   E3 policie *i.e. la police*, civil Notes at A1, A2, E3.

sober prince. So after the miserable death of *Nero* a most cruell tyrant, succeeded *Galba*, an emperor most gratious: So after the strange euent of the most drunken and licencious *Vitellus*, succeeded *Vespatian* the most continent: And vnto the monster of nature *Heliogabalus* slaine and drawne in the same faction that was *Vitellus*, succeeded *Alexander Seuerus* the most vertuous: a thing most strange, considering that he was his cosin germaine, and together with him nourished and brought vp: and that the power to commaund in soueraigntie hath this mischiefe in it, that often times it maketh of a good man, an euill; of an humble man a proud; of a mercifull man a tyrant; of a wise man a foole; and of a valiant man a coward. For what could be more notable then the first fiue yeares of *Nero* his raigne? what more excellent then his youth? or who for modestie was to be compared in the beginning to *Tiberius*? who so behaued himselfe (as saith *Suetonius*) as if he had almost beene a priuat man: and being of one called Lord, commaunded him, that he should no more by way of reproach so call him: and against slaunderous and infamous libels made of him, oft times said no more, but that in a free citie, men ought also to haue their tongues free: but speaking vnto the Senat: I haue had this good fortune (said he) to haue you for my gratious Masters, and so long as I liue I will acknowledge you for my good Lords: for a good prince (said he) must be the slaue not onely of the Senat, but also of all the citisens in generall, and often times of euery one of them in particular. Neither did he any thing in the beginning of his raigne, no not euen in the least things, without the aduise of the Senat; and yet afterwards hauing well tasted of the power of soueraigntie, hee became the most detestable tyrant that euer was for crueltie and voluptuous pleasures. So we read also that *Herod* the elder raigned six yeates as a good and iust king (as saith *Philo*) and one and thirtie yeares as a most cruell tyrant, who caused seauentie Senators of the the house of *Dauid* to be all slaine, which was indeed the whole bodie of the Senate except *Semneas*, and afterward put to death his wife a most noble gentlewoman, with three of his owne children: and now lying at the point of death, gaue commaundement to kill all the best and chiefe of the Nobilitie of the whole land, to the intent that great mourning might thereby be after his death. Which examples I haue amongst many other marked, whose beginnings were too faire to continue long: the reason whereof may well be, for that he which at the first seemeth to be so notable wise and worthie, must needs dissemble much: wherein *Tiberius* the emperour is said to haue excelled all others. Whereas of them which haue so curiously learned the art of false semblant and dissimulation, and haue their countenances at commaund, nothing that good is, true, or honest, is to be expected; but all things vaine, false, and fained, full of hipocrisie and craft: Whereas he which at the first discouereth his imperfections (albeit that he be not therein wise) yet can he not possibly be a man exceedingly mischieuous or naught: yea of such an one it is to be hoped, that he may at length proue an vpright and iust man: such an one as *Iohn* the French king is reputed to haue bene, who was of such a stomacke, as that he could by no meanes endure to looke aright vppon him whome he hated or liked not of: And yet for all that we read not of any thing by him either dishonourable or wickedly done. Neither ought it vnto any man to seeme straunge, if there haue bene but few princes for their vertues famous: for if euery where there be such a scarcitie of good and valiant men, and that kings are not chosen out of the number of such: and that they to whome their kingdomes come by succession, commonly haue their education polluted with so many vices, as that hard it is to say which of them is the greatest: it is almost a myracle if one of them shall bee able to get out of such a gulfe of all maner of vices. Yet if any such there shall be, as shall for his vertues become famous, he as a toarch vpon an high place or watch tower, filleth al
things

Princes natures much altered by soueraigntie.

The fairest beginnings of princes raignes proue not alwaies the best.

Why there be so fewe vertuous princes?

F1 cruell   F3, F4 Vitellius   F4 faction *i.e.* fashion, manner (*façon*)   18 naught *i.e.* wicked, vicious

things with the light and brightnesse of himselfe: neither is onely whilest he yet liueth highly commended: but being dead, leaueth vnto his children and posteritie also, the most fragrant and sweet smelles of his vertue and worth, who though they shall right wickedly liue, yet are they the rather borne with, for their fathers vertues sake. *Cambyses* did many most cruell and shamefull things, yet was hee alwaies both loued and honoured of his subiects, and redoubted of his enemies, and all for the great loue they bore vnto his father *Cyrus*, which was so well grauen in the harts of the people (as saith *Plutarch*) that they loued euen all such as had a great and rising nose, such an one as *Cyrus* had. And the emperour *Commodus*, albeit that he were a most cruell tyrant, and had in one day commaunded the great Prouost of Rome to kill all the beholders of the playes in the Theatre (which were not fewer than threescore thousand persons) for that they could not forbeare laughing, to see him in stead of an emperour, so cunningly to play the Fencer, as if he had bene one inded; yet was hee neuerthelesse of the people alwaies beloued, for the loue they bare vnto the remembrance of *Marcus Aurelius* his father.

Euil princes euen for their fathers vertues oftentimes of their subiects beloued.

Wherefore we see kingdomes which come by succession, seldome times to suffer chaunge or innouation, albeit that a wicked sonne succeed a good father: for that his kingdome is like vnto a great tree which hath taken as deepe root as it spreadeth branches: whereas he which commeth but newly vnto a kingdome commended nor strengthened with no vertue or power of his auncestours, is indeed like vnto an high tree: which for that it is not well rooted, is with the wind and tempest easily ouerthrowne. For which cause a tyrant the sonne of a tyrant, must needs raigne in great daunger, except he be with great wealth and the power of his neighbor princes strengthened, or by long discent of his auncestours haue obtained his kingdome. Neither can the vertues of a new prince deliuer his vngracious sonne from the conspiracies of his subiects: as it happened vnto *Hierome* a tyrant of Sicilie, who succeeded to *Hiero* his grandfather, a new prince in his kingdome, which he had by no right or claime gained, but was yet for his manifold and great vertues, of a priuat man, thought right worthy of that so great a kingdome, which hee so held almost sixtie yeares, without force or garrison, to the great contentment of all men; beloued not of his owne subiects onely, but of all his neighbour princes also, and especially of the people of Rome, to whome he was most deere: whose nephew, that he might seeme to excell his grandfather in magnificence and state, thought it better for the assurance of his estate, to strengthen himselfe with strong garrisons of men, and so afterwards wholly giuing himselfe ouer vnto riot and excesse bare himselfe proudly towards all men, and so drew all mens hatred vpon him: and as for the counsel, the most assured foundation of his grandfathers kingdome, he altogether set it at naught: & to heape vp his mishaps, without any cause why, renounced the amitie and alliance of the Romans. And so hauing lost both all the ornaments of his honour, and the stayes of his assurance, was by the conspiracie of his subiects himselfe with all his friends and kinsfolkes most miserably slaine, and his Monarchie forthwith chaunged into a Popular estate. The like end almost had *Dionysius* the younger, another king of the same countrey also, and sonne to *Dionysius* the elder, who by fraud inuaded the estate, which he of long time held with strong garrisons and fortresses, without the stay or alliance of any other forren prince: but he once dead, and this his sonne a man vnskilfull of the gouernment, and altogether giuen to riot, succeeding in his place, and banishing his vncle *Dion*, and confiscating his goods, he was by the same *Dion*, returning out of exile againe into his owne countrey, with an armie thrust out of his kingdome, and all the fortresses of his tyrannie ouerthrowne: which *Dion* not long after being also slaine, the Monarchie was againe chaunged into a

A new prince without great vertues hardly to maintaine his estate.

Popular

C 5 vertues D 4 afterwards

Popular estate. Whereby it is to be vnderstood, new princes without great vertues hardly to maintaine their estate: which although it be a thing right manifest, yet appeareth it more plainely by the example of *Herod* the elder, vpon whome *Cæsar* for the valour of *Antipater* his father, by a decree of the Senat bestowed the kingdome of the Iewes: who although he were in great fauour with *Marcus Antonius*, and *Octauianus Augustus*, yet for the better assurance of his kingdome, built most strong castles, and to gaine the good will of his subiects, bestowed great masses of money for reliefe of the poorer sort, and eased the people of a third part of their woonted tributes: but knowing how little he had for all that gained, he tooke also an oath of alleagiance of his subiects, seeking to gaine them of the better sort with extraordinarie fauours and good turnes: and yet for all that he could do, he was so hated of his subiects, that beeing become sickly, the people much reioyced thereat: which he perceiuing, it had almost driuen him into a phrensie. But he being dead, the Iewes sent fiftie ambassadors to Rome, that so eased of that regall gouernment, they might become subiects vnto the Romans, and so happily had obtained to haue bene, had not *Herod* his sonne bene then in great fauour with *Augustus* the emperour, vnto whome the elder *Herod* had before by his will left fifteene hundred talents of gold. Howbeit yet, that all the successours and posteritie of *Herod*, which were in number many, in lesse than threescore yeares, all in poore estate perished, as well for that he being but a new man, was not descended of royall race: as for that his prowesse and valour fayled in his successours.

That is nine hundred Thousand crownes.

But these conuersions and chaungings of kingdomes and Commonweales chance so much the rather, if the tyrant be too great an exactor too cruell, or too much giuen to his voluptuous and vnlawfull pleasures, or be delighted in all these together: as was *Nero*, *Tiberius* and *Caligula*: and yet of these, wantonnesse and whoredome hath ruinated moe princes than all the other causes: and so is it also much more daungerous vnto a prince for his estate than crueltie: for crueltie keepeth men in feare and awe, & bringeth a terrour vpon the subiects; whereas wantonnesse bringeth after it an hate and contempt also of the tyrant; forasmuch as euerie man deemeth the effeminat man to be also faint hearted, and farre vnworthie to commaund a whole people, which hath not power ouer himselfe. So we see that *Sardanapalus* king of Assyria, *Canades* king of Persia, *Dionysius* the younger, and *Hierosme*, kings of Sicilie, *Heliogabalus*, *Amyntas*, *Chideric*, *Periander*, *Pisistratus*, *Tarquin*, *Aristocrates* king of the Messenians, *Timocrates* king of Cyrene, *Andronicus* emperour of Constantinoble, *Rhoderike* king of Spaine, *Appius Claudius*, *Galeace Sfortia*, *Alexander Medices*, the Cardinall *Petruce* Tyrant of Sienne, *Lugrac* and *Megal*, kings of Scots, all for wantonnesse to haue lost their estates, and most of them slaine vpon the fact doing. Neither is it long since Delmendin and Delmedin, two of the greatest cities of Affrike, were by rebellion dismembred from the kingdome of Fez, and brought vnder the obeysance of the Portugals, for a maiden by force taken from her husband to whome she was betrothed, by the gouernour, who was therefore afterwards slaine: as was also *Ahusahid* king of Fez himselfe with his six children all massacred by a secretarie of his, for hauing abused his wife. Neither for any other cause did the people of Constantine (a sea towne in Affrike) chose rather to suffer the commaund of *Delcaid* a Christian renegat, than to obey the king of Tunes his sonne. And why in our time was *Muleasses* thrust out of his kingdome, and so lost his estate, but for intemperance? and yet neuerthelesse was so drowned in delights, as that returning out of Germanie, without hope that the emperour *Charles* the fift (in whom his greatest trust was) would afford him any aid, and banished as he was out of his kingdom, yet spent he an hundred crowns vpon the dressing of one peacock, as *Paulus Iouius* reporteth: and to the end he might better conceiue the pleasure of musick, stil couered

Couetousnesse, crueltie, and the voluptuousliues of princes, oftentimes the causes of the change or ruine of their estates.

Voluptuousnesse more daungerous vnto a prince than crueltie.

red his eyes, as hauing learned a double pleasure, not to bee so well perceiued by two sences at once: yet such was the iudgement of God vppon him, as that by the commaundement of his sonnes he had his eyes put out with an hot barre of Iron, by little and little drying vp the humors of them, and depriued of his kingdome also.

But for the crueltie of a prince, the estate easily chaungeth not if he be not more cruell than the wild beasts themselues, such as were *Phaleris, Alexander Phereus, Nero, Vitellius, Domitian, Commodus, Caracalla, Maximinus, Ecelinus* of Padua, and *Iohn Maria* of Millan, who were all slaine, or driuen out of their dominions, and their Tyrannical estates for the most part chaunged into estates Popular. Which befell them not so much for the crueltie by them vsed against the common sort of people (wherof no reckoning nor account is made in a Tyrannicall estate) as for crueltie committed in the person of the great and best friended, who are alwayes of tyrants to bee feared: vnto whome euen contumely and disgrace is oftentimes more grieuous than crueltie it self: wherof we haue a domesticall example of that *Bodile*, who for that he was by the commaundement of *Childeric* king of Fraunce whipped, slew not onely the king, but the queene also, being then great with child. So was also the emperour *Iustinus* the third slaine by *Atelia* generall of his armie, whose sonne he had slaine, and in despight prostituted his wife vnto his seruants. And *Archelaus* king of Macedon, was likewise slaine by him whome he had put into the hands of *Euripides* the poet, to be whipt: as was his nephew also king of Macedon, slaine by him whome hee had without punishment suffered to be abused against nature by *Antipater*, and scorned him crauing of him reuenge.

Extreme crueltie oftentimes cause of the change of the princes estate

The Aristocratike estate also of them of Mitylen, was chaunged into a Popular, for that it chaunced certaine gentlemen as they went along the streets with their bastanadoes, in sport to strike all such of the common people as they met: Whereupon one *Megacles* tooke occasion to stirre vp the comminaltie to fall vpon the nobilitie, and so to kill them. And not to seeke for examples farther, *Henry*, of late king of Sweden (but now a prisoner) was also thrust out of his kingdome, for that he not onely disdainfully reiected the request of a certaine gentleman his subiect, but also with his owne hand most cruelly stabbed him with his dagger wherwith the nobilitie and people moued, tooke him prisoner, and enforcing him to resigne his kingdome, gaue it to his younger brother, who now raigneth. And almost alwaies the tyrants-quellers haue receiued either the estate or goods of the tyrants by them slaine, or the greatest honours and preferments in the state, as rewards due to their deserts. So both the one and the other *Brutus*, obtained the greatest estates in Rome; the one of them for hauing driuen out the proud king *Tarquin*, and the other for hauing slayne *Cæsar*. And *Arbaces* gouernour of the Medes hauing brought *Sardanapalus* king of Assyria to such extremitie, as that he was glad to burne himselfe aliue together with his concubines and treasures, for reward enioyed his kingdome. So *Lewes* of Gonzaga hauing slaine *Bonacolse*, tyrant of Mantua, was by the subiects chosen their prince, his posteritie euer since by the space of about two hundred and fiftie yeares hauing enioyed that estate. And the Venetians hauing slaine the tyrant *Eceline*, obtained the seigneurie of Padua.

Rewards still giuen vnto the killers of tyrants

Some others there be, which seeke the tyrants death, and so the chaunge of the estate, hauing nothing before their eyes but the desire of reuenge, and that without either the feare of God, the regard of their countrey, or loue of their neerest and deerest friends: as he which to be reuenged of king *Roderike*, who had rauished his wife, drew the Mahometan Moores into Spaine, who draue out the king, and there vsing an hundred thousand cruelties, possessed the kingdome of Spayne, which they held by the space of seuen hundred yeares after. And some others there bee also, who neither for hope

Some for desire of reuenge, and some for the desire of honor and the deliuerance of their countrie, to haue procured the tyrants death and so the changing of the estate.

hope of bearing of rule, of preferment, or of wealth: neither for reuenge of wrongs, nor for any other priuat iniuries receiued, are yet induced to the killing of a tyrant, without hope to be able by any means to escape therefore a most sharpe and cruell death, respecting onely the deliuerance of their countrey, and the honour of the fact: such as were *Harmodius*, and *Aristogiton* in Athens, and those which slew *Domitian* and *Caligula* the cruell emperours. A thing which most commonly happeneth in the Popular estates, wherein the new tyrants by force or fraud hauing oppressed the libertie of the people, are neuer assured of themselues, or of their estate, without great and strong garrisons about them. So we see *Alexander Medices*, nephew to pope *Clement* the seuenth, & sonne in law to the emperour *Charles* the fift, by whose forces and power hee obtained the soueraigntie of Florence, and draue out them also that were of greatest power and courage in the state, to haue compassed himselfe with great and strong garrisons, and alwaies to haue gone armed, in such sort as that it seemed almost impossible to find the meanes to come neere him, and yet for all that to haue bene slaine by the conspiracie of *Laurence Medices*, not onely his neere kinsman, but his most familiar and domesticall friend also: when as the said *Laurence* had promised to prostitute vnto him his owne sister; that so he might the better deliuer the man disarmed (euen as he was kissing and embrasing his sister, whome he thought to haue rauished) to the murtherer to be slaine: which was so couertly done as that the souldiours of his guard, whome he kept for the saftie of his person, making merrie in a dining chamber fast by, perceiued nothing of the murther of their prince. And yet in so doing, the said *Laurence* neither deliuered his countrey from tyrannny (whereinto it by and by after againe fell) neither himselfe from daunger, being at length by a murtherous fellow himselfe also slaine at Venice. And *Cosmus Medices*, who after the death of *Alexander*, by the helpe of the garrison souldiours, the supportation of his friends, and fauor of the pope, obtained the same gouernment; albeit that he was reported to haue bene one of the wisest princes of his age, or of long time before him, and a right great justicier, euen by the report of his enemies themselues, and had diuers strong castles euen in the citie it selfe: yet neuerthelesse was he an hundred times in daunger of his person, by the conspiracies of his subiects against him, being not able to endure a maister ouer them, albeit that hee were both iust and vertuous. And he which now raigneth, not long since missed not much to haue bene slaine by the conspiracie of *Puccinus*, neither can bee safe without a strong garrison, so long as the citisens his subiects shall either remember or hope for the rewards of their valour and libertie. And for this cause *Dionysius* the elder of Syracusa, being chosen generall, and hauing made himselfe maister of all, and chaunged the Popular estate into a Monarchie, had alwaies forty thousand souldiors in readinesse at his call to set forward, beside a great garrison still attendant about his person, and diuers strong holds, onely to keepe the people of Syracusa with a part of Sicilia in subiection. And yet neuerthelesse was he no tyrant, as we call a tyrant, that is to say, a cruell, vitious, and naughtie man: neither was he euer amorous of other mens wiues, but to the contrarie sharply reproued his sonne (as saith *Plutarch*) for hauing taken away one of his subiects daughters, saying, That he should neuer haue one to succeed him in his estate, if he vsed such fashions: as indeed it fell out with him, being shortly after his death chased out of his kingdome.

Force and feare, things necessarie for a new prince, for the maintenance of his estate.

Now if any man shall obiect and say vnto mee, That force and feare are two euill masters for the maintaining of an estate: true it is, and yet needfull for a new prince to vse, who by force changeth a Popular estate into a Monarchie, a thing altogether contrarie vnto a Monarchy Royall; which the lesse guard it hath, the surer it is: & therefore the wise king *Numa* put from him the three hundred archers which *Romulus* his prede-

predecessour had taken vnto him for his guard, saying, That hee would not distrust a people which had willingly and of themselues put their trust in him: neither yet commaund ouer them which should distrust him. But *Seruius* hauing of a slaue made himselfe a king, beset himselfe with strong guards, and that wisely, as beeing forsaken of the Senators, who tooke his seruile gouernment in great euill part: For as iust pleasing, & gracious, as he was, yet had it bene a thing impossible for him withourguards, garrisons, and fortresses, long to haue maintained himselfe and his so new an estate, but that he should haue fallen into the hands of his enemies. There was neuer a more gratious, magnificent, noble, couragious, or courteous prince then *Cæsar*; and yet notwithstanding, all these his great vertues were not able to preserue him, but that he was by his sonne *Brutus* and other the conspirators with incredible consent and fidelitie combyned against him, in the middest of the Senat most cruelly slaine: who being before warned to take vnto him a guard for the safetie of his person, frankly answered, that he had rather to die once for all, than still to languish in feare: wherein he did not wisely so to refuse a guard, hauing pardoned his greatest enemies (whom he suffered still to liue) and desiring to chaunge into a Monarchie the free estate of the most warlike people that euer was in the world. Which his course *Augustus* his successour followed not, but first caused to be put to death all the conspiratours against *Cæsar*, (not so much in reuenge of the death of his vncle *Cæsar*, as he pretended, as so to prouide for his owne safetie) after that hee still guarded with a strong guard about him, easely kept himselfe from the violence of his enemies: And albeit that hauing quite discomfited and ouerthrowne *Sextus Pompeius*, and *Lepidus*, and ouercome *Marcus Anthonius* in battell at Actium, (who afterwards also slew himselfe) and the other citisens of greatest force and courage, either in battell slaine or otherwise taken out of the way; he might haue seemed to haue beene able to haue raigned in great securitie: yet neuerthelesse hee dispersed fortie legions into the prouinces, placed three legions in Italie, and that not farre from the citie, kept a strong guard about him for the safetie of his person: forbid the Senators without leaue to depart out of Italie, and committed the gouernment of his legions not vnto any the great Lords, but to gentlemen onely, or some of the meanest of the nobilitie. As for the creating of the officers of the citie, he diuided it betwixt himselfe and the people; yet so as that of such as stood for them, he would bring some of them by the hand vnto the people, and so recommending vnto their choice them whom he wished to haue preferred vnto the offices and honors: he tooke from the people their free choice, and had the magistrats still beholden and bound vnto him. Iustice he daily administred, without intermission, receiuing and answering euery mans request, hauing alwaies before him the records of the publike reuenues of his forces, and of the prouinces, so that he alone seemed to discharge all the dueties of all the officers. Whereby it euidently appeareth him to haue beene a sole Monarque, and soueraigne Prince, whatsoeuer faire title of a Tribune of the people, or of a Prince, was by one or other giuen vnto him. That is also reported to haue beene of him verie popularly done, in that he commaunded debts due to the Commonweale, which were growne by the ciuill warres, and the records of the debters to be torne and burnt. And yet this so mightie a Prince, endued with so great vertue & wisedome hardly escaped the hands of the wicked conspirators against him, albeit that the most desperat and daungerous sort of them were now long before dead. But after that the subiects hauing by little and little made proofe of his iustice and wisedome, tasted of the sweetnes of long peace and assured tranquillitie, in steed of cruell and bloodie ciuill warres,, and that they had to doe, rather with a father than with a lord (as saith *Seneca*) and so began to loue and reuerence him: he againe on his part

The notable wisdome of Augustus in his gouernment, for the establishing of his estate.

discharged his guard, going as a priuat man sometimes with one man, and sometimes with an other without any other companie; and so laide the foundation of that great Monarchie, with the most happie successe that euer Prince did.

How Aristocraties or Popular estates are changed into Monarchies.

Now all Monarchies newly established by the change of an Aristocratie, or Popular estate, haue as it were taken their beginning, after that some one of the magistrats, captaines, or gouernours, hauing the power of the state in his hand, hath of a companion made himselfe Lord and soueraigne, or else that some straunger hath subdued them, or that those states haue willingly submitted themselues vnto the lawes & commandements of some other man. As for the first point, and the most ordinarie change of these estates we haue examples enowe. For so *Pisistratus*, when he had got the chiefe office in the common weale, inuaded the libertie of the people: as did also *Cypselus* at Corinth, *Thrasybulus*, *Gelo*, *Dionysius*, *Hiero*, *Agathocles* at Syracusa, *Panætius*, and *Icetes* at Leonce, *Phalaris* at Agrigentum, *Phidon* at Argos, *Periander* at Ambrace, *Archelaus* in Candie, *Euagoras* in Cyprus, *Polycrates* in Samos, *Anaxilaus* at Rhegium, *Nicocles* at Sicyon, *Alexander* at Pheree, *Mamercus* at Catana, the Decemuiri at Rome, and there after them *Sylla* and *Cæsar* : the *Scaligers* at Verona, the *Bentinoli* at Bolonia, the *Manfreds* at Fauentia, the *Malatestes* at Ariminum, the *Baleones* at Perusium, the *Vitelles* at Tifernas, the *Sforces* at Millan, and diuers others of like sort, who of gouernors of cities and armies haue taken vpon them the soueraigntie.

Master of the forces, Master of the Estate.

For in matters of estate it may be holden for an vndoubted maxime, that he is master of the estate, which is master of the forces. Wherefore in well ordered Aristocratique and popular Commonweales, the greatest honours are graunted without power of commaund, and the greatest powers to commaund are not graunted without a companion therein : or if it be dangerous to diuide the power of commaund to many, as in matters of warre it is ; then the power so graunted vnto the magistrat or Generall ought to be but short.

Orders necessary for the maintenance of Aristocratique and popular commonweale.

And therefore the Romans made chiefe commaunders their two Consuls: and the Carthaginensians their two Suffets, who euery other day commaunded by turnes : For albeit that the dissention which is commonly betwixt them which are in power equall, is sometimes an hinderance for the execution of good and profitable things : yet so it is that such a commonweale so gouerned is not so subiect to be turned into a Monarchie, as it were if it had but one chiefe and soueraigne magistrat : as the great *Archon* at Athens, the *Prytani* with the Rhodians, the yearely *Generall* with the Achæans and the Ætolians, and the *Duke* at Genes. And for the same cause the Dictatorship in Rome continued no longer then the charge required, which neuer passed six monethes at the longest ; yea and sometime lasted but one day ; which time expired, the power to commaund ceased : and if so be that the Dictator did for any longer time retaine his forces, he might therefore be accused of treason. And in Thebes, so long as it was a Popular estate, the law was that the Generall of the armie should be put to death, if he retained the forces aboue a day after the appointed time : which was the cause that the great capitaines *Epaminondas* and *Pelopidas* were condemned to death, for hauing retained their forces foure monethes after the time, howbeit that they were by necessitie constrayned so to doe, neither could without the great danger of the State haue otherwise done. And so for the same reason almost all the Magistracies are annuall, in Aristocratique and Popular Commonweales. Howbeit that in Venice the six Councelours for the estate which are assistant vnto the Duke, continue but two monethes in their charge : and he that had the keeping of the principall fortresse of Athens, had the keyes thereof but for one day onely: no more then hath the captaine of the castle of Rhaguse, who chosen by lot, hath the charge but for a day, and is led into the castle hoodwinkt. It behoueth also in popular

lar & Aristocraticall Commonweales so much as possible is, to beware that the lawes and ordinances concerning the Magistrats time be not changed, neither their charge prorogued, if the necessity be not verie great: as the Romans did to *Camillus*, to whom the Dictatorship was prorogued for six monthes, which had neuer to any other person beene graunted. And namely by the law Sempronia it was straitly forbidden that the gouernments of Prouinces should be graunted vnto any for longer time than fiue yeares, which law had it beene kept, *Cæsar* had neuer inuaded the estate as he did hauing the gouernment of the Gaules by the consent of *Pompeius* and *Crassus* graunted for fiue yeares more than the law allowed of: whereunto in that point was derogated in fauour of him. Which was a notable ouersight, considering that they had to doe with the most ambitious man that euer was; who so well grounded his power to continue, that he gaue at one time vnto *Paulus* the Consull nine hundred thousand crownes, to the intent that he should not oppose himselfe against his enterpises; and vnto the Tribune *Curio*, fifteene hundred thousand crownes to take his part. The people of Rome moreouer allowing him pay for ten legions of souldiers so long as the warres in Fraunce should last. Which so great a power was ioyned with the hardiest hart that then liued, and the most valiant that euer was, and discended of so noble an house, as that in an oration vnto the people he doubted not to say, That by the fathers side he was discended from the gods; and by the mothers side from kings; and yet withall so modest, as that his great enemie *Cato* said, That there was neuer so modest a tyrant as he, and withall so vigilant: as that *Cicero* an other great enemie of his, (who conspired his death) calleth him in one of his Epistles, The monster of wisdome & incredible diligence: and moreouer so magnificall and popular as euer any was, sparing for no cost for the setting forth of playes, iusts, tournies, feastes, largesses, & other publike delights. In which doing he vpon the publike charge woone the harts of the common people, and gained the honour of a most gratious and charitable man towards the poore. And yet for all that hauing by this meanes gained the soueraigntie, he sought for nothing more than by all meanes to clip and cut off the wealth & power of the people, and to take from them their priuileges: for of three hundred and twentie thousand citisens which still liued of the publique corne which they receiued, he retained but an hundred and fiftie thousand, and sent fourescore thousand ouer the sea into diuers Colonies a farre off: and beside that tooke away most part of their fraternities, corporations, and colleges. In briefe it hath alwaies beene seene in all changes of Aristocratique and popular Commonweales, them to haue beene still ruinated, which haue at any time giuen too much power vnto the subiects whereby to exalt themselues: Which thing *Iulian* the Apostata ment by that his embleame or deuise of an Eagle shot thorow with arrowes fethered with his owne feathers, being before pluckt from her. For so do the soueraigne gouernors and magistrats of those estates, especially when too great power is giuen to him which is of too ambitious and hautie a mind. And thus much concerning the chaunge of a Popular or Aristocraticall estate into a Monarchie, wherein one of the subiects maketh himselfe Lord thereof.

To chaunge the lawes and ordinances concerning the magistrats time, or to prorogue his charge, a thing most dangerous in an Aristocratique or Popular Commonweale.

Wonderfull bribes giuen by Cæsar in aspiring to the estate.

Aristocratique and Popular Commonweals still ruinated by the subiects, hauing too much power committed vnto them.

But the chaunge of a Popular estate into an Aristocratie chanceth commonly vpon the losse of some great battell, or other notable detriment of the state, receiued from the enemies: as to the contrarie the Popular power then most encreaseth when it returneth from the warres with some great victorie ouer their enemies. Of which manner of chaunges as there are many examples, so is there none more fit than those of the Athenians and Syracusians, two Commonweales of the selfe same time: when as the Athenians by the default of *Niceas* their generall, vanquished by the Syracusians and so discomfited, forthwith chaunged their Popular estate into an Aristocratie of foure hundred

The mutuall chaunge of a popular estate into an Aristocratie, and of an Aristocratie into a Popular estate.

A3, A4 prorogued *i.e.* prolonged, extended   B3 enterprises

hundred men, who yet bare themselues for fiue thousand by the deceit of *Pisander* : so that the people complayning themselues to be so spoiled of the soueraigntie, and comming to giue voice in the councell, was thence repulsed & driuen backe by the forces which the foure hundred had in their power, wherwith they slew diuers of the people and discouraged the rest: at which verie time the Syracusians proud of their victorie (to the contrarie) chaunged their Aristocratie into a Popular estate. And within a while after the Athenians hauing heard news of the great victorie of *Alcibiades* against the Lacedemonians, tooke vp armes against the foure hundred of the nobilitie, whom they by the leading of *Thrasybulus* thrust out or slew, and so againe chaunged the Aristocratie into a Popular estate. And in like manner the Thebans ouercome by the Enophites, chaunged their Popular estate into an Aristocratie. And albeit that the Romans hauing lost two great battels vnto *Pirrhus* changed not their popular estate, yet so it was that indeed it was then a faire Aristocratie of three hundred Senators which gouerned the estate, and but in appearance and show a Democratie, or a Popular estate, the people being neuer than then more calme and tractable. But so soone as the Romans had gained the estate of Tarentum, the people forthwith began to set vp their hornes, demaunding to haue part in the lands which the nobilitie had of long time possessed. And yet neuerthelesse afterwards, when as *Hannibal* had brought the Roman estate into great extremitie, the people became as humble as was possible: but after that the Carthaginensians were ouercome, king *Perseus* ouerthrowne, *Antiochus* put to flight, the kingdome of Macedonia and Asia subuerted; then immediatly againe followed the sturres for the diuision of lands, and the turbulent seditions of the *Gracchies*, wherewith the Tribunes armed the people in most insolent manner, insulting vpon the nobilitie. In like manner the Florentines ouerthrew their Oligarchie, established by Pope *Clement* the seuenth, restoring the people againe vnto their wonted libertie: for so soone as newes was brought vnto Florence, That Rome was by the imperials sackt, and the Pope with the rest of the Cardinals and Bishops besieged; it is not to be beleeued, with what pride the headstrong people began to rage against them of the house of *Medices*; with what furie they cast downe their statues, defaced their armes, and reuersed all their decrees and lawes. The Popular estates of the Swissers indeed first tooke their beginning from the pride and insolencie of the gouernours of those places, but yet had their greatest encreasings after the victorie of Sempach, about the yeare 1377, at which time the nobilitie being with a great slaughter ouerthrowne by the rural people, there was no more talking of Aristocraties, nor of acknowledging of the soueraigntie of the empire ouer them, in what sort soeuer. But the chiefe cause of these conuersions and chaunges of these estates, is the rash vnstaidnesse and vnconstancie of the people, without discourse or iudgement moued with euerie wind; which as it is with a little losse discouraged, so is it also after any victorie intollerable; neither hath it any more deadly or dangerous enemie, than too much felicitie and prosperous successe of the affaires thereof; nor a wiser maister than aduersitie and distresse, wherewith it daunted and discouraged, learneth to rest vpon the councell of the wiser sort, leauing the helme of the estate for them to gouerne, which they themselues in such tempestuous times know not how to hold. Whereby it is to bee perceiued, nothing to be more profitable for the preseruation of a Popular estate, than to haue warres, and to make enemies for it if otherwise it haue none. Which was the principall reason that moued *Scipio* the yonger so much as in him lay, to hinder the rasing of the famous citie of Carthage, wisely foreseeing, that the people of Rome being altogether martiall and warlike, if it had no enemies abroad would at length be enforced to make war vpon it selfe. For which cause also *Onomadesme* generall of the Commonweale of Chio,

Nothing more profitable for the preseruation of a Popular estate than warres.

F9 *For* Thrasybulus (Fr 6–8) *read* Thrasylus (Fr 1–5 and L). Note at F10.

Chio, hauing appeased the ciuill warres, and driuen out the most mutinous, would by no meanes banish the the rest, albeit that he was earnestly perswaded so to doe, saying That so it would be daungerous, least (that hauing cast out all the enemies) they should fall together by the eares with their friends. Howbeit that this reason which hath place for the straunge and forren enemies, is not yet to bee receiued for the maintaining of enemies at home amongst the citisens themselues: and yet in this case hee did but that which best beseemed him, and was also most expedient. For he that will haue the vpper hand in ciuill warre, if he shall banish all them that take part with the faction contrarie to his owne, he shall then haue no hostages at all left, if the banished shall prepare new warres against him: but hauing slaine the most outragious and daungerous, and banished the most mutinous, he ought still to retaine the remnant; for otherwise hee is to feare least all the exiled together, making warre vppon him, without feare of their friends at home, should so by force ouerthrow their enemies, and chaunge the Popular estate into an Aristocratie. As it happened vnto the Heracleans, the Cumans, and the Megarenses, who were chaunged from Popular estates into Aristocraties, for that the people had wholly driuen out the nobilitie, who with their friends combining their forces, and possessed of these three commonweales, ouerthrew therein the Popular estates, and againe established Aristocraties.

Yet amongst other conuersions and chaunges of Commonweales, the chaunge of a Popular estate into a Monarchy oftenest happeneth; and that either by ciuill warres, or through the ignorance of the people, hauing giuen too much power to some one of the subiects, as we haue before said. For *Cicero* speaking of the ciuill warres betwixt *Cæsar* and *Pompey*, saith, *Ex victoria cum multa, tum certe Tyrannis existit*, Of victorie ensue many things, but especially a Tyrannicall gouernment. For that almost alwaies in ciuill warres the people is diuided: wherein if it so fall out, that the leaders of the factions bring the matter vnto the tryall of a battaile, no man can doubt but that hee who therein shall carrie away the victorie, possessed of the forces and powers, shall either for ambition and the desire of honour, or for the saftie of his person, keepe vnto himself the soueraigntie. Whereas contrariwise Tyrannicall gouernments (for the most part) chaunge into Popular estates. For that the people which neuer knoweth how to keep a meane, the Tyrannicall gouernment once taken away, desiring to communicat the soueraigntie vnto them all, for the hatred that it beareth against Tyrants, and the feare that it hath to fall againe into tyranny, becommeth so furious and passionat, as without reason or discretion to fall vpon all the kinsmen and friends of the tyrant, and not to leaue one of them aliue: whereof for the most part ensueth the slaughter, exile, & proscription of the nobilitie; in which case euerie man of valour, courage, and worth, chuseth rather to shunne the furie of the most headstrong people, as the raging of a wild beast, rather than to beare rule ouer it. As it happened at Athens, after that *Pisistratus* was slaine; at Rome, after *Tarquin* the proud was driuen out: at Syracusa, after *Hiero* slaine, and againe after that *Dionysius* was banished: at Florence, after that the duke of Athens (who afterwards died Generall in the expedition of Poitiers) was driuen out: at Milan, after that *Galuagno* the tyrant had there lost his estate, where the people of Milan for fiftie yeares after, held a Popular estate, vntill that at last it was againe changed into a Tyrannicall gouernment by the Torefans. Neither did the Swissars otherwise establish that their Popular estate (which by the space of 260 yeares hath continued euen vnto this day) but by killing of the tyrannicall deputies of the empire, tyrannizing ouer them. The like we see to haue happened in Thessalie, after that *Alexander* the tyrant of the Phereans was slaine: and in Sienna, after that *Alexander Dichi* the new tyrant, was by the conspiracie of *Hierome Seuerin* slaine, and his partakers of the nobilitie

marginalia: Popular estates most commonly to chaunge into Monarchies.

marginalia: Tyrannicall gouernments most commonly to chaunge into popular estates.

D9 *For* Hiero *read* Hieronymus.   E1 expedition *i.e. journee*, battle (repeated several times in this sense)   E5 260 yeares (Fr 3–8) 350 years (Fr 1–2). Cf. note at 424 K6.   Note at D8.

nobilitie *De Monte Nouo* cast out, slaine, and banished, the people forthwith tooke vpon it the soueraigntie. Neither is it to be doubted, but that the Florentines, after the death of *Alexander Medices* the new tyrant, would haue taken the gouernment from them of the house of *Medices*, and reestablished their Popular estate, if they had certainly knowne the tyrant to haue beene slaine: but when as almost onely *Laurence Medices* with *Caracciolus* the murtherer were priuie to the murther (supposed to bee not onely the tyrants familiar and domesticall acquaintance, but his most inward friend also) no man could by him be persuaded, that he had slaine the tyrant: but so by present flight making shift for himselfe, gaue opportunitie to young *Cosmus Medices* his cosen (who then had the forces of the estate in his power) to take vppon them the soueraigntie. But this conuersion or chaunge of Tyrannicall gouernments into Democraties, or of Democraties into Tyrannicall gouernments, most commonly happeneth, as we haue said, by occasion of ciuill warres: for if a strange enemie become lord of any Popular estate, he commonly ioyneth it vnto his owne: which is not then to be called a change, but a destruction of that Commonweal, so vnited vnto the victors; except the victor (which seldome times happeneth) restore vnto the vanquished their libertie and gouernment: as the Lacedemonians chose rather that the confederat cities of the Athenians, by them ouerthrowne in the Peloponesian warre, yea and that euen the citie of Athens it selfe also, should enioy their wonted libertie, than to be ioyned vnto the Lacedemonian estate: howbeit yet that the Lacedemonians in euerie place established Aristocraties for Popular estates, quite contrarie vnto the manner and fashion of the Athenians, who in all places went about to ouerthrow Aristocraties, and to establish Democraties or Popular estates. So that it differeth much, whether the conuersions or chaunges of Commonweales proceed from a forren and straunge enemie, or else from the citisens themselues.

The fickelnesse of the people oftentimes cause of the change of the estate.

Sometime also the people are so fickle and fantasticall, as that it is almost a thing impossible for them to hold any one estate, which it is not by and by againe wearie of: as we may say of the auntient Athenians, Samians, Syracusans, Florentines, and Genowayes; who after they had changed from one estate or forme of gouernment, would by and by haue another. Which phantasticall disease most commonly chanceth vnto such Popular estates, as wherein the subiects be too wise and of too subtill spirits, as were those whome we haue before spoken of: For amongst them euerie man thinketh himselfe worthy to be a commaunder, whereas where the subiects be more grosser witted, they the more easily endure to be by others ruled, and more easily yeeld vnto other mens aduises, than doe they whome you must with the multitude of arguments and subtiltie of wit conuince, before you shall persuade them vnto any thing: so subtillising their reasons, as that oftentimes they vanish euen into smoke; whereof ariseth an obstinacie of conceit, alwaies enemie vnto wise councels, with diuers changes of Commonweales. As a man may easily see in *Thucidides*, *Xenophon*, and *Plutarch*, the Athenians lesse than in an hundred yeares, six times to haue chaunged their estate; and since them the Florentines seuen times: which so happened not neither vnto the Venetians, nor Swissers, men not of so sharpe a wit. For who knoweth not the Florentines to be most sharpe witted men? but the Swissers to haue alwaies bene men of a more dull spirit? And yet when as they both almost at the same time, chaunged their Monarchie into a Popular estate, the Swissers haue therein so maintained themselues now almost three hundred yeres: wheras the Florentines not long after changed their estate into an Aristocratie; they which in nobilitie and wealth exceed the rest, altogether disdaining to be made equall with the common sort of the people. But the nobilitie hauing so got the soueraigntie, began also to striue amongst themselues for the

The fickle and turbulent estate of the Florentines.

the principalitie: and with mutuall hatred and proscriptions so weakned themselues and their estate, as that they were by the people taking vp armes against them easily ouerthrowne and put to flight. But the nobilitie (and so the Aristocraticall estate) thus ouerthrowne, the popular sort, and they of them especially which were called the Grandes (or great ones) began to striue and contend among themselues, for the gouernment of the state: and yet these much more cruelly than had before the nobilitie; for that they contended not by forme of iustice, or of law, but by verie force of armes, and dint of sword; who hauing with mutuall slaughters spent themselues, the middle sort of the people (for they were diuided into three sorts) began to take vpon them the mannaging of the estate: but these also falling together by the eares for places of honour and commaund, the verie basest and refuse of the rascal people, became too strong for them, filling all places with the blood and slaughter of them, vntill they had driuen out and slaine the most part of them. Now these also of the baser sort become masters of the estate, and hauing no moe enemies left with whome to striue, began at length to struggle with it selfe, and made such cruell warre vpon it selfe, that the blood ran down the streets, yea & that most part of the houses were with fire quite consumed, vntill that they of Luca moued with their great miseries and distresse, comming in great companies to Florence, exhorted them their neighbours to lay downe armes, and to seeke for peace: by whose good speeches they persuaded at last, ceased from their slaughters & butchering of one another. Whereupon to end the matter, they sent ambassadours vnto the pope, to send them some one descended of royall blood, to rule and raigne ouer them: where by good fortune there was then at Rome *Charles* of Fraunce brother to king *Lewes* the ninth, who at the request of the pope, and of the Florentines themselues, came to Florence, and with the good liking of the people in generall, tooke vpon him the gouernment, ended their quarrels, and reconciled the citisens among themselues, together with the Commonweale: and so hauing appeased the citisens, and reformed the Commonweale, being inuited to the kingdome of Naples, he left in the citie of Florence his deputies. But he was scarce well gone out of the citie, but that the Florentines wearie of the gouernment of the deputies, came againe vnto their popular gouernment, and so withall renewed their ciuill warres. For redresse whereof they sent for the duke of Athens, who hauing taken vpon him the soueraigntie, commaunded the citisens to lay downe armes, and for the safetie of his person, tooke vnto him a strong guard, so to keepe vnder the seditious and rebellious persons. But the citisens now supposing themselues so to be spoyled of their libertie, and brought into bondage by the terrour of his guard, turned their old mutuall hatred all vppon the prince, first secretly, and afterwards three conspiracies breaking forth into open force, one after another in the citie: yea at last the citisens altogether burst out into such hatred against the prince, that they besieged the pallace wherein he lay, together with the souldiours which guarded him: neither could that so strait a siege be broken vp, vntill the prince was content himselfe with all his familie to void the city: which for safegard of his life he was glad to do, not hauing yet a whole yeare gouerned the state. So the citie deliuered of the feare of a master, appointed a forme of an Aristocratie, not much vnlike vnto a Popular estate; deuising new names for their officers and magistrats, still chaunging and rechaunging them with the manner of their state and gouernment, oftentimes no better ordered, than if it had bene committed to mad men, or children without discretion: scarcely twentie yeares together keeping the same forme of state. But as sicke men in the heat of burning feuers, desire to be remoued now hither, and by and by againe thither, or from one bed to another, as if the disease were in the places where they lay, and not in the verie entrals of their bodies: euen so the Florentines were still turning and tumbling of their estate, vntill they light vpon *Cosmus Medices*, of all Physitians the most skilfull, who cured the citie of these popular diseases, by establishing therein a Monarchie, and building therin three strong citadels, furnished with good & sure garrisons; so leauing vnto his posteritie a well grounded soueraigne state, by himselfe holden by the space of almost fortie yeares: than which nothing could haue bin wished for of almightie God, better or more wholsome for such a most seditious citie. And thus much briefly concerning the Florentine state, which haply might seeme incredible, had they not bene committed to the remembrance of all posteritie, euen by the * writings of the Florentines themselues. The like tragedies we see to haue bene plaid also by the people of Affrike (who in sharpnesse of wit are said to passe the Italians) when they made proofe of Popular estates: wherof I will set downe but one or two examples amongst many: as namely the inhabitants of Segelmessa, a citie vpon the sea coast in the kingdome of Bugia, reuolting from their king, established among themselues a Popular estate, but shortly after entred into such factions and ciuill seditions, as that not able to endure either the gouernment of their king, or yet the gouernment of themselues, they by common consent laid all their houses and the walles of their citie euen with the ground, that so they might euerie one of them as kings and princes rule and raigne in their owne houses abroad in the countrey. The people also of Togoda, a citie in the frontiers of the kingdome of Fez, wearie of their Aristocratie, forsooke their countrey. For which causes the people of Affrike, not able to endure the Aristocratique or Popular estates, haue almost euery where established Royall Monarchies.

Antoninus Pogginus Machianellus.

Now albeit that Aristocratike estates seeme to many both better and more assured and durable also than the Popular, yet so it is, that the gouernors therof if they bee not of accord among themselues, are still therein in double daunger: the one from the faction among themselues, the other from the insurrection or rebellion of the people, who neuer faile to fall vpon them if they once find them at variance among themselues, as we haue before shewed of the Florentines. The like whereof happened at Vienna, at Genes, and diuers other Commonweales in Germanie also. As it also chanced in the Peloponesian warre, vnto all the cities of Greece which were then gouerned by the nobilitie or richer sort. Which is also yet more daungerous, when the gouernours giue leaue to all straungers to come and dwell in their cities or countries: who by little and little encreasing, and in wealth and credit growing equall with the naturall subiects or citisens and hauing no part in the gouernment, if they shall chance to be surcharged, or otherwise euill entreated of the gouernours of the state, will vppon the least occasion rise vp against them, and so haply chase euen the naturall lords out of their own countrey: As it chaunced at Sienna, at Genes, at Zurike, and at Cullen; where the straungers encreasing, and seeing themselues surcharged and euill entreated, without hauing any part or interest in the estate, draue out the gouernours and slew most part of them. And namely they of Lindaw, after they had slaine the gouernors, chaunged their Aristocratie into a Democratie or Popular estate: as also did the inhabitants of Strasburg, who in detestation of the Aristocraticall gouernment, which they had chaunged into a Popular, after they had driuen out, banished, or slaine their lords and gouernours, solemnly by law prouided, That no man should haue the great estate, or any other publike charge in the citie, except hee could first well proue his grandfather to haue bene some verie base fellow, and so himselfe to be descended from the meanest sort of the rascall people. Which yet is no new matter: For we read, that the straungers in the Commonweale of Corfu encreased so fast, that in the end they seised vpon all the nobilitie, whom they cast into prison, and there murthered them; chan-

Discord amongst themselues daungerous vnto the gouernours of an Aristocratie.

Multitude of straungers in an Aristocratie daungerous.

F1 Medices   H9 *For* Vienna *read* Sienna *i.e.* Siena.   K5 *For* estate *read* estates *i.e.* offices.
Notes at H1, H5.

chaunging afterwards that Aristocraticall estate into a Popular gouernment. The like hapned vnto the Aristocratique Commonweales of the Samians, the Sibarites, the Trezenians, the Amphipolits, the Chalcidians, the Thurians, the Cnidians, and them of Chio, who were all by strangers changed into popular estates, hauing with their multitude thrust out the naturall Lords and gouernours. Which is the thing most to be feared in the Venetian estate, which we haue before showed to be a meere Aristocratie, and receptacle of all straungers, who haue there so well encreased, that for one Venetian gentleman there are an hundred citisens, as well noble as base descended of straungers; which may well be proued by the number of them which was there taken 20 yeares agoe, or thereabouts: wherein were found nine and fiftie thousand three hundred fortie nine citisens, aboue twentie yeares old; and threescore seauen thousand fiue hundred fiftie seauen women: two thousand one hundred eightie fiue Religious men, 1157 Iewes: which are in all, an hundred thirtie and two thousand three hundred and thirtie persons; whereunto putting a third part more for the number of them which are vnder twentie yeares old, (taking the ordinary age and the liues of men to be 60 yeares, as the law prefineth) it amounteth to the number of about an hundred seauentie six thousand foure hundred and fortie citisens, beside straungers. In which number the nobility or gentlemen were not comprehended, who could not be aboue three or foure thousand, accounting as well them that were absent, as them that were present. And truely I cannot but maruell why the Venetians haue published, yea and that more is haue suffered to be put in print the number that then was taken. The Athenians long agoe committed the like errour, and when the citie was most populous, found that vpon the number taken, there were in the citie twentie thousand citisens, ten thousand straungers, and foure hundred thousand slaues: which open number and account the Romans would not take of their straungers, and so much lesse of their slaues: whom they would not either by their countenance or attire haue knowne from the rest of the citisens: Howbeit that some were of opinion that the slaues ought to be knowne by their apparell; yet their opinion preuayled which thought the same to be daungerous, and a thing to bee feared, lest the slaues entering into the number of themselues, should make their masters their slaues, for so *Seneca* writeth. We read in the hystorie of Cardinall *Bembus*, that the greatest assemblie of the gentlemen of Venice in his time (when as that Commonweale was most populous) was but fifteene hundred; which their fewnesse they by most certein tokens, and their attire, make still to appeare. But that which hath most maintained their seignorie against the commotion of the citisens, is the mutuall amitie and concord of the gouernours and gentlemen among themselues; and the sweetnes of libertie, which is greater in that citie than in any other place of the world: so that beeing drowned in pleasure and delights, and hauing also part in certeine honors and meane offices, whereof the gentlemen are not capable, they haue no occasion to stirre for the chaunging of the estate; as had those of whom I haue before spoken, who were not onely debarred of all offices, but by the gouernors of the State surcharged and euill entreated also.

Now all these changes of Aristocraties into popular Commonweales haue beene violent and bloodie, as it happeneth almost alwaies: whereas to the contrarie it commeth to passe that Popular estates chaunge into Aristocraties by a more gentle and insensible chaunge. As when entrance is giuen vnto straungers, who in tract of time by little and little plant themselues, and multiplie, without hauing any part in the estate and gouernment, it falleth out in the end that the naturall citisen employed in publique charges, or in the warres, or by popular diseases wasted, do so decay; the straungers

The number of the inhabitants of Venice in the yeare 1555.

The change of popular estates into Aristocraties of all others most gentle and quiet.

B3 Religious men, 2082 RELIGIOUS WOMEN, 1157 Jewes (Fr and L. The total is then correct.)

straungers still encreasing: whereby it commeth to passe, that the lesser part of the inhabitants hold the soueraigntie, which wee haue shewed to bee a right Aristocratie. Such were the changes of those Commonweals which we haue before noted, from the people vnto the nobilitie, and such as haue indeed happened vnto the Venetians, the Luques, them of Rhaguse, & of Genes, which being in auntient time Popular estates, haue by little and little as it were without feeling, changed into Aristocraties: ioyning hereunto also, that the poorer sort of the citisens hauing much a do to liue, & so wholly intentiue vnto their domesticall and priuat affaires, shun all publike charges without profit: and so by succession and prescription of time exclude themselues with their families from entermeddling with the state. And this maner of change in the estate, is of all others most gentle and easie, and least subiect vnto tumults and sturres: neither can otherwise be letted, but that it wil in time chaunge, but by keeping of strangers from entring into the citie: or by sending of them out into colonies, or else together with the rest admitting them vnto the honors and preferments in the estate: and so much the more if the people be giuen to warre. For otherwise it is to be feared, that the nobilitie not daring to put armes into the subiects hands, but being constrained to go to warres themselues, should be all at once ouerthrowne, and so the people inuade to soueraigntie: as it happened to the seigneurie of Tarentum, which in one battell against the Iapiges lost almost all the nobilitie: after which the people seeing themselues the stronger, changed the Aristocraty into a Popular estate, in the time of *Themistocles*. And for this cause the nobilitie of the Argiues being almost all slaine by *Cleomenes* king of Lacedemonia, they that remained yet aliue, fearing the rebellion of the people, of themselues receiued the comminaltie into the fellowship of the gouernment, and so of their owne accord seemed willingly to grant that which the people otherwise haue taken from them by force, & whether they would or no: by which means their Aristocratie most quietly and sweetly chaunged into a Popular estate. So one of the things that gaue aduantage vnto the people of Rome ouer the nobilitie, was the victorie of the Vientes, who in one battell slew 300 of the Fabians, all gentlemen of one house, when as not long after twelue families of the Potitij, who ascribed the beginning of their houses vnto the gods, were in one and the same yere quite extinguished & brought to naught, as *Liuie* writeth. And therefore the Venetians, better citisens than warriors, if they bee to make warre (which they neuer doe but vpon great necessitie) vse commonly to chuse their generall one of their nobilitie, their souldiors for the most part beeing strangers and mercenarie men. But this inconuenience for the changing of the estate, for the losse of the nobilitie, cannot happen in a Monarchie, if all the princes of the blood bee not slaine together with the rest of the nobilitie: as the maner of the Turks is to doe in all places where they haue any purpose absolutely to command, where they spare not so much as a gentleman: whereof haue ensued the destruction of many Commonweals in the East, and great encreasing of the Turkish empire. But this change, or rather vnion or encreasement of one estate by another, proceedeth from externall force. So in France also, when as almost all the nobilitie of France was slaine in the expedition of Fontenay, neere vnto Auxerre, by the ciuill warre betwixt *Lothaire* the eldest sonne of *Lewes* the Gentle, on the one part, and *Lewes* and *Charles* the Bald on the other: yet for all that all their three Monarchies stood still firme: and namely when the countrey of Champagne had lost so much of the nobilitie in those wars, as that for the restoring therof, the gentlewomen had especial priuilege to ennoble their husbands with whom they should marrie, and yet for all that the Monarchy in the state therof felt no change at all. And thus are the great and notable changes commonly made in Aristocratike and Popular Commonweales.

But

K1 expedition *i.e. journee*, battle   Note at I6.

Of A Commonweale.

But nothing is so much in an Aristocratie to be feared, as least some gracious man of the nobilitie, or of the people, desirous of rule & authoritie, should stirre vp the people against the nobilitie, and become leader of them himselfe. For therof ensueth the most certaine destruction of an Aristocratie, together with the nobilitie. In this sort *Thrasyllus* first, and afterward *Thrasybulus* at Athens, *Marius* and *Cæsar* at Rome, *Fra. Valori*, and *P. Sodorin* at Florence, armed the people against the nobilitie: which is also so much the more to be feared, if the great honours of the estate bee bestowed vppon most filthy and wicked men, and other vertuous men and such as haue well deserued of the Commonweale, kept backe and excluded. Which thing seemeth not grieuous onely to euerie good man, and not to be borne withall, but ministreth occasion also vnto the seditious and popular, to enflame the people against the nobilitie. Neither for any other cause did the people of the Orites by force wrest the power and gouernment from the nobilitie, than for that they had preferred vnto the chiefe honours one *Heracleotes*, a man for his euill life infamous. Which thing also was the destruction of *Nero* and *Heliogabalus*, for that they had bestowed the greatest honours and preferments of the empire, vpon most wicked and corrupt men. Which of all other things is most to be feared and shunned in an Aristocratie Aristocratically gouerned: that is to say, where the people is kept from all honours and places of commaund: which although it be of it selfe an hard thing patiently to endure, yet were it the better to bee borne, if the gouernment were committed to good men: but when it is giuen to wicked and vnworthy men, euerie audacious fellow vppon occasion offered, will easily draw the people from the nobilitie, and so much the rather, by how much the nobilitie shall be at lesse vnitie among themselues. Which plague, as it is in all estates and gouernments, so is it especially in an Aristocratie to be eschewed and fled. Now discord oft times ariseth euen of most small matters, which as sparkes raise the great fiers of ciuill warres, which at length take hold euen of the whole bodie of the estate of a citie or Commonweale. As it happened at Florence, for the refusall made by a gentleman of the noble house of *Bondelmont*, to marrie a gentlewoman to whome hee had before giuen his promise, gaue occasion to the raising of a faction amongst the nobilitie, who so wasted and deuoured one another, as that the people to end the quatrel, easily draue out all the rest, and commaunded the state of the citie. And for like occasion arose great ciuill warres amongst the Ardeates, for an inheretrix, whome her mother would haue married vnto a gentleman, and her guardions to a base obscure man: which diuided the people from the nobilitie, in such sort, that the nobilitie vanquished and put to flight by the people, tooke their refuge vnto the Romans, and the people vnto the Volsians, who were afterwards vanquished by the Romans. So also the citie & Commonweale of Delphos, for the same occasion, was chaunged from an Aristocratie vnto a Popular estate. The state of Mitelin was also chaunged from an Aristocratie into a Popular estate, vpon a suit betwixt the nobilitie and the people, Which of them should haue the tuition of two orphans. And the state of the Commonweale of the Hestiens, for a suit in matter of inheritance betwixt two priuat men. And the sacred warre which chaunged not, but euen vtterly ruinated the estate of the Phocenses, was grounded vpon the marriage of an inheritrix, whome two of their great lords stroue to haue. And that more is, the Ætolians and Arcadians, for a long time sore weakened one another with mutuall warres, and all but for a boares head: as they of Carthage and of Bizaque did also for a small frigot. So betwixt the Scots and the Picts, was raised a most cruell warre, and all but for certaine dogges, which the Scots had taken from the Picts, and neuer could be againe reconciled, howbeit that they had for six hundred yeares before liued in good peace and amitie together. And the war betwixt the duke
of

Ambition and vnworthie bestowing of the great preferments of the commonweale, thinges most daungerous to an Aristocratie

Discord among the nobilitie a thing most daungerous to the state

Small matters oftentimes the cause of great chaunges in commonweales

---

B4 Heracleotes (L) *properly* Heracleodorus (Fr) Cf. Aristotle, *Politics*, 1303a.   E2 Romans. So
E4 Mitelin *i.e.* Mitylene (Fr) Miletus (L). Fr is correct. Cf. Aristotle, *Politics*, 1304a.

of Burgundy and the Swissers, which could no otherwise be ended, but by the death of the duke himself, was all but for a wagon load of sheepe skins which he had taken from the Swissers.

Great men hardly to be called in question to giue an account of their doinges, without the daunger of the estate.

Sometime also the changes and ruines of Commonweales come, when the great ones are to be brought in question, to cause them to giue an account of their actions, whether it be for right or wrong: wherein euen they which are guiltlesse (and especially in Popular estates) not without cause alwaies feare the calumnies and doubtfull issues of iudgements, which most commonly endaunger the liues, the goods, and honour of such as are accused. And to leaue forren examples, wee haue store enow of our owne, and that of such as of late haue set on fire all the kingdome with ciuill wars when it was but spoken of, for calling them to account for two and fortie millions. And no maruell if they so feared to be brought in question for embeseling of the common treasure and reuenewes, when as *Pericles*, a man of greatest integritie, and which had most magnificently spent euen his owne wealth for the Athenian Commonweale, rather than he would hazard the account that they demaunded of him for the treasure of Athens, which he had mannaged, and so generally of his actions, raised the Peloponesian warre, which neuer after tooke end vntill it had ruinated diuers Commonweals, and wholly chaunged the estate of all the cities of Greece. Who alwaies hauing bene a good husband, and had the charge of the common treasure of that Commonweale, by the space of almost fiftie yeares, was therefore yet found neuer the richer, as *Thucydides*, a most true historiographer, and *Pericles* his most mortall enemie reporteth of him: who caused him to be banished with the banishment of the Ostracisme. And euen for the selfe same cause the Rhodians and they of Choos had their estates changed from Aristocraties into Popular estates. And albeit that *Cæsar* was of himselfe most ambitious and desirous of soueraigntie: yet was he not so much desirous to beare rule, as affraid to be called to account by priuat men, for such things as he had done, as his enemies had openly boasted that he should, so soone as hee was discharged of his charge: not the least cause that moued him to ceise vpon the estate. For what assurance could he haue of himselfe, seeing before the two *Scipioes* (*Africanus* the honor of his time, and *Scipio Asiaticus*) *Rotulus* and *Cicero*, by the iudgement of the people condemned? Now if good men were to feare, what should the wicked do? who besides that they are in hope the better to escape, the Commonweale beeing all on a broile, are also resolued, that the common treasures can neuer more easily be robbed, or good men spoiled and slaine, than in the time of ciuill warres: euer taking it for an aduantage to fish in the troubled water. And although it may fortune such wicked men also to perish (as oftentimes it happeneth them which haue bene the authors of ciuill warres, themselues to die a most miserable death) yet haue they still in their mouths that desperat saying of *Cateline*, That the fire (forsooth) which had taken hold of his house, which he could not with water quench, hee would yet quench with the vtter ruine of the same. And truly much he missed not, but that hee had vtterly ouerthrowne the Roman Commonweale, or stept into the soueraigntie, had not *Cicero* the watchful Consul, and *Ca. Antonius* his companion (although it were with much a do) slaine him so desperat a citisen, with all his fellows. Neither ought *Cicero* (by his good leaue bee it said) to haue driuen *Catiline* out of the citie, but to haue oppressed him euen there, the conspiracie once detected. For it is not to be hoped, but that he which seeth himself banished from his house, & from his country, if he haue power, wil forthwith put himself in arms, as he did. And had he gained the battell against *Ca Antonius*, hee had put the whole estate in great danger, being one of the most noble gentlemen, and best allied of all them that were in Rome. Certeine it is that by his departure out of the citie, a great and

How daungerous a matter it is in euerie commonweale to bannish a great man.

H3 Choos *i.e.* Cos   H6 *For* by privat men *read* as a private man (*privatus* in L 1–4, *privatis* in L 5).
H10 *For* Rotulus *read* Rutilius (Fr and L).   K2 much ado

and dangerous sinke of the Commonweale was so well clensed; yet had it beene better for him to haue beene there oppressed, than armed against his owne countrie. But of such great and dangerous enemies, the wiser sort aduiseth vs, to make them our verie good friends, or else vtterly to destroy them, rather than to driue them out of the citie, except we should for honour banish them: as they did in the cities of Athens, Argos, and Ephesus, where the great Lordes mightie in wealth, fauour, or vertue, were for a certeine time (which for all that neuer exceeded ten yeares) constrained to absent themselues, without any losse of goods or reputation; which was an honourable kind of banishment. Of whom so banished, not any one of them is reported to haue therefore made warre vpon his countrie. But to banish a great Lord with losse of his goods and contumely, is not to quench but to kindle the fire of warre against the estate: For that oft times such a banished man by the helpe of his friends aspireth vnto the soueraigntie; as did *Dion* banished out of Syracusa by *Dionysius* the yonger, against whom for all that he yet tooke not vp armes vntill he was by him proscribed. And *Martius Coriolanus*, who cast into exile, brought the Romans to such extremitie, as that had he not suffered himselfe to haue beene ouercome with the prayers and teares of his mother, and the other women whom the Romans had sent vnto him, the Roman state had there taken end. In like manner the banished men of the house of *Medices*, and the nobilitie of Zurich in the yeare 1336, thrust out of their cities, by the helpe and power of their friends and allies besieged their owne natiue countries, and for a long time wearied the citisens their countrymen with a most doubtfull and daungerous warre. But yet here some man may say, That it is more safetie to keepe a wicked and a daungerous citisen without the wals, than to bee troubled with such a plague in the verie enttrailes of the Commonweale. Whereto I yeeld: but yet how much greater a follie is it to let him whom thou oughtest to kill, to escape out of the citie, who once got out, is both willing and able to stirre vp, and maintaine warre? *Artaxerxes* king of Persia had cast in prison *Cyrus* the yonger, guiltie of high treason, and had commanded him in princely manner to be bound with chaines of gold; and afterwards ouercome with his mothers requests enlarged him: but he had no sooner got his libertie, but that he made most grieuous warre vpon the king, and was like enough by his brothers death to haue obtained the kingdome, or else haue vndone his countrie; had he not by the kings armie beene circumuented and slaine. I said we must kill such people, or make them our good friends: as did *Augustus*, hauing discouered the conspiracie of *Cinna* against him, and hauing him in his power attainted and conuinced by his owne letters, yet neuerthelesse pardoned him; and not so content, tooke him by the hand, and swore a bond of mutuall friendship with him, and afterwards bestowed the greatest honours and preferments of the estate vpon him, at the time that *Cinna* expected nothing but the sentence of condemnation, and so present execution; vsing these words of grace and fauour vnto him: *Vitam tibi Cinna iterum do, prius hosti, nunc insidiatori ac parricidæ; Ex hodierno die amicitia inter nos incipiat, contendamus vtrum ego meliore fide vitam tibi dederim, an tu debeas*, Cinna (said he) thy life I giue thee againe, being before mine enemie, and now a traitour and a murtherer; But from this day, let vs begin to be friends, and from henceforth let vs striue, whether I with greater trust haue giuen thee thy life, or thou with greater faithfulnesse doest ow it. After which time he neuer had a more faithfull friend; being also afterwards by him appointed heire of all his goods. *Augustus* had before put to death an infinite number of such as had sworne and conspired his death: but now had a purpose in *Cinna* to proue if by gentlenesse and mercie he could gaine the hearts of men, wherein he was not deceiued: for from that time there was neuer any found which durst attempt any thing

against

[margin: This was the Ostracisme banishment.]

[margin: Great men enemies vnto the estate, are either to be slaine, or by great kindnes to be made therunto faithfull friends.]

against him. So the Venetians also hauing taken prisoner *Gonzaga* the duke of Mantua, of all others their most mortall enemie, (who had ioyned all his forces and power with king *Lewes* of Fraunce for the ouerthrow of the Venetian state) did not onely set him at libertie, but made him Generall also of their forces; by which so honorable a kindnesse he bound, for euer after continued their most fast and loiall friend. And this is it for which *Pontius* the old capitaine of the Samnites said, That the great armie of the Romans surprised in the straites of the Appenine mountaines was either franke and freely to bee set at libertie, or else all to be put to the sword: for that so it should come to passe, that either the power of the Romans should by so great a slaughter be greatly weakned, or else hauing receiued from the Samnites so great a benefit, as the life and libertie of so many men, they should for euer after keepe good league and friendship with them.

<small>Small Commonweales more subiect vnto change than great.</small>

But these conuersions and chaunges of Commonweales do more often happen in little and small cities or estates, than in great kingdomes full of great prouinces, and people. For that a small Commonweale is soone diuided into two parts or factions: Whereas a great Commonweale is much more hardly diuided; for that betwixt the great Lords and the meanest subiects, betwixt the rich and the poore, betwixt the good and the bad, there are a great number of the middle sort which bind the one with the other, by meanes that they participate both with the one and the other, as hauing some accord and agreement with both the extreames. And that is it for which we see the little Commonweales of Italie, & the auntient Commonweals of Greece, which had but one, two, or three townes or cities belonging to them, in one age to haue suffered moe alterations and chaunges than are in many ages reported to haue beene in this kingdome of Fraunce, or in the kingdome of Spayne. For it is not to be doubted but that the extreames are alwaies contrarie one of them to the other, and so at discord and variance betwixt themselues, if there be not some meanes which may binde and ioine the one of them with the other; which we see by the eye, not onely betwixt the nobilitie and base common people, betwixt the rich and the poore, betwixt the good and the bad, but euen in the same citie also, where as but the diuersitie of places seperate but by some riuer, or wast vacant peece of ground without building

<small>Small occasions serue to raise great dissention amongst citisens, and so the change of the estate.</small>

vpon it, doth oft times set the citisens at odds, and giue occasion to the chaunging of the estate. So the citie of Fez was neuer at quiet, neither could the slaughters & murthers euer be appeased or staied, vntill that *Ioseph* king of Marocco and of Fez, of two townes standing some what distant of them one from the other by continuate building made them both one, and that now the greatest citie of Fez, whereby he gained the praise and commendation of a most wise & discreet prince; for that he so not onely ioyned houses to houses, and wals to wals, but bound also the mindes of the citisens and inhabitants of both places (before burning with an incredible hatred one of them against an other, and alwaies diuided in warres) now in perpetuall loue and friendship together. Which hapned also vnto the Clazomenians, where one part of the citie standing in the maine, and the other part in an Iland, there was alwaies discord and warre betwixt them of the Isle and the other citisens. And so at Athens they which dwelt by the hauens side commonly called Piræus, were at continuall discord and variance with them of the vpper Towne which they called Astu or the Citie, vntill that *Pericles* with long walles ioyned the Hauen vnto the Citie. For which cause also such tumults and quarrels fell betwixt the citisens of Venice, and the mariners and other the seafaring men, as had brought the citie into extreame perill and daunger had not *Peter Lauredan* with his great authoritie and wisedome appeased the same.

But most often it hapneth the chaunges of Commonweales to follow after ciuill discord,

A discord, especially if some neighbour prince shall vpon the suddein oppresse a citie or State weakned with the slaughter of the citisens or subiects, or else the citisens or subiects themselues being by the eares together: As the Englishmen haue often times vanquished and ouerrunne the French being at variance among themselues: And the king of Fez easely tooke the citie of *Tesza*, the citisens being almost all consumed and spent with ciuill warre, And in the memorie of our fathers *Philip* the second duke of Bourgondie ioyned vnto the boundes of his dukedome Dinan and Bouines, two cities in the countrie of Liege (parted in sunder but with a riuer) after that they had with long warres weakned themselues, which two cities for all that he could not before by any force subdue; howbeit that in taking of them he did but marrie the one of B them vnto the other, as saith *Philip Commines*. So also whilest the kings of Marocco were in armes together for the soueraigntie, the Gouernour of Thunes and of Telesin dismembred those two prouinces to make himselfe a kingdome of. And by the same meanes *Lachares* seeing the Athenians in combustion, in the time of *Demetrius* the besieger, stept into the Seignorie. And that more is, we read that foure thousand fiue hundred slaues and banished men inuaded the Capitoll, and missed but a little to haue made themselues lords of Rome, whilest the Nobilitie and Common people in the meane time were together by the eares in an vproar in the middest of the citie, who thereupon fell to agreement among themselues; not vnlike vnto two dogges, who readie to pull one an others throat out, seeing a wolfe, fall both vpon him. Wherfore such ciuill discord is most daungerous vnto cities or estates, especialiy if there be no societie or allyance betwixt the State so troubled, and the neighbour Princes: for that the enemie so at hand, may oppresse the state (the citisens or subiects so at variance among themselues) before that any helpe can come. Whereat we are not to maruell, for they to whom neither the huge height of steepe mountaines, neither the vnmeasurable depth of the botomlesse sea, nor the most solitarie desarts, nor the greatest and strongest fortifications, nor the innumerable multitude of enemies can serue for the staying of their ambitious and auaritious couses and desires; how should they content themselues with their owne, without encroaching vppon their neighbours, whose frontiers touch theirs, and that fit occasion presenteth it selfe for them so to do?
D which is there the more to be feared where the Commonweale is but little: as is that of Rhaguse, of Geneua, and of Luque, which haue but one Towne, and the territorie verie strait; so that he which shall gaine the towne, shall withall become master of the Estate also: which so chaunceth not in great and spacious Commonweale, wherein many castles, cities, countries, and prouinces are in mutuall helpe together combyned, so that one citie thereof being taken, or a countrie or prouince thereof spoyled, yet followeth not the ruine of the Estate, one of them still succoring an other, as many members in one bodie, which at need helpe one an other.

Yet for all that a Monarchie hath this aduantage proper vnto it selfe, aboue the
E Aristocratique and Popular estates, That in these commonly there is but one towne or citie wherein the Seigneurie lyeth, which is as an house or place of retrait for them which haue the mannaging of those estates to retire vnto; which once taken by the enemie, the estate is withall vndone: whereas a Monarke chaungeth himselfe from place to place as occasion requireth: neither doth the taking of him by the enemie bring with it the losse of the Estate. As when the citie of Capua was taken, their estate was also ouerthrowne by the Romans, neither was there so much as one towne or fortresse which made resistance against them; for that the Senat and the people which had the soueraigntie were all together taken prisoners. The citie of Sienna also being taken by the duke of Florence, all the other townes and fortresses of that Seigneurie

Commonweales most often chaunged or ouerthrowne by forrein princes, taking the aduantage of the ciuill discord of the subiects amongst themselues.

A Monarchie not so easily changed or ouerthrowne, as is an Aristocratie or Popular Commonweale.

P p at the

A3 (margin) overthrowne   C1 especially   C8 courses   D4 in great and spacious Commonweales at the same time yeelded themselues vnto him also. But the king taken prisoner, is most commonly for his ransome set at libertie; wherewith if the enemie hold not him selfe content, the Estates may proceed to a new election, or take the next of blood if they haue other princes: yea sometime the captiue king himselfe had rather to yeeld vp his estate, or else to die a prisoner, than to grieue his subiects with his too heauie a ransome. As indeed that which most troubled the Emperour *Charles* the fift was the resolution of king *Francis* then his prisoner, who gaue him to vnderstand that he was vpon the point to resigne his kingdome vnto his eldest sonne, if he would not accept of the conditions by him offered: For why, the realme and all the Estate stood yet whole without any chaunge taking, or any alteration suffering. And albeit that Spayne, Italie, England, all the Low Countries, the Pope, the Venetians, and all the Potentates of Italie had combyned themselues against the house of Fraunce, ouerthrowne our legions at Pauie, and caried away the king with the flower of the nobilitie into Spayne; yet was there not any which durst enter into Fraunce to conquer it, knowing the lawes and nature of that Monarchie. For as a building grounded vpon deepe foundations, & built with durable matter, well vnited and ioyned in euery part, feareth neither winde nor tempest, but easily resisteth all force and violence; euen so a Commonweale grounded vpon good lawes, well vnited and ioyned in all the members thereofe, asily suffereth not alteration: as also to the contrarie we see some states and Commonweales so euill built and set together, as that they ow their fall and ruine vnto the first wind that bloweth, or tempest that ariseth.

And yet is there no kingdome which shall not in continuance of time be chaunged, and at length also be ouerthrowne. But they are in better case which least feele such their chaunges by little and little made, whether it be from euill to good, or from good to better; as we haue showed by the example of the Venetian Commonweale: which at the beginning was a pure Monarchie, which afterward was sweetly chaunged into a Popular estate, and now by little and little is chaunged into an Aristocratie, and that in such quiet sort, as that it was not well by any man perceiued that the estate was at all chaunged. An other example we haue also of the Germaine Empire, which founded by *Charlemaigne* and discending to his posteritie, so long continued a true Monarchie vnder one soueraigne princes gouernment, vntill that the line of *Charlemaigne* fayling, the Emperours begun to be created by election; at which time it was right easie for the princes which had the choice by little and little to clip the Eagles wings, and to prescribe lawes and conditions vnto the Emperour to rule by; and yet right happie was he which could thereunto aspire vpon any condition whatsoeuer: whereby the state of the Monarchie began by little and little to decay, and the state of an Aristocratie to encrease in the Princes and Estates of the Empire, in such sort as that at this present the Emperours haue nothing more but as it were the bare name and title of an Emperour, the soueraigntie resting in the Estates of the Empire it selfe. So that had not eleuen most noble Princes of the house of Austria for their worthy deeds right famous, as it were in a successiue right (one of them whilest he himselfe yet liueth, still procuring an other of the same house to be designed Emperour) in some sort maintained the maiestie of the Germaine Empire, the Emperours for their estate had now long ago beene like vnto the Dukes of Venice, and happely inferiour too. The like chaunge hapned vnto the Polonians, the lyne of *Iagellon* failing: as also the Danes, after that *Christierne* their king was by them his subiects imprisoned, and his brother to be chosen king in his place, sworne to such conditions as the nobilitie would: and after that *Frederike* which now raigneth hath beene constrained to confirme the same, (as I haue before noted) whereby it manifestly appeareth, that the Nobilitie there hold

The resolution of Francis the French king, being prisoner to the Emperour Charles the fift.

The insensible change of estates best and most tollerable.

The insensible estanging of the Venetian estate, and of the state of the German Empire.

G9 thereof, easily   H10(margin) changing   Notes at G5, H5.

A hold as it were the soueraigntie, and that by little and little that kingdome will change into an Aristocratie if *Frederike* should die without children.

And albeit that the estates of Hungarie, Bohemia, Polonia, and Denmarke, haue alwayes pretended the right of election of their kings, although they haue children, (which prerogatiue they stil maintaine) yet commonly the kings their parents appointed their children vnto the succession of their kingdomes, who so chosen in their fathers places, better maintaine the rights of soueraigntie than do straungers (who haue the same oft times cut short, and so their soueraigne power in them restrained) so that the kingdomes so descending, as it were in succession from the great grandfathers vnto their nephewes, the soueraigne rights by little and little without violence returne again B from the nobilitie vnto the kings themselues: which is both an easie chaunge, & most wholsome for the Commonweale. For so *Cazimir* the Great, king of Polonia, worthily defended the soueraigne rights by him receiued from his great grandfather: but hee dead without issue, the Polonians indeed called *Lewes* king of Hungarie (and *Cazimir* his nephew) vnto the kingdome of Polonia, but with the soueraigntie therein much diminished; he for the gaining of the kingdome yeelding to whatsoeuer the estates desired. But *Lewes* dead also without heires male, *Iagello* duke of Lithuania marrying one of the daughters and heires of *Lewes*, and so with her obtaining the kingdome of Polonia, yet more impaired the soueraigne rights than they had before bene: the prinC ces of whose posteritie neuerthelesse as it were in succesiue right, for the space of aboue two hundred yeares, tooke vpon them the gouernment of the kingdome, and notably maintained the rights of their soueraigntie, vntill the death of *Sigismundus Augustus*, last heire male of that house: vnto whome by right of election succeeeded *Henrie* of Fraunce, *Charles* the ninth the French kings brother: but with oathes and conditions bound vnto the estates, so much derogating from the rights of a soueraigne Monarch, as that indeed he might haue seemed rather a prince than a king. And to say yet more, I being sent to Mets, to assist them which were thither sent with the duke, to receiue the ambassadours of Polonia, and to parle with them, it was told me by *Salomon Sboroschi* one of the ambassadours, That the estates of Polonia had yet cut much shorter D the power of the new elected king, had it not bene in the regard they had of the honor of the house of Fraunce. Thus we see Monarchies peaceably by little and little to change into Aristocraties, if so it be that the Monarchie be not by auntient lawes and immutable customes, maintained in the maiestie thereof. As we see in the creation of the pope, where the Consistorie (or Colledge of Cardinals) derogat nothing from the soueraigne maiestie that he hath in all the demaine of the church, and the sees depending thereon: no more than do the order of the knights of Malta in any thing diminish the power of the Grand maister, who hath the power of life and death, and to dispose of the reuenewes, estates, and offices of the countrey, yeelding fealtie and homage vnto the king of Spaine for the isle of Malta, which *Charles* the fift the emperour vpon E this condition gaue them. And albeit that the colledge of cardinals after the death of pope *Iulius* the second, determined in the conclaue, to moderat the popes power: yet shortly after they flew from that they had before decreed, in such sort that *Leo* the tenth, then by them chosen, tooke vpon him more power than had any pope of long time before him.

But that chaunge is of others most daungerous to a Monarchie, when as the king dying without issue, there is some one who in wealth and power exceedeth the rest; & so much the more, if he be also ambitious and desirous of rule: For no doubt, but that hauing the power in his hand, hee will, if hee can, take the soueraigntie from the other weake princes. For so *Hugh Capet* the right line of *Charlemaigne* ended, being Prouost

Kingdomes going by election and so indeede but Aristocraties, long continued in one familie, easily chaunge at length into Monarchies as by succession discending.

The most daungerous chaunge of a Monarchie.

Pp ij of

A4 children   A10 nephewes *i.e. pronepotes*, great-grandsons   E9 Capet, the   Note at D1.

of the citie of Paris, and a man of great wealth, and no lesse fauoured of the people, excluded from the kingdome *Charles* duke of Loraine, who with his sonne *Otho* were the onely men left of all the posteritie of *Charlemaigne*. Which is also to bee feared of the great Othoman princes, who although they haue their families of the *Machaloglies*, of the *Ebranes*, and the *Turacans*, of the princes house and blood, to succeed in the Turkish empire: yet for all that if the Othoman familie should altogether perish, it is to be thought, that some one of the Bassaes or other great men, in greatest fauour with the Ianzaries, and the other souldiours of the court will carrie away the estate and soueraigntie from the other princes of the aforesaid families, being but weake, and far off from the Grand Signior, which might so raise the greatest ciuill warres in the East, for the great opinion which the people hath of long conceiued of the valour and maiesty of the Othoman familie. A notable example of such change of state wee haue in the chaunge of the Lacedemonian kingdome: where *Cleomenes* the king vanquished and put to flight by *Antigonus*, the kingdome was chaunged into a Popular estate, which so continued for three yeares: during which time the people made choyce of fiue Prouosts, or chiefe magistrats, whome they called Ephori, chosen out of the people themselues: but newes being brought of the death of *Cleomenes*, slaine in Aegypt, two of the fiue Ephori conspired against the other three their companions and fellowes in office: and so as they were doing sacrifice, caused them to be slaine: which done, they proceed to the election of *Agesipolis* for their king, a prince of the royall blood. But whereas before *Cleomenes* they were woont to haue two kings: one *Lycurgus* a man gracious with the people, but otherwise none of the blood royall, by corruption and briberie caused himselfe also by the people to be chosen king, *Chilon*, a noble gentleman, discended from *Hercules*, being for his pouerty and want of ability excluded, who not able to endure so great an indignity offered vnto his house and family, procured all the magistrats to be slaine: *Lycurgus* himselfe onely escaping, who after great effusion of blood, held the soueraignty himselfe alone, hauing before almost quite destroyed the royall race of the Heraclides posterity of *Hercules*. And thus much concerning the chaunge and ruine of Commonweales, which whether they may by any meanes be forseene and preuented, let vs now also see.

These noble families are nowe also al or most of them extinguished and come to nought.

Chap. II.

¶ *Whether there be any meane to know the chaunges and ruines, which are to chaunce vnto Commonweales.*

Seeing that there is nothing in this world which commeth to passe by chaunce or fortune, as all diuines and the wiser sort of the Philosophers haue with one common consent resolued: Wee will here in the first place set downe this maxime for a ground or foundation, *That the chaunges and ruines of Commonweals, are humane, or naturall, or diuine*; that is to say, That they come to passe eitheir by the onely councell and iudgement of God, without any other meine causes: or by ordinarie and naturall meanes of causes and effects, by almightie God bound in such fit order and consequence, as that those things which are first haue coherence with the last; and those which are in the middest with them both: and all with all combined and bound together with an indissoluble knot and tying: which *Plato* according to the opinion of *Homer* hath called the Golden Chaine, that is to say, σειρὰν χρυσῆν, or by the will of man, which the diuines confesse to be free, at the least concerning ciuill actions: howbeit that indeed it is no will at all, which in any sort whatsoeuer is enforced and bound

Which

F4–5 Michaloglies (cf. 745 B2)   K2 meine causes *i.e.* mean, or intermediate, causes

Notes at I2, K7.

Which will of man is so mutable and vncertaine, as that it should be impossible to giue thereby any iudgement, to know the changes and ruines which are to fall vpon Commonweales. As for the councell of God, it is inscrutable, but that he sometime by secret inspiration declareth his will, as he hath done vnto his Prophets, causing them many worlds of yeres before to see the falles of many the greatest empires and Monarchies, which posteritie hath by experience found to be true. But this diuine power of the almightie most seldome times sheweth it selfe immediatly without the comming betwixt of meane causes; neither doth he it without greatest force and most sudden violence: as when he in one and the selfe same moment with wonderfull fire, and reuenging flames, destroyed the fiue cities with Sodome and Gomorrha: and so chaunged also the place, then full of most sweet waters and aboundance of fish, with a most stinking & lothsome taft, as that it yet is vnto all kind of fish pestilent & deadly: and as for the ground it selfe, before of wonderful fertility, he so couered it with ashes and stinking sulpher, as that he seemeth in that countrey to haue left no place for wholsome plants, or any kind of graine to grow in. So also he ouerwhelmed Bura and Helice, two cities of Greece, with such a deluge of water, and that so suddenly, that euen they also which were about to haue fled out of the cities into the ships, being by the wonderfull rising of the waters, vnable to come to the hauen, were so all drowed. By the like wrath of God a great earthquake in a moment swallowed vp three and twentie cities in Italie, where afterward the Fennes called Pontinæ burst out. As in like manner twelue cities of Asia are reported to haue bene all at once vpon the sudden with an earthquake deuoured.

Mans will still mutable, and God his iudgements inscrutable, afoord no meane for man by thē to foresee the changes and ruines of Commonweales.

God his inmediate iudgements most sudden and most dreadfull.

Wherefore seeing that mans wil is still diuers and mutable, & God his iudgements most secret and inscrutable: there remaineth onely to know, whether that by naturall causes (which not altogether obscure, but by a certaine constant order of causes and effects gouerned, kept their course) a man may iudge of the issue and successe of Commonweales. Yet by these naturall causes hauing in them this power (which are many and diuers) we meane not ciuill cau es, whereunto the chaunge and ruine of cities and Commonweales must needs immediatly follow as when good deserts goe vnrewarded, and great offences vnregarded, who knoweth not but that such a state or Commonweale must needs in short time perish and come to naught? For of all causes none is more certaine, none more weightie, and in briefe none neerer vnto the change or ruine of a citie or Commonweale, than these. But the causes which we here seeke after, are the celestial and more remote causes, yet proceeding from a certaine naturall course and force: howbeit that it be good also to behold and foresee all maner of causes whatsoeuer. For as a painter doth one way consider of a mans bodie, and the Physitian another: and the naturall Philosopher one way considereth of the mind of man, & the diuine another: so also the Polititian doth one way, the Astrologer another, and the diuine a third way, iudge of the change & ruine of Commonweals. The Politian in the ruine of a citie or Commonweale, blameth the iniuries and wrongs done by the prince vnto his subiects, the corruptnesse of the magistrats, with the iniquitie of the laws: The Astrologer considereth and beholdeth the force and power of the heauenly starres and planets, and thereof thinketh diuers motions to arise in mens minds, for the change and innouation of estates and Commonweales: But the Diuine constantly affirmeth all plagues, wars, dearth, destructions of cities and nations, to proceed from the contempt of God and of his religion, and God therefore to be angrie, and to stupifie the wisedome euen of the most wisest magistrats, and to arme euen his starres against princes. And euerie one of these haue their causes, by the helpe and concourse whereof wise men may guesse the change or ruine of a citie or Commonweale. In which point we see

By what naturall causes the changes and ruines of Commonweales are to be foreseen.

*Psal. 109.
Leuit. 27.
Iob. 12.*

Pp iij

B8 drowned   D8 Polititian doth   Note at A6.

438　THE FOVRTH BOOKE

Astrologicall predictions, not to derogat from the maiestie and power of God.

see many to erre and be deceiued, which thinke, that to looke into the starres, and to search after their secret influencies and vertues, is in some sort to diminish the maiestie and power of almightie God: whereas to the contrarie it is thereby made much more glorious and beautifull, to do so great things by his creatures, as if he did then immediatly by his owne mightie hand, without any other meane at all.

Nothing done by the necessitie of nature, it selfe being still subiect to the power of God:

Now what man is there of sound iudgement, which feeleth not the wonderfull force and effect of the celestiall bodies in nature in generall? Which yet for all that no necessitie of nature worketh, for that it may by almighty God be stil kept back and restrained, being himselfe free from the lawes of nature, which hee himselfe hath commaunded; not as by a decree of a Senat, or of a people, but euen of himselfe: who being of all others the greatest, can do nothing but that which is right and iust, for that he

Esay. 19.

is himselfe the best, and hath a * perpetuall care of all people and nations, but yet then of himselfe secure, for that he is himselfe the greatest. But as all things which had beginning haue also a loose and fraile dissoluable nature (as by most certaine and vndoubtfull demonstration is to be proued) it must thereof needs follow also, not onely

All worldly things still subiect to mutabilitie and change.

cities and Commonweals, but euen also other things, which from their first beginning haue innumerable worlds of yeares flourished, must at length in tract of time fall also and take end. And albeit that *Plato* the prince of Phylosophers, hauing not as yet the knowledge of the celestiall motions, and so much lesse of their effects (which as then was couered in most thicke darkenesse and clouds) when as he with a notable inuention had conceited such a forme of a Commonweale, as seemed vnto many to bee euerlasting, if it erred not from the lawes and orders by him set downe; yet for all that he said, That it should in time perish: as he which most manifestly saw the vanitie of all things, which as they had a beginning, so were they also to take ending; nothing being still firme and stable, besides him which was the father of all things. Which being so, there be no so notable orders, no so religious lawes, no such wisedome or valour of man, which can still preserue estates or Commonweales from ruine and most certaine destruction. By which reasons, *Secundus* (a Philosopher of the Stoike sect) greatly comforted *Pompey*, discouraged and almost desperat after the Pharsalian ouerthrow. Neither yet therefore do they which thinke the course of naturall causes to concerne the changes and ruines of cities and Commonweals, thereby bind the free will of man, and much lesse almightie God himselfe vnto a fatall necessitie: no not if we should deeme all things to be done by a continuat and interlaced course of forerunning naturall causes; seeing that euen nature it selfe is by the power of God kept in & restrained. Wherfore we oftentimes see both plants, and other liuing creatures, which by nature haue a certaine period of their liues, by some externall force to hasten or preuent the tearmes by nature presined, and so sooner to die than by nature they should. And as for mankind, we haue it oftentimes in holy writ recorded, That they which lead an vpright & vertuous life, shall liue long: whereas the wicked should shorten their dayes, and bring themselues vnto a most speedie confusion and end. Whereby it appeareth certaine prefixed bounds of euerie mans life, to be by God appoined, which by sinne may bee cut shorter, and by vertue extended farther. So kingdomes also haue their beginnings, their encreasings, their flourishing estates, their changings, and ruines: yet when these chaunges shall be, or ruines, or destructions betide them, we see it by no learning to bee perceiued or vnderstood. For as for that which *Plato* hath written, Kingdomes then to fall and take end, when as the sweet consent and harmonie of them should perish and decay, is a thing not worth the refutation: whereof yet for all that more in due place shall be said.

Now many there be, which haue thought the conuersions and chaunges of estates

and

F4 *For* then *read* them.　　K1 appointed　　K4 or ruines　　Note at H5.

OF A COMMONWEALE.   439

A   and Commonweales, to depend of the force power and motion of the superiour celestiall bodies: which to discouer, were a matter of infinit difficultie, which yet for all that
should not be so great, if Commonweales should as men and other things take their
beginning. And albeit that the state and ruine of Commonweales should wholly
next vnto God depend of those eternall lights, and of their mutuall coniunctions and
oppositions, yet could thereof no certaine doctrine be deliuered or gathered, for the
great varietie and inconstancy of them which haue obserued the force and course of *The notable er-*
the celestiall stars & orbes; insomuch, that some one hath written the same star in the *rors of the Astro-*
selfe same moment to haue beene in his direct motion, and another hath likewise *logers*
written the same to be retrograde, which yet for all that, was to bee seene in the hea-
B   uens stationarie and immoueable. So that they are by their owne rashnesse to be refelled, which vaunt themselues to be able without error, to foretell the force and power of the starres, vpon cities and Commonweales; as also what effects they shall for
many yeares to come produce, when as in the very motion of the moone, which of all
the other planets hath in it least difficulty there is not one of them which well agreeth
with one another. So *Cyprian Leouicius*, following the table of *Alphonsus*, (the euident error of whom *Copernicus* hath declared) hath made so apparant faults, as that the
great coniunctions of the superior planets were seene one or two moneths after his calculation. And albeit that *Gerardus Mercator* haue endeuoured by certaine eclipses of
C   the sun & of the moone, by antient writers set downe, more curiously than any other,
to iudge of the course and order of the whole time from the beginning of the world;
yet so it is, that all his obseruations threaten a fall, as grounded vpon a false supposition:
which can in no wise be true, For he supposeth that in the creation of the world, the
sunne was in the signe Leo, without any probable reason, following the opinion of
Iulius Maternus, contrary to the opinion of the Arabians, and of all other the Astrologers, who write, that the sunne was then in the signe Aries: being yet both therein deceiued; these, six signes; and *Mercator* too. For why it is manifestly to bee proued, not
onely by the most antient orders and customes of all people, but by the most diuine
testimonies of holy scripture also, The sunne in the creation of the world, to haue bene *The sunne in the*
D   in the signe Libra: wherby the Feast of the gathering of the fruits is commanded to be *creation of the*
kept the last day of the yere, that is to say, the two and twentith day of the seuenth mo- *bene in the signe*
neth; which *Moses* hath expresly written to haue bene the first, before the departure of *Libra.*
the people out of Aegypt. Which to the intent it might be the lesse doubted of, wee *Exod.23.ver.16*
reade to be oftentimes by him repeated: for when he had cõmanded the feast day Abib, *Exod.11.ver.2*
that is to say, The feast of weeks, which the Greeks call πεντηκοστὴν: he ioyneth herun-
to these words, וחג האסיף תקופת השנה, that is to say, And the feast of the gathering of fruits
in the end of the yere. But the last moment of the yeare past, is the beginning of the yere
following; as *Orus Apollo* writeth, the Aegyptians to haue declared the reuolution of
the yeare, by a dragon turned about into a circle. But *Iosephus*, the best interpreter of
E   antiquity, declareth the moneth Abib, which of th Chaldaies is called Niscan, and of
vs before, March, but now Aprill, to haue beene in order the first for the deliuerance
of the people out of the bondage of Aegypt: but yet the moneth which of the Chaldeis is called Ethanim, of the Hebrewes Tisri, which was our October, but afterward
fell into our September, to haue bene by nature the first. All which, not onely *Iosephus*, but almost all the Hebrew Rabines also, namely *Eleazar, Abraham, Ezra, Iona-
thas* the Chaldean interpreter, with almost all the rest, constantly affirme. Which for
that it hath great force for the discerning of the ruines of Commonweales, is of vs *The world to*
more manifestly to be explaned. The antient schoole of the Hebrewes, begin the rea- *haue taken be-*
ding of *Moses* his bookes, the Genesis, in Autumne: and *Samuel*, the most antient Ra- *tumne.*
                                        Pp iiii   bine

A1 Commonweales   C7 *For* too *read* two *i.e.* two signs of the zodiac, or sixty degrees.
D3(margin) *For* Exod. 11. ver. 2 (L 5) *read* Exod. 12. ver 2 (L 1–4).   D6 וחג האסיף תקופת השנה
E1 the Chaldaies   E1 Nisan   E2 first, for   E6 Abraham Ezræ (L) *i.e.* Abraham ibn Ezra
(cf. Fr)   Note at B8.

bine of the Hebrewes, appointeth the first Tecupa, or yearely conuersion of the yeare, in the Autumne equinoctiall: whereby it is manifest, the doctrine and customes of that most antient nation, to concurre and agree with the law of God. The same was the doctrine of the old Aegyptians and Chaldies also, concerning the beginning of the yeare, from whom all the mathematicall scienses tooke not onely their beginning, but were from them to all other nations of the world deriued also. So *Iulius Firmicus* writeth, the Aegyptians hauing receiued it from their ancestors, to haue deliuered it vnto posterity, The sunne in the beginning of the world to haue bene placed in the last part of Libra. The same was also the opinion of the Indians, who are yet worshippers of the Sunne, & of the Moone, as the Spaniards haue reported. And although the yere of the Grecians, tooke beginning from the summer Solstitium, yet neuerthelesse the people of Asia beganne their Olimpiades and the beginning of the yere from Autumne. The Romans also from the remembrance of most auntient aniquitie, began the yeare from the Ides of September, *Lex vetusta est* (saith *Liuie*) *& priscis scriptis literis, vt qui Prætor maximus sit, Idibus Septembris clauum pangat*, It is an old law (saith he) and written in old auntient letters, that he which was the great Prouost, should euer the Ides of September driue or fasten a naile. This naile *Festus* calleth *annalem*, or an annuall naile, *Qui quotannis figebatur in dextra parte capitolij vt per eos clauos numerus colligeretur annorum*, Which was euerie yeare fastned in the right side of the Capitoll, that so by those nayles the number of the yeares might be gathered. *Augustus* appointed also the Olympic games in the moneth of September. And albeit that the Astrologers (as other people also for the most part) follow a new manner of account of the yeare, set downe by *Moyses*, and begin their account of the spring diuision, yet neuerthelesse they begin their tables of the celestiall motions receiued from the Aegyptians and Chaldeies from the Autumne diuision. Which antiquities, with the authoritie of so many and so worthy men, although they make the matter manifest enough and out of all doubt: yet euen nature it selfe leadeth vs thither also, as that wee must needs confesse the beginning of the world to haue bene in Autumne. For if we grant, as we must needs, man as all other liuing creatures also, to haue bene by almightie God created in such state and perfection as that they should need no nurses; so also is it to be thought him to haue prouided for all liuing creatures, and especially for mankind, ripe fruits for him to feed vpon, and most beautifull to behold, planted in most faire gardens, as is in the sacred booke of Genesis to be seene: which can in no wise be done, but that the world must be created in the beginning of Autumne. For why, *Adam* was created about Iordan, whereas corne in the spring time yet shooteth not on eare; and the moneth Abib is so called, for that the corne in the spring time in those places runneth but vp in spindle, and the trees but scarcely bud: neither is the law of nature, or the season of the spring, or of Autumne, from the beginning of the world chaunged. Wherefore *Plutarch* in his Symposiaques, when he pleasantly questioneth, Whether egges or birds were first? resolueth birds to haue bene first created: and so whatsoeuer things els are contained in the whole world, to haue bene in all parts created perfect. For otherwise if God should haue created man a crying child, or calues for oxen, or egges for birds, he must also haue created nurses to haue suckled them, and birds to haue hatched them: which if it be absurd and foolish to say, so must also of necessitie those things bee absurd, whereof these things follow, *viz.* the world to haue bene created in the beginning of the spring, and young shoots to haue bene made for fruitfull trees, and so likewise other things to haue bene created young, and not in their perfection. Whereby it is euident them greatly to erre & be deceiued, which accounting & taking the beginning of the world from the spring, and the beginning of the day from noone, doe with

their

The auntient Romaines to haue begun the yeare in September.

F 10 although   G 3 antiquitie   I 5 on eare *i.e.* in the ear   K 2 should have

Of A Commonweale. 441

A their vaine coniectures go about to blot out and extinguish the authoritie of the sacred scriptures, as also the most auntient records of the Indians, the Chaldes, the Aegyptians, and Latines, and all forsooth because cold weather still followeth after Autumne: they fearing (as I suppose) least *Adam* being a naked child, should haue taken cold. Seeing therefore the Astrologers, euen as these men also to haue laid false principles and grounds, of the celestiall motions, and much to differ amongst themselues, concerning the course of the starres and planets, they can therefore (I say) set downe nothing certaine, concerning mans affaires, or the ruines of cities and Commonweals.

Astrological predictions vncerten.

But yet it hath lesse probalitie by the foundation of townes and cities, to iudge of the rising or falling of Commonweales: as many do also of houses before they lay the
B foundations of them, to foresee and let that they should not be burnt or rased, or sicke of the falling sicknesse: which to doe is a meere folly, differing little from extreame madnesse, as though natures most constant order should depend of mans lightnesse, and the force of the celestiall Spheres, of the will and pleasure of a base carpenter or mason. Indeed by the law it is prouided, That the value of houses burnt should bee deemed by their age and continuance, for so it is read in the old Hetruscian copie: although that *D. Cuias* a most diligent interpretor of auntient readings, be of their opinion, which for *ætatibus*, thinke it ought to be read *quantitatibus* (as who should say by their quantities, rather than by their age) whereunto the lawyer neuer had respect. For his meaning was, That houses according to the stuffe and matter they were built of,
C were to be esteemed of longer or shorter continuance: as if an house were built of clay or morter, it was esteemed to be able to last some fourescore yeates: in such sort as that if it had cost an hundred crownes at first to build, being burnt fortie yeares after, there should halfe the price thereof be abated in the estimation thereof: For as for houses built with bricke (they as *Plinie* saith) if they be built vpright are euerlasting. And so *Victruuius*, and all other builders were woont to esteeme of the losse sustained, by the age and continuance of the houses burnt. For to esteeme of them by the elle, or by the greatnesse, so a barne built of clay or straw should be esteemed more worth than smaller buildings built of marble or of porphiree, as the temple of Porphiree at Sienna, one of the least, but most costly buildings of Europe. But the deciding of such questions
D we must referre to *Victruuius*, and other builders. And as for that some thinke we are by the foundations of cities and other buildings, to iudge what shall be the state or successe of a kingdome or monarchie should lesse need the refutation: but that *M. Varro* (whome *Tullie* writeth to haue in learning excelled all other Greeks and Latins) commaunded *Tarentius Firmianus* to declare vnto him the Horoscope of the citie of Rome: for so *Plutarch* and *Antimachus Lyrius* report. Whereupon he by the progresse of that Commonweale gathering the causes thereof; and by things ensuing after, gessing at things forepast, & so by retrogradation iudging the causes by the effects, by most light and vaine coniectures affirmeth the foundation of the citie to haue bene
E laid in the third yeare of the sixt Olympiade, the one and twentieth day of Aprill, a little before three of the clocke in the afternoone, *Saturne*, *Mars*, and *Venus*, being as then in Scorpio, *Iupiter* in Pisces, the sunne in Taurus, the moone in Libra, Gemini holding the heart, or middle of the heauens, and Virgo rising. But seeing that the chiefe points of this figure belonging vnto *Mercurie*, and that this whole celestial Scheame betokeneth men of traffique, or otherwise studious of Philosophie, and all kind of learning, how can it come to passe, that these things should agree, or bee applied vnto the Romans, a people of all others most couragious and warlike? Howbeit that *Taruntius* in this his figure, or Horoscope of the foundation of Rome, is most shamefully deceiued, as hauing therein placed the celestiall orbes in a situation quite contrarie vnto nature,

The rising or falling of commonweales, not to be judged or deemed of by the foundation of the townes or cities therein.

viz.

A9 probabilitie   C5 bricke, they (as Plinie saith)   C6, D1 Vitruvius   D3–4 M. Varro
D5 Taruntius Firmianus (cf. E7)   E4 figure   Notes at C7, D1.

442 THE FOVRTH BOOKE

Taruntius Firmianus deceiued in his horoscope or figure of the foundation of Rome.

viz. Venus opposit vnto the Sunne : which yet can neuer be aboue eight and fortie degrees at the most distant from the Sunne : which yet were a thing excusable and worthy to be pardoned, if it had bene by him done by forgetfulnesse : as it happened to *Augerius Ferrerius* an excellent Mathematician, who in his booke of Astronomicall iudgements, hath set *Venus* and *Mercurie*, one of them opposit vnto another, and both of them opposit vnto the Sunne : a thing by nature impossible, and hee himselfe acknowledging that *Mercurie* can neuer be six and thirtie degrees from the Sunne. Yet true it is, that *Iohn Picus* earle of Mirandula, grounding vpon this demonstration of the celestial motions, without cause blameth *Iulius Maturnus*, for that he placed the Sunne in the first house, and *Mercurie* in the tenth, which cannot be (saith he) except the sun should be from *Mercurie* the fourth part of the circle (or three signes distant:) not hauing regard, that the globe may so be placed, to encline vnto the North, as that the sun rising, *Mercurie* may come vnto the meridian, yea vnto the tenth house two houres before noone, and yet not be thirtie degrees from the sunne. But *Plutarch* writeth *Antimachus Lyrius* to haue left recorded, the Sunne to haue bene then ecclipsed, which yet he saith to haue bene the diametre of the circle distant from the Moone. And yet there is another greater absurditie in that theame of *Taruntius*, in that hee placeth the sunne in Taurus the xxj day of Aprill, which then entred not thereinto vntill the thirtith of Aprill. Howbeit also that *Lucas Gauricus*, who collected the celestiall theames of many most famous cities, differeth altogether from this theame of Rome, by *Taruntius* before set downe : for he placeth Libra in the East, as doth also *Manlius*. But of all absurd things none is more absurd, than by the ouerthrow of cities to measure the destruction of the estate or Commonweale, whereas before we haue declared, that a city oftentimes may be ouerthrowne and laid euen flat with the ground, and yet the state and Commonweal therof remaine, as we haue before shewed of the citie of Carthage : as oftentimes to the contrarie the estate and Commonweale may perish, the walls and other buildings yet standing all whole.

Wherefore then I rest not vpon such opinions, and much lesse vpon that which *Cardan* saith, who to seeme more subtilly than others to handle these hidden and obscure matters, & to raise an admiration of himselfe with men vnskilfull of these things, maintaineth the beginnings and encreasings of the greatest cities and Empires to haue come from that Starre which is the last in the taile of Vrsa Maior, which he saith to haue bene verticall vnto the great citie of Rome at the foundation thereof, and from thence euen by the helpe and working of the same Starre translateth the Roman Empire to Constantinople, and so afterwards into Fraunce, and so from thence into Germanie:

Cardan his error detected and his opinion reiected.

which although they be so set downe but by a most brainsicke man, yet do men ignorant of the celestiall motions wonderfully admire the same, and are therfore by vs to be refuted. For perceiuing that last starre of Vrsa Maior to be daily vnto manie people verticall, though perpendicular vnto them onely which are subiect vnto the circle which that starre describeth, *Cardican* saith it should be verticall at such time as the Sun toucheth the Meridian circle : in which state he supposeth it to haue beene, at such time as *Romulus* the founder of the citie laied the foundation thereof : which could not by nature so be, *viz.* that the last starre of Vrsa maior in the same howre, that is to say at noonetide, should together with the Sun touch the verticall circle : For that starre being now in the xxj degree of Virgo, by proportion of the motion of the fixed starres, by reason of the motion of the eight Sphere, it must needs haue beene in the xix degree of Leo at such time as the foundation of the citie of Rome was laied, and the Sun in the xix. degree of Aries, as the foregoings of the Sun declare. So that that starre was the third part of the circle, or foure signes and twentie degrees distant from

---

F9 Maternus   G4 degrees   H1 Manlius (L 4–5) Manilius (L 1–3). Both forms are admissible.
I10 *For* Cardican *read* Cardan.   K1 in which   Note at F7.

OF A COMMONWEALE.

A from the verticall, when as it ought to haue beene in the same signe, and in the same degree of the signe wherein the Sunne was, if *Cardan* his doctrine were true: who yet when he knew the same starre to haue beene verticall vnto many great cities at the time of their foundation, since the beginning of the world, the Sun also then being in the Meridian; he to meet with that obiection, said the Monarchie to be due but to one of them. But why that to the Romans from whose verticall it is distant twelue degrees, rather then to the Scottish fishermen which dwell neere vnto the Orcades? or vnto them of Norway, and other the Northren people? vnto whom the same starre is not onely verticall, the sun touching the Meridian in September, but is also directly perpendicular? Yet is it also more straunge, to say the same starre to haue giuen the
B Empire to Constantinople, considering that that citie was built nine hundred yeares before that the Empire was thither translated. Ioining hereunto also that the horoscope of the citie of Constantinople found in the Popes librarie in the Vatican written in Greeke letters, calculated by *Porphyrie* (as some affirme) and copied out by *Lucas Gauricus* the Bishop, declareth the Sunne then to haue beene in the xvij degree of Taurus, the Moone in the v of Leo, Saturne in the xx of Cancer, Iupiter and Venus coniunct in the same signe, Mars in the twelft, Mercurie in the first of Gemini, Aquarius holding the verticall of heauen, and the xxiij of Gemini in the Leuant; which he setteth downe to haue beene in May vpon a Munday, two howres after the sunne ri-
C sing. An other celestiall Theame of the same Citie is also taken out of the Vatican, calculated by *Valens* of Antioch, later than the former by fortie minutes. But yet that is verie absurd which *Gauricus* the good Bishop to come to his accounut supposeth the citie of Constantinople to haue beene built in the yeare of our Lord 638, three hundred yeares after the death of *Porphyrie*: which yet it is manifest to haue flourished aboue 500. yeares before Christ: which he thinketh also to haue beene afterwards taken by the Turks armie in the yeare of Christ 1430. when as in truth it was by them woon and sackt in the yeare of our Lord 1453, the xxix day of May, being 1800 yeare before taken by the French men: wherein they raigned vntill the time of *Clyarus* king of Thracia, as *Polybius* (tutor vnto *Scipio Affricanus*) writeth; at which time it was
D called Bizance. And againe afterwards also was taken by *Pausanias* king of Lacedemonia in the Median warre. And yet more, afterwards also was besieged by *Alcibiades* generall of the Athenians. And long time after, three yeares together againe besieged by *Seuerus* the Emperour, who after he had sacked it, razed it also downe to the ground, and carrying away the rest of the citisens into captiuitie, gaue the ground whereon it stood vnto the Perinthians about the yeare of our Lord two hundred: which yet not long after was againe reedified, and by *Constantine* the great wonderfully enriched after that he had thither translated the seat of his Empire. And yet againe after that, was with fire and sword most cruelly wasted by the armie of *Galienus* the Emperour, all the citisens therein being either slaine, or else caried away into captiui-
E tie. Yet ceased it not for all that to be still the seat of the Greeke empire, vntill that the Frenchmen and Flemings vnder the conduct of *Baldwin* Earle of Flaunders seized thereon; which they held together with the Empire, vntill that about fiftie yeares after they were by the *Palæologi* againe driuen out: who hauing so recouered the citie there raigned, vntill that it was by *Mahomet* the great Turke woon. All which changes of the Empire, and ruines of the citie, *Gauricus* neuer touched; neither did *Cardan* himselfe so much as suspect them: otherwise I suppose he would neuer haue written things so absurd, and so disagreeing with themselues. But great maruell it is that this *Cardans* starre hath had such power as to graunt the Empires of the world to Italie, Greece, Fraunce, and Germanie, when as it was to them but verticall, and yet hath
had

A 5 Monarchie *i.e.* supremacy, empire   C 2 account   Notes at B1, B4, C7, D4.

had no power at all vpon the realmes of Norway and Sweden, where it is not onely verticall, the Sunne being at the Meridian in the moneth of August, but is also perpendicular: and yet neuerthelesse distant from Rome and Constantinople in latitude twelue degrees at the least. Besides that, why should he giue vnto this Starre (which some foolish Astrologers take to be Saturnia) more power than to others, both for their greatnesse & nature more notable? why doth he exclude from the gouernment of the world Regulus the greatest of all the fixe starres? whie Medusa, Spica, the great Dog, the Vultur, all most faire and beautifull starres? whie in briefe a thousand and threescore others, (for so many there are accounted beside the wandering starres) vnto whom the Hebrew Mathematicians had added thirtie six mo also? Sufficeth it for this time to haue reiected these errours so grosse, as the day it selfe is cleere.

The errour of Peter Cardinall of Arliac.

But for asmuch as it were a thing infinite to refell all mens errours in this kind of matter, I will onely touch theirs, who haue thought themselues wiser than the rest, and haue beene had in reputation as best seene in the iudgement of the heauens for the chaunges of Commonweales: such as was *Peter* of Arliac Chauncelour of Paris, and afterwards Cardinall in the yeare 1416: For he writeth the beginnings, chaunges, and ruines of religions and Commonweales, to depend of the motion and coniunction of the superiour Planets. And to mee it seemeth right straunge, whie *Iohn Picus* Earle of Mirandula hath without farther search, accounted of the shamefull errours of this man, concerning the knowledge of the Celestiall Spheres, as of most certeine & approued demonstrations; who hauing noted six and thirtie great coniunctions of the superiour planets, Iupiter & Saturne, since an hundred and fifteene yeares after the creation of the world, vnto the yeare of our Lord Christ 1385, there are not of them six true, and scarce any of them set in such place and time as they ought to be. *Leupold*, *Alcabice*, and *Ptolomee* were also of the same opinion, *viz.* the remouings of people, warres, plagues, deluges, plentie, dearth, the chaunges of Estates and Commonweales, to depend of the motion and coniuction of the Planets, and especially of the superiour planets Saturne I say and Iupiter, and so much the more if Mars be also in coniunction with them both. And so indeed as oft as they are in coniunction together, such things thereof ensue as often times draw euen the wiser sort into admiration: howbeit that no necessitie be imposed vpon man kind by the influence of the heauens. But howsoeuer that be, it is manifest the Cardinall of Arliac to haue beene most grieuously deceiued, who reckning vp those great coniunctions from the beginning, supposeth it by his account to haue beene seauen thousand yeares since the creation of the world, following therein the errours of *Alphonsus*, *Eusebius*, and *Beda*; which the great consent not of the Hebrewes onely, but of all Christians also hath long a go reiected: so soone as by the old interpretation of the Bible it was perceiued them to haue erred in their account aboue a thousand fiue hundred yeares: whereas all Churches at this present follow the more certeine account of *Philo* the Iew, who followed almost the mean betwixt *Iosephus* and the later Hebrewes: for *Iosephus* differeth 342 yeares, and *Philo* but an 160 from the other Hebrewes. Whereof it is to be gathered this present yeare, which is from the birth of our Sauiour Christ 1583, (wherin *Bodin* writ these things in Latin) to haue beene 5531, or at most 5555 since the creation of the world. Wherefore *Arliac* is deceiued, who put the coniunction of the superiour Planets seauen thousand yeres ago, in the 320 yeare after the creation of the world: which after that computation must haue happened twelue hundred yeares before that the world was made. The same man doth suppose also that at the creation of the world, the Horoscope whereof he discribeth, the first degree of Cancer to haue beene then rising, the Sunne then to haue beene in Aries, (which to be false we haue

by

OF A COMMONWEALE.   445

A by necessarie arguments before proued) the Moone and Venus in Taurus, Saturne in Aquarius, Iupiter in Pisces, Mars in Scorpio, Mercurie in Gemini: which is all false and quite contrarie vnto the nature and motion of the celestiall Spheres, which is manifest vnto euery man which shall more narrowly looke thereinto, or take account of the motions of the Planets from thence vnto these times: not to speake of that, that he placed the Sunne in the xix degree of Aries, and Mercurie in the xv of Gemini, hauing so against nature diuided the one of them from the other six and fiftie degrees, as we haue before declared: *viz.* that Mercurie when he is farthest from the Sunne, neuer to be farther off than six and thirtie degrees. Which may suffice in passing by, or show that the Hypothesis of the Cardinal of Arliac and his foundation being false, the

B rest that is thereon built cannot stand. But this he had propounded vnto himselfe, It to be a thing contrarie vnto the maiestie of the Planets, if in the creation of the world he should place them other where than euery one of them in their owne throne and chariot: which deuises of the vnskilfull, are more light and farther from the antiquitie of the Chaldeis, than that they deserue to be refelled.

But how much more certainlie and better do they, which hauing consideratlie looked thorow the antiquities of the Hebrewes, and the animaduertions of *Copernicus* (who most diligently corrected the errors of *Alphonsus*, and of the Arabians) going orderly retrograde from these oppositions and coniunctions of the Planets which we now behold, vnto the verie first beginning, iudge of the reuolution of the

C time past, as also of the chaunge and state of Commonweales; if yet by this meanes any such iudgement, free from impietie and rashnesse may be made. Neither is it to be hoped (except happelie in an innumerable sort of worlds) that the three superiour Planets shall meet together in the first point of Aries, whereof our wisards rashly diuine a generall destruction of Commonweales, as also of the whole world then to ensue by fyre from heauen. Howbeit that in the yeare of our Lord Christ 1909, there shall be a meeting together of the three superiour Planets in the ninth degree of Aries: which yet for all that is no true coniunction, as not made by the centers, but by the Orbes and Spheres of the Planets. And in the yeate 1584, Saturne and Mars shall be in coniunction in the first point and 46 minutes of Aries, and Iupiter in the same signe,

D but distant from them twelue degrees, with the Sunne and Mercurie: which coniunction shall scarce chaunce againe in the reuolution of eight hundred yeares. And in this sort it is lawfull for a man looking into the yearely course of time, by writing to commend vnto posteritie the chaunges of cities and Commonweales, and so by things precedent and alreadie forepassed to iudge also of things to come: yet sauing alwaies the maiestie of almightie God, who is himselfe bound vnto no lawes of nature, neither hath thereunto bound any of his seruants. Wherein many greatly offend, who thinke the power and influence of the celestiall Spheres to be nothing, when as yet for all that their strength and power hath alwaies beene most great and effectuall, not

E onely vpon these elements which we here see, and so vpon all other sorts of liuing creatures, but euen vpon them also which liue like beasts, as * in sacred writ is to be seene, and yet of the good nothing at all to be feared. So many stood in great doubt in the yeare 1524, wherein the three superiour Planets, Saturne, Iupiter, and Mars were in coniunction in the tenth degree of Pisces, the rest of the Planets together with the Dragons head being in Aquarius & Pisces, both of them waterie Signes. Which selfe same yeare in the moneth of Februarie were twentie other coniunctions of the Planets also among themselues, besides the sixe starres; which of all other things, was a thing most worthie the admiration. So that hereupon the Astrologers all the world ouer agreeing together for the destruction of the world, with a great feare terrifyed

Margin notes:
- How a man may without offence presage the chaunges of Cities and Commonweales.
- Iob. 39. and 40.
- Vaine feares oftentimes conceiued, vpon Astrologers vaine predictions.

Qq   the

A9–10 to show   C3 worlds *i.e.* ages, centuries   E1 (margin) Iob.   Notes at C3, C8, D2.

the minds of many weake men; in that they so constantly all with one consent affirmed, the world to be now againe ouerwhelmed with an vniuersall deluge and nundation of waters; insomuch that many miscreants caused shippes to be made for them to saue themselues in from such the rage of the waters, and especially *Auriolus* President of Tholose a most cunning lawier, but a man either ignorant, or a contemner of the lawes of God, howbeit that he heard the promises of God still preached vnto him, and the oath by him made vnto * *Noah* that he would no more destroy the world by water. And true it is that in that yeare were flouds and inundations of waters in diuers countries, but yet no such generall deluge as was foretold and feared, neither any cities or countries at all knowne to be drowned. Wherefore to affirme any thing of the chaunges and ruines of Commonweales, it sufficeth not to behold onely those great coniunctions of the three superiour Planets, but also diligently to obserue and note the meane coniunctions, which are euery two hundred and fortie, and euery twentie yeare: as also the eclipse of the Sunne, and of the Moone, with the oppositions and coniunctions of the inferiour Planets amongst themselues, and with superiour planets, and in briefe their mutuall traiections, as also the force and power of the fixe starres, and their respect towards others. True it is that many of the auntient writers haue noted either dearth, or popular diseases, great mortalitie of liuing creatures, or the remouing of people, inundations of waters, or the destruction of cities, or chaunges of kingdomes to haue followed such coniunction of the superiour planets; yet not in euery place generally, but in certaine countries and places onely, whereby they haue by a certain coniecture iudged this or that signe to be by God deputed vnto this or that countrie. And hereof according to the power of the foure elements they haue diuided the twelue celestiall signes into foure parts, and haue thereof left certaine instructions to posteritie: whereof for all that because they were not by long experience approued they could make no certaine art: as the Chaldies haue fained, who vaunted themselues to haue spent 470 thousand yeares in the practise of natiuities, the better to perswade men of the certaintie of their knowledge, and to make it thereby the more saleable. Which the Chaldean bables spred abroad farre and wide vnto all people, but vnto none more foolishly then to the Indian Chinois, who say 783 thousand and seauen hundred sixtie two yeares, to be the last yeare past since the creation of the world. Others there be which in that matter lie not so loudly and yet impudently enough. For *Linus* the most auntient writer of the Greekes, *Orpheus* and *Heraclitus*, shut vp the period of the greatest yeare within the reuolution of 360 thousand yeares, whereof they supposed an hundred fourescore foure thousand to be past. But a certaine Ægiptian priest vaunted before *Solon*, the Ægiptians his countrie men to haue an historie of twentie thousand yeares written in Hieroglyphicall letters. And a little while after *Herodotus* (called the father of historie) vnderstood from the same Ægiptians, recordes of thirteene thousand yeares to be extant in their sacred letters. *Diodorus* yonger then the rest going into Ægipt to find out the trueth, heard certaine Priests to say antiquities of three and thirtie thousand yeares old to be found amongst the Ægiptians: but when he came to wey the trueth of the matter in equall ballance, he found all their antiquitie to consist but of three thousand seauen hundred yeares: the computation of which time from the beginning of the world, agreeth altogether with *Philo*, or within little lesse then two hundred yeres. And truely *Callisthenes* perswaded by the speech of *Aristotle* his master, when as others at the sacking of Babylon greedely sought after the Persian wealth, he diligently searched out and gathered together the bookes and antiquities of the Chaldies, and there noted all the historie of the Chaldies to haue bene comprehended in 1903 yeares: which time well

* Genes. 7.

The vanitie of the Chaldean Astrologers.

H9 For Which the Chaldean bables *probably read* Which Chaldean bables (*i.e.* baubles, trifles, foolishness). Cf. L.

Note at F4.

OF A COMMONWEALE.

A well agreeth with the sacred historie, if we account the time from *Nimrod*, who first obtained the soueraigntie of the Chaldies: which historie is to be thought so much the truer, for that it is so reported by *Simplicius* a mortall enemie of the Christians, as wee haue elswhere declared. And therefore *Ptolomey*, who farthest repeating from vttermost remembrance the antiquities of the Chaldies (of them I say, which had noted the stedie courses of the celestiall Spheres) bringeth the beginnings of the celestiall motions no farther than from *Nabonassar*, and from those eclipses of the moone which happened in the time of his raigne, that is, the yeare of the world 3750: But *Ptolomey* flourished in the time of *Adrian* the emperour, about foure hundred yeares after *Nabonassar*. Wherefore it ought not to seeme straunge to any man, if he neuer so
B much as once suspected the motion of trepidation, neither vnderstood the reuolution of the eight Sphere: yea he well obserued not the Equinoctials: For hee saith, The Equinoctium to haue bene the the twentie sixt of September, after the sunne rising: which *Hipparchus* had taught to haue happened 285 yeares the same day of the moneth, about midnight, whose errours could scarcely be perceiued in the time of our ancestors: as not long ago *Io. Regiomontanus* shewed the motion of trepidation, before vnto Astronomers vnknowne. Wherefore by what meanes could they by any art conclude mens fortunes, or the chaunges and ruines of cities and Commonweales, who vnderstood not so much as the celestiall motions, and much lesse the histories of
C all nations, when as yet they scarcely knew the tenth part of the world?

Wherefore they do foolishly which attribute the Quadripartite booke to *Ptolomey*, wherein the fierie Triplicitie is giuen to Europe, and those countries which lye betwixt the West and the North; the ayrie triplicitie vnto Asia, and those places which are seated betwixt the North and the East; the watrie triplicitie vnto Affrike, and the earthly triplicitie vnto the other places. Neither haue those things followed the coniunctions of the superiour planets, which should haue followed had their rules beene true. Now if any man thinke (as many there be which think right foolishly) the places of the signes being chaunged, the force and nature of the celestiall Spheres to be chaunged also; he must surely vtterly subuert all the knowledge of the force and power of the stars
D by them before set downe and deliuered: seeing that the fix starres are found since the beginning of the world to haue passed through the fourth part of the eight Sphere: but since the time wherein the course of the celestiall Spheres began first to bee of the Chaldeis noted vnder king *Nabonassar* vnto this our time, to haue ouergone almost a whole signe, εἰς τὰ ἑπόμενα, or which is all one, the Equinoctials in the same space, to haue preuented the staies of the wandering starres, εἰς τὰ προηγούμενα, and yet neuertheleсse the force and power of the celestiall houses approued in mens natiuities, is still the selfe same that it is reported to haue before bene: which thing to be so, *Cardan* himselfe confesseth: whom yet for all that it ashamed him not to write the Britons, Spaniards, & Normans, in auntient time gentle and modest nations, to be now (the regions
E of the starres being changed) become slie, craftie, and deceitfull theeues; for that they were in auntient time gouerned by Sagittary, but now by Scorpio: vnto whom the same may be aunswered which *Cassius* did vnto a certain Chaldean Astrologer, who forbad him to fight with the Parthians before the moone was out of Scorpio: vnto whom *Cassius* pleasantly aunswered, *Non Scorpiones metuo, sed Sagittarios*, I feare not (said he) Scorpions, but Sagittaries; meaning the Parthian archers, by whom the Roman legions wherewith *Crassus* in Chaldea discomfited and ouerthrowne. And truely if *Cardans* opinion were true, the nature of all things must needs so be subuerted, which yet is still the same which euer it was: For the people toward the North are now taller and stronger, and more warlike than the rest of the people of the world; and such *Vitruuius*,

The triplicities of the cælestiall signes not to be determinatly assigned vnto certaine regions and countries, as the Astrologers appoynt.

The ieast of Cassius vnto a Caldean Astrologer.

Qq ij

B4 Hipparchus   D4 εἰς τὰ ἑπόμενα *i.e.* eastwards   D5 staies *i.e. cardines*, the points around which a thing revolves, the poles   D5 *For* wandering starres *read* fixed starres (*stellae inerrantes*).
D5 εἰς τὰ προηγούμενα *i.e.* westwards   E6 *For* wherwith *read* were with.   Notes at A3, A7.

tius, *Plinie*, *Cæsar*, *Strabo*, and *Plutarch*, haue writ them to haue beene sixteene hundred yeare agoe: and therefore them to be pleasant, drunkards, grosse witted, hoarce, gray eyed, yellow haired: but Southerne people to bee sad, small of stature, leane, weake, smooth, blacke eyed, curled haire, and cleere of voice. And yet it is manifest, the coniunctions of the superiour planets in the same celestiall house, *viz.* in Scorpio to haue showed their force (if it were any) in Asia, and Europe, and not in Affrike, which they say to be gouerned by the signe of Scorpio. For before the chaunge of the Roman empire was made, and that Popular estates transferred vnto the soueraigntie of *Cæsar* alone, the superiour planets with a great coniunction met together in Scorpio: which coniunction chaunged againe about seauen hundred yeres after: at which time innumerable legions of the Arabians hauing receiued the new doctrine of *Muhamed*, rebelled against the Greeke emperours, subdued a great part of the East Asia, abolished the orders, customes, rites, ceremonies, and lawes of the Christians, when as yet Asia is in situation contrarie vnto Europe. The same coniunction happened in the yeare of our Lord 1464, after which ensued diuers motions of the people, almost in all parts of the world. For *Ladamachus* king of the Tartars was by his subiects thrust out of his kingdome: *Henrie* the sixt, king of England was by his subiects also taken and in prison slain, *Edward* the iiij of a subiect made king: *Frederike* the third driuen out of Hungary by *Matthias Coruinus*, who of a prisoner was chosen a king: *Lewes* the eleuenth the French king, by his nobilitie and vassals besieged in his principall citie, and brought in daunger to haue lost his estate. At which time also *Alexander* (commonly called *Scanderbeg*) the king of Albania his sonne, brought vp in the Turkes court, reuolted from the Turke, and tooke vp armes against him. Yet is it worth the noting, that the great coniunctions of superiour planets, show their effects more in Scorpio, a martial signe, than in any other the rest of the signes, and so much the more if *Mars* be there also, or else some one of the other planets be also in coniunction or opposition with them. With like coniunction the same planets met together also in Sagittarie, in the yeare of our Lord Christ 74: at which time all the land of Palestine was sacked, the citie of Hierusalem burnt and rased, and eleuen hundred thousand dead in the warres: at which selfe same time were seene in Europe great ciuill warres, and foure emperours slaine the same yeare. Two hundred and fortie yeres after, another coniunction of the same planets chaunced in Capricorne, after which ensued wonderfull 'chaunges not onely of Commonweales, but euen of empires and kingdomes also: *Constantine* the Great being therein chiefe doer: who hauing put to flight and slaine foure emperors, and translated the seat of the empire from the West into the East, by a perpetuall law tooke away the vaine and superstitious worshipping of the Paynim gods. We see also, that after the coniunction of the same planets in Aquarius, in the yeare 430, the Gothes, the Ostrogothes, the Francons, the Gepiges, the Heruli, the Hunnes, & other Northerne people going out like swarmes of bees, ouerranne and ransacked the prouinces of the Roman empire, and most cruelly sacked the verie citie it selfe, sometime the seat of the empire. And againe in the yeare 1524, when as the coniunction of the same superiour planets, (yea twentie other coniunctions) had happened in Pisces, most great motions of the people ensued thereafter in many places in Europe: the people in armes against the nobilitie set all Germany on a broyle: in which warre an hundred thousand men are reported to haue bene slaine: the Rhodes by the Turkes was taken from the Christians: *Frederike*, his brother *Christierne* being driuen out of his kingdome, possessed the kingdome of Denmarke: *Gostauus* of a priuat man became king of Sweden: *Francis* the French king ouerthrowne at Pauia was taken prisoner by the Spaniards. Besides that, it is to be seene, that after the great coniunction of the same supe-

[marginal note:] The coniunctions of the superior Planets to haue oftentimes wrought great effects for the alteration and changing of Commonweales.

G6 Zadamachus   I3 *For* empires and kingdomes *read* regions (*regionum* in L 1–2, *regnorum* in L 3–5).   I7 planets   I8 Gepides   Notes at F1, F2, G7, G9, K8.

OF A COMMONWEALE. 449

superiour planets in Leo in the yeare 796 king *Charlemaigne* ouerthrew the estates of the Lombards, tooke their king, and conquered Italie. At which very selfe same time the Polonians made choyce of their first king: with diuers other notable and remarkable chaunges. So also fortie yeares after, the same coniunction happened in the signe of Sagittarie, when as the Moores sacked diuers countries, inuaded a part of Greece, and ouerran Italie: and the Danes were then vp in great ciuill warres: when as at the same time *Charlemaigne* made himselfe Lord of Germanie, tooke away the Paynim superstition in Saxonie, and chaunged all the Commonweales and principalities in Germanie, and Hungarie, which he brought vnder his obeysance. With this great coniunction happened also foure eclipses: which hath not happened since: but six hundred thirtie six yeares after, *viz.* in the yeare 1544, in which time haply there had bene moe notable changes seene, if the great coniunction which hapned the yeare following in Scorpio, had happened the same yeare. And yet neuerthelesse as it was, all Germanie was vp in armes; which warres continued seuen yeares after. In briefe, if any foreknowledge be to be had from celestiall things, for the chaunges of Commonweales, we must consider the coniunctions of superior planets, since 570 yeres, with the coniunctions, eclipses, and aspects of inferiour planets, and of the six starres at the time of the great coniunctions, and to compare them with the truth of histories, and of times with coniunctions before past; and not wholly to rest vpon opinion of them, which haue determinatly assigned the Triplicities vnto regions, which I haue by euident examples before shewed not to be of any good assurance, but rather to stay vpon the nature of the signes and of the planets. And yet for all that to referre the causes and effects of them vnto the great God of nature, and not to tie them vnto his creatures. As did *Ciprianus Leouitius*, who of a coniunction of almost all the planets, than to come together with an eclips of the sunne in the yeare 1584 by his writings (as from an oracle) denounced the end of the world euen then to come, saying, *Procul dubio alterum aduentum filij Dei & hominis in maiestate gloriæ suæ prænuntiat*, Without all doubt (saith he) it foreshoweth another comming of the sonne of God and man in the maiestie of his glorie. But seeing he had so strongly assured men then of the consummation of the world, why did he yet write his Ephemerides for thirtie yeares after, when as the celestiall signes and all Commonweales should according to his predictions haue before perished? But therein he found himselfe as wel deceiued, as was before him *Albumar*, who with like rashnesse had written, That the Christian religion should take end in the yeare 1460. And *Abraham* the Iew (surnamed *The Prince of Astrologers*) who prophesied, That in the yeare 1464 should be borne a great captaine (whom they call *Messias*) who should deliuer the Iewes his countrey men from the seruitude of the Christians. And *Arnold* the Spaniard, who with like follie prophesied of the comming of Antichrist, in the yeare of our Lord 136. But *Leouicius* might haue knowne, that since the creation of the world vnto this time, there haue beene two hundred and threescore coniunctions of the superious planets, wherein were twentie foure great ones; that is to say, such as still come againe after the reuolution of two hundred and fortie yeares, *Iupiter* and *Saturne* meeting together in the same triplicitie (as they call it) and the lesser euerie twentie yeares: and the meanest planets, as of *Saturne* and *Mars*, euerie thertie yeares in the signe Cancer: and the greatest of all, *viz.* of *Iupiter* and *Saturne* in Aries, which commeth againe about euerie eight hundred yeares Howbeit that *Messahala* calleth it the greatest coniunction of all, when as the three superior planets meet together in Aries: which yet I see not shall chaunce in the yeare 1584, as *Leouicius* supposeth, when as *Iupiter* shall be distant twelue degrees from the full coniunction of *Saturne* and *Mars*: which cannot rightly be called a coniunction so much as by their

The errour of Leouicius.

Q q iij Spheres

A1 *For* 796 *read* 769.   B6 *For* 570 *read* 1570.   C4 than *i.e.* then   D2 Albumazar (Fr and L)
D5 1464 (Fr 5–8) 1364 (L) omitted (Fr 1–4)   D8 *For* 136 *read* 1345 (Fr 5–8) *or* 1340 (L) *omitted*
(Fr 1–4).   D9 *For* two hundred and threescore *read* 270 (L only). D10 superiour   E2 Jupiter
E2 call it): and   Notes at A4, E3, E5.

Spheres. But whereas the same coniunction, yea and a greater too, together with the most darke eclipses of the sunne, and of the moone, happened in the raigne of Charles the Great, yet wee see not the world therefore to haue taken end. True it is, that the Hebrew learned men write, the destruction of all this elementarie world, and so of all mankind, & of all Commonweales, to ensue after euerie seuen thousand yeares, by the inundation of waters, or els by fire, and so to rest a thousand yeares: after which God shal againe restore that which is perished: and that this shal be done seuen times, which maketh nine and fortie thousand yeres compleat, and that then this elementarie world and the celestiall also, with all the bodies thereof shall take end, the maiestie of the great eternall God, with all the blessed spirits yet still remaining. Which they say to bee by the word of God, howbeit verie obscurely declared: when as the tilling of the ground is commaunded euery seuenth yeare to be left off: and after seuen times seuen, not onely the tilling of the ground is commaunded to be left off, but euen slaues and debtors to be set free, and euerie man to returne againe vnto his owne lands and dwelling. Truly it is by long obseruation at length knowne and found out, the motion of trepidation of the eight Sphere, to accomplish the course thereof, in the reuolution of seuen thousand yeares, and the ninth Sphere in the space of fortie nine thousand yeares. Whereof *Io. Regiomontanus* hath since within this foure and twentie yeares made plaine demonstration: of the truth of which motion neither the auntient Chaldies nor Ægyptians had any knowledge, but were thereof altogether ignorant. And albeit that the auntient learned Hebrewes, haue by the gift and goodnesse of God, had not onely the knowledge of diuine and celestiall things, but euen the hidden and secret causes of nature also reuealed and made knowne vnto them, and that from them the knowledge of most goodly things is vnto other men come: as *Porphyrie* the greatest of all the Philosophers of his time confesseth: and that this doctrine of the Hebrewes cutteth off the impietie of them which hold the eternitie of the world, or els that God was for an innumerable world of yeares altogether idle: yet doe these so learned Hebrewes attribute nothing vnto fatall necessitie, either feare any the decrees of the celestiall starres, but affirme all things to be gouerned and changed by the will and pleasure of almightie God: as by him which as oft as he will is of power to shake the nature of all things, yea euen the verie foundations of the world it selfe, as was well seene in the generall deluge, which ouerwhelmed the whole world 1656 yeares after the creation thereof.

Yet doubt I not but that some more certaine precepts might be giuen of the chaunges, and ruines of Commonweales, if a man would enter into a certaine account of the time past euen from the beginning of the world: and so comparing one thing with another, and knitting one thing vnto another, shall proceed farther, and set in order the varietie of Historiographers at varience among themselues: and also going backwards, shall of all the eclipses of the Sunne and of the Moone, euen to the beginning of the world, by most certaine demonstrations comprehend the reason of the whole time past: and compare the histories of the most true writers amongst themselues, and with the oppositions and coniunctions of the celestial starres and bodies, knit and conioyne the same with numbers, whose force in all the course of nature is greatest: which things foulded vp in infinit obscurities, and hidden and shut vp in the most secret places of nature, are to be showed not by vaine coniectures, but by most euident and manifest arguments. Which is not to be hoped for from them which are more desirous of words than of matter or knowledge: who vpon an obstinat opinion confound the beginning of the world, and beginning the yere at the spring, which they ought to begin at Autumne, and the day at noone, which they ought to begin at euen, not remembring darknesse to haue bene before light, confusion before order, and a rude confused

Chaos

G8 *For* foure and twentie *read* eighty (quatre vingts).   K7 *For* and beginning the yere *read* and begin the yere (cf. L).   Notes at G10, K6.

A Chaos before the world it selfe: beside that it is in the sacred bookes of Genesis so often repeated, *Vespere & mane dies vnus*, The euening and morning were made one day. Truely I commend many things in *Gerardus Mercator* a most pure writer for the obseruation of time: but in that I cannot commend him, that he beginneth the yeare elswhere than of Libra; whereas we haue by most certaine reasons not onely out of the most auntient customes of almost all nations; but also out of the most pure fountains of sacred scriptures, declared the yeare to haue taken beginning in Autumne. Which we will againe show by the great and notable changes of estates and Commonweals: whereby things to come may be the better and more certainly perceiued, and the greatest chaunces, alterations, and changes, seene to haue happened about Autumne, that is B to say, a little before, or a little after the Autumnall equinoctiall in September, the Sun then entring into Libra: where the law of God appointeth the beginning of the yeare. And first it is manifest, the generall deluge to haue begun and also ended in Autumne. We read also, the great earthquakes, wherewith oft times great cities, and whole countries haue bene destroyed, to haue happened in Autumne, such as was that trembling of the earth at Constantinople, wherein thirteene thousand men were lost in the yeare 1509, in the moneth of September: in which moneth, and in the same citie, the earth againe grieuously shooke in the yeare 1479. So also in the yeare of Christ 545 such an earthquake happened in September, that almost all Europe shooke therewith. The C same moneth of September, wherein the battell was fought at Actium, ten thousand men perished in the land of Palestine with an earthquake. And not long agoe, *viz.* in the yeare 1526, and 27, in the moneth of September a great earthquake happened at Puteoli. The third day of the same moneth, in the yeare of our Lord 1556, such a tempest of raine and thunder happened at Lucerne, as that a greater (as is reported) was neuer seene: which selfe same month & day the towne hall at Maidenburg in Germanie, with the citisens dauncing therein, were all together with lightning consumed. The victorie of *Augustus* also against *Antonius* in the battaile at Actium, was by him obtained the second of September, where question was of the greatest empire that euer was, and the matter tried with the greatest forces that euer were assembled in any wars D whatsoeuer: by which victorie the empire both of the East and of the West, fell into the power of *Augustus* himselfe alone. The third day of the same moneth the Macedonian empire, which had so long, aud with so great glorie flourished, was by *Paulus Aemilius* chaunged from a great kingdome into diuers Popular estates, the king *Perseus* being by him ouercome and taken prisoner. *Sultan Soliman* on the like day tooke Buda the chiefe citie of Hungarie, with the greatest part of that kingdome. The same day and moneth *Rhoderike* king of Spaine was by the Moores ouercome and chased out of his kingdome, which wrought a wonderfull chaunge in the state of all that Monarchie. On the same day and moneth reuoluing, *Lewes* the twelth the French king tooke the citie of Milan, with *Lewes Sfortia* duke thereof, whome he depriued of his E estate. The like day the emperour *Charles* the fift passed ouer into Affrike, and inuaded the kingdom of Algiers. The day following, that is to say, the fourth of September *Sultan Soliman* died before Sigeth, which being one of the strongest holds of Christendome, was by the Turkes taken the seuenth day after. The ninth of September, in the yeare of our Lord 1544, *Iames* king of Scots was by the English men slaine, and his armie ouerthrowne. The same day in the reuolution of the yeare, the councell of Possi was gathered in Fraunce, *Charles* the ninth then raigning in the yeare 1561, and a decree made for the receiuing of the new religion, which raised most great troubles in France. The same day and moneth *Alexander* the Great at Arbela ouerthrew *Darius* king of Persia, with his armie of foure hundred thousand men; and so ioyned the kingdome

The greatest and most notable chaunges of estates and Commonweales to haue commonly hapned in the moneth of September.

Qq iiij dome

A4 beginneth   B2 *For* beginning of the yeare *Bodin writes* beginning of the world (Fr).   B8 *For* 1479 (L) *read* 479 (Fr). The source is Jordanes.   C3 third day (L) fourth day (Fr 3–8) *omitted* (Fr 1–2)   C4 *For* Lucerne (L 3–5) *read* Locarno (Fr 3–8) *omitted* (Fr 1–2) "Lucarna" (L 1–2).   D2 and with Notes at C2, E3.

dome of Persia vnto his owne. The tenth of September *Iohn* duke of Burgundie, was by the commandement of *Charles* the seuenth slaine, wherof great wars arose throughout all Fraunce. The like day and moneth was *Peter Lowys* the tyrant of Placence slaine by the conspiratours. We read also, that the eleuenth of September the Palæ-ologues, the Greeke emperours tooke the imperiall citie of Constantinople, and draue out thence the earles of Flaunders, who had there possessed the empire 560 yeres. The fourteenth day of September the Swissers were with a great slaughter ouerthrowne by the French, in the expedition of Mirignan: which selfe same day also the Turkes great armie laid siege to Vienna, the Metropoliticall citie of Austria. The seuenteenth day the French armie was by the English ouerthrowne at Poitiers, and king *Iohn* of France by them taken prisoner. Which day also, (or rather the like in the reuolution of the yeare) a peace was concluded at Soissons, betwixt *Francis* the first, the French king, & the emperour *Charles* the fift, being both readie with their great armies to haue fought for the kingdome, to the great hazard of both their estates, in the yeare 1544: a thing the more to be noted, for that the same yeare, moneth, and day, was also a great coniunction of the superior planets. The same day of the same moneth, in the yeare 1575 the Christian fleet with a great slaughter ouerthrew the Turkes great fleet in the battell of Lepanto. The eighteenth day of the same moneth Boulleine was deliuered vnto the Englishmen. And the foure and twentieth of September *Constantine* the Great, in a bloudie battell ouercame *Maxentius* the emperour, in the yeare of our Lord 333, and so of a simple straunge captaine made himselfe a great Monarch (which wrought a most notable and maruellous chaunge almost throughout the whole world) and so from thenceforth commaunded the account of the yeare to bee begun in September: and in the Greeke feasts vnto that day is added, ΙΝΔΙΚΤΙΩΝΩΝ, ΚΟΝΣΤΑΝΤΙΝΙΑ-ΝΩΝ, ΕΝΤΕΤΘΕΝ, ΑΡΧΗ. Wee find also, that in the yeare 1136, in the moneth of September there was a great coniunction both of the superiour and inferiour planets, in so much that the Astrologers of the East, by their letters written from all parts (as saith the Cronicle of Saint *Denis*) threatned the world with great calamities, and the people with the chaunge of their estates, which afterwards indeed chaunced: howbeit that in that the author of the historie erred, that he saith, How that the same yeare there was an eclips of the Sun the eleuenth of Aprill, and another of the Moone the fift of the same moneth, a thing by nature impossible. It is also right memorable, that the seuenteenth day of September, in the yeare 1567 *Charles* the ninth the French king, was by his subiects assailed neere vnto Meaux, where by speedie flight, and the helpe of the Swissers he hardly with life escaped the hands of the conspiratours: the which selfe same day, moneth, and yeare, *Henry* king of Sweden was by his rebellious subiects dispoiled of his estate, and cast in prison, where he yet remaineth, without any great hope to be euer with life from thence againe deliuered. The battell Montcontour was fought also in September. And the eighteenth day of September *Baiazet* at Nicopolis with a notable ouerthrow defeated a great armie of the Christians, of three hundred thousand men. And the same day *Saladin* tooke the citie of Hierusalem, on which *Pompey* had before taken it. Pope *Boniface* the eight also was in September 1303 by the French taken prisoner, and depriued of his papall dignitie. We read also many the greatest princes and monarches of the world, to haue as this moneth died: as namely the great emperour *Augustus, Tiberius, Vespasian, Titus, Domitian, Aurelianus, Theodosius* the Great, *Valentinianus, Gratianus, Basilius, Constantine* the fift, *Leo* the fourth, *Rodolphe, Frederike* the fourth, *Charles* the fift, all Roman or Greeke emperors. And of the French kings, *Pipin, Lewes* the younger, *Philip* the third, *Charles* the fift surnamed the Wise, and *Lewes* his kinsman king of Hungaria and Polonia, with other

most

A most noble and famous Monarkes in number infinite. But that is worth the marking that *Lothaire* and *Charles* the bauld, the one the king of Fraunce, and the other the German Emperour (and both of them the sonnes of *Lewes* the deuout emperour) both dyed the xxix of September, the first of them in the yeare 855, and the other 877. So *Charles* the fift, and *Sultan Solyman*, two of the greatest Emperours that were these many ages, were both borne in one yeare, and so both also in one moneth dyed, *viz.* in September. *Antonius Pius* also and *Francis* the first the French king, both of them great & famous Monarques, were both borne in September, and died both in March the moneth opposite to September. *Octauius Augustus* was also borne in September, and so likewise in the same moneth of September dyed. Whereby it is to be vnder-

B stood, Autumne and especially that moneth wherein the world was created, *viz.* September, in a sort to carie as a marke therof the notable chaunces of many the most noble and renowmed Princes, as also the straunge chaunges which haue happened aswell vnto the whole world, as vnto particular Estates and Commonweales. The next conuersions and chaunges of cities and Commonweales we see to happen into the signe of Aries, which is an other period of the Sunne, and the third and fourth sort of chaunges to fall out about the Winter or Sommer Solstitium, or farthest stayes of the Sunne: not for that the creation of the world is to be deriued from Aries, but for the notable periods of the Sunne in those times. Wherefore *Leouicius* following the dreames of vnskilful men, ought not to refer the creation and destruction of the world

C vnto the moneth of March; and much lesse to threaten vnto the world euen a present consummation and end. But he the same man had before by his writings promised vnto *Maximilian* the Emperour the soueraigntie of all Europe, with power to correct and chastice the crueltie and tirannie of other Princes (for so he writeth) of whom for all that it beseemeth him to haue more modestly writ: But *Maximilian* was so farre from the soueraigntie which he had in his vaine hope conceiued, as that he yet liuing, and with the German hoast also looking on: *Sultan Solyman* without any empeachment hauing farre and wide wasted the borders of the Empire, besieged and forced *Sigeth* the strongest place of the Empire, yea of all Europe: showing well that he should not haue too far assured himselfe vpon the prophecie of *Luther*, who hath left

D in writing that the power of the Turkes should from thenceforth diminish, which yet more encreaseth than euer it did. But it is straunge that *Leouicius* saw nothing of the straunge chaunge of the three kingdomes his next neighbours: which sith he saw not, how could he haue such certein knowledge of the end of the world, neuer as yet vnto the Angels themselues reuealed? For all which he bringeth no other reason, but that the Christian religion must together with the world take end in the waterie triplicitie, for that Christ Iesus himselfe was borne vnder the waterie triplicitie; willing as should seeme to bring in an other deluge: Wherein he showeth no lesse impietie then ignorance, whether we respect the maximes of the Astrologers, who affirme and say that

E neuer planet ruinateth his owne house, which should yet happen vnto Iupiter being in Pisces (For certein it is in the signe Pisces in the great coniunction in the yeare 1583 and 84, and that the coniunction of these two planets in that Signe is alwaies friendly:) or that we follow the opinion of *Plato*, and of the Hebrewes, and of all other Philosophers, who generally say, That the world is to be successiuely destroied first by water, and then againe by fire: or else that we rest our selues (as indeed we ought) vpon the promises of God, who cannot lye, which he in mercie made to *Noah* neuer to drowne the world againe. But as we ought not rashly certeinly to affirme any thing of the chaunges and ruines of Monarchies and Commonweales: So can we not denie but that the effects are right great and wonderfull in the coniunction

of

What times of the yeare the notable chaunces and chaunges of the world most commonly happen in.

Leouicius taxed.

A7 *For* Antonius (L 4–5) *read* Antoninus (L 1–3).   B3 renowned   E2 these two planets *i.e.* Jupiter and Saturn (cf. L).   Note at A10.

of the higher planets, when they chaunge the triplicitie, and especially when the three superiour planets are in coniunction together: or that such their coniunction haue concurrence with the the eclipses of the Sunne or of the Moone: as it happened the day before the taking of *Perseus* king of Macedon, and the battell of *Arbella* in Chaldea, which drew after them the ruine of two great Monarches, and the chaunge of diuers Commonweals, there appeared two most great and darke eclipses of the Moone. As there did also in the beginning of the Peloponesian warre, wherewith all Grecia was on a fire, the Sunne vpon a faire day was wonderfully darkened, euen at such time as *Pericles* the Athenian Generall began to set saile.

> *Great and maruelous effects wrought by the coniunction of the superior Planets.*

But as for them which contemne the force of the heauenly starres, or els are altogether ignorant thereof; they stand as men amased, to see in the same instant such conuersions and chaunges of Commonweales, and such great and turbulent motions of the people together and at once raised. As namely *Polybius* (himselfe an Atheist) in his historie exceedingly maruelleth, That in the hundred and thirtieth Olympiade in one selfe same time there was seene vpon the sudden a new chaunge of princes almost throughout the whole world. As namely *Philip* the younger to become king of Macedon, *Achæus* to be king of Asia, which he vsurped vpon *Antiochus*, *Ptolomeus Philopater* to become king of Ægypt, *Lycurgus* the younger, king of Lacedemonia, *Antiochus* king of Syria, *Hanniball* generall of the Carthaginensians: and all these people as it were at the same instant vp in armes one of them against another; the Carthaginensians against the Romans, *Ptolomey* against *Antiochus*, the Achæans and Macedonians, against the Aetolians and Lacedemonians. And afterward also three of the most famous generals of the world, namely *Scipio Affricanus*, *Hannibal*, and *Philopæmenes*, to haue all died (as *Liuie* writeth) in one yeare. These great chaunges are more euident to be seene after the coniunction of the two superiour planets, with the Sunne, or *Mars*: as it happened in the yeare 1564, that the superiour planets were in coniunction in the signe Leo, together with the Sunne & *Mercurie*: So haue we afterwards seene strange motions and sturres almost all Europe ouer. We haue seene in the same time, in the same yeare, in the same moneth, in the same day, *viz*. the twentie seuenth of September, in the yeare 1567, the French king guarded with the Swissers, assailed and in daunger to haue bene taken by his subiects: and *Henrie* king of Sweden dispoyled of his estate, and by his owne subiects cast in prison: and euen as it were at the same time *Mary* the most noble queene of the Scots spoiled of her kingdome by her subiects, and by them imprisoned, by whome it beseemed her to haue bene deliuered: and the king of Thunes driuen out of his kingdome by the king of Algiers: the Arabians vp in armes against the Turkes, the Moores of Granado and the Flemings against the king Catholike, the Englishmen against their queene, and all Fraunce in combustion. The same coniunction of the three superiour planets happened also an hundred yeares before, *viz*. in the yeare 1464, but not so precisely, neither in the signe of Leo, but onely in the signe of Pisces, and yet by and by after all the people were seene vp in armes, and not onely the princes among themselues, but the subiects also against their princes, as we haue before said.

> *The opinion of Copernicus concerning the motion & influence of the earth, refuted.*

Now as for that which *Copernicus* (the great Astrologer of his time) saith, The changes and ruines of kingdomes and Commonweales, to depend of the Eccentrique motion of the earth, it is such, as that it deserueth no aunswere or account to bee thereof made. For that he for the ground thereof supposeth two things most absurd: the one That the influences which all Philosophers attribute vnto the starres, proceed from the earth, and not from the heauens: the other, That the earth it selfe moueth with the same motions, which all the Astrologers of former times (except *Eudoxus*) haue alwaies giuen

Notes at H5, H7, K8.

OF A COMMONWEALE. 455

A giuen vnto the heauens. And yet more straunge it is to make the Sunne immouable and the center of the world; and the earth fiftie thousand leagues distant from the center, and to make part of the heauens, & of the planets, to be mouable, and part of them immouable. Which old opinion of *Eudoxus*, *Ptolomey* hath by probable arguments and reasons refuted. Whereunto *Copernicus* hath well aunswered: vnto whome *Melancthon* hath onely with this verse right well replied, *God in the heauens hath a tabernacle for the Sunne, which commeth out as a bridegroome out of his chamber, and reioyceth as a Giant to runne his course. It goeth out from the vttermost part of the heauen, and runneth about to the end of it againe: and there is nothing hid from the heat thereof.* So also might he say, That *Iosua* commaunded the Sunne and Moone to stay their course.

B But vnto all this might be aunswered, That the Scripture oftentimes accommodateth and fitteth it selfe vnto our weake sences: as when it calleth the Moone the greatest light next vnto the Sunne, which yet neuerthelesse is the least of all the starres except Mercurie. But this doctrine of *Copernicus* might by a manifest demonstration, which no man hath yet vsed, easily be refelled, *viz.* that one simple bodie hath but one simple motion proper vnto the same: as is manifestly to be proued by the principles of naturall Philosophie: then seeing that the earth is one of the simple bodies, as the other elements be, we must necessarily conclude, that it cannot haue but one onely motion proper vnto it selfe: and yet for all that *Copernicus* hath assigned vnto it three diuers

C motions: whereof it can haue but one proper vnto it selfe, so that the other must needs be violent, a thing altogether impossible: and so by the same consequence impossible also, that the alterations and chaunges of Commonweales, should proceed from the Eccentrique motion of the earth.

But let vs now come vnto the opinion of *Plato*, who thought the chaunges and ruines of Commonweales to ensue, when as the consent of the sweetnesse which proceedeth from the harmonie thereof is interrupted and broken. Which chaunceth when in the nuptiall number (as he teatmeth it) you depart farthest from those concords which the Musitions call διὰ τεσσάρων and διὰ πέντε. As for the nuptiall number he defineth it to be, that number which beginning of an vnitie, as of a mayden inuiolate is diuided in a double or triple sort of consent, in such sort as that the male,

The most darke and obscure opinion of Plato concerning the chaunges and ruines of Commonweales.

D that is to say the odd numbers shall in continuate order be placed on the right hand, and the female, that is to say, the euen numbers on the left hand in this sort and order. As for the middle places they are to be filled with numbers perfect, imperfect, quadrate, spherique, and cubique, so that no sort of numbers be wanting. But this order of numbers may be infinite, for that the force and power of tune and consent, is in diuision as infinite, as any other dimension whatsoeuer. So that the forme of a well ordered Commonweale shall so long be firme and sure, as it shall keepe right consent

```
      1
    2   3
   4     9
  8       27
 16         81
```

E and tune, well agreeing vnto the sweet delite of the eare. The Dupla or Diapason, which is of one to two; the Sesquialtera, which is the proportion of two to three, which maketh διὰ πέντε or a fift; the Sesquitertia or proportion of three to foure, which maketh διὰ τεσσάρων or a fourth. The Tripla porportion which maketh διὰ πέντε καὶ διὰ πασῶν, which for that it comprehendeth al concords and consents is called σύςημα, or a gathering of all together. Now if you go farther as vnto that proportion which is of foure to nine, the proportion of these numbers being not harmonicall, their followeth thereof an vnpleasant discord, which marreth the whole harmonie of a Commonwealte. And this in mine opinion is that which *Plato* would say, for no man as yet hath explaned this point; so that antiquitie it selfe hath not without

cause

456 THE FOVRTH BOOKE

Nothing more obscure than the Platonicall numbers.

cause long since complained, nothing to be more obscure than the Platonicall numbers. For *Forrester* the Germaine is farre from the mind of *Plato*, when as he seeketh after triple and quadruple proportions, for that in so doing he ouerthroweth the foundations of the nuptiall number & the sides of the Triangle, which consist of the double and triple proportion. But in him is also absurd, that he thinketh the same proportion to be betwixt 27. and 64. which is of three to foure, a thing by nature impossible, and contrarie to the grounds of the Mathematiques. But *Plato* willeth vs also to fill the vacant place of the propounded triangle of the nuptiall number with such other numbers as proportionally arise of the mutuall coniunction of the male and female numbers, yet still continuing the harmonie, for that the same concords are amongst them to be found, which we haue alreadie set downe amongst the other foure first numbers: as of the mariage of two to three: *viz.* of two times three is begot the number of six, which placed in the middest filleth vp the emptie place betwixt 4. and 9. which two numbers by no meanes make any consent or harmonie, but the proportion of either of them vnto sixe, is the same which is is of three to foure, that is to say, Sesquialtera or διὰ πεντε, or a fift. And so also if the number of two be as it were maried or in proportion ioyned vnto six, or the number of three, so combyned vnto six; as *viz.* two times six, or three times six, thereof shall arise two numbers, *viz.* 12. and 18. which shall fill the emptie space of the triangle betwixt 8 and 27. So if the number of two be proportionally ioyned vnto twelue, and the number of three to eighteene (as *viz.* two times twelue, or three times eighteene) thereof shall arise the numbers of 24. and of 54. And againe, if three be ioyned vnto twelue, or that which is all one, two to eighteene, thereof ariseth the number of 36. which three proportionate numbers of 24. 36. and 54. shall fill vp the vacant place of the triangle betwixt 16. and 81. the mutuall proportion of which numbers so put into the void places of the triangle, and so filled with the numbers next, still keepe a perpetuall sweet course, although the sides of the triangle were infinitely extended, of which triange let this be the forme.

The true discord which indeed maryeth the sweet harmonie of a Commonweale.

If therefore choice be had of such proportions as make a sweet consent in the perpetuall course of numbers, the Commonwealth shall so be euerlasting: if so be that the state of Commonweales depend of harmonie. But that harmonie (as saith *Plato*) is sometime broken, so that the sweet consent thereof must needs perish, and so Commonweales at length come to ruine and decay. But to say the truth, is it not much more to be feared, lest the subiects or citisens erring or declyning from the sweet and naturall harmonie of well tuned lawes, and customes, shall in steed of them embrace most wicked and pernitious lawes and fashions? And yet for all that will I not denie but that harmonie and musike haue great force & power for the chaunging of a Commonweale, in which point both *Plato* and *Aristotle* well agree. Howbeit that *Cicero* is of opinion it to be a thing impossible, that for the musique of a Commonweal chaunged, the Commonweale should it selfe therefore take chaunge. Whereof for all that we haue a most memorable example, of the Commonweale of the Cynethenses in Arcadia, who hauing giuen ouer the pleasure of musique, shortly after fell into such sedition and ciuill warres, as wherein no kind of crueltie was forgotten, or not put in execution: whereat euery man marueling why this people was become so wilde and barbarors, seeing that all the rest of the people of Arcadia were wonderfull ciuill, courteous, and tractable: *Polybius* was the first which noted it so to haue happened, for that they had left to take pleasure and delight in musique; which from all antiquitie had beene alwaies more honored and esteemed in Arcadia than in any place of

Musike to be of great force, for the chaunging or maintaining of a Commonweale.

F2 seeketh   G7 which is of   G7 *For* three to foure (L) *read* two to three (Fr).   H9 triangle let
I2–3(margin) *For* maryeth *read* marreth (cf. 455 E7–8).   K6 barbarous   Note at K1.

OF A COMMONVVEALE. 457

of the world else, in such sort as that by the lawes and customes of that countrie euery one was vppon great paines bound to exercise him selfe therein, vntill he was thirtie yeares old, which was the meane (as sayth *Polybius*) the first lawgiuers of that people wisely deuised, to quiet and tame them, being by nature rough and barbarous, as commonly all the inhabitants of the mountaines and cold countries be. The like we may almost also say of the French nation, whom *Iulian* the Apostata in his time calleth a barbarous and fierce people and of all others most desirous of libertie, who yet now at this day are in ciuilitie inferiour to no people of all Europe, none being more tractable vnto their magistrates or obedient vnto their Princes than they, as men by nature well, but by instruction better taught, and in the iudgement of all their neighbours most skilfull in Musike. Wherein that is also worth the noting, that almost all the French songes & tunes (wherewith the countrie people are euen yet much delighted) are still Ionique or Lidian, that is to say, of the fift or seuenth tune. Which tunes *Plato* and *Aristotle* forbid the youth and women to vse: for that they be of great force and power to mollifie and effeminate the minds of men; and therefore would haue them to vse the Dorian tune, which our men call the first tune to the intent that so they might be the better instructed with a certaine pleasant modestie, mixt with grauitie, a thing proper vnto this Dorian Musike. Which prohibition might haue serued better in the lesser Asia, where they haue no other songes but of the fift or seauenth tune; and namely in the countries of Lydia and Ionia: But the people of the cold and mountaine Northern countries, which are ordinarily more sauage or at least wise lesse courteous than the people of the South and the inhabitants of the plaine countries, can no way better tame and mollifie themselues than by vsing the Lydian and Ionique harmonie. Which kind of Musike was also forbidden in the primitiue Church; wherein it was not permitted to sing Psalmes or prayses vnto God but in the Dorian or first tune, which at this present is yet in the Church most in vse. But as men which would tame wilde and sauage beasts, disarme them first of their teeth and clawes; so the Lydian and Ionique harmonie disarmeth the more outragious and barbarous people of their sauage and cruell nature, and maketh them quiet and tractable: As it is happened vnto the Frenchmen, who happely had not beene so pliant and obedient vnto the lawes and statutes of this kingdome, if the nature which *Iulian* the Emperour saieth to haue beene in them so hautie and impatient of seruitude, had not by Musique beene attempered and mollified.

Musique most honored in Arcadia.

Light musike forbidden in the primatiue church

But of all those things which we haue yet brought to iudge of the future chaunges and ruines of Commonweales, we see no rule (whether it be of Astrologie or musike) certain and sure: howbeit that we haue by them some probable coniectures, whereof yet none seemeth vnto mee more certain or easie, than that which may be drawen from numbers. For why I thinke almightie God who with wonderfull wisdome hath so couched together the nature of all things, and with certain their numbers, meanes, measures, and consent, bound together all things to come: to haue also within their certaine numbers so shut vp and enclosed Commonweales, as that after a certaine period of yeares once past, yet must they needes then perish and take end, although they vse neuer so good lawes and customes: as *Plato* with *Aristotle* therein agree. But when that period shall be, neither of them declareth: except some there be which suppose *Plato* to signifie it by certaine obscure numbers in his eight booke *De Republica*: at which rocke not onely all the Academikes, but euen almost all the sects of other Philosophers also, haue suffered shipwracke. And first of all *Aristotle* skippeth ouer this place as ouer a dich, neither doth here carpe his maister (as his manner is) when as for the obscuritie thereof he had not wherefore he might reproue him.

Numbers to be of great force, whereby to deeme the chaunge and ruine of a Commonweale.

R r *Proclus*

Note at E2.

458 THE FOVRTH BOOKE

The eight booke of Plato de Repub. most difficult and obscure.

Proclus also hauing curiously enough enterpreted seauen of *Plato* his bookes *de Republica*: would not so much as touch the eight, stayed (as I suppose) with the difficultie of the matter. *Theon* also of Smyrna (for there is an other *Theon* also of Alexandria; who writt a commentarie vpon *Ptolomee* in Greeke) a man most skilfull not in *Plato* his philosophie onely: but in the Mathematiques also: at such time as he expounded *Plato* his Commonweale there stucke fast, neither tooke vpon him to expound this place. *Cicero* in one word excuseth the difficultie of *Plato* his numbers. *Marsilius Ficinus* (in mine opinion) the sharpest of all the *Academikes* plainely confesseth himselfe not to know what *Plato* in that place ment: fearing lest it should so fall out with him as it did with *Iamblichus*, who seemeth to haue bene willing in three words not to haue manifested a thing of itselfe most obscure, but rather to haue made it darker. *Philo* the Iewe euerie where imitating of *Plato*, thought that obscure and hidden number to be fiftie, and that he saieth to be signified by the right cornered Scalenus, such an one as *Pithagoras* comprehended in the three numbers 3, 4, 5. and therunto he supposeth those wordes of *Plato* to be referred, *sesqui tertia radix quinario coniuncta: sesqui tertia* the *radix* or root ioyned vnto the number of fiue for the proportion of 3, 2, 4. is the proportion *sesqui tertia*. But in that he is deceiued for that he hath brought in a plaine number, whenas it appeareth *Plato* his meaning to haue bene to haue a solid number sought out, which should in it selfe containe all kind of numbers, excepting the numbers perfect. Yet *Philo* of these radicall numbers, 3, 4, 5, brought euerie one of them apart into themselues maketh three quadrats: whereof are made 50 numbers, all plaine: but the wordes of *Plato* make mention of the hundred cube. Beside that there be Dimetients incommensurable vnto the sides, as in the number of *Plato*: whose wordes it pleaseth mee heare to set downe, and to interpret the same: as well for that the interpretors doe in the interpretation thereof verie much differ amongst themselues: as also for that hee sayth the ignorance of that number to bee vnto the Gouernours of Cities and Common-weales almost capitall.

Sesquitertia is that which containeth all that an other thing doth, and a third part more.

Ἔστι δὲ θείῳ μὲν γεννητῷ περίοδος ἣν ἀριθμὸς περιλαμβάνει τέλειος. Ἀνθρωπείῳ δὲ ἐν ᾧ πρώτῳ αὐξήσεις δυνάμεναί τε καὶ δυναστευόμεναι τρεῖς ἀποστάσεις τίτταρας δὲ ὅρους λαβοῦσαι ὁμοιούντων τε καὶ ἀνομοιούντων καὶ αὐξόντων καὶ φθινόντων πάντα προσήγορα καὶ ῥητὰ πρὸς ἄλληλα ἀπέφηναν. Ὧν ὑπίτριτος πυθμὴν πεμπάδι συζυγεὶς δύο ἁρμονίας παρέχεται τρὶς αὐξηθείς, τὴν μὲν ἴσην ἰσάκις ἑκατόν τοσαυτάκις, τὴν δὲ ἰσομήκη τῇ προμήκει ἑκατὸν μὲν ἀριθμῶν ἀπὸ διαμέτρων πεμπάδος ῥητῶν δεομένων ἑνὸς ἑκάστων ἀῤῥήτων δὲ δυοῖν ἑκατὸν δὲ κύβων τριάδος. ξύμπας δὲ οὗτος ἀριθμὸς γεωμετρικὸς τοιούτου κύριος ἀμεινόνων τε καὶ χειρόνων γενέσεων.

which is as I interpret it, *Truly the compasse of such things which take their beginning from God, is by the perfect number comprehended: but the compas of worldly things is contained by that number wherein are found numbers exceeding, and numbers exceeded by encrease and decrease, three spaces in foure tearmes comprehended; whereof are made numbers among themselues both like, and vnlike, numbers encreased, and diminished, which may be called by their owne names, and compared among themselues: whose sesquitertiall radix ioyned vnto the number of fiue, maketh two consents thrice encreased, one equall equally: an hundred times an hundred: an other equall, on one part of it selfe longer, of an hundred dimetients, which might among themselues be compared, the numbers of fiue detracted lesse by the vnitie: but two of ineffable proportion: but an hundred Cubes of the ternarie it selfe. And this number made by Geometricall proportion, is in worldly things most mightie, to them which haue either the better or the worse beginning.* Here *Plato* is slylie led away, not vnlike the fish *Polypus*, hauing on euery side cast out his blacking like ynke, lest otherwise he should haue beene entangled and caught. Wherein truely he seemed to haue imitated *Heraclitus*, to vnderstand whose writings he said a man had need of a most skilfull interpretour. Which obscure kind of writing and speaking by *Heraclitus* deuised (when as he most often would beat into his Schollers eares that his σκότισον, that is to say speake obscurelie) is oft times vsed

Obscuritie by Plato and many the auntient writers of purpose in their writings affected.

not

F1 curiously *i.e.* carefully (cf. L)   G6 five, for   G7 For 3, 2, 4 *read* 3 to 4.   H3 there be NO Dimetients
H10 συζυγεῖς   I2 interpret   Notes at H8, K4.

OF A COMMONWEALE. 459

not of *Plato* onely, but euen of *Aristotle* him selfe also, to the intent that so hauing cast a mist before his eyes aswell of the learned as of the vnlearned, concerning the knowledge of most difficult things, and shut vp in the hidden secrets of nature, they might themselues become therefore the more admirable. Which thing we especially note in the bookes of nature; which bookes *Aristotle* boasteth himselfe of purpose to haue so writ, as that he would not haue them to be vnderstood, imitating therein *Plato* his most obscure *Timæus*: Which thing *Lucilius* writ also of him selfe, that he had rather not to be at all vnderstood, then to be reprehended or found fault with all. But let vs discouer *Plato* his deceit by those things which he himselfe writeth more plainly, that we may more certeinly iudge of those things which he souldeth vp in such obscuritie of words: for he would that those things which take their beginning from God, should be contained within the perfect number. But what thing is there at length which oweth not the first beginning of the being thereof vnto almightie God, either immediatly without any other meane cause, or else some other the meane or middle causes comming betweene. And that God himselfe without any other meane cause created the Angels, and other the celestiall bodies not onely *Plato*, but euen the *Manichies* also themselues confesse; who yet most wickedly thought all earthly things to haue had their beginning from the prince of euils. True it is that the earth brought forth plants & other liuing creatures, the waters also fishes, and foules; yet both of them by the commaundement of almightie God: But vnto the creation of Man he would also haue the * Angels present. Howbeit that *Aristotle* was of opinion the formes of all things to be in a sort diuinely infused into them, when as he writ in all things to be θεῖον τι, or some diuine thing. As for the mind of man he calleth it not obscurely or doubtfully but euen plainely θύραθεν ἐπεισιέναι: which is (as I interpret it) ὑψόθεν, θεόθεν, ὀρανόθεν, from aboue, from God, or from heauen, not out of the power of the seed, as he saith of other liuing creatures: of whom for all that *Virgil* in generall saith: *Igneus est ollis vigor & cælestis origo*, A fierie force they haue, and a celestiall beginning. Wherefore we must confesse all things to be included in perfect numbers if we will beleeue *Plato*. But let vs graunt vnto the Academikes (which yet is an impietie to do) these earthly things which we speake of, to haue had their beginning else where then from almightie God, shall therefore the perfect numbers as better, be attributed vnto heauenly things? yea the perfect numbers should rather agree vnto earthly things, for that the perfect numbers how many soeuer they be are euen, and of the female kind, for otherwise they were not perfect: neither are more than * foure within an hundred thousand: there beeing also other perfect numbers * aboue that number of an hundred thousand, but such as cannot be applied either vnto diuine, or humaine or worldlie things. Wherefore seeing that the number of six is the first of the perfect numbers, it ought by the opinion of *Plato* to agree vnto things immediately by God himselfe created; and yet we see the same number neuerthelesse to agree vnto most vile and abiect liuing creatures. For *Aristotle* writeth the Hare (by the law of God an vncleane creature, & forbidden his holie people to eate of) to liue at the most but six yeares. The like number of yeares the same man attributeth also vnto Mice. And vnto certaine kinds of flyes, as vnto waspes and Bees six yeares are by *Virgill* allotted, and their hiues are still made six cornered; all which base creatures except the Hare are engendered of putrifaction. But as saith the Poet: *Numero Deus impare gaudet*, God delighteth in an odd number. And odd numbers are attributed vnto men: For that which *Seneca* writeth: *Septimus quisque annus ætati notam imprimit*, Euery seauenth yeare imprinteth some marke into age, is to be vnderstood onely of the male sexe: for experience showeth vs euen vnto the view of the eye, that the

Plato discouered and in some sort refuted.

*Faciamus hominem: Or let vs make man.

The foure perfect numbers within an hundred thousand, are 6. 496. 628. and 8128.

Perfect numbers aboue an hundred thousand: 130811, 2096128, 33550336, 536814528.

R r ij number

C4 θύραθεν ἐπεισιέναι *i.e.* "to enter from outside" (*cf. De gen. animal.*, 736b) C5 οὐρανόθεν
C6–7 Virgil . . . saith *i.e.* in *Aeneid*, VI, 730   D6(margin) *For* 6. 496. 628. and 8128 *read* 6. 28. 496. and 8128 (L 2; misprinted in L 1, 3–5).   D9(margin) 130811 (L 5) 130814 (L 4) *properly* 130816 (L 1–3)   E1(margin) 536814528 (L 4–5) *properly* 536854528 (L 1–3)   Note at D1.

THE FOVRTH BOOKE

number of six maketh a chaunge, and leaueth a marke vnto the female kind: So that as men begin to feele the heat of youth at fourteene yeares; women wax ripe at twelue, and so holding on from six to six, still so find in themselues some notable chaunge in the disposition either of their bodies, or of their mindes. All diuine Holy-daies also are concluded in septenaries, or such other odd numbers. In many places also Diamonds grow by nature it selfe polished six square, as *Plinie* in his 33. booke reporteth, which in the mountaines of the Pyrenes is a common matter. Wherefore it is an absurd thing that *Plato* attributeth the beginning and ending of diuine things vnto perfect numbers onely. But *Porphyree* the most famous philosopher of his time, when he enterpreted that of *Plato* out of his Timæus τοῖς μὲ Ἀθηναίοις ἐννακισχίλια, writeth the estate of all Commonweales, and the life of spirits to be determined, at the farthest in the reuolution of a thousand yeares. *Plutarch* in his booke entituled περὶ τῆς ἐν τῷ Τιμαίῳ ψυχογονίας supposeth the life of Spirits to extend longer, but yet neither of them sought after the perfect numbers. But if so be that *Plato* in so great fewnesse of perfect numbers, could not tell which of them should agree to things sprung from a diuine beginning; by what numbers then should he discide so great varietie of worldly things? or if he knew that number, why did he pray and make vowes vnto the Muses that they would show him it.

Plato vainely to attribute the perfect or euen numbers vnto heauenly things.

Wherefore it behoueth a man of deeper consideration to seeke out such numbers as may signifie the conuersions & chaunges of worldly things, and which are by long experience, and not by light and vaine coniectures approued: such as I deeme the numbers of seauen and nine and their quadrate and cubike numbers: viz. 49 81, 343, 729, to be. For as the number of six (which is of all perfect numbers the first) chaungeth the manners, habit, or nature of the Female kind, so most * auncient antiquitie hath by experience proued the number of seauen in some sort to chaunge the Male kind also: and that as the numbers of seauen or nine vse commonly to giue vnto men the beginning and time of their birth, that so the number growing of the multiplying of either of them, hath beene wont to bring vnto them their end and destruction. Which same thing I transfer and applie vnto Commonweales also, so that the numbers of seauen and nine, and such as arise of their quadrate and cubike numbers, do often times bring ruine and destruction vnto Commonweales. For that which we haue alleaged out of *Seneca* and *Censorius* euery seauenth yeare to imprint some marke into the age of man, and so the daungers of mens liues & substance to happen still vpon their seauenth yeares: vnderstand that to belong especially vnto men. Of which mine opinion I haue vse and experience the authour: For it is euery sixt yeare which leaueth a most certaine note of it selfe vnto women. And first to begin withall, the strength of bodie and of mind is increased in them the sixt yeare, or else therein they die: the twelft yeare they begin to wax warme, and the eighteenth yeare are readie for husbands: and if diseases fall vpon them in their sixt yeares, they are so often times in daunger: The like whereof happeneth vnto men the seauenth, the fourteenth, and one and twentieth yeare: So that *Plato* not without cause attributeth the euen numbers vnto the female sexe, and the odd numbers vnto the male. And for this cause *Plutarch* saith, The auntient Romans to haue vsed to giue name vnto their male children the ninth day, for that the seauenth was more daungerous, and vnto their female children or daughters the eight day: for that (as saith he) the euen number is proper vnto the female sexe: And therefore I suppose them of old time to haue vsed euery eight day to do sacrifice vnto Neptune, for that the element of water agreeth vnto women, as doth the firie element vnto men: As also that they thought the number of seauen to be feared. Howbeit that the law of God commaundeth the male children to be

The numbers of seauen and nine to be of great force in the chaunge of worldly things.

* *Hippocrat. de partu septimestri.*

The number of sixe to be of great power in the female sexe, and the number of seauen in the male kind.

F10 τοῖς μὲν Ἀθηναίοις ἐννακισχίλια H8 unto them I2 Censorinus I5 use and
Notes at G8, I5.

OF A COMMONWEALE. 461

to be circumcised the eight day, which the sacred interpretors of the Hebrewes thinke to haue beene done, that so there might be one Sabaoth betwixt the birth of the child and the circumcision thereof, and so more strength might thereby be giuen vnto the child. For why, *Moyses* doth in sacred writ teach vs, God most plentifully to blesse the Seauenth day (which was the birth day of the world) with his grace and all other good things: which aboundance and stoare of his good blessings is no where seene to be giuen vnto the rest of the other dayes, by a certaine wonderfull cause of nature from all Philosophers hidden.

The seuenth day of all others most blessed.

Yet nothing seemeth in mans nature more wonderfull than that the yeare threescore three hath bene still noted to be vnto almost all old men fatall, *Observandum est* (saieth *Au. Gellius*) *in multa hominum memoria, expertumque in senioribus plerisque omnibus sexagesimum tertium vitæ annum cum periculo & clade aliqua venire, aut corporis morbis grauioris, aut vitæ interitus, aut animi ægritudinis,* It is a thing observed (sayeth hee) in the great remembrance of men, and also by experience proued in many old men, The threescore and third yeare of their age to come vnto them all with some danger and hurt, either of the body, or of some great disease, or of losse of life, or of some tormenting griefe of mind. Yea there is an epistle of *Augustus* the emperour vnto his nephew *Caius*, bearing date the ninth of the Calends of October, written to the same purpose, in this sort, *Aue mi Cai, meus ocellus iucudissimus, quem semper medius fidius desidero quùm a me abes: sed præcipuè diebus talibus qualis est hodiernus: oculi mei requirunt meum Caium: quem vbicumq̧, & hoc die fuisti, spero lætum & bene valentem celebrasse quartum & sexagesimum natalem meum: nam vt vides κλιμακτῆρα communem seniorum omnium tertium & sexagesimum euasimus, &c.* All haile my *Caius* (sayth he) my most sweet delight, whom of my faith I alwaies long for when thou art from me, but especially on such daies as this is mine eyes doe now seeke after my *Caius*, whome wheresoeuer thou hast this day bene, I hope that thou merrie and in good health, hast celebrated my threescore & fourth birth day: for as you see we haue escaped the threescore and third yeare, the common Climacteriall yeare of all old men, &c. Howbeit that *Augustus* liued vntill he was seuentie seuen yeares old; as did also *Pomponius Atticus*, who died at that age. We might recken vp an infinit number not only of the poore and baser sort, but euen of the nobler sort also, who ended their daies in the threescore and third yeare of their age: but we will onely reckon vp some such as were for their learning famous, who as at that age died, viz. *Aristotle, Cicero, Crysippus,* S. *Bernard, Boccace, Erasmus, Luthar, Melancthon, Siluius, Alexander Imolensis,* the most famous lawier of his time, Cardinall *Cusan, Linacre,* and *Sturmius*: And therfore the old Greeke diuines seeme to haue consecrated the number of seauen vnto *Apollo*, and of nine vnto the Muses, as *Plutarque* writeth.

The clymactericall yeare of 63, most commonly fatall vnto old men.

Great learned men which dyed at the 93. yeare of their age.

Now if any man will more curiously search out these things, whether it be in the sacred or profane histories, he shal find the liues of men for the most part to haue expired and taken end still in the seauenth or ninth yeares of their age: and women in the sixt. *Plato* is said to haue died at the age of fourscore and one, which is nine times nine yeares: *Theophrastus* at 84, which are twelue times seauen yeares, which period few men passe; or els they passe to xiii times seauen, as did S. *Hierom* and *Isocrates*, who liued 91 yeares. *Plinie, Bartholus,* and *Cæsar* liued fiftie sixe yeares, which is eight times seauen yeares: *Lamech* liued 777 yeares, and *Methusala* (who of all others liued the longest) 970 yeares: *Abraham* liued an hundred seauentie and fiue yeares, which are fiue and twentie times seauen yeares: *Iacob* 147 yeares, which are xxi septinaries, or spaces of seauen yeres: *Isaac* liued 190 yeares, which make xx times nine yeares: *Dauid* liued seauentie yeares, which make ten times seauen yeares. An infinit thing it were to

The seauenth and ninth yeares still daungerous or fatall vnto old men; and the sixt yeare vnto women.

Rr iij

A10 Observatum est (cf. L)　　B3 morbique grauioris　　D3 (margin) *For* 93 *read* 63.　　D4 Luther
E6 777 (L) 770 (Fr)　　E9 *For* 190 *read* 180.　　　　　　　　　Notes at D4, E3, E4.

to recken vp all which are in histories found to haue ended their daies at these aforesaid periods of seauens and nines. He also who of our auncestors and of histories is called *Ioannes de temporibus* liued 361 yeares, that is to say three and fiftie times seauen yeares. It is manifest also men to be alwaies borne in the ninth or seauenth moneth: whom the Græks therfore call ἐβδομαγενεῖς and that they which are borne either sooner or later liue not. For which cause *Hippocrates* writeth a child to be fully made and perfected in all the parts and limbs thereof the seauenth day: and afterward to take encrease: and being borne the seauenth moneth to liue: but none to haue liued being borne in the eight moneth: a child also in the seuenth yeare to haue all the teeth, and that men (as *Plinie* writeth it to haue bene euen from the farthest memorie of men obserued) hauing bene kept from meat seuen dayes, albeit they may liue longer, shall yet neuerthelesse at length die thereof. The law of God hath most religiously also both consecrated and commaunded, the seuenth day to be kept holy, as the birth day of the world, and of all that therein is: which one day of all others God almightie blessed, and which day all antiquitie hath by long experience reported to be so vnlike the other daies of the weeke, as that it is taken vp as an old prouerbe, No seuenth day to passe wherein the sunne is not at one time or other therein to be seene. Vpon which day the auntient Hebrewes constantly affirme, The rage of diuels to be restrained, wisedome to be into the minds of men infused, their bodies to be strengthened, and their fields with encrease of fruit to be blessed. The seuenth yeare also is by the law of God holy, as is also the seuenth time seuen yeare, which is the yeare of *Iubilie*: neither is it to be doubted, but that a certaine secret force is in them, both for the chaunge and ruine of Commonweales. So that it ought not to seeme straunge, if that this number of seuen be of the Hebrews called sacred or holy: which *Calum* (following *Galen*, as I suppose) calleth Perfect (where he entreateth of the rest of the Sabboth day) which hee euen to astonishment woundereth to be so often and so religiously propounded, to bee of all men obserued and kept, in so much that euen the paine of death is propounded vnto the breakers thereof: so that the whole summe of all God his lawes may seeme to bee therein contained: yet is not therefore the number of seauen a number perfect, for that it is odd and masculine: whereas all perfect numbers are euen and feminine. For why, the Mathematitians define that to be perfect, which may bee diuided into the same whole parts, whereof it is made, so that in such diuision nothing be wanting or superfluous. As 1, 2, 3, make sixe: which three numbers do also equally diuide sixe into equall parts, as it was of them made, as it is in other perfect numbers also. *Lactantius* in the same errour offended, who calleth the number of three and ten, perfect and full numbers: and also *Cicero*, who deceiued many, in calling the numbers of seuen and eight full numbers; which *Macrobius* vnderstandeth to bee solide, and others to bee perfect numbers: neither of which can truely bee said of the number of seuen: as for the number of eight it is indeed a solid, but not therefore a perfect number. With like errour is *Plutarch* himselfe deceiued, who writeth, Three to be a number perfect: howbeit that *Aristotle* deemeth the force of that number to be of great force in the whole course of nature. *Philo* was herein also deceiued, in taking ten to bee the most perfect number.

Now indeed there are but foure perfect numbers from one vnto an hundred thousand, *viz.* 6, 28, 496, and 8128, amongst which the last cannot serue for the changing of Commonweales, for that it exceedeth the age of the world: neither the two first, for that they are too little: so that but one of them can be well applied vnto the chaunges of cities and Commonweals, *viz.* the number of * 496, which is made of seuentie septenaries of yeares, and a perfect number: it being also a thing by most auntient antiquitie

Marginal notes:
- The sabboth or Seauenth day of all other daies the most blessed.
- What a perfect number is?
- *In lib. de oppificio Dei.*
- *In somnio Scipionis.*
- But four perfect numbers from one to an hundred thousand. * The number 469. the onely perfect number which can well bee applied vnto the changes of cities and Commonweales.

F 5 ἐβδομαγενεῖς two and ten (Fr) 469 *read* 496.   F 10 the farthest   K 1 that number   I 4 equall   K 2 *For* ten *read* ten thousand (L only).   I 5 (margin) opificio   I 5 three and ten (L)   K 7 (margin) *For* Notes at F 4, I 3.

quitie obserued, All cities in the reuolution of fiue hundred yeares, to suffer either some great chaunge, or els some vtter ruine. But these numbers touching the chaunge or ruine of cities and Commonweales, may be two wayes applyed, viz. vnto the princes themselues, or els vnto the continuance of their kingdomes and empires. As if a man should say, This kingdome of Fraunce to fall and take end, after that threescore and three kings had therein raigned, this number consisting of the numbers of seuen and nine, conuerted in themselues. As *Esaias*, who liuing in the time of *Romulus*, prophesied, That nine kings should more yet raigne in Iudea, and that the tenth should together with the people be led away into captiuitie, and so that kingdome to take end: As also that there should be nine kings of the Persians, or as that the seuenth king of the Romans should be thrust out of his kingdom: which number of princes well agreeth with the number of the yeares which they raigned in Iurie, viz. 182, a number consisting of six & twenty septenaries: & at Rome 244, for in the 75 septenarie, that is to say, in the 245 yere *Tarquin* the proud, last king of Rome, was thrust out of his kingdome. *Hieremie* the Prophet then liued, when as the prophesie of *Esay* was fulfilled, and himselfe prophesied, That the people should be againe deliuered in the seuentie yeare of their captiuitie, as indeed they were, and the temple againe restored. The same Prophet * *Esayas* prophesied also, The most famous citie of Tyre to be in 70 yeres after vnpeopled and left desolat, and afterwards within seuentie yeares moe after the ruine therof, to be againe restored. The same number agreeth vnto the Athenian Commonweale, wherein seauen princes, whome they call Δυνασαες, raigned also 70 yeres; the taking of which citie, and the victorie of the Athenians at Salamine, is reported to haue happened vpon the verie like day. As for the number which of the Academikes is called *fatalis numerus*, or a Fatall number, viz. 1728 (being indeed a quadrat number) seemeth to haue bene expired from the raigne of *Ninus* vnto the victorie of *Alexander* the Great, at Arbela, and the ouerthrow of the Persian empire. For *Herodotus*, *Diodorus*, *Trogus Pompeius*, *Iustin*, and *Ctesias*, begin that empire from *Ninus*. And at such time as Hierusalem ouerwhelmed with most bitter calamities, was won and rased, the temple ouerthrowne, king *Sedechias* slaine, and the people carried away into captiuitie: at the selfe same time the Ægyptians rebelled against the kings of Assyria, the Athenians shooke off the tyrannicall yoke of the *Pisistratides*, and the Romans expulsed the proud *Tarquins*. Now the temple had before stood 427 yeares, a time consisting of whole septenaries. But for that in the computation of times, there is great difference amongst the Historiographers, we will vse the Roman Fasts or Calenders, which cannot lie. Wherein we see, that from the foundation of the citie, and of the Roman Commonweale vnto the battaile of Actium, wherein *Marcus Antonius* was by *Augustus* vanquished and the whole empire brought vnder the power of one onely Monarch, and a generall peace established throughout the world, there are accounted 729 yeares, the solide number of nine. The same number of yeres passed from the conquest of the kingdome of the Lombards by *Charlemaigne*, vnto the conquest of the same countrey by *Lewes* the twelfth the French king, vpon the Venetians and the Sforces. The like number of yeares is accounted also from the ouerthrow of the kingdom of the Picts, and the great victorie of the Scots vnto the captiuitie of *Marie Steward* their queene. As also from *Egbert* king of the West Saxons (who hauing vanquished the East Saxons, made himselfe the sole Monarch of England, and called the people Englishmen) vnto queene *Marie*, who was the first woman that tooke vpon her the soueraigntie of that people in fourteene hundred and fortie yeares space. So from the raigne of *Augustus*, after the victorie by him obtained at Actium, and the temple of *Ianus* the fourth time shut vp, vnto *Augustus* the last of all the Roman emperors, slaine

The numbers of seauen and nine fatall vnto Commonweales.

* *Chap 24.*

by

C4 numerus the last.   D2 consisting   E5–6 called the people   E9 *For* Augustus the last *read* Augustulus
Notes at A7, B3, B10, C1, D2.

by *Odouacer* king of the Herules, and the empire possessed by the Gothes, there are accounted 496 yeares, which we said to be a perfect number, as consisting of seuentie septinaries; with the perfect number of six: For by the Fasts the yeare following *Odouacer* began to raigne. Wherein it is also worth the noting, that as the first emperour *Augustus* with wonderfull felicitie and wisedome, both established and encreased that so great a Monarchy, which he held more than fortie yeres: so *Augustulus* the last of the Roman emperours diminished both in name and soueraigntie, held that his empire scarce a whole yeare, which happened the tenth of the calends of September. As it happened to *Constantine* the Great, who established the seat of the empire at Constantinople: and to *Constantine* the last Christian emperour, there dispoyled of his estate, and slaine by *Mahomet* king of the Turkes, surnamed the Great. Now from the building of the citie vnto this *Augustulus*, are accounted 1225 yeares: which number consisteth of whole septinaries: which thing *Vectius* the great sooth-saier foretold, as *Censorinus* out of *Marcus Varro* writeth. The same number of yeares wee find from *Ninus* king of Assyria, vnto the death of *Sardanapalus*, whome *Arbaces* gouernour of Media dispoyled of his gouernment, and translated the kingdome vnto the Medes. Now from *Saul* the first king of the elect people of God vnto that *Sedechias* was slain, and his kingdome ouerthrowne, returneth that perfect number of 496 yeres. But whereas *Iosephus* reporteth the burning of both the Temples, and the taking of the citie, to haue chaunced the selfesame day, *viz.* the ninth day of the first moneth; he in that agreeth not with the booke of the Kings, neither with the Prophet *Hieremy*, who both otherwise report the same. So many yeares, *viz.* 496. are accounted from *Caranus* first king of the Macedons, vnto *Alexander* the Great last king of that countrey, discended of the line and issue of *Hercules*, and of *Æacus*. Some there bee which adde certaine yeares moe, and some others which detract some also. Wherefore my meaning is not to alleage any other than the records set downe by the most certaine Historiographers, and such as euery man may draw euen out of the verie fasts and calenders of the Romans themselues. Of which sort is that, that from the foundation of the citie of Rome, vnto the sacking therof by the French men, are accounted 364 yeres, which number consisteth of whole septinaries: As also from the building of the citie, vnto the slaughter at Cannas, *Terentius Varro* being then Consull (at which time the Commonweale was fallen into extreame danger) are numbred 536 yeres, that is to say 77 septinaries of yeres: And from thence vnto the slaughter by the Romans, receiued from the Germans, vnder the conduct of *Quinctilius Varro*, are passed 224 yeares, a number consisting of whole septenaries: both which ouerthrowes happened the second day of August, as is by the auntient Romans reported. Neither is that lesse memorable which *Tarapha* a most certaine Historiographer amongst the Spaniards reporteth, The Moores and Arabians to haue inuaded Spaine in the yere of Christ 707, and that also the seuenth yeare of the raigne of king *Roderike*, and to haue holden the same kingdome 770 yeares, neither could vtterly be from thence againe expulsed, before the time of *Ferdinand* king of Arragon and Castile. It is also worth the noting, that from the execution of *Aman*, and the deliuerie of the Iewes at the intercession of *Hester*, vnto the victorie of *Iudas Machabeus* against *Antiochus* the noble king of Syria and his lieutenant, there passed 343 yeares, which is the solid number of seuen, that is to say seuen times seuen septenaries: both which victories happened the thirteenth day of the moneth Adar, as the Hebrewes haue well noted. The same number of yeares passed from the time that *Octauianus* (hauing vanquished *Marcus Antonius*, and vnited the whole Roman empire vnder his owne obeysance) was by the Senat called *Augustus*, vnto *Constantine* the Great; a time notable for the straunge chaunces which then

The number perfect of 496 a number proper vnto the chaunges of Commonweales.

G10 *For* first moneth *read* fifth moneth.   I2 *For* 536 *read* 539 (Fr and L).

Notes at G2, G7, I6.

OF A COMMONWEALE.

then happened in the whole empire, as well in the lawes politique, as in matters of religion. *Tacitus* hath also noted in another singularitie, That the citie of Rome was by *Nero* burnt, on the like day that it had long before beene burnt by the Gaules, which was the fourteenth of the calends of August: wherein some haue gone so farre, as to number how many yeares, moneths and dayes, passed betwixt both those fiers.

But that the numbers of six are almost vnto women fatall, I thought it not needfull by examples to proue, least I might be thought to stand vpon trifles, only that I note, that in the yeare 1582, at such time as the prince of Orenge had receiued a mortall wound, the one and twentieth of March, being the fortie ninth yeare of his age, and that all men dispaired of his life, he yet recouered his health at his entrance into his fiftieth yeare: But *Carola Charlet* of Burbon his wife within two monethes after died, when as shee entred into the six and thirtieth yeare of her age, which is the quadrat of the number of six: euen as the prince her husband was wounded in the nine and fortieth yeare of his age, the quadrat of the septenarie or number of seuen: which I thought not to haue written, but that I was told the same by the prince of Orenge himselfe, as a thing by him noted, when as I was of councell with *Francis* duke of Alanson at Anwerpe. *[marginal: The number of sixe to be vnto women fatall.]*

But now for that we are by way of discourse come so farre, the last that remayneth is for me to aunswere some thing to them which take pleasure rather to carpe than to commend my writings: for that * I said I vnderstood not the prophecies of *Daniel* concerning the rising and ruine of Empires and kingdomes. For I doubt not but that if he (amongst others a most wise man) would in their due times haue plainly set downe such things as he by diuine inspiration had conceiued and declared, all things then whereof we now doubt, should without all doubt be vnto vs most plaine and cleere. Truely he defineth the state of his owne citie, king *Cyrus* then beginning his raigne, what time the captiuitie was ended, according to * the prophecie of *Ieremie*, (which he beginneth from the destruction of the Citie and of the Temple, and not from the raigne of *Ioachim* as some suppose) and the holie people returned. He defineth it (I say) by seauentie weekes of yeares, that is by 490. yeares, and that right plainly; when as the prophecie was made in the last yeare of the captiuitie, which was the seauentieth from the destruction of the Citie and of the Temple: that so the prophecies might in good order with the prophecies, and times with times be continued: whereas they which longer protract the times leaue an hundred and twentie yeares at one gaping. But the Prophet expresly taught, that the beginning of the time ought to be accounted from the time of the prophecie giuen, wherein the people againe returned as if it had beene before dead, and appointed vnto it selfe a Prince and other magistrates, from whence the restoring of the Citie is to be accounted, and not from the repairing of the walles and buildings. In which case *Pompee* said well: *Vrbe deserta, in parietibus Rempublicam non consistere*, That the citie being forsaken, the Commonweale consisted not in the walles thereof. But many * Historiographers from the time of *Cyrus* vnto the raigne of *Herode* the great (who hauing taken Hierusalem and slaine all the Senators together with the king himselfe, and spoiled the Iewes of their kingdome) do account 490. yeares. Others there be which recken otherwise, and so great varietie and difference there is amongst them, as that all the opinions of all of them, may well be refelled, not onely by euery one of them a part, but euen by all of them together. As for those things which *Daniel* writ concerning the Empires, he openly and plainly hath called the Medes, the Persians, and Grecians vnto the Empire of Babylon; but besides them none. The fourth Empire (by him spoken of) we haue showed not to belong vnto the Romans, seeing that question is there concerning *[marginal: * In his booke: De Methodo historiarum.]* *[marginal: * Hier. 25. & Daniel 9.]* *[marginal: A good discours of Daniel his seauentie weekes.]* *[marginal: * Iosephus Funccius. Mercator. Philo.]*

Babylon,

Babylon, which the Romans neuer subdued; which when they passing ouer the riuer Euphrates had vnfortunately attempted, they receiued many and great ouerthrowes of the most inuincible Parthians. But yet more foolishly do they who attribute that fourth Empire vnto the Germans, who neuer so much as dreamed of any the least part of the Babylonians Empire. Which things for that they be by vs else where disputed we will here let passe. Which things for all that *Frankbergerus* the Saxon and Bishop of Lipsic, by the authoritie of *Luther*, and one *Dresserus* a meere schoolman with rayling without any reason at all refelleth, whom I shall yet count an eloquent man, if he shall but learne aswell to speake, as he hath learned to speake euill: But for that the angrie man (a common fault of the wise) is angrie with me, for that I dare not rashly iudge of the diuine oracles, least in so doing I might offend in such his matters, and so farre from all mens senses: he should haue taught me why he thinketh the Prophet *Daniel* to haue there omitted fiftie empires, which I haue * noted to haue bin ten times greater than the German empire, and such as haue in them also contained a great part of the Babylonian empire? Why also *Daniel* in his first chapter hath writ of himselfe, That he liued in the first yeare of the raigne of *Cyrus* king of Persia? And yet more, why he should write himself to haue receiued that diuine oracle or prophesie in the * third yeare of the raigne of king *Cyrus*? And why in the chapter following doth he make mention of *Darius* king of Persia, who was inuested in that kingdome seuen and thirtie yeares after that *Cyrus* began to raigne? For neither *Berosus* a most true interpretor of the Chaldean antiquities, whome *Ctesias* and most of the auntient writers, haue followed: neither *Megusthenes* the Cronicler of the Persian affaires, neither *Herodotus*, called the Father of Historie, neither any of the Greeke or Hebrew historiographers, report any to haue bene before *Darius Hystaspes*: I except onely *Iosephus*, who in that place dissenteth from *Berosus*. But least we should seeme to deale to sharply, and to presse them too farre, What is the reason why *Daniel* in the eleuenth chapter of his prophesie writeth, That *Darius* should haue three Persians his successors and that the fourth should come out of Grecia, who by mightie force and strong hand should obtaine the empire? But that this was *Alexander* the Great no man doubteth, who thrust *Darius Codomænus* out of the Persian empire, whose father was *Darius Achos*, his grandfather *Darius Mnemon*, and his great grandfather *Darius Nothus*, vnto whome *Daniel* turneth his speech. Which if it be so, *Daniel* must needes haue liued two hundred and twentie yeares, if he were a youth growne when as hee was carried captiue into Chaldea, which he must needes be, for that hee then spoke both most eloquently and wisely. And thus much euerie man may most plainely gather both out of the sacred scriptures, and also out of the auntient histories of *Herodotus* and *Iosephus*. For *Cyrus* died in the 30 yeare of his raigne, *Cambyses* in the 6, *Darius Hystaspes* in the 37, *Xerxes* in the 21, *Artaxerxes* in the 44, *Darius Nothus* in the 19, *Darius Mnemon* in the 36, *Darius Achos* in the 26, *Darius Cadomanus* in the 10, all making the summe of 228 yeares. For *Daniel* was taken prisoner together with king *Ioachim*. But let the interpretors of these diuine oracles suppose all things to bee manifest vnto them, and let euerie one of them with great confidence at their pleasure determine of these Daniels weekes. Yet how can these which euen most subtilly haue discussed all these matters, defend that of the Prophets *Zacharias* * and *Aggæus*, who writ their prophecies in the end of the seauentieth yeare of the captiuitie, *Darius Nothus* as they will haue it then raigning. This is now (say those Prophets) the seauentieth yeare. And if it be so that they will haue the seauentie yeares to be accounted not from the destruction of the Temple, but from the Edict of *Xerxes*, then truly *Zerubabel* and *Nehemiah* the chiefetaines of the people must needs haue liued full two hundred and fiftie

* *In methodo histor.*

* *Chap. x.*

* *Chap. 9.*
* *Chap. 23.*

fiftie yeares, being so old when *Cyrus* began his raigne, as that they were able to conduct the people out of Chaldea into the land of Palestine: whom yet the doubt not to proue euen by the testimonie of *Nehemiah* himselfe, him to haue liued euen to the last *Darius*. Wherefore all Historiographers are here much troubled and at great variance among themselues: one saying that there were but fiue of these Persian kings: an other six: and others seauen: many eight: some nine: yea and some there be which haue deuised a tenth also. Truely *Genebrardus* in his Chronologie affirmeth there to haue bene of them onely fiue: but *Functius* saith ten. Wherefore in so great rietie of opinions one of the two may be: as *viz.* that none of them all be true, the other can in no wise be, that moe of them then one should at all be true; and which of them it is I can not affirme: neither if I could would I. And in mine opinion I haue hereof more modestly than they written, that it was not a thing to me well knowne, vnto whom for all that I will yeeld, if they can by any meanes maintaine the certaintie of their owne positions. Howbeit that *S. Hierome* hath reiected many things which are found in the writings of *Daniel*: And that the Hebrewes allow not of the rest which are not writ in the Chaldee, but in the Greeke tongue by *Theodotion*.

Wherefore these examples thus propounded, it is lawfull by a certaine coniecturall gessing to ayme at the rising and falling of Commonweales: as also for a man looking into the precedent causes of things, with the diuers coniunctions and oppositions of the Planets, to go so farre as the knowledge of such things will beare: not rashly affirming, or lightly beleeuing any thing concerning such things as are by the Almightie and euer liuing God farre set from the sense and reach of man.

How it is lawfull for a man to gesse at the rising and falling of a Commonwealth.

Chap. III.

That it is a most daungerous thing at one and the selfe same time, to chaunge the forme, lawes, and customes of a Commonweale.

Ow Cities and Commonweales arise; by what meanes they are also encreased; what diuers alterations and chaunges befall euery one of them; and by what coniectures the fall and ruine of them is to be by vs gathered, I suppose we haue sufficiently before declared. But for asmuch as the presumptions by vs alreadie noted, are not sufficient to make any certaine demonstration of, but rest vpon such grounds as are fartheft off from the senses and capacitie of the common sort of men: Neither that if they were deliuered by way of demonstration, or other more certaine rules, should they therefore inferre any necessitie at all? It remaineth that wee according to that wisedome and discretion wherewith almightie God hath of his goodnes endued men, endeuour our selues to rule Estates and Commonweales, and by all meanes to foresee and decline the chaunges and ruines of them. For why, it is one generall opinion and doctrine of all Philosophers, yea euen of them which idly dispute what is done in heauen: a wise man not to be bound or subiect vnto the power or influence of the starres: but onely they which giue the raines vnto their disordered appetites, and beastly desires, not suffering themselues to be gouerned by the rule of reason, or of other the best lawes: vnto whome *Salomon* the maister of wisedome hath sharply threatned the torment of the wheele, saying, That God should cause the wheele to passe ouer them: that is to say, the force and effect of the celestiall Spheres, which ouer the good should haue no power at all. Seeing therefore that the power & influence of the starres may by the power of God, that is, by wisdome (by the gift and goodnesse of almightie God giuen vnto men) be auoided: and that wise physitians haue found the meanes

Wise men not to be subiect vnto the power or influence of the starres, as sensual men be.

A2 they doubt not   A3 *Delete* him *or substitute* them *i.e.* Zerubbabel and Nehemiah (cf. L).
A8–9 so great varietie   D6 at all: it

meanes to chaunge the diseases, and to alter feuers contrarie vnto their naturall courses, to the intent the more easily to cure them, or at leastwise to asswage them; why should not the wise politician, or gouernour of a Commonweale, foreseeing the conuersions and chaunges which naturally happen vnto Commonweales, by good lawes and other conuenient remedies preuent the ruine therof: or if the force of the mischiefe be so great, and the destruction so certaine, as that it can by no wisdome of man bee preuented or staied, yet shall he performe that which cunning physitians doe, who by the Symptomes appearing vpon the criticall dayes, and by the causes of the disease, doe more certainlie and better guesse of the sicke mans death in what manner it shall bee: and so yet in good time giueth thereof warning vnto his ignorant subiects, lest that they should vpon the suddein be vtterly oppressed with the ruine of the falling Estate and Commonweale. And as the most skilfull Phisitions euen in the state of the disease, and the greatest griefe therof, do yet put their patients in greater comfort, if the Symptomes, be good then if the griefe or fit without them were but easie and gentle; and as to the contrarie when they see a man in the highest degree of health that may be, they are then in the greatest feare, lest he should suddenly fall vnto some extreame sicknesse, as the great phisition *Hippocrates* saith: So also a wise gouernour of a Commonweale, seeing the state on all sides beset, and almost ouerwhelmed with enemyes, yet if in so great daunger he otherwise see wise men sitting at the helme of the Commonweale, the subiects obedient vnto the Magistrats, and the Magistrats vnto the Lawes; he taketh courage thereat, and promiseth both vnto himselfe and others good successe; the ignorant people & cowards hauing in the meane time lost their patience, and lying as men plunged euen into the bothom of dispaire. In which state the Romaine commonweal stood after the third slaughter of their armie at Cannas, when as now many of the friendly and confederate cites, which before had continued in their fidelitie and allegeance, reuolted from the Romaines, following the fortune and victories of *Hanniball*: For why almost all men now despaired of the estate of the Romaine Empire: at which time of distresse, of all others no man more hurt the Commonweale than did *Terentius Varro* the Consul, who with some few hauing escaped from so great a slaughter (as wherein threescore thousand of the citisens of Rome were slaine) writ letters vnto the Senat and people of Capua, That the Roman Commonweale was vndoone, as hauing in that battell lost all the force and flower thereof. Which thing so terrified them of Capua, (although in wealth and power they farre exceeded all the rest of the Roman confederates) that they not onely themselues forsooke the Romans, but drew with them many of their allies and confederates also vnto *Hanniball*: when as in deed the Consul should haue extenuated the ouerthrow and losse receiued. Whereas *Scipio*, who was afterwards called *Africanus*, to the contrarie with comfortable speeches then cheered vp diuers of the citisens dispairing of the state of the Commonweale, and by oath constrained such as were about to haue abandoned the citie, to stay there still, and not to stirre, but resolutely to aduenture their liues for the defence of their countrie and Commonweale. Neither was the Senate terrified with the feare of so many daungers, as wherewith they were on euery side beset and inclosed, but rather seemed with greater wisdome to mannage the Estate than euer it did before. And albeit that the common people (according to their wonted lightnesse and foolish ignorance) almost in euery towne and city sung the praises of *Hanniball*, after his so many and so great victories ouer the Romans: Yet for all that, the Senat of euery citie fauoured the Romans: For so saith *Liuie*, *Vnus veluti morbus omnes Italiæ populos inuaserat, vt plebs ab optimatibus dissentiret: Senatus Romanis faueret, plebs ad Pœnos rem traheret*, One disease as it were (saith he) had infected all

Marginalia:

The ruine of a Commonweale to be by the wisdome of the gouernour preuented, or els warning thereof to be by him in due time giuen vnto his subiects.

Wisdome neuer discouraged with the daungers of the Commonweale: so long as they see the state wisely and discreetly gouerned.

What opinion wise men had of the distressed estate of the Romaine Commonweale, after the great ouerthrowe at Cannas.

all the people of Italie, *viz.* That the people still dissented from the nobilitie; the Senat still fauoured the Romanes; and the people still enclined vnto the Carthaginensians. Yea *Hiero* king of Siracusa, accounted the wisest prince of his age, did then much more carefully than before honour and reuerence the amitie and alliance of the Romaines, not doubting in what he could to helpe and releeue them; yea and in that their desperat estate amongst other things sent them a statue of Victorie (of gold) for a present; as he which had oftentimes proued the incredible wisdome of that Senat in the mannaging of their affaires. Wherein a man may see, that the wiser sort seeing the Romans so aduised and so constant in their extreme necessitie, and that their lawes were neuer more straightly kept, or martiall discipline more seuerely obserued, (as *Polybius* an eye-witnesse of those things, himselfe writeth) were alwaies of opinion that the issue of their affaires would be good: not vnlike the wise physition, who seeing fauourable Symptomes in the strongest fit of his patients disease, is yet still in good hope. Whereas Carthage to the contrarie proud of so many and so great victories, mistres of so many countries and nations, and placed in the height of all worldly felicitie, was neuer than then neerer vnto ruine and destruction: wherof were most certain tokens, for that in that Commonweale was no place left either for law or vertue, all things being done by the popular rage, or vnruly lust of the common people: so that it must needs shortly after be cast downe headlong from the highest degree of honour, and become subiect vnto the Romans, as not long after it did, *Scipio* beeing then their generall.

Wherefore the first rule for the keeping and preseruing of Commonweales in their estates, is well to know the nature of euery Commonweale, together with the diseases incident vnto them: whereof we haue more at large discoursed in the former Booke. For it is not enough to know which kind of Commonweale is better than other, but it behoueth vs also to know the meanes how to maintaine euerie one of them in their estate, if it be not in our power to chaunge the same, or that in chaunging thereof we shall put all to the hasard of vtter ruine and decay. For whie, it is better to haue an euill Commonweale than none at all: as with conuenient diet in some sort to preserue the sicke man, than by applying of medicines to an incurable disease so to take away his life quite. For as physitians say, we must neuer apply violent remedies but vnto desperat diseases; and that whenas there is now no other hope left. And this maxime taketh place in euerie sort of Commonweale, not onely for the changing of the estate, but euen for the changing of lawes, maners, and customes also: whereunto many hauing no regard haue ruinated and ouerthrowne right faire and great Commonweales, allured with the baite of some one or other good law, which they haue borrowed from some one Commonweale quite contrarie vnto their owne. For as we haue before shewed, many good lawes there be good for the maintenance of a Monarchie, and yet fit for to ruinat a Popular estate: as other also there bee good for the preseruation of the Popular liberty, & yet most fitly seruing for the ouerthrow of a Monarchy: for that those Estates by nature contrary, are by quite contrary laws both maintained and ruinated.

And albeit that some lawes there be good and indifferent to all sorts of Commonweales, yet so it is, that the antient question of right wise Politicians is not yet well resolued, *viz. Whether a new law being better, be to be preferred before an old antient law that is worse?* For the law be it neuer so good, is nothing worth if it cary with it a contempt of it selfe, or of the rest of the lawes: Now so it is, that newnesse in matter of lawes is alwayes contemptible, whereas to the contrary, the reuerence of antiquity is so great, as that it giueth strength enough vnto a law to cause it to be of it selfe obeyed, without

margin notes:
The first rule for the keeping and preseruing of Commonweales in their estates.

Violent remedies neuer to be vsed but in desperate diseases.

A notable question.

Auntient lawes though worse still of greater esteeme and reuerence than the new though better.

without the authority of any Magistrat at all ioyned vnto it: whereas new edicts and lawes with all the threats and penalties annexed vnto them, and all that the Magistrats can do, cannot but with great difficulty find intertainment: in such sort, as that the fruit we are to receiue of a new edict or law, is not oft times so great, as the harme which the contempt of the rest of the lawes draweth after it for the nouelty of some one. And to make the matter short, there is nothing more difficult to handle, nor more doubtful in euent, nor more dangerous to mannage, than to bring in new decrees or lawes. And this reason seemeth vnto me very considerable, but yet I will set downe another of no lesse weight, which is, That all the change of laws concerning the estate is dangerous: For to chaunge the customes and lawes concerning inheritance, contracts, or seruitude from euill to good, is in some sort tollerable; but to chaunge the laws which concerne the estate, is as daungerous, as to remoue the foundation or corner stones which vphold the whole weight or burthen of the buildings; in which doing, the whole fabrike is to be sore shaken, and beside the daunger of falling, receiueth more hurt by the shaking thereof, than it doth good by the new repairation, especially if it bee now become old and ruinous. For euen so it is in a Commonweale now alreadie growne old, wherein if a man neuer so little remoue the foundations that vpholdeth the same, he is in great danger of the ruine therof. For the antient maxime of the most wise politicians ought wel to be waied, *That we must not change any thing in the laws of a Commonweale which hath long maintained it selfe in good estate, whatsoeuer apparent profit may bee thereby pretended*. And for these causes the old law of the Athenians, which was afterward also receiued in Rome, and passed in force of a law, published at the request of *Publius Philo*, was the most necessarie law that could be in a Commonweale, *viz*. That it should not be lawfull for any person vpon paine of death to present any request vnto the people, without the priuitie of the Senat. Which law is yet better kept in Venice than in any place of the world els, whereas it is not permitted so much as to present any request euen vnto the Senat, without the aduise of the councell of the Sages. And yet in the Commonweale of the Locrensians, this law was much straiter, Where he which would present any request, to haue it passe in force of a law, was constrained to moue it before the people with a rope about his neck, wherewith hee was there vpon the place to be strangled, if he preuailed not to proue the law by him moued to be good and profitable for the Commonweale. Which was the cause that this estate for a most long time stood and flourished, without any thing added or diminished to or from the most antient laws and customes thereof, no man daring to propound any new law to passe, vntill that one of the citisens which had but one eie, made a request vnto the people, That he which wittingly should put out his eye which had but one, should therefore himselfe haue both his owne put out: For the making of which motion his aduersarie had giuen him cause, hauing oftentimes threatned him to thrust out his eye, and so to depriue him quite of his sight, although he were therefore to endure the penaltie of the law, which was to loose one of his owne. With the equitie, or rather necessitie of whose so reasonable a request the people moued (though with much a do) enacted the law. Whereby yet nothing was derogated from the law called *Lex talionis* (or the law of like punishment) which was then common to almost all nations: For why, it was reason that hee which had maliciously depriued another man of his sight, should himselfe be depriued of his owne sight also.

Now if any man should say, That many lawes must oft times of necessitie bee changed, as the lawes concerning victuals, or the bringing in, or carrying out of marchandise, or concerning the augmenting or diminishing of the punishment to bee inflicted vpon offendors, which are euen in a short time to be chaunged; I therein agree with him,

Auntient lawes concerning the estate of a Commonweale not to be without great daunger altered.

The extreame daunger he was in, which moued any new law amongst the Locrensians.

Lawes concerning ordinarie pollicie may oftentimes be changed but not lawes concerning the estate.

him, for that necessitie hath no law: first, if new lawes giue good hope of fruit and profit of them to arise, as of good corne yet in the blade, then are they not to be reiected: but here question is not of lawes concerning ordinarie policie, but of such as concerne the very estate it selfe. Which I both would and wish, if possibly it might be, that they should still be most firme and immutable: not for that the Commonweale ought to serue the laws, seeing that they are al made for the maintenance of the Commonweale, and of the societie of men: neither that any man wisheth the safetie and preseruation of the lawes, but for the Commonweales sake. For why, the first and chiefe law of all Commonweales, is this, SALVS POPVLI SVPREMA LEX ESTO, The welfare of the people, let that be the last law. For what reason moued *Themistocles* to fortifie the citie of Athens with walles and bulwarkes, euen the verie same reason induced *Theramenes* to persuade the Athenians to rase their walles, viz. the welfare of the people: whereas otherwise the Lacedemonians had vndone the citisens together with the citie. Wherefore no law is so sacred, but that vpon vrgent necessitie it is to be changed. And therefore *Solon* after he had published his lawes, caused the Athenians to sweare to obserue and keepe them for the space of one hundred yeare: giuing them thereby to vnderstand, that lawes could neuer be made immutable, neither were to be all at once together chaunged. *Lycurgus* also in like maner tooke an oath of the Lacedemonians his subiects, to keepe his lawes vntill his returne from the Oracle of *Apollo*, from whence he afterwards neuer returned, but went himselfe into voluntarie exile, out of his natiue countrey; so to bind his citisens so much as possible was to the perpetuall keeping of his lawes. And albeit that the iniquitie of some auntient law bee by right euident, yet is it better to endure it, vntill that it in time by little and little of it selfe loose the force, than vpon the sudden by violence to repeale it. For so did the Romans by many the lawes of the twelue tables, which they would not abrogat, but onely by not obseruing them, in that they were vnprofitable or vniust, suffered them so to grow out of vse: which they so did, least in abrogating of them, they might seeme to impaire the credit and authoritie of the rest of the same lawes. Yet after that they had by tract of time bene of long buried as it were in obliuion (which was seuen hundred yeares after that they were first published) it was at the motion of *Æbutius* the Tribune, decreed, That such of those lawes as were as it were of themselues growne out of vse, should be reputed as repealed and abrogated, to the end that no man should with them yet standing in force be entangled.

But for that the nature of man as of all other worldly things also, is most slipperie and vnconstant, running still headlong from good to euill, and from euill to worse; vices by little and little still encreasing, not vnlike vnto euill humors, which without sencible feeling encrease mans bodie, vntill it be full of them, breedeth in it many most daungerous diseases, and so at length bringeth it vnto vtter destruction. For remedie whereof new lawes must of necessitie be deuised: which must yet for all that by little and little be done, and not violently all at once. As *Agis* king of Lacedemonia vnwisely attempted to haue done: who desiring to reestablish in the Commonweale the auntient discipline of *Lycurgus*, now by the negligence of the magistrats almost grown quite out of vse, caused all the obligations and scedules of priuat men to be vppon a sudden brought out & burnt: which done, he was about to haue proceeded to the making of a new diuision of lands, to the end to haue so made an equalitie of wealth and goods amongst the citisens, as *Lycurgus* had before done: which although it were a thing desired of many in the Lacedemonian Commonweale (which had indeed so bene founded) yet so it was, that in making too much hast in the doing thereof, he not onely fell from his hope, but thereby kindled such a fire of sedition also, as burnt vp his whole house,

The cheife lawe of all Commonweales.

No lawe so sacred but that vpon vrgent necessitie it is to be chaunged.

Better to suffer euill lawes by little and little to growe out of vse, then vpon the soden with daunger to abrogate them all at once.

Neither are old lawes to be altogether sodenly without daunger abrogated: or newe lawes rashly established.

A1 *For* first, *probably read* for if (cf. L). C2–3 *For* bee by right evident *read* bee right evident.
D7 encrease IN mans bodie   Note at B6.

house, and so afterward dispoiled of his estate, and by his rebellious subiects together with his mother and other his friends and partakers strangled; made away for a sort of mad and euill minded fellowes to inuade the state, hauing so depriued his countrey of himselfe a good and vertuous prince. Whereas he should before haue made himselfe maister of the forces, or if that had not bene possible, yet to haue sounded the minds of them of the geater sort, and by meanes to haue gained them vnto him one after another, as had *Lysurgus* done before him; and then to haue forbidden them the vse of gold and siluer, that so it might haue growne into as little estimation as iron: and in some time after that, to haue forbidden all sumptuousnesse in apparell, and rich furniture, and not at once to haue encroached vpon the libertie of the people, to haue proued their patience, and chaunged their discipline: For that to vse such a violent letting of blood, before the corrupt humors purged, or so strong a medicine, before any preparatiue giuen, is not the way to cure the diseases, but to kill the diseased. Wherefore in the gouernments of Commonweales, and healing the diseases thereof, we must imitat not the Physitians onely, but euen nature it selfe, or rather the great God of nature whom we see to do all things by little and little and almost insensibly. The Venetians right wisely during the life of *Augustin Barbarin* their duke, attempted not in any thing to abridge his power, though by them much misliked and feared; least in so doing they should either haue offered some disgrace vnto him their prince, now growne old, or els haue raised some new sturres, and so haue troubled the quiet of their Commonweale. But he once dead, before they proceeded vnto the new election of *Loredan*, the seignorie caused such new lawes and decrees to be published, as whereby the power of the dukes was right greatly impeired and diminished. The same wee haue shewed also to haue bene done in the elections of the German emperours, the kings of Polonia, and of Denmarke, who of soueraigne Monarches are now brought vnto the small estates of Generals in chiefe, some of them more, and some lesse: which the more closely to hide, they haue left vnto them the imperiall and roiall markes and cognisances in their habits, in their titles and ceremonies, but in few things els in effect and deed.

Dangerous for a prince vpon the soden to displace or caste offe the anntient seruitor of his predecessours, or great magistrats of the estate.

But as it is a daungerous thing for the subiects all at once to abridge or cut short the power of a soueraigne prince or magistrat, who yet hath the power in his hand: so is it also no lesse daungerous for a prince vpon the sudden to displace or cast off the antient seruitors of his predecessours, or els at once to thrust out some part of the great magistrats and officers of the estate, and to retaine the rest, they which are new chosen or retained, resting ouer charged with enuie, and the other with euill doing or ignorance, and withall depriued of the honour and good, which they haue bought full deere. And it may be that one of the fairest foundations of this monarchy is, that the king dying, the officers of the crowne continue still in their charge, who by that means still maintaine the Commonweale in the estate thereof. And albeit that the officers of the kings house be at the pleasure of the successour to be chaunged, so ought hee yet therein to vse such discretion, as that they which are remoued haue not occasion to innouat or moue any thing as men disgraced, or at leastwise haue no power left them so to doe, albeit that they were thereunto willing. In which point the emperour *Galba* being deceiued, and hauing thrust *Otho* out of the hope hee had conceiued of the empire, to adopt *Piso* to succeed him in the gouernment, and yet for all that without disarming of *Otho*, he was shortly after by the same *Otho* (a man in great fauor with the Pretorian souldiours) slaine together with *Piso*, whome he had before adopted to succeed him in the empire and gouernment of the state. All which perils and daungers are lesse to be feared in an Aristocratike or Popular estate, for that in them they which haue the soueraigntie neuer die; howbeit that there is in them no lesse danger in chaunging of their

---

F2 made a way   F6 greater   F6 by meanes *i.e. illecebris*, by inducements   G9 either

OF A COMMONWEALE. 473

their soueraigne magistrats, or generals (as we haue before declared) or in making of lawes which may tend to the impairing of the power of the people, or which may any way seeme profitable vnto the nobilitie, and preiudiciall or hurtfull vnto the people: or in case that victuals and prouisions faile, or that some great extreame dearth arise; in which cases there is alwaies daunger of popular commotions and rebellions. So that in briefe, when question is for the displacing of great magistrats, or for the suppressing of corporations or colledges, or for the cutting short of priuileges, or the augmenting of punishments, or for the reforming of disorders amongst the people, or for the calling of great men to account, or for the reducing of religion to the former course and beginning thereof; which by succession of time, following the naturall corruption of man, hath bin altered & changed from the first puritie therof: there is no better means than to come thereunto by little and little, without forcing of any thing, if it were possible, as by way of suppression. Whereof we haue a notable example of king *Charles* the fift (euen he that was surnamed the Wise) who at such time as he was Regent in France (his father being as then prisoner in England) by the euill councell of some, ignorant in matters of estate, at one chop suspended all the officers in Fraunce, of whome also hee suppressed the greatest part, appointing fiftie commissioners for the hearing of such accusations as should be laid against them for the extortion and briberie by them committed and vsed: whereupon all Fraunce was in such tumult and vprore (for the infinit number that then were of male contents) as that shortly after for remedie thereof, hee by a decree in the high court of parliament at Paris, whereunto all the nobilitie were assembled, abrogated the former law. Which decree is yet extant in the act of that his court, to this effect and purpose, *Cùm regiæ potestati: & procurationi, quam gerimus, non modò quæ ab alijs, sed etiam quæ a nobis ipsis & in Rempublicam, & in singulos peccantur emendare consentaneum sit, rebus planè perspectis & cognitis, quæ de imperio magistratibus adempto noua lege iussimus, placet abrogari; vt quidem abrogamus, & apertè declaramus, legis illius, quæ importunis quorumdam rogationibus erepta est, nullam vim fore, & quæ acta gesta sunt, cum magno nostro dolore acta gesta fuisse; nec illam magistratuum ac honorum abrogationem, quam non iure factam esse censitemur cuiquam fraudi esse: aut cuiusquam ius ac dignitatem violare nos vlla ex parte voluisse: ac proinde legem illam iure a nobis rescindi & abrogari testamur, vt omnibus magistratibus salua omnia & integra restituantur,* Whereas by the regall power and authoritie which we beare, it is fitting for vs to correct and amend, not onely such things as by others, but euen by our selues also are trespassed against the Commonweale, or other men in particular: all things throughly looked into, and tried, our pleasure is, That what we haue by a new law commaunded concerning power and authoritie taken from the magistrats, to be againe abrogated, as indeed we abrogat, and plainely declare the force of that law (which was by the importunat suit of some wrested from vs) to be nothing: and that such things as were then done, to haue bene done to our great griefe: neither that that depriuation of offices or honours, which we confesse to haue bene not lawfully done, to bee imputed to any man: neither that our will was in any part to violat any mans right or honour: And therefore we freely protest, that new law to be of vs rightly repealed and abrogated: and that so all things safe and whole, may so againe bee vnto the magistrats restored. And thus much he. But *Charles* the ninth comming vnto the crowne, and seeing the number of officers through the libertie of the times growne almost infinit, to the great hurt of the Commonweale, in such sort, as that it seemed a thing almost necessarie to haue depriued them of their honours and fees, yet did he not so, for that it could not without great iniurie be done, when as the money they had before paid for them, could not by reason of the want of coine in the common treasurie, bee againe repaid

All alterations of lawes or other great matters in a Commonweale are best to be made by little and little.

The wise course taken of Charls the ix for the abating of the infinite number of officers in the Commonweale.

Ss iij

A2 impairing   C9 confitemur

repaid vnto them: neither if it could haue bene, could he yet be without imputation & disgrace, that was so without cause displaced. Besides that, vnto many their credit & reputation was in more esteeme & deerer than was their profit, and much the more was it to be feared, that if they should both of their money and preferment be together spoiled, least their present credit and profit being impaired, and the hope also of the recouerie of the money they had paid lost, should minister vnto many of them occasions for them to raise rebellions and new sturres in the estate of the Commonweale. Wherefore the want of money in the common treasurie profited vs then mindfull of other things, and fortune so fauoured our vnskilfulnesse and ignorance, as in auntient time it did a painter, who painting of an horse, when as he not knowing how cunningly to expresse the foame of the horses mouth, and wearie of his worke not well sorting to his mind, in an anger cast his wet spunge at it, and so by fortune expressed that which he by cunning could not do: euen so it pleased that king to lessen the multitude of his officers stil as they died, by chusing no new in their steads, when as he could not againe restore vnto them the money they had paid for their offices; neither yet if the princes wealth & power had bene so great, as with his becke or a wink of his eye, to cause all his subiects to tremble, and so to be able to doe what thing soeuer he list, should he yet seeme to do wisely by force to take away the offices and places before sold vnto his magistrats and officers: For that not onely they which haue receiued the iniurie, but euen other his subiects also, are oft times much moued and incensed with iniuries and wrongs done vnto other men: Besides that, the mightier that a man is, the more iustly and temperately he ought to behaue himselfe towards all men, but especiall towards his subiects. Wherefore the Senat and people of Basil did wisely, who hauing renounced the Bishop of Romes Religion (which they now detested.) would not vpon the sodaine thrust the Monkes and Nunnes with other the Religious persons out of their Abbies and Monasteries: but onely tooke order, that as they dyed, they should die both for themselues and their successors, expresly forbidding any new to be chosen in their places; that so by that meanes their colledges might by little and little by the death of the fellowes be extinguished. Whereby it came to passe, that all the rest of the Catthusians of their owne accord forsaking their cloister, yet one of them all alone for a long time remained therein, and so quietly and without any disturbance held the right of his couent, being neuer enforced to chaunge either his place, his habit, or old ceremonies, or religion before by him receiued. The like order was taken at Coire in the diet of the Grisons: wherin it was decreed, That the ministers of the reformed religion should be maintained of the profits and reuenewes of the church, the religious men yet neuerthelesse still remaining in their cloisters and couents, to bee by their death suppressed, they being now prohibited to chuse any new in stead of them which were dead: as I haue learned by the letters of the ambassadour of Fraunce, who was then at Coire. By which meanes both they which professed the new religion, and they which professed the old, were both prouided for: whereas otherwise it had beene an vnreasonable thing to haue thrust them, who had learned not onely to liue idly, but euen to doe nothing at all (as *Lucilius* merrily saith) hauing neither trade nor occupation to liue vppon, out of the old possession of their lands, were it neuer so vniust. Whereof beside the iniurie vnto them done, daunger might haue also ensued, least they not hauing whereof to liue, and so brought into dispaire, might haue attempted some thing against the state; and so haply drawne after them all their friends and allies also, to the great trouble of the whole Commonweale. For the same cause the king hauing giuen leaue for the free exercise of the new religion in this realme of Fraunce, and seeing that they which vnder the colour thereof were gone out of ther cloisters, demanded a portion in the

Not good for a prince to vse the greatnesse of his power in displacing of the great officers of his realme and state.

Religeous houses with great wisdome quietly suppressed at Basill and Coire.

K6 allies also

OF A COMMONWEALE. 475

A the lands and inheritance of their parents or neere kinsmen: it was decreed, and that vpon great paine, That they should againe returne vnto their cloisters: which seemed to be a thing directly contrarie vnto the law, whereby free libertie was giuen for euerie man that wold, to professe the new reformed religion. Howbeit that this was indirectly to stop the mouthes of them which departing out of their monasteries, sought to trouble the estate, and vnder the vaile and colour of religion, to trouble the most great and noble houses of this realme: besides that it had beene also necessarie in all the customes of this realme, to rase the article concerning the religions, who both by the cannon and ciuill laws, as also by all our lawes and customes, are excluded and shut out from all hope of inheritance.

B But now that which we haue said, That the multitude of officers, or of colleges, and companies, of priuileges, or of wicked men, which through the sufferance of princes, or the negligence of the magistrat, are by little and little growne to the hurt of the Commonweale, are by the same meane to be againe suppressed; hath place in all things which concerne the publike state, and hath a reference vnto the nature of the lawes, which haue no force nor effect but for the time to come. And albeit that tyrannie bee a thing most cruell and detestable, yet so it is, that the surest way and meane to suppresse the same, if the tyrant haue neither children nor brethren to succeed him, is together with the death of the tyrant to abolish also the tyrannicall gouernment; & not by force C whilest he yet liueth to striue to take from him the gouernment, with the hazard of the ruine of the whole estate, as oftentimes it chaunceth. But if the tyrant haue children, and doth what he may to destroy the good, and to put the great men one after another to death (as *Tarquin* the proud, and other tyrants following his steps vsed commonly to doe) or to suppresse the magistrats or other great officers which might stay the course of his tyrannie, to the end that hee may without let or controlement doe whatsoeuer him pleaseth: then in this case violent remedies are to bee vsed, but with such limitation and restriction as we haue before set downe, and not otherwise, least so wee might seeme rashly to arme the subiects against their princes.

The best and surest way for the suppressing of a tyrant.

We ought then in the gouernment of a well ordered estate and Commonweale, D to imitat and follow the great God of nature, who in all things proceedeth easily and by little and little, who of a little seed causeth to grow a tree for height and greatnesse right admirable, and yet for all that insensibly; and still by meanes conioyning the extremities of nature, as by putting the Spring betwixt Winter and Sommer, and Autumne betwixt Sommer and Winter, moderating the extremities of the times and seasons, which the selfe same wisedome which he vseth in all other things also, and that in such sort, as that no violent force or course therein appeareth. But if it be oftentimes daungerous to chaunge the lawes of an estate or Commonweale, as wee haue before declared: Let vs now see also, if it be not in like sort daungerous oftentimes to chaunge the magistrates, or that it is much E better to haue them perpetuall and without chaunge.

The wise politician in the gouernment of the estate is to imitate the works of God in nature who by litle and litle bringeth great things to perfection.

whether.

A8 *For* religions *read* religious *i.e.* those in monastic orders.   C6 in this case   D5 *For* which the selfe same *read* with the selfe same.

Chap. IIII.

Whether it be better in a Commonweale to haue the Magistrats still chaungeable, or else perpetuall.

Orasmuch as both cities, citisens, and Commonweales, vse commonly to be for nothing more turmoiled and troubled than by men for the obtaining of offices and honours, mee thinke this question to bee one of the most profitable and most necessarie of any that can be made in matter of estate, *Whether it be better to haue annuall or perpetuall Magistrats in a Commonweale?* Than which question I know not whether there be any amongst them which concerne a Commonweal more harder to decide, or more pleasant to vnderstand, and therefore not in any wise by vs in this place to be omitted. Which I say not as meaning to take vpon me the deciding of this question, but onely to touch the reasons which might well be giuen both on the one side and the other, leauing the resolution thereof vnto them which heretofore haue better sounded the proceeding and consequence thereof. Neither is it mine intent or purpose, either to propound and moue this question, to giue foot vnto them which would chaunge the laws alreadie receiued, which the subiects ought to hold for good and wholesome in euerie Commonweale; nor for any desire I haue to chaunge the estate of Commonweals alreadie established, which haue continued by long succession and course of yeares.

Reasons to show that magistrats ought not to be perpetuall.

Rewards for vertue ought to be vnto all men common.

Now the first and strongest reason that is to be had to make the magistrats and officers annuall, is, for that the first and principall end of euerie Commonweale ought to consist in vertue: and that the scope of euerie good and true law-giuer, is to make his subiects vertuous. Which to attaine vnto, it behoueth him to propound vnto the view and sight of the whole world, the rewards of vertue, as the marke whereat euerie man ought to aime in best sort he can.

Now most certaine it is, that honour is no other thing than the reward and prize of vertue, which neither ought nor can by the counterpoise of profit be esteemed: whereas rather to the contrarie vertue hath no more capital an enemie, than profit deuised to arise by honour. If then the honourable preferments, offices and commissions bee taken out of publique place, to be alwayes enclosed & shut vp within the particular houses of most vnworthy men, who for fauour or money carrie away the same; it is not then to be thought vertue in that estate to be the prize, the corrupt nature of man being such as is right hardly to be drawne vnto vertue, what reward or prise soeuer bee deuised for the alluring of men thereto. And thus much for the first point, which ought to moue princes and wise law giuers, to set preferments, offices, and all such other the rewards of vertue, in the eye of all the world, and so to diuide them amongst their subiects, to euery man according to his deserts, which they cannot do, if they grant them vnto men in perpetuities.

The root of sedition is by all meanes to be cut vp in a Commonweale which can hardly be where magistrats and officers be perpetuall.

Another point which the wise law giuer ought still to haue before his eyes, is, To cut vp the roots, and to take away the seedes of ciuill sedition, so to maintaine his subiects in good peace and amitie amongst themselues, and one of them with another. Which is a matter of such weight, as that many haue thought it to bee the onely end which the good law maker ought to hope after. For albeit that vertue may oftentimes be banished out of Commonweales, for men to liue in a disordered licentiousnesse of all kind of voluptuous pleasures: yet in that all men agree, that there is no more daungerous

Note at I2.

gerous a plague vnto Commonweales, than ciuill sedition and discord. Forasmuch as it draweth after it the common ruine aswell of the good as of the bad. Now so it is, that the first and principall cause of sedition, is inequalitie; as to the contrarie the mother nurse of peace and amitie, is equalitie; which is no other thing than naturall equitie, distributing rewards, preferments, honours, and all other things common vnto the subiects indifferently, and in the best sort that may be. From which equalitie the very theeues and robbers themselues may in no wise depart, if they meane to liue together. Hee therefore that shall diuide the honours and offices of estate vnto a small number of men, as needs it must be, when they are giuen for tearme of life, hee I say hath lighted the greatest flames of ielousie of one of them against another, and the greatest fire of sedition that can possibly be raised in a Commonweale.

Now if there were no more but the two reasons before alleaged, *viz.* The enioying of vertue, with the rewards thereunto due, and the auoyding of sedition, the greatest plague of a Commonweale; yet were they euen sufficient to let, that offices should not be perpetuall, but rather annuall, to the end that euerie man so hauing therein part and interest, might so also haue occasion to liue in peace. But yet there are farther reasons also, which is, that by such perpetuitie of offices and promotions, not onely the vnitie and concord of subiects, and the true rewards of vertue are so taken away, but that the due punishment by the lawes appointed for offendors are thereby also impeached, or rather quite abolished: Whereof the wise law giuer ought to haue a greater regard than of the rewards to vertue due. For that the wise and accomplished man looketh for no other reward of his vertuous actions more than vertue it selfe: which a man cannot say of vice, neither of the vitious. And for this cause the lawes both of God and man, euen from the first vnto the last, haue commaunded nothing more, than the punishment of the wicked. And what punishment should a man do vppon them, who are alwaies so high mounted, as that it is impossible to come nigh them? Who shall accuse them? who shall imprison them? who shall condemne them? Shall their companions or fellowes in power? will they cut their owne armes, or rip their owne entrals? beleeue it they will neuer be so euill aduised. What if the great ones bee also partakers of their foule robberies, villanies, and extortion? how shall they then punish the others? they will rather blush for shame, and be touched with compassion of them which are like vnto themselues, than with the hainousnesse of the offences be enduced to take of them punishment. But if any there be so hardie as to accuse, yea or but so much as to complaine of one of these demie gods, he is in daunger of his life, as a false enformer, if hee by proofe cleerer than the sunne it selfe, proue not villanies done in most obscure darkenesse: and admit that all be by them well proued, and that the guiltie magistrat be conuinced and attainted, yet so it is, that this ordinarie clause *Frater noster est*, He is our brother, shall suffice to couer and burie all the villanies, deceits, and extortion, of the most vniust magistrat that a man could imagine: So that hardly one of a thousand which had deserued punishment, should in fiue hundred yeres be brought to execution.

Perpetuitie of offices the cause of impunitie of the great officers.

But if the magistrats were annuall, it is most certaine, that the feare to be called to account, would alwaies keepe them in awe, and that they would tremble and quake as often as they heard that thundering threatning which the Tribunes of the people made to *Manlius, Priuatum rationem rerum ab se gestarum redditurum, quoniam Consul noluisset*, That he being a priuat man, should giue account of such things as hee had done, for that he would not so do being Consull. And indeed what could a man see more faire, than them which had but a little before administred iustice, and taken charge of the common treasure, with other such publike offices, after that they had put off their

Great magistrats and officers in doubt to be called to account where they are but annuall.

robes

Note at D 10.

robes of dignitie, to come in their common attire as priuat men, to giue an account of their actions done in the time of their magistracie. And this is it for which *Plutarch* hath so highly commended the custome of the auntient Romans, who animated the young men to commence their publike accusations against such as had euill acquited themselues in their publike charges, setting them on as grayhounds vpon wolues, or other wild beasts. In which doing not onely the offendors were punished, but euerie man else also vpon an emulation and strife, as it were endeuoured him to doe well; but especially they, who had themselues accused others, as well assured that there neuer wanted some, who still right narrowly looked into all their doings, so that it much concerned them to beare themselues most vprightly in the whole course of their liues. Which benefits those estates and Commonweales must neeedes want, which haue their magistrats perpetuall, or for tearme of life. For which cause the emperour *Claudius* wisely renewed an old edict or law, then growne out of vse: which was, That hee to whome the gouernment of any prouince was by lot fallen (as the maner was) should forthwith, all excuses set apart, go vnto his charge; and that the time of his authoritie and charge once expired, he should not forthwith take vppon him any other new publike charge or gouernment, to the intent that the euill behauiour or extortion of the magistrats should not by such continuation of their power and authoritie remaine vnpunished. For whatsoeuer decrees or lawes bee made, the euill magistrats would still keepe the power in their hands, and doe what they can one for another: in such sort strengthening themselues, as that is a thing almost impossible to haue of them any reason. Which was the cause that moued *Hannibal* that great captaine to present a request vnto the people of Carthage, To make their judges annuall, which before held their places for tearme of life, and that none of them should keepe his place two yeares together, as *Liuie* reporteth, whose words we thought good thus here to set downe, *Iudicum ordo ea tempestate dominabatur Carthagine, eo maxime quod ijdem perpetui iudices: res, fama, vitaque omnium in illorum potestate erat; qui vnum eius ordinis, & omnes aduersos habebat. horum in tam impotenti regno Prætor factus* Annibal, *vocare ad se Quæstorem; idem pro nihilo habuit; nam aduersæ factionis erat: & quia ex quæstura in iudices potentissimum ordinem referuntur, iam pro futuris mox opibus animos gerebant: id indignum ratus* Annibal, *viatorem ad prehendendum Quæstorem misit, subductumque in concionem non ipsum magis quam ordinem iudicum (præ quorum superbia atque opibus nec leges quicquam essent, nec magistratus) accusauit, & vt secundis auribus accipi orationem animaduertit, legem extemplo promulgauit pertulitque*, The order or companie of the judges (saith he) did at that time beare all the sway at Carthage; and well the more, for that the selfe same men were still perpetuall judges: euerie mans wealth, fame, and life, was in their power; he that had one of them of that order against him, had them al his enemies. In this their so insolent a raigne *Hannibal* being made Pretor, conuented one of the Questors, or publike receiuers before him, which made thereof no reckoning, for why, he was of the contrarie faction vnto him: and forasmuch as out of the Questors choyce was still made into the most mightie order of the judges, they still bare their hautie minds aunswerable vnto the wealth and power they were afterwards to enioy. Which *Hannibal* taking for a great indignitie, sent a sergeant to lay hands vpon the Questor, and hauing brought him into the generall assemblie of the people, accused not him more than he did the whole order of the judges (through whose pride and wealth, neither the lawes nor the magistrats were (as he said) any thing at all regarded) and perceiuing his speech to be with the good liking of the people receiued, forthwith enacted, and proclaimed a law, That the judges should be euery yeare chosen, and that none of them should be judges two yeares together. And thus farre he. For why,

it

Euill magistrats most commonly hold together.

G1 needes   H1 as that IT is a thing   H1–2 reason *i.e.* satisfaction, justice   H6–7 judices
ERANT: res   Note at I4.

it was otherwise a thing impossible to chastise them, a man still hauing them all his enemies, that should touch but one of them. For that they beeing perpetuall magistrats, and commonly allied one of them vnto another, it was impossible to hope to haue any of them punished, and much lesse to haue against them iustice, if a man had any thing to do with them: and in case a man refused one of them, hee must in so doing refuse the whole bench of them also. As not many yeares ago in the court of Paris (which at this time consisteth of an hundred and fiftie iudges) in a suit betwixt *Chr. Thuan*, chiefe iustice in that court, and *Iohn Tili*, register of the court (who tooke vpon him the defence of his daughter being absent) were, for alliance onely, threescore iudges on the one side, and two and fortie on the other, chalenged and reiected, and all vpon the same bench. And for this cause it was ordained in the assembly of the estates of the countrey of Languedoc, holden at Montpelier in the yeare 1556, where then I was, and charge there giuen to *Iohn Durande*, atturney for that country, That amongst other his instructions, he should especially moue the king, that it might please him to ordaine, that the nie kinsmen or other of alliance vnto the iudges, should not from thenceforth be admitted vnto the same bench, neither into the same court. Which same request foure yeares after, was by the estates of Fraunce presented vnto the king in the parliament at Orleance, howbeit that nothing could therein bee obtained, neither can be, so long as honours and preferments are in perpetuitie giuen in the Commonweale. For it is now two hundred and fiftie yeares since that king *Charles* the fift, and before him *Philip* the Faire had ordained, That no man should bee iudge in the same countrey wherein he was borne: as in like case *Marcus Aurelius* made an edict, That no man should be gouernour in his owne countrey. Of which law the profit was thought so great, as that he would haue the same afterwards extended euen vnto them which were but councellours or assistants vnto the gouernours of countries: which was a thing then wel put in execution, as it is at this present in Spaine, & in most of the cities in Italie, where the ordinarie iudge is most commonly a stranger. Which was also by the ambassadours of Moscouie requested of the estates of Polonia. Howbeit that the decrees of our kings concerning those matters, were quickly buried, after that the publike offices and charges began to be with vs giuen for tearme of life. And not to search further into the edicts of the Roman emperours, we find also in *Cæsar* his Commentaries, that the auntient Gaules, and namely they of Autun, had amongst them an inuiolable law, which expresly forbad the magistrats to be continued in their places aboue one yeare, and that two of one familie could not be magistrats together, nor yet one of them, so long as the other who had alreadie bene magistrat should liue. And that more is, it was alwaies expresly forbidden, That two of one familie might be councellors together, neither yet one of them, so long as the other who had alreadie so bene a councellour was aliue.

That no man should be a iudg in his owne countrie.

The ordinarie iudges in Italie straungers.

Lib. 7.

Moreouer the thing which ought of all others to be most recommended vnto all subiects in generall, & euerie one of them in particular, is the preseruation of the Commonweale. And what regard or care of the publike good should they haue, which therein haue no part? Such as are themselues excluded, and which see the common preferments and offices giuen in prey to some few in perpetuitie? How should they haue any care of that which concerneth them not, neither neere, nor a farre off? And admit that any good and honest man would say, would doe, or vndertake, any thing that were for the common good or profit, being himselfe but a priuat man, who should hearken vnto him? who should support him? who should fauour him? So that euery man leauing to thinke of the publike, entendeth vnto his owne businesse, and hee in that case should be but laughed at, and derided as a foole, which should take more care of

The great offices and preferments of the Commonweale giuen in perpetuitie breedeth a carelesues of the Common good both in the magistrats themselues and others

of the common welfare than of his owne. As for them who alreadie enioy the publike preferments and offices, they for the most part haue no great care of the common good, being now for euer assured of that which they most desired. O but how much more happie should both the subiects and Commonweale be, if euerie man in his degree and according to his qualitie, hauing enioyed conuenable preferments, and so hauing learned true wisedome by the mannaging of worldly affaires, should retire themselues from these vaine and worldly businesses, to occupie themselues in the contemplation of things naturall and diuine? For most certaine it is, that contemplation is the true mother and mistresse of al true wisedome and happinesse, which men altogether wrapped vp in worldly affaires, neuer so much as once dreamed or tasted of; and yet for all that this is the end, this is the scope, this the chiefe point of all mans felicitie.

One man to haue many offices and especially in perpetuitie, not good for the Commonweale.

And yet besides these three, there is another great inconuenience also, in that offices and preferments are in Commonweales graunted vnto men for tearme of life: that is to wit, that some few would haue all, and some one would possesse himselfe of many publike charges and offices at once; as it was in auntient time permitted them in Carthage: which for all that seemed both vnto *Plato* and *Aristotle* a thing right daungerous, For that it is an hard matter for one man well to discharge one office, but well to discharge many no one man can; and is therefore in euerie well ordered Commonweale a thing forbidden. Howbeit that the ambitious desires of men alwayes passeth beyond the prohibitions of the lawes, the most vnworthy most commonly burning with the hoatest flames of ambition; not vnlike the weake stomacke, which is alwaies more desirous of meat which it cannot disgest, than is the stomacke which can better disgest it: thinking it not to stand with their honor and reputation to stay in the meane, or to abate any of their titles and dignities, but contrariwise to mount still higher and higher. In so much that the seigneurie of Venice in some sort to satisfie the ambition of the citisens, gaue leaue vnto him which had borne a greater office, to refuse the lesse being laid vpon him: which is a daungerous course, to measure the publike charges and offices, by the foot of the subiects ambition, and not by the common profit.

Then how much more daungerous is it, to make the magistrats and publike charges perpetuall, onely to serue the ambitious desires of some, and so to make the Commonweale subiect vnto the desire and pleasure of some few? For why, it is to be feared least that they who can neuer satisfie their immoderat desires with the multitude of offices and publike charges, but had rather to burst at the table of ambition, than in time to withdraw themselues: It is (I say) to be feared least some hungrie fellowes shall at length say vnto them, Depart you hence; or if they will not so doe, plucke them away by force, not without their owne daungers, and troubling of the quiet estate of the Commonweale.

Old men in danger to be thrust off the bridges.

At the assemblies of the estates of Rome into the place called *Campus Martius*, for the chusing of their cheife magistrats, and other their great officers, certaine narrow bridges were in diuers places laid for the citisens to passe ouer by, that so the little tables wherein their voices were contained, might the better be of them receiued: at which time such as were threescore yeares old, were still warned to giue place, and not to come to giue their voices, least haply they might by the multitude of the younger sort be oppressed: and not for that such old men were cast headlong from off the bridges into the riuer, as some haue thought. But how much more seemely were it for them which haue quietly of long enioyed the great offices and preferments in the Commonweale, and which are now growne old therein, sweetly to retire themselues out of those high places, than violently to be thrust out by others? especially considering that there is no place more slipperie or daungerous, than are the places of honour and commaund. Besides that (which worse is) such ambitious men in their falling

Note at F6.

ling draw after them the fall of many others also, together with the ruine of the whole Commonweale: as did *Marius*, who hauing passed through all the degrees of honour, and bene six times Consull (which neuer Roman had bene before him) yet not so content, would needs take vpon him the charge of the wars against king *Mithridates* (which by lot was fallen vnto *Sylla*) howbeit that hee was now growne extreame old, to the intent to obtaine the seuenth Consulship, and to continue a perpetuall commaunding power vnto himselfe. But *Sylla* vnderstanding of the commission giuen to *Marius*, and of the authority by a tumultuous assembly of the people taken from him now absent (and hauing also an army with him) contrarie vnto the law and the custom of their auncestors, straight way returned to Rome with his partakers, seyzed vpon the citie, where he made a most horrible massacre; which afterwards in such sort continued, as that all Italie and Spaine was embrued with blood, not onely the captaines and chiefe commaunders of *Marius* his faction being by *Sylla* slaine, but euen his companions, friends, and kinsmen also, being most shamefully proscribed, or els banished, and so the Popular estate brought vnto an extreame tyrannie. So euen for the same occasion three hundred yeares before, the Popular estate was there chaunged into a faction of an Oligarchie; not for hauing of offices in perpetuitie for tearme of life, but onely for hauing continued the charge vnto the Decemuiri, or ten Commissioners, for two yeares together; men appointed for the reforming and amending of the lawes, who would haue so continued the third yeare also, and by force of armes still maintained their commission, encroaching vpon the libertie of the people, had they not by force of armes (though not without great daunger of the state) bene againe remoued.

Ambitious men neuer satisfied with honors, oftentimes the cause of great trobles in a Commonweale.

So by the same meanes many Popular and Aristocratique estates were chaunged into Monarchies, or at leastwise into tyrannicall gouernments; for hauing giuen the publike charges and commissions vnto their magistrats or commissioners, for longer time than was needfull, or for proroguing of them longer than by the law they should; as to *Pisistratus* in Athens, to *Philon* in the citie of Argos, to *Cypselius* in Corinth, to *Dionysius* at Syracusa, to *Panætius* at Leontium, and to *Cæsar* at Rome. Which *Æmylius Mamercus* the Dictator foreseeing, presented a request vnto the people, which passed into the force of a law, whereby it was ordained, That the Censors power from that time forward should continue but for eighteene monethes, which before was established for fiue yeares: and the next day after that he was created Dictator, deposed himselfe of his Dictatorship, being not willing to hold it more than one day; giuing this reason vnto the people of his so doing, *Vt scitas quàm mihi diuturna imperia non placeant*, That you may know (said he) how little long lasting authoritie and power please me. And for the same occasion the law Cornelia, published at the instance of one of the Tribunes of the people, prouided, That it should not be lawful for any man to seeke to haue one and the same office more than once in ten yeares. Neither missed it much but that *Gabinius* the Tribune had by the Senators themselues beene slaine in the full Senat for hauing by his request made vnto the people, procured commission for fiue yeares together to be graunted vnto *Pompey*, for the ending of the Piraticall warre: Whereof *Dion* giueth a notable reason, For that (saith he) the nature of man is such, as that a man hauing for long time borne some honourable charge, commonly hath al other men in contempt and disdaine, neither can well endure to liue in subiection after he hath for a long time commaunded. Which thing *Cassiodorus* almost in the same sence writeth, *Antiquitas, prouinciarum dignitatem voluit annua successione reparari, vt nec diutina potestate vnus insolesceret, & multorum prouectus gaudia reperiret*, Antiquitie (saith he) would the honour of the prouinces to be repaired with annuall succession, in such sort as that one man should neither grow insolent with long power, and

Continuation of great offices oftentimes the cause of the change of the estate.

Tt pre-

C7 *For* Philon (L) *read* Phidon (Fr).   D4 sciatis   E7 reperirent (Fr and L)   Note at C8.

preferment be a comfort to many. And haply it was not one of the least causes that the Assyrian and Persian empires stood so long, for that they euerie yeare chaunged their lieutenants and generals.

Great inconueniences ensuing by making of offices and dignities hereditarie.

But how then commeth it to passe, that euen children by way of complaint sue to be maintained and kept in the possession of the honours and estates that their fathers and grandfathers had? As in fact hath bene seene in the constables of Campagne, of Normandie, and of Britaigne: in the marshals De la Foy, as they tearme them, in the great chamberlaines, and other infinit, euen vnto the sergeants fees of Normandie, as I haue before noted. And namely in Aniou, Touraine, and Maine, the house of Roches had made the offices of bailifes and stewards hereditarie, had not *Lewes* the ninth reuoked them, and made them mutable and iusticiable, by his decree in the yeare 1256. The like is done in Principalities, Dukedomes, Marquisats, and Earledomes, which now are had in perpetuitie, which before were holden but by way of commission, and that during the princes pleasure, which at the first were but annuall, but afterwards perpetuall: and at last by the fauour of our kings are become hereditarie. Howbeit that other people also as well as we, haue in the same errour offended. So that there is almost no place in all Europe (except in England) where offices and dignities are not now hereditarie, in such sort as that commaunding power and authoritie, with the administration of iustice, is by right of succession fallen euen vnto women and children, and so of a thing publike made particular, and to be sold to him that wil giue most, as it must needs be, being once brought into the forme of a patrimonie, which hath giuen occasion more boldly to trucke all estates and offices, when as men see by the lawes and customes euen sacred iustice it selfe prophaned, and set to sale to him that will giue most: Of which inconueniences is proceeded the euill custome of making of all estates and offices perpetuall. For one should doe iniurie to take an office from a marchant, and not restore vnto him againe the money that he paid for it. Thus we see the dangers and absurdities one of them as it were linked in another, by the making of the estates and offices of the Commonweale perpetuall. Besides which reasons by me alleaged, we haue also the authoritie of the greatest Law makers, Philosophers, and Lawyers, as also the examples of almost all the auntient Commonweales; as namely, of the Athenians, the Romans, the Celtes, and others infinit, who haue flourished, and do yet flourish in diuers places of Italie, Swisserland, and Germanie, as also the authoritie of Sir *Thomas Moore*, chauncellour of England, who in the Commonweale by him deuised, maketh all the magistrats and officers therein annuall, some from six monethts to six monethes, and othersome from two monethes to two monethes, and all to auoid the inconueniences which I haue before spoke of. And these reasons they for most part vse, which say, That magistrats and officers should not be in a Commonweale perpetuall.

The great inconueniences ensuing of hauing the offices in a Commonweale still annuall or changable.

But now on the other side, they which maintaine it to bee more for the publike good, to make the estates and offices in a Commonweale perpetuall, alleage, That nothing can be well done in a yeares space, when as the magistrat must depart out of his charge before he well know his dutie; and hauing begun to vnderstand what belongeth vnto his place, must yet forthwith leaue the same vnto a new man; and so hee likewise vnto another, all still new men; so that the Commonweale is still to fall into the hands of vnsufficient men, and such as want experience. But suppose that the prince or the people, or they which haue the choice of the magistrats, commit not the publike charge but vnto men knowne to be of good experience yet seeing so many holy daies, dayes not iudiciall, vacations, daies of election, and of triumph, as take vp a great part of the yeares, as well the publike as mens priuat actions must therewith needs be trobled,

warres

H4 estates   I4–5 monethes   K9 *For* yeares *read* yeare.

warres begun be delaid, iudgements interrupted, actions of the wicked abolished, punishments deferred, & in briefe the Commonweal in the greatest dangers therof to be abandoned. Whereof wee haue a million of examples in all histories, both of the Greekes, and of the Latines, which had their offices annuall. And it hath oftentimes happened, that the magistrats and captaines hauing charge to make & performe some warre, were vpon a sudden called home againe, and so all was at a stay: as it happened when question was for the sending of one to succeed *Scipio Africanus*, the people, the Senat, and the magistrats, found themselues therewith greatly entangled; *Mutis* (saith *Liuie*) *contentionibus & in Senatu, & ad populum acta res est: postremo eo deducta vt Senatui permitterent: patres igitur iurati (sic enim conuenerat) censuerunt vt Consules prouincias inter se compararent*, The matter (saith he) was with great contention debated, both in the Senat, and before the people; at length it was brought to that point, as that the people committed it vnto the Senat: wherefore the Senators beeing sworne (for so it was agreed) determined, That the Consuls should diuide the prouinces betwixt them. Which was a great noueltie to sweare the Senat thereunto. But *Scipio* vnderstanding of the decree of the Senat, whereby one of the Consuls was forthwith to succeed him, without farther delay concluded a peace, more to the aduantage of the enemie than hee would otherwise haue done, if hee had not feared least his successour should haue carried away from him the glorie and honour of his victorie, as it is reported himselfe to haue oftentimes said. So the warre against king *Mithridates* was protracted aboue twentie yeares, by reason of the continuall chaunging of the Roman Generals, the enemie in the meane while (many faire opportunities by him offered, and by the Romans neglected) farre and wide extending his dominion and empire. Yea sometimes the Generall was to giue vp his charge, when hee was euen vppon the point to ioyne battell with the enemie, although he had none appointed to succeed him: as it happened vnto the great captaines *Epaminondas* and *Pelopidas*, whose charge expired euen at such time as they were to giue the enemie battell: who yet neuerthelesse seeing themselues to haue an aduantage of the enemie, and that they could not without the most manifest danger of the state leaue their charge, gaue battel, and so obtained a most glorious victorie, whereby the Thebans with their allies were preserued, and the Lacedemonians with a great slaughter ouerthrowne. But returning home, in stead of thanks and triumph, they were both accused of high treason, for that they had holden their charge longer than the time by the law appointed, & so brought vnto their triall and conuicted, were by the commissioners condemned to die: howbeit that they were afterwards by the people pardoned. Now who knoweth not how many strong places haue bene taken by the enemie, for chaunging of their captaines? how many cities and townes haue bene forced, for hauing put into them new gouernours? and especially at such time as the enemie was nie, & readie to besiege the same: as oftentimes it commeth to passe, that the fauourites carrying away the honor, the old expert captaines are excluded, who right often in reuenge thereof either go ouer vnto the enemie, or els etherwise disfurnish the place of victuals, and other things necessarie.

And yet there is another reason which might well stay the preferments and offices of the commonweale from being mutable, which reason *Tiberius* the emperour had still in his mouth, at such time as men complained him to be the first that had for many yeares together continued the estates and offices still in the same mens hands: I do it (said he) to the end that they which are already full of the blood of the people, may as Horseleeches, full and ready to burst, giue the subiects some release, fearing lest such as should come new & all an hungred, should without remorse or respect at all, draw out the rest of their blood, gnaw their bones, and sucke out the very marrow that was yet

The reason why Tiberius the Emperor would not haue the great officers often chaunged.

Tt ij   left

A8 Multis   E1 els otherwise   E6 (margin) officers   E8 without remorse or respect *i.e.* without intermission or respite (cf. Fr)   E9 gnaw

left in the subiects. And this vnto me seemeth to be a reason of right great importance: for it is an olde and true saing, *Non parcit populis regnum breue*, a short raigne spareth not the people. And yet in the raigne of *Tiberius*, offices and other places of commaund, were vsually giuen and not sold; obtained, but not craued, vpon men of desert bestowed, and not shamefully set to sale to them that would giue most: which opinion of *Tiberius* ought to bee of much more force in such places as where port sale is made of all preferments and offices of the common weale: for it is to bee presumed (as sayth *Alexander Seuerus* the emperor, & after him *Lewes* the 12) that the marchants of offices must sel by retaile, & as deere as they can, that which they had before bought in grosse.

And beside that which we haue already said, how is it possible that he should commaund with such authority as beseemeth a magistrat, which seeth that by and by after he shall but stand for a cipher (as they say) without any authority or power at all? who shall obey him? who shal feare him? who shall do his commaunds? wheras to the contrary, if the magistrats power be perpetuall, he shall commaund with dignity, hee shall boldly oppose himselfe against the wicked, and giue ayde and succour vnto the good: he shall reuenge the wrong done vnto the oppressed, and resist the violence of tyrants, and that without feare or misdoubt of being thrust out, or dispoyled of his dignity and office, as hath bene seene by some euen of the greatest princes, astonished with the constancy & immutable assurance of the magistrats, not hauing what to reproue him for: neither yet daring to displace them, fearing also the discontentment of their subiects, vnto whom the brightnes of Iustice and vertue is alwayes redoubtable, and the integrity of valiant and couragious men right commendable.

In briefe, if we would haue (as all men ought to wish to haue) magistrats wise, stout, and well experimented in the charge committed vnto them, we must wish them to bee perpetual: for why it is impossible that new magistrats should be expert in their charge the first yeare, considering that the life of man is right short, and the nature of authority and power most difficult, whether it be for the training vp of the subiects in warres, or for the maintaining of them in peace; for the administration of Iustice, or for the mannaging of the publike reuenues: all which cannot in short time of new magistrats be either throughly learned, or duly practised. For as the ruine of families commonly commeth of new seruitors, euen so the fals of Commonweales also proceedeth from new magistrats, who still bring in new deuises, councels, laws, factions, customs, edicts, stiles, iudgements, ceremonies, actions, and in briefe a new chaunge of all things in the Commonweale; whereof ensueth a contempt of the old laws & customs, as also of the magistrats themselues. All which may well be seene in the antient Commonweals of of the Greeks & Romans, wherein the new magistrats were no sooner placed, but they forthwith forged new edicts & laws, so to cause themselues to be the more spoken of; without regard whether they were profitable for the Commonweal or not: propounding only this vnto themselues, how to leaue a remembrance of their names vnto posteritie: wheras men so sicke of ambition, are still more desirous of a great than of a good name. Howbeit that it is not needfull to vse many arguments to proue & show as it were vnto the sight of the eye, that the magistrats and officers ought to be perpetuall, seeing that we haue the law of God, which cannot bee so bound vnto places or persons, but that a man therefrom may well draw an example to imitate and follow. Now it is not found, that the magistrats and officers established in the law of God were annuall: neither is it found, that they which were once prouided of honorable places and preferments in the Commonweale, were euer after againe remoued to giue place vnto new magistrats, and so to yeeld vnto ambition that which is to vertue due. So wee find also, that *Plato* would that the offices in his Commonweale should still

New lords new lawes.

F6 port sale *i.e.* public sale to the highest bidder G9 *For* reproue him *read* reproue them.
I2 factions *i.e.* manners, fashions (*façons*) Note at K9.

still for the most part be perpetuall. So that in briefe we see the reasons by vs alleaged, to be by the sacred scriptures, as also by long experience and tract of time confirmed, not by the example of small Commonweales, but euen of the greatest and most flourishing monarchies and kingdomes that now are, or euer were in the whole world, as were those of the Assyrians, the Persians, the Aegyptians, the Parthians, the Aethiopians, the Turkes, the Tartars, the Moscouites, the Polonians, the Germans, the French men, the Danes, the Swedens, the Englishmen, the Scots, the Spaniards, the Italians; excepting some few Commonweals, which are still turmoiled with the continual changing of their Magistrats, and perpetuall flouds of sedition and discord for the shortnesse of their offices.

Now it is not like so many people and nations to haue failed of the light of nature, of iudgement, of reason, & experience, seeing their estate so wisely managed, and to haue so long flourished both in time of peace and war: which could in no wise so long haue stood, had their mutable magistrats bene euery moment to haue bene anew chosen. And thus we see the reasons both of the one side and of the other, which might moue some to make their magistrats perpetuall, as some others also to make them annuall. Vnto which reasons sometime are ioyned such flourishes of eloquence, as might at the first well dasle the eyes not onely of the ignorant, but euen of the sharpest witted also, to heare the reasons of the one side, without giuing of eare vnto the reasons of the other, which are here by vs indifferently set downe, that euery man might suspend his iudgement, vntill that euerie thing were in equall ballance well weighed.

But as men oftentimes erre in the maintaining of the societies of men, and gouernment of cities and Commonweales; so doe they in two notable things also especially: whereof the one is, That they too narrowly looke into the inconueniences of a law, without weighing of the good that ensueth thereof: the other, That they runne from one extreame into another; and so as it were shunning the water, run all headlong into the fire, when as they should haue staied in the middest. *Plato* would, that the magistrats in his Commonweale should bee all perpetuall: which extremitie seemed vnto *Aristotle* blame-worthy, who therefore running himselfe into the other extremitie, and reiecting the opinion of his master *Plato*, opened a way vnto all the citisens, to all the honours and preferments of his Commonweal, saying, That otherwise to do, were to kindle the fire of sedition in the whole estate: whereas yet neither the one nor the other of them hath made any distinction at all of Commonweales, whereof the resolution of this question especially dependeth. And we haue seene euen in this our time one * of the greatest persons of this realme, and the chiefe man of his cote, who hauing embraced the opinion of *Aristotle*, hath endeuoured himselfe by all means to change all the offices into commissions, to be holden but by sufferance: who neuer had other thing in his mouth, and yet without any distinction in what forme of Commonweale this chaunge were, without harme to be receiued.

Two great errors oftentimes committed in the gouernment of Commonweales.

Michael hospitalis chauncelour of France.

Now most certaine it is, that Commonweales in nature contrarie, are by contrarie lawes and meanes to bee also gouerned and maintained (as wee haue oftentimes before said, and yet must oft times say) so that the rules and orders proper to maintaine and preserue Popular estates, serue to the readie ruine and ouerthrow of Monarchies and sole gouernments. The Popular estates are maintained by continuall chaunge of officers, to the end that euerie man according to his qualitie might haue part in the offices, according as they haue part in the soueraigntie, which can in no wise bee where offices be giuen in perpetuitie. Besides that equalitie the nurse of Popular estates is by the annuall succession of magistrates the better maintained, and the long custome of continuall commaund giue not an appetite

Commonweales in nature contrarie, by contrarie meanes to be also maintained.

Annuall magistrats best in a popular Commonweale.

D5 of his cote *i.e.* of the *robe longue*, the magistracy   D9 were without   Note at E9.

or defire to fome one or other ambitions citifen to afpire vnto the foueraigntie alone. Whereas to the contrarie in Monarchies it is not neceffarie, no nor yet wholefome, that fubiects hauing no intereft in the foueraigntie, fhould be nourifhed in ambition, it being fufficient for them to learne to bee dutifull and obedient vnto their foueraigne prince, and efpecially if the Monarchy be Lordlike or Tyrannicall: For that the fubiects in the one be the princes naturall flaues, and in the other the tyrants flaues by force, it fhould be a thing impofsible for fuch a Lordlike Monarch, or tyrant to hold their eftates, and to giue fuch yearely or fuccefsiue commanding power vnto their fubiects. And therefore tyrants, who are no leffe hated and feared of their fubiects, than they themfelues feare and hate them, hauing little or no truft or confidence in them, for moft part guard themfelues with ftraungers onely, and fome few of their owne fubiects, fuch as they know to be vnto themfelues moft loyall and faithfull, vnto whome they commit the cuftodie and guard of their owne perfons, of their eftates, of their forces, and of their wealth, without any defire at all to chaunge them, not onely for that they diftruft others, but alfo for that they would not acquaint them with the fweetneffe of power and command, leaft fo fome one or other of them therewith enflamed, fhould be defirous to difpatch the tyrant of his life, fo to obtaine his place: or els otherwife in fo doing to gratifie the fubiects. Whereas the Lordlike Monarch whome his fubiects more willingly obey as his naturall flaues, is not fo much hindred or letted from the choice of his magiftrats and officers, as is the tyrant, who is not but by force and conftraint obeyed of his fubiects; and therefore giueth not the preferments or offices of his eftates in perpetuitie, neither yet maketh them annuall; but onely beftoweth them as he feeth good, and that for fo long as pleafeth him, diuiding them amongft many at his good pleafure, without any law or decree therefore, all depending of his will and pleafure.

The pollicie and craft of tyrants.

But the Royall Monarch, who is in fuch fort to intreat his fubiects, as is the good father his louing children, albeit that he be no more bound vnto mans lawes, than are the other Monarches, yet will he neuertheleffe of himfelfe eftablifh decrees and lawes, for the placing and difplacing of magiftrats and officers, to the end they might fo bee holden; diuiding the honours and rewards of vertue not to all indifferently, without difcretion, but vnto fuch as deferue the fame; hauing ftill more refpect vnto the experience and vertue, than vnto the grace and fauour of them who are vnto him moft of all commended. And yet for all that, fhall in all things obferue and keepe the commendable mediocritie, in fuch fort, as that he fhall make many offices perpetuall, and fome changeable alfo from three yeares to three yeares; and otherfome to bee euerie yeare alfo chaunged; as namely the prefidents of the parliaments, of the finances or common receit, or gouernours of prouinces, who could neuer otherwife bee punifhed for their oppreffion and mifdemeanor, if they had their fuch great authoritie and power in the eftate and Commonweale ftill in perpetuitie. He fhall alfo diuide the honors and preferments of the ftate, vnto the richer and nobler fort, albeit that they be not men of fo great experience as are fome of the poorer and bafer fort, fo to preuent fturres and feditions: yet for all that prouided alwayes, that vnto them which of themfelues are not of fufficient capacitie be ftill affociat men of good experience in their charge, fo to couer and fupplie the defect of the others: And yet is not fo bound, vnto his own laws, but in cafe of necefsitie hee may againe difplace them whome hee hath before ordained to be perpetuall magiftrats, finding them of whome he hath fo euill made choice, for the weakeneffe of their minds or bodies, to be altogether infufficient for the publike charge to be by them fuftained, or for to couer the fhame of them which are fo infufficient, fhall giue them fome honeft meanes to difcharge themfelues of fuch their charge

The magiftrats in a royall monarchie fome perpetuall and fome annuall.

F 1 ambitious   I 10 preferments

OF A COMMONWEALE. 487

charge: as did the most wise emperor *Augustus* vnto a great number of the Senators, who vnworthy of their so honourable places, by that meane cleanely displaced themselues, without any force or sturre; or at leastwise shall appoint them deputies for the executing of their charge: yet in the meane time suffering the magistrates and officers themselues, to enioy still their titles of their offices, and woonted priuileges. And to the intent that iustice, the principall and chiefe ground of an estate of Commonweale may bee the more religiously distributed, hee shall for the administration thereof appoint perpetuall colledges and companies of Iudges, and especially of such as are without appeale to iudge of the liues, fame, and goods of the subiects: not onely that these judges should so be the better experimented (as well for hearing the opinion of diuers, as for their long exercise in iudgement:) but also that so their seuerall power might be in some sort weakened (for feare they should abuse the same) and that so being many of like authoritie and power, they should not so easily be corrupted: not vnlike to a great deale of water which is more hardly corrupted than is a little. For as *Plinie* sayth: *Nemo omnes, neminem omnes vnquam fefellerunt: melius omnibus quàm singulis creditur.* No man euer deceiued all men, neither did all men euer deceiue any man: better it is to beleeue all than one. Howbeit, yet that by the wisedome and vertue of some one good judge, a whole companie, or bench of judges of the same court is oftentimes releeued: and their factions and secret practises broken; or being otherwise good men, yet misse-enformed by false accusers and pettie foggers, cannot know or vnderstand the truth: but are by the wisedome of some one of their companie the better enformed. As I haue knowne one judge alone to haue caused the whole companie of judges to change their opinion, being before resolued and set downe to haue put a poore innocent woman to death: whom yet for all that he by most pregnant and liuely reasons clearely and fully acquited of that shee was in danger to haue beene condemned for. Who therefore well deserueth to be named: and was *Potier* a learned judge of great integritie and vertue: who hath left vnto his countrey his two sonnes inheritours of their fathers vertues: one of them Master of the Requests: and the other, Secretarie of the Finances; in vertue not inferior vnto their father. Besides that, the experience of many worlds of yeares hath giuen vs sufficiently to vnderstand many judges, by conferring their opinions together, to giue therby a better and sounder iudgement, than where they iudge euery one of them apart. Howbeit that *Aristotle* thinketh it better to haue euery judges opinion considered of apart by it selfe: and that he saith to haue beene the vsuall manner of iudgement in many the cities of the Greeks. Now the Romans to haue holden both these fashions and manners of iudgements *Asconius Pedianus* is the Authour, where he saith: *Aliam esse rationem cum vniuersi Iudices constituunt, aliam cum singuli sententiam ferunt*, It to be one manner of proceeding when all the judges together determine of a matter, and another when euery one of them deliuer their opinions apart. Wherefore causes are more indifferently and vprightly discided in Europe by a competent number of judges together: then by seuerall judges in Asia and Africke, whereas one particular judge of a Prouince according to his will and pleasure determineth of all appeales made vnto him from the other particular and inferiour judges in that prouince. And albeit that in Grand Caire (one of the greatest cities of the world) there be foure judges which haue their diuers and seperate iurisdictions, and euery one of them haue also their diuers Deputies, who judge also of causes apart and by themselues, yet are the appeales still brought vnto the first judge chiefe of the foure; who alone without any companion or assistant by him selfe at his pleasure discideth all appeales: whom it is no great matter for him to winne, that standeth in his good grace, or that hath the

Tt iiij   grea-

Marginal notes:
- That the colledges and companies of judges ought to be perpetuall.
- Better many judges then one alone.

greatest presents to giue him. Howbeit that the two Cadelescheis are the chiefe of all the judges, and may at their pleasure place or displace any of the rest of the judges, yea and all of them together also so long as it shall please the Grand Seignor. For why amongst the Turkes all power and commaund is but by sufferance and during pleasure both giuen and receiued.

<small>Good that inferiour Magistrats & officers should be perpetuall.</small>

Now we haue before said that in the royall Monarchie all the Magistrates and Officers should neither be perpetuall, neither all still mutable: For that it is not needfull to chaunge the meane officers, as Clarks, Sergeants, Vshers, Notaries, and such other like, who for that they haue no power or authoritie to commaund, cannot hurt the Estate: and yet neuerthelesse the experience of their charge which cannot but in long time and by great practise be got, requireth that they should bee perpetuall. And so might a man say of other inferiour officers also, being still subiect vnto the power and authoritie of the greater, but cannot yet oft times be chaunged without the great hurt of the Commonweale, and many priuate mens hinderance. The Senators and Councelours of estate also, whose dexteritie for the mannaging of the great affaires of the Commonweale is not but by long experience to be gotten; we see them to haue beene in Rome, in Lacedemonia, and amongst the Areopagi in Athens, perpetuall: and so I thinke they ought to be euery where else, so that in the perpetuall chaunge of mutable magistrates, the Senate should still be constant, firme, and immutable, and that vpon it the other mutable offices and magistrates should as vpon a most sure stay rest: which was not so well prouided for by *Plato*, who would haue his Senate to be euery yeare by lot chosen. But now as for such great magistrates and officers as acknowledge no commaund more than the soueraigne Princes alone, whither it be in martiall affaires, the administration of iustice, or the charge of the publique receit if the royall Monarch shall keepe them but one, two, or three yeares in their charge at the most, he shall so leaue open a way vnto his iustice, for the examining of their actions, and by the same meanes shall cause the wicked and corrupt magistrates to quake, standing alwayes in dread to be called to giue an account of their doings. And for that Magistrats and Officers are not to be chaunged all at once (for that all sudden chaunges in a Commonweale are daungerous) and that the publique actions be not interrupted, the chaunge of such great Magistrates as are in corporations and colleges together is to be made by the succeeding of them one of them vnto an other: as they doe in the Commonweale of Rhaguse, where the Senate is perpetuall, and the Senators who are also soueraigne judges, are not but euery one of them one yere in charge: who yet chaunge not all at once, but successiuely, and as it were insensiblie; and in their turne after that they haue for a certaine time liued as priuate men, returne more fresh vnto the same charge againe.

<small>That Senators and Counsellors of estate ought to be still perpetual.</small>

<small>Lib. de Legibus Cap. 174.</small>

<small>A generall and necessarie rule to be kept in euery Commonweale.</small>

But yet generally in euery Commonweale this rule hath alwayes place without exception, viz. That the perpetuall Magistrats & Officers should haue either no power at all, or else verie little power to commaund, or else some companion ioyned with them: and that they to whom great power is giuen, haue the same but for a short time, and by the law limitted to some few monethes or yeates. By which tempering and moderation of power and commaund, the difficulties and daungers shall cease, which might otherwise ensue by the suddein chaunge of all the Magistrates at once, for the interruption of publique actions. Neither need we so to feare lest the Commonweale should be without Magistrates, as a ship without a master to gouerne the same: as it often times chaunced in Rome, for the sute of the magistrates, who one of them hindered an other, or els the same day entered all into their charge, as they all at one and at the selfe same instant departed out of the same together. Neither need we to feare also

also left the wicked by briberie mounted vnto the more hie degrees of honour, should escape vncorrected: or that the ignorant or vnskilfull should carie away the preferments of the estate and Commonweale: they which before had charge, hauing for certaine yeares rested themselues, still returning againe with much greater experience then before. Now they which wish for annuall Magistrats, annuall Senators, annuall powers and commaunds, foresee not that (beside the difficulties and daungers by vs before alleaged to ensue thereof) by this meanes either rude artificers or such like ignorant and vnskilfull men, must be called vnto such publike charges as they are neuer able to discharge, or else that the Commonweale must needs be full of most wise men, and such as are of greatest experience and knowledge. Howbeit that cannot by nature be, that all men can do all things: wheras we see particular men scarcely well to discharge their particular charges; and in other some to rest great wisedome, who yet haue no skill in gouernment at all. But in doing that which wee haue said there shall not easilie any default fall out, neither shall the subiects haue any iust cause whereof to complaine; the rewards of honour being so exposed to euery mans sight, as the marke whereat euery one should ayme, though few there bee which hit the same, and the fewer officers and rewards there should be, and the dearer that they were prized, the more they should be of all desired: when as euery man should for his vertue be called vpon, and that there should be no cause of sedition, no man being excluded from the merite and reward of his vertue and sufficiencie, so that the causes of sedition so taken away, the subiects may still liue in all peace and tranquillitie. And if need be we may vse Commissioners or Syndiques, as they did in the time of *Lewes* the ix, and *Philip* the faire, for the chastising of the officers, and the calling of them to account.

Now some difficulties concerning the chaunging of Magistrats and Lawes are by vs before set downe, and more I suppose will be imagined: yet were it vnreasonable to looke into the discommodities of a law (and so for the same to reiect it) without consideration also of the profits thereof, seeing that there is no law so good (as saith *Cato* the Censor) which draweth not after it some incommodities. And in mine opinion that law may alwayes be accounted good and profitable, if the good which may ensue thereof be manifest, and greater then the harme that is to be feared thereof: wherein many often times offend, which thinke it impossible to haue all discommodities quite taken out of the lawes, the Commonweale yet neuerthelesse still standing in safetie, but so falling into such daungers as they before thought not of, straight waies blame the lawes, and often times chaunge the same, when as in truth they should haue accused & chaunged them selues. So some good Princes euill aduised often times to their harme cancell a good Law for some one incommoditie they haue seene therein. Whereof we will vse no other example then that of *Lewes* the xj, who comming to the Crowne at once displaced all his fathers auntient seruitours, and remoued also the princes his nie kinsmen from the gouernment of the state: who therefore with a wonderfull consent conspired with the enemy against him, and brought him to such a strait, as that they had almost strucke the crowne from his head, and by force wrested the roiall scepter out of his hands. But these sturres againe quieted, and all things well pacified and set in order, fearing lest his sonne should fall into the like daunger, charged him neuer to chaunge them whom he had aduaunced; and yet not so contented, made a law, whereby he decreed all offices to be perpetuall; and that such as were once preferred thereunto, should not be againe displaced, otherwise then by resignation, death, or forfaiture: And by an other Edict declaring the former, published the xx. of September in the yeare 1482 decreed, That no officers hauing forfeited their offices, for what cause soeuer, should be enforced to yeeld vp their offices, except it were so before adiudged,

No lawe so good but that it draweth after it some discommoditie.

That a good law is not to be changed for some one discommoditie ensuing thereof.

Dangerous to change all the cheife magistrats of a Commonweale at once.

D1 *For* impossible *read* possible (cf. L). Notes at B2, E4.

adiudged, and the parties condemned. Which edict hee commaunded to stand in force, not onely whilest he himselfe yet liued, but also during the raigne of his sonne *Charles*. And albeit that he could not so bind the hands of his successour, yet so it is neuerthelesse, that this his decree & law hath euer since bene inuiolably kept, although the auntient clause, *So long as it shall please vs*, remained still in all letters of office. Which words declare no perpetuall power to be giuen vnto the magistrats or officers, but by sufferance onely, except by law or custome it be otherwise prouided. Yet still remaineth that idle clause, that thereby it may be vnderstood, all power and authoritie to haue in auntient times bene giuen by our kings during their pleasure, and so to haue of the magistrats bene holden but by sufferance onely. And albeit that in the raigne of *Philip* the Faire this string was againe touched, for the giuing of offices in perpetuitie, yet for all that the matter still rested vndecided. But *Philip Valois* reuoked the commissions, and ordained, That from that time forward the royall offices should bee perpetuall; which well declareth them before to haue beene mutable at the pleasure of the kings, albeit that the officers had not forfeited them. And amongst those praises which they giue vnto king *Robert*, one of the greatest is, That he neuer displaced officer, if he had not for some foule and infamous fact before forfeited his office. Whereby it is to be gathered, king *Robert* his auncestours to haue vsed other lawes and customes.

But yet haply it may seeme vnto some, that if offices should still be giuen with that clause, *During the Prcines pleasrue*, the magistrats would better discharge their charges for the hope they should haue by this meane to continue still in their places, proceeding still from better to better, and bearing themselues vprightly, for feare otherwise to be displaced. Whereunto I agree, in a well ordered Lordly Monarchy: but the daunger should be greater to open such a gap vnder a prince on euery side beset with flatterers, and compassed in with clawbackes: For why, euerie man seeth, that princes so beset, must either make a most filthy gaine and traffique of their offices, or else take such places and power to commaund, from good men, who almost alwaies haue the courtiers life (polluted with all manner of vices) in hatred and detestation. Besides that this bestowing of offices during pleasure, sauoureth somewhat of tyranny, or of a Lordlike gouernment, rather than of a Royall Monarchy; which (so much as possible is) should by lawes, and not by the princes will and pleasure onely bee gouerned: So as many a Lordly Monarchie, where the subiects being naturall slaues adore and feare their soueraigne prince, as a god come downe from heauen, accounting his commaunds as the lawes of nature it selfe. Whereas in a Royall Monarchy, where the subiects are as children, it is needfull to rule and gouerne all things by law, as much as possible may be: for otherwise if the king shall without cause exclude some one more than some other from some office or preferment, he that should bee so excluded should hold himselfe iniured, and so rest discontented with his prince; who ought rather to be beloued than feared of his subiects: which to bee, he ought to take away all occasion of discontentment that men might haue against him; and better meanes is there none, than to leaue all that may be to the disposition of the lawes and customes, no man so hauing iust cause to complaine of the prince.

That offices in a royal Monarchie are rather to be bestowed by order of law, than by the Princes will & pleasure onely.

The learned *Budeus* who was of opinion that it were best to haue the magistrats and offices still changeable, without hauing regard vnto the law made by *Lewes* the xi. hath holden, That in auntient time the Presidents and counsellors of the parliament of Paris were but annuall: and that the solemne oath which they still take the 12. day of nouember, and the letterspatents which they still are to haue from the king for the opening of the Parliament, show sufficiently that their estates were not perpetuall, but still at the pleasure of the prince to bee reuoked, and so to bee by them holden but by sufferance;

G6 greatest   G10 the Princes pleasure

sufferance: and so by these reasons drew many to be of the same opinion with him, who had they but turned ouer the records of the court, and of the chamber of accounts, they should haue found that that Parliament which before was ambulatorie & moueable, and which had no power but by commission, was by *Philip* the long ordayned to be an ordinarie Court, with ordinarie power, circuite, and iurisdiction; in the erection whereof was expressed that it should still haue therein one or two Presidents, of whom the first was the Earle of Burgundie the kings nie kinsman, as in like sort the President in the Imperiall chamber, is alway one of the princes of the Empire. And so for a long time also the President of the court of Paris was still a martiall man and not a gowne man as he now is: and euen yet at this present the Great Prætor of the court of Paris, whom we call the chiefe President, is still honored with the qualitie and title of a martiall man, as of a knight, or as the Latins call it *Miles*, or a souldiour, although he neuer drew sword: which title the other judges of that court haue not, who then were but three score, but now are an hundred and fiftie. Whereby it is plaine the court of Paris so founded to haue an ordinarie and perpetuall power, neither to haue need of the Princes annuall rescripts, or letters patents for the disciding and determining of controuersies. Howbeit that king *Henry* the second comming into the Parliament for the publishing of certaine Edicts and lawes, which in that court could hardly find passage (hauing it put into his mouth by certaine flatterers) said openly, That the Parliament had at all no power, if it pleased not him by sending of his letters Patents euery yeare to giue opening vnto the same; which his speech astonished many. But certaine it is that the letters patents which are sent to this end, and the annuall oath which the Presidents and Councelours take, is but a matter of formalitie and custome, necessarie at such time as the parliaments were not holden but by commission: But afterwards that they were erected into the forme of ordinarie courts, such auntient solemnities are no more necessarie: for why the annuall Magistrats are to take an annuall oath; whereas they which are perpetuall Magistrats are to take it but once for all, without any needlesse reiteration of the same. So the continuall Roman Magistrats euery yeare tooke their oath, for that their power was but annuall: wheras the Senators tooke it but once for all, for that their dignitie was perpetuall and during the whole time of their liues. The same might be said of the forme of the commissions and decrees of that court, conceiued vnder the name and seale of the king, and namely of the letters missiue of the court: which although they bee conceiued in the name of the court, are yet neuerthelesse sealed with the little royall seale with the flowredeluce: howbeit that all the other magistrats, seneschals bailiefes, prouosts, and gouernours of countries, hauing power of ordinarie commaund or by commission, direct the same vnder their owne names, and their owne seales; which is yet retained of the auntient forme, euer since that the parliament was but the kings priuie councell, which councell for that it had no ordinarie power, did nothing of itselfe, and the commissions are alwaies graunted in the name of the king, as hauing the onely power to commaund in his councell, as we haue before shewed. Which forme hath bene euer since followed in the erection of other parliaments, euen vnto the court of Aides, who giue out all their commissions, vnder the kings name: which hath moued some to say, That the parliaments haue nothing but an extraordinarie power by way of commission onely. Howbeit that it sufficiently appeareth by that which is by vs before said, them to haue an ordinarie and perpetuall power, which they still hold the king beeing dead: Which if it were but a power holden vpon sufferance, (as some would haue it) it should then together with the death of the king take end, as all other powers and commissions else doe. But these courts and the ordinarie magistrats thereof, the king being

The erection of the parliament of Paris.

D 5 flowredeluce *i.e.* fleur-de-lis   Note at B 3.

being dead neither chaunge their attire, nor vse any mourning garments, or other signes of sorrow: yea that more is, the first confirmations of the new king are alwaies graunted vnto the Courts of Parliament; as hath beene alwaies vsed since the time of *Lewes* the eleuenth, in such sort as that their power is not onely ordinarie, but perpetuall also, not onely in the whole bodies of themselues, but euen in euery one of the members, officers, and ministers of the said Courts of Parliament.

The giuing of offices during the princes pleasure not to be discommended.

And yet for all that is not the manner of those Princes to be discommended, who vnto their Officers and Magistrates giue their power but by sufferance, which they (if cause be) at their pleasure againe take from them, as the kings of England haue vsed to doe. For albeit that the auntient and moderne Commonweales, especially the Popular and Aristocratique (more straitly bound vnto the lawes than are Monarchies) haue their Magistrates and officers for the most part annuall, and that none of them was againe displaced, without iust cause why; yet so it was for all that, that the people sometimes reuoked their former choice made, and placed some others whom they knew to be more fit for the charge they were to vndergoe: as it did in establishing the Dictators and others their Captaines and Gouernors, reuoking sometimes (as I say) euen their ordinarie magistrates; as it did *Octacilius* the Consul, who at the request of *Fabius Maximus* was remoued from his charge, as a man not sufficient for the managing of so great and daungerous a warre as the State had then in hand. Neither had they for the remouing of their magistrat, regard onely if he had in any thing trespassed, and so deserued to be remoued; but euen vnto the insufficiencie of him also, whither it were knowne or vnknowne when they receiued him into the Estate, or that it were befallen him afterwards; deeming also weaknesse, or age, madnesse, or other like diseases, such as let and hinder mens reasonable actions, to be sufficient also to displace them from their offices. And namely *Lucius Torquatus* chosen the third time Consul excused himselfe before the people for the infirmitie of his eyes; saying, That it was not reason to put the gouernment of the Commonweale into his hands, who could not see but by other mens eyes. But O how many are there of the blind, deafe, and dumbe, not hauing in themselues any light of nature, neither wisedome, nor experience so much as to gouerne themselues, who are not yet content to guide the sayles and tackles, but desire also to lay hands euen vpon the verie helme also of the Commonweale?

That in euery commonweale there ought to be some estates and magistrats perpetuall.

Now that which we haue said concerning the meane that ought to be kept in the chaunge and continuation of Magistrats and Officers, hath not onely place in royall Monarchies, but euen in Popular and Aristocratique estates also, where the offices almost all, or for the most part, ought to be euery yeare, or from two yeares to two yeares still mutable: as they do among the Swissers, and diuers other Commonweals. Yet neuerthelesse for the preseruation of the same, there must still be some estates in the Commonweale perpetuall: as namely those whose experience and wisdome is alwayes necessarie for the stay of the rest, such as be the Councellors of estate: And this is it, for which the Senat in Rome, in Athens, and in Lacedemonia, was still perpetuall. And why, the Senators still during their liues held their charge and places: for as the hookes and hinges whereupon great burdens rest, must of themselues be strong and vnmoueable; euen so the Senat of the Areopagi, and of other Commonweales also, were as most strong and sure hinges, whereupon as well all the mutable officers as the whole waight of the Estate and Commonweale rested & reposed themselues. The contrarie whereof is to be done in Monarchies, wherein the greater part, and almost all the estates ought to be perpetuall, except some few of the chiefe and principall: as they doe in the kindome of Spayne, where they well know how to keepe

OF A COMMONWEALE. 493

keepe this mediocritie or meane proper vnto the royall estate. And so for the same cause the Venetians which haue an Aristocratique estate, make their officers euery yeare chaungeable, and some of them from two moneths to two moneths; and yet neuerthelesse haue their Duke, the Procurators of S. Marke, the Chauncelour, and foure Secretaries for the Estate, perpetuall; which the Florentines ordayned in their Estate also (after that they were by *Lewes* the xij, deliuered from the most cruell tyrannie of Countie *Valentinus Borgia*) taking order that their Duke should from that time forward be perpetuall, to the entent that the Commonweal before in perpetuall motion and chaunge of all their estates and offices, might yet haue some thing firme and stable whereupon to rest and stay it selfe: which good order being in short time after by the most turbulent Florentines abolished, they fell againe into greater tumuls and ciuill warres then euer they were in before: whereas if they had had but a perpetuall Senate at the least, and the Senators continued in their charge, (who from six moneths to six moneths were stil chaunged and rechaunged) and had but kept a certaine meane betwixt these two extremities, of generall chaunge, and still continuing of all their offices, their estate had beene much the more assured, neither had their Commonweale beene still so tossed and turmoyled with so many and so great surges of sedition, and tempests of ciuill warres. But these things thus by vs declared, let vs now see also whether in a wise and well ordered Commonweale it be good that the Magistrates should be all at vnitie, and of one accord among themselues or not?

CHAP. V.

¶ *Whether the vnitie and concord of Magistrats amongst themselues bee good and wholesome for the Commonweale, or not?*

His question, *viz.* Whether it be good that the magistrats and officers of a Commonweale should be of accord, or els at discord and variance among themselues? may perhaps seeme altogether needlesse and vaine. For who euer doubted but that it was alwaies expedient, yea and necessarie too, that the Magistrats in euerie Commonweale should be of one and the same mind? to the end that they all together might with one consent and heart embrace and seeke after the publike good: And if so it be (as wise men haue alwaies thought) that a well ordered Commonweale ought to resemble a mans bodie, wherein all the members are vnited and conioyned with a maruellous bond, euerie one of them doing their office and dutie; and yet neuerthelesse when need is, one of them still aideth another, one of them releeueth another; and so all together strengthen themselues, to maintaine the health, beautie, and welfare of the whole bodie: but if it should happen them to enter into hatred one of them against another; and that the one hand should cut the other, or the right foot supplant the left, and that the fingers should scrape out the eyes, and so euerie member should draw vnto it selfe the nourishment of the other next vnto it; it must needs fall out, that the bodie in the end must become maimed, lame, and impotent, in all the actions thereof: euen so in like manner may a man deeme of the estate of a Commonweale, the honour and welfare whereof dependeth of the mutuall loue and good will of the subiects among themselues, as also toward their soueraigne prince. Which sweet vnitie and agreement how is it to be hoped for, if the magistrats which are the principall subiects, and such as ought by their example to bind together the rest, be at variance and discord among themselues? But euen to the contrarie the subiects shall become partakers of the factions of the magistrats, they first nourishing secret grudges, and afterward open enmi-

Reasons to show that magistrats ought to be at vnitie and concord among themselues.

Vu

enmitie, vntill that at length all breake out into open ciuill warre, all for the maintenance and vpholding euerie one of them of the chiefe of their factions, to the destruction of the Commonweale: or in case stay be made thereof, and that things fall not out altogether so euill, yet must still publike actions by such ambitious discord of the magistrats be hindred, and the Commonweale sore troubled: whereunto it shall happen as it doth vnto a maid, for whome (as *Plutarch* saith) her suters enter into such a iealousie and passion, as that desiring euerie one of them to haue her to himselfe, they so in stead of louing and embracing of her, most cruelly rent her in peeces amongst them. And what good successe may a man expect of an armie, or what victorie is to bee hoped for ouer the enemie, where the captaines and commaunders are at discord among themselues? or what iustice is to be looked for, where the judges are diuided into factions? Yea it hath bene oftentimes seene some of them to haue beene of contrarie opinions and aduise vnto others, and that vpon a verie iealousie and hatred they had among themselues, and so play as it were at hazard with the life, the goods, and honour of the subiects: as *Agesilaus* king of the Lacedemonians (albeit that hee was one of the most famous of them that euer was) to impaire the credit and authoritie of *Lysander* whome he hated, reuersed all his iudgements, and gaue sentence quite contrarie, not so much for the iniquitie of the cause (as he himselfe said) as in despight of him his enemie onely. And to make the matter short, most certaine it is, that dissentions and ciuill warres (the capitall plagues of Commonweales) take foot, root, encrease, and nourishment, of nothing more than of the hatred and enmitie of the magistrats among themselues. Whereof it followeth the vnitie and concord of them among thmselues to be vnto the subiects not onely profitable, but euen necessarie also. Which may all seeme right profitable arguments and reasons for the one side.

Contrary reasons to show that it is good for the Commonweale, that magistrats should be at discord and variance among themselues.

But now they which more subtilly reason of these matters, deeme to the contrarie, the health, and welfare of the Commonweale to be best preserued and kept by the discord of the magistrats. For why (say they) the force and nature of vertue is such, as that it cannot be contrarie vnto vertue; neither that good men, although they bee at neuer so great oddes, can yet be enemies among themselues: but being prouoked by the iniuries of the wicked their aduersaries, do still wel the more and more encrease and flourish: neither is the valour of worthy men any where more euident and manifest, than when they without bitternesse contend among themselues; and so prickt forward with an honest ambition, and enflamed with the heat of men like vnto themselues, as with a fire, are by the emulation of their competitors incited to take in hand great matters, and so still to ouercome their enemies in well doing. So when *Taxilas* king of the Indians had by his ambassadours freely and without resistance offered his kingdome vnto *Alexander* the Great, (then bearing downe all the kingdomes of the East before him) if so be he wanted wealth; and withall refused not to receiue wealth also at his hands, if hee had of it too much: *Alexander* glad of such a match, said vnto him, If we must thus contend and combat together, it shall neuer be said, that you shall take this point of honour from me, as to be accounted more magnificall, more courteous, or more royall, than my selfe: and so gaue vnto him another great kingdome, with an infinit masse of treasure. In like manner *Tullus Hostilius* king of the Romans, said vnto *Metius Suffetius* Dictator of the Albanians, *The ciuill discords which thou obiectest vnto vs, wee deem them as profitable to our citie; for we striue together, whether of vs shall better or more earnestly fight for the good of the Commonweale.*

The fruit of foes.

Now if contention and emulation be thus good and profitable amongst valiant & good citisens, and wholesome for Commonweales, how much more then ought it to be thought necessarie for most base and abiect men, for the stirring of them vp to vertue,

OF A COMMONWEALE. 495

A tue, and deterring of them from vice. For of all the great profits which men vse to reap from their enemies, none is greater than so to liue as that we seeme not to exceed them in vices, or be ouercome of them in vertues. But if such discord and contention be both honourable and profitable in a citie or Commonweale, wherein the princes and magistrats are all good men, and striue but for vertue onely; how much more then shall the contention be profitable, where the good striue against the euill? But in case that all the magistrats be euill, then is discord and contention amongst them not onely profitable, but euen necessarie also, least otherwise they beeing at vnitie and concord among themselues, and in possession of the gouernment, might freely and without feare make hauocke and spoile both of the publike and priuat affaires. In which case it cannot fall

B out better either for the subiects, or for the whole Commonweale, than if they by their mutuall hatred and accusations shall openly detect and lay open vnto the world, their owne filthinesse, their foule extortions and robberies, as the sheepe are neuer more assured, than when the wolues deuoure one another; as it happened saith *Philip Commines* in England, that whilest the great lords slew or condemned one another, the poore people in the meane while remained safe from their inuasion. Which was the wise councell of *Cincinnatus*, seeing the Consull *Appius* openly to withstand the people to hinder them for the doubling the number of their Tribunes: Let be (said *Cincinnatus*) for the moe they shall be, the worse they will agree. And right needfull oftentimes it

C was the power of the Tribunes to bee broken and weakned by their owne diuision, when as by the opposition of any one of them, all the proceedings of the rest were so hindered and stayed. And truely *Cincinnatus* therein said wisely, for so the Commonweale stood and flourished, the Tribunes oftentimes being at discord and varience among themselues, which (they being at vnitie and concord) would haue in a moment fallen: and so long it well stood vntil that *Pub. Clodius* a most wicked man, about foure hundred yeares after presented a request vnto the people, which passed into the force of a law, whereby it was ordained, That from thenceforth the opposition of one of the Tribunes should not hinder the proceeding of the rest of his fellow Tribunes. And therfore *Cato* the Censor, the beautie of the Romane wisedome (and one to whome

D was giuen the chiefe prayse for wisedome and vertue amongst the Romans) could neither endure the agreement of his seruants in his familie, nor of the Magistrats in the Commonweale, but slily and secretly still sowed hatred and sedition amongst them; that so the wicked and offendors might with their accusations as with mutuall wounds fall, and the good so gaine praise. For why, he thought it a thing almost impossible in so great an accord of slaues and of magistrats, but that the one of them should make spoile of the Commonweale, and the other of his priuat subitance, especially being in hope to escape vnpunished, and out of feare for being accused. And therefore doubted not fiftie times to accuse offendors, hee himselfe being also fortie times by others accused: howbeit that he still bearing himselfe vpon the integritie of his forepassed life, and

E the commendable things by him done, easily auoided all the slanders by his aduersaries against him faslly surmised. Neither was that Commonweale euer after fuller of good and valiant citisens, than it was in his time. Yea the Senat of Rome allotted a great summe of money to *Mar. Bibulus* to buy his Consulship, and the voyces of the people, to the intent to oppose him against *Cæsar* his knowne enemie, who had cunningly set vp *Luceius* his friend (whome the Senat would haue had excluded) that so hee might doe all things as he thought good, his friend and fellow in office agreeing thereunto. And not to go farther, we haue heretofore the witnesse of *Iulius Cæsar*, who in his Commentaries saith, The Gaules to haue had a most auntient custome amongst them, to stirre vp their great lords one of them against another, to the intent that the common *Lib. 6.*

people

D7 out of feare   E1 falsly surmised   Note at E8.

people (which were as he reporteth but slaues) might so bee safe and free from their outrages and robberies. For so one of them opposing himselfe against another, and euill controlled by the good, and the wicked by themselues; there should be no doubt but that the Commonweale should so be in much more safetie and assurance, than if they were of one accord among themselues. Whereby it is to be vnderstood, the discord of princes and magistrats to haue alwaies bene vnto Commonweals wholesom: as the meane whereby the wicked (as we said) may by the vertue of the good, or their owne mutuall accusations be weakned. Which seemed a thing profitable not onely vnto the Romans, and our auncestours, but euen vnto *Lycurgus* the wise law giuer also, who therefore himselfe set dissention betwixt the two kings of Lacedemonia, and appointed also, That there should alwaies two enemies be sent ambassadours for the state; to the intent they should not by their mutuall consent and good agreement betray the Commonweale: but that being at variance, they might still one of them bee controlled by the other. As for that which is said, the parts of mans bodie which represent a well ordered Commonweale, to bee neuer at discord among themselues, is quite contrarie; for were not the humors of mans bodie much contrarie, a man should quickly perish: the preseruation thereof dependeth of the contrarietie of hoat & cold, of moisture and drought, of bitter choller to sweet flegme, of beastly desires to diuine reason; as also the preseruation of the whole world next vnto God dependeth of the contrarietie, which is in the whole and euery part thereof. Euen so the magistrates in a Commonweale ought in some sort to be at difference among themselues, albeit that they otherwise be right good men, for that trueth, the publike good, and that which is honest, best discouereth it selfe by that which is thereunto contrarie: and is still to bee found in the middest betwixt two extreames. And it seemeth that the Romans had this principall end before their eyes, ordinarily making choyce of their magistrats that were to bee placed in the same charge, still enemies one of them vnto another; or at leastwise of quite contrarie humors and dispositions, as is in all their histories to be seene. As when the Senat foresaw that *Claudius Nero* should carrie away the Consulship, an hoat and sturring man, and withall a most valiant and couragious captaine to oppose against *Hannibal*: the Senat (I say) procured to haue ioyned vnto him for his companion or fellow in office *Liuius Salinator* an old captaine, and a man of great experience, but yet as cold and staid, as was the other hoat and terrible, and yet fit to heat the old age of *Liuius*, now a little too cold for the warres: who so ioyned and vnited together, gained a most notable victorie against *Hannibal*, which was the ruine of the Carthaginians, and the preseruation of the Roman estate. These two men also afterwards were by the people made Censors together; who still at discord, noted one of them another of infamie, a thing neuer before seene: and yet they thus still at variance, were in all mens iudgements two of the most famous and vertuous men that then were in Rome. With like wisedome the Romans ioyned together *Fabius Maximus*, and *Marcus Marcellus*, in their warres against *Hannibal*, both of them right great and most expert captaines, but the one of them being a cold, and the other an exceeding hoat man; the one alway still desirous of battell, and the other still seeking for delay; the one called the Roman Sword, and the other the Buckler; the one a fierce warrier, and the other a long lingerer: by which contrarie humors of these two so great personages the estate was not onely preserued from ruine and destruction, which must needs otherwise vndoubtedly haue ensued, but farre and wide enlarged also. If then the emulation and discord of the most vertuous magistrats be so profitable vnto a Commonweale, what then is to bee hoped for, when the good magistrats shall oppose themselues against the wicked?

And

And these reasons may on both sides seeme probable, but what in trueth is to bee resolued vpon, is not so easie to iudge which to do, not onely the qualitie of the magistrats themselues, but the diuers formes of Commonweales, is to bee also considered. And yet I suppose, that in euerie kind of Commonweale it is good that the inferiour magistrats and officers, being vnder the power and authoritie of the greater, should stil be at variance and discord among themselues, and that more in a Popular estate than in any other: For that the people hauing none but the magistrats to gouerne them, is most easie to be pilled and polled, if the magistrats bee not one of them by another controlled. And in a Monarchie it is expedient also, that euen the greatest magistrats should sometime be at oddes, considering that there is a soueraine prince to chastise and correct them; so that hee bee not mad, furious, or a child, or one otherwise subject vnto another mans power. But in an Aristocratike or Popular Commonweale it is most daungerous, that the great magistrats should bee at discord among themselues, and that especially if they bee not good men, who neuer haue any such contention or debate amongst them, as may hurt the estate or Commonweale: but such as was the honourable difference betwixt *Scipio Affricanus*, the elder, and *Fabius Maximus*: betwixt *Scipio* the younger, and *Cato*; betwixt *Liuius* and his companion *Nero*; or the contention of *Lepidus* with *Fuluius*, of *Marcus Scaurus* with *Catulus*; or of *Themistocles* with *Aristides*: whose notable contention for vertues sake was alwayes vnto the Commonweale wholesome. But if the greatest magistrats in a Popular estate bee euill and wicked men, or that their ambition be founded vppon an euill ground, it is then daungerous least that their differences bee cause of ciuill warres; as it happened betwixt *Marius* and *Scylla*, betwixt *Cæsar* and *Pompey*, *Augustus* and *Marke Anthonie*, *Thucidides* and *Pericles*. And yet much more dangerous such contentions are in an Aristocratie, than in a Popular Commonweale: For that the gouernours, which are alwaies the fewer in number in an Aristocratique estate, and yet commaund the rest, haue still to doe with the people: who vpon the first occasion take vp armes against their lords, if they once enter into quarrels. For a few lords in an Aristocratie are easily drawne into two parts, by the great magistrats, who if they fall into sedition among themselues, as also with the people, it cannot otherwise bee, but that the chaunge of the estate must thereof needes ensue; the leaders of the factions oppressing their enemies: or else the gouernment of the estate falling wholly into one mans hands, which is not so much to bee feared in a Monarchie, whereas the soueraigne prince vnder his power keepeth all the magistrats in awe.

But in euerie Commonweale it is expedient and necessarie, that the number of the soueraigne magistrats, or of them which come neere vnto the soueraigntie, should still be odd, to the end that the dissention amongst them might still be composed by the greater part or number of them; and that the publike actions be not by the equalitie of them hindred or letted. And that is it for which the Cantons of Vrie, Vnderuald, Zug, and Glaris (which of all others are most Popular) haue beene glad to make in euerie one of them three soueraigne magistrats, whom they call Amans, & not two, for that the third may easily reconcile two being at variance betwixt theselues: in stead whereof they of Schwits haue foure, as they of Geneua haue also their foure Sindiques, and they of Berne, Lucerne, Friburg, and Solure their two Auoyers: and Zuric, Basil, Schaffouse, their two Bourgomasters: as some there were which thought it better to haue of such great magistrats moe than foure, and yet in odd number also; as in auntient time the Athenians had their nine Pretors, whome they called Archontas; that so the fewer might still yeeld vnto the rest, or be in number ouercome, which cannot be where onely two beare the sway, except they had alternatiue power to commaund each of them his day by turnes, so as had the Carthaginensians Suffetes, and the Roman Consuls, so as we haue before said. And therefore by our laws also are three appointed for the common receit, that so the third might still reconcile the other two his companions at difference betwixt themselues, or els by ioyning himselfe to one of them, make that part the greater. Which odd number of great magistrats is more necessarie in a Popular or Aristocratike estate, than in a Monarchy; and the discord and dissention of them lesse in this state to be feared than in the other. For that as almightie God the Father of the whole Fabrike of the world, and of nature, doth with an admirable concord and agreement gouerne this world, composed of the contrarie conuersions and motions of the celestiall orbes among themselues, as also of the different natures of the starres and elements, and of the contrarie force and power of planets and of other liuing creatures: euen so also a king (the liuing image of God himselfe the prince of all things) should of the dissimilitude of magistrats, in some sort, at variance among themselues, keepe and maintaine the welfare of his subiects and people. And as in instruments, and song it selfe, which altogether out of tune, or all in the selfe same tune, the skilfull and learned eare cannot in any sort endure, is yet made a certaine well tuned discord, and agreeing harmonie, of most vnlike voices and tunes, viz. of Bases, Trebles, and Meanes, cunningly confused and mixt betwixt both: euen so also of the mightie, and of the weake, of the hie, and of the low, and others of the middle degree and sort betwixt both; yea euen of the verie discord of the magistrats among themselues ariseth an agreeing welfare of all, the straitest bond of safetie in euerie well ordered Commonweale. So *Cæsar* making sharpe warre vpon them of Beauuis, hauing in his armie two captaines deadly enemies one of them vnto the other, commaunded them to turne all that their hatred vpon their enemies, who so in his verie sight with great emulation gained a notable victory ouer their enemies, which their dissention had giuen vnto their enemies, had they not had a generall aboue them, who kept them both in awe. Which as it oftentimes happeneth, so did it also chaunce to *Lewes* the twelfth the French king, who gained the estates of Bolonia, and ouerthrew the Popes armie, by reason of the discord betwixt the cardinall of Pauie, and the duke of Vrbin, who through iealousie of one of them against the other, so hindred & entangled themselues, as that they gaue victorie vnto the French: into which daunger the Roman estate was like to haue fallen, by the contention risen betwixt *Fabius Maximus*, and *Minutius* the Roman generals, which had vndoubtedly giuen *Hannibal* the victorie, and the Romans the ouerthrow, had not *Fabius* for the good of the Commonweale forgot his displeasure, and by his valour deliuered his rash companion together with the Roman armie, from a most certaine and present destruction.

The contention of the great magistrats most daungerous in a popular Commonweale: and their too great friendship to be no lesse perilous also.

Wherefore the contentions of the greater Magistrates are most daungerous in a Popular estate or Commonweale, (where there is no other head to commaund them but the multitude) and especially if he seeke how to serue their owne proud and ambitious desires, rather then the common good. And therefore the Roman Senat seeing *Marcus Lepidus*, and *Q. Fuluius* mortall enemies chosen Censors together, went vnto them in great number to perswade them now at length for the Commonwealth sake to become friends, or at least wise to suspend their enmitie, so the better to attend vnto their office, being the fairest and of greatest importance in the whole Commonweale. The like whereof we read to haue beene often done by the Senat, in setting the busie Tribunes, and proud Consuls agreed, at such time as their dissentions seemed to tend vnto the daunger of the State. But as it is not good that the greatest magistrates in a Popular estate should be too great enemies; so also is it not conuenient that they

---

G2 *For* planets *read* plants. H9 *For* estates of Bolonia *read* estate of Bolonia (cf. Fr). I10 *For* if he seeke *read* if they seeke.

OF A COMMONWEALE. 499

they should be too great friends, especially if they be not good men, and that for the reasons by vs before alleaged. Which was the cause that the yonger *Cato* seeing *Pompee*, *Cæsar*, and *Crassus* so straitly allied together, and that they so conioyned, were too strong for all the rest of the people; cried out aloud the Commonweale by such combyning of the great ones to be bought and sold; foreseeing as it were out of a watch tower the stormes and tempests thereof then at hand. Yet true it is that of two extremities it is better that the great Lords and magistrats in a Popular or Aristocratique estate should be of one accord then at discord: for that being of accord, they will alwaies like better to commaund others, and so in some sort or other to preserue the Estate such as it is, than together with the Commonweale, quite to ouerthrow their owne power, whereunto their discord would bring them, when they had once giuen sayles vnto the tempest. In such sort as *Liuie* said of *Caluinus* the Campanian: *Improbum hominem, sed non ad extremum perditum, qui mallet incolumi quàm euersa patria dominari*, A wicked man (saith he) but not altogether desperate, who had rather to rule ouer his countrie yet standing vpright, then ouer the same ouerthrowne. So albeit that *Mar. Tullius* said, The three-headed alliance of *Cæsar*, *Crassus*, and *Pompee* to be a thing greatly to be feared: Yet when he saw *Crassus* the moderator with the Roman legions slaine in Chaldea, and *Iulia Cæsars* daughter *Pompee* his wife by vntimely death taken away, he cried out: *Vtinam Cn. Pompei, amicitiam cum Cæsare nunquam coisses, aut nunquam diremisses*, I would to god, O Pompee, (said he) thou haddest either neuer made friendship with Cæsar, or hauing once made it, haddest neuer broken it. For why their friendship much diminished the Popular power, but their enmitie altogether ruinated the same; one of them being in no wise able to endure his equall, nor the other his superiour, vntill that so by ciuill warre the state was quite at length ouerthrowne, and *Cæsar* become master of all. And as for that which *Cæsar* writeth, our auncestours the auntient Gaules to haue thought the dissention of their princes and great gouernours to haue beene profitable vnto their estates, I can hardly be perswaded therein: when as by the report euen of *Cæsar* himselfe, the dissention of the princes and of the estates of Fraunce, (then for the most part gouerned by Aristocraties) wrought their owne destruction; some of them praying aide of the Germans, and some of them of the Romans, being long a prey both to the one and to the other, and in the end vnto the Romans alone as the onely conquerors. Neither is it true the mutuall slaughters of the Nobilitie of England to haue beene commodious and profitable vnto the comminaltie and inferiour sort, as *Philip Comines* writeth; yea at such time as I was Embassadour in England, I vnderstood by some of the inhabitants there, them to feare nothing more then the factions of the Nobilitie and their ciuill discord: for the better appeasing and repressing whereof they haue often times vsed to assemble the high court of Parliament, whereunto all the States are assembled. And thus we haue declared in what sort the Magistrates ought to behaue them selues towards their Prince, as also how they ought to beare them selues one of them towards an other, as also towards other priuate men; and whether they ought to be at vnitie among them selues or not. Now it remaineth for vs briefly to show also, how the Prince ought to behaue him selfe towards his subiects; and whither it be expedient that he should him selfe iudge them, or be him selfe conuersant among them.

Philip. 2.

Vu iiij CHAP.

A8 then at discord *i.e.* than at discord (cf. 532 l5). B2 *For* Calvinus *Bodin writes* Calvinius *but properly* Calavius Notes at A8, C4, D5.

Chap. VI.

¶ *Whether it be conuenient or expedient for the Maiestie of a soueraigne Prince to iudge his subiects him selfe, or to be much conuersant with them.*

Kings first established to iudge his subiects.

IT may seeme vnto some that this question not before reasoned of, hath not in it any doubt, and that it is not needfull for vs farther to enter there into, considering that all the auntient and wise polytitians are of accord, that kings were neuer for other thing established than for the administration of justice, as saith *Herodotus* speaking of the Medes; and *Cicero* likewise of the Romans; as also we read that the first kings of Greece, *Æacus, Minos,* and *Radamanthus* had no title more honorable then the title of Iudges; who for they with great equity administred iustice, are by the Poets reported to haue obtayned of *Iupiter* an euerlasting power & office for iudging of the ghosts in hel. And albeit that *Homer* calleth princes the pastors, or feeders of the people. Yet so it is that the title of Iudges hath long time after him continued in the person of the princes of Athens, who had the soueraigne gouernment for ten yeares. And not onely the princes of the Medes, the Greeks, and Latins, but euen the Generals also, who were as soueraignes amongst the Hebrewes, had no other title then the title of Iudges: And at such time as they demaunded of *Samuel* (now wearied with age) a king, they ioyned thereunto, that he might iudge them, as other kings did their people: Which showeth sufficiently that the principall charge which they had, was to doe iustice themselues in person.

Reasons to show that princes themselues in person ought to administer iustice vnto their subiects.

And the principall reason that might moue the princes themselues to iudge the subiects, is the mutuall obligation which is betwixt the Prince and his subiects: For as the subiect oweth vnto his lord all duety, aide, & obedience; so the Prince also oweth vnto his subiects iustice, guard, & protection: so that the subiects are no more bound to obey the prince, than is the prince to administer vnto them iustice. Neither is it sufficient to haue it done by an other man, as by the Magistrate at the Princes command, seeing that the subiects being commaunded to yeeld their faith and obedience vnto the prince, cannot do it by their Deputies, but onely by themselues in person; and that this obligation betwixt the Prince and the subiect is reciprocall. Howbeit that it is lesse inconuenient that the vassall should giue his faith and homage vnto his Lord by his deputie, than the Lord to do him iustice by his officer, for that the obeisance of the subiect in this case cannot be called in doubt: whereas the subiect hath no warrant that the magistrat or officer shall not suffer himselfe to be by bribes corrupted, which the Prince will not do, who is therefore still aunswerable before God, vnto whom he cannot say that he hath therewith charged the conscience of his Iudges, his owne thereby being not discharged. Besides that it much and notably concerneth Commonweales, that they which hold the soueraignty should themselues doe iustice: that is to wit, the vnion and amitie of the Princes with the subiects, which cannot better be nourished and maintained than by the communion of one of them with the other, which is lost, and brought to nought, when the Princes do nothing but by their magistrats and officers: For so it seemeth vnto the subiects that their princes disdaine and contemne them, a thing vnto them more grieuous than if the prince should him selfe doe them wrong; and so much the more heauy, as a contumelie or disgrace is more hardly to be borne, than is a simple wrong or iniurie.

The great good that ensueth when princes in person themselues do iustice vnto their subiects.

Whereas to the contrarie when the subiects see their Prince to present him selfe in person vnto them to do them iustice, they go away halfe contented, albeit that they haue not that which they desired, or at least wise they will say, The king hath seene our request, he hath heard our difference, he hath taken the paines to iudge our cause. And if so be that the sub-

iects

Of A Commonweale.

A iects be by their king seene, heard, or vnderstood, it is almost incredible, how much they are rauished with contentment and pleasure, if the Prince be neuer so little vertuous, or haue any other commendable qualitie in him. Besides that there is no greater meane to giue authoritie vnto his Magistrats and officers, and to cause iustice it selfe to be both feared and reuerenced, than to see the king him selfe sitting in his regall throne to do his subiects iustice. Moreouer the Magistrats often times doe wrong and iniurie vnto the subiects by standing vpon the nice clauses, words, and sillables of the law, which they dare not passe, as being bound and subiect thereunto. And in case that they make any conscience to iudge according to the strictnesse of the law, they must yet first send their reasons vnto the Prince, and attend his aunswere, and exposition of B his Edicts and lawes made according vnto the opinion and aduise of his other officers, who will often times see the suters purses bothom in such sort as that many sutes liue longer than the parties and suters them selues, yea and some times are for euer suspended. Whereas if the Prince him selfe in person shall vouchsafe to iudge the matter, he which is the liuing law, and aboue all ciuill lawes, being accompanied with his Counsell shall doe both good and speedie iustice, as hauing respect vnto the verie ground and equitie of the matter, without farther standing vpon titles and formalities. By this meanes also so many oppositions, appeales, ciuill requests, remouing of causes, infinite decrees, one of them vpon an other, which make sutes immortall, should cease, and iustice without stay or let take course, no appeal being to be made C from the Prince. Ioyning hereunto also that the Commonweale should so be relieued of the great charges and wages which it alloweth vnto Iudges, and of their particular fees which are aboue measure heauie; besides the bribes and presents which must be giuen, which often times passe the ordinarie fees, in such sort as that the subiects in steed of hauing good and speedie iustice (which the Prince oweth them) are constrained to paie for it as for the most precious thing in the world: howbeit that oftentimes it happeneth, that the marchant is well paid, and yet the marchandise by him deliuered is right little or nothing worth. And yet there is another verie considerable point also: which is, That the parties contending are sometimes great and honourable, as that they would neuer answere before many judges, in discredit for their vnworthinesse, iniD quitie, or other like qualitie, whereby it oftentimes commeth to passe, that they end their suits and differences by combats and dynt of sword: whereas the Prince in presence might euen with the twinkling of his eye set them agreed. And were it that no other greater profit were thereby to come vnto the Commonweale, then that the prince by vse and exercise of iudgement should haue the force of right and iustice throughly engrafted in his mind; what greater or better thing could there bee wished of almightie God either for the prince or for the subiects, than that hee might most curiously and seriously learne daily to administer iustice? The knowledge of other artes and sciences, which is it selfe a thing most royall, and so most proper vnto kings. For as for the knowledge of armes, and of martiall affaires, it is well fitting a Prince against E his enemies, whereas iustice is most necessarie for him at all times, and in all places, whether it be in peace or warre.

But not to rest altogether vpon reason and arguments, we will also vse the examples herein of the most wise and noble princes. VVhat man was there amongst men to be in wisedome compared with *Salomon*? And yet we read, That the onely prayer that he made vnto God, was to obtaine wisedome wherewith rightly to iudge his people, which his prayer was so acceptable vnto God, as that he seemed therefore most plentifully, and to the great worlds wonder, to haue powred out vpon him all the treasures both of wisedome and of knowledge; that so all men might vnderstand God not onely

Examples of great Princes, who themselues in person administred iustice vnto their subiects.

D9 and sciences, THE PRINCE MAY EASILY DO WITHOUT, BUT HE CANNOT DO WITHOUT THE KNOWLEDGE OF JUDGING, which is it selfe (cf. L) Note at A7.

ly to haue inspired him with wisdome, but also that the office of right iudgement was euen by God himselfe giuen vnto kings; who was also for experience in great affaires and politike wisedome like vnto the Great *Augustus*? And yet neuerthelesse wee read that he without ceasing was still busied in the administration of iustice, insomuch that euen when he was sicke, he caused himselfe to bee carried in his horselitter to doe iustice. Howbeit that that was the ordinarie vacant time of the Roman emperours, who for the administration of iustice were commended aboue all the princes of the world, euen so farre, as that a poore old woman to whom the Great emperour *Adrian* refused to aunswere her preferring vnto him a request, excusing himself, That he was not then at leasure, *Raigne no longer then* (said she) *but discharge thee of thy charge thou bearest*. Whereunto the emperor hauing not what to answere, presently staid & did her iustice. Now then if so great a prince (whose empire was bounded with the same bounds that the course of the sunne was, and troubled with so great affaires) acknowledged the bond, To doe his subiect iustice: what ought they then to doe which hold but the scantlings of that great empire? Ought not euerie one of them to enforce himselfe in his owne person, and to studie with all his power, how to imploy himselfe for the doing of iustice? considering that (as *Plinie* the yonger saith) there is no more noble Philosophie, than to entreat of the publike affaires, and to doe iustice, putting in practise that which the Philosophers haue taught.

A notable example of the great emperour Adrian for the doing of a poore old woman iustice.

Now if the knowledge of that which is right, and the administration of iustice, bring so many & so great profits vnto princes; how much greater shal the same then be, if they shall by themselues handle but those things onely which are proper vnto their soueraigntie? For as for the rest of the ciuill affaires, a prince may well commit them vnto the magistrats: but the rights of soueraigntie, and the deciding of them, hee can in no wise put off, but together with the soueraigntie it self. Surely they are verie blind, deafe, and dumbe, which neuer but by other mens eies see, and by other mens eares heare, and by another mans tongue, and that oftentimes a straunge tongue also, speake and talke of such things as are theirs, and most proper vnto themselues. Now wee haue before shewed also, not by the examples of straunge nations onely, but euen by the examples of our auncestours also, the idle slothfulnesse of kings, who committed the mannaging of all their affairs vnto their domesticall seruants, to haue thereby brought both themselues and their posteritie vnto destruction.

To be necessarie for a prince to vnderstand of the affaires of estate.

These arguments and reasons thus by vs before alleaged, make a faire show vnto them who sufficiently vnderstand not, nor by experience know not, the secrets of soueraigntie, and hidden knowledge for the maintaining of maiestie: But vnto me looking neerer into the matter, they are not sufficient to resolue this question, nor to maintaine, That a prince ought in person himselfe to administer iustice: Yea vnto mee it seemeth not onely not necessarie, but not profitable vnto the subiects, the prince himselfe to bee vnto them the minister of iustice. True it is, that for them so to do, it should bee not onely profitable, but euen necessarie also, if the princes were themselues such as *Scylax* faigned vnto himselfe the kings of the Indians to be; that is to say, so much better than their subiects, as the gods are aboue men. For what can bee more glorious or more royall, than to see a prince by himselfe in the open sight of the people with great integritie and vprightnesse iudge and decide causes, to giue rewards vnto such as haue well deserued of the Commonweale, and to inflict punishment vpon the wicked and offendors. For he must needs be a good and wise man himselfe, which is not delighted but in the companie of good and wise men: and he must needs excell in integritie and iustice, who himselfe with great equitie administreth iustice. But shall we therfore say, that vitious princes ought to thrust themselues into the sight, and so to communi-

Reasons to show that it is not meet for princes themselues in person to administer iustice vnto their subiects.

cat

Notes at F2, F6, H2.

Of A Commonvveale.

cat their vices vnto their subiects? the least vice in a prince being like vnto a canker in a faire face: and so to doe, what were it els, than in the sight of the people to set vp an example of vice, to lead men, to draw them, yea & euen to enforce them to be naught? For there is nothing more naturall, than for the subiects to conforme themselues vnto the manners, vnto the doings and sayings of their prince; there being neither gesture, action, nor countenance in him, be it good or bad, which is not marked, or counterfaited by them which see him, hauing their eyes, their sences, and all their spirits, wholy bent to the imitation of him. So that *Plinie* well called the princes life a Perpetual Censorship, whereunto we still direct and conforme our selues. And this is a doctrine from most auntient antiquitie deliuered vnto all posteritie, first by the maister of wisedome himselfe, and after by *Plato, Cicero, Liuie,* and *Cassiodore,* repeated as an infallible rule, *That such as the prince of a Commonweale is, such will the people also be.* Yea *Theodoric* king of the Gothes, writing vnto the Senat of Rome, passeth further, vsing these words, *Facilius est errare raturam, quam dissimilem sui princeps possit Rempublicam formare,* An easier thing it is (said he) for nature to chaunge her course, than for a prince to frame a Commonweale vnlike vnto himselfe. And though examples need not in so plaine a matter, yet we haue seene king *Francis* the first, in this realme, and *Mansor,* surnamed the Great, emperour of Affrike and Spaine, who both two in diuers times, and in diuers places, began to haue learning and learned men in estimation; when suddenly the princes, the nobilitie, the cleargie, yea euen the souldiors and artificers, with all the people in general, gaue themselues so to learning, as that there was neuer found so great a number of learned men in all languages, and in all sciences, as in their time. Seeing therefore that the princes example is of so great force and power for the conforming and chaunging of his subiects manners, either to good or bad; great heed is to bee taken, that the prince, except he be by nature wel, and by education better framed and instructed, come not much abroad for the people to behold and imitat: but if he be euill & wicked, then by all meanes to be as a popular and common plague kept out of the sight of his subiects. Yet haply some man may say, That an euill prince should not therefore abstaine or withdraw himselfe from publike affaires, or from the iudgement place or Senat; for that no man was so bad, but that he hath in him some vertues or commendable qualitie; or which cannnot at leastwise dissemble some of his vices: of which his vertues & vices, his subiects may make choyce, in such sort as that they may easily decline the one, and embrace the other. But in mine opinion and iudgement, they will rather imitate his vices, than his vertues: and so much the rather, by how much the corrupt nature of man is more prone and enclined vnto vice than vnto vertue; as also for that there is but one most strait way which leadeth vnto vertue, wheras on both sides there are innumerable crooked by-wayes and turnings vnto vice, whereinto they may more easily fall, than into the straight and right way of vertue. In *Alexander* the Great were many most rare and heroicall vertues, yet so it was, that he greatly blemished the beautie of them, as also of his other noble acts, by an euill custome that hee had to bee drunke; wherein he tooke such delight, as that hee propounded a talent as a prize vnto him which could drinke most: in which beastly contention and strife fortie together with him which had gained the prize burst and perished; hee himselfe almost looking on. *Mithridates* also king of Amasia, imitating of *Alexander* the Great herein, surpassed him, that hauing set vp a prize for him that could eat and drinke most, hee (as *Plutarch* saith) gained the foule victorie in both (if to bee ouercome of intemperance and excesse be to be accounted at all a victorie.) But to counterfeit vertues, or to dissemble vices, as it hath alwayes seemed a most hard thing vnto all men, so hath it especially vnto princes, for that they of all others haue least learned to commaund their desires,

Such a prince, such a people.

That an euill prince ought not much to come abroad for the people to imitat his vices.

The subiects still readier to imitate the vices than the vertues of the prince.

600 Crownes.

A3 naught *i.e.* wicked   B4 naturam   Note at E3.

Princes of all others most hardly to counterfeit vertues, or to dissemble their vices

fires, to restraine their lusts, to bridle their affection, which he that knoweth not how to do, shall neuer be a good or cunning dissembler. *Dionysius* the younger moued with the fame and vertue of *Plato*, caused him to be sent for vnto Syracusa, who had no sooner begun to tast of the wisedome, vertue, and learning of the man, but that in a moment all minstrels, players, drunkards, bauds, harlots, and such like, were quite vanished out of the princes sight, and the court so suddenly chaunged, as if it had bene from heauen inspired. But for that *Dionysius* had but chaunged his countenance, & not his mind, and cast out the allurements of pleasures, but not pleasures themselues; hee could not long dissemble his vices, eithes yet endure *Plato*, who was no sooner gone out of the court, and disembarqued out of Sicilie, but that the prince forthwith returned vnto his woonted vices, by him before for a while forborne, but not quite forsaken: at which verie instant minstrels, dauncers, harlots, bauds, and such other vermine of the court, which had before bene driuen out were againe recalled. So much power the prince hath at his pleasure to chaunge and turne the harts of his subiects, but alwayes rather vnto vices and vanities, than vnto vertues. But I doe more willingly remember our own domesticall examples than others; king *Francis* the elder, for the healing of a wound he had receiued in his head, caused his head to be polled, when suddenly after all his houshold seruants, all the princes, all the nobilitie, the magistrats, the artificers, and people of all sorts in generall, caused their heads to be from that time forward polled also, insomuch that if any did from thenceforth vse the old fashion, and account it an vndecent thing to be polled, he was therefore of all men derided: whereas before from the beginning of this kingdome, it had alwayes bene the marke of the kings, neither was it lawfull for any but for the nobilitie and Senators, to weare long haire: all the rest of the meaner sort being befor compelled to poll themselues as slaues, vntil that *Peter Lombard* bishop of Paris (for the power and authoritie which bishops then had aboue kings) obtained, That it might be lawful for the common people to weare long haire also. True it is, that the flatterers of princes helpe much to conforme the maners and fashions of the people vnto those of the princes, they still rather counterfeiting than imitating euen the vices and defects of the prince, whome if they see laugh, they laugh also, although they know no cause why; if he be lame, they halt downe right also. *Alexander* the Great, and *Alphonsus* king of Aragon, beeing both wrie necked, the one by nature, and the other by custome, the courtly curres to counterfeit that their deformitie, held their neckes also awry; as the Courtier, and *Plutarch* in the life of *Pyrrhus* writeth. Seeing therefore the nature of man is enclined to follow the vice of the prince, were it not euen to vndoe a people, and to ruinat an estate, to thrust still into the sight of the people a prince euill brought vp; and a pottraitor of vices for them to imitat? And yet it is more daungerous for that for one vice which the prince hath, oftentimes those of his traine haue an hundred, who euerie where as they passe, may alter & marre the good disposition of the people; or like swarmes of flies & caterpillers, who hauing deuoured the leaues, and fruit, do also leaue their spaune behind them, able to infect the fields and trees be they neuer so cleane and fruitfull.

But suppose we the prince not to be vitious (a rare gift, and by the goodnes of God giuen vnto men, when as in euerie age a tollerable prince is scarcely to bee found) but to be of great vertue and perfection, yea euen a man without fault (howbeit that there is a great space betwixt them which are endued with vertues, and them which are without vices) yet is it almost a thing impossible, but that some thing shall at one time or other fall from him, which wel noted may seeme vnto the people foolish or rediculous: wherein much is derogated from the reputation and dignitie which the subiects ought to haue of him. But let vs suppose that also, him to be neither a man euill giuen, nor foolish,

F9 either yet endure I6 a portraitor (*i.e.* portraiture) K4 howbeit that

foolish; neither yet so to seeme, but to be a man endued with great vertues, and of good education; yet so it is that too ordinarie conuersation, and too great familiaritie of the subiects with the prince much diminisheth his maiestie, and withall engendreth a certaine contempt of him: of which contempt proceedeth the disobedience of the subiects vnto him and his commaunds, to the ruine of the whole estate. And now againe to the contrarie, if the prince to maintaine his maiestie shall ordinarily show himselfe vnto his subiects, in his greatnesse, with a terrible port, it may be that so hee may bee the more of them redoubted: but it is daungerous least he should be therefore the lesse loued. Whereas the loue of subiects towards their soueraigne is much more necessarie for the preseruation of an estate, than is feare; and so much the more, for that loue cannot be without feare to offend him whome wee loue; whereas feare may well be, and most often is without any loue at all, men commonly hating him whome they feare, and as occasion serueth still seeking to take him out of the way.

Too much familiarity of a prince with his subiects, not good: and alwayes to be seene of them in his maiestie, a thing vnto them dreadfull.

And truely vnto me more deepely considering of the matter, almightie God (the soueraigne prince of the whole world) seemeth to haue shewed a short way vnto worldly princes (the true images of himselfe) how they are to communicat themselues vnto their subiects, to be of them both beloued and feared: For he communicateth himselfe vnto men but by visions and dreames, and that but to a few of the elect & most perfect of them also, men of great integritie of life. But when hee with his owne voyce published the Ten Commaundements, he caused his fire to bee seene heauens high, and the mountaines to tremble with thunder and lightning, with such a dreadfull sound of trumpets, that the people strucken with feare, and falling flat vpon their faces, besought him, That hee would no more from thenceforth speake vnto them himselfe (for that otherwise they should all die) but onely to commaund such things as he pleased by his seruant *Moyses*. So that that people of all others most chosen, had but once almightie God (who sheweth himselfe but in spirit to be seene) himselfe sounding forth his lawes; when as yet for all that to allure men the more feruently to loue him, hee at all times, and in all places and countries, doth with great loue, and eternall bountie, foster and cherish all mankind, yea indeed all sort of liuing creatures, powring continually vpon them his great and infinit fauours, larges, and bountie. If therefore the wise prince ought in mannaging of his subiects, to imitate the wisedom of God in the gouernment of the world, he must but seldome times come into the sight of his subiects, and that with such a state and maiestie, as best agreeth with his wisedome, power, and greatnesse, and yet make choice of some few most wise and worthy men, with whome to communicat his secret councels, and by them to declare his will and pleasure vnto the rest, and yet incessantly to heape vpon his subiects his graces and fauours; & with great wisedome and power to protect and defend them against their enemies. In the booke *De Mundo* (or of the world) dedicated to *Alexander* the Great (and without cause ascribed to *Aristotle*, as sauouring nothing of his stile) a comparison is made of a soueraigne prince vnto God; as that the great king of Persia was stil resiant in a proud and stately pallace or castle, compassed in with three high walles, full of all pleasures and delights, neuer sturring abroad, or shewing & acquainting himselfe but with some few of his friends; who yet neuerthelesse by fiers and watches set vpon high places, stil in one day vnderstood and knew all the enemies of his empire, euen from the farthest parts of the East Indies, vnto the straits of Hellespontus. And yet neuer was there any princes vnder heauen more honoured and reuerenced, or better beloued of their subiects than they: or whose commaunds were more iust vnto their subiects, or more of their subiects regarded, or that longer preserued their empire, power, and state. So those princes also which giue themselues ouer, and became slaues vnto their vaine pleasures

How princes are to behaue themselues, to be of their subiects both beloued and feared.

Xx and

B1 without resident　　C5 *For* had but once *read* heard but once (L).　　D5 will and　　D10 resiant *i.e.* resident　　E4 *For* the enemies *read* the newes (*nouvelles* in Fr).

and delights, most commonly vsed to withdraw themselues from the sight of the multitude into some secret places, that so they might at more libertie glut themselues with all kind of pleasures. For so *Tiberius Cæsar* of all others the most cunning dissembler, made choyce of a most desert island, wherein he for many yeres liued in all kind of voluptuous and beastly pleasures. Which was of him right filthily done, but yet more wisely than they who with the most odious smell of their loathsome pleasures pollute and defile as well publike as priuat places: who besides that they offend more by giuing of euill example than by the wickednesse it selfe by them committed, doe also in the minds and conceits of men engender a neglect and contempt of themselues.

How a prince is to frame his countenance and speech when he showeth himselfe vnto the people.

Wherefore a prince that wise is, so oft as he should show himselfe vnto the people (which he should most seldome do) should so prepare himselfe, as that he may vnto all men seeme euen in his face and countenance to carry with him a certaine state and maiestie yet still mixt with modestie, but especially in his speech, which should alwaies be maiesticall and sententious, and in the manner of phrase, something different from the vulgar. Which if it shall seeme something hard for the prince to performe, or that he haue not the grace of speaking, it is best for him to speake little, or els altogether to be silent: For that we know men in so great matters, as to contemne, or feare; to hate, or loue; to be stil no lesse with opinion, than with any certaine reason, led & moued thereunto. For if the prouerbe of the wise Hebrew be true, *That the foole himselfe in holding his peace is accounted wise*, how circumspect and aduised ought a prince to be, when hee openeth his mouth to speake in publike place? considering that his words, his countenance, and lookes, are oftentimes accounted and esteemed of as lawes, oracles, and decrees. Wherein *Tiberius* the emperour, least he should in any thing offend, brought in a new fashion, as to be spoke vnto, and also to giue aunswere by writing, for what matter soeuer it was, *Moris erat* (saith *Tranquillus*) *eo tempore principem etiam presentem scripto adire*, The manner (saith he) at that time was, with writing to goe vnto the prince euen then present; to the end that nothing might escape which had not before bene well thought vpon. For it is not possible but that they which speake much in open assemblies, as in the Senat, or before the people, must many times erre: which done by a prince, shall breed contempt, or at leastwise cause him to bee the lesse esteemed: so that a Grecian (I wot not who) not vnfitly said, *That a prince if hee bee wise should vnto the people, or in open audience no otherwise speake, than hee would doe in a Tragedie*.

But I know that some of contrary opinion vnto mine, wil say, Is it not the true estate and office of a prince, to doe iustice vnto his people? to heare the complaints of his subiects? to see the requests of his own? and by the mouth of euery one to vnderstand of their iust grieuances, which are commonly suppressed, or at leastwise disguised by another man? And why then should the prince hide himselfe from his people? talke but with few, and those of his most inward friends also? or aunswere nothing vnto many, of right asking him of many things? yea not to be willing so much as to heare his subiects speake? Things altogether absurd, and not beseeming the maiestie of a soueraigne prince. Whereunto I say, that mine opinion is not, that he should so hide himselfe, as not at all to show himselfe; as the kings yet doe euen at this present in the East Indies, and namely the king of Borney, who speaketh not vnto any but vnto his wife and children; neither is seene of any, but still speaketh vnto others by one of his gentlemen through an hole by a reed or cane which he holdeth in his mouth, as he did vnto the king Catholike (as we read in the histories of the Indies:) but my meaning is, that he should not be much in the assemblies of the people, neither easie to bee spoke withall of all men, not to vse much discourse with his subiects, except with such as are

The maner of the kings of Borney.

How a prince ought but seldome times to conuerse with his subiects.

neere

Note at K6.

Of A Commonweale. 507

neere vnto him, or of his familiar acquaintance; not to take pleasure in iests and taunts, in play, or other publike exercise: For that by such things the princes maiestie and reputation, which ought by all meanes to be whole and vntouched, is greatly impaired and lightned: and so much the more, by how much the prince is of greater estate and maiestie: whereunto good and especiall regard is always to be had. For it were not seemely for a pettie prince in his estate to counterfeit the great kings of Æthiopia, of Tartarie, of Persia, or of Turkie, who suffer not their subiects so much as to looke directly vpon them, neither are so much of them redoubted and feared for their power, as for the maiesty that they hold when they show themselues vnto their subiects. Howbeit that the kings of Affrike hold yet this maiestie more, as in the historie of *Francis D'Aluarez* is to be seene, where hee speaketh of the maiestie of the Great Negus, whome we call *Prester Iohn*: and in the historie of *Leo* of Affrike, where hee speaketh of the king of Tombut, before whome his subiects appeare not, but vpon their knees, with dust vpon their heads.

Now if any man shall say, That the kings of the East, and of the South are thus to be honoured, for that their subiects are of an abiect and a seruile nature; but that they of the North, or of the West, whose subiects be of greater courage, are not able to endure such a seruitude and slauerie: this shall be in due place decided, as also what the nature of euerie region is: and yet for all that I see the kings of England, Sweden, Denmarke, and Polonia, who are situat toward the North, much better to maintaine the maiestie of their estates with their subiects, than doe the kings of Fraunce, or the princes of Italie; and the kings of Moscouia yet better than all the rest, and yet are not therefore the lesse, but well the more of their subiects obeyed.

Now the greatest daunger that can come vnto a prince, to doe all by others, is, least that they vpon whome he should so discharge himselfe, should take from him his estate and soueraigntie, and so possesse themselues thereof: which for al that hath neuer chanced in this realme, but onely vnder king *Childeric*, surnamed the Loutish: since the time that the kings of Fraunce showed themselues vnto their subiects in their maiestie but once a yeare, *viz.* the first of May; as we read in our owne histories, and also in *Cedrinus* a Greeke author, who saith, That the auntient kings of Fraunce tooke no other pleasure but to eat and drinke, leauing the mannaging of all their affaires vnto the great Master of the Pallace. But we must not draw into consequence the example of one king bereft of sence, to ground a maxime of state vpon. Yet is there well one meane to meet with that inconuenience, which is, That the prince for one lieutenant, or for one great Maister of the Pallace, should haue two or three in power and fauour equall: For in so doing he shall neuer be circumuented, their power being so diminished, one of them still bewraying or controlling the other, the kings maiestie being so still the more stately and sure. For *Tiberius* hauing made *Seianus* too great; and so *Commodus, Perennius*; *Theodosius* the second, *Eutropius*; *Iustinian, Bellisarius*; *Xerxes, Artabanus*; and *Childeric, Pepin*: committing vnto them alone the mannaging of all their affaires, with the guard of their persons, they fell into the daungers which wee spake of, being in hazard of their estates.

How the danger least a prince should be dispossessed of his estate by him whom he putteth in trust for the mannaging of his affaires, is to be preuented.

As for the administration of iustice, and the hearing of the complaints and griefes of the subiects, it shall be alwayes better prouided by good and sufficient magistrats, than by the prince in person himselfe. For who knoweth not so many good parts to bee requisit in a good judge, as are not all well to be found in the most sufficient prince in the world? Yea who knoweth not so many things to bee within the compasse of the duetie of a good judge, as may ouerslip and escape euen the most skilfull and carefull men? whereof many must needs escape the prince before he can perceiue them, and

Iustice better to be administred by good and sufficient magistrats, than by the prince himselfe.

Xx ij   so

508　　　　　　　　　　The Fovrth Booke

so many times the verie substance of the matter consisteth in that which is ouerslipped. And if one shall say, that the prince may haue about him both wise and learned councellors, according to whose aduise and councell he may determine of matters, and so giue iudgement; such as *Augustus, Traian, Adrian, Marcus Aurelius, Alexander Seuerus*, and the other Roman emperours are reported to haue had: who were alwaies accompanied with most worthy and excellent personages: truly that seemed not so hard a matter vnto the Roman princes, so brought vp and so enured thereunto, but now we liue after another manner and fashion. And who is there that seeth not, not onely the prince not to be able to endure so many dilatory pleas, so many slights of the lawyers, so many shifts of the plaintifes, such petitions and outcries of such as run from court to court? but not euen the magistrats themselues without incredible tediousnesse to be able to endure the same? all which yet they must deuoure. Yea the prince is not able himselfe to conceiue all such things as are the greatest and of most importance in the Commonweale, and how then shall he alone suffice to decide and determine so many suits and causes? But if hee shall take that charge in hand, and not well and orderly discharge the same, in stead of doing of the subiects right, hee shall doe them great iniurie and wrong. Wherein *Demetrius* (he which was called the Besieger) hath for iust cause beene blamed: who hauing receiued a great number of his subiects requests, put them into the lap of his mantle, and at the first bridge he came vnto, whereby hee was to passe ouer a riuer, shooke them all into the water: Whereof the subiects seeing themselues by him contemned, conceiued a mutuall hatred against him, so that shortly after he was forsaken of his armie, which yeelded it selfe to *Pyrrhus* together with the kingdome, which he so gained without battell. Besides that in this course taken, we should be alwaies driuen to haue recourse vnto the commissioners for instructions: and afterwards vnto the prince for iudgement of the cause: howbeit that it is sometimes hard, and oftentimes pernitious also, to seperat the instructions of the matter from the iudgement.

An hard chargeable, and daungerous matter, for subiects to prosecute their suits before the prince.

But suppose that the prince were at leisure, and that hee both could and would see, heare, and iudge all the causes of his people, yet were it a thing not beseeming the maiestie of a king to make such an ordinarie confusion of his court, where beside the subtilties, the countenances and fauours, (not there subiect to enquirie) and the contraritie of letters, commissions, decrees, and prouisions, which are there dispatched vnder the name (but without the knowledge) of the prince, whereof colour is oftentimes made for the doing of wrong: it is yet moreouer insupportable for the subiects, vnto whome iustice is due in the places where they are, to search for the same at the court, and to follow the prince still remouing from place to place; where it were better for them sometimes to loose their right, than with so great charge to follow the suit. Besides that the most honorable and worthy causes for a prince that wil himselfe intermeddle in iudgements, are the causes concerning life and honor: who shall be the accusers? who would fall into so great charges to sue the matter in the court? and into the daunger to bee slaine by the accused, if the prince should pardon the fault. For when princes vse scarcely at any time to condemne the guiltie parties, but doe oftentimes pardon and restore such as be alreadie condemned: by this meanes should ensue not onely no punishment of offences, but euen the greatest impunitie of the offendors: than which there is no more certaine token of a Commonweale in short time about to perish. Wherewith to meet, secret accusations haue bene brought in and admitted by an auntient edict of *Conan* king of Scots, which is at this day in vse in Scotland, and called the Indict: and yet is better prouided for by the ordinance of Milan (which well deserueth to bee religiously kept in euerie Commonweale) where in euerie towne there is a chest with an hole

---

H1 *For* mutuall *read* mortall (cf. Fr).　　H4 recourse　　H5 judgement of　　H8 (margin) chargeable *i.e.* costly, expensive　　I1 contraritie *i.e.* contrariety　　K1 fault　　Note at H6.

OF A COMMONWEALE.   509

A hole in it, in euery principall church, whereof the gouernours haue the key, wherein to it is lawfull for euery one secretly to put his bill of accusation against any man; wherin the crime committed, the time, the place, the partie guiltie, and the witnesses, are all of them comprised, with the reward of the moitie of the confiscation allowed vnto the accuser. Which is an easie way for the punishing of offences before ordinarie judges; a thing impossible to prosecute before the prince. For these reasons and the difficulties by vs noted, *Tiberius* the emperour hauing obtained the empire, protested in the full Senat, and afterwards by his letters made it knowne vnto the officers, That hee would take vppon him nothing which belonged vnto the iurisdiction of the magistrats; for that it was more that was required of a prince, than of a magistrat. Nei-
B ther ought it to seeme vnto any man straunge, why the office to iudge and decide matters, proper vnto the auntient kings, should now belong vnto the magistrats? for that when people as yet had no lawes, but that the kings power and will was accounted for law, it was then needfull for subiects causes to bee iudged by the princes: but after that lawes were once established, according vnto which the magistrat was bound to iudge, and due punishment by them appointed for offences, and rewards vnto such as had well deserued; that necessitie was taken away, and translated from the princes vnto the judges.

Why the office to iudge and decide matters, a thing proper vnto the auntient kings, now belongeth vnto magistrats and judges.

But here some man may say, That a prince may be so wise, so iust, and so full of vn-
C derstanding, as that he will giue no iudgement but such as is agreeable vnto equitie and reason; and the compasse of his territorie so strait, as that hee may himselfe suffice to iudge and determine all the suits of his subiects, as there bee diuers such princes in the Low countries, in Germanie, & especially in Italie: In this case should it not be a goodly and a profitable thing for the Commonweale, the prince himselfe there to administer iustice? If thou aske me what mine opinion is therein, I thinke it not profitable either for that so blessed a prince, either for those his so happie citisens or subiects, or him in person himself to sit in iudgement; not for that the subiects do so much loue and honour the maiestie of their prince, as not to dare freely enough to speake their minds, and to cause him to vnderstand their right; neither for that they could hardly haue ac-
D cesse vnto him, for the multitude of causes which he should still haue before him, hauing opened this gap: but euen for that nothing is so proper vnto a prince, as clemencie; nothing vnto a king, as mercie; nothing vnto maiestie, as lenitie. And therefore the emperor *Titus* (a man of so great courtesie, as that he was called *Humani generis delitias*, or the myrror of mankind) gladly took vpon him the office of the great bishop, because he would pronounce sentence of death vpon no man, either pollute his hands with mans blood, when as yet some other emperours who were also bishops (though not so religious as he) least of all others abstained from such capitall iudgements of life and death. Now nothing is more contrarie vnto true iustice, than pitie; neither any thing more repugnant vnto the office and dutie of an vpright judge, than mercie: hee
E not onely by the ciuill law, but euen by the law of God also being forbidden to haue pitie (euen of the poore) in iudgement: which we said to be so proper vnto maiestie, as that it cannot be therefrom diuided or seperated. So that a prince sitting in iudgement must take vpon him two contrarie persons, that is to say, of a mercifull father, and of an vpright magistrat; of a most gentle prince, and of an inflexible judge. And if the prince be by nature mild and pitifull, there shall bee none so euill or wicked, who by force of teares and prayers shall not escape the punishment by the law appointed, euen the most cruell men being oftentimes by them ouercome. So we read, that *Augustus* the great emperour, for wisedome inferiour vnto none, examining a murderer, began in this sort to question with him, *I am sure thou hast not killed thy father*: in which words he not

Not good for a soueraigne prince how sufficient soeuer, to sit in iudgement himselfe, for feare of too much lenitie, or else seueritie, to the peruerting of iustice.

Nothing more contrary vnto true iustice, than lenitie and pitie.

Xx iij   onely

B2 magistrats: for that   C6 *For* or him *read* for him.   D3–4 delicias (cf. L)   D4 myrror *i.e.* in the sense of model, paragon (but cf. 591 A4)

onely instructed the guiltie man what he was to aunswere to him both his prince and judge, but also most courteously gaue him his pardon. *Nero* also at such time as the condemnation of a man was presented to him to signe, is reported to haue said, *Vtinam literas nescirem*, I would to God I knew not letters. And therefore *Cicero* pleading before *Cæsar*, before resolued in any wise to haue put *Ligarius* to death, said, That he pleaded not before him as a judge, but as before the father of the people: and hauing somewhat appeased his anger, began thus to presse him farther, *Causas, Cæsar, egi multas, & quidem tecum, cum te tenuit ratio honorum tuorum, certe nunquam hoc modo; ignoscite iudices: errauit, lapsus est, non putauit, si vnquam posthac: ad parentem sic agi solet, ad iudices, non fecit, non cogitauit, falsi testes, fictum crimen, Dic te Cæsar de facto Ligarij iudicem esse &c. Cæsar* (saith he) I haue pleaded many causes, and that with thee, when thou stoodst vpon thine honour, but yet neuer pleaded I in this manner: pardon him my lords, he hath erred, he was deceiued, he thought it not, if euer hee shall doe so againe: so men vse to plead before a (soueraigne prince, or a) father: but vnto the judges, we say flatly, He did it not, hee neuer thought it, the crime is forged, the witnesses are false. But say *Cæsar*, thy selfe to be judge of the deed done by *Ligarius*, &c. And in this sort secretly insinuating vnto *Cæsar*, that he ought not to bee a judge, holding the place of a soueraigne: and afterwards highly commending *Cæsar* his noble acts, his valour and his clemencie, moued him so much, as that he chaunged both his colour and countenance, and was in such a sort rauished, as that he could not heare the one halfe of the oration (the shortest of all them that *Cicero* left in writing) but that he graunted more vnto the guiltie man than euer he hoped for. If then *Cæsar* himselfe, one of the greatest orators that euer was (euen in the iudgement of his capitall enemie *Cicero*) and one of the most valiant and wisest men of his time, was so ouercome by the force of eloquence, pardoning him whome he deadly hated, and had before resolued to put to death: what shall the lesse circumspect prince do, be he neuer so little enclined vnto pitie? how shall he be able to endure the filed speech of an eloquent aduocat? the pititious complaints of poore old men? the cries and sighes of distressed women? the weeping and wayling of little children? King *Agesilaus* a most famous prince of his time, ouercome by the importunat requests of a friend, writ vnto the judges, requesting them, That if the partie accused, in whose behalfe he writ, were not guiltie, hee should bee acquited by the equitie of his cause: but if he were lawfully conuict, hee should yet neuerthelesse bee for *Agesilaus* his sake discharged, and so in any case acquited But O how many should escape the penaltie of the lawes, if judges in such cases should hearken not onely vnto the princes secret letters, but euen vnto their letters pattents also: and then what may wee deeme that a prince himselfe would doo? Wherefore himselfe in person to sit in iudgement, beseemeth not the maiestie of a soueraigne prince.

The people in a Popular estate easily moued vnto pitie.

But now if it bee so hard for a prince in this case not to erre and bee deceiued, then how much more hard is it in a Popular estate, where the people suffer themselues to bee deceiued and led away with faire words, as a man may see almost in all the accusations made both in Athens and Rome, when the people giue sentence; where the innocent were condemned, and the guiltie acquited: of examples whereof all the histories are full. As *Seruius Galba* a great oratour, accused, attainted, and condemned of treason befor the people of Rome; not hauing any more to say for himselfe, but turning his speech and action, wholly framed to the mouing of pitie; and so embracing his children, and with teares commending them vnto the people, so moued the beholders, as that he easily obtained pardon, and so escaped. Whereupon *Cato* the elder, who had accused him, said That had not *Galba* abused his children and his teares, hee had beene well whipt. Whereas other noble and valiant men, who could

neither

OF A COMMONWEALE.

A neither abuse their prayers nor teares, but bearing themselues vpon their integritie, if but some lying oratour, or false enformer, had accused them, they were most vniustly condemned. And so oftentimes in like manner not oratours, but flatterers: and that not openly, but secretly, doe with diuers deceits circumuent the prince. And therefore the nobilitie of Polonia, by force wrested a priuilege from *Lewes* king of Polonia and Hungarie: That if question were of any of their liues and honours, they should not bee iudged but by the king himselfe: foreseeing, that so they might easily escape the iudgement of the king, but not the judges, who are bound vnto the stricktnesse of the lawes. And hereupon it is come to passe, that none of the nobilitie are euer there condemned to death, what offence soeuer they doe, but alwayes
B escape either by fine, or at worst, by beeing kept in prison for the space of a yeare and sixe weekes, which is now there passed into the force and strength of a law, and yet is there obserued and kept; as I haue learned of *Zamosche* the Polonian ambassadour.

But suppose the prince to bee such an one as is not easily to bee moued vnto pitie or compassion, yet then is it to bee feared, least hee in iudgement fall into crueltie. For whereas to keepe the meane is to euerie man a right hard thing, so vnto princes it is of all others most difficult, who easily suffer themselues to be carried into the one extremitie or other. If hee bee a good prince and an embracer of vertue, hee will haue
C wicked men in extreme horror & detestation, wherwith euen the wisest men are moued with a iust anger, and so oftentimes carried away with a cholerike passion. There need no better example than that of *Augustus* the emperour, who was accounted to bee one of the most wise and vertuous princes that euer was, and at his first sitting in iudgement endured as it were the paine of the condemned: and suffered not lesse (as saith *Seneca*) than did they themselues which were executed. And yet neuerthelesse this vertuous prince by continuall custome of iudging and condemning such as were conuict before him (as most necessarie it was) became too much rigorous and cruell, suffering himselfe to bee transported with passion and indignation against the wicked: in such sort, that one day sitting in iudgement, and condemning many the accused to di-
D uers punishments: his friend *Mecenas* beeing not able for the preasse to come neere him, cast a little billet of paper into his bosome, wherein hee called him an Executioner or Hangman: whereat *Augustus* suddenly staied, and finding himselfe transported with choler, and so to bee too hastie in iudgement, to stay his anger forthwith brake vp the court. And for this cause our fathers haue right wisely ordayned, That the Criminall Chamber of Parliaments should from three monethes to three monethes still bee chaunged (which for this cause is called *Tournelle*: for that all the judges of the other Chambers iudged euerie one of them by turnes, to the intent that the common custome to condemne and put men to death, should not chaunge the naturall mildnesse of the judges, and make them cruell and hard harted. Besides that it is
E a verie hard, and almost impossible thing (as saith *Theophrastus*) that a good and honest man, should not enter into choller, seeing the most detestable enormities of the wicked, and so sometimes to become as a man euen furious, and as it were out of his wits. So *Claudius* the emperour hearing one day the plaintife rehearse the great and manifold villanies of one accused, fell into such an outrage, that taking vp a knife which lay before him, hee threw it into the accused mans face, euen in full iudgement. But if the prince which intermedleth himselfe with iudgement bee by nature cruell, he shall then make a butcherie of his court; as did the emperour *Caligula*, who by one onely sentence, for diuers crimes condemned fiftie persons, euen vnto the same kind of death, and often tooke pleasure to cut off the heads of many goood men, some-

A most hard thing for a soueraigne prince sitting himselfe in iudgement, to keepe a meane betwixt too much lenitie and seueritie.

The most strange & extreame crueltie of Caligula the emperour.

time

time to proue his owne strength, and sometime to proue but the edge of his Cimitar. If therefore it bee so hard euen for the most wise, to keepe the meane betwixt mildnesse and rigour, which is necessarie for judges, it is not so easily to bee found in princes, who are most commonly extreame in their actions: for the waywardnesse of a priuat man, is indignation in a prince; and the anger of a subiect, is called furie in a king.

The best and surest meanes for the maintenance of a prince in his estate, is by all good meanes to procure the loue of his subiects: and how the same is to be obtained.

But let vs proceed farther, and suppose, that the prince haue the grauitie, the knowledge, the wisedome, the discretion, the experience, the patience, and all other the vertues requisit in a good judge: yet so it is, that he cannot be without daunger, if he shall in person iudge his subiects. For the best and fairest rule for the maintenance of the state of a Monarchy, is, that the prince, if it may be, cause himselfe to be beloued of al, without the disdaine or hatred of any. Wherunto to attaine, he hath two means, the one by appointing due punishment to be inflicted vpon the euill, & the other by giuing deserued rewards vnto the good. And for that the one of them is fauorable, & the other odious, it behoueth the prince that would be loued, to reserue vnto himselfe the bestowing of rewards; which are, estates, honors, offices, benifices, pentions, priuileges, prerogatiues, immunities, exemptions, restitutions, and other graces and fauours, which euery well aduised prince ought himselfe to graunt: but as for condemnations, fines, confiscations, and other punishments, he is not himselfe to meddle with them, but to commit them vnto his most vpright and wise magistrats, for them to doe good and speedie iustice therein. In which doing, they which receiue the benefits, shall haue good cause to loue, respect, and reuerence the prince their benefactor: and those which are condemned, shall yet haue no occasion at all to hate him, but shall still discharge their choller vpon the magistrats and judges. For why, the prince doing good to euery one, and euill to none, shall be beloued of all, and hated of none: which euen nature hath figured out vnto vs in the king of Bees, who neuer hath sting, least he should hurt any. And albeit that the sacred Scriptures teach vs, all plagues, diseases, calamities, and other worldly chaunces to depend of the wrath of God; yet in this all diuines (which more exactly entreat of diuine matters) wholly agree, none of all these things to bee done by almightie God, as by an efficient cause; but by permission onely, and to bee from him diuided, but as from a not letting cause: which cause the manner of the Hebrew phrase euerie where signifieth by the word *Hiphil*, ordinarily vsed, when it speaketh of the vengeance of God. We read also in the Poets (though somewhat otherwise) that *Iupiter* had three kinds of lightning, which they called *Manubias Albas, Rubras, Atras*. The first is white, which serueth for aduertisement, but hurteth no man, as proceeding onely from *Iupiter*, and his friendly aspect vnto the Sunne: For which cause *Seneca* saith, *Id solum fulmen placabile est, quod mittit Iupiter*, That onely lightning (saith hee) is peaceable which *Iupiter* sendeth. The other is red, and proceedeth from the aspect of *Iupiter* vnto the inferiour planets, whome they call the inferiour gods, which hurteth and blasteth fruits and beasts, but killeth no man. The third is blacke, and made by the aspect of *Iupiter* vnto the high planets and the fixe starres (which they call the high gods) which killeth, ouerthroweth and destroieth whatsoeuer it lighteth vpon. For the Theologie of the auntients belonged vnto the Bishops, the Philosophers, and the Poets, as *Marcus Varro* witnesseth in the one and twentieth booke of worldly things: wherein they all agreed, That the great God, which they thought to be *Iupiter* (to speake properly and according to the truth) could not be himselfe angrie, neither hurt nor condemne any man, but all things to be done by meane causes, and the ministerie and power of angels. And therefore the auntient Ægyptians deriued a law euen from

Prometheus

I1 *For* divided *read* derived (cf. L). Note at K2.

Of A Commonvveale. 513

A *Prometheus* their law giuer, whereby their kings were not onely forbidden to kill any man, but euen so much as to behold any execution done; least by such looking on, some print of crueltie should remaine in them the beholders. And this vnto mee seemeth a great secret of this our kingdome, and a thing of great force for the gaining of the subiects loue and good will towards the prince; all rewards, gifts, honours, offices, charges, and commaunds, comming still from the king: but penalties, and punishments alwaies adiudged and inflicted by the magistrats. For at such time as *William Poyet* (my countrey man) Chauncellor of Fraunce was accused of treason, and by the enuy of his most gratious enemies circumuented, the king who had receiued the wrong would not himselfe be iudge in the cause, neither so much as be present at the triall; yea when the
B pattie accused had refused all the judges of Paris, it was the kings pleasure, that two judges, men of great integritie, and free from all corruption, should be called and chosen out of euery court of parliament in Fraunce to try him: Whereby may be vnderstood with what an obseruation of law and iustice this kingdome standeth, when as almost at the same time *Thomas Moore* Chauncellor of England, and *Hierome Moron* Chancellor of Milan, both of them accused of treason, had for their judges, one of them euen the verie conspirators themselues, guiltie of the same treason against the prince, and the other his great enemies.

But here haply some man may say, the honour of noble personages to require, that when question is of their liues, their honour, or whole estate, the king himselfe should
C take vpon him the hearing of the matter. For when the duke of Alencon (*Charles* the seuenth his nie kinsman) was accused of treason, the court of parliament answered the king, That hee could not be tryed but in the presence of the king, and of the peeres of Fraunce, without being lawfull for them to appoint their substitutes. In like case vppon councell asked by *Lewes* the eleuenth, when question was for the triall of *Renate* of Aniou king of Sicilie, the court gaue the same aunswere, *viz.* That it could not so much as giue an interlocutorie decree against a peere of Fraunce, when question was of his honour, except the king himselfe were there present. I say for all that, that this was not for the king to iudge. For why, it is to be proued, that the king in auntient time was not in person himselfe assistant in the iudgement of treason, although it were in the
D triall of the princes, or of the peeres; as is to be found in the records of the court, a protestation the third of March 1386, made by the duke of Burgundie, as chiefe peere of Fraunce, against king *Charles* the sixt, wherein is contained, That the king ought not to be assistant at the iudgement of the king of Nauarre, arraigned of treason; and that so to be, appertained not but onely to the peeres of Fraunce, saying, The like protestation to haue beene made against king *Charles* the fift, to the intent hee should not bee present at the triall of the duke of Brittaine: and in case hee would needs passe on farther, and breake the custome of their auncestors, the peeres of Fraunce demaunded in full parliament, That an act of that their protestation might be vnto them decreed, and so afterwards it was enioyned vnto the clarke by a decree of the court, to deliuer vnto
E the peeres, and to the kings Attourney generall an act of such their protestation. So also when question was for the triall of the marquesse of Salusse, vnder the raigne of *Francis* the first, it was by liuely reasons and by the authoritie of the lawes both of God and man maintained, That the French king could not in that iudgement be assistant, seeing it concerned the confiscation of the marquisat: and albeit that the kings Attourney generall vrging the matter, the king was at the iudgement present, yet gaue hee not sentence, whereby the marquesse was himselfe condemned, and his goods most iustly confiscat, yet that iudgement for al that seemeth vnto many but extorted, and the other princes rested therewith much discontented. So also *Alexander* the Great would neuer

[margin: Not lawfull for the French king to be in person assistant in the triall of a prince or peere accused of treason.]

take

A 1 Prometheus   Note at B 8.

The king ought not to be judge, where he is himselfe a partie, as in matters concerning his owne interest.

take vpon him the person of a judge, neither thought it meet to bee assistant in the iudgement giuen against *Philotas*, *Calisthenes*, and others which conspired against his person, least he should so seeme to haue terrified the judges, or to haue taken from them the free power of iudging: as we read in *Quintus Curtius*. For if it bee contrarie vnto the law of nature, that the partie should be judge also; & That the king is a partie in all causes which concerne either the publike or his owne proper patrimonie in particular, in which case he cannot be a judge; by a much stronger reason ought the same to take place in the offence of treason, and especially in the chiefe point, where question is, the partie accused to haue attempted the honour or life of his prince. And for this cause *Lewes* the ninth would not pronounce sentence at the iudgement of *Peter Mauclere* duke of Britaine, albeit that hee was there present when the iudgement was giuen; neither likewise at the iudgement of *Thomas* earle of Flaunders. Neither yet *Philip* the Long the French king, in the cause of *Robert* earle of Flaunders attainted of treason. Yea that more is, the decrees or sentences are giuen in the name of the peers, and not in the name of the king, albeit that he were himselfe there present: as is to bee seene in the sentence giuen against *Robert* earle of Flaunders, which beginneth thus, *Nos pares Franciæ ad requestam & mandatum regis venimus in suam curiam Parisijs & tenuimus curiam cum xij alijs personis, &c.* Wee the peeres of Fraunce at the request and commaundement of the king came into his court at Paris, and with twelue other persons held court. The sentence also against *Peter Mauclere*, whereby the fee of the countie of Britaine was taken from him, is giuen by one archbishop, two bishops, eight earles, *Mathew Montmorancie* the vicount of Beaumont, and *Iohn* of Soissons, conceiued in these words, *Notum facimus quod nos coram clarissimo domino nostro Ludouico rege Franciæ iudicauimus, &c.* We make it knowne, that we before our most noble lord *Lewes* king of Fraunce haue iudged, &c. By which words it appeareth that the king, albeit that he was present, yet gaue not sentence, no not euen in trials concerning soueraigntie. So also we may see in the case of the succession of *Alphonsus* countie of Poitiers, although there were but question of the demaine, the king yet neuerthelesse gaue not therein his opinion or iudgement. Neither in like sort did king *Francis*, howbeit that he was present at the iudgement of *Charles* of Burbon the constable attainted of treason. And that more is, when question was of the fealtie and homage which the counties of Champagne ought to doe vnto the king, it was iudged by the peeres of Fraunce, and many earles, the king then present, not to iudge, but to assist them: the forme of which sentence is yet found in these words conceiued, *Iudicatum est a paribus regni, videlicet a Rhemensi Archiepiscopo, & Lingonensi, Guillielmo Catalaunensi, Ph. Beluacensi, Stephano Nouiomensi episcopis, & Odone duce Burgundiæ, & alijs episcopis, & baronibus, &c. Nobis audientibus & iudicium approbantibus &c.* Now if the prince ought to doubt to iudge the causes of his subiects, where it concerneth but their particular, and wherein he himselfe can haue no interest, to the end not to giue occasion of discontentment to them whome he should condemne, whether it were right or wrong, but ought still to maintaine himselfe in the loue and vnitie of his owne people, as in a most stately and strong tower: then how much more ought he so to doe, when hee is himselfe a partie, or the causes capitall, as for rebellion or treason? I remember, that in the triall of *Charles* duke of Burbon, one *Valier* examined in the tower of Loches, by the president *de Selua*, and the bishop of Puy, and other the conspiratours examined at Tarrare by *Iohn Brinon* president of Roan, deposed, That the occasion which caused the duke to rebell, was the aunswere that king *Francis* made vnto the articles which the duke had sent vnto the court of parliament, concerning the suit he had against the king and the regent, concerning certaine lands and demaines which the duke claimed as belonging

---

G8 personis, &c.   H2 Montmorancie, [and] the vicount   H3 *For* clarissimo (Fr 7) *read* charissimo (Fr 3–6, 8) *or* carissimo (Fr 1–2 and L), *and hence for* most noble *read* dearest (H4).   I3 to assist them *i.e.* to be present with them (cf. Fr)   Note at I4.

OF A COMMONWEALE. 515

longing vnto himselfe. Wherein had not the king in any sort medled, but left it all together vnto his judges and attourneies, he had not giuen occasion to so great a subiect to haue brought both the king himselfe, and the whole realme, into such a daungerous an estate as it was in short time after. For what good iustice soeuer the prince do, alwaies he that shall bee condemned will thinke that hee hath wrong done him.

Now to say as some men do obiect and say, That if the prince in person himselfe should take vpon him the administration of iustice, men should haue a good and quicke dispatch of their suits; and that such numbers of appeales, such exceptions and petitions, with other long delaies of iustice, should be so quite cut off; deserueth not so much as aunswere. For who is he which knoweth not at what great charge he must bee, how many circumstances and delayes, how many windings and turnings, how many repulses and griefes he must endure that hath any suit in court? Neither is it to be thought, Iudgements to be so much the better, by how much they are the shorter. For albeit that *Thucidides* (the most famous of them that were of his time, of the councel of the Areopagi in Athens) seemeth to haue beene in the same opinion that some others were, *viz.* That offences once committed, were forthwith to be punished; yet I verily suppose the opinion of *Plutarch*, yea of the Hebrewes themselues to bee the truer: for these thinke it necessarie for him that will iudge aright, to vse delaies in publike iudgements. But he in that little booke which he wrot of the slow vengeance of God, plainly teacheth men to be warned by almightie God, if they will be the true imitators of his iustice, to proceed but slowly and by little and little in the triall of capitall causes, whether it be that the truth of the matter may the better appeare, or for the drawing of some profit from the offendors before their death, or to draw them to repentance, or for their more griuous punishment (for that the punishment is the greater the longer that it hangeth ouer ones head) or the better or more iustly to iudge of another mans life, being withall in question. For right hard it is for a judge pressed with choller and desire of reuenge, hasted by some, and thrust forward by others, to doe good iustice, what knowledge or feare soeuer hee haue to iudge amisse: and what shall then the prince doe, who hath neither the one nor the other? The iudgements of the inferiour magistrats are corrected by the superiour, by way of appeale: but if the prince himselfe shall take vpon him to iudge, who shall reforme his decrees? For he that in the former iudgement hath not sufficiently declared his matter vnto the judge, or by ouersight let some thing passe; if yet he may appeale, all may wel be amended: but if the prince himselfe shall once giue iudgement, the gate is then after sentence shut vp, and no place left for appeale, or how to amend the errour. Which we say to restraine a prince from intermedling with iudgements, except he be a man of great wisedome, or vse therein the assistance of his wise and learned councellors; and the causes such as may seeme worthy the princes hearing and iudgement: following therein the councell of *Iethro*, who seeing *Moyses* troubled from morning to night in doing iustice to all men, and in all causes, You kill your selfe (said he) with taking so much paine; chuse mee out of the wisest and most discreet men of the people to ease your selfe vpon; and if there be any thing high or difficult to iudge, it sufficeth that you take vpon you the hearing thereof, leauing the rest vnto the other magistrats and judges to heare and determine. Which counsell of his father in law *Moyses* followed. So likewise wee read, that *Romulus* hauing committed vnto the Senat and the magistrats, the ordinarie administration of iustice, reserued vnto himselfe onely the hearing of matters of greatest importance. And albeit that the Roman emperours afterwards would haue their iudgements to extend something farther, yet was the emperours iurisdiction for the hearing of matters still shut vp and included within certaine bounds: which for all that the princes flatterers, or else

A vaine obiection for the shortning of suits, if the prince himselfe in person take vpon him the administration of iustice.

The quicker iustice not alwayes the better.

Causes worthy & well beseeming the princes hearing & deciding.

Note at B2.

else the princes themselues oft times went beyond, sitting in iudgement sometimes euen of light and ordinarie matters: so as did *Claudius* the emperour, (the most sottish lout that euer was) who yet would alwayes be iudging and deciding of causes and controuersies: of whome *Tranquillus* thus writeth, *Alium negantem rem cognitionis sed ordinary iuris esse, subito causam apud se agere coegit,* He compelled (saith he) another man denying the matter to belong vnto the emperours hearing, but to be onely an ordinarie matter, and so to belong to the ordinarie iurisdiction, hee compelled him (I say) euen forthwith and without more adoo, to plead the cause before him, but that so foolishly, as that the lawyers openly mocked him, therefore insomuch that one of them was so bold with him as to say vnto him in Greeke, which yet most of the standers by vnderstood, καὶ σὺ γέρων τί καὶ μωρὸς, *An old man, and a foole too*. And another tript him going out of the iudgement seat, and so gaue him a fall: yea his folly at last proceeded so farre, as that the verie pages and lackies would play with his nose as hee slept, and spot his face with inke. And into this case the prince must needs fall, who void of wisedome, thinketh it a goodly matter in the presence of the people to determine great matters, and so to make himselfe to bee of all men contemned and laughed at: than which nothing can be more daungerous in a Monarchy. Wherefore the prince which will often sit in iudgement, be present in the Senat, or much show himselfe vnto the people, him I would haue equall in vnderstanding vnto *Salomon*, in wisedome to *Augustus*, and in modestie to *Aurelius*; or els but seldome to come abroad, and more seldome himselfe to administer iustice, and that so much the lesse in the presence of straungers, who still iudge such things as seeme not commendable in a prince, not onely in his mind, but euen in the euill feature of his bodie, or vncomelinesse of his attire: and such other small imperfections (which the subiects for the loue and reuerence which they beare vnto their naturall prince easily beare with all) to be euen right great vices or deformities. Which the straungers neuer excuse, but reporting the same to the worst, still augment them in straunge places, euen to the least of his lookes, countenances, behauiours and gestures. The fame of king *Agesilaus* had with the bruit thereof filled all the lesser Asia, Greece, and Affrike, whome yet when the king of Ægypt had seene lying vpon the ground in a medow, with a course Greeke cloke on his back, and himselfe but leane, little, and lame withall, he made of him no great account, but rather had him in contempt and derision. The like is reported in the memorie of our fathers, to haue happened vnto king *Lewes* the eleuenth, who being chosen arbitrator in a controuersie betwixt the kings of Nauarre and Castile, and going vnto the frontiers of his kingdome, the Spaniards at their arriuall mocked the French men and their king, Who seemed vnto them as a pilgrim come from Saint *Iames* of Compostella, with his great cap vpon his head, set all about with brouches, and his iacket of course cloath, without any maiestie at all, either in his countenance, or in his behauiour; and they of his traine all in like sort apparrelled: (For why, he could not abide to see any man in braue attire) whereas the king of Castile and his troupe beeing come, showed themselues in most sumptuous attire, with their horses in their rich caparisons: which shewed a certaine greatnesse in the Spaniard, insomuch as that it seemed the Frenchmen to haue bene but the Spaniards seruants, but that there was a great and strong armie of them not farre off in the field, in readinesse at all assaies: which the Spaniards discouering, yeeld vnto the French king such conditions as himselfe pleased. And yet the same king *Lewes* the eleuenth considering princes by the opinion of men to bee either prayse or disprayse worthy (who commonly are led away but with the exterior show) hearing that the ambassadours of Venice were come brauely apparrelled, and well accompanied, he caused himselfe to be also most magnificently in royall robes attired,

---

F9 mocked him therefore, insomuch   G10 Augustus   G10 Aurelius

OF A COMMONWEALE. 517

A tired, and so sitting in an high chaire of Estate, admitted the embassadours vnto his presence.

Wherefore with greater reason ought a prince, when as he commeth to an enter view with another strange prince (which he ought but most seldome to doe) to shew himselfe in such sort, as that there be nothing in his attire, and much lesse in his countenance or behauiour and speech to be discommended. And that is it for which *Philip Commes* speaking of the enterview of princes, sayth, That they ought to shun it so much as they may: for that their presence alwaies diminisheth their fame, and the opinion conceiued of their persons, causeth them to bee the lesse esteemed: a thing yet more to be feared towards the strangers than towards the subiects. *(That princes ought seldome to come to an enterview of their persons.)*

B Now that which I haue said, It not to be fit for soueraigntie, or for soueraigne princes to entermeddle with iudgements; ought yet more to be obserued in a popular estate, for the great difficulties in assembling of the people, and to cause them to vnderstand reason; and then after that they haue vnderstood it, to induce them well to iudge thereof, their iudgements being oft times peruerted by seditious declamations or factions: which was the greatest occasion of the ciuill warres amongst the Romans, vntill that *Sylla* the Dictator had remitted the hearing of all causes vnto the magistrats, excepting the offence of treason, and that in the highest degree. *(The people vnfit to iudge of matters.)*

C But yet besides the inconueniences by vs before noted, nothing hath euer bene more daungerous, or more ruinated Commonweales, than to translate the authoritie of the Senat or commaund of the magistrats, vnto the prince or the people. For that the lesse the power of the soueraigntie is (the true markes of maiestie thereunto still reserued) the more it is assured; as well said *Theopompus* king of Lacedemonia, who hauing encreased the power of the Senat, and appointed fiue Ephori in title of office, as Tribunes of the people: and being therefore by his wife reproued, for that in so doing hee had much diminished his owne power: So haue I also (said he) much more assured the same for the time to come. For hard it is for high and stately buildings long to stand, except they be vpholden and staid by most strong shores, and rest vpon most sure foundations; all which consisteth in the Senat or councell, & in the good duties of the magistrats. *(That the Senat or Magistrats are not to be depriued of their authoritie & power to haue the same giuen to the prince.)*

D In which thing the Venetians, as they haue done many things wisely, so haue they done in nothing more than in that, that they which haue the soueraigntie, intermedle not with iudgements onely, but not so much as with any other thing els, which may wel by the magistrats or the Senat be dispatched: Which haply hath bene one of the chiefe meanes wherby that state hath bene so long preserued, considering that there neither is, nor euer was any Comonweal, where they which haue the soueraigntie trouble themselues lesse with that which belongeth vnto the councel or the magistrats. The Great Councel of the nobilitie, or gentlemen, wherin the whole maiestie of that Commonweal resteth, is neuer assembled but for the creating of new magistrats, or enacting of lawes, all the rest of the affaires of the estate being to be dispatched by the Senat, and

E the councell of the Ten, and of the Seuen men; and matters of iurisdiction by the other magistrats. Which if it be a thing commendable, and well appointed in Aristocratike estates, with better reason ought it to take place in Popular estates, *where the moe heads there be, the lesse wit there is, and so the worse resolution also.* Neither like I of *Xenophon* that most famous mans opinion, who speaking of the Athenian Commonweale, saith, That the more popular that the lawes are, the better they maintaine a Democratie, or Popular estate, When as (saith hee) the people hath the hearing of all matters, and that all passeth by lot and voyce: which thing indeed doth vtterly ouerthrow all Popular Commonweales. As in Athens, when as by the persuasion of *Pericles*, the hearing and deciding of matters, and the mannaging of the state, was taken

Yy from

Notes at A1, D8.

518   THE FOVRTH BOOKE

The Popular Commonweale not to be the best maintained by the most Popular lawes. from the Senat or councell of the Areopagi, to be brought backe vnto the people; the citie destitute of wit, and without councell, fell first forthwith into great broyles, and not long after into vtter ruine & decay. But amongst the Swissers, where their Popular estates haue now flourished 260 yeares, and so yet continue and grow from good to better, still flourishing both in peace and warre: those their estates are preserued and vpholden by lawes of all other least popular, nothing being almost left vnto the people more than the chusing of their officers, the other rights of soueraigntie being but sparingly and within a certaine conuenient measure communicated vnto them. Neither was the Roman Commonweale euer fairer or farther from ciuill warres, than when (the maiestie of the people saued whole) all things were done by the Senat and the magistrats: which was from the first Carthaginensian warre, vnto the conquest of the kingdome of Macedon. But after that both the *Gracchies* by their most popular lawes had taken from the authoritie of the Senat and the power of the magistrats, as much as they possibly could, all to encrease the wealth and libertie of the people; there ensued thereof a most miserable change of that Commonweale: neither did the citie of Rome euer after cease from ciuill warres and sedition, vntill that immoderat libertie of the insolent people, was by the power of one oppressed and brought vnder, and they so brought into extreame miserie and seruitude. The same inconuenience or mischiefe befell the Megarensians, who from a Popular estate fell into a most miserable Tyrannicall gouernment (as saith *Plato*) for the vnbridled libertie and insolencie of the people, taking vpon them the hearing of all things, aboue the authoritie, iurisdiction, and power of the Senat, or of the other magistrats.

The best ordered Commonwealth But the best kind of Commonweale is that, wherein the soueraigne holdeth what concerneth his maiestie, the Senat maintaineth the authoritie thereof, the magistrats execute their power, and iustice hath her ordinarie course. Whereas otherwise if the prince or the people shall take vpon themselues the authoritie of the Senat, or the commaunds, offices, or iurisdictions of the magistrats; it is much to be feared, least that they destitute of all helpe, shall at the length be spoyled of their owne soueraigne maiestie also. And in mine opinion they shamefully erre, which thinke themselues to encrease the princes wealth and power, when they show vnto him his Clawes, giuing him to vnderstand, that his will his countenance, and his looke, ought to be as an edict, a decree, and a law; to the end that there should be none of his subiects which should presume to take vpon them the hearing or deciding of any matter, which might not bee againe *The foolish saying of Caligula.* by him reuersed and chaunged: so as did the tyrant *Caligula*, who would not that the lawyers should so much as giue their councell and opinions, when as he said, *Factum vt nihil respondeant nisi Eccum,* that is to say, That is he to whome it alone belongeth to giue his opinion; meaning by himselfe: but by the word *Eccum,* which is, Behold the man; alluding to the word *Æquum,* which is, That which is right and iust. But this opinion by little and little crept into princes minds, breeding in them an incredible desire of oppression and tyrannie.

CHAP.

Of A Commonweale. 519

Chap. VII.

¶ Whether a Prince in ciuill factions ought to ioyne himselfe to one of the parties, and whether a good subiect ought to be constrained to take part with the one or the other faction: with the meanes to remedie seditions.

Ow wee haue alreadie declared, What a Soueraigne Prince ought to be in the administration of iustice towards his subiects; and if he should take vpon him the person of a judge, when, and how, and in what sort of Commonweale he ought to doe it: let vs now also see out of the tearmes of iustice, when the subiects are diuided into factions and part-takings, and that the judges and magistrats are themselues parties also, Whether the Soueraigne Prince ought to ioyne himselfe to one of the parties; & whether the good subiect ought to be constrained to follow the one or the other partie, or not. And first let vs set downe this as a maxime, All factions and part-takings to be daungerous and pernitious in euerie sort of Commonweales, and that they ought, if it be possible, by all meanes to be preuented; or if that cannot be before they bee plotted, yet to search the meanes to heale them, or at leastwise to imploy all conuenient remedies to mittigat the disease. And albeit that of ciuil seditions and part-takings there sometime commeth great good, as some one or other good law, or some other good reformation, which had not bene if the sedition had not happened; yet it is not therefore to be said, that sedition is not daungerous, although that it by chaunce and casually draw after it some good: as in mans bodie a disease chauncing, is the cause that men vse letting of blood, and purgations, and so draw away the euill and corrupt humors: so seditions oftentimes are cause that the euill or wicked men are slaine, or driuen away and banished, to the end that the rest may liue in quiet; or that euill lawes and decrees be cancelled and repealed, to giue place vnto good, which had otherwise neuer beene receiued. For which if one shall say, That seditions, and ciuill warres, are good, hee might also say, that murders, parricides, adulteries, theft, and the subuersion of estates & Commonweales are also good. For why, there is no impietie so great, no villanie so detestable, whereof no profit may redound, either to all, or to some men in particular; yea the verie villanies of wicked men almightie God vseth to draw either to the punishment of the reprobat, or to the glorie of his name. Which yet to prayse, were as if we should commend diseases; as *Fauorinus* the Philosopher highly commended the feuer quartaine: which were but to confound the difference betwixt good and euill, the difference betwixt profit and disprofit, betwixt honour and dishonour, betwixt vice and vertue; and in briefe to confound fire and water, heauen and earth together. Wherefore as vices and diseases are daungerous both vnto the bodie and the soule; so seditions and ciuill warres are hurtfull and pernitious vnto all estates and Commonweales.

All factions and part-takings dangerous vnto Commonweales.

But it may be some man will say, That seditions and ciuill warres are good and profitable for Tyrannicall Monarchies, and for the maintaining of Tyrants in their Tyrannicall estates, they being alwayes enemies vnto their subiects, and such as cannot long continue, if the subiect be once at accord amongst themselues. But we haue before declared, the Tyrannicall Monarchy to be of all others the weakest, as that which is not but by cruelties and villanies nourished and maintained; and yet commonly wee see it to fall and take end by seditions and ciuill warres: so that if we looke into all tyrannies which haue bene destroyed and ouerthrowne, we shal find it most commonly to haue happened of factions and ciuill tumults. Yea euen the most craftie and subtill tyrants,

Seditions and factions dangerous euen for Tyrannicall gouernments

Yy ij   who

who by little and little put to death, now some, and then others, to fat themselues with the blood of their subiects, and to saue their owne vnluckie life, which they lead in continuall paine and languor, neuer escape the murdering hands of conspirators; who so much the more encrease, by how much moe the tyrant putteth of his subiects to death; others which are vnto them allied, being alwaies prest and readie to reuenge the death of their so nie kinsmen: and albeit that the tirant put to death all their kinsmen, friends, and allies, yet neuerthelesse they shall so stirre vp all the good subiects against themselues. And of the goods of the subiects for tyrants to enrich themselues, is to procure their owne ruine and decay: for it is impossible that spleene should fill it selfe, or that the ouergrowing of corrupt proud flesh should fatten it selfe, but that the other members must drie, and so the whole bodie shortly after perish and consume also. And therfore the Florentines in my iudgement had no reasonable cause, why secretly to maintaine the factions of the Pistoians, whome they had before subdued: for that they foresaw not, them whome they thought might so by their mutuall broiles and contentions be weakned, & so the more easily endure the Florentines their lords, by liberty and the vse of armes to grow more fierce and couragious, than if they had liued in peace and quiet, and with aboundance of delights lost their force and strength: besides that, they therewith lost so much of their owne force, by the losse of so many good subiects, one of them by another ruinated and ouerthrowne.

<small>An especiall benefit a Monarch hath aboue other Commonweales.</small>

Now if seditions and factions be dangerous vnto monarchies, then are they much more daungerous vnto Aristocraties and Popular estates: for that Monarches may maintayne their maiesty, and as neuters decide the quarrels of their subiects; or by ioyning themselues to one of the parties, to bring the other vnto reason, or els altogether to oppresse them: whereas the people diuided in a popular estate, hath no soueraigne ouer them; no more than the lords diuided in Aristocratie haue no man to comaund them: if it be not that the greater part of the people, or of the lords, be not of the faction, which so may commaund the rest. Now when I say faction, my meaning is not of an handfull of people, or some small number of subiects, but euen of a good part of them banded against an other, able to trouble the whole estate: but if they be but few in number, hee that hath the soueraignty in hand, ought at the first to represse them;

<small>Priuat factions how they are to be suppressed.</small>

which he may doe either by commaunding them to lay downe armes, or by referring the cause of their dissention and variance vnto indifferent judges: or if the matter bee such as may require his own declaration and pleasure, then to doe the same with good aduice, and the mature deliberation of his most wise magistrats and councellours, not in any wise suspected to fauour the one part more than the other: and this to the intent that the prince, or they which haue the soueraignty, should not themselues beare the enuy or discontentment of them which should so bee condemned. But if the faction be grown so farre, as that it cannot by way of iustice, or by orderly inducements be appeased, it then behooueth the soueraigne prince, or them that hold the soueraignty in an Aristocratie or popular estate, to vse their forces for the vtter extinguishing thereof, by the punishing of some few of the ring-leaders and chiefe men in the faction; that so the punishment may touch but some few, and yet the feare come vnto all of them. Neither ought the soueraigne prince to deferre the matter so long, vntill they bee growne so strong as that they be not any more to be resisted; or that the leaders of them being for feare of punishment become desperat, shall seeke to ouerthrow the whole estate of the commonweale. For there still are, and alwaies haue bene good and valiant men, which for the welfare of their countrey doubt not to aduenture their liues; although there be many, who to the contrary had rather their countrey should perish for them. Which kind of men (the very plagues of commonweales) are vpon the sudden to bee oppressed

Note at I9.

OF A COMMONWEALE. 521

A oppressed, lest happely the whole estate of the commonweale were oft times by some one or other of them to bee indaungered; yea, although such ciuill discord rise but for some priuate displeasure of theirs.

But all this which we haue yet said, is to be vnderstood but of factions which concerne not the estate; for if the faction be directly against the state, or the life of the soueraigne prince, there is then no question whether the prince should take a part, or show himselfe an open enemy vnto such seditious, which so professe themselues of all others the greatest enemy of their prince & commonweale: for otherwise, if when the state and welfare of the commonweale, or the prince his owne life is attempted, he shall sit still but as an idle beholder, he shall so inuite and annimate not the more desperate sort B of men onely, but euen very cowards to seeke after his life also. But yet a great difference there is to bee made in the manner of punishment of the offendors: for if the number of the conspirators against the state or his person be but few, he shall suffer the Magistrats to proceed against them by order of law, and as he seeth cause himselfe to moderate the heauinesse of the punishment; which the fewer the conspirators are, is so much the sooner to be inflicted, and before that moe bee discouered, to the end that by the punishment of some few, the good subiects may stil be kept within the compasse of their allegiance and dutie, and those which were euill enclined, so terrified from their euill intended purpose. Neither yet is too strait or strict enquirie to bee made to find C out all the conspirators, least by force of torture and torment, such things bee haply wrung out, as were indeed better vnknowne than knowne. And yet it is not to be dissembled or winked at, if the partie guiltie bee once discouered to haue conspired against the life of his soueraigne, or yet to haue but bene willing so to haue done. As it happened vnto a gentleman of Normandie, who confessing vnto a frier (his ghostly father) of a purpose that he had had to haue slaine *Francis* the first the French king, but yet not daring so to do, to haue repented him now of his so wicked and detestable a purpose, was therefore of the frier so much as in him lay pardoned; who yet neuerthelesse forthwith reuealed the same vnto the king, who causing the gentleman to bee apprehended, sent him vnto the parliament of Paris to be tryed, where he was as a traitor condemned to death. Howbeit, that (in mine opinion) the king in his greater wise- D dome might haue done better to haue pardoned him, for that it had repented him of that his wicked purpose (which the law for the hainousnesse of the fact doe so seuerely punish) & so was become the betraier & accuser of himself before he was by any other accused. And it may be that it had bin better to haue executed him without making of the king acquainted therewith, so to haue disburdened him of the enuy of such a iudgment. So as did the emperour *Augustus* with *Q. Gallus*, who hauing not onely purposed, but euen desperatly also attempted to haue slaine him; and being therefore by the Senate condemned of treason, was yet by the same emperour *Augustus* (dissembling the matter as if he had thereof knowne nothing) pardoned, and so sent away vnE to his brother then gouernour in one of the prouinces: but was yet neuertheleffe vpon the way slaine, not without the secret commaundement of *Augustus* himselfe, as many men supposed, vsing therein the like subtilty: a craft that had his vncle *Caesar* before vsed, in giuing pardon to *M. Marcellus* at the request of the Senate; who yet was immediatly after slaine, as one of *Caesar* his most mortall enemies. Yet more likely it is, neyther *Caesar* (who in a certayne naturall clemency exceeded almost all other princes) neyther *Augustus* (placed in so high a seat of honour and maiestie) to haue beene willing to haue defiled or stained their so great honour & dignity with the secret murder of them whom they might most iustly haue executed. Howbeit that some of the finer sort to the contrary excuse the matter, as by them done for the safty of their owne

Yy iiij liues

Factions and conspiracies against the prince or estate, how they are to be repressed and the conspirators punished.

That in a conspiracie it is not good to make too strait enquiry to find out all the conspirators.

E2 the like subtilty & craft that (cf. L)   Note at C10.

liues; and yet so by this meanes still to maintaine the great opinion which they had before caused men to conceiue of their clemency and mercy. But if the conspirators be in number many, and that they be not all discouered, the wise prince ought to beware how he putteth to torture those that be condemned, albeit that he might euen with a becke without danger kill them all: for that for one that he should put to death, there would arise vp an hundred of their allies & friends, who it may be, haue power enough, or at least wise neuer fayle of will enough to reuenge the death of them which were of their bloud; and in case all this were not so, yet ought the prince alwayes to shunne the note and blame of cruelty, as well of his subiects as of strangers: wherein *Nero* was greatly deceiued, who hauing discouered the conspiracy against his person and estate, would needs by torture & torment know all them that were partakers therein: wherin he found so great a number of them that were, what by right, and what by wrong accused, as that the cóspirators indeed seeing themselues condemned, discharged their choller vpon the tyrants most faithfull and loyall friends: all whom hee caused most cruelly to be slayne; which was afterwards the cause of the open and generall rebellion of the captaynes and gouernours of the prouinces against him. And for this cause *Alexander* the great hauing put to death *Parmenio*, *Philotas*, and the rest which had conspired his death, by a new decree or law abrogated the auncient law of the Macedonians, whereby fiue of them that were the nearest of kinne vnto the conspirators were still to be put to death. But the best and surest way to auoyd the farther daunger of a conspiracy already preuented, is for a prince to dissemble the matter, as if he knew not the conspirators, as *Tacitus* well sayed, *Optimum remedium insidiarum, est si non intelligatur*, The best remedie of a conspiracie is not to seeme to vnderstand thereof. So when *Hanno* generall of the Carthaginensians, had purposed to haue slaine all the Senators, and chiefe men of the citie, vnder the colour of the marriage of his daughter; the Senat vnderstanding of the matter, but dissembling the same, forthwith caused an edict or law to be published, concerning the charges to be made at feasts: wherein the number of the guests, & the charges of the feast (which was not great) was most straitly appointed. By which decree of the Senat, the conspiracie intended, was without any tumult or bloodshed at all quietly suppressed. So in like manner *Eteocles* captaine of the Lacedemonians, with a strong garrison of souldiors holding the island of Chio against the Atheniensians, and vnderstanding that the garrison souldiours secretly conspiring together, had determined to kill the inhabitants their friends and allies, in whose aid they were come, and so to take vnto themselues the possession of the iland; and that the signall of the conspiratours was, for euery one of them to carrie in their hands a cane, or reed: hee (I say) vnderstanding of the matter, and accompanied with certaine of his most assured friends, & so walking about the citie, slew the first that he met withall carrying of a reed, and so suddenly gaue it out, That hee would kill all the rest that so carried reeds in their hands, and yet withall tooke order with the inhabitants of the island, that the souldiers were paid their pay: and so by the death of one onely souldiour the conspiracie was quenched before the fire could bee well kindled: and the occasion of the conspiracie so taken away, and all againe well quieted. Wherefore euerie gouernour and magistrat ought to take care, not so much to take away seditions alreadie growne, as to preuent them: For that a sedition once set on fire, is like a sparke suddenly blowne, which with the rage of the people, which setteth all the citie on a light fire before it can be againe quenched. Wherein the princes commaunds are not to be expected, who commonly know least of such things as touch them neerest. Yea oftentimes it happeneth princes wel to vnderstand the secrets, writings, doings, and sayings of other forren princes, and yet perceiue not the fire kindled at home in their own realmes,

---

H3 *For* intelligatur (Fr 7) *read* intelligantur (Fr 1–6, 8 and L).   H10 *For* Eteocles (L) *read* Eteonicus (Fr).   K5 suddenly blowne with the rage (cf. L)

OF A COMMONWEALE. 523

A realmes, in their own pallaces, yea euen in their owne bed chambers. The conspiracy of *Pelopidas* for the surprising of the castle Cadmea, and the expulsing of the Lacedemonians out of Thebes, was knowne in Athens, before that any thing thereof was discouered in Thebes, as the euent shewed. For why, but euen a little before that *Archias* the captaine of the castle was together with the garrison souldiors therein slaine, he was by letters from the bishop of Athens warned to looke to himselfe: which letters because he would not at supper read, he vsed the common prouerb; *In crastinum negotia*, To morrow will serue for our businesse. Who knoweth not the emperour *Charles* the fift to haue bene either partaker, or priuie almost to all things that were any where done by other princes, yet did he not so much as once suspect the conspiracie which

B * duke *Maurice* and *Albertus* marquesse of Brandeburg his familiar and domesticall friends, had euen fast by him contriued against him: yea and had also effected the same before he could feele or perceiue the smoke thereof. But what need forren examples? the conspiracie of *Amboise*, which set all Fraunce on fire, was diuulged in Germanie, England, and Italy, before it was once suspected by them against whome it was contriued in Fraunce: vnto whom the cardinall *Granuellan* is reported by his letters to haue first discouered the same, and yet there were aboue ten thousand persons which had therein a part. Whereby it is plaine, such conspiracies as wherein the force and power of many is to be required, to haue alwayes had most difficult and daungerous euents: for that they can neither by a few be effected, neither yet by many be concealed. Yea

C oft times it chaunceth the conspirators most secret designes to bee euen by women first reuealed. As it happened to *Philotas*, who discouering the conspiracie against *Alexander* the Great vnto a courtisan whom he loued, was together with his complices to his destruction by her bewrayed. So *Fuluia* vnderstanding of *Cateline* his conspiracie by one of his souldiors, reuealed the same vnto the Consull *Cicero*. And in our time the secret designes of the Prior of Campania (generall of the French gallies) for the sudden surprising and rifling of the citie of Venice by a souldiour reuealed vnto a courtisan, was forthwith by her discouered and made knowne vnto the Senat. Yet for all that an hard matter it is for a prince, be he neuer so wise or subtill, to preserue himselfe from the daunger of a resolute man that hath sworne his death: for that as the secret, &

D the execution thereof is but against one man onely, so is it but in one man alone enclosed, willing and resolued to sacrifice his life (how deere vnto him soeuer) to haue another mans, howbeit that he were beset round with an armie. Such an one as *Scaeuola* is reported to haue bene; who of the euent gaue first name vnto his house and familie, for that he of his owne accord had thrust his right hand into a burning fire, so to bee burnt of, for that he mistaking the man, had slaine the kings lieutenant in stead of the king himselfe. With no lesse boldnesse (or valour should I say) did a seruant of *Lazarus* the Despot of Seruia kill *Amurath* the king of the Turkes, in the middest of his legions of men, so to reuenge the death of his lord, and the dishonour done vnto the queene his wife. So *Pausanias* also in the sight of the whole armie slew *Philip* king of

E Macedon, *Alexander* the Great his father. And *Peter Aloisius* also duke of Placence, was in his owne castle by two murderers stabbed and slaine euen in the sight of his guard. And he that slew the emperour *Domitian* went to seeke him out euen into his cabinet with his arme in a scarfe: in such sort as did *Aod* kill *Eglon* king of the Moabites. And if *Cosmus Medices* duke of Florence (hauing ceized vpon the estate) had not alwaies gone armed, neither could his great guards, nether yet his strong castles haue kept him from the hands of most desperat men, who oftentimes found meanes to enter euen into his most close and secret places, to haue slain him an hundred times, what death soeuer they should therefore haue died. Yea amongst the rest of many

Yy iiij most

Princes oftentimes better to vnderstand of the conspiracies against other princes, than of such as are against themselues at home contriued.

* 1552.

Conspiracies hard to be concealed, being oft times euen by women reuealed.

The most daungerous conspiracie that can be against the person of a prince, and the hardest to bee auoyded.

A4 (margin) other mail (cf. Fr and L)   B7 above ten thousand (Fr) six thousand (L)   E6 armed *i.e.* clad in armor or Note at D8.

most desperat murtherers, there was one, who euen in the councell chamber strucke him with his dagger, thinking so to haue stabbed him (his guard standing round about him) not knowing him as then to haue had a priuie coat vpon him. And yet well hee knew that his life lay thereon, and so indeed was presently cast headlong out at a window downe to the ground.

But forasmuch as we haue before touched certaine meanes which may preserue a prince from falling into these daungers, and whereby to hinder the conspiracies which might be made against his person: Let vs now see how he ought to beare and behaue himselfe in conspiracies and factions, which are not directly against himselfe nor his estate, but amongst his great lords among themselues, or among the estates, townes, or prouinces subiect vnto him; all which he ought by all meanes to preuent, and not to neglect any thing how little soeuer it be for the meeting therewith. For as the great stormes and tempests are caused of most light and insensible exhalations and vapours: euen so seditions and ciuill warres the destructions of cities and Commonweales, are most times begun for most smal matters, and such as a man would not thinke that euen they should worke such effect. In the raigne of *Iustinian* the emperour all the cities of the Greeke empire were diuided into factions, for the maintaining of the colours of Greene & Blew, which they according to their fancies tooke vnto them in their sports and iusts, one of them brauing and contending with another: which in the end tooke such force and went so farre, as that the judges and magistrats of Constantinople, going about to punish the seditious, were letted so to doe by others of the same faction who tooke part with them, and so tooke out of the hands of the officers and executioners such as were by them led to the place of execution, and not so contented brake open the prisons also, and let loose all the prisoners, and in the same rage burnt the temple of Saint *Sophia*: and to auoid the punishment which they (hauing laid downe armes) were not to hope for, made choyce of one *Hippatius* the captaine and ring-leader of their faction, for emperour; *Iustinian* with his familie in the meane time lurking in a corner. Which tumult proceeded so farre, as that thirtie thousand men were in one day in that quarrel slaine: and had not he the leader of the faction (and he euen the new chosen emperour) there beene killed, the emperour *Iustinian* had vndoubtedly had much to do to haue saued his life; who yet at the beginning together with his other courtiers tooke great sport and pleasure therein. The like whereof happened at Syracusa also, where two of the magistrats become riuals, and so falling out for their loue, at the first gaue occasion for other men to laugh at them, but at length so diuided the whole Commonweale into two such factions, which so banded the one the other, as that the most couragious of the nobilitie being slaine, the people taking vp armes and driuing out them that were left of the nobilitie or better sort, tooke vpon it the soueraigntie, and so changed the Aristocratie into a Democratie or Popular estate. Wherefore it behoueth a prince, before the fire of sedition and ciuill warres by such sparkes be enflamed, to cast on cold water, or else quite to quench the same: that is to say, to proceed to the preuenting thereof, either by sweet speeches and persuasions, or els by open force. So as did *Alexander* the Great, who seeing *Ephestion* and *Craterus* his greatest friends, vpon a mutuall emulation to be at discord and varience amongst themselues, and so to draw the rest of his valiant captaines into parts taking with them: hee at the first with faire words, and gentle persuasions sought to make them friends together, but afterwards taking them apart, sharply rebuked them both, threatning withall to band himselfe against him which soeuer of them should first by word or deed offend the other: by which sharp reprehension putting them both in feare, made them friends together. And so our king *Lewes*, he who for his deuotion towards God, for his loue towards

Of small sparkes oft times do arise the great flames and fiers of sedition.

That the quarrels of great men ought euen in the beginning to be wisely appeased, or by force of the prince suppressed.

G 5 *For* that even *read* that ever (*jamais* in Fr).   H 6 Hippatius *i.e.* Hypatius (Fr and L)

towards his neighbours, for his charitie towards particular men, and vpright dealing towards al, is numbred amongst the Saints; vnto his great praise vsed the matter, as that all the time of his raigne there was neuer difference or contentions betwixt any the princes, which he for his integritie and wisedome himselfe in most friendly and peaceable manner quieted not. Yet of all things this is in a prince most to bee taken heed of, That in ending the differences and quarrels of the nobilitie or princes, he seeme not to be led or moued with the loue or hatred of any of them, one more than another. Wherin *Archidamus* king of the Lacedemonians, wisely prouided for himselfe, who seeing two great men his most deere friends at oddes betwixt themselues, brought them both into the temple, and there demaunded of them whome they would make choyce of to be arbitrator of the difference betwixt them? who both answering, That they would make choyce of none other but of *Archidamus* himselfe: Sweare then vnto me (said he) that you shall both abide mine award, and doe as I shall enioyne you: which they both doing, he straitly enioyned them both, Neuer to depart out of that same church, vntill they had reconciled themselues one of them vnto another, and so became sworne friends. Whereby he wisely without any offence or displeasure vnto himselfe (by giuing of iudgement betwixt them) made them friends, and so with thanks enioyed the fruit of their friendship and good agreement, than which nothing ought to be more deerer or more pretious vnto a prince: for that no fortresses are vnto princes more assured, no castles stronger, than is the loue and fidelitie of their subiects towards them. But here I speake of a good prince, and not of a tyrant which taketh pleasure to see the great men still ruinated one of them by another; neither aimeth at any other marke, but how to flesh the great ones one of them vpon another. Howbeit that it oftentimes falleth out, that the dogges falling vnto agreement among themselues, fall all vpon the wolfe: so as did the factions of the Colonnois and the Vrsins, who hauing discouered that pope *Alexander* the sixt set them still at discord and variance among themselues, so by their calamities and falles to encrease the strength and power of his bastard sonne *Borgia*; they fell to agreement among themselues, and so made head against him their common enemie.

A wise part of Archidamus in making of two great enemies friends.

The craft of tyrants in setting other men together by the eares, sometime daungerous vnto themselues.

Sometime also a tyrant seeing the nobilitie in the State to flourish with the strength and alliance of friends, and the fauour of the people, and not to seeke one of them anothers ruine, neither to haue any equall aduersaries to oppose themselues against them; doth yet secretly affoord fauour vnto some of the meaner or weaker sort, and so armeth them against the richer and stronger, and by some notable and irremissable villanie by them committed against the other, bindeth them vnto him, in such sort, as that they can neuer be reconciled againe vnto the parties by them so offended. So as *Iohn Bentiuole* the tyrant of Bononia is reported to haue done: who fearing the good agreement of them of the greater sort, easily suffered the chiefest of the house and familie of the *Marischots* (then the richest and a man of greatest credit in all that countrey) to bee of his enemies slaine, to the end that hee might so bee dispatched of him, and supported of them of the contrarie faction: all reconciliation being by that so great an outrage broken off, and all hope of mutuall friendship vtterly cut asunder: all which his tyrannicall slights and deceits, together with the fauour of the French king, yet helped him not, but that at length he was thrust out of his estate, and so by violence pluckt headlong euen out of the chiefest strength of his tyranny. But as the bond and obligation of a notable villanie is of all others the strongest, so is it also in euery Commonweale most of all to be feared, for that thereby all the hope of amitie and concord is cut off towards them which haue receiued the iniurie. As it happened to the armie of Carthage, which for want of pay reuolting against the seigneurie or state, vnder the conduct

The obligation of wicked and desperat men grounded vppon some notable villanie, in all Commonweales most daungerous, and how to be suppressed.

duct of two or three of their mutinous captaines, ceized vpon diuers strong townes & places which they rifled and ransackt: which captaines and ringleaders fearing to bee by the souldiours at one time or other betrayed and deliuered, persuaded the rest of the chiefe principall men amongst them, to kill the ambassadours of the seigneurie, and to hang vp *Hasdrubal* the Generall with the rest of the Carthaginensians which were fallen into their hands, to the end that hauing bound them by such cruelties, they should now haue no hope at al to saue their liues by composition. In which case there was no other meane for the Seigneurie to vse, but euen plaine force, so vtterly to root them out which could not otherwise be healed: as was afterwards that armie of the Carthaginensians, being by a long and cruell war at length defeated. For why, they had directly banded themselues against the seigneurie: in which case we haue said the prince must of necessitie become a partie, and show himselfe a most sharpe enemie vnto the rebellious.

How a soueraign prince is to end the quarrels and controuersies that are betwixt the nobilitie.

But if discord and contention be amongst the princes and great men themselues, & that vnder the same soueraigne prince, which yet he cannot either by his princely authoritie, neither by faire persuasion, nor hope of rewards, appease; he ought then to giue them arbitrators, men of great integritie and wisdome, and such as they themselues can like of. In which doing the soueraigne prince shall discharge himselfe of the heauinesse of the iudgement to be giuen, and of the hatred and displeasure of him or them that should be condemned. For if this manner of proceeding is and alwayes hath beene commendable for the ending of controuersies euen betwixt kings themselues, by committing their differences vnto the arbitrement of princes; and that all nations vse this manner and fashion: with how much more reason ought a wise prince (as of right hee may) cause his owne subiects to condescend thereunto, and especially them which are neere vnto him in alliance or blood, to the end that their quarrels and contentions should neuer (if it were possible) so farre passe the bounds of reason, as to come to bee tried by the sword or force of armes.

Dangerous for a prince not to shew himselfe indifferent in the quarrels and controuersies of his great subiects.

But in ending such controuersies, the prince aboue all things must beware that hee show not himselfe more affected vnto the one part than to the other: which hath bene the cause of the ruine and ouerthrow of many princes and estates. So *Philip* the first king of Macedon was not slaine, but for that he openly fauoured *Antipater* against *Pausanias* a meane gentleman, in denying of him iustice; which was the cause that *Pausianas* discharged his choler euen vpon the person of the king himselfe. Neither for any other cause did *Henrie* the sixt, king of England, stirre vp that long and deadly ciuill warre, wherewith all England was in combustion eight and twentie yeares, and wherein were lost about fourescore princes of the royall blood (as *Philip Comines* reporteth) but for that the king tooke vpon him to be captaine of them of the faction of the house of Lancaster, against them of the faction and house of Yorke: who at length hauing vanquished and ouercome their enemies, put to death the king himselfe in prison, with all the rest of his neerest kinsmen. The conspiracie also of the marquesse of Pescata, against *Charles* the emperour, was grounded vpon the fauour that the emperour bare vnto the viceroy of Naples, against the marquesse. It were but lost time to set downe in writing the cruell & bloodie warres which haue bene raised in this realme by *Robert* of Arthois, *Lewes* of Eureux king of Nauarre, *Iohn Montford*, *Iohn* of Burgundie, and diuers others of our time, which it is not needfull to rehearse, and all for the fauours of the kings, who forgetting the high degree of maiestie whereunto they were mounted, would basely take vpon them the offices of aduocats, of judges, and arbitrators; so descending from the highest vnto the lowest places, so to follow the passions of their subiects, making themselues companions vnto some of them, and vnto other some of them enemies.

But

I2 Pausanias

OF A COMMONWEALE.   527

But some will haply say, That by this meanes the king shall know newes, and keepe the parties also in awe: whereunto I also well agree, that a young king might so doe amongst his ladies and gentlewomen, to take pleasure & knowledge of news enough, but not amongst his princes and other his great lords. Now if any man shall further obiect and say, Princes to be oftentimes, yea and that against their will enforced so to doe, and to take a part, when as he which thinketh himselfe wronged, vpon an obstinat mind will not by any reason, persuasion, iudgement, or arbitrement, suffer himselfe to be ouerruled or persuaded. In which case I say, that necessitie hath no law: and yet that the prince before hee may come to that point of extremitie, as to vse his force, ought to proue all the meanes that he possibly may, for the composing of the matter in controuersie, and making of those his great subiects friends: which if it may not be, then by force and strong hand to ouerrule that which he could not otherwise doe: For that it cannot be, that he which shall be so froward or presumptuous as not to hearken vnto reason, nor his friends persuasion, can haue many to take his part, or to stand fast by him in that his so great and obstinat wilfulnesse.

When, and how a soueraigne prince is to vse his force for the appeasing of the controuersies and quarrels betwixt his great subiects

Yet might some man say, That the occasion of the quarrell may be so secret, as that no proofe can thereof be made, neither any iudgement giuen, and yet that hee which hath so receiued the iniurie, demaundeth thereof an amends: in which case the princes find themselues oftentimes much troubled, as when an iniurie or offence is vnto any man secretly offered or done, which he which did it denieth, and that the trueth cannot therein be tried but onely by bare surmises & coniectures; in this case what is amongst the common and vulgar sort to bee done? it is an easie thing to say, as that no man ought without most manifest witnesses to be condemned: but souldiours, and such as stand vpon their nobilitie, deeme their honour to be stained, and their reputation greatly impaired, except he haue satisfaction, who vpon his oath affirmeth himselfe to haue so bene by any man secretly wronged. For why, such men say, the subiects liues and goods to be all in the princes hand and power to be disposed of, but not their honour and reputation. In which case the people of the North haue for the tryall of the matter appointed combats; as is to be seene in the auntient lawes of the Lombards, of the Saliens, the Ripuaries, the English, the Burgundions, the Danes the Almaines, and the Normans; who in their customes call the Combat, *The law of appearance*: which many for all that haue as a most beastly thing reiected, as neuer receiued or practised by the Assyrians, the Ægyptians, the Persians, the Greekes, or Latines, except in lawfull warre, one man against his enemie, and that by the good leaue of the Generall of the armie; or else sometime one Generall encountering hand to hand with another, for the sparing of their subiects blood: so *Cossus* and *Marcellus* in battell hand to hand ouercame their enemies kings? Or els one king against another king, as did *Romulus* with the king of the Latines, and *Hundig* king of the Saxons, with *Roe* king of Denmarke. So also *Charles* king of Naples chalenged *Peter* king of Arragon vnto the combat, for the triall of their right vnto that kingdome, which they yet performed not. Neither is this any meane matter, when as *Corbis* and *Orsua* contending for the principalitie before *Scipio Affricanus* the Romane Generall, said, That they would haue none other judge, either of God or man, to decide their quarrell, but *Mars* onely. And yet for all that it is better to appoint combats amongst subiects, according to the auntient and lawfull manner of our aunceftors, when the persons are of like qualitie which so stand vpon their honour, and that there is some apparant coniecture of the wrong receiued (for why the auntient lawes neuer admitted combat in a plaine and euident matter, or wherein good proofe was to be had) for that to deny combat vnto noble personages standing vpon their honour, and at so great oddes as that they can by no other

The beginning of combats.

Combats when to be admitted.

B6 Yet might   C2 to bee done, it is   D3 the Persians, THE HEBREWS, the Greekes (This list is in Fr only.)   D7 kings: or els   E1 *For* meane matter *read* newe matter (cf. L).   E8 unto noble Note at B5.

528   THE FOVRTH BOOKE

other means be appeased, were but to nourish the fire of ciuill war euen in the entrails of the Commonweale, which after it is once kindled, enflameth the whole body thereof. For that two inconueniences propounded, wise men haue well taught vs, the greater ought stil to be of vs declined. Ioine hereunto also, that to change a custom which hath for many worlds of yeares bene found necessarie, is not onely an hard matter, but withall daungerous also. *Rotaris* king of the Lombards, had taken the law of Combats from amongst his subiects, but yet at their instant requests was enforced to restore the same againe into the former force; protesting withall, That it was but inhumane and naught, (as is in the lawes of the Lombards to be seene) but yet for all that necessarie to auoid greater inconueniences: For that the law of Combat being so taken away, moe good and innocent men were most cruelly and secretly slain and made away, than haply had bene, the daunger and eternall infamie of such hidden treacherie beeing still propounded to the offendors, to be tried by combat. So king *Lewes* the ninth, hauing the honour of God, and the welfare of his subiects before his eyes, was the first that forbad combats in this realme; which edect was thus, NOVS DEFENDONS BATAILLES PAR TOVT EN NOSTRE DOMAINE EN TOVTES QVERELLES, *We forbid Combats in all quarrels throughout our dominions*. And for that this edict was euill kept, *Philip* the Faire, king *Lewes* his nephew, caused the like also to bee published, whereby he vtterly forbad combats: who yet within two yeres after was at the instant request of his subiects constrayned to restore them againe, by reason of the secret murders and stabbings, yea euen of the most valiant men, who then were in euery place so slaine. *Philip* of France, surnamed the Hardie, duke of Burgundie, did not altogether forbid combats in Holland, but yet commanded them not to bee at all suffered, without the lawfull appointment of the magistrats: whereas before they were there open and common without iust cause euen to all sorts of men. But it was a thing most barbarous, that *Fronto* king of Denmarke in auntient time appointed all causes and quarrels to bee decided by combat, as the Saxon historiographer saith. Howbeit that the Russians and Hungarians otherwise vse it not, but when there is no euident proofe of the matter brought in question. But in our remembrance the prince of Melphe, the king his lieutenant in Piemont, found no remedie or meanes better, for the restrayning of the secret murders and mutinies which were ordinarie amongst his souldiors, than combat to be for them appointed, by the leaue and authoritie of the Generall; with condition, That the vanquished should not be spared, but still bee slaine by the victor, and his bodie throwne into the riuer: For which such combats hee appointed a publike place betwixt two bridges, compassed round about with the riuer: so that the hope of flight or of aid taken away, and that they must either ouercome their enemie, or there shamefully die; the souldiors afterwards began to behaue themselues more modestly, and so liue the more quietly together.

But now, when as to haue the lie giuen one, was neither by the Romans thought to be a thing iniurious, neither that our aunceftors had allowed the combat for the lie giuen to another man; it began in our age to be a thing not only contumelious, but euen capitall also; and that especially in the time of *Francus* the first the French king, who in a great assembly of his greatest peers one day said, that he was not an honest man which could endure the lie giuen him. Which he said, hauing by his heraults at armes giuen the lie to *Charles* the fift, for some dishonorable speeches he had giuen of him. Which yet since with vs is growne as it were into a law, so that none of the nobilitie or martiall men, which will put vp the lie, is accounted of, as of a man of any worth or valour, but as of a base or vile fellow. Whereof haue risen great quarrels, brawles, and murders, amongst all sorts of subiects. Which to meet withall, *Henry* the second, who not without

Combats by diuers great princes forbidden, & for the auoiding of greater inconueniences by them againe allowed.

Of the lie giuen, what is to be thought.

G5 edict   Note at H7.

out much griefe with a great number of his nobilitie, had seene a matter ended by combat, by a perpetuall law forbad controuersies or quarrels to be afterwards so tried. And to the intent that no man, who had rashly receiued the lie, should incurre the note of infamie: *Charles* the ninth reuiuing the edict made by his father, for the forbidding of combats, ioyned thereunto moreouer, That he would take vnto himselfe the honour and reputation of such as found themselues grieued, for that they might not haue the combat for the lie offered them: and yet there was neuer in Fraunce so many murders seene, as when combats were so forbidden. For who should not bee well laughed at, which for the lie giuen him should appeale vnto the judges? And yet in the opinion of the nobilitie and martiall men, he shall seeme to incurre the most heauie note of infamie, which shall not by force of armes repell such a reproach or disgrace offered him. Neither can the frowardnesse (should I say) or vanitie of so foolish an opinion easily be out of mens minds remoued.

But whereas we before said, that the combat is for the auoiding of greater inconueniences to be borne withall, my meaning is not, that it should be by law allowed, but onely in case of necessitie graunted, and that by the princes expresse letters, after the hearing of the parties, and for the auoyding of murders and seditions, which might otherwise ensue. Whereby that inconuenience shall be auoyded, which otherwise without combat could not be prouided for, that kinsmen, neighbours, and friends, should for one mans wrong in a sort be enforced to take vp armes, and so to entertaine another mans quarrell: as oftentimes it chaunceth the force and furie of wicked men, to fall vpon the heads of good and worthy subiects. But that is in the hearing of the matter especially to be respected, that combat be not graunted for the triall of any but of capitall causes, and those also whereof no manifest proofe is to be had or found out: following therein also the auntient lawes, which will, That the vanquished should bee declared infamous, and so disgraded of all his estates and honours, condemned to some shamefull death, if he will not better die of the hand of the victor. Which seueritie of punishment, and feare of infamie, might stay many as well from entring into combats, as also from leading of a quarrellous and wicked life. For *Philip* the Faire hauing forbidden combats, thought it not good otherwise to restore them againe vnto the nobilitie, but vpon the cause before knowne vnto the magistrats, as it was by the old decree of the Senat prouided. As by another decree of the same Senat giuen in the controuersie betwixt the counties of Foix and Armagnac, it was said, That combats might not take place, when question was of ciuill right and law, which is yet the custome of them of Berne. And by the lawes of Naples also, it was ordained, That combats should not take place but in cases of treason, and of casuall murder: whereas before it was lawfull in any offence whatsoeuer to chalenge the combat of the aduersarie, theft onely except: which yet I see by the custome of them of latter time, not to haue beene without good cause lawfull. Howbeit that by the lawes of Spaine no iust cause of combat is allowed. And thus much concerning priuat and particular quarrels; with the meanes to appease the same.

How, and for what cause combats are to be granted.

But if quarrels and contentions arise betwixt whole families, or betwixt whole corporations and colledges of the same citie or Commonweale, and vpon such like causes as doe betwixt priuat men: combats in that case are not to haue place, but the parties so at oddes are by way of iustice to be kept in good peace; or otherwise by force & sharpe punishment to be inflicted vpon the offendors to be kept in awe; yet for all that in such sort, as that iustice should still haue place euen in armes in the execution doing: as it was in Rome, at such time as by a decree of the Senat it was appointed and set downe, That foure hundred innocent slaues should be all put to death; with which vn-

Combats not to be admitted for the quarrels and contentions betwixt families.

Zz usuall

D5 *For* Berne *read* Béarn. D8 *For* of them of latter time *read* of our ancestors (*majorum nostrorum* in L 1–4, misprinted *minorum nostrorum* in L 5). Note at E4.

THE FOVRTH BOOKE

Seditions arising for the execution of iustice, how they are to be preuented.

usuall manner of execution the common people all inraged was about to haue taken vp armes, if the emperor *Nero* had not for the keeping of them in, dispersed the souldiours of his guard into euery quarter of the citie, so to keepe all quiet, vntill that the execution was done. Whereof *Iustinian* the emperour hauing euen in like case failed, fell into the great and daungerous sedition (whereof we before spake) which vpon the sudden set all Constantinople almost vpon a light fire. As not long ago the two most famous cities of Paris and Antwerpe, were in great tumults and vproares, at such time as the people saued from execution certaine persons for their religion condemned to die: whereof the reuolt of the Low countries against the king begun. Neither is this any new matter, but knowne to haue happened in the glory of the Roman Commonweale: when as at such time as the Consull had commanded one *Volero* a factious fellow to haue the bastenado giuen him, (as the manner of punishing of such offendors was) the people by force tooke him out of the hands of iustice, euen as hee was to haue bene stripped, and made him Tribune to defend the popular libertie against the Senat and the Nobilitie, with whome the people were still at warre, if they had no enemies abroad. For which cause the Senat and Magistrats chiefe care, was to find out forren enemies to oppose against the people: or if they wanted such, by all meanes to forge new enemies and warres, as knowing them otherwise neuer to cease from seditions & ciuill broyles. For so soone as that the Carthaginensians had made peace with the Romans, after the first Punique warres, they forthwith entred into a great daungerous ciuill warre at home among themselues: which still happened vnto them at Rome, if they were neuer so little a while without warres. We see also, that they neuer shut vp the temple of *Ianus*, which was the signe of an vniuersall peace, but twice in seuen hundred yeares space.

Nothing more hurtfull vnto a warlike people than peace.

And if we marke the histories well, wee shall find nothing to haue bene more daungerous and hurtfull vnto a valiant and warlike people, than peace: For that men accustomed to warres, and still trayned vp in armes, seeke for nothing els but dissentions and broyles, neither hate any thing more than to be at rest and quiet. And that is it for which the histories report *Ca. Marius* to haue bene the best generall of his time in the warres abroad, but the worst and most troublesome man aliue at home and in time of peace: for that he well knew not what peace & quietnesse meant. Yet whether it be better in a Commonweale to traine the people vp in peace or warre wee will hereafter declare.

Seditions in a Popular Commonweale of all others most dangerous, and how to be appeased.

Now we haue in some sort touched certaine meanes for the preuenting of seditions and part-takings: but as it is much more easie to stay the enemie from entring, than to driue him out after he is once entred; so is it more easie also to preuent seditions and tumults, than to appease the same: and yet that more hardly also in a Popular estate or Commonweale, than in any other. For why, the prince in a Monarchy, and the lords in an Aristocratie still are, and ought to be, as soueraigne judges and arbitrators of the subiects: and so oft times of their absolute power and authoritie appease and quiet all their differences: wheras in the Popular gouernment the soueraigntie lieth in the people themselues, which are so diuided into factions, who in no other acknowledge the magistrats, but as men subiect vnto their commaund and power. Wherefore in such Commonweales such seditions and factions are with the greatest care and diligence that possible is, to be at the first preuented: but if they bee once risen before they were well foreseene, then it behoueth the most wise and vertuous men in the estate to take the matter in hand: who by their great wisedome and kind speeches may againe appease the turbulent motions of headstrong and giddie common people. For as they which are sicke of a phrensie, which causeth them to skip and daunce without ceasing, cannot be cured, except the cunning musitian tune his instrument vnto their mad manner

Of A Commonweale. 531

A ner and fashion, to draw them vnto his owne, and so to fall by little and little, vntill that they be so againe made more quiet and tractable: euen so ought also the wise magistrate seeing the people in a rage, at the first to accommodate and frame himselfe vnto their disordered appetite, that so he may afterwards by little and little induce them to hearken vnto reason: and so by yeelding at first vnto the tempest, at length put into the desired hauen. For to seeke by force to stay the rage of an angry and incensed multitude, is no other thing than as if a man should by maine strength seeke to stay the force and course of an headie streame, most violently falling from the high and steepe rockes.

B And as for them which goe about by force of armes and strong hand to stay the angrie peoples rage and furie, if they bee not verie strong and well assured of the victorie, they put the estate into great perill and danger: for if the subiect become victor, no doubt but that hee will at his pleasure prescribe lawes vnto the vanquished. And admit that the prince himselfe be not vanquished, yet so it is, that if he attaine not vnto the full of his designes, he shall in so doing make himselfe contemptible, giue occasion vnto his other subiects to rebell, for strangers to inuade him, and for all men to contemne him. Which is yet more to bee feared in popular estates, and was most manifestly knowne in the seditions which happened in Rome, wherein they which would needs proceed by force, and openly resist the desires of the people (vp in furie)

That the people vp in tumult or sedition, is not by strong hand or open force to be staied or appeased

C marred all: whereas to the contrarie, they which sought by faire meanes to win them, still brought them to reason, and so vpheld the state of the citie, otherwise readie to haue fallen. *Appius Claudius* seeing the people of Rome to demaund to haue had the obligations and bands for money lent, canceled, (wherein the richer sort and vsurers had a notable interest) was of opinion, not to haue any thing of the due debt remitted. And at another time the people being reuolted from the nobilitie, hee the same man would haue had them most rigorously entreated, without any regard to haue been had of them at all; for that the people otherwise would swell with pride, and become insupportable: howbeit, *Seruilius* at the first time, and *Menenius Agrippa* at the second, withstood him, and so carried away the matter from him. Which *Agrippa* shewed in

D deed, and by a most excellent fable of mans bodie and the parts thereof (which hee so liuely set before euery mans eyes, that he caused the armes to fall out of the hands of both parties, and so sweetly againe reconciled the people vnto the nobilitie: wherby he together with the welfare of the Commonweale, and all mens loue, gained also vnto himselfe immortall fame and glorie. And if so be that wild beasts will neuer by strokes be tamed, but by the kind handling of him that tameth them: euen so the people once moued or enraged, as a beast with many heads, and of all others the wildest and fiercest, is neuer by force, but by good and kind vsage and entreatie to be gained. Wherefore in such time of common vprore and tumult, something is to be graunted vnto the people: and if the sedition be raised for famine or for dearth of victuals, some

E present distribution is to be made, and reliefe giuen vnto the poorer sort, who are not with words to bee appeased. For that as *Cato* the Censor, speaking of the people of Rome, sayd, The hungrie bellie hath no eares. Neither in that case must the magistrats spare faire words or promises, yea more than is euer to be performed. For that the matter so standing, both *Plato* and *Xenophon* giue leaue vnto the magistrates to lie, as physitions to children and their sicke patients. So the wise *Pericles*, to draw the people of Athens vnto reason, fed them with feasts, with plaies, with comedies, with songs and daunces; and in time of dearth caused some distribution of corne or money to be made amongst them: and hauing by these meanes tamed this beast with many heads, one while by the eyes, another while by the eares, and sometimes by the bellie, hee

The hungry belly hath no eares.

The wisedome of Pericles to draw the common people of Athens to vnderstand reason.

then

Zz ij

A1 *For* so to fall *probably read* so to stall *i.e.* slow down, come to a standstill (cf. Fr). C3 bands *i.e.* bonds C10 thereof, which E3 (margin) hungry then caused wholesome edicts and lawes to bee published, declaring vnto them the graue and wise reasons thereof: which the people in mutinie, or an hungred, would neuer haue hearkened vnto.

How, and when the people is to be flattered.

Yet whereas we haue said, that the people is to be flattered, and to haue something graunted vnto it: yea sometimes euen things vnreasonable; especially in popular and Aristocraticke estates, that is to be vnderstood in time of extremitie, when as it is alreadie vp in sedition: and not for that one ought still to follow the appetite and passion of the insatiable people, and without reason: But euen to the contrarie, it is so to bee gouerned, as that it be not too hard curbed, neither yet left with the reines at too much libertie. For as it is a right slipperie high standing place to serue the appetite and pleasure of the vnsteady people, so is it yet much more daungerous also, openly to oppose a mans selfe against it: so as did *Appius, Coriolanus, Metellus, Cato* the younger, *Phocion*, and *Hermiodorus*, who whilest they would haue all things of the people by strong hand, and rather breake than bow, they did either vtterly vndoo themselues together with the Commonweale, or at leastwise brought it into most great perill and danger. True it is, that for the prince or magistrats thus to temper maiestie with clemency towards an vnruly and headstrong people, without iudgement and reason, is a most hard and difficult matter: yet is there nothing more necessarie, especially in Popular gouernments, than not too much to flatter, neither yet to deale too roughly with the people. But as the Sunne goeth, rising and setting with the other starres and planets, dayly carried about with the most swift motion of the superiour celestiall spheres, and yet for all that faileth not to performe his owne naturall course by retiring backe by little and little; and that by how much the higher he is mounted vp from the Horison, the lesser hee seemeth for to be: Euen so ought the wise gouernour to doe, following in part the affections and desires of the troubled people, so much the more easily afterwards to attaine vnto the full of his designes. And albeit that a prince had the power by force to represse and reforme a mutinous and rebellious people, yet ought he not so to doe, if otherwise he may appease them. For what Physitian is there so inconsiderat, as to vse sections, and cauterisings, or burnings, if the disease might otherwise be cured? And so what prince is there so euill aduised, as by way of force and fact to proceed against his people, if with a kind word speaking hee may appease all? But especially in a Popular estate, wherein it beseemeth the wise magistrat, by all faire means to appease and quiet the passions of a troubled people, in laying plaine before their eyes the euill successe which may ensue of their so euill and disordered proceedings. We read therof many examples, but yet none more famous than that of *Pacuuius Caluinus* of Capua, who being accounted a great fauourer of the comminaltie, and an vtter enemie vnto the nobilitie of that citie, yet vnderstanding of a purpose that the people had vpon the sudden to kill all the Senators of the citie, which so cruell a murder hee greatly detested, but yet seeing the common people so resolutely set downe vpon the matter, as that they were not to be remoued, he himselfe made show also, as if he had as well as any of the rest liked of that the peoples will and purpose, yet withall gaue the Senators to vnderstand of the great daunger they were in, and of the purpose he had for the safegard of their liues, willing them to bee of good cheere, and to feare nothing. And so afterwards the Tribune or chiefe leader of the mutinous people, hauing shut vp all the Senators into a strong place, as men appointed for the slaughter: but indeed so to preserue them from the present furie, hee then with a merrie and cheatefull countenance comming forth vnto the angrie people, spake vnto them thus, *That which you men of Capua haue oftentimes wished for, That it might once be in your power to be reuenged*

Force neuer to be vsed against the people, where faire meanes may preuaile.

The commendable deceit of Pacuuius, to deceiue the angry people.

F5 unreasonable *i.e.* inequitable, unjust (cf. Fr and L)   F8 of the insatiable people, and without reason *i.e.* "of the insatiable and irrational people" (cf. Fr)   G1 daungerous   G3 Hermodorus   I5 Calvinus (L 4–5) Calavinus (L 1–3 and Fr) *but properly* Calavius   I7 understanding   K4 the Tribune *i.e.* Pacuvius himself

A uenged of the most wicked and abhominable Senat; you now haue the same put into your hands, not by vprore and tumult, by assaulting and breaking open their houses one by one, which they keepe and defend with strong companies and guards of their seruants and friends, but euen at your pleasure, and without daunger. Receiue them all shut vp in the court, where I will giue you power to pronounce sentence of euery one of their liues. But before all things it behoueth you so to satisfie your anger, as yet to deeme your owne health and welfare better than the satisfying of your rage and wrath. For a Senat you will not altogether bee without: for that you must needs either haue a king, which is a thing to be abhorred; or els a Senat, the onely Councell of a free citie. Wherefore two things rest for you to doe, the one that you take out of the way the old Senat: and the other, that
B you chuse a new. And this said, hee sat downe; and so the Senatours names beeing all put into a pot, hee commaunded the first name that was drawne out to bee read, and him so named, to bee brought out of the court. Is it your pleasure then (said hee) that this man shall first die? Whereunto all the people cried alowd, That it was well said of him, and well done. *Well, I see then* (said *Pacuuius*) *what his doome is: let him bee cast out; and now for him an euill and wicked man, make you choyce of a good and vpright Senator to bee put into his place*. Whereupon they all at the first were silent, for lacke of a better to make choyce of: but as soone as one more impudent than the rest had named one, presently a greater crie was heard than before; some crying out, That they knew him not; otherssome exclaiming as fast against him as a
C naughtie base fellow, of some beggerly trade or other, and so vnworthy of the place: The like sturre there was, when choyce was to bee made of the second, and third Senator, the base artificers and trades-men still nominating some one, and some another: in such sort, as that they now began to fall out among themselues, about the choyce, none of them beeing willing to yeeld or giue place to other, which whilest they did in euerie Senator which was named, there was no lesse trouble and sturre among themselues, than was before betwixt them and the Senatours. Whereuppon they were better contented that the old Senatours should now still hold their places, than to suffer one of them to bee preferred before another. Wherein the councell of the Tribune was right wise, and cunnningly by him put in execution:
D who after hee had by his wise dissimulation somewhat appeased the mad peoples rage, hee as it were with his finger poynted out, and layed open euen vnto euerie mans eye, the great hurt and inconuenience that was to ensue, by putting the Senators to death: as that not onely such a shamefull murder should for euer bee accounted most cruell and inhumane; but that also by the dooing thereof the Commonweale should bee without councell, as a bodie without a soule; and the fire of sedition raised also amongst the people, about the preferment, and them that were to bee preferred.

But if the people once enraged be alreadie vp in armes, it is a most hard and daungerous matter to appease them: in so much as that not long agoe there was one that
E set fire on his owne house (least the Commonweale should with the flames of sedition euen then haue perished) so to turne the citisens then together by the eares to leaue the fray, and to come to helpe to quench the fire, for feare least all should haue beene burnt. Then if any man there bee in vertue and valour exceeding the rest, who will with good speech take vppon him to persuade the people vnto peace and concord, hee onely, or else none, is the man that may appease the peoples frantike furie and rage Which thing *Virgil* most excellently expressed in these few verses following,

The mutinous people best appeased by the good persuasion of some good old vertuous personage.

C10 cunningly   E7 Virgil . . . expressed *i.e.* in the *Aeneid*, I, 148-153

Ac veluti magno in populo cum sæpe coorta
Seditio est, sæuitq, animis ignobile vulgus;
Iamq, faces & saxa volant, furor arma ministrat:
Tum pietate grauem ac meritis si fortè virum quem
Conspexere, silent, arrectisq, auribus astant:
Ille regit dictis animos, & pectora mulcet.

And as a sudden tumult rais'd amidst a people great,
When as the base and rascall sort are in the greatest heat,
And firebrands now and stones do flie, such weapons as there lye,
Then if some good graue worthy sire they fortune to espie,
They silent with attentiue eare stand listning to his lore:
He with good words their minds doth rule, and calmes the whole vprore.

Such we said *Pericles* to haue bene in Athens, *Menenius Agrippa* in Rome, and not long agoe *Peter Loredan* in Venice, who at such time as the marriners and sea-faring men banded themselues against the rest of the citisens, and in such sort massacred one another, as that neither duke, neither the Senat, nor other magistrat could come nie, but that they were by force and violence of the furious people reiected; this plaine gentleman *Peter Loredan* (I say) a priuat citisen, and bearing no office at all, showing but himselfe in the middest of these combats, and holding but vp his hand on hie, caused the weapons to fall out of euery mans hand, for the reuerence they all bare vnto the vertue of so graue a personage; and so as it were in a moment appeased all that ciuill discord. Whereby it was to be seene, vertue to be of greater power and maiestie than armes, than lawes, yea than all the magistrats together.

Peter Loredan a most notable citisen.

There is also in the reuerend feare of religion a great power for the staying of the tumultuous people. For at such time as the Florentines were fallen out into such a furie among themselues, as that the citie swome with the blood and slaughter of the citisens: and that they could by no meanes be parted, *Francis Soderin* the bishop attired in his bishoplike attire, and attended vpon with a company of priests, and a crosse carried before him, came into the middest of the furious citisens, so bandying it one against another; at the sight and presence of whome, they all for the reuerend feare of religion vpon the sudden laid downe their weapons, and so without more adoo, got themselues home euery man vnto his owne house. So also *Iadus* the Iewes high Priest, in his *Pontificalibus* met *Alexander* the Great comming towards Hierusalem with his victorious armie, with whose port and maiestie *Alexander* terrified, worshipped the High Priest, and was so farre from ransacking either of the countrey or holy citie, as that he gaue it great priuileges, with whatsoeuer the High priest els requested. With like wisedome pope *Vrban* is reported to haue turned *Attila* king of the Hungarians from the siege of Aquilia.

The reuerend feare of religion a good meane for the appeasing of the seditious people.

But sometime such is the deadly hatred of citisens amongst themselues, as that they need of the helpe of their friends and allies, yea and sometimes euen of meere strangers to set them agreed. In which case an other good old man of Florence seeing the citisens without pity to kill and massacre one another, and on all sides to burne one anothers houses, went to request the Luquois their neighbours and friends, to interpose themselues for the appeasing of these so deadly broyles, as had well neere ruinated the whole estate: Wherewith the Luquois mooued, came in great numbers, by whose good trauell and mediation all those slaughters aud broyles were well stayed and quited: a thing both commendable and profitable, not to them onely which are so set a-
agreed,

Seditions sometimes appeased by the interposition and mediation of friends.

I5 Pontificalibus (cf. 123 A8) K1 that they K8 slaughters and K8–9 *For* quited *probably read* quieted. K9–535 A1 so set agreed

Of A Commonweale. 535

agreed, but euen to them also which were the workers therein, as reaping therby great honour, together with the loue of them whom they so made friends. Yea oftentimes it happeneth, that the citisens deuided into factions, weary at length of their murders and tumults, seeke but to find an occasion for them to fall to agreement; yet being of opinion it to touch them in honour, that should first seeke for peace, therefore continue their bloody quarrels vntill that they haue vtterly ruinated one another, if some third man interpose not himself betwixt them for the making of them friends: which thing oftner happeneth in popular or Aristocratike commonweales, than in a monarchie: wherein the subiects are by the power and authority of one onely prince still to bee set at one, & reconciled amongst themselues, together with the commonweale. How- be it, that sometime it happeneth the soueraigne prince to make himselfe a party, in stead of holding the place of a soueraigne Iudge: in which doing for all that he shall be no more but the head of one party, and so vndoubtedly put himselfe in daunger of his life, and that especially when such daungerous seditions and factions be not groun- ded vpon matters directly touching his estate, but otherwise, as it hath happened al- most in all Europe within this fifty yeares, in the warres made for matters of religion: for we haue seene the kingdome of Sweden, of Scotland, of Denmarke, of England, the Cantons of the Swissers, yea and the Germaine empire also, to haue changed their religion, the estate of euery of these monarchies and commonweales yet standing en- tire and whole: howbeit that the truth is, that it was not done, but with great violence, and much bloudshed in many places.

Nothing more daungerous vnto a prince than in seditions to make himselfe a partie.

But religion by common consent once receiued and setled, is not againe to be cal- led into question and dispute, that so all the wayes and entrances vnto sedition and fac- tion may be stopped, and the assurances of vnity and peace strengthened; for that all things called into disputation, are so also but as things probable called in doubt: and what can come neerer to impiety then by probable arguments to call in doubt the lawes of God, which are by their nature immutable and eternall; and such as of the truth whereof euery man ought to be most certainly resolued and assured Besides that, nothing is so firme and stable, nothing so manifest and cleare (except it rest vpon most playne and vndoubtfull demonstrations) which may not by disputation and force of arguments be obscured or made doubtfull; and especially where that which is called into question, or dispute, resteth not so much vpon demonstration or reason, as vppon the assurance of fayth and beleefe onely: which they which seeke by demonstrations and publishing of bookes to performe, they are not onely mad with reason, but wea- ken also the foundations and grounds of all sorts of religions.

It is daungerous to call that into question which ought to be hol- den as resolued vpon.

Religion once re- ceiued and setled, to be no more called into que- stion or doubt

There is a most antient law of *Licurgus* extant, which the Florentines (of all others the sharpest disputors) established in their popular estate, *viz. Ne de legibus semel reep- ctis ac probatis disserere liceret*, That it might not be lawfull to dispute or make question lawes once receiued and allowed. For why he of others the wisest, well vnderstood, lawes disputed and reasoned vpon to bee still doubted of; which doubting brought with it an opinion of the iniquity thereof; whereof must needs follow the contempt both of the lawes and magistrats, and so consequently the ruine and destruction of the whole commonweale. But if Philosophers and Mathematicians cannot abide to haue the principles of their sciences reasoned of, what great folly, or rather madnesse is it to dispute not onely priuatly, but euen openly also of religion alreadie approued Howbeit that *Anaxagoras* maintained the snow to be blacke, and *Fauorinus* the Quar- taine feuer to bee a very good and wholesome thing; and *Carneades* hauing one day highly commended iustice, the very next day preferred iniustice before it, and that it was (without all comparison) better to be a verie knaue than a vertuous honest man:

Z z iiij

which

which they all so persuasiuely did, as that they drew a great number of men to bee indeed of their opinions. Although *Aristotle* said them which made question, whether snow were white or not, to want sence: but them which doubted whether there were a God or not, not to be with arguments refuted, but by the lawes punished: howbeit that he himselfe by necessarie demonstration proued there to be one euerlasting God, and that there could be no moe gods but he. Wherfore, all the kings and princes both of Affricke and of the East, doe most straitly forbid all men to dispute of their religion. Which like strict prohibition is also set downe by the lawes and decrees of Spaine So also the king of Moscouie seeing his people, who had receiued the rites and ceremonies of the Greekes, diuided into diuers sects and factions, by reason of the diuers preachings and disputations of the ministers: hee thereupon forbad them vppon paine of death any more to preach or dispute of religion; and withall gaue a booke vnto the bishop and parish priests, wherein was contained what hee would haue euery man persuaded of, and to beleeue, concerning matters of faith and religion, which he commaunded them vpon all feastiuall dayes to reade and publish vnto the people: with a capitall paine thereunto annexed, if by any mans exposition any thing were at all thereunto either added or diminished. And *Moyses*, when hee had most curiously written all those things which he had learned and receiued from Almightie God, and declared the same vnto the people: yet in one chapter of the law (the people yet wandering vp and downe in the desart) he commaunded the priests and Leuits aloud and distinctly to reade the law, yea, and that dayly also, that so it might bee vnderstood and knowne vnto the people of euery age and sexe: and so in another chapter forbad any thing to be vnto the lawes of God either added or detracted. Yet sayth hee not, that they should dispute thereof: but euen to the contrarie, the Hebrewes instructed by the prophets from the father to the sonne: they teaching the law of God in seuen Colledges, which then were in mount Syon, neuer yet suffered men to enter into disputation thereof, as we read in *Optatus Mileuitanus*. For why, disputation was inuented but for things probable and doubtfull; and not for things religious and necessarie, and such as euery man is bound to beleeue: which by disputation are alwaies made doubtfull. Wherefore seeing that disputations of religion bring not only the doubt and ouerthrow of religions, but euen the ruine and destruction of Commonweales also; it behooueth them to be by most strait lawes forbidden: which after long ciuill war was by the estates and princes of the Germane empire prouided for, and a decree made, that the princes should with mutuall consent defend both the Romane and Saxon religion: whereunto that was also ioyned, That no man should vpon paine of death dispute of the religions. Which seuere punishments, after that the Germane magistrates had inflict d vpon diuers, all Germany was afterwards at good quiet & rest: no man daring more to dispute of matters of religion. Moreouer, seeing that not onely all wise law-giuers and Philosophers, but euen the very Atheists themselues also (as namely *Polybius* himselfe an Atheist) are of accord, That there is nothing which doth more vphold and maintaine the estates and Commonweals than religion: and that it is the principall foundation of the power and strength of monarchies and Seignories: as also for the execution of iustice, for the obedience of the subiects, the reuerence of the magistrats, for the feare of doing euill, and for the mutuall loue and amitie of euery one towards other, it is by most strait and seuere lawes to be prouided; that so sacred a thing as is religion be not by childish and sophisticall disputations, (and especially by such as are publickely had) made contemptible, or by probable arguments made doubtful, and so at length quite taken out of the minds, both of the hearers & of the disputors together. Neither are they to be heard which thinke themselues to be able with more subtill

rea-

Lib. 3.

Disputations of religion dangerous.

Lib. 6. De militari ac domestica Romanorum disciplina.

The power of religion.

G7 curiously *i.e.* carefully, exactly   K2 (margin) disciplina

OF A COMMONWEALE. 537

A reasons to persuade all things: for that as *Papinian* most wisely said, *Summa ratio est quæ pro religione facit*, It is of all the greatest reason, which tendeth to the maintainance of Religion.

I will not here in so great varietie of people so much differing among themselues in religion, take vpon me to determine which of them is the best (howbeit that there can be but one such, one truth, and one diuine law, by the mouth of God published) but if the prince well assured of the truth of his religion, would draw his subiects thereunto, diuided into sects and factions, hee must not therein (in mine opinion) vse force: (For that the minds of men the more they are forced, the more froward and stubborne they are; and the greater punishment that shall be inflicted vppon them, the lesse good is B to be done; the nature of man being commonly such as may of it selfe bee led to like of any thing, but neuer enforced so to doe) but rather it behoueth the prince so perswaded of the truth of his religion, without fainting or dissembling to professe and follow the same, still deuoutly seruing the almightie God. by which meanes he shall both turne the will and minds of his subiects vnto the admiration and imitation of himselfe, and at length also plucke vp euen the verie rootes of all sects and opinions: In which doing he shall not onely auoid commotions, troubles, and ciuill warres, but lead also his straying subiects vnto the port of health. Whereof as there are many examples, so is there none more fit for this our purpose, than that of *Theodosius* the elder, C who at the beginning of his raigne found all the prouinces of the empire full of Arrians, whose strength and power was so growne and encreased vnder three or foure Arrian emperours their fauourers, as that their doctrine was not onely by eight councels confirmed, which were at diuers times assembled at Tyre, at Sardis, at Sirme, at Milan, Seleucia, Nice, Tarsis, and especially at Ariminum (where six hundred bishops were of their opinion: and but three of name which held the contrarie) but that they also punished other their aduersaries of opinion contrarie vnto themselues, with confiscations, proscriptions, and other most grieuous punishments. Yet would not this good emperour now come vnto the empire, either force or punish the Arrians, although that hee deadly hated them, but graunted vnto them both the Arrians (I say) D and the Catholikes, their churches, and suffered them in euerie towne to haue two bishops, of either religion one: and albeit that hee at the importunat suit and instance of the Catholike bishops, commaunded certaine edicts to bee published against the Arrians, yet was hee well contented to haue the same holden in suspence, and not put into execution; as his letters vnto *Ambrose* in these words declare, *Trade Arrianus Basilicam, mei namque sunt omnia iuris*, Giue (saith hee) vnto the Arrians a church: for that all are in my power. Which thing *Rotaris* also king of the Lombards by his law permitted. And yet neuerthelesse this emperor liuing according to his religion, and instructing his children & kinsmen in the same, wonderfully diminished the Arian sect in Europe: howbeit that they haue euer since continued, and so yet do, both in Asia and E Affrike, vnder the law of *Mahomet*, grounded vpon the same foundation. The great emperour of the Turkes doth with as great deuotion as any prince in the world honour and obserue the religion by him receiued from his auncestours, and yet detesteth hee not the straunge religions of others; but to the contrarie permitteth euery man to liue according to his conscience: yea and that more is, neere vnto his pallace at Pera, suffereth foure diuers religions, *viz*. That of the Iewes, that of the Christians, that of the Grecians, and that of the Mahometanes: and besides that, sendeth almes vnto the Calogers or religious Monkes, dwelling vppon the mountaine Athos (being Christians) to pray for him: as did *Augustus* to the Iews, to whom he ordinarily sent

Religion not to be enforced.

How a prince wel assured of the truth of his religion is to draw his subiects thereunto, being therefore diuided into sects and factions

---

A7 (margin) religion A8 (margin) therunto A9 (margin) therfore B2 behoveth
B3 fainting *i.e.* feigning, deceiving (cf. Fr) Notes at A3, A5, B2, E5.

sent his almes and perpetuall sacrifices to Hierusalem, which hee commaunded to bee there dayly made for the health of himselfe, and of the Commonweale. For why the people of auntient time were persuaded, as were the Turks, All sorts of religions which proceed from a pure mind, to be acceptable vnto the gods. And albeit that the Romans easily admitted not straunge religions into their Commonwealeas (as in the warres against them of Veios the Ædiles had in charge, *Ne qui nisi Romani dij, neu quo alio more quam patrio Colerentur*, That no gods should be worshipped but the Roman gods, neither after any other manner than after the manner of the countrey) yet for all that did they easily suffer euery man priuately within the citie to vse his owne manner and fashion, and his owne religion: yea the Romans themselues receiued into the citie the sacrifices of *Isis* and of *Esculapius*, and suffered the Pantheon to be dedicated to all the gods. Only the Iewes of all people detested straunge ceremonies: whereby they prouoked the hatred of all people against them. For at such time as *Antiochus* the Noble besieged Hierusalem, the Iewes tooke truce with him for eight dayes, wherein they might keepe holy the Feast of their deliuerance out of Ægypt, dedicated vnto the honour of the immortall God: Whereunto *Antiochus* (as *Plutarch* writeth) willingly condescended; and yet not so contented, with great reioicing brought also bulles and rammes for the furnishing of the sacrifice euen vnto the gates of the citie. Howbeit that afterwards the time of the truce expired, he tooke the citie and sacked it. But as he was about therein to haue sacrificed after the manner of the Greekes, the Priests & Leuites cursing and banning, forsooke the Temple. For which cause *Antiochus* enforced them, as contemners of the gods, to receiue the Greeke ceremonies and sacrifices, yea and caused hogges also to be killed in the temple, and the Iewes to bee enforced to eat of them, tormenting such as refused so to do with all kind of torments and tortures, which in that citie wrought the change both of the religion and state. But *Ptolomeus Lagus* (as *Agatharchides* writeth) and after him *Pompeius*, after long siege hauing taken Hierusalem (the same day that the Iewes had before taken truce with *Antiochus*) yet both of them kept their hands from sacrilege: which *Crassus* did not, neither *Flaccus*: whome yet *Cicero* denieth to haue taken any gold belonging vnto the temple; in which oration, as serued for his purpose, hee said, The gods of the Iewes to haue deliuered their seruants from the bondage of the Romans. So that the Iewes detesting the gods of other nations, caused all other people and nations most grieuously to hate and contemne them: For at such time as *Quadratus* being President of Iudea, a common souldiour had in contempt showed his tayle vnto the Iewes, as they were sacrifising in the temple, such an vprore and tumult ensued thereof, as that twentie thousand of the Iewes were there slaine. At which time the Iewes by a decree of the Senat, were driuen also out of Rome: where *Tiberius* caused such as would not remoue thence, either to chaunge their religion, or to become slaues; but this was done in Rome onely. For the same *Tiberius* forbad *Pilat*, who had determined to haue placed certain shields and escutchions in the temple of the Iewes, to place the same, or to alter any thing of their religion. But *Alexander Seuerus* the emperor in his priuat sacrifices worshipped *Abraham, Orpheus, Hercules*, and *Christ*. But when the Christians as well as the Iewes, had begun to detest those thirtie thousand gods which *Pindarus* now in his time worshipped, and so began to breed a contempt of the gods in the minds of men, the princes and magistrats began likewise with most grieuous punishments to persecute them, except they would forsweare Christ and the Christian religion, the Iewes (bearing themselues vpon the antiquitie of their religion being become their accusers and enformers against them) least they should seeme partakers of the same impietie with them. And thus as the multitude of religion and sects was innumerable, some detesting

---

F5 Commonweale (as them, least K7–8 religion) being become their accusers and enformers against K9 religions and sects Notes at F2, F4.

OF A COMMONWEALE. 539

A detesting the rites and ceremonies of others: so thereof proceeded also the diuers and manifold chaunges of Commonweales. And albeit that tyrants had before exercised incredible cruelties vpon their subiects, yet neuer thought they it lawfull for them to rule ouer mens minds before the time of this *Antiochus*, whome wee but euen now spoke of. Which was the cause that *Theodoricus* king of the Gothes (though fauouring the Arrians) would not yet enforce the conscience of his subiects, nor haue them tormented for their religion; least vnder the pretence of impietie hee should haue seemed to haue taken the spoyle of their goods, or bind their minds, which could by no threats or commaunds be constrained or bound. For so he writing vnto the Senat at Rome, vseth these words, *Religionem imperare non possumus, quia nemo cogitur vt cre-*

B *dat inuitus*, Religion (saith he) we cannot commaund, for that no man is compelled against his will to beleeue: as we read in *Cassiodore*: Which reason of all others seemeth vnto me most effectuall, for the taking away of such punishments, as are vnder the colour of religion to be inflicted vpon the subiects. Wicked and straunge rites & ceremonies, and such other as the greater part of the subiects of greatest power detest, I thinke it good and profitable to haue them kept out of the Commonweale. For the preseruation of the subiects loue amongst themselues, which is especially nourished & maintained by their consent and agreement in matters of religion: yet if the same religion be liked of by the opinion of neighbour nations, and of many of the subiects, then ought it not onely with punishments not to be restrained, but also so much as may

C be prouided, that if it may not without sedition bee publikely professed, yet that no man be forbidden the priuat exercise of such his religion For otherwise it shall come to passe, that they which are destitute of the exercise of their religion, and withall distasted of the religion of the others, shall become altogether Atheists (as wee daily see) and so after that they haue once lost the feare of God, tread also vnder foot both the lawes and magistrats, and so inure themselues to all kinds of impieties and villanies, such as is impossible by mans lawes to be redressed. Howbeit what lettteth vs to follow the councell of the most holy prophets, of whom * the one persuaded his countrimen led away into captiuitie into Chaldea, That at such time as they should bee enforced to fall downe before the idols, yet that they should with a pure mind alwayes wor-

D ship the euer liuing God: & the *other admitted the request or excuse of *Naaman* the king of Syria his seruant, but newly instructed in the true religion and seruice of God, if he were present with the king his maister sacrificing vnto a straunge god, so that hee kept his mind pure and cleane from idolatrie. For they are much deceiued, which think Commonweales to be better kept in order by mens commands and lawes, than by the feare of God his iudgements. For as the greatest tyranny is nothing so miserable as an Anarchie, when as there is neither prince nor magistrat, none that obeieth, neither yet any that commaundeth, but that all men liue as they list at libertie in all looseneffe of life, without feare of punishment. So the greatest superstition that is, is not by much any thing so detestable as Atheisme. And truely they (in mine opinion) offend much,

E which thinke that the same punishment is to bee appointed for them that make many gods, and them that would haue none at all: or that the infinitie of gods admitted, the almightie and euerliuing God is thereby taken away. For that superstition how great soeuer it be, doth yet hold men in feare and awe, both of the laws and of the magistrats, as also in mutuall duties and offices one of them towards another: whereas meere Atheisme doth vtterly root out of mens minds all the feare of doing euill. Wherfore two inconueniences propounded, Superstition (I say) and Atheisme, we must still decline the greater: yet when we may not publikely vse the true religion, which still consisteth in the worshipping of one almightie and euerlasting God: least by contemning

of

No man to be compelled against his will to beleeue.

To forbid men the priuat exercise of their religion, is to make them oftentimes to become Atheists.

* *Baruch*

* *Helisæus*.

Atheisme worse than the greatest Superstition.

B6 Commonweale, for

of the religion which is publikely receiued, we should seeme to allure or stirre the subiects vnto impietie or sedition, it is better to come vnto the publike seruice, so that the mind still rest in the honour and reuerence of one almightie and euer liuing God.

Why many sects better agree in a Commonweale than two onely.

But now, whereas some men maruell how it came to passe, that in the time of *Theodosius*, considering the diuersitie of sects and of religions that then were, they could so stand without ciuill warres, being then at the least an hundred diuers sorts of them according to the account of *Tertullian* and *Epiphanius*: whereof the cause was, the multitude and varietie of such different opinions, which so still held one of them in counterpoise with another. Now in matters of sedition and tumult, nothing is more dangerous, than to haue the subiects diuided into two opinions or factions onely, whether it be before matters of estate, or of religion, or for the lawes and customes, or other matters whatsoeuer that the subiects are so diuided. For that but one thing can by nature be contrary vnto another thing: and moe things than one to be contrarie vnto one, is a thing not to be imagined. So that where there be moe than two sects or sorts, there must needs be some in the meane betwixt the two contrarie extreames, which may set them agreed, which otherwise of themselues would neuer fall to agreement. And therfore *Solon* by law prouided, That in ciuill seditions and troubles, euery man should of necessitie take either the one or other part, and that it should not bee lawfull for any man to stand as neuter: which vnto many seemed a thing vnreasonable, considering that the greatest prayse and commendation of a good subiect is; to bee a quiet ciuill man, desirous and doing the best that he can to liue in peace. Besides that, by this means the conscience of an honest man is forced, to take either the one or other part, when as haply he thinketh both naught, and that they are both in the wrong. And that more is, it may so happen, that if in such seditions he will follow that part which hee iudgeth the better, he must beare armes euen against his father, against his brethren, and friends, which are in armes in the other side: which were the way so to compell men to commit vnnaturall murders, and to kil euen them whom we ought to defend, & to depriue them of life, by whom we our selues liue. In briefe the law of God forbiddeth him that knoweth the truth, to follow the common opinion of them which are out of the way: whereunto *Solons* law seemeth to repugne, in forcing a man to take either the one part or the other, although that they be both naught. Howbeit that a man might say vnto the contrarie, this *Solons* law to be most profitable and necessarie also vnto Popular and Aristocratike estates, wherein is no soueraigne, which standing as neuter, may determine and decide the differences of them which shall so bee at discord and variance. For men well know, that the most craftie men in time of ciuill warres, withdraw themselues so much as possibly they can out of the preasse, if they be not well assured of the victorie of the part that they themselues take (if it bee not so, that they see the daunger such, as that the publike fire is like to take hold and burne euen their own priuat houses) yea oftentimes the more subtill and deceitfull sort set the rest at dissention and debate, that so they may themselues the better fish in troubled water, and make a bridge for themselues to passe ouer, to ceize vpon other mens goods and honors: imitating therin the priests of *Mars*, whome the auntients called πυροφόρους, or *Fire-bearers*, who hauing orderly performed their solemne execrations, cast fire brands betwixt both armies standing readie ranged, and so stirred them vp to battell: but yet retired themselues in safetie out of the medley and daunger. Now if the law of *Solon* might take place, these fire makers durst not sow debate and discord among the citisens, seeing that they must themselues then run into the same danger with others. And as for other honest men which loue peace, and like neither of the one nor other faction, if they must needs be constrained to take a part, they will then enforce themselues by all means to preuent seditions,

Whether Solons law for part-taking, as that euery man should be of necessitie bound to take either the one or the other part in time of sedition, be good and profitable vnto Commonweals or not

---

F6 at the least an hundred (Fr) about 120 (L)   G1 be for matters of estate   I7 themselues take,
AND NEVER ENDANGER EITHER THEIR LIVES OR THEIR GOODS FOR THE SAKE OF A FACTION (if it bee not

Of A Commonweale.

A seditions, and in what they may to withstand them: or if they cannot be foreseene, yet to do what they may to appease them. For why, the great vertue and authoritie of good subiects is of great force to keepe the rash and mad vulgar people in some order: and to persuade them being disquieted againe vnto reason, who would euer be at ods and variance, if they were not by the good councell of the wiser sort better persuaded. By which reasons *Solons* law seemeth to be vnto cities and Commonweales profitable. Besides that, if in the leagues and societies of princes among themselues, it be good and profitable for them all, some one of them to be of greater power than the rest, or at leastwise to ioyne himselfe with them that bee of greatest power: how much more true and profitable is it in ciuill warres still to take the one or the other part: where hee

B which standeth as neuter, as he is of no man protected, so lieth he open to the common spoyle of all men. For so *Theramenes*, who all the time of the Peloponesian war, and the troubles of the Athenians, had kept himselfe quiet, and stood still looking on, but as an idle beholder, without taking part either with the one or with the other, was himselfe at the last forsaken of all, and so left vnto the mercie of the tyrants, who made him a miserable spectacle vnto all men, and in the end most cruelly put him to death. Hee therefore which will stand as neuter, whether it be in ciuill warre, or in warres amongst straungers, ought at the least to doe his endeuour to set the rest agreed: or if hee shall see the quarrels, warres, and ruines of others, to tend to the profit of the better sort, or

C the assurance of his estate, his wealth or person (as it sometimes happeneth that tyrants and wicked subiects or citisens agree not but for to ruinat the good) yet ought he which so standeth as neuter, to show himselfe in appearance desirous and forward to set them agreed: which many men haue done euen then when they most nourished and maintained such quarrels in the most secret manner they could: *A thing which God* (as *Salomon* saith) *abhorreth*: if it be not in case (as I haue said) that the concord and agreement of the euill, tend to the ineuitable ruine and decay of the good. For as for one good vertue, there are many vices one of them quite contrarie vnto another; and that for one good man, there be ten which are nothing worth: so God hath also appointed, That the euill and wicked men should euen one of them by another be brought to ruine and destruction: *I will reuenge me* (saith God, speaking by the mouth of the pro-

D phet *Ieremie*) *of mine enemies, by mine enemies*. I haue said, that good princes and good subiects ought to dissemble the good and pleasure they take in the discord and contention of other the wicked princes or citisens; for that there is nothing which grieueth a man more, than to see others in all securitie, to take pleasure and reioyce in his ruine and decay.

Thus haue we seene certaine meanes for the appeasing of tumults and seditions amongst many. For which there might yet some more particulars bee also rehearsed; as to take away the vse of belles from rebellious or seditious citisens: so as wee read to haue bene done in the rebellions at Montpelier, and at Bourdeaux, which were yet af-

E terward vnto them againe not without a great fine restored: howbeit that the greater part of the inhabitants of Bourdeaux most instantly requested, That they might not be so restored, hauing felt the commoditie that came thereby. But whether well or euill, I leaue it to the resolution of euery man of sound iudgement. The great emperour of the Turkes, with the other princes of the East, haue taken strait order, That this inuention of belles, first deuised in Italie, should not into any of their dominions or territories be receiued: whereby they haue well auoided one of the greatest occasions of ciuill tumults and broyles. The noyse and backward ringing of the belles (as when houses be on fire) being not onely proper vnto straunge accidents, and to put the mutinous people into armes, but also to trouble euen the quiet spirits of peaceable men,

Aaa   and

The daungerous estate of them that stand as neuters in time of sedition.

Prouerb. 4.

The vse of belles, why in many countries forbidden.

Note at C4 (margin).

and to thrust fooles headlong into fury: as did he, who the more to sturre vp the people rung the Tocsaine, together with the great bell at Bourdeaux, and was therefore himselfe hanged in the belrope, as he had well deserued.

The best and surest way to preuent sedition.

Another and the most vsuall way to preuent sedition, is to take away the subiects armes: howbeit that the princes of Italy, & of the East cannot endure that they should at all haue armes; as doe the people of the North and of the West: no more then they did in auncient time in Greece and in Asia. For so *Aristotle* speaking of the Barbarians, accounteth it for a strange thing, that a man should in a quiet and peaceable citie weare a sword or a dagger in time of peace: which by our lawes, as also by the manners and customes of the Germaines and Englishmen is not onely lawfull; but by the lawes and decrees of the Swissers euen necessarily commaunded: the cause of an infinit number of murders, hee which weareth a sword, a dagger, or a pistoll, being more fierce and insolent to offer vnto others iniury, as also to commit murder if any iniurie be offered him: whereas if he were disarmed, he should doe neither the one nor the other; neither should yet incurre the infamy and disgrace which followeth them, who when they are wronged, dare not to draw their weapons. The Turkes herein go yet farther, not onely in punishing with all seuerity the seditious and mutinous people, but also by forbidding them to beare armes, yea euen in time of warre, except it bee when they are to giue battell: wheras otherwise if the enemie be not nie, they lay their armes vp in their tents, or in their carriages: and yet they are accounted the best soldiours of the world: which if they doe in the field, and in time of warre, what is it to be thought them to doe in their townes, and in time of peace?

The common wearing of weapons in a peaceable Commonweale, the occasion of many euils.

Amongst many the lawdable manners and customes of the policy of Paris, there is one a very good one, and well put in execution, which is, That no car-man or porter shall weare sword, dagger, knife, or any other offensiue weapon, and that for the murders by them committed in their ordinarie quarrels which they still had one of them against another which if it might take place vpon all persons: also a thousand murders and stabbings are committed, which should neuer haue happened, neither the seditions and broyles raysed, which haue vpon this occasion bene in many places kindled. For it is not the part of a wise politician, neither of a good gouernour, to expect vntill the murder be committed, or that the sedition be raysed, before he forbid the bearing of armes, but as a good phisition preuenteth diseases: and if chaunce be that the partie be sodainly attainted with any violent griefe, he first asswageth the present paine, and that done applyeth conuenient remedies vnto the causes of the disease: euen so the wise prince ought (so much as in him lyeth) to preuent sedition, as also when they are happened to appease them at what charge soeuer: and then afterward to looke into the cause of the diseases farthest off from the effects, and so thereunto to apply remedies conuenient.

Impunitie of offendors to draw after it ruine of estates.

Now we haue before spoken of the causes which worke the chaunge of estates and commonweales, of which selfe same causes proceed also seditions and ciuill warres, as of the denyall of iustice, of the oppresion of the common people, of the inequall distribution of punishments, and of rewards; of the excesiue riches of some few in number, and extreame pouertie of the greater sort; of the too great idlenesse of the subiects, or of the impunitie of offendors: and it may be that this last point is therein of greatest consequence or importance, and yet the least of all regarded. Which as I haue before touched, so must I also oftentimes repeat the same, for that the princes and magistrats which desire to be accounted mercifull, do oftentimes turne vpon their owne heads the same punishment that the offendors deserued. And that is it for which the wise Hebrew hath so oftentimes aduised vs, Not to become suretie for another man: not for that he forbid-

---

K1 inequall *i.e.* inequitable, unjust   K3 greater sort (*but probably a misprint for* greater part)
Notes at H1, H7.

forbiddeth a charitable dealing one of vs towards another (as many haue thought) but rather to giue all men to vnderstand, That they which become sureties for wicked men, and so find meanes to deliuer them from deserued punishment, shall beare the pain of the offendors guilt therefore. As was said to king *Achab*, who had saued the life of *Benadab* the king of Syria, whom hee should haue put to death, God caused it to bee told vnto him by his prophet, That he was become suretie for another man, and that it should surely cost him his life therefore. Which being but spoken in particular vnto this one king, extendeth yet in general vnto all princes and Commonweals, who haue no more certaine cause of their ruine and decay, than the want of the due execution of iustice. To punish the rebellious, is also one of the meanes to preuent and meet with rebellions yet to come, which how it is to be done we haue before said, when as wee reasoned of punishments to be vpon corporations and colledges inflicted; which is to take place when some one corporation, or the least part of the subiects haue erred or offended; but not if all the people in generall, or the greatest part of them be in fault: For albeit that the physitian or surgeon sometimes for the preseruation of the whole bodie, cuts off a mans leg or arme, yet must he not therfore cut off the head, or any other of the principall members, if they shall chance to be infected: but therin follow the wise councell of the great Physitian *Hippocratts*, who vnto desperat diseases forbiddeth vs to apply any remedy at all. But beside the causes of seditions & rebellions, which wee haue before spoke of, there is yet another, which dependeth of the immoderat libertie of speech giuen to orators, who direct & guide the peoples hearts & minds according to their owne pleasure. For there is nothing that hath more force ouer the minds of men, than hath eloquence: So that our ancestors haue not without cause purtraied *Hercules Celtique* not as a yong & strong man with a great club in his hand, but as a reuerend bauld old man, drawing after him a great number of people enchained, & hanging by the eares with chaines, which all issued out of his mouth; to shew, that the armies and power of kings and monarchs are not so strong as the vehemencie and force of an eloquent man, who encourageth & enflameth the most cowardly & faint hearted to vanquish euen the most valiant, who striketh armes out of the hands of the most couragious, who turneth rage into mildnesse, & barbarisme into ciuility, who changeth whole Commonweals, and sporteth with the people at his pleasure. Which I say not for the prayse of eloquence, but to shew the force & power therof, which is oftner emploied to euill, than to good. For seeing that this is nothing els but a disguising of the truth, and an art to make that seeme good, which is indeed naught, & that right which is wrong, and to make a great matter of nothing, as of an Emot an Elephant (that is to say, an art to lie cunnungly) wee need not doubt, but that for one which vseth this art well, fiftie vse the same euill, & that amongst 50 Orators it is hard to find an honest man. For that to seeke after the plaine & bare truth, were a thing altogether contrarie vnto their profession, seeing that the best rule that *Cicero* giueth vnder the person of *Marcus Antonius* the Orator, is to say nothing against himself: or rather as *Aristotle* saith, So well to disguise matters, as that the deceit thereof cannot not be discouered: or to speake more plainly, to couer all things with lies and dissimulation. So that if we will but wel looke into al them which had the name to haue beene the most noble and famous Orators, we shall find them to haue beene still the stirrers vp of the people to sedition, to haue oftentimes changed the laws, the customs, the religions, and Commonweals, yea & some others of them to haue vtterly ruinated the same; in which doing they haue also almost all of them ended their dayes by violent death. Which it is not needfull here to proue by the Orators of Athens, or of Rome, but euen by those of our age, who haue so well bestirred themselues, as that vnder the colour of religion they haue troubled

The immoderat libertie of speech giuen vnto Orators a great cause of seditions and rebellions.

The force and power of eloquence.

bled all the empires both of Affrike & of the West: yea and many of them so wrested the scepters euen out of the kings hands. As it happened vnto the king of Marocco, descended (as is supposed) from the house of *Ioseph*, from whom a preacher vnder the vaile of religion tooke both the crowne and scepter: & albeit that he was commonly called the *Asse Knight*, yet preached he so well, as that he assembled an armie of sixscore thousand men to take his part. In like sort he which was first called the Sophi, inuaded the kingdome of Persia, and in short time draue out the children of *Vsun Cassan* the lawfull king, vnder the same coulour of religion. As also not long agoe *Iohn* of Leiden (who of a botcher became a preacher) ceised vpon Munster the Metropoliticall citie of Westphalia, and there taking vpon him the state of a king, was hardly after three yeares siege by the imperiall armie thence remoued. And by the selfe same meanes *Hierome Sauanarola* a preacher, incited by *Anthonie Soderin*, vppon the contention which happened among the inhabitants at Florence, about the estate, so much preuailed with his persuasions vnto the people, as that hee translated the soueraigntie from the nobilitie vnto the people, and chaunged the Aristocratie into a Democratie or Popular estate. No otherwise than had before *Ephialtes*, by the setting on of *Pericles* by his seditious orations, drawne vnto the people the soueraigntie of that state, taken from the Senat of the Areopagi; and so made the Athenian estate of all others the most Popular. And to be briefe, we haue seene all Germany in armes, and an hundred thousand men slaine in lesse than in a yeare space, after that the mutinous preachers had stirred vp the people against the nobilitie. How often hath the speeches of preachers bene heard, tending by all meanes to haue incited the princes and people to kill, massacre, & burne their subiects: as did in auntient time *Nestorius*, preaching before the emperor at Constantinople in this sort, *Giue me emperour, the earth void of heretikes, and I will giue thee heauen: destroy with me the heretikes, and I with thee wil ruinat the power of the Persians*: for which he was called the *Fire maker*: For had the emperour giuen credence vnto him, he had so put to death the greatest part, and almost all his subiects, and *Nestorius* himselfe first of all. Wherefore a knife is not more daungerous in the hand of a mad man, than eloquence in the mouth of a mutinous Orator. And yet neuerthelesse it is a meane for them which will well vse it, to reduce the people from barbarisme to humanitie, to reforme disordered maners, to correct the lawes, to chastice tyrants, to cast out vices, to maintaine vertue. And as men charme the Aspis, Vipers, and Serpents, by certaine words; euen so the Orators (as *Plato* saith) by the sweetnesse of their eloquent persuations, charme euen the most sauage and cruell people. Neither is there any other greater or better means for the appeasing of seditions & tumults, and to keepe the subiects in the obedience of their princes, than to haue a wise and vertuous preacher, by whom they may bend and bow the hearts of the most stubborne rebels, especially in a Popular estate, wherein the ignorant people beareth the sway, and cannot possibly bee kept in order but by the eloquent Orators: which for this cause haue alwayes holden the chiefe degree of honour & power in such Popular estates, causing the honourable charges & commissions, gifts and rewards, to be still giuen to whom they saw good: so that in briefe both peace & war, arms and laws, wholy depended on the pleasure of the Orators. And so to the contrarie, there is nothing more to be dreaded in a tyrant, than the Orator which hath the bent of the peoples bow, and is in credit & estimation with them, especially if he hate the tyrant, or his Tyrannicall gouernment. But forasmuch as the rules by vs alreadie set downe, ought to bee applied vnto the nature of Commonweals, and that the Commonweals, laws & customs, are likewise to bee fitted vnto the nature & disposition of euery nation. Let vs now also speake of the nature of al people, as of a thing most necessary for the good gouernment of Estates and Commonweales.

THE

Eloquence in an euill man as dangerous, as a sword in a mad mans hand.

A wise, vertuous, and eloquent preacher, of all others the fittest man to appease rebellions, and to keepe the people in obedience to their prince.

F9 botcher *i.e.* patcher, mender G1 removed his [*i.e.* Ephialtes'] seditious orations drawne (cf. L) tyrant (cf. 213 B2–3) G6–7 Ephialtes, by the setting on of Pericles, by K3 in a tyrant *i.e.* in the case of a tyrant, by a Notes at G2, H2.

545

THE FIFT BOOKE OF OR CONCERNING A COMMONWEALE.

Chap. I.

¶ *What order and course is to be taken, to apply the forme of a Commonweale to the diuersitie of mens humors, and the meanes how to discouer the nature and disposition of the people.*

Itherto we haue treated of that which concernes the generall Estate of Commonweales; Let vs now shew what may be particular to some, through the diuersitie of peoples humors, to the end that wee may accommodat the publike weale to the nature of the place; and the ordinances of man to the laws of nature, wherof many haue had small regard: but striuing to make nature obedient to their edicts, haue oftentimes troubled, yea ruined great estates. And yet those which haue written of a Commonweale, haue not treated of this question. For euen as we see a great varietie in all sorts of beasts, and in euery kind some notable alteration for the diuersitie of regions: in like sort we may say, that there is in a manner as great difference in the nature and disposition of men, as there is of countries: yea in the same climats the people of the East are found to differ much from them of the West: And in the same latitude and difference from the Equator, the people of the North differ from them of the South: And which is more, in the same climat, latitude, and longitude, and vnder the same degree, we find a difference betwixt a hilly countrey and the plaines: so ar in the same citie, the diuersitie of hills and vallies forceth a diuersitie of humors and dispositions: And townes seated vppon vneuen places, are more subiect to seditions and chaunges, than those that are built vppon an equall and plaine ground. The citie of Rome, which hath seuen hils, was neuer long without sedition. And *Plutarch* (hauing not duely examined the cause) doth wonder why there were three factions in Athens of diuers humors: those of the high citie, which they called *Astu*, demaunded a Popular State; those of the base towne required *Oligarchia*, or the gouernment of few; and the inhabitants of the Port Piree, desired an Aristocraticall State, that is, a mixt gouernment of the nobilitie and the people: whereof wee will soone shew you a naturall cause. And if *Theophrastus* find it strange that the people of Greece be so different in manners and dispositions, who would not admire to see such contrarie humors in one and the same citie? we cannot impute it to

The nature of the people is much to be regarded in the framing of a Commonweale.

Townes vneuenly built vppon mountaines and vallies, are subiect to seditions.

Aaa iiij the

the mixture of people which haue come thither from all parts, seeing that Plutarch speaketh of *Solons* time, when as the Athenians were so little mingled with any other nations, as they held for certaine, that they were issued out of the land of Attica, wherein the Orator *Aristides* doth glorie. In lik sort we say the Swissers (hauing their originall out of Sweden) to be verie different in manners, nature, and gouernment: for although they be more strictly allied than euer any nations were, yet the fiue small cantons of the mountaines, and the Grisons, are held more fierce and more warlike, and do gouerne wholy popularly: the rest are more tractable, and are gouerded by an Aristocratie, being more enclined thereunto, than to a Popular estate. It is needfull to haue a speciall care to the nature and inclination of the people, if wee will chaunge an estate as it happened in Florence, about an hundred years since, when as the Commonweale by succession of time was almost chaunged into *Aristocratia*, the citisens beeing so encreased, as they were forced thrise to enlarge the compasse of their walles. For the preuention whereof the Senat was assembled, and the matter propunded: whereas the Senatour *Vespucius* did show by liuely reasons, That an Aristocraticall estate was without all comparison the most sure, and farre better than a Popular gouernment; giuing for an example the state of Venice, flourishing vnder the commaund of few gentle men: but *Antonie Soderine* maintained a Popular estate, and preuailed; saying, That the nature of the Venetians was proportionable to an Aristocratie, & the Florentines to a Populat estate. We will soone shew if his grounds were true. We read also, that the Ephesians, Milesians, and the Siracusians were almost of the Florentines humor: for they could not endure any but a Popular estate, nor allow any one to exceed his companions, banishing euen those that surmounted in vertue: and yet the Athenians, Ephesians, and Milesians, were much more mild and tractable; so were they much neerer the East: and contrariwise the Siracusians, Florentines, and Carthagineans, were much more fierce and rebellious, beeing more Westward. The people of the East haue much more ostentation and many words, in the iudgement of all auntient writer, and euen of the ambassadour of the Rhodiots, excusing the fault of his maisters, vpon their naturall inclination, making mention also of the naturall vices of other people, *Gentes aliæ (inquit) iracundæ, aliæ audaces, quædam timidæ, in vinum ac venerem proniores aliæ sunt, Atheniensium populum fama est celerem & supra vires audacem ad conandum, Lacedemoniorum cunctatorem: non negauerim & totam Asiæ regionem inaniora parere ingenia, & nostrorum tumidiorem sermonem esse*, Some nations (said he) are cholerike, others bold; some fearfull, others prone to wine and women; the peole of Athens are said to be sudden, and exceeding bold to attempt any thing; the Lacedemonians are slow and deliberat: I will not denie, but that all the region of Asia brings forth vaine wits, and ours great talkers. The people of Athens (said *Plutarch*) were cholerike and pitifull, taking pleasure in flatteries, and enduring easily a scoffe: but those of Carthage were cruell and reuengefull, humble to their superiours, and imperious to their subiects, faint hearted in aduersitie, and insolent in prosperitie. The people of Rome contrarie vnto them were patient in their losses, constant in their victories, moderat in their passions, hating flatterers, and taking delight in graue and seuere men: so as the elder *Cato* demaunding the Censorship of the people, said, That they had need of a seuere Censor, threatning to punish vice with seueritie: yet the people desired rather to chuse him that threatned them, being but of a meane calling, than the greatest noble men that flattered them. The like they did to *L. Torquatus*, whome the people did chuse Consull without his priuitie: vnderstanding of his election, he told the people, That his disposition was such, as he could not tollerat their vices, neither could the people endure his commaundements; and therefore if they were wise, they should make

make another choyce: yet was he chosen againe by the people. That which I say may be easily discerned by the difference of the Athenian and Roman Orators: for these did more respect the maiestie of the people, than those of Athens, who abused the people with such insolencie, as one of them hauing assembled the people for matters of state, after that he had made them to attend him long, in the end he came into the pleading place, with a garland of roses, saying vnto them, That hee had resolued that day to feast his friends, and so departed: whereat the people laughed. Another time *Alcibiades* speaking to the people, let flie a quaile out of his bosome, and the people run after it, and brought it to him againe. If he had done this in Carthage (saith *Plutarch*) before the people, they would haue stoned him: the Romans would not haue suffered it vnpunished; for that a citisen of Rome was depriued of his Bourgeship, for that hee had yawned too lowd before a Censor, as *Valerius Maximus* doth testifie.

Therefore a wise gouernour of any Commonweale must know their humours, before he attempt any thing in the alteration of the state and lawes. For one of the greatest, and it may be the chiefest foundation of a Commonweale, is to accommodat the estate to the humor of the citisens; and the lawes and ordinances to the nature of the place, persons, and time. For although *Baldus* saith, That reason and naturall equitie is not restrained nor limited to a certaine place: that is to bee vnderstood, when as the reason is vniuersall, and not whereas a particular reason of places and persons receiues a priuate consideration. For which cause wee must varie the estate of the Commonweale to the diuersitie of places; like vnto a good Architect, which doth fit his building according to the stuffe hee finds vpon the place: So should a wise Politician doe, who may not chuse what people he will. As *Isocrates* said in the prayses of *Busiris* king of Ægypt, whome he esteemeth very much, for that hee could chuse a countrey and a people the fittest in all the world to gouerne. Let vs first speake of the nature of the people of the North and South, and then of the East, and West, and the difference betwixt the mountainers & those that liue in vallies, or in moorish places, or that are subiect to violent winds: then will we shew how much discipline may change the nature and disposition of men, reiecting the opinions of *Polybius*, and *Galen*, who held, That the countrey and nature of the place did rule necessarily in the manners of men. And the better to vnderstand the infinit varietie which may be betwixt the people of the North and South, we will diuide all the nations that inhabit the earth, on this side the Equator, into three parts: the first shal be of thirtie degrees on this side the Equator, which we will attribute to the burning Regions, and people of the South: & the thirtie degrees next, to those that inhabit the temperat regions, vnto the sixtieth degree towards the Pole, and from thence vnto the Pole shall bee the thirtie degrees of the nations of the North, and the regions that be exceeding cold. The like diuision may be made of regions beyond the Equator, towards the Antartike Pole: then wee will diuide the thirtie degrees of the burning regions into the moitie, the fifteene first being more moderat, betwixt the Equator and the Tropickes; the other fifteene more burning, vnder the Tropicks: and by the same meanes we will take the fifteene degrees following of the temperat region, which stretcheth vnto the 45 degree, which hold more of the South, and the other fifteene vnto the sixtieth degree, the which are more distempered in cold, and incline more to the North: and in the fifteene following, vnto the 75 degree, although that men bee much afflicted with cold, yet are there many nations and Commonweales. But as for the other fifteene adioyning to the Pole, wee must make no account of them; for that there are few men, which liue in caues like vnto brute beasts (as marchants do report, and histories haue certified.) I haue giuen the reason of these diuisions in a particular booke of the Method of Histories,

Marginalia:
- A good Architect fits his building according to the stuffe he finds vpon the place.
- A diuision of people.
- The heat is greater vnder the Tropick, than vnder the Equator.
- Olaus and Saxo Grammaticus.

548   THE FIFTH BOOKE

ries, and therefore need lesse now to enter any further into it. These points being concluded, it shall be more easie to iudge of the nature and disposition of the people. For it is not sufficient to say, that the people of the North haue force, with bignesse & beautie of the bodie, and little wit: and contrariwise, that the Southerne nations are weake, little, blacke, and haue great wits: for that experience doth teach vs, that those people which liue in the extremities of the North, are little, leane, and tamed with cold; the which *Hipocrates* doth confesse, the which we must reconcile with the rest, in setting the limits as I haue said. And the saying of *Hipocrates* shall bee vnderstood of those nations that inhabit beyond the 70 degree towards the Poles. We will also allow of the opinion of *Hippocrates*, and after him of *Aristotle*, who haue written, That the people of the North haue a flaxen and fine haire. And yet *Galen* saith, That they haue the haire red: the which we must vnderstand of those that are about the 60 degree, whereof there are many in England, whome the inhabitants say are issued from the Danes and Swedens, who inuaded England; noting them by their red haire. But from the Baltique sea vnto the 45 degree, and on this side, the people haue commonly flaxen haires. And in old times, when as nations were not so mingled as since they haue bene, they did know a Northerne man by his flaxen haire and his greene eyes; as *Plutarch*, *Tacitus*, *Iuuenal*, and in our times the Baron of Herbestein haue obserued: and as I haue discoursed in my booke of the Method of Histories, and shewed that *Amiot* in his translation of *Plutarch*, vpon the towne of Marius, tearmes them red and chesnut eyes: wheras he should haue called them greene eyes: the which is verie apparant. But those which are about the 60 degree, haue in a manner all eyes like vnto Owles, and the colour of the water lookes white in their eyes: they haue a weake sight by day, and see better in the darke, like vnto night Owles, which they call *Nictalopes*. Of this I was assured of the ambassadour *Pruinski*, a Lituanian, and of *Holster* Commissarie of the warres, borne at Ostolcome in Sweden, who is haired like a Kow, and eyed like an Owle: which colour, force, and bignesse, comes (as *Aristotle* saith) of the interiour heat: as the inhabitants of Affrike haue blacke eyes, for the little heat they haue in their interiour parts, being exhaled by the heat and drought of the sunne: whereas the cold doth keepe in the heat in the Northerne regions, if it be not so vehement as it doth in a maner quench it: for which cause those that inhabit beyond the 75 degree, are weake, little, and tamed with extreame cold, the which is so vehement, as many die; as the marchants report. And euen the baron of Heberstein writes, That the spittle freezeth sometimes before it falles to the ground, the which may seeme incredible. But it is most certaine that the Baltique sea freezeth in such sort, as whole armies passe from the maine land to the ilands; although the heat in sommer is sometimes so violent, as it burnes not onely the fruits of the earth, but also the houses and villages, as the same author writes that it hath happened in Moscouie, in the yeare 1524. The which also chanced in Polonia, in the yeare 1552, as *Thomas Cromer* writes. And the like chaunced in England, in the yeare 1556, as I haue seene by letters from *M. de Nouailles* ambassador in England for the French king: in the which he doth assure, That the heat had bene so vehement, as the flame kindled by the sunne, burnt the fruits and villages throughout a whole countrey. The which *Aristotle* doth affirme in his Problemes, That the heat is more violent in cold countries than in hoat: but that is to bee vnderstood in watry places. And whereas there is some mountaine which doubleth the heat by reuerberation; as it happened in the towne of Naim in Gascoine, the which was wholy burnt with the heat of the sunne at noone day, in the yeare 1540: and the towne of Montcornet neere vnto Laon, the which was burnt in the moneth of May, in the yere 1574, after a straunge manner, the fire flying through the streets, and through places farre distant

Marginal notes:
- Aristotle & Hipocrates agree herein.
- The difference of the people in the Northerne regions.
- In the history of Moscouie.
- The heat more vehement in sommer in cold countries than in hoat.

F6 *For* tamed *read* tanned.   G10 *For* towne *read* life (*ville* in Fr 7, *vie* in Fr 3-6, 8, omitted in Fr 1-2).   H6 Ostolcome *i.e.* Stockholm   I2 *For* tamed *read* tanned.   I8 *For* 1524 *read* 1525.   K1 for the   K5 whereas *i.e.* where   Notes at G1, G4, H1, I9.

A stant from the houses where it first began: for the situation thereof is waterish, as I haue said; and the grosseneſſe of the vapour retaines the heat, the which the maiſters of hoat houſes know full well; who to ſpare wood, caſt water into their ſtoues. The Northerne parts then being full of waters, lakes, and fountaines, the vapors which are drawne vp into the ayre, receiue and retaine the heat more violently: as in the Southerne parts it is more vehement vpon the earth. For euen as the heat is more violent in mettall than in wood, and in great wood than in ſmall bruſh: ſo the ſun hath more effect vpon the earth than in the ayre; and in a vaporous ayre in moyſt regions, than in a dry countrey, wherens the ayre is ſubtill, and without any ſencible bodies: which may be the cauſe that God hath made the Southerne countries more rainie, and leſſe waterish: and thoſe places which are moiſt in the Southerne parts, lie commonly towards the North, and are couered with mountaines towards the South, as Aquitaine (which is ſo called for the aboundance of waters) hath the Pyrenean hilles. Barberie hath mount Atlas, which is wonderfully high, out of the which the ſprings and riuers riſe all towards the North (as we read in *Leo* of Affrike) alſo the ſun caſting his beams perpendicularly vpon the countrey, would make that inhabitable, the which is one of the moſt fruitfull and beſt peopled countries in the world. And euen as in winter the places vnder ground, and the inward parts of creatures, retaine the heat which doth euaporat in ſummer: euen ſo it fares with people that inhabit the Northerne parts, which haue the inward heat more vehement than thoſe of the Southerne regions: which heat cauſeth the forces and naturall powers to be greater in the one than in the other: and which alſo doth cauſe the one to eat more, and to diſgeſt better than the other, for the cooleneſſe of the region which keeps in the naturall heat. So as thoſe armies which come from the Southerne parts into the North, are more vigorous and luſtie; as it was ſeene in the armie of *Hannibal* paſsing into Italy, and the armie of Moores and Arabians, which haue come into Europe: and of ſeuen thouſand Spaniards which paſſed into Germanie, vnder the emperour *Charles* the fift: and of fortie thouſand Gaſcoines, which went to ſuccour the king of Sweden, who obtained goodly victories. And contrariwiſe the armies that come out of the North, grow weake and languiſh, the more they goe towards the South, yea euen in ſommer; as it appeared in the Cimbrians, of whome *Plutarch* witneſſeth, That they were all molten with ſweat, and languiſhed with heat which they felt in Prouence, the which would ſoone haue conſumed them all, although they had not bene vanquiſhed by the Romans: as it happened to the French before Naples, & to the Lanſquenets which paſſed into Italie, vnder the commaund of *Charles* of Bourbon and of *George Fronſperg*, of the which after they had ſackt Rome, there died ten thouſand without any blow, before the yeare was expired, as *Guichardine* writes. This doth alſo plainely appeare in the troupes of cattell which goe out of the North into the South, they looſe their fatneſſe, and their milke, and fall away: the which *Plinie* hath noted, and the marchants find it true by daily experience. And euen as the Spaniard doubles his appetite and forces, comming out of Spaine into Fraunce; euen ſo the French looſe their appetites and languiſh, going into Spaine: and if he will eat and drinke as he doth in Fraunce, he is in daunger not to continue it long. And euen the nations of the Northerne regions fall a languiſhing and fainting of the heart, when as the Southerne winds blow: the ſame reaſon doth teach vs, why that men and beaſts, yea and birds which moſt ſuddenly feele this alteration, grow fat in winter, and leane in ſommer. If *Leo* of Affrike, and *Francis* of Aluares, (who haue written the hiſtories of Affrike and Ethiopia) had well obſerued this reaſon, which is naturall, they had not ſo highly commended the abſtinence of thoſe people: for they cannot haue any appetite, the interiour heat wanting in them. Neither muſt we blame

the

Why the ſunne is hoater on the earth than in the ayre.

What places in the South are moſt ſubiect to waters.

Why the armies of the North languiſh when they go towards the South.

Why the people of the South be abſtinent.

A9 whereas   A9 *For* bodies *read* bodie (cf. Fr).   A10 *For* more rainie *read* less rainie.   B5 *For* also *read* else *i.e.* otherwise.   B6 inhabitable *i.e.* uninhabitable   C7 *For* fortie thousand *read* four thousand.   E3 Northerne   Notes at C10, D7, E6.

550 THE FIFTH BOOKE

Why the people of the North are more hungry.

the people of the North, for that they are more hungry, and deuoure more than they of the South, considering the inward heat and greatnesse of the men. The same effects are found in the Antartike regions: for wee read in the Histories of the Indies, That *Magellan* found neere vnto the strait which he called by his own name Giants *Patagenes*, so great and mightie, that eight Spaniards armed were troubled to hold one; but otherwise verie simple. The people of the North get it by force, and they of the South by policie: so they of the middest participat of the one and the other, and are more fit for warre, by the iudgement of *Vegetius* and *Vitruuius*: and therefore they haue erected great empires, the which haue flourished in armes and lawes. And the wisedome of God hath so well distributed his graces, as he hath neuer ioined force with excellencie of wit, neither in men nor beasts: for there is nothing more cruell than iniustice armed with power.

The people of the middle regions are better tempered in wit and bodie.

The people therfore of the middle regions haue more force than they of the South, & lesse pollicie: and more wit than they of the North, & lesse force; and are more fit to commaund and gouerne Commonweales, and more iust in their actions. And if we looke well into the histories of all nations, we shall find, That euen as great armies and mightie powers haue come out of the North; euen so the hidden knowledge of Philosophie, the Mathematikes, and other contemplatiue sciences, are come out of the South: and the politike sciences, lawes, and the studie thereof, the grace of well speaking and discoursing, haue had their beginning in the middle regions, and all great empires haue bene there established;

The greatest empires were in the middle regions.

as the empire of the Assyrians, Medes, Persians, Parthians, Grecians, Romans, Celtes. And although that the Arabians & Moors had for a time ceised vpon the empire of Persia, Syria, Ægypt and Barbarie, & brought a good part of Spaine vnder subiection, yet could they not subdue Greece nor Italie. And whereas they would haue subiected Fraunce, they were vanquished, and their armie of 300 thousand men (which they had brought) defeated. In like sort the Romans haue stretched forth their power ouer all the nations of the South and East, but they preuailed little against them of the North and West: & although they were conquerors ouer all other people, yet they imploied all their forces, & had somewhat to do to make resistance against the Northerne nations, who neither had walled townes, fortresses, nor castles; as *Tacitus* saith, speaking of the Germans. And although that *Traian* had made an admirable bridge vpon the riuer of Danow, and vanquished *Decebalus* king of Daciens; yet the emperour *Adrian* his successour, caused it to bee broken downe, fearing least the people of the North (hauing such a passage open) should enter into the heart of the Roman empire: as they did after that the emperour *Constantine* had discharged the Roman legions, which guarded the riuer of Rhine and Danow:

The people of the North dispersed throughout all the Roman empire.

For soone after the Almans, then the Gothes, Ostrogothes, Vandales, Francs, Bourguignons, Herules, Huns, Hongres, Lombards; and in succession of time, Normans, Tartars, Turkes, and other nations of Scithia, inuaded the Prouinces which the Romans had held. And although the English haue had great victories ouer the French and conquered the country which lieth South to them, yet for these nine hundred yeres they could neuer expell the Scottish men out of the island; and yet it is well knowne how much more populous France is than England, and England than Scotland. We may obserue the like in the Turkes, a Northerne nation, who hath extended the greatnesse of their empire to the goodliest regions of Asia, Affrica, and Europe, hauing in a manner subdued all the ilands of the Mediterrannean sea; yet haue they bene defeated by the Tartarians, & are much trouled to make head against the Moscouits. We read, that God did threaten his people by the oracles of his prophets with the nations of the North, foretelling that warre murder, and the ruine of Commonweales should come from thence. For although that men be much diminished in numbers, force, proportion

Esai. 14.41.
Ezec. 16.51.
Dan. 8.48.
Zach. 11.

I5 For *river* read *rivers*. K6 troubled. Notes at I7, K7 (margin).

OF A COMMONWEALE. 551

A portion, vigour, and age, in respect of the auntients (a complaint of most writers by the historie of *Plinie*) so hardly vpon the face of the earth shall you now find a citie comparable to Capua (containing thirteene miles in circuit) much lesse matchable to the famous Babylon, which though it were situated foure square in a leuell soile, yet could a good foot man hardly trauell round about it in three dayes: but this notwithstanding in multitudes of people, in strength of bodies, and large proportion of members, the Northerne prouinces do at this day farre excell the Southerne. In regard whereof that militarie discipline of the Romans, which priuileged souldiours at fiftie yeares from future seruice, was not allowable amongst the Lacedemonians; who being nothing inferiour to the Romans, either for strength of bodie, or warlike experience,

B yet freed their people from the seruice thereof, at fortie: the reason being, for that they were so much the more vnable to hold out so long as the Romans, by how much the one nation approached more neere to the South than the other. So bring a Scithian from his natiue habitation to the South, and you shall find him presently to droop, and fall away with sweat and faintnesse. And therefore the pirats of the Mediterrannean finding by experience, that the English and Dutch captaines are vnfit for paines taking in those hoat countries, in their markets prize them at a verie low rate. For the people of the North are inwardly hoat, enioying a most dry aire, and therefore more thriftie than the Southerne, who inwardly are cold, according to the propertie of the South, a climat moist by nature. Wherein the Grecians deriuing, Νοτὸν, παρὰ τῆς νωτίδος, *Lacedemon more Southerly than Rome.*

C *i. ab humore*, from moisture, are to be beleeued; experience teaching vs, That when the winds blow from the South, we expect showers; but when from the North, faire weather and cleere skies. For which reason the people of the North are and haue alwaies bene great drinkers, witnesse the Greeke prouerbe, To drinke like a Scythian, the which *Tacitus* hath not forgotten, speaking of the manners of the Germans, *Diem noctemque (inquit) continuare potando nulli probrũ, ita vt crœbra inter vinolentos rixæ fiebant*, They held it no disgrace (saith he) to sit all day and night drinking: so as oftentimes there fell out iarres among these drunkards. The which is not the fault of the men, but of the region: For such as trauell from the South to the North, will eat and drinke no lesse than they that are home bred. But *Tacitus* was deceiued, in saying, That the Germans

D did drinke more and eat lesse, by reason of the coldnesse and barrennesse of the countrey. But contrariwise seeing that thirst is nothing else but an appetite of cold and moisture, and that hunger is an appetite of drought and heat; and that the people of the North haue the interiour heat much more in comparison than those of the South, they must of necessitie drinke more. In like sort the people of the Northerne regions haue their skins softer, more hairie, and subiect to sweat than the people of the South; which haue the skin hard, little haire and curled, and the skin withered with drinesse, enduring heat easile without sweating: but they cannot well beare with cold, nor wet; as appeared in the Spaniards, which died of cold in great numbers vppon the high mountaines of Peruana. And no wonder, for men bred and brought vp in hoat regi- *The reason why they of the North drinke more than in the South.*

E ons, in colder places inwardly waxe chill, whose bodies if any extraordinarie or sudden alteration of wether attache (an accident often happening in those Sotherly quarters, especially vpon the tops of those high hils) it must needes follow, that their naturall heat, both inward and outward, do vtterly forsake them: the contrarie whereof betideth the Scythian, who by nature being inwardly hoat, by cold becommeth so much the more able and couragious, by how much the cold forceth the outward heat vnto the heart, the true seat and center of liuely heat. Yea the report, how subiect the Southerne people through want of inward heat are to looseneffe and the bloody flixe, almost passeth credit, albeit most true: Whereas on the contrarie the countries situated

North.

A8 *For* fiftie *read* fiftie five (cf. 610 F1).   B6 *For* captaines *read* captives.   B8 *For* thriftie *read* thirstie.   B10 νωτίδος (L 4–5) νότιος (L 1–2) *properly* νοτίδος (L 3)   C1 i.e. ab humore
C6 probrum: crebrae ut inter vinolentos rixae (L, as in *Germania*, 22)   D8 easilie   E2 attache *i.e.* attack   Notes at A2, C4, D8.

552   THE FIFTH BOOKE

Northwards, abounding with riuers and lakes, do enure mens bodies to fogges & cold moistures, and that in such able manner, that Scythians do oftentimes defeat their enemies by their ambuscadoes hidden in deepe marishes; testified by *Herodianus*, who writeth, That the Germans infested the Romans with their missiue weapons, themselues standing safe in the middest of the waters. Which secret of nature *Galen* not well vnderstanding, seemeth to wonder at, especially for bathing their new borne infants in cold running riuers; a custome vsed in like manner by the Ausonij,

> *Natos ad flumina primum,*
> *Deferimus, sæuoque gelu duramus & vndis:*

> Our new-borne babes at first to springs we bring,
> T'endure cold stormes their bodies so enuring.

The ground of which German custome *Iulianus* surnamed the *Apostata* writeth to be, that this people held an opinion, That the true borne children would flote vpon the waters, but the base and bastards would sinke to the bottome. And euen as the people of the North doe languish soone with heat, so are they soone wearied and tyred with labour in the Southerne parts, or in a hoat season. The which was first knowne at the battell of Plombin, whereas the Celtes being inuitoned with two armies of the Romans, fought valiantly: but after they had spent their first furie, they were soone vanquished. *Polybius* saith, That to vanquish the Celtes, you must but ward their blows for a time, and yet they were held inuincible. *Cæsar* holds the same opinion of the Gaules, That in the beginning of a battell they were more than men, but in the end lesse than women. The which is more naturall to the Germans, and other people of the North (as *Tacitus* saith) who had knowne them by long experience: For the Gaules, especially those of Languedouich, hold the middle region betwixt the cold and extreame heat, although the qualitie of the Westerne region makes the country more cold. And those which are in the middest are impatient of cold or heat: the which *Cæsar* doth witnesse of the Gaules, who suffer cold more easily than the Spaniards, and heat than the Germans. And euen as the people of the middle regions hold of the two extreames in humor, so doe they agree with the one and the other in manners and complexions: and as God by his admirable wisedome doth vnite all things by conuenient meanes to their extremities. In like sort we see that hee hath obserued the same order betwixt the nations of the North and South, which can neuer concurre together for the contrarietie of manners and humors that is betwixt them. The which is a thing verie considerable, when there is any question to treat a peace, or to make a league betwixt two nations so contrarie, or to lead them both forth to the warre together; you must place that nation betwixt them that doth participat of both their natures, and that haue their affections more moderat. As *Galen* saith, That the Germans and Arabians haue not that commendable ciuilitie which is in them that are borne in Asia the lesse; the which is not onely betwixt the Pole and the Equator, but also betwixt the East Indies and Fraunce Westward: A countrey for this vertue so highly commended by *Tully*, that he doubteth not to affirme, That therein not onely rested the mirror of ciuilitie, but that from thence it hath bin deriued to all forreine nations. But I am not of their opinions, who draw their arguments of ciuilitie and barbarisme from the effects of heate and cold, finding euery day by common experience, that the Southerne people go beyond al other nations in quicknes of wit, whereas barbarisme and rude behauiour proceede from ignorance and want of education, a lesson long ago verified by *Herodotus*, who for good wits and ciuill behauiour commendeth the

                                                                                      Ægiptians

Sidenotes: Proofe to know the bastards from them that were lawfull. — The middle region participates of both the extreames. — Courtesie and humanitie comes from Asia.

F9 Natos, etc. The quotation is from Virgil, *Aeneid*, IX, 603–604.   H5 North, as Tacitus saith who Notes at G6, I10, K5.

Ægyptians before all other people of what nation soeuer. And after him *Cæsar* (in his Commentaries of the ciuill warres) gaue them the like priuilege, saying, That the Alexandrians did so artificially counterfeit the Roman engines of warre, as it seemed the Romans were but their apes, he vseth these words, *Ipsi homines ingeniosissimi ac subtilissimi*, The men themselues were verie wittie and politike: And yet Ægypt is partly vnder the Tropique, whereas the heat is more violent than vnder the Equator, by the iudgement of *Posidonius* and the Spaniards. The Romans held the like opinion of the people of Affrike, whom they called *Pænos*, who had often deceiued the Romans, and ouerthrowne their forces by policie. So *Columella* teatmes them *Gentem acutissimam*, A most subtill nation: But yet they had not such excellent wits as the Ægyptians, neither are they so neer the South. And without any further search we haue the proofe therof in this realm, where the difference is apparent in regard of the English, who complained to *Philip* of *Comines* with admiration, for that the French lost most commonly in their warres against them, and won still in their treaties. Wee may write the like of the Spaniards, who neuer made treatie for these hundred yeares with the French, but they had the aduantage: the which were long to repeate in particular. I will onely produce the treatie of Cambresis, made in the yeare 1559. It cannot bee denied but the forces of Fraunce were great and sufficient to withstand a mightie enemie, yet the Spaniard got more by this treatie, without striking stroke, than they had done before in fortie yeares, neuer hoping (as they confessed afterwards) to draw Sauoy nor Piedmont out of the hands of the French: For although the duke of Sauoie, a vertuous and a generous prince, deserued much, as well for the equitie of his cause, as for the alliance of the house of Fraunce, yet he expected not so happie an issue of his affaires: the which was cunningly handled by the Spaniard, which reaped both thankes, and the greatest fruits of this treatie, hauing so much diminished the state of Fraunce (which stretched euen vnto the gates of Milan) and set the duke of Sauoy as it were a barre betwixt Italie and Fraunce, to shut vp the passage that the French might pretend no more in Italie. It cannot be denied, that such as had the charge to capitulat for the French, did not shew so great discretion, faith, and loyaltie, as they might: but I vnderstand from one of good credit, that it was resolued in the councell of Spaine, That they should prolong the treatie all they could; for that the nature of the French was so sudden and actiue, as they would easily yeeld to that which was demanded, being tired with many iourneies, and the ordinarie tediousnesse of the Spaniard, the which was not forgotten in this treatie. It was also obserued, That in all the sittings and assemblies made by the deputies, alwaies the French were first come, and although they had set all their people to watch, that they might sometimes enter the last; yet were they still deceiued by the subtiltie of the Spaniards, and impatience of the French, who seemed by this meanes to sue for peace. This fault is not to bee imputed to them that had the charge to treat a peace, but vnto nature, which is hardly vanquished. For we read the like of the ambassadours of Fraunce, conferring with the ambassadours of the emperour, of Venice, Spaine, and Ferrare, before *Francis Sforce* duke of Milan. Our manner (saith *Philip de Comines*) is not to speake treatably, as they doe: for wee speake sometimes two or three together, so as the Duke said, Ho, one to one. Whereby we may iudge as in any other obseruations, That the nature of the Spaniard (being much more miridionall than we) is colder, more melancholike, more staied, more contemplatiue, and by consequence more ingenious than the French; who by nature cannot stay to contemplat, being cholerike and full of spleene, the which makes him more actiue and prompt, yea so sudden, as he seemes vnto the Spaniard to run, when hee goes but his ordinarie pace: for which cause both the Spaniard and the Italian desire to haue French men to serue

The nature of the French.

The Spaniard alwayes circumuents the French by treacheries.

The reason why the Spaniards circumuent the French.

The nature of the Spaniard.

A8 Pœnos (cf. Fr). E2 treatably *i.e.* moderately, gently, sedately E4 *For* any other *read* many other
Notes at A5, A7, C7, C9.

serue them, for their diligence and quicknesse in all their actions: so as yerely there go infinit numbers into Spaine; as I haue seene being at Narbone, especially out of Auuergne and Limosin, to build, plant, till their lands, and doe all manuall workes, which the Spaniard cannot doe, but would rather die for hunger, he is so slothfull and heauie in al his actions. When as *N. Strossie* Prior of Capoua, attempted to surprise Valencia in Spaine, by meanes of the French gallies, whereof he was then Admirall: the practise being discouered, the Viceroy sought to expell all the French out of Valencia, which were found to be ten thousand: for whose loyaltie the Spaniards stood bound, rather than they should depart: which shewes how greatly that countrey is peopled with French. And without doubt those which are bred of the mixture of those two nations, are more accomplished than either of them: For in the Spaniard wee desire more viuacitie and cheeretulnesse, and to haue the actions and passions of the French more moderat: and it seemes the Italian doth participat of the one and the other, Italie beeing in the most temperat situation that can be, betwixt the Pole and the Equator, and in the middest of Asia, Affrike, and Europe, bending a little towards the East & South. And euen as they which liue at the extremities of the Poles, are Flegmatike, and at the South melancholie; euen so they which are thirtie degrees on this side the Pole, are more sanguin; and they which approach neerer vnto the middest, more sanguin and cholerike; and then drawing towards the South, more sanguin and melancholike: so their complexion is more blacke and yellow, blacke being the colour of melancholy, and yellow of choler *Galen* confesseth, That flegme makes men heauie and dull; blood cheerefull and strong; choler, actiue and nimble; and melancholy, constant and graue: and according to the mixture of these foure humors, more or lesse, so many varieties there be, which *Theodore Duca* of the house of *Lascare* emperour of Constantinople hath laboured to comprehend in 92 kinds, not onely for the foure humors, but also for the three parts of the soule, Reason, Anger, & Appetite (or Desire:) but for that his opinions are not grounded vpon the proofe of any example, nor vpon necessarie reason; and for that he makes no distinction of the parts of the world, neither of moist places, hilly nor windie, from those that are drie, plaine, and temperat: neither for that he hath not denied those people which haue bene brought vp in ciuill discipline, from the rude and barbarous, in this varietie of soules and humors which he hath supposed, wee will follow that discipline which seemeth most agreeing to reason and nature, & hath beene confirmed by many examples. Auntient histories do agree, That the people of the North are not malitious nor craftie, as the nations of the South be. And *Tacitus* speaking of the Germans, saith, It is a nation that is neither subtill nor craftie, discouering their secrets as it were in jest, and then they goe easily from their promises. The like iudgement we find of the Scythians in *Herodotus, Iustin, Strabo, Plinie,* and *Vegetius,* & therefore auntient princes as well as at this day, had no other guards for their persons than Scythians, Thracians, Germans, Swissers, and Circassians. And euen the Seigneurie of Rhaguse or of Genes, haue no other guards but Germans and Swissers. And which is more, the kings of Affrike beyond mount Atlas, haue none other guard but souldiours of Europe; who although they be Mahometans, yet had they rather trust in Christians that haue abiured their faith, than in those of the countrey; the which was first put in practise by the great *Mansor* emperour of Affrike and of Spaine: and heretofore the king of Tunis had 1500 light horsemen of Christians renigadoes, and his guard of Turkish and Christian slaues, as *Leo* of Affrike saith; knowing well that the people of the North haue more force than subtiltie, and hauing receiued entertainment of any prince, they alwayes remaine faithfull for the guard of his person, and to reuenge his iniuries (although he be a tyrant) neuer aspiring to his estate. And therfore

Chereas

G9 *For* sanguin and melancholike *read* choleric and melancholike (Fr).   H1 choler. Galen
H10 *For* denied *read* divided.   Notes at G2, H2, H8, K1.

Of A Commonweale. 555

Chereas captaine of the guard to the emperour *Caligula*, hauing slaine the emperor, was presently murdered by the guard, which were Germans, who could not (as *Iosephus* writeth) forbeare reuenge. In like sort the antients haue obserued a barbarous crueltie in the people of the North: for euen *Thucidides* son to *Olorus* king of Thrace, tearmes the Thracians a most cruell nation: and *Taritus* speaking of the Germans, They doe not (saith he) put the guiltie to death after order of law, but by crueltie, as enemies. I will let passe the auntient, and content my selfe with late examples. Wee haue none more notable than that of *George* captaine of the rebels in Hungarie, beeing taken by them of Transiluania, they caused his souldiours and companions to fast three dayes, and then gaue them to eat their captaine halfe roasted, and his bowels boyled. I omit the straunge cruelties of *Dracula* duke of Transiluania, and of *Otton Trucces*, who caused the murtherer of his lieutenant to be roasted with a slow fire, during the commons warre: and of late *Grombache* a German, was condemned to haue his heart pulled out being aliue, and to haue his face beaten therewithall, by *Augustus* duke of Saxonie in the castle of Goth. We find also, that the breaking vpon the wheele was inuented in Germany, and the impaling or setting men vpon stakes aliue, in Tartaria. Neither is it lesse cruell in Tartaria, to force them that are condemned, to breake their owne neckes, or els to whip and torment them: Which makes men to thinke, that the cruelties of the king of Moscouie published and printed, are verie likely. For the lesse reason and iudgement men haue, the more they approach to the nature of brute beasts, who can no more yeeld to reason and gouerne their passions than brute beasts. And contrariwise, the people of the South are cruell and reuengefull, by reason of melancholie, which doth inflame the passions of the soule with an exceeding violence, the which is not easily suppressed. *Polybius* speaking of the warres of the Speudians, and Carthagineans, people of Affrike, he saith, That there was neuer seene nor heard of any warre, where there was more treacherie and crueltie: and yet they are but toyes in respect of the horrible treacheries mentioned by *Leo* of Affrike (and in our age) betwixt *Muleasses* and his owne children. And euen the king of Tenesme beeing solicited by *Ioseph* king of Marocco to submit himselfe vnder his obedience, which his grandfather had reiected, he slew his ambassadours; wherewith the king of Marocco beeing insenced, put a million of people to the sword in the realme of Tenesme, leauing him neither towne, castle, house, beast, nor tree. And speaking of *Homar Essuein* a minister to *Mahomet*, seeking to make himselfe king, after that he had forced the fort of Vngiasen, hee was not content to put all to the sword, but he cut & tare the children out of their mothers wombes. And the same author writes, That *Isaak* king of Tombut in Affrike, hauing taken the king of Gagao, he caused him presently to bee put to death, and his children to be guelt to serue him as slaues, doing the like vnto al the kings he takes. We read of the like cruelties or greater at the West Indies, newly discouered: for the Brasilians are not contented to eat the flesh of their enemies, but will bathe their children in their blood. But the crueltie is more remarkable, when as they doe execute any one that is condemned by law; the which should be done without passion, and free from reuenge. Yet we read of punishments that were vsed in old time among the Persians, which exceed all crueltie: and in Ægypt at this day they flea them aliue which rob by the high way, then they stuffe the skin full of haie and set it vpon an Asse, by his side that is so fleaed: Which cruelties the people that liue betwixt both these extreames can neither see nor heare without horrour: and therefore it seemes, that for this cause the Romans suffred them that were condemned, to die of hunger, and the Greeks gaue them hemlocke (which is a sweet poison) to drinke: and those of Chio did temper it with water, and the Athenians with wine, to take away the bitternesse thereof, as *Theo-*

Bbb ij   *phrastus*

Marginalia:
- The people of the North faithful to the prince that entertaineth them
- Strange cruelties of the people of the North.
- Melancholike men cruell and reuengefull.
- Terrible cruelties of the people of the South.
- The people beetwixt both extreames, not subiect to crueltie.

A5 Tacitus   B7 *For* cruell in Tartaria *read* cruell in Lithuania (Fr and L).   B8 *For* men to thinke *read* me to thinke (Fr and L).   C4 *For* Speudians *read* Spendians *i.e.* followers of Spendius.
Notes at B8, C7.

phrastus saith. We may therefore note the difference of crueltie betwixt the people of the North and South: for that the first are transported with a brutish violence, like beasts without reason: and the other (like vnto foxes) imploy all their wits to glut themselues with reuenge: and euen as the bodie cannot bee purged of melancholy but with great difficultie, so the passions and perturbations of the mind, which grow by a setled melancholy, are not easily pacified. So as they which are possessed with this humor, are more subiect vnto frensie than any others, if they find not wherewithall to satisfie their affections. And therefore there are more mad men in the Southerne regions, than towards the North. *Leo* of Affrike doth write, That in the kingdoms of Fez and Marocco there are great numbers: And euen in Grenado (which is more Southernly) there are many hospitals for mad men onely. The varietie of mad men shews the naturall humour of the people: for although there bee store of fooles and mad men in all places and of all sorts, yet those of the Southerne parts haue many terrible visions, they preach and speake many languages without learning them, and are sometimes possest with euill spirits, hauing leane bodies, more like vnto ghosts then those corpulent and sanguin men towards the North, which do nothing but dance, laugh and leape in their fooleries: and in Germanie it is called the disease of *S. Victus*, the which is cured by musick: whether that the sweet harmonie thereof doth recall the reason which was distempered, or whether that musick doth cure the infirmities of the bodie by the mind, as the phisick doth cure the mind by the bodie, or that euill spirits which do sometimes torment mad men are expelled with this diuine harmonie, delighting in nothing but in discords: or as we reade that the euill spirit hearing the sound of a harp fled, and left *Saul* in rest, which seemes to haue been the cause why *Elizeus* when he would prophecie before the kings of Iuda and Samaria, he caused one to play of an Instrument. And when as *Saul* was encountred by the holie troupe of the Prophets playing vpon instruments of musick, presently the spirit of God fell vpon him. Oftentimes euill spirits doe applie themselues to the humor of mad men: for chollerike men strike in their furie, which happens not in those that are of a sanguin complexion, and much lesse in them that be flegmatike, which haue a Lethargie, the which is a dull and sleeping furie. And for that the melancholike man is the wiser, if he chance to fall mad, his furie is the more incurable, for that a melancholike humor suffers not it selfe to be gouerned as the rest: those that be sanguin, although they be not so often furious, yet are they often mad, the which is neuer incident to wise men, for *Tully* sayth, *Furor in sapientem cadere potest, insania non potest, & furioso curator datur, non insano, quia insanus dicitur, qui suis cupiditatibus imperare nescit*: Furie may well fall into a wise man, but not madnes: a gouernor is giuen to a furious man, but not to a mad man, for he is called mad that cannot rule his owne desires. As touching that which we haue said, that the people of the South are commonly more graue, more discreet, and more moderate in all their actions: it is plainely seene not only in diuers other nations, but also in this realme, which seemes to be the cause that those which haue made the customes, haue limited them to be of full age that liue towards the North at 25. yeares, and the others at 19 or 20 yeares, except it bee in those countries which border vpon the sea, whereas the people (by reason of their trafficke) are more politike. I cannot without the note of ingratitude to mine owne countrie forget the iudgement which the auncients haue giuen of the citie of Angiers, as it is to be seene in the letters pattents of king *Charles* the 5 called the wise, the which he granted for the priuiledges of the Vniuersitie of the said citie in these words, *Quodq́, inter regiones alias Regni nostri, ciuitas Andegauensis veluti fons scientiarum irriguus, viros alti consilij solet ab antiquo propagatione quasi naturali prouidere*: For that among other prouinces of this

OF A COMMONWEALE. 557

A this our realme, the citie of Angers like vnto a flowing spring of all sciences, is wont to send forth men of great knowledge and iudgement, as it were by a naturall propagation. These letters are dated the first of August in the yeare 1373.

We haue yet another notable difference betwixt the people of the South and of the North, for that these are more chast and abstinent, and those of the South much giuen to lust, the which growes by reason of the spongious melancholie, so as all Monsters do commonly come from Affrike, which *Ptolomie* saith to be vnder *Scorpio* and *Venus*, adding moreouer, that all Affrike did worship *Venus*: and *Titus Liuius* speaking of the Numidians (who were the most Southerly of all the Romans subiects or allies) The Numidians (sayth he) were giuen to venerie more than all the other Barba-
B rians. Wee read also that the kings of Affrike and Persia had alwaies great troupes of wiues and concubines, the which is not to be imputed to their depraued customes, for that at the West Indies king *Alcazares* had 400 wiues : and the father of *Attabalipa* the last king of Peru, (who was defeated by *Pizarre*) had 200 wiues, and fiftie children : and the king of Giolo had 600 children : so many had *Hierotimus* king of the Parthians, who had also a great number of wiues : and *Surenus* Generall of that armie of the Parthians which defeated *Crassus*, had ten thousand. The Scythians and Germaines haue enough of one wife : and *Caesar* in his Commentaries sayth, that the Englishmen in his time had but one woman to ten or twelue men : and many men in
C the North parts knowing their owne insufficiencies, geld themselues in despight, cutting the vaines Parotides vnder the eares, as *Hippocrates* sayth : who seeking out the cause of this disabilitie, concludes, that is for the coldnes of the bellie, and for that they are commonly on horseback : wherein he is deceiued, for *Aristotle* holdeth, that agitation doth prouoke; and as for want of heate, it is most certaine that those which dwell in cold countries abound with heate inwardly, as it appeares by the corpulencie and strength of those Northen nations : and contrarywise those of the South are very cold. It is the nature of melancholie which abounds most in them of the South, the which being frothie, prouokes to lust, as *Aristotle* writes in his Problemes, where he demaunds why melancholike men are most lecherous : the which is notorious in the Hare, the which is the most melancholike of all other creatures, and which only con-
D ceiues being big with yong, as well the male as the female, as *M. Varro*, and other writers do witnesse, and experience hath taught vs; so as we may say they are much deceiued which haue so much extolled the pudicitie and chastitie of the Scythians, Germaines, and other Northen nations, as *Caesar* writes in his Commentaries. Among the Germaines (sayth he) it is a dishonest and villanous thing for a man to know a woman before the age of 25 yeares, which thing they conceale not : and *Tacitus* sayth, there are none but the Germaines among the barbarous nations that content themselues with one wife : yea sometimes they liue in perpetuall chastetie, as the Emperour *Henry* 2. did, and *Casimir* 1. king of Poland, and *Ladislaus* king of Bohemia would ne-
E uer marrie; the which was not for that they were chaste, but rather through a naturall weakenes : and *Ihon* 2. great Duke of Muscouia, did so abhorre women, as he did euen sound at the very sight of them, as the Baron of Herbestein doth write, speaking of the Muscouites, They neuer see their wiues (saith he) vntill the day of their marriage. The people of the North are so little subiect to iealousie, as *Altomer* a Germaine, and *Irenicus* do write in commendation of their countrie, that men and women throughout all Germanie doth bathe together pel mel, yea and with strangers, without any touch of iealousie, the which as *Munster* sayth, is not knowne in Germanie : whereas contrariwise those of the South are so passionate, as oftentimes they dye of that disease. Being sent into England with an Ambassage, I heard *Mendoza* the spanish Ambassadour

The people of the South much giuen to women.

A strange maner of gelding of men, which they vsed in Scythia & low Germanie.

Melancholike men most giuen to lust.

The people of the North enemies to women.

The people of the South much giuen to iealousie.

Bbb iij say,

B5 Giolo : Gillo (L) *properly* Gilolo (Fr)   D6 *For* 25 yeares (Fr) *read* 20 yeares (L). Cf. *De bello Gallico*, VI, 21.   E2 sound *i.e.* swoon, faint   E4 *For* Alcomer *read* Altomer *i.e.* Andreas Althamer.

say, That it was a shamefull thing to see men & women sit together at holie sermons: to whome Doctor *Dale* Master of Requests answered pleasantly, That it was a more shamefull thing for Spaniards to thinke of satisfying of their lusts euen in holie places, the which was far from Englishmens minds. We reade in the historie of the Indies that the king of Puna was so iealous, as he did cut off the priuie parts, with the noses and armes of those Eunukes that attended of his women. The people that inhabit the middle regions hold a mediocritie in all this, but the most part of them allow but one lawfull wife: and although that *Iulius Cæsar* did persuade *Heluidius Cinna* to publish the law of Poligamie (or manie wiues) to the end that *Cesarion* (whom he had by the Queene *Cleopatra*) might be legitimate, yet this lawe was reiected: and the same lawe being reuiued by *Ihon Leiden* a cobler, hauing made himselfe king of Munster in Westphalia, did more trouble their estate than all the other lawes and alterations which he made. But the Romaine Emperours made a generall lawe to all nations without any distinction, noting him with infamie that had more than one wife: and since, that punishment of infamie hath been made capitall within this realme. But the Romane lawe hath been of no force in Affrike, for the inconueniences that happened; as it is incident to all those that seeke to applie the lawes of the people of the South to them of the North, making no difference of their dispositions, wherein many haue beene much deceiued, and euen *Cardan*, who sayth, That man is wiser than all other creatures, for that he is more hote and moyst; the which is quite contrarie to the truth, being most apparant that the wisest beasts are colder than any other, in the opinion of *Aristotle*. In like sort among militarie punishments, one was, to let the souldier bloud that had offended, for that those which abound in bloud had the passions of the mind more violent and lesse obedient vnto reason. Of all beasts the Elephant is held to be the wisest, of the Antients, for that their bloud is coldest; and the most melancholike of all others, the which makes them leapers: and to this leprosie the people of the South are much subiect, the which was called by the Antients *Elephantiasis*, a disease vnknowne in Greece before *Plutarch*, or in Italie before *Pompey*, as *Plinie* writes. But he deceiues himselfe to say, that it was proper to the Egyptians, for all the coast of Affrike abounds with them; and in Ethiopia it is so common, as the leapers are not separated from the sound. But Leprosie differs from *Elephantiasis*, the which is a great swelling in the thighes and legs, and leprosie is a canker or infection ouer the whole bodie. It may be this melancholie is the cause of long life, for all the Ancients consent, that the Elephant liues three and foure hundred yeares, and Rauens more, who haue little bloud, and that very melancholie. *Francis Aluarez* reporteth, that he had seene *Abuna Mare* Bishop of Ethiopia who was 150 yeares old, and yet verie lustie, which was the greatest age that euer was found in the Censors registers at Rome. And we must not wonder if *Homer* sayth, that *Memnon* king of Ethiopia liued fiue hundred yeares, for *Xenophon* long after writes, that in the same countrie there were men that liued sixe hundred yeares: but those of the South haue verie drie bodies, and are subiect to the falling sicknes, quartaine agues, and the Kings euill. Hereby we may iudge, that the people of the South are infected with great diseases of the bodie, and notorious vices of the minde: and contratywise there are no people that haue their bodies better disposed to liue long, and their minds apter for great vertues. So *Titus Liuius* hauing much commended *Hannibal* for his heroicall vertues, These great vertues (saied hee) were accompanied with as great vices, inhumane cruelty, treacherie, impietie, and contempt of all religion: for greatest spirits are subiect to greatest vertues and vices. Wherein the auntient writers haue bene deceiued, commending so highly the vertue, integritie, and bountie of the Scythians, and other people of

the

All lawes agree not with all nations.

Melancholy the cause of wisedom

Melancholy the cause of long life.

The people of the South subiect to extreames.

G1 cobler *i.e.* sartor, mender   I5–6 Abuna Marc   Notes at F6, I1, I10, K1.

the North, and condemning the vices of the South: For he deserues no prayse for his bountie, that hath no wit, and that cannot be wicked, for that hee knoweth no euill; but he that knoweth euill, and how to put it in practise, and yet is an honest man. In like sort *Machiauel* was ouerseene, saying, That the Spaniards, Italians, and Frenchmen, were the wickedest people in the world; shewing thereby, that he had neuer read any good booke, nor knowne the disposition and differences of nations. But if wee shall looke more narrowly into the disposition of the people of the North, of the South, and of them that are betwixt both; we shall find that their natures are like vnto young men, old men, and them of middle age, and to the qualities which are attributed vnto them. In like sort euerie one of those three in the gouernment of the Commonweale vseth that which he hath most at commaund: The nations of the North, by force; those in the middest, by equitie and iustice; and the Southerne parts, by religion. The magistrat (saith *Tacitus*) commaunds nothing in Germanie, but with the sword in his hand. And *Cæsar* writes in his Commentaries, That the Germans haue no care of religion, and make no account of any thing but of warre and of hunting. And the Scythians (saith *Solinus*) did sticke a sword into the ground, the which they did worship, placing the end of all their actions, lawes, religions, and iudgements, in their force and armes. We find that combats came first from the people of the North, as wee haue said elswhere: all the lawes of the Saliens, Francons, English, Ripuaries, and other Northerne nations are full of them: And the law of *Fronton* king of Denmarke would haue all controuersies decided by single combat: Which lawes could neuer be abrogated, although that both popes and other princes haue laboured much, not considering that the naturall disposition of them of the North, is quite contrarie to them of the South. And at this present in Germany they make great account of the Reisters law, the which is neither diuine, humane, nor canonicall; but the stronger commands the weaker: as *Brennus* captaine of the Gaules said vnto the treasuror *Sulpitius*. The middle nations are more reasonable and lesse strong, they haue recourse vnto reason, vnto judges, and vnto suits. It is most certaine, that lawes and the manner of pleading are come from the people of the middle nations; as from Asia the lesse (whereas great Orators and Pleaders were in credit) from Greece, Italie, and Fraunce: whereof a certaine Poet speaketh, *Gallia causidicos docuit facunda Britannos*, Eloquent Fraunce hath taught the pleading Brittons. It is not at this day alone, that Fraunce hath beene full of suits and contentions, the which cannot be altered and taken away, vnlesse they change the nature and disposition of the people: and it is much better to decide all controuersies by law, than by the sword; the one is fit for reasonable creatures, the other for brute beasts: and to conclude, all great Orators, Law-makers, Lawyers, Historiographers, Poets, Comedians, and others which draw vnto them the hearts of men with goodly discourses and sweet words, are in a manner all of the middle nations. We see in the histories both of the Greeks and Latins, before they attempted the least warre, the matter was debated with many solemne orations, denominations, and protestations: the which the people of the North do not vse, who presently fall to armes, and euen as the one vse force only like vnto Lions, so they of the middest arme themselues with lawes and reasons. In like sort the people of the South haue recourse vnto craft and subtiltie, like vnto Foxes; or vnto religion: for eloquent discourses agree not with the grosse wits of the Northerne people, and they are too base for them of the South, who allow not of any legall reasons or rhetoricall suppositions, which hold truth and falshood in suspence, but they require certaine demonstrations or diuine oracles, which exceed any humaine discourse. So we see that the people of the South, the Ægyptians, Caldeans, and Arabians, haue brought to light the hidden sciences both

Posse & nolle nobile.

The manner of gouernment in the three temperatures.

The Frenchmen giuen by nature to pleading.

The seuerall disposition of people according to the climats.

Bbb iiij   naturall

A4 *overseene i.e.* deceived, mistaken   C10–D1 *a certaine Poet i.e.* Juvenal (cf. *Satires*, XV, 111)
D10 *For* denominations *probably read* denunciations (cf. Fr).   Note at B4.

naturall and mathematicall, which torment the greatest wits, and force them to confesse the truth: and all religions haue in a manner taken their beginning from the people of the South, and from thence haue been dispersed ouer the whole earth: not that God hath any acception of places and persons, or that he doth not suffer his diuine light to shine vpon all men; but euen as the Sunne is seene more easily in a cleere and still water than in that which is troubled and filthie, so in my opinion the heauenly light doth shine far more brighter in pure and cleane spirits, than in those which are poluted with base and earthly affections. And if it be so that the true purifying of the soule is by his heauenly light, and by the force of contemplation in the most perfect subiect; without doubt they shall soonest attaine vnto it which haue their soules rauished vp into heauen; the which we see happen vnto melancholike men, which haue their spirits setled and giuen to contemplation, the which is called by the Hebrewes and Accademiks a pretious death, for that it drawes the soule out of this earthlie bodie vnto spirituall things. It is no meruaile then if the people of the South be better gouerned by religion, than by force or reason, the which is a point verie considerable to draw the people, when as neither force nor reason can preuaile: as we reade in the historie of the Indies, that *Christopher Colombus* when he could not draw the people of the West Indies vnto humanitie by any flatterie or faire meanes, he shewed them the Moone the which they did worship, giuing them to vnderstand that she should soone lose her light: three dayes after seeing the Moone eclipsed, they were so amazed, as they did what he commanded them. So the more we draw towards the South, the more deuout we finde men, and the more firme and constant in their religion, as in Spaine, and more in Affrike: whereas *Francis Aluarez*, and *Leo* of Affrike do say, that religion is much more reuerenced and honoured there than in Europe, where among other obseruations *Leo* notes, That in one citie of Fez there are seauen hundred temples, and the greatest is 1500 paces in compasse, 31 gates, and within it 900 lamps, the yearely reuenue of which temple is 73000 ducates. But *Aluarez* reports far stranger things of the greatnes of temples, of the incredible fasts and deuotion of the people of Ethiopia, and that the greatest part of the nobilitie and the people make verie strict vowes of religion. The greatest reason that hath so long maintained Ethiopia in that goodlie and florishing estate, and that doth still hold the subiects in the obedience of their prince and gouernour, is the assured persuasion which they haue (as *Aluarez* saith) That good and euill comes not vnto them by their friends or enemies, but by the will of God. As for suites, there are fewer than in any part of the world: and which is more strange, they keepe no records in writing of any decrees, iudgements, testaments, or contracts, except the accounts of the receit and expences. Who so should seeke to gouerne those nations by the lawes and ordinances vsed in Turkie, Greece, Italie, France, and other midle regions, he should ruine their estate. In like sort he that should accustome the people of the North to the pleading of France and Italie, should finde himselfe much troubled, as it hapned to *Mathias* king of Hongarie, who sent for Iudges out of Italie to reforme the iurisdiction of Hongarie, but in a short time the people were so troubled with this canonicall pleading, as the king was constrained (at the request of his Estates) to send back his Italian Iudges into their countrie. So *Ferdinand* king of Spaine sending *Pedrarias* Viceroy to the West Indies, the which then were newly discouered, he did expresly forbid him to carrie any lawyer or aduocate with him, to the end he should not sow any seeds of sutes and pleading where as there was not yet any. But who so should seeke to roote out all sutes and processes in France and Italie, he should thrust the people into perpetuall seditions: for euen the Iudges themselues being vnable to determine and end sutes, for the difficultie and contrarietie of reasons.

F4 acception *i.e.* partiality, undue favor Note at H10.

Of a Commonweale. 561

A reasons that are of either side, they oftentimes depute arbitrators, or else they prolong the sute of purpose to giue the parties occasion to agree friendly, and to discharge their choller vpon the Iudges and aduocates, else they would fall to armes, whereby it appeares that the people of the middle region are more capable to gouerne a commonweale, as hauing more naturall reason, the which is proper to humaine actions, and as it were the touchstone to destinguish the difference betwixt good and euill, betwixt right and wrong, and betwixt honest and dishonest things. Wisedome is fit to commaund, and force to execute, the which is proper to the people of the North, but they of the South being lesse capable of gouerment, giue themselues wholly to the contemplation of naturall and diuine sciences, and to discerne truth from falshood. *Three vertues proper to three nations of the North, South, & middle regions.*

B And euen as the wisedome to know good and euill is greatest in the people of the middest, and the knowledge of truth and falshood in the people of the South, euen so those arts which consist in handie works, are greater in the people of the North then in any other, and therefore the Spaniards and the Italians admire so many and so diuers kinds of works made with the hand, as are brought out of Germanie, Flanders, and England. And as there are three principall parts in the soule of man, that is to say, the imaginatiue or common sence, reason, and the intellectuall part, euen so in euery well ordered Commonweale the Priests and Philosophers are imployed in the search of diuine and hidden sciences, being as it were the hart of the citie, the magistrates and officers to commaund, iudge, and prouide for the gouerment of the State, being as it were the reason of the citie: and the common people applie themselues to labour and mechanicall arts, the which is conformable to common sence. *Prudentia. Scientia. Ars.*

C We may conclude the like of the vniuersall Commonweale of this world, the which God hath so ordained by his admirable wisedome: As the people of the South are made and appointed for the search of hidden sciences, that they may instruct other nations: Those of the North for labour and manuall artes: and those of the middle betwixt the two extreames, to negotiat, traffique, iudge, plead, command, establish Commonweales; and to make lawes and ordinances for other nations: whereunto those of the North are not so apt for want of wisedome: neither are the people of the South, be it that they be too much giuen to diuine and naturall contemplations; or for want of that alacritie and promptnesse, which is required in humane actions; be it that hee cannot yeeld in his opinions, dissemble, nor endure the toyle which is necessarie for a man of state; or that he is soone wearie of publike affaires, or that hee is oftentimes expelled by ambitious courtiers: as it happened to the wise men of Persia, who were suddenly put from the gouernment of the state, after the death of *Cambises*: and to the Pithagorians in Italie. And it seemes this was figured by the fable of *Iupiter*, who expelled his father *Saturne* out of his kingdome: that is to say, an ambitious and politike courtier dispossessed a Philosopher giuen to contemplation: For who so shall wel obserue the nature of Planets, he shall find in my opinion, that the diuision of them doth agree with the three regions aboue mentioned, according vnto their naturall order, giuing the highest Planet, which is *Saturne*, to the Southerne region, *Iupiter* to the middle, and *Mars* to the Septentrionall parts, the Sunne remaining in the middest, as the spring of light equally common to them all. Then followes *Venus*, proper to the people of the South, then *Mercurie* to them of the middle regions: and last of all is the Moone for the North parts, which sheweth the naturall inclination of the people of the North to warre and hunting, fit for *Mars* and *Diana*: and the people of the South to contemplation, besides their disposition to venerie. And the nations betwixt both the qualitie of *Iupiter* and *Mercurie*, fit for politike gouernments: the which hath a straunge sympathie in mans bodie, which is the image of the vniuersall world, and of a

D *The disposition of the three nations in the gouerment of the world.*

Why those of the South are not fit to gouerne a state.

E *The proportion of the Planets to the people.*

well

A 5 naturall reason *i.e.* prudence naturelle, prudentia (cf. 4 K2 and note) B 9 the hart *i.e. mens*, mind, intellect. Note at E 8.

562　The Fifth Booke

In Method. hist. cap. 5.

well ordered Commonweale: for setting the right hand of man towards the North, going from the East into the West, according vnto the naturall motion of the world, and the true constitution thereof; as I haue shewed in another place: the right part which is the more strong and masculine, hauing the lyuer and the gall, which the Hebrewes attribute to the Moone and *Mars*, sheweth plainely the nature of the people of the North to be sanguin and warlike. The left side, which is the feminine part (so called by the Philosophers) and the weaker, hauing the spleene and the melancholike humor, discouers the qualitie of the people of the South. Euen so we find more women in the Southerne parts, and more men in the North: for else it were impossible that euerie man in the South countries should haue so many wiues.

More women in the South than men.

And thus much as touching the generall qualities of all people: for as for the particular, there are in all places and in all countries men of all humors, and subiect to that which I haue said more or lesse. Moreouer the particular situation of places, doth much alter the nature of the countrey. For although there is not any certaine place, whereas we may distinguish the East from the West, as we may the South from the North: yet all auntients haue held, That the people of the East are more mild, more courteous, more tractable, and more ingenious, than those of the West, and lesse warlike, Behold (saith *Iulian* the emperour) how the Persians and Syrians are mild and tractable. Who sees not the furie of the Celtes & Germans, & how iealous they are of libertie? the Romans are courteous and warlike, the Ægyptians wittie and subtill; and withall effeminat. The Spaniards haue obserued, That the people of Sina (the which are farthest Eastward) are the most ingenious and courteous people in the world: and those of Brezill, which are farre Westward, the most cruell and barbarous. To conclude, if we looke well into histories, we shall find, that the people of the West do participat much of the nature of the North; and the people of the East with them of the South in the same latitude. The naturall bountie of the ayre, and of the Easterly winds, is the cause that men are more faire, and of a bigger proportion: and it is straunge, if the plague or any other infectious disease comes from the West into the East, or from the North into the South, it continues not: whereas if they begin in the East, or in any part of the South, they are long and verie infectious: as it hath bene proued by experience in old times, and at this day the coniecture is infallible in the countrey of Languedoc, whereas the plague is ordinarie. I haue noted many examples in another place, the which I omit now for breuitie sake: yet the difference of manners and dispositions of people, is much more notorious betwixt the North and the South, than betwixt the East and the West. But the greatest chaunge in particular, is the difference of hilly places from vallies: and of vallies turned towards the North or towards the South, in the same climat or like latitude, yea in the same degree, which causeth a wonderfull difference betwixt the one and the other: as it is plainly seene in mountaines which stretch from the West to the East: as the Appenin, which diuideth in a manner all Italie in two, mount Saint Adrian in Spaine, the mountaines of Auuergne in Fraunce, and the Pyrenees betwixt Fraunce and Spaine, mount Taurus in Asia, and Atlas in Affrike, which runs from the Atlantike sea vnto the confines of Ægypt aboue six hundred leagues; mount Imaus, which diuides Tartarie from South Asia, the Alpes which begin in France, and continue vnto Thrace: and mount Calphat, which diuides Polonia from Hungarie; the which causeth them of Tuscane to be of a contrarie humor to them of Lombardie, and farre more ingenious: as also wee see them of Arragon and Valence, and other people beyond the Pyrenean hilles, to bee of a different disposition to them of Gasconie and Languedoc, who hold much of the nature of the North; and the people on this side mount Atlas are farre lesse ingenious than the Numidians, and other

The people of the East more courteous, and more ingenious than those of the West.

Remarkable particularities of places.

H1 Sina *i.e.* China　　H1 the which　　H6 South, in　　I2 in another place *i.e.* in the *Methodus*, pp. 130–131　　I10 mount Saint Adrian *i.e.* the Cantabrian Mountains　　K4 Calphat (Fr 7) Carphat (Fr 1–6, 8) *i.e.* the Carpathians　　Note at F10.

other nations which are on the other side mount Atlas: for the one are very white, and the other exceeding blacke; the one subiect to many infirmities, the other sound, cheerefull, and of long life. We must not then maruell if the Florentine (who is towards the East and South, hauing the mountaines at his backe vpon the North & West) be of more subtill spirit than the Venetians, and more aduised in his priuat affaires: and yet the Florentines in their assemblies spoile all through the subtiltie of their wits: whereas the Venetians in their councels resolue grauely, as wee haue obserued for these two hundred yeres: for those that haue least wit, yeeld to reason, change their opinions, and referre themselues to men of best iudgement: but so many great spirits being subtill and ambitious, are obstinat, and will hardly yeeld from their opinions: & for that euerie man holds himselfe able to commaund, they will haue a Popular estate, the which they cannot maintaine without quarrels and ciuill dissentions, by reason of a naturall obstinacie, proper to the people of the South, which are melancholike, and to those which for the particular situation of the place, doe participat of the nature of the South. And euen as they which goe from Bouloigne to Florence, or from Carcassonne to Valence, find a great alteration from cold to hoat, in the same degree of latitude, by reason of the diuersitie of the one vallie turning to the South, and the other to the North: in like sort shall they find a diuersitie of spirits. And therefore *Plato* gaue God thankes, That he was a Grecian, and not a Barbarian; an Athenian, & not a Theban; although there be not twentie leagues betwixt Thebes and Athens: but the situation of Athens was towards the south, inclining towards Pyrene, hauing a little mountaine behind it, and the riuer Asopus betwixth the two cities: so the one was giuen to learning and knowledge, and the other to armes. And although they had one kind of Popular gouernment, yet was there no sedition in Thebes, whereas the Athenians had many quarrels and dissentions for the state. In like sort the Cantons of the Swissers haue maintained their Popular estate verie wisely these foure hundred yeres: the which the Florentines and the Genouois could neuer (with the excellencie of their wits) doe ten yeares together, without some mutinies. For the people of the North, and those that liue vpon mountaines, being fierce and warlike, trusting in their force and strength, desire Popular estates, or at the least electiue Monarchies: neither can they easily endure to be commaunded imperiously. So all their kings are electiue, whome they expell if they insult or tyrannize: as I haue obserued of the kings of Sweden, Denmarke, Norway, Poland, Bohemia, and Tartarie, which are electiue.

That which I haue spoken of the nature of the Northerne countries, agrees with the mountaines, the which are oftentimes more cold than the regions that are farre Northward: for in many places they haue snow and yce perpetually: and euen vnder the Equator the mountaines of Peru are so high and cold, as many Spaniards died for cold, and lay long dead before they corrupted; as we read in the histories of the West Indies. *Leo* of Affrike hath no cause to wonder, why the inhabitants of the high mountaine of Megeza in Affrike are white, tall, and strong; and those of the vallie are little, weake, and blacke: for generally both the men, beasts, and the trees of the mountaine, are of a stronger constitution than the others. And old men vpon mount Atlas of 100 yeres old, are vigorus, as *Leo* doth testifie. This force and vigour doth cause the mountainers to loue popular libertie, who cannot endure to be braued; as wee haue said of the Swissers and Grisons. And in like sort the inhabitants of the mountaines of Bugia, Fez, Marocco, and Arabia, liue in all libertie, without any commaunder: not through the assurance of any places that are fortified by nature, but for that they are sauage and cannot be reclaimed. The which should serue for an aunswere vnto *Plutarchs* demand, Why the inhabitants of the high towne of Athens required a Popular estate, & those of of the low towne the gouernment of few: considering the reason that I haue giuen. He should therefore wrong himselfe verie much, that should seeke to chaunge the Popular estate of the Swissers, Grisons, and other mountainers, into a Monarchie: For although a Monarchie be farre better of it selfe, yet is it not so fit for that subiect.

We must therefore carefully obserue what euerie nation desires, and what they abhorre; and first you must draw them to a milder kind of life, before you propound a royaltie vnto them, the which is effected by quietnesse and ease, inuring them to the studies of sciences and musicke. And for this cause *Polybius* saith, That the auntient lawgiuers of Arcadia, had strictly bound the inhabitants of the mountaines of Arcadia, to learne musicke, vpon great penalties: thereby to temper the naturall sauagnesse of that people. *Titus Liuius* also speaking of the Ætolians dwelling on mountaines, the most warlike and rebellious people of all Greece, he sayth, *Ferociores Ætoli quam pro ingenijs Grecorum*, The Ætolians were more fierce than was agreeable to the humor of the Greekes: They troubled the Romans more (although they had but three townes) than all the rest of the Greekes. In like sort, the inhabitants of the mountaine of Genes defeated the Roman armies, and continued warre against them one hundred yeares, neither could they euer bring them in subiection vntill they had transported them from the mountaines into the vallies, after which time they became good & quiet subiects; as we read in *Titus Liuius*. We must not then maruell, if by the Swissers lawes euerie man is bound to weare a sword, and to haue his house furnished with offensiue and defensiue armes: which other people forbad for the most part. And contrariwise the inhabitants of vallies are commonly effeminat and delicat: and euen the naturall fertilitie of the vallies, giue the inhabitants thereof occasion to glut themselues with pleasure.

In Swisserland euery one is boūd to weare a sword.

Inhabitants of vallies are effeminate.

As for the inhabitants vpon the Sea coast, and of great townes of traffique, all writers haue obserued, That they are more subtill, politike, and cunning, than those that lie farre from the sea and traffique. Therefore *Cæsar* speaking of the inhabitants of Tournay, These men (saith he) for that they are farre from the ports of the sea, are not soft & effeminat with the marchandise and delights of straungers. And to that end *Tully* said, That the inhabitants of the riuer of Genes, were called deceiuers and coseners; & those of the mountaines, rude and vnciuill: for that these were not accustomed to traffique, to sell and to deceiue. Wherfore *Ioseph* speaking of the inhabitants of Ierusalem & Sparta, saith, That they were remote from the sea, & lesse corrupted than others. For which cause *Plato* forbids them to build his Commonweale neere vnto the sea, saying, That such men are deceitfull and treacherous. And it seemeth that the prouerbe which saith, That Ilanders are commonly deceitfull; should be applied to this that we haue spoken, for that they are more giuen to traffique, and by consequence to know the diuersitie of men and their humors, wherein the policie of trading doth consist, to dissemble his words and countenance, to deceiue, lie, and to cousen the simple for gaine, the which is the end of many marchants. And to this end the Hebrewes applie that text of Scripture, where it is said, *Non eris mercator in populo tuo*, There shall be no marchant among the people: which some do interpret a deceiuer or cousener; but the Hebrew word signifies Marchant.

Merchants giuen to lie & deceiue.

There is also a great varietie for the difference of places subiect to violent winds, which makes people to differ much in manners, although they be in the same latitude and climat: For we see plainely, that those people are more graue and staied, when the ayre is calme and temperat, than those which liue in regions beaten with violent winds: as Fraunce, and especially Languedoc, high Germanie, Hungarie, Thrace, Circassia, the countrey of Genes, Portugall, and Persia, whereas men haue more turbulent spirits, than

The violence of the wind breeds a great varietie in men.

than those of Italie, Natolia, Assiria, and Ægypt, whereas the calmnesse of the ayre make men farre more mild. We doe also see in moorish places another difference of men, contrarie in humour to them of the mountaines. The barrennesse and fruitfulnesse of places doth in some sort chaunge the naturall inclination of the heauens: And therefore *Titus Liuius* said, That men of a fat and fertill soile, are most commonly effeminat and cowards; whereas contrariwise a barren countrey makes men temperat by necessitie, and by consequence careful, vigilant, and industrious: as the Athenians were, whereas idlenesse was punished capitally: Neither by *Solons* law were the children bound to reliue the parents, if they had not taught them some meanes whereby to get their liuing. So as the barrennesse of the soyle doth not onely make men more temperat, apt to labour, and of a more subtill spirit; but also it makes townes more populous: for an enemie affects not a barren countrey, and the inhabitants liuing in safetie doe multiplie, and are forced to traffique or to labour. Such a one was the citie of Athens, the most populous of all Greece: and Nuremberg, which is seated in the most barren soyle that can be, yet is it one of the greatest cities of the empire, and full of the best artisans in the world: and so are the cities of Limoges, Genes, and Gand. But those that dwell in vallies become soft and slothfull through the richnesse of the soyle. And as they that lie vpon the sea for their traffique, and those of barren countries for their sobrietie, are industrious: in like sort those which make the frontiers of two estates beeing enemies, are more fierce and warlike than the rest, for that they are continually in warre, which makes men barbarous, mutinous, and cruell; as peace makes men quiet, courteous, and tractable. And for this cause the English heretofore were held so mutinous and vnruly, as euen their princes could not keepe them in awe: yet since that they haue treated of peace and alliance with France & Scotland, & that they haue bene gouerned by a mild and peacefull princesse, they are growne verie ciuill and full of courtesie. Whereas contrariwise the French, which did not yeeld to any nation in courtesie and humanitie, are much chaunged in their dispositions, and are become fierce & barbarous since the ciuill warres: as it chaunced (as *Plutarch* saith) to the inhabitants of Sicilie, who by reason of their continuall wars, were growne like vnto brute beasts.

But he that would see what force education, lawes, and customes, haue to chaunge nature, let him looke into the people of Germanie, who in the time of *Tacitus* the Proconsull, had neither lawes, religion, knowledge, nor any forme of a Commonweale; whereas now they seeme to exceed other nations in goodly cities, and well peopled, in armes, varietie of artes, and ciuill discipline: And the inhabitants of Bugia (which in old time was Carthage, the which in former times had contended with the Romans for the empire of the world, being the most warlike people of all Affrike) by the continuance of peace, and the practise of musike (wherewith they are much delighted) they are become so effeminat and timerous, that *Peter* of Nauarre comming thither with fourteene ships onely, the king with all the inhabitants fled, and without striking stroke abandoned the citie, whereas the Spaniards built goodly forts without any opposition. Therfore *Plato* maintained, That there were two arts necessarie in al cities, Wrestling, and Musicke; the one being the nurce of the mind, the other of the bodie. If they neglect wrestling, the force of the bodie must languish: if the studie of Musicke, they will become rude and barbarous: if both, then must both bodie and mind grow dull with idlenesse and sloth: For commonly we see those whose minds are delighted with the sweet sound of Musicke, to be verie mild and courteous. What should I speake of the Romans, & of that famous citie, which had so often triumphed ouer Europe, Asia, and Affrike, whilest that it flourished in armes and learning; which hath now lost the beautie and vertues of their fathers, through sloth, to the eternall infamie of their idle

A fertill countrey breeds effeminat people.

A barren soyle makes the people wittie.

People giuen to warre fierce and sauage.

Education alters nature.

Wrestling and Musike necessary in all Commonweales.

C7 dispositions   C7 fierce   C9 were growne like vnto   Notes at A2, B6, B7, C3, E3.

prelats. Whereby it appeares how much education preuailes: whereof *Licurgus* F
made triall, hauing bred vp two grayhounds of one litter, the one in hunting, the other
to the pottage pot, and then made triall of them before all the people of Lacedemon,
bringing forth a quick hare, and pots of meat; so as the one followed the hare, and the
other ran to the meat. It is most certaine that if lawes and customes be not well maintained and kept, the people will soone returne to their naturall dispositions: and if they
be transplanted into another countrey, they shall not be chaunged so soone, as plants
which draw their nourishment from the earth: yet in the end they shall be altered,
as we may see of the Gothes, which did inuade Spaine, and high Languedoc; and the
auntient Gaules which did people Germanie, about the blacke forrest and Francford,
with their Collonies. *Cæsar* saith, That in his time (which was some fiue hundred yeres G
after their passage) they had chaunged their manners and naturall disposition with that
of Germany.

But it is needfull to purge an errour into the which many haue fallen, hauing taxed
the French of lightnesse, imitating therein *Cæsar*, *Tacitus*, *Trebellius*, and *Pollio*. If they
tearme a certaine alacritie and promptnesse in all their actions, Lightnesse; the iniurie
pleaseth me, the which is common to all the people of the middle regions betwixt the
Pole and the Equator: for euen in like sort *Titus Liuius* doth call them of Asia, Greece,
and Syria, *Leuissima hominum genera*, Light kind of men: the which the ambassadour
of the Rhodians did freely confesse in the open Senat at Rome. And *Cæsar* himselfe
doth interpret that which he would say, acknowledging that the Gaules haue good H
wits, and prompt, and tractable. And *Scaliger* borne at Verona, writes, That there is
not any nation of a quicker & more liuely spirit than the French; be it in armes or learning, be it in the trade of marchandise, or in well speaking: but aboue all, their hearts
are generous and loyall, keeping their faith more constantly than any nation. And
Baptista Mantuanus, the most excellent Poet of his age, writes thus of the French,

> *Hoat fierie spirits haue the Gaules, their bodies passing white,*
> *And of that white haue they their names; a crimson colour bright*
> *Their womans faces garnisheth, wherewith a comely grace*
> *Being mixt, Nature out of two sundrie colours one doth raise:*
> *Frolike they are, of cheerefull hew, delight in rounds and rime,* I
> *Prone vnto Venus sports, to banqueting, and when they see their time*
> *As prone vnto Church seruice. They list not beare the yoke,*
> *Hypocrisie they flie amaine, and what is falsly spoke:*
> *Hating the sullen Saturnist, they giue themselues to game,*
> *To hunting, hawking, hils and dales theile thorow them amaine.*
> *I, they in warres delight them too, the barbed horse to ride,*
> *Their brigantines, their bow, and speare, to vse it is their pride:*
> *Whole nights abroad to sleepe on ground it is their chiefest ioy,*
> *And to be slurd with sunne, and rust, th'account it nothing coy,* K
> *With dust to be orespred, to sweat vnder the weight of armes,*
> *For countrey, kin, and eke for king, to vndergoe all harmes;*
> *Yea death it selfe to them is sweet.*   Thus farre *Mantuan*.

The French held to be constant.

The constancie of the French appeares plainely by the religion which hath bene receiued and allowed by our predecessors, for the which we haue contended these threescore yeres with such obstinacie, as no nation in the world hath endured such burnings,
spoylings, tortures, and ciuill wars, as we haue caused vnto our selues. Wherby *Cæsars*
testi-

G5 *For* Trebellius, and Pollio *read* and Trebellius Pollio.   H6 French   I7 thorow *i.e.* pass through, range over   I8 I *i.e.* Aye   I9 brigantines *i.e.* body armor   K1 slurd *i.e.* stained
Notes at H2, K9.

testimony appeares to be very true, writing, That all the nations of the Gauls was much giuen to religion, which is far from lightnesse and inconstancie. But that fierie vigour, as *Veronensis* sayth, which we see in the french, and the wonderfull alacritie in doing of things proceedes from choller: from thence grow the violent motions of the mind, from thence come murthers, when as from words they fall to blowes, and choller enclining vnto rashnes breakes forth sodenly, the which if it be restrained within the bound of reason it doth greatly increase wisedome the gouernesse of mans life, as *Galen* sayth, writing of a chollerike humor, but if it be distempered, it turnes into rashnes, which properly we call lightnes, but this inconstancie is much more proper and incident to the people of the North. We haue said (speaking in generall) that the people of the South are of a contrarie humour and disposition to them of the North: these are great and strong, they are little and weake: they of the north hot and moyst, the others cold and dry; the one hath a big voyce and greene eyes, the other hath a weake voyce and black eyes; the one hath a flaxen haire and a faire skin, the other hath both haire and skin black; the one feareth cold, and the other heate; the one is ioyfull and pleasant, the other sad; the one is fearefull and peaceable, the other is hardie and mutinous; the one is sociable, the other solitarie; the one is giuen to drinke, the other sober; the one rude and grosse witted, the other aduised and ceremonious; the one is prodigall and greedie, the other is couetous and holds fast; the one is a souldier, the other a philosopher; the one fit for armes and labour, the other for knowledge and rest. If then the inhabitants of the South be wilfull and obstinate, as *Plutarch* sayth, speaking of the Affricans, maintaining his resolutions very wilfully, it is most certaine that the other is changeable, and hauing no constancie, those of the middle regions hold the vertue of the meane, betwixt wilfulnes and lightnes, not being changeable in their resolutions without reason, like vnto the people of the North, nor yet so setled in their opinions, as they will not be altered without the ruine of an estate. *Tacitus* writing of the Germains, saith, that they hold it no dishonor to denie their word. The Eastgoths and Weastgoths being expelled by *Attila*, they required some land to inhabit from the Emperour *Valens*, swearing to imbrace the Christian religion, which hauing granted them, they treacherously seazed on *Valens*, and burnt him aliue, and the people of Gronland which are neerest vnto the Pole, being of an inconstant humor, as *Munster* saith, did easily imbrace the Christian religion, and then afterwards fell againe to their Idolatrie. And as for the Muscouites, the Baron of Heberstein saith in their historie, that he hath not knowne any nation more disloyall, which will haue all men to keepe their faith with them, and they with no man. This falshood or treacherie comes from distrust, or from feare, and both the one and the other from want of spirit and wit: for a wise and considerate man as those of the middle region be, is not distrustfull, for that he foreseeth what may happen, and with courage and constancie doth execute what he hath resolued, the which the people of the South do not so well, being fearefull, nor they of the North which want wit. And to make it manifest how distrustfull and suspitious the people of the North be, looke into the realme of Denmarke and Sweden, whereas the magistrates do hide men in the Innes to heare what is spoken. The gouernment of euery Citie is of great force in the alteration of the peoples natures and dispositions: if they be oppressed with tyrannie and seruitude, they grow faintharted and deiected: they which liue in popular estates and enioy their liberties, must of necessitie be more bold and warlike, wherein not only the nature of the heauens and regions in generall are to be considered, but also the particularities of the regions. What may grow in the minds of men from the ayre, water, winds, hills and vallies, what from religion, lawes, customes, discipline, and from the state of euery commonweale, and

Inconstancie incident to them of the North.

The difference of humors betwixt them of the North and South.

The people of the North carelesse of their faith.

The gouernment of a state alters the peoples dispositions.

568   THE FIFTH BOOKE

Great differences of people in colour in the same climats.

not to obserue the climate alone, for we see in climates that be alike and of the same eleuation foure notable differences of people in colour, without speaking of other qualities, for that the West Indians are generallie of a duskish colour like vnto a roasted quinze, vnlesse it be a handfull of men that are black, whom the tempest carried from the coast of Affrike: and in Siuill of Spaine the men are white, at Cape Bonne Esperance black, at the riuer of Plate of a chestnut colour, all being in like latitude, and like climates, as we reade in the histories of the Indies which the Spaniards haue left in writing: the cause may be the change from one countrie to another, and that the Sunne in Capricorne is neerer vnto the earth by all the eccentricall latitude, the which are aboue foure hundred thousand leagues. The transportation of Collonies works a great difference in men, but the nature of the heauens, winds, waters and earth, are of more force. The Colonie of the Saxons which *Charlemaine* brought into Flanders, differed much from all the French, but by little and little they were so changed as they retaine nothing of the Saxon but the language, the which is much altered, pronouncing their aspirations more lightly, and interlacing the vowels with the consonants: as the Saxon when he calles a horse Pferd, the Flemings say Perd, and so of many others. For alwaies the people of the North, or that dwell vpon mountaines, hauing a more inward heate, deliuer their words with greater vehemencie and more aspiration than the people of the East or South, who interlace their vowels sweetly, and auoid aspirations all they can (and for the same reason women who are of a colder complexion than men, speake more sweetly) the which was verified in one tribe of the people of Israell, for those of the tribe of *Ephraim* which remained in the mountaine and towards the North, which they called Gallaad, were not only more rough and audacious and bold than those that dwelt in the valies, of the same tribe, but did also pronounce the consonants and aspirations which the others could not pronounce; so as being vanquished, and flying from the battaile, not able to distinguish the one from the other being of one nation, they watched them at the passage of Iordain, demaunding of them how they called the passage or foord, which was named *Schibolet*, the which they pronounced *Sibolet*, which doth properly signifie an eare of corne, although that they be both oftentimes confounded, by which meanes there were 42000 men slaine. It is most certaine that at that time the Hebrewes held the purenes of bloud inuiolable, and that it was but one tribe. That which I haue said, That the nature of the place doth greatly change the nature and pronunciation of men; may be generally obserued, and especially in Gasconie in the countrie which is called Labdac, for that the people put L. in stead of other consonants. We do also see the Polonians, which are more Eastward than Germanie, to pronounce much more sweetly: and the Geneuois being more Southerly than the Venetian these men pronounce Cabre, and the Geneuois say Crabe, whereby the Venetians distinguished them that fled, hauing gotten a great victorie against the Geneuois, making them to pronounce Cabre, and killing all them that could not do it. The like did the inhabitants of Montpellier in a sedition which happened in the time of king *Charles* the fift, seeking to kill the strangers, they shewed them beanes, which the strangers called *Febues*, and the inhabitants of the countrie called them *Haues*; like vnto the Sabins, which did pronounce *Fircus Fœdus*, for *Hircus Hædus*, as *Marcus Varro* sayth. And thus much touching the naturall inclination of people, the which notwithstanding carrie no necessitie as I haue sayd, but are of great consequence for the setling of a Commonweale, lawes and customes, and to know in what manner to treat with the one and the other. Let vs now speake of other meanes to preuent the changes of Commonweales, which groweth through aboundance of riches.

The nature of the place doth commonly change the language.

CHAP.

Of A Commonweale. 569

Chap. II.
The meanes to preuent the changes of Commonweales, which happen through the great riches of some, and exceeding pouertie of others.

Mong all the causes of seditions and changes of Commonweales there is none greater than the excessiue wealth of some fewe subiects, and the extreme pouertie of the greatest part. All antient histories are full, whereas it appeares that all they which haue pretended any discontentment against the state, haue alwayes imbraced the first occasion to spoile the rich: yet these changes and mutenies were more ordinarie in old time than at this day, for the infinite number of slaues which were thirtie or fortie for one free man; and the greatest reward of their seruice, was to see themselues freed, although they reaped no other benefit but only libertie, which many bought with that which they had spared all their life time, or else with what they borrowed, binding themselues to restore it, besides the duties they did owe to them that did infranchise them: besides, they had many children, which happens most commonly to them that labour most, and liue most continently, so as seeing themselues in libertie and opprest with pouertie, they were forced to borrow vpon interest, to sell their children, or to satisfie their creditors with their fruites and labours; and the longer they liued, the more they were indebted, and the lesse able to pay: for the Hebrewes called vsurie a biting, which doth not only wast the debtor vnto the bones, but doth also suck both bloud and marrow, so as in the end the number of the poore being increased, and not able to indure this want, they did rise against the rich, and expelled them from their houses and townes, or else they liued on them at discretion. And therefore *Plato* called riches and pouertie the two antient plagues of a Commonweale, not only for the necessitie that doth oppresse the hongrie, but also for the shame, the which is more insupportable to many than pouertie it selfe: for the preuenting whereof, some haue sought an equalitie, the which many haue commended, tearming it the nurse of peace, and loue betwixt subiects; and contrariwise inequalitie the spring of all diuisions, factions, hatred and partialities: for he that hath more than an other, and sees himselfe to haue greater wealth, he will also be higher in honor, in delights, in pleasures, in diet and in apparell, hauing no great regard of vertue: the poore on their part conceiue an extreme hatred and iealousie, seeing themselues thus troden vnder foote, they thinke themselues more worthie than the rich, and yet are opprest with pouertie, honger, miserie and reproch. And therefore many antient law giuers did equally diuide the goods and lands among the subiects, as in our time *Thomas Moore* Chancellor of England in his Commonweale sayth, That the only way of safetie for an estate, is when as men liue in common: the which cannot be whereas is any proprietie. And *Plato* hauing charge to frame the Commonweale and new Colonie of the Thebans and Phociens, by the consent of the subiects which sent Ambassadors to him to that end, he departed, leauing it vnfinished, for that the rich would not impart any of their wealth vnto the poore: the which *Licurgus* did with the hazard of his life, for after that he had banished the vse of gold and siluer, he made an equall distribution of the lands. And although that *Solon* could not do the like, yet his will was good, for that he made frustrate all bonds, and granted a generall abolition of debts. And after that the vse of gold and siluer was allowed in Lacedemon after the victorie of *Lisander*, and that the testamentarie law was brought

The chiefest cause of the change and subuersion of a state

The cause of mutinies in an estate.

The two plagues of all Commonweales.

Equalitie the surest maintenance of a Commonweale.

in, the which was partly the cause of inequalitie of goods: King *Agis* seeking to bring in the antient equalitie, he caused all bonds and obligations to be brought into a publike place and there burnt them, saying, That he had neuer seene a goodlier fier: then he began to deuide his owne goods equally, but when he sought to distribute the lands, he was cast into prison by the Ephores and there slaine. In like sort *Nabis* the tyrant hauing taken the citie of Argos, published two Edicts, the one to free them of all debts, the other to deuide the lands equally: *Duas faces* (sayth *Titus Liuius*) *nouantibus res ad plebem in optimates accendendam*: Two firebrands for them that sought for innouations to kindle and incense the people against the better sort. And although the Romains haue in that point seemed more iust than other nations, yet haue they often granted a generall recision of debts sometimes for a fourth part, sometimes for a third, and sometimes for all; hauing no better meanes to pacifie the mutinies and seditions of the multitude, least it should happen vnto them as it did vnto the chiefe men among the Thuriens, who hauing gotten all the lands into their hands, the people seeing themselues opprest with debt and vsurie, and without any meanes to satisfie, they fell vpon the rich and expelled them from their goods and houses. These reasons may be held goodly in shew, when as in truth there is nothing more pernitious and dangerous to Commonweales, than equalitie of goods, the which haue no firmer support and foundation than faith, without the which neither iustice, nor publike societie can stand, neither can there be any faith, if there be not a due obseruation of conuentions and lawfull promises. If then bonds be broken, contracts disanulled, and debts abolished, what can there be expected but the vtter subuersion of an estate? for there can be no trust one in an other. Moreouer such generall abolitions do most commonly hurt the poore, and ruine many, for the poore widowes, orphelins, and meaner sort hauing nothing but some little rent, are vndone when this abolition of debts comes; whereas the vsurers preuent it, and oftentimes gaine by it: as it happened when as *Solon* and *Agis* did publish an abolition of debts, for the vsurers (hauing some intelligence thereof) borrowed money of all men, to defraud their creditors. Besides, the hope of these abolitions do incourage the prodigall to borrow at what rate soeuer, and when their credit is crackt, to ioyne with the poore which are discontented and desperate, and to stir vp seditions: whereas if the hope of these abolitions were not, euery one would seeke to gouerne his estate wisely, and to liue in peace. If it be vniust for the creditor to lose his goods, and the debter to gaine that which is not his, how much more vniust is it to take land from the lawfull owners to enrich other men with their spoyles: for they that seeke to be freed from their debts, pretend the oppression of vsurie, and the barren nature of siluer, the which cannot be in lawfull successions, so as we may rightly say, that such a diuision of another mans goods, is a meere robberie vnder a shew of equalitie, and the ruine not onely of a Commonweale, but of all humane societie. To say, That equalitie is the nurce of friendship; is but to abuse the ignorant: for it is most certaine, that there is neuer greater hatred, nor more capitall quarrels, than betwixt equals: and the iealousie betwixt equals, is the spring and fountaine of troubles, seditions, and ciuill warres. Whereas contrariwise the poore and the weake yeeld and obey willingly the great, rich, and mightie, for the helpe and profit which they expect: which was one of the reasons which moued *Hippodamus* the law giuer of the Milesians, to ordaine, That the poore should marrie with the rich, not onely to auoid inequalitie, but also to make their friendship the more firme. And whatsoeuer they say of *Solon*, it appeares sufficiently by the institution of his Commonweale, that he made foure degrees of citisens according to their reuenewes, and as many degrees of state and honours: the rich had fiue hundred measures of corne, wine, or oyle,

Equalitie of goods dangerous to a Commonweale.

Abolition of debts ruins the poorer sort.

The equall diuision of lands most iniust.

Equalitie of goods the ruine of humane societie.

Solons deuision of citisens.

in rent; the next three hundred, others two hundred, and those which had lesse might beare no office of honour. And euen *Plato* hath made three estates in his second Commonweale, one richer than another, ordaining, That euery one of the fiue thousand & fortie citisens, should leaue one of his children sole heire. And as for that which *Licurgus* did, who would haue equalitie perpetually obserued in succession, diuiding the lands by the powle; it was impossible, for that he might see before his eyes, or soone after, this equalitie quite altered, some hauing twelue or fifteene children, others one or two, or none at all: the which would be more ridiculous in those countries whereas pluralitie of wiues is tollerated, as in Asia, and in a manner throughout all Affrike, and at the new found lands, whereas it falles out oftentimes, that one man hath fiftie children. Some haue sought to preuent this inconuenience, as *Hippodamus* law-maker to the Milesians, who would not allow aboue ten thousand citisens, the which *Aristotle* did like well of, but by that meanes they must banish the ouerplus, or else execute the cruell law of *Plato* approued by *Aristotle*, who hauing limited the number of his citisens to fiue thousand and fortie, ordained that they should cause the rest to miscarrie as soone as they were conceiued, and those that were borne lame or crooked should be cast off: the which cannot be spoken without great impietie, that the goodliest creature which God hath made, should not only be made away after it is borne, but also be destroyed in the mothers womb. Whereunto *Thomas Moore* Chancellor of England seemes to agree, who would not haue lesse than ten, nor more than 16 children in one familie: as if he might commaund nature. And although that *Phidon* law-giuer to the Corinthians did seeme to foresee it more wisely, forbidding expresly to build any more in Corinth (as they made a defence not to build in the suburbs of Paris, by the kings Edict in the yeare 1558,) yet the subiects multiplying they must either erect a new Colonie, or banish them iniuriously. But in my opinion they erre much which doubt of scarcitie by the multitude of children and citisens, when as no cities are more rich nor more famous in arts and disciplines than those which abound most with citisens. It is indeed lesse to feare that by reason of so great a multitude of citisens there will be deuisions, for that there is nothing that doth keepe a citie more free from mutinies and factions than the multitude of citisens, for that there are many which be as a meane betwixt the rich and the poore, the good and the wicked, the wise and the simple, and artificers and noblemen, which may reconcile these extremes when they disagree: and there is nothing more dangerous than to haue the subiects diuided into two factions without a meane, the which doth vsually fall out in cities where there are but few citisens. Laying aside therefore this opinion of equalitie in a Commonweale alreadie framed, rauishing and taking away another mans goods, whereas they should preserue to euery man his owne, according vnto the law of nature; and reiecting also them that would limit the number of the citisens, we will maintaine that this deuision of portions ought not to be allowed but in the framing of a new Commonweale in a conquered countrie: the which diuision should be made by families, and not by the powle, reseruing alwaies some prerogatiue for one of the familie, and some right for the elder in euerie house, according to the law of God; who doth shew vs with his finger what course to take, for hauing chosen the tribe of *Leui* to giue him the right of the elder aboue the other twelue, he gaue them no lands but only houses in cities, appointing them the tenth of euery tribe (which was twelue tenths) without any labour, the which was twise as much at the least as any tribe had, all things deducted. And among the Leuites the right of the elder was reserued to the house of *Aaron*, which had the tenth of the Leuites, and all the oblations and first fruites: and to euery priuat house he assigned twise as much of the goods and lands vnto the elder as to any other of the heires,

Equalitie impossible to be kept in a state.

A cruell law made by Plato.

It is iniurious to tye a citie to a certaine number.

Great cities are lesse subiect to seditions than others.

The manner how to diuide a conquered citie.

Deuision of land by the law of God.

Ccc iiij

A6 *by the powle i.e.* by the poll or head, equally C4 *For* 1558 (Fr 7) *read* 1548 (Fr 1–6, 8 and L).
D2 reconcile E1 *For* one of the familie *read* one of the families.

heires, excluding the daughters wholie from the succession, but for want of males in the same degree, whereby we may iudge that the law of God hath directly reiected all equalitie, giuing to one more than to another: and yet he hath kept among the twelue tribes, except that of *Leui*, an equall deuision of inheritances; and among the yongers an equall deuision of the succession, except the right of the elder, the which was not of two third parts, nor of foure fiue parts, nor of all; but of the halfe, to the end that such inequalitie should not be the cause of the great wealth of some few subiects, and the extreame pouertie of an infinit number: which is the occasion of murthers among brethren, of diuisions in families, and of mutinies and ciuill wars among subiects. And to the end the diuisions thus made may remaine indifferent, there must not be any prohibition of alienation, either in a mans life, or by testament; as it is vsed in some places, if we will obserue the law of God, which ordaines, That all successions sold, shall returne the fiftieth yeare to the house, familie, or tribe, from the which it was sold: wherby the poore that are afflicted, and forced to sell to supply their necesities, shall haue means to sell the fruits and reuenewes of their lands to the fiftieth yeare, the which shall returne afterwards to them or to their heires: ill husbands shall be forced to liue in penurie, and the couetousnesse of the rich shall be preuented.

Abolition of debts pernitious. As for abolition of debts, it was a thing of a daungerous consequence, as it is said, not so much for the losse of the creditor (the which is of no great moment, when the question is of the publike state) as for that it opens a way for the breach of faith in lawfull conuentions, and giues occasions to mutines to trouble the state, hoping still to haue abolition of debts, or at the least an abatement of interests which haue bene long due, reducing them to the fiue and twentieth penie: the which hath bene obserued in Venice. We see by the law of God, that debts are not cut off, but it giues the debtor respight the seuenth yeare, and suspends the debt. But the true meanes to preuent vsurers to ease the poore for euer, and to maintaine lawfull contracts, is to obserue the law of God, which hath defended all kinds of vsuries among the subiects: For the law were *Vsurie must bee cut off.* vniust in regard of straungers, if it were lawfull for them to deliuer out money vpon interest vnto the subiect, from whome he should draw his whole estate, if the subiect might not vse the like prerogatiue vnto straungers. This law hath bene alwaies much esteemed of all lawgiuers, and of the greatest Polititians, that is to say, of *Solon, Licurgus, Plato, Aristotle*, and euen the ten commissionars deputed to reforme the customes of Rome, and to make choyce of the most profitable lawes, would not allow aboue *Tacit. lib 5. Fest. lib. 19.* one in the hundred for interest; the which they called *Vnciarium*, for that the vsurie of euerie moneth came but to an ounce, which was the twelfth part of the hundreth crowne which had bene borrowed, and the vsurer which exacted any more, was condemned to restore foure fold: esteeming the vsurer (as *Cato* said) worse than a theefe, *An vsurer esteemed worse than a theefe.* which was condemned but in the double. The same law was afterwards published anew at the request of the Tribune *Duilius* in the yeare of the foundation of Rome 396: and ten yeres after *Torquatus* and *Plautius* being Consuls, it was reduced to halfe an ounce in the moneth, and a halfe penie in the hundred: so as it did not equall the principall but in two hundred yeares. But the yeare following vsurie was quite forbid- *Vsurie forbidden in Rome.* den by the law Genutia, for the dayly seditions which happened by the contempt of those lawes of vsurie: for what moderation soeuer you make of vsurie, if it bee any thing tollerated it will soone encrease. And those which maintaine vnder a color of religion, That moderat vsurie or rents, after foure or fiue in the hundred, are honest and iust, for that the debtor reapes more profit than the creditor, abuse the word of God, which doth expresly forbid it. For although some would take light interest for the good of the debtor, yet many would abuse it. For euen

as

A as a hatchet at the first makes but a little ritt, but in the end breakes all in sunder: so the sufferance of vnlawfull things, how small soeuer, growes in the end to all impunitie: as they which haue forbidden vsurie among Christians, and yet haue allowed it for the church and hospitals; and some also haue found it conuenient for the Commonweale and the treasure; but there is nothing that giues the subiect more occasion to breake a law, than to defend a thing, and tolerat it with some exceptions. The which is an ordinarie fault among princes and prelats, seeking to exempt and free themselues from those things which are forbidden to the subiect: & who would find that bad in particular, which is publikely allowed? And for that all defences in matter of lawes are vnprofitable without some punishment, the which are not regarded if they be not duly exe- Laws are vnprofitable without penalties.

B cuted, therefore the law Genutia being ill executed, was by little and little neglected. And therefore in England they haue prouided, that when as any edict was made, they presently appointed a Magistrat or Commissarie, to see the law obserued, who continued in that charge vntill the law were disanulled. But the couetousnesse of vsurers did so exceed, as they lent after twentie foure in the hundred, vntill that the law Gabinia did moderat the greatest interest, at twelue in the hundred, vnlesse it were in venturing at sea, whereas the creditor tooke vpon him the hazard: But this law was ill executed in the prouinces, whereas they did take fortie eight in the hundred for a yeare, For the extreame necessitie of him that borrowes, and the insatiable couetousnesse of him that lends, will alwayes find a thousand deuises to defraud the law. The punishment of

C vsurie was verie seuere in the Commonweale of the Candiots: and therefore hee that would borrow seemes as if he would take it violently from the creditor: so as if the debtor did not pay the intrest, which they could not recouer by law, he was accused as a theefe and robber: the which was but a grosse shift, in regard of their sales they make at this day, the Notarie putting in this cause, *And the rest in money*. It is true, that at the first councell of Nice, the bishops procured the emperour to forbid vsurie in money and fruits: the which in regard of fruits, were so much and halfe so much more: that is to say, fiftie for a hundred. But it was not obserued, especially for fruits, whereas he that borrowes in a time of dearth is glad to pay it againe and halfe as much more after haruest. Wherein it seemes there is great reason, for hee that lends might haue gained Vsurie in fruits seemes tollerable

D more if he had sold it in a time of scarcitie, as they do commonly. Besides there is nothing deerer than that which nourisheth, nor any thing more necessarie. And there- Nothing deerer or more necessarie than that which nourisheth. fore the emperour *Iustinian* hauing rated vsurie for the countrey man at foure in the hundred in money, he decreed, They should pay but twelue in the hundred in fruits, and not fiftie in the hundred as had bene formerly vsed. *Charles* of Molins had no cause to seeke to correct the Greeke and Latine text of the law, against the truth of all copies, that hee might defend the edict of *Lewes* the twelfth, and the decrees of the court of parliament, which made equall the interest in fruits and money: but the difference is great betwixt the one and the other: for by *Iustinians* law, the poore labourer reaped great profit, being freed for thirteen bushels of corne after haruest, for twelue

E which he had borrowed in a time of dearth: and yet by this correction which Molins giues, he should be freed for a third part of a bushell, the which is verie absurd; seeing that before *Iustinians* decree, it was lawfull to take fiftie in the hundred for fruits. It is farre better to relie vpon the law of God, which doth absolutely forbid vsurie, and the creditors good deeds shall be more meritorious and more honourable to lend without A meritorious deed to lend without vsurie. profit, than to receiue of the poore laborer, in the qualitie of vsurie, a handfull of corne, for so great and necessarie a good turne. Therefore *Nehemias* (after the peoples returne from captiuitie) did forbid them to take any more vsurie, as they had done before taking twelue in the hundred, as well in money as in fruits: and according to this example

ple

B8 yeare. For   C5 *For* this cause *read* this clause.   D2 (margin) deerer   Note at C4.

574 THE FIFTH BOOKE

ple the decree of Nice was made: but after that *Calixtus* the 3, & *Martin* the 5, popes, had giuen way to rents & annuities, the which were little before that time in vse; the interest hath growne so high, as the vsurie limited by *Iustinian*, & partly practised by the Cantons of the Swissers, is farre more easie and more supportable, although the laws of Fraunce and Venice do not allow any man to demaund aboue fiue yeares arrerages past: For this sufferance of interest, without interest hath growne to be a law, wherby the vsurers doe sucke the blood of the poore with all impunitie, especially in sea towns, where there is a common bourse or banke; as at Genes, where there are some worth foure or fiue hundred thousand duckets, others aboue a million, as *Adam Centenier*, & they say that *Thomas Marin* hath twise as much. So as the marchant for the sweetnes of gaine giues ouer his traffique, the artificer scornes his shop, the labourer leaues his labour, the shepheard his flocke, and the noble man sels his land of inheritance, to make fortie or fiftie pounds a yeare rent in annuities, in stead of ten ponnds a yeare in fee simple land. Then afterwards when as the rents faile, and the money is spent, as they know which know not any other good meanes to liue, giue themselues to theeuing, or to stir vp seditions and ciuill warres, that they might robbe secretly: the which is the more to be feared, when as one of the estates of the Commonweale, and the least in force and number, hath in a manner as much wealth as all the rest; as it hath beene seene heretofore in the state of the Church: whereas the hundred part of the subiects in the Westerne Commonweales, making the third estate, had the tythes of what nature soeuer, and against the lawes of the primitiue Church (as the Popes themselues confesse) and haue seized vpon testamentarie legacies, as well mouables as immouables, Dutchies, Counties, Baronies, Lordships, Castles, houses both within and without Townes, rents of all sorts, and bonds made freely; and yet they tooke successions of all sides: they sold, exchaunged, purchased, and imploied the reuenewes of their benifices for other acquisitions; and all without taxe, subsidie, or any charge, euen in those places whereas the taxes are personall. So as it was necessarie to enioyne the Cleargie to put away such land as had bene left vnto the church within a certaine time, vppon paine of confiscation: as by a law made in England by king *Edward* the first, which did forbid all church men to purchase any land; as it appeareth in *Magna Carta*: the which hath beene since renewed by the emperour *Charles* the fift in Flanders, vpon paine of confiscation: the which seemes to haue bene forbidden in old time. For we find that earles of Flanders haue bene heirs vnto priests: which custome was abolished by pope *Vrbin* the fift. For the same reason the parliament at Paris did prohibit the Chartrens and Celestines of Paris, to purchase any more, against the opinion of the abbat of Palerme. Yet these defences were grounded vpon the chapter, *Nuper de decimis*. And at Venice it hath bene enacted, and church men were commanded to dispossesse themselues of all lands, prohibiting to leaue any legacie to a Cleargie man, nor to make a will by the mouth or writing of a cleargie man. And by a law made at the request of the states of Orleans, the twentie seuenth article, all cleargie men are forbidden to receiue a testament or last wil, in the which any thing is giuen him (the which is verie ill executed) for the abuses that were committed. Not a hundred yeares since within this realme, they would not haue laid any dead bodie in holy buriall, if hee had not bequeathed some legacie vnto the church: so as they tooke out a commission from the officiall directed to the first priest of the place: who taking a view of his goods that had died intestat, bequethed what he pleased vnto the church in his name that was dead the which was reproued by two decrees of the parliament of Paris, one in the yeare 1388, and the other in the yeare 1401. I haue also a declaration drawne out of the Treasure of France, by the which the twentie barrons of Normandy named in the act, dated in the yere 1202, declare

Annuities worse than interest.

The Clergy enriched, and others made poor.

Clergy men forbidden to purchase lands.

In old time euery man was forced to leaue something vnto the church.

F6 of interest without   G3 ten pounds (*i.e.* one hundred livres)   G4–5 as they which know not
H1 primitive   H2–3 Dutchies, Counties,   I4 prohibit   I4 Chartrens *i.e.* Carthusians
Notes at G6, I1, K2.

OF A COMMONWEALE. 575

A declare vnto *Philip Augustus*, That the goods of him that dies without making a will, belonged vnto him, hauing laine three dayes sicke before his death: and by the confirmation of the priuileges of Rochell, graunted by *Richard* king of England and earle of Poitou, it is said, That the goods of the Rochelois should not bee confiscat, although they died intestat: the which was also common in Spaine, vntill the ordinance made by *Ferdinand* in the yere 1392, bearing these words, *Que no sellauen quintos da los que mueren sin fazer testamento dexando hijos o parientes dentro del quarto grado que pueden hauer & heredar sus bienes, vz.* The fift shal not be leuied of those which die intestat, so as they haue any children, or kinsfolke within the fourth degree fit to succeede. It is no wonder then if the clergy were rich, seeing that euerie man was forced to make a wil &

The auntient rights of the duke of Normandie and earles of Poitou.

B to leaue the church a legacie, vnder rigorous paines; being also straitly defended for many yeares, not to alienat nor rent out the goods of the church, vpon paine of nullitie. By the commaundement of *Charles* the ninth a suruay was made of all the reuenewes of the church within this realme, the which was found to amount to twelue hundred and thirtie thousand pounds starling a yere rent, not comprehending the ordinarie and extraordinarie alms. But *Allemont* president of the accounts at Paris, made an estimat, That of twelue parts of all the reuenewes of Fraunce, the Cleargie enioyed seuen. And by the registers of the chamber of accompts it appeeres, that within this realme there are twelue Archbishopricks, 104 Bishopriks, 540 Abbaies, and 27400 parishes

The reuenewes of the Clergy in France.

C or cures (taking euery towne for a cure, and the least village for one where there is a parish) besides Priories and begging friers. Their reuenues had been far greater if Pope *Iohn* the 22 had not disanulled the decree of Pope *Nicholas*, who had allowed all begging friers to enioy the frutes of lands, and the Pope should haue the proprietie, the which was a grosse cunning to frustrate the vowes of pouertie, for that the propertie is fruitlesse and in vaine, as the law saith, if the vsufruct were perpetuall, as bodies and colledges be I do not speake of the well imploying of their goods, but I say that this great inequalitie (it may be) hath ministred occasion of troubles and seditions against the Clergie, throughout all Europe, when as in shew they made a cullour of religion: for if this occasion had not been, they had found out some other. as they did in time of our

The propertie of land is in vaine whereas the vsufruit is perpetuall

An occasion found out to ruine the Cleargy.

D predecessors against the Templers and the Iewes; or else they would haue required a new deuision of lands, as *Philip* the Roman Tribune did for the people, pretending that there were but two thousand men in Rome which possessed all, although they were numbred in all to be aboue three hundred thousand; and those few did so increase in wealth, as *Marcus Crassus* by a declaration of the Censors, was esteemed to be worth sixe millions of crownes: and fiftie yeares after *Lentulus* the high Priest was found to be worth ten millions of crownes. The Romains laboured to preuent these inconueniences, publishing many lawes touching the deuision of lands: among the which the law Quintia and Apuleia, would haue the conquered lands deuided among the people, the which if they had bin well executed, those seditions had bin preuented which

The cause of seditions in Rome.

E so troubled the Commonweale: but the mischiefe was, that the conquered lands were farmed out by fauour to priuat men, with a pretence of benefit to the Commonweale, vpon condition to pay the tenth of graine, and the fift of frutes, and some rent for the pastures: yet this rent and other duties were not paied, for that great men held them in other mens names: for which cause *Sextus Titius* the Tribune presented a request vnto the people, to the end that the receiuers of the reuenues might leuie the arrerages that were due, the which was granted, but being not well executed, it was a meanes to present other requests vnto the people, that the lands and reuenues of the Commonweale which priuate men held without paying any thing, might be deuided among the people: the which did greatly amaze the rich, and caused them to suborne *Thorius* the

Tribune

A8 bienes, viz.   B1 leave the church   B9 540 (Fr) 548 (L)   C5 bodies *i.e. corps*, corporations
Notes at B1, B6, C5, C9.

Tribune vnder hand, That by his intercession vnto the people the lands should remain still in their possessions, and the arrerages should be paied vnto the receiuers of the reuenues: which law they caused afterwards to be abrogated, when as the magistrates themselues held the lands, of the which they could not be dispossest, nor forced to pay without great disturbance to the state. In the end the law Sempronia was published by force, at the request of *Tiberius Gracchus*, the which differed from the law Licinia, by the which all men were forbidden (of what estate or qualitie soeuer) to hold aboue fiue hundred acres of the Commonweales land, a hundred kine, and fiue hundred sheepe and goates, and to forfeit the ouerplus: but the law Sempronia spake of nothing but of the publike lands, ordaining that euery yeare there should be three Commissioners appointed by the people to distribute vnto the poore the surplusage of fiue hundred acres that should be found in any one familie: but the Tribune was slaine the last day of the publication, in a sedition moued by the Nobles: yet *Caius Gracchus* his brother being Tribune of the people ten yeres after, caused it to be put in execution, but he was slaine also in the pursuite thereof, after whose death the Senate to pacifie the people caused it to be executed against many. And to the end those lands should not remaine waste, the poore wanting cattell and meanes to till it, it was ordained that according vnto the law Sempronia of *Tiberius Gracchus*, the treasure of king *Attalus* (who had made the people of Rome his heire) should be distributed among the poore, to whom they had giuen part of the lands: by which meanes many of the poore were prouided for. And to take away occasion of future seditions, they sent away part of the poorer sort into Colonies, to whome they did distribute countries conquered from the enemie. But there was one article in the law of *C. Gracchus* which was most necessarie, and yet it was abrogated, Prohibiting the poore to sell or make away those lands that were assigned vnto them: for the rich seeing that the poore had no meanes to entertaine those lands, redeemed them.

Lawes made for the distribution of lands.

There was also another cause of this inequalitie of goods, which was by the libertie that euerie one had to dispose freely of his goods, and to whom he pleased, by the law of the twelue Tables. All other people, except the Athenians (where *Solon* first published this law) had not free libertie to dispose of their lands. And *Licurgus* hauing deuided the lands of the inhabitants of the citie into seuen thousand parts (some say more, others say lesse) and the lands of the countrie into twelue thousand equall parts, he did not suffer any one to dispose thereof; but contrariwise, to the end that in processe of time the seuen thousand parts of inheritance might not be sold, or diminished into many members, it was decreed, That the elder of the house, or the next of kin should succeed to the whole inheritance; and, that he could not haue but one part of the seuen thousand; and he must be also a Spartaine borne. Others were excluded from the succession, as *Plutarch* saith, speaking of king *Agesilaus*, who in the beginning was bred vp straightly as a younger brother, for that hee was issued of a younger house. This for a time did entertaine the 7000 families in equalitie, vntill that one of the Ephores being incensed against his eldest sonne, presented a request vnto the Seigneurie, the which passed for a law, by the which euery man had libertie to dispose of his goods by will. These testamentarie lawes being receiued in Greece, and afterwards published in Rome, and incerted in the twelue tables, were the cause of great alterations. But the people of the East and West might not dispose of lands by testament: a custome which is yet obserued in some parts of France, Germanie, and other nations of the North. And therefore *Tacitus* writes, that the Germaines had no vse of Testaments, the which many haue vnaduisedly attributed to ignorance and barbarisme. And euen in Polonia it is expresly forbidden by the lawes of the two *Sigismonds*, according

The testamentarie law the cause of inequalitie.

In Poland and many other parts of the North, they may not dispose of lands by testament.

Notes at I9, K8.

cording vnto the antient customes, to dispose of lands by testament. The Oxiles and the Phytales had a stricter custome, forbidding them to pawne any lands. And by the custome of Amiens and other customes of the Lowcountries of Flanders, no Nobleman might sell away their seigneuries vntill they had solemnely sworne pouertie: the which is also strictly obserued in Spaine. We haue also said before, that the law of God did expresly defend all alienation of lands, either in a mans life or by testament, reseruing the right of the elder in euery familie, without any difference of noble or villain, according to *Licurgus* law in his deuision of 7000 parts in Lacedemon: and those of Caux in Normandie, as well the Gentlemen as others, do much better preserue the dignitie and beautie of their antient houses and families, the which by this meanes are not dismembred, and all the estate of the Commonweale in generall: the which is the more firme and stable being grounded vpon good houses and families, and as great and immoueable pillers, the which could not support the burthen of a great building, if they were weake, although they were many. And it seemes that the greatnes of France, Spaine, and England is supported by great and noble families, and by corporations and Colleges, the which being dismembred into peeces, will be the ruine of the State. But this opinion is more probable than necessarie, vnlesse it be in an Aristocraticall estate: for it is most certaine that in a Monarchie there is nothing more to be feared than great men, and corporations, especially if it be tyranicall. As for a popular estate which requires equalitie in all things, how can it endure so great inequalitie in families, whereas some should haue all, and others die of hunger: seeing that all the seditions which haue happened in Rome and in Greece haue been grounded vpon this point. There remaines an Aristocratie where as the noble and great men are vnequall with the common people, and in this case the right of the elder may maintaine the estate, as in the seigneurie of Sparta, whereas the seuen thousand parts equally diuided vnto the elder of euery familie, maintained the State: and as for the yonger brethren, vertue aduanced them to offices and honors according to their merits: and commonly they proued the most famous, hauing (as *Plutarch* said) nothing to aduance them but their vertues. It was the antient custome of the Gaules: and without doubt our Nobilitie would be much more esteemed, if the prohibition of selling of their seigneuries were dulie executed, according to the lawes and ordinances of this realme, and of the Empire, where it is better obserued. The like defences were made in Polonia, by the laws of *Albert*, & *Sigismond Augustus* kings in the yere 1495 & 1538, & by an edict made by *Peter* duke of Brittaine, forbidding the common people to purchase the seigneuries of noble men, vpon paine of confiscation. And although that *Lewis* the 12 disanulled those defences in the yeare 1505, yet king *Francis* the first renewed the Edict in the yeare 1535 vnder the same paine of confiscation. The meanes to vnite the nobilitie and the common people more strictly together, is to marrie the yonger children of noble houses being poore (in an Aristocraticall estate) with the Plebeians that are rich, as they did in Rome after the law Canuleia; the which is practised at this day by the Venetians, and almost in euery Commonweale, whereas the nobilitie hath any prerogatiue ouer the common people: the which is the surest way to maintaine the nobilitie in wealth, honour, and dignitie. And yet it is necessarie to moderat the dowries of women in what estate soeuer, least that meane houses be not beggered to enrich the nobles: wherein the antient lawgiuers haue been much troubled to obserue this equalitie, and to prouide that ancient houses and families might not be dismembred and ruined by the daughters. The law of God would not allow the daughters to succeed if there were any brethren: and although there were not any, yet the daughters that were heires were commanded to marrie the next kinsman of that familie: to the end

In some places noble men may not sell away their seigneuries.

Great kingdoms supported by noble families, especially in an Aristocratical estate, but they are contrarie to a Popular estate, or to a Tyranny.

Inequalitie maintained the estate of Sparta.

Laws prohibiting noble men to sell their seigneuries.

A meanes to vnite the gentry & the plebeians.

Ddd   saith

A1 Oxiles *i.e.* subjects of Oxylus, King of Elis (cf. Aristotle, *Politics*, 1319a)   A2 Phytales *i.e.* people of Aphytis (cf. *ibid.*)   A5 (margin) noble men   Notes at A8, E5.

578   THE FIFTH BOOKE

In the East parts the daughters inherit no lands.

saith the law, that the inheritance may not be drawne from the house by the daughters. This law was obserued in Greece, where as the next kinsman married the heire, neither might the daughter marrie with any other. In Persia and Armenia the daughter had nothing of the house but the moueables: a custome which is yet obserued in all the East, and almost throughout all Affrike, although that *Iustinian* the Emperour, or rather *Theodora* his wife, hauing alwayes fauored her owne sexe, reformed that custome of Armenia, terming it barbarous, not regarding the intention of the antient lawgiuers. *Hippodamus* lawgiuer to the Milesians, would not frustrate the daughters of all succession, but he ordained that the rich should marrie with the poore, wherein he did obserue the equalitie of goods, and entertained loue betwixt the couples, and betwixt the poore and the rich. It is most certaine that if the daughters be made equall with the sonnes in the right of succession, families shall be soone dismembred: for commonly there are more women than men, be it in Commonweales in generall, or in priuate families: the which was first verified at Athens, where as the pluralitie of women gaue name vnto the citie: and within these twentie yeares at Venice, (whether comes a world of strangers) there was found vpon a suruaie two thousand women more than men: whether it be that they are not subiect to the dangers of warre and trauell, or that nature is apter to produce those things that are lesse perfect. And therefore *Aristotle* said in his Politikes, That of fiue parts of inheritance the women of Sparta held three, the which came by the permission of the testamentarie law; and for this cause (saith he) they comanded absolutely ouer their husbands, whom they called Ladies. But to preuent this inconuenience at Rome, *Voconius Saxa* the Tribune, by the persuasion of *Cato* the Censor, presented a request vnto the people, the which passed for a law, whereby it was enacted, That the females should not succeed so long as there were any male carrying the name, in what degree of consanguinitie soeuer he were; and, that they might not haue giuen them by testament aboue the fourth part of the goods; nor more than the least of the Testators heires. This law retained the antient families in their dignities, and the goods in some equalitie, keeping women in some sort in awe: yet they found a meanes to defraud it, by legacies and feofments made in trust to friends, with request to restore the successions or legacies vnto the women which could not recouer them by order of law nor by petition, before *Augustus* time; who following the pernitious counsell of *Trebatius*, tooke an occasion to abrogate the law, demanding a dispensation of the law Voconia of the Senat, for his wife *Liuia*: so as this law being troden vnder foot, the Roman citisens began to be slaues vnto their wiues, who were their mistresses both in name and effect. Then might you haue seene women wearing two rich successions at their eares, as *Seneca* saith; and the daughter of a Proconsull who did weare at one time in apparell and iewels the value of three millions of crownes, the inequalitie of goods being then at the highest, after which time the Roman empire declined still vntill it was wholie ruined. By the antient custome of Marseilles it was not lawfull to giue aboue a hundred crownes in marriage with a daughter, and fiue crownes in apparell. And by the Statutes at Venice it is forbidden to giue aboue 1600 ducats to a noble mans daughter: and if a Gentleman of Venice marrie a citisens daughter, he may not take aboue two thousand ducats; nor the females succeed so long as there is any male of the familie: but in truth this law is as ill obserued as that of king *Charles* the 9, which forbids to giue vnto a daughter in marriage aboue a thousand pounds starling, and yet the ordinance of king *Charles* the 5 doth giue no more vnto the daughters of the house of France. And although that *Elizabeth* of France, daughter to *Philip* the faire were married vnto the king of England, yet had she but twelue hundred pounds starling to her dowrie. Some one will say vnto

The inequalitie of goods grows, for that the daughters being heires are married to the rich.

The law of succession at Rome, defrauded.

A commendable law at Venice.

The law of Fraunce for the marriage of daughters.

G 5 whether *i.e.* whither   Note at H 1.

OF A COMMONWEALE. 579

to me, that it was very much, considering the scarcetie of gold and siluer in those daies: but the difference also is very great betwixt a thousand pounds, and foure hundred thousand crownes. It is true that she was the goodliest Princesse of her age, and of the greatest house that was at that day. And if we will seeke higher, we shall find in the law of God that the marriage of a daughter at the most was taxed but at fiftie sicles, which make fower pounds starling of our money, in which penaltie he was condemned that had seduced a virgin, whom also he was forced by the law to bring home, if the father of the maiden so pleased: which makes me beleeue that the antient custome of the Persians is likely, for that the Commissioners deputed yearely to marrie the maids gaue the honestest and fairest to them that offred most, and with that money they married them that were lesse esteemed (that none might be vnprouided for) with this caution to them that married the deformed, Neuer to put away their wiues, but in restoring of their dowries: by the which they prouided for the marriage of maids, the modestie of wiues, the dignitie of husbands, and the publike honestie whereon wise lawgiuers should haue a speciall care, as *Plato* had. For to take from the daughters all meanes to prefer themselues according to their qualities, were to giue occasion of a greater inconuenience. And it seemes that the customes of Aniou and of Maine haue giuen them a third part in successions, of gentlemen in fee simple, the which is left to the yonger males but for terme of life, to the end the daughters should not be vnprouided for, hauing not meanes to aduance themselues like vnto the males: for the reformation of which custome they haue heretofore made great complaints: the which might as well be done, as in the custome of *Mondidier*, and in that of *Vendosme*, (an antient dependance of the countrie of Aniou, before that it was erected to a Countie or a Duchie) where as a yonger brother of the house of Aniou, hauing taken his elder brother prisoner, made him to change the custome of Aniou in regard of the Chasteleine of *Vendosme*, the which he had but for terme of life. And although that in Brittanie by the decree of Cont *Geoffrie* in the yeare 1181 the eldest in gentlemens houses caried away all the succession, and maintained the yonger at his owne pleasure: yet to preuent infinit inconueniences, *Arthur* the first duke of Brittanie enacted, That the yonger children should haue a third part of the succession for terme of life, as it is obserued in the countrie of Caux, by a decree of the Parliament at Rouen, the daughters portions being deducted. I haue hitherto treated of subiects only, but we must also take heed least that strangers set footing within the realme, and purchase the goods of the naturall subiect: and preuenting all idle vagabonds which desguise themselues like Egiptians, when as in truth they are very theeues, whom all Magistrates and Gouernors are commanded to expell out of the realme by a law made at the estates of Orleance, as it was in like manner decreed in Spaine by *Ferdinand* in the yeare 1492 in these words, *Que los Egiptianos con sennores salgan del Reyno dentro sessenta dias*: That all the Egiptians with their women shall depart out of the realme within threescore daies. This swarme of caterpillers do multiplie in the Pyrenees, the Alps, the mountaines of Arabia, and other hillie and barren places, and then come downe like wasps to eate the honie from the bees. Thus in my opinion I haue set downe briefly the fittest meanes to preuent the extreme pouertie of the greatest part of the subiects, and the excessiue wealth of a small number, leauing to discourse hereafter, If the lands appointed for the seruice of the warre may be dismembred or sold. Let vs now see if the goods of men condemned should be left vnto their heires.

The law of God for dowries.

The law of Persia.

Custome of Aniou.

Ddd ij   CHAP.

A5 sicles *i.e.* shekels (cf. Deut. 22:29) (Fr and L).   B8 successions of gentlemen   C7 For 1181 read 1185
D9 Egiptians   Notes at A2, C2, D9, E2.

Chap. III.

Whether the goods of men condemned should be applied vnto the common treasure, or to the Church; or els left vnto the heires.

His Chapter depends vpon the former, for one of the causes which brings the subiects to extreame pouertie, is to take the goods of the condemned from their lawfull heires, and especially from children, if they haue no other support nor hope, but in the succession of their parents: and the more children they haue, the greater their pouertie shall be, to whome the succession of their fathers belongs by the law of nature, and who by the law of God should not suffer for their fathers offences. By which confiscations not onely the lawes of God and nature seeme to be violated, but the children (who haply haue bene bred vp in delights) are oftentimes reduced to such pouertie and miserie, as they are thrust into despaire, and attempt any villanie, either to be reuenged, or to flie from want which doth oppresse them. For we may not hope, that they which haue bene bred vp as maisters, will serue as slaues: and if they haue not in former times learned any thing, they will not now begin, when as they haue no meanes. Besides the shame they haue either to beg, or to suffer the reproach of infamie, doth force them to banish themselues, and to ioyne with theeues & robbers: so as for one sometimes there goe forth two or three worse than hee that had lost both life and goods: so as the punishment which serueth not onely for a reuenge of the offence, but also to diminish the number of the wicked, and for the saftie of the good, produceth quite contrarie effects. These reasons briefly run ouer, and amplified by some examples, seeme necessarie to shew that the law of *Iustinian* the emperour, receiued and practised in many countries, is most iust and profitable: whereby it was enacted, That the goods of them that were condemned should be left vnto their heirs, vnlesse it were in case of high treason. Contrariwise some may say, that this is a new law, and contrarie to all the auntient lawes and ordinances of the wisest princes & lawgiuers, who would haue the goods of any one condemned, adiudged vnto the publike, without some especiall cause to moue them to the contrarie: bee it for reparation of faults, which oft times is pecuniarie, and is to be paid to the Commonweale interessed, for els there should bee no meanes to punish by fines, the which is an ordinarie kind of punishment: be it for the qualitie of the crimes, and of those that haue robbed the Commonweale, which must be satisfied out of his goods that hath offended: or to terrifie the wicked, which commit all the villanies in the world to enrich their children, and many times they care not to loose their liues, yea to damne themselues, so as their children may be heires of their robberies and thefts. It is needlesse to proue this by examples, the which are infinit: I will onely produce one of *Cassius Licinius*, who being accused and condemned of many thefts and extortions, and seeing *Cicero* (who was then president) putting on his purple robe, to pronounce the sentence of confiscation and banishment, he sent one to tell *Cicero* that he was dead during the processe, & before the condemnation, choaking himselfe in view of the judges with a table napkin, to the end he might saue his goods for his children: Then *Cicero* (saith *Valerius*) would not pronounce the sentence. It was in the power of the accused to saue his life in abandoning of his goods, according vnto the conclusions of his accusers: as *Verres* and many others in like case did: for by the law Sempronia they might not condemne a bourgesse of Rome to death, nor whip them by the law Portia. And although that *Plutarch*, and *Cicero* himselfe writes to his friend *Atticus*, That hee had condemned *Licinius,*

It seemes against the law of nature to take the succession of the father condemned from the child.

Iustinian left the goods of the condemned vnto the heire.

Wicked men wil attempt any thing to enrich their children.

OF A COMMONWEALE. 581

nius, it is to be vnderstood by the aduice and opinion of all the judges, not that he had pronounced the sentence, for those lawes were not yet made against them which killed themselues before sentence. And a hundred and fiftie yeares after, if any one being accused and guiltie of any crime, had killed himselfe through dispaire or griefe, he was buried and his testament was of force, in the time of cruell *Tiberius*, *Pretium festinandi*, (saith *Tacitus*) that is to say, Murtherers in their persons had that aduantage ouer others. But whether that he were condemned after his death, or that he died of griefe, it appeares plainely that many make no difficultie to damne themselues to enrich their children. And it may be there is nothing that doth more restraine the wicked from offending, than the feare of confiscation, whereby their children should be left beggers. Therefore the law saith, That the Commonweale hath a great interest, that the children of them that are condemned, should be poore and needie. Neither can wee say, that the law of God or nature is therein broken, nor is the sonne punished for the father, for that the fathers goods are not the childrens: and there is no succession of him whose goods are iustly taken away before he is dead. *A law in fauour of murtherers.* *The law of confiscation terrifies the wicked.*

And if any one feares that want wil driue the children to dispaire, and to all kinds of wickednesse: much more reason hath he to feare, that wicked children will abuse their fathers goods, to the ruine of good men and of the Commonweale. And therefore the law excludes the sonnes of him that is condemned for high treason, from all successions direct and collaterall, and leaues vnto the daughters (who haue lesse power to reuenge) a fourth part of their mothers goods. But there is a greater inconuenience if the goods of the condemned be left vnto their heirs, then shall the accusers and informers haue no rewards, and wickednesse shall remaine vnpunished. *Rewards are necessary for accusers.*

These be the inconueniences on either part, but to resolue of that which is most fit, is most necessarie that the true debts being either publike or priuat, and the charges of informations, should be deducted out of the goods of the condemned, if they haue wherewithall: else there should be no punishment of the wicked. Yet this clause ought not to be annexed vnto the sentence, and hath bene reproued by many decrees of the court of parliament, to the end that the judges may know, that they ought to do iustice although the condemned hath not any thing. In like sort it is necessarie that fines & amercements should be leuied out of their goods that are condemned in any summe of money, prouided alwayes, that it be taken out of their mouable goods, or out of that which they haue purchased, and not out of those lands which come by succession, the which must be left vnto the heire. And in capitall crimes, that the mouables & lands purchased, should be forfeited and sold to them that would giue most, for the charges of the processe, and the reward of informers; and the rest to be imployed to publike & charitable vses, the succession remaining to the lawful heires: in so doing you shal preuent the extreame pouertie of the children, the couetousnesse of slaunderers, the tyranny of bad princes, the euasion of the wicked, and the impunitie of offences. For to forfeit those lands which are tyed vnto the house, were no reason, seeing it is not lawfull to alienat them by testament, nor in many places to dispose therof in their life time: by the which should follow a great inequalitie of goods. And for this reason the goods and lands purchased must be sold, and not applied vnto the church or publike treasure, least that in the end all priuat mens estates should come to the publike, or to the church: for that it is not lawfull to alienat those goods which are vnited to the reuenewes of the Commonweale, or to the church. Moreouer informers and accusers must bee rewarded, not with the possessions of the condemned (which might animat them to accuse good men wrongfully) but with some peece of mony: For the desire to haue the house or inheritance of another man, the which they could not obtaine for money, would *What order is to be obserued in their goods that are condemned.* *Lands which come by succession cannot be forfeited.*

Ddd iiij be

582 THE FIFTH BOOKE

be a great occasion of false accusers to ruine the innocent. Yet must informers haue some reward, else the wicked shall continue their villanies with all impunitie. And as a good huntsman will neuer faile to reward his dogges with the intrails of the beast, to make them the more liuely: so a wise law-giuer must reward them which seize vppon the wolues and lions of the Commonweales. And for that there is nothing (after the honour due vnto God) of greater consequence than the punishment of offences, wee must seeke all meanes possible to attaine vnto it. But the difficultie is not small, to take the confiscations from the publike, to imploy them as I haue said, and especially in a Monarchy. Yet there are many reasons, the which a wise and vertuous prince will more esteeme for his reputation, than all the goods in the world gotten by confiscations. For if the publike reuenewes be great, or the charges and impositions laid vppon the subiect sufficient, the confiscations ought not to be adiudged vnto the treasure, if the Commonweale be poore, much lesse may you inrich it with confiscations. In so doing you shall open a gate for false accusers to make marchandise of the blood of the poore subiects, and for princes to become tyrants. So we see that the height of all tyranny hath bene in proscriptions and confiscation of the subiects goods. By this means *Tiberius* the emperour made the way to a most cruell butcherie, leauing to the value of sixtie seuen millions of crownes gotten the most part by confiscations. And after him his nephewes *Caligula* and *Nero*, polluted their hands with the blood of the best and most vertuous men in all the empire, and all for their goods. It is well knowne that *Nero* had no colour to put to death his maister *Seneca*, but for his wealth. Neither shall there be at any time false accusers wanting, knowing they shall neuer bee called in question for their slaunders, being supported by the prince, who reaps part of the profit. *Plinie* the younger speaking of those times, Wee haue (saith hee) seene the iudgements of informers, like vnto theeues and robbers: for there was no testament, nor any mans estate assured. And therefore by the lawes, the kings procurator is enioyned to name the informer, least the accusation in the end should proue slaunderous: the which is necessarily obserued in Spaine, before that the kings procurator is admitted to accuse any man, by an edict of *Ferdinand*, made in the yere 1492, in these tearmes, *Que ningun fiscal pueda accusar a conseio persone particular, sin dar primeramente delator*, That no fiscall or publike officer may accuse any priuat person before the Councell, but hee shall first giue in the accusers name. If confiscations haue beene alwayes odious in euerie Commonweale, much more daungerous be they in a Monarchy than in a Popular or Aristocraticall estate, where false accusers are not so easily receiued.

If any one will obiect, That we need not to feare these inconueniences in a Royall estate, hauing to doe with good princes: I annswere, that this right of confiscation is one of the greatest means that euer was inuented, to make a good prince a tyrant, especially if the prince be poore. For he that hath no pretext to put his subiect to death; if he hopes to haue his goods thereby, he will neuer want crime, accusers, nor flatterers. And oftentimes the wiues of princes kindle this fire, & inflame their husbands to al crueltie, to enioy the goods of them that are condemned. *Achab* king of Samaria could not get *Naboths* vinyard, neither for price nor praier, but queene *Iesabel* subborned two false witnesses, to condemne the innocent as guiltie of treason both against God and man. And *Faustine* did still importune the emperour *Marcus Aurelius* her husband, to put to death the poore innocent children of *Auidius Cassius*, beeing condemned for treason, whose goods the emperour left vnto his children; as the kings of Persia were woont to doe, euen in cases of high treason, and hath bene often practised in this realm. And by the lawes of Polonia, confiscation hath no place but in the highest degree of treason: and oftentimes it is giuen vnto the kinsfolkes. But it is a hard matter to recouer the

The inconueniences which grow in adiudging of confiscations vnto the publike.

Confiscations the cause of tyranny.

Confiscations most daungerous in a Monarchy.

Tyrants are enriched by false accusations, by meanes of confiscations.

F9 Monarchy   G6 confiscation   H10 persona   H10 primeramente   I6 aunswere
Note at G5.

OF A COMMONVVEALE. 583

A the goods which are once forfeited, be it by right or wrong; for they hold it for a rule, That amercements once adiudged to the crowne and receiued, are neuer restored, although the iudgement were false. The which is the more to bee feared, for that the goods of them that are condemned for treason, are forfeited to the prince, and not to the lords of the soyle, who cannot pretend any thing if another mans subiect bee condemned for treason, as they may doe in all other crimes. And although we may number as many good and vertuous kings in this realme, as euer were in any Monarchie vpon this earth, yet wee shall see that the reuenewes haue beene more augmented by confiscations and forced gifts, than by any thing else. Was there euer prince in the world in vertue, pietie, and integritie, like vnto our king Saint *Lewes*? and yet by the
B meanes aforesaid, hauing caused *Peter* of Dreux to be condemned, he did confiscat, and then vnite vnto his crowne the earldome of Dreux: as he did also vnto *Thibaut* king of Nauarre and earle of Champagne, who was in the like daunger, if he had not resigned Bray, Fortione, and Monstrueil: and *Raymond* earle of Tholouse, the countrey of Languedoc. The countries of Guienne, Aniou, Maine, Touraine, and Auuergne, are come vnto the crowne by confiscations in the time of *Philip Augustus*. The dutchie of Alencon, and the earledome of Perch, are also come by confiscations. In like case [a] Perigort, [b] Ponthieu, [c] la Marche, [d] Angoulesme, [e] l'Isle in Iourdaine, the marquisat of Saluses, and [f] all the goods of *Charles* of Bourbon, with many other priuat Seigneuries, haue bene forfeited for high treason, according to the custome of other Commonweales,
C and the antient laws. But the custome of Scotland in cases of treasons is more cruell, whereas all the goods of him that is condemned accrue vnto the exchequer, without any regard of wife, children, nor creditors.

1234.
1202.
a 1458.
b 1369.
c 1370.
d 1202.
e 1302.
f 1535.

If any man will say, That the king freeing himself of those lands which hold not immediatly of him, according to the edict of *Philip* the Faire, and giuing the most part of them which hold directly of him, vnto such as shall deserue well, the which he may do before they be incorporat vnto the crowne: hee shall not appropriat vnto the publike all the goods of priuat men, as else he might do in time. And to preuent this inconuenience, the king cannot recouer those lands which hold directly of him, offring the price to them that bought them: for so he might by purchase get all his subiects lands
D I doe therefore thinke this more conuenient, than to adiudge the confiscations vnto the people; as they did in Rome by the law Cornelia, which *Sylla* the Dictator did publish, after that he had enriched his friends and partisans with the spoyles of his enemies. But there is as small reason to giue them to the flatterers of princes, and to the horse leaches of the court, as it is vsuall in all gouerned Monarchies, which opens a gap vnto false accusers, giuing vnto the vnworthy the rewards of the well deseruing. Who doth not remember (although I grieue to remember) the blood of innocent citisens shed for gaine vnder a colour of religion, to glut these horseleaches of the court? Therefore to auoide these inconueniences of either part as much as may be, I see no better meanes than that which I haue said, That deducting the charges of the suit, his
E iust debts being publick or priuate, and the rewards of the accusers; the surplusage of his inheritance should be left vnto the heires, and that which was purchased to charitable vses: prouided alwaies that that which is giuen to the informers, or to the colleges in charitie, shall be only in money and not in lands, for the reasons that I haue formerly giuen. As for charitable works, there neuer wants meanes to imploy it, either in diuine things, or in publike works, or else about the sicke or the poore. In old time at Rome amercements were adiudged to the treasurie of Churches, to be imployed in sacrifices, and therefore they called amercements *Sacramenta*, as *Sextus Pompeius* saith: for which cause *Titius Romilius* refused the peoples bountie, which had decreed that

Informers must be rewarded with money, and not with lands.

Ddd iiij   they

B4 Bray, Fortione, and Monstrueil *i.e.* Bray-sur-Seine and Montereau-faut-Yonne   D5 *For* all governed *read* ill governed.   E9 *For* Titius (Fr 7) *read* Titus (Fr 1-6, 8 and L).
Notes at A4, B4, B4(margin).

they should restore vnto him the fine in the which he had bene condemned, saying, That things consecrated vnto God should not be taken from him. The like was also obserued in Greece for the tenth of the goods that were confiscate, the which were adiudged vnto the Church, as we may see in the sentence giuen against *Archiptolome, Antiphon*, and his consorts in Athence in the forme that followeth. The 16 day of *Prytanee, Demonicus Dalopeie* being Register, and *Philostratus* Captaine, at the pursuite of *Andron* touching *Archiptolemus, Onomaches,* and *Antiphon*, whome the Captaine hath accused that they went to Lacedemon to the preiudice of the Commonweale, and that they departed from the Camp in one of the enemies ships; the Senat hath decreed, That they should be apprehended, and that the Captaine with ten Senators named by the Senat, should determine of them, to the end they might be punished, that the Thesmothetes should call them the next day, and bring them before the Iudges, and that the Captaine or any other might accuse them, to the end that iudgement being giuen, execution might follow, according to the lawes made against traitors. And vnder the decree the sentence is set downe in this sort, *Archiptolemus* and *Antiphon* were condemned and deliuered into the hands of eleuen executioners of iustice, their goods forfaited, and the tenth reserued vnto the goddesse *Minerua*, and their houses razed: afterwards they did adiudge all vnto the publike treasor, and yet the law did allow the Iudges to dispose in their sentence as they should thinke the cause deserued for publike or charitable vses, as we haue a commendable custome in this realme. That which I haue said of successions should principallie take place, when as there is any question of lands holden in fee, for the prerogatiue and qualitie of the fee, affected to the antient families for the seruice of the Commonweal. Wherin the Germans haue well prouided, for in all confiscations the next of kin are preferred before the publike treasurie when there is any question of land in fee; wherby flatterers haue no means to accuse wrongfully, nor Princes to put good men to death for their fees which seemes to haue been the reason that by the lawes of God the amercement was consecrated vnto God, and giuen to the high Priests, if he that had offended were not in presence, or had no heires. And for that this Chapter concernes rewards and punishments, order requires that we discourse of the one and the other.

The law of Athens in cases of treason.

The law of Germanie for confiscations.

Chap. IIII.

Of reward and punishment.

IT is needfull to treate here briefly of rewards and punishments, for he that would discourse thereof at large should make a great volume, for that these two points concerne all Commonweales, so as if punishments and rewards be well and wisely distributed, the Commonweale shall be alwaies happie and florish, and contrariwise if the good be not rewarded and the bad punished according to their deserts, there is no hope that a Commonweale can long continue. There is not any thing that hath bred greater troubles, seditions, ciuill warres, and ruines of Commonweales than the contempt of good men, and the libertie which is giuen to the wicked to offend with all impunitie. It is not so necessarie to discourse of punishments, as of rewards, for that all lawes and bookes of lawyers are full of them, but I find not any one that hath written of rewards: either for that good men are so rare, and wicked men abound; or for that it seemes more profitable for a Commonweale to restraine the wicked with the feare of punishment, than to incourage the good to vertue with rewards. But for that punishmēts are odious of themselues,

The two principall foundations of euery Commonweale.

F5 *For* 16 *read* 21 (Fr only).   F6 Demonicus Dalopece (*properly* Demonicus of Alopece)
H2 affected *i.e.* allotted, assigned   Note at H3.

selues, and rewards fauourable, therefore wise Princes haue accustomed to referre punishments vnto the Magistrate, and to reserue rewards vnto themselues, to get the loue of the subiects, and to flie their hatred: for which cause Lawyers and Magistrates haue treated amplie of punishments, and but few haue made any mention of rewards. And although the word merit is taken in the best sence, as *Seneca* saith, *Altius iniuriæ quam merita descendunt,* Iniuries make a deeper impression than merits, yet we will vse it indifferently and according vnto the vulgar phrase. Euery reward is either honorable, or profitable, or both together, else it is no reward, speaking popularly and politikely, seeing we are in the middest of a Commonweale, and not in the schooles of the Academikes and Stoikes, which hold nothing to be profitable that is not honest; nor honorable which is not profitable: the which is a goodly paradoxe, and yet contrarie to the rules of policie, which doe neuer ballance profit with the counterpoise of honour: for the more profit rewards haue in them, the lesse honourable are they, and alwayes the profit doth diminish the beautie and dignitie of the honour. And euen those are most esteemed and honoured, wherein they imploy their goods to maintaine the honour. So as when we speake of rewards, we vnderstand triumphes, statues, honourable charges, estates, and offices, which are therefore called honors: for that many times the priuat estates of famous men are wasted thereby: the rest haue more profit than honour in them, as benefices, militarie gifts, immunities of all or some charges; as of taxes, imposts, wardship, exemptions from the warre; and from ordinarie judges, letters of estate, of freedome, of legitimation, of faires, of gentrie, of knighthood, and such like. But if the office be hurtfull, and without honour, it is no longer a reward, but a charge or burthen. Neither may wee confound a reward and a benefit; for a reward is giuen vpon good desert, and a benefit vpon speciall fauour. And as Commonweals be diuers, so the distribution of honours and rewards is verie different in a Monarchy, and in the other two estates. In a Popular estate rewards are more honourable than profitable: for the common people hunt only after profit, caring little for honour, the which they doe willingly giue to them that are ambitious. But in a Monarchie the prince is more iealous of honour than of profit, especially if he be a tyrant, who takes nothing more disdainefully, than to see his subiect honoured and respected; fearing least the sweet intising bait of honour, should make him aspire and attempt against his estate: or els for that a tirant cannot endure the light of vertue: as we read of the emperor *Caligula,* who was iealous and enuious of the honor that was done to God himself: and the emperor *Domitian,* who was the most base and cowardly tyrant that euer was, yet could hee neuer endure that any honour should be done vnto them that had best deserued, but hee put them to death. Sometimes princes in stead of recompencing of worthy men, they put them to death, banish them, or condemne them to perpetuall prison, for the safetie of their estates. So did *Alexander* the Great to *Parmenio* his constable, *Iustinian* to *Bellisarius, Edward* the fourth to the earle of Warwike; and infinit others, who for the reward of their prowesse haue bene slaine, poisoned, or ill intreated by their princes. And for this cause, as *Tacitus* writes, the Germans did attribut all the honour of their goodly exploits vnto their princes, to free themselues from enuie which followes vertue. And therefore we neuer see Monarches, & much lesse tyrants, to graunt triumphes and honourable entries vnto his subiects, what victorie soeuer they haue gotten of the enemie. But contrariwise a discreet capfaine, in stead of a triumph at his returne from victorie, humbling himselfe before his prince, he saith, Sir, your victorie is my glorie, although the prince were not present: for hee that commaunds deserues the honour of the victorie, euen in a Popular estate: as it was adiudged betwixt the Consull *Luctatius* and *Valerius* his lieutenant, vpon a controuersie they had for the triumph, the which

Valeri-

Difference of rewards.

Difference of reward and benefit

The difference of giuing rewards in a Popular estate and a Monarchy.

A tyrant cannot endure to haue the subiect honoured.

The honour of the souldiors victory is due vnto the captaine.

Valerius pretended to be due vnto him, for that the Consull was absent the day of the battell. So we may say, that the honour of the victorie is alwayes due vnto the prince, although he be absent the day of the battell: as *Charles* the fift, king of France was, who gaue his armes vnto one of his gentlemen, and retired himselfe out of the fight, fearing to fall into his enemies hands: And for this cause he was called wise, remembring how preiudiciall his fathers captiuitie was vnto Fraunce. The like we may say of Popular estates, that the generals victories belong vnto the people vnder whose ensigns they haue fought, but the honor of the triumph is giuen vnto the Generall: the which is not obserued in a Monarchy. Which is the chiefe, and it may be the onely occasion, why in Popular estates well gouerned, there are more vertuous men than in a Monarchy: For that honor which is the onely reward of vertue is taken away, or at the least much restrained from them that deserue it in a Monarchy, and is graunted in a lawfull Popular estate, euen in matters of armes. For as a generous and noble minded man doth more esteeme honour than all the treasure of the world; so without doubt he will willingly sacrifice his life and goods for the glorie he expects: and the greater the honours be, the more men there will be of merit and fame. And therefore the Commonweale of Rome hath had more great Captaines, wise Senators, eloquent Orators, and learned Lawyers, than any other Commonweale, either Barbarians, Greeks, or Latines: For he that had put to rout a legion of the enemies, it was at his thoice to demand the triumph, or at the least some honourable charge; one of the which could not bee denied him. As for the triumph, which was the highest point of honour a Roman citisen could aspire vnto, there were no people vnder heauen where it was solemnised with more state and pompe than at Rome: For he that triumphed, made his entrie more honourable than a king could doe in his realme, dragging the captiue kings & commaunders in chaines after his chariot, hee sitting on high attired with a purple robe wrought with gold, and a crowne of baies, accompanied with his victorious armie, being braue with the spoyles of their enemies, with a sound of trumpets and clarons, rauishing the hearts of all men, partly with incredible ioy, and partly with amazement & admiration: and in this manner the Generall went vp to the Capitoll to doe sacrifice. Aboue all (saith *Polybius*) that which did most inflame the youth to aspire to honour, were the triumphall statues or images liuely drawne of his parents and predecessors, to accompnie him to the Capitoll. And after he had done the solemne sacrifice, hee was conducted home to his house by the greatest noble men and captaines. And those which died were publikely praysed before the people, according vnto the merits of their forepassed liues. And not onely the men, but also the women, as we read in *Titus Liuius*, *Matronis honor additus, vt eorum sicut virorum solemnis laudatio esset*, There was honour giuen vnto matrons, that there might bee a solemne commendation of them as of men. I know there are preachers which will say, That this desire of honour is vaine, which euerie good man should flie: but I hold that there is nothing more necessarie for youth (as *Theophrastus* said) the which doth enflame them with an honest ambition; who when as they see themselues commended, then do vertues spring and take deeper root in them. And *Thomas Aquinus* saith, That a prince must bee nourished with the desire of true glorie, to giue him the taste of vertue. We haue no reason then to maruell, if neuer any Commonweale did bring forth such famous men, and so many, as Rome did: For the honours which were graunted in other Commonweals, came not neere vnto them which were giuen in Rome. It was a great reward of honour at Athens, and in the Olympike games, to be crowned with a crowne of gold in the open theatre before all the people, and commended by an Orator; or to obtaine a statue of brasse, or to be enterrained of the publike charge, or to be the first, or of the first

Marginal notes:
Why Popular estates haue more famous men than Monarchies.
Preferments to honour breeds men of desert.
The description of a triumph at Rome.
The honours giuen at Athens.

G9 at his choice   H7 clarons *i.e.* clarions   I6 ut earum   K6 came not   K9 entertained
Notes at F1, G3.

first rank in places of honors, for himselfe & his house; the which *Demochares* required of the people for *Demosthenes*, after that he had made a repetition of his prayses, wherin there was no lesse profit than honour. But the Romans (to giue them to vnderstand that they must not esteeme honour by profit) had no crowne in greater estimation, than that of grasse or greene corne, the which they held more pretious than all the crownes of gold of other nations. Neither was it euer giuen to any, but to *Q. Fabius Maximus*, surnamed *Cunctator*, with this title, *Patrie seruatori*, To the preseruer of his countrey. Wherein the wisedome of the auntient Romans is greatly to be commended, hauing thereby banished couetousnesse and the desire of gainefull rewards; and planted the loue of vertue in the subiects hearts, with the price of honour. And whereas other princes are greatly troubled to find money, to emptie their coffers, to sell their reuenewes, to oppresse their subiects, to forfeit some, and to spoile others, to recompence their slaues and flatterers (although that vertue cannot bee valued by any price) the Romans gaue nothing but honours, for that the captaines respected nothing lesse than profit: and euen a priuat Roman souldiour refused a chaine of gold of *Labienus* lieutenant to *Cæsar*, for that he had hazarded his life couragiously against the enemie, saying, That he would not the reward of the couetous, but of the vertuous; the which is honour, that we must haue alwayes before our eyes. But vertue must not follow, but goe before honour: as it was decreed by the auntient high Priests at Rome, when as Consull *Marcus Marcellus* had built a temple to Honour and Vertue; to the end the vows and sacrifices of the one should not be confounded with the other, they resolued to make a wall to diuide the temple in two, but yet so, as they must passe thorow the temple of Vertue, to enter into that of Honour. And to speake truely, the auntient Romans onely did vnderstand the merits of vertue, and the true points of honour. For although the Senator *Agrippa* left not wherewithall to defray his funerall, nor the Consull *Fabricius* nor the Dictator *Cincinnatus* wherewithall to feed their families, yet the one was drawne from the plough to the Dictatorship, and the other refused halfe the kingdomes of *Pyrrhus*, to maintaine his reputation and honour. The Commonweale was neuer so furnished with worthy men, as in those dayes, neither were honours and dignities better distributed than in that age. But when as this pretious reward of vertue was imparted to the vicious and vnworthy, it grew contemtible, so as euery one scorned it, and held it dishonourable: as it happened of the gold rings which all the gentlemen of Rome neglected, seeing *Flauius* a libertine to *Appius* and a popular man, created Ædile, or chiefe ouerseer of the victuals; the which they were not accustomed to giue to any but gentlemen, although he had deserued well of the people. And the which is most to be feared, good men will abandon the place wholly to the wicked, for that they will haue no communication nor fellowship with them: as *Cato* the younger did, who being chosen by lot with diuers other judges to iudge *Gabinius*, and seeing that they pretended to absolue him, beeing corrupted with gifts, hee retired himselfe before the people, and brake the tables that were offered vnto him. So did the chast women in this realme, who cast away their girdles of gold, the which none might weare that had stained their honours, who notwithstanding did weare girdles, & then they said, *Que bonne renommee valoit meux que ceinture dorée*, That a good name was better than a golden girdle. For alwaies vertuous men haue impatiently endured to bee equalled with the wicked in the reward of honour. Haue wee not seene that the onely meanes that king *Charles* the seuenth found to make a number of vnworthy men, who had gotten the order of knights of the Starre, by women or fauour, to leaue it, he decreed, That the archers of the watch at Paris, should weare a star vpon their cassockes, which was the marke of Saint *Owen*: whereuppon all the knights of

this

The Romans esteemed honour more than profit.

A worthy saying of a souldior.

The vertuous refuse honours when they are giuen to the vnworthy.

The naturall order of honour and vertue.

A7 Patriae   B2 to forfeit some *i.e.* to confiscate their possessions   E3 valoit mieux   E7 *For* women or favour *read* money or favour (Fr and L). Cf. 582 K2.   E9 *For* cassockes *probably read* caskes *i.e.* casques, headpieces (*pileus* in L).   Notes at B4, E5.

588   THE FIFTH BOOKE

this disorder left the starre. As in like case the people of Athens disanulled the law of Ostracisme, by the which the best men were banished their countrey for three yeares, when as *Hyperbolus* one of the worst and wickedest men of Athens had bene condemned by that law.

It is a daungerous and very pernitious thing in euery Commonweale, to grant honours and rewards without any difference, or to sell them for money; although that they which thinke to win honour in buying their offices, abuse themselues as much as those which thought to flie with the golden wings of *Euripides*, making that which should be the lightest of all others, of the heauiest mettall: for then the precious treasure of honour turnes to dishonour; and honour being once lost, then do they exceed in all vice and wickednesse: the which shall neuer happen if the distribution of rewards and punishments be ordered by a harmoniacall iustice, as wee will shew in the end of this worke. If a Consull be allowed a triumph, it is reason that captains and lieutenants should haue the estates and offices, the horsmen the crowns and horses, and the priuat soldiors also should haue part of the arms & spoils. And in the bestowing of offices they must also haue a respect vnto the qualitie of persons: to Gentlemen the offices of Consull, and Gouernments; to the Plebeians the Tribunes places, and other meane offices fit for their qualities and merits: and if the vertue of a meane man or of a priuate souldier be so great that hee exceeds all others, it is reason that he haue his part in the greatest dignities, as it was decreed by the law Canuleia, to appease the seditions betwixt the nobilitie of Rome and the people: but he that would make a Consull, a knight of the Order, or a master of the horse, of a base fellow that had neuer caried arms, without doubt he should blemish the dignitie of rewards, and put the whole estate in danger of ruine. In old time there was more difficultie to create a simple Knight, than is now to make a Generall: they must haue deserued well, and prepare themselues for it with great solemnitie. And euen Kings children and Princes of the bloud were not admitted to be Knights but with great ceremonies: as we may reade of Saint *Lewis*, when he made his sonne *Philip* the 3. Knight, who afterwards created *Philip* the faire Knight in the yeare 1284 and he his three children in the presence of all his Princes: and which is more, king *Francis* the first after the battaile of Marignan caused himselfe to be dubbed knight by Captaine *Bayard*, taking his sword from him. But since that cowards and housedoues caried away this price of honor, true knights neuer esteemed it: so as *Charles* the sixt at the siege of Bourges made aboue fiue hundred knights banerets, & many other knights, which had not power to raise a banner, as *Monstrelet* said. In like sort that militarie girdle which the Roman Emperours did vse to giue as a reward of honor to them that had deserued well of the Commonweale; as the coller of the order, the which they tooke away in reproch, as *Iulian* the Emperour did from *Iouinian* and other christian Captaines; and the honor of a Patrician, the which the Emperours of the East did esteeme as the highest point of honor and fauour: in the beginning it was not giuen but vnto the greatest Princes and noble men. As we read that the Emperour *Anastasius* sent the order of a Patrician to king *Clouis* in the citie of Tours, but after that it was imparted to men of base condition and vnworthie of that honor, it grew contemptible, so as Princes haue bin of necessitie glad to forge new honors, new prizes and new rewards. As *Edward* the third king of England made the order of Saint *George*, or of the Garter: and soone after the 6 of Ianuary 1351 king *Ihon* did institute the order of the Starre in the Castell of Saint Owen: and long after that *Philip* the second duke of Burgogne erected the order of the golden Fleece. and 40 yeres after him *Lewis* the 11 king of France made the order of Saint *Michaell*; as also after him the dukes of Sauoy haue instituted the order of the *Anonciado*, and other Princes haue done

Marginal notes:
- The reward of honour turnes to infamie, if it be giuen to the vnworthy.
- Harmoniacall proportion in the distribution of rewards.
- The estimation of honours in old times.
- The orders of England, France, and Bourgongne.

F2 *For* three yeares *read* ten yeares (Fr only).   G1 (margin) infamie

done the like, to honor with the title of Knighthood those that deserued well, whose seruices they cannot otherwise reward. By the first article of the golden Fleece, the which was instituted the tenth of Ianuary 1429 no man might be Knight of that order, vnlesse he were a Gentleman of name and armes, and without reproch: by the second, he might not carrie any other order of what Prince soeuer, but with the priuitie & consent of the chiefe of the order: the seuenth article wils, That all personall quarrels and dissentions of Knights among themselues shall be decided by Iudges of the order, the which is a bodie and Colledge, with a Chancellor, Treasorer, King at armes, Register, a priuat Seale of the order, and soueraigne iurisdiction, without appeale or ciuill request. *Lewis* the 11 imitating the example of *Philip* Duke of Bourgogne, who had entertained him in the time of his disgrace with his father, instituting the order of Saint *Michell* into a Colledge, the first day of August in the yeare 1469 he set downe those articles whereof I haue made mention, and all other articles specified in the institution of the Fleece: and besides in the 37 article it is said, That when any assemblie shall be made, the life and conuersation of euery Knight shall be examined one after an other, during which examination they shall depart out of the Chapter, and be called againe to heare the admonitions and censures of the Chancellor of the order: and in the 38 article it is said, That an examination and censure shall be made of the soueraigne and head of the order, which is the King, as of the rest to be punished and corrected, according to the aduice of the brethren of the order, if he hath committed any thing against the honor, estate, and dutie of Knighthood, or against the statutes of the order: and in the 42 article it is decreed, That any Knights place being voyd, the Chapter shall proceed to a new election, and the Soueraignes voice shall stand but for two: and both he and all the Knights of the order shall be bound to take a solemne oth at their entrie into the Chapter, to chuse the worthiest that they know, without respect to hatred, friendship, fauour, bloud, or any other occasion, which might diuert them from the right: which oth shall be made in the Soueraignes hands from the first vnto the last: and in the last article there is an expresse clause, That neither the King nor his successors, nor the chapter of the order may not derogate from the articles of the institution. Behold briefly the institution of the order and Colledge of honor, the goodliest and the most royall that euer was in any Commonweale, to draw, yea to force mens minds vnto vertue. It may be some one will say, that the first institution of 31 Knights in the order of the golden Fleece, of 36 in the order of France, and of 24 in the order of the Garter instituted at Windsor, cuts off the way to vertue, for that it is expresly defended in the last article of the ordinances of *Lewis* the 11 not to increase that number, although the Soueraigne Prince and the whole Chapter were so resolued; but in my opinion it is one of the chiefest articles that ought to haue bene dulie obserued: to auoid the inconueniences which we haue seene by the infinite number of the order of Saint *Michell*, for the number is sufficient to receiue them that shall deserue that honor: and the fewer there are, the more it will be desired of all men: as at a prize, the which is the more greedily desired, for that euery man hopes for it, and few carrie it. And in this number soueraigne Princes are not comprehended, to whom they present the order only for honor, for that they cannot be tyed to the lawes of the order, and retaine the rights and prerogatiues of soueraigntie. And although the number were small, yet were there but fourteene Knightes at the first institution of the order, the which are named in the ordinance: and in the time of King *Francis* the fifft the number was neuer full. So it is most certaine, that there is nothing that doth more blemish the greatnes of the honor, than to impart it to so many. And for this cause many seeing the smal account was held of the order, procured to haue their Seigneuries erected into Earledomes, Marquisats,

The law of the Golden Fleece.

The law of the order of Saint Michael.

The excessiue number of Knights of the order, haue ruined the order.

and Duchies, which number hath so increased in a short time, as the multitude hath bred contempt, so as *Charls* the ninth enacted by an edict, That after that time all Duchies, Marquisats and Counties should be vnited vnto the Crowne, if the Dukes, Marquises and Earles dyed without heires males issued of their bodies, although the said Seigneuries had not in former times belonged vnto the Crowne: the which is a verie necessarie Edict to restraine the insatiable ambition of such as had not deserued these titles of honor, whereof the Prince should be iealous. And generally in all gifts, rewards, and titles of honor it is expedient (for the greater grace of the benefit) that he only which holds the Soueraigntie should bestow it on him that hath deserued; who will thinke himselfe much more honored, when his Prince hath giuen him his reward, seene him, heard him, and graced him. Also the Prince aboue all things must be iealous that the thanks of his bountie may remaine, banishing from his court those sellers of smoke, or punishing them as *Alexander Seuerus* did, who caused one to be tyed vnto a post, as *Spartian* saith, and smothered him with smoke, causing it to be proclaimed by the trompet, So perish all such as sell smoke. He was fauored by the Emperour, who as soone as he knew the name of any one whom the Emperour meant to grace either with honor or office, he went vnto him, promising him his fauour, the which he sold at a high rate, and like a horseleech of the Court he suckt the bloud of the subiects to the dishonor of his Prince, who should hold nothing more deere than the thanks of his gifts and bountie; else if he indure that his houshold seruants steale away the fauours of his subiects, it is to be feared that in the end they will make themselues masters, as *Absolon* did, who shewing himselfe affable and courteous to all the subiects, abusing the charges of honor, offices, and benefices, giuing them vnder the fauour of the King his father to whom he pleased; he stole from him (saith the scripture) his subiects hearts, and expelled him from his royall throne. We read also of *Otho*, who hauing receiued 2500 crownes for a dispensation which the Emperour *Galba* gaue at his request, he gaue them among the Captaines of the guards, the which was a chiefe meanes for him to vsurp the State, after that he had caused *Galba* to be slaine. This gift was like vnto the Eagle which the Emperour *Iulian* caried in his Standard, the which pulled off her owne feathers, whereof they made arrowes to shoot at her. For the same occasion the last kings issued from *Meroue* and *Charlemaigne* were expelled from their estates by the Maiors of the pallace, who gaue all offices and benefices to whom they pleased without the kings priuitie or consent: and therefore *Loup* Abbot of Ferrieres did write vnto *Charles* the 3 king of France, aduising him to haue a speciall care that his flatterers and courtiers did not steale from him the thanks of his liberalitie. Some will say, that it is impossible for a Prince to refuse his mother, brethren, children, and friends: I must confesse it is a hard matter to auoid it, yet I haue seene a King who being importuned by his brother for another, said vnto him in the presence of the sutor, Brother, at this time I will do nothing for your sake, but for the loue of this man who hath deserued well, to whom he graciously granted what his brother had demanded. But if the Prince will wholie yeeld himselfe to the appetite of his followers, we may well say that he is but a cipher, which giues all power vnto others, & reserues nothing to himselfe: he must therefore know which be good and vertuous men, and that haue well deserued. And least the Prince should be forced to denie many importunate beggers, he must make choise of wise and faithfull masters of requests, to receiue euery mans petition, who may dissuade such as demaund any thing that is vniust or against the good of the State, or at the least they must acquaint the Prince therewith that he may not be surprised in his answer: By this meanes importunat beggers shall be kept backe by good men, neither shall they haue any cause to bee discontented with the Prince,

Marginalia:
- Sellers of smoke dangerous to an estate.
- It is the ruine of princes to giue too great authoritie to his subiects.
- Charles the ninth to Henry.

F8 benefit) that (*Otho*, 5).   H6 2500 crownes (Fr) 10,000 crowns (L). Suetonius gives "1,000,000 sesterces" Note at F7.

A Prince, who they will thinke vnderstands not thereof, or else he will satisfie them with pertinent reasons, wherein the Emperour *Titus* is greatly commended, for that he neuer sent away any man discontented, whether he granted or refused what he demanded, and therefore they called him, The delight of mankind. Moreouer an impudent begger knowing that his petition shall be viewed, red and examined by a wise Chancellor, or an vnderstanding master of requests will not presume to pursue a thing that is vniust; for Princes neuer want flatterers and impudent beggers, the which haue no other end but to drinke the bloud, eate the boanes, & suck the marrow both of Prince and subiect: and those which haue best deserued of the Commonweale, are commonly most kept back, not only for that their honor forbids them to flatter, and to beg the reward of vertue, which should be offred vnto them: but also for the charges and expences of the pursuite, and many times without all hope. And if their petitions be once reiected, they will not make a second attempt, no more then *Callicratidas* a Lacedemonian Captaine (one of the most vertuous of his age) who was mockt of the Courtiers of yong *Cyrus*, for that he had not the patience to court it long: and contrariwise *Lisander* a flattering courtier, if euer any were, obtained whatsoeuer he demaunded. A modest and bashfull man is amazed in this case, where as the impudent preuaile, knowing well the humor of Princes, who alwaies loue them to whom they haue done most good, and the most part hate them to whom they are most bound: and to say the truth, the nature of a benefit is such, as it doth no lesse bind him that giues, than him that receiues it: and contrariwise thanks and the acknowledging of a benefit is troublesome to an ingratefull person, and reuenge is sweet, wherof *Tacitus* giues the reason, saying, *Proniores ad vindictam sumus quam ad gratiam, quia gratia oneri, vltio in quæstu habetur*: We are more prone to reuenge then to giue thanks, for thanks is held a burthen, and reuenge a gaine. And although that many Princes neither pay, nor giue any thing but words, yet the least promise that is made vnto them they hold as a firme bond. There is yet an other point which hinders and cuts off the rewards of good men, which is, that if a wise Prince bestowes any office, priuiledge, or gift to whom soeuer, before he can enioy it, he must giue the one halfe in rewards: and oftentimes their promises are sold so deere, as they carrie away little or nothing at all, the which is an incurable disease but by seuere and rigorous punishments, for the which they must of necessitie prouide, seeing that punishments and rewards are the two firmest supports of a Commonweale. The best meanes to preuent it is for the Prince to cause the gift to be brought and deliuered, and if it were possible to be present thereat himselfe, specially if it be to a man of worth: for the gift comming in this sort from the Princes own hand, hath more efficacie and grace, then a hundred times as much giuen him by an other repiningly, or curtalled for the most part. The like censure is to be made of praise or commendations, which the Prince deliuers with his owne mouth to him that hath deserued it, the which hath more effect then all the wealth that he can giue him: and a reproch or blame is as a stabbe vnto generous minds to force them to do well. But it is impossible euer to see a iust distribution of punishments and rewards, so long as Princes shall set to sale dignities, honors, offices, and benefices, the which is the most dangerous and pernitious plague in a Commonweale. All nations haue prouided for it by good and wholesome lawes; and euen in this realme the ordinance of S. *Lewis* notes them with infamie that haue vsed the fauour of any man to procure them offices of iustice, the which was reasonablie well executed vntill the raigne of king *Francis* the first, and in England it is yet rigorously obserued, as I haue vnderstood by M. *Randall* the english Ambassador; the which was also strictly decreed by an edict of *Ferdinand*, great Grandfather by the mothers side to *Philip*, made in the yeare 1492 where as the

Tranquil. in Tito

Why good and vertuous men want rewards.

Plut. in Lisand.

Why we are more prone to reuenge than to requite.

Punishments & rewards, the two supports of a Commonweale.

The sale of offices and benefices most dangerous in a Commonweale.

forme

A 10 flatter, and   C 3 questu (Fr 7) *preferably* quæstu (Fr 1-6, 8 and L)   Note at B8.

forme of choosing of offices of iustice is set downe: *Que no se puedan vender, ny trocar officios de Alcaldia, ny Alquaziladgo, ny regimiento, ny veyntes quatria, ny fiel executoria, ny iuraderia.* It is not needfull to set down the inconueniences & miseries that a Commonweale is subiect vnto by the sale of offices, the labour were infinite being so well knowne to all men. But it is more difficult in a popular State to perswade them that this trafficke is good, then where as the richest men hold the Soueraignetie, it is the onely meanes to exclude the poorer sort from offices, who in a popular estate will haue their parts without paying any money, and yet hardly shall they obserue these prohibitions, when as the common people shall reape some benefit by choosing of ambitious men. As for a Monarke, pouertie sometimes forceth him to breake good lawes to supplie his wants, but after they haue once made a breach, it is impossible to repaire it. It was forbidden by the law Petilia to go to sayers and assemblies, to sue for the peoples fauour & voyces. By the law Papiria no man might weare a white gowne. The law Calphurnia declared him incapable for euer to beare any office that had been condemned of ambition, vnlesse he had accused and conuicted an other, and he that had caused his competitor to be condemned of ambition, he obtained his office; afterwards punishment was made greater by the law Tullia, published at the request of *Cicero,* whereby it was decreed that a Senator condemned of ambition should be banished for ten yeares, but it was not obserued by the rich, who sent their broakers into the assemblie of the States with great sommes of money to corrupt the people, so as *Cæsar* fearing to haue one ioyned with him in the Consulship that might crosse his designes, he offred his friend *Luceius* as much money as was needfull to purchase the peoples voyces: whereof the Senat being aduertised, they appointed a great somme of money for his competitor *Marcus Bibulus* to buy the peoples suffrages, as *Suetonius* doth testifie. This was vpon the declining of the popular estate, the which was ouerthrowne by this meanes; for vndoubtedly they which make sale of estates, offices, and benefices, they sell the most sacred thing in the world which is Iustice, they sell the Commonweale, they sell the bloud of the subiects, they sell the lawes, and taking away all the rewards of honor, vertue, learning, pietie, and religion, they open the gates to thefts, corruption, couetousnes, iniustice, arrogancie, impietie, and to be short, to all vice and villanie. Neither must the Prince excuse himselfe by his pouertie, for there is no auailable excuse, or that hath any colour to seeke the ruine of an estate, vnder a pretence of pouertie. And it is a ridiculous thing for a Prince to pretend pouertie, seeing he hath so many meanes to preuent it if he please. We reade that the Empire of Rome was neuer more poore and indebted then vnder the Emperour *Heliogabalus* that monster of nature, and yet *Alexander Seuerus* his successor, one of the wisest and most vertuous Princesse that euer was would neuer indure the sale of offices, saying in the open Senat, *Non patiar mercatores potestatum,* I will not indure these marchants, or buyers of dignities: and yet this good Emperour did so abate the taxes and imposts, as he that paied one and thirtie crownes vnder *Heliogabalus,* paied but one crowne vnder *Alexander,* resoluing, if he had liued, to take but the third part of it, but he raigned but foureteene yeares after that he had freed his predecessors debts, and defeated the Parthians and the people of the north, leauing to his successor an Empire florishing in armes and lawes. But his court was wisely ordred, excessiue prodigalities were cut off, rewards were equallie destributed, & the theeues of the publike treasure were seuerely punished. He was called *Seuerus,* by reason of his seueritie. He hated flatterers as a plague to all Princes, neither durst the horseleeches of the court come neere him. He was very wise in all things, but especially in the discouering of mens humors, and of a great iudgement in decerning of euery mans merits; being reuerent with a seuere kind of

Sale of offices least vsed in a Popular estate.

The inconueniences which grow by the sale of offices.

Pouertie no lawfull excuse in a prince for the sale of offices.

A worthy saying of an emperour.

The disposition of the emperour Seuerus.

F2 Alguaziladgo (as in L, misprinted in Fr)   G5 ambition *i.e. ambitus,* illegal canvassing for votes
H10 *For* arrogancie *Bodin writes* ignorance (Fr and L).   I2 available *i.e.* valid   I2 colour, to seeke
I10 one and thirtie   K9 reverent *i.e.* reverend, worthy of respect

OF A COMMONWEALE.

A of maiestie. We haue shewed before, that the softnes or simplicitie of a Prince is dangerous to an estate. After that the great king *Francis* the first became (through his old age) austere and not so accessible, the flatterers and horseleeches of the court came not neere him, so as the treasure was so well husbanded, as after his death they found seuenteene hundred thousand crownes in readie money, besides the quarter of March which was readie to be receiued: and his realme full of learned men, great Captaines, good Architects, and all sorts of handicrafts, and the frontires of his estate extending euen vnto the gates of Milan, being assured by a firme peace with all Princes. And although that he had been encountred with great and mightie enemies, and had been taken prisoner and paied his ransome, yet did he build Cities, Townes, Castles, and stately Pallaces:

The good husbandry of king Francis the first.

B but the facilitie and too great bountie of his successor *Henry* the second brought the estate indebted within little more than twelue yeares after, foure millions three hundred fortie eight thousand three hundred nintie three pounds eighteene shillings starling (as I learned out of the accounts) and the countries of Sauoy and Piedmont, with all that which they had conquered in thirtie yeares before, lost, and the rest much ingaged. I omit to speake how much France was falne from her antient dignitie and beautie, how worthie men were kept from their degrees, vertuous men troden vnder foote, and the learned contemned: and all these miseries came vpon the realme, for that he did prodigallie giue dignities, offices, benefices, and the treasure to the vnworthie, and suffered the wicked with all impunitie. That Prince then that will enioy a happie

The prodigality of king Henrie the second.

The cause of the calamities of Fraunce.

C estate let him refer the punishment of offences to the Magistrate, as it is expedient, and reserue rewards vnto himselfe, giuing by little and little according to euery ones merit, that the thanks may be the more durable; and commaund punishments to be done at an instant, to the end they may be the lesse grieuous to them that suffer them, and the feare deeper grauen in the harts of others, terrifying them from their wicked and disordred liues. These lawes of punishments and rewards being dulie obserued in a Commonweale, vertue shall be alwaies honorablie rewarded, the wicked shall be banished, publick debts shall be paied, and the State shall flourish with all aboundance. But for that the frauds of courtiers are so many, and such infinit deuises to rob the treasurie, so as the wisest Princes may be circumuented, a law was made by *Philip* of Valois, and

D verified in the court of Parliament, and chamber of accompts, whereby it was enacted, That all gifts giuen by the king should be void, if his letters pattents did not containe whatsoeuer had been giuen to him or to any of his predecessors in former times by the Princes bountie: which law although it were most profitable, yet was it abrogated two yeares after by their meanes that were interessed, finding how much it did preiudice them, so as it was enacted that it should bee sufficient to haue the derogatorie annexed to their pattents, as I haue seene in the auntient registers of the court: but that also was taken away, least any remembrance of benefits should hinder the Princes bountie.

In the yeare 1333. 11. May.

There was another law made by *Charles* the 8, whereby all gifts aboue ten pounds
E starling should be enrolled: but since they haue vsed so much fraud, as one in this realm was not ashamed to bragge in a great assembly, That he had gotten (besides his offices) fiue thousand pounds starling a yeare of good rent, and yet there was not any one gift made vnto him to be found in all the registers of the chamber, although it were apparant that he had nothing but from the king. We must not therefore wonder at great debts, seeing the treasure is exhausted after so strange a manner, as hee that hath most receiued, makes a shew to haue had nothing. For to giue so much to one man, although he deserue well, doth not onely waste the treasure of the Commonweale, but also stirre vp the discontented to seditions and rebellions. And one of the best meanes to preserue

In what sort the prince should giue.

Eee iij an

an estate in her greatnesse, is to bestow gifts and rewards on many, to continue euerie one in his dutie, and that they may ballance one another. Also an aduised prince must giue sparingly to the importunat, and offer to them that beg not, so as they bee of good desert, for some can neuer aske, nor yet take it when it is offered them. As *Antigonus* king of Asia said, That he had two friends, whereof the one could neuer be satisfied, & the other could neuer be forced to take any thing. To such men *Dionisius* the elder, lord of Siracusa, behaued himselfe wisely, For to vs (said *Aristippus*) which demaund much he giues little, and to *Plato* who craues nothing, he giues too much. This was a safe kind of giuing, retaining both the money and the thankes. Yet princes haue many other means to grace and reward a seruant, than with mony, the which is lesse esteemed by men of honour, than a good looke, an alliance, a marriage, or a gracious remembrance. And sometimes the gift is such, as it brings more profit to him that giues it, than to him that receiues it. *Charles* the fift, emperour, being come into Spaine, to requite the well deseruing of the duke of Calabria (who had refused the crowne and kingdome of Spaine, which was offered vnto him by the estates) being then a prisoner, he freed him out of prison, and married him to one of the richest princesses that was then liuing, widow to king *Ferdinand*: with the which deed the people receiued great content, the duke great honour, wealth, and libertie, and the emperour the loue of the duke, the loue of the people, and the assurance of his estate, without any charge: And moreouer by this meanes hee kept the widow from marrying with any forren prince: giuing to the duke a wife that was aged and barren, to the end that the dukes line (which made a pretence to the realme of Naples) should be extinct with him.

It is a principal point which a prince ought to respect, That his bountie and rewards be giuen with a cheerfull heart: for some are so vnpleasing, as they neuer giue any thing without reproach, the which taketh away the grace of the gift, especially if the gift be in stead of a reward or recompence. But they do much worse, which giue one & the same office, or one confiscation to many, without aduertising either the one or the other: the which is no benefit, but an iniurie. This is to cast the golden apple among subiects to ruine them. And oftentimes we see them consumed with suits, and murder one another with the sword: whereby the prince shall not onely loose the fruits of his bountie, but the loue of his subiects, and reape for thankes eternall hatred. The which is a grosse errour in matters of state, and yet vsuall among princes; not so much through forgetfulnesse of that which is past, but of set purpose, being falsly instructed from their youth, That they must be liberall and refuse no man, thereby to win the hearts of all men: and yet the end is quite contrarie to that which they haue propounded, giuing one thing to many. And to refuse no man, is not to be liberall nor wise, but prodigall and indiscreet. I would not onely haue the prince liberall, but bountifull, so as he proue not prodigall: for from a prodigall he will grow to be an exactor, and of an exactor a tyrant: and after that he hath giuen his owne, he must of force pull from others to giue. The laws of liberalitie commaund, That he should obserue well to whome he giues, what hee giues, at what time, in what place, and to what end, and his owne abilitie that giues. But a soueraigne prince must withall remememember, that rewards must goe before gifts, and that he must first recompence them that haue well deserued, before he giue to such as haue nothing deserued; and aboue all, let him measure his bountie according to his abilitie. The Romans to releeue the pouertie of *Horatius Cocles* (who alone had withstood the enemies armie, and saued the citie from sacking, and the citisens from ruine) they gaue him an acre of land, or little more; the which was much at that time, hauing but two leagues compasse about the citie. But *Alexander* the Great gaue kingdomes and empires, and thousands of talents: if he had done otherwise it had beene against his maiestie

---

G4(margin) Charles   H7 confiscation   I9–10(margin) *For* libertie *read* liberalitie.
K2 remember   Note at F1.

stie and greatnesse. *Alphonsus* the fift, king of Castile, gaue the kingdome of Portugall to *Henrie* of Boulogne of the house of Loraine, from whome are issued the kings of Portugall for these fiue hundred and fiftie yeares: it was for a reward of his vertue, marrying him to his bastard daughter. But yet was he blamed, to haue giuen away so goodly an estate, his owne not being at that time much greater. In like sort wee may say, that the custome of the auntient Romans was commendable, to nourish vpon the publike charge three children borne at one birth, for a reward of the memoriall victorie obtained by the three *Horatij* against the *Curiaty*. But *Solons* law, which would haue their children which had beene slaine in the warres for their countrey, maintained by the publike, could not continue, although it were practised throughout all Greece, as we read in *Aristotle*, for it did quite waste and consume their treasure.

<small>The beginning of the kings of Portugall.</small>

If any one suppose, that the bountie and greatnesse of a prince shall not appeare, if he giue to none but to such as shall deserue; I will yeeld vnto him. I know that bountie & magnificence is well befitting a great prince: neither must wee thinke it strange if the prince aduance one of a poore and base condition to honour and wealth, so as there be vertue and merit in him: else if the prince shall raise an vnworthie person aboue good men, or equall him in ranke with great personages, in doing good to the one hee shall wrong all the rest. That worthy saying of *Chilo* is extant, one demanding of him what God did, He casts downe the proud (aunswered he) from aboue, and raiseth the poore and deiected to the highest degree of honour. A good prince should imitat God, aduancing the poore and vertuous to honours and riches. But when as the colledge of Cardinals did admonish Pope *Iulio* the third, hauing created P. M. du Mont Cardinall, being a young boy whome he loued, saying, That it was a great dishonour to blemish so honourable an order with so base a man, hauing neither vertue in him, nor learning, neither nobilitie nor goods, nor any marke which might merit (as they said) to appproach to such a degree: But the pope (who was verie pleasant) turning vnto the cardinals, What vertue, (saith he) what nobilitie, what learning, what honor, did you finde in me, to make me pope? It is most certaine, that a vicious and vnworthy prince, will alwayes haue his friends and followers of his owne humor: as it appeares by the emperour *Heliogabalus*, who gaue the greatest offices, and inriched the most detestable villaines in all the empire: wherewith his subiects and guard being incensed, they slew that monster of mankind, with his mother, and threw them into the common priuies. But without any further search, we haue seene the proofe before our eyes, how disdainefully it hath bene taken to see the due rewards of good subiects, and vertuous men, giuen to the vicious, to straungers, and to the vnworthy, the which hath put the goodliest realme of Europe in combustion. For wee find, that the gifts in the yeare 1572 amounted to 270000 pounds starling: and the yeare following to 204400 pounds: and in the yeare 1574 there was giuen 54700 pounds: and in the six moneths following they gaue 95500 pounds starling, besides pensions which were not lesse than twentie thousand pounds starling: and the greatest part of all this treasure grew by the sale of offices, & by confiscations, which was the cause of all our miseries: and yet by the law of Fraunce, England, and Spaine, such buyers should be held infamous: which lawes should be reuiued, and that commendable custome which was practised vnder *Seuerus* maintained, who caused his name to be set vp in all publike places, whome hee meant to preferre to any gouernment, giuing leaue to all men to accuse him, yet with the paine of death to him that did it falsely, saying, That it was great shame to bee lesse carefull of the life and conuersation of a gouernour, than the Christians were of the qualities of their bishops and ministers, whome they examined with all rigour before they were admitted. The which is much more expedient than the manner of examination

<small>Bountie will befits a great prince</small>

<small>A pleasant aunswere of pope Iulius the third.</small>

<small>Aduancements bestowed on the vnworthy incense the subiects</small>

<small>A commendable custome of Alexander Seuerus.</small>

Eee iiij

B4(margin) *For* will *read* well.   Note at C2.

nation which the Venetians, Genouois, Luquois, and Florentines, do vse, after that the officer hath left his charge. For a bad and corrupt magistrat growne rich with thefts, will not sticke to corrupt a judge, to saue both his life and his goods corruptly gotten. It is better therefore to preuent a disease, than to labour to cure it, and better late than neuer, that the feare of this search might keepe officers within the bounds of their dutie. But yet *Solons* law was farre better, by the which the life of the officer was examined both before his admittance to the office, and after he had left it: as we read in the pleadings of *Demosthenes*. Hauing then examined the life and manners of such as aspire to dignities, offices, benefices, knighthoods, exemptions, immunities, gifts and rewards. If their liues be polluted and wicked, they are not onely to be reiected, but also to bee punished. And rewards are to be distributed to good men, according to euerie mans merit: and by an harmoniacall proportion you must giue the purse to the most loyall, armes to the most valiant, iustice to the most iust, the censure to the most vpright, labour to the strongest, the gouernment to the wisest, the priesthood to the deuoutest: yet hauing respect to the nobilitie, riches, age, and power of euerie one, and to the qualitie of the charges and offices. For it were a ridiculous thing to seeke a judge that were a warrior, a prelat couragious, and a souldiour with a conscience. We haue treated of Rewards, Triumphes, and Honours, which are for the most part giuen vnto men of warre: Let vs now see if it be fit to exercise the subiect in armes.

Demost. in orat. de falsa legat. & contra Timarchum.

A true distribution of offices and charges.

CHAP. V.

whether it bee more conuenient to trayne vp the subiects in armes, and to fortifie their townes or not.

IT is one of the highest questions of State, and it may be of the greatest difficultie to resolue, for the inconueniences that may rise on either part, the which I will treat of as briefly as I may, setting down what I hold most conuenient, leauing notwithstanding the resolution to the wise polititians. To follow the opinion of *Aristotle* simply, and to maintaine that a citie ought to be well fortified, well situated for the sending forth of an armie, and of hard accesse for the enemie; were not to decide the difficulties which might be obiected, whether it should haue place in a Monarchie, as well as in a Popular estate, or in a tyranie as in a monarchie; seeing that we haue shewed before that Commonweals contrarie one vnto an other, or at the least very different, must be gouerned by contrarie or very different maximes. Besides, for the well training the subiect vp in armes, there is nothing more contrarie than to fortifie their townes, for that the fortification of them make the inhabitants effeminate and cowards: as *Cleomenes* king of Lacedemonia doth witnes, who seeing the strong fortifications of a towne, he cryed out, O goodly retreat for women. And for this cause *Licurgus* the lawgiuer would neuer allow the city of Sparta to be fortified, fearing least the subiects relying on the strength of their walls should grow fainthearted, knowing well that there was no such fortresse as of men, who will alwaies fight for their goods, liues, and honors, for their wiues, children, and countrie, so long as they haue no hope in flight, or of any retreat to saue themselues. These two things then are contrarie, to haue warlike citisens, and fortified cities: for valiant and warlike men haue no need of castles, and those which dwell in strong places desire no warre. So we see the Tartarians in Scythia, and the Æthiopians and Arabians in Affrike, which are held to bee most warlike: and yet they haue no forts but tents, and some villages without wall or ditch. And euen the great Negus or
Preste-Ian

Reasons against the fortifying of townes.

OF A COMMONWEALE. 597

A *Preste-Ian*, which is the greatest lord in all Affrike, hauing (as they say) fiftie kings vnder him that doe him homage, hath no forts nor castles, but his tents, but that fort only which is built vpon the top of the mountaine Anga, whereas all the princes of the blood are kept with a sure guard, least they should draw the subiects from the obedience of their prince by seditious factions. Yet there is no prince vnder heauen more reuerenced and respected of his subiects, nor more redoubted of his enemies, than in Tartaria, and Æthiopia. Forts are held fruitlesse and of small consequence in the opinion of the greatest captaines, who hold him that is maister of the field, to bee maister of all the townes. It is well knowne, that after the battell of Arbella in Chaldea, whereas *Darius* the last king of Persia was defeated, that there was neither citie nor fort in all
B the whole Persian empire, that held out one day against *Alexander* the Great, although there were an infinit number, and the conqueror had but thirtie thousand men. After that *Paulus Æmilius* had vanquished *Perseus* king of Macedon in battaile, there was not any one towne that made resistance, but all the whole kingdome yeelded in a moment. After the battell of Pharsalia, who forsooke not *Pompey*? all the townes and strong places of the East, which before were shut against *Cæsar*, did now open their gates vnto him without any difficultie. And without any further search, it is well knowne, that after the victorie which king *Lewes* the twelft obtained against the Venetians, he was presently maister of the townes. As in like case after the battaile of Marignan, all Lombardie, and euen the castell of Milan, yeelded vnto king *Francis*; and
C vpon his taking prisoner at Pauia, he lost all on the other side of the Alpes.

But there is a more necessarie reason against the fortifying of places, it is to bee feared, that an enemie entring the stronger, and taking those strong places, hee will hold them, and by that meanes the whole countrey: whereas otherwise hauing once spoyled it, he shall be forced to leaue it. For this reason *Iohn Maria de la Rouere* duke of Vrbin, rased all the forts of his countrey, and retired himselfe to Venice, finding his forces too weake to encounter the enemie; assuring him that the duke of Valentinois comming with all the power of the church could not hold it, being hated to the death, and the duke of Vrbin beloued and respected of his subiects; as it proued true for pope *Alexander* being dead, the duke of Vrbin was receiued with great ioy of his subiects,
D and all other princes that were feudatories to the church, were either taken or slaine in their places of strength. And for the same cause the Geneuois, after the battaile of Pauia being reuolted from the king of Fraunce, besieged their fort called the Lanterne, and then rased it. As also the Milanois did the castle Iof, the which was built before the *Sforces* were lords of Milan, to the end that forreine princes should bring them no more in subiection by meanes of their fort. So the auntient Siracusians did Acradina, and the Romans the cities of Corinth, Carthage, and Numance, the which they had neuer rased, if the fort of Acrocorinth and other places, strong by nature and easie to be fortified, had not forced them vnto it, least the inhabitants should make vse of them,
E as *Philip* the younger, king of Macedonie had done, who called the cities of Corinth, Chalcide, and Demetrias, the shackles and fetters of Greece. Which forts *Titus Flaminius* rased to the ground, to free them from the seruitude of the Macedonians, and to take away all feare of tyrants. The which is another strong reason to take all occasion from princes to tyrannize ouer their subiects, as those doe which assure themselues by Cittadels, which the people called Tyrants nests; and tyrants tearmed them a scourge for villaines, in contempt and scorne of the poore subiects: as *Grislerus* lieutenant to the emperour in Swisserland did, who built a fort in the vallie of Vri, and calling it *Zwing Vri*, that is to say, the yoake of Vri, which was the first occasion that moued the Cantons of the Swissers to reuolt, as we read in their histories. And *Salomon* was the
first

Frandis Alueres in the historie of Aethiopia.

He that is master of the field, is master of the townes.

The strongest fort is the loue of the subiects.

The first cause of the Swissers reuolt.

A 1 (margin) Francis   C 1 upon

first that made a Citadell in Ierusalem, beginning euen then to intreat his subiects ill, exacting new tributes of them, giuing occasion to his successour to continue them, and for the ten tribes to reuolt, and to chuse themselues a king: for commonly Citadels breed a iealousie and distrust betwixt the prince and his subiects, the which is the nurce of all hatred, feare, and rebellion. And euen as castles and Citadels giue bad princes occasion to afflict their subiects, so townes well walled and fortified, do oftentimes cause subiects to rebell against their princes and lords; as I haue shewed elsewhere. And therfore the kings of England neuer suffer their subiects to fortifie their houses, the which is more strictly obserued in Moscouie, to auoid the rebellion of subiects, who are easily moued thereunto, trusting in their walles. And the inhabitants of Telesse in the realme of Thunis, relied so much in the strength of their citie wals, as commonly they slew their gouernours, not able to endure any commaund: so as the king of Thunis going thither with a mightie armie, he demaunded of them, Who liued? they answered him, The red wall: but hauing forced the towne, he rased it, and put all the inhabitants to the sword: as *Hannibal* did at Saguntum, *Sylla* at Athens, the emperor *Seuerus* at Bizantium, *Dagobert* at Poitiers, *Nabuchodonosor* and *Vespasian* to the citie of Ierusalem, all which were reuolted for the trust they had in their forts, eating euen their children through the tediousnesse of sieges, and in the end haue bene rased, and the inhabitants rooted out: the which would haue easily compounded, if the confidence of their strong places had not abused them. For commonly wee see, that weake townes and ill fortified, doe soone compound and send away the enemie, for some peece of money, without any infamie or dishonour: as it hath bene seene by the citie of Paris, the which was neuer taken since that *Cæsar* forced it, the which had beene long since rased, if it had bene fortified hauing bene so often threatned by the enemie: but still they haue preserued themselues by treaties and compositions, the which they had not done being well fortified, either for feare of reproach and dishonour which follow them, which treat with an enemie when they may resist: or for the obstinacie of the inhabitants, or the heads of a faction, who had rather die, than yeeld vnto an enemie, hauing no hope to escape, & seeing their houses on fire, they striue in ruining it, to quench it with the blood of their fellow citisens. But there be no cities so strong, that can long resist the canon, and much lesse famine: For if the besieged be few in number, they shal be soone wearie and tired: if there be many, they shall be the soouer starued.

If then forts and citadels make a bad prince to tyrannize, an enemie to seize vppon the countrey, subiects to be cowards towards an enemie, rebels to their prince, and seditious among themselues? we cannot say they be profitable, or necessarie; but contrariwise hurtfull and pernitious to a Commonweale.

As for the other question, Whether we should traine the subiects vp in armes, and seeke warre rather than peace: It seemes we should not call that in doubt: for we must esteeme that Commonweale most happie, whereas the king is obedient to the lawes of God and nature, the magistrats vnto the king, priuat men to the Magistrats, the children to the parents, the seruants to the maisters, & the subiects vnited together in loue, and all ioyntly with their prince to enioy the sweetnesse of peace and true tranquilitie of mind. But warre is contrarie to this which I haue said, and souldiours are sworne enemies to this kind of life. It is impossible for a Commonweale to flourish in religion, iustice, charitie, integritie of life, and in all the liberall sciences and mechanike artes, if the citisens enioy not a firme and an assured peace. And who is more enemie to a peaceable man, than a furious souldiour? to a mild countrey man, than a bloodie warrior? to a philosopher, than a captaine? to the wise, than fooles? For the greatest delight that souldiours take, is to forrage and spoyle the country, rob the peasant, burne villages,

Note at K6.

villages, besiege, batter, force and sacke townes; massacre good and bad, young and old, all ages, and all sexes; force virgines, wash themselues in the blood of the murthered, prophane holy things, rase temples, blaspheme the name of God, and tread vnderfoot all diuine and humane lawes. These are the fruits of warre, pleasing and delightfull to all souldiors, but abominable to all good men, & detestable before God. What need examples in so manifest a matter? who can thinke of them without horror? or heare them spoken of without sighing? Who knowes not the wounds of the husbandman? who sees not their miseries? who heares not their complaints? Euery mans field, cattell, and corne, wherewith we liue and draw our breath, are in the power of souldiours, that is (as many do interpret it) of robbers. If it be so, I see no reason why wee should instruct citisens in this cruell and execrable kind of life, or to arme them, but to repulse violence in time of extreame necessitie. For those which take small occasions to make warre, are like vnto flies, which cannot hold themselues vppon a smooth polished glasse, but vpon rough places. And those which seeke warre to inrich themselues with their neighbours spoyles, shall be in continuall torment, leading a miserable life: for desire hath no bounds, although in show they seeme to be contented with the desire of a kingdome: euen like vnto a slaue, who desires onely to be freed of his bands; being vnbound, he affecteth his libertie; and being free, he demaunds to bee made a citisen; after that he desires to be a magistrat; and being come to highest place of magistracie, he affects to be a king; and being a king, hee will bee an absolute and sole monarch; and in the end he will be worshipped as a God. How much more happy then is a prince, or a small Commonweale (although there be nothing little where there is content) enioying an assured rest, and a peace without enemies, without warre, and without enuie. For the bounds of a well ordered Commonweale are not limited by the sword, as *Agesilaus* boasted, but by iustice, as *Pompey* said to the king of the Parthians, when as he would haue the riuer of Euphrates to distinguish the bounds of the Roman and Parthian empires.

Warre hatefull to God and man

The subiect is not to be trained vp in armes.

This haue I briefly obiected against the fortifying of cities, & militarie discipline: but many things may be said on the contrarie part, That townes without wals lie open to the spoyle of theeues and robbers, and the liues and liberties of the citisens, to the mercie of their enemies. Moreouer a towne without walles seemes to be a bait to intice any one that would inuade it, who else would haue no desire, and lesse power, if it were well fortified: like vnto men that trauell vnarmed, they encourage theeues to kill them, to haue their spoiles. For it is manifest, that the sacke of cities is a bait for souldidiours, and he will willingly be an enemie to them that are weake, that durst not look of them being armed. Besides, the first, and in a manner the onely occasion to gather men together into one societie and communaltie, was for the tuition of euery one in particular, and of all in generall, and of their wiues, children, goods, and possesions, the which cannot be in safetie without wals. For, to say, that men will make a wall against the enemie, that may well be when as they must fight: but those which must make defence, are not commonly the fourth part of the inhabitants, for that there are alwayes more women than men, besides children, old men, sicke men and impotent, who can haue no recourse but vnto walles.

The inconueniences not to haue fortresses.

A towne vnfortified, is a bait for an enemie.

A communalty cannot be in safetie without some defence.

It is a ridiculous thing to say, That men without walls will be more valiant: if that were true, what need we any offensiue armes to affront the enemie, nay rather it should be necessarie to command euery man to fight naked, as *Isadas* did, being one of the goodliest and most valiant gentlemen of Sparta, who seeing *Epaminondas* with an armie of Thebans fighting with the Lacedemonians, and labouring to enter into their citie, he stript himselfe naked, and with a pertuisan in one hand, and a sword in the other,

---

A4 divine   D4–5 souldiours   E9 pertuisan *i.e.* partisan, a spear with a cutting edge

600   THE FIFTH BOOKE

Isadas punished for his rashnesse, and rewarded for his valour.

ther, he chargeth the enemie desperatly, whereas he did valiant exploits: for the which the seigneurie gaue him a crowne, but he was condemned in a fine, hauing so rashly abandoned his life vnto the enemie, being vnarmed. In like sort should the Senat of Sparta haue been condemned in a great fine, for that they had abandoned the people and so great a citie to the mercie of their enemies, hauing no walls; the which without doubt had then fallen into the Thebans power if they had not been fortified with ditches and rampars. If a rampar did then auaile for the safetie of the citisens, who doubts but walls will be more profitable? and if walls make the citisens cowards, mutinous, and rebels, why did they not fill vp the ditches of Lacedemon? But the euent doth shew which of the two is most profitable, for *Cleomines* king of Sparta hauing lost the battaile of Selaria, hauing no place of retreat was forced to flie into Ægypt, abandoning his estate and countrie to the enemie, who presently entred into the citie of Sparta without any resistance. And if walls make men cowards, *Lisander* hauing taken Athens, would not haue razed the walls, the which *Themistocles* and *Pericles* had caused to be built for the defence of that citie, the which was afterwards the most flourishing of all the East. To say that the enemie shall not be able to hold a countrie if there be no walled townes, I yeeld vnto it: but who shall keepe him from the spoile of cities, from burning of houses, from murthering of men, rauishing of women, and leading children into captiuitie, according to the antient warres, that is, of the stronger? all histories are full of these calamities. There is also as small reason to thinke that weake townes and without walls will compound with the enemie, and not stand out; whereas contrariwise an enemie that shall see the entrie easie, will neuer allow of any reasonable composition, which otherwise he would do, finding a difficultie to besiege and to force a town well fortified. Moreouer who sees not but a small fort doth oftentimes stay a great and mightie armie, whereof we haue too many examples: and many times those which do besiege are besieged with cold, hunger, and diseases, and for one they kill within, there are a hundred slaine without. Constantinople did indure the Turks siege eight yeares, vntill they were relieued by *Tamberlan* emperour of the Tartars, who defeated *Baiazet* king of the Turks with all his armie. Euen so the king of Fez indured a siege seuen yeares in the towne of Fauzara against the king of Marocco, whose armie in the end was consumed with the plague in the yeare 1412. And the towne of Mecna in Affrike held out also seuen yeares, whereas the enemies died for the most part, and were forced to depart with shame and losse. And in our age the citie of Metz (although it were nothing so well fortified as it is at this day) did long resist the armie of the emperour *Charles* the fift, and was a buckler vnto all France, which had been in great danger if the emperour had not found this towne well fortified, from whence he was forced to depart, being both himselfe and his armie besieged with hunger, cold, & many diseases. The citie of Tyre held out great *Alexander* seuen moneths, during which time the king of Persia had good meanes to leauie forces, and to prouide for his estate. And if walls made men faintharted and cowards, why did the Romans fortifie their citie, being the most valiant people that euer were? And it was auaileable for them to haue good walls, when as *Marcius Coriolanus*, the *Tarquins*, *Hanniball*, and others did besiege them, and burnt euen vnto their gates. And euen when as the Gaules had forced and wholie burnt the citie, their estate had been vtterly ruined if they had not retired into the Capitoll. The like had happened vnto the Pope and Cardinals after that the armie of *Charles* of Bourbon had sackt Rome, if they had not fled into the castell S. Ange, where they were besieged as long as the antient Romans were in the Capitoll. And euery man knowes that countries without forts are presently conquered vpon the first battaile that is woon within the countrie, as we reade of England, which

Weake townes must yeeld to the victors will

A strong fort is oftentimes the ruine of the enemies armie.

Leo of Affrike.

G1 Selasia   K1 availeable *i.e.* advantageous, profitable   Note at G9.

Of A Commonweale. 601

which the Saxons conquered from the antient Brittains, who were expelled, and their enemies tooke possession. After the Saxons the Danes entred, who were lords of it for the most part: then *William* the Conqueror by the meanes of one only victorie became absolute lord, and tooke possession thereof. And during the quarels betwixt the houses of Lancaster and Yorke, the realme was lost and recouered thrise in sixe moneths: as if *Henry* the sixt, *Edward* the fourth, and the earle of Warwike had plaied at base: and although that *Edward* in the end inioyed the realme, yet soone after his death his brother *Richard* duke of Glocester (hauing made himselfe king by the murther of his nephues) was defeated and slaine by the earle of Richmond, who had bin banished into France, from whence he brought some small ayde which king *Lewis* the 11 had giuen him. The which happens not in fortified countries where there is any retreat: for which cause the Romans did neuer camp but they cast vp a trench about the armie of 25 foot broad, and most commonlie with palissadoes; neither did they euer giue battaile but they left a garrison within their camp, to make good the retreat if their enemies were the stronger, the which hath relieued them in great losses, as *Paulus Æmilius* did wisely discourse vnto the armie before that he gaue battaile vnto the king of Macedon, saying, *Maiores nostri castra munita portum ad omnes casus exercitus ducebant esse, vnde ad pugnam exirent, quo iactati pugnæ receptum haberent & qui castris exutus erat, etiamsi pugnando acie vicisset, pro victo habebatur*: Our elders held a camp well fortified, a safe retreat for all euents, from the which they went forth to fight, and retired if they were beaten, and he that had lost his camp, although he had ouercome in fighting, yet was he held as vanquished. The experience of many ages, and of the antient Commonweales of the Persians, Egiptians, Greeks, Latins, Gaules, and other nations, which haue alwaies fortified and vittailed their townes, ports and places that were fit to be fortified, to assure and defend their friends, and to incounter and resist their enemies, giues vs to vnderstand, that it is necessarie to vse it; and euen the Tartars within these hundred yeares build and fortifie their places: for how valiant soeuer a nation be, yet can they not long resist nor vanquish him which is much more stronger. These reasons shall serue to prooue that it is necessarie to fortifie towns. We will in like maner hold, that the citisens must be instructed in martiall discipline, for that seeing by the lawes of God and nature we may defend our liues from violence, and our goods from spoyle, we must then conclude, That it is needful to accustome the subiects to armes, not only defensiue, but also offensiue, to protect the good, and offend the wicked. I call all those theeues and wicked which make warre vniustly, and take away an other mans goods wrongfully, and euen as wee ought to punish and take reuenge on subiects that bee theeues and robbers, so must we of strangers what royall title soeuer they carrie, this is grounded vpon the law of God and nature. Neither is it true that *Tully* writ, That no warre was iust but for the recouerie of ones owne; or, that was denounced before vnto the enemie: for the proclaiming of warre makes it not iust, but the cause must be necessarie: there can be none then more iust than to defend the liues of innocents. There are other priuate considerations besides these: for the best meanes to maintaine an estate, and to preserue it from rebellions, seditions, and ciuill warres, and to entertaine them in loue, is to haue an enemie against whom they may oppose themselues. This appeares by the example of all Commonweales, and namely of the Romans, who neuer could find a more safe and surer remedie against ciuill warres, than to affront the subiects with an enemie: for being on a time at warre among themselues, the enemie entred the towne, and seazed vpon the Capitoll, but suddenly they were reconciled, and expelled him: a while after the Veientes seeing them returne to ciuill warres, they began to wast and spoyle the Roman territories, but the Romans were soone agreed, discharging

Fff their

Marginal notes:
- The realme of England thrice conquered.
- The Romans did alwayes fortifie their campe.
- A countrey vnfortified cannot long resist a strong enemie.
- The cause makes the warre iust.
- War against an enemie, entertaines the subiects in loue.
- *Dion. Halicar. lib. 7. Liuius lib. 3.*

E2 them *i.e.* the subjects (cf. Fr)   Notes at C7, D10.

their choller vpon them, so as they neuer ceased vntill they had razed their citie, and made the inhabitants subiect. And about the same time the princes and people of Tuscane hauing conspired against the Roman state, sought to nourish seditions and diuisions among them, saying, That their power was inuincible, and would alwayes grow, if it were not made weake by ciuill warres, the which is the only poyson to make Empires and States mortall, which else would be immortall. In like case the people of Spaine being reuolted from the emperour *Charles* the fift, forcing in a manner the duke of Calabria to accept of the Crowne, being thus in armes one against an other, king *Francis* the first sent an armie which recouered Fontarabie and the kingdome of Nauarre, but sodenly this ciuill warre was pacified among the Spanyards, who with one common consent fell vpon the french, and recouered that from them which they had conquered, else the state of Spaine had been in great danger, as many haue supposed, if the french had temporized a while. And without any further search, we haue a president of this realme, the which was in great hazard in the yeare 1562, if the english had not set footing into France, hauing seazed vpon Newhauen, but presently the ciuill warres ceased, and the subiects agreed to fall vpon their common enemie, which the english perceiuing, they haue since resolued to let the french fight and ruine one another, and afterwards to inuade the realme without any difficultie or resistance. But I will returne to forraine examples, (and I would to God we had no domesticall presidents) to shew that it is a hard thing and almost impossible, to maintaine subiects in peace and loue, if they be not in war against some enemie. It is apparant in all the histories of the Romans, who after they had vanquished their enemies, presently fell to mutinie, for which cause the Senat entertained warre, and deuised enemies when they had none, to keepe them from ciuill warres, the which they continued vntill they had extended their frontiers vnto the ilands of Orcades, to the Atlantike sea, to the riuers of Danubius and Euphrates, and to the deserts of Arabia: and hauing no more enemies to make head against them, they murthered one an other most cruelly, and so much the more, for that they were growne mightie, and had few enemies, as in the ciuill warre betwixt *Cæsar* and *Pompey* for rule, whereof *Cicero* speaking said, *Bellum pium ac necessarium visum est, ciuibus tamen exitiabile, nisi Pompeius vicerit, calamitosum etiam si vicerit*: It seemes, said he, to be a godly and necessarie warre, yet fatall vnto the citisens vnlesse that *Pompey* win, and lamentable if he do win: But it was more cruell betwixt *Augustus* and *Marc Anthonie*: for which cause the emperour *Augustus* hauing changed the popular estate into a Monarkie, was not so ill aduised as to discharge the fortie legions, but he sent them into prouinces, & vpon the frontiers of barbarous nations, to entertaine them in martiall discipline, and to preuent all occasions of ciuill warres at Rome. But the emperour *Constantine* the great (following the counsell of some Bishops and ministers vnacquainted with matters of State) discharged the legions, which made them forget the antient militarie discipline, and opened a gate to barbarous nations, who inuaded the Roman empire of all sides, whereby it appeeres that lawes, iustice, religion, subiects, and the whole estate next vnder God, is in the protection of armes, as vnder a strong shield. There is yet an other reason of great moment, to shew that it is necessarie to entertaine martiall discipline, and to make warre, for that there is no citie so holy, nor so well gouerned that hath not in it many theeues, murtherers, idle persons, vagabonds, mutins, adulterers, and diceplayers, which leade a wicked life, and corrupt the simplicitie of good subiects; neither can lawes, magistrates, nor any punishment keepe them in awe. And euen it is commonlie said that gibets are set vp but for beggers, for that statutes and ordinances in many places are like vnto spiders webs, as *Anacharsis* said vnto *Solon*, for that none but weake flies are taken in them, and great

Ciuill warres the ruine of states.

Newhauen taken by the English caused the ciuill wars of Fraunce to cease.

Rest the cause of ciuill ware in a warlike citie.

The first occasion to ruine the Roman empire.

Armes the defence of states.

A meane to purge the Commonweale of vagabonds and idle persons.

G3-4 president *i.e.* precedent   G5 Newhaven *i.e.* le Havre   H6 *For* Arabia *Bodin writes* Africa.
Notes at H6, K2.

great beasts breake easily through them. There is no better meanes then to purge the Commonweale of this infectious filth, then to send them to the warre, the which is as it were a purging medicine to expell corrupted humors out of the vniuersall bodie of the state. This was the principall occasion which moued *Charles* the wise king of France to send succors so willinglie vnto the bastard of Castille vnder the conduct of *Bertrand* of Guesclin Constable, the which purged France of an infinite number of theeues: Euen so did *Lewis* the 11 to the Earle of Richmond; and both the one and the other not only purged France of idle persons, but also returned with honor to haue setled two kings in their estates, from the which they were expelled. Moreouer, the militarie discipline of the Romans which should be common to all nations, made a coward valiant, an intemperat man modest, a slothfull man actiue, a prodigall man frugall, and a licentious man continent: neither is it sufficient for a captaine or souldier to know how to fight, but there are many other excellent arts which be companions to this vertue, that is to say labor in busines, resolution in dangers, temperance in desires, industrie in action, speed in execution, and counsell in prouiding, these are necessarie for the arte of warre. The subiect then being instructed in militarie discipline, is not infected with lust, licentiousnes, impietie and sloth, but being wicked and impious, they inure themselues to all kinds of vertue if they learne the precepts of the Roman militarie discipline and arte of commanding. Besides, there is nothing that containes the people within the dutie of honor and vertue more then the feare of a warlike enemie. The people of Rome (saith *Polibius*) were neuer more vertuous, nor the subiects more obedient vnto the magistrates, nor the magistrates vnto the lawes, then when as *Pyrrhus* at one time, and *Hanniball* at an other were at the gates of Rome; but after that *Perseus* and *Antiochus* were vanquished, hauing no enemie left whom they might feare, then vices began to take roote, and the people fell into superfluities and delights, wich corrupted all good manners, and blemished the beautie of their antient vertue. O how wisely did *Scipio* oppose himselfe in open Senat, that the citie of Carthage should not be razed, foretelling they either should haue ciuill warres, or that the vertue of the Romans would soone decay, hauing no enemy to contend withall, for euen as moderate libertie puffes men vp, and makes them proane to all vices, so feare retaines them in their duties: and we must not doubt but the great politian and gouernour of all the world as he hath giuen to euery thing his contrarie, so hath he suffred warres and hatred among nations to punish one by an other, and to keepe them all in feare, which is the only comptroller of vertue, as *Samuell* in an oration which he made vnto the people said, That God had stirred them vp enemies, to keepe them in awe, try them, and punish them. And that I may conclude briefly, if there be no respect had of so many commodities, yet let vs haue a care of the health and necessitie of the Commonweale, least it grow wast and desolate through the spoiles and insolencie of the enemie, for when as the enemies forces are neere, although there be no inuasion, yet the flocks are forsaken, the tillage is abandoned, and all trafficke ceasseth; and oftentimes the whole yeares fruits are lost at the rumor of any danger, or the terror of warre. Who will then doubt but the subiects should be trained vp in armes, in the which there is not only much glorie and profit, but also the health of the citisens, the help of their neighbors, the fortunes of the subiects, and the securitie of them all. By these reasons it appeares, that they are much abused which thinke that the only end of warre is peace. And if it were so, what better meanes were there to haue peace in despight of the enemie, then to let him know that you haue meanes to make warre? Neuer wise Prince nor good Captaine made a peace vnarmed, and as *Manlius Capitolinus* said, *Ostendite modo bellum, pacem habebitis, videant vos paratos ad vim, ius ipsi remittent*: Shew them warre

The martiall discipline of the Romans, was a schoole of vertue.

The praise of militarie discipline.

The feare of enemies keepe subiects in awe.

The prouidence of Scipio the younger.

Wars allowed of God.

The way to haue a peace, is to prepare for force

C 9 For moderate *read* immoderate (*effrenee*).

warre said he, and you shall haue peace, let them see you readie for force, and they will do you right. These reasons are partly true and partly probable, and may of either side dazle the eyes of the cleerest sighted if they looke not neerely vnto them. To the end we may resolue something, let vs distinguish of Commonweales. I hold then that in a popular estate it is necessarie to traine the subiects vp in armes, to auoid the abouenamed inconueniences, vnto the which a popular estate is by nature subiect; and if the people be warlike and mutinous by nature, as the nations of the North be, being trained vp to armes and martiall discipline, it shall be expedient to affront them often with their enemies, and not to admit any peace but vpon good termes, as a dangerous thing to a warlike nation. And a peace being concluded, you must notwithstanding entertain your souldiers vpon the frontiers, as the emperor *Augustus* did, although he had changed the popular estate into a Monarchie: or else send them to Princes that are in league, to be entertained in the art of warre; as the Swissers haue wisely done, being a people bred in the mountaines apt to warre, and hardly maintained in peace, inioying a popular libertie; and by this meanes they haue alwayes had souldiers nourished and entertained at another mans cost, besides their publike and priuat pensions (which haue been great, as I haue formerly shewed) and the assurance of their estate, by means of alliances contracted with so mightie a king. And as for forts, it is not needfull in a popular estate to haue their townes too well fortified (except it be the chiefe citie, which is the seate of the popular estate) and much lesse any Castels or Citadels, least some one thrust on with an ambitious desire of rule surprise them, and change the popular estate into a Monarchie: as *Denis* the tyrant did, hauing surprised Acradina the fort of Siracusa by fraud. Or else the enemie may take them & fortifie them, as the Lacedemonians did, hauing razed the walles of Athens, they left a garrison in the Castell: and doing the like vnto the popular estate of Thebes, they tooke their fort called Cadmee, leauing a garrison in it. For there is no meanes to subiect a people, or to change a Democratia into a Monarchie but by Cittadels, so did the tyrants in old time: and in our age *Cosme de Medicis* duke of Florence had made two Cittadels in Florence, with a garrison of strangers, hauing found by experience that it was impossible to change the popular estate into a Monarchie, and to assure his life among the people: and therefore the Cantons of Vri, Vnderuald, Glaris, and Appenzell, which are all popular, haue no walles, like vnto the rest which are gouerned Aristocratically. We will giue the same censure of *Aristocratia* in regard of fortresses, as of a popular estate, the which is so much more to be feared, for that it is more easie for one of the commanders to win the common people to his will, and to incense them against the chiefe men. But as for royall Monarchies, if their bounds and limits be large, it is not expedient for the Prince to build Cittadels, not places of strength, but vpon the frontiers, to the end the people may be without feare of tyranizing; and yet hauing fortified the frontiers of his estate with places impregnable, the subiects will stil thinke it is against the enemie, and the Prince at neede may vse them against all enemies, both strangers and subiects in case they rebell: the which nature hath taught vs, which hath armed the head and the extremities of all beasts, leauing the middest, the bowels, and the other parts vnarmed. But the Monarke is ill aduised that doth inuiron a towne with mightie walls, if he doth not withall build a good Cittadell, for that nothing doth more animate the subiects to reuolt, the which they would not so easily attempt, seeing before their eyes Cittadels well fortified. It is also necessarie as well in a Monarchie as in an Aristocritie, that the gouernor of the towne depend not of the captaine of the Cittadell, nor the captaine of the gouernor, neither that the captaine of the Cittadell be a Prince, or a great man: the which is well obserued in Turkie, according to the

rule

Sidenotes:
- A resolution of the question.
- In a Popular estate the subiects must be trayned vp in armes.
- In a Popular estate onely the capitall citie must be fortified.
- Citadels not to be built in a Popular estate.
- Citadels the cause of tyrants.
- Citadels more dangerous whereas few do gouern.
- To fortifie the frontiers, is according to the law of nature.

l3–4 a popular estate, FOR THERE IS NO LESS DANGER THAT ONE OF THE LORDS WILL MAKE HIMSELF SOVEREIGN, AND MASTER OF HIS COMPANIONS, THAN IN A POPULAR ESTATE; the which   l7 nor places Note at G8.

rule of the antient Sultans of Egipt, as also our kings do, but the Venetians more strictlie then all others, for that they are forced to fortifie their townes, to defend the subiects against their enemies, and fearing the rebellion of their subiects, who haue no share in the gouerment, they haue strong Cittadels in their townes, whither they do euery yeare send new Captaines besides the Potestates or Gouernors, least that he should hold the Cittadell as his inheritance. And those of Rhagouse (which haue but one citie and a small territorie) are forced to change their Captaine euery day, who is brought into the fort with his face couered. In like sort the Athenians changed the Captaine of their fortresse euery day, the which was one of the nine Archontes, for the distrust they had that one of the subiects should make himselfe lord. For the preuenting whereof, it shall be needfull to remoue Cittadels from the capitall townes in a popular estate, or an Aristocraticall estate, as the Venetians haue done wisely at Venice, to take all occasion from the duke, and to free the gentlemen from suspition of any alteration in the state. It was wisely prouided in England, Turkie, Muscouie, and in a manner by all the kings of the East and of Afftike, that no subiect should fortifie his house in the countrie, for if the maister of a priuate castell be a great man, he will soone take an occasion to reuolt, if he be poore, to rob; and for this cause the imperiall townes of Germany haue oftentimes razed gentlemens castels, that rebels and theeues might haue no retreat, the which the Swissers haue done throughout all their countrey, hauing expelled the antient lords. But this were a dangerous thing in an antient Monarchie to ruine priuate mens castels which are of strength, but well they may prohibit their subiects not to build any more without licence from the Soueraigne, who may not easily grant it, for that it is sufficient to haue a house able to defend him from theeues, and thus much for fortifications. But the question is not small, if in Aristocratia, the better sort only, which command, are to be trained vp in armes, or all the people, or else wholie to banish the arte of warre. If the common people do once become souldiers, it is to be feared they will attempt to change the state, to haue a part in the gouerment, if they be not alwayes imployed against the enemies, as I haue shewed before by many examples; and if none but the better sort be armed, they shall be soone defeated, and will cause a necessarie change of their estate: but if they will quite banish the arte of warre out of their Commonweale, they shall remaine a skorne and pray to all their neighbors, if they be not strictly allied vnto the strongest, or else if they haue not townes that be inaccessible and forts impregnable, as the Venetians, who fearing the aboue named inconueniences, haue banished the arte of warre out of their Commonweale, as Cardinall *Contarenus* saith: the which is rather to be attributed to sloth, then to any set or positiue law, for that within these two hundred yeares they were verie warlike, and obtained great victories of the Genuois, but pleasing themselues with the continuall fruits of peace and ease, they haue neglected the practise of armes, imploying strangers in their wartes: neither can they indure any gentleman of the seigneurie to be a commander, but if they know any Venetian gentleman that aspires to the warres, and that followes the courts of other Princes, by and by they call him home, desiring rather to haue an Almain a Bargamasco, or a stranger for their generall, if they make warre by land, than one of their owne lords, and an armie of strangers rather than of subiects: but withall they send a Prouidador or Commissarie, by whose councell the Generall is gouerned. And although there be many inconueniences, to haue a Commissarie commaund a Generall, a citisen strangers: one that vnderstands nothing in matters of warre, them that are bred vp in armes: yet by this meanes they auoid many other daungers which are not lesse: the which we haue seene fall out in their Commonweale, whereas they vsed none but their own subiects and forces. Their

Citadels in townes of strength, keepe the subiects from rebelling.

Distrust of noblemen in an Aristocraticall estate.

Citadels not to be built in the chiefe citie of a Popular estate, nor in a Seigneurie.

The Venetians do not practise armes in their Commonweale.

Why the Venetians neglected armes.

Fff iij   histories

C4 theeves. And thus   E2 an Alvian, a Bargamasco (*i.e.* Bartolommeo d'Alviano and Bartolommeo Colleoni of Bergamo)   E9 For whereas *read* whenas *i.e.* when.   Note at B6.

606 THE FIFTH BOOKE

Why the Venetians imploy strangers in their warres.

histories are full of conspiracies, seditions & ciuil wars, which they had in the middest of their city. The Carthagineans, being not yet wel instructed in the art of war, were wont to send for Lacedemonian captaines, which should lead a Carthaginean armie vnder a Generall of Carthage; yet would they neuer haue both Generall and armie strangers, least their Commonweale should fall into the power of straungers. If warre be not to be vndertaken, but for the repelling of iniuries, and to enioy peace, and that it sufficeth to make a Commonweale happie to keepe their owne, to haue their places neere vnto their enemies well manned and fortified, and to enioy the fruits of a desired peace;

The seigneury of Venice most happy.

without doubt the Seigneurie of Venice may iustly tearme it selfe happie, which hath not onely the seat of their empire by nature and art inexpugnable, but also haue their townes and fortresses vpon the continent so well fortified, as they neither need to feare the inuasions of their enemies, nor the rebellions of their subiects: caring little for any new conquests, or to extend their bounds. We see the Venetians do flie from all occasions of warre, as from the plague, and they neuer enter into it but by constraint, and seeke for peace at what price soeuer, euen with the losse of their reuenewes; as we may see in the treatie which they made with pope *Iulio* the second, the emperor *Maximilian*, and the king of Naples, in the yere 1508, their ambassadours being humbled at their feet, yeelding to all which they demanded. As they did in like maner to *Sultan Selim* in the yeare 1570, abandoning the holy league to purchase his peace, after they had lost a goodly kingdome. And euen as beasts which haue no offensiue armes, as hares that haue no gall, as Stagges and Does seeke to saue themselues from the hounds and hawke, by flight; so they are not to be blamed, nor that Commonweale to bee lesse esteemed, which sues for peace, hauing no meanes to resist: the which would be dishonourable to a warlike nation, or for a conquering prince, who cannot demaund a peace

The Venetians desire peace with their losse.

A generous prince demands neither peace nor warre.

of his enemie without blushing. There was nothing that did so long protract the conclusion of a peace betwixt king *Henrie* the second, and the emperour *Charles* the fift, as a certaine rumor spred abroad, That the emperour demaunded a peace: which was to get the highest point of honour, which a generous prince may desire, yea if he were entred into anothers countrey. As the same emperour did in the yeare 1544, hauing thrust all the forces of the empire, and his owne, into this realme, with those of the king of England on another side, who had alreadie diuided the realme betwixt them (as *Sleidan* saith) if the pope had not forced the emperour to make a peace: which the king would neither demaund, nor accept, but with reasonable conditions. Although that *Lewis* the eleuenth demaunded it of *Edward* the fourth, king of England, as soone as he was entred into Picardie, and bought it deerely, caring little that the earle of Lude and other his fauourites called him cowardly king. But his father *Charles* the seuenth did a stranger thing for to obtaine a peace of the duke of Bourgongne, his vassall and naturall subiect; he sent the constable of France, the chauncellor, a marshall of France, and many other great personages, to treat a peace with him, who in open assembly, and in the name of the king their maister, craued pardon of the duke, for the death of *Iohn* duke of Bourgongne, confessing openly, That the king had done ill, being young, indiscreet, and ill councelled; intreating the duke, that he would forget his discontent: the duke said, That he did pardon the king for the honour of God, and compassion of the people of Fraunce, and to obey the councell of the pope and other christian princes that had intreated him. A slaue could not behaue himselfe more humbly and abiectly vnto his maister, than the king did vnto his subiect, to restore the realme to his first beautie, and to expell the English, as he did soone after. The Romans would rather haue lost their estate, than once to haue dreamt of it: For wee cannot find that at any time during seuen hundred yeares, that they had warres with all nations, that they

Lewes the eleuenth reproched by his subiects for demaunding of a peace.

Charles the seuenth demaunds a peace basely of the duke of Bourgongne.

G5 revenewes *i.e. domaine*, which may also mean territory (cf. note at 650 G10)   G10–H1 as hares, OR that have   H1 *For* Does *read* Doves.   K1 (margin) demaunds   K7 expell

Notes at H8, K4.

OF A COMMONWEALE.

they euer demaunded peace but of the Gaules, who held them besieged in the Capitol, after they had burnt their citie: and of *Coriolanus*: But contratiwise being vanquished by the power of king *Perseus*, they would neuer accept of any peace of the victor, vnlesse he would submit himselfe and his kingdome vnto their mercie, although he offred to pay them tribute. And when as king *Pyrrhus* (after that hee had obtained two notable victories, and was maister almost of all Italie) sent his ambassadour to Rome, to treat a peace vpon reasonable conditions: they were aunswered, That the Romans would not treat of any peace, except that *Pyrrhus* did first depart out of Italie; and that they did contend with him for their honours and dignities, not for their liues and fortunes. The king receiuing this aunswere, said, That the Romans could not liue in quiet, neither conquerors, nor conquered. This was the aunswere of a valiant people, who knew their owne forces to be able to make head against an enemie: the which would be very much vnbefitting a weake prince, who must (like vnto a wise pilot) strike sails, & yeeld vnto the tempest, that he may recouer a safe port, & not to make necessitie subiect to ambition: as the Vauoide of Transiluania did, who said openly, That he had rather bee slaue vnto the Turke, than allied vnto *Ferdinand*, and so afterwards it fell out. Wee haue an example of the great Knez of Moscouie, who seeing the Procope of Tartaria entred into his countrey with eighteene legions, knowing well that he was vnable to make resistance, he went to meet him vnarmed, and humbling himselfe before him, he saued his people and his estate from an ineuitable ruine, yet holding his countrey by yeelding homage to the Procope. But being at this day equall or greater in forces, & freed from the seruitude of the Tartar, all princes would scorne him, if he should demaund a peace, especially hauing receiued an iniurie. For that prince that beares an iniurie, will soone endure to haue a law prescribed him; and if he once suffer his enemie to giue him a law, he shall soone be reduced into slauerie. But howsoeuer, a mightie prince (if he be wise and valiant) will neuer seeke for war nor peace, if necessitie (which is not subiect to the lawes of honour nor force) doth not constraine him, neither will he euer giue battaile, if there be not more apparant profit in the victorie, than of losse if the enemies should vanquish: as the emperour *Augustus* said, who for this reason neuer gaue battaile but vpon necessitie. But it is not vnfitting a poore prince, or a small seigneurie, or for him that makes no profession of armes, to demaund peace in his losse. As pope *Iulio* the third, who demaunded peace of king *Henrie* the second, calling him before God, to iudge of the wrong which hee had done him: The king graunted him a peace, and said, That he would appeare before God; but hee doubted the pope would not shew himselfe. Wherewith the pope, who was of a pleasant disposition (seeing the letters which were signed by the king in the campe lying at Metz, in the yeare 1552) was very glad, although in shew he seemed to bee grieued, saying, That it was not the king that had indited those letters, but the capitall enemie of the church. And as the greatnesse of courage and magnanimitie is the light of all other vertues, and which doth aduance princes to the highest point of honour; so is it the onely vertue which doth most daunt an enemie, although he be mightie and warlike, and oftentimes giues the victorie without blowes: as *Furius Camillus* hauing sent home the children of the Falisques, whome their Schoolemaister had brought into his campe, he conquered their citie without striking stroke. And *Fabricius* hauing sent vnto king *Pyrrhus* the Physitian which offred to poison him, refusing halfe his kingdomes and his treasure, (although he were one of the poorest gentlemen in Rome) and causing their ransomes to be paid, whome *Pyrrhus* had freely set at libertie, beeing loath the Romans should be bound in any respect vnto so great a king. Or as *Scipio* who hauing conquered a good part of Spaine with little paine, sent backe a ladie of sin-

Fff iiij   gular

The Romans neuer demanded a peace of any but twice.

The Romans of an vndaunted resolution.

It is no dishonor to submit in time of necessitie.

When a prince should giue battaile.

A shew of courage doth many times daunt an enemie.

gular beautie vnto her husband, prince of the Celtiberians, imitating the example of *Cyrus*. These vertuous acts tooke from their enemies all courage, to make any more warre against so valiant and magnanimious a people, who could neither bee vanquished by honour, nor vanquished by treacherie: the which was more apparant after the battaile of Cannes, *Hannibal* hauing appointed eight thousand Roman prisoners to be ransomed for an hundred crowns a peece one with another, hoping that the Romans who had lost so many men, would willingly pay their ransoms: but the Senat decreed, That no one should be redeemed at any rate, giuing all to vnderstand, That either they must vanquish, or be slaues to the enemie: Wherewith *Hannibal* was so amased, and daunted, as he dispaired euer to vanquish the Romans. And contrariwise the Romans did assure their estate, which was much shaken and abandoned of all friends and allies. For the Senat did well imagin, that *Hannibal* hauing sucked so much blood of the Romans, he would also exhaust their treasure, in drawing from them eight hundred thousand crownes, and restoring vnto them the veriest cowards of all the Roman armie; making euery one to resolue either to vanquish or die, hauing lost all hope of libertie, whereby they became fearefull and inuincible. And euen as they neuer fainted in their losses; so were they neuer proud nor arrogant in their victories. For when as *Antiochus* the Great hauing lost a goodly armie, sent his ambassadours to both the *Scipioes*, offring to accept of what conditions the Romans pleased: Whereunto *Scipio* the African made an answere worthy of a great and vertuous prince, That the Romans lost no part of their courage when they were vanquished, nor of their modestie, when they did vanquish, demaunding no harder conditions after their victorie than before. But the aduantage which the Romans had, was, that they made warre in their enemies countrey, hauing magazins of souldiors in Italy, to supply their armies if they were defeated: or if they conquered those countries where they made warre, they might add them to their empire, & plant them with their owne colonies. A wise prince will neuer attend an enemie in his own country, if he may stop his entrie, vnlesse he hath another army ready, or a sure retrait into some places of strength, els he hazards his whole estate vpon a victorie; as *Antiochus*, *Perseus*, *Iuba*, and *Ptolome* the last king of Ægypt did against the Romans: *Darius* against *Alexander*, and oftentimes the French against the English. And for this cause *Lewis* the grosse vnderstanding that the emperour *Henry* came with a mightie power to make warre in Fraunce (the king hauing receiued Pope *Gelasius* into his protection, and suffered him to excommunicat the emperor) he gathered together an armie of two hundred thousand men, as *Suggerius* abbat of Saint *Denis* in Fraunce hath left in writing, and went as farre as the Rhin vpon the territories of the empire, which was the onely cause that made the emperour to lay aside armes, and to accept of what peace it pleased the king. In like sort *Philip Augustus* aduertised that the emperour *Otho* the second, the king of England, with the potentats of the Low countries, came into his realme with a mightie armie, he fortified his places, marched out of his frontiers, and defeated them in battaile. And if king *Francis* the first, when as he lost his armie before Pauia, and himselfe taken prisoner, had receiued such an ouerthrow in the hart of Fraunce, this realme had bene in great daunger; but chauncing in Italie, the conquerors contented themselues with the victorie; and the subiects in the meane time had leasure to rally their forces, and to fortifie their frontiers.

Many hold opinion, That a soueraigne prince should not hazard his person on a day of battaile, especially if the enemie be entred into the hart of his realme: It is true, if he be a coward and base minded: but hauing the reputation of a valiant and generous prince, he doubles the courage and force of his armie, and so much the more if he be beloued of his armie, and his presence works a wonderfull effect, when he is seene of them

---

F4 *For* nor vanquished by treacherie *read* nor vanquish by treacherie (Fr and L).   I5 in Fraunce

them all, and euerie one seene of him, for oftentimes shame retaines a flying armie, seeing the presence of their king, and fearing least he should fall into some daunger, *Vrget enim (vt ait Maro) presentia Turni*, The presence of *Turnus* (as *Maro* saith) doth vrge them to fight. As it happened to *Cæsar* before Therouenne; and in Spaine, fighting for his life against *Pompeis* children, where the battaile had bene lost if he had not bene present. And many beleeue that the victories which *Edward* the fourth got in nine battails, was, for that he did alwaies fight on foot. How many princes and great men do willingly follow the kings person, which else would not march vnder any others commaund. For when as *Eumenes* was very sicke his armie refused to fight, vnlesse he were brought into the campe in a litter; such confidence they had in his presence. Yet would I not that a soueraigne prince or a Generall, should do the office of a priuat souldiour, putting his life rashly in daunger; as it is said of *Pelopidas*, *Marcellus*, *Gaston de Foix* duke of Nemours, and many others, whose death hath drawne after it the hazard of the state.

How a prince or Generall should carry himselfe in a battaile.

I will not here treat of the art of warre, which many haue handled, but onely that which concernes the state. I conclude then, that a prince hauing well manned and fortified his frontiers, if he doubts that the enemie will enter into his countrey, let him preuent him, and put the warre as farre from him as he may: and if he be entred, not to hazard his estate and person rashly vpon the euent of a battaile, especially if hee haue to deale with a warlike people, who commonly get the victory being brought to dispaire, knowing well, that there is no meanes for them to escape death in anothers countrey, if they be vanquished, hauing neither fort, retreat, nor any succour. Amongst many we haue a lamentable example of our king *Iohn*, who chose rather to hazard his life, his nobilitie, and his whole estate, in a doubtfull battaile at Poitiers, than to graunt a peace vnto the prince of Wales, and the English armie, who demaunded only to depart with their liues: there did ten thousand desparat men defeat an armie of fortie fiue thousand French, and led away the king captiue. *Gaston* of Foix committed the like errour, hauing defeated the enemie at Rauenne, seeking to pursue a squadron of Spaniards that fled, he lost his life, and left all that hee had conquered in Italie in prey to the enemie. What should I speake of auntient examples, the histories are full of them: but there is none more famous than that of *Cæsar*, whose armie was in despaire through famine & want, being enuironed both by sea and land with the enemies townes and legions, and had soone perished for hunger, if they had not vanquished, yet would *Pompey* needs giue that battell of Pharsalia, hauing twice as many men as *Cæsar*. In so great a despaire of things, the Generall of the Volsques did incourage his armie with a briefe speech, after this maner, *Armati armatis obstant virtute pares, sed necessitate superiores estis*, Armed men stand against armed men, equall in vertue, but in necessitie you exceed them. And another captaine of the Samnites said, *Iustum est bellum quibus necessarium, & pia arma quibus nulla nisi in armis relinquitur spes*, That war is iust to whome it is necessarie, and those armes religious to them that haue no hope but in armes. And therefore *Fabius Maximus* (the last of that familie) endured all the scornes and disgraces of his enemies, rather than he would commit the fortune of the Commonweale to a doubtfull battell: and in the end he reaped the honor, To haue preserued his countrey. Whereas *Hannibal* hauing hazarded a battaile against *Scipio*, who went to besiege Carthage, to draw the enemie out of Italie, lost both his armie and the estate. It is no good consequence to say, that the Romans fought three battails with *Pyrrhus*, and as many with *Hannibal*, in the heart of Italie, for that they had magazins of men of warre, as well out of their owne countries, as from their allies: the which they could not want, for that by the laws euerie one was forced to carrie armes at seuenteene yeares of age, and were not freed

It is daungerous to fight with a desperat army.

Necessitie of an inuincible force.

No prince should fight a battaile, but constrained.

from

Plut. in Gracchis. from them vntill fiftie fiue: neither was it lawful for any man to demaund an office or benefice, that had not carried armes ten yeares. And at one time there were two thousand citisens excluded from the Bourgeship, for that they had bene foure yeares together absent from the warres, except they which had bene dispensed withall vpon some iust cause (as *Titus Liuius* saith) to the which discipline they were at the first constrained by the incursions of their bordering neighbours, being iealous of their greatnesse: But hauing afterwards brought all the people of Italie vnder their subiection, or treated alliances with them, and finding that a people giuen to armes, could not liue idly in peace without ciuill warres, they found it expedient for the good of the Commonweale, to seeke out new enemies, making warre sometimes to reuenge the wrongs done vnto their confederats: and sometimes defending them against their enemies, graunting triumphes, honourable estates, and great rewards to valiant captaines. The which was wisely ordained by the Senat, as an healthfull remedie against ciuill warres; the which *Bebius* the Tribune of the people did obiect vnto the Fathers, That warre was sowne vpon warre, that the people might neuer be at quiet: and therefore there was no distinction betwixt militarie charges and offices of iustice: So as one and the selfe same citisen, might be a valiant Captaine, a wise Senator, a good Iudge, and a great Orator: as it is said of *Cato* the Censor, who was well skilled in tillage, as it appeareth by his bookes, yet was he not ashamed to leaue his armes to goe to the plough; or to leaue the plough to plead, sometimes to be a Iudge, to sacrifice, or to play the Oratour before the people or Senat. And *Cæsar* was high Priest, and in *Tullies* opinion a most excellent Orator, and the best captaine of his age. There were many not onely in Italie, but also in Greece, that excelled in the art of warre and policie. We read in *Iulius Pollux*, That the Athenians were bound to go to warre at fourteene yeares, and continued vntill threescore. Therefore *Aristides, Pericles, Phocion, Leosthenes, Demetrius* the Phalerian, *Alcibiades, Themistocles,* and infinit other Grecians, were like vnto the auntient Romans, and did excell in the art of warre and policie. But the wisest politicians did seperat the art of warre from other vocations. In the Commonweale of Creet euerie man was not allowed to carrie armes, but certaine speciall persons: nor in old times in Fraunce, whereas the horsemen had this charge, and the Druides were exempt. In Ægypt none but the Calasires were men of warre: the which *Licurgus* did allow. And therefore *Plato* diuided the citisens into three orders, Keepers, Men at armes, and Labourers: imitating the Ægyptians, who made three seuerall kindes of estates. By little and little the Athenians made a distinction of Armes, Policie, and Iustice; and so did the Romans. And truely in this short course of our life, there are few that doe excell in politike arts, but in both not any. It seemes that *Augustus* did first take from Senators, Proconsuls, and Gouernours of Prouinces, the power to weare armes: so as in succession of time they called offices without armes dignities; as wee read in *Cassiodorus, Quamuis inquit, omnia dignitatum officia manu secludantur armata, & ciuilibus vestibus induti videantur, qui districtionem publicam docentur operari: tua tamen dignitas à terroribus eruatur, quæ gladio bellico rebus etiam pacatis accingitur: arma ista iuris sunt, non furoris,* Although (saith hee) that all offices of dignitie bee excluded from armed hands, and that they seeme to bee attired with ciuill garments, that are taught to labour in the difficulties of the Commonweale: yet the dignitie seemes to be pluckt from terrours, the which is guirt with a warlike sword, euen in the qnietest times: these be the armes of Iustice, not of Furie. And consequently all nations by degrees, haue separated souldiours from schollers and men of justice, beeing a difficult thing to excell in one art, but impossible in all; nor worthily to exercise many victories. Moreouer it was a thing almost impossible, to traine all the subiects of a Commonweale

The Romans sought occasion of warre.

Plut. in Phocione.

Plut. in Licurg.

Herodot.

In Phocione.

Dion. lib. 53.

In forma Comitiuæ, Written to the Gouernour of a Prouince.

F1 neither   G2 honourable   I2 allow *i.e.* approve   I8(margin) Dion.   I9 omnia (L 5) properly omnium (L 1–4 and Fr). Cf. Cassiodorus, *Variarum,* XII, 1.   I10(margin) comitivæ K4 *For* yet the *read* yet thy (cf. I10).   K5 quietest   K8 *For* victories *read* vocations (cf. Fr).
Note at H7.

OF A COMMONWEALE. 611

weale vp to armes, and to maintaine them in the obedience of the laws and magistrats. This was haply the cause which made king *Francis* the first, to cast the seuen legions of foot, which he had erected within this realme, in the yeare 1534, euery legion containing six thousand foot. And although that his sonne *Henry* did renew them twentie yeares after, yet was he forced to alter his opinion, seeing the Commonweale troubled, and mutinies growne in many places, by meanes of those legions. And yet in the opinion of straungers, and of those that haue iudicially examined the goodly ordinances that were made to that end, there was neuer any thing better instituted for the art of warre, the which is as necessarie in this realme, as in any part of the world, being enuitoned with warlike and mightie nations, which make a common practise to spoyle: like to a countrey of conquest. Yea if they had entertained but foure legions of foot, besides the troopes of horse, for the defence of the realme, and placed them as it were in garrison vpon the frontiers, they had prouided wisely for the safetie of the Commonweale. Fraunce is not the twentieth part of the Roman empire, for the guard whereof *Augustus Cæsar* said, That fortie legions did suffice, being but fiue thousand men in a legion. The foure legions of foot and troopes of horse, paied in time of peace, according to the ordinance of king *Francis* the first, would not haue cost three hundred and fiftie thousand pounds starling, and yet is it halfe as much more as the legions had in *Augustus* his time: and the whole pay of the men at armes of Fraunce, in the yeare 1560, came but to 235300 pounds starling, as well the old bands, as the men at armes. And *Augustus* entertained fortie legions of horse and foot, besides his and the citie guards, and two nauies for the defence of both seas, keeping the empire safe from forren and ciuill warres, and all for twelue hundred thousand pounds starling a yeare, with an excellent description of all orders: the which other princes should propound vnto themselues, to imitat such as *Orosius, Dion, Tranquillus*, & other writers haue described it in their monuments: and yet was it not lawfull for the Roman souldiours (notwithstanding their small entertainment) to rob and spoyle: as we see at this day. This was the meanes to maintaine martiall discipline, to defend the rights of citisens, and allies, and to repell the enemie: Else if you be prest with warre, you shall be forced not only to abandon your neighbours, but also your countrey: or else in this extremitie you must vse vntrained souldiours, who become captaines before they were euer souldiours: or else forced with necessitie you must beg and buy forren succours at a deere rate. I doe not thinke that forren succours are to bee reiected, as many suppose: for there is no great empire can be augmented without the succours of confederats, neither can they long resist the violence of an enemie: but I allow of those succours which come from allies, that are vnited together in an offensiue and defensiue league, as the Cantons of the Swissers be: or at the least in a defensiue league, as they bee with the house of Fraunce. For by this meanes they are not onely the more strengthned, but they also take from the enemie those succours which he might draw from them, and the occasion from all men to make warre against either of them, vnlesse hee meane to be a professed enemie vnto them both. But I desire that the confederats should be tied by a mutuall bond, and altogether equall, to auoid the reproaches, quarrels, and inconueniences that grow of inequalitie. Those leagues and treaties be vnequall, when as one is bound to pay the diets or assemblies of their allies, although they did raise but one companie of souldiours, and notwithstanding bee tied to pay them a continuall pension, besides their entertainment in the time of warre, and succours of horse and foot at need without pension or pay. These treaties did our kings of Fraunce make with the Cantons of the Swissers, least other princes should draw them to their succours. It is also necessarie in an offensiue and defensiue league which is equall, That the

The entertainment of legions, very necessarie in a state.

Augustus kept fortie legions continually in pay.

The inconueniences, not to haue trained bands.

It is good to haue mightie friends and allies in an equall league.

con

A2 Francis   A2 to cast *i.e.* to dismiss, disband   A7 judicially *i.e.* judiciously   C1 horse and
C5 themselues to imitat, such   D4 augmented   Notes at A4, C3.

612 THE FIFTH BOOKE

conquests should be common (as it hath alwaies been among the Cantons, when as they haue made warre in common) and that whatsoeuer is conquered by the one, should be priuate, wherein the antient Italians were circumuented by the Romans in their treaties, for the Romans hauing made an offensiue and defensiue league with their neighbors the Italians, they had alwayes for one Romaine legion two from their allies readie paied, and the Generall of the armie was alwaies a Romaine; and yet their allies had no pension nor entertainement from the Romans, nor any part of their conquests which were made in common, nor in dignities and offices, except some townes of the Latins; which was the cause of the sociall or confederats warre in Italie against the Romans, who were reduced to that extremitie, as they were forced to giue the right of a citisen, with part of their offices, and their voyces at elections, almost to all their allies in Italie. The Athenians with the like fraude did circumuent their neighbors and confederats, from whom they did exact tributes contrarie to their treaties, neither did they euer vndertake any warre but one without the forces of their allies, whereupon most of them fell off vnto the Lacedemonians when occasion was offred.

Polibius and Liuie.
The Romans circumuented their allies in Italy in their treaties.

It may also be doubted whether it be fit to haue many allies, or mercinarie souldiers of diuers languages, for the difficultie there is to speake vnto them, and to incourage them by orations, a thing very necessarie in warre. But experience hath taught vs, that diuers nations and diuers tongues are easie to gouerne and leade, as *Anniball* did shew, hauing an armie consisting of Carthaginians, Mauritanians, Numidians, Spaniards, Italians, Gaules, and Greeks, and yet in fifteene yeares space he neuer had mutinie in his camp, & obtained great victories; but if such an armie be once mutined, there is no meanes to pacifie it: this is the opinion of *Polibius*, a captaine of great experience, and Schoolemaster to *Scipio Affricanus*. That which we haue spoken touching the succors of allies, is not to be vnderstood that an estate should wholie relie vpon them, but a well gouerned Commonweale must be supported by her owne forces, and alwayes be stronger than the succours she hath from her allies: for he alwayes commands the state that is master of the force, and will make himselfe an absolute lord vpon the least occasion, if he haue any desire, the which neuer wants in ambitious minds. And if allies and confederates be to be feared in an others countrie when they are the stronger, what assurance can we haue of strange forces, which haue no offensiue nor defensiue league with vs? there is no doubt, but in danger they will be more carefull of their owne liues than of an other mans, and will attribute vnto themselues the profit and honor of the victorie, exhausting their treasures, and growing souldiers at their cost whom they serue. How often haue we seene the stranger being the stronger, make himselfe absolute lord ouer them that called him? We haue in our age the example of *Cairadin* that famous pirat, called in by the inhabitants of Alger, to expell the Spaniards out of their fort; hauing vanquished them, he slew *Selim* their king with all his familie, and made himselfe king thereof, leauing the state to *Ariadin Barbarousse* his brother. And *Saladin* a Tartar being called by the Caliph and the inhabitants of Caire to expell the Christians out of Soria, after the victorie he slew the Caliph; and made himselfe absolute lord, and least that they of the countrie should attempt any thing against him, he alwayes imployed Tartarians and Circassians (that were slaues) in the warre, and for his guard, forbidding all others to beare any armes: and by this meanes he and his successors inioyed that kingdome, vntill that *Sultan Selim* Emperour of the Turks made himselfe lord thereof. By the same means the Herules, Gothes, and Lombards became lords of Italy, the French of Gaule, the English Saxons of Brittaine, the Scottishmen of Scotland, hauing expelled the Brittons and the Picts, who had called them to their succours; and the Turke of the empire of the East and the realme

Forren forces being the stronger, make themselues maisters ouer them that call them to their succours.

Note at H2.

OF A COMMONWEALE. 613

A realme of Hongary, being intreated by the Emperours of Constantinople and the states of Hongary. And the Emperour *Charles* the fift had reduced Germanie into the forme of a Prouince, and made it hereditarie by the same fraude that the rest, when as a part of Germanie vnder colour of religion called in the Spaniards and Italians, for hauing subdued the princes of Saxony, he labored to subiect the rest vnder the spanish empire, intending to make *Philip* his sonne king of Germanie, if *Henry* the second had not freed them with the forces of France, who for this cause was called by the Germaines in their printed bookes the protector of the Empire, and the deliuerer of the Princes. The which the princes of Germanie hauing foreseene, did bind the Emperour *Charles* the fift in the twelft article of his oth, that he should neuer bring an armie of strangers into Germanie; but since the Emperours death the Electors did sweare neuer to choose a forraine prince Emperour; yet if the States of the countrie cannot agree vpon a soueraigne prince, it is better to haue a prince from a farre countrie than a neighbour. And for this cause the Ætolians made *Antiochus* king of Asia their Generall for a yeare, the Tarentines king *Pyrrhus*, the Polonians *Henry* Duke of Aniou; *Leo* king of Armenia one of the children of *Andrew* king of Hongarie, to giue him his daughter and his estate: else it is to be feared that a neighbour prince chosen Generall but for a yeare, will make himselfe perpetuall, or if he be perpetuall, will grow hereditarie, taking from the subiects their right of election: or if the estate be giuen to one that is a king and to his heires, it is to be doubted he will make it a tributarie prouince to free his owne countrie from taxes and impositions, which happilie was the cause why they did not choose the Emperours eldest sonne king of *Polonia*, for it is not to be expected that he will euer beare that affection to strangers that he doth vnto his owne, but will easily abandon an others estate at need, to defend his owne. To conclude, in my opinion a Commonweale well ordained, of what nature soeuer, should be fortified vpon the approches and frontires, in the which forts there should be good garrisons trained vp dayly to armes, hauing certaine lands appointed for souldiers the which they should enioy only for their liues, as in old time the fees and feudataries were, and at this day the Timars and Timariots in Turkie, the which are giuen vnto souldiers like vnto benefices, vpon condition they should be readie with horse and armes whensoeuer occasion of warre required: which lands neuer go vnto their heires, but are bestowed by the princes free gift vpon the most valiant souldiers, with a clause not to alienate them, that souldiers might not rob and steale as now they do with all impunitie. And vntill that these lands in fee may be disposed according to their first institution, it shall be fit to erect some legions of foote and horse according to the estate and greatnes of euery Commonweale, that they may be bred vp in martiall discipline from their youth in garrisons vpon the frontires in time of peace, as the antient Romans did, who knew not what it was to liue at discretion, and much lesse to rob, spoile, and murther, as they do at this day, but their camp was a schoole of honor, sobrietie, chastitie, iustice, and all other vertues, in the which no man might reuenge his owne iniuries, nor vse any violence. And to the end this discipline may be obserued, as they do at this day in the Turks armie, it is necessarie that good Captaines and souldiers be recompenced, especially when they grow aged, with some exemptions, priuiledges, impunities, and rewards, after the manner of the Romans. And although the third part of the reuenues be imployed about the entertainement of souldiers, it were not too much: for thereby you should be assured of men at need to defend the state, especially if it be enuied and enuironed about with warlike nations, as those people be that are scituate in the temperate and fertile regions of France, Italie, Hongarie, Greece, Asia the lesse, Soria, Egipt, Persia, and the ilands lying in the Mediterranean sea: for the nations lying

The conclusion of the proposition.

Ggg

E4 *For* impunities (Fr 7) *read* immunities (Fr 1-6, 8 and L).

Those which inhabit in fertill countries, being enuironed by greedy enemies, haue need to bee warlike.

lying vpon the extremities of hot and cold, as the Ethiopians, Numidians, Negros, Tartars, Gothes, Muscouites, Scottishmen, and Swedens, haue no neede of great forts, nor to entertaine any legions in time of peace, hauing no enemies but such as they make themselues; the people of the North being by nature too warlike, all horsemen, or for the most part, and giuen to armes, without any need to traine them vp in it, vnlesse it be to discharge the countrie, or as I haue said, for that they cannot be kept in peace. And to the end the state may not be brought in danger by any treacherous and faithlesse allies, or that strangers suck not the bloud of the subiects growing warlike at an others charge, being readie to inuade the estate, let all offensiue and defensiue leagues and alliances be equall, receiuing as great succours at neede as they shall be bound to giue; and yet the succours of the confederate must not be such as they may force or prescribe a law. Moreouer, it must not be allowed for all other subiects to carrie armes, least the laborer and handicrafts man should take a delight in theeuing and robbing, leauing the plough and shop, hauing no experience of armes, and when as they are to march against an enemie, they forsake their coulors and flie at the first charge, putting a whole armie in disorder, especiallie the handicrafts man, and they that sit alwaies, being bred vp in the shadow, whom all antient and wise Captaines haue held vnfit for warre, whatsoeuer Sir *Thomas Moore* saith in his Commonweale. Seeing that wee haue discoursed of men of warre, of forts and of succors that are drawne from them that are in league, let vs now speake of the suretie of treaties and leagues betwixt Princes and Commonweales.

Handicraftsmen vnfit for warre.

Chap. VI.

Of the suertie of alliances and treaties betwixt Princes and Commonweales, and of the lawes of armes.

His treatie depends of the former, the which ought not to be omitted, seeing that neither lawyer nor polititian hath euer handled it: and yet there is nothing in all affaires of state that doth more trouble Princes and Commonweales, then to assure the treaties which they make one with an other, be it betwixt friends or enemies, with those that be newters, or with subiects. Some assure themselues vpon their simple faith mutuallie giuen, others demaund hostages, and many require some places of strength: some there are which rest not satisfied if they disarme not the vanquished for their better assurance, but that which hath been held the strongest assurance, is, when it is confirmed by alliance and neerenes of bloud. And euen as there is a difference betwixt friends and enemies, the conquerours and the conquered, those that are equall in power and the weake, the prince and the subiect, so in like sort their treaties must be diuers, and their assurances diuers. But this maxime holds generall and vndoubted, that in all kinds of treaties there is no greater assurance then that the clauses and conditions inserted in the treaties be fit and sortable for the parties, and agreeing with the subiect that is treated of. There was neuer any thing more true then the aduice of that Consull which said in open Senat, *Neminem populum diutiùs ea conditione esse posse, cuius eum pœniteat*, No people can continue long in that estate whereof they are wearie. The question was touching the Priuernates whom the Romans had vanquished, for that they had broken the league, they demanded of their Ambassador what punishment they had deserued? The paines, answered he, of such as should liue in libertie. Then the Consull replied, If we pardon you, shall we be assured of a peace?
the

Plantius Consul, apud Liuium li. 8

Notes at F5, H8, I3.

the Ambassador answered, *Si bonam dederitis, & fidam & perpetuam, sin malam haud diuturnam:* If you giue vs a good peace, you shall haue it kept faithfullie and perpetually; if a bad one, it shall be soone broken. The yonger Senators found these answers too proud and haughtie, but the wiser sort said, That this people which contended only for their libertie deserued to be made citisens of Rome, else they would neuer be good subiects, nor trustie friends: and according to this aduice the decree of the Senat did passe in force of a priuiledge, and was confirmed by the people; and yet had they yeelded themselues to the mercie of the Romans, as all the other cities of the Latins their allies had done, who had conspired against the Romains. The assurance which the antient Romans tooke of those whom they would make subiect after they had vanquished them, was to seaze vpon all their places of strength, to put in garrisons, to receiue hostages, and to disarme the vanquished. *Mos autem, inquit Liuius, Romanis vetustus erat, cum quo nec fœdere nec æquis legibus iungeretur amicitia, non prius Imperio in eum tanquam pacatum vti, quam omnia diuina humanaque dedidisset, obsides accepti arma adempta, præsidia vrbibus imposita forent:* It was an antient custome among the Romans towards those with whom they had not ioyned in league, nor contracted friendship vpon equall tearmes, neuer to gouerne them peaceably, vntill they had yeelded vp all, deliuered hostages, disarmed them, and put garrisons into their townes. For we may not thinke euer to keepe that people in subiection which hath alwayes liued in libertie, if they be not disarmed. To take away part of their libertie, is to incense them more, than if they were wholie subiected: as *Lewis* the 12 did vnto the Geneuois, who had put themselues vnder his protection when they were in danger, which being past, they reuolted, and allied themselues vnto his enemies; against whom he went in person, besieged them, and forced them to yeeld; then he condemned them in two hundred thousand crownes, putting a strong garrison into their fort called the Lanterne; yet he suffered them to liue after their owne lawes and with their old magistrates, taking only from them the stamp of their coine. It had been farre better either to haue made them good subiects, or to haue restored them to their perfect libertie: for king *Lewis* the 11 to whom they had giuen themselues, made answere, That he gaue them vnto the diuell refusing to receiue a yearely pension for the protection of such disloyall allies, who had reuolted from king *Charles* the 6, hauing receiued them into his protection to defend them against the Venetians. And the Earles of Sauoy receiued those of Berne into their protection, beeing opprest by the lords of Bourdorg; but the feare being past, they desired nothing more than to be freed from their protection, the which the Earle willinglie granted, chusing rather to haue faithfull fellowes, than faithlesse allies. But king *Francis* the first in my opinion committed a greater error, who refused two hundred thousand crownes in his necessitie, the which the Geneuois offred him to be freed from his protection, giuing him to vnderstand that vpon the first occasion they would reuolt, as they did after the battaile of Pauia, and afterwards expelled the garrison which remained in their fort, and razed it to the ground: he should either haue made them faithfull and free confederats, being tied together by an equall league; or els haue made them subiects, and so haue taken from them the gouernment of their estate.

But some one will say, that it is a breach of faith to infringe the treaties, and to change the protection into a soueraignetie. I answere, that it is and alwayes shall be lawfull for the Patron to make himselfe absolute lord, if the client be disloyall. We read that *Augustus* made those people subiect which had abused their libertie. And therefore king *Charles* the 9 (hauing discouered the secret practises of the Spaniards with the inhabitants of Thoul, Metz, and Verdun) was inforced somewhat to re-

straine

A free people is neuer kept in subiection, vnlesse they be disarmed.

A Popular estate must either be wholly subiected, or set at free libertie.

straine their liberties, for in all treaties of protection there is an expresse clause, That those which are in protection shall retaine their estate and soueraigntie: but there is no great assurance if the Protector holds his clients forts, for that he may make them subiect when he pleaseth. Who knowes not that the cities of Constance, Vtrech, Cambray, Vienna in Austria, and many others which haue put themselues in the protection of the house of Austria, haue now lost their liberties. The kingdome of Hongarie hath runne the same fortune: for after the death of king *Ihon*, the estates of the countrie sent Ambassadours to the Turke to receiue their yong king and the realme into his protection, fearing least *Ferdinand* should make himselfe lord thereof, pretending the realme to belong vnto him by vertue of certaine treaties made betwixt the house of Austria, and the kings of Hongarie; but those treaties had no sure ground, for the realme being electiue, the king could not take this prerogatiue from the people without their consent: and if the house of Austria lying so neere and being so famous for their glorious deeds, had made offer of any one of their princes to haue bin chosen, they had caried it without any difficultie; but the estates had rather make choise of *Mathew Coruin* for their king, than to lose the right of election: and although that the new king and the estates of the countrie did ratifie the former treaties with the house of Austria, yet were they not kept, for that they seemed to be made by force against all law and reason, wherefore they did chuse rather to put themselues vnder the Turks protection; who soone after made himselfe absolute lord, knowing well that *Ferdinand* would carrie it, who notwithstanding had some part, but he was forced to agree with the Turke, paying yeerely a good summe of money, which the Emperour tearmes a Pension, & the Turke a Tribute, vanting that the Emperor is his Tributarie. But there is a great difference betwixt a pensionar and a tributarie, for tribute is paied by the subiect, or by him who to inioy his libertie paies that which is promised vnto him which hath forced him thereunto. A pension is voluntarily giuen by him that is in protection, or by him that is equall in a treatie of alliance to haue peace, and to withhold the pensionar from ioyning with his enemies, or to haue succours when he shall require them; as in the treaties of equall league betwixt the kings of France, and the Cantons of the Swissers, vpon that condition that our kings might at their pleasures leauie an armie of Swissers for the defence of this realme, and should likewise help them against the incursions of their enemies: and for that it was needfull to make many leuies of Swissers for the guard of this crowne: fearing also least the enemies thereof should draw them from the societie of the French, our kings haue willingly graunted a thousand crownes yearely pension to euery Canton, notwithstanding that king *Francis* the first, three yeares before the treatie, had gotten of the Swissers at Marignan one of the goodlyest victories that euer Prince obtayned. And although we haue sayd, That protection rightlie was that, when as one takes the defence of an other freely without any reward, for that the mightie are bound to defend the weake against the iniuries of their enemies: yet for the assurance of treaties and protections, they vse to receiue a pension from him that puts himselfe into protection, to the end that the Protector beeing bound not onely by his oath, but also in receiuing a pension, should bee more readie to succour his adherent a need. This was held by the Antients, against the honor and maiestie of the Empire: but since that, they haue confounded honestie with profit, they haue begun to make marchandise of protection; whereof *Saluian* of Marseilles doth greatlie complayne, saying, That the weake putting themselues in the protection of the mightie, giue all they haue to be protected. It is well knowne that they of Luques, Parma, Sienna, and manie others, pay great pensions to be protected: And oftentimes a pension is payed to the

Imperiall cities made subiect vnder colour of protection.

Hungary made subiect vnder shadow of protection.

The difference betwixt tribute and pension.

Why the king of France gaue pension vnto the Swissers.

The mighty are bound to defend the weake.

the protector, not so much to warrant him from his enemies, as from the protector himselfe: as it happened after the battaile of Pauia, all the potentates of Italie turned their vowes to the Spanyard, and to free themselues from inuasion, they put themselues into their protection. Amongst others the Luquois payed vnto the Emperour *Charles* the fift, tenne thousand ducates: the Siennois fifteene thousand, and the duke of Ferrare fifteene thousand, the which he paied to the Viceroy of Naples, vnder colour of lending, without hope of restitution, being in the protection of the French. But it is shamefull and dishonourable, to take into protection, to receiue a pension, and to abandon the client in his great need. Not long since *Sigismund Augustus* king of Poland had taken the protection of the inhabitants of Lifland, against the king of Moscouia: but hauing made a league with the Moscouite, he is not onely said to haue abandoned his clients, but to haue betrayed them vnto their enemie. But if he that is in protection as a soueraigne, and in subiection as a vassall and subiect, demaunds aid of his protector, he hath double reason to defend him, especially if they attempt any thing against his honour and person: as it happened in the yeare 1563, in the Moneth of March, when as the Inquisition at Rome sent out a Citation against the queene of Nauarre, to appeare personally at Rome within six monethes, and not by any procurator, vpon paine of confiscation of all her goods, estates, and seigneuries. King *Charles* the ninth tooke her into his protection, saying, That she was neerely allied vnto him in blood, that she was a widow, and tied to the house of Fraunce, a vassall and subiect vnto the king; and that by treaties of popes, and generall councels she might not be drawne out of the realm for what cause soeuer: seeing that pope *Clement* the seuenth sent two cardinals into England, to heare king *Henrie* the eight, touching the diuorce betwixt him and *Katherine* of Spaine. And for that the Citation and threat made vnto such a princesse, toucht his honour and the estates, the king of France did aduertise all his neighbour princes and allies, by his ambassadors, giuing the popes legat to vnderstand, That his maister should not take it ill, if hee did punish those that were the cause of this enterprise: as *Lewis* the young did in the like case to *Thibaud* earle of Champagne, who had caused the earle of Vermandois to be censured by the pope: intreating the pope moreouer, to reuoke his sentences giuen as well by himselfe, as by his deputies: else he should not hold it strange if hee vsed the meanes which had bene accustomed in like cases.

It is dishonourable to abandon him you haue taken into protection.

By the commandement of pope Pius the fift.

But it falls out oft, that those which are receiued into protection, after the daunger is past, make warre against their protectour: We haue many examples, and without further search, in our memorie we haue seene many princes of Germany cast themselues into the protection of king *Henrie* the second, to be freed from the captiuitie and slauery which did threaten them: the king receiued them into protection, and in stead of taking any pension, he gaue them two hundred thousand crownes towards their wars, and leuied an armie of threescore thousand men at his owne charge for the libertie of the empire. And although by the 34 article of the treatie of Protection, it was concluded, That the confederat princes should suffer the king to seize vpon the imperiall townes, speaking French, yet the emperour was no sooner chased away, & the empire restored to her former beautie, by meanes of the French, but the chiefe of the confederats and adherents, forsooke the kings protection: and which is more, tooke armes against their protectour. And at an imperiall diet, held in the yere 1565, it was decreed, To send an ambassage into Fraunce, to demaund those three imperiall townes which are in the protection of France, Thoul, Verdun, and Metz, although that Verdun hath for these hundred and sixtie yeares bene in the protection of Fraunce, paying thirtie pound starling onely for a yearely pension. But this imperiall decree tooke no effect, and

The Duke of Saxonie. The Lantgraue of Hesse. The Marquesse of Brandebourg.

Ggg iij

A6 *For* duke of Ferrare fifteene thousand *read* duke of Ferrare fifty thousand.   D9 threescore

and the king was aduertised by letters of the first of December 1559, from a pensioner of his, That the estates of the empire would be wel pleased, to haue the king hold those townes of the empire, doing homage for them: which shewed, that he held not these townes but vpon good and iust considerations. And for that the protectour cannot be inuaded by him that is in protection, being alwayes the weaker: those which put themselues into protection, haue need of greater securitie than the protectors, least vnder a colour of patronage they loose their liberties.

Those which are in protection haue need of greater securitie than the protector.

Some one may obiect, That it is an absurd thing to demaund securitie of the protector, seeing that the client puts himselfe in his protection: and by an auntient decree of the court of parliament, the vassal demaunding securitie against his lord, was reiected. But the deceit and treacherie of man hath so farre extended, as the wisest haue held it necessarie to succor the vassall against the violence of his patron, whom the soueraigne prince shall take into his safegard, if there be iust cause: with greater reason the client is to seeke all the securitie that may be from the protector. The first assurance depends vpon reasonable conditions annexed vnto the treatie: the second of the letters of protection, which the protector must deliuer vnto the clients, to testifie, That all the rights of soueraigntie and maiestie remaine absolute vnto the client: and this is to be done in Monarchies, at the comming of a new prince: for the protection is dissolued by the death of the client, as well as of the patron: neither is the succession tied vnto the protection. And therefore the inhabitants of Mets, after the death of *Henry* the second, demaunded to haue new letters of protection from *Charles* his sonne: not for that they should be more safe from their enemies, but to shew that they were not in subiection, the which is generall in all treaties made betwixt princes, and it hath beene alwayes obserued, to renew leagues and alliances, which else should be dissolued by death. So *Perseus* king of Macedon, after the death of his father, sent an ambassage to the Senat of Rome, to renew the league they had with his father, and to the end he might be called king by the Senat. But when as the Senat offered to renew the same conditions of the league which they had with *Philip* his father, *Perseus* refused them, saying, That the treatie made with his father, did nothing concerne him: and if they would contract a new league, they must first agree vpon the conditions. So *Henrie* the seuenth, king of England hauing receiued the duke of Suffolke from the Archduke *Philip*, father vnto the emperour *Charles* the fift, vpon condition, That he should not put him to death, he kept his faith; but he being dead, his sonne *Henry* the eight caused his head to bee cut off, saying, That he was not tied vnto the treatie which his father had made.

The assurance of the league of protection.

A league made with the father binds not the sonne.

But for that protections are more daungerous for the adherents or clients, than all other treaties, it is needfull to haue greater securitie: for oft times wee see, that for want of securitie the protection is chaunged into a seigneurie. And sometimes hee thinkes himselfe well assured, that makes the wolfe the keeper of his flocke. And therefore protections must be limited to a certaine time, especially in Popular and Aristocraticall estates, which neuer die. And therefore the inhabitants of Geneua hauing put themselues in the protection of them of Berne, would not haue the protection continue aboue thirtie yeares, the which did expire in the yeare 1558, and then the Geneuois made an equall league with the Bernois, the which was not without great difficultie, being almost brought into subiection, by the practises of some citisens that were executed. Since the first impression of these books, a Printer of Geneua put them suddenly to the presse, making an aduertisement in the beginning, wherein hee doth controll some places: but he deserues to be punished by the Seigneurie: First, for that hee hath attempted against another mans workes, who hath spoken as honourably of Geneua, as of any Commonweale whatsoeuer. Secondly, for that he hath infringed the ordinances

---

G9 For the succession *probably read* the successor (cf. Fr). Note at I4.

nances of the Seigneurie of Geneua, published the fift of Iune, 1559: whereby it is expresly defended, To make any inuectiue against such authors as are set forth. For if the author deserued any reproachfull words from the Printer, he should not haue printed them, and much lesse set them to sale. But as for his reprehensions all men of iudgement haue esteemed them as they deserue. And heretofore this good Printer hath bene aunswered, who maintaines, That it is lawfull for the subiect to kil his prince, kindling by this meanes the fire of sedition and rebellion in all places. And whereas hee saith, That Geneua hath not bene in the protection of Berne, the author refers himselfe vnto the treatie that was made in the yeare 1536. But the fault growes, for that they knew not what protection was, which our auntient treaties call *Auouoison*, and in Latine *Aduocatio*. The like may be said of Rotuille, and of Mulhouse, which are allied with the Cantons of the Swissers, but it is an alliance of protection. As in like case the abbat and towne of Saint Gall, which are also allied, but yet in the protection of Zurich, Lucerne, Swits, and Glaris, as I haue seene by the treaties which the abbat of Orbez, (hauing remained long ambassedour in Swisserland) imparted vnto me from the first vnto the last: those of Valdaost, were in like daunger to them of Geneua, for the Valoisians would haue made them subiect, vnder a colour of protection, in the yeare 1559, if the king of Fraunce had not defended them. And euen as the vassall is freed from the fealtie and homage which he oweth vnto his lord, if hee bee ill intreated by him, as it was adiudged by the court of parliament, for the lady of Raiz against the duke of Brittaine: in like sort the client is exempt from the power of the protector, if he doth infringe and breake the lawes of protection. But the chiefest caution and assurance, is, when as the protector is not ceised of the places of strength, nor hath not any garrisons in his clients townes. There is nothing more true, than what was spoken by *Brutus* the Tribune of the people, vnto the nobilitie of Rome, That there was one onely assurance for the weake against the mightie, which was, That if the mightie would, they could not hurt them: for that ambitious men that haue power ouer another, neuer want will. And therefore it was wisely prouided by the Scots, when as they came into the protection of the English, made in the yeare 1559, That the queene of England, who tooke their protection, should giue hostages, the which should be chaunged euery six moneths: and that she should not build any forts in Scotland, but with the consent of the Scottish men. Wherein the Athenians did erre, who hauing put themselues first into the protection of *Antipater*, then of *Cassander*, of *Ptolomey*, and in the end of *Demetrius* the Besieger, they suffered their protectors to seize vpon their forts, and to put in garrisons, who presently made themselues soueraigne lords. The which *Demosthenes* had well and wisely foreseene, when as one commended vnto him the mildnesse and courtesie of *Antipater*: hee aunswered, Wee desire no lord and maister, how mild and gratious soeuer: and him did *Antipater* pursue euen into Italie, and slue him. But the Athenians were circumuented by the same fraud as they had done their associats: For the Persians being expelled out of Greece, all the cities of Greece made an equall league, for the defence of their estates and liberties, concluding, That they should haue one common treasurie in *Apolloes* temple, whither all the associats should yearely bring their money, that an account might bee giuen of the receits and expences by a common consent. Euerie citie sent ambassadours for the swearing of their league: *Aristides* surnamed the Iust, came for the Athenians, who after solemne sacrifice, did cast peeces of burning yron into the sea, calling heauen and earth, and all their gods, to witnesse, and saying, As this fire is quencht in the water, so let them suddenly perish, that shall breake their faith. But the Athenians seeing the common treasure great, fortified their citie ports, & passages therewith, and made pro-

The client is freed from the protection, if the protector make any breach.

The league broken by the fraud of the Athenians

620　THE FIFTH BOOKE

The cities of Greece subiected vnder colour of alliance.

uision of nauie, ships, & gallies well armed. And then finding themselues the stronger, they changed the equal league into protection, & protection into subiection. So as the appellations of all the confederat cities came vnto Athens; as we read in *Xenophon*, & all charges and impositions were taxed by the Athenians, who had freed themselues from all imposts: the which chanced for that the Athenians trained their subiects vp in arms, at their confederats costs. And so did the Lacedemonians to all their confederats, whom vnder colour of an equall league, they imperiously forced to obey: for that for the most part they were all mechanike people. And contrariwise in Lacedemon there was not any Spartan that was an Artisan, being against *Licurgus* his lawes: so as the citie of Sparta was farre more mightie, and held in a manner all their other allies in subiection; as we read in *Plutarch*. We see that the Latines fell almost into the like difficultie, after that they had made an equall league with the Romans, against whom they tooke armes: for that the Romans commaunded them imperiously as their subiects: whereof *Setin* captaine of the Latines complained, saying, *Sub vmbra fœderis æqui seruitutem patimur*, We are (saith he) slaues vnto the Romans, vnder colour of an equall league. And a little after, *Consilia populorum Latinorum habita, responsumque non ambiguum imperantibus milites Romanis datum, absisterent imperare ijs, quorum auxilio egerent: Latinos pro sua libertate potius quam pro alieno imperio arma laturos*, The Latines hauing held a councell, and giuen a plaine aunswere to the Romans which commaunded the souldiours, they wished them to forbeare to commaund them whose aid they needed: the Latines would rather take arms for their owne liberties, than for anothers rule and empire. We read, that *Licortas* captaine generall of the Acheans, vsed the like complaints to *Appius* the Consull, after that the Acheans had treated an equall league with the Romans, *Fœdus Romanorum cum Acheis specie quidem æquum esse: re precariam libertatem, apud Romanos etiam imperium esse*, The league which the Romans haue with the Acheans, in shew it is equall, but in effect it is an intreated libertie, and with the Romans it is emperie or absolute command. For the same cause the Samnites made warre against the Romans, renouncing their league: for that vnder a colour of societie, they would commaund absolutely ouer them. And for the same reason the cities of Italie allied vnto the Romans by an equall league, reuolted from their alliance for that the Romans drew from them an infinit succour of men and money, so that in all their warres they had two of their allies for one Roman, and by that meanes conquered the greatest empire that euer was, and yet their associats had no part of the conquest, but some pillage, after that the Romans had taken what they pleased: which was the cause of the confederats warre in Italie, the which had no end, vntill that the allies were made citisens of Rome, to haue part of honours and offices. And yet what equall league soeuer the Romans made, they were still the stronger, m held their allies as it were in subiection. How imperiously the Romans behaued themselues towards their confederats, the speech of the Consull *Appius* vnto the Generall of the Acheans, contending for the libertie of the Lacedemonians, is a sufficient testimonie, saying, *Dum liceret voluntate sua facere gratiam inirent, ne mox inuiti & coacti facerent*, Whilest they might do it of their owne free will, they should deserue thankes; else they should be soone forced thereunto against their wills. And in the treatie made with the Ætolians (to whome they would not graunt any peace, vnlesse they submitted themselues wholly vnto their mercie) there are these words, *Imperium maiestatemque populi Romanorum gens Ætolorum conseruato sine dolo malo; hostes eosdem habeto quos populus Romanus, armaque in eos ferto: & bellum pariter gerito, obsides arbitrio Consulis 40, & talenta quinquaginta dato*, You Ætolians shall maintaine the empire and maiestie of the people of Rome, without any fraud or guile, their enemies shall be yours, you shall carry arms, and

The cause of the sociall warre.

Liui. lib. 56.

F3 appellations *i.e.* appeals　　G6 Concilia　　I5 (margin) *For* lib. 56 (Fr 6-8) *read* lib. 36 (Fr 1-5 and L).　　I6 and offices　　I7 stronger, & held　　K5-6 *For* Romanorum *read* Romani (cf. Fr).　　K8 *For* quinquaginta *read* quingenta (Fr and L).

and make warre against them with the people of Rome: you shall giue fortie hostages at the Consuls discretion, and fiftie talents. They left them the free gouernment of the state, but with such conditions, as they were little better than subiects; hauing vnfurnished them of men and money, and taken the best amongst them for hostages. These words of the league, *Maiestatem Romanorum conseruato*, Maintaine the maiestie of the Romans; shewes, that the league betwixt the Romans and the Ætolians was vnequall, and that the one did respect the maiestie of the other with all honour. And although the Romans gaue lawes vnto the Ætolians, yet they did enioy their estate and soueraigntie: as they did in all Greece, which they freed from the power of the kings of Macedon. And after that they had vanquished and taken *Perseus* king of Macedon, they freed all the people, and discharged them of the moitie of their imposts, suffering them to gouerne their owne estates: and for their better assurance, they commaunded vpon paine of death, That all Gouernours, Captaines, Lieutenants, Presidents, Councellours of state, Gentlemen in ordinarie, and euen the kings Pages and Footmen (*qui seruire regibus humiliter alijs superbe imperare consueuerunt*, Which had beene accustomed to serue their kings humbly, and to commaund others imperiously) to depart out of Macedon, and to passe into Italy. And not content therewith, they diuided Macedon into foure prouinces, forbidding vpon paine of death, That the one should haue no accesse, communication, traffique, commerce, nor alliance of marriage, with another: and moreouer, that the moitie of those charges which were paid to the king, should be carried yearely into the treasurie of Rome. And so the people of Macedonie receiued a law from the victor, and remained tributaries, yet they enioyed the gouernment of their estates. The Consull *Mummius* vsed the like policie, hauing subiected the estate of Achaia, he rased Corinth, and abolished the societies & communalties of Greece; yet he suffered the free people to enioy their laws and magistrats, easing them of part of their tributes: the which was a subtill meanes to draw vnto the amitie of the Romans all the people which had bene held in slauish subiection, and to make tyrants to tremble, or at the least to force soueraigne kings and princes to gouerne their subiects iustly, seeing that the prize and reward of the Romans victorie, was the liberty of people, and ruine of tyrants. Whereby they reaped the greatest honour that men might in this world, To be iust and wise.

Macedonie made tributarie to the Romans.

The fruits of the Romans victories

It is also a double wrong which the lord receiues from his subiect, hauing put himselfe in the protection of another, and from him that hath receiued him, if hee hold not of him by fealtie and homage, or hath some liuing in the protectors countrey. And for that *Charles* of Lorraine bishop of Metz, put himselfe into the protection of the empire, and obtained a safegard for him and his, of all that which he held in the country of Messin, in the yeare 1565, the king of Fraunce his lieutenant opposed himselfe to the publication of this safegard: whereby he (hauing recourse vnto the empire) brought in question his obedience due vnto his prince, the protection of Metz, & his kings right. And yet many princes receiue all that seeke it, without discretion, the which is the cause of many inconueniences, if the protection be not iust. It is a daungerous thing to vndertake the protection of another prince, but it is more dangerous to vndergoe it without a iust cause, being the chiefe subiect of all wars, & the ruine of cities and kingdoms, when as subiects fall from the obedience of their naturall prince, to obey another. And generally all treaties of alliance made with a prince or warlike people, draw after them a subiection and necessitie to take armes alwayes for his succour, and to run the same fortune: as the Romans confederats, who by their treaties were bound to furnish men and money for their succours, and all the profit and honour of the conquests came vnto the Romans. They make no such treaties at this day, yet the victor prescribes a law vn-

---

A2 *For* fiftie talents *read* 500 talents (cf. 620 K8 as corrected and Livy, XXXVIII, 8–11).

Note at E9.

vnto the vanquished. And therefore many haue bene of opinion, That it was expedient for a prince to be a Neuter, and not to meddle with any other princes warres: the chief reason is, That the losse is common, but the fruit of the victorie is his only whose quarrell they maintaine; besides, he must declare himselfe an enemie to those princes which haue not wronged him: but he that shall stand indifferent, is oftentimes a means to reconcile enemies: and maintaining himselfe in the loue of them all, hee shall reape thanks and honour of euerie side. And if all princes be in league one against another, who shal mediat a peace? Moreouer it seems there is no better meanes to maintaine the greatnes of an estate, than to see the neighbor princes ruine one another. For the greatnes of a prince (to speake properly) is nothing els but the ruine & fall of his neighbors: & his strength is no other thing, but the weaknesse of another. And therfore *Flaminius* said vnto the Consull *Attilius*, intending to ruine the citie of the Aetolians, That it was not so expedient to weaken the Ætolians, as to oppose against the greatnesse of young *Philip* king of Macedon. These reasons may helpe them that defend neutralitie: but it seemes they are subiect to greater inconueniences. First in matter of state it is a maxime, That he must either be the stronger, or of the stronger faction (and this rule doth not admit many exceptions, be it in the selfe same Commonweale, or among sundrie princes) els hee must alwayes remaine a prey at the victors discretion: as the Roman ambassadour said vnto the Acheans, whome *Antiochus* king of Persia persuaded, That they would remaine neuters betwixt him and the Romans. And it seemes, that whosoeuer will maintaine himselfe, must of necessitie bee a friend or an enemie Whereof we haue an example in *Lewes* the eleuenth, king of Fraunce, against whom they made warre of all sides, so long as he continued a newter: but after that he had allied the Swissers more strictly among themselues, & the citie of Strausbourg with them, and that he had entred into that league, neuer any enemies durst assault him, (as *Philip de Commines* saith:) for neutralitie, *Neque amicos parat, neque inimicos tollit*, It neither purchaseth friends, nor takes away enemies: as an auntient captaine of the Samnites said. And the like conclusion was made among the estates of the Ætolians, by *Aristemus* their Generall, saying, *Romanos aut socios habere oportet, aut hostes, media via nulla est*, We must haue the Romans either confederats or enemies, there is no meane. We haue infinit examples in al histories: *Ferdinand* king of Aragon found no better means to pull the kingdome of Nauarre from *Peter* of Albret, than in persuading him to bee a neuter betwixt him and the king of Fraunce, that hee might bee abandoned at need. And the inhabitants of Iabes remaining neuters, and not ingaging themselues in the warre which the people of Israel made against the tribe of *Beniamin*, they were all slaine, and their townes rased. As also the Thebans fell into great daunger, being neuters, when as king *Xerxes* came into Greece. As in the like case the towne of Lays in Soria, was surprised, spoiled, sacked, and burnt, by a small troupe of the tribe of *Dan*: for that (as the historie saith) they were not in league with any soueraigne prince or state. And without any further search, the Florentines after they had left the alliance of the house of Fraunce, refusing to enter into league with the pope, the emperor, the king of England, and the king of Spaine, against the king of Fraunce, they soone felt the fruits of their neutralitie.

But it were an vniust thing, will some one say, to ioyne in league against France, with whom they had been so strictly conioyned: I confesse it, so should they not haue left it at need as they did; for the league is not only broken if thou beest an enemie to my associates, or if thou ioynest with my enemies, but also if for feare thou doest abandon thy associates, being bound by the league to succour them; as a Roman Ambassador said, *Si socios meos pro hostibus habeas, aut cum hostibus te coniungas*, If thou takest

my

G9 *For* king of Persia *Bodin writes* king of Asia. and L). Cf. Livy, IX, 3. H6 (margin) *For* lib. 5 (Fr 6-8) *read* lib. 9 (Fr 1-5 H8-9 Aristenus

Of A Commonweale. 623

A my associates for thine enemies, or ioynest with mine enemies. Yet some may say, that neutralitie may well be granted with the consent of other princes, which seemeth to be the best support without any feare of the victors. The estates of Lorraine, Bourgongue and Sauoy haue maintained themselues in a free peace, so long as they had an alliance of tranquilitie, but after that the Duke of Sauoy had once vnited himselfe to the Spanish faction, he was expelled his countrie by the french. But there is a great difference to be a neuter without the friendship either of the one or the other, and a neuter allied to both parties, and these are farre more assured, than if they were enemies to both factions: for they are free from the victors inuasion, and if there be any treatie of peace betwixt both parties, they are comprehended of either side. And if neutralitie be com- *The difference of neutralities.*
B mendable in that manner, as I haue said, it is farre more commendable in a Prince that doth exceede all others in power and dignitie, that he may haue the honor to be the vmper and moderator; as it happens alwaies, that quarrels betwixt Princes are decided by friends that stand indifferent, and especially by those which exceede the rest in power and greatnes, as heretofore many Popes which knew well how to mainetaine their ranke, and reconcile Christian Princes, haue reaped honor, thanks, and assurance *In what case one should be neuter* for their persons and estates, and those which haue followed either the one or the other partie, haue drawne after them the ruine of other Princes. It was thought very strange in Spaine that Pope *Alexander* the 6 a naturall Spanyard, should enter into league
C with *Lewis* the 12, king of France against the Spanyards; and when as the Spanyards had the better in Italie, he told the french Ambassador that he would remaine a neuter, and be a common father to both parties, but it was too late now to make a shew to quench that fier which he himselfe had kindled. As in the like case the Duke of Alua Viceroy of Naples being aduertised of a request made by the Procurator of the chamber of Rome against the Emperour, touching the confiscation and reunion of the reaime of Naples to the reuenues of *S. Peter*, he did write vnto Pope *Theatin*, who had entred into league with the house of France, that he should remaine as neuter for the dignitie which he had aboue all other Christian Princes, but the truce being broken, the armies in field, and their ensignes displayed, the end was miserable, for the Pope renounced the league, leauing the french in their greatest neede, and it was concluded by
D a treatie which he made with the Spanyard that he should continue newter. Neuer was the hatred of any Prince so pernitious vnto his enemie, as the fauour of *Theatin* was then vnto the french, without the which they had not bin reduced to such extremitie, as in one day to lose all they had conquered in thirtie yeares. It is more strange, for that the memory is more fresh of the like errors committed by pope *Clement* the 7, fauoring one of these princes against the aduice of *Lewis Canosa* his Ambassador, who aduertised him by letters written out of France, that the greatnes and suertie of his estate was to shew himselfe a neuter: so soone after he see himselfe prisoner to the imperials and the citie of Rome sackt after a strange manner, and both himselfe and his
E Cardinals ransomed at the victors discretion. I enter not into the worthines of the fact, neither is it in question to know who deserued most fauour, but only, that hee which alone may be iudge and moderator of honor, should neuer make himselfe a partie, although he were assured that he should incurre no danger, much more when his estate is in question, and that he can haue no securitie but hazard by the victorie. There are others who to win fauour of all sides forbids their subiects by publike proclamations to giue ayde or succour to the enemies of their associates, and yet vnderhand they suffer them to passe, yea sometimes they send them, so did the Ætolians, saith *Titus Liuius, Qui iuuentutem aduersus suos socios, publica tantum auctoritate dempta, militare sinunt, & contrarie sæpe acies in vtraq, parte Ætolica auxilia habent,* Which
suffer

A3 Bourgongne   D8 see *i.e.* saw   E5 forbid   Note at A4.

THE FIFTH BOOKE

Allies are sometimes dangerous.

suffer there your yong men vnderhand to goe to warre against their owne confederates, and oftentimes troupes of Ætolians are seene in either armie. Such allies are more dangerous than enemies. But it may be some one will say that it is dangerous to suffer a Prince so to increase in power as he may giue law vnto the rest, and inuade their estates when he pleaseth. It is true, and there is no greater occasion then that, to induce a neuter to seeke by all meanes to hinder him; for the suretie of Princes and Commonweales consists in the equall counterpeeze of power. So when as the Romans made warre against king *Perseus*, some fauored the king, others supported the Romans, *Tertia pars* (said *Titus Liuius*) *optima eadem & prudentißima, si vtique optio domini potioris daretur, sub Romanis quàm sub Rege esse mallebat : si liberum inde arbitrium neutram partem volebat altera oppressa fieri potentiorem : ita inter vtrosque conditionem ciuitatum optimam fore, protegente semper altero inopem ab alterius iniuria, & illibatis vtriusque partis viribus parem esse*: A third part, saith *Titus Liuius* being the best and the wisest, if they were to make choise of their lord, had rather subiect themselues vnto the Romans than vnder the king, but if they might haue their free will, they would haue neither of them superior, with the ruine of the other, so as betwixt both the cities should be secure, the one alwayes protecting the weake from the iniuries of the other, and they both should remaine equall, their forces being not impaired: So as the wisest haue held opinion, that there was nothing better for the suretie of estates, then to haue the power of great Princes as equall as might be; yet those which were of this opinion, when as the Romans and Macedonians were in warre, remained neuters, although they were tyed to the power of the Romans, and to the king of Macedon, and it succeeded well for them: for there is a difference in wishing the parties to be equall, and in making himselfe a partisan. It is therefore commendable for the greatest

It is honourable for great princes to be neuters.

and mightiest Princes to remaine neuters, although it be not so concluded betwixt other Princes, as I haue said before. And this is necessarie for the common good of all Princes and States, which cannot be reconciled but by their common allies, or by them that are neuters. But those that be neuters do many times kindle the fier in stead of quenching it; the which may be excusable, if the preseruation of their estate depends vpon the warre which they entertaine betwixt others; but it can hardly be concealed, and the matter once discouered, the parties most commonly agree to fall vpon their common enemie, as it happened to the Venetians, who were alwayes wont to sow diuision among their neighbours, and to fish in a troubled water. *Lewis* the twelfth discouering it, he allied himselfe with all the other Princes, and then they all iointly made a

A generall league against the Venetians.

league against the Venetians, who were reduced to that extremitie, as they yeelded Creme, Bresse, Bergame, Cremona, and Guiradadde, being members of the Duchie of Milan, vnto the french king, and to the Pope Fauence, Rimini, Rauenne, and Ceruie, being of the patrimonie of *S. Peter*: to the Empire Padoua, Vincentia, and Verona: to the Emperour the places of Friuli and Treuisan, being the inheritance of the house of Austria: to *Ferdinand* the ports and places ingaged by the kings of Naples to the seigneurie of Venice, and to call home their magistrates from the imperiall townes, and out of all the countrie which they held vpon the firme land. Whereas before the warre the Pope would haue been contented with some one place, but this tooke not effect, for Dominike *Treuiran* Procurator of *S. Marke* stayed the Senat, saying, That the Venetians were alwayes accustomed to take townes and castels, but hauing once taken them, it were absurd to restore them. It is therefore more safe for him that remaines a neuter to meditate a peace, than to nourish warre, and in so doing to purchase

It is most safe for a neuter to mediat peace.

honor and the loue of others with the assurance of his owne estate, as the Athenians procured a peace betwixt the Rhodians and *Demetrius* the besieger, to the great content

tent

F7 counterpeeze *i.e.* counterpoise   F10–G1 arbitrium ESSET, neutram   H6 other Princes, AND FOR THE WEAKER ALSO, WHEN IT IS SO AGREED BETWIXT OTHER PRINCES, as I   K4 Dominike Trevisan   Notes at K7.

tent of both parties, who were tyred with warre, and yet were loth to demaund a peace one of another: by which meanes the Athenians did reape great honor and profit to their estate. The which is so much the more necessarie, if he which is a neuter be allied to them that are in warre, and hath occasion to draw succors from his allies: as our kings haue alwayes done betwixt the Catholike and Protestant Swissers, and betwixt the Grisons and the Swissers, as well for the lawes of friendship, as fearing that in the meane time he should want the ayd of his confederats. And sometimes those which are wearied with the warre, stirre vp a third partie being a neuter, for the desire they haue of peace, and the shame they haue to seeke it: as the Florentines not able to subdue the Pisans, by reason of the Venetian succors, who desired nothing more than to retire themselues, they did procure the duke of Ferrare vnderhand to mediate an agreement. It is the greatest point of honor that a Prince can attaine vnto, to be chosen judge and vmpier of other princes quarrels, as in old time the Romans were, for the great opinion which was held of their vertue & integritie: & since, this prerogatiue hath been giuen vnto the Popes among other Christian Princes, who oftentimes haue been chosen iudges and arbitrators of all their controuersies: as in the treaties betwixt king *Charles* the 5, and *Charles* king of Nauarre, made in the yeare 1365; and betwixt *Philip Augustus* and *Richard* king of England: If the Pope were not a partie, as *Innocent* the 4 was against the Emperour *Frederick* the 2, then the Emperour made choise of the Parliament of Paris for arbitrator, which was the Senat of Peeres and Princes, and the Councell of France. And Pope *Clement* the 7 making a league with the kings of France and England against the Emperour in the yeare 1528, he caused it to be inserted in the treatie, That if it were needfull to conclude a peace with the Emperor, he should haue the honor to be arbitrator. *Paule* the 3 did the like betwixt the king of France and the Emperour in the treaties of Marseilles and Soissons. One of the most necessarie things for the assurance of treaties of peace and alliance, is to name some great and mightier Prince to be iudge and vmpier in case of contrauention, that they may haue recourse vnto him to mediate an agreement betwixt them; who being equall, cannot with their honors refuse warre, nor demaund peace. But to the end that other Princes be not driuen to that exigent, it shall be necessarie for them all to ioyne together in league, to keepe downe the power of any one that might bring the weaker into subiection: or else if they be in league, to send Ambassadors to mediate a peace before the victorie, as the Athenians, the Rhodians, the king of Egipt, and the seigneurie of Chio did, betwixt *Philip* the yong, king of Macedon, and the Ætolians, fearing the greatnes of the king of Macedon, as we reade in *Titus Liuius*. And for this cause after the taking of king *Francis* the first before Pauia, the Pope, the Venetians, the Florentines, the Duke of Ferrare, and other Potentates of Italie, made a league with the king of England for the deliuerie of the king of France: not for that the afflicted fortune of the French did moue them vnto pitie (as it is vsuall to kings, to whom the name of maiestie seemes holie) but for feare of the imperiall Eagle, which hauing couered a great part of Europe with her wings, might gripe and teare in sunder those pettie princes with her tallents: and yet they themselues had not many yeares before ioyned in league with the Emperour against king *Francis* after the battaile of Marignan, and restored *Francis Sforce* to the Duchie of Milan; hauing found by experience how dangerous the neighbourhood of a mightie Prince was, for if he be iust and vpright, his successor will not resemble him, for which cause *Methridates* king of Pontus seeing the Roman empire to reach vp to heauen, he entred into league with the kings of Parthia, Armenia, and Egipt, and with many cities of Greece against the Romans, who had seazed vpon the greatest part of Europe vnder coulor of iustice, causing in one day

_{It is honourable for a prince to be an vmpire in other princes quarrels.}

_{Why many princes made a league against the emperour after the battaile of Pauia.}

_{It is dangerous to be neighbour to a mightie prince.}

Hhh   fortie

C8, D2 For meditate *read* mediate (cf. note at 624 K7).   C10 exigent *i.e.* exigency, extremity
E2 tallents *i.e.* talons   E6 Mithridates

fortie fiue thousand Roman citisens to be slaine throughout all Asia, by a secret conspiracie, but it was then too late to make a league against a power which was inuincible. And therefore at this day if great Princes conclude a peace, all others seeke to be comprehended therein, as well to assure their estates, as to hold those great princes in an equall counterpeize, least that the one by his greatnes oppresse the rest: as in the treatie of peace made at Cambray in the yeare 1559, all estates and Christian Princes were comprehended by the king of France, or the Catholike king, or by them both togither, and any others that the two kings should name within sixe moneths. But they must be named particularly, and not in generall tearmes by the names of allies or neuters, for if there be not a speciall expression, they may iustly pretend ignorance; for that affaiers of state are sometimes managed so secretlie and so sodenly, as a league is made before the enterprise can be discouered, notwithstanding all the diligence of Ambassadors to learne out the conditions of the treatie: as it happened in the treatie of Cambray made in October 1508, whereas the Pope, the Emperour, the Empire, the king of France, the king of Arragon and Naples, the king of Castill, the Dukes of Lorraine, Ferrare, and Mantoue, entred into league against the seigneurie of Venice, the which was concluded before the Venetians had any notice thereof, although they had ambassadors in a manner with all these Princes: and without doubt if they had had any intelligence thereof, they might easily haue preuented it, seeing that after the conclusion thereof, and the warre begun, they found meanes to withdraw the Pope, and to make him a mortall enemie to the French, which was the only meanes to preserue their estate from ineuitable ruine. The like happened vnto the protestant Princes, against whome the treatie of Soissons was made in September in the yeare 1544, betwixt the king of France and the Emperour, where by the first article it was agreed, that the two princes should ioyne their forces together to make warre against them, the which they could neuer beleeue, vntill they had seene the preparations made against them. They might easily haue preuented the storme which fell vpon them: for that the Emperour had no great desier to make warre against them, and the king lesse, who did secretly fauour them; so as in giuing the Emperour some succors, or sending an ambassador vnto him, they had been comprehended in the treatie, for they had no enemie but the Pope, who was then a neuter betwixt the Emperour and the King. Sometimes the league is so strong, and the hatred so great, as it is a hard matter to hinder it, and much more to breake it, being concluded. King *Francis* the first was well aduertised of the league made betwixt the Pope, the Emperour, the king of England, the Venetians, the Dukes of Milan and Mantoue, the Commonweales of Genes, Florence, Luques, and Sienna, all confederates against his estate; yet could he not preuent it, but in quitting the duchie of Milan. Those which had concluded a peace and perpetuall amitie with him, and those which were tied vnto him by a defensiue league, brake their faith, and made open warre against him: the which was not held strange, for many make no esteeme of the breach of faith in matter of treaties betwixt princes, especiallie if they may reape any profit thereby: yea some are so treacherous, as they sweare most when as they intend most fraud, as *Lisander* was wont to say, That men must be circumuented and deceiued with oathes, and children with toyes; but he felt the grieuous punishment of his disloyaltie. Doubtlesse, periurie is more detestable than atheisme, for that the atheist who beleeues there is no God, is not so wicked and impious, as he that knowes there is a God which hath a care of humane things, yet vnder coulor of a false and counterfeit oath, is not ashamed to skorne and abuse his deitie: so as we may rightly say, That treacherie is alwayes ioyned with impietie and basenesse of mind; for hee that willinglie forsweares himselfe to deceiue another,

shewes

shewes plainely that he skornes God, and feares his enemie. It were better neuer to call the immortall God, or him they hold to be a God, to be a witnes of their fraud, but only themselues; as *Richard* Earle of Poitiers sonne to the king of England did, who giuing a confirmation of the priuiledges of Rochell, vsed these words, *Teste meipso*, My selfe being witnes. Seeing then that faith is the only foundation and support of iustice whereon not only Commonweales, but all humaine societie is grounded, it must remaine sacred and inuiolable in those things which are not vniust, especially betwixt princes: for seeing they are the warrants of faith and oathes, what remedie shall the subiects haue against their power for the oathes which they take among themselues, if they be the first which breake and violate their faith. I speake of iust things, for it is a double impietie to sweare to do a wicked act, and in this case he that breakes his oath is no treacher, but deserues reward. And in like case, if the Prince hath promised not to do a thing which is allowable by the law of nature and iust, he is not periured although he make breach thereof; neither are priuate men tyed by their oath, if they haue promised to do more than is allowable by the Ciuill law. Those things which are by nature vniust and vnlawfull no man may promise, neither may any man vrge them if they be promised. But wise Princes ought not to sweare any thing vnto other Princes that is not allowable by the law of nature and nations, nor force any Prince that is weaker then themselues to sweare to vnreasonable conditions. And to take away all ambiguitie of words, it shall be needfull to shew what is vniust, else he that is bound will take the word iust in generall to make vse of it in some speciall case, as in the treatie made in the moneth of May, in the yeare 1412, betwixt *Henry* king of England and his children on the one part, and the Dukes of Berry, Orleans, and Bourbon, the Earles of Alancon and Armaignac, and the lord of Albret on the other part, who sware to serue the king of England with their bodies and goods in all his iust quarrels when they should be required. There was no expresse reseruation of their soueraigne, against whom the king of England meant to imploy them by vertue of this contract, the which he could not do. There is neuer any iust cause to take armes against ones prince or countrie, as an auntient orator said, yet are not those princes free from the note of treacherie, which infringe their faith in matters which they haue sworne to their preiudice, being forced thereunto by the victor as some Doctors haue maintained, being as ill informed of the estate of Commonweales, as of auntient histories, and of the ground of true iustice, discoursing of treaties made betwixt princes, as of contracts and conuentions among priuat men, the which is an opinion of most dangerous consequence, which error hath taken such roote within these two or three hundred yeares, as there is no league (how firme soeuer) made betwixt princes, but it is broken, so as this opinion goes now for a grounded maxime, that the prince which is forced to make a league or peace to his hurt and preiudice, may go from it when occasion is offred. But it is strange that neither the first lawgiuers and lawyers, nor the Romans who were the patrons of iustice, did neuer thinke of this shift and euasion. For it is manifest, that most treaties of peace are made by force, either for feare of the victor, or of him that is the stronger; and what feare is more iust then of the losse of life? yet neuer any prince or lawgiuer did refuse to performe that which he had promised vnto the victor, as if it had been forced. *Quæ enim viro forti, inquit Tullius, vis potest adhiberi?* What force can be vsed, sayth *Tully*, to a valiant and resolute man? It appeared in the Consull *Marcus Attilius Regulus*, who being taken prisoner by the Carthaginians and sent to Rome vpon his word, swearing that he would returne vnlesse he could procure some noblemen that were captaines to be set at libertie, from the which he disswaded the Senat, yet did he not refuse to returne, although it were to an assured death,

Faith betwixt allies must be kept.

It is no disloialtie to breake an vnlawfull oath.

A daungerous opinion in treaties.

A resolute man can not be forced

B2 treacher *i.e.* deceiver, cheat   C9 orator said. Yet   E8 *For* captaines *read* captives.
Notes at A8, B4.

death, nor yet the Consull *Mancinus* to the Spanyards, when as he could not perswade the Senat to the conditions of peace. What grauer schoolemasters of the lawes of armes, what better interpreters of the Roman lawes can we desire, than the Roman Consuls? they went willingly vnto torments rather than they would treacherously breake their faith. The Consull *Posthumius* and his companion with sixe hundred Captaines, Lieutenants and Gentlemen of the Roman armie, being surprized by the enemie in the straights of the Appenine hills, whereas they could neither aduance, retire, nor yet fight; being set at libertie vpon their words, and hauing disputed of the law of nations in open Senat, and before all the people, touching accords and treaties made in warre; they did neuer pretend force nor feare, but it was only said, that they could not treat of any conditions of peace with the enemie, without an especiall charge and commission from the people of Rome: whereupon the Consuls which had sworne the peace, and those which had giuen themselues as hostages for the whole armie, yeelded themselues willinglie to the enemie, to dispose of their liues at their pleasure, and so they were delinered vnto them by the Heralds.

The treatie of Madril.

In the treatie of Madrill, made the 14 of February 1526, it was said, That king *Francis* the first being come vnto the first towne of his realme, he should ratifie the articles which he had sworne in prison, and cause them to be ratified by the Daulphin of France when as he came to age: and by the last article it was agreed, That if the king would not obserue the peace which he had sworne, he should returne prisoner into Spaine, giuing his two sonnes *Francis* and *Henry* for hostages. Being at libertie, all Princes offred themselues, and ioyned with him in league against the Emperour *Charles* the fift, to pull downe his power whom they had raised vp to heauen. The king hauing assembled all his princes and noblemen in his court of Parliament to resolue what was to be done touching the treatie of Madrill: *Selua* the first president, seeking to prooue that the king was not tyed vnto the treatie, he grounded himselfe vpon the authoritie of Cardinall *Zabarella*, who held, That whatsoeuer was done by force or feare, was not to be ratified; confirming it by the example of *Ihon* king of Cipres, who being taken prisoner by the Geneuois, gaue his sonne for hostage, and yet kept not his promise. I wonder the President of so great a Senat did not blush not only to commend a man that was ignorant of the lawes of armes, but also to arme himselfe with such foolish arguments, yet this was the chiefest ground of the breach of the treatie of Madrill, adding thereunto, that the king could not giue away or renounce the soueraigntie of the Lowcountries, nor the duchie of Burgongne, without the expresse consent of the estates. This indeed was sufficient to breake the treatie, the rest were impertinent. But all these obiections were neuer brought in question by the antients, they neuer required, That a prince being set at libertie out of his enemies power, should ratifie that which he had sworne being a prisoner: a ridiculous thing, that were to call the treatie in question, and leaue it to the discretion of him that was a prisoner, whether he shall obserue that which he hath sworne or not. Moreouer the antients neuer regarded the breach of treaties, when as they tooke hostages: for that he is not tied to any lawes of the treatie, nor to any other, neither is he forced to sweare; for hostages are giuen to be pledge for him that is captiue, and to suffer, if he shall make a breach of the conditions agreed vpon. And were not he simple, that hauing a good pledge, should complaine of his debtor, that he hath broke promise with him: therefore the Consull *Posthumius* maintained before the people, That there was no contrauention in the treatie made betwixt him and the Samnites, seeing it was no treatie of peace, or league, but a simple promise, the which did bind them onely which had consented thereunto, *Quid enim (inquit ille) obsidebus aut sponsoribus in fœdere opus esset, si præcatione res transigitur?*

Treaties made by a prisoner may not be broken.

An oath is needlesse where hostages are taken.

F6 Gentlemen   G5 delivered   G6 Madrill *i.e.* Madrid   K2 *For* any other *read* any oath.
K9 obsidibus   K9 precatione   Note at H10.

OF A COMMONWEALE. 627

A *tur? Nomina Consulum Legatorum, Tribunorum militum extant: si ex foedere res acta esset, præterquam duorum foecialium non extarent,* What need (saith he) should there bee of hostages and sureties in a league or peace, if it be concluded by intreatie? the names of the Consuls, Lieutenants, and Tribunes, which vndertooke it, are extant: if it be ended by a league, there should be no names ioyned vnto it, but of the two heraulds. Whereby it appeares, that king *Francis* the first, and the king of Cipres, who left their children for hostages, were absolued of their promises by their enemies themselues, for that they had pledges, and did not trust in their prisoners oath. And by the law of arms a prisoner which hath his libertie giuen him vpon his word, is bound to returne to prison againe. And by a proclamation made by the Senat of Rome, all prisoners were
B enioyned vpon paine of death (the which were verie many, being let goe vppon their words by king *Pyrrhus*, to goe visit their friends) should returne at a certaine day, but no man gaue any hostage. And if the prisoner be held in bonds, he may escape, neither is he bound to him that tooke him: as king *Francis* the first said vnto *Granuella* the emperours ambassadour. For as a Roman Consull was wont to say, *Vult quisque sibi credi, & habita fides ipsam obligat fidem,* Euery man desires to be beleeued, & a trust reposed, binds the faith it selfe.

A prisoner taken in the war, being kept, may escape without blame.

If any one say vnto me, That the king had sworne to returne, if the treatie tooke not effect: and that king *Iohn* returned prisoner into England, for that he could not accomplish the conditions of the treatie, by which he had giuen a great part of the realme
C to the English, and promised three millions of crownes: I aunswere, that there was no fault in the king, for the estates opposed against the alienation of the reuenues of the crowne: and as for his returne, neither he nor king *Iohn* were tied vnto it, seeing they had taken their children for hostages. And therefore king *Francis* seeing that the emperour would not remit the vniust conditions of the treatie, with the councell and consent of his princes and subiects hee proclaimed a new warre against him: wherewith the emperour being moued, said, That the king had carried himselfe basely, and that he had broken his oath, and that hee would willingly hazard his life with him in single combat, to make an end of so great a warre. The king being aduertised by his ambassadour, That the emperour had touched his honour and reputation; hee caused all the
D princes to assemble in his court of parliament; and after that hee had called *Perrenot Granuelle* ambassadour for Spaine, he said vnto him, That *Charles* of Austria (hauing said vnto the herauld of Fraunce, That the king had broken his faith) had spoken falsly, and that as often as he should say so, he did lie: and that hee should appoint a time and place for the combat, where he would meet him. The king of England finding in like sort that he was touched, vsed the like chalenge, and with the like solemnities. It was done like generous princes, to let all the world vnderstand, that there is nothing more foule and impious than the breach of faith, especially in princes. Neither was there euer prince so disloyall, that would maintaine it to be lawfull to breake their faith. But some haue pretended that they haue bene circumuented in their treaties, by the fraud of
E their enemies: others, that they haue erred in fact, or haue bene seduced by euill councell: or that things were so chaunged, as the wisest could not haue foreseene them: or that it should be impossible to obserue the treaties without the ineuitable losse, or apparent daunger of the whole state. In which cases they would pretend, That an oath doth not bind, the condition or the cause of the oath being impossible or vniust. Some there be which maintaine, That the pope may dispence not onely with the oath of other princes, but also of himselfe: but they haue bene confuted by other Canonists. So pope *Iulio* the second finding no meanes to breake his faith with king *Lewis* the twelft, that he might fly from the treatie of Cambray, he did not say, that hee was not tied to

The French king defies the emperour.

The king of England defies him.

Hhh iij his

[627ᵛ] THE FIFTH BOOKE

his oath, but he tooke occasion to aduance a factor in Rome to the bishoprike of Arles in Prouence, without the priuitie of the king or his ambassadour, which did reside at Rome: wherewith the king being incensed (as the case deserued) he caused all the fruits which the beneficers of Rome had in Fraunce, to be seized on: then the pope hauing found what he sought for, declared himselfe an open enemie vnto the king. So *Guicchardin* writes, That pope *Iulio* was woont to bragge, That all the treaties which hee made with the French, Spaniards, and Germans (all which he called barbarous) was but to abuse them, and to ruine one by another, that he might expell them all out of Italy. There are others which curse and condemne traytors, yet they loue the treason, and hold the fruits thereof sweet: as it is written of *Philip* king of Macedon: and the Lacedemonians condemned *Phebidas* their captaine, for that contrarie to the tenor of the treatie made with the Thebans, hee had seized vpon their castle called Cadmee, & yet they kept the place still, as *Plutarch* writes. Some which can find no iust cause nor colourable to falsifie their faith, and haue any respect to their honour, they aske aduise and councell of lawyers: as the marquesse of Pesquiere, who aspiring to make himselfe king of Naples, caused many consultations to bee made vnder hand, to know if hee which were vassall to the king of Naples, might (with his faith and honour saued) obey the pope, who was soueraigne lord of the realme of Naples, rather than the king, who was but a feudatarie: hauing two strings to his bow, for he made his account, that if the warre were attempted by the duke of Milan with the popes consent, against *Charles* the fift, should succeed well, he should then be king of Naples: but if hee should faile, then would he begge the dutchie of Milan, as a reward for his seruice, the duke beeing conuicted of rebellion. But this conspiracie being discouered, hee caused *Maron* the dukes chauncellour to be apprehended and put into the castle, and making of his processe, he suffred him to escape, fearing he should speake too plainely, if he were ill intreated: and soone after he died of thought, knowing well that his treacherie and disloyaltie was discouered, and inexcusable, seeing that he betrayed both the emperour and the duke, and all those of the league by the same meanes: the which is the most detestable treacherie of all others. Yet do I not blame him, that to assure himselfe hath two strings to his bow, so as it be done with a respect to his faith and honour: as it is reported of *Themistocles*, who secretly aduertised the king of Persia, That vnlesse he departed suddenly out of Europe, the Greekes had resolued to breake the bridge which hee had made vpon the sea Hellespont, to passe his armie out of Asia into Europe: desiring him to keepe it secret. This he did to assure himselfe of the fauour of the king of Persia, if he did vanquish; or to haue the honour to haue expelled him out of Greece, if hee marched away, as he did. But these subtill deuises beeing discouered by princes that are in league, do oftentimes cause good friends to become sworne enemies: as the Epirots, who agreed with the Acheans their confederats, to make warre against the Ætolians, and yet they did signifie by their ambassadour, That they would not take armes against them. Another time they plaid the like part with *Antiochus*, promising him al friendship, so as they might not be in disgrace with the Romans, *Id agebatur (inquit Titus Liuius) vt si rex abstinuisset Epiro, integra sibi essent omnia apud Romanos, & conciliata apud regem gratia, quod accepturi fuissent venientem*, That was done (saith *Titus Liuius*) that if the king did forbeare to enter into Epirus, they should continue in fauour with the Romans, and they should purchase grace with the king, that they would haue receiued him if he had come. But their councels being discouered, they procured to themselues a miserable slauerie with the flight of *Perseus*. The lawyers hold it for a maxime, That faith is not to be kept with them that haue broken their faith. But they passe on further and say, That by a decree made at the councell of Constans, it was ordained, That no

faith

Plu. in Epaminonda.

G3 (margin) Epaminonda   G10 *For* warre were attempted *read* warre attempted.   H3 *For* Maron *read* Moron *i.e.* Girolamo Morone.   H6 of thought *i.e.* of sorrow, grief   Note at I10.

faith should be kept with the enemies of the faith: for that the emperour *Sigismond* hauing giuen his faith to *Lancelot* king of Bohemia, and a safe conduct to *Iohn Hus*, and *Ierosme* of Prague, would not suffer any to proceed against them: but to free him of that doubt, there were many Lawyers, Canonists, and Diuines, especially *Nicholas* abbat of Palerme, and *Lewis du Pont* surnamed Romain, which concluded in this opinion, the which passed for a decree, and was confirmed by the councell. So as *Iohn Hus* and his companion were executed, although that neither the councell nor the emperor had any iurisdiction ouer them: neither was the king of Bohemia (their naturall lord) of their opinion, to whom notwithstanding the emperour had giuen his faith, but they regarded it not. Whereat we must not maruell, seeing that *Bartol* (the first lawyer of his age) maintaines, That faith is not to be kept with priuat enemies, but with captains in chiefe. According to which decree the cardinall Saint *Iulian* was sent Legat into Hongarie, to breake the treaties of peace concluded with the Turke: against the which *Humiades* father to *Mathew Coruin* king of Hongarie opposed himselfe vehemently, shewing that the peace was concluded with very reasonable and profitable conditions for the Christians, notwithstanding the Legat shewed him this decree made by the Councell, by the which they might not hold no faith with the enemies of the faith. The Hongarians building thereon, brake the peace. But the Emperour of the Turks hauing notice of this decree, and of the breach of the peace, leauied a mightie armie, and hath neuer ceased since, both he and his successors, to increase in power, and to build that great Empire vpon the ruine of Christendome; for euen the Emperour *Sigismond* himselfe was chased away with all the armie of Christians, and the Ambassador which had carried this decree, was in his returne slaine by certaine theeues that were Christians, whereby it appeared that God was displeased with that decree, for if it be lawfull to breake ones faith with infidels, then is it not lawfull to giue it; but contratiwise if it bee lawfull to capitulate with infidels, it is also necessarie to keepe promise with them. The Emperour *Charles* the fift made a league of friendship by his Ambassadour *Robert Inglish* with the king of Persia, who was pursued by the Sangiac of Soria euen vnto the frontiers of Persia, and yet he had no other reproch to make against king *Francis* the first but that he had made a league with the Turke. It is well knowne that the kings of Poland, the Venetians, Geneuois, and Rhagusians haue the like with them. And the same Emperour *Charles* the fift gaue his faith vnto *Martin Luther* (whom the Pope had cursed as an enemie to the Church) to come to imperiall diet at Wormes, in the yeare 1519, whereas *Echius* seeing that hee would not abiure his opinion, alleaged the decree of Constance, according to the tenor whereof hee vrged them to proceed against him, without any respect to the faith which the Emperour had giuen. But there was not any prince which did not abhorre this request of *Echius*, and detested his decree. And therefore the emperour to maintaine the publike faith, sent *Martin Luther* backe safe to his owne home, with certaine troupes of horse. I know not how it came in the fathers minds at the councell of Constans, to take all faith from heretikes, when as the pope himselfe at his first installing, doth take an oath of the Iewes, suffring them to enioy their religion with all libertie. Yea and many times the princes of Germanie and Italie do admit Iewes to be witnesses in their suits, the forme of the Iewes oath is set downe in the decrees of the Imperiall chamber, *Lib.* 1. the 86 chapter, where it is said, That they should sweare to keep their faith with the Christians as loyally as their predecessors did with the Gisans that were Idolaters. So *Iosua* commaunder ouer the Israelites, hauing bene circumuented by the Gabionites beeing Pagans and Infidels, in a treatie which he had made with them, to saue them, and foure townes

If faith be to be kept with enemies of the faith

L. conuentionum F. de Pactis.

Faith must be kept with Pagans and Idolaters.

townes which they had : and hauing afterwards difcouered their fraud, beeing perfuaded by the Captaines of the Ifraelites to breake the peace, he would not do it, faying, That they had giuen their faith, to the end faith the text, that the furie of God whom they had called to witneffe fhould not fall vpon them. As for that which we faid, That no faith is to be kept with them that haue broken their faith: it is but agreeable with the law of nature, and all hiftories are full of them. And in our time *Sinan Bafcha* hauing capitulated with them of Tripoli in Barbarie, and fworne by his maifters head to fuffer the knights of Rhodes to depart with their baggage after, that the towne was yeelded, notwithftanding his oath, he made all the inhabitants flaues, except two hundred which he fet at libertie at the requeft of *Aramont* the french Ambaffador: and being challenged of his oath, he anfwered, That no faith was to be kept with them, for that they had fworne at Rhodes neuer to carrie armes againft the Turks, reproching them that they were worfe than dogs, which had nether God, faith, nor law, the which might haue been refelled by them of Tripoli, but that might ouercame right, for that they were not tyed to the oath taken by the knights of Rhodes ; nor, if the Tripolitans had formerly fworne, could he now take reuenge thereof by this new accord. For former periurie and treacherie may not be repeated nor reuenged when as they haue once concluded a peace and agreement together, elfe there fhould neuer be any affurance of peace, nor end of treacherie. But if one Prince hath broken his promife and deceiued an other, he hath no caufe to complaine if he be requited with the like : as the Romans hauing vanquifhed the Epirots (who had broken their faith with them, and put garrifons into their townes during the warres of Macedonie) prefently after the taking of *Perfeus*, they made it to be giuen out that they would alfo fet the Epirots at libertie, and withdraw their garrifons, inioyning ten men of the chiefe of euery citie to bring all the gold and filuer, and then fodenly they gaue a watchword to the garrifons to fack and fpoile the cities, the which was done, and in this fort they fpoyled 70 cities. In the punifhment of this treacherie, the Romans behaued themfelues more cruelly than was needfull, for that the reuenge fhould not extend but to them that had committed the periurie; and this diffembling was againft the antient honor of the Romans. But if periurie were couered by a new treatie, it were not lawfull to reuenge it : yet there are fome fo bafe and treacherous as when they fweare, they haue no thought but for to fweare and breake their faith, as *Charles* Duke of Bourgongne gaue a fafegard to the Earle of S. Paul Conftable of France to fell him difhonorablie to *Lewis* the 11 king of France. But *Antony Spinola* Gouernor of the Ifle of Corfica for the Geneuois, committed a fouler act, adding crueltie to his periurie; for hauing called all the Princes of the ifland together vnder colour of councell, and inuiting them to a banquet, he commanded them to be flaine, the hiftorie is frefh. And the banifhed men of Cynethe a citie of Greece, being called home, and receiued by a new treatie made with them which had expelled them, they fware to forget all iniuries paft, and to liue together in peace and amitie : but in fwearing (faith *Polybius*) they ftudied of nothing els, but how to betray the citie, as they did, to be reuenged of the iniurie (which they had couered by a new accord) expelling all their enemies. But God to reuenge their difloyaltie, fuffered the Arcadians, to whome they had betrayed the citie , to kill all thofe which had put it into their hands. Oftentimes princes and feigneuries forfake their leagues for feare , who commonly doe follow the victors partie : as after the battaile of Pauia, all that were in league with the king of Fraunce in Italie, forfooke him : and after the battaile of Cannes, almoft all the Romans affociats in Italie left them : and euen the Rhodians after the taking of the king *Perfeus* (with whome they were in league) they made a proclamation, That no man vpon paine of death, fhould fay or doe any thing in fauour of him.

Faith is not to be kept with them that haue broken their faith.

Periurie couered by a new treatie, may not be repeated.

Fraud circumuented by fraud.

Feare is oftentimes the caufe of a breach.

Of A Commonweale. 629

A Feare may well excuse base minded men from giuing aid, but not from periurie: but what colour or excuse can he haue, that comes to capitulat with an intent to deceiue and circumuent? It is inexcusable to men, and detestable before God. And yet the emperour *Maximilian* the first was wont to say, That he made no treaties with the French, but to abuse king *Lewes* the twelft, and to bee reuenged of seuenteene iniuries which he had receiued from the French, although he could not specifie one: for euery man knowes, that for these two hundred yeres, Europe neuer had prince more religious than *Charles* the eight, nor more vpright and iust than *Lewis* the twelfth, who raigned in the time of *Maximilian*. Yea the last, who alone among all others, was called Father of the people, did shew how loyall he was both in deed and word, hauing treated **B** a peace with *Ferdinand* king of Arragon, from whome hee had receiued many wrongs and losses, yet when as *Ferdinand* was come vnto the port of Sauonne, the king of Fraunce entred into his gallie, accompanied onely with two or three noble men, *Ferdinand* beeing amazed at his great assurance and bountie, went out of his gally, and lodged in the castle of Sauonne. It was in the power of the king of Fraunce to retaine him (as *Charles* of Bourgongne did in the like case to *Lewes* the eleuenth at Peronne) but hee was so free from any so vild a disposition, as he omitted no pompe nor magnificence to giue him all the content that might bee. ¶ The confidence of both kings is disallowed by treacherous men, who shew plainely how per-**C** fidiously they would haue dealt: but to all good men it must needs seeme commendable, which detest that in others, which they themselues hold dishonest. But if princes being in warre, haue made a truce, and concluded a parle, they must come vnarmed, least the one (being secretly armed) should by fraud murther his enemie, as *Iphicrates* the Athenian did *Iason* the tyrant: or as *Mithridates*, who slue the prince of Armenia his sisters sonne. Or if the one comes weakely accompanied and with small force, then must he take hostages from the other, or some places of strength, before he approach, as it is commonly vsed. So did king *Perseus*, who being come with a great traine vnto the frontiers of his realme, and would haue passed the riuer which diuided the two kingdomes, *Q. Martius Philippus* the Roman ambassadour required hostages, if hee meant to passe with aboue three in his companie: *Perseus* gaue the chiefe of his friends, **D** but *Martius* gaue not any, for that he had but three men with him. If there be question to giue hostages for the deliuerie of some great prince that is a prisoner, it must be done with equall forces on either side; and in deliuering the hostages, to receiue the captiue at the same instant; as they did when as king *Francis* the first came out of Spain from prison: else it were to be feared, that a disloyall prince would hold both prisoners and hostages: as *Triphon* the gouernour of Soria did, hauing taken *Ionathan* by treacherie, he promised to set him at libertie for threescore thousand crownes, and his two sonnes hostage: hauing deliuered him the ransome and hostages, hee kept the money and slue the hostages with the prisoner: commaunding his pupill the king of Soria to **E** be cruelly murthered. We must by all meanes shun these pestilent kind of men, and not contract any league or friendship with them, vnlesse it be forced. Yea if they had contracted mariage, yet there is no assurance, if the prince be treacherous and disloyall: as *Alphonsus* king of Naples was, who slue *Cont Iames* the duke of Millans ambassadour. Such a one they write was *Caracalla* emperour of Rome (who neuer shewed a good countenance, but to such as he meant to murther) hauing made a peace with the Parthians, he demaunded the kings daughter, the which was graunted him: so as hee went into Persia wel accompanied to marie her, being all armed vnder their garments, who vpon a signe giuen, when as they thought of nothing but of good cheere, he caused all the noble men that were at the marriage to be slaine, and so fled away: being not

ashamed

Marginalia:
- A: Feare cannot excuse periurie.
- C: What is to be obserued betwixt princes going to parle.
- D: In what sort hostages are to bee giuen for a prince that is prisoner.

B7 vild *i.e.* vile, base, wicked   B9 disallowed *i.e.* disapproved, censured   Note at C1.

[629ᵛ] THE FIFTH BOOKE

ashamed to boast, That it was lawfull to vse his enemies in that sort. This murther was not so cruell, as the excuse was detestable and odious: but God did not let his disloyaltie to be long vnpunished, suffering one of his houshould seruants to murther him as he was at the stoole, and to enioy the empire for his reward. They say, that *Cæsar Borgias* sonne to pope *Alexander* the sixt, was like vnto this monster, whome *Machiauel* doth produce for the paragon of princes: he had learned of his father to poyson such as he inuited to a banquet: it cannot be said, Which did exceed other in treachery: *Alexander* the father neuer did that which he said, and *Cæsar* his sonne neuer spake that which he did: and both of them did religiously hold, That faith was to be giuen to all men, but to be kept with no man. *Cæsar* gaue his faith, and sware great oathes for the assurance of the peace which he had made with the princes that were in league against him: and hauing drawne them together vpon his faith, hee murthered them cruelly whereat his father laughing, said, That he had shewed them a Spanish tricke. But it was an extreame folly for the princes to put their liues into the hands of the most disloyall and perfidious man liuing, and knowne for such a one: and euen at such a time as he was but subiect to the pope, and had no power to giue his faith to them he put to death: so as the pope might haue excused them as his subiects and vassals, without any note of treacherie. But the pope was poisoned with the same poison which hee had prepared for his friends and companions: and his sonne escaping the force of the poyson, was ouerreacht with the same fraud that he had circumuented his enemies. For when as *Consaluus* Viceroy of Naples had giuen him his faith (not being so skilfull in the law of armes and herauldry, as he was to commaund in warre) *Borgias* came to Naples, which when as king *Ferdinand* vnderstood, he commanded him to keepe *Borgias* prisoner: the Viceroy shewes his charge, and *Borgias* did vrge him with his oath and faith: but the Viceroy could not giue his faith without the kings expresse commission, much lesse release a subiect that is captiue, when as the king forbids it. Neither should *Borgias* haue entred rashly into his enemies countrey. We read that *Albret* earle of Franconie committed the like errour to the duke of Valentinois: for beeing besieged by the emperour *Lewis* of Bauiere, *Othon* the Archbishop of Ments persuaded him to come vnto the emperour vpon his faith, swearing, That if hee were not reconciled to the emperour, he should returne safe with him vnto his castle. This good bishop being gone forth, made shew as if he had forgotten something in the castle, and returned backe with the earle. After that he had deliuered the earle into the emperors hands, being vrged of his promise, he said, That he was returned: like vnto the souldiour in *Polybius*, who notwithstanding his shift, was sent backe by the Senat of Rome, with his hands, and feet bound to the enemie. But although the Archduke could not giue his faith vnto a rebell, without warrant from the emperour, yet for that hee had fraudulently drawne a man into danger, who was ignorant of the laws of armes (otherwise than *Consuluus* had done) he was not free from the foule crime of treacherie: like vnto *Paches*, who persuaded *Hippias*, that he should come forth of his castle to a parle, swearing, That he should returne safe: the captaine being come forth, the castle was easily taken: then did he bring *Hippias* backe safe into the castle according to his promise, and there slue him. In like sort *Saturnius* the Tribune with his complices, hauing seized vpon the capitoll by conspiracie and rebellion, comming forth vpon the Consuls faith and safegard, they were slaine, and their memorie condemned. The like chance happened in Luques in the yeare 1522, when as *Vincent Poge* and his companions had slaine the Gonsalonier in the palace, the magistrats gaue them their faith and assurance, that they should not be called in question for the fact, so as they would depart the citie: for that they were then in armes, and the stronger: yet soone after they were pursued

and

The treacherous disposition of pope Alexander the sixt, and Cæsar Borgias his sonne.

Treacherie paied with treachery.

G7 *For* excused *read* executed.   H7 *For* Albret *read* Albert.   H9 Ments *i.e.* Mainz   I6 *For* Archduke *read* Archbishop.   I9 Consalvus   K3 Saturninus   Note at K3.

OF A COMMONWEALE.

and punished as they deserued. And to the end that by the promise of magistrats, the publike faith and assurance should not be broken, the Seigneurie of Venice made a decree in the councell of ten, published in the yere 1506, That no gouernor nor magistrat should giue any safeconduct to a banished man: the which was reserued for the Seigneurie onely; who by another decree made in the yeare 1512, did forbid to take any one prisoner, to whome the Seigneurie had giuen a safeconduct: not that princes and soueraigne states are bound to giue their faith vnto subiects, and much lesse vnto banished men; but hauing once giuen it they must keepe it inuiolable. We haue no better schoolemasters of the lawes of armes, and of the publike faith, than the auntient Romans, and yet we read that *Pompey* the Great did capitulat with pirats, giuing them a sure retreat in some townes & prouinces, to liue there vnder the obedience of the Romans: for he was aduertised, that the pirats had nine hundred sayle of ships, and aboue fiue hundred townes vpon the sea coast, commaunding the whole sea, so as the gouernours could not passe to their prouinces, nor marchants traffique: and that so great a power could not be defeated, without exposing the estate of the people of Rome to apparent daunger; the maiestie whereof stood and was absolute by meanes of this treaty: and if he had not kept the faith which he had giuen them, or if the Senat had not ratified the treatie, he had polluted the honour of the Romans, and blemished the fame of so worthy an exploit. Not that I would haue states to enter into any league, or haue any commerce with pirats and theeues, (for that they ought not to bee partakers of the law of nations, as I haue said before.) And although that *Tacferin* chiefe of an armie of theeues in Affrike, sent ambassadours to Rome, to the end they should appoint lands & places for him and his to inhabit, else he would proclaime perpetuall warre against the Romans; yet the emperour *Tiberius* taking this for an indignitie, would not so much as heare his ambassadours, saying in open Senat, That the auntient Romans would neuer heare, nor treat in any sort with *Spartacus* the slaue, by his profession a Fencer, and captaine of the theeues, although he had gathered together threescore thousand slaues, and defeated the Romans in three battailes: but after that he had bene vanquished by *Crassus*, all that escaped were hanged. Whereby it appeares, that it is dishonourable for a prince or state, to treat with theeues: but hauing once plighted their faith vnto them, it is against their dignitie to breake it. There is a rare example of the emperour *Augustus*, who made a proclamation, That whosoeuer could bring vnto him *Crocotus*, captaine of the theeues in Spaine, should haue 25000 crownes: whereof he being aduertised, he went and presented himselfe to *Augustus*, and demaunded the reward: the which the emperour caused to be giuen vnto him, and withall pardoned him, to giue an example to others, that they must keepe their faith, without any respect to the parties merit.

It is dishonourable for a prince to deale with theeues.

A notable deed of the emperour Augustus.

There is great difference, whether faith be giuen to a theefe, a friend, an enemie, or a subiect: for a subiect which ought to maintaine the honour, estate, and life of his soueraigne prince, if he proue treacherous and disloyall vnto him, and that hee hath giuen him a protectiõ, or if he come to capitulat with him, if the prince doth infringe his oath with him, he hath not so great cause to complain as a theefe, if the theefe be not his subiect: as the legion of Bulgarian theeues, which being come into France to dwell there, king *Dagobert* gaue them his faith, finding it daungerous suddenly to breake such a troupe of loose and desperat men: but soone after vpon a certaine day, a watchword being giuen, they were all slaine. But there is a great difference, whether a soueraigne prince doth capitulat with his friends or his enemies, & that those subiects which haue rebelled against his maiestie, be comprehended in the treatie: Many haue made a question, if the prince breaking his faith with those rebels, and seeking reuenge of them,

whe-

D2-3 Crocotus: Crocotas (Fr) *more accurately* Coracotas (L). Cf. 2 G10-H1.   Notes at B10, E6.

whether the enemie be thereby wronged, and if the assurance giuen, or the truce, bee thereby broken? as it oftentimes falles out, the which doth most afflict princes: as *Titus Liuius* saith of *Philip* king of Macedon, *Vna res Philippū maxime angebat, quod cum leges a Romanis victo imponerentur seuiendi ius in Macedonas, qui in bello ab se defecerant ademptū erat*, One thing tormented *Philip*, that hauing laws prescribed him by the Romans, he might not tyrannize ouer the Macedonians who had fallen from him during the wars. I hold that in this case the treatie is broken, and that the enemie or the prince which hath contracted securitie for an other princes subiects, may take it for an iniurie, & seeke his reuenge, although the subiect were guiltie of treason in the highest degree. As the Barons of Naples, who went to Naples vpon assurance giuen, and an oath taken by *Ferdinand* king of Naples, vnto the Pope, soueraigne lord of Naples, the king of Spaine, the Venetians, and the Florentines, who were bound, and had all sworne to entertaine the treatie, yet they were imprisoned by *Ferdinand* king of Naples, who put them all to death, although he had receiued them vnder his fathers assurance and his owne. But there is no breach of the treatie if a priuat person seekes reuenge of former wrongs of them that are comprehended in the treatie vnlesse; he hath precisely promised that he shall not suffer any pursuit to be made against them for any thing that had been committed before the treatie; or that assurance was giuen them in generall tearmes to returne vnto their houses. For a generall clause in generall tearmes hath the same force that a speciall clause in a speciall case, which may not be stretcht from the places, times, persons and cases, contained in the articles of the treatie or safeconduit: all which notwithstanding were neglected by pope *Leo* the tenth, who hauing giuen his faith and a pasport vnto *Paul Baillon* (who had expelled his nephew out of Perouze) when he came to Rome he was committed prisoner, and his processe made, not only for his rebellion, but for many other crimes, for the which he was conuicted and executed. The historie reports, that the pope had not only giuen his faith vnto him, but to all his friends in generall: true it is they were all his vassals. He did the like vnto *Alphonso* Cardinall of Sienne, being accused that he had attempted to poyson the Pope: to draw him into his snares he gaue him his faith, and to the Ambassador of Spaine in the name of the Catholike king; yet he came no sooner to Rome but his processe was made: whereupon the ambassador of Spaine complained greatly, but the Pope (who wanted no lawyers) answered him, That a safegard or protection how ample soeuer, is of no force, if the crime committed be not expresly set downe: so as presently after the Cardinall was strangled in prison. But the Spanish Ambassador could not stipulate a protection for any one without a commission from his maister, as we haue shewed before: the ignorance whereof hath oftentimes been a great plague and ruine to princes. Pope *Clement* the 7 circumuented the Florentines in our age with the like fraude, hauing promised the Spanish Ambassador to maintaine their estate free: but hauing seazed of the citie, he made it subiect to *Alexander* his brothers bastard, who put the chiefe men to death, after the proscription of many, saying, That treason was alwayes excepted: the which was a friuolous and idle excuse, seeing that he was neuer lord of Florence. Therefore in all treaties it is most safe to set downe particularly the number and qualitie of the iudges, for the differences that may arise among the associates, so as the number be equall of either side; with authoritie to the arbitrators to chuse an vmpier, if they cannot agree among themselues: as in the league made by the foure first Cantons in the yeare 1481, where it was sayd in the fourth and fift Article, that in all controuersies they should chuse an equall number to determine of them. And in the alliance betwixt the house of Austria and the twelue Cantons, the Bishops of Bohemia and Constance are named: but in the treatie betwixt the king of France and the Swissers,

Swissers, in the yeare 1516 in the 17 Article it is said, that in matters of controuersie, euery one should chuse two arbitrators, and if they could not agree, the plaintife should chuse a fift out of the Valesiians or from Coire to be vmpier, who might not alter any thing of their opinions, but chuse the one of them. It were more conuenient that the fift had been chosen by the foure which could not agree, for that the Swissers were alwayes demanders, and named whom they pleased, so as the king had alwayes the worser cause.

There is an other point which doth commonly deceiue Princes, which is, to treate with Ambassadors, deputies, or Lieutenants, without an especiall commission: for notwithstanding any promise which he shall make to haue it ratified by his maister, yet is there no assurance, for that the Prince which promiseth stands bound for his part, and the other remaines at libertie to accept or reiect the conditions of the treatie; and happelie in the meane time there falls out some accident which breeds an alteration: as it happened betwixt the Samnites and the Numantines, and (without any farther search) to *Lewis* the 12, who treated a peace with the Archduke *Philip* passing through France in the yeare 1503, by vertue of an ample Commission which he had from his father in law, promising moreouer to cause him to ratifie it: but *Ferdinand* attended the issue of the warres of Naples, whereas the French were vanquished in two battailes, and expelled the realme, so as he refused to ratifie what his sonne in law *Philip* had concluded with the king of France, saying, that the Archduke had no especiall commission. At the least there must be a time prefixt for the ratifying of the treatie, or a resolute clause for the want thereof: for in matters of State, and of treaties betwixt Princes and Commonweales, a silent ratification is not sure. And this was the cause of the breach of the treatie of Bretigny, the which *Charles* the fift then Regent of France had not ratified touching the soueraigntie of Guienne. And the same occasion made them of Carthage breake the peace betwixt them and the Romans: for after the first warre, they had made two treaties, in the first all the associates of both nations were comprehended in generall teatrmes only; and it was said, that the treatie made with *Luctatius* the Consull should hold if the people of Rome did like of it, the which they would not ratifie, but sent an expresse commission into Affrike with the articles they would haue concluded, and *Asdruball* Generall of the Carthaginians confirmed them. In this treatie the Saguntines were expresly comprehended, as allied vnto the Romans, but this treatie was not expresly ratified by the Carthaginians; vpon which point the Senat of Carthage stood, maintaining that *Hanniball* might lawfully make warre against the Saguntines: and yet the Carthaginians hauing obserued the treatie made by their Generall in all other clauses, they had ratified it in fact, which is more than words. It is therefore the more sure not to conclude any thing without an especiall commission, or expresse ratification, for there neuer wants excuses and deuises to couer their disloyalties, the histories are full of them, as of the Calcedonians against the Bizantines, of *Cleomenus* against the Argiues, and of the Thracians against the Thessalians, who when as they had concluded a truce for certaine dayes, they spoyled their fields by night: and as the Flemings, who fearing to pay two millions of florens into the popes treasurie, (as it was cōcluded by the treatie of peace, if they did rebell against the king of France) they councelled *Edward* the third, king of England, to quallifie himself king of France, and then they would take armes for him, the which was done. Others distinguish vpon the word, as king *Lewis* the 11, who making a shew that he had need of the good councell and aduice of *Lewis* of Luxembourg Constable of France, he said, That he wanted his head. And the Emperour *Charles* the fift by a subtill alteration of a letter denied that which others thought hee had affirmed, writing touching the deliuerie of

*Iii

the

C1 *For* resolute clause *Bodin writes* resolutive clause *i.e.* one canceling the rights of the party which fails to ratify.
Notes at D9, E1.

[631ᵛ] THE FIFTH BOOKE

the princes of Germanie out of prison. But *George Cornarus* found a more subtill interpretation, seeing that he could find no meanes to breake the treatie made with the king of France, said, That the treatie was made with the king for the preseruation of his estate, and not to recouer them when they were lost. But when all failes, and that there is no other excuse, he that is the stronger, is in the right, and the weaker hath wrong, as *Atabalippa* king of Peru (being prisoner to *Francis Pizarre*, Captaine of the Spanyards) he promised the value of ten millions and three hundred thousand ducats for his ransome, the which he payed: the Spanyards hauing resolued to put him to death, said, That there was no meanes for his libertie, vnlesse he became a Christian: he to saue his life was baptized, but with much griefe of mind, saying, That the immortall sonne was to be preferred before mortall gods, but terrified with such imminent danger, he imbraced the Christian religion. What shall I say more? The Spanyards hauing a king that was penitent, confessing and obedient to all their lawes, they put him to death, without any regard of faith or oath, like vnto the wicked Millanois, whom it were a sinne to name, who hauing taken his enemie at an aduantage, set a dagger at his throat, threatning to kill him, if he did not aske him pardon for all the iniuries he had done him, the which was done: then he threatned him with death if he did not denie God; he abiured God and all his works with horrible execrations, but his aduersarie not satisfied therewith, caused him to repeate those curtesies often, least they should be counterfet, and then he slue this blasphemer, saying, That he was reuenged both of bodie and soule. Behold the reward which this denier of God receiued, for putting his trust in the promises of a murtherer. In the treatie made betwixt king *Lewis* the 11 and *Charles* Duke of Bourgongne, in the yeare 1475, he made the king to sweare first by the word of a king, then by the faith of his bodie, and by his creator, by the faith and law which he had taken in his baptisme, and vpon the Euangelists and the Canon of the Masse, and in the end vpon the true Crosse. I omit to write what he profited by this oath, and what succeeded. But the Earle of S. Paule would not giue any credit to all this, when as the king gaue him a safeconduit, vnlesse he would sweare by the crosse of *S. Lau*, which was kept at Angers, the which he refused to do, hauing resolued to put him to death, and fearing aboue all things this crosse, whereupon the lord of Lescut required him to sweare before he would come vnto his seruice, and he kept his oath. The like was done in the treatie of peace betwixt *Charles* Regent of France, and the king of Nauarre, when as the Bishop of Lizieux said Masse in a tent pitcht betwixt the two armies, and receiued the oath vpon the hoste: for better assurance of the treatie, the Bishop diuided the hoste in two, giuing the one halfe to the king of Nauarre, the which he refused, excusing himselfe that he had broke his fast, neither would the Regent take the other part, so as either suspected the other of periurie. The Auntients vsed sacrifices with effusion of bloud, with many imprecations and execrations against the breakers of the league: and the kings of Parthia and Armenia when they entred into any offensiue and defensiue league, they tied their thombs, and drawing forth the blood, they suckt it one after an other: as in the like case the king of Calange at the East Indies, making an alliance with the Portugalls, drue blood from his left hand, and rubd his face and tongue therewith. But there is no assurance in any oathes if the Prince be disloyall: and if he be iust, his simple word shall be a law vnto him, and his faith an oracle. It is forbidden by the holie scriptures to sweare by any but by the name of the eternall God, for it is he alone that can reuenge the breakers of their faith and the scorners of his name, and not they which haue neither power nor care of humane things, the which the thirtie Ambassadors of Carthage feared when as the Romans had agreed to graunt them a peace, an auntient Senator (knowing the disloyaltie

of

A new kind of oath.
Philip Comines.

Tacit. Lib. 4.
In the historie of the Indies.
If the prince bee disloyal, his oath is not to be regarded.

Notes at G4, H2, H9, I7.

A of the Carthaginians) asked them in open Senat, By what gods they would sweare: they answered, that they would sweare by the same gods which had so sharply punished their disloyaltie. For he offends no lesse that thinks to mock God, than he which doth it in deed, neither is he to be credited although he hath sworne. The princes partisans of the houses of Orleance and Bourgongne did sweare sixe treaties of peace in lesse then twelue yeares, and not any one was kept, as we read in our histories. And for that among all the treaties made among princes, there is not any one that hath more need of assurance, and that is more difficult to entertaine, than that which is made with the subiect, hauing conspired against his prince; I am of opinion that in this case the treatie should be made with neighbour princes, to warrant the subiects, or else spee-

B dily to depart the countrie. And if any one will obiect that the subiect ought not to haue any safegard or protection from his lord, as it was adiudged by a decree of the court of Parliament for the Earle of Tonerre, I confesse it: But I say, the subiect must either do thus, or else depart the countrie, when they haue to do with a soueraigne Prince. For there is no greater torment vnto a Prince, than to be forced to capitulate with his subiect, and to keepe his faith with him. *Lewis* the 11 gaue a good testimonie thereof to the Duke of Nemours, to the Earle of S. Paul, to the Duke of Brittanie, to the Earle of Armaignac, and to all his subiects that had rebelled, all which almost hee put to death; and the historie of Flanders puts his owne brother in the number, affirming that he was poisoned. And not long since the yonger brother to the king of Fez

C besieged the king his brother with an armie, and forced him to conclude a peace with such conditions as he pleased, and then he entred into the Castell with a small traine to do his homage, but sodenly he was strangled by the kings commandement, and cast out at a window in view of his armie, which hauing lost their head, yeelded presently. In like sort the Duke of Yorke hauing taken armes against *Henry* the sixt king of England, hauing gotten the victorie he made an agreement with the king vpon condition that after his decease the Crowne should come vnto the house of Yorke; and the prince of Wales, sonne to king *Henry* the 6 should be excluded, and in the meane time he should remaine Regent of England: but soone after being taken he was beheaded with his accord, being crowned with a crowne of white paper. You must not gall the Lion

D so hard as the bloud may follow, for seeing his owne bloud and feeling the smart, if he haue his libertie he will be reuenged: I would I had not so many examples as haue bin seene in our time. But when as I say it is necessary that neighbour princes and allies be comprehended in the treatie made betwixt the prince and his subiects as pledges and warrants, I do not meane that it shall be lawfull for forraine princes to thrust their neighbours subiects into rebellion, vnder coulor of protection or amitie: and in truth the beginning and spring of all the warres betwixt king *Francis* the first, and the Emperour *Charles* the fift, was for the protection of *Robert de la March*, whom king *Francis* receiued, as *du Bellay* hath well obserued. But a wise prince may meditate an accord betwixt another prince and his subiects, and if he finds that the outragious proceeding

E of a Tyrant against his subiects be irreconcileable, then ought he to take vpon him the protection of the afflicted with a generous resolution: as that great *Hercules* did, who purchased to himselfe immortall praise and reputation, for that he tooke vpon him the protection of afflicted people against the violence and crueltie of tyrants (which the fables call monsters) whom he went through the world to conquer: wherein the auntient Romans did also exceed all other nations. And without any more search, king *Lewis* the 12 receiued into his protection the Bentiuoles, with the houses of Ferrara and Mirandula, against the oppression of pope *Iulio* the 2: but he caused to be inserted into the protection, That it was without preiudice to the rights and dignity of the Ro-

Iii ij   man

The maner how to capitulat betwixt the prince and the subiect.

Meierus.

In what case a forrien prince may take vpon him the protection of another princes subiects.

D9 *For* meditate *read* mediate (cf. note at 624 K7).   Note at A4.

man church: and for the same cause king *Henry* the 2 tooke the protection of the same princes of Mirandula against the violence of pope *Iulio* the 3, and of many princes of Germanie against the Emperour *Charles* the 5 for the libertie of the Empire, and entertained the league of the sea townes which the Emperour sought to breake, & to change the Empire into an hereditarie kingdome else he which persuadeth: another Princes subiects to rebell vnder culour of protection (which should be as a holie anchor for people vniustly tyranized) he doth open the gate of rebellion to his owne subiects, and brings his owne estate into danger, with an euerlasting shame and dishonor. And therefore in all societies and leagues among princes it is alwaies excepted, That the one shall not take the protection of anothers subiects, whether the cause be iust or vniust. The only reason which hindred the treatie of peace betwixt king *Antiochus* the great, and *Ptolomie* king of Egipt, was the protection of *Acheus*, who of gouernor of Asia had made himselfe king, and had withdrawne it from his soueraigne prince, as *Polibius* saith. And for this cause *Sigismond Augustus* king of Polonia, to haue peace with the king of Muscouie, was forced to leaue the protection of *Rigie* in Liuonia. And whatsoeuer some say, that it is lawfull for the vassall to free himselfe from the subiection of his lord, if he be ill intreated; it is to be vnderstood of an vndervassall, which hath recourse vnto his soueraigne lord, and not of a leege vassall which holds immediatly, and without the meanes of any other vassall, who in some other respect may be a soueraigne: as the subiects of Guienne and of Poitou rebelled iustly against the king of England vassall to the king of France, for that he denied them iustice, and for that cause he was depriued of those fees which he held on this side the sea, according to the Canon law, although that many are contented to take away the iurisdiction only. And of late daies the Geneuois expelled the Marquis of Final out of his estate at the complaint of his subiects, and tooke them into their protection: who whenas hee complained vnto the Emperour of the wrong which was done vnto him, the Geneuois aunswered, That they had freed but their owne subiects from the tyrannie of the Marquis: yet hee preuailed against them, notwithstanding they pleaded that hee was their vassall. Else euery one might vnder colour of ill vsage rebell against his lord, and put himselfe in the protection or subiection of another: as some subiects of the Duke of Sauoy, hauing been thirtie yeares or thereabouts vnder the seigneurie of Berne, seeing now that they would turne them ouer to their antient lord, they beseeched the Bernois instantly, not to abandon them, being afraid of ill vsage: but they were denied their request, as I haue vnderstood by letters from the Ambassador *Coignet*. And although that hee that is banished by his prince may be receiued into protection by another prince, or into subiection, without any breach of the treatie (which forbids the receiuing of another princes subiects into protection) for that those which are banished for euer, are no more subiects: but if those banished men would attempt any thing against their auntient Lord, the prince which hath receiued them ought not to suffer them. And therefore the princes of Germanie sent Ambassadors to king *Henry* the 2, to requite him not to receiue *Albert* Marquis of Brandebourg into his protection, being banished by a decree of the Imperiall Chamber: the king made answere in the moneth of August, in the yere 1554, That although the house of France had alwaies been the support of afflicted princes, yet would he not shew any fauour vnto the Marquis against the holy Empire. Yet notwithstanding if the prince exceeding others in power and dignitie, be duly informed that another princes subiect be tyrannized, he is bound not only to receiue him into protection, but also to free him from the subiection of another; as the law takes the slaue out of the power of a cruell maister: but it more befitteth to free the subiect from the subiection of another, and to set him at libertie, than to subiect

ieft him to himselfe, as the Romans did all Greece and Macedonie, which they deliuered from the dominion of kings, to set them at full libertie. So did pope *Agapet* (who freed the successors of *Gautier d'Iuetot* from the subiection of the kings of France, for that king *Lothair* had slaine him with his owne hand in the Church, at what time as he craued pardon of him) to giue example to other princes not to vse any such cruelties to their subiects: and for the like crueltie *Henry* king of Sweden was expelled his estate by his owne subiects, in the yeare 1567. But it was held very strange that pope *Iohn* the 22 in the treatie made betwixt *Philip* the long king of France and the Flemings, caused it to be set downe, That if the king did infringe the treatie, it might be lawful for his subiects to take armes against him, to the which the Princes and Barons of France did oppose, causing that clause to be razed; and it was more strange that it should come out of the mouth of a french pope, a naturall subiect to France, and who had once been Chancellor. But the prince may well sweare that if he breake the treatie made by him, his subiects shall be freed from their obedience, as it was in the treatie of Arras, and hath been vsed among our first kings of this realme: as in the treatie which was made betwixt *Lewis* and *Charles* the bald brethren, the oath which either of them made was with this condition, That if it chanced, which God forbid, that I should breake my oath, I then absolue you from the faith which you owe me. *Lewis* sware first in the Roman toung these words which follow, the which the President *Fauchet*, a man well read in our Antiquities, did shew me in *Guytard* an historian and prince of the bloud, *Pro deo amur, & pro Christian poblo & nostro commun saluament dist di en auant, inquant des sanir podir medunat, si saluerio cist meon fradre Karle, & in adiudha, & in cad vna causa si com hom par dreit son fradre saluar dist, ino quid il vn altre si faret. Et abludher nul plaid nunquam prindraÿ qui meon vol cist, meon fradre Karle in damno sit:* That is to say, For the loue of God and the Christian people, and for our common health from this day forward, so long as God shall giue me knowledge and power, I will defend my brother *Charles*, and will aide him in euery thing as any man by right ought to saue his brother, and not as another would do: And by my will I will haue no quarrell with him, if my brother *Charles* doth me no wrong. King *Lewis* hauing made an end of this oath, king *Charles* spake the same words in the Germaine toong thus, *In God est &c.* Then both the armies subiects to the two princes sware thus, *Si Ludouigs sagrament que son fradre Carlo iurat, conseruat, & Carlus meo sender de sue par no lostaint, si io retornar non lutt pois, ne io veuls cui eo retornar ne pois, in nulla adiudha contra Ludouig:* That is to say, If *Lewis* keepes his oath made with his brother, and *Charles* my lord for his part doth not hold it, if I cannot preuent it, I will not returne with him in peace, nor do him any obedience. The subiects of *Charles* sware in the Roman toong, and the subiects of *Lewis* in the Dutch. But to returne to our purpose: it is dangerous to take the protection of another, especially of those which are subiect to princes allies, but vpon a iust cause, so is it more strange to leaue an associat in danger. But it is a question, whether a prince may take the protection of another prince vniustly oppressed, without breach of the league: for it is most certaine that we aide priuate allies and common allies, if they be wronged by one of the allies: but he that is not comprehended in the league, may not be defended against him that is allied, without breach of the league: on the other side it is a thing which seemes very cruell, to leaue a poore prince to the mercie of one more mightie that doth oppresse him and seekes to take his estate from him.

If one that is in league may succour him that is not allied against his associat, being wrongfully oppressed.

The Senat of Rome was much troubled herewith, for that the Capouans being assailed, & vniustly oppressed by the Samnites, had recourse vnto the Romans, who had a good desire to aid them: considering withall, that the Samnites would be too migh-

*Iii iiij tie

C2 *For des* Bodin *writes* ds *i.e.* deus.   C2 podir me dunat   C4 prindrai   D3 ne io veuls (L) ne io ne veuls (Fr)   D3 retornar me pois   D4 contra Ludovig (Fr) contra Ludovig nunli iver (L)
D7 in the Dutch *i.e.* in German   Notes at C1, D7, E1.

tie & insupportable, if they had once seized vpon the Seigneurie of Capoua, and that it was a meanes to subdue the Romans: notwithstanding it was resolued by the Senat not to giue any succours vnto the Capouans, considering the league which they had sworne with the Samnites, *Tanta vtilitate* (saith *Titus Liuius*) *fides antiquior fuit*, Faith was of more respect than so great a benefit. I will set downe word by word, the aunswere which was made vnto the six ambassadours, the which deserues to bee grauen in letters of gold, *Legatis Campanorum auxilia contra Samnites petentibus, Consul ex authoritate Senatus sic respondit: Auxilio vos Campani dignos censet Senatus: sed ita vobiscum amicitiam iustitui par est, ne qua vetustior amicitia ac societas violetur: Samnites nobiscum foedere iuncti sunt: itaque arma Deos prius quam homines violatura, aduersus Samnites, vobis negamus: Legatos sicut fas est, precatum ad Socios mittemus, ne qua vobis vis fiat*, The Consull with the authoritie of the Senat did aunswere in this sort vnto the ambassadours of the Campanois, demaunding succours against the Samnites. The Senat holds you of Campania to be worthy of succours, but it is fit so to ioyne friendship with you, as a more auntient league and societie may not be violated: the Samnites are linkt vnto vs in league, and therefore we denie you armes against the Samnites, whereby we should wrong the gods rather than men: but we will send ambassadours (as we may lawfully) to request our associats, not to offer you any violence. The ambassadours of Capoua had a secret charge, to offer the subiection of Capoua vnto the Romans, in case they should refuse to giue them succours: who seeing themselues reiected, made this offer, *Quandoquidem nostra tueri non vultis, vestra certe defendetis: itaque populum Campanum vrbemque Capouam, agros, delubra Deum, diuina humanaque omnia in vestram P. C. populique Romani ditionem dedimus. Tum iam fides agi visa, deditos non prodi*, Seeing you will not protect vs and ours, yet at the least you shall defend your owne: we yeeld therefore into your power O reuerent fathers, and of the people of Rome, the people of Campania, and the citie of Capoua, with their fields, churches, and all diuine and humane rights. Now is your faith ingaged, not to betray them that yeeld vnto you. Whereby it appeares, that the stranger is not to be succoured against the allie, vnlesse he yeeld himselfe a subiect vnto him whose protection he pretends: for in that case euery one is bound to defend his subiects against the iniuries of the mightie. If the Athenians had made the same aunswere to the Corcyrians, demaunding aid against the Corinthians their allies, they had not fallen into a warre which set all Greece on fire for the space of twentie eight yeres, and was not ended, but with the ruine of the Athenians, who were made subiect vnto the Lacedemonians, as they had deserued, what colour of iustice soeuer they pretend, that the league ought to cease if one of the associats doth make warre vniustly against a straunger. If this interpretation might take place, there should be no league nor alliance vnbroken. And therefore in contracting of leagues and new societies, the more auntient associats (although they are held to be excepted by law) must be precisely excepted: so as no aid is to be giuen vnto the latter confederats against the more auntient, vnlesse they haue first begun the warre. As in the league made betwixt the house of Fraunce and the Cantons of the Swissers, in the yeare 1521, in the which the auntient allies were excepted: but there was a derogatory clause, in these words, If the auntient allies did not make warre against the king of Fraunce, which was the principall subiect of the treatie. But it may so fall out, that three princes being in league, one may make warre against the other, and require aid of the third. In this case there are many distinctions. If the treatie of alliance be but of amitie and friendship, it is most certaine that he is not in that case bound to giue any succours, if the treatie imports a defensiue league, he must aid the most auntient ally by a precedent alliance: If the associats be of one standing, he owes succours vnto him that

A stranger is not to be succoured against an ally, vnlesse hee make himselfe a subiect.

F6 *For* the six ambassadours *read* the ambassadours (no numeral in Fr or L, or in Livy, VII, 30–31).
F9 institui

Of A Commonweale. 634

A is vnited vnto him by an offensiue and defensiue league. If it be offensiue and defensiue of all parts, he must not succour neither the one nor the other: but he may well mediat a peace, and cause their quarrels to bee compounded by their common allies: as it is commonly vsed, making warre against him that will not referre his cause to arbitrators, or yeeld to their arbitrement, as it is expresly set downe in the treatie of Stance, made betwixt the eight Cantons. Arbitrements are not to be reiected, how great soeuer princes be: as *Henry* king of Sueden did vpon the controuersies hee had with the king of Denmarke, who offered to referre his cause to *Henry* the second, king of Fraunce: the which the king of Sueden refused, saying, That he was as great a king as the rest. But the Romans, who exceeded all nations in riches and power, if they had any controuersie
B with their allies, they referred it to the arbitrement of their common confederats, *Romanus Legatus* (saith *Titus Liuius*) *ad communes socios vocabat*. And if it be not lawfull by the law of armes, to allow of the combat, when there is any proofe by witnesse or otherwise, what an iniustice were it, to suffer two princes or states to enter into warre, if a third may reconcile them, or els ioyne with him that is wronged. It were a simple part to suffer his neighbours house to burne, the which hee might quench with his honour. Moreouer it may be doubted, whether the league be broken, if thou shalt offer violence to any confederats father or brother, being not comprehended in the league. If they bee subiects, there is no question: if they bee absolute of themselues, it may be doubted; for that the father and the sonne are held to be all one: but in my opinion
C there is nothing done against the league, vnlesse the fathers person were excepted in the treatie. And although the father may pursue an iniurie done vnto his sonne by action, yet may he not attempt warre by the law of armes, for a sonne that is out of the fathers iurisdiction, and not excepted in the treatie, although hee bee wronged by his confederats: for that the fathers power hath nothing common with the lawes of armes and maiestie, much lesse may the league be broken for brethren that are wronged. But to auoid all these inconueniences, the most safest way is, to limit all leagues to a certaine time, to the end they may add or take away from the treatie, or giue ouer the league altogether, if they thinke it expedient for them: and especially betwixt Popular estates and those which are gouerned Aristocratically, the which neuer die. For in Monar-
D chies societies and leagues are dissolued by the death of princes, as wee haue said. Yet princes making treaties with Seigneuries and Popular states, haue beene accustomed to continue the time of the league after the princes death: as it was in the league betwixt the Cantons of the Swissers, and *Francis* the first, where the time was limited for the kings life, and fiue yeares after, and since it hath alwayes so continued: but that condition did bind the Swissers, and not *Francis* his successor, who might at his pleasure hold, or go from the league: for that an oath is personall, and to speake properly, cannot be taken for the successor.

But some one will say vnto me, That the first clause in all the auntient treaties and leagues, which the Romans made with other states and Seigneuries, was, That they
E should be perpetuall. And therefore the Hebrewes did call the strongest and best assured alliances, treaties of salt, for that salt of all things compounded of the elements, is least corruptible: as they also call a statue or image that is euerlasting, A statue of Salt, not that the holy Scripture meanes, that *Lots* wife was turned into a salt stone, as many beleeue. But in my opinion there is nothing more pernitious in treaties than to make them perpetuall: for he that feeles himselfe any thing ouercharged with the treatie, hath reason to breake it, seeing it is perpetuall: but if it be limited, hee hath no cause to complaine. Moreouer it is easie to continue leagues and alliances alreadie made, and to renew them before the time prefixt be expired: as hath beene alwayes done with

Iii iiii   the

B5–6 a simple part *i.e.* a foolish act   B6–7 with his honour *i.e.* without prejudice to his honor
B7 whether   Notes at C5, E1.

the Cantons for these fiftie yeares: and although we were assured of a perpetuall amitie and friendship, and that there should bee no cause of griefe or dislike, yet friendships grow cold, and haue need to be reuiued and quickned by new treaties. And therefore in the treatie betwixt the Vallesians and the fiue small Cantons, it is set downe in the last article, that the league should be renued euery tenth yeare. And in the treaties betwixt the eight Cantons it is said, that the alliances should be renued euery fiue yeares. The Romans did sweare a league and perpetuall amitie with the inhabitants of Laurentum, and yet was it renewed euery yeare, *Cum Laurentibus (inquit Liuius) renouari fœdus iussum, renouaturque ex eo quotannis post diem decimum Latinarum*, Beeing commaunded (saith *Liuie*) to renew the league with the Laurentines, it was thereupon renewed euerie yeare after the tenth day of the Latines. And the same author saith, *Adire iussi sunt Legati Romani Cretam, & Rhodū & renouare amicitiam simul, speculari num solicitati animi sociorum ab rege Perseo fuissent*, The Roman ambassadours were commaunded to go to Creet and Rhodes, to renew the league, and to discouer if their confederats minds had bene corrupted by king *Perseus*. There was a league of perpetuall friendship made in the yeare 1336, betwixt *Philip* of Valois, and *Alphonso* king of Castile: and afterwards it was renewed betwixt king *Iohn* and *Peter* king of Castile, in the yeare 1352: and betwixt *Charles* the fift, king of Fraunce, and *Henrie* king of Castile: and yet euerie one of these leagues was made perpetuall for the associats and their successors. As was also betwixt the houses of Scotland and Fraunce, for these three hundred yeares, that they haue continued in good and perpetuall league and amitie, vnto the yeare 1556. There is also another reason why the time of leagues and alliances should be limited, for that there is an ordinarie clause annexed to all treaties, Not to make any peace or truce, or to enter into league with a common enemie, or with them that are not comprehended in the treatie, without the consent of all the associats, or of the greatest part: But if one of the allies will not consent thereunto, must the rest be ingaged in his hatred, and in a continuall warre, if the league bee perpetuall? That were against all diuine and humane lawes, if the occasion of this hatred doth cease, and that a peace may be made without the preiudice to the allies. But this clause is ill practised, for if any one of the associats hath an intent to goe from the league, hee is so farre from demaunding the consent of the rest, as sometimes he doth treat so secretly, as all is concluded before that any thing can be discouered, and oftentimes they abandon their associat vnto their enemies. We haue a notable example in our memorie, of the treatie of Chambort, made in the yeare 1552, betwixt the king of Fraunce of the one part, and the duke *Maurice*, the marquesse *Albert*, and the Lantgraue of Hesse on the other; where it is said in the two & twentieth article, That if any of the associats should make any peace or agreement, or haue any secret practise with the emperor, or his adherents, without the consent of his other allies, he should be punished as a periured, without all remission, in the view of all the armie. And yet within six moneths after, the elector *Maurice* agreed with the emperor at a treatie at Passau, neither aduertising king *Henrie* (who was chiefe of the league) nor yet comprehending him in the treatie. Against whome the marquesse *Albert* exclaimed, saying, That it was a base and villanous act, calling the duke traitor, and disloyall to his countrey, the emperour, and the king of France. And yet he did worse than his companion: for after that he had drawne great summes of money from the king, he turned to the emperour, and made open warre against the king: so as the imperiall souldiors called *Maurice* Bachelor, or Graduat, & *Albert* Doctor, for the notable tricks which he plaied. And of late memorie the Seigneurie of Venice concluded a peace with *Sultan Selim*, so secretly, as it was published at Constantinople, at the comming of the French ambassadour, before that any one of the

Treaties betwixt the kings of France & Spaine

The league betwixt the French and Scots.

The treatie of Chambort.

The princes of the empire in the protection of the king of Fraunce.

Why Marquesse Albert was called Doctor.

G2 amicitiam, simul speculari   18–9 For without all remission *read* without any remission.

the confederats of the holy league was aduertised thereof, although it were expresly forbidden in the treatie, that not any one of the confederats might make a peace or truce with the Turke, without the consent of all the rest. So the auntient Romans hauing to doe with faithlesse and disloiall people, they did not willingly conclude a peace, but a truce for many yeares, as they did with the Veientes, *Veientibus pacem petentibus in annos centum induciæ datæ,* The Veientes requiring a peace, they had a truce graunted them for an hundred yeares. And in another place, *Induciæ Veientibus pacem petentibus in annos 40 datæ,* A truce of fortie yeares was graunted vnto the Veientes, who demaunded a peace. And in another place, *Cum populo Cerite inducias in centum annos factas,* There was a truce made with the people of Cerites for an hundred yeares. And in another place, *Hetruriæ populi pacem petentes in annos 30 inducias impetrarunt,* The people of Hetruria demaunding a peace, they obtained a truce for thirtie yeares. For alwayes a truce is more holy, and lesse violable than a peace. And if wee shall well obserue the end of those which haue broken any truce, we shall find that it hath bene miserable, and many times the ruine of states. So the Romans haue alwayes punished seuerely the breakers of any truce: the first example was showne vpon the person of *Metius* Dictator of the Albanois, who was pulled in peeces with foure horses, and the citie of Alba rased: the people of Veientes were rooted out, hauing rebelled seuen times against the articles of the truce: the citie of Carthage was burnt to ashes: the people of Capoua slaine for the most part, and the rest made slaues: the inhabitants of Corinth massacred, and their citie burnt to ashes: the Samnites were ruined, hauing infringed their faith seuen times, as we read in *Titus Liuius, Strabo*, with infinit others, which were impossible to set downe in particular, which carrie an euerlasting testimonie of Gods iust iudgements against treacherous and disloyall princes, and faithlesse people, which mocke at oathes. As for treacherous and disloyall subiects, they were neuer vnpunished, *In Veliternos veteres ciues grauiter sæuitum quod toties rebellarent, muri disiecti, Senatus abductus,* They punished the Veliternians (who were auntient citisens) verie seuerely, their walles were cast downe, and their Senat carried away. And after the second Punike warre, the Roman subiects which had bene traitors were excepted, *Perfugæ (inquit Liuius) bello punico 380 Romam missi, virgis in Comitio cæsi, & de Saxo deiecti,* In the Punike warre 380 runnawayes (saith *Liuie*) beeing sent to Rome, were whipt in the open assemblie, and cast downe the rocke. And if the enemie hauing giuen hostages, did infringe their treaties, the hostages were publikely put to death: as it happened vnto three hundred hostages of the Volsques, which were slaine: and in like case the hostages of the Tarentines, *Fugientes retracti, ac virgis diu cæsi, de Tarpeio deiecti sunt,* Fleeing they were fetcht backe and being beaten long with rods, they were cast from the mount Tarpeia (saith *Titus Liuius*.) But since that they haue made a trade of the breach of faith, they haue also made a conscience to put hostages to death: as *Narses*, who pardoned the hostages of the Luquoies, hauing broken their faith: and *Charles* duke of Bourgongne had no sooner set three hundred hostages of the Leegeois at libertie (the which he might iustly haue put to death, whatsoeuer *Comines* saith) but they attempted a new warre against him.

The clause that hostages should be subiect vnto capitall punishments, was vnknowne to the auntients, for it was alwayes lawfull not only to kill hostages that fled, but also if they that had giuen hostages had infringed their faith. But since they haue thought it fit to expresse those words in their promises, least that hostages should pleade ignorance of the law of armes, or that it should seeme too cruell that one should suffer for anothers offence. I will not denie but the Romans haue somewhat blemished the brightnes of their auntient integritie and iustice, the which happened vnto them not so much

much through their owne fault, as by the Grecians and Carthaginians, whose treacherie they had often tried: witnes that which *Liuie* writes of the Ambassadors that were sent into Greece, when as they made report of their charge in open Senat, he saith thus, *L. Martius & Attilius Romam reuersi, nulla alia re magis gloriabantur, quam decepto per inducias & spem pacis Rege, quæ magna pars Senatus probabat: sed veteres moris antiqui memores, nouam istam sapientiam improbabant, nec astu magis quam vera virtute bellage ßisse maiores, denunciare bella, & sæpe locum finire, quo dimicanturi essent. L. Martius* and *Attilius* being returned to Rome, gloried in nothing more, than that they had circumuented the king with a truce, and the hope of peace: the which the greatest part of the Senat did allow of, but the most auntient (remembring their customes of old) did disallow of this new kind of wisedome, for that the auntients did not make warre by craft and pollicie, but by vertue, proclaiming warre, and oftentimes appointing the place where they would fight. Yea they were accustomed to renounce their alliance and friendship that had wronged them, before they would begin any warre. *Veteres,* saith *Suetonius, bellum indicturi, renunciabant amicitiam,* The auntients when they would make warre against any one, they renounced his friendship: a custome which was obserued among priuat men, euen in the time of the Emperour *Tiberius:* for *Germanicus* being grieuously wronged by *Piso* gouernor of Soria, sent him word that he renounced his friendship: and *Henry* the 5 king of England sent word to *Lewis* duke of Orleance by his ambassador, That he could not defie him, vnlesse he renounced his friendship, and sent back the alliance. And at this day those which be brethren in armes, and princes which do weare one anothers order, they send back the order before they make warre. But the Greeks who had taught the Romans their deceits and disloyalties, were punished, as we may see in *Liuie,* where he saith, *Phocenses cum pacti essent nihil hostile se a Romanis passuros portas aperuerunt, tum clamor est sublatus a militibus, Phocenses nunquam fidos socios, impune eludere: ab hac voce milites vrbem diripiunt, Æmilius primo resistere, captas, non deditas vrbes diripi,* The Phocenses when they had contracted that they would not indure any hostile acte of the Romans, they opened their gates; then began there a crie among the souldiers, that the Phocenses being neuer faithfull associates did laugh at them vnpunished: at this crie the souldiers spoile the towne, at the first *Æmilius* made resistance, saying, That they vsed to spoyle cities that were taken by force, and not that yeelded. But the Romans to repaire this error, left their citie in full libertie, and restored them the lands they had taken from them. So *Polibius* who was a Greeke borne, and gouernor to *Scipio* the Affrican, speaking of the Greeks, saith, That a word among the Romans was sufficient, but in Greece for the lending of a hundred crownes they must haue ten notaries, and twise as many seales, and yet would they breake their faith. But it is far worse at this day, where there is no assurance neither in letters, seales, nor safegards, yea ambassadors are not assured, for we haue seen *Rincon* and *Fregose* ambassadors to the king of France slaine by the officers of the Emperour *Charles* the 5, and yet no iustice was done of them: whereas the Romans deliuered *Minutius* and *Manlius* to their enemies, and at another time *Fabius* and *Apronius,* to dispose of them at their pleasures, for that they had somewhat wronged the ambassadors, the which is forbidden by the law of armes. If faith be not kept with ambassadors, what shall we hope of others? yea some haue gloried in killing them, as *Helene* Queene of Russia, being intreated by her enemies to make a league, to the end she might marrie with their king, she buried all the ambassadors aliue; and before they were aduertised thereof, she sent them word that she would haue ambassadors of greater worth, whereupon they sent her fiftie more of the noblest of the whole countrie, all which she caused to be burned aliue, and vnder promise of marriage she murthered

OF A COMMONVVEALE. 636

A murthered fiue thousand which she had made dronke. It is not needfull heere to reheatse how many cities and people haue been ruined and rooted out for the breach of faith with ambassadors, who are and ought to be sacred and inuiolable. And ambassadors are also to be warned that they exceed not their charge, nor speake not any thing to the dishonor of the prince or people to whom they are sent, for a wise ambassador will alwaies deliuer his charge, if in things that be odious sparingly, and in those that be pleasing full, to the end that he may entertaine princes in friendship, and appease hatred; for that princes do oftentimes fall into mortall quarrels through the indiscretion of ambassadours. Amongst many we haue the example of *Stephen Vauoide* of Valachia, to whome the Procope of Tartaria sent an hundred ambassadours, threatning to waste
B all his countrey with fire and sword, if he sent not backe the Procopes sonne, whom he had taken prisoner. The Vauoide incensed at these threats, put them all to death, except one whome he sent home maimed of his members, to bee a messenger of this strange calamitie. Others reuenge not iniuries done vnto them by ambassadours so indiscreetly, but yet as cruelly, least they should seeme to haue broken their faith, dismissing them, and yet sending others after them to kill them: as *Tuca* queene of Sclauonia did, who sent some to murther the yongest of the three Roman ambassadours, hauing threatned her, the which was afterwards the cause of her ruine, and of her estate. But the fact of the king of Moscouie was most barbarous, who seeing an Italian ambassadour to put on his hat before he was bidden, he caused it to bee nailed fast vnto his head; a
C most cruell and barbarous deed, yet was there an error in the ambassador, who should hold the ranke and dignitie of the prince his maister, so as it bee not with the contempt of the prince to whome he is sent: for sometimes ambassadours relying vpon the greatnesse of their maister, forget themselues to meaner princes, especially men that are bred vp in Popular estates, accustomed to speake with all libertie, thinke they may doe so with Monarches, who are not accustomed to heare free speeches, and much lesse that the truth should be spoken vnto them: for which cause *Philip* the young, king of Macedonie, seeing the Roman ambassadour question too boldly with him, hee could not forbeare to braue him with reproaches. And *Popilius* the Roman Legat vsed *Antiochus* king of Asia with greater presumption, making a circle with a rod about the kings
D person, willing him to giue him aunswere, before he went out of that circle: here *Liuie* saith, *Obstupefactus est rex tam violento imperio*, The king was amazed at so violent a commaund: and yet he did what the Romans commanded, hauing tried their power. *Marius* the elder vsed the like libertie towards *Mithridates* king of Pontus or Amasia, who although he neither were ambassadour, nor had any publike charge, yet he said vnto the king, That he must obey the commaundement of the people of Rome, or be the stronger. Then did *Mithridates* find that true which was spoken of the Romans, That they were of a freer speech than any other nation. And sometimes too great libertie without any iniurie offends princes. For which cause *Marc Anthonie* caused an ambassador which was sent from *Augustus* to be whipt, for that he talked too free-
E ly to queene *Cleopatra*. But those princes are wisest, which hauing receiued any affront from ambassadours, demaund reparation from their maisters: as *Charles* earle of Charolois, said vnto the ambassadours of *Lewis* the eleuenth, That his Chauncellour had braued him, but the king would shortly repent it; and so it fell out: for the same yere he imbarqued the king in a most daungerous warre, with the hazard of his estate. And therefore king *Francis* the first, doubting that he should heare something of an herauld which was sent from the emperour *Charles* the fift, that might bee some impeach vnto his maiestie, he caused a gibet to be set vp before the court gate, when he heard that hee approached, letting him vnderstand, that he would hang him, if he opened his mouth,
for

C8 ambassadour   C9 to brave   D2 violento (Fr 5–8 and Livy, XLV, 12) violenti (Fr 1–4 and L)
D6 *For* commaundement *read* commaundements (Fr and L).   Note at C9.

for hauing giuen the emperour the lie, he knew well that the herauld could not bring him any aunswere, without some touch to his honour and dignitie. Some there bee that will attempt warre against their associats for any small iniurie: as the Scots did in old time against the Picts, for taking away their dogges, hauing liued together almost six hundred yeares in great peace and amitie. A good prince must trie all meanes, and dissemble many things, before he come to armes. I do not agree with *Bartol*, who saith, That the peace is not violated, if any one hath vndertaken that hee shall not bee wronged, and yet his things are stolne away by him with whome he hath made a peace: for that there was nothing that did sooner moue the antient Romans to make warre, than for things taken away, and iniuries done. *M. Aurelius* the emperour said well, *Putasne non aliter vim inferri quam si homines vulnerentur: vis est etiam cum quod per Iudicem debuit per te ipse arripis*, Doest thou thinke that violence is not offered, vnlesse that men be wounded. It is violence, when thou takest that of thine owne authoritie, which thou shouldest recouer by law. But some make breach of their faith, by a craftie interpretation of the law. As that which *Bartol* proues, If by the truce it be lawfull for a French man to passe into England, vpon condition, That if after the truce he be found within their limits, it shall be lawfull to kill him: if before the end of the truce he depart out of England, and by a storme is driuen backe into England after the truce expired: in this case he saith, they may lawfully kill him. In my opinion they may ransome him by law, but not kill him: for that he doth nothing against the truce, that by tempest is cast vpon his enemies countrey. It would seeme vniust and iniurious, to repaire that which
happens accidentally with
the losse of life.
(***)

Finis Libri quinti.

Note at F2.

THE SIXT BOOKE OF OR CONCERNING A COMMONVVEALE.

Chap. I.

¶ Of Censuring or Reformation, and wheher it be expedient to inroll and number the subiects, and to force them to make a declaration, or giue a certificat of their priuate estates.

Itherto wee haue described at large the first part of the definition of a commonweale: that is, the true gouerning of many families with absolute power, and that which depends of the said definition. It remaynes now to speake of the second part: that is, of that which is common to an estate; and which consists in the managing of the treasure, rents, and reuennues, in taxes, imposts, coynes and other charges for the maintenance of a commonweale. And for the better vnderstanding hereof, let vs first treat of Censuring. *Census* in proper tearmes is nothing else but a valuation of euery mans goods: and for that wee are to treat of reuenues, it is verie needfull to speake of censuring, and to shew, that of all the Magistrats of a commonweale, there are not many more necessary: and if the necessitie be apparant, the profit is farre greater, be it either to vnderstand the number and qualities of the citisens, or the valuation of euery mans goods; or else for the well gouerning and awing of the subiect. And calling to mind the farthest bounds of antiquity, I doe much wonder, how so goodly a charge, so profitable and so necessarie, hath bene laid aside so carelesly, seeing that all the ancient Greeks and Latines did vse it, some yearely (saith *Aristotle*) others from three, foure, or from fiue yeares to fiue yeares, making an estimation of euery mans wealth and priuate estate: whereof *Demosthenes* hauing made an abstract out of the publike registers, said (speaking vnto the people) that all the reuenues of the countrey of Attica did amount vnto threescore thousand talents, or thirtie six millions of crownes. Euen so the Romans (who did imitate the Grecians) could wel imbrace this custome, and bring it vnto Rome: for which cause king *Seruius* is much commended in histories. And although the people of Rome had disanulled and abolished all the edicts and ordinances of their kings, after they had expelled them, yet this law of censuring or surueying continued still, as the foundation of their treasure, imposts, and publike charges, &c. was continued in the Consuls persons. But after that the Consuls were distract & drawne away for warlike imployments, they then created Censors,

The commendation of censuring, or estimating the subiects estates.

Censors vsed by the Greeks and Romans.
Liu. anno 310. ab v. c.

three-

threescore and six yeares after that the Consuls had executed it. *L. Papirius*, and *L. Sempronius* being the first that were called *Censores*, and they held the office fiue yeares: but ten yeares after *L. Aemilius Mamercus* limited the time of the Censors office to eighteene moneths. And soone after, this custome was followed by all the cities of Italy, and namely by the Roman Colonies, who brought their Registers and Inrollments to Rome. Afterwards this charge was still continued; and euen *Cæsar* the Dictator tooke the paines to go from house to house to supply the Censors charge, although he called himselfe *Magister morum*, or Master of the manners. And as soone as the Emperour *Augustus* was returned to Rome, after his victorie against *Marc Anthonie*, the Senate by a publike decree gaue him the office of Censor, calling him *Præfectus morum*, or Controller of manners, who thrice numbred the citisens of Rome, and valued euerie mans goods: and not onely of the Citisens of Rome, dispearsed throughout the whole empire, but of all the subiects of euerie prouince: And was there euer Emperour that left so goodly an estate of an empire, as he did?

[margin: Cæsar and Augustus were both created Censors.]

Afterwards it was discontinued vnder the tyranny of *Tiberius* and *Caligula*, and reuiued againe by *Claudius* the Emperour, which made the 74 Lustre. It was left againe vnder *Neron*, and continued againe vnder *Vespatian*, who made the 75 Lustre: and then it left vnder the tyranny of *Domitian*, who called himselfe Perpetuall Censor, and yet made no suruey. A hundred and fiftie yeres after, or thereabouts, the Emperour *Decius* caused the Senate to declare *Valerian* Censor, with ample authoritie. And since that this office was laid aside, the empire hath alwaies declined. True it is, that the Emperours of Greece did erect an office, which they called *Magistrum Census*, or The master of inrollments, who kept the publike registers containing all testaments and publike acts, with the names and ages of euerie person; yet not with such dignity and power as the auntient Censors. But it is certaine, that all townes subiect to the Roman empire, had their Censors, euen vnder *Traian* the Emperour, and that the Senators of euerie towne were chosen by the Censors, as wee may read in an epistle written by *Plinie* the younger to the Emperour *Traian*. And (not to goe out of this realme) we read, that king *Childebert*, at the persuasion and instance of *Maroueus* Bishop of Poitiers, made an edict, commaunding all his subiects to be inrolled, and their goods to bee valued; the which is yet sometimes put in practise at Venice, Genes, and Luques, whereas there bee Censors created: and namely at Venice in the yeere 1566 they made three Magistrats to reforme the peoples manners, whom they called, *I Seignori sopra il ben viuere de la citta*: The Magistrats for the well liuing of the citisens: for that the name of Censor in a free citie abounding with all kind of delights, seemed harsh and seuere.

[margin: Lustrum.]

Few yeares before the creation of this Magistrat, hauing set forth my booke of the Method of Histories, I did therein much maruell, that in so great a number of officers, wherein the Venetians did exceed other cities, they had forgotten Censors, which were most necessarie. The commonweale of Geneue in stead of Censors haue deputed ten Antients, the which are chosen as magistrats, whereof foure are of the counsell of threescore, and six of the counsell of two hundred; which hold the subiects of that state in such awe, as few offences remaine vnpunished: so as without doubt this commonweale will flourish, if not through armes and wealth, yet by their vertues and pietie, so long as they shall maintaine the authoritie of those Auntients. Whereby it doth plainely appeare, that the best and most flourishing cities could not long subsist without Censors: wherein many ignorant diuines abuse themselues, in thinking that *Dauid* was grieuously reprehended by God, and punished,

[margin: Censors in effect created at Venice.]

[margin: Censors not to be wanted in a well ordred commonweale.]

Notes at F4, F6, H9.

OF A COMMONWEALE. 639

A punished, for that he commaunded his people should bee numbred; when as God commaunded *Moyses* the Emperour of the Israelites to doe it after their departure out of Egypt, and againe before they entred into the land of promise; and not onely to number them, but to note euerie family, and to take the name of euerie particular person before they had conquered anie thing, the which hee should leaue to posteritie: but the fault which *Dauid* committed, was in forgetting Gods commaundement, charging him, that when he did number the people euery one should offer vnto God two groats of siluer (as *Ioseph* hath verie well obserued) being commaunded in the text of the law, to exact that holy tribute for an expiation of their sinnes, so often as he should please to haue the people numbred: then he adds, Least

B a plague should be among the people. But in my opinion heerein was the greater offence, that the prince too arrogantly trusting more in the force of his legions, than in the power and helpe of the Almighty, did not number all his people, but those onely that were able to beare armes, omitting the tribe of *Leui* (which attended the sacrifice) and the tribe of *Beniamin*. And whereas the law commaunds euerie one to put halfe a sickle, or two siluer groats; that is done in my opinion, to abolish the impietie of the heathen, who taking the number of their subiects, offred a piece of siluer for euerie one vnto their gods: as also God commaunded they should sprinckle the bloud of the sacrifice aboue, and of eyther side of the altar, forbidding them expressely, not to offer any more bloud vnto their deuils, that he might call his

C people from the inhumane and hatefull worship of deuils. And it seemes that king *Seruius* had borowed this ceremony from the people of the East, when as hee commaunded a boxe to be set in *Iuno Lucinas* temple, into the which they put a *denier* for euerie one that was borne: and another in the temple of *Iuuenta*, where they did also put a *denier* for euerie one that had attayned to seuenteene yeres of age, at what time they put on a playne gowne without purple: and the third was in the temple of *Venus Libitina*, into the which they put a *denier* for euerie one that died: which custome continued inuiolable, euen when as the office of Censor was neglected.

D We read, that the Athenians were inrolled in the publike registers at the age of 14 yeeres, yet wee find no mention made of the tribute. But the numbring of the people which God commaunded to be made, was but of such as could cary armes, from 20 yeeres vpward; in the which it seemes that old men aboue 60 were not comprised, & yet they were found by pole to amount to six hundred thirtie thousand fiue hundred and fifty, besides the tribe of *Leui* which made twentie two thousand, from a moneth old vpward, which was in all six hundred fifty two thousand fiue hundred and fiftie. And fortie yeeres after the number was taken, when as all those which came forth were dead, except *Moyses, Iosua*, and *Caleb*, they were found to bee six hundred twentie foure thousand seuen hundred seuenty three, comprehending the Leuits, besides the women, slaues, old men, and youth vnder twentie

E yeres, which were at the least twice as many. But *Titus Liuius* speaking of the number of the citisens that were found in Rome, sayth in his third booke, *Censa sunt ciuium capita 415 millia, preter orbos orbasque*, the number of the citisens is 415000 besides the blind. *Florus* in his 59 booke saith, *Censa sunt ciuium capita 313 millia 823 preter pupillos & viduas*, the citisens are numbred at 313823 besides widdowes and pupils. Fiue yeeres after he sayth, *Censa sunt ciuium capita 390 millia 936*, The number of the citisens is 390936. And in the following suruey, 394356. And in the next inrollment 450000 and in the other after that 150000. I omit the former surueyes, which are all greater than this last: but it seemes the Citisens of Rome were not

Iij ij excluded,

Num. 1, 2, 3, 4, 21, 26.

The numbring of the people appoynted by God.

The number of the Israelites.

Exod. 12.

A2 (margin) *For* 1. 2. 3. 4. 21. 26 (Fr 7) *read* 1. 2. 3. 4. 26. 31 (Fr 1–3, 5–6, 8).   A3 Egypt
E6, E7 *For* 390936 *read* 390736 (Fr only).   E7 *For* 394356 *read* 394336 (Fr only)   E9 Citisens *i.e.*
female citizens (*bourgeoises* in Fr 1, 5–7, but misprinted *bourgeoisies* in Fr 2–4, 8)   Notes at D4, E1.

excluded, as it may appeare in that which I haue noted, for that there were none but widowes and orphelines excepted: and yet *Florus* saith in his 27 booke, *Censa sunt 137000 ciuium, ex quo numero apparuit quantum hominū tot preliorum aduersa fortuna populi Romani abstulisset:* The number of the citisens were 137000: wherby it appeares how many men the Romanes lost in their vnfortunate warres. And in the former view he sayth, *Censa sunt tiuium capita 270 millia:* The check-roll of all the citisens comes to 270000. as if he would inferre, that the losses which they had receiued against *Hanibal*, had carried away 133000 citisens: for if the women had beene comprehended which went not to the war, there had remayned none but women, for that they be alwayes as many or more than men, as I haue before shewed. And in Athens there was a suruey taken, wheras the number of women was greater than that of men, as *Pausanias* saith. But the scruple is decided by *Titus Liuius*, where he saith, speaking of the seuenth inrollment, *Ciuium qui puberes essent, supra centum decem millia erant: mulierum autem & puerorum, seruorumq; & mercatorum, & sordidas artes exercentium (siquidem Romanorum nemini cauponariam, aut operosam artem tractare licuit) triplo plus quàm turba ciuilis.* The citisens of full age were aboue 110000 of women, children, slaues, marchants: and of those which vsed base trades (for no Roman might be a victualer or handycrafts man) the number was thrice as many as of the ciuill sort: whereby it appeares, that marchants, handycraftsmen, women, nor children, were not registred: as for slaues they were not nūbred among the citisens, but among moueable goods, the which were commonly fiftie for one: and euen in Athens there were found a hundred times more slaues than free men, by a suruey that was taken, whereas for ten thousand strangers, and twentie thousand citisens, there were foure hundred thousand slaues. And of the number that was taken at Venice about thirtie yeares since, there were found two thousand women more than men, as I haue formerly noted.

The profit that may be gathered by the numbring of the people.

The benefits which redounded to the publike by this numbring of the people, were infinite: for first they knew the number, age and qualitie of the persons, and what numbers they could draw foorth, either to go to the warres, or to remaine at home; either to bee sent abroad in colonies, or to bee imployed in publike works of reparations, and fortifications: thereby they shall know what prouision of victuals is necessarie for euerie citie, and especially in a time of siege, the which is impossible to preuent, if they know not the number of the people. And if there were no other benefit but the knowledge of euerie mans age, it cuts off a million of sutes and quarrels the which are inuented touching the minoritie and maioritie of persons:

A meanes to cut off sutes.

for which cause king *Frauncis* the first commaunded his chauncellour *Poyet*, to puplish an edict, inioyning all curats to keepe a register of all such as should bee borne: but for that the registers are not kept as they ought, this law is ill obserued. And in regard of the quality, we see an infinit number of sutes touching the nobility, which should be auoyded by this meanes: and the sutes of forgerie & falshood, for the disguising and concealing of names of the parents, countrie, estate, and qualitie, of euerie one, whether hee bee a citisen or a stranger, a bastard or lawfully borne, a nobleman or a patrician, a plebeian or a nobleman, and of what name & house he comes, for want of registers and censors can hardly be found out.

The citisens estates are knowne by the Censors.

This appeared plainely, when as *Pericles* numbred the citisens of Athens, for the prerogatiues and priuiledges they had aboue strangers, where there were found thirteene thousand three hundred and sixty citisens, and fiue thousand strangers which carryed themselues as citisens, and were sould for slaues by a publicke decree. Moreouer, to order and gouerne the bodies & colleges of citisens according to

The citisens order is knowne.

to the estate and age of euerie person, as they did vse in Rome and in Greece, it is more than necessary to know the number of the subiects; to gather their voices in elections the number is also requisite; to deuide the people into tens, hundreds, and thousands, it is also necessarie to know the number of them. But one of the greatest and most necessary fruits that can bee gathered by this censuring and numbring of the subiects, is the discouery of euery mans estate and faculty, and whereby he gets his liuing, therby to expell all drones out of a commonweale, which sucke the hony from the Bees, and to banish vagabonds, idle persons, theeues, cooseners, & ruffians, which liue and conuerse among good men, as woolues do among sheepe, spending their liues in theeuing, dising, robbing, drinking and whooring; who although they walke in darkenesse, yet hereby they should bee seene, noted and knowne. And as for the valuation of goods, it is no lesse necessarie than the numbring of persons. *Cassiodorus* speaketh thus, *Orbis Romanus agris diuisus censuq; descriptus est, vt possessio sua nulla haberet incerta, quam pro tributorum susceperat quantitate soluenda*, The Romane territories were deuided, and euery priuate mans land laid out, that no mans possession should bee vncertaine, the which he had taken for the payment of a certaine rent or tribute. If then a suruey were taken of all the Roman empire, and the lands distributed accordingly, that it might bee knowne what burthen euery one was to beare in regard of the goods he inioyed; how much more necessary is it now, when as there bee a thousand sorts of imposts in euery commonweale, which the auntients did neuer know? This poynt is of such consequence, as it should suffice, if it serued for nothing else, but to cause euery one to bring in a declaration of his goods and reuennues: as was done in Prouence in the yeare 1471: whereby it did afterwardes plainely appeare that the commons were oppressed by the cleargie and nobilitie, if it had not beene prouided for by an edict made by *Frauncis* the first, in the yere 1534, and by another of his successors: wherupon the three estates of Prouence (beeing growne into great sutes) were called before the Parliament at Paris, where a prouinciall decree was made, That all men of what qualitie soeuer, should pay their charges & imposts according to the register made in the yeare 1471, when as there were three thousand houses charged with a soulz vpon the pound, without respect of families or persons, but to the lands subiect to contribution. They were also constrained in the yere 1516 to make a suruey and declaration of all the benefices of this realme, in regard of the tithes, the which by reason of the daily alterations and changes require a newe suruey or numbring: for some Incumbent payes more than a moytie of his benefice, when as another payeth not the thirtith part for the tithes. The like was required by *Marillas* the kings aduocate for the subsidie of Prouence.

By this meanes the poore mens iust complaints shall be releeued, whom the rich are accustomed to ouercharge, and to free themselues throughout all the realme of Fraunce, as well as in Prouence & Languedocke: By this meanes, mutinies (which are vsuall in euerie commonweale, for the vnequalitie of charges) shall cease: and moreouer all sutes depending before Iudges for reliefe, should be quite cut off: by this meanes the concussions, malice or fauour of the assessors and other officers, who haue charge to make an equall distribution of the tribute or impost, shall bee discouered, or at least the controuersie shall be decided by the Censors register: or else they might put in practise of the custome of the antient Athenians, wheras if any one were ouercharged that had lesse wealth than another, hee might force him that was lesse taxed to take his charge, or to change estates with him: as *Isocrates*, who lost against *Lysimachides*, and wonne against *Megalides*.

It expels vagabonds & idle persons out of an estate.

A meanes to equall the charges and imposts according to euery mans estate.

A meanes to auoid concussion and fauour in them that make deuision of the subiects

---

B4 *For* nulla (L 4–5) *read* nulli (L 1–3 and Fr). Cf. Cassiodorus, *Variarum*, III, 52.   B4 haberetur
C8 *For* prouinciall *read* prouisionall.   D6 Marillac   E3 concussions *i.e.* extortions
Notes at C1, D3, D7, E2.

By this meanes yow shall know who be miserable, who prodigall, which be banquerouts, who rich, which poore, who cooseners, which vsurers, & by what gaines some get so much wealth, and others are oppressed with so great want, and how to redresse it: for that by the extreame pouerty of some, and the exceeding wealth of others, we see so many seditions, trouble, & ciuill warres arise. Moreouer, all edicts and decrees, and generally all iudgements and sentences touching fines & amercements, should be ordred, and justice equally administred, when as euery mans estate were knowne, seeing that the punishment may not exceed the offence. Also, all deceits in mariages, in bargaines and sales, in all priuat & publike negotiations should be discouered and knowne.

I omit a multitude of sutes touching successions, diuisions, and morgages, the which are concealed for the most part, and should bee made plaine by the registers without search, the which should ease the subiects charge, and preuent the falshood of witnesses. It may bee some will say vnto me, That it were a hard thing to expose the pouertie of some to be scorned, and the wealth of others to bee enuied. Behold the greatest argument that can bee obiected to hinder so good and commendable a thing. But I answere, That all enuy will cease against those whom they hold to bee rich and are not, and the mockerie against such as haue wealth and were held poore. And shall the enuie of the malicious, or the derision of the scorner, hinder so good and commendable a thing. Neuer wise prince nor good law-maker did regard enuie or scorne, when there is question of good lawes. Although this law (whereof question is made) concernes onely moueable goods and not lands. To say, that it is neither good nor comely to know priuate mens wealth or wants, the course, traffike and negotiation of marchants, which consists most commonly in bookes of credit, nor to lay open the secrets of families; I answere, that there are none but cooseners & deceiuers that are loth to haue their liues laid open, & their actions knowne: good men that feare not the light, will bee alwaies glad to haue their estates knowne, with their qualities, wealth and maner of liuing. An Architect said one day to *Liuius Drucius* the Tribune, That he would make the lights of his house in such sort, as no man should ouer-looke him: To whom *Drusus* answered, I pray you make it in such sort as euery one may looke into it & see mine actions. *Velleius Paterculus* who writes the historie saith, that this man was *sanctus & integer vitæ*, of a holy & vpright life. But the office of Censor is chiefly against the wicked: And in old times euery Roman kept a register of his actions and expences, and of all his goods: But vppon the declining of the empire, when as vices began to spring vp, they neglected it, saith *Asconius*, for that many were condemned by their registers. And I find not that euer any but tyrants theeues and bankerouts hated the office of Censor, and haue hindred all they could the valuation of goods, as I haue noted of *Tiberius, Caligula, Nero*, and *Domitian*. It is therefore a meere mockery, to pretend that this would bee a meanes for tyrants to oppresse their subiects with exactions: for there is no tyrant so cruell, but he wil more willingly take from the rich than from the poore; wheras for want of a Censor the poore are pinched, and the rich saue themselues. We also see that by the practises of the vsurers & the rich citisens of Rome, of six Censors chosen successiuely in one yeare, not anie one could intend his charge: whereupon the Tribunes making their complaints before the people said, That the Senatours feared the registers and publike informations, which discouered euerie mans estate, and their actiue and passiue debts, whereby they should find, that some of the Citisens were oppressed by the others, and ruined by the vsurers. And then the tribunes protested, that they would not suffer any debtour to bee adiudged to his creditors, nor inrolled to go to the

[margin: A notable answere of a Tribune.]
[margin: The Censor hatefull to the wicked]

F2 For gaines read games i.e. tricks, stratagems (*jeu* in Fr). H8–9 Livius Drusus I8 tyrants, USURERS, theeves (Fr and L) Notes at G1, H1.

Of A Commonvveale. 643

the warres, vntill they had first seene a declaration of the debts, to the end they might prouide as they should find it needfull. Then did the debtors flocke together about the Tribune, to giue him ayd and assistaunce. Why should a good creditor feare to haue his debts and contracts viewed, or his lands (lawfully purchased) knowne? why should he hinder the knowledge of his goods, lawfully gotten by his industie and labour? It shalbe alwaies honorable vnto him; and if he be an honest man, if he loues the preseruation of the common weale, and the reliefe of the poore, he will make no difficultie to giue a declaration of his goods for the reliefe of the publike, if need shall require. If he be wicked, if hee bee an vsurer, an extortioner, a publike theefe, and a robber of priuate men, he hath reason to oppose himselfe all he can, that his goods, his life, nor his actions may be knowne: but there is no reason to aske the vinteners aduice if they shall suppresse alehouses; or the strumpet, if they shall put downe the stues; nor of bankers, if they shall abolish vsurie; nor of the wicked, if they should haue Censors.

The auntient Greeks and Latines haue alwaies spoken of censuring, as of a diuine thing, the which hath always preserued the greatnesse of the Roman empire so long as Censors were in credit. *Titus Liuius* speaking of king *Seruius*, who first ordained that euerie one should giue a certificate of his goods, saith, *Censum instituit rem saluberrimam tanto imperio*, He instituted the office of Censor, a wholesome thing for so great an empire. But after that Censors were created in the Consuls place, and that by little and little they began to take knowledge of the life and manners of euerie one, then began they to respect the Censors, and to reuerence them more than all other magistrats: whereof *Titus Liuius* saieth, *Hic annus Censuræ initium fuit, a parua origine ortæ, quæ deinde incremento aucta est, vt morum disciplinæq; Romanæ penes eam regimen, Senatus, equitumq; centuriæ, decoris, dedecorisq; discrimen sub ditione eius magistratus, publicorum ius, priuatorumq; locorum vectigalia populi Romani sub nutu atque arbitrio essent*, This yeare was the beginning of the Censors office, springing from a small matter, the which was afterwards so augmented, as hee controlled the manners and discipline of the Romans, the assemblies of the Senate, and of knights, also the distinction of honour and infamie were subiect to this magistrat; and the publike rites, with the reuenues of priuat places belonging to the people of Rome, were censured by him. The Censors office then was to receiue the number of the persons, and the valuation of their goods, to be superintendant of the treasure, to farme out the imposts, customes, and all the reuenues of the commonweale, to reforme abuses, to place and displace Senatours, to dismisse the men at armes, and to censure the life and manners of euerie one. *Plutarch* speakes in a higher stile, tearming the office of Censor, Most sacred and mightie. It may be some will say, that the charge was ouer great: yet two Censors were sufficient in so great an empire. But their charges may be deuided: for to place and displace Senators, that charge was giuen vnto the Censors, to ease the people, saith *Festus*: the which could not be done in a monarchie, whereas the prince makes choyce of all magistrats, especially of his counsell. Yet it were necessarie, that the ouerseers of the treasure should be true Censors, that is, men without blame or reproch: for you must always commit the purse to the most trustie, and the reformation of abuses to the most vpright. As for the reformation of abuses, it is the goodliest thing that euer was inuented in any commonweale, and it hath best maintained the greatnesse of that empire: for euen as the Censors were alwayes chosen out of the most vertuous men of the commonweale, so did they striue to conforme the subiects to the true patterne of honour and vertue. This was done from fiue yeres to fiue yeres: & after that they had setled the estate of

The opinion of the auntients touching Censors.

The charge of the auntient Censors.

The Censors reformers of abuses.

the

A5 industrie B8–9 saluberrimam B9 tanto FUTURO imperio (Fr, L, and Livy, I, 42)
C3–4 fuit, REI a parva (Fr, L, and Livy, IV, 8) C4 deinde TANTO incremento C6 locorum, vectigalia Note at C10.

the treasure, and farmed out the reuenues. And if they discontinued this charge (as oftentimes it fell out by reason of the tediousnesse of the warres) then did it plainely appeare, that the people grew corrupted in manners, and that commonweale declined, like vnto a bodie which leaues his ordinarie purging: this was manifest during the second Punike warre, when as they had no time to attend that charge conueniently, but as soone as *Hannibal* was retired into the territories of Naples, then the Censors (saith *Titus Liuius*) *Ad mores hominum regendos animum aduerterunt, castigandaque vitia, quæ velut diutinos morbos ægra corpora ex sese gignunt, nata bello erant*, The Censors applyed themselues to reforme mens maners, and to punish vices, the which had sprung vp by reason of the warres, as continuall feauers doe in sicke and corrupt bodies. And yet they dealt not with any abuses, but such as were not to be censured by the Iudges: for the magistrats and the people tooke knowledge of murthers, paricides, thefts, concussions, and such like crimes, the which are punished by the lawes. Is it not sufficient, will some one say, to punish crimes and offences by the law? My answere is, That the lawes punish those offences onely, which trouble the quiet of a commonweale: and yet the greatest offendors doe easily escape the punishment of the law, euen as great beasts do easily breake through the spiders web. And who is so ill aduised, as to measure honour and vertue by the lawes? *Quis est* (saith *Seneca*) *qui se profitetur legibus omnibus innocentem? vt hæc ita sit, quàm augusta est innocencia ad legem bonum esse: quanto latiùs patet officiorum quàm iuris regula? quàm multa pietas, humanitas, liberalitas, iusticia, fides exigunt, quæ extra publicas tabulas sunt!* What is he that professeth himselfe an innocent by all lawes? how strict is innocency, to bee good according to the lawe? how much larger are the rules of dutie than of law? how many things doe piety, humanity, liberalitie, iustice, and faith, challenge at our hands, the which are not inserted in the publike tables? It is manifest, that the most detestable vices, and that most corrupt a commonweale, are neuer called into iudgement. Treacherie is not punished by the law, beeing one of the most abominable vices: But the Censors (saith *Tully*) were not so curious of any thing, as to punish periury. Drunkennesse, gaming, palliardise, and loosenesse of life, are suffered with all impunity; and who can redresse these disorders but the Censor? We see most commonweales swarme with vagabounds, idle persons, and ruffians, who by their deeds and examples corrupt good citisens; and there is no meane to expel this vermine, but by the Censor. There is yet one speciall reason which shewes that the Censors office is now more necessarie than euer: for that in old times the master of euery family had absolute commaund, the father ouer his children, the master ouer his slaues had absolute power of life and death, without any appeale; and the husband had the like authority ouer the wife in foure cases, as wee haue shewed elsewhere: but all this now ceasing, what iustice may we expect of the impiety of children against their fathers and mothers? of the ill gouernment of maried couples? of the contempt of masters? How many virgins doe we see sold and dishonoured by the parents themselues, or that rather suffer them to liue loosly than to be maried, thinking it better to cast forth their children, or to kill them, than to nourish them? and how can all this be preuented but by a Censor?

    I dispute not of the conscience to God, the which is the chiefest and most principal thing that ought to be cared for in euerie family & common weale; the which care although it hath beene alwayes committed vnto Bishops, ministers, and other spirituall officers, yet the magistrat ought to haue a speciall regard that it be aboue all things held in reuerence: for although the law of God commaunds that euerie one appeare before him at the three great feasts of the yeare at the least, yet there are
some

Marginal notes: The greatest vices are punished by the Censors. — A necessarie reason to confirme the Censors office.

G9 ut hoc ita sit (Fr and L) G9 *For* augusta *read* angusta (cf. H2). G10 officiorum
Notes at F1, H5, I3.

OF A COMMONWEALE. 645

A some which neuer goe, and so by this contempt of religion, hath sprung vp by little and little, the detestable sect of Atheists, which haue nothing but blasphemy in their mouthes, and contempt of diuine and humane lawes; whereby do follow infinite murthers, paricides, poysonings, treasons, periuries, adulteries, and incests: neither is it to bee expected, that eyther prince, or magistrat shall reduce those subiects vnder the obedience of the lawes, that haue trodden all religion vnder foot. But this depends of the ouerseears or Censors, who vse diuine lawes when as mans decrees are of no force: for that *Legum metus non scelera, sed licentiam comprimit*, The feare of lawes doth not suppresse the crimes, but the libertie. There haue beene and are at this day infinite numbers, who although they offend not the princes lawes,
B yet liue they most wickedly, and as *Lactantius* said well, *Possunt enim leges delicta punire, conscientiam munire non possunt*. Lawes may well punish offences, but they cannot fortifie and amend the conscience. And as for the bringing vp of youth (the which is one of the chiefest charges of a commonweale, whereof as of yong plants they should haue the greatest care) wee see it is neglected, and that which should be publike, is left to euery mans discretion, vsing it at his pleasure, some in one sort, some in another, the which I will not touch heere, hauing treated thereof in another place. And for that *Licurgus* said, That thereon consisted the foundation of a commonweale; he appoynted the great *Pedonome* to be Censor of the youth, and to gouerne them according to the lawes, not at the parents discretion: for as the
C scope and end of a citie is all one, so the education of all the citisens, according to *Aristotles* opinion, should be all one: and so did the Atheniens decree by a publike edict, made at the request of *Sophocles*, knowing well, that in vaine were lawes made, if youth (as *Aristotle* said) were not instructed in good manners. All this depends on the care and vigilancie of Censors, first to haue a care of the manners and behauiour of schoolemasters.

I will passe ouer with silence the abuses which are committed in suffering of commedies and enterludes, the which is a most pernitious plague to a commonweale: for there is nothing that doth more corrupt the citisens good manners, simplicitie,
D and naturall bountie; the which hath the more power & effect, for that their words, accents, gesture, motions, and actions, gouerned with all the art that may be, and of a most filthy and dishonest subiect, leaues a liuely impression in their soules which apply thereunto all their sences. To conclude, wee may well say that the Commedians stage is an apprentiship of all impudencie, loosenesse, whooredome, coozening, deceit and wickednesse. And therefore *Aristotle* did not without cause say, That they must haue a care least the subiects went to commedies: he had said better, That they should pull downe their theaters, and shut the commedians out of the citie gates: *Quia* (said *Seneca*) *nihil tam moribus alienum, quàm in spectaculo desidere*: For there is nothing more contrarie to good manners, than to haunt plaies. And
E therefore *Philip Augustus* king of Fraunce, did by a publike edict banish all players out of his realme. If any one will say, that both Greeks and Romans did allow of plaies: I answere, that it was for a superstition they had vnto their gods; but the wisest haue alwaies blamed them: for although a Tragedie hath something in it more stately and heroike, and which doth make the hearts of men lesse effeminat, yet *Solon* hauing seene the Tragedie of *Thespis* plaied, did much mislike it: Whereof *Thespis* excusing himselfe, said, It was but a play: No (replyed *Solon*) but this play turnes to earnest. Much more had he blamed Commedies, that were then vnknowne: and now adayes they put at the end of euerie Tragedie (as poyson into meat) a comedie or jigge. And although that comedies were more tollerable a-

meng

Commedies and playes pernitious to a commonweale.

B7–8 in an other place *i.e.* in the *Oratio de instituenda in Republica juventute*, reprinted in Bodin, *O.P.*, I
Notes at E2, E7, E9.

mong those that dwell in the Southerne parts, beeing more heauie and melancholy by nature, & for their naturall constancie lesse subiect to change; yet should they be vtterly defended to those that liue towards the North, being of a sanguine complexion, light and inconstant, hauing in a manner all the force of their soule in the imagination of the common and brutall sence. But there is no hope to see playes forbidden by the magistrats, for commonly they are the first at them.

It is the proper charge of the graue and wise Censors, who will bee carefull to entertaine the honest Gimnasticall exercises, to keepe the bodie in health: and of musike to restraine the appetites vnder the obedience of reason: I meane musike, which doth not onely signifie harmonie, but also all liberall and honest sciences; hauing a speciall care, that this naturall musike be not altered, nor corrupted, as it is at this day, seeing there is no thing that slips more sweetly and insensibly into the interiour affections of the mind. And if we may not preuaile so much as to haue the Ionique and Lidian songs, that is to say, the fift and seuenth tunes banished out of a commonweale, and defended from all youth (as both *Plato* and *Aristotle* said it was necessarie) at the least let not the Diatonie musike (which is more naturall than the Chromatique or Enharmonique) be corrupted by other medlies: and that the Dorien songs, or of the first tune (the which is proper to sweetnesse and seemely grauitie) be not disguised into manie tunes, and so deuided, as most part of musicians become fooles or mad men, for that they cannot tast of a naturall musicke, no more than a weake stomake corrupted with delicates, can digest good and substantiall meat. All this depends of the Censors dutie: for that neither Iudges nor any other officers will euer regard it.

Two meanes to maintaine a citie.

They also complaine of excesse in apparell, and that the sumptuarie lawes are trodden vnder foot. It shall nueer be reformed, if there bee not Censors to see the lawes executed, as in old time the *Nomophylaces*, or Law keepers, did in Athens. And therefore an auntient Oratour said, That the Tribune which first restrained the Censors authoritie, had ruined the commonweale: It was *Clodius*, one of the wickedest men of his time, which law was sixe yeares after disanulled by the law *Cæcilia*.

Seeing then that to censure is so goodly, profitable, and necessarie a thing, let vs now see, if Censors ought to haue any iurisdiction: for it seemes it should be but a iest without some iurisdiction. Yet I say, that the Censor ought not to haue any iurisdiction at all, to the end that his charge be not intangled with sutes and controuersies. In like sort, the auntient Roman Censors had no iurisdiction; but a looke, a word, and a dash with a pen, was more bloudie, and touched more to the quick, than all the decrees and iudgements of the magistrat. When as they made their scrutiny or suruey, you should haue seene foure or fiue hundred Senators, the order of horsemen, and all the people stand trembling before them: the Senatour fearing lest he should be put from the Senat; the horseman from his horse, & rankt among the baser sort: and the simple citisen to be rased out of his order and from his line, and placed among the tributaries: as *Titus Liuius* doth testifie, That 66 Senators were rased at one time out of the register, and excluded the Senat. And yet left this great honour and authoritie of the Censors should make way to a tyranny, if they were armed with power and iurisdiction, or if any should be condemned without hearing; it was therefore wel aduised they should haue nothing but the censuring and reformation. And therefore *Tully* said, That the iudgement of the Censors did onely make men blush: and for that it did but touch the name, the Censors correction was called *Ignominia*, Ignominie; the which differs from infamy,

The Censors ought to haue no iurisdiction.

The Censors haue no power nor iurisdiction.

G6 Diatonic   H1 delicates *i.e.* delicacies   H5 never   Notes at G3, I2.

OF A COMMONWEALE.   647

infamy, depending vpon the Iudge that hath publike iurisdiction, and in causes that make men infamous. And therefore the Pretor did note them as infamous, that were cassiered with ignominy, the which had beene ridiculous, if they had beene infamous. And yet the doubt which Lawyers haue made, If ignominious men should suffer as the infamous; shewes plainly, that Ignominy and Infamy is not all one, as manie haue supposed. *L. 1. de ijs qui notant infam.*

By the auntient custome of Greece, it was lawfull to kill any one, or any of his children that was noted infamous, as the Orator *Libanius* saith in his pleading for *Halirhotius*. Now although the Censor had rased any Senator out of the Register booke, yet if he would make petition vnto the people he was admitted, and sometimes absolued and restored: but if there were any accuser that did second the Censor, or if the Censor himselfe would accuse any as a priuate man, if the accused were found guiltie, and condemned by the people, or by Commissioners deputed by the people, then was he not onely ignominious, but also infamous, and declared incapable euer to beare office: and therfore those which were censured, they were not iudged, but yet they were as a man may say, foreiudged: and if the Censor were an eloquent man, he would oppose himselfe as an accuser of those that would seeke to bee restored against his censure: as *Cato* did against *Lucius Flaminius*, making an oration against his filthy and disordred life, hauing rased him out of the register of Senators. But those that were better aduised, and had some hope of restitution, sued for some office, or honorable commission from the people, the which if they obtained, they were freed from all censure of ignominie, or else they were restored by the other Censors fiue yeares after: if hee did performe neither the one nor the other, he was not admitted into the Senat: neither could a horseman recouer his horse nor his ranke. And (*Vlpianus* speaking of these men) doubts whether they are to be admitted as witnesses. And for the better confirmation hereof, *Cicero* brings in an example of *Caius Geta*, who was excluded the Senate by the Censors, and yet afterwards he was chosen Censor: and a little after speaking of censuring, he saith, That the auntients would haue the Censors office to carrie a certaine feare, and not a punishent. The which was partly the cause why the *Claudian* law was disanulled, the which would not haue any Senator excluded the Senat, nor rased out of the registers, if he were not accused before both by the Censors, and condemned by either of them, the which had imbased the office of Censor, being so reuerend, as the Senate of Rome would not permit the Censors (after their charge expired) to bee accused, or called in question for anie thing that they had done during their charge: the which was lawfull against all other magistrats. And it seemes for the same reason the Emperour *Constantine* did teare the libels of accusation propounded against the Surueilans or Ouerseers at the Councell of Nice, saying, That he would not iudge them that were Censors of euerie mans life. And for the same cause *Charlemaine* in his constitutions hath made a Canon, That no prelate should be iudged without 72 witnesses, freeing the Pope from the censure of any man: the which hath bene obserued vntill the councell of Constance, where it was decreed, That the Pope should be iudged by the Councell. I will not heere dispute if the ecclesiasticall iurisdiction be well grounded; but it is to be feared, that hauing presumed so much, they are likely to lose both iurisdiction & all ecclesiasticall censure, the which hath alwaies bene of great consequence: for euen as the auntient Druides (who were antient Iudges and Prelats in Gaule) did excommunicat kings and princes that would not obey their decrees, euen so the ecclesiasticall censure amongst Christians, hath not onely maintained discipline and good manners for many

A censure is no iudgement.

Pro Cluentio.

Cæsaris Comment.

A2 (margin) notantur   C5 And Vlpianus (speaking   C10 punishment   D2 before both of the Censors   D3 either of them *i.e.* each of them (cf. Fr and L)   Notes at A2, C6.

many ages, but hath also made Tyrants to tremble, and reduced Kings and Emperours vnto reason, pulling oftentimes their crownes from their heads, and their scepters out of their hands, forcing them to make peace or warre, to chaunge their dissolute life, to do justice, and to reforme the lawes. All the histories are full, but there is none so famous, as of Saint *Ambrose*, who did censure *Theodosius* the Great, and *Nicholas* 1 Pope, who censured *Lothaire* King of Italy: and *Innocent*, who did excommunicate *Lewis* 7 King of Fraunce, to whom for three yeres space no priest durst administer the Sacrament.

True it is, that the abuse of a censure of so great consequence, hath made the ministers, the discipline, and their censure to be contemned, the which consisted in interdiction, suspension, and excommunication: for many vppon light causes, and without cause did excommunicate, yea they haue set downe 39 causes wherin a man did incurre excommunication *ipso facto*, without iudgement or sentence; and which is more, they did excommunicate Corporations, Colleges, Vniuersities, Emperours, Kings, and Kingdomes, without distinction of age, sexe, innocents, or mad men, although since (but too late) they haue somewhat corrected this abuse: but in this kingdome it was decreed by the statutes of Orleance, that they should not vse any excommunication, but in crimes and publike scandall. The Prelats, Bishops, and Popes, haue alwayes pretended the censure of manners and religion to belong vnto them, as a thing whereof judges and magistrats take no knowledge, but in case of execution. And since the auntients and ouerseers haue vsed the like prerogatiue in many places, a thing which is verie necessary, if there be no Censors, as well to reforme the peoples manners, and to watch ouer them, as to countenance the dignity of Pastors Bishops and Ministers, whom we cannot esteeme and honour too much, for the charge and dignitie which they beare; God did wisely prouide, making choice of his ministers, and giuing the prerogatiue of honour vnto the tribe of *Leui*, aboue all the tribes, and to the family of *Aaron*, of the which the Priests only were, aboue all the Leuits, giuing them the tenths of cattell, fruits, and of all heritages, with great honours and priuiledges: and by an article of the law of God it is said, That he that shall disobey the sentence of the high Priest, shall be put to death. And they that shall abase the estate of the Ministers, Bishops, and Auncients, and seeke to take from them, all ecclesiasticall censure, with their goods and honours, to see them poore and scorned, they contemne God, and regard not religion, the which is a matter verie considerable: and it was partly the chiefe cause, why the chiefe Minister of Losanna forsooke the towne, for that the heads of the Cantons could not indure that the Antients should haue the censuring of manners: yet the one is most necessarie in euerie well gouerned commonweale, either to create Censors, or to submit themselues to the censure of the Bishops.

Deut. 17.

The pouertie and contempt of the ministers makes religion to bee contemned.

The Seigneurie of Geneue reserues this prerogatiue to their Bishops, Ministers, and Auntients, to haue the priuiledge of a Corporation, and to censure the liues, and manners of men in their consistorie, and yet without any iurisdiction to commaund, or to execute their sentences, either by themselues, or by the officers of the Seigneurie, but for disobedience they excommunicate him, a matter of greater consequence: for the person excommunicated, after a certayne time is pursued criminally before the magistrate, by the Inquisitour of the faith, as in the catholike church, but not so soone: for there hath beene some one excommunicate fifteene yeeres, and afterwards conuented before the Inquisitor of the faith, who meant to proceed against him, hee hath appealed to the Parliament, where his appellation was

OF A COMMONWEALE. 649

was reiected, & he condemned in a fine, decreeing, that he should be seized on, and carried to the Bishops prison, commaunding the Inquisitor to proceed in his triall, euen vnto a definitiue sentence, and to certifie the Court. It was in those daies, when as it was lawfull to excommunicate any man euen for pettie debts, although the debtors had made it knowne that they had not any thing. But after the edict made at Orleance, and confirmed by the Parliament, the Bishops and Auntients could not vse such censures within this realme. At Lions Mr *de Moulin* was much discontented against the consistorie, saying, That vnder colour of their censure they attempted vppon the temporall iurisdiction, and yet hee blamed it in the catholike church. But taking away suspension, interdiction, and excommunication, the ecclesiasticall censure is of no force, and by the same inconuenience, good manners and discipline is abolished: but there is no reason, that for disobedience in slight matters, they should vse such censures.

The auntient Censors did set notes and marks vppon the registers against those that deserued it, to aduertise their successors in their charge of those that were so noted, if they did not amend. In my opinion that should suffice, and not to proceed against them by any amercements, or to excommunicate them for want of paiment. I leaue it to the wise to decide, whether it bee better to diuide the temporall censure (touching maners & other things aboue specified) from the ecclesiasticall censure, or to ioyne them together. But yet it were better to allow both to the Bishops & Antients, than to take all from them, and thereby to depriue the commonwale of that which is most necessarie: for wee see those estates which doe vse it, to flourish in lawes and good manners: we see whooredome, vsurie, mummeries, and excesse in all things rooted out, the blaspheamer, ruffian, and idle vagabound banished; and without doubt, those commonweales which shall vse such censure, shall continue and flourish in all vertues: they which neglect lawes, vertue, and religion, will bee contemned, as it happened in Rome not long before the ruin of the empire; when as in stead of Censors, they created an office which they called The Tribune of Plaisirs, as we may note in *Cassiodorus*. But for that the Censors office was first instituted in regard of taxes, subsidies and imposts, and to make a stocke for publike necessities, let vs also speake of treasure.

Chap. II.

Of Treasure.

IF Treasure be the sinewes of a commonweale, as an auntient Orator said, it is verie necessary to haue the true knowledge thereof, first to see by what honest meanes to gather money together; secondly, to imploy it to the profit and honour of the commonweale; and lastly, to spare and to reserue some part for all needfull euents, least the publike treasurie being exhaust, the commonweale might bee oppressed with sudden calamitie. We will therefore handle these three poynts euerie one in order.

Mony the sinewes of a Commonweale.

Touching the first poynt. There are many craftsmasters in matters of imposts, which know many meanes to raise vp great summes of money, but they neuer had the true knowledge of honour and honestie. But leauing these cunning politicians I will follow those, who as they haue had a great care of the treasure, so haue they sought by honest meanes to increase the reuenues of the commonweale, least the citie by want should be drawne into danger, and the prince forced by vnlawfull meanes

Kkk to

Note at C6.

650   THE SIXT BOOKE

to sucke the priuat wealth and bloud of his subiects, as it hath happened to those that seemed best acquainted with politike affaires: amongst the which the Lacedemonians are named, whom not content with their owne territories, as their master *Licurgus* had taught them, taking from them all vse of gold and siluer, inioyning them to make money of iron, least that strangers should grow in loue with the Lacedemonians countrie, or they with that of strangers, supposing thereby not onely to free his citisens from iniuries, but also from forraine vices: But they had no sooner past their frontiers but they fell to borrowing, some of the king of Persia, as *Lysander* and *Callicratides*: some of the king of Egypt, as *Agesilaus*, and *Cleomenes*, kings of Lacedemon. For which cause the Seigniorie of Sparta hauing soone wonne all Greece, and gathered together a great masse of treasure, they decreed, That all the gold and siluer which they had taken from their enemies, should be kept in the publike Treasurie, to serue them at their need, with defence not to vse it for anie priuat occasion: but their treasure without ground or supply beeing soone wasted, they were forced to returne to borrowing to make warre (the which is not entertayned and maintayned by diet, as an auntient Captaine said) whereby their commonweale decaied vnder king *Cleomenes*. Euerie commonweale therefore must prouide to haue their treasure built of a sure and durable foundation. There are onely seuen meanes in generall for the making of a publike treasure, in the which all other are conteined. The first is, by the reuenues of the commonweale: The second, by conquest from the enemie: The third, by the liberalitie and gift of friends: The fourth by the pensions & tribute of their alies: The fifth, vpon traffike: The sixt, vpon marchants, which bring in and carrie out marchandise: And the seuenth vppon the subiects imposts.

Touching the first, which growes by the reuenues, there is not any seemes to mee more honest & sure. So we read that all the antient monarchs and law-giuers, which builded new cities, or transported new colonies, they assigned (besides the streets, temples, theaters, & the possessions of priuat men) certaine places fit for the commonweale, and free to all in generall; the which were called Commons, and let out to priuate men for a certaine time, or for euer, paying a yeerely rent into the Treasurie or Exchequer, to supply the charges of the commonweale. We read that *Romulus* the founder of Rome & of the Roman commonweale, diuided all the lands into three parts; appoynting a third for the temporall of the Church, a third for the rents of the commonweale, and the surplusage to be deuided among priuat men, the which at that time were three thousand citisens, euerie one of the which hauing two iournies, or acres of land: so as of eighteene thousand iournies or acres of land, lying in the territories of Rome, they reserued six thousand for the sacrifices, six thousand for the reuenues of the commonweale and intertainment of the kings house, and six thousand for the citisens. Yet *Plutarch* sets downe twise as manie citisens, and saith that *Romulus* would set no limits of the territorie of Rome, lest it should be seene what he had vsurp'd from his neighbours, and that his successor *Numa* diuided the reuenues to poore citisens: but the first opinion is the more likely and the more common; for the deuision of two iournies or acres continued a long time, as *Pliny* saith, speaking to *Cincinatus* the Dictator, the which was two hundred and threescore yeares after *Romulus: Aranti sua duo iugera Cincinato viator inquit, vela corpus & audi mandata Senatus: Cincinatus* plowing his two acres, Passenger (saith he) vncouer thy bodie, and heare the commaundements of the Senat. And *Denis Halicarnasseus* holds the first opinion; hee was in houshould with *Marcus Varro*, the true Register of all Roman antiquities. But since by the law *Licinia*, euerie citisen was allowed to haue

seuen

Polib. l. 6. de milit. ac domest. Rom. disciplina.

War is not maintained by a diet.

Seuen meanes to gather treasure.

Reuenues the chiefest meanes to make a treasure.

The deuision of the lands about Rome.

The first beginning of publike rents.

G2 silver   K4–5 *For* speaking to *read* speaking of (cf. Fr).   Notes at G10, H8, K7, K8.

seuen journies or acres of land. If it be true which wee read in *Pliny*, or *Collumella*: *Post exactos Reges Liciniana illa septem iugera, quæ plebis Tribunus viritim diuiserat, maiores questus antiquis retulêre, quàm nunc nobis præbent amplissima veruacta*, After the expulsion of the kings, those seuen acres which the Tribune deuided to euerie one by the law *Licinia*, did yeeld our auncestours more profit, than now our large fields. And the oration of *Marcus Curius* is well knowne, noting him as a pernitious citisen that could not be contented with seuen acres. In this diuision *Romulus* did imitate the Egyptians, who in old time diuided all the reuenues of Egypt into three parts: The first was for the sacrifices and sacrificers; The second, to entertaine the kings house, and to defray the publike charges; And the third for the Calasiris, the which were the men of warre, alwaies entertained to serue at need: all the other citisens were either husbandmen, or slaues. Wee read also, that *Ezechiel*, in reforming the abuses of the princes of the Hebrewes, appoynted certaine lands for the sacrifices, some common for the people, besides the reuenues for the entertainement of the kings house, and to serue for publike expences. To the end (saith hee) that the princes shall no more grieue my people with exactions and imposts. Although from the beginning of the Israelits kingdome, the kings had some reuenues; for the towne of Ziceleg, with some land being giuen to *Dauid* by king *Achis*, continued for euer as part of the kings reuenues, and was neuer alienated. Of the regall reuenues some are publike, some are priuate, the last may bee sould and made away, the first neuer. And to the end that princes should not bee forced to ouercharge their subiects with imposts, or to seeke any vnlawfull meanes to forfeit their goods, all Monarchs and States haue held it for a generall and vndoubted law, That the publike reuenues should be holy, sacred, and inalienable, either by contract or prescription. In like sort, kings (especially in this realme) graunting their Letters pattents for the reunion of crowne lands, declare, that they haue taken an oath comming to the crowne, in no sort to sell or make away the reuenues: and although it were duely and directly made away, were it for euer, yet is it alwayes subiect to bee redeemed, and in such sort as the prescription of a hundred yeares, which giues a iust title to the possessor, doth not touch the reuenues of the crowne. The edicts, decrees, and ordinances of this realme are notorious, not onely against priuate men, but euen against princes of the bloud, who haue beene put from the deuision of the reuenues, & the prescription of a hundred yeres. And this is not peculiar to this realme alone, but common to the kings of England, Spayne, Poland, and Hungarie, who are accustomed to sweare not to alienate the reuenues of the crowne. The which is also obserued in popular & Aristocritall states: and euen at Venice the law allowes no prescription (the which many would limit to six score yeares:) nor yet the Cantons of the Swissers: for king *Henry* 2 hauing requested the Siegniorie of Lucerne to ingage themselues for a certaine summe of money, *Hugo* the chiefe magistrat made answere vnto the Ambassador, That both the Senat and Commons of Lucerne had sworne, neuer to pawne nor ingage their lands. Wee read also, that the same ordinances were religiously obserued in two the most goodly commonweales that euer were, Athens and Rome, whereas two great personages, *Themistocles* and *Cato* the Censor, caused all the publike reuenues to bee seized on, the which had through tract of time, and sufferance of magistrats beene vsurped by priuate men, saying in their orations, *Nec mortales contra deum immortalem, nec priuatos contra Rempub. præscribere posse*, That mortall men could neuer prescribe against the immortall God, nor priuate men against the commonweale. And therefore the court of Parliament vppon a ciuill request obtained by the kings Proctor generall, against

The publike reuenues by nature are inalienable.

Nulla præscriptio occurrit Regi.

Plut. in Catone Censorio, & Themist.

a decree

652   THE SIXT BOOKE

a decree made in fauour of the successors of *Fælix* of Nogaret, to whom king *Philip* the faire 260 yeares before had giuen the lands and Seigniorie of Caluisson, for his vertues and well deseruing of the commonweale, whereby it was reuoked vnto the Councell: shewing therby that prescription hath no place, when there is any question of the reuenues of the crowne. And the court of Parliament at Rouan, by a sentence giuen the 14 of Februarie, 1511, betwixt the kings proctor and the religious of S. *Omer*, adiudging the possession of certaine goods vnto the king, allowing the religious to releeue themselues by some other meanes, and to proue it duely, by way of inquest, *and for cause*, which words (and for cause) are not to bee vnderstood for the poore subiects of the countrie onely, but generally for all. And oftentimes the treaties made betwixt princes haue no other difficulties, but for the preseruation of the reuenues, the which princes cannot alienate to the preiudice of the publike. *Henry 8* king of England in a treatie made with the Pope and potentates of Italy, in the yeare 1527, caused this clause to be added, That they might not giue away any thing of the crowne of Fraunce, for the redeeming of king *Frauncis*: and vpon this poynt the breach of the treatie of Madrid was grounded, for that the auncient custome of this realme, conformable to the edicts or ordinances of other nations, requires the consent of the three estates: the which is obserued in Poland, by a law made by *Alexander* king of Poland, according to the disposition the common law, vnlesse the sale were made at such time as the enemy had inuaded the countrie: and that the forme be obserued from poynt to poynt, as in the alienation of pupils goods (the commonweale being alwayes regarded as a pupill) and if there be any thing omitted, it is all of no force, or at the least it is subiect to rescission, without restitution vnto the purchasor of the thing purchased. Neyther can the prince challenge that vnto himselfe which belongs vnto the publike, no more than a husband can his wiues dowrie, wherin the prince hath lesse right; for the husband may abuse the fruits of his wiues dowrie at his pleasure, but a prince may well vse, but not abuse the fruits of a publike dowrie: as the citisens that were in societie with the Athenians complained, that the publike money was to be put in *Apolloes* treasury, and not to be wasted by the Athenians.

L. si secundum C. de iure Reip.

Our kings haue and doe acknowledge, that the proprietie of the crowne lands is not the princes: for king *Charles* the 5 and 7, would not haue the crowne lands pawned, vnlesse the Parliament at the instance of the kings Proctor had so decreed, as we may see in the auntient registers of the court of Parliament, and chamber of accounts; and the reason is, for that the reuenues belong vnto the commonweale, as wise princes haue alwaies acknowledged: & when as king *Lewis* the 8 died (hauing giuen much by his testament to poore widdowes and orphans) hee commaunded all his jewels and moueables to be sould to performe his legacies, least that any thing belonging to the crowne should be sould, as hauing no interest in it. And for this cause *Pertinax* the Roman Emperour caused his name being written vppon the publike lands, to be rased out, saying, That it was the very inheritance of the commonweale, and not the Emperours, although they enioy the rents for the maintenance of their houses and the commonweale. And we doe also read, that *Antonius Pius* liued of his owne inheritance, applying nothing that belonged to the publike, to his priuat vse: whom king *Lewis* 12 (called the father of his countrie) doth seeme to imitate, who would not mingle his patrimony & reuenues, with that of the publike; erecting the chamber of Blois for his lands at Blois, Coussy, and Montfort: and yet many haue erroniously confounded the publike with the princes priuate lands. Neyther is it lawfull for soueraigne princes to abuse the fruits and reuenues of

The publike reuenues and the princes patrimony differ.

F7 *For* goods *read* woods (*bois* in Fr).   F9 duely, OTHERWISE THAN by way of inquest (Fr only)
G9 disposition OF the common   K3 *For* Antonius (L 1-2) *read* Antoninus (L 3-5 and Fr).
                                                                        Note at F1.

Of A Commonweale.

A of the crowne lands, although the commonweale be in quiet and free from all trouble; for that they haue the vse onely, and ought (the commonweale and their house being maintained) to keepe the surplusage for publike necessitie: although that *Pericles* said to the Ambassadours of the confederats, That they had no interest in the imployment of the treasure, so as they were maintayned in peace: for it was contained in the treatie of aliance, that the money which should be raised in the time of peace, should be gared in *Apolloes* temple, and that it should not bee imployed but by a common consent. But there is great difference betwixt the Treasurie or Exchequer in a monarchy, and in popular states: for a prince may haue a treasurie of his priuate patrimony, the which was called *Fiscus* by the Auntients, and that of
B the publike reuenues *Aerarium*: the one being diuided from the other by the auntient lawes, the which can haue no place in a popular or Aristocraticall estate. Yet there neuer wanted flatterers to persuade princes to sell the reuenues of the crowne to make a greater benefit; the which is a tyrannical opinion, and the ruine of a commonweale: for it is well knowne, that the publike reuenues consist chiefly in that which Dukes, Marqueses, Earles, and Barons did sometimes possesse, the which, either by succession, dowrie, or by confiscation, haue come vnto the state in Lordships, coppiholds, in fees, alienations, sales, seazures, rents, amercements, rights, confiscations, and other regalities, the which are not subiect to imposts and ordinarie charges, and oftentimes are gotten by them which are free from all charges.
C Moreouer, commissions graunted to sell the publike reuenues, for the making of money speedily, allow it to be sould for ten yeares purchase, when as priuate lands in fee with iustice are sould for thirtie yeares purchase, and those that haue dignities at fiftie yeres and more: so as some with purchase of the publike lands, reape in one yeare more profit by the iurisdiction, than they paid for the land. Others haue paid nothing at all, taking the valuation of the reuenue by extracts from the Chamber of accounts, giuen in by the receiuers in ten yeares, who oftentimes haue not receiued any thing, for that the profit of inferiour iustice is made in the chiefe and regall court. As for sales, the purchaser hath more profit, than the interest of the money
D which they haue payed can amount vnto: as also the receiuers of the reuenues are not accustomed to giue any account of casualties, but for a small part. But in farming out the crowne lands, the farmours are lyable to subsidies, and are charged according to their abilities.

There are infinite more abuses which the commonweale sustaines by the sale of their reuenues, but the greatest is, that the money which is made is not put out to rent (like vnto those that thinke to be good husbands) but is most commonly wasted and giuen vnto them that haue least deserued, and so for want of money to redeeme this land, the commonweale falles to decay: then doe they also sell the commons wherby the poore are releeued. It were more fit to sell the waste lands of the com-
E monweale, the which no man will hire, and brings no benefit to the commonweale, to the end the Treasury may bee enriched, and that the citisens may profit by the tilling thereof: but if they may haue a farmour, it is not lawfull to sell it, although that *Aristotle* commends them of Constantinople, who sould their lands for a continuall rent, the which is a meere alienation, and money taken before, diminisheth the rent: the which was expressely defended by an edict made by *Charles* the ninth. And although that afterwards he made an other edict for the renting out of waste lands, and paying of fines, by the persuasion of such as sought to make money: yet the Parliament of Paris vpon the verification of the said edict, decreed, That the rents should not be redeemed, and that there should bee no fine payed at

the

Margin notes:
- Ascenius et vlp. in l.2. §. hoc interdictum. Ne quid in loco pub.
- By the edict of Francis I, in the yeare 1544.
- The great preiudice that comes by publike sales.
- The waste lands may be sold.

A7 For gared *perhaps read* garded *or even* stored (*mises en depost* in Fr). B2 (margin) loco B7 the state; in

654　　　　　　　　　　　　　　　　　　The Sixt Booke

the beginning; and for that the Commissioners for this sale did sue vnto the King that it might bee lawfull to giue money at the entry, the Court (all the Chambers being assembled) decreed, That the purchasers might not giue aboue a third of the summe at the entry, in regard of the value of the lands: the which third part should be receyued by the Receyuers of the reuenues apart, to bee imployed to redeeme the reuenues that were sould, imposing a quadruple penaltie to bee leuied, as well vppon the receyuers, as of those that had gotten any assignation of the said money. And it is not heere needfull to relate what losses the king and commonweale haue sustayned by such alienations of waste lands. King *Frauncis* the second comming to the crowne, commaunded his Proctors and magistrats to redeeme the publike reuenues from priuate occupiers: wherein he complayned, that the crowne lands and reuenues were so dismembred and wasted, as that which remayned did not suffice for the charges that were laid vpon them. But our king hath farre greater cause to complayne now, when as there scarce remaynes any thing that is to bee sould. In the generall accounts of the treasure made in Ianuary, in the yeare 1572, there was no receit made of any reuenues, although there were six & thirtie thousand crownes a yeare in the receit, when as king *Frauncis* died, as it appeareth by an account of the treasure made in the yeare 1569: and by the same estate the alienation of the reuenues, impositions, and subsidies amounted to fourteene millions nine hundred sixtie and one thousand foure hundred and seuentie liures, fifteene soulz, and eight deniers; not comprehending twelue hundred thousand liures for the fourth and halfe fourth, and foure hundred and fiftie thousand liures, in regard of fifteene liures vppon the strike of salt, the which the country of Guienne redeemed in the yeares 1549 and 1553. whereby is plainely appeares, that the kings reuenues are almost all ingaged and made away, for fifteene or sixteene millions at the most, the which is worth aboue fiftie millions: for that Earledomes, Baronies, and other Seigniories haue not beene sould for aboue nine yeares purchase: and if it were redeemed and let to farme, it would amount yearely to almost three millions, the which would suffice to entertaine the kings house in state, and to pay most of the officers their wages, not medling with any of the other ordinarie or extraordinarie charges. And if wee may compare a small kingdome with a greater, the reuenues of the crowne of England, comprehending the land subsidies, taxes, customes, imposts, and all other charges, amount to little more than sixscore and ten thousand pounds starling a yeare, hauing a good part of the temporall lands of the church annexed vnto it, and yet the Queene doth maintayne her Court and the estate of her realme verie royally, and redeemed the reuenues.

True it is, that a setled peace for these fifteene yeres hath much preuailed for the maintenance of the state of England; and warre for the ruine of Fraunce, if God had not sent our King *Henrie* 3 from heauen to restore it to his first beautie. But we must obserue that for the preseruation of the reuenues of a commonweale, most commonly that of a monarchy is better hnsbanded than in a popular state, or in that which is gouerned by few of the better sort; whereas the magistrats and ouerseers of the treasure conuert the publike to their owne priuate profit: and euery one striues to gratify his friends, or to purchase the peoples fauour with the preiudise of the commonweale: as *Cæsar* did in his first Consulship, who deuided the territory of Capua among the people, and abated the rents of the farmes a third part, after that hee had beene well bribed. And ten yeares after *Quintus Metellus* Tribune of the people, to winne their fauour, published a law to take away the toles in all the ports of Italy. In like sort, *Pericles* to haue credit with the people of Athens, made distribu-

Margin notes:
- 7. May 1566.
- In the yeare 1559
- In the yeare 1572
- What the alienation of the reuenues of Fraunce amount vnto. A liure is two shillings.
- The reuenues of the realme of England. Herein the Author is deceeiued.
- In a popular state the reuenues are ill husbanded.

G8 For 1569 *read* 1560.　G9–H1 fourteene millions ... eight deniers: 14,961,087 livres 15 sous 8 deniers (Fr) 14,960,087 livres (L)　H4 it plainely　I10 For his first beautie *probably read* its first beautie (cf. Fr).　K2 husbanded　　　　　Notes at F4(margin), I8, K4.

A distribution of great summes of money, the which had come into the treasure. This happens not in a monarchie, for Monarchs which haue no more certaine reuenues than their lands, and that haue no power to impose subsidies or other charges vpon their subiects but with their owne consents, or vppon vrgent necessitie, are not so prodigall of their crowne lands. It is not needfull to discourse any further of reuenues, being impossible to order it better than was by the edict of king *Charles* 9 if it were duely executed.

The second meanes to gather treasure together, is by conquest vpon the enemy to recouer the treasure wasted in warre: So did the antient Romans; for although the sacke and spoyle of townes forced, belonged to the Captaines and souldiers, yet
B the treasure was carried into the treasurie of Rome. And as for the townes yeelded or taken by capitulation, the armie had but their pay, and sometimes a double pay, (before that the discipline of war was corrupted) & the treasure of the vanquished was carried to Rome, if they had not otherwise capitulated. All the gold and siluer (saith *Titus Liuius*) and all the brasse that was taken from the Samnites, was carried to the treasurie. And speaking of the Gaules beyond the Alpes, he saith, That *Furius Camillus* catryed into the Capitoll 170000 pounds of siluer which hee had taken from them: and that *Flaminius* caused to bee brought out of Spaine of the spoyles of Greece, the value of three millions & eight hundred thousand crownes, besides siluer, rich moueables, armes and ships. *Paulus Aemilius* brought thrice as
C much out of Macedony. *Cæsar* caused aboue fourtie millions to be deliuered into the publike treasurie, by the report of *Appian*. Wee may see from the 33 booke of *Titus Liuius* to the 34, infinite treasures brought to the Treasurie of Rome of the spoyles of conquered nations. And although all were not brought in by the Generals, yet fearing to bee charged with corruption, or to bee frustrate of their tryumphs, they alwayes deliuered in great summes: for *Scipio Asiaticus* was accused and condemned of corruption, in a great fine, and yet he brought into the treasurie aboue two millions of gold: and *Scipio* the Affrican his brother, was also included in the accusation, although he had brought aboue fiue millions of gold of his
D conquests into the treasurie, besides the value of ten millions and fiue hundred thousand crownes: wherein king *Antiochus* was condemned: by meanes of the victorie they had obtayned, and yet both of them were exiled and died poore. And although that *Lucullus* was the first (as *Plutarch* saieth) that inriched himselfe with the spoyle of his enemies, yet did he bring more into the Treasurie than any of the rest, except *Cæsar*: the which I thought fit to obserue, for that commonly wee imploy the treasure for the charge of the warres, and yet in all victories and conquests there neuer comes a crowne into the Exchequer, and oftentimes the sacke & spoile is giuen before the townes be taken or yeelded.

The Romans were not contented with their treasures and spoyles, but they con-
E demned the vanquished to loose a part of their territories, the which commonly was the seuenth part. Since, some haue bene condemned to loose a fourth or a third part of their lands, as in Italy, beeing subdued by *Odocres* king of the Herules. And soone after *Hortarius* king of the Lumbards condemned the vanquished to pay him yerely the moytie of their reuenues: as also the Romans had done vnto the Doriens long before. But *William* the Conqueror, after he had conquered the realme of England, declared all the countrey in generall, & euery mans inheritance in particular forfeyted vnto him by the law of armes, intreating the Englishmen as his farmours. Yet the Romans haue alwayes shewed themselues courteous and affable in that poynt, sending Colonies from their citie to inhabit the conquered countryes, distributing

The second meanes to gather treasure.

The punishment of the vanquished.

B8 *For* brought out of Spaine *read* brought to the treasury (*à l'Espargne*). C2 *For* 33 booke *read* 23 booke (Fr). D9 (margin) punishment E2 Odocres *i.e.* Odoacer E4 *For* Doriens *read* Boians *i.e.* Boii. Notes at A9, E8.

to euery one a certayne quantitie: and by this meanes they freed their Citie from beggers, mutinies, and idle persons, and did fortifie themselues with their owne men against the vanquished, the which by little and little did linke themselues in marriages, and did willingly obey the Romans, who by this meanes also haue filled the world with their Colonies, with an immortall glory of their iustice, wisdome, and power: wheras most part of conquering princes plant Garrisons, which serue onely to spoyle and oppresse the subiects. If our kings after the taking of Naples and Milan had practised this course, they had yet continued in obedience to our kings. And it is no maruell if they reuolt against the Spanyard vppon the first occasion, as well as the countrey of Flaunders hath done, hauing nothing but Garrisons there without Colonies. Yet wee find, that *Sultan Mahumet* king of the Turkes, found meanes to inrich his treasure by meanes of Christian slaues, which hee sent in Colonies into conquered countries, giuing to euery one fifteene acres of land and two oxen, and seed for one yeare: and at the end of twelue yeares he tooke the moytie of their fruits, the which hee continued for euer. *Amurath* the first dealt more mildly with the Timariots, giuing them certayne lands and rents, to some more, and to others lesse, vpon condition they should attend him in the wars when they were called, with a certayne number of horse: and if the Timariot chanced to die, the fruits should acrue vnto the Prince, vntill that hee had aduaunced some other, by way of gift. And generally the tenth of all successions belonged to the prince (the which grew by the law of armes, and by the princes conquering another mans countrey) and not by way of imposition vppon the auntient subiects. Whereby it appeareth, that the greatest and clearest reuenues which the Turke hath, are in manner casuall, and the warre is defrayed without any new charge.

The kings of Castile haue done in manner the like at the West Indies, and namely the Emperour *Charles* 5, hauing conquered Peru, gaue the lands to the Captaines and Spanish souldiers by way of gift onely; and beeing dead, they returned to the Emperour, vntill that another were aduaunced in his place: taking moreouer the fift of all the pearle and mynes; so as euerie two yeares there comes clearely into the kings treasurie in Spayne, neere foure millions of gold, the which is called, The port of Ciuill. But it is reason, that the conquests which are made vpon the enemie, and which augment their treasure, should also ease their subiects: as they did in Rome after the conquest of the realme of Macedon, the Romans were freed from taxes, imposts, and subsidies.

The third meanes to augment the treasure, is by liberalitie of friends or subiects, be it by legacie, or by donation during life: the which wee will speake briefly of, for that it is vncertaine, besides there are few princes that giue, and fewer that receiue without requitall: for if a prince giues to one that is more rich and mightie, it seemes it is for feare, or vpon some bond, & somtimes he that receiues it, accounts it as a tribute. The Emperour of the Turkes sets to the view of all the world, as well those presents which are sent him from his friends, as those that come from tributaries, to shew how much hee is feared of strangers; defraying the Ambassadors charges with great bountie, the which neuer prince nor people did. But we find that the Auntients vsed an other kind of bountie and liberalitie than they doe at this day: for at this day they giue not often but to such as are in greatnesse and prosperitie, and the Auntients gaue in aduersitie. When as *Hannibal* had in a manner quite vanquished the Romans, and taken from them almost all Italy, the king of Egypt sent the value of 400 thousand crownes to Rome in pure gift; the which the Romans refused, giuing great thanks to the king. They did the like
to

The great benefit which growes by Colonies.

Pessimus diuturnitatis custos est metus.

The Turks order to make mony, & for the warre.

The Emperors order at Peru.

The third meanes to gather treasure.

The magnificence of the Emperours of Turky.

F2 For mutinies *probably read* mutines *i.e.* seditious persons (cf. Fr).   I1 Civill *i.e.* Seville
I6 (margin) meanes   Notes at F5, K3.

to *Hierom* king of Sicile, who gaue them a crowne of gold waying 320 pound, and a Victorie of gold, with fiue thousand bushels of wheat: but they accepted nothing but the image of Victory as a happy presage. They shewed the same resolutions to the Ambraciotes, and to many other Princes and Seigniories, who at that time offered them great presents, although they were in extreme necessitie: so as there was a combate of honour, in the one to giue, and in the other to refuse. But the Romans haue surmounted all other nations in courage and resolution in their aduersities: as for other princes and people they were not so nice to take, yea oftentimes they demaunded; as the Seigniorie of the Rhodes, when their Colossus fell downe & brake some of their ships, they sent Ambassadors to kings and princes to beg, hauing small meanes, and it succeeded well: for king *Hierom* sent them threescore thousand crownes in guift, and many others imitated him: yea the king of Egypt gaue them in gold the value of eighteen hundred thousand crowns, and in siluer much more, with twentie thousand bushels of wheat, and three thousand beasts for sacrifices, besides great store of stuffe, and an infinite number of Architects and workemen the which hee entertayned at his owne charge for the building of a Colledge: so as the Seigniorie of Rhodes for an old broken image, and some crased ships, were greatly enriched by the bountie of other princes. *A good policie of the Rhodiots.*

It was common to the kings of Egypt to glorie in their bountie to others: for wee read in a manner the like of *Ptolomie* the first, toward the citie and inhabitants of Ierusalem, to whom he sent the value of two hundred threescore and sixteene thousand crownes, to redeeme a hundred thousand slaues of their nation; and ninetie thousand crownes for the sacrifices, besides a table of massy gold to set in Gods Temple: and the great presents he gaue to the 72 Interpreters, which translated the Bible out of Hebrew into Greeke. And as it was and will be alwayes tollerable for pettie princes and small Siegniories to accept the honorable gifts of great princes and monarchs: so was it conuenient for the Romans to refuse such liberalities (and to beg it had beene infamous) and to accept, by guift or legacie, great realmes and royall successions; which they gaue them which had raigned peacefully vnder their protections, for an honest recompence of their justice, when as they died without heires males lawfully begotten. By this meanes *Ptolomie* king of Cyrene, *Attalus* king of Asia, *Eumenes* king of Pergame, *Nicomedes* king of Bithinia, *Coctius* king of the Alpes, and *Polemon* king of Pontus, left the people of Rome heires of their goods & kingdoms. As for guifts from the subiect, the which the antients called oblations, there were few or none at all: for charitable gifts which be voluntarie, are now demaunded: and although the kings of Spaine, England and others vse intreaties to obtaine them, yet most commonly there is more force in these requests, than in commissions and letters of commaundement. I vnderstand by the word Gift, that which is liberally offered by the subiect vnto his prince; as the gold which they called *Coronarium*, the which the Iewes gaue vnto the Emperours, to be maintayned in the priuileges of their religion; and the magistrats of the townes and communalties of the empire: the which in time proued a forced subsidy, vntill that this force was taken away, the guifts remaining voluntary to gratyfie the Emperour, when as hee had obtayned any victorie against his enemies. *Ioseph in antiq*

Six kingdomes giuen to the Romans by legacie.

Voluntary gifts of the subiects.

The like may bee sayed of the imposts which in Spayne they call Seruice, the which was freely graunted to the kings of Spayne to entertayne their estate more honorably; and since it was almost conuerted into an ordinary charge. Wee find likewise *Seruice of Spaine.*

A1 *For* Hierom *read* Hieron (Fr) i.e. Hiero.   B5 *For* beasts *read* bushels (cf. Fr and L).
C1 *For* Ptolomie the first (Fr) *read* Ptolomie Philadelphus (L).   C2-3 two hundred threescore and sixteene thousand crownes (Fr) 176,000 crowns (L)   C4 massy i.e. solid   Notes at A2, D6, D10.

likewise that the kings of Persia contented themselues with the voluntary gifts and presents of diuers kinds that came from their subiects: but *Darius Histaspes* (he that got the kingdome by the neying of his horse) chaunged those kinds into coynes of gold and siluer, and the gifts into tributes and necessary charges, appoynting Treasurers and Receyuers in euerie gouernment (which were 127 in number) to make a diuision of the taxes and subsidies, which amounted then to foureteene thousand fiue hundred and threescore Euboique talents, the which is valued at ten millions one hundred fourescore and twelue thousand crownes. But this antient custome of Persia is maintayned at this present in Æthiopia, whereas the gouernours of fiftie gouernments bring vnto the *Negus*, king of Æthiopia, the gifts and oblations of his subiects in graine, wine, cattell, handy works, gold and siluer, without any other commission, or letters patents: so as for the greatnes of his maiesty, it is more befitting to haue them obedient vnto him, than to send foorth his commissions to exact and beg of his subiects. As for successions and testamentary legacies giuen to princes by their subiects, it is at this day very rare, and yet in old time it was one of the greatest meanes whereby princes did augment their treasures: for wee read that the Emperour *Augustus* hauing giuen by will the value of eleuen millions and two hundred thousand crownes to be distributed among the people of Rome, and the legions; he withall protested, that he left not to his heyres but three millions and seuen hundred thousand crownes, although he shewed, that he had receyued from his friends not many yeares before his death, the summe of thirtie and fiue millions of crownes. True it is, that hee was accustomed to leaue vnto the children of the Testators, the legacies and successions that were giuen him, neuer taking any thing of their testaments whom he had not knowne: wherewith *Cicero* reproched *Marc Antonie* in open Senat, That hee had inriched himselfe by their testaments whom hee had neuer knowne; and yet *Cicero* confesseth that hee himselfe had gotten by testaments a million of crownes. But tyrants tooke all without any distinction: for there was no better meanes for any one to assure his testament, than to giue somewhat vnto the tyrant: but if the testament were imperfect, the tyrant seazed vppon the whole succession, the which is reproued by the law, for which cause the custom to make Emperours and Princes their heyres, ceased.

The fourth meanes to augment and intertayne the treasure, is by pensions from their alies, which are payed in time of peace, as well as in warre, for protection and defence against their enemies; or else to haue counsell, ayd, and comfort at need, according to the tenor of the treatie. I say, that a persion is payed by friends and alies; for a soueraigne prince which hath capitulated with another to pay him some thing yearely to haue peace without any treatie of amitie or alyance, is a tributary: as *Antiochus* king of Asia, the Seigniory of Carthage, the kings of Sclauonia, and many other princes and states were tributaries to the Romans, the kings of Arabia and Idumea to *Dauid*, and the princes of Asia to the kings of Persia. And for this reason the treaties of aliance betwixt the house of Fraunce, and the Cantons of the Swissers, specify, That the king shall giue an ordinary pension of a hundred pounds to euery Canton for a peace, and two thousand for an aliance, besides all extraordinary pensions, and their pay in time of warre, & they to do him seruice in his court for the guard of his person: which doeth shew, that the Swissers and Grisons are pensioners to the king, considering the mutuall aliance, and the seruice they owe for this pension. In like sort he is no tributary that corrupteth his enemies Captaynes, as *Pericles* did to the Lacedemonian Captaynes, not (as *Theophrastus* sayd) to purchase a peace, but to deferre the warre. But wee may say, that the Cantons neuer made

---

G9–10 *For* three millions and seven hundred thousand crownes *read* 3,750,000 crownes (Fr).
Note at H6.

OF A COMMONWEALE.   659

made a more profitable league for their estate, both to inrich themselues, & to traine their subiects vp in armes at another mans cost, and also to send swaggerers and idle persons out of their countrie. By the account of him that payed the Cantons, the ordinary and extraordinarie pensions came yearely at the least to six score or seuen score thousand liures: and in the yere 1573 they came to two hundred eighteene thousand liures. The pensions that were payd to the Germaine Commaunders the same yeare, amounted to six score and twelue thousand liures, besides their entertainement in warre. *The Swissers pensions came to 14000. pound sterling a yeare.* *21800 pound.* *12300 pound.*

It is necessarie for great princes to giue pensions to the Secretaries, spies, Captaines, Orators, and houshold seruants of their enemies, to discouer their counsels and enterprises: and experience hath often taught, That there is no greater meanes to maintayne his estate, and to ruine his enemies: for the strongest place is easily taken, so that an asse laden with gold may enter it; as *Philip* the first king of Macedon said, who by his gifts & liberalitie subiected almost all Greece vnto him. And the kings of Persia had no better means to keepe the forces of Grece out of Asia, than by goodly pensions: for it is hard that he which receiueth should not doe some seruice in requitall of his money; for he is tyed by bond, or forced through shame, or mooued with hope of a greater benefit, or with feare least hee that had corrupted him should accuse him: for princes do seldome giue any great pensions vnto strangers, vnlesse they first sweare against their natiue countrie: as a Germane prince sayd at a dyet at Wormes in the yeare 1552. There was the same yeare a prince, who since is dead, the which offered to an Ambassador in his masters name, that for two thousand crownes a yeare pension, he would discouer vnto him all the secrets, practises, and negotiations of his countrie, and to imploy all his meanes to preuent any thing that might be done in preiudice of him that should pay the pension. These men are much to be feared, especially in a popular estate, in the which it is more easie for a few priuat men that gouerne the commonweale to betray it, than in a monarchy, wherein the prince accounts all that is publike his owne, and therefore hath care of it as of his owne. But such rewards and corruptions can neuer bee profitable to them that giue it, if it bee not kept secret, the which is impossible, if there be many. *Plut. in Lisand. & Agesilao.* *Whereunto pensioners are bound.*

The kings of Persia and Macedone gaue none pensions but a small number of Orators and Captaynes of the Grecians: and the king of Egypt for seuen thousand crownes pension, which he gaue to *Aratus*, had the whole estate of the Atheians at his deuotion. And therefore it seemes strange to me, why our kings (besides the ordinary pension of the Swissers) haue giuen extraordinarily to about two thousand of them which exceeded the rest in credit and dignitie; as king *Henrie* the second did, the which were knowne by their names and surnames, and gaue their acquittances; beside the priuate pensions, the which were payed by roll, and came yerely to 49299 liures: happely it had bene better to haue giuen the moity of these pensions to few men of authoritie, and secretly without any acquittance: for sometimes a pensionar had rather lose the greatest reward of any prince, than to giue a note of his hand for the receit of the money: as that English lord *Hastings*, to whom king *Lewis* 11 gaue 2000 crownes pension, the bringer demaunded an acquittance for his discharge onely vnto the king, as he said; whereunto the lord *Hastings* answered, That he would receiue his pension, but he would giue him no acquittance: the which the king demaunded earnestly, to make vse of it in time, and to bring him in suspition of a traitor to his countrie. There are also some things not only secret, but also dishonest, for the which pensions are giuen, although some hold nothing foule nor vnlawfull that is done for the benefit of his country; for my part I hold this fact *4929 pound 4 shillings.*

no

A8(margin) *For* 12300 *read* 13200.   D3 *For* Atheians *read* Achaeans.   D10(margin) *For* 4 shillings *read* 18 shillings.

660 THE SIXT BOOKE

no lesse odious, that shall suborne the houshould seruants of princes to murder their
masters, or if they cannot kill them by force, to poyson them, than hee that shall take
a reward for so fowle a fact. Wherein *Pericles* was commended, who giuing vp his
accounts, set downe an article of ten thousand crownes disbursed without warrant,
shewing neither acquittance nor cause of it: the which the people allowed without
any further inquiry, knowing well the wisdome and loyaltie of the man in the gouernment of the commonweale. It is most certaine, that a secret pensionar giuing
an acquittance, is always in feare to be discouered, whereby hee shall neither dare,
nor be able to doe any thing in fauour of him that giues him a pension. Besides, it
is dangerous when pensions are giuen publikely, the iealousie of such as haue none
will be a cause of quarrels and partialities, as hath oftentimes happened in Swisserland, in such sort, as those which had lesse than others, or none at all, were very vehement to haue the priuat pensions put into the recciuers hands with the generall pensions: the which the king denyed, saying, That he would rather restraine his
liberalitie.

Plut. in Pericl.

The fift meanes to gather together treasure, is by trafike, which the prince or the
state vseth by his factors; although there be few princes that doe vse it: and by the
lawes of this realme, England, and Germanie, it is not lawfull for the gentry to trade
in marchandise, else must he lose his qualitie: and by the law *Claudia*, no Senator of
Rome might haue a vessell at sea contayning aboue fourtie bushels. *Quæstus omnis
(inquit Liuius) patribus indecorus visus est*, All gaine (saith *Titus Liuius*) was held vnseemely for the fathers. And afterwards by the Emperours decrees it was generally defended for all gentlemen and souldiers, and by the Canons for all church men
to trade in marchandise. And the Persians in a mockery called *Darius*, Marchant,
for that he forced them to those charges, which at the first they gaue him voluntar-
rily. But yet in my opinion it is more seemely for a prince to be a marchant, than a
tyrant; and for a gentleman to traffike, than to steale. Who is ignorant, that the kings
of Portugall being restrayned within straight limits and not well able to maintaine
their estates, yet loth to oppresse their subiects, haue for these hundred yeares traded
without reproch, and to the great inriching of their states? In the yeare 1475 they
discouered the rich myncs of gold in Guinee, vnder the conduct of *Iohn* bastard of
Portugall; and twelue yeares after the spices of Calicut, and of the East; and continuing their course to the Indies, haue so wel traffiked there, as they are become lords
of the best ports of Affrike, and haue seazed vppon the Ile of Ormus in despite of
the king of Persia: they haue taken a great part of the kingdome of Marocco, and of
Guinee, & forced the kings of Cambai, Calecut, Malache, and Canauor to do them
homage, treating a league & commerce with the great *Cham* of Tartaria: they haue
pulled from the Turks & Sultans of Egypt the greatest riches of the Indies, and filled
Europe with the treasures of the East, passing euē to the Molucques: which the kings
of Castile pretend to belong to them, by a deuision made by pope *Alexander 6*, notwithstanding the marchants of Genua & Florence desired to free it for 350000 duc-
cats, which *Iohn 3* king of Portugal had paid vnto the emperor *Charles 5*, & to giue
100000 ducats more that they might haue free passage to those ilands which, the K.
of Portugal would not yeld vnto, making acount of the profit he draws from thence
as of an infinit treasure, besides the gaine that comes to his subiects, hauing much impaired the wealth of the princes of the East, & of the Venetians, who haue indured
so great a losse, as of all the calamities they indured during their warres with king
Lewis 12, they receiued no such losse as from the Portugals, taking from them their
gayne of the Easterne parts.

The fift meanes
to gather treasure.

The traffike of the
kings of Portugal

Neyther

G 10 Quæstus   I 6 Cananor   K 3 ilands; which the   Note at G 5.

OF A COMMONWEALE. 661

Neither doth the Trade of Marchandize ingrosse dishonour, or imbase the the Signiories and nobilitie of Italie, neither did *Tully* disallowe of it, but of such as sold by retayle, whome hee tearmed *Sordido*. As for the traffique which Princes practise vpon their Subiects, it is no traffique, but an impost or exaction: which is, to forbid them to trade, and to put his subiects corne and wine into his receiuers handes, to pay them at an vnder rate, and to sell it vnto strangers, or to the Subiects themselues, at his owne pleasure. This was one of the reasons which made *Alphonso* King of Naples most odious; for that he gaue his Swine to his Subiects to make fat, and if by chaunce they died, he made them pay for them: he bought the oyle in Apulia, and gaue his owne price; and the wheat in grasse, and sold it againe at the higgest price he could, forbidding all others to sell vntill he had sold his. But of all the traffiques and marchandize which Princes vse, there is not any more pernitious nor base, than the sale of honors, offices, and benefices, as I haue formerly sayd, the which may neuer be tolerated, but in the extreame necessitie of the Common weale, as the Venetians did, hauing spent in seuen yeres, that *Lewis* 12 made war against them, fiue Millions of Duckats, whereof they had made 50000 Duckats of the sale of Offices. The like reason mou'd King *Frauncis* 1 in the yere 1527, to diuide the Ciuile from the criminall Magistrates, setting all Offices to sale to them that would giue most. The which was more sowle and dishonorable in Pope *Adrian*, who three yeares before, not onely sold offices, but also benefices, as he did the Bishopricke of Cremona for 20200 Duckats, and had also resolued to leaue two hundred and twentie thousand Duckats, by halfe a Duckat for euerie chimney within the territories of the Church, making his pretext of warre against the Turke. But for that these traffiques are so filthie, and of such dangerous consequence, the which being once begun, doe neuer cease, it were better to trie all other meanes, than once to giue way vnto them.

The sixt means to encrease treasure, is vpon the marchandize that are brought in, or carryed out, the which is one of the antientest and most vsuall in euerie Common-weale, and grounded vpon equitie; which kind of custome the Latines called *Portoria*, as they did the tribute of the publique farmes *Decimas*, and of pastures *Scripturam*, and it is reason, that hee that will gaine by another mans subiects, should pay some right to his Prince or Common weale. Wherof there be diuers kindes, the which were reduced within this Realme to one impost of twenty Deniers vpon the liure or pound, by an Edict made by King *Henrie* the 2. and after reuoked, lest the customes and imposts should bee confounded, the which might prooue preiudiciall. King *Charles* 5 abated the custome halfe, but afterwardes he restored it, the which was the twentieth part of the price, or fiue in the hundred, and so the ancient Romanes tooke for custome of forraine marchandize: but afterwards the Emperours exacted the eight part, the which they called *Octuarium vectigal*, as in our time they haue demaunded the twelfe part of the price. The Emperour of Turkie takes ten of the hundred of all Marchant strangers going out of Alexandria, and of his Subiects fiue in the hundred. But in this Realme the contrarie is practised touching the salt, for the which the stranger payes nothing, but the duties of a Marchant, and the subiect payes *fortie* and *fiue liures* vpon the *measure*, contrarie to the Marchants rights. And although the Salt of France bee the best and most plentifull in all Europe, wherewith the lowe Countreys, England, and Denmarke doe store themselues, yet is it farre deerer to vs, than to them: for since that the Store houses of Salt

The Gentlemen of Italie trade in marchandise.

The tyrannicall and base traffique of king Alphonso.

The most pernicious traffick.

The sixt meanes to make money.

Anno 1551. 1556.

Lll were

A1 in grosse A3 Sordidos A8 (margin) base traffique A10–B1 in grasse *i.e.* in the blade
B1 highest B7 *For* 50000 *read* 500000. C2 *For* leave *read* levie. E1 Octauarium E6 *For*
contrarie to *read* in addition to (contre in Fr 7, outre in Fr 1–6, 8).   Notes at A10, D3.

were let out, and the officers of the Custome suppressed, the measure of Salt which the Marchant sold for ten shillings starling, is now come to fiftie foure shillings: and since these warres, to eight pounds besides the Kings rights, and the carriage: so as all comprehended, it hath been sometimes sold for a hundred and eighteene Crownes the measure, whereby the poore subiect hath beene ruined and the stranger enriched, yea sometimes the stranger brings it againe secretly to sell in France. This priuiledge was giuen vnto strangers by *Francis* the 1. that they might bring commodities and money into this Realme, rather than into Spaine: notwithstanding since it hath been verie manifest, that the stranger cannot be without the Salt of *France*: for *Charles* the 5. hauing forbidden his subiects of the lowe Countreys not to fetch any Salt in France, the estates of the countrey made it knowne, that their fish (which is their greatest marchandize) grew drie, and was spoyled with the salt that came from Spaine and Bourgongne, getting leaue with great importunitie to fetch their salt out of France, being the sweeter. It is most certaine that no salt can bee made of salt water on this side the 47 degree, by reason of the cold: and the salt of Spaine is too corosiue: so as if the stranger payd but a fourth part of that which the subiect payes for the Kings rights, there would come an infinite masse of money into the Treasorie, for we often see the ships of England and the low Countreys come into France, onely with their ballast (hauing no commodities to exchange with them) to buy salt, wine, and corne, the which abound in this Realme, and will neuer fayle; whereas the Mynes of mettall, which growe in the bowels of the Earth, are wasted in few yeares: yet strangers seeke it in the center of the earth to bring into this Realme, and to carrie away commodities necessarie for the life of man: which a wise Prince should not suffer to be transported, but for the ease of his subiects, and encrease of his Treasure, the which cannot be done without raysing of the foraine custome: for the greater the forraine custome shall be, the greater benefite shall come into the Exchequer: and if the stranger fearing the impost, shall buy the lesse, then the subiect shall haue it the better cheape; for all wares, the greatest treasures will be where there are most thinges necessarie for the life of man: although there be neither Mynes of gold nor siluer, (as there are fewe or none at all in this Realme,) yet notwithstanding doth feed a great part of Europe as King *Agrippa* sayd; and the countrey of Egypt hath neither Mynes of gold nor siluer, and yet both Affricke and Europe, are much releeued with corne which growes there. If any one will say, that by the treaties of traffique betwixt Princes, they cannot raise a forraine custome, I must answere, that this may take place amonge those which haue treated with that condition, but there are few of them; and yet it hath neuer been much regarded: for euen in the lowe countreys and in England, the french Marchants were forced in the yeare 1557 to pay a crowne vpon euerie tunne of wine that came into the port, and the subiects payd nine french crownes for the impost, without any regard to the treatise of trafficke. And the yeare following, the the Queene of England did raise the forraine custome a third part, imposing thirteene shillings and a pennie vpon euerie peece of cloth, the which is a matter of great consequence: and I haue been assured from a Marchant of Antwerpe, that in the yeare 1555 there came in lesse than three moneths into the lowe countreys a hundred thousand peeces of cloth, accounting three karsies or three cottons to a cloth. It is therefore expedient to raise the forraine customes to strangers of such commodities as they cannot want, and by that means increase

the

The mynes of Fraunce are neuer wasted.

Impost in England vpon wine.

F3 eight pounds, besides   H10 *For* all wares *read* allwaies (*tousjours* in Fr).   I10(margin) England
I10 *For* 1557 *Bodin writes* 1555.   K2 treatise *i.e.* treaty   K9 cannot want *i.e.* cannot do without
Notes at F4, H3, K2, K7.

OF A COMMONWEALE 663

the treasure and ease the subiects; and also to abate the custome of marchandise comming in, if the subiect cannot passe without them, you must raise the custome of things made by hand, and not to suffer any to bee brought out of strange countreys, and not to suffer any raw stuffs to be caried out of the land, as iron, copper, steele, wooll, flaxe, raw silke, and such like, that the subiect may haue the benefit of the workmanship, and the prince the forraine custome, as *Philip* king of Spaine, had forbidden his subiects by an edict made in the yere 1563, to requite the queene of England, who had made the like three moneths before, the like edict was made in France by King *Henrie* the second in the yeare 1552, concerning wools: but there was a Florentin, who hauing gotten a pasport by a courtiers means, caried away more wooll at one instant, than all other marchants had done before in a yere; and hauing it made into cloth at Florence, hee returned it into France, by the which he gained infinitly, the workmanship exceeding the stuffe fifteen parts: the which is a great incongruitie in matter of state and reuenewes, to forbid a traffique vnto the subiect, and then giue leaue vnto a stranger: for both king & Commonweale in generall receiue an irreparable losse, and the marchants in particular are ruined. Behold six means to gather together treasure without oppression of the subiects, vnlesse the custome of forrain marchandise that be necessary for the life of man were excessiue. The seuenth means is vpon the subiect, the which they must neuer vse, vnlesse all the rest faile, and that necessitie forceth them to haue a care of the Commonweale, being sodenly oppressed either by the enemie, or by some other vnexpected accident; in this case seeing the defence of euerie one in particular, depends vpon the preseruation of the generall, it is fit that euerie man straine himselfe; then are impositions laide vpon the subiects most iust and necessarie, and those charges which are then imposed vpon the citisens are religious and godly, without the which the citie were quite ruined. But to the end this extraordinary charge imposed during the warre, may not continue in time of peace, it is fit to proceed by way of borrowing; for that money is easilier found, when as he that lends hopes to receiue both his money againe, and thanks for his willingnesse. For when as *Hannibal* was in Italie, and did besiege euen Rome it selfe, the senate hauing consumed their treasure, would not impose new tributes vpon their subiects and confederats, (a verie daungerous thing, being then prest by the enemie) but the senators with one consent, brought their gold and siluer vnto the receiuers, being followed by the people with great ioy. And *Titus Liuius* saith; *Senatores pro se quisque aurum, argentum, æs in publicum conferunt, tanto certamine iniecto, vt prima inter primos sua nomina vellent in publicis tabulis esse, vt nec Triumuiri mensarij accipiendo, nec scribæ referendo sufficerent.* The senators bought their gold and siluer into the publicke with great contention, who should bee inrolled, so as the receiuers were not sufficient to tell it, nor the registers to inroll them. After the victorie obtained against the Carthaginiens, the senate decreed to pay what had been borrowed; but for that there was not sufficient in the common coffers to satisfie them, the creditors presented a request to haue part of the citie lands assigned vnto them, the which shuld be valued by the consuls, vpon condition, that it might be alwaies redeemed, and to pay an asse of smal rent to the receiuers for euerie acre, only for a marke, and as a witnes that it was the city lands, the which was done. If the commonweale hath not wherwithall to pay, neither in mony nor lands, & the enemy doth presse it, then is there no redier means, than to make choise of those which are ablest to bare arms, which shuld be armed

No raw stuffs to be transported.

A trade forbidden to the subiects, and allowed to strangers, is the ruine of a countrey.

The seuenth means to make money.

The honestest means in time of publicke necessitie to make money.

Ceassing vsed in old time.

664   THE SIXT BOOKE

Liuius lib. 26.

armed and entertained at the charge of others, as the antient Romaines did, so as the common good and health of the citisents was defended by some, with the wealth of others. This kind of tribute is called rash and extraordinarie. From hence these extraordinarie charges first tooke their beginning, the which afterwards became ordinarie. As we read that *Denis* the tyrant, sometimes sought occasions of war, or of fortifications, to the end he might haue cause to raise new imposts, the which he continued, after that he had treated with the enemie, or discontinued the fortresses begun.

Detestable inuentions of a tyrant.

If my wishes might take place, I would desire that such detestable inuentions might be buried with the author. There be three kinds of tributes that bee leuied of the subiect, some extraordinarie; others ordinarie; and the third which holds of both, and is called casuall: vnder which kinds is contained as well the reuenewes that rise of iurisdictions, seales, coynes, waights, and measure, as the money that is receiued vpon things sold, of what nature soeuer, or by gifts, legacies, or successions, or by the sale of offices, or in manner of a taxe, be it in the regard of euerie mans person, (which kind of tribute is called *Capitatio* by the Latines:) bee it in respect of the moouable or immoouable goods, and of fruits which grow aboue or within the earth, as mynes and treasures, or that which is gathered at ferries, or passages, the which is rightly called *Portorium vectigal*, or of any other imposition that may be imagined, how filthie and beastly soeuer, for tyrants alwaies thinke the sauor of them sweet; as that tribute which was vsually exacted from professed whores at Rome; and the sauing of vrine commaunded by *Vespasian*, the which his sonne taking vnworthily, the father held the first money that hee receiued next of that tribute, to his nose, asking him if it smelt ill, and hee denying it, *Atqui inquit è lotio est*, But sayth he, it comes of the vrine. Of which charges and impositions, the most ancient are reputed reuenewes, as the forraine custome; others are ordinarie, as taxes; and the last are extraordinarie, the which the Latines called *temerarium tributum*, a rash tribute: as subsidies imposed vpon free townes and priuiledged persons, tenths, charitable gifts equiualent to tenths, the which are leuied by commission. And to speake properly, the taxes, ayds, grants, tolles, and such like were meere subsidies and extraordinarie charges, before *Lewis* the ninth, who first leuied the taxe, as president *le Maistre* hath obserued: but hee doth not say, that it was as a necessarie subsidie during the warres; and that hee made an ordinarie receit thereof; but contrarywise adressing himselfe to *Philip* his eldest sonne and successor, he vseth these words in his testament, the which is yet found in the treasurie of France, and is registred in the chamber of accounts: *Fili, religiosus imprimis erga Deum esto: benignus & liberalis aduersus egentes, legum ac morum huius imperij custos ac vindex acerrimus: à vectigalibus & tributis abstineto, nisi te summa vis necessitatis ac vtilitatis publicæ iustissima causa ad hoc impellat, sin minus, tyrannum te potiùs, quàm regem futurum putato, &c.* Sonne, be first deuote and religious towards God, be mild and charitable to the poore, obserue the good lawes and manners of thy realme seuerely, exact no taxes nor subsidies of thy subiects, vnlesse that vrgent necessitie or the profit of the Commonweale presse thee vnto it; if thou doest otherwise, thou shalt be esteemed a tyrant and no king, &c. Some one will say vnto me, That king *Clotaire* did exact the third part and reuenewes of churches: and *Chilperis* the 8 part of euery mans wine growing, and it seems that the impost of the 8 part of the wine, the which now is imposed vpon vinteners, tooke his beginning from hence: and that *Lewis* the yong during 4 yeres, tooke the

Three kindes of impositions.

S. Lewis his testament.

F2 citisens   H2 *For* saving *read* flowing (*effusio*).   I4 that hee NEVER made an ordinarie receit (Fr)
K6 third part OF THE RENTS and revenewes (Fr)   K7 Chilperic   Notes at H6, H7.

the twentieth part of his subiects reuenewes in the yere 1167; yet it is most certaine that this was but an extraordinarie subsidie during the warre, as that *temerarium tributum* imposed by king *Charles* the sixt, for it was decreed in our open Parliament, called by *Philip* of Valois in the yeare 1338, that no impost should bee raised vpon the people without the consent of the three estates: and in stead of three hundred and fortie thousand pounds starling, which king *Lewis* the eleuenth did leuie the yeare that he died, besides the ordinarie reuenewes of the crowne, the deputies of the three estates held at Tours, offered vnto *Charles* the eight, his sonne comming to the crowne, in manner of a beneuolence for two yeares, the like graunt that was made vnto *Charles* the seuenth, and for his entrance a hundred thousand crownes to bee paide for once onely, the which he might not afterwards challenge as a due, nor call the graunt a taxe or impost. The which hath been alwaies, and is still obserued in Spaine, England, and Germanie: as *Philip Comineus* said in open parliament, in the raigne of *Charles* the eight, That no prince had power to lay any imposition vpon his subiects, nor to prescribe that right without their consents. And wee see in all commissions sent out for the leuying of taxes, and subsidies, the king vseth that antient protestation to free them, as soone as necessitie would suffer him.

No Prince can lay any subsidie vpon his subiects without their consents.

And althogh that *Philip* the long did exact but the fift part of a peny vpon euery two shillings worth of salt that were sold, yet he publickly protested to discharge the subiects of it. *Philip* of Vallois vsed the like protestation, being forced by the extremitie of warre to double the sayd custome, declaring by his letters patents in the yeare 1328, that he meant not to haue the imposition vpon the salt incorporate to the reuenewes; and yet there is no custome seems more easie than that of salt, the which is common to all the subiects: yet in the popular estate of the Romaines, and in the hottest of their Punicke warres, the impost of salt being set on foot by *Liuius* and *Claudius* censures; *Liuius* was called *Salinator* in derision: but a peace being graunted to them of Carthage, it was taken away againe: either for that there was nothing more necessarie for the life of man, or for that it was done without the peoples commaund. And for that the lightest kinds of tributes and imposts seeme heauie and burdensome vnto the poore and weake, yet could not the senators maintaine the treasurie of Rome without new impositions: the people being freed from all taxes and customes by the law Valeria, after the expulsion of their kings: therefore *C. Manlius* the Consull made a law with the authoritie of the Senate, (the Armie lying at Sutrium) that such as were made free, should pay the twentieth part of all their substance into the Exchequer: with which tribute, although the citisens were nothing oppressed, yet being vnderstood, the Tribune made a defence vpon paine of death, That no man should attempt the like without the peoples priuitie. And *Augustus* made the law Iulia, That whatsoeuer should come to any one by inheritance, legacie, or gift for death, the twentieth part thereof should belong vnto the common treasure, both these impositions were profitable to the Commonweale, and pleasing to either of them: to the one, for that they possesse anothers inheritance; and to the other, for that they obtaine their liberties. But for that the emperours which succeeded *Augustus* exacted the twentieth part of all inheritances and legacies, *Traian* therefore abrogated the said law Iulia, the which many haue labored to reuiue, changing the name of it: yet had they not then the hundred part of those tributes, which since the necessity of some, and the couetousnesse of others haue inuented. And when as *Samuel* prince of

The beginning of the custome of salt.

Liuius lib. 2.

The tribute of the twentieth part most pleasing.

the

C7 For censures *probably read* censors (cf. Fr and L).   E2 treasure; both

666 THE SIXT BOOKE

the Israelites spake vnto the people, who demaunded a King of him, he added threats of bitter tributes, *Ergo inquit regem habituri estis qui decimas fructuum, imperaturus est*, Therefore sayd he, you shall haue a King which shall command the tenths of your fruits. Neither did *Cipselus* the first Tyrant of Corinth, exact any other tribute of his subiects, but the tenths of their fruits: there were then no taxes, subsidies, tolles, and a thousand such like. So the greatest part of the Inuenters of these new Imposts haue lost their liues; as *Philistus* parasite to *Dyonisius* the tyrant, who being drawn out of the tyrants castle, was slaine by the people of *Syracusa*: and *Parthenius* or *Proclerus*, who was slaine by the people of *Treues*, for giuing counsell to king *Theodoret* to oppresse his subiects with new subsidies: and of late daies *George Prescon* Parasite to *Henrie* king of Sueden, was cruelly put to death in the kings pallace, and the king himselfe expelled his estate. What shall I speake of *Achaus* King of the Lidiens, whom his subiects did hang by the feet with his head downeward into a riuer, for the subsidies which hee imposed vppon his people: and *Theodoric* king of France lost his crowne for it. How comes it that the Netherlanders haue reuolted from the Spaniard, but for that the duke of Alua would exact the tenth pennie of euerie thing which was sold, whereby he would haue gathered an infinite treasor, or rather the wealth of all the countrey, being most certaine that one thing might be sold often in a short time, and well knowne that the marchandise sold in one day amounted to seuentie thousand ducats, as a Spaniard himselfe did write. The Histories are full of these examples, for nothing doth sooner cause changes, seditions, and ruines of States, than excessiue charges and imposts. But as the Prince must haue a care not to impose any charges, but when warre doth force him, so must he take them away when he hath obtained a peace: yet must they not runne from one extreame vnto another, and abolish all imposts and taxes, hauing neither lands nor reuenewes to maintaine the Common weale; as *Nero* the Emperour would haue done, who hauing wasted all the treasure, sought to abolish the tributes, whereof the Senate being aduertised, they thanked him for his good will to the people, yet they dissuaded him from doing it, saying it would be the ruine of the Commonweale. Many seditious citisens, and desirous of innouations, did of late yeares promise immunitie of taxes and subsidies to our people: but neither could they doe it, or if they had could, they would not, or if it were done, should we haue any Commonweale, being as it were the ground and foundation of a Commonweale. There were more reasons to haue the excessiue gifts cut off and reuoked and that an account should be made of the treasure wasted: but to take away all impositions before that the reuenewes bee redeemed and the debts payd; it were not to repaire, but to ruine the state. And most of these men which seeme to vnderstand the affaires of state so well, are greatly abused with an old inueterate opinion, that all charges and imposts must be reduced to that proportion that they were in the time of king *Lewis* the 12, and consider not that since that time gold and siluer hath come in so great abundance from the new found Lands, namely from Peru, as all things are growne ten times deerer than they were; as I haue prooued against the Paradox of *Malestroit*: the which may bee easily seene in the antient customes and contracts of this Realme, where wee shall find the value of fruits and victuals to bee ten, yea twelue times lesse than it is at this day. Wee find in the Registers of the chamber of Accounts, That the Chancellor of France in the time of S. *Lewis*, had for the charges of himself, his horses, and seruants, seuen soulz Parisis allowed him

The tenths of the subiects fruits was the first tribute.

Inuenters of new impositions most commonly slaine.

All Impositions are not to be abolished.

Abundance of gold and siluer hath made things decre.

F2–3 fructuum VOBIS imperaturus est (cf. L)   F10 *For* Theodoret *read* Theodebert.   H1 *For* seuentie thousand *read* 700,000 (L only).   Notes at I5, K7.

him a day; the which is not eight pence halfe-penie of our money: and if hee stayd in any Abbey, or other place where he spent nothing for his horses, it was then abated in his wages. I haue shewed that *Charles* the 5. king of France payd but 31000 crownes for the countie of Anxerre: and that the duchie of Berrie was bought by *Philip* the 1 of Herpin, for threescore thousand crownes: and the countie of Venice and Auignon were engaged for fortie thousand Florins. To conclude, I haue made manifest that many Earledomes, Baronies, and great Signiories haue beene sold a hundred or sixe score yeares since, twentie times better cheape than they are nowe, for the aboundance of gold and siluer that is come frō new found Lands: as it happened at Rome, whenas *Paulus Æmilius* brought such infinit store of gold and siluer from the realme of Macedon, suddenly the value of lands did rise to bee treble in price: and at what time *Cæsar* brought the treasure and spoyles of Egypt to Rome, then did Vsurie fall, and the price of lands did rise: euen as it happened to the Spaniards after the conquest of Peru by *Frauncis Pizara*, a small vessell of wine in that country cost 300 ducats, a Spanish cape of Frizado a thousand ducats, and a Iennet sixe thousand; the which was by reason of the aboundance of gold and siluer which they found at Peru, and brought into Spaine: and namely of the ransome of king *Atabalipa*; who paid the value of ten millions, three hundred twentie and sixe thousand ducats, besides twise as much that came to priuate men, captaines, soldiors, and euen to the receiuers themselues, as *Augustus Zarata* master of the Accounts to the king of Spaine doth testifie. Since great store of gold and siluer hath beene brought out of Spaine into France to buy corne and other necessarie commodities, which are transported into Spaine in great abundance, so as the prices of all things haue risen: and so by consequence the wages of officers, the pay of souldiors, the pensions of captaines, and in like sort euerie mans employment, and by the same reason the rents of Farmes, haue risen; for he that had but ten pounds a yeere rent, hath now a thousand of the same fruits he then gathered: wherein they are greatly abused that would reduce the prices of corne and victuals to the antient orders. We must then conclude, that the account of the reuenewes vnder king *Charles* the 6 in the yere 1449, which came but to fortie thousand pounds starling; was not much lesse (in regard of the value of things) than the reuenewes of fourteen hundred thousand pounds starling, the same yeare that *Charles* the ninth died, in the yeare one thousand, fiue hundred, seuentie & foure; and yet the people complained at both times that they were oppressed with tributes. And the ransom which king *Lewis* the 9 paid to the sultan of Egypt of fiftie thousand pounds starling, was not much lesse than that of king *Francis* the 1 of three millions of crownes: and although that king *Iohn* were set at the same ransome by the king of England, yet was it held so excessiue, as they were six yeares in leuying of it; but *Frauncis* the same yeare a peace was concluded, sent his ransome into Spaine. We must iudge the like of the yearely pension of 900. pounds, that was asigned vnto *Charles* the faire, sonne to *Philip*, not to be lesse, than that of ten thousand pounds starling yearely, that was giuen first to *Henrie*, and then to *Frauncis* dukes of Aniou from king *Charles* the 9 their brother. And much more honourable might they liue with that pencion, which I made mention of vnder *Philip*, than with that which *Charles* the 9 gaue vnto his brethren. Nor the Dowries of 400000 crownes asigned to euerie one of the daughters of king *Henrie* the 2, were not so great as those of sixtie thousand crownes asigned to the daughters of

The great treasure taken at the Conquest of Peru.

The Reuenewes of France vnder Charles 6 & 9.

The Lord of Ieinuille in the life of Lewis. 9.

LII iiij France

A4 Auxerre   A6 the countie of Venice *i.e.* the Venaissin   B6 Jennet *i.e.* a small Spanish horse
D6 (margin) Joinville   Notes at C8, C9, D8, E5, E7.

France by the law of king *Charles* the 5. The like may be spoken of other people, as in old time in the East, so at this present in the West. For we read in *Strabo*, that *Ptolomie* the piper, the last king of Egypt of that race, did raise vpon the countrey of Egypt the value of seuen millions, and fiue hundred thousand crownes a yeare, and sultan *Solyman* did leuie but a hundred thousand ducats of the same countrey, as appeared by an extract of the reuenewes made by *Gritty* a Venetian, in the yeare 1520, when as the estate of the whole reuenewes came not to aboue foure millions; for foure yeares after he raised it vnto six millions, as *Paulus Iouius* saith, and now he leuieth aboue twelue millions yearly, for the great abundance of gold and siluer, that is brought out of the West and East; which summe notwithstanding may seeme but little, for that we read in *Plutarch*, that the dictator *Silla* did taxe the charges of Asia the lesse, before the conquests of *Lucullus* and *Pompee*, at twelue millions of crownes, the which is not aboue the sixt part of the Turks empire.

The reuenewes of Egypt vnder Ptolomie.

The Turks reuenewes.

Sometimes the bountie of the land, and the great trade, and oftentimes the vnreasonable greedinesse of princes to heape vp treasure, make some richer than others: It is well knowne that *Charles* the fift gathered more reuenewes out of the duchie of Milan; then king *Francis* the first, at the same time did leuie in this his realme, which flowed in all abundance; who doth not know that he commaunded more out of the lowe Countreys, than the reuenewes of England were esteemed in those daies. Some one not long since, (seeking to perswade *Charles* the ninth to encrease his taxes) did pernitiously maintaine in open counsell, that *Cosme* duke of Florence did raise out of his estate six millions, hauing but a small territorie: the which was false, for hee receiued out of the estate of Florence, but twelue hundred thousand crownes, and out of that of Sienna two hundred thousand at the most. But a new prince shall doe wisely at his first entrance, to cut off the extraordinarie exactions of his predecessor, or at the least a great part of them, as well in regard of his owne dutie, as to get the good will of the people, if he be required; yea before he be required, and not to imitate *Roboam*, who following the wicked counsell of wicked men, did not onely refuse the humble petitions of his subiects, but vowed openly that he would bee crueller than his father had been, whereupon ten tribes fell from him, and created them a new king. True it is, that to hold a certaine estate of impositions, they must be made in their proper kinds, as in corne, wine, and oyles; and as for marchandise in siluer, it is the forme which the kings of Poland haue alwaies, and doe still vse, and the king of Ethiopia receiues cloth and other marchandise for his custome. But to require to haue taxes and subsidies quite taken away, or reduced to the antient custome, without any regard of the value of things, or the changes that haue happened; this were not to relieue, but to ruine an estate.

The reuenewes of the Duke of Florence.

It is an ordinarie thing in changes from a tyrannie to a popular estate, to abolish all imposts, taxes, and subsidies for a signe of libertie, as they did in Rome, at the request of the consull *Valerius*, after they had expelled their kings: but euerie man was faine to goe to the warre at his owne charge, then afterwards to pay the soldiors, and afterwards to taxe themselues by the raising of new imposts. True it is, that the Romaines did therein shew themselues verie iust: for at that time there were none that bare the charges, but the noble and the rich, the poorer sort went free; and now adaies we see none but the poore pay, and the rich goe scot-free. The like was in Suisserland, and at Lindaw, after they had expelled

their

F8 *For foure yeares* Bodin *writes* twelve years (Fr).   H9 required *i.e.* requested, asked   I4–5 marchandise, in silver; it is   K4 faine *i.e.* constrained, obliged (cf. note at 135 C2)

Notes at F1, H10, K7.

their Lords. Other doe free the chife cities and great Lords, and charge the weaker sort: as the Athenians did, when they were the stronger, they did free their owne citie against the tenor of the allyance made with the other cities of Grece, and in stead of sixtie tallents, they so augmented it, as in lesse than threescore yeares they made them pay twelue hundred yearly, the which amounts to 720000 crownes. And when as *Themistocles* captaine of the Athenians, demanded the tribute of the Adriens, saying; That hee would bring with him two mightie gods, Force and Loue: they answered, That they had two more mightie, Pouertie and Impossibilitie.

The reuenewes of the Athenians.

Plut. in Themist.

And commonly the greater cities lay the burthen vpon the champian countrey, and the richest peasants vpon the poorer, as it hath been heretofore in this realme, whereas the great cities were freed; and in old time the citie of Babilon (the greatest that euer was) remained free from all charges: the which is done lest the greater should hinder the imposts. But it fals out as in mans bodie, whereas the strongest and noblest members cast all superfluous and vicious humors vpon the weaker, and when as apostume is so swolne as the weaker part can endure no more, then must it breake or infect all the members: euen so it fals out when as the rich cities, the nobilitie and the clergie, lay all the charge vpon the poore labourer, he sinks vnder his burthen like vnto *Æsops* Asse, and the horse which would carrie nothing; that is to say, the nobilitie and the clergie, are forced some to carrie the tenths and extraordinarie subsidies, others to sell their goods, to make warre at their owne charge, and to pay the taxes and imposts directly or indirectly. For the like cause, the nobilitie and clergie of the realme of Denmarke haue been forced to taxe themselues since the yeare 1563, to maintaine the charges of the warre; but it was vpon condition, that the king should not meddle with the money. The nobilitie and clergie of England, euerie man (according to his abilitie) was subiect to taxes & subsidies, according to the antient custome of the Grekes and Romaines; yea almost of all nations, except our nation the French, with whom, as *Cæsar* saith rightly: *Nihil est plebe contemptius*, Nothing is more contemptible than the common people.

The French contemne the common people.

To remedie this inconuenience, the antients did wisely order, That all charges should be reall, and not personall; as it is put in practise in Languedoc, and since in Prouence by prouision, according to the disposition of the lawes, to the end that the rich and the poore, the noble and the peasant, the priest and the laborer, should pay the charge of their land that is to be taxed: the law exempts neither bishop nor nobleman. In other gouernments, if there be a clergieman, a noble man, a counsellor, & a vigneron, the last paies for all and the others are free, not only for their fees, but also for other tailable lands. If then necessitie force the prince to raise some extraordinary imposts, it is needfull it should be such as euerie one may beare his part, as is the impost of salt, wine, and such like things. And to take away occasion of seditions, which doe often chaunce for the impost of small things sold by retaile, it were expedient to conuert that impost into a generall summe, as it was put in practise by *Charles* the fift, with the consent of the estates, for the freeing of king *Iohn*, the which was 12 deniers vpon euerie liure, or two shillings of goods that were sold; the which was changed to an equiualent, first in the countrey of Languedoc in the time of king *Lewis* the eleuenth, yeelding for the said impost 6000 pounds starling yearly: and the like hath been also done in Auuergne for the salt, the which the countrey hath exchanged into a certaine summe: and for the same reason the impost which was taken vpon all small

Taxes must be reall to ease the poore.

Vniust distribution of subsidies in France.

Not pennie farthing.

A7 Adriens *i.e.* Andrians, people of Andros   A10 champian *i.e.* open, level   B6 apostume (*or perhaps* a postume) *i.e.* an abscess

THE SIXT BOOKE

Iauelleur or Gabelleur.

small wares, haue ben abolished in many Commonweales, for the complaints, seditions, and exclamations of the poore people against the toll-gatherers, who alwaies tooke more in the kinde than they ought. But if any one shall demaund of me, which kind of imposts are most pleasing vnto God, most profitable to the Commonweale, and most desired of good men, for the reliefe of the poore: it is that which is layd on those things which serue onely to corrupt the subiects, as

What impost is most honourable, profitable, and necessarie.

all kinds of dainties, perfumes, cloth of gold and siluer, silkes, cipresse, laces, rich colours, womens painting, pearles, precious stones, and all kinds of works of gold, siluer or enamell, & such like things, which are not to be forbidden: for such is the nature of man, as they esteem nothing more sweet & goodly than that which is strickly forbidden them; and the more superfluities are defended, the more they are desired, especially of men that are simple and ill bred: you must therefore raise them so in price, by means of the impost, as none but the rich and those that are curious shalbe able to buy them. And therefore these princes that liue towards the North, lay great imposts vpon wine, the which although it be dere, yet their subiects are so desirous thereof, as they drinke themselues drunke. And for this cause *Cato* the censor was commended, for that he layd a great impost vpon the sale of slaues, that should exceed fiftie crownes price, for that such marchandise could not be warranted.

The wisedome of the emperor Augustus.

The emperour *Augustus* did more wisely, who to correct the disordinate lust of his subiects, made lawes for marriages, by the which he imposed a taxe in manner of a fine, vpon those that did not marrie after the age of 25 yeares, or that were married and had no children, inioyning them to bring a part into the treasurie of such successions or legacies as were casually left them, giuing goodly immunities and priuiledges to such as had children: by which lawes *Augustus* purchased the commendation of a wise prince. For hereby he did both punish whoredome, adultery, & sodomie, and also force euery one to seek him a lawfull wife and children, taking away nothing of any mans present estate, but onely the tenth part of that inheritance which came vnto him accidentally from his friends, filling the treasury with money, and the Commonweale with good and vertuous citisens. Which law *Iustinian* the emperour did vnaduisedly blame, and likewise *Constantin*, who abrogated the law for punishing them that liued vnmaried, or that had no children. But the emperors *Honorius* and *Theodosius* gaue the priuiledge of children to all subiects, which was to giue way to adulteries and to all detestable vices, causing marriages and the procreation of children to grow in contempt, whereby the citie grew bare of citisens, and the empire being found in a manner wast, was seazed on by a deluge of Gothes, and other barbarous nations of the North. These kinds of impositions which are inuented for the punishment of vice, seeme not onely iust, but verie profitable.

An impost vpon sutes.

There was also another impost of ten shillings vpon euerie sute in law that was not criminall, to punish those that were too apt to plead the which many haue found strange, and in the end haue taken it away: but there was neuer any more needfull in this realme, where there are more sutes than in all the rest of Europe, the which haue much increased since the time of king *Charles* the sixt, when as an edict was made, to take away the antient custome, by the which no

The cause of many sutes in France.

man was condemned to pay any charges that had lost his sute: for in former times they were not so apt to plead: and it may be, our antient fathers, knowing the dispositions of the French, had brought in this custome (although it were vniust of it selfe) to diuert the subiects from attempting of sutes rashly. And although

---

F3 in the kinde *i.e. en espèce*, in kind, in commodities   F7 cipresse *i.e.* crêpe (Cf. Fr. The term was also applied to other light fabrics.)   G4 curious *i.e. frians*, fond of delicacies

Notes at F2, G7, G9, H5, I1.

A though the Romaines in a free Commonweale could hardly beare any imposition or tributes, yet did they willingly endure a taxe set vpon sutes and controuersies, much more heauie than that which was imposed in the time of *Charles the ninth*, by the which, he that did attempt a sute against any man, was forced to consigne two crownes into an officers hands; the which hee should receiue againe from the aduerse partie, if he did recouer his suit, or if he were vanquished, to loose them as a punishment of his rashnesse: but the Romaines tooke the tenth part in all ciuile causes, and the fift in criminall, as *Pompeius Festus* doth witnesse: yet *Marcus Varro* writes, that either of the parties did lay downe fiue hundred asses, which coms to about 10 shillings of our mony; and he which won,
B recouered his money which he had consigned, and this was besides the thing for which they contended, the which was called *Sponsio & sacramentum*, and if any one refused to consigne, hee yeelded to the other. The Hebrews did alwaies cause him that did willingly denie a debt, to pay it double, as wee read in their pandects. And although the consignations which were made in Rome vpon suits were diuers, yet the emperour *Caligula* extorted against reason, the fortieth pennie of all that was demaunded by law, without any prefixion or limitation, whether the cause were iust or vniust. But of all marchandise which tend to pleasure, lust, and pompe, the imposition is honest and profitable, seruing to no other end but to corrupt the simplicitie of the subiect, the deerest of all (which
C is Amber gris) the which is valued but at twelue pounds starling, should be prised at 300 crownes.

The extorsion of Caligula.

The law sets no impost vpon marchandise, but vpon spices, and such pretious marchandise, as are specially named, as skins of Parthia and Babilon, silkes, fine linnen cloth, painting, Indian haire, wild beasts, and Eunukes. Such impositions are alwaies commendable, and farre more supportable without comparison, than that which is layd vpon the asse, the oxe, wine, and such like. And all good princes haue abhorred that impost which they called *Capitatio*, for to lay a charge vpon mens persons for their worke, were to make warre to good wits, if they haue not some great trade, and by that means haue gathered together great
D wealth, for the which they must beare some charge; the which is not properly *Capitatio*, but with the weaker sort they must deale mildly, especially with the husbandman, which doth not till his own land. Neither are those impositions to be allowed which employ all their studies to inuent new taxes & exactions, seeking by all means to incorage princes thereunto; as that multiplier (whose name I concele for honors sake) who not many yeres since at a parliament held at Blois, made a declaration, That the king (besides al other ordinary charges) might with oppression or grieuance of poore or rich, raise thirtie millions: the king sent this man to the three estates, to expound the heauenly gift of God.

Interdum & de vectigal.

And although we had many excellent wits and of great iudgement, yet had
E he abused many with his opinion, if we had not laid open his errour and deceit. He supposed that France was two hundred leagues long from Bologne to Marseilles, and as much from Mont *S. Bernard*, to *S. Iohn de Luz*; and by this he concluded that France had fortie thousand leagues in square, and that euerie league contained fiue thousand acres of ground, which amounted to two hundred millions of acres, of the which he abated the one halfe for waters, waies and wast land, and of the rest hee would haue the king take a soulz for an acre, the which amounts to fiue millions: then he made an estimate of six hundred thousand townes and villages, and in them twentie millions of fiers, of the which he
would

A soulz is not a pennie farthing.

B7 by law *i.e.* through lawsuits   C4(margin) l. interdum. de vectigalibus (*i.e. Digest*, 39, 4, 16, 7)
D3 *For* impositions *probably read* impositors *or* impostors (*impostores* in L).   D7–8 *For* with oppression *read* without oppression.
Notes at B2, B9, C7.

would haue the king take six pence of euerie fier, which comes to six millions and two hundred and fiftie thousand liures. Moreouer he made an account of fifteen millions of all sorts of marchandise, of the which he tooke a soulz of the marchant for euerie thousand liures, making the former twelue millions. And vpon the said six hundred thousand townes and villages, one with another eleuen soulz apeece, the which comes to twelue millions, and six millions and a hundred of liures more, which then the foure tenths came vnto, all which make thirtie millions, besides the aids, taxes, customes, grants, imposts, subsidies, and reuenewes of the crowne, which came then to fifteen millions, wherein his deceit was verie apparent; first making France square, the which is in fourme of a Lorange much lesse than a square; next he makes the fertill land equall to that which is wast and fruitlesse (although there is not any land, be it neuer so fertill, whereas two third parts at the least lyes not wast) taxing the nobilitie and the clergie as well as the rest. And as for 600000 townes and villages, it is an impudent lye; for that by the extracts drawne out of the chamber of accounts, and brought to Blois to the estates, there were found to be twentie seuen thousand and foure hundred parishes in France, taking the greatest towne but for one parish, and the smalest villages hauing a parish for another: and in truth the number of parishes taken by king *Henrie* the second in the yeare 1554, came but to 24824 parishes, besides Bourgogne & Poictou, and the impost of three pounds starling vpon euerie parish, came but to threescore and fourteen thousand foure hundred eightie one pounds. *Ierosme Laski* a Polonois, father to the Palatin *Laski*, whom we haue seen Ambassador in France, inuented another manner of meanes than this former, to encrease the treasure, giuing aduise to raise three imposts vpon the subiects, and to make three mounts of pietie (for so he calleth them.) The first was in taking the moitie of euerie subiects reuenews, for once: the second was the twentieth part of his reuenewes yearely; and the third was to haue the eight part of things sold in grosse, or by retaile. But his aduise was reiected as pernitious and most impossible: for in matter of impositions there is nothing that doth more kindle seditions, than to charge the subiect with many things at once, especially a war-like people, and bred vp in libertie, as those of Polonia bee. And yet he gaue a goodly name to a wicked and pernitious inuention, calling the grounds of such impositions, Mounts of pietie. For the mounts of pietie in the cities of Italie are profitable, honest, and charitable, & inuented to ease the poore; and those of *Laski* do ruin them. There are mounts of pietie at Florence, Sienna, Luques, and other cities, wheras he that hath one daughter, the day of her birth hee may put what summe he will into the mount of pietie, vpon condition to receiue ten times as much to marrie her withall, when shee comes to the age of eighteene yeare; but if she dies before, then doth it accrue vnto the mount, vnlesse the father hath other daughters, to whom the portion shall come succesiuely. Another mount of pietie is, for the lending of money to poore men at fiue in the hundred, giuing a sufficient pawne, and not aboue ten crownes; if the debter paies not his ten crownes at the time prefixt, the pawne is sold to him that wil giue most, and the surplusage deliuered vnto the debtor: this is done to preuent excessiue vsuries, (wherewith the poore in those countreys are ruined) and the seazure and selling of moouables at an vnder price.

Notwithstanding I find that the emperour *Antonine* surnamed the *Pius* or godly, inuented a better mount of pietie, which was to deliuer out the money that

---

F1 six pence *i.e.* sixpence sterling or five sous livres (Fr) *properly* 5,000,000 livres (L)   F1-2 six millions and two hundred and fiftie thousand G1 *For* Lorange *read* Lozange *i.e.* a rhombus, diamond.
G10 *For* 24824 *read* 24827 (Fr and L).   Notes at F7, H1, I3.

that came cleere into the treasurie, all charges paid for fiue in the hundred vpon good and sufficient caution. By whose example *Seuerus* restored the treasure that was wasted, and the marchants and poore men gained much by traffique: and the publicke in a great summe did also gaine much: for if they lent a million, at the yeares end they did get fistie thousand crownes for the publicke, and priuate men got twise as much by traffique: and besides all this, the greatest benefit that did arise, the publicke treasure was assured out of the pawes of theeues and horse leeches of the court. And for this reason onely as it seems, the emperour *Augustus* long before, was accustomed to lend the money which came cleere into the Exchequer, without any interest, giuing good assurance of land; and vpon a penaltie to forfeit the double, if it were not paid at the day: by this means the publicke treasure was not idle, nor wasted by the princes prodigalitie, nor exhausted by theft, but a great benefit redounded to all in generall, and to many in particular. And here some one may obiect, that although *Augustus* did not lend the publicke money for interest, yet hee imposed a penaltie of the double, if it were not paid at the prefixed day, the which is greater than any vsurie, and therefore forbidden by the law. In my opinion, that penaltie is then disallowed by the law when we stipulate any thing fraudulently, and aboue the lawfull interest: but he that hath taken the publicke money, and restores it not at the appointed day, he commits theft; it is therefore the penaltie of theft, and not of vsurie.

A commendable institution made by Antoninus Pius.

Tranquil. in August.

A forfeiture of the double forbidden by the law. l. pecun. de vsur.

Those princes therefore did wisely in old time, which prouided for the necessitie of the Commonweale, and the profite of priuate men. But the contrarie is vsed in our daies; for princes in stead of giuing out vpon reasonable interest, borrow and pay vnreasonable vsurie: and not onely princes, but also lords and Commonweales, some more, some lesse: those which haue been held the most frugall, as the Venetians, borrow alwaies at fiue in the hundred, without any hope to recouer the principall, or at foureteene in the hunded, so long as the creditor shall liue. The colledge of Saint *George* at Genes takes money of all men at fiue in the hundred, and deliuers it out againe at the highest interest to princes and marchants; whereby they are so enriched, as they haue redeemed the Isle of Corsica, and the lands of the Commonweale. Priuate men had rather take fiue in the hundred of the colledge, to bee assured of their principall, than much more of priuate men, who oftentimes become Bankerupts: the Venetians haue alwaies lost, and shall loose, so long as they shall take eight in the hundred or more: or else they must abate their interest, as they haue by little and little abated Mount Vecchio, cutting the creditors so short, as they dare not so easily put in their money as they were woont.

The ruine of princes is to take vp at interest.

This meanes was also brought into Fraunce by the cardinall of Tournon, at such time as hee was in credit with king *Frauncis* the first, whom he persuaded (by the instigation of certaine Italians) that there was no other meanes to draw the money from all parts into Fraunce, and to frustrate the enemie hereafter, than to settle a banke at Lion, to take euerie mans money, and to pay him eight in the hundred, so as in short time hee should get into his hands all the money of Italie and Germanie: but in effect the cardinall sought to assure an hundred thousand crowns which he had in his coffers, & to get all the interest he could. Letters patents being granted, at the opening of the bank, euery man came running from France, Germanie and Italie, so as king *Frauncis* the first, when he died, was found indebted to the banke of Lion, fiue hundred thousand crowns,

The originall of the banke of Lion.

A1 paid, for   C8 hundred, so long   D5 take AT eight in the hundred *i.e.* borrow money at eight per cent (cf. Fr)

674　THE SIXT BOOKE

the which he had in his coffers and sometimes more, and a peace concluded with F all the princes of the earth. But the raigne of *Henrie* his sonne grew most lamentable, for hauing wasted his fathers treasure, and standing in need of money in the yeare 1554 borrowed at ten, twelue, and sixteene in the hundred, of the Caponyes, Albicis, and the Foucquers of Germanie, and when he was not able to pay the interest, he promised the creditors interest vpon interest. The emperour *Charles* 5 did the like for his part; true it is, he payd but ten and twelue in the hundred. And the same yeare *Henrie* the eight king of England, borrowed a hundred thousand crowns of the German marchants at twelue in the hundred: euerie one hoping to draw money and wealth vnto him by the desire of vsurie. And whereas our king *Henrie* the second thought to draw most money vnto him G by paying of more interest than the emperour or king of England, he began to loose his credit, for the wisest husbands concluded that in the end he would not be able to pay neither principall nor interest; for the interest of sixteene in the hundred, came at the least to eighteene in the hundred, detaining the interest which he could not pay: whereas the emperour made shew that he would free himselfe, giuing cities and communalties for cautions, paying the old debts with new borrowing, and euerie man lent him seeing him pay so willingly. But at this day many will free both principall and interest, to haue but thirtie paid them for a hundred; so as after the death of *Henrie*, all was filled with the complaint of creditors: and such princes and Signiories as had money in the banke at Lion, H were much altered, and not onely the Signiories of the Cantons, the princes of Germanie and others had their parts there, but also Bashas & marchants of Tur-

The Bashas of Turquie had money at interest in the bank at Lion.

kie were there in their Factors names for aboue fiue hundred thousand crownes; and nothing did more with-hold the great Turke from succoring of the French in their last voyage of Naples, vnder the duke of Guise, than the not paying of foure thousand crownes for interest to *Rustan* Basha, besides the ten thousand which *la Vigne* the ambassador carried him in the yeare 1556, fearing to loose his principall, as I haue learned by letters and instructions from *la Vigne*, for many did not buy rents for a certaine summe of money, but would haue the interest pure and simple, and vppon condition that they should haue their principall I

The policie of Italian vsurers.

againe: as many Italians doe with priuate men, to whom they lend their money simply hauing them bound both bodie and goods, without making any mention of interest, and yet by a verball agreement, they promise sixteene or twenty in the hundred; if he faile to pay the interest, they seaze vppon bodie and goods for the principall: and although the interest be paid, if they haue need of their principall they proceed by way of execution against the debtor, for he hath neuer any quittance nor witnes for the interest which hee receiueth. Behold by what meanes they draw the money out of this realme.

There are other trickes which I forbeare to touch, but for this cause king *Lewis* the ninth in the yeare 1254, and *Philip* the Faire in the yere 1300 did banish all K

Antient laws against Italian vsurers.

Bankers and Italian marchants out of Fraunce, confiscating their goods: and to discouer the debts that were owing them, it was decreed that the debtors shuld be freed from all arrerages and interests, paying the principall to the treasurers. And since, in the yeare of our Lord one thousand three hundred fortie and seuen, *Philip* of Valois for the like cause did forfeit all their goods: for it was verified by the processe that was made, that for foure and twentie thousand pounds starling, they had in few yeares profited two millions and foure hundred and fortie thousand pounds starling: and in hatred of such
vsurie

F1 *For* sometimes *read* foure times.　　H2 *For* altered *probably read* aliened *i.e.* alienated, estranged (cf. Fr).　　H6 voyage of Naples *i.e.* expedition to Naples
Note at F5.

vsurie the Lombards letters haue been alwaies taxed in the Chancery at double: and although these people haue been often banished the realme, yet there were neuer more in any place, nor will euer bee wanting, so long as princes take vp at interest. Since and before that the banke of Lion was broken, most of the cities of this realme haue lent vnto the king vpon the reuenews, customes, imposts, and tenths for reasonable interest, and those which held themselues to be of best iudgment in matters of state and treasure, aduised it for two ends, the one to haue money at need; the other to bind the cities and communalties more vnto their prince, yet we haue neuer seene more rebellions since the establishment of this realme. And as for the treasure, it hath been so well husbanded, as in lesse than twelue yeares that king *Henrie* the second raigned, hee did owe more than his predecessors had leuied fortie yeares before, for all charges: for by an account made in the yeare 1560, king *Francis* the second, successor to *Henrie*, did owe two millions three hundred twelue thousand six hundred and ten liures, eighteen soulz six deniers, of money lent freely, for the which he paid no interest: and fifteene millions nine hundred twentie six thousand fiue hundred fiftie and fiue liures, 12 soulz and 8 deniers, for the which he paid interest: and he ought more for arrerages seuen hundred threescore and fifteene thousand, nine hundred threescore and nineteene liures, foure soulz, and foure deniers: besides the debt of *Ferrara*, and other debts for marriages, which came to eight millions fiue hundred and fourteen thousand fiue hundred fourescore and twelue liures, eighteene soulz and eleuen deniers: and other remainders due, to the summe of fifteene hundred threescore and foure thousand, seuen hundred fourescore and seuen liures, two soulz, and six deniers: so as by the last article the king remained indebted one and forty millions, a hundred fourescore three thousand, one hundred threescore and fifteen liures, three soulz, six deniers: comprehending fourteene millions nine hundred threescore and one thousand seuen hundred fourescore and seuen liures fifteene soulz and eight deniers, for the aides, reuenewes, and customes engaged, to cities, corporations, and colledges, and to priuat men: amongst the which the citie of Paris hath had yerely three millions one hundred & so many thousand liures, comprehending the tenths: moreouer the clergie hath furnished aboue threescore millions in the time of king *Francis* 2, and *Charles* 9. Although the emperour *Charles* 5, and his successor haue run the same fortune, for that they took vp at interest, being indebted aboue fifty millions, for the which all the lands, and reuenews of Naples and Milan were engaged to the Genewais and other priuate persons, who now are called in question, for that they had taken of the king of Spaine in his necessitie thirtie and fortie in the hundred; and to effect it, they haue caused the catholicke king to be censured by an admonition from the Pope, if he continued those excessiue vsuries; who embracing this occasion, defrauded his creditors of ten yeres interest. We must not think that the Spaniards will suffer themselues to bee easily gulled by the bankers of Italie, as the French do, who suffer them to inioy the farmes & al the best reuenews of France, the taxes, imposts, customes and doanne of Lion, by meanes of which farmes they ransome the subiects, and transport the coynes, contrary to the laws of this realme, which forbid to suffer strangers to enrich themselues by the reuenews of the crowne: nay, it hath been more insupportable to preferre them before naturall subiects, which offered much more, & yet they had an abatement of twentie thousand crownes at one instant out of the custome of Lion, to the perpetuall infamie of the French: and least they should be molested and drawn in question of

The debts of king Henrie the second.

The debts of Spaine.

theft,

B9 *For* foure soulz *read* fourteen soulz (Fr).   C1–2 *For* eighteene soulz *read* eight soulz (Fr).
Note at B1.

676   THE SIXT BOOKE

theft, they haue gotten an euocation of all their causes to the priuie councell. The originall of all these miseries growes from *Frauncis* the first, who began to take vp money at intrest, hauing 1800000 crownes in his coffers, and peace within his realme: no well aduised prince will euer take that course, for thereby hee shall ruine the foundation of his treasure, if he will keepe his faith and pay; but if he will not, or cannot pay, then must he breake and loose his credite, which is the ruine of an estate: for he must borrow, leuie taxes, impositions, and in the end by slaunders, and tyrannies forfeit his subiects goods. Then is it most fit and necessarie for a prince to borrow money vpon interest of his allies and subiects, *Means to assure the estate of a desperat prince.* if that hee bee in danger to loose his estate, by some generall reuolt, or the conspiracie of some great men against him; for extreame remedies are to be sought in extreamest dangers: as we read that *Eumenes* did, who borrowed a great sum of money at extreame interest, of those that had conspired his death. *Agrippa* king of Iudea, recouered his realme by the meanes of his creditors, who troubled both heauen and earth for the assurance they had to bee payd: and this was also the chiefe meanes to restore *Edward* the fourth king of England, being expelled his kingdome. But if the princes creditors haue assurance to bee paid by his successors, or that they haue lands in pawne, then this course is vnprofitable. I haue set downe the meanes which in my opinion are profitable and honest to gather together treasure, the which is the first point of this chapter: the second is how to employ the treasure of the Commonweale well and honourably, the which wee haue partly toucht in the chapter of rewards and punishments. Let vs adde hereunto what remaines.

Means to employ the treasure. In old time the first article set downe in the expences of the treasure, was for almes deeds; the second for the kings house; and the third for reparations: but the order is quite changed. As for almes-deeds, the wise and antient princes of the Hebrews, haue left this discipline to posteritie, the which they receiued from the holy Prophets, who sayd, That the surest preseruation and defence of treasure, were Almes deeds, and liberalitie to the needie; the which they restrained to the tenth part of euerie mans goods, which should bee employed vpon the ministers of the church and the poore. And if we will looke aduisedly into it, we shall not find any prince, state, or family that hath flourished more in riches, honours, and all happinesse, than those which had most care of the poore and needie. In old time there were no princes vnder heauen more charitable than our kings of Fraunce, since *Robert* sonne to *Hugh Capet*, who gaue the first *The charity of the kings of Fraunce to the poore.* example to his subiects and successors to be charitable to the poore, feeding a thousand daily, giuing them horses to follow the court, to blesse him and pray for him; and to speake truly, there was neuer king in this realme that raigned longer and in greater peace. We may iustly say of our kings, that there is no race vnder heauen that hath so entertained the greatnes of their maiestie in armes and laws, and out of the which there hath issued more princes, or that haue raigned longer without offence to all other princes, Christians, Turks, Tartars, Persians, Indians, and Ethiopians. What prince euer was more charitable to the poore, than *Lewis* the ninth, who hath founded twentie eight hospitals and colledges in this realme; and had commonly in his traine six score poore folks, and in Lent twelue score, feeding them with meat from his owne table? he also liued in great honor, being feared of his enemies, reuerenced of his friends, honored of his subiects: and after that he had raigned 44 yeres, he left fiue sonnes, and foure daughters, and a kingdome flourishing in armes and laws to his successor, recommending

H4 expences   K2 longer; without

mending vnto him aboue all things to be deuout to God, and charitable to the poore. Neither may we forget *Iames* the fift king of Scotland, who was called *Rex egentium*, The king of the needie; who as he exceeded all the princes of his time in bountie, so did he surmount all his predecessors in riches. And contrariwise we see great families, states, realmes, and empires come to pouertie and ruine, hauing contemned the poore, and abandoned the subiect to the spoile of the souldior, and the thefts of toll-gatherers: when as king *Henrie* the second in the yeare 1549, did exact that extraordinarie tribute which they called *Taillon*, he promised not to employ that money to any other vse, than to the entertainment of his men at armes, and not to confound it with the ordinarie receits, that the subiect might be freed from the spoile of souldiers. The like was said, when as the realme was charged with the paiment of 50000 footmen in the time of king *Frauncis* the first, the which should be leuied vpon walled townes and their suburbes, which felt nothing of the oppression of the souldier; but notwithstanding since they haue made it equall to towne, village, and hamlet in the yere 1555, whereby the poore countreyman hath ben doubly oppressed, for they pay, and are spoiled of all sides. And yet with all these charges, they would hold themselues happy, if they might bee freed in prouiding corne and victuals for the souldiors at an vnder rate, what may then bee hoped for in those cities whereas the souldiers robbe and spoile the poore subiects with all impunitie, and insult more ouer the citizens than against the enemie? but for an excuse, they pretend they are not paid, neither would they be, to the end they might haue some colour for their thefts. There is no meanes to redresse these calamities, and to restore in some sort militarie discipline, which is now quite decaied, but in paying the souldiers: for as *Cassiodorus* said, *Disciplinam seruare non potest ieiunus exercitus, dum quod deest semper presumit armatus*, A fasting armie can neuer obserue good discipline, for what they want, they will presume to take by force: the which cannot bee done vnlesse there bee a great care had of the treasure. The kings house therefore entertained, the souldiers and the officers payd, and due rewards giuen to them that deserue them, it is great reason the poore should be remembred. And if the treasurie bee well furnished, a part would be employed to repaire townes, to fortifie vpon the frontiers, to furnish places of strength, make the passages euen, build bridges, fortifie the ports, send ships to sea, build publicke houses, beautifie temples, erect colledges for honor, vertue, and learning: for besides necessitie of reparations, it brings great profite to the Commonweale. For by this means arts and artificers are entertained, the poore people are eased, the idle are set to worke, cities are beautified and diseases expelled: finally hatred against princes (which doth often times stirre vp the subiects to rebellion) is quite suppressed, when as the impositions which he hath leuied, redounds not only to the general, but also to euery priuat mans good. And therefore the emperour *Alexander Seuerus* was accustomed to leaue many imposts and tolles to cities, to be employed in the necessarie reparations thereof.

This which I haue sayd is more expedient in an *Aristocratia*, or a Popular state, than in a Monarchie; for that the subiects being many, are with more difficultie maintai ed in peace and vnion by few commaunders: vnlesse the multitude being employed in the publicke works, may make some gaine, and not to inure them to the distribution of corne and money, as they vsually did in Popular states, and especially the Tarentins: the which is not only the ruine of the treasure, but likewise of the citie. So *Pericles* was also blamed, hauing first

The souldior must be payd to preuent all thefts and insolencies.

The benefit of reparations and fortifications.

first accustomed the Atheniens to these distributions: the which he did to gaine the peoples fauor. But when he was once master of them, he emploied the publicke treasure, not only to fortifie the citie, but also to beautifie it, and to fill it with good artificers: yet durst hee not attempt this before the citie was in peace and their treasure full, hauing then a hundred thousand tallents; that is to say, threescore millions of crownes, if we may beleeue *Demosthenes*: which summe because it is vnreasonable, it may be, we should read a hundred tallents, which make threescore thousand pounds, for that wee shewed before, that the Athenians (when as they had charged their allies with great tributes) did neuer leuy aboue two thousand tallents yearely at the most, and in *Pericles* time they did scarce exact a thousand tallents. And being accused by his enemies to haue misemploied the publicke treasure, hee made this resolute answere vnto the people, That if they were not well pleased with the walles, fortresses, and temples which hee built, hee would take the charge vpon himselfe, vpon condition, that his name should be grauen thereon, and that it was his gift: but the people allowed the charge, knowing well that all men in generall, and euerie man in particular, reaped profit and honour thereby, for that the marchant did gaine in furnishing of stuffe; sea men, and those that brought it, for their carriage; and artificers in working it; so as the profit was distributed to all sorts of people, and the glorie of their stately workes, gaue a perpetuall testimonie to posteritie of the greatnes of this Commonweale. But the greatest benefit, and which doth most import the preseruation of an estate is, That the two greatest plagues of a Common weale, Idlenesse and Pouertie, are banished: a verie necessarie thing in a popular and aristocraticall state; and especially in those countries, where they haue great spirits, and but barren soyle, as at Athens: if idlenesse get footing in such a countrey, it will neuer be without mutinies and thefts, which *Solon* foreseeing, he did inflict great punishments vpon idle persons: and so did *Amasis* king of Egypt, who condemned idle men to be put to death, if they had not wherewithall to liue, knowing the Egyptians to be the most ingenuous in the world, and the most subiect to mutinie, if they were not employed. We see Piramides built in that countrey almost three thousand yeares since, lest the pleople should haue languished with idlenesse: we haue also presidents of the wisest emperours of Rome, which haue in like sort emploied their treasure, & giuen the subiects example to imitate them: as *Augustus*, who did iustly vant, That he had found Rome built with bricke, but that he had left it built with marble: and in truth he employed foure millions and fiue hundred thousand crownes in building of the Capitoll alone: he was followed by the emperour *Vespasian*, who made great and excellent workes throughout the whole empire, rather to entertaine the meaner sort, than for any other end: for when as an excellent workeman promised him to set vp pillers in the Capitoll, of an excessiue greatnes, with small charge and few labourers; he recompenced him verie well, saying, Let me I pray you, nourish the poore: and yet he protested in open senate comming to the empire, That there was need of a milliart of crownes to free and restore that Common weale.

What shall I say of the emperour *Claudius*, who enioying an assured peace, caused the chanell of Fucina to be made, to accommodate the citie with good waters, employing dayly thirtie thousand men for eleuen yeares together. And without search of antient histories it is well knowne that the signiorie of Venice doth entertaine continuall in their Arsenall, three or foure thousand persons

---

F8 *For* pounds *read* crowns (as at F6).   H9 ingenuous *i.e.* ingenious (cf. Fr)   I1 the people
I2 presidents *i.e.* precedents

OF A COMMONWEALE.

A. sons which get their liuing by the labour of their hands, the which doth much content the citisens, seeing the publicke treasure employed so charitably. But these employments are goodly and befitting a great prince which is not indebted, when the reuenewes are not pawned, when as the Commonweale is in perfect peace, when the soldiers are paide, and rewards duly administred to euerie one: otherwise to increase the subsidies to build great pallaces, more stately than necessarie, being indebted, and to suffer the buildings of his predecessors to runne to ruine, thereby to purchase vaine glorie, that were to leaue a marke of his tyrannie, and a perpetuall testimonie to posteritie, That he hath built with the bloud of his subiects: and often times the subiects ruine the buildings of ty-

B. rants, to deface their memory from off the earth, wheras they shuld by vertuous and charitable actions, graue their names in heauen. The golden pallace of *Nero*, which comprehended a great part of Rome, was contemned by his successors, who would not vouchsafe to lodge in it, for the crueltie and villanie of him that had built it; and soone after it was ruined, as being made of spoiles, exactions and confiscations, the which follow a prodigall prince at the heeles: for of necessitie, of a prodigall he must become an oppressor, and of an oppressor a tyrant.

There were neuer two tyrants more cruell and prodigall, than *Nero* and *Caligula*; for the first, in fifteen yeares that hee raigned, had giuen away the value of fiftie and fiue millions of crownes: and the last, in one yere had wasted three-

C. score and seuen millions, so as hauing not wherewithall to defray his houshold charges, he was forced to beg the offrings in his owne person: then falling to prescriptions of priuate men, after that he had wasted the publick tresure, he filled all with cruell confiscations. This miserie of excessiue prodigalitie happens often to princes, through forgetfulnesse of the gifts which they haue bestowed, not well vnderstanding the botome of their treasuries. And for this cause, it was wisely decreed by *Frauncis* the first, that euerie yere the generals of the treasure, should send vnto the treasurer, two briefes of the publicke reuenewes of euery prouince: the one by coniecture the first day of the yeare; the other a true note of the yeare that was past: and in like case the treasurer should make two briefs

D. of the whole treasure in generall, to the end that the king and his counsell might plainly know what money was in his coffers, thereby to gouerne his gifts, rewards, and expences: but most commonly hee that hath power to dispose of it, seeth nothing. I will put for an example an estimate of the treasure which was made in Ianuarie in the yere 1572, where in a chapter of the receit, there was an article set downe of 200000 pounds starling of casuall things: and by a true account made in the end of the yeare, it was found, that they amounted to two hundred and fourescore thousand pounds starling, and yet it was verified, that there was but fiftie thousand pounds employed to the kings profit. Such was the calamitie of those times when as children and women ruled. But in my o-

E. pinion, the king had done better, if he had seen the generall account of his reuenews, the which is contained in two sheets of paper, and withall had had a register of his gifts and rewards: or if his priuie gifts be not inrolled, that he had a small briefe or remembrance of that which he had giuen, to whom, and wherefore: which are three chiefe points, whereof a prince must be verie carefull, to the end, that if he will be liberall, it should be to such as deserue it. And to this end, it were expedient the prince had a briefe register of affaires of state, and a rolle of the worthiest men of his realme, for there is no memorie so perfect, but may be confounded with the multiplicitie of affaires, whereby he shall commit

Mmm iiij great

Side notes:
- A tyrant builds with the bloud of his subiects.
- The strange prodigalitie of Nero and Caligula.
- Articles of parties casuall in the yeare 1572.
- A prince should haue a list of matters of state and of his chefe men.

C2-3 prescriptions *i.e.* proscriptions

Notes at B6, C6

great incongruities in matters of state: for a briefe note of affaires shall put him in mind of that which he hath to do, and of all enterprises, the which oftentimes remaine imperfect and ill executed through forgetfulnesse. There is no better example hereof, than that of king *Lewis* the eleuenth, who was held one of the most politicke princes of his age, yet hee ran willingly into the snare of *Charles* earle of Carolois, hauing forgotten that hee had sent his ambassadors into the countrey of Liege, to stirre them to warre against him: the earle aduertised hereof, detained him prisoner: the which had not happened, if he had kept a register of his former actions. If any flatterers of the court will object, That the register would be too great, that the prince should be too much troubled, and that hee could not liue long: why then haue those princes and great monarchs which haue been so carefull of matters of state, and gouerned the whole world with their lawes, liued so long? as *Augustus, Tiberius, Vespasian, Traian, Adrian*, and the *Antonines*, all Romaine emperours and politicke gouernours, who themselues made registers of their owne affaires, imitating the example of *Augustus*, who liued 74 yeares, leauing three Bookes written with his owne hand; the first was his deeds and publicke actions; the second was his testament; the third was an estate of all the Romaine empire, wherein was contained a particular estate of euerie prouince, what troupes of souldiers, what treasure, what armes, what shipping, and what munition, with a diligence worthie of a great monarch: yet for all this he did not omit to doe iustice ordinarily and to heare all commers, reading all the bookes of politike gouernment, that he could get, as *Suetonius* saith, remembring that which *Demetrius* the Phalerien said vnto *Ptolome Philadelph* king of Egypt, that he should find goodly secrets in bookes, which no man durst tell him. *Vespasian* in like sort, made an excellent abridgement of the empire, and yet he liued 70 yeares.

The diligence of Augustus.

The empire of Persia was greater than that of the Romaines, stretching from the farthest bounds of India, vnto Hellespont, and the desert of Libia, hauing vnder it 127 Prouinces, and yet the kings of Persia carried with them continually a register of their affaires of state and of their gifts: and whenas *Darius Longuemau* had escaped the conspirators hands, by the aduertisement which *Mardocheus* had giuen him, the king a while after reading this register by night, and finding that *Mardocheus* had receiued no reward for so great a seruice done vnto the king hee caused him to bee sent for, giuing him great honours and preferments. But without any further search, the king of Spaine doth vsually looke vpon a register of his affaires, carrying an abridgement of letters which he writes to gouernors, captaines, and ambassadors, if the matter be not verie secret. For the same cause *Charles* surnamed the wise, king of France, made a Register of his priuie councell, and the first was *Peter Barrier*, who was not busied (as at this day) with expeditions and acts of iustice, but onely to inroll the affaires of state. But aboue all it is necessarie for a prince to haue a register in his counsell, of gifts, offices, benefices, & exemptions: the which is most commonly in the hands of a secretarie and yet the hundred part of the gifts are not entred. For the redressing whereof, there are two antient lawes, the one made by *Philip* of Valois, of the which I haue formerly made mention, by the which the gift was reuoked, if the donatarie made not mention of the benefits graunted to him and his predecessors: the other is of *Charles* the eight, whereby all gifts aboue ten pounds were of no force, if they were not verified in the chamber of accounts. The first law was soone taken away by another, saying, That it was sufficient

Good lawes abrogated.

by

I8 Register *i.e.* Registrar   Note at K3.

OF A COMMONWEALE. 681

A by the Letters of gift, if it were derogated from the first decree. And as for the law made by *Charles* the eight, it is out of practise, vnder color of secret gifts and pentions, the which must not be knowne: so as the antient laws (decreeing, that the articles set downe in the chapter of expences, shall not bee allowed without an order, a commaundement, and a discharge) are now of little or no force in that respect: for the treasurer is discharged, bringing the kings hand onely, without any mention of him to whom the reward was giuen, nor wherefore. There was yet a law made by king *Frauncis* the first, and confirmed by his successor, wherby it was decreed, There should be foure keys to the place where the treasure was kept, whereof the king should haue one, and the rest should be in Com-

B missioners hands appointed by him: and the distribution of money should bee made by the kings commaundement, in the presence of the treasurer and comptroller of the Exchequer: But king *Henrie* the second by a speciall edict discharged the treasurers and officers of the treasurie, that afterwards they might not be called to any account. True it is, that one of these commissioners had giuen him at one time a hundred thousand crownes, if the common report were true; the which was much at that time, but little in regard of prodigalities practised of late. For after that king *Frauncis* the first had ordred it by sparing, all the publike treasure lay open to the spoile of great men and flatterers. But an edict made in fraud should be no hindrance, but that such as had mannaged the publike trea-

C sure might bee called to an account; as it was required at a Parliament held at Orleans; and that excessiue gifts should be reuoked or at the least cut lesse: as the Emperour *Galba* did, who reuoked *Neroes* gifts, leauing but the tenth part to the donatorie; not that they should enquire too curiously of all gifts bestowed by the prince, the which might prooue verie dangerous.

The reuocation of excessiue gifts is necessarie.

Charles the seuenth did limit by a law, what summe of money the king might take yearely to dispose of at his pleasure: which summe being verie little, seemed in those daies exceeding great. There is nothing more profitable for the prince, nor necessary for the subiects, than to haue the rewards which they giue, knowne and examined by their officers: for that princes shall alwaies maintaine their fa-

D uors, giuing liberally, and the officers shalbe subiect to the hatred and dislike of such as haue their gifts reuoked or cut lesse: so as by means of recouerie, the money should returne into the treasurie againe, and few would beg, yea they would scarce take it when it should be offered them, if they knew their gifts shuld be reuoked or examined in the chamber of accounts If bountie be commendable and worthie of a great and rich Monarch, it is ill beseeming a poore and needie prince, for he must flea his subiects, and racke them to the verie bones. King *Frauncis* the first, leauing a goodly kingdome, flourishing in armes and laws, and in all arts and sciences, to his successor, with seuenteen hundred thousand crowns in treasure, and the quarter of March readie to be receiued; yet did he not giue

E away the hundred part in rewards in 32 yeares that he had raigned, as his sonne *Henrie* did in two: for he had scarce closed his eyes, when as the confirmation of offices (which is due to the king at his first comming to the crowne) whereof an infinit masse of money was then made, was giuen to one horse leech in court. And although that *Frauncis* the father gaue pensions to Germans, English, Italians, Suisses, Albaneses, Spaniards, and Grisons; yet all his pensions, besides the Cantons were but 13000 pounds starling a yere at the most, as I haue seene by an extract out of the chamber of accounts, the which was made the yeare that hee dyed: and in the same extract there is but 42769 pounds, foure

Bounty not fit in a poore prince.

An infinit masse of money giuen to a woman.

The bounty of great King Frauncis.

foure shillings starling, which hee gaue in pension to his subiects, princes of bloud, knights of the order, captaines in great numbers, lieutenants, councellors of state, men of iustice, ambassadors, scollers studying, and many excellent workmen, and learned personages. O noble prince, who could so well make choise of worthy persons, and moderat his bountie.

We haue entreated of two points of this chapter: first how a Commonweale should gather together, and then how they shall employ: the last point is, what reserue they shall make for any necessitie, that they be not forced to begin warre by borrowing, or subsidies; whereof the Romanes were verie carefull: for although they had continuall warres vntill *Augustus* time, after the defeat of *Marc Anthonie*, yet had they neuer toucht the treasure which grew of the twentieth pence of slaues infranchised, vntill that *Hannibal* had reduced them to extreame want; then was there found foure hundred and fiftie thousand crownes in their treasurie, the which was one of the chiefest meanes to saue their estate.

<small>Rescruation of treasure.</small>

<small>The treasure of the Romaines called Sanctius aerarium.</small>

The emperour of Turkie obserues this order carefully, for besides the treasury of ordinarie receits, which is in the princes Seraigle, there is another in the castle of seuen towers at Constantinople, where the antient treasure is reserued, the which they meddle not with, if the necessitie bee not verie vrgent. Our Ancestors were accustomed in time of necessitie, when the treasure was wasted to haue recourse to the kings forrests, where there was an infinit number of tall timber-trees fit for all vses, of the which they made great summes of money; but during the ciuile warres, they are so cut downe, as hereafter they will bee onely fit to make faggots: whereby the commonweale is much damnified, and will be more dayly, vnlesse there be some speedie remedie: for there is such want of timber, as they shall bee forced to fetch it out of other countreys for their ships and buildings; they do also cut them downe so hastily, as the trees cannot grow to beare any fruit to feed our swine; and in the end we shall be forced to fetch wood from other parts for firing. And for that it hath been alwaies held a matter of some difficultie to keepe treasure safely, beeing verie hard for princes to shake off importune beggars: therefore the kings of Persia and the Romaines, that they might preserue this holy treasure from stelth, they reduced a great part of their money into thicke brickes. It is also sayd, that *Charles* the fift king of Fraunce, had caused the great Hart in the pallace at Paris to be made after the same forme that they should cast one all of gold, of the treasure which he had gathered together. And the better to assure it against theeues, the antients did lay their treasure in temples, as the Greekes in the temple of *Apollo*, *Delphique*, and *Deliaque*: the Romaines in the temple of *Saturne* and *Opis*: the antient Gaules in hallowed Lakes: the Hebrews sometimes in temples, sometimes in sepulchres: for wee read that the high priest and king of the Iewes, *Hircanus*, found great treasures in *Dauids* sepulchre. But seeing there are no sepulchres so religious, no temples so holy, that theeues will not force and enter: therefore the kings of *Morocco* hauing moulten a great quantitie of gould in forme of a bowle, pierced through with a barre of yron, they did hang it on the toppe of the pinnacle of the great Church at *Marocco*. The antient Egyptians fearing to giue occasion to their neighbours and enemies to inuade their estate, and make warre against them for their treasure (as they did to king *Ezechias*, hauing shewed his treasures to the ambassadors of the king of *Assiria*) employed it for the most part in

<small>The Turks treasure.</small>

<small>The means how to keepe treasure.</small>

<small>Isaie 30.</small>

I4–5 made; AND after the same forme K4 bowle *i.e.* ball, globe K8 as they did to *i.e.* "as was done to" (Fr) K9(margin) Isaie 39

OF A COMMONWEALE. 683

A in building of their Pyramides, beautifying of cities, bringing of riuers, and repayring the bankes of Nile. The law of God forbids to heape together much gould and siluer; lest that thereby the prince should bee allured to oppresse his subiects, or the enemie to inuade the citisens; inuiting the prince thereby to bee charitable to the poore and needie: yet a meane is to bee vsed.

<small>Deut. 17.</small>

No man in my opinion will allow of the insatiable couetousnesse of *Iohn* 22 Pope of Rome, in whose coffers they found (hee being dead) twentie three millions of gold, as many haue written; or of *Sardanapalus*, who left fortie millions of crowns; or of *Cyrus*, who left fiftie millions; or of *Tiberius Cæsar*, who
B had gathered together seuentie seuen millions, the which his successor wasted in one yere; or of *Darius Ochus* the last king of the Persians, in whose treasury *Alexander* the great found fourscore millions of gold. We read in the holy scripture that *Dauid* left sixscore millions, the which is the greatest treasure that was euer heard of: but there is some question touching the valuation of their tallent; for they write that he had gathered together a hundred thousand tallents of gold, and a thousand thousand tallents of siluer, which summe, if it bee accounted by tallents of Attica, although they be small it will seeme wonderfull: our interpreters of the Bible doe falsely thinke them Attike tallants. I find *Siclum* in the scriptures to be taken two waies, the which the Greeks call *Statera*, and the Latines
C *Talentum*, one waie it is a pound of six ounces, as in the first booke of *Paralip* the 21 chapter; another way it is taken for halfe an ounce, as in the first booke of *Samuel*, the 24 chapter. If *Dauids* treasure be numbered by the sicle or tallent of halfe an ounce, the summe will not seeme great; if it be referred to six ounces, it will comprehend fiftie thousand pound waight of gold, and ten times as much in siluer: but if it be valued by the Attike tallent, the wealth of the Romanes neuer came nere it; as we may see by an extract out of the treasury vnder the empire of *Traian*, at which time it was at the greatest; for the whole sum of their treasure (the which was kept in Egypt) came but to 74 thousand tallents, the which amounts to 44 millions, and foure hundred thousand crownes; vnlesse they had
D another treasurie at Rome, as it is likely, (although it appeare not by the extract) hauing 200000 foot, and 40000 horse in garrisons on the frontiers of the empire and in the prouinces entertained: three hundred Elephants for the warre, two thousand chariots for warre, and munition to arme 300000 men, fifteen hundred galleys of three and fiue owers on a side, besides two thousand vessels for the sea, and furniture to arme and rigge twise as many, with fourescore great ships stately adorned.

<small>22. Paralip. li.1. The greatest treasure that euer was.</small>

<small>The treasure of the Romaines.</small>

But our kings of *Fraunce* haue not offended in this point against the lawes of God, by heaping vp of too great treasures, and it is not to be feared that they will hereafter breake it: for they which say, that king *Charles* the fift left in his treasu-
E rie eighteene millions of crownes, are much deceiued, for he found the coffers empty, he paid his predecessors debts, he redeemed the reuenews of the crown, conquered Guienne from the English, purchased the countie of Anxerre, and a great part of the earledome of Eureux, restored *Henrie* king of Castill being expelled his realme, maintained and succored the kings of Scotland, against the kings of England, and raigned but 17 yeares, and yet he did not leuie for all charges aboue 43756 pounds starling yerely, comprehending the reuenews of the crowne lands: although that in his time the ayds and custome of 8 shillings vppon euerie fire were laid vpon the subiects: and his successor fortie yeares after
did

B1 *For* seuentie seuen *read* sixtie seuen (Fr). In L the figures from A8 to B3 vary widely. D4 to arme 300000 men E3 Auxerre Notes at A10, D10, E2, E7.

684   THE SIXT BOOKE

The reuenews of Fraunce vnder Charles the 5, 6, 7, Lewis the 11, and Charles the 8.

did leuie but 45000 pounds starling: and *Charles* the seuenth, the yeare that he died, receiued for all charges and reuenews, but 170000 pounds starling, as it appeares plainly in the chamber of accounts, & yet had he imposed the tax in forme of an ordinarie impost, the which at that time came but to 1800 pounds: and twentie yeares after when as *Lewis* the eleuenth died, the whole receit came but to 470000 pounds, the which was reduced to 120000 pounds, at the request of the Parliament, held at Tours at the comming of *Charles* the 8 vnto the crowne,

Diminution of halfe the charge at the comming of Charles 8.

besides the reuenews of the crowne which amounted yearely by estimation to 100000 pounds: so as the whole reuenews when as *Charles* the eight died, came not to aboue 250000 pounds. The like request was made vnto king *Charles* the ninth, by a parliament held at Orleans, at his comming to the crowne: but the necessitie was found so great as there was more need to augment than to diminish the the charge. Yet there was great hope to free the king out of debt, and to take away the subsidies & extraordinary charges, (if the realme had not ben plunged in ciuile warre) considering the good order was taken the first yeare: for the interest was moderated to fiue in the hundred, all officers wages for that yeare were diminished and halfe taken awaie, and the confirmation of offices graunted them freely. And as for the expences, all was so well ordred, as by the accounts of that yere, there came into the kings coffers 230577 pounds starling: so as in few yeares all had been discharged, without any diminution of the kings houshold seruants, the which were six hundred, besides such as were entertained for hunting & hawking, for they may well be spared without deminution of the maiestie of a king or the dignity of his house, by cutting off his ordinary traine and houshold seruants, the which oftentimes doth cause strangers to contemne him, and his subiects to rebell against him: as it chanced vnto *Lewis* the eleuenth, who hauing put the nobilitie from him & discharged the gentlemen of his house, vsed his taylor for an herald at armes, his barbar for an ambassador, and his Phisition for chancellor, (as *Antiochus* king of Syria did his phisitian *Apolophanes*, whom he made president of his counsell) & in mockerie of other kings, he ware

The basenesse of Lewis the eleuenth in his apparell.

a greasie hat, and very courfe cloth in his apparell: and euen in the chamber of accounts, there is set downe in a note of expences two shillings for a new paire of sleeues to an old dublet: and in another Item three halfe pence for a box of grease to blacke his boots withall; and yet he raised the charges more than his predecessor did by 300000 pounds starling a yeare, and sold much of the reuenews. As for the officers of the crowne, it was wisely aduised at the estates of Orleans, to reduce them to the antient number, as they were in the time of king *Lewis* the twelfe, by suppression without any disbursement. But there were some good husbands which gaue them afterwards to vnderstand, that the suppression of offices was a decrease of parties casuall, wherby the number was afterwards much augmented: And *Balley* president of the accounts told the king boldly and plainly, being at S. *Maur des fosses*, that the suppression of those officers which had been created by the new law, was both pernitious to the publicke, and hurtfull to his treasure, seeing but for three augmentations in the chamber of accounts

Anno 1566. 20 Maie.

onely, they had payd aboue threescore thousand pounds starling: but he doth not say that it is like vnto cold water which encreaseth the fit to him that hath a burning Feuer: for it is well knowne that the king or people pay wages to most of these officers after ten or twentie for the hundred, which was the principall cause of the suppression of subalternall offices by a law made by *Fraun-cis* the second. Moreouer they set not downe the prerogatiues which belong

to

F3 the tax *i.e.* the *taille*   G5 good order THAT was taken (cf. Fr)   G6 hundred   K4(margin) *For* 20 Maie (Fr 7) *read* 10 Maie (Fr 1-6, 8 and L).   K8 subalternall offices *i.e.* alternating offices, whose duties were performed by two incumbents in turn

OF A COMMONWEALE.   685

A to the officers of the chamber of accompts, that is to say, their ordinarie wages, their rights of wood, their liuerie at Easter, their rights at Hallontide, their roses, their prerogatiue of herings, their rights at Twelfetide, their rights of the stable of vertue, and of white salt, besides paper, parchment, pens, counters, purses, waxe candles, red waxe, penkniues, bodkins, scrapers and strings: they did not shew also that the other profits of offices came to much more than their wages: they will not confesse that whereas there be now seauen chambers of accompts, there was then but one; and whereas now there be two hundred officers or thereabouts in the chamber of accompts at Paris, there was wont to be but one Treasorer of France President of the chamber, and foure masters of accompts that were Clarks, by an erection that was made at Viuiers in Brie in

B the yeare 1319, afterwards they added foure lay men, which sufficed for all that were accomptable: the kingdome of Nauarre, and all the Lowcountries being then in the hands of the kings of France. And yet we haue seen in our daies, that those which haue stollen the kings treasure and the subiects wealth, haue escaped, being indebted in great sommes of money; and infinit others which haue neuer accompted. And which is more, not long since an accomptant had gotten into his possession a great and notable somme of money, wherewith he stood charged by his accompt, who by collusion with a nobleman that should haue a third part, he obtained the rest by gift, and for his discharge, he produced the kings bil signed to the nobleman. So as to call accomptants

C to their duties, they must oftentimes depute Commissioners with double charges, and the fault cannot be imputed to any other, but to those officers that are created to that end. And although that all treasorers, receiuers, comptrollers, and other accomptants should make a good and loyall accompt, and pay what remaines due; yet notwithstanding there is so great a number in this realme, as a third part of the receit is spent in gages, charges, vacations, riding voyages, and the conduct of money; as hath been well verified by the estates of the countrie of Languedock in the yeare 1556, where I was then present: who for that cause deputed *Martin Durant*, Syndic or Procurator of that countrie, to present a request vnto the king to be discharged of all officers of receit, making offer to bring all the money that was to be leuied vpon the subiect freely into the kings cofers, without any charge either for officers wages, or for carriage:

D shewing also particularly that the third part of the receipts went to officers, promising to deliuer vnto the king a full crowne, whereas hee did not receiue foure shillings, whereby he should saue 20000. pounds starling yearely in the two generalities of Languedoc, only for ordinarie charges: for then the charge of Languedoc came to threescore thousand pounds yearely. But since the officers of the finances or treasor are so increased, as *Maximinus Lullier*, Prouost of marchants at Paris, and President of the chamber of accompts, said in open Parlament at Blois, That of the crowne there came not eighteene pence cleere into the kings cofers: the which seemes incredible, yet he was held a man most expert in accompts. We must then conclude, that the subiect

E was much opprest by the polling of officers, seeing they made these offers: which we may not thinke new, for that in old times they had no other receiuers but the Viconts, Bayliffes, and Seneshals. That request made by the Syndic of Languedoc did much please king *Henry*, but it displeased the flatterers in court, and the officers of the accompts, so as it was reiected, for the friuolous difficulties they made which had interest therein, the which is not heere needfull to rehearse, so as it was concluded that receiuers and treasorers were necessarie. Seeing then that accomptants and masters of accompts is a necessarie euill (as *Alexander Seuerus* said) The fewer there are, the better shall it be for the Commonweale; for the kings treasure will still decrease when it passeth through the hands of so many officers. These were the complaints and expostu-
lations

Marginal notes:
- The right of the officers of the chamber of accounts.
- Erection of the chamber of accounts.
- An offer made by the estates of Languedoc, to king Henry the second.

Nnn

A2 Hallontide *i.e.* the season of All Saints   A3 Twelfetide *i.e.* Epiphany   A3 stable, of   A3 For vertue *read* glass (*verre* in Fr 1–6, 8, misprinted *verru* in Fr 7).   C5 gages *i.e.* wages
C5 vacations *i.e. vacations*, emoluments   C5 riding, voyages,   D10 polling *i.e.* thieving
Note at B4.

686　　　　　　　　　　　　The Sixt Booke

lations which the estates of France made vnto king *Charles* the 6 in the yeare 1412, for that he had fiue Treasorers, and that in old time there were but two: and that in like sort there were but three Iudges of the reuenues in the yeare 1372, and now there are almost three hundred within this realme. And in the yeare 1360 there was but one Receiuer generall, who did reside at Paris, & now there are 34, what would they now say to see so great a multitude. The Romans in old time had but one receiuer in euery Prouince: all customes and duties were let out to farme, and the farmers brought in their rents to the receiuer. The first office that was giuen to gentlemen of good families, and that aspired to greater dignities, was the office of Questura, or Receiuer for a yeare only, and without any comptroller to make triall of their diligence and loyaltie.

A meane to make deceiuers true and iust.

He that was found guiltie of extorsion, was declared incapeable neuer to beare any honorable charge, besides infamie and the losse of his goods, the which was a wise course to assure their treasure. But it is a strange thing and very absurd in this realme, to see so many men giue money to their maister to pick his purse. The Emperour of Turkie doth otherwise, for he neuer sels office, and for so great an Empire there are verie few

The order of the receit in Turkie.

Treasorers: the Collectors (which they call Protogeres) giue the money vnto the Subachis (which are as it were the Viconts of Normandie, who in old times had the same charge) then they deliuer it to the Sangiacs (who are as it were gouernors of the countrie) who conuey it vnto the Bellerbeis, and they send in safety vnto the Desterderlers, which are two generals of the Treasor, the one in Asia, and the other in Europe, who deliuer it to the great Comptroller, and he giues it to *Casmander Baschi*, great maister of the treasor, who hath ten commanders or deputies vnder him for extraordinarie payments, there is but one treasorer, and for all officers of accompts, there are but 25 Comptrollers which examine the accoumpts. One thing is worthie obseruation, that they haue no treasorers nor receiuers but Eunukes, after the Persian and old Grecian manner, and that wisely, for they that neither haue children, nor can be seduced with the flatteries and inticements of women, it is not to be feared that they will steale the publike treasor with the hazard of their liues and fame. As for Treasorers in France, it is more then necessarie that such offices be giuen to gentlemen of honor and of noble houses, as it was vsuall in old time, and is yet practised in England for the reason that I haue said. By an Edict made by king *Henry* the second in September in the yeare 1554 it was decreed, that the chiefe Treasorers should take their places before the Stewards of the kings house, of the councellers of the court of Parliament, of the accompts and aides, if they be not in their assemblies: and by an Edict made by *Charles* the 9, he commaunds all vassals which hold directly of the king, to do homage and fealtie vnto the Treasorers of France, the which would much discontent an infinite number of Dukes, Earles, Barons, and great personages, who would not for any thing kneele before a base fellow that had bought his office. Thus much concerning treasure, and for that it consists in coyne of gold, siluer, copper and buillon, it is necessarie to write something thereof.

Chap.

F5 *are* 34: *what*　　F10 *comptroller, to*　　G9–10 *Desterderlers*　　H2 *under him: for*　　H10 *England, for*　　I3 *For of the councellers* read *[and before] the councellers.*　　I9 buillon *i.e.* billon, silver mixed with a high proportion of base metal (cf. 695 B2–3)　　Notes at F6, F8.

Chap. III.

Of Coines, and the meanes how to preuent that they be not altered, nor falsified.

Ooking well into the best grounds, and strongest supports of a Commonweale; in my opinion, hee must exactly vnderstand this point, that will wisely settle an estate, or reforme the abuses: for that there is nothing that doth more trouble and afflict the poore people, than to falsifie the Coines, and to alter the course thereof: for both rich, and poore, euerie one in particular, and all in generall, receiue an infinit losse and preiudice, the which cannot precisely in euery point bee described, it breeds so many inconueniences. The Coine may not be corrupted, no not altered, without great preiudice to the Commonweale: for if money (which must rule the price of all things) be mutable and vncertaine, no man can make a true estate of what he hath, contracts and bargaines shall be vncertaine, charges, taxes, wages, pensions, rents, interests, and vacations shall be doubtfull, fines also and amercements limited by the lawes and customes shall be changeable and vncertaine: to conclude, the estate of the treasure and of many affaires both publike and priuate shall be in suspence: whereof the Edict made by *Gratidianus* the Tribune at Rome is a good argument, who (contrarie to the opinion of his fellow Tribunes) set a certaine price of a kind of coyne called *Victoriatus*, vpon a penaltie, whereby he purchased so great glorie to himselfe and his posteritie, as they did erect his statues in euery streete, and offred frankinsence and waxe vnto them. And *Tully* saith, *Neminem vnquam multitudini ob id vnum fuisse cariorem*, Neuer any man (for that cause only) was deerer to the people. The Prince may not make any false money, no more than he may kill or rob, neither can he alter the weight of his coyne to the preiudice of his subiects, and much lesse of strangers, which treate with him, and traffick with his people, for that he is subiect to the law of nations, vnlesse he will lose the name and maiestie of a king, and be tearmed a counterfetter of money: as *Dante* the poet called *Philip le Bel*, for that he did first among our princes corrupt the coyne, and mingle copper with siluer, which was the cause of great troubles among his subiects, and a pernitious president to forraine Princes: whereof he repented himselfe too late, restoring the coyne, and inioyning his sonne *Lewis Hutin* not to abate the goodnes of his coynes. And for this cause *Peter* the 4 king of Arragon did confiscate the estate of the king of Maiorque and Minorque, whom he pretended to be his vassall, for that he had abated the coyne: and yet the kings of Arragon themselues did erre in that point, so as pope *Innocent* the 3 did forbid them as his vassals not to vse it: whereupon the kings of Arragon comming to the crowne doth sweare not to change the waight and price of their money, which hath been allowed. But it is not sufficient to make such protestations, vnlesse the value and waight of money be ordred as it ought, to the end that neither prince nor subiect may falsifie it if they would, the which they will alwayes do, hauing the meanes, what punishment soeuer be inflicted. The ground of all these counterfet coyners, washers, clippers, and boylers of money, growes by the mixtures which are made of mettals, for one mettall being pure and simple cannot be supposed for another, differing by nature in colour, waight, substance, and sound. To preuent all these inconueniences, you must ordaine that in euery Commonweale the coynes be of one mettall without mixture, and publish the Edict of the Emperour *Tacitus*, who defended vpon losse of life and goods, to mingle gold with siluer, nor siluer with copper, nor copper with tinne or lead.

Daungerous to a state to alter the coine.

The prince cannot alter his coyne.

Coynes should be simple without any mixture.

lead. But we may except from this law the mixture of copper with tinne, which makes the sounding mettall, whereof bels and ordinance are cast, not so much vsed in old times as now: for it is not necessarie to mixe the twentieth part of lead with pure tinne to make it more malliable, seeing it may be cast and put in worke without any such mixture, the which hurts the bountie of the tinne, and can neuer be drawne from the lead. This law must not only hold in coynes, but in all plate and works of gold or siluer, in the which falsehood and corruption is more ordinarie than in coynes, for that the triall is not so easie, and oftentimes the workemanship is as deere as the substance it selfe: wherein *Archimides* is much deceiued, seeking to find out what the goldsmith had stolne out of that great crowne of king *Hieron*, and not to deface the fashion, (for as then they had no vse of the touchstone) he tooke two lumps or masses one of gold, and another of siluer, putting either of them into a vessell full of water, and by the effusion of the water he iudged the proportion of the gold and siluer, then filling it againe with water, he put the crowne into it, the which cast forth lesse water then the masse of siluer, and more then that of gold, whereby he coniectured that the goldsmith had stolne a fift part: but his iudgement was vncertaine, for he supposed the mixture or allaie to be of pure siluer, when as the goldsmith to make the gold more firme, and to giue it the better luster, makes it most commonly of copper, being also of lesse charge, the which is much lighter then siluer, which makes the gold looke paler; and so by consequence copper hath a greater bodie then siluer in a masse of an equall waight, and differs as much as thirteene do from eleuen: and if the allaie or mixture were of copper and siluer, it was impossible to make a true iudgement, vnlesse he could distinguish how much there was of either; and although it were knowne, yet shall he erre insensibly in measuring the drops of water, through the difference of the masse and proportion of the mettals: there is no refiner nor goldsmith in the world so cunning that can precisely iudge by the touchstone how much siluer or copper is mixt with gold, if the allaie be not of one pure mettall. And although that goldsmiths and iewellers haue falsly complained that they cannot worke in gold vnder two and twentie Carrats without losse, or in fine gold aboue 23 Carrats and three quarters, according to the decree of king *Francis* the first published in the yeare 1511: yet notwithstanding all good orders they make worke at twentie, yea oftentimes at nineteene Carrats, so as in twentie foure marks there is fiue marks of copper or siluer, the which in time is made into base money by those which vse to counterfet. It is therefore necessarie to obserue the same proportion and mixture in gold that is wrought, as in coynes vpon the like penalties, to the end that the vse of gold in plate and moueables may be pure. And for that it is impossible (as refiners say) to refine gold to 24 Carats, but there must be a little of some other mettall with it; nor siluer at twelue deniers, but there must be some allaie, and euen the purest refining according to the lawes is of 23 Carrats and three quarters, and hath a fourth part of a Carrat of allaie, and of siluer eleuen deniers, two graines and three quarters, such are the royals of Spaine, or else eleuen deniers and eighteene graines, as is the siluer at Paris, the which is of all others the best, for that it hath but a fortie sixt part of copper mixt with it. And in the best Spanish siluer there is a thirtie sixt part of copper, and without any great charge (besides the difficultie and length of time) they may worke gold in plate, or in coyne of 23 Carrats, and siluer of eleuen deniers twelue graines pure, without any allaie: for in so doing, the proportion of gold to siluer shall be equall, for the allaie shall be alike in the one and the other, that is to say, that in 24 pounds of siluer at eleuen deniers and twelue graines; and in 24 pounds of gold at 23 Carrats: there is a pound of other mettall in the gold which is not gold, and so likewise in the siluer which is not siluer, be it copper or any other mettall,

Archimides error in triall of mettals.

H10 *For* 1511 (M.D.XI in Fr 7) *read* 1540 (M.D.XL in Fr 1–6, 8 and L).   K1 the silver at Paris *i.e.* the silver with the Paris stamp (cf. Fr)   K5 *For* without any allaie *read* without any variation (cf. note at I9)   K6 allaie *i.e.* degree of purity   Notes at H3, I9.

Of A Commonweale. 689

A mettall, and such siluer is called in this realme, the kings siluer, in the which the 24 part is copper, and by this meanes the coynes of gold and siluer shall be stronger, and more durable, whereby they get much in the working in the fier, and in sodring, and they keepe it from wasting and brittlenes.

And to the end the iust proportion of gold to siluer, obserued in al Europe & neighbour nations, (of twelue for one, or thereabouts) may bee also kept in the weight of money: it is needfull to coine money of gold and siluer of the same weight of sixteen, two and thirtie, and threescore and foure peeces to the Marke, without any alteration either in raising or abating; to auoid on the one side the difficultie of stamping it, and on the other side the brittlenesse of fine gold and siluer, if the coine were lighter than

B one denier. Whereas on the other side also, if they make any coine weighing aboue halfe an ounce, it is easily counterfeited, by reason of the thicknesse thereof: as we see in the Portugueses of gold, and the Dollers of siluer, which weigh aboue an ounce: as also that coine of three Markes and a halfe, which the emperour *Heliogabulus* caused to be made: and that which was coined with the stampe of Constantinople, weighing a marke of gold, whereof the emperour *Tiberius* presented fistie to our king *Childeric*. By which meanes neither chaungers, nor marchants, nor goldsmiths, shall euer be able to deceiue the common people, which is ignorant of the bountie and weight: for they shall be alwayes forced to giue twelue peeces of siluer for one of gold; and euery one

C of the peeces of siluer, shall weigh as much as the peece of gold of the same marke: as we see in the single Royals of Spaine, which weigh as much as the French Crowne, which are (according to the weight set downe in the yeare 1540) two deniers sixteene graines; and that twelue single are iust the value of a French Crowne. Why then may not all coynes of gold and siluer be equall in weight? and all of one weight of both mettals haue one stampe, or caracture? Why may there not be the same likenesse & proportion of both mettalls? If this might be effected (as I hope it will) all meanes to falsifie money would be taken away. And to the end the simpler sort may not be abused in the chaunge of the said peeces, as well of gold, as of siluer; nor to take the single for the double (as they do oftentimes in Royals of Spayne, and in the new coyne of

D king *Henry* the second) it is needfull that the stampes be diuers, and not alike as those of Spaine. And yet as touching siluer, to the end they shall hold the certaine titles of Soulz, pettie Denier, and Liure, as it is specified in the edict of king *Henry* the second, made in the yeare 1551; and by reason of the payment of rents, amercements, and the lords rights, according to the customes and ordinances; the Soulz shall be of three Deniers weight of the kings siluer (as it is said) and of sixtie three to the Marke: so foure shall be worth a Liure, as it hath gone heretofore, the which is the iustest price that can be giuen: and euery peece may be diuided into three, so as euery one shall weigh a Denier, and shall goe for foure small Deniers or Pence, and shall be called a common Denier, to the end the Soulz may alwayes be worth twelue Deniers: & that the com-

E plaints of the lords for their rents and rights, beeing vsually paid in blanch, or copper money, may cease, being now conuerted vnto Soulzes, such as they were in the time of Saint *Lewis*, that is, sixtie foure to a Marke of the kings siluer. And as for other growing out of annuities, purchased for money, the rent must be paid according to the value of the Soulz which it held at that time, when as the rent was purchased; the which was but foure Deniers an hundred yeares since, and is now but the third part of the auntient Soulz: the which it will be needfull to put in vse. Such was the Drachma, or Groat of siluer, vsed throughout all Greece, which was the eight part of the ounce, which wee call a Gros, and of the same weight with the Soulz which Saint *Lewis* caused to be coined, the which were called Gros Tournois, or of Tours, and Soulz Tournois: By the

Nnn iij   which

A3 working, in   C10 *For* Henry the second (Fr 7) *read* Henry the third (Fr 5–6, 8 and L) *omitted*
(Fr 1–4).   D5 *For* sixtie three (Fr 7) *read* sixtie four (Fr 1–6, 8 and L).   Note at D10.

which Soulz Tournois, or of Tours, all antient contracts are ordered, and many treaties not onely within the realme, but also among straungers: as in the treatie made betwixt the Bernois, and the three small Cantons of the Swissers, where it is said, That the Souldiors pay, should be a Soulz Tournois. The like was in this realme, and for that cause it was called Sold, and it was like vnto the pay of the Romans, as *Tacitus* said, and of the Grecians, as we read in *Pollux*. For the Drachma, or Groat, is of the same weight with the Soulz Tournois. The Venetians haue followed the antients, and haue made the ounce of eight Groats, or Drachmaes, and the Drachma of 24 Deniers, and the Denier of two Halfepence, or twentie foure graines: as we vse in France, from which order we may not stray, as being most auntient in all Greece, and the Orientall regions.

Drachma Attica seuen pence starling.

True it is, that the auntient Romans hauing their ounce equall with the Greeks, that is to say, of 576 graines, they diuided it into seuen Deniers of their money, and their Denier was in value an Atticque Drachma, or groat, & three seuen parts more. Wherin *Buda* was deceiued, saying, That there were eight Deniers in the ounce, and that the Romans Denier, or Peny, was equall with the Attique Drachma, and the Roman pound like vnto the Attique Myne; being most certaine that the Roman pound had but twelue ounces, and the Greeke Myne sixteene ounces, according to the marchants pound weight within this realme: the which *George Agricola* hath well obserued by the calcull of *Plinie*, *Appian*, *Suetonius*, and *Celsus*. But at this day it is straunge to see the great diuersitie of pounds and ounces in all nations, nay in one and the same kingdom there are in a manner an infinit sort of pounds: whereof I will make mention of some few. An hundred weight at Paris, make 116 pound at Lion, at Rouan $96\frac{2}{3}$, at Tholouse 121 pound, at Marseilles 123, at Geneua 89, at Venice $165\frac{1}{2}$, at Genoa 155, at Basil 98, at London $109\frac{1}{2}$. That of Paris and Strausbourg agrees, so do they of Basil, Nuremberg, and Francford, and they of Thoulouse, Mompellier, and Auignon, agree in the same pound weight: but they of Tours haue a lighter pound, for fifteene ounces at Paris makes sixteene at Tours. The like difference of weight is to be obserued in the East, and in Affrike, for 100 rowls at Thessalonica, make 91 pounds at Paris: 100 rowls at Damasco, make 120 pounds at Paris, 100 rowles in Siria, make at Paris 503 pounds and foureteene ounces: the like may be written of many others. But the lightest pound weight of all, is that of Naples, for there an hundred pound weight, make but seuentie foure at Paris. But all this diuersitie of weight may easily bee reconciled in coynes, if they coine their peeces of gold and siluer of the same weight, the same name, and the same bountie, that is to say, that there be no more abatement in the gold, than in the siluer, whereby they can neither raise nor abate the price; as they do oftner than there are monethes, either at the peoples pleasure, or of those that haue authoritie and credit with princes, who borrow all the money they can, and then they raise the price of money: so as one hauing borrowed an hundred thousand crownes, raised it suddenly six pence in the crowne, whereby he gained two thousand and fiue hundred pounds starling. Another abated the course of money in March, and raised it againe in Aprill, after he had receiued the quarters rent. By this meanes also you shall cut off all falsifying and counterfeiting of coines, and the most ignorant shall know the bountie of the one and the other coine by the sight, the sound, and weight, without either fire or touchstone. For seeing that all nations for these two thousand yeares and more, haue alwaies kept, and still do keepe an equall proportion from gold to siluer, it will bee impossible either for the subiect or the prince, to raise, pull downe, or to alter, the prices of coines of gold or siluer, if base money bee banished the Commonweale, and gold set at 23 carats. And yet for that the smallest coines are profitable to the poorer sort, it is needfull to

coyne

G5 Buda *i.e.* Guillaume Budé G10 calcull *i.e.* calculation H5 so do they of BERNE, Basil
H9 rowls *i.e. rotuli* (The rotl or rotolo is a Mediterranean measure of weight.) H10 *For* 120 pounds *read* 420 pounds. Notes at F6, F9, G4, H5, I1, I3.

A coyne a third kind of money of copper, without any other mixture, as they haue begun, and as it is practised in Spaine and Italie: or else diuide the marke of siluer in 15036 peeces, euerie peece weighing nine graines, that the poore may buy the smallest things therewith. For whereas the queene of England hath banished all base and copper money, and reduced all her coines to two kinds onely, the least peece of money, which is a peny, being in value about ten Deniers, shee takes from her subiects the meanes to buy any thing at a lesse price; and which is worst, they cannot giue lesse alms to a poore bodie, than of a peny, which holds many from giuing, as I haue shewed in the Paradox against *Malestroit*: the which the Chauncelour of England caused to be translated in the yeare 1569, hoping to redresse it. But it were farre more expedient, to haue no

B other coine but of gold and siluer, if it were possible to coyne any money lesse than the penie, and that they would diuide the Marke of siluer (as in Lorraine) into a thousand peeces, which they called Andegauenses: for that *Rene* duke of Aniou and of Lorraine caused them to be coined, two hundred whereof make but sixpence; and fortie, one Soulz of our base money: and yet they are of reasonable fine siluer. But making it but halfe so little, it would be more firme, and of the same hieght that I haue spoken, and they may be cut and stamped at one instant. For the price of copper being vncertaine in all places, it is not fit to make money of, the which must alwayes be kept as certaine as may be: besides, there is no mettall so subiect to rust, the which doth consume both the stampe and substance: and contrariwise neither gold nor siluer do euer rust. And

The French copy saith 8000.

C as for the price, we read, that during the Punike warres, the pound of siluer was worth eight hundred and fortie pound weight of copper, after twelue ounces to the pound; & then the Denier of pure siluer, which was but the seuenth part of an ounce, was raised from ten pounds of copper to sixteene (as *Plinie* saith) which was after the rate of eight hundred ninetie six pounds of copper, for one pound weight of siluer, the pound weighing twelue ounces. Afterwards the least coine, which was a pound of copper, was halfe abated by the law Papiria, so as the price of copper was double that which it was before: and when as siluer came in great aboundance, it was reduced to a fourth, remaining in the same value, which was 224 pound of copper for a pound of siluer: the which is neere the estimation of copper in this realme, whereas one hundred pounds,

Fest. lib. 17. in verb. sestertius.

D at sixteene ounces to the pound, are worth but thirtie six shillings starling: and in Germanie it is better cheape, although their mouables are thereof; yea in some places the churches are couered with copper: but in Italy it is deerer, and in Spaine and Afftike much more, for it is very scant there.

Some one may obiect, That the aboundance of siluer may also cause an abatement of the price, as we read in *Titus Liuius*, that by the treatie made betwixt the Ætolians and Romans, it was said, That the Ætolians should pay for ten pounds of siluer one pound of gold: and yet by a law made by *Constantine*, the pound of gold is esteemed at 41 pound ⅖: for he would haue them pay fiue Soulz of gold for one pound of siluer, making seuentie two Soulz of gold in a pound; so as fiue Soulz is iust the fourteenth

E part of a pound, and two fifts more: and now the price is twelue for one, or little lesse. True it is, that heretofore the * Marke of pure gold was esteemed one hundred eightie fiue Liures; and the * Marke of siluer fifteene Liures fifteene Soulz Tournois: so as for one Marke of pure gold vnwrought, they must haue eleuen Markes, fiue ounces, twentie three Deniers, and fiue graines, of the kings siluer vnwrought. Towards the North, where there are many mynes of siluer, and few of gold, gold is somewhat deerer. The pope of Rome more greedie of gold than of siluer, did value the Marke of gold at 12 Markes and foure fifts of siluer: the which is at this present the price of gold and siluer, and was almost two thousand fiue hundred yeares since. For wee read in *Herodotus*,

* 18. lib.
* 10. sh.
31. sh. 6. d.
starling.

that

A2 silver pound ⅖ (cf. *Code*, 10, 78(76), 1).   A2 For 15036 read 1536.   B6 hieght *i.e.* loy, standard   D9 For 41 pound ⅖ read 14
Notes at A6, B2, B5, B8, C4.

that the pound of gold was valued at thirteene pounds of siluer: and the Hebrewes in their Pandects, set a Denier of gold for fiue and twentie of siluer, the coines of gold being double to them of siluer; which were twelue and a halfe for one. Wee read also, that in the time of the Persians, & when as the Commonweals of Greece did flourish, that an ounce of gold was worth a pound of siluer: for *Stater Doricus* of the weight of an ounce, was valued at a pound of siluer, as *Iulius Pellux* saith. And in *Augustus* his time, the king of the Indians, had the same estimation of gold to siluer, the which was then brought to Rome: and therefore hee commended the iustice of the Romans; as wee read in *Plinie*. Whereby we may coniecture, that the price of these two mettals holds in a manner throughout all Europe, after the auntient estimation. But the value of gold was raised vnder the last emperours, by reason of the spoyle therof which had bene made for the guilding of things: as *Nero* his great pallace all guilt, the which had galleries of one thousand paces long: and after him *Vespasian*, who imploied seuen millions and two hundred thousand crownes, to guild the Capitoll. And *Agrippa* couered all the temple Pantheon with copper, and then guilt it, to keepe it from rusting. And oftentimes siluer is guilt, although of it selfe it will neuer take rust. Doubtlesse we may well allow the holy ornaments to be of gold, for that the law commaunds it: but to haue vessels of gold, beds, bookes, yea and their bridles guilt, argues the madnesse of frantike men: the which if the prince doth not punish very seuerely, the price of gold must of necessitie rise: whereof our nation did vehemently complaine vnto the prince, at the estates held at Blois. Moreouer siluer hauing no hold, is little imployed to siluer withall: besides, the mynes of the North yeeld great store of siluer, & no gold: yet the alteration of price which is made, in processe of time is insensible, which can be no let but the valuation of coines made of these two mettals shall be equall in all states, banishing away all base money. Moreouer a generall traffique dispersed more now ouer the face of the whole earth than euer, cannot allow of any great alteration of gold and siluer, but by a common consent of all nations. But it is impossible to hold the price of things, retaining this base money, the which is altogether diuers and vnequall: for euen as the price of all things doth fall, as the value of money decreaseth, (as the law saith) so doth it rise in raising the price of mony. And it must rise & fall, for that there is no prince which holds the laws of mynting equall with other Commonweals, nor yet in his owne: for that the Aloy of the Soulz differs from that of the Teston, and of pettie Deniers Doubles, Lyards, & peeces of six, and three blankes, the which continue not long in one estate. The first beginning in this realme to abase the siluer coine, and to mixe the 24 part of copper therewith, was to giue occasion to marchants to bring siluer into this realme, where there is none growing: for eleuen Deniers and a halfe in Fraunce, was as much as twelue Deniers in another countrey. But this deuise was needlesse, considering the great riches of Fraunce, the which they will alwaies fetch bringing gold and siluer from all parts. This mischiefe tooke deeper root in the time of *Philip* the Faire, who did impaire the blanched money the one halfe, in the yeare 1300, adding as much copper vnto it, as there was siluer: a while after it was brought to a third, so as the new Soulz was worth but a third part of the auntient. And in the yeare 1322 the Aloie of Soulzes was so weake, as the Marke of siluer was worth 80 * Liures Tournois, and had 1600 peeces for a Marke of copper. True it is, that in the same yeare that *Charles* the seuenth recouered his crowne which had beene taken from him, he caused a new coine to be made in the moneth of October, the which was strong and good, so as the Marke of siluer was set at eight * Liures: but in the yeare 1453, he caused Soulzes to be coined of fiue Deniers of Aloie, and since they haue still decreased: so as king *Francis* the first, in the yeare 1540, caused some to bee coyned of

threee

A wonderfull masse to guild the Capitoll,

* 8. lib sterling.

* 16. shil.

F5 Stater Daricus   F6 Julius Pollux   I3 pettie Deniers, Doubles,   I10 blanched money *i.e. monnoye blanche*, silver coinage (cf. note at 689 D10)   K3 *For* 1322 (Fr 7) *read* 1422 (Fr 1–6, 8).
K6 *For* October *Bodin writes* November (Fr only).   Notes at F7, G5, G9, H3, I6, K4.

A three Deniers of sixteene graines: king *Henry* at three Deniers and twelue graines: so as the auntient Soulz of the kings siluer was worth almost foure: and king *Charles* the ninth brought it to three Deniers, the estimation still continuing alike: for that the price of the crowne did arise. And in the yeare 1577, vnder king *Henry* the third, they decrease almost halfe in weight, and a fourth part in goodnesse, from those of *Francis* the first. Other princes haue done no better; for the Crutzer of Germany, which in old time was siluer at eleuen Deniers & foure graines, is now at foure Deniers and sixteene graines: the Soulz of Wirtzburg, and the Reichs groschem at six Deniers, that is halfe siluer, and halfe copper. The Scheslind, the Rape, the Denier of Strausbourg, at foure Deniers and twelue graines: the Rapephening at foure Deniers three graines, and the
B Florines of siluer at eleuen Deniers foure graines: as also the peeces bee of fiue and of ten Crutzers, the Soulz of Flanders or Patars, whereof twentie are worth twentie and foure of ours, are but three Deniers and eighteene graines of Aloie, and more than two third parts is copper: the peece of foure Patars is at seuen deniers ten graines: the Brelingues of Gueldres, are at eight deniers, and the third is copper. In former times the Soulz, or Groat of England, was at ten deniers twentie two graines: and neuer did all this base coine continue aboue twentie or thirtie yeares at one rate or standard, or at the same weight; and from thence growes the difference of the great Liure Tournois, of the lesse, and of the meane, the Liure or pound of Normandie, the Liure of Brittanie, and the Liure of Paris, the which are all different, as wee may yet see it in the
C taxes of the popes chamber. And in Spaine the Liure or pound of Barcellona, Toledo, Molorque; In England the pound starling is worth ten of ours: And in Scotland there are two sorts of Pounds, the one starling, the other ordinarie. There is no prince in Italie, that hath not his Pound different from others: as in like case the Marke hath generally eight ounces: but the ounce of the Low countries is weaker by six graines than ours, and then that of Cologne by nine graines, that of Nuremberg six graines, and contrariwise that of Paris is stronger by an ounce. The Marke of Naples hath nine ounces, that of Salerne hath ten: and there is no towne almost in all Italie, but differs in his Marke, which makes the value of their coines so diuers, being so different in their weight & standard: the which troubles the poore people much, who loose great-
D ly by exchange, and generally they which vnderstand not the poier, as they say, or the difference, as the Banquers speake: that is the value of money of exchange from one place to another. And therefore they say of a man that is well practised in affairs, That he vnderstands the poier, as a matter of hard conceit. For they haue made the matter of coines so obscure, by reason of their mixtures, as for the most part they vnderstand nothing therein. For euen as artisans, marchants, and euery one in his facultie, disguiseth oftentimes his worke: and as many Physitians speake Latine before women, vsing Greeke caracters, and Arabike words, and Latine words abridged, yea some times they blot their paper that it may not be read, fearing that if their secrets were discouered, they should be little esteemed: so these Mynt-maisters, in stead of speaking plainely, and to
E say, that the Marke of gold of twelue parts, hath two of copper, or of some other mettall, they say, It is gold of twentie carats: and in stead of saying, that a peece of three blankes is halfe copper, they say it is siluer of six deniers fine, two deniers of weight, and fifteene deniers of course, giuing to deniers and carats, the essence, qualitie and quantity, of gold and siluer against, nature. And in stead of saying, the Marke hath threescore peeces, they say, it is of fiue Soulz currant. Againe they make some coines certaine or stable, some vncertaine and variable, and the third imaginarie, when as nothing can bee called firme in matters of coine, hauing so diminished the weight, and impaired the bountie of the gold and siluer. For the Ducat which goes currant at Venice, Rome, Naples,

A Liure is two shillings starling

A1 *For* three Deniers of sixteene graines *read* three Deniers and sixteene graines. E5 silver, against nature
Notes at A6, C2, C6, C7, C8, D1, E1, E4.

Naples, Palermo, and Messina, is an imaginarie coyne; it was in old time the same peece of gold weighing an Angell, or else a Medin of Barbarie, or an Imperiall of Flanders, almost of the same weight and touch with the auntient Ducat, worth ten Carlins of siluer, and the Carlin ten Soulz of the countrey, at 46 peeces to the Marke of gold, and six to the ounce, the which they diuide into thirtie Tarijs, and the Tarij into twentie graines, the which is one grosse vpon the ounce, more than the common ounce, which hath but eight grosse. The law calleth this coine of gold Solidus, the which (as the Angell) hath fortie eight peeces for the marke, and seuentie two for the Roman pound at twelue ounces, the which hath long time bene currant; as it appeareth by the lawes among the Grecians, Germans, English, French, and Burguignons, and it is nothing els but our French Crowne of the Sunne. But our Mynt-maisters hauing not well vnderstood the word *Solidus*, haue within these fiftie yeares set the Sunne vppon it, tearming it erroneously *Aureum Solarem*: but the common people retaining their old speech, call it yet the Crowne Sold, of *Solidus*; the which in old time weighed four deniers, as the Angell. But since princes by little and little, and by graine and graine, haue brought it to three deniers, the which is the old Crowne. And in the time of king *Iohn* the old Crowne being diminished by little and little, as by the auntient Crowne Sold of three graines, they did coyne Crownes of two deniers and twentie graines weight, of the same standard with the auntient, the which they called Francs, on foot, and on horsebacke (for then they called all French men Francs, as yet in all the East all the nations of the West are called Franques) at which time the Crowne of Burgongne, which they call Ride, was also coyned of the same weight and goodnesse: the which haue continued vntill the time of *Charles* the eight, that the Franc Crowne was diminished six graines in weight, and three quarters of a Carat in finenesse: for the old Crownes were of twentie three and three quarters of a Carat, and the Crownes with the Crowne at twentie three Carats. Afterwards king *Francis* the first correcting somewhat the Crowne with a Crowne, caused the Crowne Sold to be coined at two deniers and sixteene graines, and of the same goodnesse with the other, hauing an eight part of Aloie put to it: the which continued vnto king *Henrie*, who added foure grains of weight vnto it: and by *Charles* the ninth it was diminished fiue graines, in the yeare 1561. But the old Crownes, or Ducats of Venice, Genes, Florence, Sienna, Castile, Portugall, and Hongarie, haue kept twentie three Carats three quarters, and two deniers, and eighteene graines of weight, vntill the yeare 1540, that the emperour *Charles* the fift impaired the fioenesse of the Crownes of Spaine, of one Carat and three quarters, and three graines in weight, causing them to be coined at twentie two Carats, and two deniers fifteene graines of weight. The Crownes of Castile, Valencia, and Arragon, the which they call Pistolets, giuing an ill example to other princes to do the like: as the princes of Italie did, who haue caused some to be made at twentie two Carats & vnder, weighing two deniers and sixteene grains, as be the Crownes of Rome, Luques, Bologne, Salusses, Genes, Sienna, Sicile, Milan, Ancona, Mantoue, Ferrara, Florence, and the new Crownes of Venice. True it is, that Pope *Paul* the third, began to make Crownes to be coined in his name at twentie one Carats and a halfe, and two deniers, and foureteene graines of weight; and those of Auignon, which were made at the same time vnder the name of *Alexander Farneze* legat and the Popes nephew, are baser, and fiue deniers lighter in weight; the which brings an infinit losse to the subiect, and benefit to counterfeit coyners, myntmen, and marchants, which draw the good money out of the countrey, and coine baser in another place. The which is more ordinarie in siluer coine of high value, and aboue eleuen deniers pure, as the Royals of Castile, which hold all eleuen deniers three graines of pure siluer: out of the which other princes heretofore

---

F1–2 the same peece of gold *i.e.* a real gold piece   I4 finenesse   K4 nephew *i.e.* grandson
Notes at G3, G7, H8, I5.

OF A COMMONWEALE. 695

tofore haue gained verie much: for being conuerted into French Teſtons out of ten thouſand pounds ſtarling, they did gaine ſix hundred and fiftie pounds, nothing impairing the goodneſſe of the Teſton of Fraunce, which holds ten deniers 17 grains of fine. And by the ſame meanes the Swiſſers which conuerted the teſtons of France into teſtons of Soleure, Lucerne, and Vnderuall, gained vpon euery marke one and fortie ſoulz and eleuen deniers tournois: and for thoſe of Lucerne, Soleure, and Vnderuall, were but of nine deniers and eighteene graines, which is in the whole marke 23 graines of pure ſiluer leſſe then thoſe of France, the which were worth 25 ſoulz tournois. And as for the waight, thoſe of France are at the leaſt of 25 teſtons, and fiue eight parts of a teſton to the marke, ſo as the teſtons of Soleure are lighter in waight three eight parts of a teſton in the marke, the which was worth foure ſoulz three deniers tournois. And for that the teſtons of Soleure & Lucerne cannot be valued but for ſiluer of baſe aloye, the which they call Billon, being vnder ten deniers of fine ſiluer, after the eſtimation of fourteene liures ſeuenteene ſoulz foure deniers tournois, the marke of pure ſiluer, and the teſtons of France for that they were aboue ten deniers of fine ſiluer were valued for ſiluer of high aloye, the which are worth after the ſame proportion fifteene liures thirteene ſoulz tournois, the marke of fine ſiluer; and by reaſon of the difference of the bountie of the ſiluer the ſaid teſtons were leſſe then thoſe of France 41 ſoulz eleuen deniers tournois in the marke, abating for euery peece of the ſaid teſtons one ſoulz eleuen deniers. Thoſe of Berne for that they were of nine deniers twentie graines of fine ſiluer for the marke were worth one denier tournois in euery peece more then thoſe of Soleure, in gayning therefore but twelue pence vpon a marke it is a great gaine. The Flemings do the like, conuerting the teſtons of France in royalls of Flanders. Euery Prince hath prouided well by his lawes that neither gold nor ſiluer ſhould be tranſported vnto ſtrangers vpon grieuous puniſhments, but it is not poſsible to haue them well executed, but that much will be tranſported both by ſea and land. And although none ſhould be tranſported, yet the ſubiects ſhould alwayes haue good means to melt, alter and falſifie both gold and ſiluer coyne, if there be diuerſitie of ſtandards; which growes either by licenſes graunted to ſome goldſmiths, or done againſt the lawes; for they purſe vp that which wants in the fines of the ſiluer which they worke, as well for the abatement which is allowed them, as for the enamell and ſolder which they vſe, mocking the lawes which are made vpon the price of the marke of gold and ſiluer, ſetting what price they pleaſe vpon their works, ſo as it is alwaies ſold at a higher rate by the goldſmith then the lawes do allow, ſiluer by fortie and fiue ſoulz, and gold at twelue or thirteene liures vpon the marke, ſo as gold and ſiluer is bought dearer from the goldſmith and marchant, then from the mint maſter, who cannot exceed the kings lawes, neither in buying of ſtuffes nor in coyning. And as ſoone as the gold or ſiluer is coyned into money of better waight and goodnes then that of neighbor princes, preſently it is molt by the refiners and goldſmiths to put into plate, or to haue it coyned by ſtrangers after their ſtandard, wherein the changers ſerue as inſtruments, and vnder colour of furniſhing the people with money, trafficke with the goldſmiths and marchant ſtrangers: for it is certaine and hath been found true, that within theſe 25 yeares that the pettie ſoulz was decried, there hath been coyned in this realme aboue two millions fiue hundred thouſand pounds ſtarling, beſides the peeces of three & ſixe blanks, which are no more to be found, for that the refiners and goldſmiths found profit in them, ſo as they which haue great ſtore of gold and ſiluer plate, can make more vſe of it; for hauing bought it deere from the goldſmiths, they are loth to ſell it with ſo great loſſe: and euen king *Charles* the 9 loſt much, hauing exchanged his plate into coyne, whereas before the ſtandard of money coyned was equall with that of the goldſmiths,

margins: 4. ſh. 2. d. ob. · Billon. · 25. Millions of Liures.

ſo as

A6 *For* and for those *read* for those.   B8 leſſe then thoſe of France BY TWELVE SOUS EIGHT DENIERS TOURNOIS IN THE MARK OF TESTONS. AND SO THE TESTONS OF SOLEURE ARE WORTH LESS THAN THOSE OF FRANCE BY 41 ſoulz eleven   C10 purſe up *i.e.* pocket, appropriate   C10 fines *i.e.* fineness
E6 can make NO more uſe   Notes at B9, D1, D4, D5, E3.

so as they could lose nothing in plate but the fashion, the which continues yet as a prouerbe, It is siluer plate, there is nothing lost but the fashion. Therefore to preuent all these inconueniences, the standard of coyned money, and of works of gold and siluer, must be all one, that is of three and twentie Carats without any alaie or mixture, in gold; and eleuen deniers, and eleuen graines in siluer. They had found some meanes to reforme these abuses, letting out to farme the reuenues of the mint, and the confiscations and amercements that should grow by forfeitures, the which was let out in the yeare 1564 for fiue thousand pound starling a yeare: yet it was abolished at Moulins in the yeare 1566, and the mints were farmed out to such as offred to coyne the greatest quantitie of marks of gold and siluer: by this meanes some branches were cut off, but the rootes of these abuses remained still, so as the fraud will neuer cease. The root of abuses is the confusion of three mettals, gold, siluer, and copper; which ceasing, neither shall the subiect nor the stranger be able to commit any fraud, but it shall bee soone discouered. But euen as copper and brasse money was not allowed in this realme, for that there was none coyned, so billon or mixture being forbidden, the strangers base money shall be also banished the realme: but so long as the Prince or Commonweale shall coyne base money, there is no hope that strangers subiects will euer cease to counterfet in priuat, or to receiue all strange coynes. There is also another benefit both to the generall and particular, which growes (as I haue said) by the defence of the mixture of mettals, whereby they shall auoide hereafter the losse of siluer, the which is accounted for nothing in gold of 14 Carats and vpward, and is lost for the charges of the refining, the which is done by strong water: for they must haue sixe shillings starling at the least, yea eight to deuide a marke, yet the losse is very great in a great somme, as all the florins of Germanie are but sixteene Carats, or sixteene and a halfe at the most, so as in a hundred thousand marks there are thirtie three thousand marks losse, and of fourteene Carats fortie thousand marks and more. And besides that which I haue said, the abuses of officers of the mint shall cease in regard of the abatements, cut of the which the officers were payed their wages; for the abolishing whereof, *Henry* the 2 king of France ordained, that they should be payed by the receiuers of the same places: which decree although it were holie and good, yet was it afterwards disanulled by king *Charles* the 9, for that the chamber of accompts at Paris gaue the king to vnderstand that hee lost yearely aboue a thousand pounds starling, whereas hee should reape profit by his mints; for now the officers were paied, and did in a manner nothing. But the true meanes to preuent all, is to suppresse all the officers of mints, but only in one towne, where they should coyne all sorts of moneys, and to cause them to be payed by the receiuer of the place, the lords right remaining: the which notwithstanding the auntients did not know, and there was nothing deducted out of the money, no not the right of Brassage, as it were verie necessarie, or rather that a taxe were laied vpon the subiect for the coyning of money, thereby to take away the lords right, or any other duties, as they did in old time in Normandie, and at this day in Polonia, to preuent the notable losse which the subiects do suffer. By this meanes also the diuersitie of the price of the marke (which breedes a million of abuses) shall cease, and forraine coynes shall not be receiued but only to melt, without reckning of any thing for the lords rights, notwithstanding letters of permission obtained by neighbour Princes, to deliuer forth their money in his realme at the same rates as in their owne territories. And for the taking away of all occasions for the falsifying, altering, or changing the standard receiued for coynes of gold & siluer, it shall be needfull to haue all the money coyned in one citie only, whereas the iudges of the mint shall remaine, and to suppresse all others (if the monarchie or Commonweale haue not so large limits, as of necessitie they

---

F5 eleven graines (Fr 3–8) *properly* twelve graines (Fr 2) *omitted* (Fr 1). Cf. 688 K5–9.   G7 *For* strangers subjects (Fr 7) *read* strangers and subjects (Fr 1–6, 8).   I6 the lords right *i.e. seigneuriage*, the sovereign's levy upon the fabrication of coinage   I8 Brassage *i.e.* the fee paid to mint officials for expenses of fabrication

Notes at F4, H2, K4.

they must haue more) in which place all the refiners shall worke, with a prohibition vpon paine of death not to refine in any other place, for from them come the great abuses, and to giue notice vnto the ordinarie iudges by preuention to punish all abuses that shall be committed; for it is well knowne what abuses there haue been in this realme in the coyning of money. It is therefore necessarie to imitate the Romans, who for all the subiects of Italie had the temple of *Iuno* only where they did coyne three sorts of money pure and simple, gold, siluer, and copper, and there had three maisters of the mint, who caused it to be refined and stampt publickly, in view of all the world. And to the end that no man should be abused in the price of the coynes, there was also a place appointed where to take the essay or triall of money, at the request of *Marius Gratidianus*. We reade also that in this realme by a law made by *Charlemaigne*, it was forbidden to coine any money but in his Pallace, although his Empire stretched ouer all Germanie, Italie, and the greatest part of Spaine: but since that king *Philip* the faire, *Charles* his sonne, and king *Iohn* had established many mints in this realme, and many masters, prouost and other officers in euery mint, abuses haue also multiplied. But here some one may obiect, that the Persians, Greeks and Romans did coyne money of pure gold, siluer and copper at the highest value that could be, and yet did they falsifie it, as we reade in *Demosthenes* oration against *Timocrates*. I answere, that it is impossible to purge the Commonweale cleane of these people, but for a thousand that are now you shall not then find ten, the value of gold and siluer being knowne to euery man as I haue declared. And if there be any prince so ill aduised as to alter the bountie of his money to gaine thereby, as *Marc Anthonie* did, who coined siluer that was very base, it will be soone reiected, besides the blame he shall receiue of all men, and the hazard of the rebellion of his subiects, the which was great at such time as *Philip* the faire imbased the money. Whatsoeuer the reasons be, it is most certaine there were neuer fewer coyners of counterfet money than in the Romans time, whenas they had no money either of gold or siluer but of a high standard; and therefore *Liuius Drusus* the Tribune was blamed, for that he had presented a request vnto the people to haue an eight part of copper mingled with the siluer money, or as the mintmen say, they should coine money of ten deniers and twelue graines fine: which shewes that euen in those daies they would not admit any confusion or mixture of gold or siluer, and that their siluer was of the highest rate, as also their gold, as we may see in their medalles of gold, the which are of 23 carats and three quarters; and we find some marked with the Emperour *Vespasian*, where there wants but the 32 part of a Carat but it had been 24 Carats; the which is the purest and finest gold that can be seene. But it sufficeth for the reasons that I haue alledged, that the gold be of 23 Carats, and the siluer at eleuen Deniers and twelue graines pure. And let them not excuse themselues that they cannot command the fire, and therefore they demaund a fourth or an eight part of alaie: the which is the cause of many abuses. Yet some may say that it is more expedient to coine dobles and deniers of baser siluer, to auoide the heauines of copper money. I say, that if it be allowed to coyne base money how small soeuer, that it will proue very preiudiciall, and will be practised in liards and soulzes. And although they did coyne nothing but Dobles and Deniers, yet should they alwaies open a gap for coyners to deceiue the common people for whom this money is made, in the which he hath no knowledge, neither doth he care to haue any, for the small value, without inquiring of the bountie thereof. I haue a letter of *Iames Pinatel* written to king *Henry* the 2, in the which are these words: Sir, I thought good to aduertise you that within these sixe moneths they haue coyned in one of your mints, soulzes that are too base by foure shillings in waight vpon euery marke, and foure soulz in the goodnes of the mettall: when it shall please your

---

B5 provosts (cf. Fr)   D8 *For* of alaie *read* of variation from standard (remede). Cf. note at 688 I9.
Notes at A5, C2, E8.

your Maiestie I will shew you the worke, and I will acquaint you with the losse which you and your subiects do receiue, the which will grow greater if you preuent it not with all rigour. It was at that time that he coyned the peeces of sixe blanks, or three pence by the kings commandement, of foure deniers of siluer, and two deniers of copper, and foure deniers and foureteene graines of waight; the which was the best mixture of base money that was then in France, so in like sort they were soone molten, and few of them are now to be seene. Euery man knowes that the losse which the king and the subiect receiued of two shillings fiue pence vpon the marke, came to aboue fiue and twentie in the hundred, and yet the same *Pinatel* (hauing gotten vnder hand a commission from the generals of the mint, in the yeare 1552) caused Dobles and Deniers to be coined at Villeneufue of Auignon, and at Villefranche of Rouergue, which were valued but at twelue soulz the marke; and that it was verified that by this meanes he had stollen little lesse than fortie thousand pounds starling, and had purchased his pardon for fiue thousand pounds, the which he gaue vnto a Ladie, a fauorite of the kings, who did only defer this wicked mans punishment, but not quite free him. I conclude therefore that we must not by any meanes allow of any mixtures, no not in the smallest coynes, if we will purge the Commonweale of all counterfet money. By this meanes also the domage shall cease which the poore receiue by the decrying of money, or deminution of the price thereof, after they haue made them baser; neither shall they haue any credit with princes which suggest vnto them the profit that they may receiue by their mints, as a certaine officer of the mint did, who gaue the councell of the treasor to vnderstand, and did also write vnto king *Charles* the 9, That he might make a great proffit of his mints for the ease of his people: and in truth by his computation it was found that euery marke of pure gold wrought would yeeld vnto the king sixteene shillings starling, whereas he receiued but two shillings sixe pence, and foure deniers: and for the marke of siluer wrought the king should get foure shillings, whereas now he gained but sixteene deniers being wrought in testons. He aduised to coine money of the kings siluer of twelue soulz tournois currant, and of thirtie peeces to the marke, of the waight of sixe deniers nine grains, the halfe and the quarters after the rate; and of gold coines of 24 Carat, and one Carat of alaie, of thirtie peeces to the marke, & of the same waight with the siluer of six liures tournois. He would also haue them coine small base money of three deniers of goodnes, and 320 to the marke, and of three deniers currant, and all other kind of billon or base money vnder ten deniers fine, rating the marke at foureteene *liures tournois. This was his aduice, but it was reiected as it deserued, for it is a very ridiculous thing to thinke that the king can draw so great a profit from his mints, and yet ease his people, if that be true which *Plato* saith, That no man gaines but another looseth: and the losse by an ineuitable necessitie fell vpon the subiect, seeing the stranger felt not of it. It is very necessarie that some great prince should mediate that by his ambassadors with other princes, to the end that all by a generall consent should forbid the coining of base money, setting the value of gold and siluer as it hath been formerlie said, and vsing the marke at eight gros or drachmas, and of 570 graines to the ounce, the which is the most common; and therefore should not be of any great difficultie, for that the Catholike King and Queene of England haue alreadie banished all base money, and all the coines of gold in Spaine (except the Pistolets, and the money of Portugall) are at the highest value, and their coines of siluer at eleuen deniers and three graines, the which is the highest that is. And it should be good to haue the money cast in forme of a medall, as the auntient Greeks, Latins, Hebrews, Persians and Ægiptians did, for the charge should be much lesse, the facilitie greater, and the roundnesse more perfect, to preuent all clippers, it should

Billon.

*28.sh.starling.

G8 domage *i.e.* damage H10 *For* one Carat of alaie *read* one Carat of tolerance (*remede*). Cf. note at
688 I9.   Note at F4.

OF A COMMONWEALE. 699

A should not be subiect to bow and breake, and the marke would continue for euer, we should not be troubled with hammering, neither should there be any need of a cutter, of the cisers, or of any helpe at the waight, which falls not out so in that which is stampt; moreouer, they shall make more in one day than they can do now in a yeare. They should also take away all meanes from false coyners to mingle mettals so easily as they do with the presse and the stamp, whereas the peece stretcheth out in breadth which couers the thicknes, whereas the mould would make all medalls of the same mettall equall in bignes, waight, breadth and forme: whereas if a counterfetter would mixe copper with gold more than the allowance of 23 carats, the volume of copper which is in an equall waight twise as big and an eight part more, than that of
B gold, or twise and an eight part lighter than gold in an equall masse, would make the medall much greater, and discouer the falsehood. For it is most certaine, that if a masse of gold equall to a masse of copper doth waigh 1550 ferlins, that of copper shall waigh but 729 ferlins, the which is as seauenteene to eight in a grosse waight; as I haue learned of *Francis de Foix* that great *Archimedes* of our age, who first discouered the true proportion of metalls in waight and quantitie. We will hold the same opinion of siluer, which hath a greater masse than gold in an equall waight, and that gold is heauier than siluer in an equall masse, once more and foure fiue parts, which is 1551 in comparison of 998, or of nine to fiue: and of copper to siluer, as of eleuen to thirteene, or
C precisely, as 729 to 998, which approch neerer in waight and substance than the rest, except lead, the which is heauier than siluer, and differs as fifteene to foureteene, or more precisely, as 998 to 929; but they can make no vse of it to counterfet, for that it flies from all other mettalls but from tinne: and much lesse can they vse tinne, being a poison to all other mettalls, and cannot be cast for siluer, for that it is lighter as much as nine is to thirteene, or precisely as 600 is to 929: and much lesse being disguised for gold, the which is heauier than tinne in an equall masse, or of a lesse volume in an equall waight, as much as is betwixt eighteene and seauen, or iustly betwixt 1551 and 600, the which is twise and two seauen parts heauier. As for yron, those that do counterfet can make no vse of it by melting, for that it will not be mixt neither with gold nor siluer; and the brasing of plates vpon iron is not hard to discouer. *Plinie* calles it
D *Feoruminatio*, and we, brazing or soldring, the which the counterfetters of his time did vse. The Seigneur of Villemor, Commissarie of the warres, did shew me an auntient medall of iron couered with siluer, yet the waight and the bignes doth easily discouer the falsehood, if they looke narrowly into it, for that siluer is heauier than iron in an equall masse, or lesse in quantitie being of equall waight, as much as is from foure to three, or precisely from 998, to 634. And as for gold, it is impossible that this ferrumination and soldring can any thing auaile coyners, seeing that gold is lesse of bodie than iron in an equall waight, or more heauie in an equall masse, as much as is from sixe to nine, or of 1556 to 634. It is not to be feared that quicksiluer can falsifie these two met-
E tals, although it approcheth as neere to gold in waight as three to foure, or 1558 to 1551, for that they haue not so great knowledge to fixe it, but it euaporates into smoke. And thus much as touching the forme of coynes, and the profit that shall come by casting, as it was in old time, and vntill their mines of gold and siluer were worne and spent, and these two mettals worne, lost, hidden, and dispersed, then were they forced to make their money so thin, as they could not marke them but with the hammer, the which hath since been the occasion of many abuses; but euen as the first man hauing little gold and siluer, stampt it with the hammer, and afterwards hauing greater store began to cast it, in like sort must we now returne to casting. They began to come with a mill, but by proofe it appeared that it did not marke well, and that there was al-

Ooo ij   waies

B3 1550 (Fr 3–8) *properly* 1551 (Fr 1–2 and L)   C8 *For* two seauen parts *read* four seauen parts (cf. Fr).   D1 Ferruminatio   D9 *For* 1556 (Fr) *read* 1551 (L).   D10 *For* 1558 *read* 1158 (Fr and L). Notes at A3, C1, E8.

waies thirtie marks of clippings vpon a hundred marks of substance, whereas there is but one or two at the hammer, and the sound also did differ from that which was stampt: and which is more, the peeces were found not to be alwaies of one waight, for that the plates were sometimes drawne thinner of one side then of another. As for that which I haue said, that the marke of gold and siluer should be diuided into peeces equall of waight, without fraction of peeces vpon the marke, nor of deniers vpon the peece, nor of graines vpon the denier, the profit is very apparant, as well for the changes of marks of peeces, as for the value, waight, and vndoubted course: so did the auntients for the peece of gold or siluer waighing foure drachmas, the which is halfe an ounce, shall be equall to the sicle of the Hebrews, and the peece of two drachmas or of 32 to the marke shall be equall to the stater Atticus, to the old Philip, to the rose noble, and to the medalls of gold of the auntient Romans, which the law called Aureus: and the peece of one groat, sold tournois or drachma of 64 to the marke, shall be equall to the Attique drachma, and to the Zuza of the Hebrews, the which in Greece, and throughout all the East was a hirelings daies worke. True it is that the siluer pennie of the Romans was more in waight than three seuen parts, then a souldiers daies pay in *Augustus* time, the which is a little more then a single roiall of Spaine. And if the alterations and changes which are made sodenly be hurtfull and pernitious, they may proceed by little and little, causing money to be coined as I haue said. Vpon these difficulties (being deputed for the Prouince of Vermandois, at a Parliament held at Blois) I was called with the first President and three Generals of the mint, and *Marcel* Superintendent of the Treasure, to repaire the abuses of money, and in the end all that I haue heere said was held to be very necessary, and yet the difficultie and diseases of the Commonweale which were incurable, would not at that time allow of it: which was as much to say, that it were better the sick should perish in languishing, than to cause him to drinke a troublesome potion to cure him. I confesse that siluer mixt will come but to a moitie, being purified to eleuen deniers, twelue graines; but it will continue for euer if the standard be once setled as I haue said, if it be not done the Commonweale must needs come to ruine.

Billon.

Chap. IIII.

A Comparison of the three lawfull Commonweales, that is, a popular estate, an Aristocraticall, and a royall; and that a royall Monarchie is the best.

Ee haue hitherto in my opinion discoursed at large of all the parts of a Commonweale, it remaines for a conclusion to know the commodities and discommodities of euery kind of State, and then to make choise of the best, the which was necessarie to reserue vnto the end, after that we had discoursed both in generall & in particular of all the points of a Commonweale. Seeing then there are but three sorts of Commonweales, that is, when as the whole people, or the greatest part commaunds with absolute power, or else the least part of the citisens, or one alone; and that either of the three may be honest and commendable, or vicious, we must not only flie that which is most vicious, but also chuse the best. The tyrannie of one absolute prince is pernitious, & of many much worse: but there is no tyrannie so dangerous as that of a multitude; for so doth *Cicero* call

---

F8 of marks, AND of peeces   F8–9 auntients, for   H8 have said: if   K5 absolute power *i.e. puissance souveraine*, sovereign power   Notes at G6, G9, H6.

OF A COMMONWEALE.

call it: yet is it not so bad as Anarchia, where there is no forme of a Commonweale, no man commands, and no man obeyes. Let vs therefore flie those that be vicious, and make choise of the best of these three lawfull gouernments: and to the end that all may be made plaine, I will set downe the commodities and discommodities of euery one apart. First, some one may say, that a popular estate is the most commendable, as that which seekes an equalitie and indifferencie in all lawes, without fauour or acception of persons, and which reduceth their ciuill constitutions to the lawes of nature: for euen as nature hath not distributed riches, estates and honors more to one than to another, so a popular estate tends to that end, to make all men equall, the which cannot be done, but by imparting riches, honors & iustice equally to al men without priuilege or prerogatiue whatsoeuer; as *Licurgus* did, hauing changed the royall estate into a popular, he burnt all obligations, banished gold and siluer, and diuided the lands by equall lots; then tooke he great pleasure to see the shocks of corne equall in the field, thereby cutting off couetousnes and arrogancie, two of the most pernitious plagues of a Commonweale, and not only those, but he also banished rapine, theft, extorsion, slanders, partialities and factions, which can haue no place when all are equall, and that one can haue no preheminence ouer another. If then societie betwixt man and man cannot be maintained without friendship, and that the nurse of friendship is equalitie; seeing there is no equalitie but in a popular state, of necessitie that forme of Commonweale must be the best: in the which a naturall libertie and iustice is equally distributed to all men without feare of tyranie, crueltie, or exaction; and the sweetnes of a sociable life seemes to draw men to the felicitie which nature hath taught vs. There is one point that seemes very considerable, to shew that a popular estate is the goodliest, the most excellent, and the most perfect, which is, That in a Democraty there haue alwaies been greater commanders in armes, and worthier men in lawes, greater orators, philosophers and handicrafts men than in the other two estates: whereas the faction of few great men among themselues, and the iealousie of a Monarke keepes the subiects from all noble attempts. And it seemes that the true marke of a Commonweale consists in a popular estate only, in the which the whole people inioyes the publick, diuiding the common treasure amongst them, with the spoiles, rewards, honors and conquests, whereas few noblemen in Aristocratia, and one in a Monarchie seeme to conuert all the publicke good to their owne priuate commodities. To conclude, if there be nothing more to be desired than to haue the magistrates obedient to the lawes, and the subiects to the magistrates, it seemes it is best obserued in a popular state, whereas the law alone is ladie and mistres ouer all. These reasons are produced by popular men to maintaine a popular estate; they haue a goodly shew, but in effect they are like vnto spiders webs, the which are very subtill and fine, but haue no great force: for first of all, there was neuer Commonweale where this equalitie of goods and honors was obserued, as we haue shewed before concerning goods; and as for honors, they should do therein contrarie to the law of nature, which hath made some more iudicious and more ingenious than others, and by consequence hath ordained some to gouerne, and others to obey; some she hath made wise and discreet, others foolish and mad; to some she hath giuen excellencie of wit to gouerne and command, to others force of bodie to execute their commandements. And as for the naturall libertie they so much preach of in a popular estate, if that were of force, there should neither be magistrates, lawes, nor any forme of state whatsoeuer; else there should be no equalitie: and yet there is no forme of Commonweale which hath so many lawes, so many magistrates, nor so many comptrollers as a popular estate. And as for the publick reuenues and treasor, it is most certaine that there is no Commonweale where it is worse gouerned than by the people, as we haue

Reasons for a Popular estate.

Reasons against a Popular estate.

declared

702   THE SIXT BOOKE

declared elsewhere. Whereof amongst many others, *Xenophon* is a worthy witnesse: I cannot (said he) allow of the Athenians estate, for that they haue followed that forme of Commonweale, whereas the wicked are alwayes in greatest credit, and men of honour and vertue troden vnder foot. If *Xenophon* (who was one of the greatest captaines of his age, and who then carried away the prize to haue happely ioyned the mannaging of affaires with armes and Philosophie) hath giuen such a censure of his Commonweale, which was the most popular, and amongst the popular the most esteemed, and best ordered; or to speake more properly, the least vicious (as *Plutarch* saith;) What iudgement would he haue giuen of other Democraties, and Ochlocraties? Wherein *Machiauel* is much deceiued, to say, That a Popular estate is the best: and yet forgetting his first opinion, in anther place hee said, That the onely meanes to restore Italie to her libertie, is to haue one prince, labouring to frame the most Tyrannicall estate in the world. And in another place he confesseth, That the estate of Venice is the goodliest of all, the which is more Aristocraticall: so as no man can iudge what this wicked and inconstant man meanes. If we shall beleeue *Plato*, wee shall find that he hath blamed a Popular estate, tearming it, A Faire where euery thing is to bee sold. We haue the like opinion of *Aristotle*, saying, That neither Popular nor Aristocraticall estate is good, vsing the authoritie of *Homer*, οὐκ ἀγαθὸν πολυκοιρανίη. And the Orator *Maximus Tirius* holds, That a Democraty is pernitious, blaming for this cause the estate of the Athenians, Syracusians, Carthagineans and Ephesians: for it is impossible (saith *Seneca*) that he shall please the people, that honours vertue. And therefore *Phocion* (one of the wisest, and most vertuous men that euer was) was alwaies opposit to the people of Athens, and the people to him: and as on a certaine day the Athenians allowed of his counsell, he turned to his companions, saying, *Quid malũ mihi accidit, vt populi sensus cum meis congruerent*, What ill haue I done, that the people concur with me in opinion? And how can a multitude, that is to say, a Beast with many heads, without iugemẽt, or reason, giue any good councel? To aske councell of a multitude (as they did in oldtimes in Popular Commonweals) is to seeke for wisdome of a mad man. The which *Anacharsis* seeing, & that the magistrats and antients deliuered their opinions in open assembly, and then the people concluded; he said, That in Athens wise men propounded, and fooles disposed. And admit one might draw a good resolution from a multitude, who is he so sencelesse, that would thinke it fit to publish a matter of state in an open assembly? Is it not to prophane holy things? and yet holy things beeing prophaned, may be purified: but a secret concerning affaires of estate, being once published and spred abroad, there can nothing be expected but preiudice and dishonour to the Commonweale. And for this cause especially the Commonweale of Athens, of Siracusa, and of Florence, haue bene ruined. I omit the difficultie to assemble the people in one place, the disorder that is in a multitude, the varietie and inconstancie of people gathered together of all sorts: and yet (if it please not the magistrat) neither shall Senat nor people be assembled: as it happened in *Cæsars* Consulship, who to preuaile in his attempts (hauing terrified *Bibulus* his companion, and drawne his sword vpon him) he would not suffer the Senat to be assembled so long as his office continued. And if the Tribune were vnited with the Consull, neither there the Senat nor the people could be assembled: so as the authoritie of the Senat, and the soueraigne maiestie, was by this meanes subiect vnto six or seuen: whereby the state was brought into great danger, in not resoluing speedily in vrgent affaires. For by the lawes of *Solon*, and of the twelue tables, the people must bee assembeld three times, before they should allow of any law that was published. Oftentimes it chaunced, that the flying of a bird on the right hand, or the crying of a rat, or the falling sicknesse (it may be of some drunken man) hindred

the

A Popular estate condemned of many great men.

G1 *another place*   H4 *For* accidit *Bodin writes* excidit *i.e.* slipped out, "escaped my lips."
K3 *For* neither there the Senat *read* neither the Senat.   K7 assembled   Notes at K2, K8.

OF A COMMONWEALE. 703

the assembly; or at the least protestation of some stamering sooth-sayer, or the opposition of a magistrat, all was dissolued. Whereof *Cicero* and *Cato* himselfe complained verie much, for the power and fauour of competitors (which were alwaies many in number) to haue offices, and being enemies one to another, hindred the assembly of the people, or troubled it being assembled; and the magistrats which were in office supported them, to continue their power: so as sometimes a whole yeare was spent without the creation of a new magistrat: as it happened when as *Pompey* the Great was chosen Consull alone. And therefore the Grisons, who maintaine a Popular estate, assemble the people but euery two yeares at Coire, for the creating of new magistrats, and the making of new lawes. For there is nothing more daungerous, nor more contrarie to a Popular estate, than to continue magistrats long in their office. What is more absurd, than to allow of the rashnesse of a light and inconstant multitude for a law, who in discerning and giuing of honours, are commonly carried away with a blind and inconsiderat violence, rather than with any setled iudgement? What is more foolish, than in the greatest extremities of a Commonweale, to seeke councell from a mad multitude? for the magistrat can do nothing without commaund, and if they might they would not; neither dare they, being terrified with the peoples furie, who impute all mischaunces, and their owne errours, vnto the magistrats. So as *Philip* the first, king of Macedon, hauing inuaded and spoyled the confines of Attica, there was not any magistrat that durst assemble the estates, the people came to the place of assemblies vncalled, whereas they found no man that durst speake vnto them, as *Demosthenes* writeth. The like happened at Florence, when as the emperours armie approached to besiege them, at the instance of pope *Clement* the seuenth, al the people were so amazed, as they knew not what to resolue: For by the lawes of Florence, all the citisens should assemble before the Towne house, to resolue vpon the articles propounded by the chiefe magistrat, and then they were quite daunted. It is the weaknesse of a multitude (saith *Titus Liuius*) to waxe proud, and to insult with all licentiousnesse in prosperitie, and to be deiected and amazed with any aduersitie. And how is it possible that the soueraigne maiestie of an estate shall be maintained by a multitude, guided by a magistrat, who oftentimes must keepe them in awe by seueritie, *Et in qua regenda plus pœna, quam obsequium valet* (said *Titus Liuius*) In the gouernment whereof punishment more than obedience preuailes. So *Phocion*, seeing that the Athenians would not giue him audience, he cried out, *O fustuarium Corcyræum, quouis talento pretio sius*, O scourge of *Corfu*, more pretious than any talent: Which shewes the maiestie doth perish and decay in a multitude, whereon the chiefe ground of a Commonweale consists. But passing on, all men that haue written of estates, do hold, That the chiefe end of all Commonweales, is to flourish in pietie, iustice, valour, honour, and vertue; by the which humane society is preserued. But a Popular estate hath bene alwaies opposit, and an enemie to all good men. For the preseruation of a Popular estate (if we shall beleeue *Xenophon*) is to aduance the most vitious and vnworthy men to offices and dignities. And if the people should be so ill aduised, as to giue offices of honour vnto vertuous men, they loose their power: for that good men would fauour none but the good, which are alwayes fewer in number: and the wicked and vicious (which is the greatest part of the people) should be excluded from all honour, and by little and little banished: so as in the end wise men should seize vpon the estate, and take that from the people. The Athenians therefore (said *Xenophon*) gaue audience to the most wicked, knowing well, that they would speake pleasing things, and profitable to the vicious, as most of the people be. I cannot (said *Xenophon*) but blame the Athenians, to haue chosen the most vicious forme of a Commonweale: but hauing chosen it, I doe much esteeme them they doe so

The Grisons assembled euery two yeares.

A multitude is amazed in danger.

A multitude cannot maintaine a maiestie.

The end of Popular estates, is to banish vertue.

Xenophon giues a true iudgement of a Popular estate.

Ooo iiij

care-

carefully maintaine it, in reiecting, chasing away, and banishing the noble, wise, and vertuous; & aduancing the impudent, wicked, & vicious: for the which vice thou so much blamest (saith he) is the preseruation of a Popular estate. And as for iustice, the people (saith hee) haue no regard of it, so as they may get profit by their iudgements, which they sell to them that will giue most, seeking by all meanes to ruine the rich, the noble, and the vertuous, whome they torment continually, for the capitall hatred they beare against all good men, being contrarie to their naturall dispositions. And therefore a Popular state is the sinke and refuge of all turbulent spirits, mutines, seditions, and banished men, which giue councell, comfort, and aid, vnto the people to ruine great men: For as for the lawes they haue no respect of them, for that in Athens the peoples will is a law. This is *Xenophons* opinion, touching the Commonweale of Athens, who saith, it was the best ordered of al the Popular Commonweals in his time: neither would he haue them to change any thing to maintain the people in their greatnes. The like censure *Marcellus* the lawyer hath of a strumpet, saying, That shee hath not well done to haue abandoned her honour; but hauing lost all modestie, it was not ill done, to get what she could by her trade. So *Xenophon* concludes, That a Popular estate is nothing worth, but to maintaine it so being once setled, they must banish all honor and vertue: that is to say, the greatest tyranny is not so daungerous, as a Popular estate thus gouerned.

<small>Impunitie of vice in a Popular estate.</small>

But there is yet one plague more capitall in Popular estates, the which is, Impunitie to the wicked, so as they be citisens, that is to say, pettie kings: and euen in the Popular estate of Rome, it was forbidden to all magistrats vpon paine of death, To condemne to death, or to banish any citisen, nor to depriue him of his libertie or priuilege of a citisen, nor to whip him with rods. For it is a setled law almost in all Popular estates, *Ne ciuis quisquam quantumcumque scelus siue in deos, siue in homines admiserit, capite feriatur*, That no citisen should die the death, what offence soeuer he had committed either against the gods, or men. Therefore *Verres* (omitting the rest) being accused and condemned of theft, and of a hundred thousand concussions, extortions, and false iudgements; was thought to be seuerely punished, for that hee was enioyned to depart out of Rome: and why, for that Popular states would haue their libertie defended with the lenitie of lawes, and not with the sharpnesse of punishments. And yet they banished *Rutilius, Metellus, Coriolanus*, the two *Scipions*, brethren, and *Tully*: as in Ephesus they banished the vertuous *Hermodorus*: in Athens they expelled *Aristides* the iust, *Themistocles* died in exile, *Miltiodes* in prison, *Socrates* by poyson. And although that *Phocion* the most iust and vertuous man of his age, had bene chosen Generall fortie and fiue times, without any reproach or blame, yet (without any accusation or information against him or his companions) a base pleader, of the scumme of the people, steps vp before the multitude, and demaunds, If they would haue *Phocion* and his companions put to death: wherewith all in generall did arise vp, and holding vp their hands, condemned him, not excluding any slaue, woman, nor straunger from this condemnation, for the which many ware garlands of flowers. Which *Phocion* hearing, said, *Me quidam a vobis damnari facile patior: sed cur isti?* For my part, I am contented to bee condemned by you: but why these men? To whome the people being mad, aunswered, *Quoniam tibi sunt amici*. Neither was the furie of this mad people pacified, vntill they were all without sentence, accusation, or cause, put to death. Neither is there any hope, if a multitude begin once to insult ouer the good, that either shame or reason shal reclaime them from their furie and madnesse. Yet notwithstanding the wicked do commonly escape the peoples hands: which *Demosthenes* seeing, and that they had absolued *Antipaphon*, a most capitall offender, he proceeded, and caused him to be condemned.

<small>The most vertuous are banished, and the wicked escape, in a Popular estate.</small>

F8 *For* seditions *read* seditious.   I4 Miltiades   I10 from this condemnation *i.e.* from the assembly which passed the sentence   K2 quidem   K9 Antiphon

ned, and afterwards put to death by a decree of the Areopagits, little regarding the people, for the which he was not blamed. Whereby it appeares, that there was neither iustice nor maiestie in a Popular estate. And as in a Popular Commonweale thus gouerned, all offices are sold to them that will giue most, so the magistrats sell by retaile that which they haue bought in grosse. And euen *Marius* durst carrie bushels of siluer into the assemblies at Rome, to purchase the peoples voices: the like wee read of *Pompey*. It is no maruell then if we read of infinit corruptions and concussions in Rome: but it was more fowle and odious in Athens, whereas when *Stratocles* and *Damoclides* entred into their offices, they did openly brag, That they went to a golden haruest. If offices, lawes, iustice, and honours, were so vnworthily sold in these great Commonweales, being inriched with the spoyles of other people; what shall we iudge of Popular estates opprest with want and need? Wee haue the example of the Megarences, who hauing expelled their prince *Theagines*, established a Popular estate so licentious, as it was lawfull for the poore to goe and spoyle the rich, as it is in *Plato*. Euen so wee read, that the Swissers did long after they had expelled the nobilitie. If they would haue any one spoyled by the multitude, they did set the picture of a man with boughes vnder him at his doore, and then was he presently stript of all that he had, were he the richest or most innocent citisen. And they which doe so highly commend the Popular estate of the Romans, should rather haue extolled the worthy deeds of noble and valiant men, than the cities forme: they should set before their eyes the seditions and ciuill warres, wherewith that citie had bene shaken, and represent the people of the one side of a mountaine, and the nobilitie of another, diuided three times; and many times the furious Tribunes with their turbulent Orations, to threaten death or banishment to the best citisens: Sometime *Saturnine* the Tribune, with a rabble of rascals, slaues, and artisans, armed with staues and stones, to come into the open assembly of the people, and to expell the honester partie, and kill him that was chosen Consull by the peoples suffrages. The which the Tribunes alone did not, being enraged against the Consuls, but euen the Consuls among themselues. How many murthers of citisens haue beene seene in the middest of the citie, in the field of *Mars*, in the court, in the temples of their gods, yea in *Iupiters* capitoll, *Tiberius* and *Caius Gracchus*, *Drusus*, *Saturninus*, and *Sulpitius*, were cruelly slaine: when as the Consull *Cassius* made a proclamation, That all the Latines, and Heniques, which had no houses within Rome, should depart the citie. *Virginius* his companion made a decree to the contrarie, not so much to crosse his companions authoritie, but to set the citisens and straungers together by the eares in the middest of the citie. What was more vnworthy, or more contrarie to ciuill societie, than to see a citisen vnder an innocent gowne, to come armed to the assembly, to sue for offices, as if they went to warre, and oftentimes the contrarie factions fell to blowes. And *Tully* saith, *Lapidationes in foro sæpe vidimus, non sæpe, sed tamen nimis sæpe gladios*. We haue oftentimes seene stones cast in the assembly of the estates, and swords drawne, not so often, but yet too often. And a little after, *Meministis (inquit) corporibus ciuium Tiberim compleri: cloacas refarciri, e foro spongijs effundi sanguinem*, You remember (said he) that the riuer of Tiber hath bene filled with the bodies of citisens, that the common priuies haue bene stuffed full, and the blood suckt vp in the market place with sponges. To conclude, if we shall rip vp all the Popular estates that euer were, we shall find, that either they haue had warre alwayes with the enemie, or within the state: or else that they haue bene gouerned in shew by the people; but in effect by some of the citisens, or by the wisest among them, who held the place of a prince and monarch. Whilest that the Commonweale of Athens did flourish, it was gouerned by the Senat of the Areopagits: and when as their power and authoritie was restrained

Popular estates exceed in all licentiousnesse.

strained, *Pericles* (saith *Thucidides*) was a very Monarch, although in shew it were Popular. And *Peter Soderin* (in an Oration hee made vnto the people of Florence, to change the estate) said, That in the time of *Laurence de Medicis*, the Commonweale in shew was Popular, but in effect a meere Tyranny, for that *Laurence* gouerned all alone: but he doth not say, that it was neuer more flourishing, and that before they were neuer ten yeares free from seditions, and the most bloody factions that euer were. In like sort the Popular estate of the Romans, which had bene afflicted with so many forren and intestine warres, was it not maintained and flourished both in armes, and laws, by the Senat, and was not the authoritie thereof supported, by *Menenius Agrippa, Furius Camillus, Papirius Cursor, Fabius Maximus, Scipio, Cato, Scaurus, Pompey*, and diuers others? who maintained the beautie of the Senat, and restrained the people, keeping them within the bounds of honour? We do also read, that *Pelopidas*, and *Epaminondas*, were as it were lords of the Popular estate of the Thebans, after whose death the people found presently, that they had lost their chiefe pilots: as it happened in the like case vnto the Athenians, after the death of *Pericles*, Then (said *Plutarch*) the people did float vp and downe, like a ship without a helme: and as euery one would gouerne and commaund, some to set saile, others to go to harbrough, a storme came (saith *Polybius*) and the ship perished. And although the Athenians, after they had lost the soueraigntie of Greece, gouerned their citie & territorie popularly, yet *Demosthenes* spake plainely, and openly before the people, That the estate of Athens was vnder the power of Orators and Pleaders, of whome the captaines depended, who had at the least three hundred men bribed, to passe whatsoeuer they pleased for money. A common disease (saith *Plutarch*) in all Popular estates. *Liuius* writeth thus of the Popular estates of the Tarentines, *In potestate Iuniorum plebem, in manu plebis, rem Tarentinam esse*, The estate of Tarentum was in the peoples hands, and the people in the power of the younger sort. And a little before the declining of the Popular estate of Rome, *Crassus, Cæsar*, and *Pompey*, whome they called a triple head, gouerned and held all the Senat and people in their power and subiection: but two of them being slaine, the third became an absolute Lord. Whereby we may gather, that a Popular commaund cannot subsist without a wise pilat and gouernor, and leauing it to the most sufficient, in the end they make themselues masters, and the people serues but for a maske.

But some one will say, Doe we not see that the Cantons of the Swissers haue setled a goodly Popular estate, & haue continued their gouernment aboue three hundred and fiftie yeares, and by this meanes haue not onely preserued themselues from tyranny, but haue also chased away tyrants their neighbours? The aunswere hereunto is double: First, the situation of the countrey, and the disposition of the people agrees best with a Popular estate. Secondly, the most seditious, & mutinous, go to the seruice of other forren princes: and the rest of the common people being more mild & tractable, are easily kept in awe. Moreouer all the heads of the Cantons & Popular states, hauing entred into an offensiue and defensiue league, are strictly tied and vnited together; like vnto those that goe by night, or that are in a slipperie or daungerous way, holding one another by the hand: and in this sort they maintaine themselues against the power of Monarchs, as in old time the Athenians and Thebans did. Besides, the foundation of their Popular estate was built and cimented with the blood of the nobilitie, and of the chiefest, especially at the battaile of Sampac; then afterwards at that at Basil, when as king *Lewes* the 11 (beeing then but Daulphin) had the victorie: then all the nobilitie of the countrey, which had followed him, were banished, and the rest retired themselues willingly, after the treatie of the ten Cantons, made in the yeare 1510, and at the chaunge of religion in the yeare 1529: so as there remaines but a very few at Berne and Zurich,

---

F2 *Peter Soderin properly* Paolantonio Soderini (cf. note at 544 G2)   F3 Medicis   G7 harbrough *i.e.* harbor   K5 *For* the chiefest *Bodin writes* the richest (Fr and L).   Notes at G2, H1.

Of A Commonweale.

A Zurich, whereas the estate is Aristocraticall. And not only the Cantons, but also those at Strausbourg, Lyndaw, Sienne, Genes, and Florence (to settle a popular libertie) slue or banished the nobilitie: as they haue done in many townes of Germanie. After they of Florence had made away their nobilitie, they diuided themselues into three factions, the greater, the meane, and the popular: and as the greater sort entred into factions, and slue one another, the meaner thought to become maisters, who were so incensed one against another, as the whole citie was nothing but fire and blood, murthering one another, vntill that the scumme of the people tooke vpon them the gouernment, they alwayes hated them that looked like gentlemen, or that ware a sword, or that had gotten to any degree of honour, in what Commonweale soeuer, or that had gathered

B together more riches than the rest: which made them of Strausbourg (after they had slaine all the nobilitie, to settle a Popular estate) to decree, That whosoeuer did aspire to be Grand Bourgmaster, should proue that his grandfather was a day labourer, an artificer, a butcher, or of some such like condition. And the auntients (to assure Popular estates) did striue to equall all citisens in goods, honours, power, and rewards: and if any one were more vertuous, more iust, or more wise, than the rest, he was banished, as I haue shewed before, seeking to make an equalitie, if it were possible: and euen *Plato* did wish, That wiues and children should be common to all, to the end that no man might say, This is mine, or, That is thine: for those words of *Meum*, and *Tuum* (said he) were the breeders of discord, and the ruine of states. By the which there will grow many ab-

C surdities: for in so doing, a citie shall be ruined, and become a houshold (as *Aristotle* said) although that a houshold or familie (which is the true image of a Commonweale) hath but one head. And for this cause an auntient * lawmaker, beeing importuned by some one, to make his country a Popular estate: Make it (saith he) in thine owne house. And if they say, That it is a goodly thing so to vnite citisens and a citie, as to make one houshold of it, they must then take away the pluralitie of heads and commaunders, which are in a Popular estate, to make a Monarch, as the true fathers of a familie; and to cut off this equalitie of goods, power, honour, and commaundement, which they seeke to make in a Popular estate: for that it is incompatible in a familie. But the greatest inconuenience is, that in taking away these words of Mine, and Thine, they ruine

* *Bias.*

D the foundation of all Commonweales, the which were chiefly established, to yeeld vnto euery man that which is his owne, and to forbid theft; as it is commaunded by the word of God, who will haue euery man to enioy the proprietie of his owne goods: and we may not say, that nature hath made all things common, for the law of the mother is not contrarie to the commaundement of the father (as *Salomon* said) figuring by an Allegorie the commaundements of God, and the law of nature. But the true popular libertie consisteth in nothing else, but in the enioying of our priuat goods sincerely, without feare to be wronged, in honour, life, wife, or familie, the which euen theeues & robbers labour to keepe. And as for the power of commaund, which popular men would make equall, there is lesse reason than in goods: for discretion and wisdome is

Taking away the proprietie of goods, we ouerthrow a Commonweale.

E not equally giuen to all men, and in a Popular estate they must of necessitie chuse the most sufficient magistrats, to commaund, and to administer iustice. Moreouer, whereas there is no forme of soueraigntie, nor of a Commonweale, yet are the people constrained to chuse a magistrat or captaine to commaund them, and to doe iustice: as in the countrey of Gusula in Affrike, where there is neither king, nor any forme of a Commonweale, the people on their Faire day chuse a captaine to doe iustice, and to assure the course of traffique. And on the frontiers of the kingdome of Fez, the inhabitants of the mountaine of Magnan (who in like sort haue no forme of a Commonweale) if they see any straunger to passe by, which seemes to excell the rest in wisedome, him

Wisdome is not equall in all men, to impart offices equally.

they

A8 government: they   C7 true father   D7 *For* sincerely *probably read* securely (*en seureté* in Fr, *tranquille* in L).   E10 they   Notes at B6, C1.

A rule in Popular states. they stay by force, to administer iustice vnto them. It is a maxime in Popular states, That when as the persons are equall which are to vndergo a charge, to cast lots: and if one exceeds another, then they chuse the most sufficient. And who doth not see the great difference among men, that some haue lesse iudgement than bruit beasts; and others haue such cleere marks of diuine light, as they seeme rather angels than men? and

An error in equalitie. yet those which seeke equalitie, will haue the soueraigne power of life, honour, and goods, giuen vnto furious, ignorant, and mad men, as well as vnto iudicious and wise men: for the voices in all assemblies are numbred, without any due consideration of euerie mans worth: and alwayes the number of fooles, wicked and ignorant men, doth farre exceed the good, if that be true which *Salomon* saith, That there is not one among a thousand: the which is confirmed by the Poet,

A good man and a wise, one such as out of all mankind,
Though Apollo sought and searcht himselfe, yet could he scarcely find.

And yet there is a naturall reason, which doth teach vs, that the equalitie they seeke, doth ruine the grounds of all loue and amitie, the which can hardly subsist among equals, for that there are neuer more quarrels & dissentions, than among them that are equall; either for that the one seekes to supplant the other, or for that the one may liue

All nations haue need one of another. without the other. And it seemes that God hath imparted his benefits and graces, to countries and nations, in such a measure, as there is no man but hath need of another: to the end that through mutuall courtesie and good offices, euerie nation in particular, and all in generall, should be constrained to contract alliances and friendships together: as it is seene in a mans bodie, the which is the figure of a wel ordered Commonweale, there is no member but receiues helpe and succour from the rest, and that which seems most

Equalitie and friendship are incompatible. idle, disgests the nourishment for all the rest: as *Menenius Agrippa* a Roman Senator, did wisely shew vnto the common people, which were fallen from the nobilitie, & did seeke to equall themselues vnto them in power and authoritie. Popular gouernments in the beginning seeme pleasing and goodly, contrarie to Monarchies: the which are like vnto great riuers, which at their first springs haue small and weake currents, but increasing by their long course, their streames grow bigger, & more rough, and run with more spacious chanels, the farther they are from their heads and springs. But Popular states are like vnto the wind, the which is most vehement where it riseth, but at the length it is broken and groweth weake. I haue discoursed hereof the more at large, to shew the inconueniences which follow a Popular estate, to the end I might reduce them to reason which seeke to withdraw the subiect from the obedience of their natu-

A Popular estate a pernitious tyranny, if not wisely gouerned. rall prince, through a false hope of libertie, in framing of Popular states: the which in effect is nothing else, but the most pernitious tyranny that can be imagined, if it bee not gouerned by wise and vertuous men. And therefore among the Cantons of the Swissers (those which are best ordered) although they haue established a forme of Popular Commonweale, yet they gouerne themselues Aristocratically, hauing two or three councels, to the end the people deale not in affaires of state as little as may be; assembling seldome but by quarters, or parishes, which they call Schaffes (as in old time the inhabitants of Mantinea a Popular state did) fearing the tumults and rebellions which

Generall assemblies are dangerous in Popular estates. fall out commonly when they are altogether. But seeing it is not in the power of good citisens, nor of wise polititians, to change a Popular estate into a Monarchie: the chiefe grounds then of a Popular estate consists in the strict obseruation of lawes and ordinances, being of it selfe quite different and disagreeing from the lawes and order of nature, which giues the commauud vnto the wisest: a thing verie incompatible with the people:

I9 governed   K9 commaund

people: for if a multitude (being impatient of command) haue not good lawes and statutes before their eyes, as lights to guide them, the estate will be soone ruined. And therefore the Swissers do obserue their lawes verie seuerely, else their estate had not bene so durable: for euen as weake & crased bodies fall soone into diseases, if they leaue the good diet and order prescribed them by the Physitian; so is it in a Popular state, if they doe not obserue their laws and ordinances. And thus much to satisfie them which are not contented, although the greatest men that euer were, haue disallowed of a Popular estate.

Let vs see now if an Aristocraticall gouernment bee any thing better than the rest, as many hold opinion: for if a mediocratie be commendable in all things, and that we must flie all vicious extreames; it followes then, that these two vicious extreams being reiected, we must hold the meane, which is an Aristoctitie, or a certaine number of the most apparant citisens: as if there were ten thousand citisens, let them make choyce of an hundred; the which were a iust proportionable number betwixt one & a thousand: increasing or diminishing the number according to the multitude of the subiects, wherin they shall hold that commendable & desired mediocritie betwixt a Monarchy and a Democratie. There is yet another argument of no lesse efficacie, to proue that an Aristocraticall estate is the best, which is, That the power of soueraigne commaund, by naturall reason, is to be giuen to the most worthy: and dignitie cannot consist but in vertue, in nobilitie, or in riches, or in all three together. If then wee desire to chuse one of the three, or to ioyne them all together, the estate shall bee alwaies Aristocraticall: for the noble, rich, wise, and valiant men, make alwayes the least part of the citisens, in what place soeuer; by naturall reason then that gouernment must bee Aristocraticall, when as the least part of the citisens commaund the state, or whereunto the best and most vertuous men are admitted.

Reasons for an Aristocraticall estate.

A man may also say, that the soueraigntie should be giuen onely to the most rich, as to them that haue most interest in the preseruation of the whole state. Without doubt the most rich haue the greatest interest, and beare a greater charge than the poore, who hauing little to loose, abandon the Commonweale at need. And therefore *O. Flaminius* did wisely commit the gouernment of the cities of Thessalie, to the most rich, as to them that had most interest in the preseruation of the state. Moreouer it seems that necessitie doth guide vs to an Aristocraticall estate: for although that in a Popular estate, and in a Monarchy, the monarch or the people in shew haue the soueraigntie, yet in effect they are forced to commit the gouernment to the Senat, or priuie Councell, who consult, and many times determine of greatest affaires: so as it is alwaies an Optimacie. And if the monarch, or people, be so ill aduised as to gouerne otherwise than by a wise councell, there can nothing bee expected but an ineuitable ruine of the state. I omit other reasons lesse necessarie, as euery one may coniecture, to conclude, that an Aristocratie is the most commendable state. And yet I say, that all together are not sufficient to proue it: for as for that commendable mediocritie which we seeke, it is not reall, diuiding things in the middest, but consists in reason: as liberalitie a meane betwixt two vicious extreames, yet doth it approach neerer vnto prodigalitie than vnto couetousnesse. The meane which they seeke betwixt one and all in generall, is reall; neither can it euer be alike, for that there are some cities which haue not a thousand citisens, and others that haue aboue three hundred thousand: so as an Aristocraticall estate shall be alwaies mutable and variable, for the vncertaintie of the number: and it will often fall out, that a great Aristocraticall estate shall haue more commaunders, than a Popular state in a small citie shall haue citisens: as if there be foure hundred thousand citisens, to obserue a true Geometricall proportion, there must be foure thousand gouernours or commanders:

The gouernment of a Commonweale must be giuen to them that haue the most interest in the preseruation thereof.

Ppp

B3 *apparant* i.e. prominent, outstanding   B4 *For* one & a thousand *read* one & ten thousand.
Notes at A3, C6, E8.

commaunders: so as by a necessarie consequence, the inconueniences which are incident to a Popular estate, will also fall out in an Aristocratie, by reason of the multitude of lords: for the more gouernours there be, the more factions will grow, their consultations will be more hard to determine, and are sooner discouered. And therefore those Aristocraticall estates are more durable and assured, that haue fewest lords: as the Lacedemonians, who had but thirtie gouernours, and the Pharsalians twentie; they did long maintaine their estates, whereas others decaied soone. It is not then the middle number betwixt one and all, which makes that commendable meane, seeing that there be as many kinds of vicious Commonweales, as of commendable and vertuous.

As for the other point, That they must giue the soueraigntie vnto the most worthy, It is true; but the argument makes more for a Monarchy, than for an Aristocratie: for among the most noble, the most wise, the most rich, and the most valiant, there is alwayes some one that doth excell the rest, to whome by that reason the soueraigntie doth belong: For it is impossible to find them all equall in all respects. And as for the Senat, or Councell, we haue shewed before, that it is diuided from maiestie, and hath no power to commaund, in what estate soeuer: else doth it loose the name and marke of a Senat, the which is ordained to no other end, but to giue councell to them that haue the soueraigntie, to whome belong the resolution & decision of the councell. But *Plato* had another argument for an Aristocratical estate, saying, That it was verie hard to find any one man so wise and vertuous, as was requisit for the gouernment of an estate, and by that meanes a Monarchie were not sure. But this argument is captious, and may be vsed against himselfe: for if it be hard to find any one prince so wise as he desireth, how shall they find out so great a number as is needfull in a Seigneurie. And *Peter Soderin* Gonfalonier of Florence, speaking vnto the people against an Aristocraticall estate, he vsed the same argument which *Mæcenas* did before *Augustus* against *Marcus Agrippa*, saying, That the gouernment of few lords, is the gouernment of few tyrants: and that it was better at all euents to haue but one tyrant. For if any one will say, that among many there will haply be some number of good men, we must then rather chuse a Popular estate, for that in a great number there will be found more vertuous than in a lesse. But both the one and the other is vnprofitable: for as well in all Aristocraticall and Popolar estates, as in all corporations and colledges, the greatest part doth still ouer-rule the sounder and the better: and the more men there be, the lesse effects are there of vertue and wisedome (euen as a little salt cast into a great lake, looseth his force:) so as the good men shall be alwayes vanquished in number by the vicious, and ambitious: and for one tyrant there shall be a hundred which will crosse the resolution of the lesser but of the sounder part: as it is alwaies seene as well in the diets and assemblies of the princes of Germanie, whereas the spirituall princes of the empire, being the greatest number, haue alwaies crost the princes temporall: so as by their means the emperour *Charls* the fift, caused the empire to declare it selfe an enemie to the house of France, the which had not bene so in many ages: to the end the temporall princes should haue no hope of any succours from Fraunce in their necessities, whereinto they soone after fell. And to make short, it hath bene alwayes seene, that the more heads there be in a Seigneurie, the more controuersies arise, and lesse resolution. And therefore the Seigneurie of Venice to auoid these inconueniences, commits all affaires of state to the mannaging of a dozen persons, and most commonly to seuen, especially to keepe their affaires secret, wherein consists the health and preseruation of an estate.

But let vs suppose, that a priuie Councell in an Aristocraticall estate, bee so secret, as nothing is discouered; yet is it a difficult thing for few commaunders to maintaine their estate against a multitude, which hath no part in honourable charges: for that most
com-

F5(margin) estates   H3 Peter Soderin *properly* Paolantonio Soderini (cf. note at 544 G2)
Notes at H5, I6.

OF A COMMONWEALE.　711

commonly the lords scorne and contemne the popular, and the poore carrie alwaies a capital hatred against the great: so as vpon the least dissention among the nobles (the which is ineuitable if they be men of faction, and giuen to armes) the most factious and ambitious flieth vnto the multitude, and ruines the state: as I haue noted before of the Seigneuries of Genes, Florence, Cologne, Zurich, Strausbourg, Lindaw, and the auntient Phocians, Samians, Therenecians, Amphipolites, Corcyrians, Cnidians, Mytelenians, and Hostienses; in the which the multitude hath expelled, banished, spoyled, and slaine the nobles. And what guard soeuer they keepe, yet do they liue in continuall distrust, and sometimes in such feare, as they doe not assemble together but in places of strength: as in the citie of Benizete, lying in the realme of Telesin in Barbarie, all the lords and commaunders keepe themselues in forts, fearing the people should mutine against them, or that one of them should murther the rest. So in old time the inhabitants of Miletum, after they had expelled their two tyrants, they fell cruelly to armes among themselues, the nobles against the people: but in the end the rich hauing vanquished the poore, they framed an Aristocraticall estate, where they liued in such feare, and distrust, as they went into ships to hold their councels, fearing (saith *Plutarch*) to be surprised and slaine by the people: like vnto the lords of the Samiens, who were all massacred by the multitude, at such time as they were in councell. So as in an Aristocraty the lords dare not traine the people vp to armes, nor put weapons into their hands: neither can they go to the warre, but they are in daunger to loose the estate, if they bee once defeated: neither can they assure themselues of straungers, fearing they should bee subiected by them. To which daungers a Popular estate is not subiect, euerie one hauing a part in the state. An Aristocraticall estate then, is not onely in daunger of forraine enemies, but of the people, whome they must content or keepe in awe by force: to content them without making them partakers of the gouernment, were very hard; & to admit them to charges of honour, without alteration of the state, from an Aristocratie to a Popular, were impossible: to keepe them in subiection by force, that were not safe, although it might be done; for that were to shew an open feare and distrust of them whome they must win by loue and courtesie: else vpon any forraine war against the state, or among the gouernours themselues, the people will bee easily drawne to armes, and to shake off their yoake. And therefore the Venetians to maintaine their Aristocraticall estate, impart some small offices vnto the people, contract alliances with them, borrow of them to bind them to the maintenance of the state; and disarme them quite: and to make them more mild and pliable, they giue them full scope and libertie to all sorts of pleasures: and sometimes they make their richest citisens bourgesses. If they haue any warre against the straunger, they soone compound it at what price soeuer: and aboue all things they labour to quench and pacifie all partialities and hatred among the gentlemen: so as the rich being drunke with delights, and the poore hauing meanes to traffique, and to exercise themselues in mechanike arts, with the commoditie of the place, lying vpon the sea, being by nature strong, they haue no great occasion, & lesse power to rebell. By these meanes the Venetians (next vnder God) haue maintained their estate, and not by the forme of an Aristocraticall gouernment, as many do hold. And although the nature of the situation of Venice, the honour of the people, the wisedome of the Seigneures, and the lawes, be fit for an Aristocraticall estate, yet is it not aboue foure hundred yeares, that they haue instituted this forme of Commonweale, neither could they auoid many seditions and ciuill warres; as of the Bochonians, Faleriennes, Tepoliennes, Baiamontaines, and the cruell factions of the Iustinians, the Sceuoles, Seliens, Bassiens; the murther of eighteene dukes, and of a great number of Senators, as we may read in their histories. Wherein *Paulus Iouius* was deceiued, who

The cause that doth most ruine Aristocraticall estates.

The commanders in an Aristocraticall estate are in continuall feare and distrust

How the estate of Venice hath bene preserued.

Gianot. Donat. de Repub. Venet.

Ppp ij

A5 Genes, SIENA, Florence (Fr and L)　A6 Therenecians *i.e.* Troezenians (misspelled in Fr 7)
A10 *For* Benizete (Fr 7) *read* Benizenete (Fr 1–6, 8) *or* Benizeneta (L).　D4 libertie　D5 all sorts
E3 *For* honour *read* humour (cf. Fr).　Notes at B1, D3, E7.

who held, That the estate of Venice had continued eight hundred yeares: and *Paulus Manutius*, and *du Moulin*, haue erred more, saying, That it had bene of twelue hundred yeares standing: for it is well verified by the auntient registers of their Seigneurie, that before *Cebastian Cian* duke of Venice, in the yeare 1175, it was a meere Monarchy: and yet there hath not bene any Aristocraticall estat, to our knowledge, that hath so long continued, but haue bene for the most part chaunged into cruell Tyrannies, or bloodie Popular estates, as we haue shewed elsewhere. And to make it more apparant, I will produce for a new example the state of Genes, who hauing peace with the Venetians, by meanes of the protection of Fraunce, soone after the Adornes, and Fregoses, diuided the state (the which at that time was Aristocraticall) into two factions, whence ensued many murthers of the chiefe men: so as the people fell to armes, freed themselues from subiection, and tooke the gouernment of the state from the gentlemen: and in succession of time made a law, whereby none might bee duke of Genes, vnlesse hee were a Plebeian: and since they haue published another law, prohibiting the nobles to haue aboue a third part of all other offices. And soone after in a sedition they expelled all their gentlemen, chusing eight Tribunes, and after they had reiected the protection of Fraunce, they chose a Dyer of silke for their duke, whome king *Lewes* the twelft caused to bee hanged, after that hee had taken the citie: but when as *Andrew Doria* reuolted, and that hee had power to dispose of the state at his pleasure, hee made choyce of all such as had six houses within the citie, and of some others of name and marke, which were not so rich, and diuided them all into eight and twentie tribes, the which they called *Alberghi*, making them gentlemen, and giuing them the gouernment of the state, and debarred the rest of the common people, onely with this exception, To haue libertie euerie yeare to make ten of the Plebeians gentlemen, and to receiue them into the number of the nobilitie: the which notwithstanding was not well executed. So of foure and twentie thousand citisens, there were not aboue twelue hundred, or thereabouts, that had any part in the state: and of this number it was decreed, That euery yeare there should be a great Councell made of foure hundred, the which should chuse the Duke and the eight Gouernours, which they call the Seigneurie, to manage all affairs of state for the space of two yeres that they should be in charge, vnlesse matter were of great importance, then to assemble the Senat of an hundred gentlemen. And as for the duke, hee might not bee chosen but out of the noblest families, with a guard of 500 Lansquenets, besides the generall of the armie, and the fortie centiners. I omit other officers, as the Procurators of the Seigneurie, the Podestat, or Maior, the Iudges of the Rota, the seuen extraordinarie Iudges, the fiue Syndiks, the Censors, and the officers of Saint *George*. The estate of Genes hath continued in this sort 43 yeares, vnder the protection of the house of Austria. From the yeare 1528, vnto the yeare 1549, that *Iohn Flisco* beeing chosen duke of Genes after *Benedict Gentil*, would haue made his power perpetuall, and to effect it, he laboured to subiect the Seigneurie of Genes vnto the crowne of France, hauing alreadie defeated *Andrew Dories* armie, & slain his nephew, he fell into the sea leaping from one gally to another, the which ouerthrew all his desseins. Since the seigneury hath taken again the forme established by *Andrew Doria*, the which was cotinued vnto the yere 1574, that it was diuided into two factions; the one of the antient, the other of the new gentlemen, who are yet at ciuill war: and the antient seeing themselues expelled by the new, haue ceized vpon the places of strength, and forts without the citie, being in danger to be quite ruined, or at the least to fall into a Popular estate, as they did in the yeare 1506. The sedition happened for the qualitie of their nobilitie: for after that *Andrew Doria* had setled the state (as I haue said) & excluded the Plebeians from being dukes of Genes, the gentlemen of the antient houses

Anno. 1506. The estate of Genes, and the change thereof.

I7 *For* 43 yeares (Fr 7) *read* 44 yeares (Fr 1–6, 8) *or about* 50 yeares (L). I7 Austria, from
K2 desseins *i.e.* designs   Note at H6.

houses (which were but foure, the *Dorias*, the *Spinolas*, the *Grimoaldes*, and the *Fiesques*) caused their genealogies to be drawne and registred in publicke acts, diuiding themselues by this meanes from the Plebeians that were newly ennobled; who disdaining thereat, and finding themselues the greater number and the stronger, they haue chased away the antient houses, and if they be not soone reconciled, the people in the end will expell them all.

<small>The cause of factions at Genes.</small>

I haue shewed before, that the great Councell or Senat in an Aristocraticall estate, ought to be perpetuall, to the end there may be some firme ground, or foundation whereon the annuall change of all officers may relie. And as for the Duke, it were strange if he should not ceaze vpon the Soueraigntie, hauing fiue hundred men for his guard, seeing that he hath two yeares to remaine in charge: considering the factions that are made to attaine vnto this dignitie of honour. We see then that the chiefe ground and support of an Aristocratie, consists in the mutuall loue of the commanders: for if they agree and be of one mind, they will maintaine themselues, and gouerne much better than the people: But if there be any factions among them, then there is no State so difficult to maintaine, for the reasons before mentioned; especially, if the Commanders be martiall men: for souldiers hate nothing more than peace. And we may not marueile if the Aristocratie of the Venetians, Rhagusians and Luquois, haue continued some ages: for they are not giuen to armes, neither haue they any thing in greater recommendation than their trafficke and commoditie. And to conclude briefly, there is no forme of Aristocratie more perfect and goodly, nor more assured, than whereas they make choise of men of vertue and reputation to commaund; or at the least that they be not infamous: and if any one dies, to substitute another in his place by election, as they do vse at Geneua. If any one of the Councell of 25 dies, the most antient of the 60 succeeds him most commonly, although it be done by election: and the most antient of the great Councell of 200 comes into the Councell of 60, and the two hundred chuse one of the honestest Burgesses or citisens that is without reproch. Whereby few command and gouerne the state, and yet euery man hopes to attaine vnto it, not by mony nor ambition, but by honour and vertue. This may properly be called an Aristocratie, the which is least subiect vnto dangers, and to the rebellion of Lords or subiects.

<small>The ground and support of an Optimacie.</small>

<small>The best kind of Optimacie.</small>

Such a Seigneurie will obserue the lawes duly, and administer iustice vprightly: if they be contented with their estate, and seeke not ambitiously to wrest from another, as the Lacedemonians did. For it is impossible that a Seigneurie of few Lords and Commanders, should get and maintaine a great Empire, as a Monarke may: also the ruine and change of so great a Seigneurie is not so much to be feared, as of a great and mightie Monarchie, which draweth after it the ruine of the greatest familes, and oftentimes of allies and of neighbour States that are in his protection: Like vnto a great building which raised on high, blind the sight of others, and falling, ruines with her weight those that are neere it, with a fearefull noyse to them that heare it. Behold he commodities and discommodities of a popular and Aristocraticall estate. Now we are to speake of a Monarchie, which all great men haue preferred before all other Commonweales: yet we find it is subiect vnto many dangers, whether the change of the Monarke be from bad to good, or from good to better: although there were no other thing but the change of him that hath the Soueraigntie: yet is it much to be feared in all states: for we commonly see in the change of Princes, new desseines, new lawes, new officers, new friends, new enemies, new habits, and a new forme of liuing: for most commonly all Princes take a delight to change and alter all things, that they may be spoken of; the which doth many times cause great inconueniences, not only

<small>The discommodities of a Monarchie.</small>

<small>*Plato lib. 4. de Legib. Mutationes in republica putat esse perniciosas.*</small>

<small>A3–4 disdaining *i.e.* taking offense   C5 the 60 (Fr 3–8 and L) the 75 (Fr 1–2). Cf. note at 233 B3.
D7 families   E5(margin) lib. 4. de Legib.: lib. 7. de legib. (Fr) lib. 7. de Repub. (L). Cf. *Laws*, VII, 797–798.   E8 all Princes   Notes at A6, C9, D6, E3.</small>

to the subiects in particular, but also to the whole bodie of the state. But if this were not, and the Prince were as wise and vertuous as might be desired, yet the leagues and treaties made with his Predecessor end with him: whereupon alliances being ended, Princes fall to armes, and the stornger assailes the weaker, or prescribes him a law. The which cannot chance in popular and Aristraticall estates, when as they make perpetuall leagues, for that the people dies not; so as other Princes and priuate men desire rather to contract with a Seigneurie than with a Prince, for the assurance of treaties and bonds, wherunto the successors of Princes are not tied, vnlesse they be their heires, as manie maintaine and practise. The other inconuenience in a Monarchie is, the danger to fall into ciuill warre by the diuisions and factions of such as aspire vnto the crowne, especially if it be electiue, the which doth oftentimes draw after it the ruine of the state: Yea, in a successiue right there is no small danger, if there be many in one degree, who many times kill one another, or at the least diuide the subiects. We haue too many examples before our eyes: and oftentimes the lawfull successour is expelled by an vsurper. But admit there were no contention for the Monarchie, yet if the Monarke be a child, there will be some diuision for the gouernement, betwixt the mother and the Princes, or betwixt the Princes themselues. And God (to be reuenged of his people) threatens to giue them for Princes children and women. And although the infant haue a tutor by the appointment of his predecessour, or by the custome, yet is it to be feared, that he will make himselfe absolute Lord: as *Triphon* did, who cruelly slue his pupill the king of Siria, to make himselfe king. The which is more to be feared, if the tutor marrieth the pupils mother, as *Lewis Sforce* did, who by that meanes murthered the young prince, and made himselfe duke of Milan. And although for the auoiding of this danger, they giue the gouernement to the neerest of kinne, and the nourishment of the infant to the mother; yet haue there bene murthering mothers since, who haue not onely sold and betrayed the state, but euen the liues of their children, as the mother of *Charilaus* king of Lacedemon did. And sometimes the tutor continues his gouernment, and leaues nothing vnto the king but the title, as the duke of Northumberland did to *Edward* the sixt king of England: and *Appelles* to young *Philip* king of Macedon, who could not inioy his estate, vntill he had slaine his tutor. And if the prince comes to the crowne being yong and out of gouernment, there is no lesse danger: for then when as he should haue a dozen wise maisters to restraine his licentious appetits, the which are then most violent, he is altogether free and at liberty: so as commonly the courts of yoüg princes abound in follies, maskes, and licentiousnesse, and the subiects follow the princes humor; so as for one vice there multiplies ten, as I haue said before. If the prince be warlike, he will hazzard his subiects, his estate, and his person, to make proofe of his valour. And although he come vnto the state being of a competent age and wise, the which is rare, and the greatest gift which a people can craue at Gods hands: yet souraigntie hath his mischiefe, most commonly the wise become foolish, the valliant cowards, and the good grow wicked. It were time lost to repeat examples, the which are too ordinarie. To conclude, if the prince be subtill and wicked, he will plant a tyrannie: if he be cruell, he will make a butcherie of the commonweale; or a brothell house if he be licentious, or both together: if hee be couetous, he will pull both haire and skinne from his subiects: if he be prodigall, he will sucke their bloud and marrow to glut some dosaine of horseleeches that are about his person. And yet he will do worse than all this, if he be a sot and ignorant, as we haue sayd elsewhere. Yea, so much the more is a tyrannie to be feared, for that a tyrant hath no maister nor companion to oppose against him. These bee the dangers of a Monarchie, the which in truth are great, but there is greater perill in an Aristocraticall estate,

---

Isaie. cap. 5.

The tutors to Monarchs do oftentimes make themselues absolute Lords.

Plutar. in Licur.

Polib. lib. 7.

Soueraigntie altereth the humors of princes.

F4 stronger   F5 Aristocraticall   H2(margin) themselves   H10(margin) *For* lib. 7 *read* lib. 5
(cf. Fr).   I9 hath this mischiefe (cf. Fr and L)   K1(margin) humors   Notes at H9, I6.

state, and much more in a Popular: for the dangers which we haue set downe for the most part cease, when as the Monarchie comes by right of succession, as we will shew hereafter. But seditions, factions, and ciuill warre, are in a manner continuall: yea, sometimes greater for the attaining vnto offices, in Aristocraticall and Popular commonweales, than for the state in a Monarchie; the which admits no sedition for offices, nor for the state, but after the death of the prince, and that very seldome. But the chiefe point of a commonweale, which is the right of soueraigntie, cannot be, nor subsist (to speake properly) but in a Monarchie: for none can be soueraigne in a commonweale but one alone: if they be two, or three, or more, no one is soueraigne, for that no one of them can giue or take a law from his companion. And although we imagin a bodie of many lords, or of a whole people to hold the soueraigntie; yet hath it no true ground, nor support, if there bee not a head with absolute and soueraigne power, to vnite them together: the which a simple magistrat without soueraigne authoritie cannot do. And if it chance that the lords, or the tribes of the people be diuided (as it often fals out) then must they fall to armes one against another. And although the greatest part be of one opinion, yet may it so happen, as the lesser part hauing many legions, and making a head, may oppose it selfe against the greater number, and get the victorie. We see the difficulties which are, and alwayes haue bene in Popular states and seigneuries, whereas they hold contrary parts, and for diuerse magistrats: some demaund peace, others warre, some will haue this law, others that; some will haue one commander, others another; some will treat a league with the king of France, others with the king of Spaine, corrupted or drawne some one way some another, making open warre: as it hath bene seene in our age among the Grisons. Moreouer, sometimes it happens by the custome of the countrey, that a law, the prince, or a magistrat, is not admitted, if all that haue voices giue not their consent: as in Polonia whereas the lesser part must change their opinion, and ioyne with the greater number, either by loue or force, and for this cause they come armed to the field to chuse their king, and to force the lesser part to consent: the which cannot happen where there is a soueraigne head, of whom depends the resolution of all things. Moreouer, in a Popular and Aristocraticall estate, alwayes the greater number will bee beleeued, although the wiser and the most vertuous bee fewest in number; so as most commonly the sounder and the better part is forced to yeeld vnto the greater, at the appetite of an impudent Tribune, or a brasen faced Orator. But a soueraigne Monarch may ioyne with the sounder and the better part, and make choise of wise men, and well practised in matters of state: whereas necessitie doth force them in other commonweales to admit wise men and fooles and altogether to offices and councell. It is also impossible for a Popular state, or an Aristocratie, to command with soueraigne power, or to do any act which cannot bee done but by one person onely: as to conduct an armie and such like things: but they must create magistrats and commissaries to that end, who haue neither the soueraigne power, authoritie, nor maiestie of a Monarch. And what power soeuer they haue by vertue of their places, yet Popular and Aristocraticall commonweales, finding themselues imbarked in any dangerous warre, either against the enemie, or among themselues, or in difficultie to proceed criminally against some mightie citisen, or to giue order for the plague, or to create magistrats, or to do anie other thing of great consequence, did vsually create a Dictator, as a soueraigne Monarch: knowing well that a Monarchie was the anckor whereunto of necessitie they must haue recourse, *Trepidi patres*, saith *Titus Liuius, ad summum anxilium decurrunt. Dictatorem dici placet*, The fearefull fathers flie vnto their last refuge, they thought it best to name a Dictator. And when as *Hanniball* made all Italie to tremble,

Comparison of dangers.

Commodities of a Monarchie.

In Popular and Aristocraticall estates the lesser part is always ouer-ruled by the greater, the which is contrarie in a Monarchie.

Liuie lib. 3.
Lib. 2.
Lib. 7.
Lib. 4.

Ppp iiij   Ad

C7 cause   D6 *For* wise men and fooles and altogether *read* wise men and fools all together (cf. Fr).
E7 auxilium   Note at A1.

THE SIXT BOOKE

Liuie lib. 22.   *Ad Dictatorem dicendum remedium iamdiu desideratum Ciuitas confugit*, The citie fled vnto the remedie so long desired, which was to name a Dictator. And the reason was, for that they held the Dictator for a god, and his commandements for oracles, *Dictatoris Edictum pro numine semper obseruatum*, The Dictators Edict was always religiously obserued. And euen the enemies besieging the citie of Rome, abandoned the siege, hearing that they had created a Dictator, *Tantus erat Dictatoris terror apud hostes, vt eo creato statim a menibus discesserint*, So great was the feare of a Dictator with the enemies, as he was no sooner created, but they departed from the wals. For oftentimes euen the Consuls and their commaundements were neglected and troden vnder foote: and such as had offended retired to their companions, that is to say, to the people, to whom they might appeale. The which *Appius* the Consull seeing, hee sayd, *Minas esse Consulum non imperium, vbi ad eos qui vna peccauerunt prouocare liceat agedum, Dictatorem a quo prouocatio non est creemas*, They were but the threats, sayd he, of Consuls without any commanding power, seeing they might appeale vnto them who had offended in the like manner, Go to then, let vs create a Dictator from whom there is no appeale. The impunitie of vices, and the contempt of magistrats in a Popular estate, doth sufficiently shew that Monarchs are necessarie for the preseruation of the societie of mankind, seeing that the Romans who for the error of one Prince, had all kings in hatred, made a Dictator for the conduct of all their great affaires. So did the Lacedemonians in their extremities create a magistrat with power like vnto the Dictator, whom they called Harmoste: and the Thessaliens, him whom they called Archus: as in the like case the Mityleniens their great Æzimnere; to whom the great Prouidador of the Venetians may be in some sort compared: finding by experience that an absolute power vnited in one person, is more eminent and of greater effect, and that the same power imparted to two, three, or many lords, or to a whole communaltie, declines and looseth his force, like vnto a fagot vnbound and diuided into manie parts. And therefore *Tacitus* saith, that for the execution of great exploits the power of commanding must be restrained to one alone: the which is confirmed by *Titus Liuius*, who sayd, that three Tribunes created with Consularie power, gaue a sufficient testimonie that the force of command imparted to manie, is fruitlesse: and especially in millitarie causes, the which *Hanniball* did find, hauing against him an armie of 60000 men, commanded by two Consuls, *Paulus Æmilius*, and *Terentius Varro*, whom hee defeated: and *Amurath* against the Christian Princes at the battell of Nicopolis: and the emperour *Charles* the fift against the two commaunders of the protestants. And we may not marueile if the duke of Vrbin with a few hierlings made head against so mightie an armie, led by the chiefe commanders or generals, the which depended not one of another, that is to say, *Rance Vitelli*, and *Laurence de Medicis*: for euen *Leo* writes in his historie, that the people of Affricke hold it for an infallible Maxime, that a prince which is but weake in forces, shall always defeate a stronger armie that hath two generals. For whilest that *Cleomenes* king of Lacedemon did gouerne absolutely alone, he obtained great and goodly victories, and was neuer vanquished: but after that hee had called home the king which was banished to impart his soueraigne authoritie vnto him, soone after he was ouerthrowne and put to flight. And for this cause *Aristides* the iust, being chosen generall with *Miltiades* to commaund the armie either of them his daie, (as the Romane Consuls were wont to do) he resigned all his power and authoritie to his companion, who gaue the Persians a great ouerthrow. There are a thousand such like examples, which do shew vs the necessitie to haue one head or commander, not onely in warre (where there is greatest danger) but also to obey one soueraigne prince in a Commonweale: for euen as an armie is ill led, and most commonly

Margin notes:
- *Liuie lib. 22.*
- *Lib. 6.*
- *Lib. 5.*
- *Liuie lib. 2.*
- *Dionys. Halic. lib. 6.*
- *Plurium imperium in bello inutile.*
- *An antient opinion of the Affricans.*
- *Plut. in Aristide.*
- *One soueraigne commander most necessarie.*

F7 a mœnibus discesserint   F8(margin) *For* Lib. 5 *read* Lib. 6 (cf. Livy, VI, 28).   G2–3 liceat: agedum   G3 creemus   H2 Æzimnete   I2(margin) inutile   I6 *For* led by the chiefe *read* led by three chiefe (Fr).   I7 Rance, Vitelli (*i.e.* Lorenzo Orsini and Vitello Vitelli)

ly defeated that hath many Generals; euen so is a Commonweale that hath manie lords, either by diuision, or a diuersitie of opinions, or by the diminution of power giuen to manie, or by the difficultie there is to agree and resolue vpon any thing, or for that the subiects know not whom to obey, or by the discouerie of matters which should be kept secret, or through altogether. And therefore whereas we sayd before, that in a well ordered state, the soueraigne power must remaine in one onely, without communicating any part thereof vnto the state (for in that case it should be a Popular gouernment and no Monarchie) and that all wise Politicians, Philosophers, Diuines, and Historiographers haue highly commended a Monarchie aboue all other Commonweales, it is not to please the prince, that they hold this opinion, but for the safetie and happinesse of the subiects: And contrariwise, when as they shall limit and restraine the soueraigne power of a Monarch, to subiect him to the generall estates, or to the councell, the soueraigntie hath no firme foundation, but they frame a popular confusion, or a miserable Anarchie, which is the plague of all states, & Commonweales; the which must be duly considered, not giuing credit to their goodly discourses, which perswade subiects, that it is necessarie to subiect Monarchs, and to prescribe their prince a law; for that it is not onely the ruine of the Monarch, but also of the subiects. It is yet more strange, that many hold an opinion that the prince is subiect to his lawes, that is to say, subiect to his will, whereon the ciuill lawes (which he hath made) depend; a thing impossible by nature. And vnder this colour and ill digested opinion, they make a mixture and confusion of ciuill lawes with the lawes of nature, and of both ioyntly with the lawes of God: so as they suppose, when as the prince forbids to kill, to steale, or to commit adulterie, that it is the princes law. But for that we haue layd open this poynt at large, I will now passe it ouer. It shall suffice that we haue made apparant demonstration, that a pure absolute Monarchie is the surest Commonweale, and without comparison the best of all. Wherein many are abused, which maintaine that an Optimacie is the best kind of gouernment: for that many commanders haue more iudgement, wisedome, and councell then one alone; But there is a great difference betwixt councell and commandement: The aduice and councell of many graue and wise men may be better than of one, as they say commonly that many men see more than one alone: but to resolue, to determine and to command, one will alwayes performe it better than many: and then he which hath aduisedly digested all their opinions, will soone resolue without contention, the which many cannot easily performe: Besides ambition is so naturall among commanders that are equall in power, as some will rather see the ruine of the Commonweale, than acknowledge any one to be wiser than themselues: Others know what is good, but shame keepes them from changing of their opinions, fearing to loose the least point of their reputations: So as it is necessarie to haue a soueraigne prince, which may haue power to resolue and determine of the opinions of his councell.

Aliud est consulere aliud imperare.

If then a commonweale be but one body, how is it possible it should haue manie heads, but that it must proue a monster, as the emperour *Tiberius* sayd vnto the Senate, else it were no bodie, but a hideous monster with many heads. But some one will say that new princes make new lawes, new institutions, new ordinances: we will confesse that it happens in some, who to shew their power make lawes sometimes without any reason, but this is more frequent and vsuall without comparison in Popular and Aristocraticall estates: For new magistrats so often created, and which play the pettie kings in their Commonweales, would bee loth the yeare should passe away without giuing some cause to speake of them, either for good, or euil: for proofe whereof we find more lawes published at Rome and at Athens, then throughout all the world:

One body cannot haue many heads.

For

A7 *For* unto the state *read* unto the estates (cf. Fr).   E7 Commonweales   Note at A7.

For alwayes through iealousie one vndid what another had made: and all, as they said, was to make themselues famous, and to rob the honour of their companions, with the preiudice of the Commonweale. But to auoid these inconueniences, and insatiable ambitions in an Optimacie, or Popular state, you must not in any sort suffer the law or ordinance to carrie the name of the magistrat, as they vsed in Rome and Athens, which was the cause of so many lawes. And to say that treaties and leagues die with the Prince, that happens not alwayes, for most commonly they are continued and prorogued by an expresse clause, some yeares after the death of the prince, as it hath bene alwayes obserued betwixt the house of France and the Cantons of the Suissers, the which haue beene for the kings life, and fiue yeares after. Moreouer, we haue formerly shewed, that it is expedient allyances and leagues should not bee perpetuall; and for this cause states and commonweales do oftentimes limit their treaties to a certaine time. And as for bonds and treaties of peace, they are accustomed for their better assurance to haue them confirmed by the estates, or published in soueraigne courts, and oftentimes they bind in particular the greatest noblemen: although there bee farre greater assurance in matter of obligation and promises made by a prince than by a multitude: and the rather for that the lawes of honour are in much more recommendation to a soueraigne prince, than to a multitude of artisans or marchants, who are kings in a name collectiue, and nothing in particular. And as for the troubles which the gouernement of a young king do cause, that happens rarely, and is more incident at the election of magistrats: For at the chusing of a Gonfalonier of Genes for two yeares onely, the Commonweale is euer in combustion. There is no reason to ballance the cruelties and extorsions of a tyrant, with the actions of good princes: we know wel that a peaceable Optimacie and wisely gouerned, if it may be, is better than a cruell tyrannie. But the question is, whether it be better to haue a iust and vpright king, or manie good lords: and whether a tyrannie of fiftie tyrants be not more dangerous, than of one tyrant alone: And if there be not much more danger in Popular and Aristocraticall estates, than in a Monarchie. Yea it is most certaine that a tyrannicall Monarchie is sometimes more to be desired than a Democratie or Optimacie, how good soeuer: For if many wise and skilfull pilots hinder one another in striuing to gouerne the helme; euen so will many lords do, euery one seeking to gouerne the Commonweale, be they neuer so wise and vertuous. Although it be not needfull to insist much vpon this proofe, that a Monarchie is the most sure, seeing that a familie which is the true image of a Commonweale can haue but one head, and that all the lawes of nature guide vs vnto a Monarchie, whether that we behold this little world which hath but one bodie, and but one head for all the members, whereon depends the will, mouing and feeling: or if we looke to this great world which hath but one soueraigne God: or if we erect our eyes to heauen, we shall see but one sunne: and euen in sociable creatures, we see they cannot admit many kings, nor many lords, how good soeuer. *Solyman* emperour of the Turkes vsed this example, hearing the great cries and acclamations of ioy which the whole armie made vnto *Sultan Mustapha* his son returning out of Persia, he put him to death through iealousie, causing him to be strangled in his withdrawing chamber, and his dead body to be cast out before the whole armie: then he made a proclamation, that there was but one God in heauen, and one *Sultan* vpon earth: Two dayes after he put *Sultan Gobe* to death, for that he had wept for his brother; and *Sultan Mehemet* the third brother, for that he fled for feare; leauing but one sonne liuing, to auoid the danger of many lords. We also see that all nations of the earth from all antiquitie, euen when they were guided by a naturall instinct, had no other forme of gouernement than a Monarchie, that is to say, the Assirians, Medes, Persians

Of a Commonweale. 719

A Persians, Ægyptians, Indians, Parthians, Macedonians, Celtes, Gauls, Scythians, Arabians, Turks, Moscouits, Tartars, Polonians, Danes, Spaniards, English, Africaus, and Perusians, where there is no mention of any Optimacie, or Popular estate. Yea all the auntient people of Greece and Italie, before they were corrupted with ambition, had none but kings and monarches, as the Athenians, Lacedemonians, Corinthians, Acheans, Sicyonians, Candiots, Sicilians, Ethiopians, Latines, and Hetrusques, the which haue flourished in arms & laws, foure, fiue, six, & seuen hundred yeres; yea some haue continued eight or nine hundred yeares, others twelue or thirteen hundred yeres. And yet some wonder that the Popular estate of the Romans, or the Seigneuries of Lacedemon, and Venice, had continued foure hundred yeres, or thereabouts, after they B had expelled their kings: doubtlesse they haue reason to maruel, to see two or three Commonweales among a hundred, able to continue any time, beeing instituted against the order of nature: but no man is amazed to see many great & mightie Monarchies continue a thousand, or twelue hundred yeares, for that it is according to the right lawes of nature. And although the name of a king were hatefull vnto the Romans, yet many of them in particular affect to be soueraignes: for not many moneths before *Augustus* his birth, it was found out by oracles, that nature should soone bring forth a great Monarch of the Romans. For this cause the Senat decreed, That all infants should bee slaine that were to be borne that yeare: but euery one in particular did hinder the carC rying of this decree into Saturnes temple, for that euery one (saith the historie) did hope his sonne should be a Monarch. In like sort the princes of Persia being assembled together to consult which forme of gouerment were the better, they concluded, a Monarchy. The same argument was called in question by *Augustus* among his friends, being desirous to liue at rest, and to leaue the state, after that hee had put the nauie of *Marc Anthonie* to flight: but it was resolued, That a Monarchy was the most safe without all comparison, and the effects did verifie it: for in former times the Romans could not liue ten yeares together without ciuill warres, or some sedition: and *Augustus* maintained them quietly in peace almost fiftie yeares, the which continued long after his death. Experience is the mistresse of all things, and as the touchstone, resolues all D doubts. Therefore the Capadocians hauing lost their king, they were persuaded by the Romans, to take a Popular estate: but they refused it, and demaunded a king: so as the Romans gaue them power to chuse one, and they aduanced *Ariobarzanes*; finding the calamities of Popular states. To conclude, if we seeke authoritie, we shall find that the greatest schollers that euer were, haue held a Monarchy to be the best: as *Homer*, *Herodotus*, *Plato*, *Aristotle*, *Xenophon*, *Plutarch*, *Philon*, *Apolonius*, Saint *Ierosme*, *Cyprian*, *Maximus Tirius*, and many others. And euen in the law of God, it is said, When as the people shall chuse a king, like vnto other nations, he shall not take a straunger: Wherby he not onely sheweth, that God approueth a Monarchy, teaching a king how hee should gouerne, but also that other nations in those dayes had nothing but MonarE chies, as *Samuel* saith: He also made *Moyses* king ouer his people, for so hee is called in the law of God. And although that God gouerned his people for a time without a king, sending them alwaies by an especial fauor certaine captains, as princes & judges to free them from the subiection of their neighbors, whome the holy Scripture calls Messies, and Sauiours: yet was there neuer any Optimacie, or Popular estate among them, but contrariwise they were a long time without either prince or magistrat, beeing guided onely by the grace of God, who for this cause is called their king. And after their returne out of Babilon, they were still subiect to the kings of Persia, or of Ægypt, or of Syria: vntill that *Iudas Machabeus* of the familie of the Azmoneans, descended from *Aaron* (hauing rebelled against *Antiochus* the Noble, king of Syria) brought the office

Examples of the greatest Monarchies of the world.

Sueton. in August.

Sam. 1. 12. Deut. 33.

Nehem. 10.

Sam. 2. c. 12.

A Monarchy allowed by the law of God.

D3 seeke   E5 contrariwise   E6(margin) For Sam. 2. c. 12. (Fr 7) read Sam. 1. c. 12. (Fr 1–6, 8 and L).   Notes at C8, D6.

fice of high priest, and the soueraigntie vnto his house, who were afterwards subdued by the Romans. For as for their Senat, which consisted of seuentie one, the king making the seuentie two, and the most part of the line of *Dauid*; they busied not themselues in any thing else, but in iudging of causes of great consequence, as of the high priest, or of some tribe, or of crimes of high treason, or of false prophets: & for this cause they were onely called Iudges, whome by the corrupt Greeke word they called Sanedrim. The Caldean interpretor saith, That although they had power to make lawes, euen vnder kings, yet was it no soueraigne authoritie. True it is, that *Rabin Magmon* calling them Doctors or Informers, saith, That they had also power to create twentie three criminal Iudges, whome they called Iudges of soules; and seuen Iudges for ciuill causes, whom they tearmed Iudges of goods in euerie citie; and ten Iudges for gouernment, among the which there was one priest, or as *Ioseph* saith, two Leuites assistant to euery magistrat: and three other Arbitrators, whereof either of the parties did chuse one, and the two that were chosen did name a third. The which I haue particularly set downe, to confute their opinion, which maintaine with *Ioseph* the Historian, That the Hebrewes haue vsed a kind of Aristocraticall gouernment, taking the Senat of seuentie one for soueraigne lords: all whome *Herod*, the eldest sonne of captaine *Antipater* put to death, for that they had condemned him, and had executed him, but for the fauour of *Hircanus* king and high priest, who gaue him his pardon, or at the least staied the decree of the Senat; and afterwards he murthered his sauiour. Which sheweth plainely, that the Senat had no soueraigne power, and that it was no Optimacie: although that *Iosephus* brings in the Iewes complaynig, *Quod Hircanus & Aristobulus formam Reipub. in regnum mutarent*, That *Hircanus*, and *Aristobulus*, had chaunged the forme of the Commonweale into a Monarchy. In my opinion these reasons, with many others (which are not needfull to be here particularly exprest) are sufficient to shew, that of the three kinds of lawfull gouernments, a perfect Monarchy is the most excellent: and among the disordered, the Democratie the most vicious. A lawfull Monarchy (as a strong and able bodie) may easily be maintained: but Popular states, and Aristocraties, as feeble and weake, and subiect to many infirmities, must be preserued by diet and good gouernment. And for that it is not alwayes in the power of wise and politike states-men, to chuse the best kind of gouernment, nor to alter and change the worst, they must in this case doe like vnto skilfull shipmaisters, which yeeld vnto the tempest; they strike their sailes, and cast forth euen their most pretious marchandise, to attaine vnto a safe port. Euen so a wise man that seekes to change a state from bad to good, or from good to better; he must first insinuat with the greatest, and by obsequious obseruation draw them to his will. But if he be not assured to effect it, let him not attempt it: as *Dion* did, who ruined the Tyranny of Siracusa, suddenly to erect an Optimacie, by the councell and aduice of *Plato*: and not able to effect it, he was slaine: so as it became an estate of a turbulent multitude, much more miserable without all comparison than any tyranny. As also the Pithagorians did, who laboured suddenly to change all the Popular estates of Italie, into meere Optimacies, hauing not force sufficient to effect it, but they were all slaine, or banished. But if this Popular infirmitie cannot be cured by any physicke, it must bee borne withall, beeing better to haue a bad Commonweale than none at all; and attend the time vntill the tyranny of one, of few, or of many, be mounted to the highest precipice or downfall, from whence at the first storme they may be cast downe, or fall of themselues. Else if the tyrant be but shaken, and not quite ouerthrowne, he will commit horrible murthers of the best citisens, to fortifie and settle his tyranny. For a tyrant that hath once escaped the hands of such as had conspired against him, he becomes mad and furious, like vnto a wild beast that sees his owne blood.

Lib.6.c.6.antiq.

Ioseph.de antiq. lib.14.c.5.

A tyrant is insupportable that hath escaped any conspiracie.

F8 Maymon G1 government H2 complaynig H6 perfect Monarchy *i.e. droite Monarchie*, one conducted according to the precepts of natural law

OF A COMMONWEALE. 721

A blood. We haue too many examples, and without any further search, we haue seene *Cosmo de Medicis* (whome the banished men of Florence called Tyrant, although hee were esteemed of many others to be a good and a wise prince) build forts, & increased his Monarchy with the ruines of such as had conspired against his life and state, and yet neuer any one conspiracie tooke effect. Besides, a Tyrannie is much more insupportable, if the tyrant hath no large limits and great territories: for being poore and hungry, he oppresseth and deuours his subiects continually; & if he be cruell, he soone attaines to his desire: whereas a rich and mightie Monarch hath wherewithall to glut his appetite, and if he be cruell hee will stand in feare that some one in so great a multitude will take reuenge. Euen then as the subiects are happie vnder a great and mightie Monarch, if he haue any sparke of iustice before his eyes: so a small estate is best befitting

The subiects are happy vnder a great Monarch.

B an Aristocraticall gouernment, who will maintaine their subiects more happily than a poore tyrant should do. We see eighteene Cantons of the Swissers, besides the Grisons, whose gouernments are Popular, and Aristocraticall, hauing in length from Geneua vnto Constance but two hundred and fiftie thousand paces, and a hundred and threescore in bredth from the Alpes vnto mount Iura, most of which countrey is full of rockes, and very barren; yet haue they maintained their subiects a long time in great happinesse: but if they should enuie and desire their neighbors estate, they should soone loose their owne. And contrariwise the greater the Monarch is, the more goodly and

C flourishing it is, and the subiect more happie, liuing in an assured peace. But if it chance to be diuided into Democraties, or Optimacies, or into many tyrannies, the people are either tyrannised, or in sedition among themselues, or in continuall warre against their neighbours. Seeing then a Monarchy is the most sure of all Commonweales, and amongst all Monarchies a Royall is the goodliest: let vs say, whether it bee better to haue it by a successiue right, or by election.

CHAP. V.

D *That a well ordered Commonweale dependeth not either of lot, either of choyce, and much lesse of women; but by discent to be deriued from a most honourable stocke: and that it ought to be giuen but to one alone, without partition.*

E IT is not enough to say, that a Royall and lawfull Monarchy is better than either a Democratie, or an Aristocratie, except a man say also, such a Monarchy as is by successiue right diuolued vnto the next heire male of the name, and that without partition. For albeit that the lawfull Monarchy be alwayes to bee preferred before other Commonweals, yet neuerthelesse so it is, that amongst Monarchies that which commeth by a successiue right vnto the heires males, of name, neerest in blood, and without partition, is much more commendable and sure, than are the other which come by lot, or by choyce, or will, to the heirs male, but not to the neerest; or vnto the neerest, but yet by the mothers side; or that is the neerest by the fathers side, but yet is to make partition of the whole Monarchy with other the coheires; or else of some part thereof. All which it is needfull for vs by necessary reasons, and examples, to declare; to take away the opinion that many imprint into another princes subiects, and by that meanes entertaine rebellions, so to chaunge well ordered Monarchies, and to moue as it were both heauen and earth. All which they do vnder the vaile of vertue, of pietie, and of iustice. Yea some there are to

What Royall Monarchie is best.

Qqq be

B5 *For* two hundred and fiftie thousand paces (Fr 7) *read* 240,000 paces (Fr 1–6, 8 and L). B9 *For* Monarch *read* Monarchy (Fr). E2 *For* or will, to the heirs *read* or well to the heirs *i.e.* "or else to the heirs" (Fr). Cf. 116 G2 and 250 G4.

be found, which haue bene so bold, as to publish bookes, and to maintaine against their naturall prince, come vnto the crowne by lawfull succession, That the right of choyce is better in a Monarchy: as was done in England the seuenth of September, in the yere 1566, the queene then present at the disputation of the schollers of Oxford; the question being, That it were better to haue kings chosen by election, than by succession. Which new doctrine not a little troubled, not the queene onely, but euen the nobilitie also of that kingdome, then there present. For why, from such beginnings wee see the subiects to proceed vnto mutinies, vnto rebellions, and at length euen vnto open wars. And who is he that would not be moued to heare the inuectiue speech of an eloquent man, detesting the cruelties, the exactions, and rapines of a tyrant? who neither hath the honour of God, neither the truth, neither iustice, in regard: who driueth away the good men, and ioyneth himselfe vnto the euill: and in the end ioyneth thereunto this exclamation, O how happie is that Monarchy, wherein the estates of the people make choyce of a iust and vpright king, who aboue all things feareth God, and honoureth vertue: who regardeth the good, and chastiseth the euil: who vnto the honest appointeth due rewards, and vnto the wicked condigne punishments: who abhorreth flatterers, who keepeth his faith and promise; who banisheth the blood suckers and deuisors of new exactions out of the court, who spareth his subiects blood as his owne, who reuengeth the wrong done to others, and pardoneth the iniurie done vnto himselfe; and who in briefe more esteemeth of religion and vertue, than of all other things in the world. And so hauing set these prayses, with the counterpoise of a tyranny repleat with all vices, the vulgar sort forthwith conceiueth an opinion, that there is nothing more happy, than the Monarchy which falleth into election: yea and not they of the simpler sort onely, and such as haue small vnderstanding in the knowledge of matters of policie, but euen they also which are accounted of all others the most sufficient, are oftentimes deceiued, and much mistaken, in regarding nothing but the apparant good on the one side, without respect vnto the innumerable absurdities and inconueniences which are to be found on the other. For euen *Aristotle* himselfe is of opinion, That Monarchs should be created by election, calling the people barbarous, which haue their kings by right of succession. And for which cause he deemed the Carthaginensians more happy than the Lacedemonians, for that these had their kings by succession from the fathers to the sonne in the stocke and line of *Hercules*, whereas the others still had them by election and choyce. But so he might call the Assyrians barbarous, the Medes, the Persians, the Ægyptians, the people of Asia, the Parthians, the Armenians, the Indians, the Affricans, the Turkes, the Tartars, the Arabians, the Moscouites, the Celtes, the Englishmen, the Scots, the Frenchmen, the Spaniards, the Perusines, the Numidians, the Ethiopians; and an infinit number of other people, who still haue, and alwayes before had, their kings by right of succession. Yea and wee find in Greece (the countrey of *Aristotle* himselfe) that the Athenians, the Lacedemonians, Sicyonians, the Corinthians, the Thebans, the Epirots, the Macedonians, had more than by the space of six hundred yeates, had their kings by right of lawfull succession, before that ambition had blinded them to chaunge their Monarchies into Democraties and Aristocraties. Which had likewise taken place in Italie also, whereas the Hetruscians and Latines for many worlds of yeares had their kings still descending from the fathers to the sonnes. Now if so many people and nations were all barbarous, where then should humanitie and ciuilitie haue place? It should be onely in Polonia, in Denmarke, and in Sweden: for that almost these people alone haue their kings by election: and yet of them almost none, but such as were themselues also royally descended. *Cicero* saith, humanitie and courtesie to haue taken beginning in the lesser Asia, and from thence to haue

haue bene diuided vnto all the other parts of the world: and yet for all that the people of Asia had no other kings, but by succession from the father to the son, or some other the neerest of kin. And of all the auntient kings of Greece, we find none but *Timondas*, who was chosen king of Corinth, and *Pittacus* of Nigropont. And at such time as the royall name and line failed, oftentimes the strongest or the mightiest carried it away: as it chaunced after the death of *Alexander* the Great, who was in right line descended from *Hercules*, and the kings of Macedon, who had continued aboue fiue hundred yeares: whose lieutenants afterwards made themselues kings, *Antipater* of Macedon, *Antigonus* of Asia the lesse, *Nicanor* of the vpper Asia, *Lysimachus* of Thracia: so that there is not one to be found among them, which was made king by election. So that euen Greece it self (the nurse of learning & knowledge) shuld by this reason, in the iudgement of *Aristotle*, be deemed barbarous. Howbeit that the word *Barbarous*, was in auntient time no word of disgrace, but attributed vnto them which spake a strange language, and not the naturall language of the countrey. For so the Hebrewes called also the auntient Ægyptians, then of all nations the most courteous and learned, *Barbarous*, that is to say, עם לעז, for that they vsed the Ægyptian tongue, and not the Hebrew.

Psal. 113.

But in all Monarchies which go by election, there is one daunger thereunto alwaies incident, which is, that after the death of the king, the estate remaineth a meere Anarchy, without king, without lord, without gouernment, still in danger of ruine; as a ship without a maister, which oweth the wracke of it selfe vnto the first storme or wind that ariseth: theeues and murderers in the meane time at their pleasures committing their murders, and such other their most hainous outrages, with hope of impunitie; as the common manner is after the death of the popes, of the kings of Tunes, and in former times after the death of the Sultans of Ægypt. For there haue bene such as haue committed fiftie sundrie murders, and yet haue alwayes had the popes pardon therefore: the popes at their first entrance into the papacie, still pardoning all men their offences whatsoeuer: and so murders and reuenges commonly referred vnto the popes death, remaine then vnpunished. So that in the yeare 1522, there were two executed at Rome, whereof the one tearmed himselfe *Pater noster*, and the other *Aue Maria*, who at diuers times had stabbed and murdered an hundred and sixteene men, as was then proued. And the first thing that they commonly doe, the Papall seat being vacant, is to breake open the prisons, to kill the gailors, to enlarge the offendors, to reuenge iniuries by all meanes: which continueth vntill that the colledge of cardinals haue agreed of a successor, wherein sometime they haue beene at such discord and variance among themselues, as that the seat hath bene vacant two yeres and foure moneths together: as it chanced after the death of *Clement* the 5: yea & sometime 10 yeres, as after the election of the duke of Sauoy surnamed *Fœlix*. We read also oftentimes two or three popes, and as many emperors, to haue bene chosen at once; and the empire to haue stood vacant a yeare or two together, yea whole eighteene yeares, after that *William* countie of Holland the emperour, was slaine. And albeit that the princes electors made offer of the empire vnto the king of Spayne, *Alphonsus* the tenth, yet so it was that he would not accept thereof, for the manifest daunger that he was to put himselfe into by taking vpon him such an estate, exposed vnto the will and pleasure of the subiects, vnto the enuie of princes, and the violence of murtherers: all which time of vacancie the wicked neuertheleffe are out of frame in all kind of loose libertie. Which in some sort to remedie, the Polonians (who haue their kings by election) double the penalties for the offences committed during the choyce of the king, as I haue learned of *Zamoschy* now Chauncellour of Polonia, but as then ambassadour in Fraunce. So wee read also that during the elections of the Sultans of Ægypt (before it was by the Turkes subdued, and

Great daungers incident vnto an estate or kingdome, where the king or other soueraigne prince, is to be chosen by election.

The great disorders in Rome, in the vacancie of the papacie, and before the new pope be chosen.

Qqq ij   by

B2 Aristotle   B6 עם לעז   B6(margin) For Psal. 113 (L 4–5 and as in the Vulgate) *Bodin writes* Psal. 114 (L 1–3, Fr, and as in the Hebrew text).   C7 referred *i.e.* deferred, postponed   E3 such Note at A9.

by them vnto their empire vnited) the poore subiects, and the best townes and cities in the whole kingdome, were sacked and rifled by the Mammalukes: vntill that some one of them by the consent of all the rest was chosen Sultan.

No lesse dangerous in the vacancy of a kingdome, to make choyce of a soueraigne gouernor than of a king himselfe.

Now if some (to remedie the matter) shall say, That in the meane time there might a gouernour be established: he is therein deceiued, it being a no lesse hard matter, to make choyce of a lieutenant or gouernour, than of a king. But admit he might so bee made without any contradiction, by the consent of all the estates to whome it belongeth, to name their gouernour, yet who should be the suretie and warrant for his faith? Who should let him (hauing the power in his hand) to inuade the estate? who should disarme him being not willing thereunto? Wee see how *Gostauus* father of *Iohn* king of Sweden behaued himselfe, who of a gouernour made himselfe a king, without expecting of any other election at all, and so left the regall power by strong garrisons confirmed vnto his posteritie. And to leaue the gouernment vnto the Senat, as they do in Polonia, and did of auntient time in Rome, is no lesse daungerous, least in the meane time some of the stronger and bolder sort should possesse themselues of the fortresses and stronger places: as did *Pompey Columna*, and *Anthonie Sauelle*, who ceized vppon the Capitoll at Rome, proclaiming vnto the people libertie. And in the time of such vacancie ciuill warres and dissentions are impossible to be auoided, not only amongst the most warlike nations, but euen amongst the church men also: so that it was neuer possible to prouide so well, but that two and twentie popes had their heads chopt off,

Many popes slaine or poisoned, about their election.

and many moe of them by strong factions driuen out of their seats: not to speake in the meane time of them (in number almost infinit) who haue by poyson (the common death of the bishops of Rome) perished. Yea we read that euen in the primitiue church, *viz.* in the yeare of our Lord 356, there were six hundred persons slaine in the verie citie of Rome, about the election of *Damasus* and *Vrsicinus*, whether of them should bee pope. Neither was that onely done at Rome, but almost in euerie towne and citie,

Why the choyce of bishops, and ecclesiasticall preferments was taken from the people.

which had in them any bishops, all places were so filled with so many of Laodicia, that from thence forward it should not be lawfull for the people, to meddle with the choice of the bishops and prelats, or the bestowing of the ecclesiasticall preferments. Wherefore *Athanasius*, and *Augustine* both bishops, appointed whome they would haue to succeed them in their bishoprikes, the one at Alexandria, and the other at Hippona. What should I speake of the Roman ciuill warres, and after them of the Germans, about the choice of their emperours? their bookes, their histories, and all their monuments, are full thereof. Wherein we cannot without iudignation and horror, remember the miserable wasting countries, the mutuall slaughter of citisens, and sacking of most noble cities, mischiefs still done either by the one side or the other.

The publike demaine most commonly dissipated or embeseled by princes electiue.

And yet there is another inconuenience also, not to be omitted, which is, That kingdomes going by election, haue nothing in them which at one time or other is not subiect vnto all mens spoiles: so that euen the publike demaines, and such as before were common, and wherein euerie man had a common interest: we see them in a little time conuerted euen vnto particular mens vses: so as we see it to haue happened in the demaine of Saint *Peter* at Rome, as also in the demaine of the German empire. For the princes elect knowing wel that they cannot long raigne, nor that they cannot leaue vnto their children any thing of the estate, more than what they thinke they can by deceit and fraud purloine and hold, care not to giue any thing vnto the magistrats their friends: or by open sales and donations, to make their owne profit of the publike reuenues and possessions. So *Rodolph* the emperour for money exempted all the towns and cities of Tuscanie from the fealtie and obedience which they ought vnto the German empire: *Robert* also the emperour, gaue three of the imperiall townes vnto his sonne:

H7 so many AND SO GREAT MURDERS, THAT IT WAS NECESSARY TO PROVIDE BY THE COUNCIL of Laodicia (cf. L)   I4 indignation   I5 wasting OF countries   K5 care not to give *i.e.* do not mind giving   Note at F7.

sonne: *Henry* the first ceased vpon Saxonie: *Fredericke* the second enfranchised Nuremberg: *Otho* the third enfranchised Isne: *Lewes* of Bauiere did the like for the towne of Egre: *Henry* the fift sold all he could: and *Charles* the fourth being not able to pay the hundred thousand crownes which he had promised to euery one of the princes electors, sold vnto them all the tributes of the empire, to haue them to chuse his sonne *Charles* emperour, as he indeed was: but afterwards againe thrust out euen by the same princes who had before made choice of him. So that the principall and strongest sinewes of that Commonweale being cut in sunder, the whole body of the empire became so weake and feeble, that *Charles* duke of Burgundie doubted not to wake warre vpon the Germaine princes.

Another point there is also well worth the consideration, which is, That a man of base degree suddenly mounted vnto the highest degree of honour, thinketh himselfe to bee a god vpon earth. For as the wise Hebrew saith, There is nothing more intollerable than the slaue become a lord. And on the other side such is the feruent loue of the father toward his sonnes, that he will rather confound heauen and earth together (if he haue power so to do) than not to leaue vnto them the crowne, but to let it rest in the voyces and choice of the ignorant people,

Nothing more intollerable than a man of base degree suddenly mounted vp vnto great honor.

But let vs yet go further, for why these are not the greatest inconueniences. For where the people is to chuse their king, they must either make choice of a stranger, or of a naturall subiect: Now if choice bee to bee made out of the naturall subiects, then euery the most impudent and audatious fellow will by all right and wrong seeke to aspire vnto the soueraigntie: and if there bee many of them of equall power and grace, it is impossible but that there should be great factions, wherin the people should become partakers: or in case they were not equall, neither in vertue nor wealth, yet so it is that they would presume themselues to be equall, and neuer agree one of them to obey another, but wishing rather to endure the commaund euen of strange and wicked princes, than of another subiect their equall. As it happened in Armenia (as *Tacitus* reporteth) where the nobilitie could endure none to bee their king but a meere stranger. And of late in Polonia *Sigismundus Augustus* the king beeing dead, and a controuersie arising amongst the nobilitie, euery one of them longing after the kingdome; a decree was made whereby all the naturall subiects were embarred from obtaining of the kingdome: as I learned of the Polonian embassador, whom I was commanded to attend after they were entred into the confines of this kingdome, to conduct them vnto *Henry* the king.

Another great inconuenience about the election of soueraigne princes.

No accord where euery man would be a lord.

And in the remembrance of our fathers when as the Ægyptian Sultans were chosen by the voyces of the pretorian souldiers or Mammalukes, & they not able to endure one of them to be greater than another, had slaine diuerse of their Sultans: they at last to stint the strife, by their common consent sent their embassadors vnto *Campson* king of Caramania to become their Sultan, and to take vpon him the kingdome of Ægypt being by them offred him. With the same calamities the Germaine princes also troubled, after diuerse murthers of the emperours of their owne country, oftentimes made choyce of strangers, yea and those right small princes: as of one *William* earle of Holland, and of *Henrie* earle of Lutzembourg, one while also making choice of the king of England, and another while of the king of Spaine: yea, sometime such forraine princes refusing that same empire so offered them: For so *Alphonsus* the tenth king of Spaine refused the imperiall crowne by the princes electors offered him, which afterwards stood emptie aboue eighteene yeares, as we haue before sayd. *Sigismund* also the first king of Polonia, refused the kingdome of Hungarie, of Bohemia and Denmarke, being thereunto inuited by the Estates. So also *Lewes* the twelfth refused the

The imperiall crowne of diuers strange princes refused.

Qqq iij Seignorie

A 5–6 *For* his sonne Charles *Bodin correctly writes* his sonne Wenceslaus (L). Cf. 728 G 9.   A 9 make warre   Note at D 2.

726　　　　　　　　　　THE SIXT BOOKE

Seignorie of Pisa: and the antient Romans (as saith *Appian*) refused diuerse people which would haue submitted themselues vnder their obeysance. But admit that the strange prince do not refuse a kingdome so offered him: which if it bee farre off from the bounds of his owne kingdome, hee must than either leaue his owne, or gouerne the strange kingdome by his deputies or lieutenants: both things absurd and inconuenient. For who is he so foolish that had not rather to looke to his owne things than to other mens? and what nation or people can with patience endure to be gouerned by deputies? so to haue him whom they would not, and to want him whom they made choice of. So *Lewes* king of Hungarie at the request of his wife daughter to *Casimire* king of Polonia, tooke vpon him the kingdome of Polonia conferred vnto him by the voyces of the people: into which kingdome he was inuested, and receiued with the greatest acclamations, and applauses of all men that might be: who yet shortly after, whether it were for that he found himselfe offended with the sharpnesse of the Polonian aire: or that he was allured with the pleasures and delights of Hungarie, or that he was by the vowes and requests of his owne people recalled: returned home, leauing his wife vnto the Polonians (her countremen) with a traine of the Hungarians to attend vpon her: where so it was that the Polonians mindfull of the Great *Casimire* her father, for a space endured the womans soueraigntie, but could in no wise endure her traine of Hungarians. And so also not long ago *Henry, Charles* the French kings brother called vnto the kingdome of Polonia, his brother being dead, withall speed returned vnto his owne naturall kingdome: howbeit the Polonians would by no meanes endure the gouernement of his deputies or lieutenants, but by voyce chose vnto themselues a king: although that they could by no right or reason do so, but by the consent of *Henry*, vnto whom they had giuen all the soueraigne rights, whereunto they had not annexed any clause or condition (when as question was of the kingdome of France to fall vnto him) that hee should not in his absence by his deputies or lieutenants gouerne that kingdome bestowed vpon him: as hath bene alwayes lawfull for all princes to do. For it is an old axiome, a donation once consummate and perfected not to admit any moe conditions. But admit both the kingdomes confine together, as doth Polonia and Hungarie; what doubt is there but that he will, if he can, make one kingdome of two? or change an Aristocratique estate into a right Monarchie: yea, and that by force of armes, if the nobilitie or people shall withstand him, whereof we haue an example of the Emperour *Charles* the fifth, who after the ouerthrow of the Germaine princes had changed the Aristocracie of the Germaines into a kingdome, and had caused his sonne *Philip* to be sent for out of Spaine into Germanie, to haue made him king of the Germaines, had not *Henry* the second the French king most mightily withstood him, and so broken his designes. The occasion of *Iulius Pflugius* the Bishop is yet extant wherein hee laboureth to persuade that one thing especially, viz. that the most sure foundations of the Germaine empire might be layd. And in case that the prince cannot ioyne the kingdome which he hath got by election confining vpon him, vnto his owne naturall kingdome: yet will he so much as in him lieth draw all the profits, fruits, and reuenues of the strange kingdome vnto his owne: and hauing taken away the voyces from the nobilitie whom hee hath in his power, shall appoint or cause them to chuse whomsoeuer pleaseth him to succeed him: as the kings of Denmarke, of Thunes, yea and the Germaine emperours also themselues by a custome of long receiued from their ancestors haue vsed to do: in such sort as that the rights of elections by voyces, seeme to be vtterly taken away. So *Ladislaus* king of Bohemia, the sonne of *Albertus*, and the emperour *Fredericke* the third his nephew, by the voyce of the people chosen king of Hungarie by a certaine bond of fealtie, left

that

Marginalia:
- A strange kingdome hard to be gouerned by lieutenants or deputies.
- Charles the fift about to haue made his sonne Philip king of Germanie.
- Kingdomes electiue oftentimes changed into hereditarie.

G10–H1 with all speed　　I7 *For* occasion *read* oration (cf. L).　　K9 Hungarie, by　　Note at H9.

OF A COMMONWEALE.   727

A that kingdome vnto his nearest kinsmen all most hereditarie. And albeit that Matthias Coruinus the sonne of the noble Huniades (Ladislaus being dead without issue) by the voyces of the people obtained that kingdome (they alwaies pretending that the right of the choice of the king belonged to them; and that the succession of the next of kinne was not to take place) yet for all that Fredericke his nearest kinsman was about both with his owne power, and the strength of the whole empire to haue inuaded that kingdome, and had vndoubtedly so done, had not Matthias by his promise put him in hope of the kingdome for himselfe and his posteritie: if he should himselfe die without issue, as by chance he did. Howbeit, yet neuerthelesse that Matthias being dead, the Hungarians made choice of another Ladislaus king of Bohemia and Polonia also: with-

B out regard of the conuention and agreement before made with Fredericke, which was the cause of a most great and cruell warre for the kingdome of Hungarie: which could by no meanes be appeased: vntill that by all the degrees of the people of that kingdom it was decreed that it should from thenceforth be hereditarie: and that after the death of Ladislaus Maximilian the sonne of Fredericke should succeed in that kingdome, as indeed he did: But his nephew being left vnder age, and the estates of the kingdome pretending them to haue the right to make their choice of his gouernours; against Fredericke who sought to step into the gouernement of Hungarie, and to take vpon him the guard and protection of the yong king his nephew: the people of Hungarie, yea, and the sister of Ferdinand (the yong kings mother) chose rather to cast themselues in-

C to Solyman the great Turkes lappe, and so to betray both king and kingdome, rather than to endure the gouernement of the emperour Ferdinand in such sort, that they for the maintenance of the right of their election, are now fallen into the perpetuall seruitude of the Turke: hauing not onely lost the right of their election, which they so striue for; but in hazard also to loose their lawes, libertie, and religion: as the common custome of all strange princes is (as much as in them lieth) to change the lawes, customes, and religion of the people by them subdued, or oppressed, and to enure them, or otherwise to enforce them to embrace and follow their fashions, manners, and religions: and was as should seeme the principal cause why God forbid his people to make choice of a strange prince to raigne ouer them.

The Hungarians for the maintenance of their electiue right now fallen into the perpetuall seruitude and slauerie of the Turk.

D And yet in matter of election the way being open to manie competitours, if the matter be to be tried by force, alwayes the most wicked and deceitfull: or else the most hardie and aduenterous, put all vpon hazard to attaine thereunto: And if it hap the most vertuous to be chosen, his life is still in danger of the competitours being of greater power: as in Germanie it hath bene seene: where within this 360 yeares, since that Monarchie fell into election, there haue bene eight or nine emperours slaine or poysoned, and among others, William of Holland, Rodolph, Albert, Henry the seuenth, Fredericke the second, Lewis of Bauaria, Charles the nephew of Henry, and Gunther: besides all them who were most shamefully thrust out of the imperiall seate. And of 15 Sultans which were chosen kings of Ægypt, there were seuen of them slaine: namely,

Princes by election created still to be in great danger.

Diuerse electiue emperours and princes murthered, or els shamefully deposed.

E Turqueman, Melaschall, Cothus, Bandocader, Mehemet, Cercasse, and Giapalt. And of the Romane emperours after the death of Augustus, there were seuen one after another massacred, poysoned, or strangled: and that three of them in one yeare, oppressed onely by the conspiracie of citisens. Yea, the pretorian souldiers sometimes slew the emperours to haue a new, onely vpon hope of gifts and largesses. But still hee of whom the Senators made choice, displeased the legions and men of warre: yea oftentimes euery armie created an emperour, in such sort as that at one time there were thirtie Romane emperours chosen in diuerse places, and among them one woman, viz. Zenobia: all the empire being in ciuill warres and combustion who should carry away the state,

Qqq iiij   no

A1 *For* all most *read* almost.   B7–8 *For* against Fredericke *read* against Ferdinand.
C2 Ferdinand: in such

no end thereof being to be found vntill that the rest were by the power of one all oppressed. Neither was there any assurance in the estate, if the sonnes either lawfull or adoptiue succeeded not their fathers without election, so as did *Tiberius, Titus, Traian, Adrian, Antoninus Pius, Marcus Aurelius*, and *Commodus*. But if any of the emperours gaue not order for the adopting of his successour, in case hee had himselfe no children, the commonweale alwayes fell againe into ciuill wars. And for this cause the emperour *Adrian* fearing lest the estate should fall into election, he himselfe hauing no children, thought it not enough to adopt *Antoninus Pius*, but also caused him to adopt *Marcus Aurelius*, and *Ælius Vetus*: following therein the wisedome of *Augustus*, who to preuent the warres oftentimes arising about election, adopted his two little nephews *Caius* and *Lucius*: who both dying without issue, hee adopted also his third nephew *Agrippa*, and with him *Tiberius* his sonne in law: yet with condition that hee should first adopt *Germanicus*. And they which were so adopted and appointed heires of the empire, were called *principes iuuentutis*, or princes of the youth: and afterward of the Germaines; *reges Romanorum*, or kings of the Romans: to the end that euen in estates and Monarchies going by election, there might yet be some certaine successor. For so *Henry* the third the emperour whilest he yet liued caused his sonne to be chosen king of the Romans, and his grand child to be also by him adopted. And *Charles* the fourth after that caused his sonne *Wenceslaus* by the electors to bee designed to the empire, but not without a great summe of money: vnto whome succeeded his brother *Sigismund*, who afterward adopted his sonne in law *Fredericke* the third; who againe caused *Maximilian* his sonne to be adopted emperour. Neither was it to be doubted but that *Philip, Maximilian* his sonne, should haue raigned ouer the Germaines, had not his vntimely death preuented his fathers hope. And all bee it that the estates and princes of the empire, the imperiall seate being as then vacant, had many great princes competitors in the same; yet so it was that they deemed the grand child of *Maximilian* (*Charles*, then a very yong man, and neerest vnto *Maximilian* in bloud) by a certaine successiue right worthie to be preferred before the rest of the princes. And allbeit that the Bohemians, the Polonians, the Hungarians, Danes, and Tartars, will by no meanes suffer the election of their kings to bee taken from them; yet they thinke that their kings sonnes ought still in their choice to be preferred before all others, that so by the benefit of succession all the occasions of ciuill wars might bee preuented and taken away. For which cause *Sigismundus Augustus* king of Polonia and last of the house of Iagellon, hauing but two sisters, assembled the estates of the kingdome to consult concerning his successor; hauing before vnited the dukedome of Lituania vnto the kingdome of Polonia: whereunto for all that the estates would not consent, fearing to loose their right of election; or that he should haue giuen them a king contrarie to their good liking. And at the same time as it were, the parliament of England was holden at London in October 1566, where the estates preferred a request vnto the Queene for the prouiding of a successor vnto the crowne, to auoid (as they sayd) the euident dangers whereinto the kingdome was like to fall, if it were not foreseene and prouided for; and that they were resolued not to speake of any subsidie, or other thing whatsoeuer, vntill that matter were determined. With which request howbeit that the Queene was much troubled; saying, That they would make her graue before she were dead: yet so it was that she promised them therein to follow the counsell and aduise of such as were the wisest in her land. For a kingdome going by succession still falleth into election when there is none left neere of kin, neither of the fathers side nor of the mothers; in which case it is necessary to prouide before that the matter so fall out, whereas otherwise the estate is in great hazard to be quite ouerthrowne: as it happened vn-

to

OF A COMMONWEALE.

A to the estate of Milan in the yeare 1448, after the death of *Philip Maria* the last of the heires male of the house of Anglerie, which in successiue right had holden Milan foure hundred yeares: when as the people seeing themselues in full libertie without any lord or soueraigne, resolued to maintaine a Popular estate: razed the castle Ioue, burnt the last dukes testament, chose twelue Senators; and after that hauing made choice of *Charles Gonzaga* for their generall, most cruelly butchered all them which tooke part with *Frances Sforce*, who being a man but basely borne aspired to the soueraigntie, as hauing maried the base daughter of *Philip* the last duke, as also by the adoption which the duke had made of him. At which selfe same time the emperour *Fredericke* the third claimed that dutchie, as a fee deuolued to the empire for default of heires
B males. And *Charles* of Orleans on the other side claimed it as belonging vnto him in the right of his mother *Valentine*, both the naturall and lawfull sister of the last duke. During which quarrels the Venetians (as their vsuall manner is) to fish in troubled water, without any right at all, possessed themselues of Cremona, Laude, & Placence, all members of the dutchie of Milan. The duke of Sauoye tooke also Nouarre and Versel: *Sforce, Pauie*, and *Derthone*: and the people of Milan vnable now to mannage their estate at home, or to defend their territorie abroad; and yet abhorring the gouernement of one, and not well knowing vnto what Saint to commend themselues, voluntarily submitted themselues with their citie vnto the Venetians, by whom for all that they were reiected. So that in fine all the Christian princes and states their neigh-
C bours, were vp in armes and together by the eares for the estate; and for all that the last duke prouided not for his successor as he ought to haue done, in following that which was resolued and agreed vpon at the treatie of the mariage made betwixt *Lewes* duke of Orleans and *Valentine* his sister: neither in taking vnto him *Charles* of Orleans his nephew, and right heire of his dukedome so to haue adopted him, and brought him vp neere vnto his person, but adopted *Sforce* who had maried his base daughter, being but the first gentleman of his house.

The dutchie of Milan dismembred the line of the viscounties of the house of Anglerie failing.

But the royall stocke being extinct, the last thereof may by right adopt vnto himselfe his successor, except the nobilitie or people claime the right of the choice of their prince to belong vnto themselues. For if the last prince of the bloud shall appoint no
D man to succed him, the soueraigntie is to fall vnto the people. It beeing a common matter for Monarchies neuer to fall into election, but when the Monarch dying without heires hath not prouided a successor. For so the line of *Charles* the great beeing vtterly extinct, when as the last king of the Germaines had adopted none to succeed him, *Henry* the Faulconer duke of Saxonie was by generall consent of all men created emperour: wherein for all that the Germaine writers are at varience among themselues: one of them thinking *Arnulphus*; and another *Charles* the sonne of *Lewes* king of the Germaines to haue bene chosen emperour, and that not by the voyces of the people, but of the fiftie princes onely: and that electiue right to haue beene at length conferred vnto seuen of them who were thereof called the princes electors: and that
E to haue happened about the yeare 1250. But let vs now come vnto our owne histories. Many there be which haue reported the kings of France in antient time to haue bene created by choyce, and so that kingdome to haue fallen into election: but all that vntruly. For why that must needs haue bene done in the raigne of the Merouignes, or the Carlingues, or of the Capets.

Whether the last of the royall stocke may by right adopt vnto himselfe his successor.

About what time the seuen princes electors were first appointed for the choice of the emperour.

The error of them which haue thought the kingdome of France to haue in antient time gone by election, reiected.

Now concerning the first line which is of the Merouignes; Agathius a Greeke author of great authoritie and antiquitie (for he flourished about the yeare 500) writeth the French nation hauing chosen the best forme of a Commonweale that was possible (that is to say the royall Monarchie) to haue therein surpassed all their neighbours:

A2 the house of Anglerie *i.e.* the Visconti. B2 naturall and lawfull *i.e.* actually begotten and legitimate   C1 *For* and for all that *probably read* and all for that *i.e.* "and all because" (cf. Fr).   D9 *For* fiftie princes *read* fiftie four princes (Fr and L). Cf. 733 D2.   Note at B6.

bours: neither to haue had any other kings but by the right of succession. And the same author in another place sayth, *Theodebert* the sonne of *Theodoric* and nephew to *Clodoueus*, being yet vnder age and the gouernement of his tutor, to haue beene called vnto the crown according vnto the maner and fashion of their ancestors. *Cedrinus* also another Greek author, and he also very antient (who writ in the yeare 1058 in the time of *Philip* the first the king of France) reporteth the French men to haue had no other kings, but by a successiue right, after the antient manner of their ancestors. Wherein he sheweth the aforesayd three lines of the kings of France to haue vsed the right of succession. And if so bee that first *Charles*, and after him *Carlomaine* the children of *Pipin* caused themselues to be both chosen by the nobilitie (as indeed they were) yet was not that done but onely so by the power and fauour of the nobilitie to assure their estates, & to stop the mouths of such as were yet left of the house of the *Merouignes*, as in like case some of them did also of the house of *Capet*; who had thrust out them of the house of *Charlemaigne*. As for that which is reported of *Otho*, him by the consent and voyces of the nobilitie to haue bene created king: he at the time of his death hauing called together the princes of the kingdome, protested him to haue so done, not so much that he himselfe might reigne, as to keepe the kingdome and the Commonweale wherewith he was put in trust, in safetie vnto *Lewes* the Stammerer to whom he was appointed tutor. *Robert Otho* his brother in chalenging the kingdome as it were in the right of succession after him, was slaine in the battell of Soissons. *Rodolph* also sonne vnto the duke of Bourgundie caused himselfe also to be chosen, to exclude *Charles* the Simple, from whom in the castle of Berone wherin he then was kept prisoner, *Harbert* countie of Vermandois had in fauour of this *Rodolpe* extorted his resignation of the crowne. And after that *Hugh Capet* had wrested the scepter out of the hands of *Charles* of Loraine, he caused his sonne *Robert* whilest hee himselfe yet liued, to bee crowned; and he likewise his sonne also, *Henry* the first; and *Henry*, his sonne also: and so vntill that one of the daughters of *Baldwin* earle of Holland and regent of France, descended from the eldest daughter of the aforesaid *Charles* of Loraine, and so lineally from *Charlemaigne*, was maried vnto *Philip* the first, and was mother vnto *Lewes* the Grosse: wherby the secret grudgings & hatred of the people against the *Capets* were appeased, & the fire of ioy and blisse kindled, to see one of the race of *Charlemaigne*, and so of the bloud of Saint *Arnulph*, ioyned with the stocke of *Capets*. And if any coniecture there be, wherfore any man should thinke the kings of France to haue bene by election created; it may best seeme to be drawne from the manner of the coronation of the kings: For before the king that is to crowned take his oath, the two Bishops of Laon and Beauuois standing on both sides of the king, and lifting him vp a little from his throne, and then turning themselues vnto the people there present, demaund of them whether they will haue that man to reigne ouer them or not: whereunto they giuing their consent, the Archbishop of Reims taketh his oath. So that they which write the kingdome of France to go by election, haue had no further regard but onely vnto the manner and forme of the chusing of the king (if it ought at all to bee called a choice) the manner whereof is yet to bee seene in the Librarie of Beauuois, and which I haue also taken out of the Librarie of Rheimes, and deserueth well to be set downe at large, whereby it is to bee vnderstood, in what sort our kings haue beene in antient time crowned.

The antient manner of the coronation of the kings of France.

The title of the antient written booke of Rheimes is this, LIBER IVLIANI AD ERRIGIVM REGEM: *The booke of Iulian vnto king Errigius*: (meaning *Errichius* the father of *Philip* the first.) The words of the booke are these, *Anno 1058 indictione xij Henrico regnante xxxij, & iiij Cal. Iunij, in die Pentecostes Philippus*

F2 nephew *i.e.* grandson   H2 *For* Berone *read* Peronne.   I5 to BE crowned   K8 meaning Errichus (cf. L)   Note at K9.

A *lippus rex hoc ordine in maiore ecclesia ante altare sanctæ Mariæ à venerabili Archiepiscopo pr consecratus est incoata Missa antequam epistola legeretur,Dominus Archiepiscopus vertit se ad eum, & exposuit ei fidem catholicam,sciscitans ab eo vtrum hanc crederet, & defendere vellet: quo annuente delata est eius professio;quam accipiens ipse legit, dum ad huc septennis esset,eique subscripsit: erat autem professio eius hæc: EGO Philippus,Deo propitiante mox futurus rex Francorum,in die ordinationis meæ promitto coram Deo, & sanctis eius,quòd vnicuique de vobis commissis canonicum priuilegium,& debitam legem,atque iustitiam conseruabo,& defensionem adiuuante Domino,quantum potero, exhibebo,sicut rex in suo regno vnicuique Episcopo & ecclesiæ sibi commissæ per rectum exhibere debet: populo quoque nobis credito me dispensationem legum in suo iure consistentem,nostra auctoritate concessurum. Qua perlecta posuit eum in manus Archiepiscopi, ante stante Archi-*
B *episcopo Suessionensi,&c. Accipiens Archiepiscopus baculum S. Rhemigy, disseruit quietè & pacifice,quomodo ad eum maxime pertineret electio regis & consecratio, ex quo sanctus Rhemigius Ludouicum baptizauit & consecrauit.disseruit etiam quomodo per illum baculum hanc consecrandi potestatem & totum Galliæ principatum Ormisdas papa sancto dederit Rhemigio: & quomodo victor Papa sibi & ecclesiæ suæ concesserit. Tunc annuente patre eius Henrico,elegit eum in regem post eum. Legati Romanæ sedis,cùm id sine Papæ nutu fieri licitum non esse dissertum ibi sit: honoris tamen & amoris gratia tum ibi affuerunt: Legati Lotarius Sol; Archiepiscopi,Episcopi,Abbates,Clerici ; Dux Aquitaniæ,filius,Lega-*
C *tus Ducis Burgundiæ,Legati Marchionis,& Legati Comitis Andegauensis : post Comites Vandensis,Vermadensis,Ponticensis,Suessionensis, Aruernensis,post milites & populi tam maiores quàm minores vno ore consentientes laudauerunt, ter proclamantes : LAVDMVS, VOLVMVS, FIAT.* In the yeare 1058, the twelft of the indiction, of the raigne of king *Henry* the xxxij, the iiij of the Calends of Iune, on Whitsunday, king *Philip* was in the great church,before the altar of blessed *Marie*, by the most reuerend Archbishop in this order crowned: Masse now alreadie being begun, & before the reading of the Epistle: the Lord Archbishop turning himselfe vnto him , declared vnto him the Catholike faith, asking him whether he beleeued the same, and would also defend it? Whereunto he graunting, his profession of the same was brought forth,
D which he taking read it,(being as then but seuen yeares old) and subscribed to the same, whose profession was this, I *Philip*,by the grace of God,by and by about to be the king of France,vpon the day of my inuesting do promise before God and his saints, to keep canonicall priuilege,with due law and iustice to euery one of you the committies: as also so much as in me lieth by the helpe of God,to defend you, as a king in this kingdome of right ought to doe vnto euerie Bishop, and to the church committed to his charge: as also by our authoritie to graunt vnto the people committed vnto vs,the administration of our lawes,standing in their full power. Which profession so read, hee put it into the Archbishops hands,&c. (Here are twentie Bishops and many Abbats by name reckoned vp,and immediatly after) The Archbishop taking the staffe of Saint
E *Rhemigius*,calmely and quietly declared, How that vnto him especially belonged the choice and consecrating of the new king , euer since that *Rhemigius* baptized and consecrated king * *Lewes*: declaring also,how by that staffe of *Hormisdas* the pope gaue vnto Saint *Rhemigius* this power of consecrating the kings, with all the kingdome of Fraunce: and how the Pope *Victor* graunted the same also vnto him and his church. And so his father *Henrie* consenting thereunto,chose him to bee king after him. The Legats of the See of Rome hauing there reasoned it,not to be a thing lawfull without the licence of the Pope,were yet for loue and honours sake there present : as were also other ambassadours, as *Lotarius Sol*,with other Archbishops,Bishops,Abbats, Clarks, the young Duke of Aquitane,the ambassadours of the Duke of Burgundie,the ambassadours

The archbishops of Rheims pretend to haue the choyce of the French kings.

*This Lewes is rather to be called Clodoueus, otherwise in antient time called Hludwich.

A1–2 Archiepiscopo   B1 posuit eam   B6 Victor   C1 Vandensis (L) Vadensis (Fr)
C1 Arvernensis, H. DE ILLA MARCHIA, VICECOMES LEMONICENSIS: post milites (*i.e.* "[Heldebert] of La Marche, and the Viscount of Limoges")   C2–3 LAUDAMUS   D4–5 in his kingdome
E2 staffe, Hormisdas   Notes at A7, B8, E9.

sadours of the Marquesse, the ambassadors of the Earle of Angiers, after them the Earls of Vandosme, Vermandoise, Soissons, and Auuerne: after that the souldiors, and people, as well the greater as the lesser, with one consent commended him, crying out thrice aloud, *We prayse him, We will haue him: Let it be done*. These things wee haue word for word written, the which were neuer yet put in print. They therefore which thinke the kings of Fraunce to haue beene in auntient time created by the voyces of the people, vnderstand not the bishops of Rheimes to haue affirmed, that to haue bene giuen vnto them by a certaine singular priuilege from the bishops of Rome: howbeit that it can in no wise agree with the faith & obedience which the archbishops of Rheims haue vsed to giue vnto the kings of Fraunce. Wee read also, that *Charles* (he which for want of wit was surnamed the simple) was crowned by *Fulke* the archbishop of Rheims, in the right of his neerenesse of blood, and not in the right of any election by voyces. Whereby *Otho* so chosen, pretended himselfe to be king: and vnto whom complaining of the iniurie done him by the archbishop in crowning of *Charls*: *Fulke* aunswered, That he had made choyce of *Charles*, according to the manner and custome of his auncestors, who had not vsed to chuse kings, but of the royall stocke & race of kings. Whose letters written vnto that effect to *Otho* are yet extant. Wherby it appeares, that if euer any man had the right of election, it belonged vnto the archbishop of Rheims, or that at leastwise he was in the possession thereof: and yet for all that, that he could not make choyce of any other king, but of the princes of the blood. But to shew that the right of the crowne of Fraunce still descended vnto the heire male next of blood and name, it appeareth not onely by the authoritie of them whome wee haue before noted, but yet more also by the cruell and bloodie warre, that was betwixt *Lotaire*, *Lewes*, and *Charles* the Bauld, grounded vpon this, That their father had giuen the better part, and the regall seat of Fraunce, to *Charles* the Bauld his youngest sonne: howbeit that all the three brethren were kings, gouerning their diuided kingdoms with royall soueraigntie. And for that *Henry* the first, king of Fraunce, the younger sonne of *Robert*, had bene chosen by his father and his elder brother the duke of Burgundie reiected: he fearing least the children of his elder brother, should in their fathers right lay claime vnto the crowne, and so put all France into ciuill warres, as it had before bene in the wars betwixt him and his brother; to preuent the same, hee caused his son *Philip*, so soone as he was but seuen yeares old, to be crowned king of Fraunce. Which yet was done without any forme of election at all: except perhaps, that some would absurdly say, The election of the kings to belong vnto the archbishops of Rheims, as giuen them by the pope, mistaking the consecration, for the creation of them. Howbeit that the verie consecrating of them, properly belonged not vnto the archbishops of Rheims alone: king *Lewes* the Grosse being consecrated by the archbishop of Sens, in the citie of Orleans. Besides that the archbishops of Rheims foolishly pretend them to haue that from the pope: wherein the popes themselues haue no right, no more than they haue vnto the empire, which they haue made subiect vnto their elections; and by thrusting the sickle into another mans haruest (as saith *Albericus* the lawyer) haue against al right made lawes concerning the estate of princes, binding the emperour to giue vnto him the oath of fidelitie: chalenging vnto himselfe the power to depose him; as all other kings also. Howbeit that the bishops of Rome do themselues by their decrees confesse, the French kings to be altogether free from the popes obedience & seruitude: neither to acknowledge any one greater than themselues, next vnto God. And that is it for which they say in this realme, *That the king neuer dieth*. Which auntient prouerb sheweth well, that the kingdome neuer went by election, & the kings thereof hold their scepters neither of the pope, neither of the archbishop of Rheims, nor of the people, but of

How it is to be vnderstood. That the king neuer dieth.

F1 the Marquesse *i.e.* the Marquis Baldwin, Count of Flanders   F2 *For* Vandosme *read* Valois (cf. 731 C1).   F2 Vermandoise, PONTHIEU, Soissons (cf. 731 C1)   G3 pretended   Notes at I2, K4.

OF A COMMONWEALE. 733

onely of God alone. And I remember a lawyer, a most famous pleader of his time, who to serue the cause he had in hand, said in his pleading, That the people of Fraunce had giuen the power vnto the king: alleaging therefore the words of the great lawyer *Vlpian*, where he speaking of the Roman emperour saith, *Lege Regia de eius imperio lata, populus ei & in eum omnem suam potestatem Contulit*, By a royall law concerning his power, the people conferred vnto him and vpon him all his power: whereat the kings people suddenly arise, requesting the court in full audience, That those words might be rased out of the plea; shewing that the kings of Fraunce had neuer receiued their power from the people. Yea the court therefore sharply reproued the said lawyer, causing the words, at the request of the Attourney generall, to bee rased out of the plea, forbidding him any more to vse such speeches: who neuer after, as euery man knoweth, pleaded cause in that court. But yet this is made more plaine by the solemnitie commonly vsed at the kings burials, where the kings garments, weapons, scepter, and armes, are so soone as the king is buried cast away; an herauld at armes with a loud voyce proclaiming thrice, *Rex est mortuus*, or, The king is dead. And euen he the same man, presently after aduancing a banner with the Lillies in it, the proper armes of this nation, crieth likewise, *Viuat Rex N. eique vitam diuturnam ac felicem Deus largiatur*, God saue king N. and graunt him long and happy life. The like manners and customes vse the English, the Scots, and Spaniards, with whom (as with vs) the kingdom is by right of succession giuen vnto the neerest of kin. The like ceremonies are vsed also amongst the Bohemians, the Danes, and Polonians, but yet not before that another king be by voyces created.

But now those daungers which we haue said to follow the election of a prince, belong not more vnto the kings and princes themselues, than vnto them that chuse them: for if the king be to be chosen by the voyces of the whole people, all must needs be full of seditions, factions, and murders. But if the nobilitie, or some other estate onely, shall chalenge vnto themselues alone the right of chusing of the prince, the rest of the estates will grudge and repine thereat, that which is of right due to all, to be giuen to some few. yet could nothing be deuised more commodious or expedient for the auoiding of the factions of the seditious, and of ciuill warres, than to take from the multitude of princes and magistrats, the election of the soueraigne prince or king, & to communicat it with some few. For so the German princes (who in auntient time were fiftie foure, and now almost foure hundred) haue giuen all the right of their voyces, for the chusing of the emperour, vnto the seuen Princes Electors. Neither yet in so great fewnesse of them, doe they still well agree, but sometime being at discord among themselues, haue chosen two emperours at once: as namely *Albert* of Austria, and *Lewes* of Bauaria, who for the space of eight yeares made most cruell warres, which of them should as emperour rule and raigne one of them ouer the other, all that while one of them still spoiling and ruinating the townes, castles, and villages, of the others fauourits and part-takers. So in like manner the cardinals (who were but twelue) after the death of pope *Clement* the 4, for the great dissentions and factions of the mightie, differred the election of the next pope three yeares: and in fine chose the archdeacon of Leedes, who was then gone to Hierusalem, and was afterwards called *Gregorie* the tenth: & who for that cause bound the colledge of cardinals vnto most strait laws in the choyce of the pope, and yet could he not so prouide, but that after his death, they at once made choyce of three popes, and oftentimes of two; insomuch that at the last it was needfull to shut them vp, and to starue them with hunger, if within a certaine appointed time, they did not denounce him pope, who had at the most two parts of the voyces: which yet is more straitly kept in the chusing of the Grand Maister of the Knights of the order of Saint *Iohn*:

Rrr for

Election no lesse daungerous vnto the electors, than vnto the kings and soueraigne princes themselues so elected.

Election of princes better to bee made by some few, than by many.

D3 *For almost foure hundred Bodin writes* about two hundred (*fere ducenti*). Cf. 236 H4 and K1.
E2 *of Leedes i.e. Leodiensis, of Liège*. Notes at A6, E8.

THE SIXT BOOKE

The strait order obserued in chusing the Grand Master of the knights of Malta

fot they mure vp the twentie foure electors, before nominated by the knight, without either meat or drinke, who must chuse one who is not of that number of the twentie foure, and that within a short time limited them. There haue bene seene also such factions, suits, and murders, to haue happened in this realme, about the election euen of the inferiour bishops, as haue oftentimes troubled the state euen of the most famous cities, and wherein he that was the most vitious and ignorant most commonly carried away the matter: than which no greater cause seemeth to haue beene, wherefore the voyces for the chusing of bishops haue bene taken from the colledges of priests and monkes, and giuen to princes: as the Chauncellour *Prat* declared, at such time as question was in parliament, for the verifying of the agreement made betwixt king *Francis* the first, and *Leo* the tenth: For which cause also the bishops and abbats in Moscouie, are drawne out by lot.

Euill men more commonly preferred than the good, where men are by election promoted.

And yet neuerthelesse the onely colour that men haue to maintaine election, is to say, That the more worthy men are so chosen to be emperors, popes, bishops, and prelats. Wherein I referre them vnto the histories of all ages, which will say the contrarie: and that there haue seldome bene more vicious and wicked men, than were the most part of them who were by choyce and election preferred; which wee need not now by examples to verifie: but thus much onely I say, that if the right of succession had taken place, *Nero, Heliogabalus, Otho, Vitellius*, and such others, the monsters of nature, had neuer come vnto the Roman empire: *Augustus, Traian, Adrian*, both the *Antonines*, with other the emperours excelling in vertue and wisedome, who by adoption (as by the lawfull right of succession) obtained the empire, should haue beene excluded. But were it so that the better princes were still to bee chosen by the suffrages and voyces of the nobilitie, or of the people, or of other the wiser sort: yet so many and so great inconueniences are on euery side attending, as that it were better to want good princes (howbeit that we cannot by this meanes haue them) than to haue them with so great daunger of the subiects created and chosen, especially so long as the right of succession may take place.

A good meanes, the line of Monarchs failing, to preuent the dangers still attending vpon election.

But the line of the monarchs sayling, and the right deuolued vnto the estates: in this case it is much surer to proceed by lot, hauing made choice of the most worthiest persons, or of such as be equall in nobilitie, or in vertue, or in power, to the end that one of them may be drawne by lot, rather than to enter into tearmes of election: prouided that the name of God be first called vpon, in following the forme of the auntient Hebrewes, who still said, Lord God direct thy lot, to the end that all sorcerie and witchcraft may be from hence absent. So the great Prophet *Samuel*, when question was for the making of a new king, caused all the people to bee assembled, and the lot to be drawne for all the twelue Tribes, which falling vppon the Tribe of *Beniamin*, and lot cast also vpon the families of that Tribe, in the familie of *Cis* the lot fell vpon *Saul*, whome *Samuel* by the commaundement of God had before annointed, to the end that the people should not thinke that the kingdome was vnto him by chaunce onely fallen.

Some kings first chosen by lot, & yet their children to haue obtained their kingdomes as by a successiue right.

But after that the Monarchy is once established, men haue commonly had regard vnto the prerogatiue of successiue right, without vsing either of election, or lot. So the seuen great princes of Persia, *Cambyses* being dead without issue, vsed lot, or rather the neying of an horse for the chusing of their king. Yet wee see *Darius* hauing once by lot got the kingdome, the soueraigntie of the state to haue bene afterward by successiue right deriued vnto his posteritie.

The successiue right of the eldest sonne, common to al people

Now it is not enough that successiue right take place in the descending of a kingdome, but that the neerest of kin vnto the soueraigne monarch succeed him also: my meaning is, among the males, and those of his name, which is (to speake properly) the elder, as the first descended of him. For so the order of nature willeth that the elder

should

F1 for they   F1 *For* by the knight *read* by the knights (cf. Fr).

OF A COMMONWEALE. 735

should goe foremost next after the father, and that the rest should every one of them follow in their degree, and so by consequence, that he should be preferred before the others. And this law a man may say to be naturall, and such as hath beene alwayes almost to all people common. For so said *Perseus*, that by the right of nature common vnto all nations, and by the custome inuiolably obserued in the kingdome of Macedon, the elder was still to succeed into that kingdome. And for that reason (as saith *Diodorus*) *Alexander* the Great carried away the crowne of that kingdome, from the rest of his brethren. As the manner was also in the kingdome of Parthia, where the eldest of the house of *Arsaces* their first king, and the neerest of his blood succeeded: following therein (saith *Iustin*) the auntient custome of the Parthies. In like manner amongst the Hebrewes, the kingdome of Iuda was giuen to *Ioram*, for that (as saith the Scripture) he was the eldest. And so *Herodotus* himselfe (the most auntient of all the Greeke historiographers) saith, That generally in all kingdomes the custome was, that the elder should by right of succession haue and enioy the scepter and diadem: yea and more than foure hundred yeres before *Herodotus* (as saith *Corninus Messala*, in his booke dedicated to *Augustus* the emperour) *Ilus* as the elder brother, was preferred vnto the kingdome of the Latines, before *Assaracus* the yonger brother. We read them also of the West Indies (although men of all others most deuoid of humanitie) to haue also vsed this same natural law, for the eldest to succeed before the younger. And that when *Francis Pizarra* Generall of the Spaniards, conquering the kingdome of Peru, caused *Attabalippa* the king to be put to death: all the people thereat reioyced, to see him die that had caused his elder brother to be slaine, so to become king himselfe, contrarie to the custome of the countrey, and his fathers will conformable thereunto: who hauing two hundred children, yet by his will appointed that *Gaca* his eldest sonne should alone succeed him in his kingdome, without diuiding of the same. And albeit that the children were twins, yet so it is, that the prerogatiue of the kingdome is to be kept vnto him that is first borne, & so to be left, witnessed by most manifest proof: least such like quarrell should arise for the prerogatiue of birthright, as did betwixt *Iames* king of Scots, and the duke of Albanie, being twins: which kingdome the duke complained to bee wrongfully taken from him: king *Iames* maintaining the contrarie, for that he was the first borne. And so alwayes when men would force and violat this naturall successiue right, great troubles and ciuill warres haue thereof ensued: as it happened for the kingdom of Alba, inuaded by *Æmulius*, being of right due vnto *Numitor* the elder brother: & to *Aristobulus* king of Iudea, thrust out of the kingdome by the sentence and doome of *Pompey* the Great, to make an end of the ciuill warres and seditions: the kingdome being so restored vnto his elder brother *Hircanus*, without respect to that which *Aristobulus* alleaged, his said brother not to haue bene fit to beare armes, neither yet to gouerne a kingdome. A reason and colour for which the fathers and fauourits haue oft time troubled the right of their children, to set the crowne due vnto the elder, vpon the head of the younger. As did *Ptolomey* the first of that name king of Aegypt, who contrarie vnto the law of nations (as saith *Iustin*) preferred the younger brother vnto the kingdome before the elder, which was the cause that one of them slue the other. In which errour *Ptolomee* surnamed *Physcon* offended also, who persuaded by his wife *Cleopatra*, preferred the younger brother before the elder: but was no sooner dead, but that the people expulsed the younger, and restored the scepter vnto the elder. *Anaxandrides* also king of Lacedemonia, preferred *Dorieus* before *Cleomenes* his elder brother, for that he was the more ciuill: and yet the historie saith, that the people thereof grieuously complained, as of a thing done contrarie to the law of nations. And albeit that king *Pyrrhus* said, That his will was, that he of his children should succeed him, which

Great troubles to haue still arisen, where the naturall successiue right of the eldest hath bene violated, and the yonger brother preferred.

Rrr ij   had

D3 Amulius

736　THE SIXT BOOKE

had the sharpest sword; meaning thereby the most valiantest of them: yet the people
after his death preferred the eldest, although vnfittest for warres. For whatsoeuer valour, courtesie, beautie, or wisdome there be in the yonger more than in the elder; yet should not the father therefore, contrarie vnto the law of nations, preferre the younger before the elder: howbeit that the exteriour forme and feature of the bodie hath deceiued many. Foolishly therefore do those parents, which ouercome with the flatterie of their younger sonnes, and disinheriting the elder of their kingdomes, haue incensed their children most cruelly to murther one another: so as did the father of *Atreus*, and *Thyestes*, who willing to preferre the younger before the elder, as the fitter for the mannaging of the affaires of state, so filled and foyled his house with most cruell and horrible tragedies. But more foolelishly doe they, which search into the natiuities of thier children, so to bestow the kingdome vpon him whom the starres seeme to fauour most: as did *Alphonsus* the 10, king of Castile, who by this means would haue preferred the yonger brother before the elder: who for the disgrace so offered him, slue his yonger brother, and caused his said father for griefe to die in prison. In like case almost *Gabriel* the yonger sonne of the Marquesse of Salusse, by the consent of his mother cast his elder brother into prison, pretending that he was out of his wits: who yet breaking out of prison, recouered his principalitie, & hauing chased out his brother, coupt vp his mother in the same prison, wherein hee himselfe had but a little before beene shut vp. And not to seeke further from home, wee haue seene all this realme on fire with ciuill warres, for that *Lewes* the Deuout, at the intreatie of his second wife, had preferred *Charles* the Bauld, before *Lothaire* his elder brother. Wherefore pope *Pius* the second did wisely, in reiecting the request of *Charles* the seuenth the French king, desirous to haue preferred *Charles* his yonger sonne before *Lewes* the 11 his elder brother: howbeit that the king had reason so to do, considering that *Lewes* had without any iust occasion, twice taken vp armes against him, so to haue taken from him the crowne, and to haue pluckt the scepter out of his hand.

Great murders & ciuill warres to haue ensued, for hauing preferred the yonger brother before the elder.

Now it is so farre from that the first begotten, or eldest sonne, should for cowardise or want of courage, be imbarred to succeed vnto the crowne, as that if he be misse shapen and deformed also, yet ought not the prerogatiue he hath vnto the crowne by his birthright for that to be taken from him. Howbeit that it much concerneth the Commonweale to haue kings that be not deformed. Whervnto *Lycurgus* and *Plato*, would great regard to be had, and especially *Lycurgus*, who willed the deformed children to be slaine. But the * law of God hath decided this doubt, commanding the younger not to be preferred before the elder, for what loue or fauour soeuer. Which is not onely to take place when question is of the right of the elder, but also when the next heire male of the fathers side is to succeed vnto the crowne, albeit that he bee deformed. For one ought not for one inconuenience to break so good a law, or to open a gap so dangerous vnto Monarchies: which to be so the estates & people of Hungarie shewed by a most notable example: contrarie vnto the will & disposition of *Ladislaus* their king, who hauing no issue, adopted *Alme* his brothers yongest son, so to make him king after him, reiecting *Coloman* his elder brother, whom he in a sort banished, sending him a great way off, to studie in Paris: causing him also afterwards to enter into the orders of priesthood, & withall bestowing vpon him a bishoprike, so to take from him all the hope for him to succeed vnto the crowne. For he was a man altogether deformed, goggle eyed, euill spoken, lame, & crooked backed; & yet for all that *Ladislaus* being dead, the estates of that kingdom draue out the yonger, refusing to haue any other king but the elder brother, whome they called home, and by their ambassadors afterward obtained of the pope, to haue him dispenced with, and discharged of his orders, and married also.

* Deut. 21. The elder brother euen by the law of God to be preferred before the yonger.

A notable example.

In

F10 filled and foyled *i.e.* fouled, defiled (reading "filled" as a variant of "filed"). Cf. L.

Notes at G7, H2, H7.

A In like case *Agesilaus*, a lame dwarfe, hauing by the meanes of *Lysander* a prince of the same bloud excluded *Leotichides* as *Alcibiades* his bastard, succeeded into the kingdom, not as the kings son, but as next of the fathers side, and of the bloud of *Hercules*: his aduersaries in vaine complaining the kingdom to hault. And howbeit that *Lysander* who had preferred *Agesilaus* to the kingdome afterwards did what he might to haue abrogated the antient royall law, and to haue published an edict whereby the nearest of bloud should not haue succeeded into the kingdome, but that the most sufficient of the bloud royall should still be chosen; yet was there none found of his opinion.

Some there bee which would adiudge kingdomes vnto the yonger being borne kings sons, their elder brethren being borne before that their fathers were king: as was B iudged for *Xerxes*, declared king against *Artabazus* his elder brother begot by *Darius* before the kingdom of Persia fell vnto him: which iudgement was yet grounded vpon equitie: For that the kingdome was but lately fallen, not by any successiue right, but euen by lot or rather as it were by chance vnto *Darius*. But where the kingdome is descended by a lawfull succession from former ancestors, the eldest or neerest of the fathers stocke is to succeed, although he be borne before his father was possessed of the kingdome. Whereby is vnderstood what is to be iudged of the question, which *Bartholus* writeth to haue happened in his time; as whether *Philip* earle of Valois his son borne before his father was king of France, should as king succeed him in the king-C dome; or else his yonger sonne which he had after that he was king? Howbeit that I read in our histories him to haue left behind him none but his onely sonne *Iohn*. But this same question might well haue bin disputed in the time of king *Charles* the second, who before he was king had his sonne *Lewes*: who yet without any question obtained the kingdome, although he had his brother *Charles* borne whilest his father was king. For now question was of an antient kingdome deuolued vnto the next of name: wheras otherwise the yong sonne of a king conquering a new kingdome should be preferred before his other brethren borne before their father was a king. For as the children of base men are not ennobled, being borne before their father was made noble; neither he to be accounted a priests sonne, which was borne before his father was a priest: so D he also which is borne of a father before that he was king, nor capable of the kingdome by right of succession, cannot pretend any right to the crowne, although he be the eldest or neerest of kin: but if he be enabled to attaine thereunto by lawfull succession, the kingdome of right belongeth vnto him, how be it that hee were not the sonne of a king. As was obserued in the kingdome of Persia whereinto *Artaxerxes* succeeded, although he was borne before his father was king: as claiming the kingdome from his great grandfather. And albeit that his mother *Parysatis* thrust all Asia into ciuill warre to turne the estate vnto her best beloued sonne the yong *Cyrus*, yet so it is that by the iudgement of God he was in battell by his elder brother ouerthrowne and so slain. In like sort and vpon the same doubt which happened about the succession of the king-E dome of Hungarie, *Geica* the elder brother borne before his father had obtained the kingdome, was by the consent of all the estates proclaimed king: which neuer after was called in doubt, in what kindome soeuer. Whereas otherwise there would ensue many intollerabe absurdities: for if the king should leaue but one sonne borne before that he was king, he could not succeed him. But yet whereas we haue sayd, The soueraigntie to be due to euery one that is next of kinne; extendeth farre, not onely vnto them who the eldest being dead come in stead of the eldest, but vnto their infinit posteritie also. For so *Demetrius* reasoned in the Senat at Rome, his brother *Antiochus* king of Syria being dead: for as (sayd he) the right of nations hath before giuen the kingdome vnto mine elder brother, euen by the selfe same right ought I now to

Whether a kingdome ought to descend vnto the yonger sonne borne whilest his father was king; or to the elder, borne before his father had obtained the kingdome.

succeed

B1 Artabazus (L) Artabazan (Fr) *i.e.* Artabazanes C2 *For* Charles the second (L 4–5) *read* Charles the seventh (L 1–3 and Fr). E2 what kingdome soever E3 intollerable

738   THE SIXT BOOKE

succeed him in the same.

Whether the elder brothers son (his father being dead before he was king) bee to succeed into his grandfathers kingdome before his vncle, his grandfathers yonger sonne.

But it may de doubted if the grandfather yet reigning, the eldest sonne shall die leauing a sonne, the grandfathers nephew; Whether the kingdome be due vnto the next brother or to the nephew, who is one degree farther off. Vpon which question many haue resolued it to be due vnto the next brother. And indeed *Scipio Africanus* willing as an vmpire to haue appeased the like controuersie betwixt *Corbis* and *Orsua* the vnkle and the nephew, for the kingdome of Numidia, and not knowing what in this point to resolue vpon, appointed the kingdome to be tried by combat betwixt them two: they both of themselues refusing to haue any other god or man for iudge but Mars: In which combat *Corbis* being both the elder and the cunninger ouercame his nephew, as *Liuie* writeth.

Liuius li. 38.

Which like kind of combats betwixt the vncle and the nephew haue ofted in antient time beene vndertaken among the Germaine princes: which was the onely cause that stirred vp *Barnard* king of Italie to take vp armes against the emperour *Lewes* the Deuout; alleadging that the empire of right belonged vnto him as the onely sonne of *Pepin* the eldest sonne of *Charlemaigne*, and not to *Lewes* the Deuout the yonger brother of *Pepin*: howbeit that *Lewes* yet caried it away, though not so much by right as by force of armes, and so preuailing against *Bernard* kept him shut vp in perpetuall prison. And euen yet at this present the kingdome of Moscouie is alwayes giuen vnto the yonger brother, after the death of the grandfather, without respect vnto the children of the elder brother: and that more is, the yonger brother succeedeth in the kingdome vnto the elder brother, although the elder brother being king leaue behind him a sonne yet vnder age: For so *Basilius* the Great, king of Moscouie succeeded in the kingdome after his elder brother who had children. For which reason also *Henry* of Lancaster the sonne of *Iohn* of Gaunt deposed *Richard* the eldest sonne of *Edward* the Blacke prince: alleaging that his father beeing by death preuented, he could not succed *Edward* his grandfather in the kingdome: which yet was but an vniust quarrell pickt. So in like case *Robert* of Naples the yonger brother, by the sentence of the Pope and of the colledge of cardinals, obtained the kingdome of Naples: the sonne of the elder brother king of Hungarie being so excluded. An vsuall matter amongst the Vandals, as *Procopius* writeth: for so *Honorius* got the kingdome of *Gensericus* his grandfather, howbeit that *Gerso* his eldest sonne dying had left sonnes; which he obtained not so much by his grandfathers will, as by the antient law of almost all the Nomades and Northren nations.

The manner and order of the succession of the kingdome of Moscouie.

And which I see to haue bene common euen vnto our ancestors also: for so *Gontran* preuailed against *Childebert* the eldest sonne of *Sigisbert* in the obtaining of the kingdome of France. So *Mauld* ouercame *Robert* her nephew, the son of *Robert* her elder brother, for the countie of Arthoise, the Senat of France desciding the matter; and so obtained her fathers whole inheritance. *Henry* also sonne to *Theobald* earle of Champaigne in like sute ouercome his eldest brothers sonne. But when *Iohn Montfort* in like sute for the dukedome of Britaine was ouerthrown, by his aunt the daughter of *Vide* of Britaine; what by right he could not, he by force obtained, not without a most cruell and bloudie warre. And so (as we sayd) *Robert* the sonne of *Charles* the second, by the iudgement of the Pope obtained the kingdome of Naples, *Charles* his nephew the elder brothers sonne, king of Hungarie, in vaine reclaiming. *Sanxius* also the sonne of *Alphonsus* the tenth king of Castile, his father fauouring of him thrust his elder brothers sonnes out of the hope of the kingdome. *Iohn* also hauing slaine *Arthure*, *Godfrey* his elder brothers sonne, tooke vpon him the kingdome of England. Vnlike was the quarrell of *Siluius*, who after the death of *Ascanius*, in the right of his mother tooke from *Iulus*, *Ascanius* his sonne, the kingdome of the Latins: For that *Lauinia* had *Siluius*

F2 it may be   F3 nephew *i.e.* grandson (repeated several times in this sense)   F5 (margin) succeed
G1 (margin) *For* 38 (L) *read* 28 (Fr). Cf. Livy, XXVIII, 21.   G2 often
Notes at F5, G8, H4, H10, I5.

OF A COMMONWEALE. 739

A *nius* by *Æneas* but not *Ascanius*. But not fewer, yea and I know not whether moe nephews to haue obtained their grandfathers kingdomes, their vncles yet liuing, according to the antient law of the Lacedemonians. As for *Lycurgus*, he gaue vnto *Charilaus* his eldest brothers sonne, his kingdome, which he might easily haue taken vnto himselfe, the childs mother consenting thereunto. *Arcus* also the elder brothers sonne, after the death of his grandfather obtained the same kingdome, his vncle *Acrotatus* yet liuing. So also *Iohn* the sonne of *Ferdinand* succeeded to *Alphonsus* his grandfather king of Portugall, *Henry* his vncle being yet aliue. And not long after *Sebastian* the son of *Iohn* the eldest brother tooke vpon him the kingdome of *Emanuel* his grandfather, and not *Henry* his vncle, *Lewes* of Niuers also after the death of his grandfather got
B the counties of the Low countries his vncle yet liuing and looking on. But *Robert* the second, king of Naples (whose father by the sentence of the Pope had ouercome his elder brothers sonne) when question was betwixt the vncle and the nephew for the countie of S. Seuerine, by the councell of the lawyers gaue sentence on the nephews side. The like sentence was giuen by the iudges of the court of Paris betwixt the heires of *Iohn Vasse* the sonne of the earle of Foix, and the heire of *Francis Phebe*, who being the sonne of the elder brother had got his grandfathers inheritance, his vncle yet liuing. So also was it iudged for the dukedome of Britaine against *Iohn Montfort*. Others haue left it as a thing doubtfull to be tried by combat. For as *Scipio Africanus* permitted the combat betwixt *Orsua* and *Corbis* whom hee could not by law appease: the same we
C read to haue happened first vnder *Otho* the Great, and after that vnder *Henry* the first in Germanie; and the vncle to haue bene ouercome by their brothers sonnes. But the nephew of *Agathocles* king of Syracusa slew his vncle, going about to haue taken vpon him his grandfathers kingdome.

Neither want there probable reasons on both sides. For the nephew it auaileth that his father being dead he falleth into the power of his grandfather, & so is made his heire by the law of the twelue tables: and together with his vncles is admitted into his portion of his grandfathers inheritance, he dying intestat. And if the father substitute an heire vnto his sonne, that substitution ceaseth if the sonne beget children, onely vpon the coniecture of the fathers kind affection towards his sonne, as *Papinian* the
D lawyer hath answered. Yea, by the Roman lawes brothers sonnes are admitted vnto their vncles inheritance: but then how much more true and iust is it for them to bee admitted vnto the inheritance of their grandfathers? That is also moreouer, that by the antient customes of Fees the nephew may by right receiue the whole benefit, his vncles being quite excluded. But no reason is more effectuall, than that an inheritance neither entered vpon, neither so much as yet fallen, is not onely deriued from the grandfather to the nephews; but euen the verie vncertaine hope of a matter in trust being so but vnder a condition conceiued.

Reasons for the succession of the nephew before his vncle.

Neither yet for all this is the vncles cause on the other side altogether without reason, if a man will but more neerly looke into these matters, and without guile inter-
E pret the law of the twelue tables. For why this law still admitteth the nearest of kinne vnto the inheritance: but now the sonne is nearer vnto the father than the nephew, who but by a false supposall and fiction is deemed to be the same person with his dead father. But admitting that a faigned supposall is in some cases to bee borne withall: yet seemeth it not reason that such a false fiction should preuaile against the truth, especially vnto another mans harme or preiudice of his right. Neither doth the kindnesse of nature suffer the sonnes to be spoyled of their fathers wealth and goods, that all might be giuen vnto the nephew, who is farthest off from the grandfather: which must needs be not onely in the obtaining of a kingdome, but also of a dukedome, or of an earle-

Reasons for the succession of the vncle before his nephew.

Rrr iiij dome,

A5 *For* Arcus (L 4–5) *read* Areus (L 1–3).   A10 Henry his uncle. Lewes   C2 and the uncles
C8–9 substitute an heire *i.e.* name an alternate heir, in case the son should die   Note at D5.

dome, or of an indiuisible fee, by reason of that imaginarie fiction whereof wee haue spoken, the nephew to be supposed to represent the person of his dead father. And so farre it was from that the Roman lawes should suffer the sonnes to be disturbed by the nephewes, as that things committed euen but vpon trust come not vnto the nephewes before that all the sonnes one of them substituted vnto another, be dead. But admit that the sonnes, contrarie vnto the lawes both of nature, and of the Romans, may be disinherited, that so way may be made for the nephew (which we see in indiuisible succession to be still done) yet is it an vnreasonable, and vniust thing, an infant, a child, or one vnder age, of no experience in matters of warre, or in the other ciuill and weightie affaires of the Commonweale, to be called vnto the soueraigntie of a kingdome; and another neerer than he, that excelleth both in yeares and wisedome, to be in the meane time debarred of his fathers kingdome. For which reason the lawyers haue giuen the tuition of the fathers enfranchised slaue vnto the vncle, the nephew being excluded: but by how much more then is the tuition of the kingdome to be committed vnto the vncle, rather than vnto the nephew? And last of all so it is, that vncles vnto whom the tuition of their yong royall nephewes is almost still committed, commonly thinke of nothing else, but of the murthering and killing of them: whereof innumerable examples (and yet not all) are in histories reported, all which if I should goe about to gather together, I should so become tedious. Besides that, it is in sacred writ set downe, * *That Commonweale to be miserable and vnfortunat, where children beare rule.*

* *Esay. 3.*

Howbeit that the old receiued custome of our auncestours, and iudgements in this case often giuen, haue called me backe from this opinion. For those inconueniences which we haue spoken of, happen but seldome: which being such, the lawmakers are not greatly to respect. For if we would rehearse all the kings of Fraunce euen from the time of *Charles* the Great, we shall scarcely, or els not at all, in the space of twelue hundred yeares, find the vncle and the nephew, after the death of the grandfather, to haue met together as competitors in the succession of this kingdome. Wee read it in the space of about fiue or six hundred yeares to haue happened once in England, once in Castile, twice in Portugall, and once in Sicilia. Wherefore let the sentence as well of the auntient, as of the later lawyers preuaile for the nephew against the vncle: not onely in direct, but euen in oblique, and collaterall succession also. Which we haue somewhat the more curiously reasoned of, for that succession of the kingdome of Fraunce, which seemeth to be euen neere at hand. But if cosin Germans, or the vncle and the nephew, shall in the right of themselues without any fained supposall of representation, lay claime vnto the crowne of a king their kinsman, dead without heires male, be it that they were fiftie degrees off, yet he that is descended of the elder, albeit that hee were himselfe the younger, shall carry it away from the elder: as it may and hath oftentimes enow happened in this realme. And yet neuerthelesse in particular successions in collaterall lines, they shall equally diuide the diuisible inheritance into parts: but if the inheritance be indiuisible, the elder of the two in like degree is to bee preferred before the younger, and to enioy the right of his eldership, albeit that the younger bee descended from the more auntient auncestors: as was adiudged in the court of Paris, betwixt *Villiers*, and *Baynecourt*, cosens germans, for the inheritance of *Francis Bloqui*, without any regard vnto the race of the elder auncestours, considering that they came vnto the succession of their chiefe or head, and not by false supposall, or by the way of representation.

And yet is it not sufficient, that the next heires male of name succeed, but it is needfull also, that the kingdome, how great soeuer it be, with all the soueraigne rights thereof, bee wholly giuen to one without partition: as *Gensericus* king of the Vandales wisely

K5 of their chiefe or head *i.e. de leur chef*, in their own right   Notes at G1, K9.

Of a Commonweale.

A wisely appointed. For otherwise if a Monarchy be diuided, it is no more to be accounted a Monarchy, but rather a Poliarchy, or Monarchy diuided into many Monarchies. Which was not by the law Salique with vs (as some suppose) prouided for, or fooreseene. For we find that *Aribert*, brother to *Dagobert* the eldest sonne of *Clotaire* the second, was also king with his brother, one of them holding nothing of the other. *Clodoueus* also the eldest sonne of *Dagobert*, was king of Paris, and *Sigebert* his brother king of Metz. And after the death of *Clodoueus* his foure sonnes diuided the realme into foure kingdomes: for *Childebert* was king of Paris, *Clodoueus* king of Orleans, *Clotaire* of Soissons, and *Theodoric* of Metz. But the rest being dead, all in fine came to *Clotaire*, whose eldest sonne *Cherebert* was king of Paris, *Chilperic* of Soissons, *Gontran*
B of Orleans, and *Sigebert* of Metz, all kings: which multitude of kings were scarece euer quiet from ciuill warres. For which it was wisely prouided by the successors of *Hugh Capet*, who ordained three kings of great consequence for the maintaining of this Monarchy in the greatnesse thereof. First they excluded the bastards of the house of Fraunce, from all entrance vnto the kingdome, not allowing them so much as to be accounted in the number of their naturall children: that so from thenceforth they might thinke of the begetting of lawfull children, their base borne children being now quite excluded from the crowne. Howbeit that it was permitted vnto the bastards of other princes of the blood, and of other noble houses, to be by their fathers auouched, and to beare the name, the armes, the stile and noble titles of their naturall fathers: prouiding
C also better, by taking away of the masters of the palace, whose power was now become dreadfull vnto the people, and daungerous vnto the kings. Secondarily they ordained all the soueraigne royall rights, to be wholly and entirely giuen to the eldest brother alone, and from thenceforth not to be communicated with the younger brethren, but to be all enforced to yeeld vnto their elder brother all obedience and fealtie. And lastly, that such lands as by the kings appointment were assigned vnto the kings sonnes, to be holden in fealtie, they dying without heires male, should againe freely returne vnto the crowne. And the kings sisters to haue their dowrie in money onely: that so not onely the rights of soueraigntie, but euen the crowne lands also, might so much as possible was be kept whole & entire vnto the eldest brother. And as for the bastards of France,
D we find them in former times to haue had their parts in the kingdome together with the kings other lawfull sonnes: as the bastard brother of *Charles* the Simple, had part in the kingdome, and so after the manner of our aunceftors was called a king. True it is, that *Theodoric* the kings bastard was excluded, for that he was begot of a bondwoman, who yet neuerthelesse demaunded his part of the kingdome, vnto whome for all that aunswere was giuen, That he must first be made a free man.

And as for diuiding of a Monarchy, I haue said, that being diuided, it is no more a Monarchy, no more than a crowne or robe diuided into parts, is any more to bee accounted a robe or a crowne: the inuiolat nature of vnitie being such, as that it can abide no partition. Neither find we the auntient kings of Persia, Ægypt, Parthia, or Assyria,
E at any time to haue diuided their most great and spatious kingdomes: neither yet any other kings to haue vsed any such partition of their realmes. *Iosaphat* king of the Iewes hauing six sonnes, left his kingdom whole and entire vnto his eldest sonne *Ioram*, assigning vnto the rest certaine yearely annuities, or pensions. The first that opened this daungerous gap, was *Aristodemus* king of Lacedemonia, who yet diuided not his kingdome vnto his two sonnes, *Proculus* and *Euristhenes*, but left the kingdome vndiuided vnto them both: and so thinking to haue made them both kings, tooke from them both all soueraigne authoritie and power. After whose example the kingdome of the Messenians, neere vnto the Lacedemonians, was by the father giuen vndiuided vnto

Leucippus,

That a kingdom how great soeuer is not to be diuided, but to be wholly giuen to one without partition.

Three things of great consequéce ordained for the maintainance of the kingdome of France in the greatnesse therof.

A Monarchy diuided, no more to be accounted a Monarchy.

A1 For   B3 *For* three kings *read* three things.   Notes at C2, E2.

Leucippus and *Amphareus*, being brethren: the chiefe cause why those two kingdoms were chaunged into Aristocraties. And yet two inconueniences propounded, it is better two kingdomes to be giuen vnto two kings, than one kingdome to be giuen to many: as it hath sometimes happened, the father to haue diuided vnto his sonnes diuers kingdomes, before they were into one vnited: for so *Iames* king of Aragon appointed *Peter* his eldest sonne to be king of Aragon, and *Iames* his younger sonne to bee king of Maiorque: howbeit that afterward the elder brother tooke the yonger prisoner, and in prison starued him, whome much lesse he would haue endured to haue bene partner with him in the kingdome, and so vnited both the kingdomes into one. So it befell also the children of *Boleslaus* the second, king of Polonia, who hauing diuided the kingdome vnto his foure sonnes, and leauing nothing vnto the fift, kindled such a fire of sedition, as could not afterward be quenched, but with much blood of the subiects. Yet this diuision of kingdomes is well to bee borne withall, when it is made by him which hath conquered them, who may giue his conquests got by his owne prowesse and valour, vnto his yonger sonnes, as he seeth good, according to their age or deserts: leauing yet still vnto the eldest, the auntient kingdome or territorie: as did *William* the Conquerour, who left the dukedome of Normandie, and the other countries which he had from his father, vnto his eldest sonne *Robert Curteyse*, who succeeded him not in the kingdome of England, for that he was not the sonne of a king (as saith the Norman historie) but left that kingdome which he had conquered vnto *William Rufus*, which hee had not as yet vnited vnto his other countries: leauing vnto *Henrie* his third sonne nothing but a yetely pension: and yet for all that *Robert* the eldest brother, desirous also to haue had the kingdome from *Henry* the third brother, who after the death of *William Rufus* his brother, had ceised thereon, in seeking too greedily thereafter, lost both the one and the other: and being taken by the third brother (who now carried away all) was by him cast in prison, and so depriued of his sight there miserably died. And albeit that this disposition of the Conquerours was right iust, as grounded both vppon reason and authoritie, yet had it bene much more saftie, to haue left the whole kingdome, and all the soueraigne rights thereof vnto one alone: as was done amongst the children of *Charles* Countie of Prouince, and of *Philip Valois* king of Fraunce, where the eldest had all: which is by farre the surest for the estate, without respect vnto the other legitimat children, which are not to haue place, where question is of soueraigntie, or of demaines vnited to a Monarchy. For if honourable fees be not to be diuided, by how much lesse can kingdomes themselues, and souераigne rights so bee? As dukedomes, counties, and marquisats, yea and in many places baronies also, are not suffered to fall into partition: prouided yet that the yonger brethren bee in some sort recompensed: which recompensing is not in a Monarchy, which suffereth neither diuision nor estimation to take place. But well of long time the vse hath bene, to giue certaine lands and fees for the maintainance of the younger brethren of the house of Fraunce: which haue bene again adiudged vnto the crowne, they which had them being dead without issue: as was decided for the inheritance of *Robert* earle of Cleremont brother to saint *Lewes*, vnto whome that inheritance was adiudged: his other brethren *Charles* and *Alphonsus* earle of Poitiers both excluded. The like iudgement being also giuen against *Charles*, concerning the succession into the inheritance of *Alphonsus*, dying also without issue: *Charles* his brother enioying no part thereof, the inheritance by a decree of the Senat, being adiudged from him, and giuen vnto the crowne. For which cause the succeeding kings better aduised, and to the intent that the matter should bee no more doubted of, haue prouided, that in the letters patents concerning the lands and pensions giuen vnto their younger brethren, it should expresly be comprised, that they dying

without

without heires male, those lands vnto them so giuen should againe returne vnto the crowne: as was done in the graunt of the lands giuen to *Lewes* duke of Aniou, king *Iohn* his sonne. And albeit that *Renate* the yonger sonne of *Lewes* the third, duke of Aniou, succeeded his elder brother into the inheritance, yet was it rather by sufferance, than for any right he had so to doe as heire male. For otherwise the earle of Niuers after the death of *Charles* duke of Bourgundie (his nie kinsman dead without any heires male) might iustly haue claimed the dutchie, considering that in the letters patents of *Philip* the Hardy, the dukedome of Bourgundie was giuen vnto him and to his children, as well females as males, without any exception of sexe. Yet pretended the earle no right thereunto, but the duke being dead, king *Lewes* the eleuenth in his owne right claimed the dukedome of Bourgundie. True it is, that the French kings in that point sometime fauour the princes of the blood, suffering them to enioy the inheritance of their kinsmen, dying without heires male. So *Philip* of Valois obtaining the kingdome, resigned the earledome of Valois vnto his younger brother *Charls*. And *Charles* the sixt the French king being dead, *Charles* of Angoulesme succeeded vnto the dutchie of Orleans, and yet his sonnes sonne *Iohn* of Angoulesme succeeded not vnto the said dutchy of Orleans, *Lewes* the twelft hauing got the kingdome, annexing the same dukedome vnto the crowne. For they are deceiued which write *Peter* of Burbon, lord of Beauieu, to haue succeeded his brother *Iohn* into the lands which hee had receiued from the kings his aunceftors, by lawfull right rather than by the graunt and fauour of king *Lewes* the eleuenth, whose sister *Anne* the said *Peter* had maried, whom he most entirely loued. And so *Lewes* the twelft was content also, that *Susan* of Burbon the onely daughter of *Peter* of Burbon, marrying *Charles* of Burbon, should hold such lands, long before giuen to the crowne: but the said *Susan* beeing dead without issue, those lands were forthwith ceized vpon, and againe annexed vnto the crowne, namely the counties of Auergne, and Clermont, and the dukedome of Burbon, howbeit that it was not in the letters patents comprised: which thing is thought especially to haue moued *Charles* of Burbon to haue entred into rebellion against the king. So also we find, that after the death of *Iohn* the third, duke of Alanson, the dutchy of Alanson was at the motion of the kings Attourney generall ceized vpon for the king; howbeit that the duke had left two daughters his heires, vnto whome were reserued onely the lands by their father purchased. All which was done to the intent so much as was possible, to keepe the kingdome vndiuided, and so to come whole and entire vnto the kings, and not rent and torne, with the parts thereof as the limmes pluckt away: as it hath also bene wisely foreseene, and prouided for, in the dutchies of Sauoy, Milan, Loraine, Mantua, and Cleue, which indiuisibly belong vnto the next of kin. And albeit that the German princes do equally diuide all the fees of the empire, excepting the princes electors, yet is that contrarie vnto the custome and manner of their auncestours (who as *Tacitus* writeth) gaue all their lands and inheritances vnto the eldest, and their mouables & money onely vnto the rest. And so we read *Abraham* the Patriarch to haue done, giuing his whole inheritance vnto his eldest sonne, and money vnto the rest, whome hee sent from him whilest he himselfe yet liued.

<small>The reason why women inherit not lands by their aunceftors descending vnto them, which lands sometime belonged vnto the crowne of Fraunce.</small>

But haply here some man may say, it to be expedient if the Monarchie be great, as were those of the Persians, the Romans, the Frenchmen, and the Spaniards; and that the prince or monarch haue many children, or that there be many competitors, that then the surest way is to diuide it: so as did *Augustus, Marcus Antonius, Sextus Pompeius*, who by lot diuided the Roman empire, and so of one great Monarchie made three. And this expediencie should seeme vnto me good, if that princes after that they had bounded out their frontiers, could bound out also their desires. But there are no mountaines

<small>Great kingdoms and monarchies, not to be with any safetie diuided into many.</small>

mountaines so high, no riuers so broad, nor seas so deepe, that were euer yet able to stay the course of their ambitious and insatiable desires: as these three great men of whom I but euen now spoke, by proofe shewed: not onely the island of Sicilia (although it were but a most strait prouince) but euen the ayre which we breath, together with life it selfe, being taken from *Sextus Pompeius*, the bonds of confederacie being in short time broken amongst the confederats. Neither could *Antonius* endure the gouernment of *Augustus*, neither *Augustus* the gouernment of *Anthonie*, although he were a great way off from him. So that one of the three being before slaine, the other two could neuer be at quiet, vntill they had one of them quite ruinated the other. And if at any time it haue happened, some of the emperours of the East, and of the West, in so great an empire to haue liued in peace, it was not long, but almost a miracle, neither such as to be drawne into examples for vs to imitate: whereas to the contrarie for one example of them, which haue in vnitie and concord gouerned together, there are to be found an hundred which haue massacred one another. Whereof there is no more notable example, than the mightie *Othoman* familie, wherein many most horrible murders haue bene for the empire committed, the parents not sparing their owne children, neither the children their parents: insomuch that within this two hundred yeares past, they haue not ceased still to kill one another, vntill there be but one of them left aliue. And in the little isle of Gerbe, six kings haue in lesse time than fifteene yeares beene slaine one of them by another, being not able to endure a companion or partaker one of them with another in the soueraigntie. And albeit that *Galeace* the second, and *Barnabas*, two most louing brethren, brought vp euen from their cradles together, hauing oftentimes endured like daungers; being both banished, and both at one and the selfe same time called home againe, and both two established lieutenants of the empire, and alwayes companions in armes together; had equally diuided the principalitie of Milan betwixt them, which they so held and defended, as that it seemed a thing impossible to seperat them asunder: yet at length *Galeace* onely for the ambitious desire of soueraigntie, most cruelly slue his said brother, together with all his children. So *Abimelech* the bastard slue threescore and nine of his brethren, that he might all alone raigne. And *Berdeboc* king of Tartarie with like slaughter, and for like cause, slue his twelue brethren. *Sephadin* also caused the ten sonnes of his brother *Saladin* to be all murthered, that he might himselfe alone raigne in Ægypt. The successors of *Alexander* also most part of them slue one another, not sparing either their parents, or children. For as for one brother to kill another, it was so common a matter (as *Plutarch* writeth) as that it seemed almost a miracle vnto the ambassadour of *Ptolomey*, that *Demetrius* standing on the right hand of *Antigonus* his father, with a boare speare in his hand, could abstaine from killing of his father. But yet greater was the crueltie of king *Deiotarus*, who at one time slew twelue of his sonnes, for no other cause, but so the better to assure his kingdome vnto the thirteenth, whome he best loued. For alwayes amongst equals, the ambitious desires they haue to be one of them greater than another, still armeth them one against another: Wheras in a Monarchy, where there is but one soueraigne, and vnto whom the princes of the blood are all subiect, being prouided of yearely pensions, or lands giuen them for their maintenance; it is certaine, that to haue alwaies some farther fauour from their soueraigne, they will still yeeld them more obeysance. And therefore our kings which haue bene better aduised, haue not giuen vnto their brethren, or the princes of the blood, the places of lieutenants generall of their armies, either of the high constable: but rather vnto some other of the meaner nobilitie, such as were *Bertrand*, *Gueschlin*, *Oliuer Clisson*, *Simon* earle of Montfort, with others of like qualitie, men of great seruice, and vnder whome the princes of the blood might match; and yet neuerthelesse

Soueraigntie admitteth no partnership.

Places of too much power and command, not to be committed vnto princes of the blood, or otherwise great lords.

without

OF A COMMONWEALE. 745

A without all hope of aspiring to the soueraigntie. So as did the auntient Romans, and namely *Augustus*, who amongst other the secrets of his gouernment, had this for one, Not to giue the place of a Generall, or of a Gouernour of the frontiers, and especially of Ægypt, vnto any the noble Senators of auntient houses, but onely vnto men of meaner estate. And albeit that the kings of the Northerne parts haue as it were alwaies called the princes of their blood vnto their councell; yet so it is, that other Monarches keepe them backe so much as they can: whether it be for the distrust they haue in them, or to keepe their councell in such libertie, as that it may not be diminished by the greatnesse of the princes of the blood: or that it is to take away the ambition and iealousie which is ineuitable amongst princes of the same blood, if the king shall chance to fauor
B one of them more than another. And although there be many princes neere vnto the *Othoman* blood, as namely the *Michaloglies*, the *Ebranes*, the *Turacanes*; yet are they neuer of the priuie councel, either yet admitted to any great place of honor, or command. And in the Monarchy of the Æthiopians (which is one of the greatest, and most auntientest in the world) there is no prince of the blood, which commeth neere the court, but are all trained vp in all honour and vertue, within a most strong castle, built vppon the mountaine Anga (one of the highest in all Affrike) kept with a perpetuall & strong garrison: from whence at such time as the king dieth, he which excelleth the rest in vertue, is from the mountaine called vnto the kingdome. Which (as they say) was first
C ordained by one *Abraham* king of Æthiopia, by diuine reuelation, to auoid the factions and ciuill warres of princes among themselues; as also the massacres which oft times happen in other kingdomes, about the soueraigntie; as also to haue alwaies princes of the blood roiall, whome they call *The Children of Israel* (assuredly supposing them to be of the blood of the Hebrewes: beside that, the Æthiopian language taketh much of the Hebrew) to the intent the estate should not fall into combustion, the kings line fayling: or els for that the princes of the blood should not at libertie seeke to aduance themselues by force: or being aduanced, should not seeke to inuade the estate. For a man may hold it for a maxime, That in euery Commonweale, if too much power be giuen vnto a prince or great lord of the blood, it is alwayes to be feared, least he should
D at one time or other ceize vpon the estate; seeing that euen the basest companions mounted vnto hie degree, are not without cause to be feared. So *Sultan Solyman* made *Abraham Bassa* of a slaue so great, by heaping honors vpon honours vpon him, as that in fine fearing his power, he was glad to cause his throat to be cut as hee was sleeping, and afterwards found him be worth thirtie millions of gold. But this is more to bee feared in a little kingdome or estate, than in a great: for that the subiects coupt vp as it were all in one place, are the more easily kept vnder by the power of the stronger. So when *Iames Appian* prince of Sienna, too much fauouring *Peter Gambecourt*, a man of base degree, had made him too great in honour and wealth, he was by him (before he was aware) thrust out of his estate. The like pranke *Calippus* serued *Dion*; *Brutus*, *Cæ-*
E *sar*; *Macrin*, *Caracalla*; *Maximinus*, the emperour *Alexander*; *Philip*, the yong *Gordianus*: and an infinit number of others, who exalted from most base degree, haue driuen out their maisters by whome they grew, and so made themselues lords. Who would haue thought that *Agathocles* a Potters sonne, of a common souldior chosen a Generall, durst haue slaine all the nobilitie and richer sort of the citisens of Syracusa, & made himselfe a king? Now if such a base companion as he durst doe so much, how much more warily is it then to be foreseene, that too great a commaund or power bee not giuen vnto princes or great men, either at home, or in seruice abroad? And this is it for which many haue holden, that by law the poynts reserued vnto the maiestie of a soueraigne prince, are neuer to bee communicated vnto a subiect, no not so much as

Sss by

A right strange custome vsed among the Æthiopians.

Master of the forces, master of the estate.

D3 he was glad *i.e.* he was constrained (cf. note at 135 C2)

by commission, to the intent that no gap by any way be opened for the subiect to enter by into the soueraigne estate of his prince.

That a Monarchy, in the opinion of the author ought to descend onely vnto the heires male.
* *Genes.* 3.

* *Esay.* 8.

We haue said also, that a Monarchy ought to descend vnto the heires male, considering that the rule and gouernment of women, is directly against the law of nature, which hath giuen vnto men wisedome, strength, courage, and power, to commaund; and taken the same from women. Yea the * law of God hath expresly ordained, That the woman should be subiect vnto the man, and that not onely in the gouernment of kingdomes and empires, but also in euery particular mans house & familie: he * threatning of his enemies, To giue them women to be mistresses ouer them; as of all miseries and calamities the worst. Yea and the law it selfe forbiddeth women all charges and offices proper vnto men; as to iudge, to sue, and other such like things: and that not onely for lacke of wisedome (as saith *Martian*, when as amongst all the goddesses onely *Pallas* had no mother, but was borne of *Iupiters* braine, to shew that wisdom proceeded not from women) but also for that mens actions are contrarie vnto their sexe, and to feminine modestie and chastitie. Neither was there any thing which more incensed the Senat of Rome, against the emperour *Heliogabalus*, than to see his mother to come into the Senat, though she came but only to see, & not to say any thing. Which was also thought a right strange thing to our auncestors, that *Maud*, grandmother to *Philip* the Long, should be assistant vnto *Robert* Contie of Artoise, and *Margret* Countie of Flanders, at the iudgement of the Countie of Clairmont. Now if it be an absurd and rediculous thing, for women to busie themselues in mens publike actions and affaires, belonging properly vnto men: much more vnseemely is it, those things which belong vnto soueraigntie, to lie open vnto womens pleasure. For first the woman vnto whome the soueraigntie is deuolued, of these two things must doe one; either shee must marrie, or else continue vnmarried, and so her selfe rule. If shee shall marrie, yet is it stil a Gynecocratie, or womans gouernment; for that the marriage is made with that condition, That the soueraigntie is still with the woman, and not with the husband: as was expresly excepted at such time as *Isabella* queene of Castile marde *Ferdinand* king of Arrogon: and in our time, betwixt *Mary* queene of England, and *Philip* prince of Spaine, whome they called the queenes husband. And in like case in the matrimoniall contracts betwixt *Sigismund* archduke of Austria (who was afterward emperour) and *Mary* queene of Hungarie, whome the subiects in scorne called *King Marie* In which case the husband is chiefe of his familie, and maister of his domesticall houshold; and yet for all that in publike affaires remaineth subiect vnto his wife. For why, the publike power (as saith the law) is neuer bound vnto the domesticall power. And for this cause the Consull *Fabius* caused his father (the great *Fabius*) to alight from his horse to doe him honour, as to the Consull in publike: who yet for all that by vertue of his fatherly power, might without giuing cause or reason why, haue put him to death at home in his owne house. But if the queene shall remaine vnmarried (which is the most true womans soueraigntie) the Commonweale must needs so be in great daunger: For that the people being of a great and couragious spirit, will deeme a womans gouernment but ignominious, and not long to be endured; some both by their speaking & writing, scoffing and deriding their sexe, othersome their womanly wantonnesse, and others their womannish intollerablenesse: whereas nothing is more daungerous vnto an estate, than to haue them which beare the soueraigntie contemned and derided of their subiects, of the maintenance of whose maiestie, dependeth the preseruation both of the lawes, and of the estate, which should bee troden vnder foot for the womans sake, against whome there shall neuer want mockings, reproaches, slaunderous libels, and so in fine rebellions & ciuill war, especially if she (impatient of such vnworthy reproach) shall

This French opinion is by the examples of many worthy women, and experience of their most happy gouernments so fully refelled, as that there needeth no further reasons to be vsed, to proue the contrary.

All these dangers with many mo incident vnto womens soueraigntie, are and haue bene right well auoided and preuented, by the wisedom of worthy women, who with no lesse discretion, than many men, haue maintained the maiestie of their soueraigntie, with the reputation of their sexe.

F5 power to commaund　　H8 married Ferdinand　　H9 Arragon　　Notes at G8, H3, I2, K9.

OF A COMMONWEALE.

A shall seeke to bee thereof reuenged, which can hardly without ciuill tumult bee done. But if she shall chance to beare but the least extraordinarie fauor to any one of her subiects, beside the enuie which he is to endure, to whome such fauour is showne, men will still on her part misconster the same. For if the wisest, and most chast haue euen in that respect had much adoe to keepe themselues from false reports, much lesse can a soueraigne princesse couer her fauours; no more than can a light firebrand set vpon an high watch tower: which may serue for cause enough to kindle the fire of iealousie among the subiects, and to arme them one of them against another. Besides that, it is almost naturall vnto women, to take pleasure & delight in the number and quarrels of their suters. But if the subiects be so minded, as by force or otherwise to suffer in the soueraigne

B estate a womans gouernment, then is it not to be doubted, but that euerie one of the subiects shall be constrained to endure the like in their owne priuat houses also. For it is a rule in policie, that whatsoeuer thing is found good, and sufferable in publike, the same is to be drawne into consequence and example in particular. Which was the cause the Persian princes preferred a request vnto *Darius Memnon* (whome the holy Scripture calleth *Assuerus*) That the disobedience of the queene *Vasthi* his wife, should not remaine vnpunished, least her pride should giue occasion vnto the other subiects wiues to be disobedient vnto their husbands. For as the familie is out of order, where the woman commaundeth ouer the husband, considering that the head of the familie hath lost his dignitie to become a slaue: euen so a Commonweale (to speake proper-

C ly) looseth the name, where a woman holdeth the soueraigntie, how wise soeuer shee be; but so much the more if she be vniust withall, and not able to rule her owne immoderat lusts and desires. I suppose there is none which knoweth not what tragedies *Ione* queene of Naples (who of her vnchastitie was called *Lupa*, or a shee wolfe) stirred vp of her selfe, who most cruelly murthered three kings her husbands, and was therefore her selfe also strangled, as she well deserued. I speake not of the horrible and brutish lusts of *Semyramis*, the first that by a straunge meanes set foot into the Assyrian Monarchy. For hauing obtained of the king, to haue the soueraigne commaund but for one day, she the same day commaunded the king himselfe to be slaine. What should I say of *Athalia* queene of Iuda, who seeing her husband slaine, put to death all the princes

D of the blood (excepting one which escaped) and so by force held the soueraigntie, vntil that she was at last by the people her selfe also murthered. With like wickednesse also *Cleopatra* slue her brother, that so she might alone enioy the kingdom of Ægypt. There was also one *Zenobia*, who stiled her selfe an empresse (together with the thirtie vsurping tyrants) and was by the emperour *Aurelian* ouercome. And in like case did *Hirene* empresse of Constantinople, coupt vp at last into a monasterie her selfe. In briefe I find no people to haue liked of the soueraigntie of womans gouernment: howbeit that many haue endured the same: as did the Neapolitans the gouernment of *Constance*, last of the race of the Norman kings, that raigned in Naples. And after that of *Ioland* the daughter of *Iohn Brenne*, married to the emperor *Frederike* the second, who

E gaue that kingdome to *Manfred* his base sonne, whose daughter *Constance* marrying into the house of Aragon, kindled the fire of the warres which continued two hundred yeares, betwixt the houses of Aniou and Aragon; and could neuer bee quenched but with the great effusion of the blood of many most valiant and worthy men; and all for hauing giuen an entrance vnto a daughter into the succession of the kingdome of Naples. But when the colledge of cardinals saw the Christian Commonweale, and especially Italie, to haue endured so many and so great slaughters, in so long and such mortall warres, and all for distaffe soueraigntie; it was by them decreed, That from that time forward, the kingdome of Naples should no more descend vnto wo-

Sss ij   men

A4 misconster *i.e.* misconstrue   B5 Darius Mnemon (cf. 466 I1)   B8 to be disobedient
C2 *For* unjust *read* unchaste (*impudique*).   Notes at A10, C6, D6.

Marginal notes:
- (B) What so is good in publike, is alwayes good in particular.
- (C) The euill examples of some few ought not to bee preiudiciall vnto others that be good.

men; as in the inuestiture made to *Alphonsus* king of Arragon, in the yeare 1455, and afterward to *Ferdinand* king of Arragon, in the yeare 1458, it is expresly set downe, That the daughters should not succeed vnto the kingdome of Naples, so long as there were any heires male, either in the direct or collaterall line, euen vnto the fift degree. But that gap for the succession of daughters being opened in Italie, was afterwards also put in practise in the kingdomes of Hungarie, and of Polonia, which fell to *Marie* and *Hedwige*, the daughters and heires of *Lewes* king of Hungarie, and of Polonia; which had neuer before bene seene. At which selfe same time almost, *Mary Volmar* (contrary vnto the lawes and auntient customes of the countries) succeeded into the kingdomes of Norway, Sweden, and Denmarke. The like example was after also followed in the kingdome of Castile, whereinto *Isabel* of Castile succeeded her father, hauing gained the fauour of the nobilitie: who albeit that shee was one of the wisest princesses that euer were, yet did the estates of the countrey thereof complaine, and the people thereat grudge, complayning themselues, Neuer before to haue endured a womans gouernment. And whereas she alleaged *Socina* the daughter of *Alphonsus*, to haue before in like manner brought the kingdome of Castile vnto *Sillon* her husband: aunswere was thereunto made by the subiects, That to haue bene done rather by force, than by any right; and that from that time the estates of Castile had protested, That it was contrary vnto the lawes of the country. Which hasted the marriage betwixt *Ferdinand* and the said *Isabella*, so to keepe the people vnder. And albeit that *Henry* king of Castile, had by his last will and testament at the time of his death declared, That the kingdome of Castile after him belonged vnto *Lewes* the ninth the French king, in the right of his mother *Blaunch* of Castile; and that the barons of Castile had writ vnto the said French king, that he should come to take possession of the kingdome: yet so it was, that hee neuer durst vndertake to lay claime vnto the same, howbeit that he had the consent of the nobilitie of the kingdome by letters vnder their hands and seales, which are yet to bee seene in the records of Fraunce. Now by the same craft that *Isabel* had wrested vnto her selfe the kingdome of Castile, did *Ferdinand* the sonne of *Leonore* also gaine the kingdome of Arragon: as did also after him the earle of Barcelone, hauing married *Petronella* the daughter of the king of Arragon. Which happened also in the kingdome of Nauarre, whereunto *Henry* the Large, earle of Champaigne succeeded in the right of his wife, the king of Nauarres daughter: whose daughter and heire *Ioane*, married vnto *Philip* the Faire the French king, brought vnto him the earledome of Champaigne, with the kingdome of Nauarre: but the heires male of *Philip* the Faire failing, that kingdome of Nauarre in the right of three women fell vnto the houses of *Eureux*, of *Foix*, of *Albert*, and of *Vendosme*: so that this kingdome in lesse than foure hundred yeares, was transported into six strange houses, and vnto seuen straunge princes, the queenes husbands. But yet by the way it is worth the noting, foure women all of one name to haue opened the way vnto womens soueraigntie, in the kingdomes of Hungarie, of Norway, of Sweden, of Denmarke, of England, and Scotland. True it is, that *Maud* daughter to *Henry* the first, king of England, before brought the kingdome of England vnto the house of Aniou in Fraunce: but that was after the death of * *Stephen* earle of Bolloine nephew o *Henry*, in the right of his sister *Adela*; in such sort, as that a cosin descended of a daughter was preferred before the kings own daughter: which daughters sonne yet succeeded king *Stephen*, in such sort as that no womans gouernment seemed at all to haue bene. For which reason *Edward* the the third, king of England, vpon the difference which he had for the crowne of Fraunce, alleaged the kingdome of Fraunce by the right meaning of the law Salique, to belong vnto him: saying, That law to stand in force and take place, when the next heire male descended

of

The kingdoms of Hungarie, Polonia, Sweden, Norway, & Denmarke, Castile, Arragon, Nauarre, and England, to haue fallen into Gynecocraty, or womens soueraigntie.

* But what troubles ensued vpon this intrusion of Stephen, and the wrongfull excluding of Maud, the Cronicles will declare.

F1 1455 (L 4–5) 1345 (Fr 5–8) 1445 (L 1–3 and Fr 1–4) *properly* 1443   I6 *For* Albert (Fr 7) *read* Albret (Fr 1–6, 8 and cf. L).   I6–7 in lesse than foure hundred yeares (L) in less than 300 years (Fr)
I10 Hungarie   K3 nephew to   Note at I8.

OF A COMMONWEALE.

of the daughter (as was he frō *Isabel* sister to *Charls* the Faire) was preferred before him, who was descended of the heirs male farther off. Which exposition for all that was reiected by the councell of France, as neuer to take place, but when heirs male of the same name and stocke, in what line and degree soeuer it were vtterly failed: & that the kingdome were in daunger to fall into election. And so albeit that the emperour *Charles* the fift marrying of his sister vnto *Christiern* king of Denmarke, and caused this clause to be inserted into the matrimoniall contracts: That the males fayling, the eldest daughter issuing of that marriage, should succeed vnto the kingdome: yet so it was neuerthelesse, that the estates of that countrey had thereof no regard, for that the kingdome went by election: yea so farre off was it, that such the kings priuat agreement could take from the nobilitie of Denmarke, the power to chuse their kings: or yet neuer any one of the same kings three daughters to raigne ouer them: as that the said king himselfe was by the estates thrust out of his kingdome banished, and so afterwards also miserably died in prison. The Polonians also after the death of *Sigismundus Augustus*, excluded not onely the kings sister, but euen his nephew the king of Sweden his sonne also, who gaue a million of gold vnto the Commonweale, to haue his sonne afterward chosen: howbeit that their predecessours had before receiued *Hedwig* the daughter of *Lewes*: and that when as there was no heire male, neither in the direct nor collaterall line of the house of *Iagellon*, they neuerthelesse made choyce of *Henrie* of Fraunce.

Now if the princesse the inheritrix shall marrie (which is necessarie, so to haue an assured successour) her husband must either be a straunger, or a subiect: if a straunger, hee will instruct the people in straunge lawes, in straunge religion, in straunge manners and fashions: yea and giue the honourable places and commaunds vnto straungers also. But as for a subiect, the princesse would thinke her selfe much dishonoured, to marrie her seruant, seeing that soueraigne princes still make great difficultie to marrie a subiect. Ioyne hereunto also the iealousie that is to be feared, if shee shall marrie him whome she best loueth, reiecting the more noble and greater lords, who alwaies contemne them which are of base degree.

The inconueniences by the author supposed to ensue of a Gynæcocratie, or womens soueraigntie.

And not to speake of many difficulties which fell out about these matters, euen the verie same, yea and greater too, presented themselues at the treatie of the marriage agreed vpon betwixt *Philip* prince of Castile, and *Mary* queene of England: wherein the first article contained, That no straunger being not a naturall English man borne, should bee preferred to any office, benefice, or charge whatsoeuer. And in the fourth article it was set downe, That *Philip* prince of Castile should not carrie the queene his wife against her will out of the realme of England, neither the children begot betwixt them two: the which articles were confirmed by the estates of the land, the second of Aprill, in the yeare one thousand fiue hundred fiftie three, where beside that which I haue said, it was also more solemnly prouided, That the queene alone and of her selfe should enioy all the royalties, and soueraigne rights of the said realms, lands, countries, and subiects, absolutely; without that her husband should by the courtesie of England pretend any thing vnto the crowne and soueraigntie of the realme, or other right whatsoeuer: and that the letters and mandates should be of none effect, if they were not signed by the queene, whatsoeuer signe or consent they had of her husband: and yet without which the consent of the queene should suffice. I haue also learned by the letters of *Nouaile* ambassadour of Fraunce, who then was in England, that it was also decreed, That no Spaniard should haue the keeping of any fortresses or strong holds belonging vnto the Crowne of England, either on this side, or beyond the sea: neither that the Englishmen should by the Spaniards be constrained to goe vnto the wars out of the realme.

Sss iiij

And

C10 themselves   D7 *For* one thousand fiue hundred fiftie three (Fr 5–8) *read* 1554 (Fr 1–4 and L).
Notes at B9, C9.

750 THE SIXT BOOKE

And albeit that a most gallant & mightie prince flourishing with kingdoms, wealth, youth, and friends, had married an old woman (for why, he seemed not to haue married a wife) and such an one as by whome he was not to hope for any issue, yet could not the Englishmen patiently endure the Spaniards to set any foot into England, with whome for all that they had neuer before had any hostilitie, but had alwayes bene great friends. Yea the emperour *Charles* the fift on the other side wisely foreseeing all things, and fearing least some treason might be wrought against the prince his onely sonne, whome alone he had begot vnto the hope of so great an empire, required to haue fiftie young noble English gentlemen deliuered vnto him to be kept as hostages, so long as his sonne *Philip* was in England: howbeit that as such distrust drew after it the hatred of the English nation, so was also that article taken away, and nothing thereof obtained. But the marriage made, shortly after aboue 18 hundred English men, for religions sake went out of their countrey, into voluntarie exile and banishment. And yet beside all this, the same was, how that the English men had conspired at one and the very selfe same instant, to haue slaine all the Spaniards: for that (as the report went) they vnder the colour of a marriage, and of religion, went about to aspire vnto the soueraigntie of England. Neither was it to haue bene doubted, but that the conspiracie of the English men had sorted to effect, or els that the Spaniards had effected their designes, and so taken vnto themselues the soueraigntie, had not the death of the queene (very profitable for the kingdome) giuen an end vnto the designes both of the one and of the others.

The great daungers strange princes commanding in a straunge countrey, are still exposed vnto.

For neuer strange prince can be assured of his life, commaunding in a strange countrey, if he haue not strong guards, for the assurance of his person, and sure garrisons for the keeping of his castles and strong holds. For being maister of the forts, hee must needs be also maister of the estate: for the more assurance whereof hee must always aduance straungers; a thing intollerable to euery nation in the world. Whereof wee haue a million of examples, out of which we will remember but one of our own: what time king *William* raigned in Sicilie, in the yeare 1168, the people of the kingdome of Naples were so incensed to see a French man promoted to the honour of the Chauncellourship amongst them, as that they conspired at once to kill all the Frenchmen that then were in the kingdomes of Naples and Sicilie, as indeed they did. But if the domesticall seruant of a straunge prince, shall chaunce to kill a naturall subiect in a strange countrey, or passe himselfe in any insolence, dannger by and by hangeth ouer all the straungers heads, the least quarrell that may be seruing to cut the strangers throats, if they be not all the stronger. As it happened in Polonia during the raigne of the daughter of *Cazimire* the Great, king of Polonia, and wife to *Lewes* king of Hungarie, chosen also king of Polonia, to the great contentment of all the estates of that realme: and yet neuerthelesse for one Polonian slaine by an Hungarian gentleman, all the people of Cracouia ranne vpon the Hungarians, and in that hurle slue them all, except such as by chaunce saued themselues in the castle, who yet were there besieged together with the queene: neither was there any meanes to appease the peoples rage, but that the queene the inheritrixe and mistresse of Polonia, must with all the Hungarians her followers void the realme. But yet greater butcherie was there made of them of Austria, in Hungarie, when *Mary* the eldest daughter of *Lewes* king of Hungarie, had married *Sigismund* archduke of Austria, who going about to take vpon him the gouernment, was by his wiues mother (a most ambitious woman) driuen out of the kingdom: who not able to endure to see him raigne, to be sure to shut him quite out, was about by her ambassadours to haue called in *Charles* the French king, and so to haue put the kingdome into the power of the French. Which the Hungarians perceiuing, sent for

Small occasions serue to stirre vp the natural people of any countrey against strangers dwelling amongst them.

Charles

H4 *For* maister of the forts *read* maister of the forces (Fr). Cf. 197 C3(margin) and 745 C8(margin).
I3 daunger
Notes at G1, I5.

Charles the king of Naples, and vncle to *Mary*, *Sigismund* his wife, to take vppon him the gouernment of the kingdome of Hungarie: who was no sooner come, but that he was by the practise and commaund of the cruell queene Mother (whome hee least feared) slaine: which murder was with like crueltie also reuenged, shee her selfe being by like treason by the gouernour of Croatia slaine, and her bodie throwne into the riuer. After whose death *Sigismund* returning with a strong armie, put himselfe in full possession of the kingdome, wherof he now disposed at his pleasure, and filled all places with the slaughter of them which were of the faction against him. But let vs come to our owne domesticall examples, and vnto those wounds which but lately receeiued, bleed with the least touching, neither can but with most bitter griefe be felt. *Frances* duke of Alanson being sent for, came to take vpon him the gouernment of the Low countries, where he was with great ioy and triumph receiued: but hauing no strong garrisons, no strong castles, nor cities to trust vnto, neither could by my intreatie (who foresaw what would afterwards happen) be persuaded so to haue; receiued such a slaughter and disgrace, as I cannot without much griefe remember the same. And to go farther, we haue examples of the Scots yet fresh in memorie, who for the space of seuen hundred yeares, had with the straitest alliance that might be, bene allied vnto the house of Fraunce, and from thence receiued all the fauors that it was possible for them to hope for: yet when *Mary* queene of Scots had married *Frances* the Dalphin of France, and that the Frenchmen went about to dominier ouer the Scots, they forthwith chose rather to cast themselues into the lap of the English, and so to put themselues into the protection of them with whome they had not before so well agreed, than to endure to see the Frenchmen to commaund in their countrey: neither ceased they vntill that by the helpe and power of the English, they had driuen the Frenchmen againe quite out of Scotland. Neither are strange princes to hope, by reason to rule the desires of soueraigne princesses their wiues: from whom if they will seeke to be diuorsed, they must also banish themselues. For what prince euer bare himselfe more modestly, than did the wise emperour *Marcus Aurelius*? And yet when he with too much patience bare with the wantonnesse of his wife *Faustine* (as some of his friends thought) who for her too dissolute life would haue persuaded him to haue bene diuorced from her; Then must we (said he) againe vnto her restore her dowrie: which was euen the Roman empire, howbeit that he had the empire in the right of himselfe also, by the adoption of *Antoninus Pius* the father of *Faustine*.

And yet there is another daunger also, if the princesse heire vnto a soueraigne estate be disposed to marry a straunger; which is, that the neighbour princes and people also, as wooers, enter into diuers iealous conceits one of them against another: & so striuing for another bodies kingdome, oftentimes turne the queene from marrying at all. Yea sometimes also seeking euen by force of armes to haue her: as did the wooers of *Venda* queene of Russia, who hauing long fought who should haue her, the victor thought at last by force to haue obtained that which he by long sute and entreatie could not gaine: howbeit that she seeing no other remedie, but to fall into his hands, for despight drowned her selfe, chusing rather to loose her life, than by force to loose her chastitie. Neither are queenes marriages so easily made as are kings: for why, kings are oftentimes deceiued with painted tables, and counterfeits, marrying them by their deputies whom they neuer saw: whereas queenes will most commonly see the men themselues aliue, talke with them, and make good proofe of them: yea and oftentimes refuse them also after that they haue seene them. For neither would *Isabel* queene of Castile, marrie *Ferdinand* before she had seene him: neither could *Elisabeth* queene of England be by any man persuaded to promise marriage vnto any man, but vnto himselfe present. And

Neighbor princes iealous of the marriage of a soueraign princesse their neighbour.

Women commonly more curious in choice of their husbands, than are men in choyce of their wiues.

Sss iiij   so

C10 life, would   E4 tables *i.e.* pictures   Notes at C2, C5.

so it was aunswered vnto *Henry* king of Sweden, seeking the long ambassage of *Iohn* his brother, who now raigneth, to haue married her: aunswer (I say) was made, That of al the princes in the world, there was none vnto whome (next vnto almightie God) shee was more in kindnesse beholden, than vnto the king of Sweden, for that hee alone had requested to haue had her for his wife, whilest she was yet a prisoner, and so out of prison to haue brought her vnto a kingdome: neuerthelesse to haue so resolued and set downe with her selfe, neuer to marry any man whom she had not before seene. Which aunswere made also vnto the archduke of Austria, suing vnto her for marriage, in part brake off the hope which both of them had conceiued of marriage, both of them fearing in presence to suffer the disgrace of a deniall; and especially he, least he should be enforced with shame to returne home. As afterwards it happened vnto *Francis* duke of Alanson, seeking to haue aspired vnto the same marriage, who although hee had twice passed ouer into England, and thought the queene by long and honourable ambassages, as it were affianced vnto him, yet returned hee, fed vp but with a vaine hope, and the matter left vndone.

Now if the law of nature be violated in the soueraigne gouernment of women, yet much more is the ciuill law, and the law of nations thereby broken, which will that the wife follow her husband, albeit that he haue neither fire, nor dwelling place. Wherein all the lawyers and diuines in one agree; and that she ought to reuerence her husband: as also that the fruits of the wiues dowrie, yea euen of all the wiues goods, belong vnto her husband; not onely such as arise of the lands themselues, but euen such as fall vnto her by escheat, or confiscation of the goods of the condemned; howbeit that such goods be a thousand times better, or more worthy, than the wiues fee brought in dowrie vnto her husband: yet neuerthelesse do all such things in proprietie belong vnto the husband, what lordship soeuer that it be, which is so fallen by escheat or confiscation: as also all fruits of dowrie, and the rights of patronage depending of the wiues dowrie: which we see to haue bene vsed not of priuat men onely, but euen of kings also: as if a straunger shall marrie a queene, the profits of the kingdome shall belong vnto the husband, although the soueraigntie, and kingdome it selfe belong still vnto the wife. For so the interpretors of the law decide it, and that by the example of *Isabella* and *Socina*. Moreouer it is holden in law, That the wiues vassall ought to succour the husband before the wife, in case they be both of them in like daunger: all which is directly contrarie to such conditions, and lawes, as princes straungers are enforced to receiue from their wiues, being princesses inheritors. Besides that, honor, dignitie, & nobilitie, dependeth wholly of men, and so of the husband, and not of the wife: which is so true by the receiued customes and laws of all people: as that noble women which marrie base husbands in so doing loose their former nobilitie: neither can their children chalenge vnto themselues any nobilitie by the mothers side: which *Ancaran* the lawyer saith to take place euen in queenes which marrie base men, no princes: of which opinion the rest of the lawyers are also.

The beginning of womens soueraigntie.

All these absurdities and inconueniences follow womens soueraigntie in gouernment, which thereof tooke beginning: for that they which had no male children, had rather their daughters should succeed in their lands and fee, than such as were not of their stocke and house, and especially the heires male failing, both in the direct & collaterall line: after which point so by them gained, they began to succeed also vnto lands and fees in the right line, and were preferred before the males in the collateral line: which manner of inheriting was by little and little permitted to be vnderstnod, and extended also vnto Honours, Dignities, Counties, Marquisats, Dutchies, Principalities, yea and at last euen vnto Kingdomes. Howbeit that by the lawes of Fees, women were

Of a Commonweale. 753

were excluded from all succession in fee, although there were no heires male either in the direct or collaterall line, except it were so expresly set downe in the inuestiture of the fee. But the law Salique cutteth the matter short, and expresly forbiddeth, That the woman should by any meanes succeed into any fee, of what nature or condition soeuer it were: which is no late, new, or fained law, as many suppose, but written and enrolled in the most auntient lawes of the Saliens, the words of which law are these, *De terra vero Salica nullo portio hæreditatis mulieri veniat: sed ad virilem sexum tota terræ hæreditas perueniat*: In English thus, But of the land Salique no portion of the inheritance shall come vnto a woman: but all the inheritance of that land shall come vnto the male sexe. And so also in the edict or decree of *Childebert* king of Fraunce, is euen the very same comprehended which is in the lawes Salique, where the nephewes being in direct line, by way of *representation together called vnto the succession of their grandfather, the women are still excluded. And yet if there had bene no law Salique, at such time as contention was for the kingdome of Fraunce, betwixt *Philip* earle of Valois, and king *Edward* of England: *Philip* alleaging for himselfe the law Salique, according to the law Voconia; and *Edward* defending his cause and right by the antient Roman lawes, concerning inheritance: a decree was made by the generall consent of all the Senators and princes of Fraunce, *Ne quis in ea disceptatione peregrinarum legum auctoritate vteretur: sed legem quisque Salicam pro suo iure interpretari studeret, viz*. That no man in that controuersie should vse the authoritie of forraine lawes; but that euery man according to his right should interpret the law Salique. And why so if there had bene no Salique law at all? And howbeit that after the death of *Lewes Hutin* the king of Fraunce, the duke of Burgundie called *Iane* the daughter of *Hutin*, vnto the succession of her fathers crowne and kingdome: yet was it by the generall consent of all the estates assembled in parliament at Paris, resolued to the contrarie, As that daughters should not succeed vnto the crowne: & so the opinion of the duke was reiected. About which time, or a little before, *Baldus* called the law Salique, or the custome for the males onely to succeed vnto the crowne, *Ius gentium Gallorum*, The law of the French nation. Neither is it long agoe, since that in a suit in the parliament of Burdeaux, betwixt certaine gentlemen about the right of their gentrie; a will was brought out, written in most auntient letters, wherein the testator diuided vnto his sonnes his Salique land; which the judges interpreted to be his prediall fees, or reuenewes in land. Which was alwayes in Germanie obserued also, vntill that the emperour *Frederike* the second gaue this priuilege as a singular benefit vnto the house of Austria, That the line of the males failing, the daughters or females might succeed. Which thing the emperour could not doe, without the expresse will and consent of the estates of the empire. For which cause *Othocarus* king of Bohemia, being also of the house of Austria, without regard of *Frederikes* graunt, by right of kindred claimed the dukedome of Austria, and leuied a strong army against *Rodolph*, who by vertue of *Frederikes* graunt, claimed the dukedome as belonging vnto himselfe. Which priuilege for women so to succeed, was afterwards extended vnto the princes of the house of Bauiere also. Yet was there neuer people so effeminat, or cowardly, as vnder the colour of succession in fee, to endure that women should step into the soueraigntie: and yet lesse in Asia, and in Affrike, than in Europe. Howbeit that with whatsoeuer madnesse other princes and people haue bene astonied, which haue endured womens soueraigntie, yet haue the Frenchmen (God be thanked) by the benefit of the law Salique, alwayes hitherto preserued themselues from this disgrace. For why, this Salique law which *M. Cirier* Councellour of the parliament, said to haue bene made with a great quantitie of the salt of wisdome, was not onely alleaged and put in practise, in the raigne of *Philip Valois*, and of *Charls* the

* Representation is, when diuers children together represent their dead fathers person, and so in his right, together with their vncles succeed into their grandfathers inheritance

Poore French shifts, for the auouching and proofe of the Salique law.

the Faire, against whome the daughters pretended no claime vnto the kingdome: but also in the time of *Clothaire, Sigebert*, and *Childebert*, who were all preferred before the kings their predecessours daughters, who neuer laid claime vnto the crowne. And that is it for which *Baldus* the notable lawyer, speaking of the house of Burbon, holdeth, That the male of the same blood and name, beeing a thousand degrees off, should sooner succeed vnto the crowne and kingdome of Fraunce, than any woman much neerer. Which is not onely to take place in kingdomes, but euen in dukedoms and other principalities also, which haue the marks and rights of soueraigntie belonging vnto them. Which lawes also we see all people, excepting some few, to haue alwayes before embraced. And so the princes of Sauoy, by the authoritie of this Salique law, haue alwayes excluded the women from the gouernment: for so wee read *Constance* the daughter of the duke of Sauoy, to haue by *Peter* of Sauoy her vncle bene excluded from the gouernment: and that euen by the sentence and doome of the iudges and arbitrators, chosen for the deciding of the matter in the yeare one thousand two hundred fiftie six. Yet doubt I not but that many are afraid of womens soueraigntie, who yet indeed doubt not to shew themselues most obedient vnto womens lusts. But it is no matter (as old *Cato* was woont to say) whether that the soueraigntie it selfe be giuen to women, or that the emperours and kings bee themselues obedient vnto womens pleasures and commands.

Seeing then it appeareth plainely enough (as I suppose) the estate of a Monarchy to be of all other estates most sure; and amongst Monarchies, the Royall Monarchy to bee best: as also amongst kings them to excell which bee descended from the race and stocke of kings: and in briefe, that in the royall race the neerest of the blood is still to be preferred before the rest that were farther off: and that the soueraigntie (the female sexe excluded) ought to bee still vndiuided. Let vs now also at last see how it ought to be gouerned, as whether by iustice Distributiue, Commutatiue, or Harmonicall. For why, the fairest conclusion that can bee made in this worke, is to conclude of iustice, as the foundation of all Commonweales, and of such consequence, as that *Plato* himselfe hath entituled his bookes of Commonweals, *Bookes of Law, or of Iustice*, howbeit that he speaketh in them rather like a Philosopher, than a Lawgiuer, or Lawyer.

(*⁎*)

Iustice the foundation of all Commonweales.

CHAP.

Chap. VI.

Of the three kinds of Iustice, Distributiue, Commutatiue, and Harmonicall: and what proportion they haue vnto an estate Royall, Aristocratique and Popular.

Et vs then say in continuing of our purpose, that it is not enough to maintaine, that a Monarchy is the best estate of a Commonweal, & which in it hath the least inconuenience; except wee also (as we said) add thereunto, a Monarchy Royall. Neither yet sufficeth it to say, that the Royall Monarchy is most excellent, if we should not also shew that vnto the absolute perfection thereof it ought to be fast knit together by an Aristocratique and Popular kind of gouernment: that is to say, by an Harmonicall mixture of Iustice, composed of Iustice Distributiue, or Geometricall; and Commutatiue, or Arithmeticall: which are proper vnto the estates Aristocratique, and Popular. In which doing, the estate of the Monarchy shall be simple, and yet the gouernment so compound and mixt, without any confusion at all of the three kind of Estates, or Commonweales. For wee haue before shewed, that there is great difference betwixt the mingling, or rather confounding of the three estates of Commonweales in one (a thing altogether impossible) and the making of the gouernment of a Monarchy, to bee Aristocratique and Popular. For as amongst Monarchies, the Royall Monarchy so gouerned (as I haue said) is the most commendable: euen so amongst kingdomes, that which holdeth most, or commeth neerest vnto this Harmonicall Iustice, is of others the most perfect. Which things for that they may seeme obscure, neither are to my remembrance by any mans writings declared; I must endeuor my selfe that they may by manifest and plaine demonstration be vnderstood. Iustice therefore I say to be *The right diuision of rewards and punishments, and of that which of right vnto euery man belongeth*; which the Hebrewes by a straunge word call *Credata*: for the difference betwixt this and the other Iustice giuen vnto men by God, whereby we are iustified, which they call *Tsedaca*. For that by these, as by most certaine guides, wee must enter into this most religious and stately temple of Iustice. But this equall diuision which we seeke for, can in no wise be accomplished, or performed, but by a moderat mixture, and confusion of equalitie, and similitude together, which is the true proportion Harmonicall, and whereof no man hath as yet spoken.

Plato hauing presupposed the best forme of a Commonweale, to be that which was composed of a Tyrannicall and Popular estate: in framing the same, is contrarie vnto himselfe, hauing established a Commonweale not onely Popular, but altogether also Popularly gouerned; giuing vnto the whole assembly of his citisens, the power to make, and to abrogat lawes, to place and displace all manner of officers, to determine of peace and warre, to iudge of the goods, the life, and honour, of euery particular man in soueraigntie: which is indeed the true Popular estate, and Popularly also gouerned And albeit that he had so (as we say) formed his Commonweale, yet neuerthelesse hee said, That the Commonweale could neuer be happie, if it were not by Geometricall proportion gouerned; saying that God (whome euerie wise lawmaker ought to imitat) in the gouernment of the world alwayes vseth Geometricall proportion. The same *Plato* hauing also (as some say) oftentimes in his mouth these three words, ἀεὶ τοῦ

That a Royall Monarchy ought to be knit together with a certaine kind of mixture of the Aristocratike & Popular gouernment, the royalty yet standing whole and pure, without any mixture of those estates.

The definition of Iustice.

τον Θεον γεωμετρεῖν, which is to say, *God always to be playing the Geometritian*: which words indeed sauour well of *Plato* his stile, howbeit that they be not in all his works to be found.

Now certaine it is, that Distributiue, or Geometricall Iustice, is most contrarie vnto the Popular estate and gouernment by *Plato* set downe: the people still seeking after nothing more, than for equalitie in all things; a thing proper vnto Commutatiue, or Arithmeticall Iustice. Which was the cause for which *Xenophon* (*Plato* his companion, and both of them iealous one of anothers glory) being of opinion, That Commonweales ought to be framed, and the lawes administred according vnto Arithmeticall proportion and equalitie, bringeth in *Cyrus* yet a boy, corrected and chastised, for that he being chosen king, had chaunged but the seruants garments, appointing better apparell vnto them of the better sort, and meaner vnto them of the meaner sort: as hauing therein regard vnto decencie, and the proportion Geometricall. After which chastisement, *Cyrus* is by his maister taught, to giue vnto euery man that which vnto him belongeth, and to remember that he was a Persian borne, and was therefore to vse the Persian lawes and customes, which gaue vnto euery man that which was vnto him proper: and not the manners and fashions of the Medes, who thought it meet, that to be vnto euery man giuen, which was decent and conuenient for him. Which writings of *Xenophon*, *Plato* hauing read, and knowing right well that it was himselfe, and not *Cyrus*, which had bene corrected; forthwith reproued the Cyropædia, without naming of any partie. This diuersitie of opinions, betwixt *Xenophon* and *Plato* (famous among the Greeks) was the cause of two great factions, the one of the Nobilitie and richer sort, who held for Geometricall Iustice, and the Aristocraticall estate; the other of the baser and poorer sort, who maintained Commutatiue or Arithmeticall Iustice, and therefore wished to haue had all estates and Commonweales Popular. Now of these two factions arise a third, which was of opinion, That in euerie Commonweale Arithmeticall Iustice was to be kept in iust equalitie, when question was of the goods of any one in particular, or for the recompensing of offences and forfeitures: but if question were of common rewards to be bestowed out of the common treasure, or for the diuision of countries conquered, or for the inflicting of common punishments, that then Distributiue, or Geometricall Iustice, was to be obserued and kept, hauing regard vnto the good or euill deserts, and the qualitie or calling of euery man: insomuch that these men vsed two proportions, and yet for all that diuersly, sometime the one and sometime the other: as *Aristotle* said it ought to be done, but yet not naming either *Plato* or *Xenophon*, who yet had both first touched this string.

But as for Harmonicall Iustice, not one of the auntient writers either Greekes or Latines, neither yet any other, euer made mention, whether it were for the distribution of Iustice, or for the gouernment of the Commonweale: which for all that is of the rest the most diuine, and most excellent and best fitting a Royall estate; gouerned in part Aristocratically, and in part Popularly. But forasmuch as this point we heare speake of, euill vnderstood, draweth after it a number of errours, whether it be in making of laws, or in the interpretation of them, or in all sorts of iudgements; and to the end also that euerie man may vnderstand, that this third opinion of *Aristotle* can no more be maintained than the other; it is needfull for vs to borrow the principles of the Mathematitians, and the Lawyers resolutions. For why, it seemeth that the Lawyers for not regarding the Mathematitians, and Philosophers, as not hauing iudicial experience, haue not declared or manifested this point, which is of right great consequence (as I haue said) and that as well for the administration of Iustice, as for the maintaining of the affaires of state, as also of the whole Commonweale in generall.

Now

Plato couertly by Xenophon reproued, for appointing his Commonweale to be gouerned by Geometricall Proportion.

Harmonicall Iustice of all others the best.

F1 γεωμετρεῖν   H6 arise *i.e.* arose   H10 for the   Note at G1.

OF A COMMONWEALE. 757

Now the Geometricall proportion is that which is made of an vnequall excesse of like magnitudes among themselues: but the Arithmeticall proportion is euery way both in progression, and excesse equall: and the Harmonicall proportion is of them both, by a wonderfull cunning (confused and combined together) made, and yet is vnto them both vnlike: the first of these proportions is semblable, the second is equall, & the third is in part equall, and in part semblable; as is to be seene by the examples in the margent set: where the proportion is treble of 3 to 9, and of 9 to 27, and of 27 to 81: and the proportion Arithmeticall following, beginneth of the same number of 3, and the same difference of 3 to 9: but the difference of 9 to 15 is not like, but yet equall: for betwixt these numbers there are alwayes six differing. And the proportion Harmonicall beginneth of 3 also, but the differences are not alwayes alike, neither altogether equall also, but therein is both the one and the other sweetly mixt and combind together, as may well by Mathematicall demonstrations be vnderstood, whereinto it is not needfull for vs further at this time to enter: howbeit that certaine markes of them manifest enough, are in the auntient Roman lawes to be found; and by numbers in Geometricall proportion set downe and reported. But the difference of the Geometricall and Arithmetical proportion, is in this to be noted, That in the proportion Arithmeticall are alwayes the selfe same reasons, and the differences equall: whereas in the Geometricall proportion they are alwayes semblable, but not the selfe same, neither yet equall: except a man would say, that things semblable are also equall; which were nothing else, but improperly to speake: so as *Solon* did, who to gaine the hearts both of the nobilitie, and of the people of Athens, promised to make them lawes equall for all sorts of men: wherein the nobilitie and better sort of the people thought him to haue meant the Geometricall equalitie; and the common people, the Arithmeticall; and so to haue bene all equall: Which was the cause that both the one and the other by common consent made choyce of him for their lawmaker. Wherefore the Geometricall gouernment of an estate is, when like are ioyned with like: as for example, by the laws of the twelue Tables, the Patricij, or Nobilitie, was forbidden to marrie with the comminaltie, and order taken, that noble men should marrie none but noble women: and they of the baser sort such also as were of like condition with themselues, slaues also marrying with slaues, as differing from both the other sort. Which law is also yet inuiolably kept among the Rhagusians. So were to be deemed also, if the law were, that princes should not marrie but with princes, the rich with the rich, the poore with the poore, and slaues with slaues, by a Geometricall proportion. But if it were by law prouided, that marriages should be made by lot; that law would bee vnto the people most acceptable and pleasing, to make all equall: for that so the noble and rich ladies should by lot oftentimes fall vnto the poore and baser sort of men; the slaue might marrie the prince, the base artificer might haue to wife a woman honourably descended, most vnlike to his estate: So that by lot should the Popular equalitie bee preserued, agreeing with the Arithmeticall proportion: but the wealth and dignitie of the nobilitie and richer sort be quite ouerthrowne. And that is it for which *Euripides* saith, A lawfull equalitie to be most agreeable vnto mans nature, τὶ γὰρ ἴσον νόμιμον ἀνθρώποις ἔφυ. But both these formes of gouernment according to either Arithmeticall, or Geometricall proportion, draw after them diuers inconueniences: For in the one the poorer and vulgar sort are cast downe, and in the other the nobilitie and richer sort are contemned and disgraced. Whereas the Harmonicall manner of gouernment, with a most sweet consent, preserueth both (so much as possibly is) not confounding all sorts of people hand ouer head together. And not to go out of the example by vs propounded of marriages, he that would keepe the Harmonicall gouernment, should not require

Ttt

Three kinds of proportion. Proportion Geometricall, 3, 9, 27, 81. Proportion Arithmeticall, 3, 9, 15, 21, 27. Proportion Harmonicall, 3, 4, 6, 8, 12.

The difference betwixt Geometricall and Arithmeticall proportion.

The Geometrical gouernment of an estate.

The gouernment of an estate by Arithmeticall proportion.

The gouernment according vnto the Geometricall or Arithmetical proportion hurtfull, the one vnto the common people, and the other vnto the nobility: whereas the Harmonicall gouernment preserueth both the one and the other.

D3 with princes *Phoenissae*, 538. E2 For τὶ γὰρ (L 4–5) read τὸ γὰρ (L 1–3 and Fr 5–8) omitted (Fr 1–4). Cf. E8 hand over head *i.e.* indiscriminately, pell-mell (cf. 758 I9) Note at B4.

quire in the marriages of the nobilitie, the noble descent too farre set both on the one side and the other: as many of the Germans most daungerously doe, who most curiously search out their great great grandfathers fathers, of like nobilitie on both sides, to ioyne together their nobilitie in marriage: which is too farre to remoue and seperat the nobilitie, not from the baser sort onely, but euen from it selfe also; considering that they content not themselues, that the gentleman be noble by the father onely, as it sufficeth in the kingdome of Polonia, by the decree of *Alexander* king of Polonia: or by the father, and the grandfather, as is sufficient in this realme, by a law of king *Frances* the 1: or by father, and mother, and grandfather, on both sides, as is set downe by the new decrees of the knights of Sauoy: but they will that the right gentleman shew that hee is descended of two hundred and threescore noble persons, if the interpretation that many giue of a right gentleman be true: Some others will haue seuen degrees of nobilitie to suffice, deriued from the fathers and mothers side without disparagement. But such lawes are daungerous, and full of seditions: and for this cause the law concerning marriages, which *Appius* the Decemuir is said to haue put into the Twelue Tables, was at the motion of *Canuleius* the Tribune as daungerous, repealed: for that thereby the subiects loue was rent in sunder, and the citie by seditions ouerthrowne: which tumults and seditions the law being once abrogated, and alliances made betwixt the nobilitie and the comminaltie, vpon the sudden ceased: howbeit that noble women haue seldome married from the nobilitie, but noble men haue oftentimes married with meane women: for that nobilitie is still to bee obtained from the father. And indeed it best agreeth with Harmonicall proportion, if a rich base woman marrie with a poore gentleman; or a poore gentlewoman with a rich common person: and she that in beauty and feature excelleth, vnto him which hath some one or other rare perfection of the mind: in which matches they better agree, than if they were in all respects equall: as amongst marchants there is no partnership or societie better, or more assured, than when the rich lazie marchant is partner with the poore industrious man; for that there is betwixt them both equalitie, and similitude: equalitie, in that both the one and the other haue in them some good thing: and similitude, in that they both two haue in them some defect or want. And this is it for which the auntient Greekes aptly fained, Loue to haue bene begotten of *Porus* and *Penia*, that is to say, of *Plentie* and *Pouertie*, loue growing betwixt them two: so as in song the Meane betwixt the Base and the Treble, maketh a sweet and melodious consent and harmonie. For why, it is by nature to all men engrafted, for them still to loue most, the thing themselues want most: so commonly the foule seeketh after the faire; the poore, the rich; the coward, the valiant: whereas if the rich and noble should likewise marrie with the noble and rich, they should one of them make lesse account and reckoning of the other, for that one of them little wanted the others helpe. For as the maister of a feast ought not without discretion to place his guests hand ouer head, as they first came into the house, without any respect had of their age, sexe, or condition: so also ought he not to set all his best guests in the highest and most honourable places: neither all the wise men together with the wise, neither old men with old men, nor young men with young men, women with women, nor fools with fooles: following therein the Geometricall proportion, which seeketh after nothing else but the semblablenesse of things; a thing of it selfe foolish and vnpleasant. But the wisest maister of a feast will place and enterlace quiet men betwixt quarrellers, wise men amongst fooles; that so they may by their talke in some sort as with a medicine be cured: so betwixt cauillers shall he set a quiet man, and vnto an old babler ioyne a still and silent man, so to giue him occasion to speake, and teach the other to speake lesse: by a poore man he shall place a rich, that so hee may extend his bountie

---

G3 disparagement *i.e.* marriage with anyone of lower rank Note at I6.

OF A COMMONWEALE.   759

A bountie vnto him, and he againe for the same of the other receiue thanks: so amongst seuere and tetricall men, he shall mingle others of a more ciuill and courteous disposition; in which doing he shall not onely auoid the enuie and heart-burning of such as might complaine themselues to be placed in too low places, or not in such order as they desired (a thing hardly to be auoided where question is of degree and place;) but also of such a most beautifull harmonicall, and orderly placing, shal arise a most sweet consent, as wel of euery one of the guests with other, as also of them altogether. Which beautifulnesse of Harmonicall order, he which will with Geometricall semblablenesse, or Arithmeticall confusion, inuert or trouble, he shall so take from out of the feast all the profit, all the sweetnesse, and loue, which should still be amongst guests. And for this
B cause men say, *Scipio Africanus* to haue bene blamed by the wiser sort of men, and such as saw farthest into matters of state, for that hee first of all others had made lawes concerning the Theatre, giuing therein the first places vnto the Senators, and so in the beholding of the playes separating them from the people; when as by the space of 558 yeares before, euen from the foundation of the citie, the Senators had indifferently together with the poore stood to behold the playes: which sepation so made, much alienated the one of them from the other, and was the cause of many great and daungerous tumults and broyles afterwards in that Commonweale. Neither is it enough that the lawes and magistrats constraine the subiects for feare of punishment to forbeare to wrong one another, and so to liue in peace; but they must also bring to passe, that al-
C though there were no lawes at all, yet they should be at vnitie among themselues, and one of them still loue another. For that the foundation of marriages, as all other humane societies, which are almost innumerable, resteth in loue and friendship, which cannot long continue without that Harmonical & mutual concord which I haue alreadie spoke of: and which cannot possibly either by Geometrical or Arithmeticall Iustice & gouernmēt be done, for that the proportion both of the one & of the other, is for most part disioyned aud separat: wheras the nature of the Harmonicall proportion alwaies vniteth together the extreams, by reason that it hath accord both with the one and with the other: as by the examples propounded we are taught.

Scipio blamed for hauing vsed the Geometricall proportion in the placing of the Senators in the Theater.

Loue the foundation of all humane societies, not to be preserued by Geometricall, or Arithmeticall, but by Harmonical proportion of iustice

Now the equall gouernment and by proportion Arithmeticall, is naturall vnto Po-
D pular estates, who would that men still should equally diuide estates, honours, offices, benefits, common treasures, countries conquered: and if lawes be to be made, or officers ordained, or that iudgement be to be giuen of life and death, their desire is, that all the people should thereunto be called, and that the voice of the greatest foole and bedlem should be of as great weight and force, as the voyce of the wisest man: in briefe, the more popular sort thinke it best, that all should be cast into lot and weight: as the auntient Greekes, who in three words set forth the true Popular estates, πάντα ζυγοῖς καὶ κλήροις, which is to say, *All by lot and ballance*: or else to measure all things by a most right rule, and euery way with Arithmeticall proportion equall. Which for that it is most stearne and inflexible, is after our phrase called *Right*, and to do iustice, is said, *To*
E *do Right*: which maner of speech seemeth to haue bene taken from the Hebrews, who call their bookes of Law and Iustice, ספר הישר, that is to say, *The Booke of Right*, or as the Chaldean interpretor translateth it, *The Booke of Rightnesse*: either for that the way of vertue and iustice hath no windings or turnings, nor suffereth vs this way or that way to turne out of the right way; or else for that it is the selfe same vnto all men, without respect of any mans person, not to bee moued with loue or hatred towards any man. Such an one as many haue though *Policletus* his rule to haue bene, so straight and hard, as that it might more easily be broken than bowed either vnto the one side or the other: vnto the patterne & straightnesse whereof all artificers directed their rules. Such

The equall gouernment of Arithmeticall proportion, best fitteth Popular estates.

Ttt ij   is also

A2 tetricall *i.e.* harsh, unpleasant   B6 separation   B6–7 alienated   C7 and separat
E2 ספר הישר   E7 have thought   Note at E7.

760   THE SIXT BOOKE

is also the forme of a Popular gouernment, when all goeth by lot, and by strait and immutable lawes, without any iust and indifferent interpretation, without any priuilege or acception of person: in such sort, as that the nobles are subiect euen vnto the selfe same punishments that the baser sort are; the fines and penalties being alike vppon the rich and vpon the poore, and the like reward appointed for the strong, and for the weake, for the captaine, and for the souldiour.

The Geometrical proportion best to agree with the Aristocraticall

But now to the contrarie, the Aristocratike gouernment according to Geometricall proportion, is like vnto the Lesbian rule, which being made of lead, was euerie way so pliant and flexible, as that it might be vnto euery stone so aptly fitted and applied, as that no part (so much as possible was) might thereof be lost: wheras others, who were woont to apply the stone vnto the straight rule, oftentimes lost much thereof. So say some, that judges ought in iudgement to apply the lawes vnto the causes in question before them, and according to the varietie of the persons, times, & places, so to decline from that inflexible straightnesse. Howbeit in mine opinion, as it is impossible for a rule so pliant euery way, as was the Libian Rule, to keepe the name of a rule: so must also the strength and name of the law perish, which the judge may at his pleasure euery way turne like a nose of waxe, and so become the master and moderator of the law, whereof indeed he ought to be but the vpright minister.

Wherefore a little to decline from that inflexible straightnesse of *Polycletus* his rule, as also from the vncertaine pliantnesse of the Lesbian rule, that is to say, from the Arithmeticall, and Geometricall proportion of gouernment of estates; a certaine third kind of rule is by vs to be deuised, not so stiffe, but that it may bee easily bowed when need shall be, and yet forthwith become also straight againe: that is to say, Harmonicall Iustice: which I thinke may well bee done, if wee shall conclude and shut vp the gouernment of estate within those foure tearmes which wee haue before combined, viz. the Law, Equitie, the Execution of the law, and the Office or Dutie of the Magistrat or Iudge: whether it be in the administration of iustice, or the gouernment of the estate: which haue amongst themselues the same proportion which these foure numbers haue, viz. 4, 6, 8, 12. For what the proportion is of 4 to 6, the same the proportion is of 8 to 12: and againe the same reason is of 4 to 8, that there is of 6 to 12. So the Law also hath respect vnto Equitie; as hath the Execution of the Law, vnto the Dutie of the Magistrat: or els contrariwise, For Execution serueth vnto the Law, as doth the Dutie of the Magistrat vnto Equitie. But if you shall transpose these numbers before set in Harmonicall proportion, and so make the Magistrat superiour vnto Equitie; and the Execution of the Law, to be aboue the Law it selfe; both the Harmonie of the Commonweale, and musicall consent thereof, shall perish. As for Geometricall proportion, the tearmes thereof being transposed, is yet alwayes like vnto it selfe, whether it be in continuall proportion, as in these foure numbers, 2, 4, 8, 16; or in proportion disioyned, as 2, 4, 3, 6: conuert the order of the numbers, and say, 6, 3, 4, 2, or 3, 2, 4, 6; or in what order soeuer you shall place them, there shall alwayes be the same proportion of the first vnto the second, which is of the third vnto the fourth; and againe of the first vnto the third, which is of the second vnto the fourth. And albeit that a continuat proportion is more pleasing than that which ariseth of diuided numbers, yet maketh it of it selfe no consent; as for example, 2, 4, 8, 16: and much lesse if it consist of Arithmeticall proportions, whether that they be diuided in this sort, 2, 4, 5, 7, or els ioyned as 2, 4, 6, 8: both which proportions as farre differ from Harmonicall proportion, as doth warme water from that which is most cold, or else scaulding hoat. And so in like case may we say, that if the prince, or the nobilitie, or the people, all together hauing the soueraigntie, whether it be in a Monarchy, in an Aristocratike, or Popular estate, gouerne

The Law. 4.
Equitie. 6.
The Execution of the Law. 8.
The Office of the Iudge. 12.

Geometricall or Arithmeticall gouernment alone, no fit meane to maintaine a Commonweale.

F2 without any just and indifferent interpretation *i.e.* without any interpretation based on equity (cf. Fr)
G5 Lesbian Rule

gouerne themselues without any law, leauing all vnto the discretion of the magistrats, or else of themselues distribute the rewards and punishments, according to the greatnes, qualitie, or desert, of euery man; howbeit that this manner of gouernment might seeme in apparance faire and good, as not hauing therein either fraud or fauour (a thing for all that impossible:) yet for all that could not this maner of gouernment be of any continuance, or assurance, for that it hath not in it any bond wherewith to bind the greater vnto the lesser, nor by consequence any accord at all: and much lesse shall it haue of suretie, if all be gouerned by equalitie and immutable lawes, without applying of the equitie thereof according vnto the particular varietie of the places, of the times, and of the persons: if all honours and rewards shall be giuen to all men indifferently, by Arithmeticall proportion alike, without respect of honour, person, or desert: in which state of a Commonweale all the glorie of vertue must needes decay and perish. Wherefore as two simple medicines in the extremitie of heat & cold, and so in operation and power most vnlike one of them vnto the other, are of themselues apart vnto men deadly & daungerous; and yet being compound & tempered one of them with the other, make oftentimes a right wholesome and soueraigne medicine: so also these two proportions of Arithmeticall and Geometricall gouernment, the one gouerning by law onely, and the other by discretion without any law at all, do ruinat and destroy estates and Commonweales: but being by Harmonicall proportion compounded and combined together, serue well to preserue and maintaine the same. *A fit comparison. Harmonicall Iustice compounded of Arithmeticall and Geometricall proportion of gouernment, best for the preseruation of a Commonweale.*

Wherefore *Aristotle* is deceiued, in deeming the Commonweale then to be happy, when it shall chaunce to haue a prince of so great vertue and wisdome, as that hee both can and will with greatest equitie, gouerne his subiects without lawes. For why, the law is not made for the prince, but for the subiects in generall, and especially for the magistrats; who haue their eyes oft times so blinded with fauour, hatred, or corruption, as that they cannot so much as see any small glympse of the beautie of equitie, law and iustice. *Lawes necessarie for the good gouernment of a Commonweale, although the prince be neuer so wise or vertuous.*

And albeit that the magistrats were angels, or that they could not in any sort bee misseled or deceiued, yet neuerthelesse were it needfull to haue laws, wherewith as with a certaine candle, the ignorant might be directed in the thickest darknesse of mens actions; and the wicked for feare of punishment also terrified. For albeit that the eternall law of things honest and dishonest be in the hearts of euery one of vs, by the immortall God written, yet were no penalties so in mens minds by God registred, whereby the wicked might be from their iniurious and wicked life reclaimed. Wherefore the same immortall and most mightie God, who hath euen naturally engrafted in vs the knowledge of right and wrong, with his owne mouth published his laws, and thereunto annexed also penalties: before which lawes no penalties were appointed, neither any law maker so much as once before remembred or spoken of. For proofe whereof let it be, that neither *Orpheus*, nor *Homer*, nor *Musæus*, the most auntient Greeke writers; neither any other which were before *Moyses* (who was more auntient than all the Paynim gods) in all their workes so much as once vse the word *Law*: kings by their hand, their word and soueraigne power, commaunding all things. *No mention of law, before the law of God was giuen.*

The first occasion of making of lawes, was the chaunging of Monarchies into Popular and Aristocratique Commonweales: which they first did at Athens, in the time of *Draco*, and afterward of *Solon*: and in Lacedemonia, in the time of *Lycurgus*, who tooke from the two kings the soueraignty. Whose examples the other cities of Greece and Italie set before themselues to behold and imitate, *viz*. The Dorians, the Ionians, the Cretensians, the Locrensians, they of Elis, Crotona, Tarentum, and Rome, with diuers other townes in Italie: in which cities the people were euer at variance and discord *The first occasion of the making of lawes:*

with

Note at C6.

Laws hatefull vnto the rich and mightie.

with the nobilitie; the poorer sort still seeking to be equall with the noble and richer: which could not possibly be, but by the equalitie of lawes; which lawes they of the richer on the contrarie side vtterly reiected, seeking by all meanes to be therefrom free & priuileged: as they who with their wealth & power defended the Commonweale; and therefore thought it reason in honours and preferments, to bee aboue them of the inferiour sort: who indeed hauing so got the great estates and principall charges in the Commonweale, alwayes fauoured the richer sort, and them that were like vnto themselues, still contemning and oppressing the poore. Whereof proceeded the hard speeches and complaints of them of the meaner sort: which that they might in the citie of Rome haue some end, *Terentius Arsa* Tribune of the people, in the absence of the Consuls, blaming the pride of the Senators before the people, bitterly inueyed against the power of the Consuls; alleaging, That for one lord now there were two, with an immoderat and infinit power, who themselues loosed and discharged from all feare of lawes, turned all the penalties thereof vpon the poore people. Which their insolencie that it might not still endure, he said, He would publish a law for the creating of Fiue men, for to appoint lawes concerning the power of the Consuls, who from thenceforth should not vse further power, than that which the people should giue them ouer themselues, and not to haue their lust and insolencie any more for law. Six yeres was this law with great contention and strife betwixt the nobilitie and people debated, and at length in the behalfe of the people established. But here it shall not bee amisse out of *Liuie* to set downe the very speeches and complaints of the nobilitie, accounting it better to liue vnder the soueraigne power of a king without law, than to liue in subiection vnto the law, *Regem hominem esse à quo impetres vbi ius, vbi iniuria opus sit, esse gratiæ locum, esse beneficio, & irasci, & ignoscere posse, inter amicum & inimicum discrimen nosce, leges rem surdam & inexorabilem esse, salubriorem melioremque inopi quam potenti, nihil laxamenti nec veniæ habere si modum excesseris: periculosum esse in tot humanis erroribus sola innocentia viuere:* The king (they said) to be a man of whom thou maiest obtaine something where need is, in right or wrong: fauour to bee able to doe something with him, as desert also, who knew both how to bee angry, and to grant pardon: as also to put a difference betwixt a friend and a foe: as for the law it to bee but a deafe and inexorable thing, whholsomer and better for the begger than the gentleman; to haue no release nor mercie, if thou shalt once transgresse the same: it to be a very daungerous thing in so many mens frailties, to liue only vpon a mans innocencie: Thus much *Liuie*. After that the lawes of the Twelue Tables were made, where amongst others there was one very popular, and quite contrarie vnto the commaund and power of the nobilitie, and was this, *Priuilegia nisi commitijs centuriatis ne irroganto: qui secus faxit, Capital esto,* Let no priuileges be graunted but in the great assemblies of the estates: who so shall otherwise do, let him die the death. By which strict lawes the judges and magistrats for a time so gouerned the people, as that there was no place left for pardon or arbitrarie iudgement, to be giuen according vnto equitie and conscience without law. As it also happened, after that king *Frauncis* the first had subdued Sauoy, the new Gouernours and Magistrats oftentimes gaue iudgement contrarie vnto the custome of the countrey, and written law, hauing more regard vnto the equitie of causes, than vnto the law. For which cause the estates of the countrey by their ambassadours requested of the king, That from thenceforth it should not bee lawfull for the Gouernours or Iudges, to iudge according vnto arbitrarie equitie: which was no other thing, than to bind them vnto the strict lawes, without turning either this way or that way, than which nothing can be more contrary vnto the minds and proceedings of fauourable or corrupt judges. And therefore *Charondas* the Carthaginensian lawgiuer

Nothing more contrary vnto the minds & proceedings of fauourable or corrupt judges, than to haue their iudgements bound vnto the strictnesse of the law.

H5 discrimen nosse (Fr, L, and Livy, II, 3)   H8 need   I1 wholsomer

Of A Commonweale. 763

A giuer (a man very popular) forbid the magistrats in any thing, to depart from the words of the law, how vniust soeuer they seemed for to be. *Francis Conan* Maister of the Requests, being commaunded to heare the aforesaid ambassadour of the Sauoyans, writeth himselfe to haue greatly maruelled, that they should request so vnreasonable a thing: as *viz.* That it should not be lawfull for their magistrats to iudge according to the equitie of the cause, but the strictnesse of the law: and reprehendeth also *D. Faber,* for saying, That in this realm there are none but the soueraigne courts, which can iudge according to the equitie of the cause: saying moreouer, That he himselfe doubted not so to do, when as yet he was the least judge in Fraunce. Howbeit that the ambassadors thought their judges by the strict obseruing of the lawes, to bee better kept within the compasse of their duties, if the colour of equitie being taken away, they should still

B iudge according to the very law. *Accursius* not so elegantly as aptly vnto that he meant it, willed the vnlearned judges, strictly to stand vpon the very words of the law: like vnskilfull riders, who doubting to be able to sit the horse they are mounted vppon, for feare of falling hold fast by the saddle. *(The good counsell of Accursius vnto vnlearned judges.)*

But for the better vnderstanding and explaining of this matter, it is to be considered, that the word *Equitie* is diuersly taken. For Equitie referred vnto a soueraigne prince, is as much as for him to declare or expound, or correct the law: but referred vnto a magistrat or iudge, is nothing else, but for him to asswage and mitigat the rigor of the law: or as occasion shall require aggrauat the too much lenitie thereof: or else to supply the

C defect thereof when as it hath not sufficiently prouided for the present case offered, that so the purport and meaning of the law saued, the health and welfare both of the lawes and Commonweale may be respected and prouided for. In which sence not the soueraigne courts onely, but euen the least judges of all haue power to iudge & pronounce sentence according vnto the equitie of the cause; whether it be by vertue of their office, or that the proceeding before them is by way of request; or that the prince hath sent them some commission, or other letters of iustice for such their proceeding, which they may either accept or reiect: following therein the lawes of our kings, and the clause of the letters carrying these words, *So farre forth as shall seeme right and iust*: or that the prince by his expresse rescript or edict committeth any thing vnto their conscience by

D these words, *Wherewith wee charge their conscience*: as oft times wee see those things which for the infinit varietie of causes, cannot by lawes be prouided for, to bee by the prince committed vnto the religion and conscience of the magistrats, without any exception of such judges or magistrats: in which case the least judges haue as much power as the greatest: and yet neuerthelesse they cannot (as may the soueraigne courts) frustrat appeales, neither quite and cleane absolue and discharge the accused, but onely vntill they be commaunded againe to make their appearance in iudgement, after the manner and forme of the Lacedemonians (as saith *Plutarch*) when they are any way attainted of crime: neither can they also releeue, or hold for well releeued, a man appealing from a judge royall: nor other such like thing. Neither is it any noueltie, many

E things to be in iudgement lawfull for the greater magistrats or judges, which are not lawfull for the lesser: when as in the Pandects of the Hebrewes we read it to haue bene lawfull onely for the court of the wise and graue Senators (which they properly call *Hacanim*, and corruptly *Sanadrim*) to iudge of causes according vnto equitie: but not for the other lesser judges also. *(How euen the meanest judges may haue power to iudge according to the equitie of the cause without law. Many things in iudgements lawfull for the greater magistrats or judges, which are not lawfull for the lesser.)*

But now whereas by the orders and customes of all the cities of Italie, it is prouided, *That the Iudges may not swarue from the very words of the law*, excludeth not thereby either the equitie, or yet the reasonable exposition of the law: as *Alexander* the most famous lawyer of his time, according to the opinion of *Bartholus*, aunswered: who in *(The judge bound vnto the verie words of the law, is not yet therby embarred to vse the equitie of the law or yet the reasonable exposition thereof)*

that

Ttt iiij

A3 ambassadours (cf. 762 K4–5)   B2–3 unto that he meant it *i.e.* "unto that which he meant" ("it" probably a misprint)   B4 to sit the horse they are mounted uppon *i.e. equitare* (The connection with *aequitas* is obvious.)   E4 Hacanim (L) Hacamin (Fr 1–4, 6–8) *properly* Hacamim (Fr 5)

that respect put no difference betwixt the great magistrat and the little. For that to say truely, the law without equitie, is as a bodie without a soule, for that it concerning but things in generall, leaueth the particular circumstances, which are infinit, to be by equalitie sought out according to the exigence of the places, times, and persons: whereunto it behoueth the magistrat or judge so to apply the laws, whether it be in tearmes of iustice, or in matter of estate, as that thereof ensue neither any inconuenience nor absurditie whatsoeuer. Howbeit yet that the magistrat must not so farre bend the law, as to breake the same, although that it seeme to be right hard: whereas it is of it selfe cleere enough. For so saith *Vlpian, Dura lex est: sic tamen scripta*, An hard law it is (saith he) but yet so it is written. A hard law he called it, but yet not an vniust law: for why, it is not lawfull rashly to blame the law, of iniustice. But yet it is another thing, if the law cannot without iniurie be applied vnto the particular matter that is in question: for that in this case (as the lawyer sayth) the law is by the decree of the magistrat to be qualified and moderated. But when he saith the Magistrat, he sufficieutly sheweth that it belongeth not vnto the other particular judges so to do, but onely vnto the Pretor, as graunted vnto him by the Pretorian law, at the institution of his office: whereby power was giuen him to supply, expound, and correct the lawes.

That the magistrat ought not to breake the law although it seem vnto him hard.

But forasmuch as that greatly concerned the rights of soueraigntie, princes afterwards (the Popular estate being taken away) reserued vnto themselues the expounding and correcting of the laws, especially in cases doubtful, arising betwixt the Law and Equitie; about the true vnderstanding and exposition of the law. And therefore the judges and gouernours of prouinces, in auntient time doubting of the law, still demaunded the emperours aduise and opinion, when as the case presented, exceeded the tearmes of equitie arising of the law: or that which seemed vnto them iust, was contrarie vnto the positiue law: in which case if the prince were so farre off, as that his exposition was not in time conuenient to be had; and that to delay the cause, seemed vnto the estate daungerous; the magistrats were then to follow the very words of the law. For that it belongeth not vnto the magistrat to iudge of the law (as saith a certaine auntient Doctor) but onely to iudge according vnto the law: and for that in doing otherwise, he shall incurre the note of common infamie. And to this purpose I remember that *Bartholemew*, one of the Presidents of the enquiries in the parliament of Thoulouze, in that the councellors of his chamber, his fellow judges, would haue giuen iudgement contrarie vnto the law: he hauing caused all the rest of the judges of the other courts to bee assembled, by an edict then made at the request of the kings subiects, compelled the iudges his fellowes, in their iudgements to follow the law: Which law when it should seeme vnto the court vniust, they should then for the amending thereof, haue recourse vnto the king, as in such case had bene accustomed: it being not lawfull for the judges sworne vnto the lawes, of their owne authoritie to depart therefrom, seemed they vnto them neuer so iniust or iniurious. Whereby it appeareth the magistrat to stand as it were in the middle betwixt the law and the equitie thereof: but yet to bee himselfe in the power of the law, so as is equitie in the power of the magistrat: yet so as nothing be by him deceitfully done, or in preiudice of the law. For why, it beseemeth the iudge alwayes to performe the dutie of a good and innocent vpright man. For where I say that cases forgotten by the lawmaker, and which for the infinit varietie of them, cannot be in the lawes comprised, are in the discretion of the magistrat, it is yet still to bee referred vnto equitie, and that the judge ought still to be (as we said) an vpright and iust man, not in any thing vsing fraud, deceit, or extortion. Wherein *Alexander* the most famous lawyer seemeth vnto me to haue bene deceiued, in saying, That the judge which hath the arbitrarie power to iudge according to his owne mind, may if hee so please

To whome it belongeth to correct the law.

The magistrat to be in the power of the law, so as is equitie in the power of the magistrat.

F3-4 equalitie *i.e.* equity (cf. Fr and L)   G4 sufficiently   Notes at G1, I4, K1.

OF A COMMONWEALE. 765

A please iudge vniustly: an opinion contrarie vnto the law both of God and nature, and of all other lawyers also reiected: who are all of aduise, That a judge hauing arbitrary power to iudge according to his owne good liking, is not to be fined, howbeit that he haue vniustly iudged: prouided that he haue therein done nothing by fraud or deceit. And by the law of *Luitprand* king of the Lombards, it is set downe, That the magistrat shall pay fortie shillings for a fine, if he iudge contrarie vnto the law, the one halfe vnto the king, & the other halfe vnto the partie: but if he shal vniustly iudge in that belongeth vnto his place and office without law; he is not therefore to be fined: prouided yet that he haue therein done nothing fraudulently or deceitfully: as is yet also obserued and kept in all the courts and benches of this realme. Howbeit that the auntient Romans
B thus held not themselues content, but caused their judges to sweare, Not to iudge contrarie vnto their owne conscience: and still before that they pronounced sentence, the Cryer with a lowd voyce cried out vnto them, *Ne se paterentur sui dissimiles esse*, That they would not suffer themselues to be vnlike themselues; as saith *Cassiodore*. And in like case the judges of Greece were sworne to iudge according vnto the lawes: and in case there were neither law nor decree, concerning the matter in question before them, that then they should iudge according vnto equitie, vsing these words, δικαιοτάτη γνώμῃ. Whereunto that saying of *Seneca* alludeth, *Melior videtur conditio bonæ causæ si ad iudicem quàm si ad arbitrum quis mittatur: quia illum formula includit, & certos terminos ponit: huius libera, & nullis astricta vinculis religio, & detrahere aliquid potest &*
C *adijcere, & sententiam suam non prout lex aut iustitia suadet: sed prout humanitas aut misericordia impulit regere*, The estate of a good cause (saith he) seemeth better, if it be referred vnto a judge, rather than to an arbitrator: for that the prescript forme of law encloseth him in, and prescribeth vnto him certaine limits and bounds; whereas the others free conscience, and bound to no bonds, may both detract and add something, and moderat his sentence, not as law and iustice shall require, but euen as courtesie and pitie shall lead him. Which so great a power the wise lawmakers would neuer haue left vnto the judges, had it bene possible to haue comprehended all things in lawes: as some haue bene bold to say, That there is no case which is not contained in the Roman law: a thing as impossible, as to number the sand of the sea, or to comprehend that which
D is in greatnesse infinit, in that which is it selfe contained within a most little compasse, or as it were within most strait bounds shut vp. And therefore the court of parliament at Paris, fearing least men should draw into the consequence of lawes, the decrees that it should make; caused it to be registred, That if there were any notable doubt, or that the matter so deserued, their decree or sentence should not bee drawne into consequence, or be in any wise preiudiciall, but that it might bee lawfull in like case to iudge otherwise: & that for the infinit varietie of things doubtfull: wherby sometimes it commeth to passe euen contrarie, or most vnlike iudgements to bee giuen euen of the selfe same or verie like cases, and yet both most iust: as sometimes it chaunceth two trauellers comming from diuers countries, to ariue at the same place, by wayes altogether
E contrarie. Neither ought the judges or lawmakers to ioyne their reasons vnto their iudgements or lawes, a thing both daungerous and foolish, as giuing thereby occasion vnto the subiects, to forge therof new suits and delaies, or exceptions of error, or otherwise to deceiue the lawes. And that is it for which the auntient lawes and decrees were most briefly set downe, and as it were but in three words, which so cut off all the deceits that could against the same lawes be imagined or deuised. Wherefore it is a most pernitious thing, to gather together the decrees or iudgements of any court, to publish the same, without hauing red them in the records themselues, or knowing the reasons that induced the court to make the decree, which the judges oftentimes cause to bee recorded

Why so many things are by the wise lawmakers left vnto the conscience and discretion of the judge.

How it commeth to passe, that euen contrarie or most vnlike iudgemēts may be giuen of the same or verie like cases, and yet both iust.

That the reasons of lawes and iudgements ought not to bee vnto them ioined

Note at E1.

ded apart from the sentence or iudgement, least any should be thereby deceiued. Howbeit that it is a thing of it selfe also verie daungerous, to iudge by example and not by lawes, such iudgements being still to be chaunged euen by the least and lightest varietie and chaunge of the circumstances, of the persons, or of the places, or of the times: which infinit varieties can in no lawes, no tables, no pandects, no bookes, be they neuer so many or so great, be all of them contained or comprehended. And albeit that *Solon* was wrongfully blamed for making so few lawes, yet *Lycurgus* neuerthelesse made fewer, yea so few as that he forbad them to be at all written, so to haue them the better remembred; leauing most part of causes vnto the discretion of the magistrats. As did also Sir *Thomas Moore* Chauncelour of England, leauing in his *Vtopia* all penalties, excepting the punishment for adulterie, vnto the discretion of the magistrats: than which nothing can (as many thinke) be better or more profitably deuised, so that the magistrats and judges be still chosen not for their wealth and substance but for their vertue and knowledge. For it is most apparant euen to euerie mans eye, that the moe lawes there bee, the more suites there are about the interpretation thereof.

Few laws made by the auntient lawmakers.

Moe lawes, moe suits, and moe fees.

Wherefore *Plato* in his bookes of Lawes, forbiddeth lawes to bee written concerning the execution of the law, or concerning iurisdiction, traffique, occupations, iniuries, customes, tributes, or shipping. Which although we cannot altogether be without, yet might we of such laws cut off a great part. Which is also in this realme of Fraunce to be seene, which hath in it moe laws and customes than all the neighbor nations; and so also moe suites than all the rest of Europe beside: which began then especially to encrease, when as first king *Charls* the seuenth (as I suppose) and other kings after him, to the imitation of *Iustinian*, commanded heapes of lawes to be written, with a whole traine of reasons for the making of the same: contrarie vnto the auntient manner of the lawes and wise lawmakers: as if his purpose had bene rather to persuade than to command lawes. And this is it for which a certaine craftie corrupt judge (whom I remember to haue bene banished for his infamous and bad life) seeing a new edict or law (whereafter he still gaped) brought to be confirmed, commonly said, Behold ten thousand crownes in fees, or as some others say, Behold moe suites and heapes of gold. For why, the Frenchmen are so sharpe witted in raising of suits, as that there is no point of the law, no sillable, no letter, out of which they cannot wrest either true or at least wise probable arguments and reasons, for the furthering of suites, and troubling euen of the best judges of the world. Howbeit the iust and vpright judge, which shall not bee constrained to sell by retaile what others haue bought in grosse, may with a right few and good lawes gouerne a whole Commonweale: as was in Lacedemonia, and other flourishing Commonweales to be seene, who but with a few lawes right well maintained themselues; others in the meane time with their Codes and Pandects beeing in few yeates destroyed, troubled with seditions, or with immortall suites and delaies. For we oftentimes see suites of an hundred yeares old, as that of the Countie de Rais, which hath bene so well maintained, as that the originall parties and the beginners thereof are dead, and the suite yet aliue: Not vnlike that old woman *Ptolomais*, of whome *Suidas* speaketh, who so long, and with such obstinacie of mind and delayes maintained her suite, that she died before that it could be ended.

The Frenchmen much giuen to suits in law.

The cause of the multitude of suits in Fraunce

Now certaine it is, that of the multitude of laws, with their reasons annexed vnto them, and in this realme published since the time of *Charles* the seuenth, is come the heape of suites; not so many being to be found in a thousand yeres before, as haue bene within this hundred or sixscore yeares, and yet all forsooth full of reasons: howbeit that there is not one reason set downe in all the lawes of *Solon, Draco, Lycurgus, Numa*, nor in the Twelue Tables, neither yet commonly in the law of God it selfe. And howbeit

No reasons annexed vnto the auntient lawes.
a

---

l 4 others *i.e.* other judges, who buy their offices   Note at F 1.

OF A COMMONWEALE. 767

A beit that some may say, That the infinit multitude of people which aboundeth in this realme, may helpe to encrease the multitude of suits: so it is, that there were a great many moe in the time of *Cæsar*, and yet moe than there was then about fiue hundred yeares before, as he himselfe writeth in the sixt booke of his Commentaries. And *Iosephus* in the Oration of *Agrippa*, sayth, That there were aboue three hundred nations in Gaule: And yet neuerthelesse *Cicero* writing vnto *Trebatius* the lawyer (then one of *Cæsars* lieutenants) meerely saith, him to haue gained but a few in France to his occupation. Wherefore they which haue brought in such a multitude of lawes, as thinking thereby to cut vp all deceit by the roots, and so to restraine suits: in so doing imitat *Hercules*, who hauing cut of one of *Hydraes* heads, see seuen others forthwith to

B arise thereof. For euen so one doubt or suit being by law cut off wee see seuen others of new sprung vp, of that heape of words and reasons without reason heaped together in persuading of the law: it being indeed a thing impossible in all the bookes of the world to comprehend all the cases which may happen, and ten thousand suites arising vpon euery reason of the law giuen. So that *Seneca* thereof said well, *Nihil mihi videtur frigidius quam lex cum prologo: iubeat lex, non suadeat*, Nothing (saith he) seemeth vnto me more cold, than a law with a prologue: let the law commaund, and not persuade: except the reason of the law be from it inseparable. And howbeit that the Decemuiri, or Ten Commissioners, appointed by the Romans to reforme the lawes, and

C to establish new, had twelue tables comprehended whatsoeuer could by mans wit bee foreseene: saying and thinking also them to haue therein comprised all occurrents that might happen: yet shortly after they found themselues farre from their account, and so many things to be wanting in those their laws, as that they were enforced to giue power to the Prouost of the citie, to amend the lawes, to heape lawes vpon lawes, to abrogat the greater part of the lawes of the twelue tables: and in briefe to leaue vnto the magistrats discretion the greater part of the iudgements concerning mens particular causes or interest. And howbeit also, that in respect of publike causes, they did what they might to haue shut vp the judges within the barres and bonds of the lawes, yet so it was, that in fine they seeing the inconueniences which continually fell out in all mat-

D ters, in seeking to doe equall iustice to all men, according to the Arithmeticall proportion, were constrained (after that the Popular estate was chaunged into a Monarchy) to make a great Prouost in the citie of Rome, to whom they gaue power accordingly to iudge of all the crimes committed in Rome, and within fortie leagues round about the citie: which power was also giuen vnto the Proconsuls, and other gouernours of prouinces euery one of them within the compasse of his owne iurisdiction. Now he which extraordinarily iudgeth of offences, is not in his iudgements bound or subiect vnto the lawes, but may giue such iudgement as shall seeme vnto himselfe good; prouided yet that he therein exceed not measure, as saith the law: which measure consisteth in the Harmonicall proportion which we haue before spoken of.

E Yet such extraordinarie power by the prince giuen vnto the magistrats, whether it be for iudgement, or for mannaging of wars, or for the gouerning of a citie, or for any thing else doing, hath many degrees: for either his power is giuen him next vnto the prince, greater than which none can be: or else power is giuen him by vertue of his office, so that he may iudge as he seeth cause, or else may iudge in such sort as might the prince himselfe; which power little differeth from the highest, and such as can in no wise by the highest magistrat vnto another magistrat or Commissioner be giuen. But if in the princes rescript or commission it be contained, That the appointed magistrat shall iudge of the cause in question according as reason, equitie, religion, or wisedome, shall lead him, or some other such meane of speech, in all these cases it is certaine, that his

power

By lawes to prouide for all inconueniences, a thing impossible:

Many degrees of extraordinary power, by the prince graunted vnto the magistrat.

A2–3 many moe *i.e.* many more people (cf. *De bello Gallico*, VI, 24)   B10 had IN twelve tables
D2 *For* accordingly *read* extraordinarily (Fr and L, and cf. D6).   E2(margin) graunted
Note at A7.

power is stil limited and referred vnto the iudgement of an honest man, and the tearms of equitie: whereunto the prince himselfe ought to referre all his owne iudgements also. Wherein many are deceiued, which thinke it lawfull for the prince to iudge according to his conscience; but not for the subiect, except it be in matters and causes criminall: in which case they are of opinion, that the magistrat may as well as the prince iudge according to his conscience: which if it be right in the one, why is it not right in the other? and if it be wrong in the one, why should it not be so in the other? when as indeed it is lawfull for no man in iudgement to swarue from equitie and conscience, and that iniurie like an Ape is alwayes like vnto it selfe, filthy still, whether it bee clothed in purple, or in a pied coat. And in iudging it is one thing to bee freed from the law, and another to be freed from conscience.

Not lawful for any man in iudgement to swarue from equitie and conscience.

But if the varietie of a fact in question be not knowne but vnto the prince himself, or magistrat alone; neither the one nor the other can therein be iudge, but witnesses onely: as *Ko* (the great lawyer) answered vnto the Gouernour of Bolonia Lagrasse, who without any other witnesse had seene a murder done, telling him, That hee could not in that case be iudge. Which selfe same aunswere was also giuen vnto king *Henry* the second of Fraunce, by the judges who were extraordinarily appointed to iudge of diuers causes at Melun, where the king hauing himself taken an Italian (one with whom he was familiarly acquainted) in a fact deseruing death, committed him to prison; who soone wearie of his imprisonment, preferred a request vnto the judges, That forasmuch as he was not conuict of any crime, neither yet so much as by any man accused, hee might therefore as reason would, be discharged and set at libertie. Whereupon *Cotellus* chiefe judge of the court, with three other of the judges went vnto the king, to vnderstand of him what occasion he had for the imprisonmẽt of the man, or what he had to lay vnto his charge? Whom the king commaunded to bee forthwith condemned, for that he himselfe had taken him in such a fact as well deserued death, which yet hee would not discouer. Wherunto the chiefe judge aunswered, *Nos iurati sumus, nisi sceleris conuictum, & ex animi nostri sententia damnaturos esse neminem*, We are sworne (said he) to condemne no man except he be of some capitall crime conuict, and according to our conscience. With which aunswere the king (otherwise a most curteous and gentle prince) much moued, for that the judges seemed to doubt of his fidelitie and credit, deepely swore, That hee himselfe had taken the villaine in a fact deseruing death. Wherefore *Anne Montmorancie* Great Constable of Fraunce, perceiuing the judges to be bound by their oath, to iudge but according vnto the laws, and that in performing the kings command they should rather seeme manquellers and murderers, than vpright judges: taking the king a little aside, persuaded him to deferre the execution of the man vntill night, least the people might hap to be troubled with the nouelty of the matter. And so the guiltie partie the night following was by the commaundement of the king thrust into a sacke, and in the riuer drowned. Yea the same king also in a ciuill cause, serued but as a witnesse in the great suit about the inheritance of *George* of Amboise, where he was before the judges sworne as a priuat man, and his testimonie accounted but for one. Wherefore *Paulus Tertius* was not without cause blamed, for that he being Pope, had caused a certaine gentleman to be put to death, who had confessed vnto him (being then a Cardinall) a secret murder by him done: which thing yet the same gentleman afterward constantly denied him to haue either said or done. Howbeit it were much better and more indifferent, the prince or the magistrat to iudge according vnto their consciences in ciuill, than in criminall causes: for that in the one, question is but of mens good; wheras in the other still mens fame, yea oftentimes their liues, and whole estates is in daunger: wherein the proofes ought to bee more cleerer than

Whether a prince or magistrat may be iudge of a fact the truth thereof beeing vnto none other knowne but vnto themselues alone.

G2 *For* varietie *read* veritie (cf. Fr).

OF A COMMONWEALE.

than the day it selfe.

But yet the difference is right great, and much it concerneth, whether the magistrats in their iudgements be bound vnto the lawes or not, or else be altogether from the laws loose & free: for that in the one, question is onely of fact; but in the other, of law, equitie, and reason, and especially when question is of matter of great importance or consequence, and wherein the law is to be expounded: which in auntient time was giuen in Rome vnto the Great Prouost, as we haue before said; but by the law of God was reserued vnto the High Priest; or vnto him that was by God chosen to bee soueraigne judge of the people: or in their absence vnto the *Leuites*. Which power in the latter times of the Iewes Commonweale (and about two hundred yeares before Christ, vnder the latter princes of the house of the *Asmoneans*) was by custome, but not by law, giuen vnto the Senat of the wise Sages. As amongst the Celts our auncestours, the Priests and Druides, for that they were the makers of the sacrifices, and keepers of the holy rites, were made also the keepers and guarders of Iustice, as of all other things the most sacred. The president or chiefe of which Druides (as *Ammianus* reporteth) still carried about his necke a pretious stone, hanging downe vnto his breast, with the picture of *Truth* engrauen in it. Which most auntient custome of the Hebrewes, and of the Ægyptians, euen yet continueth in all Asia, and in the greater part of Affrike also, viz. That the Priests should haue Iustice in their hand, and the Great Bishop the exposition of the Lawes, and the deciding of the most high and difficult causes. So the Great Bishops, whome the Turkes call their Muphti, hath himselfe alone the expounding or declaring of the doubts arising of the obscure lawes, especially when question is betwixt the written Law and Equitie it selfe. Which exposition of such doubtfull lawes, the Roman emperours reserued vnto themselues, as proper vnto the soueraigntie of their imperiall maiestie. So the Persian kings had also their Muphti, as the sanctuarie both of their publike and priuat lawes, who was still resiant in the great citie of Tauris. So had the Tartars theirs in the famous citie of Samarcand: and the kings of Afrike euerie one of them their Great Bishops also: who at Athens were called *Nemophylaces*, and in other places *Thesmothetæ*. Whereby it is to be vnderstood, that such masters and interpreters of equitie when law faileth, ought still to be most wise and vpright men, as also in most high authoritie and power placed.

And now verily if the lawes of Arithmeticall Iustice might take place but euen in priuat iudgements onely, as when question is of the exchange of things, then no doubt should in such priuat iudgements be seene, but all the question should consist in fact onely: so that no place should be left for the opinion of the judges, neither yet for equitie, things being holden and shut vp within most strict and strait lawes: which wee said could not be done, and if it could, yet will we forthwith shew the same to bee most vnfit and absurd. But yet first let vs shew, that publike iudgements neither can nor ought to be handled or made according to the Geometricall lawes or proportion of Iustice. Which neuer to haue bene before done, is manifest by all the lawes which carry with them amercements or fines, which are to be found in the laws of *Drato*, *Solon*, or of the Twelue Tables: as also by the lawes and customes of the auntient Saliens, Ripuaries, Saxons, English, and French men, where almost all the penalties are pecuniarie, and the same fines most often indifferently set downe as well for the rich as for the poore, according vnto equall Arithmeticall Iustice. All which lawes were to be repealed if pecuniarie amercements and fines were according to the opinion of *Plato*, after the Geometricall proportion of Iustice, to be of the offendors exacted. These words also, *Ne magistratibus mulctam pœnamue lenire liceas*, That it should not bee lawfull for the magistrat to mitigat the fine or penaltie: a clause most commonly annexed vnto all penall

The exposition of the law, to whom it was by the law of God reserued.

The exposition of the lawes, and the deciding of most high and difficult causes both in Asia and Afrike, reserued vnto the Mahometan Priest.

Arithmeticall Iustice vnfit to bee vsed euen in priuat iudgements.

Geometricall proportion of iustice in publike or penall iudgements, not to be admitted.

Vuu

C1 *For* Great Bishops *read* Great Bishop.   C6 resiant *i.e.* resident   C7 Tauris *i.e.* Tabriz
C8–9 Nomophylaces   E8 liceat

770 THE SIXT BOOKE

nall edicts and laws; were to no purpose, but to be quite omitted, & the matter left vnto the discretion of the magistrat, at his pleasure to aggrauat or ease the fine or penaltie. Yea that law common vnto al nations, whereby it is prouided, *That the partie condemned not hauing wherewith to pay the fine due for the fault by him committed, should satisfie the same with corporall punishment to be inflicted vpon him*, were also to bee abrogated and taken away.

An obiection against Arithmeticall proportion in exacting of fines.

But here perhaps some man will obiect & say, It to bee great iniustice to condemne a poore man in a fine of 65 crownes, for a foolish rash appeale by him made vnto any the higher courts (as the maner with vs is) and yet to exact no greater fine for the same offence of the richest of all. For why, Geometricall proportion of Iustice, which exacteth sixtie crownes for a fine, of him which is in all but worth an hundred crownes, requireth threescore thousand crownes of him which is worth an hundred thousand crownes. For that the like Geometricall proportion is of threescore to an hundred, that is of threescore thousand to an hundred thousand. Thus we see the rich man by Geometricall proportion of Iustice, to be much more grieuously fined than the poore: and so contrariwise the Arithmeticall proportion of Iustice, in the imposing of penalties and fines, to be the meanes for the rich to vndoe the poore, and all vnder the colour of iustice. Which inconueniences our auncestors foreseeing, by laws gaue leaue vnto the iudges, beside the ordinarie fines, to impose extraordinarie fines also vpon offendors, if the weightinesse of the cause so require: which maner of proceeding the antient Greeks also vsed, calling this extraordinarie manner of amercement or fine, ζημίαν επωβελίας,

Harmonical proportion of iustice best.

as *Demosthenes* writeth, and which is yet vsed by the Roman lawes: which draweth very neere vnto the true Harmonical Iustice, if by the same lawes it were permitted vnto the iudges, or at leastwise vnto the soueraigne courts to deminish also the fine, hauing regard vnto the equalitie and condition of the poore and simple, as they alwayes do in the parliament at Roan. And whereas the receiuers of the fines requested of the the king, That it might bee lawfull for the iudges to encrease, but not to diminish the fines imposed vpon such as should rashly appeale *Lisoires* the President, and *D. Amours* the kings Attourney, were deputed & sent from the parliament at Roan vnto the king, to make him acquainted with diuers things concerning the demaine, & generall reformation of Normandie (wherein I then was a partie for the king) and amongst other things, to request him, That it might please his maiestie, not to constraine them to condemne all such as should rashly appeale vnto the superiour courts, in the selfe same fine of threescore pound Paris: which vnto me seemed a thing vnreasonable, hauing also in antient time before bin done, by an edict of the emperor *Claudius*. In which doing the true Harmonicall Iustice should be obserued and kept, which in part equall, in part semblable, are alike; there should be an equalitie betwixt men of the middle sort of wealth, according to the Arithmeticall proportion of Iustice: and a Geometricall proportion also betwixt the great lords and the poorer sort: Whereof the former should in this case be left vnto the disposing of the law, and the other vnto the conscience and discretion of the iudges. For there is nothing more vniust, than the perpetuall equalitie of fines and punishments. For proofe whereof let the law but lately made by king *Charls* the ninth concerning apparell, serue for an example: whereby a fine of 1000 crownes was imposed vpon all such as should either much or little transgresse the same, without respect of any the offenders abilitie, age, or condition: with prohibition for the iudges in any sort to mitigat or lessen the same. Which law concerning all men in generall, and yet made by Arithmeticall proportion of Iustice, was shortly after by the iniquie of it selfe rent in sunder, and by the magistrats themselues, as well as by other priuat men neglected. Whereas the law of *Philip* the Faire concerning apparell was much more

Nothing more vniust, than the perpetuall equalitie of fines and punishments.

F5 punishment H5 *For* the equalitie *read* the qualitie (*la qualité*). Cf. 73 B2, 776 H8, 784 I10.
I4 *For* unreasonable *read* reasonable (cf. L). K7 iniquitie Notes at F8, I6.

more iust and indifferent, as neere approaching vnto Harmonicall Iustice: and appointing diuers punishments, according to the diuersitie of the offendors; as vnto a Duke, an Earle, a Baron, and a Bishop, a fine of an hundred pound, the Banaret fiftie pound, the Knight and pettie Landlard fortie, Deanes, Archdeacons, Abbats, & other clarkes, hauing dignities or ecclesiasticall preferments, 25 pound: vnto the other lay men offending, of what estate soeuer they were, if they were worth a thousand pound, was appointed a fine of twentie fiue dound: and if they were worth lesse, they were to pay an hundred shillings: the other clearkes without dignitie or promotion, were they secular or religious that offended against the law, paid the fine of an hundred shillings, as did the others. Wherein we see vnequall punishments appointed for persons vnequall, following therein Geometricall Iustice: and yet for all that we see also equall punishments for persons vnequall, following therein Arithmeticall Iustice: and both the one and the other so mixt together, as that thereof ariseth also that Harmonicall Iustice which we so much seeke after. The same proportion is obserued in the law, allowing of euery mans apparell and attire also: as where it is said, That no woman citisen should weare a chaine: also that no bourgesse or common person of either sexe, should weare any gold or pretious stones, neither girdles of gold, nor any crowne of gold or siluer, or any rich furres; which is not forbidden the nobilitie, and yet in them also there is some difference: as in that it is said, That the Duke, the Countie, the Baron, which hath six thousand pound land, may make themselues foure new sutes of apparell in a yeare, but no more; and their wiues as many: and gownemen, and clearkes, which haue no dignities nor preferments, should not make them gownes of cloath aboue sixteene shillings the elne Paris; & for their followers not aboue twelue shillings. Many other such like articles there were, and yet was there no mention neither more nor lesse either of silke or veluet, or other such like thing. So that hee which would in penall lawes particularly keepe Geometricall Iustice, in setting downe the penalties according to the equalitie of the offences, and abilitie of the offenders, shall neuer make penall law: For that the varietie of persons, of facts, of time, and place, is infinit and incomprehensible; and such as should alwaies present vnto the judges, cases stil much vnlike one of them vnto another. So also the perpetuall equalitie of penalties according to Arithmeticall proportion, is as vniust and vnreasonable, as if a Physitian should prescribe the same medicine to all diseases: as is to bee seene by the lawes of the Romans concerning the charges to be bestowed at feasts & banquets: wherby the morsels were equally cut vnto all euen alike, and the penaltie also equall without respect of rich or poore, of noble or base: amongst whome yet it had bene no hard matter to haue kept the Geometricall proportion, as neerest vnto true iustice, euery mans wealth beeing with them enrolled in the Censors bookes: whereas with vs at this present it were a thing most hard, or rather impossible so to do, as hauing no Censors, by whom mens wealth might be reasonably knowne. But the Popular estate of the Roman Commonweale still sought after the Arithmeticall equalitie of lawes and penalties. Which equalitie the estate being chaunged into a Monarchie, the princes by little and little changed, and so moderated the penalties before vpon the nobilitie imposed; as is by the rescript of *Antoninus Pius* vnto the gouernour of one of the prouinces to be seene: who had in hold a noble gentleman conuict before him, for murdering of his wife by him taken in adulterie: wherin he willed him to moderat the penaltie of the law Cornelia; and if the murtherer were of base condition, to banish him for euer, but if hee were of any dignitie or reputation, that then it should suffice to banish him for a time.

Now it is a notable difference in termes of iustice, that the qualitie and condition of the person should in iudgment deliuer him from death, who should otherwise haue

Geometrical proportion of iustice not possible to be kept in the making of penall lawes.

Arithmeticall equalitie in the appointing of penalties, vnreasonable and vniust.

A7 twentie five pound (*i.e.* twenty-five livres)   E1 chaunged into

772 THE SIXT BOOKE

The qualitie and condition of the person to be in the making of penall lawes, and inflicting of punishments much respected.

bene condemned: for the murtherer sayth the law, ought to be put to death, if hee be not a man of some dignitie and honour. And the Law *Viscellia* willeth that the stealers of beasts, if they bee slaues, should be cast vnto the wild beasts; but if they were freemen, they should be beheaded, or condemned into the mynes: but if they were of any nobilitie, it should then suffice to banish them for a time. In like sort also, that the burners of villages or houses should bee giuen vnto the beasts, if they were men of base condition: but if they were of any noble house, then to be beheaded, or els confined. And generally, the slaues were euer more seuerely punished, than were men by state and condition free: for these were neuer beaten with rods, or with small cudgels, whereas the slaues were still beaten with clubs, or els whipt with whips made of small coards. Howbeit that *Plato* sayth, That the free Citisen ought to bee with greater seueritie punished, than the slaue; for that as (sayth he) the slaue is not so well taught as is hee: which his opinion sauoreth indeed of a Philosopher, rather than of a Iudge or of a Lawyer; yea the law of God deliuereth from death the master, who in too seuere correcting of his slaues, shall by chaunce kill him. And therfore it ought not to seeme strange, if the father were by the people of Rome openly stoned, for whipping his son with whippes as a slaue, as *Valerius* writeth. And indeed amongst free borne men, the Citisen is lesse to be punished than the stranger, the noble lesse than the base, the magistrat lesse than the priuat man, the graue and modest lesse than the vicious and dissolute, and the souldier lesse than the countreyman. Wee must not (sayeth *Labeo* the Lawyer) suffer a base fellow to enter an action of fraud against a man of honour and dignitie: neither an obscure and loose prodigall man against a modest man of good gouernment; yea the auntient Romans neuer condemned any Decurion, or Captain of ten men (for what fault soeuer hee had committed) into the mynes, or to the gallowes. The night theefe sayth the law, if hee shall with weapon stand vpon his defence, is to be condemned into the mynes; but men of reputation and qualitie offending, to bee onely for a time banished, and souldiers with disgrace casiered. Neither

Geometricall proportion of punishing, common almost vnto all people.

must wee thinke this Geometricall manner of punishing to haue bene proper vnto the Romans, or to any other people in particular onely, but to haue beene common almost vnto all other people also, as namely vnto the French, the Saliens, the English, and the Ripuaries: and yet must wee doe as doe the barbarous Indians, which for the same offences set downe most grieuous punishments as well for the noble as the base, without any proportion at all; and yet in the manner of the executing thereof make great difference: for of the baser sort they cut off their noses and eares, and for the same offence cut off the noble mens haires, or the sleeues of their garments: a common custome amongst the Persians, where they whipped the garments of the condemned, and in stead of the hayre of their heads, pluckt off the wooll of their caps.

Aristotle his opinion concerning the execution of Geometricall and Arithmeticall Iustice, reiected.

Neither are wee to stay vppon the opinion of *Aristotle*, who would Geometricall iustice to take place in bestowing of rewards, and diuiding of spoyles: but Arithmeticall iustice equally to bee executed in the inflicting of punishments, which is not onely to ouerthrow the principles of Philosophy, which will that things contrarie, as reward and punishment, should be ordered by the same rules, but also the resolution of all the greatest Lawyers and Law-makers that euer were: with whom also the Canonists, the Orators, the Historiographers, and Poets in opinion agree, and haue alwaies

Nobilitie in penalties to be inflicted, fauoured euen for the vertues of their auncestors: and the iniuries vnto them done, more seuerely punished

more easily punished the noble than the baser sort: (howbeit that the most easie punishment of all may vnto a noble man seeme most great) that so others may bee the more enflamed vnto vertue, and the loue of true nobilitie, when as they shall vnderstand the remembrance of the infinit rewards of the vertue of most famous men, and such

---

F9 were never beaten BUT with rods (*i.e.* "were beaten only with rods"). Cf. Fr. G2 for that (as sayth he) Notes at F10, G4, I1, K9.

such as haue well deserued of the Commonweale being also dead, yet still to redound vnto their posteritie. But here I measure nobilitie by vertue, & not by mony, the flowre of youth, the princes fauour, or euill meanes whatsoeuer obtained. The auntient nobilitie of *M. Æmilius Scaurus* (as saith *Valerius*) saued his life euen in flourishing time of the Popular estate: which respect of nobilitie was yet much better kept after the change of the estate; for then they began by little and little to behead the nobilitie with a sword, after the manner of the Northerne people, in stead that the Romans before vsed the hatchet in the execution of all sorts of men. And for that the Centurion sent to execute *Papinian* (the most famous lawier, *Traian* the emperours neere kinsman, and before proclaimed the defendor both of the emperours and of the empire) had with an hatchet cut off his head, he was therefore sharply reproued by the emperout *Caracalla*, telling him, That he ought to haue executed his command with a sword, as which had lesse paine, and also lesse infamie. Wherein *Gouean* the lawyer was deceiued, who writeth more griefe to haue bene in the execution with the sword, than with the hatchet, Men die (saith *Seneca*) more easily with no kind of death, than being beheaded with the sword. And by the same reason and proportion of Iustice, hee that wrongeth a noble man is more grieuously to be punished, than hee which wrongeth a common person; & he which doth iniurie vnto a citisen, than he which doth iniurie vnto a stranger. For in the lawes of the Salians, if a Saxon or Frizlander had any way wronged a free borne Salian, he was almost foure times more grieuously fined, than if a Salian had wronged a Saxon or a Frizlander. So also by the lawes of *Alphonsus* the tenth, king of Castile, a wrong done vnto a noble man was fined at fiue hundred shillings, and a wrong done vnto a common person at three hundred. And by the like law of *Charles* the Great, he that had slaine a subdeacon was fined at three hundred shillings, if a deacon at foure hundred shillings, if a priest at fiue hundred, if a bishop at nine hundred: which penalties (the authoritie of the bishops being encreased) were doubled. I here speake not of the equitie or iniquitie of these lawes, but vse them onely as examples, to shew that Arithmeticall Iustice by the lawes of many nations, neither hath had, neither yet ought to haue place, when question is of fines and punishments; and that men of honour, and of marke, ought more easily to be punished, and their iniuries more seuerely reuenged, than those done to the common sort: wherat they yet oftentimes grudge & murmure, and thinke themselues to be therein greatly wronged. Yea *Andrew Riccee* a Polonian writeth it to be a great iniustice, That the nobilitie offending are not punished with the same punishment that the common people are; the rich as the poore, the citisen as the straunger, without any respect of degree or persons: than which nothing could bee more absurdly written, of him which would take vpon him to reforme the lawes and customes of his owne countrey and Commonweale. The like complaint was against *N. Memmius* Maister of the Requests in court, for that he being by the king appointed judge in the triall of *Vlmeus* the president, had suffered the man conuicted of most capitall crimes to escape the punishment thereunto due, and yet had condemned his clearke to be hanged, who had but done his maisters commaundement: Which king *Francis* vnderstanding, merirly said, Theeues by a wicked consent to releeue one another. Howbeit that *Memmius* a man most famous not onely in his issue, but also for his wealth, honours, vertue, and deepe knowledge in the law, is releeued euen by the equitie of his sentence; whereby he depriued the said president of all his honours and goods, and afterward hauing caused him to bee most shamefully set vppon the pillorie naked, and marked in the face with an hoat yron, to bee banished. But for that his clearke and domesticall seruant, and minister of such his villanies, was but a base and obscure fellow, hauing neither goods nor office to loose, neither much

Vvu iij   regard

regard of his good name, he could not otherwise worthily be punished than by death, hauing so well deserued the same. Whereas had he bene his slaue, he had bene more to haue bene fauoured, for that then he must of necessitie haue obeyed his maister. Neihad the president bene so grieuously punished, had he not being a judge, vnto his most base and corrupt dealings ioyned also most shamefull forgerie and extortion, and that in the administration of iustice, which he had as then in keeping. For this prerogatiue hath alwayes by our auncestours bene reserued vnto the nobles, and such as otherwise are in honourable place, That being for any offence or crime condemned to die, they should not therefore be hanged, for the infamie of the punishment: wherein all writers agree. Howbeit that concerning other punishments they are not all of one opinion, *Seneca* (as we said) accounting heading for the easiest: and the Hebrewes in their Pandects, in the Title of Punishments, appointing stoning for the most grieuous, the second burning, the third beheading, and the fourth strangling. Howbeit that they deeme him most infamous, and by the law of God accursed, which is hanged on the tree.

Hanging the most shamefull death, heading the easiest, stoning the most grieuous.

and in this *Bartholus* (the famous lawyer) is deceiued, saying, That the manner and custome in France, was to hang the noble or gentlemen condemned: and that that punishment was not there accounted villanous or infamous, seeing that in his time (which was in the raigne of *Philip* the Long, about the yeare of our Lord 1318) the nobilitie of Fraunce was as famous and as honourable, as the nobilitie of any place of the world. Yet true it is, that the noble man which is a traytor vnto his prince, deserueth to be hanged; so to be more grieuously punished than the base companion, who offendeth not so much as he, as not so straitly bound to preserue the life and estate of his prince. For the more a man is obliged and bound in fidelitie vnto his prince, the more grieuously he is to be punished aboue the common person: *Viri fortes* (saith *Cicero* speaking of *Catilin* the rebell) *acerbioribus supplicys ciuem pernitiosum quam acerbissimum hostem coercendum putant*, Worthy men (saith he) iudge the daungerous citisen to bee with greater punishment chastised, than the cruellest enemie that is. And therefore *Liuie* saith, the fugitiue traytors during the Carthaginensian warre, to haue beene more seuerely punished, than the fugitiue slaues: and the Roman traytors more sharply than the Latines, who were then still beheaded, but the Roman traytors hanged. Howbeit that in all other offences the Romans were more easily punished than others. For *Scipio Africanus* (saith *Florius*) caused the Roman souldiour not keeping his ranke, to bee beaten with a vine, but other souldiors with a trunchion or cudgell of other sadder wood: the vine (as saith *Plinie*) being the dishonour of the punishment.

Noble men for treason against their soueraigne prince, why to be more seuerely punished than other meaner persons.

Yet whereas we said, That the punishment of noble men ought to bee more easie than the punishment of the base and obscurer sort, that so others might bee the more stirred vp vnto vertue; it is a common opinion, and almost of euerie man receiued: but not yet altogether true. For that in right Geometricall proportion, the noble man for his offence hauing lost his honour and reputation, is as grieuously indeed punished, as is the base companion that is whipt, who cannot indeed of the honour and reputation which he hath not, loose any thing: as children and women are no lesse hurt with a soft ferula, than are the strong with cudgels or whips. And therefore *Scipio* commaunding the Roman souldiors to be beaten with the vine, euen for the same cause for which he commaunded the Latine souldiors to be beaten with cudgels, followed therein the equalitie, or rather the Geometricall proportion of punishment. For which cause *Galba* the emperour caused the Gibbet to be painted white, and set higher than the rest, to lessen the paine of a citisen of Rome, complayning that hee should bee hanged as other theeues were: howbeit that he had poisoned his pupill. So if a Physitian or an Apothecarie shall poyson a man, he is more grieuously to be punished than if another man had

The noble man for his offence hauing lost his honour and reputation, to be as grieuously punished, as the common person that is whipt.

G5 And in this   H5 *For* acerbioribus (L 4–5) *read* acrioribus (L 1–3). Cf. *In Catilinam*, I, 1.
H6 putant (L 4–5) putarunt (L 1–3)   I2 Florus   I3 sadder *i.e.* heavier, more solid   I4 *For* being the dishonour *read* taking away the dishonour (estoit *in* Fr 7, ostoit *in* Fr 1–6, 8).

OF A COMMONWEALE. 775

had done it. And so in the same proportion of iustice, the judge which doth iniurie, the priest which committeth sacrilege, the notarie or register which committeth forgerie, the goldsmith which coyneth false money, the guardian which rauisheth his pupill, the prince which breaketh his faith and league; and generally whosoeuer offendeth in his owne vocation, and in such things as whereof he is himselfe a keeper, ought to bee therefore the more grieuously punished than others: for that his offence is therein the more grieuous. And therefore *Metius* the Dictator of the Albans, was by the commaundement of *Tullus Hostilius*, with foure horses drawne in peeces, for hauing broken his faith with the Romans. And *Solon* hauing caused his lawes to be published, and sworne by all the Athenians, appointed the Areopagits to be the keepers and interpretors thereof; and if they should breake the same, to pay therefore a statue of gold of the weight of themselues. Now had *Aristotle* himselfe neuer so little a while bene a judge, or looked into the lawes of his countrey, he would neuer haue written, That the equal Arithmeticall Iustice were to be obserued and kept in the inflicting of punishments: but that in all things, and especially in matters of punishments, the Geometricall proportion of Iustice were much better and more tollerable; as neerer vnto the Harmonicall Iustice which we seeke after, being partaker of both. Neither by this Harmonicall proportion is more fauour shewed vnto the noble than vnto the base, howbeit that vnto many it seeme contrarie. For proofe whereof, let it be, that a rich man and a poore being guiltie of the selfe same crime, the rich man is in shew more grieuously fined than the poore: howbeit that in truth the one is not more heauily fined than the other, but both of them indifferently according to their wealth and abilitie. There is with vs a most auntient law extant, whereby the poore common persons which make resistance against the magistrat commaunding them to be apprehended, are fined at threescore shillings; but the noble man at a thousand and two hundred. And for that money is more plentie in one place than in another, and in this our age than in antient time, wise lawmakers haue bene constrained to chaunge their pecuniarie punishments or fines, according to the varietie of times & places. In the flourishing time of the Roman Commonweal, & namely vnder *Traian* the emperor (who is reported to haue extended the bounds of that great empire fartheft) he was by the law accounted a poore man, which was not worth fiftie * crownes, that is to say a crowne of gold. Which decision of the Romans, the Hebrewes in their Pandects following, haue forbidden all them that are so much worth to begge. The customes of Fraunce in many places, call him a poore man, who with two or three witnesses of his owne parish, hath sworne himselfe to be poore.

But when the lawes of the Twelue Tables were made, the pouertie of men was so great, as that he was accounted a right rich man, which was worth a pound of gold. And therefore the Decemuiri by those lawes set downe a fine of twentie fiue Asses, or small peeces of brasse, for him which should with his fist giue any man a blow vppon the face: which was an heauie penaltie (as the world then went) for that it was by Arithmeticall proportion indifferently exacted of all men alike. But after that mens wealth encreased, one *Neratius* a rich fellow (as the time then was) and most insolent withall, tooke a pleasure to giue such as he thought good, as he met them in the streets, a good and sound buffet or box; on the eare and so by and by commaunded a slaue, which carried a bagge full of such small coyne after him, to pay vnto him whome hee had so strucken twentie fiue of those small brasen peeces, the fine set downe in the xij Tables: which was the cause that the law was abrogated, and order taken, that from thenceforth euery man should esteeme the iniurie vnto himselfe done, yet with power still reserued vnto the magistrat, to do therein as should seeme vnto him reasonable.

Vuu iiij Whereby

He which offendeth in his owne vocation, or in such things as wherewith he is put in trust, to be therefore more seuerely punished than other offending in the same.

Harmonicall Iustice to be indeed vnto all men indifferent, howbeit that at the first shew it seeme more fauourable vnto some than vnto others.

Fines oftentimes to be changed, according vnto the varietie of times and places.

* A crowne was then as much worth as the Rose noble is now.

Who was by the auntient Roman lawes to be accounted a poore man.

The insolency of Neratius, the cause why the lawes of iniuries were changed in Rome.

D1 *For* a crowne of gold *read* a pound of gold (L). E4 box on the eare; and

776　　　　　　　　　　　　THE SIXT BOOKE

Whereby it was then plainely perceiued and knowne Arithmeticall proportion not to be good in the imposing of penalties and fines. So also by the auntient customes of the Normans, he that strucke a common person with his fist, was fined at a shilling; but he that strucke him with his open hand, was to pay the fine of fiue shillings: but were he a gentleman that had receiued such iniurie, he was not to redresse the same by law, but by force of armes and combat: whereby it oftentimes came to passe, that hee which had before receiued the iniurie, was also in the quarrel slaine, without any punishment therfore, and that by the sufferance of the law. The like we may say of the Athenian law, which condemned him in an hundred crownes fine, which should presume to cause a galliard to be daunced in the Theatre: which *Demades* the Orator well knowing, yet to make his playes which he gaue vnto the people more gratious, amongst the musitians brought in also vpon the stage a dauncing trull there to daunce; yet before she entred, paying the aforesaid fine of an hundred crownes by the law set downe, which was indeed nothing else but a mockerie of the law, and a cause for others also to tread both it and the rest vnder foot. Which inconueniences the Polonians to auoid (for that almost all the penalties of their lawes are fines in money) alwaies ioyne vnto their lawes these or like words, *Lex hæc quia pœnalis est annua esto*, This law for that it is penall let it be but for a yeare in force.

Demades at Athens wilfully transgresseth the law, and paieth the fine.

But beside these chaunges of penalties and fines, some others haue beene constrained to chaunge such pecuniarie penalties or fines into corporall, yea euen into capitall punishments also: and that especially when the countrey groweth rich, so that men begin to contemne the fines, or that the offence groweth too common: in which cases the Hebrew lawyers are of opinion, That the penalties of the lawes are to bee encreased, and punishment with rigour executed. And therefore the law of the Britons appointeth theeues to be hanged, yeelding therefore this reason, *Ne eorum augeatur multitudo*, Least the multitude of them should be encreased. An vniust law indeed, and the reason thereof foolish; and such a law as by the antiquitie of it selfe is almost growne out of vse, for that it hath no distinction either of place, or of the equalitie of the persons offending, or of the age, or of the sexe, or of the time, or of the felonie committed; but punisheth all felons alike. When as in all executions of punishments, the lighter offences are the more lightly to be punished, yea and oftentimes also pardoned: as only in respect of age, the indifferent and equall law would that men should in all iudgements pardon youth, or at leastwise more easily punish it. So ought the iudges also more fauourably to chastise women than men: either for that their passions are more vehement than men, or that for want of reason, discretion, and learning, they are lesse able to gouerne their affections: or for that they be more tender and daintie, and therefore haue the sharper feeling of punishment than men. Which beeing so, a man may deeme the law of the Venetians vniust, which for the first felonie committed, condemneth the woman to be whipt, and marked with an hoat yron; and after that her hand cut off: and for the second offence, to haue her nose and lips cut off: whereas the man by the same law, and for like fact, is to lose but one of his eyes and his hand. By which law women, contrarie vnto equitie, are more seuerely punished than men: & the means whereby to get their liuing being taken from them, they both haue more occasion to steale than before whilest they had their limmes. Wherefore better it were according to Arithmeticall Iustice (howbeit that in matters of penalties it be vniust) to punish them both alike: or else according to Geometrical Iustice, which commeth much neerer vnto the true Harmonicall Iustice, which hath regard in particular to all the circumstances concurring. But that law and judge is verie vniust, which more seuerely punisheth the tender and feeble, young folkes or women, the sickly or old, than the

Penalties & fines sometimes changed into corporall and capitall punishments, and why.

Why women are more fauourably to be punished than men.

The iniquitie of the Venetian law in the punishing of women.

strong

H4 Britons *i.e.* Bretons, people of Brittany
73 B2, 770 H5, 784 I10.　　I3 judges also

H8 For the equalitie *read* the qualitie (*la qualité*). Cf. Notes at F8, H10.

OF A COMMONWEALE. 777

A strong and lustie. And in briefe all lawes carrying with them penalties certaine, and such as it is not lawfull for the magistrat according to the exigence of the cause, to moderat or aggrauat, are vniust. Wherein euen the wisest and best experienced may well be deceiued, if they haue not this Harmonicall Iustice still before their eyes. For where is there in the world so great wisedome, so great iustice, such a number of learned lawyers, as in the court of parliament at Paris? who yet without any restriction or limitation at all, published a law against falsifiers and forgers, made by king *Francis* the first, whereby capitall punishment was appointed for forgerie, whether it were in ciuill or criminall causes, without distinction of forgers, judges, clearkes, notaries, souldiours, or plaine countrey men. Which law for all that by the wise conniuence of that court

All lawes carrying with them penalties certaine, which may not by the judge or magistrat be in some sort moderated or aggrauated, to be vniust.

B is since growne out of vse: howbeit that the penaltie thereunto annexed yet remaineth to terrifie forgers withall: whome for all that the court punisheth with arbitrarie punishment, according to discretion, and not according to the rigour of the law, in such sort as that scarcely one of fiftie is condemned to die. For why, the same court shortly after perceiued the intollerable inconueniences and absurdities which that law drew after it, punishing with death him that had falsified but the least scedule of an hundred shillings, as well as him that had falsified the decrees of the court, or the kings seale, or borne false witnesse to condemne the innocent; as also for a meere ciuill cause, where question were but of fiue shillings: and all without regard or difference of persons. Nei-

C ther is the law of Venice any better or vpright, which appointeth no lesse punishment for falsifying and forgerie, than the cutting out of the tongue: without any distinction of the manner of the forgerie, or respect of the degree, sexe, or age of the offendor, or other circumstances whatsoeuer. But the law of Milan sauoureth more of equitie and Harmonicall Iustice: for it willeth, That he which forgeth or falsifieth an act or beareth false witnesse in a matter which exceedeth not twentie crownes, shall for the first time be condemned in foure times the value, and three dayes shamefully to bee carried about with a paper myter vpon his head: and for the second time to haue his hand cut off: and for the third time to be burnt. But if the cause exceeded twentie crownes, and so vnto the summe of fiue hundred, that then he should for the first time haue his hand

D cut off, and for the second time be burnt. But if so be that the matter exceeded fiue hundred crownes, that then the judge for the first time might deale with him according to his discretion, but that for the second offence the forger should be burnt. Wherein both the Geometricall & Arithmeticall proportion of iustice are in some sort mixt, as in the measure and proportioning of the fine: but without any regard of sexe, age, or condition, which it beseemed a lawmaker especially to haue marked. The law of God (of all other lawes the best) commaundeth the man conuict of false witnesse bearing, to endure so much losse himselfe, as he would haue done hurt vnto the other: as if he would by his false witnesse take from another man an hundred crownes, hee should bee forced himselfe to pay the selfe same summe: or if hee went about by his false testimonie to

The false witnes, how he is by the law of God to be punished.

E take away another mans life, that he himselfelfe should therefore loose his owne life: as for the rest they were referred vnto the conscience of the judges. Neither is it enough for this equalitie of punishment to aunswere as did *Draco* the Athenian lawgiuer, who being asked, Why he appointed death as well for stealing of an apple, as for killing of ones father: aunswered, That he would haue appointed a more grieuous punishment for killing of a mans father, if he had knowne any punishment worse than death. But *Lycurgus* left all kind of punishment, yea and that concerned euery man else as well in publike as in priuat iudgements, vnto the discretion of the magistrats: whom he doubted not to excell in all fidelitie and integritie, so long as they should keepe his lawes and customes: but yet haply fearing that in restraining of the magistrats power vnto the

strait

A1 with them   D10 he himselfe should   E6 that concerned every man *i.e.* "that which concerned every man," his interest, compensation, or damages (cf. L)   Note at D5.

strait bonds of lawes and penalties, should so fall into such absurdities and difficulties of iudgements, as we haue before spoke of: and wherewith they are in Popular estates, but especially in Italie, much troubled. By the law of the Venetians hee that shall so strike any man, as that he shall draw blood of him, is therefore to pay twentie fiue pound: but if he kill him, he is therefore to be hanged. Which law if it might euery where take place, how many men should we find like vnto *Neratius*, who vppon such a price would soundly buffet and bastinado such as they liked not of, as they met them. But how much more wisely did the emperour *Adrian* in like case take order, appointing him that went about to kill a man, although indeed he killed him not, to bee therefore worthy of death: and yet that he which had indeed slaine a man, without any purpose so to haue done, should be therefore acquited. For that offences are to be weighed according to the will and purpose of the offendor, and not according to the euent of the fact: howbeit that the purpose and endeuor is more easily to be punished, than the effect and deed it selfe; and the conceit of a villanie lesse than the villanie it selfe done: wherein all the diuines with the lawyers agree. Howbeit that in truth hee more greeuously offendeth against almightie God, which persuadeth another man to do a villanie, than he which doth it: for that beside the wickednesse first by himselfe conceiued, he leaueth also the liuely impression thereof engrauen as it were in another mans hart: whereas he which of himselfe doth amisse, carried headlong with the force of lust or anger, seemeth scarcely to haue bene willing to haue done it: and hee which hath against her will enforced an honest woman, whome hee could not otherwise persuade, yet leaueth her soule and spirit pure and cleane. But judges doe one way punish and consider of offences, and Philosophers another: they punish such offences and transgressions onely as are sensibly to be seene, and which a man may as it were with his finger touch, and such as trouble the common rest and quiet: but these men (*viz*. the Philosophers) enter euen into the most secret thoughts & cogitations of mens minds: wherein Sir *Thomas Moore*, sometime Chauncellour of England, is also deceiued, who maketh the intent equall to the effect: and the will vnto the deed done.

The wise law of Adrian the emperour.

Offences how they are to be weighed and punished.

Iudges and Philosophers diuersly do consider offences.

But if an offence be not onely intended, but effected also, and so the effect ioyned vnto the intent, we must not in the punishing thereof vse Arithmeticall proportion of iustice: as in the law of Milan, hee that shall without the citie steale the value of a crowne or more, is therefore to be put to death; but if lesse, the punishment is left vnto the discretion of the judges: and yet for all that in this realme he is punished with death as a theefe which hath by the high way robbed any man, whether hee had money or none: as I haue indeed seene one hanged for taking but eighteene pence from a traueller by the high way. The Roman lawes commaund notable theeues and robbers to be hanged, and so left hanging vpon the gibbet: which then was accounted the most grieuous punishment: but they then by the word *Latro*, vnderstood him whom we cal an *Assasin*, or Murtherer, which killeth men vpon the high way: but as for him which but robbeth passengers, the law calleth him *Grassatorem*, and willeth him also to bee condemned to death, but yet not hanged as the murtherer. Which wee haue here the more precisely set downe, to note the errour of *Accursius* and some other the learned lawyers, who call him also *Latronem*, or a robber, whome the Latines call *Furem*, or a theefe; making them as it were all one: and hauing in part therein giuen occasion for men to punish theeues with more grieuous punishment than haply were meet and conuenient, *viz*. with death.

Arithmeticall Iustice not to be vsed in the punishing of offences

The vnreasonable law of the Venetians for the punishing of theft.

The like absurditie is seene almost in all the lawes of Italie: as in that of Venice concerning theft, which willeth to put out one of his eies which shal steale any thing worth aboue fiue pound, vnto ten; and from ten vnto twentie, to put out one of his eyes, and

to

I1–2 the value of a crowne (L) the value of half a crown (Fr)   Notes at I9, I10.

OF A COMMONWEALE.   779

to cut off one of his hands: and from twentie vnto thirtie to put out both his eyes, and from thirtie to fortie to loose his eies & an hand: but if he shall steale aboue the summe of fortie pounds, then to be punished with death. An vnreasonable law truly, not onely for the rigour and hardnesse thereof, and the confused manner of the persons so to be equally punished, but euen in this respect also, that he which hauing the meanes out of a great masse of gold, to steale a thousand pounds, and yet contenteth himselfe with fiftie, shall therefore be punished with death: and hee that breaketh an emptie chest, with an intent to haue taken away a great summe of money if he could, shall yet escape vnpunished. The same punishments almost are also set downe by the law of Parma. Yet hath it oftentimes seemed vnto me a thing right straunge, why some which vse so seuere punishment against theeues, yet punished murders but by fines in money. For we see plainely, that the paine of death is too cruell to reuenge a simple felonie, and yet not sufficient to restraine the same: and yet the punishment of him that doth both rob and kill, to be but like: in which doing he hath more suretie to commit the murther, as also more hope to conceale the same. So that where the punishment for theft and murder is alike, there it is more safetie to kill a man, than simply to rob or steale. And yet more straunge and absurd are the lawes of the Polonians, the Danes, the Swedens, and Moscouits, and especially the law of *Casimir* the Great, king of Polonia, which for the fine of thirtie crownes, acquiteth one gentleman that hath slaine another: and if he haue maimed him of an arme or of a legge, then to bee acquited for fifteene crownes. But if a base fellow shall kill a gentleman, the fine is double, and if he shall kill a base or common person, the fine is but ten crownes, without any other corporall punishment, although he had laine in wait to kill him. Which impunitie for the killing of men being suffered, or rather by law allowed, innumerable murders thereof ensued. Howbeit that afterwards the kingdome encreasing in wealth, the penaltie of the law was doubled in the raigne of *Sigismund* the first, and order taken, that the murderer beeing apprehended, should beside the fine be also kept prisoner in the common gaile for a yere and six weekes. But that which was in that law worst of all, and the head of all mischiefe, was, that after three yeares the offendor might prescribe against the murder by him committed, whatsoeuer it were: neither could the lord which had slaine his vassall farmer (whome they call *Kmeton*) be therefore either ciuilly or criminally called into question or sued. For a like edict or law made at Milan (at such time as the Torresans held that Seigneurie) whereby it was decreed, That a gentleman might for a certaine fine be acquited for the killing of a base or common person: the common people therwith enraged, rise vp all in a mutinie, & hauing driuen out the nobilitie possessed themselues of the Seigneurie. As for the author of the law *Napus Tarresan*, he by them cast in prison, there miserably died eaten vp with lice, and that worthily, for hauing therein so much contemned the law of God, which forbiddeth to haue pitie vpon the wilfull murderer, commaunding him to be drawne euen from his sacred alter and put to death: yet leauing vnto the discretion of the magistrat the manner of his execution, according to the greatnesse of the murder committed; to the end that the equalitie of capitall punishment common to all murderers by Arithmeticall proportion of iustice, should so by Geometricall proportion be moderated, hauing respect vnto the circumstances of the place, of the time, and of the persons, which are infinit. For men right well knowe, that he which wilfully killeth a man (as lying in wait for him) is more grieuously to be punished, than he which killeth a man in his rage and choler: and hee which killeth by night, more than he which killeth by day: and he which poysoneth a man, more than he which killeth him with the sword: and the murderer by the high way worse than those: as also he that shhall kill a man in a sacred place, more than in a prophane:

Equalitie of punishment for vnequall offences, the occasion to haue the greater offences committed.

An vnreasonable law for the punishing of murder.

Hainous offences to deserue more grieuous punishments.

B1 punishment   B5 (margin) have the   B6 safetie   C9 prescribe against the murder *i.e.* cease to be liable for it on account of lapse of time   D6 Napus Torresan   E9 that shall

prophane: and before his prince, more than in any other place: (which is the onely irremissible case, by the laws of Polonia) & he that shal kill the magistrat executing of his office, more than if he were a priuat man: and he that shall kill his father, more than he which shall kill the magistrat: and he which shall kill his prince, more than all the rest. Of which varietie of cases ariseth an incredible varietie of capitall punishments to bee vpon the offendors inflicted. The same we may say also of such persons as are still vnder the guard and protection of other men, of whome they cannot possibly be aware; as the pupill of his tutor, the wife of her husband, the sicke patient of his physitian; the guest of his hoast, betwixt all whome faith is much more required: in which cases the murderers are still more grieuously to be punished. As in like case the breakers of houses, and they which by ladders clime into houses by night, deserue to be more seuerely punished, than such as shall steale in, the doores standing wide open. And therefore in Tartarie and Moscouie the least theft of all is punished with death: for that there are but few townes and houses for them to keepe themselues and their goods in. And in the West Indies, before the comming of the Spaniards, the theefe was still aliue vpon a sharpe stake impaled, for whatsoeuer theft it was. For why, all their gardens and grounds are bounded about but with a thrid, beyond which to passe was accounted a great crime: and yet greater than that it was to breake the thrid; and that in secret also than openly and in euery mans sight. Howbeit that in other crimes, as whooredome, adulterie, incest, and such other like, the offences publikely committed, are more seuerely to be punished, than such as are in secret done: for that the euill example and scandall thereof, is worse than the offence it selfe. Wherein both the diuines and lawyers all agree.

Open offences to be openly punished.

All these circumstances, with a million of others like of diuers sorts, cannot all after one fashion be cut, or by the selfe same law be iudged, according to the vnequall equalitie of Arithmeticall Iustice: neither can they in speciall lawes and articles bee all comprehended, were the volume of the law neuer so great: so as is in Geometricall Iustice requisit, which leaueth all vnto the magistrats discretion, without any law at all. And yet for all that is this Geometricall Iustice lesse vniust than the other, which leaueth nothing vnto the power and authoritie of the judge, more than the examination of the fact, and the numbring of a sort of beanes, as at Athens: or of tables of diuers colours, with letters of absolution or condemnation set vpon them, as at Rome: or of certaine balles and lots, as at Venice: without any power to iudge at all. For why, it is the law, and not the judge, which appointeth the same punishment for all: of which equalitie of iustice ariseth the greatest iniustice, some such being condemned, as deserued much lesse than the penaltie of the law being equal vnto all: and some others againe acquited, which deserued ten times more: besides that, sometimes also diuers most vnlike crimes some great, some lesse, and some almost none at all, are vnder one law passed, and so with the selfe same paine punished. As by seuen articles of the Salique law, robbers, poisoners, adulterers, burners of houses, and such as haue slaine or sold a natural French man, or haue digged vp the bodie of the dead, are all condemned in the selfe same fine of two hundred shillings. Which law altogether ouerthroweth the foundation of iustice, grounded especially vpon that, That the punishment should still bee equall vnto the offence done. Which the auntients declared by this word, ἀντιπεπονθὸς, that is to say, The law of Retribution, or of equall punishment: which first written in the law of God, set downe in the lawes of *Solon*, transcript into the lawes of the Twelue Tables, commaunded by the Pythagorians, practised by the Greeke and Latine cities, and for the antiquitie thereof reuerent; is yet by *Fauorinus*, *Aristotle*, and many others, without iust cause impugned; they too grossely taking these words of the law, *A tooth for a tooth*,

Arithmeticall equalitie in the administration of iustice, and the punishing of offences, the cause of great iniustice.

That the punishment ought to be equall vnto the offence done.

F7 of whome they cannot possibly be aware *i.e.* "against whom they cannot possibly be on their guard"
G7, G8 thrid *i.e.* thread   K7 For commaunded *read* commended (*louee, laudata*).   Note at H6.

OF A COMMONWEALE.   781

A *a tooth, a hand for a hand, and an eye for an eye.* For who is so simple, as to think, that he which hath malitiously put out his eye which had but one, to suffer the like if but one eye be therefore taken from him also? Wherefore hee is to bee quite depriued of his sight, that is to say, requited with like; which cannot be, but by putting out of both his eyes: except the blind man may otherwise be satisfied. As was decreed by the people of Locris, at the request of one which had but one eye, which his enemie threatned to put out, vpon the penaltie therefore to loose another of his owne. Wherefore then to render like for like, is to make him also starke blind, who had made another man blind. So that to requite like with like, is indeed nothing els, but to punish offences with punishments aunswerable vnto them: that is to say, great offences with great punish-
B ments, meane with meane, and so little offences also lightly: which they also meant, when they said, *A hand for a hand, a tooth for a tooth, and an eye for an eye.* And so the auntient Hebrewes, the best interpretors of God his law, haue vnderstood it, expounded it, and also practised it: as is in their Pandects to be seene in the Title of Penalties. Yea *Rabi Kanan* denieth the law of like punishment to haue any where in the cities of the Hebrewes taken place, in such sort, as that he should haue an eye put out, which had put out another mans eye: but the estimation of the eye put out, was vsually by the discretion of the judges in money valued. For proofe whereof let it be, that before the law of like punishment, there was a * law, wherby it was ordained, That if two men
C fighting, one of them should hurt another, but not yet vnto death, hee which had done the hurt, should pay the Physitians for the healing thereof. But to what end should he so pay the Physitian, if he which did the hurt were in like sort to be himselfe wounded? It should also thereof folow more absurdly, that many delicat and tender persons, in receiuing of such wounds as he had giuen to others, should thereof themselues die and perish. Besides that also, he which had the harme done him, hauing lost his hand wherewith he should get his liuing, if the others hand were also to be for the same cut off; he so wanting his hand wherewith to get his liuing, might haply so starue. Wherfore such a literall exposition of the law of like punishment, by *Aristotle* and *Fauorin* deuised, is but vaine and deceitfull. But *Aristotle* who so much blameth the law of like punishment, is himselfe in such errours entangled as he sought to eschew. For he saith,
D That in punishing of him which hath deceiued his companion, or committed adultery, we are not to respect whether he were an honest man, or an euill liuer before or not; but to punish the offence with Arithmeticall equalitie, or Commutatiue Iustice, as hee tearmeth it. But what indifferent equalitie shall that be of the same punishment, if it shall by Arithmeticall proportion be inflicted vpon persons of qualitie and condition so farre vnlike? Or what Shoomaker is so ignorant or foolish, as to shape one fashioned shoo, or of the same last, to euery mans foot? Creditors also in time equall, but in the summe of their debt vnequall, are of the goods of their broken debtor to bee paid by proportion Geometricall: as if thirtie crownes bee made of the goods of the broken
E debtor; he of the two creditors to whome there is but an hundred crownes due, shall receiue ten crownes; whereas the other creditor to whome there is two hundred due, shall receiue twentie: who if they were by Arithmeticall proportion to be paid, should each of them receiue fifteene. And yet in this case question is but of a meere ciuill particular cause resting in exchaunge; which in the opinion of *Aristotle*, is alwaies by Arithmeticall proportion to be ordered: which is not onely in this case here propounded false, but euen in all other also, wherein question is of that which vnto euery man properly belongeth, as we shall forthwith declare. Yet where *Aristotle* saith in punishing of offences no regard ought to be had, whether the offendor were before good or bad: it sufficiently sheweth him to haue had no knowledge of the order and manner of

How the word of the law, A tooth for a tooth, a hand for a hand, and an eye for an eye, are to be vnderstood.

* *Exod. 21.*

Arithmeticall proportion of iustice not indifferent in punishing of persons of condition and qualitie farre vnequall.

Arithmetical proportion of iustice not to be admitted euen in meere ciuill causes.

Aristotle impugned for saying, no regard ought to be had, whether the offendor were before the offence committed, good or bad.

Xxx   iudge-

C4 *For* as he had given *read* as they had given (cf. L).   E5 (margin) Aristotle

iudgements, or of iudiciall proceedings. For why, nothing is more diligently enquired after by the judges, than what the former life of the partie accused hath bene. Neither is it any new matter, when as the Persians, long before *Aristotles* time, not only enquired after the whole liues of them which were accused (as yet they still doe) but if their good deserts were greater than their offences, they fully acquited them also: as *Xenophon* writeth. And for the same cause the theefe taken in the third theft, is almost euery where condemned to die, howbeit that the third theft be much lesse than the first: and so he also which hath the more often offended, is more seuerely to be punished than he which hath more seldome gone astray. Wherein *Aristotle* is againe deceiued, in that he deemeth a stolne thing ought by Arithmeticall proportion to bee made euen with particular interest of him from whome it was taken or stolne. Whereas the lawes of *Solon*, the lawes of the Twelue Tables, and the emperours by their lawes, condemne him which hath stolne any thing, to restore the double or the treble, yea and sometime foure fold the worth of the thing stolne, beside the perpetuall infamie thereof ensuing. Yea the law of God willeth, That for an oxe stolne, restitution should bee made fiue fold vnto him from whom he was so stolne: both for that a more profitable beast is not by God giuen vnto man, as also for the necessitie there is to leaue such beasts oft times in the field: where they roaming vp and downe, haue for their more assurance the greater penaltie set vpon them being stolne: and hereunto some other people haue ioyned corporall punishment, yea euen vnto the paine of death.

Arithmeticall Iustice to faile euen in meere ciuill causes.

And not to speake of criminall causes onely, but of meere ciuill causes also, one in the selfe same fact gaineth the cause, & in another place looseth the same: one hath interest for his debt, and another hath nothing: and amongst them which shall in the same case haue interest, some one shall pay ten times so much as another: which for that they bee matters common vnto all such as haue any experience in iudiciall causes, there need not many examples; one therefore shall suffice for the manifesting of the matter. A Lapidarie breaketh a diamond which he by couenant should haue enchafed in a ring; he is bound to pay the price of the stone be it neuer so great, yea although hee therein haue vsed no fraud or deceit, but euen for that onely that he tooke it vpon him to do it as a workeman: whereas yet had he bene a man of another condition or occupation, hee should not haue paid the price of the pretious stone so broken, except hee had before taken the daunger thereof vppon him, or by fraud or deceit broken the stone.

Harmonicall Iustice to haue place when question is but of priuat mens right and interest as well as when question is of penalties and fines.

Now all the lawes both auntient and new, with the common course and experience of iudgements, teach vs that Harmonicall proportion of iustice ought as well to take place when question is but of priuat mens right and interest, and so in pure ciuill causes, as well as when question is of penalties and fines: as also that Arithmeticall equalitie and proportion is therein most of all vniust. And therefore *Iustinian* the emperor publishing the law concerning vsurie, ordained, That the nobilitie should not take aboue fiue in the hundred, the marchants eight in the hundred, corporations and colledges ten, and the rest six in the hundred: and particularly that none should exact of the husbandman aboue fiue in the hundred. Which law let it seeme in *Aristotle* his iudgement vniust, yet doth it carrie a good shew of that Harmonicall Iustice which wee seeke after, tempered of Arithmeticall and Geometricall proportion: Arithmeticall equalitie being therein obserued amongst the noble men, who are all vnder one article comprised, the great, the meaner, and the least: the marchants in another both rich and poore: and the countrey men in another article, howbeit that they much differ one of them from another: and the rest of the subiects all in another article beeing of diuers qualities and conditions also: And then the Geometricall proportion shewing it selfe betwixt the nobilitie and the marchants, betwixt the marchants and the colledges, and

againe

againe a certaine of the other subiects compared among themselues, and with their superiours. And this proportion of Harmonicall Iustice is also in some sort kept, and yet cut somewhat short by the law of Orleans, established by *Charles* the ninth at the request of the people: whereby the debtor condemned for money too long detained, is bound to pay after eight in the hundred interest vnto marchants, and vnto other lesse; but vnto husbandmen, persons hired, and all sorts of labourers, the double of the money due: both the chiefe points of which law is now growne out of vse, howbeit that it was with the greatest consent of the courts published. For why, that which concerneth euery priuat mans right and interest, consisteth in matter of fact, & not in matter of law; as *Paulus* the lawyer most wisely aunswered, which his one reason hath euen by the root ouerthrowne all the long discourses of all the interpretors, so diuers and so vnlike themselues, concerning euery priuat mans right and interest: all which *Iustinian* the emperour had thought himselfe to haue beene able to haue comprehended vnder one law. And therefore that which toucheth euery priuat mans right and interest how farre it concerneth him, is by our lawes wisely left vnto the discretion of the judges, for that it can no more certainly by positiue law be defined or set downe, than can the great Ocean sea into a small chanell be enclosed or shut vp. But yet the inequalitie is much greater in the law of Venice, which forbiddeth to take interest either in commodities or in money, aboue six in the hundred: which although it be a thing tollerable, and is called of the Latines *Vsura ciuilis*, or, Ciuill interest: yet is that law not so long agoe made, now againe growne out of vse, and not either publikely or priuatly kept: for that it in euery respect containing Arithmeticall equalitie, regardeth not the most vnlike condition and qualitie of persons.

That which toucheth euery priuat mans right & how farre it concerneth him, is not possible to be set downe in law, but better to be left vnto the discretion of the judge.

And howbeit that in the particular contracts and conuentions, and exchaunge of things, that Arithmeticall proportion of equalitie be best to be liked; yet is it not euen therein alwayes obserued and kept, the very countrey men and labourers, by a certaine naturall reason well deeming, that they ought oftentimes to take lesse for their hier of the poore than of the rich, howbeit that they take as great paines for the one as for the other. So the Surgeon which taketh of the rich man fiue hundred crownes to cut him of the stone, haply taketh of the poore porter no more but fiue: and yet for all that in effect taketh ten times more of the poore man than of the rich: For the rich man being worth fiftie thousand crownes, so payeth but the hundred part of his goods, whereas the poore man being but worth fiftie crownes, paieth fiue, the tenth part of his substance. Whereas if we should exactly keepe the Geometricall or Arithmeticall proportion alone, the patient should die of the stone, and the Surgion for lacke of worke starue: whereas now by keeping the Harmonicall mediocritie it goeth well with them both, the poore man cured with the rich, and the Surgion so gaining wealth, and the other their health. After which proportion euen the judges themselues haue vsed to esteeme their paines, and therefore to demaund their honourable fees: which we see to haue alwayes bene lawfull for them to doe, so that therein they exceed not measure. As I remember it to haue happened vnto a certaine Prouost of Paris, whose name I will easily passe ouer, who for adiudging the lawful possession of a litigious benefice, hauing for his owne fees set downe thirtie crownes, whereas his duetie was but three, and appeale therefore by the partie grieued made vnto the higher court, was thither sent for; where he being by *Ranconet* President of the court hardly charged for the wrong by him done: aunswered, That it was a good fat benefice that he had giuen sentence for: and that forasmuch as he did many such things for poore men without any fee at all, that it was but right and reason that the richer when they came should make him an amends therefore in paying of him deeper fees. Whereunto the President pleasantly said,

Arithmetical proportion of justice not alwayes obserued euen in particular contracts and conuentions, wherein it is yet best of all to be liked.

Harmonicall proportion to be vsed by the iudges euen in taking of their fees.

said, Him in so doing to serue them as his Taylor did him, who tooke of him twice as much for the making of him a veluet gowne, as he did for making of him one of cloth. So the law of Milan, which appointeth, That the judge may for his fee take the hundred part of the value of the suit, so that hee exceed not two hundred crownes, would seeme vnto *Ranconet* vniust: euery corrupt judge so without any proportion at all, extorting from all men, what he saw good. For that such the suit may be for a slight matter but of ten crowns, as that therein oftentimes more paines is to be taken by the judge than in a suit of ten thousand crownes: the marchant so still gaining by the rich, what he looseth by the poore.

Arithmetical proportion most necessarie to be obserued in the whole gouernment of the Commonweale.

Wherefore both in making of lawes, and in deciding of causes, and in the whole gouernment of the Commonweale, we must still so much as possible is, obserue and keepe that Harmonicall proportion, if we will at all maintaine equitie & iustice: whereas otherwise it will be right hard for vs in the administration of iustice, not to doe great wrong. As doth the law of inheritance, which adiudgeth all vnto the eldest, whether he be noble or base; of auntient time vsed by *Lycurgus* in the inheritances of the Lacedemonians, and with vs in the countrey of Caux. Lesse vniust, and yet vniust too, is the law which giueth all the noble mans inheritance vnto his eldest son; and an annuitie of the third or of the fift part vnto the younger brethren, for them to haue during their liues as they doe at Amboise and Aniou; and yet dealing therein more fauourably with the women, who hold that vnto themselues in proprietie, which the yonger brethren haue but for tearme of life. Neither is the custome of the Germans much lesse vniust, who hauing abrogated the old law, whereof *Tacitus* maketh mention, diuide the inheritance equally amongst their sonnes, making the eldest and the youngest both equall in the succession of their inheritance, according vnto Arithmeticall proportion, without any difference of persons at all. But how much more vprightly and

Harmonical proportion of iustice euen by the law of God obserued in the conferring of inheritance, & inflicting of punishments.

iustly hath the law of God dealt herein? which following the Harmonicall proportion of iustice, giueth onely vnto the sonnes the land, and vnto the daughters part of the mouables, or money to marry them with; to the end the houses should not by them be dismembred: and amongst the males allotteth two parts vnto the eldest, and to the rest euerie one of them a part: and the father dying without heires male, the same law commaundeth the women to diuide the inheritance indifferently amongst them, and yet to marrie with the next of their house or tribe, that the land might not bee carried out of their stocke and kindred. Wherein Geometricall proportion is to be seene betwixt the eldest and the rest, as also betwixt the males and the females: and Arithmeticall equalitie betwixt the younger brethren, as amongst the daughters also. So when it is said by the law of God, That he which hath deserued to bee chastised or beaten, shall be punished according to the fault by him committed; yet is it by the same law forbidden to giue him aboue fortie stripes. Which law is made according to Harmonicall iustice: For why, it is left vnto the discretion of the judge, after such a proportion, to iudge vnto fortie stripes, according vnto the equalitie of the persons and of the offences committed: Wherein the Arithmeticall equalitie is also seene, in that it is forbidden the magistrat to exceed fortie stripes, the certain number by the law appointed. Wherin he that hath the more offended, and yet hath not deserued death, is no more punished in this respect of fortie stripes, than he which hath lesse offended. Whereof the law yeeldeth this reason, least the partie condemned, lamed with many stripes, should so become vnprofitable both vnto himselfe and the Commonweale. For that it might haue bene obiected, That he which more grieuously offended, was the more grieuously also to haue bene punished, euen aboue the said number of fortie stripes: howbeit that indeed it is better to stay within a measure, than through too much seueritie to do any

---

F10(margin) *For* Arithmetical *read* Harmonical (cf. G2).   G9 their lives, as   I10 *For* the equalitie of the persons *read* the qualitie of the persons (cf. 73 B2, 770 H5, 776 H8).

Notes at F5, G9, H1, I5.

any thing vniuſtly, which vnto vs is a certaine argument drawne from the law of God, That the true iuſtice, and the faireſt gouernment, is that which is by Harmonicall proportion maintained.

And albeit that the Popular eſtate more willingly embraceth the equall lawes and Arithmeticall Iuſtice; and the Ariſtocratike eſtate contrariwiſe loueth better the Geometricall proportion of iuſtice: yet ſo it is, that both the one and the other are for the preſeruation of themſelues conſtrained to intermingle with themſelues the Harmonicall proportion. Whereas otherwiſe the Ariſtocraticall Seignorie excluding the common people farre from al eſtates, offices, and dignities, not making them in any ſort partakers of the ſpoyles of their enemies, nor of the countries conquered from them; it cannot be that the eſtate can ſo long ſtand, but that the common people beeing neuer ſo little moued, or neuer ſo ſmall occaſion preſented, ſhall reuolt, and ſo chaunge the eſtate, as I haue by many examples here before declared. And therefore the Venetian Seignorie, which is the moſt true Ariſtocratie (if euer there were any) gouerneth it ſelfe Ariſtocratically, beſtowing the great honours, dignities, beneficies, and magiſtracies, vpon the Venetian gentlemen; and the meaner offices which haue no power belonging vnto them, vpon the common people: following therein the Geometricall proportion of the great to the great, and of the little to the little. And yet to content the common people, the Seignorie hath left vnto them the eſtate of the Chaunceilour, which is one of the moſt worthy and moſt honourable places in the citie, and perpetuall alſo: and more than that, the offices of the Secretaries of the eſtate alſo, which are places verie honourable. Yea moreouer an iniurie done by a Venetian gentleman vnto the leaſt inhabitant of the citie, is right ſeuerely corrected and puniſhed: and ſo a great ſweetneſſe and libertie of life giuen vnto all, which ſauoureth more of popular libertie than of Ariſtocraticall gouernment. And that more is, the creation of their magiſtrats is made part by choyce, and part by lot: the one proper vnto the the Ariſtocratique gouernment, and the other vnto the Popular eſtate: ſo that a man may well ſay, that the eſtate of that Seignorie is pure and ſimply Ariſtocratique, and yet ſomewhat gouerned by Proportion Harmonicall, which hath made this Commonweale ſo faire and flouriſhing.

Now we haue oftentimes ſaid, and muſt yet againe ſay (for that many haue vppon this rocke ſuffered ſhipwracke) that the eſtate of a Commonweale may oftentimes be the ſame with the gouernment thereof, but yet more often quite different from the ſame. For the eſtate may be Popular, and yet the gouernment Ariſtocraticall: as in Rome after the kings were driuen out (wee ſaid) the eſtate of that Commonweale to haue bene Popular, for that then all the ſoueraigne rights were in the power of the whole people in generall; and yet the manner of the gouernment of that citie and Commonweale to haue bene from the Popular gouernment moſt farre different. For that the Senators alone enioyed the great beneficies, honours, dignities, and places of commaund: all the wayes and entrances thereunto being by the nobilitie holden faſt ſtopt vp againſt the comminaltie, yea and that ſo ſtraitly, as that it was not lawfull or permitted for any of the common ſort to marrie with any of the nobilitie; either for any noble woman to marrie but with ſome one of the nobilitie, but the noble ſtill marrying with the noble, & the baſe with ſuch as themſelues were: and the chiefe and principall voyces which were giuen in their greateſt aſſemblies of eſtate, and moſt regarded, were ſtill taken by their wealth and yeares. So that the eſtate being then Popular, and the manner of the gouernment Ariſtocraticall, according to Geometricall proportion, the people oftentimes reuolted from the nobilitie: neither was the eſtate euer quiet from ciuill tumults and ſeditions, vntill that the common people had by little and little

The Ariſtocratique and Popular eſtates, not to be maintained by Geometricall or Arithmeticall iuſtice, without a mixture of Harmonicall iuſtice alſo.

The eſtate of Venice Ariſtocratique, and the gouernment for moſt part Harmonicall.

That the eſtate of a Commonweale may be of one ſort, and yet the maner of gouernment of another.

got

got to be partakers also in the greatest benefices, honours, offices, and places of commaund, that were in the Commonweale: and that it was permitted them also to allie themselues in marriage with the nobilitie, as also to haue their voyces as well as they. And so long as this Harmonical gouernment (that is to say intermingled with the Aristocratique and Popular estate) continued, the Senat yet bearing the greater sway, so long that Commonweale flourished both in armes and lawes; but after that the gouernment (through the ambition of the Tribunes) became altogether Popular, and as the heauier weight in a ballance ouerweighed the lighter, all then went to wracke: no otherwise than as when the sweet harmonie of musicke being dissolued, and the harmonicall numbers altered into numbers of proportion altogether equall and like, therof followeth a most great vnpleasant and foule discord: the like whereof there raised amongst the citisens neuer ceased, vntill that the estate was quite thereby chaunged, and indeed vtterly ouerthrowne. So may wee also iudge of all other Commonweales; neither haue wee thereof any better example than of the popular estates of the Swissers, which the more that they are popularly gouerned, the harder they are to be maintained, as the mountayne Cantons, and the Grisons: whereas the Cantons of Berne, Basil, and Zuricke, which are gouerned more Aristocratically, and yet hold the Harmonicall meane betwixt the Aristocratike & Popular gouernment, are a great deale the more pleasing, and more tractable, and more assured in greatnes, power, arms and lawes.

The Royall estate Harmonically gouerned, to be the fairest, the happiest, and most perfect.

Now as the Aristocraticall estate founded vppon Geometricall proportion, and gouerned also aristocratically, giueth vnto the nobilitie and richer sort the estates and honours: and the Popular estate contrariewise grounded vppon Arithmeticall proportion, and gouerned popularly, equally deuideth the monies, spoyles, conquests, offices, honours, and preferments vnto all alike, without any difference or respect of the great or of the little, of the noble or of the base and common person: So the royall estate also by a necessarie consequence framed vnto the harmonicall proportion, if it be royally ordered and gouerned, that is to say, Harmonically; there is no doubt but that of all other estates it is the fayrest, the happiest, and most perfect. But here I speake not of a lordly monarchie, where the Monarch, though a naturall prince borne, holdeth all his subiects vnderfoot as slaues, disposing of their goods as of his owne: and yet much lesse of a tyrannicall monarchie, where the Monarch being no naturall Lord, abuseth neuerthelesse the subiects and their goods at his pleasure, as if they were his verie slaues; and yet worse also when he maketh them slaues vnto his owne cruelties. But my speech and meaning is of a lawfull King, whether he be so by election, for his vertue and religion, by voyce chosen, so as was *Numa*; or by diuine lot, as was *Saul*; or that he haue by strong hand and force of armes, as a conquerour got his kingdome, as haue many; or that hee haue it by a lawfull and orderly succession, as haue all (except some few) who with no lesse loue and care fauoureth and defendeth his subiects, than if they were his owne children. And yet such a King may neuerthelesse if he will, gouerne his kingdome popularly and by equall Arithmeticall proportion, calling all his subiects indifferently without respect of persons vnto all honours and preferments whatsoeuer, without making choyce of their deserts or sufficiencie, whether it be that they be chosen by lot or by order one of them after another: howbeit that there bee few or rather no such monarchies indeed. So the King may also gouerne his estate or kingdome Aristocratically, bestowing the honorable estates and charges therein with the distribution of punishments and rewards by Geometricall proportion, making still choice of the nobilitie of some, and of the riches of others, still reiecting the base poorer sort, and yet without any regard had vnto the deserts or vertues of them whom hee

A Royall estate, and yet gouerned Popularly and according to Arithmeticall proportion.

K7 punishments   Note at H2.

he so preferred; but onely vnto him that is best monyed or most noble. Both which manner of gouernments, howbeit that they bee euill and blameworthy, yet is this Aristocratique and Geometricall proportion of gouernment much more tollerable and more sure, than is that popular and turbulent gouernment, scarcely any where to bee found, as neerer approching vnto the sweet Harmonicall gouernment. For it may be, that the king to assure his estate against the insurrection of the base common people, may haue need to strengthen himselfe with the nobilitie, which come neerer vnto his qualitie and condition, than doth the base artificers and common sort of people, vnto whom he cannot descend, neither with them wel haue any societie at all, if he will in any good sort maintaine the maiestie of his royal estate and soueraigntie, as it seemeth he must of necessitie do, if he shall make them partakers of the most honourable charges of his estate and kingdome. But such an Aristocratique kind of gouernment is also euill and dangerous, not vnto the common peaple only, but euen vnto the nobilitie & prince also : who may so stil stand in feare of the discontented vulgar sort, which is alwayes farre in number moe than is the nobilitie or the rich : and hauing got some seditious leader, and so taking vp of armes, becommeth the stronger part, and so sometimes reuolting from their prince, driueth out the nobilitie, and fortifie themselues against their princes power: as it happened among the Swissers, and in other auntient Commonweales by vs before noted. The reason whereof is euident, for that the common people is not bound by any good accord either with the prince, or with the nobilitie, no more than these three numbers 4, 6, 7: where the first maketh good accord with the second, that is to say, a fift: but the third maketh a discord, the most irkesome and vnpleasant that may bee, marring wholly the sweet consent of the two first, for that it hath not any Harmonicall proportion either vnto the first or vnto the second, neither vnto both together.

A Royall estate gouerned Aristocratically, and according to Geometricall proportion.

But it may be, and commonly so is, that the prince giueth all the greatest honours and preferments vnto the nobilitie and great lords, and vnto the meaner and baser sort of the people the lesser and meaner offices onely; as to be clearkes, sergeants, notaries, pettie receiuers, and such other meane officers of townes, or of some small iurisdictions. Wherein he shall so keepe the Geometricall proportion, and Aristocraticall gouernment. Which manner of gouernment for all that is yet faultie, howbeit that it be more tollerable than the former Popular Arithmeticall gouernment, as hauing in it some equall and semblable proportion: For as the office of the Constable is proper vnto a great Lord, so is also the office of a Sergeant vnto a poore base fellow. But forasmuch as there is no sociable bond betwixt the prince and the porter; so also is there not any similitude betwixt the office of the Great Constable and of a Sergeant: no more than there is amongst these foure numbers disposed by proportion Geometricall disiunct, 3, 6, 5, 10: where the two first haue the same reason that the two last haue, and the reason of the first vnto third, is that of the second vnto the fourth: yet the reason of the second vnto the third is discordant and different from the others, and so disioyneth the extreames, which so maketh an absurd and foolish discord. And so also are the orders of citisens and subiects, disioyned one of them from another, so that no fast or sure band can bee found amongst them. For that the nobilitie thinketh it an indignitie for them to bee busied with the small offices of the comminaltie: and the common people againe take it in euill part themselues to be excluded from the greatest honours of the nobilitie. As in Rome it was not otherwise lawfull for any of the nobility, whom they called *Patricij*, to sue for the Tribuneship, but that first he must renounce his nobilitie, & become a commoner: for as then the Consulship belonged

Geometrical proportion in distributing of offices, not good.

Xxx iiij onely

onely vnto the nobilie, and the Tribuneship vnto the comminaltie. Which power once granted vnto the people, they forthwith let their weapons fal, and all the sedition & tumults before common betwixt them and the nobilitie ceased: For why, the common sort thought themselues now equall with the best, wherin the welfare of that citie consisted: whereas otherwise the force of the furious multitude could by no violence haue bin withstood. For what the proportiō was of the Consulship vnto the Tribuneship, the same the proportion was of one of the nobilitie vnto a commoner: & againe, the same respect was of a noble man vnto the Consulship, that was of a commoner vnto the Tribuneship, in Geometricall similitude. But forasmuch as it was not lawfull neither for a noble man to obtaine the Tribuneship, neither for a commoner to enioy the Consulship, the people was disioyned from the nobilitie, and a perpetuall discord betwixt the Consuls and the Tribunes still troubled the citie: in such sort, as in these numbers thus placed is to be seene, 2, 4, 9, 18: wherein are found two eights by Geometricall proportion disiunct, and which yet mixed together make the most hard discord that is possible, by reason of the disproportion which is betwixt 4 and 9, which is intollerable, and marreth all the harmonie. So was there also almost a perpetuall discord betwixt the nobilitie & the people, vntill that the Consulship, the Censorship, the Pretorship, and the chiefe Benefices, excepting some few, were communicated vnto the people also. Whereas might it with the same moderation haue beene lawfull for the nobilitie to haue obtained the Tribuneship also, yet so as that the number of the commoners in that societie of the Tribunes might yet still haue bene the greater, and the nobles not enforced to renouce their nobilitie: no doubt but that the estate so Harmonically gouerned had bene much the more assured, better ordered, and of much longer continuance than it was, by reason of the sweet agreement of the citisens among themselues, and that Harmonicall mixture of the offices and places of authoritie and commaund in the estate and Commonweale: as in these foure numbers by Harmonicall proportion conioyned, is plainely to be seene, 4, 6, 8, 12: where the proportion of the first number vnto the second, and of the third vnto the fourth, is a *Diapente*, or a fift: and againe the proportion of the first vnto the third, and of the second vnto the fourth, is a *Diapason*, or an eight: and the proportion of the second vnto the third, a *Diatessaron*, or a fourth: which with a continuall proportion ioyning the first with the last, and the middle to both, and so indeed all to all, bringeth forth a most sweet & pleasant harmonie. But it was so farre off, that gentlemen of auntient houses were in Rome receiued into the Tribuneship (if they first renounced not their nobilitie, and caused themselues to be adopted by some base commoner) as it was for the base commoners to aspire vnto the Consulship: which they neuer did, except they had before obtained the greatest honours of the field, as did *Marius*; or else by their eloquence, as did *Cicero*; or by both together, as did *Cato* the Censor. Which yet was a matter of such difficultie, as that *Cicero* boasteth of himselfe vnto the people, That hee was the first new man (now they then called him a new man, who the first of his house and familie had obtained honours) who of them of his ranke had obtained to be Consull: and that the people vnder his conduct had cut in sunder and for euer after laid open for vertue that honourable place, which the nobilitie had before with strong garrisons holden, and by all meanes shut vp. So that it ought not to seeme strange if the Commonweale were then troubled with the seditions of the people, when as in such a multitude of the common sort, so few of them euen in *Cicero* his time aspired vnto those so great honours, the nobilitie of great and auntient houses commonly still enioying of them.

Wherefore it becommeth a good gouernor in a Popular or Aristocratique estate, and especially a wise king in his kingdome, to vse Harmonicall proportion in the gouernment

The reasons why the Consuls and Tribunes were alwayes at discord in Rome.

The Royal estate gouerned Harmonically, the fairest and most perfect.

H2 renounce   K6 *For* aspired vnto *perhaps read* attained vnto (*pervenirent* in L). K9–10 government
Notes at I9, K4, K6.

uernment thereof, sweetly intermingling the nobilitie with the comminaltie, the rich with the poore; & yet neuerthelesse with such discretion, as that the nobilitie still haue a certaine preheminence aboue the base comminaltie. For why, it is good reason that the gentleman excelling in deeds of armes and martiall prowesse, or in the knowledge of the law, as wel as the base common person, should in the administration of iustice, or in the mannaging of the wars, be preferred before him. As also that the rich in all other respects equall vnto the poore, should be preferred vnto such places and estates as haue more honour than profit: and the poore man contrariwise to enioy those offices and roomes which haue more profit than honour: both of them so resting reasonably contented, he which is rich enough seeking but after honour, and the poore man after his profit. For which cause and consideration, the wise Roman Proconsull *Titus Flaminius* taking order for the Thessalian Commonweale, left the gouernment and soueraigntie of the townes and cities by him conquered, vnto them of the richer sort and of best abilitie: wisely deeming, that they would be more carefull for the preseruation and keeping of them, than would the poore, who hauing not much to loose, had no great interest therein. Now if two or three magistrats were to bee chosen, it were better to ioyne a noble man with a commoner, a rich man with a poore, a young man with an old: than two noblemen, or two rich men, or two poore men, or two young men together; who oftentimes fall out into quarrels betwixt themselues, and so hinder one another in their charges: as commonly it happeneth betwixt equals. Besides that, of such a coniunction of magistrats of diuers state and condition (as wee now speake of) should arise this great profit, That euery one of such magistrats would seeke to maintaine the prerogatiue & right of them of their owne estate and such as themselues were: As in our soueraigne courts, and in other corporations and societies also, by our customes composed of men of all sorts, we see iustice and right to bee commonly better, and more vprightly vnto euery man administred, than if they wholly consisted of noble men, or of commoners, or of clergie men, or of any one estate alone.

Iustice better administred by magistrats of diuers sort & condition, than by men all of one estate and degree.

But now in ciuill societies there is no meane better to bind and combine the little ones with the great, the base with the noble, the poore with the rich, than by communicating of the offices, estates, dignities, and preferments, vnto all men, as well the base as the noble, according vnto euery mans vertues and deserts, as wee haue before declared. Which deserts both now are & euer were of most diuers sort & condition: so that he which would stil giue the honorable charges and preferments of the estate vnto vertuous and religious men onely, should vtterly ouerthrow the whole Commonweale: for that such vertuous and deuout men are alwayes in number much fewer than the euill and wicked, by whome they might easily be ouercome and thrust out of their gouernment. Whereas in coupling the poore vertuous men (as I haue said) sometime with the noble, and sometime with the rich, howbeit that they were deuoid of vertue; yet so neuerthelesse they should feele themselues honoured, in being so ioined with the vertuous, mounted vnto honourable place. In which doing all the nobilitie shall on the one side reioyce to see euen bare nobilitie rspected, and a place for it left in the Commonweale, together with men excelling in vertue and knowledge: and all the baser sort of the common people on the other side rauished with an incredible pleasure to feele themselues all honoured, as indeed they are, when they shall see a poore Physitians sonne Chauncellour of a great kingdome; or a poore souldior to become at length Great Constable: as was seene in the person of *Michael D' l' Hospitall*, and *Bertrand Guescheling*: who both of them, with many others, for their noble vertues were worthily exalted euen vnto the highest degrees of honours. But all the subiects grieue and take it in euill part, when as men neither for the honour of their house, nor for any their

Diuers sorts of deserts, and that vertuous men onely are not to be preferred vnto the honourable places and charges of the Commonweale

---

B3–4 of best abilitie *i.e.* of greatest wealth (cf. Fr and L)   D4 utterly   E1 respected
Notes at A6, D10.

790　　　　　　　　　The Sixt Booke

Vnworthy persons not alwayes to be excluded from certaine offices and places of commaund in the Commonweale.

their vertues noble, but rather for their loose and lewd liues infamous, shall be placed in the highest degree of honour and command: not for that I thinke it necessarie the vnworthy citisens or subiects to be altogether kept from all offices & places of command (a thing which can in no wise be) but that euen they such vnworthy persons may bee sometimes capable also of certaine offices; prouided alwayes that they bee in number but few, that their ignorance or wickednesse may not take any great effect in the estate wherein they are. For we must not onely giue the purse vnto the trustiest, armes vnto the most valiant, iudgement vnto the most vpright, censure vnto the most entire, labor vnto the strongest, gouernment vnto wisest, priesthood vnto the deuoutest, as Geometricall Iustice requireth (howbeit that it were impossible so to doe, for the scarcetie of good and vertuous men:) but we must also, to make an harmonie of one of them with another, mingle them which haue wherewith in some sort to supply that which wanteth in the other. For otherwise there shall be no more harmonie than if one should separat the concords of musique which are in themselues good, but yet would make no good consent if they were not bound together: for that the default of the one is supplied by the other. In which doing, the wise prince shall set his subiects in a most sweet quiet, bound together with an indissoluble bond one of them vnto another, together with himselfe, and the Commonweale. As is in the foure first numbers to bee seene: which God hath in Harmonicall proportion disposed to show vnto vs, that the Royal estate is Harmonicall, and also to be Harmonically gouerned. For two to three maketh a fift; three to foure, a fourth; two to foure, an eight: and againe afterwards, one to two, maketh an eight; one to three, a twelft, holding the fist and the eight; & one to foure, a double eight, or *Diapason*: which containeth the whole ground and compasse of all tunes and concords of musicke, beyond which he which will passe vnto fiue, shall in so doing marre the harmonie, and make an intollerable discord. So may one say of a point to a line, as also of the plaine superficies, and of the solid bodie also of any thing. Now the soueraigne prince is exalted aboue all his subiects, and exempt out of the ranke of them: whose maiestie suffereth no more diuision than doth the vnitie it selfe, which is not set nor acccounted among the numbers, howbeit that they all from it take both their force and power. But the three estates stand orderly disposed as they are, and as they alwayes haue yet beene in euery well ordered Commonweale, viz. the Ecclesiasticall order first for the dignitie which it beareth: & the prerogatiue of the ministerie and function thereof towards God, being yet composed both of noble and of base. Then after them follow the Martiall men, in whose protection all the rest of the subiects in some sort rest: which order and estate is also composed both of the noble and vnnoble. And in the third and last, are set the common people of all sorts and vocations, as schollers, marchants, artificers, and labourers: euerie one of which estates hauing part and interest into the offices and honourable charges of the Commonweale, with great respect and regard still to bee had vnto the merits and deserts, as also vnto the qualitie of the persons, there may therof be formed a pleasant harmonie of all the subiects among themselues; as also of them altogether with their soueraigne prince. Which is also declared, and in some sort figured euen in the nature of man himselfe, being the verie true image of a well ordered Commonweale: and that not in his bodie onely, which still hath but one head, and all the rest of the members aptly fitted thereunto; but euen in his mind also, wherein Vnderstanding holdeth the chiefe place, Reason the next, the Angrie Power desirous of reuenge, the third,

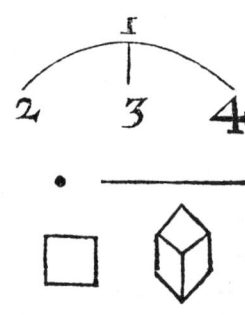

The order of the three estates in a well ordered Commonweale.

The well ordered Commonweale in some sort figured euen in the nature of man himselfe.

Of A Commonvveale. 791

A third, and brutish lust and desire the last. Whereof the mind or vnderstanding like vnto the vnitie in numbers indiuisible, pure, and simple, is of it selfe free from all concretion, and from all the other faculties of the soule apart separated and diuided: the angry power with desire of reuenge resting in the heart, representeth the souldiors and other martiall men: and sensuall lust and desire resting in the liuer vnder the midriffe, betokeneth the common people. And as from the liuer (the fountaine of bloud) the other members are all nourished, so husbandmen, marchants, and artificers doe giue vnto the rest of the subiects nourishment. And as many men for lacke of vnderstanding liue like beast, smoued with that only which is present and before them, without mounting any higher vnto the contemplation of things intellectuall and diuine, whom the sa-

B cred scriptures call also beasts: euen so also the Aristocratique and popular Commonweales without vnderstanding, that is to say, without a prince, are in some sort able to maintaine and defend themselues, though not long: being indeed about to become much more happie if they had a soueraigne prince, which with his authoritie and power might (as doth the vnderstanding) reconcile all the parts, and so vnite and bind them fast in happinesse together: for why no gouernment is more happie or blessed, than where the reasonable soule of man is gouerned by wisedome, anger and desire of reuenge by true valour, lust by temperance; and that vnderstanding bearing the rule, and as it were holding the reines, guideth the chariot, whereafter all the rest follow whether soeuer he will lead them: for so all honestie, all the lustre of vertue and dutie

C shall euery where flourish. But when the power and commaund of vnderstanding beaten downe and quite ouerthrowne, anger as a mutinous and vnruly souldior, and intemperat lust as a turbulent and seditious people, shall take vpon them the gouernement, and so inuading the state, shake wisedome and vnderstanding, and thrust it out of place: euery Commonweale must needs euen like the powers of the soule and mind needs so fall into all manner of reproch and filthinesse of vices. So that nothing is more like vnto a well gouerned Commonweale, than that most faire and fit comparison of the soule and the powers thereof, there being therein so established a most Harmonicall proportion of iustice, which giueth to euerie part of the soule that which vnto it of right belongeth. The like whereof we may say also of the three estates of a

D Commonweale, guided by Wisedome, Fortitude, & Temperance: which three morall vertues vnited together, and with their king, that is to say, the intellectuall and contemplatiue vertue, there is thereby established a most faire and Harmonicall forme of a Commonweale. For that as of vnitie dependeth the vnion of all numbers, which haue no power but from it: so also is one soueraigne prince in euerie Commonweale necessarie, from the power of whome all others orderly depend. But as there cannot bee good musicke wherein there is not some discord, which must of necessitie be intermingled to giue the better grace vnto the Harmonie (which the good Musitian doth, to make the consent of the fourth, the fift, and the eight, the more pleasing and tunable, some discord running before which may make the consent much more sweet vnto the

E eare; as do also cunning cookes, who to giue the better tast vnto their good meates, serue in therewith certaine dishes of sharpe and vnsauerie sauces; and as the cunning painter, to grace his picture, and to giue a better show vnto his brighter colours, still shadoweth the same with blacke, or some other darke colour (for that the nature of all things in the world is such, as to loose their grace, if they tast not sometime of disgrace; and that pleasure alwayes continuing becommeth vnsauorie, daungerous and vnpleasant): So also is it necessarie that there should be some fooles amongst wise men, some vnworthy of their charge amongst men of great experience, and some euill and vitious men amongst the good and vertuous, to giue them the greater lustre, and to
make

Ionas the last, and Psal. 49.

One soueraigne prince alwayes most necessarie in a Commonweale

That the bad are to be mingled with the good, for the making of a good Harmonicall proportion in a Commonweale

---

A9 beasts, moved   C5–6 must needs even like the powers of the soule and mind so fall   D1 which three   D8 Harmonie, which   E3 to give

make the difference knowne (euen by the pointing of the finger, and the sight of the eye) betwixt vertue and vice, knowledge and ignorance. For when fools, vitious, and wicked men, are contemned & despised, then the wise, vertuous, and good men, receiue the true reward and guerdon for their vertue, which is honour. And it seemeth the antient Greekes in their fables, to haue aptly shadowed forth vnto vs that which wee haue spoken of these three kinds of Iustice, giuing vnto *Themis* three daughters, *viz*. ἐυνομία, ἐπιείκεια, εἰρήνη: that is to say, *Vpright Law, Equitie*, and *Peace*: which are referred vnto the three formes of Iustice, Arithmeticall, Geometricall, and Harmonicall: howbeit that peace which shadoweth forth Harmonicall Iustice, is the onely scope and summe of all the lawes and iudgements, as also of the true Royall gouernment: so as is Harmonicall Iustice the end both of Arithmeticall and Geometricall gouernment also.

The three daughters of Themis to represent the three proportions of Iustice.

But these things thus declared, it remaineth for vs to know (as the chiefe point of this our present discourse) Whether it be true that *Plato* saith, God to gouerne this world by Geometricall proportion: For that he hath taken it as a ground, to shew that a well ordered Commonweale ought (to the imitation of the world) to be gouerned by Geometricall Iustice: Which I haue shewed to be contrarie, by the nature of the vnitie, Harmonically referred vnto the three first numbers: as also by the intellectuall power, compared vnto the three other powers of the soule: and by a point compared to a line, a plaine superficies, or other solid bodie. But let vs goe farther, for if *Plato* had looked neerer into the wonderfull Fabrike of the world, hee should haue marked that which hee forgot in his *Timeo*, *viz*. The Great God of nature to haue Harmonically composed this world of Matter and Forme, of which the one is maintained by the helpe of the other, and that by the proportion of equalitie and similitude combined & bound together. And for that the Matter was to no vse without the Forme, and that the forme could haue no being without the matter, neither in the whole vniuersall, neither yet in the parts thereof: he made the world equall to the one, and semblable to the other: equall vnto the matter whereof it is made, for that it comprehendeth all: and semblable or like vnto the forme, in such sort as is the Harmonicall proportion composed of the Arithmeticall and Geometricall proportions equall to the one, and semblable to the other, being one of them separate from another vnperfect.

The world to bee made and gouerned also by Harmonicall, and not by Geometricall proportion, contrarie to the opinion of Plato.

And as the Pythagorians sacrificed the great sacrifice Hecatombe, not for the sustendure of the right angle, which dependeth of the two sides (as many thinke) but for hauing in the selfesame figure found the equalitie and similitude of two other figures, the third figure being equall vnto the first, and like vnto the second: so do we also owe the immortall euerlasting sacrifice of praise and thanksgiuing vnto almightie God, for that he hath by an admirable bond of Harmonie, bound together this world of matter and forme, equall to the one, and like to the other: equall indeed to the matter, so that there is nothing thereof wanting, or yet superfluous: but yet like vnto that euerlasting forme, which he the most wise workeman had in his mind before conceiued, before he made that so great and excellent a worke: as we read in the holy * Scripture.

Gen. 2.

And as for the motion or mouing of the celestiall Spheres, wee see that God hath made one motion equall, which is the swift motion of the superiour Sphere: and another vnequall, which is the motion of the Planets (contrarie vnto the former:) and the third the motion of Trepidation, which containeth and bindeth together both the one and the other. And so if we should enter into the particular nature of other worldly

---

I3 the sustendure *i.e.* the hypotenuse   Notes at I3, I4.

ly creatures also, we should find a perpetuall Harmonicall bond, which vniteth the extreames by indissoluble meanes, taking yet part both of the one and of the other. Which coherence is neither agreeable vnto Arithmeticall nor Geometricall, but euen proper vnto the Harmonicall proportion onely: wherein the sweetnesse of the consent consisteth in tunes aptly mixt together: and the harsh discord, when as the tunes are such as cannot fitly be mingled together. So we see the earth and stones to be as it were ioyned together by clay and chaulke, as in meane betwixt both: and so betwixt the stones and mettals, the Marcasites, the Calamites, and other diuers kinds of minerall stones to grow: So stones and plants also to be ioyned together by diuers kinds of Corall, which are as it were stonie plants, yet hauing in them life, and growing vppon roots: Betwixt plants and liuing creatures, the Zoophytes, or Plantbeasts, which haue feeling and motion, but yet take life by the roots whereby they grow. And againe betwixt the creatures which liue by land onely, and those which liue by water onely, are those which they call *Amphibia*, or creatures liuing by land and water both, as doth the Beuer, the Otter, the Tortoise, and such like: as betwixt the fishes and the fouls are a certaine kind of flying fishes: So betwixt men and beasts, are to bee seene Apes and Munkies; except we shall with *Plato* agree, who placed a woman in the middle betwixt a man and a beast. And so betwixt beasts and angels God hath placed man, who is in part mortall, and in part immortall: binding also this elementarie world, with the heauens or the celestiall world, by the æthereall region. And as a discord sometimes (as we said) giueth grace vnto the sweetest Harmonie: so God also hath here in this world mingled the bad with the good, and placed vertues in the middest of vices, bringing forth also certaine monsters in nature, and suffering the eclipses and defects of the celestiall lights: as also the Surd reasons in Geometricall demonstrations: to the end that thereof might arise the greater good, and that by such meanes the power and beautie of Gods workes might be the better knowne, which might otherwise haue beene hid and folded vp in most thicke and obscure darkenesse. And therefore it is, that God hauing hardened *Pharaoes* heart, which the wise Hebrewes expound to be the enemie of God and Nature, saith thus vnto him, *Excitaui ego te vt demonstrarem in te ipso potentiæ meæ vim ac decus, vt toto terrarum orbe gesta mea omnium vna commemoratione prædicarentur*, I haue stirred thee vp (saith he) that I might in thee declare the force & glorie of my power, that so all my acts might with one report of all men bee praised throughout the whole world. And these things truely belong vnto the most true report of the things then done in Ægypt: but there lieth hidden therein a more diuine meaning than that, concerning the great *Pharao*, the worker and father of all mischiefe, whome the sacred Scriptures declare by the name of *Leuiathan*: and yet in this all the diuines agree, this of all others the greatest enemie of God and man, to bee still by the becke, word, and power of God, kept in and restrained: and all the force and power of those mischiefes and euils by him and his wrought (which we so much both fret and maruell at, and without which the power of the good should neither bee, neither yet be at all perceiued) to be shut vp within the bounds of this elementarie world: and aboue the same to be nothing but that which is holy and cleane from all filth and wickednesse; in such sort, as that that little staine of euils here shall much more profit than hurt. Whereof *Augustine* speaking, saith well, *Qui Deum immortalem vllum mali dedecus perpessurum negat, nisi maius bonum consequi certo sciret*, Who denieth that the immortall God would euer suffer any euill or wickednesse to bee done, but that hee most certainly knoweth a greater good to ensue thereof. Wherefore as of Treble and Base voyces is made a most sweet and melodious Harmonie, so also of vices and vertues, of the different qualities of the elements, of the contrarie motions of the celestiall

The Harmonical bond wherewith the world and the parts thereof are indissolubly bound and vnited together.

stiall Spheres, and of the Sympathies and Antipathies of things, by indissoluble meanes bound together, is composed the Harmonie of the whole world, and of all the parts thereof: So also a well ordered Commonweale is composed of good and bad, of the rich and of the poore, of wisemen and of fools, of the strong and of the weake, allied by them which are in the meane betwixt both: which so by a wonderfull disagreeing concord, ioyne the highest with the lowest, and so all to all, yet so as that the good are still stronger than the bad; so as hee the most wise workeman of all others, and gouernour of the world hath by his eternall law decreed. And as he himselfe being of an infinit force and power ruleth ouer the angels, so also the angels ouer men, men ouer beasts, the soule ouer the the bodie, the man ouer the woman, reason ouer affection: and so euery good thing commaunding ouer that which is worse, with a certaine combining of powers keepeth all things vnder most right and lawful commands.

Almightie God in the gouernmēt of the world, to be of all worldly princes imitated in the gouernment of their estates and kingdomes.

Wherefore what the vnitie is in numbers, the vnderstanding in the powers of the soule, and the center in a circle: so likewise in this world that most mightie king, in vnitie simple, in nature indiuisible, in puritie most holy, exalted farre aboue the Fabrike of the celestiall Spheres, ioyning this elementarie world with the celestiall and intelligible heauens; with a certaine secure care preserueth from distruction this triple world, bound together with a most sweet and Harmonicall consent: vnto the imitation of whome, euerie good prince which wisheth his Kingdome and Commonweale not in safetie onely, but euen good and blessed also, is to frame and conforme himselfe.

(***)

Laus Deo vni & trino in secula seculorum. Amen.

Imprinted at London by Adam Islip. 1606.

F7 *For* of all others *read* of all things (L).   Note at G3.

NOTES

For an explanation of the abbreviations and symbols used below and also of the basis of the textual criticism, see Appendix D above. The French and Latin editions referred to by symbol (Fr 1, Fr 2, L 1, L 2, etc.) are identified in Appendix C. In order to avoid a series of separate footnotes to these notes, I have used square brackets to incorporate sources, dates, and other materials that appear in the margins of the French and Latin versions, into the body of the notes. In the process the great majority of the references to sources have been expanded and made more explicit, since Bodin usually refers to his sources only in general terms.

Book I

CHAPTER 1 (PAGES 1–8)

1 E5 *law of Armes* || Fr adds: "... unless perhaps this were done by a forced necessity, which is not subject to the authority of human laws."

2 G10 *ten Sesteritees.* Inexact. Bodin actually writes *decies sestertium,* i.e., 1,000,000 sesterces or 1,000 sestertia. Cf. 630 D3 and Dio Cassius, *History of Rome,* LVI, 43.

3 B1–2 *Which as it may serve ... of a Commonweale.* Misleading. Bodin's distinction here is not between "Citie" and "Commonweale," but between "description," which concerns accidental characteristics, and "definition," which gives the essential features common to every example of the thing defined. For Bodin the word *civitas,* which Knolles frequently renders as "citie," is practically synonymous with *respublica.* While a distinction is made between them at 49 D10–E2, it is ignored thereafter.

3 B8 *which a good man will never consent unto.* From Fr, but L expands: "This doctrine is contrary to all the precepts of all theologians and philosophers, who deem the just to be always blessed, even if they suffer all the blows of fortune; and the unjust to be most miserable, even in the greatest prosperity and good fortune."

4 I8 *the mind.* Imprecise. Bodin's terms here are *animus* or *âme inférieure,* which are then contrasted with "the understanding and mind it selfe" (*mens* or *la partie intellectuelle*) at K1.

4 K2 *Wisedom, Knowledge, and true Religion.* Bodin's terms are *prudence* or *prudentia, science* or *scientia,* and *vraye religion* or *religio,* while the "true wisedome" composed of all three (K7) is *sagesse* or *sapientia.* This sharp division of all knowledge into three categories is a basic feature of Bodin's thought. See, for example, chapter I of the *Methodus.* Knolles failed to appreciate the significance of these categories, and more than once he failed to distinguish them in his translation. Occasionally Bodin's classification varies, as at 561 A7–B5, where *prudentia* and *scientia* are contrasted with *ars,* manual skill or artistic ability.

5 B2–3 *armes for souldiers ... enemie and robber.* From L. Fr shows less concern for the justice of the cause: "And to subject enemies and extend frontiers by conquest, offensive weapons are provided."

5 B7 *nurturing.* I.e., training, educating, while "education" (B8) is used conversely in the sense of raising or nurturing.

6 H1 *the action of the mind.* I.e., *mentis agitatio,* whereas the "action of the mind" attributed to Aristotle (H10) is *mentis actio.*

7 B2 *elementarie region* || Fr adds: "... which feels a wonderful change as a result of the waning of this light [of the moon] ..."

CHAPTER 2 (PAGES 8–14)

9 D4 *or many other particular assemblies.* Faulty. "... or several individuals ..." (Fr).

9 E9 *soveraintie of power.* Bodin writes *puissance souveraine* and *summa potestas,* but here, as elsewhere, Knolles's rendering of these terms lacks precision. Cf. 10 F8.

11 A10–B1 *common unto all the citisens together, or by use and profit.* Incomplete. L reads: "... common unto all the citizens either by ownership (*nexu & mancipio*) or by usufruct (*usu & fructu*) ..."

12 F5 *garments still taken from him* || Fr adds: "This word [*robes*] shows well enough in our language that garments have always been the property of every individual, for he who robs (*desrobe*) is called a thief. However, in Italian the word *roba* means other movables as well as garments."

CHAPTER 3 (PAGES 14–20)

14 H2 *for as much as that libertie.* Inexact. Fr reads: "... when (*quand*) that liberty ..." The word "yet" (H4) is added by Knolles.

16 I9–10 *That he divided ... power of others.* Obscure. "... That he divided the title of persons *quae sunt in potestate* from those *quae sunt*

in manu . . ." (Fr). Bodin's source is the *Tituli ex corpore Ulpiani*, edited by Jean du Tillet and first printed at Paris in 1549.

17 C5–6 *who besides the persons . . . in the fact.* I.e., ". . . who had killed adulterers outside the [classes of] persons specified in the laws when they were caught in the act." (L). Cf. Justinian, *Digest*, 48, 5, 25(24).

17 D7 *altogether unpunished* ǁ Strictly, ". . . almost unpunished . . ." (Fr and L). Fr adds: ". . . especially in this Realm [of France] . . ."

19 C9–10 *whom both God and mans law doth call his house-fellow.* As in L 1, 3–5, but L 2 and Fr read more accurately: ". . . whom the [Roman] law calls 'sharer of the earthly and heavenly house.'" Cf. Justinian, *Code*, 9, 32, 4.

CHAPTER 4 (PAGES 20–31)

20 K8 *according to his abilitie.* Faulty. ". . . as long as they [i.e., the children] are helpless . . ." (Fr).

21 E1 *the law Servia.* Both Fr and L quote this law (*Si parentem puer verberit, ast olle plorassit: puer divis sacer esto*) and discuss its meaning marginally.

23 A6–7 *being Tribunes.* Strictly, ". . . being Magistrates . . ." Cf. Fr.

25 D4–5 *in reward of his emancipation* ǁ Addition in Fr and L. L reads: ". . . for example, in order to buy an office . . ."

25 E3–5 *or yet be expressed . . . dying before him.* Obscure. ". . . or even if it is stipulated in the son's emancipation, lest the gift should prove detrimental to the father, that if the son should die first the father will retain the full right to his lawful inheritance." (L).

26 K2 *the laws of England* ǁ Fr adds: ". . . published in 1563 . . ." Cf. England, Statutes, *Anno quinto reginae Elizabethae* (London, 1563).

27 A4 *unto the Duke of Wittemberg, ambassadour for the French.* Faulty. ". . . to the Duke of Württemberg for the ambassadors of France . . ." (Fr).

28 K3 *longed for* ǁ L adds: ". . . just as Philip, King of Macedon, reproached his children because they had assumed their inheritance while he was still alive."

28 K8 *to be restrayned* ǁ Fr adds: "Would that this [law] should apply everywhere, that we might see children obedient and attentive to their parents. How greatly they would fear to offend them!"

29 B6 *adopted for her owne* ǁ L adds: "At Aegina it was lawful not only to adopt sons, but also to make them heirs if the father had no natural children begotten in lawful marriage."

29 C3–4 *As also all the people of the East made little or no difference.* As in Fr, but in L the comparison is chronological: "However in earlier times there was almost no difference . . ."

29 D1 *people of Asia* ǁ Fr adds: ". . . a custom which they observe even now, and which is kept almost everywhere in Africa."

29 D3 *Thus having confirmed the matter by course of historie.* Error. Bodin writes: "We have given the reason in the *Method of Histories* [i.e., the *Methodus*], ch. 5." (Fr).

30 F3 *or neere kinsmen* ǁ L adds: "Aulus Gellius is wrong in saying that women could not adopt because they were not allowed into the assembly, since adoption was done without an assembly."

30 H6–7 *whereby his owne . . . his adoptive father.* Inexact. ". . . for that of his own father [Octavius] was reduced [to Octavianus], and put after the name of his adoptive father." (Fr).

31 D8 *any children, either naturall or legitimat.* Inexact. ". . . any natural *and* legitimate children . . ." (L). Bodin uses the term "natural children" in the sense of actually begotten children, whether legitimate or not.

CHAPTER 5 (PAGES 32–46)

32 H1–6 *Now every Slave . . . of the Hebrewes.* As in Fr, but L revises the classification: "Slaves are of five kinds. The first is of those who are called slaves by nature, born of a woman slave. The second is of those who are taken by enemies; these were made slaves by the ancient law of war. The third is of those who have been condemned to public works, who are called slaves of punishment (*servi poenae*). The fourth is of those who have voluntarily gone into slavery, and especially those who have received money for their liberty. The last type is of those who have been sold by pirates or brigands, and are possessed by their purchasers in good faith. We have said before that liberty cannot be infringed by brigands, and hence not even by those who knowingly buy a free man from a brigand, or by those who have won another man's freedom in games of chance, as was formerly the practice among the Germans." (12 lines).

34 H5–7 *In like sort . . . deserveth death.* Based on Fr, which reads ". . . make war unjustly upon . . ." for ". . . unjustly lie in wait for . . ." L is more explicit: "In the same and even a worse position are those who wage war on others unjustly, and who lie in wait for another man's goods, life, and liberty. These men, even if they pose as kings and princes, are nevertheless more properly to be accounted thieves."

34 H10 *in so saying* ǁ Addition in L (a philological digression, 5 lines). Inserted marginally in Fr 1–6, 8, but not in Fr 7.

Notes to Book I

35 D5 *some well learned men.* The margin refers to George Buchanan (Fr only).

40 H7 *draw everie man unto labour* || Fr adds: "At almost the same time, by letters patent of King Dagobert, which are in the treasury of St. Denis-en-France, all subjects were forbidden to take away or harbor slaves from the Abbey of St. Denis. Later when the slaves had the status of mainmortables, the Abbot Suger freed the men from mortmain also, on condition that they went to another district (*pays*). I have seen this in the charter which he issued in 1141, when he was regent of France." (8 lines). Cf. 41 B9–C1, which is from L.

40 H10–I3 *To the imitation ... the yere 1250.* From L, but Fr gives more detail: "So that by 1200 (*sic*) servitudes were virtually abolished throughout the world, except in the West Indies, which at their discovery were full of slaves, who could be killed without any penalty at all. Moreover, those vanquished in war were not put to ransom, and the thief was enslaved to the man whom he had robbed, and anyone could sell himself and his children into slavery." (7 lines).

41 B5 *as another mans goods* || Fr adds: "... as it would seem by the next article, where it is said that the burgesses will pay like the nobles for the serfs that they hold. This refers to successions which they inherited."

42 I8–10 *Narbona ... Romans.* As in Fr. L adds Valence to this list.

43 C9 *for slaves* || Fr adds: "... because [the Jews] had Christian servants and chambermaids, (for so reads the old history of St. Denis-en-France) in contravention of the law, which forbids it [*Code*, 1, 10, 1]. But the word servant (*sergent*), which some call *servientem*, does not mean a slave, or serf, which is *mancipium*, in the sense that it is understood in an article of the estates held at Tours, in which it is stated that in ancient times we were called free (*francs*), but now we are serfs." (7 lines).

44 G8 *unto their nephewes in the fourth degree.* Fr reads: "... and their children up to the third degree [i.e., great-grandchildren] ..." L reads: "... unto the grandchildren, but the great-grandchildren and their posterity are accounted base ..." Possibly a deliberate alteration by Knolles.

44 K3–4 *But concerning the Spaniards ... at the first.* As in Fr, but L is stronger: "But it is almost characteristic of the Spaniards to deal courteously in the beginning with those whom they mark out for slavery or slaughter."

CHAPTER 6 (PAGES 46–69)

47 C10 *theefe and robber* || Addition in L (etymology of the Hebrew term, 3 lines).

47 D5–6 *an opinion by me ... elswhere refelled.* For his refutation of the hypothesis of a "Golden Age" see *Methodus*, ch. 7. The earlier work reveals, however, that Bodin himself had shared this same "error" to the extent of believing (pp. 214–215) that some early kingdoms were founded on justice, others on force.

47 E7–9 *in such sort ... in great power.* From Fr, but L substitutes: "... and afterwards his son, bearing himself as a king, found it necessary to maintain the kingdom acquired by brigandage by means of equity and justice."

48 H10 *straunger slaves be not so* || Fr adds: "... which is sufficient proof that [the former] is also a subject of the Commonweal, even though he is the slave of a private man."

49 B2 *free of that wherein he is borne.* I.e., "... a free subject of that Commonweal wherein he is born ..." (Fr).

50 F6–G5 *for the word citisen ... citisen may well be.* A confused passage, following Fr 3–8. In contrast, Fr 1–2 read: "For the word burgess (*bourgeois*) means something more special for us than the word citizen, and is properly the natural subject and citizen, inhabiting a town, who has the right of a corporation and college, or certain other privileges which are not communicated to those of the open country. I have said natural subject, because the naturalized subject, though dwelling in the town and enjoying the right of a burgess, is called in many places a simple citizen; whereas the former is called a burgess, and has some particular privilege. Thus at Paris only a natural burgess, born in Paris, can be Provost of the Merchants, and at Geneva, the citizen cannot be syndic of the town, nor councilor of the privy council of twenty-five, but a burgess may well be."

The reason for the reversal in terminology lies in the Geneva edition of 1577, which flatly contradicts Bodin's original statement respecting Geneva: "On the contrary at Geneva the burgess may not be syndic of the town, nor councilor of the privy council of twenty-five, for there the burgess is not born in Geneva, but is a stranger, received by the Seigneurie, to enjoy certain privileges which inhabitants do not have. But the citizen, born in the town of another citizen or of a burgess, may well be [syndic or councilor]." This passage is directly reflected in Fr 3–8, which add at G5: "... for the citizen is he that is born of the citizen or burgess, and the burgess is he that is received into citizenship." On this and other alterations prompted by the Geneva edition, see M. Reulos, "L'Edition de 1577 de *La République*," *Bibliothèque d'humanisme et renaissance*, XIII (1951) pp. 342–354.

In L the point is condensed: "For properly a burgess (*civis urbanus*) is he who is surrounded by the walls and buildings of a town (*urbs*); but

A 107

Notes to Book I

in the best legal sense it is he who is born, not made, a citizen, and who enjoys a certain privilege peculiar to urban citizens. For example, at Paris . . ." Rousseau's remarks on Bodin's "error" (*Social Contract*, I, 6) suggest that he read the *République* in one of the early French editions.

50 G6 *of Germanie* ‖ Fr adds: "However by our customs and ancient edicts, the word *bourgeois* signified commoner (*roturier*), whom the nobles call *vilain* because he inhabits a town (*ville*). For in former times the nobility remained in the country. Even yet the *garde bourgeoise* and the *garde noble* are distinguished in our customs, and the *bourgeois* contrasted to the noble."

50 I8-10 *That he which hath caried . . . out of the citie*. Imprecise. ". . . That he which hath carried out of the town (*ville, urbs*), that which was by the law forbidden to be carried out of the city (*cité*), and hath carried the same into another town (*ville, urbs*) of the same province, is neither to be said to have carried the thing out of the city (*civitas*) . . ." Cf. Fr and L.

50 K3 *unto the same prince* ‖ Fr adds: "The Hebrews have kept the same distinction between town and city, for they call the town קירית, that is to say 'the walled' (*la murée*) and the city עיר." Bodin apparently derives קירית from the same root as קיר, "wall," whereas the accepted derivation is from קרה, "to meet," which gives the sense "meeting place."

51 B3-4 *unto the seignorie of Venice* ‖ Fr adds: ". . . or unto the Lords of the Leagues [i.e., the Swiss] . . ."

51 B9 *use this word (Citie)*. Inexact. ". . . use the word Commonweal (*Republique, Respublica*)."

52 I7 *above an hundred yeares before*. Faulty. ". . . even before the hundredth year [had expired]." (L). He refers to *Digest*, 7, 4, 21.

54 F7-8 (*as who should say, Men made partakers of their immunities*). Knolles varies the figure. Bodin writes: ". . . because they took the same offices (*eadem munera . . . caperent*) . . ."

54 H1-2 *Thus we see two sorts . . . or countrey citisen*. As in Fr, but L is more complex: "Therefore there is a difference between the urban citizen and the rural citizen, and again the latter is different from the municipal citizen. Hence it ought not to seem strange that Caesar gave legacies to the Roman people apart from the tribes, for the rural tribes constituted part of the Roman people, and had equal voting rights with the urban ones."

54 K1-2 *before that it was permitted*. Inexact. Bodin writes: ". . . although (*ores que*) it was permitted . . ."

55 B10 *citisens with them* ‖ Fr adds: "And even the affranchised, who were called Junian Latins, were really subjects and citizens, except that they could not dispose of their goods." They were called Junian Latins because their status was regularized by the *lex Junia Norbana*.

55 C7-9 *470 townes . . . 260 tributaries*. Knolles follows Fr, but in L the list is entirely different, and both versions are at variance with Pliny's figures. Cf. *Natural History*, III, 1 and 3.

55 D10 *the peoples leave* ‖ Fr adds: ". . . and especially if an appeal were launched by a citizen to the Roman people or to the Emperor, even though governors of provinces had the right of *haute, moyenne, & basse justice* [*Digest*, 2, 1, 3] over all provincial subjects."

56 G6 *S. Paul*. L begins: "And Paul himself, easily first (*princeps*) among Christians of his time . . ."

56 I2-3 *soveraigne power and jurisdiction*. Bodin's terms here are *merum imperium ac jurisdictio* and *haute justice*.

56 I10 *onely over their slaves*. Strictly, ". . . only over slaves . . ." (Fr and L). Cf. *Digest*, 2, 1, 12.

56 K7 *our Saviour Christ Jesus*. The words "our Saviour" are added by Knolles.

57 E7 *exempted from taxes and tallages* ‖ L adds: ". . . as is the case among the English, Spaniards and Germans . . ."

58 H7-I1 *Wherefore seeing . . . unto strangers*. As in Fr, but L revises, omitting the idea of mutual obligation: "Therefore since the same man cannot be regarded as citizen and stranger, or as ally and subject, it must follow that the true citizen either is born [in that status], or else submits himself to the rule and sovereign power of another man."

59 B1 *bound unto the Senat and the lawes of the people of Rome*. Strictly, ". . . bound unto the laws of the Senate and people of Rome . . ." (L).

59 E1 *hundred thousand pound*. I.e., 100,000 *livres tournois*. Later, in the chapter on finance, Knolles generally converts amounts in livres into sterling at the rate of ten livres to the pound.

60 F8 *as was by him provided*. Inexact, perhaps deliberately so. ". . . to be attended to by him (*pour y estre par luy pourveu*) . . ." L is stronger: "For this was brought about by Henry II, King of France, while he exercised power in Scotland on behalf of his daughter-in-law."

60 F9 *as the Swissers* ‖ L inserts: ". . . who have divided rule (for there are thirteen commonweals, each one of which has the supreme right of ruling over its own people) . . ."

60 G2-3 *in such sort as that one of them*. Strictly, ". . . unless it happens that some of them . . ." (Fr).

Notes to Book I

64 F10–G1 *five hundred thousand of definitions of citisens*. A compromise. Fr reads: "... fifty thousand definitions of citizens ..." But L substitutes: "... the variety of citizens should be infinite ..."

64 H2–3 *fearing the rebellion of many subjects, with a few of the great states*. Faulty. "... fearing the rebellion of the many [who were] subject to few lords ..." (Fr).

64 H5–8 *It is then ... citisen from a straunger*. As in Fr, but L reads: "Therefore the true and proper distinction between a citizen and a stranger is that the one is subject to public power and authority, the other can refuse the commands of a foreign prince. The prince is bound to protect the citizen from the wrongs of enemies and citizens alike; but not to protect the stranger, unless he is requested to do so, and impelled by the duties of humanity."

65 C5 *of their father that survived*. Strictly, "... of *his* father who has survived him?" (Fr).

66 F10 *subjects of Milan* ‖ Addition in L(margin) and Fr. Fr reads: "... to which ordinance [of Charles V] Jean Baptiste de Plot has set down fifty limitations, which are badly carried out."

66 G8–9 *to have reason of their debtors* ‖ I.e., "... in order to have satisfaction from their debtors." Following Fr, which then adds: "And even in the mountains of the Grisons and Switzerland, where the poet du Bellay says that parricides should be confined, it is not permissible to mortgage one's land."

66 H8–9 *for otherwise ... or naturall subject*. Confused. "For otherwise, in order to have the stranger's children succeed, it is requisite that they be born in France, and of [a mother who is] a citizen (*bourgeoise*) or natural subject." This sentence, based on Fr, corresponds to the following one (H9–I2), which is from L.

67 A2 *Visier Bassaes* ‖ Fr adds: "Besides what I have said, it is permitted to all strangers who die outside France to dispose of goods acquired in France by testament. This demonstrates clearly that strangers are treated much more graciously in France than they were in Greece, or Rome, or in all the East."

67 C1–2 *subjects of the empire* ‖ Addition in Fr (margin) and L. L reads: "... and the Parlement of Paris has repeatedly judged [that this right of reprisal is not to be used against citizens], even in the religious war which recently devastated the whole of France." The date given for this statement is 1567 in L, 1569 in Fr.

CHAPTER 7 (PAGES 69–84)

70 F5–6 *and the reason is, for that unto dutie no hire is due*. As in Fr, but L differs: "... because he did promise. But even if he has not promised, and the thing is done in the line of duty, no reward is due." Cf. *Digest*, 17, 1, 1, 4.

70 G5 *their adherents* ‖ L adds: "This is related to the statement of Festus [ed. Müller, p. 233] that it began to be called patronage (*patrocinia*) when the *plebs* were divided among the fathers (*patres*) in order to be protected by their resources."

70 K8–9 *things common to the free borne clients, with the vassals or adherents*. Faulty. The contrast is between the "client"(L) or "adherent" (Fr) on the one hand and the "vassal" on the other.

72 I7–8 *I doubt not ... are not straungers unto us, &c*. I.e., *are* strangers to Rome (cf. Fr). Confusion arises because L quotes a version of *Digest*, 49, 15, 7, which begins *Non dubito quin foederati, & liberi nobis externi non sint* and then remarks marginally that the Florentine version omits the second negation. Cf. *Digestorum seu pandectarum libri quinquaginta ex Florentinis pandectis repraesentati* (Florence, 1553), III, 1585–1586. The next sentence (I8–K2) follows Fr, but L continues quoting directly from the *Digest* (13 lines).

72 K6 *more honourable than the other* ‖ Fr adds: "And this phrase does not signify *communiter*, as the adversary of Cornelius Balbus said [*Pro Balbo*, 16], nor does it signify 'without fraud and deceit,' as Carolus Sigonius says [*De antiquo jure Italiae*, Bk. I, ch. 1]."

72 K8–74 F6 *And the more cleerely ... give nor take lawes*. From Fr only. In L this passage is transferred to Book V, ch. 6. Cf. note at 614 I3.

76 K9–77 A2 *The Valesians ... for league defensive*. Inexact. Fr reads: "... the Valaisans in the year 1528 [1527 in L], in addition to the ancient particular treaty made between them and the people of Berne in defensive alliance in the year 1475."

77 C1 *their assemblies*. Faulty. Bodin's word is *ressort*, which may mean simply an appeal, or else the extent or province of a jurisdiction. The common phrase *ressort et souveraineté* is similarly mistranslated at 79 A4, 79 A5–6, 80 F1, 81 B1–2, 81 C9–10, possibly through confusion with the English word "resort." Later, however, Knolles renders the term properly. Cf. 126 I4–5, 129 A7, 139 C6, 237 D4 ("jurisdiction"); 158 H7 ("precinct"); 491 A5 ("circuite"); 155 C2, 168 H2, 170 F4–5 ("appeals" or "appeal"), *et alia*.

77 E1 *to depend* ‖ Addition in Fr and L. Fr reads: "This has not been without great difficulty. For example, the King was warned by letters from his ambassador, who was at Soleure in 1565, that the Bishop of Terracina, the Papal nuncio, was stirring up enough sparks to kindle a fire among them, but the King poured on cold water to extinguish it."

79 D3 *given unto them succours* ‖ L adds: "From this it is manifest that the Lacedemonians had previously been admitted into the Amphictyonic treaties of alliance. But whenever allies differ among themselves, the decision is left to the common allies, even if this is not expressed in the treaty."

81 B5 *every yeare chosen* ‖ L adds: "For the fewer the cities, the more easily are they all fused into one Commonweal."

81 D1–3 *Now it seemeth . . . empire of the Germans*. This statement is at variance with Bodin's earlier opinion that both the Latin and Tuscan leagues were unitary states, while the three Aetolian cities remained separate entities. Cf. *Methodus*, p. 166.

81 E1 *straunge princes, as* ‖ *Henrie*. L inserts: ". . . William, Count of Holland . . ."

82 G8 *pention yearly* ‖ L adds: "I myself have no doubt that the German princes would try to win back the Swiss to their rule if they could."

82 H8–10 *but the Swissers . . . states of the empire*. As in Fr, but L introduces a qualification: "Nevertheless I am not of the opinion that the Swiss are for this reason subject to German rule (*imperium*), but rather that they acknowledge the dignity (*majestas*) of the Germans to be superior, and even the Emperor himself [to be superior], who is subject (*in fide ac ditione*) to the German Empire."

82 K9 *the See of Rome, the Pope, and the empire*. As in Fr, but L omits "the See of Rome" and adds "the House of Austria."

83 A10 *not subject to the Swissers*. As in Fr, but L reads: ". . . not subject to the Germans . . ."

CHAPTER 8 (PAGES 84–113)

84 H9 *the Italians Segnoria* ‖ Fr adds: ". . . which word they use in respect of private men as well as in respect of those who conduct all the affairs of state in a Commonweal."

85 A2–3 *and therein defended by the power of another*. Faulty. ". . . and keeper of the power of another." Knolles reads *gardé* in place of *garde*.

85 B3 *magistrats or officers*. Inexact. Bodin writes ". . . commissioner or officer . . ." (Fr) and ". . . commissioners or magistrates . . ." (L). Similarly at B10 for ". . . officers or magistrats . . ." read ". . . commissioners or magistrates . . ." For the definitions of these terms, see Book III, ch. 2, and Appendix B, no. 9.

85 B5 *or suffer them to hold it*. Faulty. ". . . or hold it in suspense (*en souffrance*) . . ."

85 D9 *new officers* ‖ L adds: ". . . or the driving of a nail [to mark the passing of the year]."

86 F1–2 *it was not enough for him to be a noble Senator onely*. L adds an explanatory marginal note: "A *novus* was a man who was first [of his family] to obtain an office in the Commonweal. A *nobilis* was the son of a *novus homo*. A *patricius* was a man who derived his origin from the fathers enrolled by Romulus."

86 H3–4 *and much more . . . limitation of time*. Inexact. ". . . which [type of grant] is much greater than if the power were revocable at the pleasure of the people, without limitation of time." (Fr, but Fr 7 faulty).

88 F9 *or lieutenant* ‖ Fr and L add: ". . . or commissioner . . ."

88 H7 *hath given the power* ‖ L adds: "However, the ratification of the magistrate in the more important matters pertaining to his jurisdiction is not made retroactive (*retrotrahitur*), as is that of the prince who has supreme power in the Commonweal."

89 D1 *of right*. Bodin specifies: ". . . by hereditary right . . ." (Fr and L).

89 D9 *Is he a just judge*. Bodin writes merely: "Is he a judge?" (Fr and L).

90 F5 *growne out of use* ‖ Fr qualifies: ". . . unless the King assembles the Estates, as I have learned from a Spanish gentleman."

90 H8 *by the high court of Parliament*. Imprecise. Fr reads: ". . . by the upper chamber of Parliament . . ." L reads: ". . . by the higher court, which is composed of bishops and noblemen . . ."

90 I8 *and of nations*. Abbreviated and inexact. Fr reads: ". . . and to many human laws common to all peoples." L reads: ". . . as well as [to] the law which is common to all peoples (*lex omnium gentium communis*), which has grounds (*rationes*) separated from divine and natural law."

91 B4–5 *The reason . . . given to none*. Or: ". . . The account is not correct unless it is rendered to none (*Non aliter ratio constat, quam si nulli reddatur*)." Tacitus, his source, reads *uni* in place of *nulli*. For the circumstances, see *Annals*, I, 6.

91 E1 *And for this cause Tiberius*. As in Fr, but L begins: "For when the sovereignty of the Roman people seemed to have been transferred to the absolute rule of one man, from whom privileges had to be requested, Tiberius . . ."

92 F7–8 *so neither can a soveraigne prince* ‖ L adds: ". . . nor indeed [can] a magistrate or any private man . . ."

92 G2 *franke good will* ‖ Addition in Fr 4 only: "We shall make the same judgment about the customary laws, though many have written that the Prince is bound by them. The question was

Notes to Book I

raised in relation to the Duchy of Brittany, particularly where the custom regulates matters which concern the sovereign prince. But I hold that if the prince is not in any way subject to the civil laws, much less is he subject to customs, which depend upon the will of his subjects, and are often contrary to divine and natural law." (8 lines). Omitted in Fr 1–3, 5–8.

92 G3–6 *neither is it in their power . . . feare and reverence.* As in Fr, but L is more concise and more explicit: "Those who attempt to break down or weaken these [divine and natural laws] shall not escape the judgments of the divine majesty."

92 H4–6 *If the prince . . . made unto himselfe.* Following Fr, but L is more direct: "If the prince binds himself by an oath to himself, the obligation of the oath cannot stand, for the reason that we have given."

92 I3 *that made the promise* ‖ L adds: "And although Alexander of Imola stated in almost all his commentaries and responses that covenants which would have had no force acquire it by the force of an oath alone (which opinion he can support neither by likely reasons nor by authority), yet even he denies [*Consilia*, Bk. 6, consilium 224] that Princes are bound by their own edicts and laws, even when they have confirmed them by an oath." (6 lines).

92 K1–2 *in that which toucheth the diminishing of his majesty.* As in Fr, but L reads: ". . . not only in matters which relate to his rights of sovereignty, but even in those which concern his private advantage and domestic affairs."

93 A2–3 *which to bee true . . . no need of money.* Obscure. "While this is true, and can be confirmed by reason and authority, nevertheless there is no need of money . . ." (L).

93 B5–6 *further than standeth with his profit, except he be their heire.* The first clause is in L only, the second in Fr only.

93 E1 *to revenge the pope.* This may be a misprint for: ". . . to reverence the Pope (*Pontificis maximi majestatem comiter observaturum*) . . ." Fr reads: ". . . to obey the Pope . . ."

93 E1–2 *to defend the widdowes, the fatherlesse, and poore.* As in Fr, but L adds another category: ". . . to embrace with all charity the orphans, the poor, and strangers."

94 F1–3 *I say yet . . . equitie of them ceasing.* From Fr, but L offers a different explanation: "The name of Kings is sacred and majestic, but many are kings in name rather than in reality, as is reported of the kings of Denmark and Bohemia. We shall make the same judgment about the kings of the Epirots also."

94 F10 *nobis commissis.* When the quotation is repeated and expanded later on, this phrase is given as *vobis commissis* (731 A7), but both forms represent a corruption of the original text. See the notes at 730 K9 and 731 A7.

94 H3–4 *but I have seene . . . in Avergne.* As in Fr, but L substitutes: "However both savor somewhat of ecclesiastical authority. But I shall propose, for all kings to study and imitate, the purest and best formula that can be devised, which has been copied out of the most ancient archives of a library in Auvergne."

95 A4–5 *but the condition . . . chiefe in a Commonweale.* Imprecise. ". . . but the condition of a *princeps*, that is, the [man who is] first in a Commonweal." The comment on the oath (A 3–5) appears in L only. In Fr the oath itself is worded differently at 94 K1–2. The concept of the principality is explained below, pp. 99, 196–197.

95 A8–10 *& albeit that . . . stayed & grounded.* As in Fr, but L substitutes: "For if derogation is made from the laws of the realm (*leges imperii*), this is usually repaired by the magistrates on the death of the prince, whether it be any decree repugnant to the *leges imperii*, or any infringement of the right of sovereignty, or any usurpation of lands belonging to the Commonweal."

95 E6–7 *furthest from reason* ‖ Addition in Fr 4 only: ". . . and also pernicious. There have been found some who, under a pretext of this kind, have wished to make the kingdom elective, with power in the estates to wrest the scepters and crowns from the true heirs in order to give them to the most factious and ambitious. This brings about the inevitable ruin of monarchies which are based on the right of succession as though upon a most sure foundation, as I pointed out to the Estates of France held at Blois in 1576, having been chosen deputy by the estates of the country of Vermandois. For it is quite certain that the whole people has no other voice than a supplicative one, the Privy Council has a deliberative voice, those who have access to the Council without a place on it have a consultative voice, and the King alone has a definitive voice. Otherwise, if the decision depends on many, the marks of sovereignty are lost, and the monarchy is nothing more than an aristocracy or democracy, abandoned to the mercy of the most wicked and factious." (16 lines). Omitted in Fr 1–3, 5–8.

96 K9–97 A2 *That the estates of England . . . high court of parliament.* L applies this statement to both England and Spain.

97 A5–7 *for that it is not . . . goods from him.* From Fr. L reads: ". . . since no one is so wicked a tyrant as to think it right for him to plunder another man's goods."

97 B10–C1 *power to condemne, as* ‖ *king Henrie the sixt.* Addition in Fr and L. Fr reads: ". . . as Thomas and Henry Howard were condemned by

Notes to Book I

the estates at the indictment of Henry VIII, King of England; and in addition King Henry VI . . ." Doubtless a deliberate omission by Knolles.

97 C10 *should be from the estates in bodie together seperated*. Awkward. ". . . should be in the Estates as a separate body . . ." (Fr).

97 D6 *the conclusion of the treatie*. Imprecise. Bodin writes *verification*, the term applied to the registration of instruments by the Parlement of Paris. (Fr).

97 E5 *the courtesie of England*. A marginal note in Fr and L explains that this is the right of the husband to the usufruct of his wife's goods after her death.

98 H7 *commonly used in every place*. Faulty. ". . . [used] in all the *pays coutumier* . . ." (Fr).

99 B4 *to keepe the lawes* || Addition in Fr 4 only: ". . . as is still done in the Commonweals of Switzerland, and at Geneva, where each man in the presence of the Syndics swears, with raised hands, to keep the laws and ordinances." Omitted Fr 1–3, 5–8.

99 B7 *done in all lawes* || Fr adds: ". . . even though they were iniquitous and absurd, which is not to resolve the difficulty."

99 C3 *by the lesser to the greater* || Addition in Fr 4 only: ". . . which cannot be said of a whole people having the sovereignty when they swear before a simple magistrate, as was done at Geneva in the year 1560, when the whole people swore to keep the laws that were then published." Omitted Fr 1–3, 5–8.

99 D7 *sacrificed in the Capitoll* || Fr adds: "Thus Trajan sometimes took the Consulship, in addition to his Imperial title, as did the other Emperors also."

99 D10–E2 *which forme of a Commonweale . . . as amongst the Venetians*. Mainly from L. In Fr the concept is more confused: "This form of Commonweal was Aristocratic in appearance, but Monarchical in effect, and was called a principate."

100 F1 Οὐκ . . . βασιλεύς. The three major errors in this line (*Iliad*, II, 204–205) also occur in L 1, a fact which suggests that neither Knolles nor his printer was familiar with Greek. For an accurate version, see 196 I4.

100 G2 *in the name of a soveraigne prince*. Inexact. ". . . in the quality of prince [i.e., *princeps*] . . ." (Fr).

100 I10 *seemes not to have*. Strictly, ". . . seems not to have had . . ." (L). Sigismund Augustus died in 1572.

101 A6–7 *the majestie of absolute soveraigntie*. Combining *jus majestatis*, as in L, and *souveraineté absolue*, as in Fr.

102 G10 *danger of the law*. I.e., "force of the law," but Bodin actually writes: ". . . force of the judgments . . ." (L).

103 D5 *latter edicts and derogations*. Strictly, ". . . latter edicts and laws." (L).

104 F6 *for a man so to doe*. Strictly, ". . . for a man to do anything . . ." (L). The statement is a general one.

104 H9 *made with them*. As in Fr, but L clarifies: ". . . made with private men . . ."

105 D2 *or from them derogat* || Fr adds: ". . . provided that the derogation from the law, while bringing profit to some, does no harm to others without just cause."

105 D5 *more profitable*. As in Fr, but L substitutes: ". . . less profitable . . ." Similarly Fr reads: ". . . most upright and honest . . ." at D6. But L becomes: ". . . less honest and less just . . ."

105 E3 *for under the colour of profit that these flatterers and scrapers carrie things*. Faulty. ". . . for under color of the profit which these flatterers and scrapers obtain (*emportent*) . . ."

106 G3–5 *or for the varietie . . . God and nature*. Based on Fr, which reads: ". . . depend always of the civil laws . . ." (G4). L is clearer: ". . . or [concerning laws] which contain penalties, of which we have an infinite variety. For although [the principle of] avenging crimes is derived from nature, yet the rigor or laxity of the penalties depends upon the laws and ordinances of men."

107 B6 *unto his promises* || Fr and L add: ". . . as the Master of the Sentences [Peter Lombard] says."

107 C4 *of late*. Error. ". . . long ago (*pridem*) . . ."

107 D10–E2 (*although that it was not needfull for him so to have done, considering that he was long time before in all other things dispensed with from the lawes*). Based on Fr, which omits the words "in all other things." L differs: ". . . [because] although in all other things he was freed from the laws of the country, yet in his own affairs he could not be the author of a measure for his own advantage."

107 E5 *Philip the second*. The name occurs in L only. Bodin means Philip III, and a marginal note in Fr and L gives the date 1282.

107 E6 *unto the customes of the civil law*. Imprecise. L reads: ". . . unto *lex civilis* . . ." But Fr reads: ". . . unto the customs concerning the redemption of family lands (*retraict lignager*)."

108 F1 (*in some cases*). Added by Knolles. However Bodin's statement has a marginal reference to *Code*, 4, 38, 14, and refers specifically to *retrait lignager*, not to Roman law in general.

Notes to Book I

108 K3 *unto the Roman laws* ‖ Fr adds: ". . . and even less unto his own . . ."

109 D7–8 *by confiscation.* Bodin writes: ". . . by legitimate confiscation . . ." (Fr and L).

111 B7 *of full age* ‖ Fr adds: ". . . when it is a matter of their private interest."

111 B10–C1 *in that they confound . . . but all one in a popular or an Aristocraticall state.* As in Fr, but L revises: ". . . having confused the affairs of the prince with those of the Commonweal, which are judged according to the same law in a popular state, but not in the others [i.e., aristocracy and monarchy]."

CHAPTER 9 (PAGES 114–153)

114 F5–7 *This question . . . all Europe and Asia.* From Fr, but L enlarges: "We are to treat this question in a separate chapter, because it concerns the rights of sovereignty, and ought not to be carelessly confused with the right of protection or clientage, of which we have spoken before. For the feudal or fiduciary right is more inviolable than the right of protection (*patrocinium*) which the authorities also call the right of patronage (*patronatus*). This latter is the older, but the former, which originated from the Lombards, now seems to encompass all peoples with a mutual bond of fealty." (8 lines).

114 G7 *or base charges* ‖ L adds: "And since benefactions of this kind were customarily granted on account of military service, and war against enemies, they were at first called *militiae ex casu*, and afterwards, from the giving of faith (*fides*), were known as fees (*feuda*), On this account it seems to be spelled F.E.D.U.M., because a man who gave his faith used these words: *fidelis ero domino vero meo*, and when the words were contracted into letters, the name *feudum* was obtained. But it may be more correct to derive it from the treaty (*foedus*) contracted on the one side and the other." (7 lines). Bodin uses the phrase *militia ex casu* several times in L, and Knolles clearly did not understand it (cf. note at 395 B3). The term itself occurs in the *Novellae* of Justinian, and its precise meaning was a matter for speculation. Some commentators considered it identical with the *feudum*, but this notion was contested by Lelio Torelli, the learned editor of the Florentine pandects, in his tract entitled *De militiis ex casu*, written in 1542 and printed in Antonio Agustín's *Emendationes et opiniones* (Basel, 1544).

115 A9–D10 *Which that it may . . . last sort are the right slaves.* This passage is mainly from L, but the sentence at C1–4 is from Fr and is inconsistent with L. Fr lists only six "degrees of inferiors," omitting the last two and not distinguishing between protection with and without pension. Moreover, at the beginning (B1–C4) Fr reverses the order as follows:

"The first is the tributary prince, who is inferior in the treaty to the man to whom he owes tribute, yet nevertheless he retains the entire right of sovereignty, without any other submission to him to whom the tribute is paid. And although he seems to be more heavily burdened than he who is in protection, yet in reality he is superior, for in paying the tribute which he has promised in order to have peace, he is acquitted, and has no need of anyone else in order to defend his estate. The second is the prince who is in protection or *advouaison*, who is inferior to his protector, as we have said, and inferior to the tributary prince, in that he cannot safeguard himself from invasion by his enemies without aid and protection. He puts himself under the shield of another man, and is called an adherent, or *advoué*. The protection is called *advouaison*, which we have discussed earlier." (14 lines).

117 B7 *who seemed alwayes to keepe the state of soveraigntie.* As in L, but Fr reads: ". . . whom even the Queen of England admits to be a sovereign Prince."

118 F3–5 *but onely conditionall . . . which he did not.* As in Fr, but L substitutes: ". . . [but] upon the condition that he [Philip] should undertake to protect him against John, King of England. Whether he did this or not is doubtful, yet he avenged the murder of Arthur."

118 G5–6 *Girald, whome some call Vitald.* "Girald" is probably a misprint for Gitald. Bodin writes "Guytard" and "Witard" in Fr 1–4, "Guytald" and "Witald" in Fr 5–8, "Vitaldus" in L, while the usual form is Nithard. His history, *De dissensionibus filiorum Ludovici Pii*, was not printed until 1588.

118 I9 *cannot abide.* More probably, ". . . cannot maintain (*soustenir*) . . ."

118 K6–7 *although Argentraeus otherwise thinke* ‖ Addition in L. "For he [Argentraeus] reprimands Gregory the bishop, Haimo [i.e., Aimoin] and Sigebert, with whom I agree, for lying, and yet Vitaldus [i.e., Nithard] wrote the same things as they. It is even more absurd that he thinks Peter of Dreux, who was the King's subject and kinsman, to be the first who submitted the sovereignty of a foreign principality to the rule of France. Nor could his children and descendants exempt themselves by treachery from the perpetual, and indeed natural, obligation which had been contracted with the Kings of France. As for the fact that he tries to absolve the Dukes of Brittany, who joined with the English in a wicked conspiracy for the downfall of this realm, from a charge of high treason; that he cannot abstain from invective and abuse when he writes of the kings of France and of all other princes;

that he generally heaps every kind of praise *ad nauseam* upon his own [Breton] countrymen, even though he uses a French surname; that he generally disparages and glosses over the victories of the French; that, finally, he wishes to be the sole authority, and impugns the honesty of the most ancient and most trustworthy writers—all of this certainly seems to be an abuse of literary pursuits. For the writer of histories should take the greatest care lest he seem to alienate the subjects from their obedience and allegiance to their prince, and to incite them to rebellion. But let us return to the main point." (21 lines). Bertrand d'Argentré, seneschal of Rennes, was an able jurist who defended feudal rights and customary law against the attacks of Charles du Moulin. In Fr he is mentioned favorably (cf. 118 I8–9). The occasion for Bodin's perceptibly harsher judgment of him in L was the publication in 1582 of his *Histoire de Bretagne*, which revealed the Breton jurist as a credulous and superficial historian.

126 H9 *the emperour holdeth them also of the pope*. From Fr, which uses the past tense, but L substitutes: "... the Kings of Spain have acknowledged that they hold them in fealty from the Bishops of Rome."

126 H10 *did fealtie and homage*. I.e., did fealty and homage for the islands just mentioned (cf. Fr).

133 B6 *the princes of East Frizeland*. This agrees with L, which reads *princeps*, but Fr reads: "... the princess of East Friesland ..." Anne of Oldenburg, princess of East Friesland and regent from 1540 to 1558, died on November 10, 1575.

135 C2–3 *as that hee was glad ... to use his owne power*. I.e., "... that he was obliged to go out of the kingdom, in order to use his own power freely ..." Cf. Fr and L. Knolles uses "glad" in the sense of "constrained" or "obliged." For further examples of this usage see 258 I4, 261 B3, 405 B7–8 and note, 745 D3. He also uses "fain" in the same sense, as at 668 K4. Cf. *O.E.D.*, s.v. "fain," adj., sense 2.

136 H6 *al Christian kings*. Strictly, "... all consecrated kings ..." (Fr and L).

136 I6–7 *that the pope hath in power ... really and indeed*. I.e., the pope has jurisdiction over the emperors by lawful authority (*ipso jure, par puissance*), over other kings in fact (*reipsa, reellement & de faict*).

141 B6 *have seemed prejudiciall* ‖ Fr adds: "However the Emperor Ferdinand showed no concern whatsoever, no matter what remonstrances la Forest, the French ambassador, made to him."

142 F1–4 *Comitatus Perusiae ... terris, &c*. I.e., "The County of Perugia, Reate, Salvia (?), Interamna, Campania, and also Rome, Ferrara, etc.; the March of Ancona, the lands of Countess Matilda, and whatever lies on this side of Radicofani [in Tuscany] down to Ceperano [on the frontier of Naples], the Exarchate of Ravenna, the Pentapolis, together with other lands, etc."

142 H1 *Innocent the fourth*. L 2 substitutes "Innocent III," but Bodin should have written Honorius III.

144 I6 *by the power (should I say) or by the outragiousnesse*. Bodin's terms here are *potentia* and *impotentia*. The former signifies a power based on personal ascendancy, in contrast to *potestas*, power arising from legitimate authority.

145 D1–2 *any prince in the world* ‖ Addition in Fr and L. Fr reads: "I have seen the letter which is still found in the Treasury of France, in the chest marked *Anglia*."

145 D10 *certaine of his bastards*. The word "his" is added by Knolles.

150 F2 *drew him over* ‖ L adds details: "'*Major ad minorem*,' he said, 'Perseus to Philip.' For Martius was very tall and Perseus very short, and the latter's father was also called Philip. Perseus, smiling, crossed the river." In talking of stature, Bodin confused the main point. Cf. Livy, XLII, 39.

151 C9 *of Ferrier & Faur* ‖ Fr 1–4 add: "... some of the most worthy persons ever to be employed in the capacity of Ambassadors." Omitted Fr 5–8. This is the same Gui du Faur, Sieur de Pibrac, to whom the *République* is dedicated. Arnaud du Ferrier had occupied a chair of law at Toulouse, and may have been one of Bodin's teachers.

152 G3 *the yeare 1555*. As in Fr, but clearly erroneous. Omitted in L.

152 G5–6 *while king Philip was married unto the queene*. As in Fr, but L reads: "... while Philip of Spain was king of England."

CHAPTER 10 (PAGES 153–182)

153 D7 *the custome of tyrants*. As in Fr, but L reads: "... the custom of princes?" Cf. I Samuel 8:11–18.

154 F10 *except the soveraigne government were also spoken of*. Faulty. "... unless it is a question of [its] government (*gubernatio*)." (L only). For Bodin's distinction between form of commonweal and form of government, see 199 D10–200 F6.

156 F7–G1 *The same opinion ... and the magistrat*. As in Fr, but L is briefer, and omits the reference to rewards: "The same thing remains to be judged concerning punishments, which we see to be imposed by the magistrates."

156 I2–3 *all his subjects in generall* ‖ L adds:

Notes to Book I

"... or at least the greatest part of the citizens..."

156 I7 *the meniall people* ‖ L adds: "... because it bound neither the patricians nor the nobles. But since this matter gives occasion for civil discords, the greatest care must be taken that *plebiscita* should find no place in a Commonweal unless the whole people is bound by them. This had to be done at Rome."

158 I3–4 *and if the matter concerne the high points of soveraigntie, as is the majestie of the Commonweale.* Awkward. The first clause is from Fr, while L reads: "... if a matter of importance or the sovereignty (*majestas*) of the Commonweal seems to be involved."

159 A4 *his nephew.* L gives *nepos*, while Fr reads: "... his son..." The actual relationship has been disputed.

160 F10 *and particularly to others, to whome they be graunted.* Mistranslation. "... to the exclusion of all others (*privativement à tous autres*)."

160 H7 *of other former princes.* These words are inserted by Knolles.

161 C4 *to amplifie their lawes.* Possibly corrupt. Bodin writes: "... to transcribe their laws (*ad leges describendas*)..."

161 D8–10 *So ought the law ... the author.* Based on Fr, which omits the parenthesis. L enlarges: "To this point therefore belongs the ancient law which some call Laetoria, others Plaetoria, but which I think to be Praetoria, which Papinian shows to have been proposed concerning the jurisdiction of the Praetor."

162 H2–3 *under that soveraigne law.* Strictly, "... under the law of the sovereign..." (Fr), i.e., under the lawmaking authority of the sovereign.

163 B9 *the people commaunded* ‖ L adds: "By the word *centuriae* it is sufficiently understood that this was ordered by the whole *populus*, and not by the *plebs* alone, since the assembly of the *plebs* was not held by centuries, but by tribes."

166 H1 *even unto the meanest offices.* Condensing Fr, which reads: "... even unto the measurers, surveyors, hog inspectors, and other similar officials who are established in their office by perpetual edict."

169 C2 *of the imperiall cities* ‖ Fr adds: "It will not do to say that appeals brought against bailiffs, seneschals, and other inferior judges are not made directly to the Courts of Parlement, or to the Imperial Chamber; but that the appeal devolves upon the King, or the Emperor, who sends the case to judges appointed by him, who are in these circumstances his lieutenants; and that for this reason there can no more be an appeal from the lieutenant of the Prince than from the Prince himself. For although in terms of [civil] law there is no appeal from the lieutenant to the man who appointed him to his place [*Digest*, 49, 3, 1], yet all the authorizations to proceed with an appeal (*reliefs d'appel*) read that the condemned are appellants to the King and to the Courts of Parlement, which are termed ordinary judges of matters dealt with by ordinary procedure (*juges ordinaires des ordinaires*) and not extraordinary judges only, especially in view of the fact that they hear many cases as a court of first instance. Besides this, we see that even the lowest presidial magistrates are judges of last resort in certain cases." (17 lines).

169 D6 *paine of false judgement* ‖ Fr adds: "... according to the common [i.e., civil] law [*Digest*, 42, 1, 14 and 48, 19, 4], as well as by the ordinances of this Kingdom. And although many judges have been accustomed to use the words 'in sovereignty' in their judgments, nevertheless this is an abuse of the word, which is applicable only to a sovereign prince."

170 F7–8 *wherein is also fealtie and homage comprised.* As in Fr, but L enlarges: "Within this word sovereignty (*majestas*) are included all the things which we consider highest and most important in the Commonweal, yet the reservation of final appeal is generally stated in express terms."

171 A2 *it was long doubted.* Bodin gives the date of this incident as 1571 (Fr and L).

171 C2 *given false judgement* ‖ Fr adds: "By the same letters one may see that the exception [*exception* in Fr 1–6, 8, *execution* in Fr 7] of the reserved matters implies the confirmation of final appeal and sovereignty."

171 C4–5 *if the matter exceed the summe of 50 crowns.* Bodin actually writes: "... when the value of the suit does *not* exceed the sum of 50 crowns..." (L only), but this is an error. Cf. 237 D4–6 and *Methodus*, p. 207.

172 I10–K1 *although that they examine the pardon graunted* ‖ Obscure. Bodin distinguishes between *lettres de remission*, used in capital cases, and *lettres de pardon*, used for less serious offenses. The latter could be examined by the magistrates; the former could not. L adds an illustration to show when a pardon might be granted: "... as when, for example, a man innocent of crime confesses that by some accident he has been present at a murder along with the assassins."

173 A5–6 *begin sute of execution* ‖ L adds: "However this law is not peculiar to France, and is established with the greatest equity, in order that litigation may be plucked out by the roots, when it is manifest from the court records that the defendant must pay. For besides ourselves the English, Germans, Spaniards, Italians,

Greeks, Africans, Asians (and, I should think, other peoples also) use this law."

173 C5–7 *As for Governours ... have not that power by privilege, or by office, but by commission.* As in Fr, but L revises: "But the deputies of a prince, or the regents of a kingdom, assume the rights of sovereignty not as a favor from the prince, but in the right of a magistracy or of a public commission."

173 C7 *as the deputies or lieutenants of their princes.* Inexact. "... as the Princes [who are] deputies and lieutenants of the [German] Empire." (Fr).

173 E9 *having to friend.* Strictly, "... having as head..." (Fr). He refers to Charles, Cardinal of Bourbon, who was Archbishop of Rouen from 1550 to 1582.

174 F4–5 *but was since taken away by king Henry the third.* From L only, which actually reads: "Here the reader is to be advised that when I was writing this in Latin, that privilege had been taken away by King Henry III."

174 I7 *law of God appointed* ‖ L adds: "... [and] which is the old punishment appointed by the Twelve Tables and by the laws of almost all peoples."

177 E7 *in the Parliament at Orleans.* Strictly, "... at the request of the Estates of Orleans ..." (Fr).

178 G7–8 *as that the people was from that time discharged of all taxes and payments.* From Fr, but L substitutes: "... that the prices of land rose sharply."

178 H10–I2 *but yet an abuse ... to be reformed.* From Fr, with a marginal reference to *Code,* 8, 52(53), 2. L reverses this opinion: "... for long duration of time may bring it about that what has grown old by harmful usage and precedent may have greater sway than the law itself."

179 C8–D6 *A thing truely ... vaile of errour.* Mainly from L. Fr is briefer and does not moralize: "This [right of wreckage] was not at all in use among sovereign princes in ancient times, yet today it is common to all who have ports on the sea."

179 E2–5 *Which law ... right lawfully do.* Faulty translation. Doria's two galleys were wrecked and then confiscated (Fr and L), while anchorage on shore is a new and separate point. Fr reads: "We shall say the same of the duties (*droits*) which are levied for merely casting anchor upon land." L reads: "But it is not lawful even to cast anchor upon foreign shores without the prince's leave, yet formerly this belonged to the *jus gentium*."

180 H3–7 *The other rights of receipt ... the case of privileges.* Here Knolles, departing from his usual French edition, follows closely the text of Fr 1–2, but later editions (Fr 3–8) alter this as follows: "There are indeed 150 rights of the treasury, belonging for the most part to the sovereign prince, which it is not necessary to set down in detail here, and which the lawyers have examined sufficiently and perhaps too much [cf. G9–H3, which follows L]. Nevertheless the power to grant the right of holding a fair, which was in ancient times a mark of sovereignty [*Code* 4, 60, 1] just as it is at present, is comprised under the heading of privileges, and not under the rights of the treasury, and many other similar ones mentioned above [can be treated in similar fashion]." (8 lines).

180 I1–5 *howbeit that the princes ... Marque or Reprisal.* From Fr, but L differs and enlarges: "For whenever anyone suffered harm from enemies, it was lawful for him to carry away whomsoever he could of the enemy as captives, even in time of truce. In wartime, even if no injury had been inflicted by the enemy, the taking of captives was barred to none. But in times of peace or of truce, lest the truce be violated under pretense of an injury received, princes reserved this right to themselves, so that it was not lawful to lay hands upon enemies or strangers, while they were dwelling among the citizens, except after the matter had been investigated judicially. Yet it would have been better to grant this right to governors of provinces and to the authority of the higher courts, as in this realm ..." (10 lines).

180 K7 *in his life.* Probably a misprint. Read "... in his stile ..." (i.e., style) or "... in his title ..." Bodin writes *en sa qualité*.

181 A5 *June 1465* ‖ Fr adds: "This opened the way for the King to obtain the County of Provence."

181 C3 *spred their language and religion.* As in L, but Fr mentions language only.

181 C10 *our conscience.* Inexact. "... their conscience." (Fr).

181 D8–E1 *but to arrogat ... proper unto himselfe.* From L, but Fr is more specific: "Some also take the title of Sacred Majesty, like the Emperor; others, of Excellent Majesty, like the Queen of England by her edicts and letters patent."

182 F4 *in number infinit.* Condensing L, which reads: "... for of individual instances (*singularia*), which themselves are infinite, no science or discipline can be formulated."

182 I1 *my booke De Imperio.* One of Bodin's early legal treatises. In his will he asked that his manuscripts of these treatises be destroyed, and this was done in his presence before he died. Cf. G. Ménage, *Vitae Petri Aerodii quaesitoris andegavensis ...* (Paris, 1675), p. 143.

Notes to Book II

Book II

CHAPTER 1 (PAGES 183–197)

183 C8 *but some part*. Strictly, "... the lesser part..." (Fr). Cf. 184 F8 and Appendix B, no. 6.

184 K1 *of a Monarchie and Democratie*. Bodin writes: "... of tyranny and democracy..." (Fr and L); Plato himself writes "monarchy" (*Laws*, 693 D), but Aristotle represents him as having said "tyranny" (*Politics*, 1265b).

185 D8–E3 *and who should those subjects bee ... a state popular*. From Fr, but L reaches a harsher conclusion: "But how shall the citizens allow themselves to be bound by authority when they are unwilling? How will they be able to restrain the man ruling them? For if they obey of their own accord, their sovereignty is weakened and collapses. But if both sides refuse commands, and if there is nobody to obey or command, it will be not a Commonweal but an anarchy, which is worse than the cruelest tyranny."

186 F8 *twentie yeres*. Imprecise. Bodin writes "... twenty-one years..." in Fr and "... more than twenty years..." in L. The dates usually given are 431–404 B.C.

188 G10–H1 *Bethudere*. Here, and again at 361 A4, Bodin's spelling is "Bethudete" in Fr, "Bethudeta" in L. In Alvarez's *Description de l'Ethiopie*, Bodin's probable source for the term, it is spelled "Betudete."

191 E2–3 *many have both thought and writ*. L explicitly mentions du Haillan, who modified his opinion in a later (1580) edition of *De l'estat et succez des affaires de France*. It seems clear that Bodin's criticism brought about the change. For the relevant passages, see W. F. Church, *Constitutional Thought in Sixteenth-Century France* (Cambridge, Mass., 1941), pp. 121–122.

193 A1 *which booke is now lost* ‖ Addition in Fr and L. L reads: "However [Aristotle] called Plato's Commonweal neither an aristocracy nor a democracy, but a mixture of both, or πολιτεία [*Politics*, 1265b]."

193 B2 *him to say* ‖ L adds: "Indeed when Socrates read Plato's *Phaedrus* he was astonished, and exclaimed, 'How many falsehoods this young fellow has devised about me!'"

193 B9 *59 entire parts* ‖ I.e., 59 divisors. Cf. Plato, *Laws*, 738 A. L adds: "However the number 180, [which is] four times smaller (*quadruplo minor*), has 60 divisors." Possibly the text is faulty here.

195 B3 *of a popular estate* ‖ Fr adds: "... which the ancients properly called Commonweal (*Republique*)."

195 D6 *nobilitie was excluded* ‖ L adds: "In this way the *plebs* remained quiet for a time, while the greater magistrates—I mean the Consuls, Praetors and Censors—were chosen in *comitia centuriata*, that is, by the optimates, and the lesser magistrates in *comitia tributa*, that is, by the *plebs*." This sentence replaces the opening sentence (A4–B2), which follows Fr. The entire paragraph as written in Fr is considerably revised in L.

196 G9–10 *whereof no knowledge is to be had*. Bodin actually writes: "... but [the concept of] infinity should always be rejected in every science and doctrine." (Fr, cf. L).

197 C10 *above the rest*. Imprecise. Bodin specifies: "... above the rest in dignity..." (L).

CHAPTER 2 (PAGES 197–204)

199 B1–2 *wholly in the queene* ‖ Fr 1–4 add: "... otherwise neither the one nor the other would have been sovereign." Omitted Fr 5–8.

199 C9–10 *and Lepidus unfit for government, had submitted his authoritie unto Augustus*. As in L, but Fr reads: "... which were reduced to two, after Augustus had despoiled Lepidus..."

202 F2 *as not holden of him* ‖ Addition in Fr and L. Fr reads: "... no more than [in the case of] the Romans, who never knew this direct lordship. These words *dominium directum* and *dominium utile* are nowhere to be found in the whole of the Roman law, not even in the *Code*, or in the *Authentics*." The *Authentics* are a collection in Latin of the *Novellae* of Justinian. In L this passage occurs at 201 E4, and the expressions "direct soveraigntie" (201 E6), "soveraigntie" (202 F2), and "soveraigne right" (F3–4) all refer to this earlier concept of *dominium directum* or *droite seigneurie*, rather than to *majestas* or *souveraineté*.

203 A8 *of Lorains daughter* ‖ Fr adds: "However M. de la Mothe, Counselor to the King in the *Grand Conseil*, showed me that the Duchy of Bavaria and several others have descended in former times in the female line."

203 B2–4 *But how soever ... parts of Europe*. From Fr. L withdraws the reference to Germany and the North and substitutes: "From this it is seen that the traces of lordship have remained in Asia and Africa, but are now very scarce in Europe."

203 E4 *I aunswere, that of auntient time it was indeed against the law of nature*. Inexact. "... I answer that it is indeed *to some extent* against the law of nature..." Knolles apparently misreads *aucunement* as *anciennement*.

203 E5–8 *but if the consent ... is tyrannicall*. Following Fr, but L places more stress on human

A117

nature: "But since the violence or inborn cupidity of men is such that they cannot live for long in ease and tranquillity, but constantly wage wars, for the most part without just cause, is it not right that those who wage war on others unjustly should be punished when defeated by loss of their goods, by death, or by servitude? This is the just law of lordship [*Digest*, 49, 15, 19], provided that cruelty is avoided, and it is also sanctioned by the laws of the Scriptures." (8 lines).

CHAPTER 3 (PAGES 204–210)

205 C2–3 *as it most commonly doth*. From L, but Fr reads: ". . . as did all the ancient kings, as Thucydides has well noted . . ."

205 C3 *as this of ours*. From L, but Fr reads: ". . . without regard for the daughters, or the males descending from them, as is done in this kingdom by the Salic law . . ."

205 C3 *by election*, || *as in many kingdomes*. Fr inserts: ". . . as Aristotle writes to have been the practice in heroic times (however in this he is contrary to Thucydides and to the truth of the histories); and as is also done in many kingdoms . . ."

205 D1 *afterward queene* || Fr adds: ". . . and in addition the testament was confirmed and ratified by the people . . ."

205 D3 *or by chaunce* || L adds: ". . . as the kingdom of the Israelites [was given] to Saul; or . . ."

205 E3 *by the Mamalukes* || Fr adds: ". . . and Charles of France, the brother of St. Louis, whom the Pope sent to the Florentines, who were asking for a prince of the blood royal; and the Viscounts of Anglerie [i.e., the Visconti] were chosen lords of Milan for their nobility, although they were strangers . . ."

206 K6–7 *Herodotus . . . Xenophon*. Fr omits Berosus from this list, while L adds Manetho, Ephorus, and Theopompus.

207 B9–10 *who hath his proper difference seperated from a Monarch Royall*. From Fr, but L substitutes: ". . . whom we have shown to differ from kings not in genus but in form."

207 E7 *majestie of a king* || Fr adds: "Besides, the name 'King' can be proper only to him who is sovereign absolutely."

208 I2–3 *by which things . . . it selfe the chiefest*. Awkward. "It is certain that these things detract from the authority (*imperium*), which is supreme, of another man's sovereignty . . ." (L).

208 I9 *majestie of a superiour* || L adds: ". . . [because] these are proper to magistrates. But even royal power, which is the highest, cannot be conferred, except upon subjects, and certainly not upon a man who possesses the marks of sovereignty in his own right."

209 C8–9 *not easily with the wings of aspiring ambition to be passed*. This embellishment is added by Knolles.

210 F6 *thence againe* || Fr adds: ". . . and the Kingdom of Norway [has been] made hereditary, and even subject to feminine rule. For this reason it was claimed by the dowager of Lorraine and the Countess Palatine, daughters of Christian, King of Denmark, who showed that Margaret of Wolmar [i.e., of the house of Waldemar] was queen of the three kingdoms, Norway, Sweden and Denmark, by right of succession." (6 lines).

CHAPTER 4 (PAGES 210–218)

211 E7 *a most just prince* || Fr and L add: ". . . and a great prophet . . ."

212 F3–5 *at such time as M. Valerius Messala, was by a decree of the Senat, and of the people of Rome, called Father of his countrey*. Knolles follows Bodin (L only), but in fact Messala was deputed by the Senate to greet Augustus with this title. Cf. Suetonius, *Augustus*, 58.

213 B2–3 *most of tyrants to be in others feared*. I.e., ". . . most to be feared by tyrants [when found in other men] . . ." Cf. L.

213 E2 *raking officers*. Bodin's word is *corratiers*, which means agents or intermediaries, especially in a pejorative sense. Knolles translates it as "extorcioners" at 217 B6.

214 I10 *Julius, his mothers Mathematician*. Faulty. Bodin writes: ". . . Julius Maternus [*maternus* in L 1, *Maternus* in L 2–5], the mathematician . . ." But this in turn seems an error for Flavius Maternianus, commander of the city guards, who informed Caracalla of a prophecy made by a seer in Africa. Cf. Dio Cassius, *History of Rome*, LXXIX, 4.

216 F8 *unto others commendable* || Fr adds: "We shall discuss later to what extent governments should differ according to the differences between peoples. For the present it is sufficient to have mentioned [this point]."

216 K7 *an untamed beast* || Fr inserts: ". . . as is done at the changing of a popular estate into a monarchy . . ."

217 B3 *That of a craftie and subtill man is made a good king*. From L. The paradox is clearer in Fr, which reads *De meschant homme bon Roy*. Cf. 218 H3–4.

217 C9 *and of some called Charles do nothing*. Strictly, ". . . and of a Charles Fait-neant." (Fr only). Who is meant here is not clear. Perhaps Bodin is confusing Louis Fainéant with his uncle and heir, Charles of Lorraine, who was

supplanted by Hugh Capet in 987. Cf. 229 D2 and note.

217 D6–7 *almost a thousand Sestertioes.* Faulty. Bodin writes *fere millies sestertium*, i.e., almost 100,000,000 sesterces or 100,000 sestertia.

218 H6 *our auncestors called evill.* Bodin's terms here are *mauvais* and *malus*, while in the proverb he writes *meschant, callidus, improbus, malitiosus*.

CHAPTER 5 (PAGES 218–230)

219 D4–7 *against whome . . . Solon onely.* Confused and inexact. The first part is from Fr, which reads: ". . . and the murderers who slew the tyrants of Athens [i.e., the children of Pisistratus?] did not proceed by judicial means." The second part is from L, which reads: "But Harmodius and Aristogiton slew the children of Pisistratus by private authority, the law of Solon having been disregarded." (L 2–5). Knolles's version corresponds to L 1, in which a comma is misplaced.

220 K1–221 B8 *For it is great difference . . . his subjects and people.* Fr and L differ significantly here. Whereas Fr discusses intervention by "a foreign Prince," L extends this right to the "stranger" (*peregrinus*), whether sovereign or not. The recapitulation at 221 B6–8, permitting "any straunger" to kill a tyrannical monarch, occurs in L only.

224 H2 *to kill the magistrat* || Fr adds: ". . . or the commissioner who has power to command . . ." Cf. *Digest*, 48, 4, 1.

225 B1(margin) *Sledan. lib. 4.* "Lib. 4" is not in Fr or L. The correct reference is Book 8. Cf. Sleidan, *History of the Reformation* (London, 1689), p. 148.

225 B7–10 *And yet it is most certaine . . . which was not done.* From Fr. L elaborates: "However if the Emperor Charles had oppressed the Commonweal and the citizens with tyranny he could lawfully have been slain, as we have shown above, since he did not have the rights of sovereignty. But Luther did not employ this distinction and I am inclined to think that he did not understand it. He did not reflect that Charles was in the same relationship with the Commonweal as all princes, except some very few, but rather he answered just as though Charles alone held supreme authority." This alteration seems to have been prompted by the Geneva edition of 1577, the Preface of which criticizes Bodin for misrepresenting Sleidan's version (A9–B2) of Luther's attitude to resistance. Cf. Reulos, pp. 352–353.

225 D4–7 *lawful it is . . . life or honour.* Based on Fr, which actually reads ". . . to ward off (*parer*) the blows, [and] suffer death . . ." at D6. L changes the emphasis: "Everyone may refuse his commands which conflict with the laws of God and nature, and [you ought] to meet death courageously rather than obey, if you cannot save yourself by flight."

227 B3–4 *revived to ratifie his other evill acts.* Inexact. ". . . revived because of the ratification of his acts." (Fr).

228 H5 *to accept in stead of the whole.* Inexact. ". . . to obtain a release (*acceptilatio*) from the whole amount . . ."

229 D2–4 *And Hugh Capet . . . Charlemaigne.* Combining Fr and L, but L enlarges: "Hugh Capet did the same to Charles, whom he had captured in this city of Laon, after a long siege, through the treachery of the bishop of Laon. He imprisoned him in the castle of Orleans, so as not to begin his reign by the murder of a blood relation, and to show that the royal stock was to be spared."

229 D10–E1 *and the Commonweale* || Addition in Fr and L. Fr reads: ". . . and the Queen of England [holds] her cousin, who has always claimed that the two Kingdoms belong to her." L enlarges: "And Queen Elizabeth of England did the same to Mary Queen of Scots, whom the Scots claim to be the rightful ruler of the whole island. She has held her in captivity for a long time, for her own safety and that of her Commonweal, but it seems that she wishes eventually to restore her liberty and her rights in both kingdoms, which we hope will be done soon."

CHAPTER 6 (PAGES 230–244)

230 I5 *government of good men* || L adds: "For those men, says Cicero [*Pro Sestio*, 45], who wished what they did and said to be pleasing to the multitude, were of the popular party, but those who acted so that their plans might be approved by all the best men, were considered to be of the optimates. This is what he said to further his argument."

230 I7–8 *but to the government thereof.* Faulty. ". . . as is requisite in order to know the government thereof." (Fr).

232 K4 *by lot given.* Bodin's phrase is *par forme* [*force* in Fr 7] *de baloter*, i.e., voting by means of *balottes*. The *balotte* was a small ball used either for voting or for drawing lots, but L shows that Bodin is thinking of it here as a voting procedure.

233 B3–E5 *The same yeare . . . vertue and integritie only.* This description of Geneva differs in several details from the original version in Fr 1–2. The revisions, which first appear in Fr 3, are clearly due to amendments inserted in the Geneva edition of 1577. Cf. Reulos, pp. 345–346.

234 F3–235 B4 *Which neverthelesse differ . . . better lawes and orders than the rest.* This passage

is omitted in Fr 1, and Moreau-Reibel has pointed out (*Jean Bodin et le droit public comparé* [Paris, 1933], p. 253) that Bodin obtained much of it from Josias Simler's *De republica Helvetiorum*, first published at Zurich in 1576 and then by du Puys at Paris in 1577.

234 G2–3 *and by the Senators or magistrat.* Faulty. "... whether they [i.e., those elected] are senators or magistrates ..." (Fr and L).

234 I9 *at Berne for a yeare* ∥ Fr and L add: "... and at Lucerne for six months."

234 K2 *and xxvi others.* Error. Fr and L read: "... xxxvi others ..." But both Fr and L then indicate that the combined total of these thirty-six and the Senate of twenty-six is a body of sixty.

236 H1–5 *insomuch that ... the imperial cities.* From Fr. L substitutes: "But it almost always happens that those who possess the right of election in the Commonweal encroach upon the rights of sovereignty. We have said that this happened especially in the Commonweal of Venice, where sovereignty was of the royal type, and in the same way also the electors of the German Emperor gradually transferred the rights of sovereignty into their own hands."

236 I1–2 *privatly over the emperour himselfe, and over all.* Strictly, "... to the exclusion of (*privativement à*) the emperor, and of all ..."

237 B5–9 *Howbeit yet many are of opinion ... one divided from another.* In L Bodin remarks that he formerly held this view himself, "... but I gave up this opinion when I perceived more clearly that the Estates of Germany have the supreme sovereignty ..."

237 D6 *as to all the appeales of the subjects of the empire.* Inexact. "... [which chamber is] common to all the subjects of the Empire." Knolles reads *comme* instead of *commune*. L is more specific: "The same court is the source of commands, orders, and letters of execution to the princes, the magistrates, and the Senate of each city or province."

237 D7 *twentie foure judges, and one prince of the empire.* Inexact. Fr reads: "... 23 judges, and one prince of the empire ..." L reads: "... 24 judges, of whom the chief is one of the princes ..."

238 F4–5 *than if they were but of themselves onely.* Strictly, "... than if there were but the estates only." (Fr).

240 G6 *the head, deserveth* ∥ L adds: "... and this is also due to the House of Austria, greatly renowned for its glorious deeds."

240 I8–9 *Ausburg, Nuremberg, Wormes.* As in Fr. L omits Augsburg and adds Ulm.

240 K6 *two Censors.* The word "two" is not in Fr or L, and may be a misprint for "the." Cf. *Methodus*, p. 208.

241 B4–5 *and now of late to hold of the empire.* Faulty. "... and to hold immediately (*nuement*) of the Empire ..."

242 K3 *six thousand.* As in Fr. In L the example suggests 9,000 rich out of 10,000 citizens.

243 C4 *the second sort.* Bodin writes: "... the third sort ..." (Fr), but this is clearly a mistake. Cf. Aristotle, *Politics*, 1292b.

CHAPTER 7 (PAGES 244–252)

245 D10 *in giving of their voices* ∥ L adds: "... which could occur if 51 citizens of every century agreed ..."

245 D10 *fourescore centuries.* As in Fr. Here L reads "... 85 centuries ..." but reverts to "... 80 centuries ..." at E5. Bodin does not mention the equites, who voted first in eighteen centuries and whose support was needed to give the first class its absolute majority.

246 F8 *maintainers of their liberties* ∥ L adds: "But this could not be done unless the votes of all men were made equal."

246 G3 *assemblies of the common people* ∥ L adds: "This was the first time that the names *plebs* and *populus* were distinguished. The *populus* included the Senate, the patricians, and the plebeians."

249 C8–9 *the nobilitie, or a few of the better sort.* Imprecise. Fr reads: "... the nobility, or a few rich men ..." L substitutes: "... the better sort (*optimates*) ..." Similarly at 251 D9 Bodin writes "... the nobility and the rich ..." in Fr, "... the optimates ..." in L.

249 C10–D1 *upon the poorer and baser sort, aswell as upon the rich, without favour or respect of persons.* As in Fr, but L substitutes: "... upon the plebeians only ..."

250 K2–6 *For the true nature ... or favour of any man.* From Fr, but L revises and expands: "For the chief point of democratic liberty is that all men may be made equal in everything. Nor are they willing to obey except on the condition that they in turn shall command those whom they obey. And not even in this manner can they be kept to their duty, unless they are made more pliant by the imposition of very necessary and just precepts, or else cajoled by gifts and flattery. But since a large number cannot stand out above the crowd in virtue, wealth, and nobility, it generally happens that the multitude pursue the noble, the rich, and the virtuous with a certain envy and meanness of spirit." (9 lines).

251 E8 *among themselves, together with the Commonweale.* Strictly, "... among themselves *and* with the Commonweal (*inter se & cum*

Notes to Book III

Republica)." The harmony between the whole and its parts, and of the parts among themselves, is a favorite figure of Bodin's. Cf. 364 F5 and the note at 361 B4.

252 G4 *the officers, colleges, and corporation*. Inexact and incomplete. ". . . the commissioners (*curatores*), colleges, corporations, and orders of citizens . . ." (L only).

Book III

CHAPTER I (PAGES 253–278)

253 D5–7 *and yet performed great matters . . . close and covert*. Inexact. ". . . and yet [all these men] performed great matters, albeit that *they* were beset with many great and right puissant enemies: and were therefore the more redoubted, for that *their* designs were so close and covert . . ." (Fr).

255 C3–4 *Seeing therefore . . . Aristocraticall estates*. As in Fr, but L drops the distinction: "Therefore since a senate is so necessary in every Commonweal . . ."

256 F3–4 *Let credit be given to no man upon his oath*. Unlikely in this context. Read: "Let no fealty be sworn to any man . . ." The words "manumised mens" (F4) are inserted by Knolles.

256 G4 *wise men, and fearing God*. As in Fr, but L enlarges: ". . . who surpass the others in wisdom (*sapientia*), prudence (*prudentia*), and science (*scientia*). *Sapientia* distinguishes piety from impiety; *prudentia*, honor from baseness; *scientia*, truth from falsehood." Cf. 4 K2 and note. L also comments marginally on the Hebrew equivalents for these terms.

257 E5 *Sir Thomas Moore* ‖ Fr and L add: ". . . Chancellor of England . . ."

258 K3 *who now governeth the kingdome of Polonia*. As in L. Fr 1 reads: ". . . who is at present King of Poland . . ." But Fr 2–8 amend this to: ". . . who has usurped the Kingdom of Poland . . ." The change illustrates French reluctance to admit the validity of Henry III's deposition by the Estates of Poland after his precipitous return to France in 1574.

259 B6 *Aediles*. Strictly, ". . . Curule Aediles . . ." (L).

265 A2 *is enclosed within the compasse and circuit of a mile*. Inexact. Fr reads: ". . . is enclosed within the compass and circuit of the suburbs (*la banlieue*) . . ." L reads: ". . . has authority no further than the first milestone from the city."

265 B7–C7 *But there is a notable difference . . . princes commaund* ‖ Fr and L differ here. For the first part (B7–C1) Knolles follows Fr, while L reads: "In this point only [Commonweals] differ, that what is decided in the smaller council or Senate in popular or aristocratic states is usually set in order by the magistrates without orders from the people or nobility. What the smaller council finds doubtful or important is customarily brought to the Senate to be decided there. What the Senate cannot order without infringing sovereignty is referred to the assembly of the people or nobility."

In the second part (C1–7) Knolles follows L, while Fr reads: "But in a Monarchy, advice and deliberation are carried on in the Senate, and resolution in the small council." Fr then adds: "This may be seen at every point in Titus Livius. When question arises of peace or war, or of other important matters which concern the sovereignty, the deliberation occurs in the Senate, and the matter is resolved by the people, as I have shown by many examples above in the chapter 'Of the marks of sovereignty.' Similarly, when war was declared on the Romans by the Tarentines, the Senate, as Plutarch says, advised the action, and the people of Tarentum gave their command." (8 lines added).

266 I10–K1 *in the raigne of Charles the ix*. Bodin gives the precise date: 15(L) or 16(Fr) August 1563.

267 B3–C7 *In like case . . . by the greater part*. From Fr, but L revises this passage: "But in order to weaken the prestige and dignity of the Parlement, Charles IX commanded the most recent transactions of the court to be brought to him and canceled in his presence. After his death the Privy Council, which had become greatly enlarged, began to be so encumbered with the determination of suits that it now appears to be an ordinary court of judges. For Henry III, as I said previously, created a new Senate, smaller than before, which he called the Council of State, because he knew that the opinions of the wise were being overcome not by the weight [of opposing arguments], but by numbers . . ." (9 lines).

268 F1 *of twentie* ‖ L adds: ". . . and nowadays there are scarcely a dozen."

270 H7–8 *profitable or hurtfull*. As in Fr, but L enlarges: "There ought to be the same distinction also between things profitable and unprofitable, for almost always the one type are joined with justice, the other type with injustice."

271 D4–9 *Into which difficulties . . . to be judged upon*. Inexact, but Fr and L differ here as to the Venetian practice. Fr reads: "The Venetians also find themselves in the same difficulties, and this often forces them to give opinions orally, and to give up the use of ballots, which they employ even when the question concerns property, life, and honor, in the fashion of the ancient Greeks and Romans. This cannot be done without injustice, because of the infinite variety of cases which come up for judgment."

A 121

L reads: "But when the Venetians fall into these difficulties, they are forced to give up secret voting and give their opinion aloud. They are also accustomed to do this when the judgment concerns life, honor, and property. Indeed this [type of judgment] cannot be reached by secret voting and tablets, which the judges of the Greeks and Latins also used, without the greatest injustice." On the relation between "lots" (D5 and D7) and "ballots," see the note at 232 K4.

275 B1 *charge of the common treasure* || Addition in Fr 4 only: "... and by the command (*commission*) of the people which provided that Caesar's army should be paid out of the treasury, and countless other similar [examples]." Omitted in Fr 1–3, 5–8.

275 B9–C1 *for so it was . . . to the number of fiftie*. From Fr, but L revises: "For if there were fewer than 400 senators, or even 200 after the *lex Julia* . . ." Dio Cassius, the source given for this statement, gives no precise figure. Cf. *Roman History*, LIV, 35, and LV, 3.

275 C7 *if the commission be not on foot*. Inexact. ". . . if the commission be not at the foot [of the document]." (Fr). Cf. 325 E1–2 and 337 A7–8.

277 A1–4 *But the king being dead . . . into the councell*. From Fr. L substitutes: "The others, the magistrates, are created by law, and confirmed by a charter signed by the king and sealed with the great seal. They do not depend on the pleasure of the prince, who cannot compel them to vacate their magistracy unless they have committed a capital crime, and have been convicted in a public trial."

277 C6 *Rome, Lacedemonia, and Pharsalia*. As in Fr, but L adds Massilia and the Athenian Areopagites to this list.

CHAPTER 2 (PAGES 278–293)

278 F8–K1 *As in the whole . . . Magistrats or Officers*. The introduction to this chapter in Fr is considerably rearranged and expanded in L, but the differences seem of slight importance. Knolles takes the first part (F8–H3) chiefly from L, the remainder from Fr.

278 G8–9 *vertue of commissi[on] onely* || L adds: "We are to use foreign or barely Latin words here, forsaking [Latin] lest the obscurity of the words increase the difficulty of the matter. However many have made the word *officialis* Latin by usage. Paulus himself, following Suetonius, calls public charges *officia* [*Digest*, 50, 16, 18]."

279 A7–8 *For he saith . . . should be magistrats*. From Fr, but L substitutes: "For he defines a magistrate as the ordinary official (*potestas*) of the Roman people. But definitions must have universal application; individual instances can be neither defined nor comprised in any discipline. Moreover the word *potestas* almost always meant provincial magistrates, as we shall show later."

279 C5–8 *For when Lentulus . . . the Senat of law*. Bodin cites this incident again at 295 D7–8 and at 298 G10–H1. The third time he correctly attributes it to M. Lucullus. Cf. Cicero, *Ad Atticum*, IV, 2.

279 E9 *even unto the Aruspises* || Mistranslation or misprint. Read: ". . . and [power] to take the auspices." (Fr and L). L adds: "[But] it is almighty God who has the charge of human affairs." Cf. E6.

282 H4–6 *For the suspending . . . but even in a Monarchie also*. From L, but Fr reads: "For the suspension of all magistrates gives infinite power to commissioners, and cannot be done without danger, except in a monarchy." The adverse judgment on Charles V's experiment (I1–3) occurs in L only.

283 A7 *yet unto others it may seeme strange*. Following L. Fr is more pointed: "As for the jurisconsults who never stir from the Schools, they may be pardoned [for failing to understand it]."

283 C2–3 *Which the Latines properly called Curatio, which is to say a Commission*. As in Fr. L reads: "The ancient Latins called it *curatio*, which Suetonius in the *Life of Augustus* [89] seems to call *commissio*. 'He warned the Praetors,' he writes, 'not to suffer his name to be made common by *commissiones*.'" Suetonius, however, is using the word in an entirely different sense. Cf. 346 G3–5.

283 C7–9 *both which Aristotle . . . never intermedling therein*. From Fr, but L generalizes: "Aristotle nowhere makes this distinction, nor do the other philosophers, who wrote about the Commonweal without taking the slightest part in its management. Diogenes Laertius considered all those whose *Lives* he wrote to have been inept at conducting political affairs."

284 F8–9 *as to judge according to the latter proceedings, and to leave the former*. Inexact. ". . . [but] to judge later suits (*proces*) and leave aside earlier ones [is another matter] . . ." (Fr only).

284 H5–6 *are afterwards Commissioners*. Inexact. ". . . are appointed Commissioners . . ." Knolles apparently read *depuis* in place of *deputés*.

288 G1 *to the contrarie*. This phrase is added by Knolles and seems to distort Bodin's meaning.

288 I4–7 *and not for that commissions . . . any officers ordinarie power*. From L, but Fr is longer: "On this point many [jurisconsults] have taken great pains to seek out the reason, and finally have reached agreement, resolving that it is

because offices are agreeable and commissions odious; or else that the ordinary way, as they term it, is agreeable, and the extraordinary way odious. This [reason] cannot hold, either in the punishment of crimes, which is done most frequently and most satisfactorily by extraordinary means, or in the privileged treatment of persons or of actions which call for the use of extraordinary procedure [*Digest*, 50, 13, 1]. Others have thought that it is because the prince never dies, which we have refuted above. Besides, this could not apply in kingdoms which are transmitted by election, although long ago even in this realm the prince was not called king before his coronation, as du Tillet has noted. Moreover if this reason were admissible it would follow that in popular and aristocratic Commonweals commissions would be perpetual, for neither the people nor the lords as corporate bodies ever die [*Digest*, 5, 1, 76], unless they are suddenly exterminated. The true reason for this difference arises from the fact that offices are perpetual, or at least they always have a specified duration, and are based upon an edict giving power to continue the charge; whereas commissions cease when the charge has been executed, and do not rest upon laws, as we have said." (25 lines).

289 B5-7 *as were other . . . any law at all.* From L, but Fr reads: ". . . and what is more there is in the registers of the Parlement of Paris the creation by express edict of an office of inspector of hogs, verified in the month of July of the same year [1544]."

291 B8-9 *which is not . . . committed unto him.* Inexact. ". . . which would not even be permitted in the case of a private man who might have given a general charge [to someone]." (Fr only). He refers to *Digest*, 12, 6, 6 and 17, 1, 46.

291 D1-2 *state and Commonweale* ‖ Fr adds: "We shall discuss later whether the subject should take on an unjust commission, or whether he should reject it, and how he should behave in such cases. For what we have said concerns just and reasonable commissions only, and [is given] to show the difference between commissions and offices."

291 D9 *without appeale unto any other magistrat.* Faulty. ". . . without any title (*appellation*) of magistrate . . ."

292 F3 *both Sigonius* ‖ *and Gruchius.* Fr does not mention Grouchy, and Fr 2-4 add: ". . . [Sigonius] would have had more honor by writing of something other than the law of the Romans, especially where he handles 'Concerning judgments.'" Fr 5-8 omit the words "would . . . Romans."

292 H2-3 *The word Imperator, signifieth properly a generall or chiefe captaine.* As in Fr, but L expands: "However Cicero spoke like an orator to advance his cause, since the majority of magistrates and commissioners were created not by the whole *populus*, but by the *plebs* without the patricians, voting by tribes and not by centuries, as we have shown before. For the word *imperator* is properly used of the man whose commands the army is bound to obey, while *dux* is applied to the man who, because he is active and skilled in military science, draws up the army in battle array, pitches camp, besieges fortresses, and yet is under the *imperator*. Thus Cicero writes that war was waged against the Romans in Africa with Xanthippus the Lacedemonian as military leader, but Hasdrubal as commander-in-chief." (9 lines).

CHAPTER 3 (PAGES 293-309)

293 B5 *in a Commonweale* ‖ L adds: "It matters little which words we use, if Latin ones are lacking, provided that we understand the thing itself." This refers to the word *officialis* (cf. note at 278 G8).

293 C1 *before any lawyers or Officers.* Inexact. ". . . before any laws or offices . . ." Cf. Fr and L.

294 G1-3 *Howbeit that many . . . to be his, say.* Inaccurate. "In this point those who have forged (*supposé*) the books *On the Latin Language* under the name of Marcus Varro are mistaken, when they say . . ." (Fr). Cf. 297 C2-8.

294 I7-8 *as Plutarke reporteth* ‖ L adds: "The Hebrews comprehend all public persons who have *imperium* by the one word judges (שופטים). The rest they call שומרים, that is, underofficials (*ministri*)."

295 A1-6 *We must therefore . . . Wherefore we have said.* Faulty, owing to a misprint in Fr and a different construction in L. Fr reads: "We must therefore confess that of persons with a public and ordinary charge, some are magistrates, others are not. And since negation [*negation* in Fr 1-5, *negotiation* in Fr 6-8] makes a division faulty by its very nature, we have said . . ."

295 A9 *ministers unto the magistrats* ‖ L adds: "But since we are hampered by lack of words, we have decided that this word [*officiales*] should be applied to the whole class, in order to use the word *ministri* in its proper place, and also to make this discipline conform to legal, political, and military usage. For we [French] call those who occupy public and ordinary charges, whether with or without *imperium*, *officiarii* in the popular tongue [i.e., *officiers*]." (7 lines).

296 H1-298 F8 *And in that . . . foundation of the citie.* Mainly from L, which revises and extends the corresponding passage in Fr.

296 H9 *but for the publike crimes sake.* Obscure. ". . . but [infamy arose] out of the ground for the public accusation (*crimen*)." Cf. K8-9, which is from Fr.

297 C3 *which are in his name carried about in the Latine tongue.* Strictly, ". . . which are circulated concerning the Latin language . . ." (L). He refers to Varro's *De lingua Latina.*

297 C4–5 *many things to be in them spoken by contraries.* Inexact. ". . . the word *multa* to be called by the contrary (*per antiphrasim*)." I.e., *multa* (or *mulcta*), a fine or loss, is contrary to *multus,* much.

298 F9–10 *amongst the rest made one, whereby he giveth unto all magistrats jurisdiction and divination.* Based on Fr, but L is more precise: ". . . sings thus of the magistrates, 'Let the magistrates punish disobedient citizens by fines, imprisonment, or whipping, unless forbidden to do so by an equal or greater magistrate, or by the people, to whom let there be appeal. When a magistrate has pronounced sentence, let there be a hearing before the people concerning the penalty.' A little later he adds, 'let all magistrates have judgment or divination.'" Cicero actually writes "judgment *and* divination" (*De legibus,* III, 3).

298 G10–300 K7 *For that which Lucullus . . . authoritie and magistracie.* From L. This discussion is almost entirely lacking in Fr, which merely reads: "It is true that bishops have a much more extensive cognizance than the early priests, for they may imprison in their court, and condemn to torture, although magistrates execute their sentences. The ancient priests did not have this power, nor did they have cognizance of marriages, or of many other matters which the bishops have now, as we shall say in due place." (7 lines).

300 F9–10 *by retracting the cause, to reject the witnesses; and so when as no moe could justifie the matter, freely.* Incomplete translation of an obscure passage in L, which probably should read: ". . . to reject the witnesses, when the case is retried (*causa retretata*), in order that they might not be arrayed against him, and by destroying the testimony, when none could testify further [*or possibly with* Knolles: when no more could testify], freely . . ."

302 I4–5 *that hee alleageth of Appius the Consull.* Strictly, ". . . that which Appius the Consul said . . ." (L).

304 F3–4 *As for the Questors . . . that they had not.* From Fr, but L expands: "There is a doubt about the Quaestors. Marcus Messala deprives them of all power of summons and apprehension. Asconius shows that they lacked not only a sergeant, but even an official chair such as the Curule Aediles used. However he says that these Quaestors exercised jurisdiction on their benches. Therefore we must admit that they had taken over a small part of the Praetor's jurisdiction, which they could exercise without *imperium* in the same way as the Curule Aediles, as the priests, or as specially appointed judges (*judices dati*), whose sentences were carried out by magistrates [*Digest,* 42, 1, 15, pr.]." (8 lines).

304 K1–2 *Pretor of the citie judged* ‖ L adds: ". . . and later the Prefect of the city (*Praefectus urbi*) . . ."

305 A2 *which many have rashly abused for infamie.* As in L, but Fr is specific: ". . . which Doctor Cujas has taken for infamy." Cujas later denied this allegation (*Observationes et emendationes,* XVIII, 38).

307 C1–5 *There are also . . . other cities also.* From Fr. L qualifies, stressing the variations between peoples: "Now as for our statement that there are certain public charges which cannot be exercised without loss of respect, I find that this varies according to the diversity of laws and customs. As an example the Romans, by a decision of the Censors, kept the executioner outside the walls of the city. The people of Toulouse have the same rule even now. But the ruling of the Censors affected only those who strangled the condemned with a rope, and not to the lictors, who either beat the victims to death with clubs while they hung from a frame, or beheaded them. By our customs, however, the one method is as disgraceful as the other. He who attempted suicide, Festus says, was also considered to be on a level with the executioner. And while the offices of sergeants and attendants were formerly servile, they are now deemed honorable." (12 lines).

308 G7–8 *By lot . . . degrees of the people.* Obscure, combining Fr and L. L reads: "By lot the citizens are drawn from one, or more, or from all classes [of society] . . ." The whole passage (G1–I9) is modeled closely on Aristotle, *Politics,* 1300a–b.

308 K8–9 *But by this division cannot the diversitie of magistrats and officers be judged.* As in Fr, but L is more explicit: "Here he comprehends all who are appointed to public charges (I exclude divine matters), whether they obtain them by ordinary means or as extraordinary commissioners, whether they obey or command, within the term ἄρχοντες, that is, *magistratus.*"

309 A8–B6 *But better it were . . . particular persons onely.* From Fr. L expands this into a careful summary of the entire discussion: "I think it is more convenient to say that public charges concern either divine matters or human matters. Those which concern human matters are either ordinary, which are called offices, or extraordinary, as are commissions. The ordinary charges are either honorable or subordinate. The honorable ones are accompanied either by *imperium* alone, or by jurisdiction alone, or by both, or else they lack both. To the latter class belong ordinary ambassadors of the Commonweal and senators. To the former belong judges

and magistrates. Commissioners are divided in the same way. Of the charges which refer to subordinate matters, and which are devoid of honor, some are ignominious, some are exercised without any ignomy. The individual branches of this division may be divided in turn, for magistrates are said to be either greater (who are bound only by the authority of the sovereign) or lesser. The latter are again of two kinds: some are bound by the commands of the greater magistrates, but command the lower magistrates; the others have authority over private men only." (17 lines).

CHAPTER 4 (PAGES 309–325)

310 H1–2 *or for some particularitie . . . divers sorts.* Inexact. ". . . or for a general pardon (*abolition*), or a particular one, or a remission, or letters of pardon, which are different things . . ." (Fr).

310 H7–8 *letters of jurisdiction or commaund, or letters of justice or state.* Confused. As the following discussion shows, letters of "jurisdiction" (L) and of "justice" (Fr) are synonymous, as are letters of "command" (Fr) and of "state" (L).

312 I5–6 *of God and nature* || Addition in Fr and L. Fr reads: ". . . as if the prince should command the magistrates to put to death the innocent or kill the children . . ."

316 G7–8 *sometimes wel eased, which have used these restrictions.* Strictly, ". . . have sometimes been well contented that these restrictions have been used [by the magistrates] . . ." (Fr).

317 B9 *should never sort to good end.* Strictly, ". . . should never reach *any* conclusion." Cf. Fr and L.

321 B5–7 *But if any man . . . to be embarred.* Awkward. "But if anyone under some show of truth shall deceive (*obrepserit*) the prince, he is to be barred from the profits and advantages contained in the [prince's] rescript." Following L 3–5; L 1–2 are corrupt.

321 C5–8 *and especially in popular estates . . . ruine of the Commonweale.* Mainly from L. Fr is more explicit: ". . . and especially in popular states, where the inequality caused by privilege gives rise to popular seditions, and frequently to the ruin of Commonweals."

321 E4 *worldly Souldiours.* Strictly, ". . . forensic soldiers . . ." (Fr and L).

322 H1–2 *some most pernitious and daungerous unto the state.* From Fr, but L specifies: ". . . the interpreters of papal law . . ." with a marginal reference to John Andreae, Panormitanus (Nicolo Tedeschi, Archbishop of Palermo), and Felinus Maria Sandaeus.

322 I6 *by the parliament at Blois.* Strictly, ". . . by the assembly of the Third Estate at Blois [in 1576] . . ." (Fr).

322 K7 *For in him it is to be presumed.* Strictly, "For in the former case (*car en luy*) it is to be presumed . . ."

323 E5–6 *and all for the false opinion that the people have of the equitie and integritie of the judges.* Inexact. ". . . and why so? Because the magistrates themselves are the authors of the revolt, through [their] false opinion of right and justice . . ." (L).

323 E8–324 F10 *an honest speech . . . thy prince thy selfe.* As in L, but Fr differs: "That is all very well as a remonstrance, but if the will of the Prince is firm and unalterable, should one endanger the state? Should one allow oneself to be compelled? It would be more honest to give up one's place and office. But is there anything more dangerous and more pernicious than the subject's disobedience to and contempt for his sovereign?" (6 lines).

CHAPTER 5 (PAGES 325–342)

326 F4 *to enforce or punish them,* || *which Demosthenes.* Incomplete. Fr adds: "In this consists the execution of commands, which Demosthenes . . ." L adds: "But this is done by the infliction of penalties, which Demosthenes . . ." Fr 7 is corrupt at this point.

326 H4 *owne hands and seales* || L adds: "But this is permitted only to those judges who, either alone or with a colleague, have a right to command from some other source; and not to private citizens if they have been appointed judges by magistrates."

326 K10–327 A2 *But the last and highest degree . . . highest marke of soveraigntie.* As in Fr, but L narrows this "highest degree" by omitting the power to impose the death penalty: "But to deliver from punishment those who are condemned is proper to sovereignty . . ."

327 C5 *a notable question, which is not yet well decided.* For the history of this question, see the penetrating study by M. P. Gilmore, *Argument from Roman Law in Political Thought, 1200–1600* (Cambridge, Mass., 1941).

329 A1 *penaltie of the law.* Strictly, ". . . power (*potestas*) of the law . . ." This is still part of the quotation from Marcianus, of which Knolles quotes only the first part in Latin. Cf. *Digest*, 48, 16, 1, 4.

329 B4–6 *for that the law . . . or such like.* Faulty. ". . . because [if voting tablets had been used] the law itself, not the people, would have been the arbiter of the punishment. The sentence was usually of this sort, or similar . . ." (L).

Notes to Book III

329 C6–D2 *Whatsoever . . . themselves be present.* Mainly from Fr. L quotes directly from the *Digest*, 1, 21, 1, pr. (10 lines).

330 I9–K1 *And thus much . . . to search farther.* Imprecise. The point disputed by Lothair and Azo is classified as a subordinate thesis (*hypothesis*), which must then be extended into a general proposition (*ad thesim & quaestionem infinitam*). Cf. L.

331 C2 *king Lewes* ‖ Fr adds: "Others are established in the form of fiefs, like many sergeantships in Normandy which are termed enfeoffed."

331 C9–10 *And in the records . . . at once in the armie.* As in L, but Fr gives details: "And in the records of the *Chambre des Comptes* I have seen an extract of the following article from the Counts of Caux in Normandy: Total of the establishment—17 *chevaliers*, 106 *escuyers*, 25 *arbalestriers*, and 365 [others], partly sergeants, partly constables." Omitted in Fr 1–4.

332 K2 *albeit that the honour and dignitie of the office be not proper.* Inexact. ". . . albeit that the office [*office* in Fr, *honor ac dignitas* in L] be not proper . . ."

333 A9–10 *as a thing put in trust unto the magistrat.* Inexact. ". . . just as something put in trust remains the property of the owner, and [to show] that the guardianship [of offices] is entrusted to those who are invested in them." (Fr).

333 E4–9 *Now such proportion . . . or justice of the cause.* From Fr. L revises and expands: "And so we see that the lawyers speak of the hearings (*cognitiones*) and decrees of the prince, not of his jurisdiction or judgments. The books of Paulus, *Libri decretorum in cognitionibus prolatorum*, refer to this point. Likewise whenever a magistrate or specially appointed judge investigates and decides at his own discretion outside the law and, as it were, freed from chains, he does not proceed by law, nor is he said to carry out the *legis actio*. Festus properly defines an arbiter [ed. Müller, p. 15] as one who possesses power (*potestas*) over the whole affair. And thus Cicero [*Pro Roscio Comoedo*, 4] reproached his adversary for having confused a judge with an arbiter: 'Were you taking the same man as arbiter and judge? Were you giving the same man unlimited freedom of action, and also binding him within the strictest formula?' Here it is a question of an arbiter appointed by law, not of one freely accepted. Even Aristotle himself distinguished in the same way between δικασταί, judges, and διαιτηταί, arbiters [*Politics*, 1268b]."

334 K2–7 *For whereas . . . jurisdictio est.* Faulty. "For whereas the Romans had properly separated the office of Proconsul's lieutenant, whom they called *legatus*, from the deputy in the quality of particular commissioner, whom they called *judex datus*, and also from him to whom power to command was given by the magistrate, whom they called *is cui mandata jurisdictio est . . .*" (Fr).

335 C2 *be comprehended* ‖ Fr adds: "And even though there are some penalties and fines appointed by the edicts which have a prohibition against reducing them, nevertheless this is often contravened by the magistrates. An example is the edict concerning forgers, made by King Francis I, which imposed the death penalty whether the offense concerned civil or criminal causes. The Parlements, Bailiffs, and Seneschals, who published, verified, and registered it without qualification, do not keep it at all, having found in the course of time that it was unjust, because the infinite variety of cases does not permit homogeneity of decisions." (10 lines).

337 A8 *be not on foot.* Faulty. Read: ". . . be not at the foot [of the document]." (Fr). Cf. 275 C7 and note, and 325 E1–2.

339 B9 *who were afterwards.* Faulty. ". . . who were at that time (*alors*) . . ." The date given is A.U.C. 304 in Fr 1–4 and L, 303 in Fr 5–8. Cf. Livy, III, 55.

339 C1–2 *were called Consuls* ‖ L adds: "Marcus Tullius [Cicero] shows this sufficiently in his law [*De legibus*, III, 3] conceived in these words: 'Let there be two [men] with royal power, and let them be called Praetors, Judges, and Consuls from [their functions of] leading (*praeeundo*), judging, and taking counsel (*consulendo*).'"

339 E2 *paid unto the judge* ‖ Addition in Fr and L. L reads: "Our countryman [Gui] Pape is wrong in writing that the wound was inflicted during a judicial examination, for it is unheard of that defendants should be examined while wearing their swords."

340 G6 *coughed and spauled.* I.e., spat. Inexact. ". . . breathed and yawned . . ." (Fr). Cf. 547 B1–2.

341 C4 *enclining neither unto crueltie nor mercie.* As in L, but Fr reads: ". . . and do not give way at all to pity, to which men are naturally more prone than to rigor . . ."

342 I7–8 *And thus much concerning the power and authoritie of Magistrats over particular and privat men.* This concluding sentence is added by Knolles.

CHAPTER 6 (PAGES 343–361)

344 H8–9 *in the absence of the king, oftentimes in judgement used this forme of speech.* Based on Fr, but L is more specific: ". . . was accustomed, as occasion arose, to use the following formula, after all the votes of the judges had been taken, if he thought the question was to be decided otherwise . . ."

344 I4 *the king that so commaundeth* || Fr adds: "That is why he who delivers the king's word speaks in this fashion: 'The King commands you that on the folded portion of these letters it shall be stated they have been read, published, and registered, having been heard at the motion of his *procureur*, without adding thereto, he requesting or consenting.'"

345 A8 *So a controversie arising*. Bodin is more specific here: "And indeed I remember that when I was young a controversy arose . . ." (L). Fr and L give the name of the magistrate in question, Gilles le Maistre, who became first president in 1551 and died in 1562.

345 E1 *the soveraigntie of his person*. Strictly, ". . . the character (*personne*) of sovereign . . ." (Fr only).

348 H9–13 *seeing that that . . . themselves or not*. Mainly from Fr, but awkward. L revises: "This should be understood of the Consul on the day when he has the fasces and the right to command. For although the Praetors always had the fasces and *imperium*, since they conducted affairs by means of divided offices, the Consuls shared the same office and never had the fasces both on the same day, as Verrius Flaccus writes [in Festus at the word *majorem*]." Cf. Festus, *De verborum significatione*, ed. Müller, pp. 160, 161.

348 K4 *power to commaund* || Addition in Fr 3–4 only: "Since the second edition Cujas, who works wonders in his chair [of Roman law at Bourges], has caused it to be understood [cf. *Opera* (Venice-Modena, 1758–1783), IX, col. 1044] that Bodin thinks it was necessary for the Consul to enfranchise in the presence of his colleague, which is exactly the opposite to what [Bodin] believes." Omitted in Fr 1–2, 5–8. For the reply of Cujas, see his *Observationes et emendationes*, XVIII, 38.

348 K8 *proceed on further* || L adds: "But the *imperium* of the Praetors was common to all, although they had a divided jurisdiction."

351 B8–9 *if any other monster were borne*. Preferably, ". . . if any other portent (*monstrum*) were announced . . ."

351 C7 *subject to revocation* || L adds: "Those who were chosen magistrates under faulty auspices often retained their authority without anyone objecting, but sometimes they were compelled to give up their office."

351 D3 *unfortunat and contrary* || Fr adds: "And in order that the multiplicity of oppositions and auspices might not conflict with one another, it was not lawful to take the auspices, or to announce the results, or to stay the proceedings, more than once on any one day."

352 F7 *and broken off* || Fr adds: "Although this [cancellation of actions (cf. *Digest*, 5, 1, 58)] is not rigorously observed, it ought to be if the matter concerns life or honor."

353 A5 *Ex quo provinciam ingressus est*. I.e., "From the time when [the proconsul] entered the province." The reference is to *Digest*, 1, 16, 4, 6. Cf. Cujas, *Observationes et emendationes*, I, 1, and his reply to Bodin, *ibid.*, XVIII, 38.

354 G1–3 *And albeit . . . ordained and appointed*. Fr specifies that this edict was verified on June 13, 1499 (misprinted 1419 in Fr 7). But Charles VIII died in 1498, and L substitutes: "In the reign of Charles VII [*sic*], the Senate, which was called the Great Council, decided matters of state. Nevertheless by a law of Louis XII it was provided [*in the margin*: in the year 1499] . . ."

355 B8–9 *but jurisdiction not so, as many have thought*. Misleading. Bodin means: ". . . although many have thought that jurisdiction *can* be exercised jointly . . ." (cf. Fr and L). The authorities cited marginally are Bartolus, Baldus, Antonius de Butrio, Alexander of Imola, Panormitanus, Dominicus de Sancto Geminiano, and Felinus.

357 B3–358 F1 *which the Lawiers . . . being before lost*. Mainly from L. Fr 3–8 differ considerably, and Fr 1–2 omit almost the whole of the passage.

357 B8 *with a straunger* || L adds: "In the same sense κύρια δόγματα is rendered by Marcus Tullius [Cicero] as 'established and approved (*certa ac rata*) doctrines of the Philosophers.'"

357 C4 *or edict peremptorie* || Fr adds: "This error [concerning the word *fatalia*] has remained until now to be corrected. Since the first edition of this book Doctor Cujas, not being able to deny that it was a notable error to call days of assignation and days prefixed *dies fatales*, has striven to make his pupils understand [cf. *Opera*, IX, col. 1044] that Bodin did not correct the error in the word [by substituting] κυρίας ἡμέρας in place of κηρίας ἡμέρας, which is the reading in all the editions of the *Authentics* printed in the last fifty years. *But Cujas has never shown that there was ever a lawyer, or anyone speaking Latin, who called prefixed days* dies fatales, *and he has not denied that* κηρίας ἡμέρας *has been found in all the books printed in the last fifty years*. But to show Cujas why the interpreters have believed that one should read κηρίας, it is clear that the words κῆρ and κήρ, the one signifying 'heart' or 'soul,' the other 'fatal destiny,' which the Hebrews also call קיר, are both derived from κηρῶ τὸ στερίσκω, [i.e., 'to harm, in the sense of deprive'], for there would be no ground for saying *fatales dies* if the world κήρ did not signify *fatum*.' (18 lines). The sentence printed here in italics appears in Fr 3–4 only. קיר, which does not occur elsewhere with this meaning, would seem to be a simple transliteration from the Greek κήρ. Cujas made a further rejoinder in his *Observationes et emendationes*, XVIII, 38.

357 D10–E3 *But that Justinians ... it is plaine.* From L. Fr differs here: "I wished to note these points in order to reply to Cujas, who finds it strange that Bodin should think the laws of the *Code* to have been in Greek. He has not seen in the second law under the title 'De veteri jure' [i.e., *Code*, 1, 17, 2, 21] that Justinian expressly desired it. And who is so dull-witted as to think that the Greeks neglected to translate from Latin the laws of the Theodosian and Hermogenian Codes, from which the Justinian Code was for the most part composed? They even translated the *Institutes* into Greek, and most of the laws of the *Pandects* in their *Basilicon*, especially during the decline of the Empire, when they wished to enhance the splendor of the Greek language by teaching the law to students in Greek." (12 lines).

357 E6 *Greeke word φεύγοντα* || Fr adds: "And because the Emperors Justinian and Leo issued their new ordinances in Greek, those who translated them into Latin used Greek phrases, being unfamiliar with Latin."

358 F1 *into Greeke* || L adds: "... as though they had been brought home from exile ..."

360 G6–7 *so that they are to be blamed which otherwise either thinke or write.* As in L. Fr 3–8 read: "... and he who has written to the contrary has not carefully examined the registers of Geneva." Omitted in Fr 1–2. This is another reference to the Geneva edition of 1577, which alters Bodin's version of the incident. Cf. Reulos, pp. 347–348.

360 I3–5 *And thus much ... towards an other.* From Fr, but L substitutes: "Let this be sufficient concerning offices, *imperium*, and the general authority of magistrates, [for these are the points] which I have considered to be capable of universal application." The entire paragraph (360 I3–361 A8) is omitted in Fr 1–4.

360 K5 *or chiefe Mareschall* || L adds: "... and the next to him is the Admiral of the fleet."

360 K9 *great Bishop* || L adds: "... and [is] the arbiter of doubtful laws, and supreme judge."

CHAPTER 7 (PAGES 361–386)

361 B4–D3 *Now after that ... colledges together.* Following Fr, but L recasts these opening sentences so as to obtain more rigorous definitions: "A college is a lawful association of three or more persons of the same condition, while a corporation is a union of several colleges. A university (*universitas*) is an aggregate of all the families, colleges, and corporations of the same town, associated together under the same law [cf. Appendix B, no. 10]. A Commonweal has one feature more than a university, in that it encompasses the multitude of all the citizens and towns within the sovereignty of the realm. I have thought it necessary that these definitions, which have been omitted by all who have written about the Commonweal and about public law, should be added to this discipline, for without settled definitions nothing firm and enduring can be established. One can narrow down the whole human race by successive stages into Commonweals divided in territory and sovereignty, and [proceed] from these to *universitates*, then to corporations, then to colleges, and finally to families, and from these to individuals, so that the difference between these [social units] seems not much greater than that between the whole and its parts." (17 lines). It is to be noted that while L defines *universitas* narrowly, Fr uses *communauté* as a general term for several types of social unit (cf. C10–D1).

363 E2 *one of them with another* || L adds: "... and not φειδίτια, which Plutarch has derived from 'parsimony' [φειδώ]."

365 D3–4 *albeit that they have neither common treasure.* As in L, but Fr specifies "some common treasure" among the things which are requisite in order to have a college.

366 F2–4 *And as for the fellowes ... in their affayres.* From Fr, but L alters this: "But it is not necessary for the fellows to be equal in power and authority, or of like condition."

366 F8–G4 *But if this head ... the principall.* From Fr. L diverges: "If [this head] has the right to punish the whole body, it is not called a college, but a lordship (*dominatus*) in he case of a supreme prince, and a family or a school in other cases, provided only that its assembly is held in such a way that there are no fellows. For that assembly over which the Pope presides cannot be termed a college, since he has supreme power of life and death, not only over individuals, but also over the whole body. If he does not have it by legal right, he seems to have it in actual fact." (7 lines).

366 H9 *showing indeed no Philosophie in so saying.* Inexact. "There is no philosopher who has said this ..." (Fr, but Fr 7 corrupt). The lawyer in question is Bartolus.

367 D2 *if it be well ruled.* As in Fr, but L expands: "... that is, one should bring it about that reason rules and that the desires obey reason. In this way everything will be given its due, which is the most important constituent part of justice."

370 G1–3 *yet still provided ... their common society.* Confused. Fr reads: "... provided that two thirds have been present at the meeting, although they were not of one opinion on matters concerning the community." L substitutes: "... provided that two thirds of the college consent to the decree." There is a corresponding discrepancy at 371 C7–9, where Knolles follows

Notes to Book III

Fr, but L substitutes: "... but it has been defined as the greater part when at least two thirds (*duae partes ad summum*) agree at the same time, whether the rest be present or absent." But Fr and L agree at 371 D1–4, so that Fr is the more consistent of the two. Cf. 247 B9–C2. Bodin's authorities are *Digest*, 3, 4, 3 and 3, 4, 4, and the glosses on these titles.

371 B1 *chaunged their opinions* ‖ L adds: "Yet if they had not changed [their opinion], nothing firm and durable could have been decided while our college [i.e., the Third Estate] was opposed."

373 B4 *if it be so reserved unto him.* Possibly "reserved" is a misprint for "referred." Bodin actually writes: "... if there is any opposition." (Fr only).

374 H1–I3 *For we see ... all indeed guiltie.* This illustrative passage, which first appears in Fr 1, is modified once in Fr 3, again in Fr 5, and again in L, an indication of Bodin's uncertainty on the point.

374 I2–3 *none of them is guiltie ... yet are they all indeed guiltie.* Knolles reconciles a divergence in the texts. The first part is from L, the second from Fr.

376 F6 *murtherer of his countrey* ‖ L adds: "For having practiced similar cruelty against the people of Abydus, Philip II, King of Macedon, was compelled to serve the Romans and pay them tribute."

376 I8–K10(margin) *This Frederike ... Ecco, la fica.* The explanation is added by Knolles. The story is corroborated by Littré, who attributes it, however, to Frederick Barbarossa. Cf. *Dictionnaire de la langue française* (Paris, 1885), s.v. "figue."

379 A3–7 *By these examples ... to be taken heed of.* As in L, but Fr is more specific: "If one passes judgment on these three princes, it will perhaps be said that the one was too severe in the punishment of a community; the other aimed at too much lenity, for a rebellion passed over too indulgently soon brings on another. The third tempered the other two, holding the middle course between gentleness and cruelty, which is the means to attain that true justice which the law wishes to be observed [*Digest*, 48, 19, 11] in the punishment of crimes, particularly where it is a question of punishing a multitude, whether organized as a community or not." (9 lines).

380 G3 *mirrour of the world.* Possibly a misprint. Bodin writes: "... mistress (*domina*) of the world ..."

380 I2 *Cato the Censor most grievously said.* More precisely, "... Cato the Censor, a most authoritative witness (*gravissimus testis*), said ..." Knolles may mean "grievously" in the sense of "harshly" or "severely," or possibly in the sense of "impressively" or "weightily."

382 G8 *in peace and obedience* ‖ Fr adds: "... and Valens and Valentinian did so even more, although one was Arian, the other Catholic."

383 A9 *of Philip the faire* ‖ L adds: "... and not long ago against those who revived the religious sects ..."

383 E2 *the popular estate was established.* Imprecise. "... the assemblies of the people (*les estats du peuple*) were re-established ..."

384 G7–8 *it cannot be better done, than by the estates.* Combining Fr and L, which differ. Fr reads: "... this can only be done by the estates ..." But L is less emphatic: "... this is usually done best of all by colleges and corporations."

385 A8–B1 *But how necessarie ... tributes & servitude.* From L. Fr is more detailed: "I shall not deny that there are abuses and thefts, which have been well demonstrated by the abstracts of the Estates of Brittany for the year 1567 [1567 in Fr 1–4, 1566 in Fr 5–8]. I am also well aware that the pensions of the Estates of Languedoc amounted to more than twenty-five thousand francs, without counting the expenses of the Estates, which were scarcely less. But it cannot be denied that in the reign of King Henry [II] Languedoc yielded by this means 100,000 livres every year, and Normandy 400,000, which equaled the provinces which have no Estates. Yet it is quite certain that *élections* cost the King and the subjects twice as much as estates, and in taxation matters the more officers there are the more corruption. Besides, the complaints and grievances of provinces governed by *élection* are never seen, read, or presented, or else they are disregarded, whatever they may be, as merely individual grievances." (16 lines).

CHAPTER 8 (PAGES 386–405)

386 I7 *Chap. VIII.* This entire chapter appears only in the Latin editions.

389 A6 *Nimrod the great robber, most notably attended.* More probably, "... Nimrod, the most renowned robber, attended ..." (reading *nobilissimus*, as in L 2, rather than *nobilissime*, as in L 1, 3–5).

390 F8 *faire furnitures for horses.* Bodin's term is *phalerae*, which can mean trappings for horses, but which also stands for the ornamented metallic plates worn by men as a military decoration.

390 I3–8 *For Cicero ... and gentlemen.* Faulty and incomplete. "For Cicero had six competitors for the Consulship [Asconius Pedianus, *Orationum Ciceronis quinque enarratio*, 73], two patricians and four plebeians. Of the latter two were from office-holding families (*nobiles*), two were the first of their families to obtain a magistracy. Only Cicero was born into the equestrian order.

Therefore the fathers of this Cicero, of Marius, of Cato the Censor, of Quintus Pompeius, of Curius, of Philo, and of Genutius, were baseborn men from the *plebs*, they themselves were *novi homines*, and their sons were *nobiles*."

393 C8–9 *for the Greeks . . . and we an horseman.* Faulty. ". . . for κέλης ἵππος, a riding horse, is the unharnessed one (ὁ ἄζυξ), which the Latins call *sellarius*." *Sellarius* may mean either a horseman or a riding horse. Cf. *Methodus*, pp. 344–345.

394 G2–3 ὁ μὲν γὰρ ἐσθλὸς . . . δυσγενὴς εἶναι δοκεῖ. Bodin adds a marginal translation into Latin: "A good man is noble in my opinion, but a wicked man seems base, even if born of a greater father than Zeus himself." This quotation and also those at 395 C8–9 and D9 are fragments preserved in the *Florilegium* of Stobaeus and reproduced in A. Nauck, *Tragicorum Graecorum fragmenta* (Leipzig, 1889), Nos. 22, 336, 527.

395 B3–4 *he which by some chaunce or casualtie hath obtained some great place of service, or other fee.* Inexact. Read merely: ". . . he which hath obtained a fee (*militia ex casu, sive feudum*) . . ." At D1–2 Bodin again writes *seu feuda, seu beneficia, seu militiae ex casu.* Cf. note at 114 G7.

399 C5–7 *For that divine law . . . a naturall Israelite.* Inexact. "For the divine law which forbade lending at interest to citizens [i.e., Israelites] does not seem to have forbidden doing so to strangers [Deuteronomy 23:19–20], to the end that it might not be lawful to buy anything which would be sold at retail to a citizen of Israel at a higher price."

399 D7 *in like manner also* ‖ L adds: ". . . just as there are many prohibitions of this kind, which apply to the holy people but not to others [*in the margin*: such as the rules which have been handed down concerning sacrifices and the selection of foods]."

402 K3 *cloath, ropes,* ‖ *garments.* Bodin inserts: ". . . wickerwork (*vimina*) . . ."

405 B7–8 *in so much that Cicero the Consull was glad to call.* Condensed. ". . . and when the people and the knights broke into an uproar of mutual abuse, they so disturbed the whole theater and the plays, that it was necessary for Cicero the Consul to call . . ." For Knolles's usage of "glad," see the note at 135 C2.

Book IV

CHAPTER I (PAGES 406–436)

406 I1–2 *either by the strength of some stronger than themselves, or by the power of some others, who.* Awkward, but based upon L. Fr reads more smoothly: ". . . by the violence of the stronger, or by the consent of some, who . . ."

406 I3–5 *to be by them disposed of . . . betwixt them agreed upon.* Following Fr. L drops this suggestion that the surrender of liberty may be either with or without conditions.

408 G6–10 *which hath alwaies . . . part of the subjects.* From Fr, but L enlarges: "But Alphonsus died childless, and the province of Narbonne and Septimania [i.e., Languedoc], which by feudal right and the laws of sovereignty was held from the kings themselves, returned to the king on the dissolution of the fee. In this way *dominium utile* was merged with *dominium directum*. Therefore Languedoc was a province of this kingdom, not a Commonweal. If, however, the province had been torn away from this kingdom, it would have been subject to the conditions laid down by the treaty, since it had not entered into the treaty on equal terms."

409 E5–6 *in the number of two* ‖ Fr adds: "In this respect Aristotle is mistaken in making a kingdom of Lacedemonia, where two sovereign princes ruled before the time of Lycurgus."

409 E8–9 *suspence and sufferance* ‖ L adds: ". . . until the question of sovereignty is decided. In this period commissioners are appointed for the Commonweal, or else the magistrates govern the Commonweal by themselves, without a commissioner."

410 H2–3 *The last point . . . quite extinguished.* As in Fr, but L clarifies: "Thus it may be that after the Commonweal is abolished the people retain their family laws, associations, and dealings with one another. But when the whole people is destroyed the Commonweal must needs perish also." The paragraph from G4 to H1 occurs in L only. These changes were undoubtedly suggested by the comments of Ferrier, pp. 14–16.

410 I7–8 *corruptly Stamboll, the choyce seat of the Turkish emperours.* All but the word "Stamboll" is added by Knolles.

411 B8 *a Sadler.* Probably a misinterpretation of *sellularius opifex*. John of Leyden was actually a journeyman tailor. Cf. 544 F9 and 558 G1.

412 K1 *whome the Histories for the most part call Ninus.* Based on Fr, but omitted in L after criticism by Ferrier, pp. 19–20.

413 A1–2 *more than the figure onely* ‖ L adds: "Two governors divided his kingdom between themselves. One obtained the kingdom of the Assyrians, who were also called Chaldeans, the other the kingdom of the Persians. Eventually both were left to King Cyrus, whose son Cambyses died without issue. This gave the princes an opportunity to conspire against the Magi, who had invaded the royal palace, and when these were slain ten princes came to an agreement that he might rule whose horse neighed before sunrise. In this way Darius acquired the kingdom, and thenceforth his

Notes to Book IV

descendants held that great empire until the time of Alexander the Great, who conquered the Indian and Scythian kings, and annexed their kingdoms to his ancestral lands and those which he had acquired by his own virtue. If we look at other peoples, we shall find that kings ruled everywhere in those times." (13 lines).

413 A2-4 *the princes of the Medes ... and Lacedemonians*. As in Fr. L omits the Hebrews and adds Ethiopians, Greeks, Lydians, Cretans, and Latins.

413 E3 *a good captaine* ‖ L adds: "Likewise the Israelites, although they had a most excellent prince in Samuel, asked him [I Samuel 8:20] for a leader of the army."

422 F10-G1 *overcome by the Enophites*. As in L, but Fr reads more correctly: "... after the battle of Oenophyta, which they lost ..." The victors were the Athenians. Bodin's source here appears to have been Aristotle, *Politics*, 1302b.

423 D8 *Pisistratus*. Inexact. "... the Pisistratidae ..." (Fr and L).

424 K6 *almost three hundred yeres*. As amended by Knolles. Bodin writes "... 360 years ..." in Fr, "... almost 400 years ..." in L, both of which conflict with the revised figure at 423 E5. For further evidence of his uncertainty, see 518 F4 and 706 I3-4. Probably he is reckoning from the treaty of 1315 between Schwyz, Uri, and Unterwalden (cf. 76 I7-8).

426 H1-2 *Royall Monarchies*. Inexact. The word "Royall" is added by Knolles and is inconsistent with Bodin's argument in Book II, ch. 2.

426 H5-6 *the one from the faction among themselves, the other from the insurrection or rebellion of the people*. As in Fr, but L substitutes: "... the one from [external] enemies (*hostes*), the other from the plebeians."

428 I6 *the rest of the nobilitie* ‖ L adds: "... and not even then does a monarchy come to an end, if some capable captain or commander sets himself up as a prince."

432 G8-10 *which bind the one ... both the extreames*. From Fr, but L expands: "... which join together the extremes, or else divide into several factions. Now if there are more factions than two, the third links the other two in friendship, or by an alliance with one of them breaks down and conquers the other."

434 G5 *nature of that Monarchie* ‖ L includes the name of the Constable, Charles, Duke of Bourbon, in the anti-French alliance (F10-G2) and then adds: "... and the band of wickéd citizens who conspired with Charles of Bourbon, the victor, did not bring about any change (*conversio*) of the Commonweal, nor even any disturbances."

434 H5-7 *which at the beginning was a pure Monarchie, which afterward was sweetly chaunged into a Popular estate, and now by little and little is chaunged into an Aristocratie*. As in Fr 3-8 and similar to L, but Fr 1-2 read: "... which at the beginning was popular, and little by little changed into an aristocracy ..." Bodin inclines towards this latter view in the *Methodus* (p. 188).

435 D1-2 *Thus we see Monarchies peaceably by little and little to change into Aristocraties*. As in Fr, but L differs, adding another stage: "In this way, therefore, the rights of sovereignty pass from the control of one man to the optimates, and from them to the people ..."

CHAPTER 2 (PAGES 436-467)

436 I2 *Chap. II*. In this chapter Fr and L differ sharply, the later version being both amended and expanded very considerably. Many of the emendations may be traced directly to the criticisms advanced in Ferrier's *Advertissemens à M. Jean Bodin sur le quatriesme livre de sa Republique*, while a few of the additions in L represent material drawn from Bodin's own answer to Ferrier in the *Apologie de René Herpin pour la Republique de I. Bodin*, which was written in 1580.

436 K7-9 *or by the will of man ... enforced and bound*. Following Fr, but L expands: "... and Zeno [has called it] fate, the other Stoics providence (*pronoea*), and Augustine (following Panaetius and Seneca, I believe) has called it God. But they err seriously who interchange nature and God, as though God were bound by the laws of nature, just as the fables relate that Jupiter is bound by the decrees of Adrastia [i.e., Nemesis]. However Augustine was correct in writing that either there was no fate, or God himself was fate, since nothing is constant, nothing sure, nothing immutable, except God.

"But by the common consent of the Hebrews and the more learned divines, the will (*voluntas*) which God bestowed on mankind is free, and released from all necessity. For if there were certain celestial and necessary causes of our wills and desires, not only would the human will be unfree, but it would not even be a will. It would be absurd to say that a man wills something when he acts under any constraint. This indolent and spiritless doctrine of the Stoics and fatalists was completely abandoned long ago by Poseidonius himself, the principal Stoic of his time, and by all the best philosophers, as well as by the more skilled divines. Even Philip Melanchthon, who contended very strongly that the will is unfree, admits that man's will is free in human and civil affairs." (20 lines).

437 A6-C2 *But this divine power ... earthquake devoured*. This passage occurs in L only, and all the examples cited—Sodom and Gomorrah,

Bura and Helice, the twenty-three Italian and the twelve Asiatic cities—are among those mentioned by Ferrier (pp. 16–18), who even recommended their inclusion in the *République*.

438 H5 *father of all things* || L adds: "... even though Sophocles, referring to the whole species of gods, may have written [*Oedipus at Colonus*, 607–608] 'The gods alone feel neither old age nor death.'"

439 B8–9 *after his calculation*. As in Fr, but L places the calculated dates *after* the actual conjunctions.

441 C7–8 *For to esteeme of them by the elle, or by the greatnesse*. Condensing Fr 3–8, which read: "Since the second edition, Bodin has been informed that Cujas has persisted in his interpretation, according to which he would have buildings valued by the yard. If this were true..." Omitted in Fr 1–2. For Cujas's original statement, see *Observationes et emendationes*, VI, 3. For his reply to Bodin, see *ibid.*, XVIII, 38.

441 D1 *we must referre to Vitruvius*. Here Fr and L quote marginally a substantial passage from *De architectura*, II, 8, 8–9.

442 F7 *can never be six and thirtie degrees from the Sunne*. Here, and also at 442 G4 and 445 A9, Fr reads "thirty-six degrees." Ferrier criticizes this (p. 10), and L accordingly substitutes "thirty degrees." Bodin discusses the question in his *Apologie*, fol. 24ᵛ.

443 B1 *nine hundred yeares*. Imprecise. Fr reads: "... more than 900 years..." L reads: "... about 1000 years..."

443 B4 *(as some affirme)*. Condensing L, which diverges from Fr for several lines: "... as some inconsistently and rashly affirm, since Porphyry maintained very strongly that the world is eternal, while the horoscope of the city is dated the 5838th year of the world, in May, on a Monday, two hours after sunrise, as indeed Gauricus copied from the Vatican [Library]. To it he adds these words: *Subtrahe 5200. anni mundi, Byzantii 3838. post Christum 638.*" This chronology is vigorously attacked in the *Apologie*, fol. 20–20ᵛ.

443 C7 *1453, the xxix day of May*. Knolles gives the correct date. Fr gives May 30, 1453, but Ferrier suggests May 28 or 29, 1452 (p. 30). The *Apologie* counters with May 29, 1453 (fol. 20), but L, apparently following Ferrier's suggestion, gives May 30, 1452.

443 D4 *and carrying away the rest of the citisens into captivitie*. As in L. Fr reads: "... and put all the inhabitants to the sword." Ferrier criticized this (pp. 31–32), and Bodin accordingly modified it, but cf. 410 I4–6, where Fr and L are substantially the same.

444 G7–8 *motion and conjunction*. Inexact. Bodin writes only: "... conjunctions..." (Fr and L). The fault is repeated at H7.

445 C3–4 *the three superiour Planets*. As in L, but Fr reads: "... the two highest planets..." i.e., Jupiter and Saturn.

445 C8–9 *which yet for all that is no true conjunction, as not made by the centers, but by the Orbes and Spheres of the Planets*. As in L. Fr speaks of this case as a true conjunction, but Ferrier contests the point (pp. 36–37), and L qualifies the original assertion.

445 D2 *eight hundred yeares*. As in L. Fr reads: "...953 years and 91 days..." Ferrier rejected this in favor of a cycle of about eight hundred years (pp. 37–38). Bodin's acceptance of this view necessitated a drastic revision of the following passage (445 D2–446 F10), which Knolles takes from L and which, as originally written, was closely dependent upon this figure. Fr 1–4 read as follows:

"If one subtracts this number [953 years and 91 days] from the age of the world, working backwards [from the time] when a major conjunction occurred, one will find similar effects and changes. *For example if we take the year 1524, which was the 5496th year of the creation in the calculation of Philo the Hebrew, we find that by subtracting 953 years and 91 days four times, the great conjunction of Saturn, Jupiter and Mars in Pisces occurred 1682 years and three months [from the creation], at which time the great flood occurred.* Such [a conjunction] there was in the year 1524, when all the astrologers of Asia, Africa and Europe predicted another general deluge, and many unbelievers were found who built arcs to save themselves, notably President Auriol at Toulouse, even though they were reminded of God's promise, and his oath never again to cause men to perish by flood. It is quite true that the year brought great tempests and floods of water in many countries. *However not one Astrologer has taken heed of the conjunction which I said to have occurred in the year of the flood, and which they thought to have occurred 2242 years after the creation. They suppose that [the flood] came after the third great conjunction, which is impossible.* For the age of the world up to the flood, that is to say 1656 years, is well demonstrated by the text of the Bible, but the error and obscurity in chronology is between the flood and the first Olympiad. *If therefore we add 36 years to Philo's reckoning, the great conjunction will be found in the year of the flood.* Josephus adds 200 years more than Philo; the other Hebrews 160 years fewer. If the Arabs and Alphonsus had taken the true calculation of the age of the world in this manner, and had noted the great conjunctions by working backwards, and had related both to the truth contained in histories, it might have been possible to confirm more exactly the age of the world, and to obtain a more certain knowledge of the changes and ruins of Commonweals [produced] by the celestial motions. But those who have conjectured the horoscope of the world at their pleasure, as I have said, and who have based the conjunctions upon a false principle, cannot possibly either know anything about conjunctions or establish anything concerning the changes of Commonweals." (41 lines). The sections italicized here are either omitted or rather awkwardly revised in Fr 5–8.

446 F4–5 *President of Tholose.* As in Fr. After Ferrier asserted (pp. 39–40) that Auriol was neither "president, nor counselor, nor judge," but only a doctor regent in canon law at the University, L qualifies him as: ". . . [a man] very skilled in human law . . ." In point of fact, however, the *Dictionnaire de biographie française*, ed. J. Balteau, M. Barroux, and M. Prevost (Paris, 1933–   ), states that Auriol did become first *conseiller-clerc*, then *président*, of the Parlement of Toulouse.

447 A3–4 *as wee have elswhere declared.* See the *Methodus*, p. 320.

447 A7 *Nabonassar.* As in L. Fr gives: ". . . Sennacherib, King of Assyria . . ." But Ferrier suggested (p. 41) that this should be Nabonassar, and Bodin made the change.

448 F1 *Plutarch.* As in L. Fr omits Plutarch, but includes Tacitus in the list.

448 F2–3 *gray eyed.* Inexact, or possibly a misprint for "green-eyed" (cf. 548 G7 and H1). Bodin's terms are *verds* and *caerulei*. For a fuller discussion, see *Methodus*, pp. 90–92.

448 G7 *Henrie the sixt.* Bodin erroneously writes: ". . . Henry V . . ." (Fr and L), but Knolles corrects him.

448 G9 *a prisoner.* Possibly a misprint. Bodin actually writes: ". . . a private man . . ." (L).

448 K8–9 *taken prisoner by the Spaniards* || Fr adds: ". . . and strange floods of waters occurred in many places."

449 A4–10 *So also fortie yeares after . . . happened also foure eclipses.* As in Fr, but L associates all these events directly with the conjunction of A.D. 769 (448 K9–449 A1, with date corrected).

449 E3 *and the meanest planets, as of Saturne and Mars.* Faulty. ". . . and the intermediate [conjunctions], of Saturn and Mars . . ." (L).

449 E5 *about everie eight hundred yeares.* As in L. The corresponding figure in Fr is nine hundred years, but Ferrier suggests eight hundred years (pp. 35–36), and Bodin adopts the suggestion.

450 G10 *altogether ignorant* || Fr adds: "Nevertheless this is clearly symbolized for us by the ten curtains of the Tabernacle, which represent the ten moving Spheres, and which were formerly supposed to be only eight in number, as well as by the explicit text of the law of God, which speaks of rest in the seventh year and of the return of inheritances after forty-nine years. Leo the Hebrew relates this to [periods of] seven thousand and forty-nine thousand years." (6 lines). Part of this corresponds to the sentence at F10–G4, which follows L.

450 K6 *matter or knowledge* || L adds: ". . . who, on leaving the schools, chase after syllables . . ." This is a favorite theme of Bodin's. For even harsher comments on the grammarians and their methods, see *Methodus*, pp. 7–8.

451 C2 *the yeare 1526, and 27, in the moneth of September.* Faulty. L reads: ". . . the year 1527, on the 26th of September . . ." Fr reads: ". . . the 26th [of September], 1537 . . ."

451 E3 *the seventh day after* || I.e., on September 7 of the same year (cf. Fr and L). Fr then adds: "On the following day [September 8] Sigismund, father of [Sigismund] Augustus, King of Poland, put to flight the Muscovite army."

451 E3–4 *The ninth of September, in the yeare of our Lord 1544.* Badly confused. For "1544" Bodin writes 1564 (L only). As written in L 1–2 this figure refers to the capture (actually in 1566) of Szigeth in the preceding sentence, but in L 3–5 the punctuation is faulty. Knolles, probably thinking of James V (who died in 1542), amends Bodin's figure to 1544, but Bodin is thinking of James IV, slain at Flodden Field on September 9, 1513.

452 G1 *Which day also.* As in L, but Fr reads: ". . . the preceding day . . ." i.e., September 16. Modern authorities give September 18.

452 H3 *from thenceforth commaunded the account of the yeare to bee begun in September.* Inexact. Bodin actually writes: ". . . commanded that from thenceforth the reckoning of the years should be begun from September of the year 333." Cf. Fr and L.

453 A10–C2 *Whereby it is to be understood . . . consummation and end.* From L. Fr differs in some respects: "We read also that the greatest earthquakes have occurred in September, as Nicolas de Livre has well noted in his book *On the motion of the earth* . . . [Several examples follow, already given in L at 451 B4–C6.] . . . On the 17th of September, the bridge over the Tiber fell, killing 560 persons, in the year 1444. Sometimes these remarkable changes occur at the end of August, when the September moon precedes the sun's entry into Libra. All these examples show that just as the world was created in September, with the sun in the first degree of Libra as we said, so too the important changes occur in September, and not in March, the month

A 133

appointed by Leovicius for the end of the world. The law of God calls [such men] false prophets, and forbids us to fear those who predict and assure us of things which never happen." (31 lines in all). Nicolas de Livre, Sieur de Humerolles, was a friend of Bodin's whose *Discours du tremblement de terre en forme de dialogue* (Paris, 1575) was translated from the Italian of Lucio Maggio. Bodin himself contributed a preface in Latin verse.

454 H5 *after the conjunction of the two superiour planets, with the Sunne, or Mars.* Inexact. Bodin writes: "... after the conjunction of the *three* superior planets, in the signs of the Sun [Leo] or of Mars [Scorpio]." (Fr only).

454 H7 *the Sunne & Mercurie* || Fr 1–4 add: "... which had not happened for almost eight hundred years." Omitted in Fr 5–8.

454 K8 *and not from the heavens* || L adds: "... that is, that terrestrial things rule over celestial, and transitory things over eternal."

455 A3–4 *part of them immovable* || L adds: "[By so doing] he thought that he could undermine the precepts of all philosophers and divines, and the human senses, the foundations of all sciences."

455 A6–9 *God in the heavens ... the heat thereof.* The quotation is from Psalms 19:4–6. In Fr Bodin quotes from the metrical version by Clément Marot. Condensed in L.

455 C1 *a thing altogether impossible.* As in Fr, but L explains more fully: "But nothing which is violent can be of long duration, or at least that motion which is in addition to its natural one must proceed from elsewhere than from itself. For as Copernicus would have it, the whole earth must rotate rapidly in twenty-four hours, and then must revolve around the sun in the space of a year, as well as [undergoing] the motion of trepidation. Besides these motions the single particles of earth, like everything which remains stationary by the pressure of its own weight, must sink straight downward by a certain natural impulse. There is also the motion when the earth shakes violently and parts asunder, whence come subsidences and chasms. From this it is clear by the doctrine of Copernicus himself that earth, which is heavy, inert, and dense because of its own weight, has five entirely different and conflicting motions." (12 lines).

456 K1 *therefore take chaunge* || L adds: "... but rather [he thinks that this occurs] through a change in the habits and mode of life of the citizens." For "citizens" Cicero actually writes *nobiles*, "aristocrats" (*De legibus*, III, 14).

457 E2–460 G8 *although they use never so good lawes ... that they would show him it.* Fr omits almost the whole of this passage and reads instead: "It is necessary to demonstrate [this point], which no one has done before, in order to reach some understanding of the changes and downfalls of Commonweals, and to show that human affairs do not happen fortuitously. Nevertheless God sometimes departs from the ordinary course of natural causation, and acts outside it, to the end that men should not believe that all things occur by a fatal destiny." (7 lines). A similar denial of fortuity and destiny occurs in the *Methodus*, pp. 235–236. Part of the longer version found in L (457 E7–458 K4) is adapted from the *Apologie*, fol. 41–41^v.

458 H8–I1 Ἔστι δὲ θείῳ ... χειρόνων γενέσεων. This quotation, which has given rise to a great deal of speculation as to its meaning, is from Plato's *Republic*, 546 B-C. Bodin's own contribution to this debate is examined with care in A. Diès, "Le Nombre de Platon. Essai d'exégèse et d'histoire," Académie des Inscriptions et Belles-Lettres, *Mémoires*, First Series, XIV Part I (1940), pp. i–v, 1–141.

458 K4 *is slylie led away.* Strictly, "... has slipped away (*elapsus est*) ..." Possibly Knolles wrote "fled away."

459 D1 *the perfect numbers.* Here Bodin uses the term in the sense of a number equal to the sum of all its divisors, including unity. Of the four above 100,000 which he cites in the margin, three—properly 130816, 2096128, and 536854528—are now known not to be perfect numbers, though they were commonly believed to be in the sixteenth century. Cf. L. E. Dickson, *History of the Theory of Numbers* (Washington, 1919), I, 8–9.

460 G8 *that they would show him it* || L adds: "However it is necessary [to understand] from the words of Plato that he wished to express not some one number only, but a whole geometrical figure, in the sides and dimensions of which would be contained the whole variety of numbers set out in the following table ... [L gives a table, in seventeen columns, of various types of number series and then goes on for two further pages to discuss the geometrical implications of Plato's passage.] ... We have pursued these points in greater detail to make it clear from the individual enumeration of the component parts that no figure constructed by geometrical means can be fitted to the numerical relationships which Plato set down, in such a way that we may ascertain from these the cycles and limits of human affairs. Finally, that Plato himself was forgetful at this point is shown clearly enough by the geometrical surds which he wished to be contained in that figure, for this is clearly inconsistent with numbers and arithmetical relationships." (95 lines and one page for the table). The Abbé Diès has shown (pp. 59–60, 66, 69) that the table is taken with only minor changes but with-

out acknowledgment from Jacques Lefèvre d'Étaples's commentary on Aristotle's *Politics*.

460 I5 *use and experience the authour* ‖ L adds: ". . . than which there can be no better nor surer teacher."

461 D4 *Crysippus*. Included in Fr, but omitted in L after a correction by Ferrier (p. 52).

461 E3 *Theophrastus at 84, which are twelve times seaven yeares*. Knolles alters the figure. Fr reads: ". . . Theophrastus at 83, which are twelve septenaries . . ." L omits this example after criticism of its inaccuracy by Ferrier (p. 53).

461 E4–5 *or els they passe to xiii times seaven, as did S. Hierom and Isocrates, who lived 91 yeares*. As in Fr, but L expands, adding new examples: "Petrarch [completed] ten septenaries, and died on the anniversary of his day of birth; Galen, ten [septenaries]; Staseas the Peripatetic, twelve; Eli, fourteen; Hippocrates, fifteen; St. Jerome, King Hiero of Syracuse, and Isocrates, thirteen."

462 F4–6 *It is manifest also . . . later live not.* From L. Fr differs: "Why does [death] occur in these years rather than in others? Why does the seventh male [child] cure the scrofula? For even the Greeks discovered this wonder of nature, and applied the term 'Hebdomagenes' to the seventh male child, *as some have thought, or else to him who was born in the seventh month*." The words italicized here are omitted in Fr 1–2. Modern Greek lexicons explain ἑβδομαγενής as "born on the seventh day of the month." It was an epithet of Apollo.

462 I3–4 *into equall parts*. Strictly, ". . . into integral parts . . ." (L). Cf. note at 459 D1.

463 A7 *converted in themselves* ‖ Fr adds: ". . . or else that an empire would last 1225 years from its foundation, as did that of the Romans, a number which makes 175 septenaries; or else that the number of years and of kings is a square or a cube of a multiple of seven or nine." (5 lines).

463 B3 *at Rome 244, for in the 75 septenarie*. As in L, but clearly intended to read: ". . . in the 35th septenary . . ." In place of "244" Fr reads: ". . . 144 years, which is the square of twelve . . ." Ferrier had corrected this to 244 (pp. 57–58), and the *Apologie* admits the error (fol. 39ᵛ).

463 B10 *to be againe restored* ‖ Fr adds: "But to show that this involves no necessity, we behold a great King who is the sixty-third, and monarch of two great Kingdoms [i.e., France and Poland], whom God maintains by His favor against human power, the power both of his own subjects and of foreigners. *It is true that there are three kings in this reckoning whom many do not count as kings at all, namely Odo (or Eudes), Charles the Fat, and Rudolph (Raoul)*." (7 lines). The sentence italicized here is omitted in Fr 1–4.

This passage, omitted in L, is in sharp contrast with Bodin's later predictions of Henry III's ruin, but the King's misdeeds, notably the murder of the Guises, were a major factor in Bodin's changed attitude. Cf. J. Moreau-Reibel, "Bodin et la Ligue d'après des lettres inédites," *Humanisme et renaissance*, II (1935), 422–440, and the published *Lettre de Monsieur Bodin* (Paris, 1590), pp. 16–17.

463 C1 *raigned also 70 yeres* ‖ Fr adds: "The democracy also, from the battle of Salamis and the rout of the Persians—at which time the Athenians had the sovereignty of almost all Greece—down to the overthrow of the popular estate, lasted seventy years, as Appian says."

463 D2 *proud Tarquins* ‖ Fr adds: "Now when this great number which the Academics call 'Fatal' was fulfilled, the change occurred in the following year in the 247th septenary, which is 1729. In the same way we find that when the perfect number 496 has elapsed, changes ordinarily occur in the year following, which is the 71st septenary." (7 lines).

464 G2–3 *1225 yeares: which number consisteth of whole septinaries*. From L. Fr 3–8 read: ". . . 1325 years, a square number . ." Ferrier branded this as an error (p. 62), and the *Apologie* admits the mistake (fol. 39ᵛ), but Fr 1–2 read correctly enough: ". . . 1225 years, a square number and also made up of whole septenaries."

464 G7–H8 *Now from Saul . . . fasts and calenders of the Romans themselves*. Mainly from L. Fr gives considerably more detail at this point: "[In this Assyrian chronology] Funck gives three years more, others six years less; so that by halving the difference this great number is complete. From the time that Arbaces, Governor of the Medes, made himself king, to the last king who was driven out by Alexander the Great, are found 496 years. This same perfect number is found not only from Augustus to Augustulus, but also from Augustulus to the time that Charlemagne was designated Emperor of the West in Rome. What I have written is borne out by the *Fasti* of Onuphrius, who paid no attention to [the significance of] numbers, but only to chronological precision. We also find this perfect number of 496 from the foundation of Alba Longa to its destruction, and the overthrow of the Alban Commonweal by Tullus Hostilius. Likewise Genebrard, professor of the Hebrew language, writes that there were 496 years from Saul, first king of the Hebrews, to Zedekiah, the last, who, after seeing the ruin of his estate and the captivity of his people, was led away a captive. Gartze gives ten years more, the Talmudists a great deal less, but all agree that from the return of the Hebrews, and the re-establishment of their Commonweal under Zerubbabel, who led the people back from captivity, to the

year that Herod the Idumean was appointed king by the Roman Senate, there were 496 years [but cf. 465 B8–E7, which is from L]. They also agree that the first and second temples were burnt on the same day and month, that is, the ninth day of the fifth month, which Josephus singled out as a miracle. It is true that the histories are not in agreement about what happened, because a part of the month, as reckoned by the Hebrew method, does not coincide with the Greek month, nor does this in turn agree with the Latin month. This same number of 496 is found from Caranus, the first king of Macedon, to the last year of the reign of Alexander the Great, the last king of that country of the line of Hercules and Aeacus. Funck gives eight years less, the others add twelve years more. The same perfect number of 496 is seen from the slaying of Syagrius, the last Roman Proconsul in France, to the year that Hugh Capet became King of France. It occurs again from Hugh Capet to the year that Charles VIII crossed the Alps, and stirred up not only all the states of Italy, but the whole Empire of the East as well. Yet this [instance] is not so well verified as the others, because of the differences among historians and the unreliability of the histories. The man who is followed most widely, Paulus Aemilius, who undertook to write the history of France, erred by ten whole years in a single section, as du Tillet has shown. But the examples that I have given are sufficient to show the mysterious influence of these numbers upon the important changes in Commonweals. If the whole chronology of every Commonweal were properly calculated, one could find countless examples, just as they are seen at a glance in the Roman *Fasti*." (56 lines).

464 I6 *auntient Romans reported* || Fr adds: "... and from the conflagration of Carthage to the conflagration of the city of Rome under Totila, King of the Goths, there are 700 years."

465 A6–467 B6 *But that the numbers of six . . . in the Greeke tongue by Theodotion*. These paragraphs are omitted in Fr.

CHAPTER 3 (PAGES 467–475)

471 B6–8 *giving them thereby . . . all at once together chaunged*. As in Fr, but L substitutes: "... either because he thought that none of those who took the oath would live any longer, or else that it might be understood that laws could not be made entirely immutable."

CHAPTER 4 (PAGES 476–493)

476 I2–3 *than profit devised to arise by honour* || Faulty. "... than profit divided (*divisé*) from honor." (Fr). L adds: "... if indeed profit be separate from honor, to which it is joined by nature itself."

477 D10 *in five hundred yeres*. Imprecise. Fr reads: "... in fifty years ..." L reads: "... in an age (*uno seculo*) ..."

478 I4 *promulgavit pertulitque*. In L the quotation stops here, whereas in Fr it goes on to give the provisions of the law, which are translated at K8–9. Cf. Livy, XXXIII, 46.

480 F6 *true wisedome*. Loose translation. Bodin is contrasting two distinct types of "wisedome" for which he uses different terminology, knowledge of human affairs at F6 (*prudence, prudentia*) and knowledge of natural and divine matters at F9 (*sagesse & pieté, verissima sapientia ac beata vita*). Cf. note at 4 K2.

481 C8 *Panaetius at Leontium* || Fr adds: "... to Phalaris, in Ionia ..." which appears to be a confusion of two examples cited by Aristotle (*Politics*, 1310b).

484 K9 *that Plato* || *would that the offices in his Commonweale* || Knolles suppresses two compliments to Plato. Fr reads: "... that Plato, who attained the foremost place among philosophers, would ..." L reads: "... in that Commonweal which men called divine ..."

485 E9 *and the long custome of continuall commaund give not an appetite*. Careless construction. To clarify, revise from E4: "Popular estates are maintained by continual change of officers, to the end that every man, according to his quality, may have part in the offices just as he has in the sovereignty; and [to the end] that equality, the nurse of popular estates, may be maintained as well as possible, by means of annual succession of magistrates; and [to the end] that the custom of long continued command should not give an appetite ..." As in Fr, but punctuation is faulty in Fr 7.

487 C4 *woman to death* || L explains: "... on an accusation of heresy, as was the practice at the time ..." Since the judge in question, Jacques Potier, Sieur du Blancmesnil, died in 1555, the incident throws a ray of light on Bodin's early years and gains in significance from a recent suggestion that Bodin himself may have been involved in two heresy trials in the same period. Cf. E. Droz, "Le Carme Jean Bodin, hérétique," *Bibliothèque d'humanisme et renaissance*, X (1948), 78–79.

487 D9 *deliver their opinions apart* || Fr 2–8 add: "Carolus Sigonius has interpreted this [statement of Asconius Pedianus] in an entirely different sense." Omitted in Fr 1. Bodin gives a marginal reference to Sigonius' *De judiciis*, Bk. II, ch. 2, which should read Bk. II, ch. 22.

489 B2–3 *and in other some to rest great wisedome, who yet have no skill in government at all*. Imprecise. "Some have the greatest wisdom in deliberations, but no capacity to command." (L).

Notes to Book IV

489 E4 *whom he had advaunced* ‖ L adds: "... and forbade him to pursue letters, that he might not think himself a wise man: for he knew that those princes who have become proficient in learning reject the advice of others."

491 B3-4 *which title ... an hundred and fiftie.* From L. Fr gives a more detailed description: "In addition there were eight clerks and twelve laymen, four persons for the *Requestes du sang*, and two chambers of Inquests, in which there were eight laymen and eight clerks to judge, and twenty-four *rapporteurs*. Those who wore the long gown were called clerks whether married or not, and the rest were laymen." (5 lines).

492 H8 *other mens eyes* ‖ L adds: "However nothing hindered him from foreseeing everything by means of his keen understanding, and from giving excellent advice on public questions."

CHAPTER 5 (PAGES 493-499)

495 E8-496 F2 *The Gaules ... outrages and robberies.* As in Fr, but L quotes directly, and at some length, from *De bello Gallico*, VI, 11 (9 lines).

496 H2 *they otherwise be right good men.* The word "otherwise" is inserted by Knolles (cf. Fr).

496 I4 *against Hannibal.* Inexact. Bodin correctly writes: "... against Hasdrubal ..." (Fr and L). At H10 L reads: "... against Hannibal and Hasdrubal ..."

497 E3 *betwixt themselves* ‖ L adds: "... and the Commonweal is less liable to sedition than if the supreme authority were given to two."

499 A8 *at discord* ‖ L adds: "... even if [their concord] is devoted entirely to the advancement of their private aims and interests."

499 C4-5 *untill that so by civill warre the state was quite at length overthrowne, and Caesar become master of all.* Knolles departs from Bodin's text, which only reads: "... they found it necessary to determine by civil war which of the two should command over the other." (L).

499 D5 *at such time as I was Embassadour in England.* From L. Bodin was a member of Alençon's embassy in 1581, but never a resident ambassador. The statement that the English parliament was assembled frequently in order to diminish factions also appears in Fr, but there the Earl of Rutland is named as the source of the information. Edward Manners, third Earl of Rutland, had visited France in 1570-1571.

CHAPTER 6 (PAGES 500-518)

501 A7-8 *by standing upon ... and subject thereunto.* As in Fr, but L introduces alternative reasons: "... either through favor, or hatred, or fear, or even under the compulsion of unjust laws."

502 F2 *even by God himselfe given unto kings.* Strictly, "... given by God unto kings themselves." (L).

502 F6 *the ordinarie vacant time.* Mistranslation. Read: "... the ordinary occupation (*vacation*) ..." (Fr). Later Knolles translates the term correctly as "vocation" (610 H8).

502 H2-3 *handle but those things onely which are proper unto their soveraigntie.* Faulty emphasis. Read: "... handle those very things which belong to sovereignty?" (L, and cf. Fr).

503 E3-4 *almost looking on* ‖ L adds: "Not only the Greeks, but even other princes, to their shame, strove to imitate this practice."

506 K6-7 *unto the king Catholike.* Inexact. "... unto the ambassador of the king Catholic ..." (Fr).

507 C7-8 *since the time that.* Strictly, "... during the time that ..." (Fr). L adds a further comment to this statement: "Certainly the peoples of France were never more obedient, nor was the sovereignty of the kings more majestic, than under those early kings."

507 D7 *or controlling the other* ‖ Fr adds: "... as did the Emperors of Constantinople, who divided the office of Great Provost of the Palace into two or three provostships of equal power, and gave the superintendence of justice and the laws to a Chancellor."

507 E6-7 *the most sufficient prince in the world.* Strictly, "... the most sufficient men in the world?" (Fr). Cf. E7-9, which is based on the corresponding sentence from L.

508 H6-7 *from the judgement* ‖ L adds: "But who would not prefer freedom from suits and contentions? What princes, however willing they may be, can afford sufficient time away from their own affairs to handle these matters?"

512 K2-4 *For the Theologie of the auntients belonged unto the Bishops, the Philosophers, and the Poets.* From Fr. L expands and clarifies: "But the [Greek and Roman] theology of Jupiter was threefold, and was a matter for both philosophers and priests, no less than for poets. Its first aspect related to the universe and the causes seated in nature; the second pertained to the Commonweal, which is maintained by religious rites and sacrifices; the third concerned the theater." Cf. St. Augustine's summary of Varro's views in *De civitate Dei*, VI, 5.

513 B8 *his great enemies* ‖ Addition in Fr and L. Beginning from "accused of treason" (B6), Fr continues as follows: "The latter [Morone] was judged by those appointed by the Marquis of Pescara, the leader of the conspiracy against the Emperor [Charles V]; while Thomas [More]

A 137

had his adversary for judge, a man who had grabbed his office and who had appointed commissioners at his own discretion to prepare for the trial. The King named twelve judges to give a verdict, following the custom of the country, and these had no sooner said 'Guilty,' that is, worthy of death, than the new Chancellor pronounced the sentence. I have learned this from the letters of Cajetanus, the Papal legate. This conviction gave the King of England a very bad reputation both at home and abroad, more for the form of the procedure employed than for its actual grounds. This would not have happened if the King had refrained from interfering with the judgment as scrupulously as the King of France did when his Chancellor was tried." (14 lines). L gives rather less detail on More's trial, but is more openly critical of its basic injustice.

514 I4–7 *Judicatum est ... approbantibus &c.* I.e., "It has been judged by the peers of the Realm, namely, by the Archbishop of Reims, the Bishop of Langres, the Bishops William of Châlons, Philip of Beauvais, Stephen of Noyon, by Odo, Duke of Burgundy, and by other bishops and barons etc., in our hearing and with our approval of the sentence, etc." Bodin also gives the date: July, 1216 (Fr and L).

515 B2 *any suit in court* ‖ Fr adds: "And as for appeals, this is one means of correcting and changing unjust judgments."

517 A1–2 *unto his presence* ‖ L adds: "For this reason Tarquinius Priscus is praised, because he introduced from Etruria the fasces, robes of state, curule seats, rings, decorations, military cloaks, the *toga praetexta* and *toga picta*, golden triumphal chariots, and other regal ornaments, as a means of giving prominence to the majesty of the prince."

517 D8–9 *the creating of new magistrats, or enacting of lawes.* As in L, but Fr reads: "... creating magistrates, [passing] general ordinances, and granting pardons, which [three functions] are the principal marks of sovereign majesty ..."

518 I10 *oppression and tyrannie* ‖ Addition in Fr and L. Fr 3–8 read: "Having concluded this question, let us now discuss whether the prince ought to take sides in civil factions." Omitted in Fr 1–2.

CHAPTER 7 (PAGES 519–544)

519 D4 *glorie of his name* ‖ Fr adds: "... which [villainies] are not by any means committed against His will, as the Hebrew sage says."

519 E1–520 G1 *But it may be ... perish and consume also.* From Fr. In L this passage is rewritten as follows: "Now if anyone thinks that [civil wars] are useful to tyrants, he is indeed deceived. For even if the tyrant is supported by the mutual accusations of the citizens one against another, and most of all by the proscription and overthrow of the more powerful ones, and is correspondingly weakened by the citizens' concord and unity, nevertheless it still does not follow that tyranny is strengthened by civil wars. For by their civil strife the citizens must necessarily destroy either the tyrant or themselves. If the tyrant wishes to arm one part of them against the rest, it is to be feared that he will either fall in the fighting, or else be struck down by the very men that he has armed. But if we suppose that tyrants delight in the greatest possible strife among the citizens, and idly view the struggle from their castle, as though from a watchtower, we must then admit that they will never retain the obedience of those whom they have armed. Nor is there any tyrant so demented as to prefer to rule a ruined Commonweal rather than one that is intact. Therefore while tyrants have many fears, the greatest is that the citizens may take up arms, and [to avoid this] they try in every way to disarm them, as if they were wild beasts, which are not quiet unless their teeth and claws have been removed. We find that nothing has brought about more downfalls of tyrants than civil wars. Even if the tyrant's power is seemingly increased when the city is emptied of citizens, yet it is actually lessened, because the winning faction first rejoice in victory over [other] citizens in order that in the end they may triumph more easily over the tyranny itself." (22 lines).

520 I9–10 *the soveraigne prince, or them that hold the soveraignety in an Aristocratie or popular estate.* Inexact. Fr reads simply: "... the Sovereign ..." But L substitutes: "... the prince in a monarchy, or the greatest magistrate (*Praetor maximus*) in a popular estate ..."

521 C10 *condemned to death* ‖ Fr adds: "... as I have learned from M. Canaye, an advocate in the Parlement, and one of the leaders of his profession."

523 D8 *Amurath.* Bodin writes Bajazet (Fr and L), but Knolles corrects his error.

527 B5 *obstinat wilfulnesse* ‖ L adds: "Nevertheless the prince should strive by every means to prevent the subjects from becoming stronger than himself."

528 H7 *the Saxon historiographer.* Faulty. "... Saxo the historian ..." (Fr). Bodin refers to the Danish writer Saxo Grammaticus.

529 E4–7 *but the parties ... in the execution doing.* Based on Fr, but L expands: "... for the very meaning of the word combat (μονομαχία) or duel is inappropriate [to groups of citizens]. Although King Tullus Hostilius decreed a combat of three Horatii against three Curiatii, this was justifiable for the sake of ending the war between the Albans and the Romans. Nor

does it matter how many fight against a foreign enemy. But quarrels of citizens among themselves are another matter. One should have regard for their lives, honor, and fortunes, and proceed by legal means if one of them harms another; and since there are certain family laws [cf. 13 A4–14 G1], and individual statutes for each college, these should be carefully examined by the judges. The greatest care must be taken to station armed guards everywhere, if any apprehension of civil sedition arises. This frequently happens when the lives of powerful or popular citizens are at stake, or when punishments are to be inflicted in accordance with laws or customs that are seldom invoked." (14 lines).

537 A3 *of Religion* ‖ L adds: "However Aristotle most properly wrote that orators who try to prove their contentions and geometricians who endeavor to persuade are both acting absurdly, because probable things cannot be demonstrated, and definite and necessary things ought not to be urged by means of arguments." Bodin gives as a marginal reference *Ad Theodecten* (i.e., the *Rhetoric*), but cf. *Nicomachean Ethics*, 1094b.

537 A5–6 (*howbeit that . . . God published*). From Fr, but L enlarges: "However there cannot be more than one truth, and to arrive at that religion which is true, and which is promulgated by the voice of almighty God, we should proceed not by disputations, but by incessant prayers to the eternal God, the father and ruler (*parens ac princeps*) of all the gods."

537 B2 *never enforced so to doe* ‖ L adds: "This was my advice to Elizabeth, Queen of England, and to her Lords and Council, when Campion the Jesuit and the [other] Catholics were being tried on capital charges."

537 E5–6 *that of the Christians, that of the Grecians.* Strictly, ". . . that of the Christians, of the Roman and the Greek rite . . ." (Fr). L adds two other religions to this list, those of the Ethiopians and Persians.

538 F2–540 F3 *For why . . . ever living God.* Apart from the reference to Theodoric (539 A5–B2) the whole of this passage is omitted in Fr 1–4, and only small portions of it (539 A5–B2, C2–7, D6–10, E6–8) appear in Fr 5–8.

538 F4 *unto the gods* ‖ L adds: "How wise this was I do not discuss. But if any had taken an oath according to his own religious rite, that oath was recognized by the [Roman] laws." Cf. *Digest*, 12, 2, 5, 1.

541 C4(margin) *Proverb.* 4. The numeral is erroneously added by Knolles. The correct reference is Proverbs 6:16–19.

542 H1–2 *what is it to be thought them to doe in their townes, and in time of peace.* Misinterpreted. Bodin writes: ". . . what is to be done [by Europeans] in towns, and in time of peace?" (Fr, and cf. L).

542 H7–8 *which if it might take place upon all persons: also a thousand murders and stabbings are committed, which should never have happened.* Inexact, owing to an unusual construction in Fr. Read: ". . . if this applied to everyone, a thousand murders and assassinations [which] are committed [now] would never happen . . ."

543 A9–10 *due execution of justice* ‖ L adds: "This [impunity of offenders] is openly displayed to the appellants by many corrupt magistrates and judges, in order to entice others to their jurisdiction for the sake of a most shameful gain. For this reason it is wisely provided by the laws of the Empire that in private suits anyone can appeal to the Imperial Chamber provided that the amount in question exceeds fifty crowns, but this is not allowed in criminal cases. Nor in Scotland is there any appeal from the judges of criminal trials, which are usually carried out with the greatest secrecy. In certain provinces of lower Germany crimes which cannot be proved by unquestionable evidence are punished on the basis of conjectures. This judicial principle has continued from the time of Charlemagne down to the present, and has been found a most useful method of punishing the most atrocious crimes, which are generally committed in secret, and of deterring evil men from a life of crime. This was the origin of the practice, unknown to the ancients, of varying the penalty according to the type of proof, which has long been an established custom with us." (16 lines). The consequences of convicting on presumptive evidence alone are forcefully demonstrated in Bodin's *Démonomanie des sorciers*, first printed in 1580. After a thorough consideration of the problem of proof in sorcery cases (Book IV, ch. 4), he concludes that in general presumptive evidence ought to be admitted because of the seriousness of the crime of sorcery and the difficulties of obtaining more positive proof.

544 G2 *Anthonie Soderin.* As in Fr, but L substitutes Piero Soderini. Paolantonio Soderini (1448–1499) was a follower of Savonarola, and spoke against Vespucci in favor of a popular estate (cf. 546 G8 and Guicciardini, *History of Italy*, Bk. II, ch. 2). His brother Piero Soderini (1452–1522) also took part in the reform of the constitution, and was elected Gonfalonier for life in 1502. Bodin clearly confuses the two men (cf. 706 F2 and 710 H3).

544 H2–3 *incited the princes and people to kill, massacre, & burne their subjects.* Confusion of Fr and L. Fr reads: ". . . incite Princes to kill, massacre and burn their subjects." L reads: ". . . incite princes and peoples to violence, slaughter and civil war."

Book V

CHAPTER I (PAGES 545–568)

545 B1 *The Fift Booke.* At this point the character of the translation itself changes abruptly, and the change continues throughout the next nine chapters. The precise nature of this change, and the possible reasons underlying it, have already been discussed in the Introduction, section IV (above, pp. A 48–A 49).

545 D8 *and the plaines* ‖ L adds: "And to show how much difference there is in the nature of places, we find that some are healthful, others are pestilential, and many other characteristics vary from place to place."

546 F4 *Aristides doth glorie* ‖ L adds: "... in his *Panathenaea*, in which he calls the Athenians the noblest of all mortals, because he thought that they were autochthonous and earthborn." Cf. *Methodus*, pp. 318, 334.

546 F9 *than to a Popular estate* ‖ L adds: "... and these [aristocratic cantons] are accustomed to check, by means of stricter laws and religious restraints, the unbridled liberty which suits the wildness of rustic folk."

546 G8–10 *That the nature... to a Popular estate.* As in Fr, but L expands the argument: "... That a popular estate, even if it seemed not to be as commendable as an aristocracy, was nevertheless more convenient for Florence and closer to the Florentine nature and disposition; that a legislator must necessarily frame the constitution of a Commonweal to the habits and nature of each nation; that the Venetians cherished aristocracy as befitting their character, while the minds of the Florentines were fundamentally disposed towards popular liberty; and that nothing which was done contrary to nature would be stable or long-lasting." (8 lines).

546 G10 *if his grounds were true* ‖ L adds: "Likewise it is evident that the most important reason why the people of the Netherlands revolted against Spanish rule was that they could not stand Spanish ways, which are most unlike their own. But the Spanish sky is separated by almost twelve degrees of latitude from the most distant stretches of the Low Countries, and this is the principal source of the differences in character." (6 lines).

547 C10–D1 *the manners of men* ‖ L adds: "For although vices can arise from natural causes, yet their eradication—as when a man who is inclined towards such vices is actually reclaimed from them—is not dependent on natural causes, but on will, effort, and discipline. All of these have no place if we admit necessity." (5 lines).

548 G1 *flaxen and fine haire* ‖ L adds: "... for so Lucan says [*Pharsalia*, II, 51], 'The blond Suevi come down from the extreme North.'"

548 G4 *by their red haire* ‖ L adds: "... and they, just like the French, believe that one should beware of such people, and all the more if the other signs of depravity are present, as in those lines of Martial [*Epigrams*, XII, 54], 'Red-haired, swarthy-faced, short of foot, and one-eyed [L reads *luscus* instead of *laesus*], you are a marvel, Zoilus, if you are a virtuous man.'"

548 H1 *which is verie apparant* ‖ L gives further illustrations: "For so Juvenal says [*Satires*, XIII, 164–165], 'Who does not know the cerulean eyes of a German, and his blond headdress, twining the moist ringlets into horns?' because they used to twist their hair and beard into ringlets and knots in the ancient Greek fashion. As Horace says [*Epodes*, XVI, 7], 'Nor could Germany conquer with her fierce, blue-eyed men,' and Tacitus [*Germania*, 4], 'Fierce blue eyes, reddish hair.'" (6 lines).

548 I9 *as Thomas Cromer writes* ‖ Fr 1–4 add: "... and as Count Gorka, who came as ambassador to France, assured me." Omitted in Fr 5–8. Gorka was one of the ambassadors sent to meet Henry, Duke of Anjou, on his election to the Polish throne in 1573. Bodin means Martin Cromer rather than Thomas Cromer, and he identifies the Polish historian correctly in the *Methodus*.

549 C10 *yea even in sommer.* More probably, "... especially (*mesmement*) in summer..." Bodin seems to use *mesmement* consistently in the now obsolete sense of "especially" or "particularly," while Knolles sometimes translates it as synonymous with *même*. Cf. 586 G3 and note, 606 H8 and note.

549 D7 *as Guichardine writes* ‖ L adds: "Yet they met with no mishap except from drunkenness, which is lethal in the South."

549 E6 *and leane in sommer* ‖ L adds: "However it is characteristic of islands and of coastal regions that the coldness of the air is warmed by the surging of the sea. Although I doubted this, I found it to be true when I crossed over to England, where the climate is milder than in France. For when the ocean is tossed about by the winds, it grows so warm that the water seems to be heated over a fire. As a result the men and their herds suffer no damage from the cold and frost." (7 lines).

550 I7 *Huns, Hongres,* ‖ *Lombards.* Both Fr and L insert the Gepidae in this list. For Bodin the "Huns" (as in L) and the "Hongres" (as in Fr) are the same people.

550 K7–9(margin) *Esai., etc.* These references are incomplete and also faulty, owing to misprints in Fr and L. The references which Bodin seems to have intended are: Isaiah 14:31; 41:25; 49:12; Jeremiah 3:18; 4:6; 6:22; 13:20; 15:12; 16:15; 23:8; 25:9; 46:20, 24; 47:2; 50:3, 9, 41;

Notes to Book V

51:48; Ezekiel 8; 48; Daniel 11; Zechariah 2:6; and the Book of Wisdom.

551 A2–5 *so hardly upon the face . . . in three dayes*. As in L, but Fr cites other evidence: "... and although we find that there are no longer any armies of 500,000 or 600,000 or even 2,500,000 fighting men, as we read in the sacred and profane histories; nor any longer a town similar to Crotona, which was twelve [sic] leagues in circuit, or to Babylon, which was thirty, [though built] on a square plan; nor any men of seven, eight and nine cubits in height, as are found in the histories of the Hebrews and Greeks ..." (8 lines). Cf. *Methodus*, p. 318. The reference to Crotona is from Livy, XXIV, 3.

551 C4 *To drinke like a Scythian* || L adds: "... which [proverb] the knowledgeable banqueter in Athenaeus [*Deipnosophistae*, X, 427] used, when, by a slight change of the word which cannot be understood except in Greek, he said to the boy pouring in water, 'ἐπισκύθισον, make it Scythian [i.e., strong]' instead of 'ἐπιχύτισον, fill it up.'" Cf. *Methodus*, p. 94.

551 D8 *with cold, nor wet* || Addition in Fr and L. L reads: "And while the Romans, though most practiced in warfare, passed the whole winter in inactivity, as did the Carthaginians and Greeks; the Scythians, on the other hand, wage war all the more fiercely when everything freezes hard. Indeed they even cross the rivers and range over the seas, which are then solid with ice."

552 G6 *sinke to the bottome* || L adds: "However nowadays, when women are suspected of witchcraft, German judges have them bound hand and foot and placed in water. Those who sink are declared innocent; but those who float are held guilty of sorcery."

552 I10 *that commendable civilitie*. Imprecise. Galen's concern, according to Bodin, was with *temperance* or *temperatio*, i.e., moderation or fit proportion of bodily humors, while Cicero's "civilitie" (K2–4) is *civilité & courtoisie* or *humanitas*, i.e., refinement or urbanity of manners.

552 K5–6 *who draw their arguments of civilitie and barbarisme from the effects of heate and cold*. Strictly, "... who think that barbarism and wildness proceed from extremes either of heat or of cold." (L). In Fr this opinion is specifically attributed to Aristotle.

553 A5 *wittie and politike* || L adds: "And when Marcus Antonius had sampled the urbanity, the charms, and the delights of the Egyptians, he despised the manners of the Romans as those of rustics."

553 A7 *and the Spaniards* || L adds: "The reason is obvious: that the Sun stays [overhead] longer (*Solis statio diuturnior*), and the circumference of the Tropic is less than that of the Equator."

553 C7–8 *to shut up the passage that the French might pretend no more in Italie*. Based on Fr, but L substitutes: "... so that the French retained nothing in Italy except the territory of Saluzzo, and this also the Spaniards attempted to seize by various deceits while the civil war was raging in France."

553 C9 *did not shew so great discretion, faith, and loyaltie, as they might* || The meaning is: "... *did* show all the discretion, faith and loyalty that they could ..." Cf. Fr, L, and a similar construction at 4 G4. L adds a qualification: "... even if some of them were reputed to have agreed upon a price for their release from captivity which was to the public disadvantage." The Constable Anne Montmorency and the Marshal St. André, both taken prisoner at St. Quentin in 1557, were among the French plenipotentiaries appointed to discuss terms of peace.

554 G2–3 *the French more moderat* || L adds: "For this reason the many precepts of Lycurgus and Plato concerning gymnastics and the exercising of citizens ought to be applied to the Southerners in order that their bodies, which are debilitated by great intelligence and assiduous contemplation, may be strengthened and made more active. Those who abound in yellow bile detest quiet, for the bile drives them hither and thither against their will; those who are able to devote themselves to contemplation become very adept at managing affairs (*prudentissimi*). The wildness and stupidity of the Northerners is remedied by literary pursuits, for continual toil makes men more brutal, as Aristotle writes in Book VIII of the *Politics* [1338b]. That nature is better which, avoiding the extremes of inadequacy and excess, adheres firmly to the golden mean in regard to both physical and mental capacity, as does the Italian nature." (12 lines).

554 H2 *constant and grave* || L adds: "But what [Galen] neglects to say is that strength arises from blood. Hence Festus [ed. Müller, p. 266] writes that *robustus*, strong, is derived from *rubor*, redness. Fortitude and strength of mind come from yellow bile. This is not because the abundance of blood and of humors produces strength by itself, but because blood, which is thicker and more abundant in fibers, enlarges and hardens the muscles from which strength is engendered."

554 H8 *no distinction of the parts of the world* || L adds: "... which Hippocrates, in his book *De aere, aquis, et locis*, thinks to be most necessary of all for the thorough understanding of the nature of men ..."

554 K1 *beyond mount Atlas*. Strictly, "... on this side of Mount Atlas ..." (Fr and L).

Notes to Book V

555 B8 *and torment them* ‖ Fr adds: "... and finally to hang them nevertheless."

555 C7–8 *(and in our age) betwixt Muleasses and his owne children*. Misleading. "... and [those reported by Paulus Jovius] in our time betwixt Muley Hassan and his own children ..." (Fr). Both Fr and L name Jovius marginally as the source. L enlarges: "Indeed in recent years the children of Muley Hassan, King of Tunis, not only drove him from his kingdom with the greatest filial disloyalty, but also most cruelly put out his eyes." Cf. *Methodus*, p. 101.

556 G5 *possest with evill spirits* ‖ L adds: "The inhabitants call this [Southern] type of fury divine, as though a madman might see what a wise man does not, and he who loses his human faculties might attain divine ones."

556 I7 *his owne desires* ‖ L adds: "But how many men have their passions under control? How many restrain their desires? Certainly none but the wise man. But sometimes madness (*insania*) passes into fury (*furor*), and this kind of fury is pacified by flogging. For in London there is a large number of madmen (*furiosi*) assembled in one building, who are severely beaten with whips at full moon, when the force of their fury increases by reason of the swelling of their heads. When I expressed pity at this, I was told by the keepers that this was wholesome treatment for fury." (8 lines).

558 F6 *of his women* ‖ L adds: "Here someone may object that if the Scythians are so impotent in love-making, whence came such a multitude of robust men as there is in the North? I attribute this to continence, and I think that scarcity of children and dissimilarities [from the parents] arise from frequent and promiscuous intercourse. For this reason the laws of Lycurgus forbade husbands to remain all night with their wives. It is well known that the less frequently a man has intercourse with his wife, the more numerous and stronger will be the children that he begets. Very often women who sleep apart from their husband will bear twins after a single copulation. Thus it happens that although all men are somehow linked with the beasts in this respect, those who are closer to the bestial nature, like the Scythians, derive greater enjoyment from the pleasures which are in accordance with nature. They also bear offspring similar to the parents, so that Tacitus writes [*Germania*, 4] that all Germans resembled one another. This is because they have very little inclination to unnatural intercourse, or to liaisons with foreigners, and not because they all live in a uniform climate, as Hippocrates writes, since every country has its own distinctive climate. Therefore the large number of people is the result of a pleasure which is tempered and in harmony with nature. Hence Jornandes called lower Germany a factory of men. From there have emerged almost infinite hordes of people. Indeed we find to our astonishment that in the country of Zeeland and Holland, where the ancients place the Cimbri and Batavi, sheep conceive three or four times every year, and sometimes bear triplets and quadruplets [or: bear twins three and four times a year], while in the South they conceive once, or at most twice, and bear only one lamb. It is also incredible, but true, that in the North the number of males is everywhere either equal to or greater than the number of women, but in the South there are many more females than males in every kind of animal. For Caesar's statement [*De bello Gallico*, V, 14] that frequently twelve Britons were satisfied with one wife, together with the discovery that individual Indians have bevies of wives, demonstrate that there is an abundance of women [in the South] and a shortage of them [in the North]." (33 lines).

558 I1–2 *But Leprosie ... whole bodie*. Condensed from L only. The full passage reads: "Here we should be warned that by a serious error leprosy is confused with elephantiasis, not only by the ignorant, but even by those who have won the highest reputation for learning. Elephantiasis is a massive swelling of the legs, but leprosy is a cancer of the whole body. The error has arisen from the translators of Galen, who render λέπρα and ἐλεφαντίασις, two separate diseases, as *lepra*. Galen does write that two sufferers from elephantiasis contracted leprosy as a result of eating vipers, yet both Aristotle and the schools of physicians constantly assert that this type of diet cures leprosy." (11 lines).

558 I10 *those of the South have verie drie bodies*. Condensed from L only, which actually reads: "Likewise Leo Africanus reports that in Numidia he saw many centenarians who showed no appearance of old age, but nothing more desiccated could have been imagined. Cicero writes [*De senectute*, 10] the very same thing of Masinissa, King of Numidia, who, at the age of 90, would not mount a horse if he had begun a journey on foot, nor dismount if he was mounted. Nor could he be induced to cover his head in any rain or cold. Then he adds that his body was excessively dry." (8 lines).

558 K1 *the falling sicknes, quartaine agues, and the Kings evill*. As in Fr, but L substitutes: "... insanity (*furor animi*), leprosy, epilepsy [i.e., the falling sickness], and dysentery."

559 B4–5 *And Caesar writes ... and of hunting*. From Fr, but L enlarges on the point: "... and Campanus says of the Germans in his *Speech*: 'Your ancestors did not go to a temple unless they were armed.' And Caesar says of the Germans [*De bello Gallico*, VI, 21]: 'They have no druids to regulate divine worship, no zeal for sacrifices. They reckon among the gods only

those that they see and by whose offices they are openly assisted, such as the Sun, the Moon, and the Fire-God (*Vulcanus*). Of the rest they have learnt not even by report.' From this it may be understood that those who are slow of mind are swayed by their senses only, like beasts, and are concerned only with that which is before them, and which can be perceived by the senses. It ought not to seem strange, therefore, if many Germans who have left the Roman faith still hold fast to their images, in order that the figures of the deities displayed before them may induce reflection upon divine matters. For less intelligent men take the things that they see for the deity itself." (12 lines). Joannes Antonius Campanus, Bishop of Crotona and Teramo, was the author of *Oratio . . . ad exhortandos principes Germanorum contra Turcos et de laudibus eorum* (Rome, ca. 1471).

560 H10 *vowes of religion* ‖ L continues here: ". . . of the infinite multitude of monks and priests, and of the fact that he had seen 2355 priests ordained at one ceremony. These things make it clear that nowhere is religion held in greater veneration than in Ethiopia."

561 E8 *politike governments* ‖ L adds: "Caesar reports that the ancient Scythians and the Germans devoutly worshiped Mars and Diana (just as the Southerners worshiped Venus, whom they called Astarte), and were extremely fond of hunting. Indeed, the Germans always speak of the Moon [*der Mond*] in the masculine gender, a point which Antoninus Caracalla thought to be not only important, but even necessary, for maintaining authority over women." (7 lines).

562 F10 *so many wives* ‖ L adds: "I omit what the ancients have reported concerning the movement of the male [foetus] to the right side of the womb."

563 A3 *cheerefull*. Bodin writes *alaigres* and *alacres*, which suggests lively or active rather than joyous. Neither meaning seems consistent with his other remarks on Southerners.

563 A8 *those that have least wit*. Strictly, ". . . those that have less wit (*esprit*) . . ." (Fr).

564 G4-5 *They troubled . . . rest of the Greekes.* As in Fr, but L expands: "They were so given to hiring themselves out as mercenaries that the same nation often constituted opposing armies, which fought with each other on behalf of rival employers. Even the Romans, against whom they waged war for a very long time, found them almost invincible. Yet they had a popular estate comprising three towns only. This should not seem strange to anyone who knows the nature of the mountains in which the Aetolians live." (6 lines).

564 G9 *in Titus Livius* ‖ L adds: "Indeed the Marsians, the ancient inhabitants of the Apennine mountains, are reported to have been the fiercest people in all Italy; hence the proverb 'No one has conquered without the Marsians.' Likewise Livy says [IX, 13] that the Samnites dwelt in villages in the mountains, and no people waged war longer against the Romans. I pass over the fact that Gustavus, in order to seize the kingdom of Sweden, recruited an army in the mountains of Dalecarlia." (6 lines).

564 H1-4 *And contrariwise . . . with pleasure.* As in Fr, but L is more explicit: "For such is the inheritance and upbringing [of the Swiss] that they would give up their lives rather than suffer their weapons to be taken from them. The contrary is found in those who are born in villages and plains, especially in the more fertile regions. This is because character is often formed not so much by the family stock as by those things which are furnished by the very nature of the place and by the mode of life, for by these things we are nourished and sustained." (6 lines). Although Bodin cites no authority, the last sentence is from Cicero, *De lege agraria*, II, 35.

564 H9-12 *And to that end Tully . . . and to deceive.* From Fr, but L quotes Cicero as follows: "Tullius says [*De lege agraria*, II, 35]: 'The Carthaginians are given to fraud and lying, not so much by race as by the nature of their position, because their ports brought them into touch with merchants of many lands, and their love of gain gave them a love of cheating. The Ligurians are mountain men, rugged peasants. The land itself makes them so, yielding nothing except after much cultivation and heavy toil. The Campanians are proud, as a result of the fertility of their lands, the abundance of their crops, and the size, layout, healthfulness and beauty of their city.' These are Cicero's words, and they confirm what we have said." (7 lines).

564 I7-8 *diversitie of men and their humors* ‖ L adds: "Indeed practical wisdom (*prudentia*) is acquired by learning to distinguish the character of different peoples, so that Homer calls Ulysses a most prudent man because he had seen the ways and the cities of many men."

564 K7 *beaten with violent winds* ‖ L adds: "The reason is clear. A quiet mind cannot exist in a man who is tossed back and forth. This is evident from the fact that no one can think amid commotion and uproar. Contemplation must be performed by a mind cleansed and free from perturbation, and even the body should be at rest. Also the more insane a man becomes, the more he is tossed about by the motion of his mind and body."

565 A2 *farre more mild* ‖ L adds: "Likewise it is well known that no people in France are fiercer than those of Narbonne and Aquitaine, even though they are more southerly than the people of central and northern France (*Celtae ac Belgae*),

because in that area the Altanian (for Pliny calls the winds by the same names that the inhabitants use) and the Circian winds blow almost continually and very strongly. This produces a certain wildness, and restless agitation of the mind." (5 lines). Altanus is described as a wind from the south-southwest; Circius, from the west-northwest.

565 A2–3 *another difference of men*. As in Fr, but L specifies: "... a certain weakness (*mollities*) of body and mind alike ..."

565 B6 *and so are the cities of Limoges, Genes, and Gand*. As in Fr, but L substitutes: "Almost the same is our Limogaea, for so the inhabitants pronounce it, from a word which is clearly Greek—not from λοιμός, 'plague,' since it is situated in the mountains, and supplied on every side with wholesome waters—but from λιμός, 'famine,' because it is necessary to bring in grain from outside or else die of hunger on account of the barrenness of the countryside. Yet it has the greatest number of highly skilled artisans of any city in France, except Paris and Toulouse." (7 lines). On the derivation of Limoges from λιμοῦ γαῖα, "land of hunger," see the Latin text of the *Methodus* (O.P., I, 249).

565 B7 *richnesse of the soyle* || L adds: "For when the waters and very fertile snows flow down from the mountains into the valleys, they must needs produce a fertility which can make up for the barrenness of the mountains. Of this nature are the valleys of Mount Atlas, from which the ancients reported harvests of a hundred for one, and Leo Africanus of fifty for one not long ago. Strabo writes that in the valleys of Mount Taurus grew clusters of grapes two cubits in size, and that seventy pecks (*modii*) of figs were gathered from one tree. Virtually the same things are reported of the area around Damascus, in the valleys of the mountains of Lebanon. We know the Limagne in Auvergne, the Turin district, or rather the whole of Piedmont, Val d'Or in the Pyrenees, Tempe in Thessaly, situated among mountains, and likewise the valley of Sitten, and those of the Carpathians. These abound with an incredible fertility. Amid such plenty, and in such pleasant regions, it must follow that the inhabitants will be abandoned to pleasures and delights. Of this nature were the Sybarites, placed in the middle of enclosed valleys, who were inflamed, as Athenaeus writes [*Deipnosophistae*, XII, 518–521] with a passion for sensual pleasures, and who saw neither the rising nor the setting sun." (16 lines). This addition is modeled closely upon a passage in the *Methodus*, p. 141.

565 C3 *keepe them in awe* || Fr adds: "... and it was even necessary to accommodate the English merchants separately, as the city of Angers was compelled to do, having one house in common for the merchants of every nation, and a separate one for the English, because they could not get on with the rest." (5 lines). L omits the flattering reference to Queen Elizabeth (C4–5).

565 E3 *if the studie of Musicke*. More precisely, "... if they reject music (that is, the cultivation of the Muses) ..." (L).

566 H2 *Scaliger borne at Verona* || L adds: "... no less distinguished for his erudition than for his descent and progeny ..."

566 K9 *caused unto our selves* || L adds: "... in order that each one of us might hold firmly to his own religion."

567 A10 *people of the North* || L adds: "But they are greatly deceived who twist this lightness—or rather quickness of spirit—into either inconstancy or perfidy. I have no doubt that there are and always have been light and perfidious men everywhere, but this is relative to the norm [for the region]. Galen attributes constancy to the melancholic temperament, and lightness to those who are sanguine, and hence fleshy from [abundance of] blood. For the sanguine humor is the contrary one to the melancholic, and therefore the two must produce contrary effects. That the sanguine temperament predominates in Northern peoples is shown sufficiently by the reddish color of their faces, which is most apparent in those who suffer from skin disorders (*lepra*). These are all red in the North, but are called ἀλφός from their whiteness in the South. Therefore since Northerners are stronger than the others (Festus notes that *robur*, strength, is derived from *rubor*, redness), they clearly correspond to the period of youth, just as the melancholic temperament most closely resembles old age, and it follows that the Northerners are lighter than others, for not only Aristotle but also experience itself show us that lightness is characteristic of adolescents, who suddenly desire new things and then quickly loathe them. Likewise they are bold, hot-tempered, merry and spendthrift, all of which qualities accord with the Northern temperament, while Southerners are just the opposite." (20 lines). On the characteristic temperaments of the young and old, cf. *Methodus*, p. 125, and Aristotle, *Rhetoric*, 1389a–b.

567 C7 *denie their word* || Fr adds: "... but he was not yet acquainted with the English, Danes and Normans, who originated from that country [i.e., Germany], and who incline even more towards Northerly characteristics."

567 C10–D3 *and the people ... to their Idolatrie*. Condensed from L, which embarks at this point on a long discussion of inconstancy in religion: "Although constancy should shine the brightest in religion, once it has been adopted, the Goths quickly embraced the Christian religion when they came into Italy, and soon took up Arianism.

Notes to Book V

The Greenlanders, who are nearest the Pole, being of an inconstant disposition, as Munster says, easily embraced the Christian religion, and afterwards lapsed into idolatry. The Turks eagerly embraced the rites and deities of the Arabs when they first came from Scythia to Asia Minor. The Tartars embraced Christianity, and soon after Islam, without any compulsion. The Bohemians and Saxons were the first to forsake the Roman rites; how wisely I shall not discuss, nor is the question relevant at this point. Immediately the whole of Saxony, the Baltic cities, Denmark, Norway, Sweden, the Swiss, who are descended from the Swedes, and later England and Scotland also, broke away. Upper Germany, which is further from the North, resisted to some extent, and the whole of it did not repudiate the old rites. France has now been fighting on behalf of the Roman rites for sixty years, and refuses to be parted from them. Indeed Sleidan himself, who criticizes the lightness of the French, admits that he witnessed nine years of most painful burnings at the stake and quarterings in France, and none in Germany. Nor did the new doctrines of Luther, which had been approved, satisfy the Germans for very long, but almost at once they absorbed the opinions of the Anabaptists, John of Leyden, Zwingli, Carlstadt [*Carlestadius* in L 3–5, *Selestadius* in L 1–2], Osiander, Westphal, the Davidists, Stancari, the Adamites, the Waldenses, the Interimists, and countless other sects. The southerly peoples of Asia and Africa do not give up an established religion except as a result of prophecy or force of arms. We marvel at the incredible steadfastness of the Jews, which drove Antiochus the Noble almost to insanity. Having spread from the South far and wide throughout the world, they now wander about in great servitude and poverty, yet for almost four thousand years they have observed very strictly the law of Moses.

"In the sayings and deeds of men, as in all things, I have always approved that golden mean called constancy, which lies midway between stubbornness and lightness. Yet many, like Nonius Marcellus [*De conpendiosa doctrina*, 432–433], distinguish between steadfastness (*pertinacia*) and stubbornness (*pervicacia*), considering one a merit and the other a fault. However this may be, a steady continuance in one opinion has certainly never been approved by the wise. Just as in navigation it is sound practice to yield to a tempest, even if [by so doing] you cannot make port, so also in human affairs, which are changeable and contradictory (I exclude divine matters), I think it is honest to change one's opinion. Those people who defend their opinion so stubbornly that they think it a disgrace to be contradicted, and a dreadful thing to be overcome, or who prefer to give up their lives rather than their established beliefs, are helping neither themselves nor their Commonweal. The Southerners are of this sort, while the Scythians are the most fickle." (43 lines). This addition follows, with omissions and slight modifications, a corresponding passage in the *Methodus*, pp. 126–128.

L goes on to give a slightly fuller comparison of Northern and Southern characteristics (cf. 567 A10–C1, which is from Fr), again following the *Methodus*, pp. 124–125. Then L develops another point omitted in Fr: "Those who have less intelligence [i.e., Northerners] are carried hither and thither without cause, and resemble children, who contract friendships easily and lay them aside easily, while men advanced in years do not. The more intelligence a man has, the less readily is he drawn into friendships, hatreds, or new opinions, yet when he has acquired them, he is that much more reluctant to give them up." (6 lines). Cf. *Methodus*, p. 125.

567 E6 *wherein not only the nature*. Condensing L, which actually reads: "There is no need to give examples, since they are obvious, and it would be endless to pursue them. From them it may be understood that not only the nature . . ."

568 F8–10 *and that the Sunne . . . thousand leagues*. As in Fr, but L casts doubt on this explanation: "If they were black only under Capricorn, I should think that that black coloring is to be ascribed entirely to the heat of the sun, for the sun is nearer the earth in Capricorn by the full extent of its eccentricity [*tota eccentrici latitudine*, and cf. Fr] which comprises almost 800,000 miles, but at the River Niger on this side of the equator all men are just as black."

CHAPTER 2 (PAGES 569–579)

569 C10 *than povertie it selfe* ‖ L adds: "Nevertheless to seek one's living by spinning and weaving or manual labor is not so much to be feared as the baneful plague [of poverty] which arises from that sense of shame, and which brings utter ruin upon families and Commonweals alike."

572 F6 *but of the halfe*. Faulty. ". . . but a portion twice as great as that of [each of] the others . . ." (L). Cf. 784 H9–10.

572 F10–G1 *there must not be any prohibition*. Inexact. ". . . there need not be any prohibition . . ." (Fr).

572 G3 *from the which it was sold* ‖ Additions in Fr and L. Fr adds: ". . . as well as the right of *retraict lignager*, instituted by the law of God." *Retrait lignager* was the right of a relative to recover entailed family land which had been sold, by reimbursing the purchaser.

L adds: "For by this means the sale was of fruits, not of lands, an estimate being made of the annual revenue. But [among the Hebrews] the year in which the restitution of persons and lands was made was a common limit for everyone, so arranged that if three years remained until the year of Jubilee, the revenue for three years was estimated."

572 K8 *which doth expresly forbid it.* Condensing Fr and L. L reads: "... which forbids all kinds of usury so expressly that no one ought to call it in question, unless he thinks that he can plainly contravene the pronouncements of God by vain subtleties."

573 C4–5 *in regard of their sales they make at this day, the Notarie putting in this clause.* Imprecise. "... compared with what is done [now] in [feigned] purchases at a monetary loss, and [also] with the clause of the notaries which reads . . ." (Fr, and cf. L).

574 G6 *robbe secretly.* Strictly, "... rob in safety." (Fr, but misspelled in Fr 6–7).

574 I1–3 *the which seemes ... Urbin the fift.* As in Fr, but L clarifies: "Yet this law [of Charles V] seems to have been passed earlier, since in former times the earls of Flanders confiscated the inheritances of priests until Pope Urban V forbade the practice on pain of excommunication."

574 K2 *that were committed* ‖ L adds: "For who doubts that as a result of their liberty to write down testaments without employing eye-witnesses or even hearsay witnesses [*in the margin:* as is permitted by Canon Law, title "De testamentis," chapter "Cum esses"], a great many bishops and priests have gained possession of the estates of private men?"

575 B1–2 *straitly defended for many yeares, not to alienat nor rent out the goods.* Faulty. "... strictly forbidden to alienate, or to lease for a long period of years, the goods ..." (Fr).

575 B6 *extraordinarie alms* ‖ L adds: "But this was a conservative estimate, for fear that the true figure should arouse envy and endanger the ecclesiastical order."

575 C5–6 *and colledges be* ‖ L adds: "But not long ago the mendicant orders would have been permitted by a decree of the Council of Trent to possess lands, had the French not repudiated that Council."

575 C9–10 *as they did in time of our predecessors against the Templers and the Jewes.* Based on Fr, but L is more openly critical: "... just as the Templars, in the time of our ancestors, were dispossessed, in the most unjust and most infamous manner, of their ancient holdings, which seemed to be too extensive."

576 I9 *issued of a younger house* ‖ L adds: "Plato strongly recommended this practice of Lycurgus in his 125th law [cf. *Laws*, 740], and wished the entire inheritance to descend to one of the children whom the father should choose, with alienation forbidden."

576 K8 *ignorance and barbarisme* ‖ L quotes verbatim from Tacitus (*Germania*, 20) and then adds: "And even though Germany has largely adopted the testamentary laws of the Romans, our ancestors forbade bequests of paternal family lands beyond a sixth part or a fourth part at the most, and granted them by lawful right to the nearest of kin in every case."

577 A8–9 *according to Licurgus ... do much better preserve.* Careless combination of Fr and L. Fr reads: "Now it seems that the eldest, in succeeding to the whole inheritance, as did the 7000 Spartans in Lacedemonia, and as do the people of Caux in Normandy, both noble and base, do much better preserve ..."

577 E5–7 *wherein the antient lawgivers ... by the daughters.* As in Fr, but L substitutes: "... and also in order that by the regulation of dowries women might be more easily compelled to modesty and obedience to their husbands. We see that those given very large dowries inevitably rule their husbands in shameful fashion, and that the husbands, losing their honor and dignity, are subservient to their wives. Restraints are therefore to be placed on [woman's] headstrong nature and on this untamed animal, as Cato the Censor used to say [cf. Livy, XXXIV, 2], for once they have achieved equality, they will quickly dominate." (7 lines).

578 H1–2 *whom they called Ladies.* Careless. "... who called them Ladies (*dames, dominae*)." (Fr, and cf. L).

579 A2–3 *foure hundred thousand crownes.* L explains that this was the figure established by decree as the dowry for the daughters of Henry II. Cf. 667 E7 668 F1.

579 C2–6 *and in that of Vendosme ... terme of life.* From Fr. L notes that this change in the custom of Vendôme "... instigated other eldest sons to come to equitable agreements that [younger sons] should possess this third in right of ownership."

579 D9–10 *threescore daies* ‖ L adds: "They are wrong in calling themselves Egyptians, since they have always differed from the Egyptians in customs and language. Nor is it likely that they have journeyed across the entire Mediterranean sea from a most fertile region to the remote and barren shores of Spain."

579 E2–4 *Thus in my opinion ... wealth of a small number.* From Fr, but L enlarges: "But nothing in a Commonweal is so harmful as a multitude of vagrant idle poor, who plunder the

goods of private men, and place all their hopes of betterment in the overthrow of the Commonweal. Amasis, King of Egypt, warded off this plague very successfully by a strict enactment that idle men who had nothing that they could call their own should be executed like robbers." (7 lines).

CHAPTER 3 (PAGES 580–584)

580 H10–11 *who would have the goods . . . to move them to the contrarie.* Faulty. ". . . who have desired, and not without the best of reasons, that the goods of the condemned should be adjudged to the public [treasury]." (Fr).

580 K6 *according unto the conclusions of his accusers.* Imprecise. ". . . to the extent of meeting the claims and demands of his accusers." (Fr).

582 G5 *princes to become tyrants* || L adds: "There also comes to mind the argument of Plato, who prohibits the alienation or confiscation of ancestral lands in his *Laws*, ch. 528 [cf. *Laws*, 741], in order that the equality of property which he had devised in his imagination should not be destroyed."

583 A4–5 *and not to the lords of the soyle.* Condensed. Bodin actually writes: ". . . to the exclusion of the other lords, whether they hold from the Crown, or whether they are sovereign . . ." (Fr).

583 B4–5 *and Raymond earle of Tholouse, the countrey of Languedoc.* As in Fr, but L explains more fully: ". . . and Raymond, Count of Toulouse, gave the whole of Languedoc and the district of Toulouse to Alphonse, brother of St. Louis, nominally as the dowry which he had promised him, with the condition that if Alphonse died childless, the lands should come under royal control. He is said to have done this more from fear than by his own volition, in order to find, under the pretext of fulfilling his promise, some solution to the civil wars which were wearing him down." (6 lines).

583 B4–10 (margin) *1234 . . . 1535.* Knolles confuses these dates. Bodin gives them as follows: Dreux, 1230; Bray and Montereau-faut-Yonne, 1234; Guienne, Anjou, Maine, Touraine, and Auvergne, 1202; Alençon and Perche, 1458; Périgord, 1396; Ponthieu, 1370; la Marche, 1302; Angoulême, 1302; Saluzzo, 1535; the property of Charles of Bourbon, 1527. No date is given for l'Isle-Jourdain (Fr and L).

584 H3 *service of the Commonweal* || L adds: "This applies in our customs when a fee is forfeited through the perfidy of a vassal who forswears his lord, for when the vassal dies the forfeited fees are restored to his kinsmen. [*In the margin:* This was decided in the Parlement of Paris against the Marshal de Saint-André and in favor of the Lord of Parthenay in 1556]."

CHAPTER 4 (PAGES 584–596)

586 F1–2 *the day of the battell* || L adds: "And when Livius Salinator and Claudius Nero had jointly won a notable victory over Hasdrubal by virtue of their consular authority, the triumph was nevertheless granted to Livius, because the battle was fought on a day when he had the fasces and command, and the victory was said to have been gained under the auspices of Livius." Cf. 348 I3–6.

586 G3 *even in matters of armes.* Read: ". . . especially (*mesmement*) in matters of arms." Cf. note at 549 C10.

587 B4–5 *nothing lesse than profit* || L adds: "And just as the rewards of virtue were considered that much greater, the further removed they were from profit and gain, so also they thought no punishment worse than ignominy. The profits from the victories almost always went to the treasury or to the common soldiers."

587 E5 *reward of honour* || L adds: "However [the virtuous man] does not seek honors unless impelled by duty; and if he does, it is not for his own advantage, but for that of others. If successful, he does not boast; nor is he distressed by failure, but bears it calmly. If he does feel any regret, he grieves not for himself but for the Commonweal."

589 D3 *24 in the order of the Garter.* Bodin writes "40" (Fr and L), but Knolles corrects him.

590 F7 *Prince should be jealous* || L adds: "But since a prince is very often compelled by persistent requests to derogate from an edict, the Parlement of Paris is accustomed to reject his rescripts [of derogation]."

591 B8–9 *them to whom they have done most good* || L adds: ". . . that is, actors, hangers-on, flatterers, harlots and sodomites."

593 C5–6 *terrifying them from their wicked and disordred lives.* Drastically condensing a passage added in L, which reads: "For while punishments have many advantages, the pain inflicted on the wrongdoer in order to make him a better man is the least of them. In capital punishment it has no place at all. There is a greater advantage in respect of the one sinned against, in that amends are made in every way possible, either for the violated majesty (although really it is inviolable) of immortal God, or for the wrong done to human dignity. Certainly no one ought to demand this for his own sake alone if he would imitate the great Augustus, who appeared to suffer punishment when he exacted it. Even though [the punishment] usually brings comfort to those who have suffered great wrongs, it is more important to see that from thenceforth it should bring security both for the one wronged and for everyone else; and also that it should

Notes to Book V

decrease the number of the wicked. The greatest advantage of all, however, lies in the example, in that the dread of poverty, infamy, torture and even death may restrain others from a life of villainy." (15 lines). There is a similar discussion of the benefits resulting from punishment in the *Démonomanie* (Bk. IV, ch. 5), which, however, asserts that the first and foremost consideration is the appeasement of divine wrath.

594 F1-2 *to continue everie one in his dutie*. This should read: "... in order to please everyone [*à fin de contenter un chacun* in Fr 1-6, 8, but misprinted *à fin d'y continuer un chacun* in Fr 7] ..." Cf. L also.

595 C2 *P. M. du Mont*. Faulty. Knolles reads "P. M." as the initials of Cardinal del Monte, but in fact these letters, which appear in L only, are in apposition with Julius III, and stand for *pontifex maximus*.

CHAPTER 5 (PAGES 596–614)

598 K6 *an assured peace* || Addition in Fr and L. L reads: "But soldiers generally disturb this [state of peace], because peace is always an enemy to war, and soldierly virtues are despised when the Commonweal is at peace."

600 G9 *according to the antient warres, that is, of the stronger*. Careless. "... according to the law of ancient warfare, that is, the right of the stronger?" (Fr).

601 C7-8 *for how valiant ... more stronger*. From Fr, but L differs: "... since they were very often caught off their guard by unforeseen attacks of the enemy. We see that by this means even the most powerful are overcome by the most cowardly."

601 D10 *the lives of innocents* || L adds: "... or one's own life. For he who does not protect the life, civil rights, or property of innocent men, or who does not repel if he can the wrong done unto others, is only slightly less at fault than if he had inflicted the injury himself. This principle of individual conduct extends to societies, so that we avenge those who have been wronged by means of armed forces when other methods fail. But this cannot be done without the military arts." (6 lines).

602 H6 *deserts of Arabia* || L adds: "But they did not think it right to wage war on anyone unjustly, and after they had subdued their neighbors and increased their resources no one could attack them with impunity. Consequently they determined, with incredible virtue and courage, to revenge the wrongs inflicted on their allies and confederates and to deliver the oppressed from tyranny, both to have a worthy occasion for war and to prevent the citizens from lapsing into idleness or warring among themselves. Thus they considered that they should fight for the honor of their Empire, for glory, of which they were more desirous than other peoples, and for the rights not only of allies but even of those with whom they were not associated in any way, if these were wronged by the more mighty. For where can blood be shed to better effect? Where can one lay down life more honorably? Where can one gain truer and more enduring glory? They also waged war frequently on behalf of merchants and shipowners who had been mal-treated, or when danger threatened the safety of weaker peoples. Most of all they fought for their allies, on whose behalf they were so zealous in exacting vengeance for injuries that the fear which they aroused in the hearts of barbarous nations and cruel tyrants restrained even the most powerful from wrongdoing, and held the good to their duty.

"Indeed they awarded the crown of all the virtues to courage, to which they also gave the fitting name *virtus*. Thus Caesar, writing of a mutiny of the soldiers, says [*De bello Gallico*, VII, 52]: 'I value discretion (*modestia*) in a soldier more highly than courage (*virtus*).' For this reason they were trained in the military arts from the games of their childhood. At the end of childhood they became soldiers; in the early twenties, centurions; as young adults, military tribunes; at maturity, commanders-in-chief. Nor did they acquire their military knowledge from the precepts and writings of others, but rather from their own commands; not by defeats, but by victories; not by flight, but by triumphs. Thus it should not surprise anyone that the Romans waged more wars than other peoples had even read about, and acquired more provinces than others even aspired to." (31 lines).

602 K2 *under a strong shield* || L adds: "For when a Commonweal is engaged in a war, the other arts and disciplines must go into hiding, as though paralyzed with fear. They will be of no use amid the noise of trumpets and drums, but will give place to the art of war."

604 G8 *so mightie a king* || L adds: "[I shall add] this point only, that those who discourage [the Swiss] from military training under the pretext of religion are working for the overthrow of their government. However war itself is not only approved by divine law, but even commanded, provided that it is just. Certainly the ancient Romans resolved to go to war only after the most solemn religious ceremony. Livy says [XXXI, 9], 'The Roman Commonweal was particularly concerned with religion at the beginning of new wars, holding public supplications and offering prayers at all the seats of the gods.'" (7 lines).

605 B6 *house in the countrie* || Fr adds: "... this is the safest course for newly established monarchs ..."

Notes to Book V

606 H8–9 *yea if he were entred.* Read: "... particularly (*mesmement*) if he were entered ..." Cf. note at 549 C10.

606 K4 *to obey the councell of the pope.* Inexact. "... to obey the Council [of Basel] and the Pope ..." (Fr).

607 A2 *had burnt their citie* ‖ L adds: "Certain unskilled historians have written that the army of the Gauls was later vanquished so completely by the generalship of Furius Camillus that not a single man survived the slaughter, as though Furius, an exile, lacking an army, money, and advisers, could have achieved more than the Roman legions and resources aided by the armies of their allies. But Callimachus and the whole history of the Greeks show that the armies of [these] Gauls conquered Greece and founded the Kingdom of Thrace." (8 lines). L then omits the reference to Coriolanus.

607 C6–7 *if necessitie (which is not subject to the lawes of honour nor force) doth not constraine him.* Faulty. "... if necessity (which is not subject to the laws of honor) do not force him ..." (Fr).

607 E9 *who having conquered a good part of Spaine with little paine, sent backe a ladie.* Inexact. "... who conquered a good part of Spain without trouble, *because* he had sent back a lady ..." (Fr).

610 H7 *warre and policie* ‖ Fr adds: "This was well suited to warlike and conquering peoples."

611 A4–5 *twentie yeares after.* Based on L, which, however, also gives the date 1552. Fr correctly reads: "... eighteen years after ..."

611 C3–4 *with an excellent description of all orders.* Obscure. Bodin probably means: "... [which were raised] by a most excellent assessment (*descriptio*) of all orders." Cf. L.

612 H2 *obtained great victories* ‖ L adds: "And also we often see our armies, composed of Swiss, Italians, Germans, and French, accomplish a task promptly, and still maintain concord [among themselves]."

614 F5–7 *unlesse it be ... cannot be kept in peace.* As in Fr, but L substitutes: "I except the popular estate, which, wherever it is situated, cannot be very long without military discipline and the waging of war."

CHAPTER 6 (PAGES 614–636ᵛ)

614 H8 *This treatie depends of the former.* The chapter begins with these words in Fr, but in Fr 1 (and also in two of the editions of 1577) this chapter is numbered as Book I, ch. 8. As originally written, then, it was to be read in close conjunction with the discussion of alliances and protection in Book I, ch. 7. The change in position reflects Bodin's rather loose arrangement of topics and also accounts for the long addition in L at 614 I3.

614 I3 *or with subjects* ‖ L adds a long explanation of various types of treaties: "To give these matters greater clarity, we must employ definitions of each part. The law of arms (*jus fetiale*) is so called from *fides*, and the *fetiales* because they had charge of public faith between peoples, in order that the good faith (*fides*) of the peace might be established by means of a treaty (*foedus*). So Varro writes in the extant portion of his *De lingua latina* [V, 86], and in his second book 'On the life of the Roman people' [in Nonius Marcellus, *De conpendiosa doctrina*, 529] he says: 'They undertook wars slowly and without presumption, because they thought they must wage no war that was not just; and they would send beforehand four *fetiales* whom they called Orators.' But a treaty (*foedus*), which Varro says was also called *fidus* by Ennius, is a public covenant, undertaken in perpetuity, of princes or peoples among themselves. *Sponsio* is an agreement reached by military commanders or their deputies without the command of the people; its terms and results depend upon whether or not the princes or peoples ratify what has been promised. *Pactio* is a temporary covenant of princes or peoples, which very often is left to the authority of magistrates or commanders, who may in their own right postpone wars for a short time, or hold them in suspense by a truce for some days. In ancient *foedera* no names were inscribed except those of the *fetiales* on both sides; in *sponsiones* the names of commanders or their deputies were inserted, as that Roman consul argued who had made peace with the Samnites without a command from the Roman people. From his speech [cf. Livy, IX, 8–9] and from [other] historical sources we have gathered and set down the difference between *foedus* and *sponsio*, and the difference of both from *pactio*, though the terms are sometimes confused by governments.

"But there are three kinds of *foedera*—those made with friends, or with enemies, or with those who are neither friends nor enemies. With enemies we contract a long truce, or perpetual peace, or friendship. Moreover in peace negotiations the wrongs suffered are either passed over in silence, as usually happens, or they are recounted. When complete forgetfulness of wrongs is agreed upon it is customary to deal with boundary questions, or the return of captives, or the rights of sovereignty, or trade and hospitality. With friends either treaties of limited duration are renewed or altered, or the controversies of private men are settled. With other peoples friendships are contracted by means of either equal or unequal alliance. The latter is of two kinds. The first is when one people publicly declares that it respects the majesty and admits the superiority of the other, and that it commits itself to the other's protection and, as it were, wardship (*tutela*). This type is called *patrocinium*.

The second type is when a people acknowledges a superior and promises willingly to respect its majesty, but yet does not submit to its protection. Those who recognize a superior in a treaty either pay an imposed tribute or a [voluntary] pension, or else they are freed from all pensions or tributes. Those who are allied by the type of agreement which the Latins call *aequum foedus* retain the honor of their sovereignty undiminished in any way whatsoever, since neither one is bound to acknowledge the other as a superior, nor yield to the other the prerogative of honor, even if one shall undertake to contribute more than the other for their mutual aid. Those who make a capitulation (*deditio*), either voluntarily or under compulsion, do come into protection (*in fidem*), but not into league (*in foedus*) and differ in no respect from subjects. Thus of the Campanians who had surrendered to the Romans Livy writes: 'Those who have come into protection not by treaty but by capitulation are in a different position.' But among all confederated princes or peoples there is a common association, friendship, rights of lodging and of commerce, so that one may enter the territory of the allies, transact business, and trade freely back and forth, either in some commodities or in all, and this either without the payment of any duty, or with a fixed duty that is levied upon merchants according to the treaty. Of these confederates there are two kinds: the first are those who agree to aid each other if they are attacked by enemies; the second type are those who promise also to provide troops and resources for invading the enemies of their allies, and this may be with certain exceptions, or without any exception. But the closest alliance of all is when we have the same enemies and the same friends as our allies. In this kind of alliance and friendship princes usually exchange with each other some badge of honor of their country, such as a military belt or a necklace. Sometimes also alliances and treaties are confirmed by marriages.

"Yet a more inviolable alliance and promise is that which is given and received in turn as one king to the other, one man to the other, and one people to the other, as were the old treaties of the French with the Spaniards and the Scots. The force of these words, if it was not understood before, was certainly perceived when Edward IV, King of England, having been deprived of his kingdom, appealed to the French through ambassadors for the assistance stipulated by treaty. The ambassadors were told that the treaty had been contracted with the king and the kingdom of England, and that war could not be waged against the new king of England or the kingdom without violating it. This is the force of the words *Cum rege populove*. But when a promise is given as one king to another, and one man to another, a king may lawfully seek aid even when driven out of his kingdom. In order that these treaties may be more inviolable, they are often promulgated in the senate or the higher court, or in the assembly of the nobility or the people, as is provided in the treaty [of Arras] made between Louis XI, King of France, and Maximilian, Archduke of Austria, in 1482. There is also one kind of treaty which we call neutral, and this is generally made by those who are situated in between enemies, in order to be safe from both sides. An example is the treaty with the people of Franche-Comté, to which the Bassigny district was added at the request of the Swiss in 1555. Again, all treaties are either perpetual, or for a fixed period, or are valid for the lifetime of the princes in the alliance. Yet it is more often specified that when either prince dies there shall be an opportunity for an alliance with his successor for three or four years, as is provided in the treaties between the French and the Swiss.

"From this it may be seen that the Roman ambassadors to Antiochus the Great did not classify treaties with sufficient care when they said [Livy, XXXIV, 57]: 'There are only three kinds of treaties: the first is when conditions are dictated to those defeated in war; the second is when equals in war come into peace and friendship by means of an equal league; the third is when those who have never been enemies contract a treaty of friendship, neither imposing nor receiving conditions.' Now that these matters have been settled, let us discuss the assurance of treaties." (101 lines). Substantial sections of this passage coincide with the discussion at 72 K8–74 F6, which occurs in Fr only.

618 I4 *the treatie which his father had made* || L adds: "It must therefore be so provided that he who demands a promise demands it for himself and for his heirs and successors in the kingdom, and that he who promises does so on his own behalf and for his heirs and successors, in order that the obligation may be effectual." L refers marginally here to the *Digest*, 45, 1, 4, and 2, 14, 40.

621 E9 *yet the victor prescribes a law*. Faulty. "... unless the victor prescribes a law..." Knolles apparently reads *si est-ce que* instead of *si ce n'est que*, as in Fr.

623 A4–5 *have maintained themselves in a free peace, so long as they had an alliance of tranquilitie*. Awkward combination of Fr and L. Fr reads: "... have always maintained themselves so long as they have had an alliance of neutrality..." L reads: ".. which flourished in peace and tranquillity as long as they abstained from the wars of neighboring princes with the latter's express consent..."

624 K7 *to meditate a peace*. The sense is clearly "to mediate a peace" (cf. Fr), but this usage is repeated several times. Cf. 144 G3.

624 K7–8 *than to nourish warre... his owne estate*. As in Fr, but L substitutes: "... or at

Notes to Book V

least to pretend to, if other peoples' wars are profitable to your Commonweal, and peace would be harmful. Yet no one can dissemble or play a part for very long. But if matters incline towards peace, that is, if it appears that those who have waged war on one another for a long time are weary of the losses they have sustained, then especially you must strive in every way to bring it about that the peace shall seem to have been made at your instigation and persuasion." (6 lines).

626 A8–9 *what remedie shall the subjects have against their power.* Inexact. ". . . what remedy shall the peoples subject to their power have . . ." (Fr).

626 B4–5 *neither are private men tyed by their oath, if they have promised to do more than is allowable by the Civill law.* Based on L. Fr, which is vague but more consistent with B2–4, reads: ". . . for even the subject is not perjured who contravenes the oath he has made in a matter which is permitted by law." This statement is supported in both versions by an extensive marginal reference to legal authorities.

626ᵛ H10 *so great a Senat* ‖ Incomplete. L inserts: ". . . than which none is more illustrious in the whole world . . ." The criticism of de Selve occurs in L only.

627 D6 *with the like solemnities* ‖ Fr 1–2 add: "But afterwards the Emperor was unwilling to hear anything more of the matter, as du Bellay has very well written, laying bare the lies of those [Sleidan and Guicciardini] who have written the contrary." Omitted in Fr 3–8.

627 D8 *especially in princes* ‖ L adds: ". . . because nothing maintains Commonweals more firmly than faith, and when this is destroyed it must follow that justice, one of the fairest virtues, and with it human society, are also destroyed."

627 E4–5 *In which cases . . . impossible or unjust.* From Fr, but L enlarges on this point: "In short everything is defended as having been done justly provided that it is done under obligation, or under compulsion, or through lack of prudence, or as a result of an unexpected event. When these reasons arise, they are used as a pretext for breaking faith, yet it can never be just to do this unless what you have promised is naturally unjust, or cannot be carried out. I know that the flatterers of princes, who discuss these things too indulgently, diligently seek out every pretense for perjury. But those who reason more forcefully think that the keeping of promises must be preferred before all questions of profit whatsoever, if, after verbal quibbles have been set aside, the terms of the agreement are clear and without doubt." (10 lines).

627ᵛ I10–K1 *Another time they plaid the like part with Antiochus, promising him al friendship.* As in Fr, but L substitutes: "In the Macedonian war [the Epirots] promised that they would be friendly to the side of Perseus . . ." The sentence at K6–7 occurs in L only. However comparison with Livy, XXXVI, 5, shows that the version in Fr is correct.

628 B1–2 *captains in chiefe* ‖ L adds: "More detestable than this is the barbarism, or rather obtuseness, of the sort of men who try to undermine by such arguments the foundation of justice —that is, keeping faith—and who are and have been engaged in its utter destruction. But since that dictum of Bartolus is too pointless and trivial to deserve a lengthy refutation, let us return to the main point of this discussion." (6 lines).

628 C7 *keepe promise with them* ‖ Addition in Fr and L. L reads: "For these things follow logically one from the other. Therefore they ought to have inquired beforehand whether or not it was right to make an agreement with an infidel prince."

628ᵛ G10 *requited with the like* ‖ Fr 1–4 add: ". . . before a new treaty is entered into." Omitted in Fr 5–8.

629 C1 *which detest that in others, which they themselves hold dishonest.* Faulty. ". . . which do not think it right to suspect other men of that which they themselves detest." (L).

629ᵛ K3–5 *In like sort . . . memorie condemned.* As in Fr, but L expands: "When Gaius Marius was Consul he gave his faith to the Tribune Lucius Saturninus, who had slain the Consul-elect Memmius [*Memmius* in L 3–5, *Mummius* in L 1–2] in the Campus Martius, in order to draw him out of the Capitol which he together with other traitors had seized. The Tribune accepted the assurance of a man who was both Consul and friend, but no sooner had he emerged from the Capitol than he was slain by Gaius Rabirius. Thirty years afterwards the latter was accused of treason by Titus Labienus, a Tribune. The condemned man appealed from the *quaestores parricidii* to the people. Cicero, as Consul, undertook the defense of the accused and displayed all his oratorical powers before the people. In concluding, he says [*Pro Rabirio perduellionis*, 10]: 'If faith was given to Saturninus, as you have so frequently said, it was not given by Gaius Rabirius, but by Gaius Marius, and he was its violator if it was not kept. O Labienus, how could this faith be given without a *senatusconsultum*? Are you such a stranger to this city, so inexperienced in our traditions and customs, that you do not know this?' For there can be no derogation from public right through the covenants of private men. If anyone forgets his grievances and comes to an agreement with an adversary, he does not break faith if he is commanded by an edict to kill this man, because

A151

public right takes precedence. Yet I cannot approve Bartolus' gloss on the law 'Opprimendorum' in the title 'Quando liceat sine judice' [*Code*, 3, 27, 2] that it is lawful to kill a banished man with whom you have previously made an agreement. One may indeed do this without punishment, according to the customs of Italy, but not without loss of reputation; and if it is lawful, it is nevertheless not honest, for Paulus says, *non omne quod licet honestum est*." (23 lines).

630 B10–C1 *for that they ought not to bee partakers of the law of nations, as I have said before*. As in Fr, but L expands: "... nor [would I consider] him guilty of perjury who agrees with robbers to pay a ransom for his liberty, and then does not bring it, even if he has sworn to do so; because they are not in the category of enemies, and they ought not to enjoy the advantage of the rights and laws which they attempt to overthrow. Yet a Commonweal which has given faith to robbers can scarcely break it without loss of honor, even though it may not be guilty of perjury if it departs from the oath." (6 lines).

630 E6 *they were all slaine* ‖ L adds: "He preferred profit before honor. The Romans did otherwise, either not giving their faith, or not breaking it once given. When Titus Manlius, the first to bear the name Torquatus, was still a youth he compelled the Tribune Pomponius to swear at the point of a sword that he would renounce the accusation which he was bringing against Manlius' father. Even though the Tribune had sworn under the pressure of fear, he brought the matter before the people, and explained why it was necessary for him to abandon the case. Such, says Cicero [*De officiis*, III, 31], was the force of an oath in those times." (8 lines).

630 E6–7 *But there is a great difference, whether a soveraigne prince doth capitulat with his friends or his enemies, & that those subjects*. Inexact. Bodin writes: "However the difficulty is far greater if the sovereign prince capitulate with his friends or enemies, and those subjects . . ." (Fr).

630ᵛ G5 *his owne* ‖ L adds: "For clearly the Romans would not have protected the Macedonian fugitives against Philip by means of the same guarantee, if it had been lawful for a prince to break his pledged faith without punishment."

630ᵛ K5–6 *the league made by the foure first Cantons in the yeare 1481*. As in Fr, but L substitutes: "... the league which our kings made with the Swiss in the year 1481 . . ."

631 D9 *the histories are full of them*. Inexact. "... the books of Polyaenus [i.e., the *Stratagemata*] are full of them . . ." (L only).

631 E1 *fields by night* ‖ L adds: "More shameful was that ruse of Pericles, who promised his enemies that their lives would be spared if they threw away their steel; but when they were disarmed he ordered those who had even iron clasps on their clothing to be slain."

631ᵛ G4 *faith or oath* ‖ L adds: "... so that the saying of Marcus Varro [in Nonius Marcellus, *De conpendiosa doctrina*, 81] could justly have been applied: 'He who can, demands the more, as the great fish eats the lesser and the hawk kills the birds.'" Cf. *Methodus*, p. 214.

631ᵛ H2 *promises of a murtherer* ‖ Addition in Fr and L. Fr reads: "But the more strange new oaths there are, the less assurance there is." L reads: "But once a man has cast aside the fear of his deity, the more strictly he binds himself by oath the less is he to be trusted."

631ᵛ H9 *the crosse of S. Lau*. The name is introduced by Knolles. Bodin calls it simply "the true cross of Angers" (Fr). It was given to the Cathedral chapter by Fulk V, Count of Anjou and King of Jerusalem.

631ᵛ I7–9 *The Auntients . . . breakers of the league*. As in Fr, but L enlarges: "Among the ancients, some sanctified treaties by slaying victims, others by joining their hands, still others by casting stones, or plunging glowing iron into cold water, while chanting dire execrations. Caesar writes [*De bello Gallico*, VII, 2] that our ancestors entered into treaties in the most binding fashion [by swearing] before their assembled war standards. To join together in the strictest pledge of union, [people] wounded themselves and squeezed out the blood, mixed it with wine, and drank cups of this mixture simultaneously. Clearchus the Lacedemonian and Tissaphernes the Persian moistened their swords with the blood of the victims." (8 lines).

632 A4 *although he hath sworne* ‖ L adds: "But a good man is to be trusted even without being sworn, and indeed the Athenians stopped Xenocrates from swearing as he was approaching the altar to take the oath."

632ᵛ G7–9 *it is to be understood . . . may be a soveraigne*. As in Fr, but L expands and clarifies: "This error should be eradicated, for the rights of subjects are one thing, and the rights of vassals are another, as we have shown above. Vassals are bound by a certain territorial obligation, and although this adheres in some way to the person, nevertheless the vassal can exempt himself from it whenever he pleases, provided he does so without fraud, even if the lord is unwilling [to release him]. The subject cannot be released from the bond of obedience which he owes to his prince except by the prince himself." (6 lines).

632ᵛ H2 *according to the Canon law*. Faulty. Bodin writes: "... according to the common law (*le droit commun*) . . ." By the *droit commun* Bodin generally means the Roman law, but in this case there is a marginal reference to the constitution of the Emperor Frederick I, "De pace Constantiae," which is included among the *Consuetudines feudorum*, a work sometimes appended to early editions of the *Corpus juris civilis*. There is an edition with critical apparatus by Cujas entitled *De feudis libri V* (Lyon, 1566), but Bodin's references to this work are numbered so as to coincide with an earlier edition appended to the *Novellae* of Justinian (Paris, 1552).

632ᵛ K3–5 *That although . . . holy Empire*. As in Fr, but L expands and clarifies: "That he and his ancestors were and always had been friends of the Germans, and that it had never been possible to draw them from their friendship and alliance with the German Empire. But since he considered that all princes were united either by marriage connections and kinship, or at least by similarity of position and, as it were, by a certain association, it should not seem strange if he saw fit to grant hospitality to a German prince who fled to him under adverse circumstances. He wished to assure them, however, that he would never assist anyone against the sovereignty of the German Empire." (9 lines).

633 C1–D6 *Pro deo amur . . . do him any obedience*. These are the famous Strasbourg Oaths, among the oldest specimens of the French language. The corrections have been inserted in order to give Bodin's version of the oaths, but several minor variations between editions have been left unrecorded. Modern versions differ considerably from the form given here, but the latter should rather be compared with the facsimile of the manuscript reproduced in E. Koschwitz, *Les plus anciens monuments de la langue française* (Leipzig, 1907).

633 D7 *in the Dutch* ‖ L adds: "The Romans and other peoples employed sacrifices [*sacrificia* in L 1–3, *beneficia* in L 4–5] and slaughtering of beasts, prayers and imprecations [for assuring treaties]."

633 E1 *without breach of the league* ‖ Bodin adds the qualification: ". . . if the prince who receives the wrong is not comprehended in the league . . ." (Fr). In L the passage from D10 to E4 is expanded and clarified as follows: "But it may be asked whether or not you should go to the aid of a foreign prince who has been wronged by your ally and needs help. We have said that we ought to help those who have suffered a wrong, even if they are linked with us by no other connection than that which ought to exist between men, against those with whom we have no association and no treaty. Much more should we aid allies, not only against strangers, but even against allies, if the latter will not refrain from wrongdoing even when they have been warned. Yet it is doubtful whether we also ought to aid strangers unjustly oppressed against [our own] allies. If [the strangers] were allies, we should be bound to do this very thing. And if any of our subjects harms anyone among our allies, he incurs the penalty of treason [marginal reference to *Digest*, 48, 4, 1, and Bartolus' gloss upon it], but not if he harms a stranger." (12 lines).

634 C5–6 *for that the fathers . . . brethren that are wronged*. Condensed from L, which reads: "[This applies] even if he has not been emancipated, because paternal authority [*Digest*, 36, 1, 14] has nothing in common with the laws of arms or of sovereignty. This is when the son governs a kingdom apart from his father's. Much less therefore may the league be broken for brethren that are wronged, even though he who kills a brother forfeits his fee by reason of the animosity of his lord, according to the first chapter of the title 'Whether he who kills a brother' [in the *Consuetudines feudorum*]. Therefore a better way to meet these inconveniences, although it is very difficult to avoid them altogether, is to mention by name (*excipere*) not only subjects and allies, but also kinsmen." (8 lines). Fr omits the passage from B7 to C6.

634 E1 *should be perpetuall* ‖ Addition in Fr and L. Fr reads: ". . . and [will say] that it is a bad omen to limit friendship to a specified period, seeing that animosity ought to be temporary and friendship perpetual."

635 C2 *seven times* ‖ L adds: "In the end the last remnants of the Samnites were exterminated or banished from Italy by Lucius Sulla during the Social War. Even though four thousand threw down their arms and surrendered [Strabo, V, 249], he accepted their surrender and nevertheless ordered them to be slain, in contravention of the law of arms."

636 C9 *brave him with reproaches* ‖ L adds details: "For when the Roman ambassador [Marcus Aemilius Lepidus] asked Philip whether the people of Abydus had attacked him first, his speech, to a man unaccustomed to hear the truth, sounded more insolent than it ought to have been in the presence of a king. Philip replied: 'Your youth, your fine appearance, and the Roman name make you too arrogant.'" Cf. Livy, XXXI, 18.

636ᵛ F2–H4 *Some there bee . . . losse of life*. This passage occurs in L only. The final lines (G5–H4) may well have been suggested by Bodin's own experience in the Low Countries in 1583. Returning home from Antwerp by sea, his ship put back to Flushing, where the governor of the town detained Bodin for lack of a passport. Cf. *Calendars of State Papers Foreign, 1583 and Addenda*, No. 138.

Book VI

CHAPTER I (PAGES 637–649)

637 B6 *Chap. I.* This chapter is translated almost entirely from Fr, and consequently fails to reflect several extensive additions and modifications in L.

637 C1–4 *Hitherto . . . the said definition.* Following Fr, but L begins differently: "We seem to have opened to view the origins of Commonweals, their increase and growth, changes in forms of government, the rights of sovereignty, the structure of magistracies, the classes of citizens, the techniques by which Commonweals are consolidated, and the laws of arms."

637 C6–7 *the treasure, || rents, and revennues.* Bodin includes in this list "the public lands" (*le domaine,* or *agri communes,* [*et*] *loca publica*), but Knolles generally makes no distinction between *domaine* and *revenus,* translating both as "revenues." Cf. note at 650 G10.

637 E2 *millions of crownes* || L adds: "What better means could ever have been devised for finding out not only the public wealth but also all the goods of individual citizens? Plato was especially concerned to have a census of everyone, in which the names of newborn citizens would be publicly inscribed on a white wall, and those of the deceased would be deleted. I should like the cancellation to be made in such a way that the names of the dead could still be read." (6 lines).

637 E4(margin) *310. ab u.c.* This date is misplaced. It refers to the creation of separate Censors at E9 (cf. Fr).

638 F4 *to eighteene moneths* || L adds: ". . . because he disliked long-lasting authority in a free commonweal. Yet the law was repudiated by the Censors themselves, and Mamercus the Censor [*sic*] branded with a type of ignominy for attempting to diminish that authority in any respect at all." Livy records (IV, 24) that Mamercus was Dictator when he carried this law.

638 F6 *to Rome* || Addition in L and margin of Fr: "Livy writes [XXIX, 37] that Nero and Livius Salinator received the census lists of twelve colonies from the Censors of the colonies, in order that there might be documents in the public registers to show the number of soldiers and the amount of wealth in these colonies."

638 H9 *an epistle written by Plinie the younger.* Fr and L add marginally an extensive quotation from the *Epistles,* X, 112 (about 7 lines).

639 D4–5 *six hundred thirtie thousand five hundred and fifty.* As in Fr, but the Bible gives 603,550. Cf. Exodus 38:26 and Numbers 1:46.

639 E1–4 *which were at the least twice . . . besides the blind.* From Fr, but L diverges: "We have shown above that women everywhere outnumber men, but especially in the southern regions. Those under twenty made up about a third of the population, since man's life is generally limited to 63 years. That the Romans also did not count women, slaves, and handicraftsmen in the number of the citizens may be seen from what Dionysius, Florus, and Livy write. When Romulus began to reign, there were numbered 3000 citizens; but at his death there were 46,000 *pedites* and 1000 *equites*. Under King Servius there were counted 80,000 who could bear arms, as Fabius Pictor writes. At the next lustrum there were 132,419; then 262,322; then 273,000; then 278,222." (12 lines). L condenses the next few lines (639 E4–640 F2), omitting the rather tentative suggestion in Fr that female citizens (*bourgeoises*) were included in the census and reasoning more positively from Florus' statements (640 F2–7) that ". . . the Romans made no account of women in the census, or else they were not included in that number [of 137,000 citizens]." For further change in L on this point, see the note at 640 G9.

640 G9–H1 *whereby it appeares . . . fiftie for one.* As in Fr. L expands: "This reveals how many persons there would have been if account had been taken of female citizens and children, and if those inhabitants who were not citizens had been registered. The citizen who was *incensus*, that is, who had not made a declaration before the Censors, was passed under the yoke like a slave. 'The greatest forfeiture of civil rights,' says Ulpian in the *Tituli* [title 11], 'is when citizenship and liberty are lost, as when someone becomes *incensus*.' Sometimes the Censors were compelled to visit not only the Roman colonies in Italy, of which there were 24, but even the provinces, to obtain a better account of the citizens scattered through the provincial colonies. Here someone may say that since it was necessary to make a declaration before the Censors not only of every citizen, but even of every slave and animal, and of lands also, both urban and rural, how could it happen that female and juvenile citizens, as well as handicraftsmen, who were free men but foreigners, were not counted? In my opinion the census was taken of everyone, for so Dionysius of Halicarnassus writes in his fourth book, but the Censors were accustomed to add up only the number of citizens who could bear arms, and this concise total was the one set down in the annals of the historians." (20 lines).

640 I6–7 *king Frauncis the first commaunded . . . to keepe a register.* Inexact. ". . . King Francis I, at the suggestion of Chancellor Poyet, my fellow Angevin, commanded the parish priests in a published edict to keep a register . . ." (L).

640 I8 *this law is ill observed* || L adds: ". . . even though Henry III ordered the same law to be renewed."

NOTES TO BOOK VI

641 C1–2   *as it should suffice, if it served for nothing else, but to cause*. Faulty. "... that it should suffice, even if there were no other reason, to cause..." (Fr).

641 D3   *in regard of the tithes* ‖ I.e., the *décimes*, paid by the clergy to the Crown. L adds: "... which the bishops themselves had voted to the king and Commonweal when it was in financial difficulties."

641 D7   *Provence* ‖ L adds: "The whole district of Alet in Languedoc has been assessed even more carefully. The size and value of each field was taken, and a threefold [classification made] of three kinds of land, that is, good, medium, and poor, and a threefold estimate made of each kind [L is obscure here: *ac triplici trium agrorum, optimorum inquam, mediocrium, ac sterilium, & cuiusque generis triplici ratione inita*]. I learned of this survey from the assessors themselves when I attended the Estates of Languedoc in 1568." (6 lines).

641 E2   *before Judges for reliefe*. Faulty. "... before the Judges of [the Court of] Aids..." (Fr).

642 G1–3   *the which are concealed ... without search*. Following Fr. L differs and expands: "Which of these are prior to and to be preferred before the others could be explained from the register of every man's property that I have mentioned. On the other hand ignorance of these matters envelops not only public business but even each man's private transactions in the deepest obscurity. Thus Livy, writing of the time when continual changes in ownership had gone so far that it was scarcely known who owned which land, says in his seventh book [VII, 22]: 'Since the multitude of transactions had changed the pattern of ownership, it was decided to hold a census.'" (8 lines).

642 H1–2   *this law (whereof question is made)*. I.e., the law which is cited at G4–5 as an argument against a public census. Both Fr and L have a marginal reference to *Code*, 10, 35(34), 2, 2, opposite the objection.

643 C10–D2   *and the publike rites ... were censured by him*. Or, with altered phrasing at C6–7, read: "... and jurisdiction over public and private sites, and the revenues of the Roman people, were subject to his discretion." Cf. Fr and L.

644 F1   *farmed out the revenues* ‖ L adds: "Then if any fortresses, harbors, walls, or military roads required repairs or replacement, that was also a concern of the Censors. As the final event of the Censorship, the whole people was purified by solemn sacrifice in the Campus Martius, the classes of citizens were drawn up, and if anyone was leading a dissolute life, this was noted accordingly in the public registers, with the result that good citizens considered this mark even more to be feared than a judicial decision." (6 lines).

644 H5   *in the publike tables* ‖ L adds: "Thus spoke [Seneca]. Although he was ignorant of divine laws, he was not unaware of those which we have grasped from nature itself. For if anyone should wish to open the folded tablets of his own mind, he would learn at once that a good man is he who assists whom he can, and injures no one unless provoked by injustice [cf. Cicero, *De officiis*, III, 19]. These things are not included in the laws of any nation. Indeed we see many destructive and ruinous commands and prohibitions, which no more deserve the name of laws than if a madman decreed them by his own authority." (9 lines).

644 I3   *by the Censor* ‖ L adds: "For the Censors carefully sought out the way that each man behaved at home, and even in his hidden retreats, towards his wife, children, slaves, and relatives. On this account if a suitable name were sought for the censorship, I would not hesitate to call it the directress of commonweals, the producer of all virtues, the mother of good citizens, the scourge of the wicked, because it alone seems able not only to cut around the roots of the more serious crimes and depravities, but even to pluck out the fibres, strip off the stems, and destroy the very seeds of the vices [which underlie them]." (9 lines).

645 E2–3   *I answere ... alwaies blamed them*. As in Fr, but L expands: "I answer that the Romans dedicated the *ludi Apollinares*, *ludi Seculares*, *ludi Circenses*, and games of this type to the majesty and honor of the gods whom they revered most highly, and did not establish them as an infamous example of wantonness. But after Rome began to be infested with the vices of neighboring peoples, actors (*histriones*) also gradually crept into the city from Histria, as Verrius Flaccus writes [cf. Festus, ed. Müller, p. 101] and opened the way to shamelessness in the games. But if these games could have been forbidden without infringing religion, I have no doubt that the Censors, in their supreme dignity and wisdom, would have banished all the public performances from the Commonweal. Indeed I am able to make this inference from all the wisest authors. For Seneca writes [*Epistulae morales*, 7] 'Nothing is so contrary to good habits as to linger in the theater.' Even Aristotle warns [*Politics*, 1336b] that every care must be taken lest the citizens attend performances of comedies [cf. D5–9, which follows Fr]. What of Augustine? He says, 'Everything in the theater is opposed to piety and virtue.' I note that this opinion was shared by Tertullian, Chrysostom, Cyprian, Valerius, Polydore [Vergil], and that prince of lawgivers, Solon himself. Are not these men teachers of the greatest authority? Is it strange, then, that theatrical performances were prohibited by the Council of Carthage, since even the ancient Greeks, who had acquired no notion

Notes to Book VI

of true piety, considered them dangerous to Commonweals?" (21 lines).

645 E7 *turnes to earnest* ‖ L adds: ". . . and hence the statement of Cicero [*De legibus*, II, 15] that ancient Greece severely punished the actors of this type of play."

645 E9 *although that comedies were more tollerable.* Strictly, ". . . although *plays* were tolerable . . ." (Fr). Cf. L, which stresses that ". . . plays (*spectacula*) are dangerous for every kind of men . . ." though less so for Southerners.

646 G3–H2 *And if we may not prevaile . . . good and substantiall meat.* Following Fr. L expands this passage, revising several details and insisting even more strongly on the danger of mental derangement inherent in mixing diatonic music with chromatic or enharmonic (27 lines).

646 I2–8 *let us now see . . . judgements of the magistrat.* As in Fr, but L enlarges: "But it may be asked whether the censors should be given the power to command (*imperium*), and, if this is given, whether or not they should also have jurisdiction. For without *imperium* or jurisdiction the censorship might seem useless. Yet if my opinion were sought, I should like them to have neither *imperium* nor jurisdiction, lest this most troublesome office, which demands the greatest effort and vigilance, might also become involved in the intricacies of lawsuits. For the judicial function is one thing, censorship another. We find that the Roman censors had *imperium*, but only to convoke the assembly of the people, to muster the army of the city, to hold the lustrum, and to summon each man to the registration. This could not be done without edicts, and no one who lacked *imperium* could issue edicts, summon, or muster an army, unless he sought assistance from someone who had *imperium*. But since there is no need of an army and a lustrum, I think it would be sufficient to proclaim by a magistrate's edict, with penalties attached, that everyone should be enrolled in the public registers. But someone may say: 'What will happen if the censors cannot command, compel, or judge?' I think that the glance, the reprimand, and the note of ignominy of the [Roman] Censors were more severe than all the decrees and judgments of all the magistrates." (19 lines).

647 A2–3 *that were cassiered with ignomy.* As in Fr, but L clarifies: ". . . that were dismissed with ignominy by their commander [cf. *Digest*, 3, 2, 1]. For the commentators on the law call this infamy of fact [in the glosses on *Digest*, 23, 2, 43, 12]. The edict [of the Praetor] contains nothing concerning those who are noted by the Censors."

647 C6–10 *Cicero brings in an example . . . and not a punishment.* Following Fr, but L quotes directly from *Pro Cluentio*, 42–43 (12 lines), and a similar direct quotation is also printed marginally in Fr. Cf. also 305 D5–306 F3.

648 F6–10 *and Innocent . . . their censure to be contemned.* Following Fr (but the reference to Innocent II at F6–8 is omitted in Fr 1–4). L expands, criticizing the papacy more sharply: "By this means they compelled both [Theodosius and Lothair] to do penance, and to crave pardon. But since many popes misused so great a power too ostentatiously, they dulled the edge of the ecclesiastical sword, which has gradually become so blunt that for many princes nothing is more contemptible than the popes themselves and their interdictions. For what reason did Pope Innocent excommunicate King Louis VII of France for three entire years? Because he had taken as his wife a first cousin, far removed from the [prohibited] degree of kinship, whom he could rightly marry according to divine and human law [Leviticus, ch. 18, and *Code*, 5, 4, 19]. Nevertheless he divorced her. Why was his son Philip Augustus thought worthy of the same excommunication, except that he was considered to be a relation by marriage (*affinis*) of the very woman whom he had married with papal consent? Yet he was compelled to repudiate her by the pope himself, to the great indignation of all princes. However nowadays the censure of these same popes who ought to have prohibited incestuous marriages would be the same as that which is reported of Jupiter, almost [sanctioning] marriage with a sister (*pene soror et conjunx*)." (18 lines). For the dual relationship of Jupiter and Juno in Roman mythology, see Virgil, *Aeneid*, I, 47; Ovid, *Metamorphoses*, III, 266; and Horace, *Carmina*, III, 3, 64.

648 G9–H6 *The Prelats, Bishops . . . which they beare.* As in Fr, but L diverges, abandoning the reference to Protestant practice: "Certainly the bishops have borne themselves as judges of religious matters and censors of morals, because the laws and magistrates customarily punish only the offenses which burst into the open and trouble the citizens, and not even all of these, but only those within their reach. Therefore, since morals and religion fall within the same sphere, or very closely related spheres, I should prefer both to be entrusted to the bishops, if only they were the sort of men they ought to be, that is, men who surpass all others in integrity, honesty, piety, sanctity, wisdom, and prudence in managing affairs. In this way the greatest honors would be heaped upon the most sacred order." (10 lines).

649 C6–7 *they which neglect lawes, vertue, and religion, will bee contemned.* Careless. ". . . and when censorship is neglected, laws, virtue and religion will be contemned . . ." (Fr).

CHAPTER 2 (PAGES 649–686)

650 G10 *the revenues of the commonweale.* Bodin's terms here are *domaine* and *agri publici*. But the concept of the *domaine* represented many sources

of income other than that arising from crown lands, and hence Knolles regularly—and sometimes quite inappropriately—renders the concept by the more general word "revenues." Cf. 606 G5, 627 C2–3, and the note at 637 C6.

650 H8–I1 *certaine places . . . a certaine time, or for ever.* Faulty. ". . . certain places belonging to (*propres à*) the Commonweal, and common to all in general, which were called Commons [*Digest*, 50, 16, 115]; and [also assigned] a certain *domaine*, leased or granted to private men for a limited time or in perpetuity . . ." (Fr, and cf. L).

650 K7–8 *Cincinatus plowing . . . of the Senat.* Faulty translation. "An apparitor said to Cincinnatus, as he was plowing his two *jugera*, 'Cover thy body, and hear the commands of the Senate.'" Cf. Pliny, *Natural History*, XVIII, 4.

650 K8–10 *And Denis Halicarnasseus . . . all Roman antiquities.* As in Fr, but L substitutes other authorities: "Likewise Festus Pompeius writes [ed. Müller, p. 53] that it was called *ager centuriatus*, because it was divided into lots of 200 *jugera* when Romulus gave 200 *jugera* to every hundred citizens. And Marcus Varro says [*Res rusticae*, I, 10]: 'Before the Punic War our ancestor paid for two *jugera*, because these were reputed to have been apportioned to each man by Romulus. Because these descended to the heir, they were called the *haeredium*.'" (5 lines).

651 D5 *the revenues of the crowne* || I.e., the *domaine*. L adds: "Thus Andrew, King of Hungary, was summoned before Pope Honorius III, because he had alienated part of the public lands, in the year 1221."

652 F1 *Fœlix of Nogaret.* Inaccurate. ". . . [Guillaume de] Nogaret de St. Félix . . ." Cf. Fr.

654 F4(margin) *7. May 1566.* This should read "12 July 1566" (as in L, but misprinted 12 July 1556 in Fr). The date "7. May 1566" refers to the preceding decree of the Parlement (653 E8–9). Cf. Fr and L.

654 I8–10 *True it is . . . to his first beautie.* As in Fr. L omits this sentence and substitutes: "So far is [the Queen of England] from burdening the subjects with taxes that she even discontinued the extraordinary tributes which had usually been levied every third year. When we were there on an embassy, we watched with the greatest pleasure the estates of the people. Fifty thousand sestertia were offered by the people as a subsidy towards the necessary expenses of the Commonweal, but the Queen refused half this sum, and thanked the people." (7 lines).

654 K4–6 *and every one . . . the commonweale.* As in Fr, but L is more explicit: "In this way it happens that the magistrates, with the consent of the people, or certainly without opposition from them, and often even with the connivance of the optimates, make perpetual leases of the lands to their own advantage or that of private individuals. This is done under the pretext of a small rental, but eventually they obtain exemption from this also. Everything is easily taken away from the people, if only a man wins their favor, and distributes some grain or money or public land among the *plebs*." (7 lines).

655 A9 *treasure wasted in warre* || Fr adds: ". . . as a warlike and conquering people ought to do." Omitted in L, and Fr 7 is corrupt here.

655 E8 *courteous and affable.* Strictly, ". . . courteous and well advised . . ." (Fr).

656 F5–6 *wisdome, and power* || L adds: "Livy says [Epitome of Bk. LX] 'When Gaius Gracchus had been made Tribune for a second year in succession, he proposed agrarian laws providing for the foundation of several colonies in Italy, and one on the site of the demolished city of Carthage.' Again, 'They established a Latin colony in the region of Thurii, to which went 3000 *pedites* and 300 *equites*, a small number for the amount of land.' [Livy, XXXIV, 53; XXXV, 9]. Asconius writes that the Romans founded more than 53 colonies in Italy, and Pliny enumerates many more outside Italy." (7 lines).

656 K3 *nor people did* || Additions in Fr and L. Fr reads: "Hence he is the only prince at whose court almost all other princes maintain resident ambassadors." L reads: "He does not deign to send ambassadors to any other princes, except when he begins his reign, and even then not to all."

657 A2 *five thousand bushels of wheat.* Inexact. Fr reads: ". . . 5000 *muids* . . ." L reads: ". . . 300,000 *modii* of wheat and 200,000 of barley . . ." as does Livy (XXII, 37). The *muid de Paris* was roughly equivalent to a quarter, rather than a bushel, and the *modius* was about a peck. But Bodin also was careless about units of measurement. At B4–5 the "three thousand bushels for sacrifices" are given as ". . . 3000 *muids* . . ." in Fr, ". . . 3000 *modii* . . ." in L. For the original figures, see Polybius, *Histories*, V, 89.

657 D6 *there were few or none at all.* Inexact. ". . . there are at present few or none at all . . ." (Fr). While Fr cites the examples of "Spaine, England and others" (D7–8), L singles out Spain and France as countries in which gifts to the Crown have become compulsory levies.

657 D10–E6 *as the gold which they called Coronarium . . . against his enemies.* From Fr. L revises: "The ancient Romans received the *aurum coronarium* in moderation, and only in order to celebrate a victory gained over their enemies. Their descendants exacted it like an ordinary tax [*Code*, 10, 76(74), 1] although they called it oblations. When King Philip had been

Notes to Book VI

conquered and Greece liberated from its fear of servitude, Flamininus sent 114 golden crowns to Rome as gifts from the [Greek] cities. And Philip, having accepted the conditions of peace laid down by the ten Roman ambassadors, placed a gold crown weighing 100 pounds on the Capitol. The Rhodians, to forestall the Senate from taking more severe measures against them, sent a golden crown weighing 200 pounds to Rome. Later on the *aurum coronarium* began to be exacted as an ordinary tribute [*Code*, 1, 9, 17, and *Theodosian Code*, 12, 13, 4] from the *decuriones* of the cities and from the colleges of the Jews." (12 lines).

658 H6–7 *by testaments*. Strictly, ". . . by testaments of his friends alone . . ." (Fr).

660 G5 *liberalitie* ‖ L adds: "We have spoken above of the deceits of the Athenians and the practices of the Romans in enriching their treasury and improving their city, walls, harbors and fleets, with the money contributed by their allies."

661 A10 *he bought the oyle in Apulia*. Strictly, ". . . he bought *all* the oil in Apulia . . ." (Fr).

661 D3–4 *Wherof there be divers kindes*. Knolles omits the names. Fr reads: "From this have arisen the *droit de rêve*, the *haut passage* or *domaine forain*, and the *traite foraine* . . ." All were duties on exports.

662 F4–5 *a hundred and eighteene Crownes the measure*. This figure is suspect. Fr reads: ". . . 360 livres . . ." i.e., 36 pounds sterling. Why Knolles changes the unit of currency at this point is not clear.

662 H3 *are wasted in few yeares* ‖ Addition in Fr and L. Fr reads: ". . . and can only be replenished (*renaistre*) over many centuries." Cf. *Response* (ed. Hauser), p. 36.

662 K2 *treatise of trafficke* ‖ L adds: "The quantity of wine that pours into England and the Low Countries from France might seem incredible, yet it is a fact. I have no better evidence of this than the fact that in 1578 one Lauda, a merchant of Cambrai, was responsible for exporting 33,000 *modii* of wine [from France] into the Low Countries by overland transport, even though he found that the routes were difficult and in many places blocked by the enemy. The value was four crowns per *modius* at the least. From this it may be understood how much more must be brought in by sea. Other merchandise I shall not mention." (9 lines).

662 K7–8 *three karsies or three cottons*. Types of coarse woolen cloth which were apparently produced in standard sizes.

663 A4 *strange countreys* ‖ L adds: ". . . but the duty on raw, unworked materials which we import from foreign countries is to be removed, or reduced as far as possible, because one must look to the profit and advantage of the citizens before that of foreigners."

663 E2–7 *but for that there was not sufficient . . . the which was done*. As in Fr. L expands, quoting verbatim the relevant passage from Livy (XXXI, 13) and adding: ". . . So Livy writes. I have set this down word for word, because this method of raising money and discharging a promise seemed to me the most profitable of all." (12 lines).

664 H6 *of the urine* ‖ L adds: "And because his muleteer dismounted too often to shoe the mules, [leaving] an opportunity for men to approach the emperor, he bargained with the muleteer, who was bribed for his action, for a share of the money [cf. Suetonius, *Vespasian*, 23]. 'He was not content,' says Suetonius [*Vespasian*, 16], 'to revive the imposts repealed under Galba, but added heavy new ones, and raised the tributes of some provinces, and even doubled them. He openly carried on transactions that would have shamed even a private man, buying up certain things for the sole purpose of selling them later at retail. He did not hesitate to sell offices to candidates, nor [acquittals] to accused men, whether guilty or innocent. It was even believed that he deliberately made a practice of advancing the most rapacious of his collectors of revenue to higher offices, that they might be richer when he later condemned them. Indeed it was commonly said that he used these men like sponges, because he soaked the dry ones, and then squeezed out the wet ones.' A little later he adds: 'There are some who believe that he was induced into pillage and robbery by the extreme poverty of the privy purse (*fiscus*) and the public treasury (*aerarium*). He gave evidence of this at the very beginning of his principate, when he declared that to enable the Commonweal to continue he required forty million sestertia' (that is, 1,000,000,000 crowns). This is Suetonius' account. But if the emptiness of the public treasury forced this prince, who was most prudent in other respects, to such loathsome and shameful practices, what are we to expect that tyrants will or will not do when they are pressed by want?" (18 lines).

664 H7 *are reputed revenewes*. I.e., are classified as part of the *domaine* of the Crown rather than as taxes. The sentence from H6 to H10 occurs in Fr only.

666 I5 *foundation of a Commonweale* ‖ Addition in Fr and L. L reads: "For if customs and taxes were abolished, what would be left over to enable the prince to maintain the Kingdom? We have shown before that almost all public or *domaine* lands [*Fr* adds: and the greater part of the *aides* and *gabelles*] have been alienated, and that the fees (*militiae ex casu*) and military lands, which

Notes to Book VI

formerly were granted to the nobility for the purpose of waging war, are now owned outright by baseborn men or even by colleges." (6 lines).

666 K7 *lesse than it is at this day* ‖ Fr adds: ". . . and consequently rentals and the price of lands to be twelve times less than at this day."

667 C8 *he that had but ten pounds a yeere rent, hath now a thousand.* Faulty. ". . . he that had but ten pounds (100 livres) a year rent has now a hundred (1,000 livres) . . ." (Fr).

667 C9 *he then gathered* ‖ Fr adds: "For an annual income of a *muid* of wheat could be obtained in 1522 for 100 to 120 *livres tournois*, while now it costs almost as much to buy [one *muid*] outright. I have noted this from the registers of the Châtelet of Paris. Indeed the *muid* of wheat (Paris measure) was purchased for 320 livres and more in 1564 and 1573 [1563 in Fr 5-8] when wheat was scarce. And anyone who looks up the customary laws of France will find that even the Paris *muid* of wheat was ordinarily worth one-fourth less than it was in 1522." (9 lines).

667 D8-9 *and although that king John were set at the same ransome.* As in Fr, but L revises: "When King John was captured by the English [his ransom was set] at almost 200,000 sestertia, but that of Francis I was 80,000 sestertia. The latter paid a smaller amount, because he married the sister of the Emperor Charles V, and gave up his rule over the Low Countries."

667 E5 *their brother* ‖ L adds: ". . . first because of the prices of commodities, and then because the *livre tournois* of King Philip's reign was almost four times more valuable than that of Charles IX's reign."

667 E7 *unto his brethren* ‖ L adds: "For this reason it was necessary to increase it somewhat. For when, as Master of Requests to Francis, Duke of Anjou and Brabant, I drew up the accounts of receipts, I discovered that 14,000 sestertia (i.e., 612,000 *livres tournois* or 204,000 of our crowns) had been collected by the receivers in the year 1582 from the grants which he had received through the kindness of the King."

668 F1 *Charles the 5* ‖ L adds: ". . . first because the crowns of that time were somewhat better than ours, and also because the prices of commodities were ten times lower in Charles V's reign than they were when Charles IX was king."

668 F1-2 *The like may be spoken of other people, as in old time.* Incomplete. Fr reads: "The like may be spoken of other peoples where gold and silver were plentiful, as in old time . . ."

668 H10 *the wicked counsell of wicked men.* Inexact. Bodin writes: ". . . the wicked counsel of the young men . . ." (L). Cf. I Kings 12.

668 K7 *but the noble and the rich.* Strictly, ". . . but the rich, [whether] noble or base . . ." (Fr). Knolles borrows from L, which differs at this point and does not refer specifically to the Romans.

670 F2 *against the toll-gatherers.* Bodin writes: ". . . against the *Javeleurs* or *Gabeleurs*, for the word *gabelle* (a tax on a commodity) came from *javelle* (sheaf, handful)."

670 G7-9 *And for this cause Cato . . . could not be warranted.* As in Fr, but L enlarges: "With like prudence Cato the Censor, in order to delay as long as possible the ruin of a Commonweal which was on the point of being destroyed by luxury, ordered his attendants to enroll in the censorial registers all ornaments, women's apparel, and vehicles worth more than 15,000 *asses*. Likewise he ordered that slaves under twenty who had been bought since the previous lustrum for less than 10,000 *asses*, or more [*sic* in L, but delete "less than." Cf. Livy, XXXIX, 44.], were to be assessed at ten times more than they were worth. All these things were to be taxed at three *asses* per thousand." (8 lines).

670 G9 *could not be warranted.* I.e., justified. However Bodin's wording (*on ne pouvoit lors defendre telle marchandise*) suggests the more probable reading of: ". . . could not be prohibited." Cf. F9 and G1.

670 H5 *to such as had children.* Strictly, ". . . to such as had more children than the rest." (Fr and L).

670 I1-3 *Which law Justinian . . . or that had no children.* Following Fr, but L enlarges: "First Constantine [*Code*, 8, 57(58), 1], and then Justinian the Emperor [*Code*, 6, 51, 1], by a most dangerous example either abolished or in large part derogated from these laws concerning *bona caduca*, that is, the *lex Julia* and the *lex Papia Poppaea*. For when the tremendous usefulness of the *lex Julia* had been confirmed, the Consuls Papius and Poppaeus added various provisions to it, decreeing heavier penalties for the childless and larger rewards than the *lex Julia* gave for those with large families." (7 lines).

671 B2 *Sponsio & sacramentum* ‖ Fr adds: ". . . which each of the parties consigned if one of them demanded it . . ."

671 B9-C2 *serving to no other end . . . 300 crownes.* Here Knolles switches over abruptly from L to Fr, and in doing so he omits Bodin's reference in both Fr and L to the schedule of 450 types of merchandise established in 1542. L reads: "But while merchandise generally was valued at a low figure by the edict of King Francis I [concerning the *imposition foraine*], those kinds which are imported for the corruption of the citizens were priced much more cheaply than was fitting. Thus ambergris, the most

expensive commodity mentioned in the edict, is reckoned at just under three sestertia per pound, whereas it ought to have been ten sestertia, in order to bring a greater revenue into the treasury. The prices of things useful to the citizens should have been set very low or at zero, to enable the impost to be paid more easily, and to induce foreign merchants to bring in these commodities in greater quantities." (9 lines).

671 C7 *wine*. Faulty. Bodin writes *tonlieu* (Fr 1–6, 8), which was the tax paid for the right to display goods in markets. Fr 7, however, corruptly gives *tonelier*, which Knolles reads as *tonnelier*, a cooper.

671 C7–8 *And all good princes have abhorred that impost which they called Capitatio*. As in Fr, but L explains in detail: "The *Capitatio* also, which had been introduced by tyrants, was abolished by Servius, King of Rome, but Tarquin the Proud renewed it, exacting ten *denarii* for every head. Constantine abolished it completely. It was the tax which every *paterfamilias* had to pay to the treasury for every member of his household, even if they had no property, a practice which is uncommon with us. There was also a *capitatio annonaria*, imposed upon those who possessed land according to the number of teams and laborers employed in its cultivation." (8 lines).

672 F7–8 *all which make thirtie millions*. As in Fr. The calculation is faulty in several respects, a point which is stated specifically in L: "All of these come to about 300,000 sestertia, and he was unable to reach the figure of 700,000 sestertia except by adding the *décimes*, and the ancient customs, taxes, and imposts, which was contrary to what had been proposed at the start." Bodin takes the value of the sestertium as approximately 43.7 *livres tournois*. The passage from 671 D3 to 672 H2 is omitted in Fr 1–2.

672 H1–2 *threescore and fourteen thousand foure hundred eightie one pounds*. Knolles derives this figure by multiplying 24,827 by 3, but Bodin gives the actual figure of receipts as: ". . . 87,859 livres." (Fr only). Moreover, Knolles's figure of three pounds sterling per parish is inexact; Bodin gives 31 livres (Fr and L).

672 I3 *the grounds of such impositions*. Strictly, ". . . the funds of such impositions . . ." Knolles confuses *le fond* and *le fonds*. This confusion recurs at 679 C6.

674 F5 *the Foucquers of Germanie*. I.e., the Fuggers, but the name is introduced by Knolles. Bodin writes merely *les participes d'Allemagne* (Fr only).

675 B1–2 *hee did owe more than his predecessors had levied fortie yeares before, for all charges*. Imprecise. Fr reads: ". . . he owed more interest [annually?] than his predecessors forty years before levied for all charges." L revises: ". . . he owed more than his ancestors had exacted from the subjects in forty years, and almost all of this debt was contracted during the twelve years that he reigned as a result of interest (*usurae*)."

677 B9 *at an under rate* || Fr and L add: ". . . as has been done for some years."

677 C8–9 *great care had of the treasure* || L adds: "But very often we see princes begin a war by borrowing at interest. Nothing can be more ruinous than this."

677 D1 *poore should be remembered* || L adds: ". . . not only because of that bond of humanity which we have in common with them, but also in order that the poverty of the subjects may not trouble the Commonweal, as we have said before."

679 B6 *at the heeles* || L adds: "However the tyrants' practice of constructing proud and useless public works is more acceptable than the squandering of gifts upon the most unworthy men."

679 C6 *the botome of their treasuries*. Strictly, ". . . the funds (*le fonds*) of their treasuries." Cf. note at 672 I3.

680 K3 *are not entred* || Fr adds: "Now if the prince has no register of benefactions, or if he does not remember his gifts, more often than not he will give to those who have deserved nothing, or who have merited punishment rather than reward."

681 A1 *by the Letters of gift, if it were derogated from the first decree*. Read: ". . . if derogation were made from the first decree by the letters of gift." (Fr). Cf. 593 D2–9.

681 C5 *the which might proove verie dangerous*. Condensed from L, which actually reads: "[Revocation of gifts] is a matter full of danger, as we have said above, yet sometimes it is a highly necessary measure against embezzlers of public funds."

681 D7 *to the verie bones* || Fr adds: ". . . and as the Emperor Hadrian used to say, the treasury can no more expand than can the spleen, without causing the rest of the body to dry up." Cf. the Latin edition of the *Methodus*, O.P., I, 194. The source of this remark is Aurelius Victor (*Epitome de Caesaribus*, 42), who, however, attributes it to Trajan.

681 E6(margin) *given to a woman*. I.e., to Diane of Poitiers, but Bodin is less specific, and merely writes: ". . . given to one person only (*une seule personne*)."

683 A10 *fiftie millions* || Fr adds: ". . . or of the Athenians, who accumulated sixty millions, if there is no mistake in the figure."

683 D10 *hereafter breake it* || L adds: "The prince who is well formed by education will

never be tormented either by the desire to increase his wealth, or by the fear of losing it. Nor will he think that it is to be despised and thrown away, but rather he will regard it as the handmaid of benevolence and generosity. In the process of accumulating wealth many people lose their senses, and live in constant fear of losing what they have acquired." (6 lines).

683 E2 *paid his predecessors debts* || Fr 1–4 add: "... and paid his father's ransom..." Omitted in Fr 5–8.

683 E7 *43756 pounds starling*. Knolles intends "43750 pounds sterling." In L the figure is: "... scarcely 10,000 sestertia (that is, 437,500 *livres tournois*), or not even that..." But Fr reads: "... he did not levy above 300,000 livres yearly for all charges..."

685 B4 *have escaped* || Fr 1 adds a list of names here which is omitted in Fr 2–8 and L: "... and among others, Herouel, Sapin, Maigret, Spifame, Morlet, Carré, la Guette, [and] Tartereau..."

686 F6 *so great a multitude* || Addition in Fr and L. Fr reads: "... now that the Kingdom has been reduced by a half?" Perhaps a deliberate omission by Knolles.

686 F8 *to the receiver* || Fr adds: "Moreover there were not so many accounts postponed and undecided as one sees nowadays."

CHAPTER 3 (PAGES 687–700)

687 A2 *Chap. III*. This chapter is undoubtedly the most difficult of all to translate. Bodin's argument is at once highly technical and loosely constructed, and his precise meaning is often in doubt. Knolles's translation, which for the most part follows Fr closely, tends to go astray on technical terms, or else to omit them altogether. There is another English version of this chapter embodied in G. A. Moore's edition of *The Response of Jean Bodin to the Paradoxes of Malestroit and the Paradoxes* (Chevy Chase, Md., 1946). Moore errs, however, in stating that "Bodin practically copied parts of the *Response* into the sixth book of the *Republic*" (p. ix); actually the copying was the other way round. The first edition of the *Response* was printed in 1568, but the discussion of coinage in the *République* of 1576 is entirely rewritten, and bears scant resemblance to the earlier work. However when a second edition of the *Response* was printed in 1578, Bodin incorporated in it virtually the whole of Book VI, ch. 3 of the *République* and dropped the considerably shorter corresponding section of the 1568 edition. The extent of the change may be seen by comparing Moore's translation of the 1578 edition (pp. 60–84) with Hauser's reprint of the 1568 edition (pp. 41–50). In the Latin version of the *République* the discussion of coinage is extensively revised once more, and its length is reduced by about one third by the omission of much technical detail, particularly that relating to France. Hauser's edition of the *Response* contains much useful information about coinage, but the version of Book VI, ch. 3 of the *République* which he includes in it (pp. 113–129) is both inaccurate and incomplete.

687 C1 *contrarie to the opinion*. Inexact translation. "... in conformity with the opinion of his colleagues (*de collegarum sententia*)..." (L only). Cicero records that the edict was drawn up jointly and was to be published jointly, but that Gratidianus, breaking the agreement, published the law individually and prematurely (cf. *De officiis*, III, 20). Gratidianus was Praetor, not Tribune, at the time.

687 C5 *deerer to the people* || Addition in Fr and L. L reads: "From this it may be understood how much the Commonweal is harmed when the coinage is debased by the prince himself, by public law and authority."

687 C9 *law of nations* || L adds: "... by which the value of gold and silver is established..."

687 E4 *boylers*. Strictly, *billoneurs*, which can mean those who melt down coins, but which usually stands for persons engaged in any type of illegal trade in money.

688 H3–5 *yet shall he erre ... proportion of the mettals*. Inexact. "... yet the imperceptible error which occurs in measuring the drops of water makes a great difference in [the calculation of] the volume of the metals." (Fr).

688 I9 *and hath a fourth part of a Carrat of allaie*. Faulty. "... with one eighth [of a carat] of variation (*remede*)..." *Le remède* was the limit within which coins might legally vary in weight or in fineness from the prescribed standard. Knolles misunderstands the term, and it is mistranslated throughout the chapter. L explains the concept more fully: "... with an impairment [i.e., tolerance] of one eighth of a carat, that is, if a quantity of this kind of gold were of 192 parts, 3 parts of gold would be missing."

689 D10–E1 *beeing usually paid in blanch, or copper money*. Faulty. "... which were formerly paid in silver coinage of high quality (*forte monnoye blanche*)..." Bodin is evidently using the term *monnoye blanche* in contrast to the debased *billon* which replaced it, but Knolles takes it as copper money which has been artificially whitened, or silvered over. For this latter meaning, cf. Cotgrave.

690 F6 *as we read in Pollux* || L adds: "... and the daily labor of artisans and country laborers was generally valued at this figure in the Holy Scriptures [St. Matthew 20:1–13]."

Notes to Book VI

690 F9 *as we use in France* ‖ Fr 1–4 add: ". . . and as is done in Spain and Africa . . ." Omitted in Fr 5–8 and L. Cf. the notes at I1 and I3.

690 G4 *& three seven parts more*. As in Fr. One would expect to read: ". . . and one-seventh more." But Bodin repeats the same fraction at the end of the chapter (cf. 700 G6 and note).

690 H5 *That of Paris and Strausbourg agrees*. Incomplete. "Those of Paris, Strasbourg and Besançon (*Vezuntini*) are the same . . ." (L only).

690 I1 *the like may be written of many others*. Condensing L, which actually gives others: ". . . 100 pounds in the Aegean Islands make 91 pounds at Paris; on the coast of Africa 116 pounds are equivalent to 100 pounds at Paris; in Asia Minor 100 *rotuli* make 123 pounds four ounces at Paris." The passage from G10 to I3 occurs in L only.

690 I3 *foure at Paris* ‖ Addition in L. (Some towns, such as Oran in Africa, have as many as four different pounds for weighing different types of commodities, 10 lines.)

691 A6 *about ten Deniers*. Bodin writes: ". . . eight deniers or thereabouts . . ." (Fr), but Knolles, taking the livre at two shillings sterling, makes the appropriate correction.

691 B2–3 *divide the Marke of silver (as in Lorraine) into a thousand peeces*. Knolles confuses Fr and L. Fr reads: ". . . divide the mark of silver . . . [into] 8000 pieces . . ." L reads: ". . . divide the *ounce* of silver into 1000 coins . . ." Thus the discrepancy noted marginally at B3 disappears.

691 B5–6 *But making it but halfe so little*. More strictly, "But by making only half as many . . ." Cf. Fr.

691 B8–9 *as certaine as may be* ‖ L adds: ". . . and this especially on account of the rules of commerce which are common to all peoples in their dealings with one another."

691 C4–5 *which was after the rate of eight hundred ninetie six pounds of copper, for one pound weight of silver*. As in Fr. L omits this figure, which is faulty, and then substitutes "210 pounds" i.e., one fourth of 840, in place of 224 pounds at C9.

692 F7–8 *the which was then brought to Rome*. Faulty. ". . . which was then current at Rome [reading *ferebatur* as in L 1, 3–5 rather than *feriebatur* as in L 2]."

692 G5–6 *to keepe it from rusting* ‖ Addition in Fr and L. Fr adds: ". . . as is done also with iron, which is gilded to keep it from rusting." L enlarges: ". . . which [gilding] has preserved the copper from corrosion, and the temple from the weather and from decay, for more than 1600 years down to the present time. And had the copper not been gilded, it would eventually have corroded and let in the rains."

692 G9–10 *the price of gold must of necessitie rise*. As in Fr, but L explains: ". . . gold will necessarily become not merely scarce but almost unobtainable everywhere, since in gilding things there is a constant and irretrievable loss of gold."

692 H3 *no gold* ‖ Fr adds: ". . . and those of the New World yield much more silver than gold."

692 I6 *where there is none growing* ‖ Fr adds: ". . . which was to give away to the foreigner the twenty-fourth part of the silver."

692 K4 *and had 1600 peeces for a Marke of copper*. Faulty. Bodin writes: ". . . and there were 1600 coins of silver alloy to the mark (*& avoit seize cents pieces pour marc d'œuvre*)."

693 A6–C10 *Other princes have done no better . . . their weight & standard*. From Fr. L omits the details and alters the emphasis: "We see that our kings were virtually compelled to do this by the example of neighboring princes, particularly those of Switzerland, Germany, and the Low Countries. Since they always issue silver coinage baser than ours, they were stripping our people and our cities of silver coinage, in order to produce their own from it and send back their coins to us as a result of the requirements of trade." (6 lines).

693 C2 *ten of ours*. Bodin writes: ". . . eight of ours . . ." (Fr), but Knolles retains his usual conversion rate. Cf. note at 691 A6.

693 C6 *and then that of Cologne by nine graines*. Faulty. ". . . and that of Cologne [is weaker than ours] by nine grains . . ." (Fr, but Fr 7 corrupt).

693 C7 *stronger by an ounce*. As in Fr, which is misleading. Bodin seems to mean: ". . . stronger by one ounce [in the pound]." Cf. 690 H7–8, which is based on L.

693 C8 *nine ounces*. Knolles's correction. Bodin writes: ". . . nine *gros* . . ." (Fr), but this seems erroneous, for the *gros* was commonly $\frac{1}{8}$ of an ounce, or $\frac{1}{64}$ of a mark. Bodin makes a similar slip at 698 K1 which Knolles does not amend.

693 D1–2 *the poier, as they say, or the difference, as the Banquers speake*. Bodin merely writes *le pair, comme parlent les banquiers*. *Le pair* was the rate of exchange between currencies that was indicated by the actual amount of precious metal in the coins. At a later date the English term was "par" or "par of exchange." Cf. *O.E.D.*, s.v. "par," sb. 1, sense 2a.

693 E1 *Marke of gold*. Inexact. ". . . mass of gold [*masse* in Fr 1–4, *mace* in Fr 5–8] . . ."

693 E4 *fifteene deniers of course*. I.e., of actual value in circulation. Whereas the "par" indicated

a rate of exchange based on the intrinsic value of the metal in the coins, the "course of exchange" was the rate at which transactions actually took place, the market value.

694 G3–6 *but the common people . . . which is the old Crowne*. Based on Fr. L differs and expands: ". . . as though *solidus* were derived from the sun (*sol*). But the [Roman] law calls it *solidus* because it is made from the purest gold. There is nothing in the whole of nature more solid or more compact than gold, since all other bodies have certain empty spaces. And just as the *aureus*, which in the reign of Augustus weighed the same as the Attic *stater*, the *Philippeus*, or the English rose [noble]—all of two drachms—gradually began to be impaired during the decline of the Empire as a result of the capital offenses of the directors of the mint, until at the time of Constantine it was one third lighter than the old one; so too the *aureus solidus* of Constantine (which is like the English Angel, and was very common among our ancestors) was gradually diminished in weight, and continues to be impaired by the thefts of the masters of the mint." (12 lines).

694 G7–8 *being diminished by little and little, as by the auntient Crowne Sold of three graines*. Faulty. ". . . being gradually diminished by three grains, like the ancient Crown Sold . . ." (Fr).

694 H8–9 *having an eight part of Aloie put to it*. Faulty. ". . . save for an eighth [of a carat] of tolerance (*remede*)." Cf. note at 688 I9.

694 I5–7 *causing them to be coined . . . they call Pistolets*. Faulty. ". . . causing the crowns of Castile, Valencia, and Aragon, which are called Pistolets, to be coined at 22 carats, and at 2 deniers 15 grains weight." (Fr).

695 B9–10 *one soulz eleven deniers* ∥ Fr adds: ". . . and $\frac{9}{26}$ of a denier." Clearly Bodin should have written: ". . . one sou, *seven* deniers and $\frac{9}{26}$ of a denier." The entire calculation is faulty in several respects, and the passage from 694 K7 to 695 C4 is greatly condensed in L.

695 D1 *the abatement*. Strictly, ". . . the variations from the standard (*les remedes*) . . ." Cf. note at 688 I9.

695 D4–5 *silver by fortie and five soulz, and gold at twelve or thirteen livres*. Inexact. ". . . silver by forty or fifty sous, and gold by 12 or 13 livres . . ." (Fr).

695 D5–6 *bought dearer from the goldsmith and marchant, then from the mint-master*. More probably, ". . . bought dearer by the goldsmith and merchant, than by the mint-master . . ." Cf. Fr.

695 E3 *decried*. I.e., depreciated, devalued. Presumably he refers to the *Ordonnance de Fontainebleau* of January 14, 1550/1. Cf. *Response* (ed. Hauser), pp. 26, 103.

696 F4 *without any alaie or mixture*. Strictly, ". . . without variation from the standard (*sans remede*) . . ." Cf. note at 688 I9.

696 H2 *the which is done by strong water*. Incomplete. ". . . which is done by *ciment Royal*, or by nitric acid (*eau de depart*)." Cotgrave explains that *ciment royal* was the term for a type of cement compounded by the mint men for assaying gold.

696 K4–5 *to deliver forth their money in his realme*. Strictly, ". . . to deliver forth their money at another man's expense . . ." Bodin writes *pour exposer au prix d'autruy leurs monnoyes*, but Knolles clearly misreads *prix* as *pays*.

697 A5 *in the coyning of money* ∥ Additions in Fr and L. Fr adds: ". . . and in the *boites*, because of the small number of judges with exclusive cognizance [of these matters], particularly after the suppression of the *generaux subsidiaires*." The *boites* were the sealed boxes in which coins were conveyed from the place of fabrication to the Cour des Monnaies. The *généraux subsidiaires* were provincial officials who assisted the officials of the Cour des Monnaies. L adds: "I believe that [having only one mint] may seem a novelty to the mint-masters, especially to ours, who have almost twenty workshops for making coins."

697 C2 *as Marc Anthonie did*. As in Fr, but L modifies: ". . . as Marcus Antonius was reproached for doing during the Triumvirate, but I believe that this reproach originated from his opponents."

697 E8 *soulzes that are too base by foure shillings in waight*. Faulty. ". . . *douzains* that are too base by 20 sous in weight . . ." i.e., by *two* shillings sterling. Though the *douzain* had a nominal value of twelve deniers or one sou, it differed in practice owing to variations in weight and fineness.

698 F4–5 *of foure deniers of silver, and two deniers of copper*. Faulty. ". . . of four deniers in fineness, with two grains of permitted variation from the standard (*deux grains de remede*) . . ." Cf. note at 688 I9.

699 A3–4 *of the cisers, or of any helpe at the waight, which falls not out so in that which is stampt*. Inexact. ". . . and there would be no loss from the clipping, and no variation (*remede*) in the weight, while it is necessary to allow at least two *ferlins* [of variation] in the mark for coins that are stamped." (Fr). Cf. note at 688 I9.

699 C1–2 *except lead, the which is heavier than silver, and differs as fifteene to foureteene, or more precisely, as 998 to 929*. There is a confusion here which arises from discrepancies between editions.

A 163

Apart from several misprints, the figures for these two metals in Fr 1–4 are 866 for silver and 929 for lead; in Fr 5–8 they are 998 for silver and 929 for lead; in L they are 929 for silver and 998 for lead. Thus at C2 and again at C5 Knolles follows the ratios given in L, but elsewhere he follows Fr 5–8. Those given in L were repeated later in the *Universae naturae theatrum* (Lyon, 1596), p. 260, but it should be noted that the figures in the early French editions (Fr 1–4) give the most accurate set of specific gravities.

699 E8–9 *They began to coine with a mill, but by proofe it appeared.* As in Fr, but L enlarges: "In our own time, by a most ingenious method, in fact by a very clever invention of the French, coins have begun to be punched out in a circular shape and stamped in a single operation, and this very rapidly. But this method fell into disuse, because it was found by experience that . . ." At an earlier stage Bodin had favored this process (cf. *Response* (ed. Hauser), pp. 42, 130). The coins that were produced by this method have a strikingly modern appearance.

700 G6 *was more in waight than three seven parts, then a souldiers daies pay.* Inexact. Fr reads: ". . . was heavier *by* three sevenths. This [*denarius*] also was a soldier's day's pay . . ." Presumably Bodin should have written "heavier by *one* seventh." Cf. 690 G4 and note.

700 G9 *coined as I have said* || Fr adds: ". . . in order that everyone shall have an opportunity to get rid of debased coinage with a minimum of loss." There is a misprint in Fr 7 which obscures the meaning.

700 H6–9 *I confesse . . . come to ruine.* As in Fr. L substitutes: "But shortly afterwards I learned that corrupt officials had stepped in to prevent these proposals that I have outlined from being enacted. Indeed they have produced silver coinage baser than before, and by this means have amassed almost 10,000 sestertia. I have no doubt that if the debased coinage were prohibited by law and surrendered to the mint officials at a fair price, the subjects would suffer no slight loss, for which each prince individually ought to provide some measure of compensation. But every good man should consider this a very slight inconvenience to set against such outstanding advantages." (8 lines).

CHAPTER 4 (PAGES 700–721)

702 K2–3 *And if the Tribune.* Strictly, "And if the majority of the Tribunes . . ." (Fr).

702 K8 *the flying of a bird on the right hand* || L adds: ". . . for the Romans, contrary to the practice of all [other] peoples, considered the left side more auspicious than the right . . ." There is a marginal reference to Cicero, *De divinatione*, II, 39. Cf. *Methodus*, p. 120.

703 D7 *in pietie, justice, valour, honour, and vertue.* Combining Fr and L. Fr reads: ". . . in honor and virtue . . ." L substitutes: ". . . in piety, justice, valor (*fortitudo*), and especially in practical wisdom (*prudentia*) . . ."

705 E1 *effundi.* As in L, but modern editions of Cicero read *effingi*, "to be wiped up" (*Pro Sestio*, 35).

705 E4 *with sponges* || L adds: "Methinks I see the Tribune Sulpicius trampling under foot the decrees of the Senate and the commands of the magistrates, at the instigation of Marius, in order to take away Sulla's province; and calling the *plebs* to arms by seditious speeches, as though by the firebrands of the Furies. I see disorderly meetings of all classes and of all ages troubling the city. I see Sulla returning with his army, fouling the city itself with the blood of the citizens, tearing down some houses, setting others ablaze. I see the swarming soldiers slaying those they meet, without any regard for sex, years, or station. Everywhere the flashing of swords blinds the eye; everywhere is heard the clangor of arms, the crashing of falling roofs. Every street resounds with the crying of children, the wailing of women, the shouting of soldiers, the groans of the dying. Murder is mingled with rape, and rape with murder, until at length the entire city overflows with the blood of its own citizens. Later, when Sulla withdraws, Marius returns, seizes the fortresses, throws the assembly into disorder, creates magistrates at his own pleasure, turns out the supporters of Sulla and puts them to flight, and requites murder with murder. Soon afterwards Sulla again returns with his army and ranges over the whole of Italy, inflicting unheard of cruelties, slaughtering citizens on every side, and even dancing with joy at the obsequies of the Commonweal." (20 lines).

706 G2 *bounds of honour* || Addition in Fr (margin) and L. L reads: "On this account Livy writes [XXXVIII, 51]: 'The city which is mistress of the world lies under the protection of Scipio. His will takes the place of the senate's decrees and the people's commands.'"

706 H1–2 *at the least three hundred men.* Bodin writes: ". . . three hundred men at the most (*pour le plus, ad summum*) . . ." But *ad summum* is occasionally used in the opposite sense. Cf. notes at 370 G1 and 733 E8.

707 B6 *he was banished* || L adds: ". . . or else he was crushed by accusation and slander, lest they should appear to be too openly declaring war against virtue."

707 C1–2 *and become a houshold (as Aristotle said).* As in Fr, but L suggests other reasons: ". . . not because it is to be feared that a Commonweal will become one and the same family, as Aristotle thought, but because Commonweals were

Notes to Book VI

established principally in order that [men] should preserve what was their own [cf. Cicero, *De officiis*, II, 21], and because there is no more fertile source of discords than the community of all things."

709 A3 *the Swissers do observe their lawes verie severely* ‖ L adds: ". . . contrary to the manner of ancient democracies. No mercy may be expected in capital crimes. Even if the cantons suffer the severity of the laws to be relaxed out of consideration for [foreign] princes and allies, and punish somewhat more lightly, nevertheless it is exceedingly difficult for the condemned to escape from their punishment."

709 C6 *A man may also say, that the soveraigntie should be given onely to the most rich.* As in Fr, but L substitutes: "But if all the citizens are vicious or cowardly, so that there are no degrees of goodness, but only badness, then it is certainly better to establish a form of government on the basis of wealth and property [reading *censu* as in L 3–5 rather than *sensu* as in L 1–2] . . ."

709 E8 *shall have citisens* ‖ L adds: "Indeed the popular Commonweal of the canton of Schwyz has not many more citizens than the number of optimates at Venice."

710 H5 *used the same argument which Maecenas did before Augustus against Marcus Agrippa.* As in Fr, but L attributes this argument against aristocracy to Agrippa, whom Dio Cassius represents as having advocated the restoration of the republic. Cf. Dio's *Roman History*, LII, 2–40.

710 I6–7 *as well in the diets and assemblies of the princes of Germanie.* Imprecise. ". . . as well in the Diets of the ten circles of Germany, as in the Imperial Diets . . ." (Fr).

711 B1 *keepe themselves in forts.* Strictly, ". . . keep themselves in the fortress . . ." (Fr). L explains more clearly: ". . . all the optimates have their dwelling in the same fortress, not only to be safe from the plebeians, but also so that no one of the patricians should be able to seize the citadel and establish a tyranny."

711 D3–4 *disarme them quite* ‖ L adds: ". . . in order that they may be unable to do harm even if they wish to. They also have very strong fortresses in their towns, the more easily to retain the obedience of those who are more distant from the city."

711 E7 *Tepoliennes, Bajamontaines.* Both these names seem to refer to the followers of Bajamonte Tiepolo, who conspired against the government with the aid of the Querini in 1309. Cf. *Methodus*, p. 278.

712 H6 *So of foure and twentie thousand citisens.* Faulty. "So of eighty thousand (*quatre vingts mil*) citizens . . ." L alters this figure to "seventy thousand citizens" of whom "scarcely two thousand" had the sovereignty.

713 A6 *will expell them all* ‖ L adds: "For nothing is truer than that saying of Lucan [*Pharsalia*, I, 92–93]: 'There shall be no trust among fellows in sovereignty, and all power will be impatient of a partner.'" Cf. 198 G4–9.

713 C9–D5 *This may properly be called an Aristocratie . . . as a Monarke may.* From Fr, but L clarifies and expands: "This is the truest aristocracy, which makes a practice of summoning all the ἄριστοι, that is, the best men, into the government, whether they be poor or rich, plebeian or noble. This means that since the avenue to honors and command is barred to no one, except to someone who has stained his honor and reputation by some shameful deed, there can be no contention between the *plebs* and the optimates over honors and authority. Moreover by this means there will be room for the best laws and the highest virtues in a Commonweal. Another very good point is that in this Commonweal [i.e., Geneva] there is an annual censorship of the Elders, in order that those who have been advanced to offices under a pretense of virtue may soon be found out, and that those who rely on their authority and behave in an insolent manner may be deprived of office with perpetual infamy and shame. The Lacedemonians had the highest regard for virtue in the creation of optimates, and gave no preference to wealth or nobility, but those who had mounted to the highest degree of honor could not be displaced by any form of censure. Nevertheless by means of this aristocratic form of government the Lacedemonians flourished for about five hundred years, greatly renowned for their military and domestic discipline. But when they began to covet the government of other peoples, they lost their own. The Genevans, as a people who suffer the military arts to lie neglected, not only do not desire foreign territories, but consider that they are very well off if they can look out for themselves and preserve their own sovereignty, which has almost the same boundaries as the walls of their city." (22 lines).

713 D6 *of so great a Seigneurie.* Misleading. Bodin writes: ". . . of a small seigneurie . . ." (Fr).

713 E3–4 *whether the change of the Monarke be from bad to good, or from good to better.* As in Fr, but L substitutes: ". . . whether a better or a worse [monarch] succeeds."

714 H9 *Edward the sixt.* Bodin writes: ". . . Edward V . . ." (Fr and L), but Knolles corrects him. L makes a further suggestion: "The Duke of Northumberland, in order to smooth his son's path to the throne, is reported to have removed King Edward V [*sic*] of England by poison."

714 I6–7 *he will hazzard his subjects, his estate, and his person, to make proofe of his valour.* As in Fr, but L substitutes: ". . . he would rather

Notes to Book VI

declare an unjust war than fail to make proof of his spirit and valor."

715 A1 *much more in a Popular* || L adds: "But it is unjust in finding fault with anything to pass over the advantages and reckon up the defects. I confess that some evil is inherent in regal authority, but without that evil we shall not have the benefits which are sought after in this form of government."

717 A7–8 *for in that case it should be a Popular government and no Monarchie*. As in Fr, but L suggests an alternative: "... otherwise the sovereignty of the kingdom must degenerate into either a pestiferous anarchy or a popular disorder ..."

718 H2–3 *There is no reason to ballance the cruelties and extorsions of a tyrant, with the actions of good princes*. From Fr, but L differs and expands here: "Finally, as for the complaint that tyrants do many things that are intemperate, cruel, wanton and wicked, I do not deny it. For what would be more divine than monarchy, if everything were ruled by reason? Nevertheless any tyranny whatsoever seems more endurable than the domination of the people, because tyrants realize that they proceed at their own peril, but a raging and impetuous people has regard neither for itself nor for anyone else." (6 lines).

718 H7 *one tyrant alone* || L adds: "... for the desires of one tyrant can eventually be sated, but not those of many."

719 C8–9 *long after his death* || L adds: "From this fact it was realized that the royal type of state, formerly favored, had been rejected, as Cicero writes [*De legibus*, III, 7], not so much for the defects of kingly government as for the vices of a king."

719 D6 *and many others*. A marginal note in Fr 2–8 and L specifically mentions Bartolus' *Tractatus de regimine civitatis*. Omitted in Fr 1.

CHAPTER 5 (PAGES 721–754)

722 G10 *of religion and vertue*. Inexact. "... of the honor and glory of virtue [following L, but Fr reads *qui sur tout a la religion d'honneur devant ses yeux*] ..."

722 K1 *by right of lawfull succession*. Bodin adds a marginal note in Fr and L. Fr reads: "So writes Thucydides, contrary to Aristotle's opinion that in heroic times kings obtained their thrones by election."

723 A9 *Asia the lesse* || Fr inserts another, "Ptolemy of Egypt," whom L omits.

724 F7 *by the consent of all the estates*. Based on L, but Fr reads: "... without assembling the estates ..."

725 D2 *of the Polonian embassador*. Strictly, "... of the Polonian embassadors ..." (L), but Fr is more specific: "... as I learned from Lord Herburt, one of the thirteen ambassadors from Poland ..."

726 H9 *any moe conditions* || Fr adds: "Moreover the Emperors of Rome and later of Germany, elected in the same way as the rulers of Poland, have governed their empires through lieutenants over a very long period."

728 G2 *Tiberius his sonne in law*. Bodin writes: "... his stepson (*privignum*) ..." But in fact Tiberius was also Augustus' son-in-law.

728 H9 *the Bohemians, the Polonians, the Hungarians, Danes, and Tartars*. Fr includes the Swedes in this list, while L omits the Hungarians.

728 K6 *For a kingdome going by succession* || Bodin adds: "... as the Kingdom of England has always done ..." (Fr). Undoubtedly a deliberate omission.

728 K9 *quite overthrowne* || L adds: "When I went over to England on an embassy on behalf of Francis, Duke of Anjou, a few years ago [i.e., in 1581], the assembled Estates of the people were forbidden, subject to the penalty of treason, to talk about a successor to the throne. This was a means of providing for the safety of the ruler, but not of the people. Nevertheless I maintained that the interests of both could be protected, first by the adoption of the King of Scotland, then by a marriage of [this] prince to the Lennox [heiress] and a very close treaty connection, that there might be everlasting harmony between the two peoples of this island. This was my speech to the Queen. To the inexperienced it may seem that this plan would be detrimental to France, but to me it seems likely to be extremely profitable because of the most ancient and most inviolable treaty between the Scots and the French, and very wholesome also for both of the kingdoms bounded by the waves of the same ocean. For the prince should desire nothing more dearly than that at his death the people should enjoy the greatest peace and tranquillity. Nero, on the other hand, often wished that his death might be followed by a world-wide conflagration." (17 lines). The *Lenoxia* to whom Bodin refers must be the daughter of Charles Stuart, Earl of Lennox, the ill-fated Lady Arabella Stuart, who was James's first cousin and next in the line of succession.

729 B6 *Pavie, and Derthone* || Fr adds: "... and Charles of Orleans [took] Asti."

730 K9–731 C3 *Anno 1058 ... VOLUMUS, FIAT*. There is a more extensive and more accurate version of this passage in the *Recueil des historiens des Gaules et de la France*, ed. Dom M. Bouquet *et al.* (Paris, 1738–1904), XI, 32–33, which at some points differs considerably from

that given by Bodin. Both versions, together with other documents relating to this coronation, are printed in *Le Ceremonial françois*, ed. D. Godefroy (Paris, 1649), I, 119–124.

731 A7 *unicuique de vobis commissis*. As in Fr and L, but the wording is corrupt. The version in the *Recueil* reads *unicuique de vobis et de Ecclesiis vobis commissis*. Hence at D3 for ". . . to every one of you the committies . . ." understand ". . . to every one of you and to every one of the churches committed to your charge . . ." Cf. above, 94 F10 and note.

731 B8 *licitum non esse*. The version in the *Recueil* omits this negative, and the lines B7–9 read as follows: ". . . elegit eum in Regem. Post eum, Legati Romanae Sedis, cum id sine Papae nutu fieri licitum esse disertum ibi sit, honoris tamen & amoris gratia tum ejus ibi affuerunt Legati. Post hos, Archiepiscopi & Episcopi . . ."

731 E9 *the young Duke of Aquitane, the ambassadours of the Duke of Burgundie*. Inexact. ". . . the Duke of Aquitaine, [and Hugh,] the son and ambassador of the Duke of Burgundy . . ." For this reading, see the version in the *Recueil*.

732 I2 *crowned king of Fraunce* || Addition in Fr and L. Fr 5–8 read: "However many maintain that Robert [Duke of Burgundy] was younger than Henry. The ancient historian Glaber holds this view, and says that their mother favored the younger son." Omitted in Fr 1–4, which contain instead the passage given in the note at 736 H2.

732 K4 *other kings also* || Fr adds: "M. le Cirier, a Counselor in the Parlement, and a man of honor and knowledge, could not bear patiently this [claimed right of deposition], and in his book *De jure primogeniturae* he commended the opinion of Albericus."

733 A6 *all his power*. More precisely, ". . . all its power." Cf. 88 G7–8 and *Digest*, 1, 4, 1, pr.

733 E8 *at the most two parts of the voyces*. Bodin writes *ad summum duas suffragiorum partes*, which in this context should mean "at least two thirds of the votes." But Bodin seems to use the phrase *ad summum* in both of these senses. Cf. notes at 370 G1 and 706 H1.

736 G7 *out of his wits* || Fr adds: ". . . as it sometimes happens in the most illustrious families of Germany."

736 H2 *before Lothaire his elder brother* || Addition in Fr 1–4: "The same thing was done by King Robert of France, who preferred Henry I before his elder son, who was of a slack and cowardly disposition, and who contented himself with [the Dukedom of] Burgundy." Omitted in Fr 5–8 and L, which modify this view. Cf. note at 732 I2.

736 H7 *out of his hand* || Fr adds: "It is true that Louis XI was greatly devoted to the Popes, going so far as to raise a powerful army with which he defeated the Swiss at Basel and expelled the Council, which had excommunicated Pope Eugene and declared him unworthy of the Papacy. However with the aid of Louis XI he later re-established himself by force, and even excommunicated all the Cardinals, Bishops and Archbishops that had attended the Council. He ruled for fifteen years after that without absolving those whom he had excommunicated, while remaining excommunicated himself." (9 lines).

738 F5–G1 *And indeed Scipio Africanus . . . as Livie writeth*. Here Knolles is confusing two separate incidents, the quarrel between Corbis and Orsua for rule over Ibes in Spain (Livy, XXVIII, 21) and a similar rivalry, possibly that of Jugurtha with his cousins, for the kingdom of Numidia. It would appear from Fr that Bodin shares this confusion, but L omits the reference to Numidia.

738 G8 *in perpetuall prison* || L adds: ". . . and obtained the kingdom by the same authority that prevailed among the ancient Germans, Vandals, English and Scots."

738 H4–5 *Richard the eldest sonne of Edward the Blacke prince*. Strictly, ". . . Richard, the son of the eldest son, [Edward the Black Prince] . . ." Cf. Fr and L.

738 H10–740 I3 *for so Honorius . . . to be even neere at hand*. Following L. This passage is largely omitted in Fr, which reads as follows at this point: "And even in private successions representation [of dead children] in the direct line of descent did not occur in any of the Northern countries, nor in Flanders, Artois, Picardy or Normandy. Nor did it occur in many of the *coutumes* of France, but these have gradually been changed, especially since the dispute over the County of Artois between Maud and her nephew Robert, and since the more common opinion of the lawyers and the practice of those peoples which grant scepters and crowns to the children of the elder sons by representation, have come into fashion. This was done in ancient times. For even Lycurgus, a younger son who could have seized the crown, kept it for his nephew Charilaus, the son of his elder brother, according to the ancient custom of Lacedemonia, which required that there be two kings descended from Procles and Eurysthenes of the lineage of Hercules." (15 lines). The question is given greater prominence in L because the death of the Duke of Alençon in 1584 had left Henry of Navarre and his uncle Charles, Cardinal of Bourbon, as the nearest heirs to the French throne.

738 I5 *the eldest sonne of Sigisbert*. Strictly, ". . . the son of Sigebert the eldest son . . ." (L).

NOTES TO BOOK VI

739 D5–8 *than that an inheritance ... under a condition conceived.* This is a reference to *Code*, 6, 52, 1, which permitted both legacies and *fideicommissa* left to children, grandchildren, or great-grandchildren to be transmitted by the recipients to their children before the will of the first testator had been opened.

740 G1 *neerer than he.* This phrase is added by Knolles.

740 K9 *Gensericus.* This is printed as *Geric* in Fr, *Georgius* in L, but Knolles's amendment seems correct. Cf. Procopius, *History of the Wars*, III, 7.

741 C2 *Secondarily.* As in L 3–5, but L 1–2 and Fr number this as the third point, the second being the curbing of the mayors of the palace. In L, therefore, there are four distinct provisions, while Fr groups the third (C2–5) and fourth (C5–10) together in a more abbreviated form.

741 E2 *partition of their realmes* || L adds: "However cities and lands were given in usufruct to the other children by the first-born."

743 B6 *his sonnes sonne.* Bodin actually writes *son arriere-neveu* (Fr only), but both he and Knolles seem to be at fault on genealogy here.

746 G8–9 *that Maud, grandmother to Philip the Long, should be assistant unto Robert Contie of Artoise.* Inexact. "... that Maud [Countess of Artois], the mother-in-law (*belle mere*) of Philip the Long, should be present at the judgment of [her nephew] Robert, Count of Artois ..." (Fr).

746 H3 *womens pleasure* || L adds: "... [and] it is most absurd of all [for women] to hold scepters."

746 I2–3 *In which case.* As in Fr, but L is more outspoken: "These contracts were concluded upon very unjust terms, because ..."

746 K9 *impatient of such unworthy reproach.* Bodin writes merely: "..., impatient of reproaches ..." (L).

747 A10 *so minded.* Weakened. Bodin writes: "... so cowardly ..." (Fr, and cf. L).

747 C6 *as she well deserved* || Fr adds: "A few years ago we saw tragedies no less strange, and a whole Kingdom aflame over similar events." This is undoubtedly a reference to Scotland. Omitted in L.

747 D6–7 *In briefe I find no people to have liked of the soveraigntie of womans government.* Weakened. L reads: "Nor has any people been so incorrigibly slothful as to approve of gynaecocracy ..." Fr reads: "In brief, there was found no people so effeminate as to approve of gynaecocracy, until the line of the Norman kings of Naples failed ..."

748 I8 *the queenes husbands* || Addition in Fr and L. L reads: "Although we read that the Kingdom of England descended in the female line in the time of Domitian [Tacitus, *Agricola*, 16], nevertheless for more than 1500 years it suffered no womanly rule until Mary, the sister of King Edward V [*sic* in L and Fr 1–5, but corrected in Fr 6–8], King of England, took over her brother's sovereignty, approximately ten years after Mary, the daughter of James V, King of Scotland, received the government of that kingdom. We read that previous to this the latter country had devolved upon 105 kings in an unbroken line, without female succession. Indeed at one time when King Bitricus had been poisoned by his wife, the senate and people of Scotland passed a perpetual law which forbade the wives of kings to be called queens, or to be seated with their husbands in public." (10 lines).

749 B9 *choyce of Henrie of Fraunce* || Addition in Fr and L. Fr reads: "Now although elections of monarchs are dangerous for the reasons which we have given above, yet when the male line fails they are more acceptable than to see the kingdom fall to the distaff side, because [then] it is necessary to endure a pure gynaecocracy, contrary to the laws of nature." (6 lines).

749 C9 *And not to speake of many difficulties which fell out about these matters.* With these words Knolles covers up a long discussion of English affairs which occurs in both Fr and L. L reads: "But what if she is rejected by the subject whom she desires? We find that this has happened in our own time in the case of Mary, Queen of England. The Earl of Devonshire, a member of the Courtenay family, whom she released from prison and dearly loved, and whom she wished to marry, spurned her because he sought to marry her sister Elizabeth. This is said to have been the cause of his banishment and eventually of his death also, even though he was descended from the kings of France on his father's side, and from the kings of England on his mother's. There is none now who can trace his paternal descent back to the kings of England except Somerset, the Earl of Worcester, whose son not long ago [in the year 1573] participated at the baptism of the daughter of King Charles IX [*Fr adds*: in the name of the Queen of England]. He traces his descent from John of Gaunt, son of Edward III, King of England, but not by lawful wedlock. [In the year 1565] there was common talk that the Estates ought to designate the Earl of Huntingdon as [next] King of England, and place after him the Duke of Norfolk, on the ground that while the latter was the most popular and the most wealthy, the former was descended from the kings of England on his mother's side. This plan was secretly encouraged through the ambassadors, in order that no neighboring prince should seek to marry the Queen and join the resources of so great a kingdom with his own, for it seemed that such a union could not be effected

without endangering or ruining the neighboring countries. When the Queen heard of this she informed the princes through the ambassadors that she would never debase her prerogatives of sovereignty and dignity so far as to allow herself to be defiled by marriage with a subject, but would make choice of a foreign prince who had neither the wealth nor the power to harm his neighbors [*Fr adds*: and that she would give nothing of her own property or troops to her husband, since she wished to make use of him only to leave a successor]. Not long afterwards, when Ferdinand, Archduke of Austria, sent ambassadors to England, the Queen seemed about to agree to marriage most willingly, but in the marriage treaty it was provided in the first article that no Catholic religious services were to be held in England; that the man who married the Queen was not to be called king; that magistracies, benefices, commands and commissions were not to be conferred on foreigners; that if the Queen died before her husband, he might not take anything out of the kingdom or call anything his own. Since these conditions seemed quite intolerable to the Archduke, or, to be more accurate, since he feared that he would not be acceptable to the Queen and the people, the ambassadors departed without accomplishing their mission. Yet nothing has been requested more anxiously and more often by the Estates of England, than that the Queen should marry, or appoint a successor to the throne, for they are well aware that if the succession were doubtful at the death of this most wise princess, the kingdom would be greatly troubled by civil wars. On the other hand, the Queen cannot appoint a successor without danger [to herself]." (41 lines).

750 G1–2 *nothing thereof obtained* ‖ Addition in Fr and L. L reads: "But in order to hasten the arrival in England of this prince whom she wished to marry, the Queen is reported to have sent him 300,000 crowns."

750 I5 *all the stronger* ‖ L adds: "Hardicanute, King of the Danes, had subjected England to his rule, and had crushed the people with a most mighty army, yet in one conspiracy the English slew all the Danes, and not long afterwards [in the year 1041], they poisoned the king himself."

751 C2 *of them with whome they had not before so well agreed*. Weakened. Bodin writes: "... of their ancient enemies ..." (Fr).

751 C5 *out of Scotland* ‖ Addition in Fr and L. Fr reads: "Since then we have seen the outcome of Mary Stuart's second marriage with [Lord Darnley,] the son of the Earl of Lennox, which ought to serve as a warning to all peoples." In L the tone changes: "Here I pass over the many great disasters which ensued from the marriages of the most illustrious princess Mary."

752 H7–8 *which we see to have bene used not of privat men onely, but even of kings also: as if a straunger*. As in L, but Fr omits this, reading instead: "Nevertheless in the treaty of marriage made between Philip of Castile and Mary, Queen of England, we see quite the contrary, even though many [lawyers] are of opinion that if a stranger ..."

753 A10–B1 *And so also ... in the lawes Salique*. Inexact. "And so also in the edict of Childebert, King of France, which is included among the Salic laws ..." (L, and cf. Fr).

753 B2 *by way of representation together called*. The notion that the grandsons succeed *jointly* is introduced by Knolles, who also adds the marginal definition.

754 G5–6 *are afraid of womens soveraigntie*. Weakened. Bodin writes: "... have a great horror (*perhorrescant*) of women's sovereignty ..." (L only).

CHAPTER 6 (PAGES 755–794)

756 G1–2 *had chaunged but the servants garments ... of the meaner sort*. Faulty. "... had ordered the garments [of his playmates] to be changed so that the larger ones were given to the bigger [boys] and the smaller ones to the shorter [boys] (*ampliora grandioribus, minora brevioribus*)." Cf. Xenophon, *Cyropaedia*, I, iii, 17.

757 B4–5 *howbeit that certaine markes of them manifest enough, are in the auntient Roman lawes to be found*. As in Fr, but L modifies this: "Geometrical and arithmetical ratios occur frequently in the writings of jurists [*Digest*, 28, 5, 82(81), pr.; 28, 5, 88(87); and 28, 2, 13, pr.], and are easily identified. But harmonic ratios are not so clearly perceived [*Code*, 4, 32, 26, 2]."

758 I6 *if the rich and noble should likewise marrie with the noble and rich*. As in L 1, 3–5, but L 2 reads: "... if the rich and noble should marry with the baseborn and rich ..."

759 E7 *Policletus his rule*. In Fr and in the *Methodus* (p. 4) Bodin contrasts the pliant Lesbian rule (cf. Aristotle, *Nicomachean Ethics*, 1137b) with the inflexible "rule of Polycletus," but in L, as though in recognition of his earlier misuse of this latter term, he adds the following explanation at E9: "Yet it is more correct for the rule (*canon*) of Polycletus to be understood as the book which that celebrated sculptor produced on the subject of his art. In this book he dealt most acutely with everything that should be noted in fashioning a statue of man, the shape of each individual part from the largest to the smallest, their position, and their proportion among themselves. In our time Albert Dürer has most carefully written a similar book. But in addition to this Polycletus publicly displayed at

the same time a statue of his own making in which all these points were most scrupulously observed, lest he should seem to recommend anything to others which he could not achieve himself. This statue itself he also called a canon, that is, a rule, and from it other craftsmen were accustomed to fashion their statues. Yet let us admit the rule of Polycletus to have been the straightest of all, and even made of iron soaked in vinegar, that it might be inflexible." (14 lines).

761 C6–7 *of equitie, law and justice.* Strictly, ". . . of right and justice (*jus ac justitia*)."

764 G1 *not lawfull rashly to blame the law.* Faulty. ". . . not lawful for the subject to blame the law . . ." (L). Bodin writes *subdito*, but Knolles apparently reads *subito*.

764 I4 *at the request of the kings subjects.* Faulty. ". . . at the request of the Crown lawyers (*gents du Roy*) . . ."

764 K1 *the power of the magistrat* ‖ Fr adds: ". . . which [equity] extends so far as to supply what is wanting in the law, or to extract a principle from it, for the correct interpretation of the law is nothing else than the law itself."

765 E1–2 *Neither ought the judges or lawmakers to joyne their reasons unto their judgements or lawes.* Based mainly on L. Fr gives more detail: "In such a case [the Parlement] causes its reason to be inserted in the register, or else it inserts in the text of the *arrêt* the clause *Sans tirer à consequence*, 'without creating a precedent.' But since this clause may throw the parties into confusion, it is seldom included. Even less frequently does the Court give the reason upon which it has based its *arrêt*, a practice followed by many judges and lawmakers who insert reasons in their laws and judgments . . ." (7 lines). The entire discussion of French procedure (765 D2–766 F6) is omitted in Fr 1–2.

766 F1 *thereby deceived* ‖ Addition in Fr 3–8: "For not knowing the reason of the Court, [people who publish decisions] make a single *arrêt*, which is a hypothesis or particular instance, into a general law, which is the thesis [i.e., general proposition. Fr reads *l'arrest* here, but this seems a misprint for *la these*]. I have seen this happen in a small and unimportant suit, in which the litigants differed as to the interpretation of the customary law. If at this point the court had given an interlocutory sentence to have the matter determined by a public inquiry to ascertain the custom, as is often done in such cases, the litigants would have been ruined. Upon application the Court decided the suit definitively, and caused it to be stated in the register that this was done without derogation from or prejudice to the customary law. Nevertheless those who knew nothing of the Court's reasons wrote that the Court had ruled on the customary law. Then people have the *arrêts* printed to be used as law." (13 lines). Omitted in Fr 1–2.

767 A7–8 *meerely saith, him to have gained but a few in France to his occupation.* Inexact. ". . . says that he was earning very little from his occupation." (Fr). Cf. Cicero, *Epistulae ad familiares*, VII, 13.

770 F8 *a fine of 65 crownes.* As in L. Fr gives this figure as 60, which is more consistent with the examples that follow, but in Fr all the amounts are given in livres. Cf. I4, where the figure occurs in Fr only.

770 I6–7 *which in part equall, in part semblable, are alike.* Inexact. ". . . which is in part equal, in part semblable." (Fr, but Fr 7 is corrupt, omitting the verb.)

772 F10–G1 *beaten with clubs, or els whipt with whips made of small coards.* Strictly, ". . . whipped with scourges (*courgees*) or with small cords." (Fr).

772 G4 *delivereth from death.* Strictly, ". . . delivereth from punishment . . ." (L only). There is a marginal reference to Exodus 21.

772 I1–4 *and yet must wee doe . . . great difference: for of the baser.* Faulty. "But we must *not* do as do the barbarous [West] Indians, who for the same offense punish base men much more grievously than noblemen, without any proportion whatsoever. For of the baser . . ." (Fr). The distinction between the penalty appointed and its execution is introduced by Knolles.

772 K9 *infinit rewards.* The adjective is misplaced, owing to a misprint in L 5. Read: ". . . unto their infinite posterity." at 773 A2. More accurately, ". . . when they shall understand that the rewards of the virtue of famous men, and the memory of those who have deserved well of the Commonweal, extend even after their death unto their infinite posterity." (L).

773 B5–6 *beheaded with the sword* ‖ L adds: "Yet the Italians and Spaniards, like the people of Narbonne and Aquitaine, behead with axes. In the Low Countries the practice is to cut the throats of noblemen with a sword, as if they were cattle."

776 F8 *sufferance of the law* ‖ L adds: "But nothing is more to be avoided in the making of laws than giving the rich and powerful freedom to transgress by means of a crafty interpretation of them."

776 H10–11 *When as in all executions of punishments, the lighter offences are the more lightly to be punished, yea and oftentimes also pardoned.* Faulty and incomplete. "But in all exactions of punishment, *minors* are punished more lightly [*Digest*, 50, 17, 108], and often they crave

Notes to Book VI

pardon. However in their case it is not [really] a lighter punishment or a pardon, for whoever does anything as a result of youthful error, impulse, or inconstancy is considered to have transgressed very little, or not at all." (L). The remainder of the sentence (I1–3) is taken from Fr.

777 D5 *to have marked* ‖ Fr adds: ". . . and if the forgery is for the value of 10,000 crowns or more, the punishment is no greater than for 500 crowns."

778 I9 *upon the high way* ‖ Addition in L (derivation of the word *latro*, 3 lines).

778 I10 *calleth him Grassatorem* ‖ L adds: ". . . as indeed the lawyers define him [*Digest*, 48, 19, 28, 10], following Cicero, who says [*De fato*, 15] 'Sometimes a well-dressed traveler gives a vagabond (*grassator*) the inducement to rob him.'"

780 H6–8 *neither can they in speciall lawes . . . without any law at all.* Mainly from Fr, which is contradictory. To clarify, L rephrases H4–9 as follows: "Therefore this great variety of cases cannot be decided according to one single law common to all, and if you wish to include everything in laws, this cannot be achieved in any number of books. Nor, on the other hand, should everything be left to the discretion of the magistrates, though the latter course is more just than the former."

782 F4 *as yet they still doe*. Misleading. Bodin writes: ". . . as is still done everywhere . . ." (Fr).

782 F10–G1 *a stolne thing ought by Arithmeticall proportion to bee made even with [the] particular interest of him from whome it was taken or stolne* ‖ I.e., the compensation or damages ought to be made equal to the value of the thing stolen (cf. Fr and L). Both Fr and L add an example to illustrate this point. Fr reads: "To show this he sets down three quantities—2, 4, 6—which he supposes to have been equal in this fashion—4, 4, 4. Insofar as he that [now] has six units has stolen two of them from the first man, he has created inequality, which the judge (who is in the middle position) restores to equality. Now if this were in force, a thief would always be discharged by returning the thing stolen, even though he had repeated his crime a hundred times." (6 lines). Cf. Aristotle, *Nicomachean Ethics*, 1131b–1132b.

784 F5–6 *every corrupt judge so without any proportion at all, extorting from all men, what he saw good.* Inexact. ". . . since he, the most corrupt judge of all, used to extort everything from everyone without any proportion at all." (L). Fr 3–8 support this reading, and the comment is omitted in Fr 1–2.

784 G9 *at Amboise*. Faulty. Bodin's term here is *Ambiani;* i.e., the people of the Amiénois (L only).

784 H1 *for tearme of life* ‖ L adds: "More unjust is the law of the English and Scots, which grants all the lands of noble families to the first-born son, and only money to the rest. It also allows one third of this money, together with the usufruct of one third of the lands, to the wife who survives her husband. Nor is it lawful to leave [her] more than a third of the money by testament." Perhaps omitted by Knolles out of deference to his patron, Sir Peter Manwood.

784 I5 *amongst the daughters also* ‖ L adds: "Of all the laws concerning successions which have been proposed anywhere on earth, this one ought to seem the most equitable and the most sacred."

785 B1–2 *never so little moved*. Strictly, ". . . never so little trained to war (*aguerri*) . . ."

786 H2–3 *estates and honours* ‖ Fr adds: ". . . leaving nothing to the poor but subjection and obedience . . ."

788 I9–K1 *That hee was the first new man . . . who of them of his ranke had obtained to be Consull*. Inexact. ". . . That he was the first new man for a long interval, and the first of their times . . . to have been made Consul." (L). Cf. *De lege agraria*, II, 1, where the phraseology differs slightly from Bodin's.

788 K4 *shut up* ‖ L adds: "Indeed Sallust says [*Catilina*, 23], 'On previous occasions the greater part of the nobility was inflamed with jealousy, and considered the Consulship to be in some way defiled, if a *novus homo*, however outstanding, should obtain it.' When the nobility had been thus overcome after many storms, the Consulship was entrusted to a new man. Likewise Livy writes [XXXIX, 41] of Cato the Censor: 'The nobility opposed his candidacy.' Again [*ibid.*], 'They were angry to see a new man Censor.' The children of those who were the first of their family to hold offices and commands were called *nobiles*." (7 lines).

788 K6 *so great honours* ‖ L adds: "And when they had been promoted [to high office], they looked down on the common people. Livy says: 'When these plebeian *nobiles* were consecrated, forthwith they despised the *plebs*.'"

789 A6 *be preferred before him* ‖ L adds: ". . . because of that reputation for virtue and excellence which he has acquired from his ancestors, in order that others may also be inflamed with a more ardent desire for virtue."

789 D10 *mounted unto honourable place*. Condensed. ". . . and the latter [should likewise feel honored] to mount to a position of honor." (Fr).

792 I3–4 *which dependeth of the two sides*. Fr 1 reads *qui pent les deux costez*, but Fr 2–8 sub-

A171

stitute *qui peut les deux costez*, "which is equal in power to the two sides," i.e., the hypotenuse when squared is equal to the squares on the two sides. For this usage of *pouvoir*, compare *O.E.D.*, s.v. "power," sub. 1, sense 11. It would seem probable that Knolles was temporarily following Fr 1 (or one of the two 1577 editions which have the same reading and the same diagram). Cf. note at I4.

792 I4-7 *for having in the selfesame figure found the equalitie and similitude of two other figures, the third figure being equall unto the first, and like unto the second.* Both Fr and L explain this marginally. Fr reads: "Let this demonstration make it clear. To a given triangle (3) let a similar one be given (2), according to Book VI, [proposition] 18 [of Euclid]. Then let the rectangular parallelogram (1) be constructed equal to triangle 3, as in Book I, [proposition] 42. Triangle 3 will be equal to rectangle 1 and similar to triangle 2." Knolles's diagram closely resembles that in Fr 1, but Fr 2-8 have more accurate diagrams with proportions similar to those shown below.

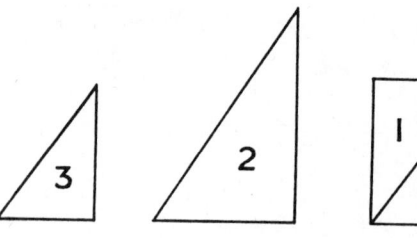

794 G3-4 *Wherefore what the unitie is in numbers, the understanding in the powers of the soule, and the center in a circle.* As in L, but Fr gives these correspondences as follows: "And just as the unity is to the three first numbers, the intellect to the three parts of the soul, and the indivisible point to the line, plane surface, and solid body . . ." Cf. 790 H7-9 and 792 G7-10. At all of these points L omits the comparison of point, line, surface, and solid body.

INDEX NOMINUM

For both the Index Nominum and the Index Rerum I have felt it more convenient to index the endnotes (pp. A105–A172) according to the page in the main text at which each note originates. All index references to these notes are designated by the symbol N (or NN if the reference relates to two or more notes on the same page). To illustrate, 567&NN means that the name or matter in question may be found on page 567 and also in two—or more—of the endnotes to that page (which will be found on pp. A144–A145), while the form N114 is used for a reference that occurs in the endnotes to page 114 but not in the text itself at that page. Textual corrections at the foot of each page have been indexed as an integral part of the page itself. References in the A series pagination (e.g., A40, A78) are used only for the editor's Introduction and Appendixes. Small Roman numerals (e.g., iii, v) refer to Knolles's Dedication and Preface. The twelve unnumbered verso pages at the end of Book V are designated 625^v, 626^v, etc.

In the Index Nominum I have attempted to establish the identity of all the peoples, persons, and places that Bodin mentions. But there are difficulties. Bodin used some sources in which fact mingled with myth, as in his authorities on Scotland. His classical texts were edited far less meticulously than ours today. There were areas of confusion in his vast historical knowledge, such as the successions in certain duchies and counties of France. Sometimes he lapsed when he trusted his prodigious memory a little too far. Many of the contemporary figures that he mentions have retreated into the obscurity of history. Clearly in a task of this kind one must settle for less than perfection. Yet a surprisingly large proportion of the apparently most obscure names did yield to a few days of concentrated effort in the stacks of Widener Library at Harvard. Where substantial doubts remain, I have generally left the entry with a query.

The variety of spelling encountered in the 1606 version is breathtaking. In indexing I have listed in parentheses only the main variants that occur; many minor ones, as well as those clarified or corrected in textual corrections at the foot of the page, have been omitted. Diversity in spelling requires numerous cross references, but there would have been far more had it not been decided at the start to eliminate many that fell within a few lines of the entry to which they referred.

A few simple abbreviations have been adopted as follows: emp. = emperor(s), k. = king(s), q. = queen(s), archd. = archduke(s), d. = duke(s), ct. = count(s), ctss. = countess, card. = cardinal, archbp. = archbishop, bp. = bishop(s).

Aaron, 392, 571, 648, 719
Abimelech, 744
Abraham, the patriarch, 47, 461, 538, 743
Abraham, k. of Ethiopia, 745
Abraham, pasha, *see* Ibrahim
Abraham bar Hiyya (Abraham Judaeus), 449
Abraham ibn Ezra, 439
Absalom (Absolon), 590
Abu Chemmu (Abuchemo), k. of Tlemsen, 410
Abuna Marc, *see* Mark
Abu Sa'id Othman (Abusahit, etc.), k. of Fez, 410, 416
Abu Zayyan (Abyamein), k. of Tlemsen, 410
Abydus, N376, N636
Academics, 7, 193, 457–459, 463&N, 560, 585
Accursius (Acursius), 48, 295, 763, 778
Acerrani, 76
Achab, *see* Ahab
Achaeans (Achaia), 79–81, 177, 187, 207, 258, 260, 268, 386, 420, 454, 620–622, 627^v, 659, 719
Achaeus, 454, 632^v, 666
Achilles, 35, 196
Achish (Achis), 651
Acilia, gens, 391

Acron, Helenius, 260
Acrotatus, 739
Actium, battle of, 98, 196, 263, 419, 451, 463
Actius, *see* Visconti, Azzo
Acursius, *see* Accursius
Adalbert (Albert), marquis of Franconia, 629^v
Adam, 15, 440–441
Adamites, N567
Adela, mother of Stephen, k. of England, 748
Adelaide (Adella), q. of France, 160
Adelstan, *see* Athelstan
Adherbal, k. of Numidia, 121
Adolphus, emp. of Germany, 221, 237
Adolphus, d. of Holstein-Gottorp, 81, 84, 209, 241
Adorni (Adornes), 712
Adosinda (Socina), wife of Silo, k. of Asturias, 748, 752
Adrastia, N436
Adrian, emp., *see* Hadrian
Adrian VI, pope, 661
Aeacus, Aeacidae, 392, 464&N, 500
Aebutia, gens, 391
Aebutius, tribune, 25, 336, 471
Aegean Islands, N690
Aegeus, 29

Aegina, Aeginetans, N29, 186
Aegypt, Aegyptians, *see* Egypt, Egyptians
Aelia, gens, 391
Aelius Tubero, Quintus, 10
Aelius Verus, *see* Verus
Aemilia, gens, 391
Aemilia de censoribus, lex, 301, 350
Aemilius, Paulus, or Paolo Emilio, N464
Aemilius Lepidus, Marcus, consul 187 B.C., 497–498, N636
Aemilius Lepidus, Marcus, triumvir, 199&N, 409, 419
Aemilius Lepidus Livianus, Mamercus, 347
Aemilius Mamercus or Mamercinus, Mamercus, 85, 281, 481, 638&N
Aemilius Paulus, Lucius, consul 216 B.C., 716
Aemilius Paulus, Lucius, consul 50 B.C., 421
Aemilius Paulus Macedonicus, Lucius, consul 182 B.C., 18, 30, 150, 178, 285, 451, 597, 601, 655, 667
Aemilius Regillus, Lucius, 635^v
Aemilius Scaurus, Marcus, 391, 396, 706, 773
Aemilius Scaurus (*error for* Lepidus), Marcus, consul 78 B.C., 497

A173

Index Nominum

Aeneas, 739
Aenobarbus, *see* Barbarossa
Aequi, 163
Aerodius, Petrus, or Pierre Ayraut, N182
Aeschines, 283, 289, 308
Aesculapius (Esculapius), 538
Aesop, 669
Aethiopia, Aethiopians, *see* Ethiopia, Ethiopians
Aetolians, 81&N, 163, 261, 268, 420, 429, 454, 564&N, 613, 620-621, 623-625, 627^v, 691
Africa, Africans (Affrike, Affrick, etc.), political institutions of, 47, 188, N203, 204, 222, 426, 507, 722; nature of peoples, 548, 553-555, 557-558, 560, 563, 567&N; slavery in, 38, 42-44; influence of stars on, 447-448; mentioned, 18, N29, 40, 45, 52, 66, 147-148, 164, N173, 177, 181, 201, 203, 218, 285, N292, 322, 386, 400, 411, 413, 416, N445, 451, 487, 503, 516, 536-537, 544, 549-550, 562, 565, 568, 571, 578, 596, 600, 602, 605, 630-631, 660, 662, 690&NN, 691, 707, 716, 719, 745, 753, 769
Africanus, *see* Scipio
Agamemnon, 10, 35, 196
Agapet II, pope, 633
Agatharchides, 538
Agathias (Agathius), 729
Agathocles, 420, 739, 745
Agde, 176
Agesilaus, 207, 215, 221, 494, 510, 516, 576, 599, 650, 737
Agesipolis, 436
Aggaeus, *see* Haggai
Agis, 187, 221, 471-472, 570
Agraria, lex, *see* Sempronia agraria
Agricola, George, 690
Agrigentum, 374, 420
Agrippa, *error for* Herod the Great?, 312
Agrippa, Herod I, k. of Judea, 676
Agrippa, Herod II, 662, 767
Agrippa, Menenius, *see* Menenius
Agrippa, Marcus Vipsanius, 30, 263, 692, 710&N
Agrippa Postumus, 728
Agrippina, 30
Agustín, Antonio, N114
Ahab (Achab), 224, 543, 582
Ahiah (Aiah), 360
Ahasuerus (Ahashuerosh, Assuerus), 102, 747
Aiguemont, *see* Egmont
Ailly, Pierre d' (Peter of Arliac), 444-445
Aimoin of Fleury (Aymon, Haimo), N118, 208
Aix, 266
Alamant (Allemand, Allemont), François, 169, 346, 575
Alanson, *see* Alençon
Alaric, 108

Alba Longa, Albani, N464, 494, N529, 635, 735, 775
Albania, Albanians, 235, 448, 681
Albany, Alexander Stewart, d. of, 735
Albergati (Albergat), Fabio, vi
Albericus, 732&N
Albert I, emp. of Germany and d. of Austria, 727
Albert II, emp. of Germany and d. of Austria, 726
Albert, k. of Poland, *see* John Albert
Albert II, *error for* Frederick I, d. of Austria, 733
Albert V, d. of Bavaria, 13, 84
Albert Alcibiades, margrave of Brandenburg, 312, 523, 632^v, 634^v
Albert, earl of Franconia, *see* Adalbert
Albizzi family (Albicis), 674
Albret, 13, 626, 748
Albumazar, 449
Alcabice or Alchabitius, 444
Alcazares, 557
Alcetas, 214
Alciati, Andrea, 135, 334, 389
Alcibiades, 18, 172, 422, 443, 547, 610, 737
Alcimus Siculus, 17
Alemdin or Almedin (Dalmendin), 416
Alençon (Alanson), 583&N, 743. *See also* Francis *and* John, d. of Alençon
Alet, N641
Alexander II, pope, 142-143
Alexander III, pope, 40, 145
Alexander IV, pope, 144-145
Alexander VI, pope, 126, 129, 525, 597, 623, 629^v, 660
Alexander the Great, 2, 57-58, 62, 104, 121, 204-206, 208, 229, 254, 410, N413, 451, 463, 464&N, 466, 494, 503-505, 513-514, 522-524, 534, 585, 594, 597, 600, 608, 683, 723, 735, 744
Alexander, emp. of Rome, *see* Severus, Alexander
Alexander Jagellon, k. of Poland, 652, 758
Alexander, prince of Albania, *see* Scanderbeg
Alexander of Imola, A71, N92, 131, 295, 299, N355, 461, 763-764
Alexander de Medici, *see* Medici
Alexander, tyrant of Pherae, 213, 417, 420, 423
Alexandria, 36, 57, 62, 375, 553, 661, 724
Algiers (Alger), 148, 451, 454, 612
Allemand, Allemont, *see* Alamant
Allen, J. W., A66
Almaigne, Almans, *see* Germany, Germans
Almansor (Mansor), caliph of Cordova, 503, 554

Álmos (Alme), 736
Alphonsus V, k. of Aragon, I of Naples, 31, 90, 93, 126, 748
Alphonsus, k. of Aragon, *error for* Ferdinand II, k. of Naples, 504
Alphonsus I, k. of Castile, 748
Alphonsus V, *error for* VI, k. of Castile, 595
Alphonsus VI, k. of Castile, 148
Alphonsus X, k. of Castile, 81, 108, 723, 725, 736, 738, 773
Alphonsus XI, k. of Castile, 124, 634^v
Alphonsus I, k. of Naples, *see* Alphonsus V, k. of Aragon
Alphonsus II, k. of Naples, 123, 661
Alphonsus, *error for* Ferdinand I, k. of Naples, 629
Alphonsus V, k. of Portugal, 739
Alphonsus, d. of Ferrara, *see* Este, Alfonso I d'
Alphonsus, ct. of Poitiers and Toulouse, 408&N, 514, N583, 742
Alphonsus, card. of Siena, *see* Petrucci, Alfonso
Alphonsus, astronomical tables of (compiled under Alphonsus X, k. of Castile), 439, 444, 445&N
Alps (Alpes), 134, 137-138, 143, 407, N464, 562, 579, 597, 655, 657, 721
Althamer, Andreas, 557
Althusius, Joannes, A18, A28
Alva, Fernando Alvarez de Toledo, d. of, 623, 666
Alvarez, Francisco, A48, 147, N188, 202, 507, 549, 558, 560, 597
Alviano, Bartolommeo d', 605
Aman, *see* Haman
Amasia, 410, 503, 636
Amasis, k. of Egypt, 401, N579, 678
Ambiani, N784
Ambiorix, 222
Amboise, 523, 784&N
Amboise, George d', 768
Ambracia, Ambraciots, 420, 657
Ambrose, St., bp. of Milan, 45, 314, 537, 648
Ambrun, *see* Embrun
America, *see* North America
Amiénois, N784
Amiens, 66, 119-120, 577
Amiot, *see* Amyot
Ammianus Marcellinus, 769
Ammonites, 35
Amorites, 35, 410
Amos, 84
Amours, Nicolas d', 770
Amphareus, *see* Aphareus
Amphictyonic League, 79&N
Amphipolites, 427, 711
Amulius, 735
Amurath I, k. of the Turks, 523, 656

A174

Index Nominum

Amurath, *error for* Bajazet I, k. of the Turks, 716
Amyntas, k. of Macedonia, 416
Amyot (Amiot), Jacques, 548
Anabaptists, 12, 380, 411, N567
Anacharsis, 157, 602, 702
Anagnini, 76
Anastasius I, emp. of the East, 19, 29, 208, 314, 382, 588
Anatolia (Natolia), 565
Anaxagoras, 535
Anaxandrides, k. of Sparta, 735
Anaxarchus, 104
Anaxilaus, tyrant of Rhegium, 420
Ancarano, Pietro de, 752
Ancona, 141, 142&N, 694
Ancus Martius, 179
Andreae, John, canonist, N322
Andrew II, k. of Hungary, 140, 613, N651
Andron, 584
Andronicus I, emp. of Constantinople, 214, 416
Andros, Andrians, 669
Androtion, 273
Anga, Mount, *see* Angua
Angers (Angiers), A3–A5, A7–A8, 371, 556–557, N565, 631ᵛ&N
Angiers, earl of, *see* Geoffrey, ct. of Anjou
Anglerie, house of, N205, 729. *See also* Visconti
Anglo-Saxons (Saxons, English Saxons, East Saxons, West Saxons), 463, 601, 612
Angoulême, 583&N, 743
Angua (Anga), Mount, 597, 745
Anjou, 13, 28, 116, 482, 579, 583&N, 784
Anjou, house of, 134, 139, 165, 230, 579, 731–732, 747–748. *See also* Charles; Francis; Fulk; Geoffrey; Henry; Lewis; *and* René, d. and ct. of Anjou
Anne, q. of France, 160
Anne, duchess of Bourbon, 743
Anne of Oldenburg, princess of East Friesland, N133
Anniball, *see* Hannibal
Anthony of Bourbon, k. of Navarre, 199
Anthony, d. of Lorraine, 170
Anthony, ct. of Vaudémont, 132
Antigonus, k. of Asia, 58, 104, 149, 208, 245, 253, 260, 281, 594, 723, 744
Antigonus Doson, k. of Macedon, 80–81, 187, 436
Antimachus Lyrius, of Teos, 441–442
Antioch, 51, 443
Antiochus I, Soter, k. of Syria, 209
Antiochus III, the Great, k. of Syria, 73, 378, 422, 454, 608, 613, N614, 622, 632ᵛ, 655, 658, 684
Antiochus IV, the Noble, k. of Syria, 392, 464, 538–539, N567, 603, 627ᵛ, 636, 719, 737

Antiochus VI, Theos, k. of Syria, 629, 714
Antiochus, philosopher, 27
Antipater, regent of Macedon, 619, 723
Antipater, *error for* Attalus, 417, 526
Antipater, father of Herod the Great, 416, 720
Antipater, philosopher, 27
Antiphon, an Athenian, 704
Antiphon of Rhamnus, Athenian orator, 584
Antonia, gens, 70, 391
Antonine emperors, 680, 734
Antoninus Pius, emp. of Rome, 30, 57, 135, 198, 366, 382, 453, 652, 672, 728, 751, 771
Antoninus of Forciglioni, St., archbp. of Florence, 426
Antonius, Marcus, the orator, 543
Antonius, Marcus, the triumvir, 39, 57, 98, 199, 372, 388, 393, 409, 413, 416, 419, 451, 463–464, 497, N553, 602, 636, 638, 658, 682, 697&N, 719, 743–744
Antonius de Butrio, N355
Antonius Hybrida, Caius, 350, 430
Antwerp (Anwerpe), A10, A29, 465, 530, N636ᵛ, 662
Aod, *see* Ehud
Apelles (Appelles), a Macedonian, 714
Apelles, painter, 400
Apennine mountains (Appenin, etc.), 164, 432, 562, N564, 626ᵛ
Aphareus (Amphareus), 186, 198, 742
Aphytis, 577
Apion (Appian), 293
Apollo, 187, 461, N462, 471, 619, 652–653, 682
Apollonia (Appollonia), 249
Apollonius of Tyana, 399, 719
Apollophanes, 684
Appenzell (Apenzel, etc.), 60, 76, 78, 247, 250, 268, 604
Appian, *see* Apion
Appian, historian, 39, 208, 303, N463, 655, 690, 726
Appiano, Jacopo d', 745
Appius Claudius, consul 460 B.C., 495
Appius Claudius, decemvir, 337, 416, 758
Appius Claudius, consul 349 B.C., 391
Appius Claudius, consul 212 B.C., 375
Appius Claudius, consul 185 B.C., 620
Appius Claudius Caecus, censor 312 B.C., 48, 246, 301, 350, 587
Appius Claudius Regillensis, consul 495 B.C., 531–532,˙716
Appius Claudius Sabinus, consul 471 B.C., 302&N, 345, 377
Appuleius or Apuleius, 9
Apronius, Cnaeus, 635ᵛ
Apuleia, lex, 575

Apulia, 273, 661&N
Aquila, tribune, 220
Aquileia (Aquilia), 534
Aquilia, gens, 391
Aquinas, St. Thomas, A25, 357, 586
Aquitaine, 170, 254, 549, N565, N773
Aquitaine, Widdo, or Gui, d. of, 731&N
Arabia, Arabians, 39, 205, 361, 393, 400, 412, 439, 445&N, 448, 454, 464, 549–550, 552, 559, 563, N567, 579, 596, 602, 658, 719, 722
Aragon (Arragon), 31, 90, 92–93, 96, 122, 125–127, 139–140, 176, 199, 230, 383, 464, 504, 527, 562, 622, 625ᵛ, 629, 687, 694&N, 742, 746–748
Aramont, Gabriel de Luetz, baron d', 628ᵛ
Aratus, 80, 110, 213, 221, 227, 659
Arbaces, 412, 417, 464&N
Arbela (Arbella), battle of, 451, 454, 463, 597
Arcadia, Arcadians, 429, 456–457, 564, 628ᵛ
Arcadius, emp. of the East, 29, 227
Archelaus, k. of Macedon, 417
Archelaus, tyrant of Candia, 420
Archeptolemus (Archiptolemus, Archiptolome), 584
Archias, polemarch of Thebes, 523
Archias, Licinius, 65
Archidamus, k. of Sparta, 525
Archimedes, 688, 699
Arco (Arques), 133
Ardeates, 429
Areus, k. of Sparta, 739
Argentraeus or Bertrand d'Argentré, seneschal of Rennes, 118&N
Argos, Argives, 198, 420, 428, 431, 481, 570, 631
Argyll (Argueil), 117
Ariander, 177
Arians, Arianism (Arrians), 382&N, 537, 539, N567
Arias de Avila, Pedro (Pedrarias), 560
Aribert, *see* Chariberg II
Aricini, 76
Ariminum, *see* Rimini
Ariobarzanes, 719
Aristaenus (Aristenus), 622
Aristides, "the Just," 105, 215, 249, 251, 392, 413, 497, 610, 619, 704, 716
Aristides, Aelius, rhetorician, 546&N
Aristippus, 594
Aristobulus, princes of Judaea, 196, 720, 735
Aristocrates, k. of the Messenians, 416
Aristocrates, an Athenian, 157
Aristodemus, 186, 198, 741
Aristogiton, 219&N, 221, 418

A175

Index Nominum

Aristotle, on the *summum bonum*, 4, 6&N, 761; concept of the polis, 8, 10, 50, 154–156, 571, 707&N; the citizen, 53; types of state, 184&N; the mixed state, 192, 193&N; on monarchy, 200, N205, 206–207, 225, N409, 719, 722&N, 723; on aristocracy, 242, 243&N, 702; on democracy, 248–250, 702; on magistracies, 278–279, 283&N, 294, 480, 485, 487; on slavery, 33, 387; on numbers, 457–459, N460, 462; on music, 456–457, 646; on education, 645&N; on temperament and climate, 548, N552, N554, 557–558, N567; on justice, 756, 772, 775, 780–781; 782&N; on punishing heresy, 536; compared to Bodin, A9, A25, A28; and Peter Ramus, A3, A25, A27; conflicting attitudes of Bodin and Knolles towards, A41, A52, A55; study of, prescribed in Oxford, A54–A55; mentioned, A42, A69, A90, v, 19, 47, 69, 121, 166, 186, 204, 265, N308, N333, 357, 362, 392–393, 395, 397, 399, N422, 429, 446, 461, N481, 505, N537, 542–543, N558, 572, 577–578, 595–596, 637, 653, N759

Aristotle of Argos, the dialectician, 213

Arles, 42, 131, 134–135, 138–139, 627ᵛ

Arliac, Peter of, see Ailly, Pierre d'

Armagnac, Bernard VI, ct. of, 529

Armagnac (Armaignac), Bernard VIII, ct. of, 626

Armagnac (Armaignac), Jean V, ct. of, 632

Armenia, Armenians, 121, 578, 613, 625, 629, 631ᵛ, 722, 725

Arnaud (Arnald) de Corbie, 173

Arnobius, 17

Arnold, *error for* Renaud III?, ct. of Burgundy, 122

Arnoldus de Villa Nova, 449

Arnulph, St., 730

Arnulphus, emp. of Germany, 729

Arpinum, Arpinates (Arpinas, Arpine), 54, 76, 390

Arques, see Arco

Arragon, see Aragon

Arras, 122

Arras, treaties of, 122, 170, N614, 633

Arsaces, k. of Parthia, 735

Artabanus, 200, 507

Artabazanes or Ariabignes, 737

Artabazus, 413

Artaxerxes I, k. of Persia, 202, 466. *See also* Darius Longimanus

Artaxerxes II, k. of Persia, 58, 431, 737. *See also* Darius Mnemon

Artaxerxes III, k. of Persia, *see* Darius Ochus

Artemidorus, 18

Arthur I, d. of Brittany, 116, 118&N, 140, 579, 738

Arthur II, d. of Brittany, 120, 127, 167

Artois (Arthoise, etc.), 66, 127, 170, 526, 738&N, 746

Arzila (Arzille), 410

Ascanius, 738–739

Asconius Pedianus, 303, N304, 329, N390, 487&N, 642, 653, N656

Asdruball, *see* Hasdrubal

Asellius, 351

Asia, Asians, 22, 29, 39, 42, 44, 66, 71, 114, 119, 147–148, 152, N173, 177, 181, 200–202, 203&N, 204, 206, 209, 222, 262, 322, 360, 381, 437&N, 440, N445, 447–448, 487, 537, 542, 546, 550, 554, 562, 565, N567, 571, 625ᵛ, 686, 722–723, 737, 753, 769. *See also* Asia Minor

Asia Minor, 51, 56, 81, 104, 111, 149, 164, 172, 186, 209, 253, 314, 367, 378, 407, 411–412, 422, 454, 457, 516, 552, 559, 566, N567, 594, 613, 622, 627ᵛ, 632ᵛ, 636, 657–659, 668, N690, 722–723

Asmonaeans (Azmoneans, etc.), 196, 392, 719, 769

Asopus, river, 563

Aspremont or Apremont, 59, 132

Assaracus, 735

Assemberg, 83

Assuerus, *see* Ahasuerus

Astarte, *see* Venus

Asti, 114, N729

Assyria, Assyrians (Asiria, Assiria, etc.), 47, 148, 152, 200, 204, 206, 208, 223, 389, 412, N413, 416–417, N447, 463, 464&N, 482, 485, 527, 550, 565, 682, 718, 722, 741, 747

Atabalipa or Atahualpa (Atabalippa), k. of Peru, 557, 631ᵛ, 667, 735

Atelia (?), 417

Atella, 375

Ateria Tarpeia or Aternia Tarpeia, lex, 296

Aterius or Aternius, Aulus, 298

Athaliah, 747

Athanasius, 724

Athelstan (Adelstan), 116

Athenaeus, 17, 268, N551, N565

Athenagoras, 382

Athens, Athenians (Athence, Atheniensians), as a monarchy, 206, 225, 413, 500, 719, 722; the lawgivers, iv, 21, 103, 161, 259, 268, 383, 395, 471, 757, 761, 775, 777; the Pisistratidae, 219&N, 418, 481; as a democracy, 193, 246, 421–424, 429, 531, 534, 543–544, 717–718; defects of democracy at, 510, 517, 702–706; Thirty Tyrants, 110, 227, 230, 263; popular assembly, 162, 168, 172, 245, 256, 280–281, 294; procedure in assembly, 48, 247, 273, 344, 470; senate, 157, 267, 277; Areopagus, 261, 271, 277&N, 278, 488, 492, 515; magistracies, 243, 249, 284, 308, 326, 392, 482, 645–646, 769; Archons, 86, 197, 354, 420, 497, 605; laws and customs, 18, 29, 36, 102, 380, 392, 555, 576, 584, 586, 610, 639, 641, 776, 780; ostracism, 251, 431, 588; citizenship and aliens, 48–49, 53, 58–60, 62, 64–65; population, 38, 427, 578, 640; nature of the people, 399, 545, 546&N, 547, 563, 565; public finance and coinage, 177, 182, 651, 654, 678, N683; external relations, A70, 51, 214, 598, 612, 619–620, 624–625, 652, N660, 669; Peloponnesian War, 101, 186, 430, 443, 454, 541, 604, 633ᵛ; domestic history, 105, 432–433; force of numbers in history of, 463&N; mentioned, 18, 37, 297, 394, N422, 522–523, N632, 706

Athens, Walter of Brienne, d. of, 423, 425

Athos, Mount, 537

Atilia, gens, 391

Atilia (Attilia), lex, 351

Atilius Regulus (Attilius), Marcus, consul 267 B.C., 626

Atilius Regulus Serranus (Serranus), Marcus, consul 257 B.C., 401

Atilius Serranus (Attilius), Aulus, consul 170 B.C., 622, 635ᵛ

Atilius Serranus, Caius, curule aedile 193 B.C., 404

Atinia, lex, 274

Atlantic (Atlantike), ocean, 562, 602

Atlas, Mount, 549, 554&N, 562–563, N565

Atreus, 198, 736

Attabalippa, *see* Atabalipa

Attalus I, k. of Pergamus (Asia), 81

Attalus III, k. of Pergamus (Asia), 111, 407, 576, 657

Attica, 546, 637, 703

Atticus, Pomponius, 59, 103, N279, 461, 580

Attila, k. of the Huns, 202, 534, 567

Attilia, Attilius, *see* Atilia; Atilius

Audenarde or Oudenarde, 376

Augsburg (Ausbourg, Auspurge, etc.), 13, 82, 84, 133, 235, 237–238, 240&N

Augustine, St., 298, N436, N512, N645, 724, 793

Augustulus, Romulus, emp. of the West, 463, 464&N

A176

Index Nominum

Augustus (Octavianus, Octavius), emp. of Rome, life and character, 30&N, 413, 452–453, 461, 502, 516, 607, 658, 719; career until made emperor, 39, 199&N, 291–292, 409, 451, 497, 636, 638, 734, 743–744; constitutional position as emperor, 91, 98, 107, 157, 196–197, 201, 212&N, 710; and the Senate, 61, 259–261, 266, 275, 396, 487; administrative policies, 39, 57, 149, 205, 262–263, 329–330, 343, 346, 384, 419, 440, 508, 602, 604, 610–611, 615, 673, 678, 680, 728&N, 745; and the Jews, 366–367, 416, 537; clemency and integrity as a judge, 2, 36, 341, 431, 509–511, 521, N593, 630; legislation, 17, 158, 391, 405, 578, 665, 670; mentioned, 24, 54, 160, N283, 463, 464&N, 682, 692, N694, 700, 727, 735
Augustus, elector of Saxony, 555
Aurelia, gens, 391
Aurelia, lex, 266, 308
Aurelianus, emp. of Rome, 30, 375, 452, 747
Aurelius Antoninus, Marcus, emp. of Rome, 30, 104, 198, 201, 262, 415, 479, 508, 516, 582, 636^v, 728, 751
Aurelius Victor, Sextus, N681
Auriol, Blaise d', N445, 446&N
Ausimum or Osimo (Ausun), 141
Ausonii, 552
Auspurge, Ausbourg, etc., see Augsburg
Austin, John, A19
Austria, Austrians, A61, 151, 452, 750
Austria, house of, 13, 78, 82&N, 83–84, 89, 167, 210, N240, 434, 616, 624, 630^v, 712, 753
Austria, duchy of, d. of, archd. of, 90, 119, 121–122, 170, 209, N614, 627, 746, 750, 752. See also Charles V; Ferdinand I; Maximilian I; and Sigismund, emp. of Germany; Philip I, k. of Spain
Autun (Austun), 54, 58, 79, 207, 479
Auvergne (Avergne), 54, 79, 94&N, 554, 562, N565, 583&N, 669, 743
Auvergne (Auverne), William, ct. of, 731–732
Auxerre, 428, 667, 683
Avaricum, 79
Aventine, Mount, 195
Avignon, 143, 145, 667, 690, 694, 698
Aymon, see Aimoin of Fleury
Azariah (Azarias), son of Nathan, 360
Azariah (Azarias), grandson of Zadok, 360
Azmoneans, see Asmonaeans

Azo (Azon), jurist, 327, 329, 330&N, 333–334, 768

Baal (Bahal), 224
Babington, Anthony, A11
Babington, Francis, rector of Lincoln, A53
Babylon (Babilon), 10, 152, 223, 446, 465–466, 551&N, 669, 671, 719
Bactrians, 215
Baden (Bade), in Aargau, 73, 77, 83
Baebia, lex, 281, 284
Baebius (Bebius), Quintus, tribune, 610
Baeotians, see Boeotians
Baglioni family (Baillions, Baleones), 130, 420
Baglioni, Giovan Paolo (Paul Baillon), tyrant of Perugia, 630^v
Bahal, see Baal
Bailly (Balley), Jean, 684
Bajamontaines, see Tiepolo
Bajazet I, k. of the Turks, 221, 452, 600
Bajazet, error for Amurath I, N523
Balbus, Lucius Cornelius, 61, N72, 255, 263
Baldus, jurist, A71, 17, 103, 108, 137, 150, 155, 171, N355, 359, 547, 753–754
Baldwin V, ct. of Flanders, 730, 732
Baldwin IX, ct. of Flanders and emp. of the East, 443
Baleones, see Baglioni family
Baliol, John, k. of Scotland, 117
Balley, see Bailly
Baltic (Baltique) Sea, 66, 548
Baltic towns, see Hanseatic towns
Bamberg, 84
Banaia, see Benaiah
Bandocader or Malik al-Zahir Rukn al-din Bibars Bundukdari, sultan of Egypt, 727
Baptista Mantuanus, 566
Bar, 170
Barbarigo, Agostino (Augustin Barbarin), doge of Venice, 472
Barbarius or Barbatius, Philippus, 68
Barbarossa, Khair Eddin (Hariadenus Aenobarbus, Ariadin Barbarousse, etc.), 2, 410, 612
Barbarossa, Cairadin (error for Horush), 612
Barbarus, Hermolaus, 258
Barbary, 36, 44, 141, 381, 411, 549–550, 628^v, 694, 711
Barcelona, 125, 693, 748
Bardylis (Bargulus), pirate, 3
Barnabus, see Visconti, Bernabò
Barnagais (Barnagas), lord of Arquiquo, 148
Barnard, see Bernard
Barrier, Pierre, 680
Barthélemy (Bartholomew, etc.), Jean(?), 317, 764

Bartolus (Bartholus), A71, 40–41, 91, 135, 295, 299, N355, N366, 394–396, 408, 461, 628&N, N629, N633, 636^v, N719, 737, 763, 774
Baruch, 539
Baseggi family (Bassiens), 711
Basel (Basil, Basill), 76–78, 149, 234, 264–265, 474, 497, 690, 706, N736, 786
Basel, Council of, N606, N736
Basil, St., 40
Basil (Basilius), k. of Muscovy, 149, 738
Basilius, emp. of the East, 452
Bassefontaine, bp. of Limoges, see L'Aubespine
Bassiens, see Baseggi
Bassigny, 73, N614
Batavi, N558
Báthory (Bathor), see Stephen, k. of Poland
Baume, see La Baume
Bautru des Matras, Jan, A12
Bavaria (Bauyere, Baviere), 13, 83, 84, 158, N203, 753. See also Lewis of Bavaria, emp. of Germany
Bayard, Pierre du Terrail, chevalier de, 588
Bayencourt (Baynecourt), sieur de, 740
Bayonne, Jean V de Monstiers, bp. of, 248
Béarn, 120, 133, 529
Beaucaire, 135
Beaujeu (Bellojoci), 133–134, 743
Beaumont, Raoul, vicomte de, 514
Beauvais (Beauvis, Beauvois), 79, 94, 498, N514, 730
Bebius, see Baebius
Bede (Beda), 444
Bedford, John, d. of, 173
Belgae, N565
Belisarius (Bellisarius), 507, 585
Bellièvre, Pomponne de, seigneur de Grignon, 248
Bellojoci, see Beaujeu
Belluga, Peter, 90, 136
Bembo, Pietro, card., 190, 427
Benadab, see Benhadad
Benaiah (Banaia), 360
Benedict XII, pope, 140, 146
Benedict XIII, pope, 145
Benevento, 123, 139
Benhadad II (Benadab), k. of Syria, 543
Beni Iezneten (Benizenete, etc.), 711
Benjamin, tribe of, 56, 360, 622, 639, 734
Bentivogli, rulers of Bologna, 420, 525, 632
Beotia, see Boeotia
Berdeboc or Birdibek, k. of Tartary, 744
Bergamo, 605, 624
Bernard (Barnard), k. of Italy, 738
Bernard of Clairvaux, St., 461

A177

Index Nominum

Berne, Bernese (Bernois, etc.), A80, 52, 58, 60, 68, 74, 76&N, 77–78, 82, 149, 234, 241, 250–251, 264–265, 360, 497, 615, 618–619, 632ᵛ, 690, 695, 706, 786
Berosus, 206&N, 466
Berry (Berrie), 170, 176, 626, 667
Besançon, N690
Bias, 707
Bibbiena (Bibiene), Bernardo Dovizi, card., 150
Bibulus, Calpurnius, 495, 592, 702
Bichi (Dichi), Alessandro, ruler of Siena, 423
Bienne or Biel, 77
Bigot, Emery, avocat du roi, 174
Bishop, George, A59, A62
Bithynia, Bithynians, 51, 61, 111, 121, 407, 657
Bitricus, k. of Scotland, N748
Bizance, Bizantines, etc., see Byzantium, Byzantines
Bizaque, see Byzacium
Black Forest, 566
Blanche, daughter of Louis IX, 127
Blanche of Castile, 127, 173, 748
Blancmesnil, see Potier
Blois, 41, 176, 180, 652
Blois (Bloyse), Estates General of, A7–A9, A72, N95, 322&N, 370, 403, 671–672, 685, 692, 700
Bloqueaux (Bloqui), François, sieur de, 740
Boccaccio (Boccace), Giovanni, 461
Bocconi (Bochonians), 711
Bodillon or Bodilo (Bodile), 417
Bodin, Guillaume, A3
Bodin de Montguichet, Jean, A7
Boeotia, Boeotians (Beotia, Baeotians), 75, 360, 386
Boethius, Anicius Manlius Severinus, 54
Boethius, Hector, 88
Bohemia, Bohemians, A61, 13, 27, 65, N94, 134, 150, 209, 413, 435, 557, 563, N567, 628, 630ᵛ, 725–728, 733, 753
Boii, 655
Boleslas II, error for III, k. of Poland, 742
Bolloine, Bologne, see Boulogne
Bologna (Bolonia, Bononia, Boulongne la Grace, etc.), 64, 70, 76, 144, 327, 420, 498, 525, 563, 694, 768
Bonacossi (Bonacolse), Passerino, 417
Bondelmont, see Buondelmonti
Boniface VIII, pope, 145, 383, 452
Bonne Esperance, cape, see Good Hope
Bononia, see Bologna
Bononia, Henry of, see Henry of Burgundy, ct. of Portugal
Bordeaux (Bourdeaux, Burdeax), A84, 62–63, 266, 356, 359, 369, 378, 541–542, 753

Borgia, Cesare, d. of Valentinois, A70, 376, 493, 525, 597, 629ᵛ
Borgia, Lucrezia (Lucrece), 129
Borneo (Borney), 506
Borso (Borsus), d. of Ferrara, see Este
Borysthenes (Boristhenes), see Dnieper
Bouillon (Buillon), 59, 140, 144, 148
Boulogne (Bolloine, Boulleine, Bologne, Boulongne), 132, 452, 671, 748
Boulogne, Henry of, see Henry of Burgundy, ct. of Portugal
Boulongne la Grace, etc., see Bologna
Bouquet, Dom Martin, N730
Bourbon (Burbon), house of, 134, 171, 465, 626, 743, 754. See also Anthony of Bourbon; Charles, card. of Bourbon; Charles, d. of Bourbon
Bourbonnais (Burbonnois), 41
Bourdeaux, see Bordeaux
Bourdin, Maurice, see Gregory VIII, antipope
Bourdorg, see Burgdorf
Bourges, A4, A8, 54, 79, N348, 588
Bourgongne, Bourguignons, etc., see Burgundy, Burgundians
Bouvines (Bovines), 433
Brabant, 132, N667
Brandenburg (Brandebourg, etc.), 312, 523, 632ᵛ
Bray-sur-Seine, 583&N
Brazil, Brazilians (Brezill, Brasiles, etc.), 35, 555, 562
Bremen (Breme, Bresme), 84, 241
Brenne, John, see John of Brienne
Brennus, 559
Brescia (Bresse, Brixia), 66, 375, 624
Bretigny, treaty of, 121, 254, 631
Bridgewater, John, rector of Lincoln, A53
Brie, 685
Brinon, Jean, 514
Britain, Britons (Brittaine, Brittaines, Brittons, Great Britain), A18–A19, A40, 395, 447, N558, 559, 601, 612. See also England, English
Brittany, Bretons (Brittaine, Brittanie, Britaine, Bretaigne, Britaigne), 13, 60, N92, 116–117, 118&N, 120, 127, 140, 167, 171, 176, 180, 384, N385, 482, 513–514, 577, 579, 619, 632, 693, 738–739, 776
Brixia, see Brescia
Bruno (Brunon), see Leo IX, pope
Brunswick (Brunsvich, etc.), 83, 131, 241
Brussels (Bruxels), 239
Brutus, Lucius Junius, consul 509 B.C., 28, 260–261, 417
Brutus, Lucius Junius, tribune 494 B.C., 619

Brutus, Marcus Junius, praetor ca. 142 B.C., 63
Brutus, Marcus Junius, assassin of Caesar, 33, 219, 417, 419, 745
Buchanan, George, N35
Buda or Budapest, 451
Budé (Budeus), Guillaume, 490, 690
Budelius, Renerus, A83
Bugia, 147, 426, 563, 565
Buillon, see Bouillon
Bulgarians, 630
Buondelmonti (Bondelmont) family, 429
Bura, 437&N
Burbon, Burbonnois, see Bourbon; Bourbonnais
Burdeaux, see Bordeaux
Burgdorf (Bourdorg), 615
Burghley, William Cecil, lord, A7
Burgundie, free, see Franche-Comté
Burgundy, Burgundians (Bourgongne, Bourgundie, Bourguignons, Burgundions, etc.), 59, 122, 127, 132, 143, 171, 177, 202, 208, 376, 384, 527, 550, 623, 626ᵛ, 632, 662, 672, 694, 743. See also Charles the Bold; Eudes; Hugh; John; Philip; Robert; and Rudolph, d. of Burgundy
Burke, Edmund, A23
Burrus (Burra), Afranius, 319
Bursec (Buzac), Étienne d'Olmières, called, 385
Busiris, k. of Egypt, 215, 547
Byzacium (Bizaque), 429
Byzantium, Byzantines (Bizance, Bizantines, etc.), A51, 18, 410, 443, 598, 631. See also Constantinople; Greece

Caboche, 223
Cadalus (Cadol), bp. of Parma, see Honorius II, antipope
Cadde, Cade, League of the, see God's House, League of
Caecilia, gens, 391
Caecilia de censoribus, lex, 646
Caecilius, Sextus, 98
Caecilius Metellus, see Metellus
Caepio, Ruscius, see Ruscius
Caerites (Cerites), 76, 635
Caesar, Caius Julius, as authority on the Gauls, 17, 22, 35, 71, 79, 178, 207, 222, 393, 479, 495, 499, 552, 564, 566, N631ᵛ, 647, 669, 767; on the Germans, 362, 559&N, N561; on the Britons, 557, N558; on the Helvetians, 50; on the Alexandrians, 553; character of, 220, 226, 253, 263, 419, 421, 521, 610; early career of, 57, 188, 205, 261, 274, 352, 356, 372, 429, 495, 592, 654, 702; and Pompey, 291, 423, 497, 602; and the triumvirate, 499, 706; dictatorship of, 30, 51, N54, 56, 86, 175, 220, 259–260,

A178

Index Nominum

384, 391, 416, 420, 430, 448, 481, 510, 558, 638; as military leader, 162, 290, 498, N602, 609, 655, 667; death of, 110, 219, 254–255, 417, 461, 745; mentioned, 3, 33, 47, 88, 199, 227, N275, 298, 448, 587, 597–598
Caesar, Caius, grandson of Augustus, 30, 461, 728
Caesar, Lucius, jurist, 348
Caesar, Lucius, grandson of Augustus, 30, 728
Caesarion, 558
Cahors, 176
Cairadin, see Barbarossa
Cairo (Caire, Grand Caire), 487, 612
Caius, see Caesar, Caius
Cajetan, Tommaso de Vio, card., 93, N513
Calabria, Ferdinand, d. of, 379, 594, 602
Calais, 72, 127
Calange, 631^v
Calatia, 375
Calavius, Pacuvius, 499, 532
Calcedonians, see Chalcedonians
Caldea, Caldeans, see Chaldea, Chaldeans
Caleb, 639
Calembourg, see Kalundborg
Calicut (Calecut), 20, 147, 660
Caligula, emp. of Rome, 30, 99, 169, 196, 213, 215, 226, 244, 324–325, 366, 416, 418, 511, 518, 555, 582, 585, 638, 642, 671, 679
Calixtus II, pope, 143
Calixtus III, pope, 574
Callicratidas (Callicratides), 207, 591, 650
Callimachus, N607
Callippus (Calippus), 745
Callisthenes (Calisthenes), 121, 446, 514
Callistratus (Calistratus), jurist, 305–306
Calpurnia, gens, 391
Calpurnia de ambitu (Calphurnia), lex, 592
Calvin, Jean, 224–225, 462
Calvinism, Calvinists, A4, A18–A19, A69
Calvisson, 652
Cambar, 147, 660
Cambrai (Cambray), 66, 122, 135, 616, N662
Cambrai (Cambray), treaty of (1508), 625^v, 627
Cambrai (Cambray, Cambresis), treaty of (1559), see Cateau-Cambrésis
Cambridge, A62, A65, v
Cambyses (Cambises), k. of Persia, 204, N413, 415, 466, 561, 734
Camden, William, A43, A58, A62
Camillus, Marcus Furius, 14, 282, 421, 607&N, 655, 706

Camillus, Furius, *error for* Aulus Cornelius Cossus, 219
Campagne, see Champagne
Campania, Campanians, 142&N, 189, 274, 375, 499, N564, N614, 633^v. *See also* Capua, Capuans
Campania, the Prior of, *see* Strozzi
Campanus, Joannes Antonius, N559
Campion, Edmund, A10, A40, N537
Campson Gaurus or al Ashraf Qansuh al-Ghauri, sultan of Egypt, 205, 410, 725
Canades (*error for* Cobades?), k. of Persia, 416
Cananor or Cannanor (Canor), 147, 660
Canary Islands (Canaries), 61, 126, 140
Canaye, Jacques de, N521
Candie, Candiots, *see* Crete, Cretans
Cannae (Cannas, Cannes), 38, 165, 189, 464, 468, 608, 628^v
Canor, *see* Cananor
Canossa, Ludovico di, 623
Cantabrian mountains, 562
Canterbury, A57, A60, 116, 140, 176, 267
Canuleia, lex, 243, 249, 391, 577, 588
Canuleius, Caius, 413, 758
Canute IV, k. of Denmark, 117
Cape Province, A18
Capet family, 209, 729–730. *See also* Hugh Capet, k. of France
Capito, Wolfgang Fabricius, 137
Capitolinus, *see* Sestius Capitolinus
Cappadocians (Capadocians), 20, 719
Capponi family (Caponyes), 674
Capua, Capuans (Capoua, Capouans), 319, 375, 433, 468, 532–533, 551, 633–633^v, 635, 654. *See also* Campania, Campanians
Capua (Capoua), the Prior of, *see* Strozzi
Caracalla, Antoninus, emp. of Rome, 214&N, 226, 318–319, 375, 417, N561, 629, 745, 773
Caracciolo, Giovanni, prince of Melfi, 528
Caracciolus, assassin, *see* Scoronconcolo
Caramania, 56, 725
Caranus, k. of Macedon, 464&N
Carcassonne, 563
Cardan, Jerome, 442–443, 447, 558
Carinthia, duchy of, 89–90
Carloman (Carlomaine), k. of the Franks, 730
Carlstadt, Andrew Bodenstein of, N567
Carmelites, A3–A4, A12, A23
Carneades, A70, 535

Carobert or Charles, k. of Hungary, 150, 738
Carola Charlet, *see* Charlotte
Carolingians (Carlingues), 729
Carolois, *see* Charolais
Carpathian mountains, 562, N565
Carré, an embezzler, N685
Carthage, Carthaginians (Carthaginensians, etc.), government and magistracies, 166, 261–262, 265, 420, 442, 478–480, 498, 606, 722, 762; history and laws, 61, 148, 429, 522, 525–526; relations with Rome, 52, 162–164, 362, 422, 454, 469, 496, 530, 597, 603, 609, 612, 626, 631–632, 635, N656, 658, 665; nature of the people, 546–547, N551, 555, N564, 565, 635^v; mentioned, 178, 422, N464, 518, 663, 702, 774. *See also* Poeni; Punic Wars
Carthage, Council of, N645
Carthusians (Chartrens), 474, 574
Carvilius Maximus Ruga, Spurius, 19
Casimir I, k. of Poland, 557
Casimir III, the Great (Cazimire, etc.), k. of Poland, 64, 163, 381, 435, 726, 750, 779
Casmander, pasha, 686
Cassander, k. of Macedon, 619
Cassia, gens, 391
Cassia, lex, 391
Cassia tabellaria, lex, 344
Cassiodorus (Cassiodore), Magnus Aurelius, 10, 30, 100, 168, 259, 263, 394, 481, 503, 539, 610, 641, 649, 677, 765
Cassius, father of Cassius Viscellinus, 23
Cassius, Avidius, 582
Cassius Longinus, Caius, consul 171 B.C., 292
Cassius Longinus, Caius, praetor 44 B.C., 219, 447
Cassius Longinus, Caius, consul 30 A.D. and jurist, 38, 305, 374, 396
Cassius Viscellinus, Spurius, 705
Castelnau, Michel de, sieur de la Mauvissière, A34
Castile, (Castill, Castille), 81, 124, 126–127, 136, 148, 173, 199, 229, 383, 464, 516, 595, 603, 625^v, 634^v, 656, 660, 683, 694&N, 736, 738, 740, 746, 748–749, 773
Catana, 420
Cateau-Cambrésis (Cambray, Cambresis), treaty of (1559), 162, 553, 625^v
Catharo, *see* Cattaro
Catherine, *see* Katherine
Catholics, Catholicism (Roman rites, etc.), A5, A7, A9–A13, A40, A53, 60, 77–78, 84, 381, 382&N, 474, 536, 537&N, N567, 625, 731. *See also* Rome, Church of

A179

Index Nominum

Catilina (Cateline, Catilin, etc.), Lucius Sergius, 24, 54, 56, 160, 328, 350, 352, 397–398, 430, 523, 774
Cato, *error for* Caius Flavius Fimbria?, 243
Cato, Marcus Porcius, the Censor, A70, 16, 19, 28, 36, 172, 181–182, 312, 327, 380&N, 390&N, 400–401, 489, 495, 497, 510, 531, 546, 572, N577, 578, 610, 647, 651, 670&N, 706, 754, 788&N
Cato Uticensis, Marcus Porcius, 162, 286, 294, 350, 421, 499, 532, 587, 703
Cattaro (Catharo), 235
Catulus, *see* Luctatius
Caulis, *see* Du Choul
Caux, N331, 577&N, 579, 784
Cazimir, Cazimire, *see* Casimir
Cecropidae, 392
Cecrops, 205
Cedrenus (Cedrinus), Georgius, 507, 730
Celestines, 574
Celsus, the philosopher, 382
Celsus, Cornelius, A73, 690
Celsus, Juventius, 287
Celtae (Celtes), 22, 43, 393, 413, 482, 550, 552, 562, N565, 719, 722, 769
Celtiberians, 608
Censorinus, author, 347, 460, 464
Censorinus, Lucius Marcius, 52
Centurione (Centenier), Adamo, 574
Ceperano, 142&N
Cercasse or Barkuk al-Daher, sultan of Egypt, 727
Ceres, 339
Cerites, *see* Caerites
Cervia (Cervie), 624
Cesarini, Giuliano (St. Julian), card., 628
Ceylon, 205
Chaerea (Cherea, Chereas), Cassius, 213, 555
Chaeroneia (Cherronea, etc.), 48, 246
Chalcedonians (Calcedonians), 631
Chalcis, Chalcidians (Chalcide), 427, 597
Chaldea, Chaldeans (Caldea, Caldeans, Chaldies, etc.), 18, 199, N413, 439–441, 446–447, 450, 454, 466–467, 499, 539, 559, 597
Chaldean (Caldean) Interpreter, the, *see* Jonathan ben Uzziel
Châlons, 41, 514&N
Cham, *see* Ham
Chambord (Chambort), 83, 634ᵛ
Champagne (Campagne, Champaigne), 20, 66, 331, 428, 482, 514, 583, 617, 738, 748
Charibert I (Cherebert), k. of Paris, 741
Charibert II (Aribert), k. of Aquitaine, 741

Charilaus, k. of Sparta, 714, N738, 739
Charlemagne or Charles the Great (Charlemaigne, etc.), emp. of the West, 39, 118, 137–139, 142, 146–147, 151, 198, 229, 236, 256, 283, 434–436, 449–450, 463, N464, N543, 568, 590, 647, 697, 729–730, 738, 740, 773
Charles IV, emp. of Germany, 13, 91, 122, 128–130, 132, 134–135, 142–143, 725, 727–728
Charles V, emp. of Germany, position as Emperor, 81, 93, 123, 128, 144–145, 225&N, 238–239, 710, 728; policies in Germany, 84, 237, 523, 716; in Italy, 66&N, 67–68, 87, 172, 526, 617, 627ᵛ, 668; in the Low Countries, 59, 378–379, 574&N, 662; in Spain, 435, 594, 602; in the New World, 42–43, 46, 203, 656; financial policies, 674–675, 694; relations with France, 72, 150, 434, 452, 528, 606, 613, 626ᵛ, 627&N, 631, 632–632ᵛ, 634ᵛ, 635ᵛ–636, N667, 726; as vassal of France, 121–122, 124–127; foreign relations elsewhere, 82, 141, 360, 451, 628, 660, 749–750; mentioned, A42, 83, 135, 170, 253, 410–411, 416, 418, 452–453, N513, 549, 600, 618
Charles I, the Bald, k. of France, 118, 131, 138–139, 151, 428, 453, 633, 729, 732, 736
Charles II, the Fat, k. of France, N463
Charles III, the Simple, k. of France, 217, 590, 730, 732, 741
Charles IV, the Fair, k. of France, 108, 667, 697, 749, 754
Charles V, the Wise, k. of France, 30, 41, 61, 87–88, 117, 120, 124, 127, 155, 170, 173, 176, 254, 266, 282&N, 452, 473, 479, 513, 556, 568, 578, 586, 603, 625, 631–631ᵛ, 634ᵛ, 652, 661, 667, 668&N, 669, 680, 682–683
Charles VI, k. of France, 31, 98, 117, 122, 124, 127, 129, 134–135, 167, 173, 377, 513, 588, 615, 665, 667, 670, 683–684, 686, 743, 750
Charles VII, k. of France, 31, 41, 61, 95, 111, 122, 124, 127, 145, 167, 170, 175, 229, 263, 267, 288, 334, 352, N354, 358, 452, 513, 587, 606, 652, 665, 681, 684, 692, 736–737, 766
Charles VIII, k. of France, 66, 95, 112, 119, 148, 167, 175, 180, 228, 255, 263, 267, 334, 354&N, 358, 376, 385, N464, 490, 593, 629, 665, 680–681, 684, 694
Charles IX, k. of France, A8, 64, 66, N77, 88, 91, 96, 106, 141, 152, 170, 177, 264, 266, N267,

284, 289, 314, 343, 435, 451–452, 454, 473, 529, 575, 578, 590, 615, 617–618, 653, 655, 667&N, 668&N, 671, 675, 684, 686, 693–696, 698, 726, 737, N749, 770, 783
Charles, k. of Hungary, *see* Carobert
Charles I, k. of Naples and ct. of Anjou, 122, 134, 139, 150, 205&N, 229, 377, 425, 527, 742
Charles II, k. of Naples, 122, 738
Charles III, k. of Naples, 751
Charles II, the Bad, k. of Navarre, 120, 155, 218, 513, 625
Charles of Angoulême, *see* Charles, d. of Orleans
Charles, d. of Anjou, *see* Charles I, k. of Naples
Charles of Berry, d. of Guienne, 736–737
Charles, card. of Bourbon, N173, N738
Charles, d. of Bourbon, Constable of France, N434, 514, 549, 583&N, 600, 743
Charles the Bold, d. of Burgundy, 110, 320, 430, 628ᵛ–629, 631ᵛ, 635, 636, 680, 725, 743
Charles, ct. of Charolais, *see* Charles the Bold, d. of Burgundy
Charles, d. of Lower Lorraine, N217, 229&N, 436, 730
Charles I, d. of Lorraine, 132, 203
Charles II, d. of Lorraine, 170
Charles of Lorraine, card. bp. of Strasbourg, bp. of Metz, 621
Charles Martel, Mayor of the Palace, 30
Charles, d. of Orleans, 626, 729&N, 743
Charles, ct. of Provence, 742
Charles III, d. of Savoy, 133
Charles, ct. of Valois, 743
Charlotte (Carola Charlet) of Bourbon, princess of Orange, 465
Charolais (Carolois, Charrolois, etc.), 127, 636, 680
Charondas, 762
Chartrens, *see* Carthusians
Chartres, 79
Chartres, treaty of, 127
Châtel-sur-Moselle (Chastelet), 170
Chauviré, Roger, A34, A66
Cherea, Chereas, *see* Chaerea
Cherebert, *see* Charibert I
Cherronea, *see* Chaeroneia
Childebert I, k. of the Franks, 208, 741
Childebert II, k. of the Franks, 151, 638, 738, 753&N, 754
Childeric I, k. of the Franks, 416
Childeric II, k. of the Franks, 417
Childeric III (Childerike), k. of the Franks, 137, 507
Childeric, *error for* Chilperic I, k. of the Franks, 689

Index Nominum

Chilon, Spartan prince, 436
Chilon (Chilo), Spartan sage, 595
Chilperic I, k. of the Franks, 664, 741
China, Chinese (Sina, Indian Chinois, etc.), 67, 446, 562
Chios (Chio), 242, 422–423, 427, 522, 555, 625
Chosroes (Cosroe), k. of Persia, 30
Christ, see Jesus Christ
Christendom, the Christian Commonweal, Christian princes or kings, A41, A61–A62, iii, 39–40, 92–93, 136–137, 141, 145, 152, 174, 240, 393, 451–452, 623, 625–625ᵛ, 628, 676, 716, 729, 747
Christians, Christian Church, Christian religion, A12, 38, 40, 42, 43&N, 44, 56&N, 136, 150, 298, 300, 357, 364, 382–383, 416, 444, 447–449, 453, 464, 537&N, 538, 554, 567&N, 573, 588, 595, 612, 628, 631ᵛ, 633, 647, 656
Christian I (Christiern), k. of Denmark, 194, 241
Christian II (Christierne, etc.), k. of Denmark, 100, N210, 229, 434, 448, 749
Christian III (Christiern, etc.), k. of Denmark, 100, 229
Chrysippus (Crysippus), 461
Chrysostom, Dion, see Dion
Chrysostom, Joannes, 381, 399, N645
Chur, see Coire
Church, William Farr, N191
Cian, Cebastian, see Ziani, Sebastiano
Cicero, Marcus Tullius (Tully, Tullius, etc.), personal and political career, 54–56, 160, 245, 328, 350, 372, 390&N, 397, 404, 405&N, 430, 461, 523, 580, 592, 658, 704, 788; legal pleadings, 510, 538, N629; as moral and political philosopher, 14, 27, 47, 67, 184, 193, 200, 216, 225–227, N230, 256, 298 &N, 323, 378, 456&N, 503, 556, N564, 601, N644, 700, N707, 774; on the Roman constitution, 103, 157, 175, 188, N279, 291–292, 329, N333, 335–336; on magistracies, 286, 292&N, 303, N339, 340, 347–348; on the Censors, 305, 644, 646, 647&N; on the Senate, 260, 266, 274; on citizenship and aliens, 48, 55, 58–61, 65; comments on Roman history, 423, 499–500, 602, 687&N, 705&N, N719; on Caesar, 421, 610; on Sulla, 86, 220; on social status at Rome, 31, 369, 388, 396, 398–400, 661; on Roman laws and customs, 307, 626, N630, N702, 703, N778; on foreign laws and customs, 3, 35, 232, 552&N, N558, 564&N, N645, 722, 767&N; on oratory, 543; on numbers, 458, 462; mentioned, A27, A30, A56, 17, 24, 50, 279, N357, 391, 441
Cilli (Cilia), 90
Cimbri (Cimbrians), 549, N558
Cincinnatus, Quinctius, 11, 85, 401, 495, 587, 650&N
Cinna, Helvius (Helvidius), tribune, 558
Cinna, Lucius Cornelius, 39, 398
Cinna Magnus, Cnaeus Cornelius, 431
Cinque Ports, A57
Cipres, see Cyprus
Cipselus, see Cypselus
Circassia, Circassians, 554, 564, 612
Cirier, see Le Cirier
Cis, see Kish
Città di Castello (Tifernas), 420
Clairmont, see Clermont
Claudia, gens, 388, 391
Claudia de senatoribus, lex, 398, 660
Claudia de sociis, lex, 54
Claudian law, see Clodia de censoribus, lex
Claudius I, emp. of Rome, 30, 244, 341, 345, 381, 411, 478, 511, 516, 638, 678, 770
Claudius, tribune, see Clodius Pulcher
Claudius, Appius, see Appius
Claudius Marcellus, see Marcellus
Claudius Nero, see Nero
Clazomenians, 432
Clearchus, N631ᵛ
Clement II, pope, 142
Clement III, pope, 143
Clement IV, pope, 146, 733
Clement V, pope, 137, 144–145, 723
Clement VI, pope, 146
Clement VII (Giulio de' Medici), pope, 123, 144, 150, 418, 422, 617, 623, 625, 630ᵛ, 652, 703
Cleomedon, 102
Cleomenes (Cleomenis, Cleomines), k. of Sparta, 39, 51, 187, 428, 436, 596, 600, 631, 650, 716, 735
Cleopatra, q. of Egypt, 558, 636, 747
Cleopatra, q. of Egypt, wife of Ptolemy Physcon, 735
Clermont (Clairmont, Cleremont), 742–743, 746
Cleves (Cleve), 83, 743
Clisson, Olivier de, 744
Clodia de censoribus, lex (the Claudian law), 647
Clodiae, leges, 160, 279
Clodius Pulcher (Claudius), Publius, 31, 38, 56, 65, 103, 160, 260, 286, 298, 383–384, 495, 646
Clodoveus, see Clovis
Clodoveus, error for Clodomir, k. of Orleans, 741
Cloelia or Cluilia, gens, 391
Clotaire I (Clothaire, Lothair, k. of the Franks, 633, 741, 754
Clotaire II, k. of the Franks, 272, 664, 741
Clovis or Clodoveus I, k. of the Franks, 118, 198, 208, 588, 730–731, 741
Clovis or Clodoveus II, k. of Paris, 741
Clyarus, k. of Thrace, 443
Cnidians, 86, 235, 241, 427, 711
Coctius, 407, 657
Coconato, Annibale Radicati, ct. of, A8
Codrus, k. of Athens, 211
Coignet, Mathieu, sieur de la Thuillerie, 632ᵛ
Coire or Chur, 264, 474, 631, 703
Cold-Ashby, A52
Coligny (Colineus), François de, sieur d'Andelot, 332
Colleoni, Bartolommeo, 605
Cologne (Cullen), 93, 426, 693&N, 711
Coloman or Kalman, k. of Hungary, 736
Colonna family (Colonnois), 525
Colonna, Pompeio (Pompey Columna), card., 724
Colophon, 249
Columbus (Colombus), Christopher, 560
Columella (Collumella), Junius Moderatus, 36, 553, 651
Commines (Comines, Comineus), Philippe de, 97, 119, 148, 229, 255, 270, 385, 433, 495, 499, 517, 526, 553, 622, 631ᵛ, 635, 665
Commodus, Aurelius, emp. of Rome, 30, 41, 177, 214, 415, 417, 507, 728
Compostella, see Santiago
Comum, see Novum Comum
Conan, k. of the Scots, 508
Conan, see Connan
Concordia, 141
Condé, see Lewis of Bourbon, prince of Condé
Connan (Conan), François, 157, 275, 763
Conrad II, error for III?, emp. of Germany, 122
Conrad IV, emp. of Germany, 143
Conradin, son of Conrad IV, emp., 229
Conring, Hermann, A83
Consalvus, see Gonsalvo de Cordova
Constance, q. of Naples and Sicily, 747
Constance, daughter of Manfred of Sicily, 747
Constance of Savoy, 754
Constance, city of, 616, 630ᵛ, 721
Constance, Council of, 132, 203, 627ᵛ, 647

A181

Index Nominum

Constance, Diet of, 128
Constance, Peace of, 131, 176
Constans, Flavius Julius, emp. of Rome, 382
Constantine the Great, emp. of Rome, 25, 40, 44, 176, 227, 320–321, 443, 448, 452, 464, 550, 602, 647, 670&N, N671, 691, N694
Constantine V, emp. of Byzantium, 452
Constantine XIII, emp. of Byzantium, 464
Constantine, k. of Scotland, 116
Constantine, Donation of, 147
Constantine, town of, 416
Constantinople, A34, A51, 18, 137–138, 146, 152, 198, 214, 221, 228–229, 242, 359, 381, 410, 416, 442–444, 451–452, 464, N507, 524, 530, 544, 554, 600, 613, 634^v, 653, 682, 689, 747. *See also* Byzantium; Greece; Istanbul; Pera
Contarini (Contarenus), Gasparo, card., 166, 168, 184, 186, 188, 190–191, 193, 605
Conti, Lorenzo, A82
Copernicus, Nicholas, A54, 439, 445, 454, 455&N
Coracotas, *see* Corocotta
Corbeil, 373
Corbie, Arnald de, *see* Arnaud
Corbis, 527, 738&N, 739
Corcyca, *see* Corsica
Corcyra, Corcyraeans (Corfu, Corcyrians, etc.), 186, 235, 426, 633^v, 703, 711
Corfu, *see* Corcyra
Corinth, Corinthians, 58, 206, 226, 413, 420, 481, 571, 597, 621, 633^v, 635, 666, 719, 722–723
Coriolanus, Marcius, 431, 532, 600, 607&N, 704
Cornaro (Cornarus), Giorgio, 631^v
Cornelia, mother of the Gracchi, 30
Cornelia, gens, 391
Cornelia, lex, on privileges, of Gaius Cornelius, 90, 160, 275
Cornelia, lex, on requests to the people, of Sulla, 276
Cornelia agraria, lex, of Sulla, 583
Cornelia de falsis, lex, of Sulla, 300
Cornelia de magistratibus, lex, of Sulla, 481
Cornelia de praetoribus octo creandis, of Sulla, 281
Cornelia de sicariis, lex, of Sulla, 37, 771
Cornelius, Gaius, 276, 336. *See also* Cornelia, lex, on privileges
Cornelius Balbus, *see* Balbus
Cornelius Scipio, *see* Scipio
Cornelius Sulla, *see* Sulla
Cornu, Paul-Louis, A7
Corocotta (Coracotas), 2, 630
Corse, Sampetre, *see* Sampiero d'Ornano

Corsica (Corcyca), 125–126, 139–140, 179, 218, 628^v, 673
Coruncania, gens, 391
Corvinus, Matthias, *see* Matthias
Corvinus Messala, *see* Valerius Messala Corvinus
Cos, 430
Cosmo (Cosmus), *see* Medici, Cosmo de'
Cosroe, k. of Persia, *see* Chosroes
Cossus, Cornelius, 527
Cotelle (Cotellus), 768
Cotgrave, Randle, A89, N689, N696
Cothus or Malik al-Mozaffar Saif al-din Kotuz, sultan of Egypt, 727
Cotignac, Jean de, 258
Cotta, Lucius Aurelius, 350
Coucy (Cousi, Coussy), 180, 652
Courtenay family, N749. *See also* Devonshire
Cracow (Cracovia), 140, 179, 750
Cranmer, Thomas, archbp. of Canterbury, A53
Crassus, Marcus Licinius, the triumvir, 9, 38, 199, 421, 447, 499, 538, 557, 575, 630, 706
Crassus, Publius Licinius, consul 171 B.C., 292
Craterus, 524
Crema (Creme), 624
Cremona, 624, 661, 729
Crete, Cretans (Creet, Cretensians, etc., also Candie, Candiots), 12, 186, 218, 260, 364, N413, 420, 573, 610, 634^v, 719, 761
Crèvecoeur (Creveceur), 135
Croatia, 90, 208, 751
Croizile (Crozile), merchant of Tours, 66
Cromer, Martin, 32, 548&N
Crotona, N551, N559, 761
Crysippus, *see* Chrysippus
Ctesias, 463, 466
Ctesiphon, 283
Cujas (Cujacius), Jacques, A71, 279, N305, N348, 353&N, NN357, 441&N, N632^v
Cullen, *see* Cologne
Cumae, Cumaeans (Cumes, Cumani, Cumans), 76, 187, 423
Cunio (Cuneus), William of, 408
Curdes, *see* Kurds
Curia, gens, 391
Curiatii, N529, 595
Curio, Scribonius, 421
Curius Dentatus, Marcus, 390&N, 401, 651
Curtius Rufus, Quintus, 514
Cusanus (Cusan), Nicholas, card., 461
Cyanee, Sebastian, *see* Ziani
Cybele, 340
Cynaetha, Cynaethians (Cynethe, Cynethenses), 456, 628^v
Cynus or Cino da Pistoia, 155
Cyprian, bp. of Carthage, N645, 719

Cyprus (Cipres), 58, 104, 286, 420, 626^v–627
Cypselus (Cipselus), tyrant of Corinth, 420, 481, 666
Cyrene, 37, 111, 407, 416, 657
Cyrus the Elder, k. of Persia, 204, 215, 400, N413, 415, 465–467, 608, 683, 756&N
Cyrus the Younger, 431, 591, 737

Dacia, Dacians, 17, 412, 550
Dagobert I, k. of the Franks, N40, 118, 376, 383, 598, 630, 741
Dale, Valentine, A8, 96, 558
Dalecarlia, N564
Dalmendin, *see* Alemdin
Damascus (Damasco), N565, 690
Damasus I, St., pope, 724
Damasus II, pope, 142
Damoclides, *see* Dromoclides
Damocritus, 207
Damon, of Athens, 251
Damonax, *see* Demonax
Dampierre, ct. of, *see* Du Val
Dan, tribe of, 622
D'Andelot, *see* Coligny
Danes, *see* Denmark
Daniel, 101–102, 465–467, 550&N
Dante Alighieri, 687
Danube (Danow, Danubie, Danubius), 412, 550, 602
Danus (*error for* Joannes, usurper of the West?), 67
Danzay (Danezay, Danzai), Charles Quissarme, seigneur de, 66, 117, 209, 241
Darius I, Hystaspes, k. of Persia, 177, 204–205, 207, N413, 466, 658, 660, 734, 737
Darius II, Ochus or Nothus, k. of Perisa, 466, 683
Darius III, Codomannus, k. of Persia, 229, 451, 466–467, 597, 608
Darius Longimanus (Longuemain) or Artaxerxes I, Longimanus (?), k. of Persia, 680
Darius Mnemon or Artaxerxes II, Mnemon, k. of Persia, 102, 466, 747
Darius Ochus (Achos) or Artaxerxes III, Ochus, k. of Persia, 466
Darnley, lord, *see* Stuart, Henry
Dauphiné (Daulphinie), 41, 173, 384
David, k. of Israel, 148, 223–224, 228, 461, 638–639, 651, 658, 682–683
David II, k. of Scotland, 117
David, house of, 414, 720
Davidists, N567
Decebalus (Decebald), k. of Dacia, 412, 550
Decia, gens, 391
Decius, emp. of Rome, 638
Decius Mus, Publius, consul, 340 B.C., 211
Decius Mus, Publius, consul 312 B.C., 388

Index Nominum

Deiotarus, 744
Delcaid, *see* Nabil
Della Rovere, Francesco Maria (John Maria), d. of Urbino, 597
Della Scala family (Scaligers), lords of Verona, 420
Della Torre family (Toresans, Torresans), lords of Milan, 423, 779
Della Torre (Torresan), Nappo, 779
Delmedin, *see* El Madina
Del Monte (Du Mont), Innocenzo, card., 595&N
Delphi, Delphians (Delphos, Delphiens), 20, 79, 429
Demades, 776
Demetrias, in Thessaly, 597
Demetrius, k. of Croatia, *see* Zvonimir
Demetrius I, Poliorcetes, k. of Macedon and Asia, 58, 80, 214, 229, 245, 260, 281, 400, 406, 433, 508, 619, 624, 744
Demetrius I, Soter, k. of Syria, 737
Demetrius Phalereus, 297, 392, 610, 680
Demetrius, pirate, 2
Demochares, 587
Demonax (Damonax), 380
Demonicus of Alopece, 584
Demosthenes, 17, 47–49, 65, 102, 157, 168, 172, 246–247, 260, 273, 281, 283, 308, 326&N, 357, 587, 596, 619, 637, 678, 697, 703–704, 706, 770
Denis, *see* Dionysius
Denmark, Danes, 31, 41, 61, 66, 82–84, N94, 100, 117, 163, 166, 178, 194, 208–209, N210, 221, 229, 241, 288, 293, 413, 434–435, 448–449, 472, 485, 507, 527, 528&N, 535, 548, 559, 563, 567&NN, 601, 634, 661, 669, 719, 722, 725–726, 728, 733, 748–749, N750, 779
Dentatus, Lucius Sicinius (Siccius), 389–390
Derthone, *see* Tortona
Derval (Ervall), 165
Desmond, earl of, 141
Des Roches (Roches) family, 482
Devonshire, Edward Courtenay, earl of, N749
Diana, 37, 368, 561&N
Diane de Poitiers, duchess of Valentinois, N681
Diaz de Aux (Didato), Martin, 90
Dichi, Alexander, *see* Bichi
Dickson, L. E., N459
Didato, Jean Baptiste, 360
Didato, Martin, *see* Diaz de Aux
Didius Julianus, *see* Julianus
Diès, Auguste, N458, N460
Dijon, 165, 266
Dinant (Dinan), 433
Dio, *see* Dion, of Syracuse
Dio Nicaeus, *see* Dion Cassius

Diocletian, emp. of Rome, 25, 30, 33
Diodorus Siculus, 29, 65, 69, 205, 446, 463, 735
Diogenes the Cynic, 225–226
Diogenes Laertius, 283&N
Dion (Dio), of Syracuse, 221, 410, 415, 431, 720, 745
Dion Cassius (Dio Nicaeus), the historian, N2, 36, 99, 152, N214, N275, 481, 610–611, N710
Dion Chrysostomus (Chrisostome) 160
Dionysius (Denis, Dionisius, Dyonisius), tyrants of Syracuse, 58, 104, 210, 226, 384, 415–416, 418, 420, 423, 431, 481, 504, 594, 604, 664, 666
Dionysius (Denis) of Halicarnassus, 8, 11, 17, 23, 154, 156–157, 184, 188, 207, 273, 275, 294, 297–298, 362, 389, 397, 399, 601, N639, N640, 650, 716
Ditmarsh (Thetmarsh, Tietmarsh), 241
Djerba (Gerbe), island of, 744
Dnieper, river, 148
Doeg, 324
Dombes, 133
Dominicus de Sancto Geminiano, N355
Domitia, gens, 391
Domitia de sacerdotiis, lex, 245
Domitianus, Flavius, emp. of Rome, 216, 227–228, 269, 367, 381, 417–418, 452, 523, 585, 638, 642, N748
Doria family, 713
Doria, Andrea, 179&N, 232–233, 712
Dorians, 363, 646, 761
Dorieus, 735
Douay, A53
Dowdall, Harold Chaloner, A46, A89
Dózsa, George, Hungarian rebel, 555
Draco, 761, 766, 769, 777
Dracula, *see* Vlad Dracul
Dragut, Arraiz (Dragut Reis), 2
Drepanius, Latinus Pacatus, 105
Dresser (Dresserus), Matthias, 466
Dreux, 14, 583&N
Dromoclides (Damoclides), 705
Droz, E., N487
Drusus, *see* Livius Drusus
Du Bellay, Guillaume, N627, 632
Du Bellay, Joachim, N66
Du Choul, Guillaume, 177
Du Faur, Gui, sieur de Pibrac, A9, A69, A71, 151&N
Du Ferrier, Arnaud, 151&N
Du Guesclin (Guescheling, etc.), Bertrand, 603, 744, 789
Du Haillan, Bernard de Girard, sieur, N191
Duillia, lex, 168, 281
Duillius, Marcus, 572
Du Mont, *see* Del Monte

Du Moulin (du Molin, of Molins, Molinaeus, etc.), Charles, A71, 108, 116, N118, 137, 334, 573, 649, 712
Du Pont, Lewis, *see* Pontano
Du Prat, Antoine, 116, 734
Du Puys, Jacques, A74, A78, N234
Durand, Jean, *error for* Guillaume, bp. of Mende, 146
Durand (Durande), Jean, *error for* Martin?, 479
Durand (Durant), Martin, procureur général de Toulouse, 685
Dürer, Albert, N759
Dutch, *see* Low Countries
Du Tillet (Tili, Tillet), Jean, sieur de la Bussière, N16, 181, N288, 479
Du Tillet, Jean, bp. of Meaux, N464
Du Val, Jacques, ct. of Dampierre, A72
Dyonisius, *see* Dionysius

Easterlings, *see* Hanseatic towns
East Frizeland, *see* Friesland
Eastgoths, *see* Ostrogoths
East Indians of China, *see* China
East Indies, 148, 505–506, 552, 631ᵛ. *See also* Indies
East Saxons, *see* Anglo-Saxons
Ebranes, 436, 745
Eccelino da Romano (Eceline, Ecelinus), 417
Eck (Echius), Johann Maier, 628
Edmund (Edmond), k. of Sicily and earl of Lancaster, 122
Edward I, k. of England, 60, 97, 574
Edward II, k. of England, 578
Edward III, k. of England, 117, 120–121, 135, 181, 588, 631, 738, 748, N749, 753
Edward IV, k. of England, 73, 148, 448, 585, 601, 606, 609, N614, 676
Edward VI, k. of England, A52, 112, 205, 714&N, N748
Edward, the Black Prince, 609, 738&N
Edward, Prince of Wales, son of Henry VI, 632
Egbert, k. of the West Saxons, 463
Eger (Egre), 131, 725
Eglon, k. of the Moabites, 523
Egmont (Aiguemont, etc.), Lamoral, ct. of, 83, 290
Egubin, Augustin, *see* Steuco
Egypt, Egyptians (Aegypt, Aegyptians), monarchical government, 200, 204, 206, 208, 311–312, 413, 485, 719, 722, 735, 741, 747; laws and customs, 17, 28–29, 65, 71, 256, 389, 512–513, 527, 555, 601, 769; revenues, loans, gifts, coinage, 110, 177, 650–651, 656–657, 659, 667–668, 682–683, 698; social classes, 69, 393, 610;

A183

Index Nominum

Egypt—continued
nature of the people and climate, 553&N, 558–559, 562, 565, 613, 723; astrology of, 440–441, 446, 450; as origin of Gypsies, 579&N; and the Jews, 148, 220, 381, 439, 538, 639, 793; and Rome, 57, 313, 745; foreign relations, 463, 625; in post-classical times, 147, 167, 205, 213, 343–344, 389, 410, 550, 605, 660, 662, 667–668, 725, 727, 744; mentioned, 62, 436, 516, 562, 600. *See also* Amasis; Busiris; *and* Ptolemy, *k. of Egypt*

Ehud (Aod), 523

Eleanor (Leonore) of Aragon, q. of Castile, 748

Eleazar ben Shammua, 439

Eli, high priest of Israel, N461

Elias or Elijah (Helias), 94

Elihoreph (Eliphore), 360

Elis, 577, 761

Elisha (Elizeus, Heliseus), 539, 556

Elizabeth I, q. of England, A8, A10–A11, A29, A34–A35, A40, A52–A53, A56, N26, 68, 96–97, 112, N117, 152, 205, N229, N537, 565&N, 619, 654&N, 691, 722, 728&N, N749, 751–752

Elizabeth of York, wife of Henry VII, k. of England, 148

Elizabeth of France, *see* Isabelle

Elizeus, *see* Elisha

El Madina (Delmedin), 416

Emanuel, k. of Portugal, 148, 739

Embrun (Ambrun), 173, 176

Emmanuel Philibert, d. of Savoy, 41, 553

Empire, German Empire, etc., *see* Germany

Endobald (Endobalde), 272

Engadine, 248

England, English, the monarchy, 97–98, 128, N152, N181, 222, 507, 651, 719, 722, 746, 748&N; succession to the throne, 112, 728&NN, 733, 740, N749; Parliament of, 90, 96&N, 97–98, 101–102, 192, 371, 384, 499&N; taxation and revenues of the Crown, N57, 654&N, 657&N, 665, 668–669; magistracies, 258, 293, 311, 482, 485, 492, 573, 591, 595; Privy Council, 267–268, 272; laws and customs, A46, iii, 26&N, 33, 39, 61, 65–66, N173, 178, 181, 202, 398, 400–401, 527, 542, 557–559, 577, 588, 598, 605, 660, 769, 772, N784; climate and temperament of the people, 548, N549, 553, 557, 561, 565&N, N567; early history, 600–601, 612, N750; civil wars, 495, 526; Reformation, 535, N567; coinage, 693–694, 698; imports, 661, 662&N, 663;
relations with France, 62, 72, 111, 116, N118, 119–121, 127, 152, 170–171, 254, 433–434, 452, 523, 602, 608, N614, 622, 625–625ᵛ, 632ᵛ, 636ᵛ, 681, 683; captivity of k. John of France, 88, 282, 473, 609, 627, 667&N; relations with Scotland, 59–60, 117, 133, 550, 619, 751–752; with Ireland, 117&N; with the Papacy, 126, 359; Bodin's visit to, A10, A29, A32, A37, A72; Bodin's arrest sought by, A11; Bodin's attitudes towards, A34, A40–A41; Bodin's reputation in, A31, A39, A52, A61–A64, A66; mentioned, A7, A42–A43, A51, A59, v, 3, 66–67, 140, 205, 229, N257, 410, 448, 451, 454, 463, 513, 551, 686, 691, N738, N750. *See also* Britain, Britons; Edward; Henry; John; Richard; *and* William, *k. of England*; Elizabeth *and* Mary, *q. of England*

England, Church of, A54, A56

English Saxons, *see* Anglo-Saxons

Ennius, N614

Epaminondas, 420, 483, 599, 627ᵛ, 706

Epaphroditus, 228

Ephestion, *see* Hephaestion

Ephesus, Ephesians, 37, 251, 367, 431, 546, 702, 704

Ephialtes (Ephialtis), 392, 544

Ephorus of Cumae, N206

Ephraim, 29, 568

Epidaurians, of Epidaurus in Illyricum, 235. *See also* Ragusa

Epidaurians, of Epidaurus in the Peloponnesus, 232

Epiphanius, 383, 540

Epirus, Epirots, 93, N94, 206, 214, 627ᵛ&N, 628ᵛ, 722

Erasmus, Desiderius, 461

Eric (Henry) XIII, k. of Sweden, VII of Denmark, d. of Pomerania, 31

Eric (Henry) XIV, k. of Sweden, 194, 209, 226, 229, 417, 452, 454, 633, 634, 666, 752

Erigius, Errigius, Errichus, *see* Henry I, k. of France

Ernest, archd. of Austria, 209

Ervall, *see* Derval

Esculapius, *see* Aesculapius

Esaias, Esay, Esayas, *see* Isaiah

Esdras, 152

Essenes (Essei), 224

Essuein, Homar, *see* Omar

Este, Alfonso I d' (Alphonsus), d. of Ferrara, 129

Este, Borso d' (Borsus), d. of Ferrara, 129

Este, Nicolo II d', lord of Ferrara, 129

Esther (Hester), biblical, 102, 381, 464

Esther or Esterka, favorite of Casimir the Great, 381
Eteonicus, 522

Ethelwolf (Etelpe), 116

Ethiopia, Ethiopians (Aethiopia, Aethiopians, etc.), 11, 60, 147–148, 150, 188, 202, 204–205, 222, 243, 361, N413, 485, 507, N537, 549, 558, 560&N, 596–597, 614, 658, 668, 676, 719, 722, 745

Etruria, Etruscans (Hetruria, Hetruscians, Hetrusques, etc.), 181, 208, 290, N517, 635, 719, 722

Euclid, N792

Eudes or Odo (Otho), k. of France, N463, 730, 732

Eudes III (Odo), d. of Burgundy, 514&N

Eudes IV, d. of Burgundy, 491, 753

Eudoxus, 454–455

Eugenius IV, pope, N736

Eumenes of Cardia, k. of Asia, 149, 609, 676

Eumenes II, k. of Pergamum, 33, 111, 121, 262, 407, 657

Euphrates, river, 412, 466, 599, 602

Euripides, 19, 35, 394–395, 417, 588, 757

Europe, Europeans, A7, A13, A16, A20, A31, A51, A58, A61, A65–A66, A78, 34, 39, 42, 44, 69, 114, 119, 123, 181, 201–202, N203, 322, 360, 381, 385–386, 441, N445, 447–448, 451, 453–454, 457, 482, 487, 535, 537, N542, 549–550, 554, 560, 565, 575, 595, 625, 627ᵛ, 629, 660–662, 670, 686, 689, 692, 753, 766

Eurysthenes (Euristhenes), k. of Sparta, 198, N738, 741

Eusebius of Caesarea, 444

Eutropius, 507

Euxitheus (Euxithenes), an Athenian, 65

Evagoras, k. of Cyprus, 58, 420

Eve (Eva), 15

Evreux, 526, 683, 748

Ezechias, *see* Hezekiah

Ezekiel (Ezechiel), 152, 223, 651

Faber, Jean, jurist, A71, 763

Fabia, gens, 391, 428

Fabius, Quintus, 635ᵛ

Fabius Ambustus, Marcus, 103

Fabius Buteo, Marcus, 166, 277

Fabius Gurges, *error for* Quintus Fabius Maximus, consul 213 B.C., 28

Fabius Maximus, Quintus, consul 213 B.C., 746

Fabius Maximus Cunctator, Quintus, 85, 340, 492, 496–498, 587, 609, 706, 746

Fabius Maximus Rullianus, Quintus, 48, 85, 172, 246, 290

Fabius Pictor, Caius, 400

Fabius Pictor, Quintus, N639

Index Nominum

Fabius Vibulanus, Marcus, 302
Fabricia (Fabritia), gens, 391
Fabricius Luscinus, Caius, 587, 607
Faenza (Favence, Faventia), 420, 624
Fair Promontory, the, near Carthage, 362
Falieri (Faleriennes), 711
Faliero (Falier, Falerius), Marino, doge of Venice, 191, 221
Falisci (Falisques), 607
Fanzara (Fauzara), 600
Farnese, Alessandro, card., 123, 694
Farnese, Pierluigi (Peter Aloisius or Louys), d. of Parma, 452, 523
Fauchet, Claude, 633
Faur, see Du Faur
Faustina (Faustine), 582, 751
Fauzara, see Fanzara
Favence, Faventia, see Faenza
Favorinus, 519, 535, 780–781
Felinus Maria Sandaeus, 133, 299, N322, N355
Felix V (Foelix), formerly Amadeus VIII, d. of Savoy, antipope, 723
Felix, procurator of Judaea, 56
Felix (Foelix) of Nogaret, see Nogaret
Ferdinand, emp. of Germany, 82, 84, 121, 123, 131, N141, 144, 151, 209, 238–239, 607, 616, 727, N749, 752
Ferdinand I, k. of Aragon, 126, 748
Ferdinand, II of Aragon, V of Castile, III of Naples, k. of Spain, 122, 126, 199, 383, 464, 560, 575, 579, 582, 591, 594, 622, 624, 629–629ᵛ, 631, 746, 748, 751
Ferdinand I or Ferrante, k. of Naples, 630ᵛ, 748
Ferdinand, prince of Portugal, error for?, 739
Ferdinand, d. of Calabria, see Calabria
Ferrara, 62, 65, 114, 129, 142&N, 144, 154, 158, 182, 553, 617, 625–625ᵛ, 632, 675, 694
Ferrier, Arnaud du, see Du Ferrier
Ferrier, Auger (Augerius Ferrerius), A34, A89, vi, N410, N412, N436, N437, 442&N, NN443, NN445, N446, N447, N449, NN461, N463, N464
Ferrières, 590
Festus, Sextus Pompeius, 16, N70, 76, 84, 156, 166, 273, 291, 297, 305, N307, N333, 348&N, 362–363, 440, N554, N567, 572, 583, 643, N645, N650, 671, 691
Fez (Fes), 46, 147, 205, 209, 361, 410, 416, 426, 432–433, 556, 560, 563, 600, 632, 707
Ficino (Ficinus), Marsilio, 458

Fieschi (Fiesques), 713
Fiesco, Antonio (Anthonie Flisque), 130
Fiesco, Giovanni Luigi (John Flisco), 712
Figulus, Caius Marcius, 351
Filmer, Sir Robert, A64–A66, A84–A85
Finale (Final, Finall), Alfonso II, marquis of, 130, 632ᵛ
Firmanus, Tarutius (Taruntius Firmianus), 441–442
Firmicus Maternus, Julius, N214, 439–440, 442
Flaccus, see Valerius Flaccus
Flaccus, Verrius, N348, N645
Flamininus (Flaminius), Lucius Quintius, 36, 309, 647
Flamininus (Flaminius), Titus Quintius, 187, 232, 597, 622, 655, N657, 709, 789
Flaminius the consul, error for Spurius Postumius Albinus, 380
Flanders, Flemings (Flaunders), A10, A29, A38, A51, 122, 127, 135, 170, 376, 378, 443, 452, 454, 514, 561, 568, 574&N, 577, 631–633, 656, 693–695, 732, N738, 746. See also Low Countries
Flavius, Cnaeus, 587
Fleming, Richard, bp. of Lincoln, A52
Flisco, Flisque, see Fiesco
Floard or Flodoard, 118, 132, 146
Flodden Field, N451
Florence, Florentines (Florens, Florentins), forms of government, 165, 168, 172, 185, N205, 243, 407, 410, 422–426, 493, 544, 546&N, 604, 702–703, 706, 710; political history, 216, 220, 418, 429, 523–524, 534, 630ᵛ, 721; political institutions, 85, 207, 211, 277, 280, 282, 333; laws and customs, 64, 69, 158, 181–182, 389, 393, 535, 596, 672, 707; nature of the people, 563; revenues, 668; external relations, 123, 129–130, 150, 154, 359, 376, 433, 520, 622, 625–625ᵛ, 660; mentioned, 144, 258, 663, 694, 711
Florentine Pandects, 72&N, N114
Florus, Lucius Annaeus, 38, 197, N636ᵛ, 639&N, 640, 774
Foelix, see Felix
Foix, 529, 739, 748
Foix, François de, ct. of Candale, 699
Foix, Gaston de, see Nemours
Foix, Paul de, 152
Fontainebleau, N695
Fontarabie, see Fuenterabia
Fontenay or Fontenoy-en-Puisaye 428
Formiani, 76
Forster (Forrester), Valentin, 456
Fossombrone (Fossabrum), 141

Foucquers, see Fuggers
France, French, monarchy of, 90, 95, 98, 112–113, 191–192, 217–218, 222, 428, 507&N; regency, 86–87; limits on royal power, A16–A17, 101, 110–111, 169–172; succession to the throne, 128, 434, 729–733, 740, 742–743, 753–754; the Estates General, 95&N, 96, 370–371, 665; councils, 263–264, 269–270, 272, 276–277; courts and judicial procedure, 102, 108, 169, 181, 266–267, 310–311, 354, 356, 371, 490–492, 513–514, 766–767, 774; magistracies, 167, 188, 280, 288–289, 326, 331–332, 489–490; superior position of kings of France, 119–120, 122–126, 135, 138, 142, 145–146, 150–152; foreign alliances, 73–74, 82–83, 124; relations with Brittany, 117, 118&N; nature of the people, 457, 553–554, 559, 564, 565&N, 566, 567&N; slavery, 39, 41–42; citizenship and aliens, 63, 65, 66&N, N67; dowries and inheritances, 576&N, 578, N738; clergy, 474–475, 575; chivalric orders, 588–590; coinage, 688–698; prices, 667&N; trade, 661, 662&N, 663; royal finances and treasury, 670–677, 679–686; the royal *domaine*, 652–654; mystic numbers in French history, N463, N464; in classical times, 17, 22, 54–55, 57, 208, 260, 443, 499, 610; Bodin addresses French version to, A31; mentioned, *passim*. See also Gauls; Celtae; Franks
Francford, Franckford, see Frankfurt
Franche-Comté (Franche-countie, the free counties, free Burgundie), 73, 132, 134, N614
Francis I, k. of France, personal qualities, 217, 453, 503–504, 588; constitutional changes, 167, 170, 172, 181, 263, 267, 289, 591, 661, 734; domestic policies, 62, N335, 378, 513–514, 577, 611, 640&N, 662, 758, 773, 777; fiscal and monetary policies, 176, 593, 641, 653, N671, 673, 676–677, 679, 681, 688, 692–694; relations with Charles V, 121–122, 150, 378, 528, 602, 628, 632, 636; captivity of, 173, 434, 448, 625, 626ᵛ, 629, 652, 667&N; relations with the Swiss, 74, 77–78, 616, 634; other foreign relations, 597, 608, 615, 625ᵛ; mentioned, A3, 222, 289, 452, 521, 589, 668, 762
Francis II, k. of France, 112, 171, 654, 675, 684, 751
Francis the Dauphin, son of Francis I, 626ᵛ

A185

Index Nominum

Francis, d. of Alençon, Anjou, and Brabant, A8–A11, A29, A34–A35, A72, 171, 378, 384, 465, N499, 667&N, N728, N738, 751–752
Francis II, d. of Brittany, 176, 180
Francis of Lorraine, d. of Guise, 674
Francis I, d. of Lorraine, 170
Francis Phoebus (Phebe), k. of Navarre, 739
Francis Sforza (Sforce), see Sforza
Francis Valori, see Valori
Franciscans, A12, 222
Franckenberger (Frankberger), Andreas, vi, 466
Franconia, 84, 629^v
Frankfurt (Francford, Franckford), A45, A78, 381, 566, 690
Franks (Francons, Francs, etc.), 202, 448, 550, 579
Frederick, pope, see Stephen IX
Frederick I, Barbarossa, emp. of Germany, 108, 117, 131, 143, 150, 208, N632
Frederick II, error for I, emp. of Germany, 376&N
Frederick II, emp. of Germany, 40, 65, 67, 139, 142–144, 179, 368, 625, 725, 727, 747, 753
Frederick III, emp. of Germany, 241, 448, 452, 726–729
Frederick III, error for Wenceslaus, emp. of Germany, 128
Frederick I, k. of Denmark, 100, 448
Frederick II, k. of Denmark, 82, 100, 194, 209, 229, 434
Frederick of Austria, ct. of Tyrol, 82
Frederick, ct. of Vaudémont, 132, 203
Free Burgundie, the free counties, see Franche-Comté
Fregosi (Fregoses), 712
Fregoso (Fregose, Fregosius), Cesare, 68, 635^v
Freiburg (Friburg), canton of, 52, 58, 149, 234, 241, 264, 497
French, etc., see France
Friedrich, Carl Joachim, A18
Friesland, Frieslanders (East Frizeland, Frizlanders), 133&N, 773
Friuli, 624
Froissart (Frosard), Jean, 331
Frondsberg or Frundsberg (Fronsperg), George von, 549
Fronto, Titus Catius Caesius, 216
Frotho or Frode (Fronto), k. of the Danes, 528, 559
Fucinus (Fucina), canal, 678
Fuenterabia (Fontarabie), 602
Fufia (Fusia), lex, 247
Fuggers (Foucquers), 674&N
Fulk V, ct. of Anjou and k. of Jerusalem, N631^v
Fulk (Fulke), archbp. of Reims, 732
Fulvia, 523
Fulvia, gens, 391

Fulvius, Quintus, 24
Fulvius Flaccus, Cnaeus, 296
Fulvius Flaccus, Quintus, 189, 274, 319, 375
Fulvius Nobilior, Marcus, 497–498
Funck (Funccius, Functius), Johann, N464, 465, 467
Fundani, 76
Furia, gens, 391
Furius, Marcus, 369
Fusia, lex, see Fufia

Gabinia, lex, on piracy, 162, 281, 285
Gabinia, lex, on usury, 573
Gabinius, Aulus, 90, 481, 587
Gabionites, see Gibeonites
Gabriel, marquis of Saluzzo, 736
Gaca, see Huascar
Gaditani, 60
Gago or Gao (Gagao), error for Gober, 555
Galba, Sulpicius, emp. of Rome, 30, 262, 282, 414, 472, 590, N664, 681, 774
Galba, Servius (Sergius), see Sulpicius Galba
Galeazzo (Galeace, Galeas), see Sforza; Visconti
Galen, N461, 462, 547–548, 552 &N, 554&N, N558, 567&N
Gallaad, see Gilead
Gallienus (Galienus), emp. of Rome, 443
Gallius (Gallus), Quintus, 521
Gallograeci or Galatians, 164
Gallus, Caius Sulpicius, 80, 187
Galvagno, lord of Milan, 155, 423
Gambacorti (Gambecourt), Pietro, 129, 745
Gand, Gantois, see Ghent
Gaoga, 47, 147
Gartze, Johann, N464
Gascony, Gascons (Gascongne, Gascoines, etc.), 42, 548–549, 562, 568
Gaul, Gauls (Gaule, Gaules), 35, 69, 79, N94, 222, 421, 465, 479, 495, 499, 552, 559, 566–567, 577, 600–601, 607&N, 612, 647, 655, 682, 719, 767. See also France
Gaunt, see Ghent
Gaurico (Gauricus), Luca, 442, 443&N
Gautier, sire d'Yvetot (Ivetot), 633
Gegania, gens, 391
Geica, see Géza
Gelasius I, pope, 136
Gelasius II, pope, 608
Gelders, see Guelders
Gellius, Aulus, 17, N30, 54, 297, 304, 461
Gellius Publicola, Lucius, 267, 305
Gelon (Gelo), tyrant of Syracuse, 205, 420
Genebrard, Gilbert, N464, 467

Geneva (Geneve), A4, A8, A33–A34, A64, A71, A79–A80, A85, 50&N, 58, 60, 74, 77, NN99, 197, N225, 233&N, 234, 250, 265, 277, 299, 359, 360&N, 381, 433, 497, 618–619, 638, 648, 690, 713&N, 721
Genghis Khan, 209
Genoa, Genoese (Genes, Genua, Genevois, Genouois, Genewais, Genowayes, etc.), 27, 42, 64, 68, 119, 129–130, 134, 148, 152, 177, 188, 197, 232–233, 242, 245, 259, 269, 277, 284, 308, 359, 376, 420, 424, 426, 428, 554, 563–565, 568, 574, 596–597, 605, 615, 625^v, 626^v, 628–628^v, 632^v, 638, 660, 673, 675, 690, 694, 707, 711–713, 718
Gensericus, k. of the Vandals, 738, 740
Gentile, Benedetto, doge of Genoa, 712
Genutia, lex, on usury, 572–573
Genutius Aventinensis, Lucius, 390&N, 391
Genzo (Gerso), son of Gensericus, 738
Geoffrey II, Martel, ct. of Anjou (Angiers), 731–732
Geoffrey II (Godfrey), d. of Brittany, 579, 738
George, Hungarian rebel, see Dózsa
George of Amboise, see Amboise
Gepidae (Gepides), 448, N550
Gerasa, 39
Gerbe, see Djerba
Gergoie (Gergoye), 79
Germaine de Foix, 126
Germanicus Caesar, 635^v, 728
Germany, German Empire, Germans (Almaigne, Almans, the Empire, etc.), form of government, 191, 221, 236–241, 434, 613, 726; position of the Emperor, A20, A35, 82&N, 93, 100, 122–123, 128, 130, 150–151, 181, 197, 203&N, 204, 225, N236, N237, 368, 453, 472, N726, 733; succession to imperial crown, 210, 723, 725, 727–729, 738; vassalage to the Empire, 117, 129, 132–136, 141–145, 148, 208–209; revolt of the Swiss, 76, 82&NN, 83, 407, 423; foreign relations, 68, 139, 416, 523, 553, 617, 621, 625–625^v, 627^v, 632^v&N, 659, 681; internal constitutional structure, 59, 81, 84, 131, 154, 171, 176, 178, 241&N, 247, 277, 371, 385, 426, 665, 707, 710&N, 724–725; Imperial Chamber, 169, N237, 491, N543; judicial procedures, 322, N543, N552, 628; magistracies, 64, N173, 293, 344, 482, 485; nature of the people, 29, 37, 270, 299, 362, N548, 550–552,

Index Nominum

Germany—continued
554–557, N558, 559&N, 561 &N, 562, 564–566, 567&N, 568, 585; laws and customs, 13, 30, 32&N, 39, 50, N57, 62, 65, 108–109, 381, 395, 400, 509, 527, 542, 559, 576&N, 577, 584, 605, 660, 739, 743, 753, 784; finance and coinage, 673–674, 691, 693&N, 694, 696–697; religious questions, A61, 380, 535–536, 544, N567; influence of stars, 442–443, 448–449; not the fourth Empire, 466; editions published in, A44–A45, A78; mentioned, A31, 39, N83, 91, 118, 124, 138, N173, 202, 376, 383, 399, 410, 422, 451, 453, 464, 499, 549, N612, 631ᵛ, N674, N736, N738. *See also* Italy, Italians

Gerso, *see* Genzo

Geta, Caius Licinius, 305, 647

Geta, Septimius, 318–319

Géza (Geica), k. of Hungary, 737

Ghent, Ghenters (Gand, Gaunt, Gantois), A51, 122, 320, 376, 378, 401, 565

Ghiara d'Adda (Guiradadde), 624

Giannotti (Janot), Donato, 190, 711

Giapalt or Ashraf Janbalat, sultan of Egypt, 727

Gibeonites (Gabionites), 628

Gilead (Gallaad), 568

Gilippus, *see* Gylippus

Gilmore, Myron Piper, N327

Gilolo or Halmahera, 557

Giora, 39

Giovio, Paolo, *see* Jovius

Girald, Gitald, *see* Nithard

Giustiniani (Justinian) family, of Genoa, 242

Giustiniani (Justinians), of Venice, 711

Glaber, Raoul, of Cluny, N732

Glarus (Glaris), canton of, 60, 76, 78, 82, 149, 247, 250–251, 497, 604, 619

Gloucester (Glocester), Richard, d. of, *see* Richard III, k. of England

Gnesen (Gnesne), 140, 176, 258

Gnostics (Gnostici), 383

Gobe (*error for* Djihanghir?), son of Solyman the Great, 718

Godefroy, Denis, N730

Godfrey of Bouillon, k. of Jerusalem, 140, 148

Godfrey, *see* Geoffrey II, d. of Brittany

God's House, League of (League of the Cadde, Cade), 83, 248

Gomorrah (Gomorrha), 437&N

Gondelphfingen, *see* Gundelfingen

Gonsalvo de Cordova (Consalvus), Hernandez, 629ᵛ

Gontran or Guntram, k. of Burgundy and Orleans, 738, 741

Gonzaga, Carlo, 729

Gonzaga, Gian Francesco II, marquis of Mantua, 432

Gonzaga, Luigi I, lord of Mantua, 417

Good Hope (Bonne Esperance), Cape of, 568

Gordianus I, emp. of Rome, 411

Gordianus III, emp. of Rome, 745

Gorgones (Gorgonides), in the Canary Islands, 126

Gorka, Andreas, ct., N548

Gorze (Gosen), 133

Gostavus, *see* Gustavus

Gotha (Goth), 555

Goths (Gothes), 30, 108, 168, 202, 235, 259, 321, 448, 464&N, 503, 539, 550, 566, N567, 612, 614, 670. *See also* Ostrogoths; Visigoths

Goveanus (Govean, Jovean), Antonius, 279, 773

Gozo, island of, 44

Gracchi (Gracchies), 30, 350, 422, 518. *See also* Sempronius Gracchus

Granada (Granado, Grenado), 126, 454, 556

Grand Caire, *see* Cairo

Grand Signior, *see* Turkey

Granvelle (Granvellan), Antoine Perrenot de, 239, 523

Granvelle (Granvella, Granvellan), Nicolas Perrenot de, 67, 627

Gratianus, emp. of Rome, 40, 452

Gratidianus, Marcus Marius, 687&N, 697

Great Britain, *see* Britain

Greece, Greeks (Graece, Graecia, Grecians, Greekes, Grekes, Greek Empire, etc.), forms of government, 154, 186, 210, 226, 232, 235, 241, 381, N413, 426, 432, N463, 500, 577, 719, 722–723, 761; magistracies, 103, 268, 271&N, 280, 308, 311, 335, 340, 372, 483–484, 487, 765; senates and councils, 255–257, 260, 263, 265, 273; censorship, 637, 641, 643; treasure and coinage, 177, 650, 682, 686, 689–690, 692, 694, 697–698, 700; laws and customs, 17, 30, 32, 35, 48, 56, 65, 71, 219, 362–363, 392–393, 397, 400, 440, N462, N503, 527, 538, 542, N548, 555, 559, 576, 578, 584, 595, 601, 645&NN, 647, 669, 770; nature of the people and climate, 200, 251, 545, N551, N557, 558, 564, 566, 610, 613, 635ᵛ; idea of justice and the mean, 758, 780, 792; Peloponnesian War, 430, 454, 633ᵛ; alliances, 75, 79, 619, 669; external relations, 204–205, 597, N607, 622, 625, 627ᵛ, 659; relations with Rome, 80, 161, 262, 386, 621, 633, 655, N657; and prophecies of Daniel, 465–466; as the Eastern Empire (*see also* Byzantium; Constantinople), 19, 137, 139, 310, 343, 357, 443, 448, 452, 524, 638; Greek Orthodox Church, 536–537; post-classical Greece, 44, 66, 258, 358, 449, 550; mentioned, 9, 16, 62, N67, N173, 208, 217, 231, 276, 411–412, 437, 516, 560, 563, 565, 586, 612, 628ᵛ, 706

Greenland, Greenlanders (Gronland), 567&N

Gregorius, Peter, A28

Gregory I, pope, 137, 151

Gregory VI, pope, 142

Gregory VII or Hildebrand, pope, 143, 208

Gregory VIII (Bourdin), antipope, 143

Gregory VIII, pope, 146

Gregory IX, pope, 146

Gregory X, pope, 146, 371, 733

Gregory XI, pope, 129, 146, 368

Gregory XII, pope, 146

Gregory, bp. of Tours, 118&N

Grenoble (Gratianople), 266

Grey, Sir William, 13th baron Grey de Wilton, 72

Grimaldi family (Grimoaldes), 713

Grisons (Grises), N66, 74, 78, 83, 165, 233, 241, 247–248, 250, 265, 407, 474, 546, 563–564, 625, 658, 681, 703, 715, 721, 786

Grissler or Gryssler (Grislerus), bailiff of Uri, 597

Gritti (Gritty), Luigi, 668

Gronland, *see* Greenland

Grouchy or Gruchius, Nicolas, 283, 292&N

Grumbach (Grombache, etc.), Wilhelm von, 82, 555

Guelders (Gelders, Gueldres), 123–124, 693

Gueschlin, Guescheling, Guesclin, *see* Du Guesclin

Gui (Vide) de Bretagne, ct. of Penthièvre, 738

Guicciardini (Guichardine, etc.), Francesco, 129, N544, 546, 549, N627, 627ᵛ

Guiche, *see* La Guiche

Guienne (Guyenne), 66, 116, 120, 378, 583&N, 631, 632ᵛ, 654, 683

Guinea (Guinee, Guynee), 147, 660

Guines (Guynes), 72, 107, 116

Guiradadde, *see* Ghiara d'Adda

Guiscard, Robert, 139

Guise, François de Lorraine, d. of, 674

Guise, Henry, d. of, A11, N463

Guise, Louis, card. of, A11, N463

Guitard, *see* Nithard

Gundelfingen (Gondelphfingen), 239

Gunther of Schwartzburg, 727

Gustavus I (Gostavus), k. of Sweden, 209, 448, N564, 724

Index Nominum

Gusula, *see* Guzzula
Guyenne, *see* Guienne
Guynee, *see* Guinea
Guynes, *see* Guines
Guytald, Guytard, *see* Nithard
Guzzula (Gusula), 707
Gylippus (Gilippus), 207

Hadrian (Adrian), emp. of Rome, 21, 27, 30, 37, 54, 159, 169, 201, 262, 266, 355, 359, 367, 447, 502, 508, 550, 680, N681, 728, 734, 778
Haggai (Aggaeus), 466
Haillan, *see* Du Haillan
Haimo, *see* Aimoin
Hainault (Henault), 66, 173
Halirrothios (Halirhotius), 647
Halle (Hale), 135
Ham (Cham), 47
Haman (Aman), 464
Hamburg (Hambourg), 84, 241
Hananel (Kanan) ben Hushiel, 781
Hannibal (Anniball, Haniball, etc.), 165, 189, 211, 285, 291, 304, 422, 454, 468, 478, 496&N, 498, 549, 558, 598, 600, 603, 608–609, 612, 631, 640, 644, 656, 663, 682, 715–716
Hanno, Carthaginian general, 522
Hanno, Carthaginian navigator, 61
Hanseatic towns (Baltic towns, Easterlings, Hauns cities, Sea towns, Vandales), 66, 74, 82, 84, N567, 632^v
Harbert, *see* Herbert
Hardicanute, k. of England, N750
Hariadenus Aenobarbus, *see* Barbarossa
Harmodius, 219&N, 221, 392, 418
Harris, William, fellow of Lincoln, A53
Harris case, A18
Hart, William, scholar of Lincoln, A53
Hasdrubal, son of Hanno, N292
Hasdrubal (Asdruball), son-in-law of Hamilcar Barca, 631
Hasdrubal, son of Hamilcar Barca, brother of Hannibal, 348, N496, N586
Hasdrubal, *error for* Gisco, 526
Hastings, William, lord, 659
Hauns cities, *see* Hanseatic towns
Hauser, Henri, A7, A83, A89, N687
Hearnshaw, F. J. C., A38
Heberstein, *see* Herberstein
Hebrew, the wise, *see* Solomon
Hebrews, *see* Jews
Hedui or Aedui, 149
Hedwig, q. of Poland, 748–749
Heidelberg, 238
Heldebert, ct. of La Marche, 731
Helene, q. of Russia, *see* Olga
Helfenstein (Helfustein), Georg von, baron of Gundelfingen, 239
Helias, *see* Elias

Helice, 437&N
Heliogabalus or Elagabalus, emp. of Rome, 205, 214, 218, 414, 416, 429, 592, 595, 689, 734, 746
Heliseus, *see* Elisha
Hellespont (Hellespontus), 10, 75, 505, 627^v, 680
Helvetians, 50. *See also* Switzerland
Henault, *see* Hainault
Henry I, the Fowler, emp. of Germany, 236, 725, 729, 739
Henry I, *error for* Henry II, emp. of Germany, 132
Henry II, emp. of Germany, 557
Henry III, emp. of Germany, 142, 728
Henry IV, emp. of Germany, 143
Henry V, emp. of Germany, 129, 133–134, 142–143, 375, 608, 725
Henry VI, emp. of Germany, 327
Henry VII, emp. of Germany, 81, 725, 727
Henry I, k. of Castile, 748
Henry II, the Bastard, k. of Castile, 127, 136, 603, 634^v, 683
Henry I, k. of England, 97, 229, 742, 748
Henry I, *error for* Henry II, k. of England, 209
Henry I, *error for* Henry III, k. of England, 268
Henry II, k. of England, 140
Henry II, *error for* Henry III, k. of England, 120
Henry III, k. of England, 122
Henry IV, k. of England, d. of Lancaster, 83, 626, 738
Henry V, k. of England, 31, 95, 127, 635^v
Henry VI, k. of England, 97&N, 448&N, 526, 601, 632
Henry VII, k. of England, earl of Richmond, 601, 603, 618
Henry VIII, k. of England, A40, A52, A56, 96, N97, 111, 116, 141, 199, 205, N513, 617–618, 625, 652, 674
Henry, *error for* Edward I, k. of England, 119
Henry I (Erigius, Errichus, etc.), k. of France, 94, 209, 730–731, 732&N, N736
Henry II, k. of France, constitutional issues under, 264, 298, 332, 345, 491, 686, 768; domestic administration, 41, 217, 378, 528, 611, 663, 672; finance and coinage, N385, 593, 661, 674, 675&N, 677, 681, 685, 689, 693–694, 696–698; relations with the Empire, 27, 72, 83, 151, 179, 238–239, 606, 613, 617–618, 625^v, 632^v &N, 634^v, 726; with the Swiss, 74, 78, 251, 360, 651, 659; with Scotland, 60&N; with Ireland, 141; with the Papacy, 607, 632^v; mentioned, A3, 223, N579, 626^v, 634, 667
Henry III, k. of France and Poland, d. of Anjou, A8–A9, A11, A21, A29, A34–A35, vi, 87–88, 94, 166, 174&N, N258, 264, N267, 343, 370, 435, N463, N548, 590, 613, N640, 654, 667, 689, 693, 725–726, 749
Henry IV, k. of France and Navarre, A11, N738
Henry I, the Large, k. of Navarre, ct. of Champagne, 738, 748
Henry I, the Cardinal, k. of Portugal, 148, 739
Henry, k. of Sweden, *see* Eric
Henry, d. of Anjou, *see* Henry III, k. of France
Henry, ct. of Champagne, *see* Henry, k. of Navarre
Henry, son of Henry II, k. of England, 209
Henry, d. of Lancaster, *see* Henry IV, k. of England
Henry, ct. Palatine, *error for* Henry, d. of Lower Bavaria, 81
Henry, d. of Pomerania, *see* Eric
Henry of Burgundy (Bononia, Boulogne), ct. of Portugal, 126, 148, 595
Henry, prince of Portugal, *error for* ?, 739
Henshaw, Henry, rector of Lincoln, A53
Hephaestion (Ephestion), 524
Heracleans, 423
Heracleodorus, 429
Heraclidae (Heraclides), 206, 392. *See also* Hercules
Heraclitus, 446, 458
Herberstein (Heberstein, Herbestein), Sigismund, baron von, 548, 557, 567
Herbert I (Harbert), ct. of Vermandois, 730
Herbert IV, ct. of Vermandois, 731–732
Herburt, Jan, castellan of Sanok, N725
Hercules, 58, 186, 198, 206, 220, 436, 464&N, 538, 543, 632, 722–723, 737, N738, 767. *See also* Heraclidae
Herispo, ct. of Brittany, 118
Hermeas, 378
Hermodorus, of Ephesus, 251, 532, 704
Hermogenian Code, 357&N
Hermolaus Barbarus, *see* Barbarus
Hernici (Herniques), 54, 163, 705
Herod I, the Great, k. of Judea, 393, 414, 416, N464, 465, 720
Herod Agrippa, *see* Agrippa
Herod Antipas, 416
Herodianus, 178, 228, 552
Herodotus, 20, 47, 177, 184, 186, 193–194, 196, 206, 397, 446, 463, 466, 500, 552, 554, 610, 691, 719, 735
Herouel, an embezzler, N685

Index Nominum

Herpin or Eudes Arpin, ct. of Berry, 667
Heruli (Herules), 30, 202, 448, 464, 550, 612, 655
Hesse (Hess), house of, 13
Hesse (Hessen), Philip, landgrave of, 78, 83, 634ᵛ
Hester, *see* Esther
Hestiaea or Oreus, people of (Hestiens, Hostienses, Orites), 429, 711
Hetruria, Hetruscians, Hetrusques, etc., *see* Etruria
Hezekiah (Ezechias), 682
Hicetas (Icetes), tyrant of Leontini, 420
Hieremie, Hieremy, *see* Jeremiah
Hiero (Hieron) II, k. of Syracuse, 205, 415, 420, N461, 469, 657, 688
Hierome, *see* Jerome, St.
Hieronymus (Hierome, Hierosme), k. of Syracuse, 226, 254, 415–416, 423
Hierotimus, k. of the Parthians, 9, 557
Hierusalem, *see* Jerusalem
Hildebrand, *see* Gregory VII, pope
Hipparchus, astronomer, 447
Hippias, Arcadian captain, 629ᵛ
Hippo (Hippona), 724
Hippocrates (Hipocrates, Hypocrates), 379, N461, 462, 468, 543, 548, N554, 557, N558
Hippodamus (Hyppodamus), 69, 393, 570–571, 578
Hippotae, 360
Hircanus, *see* Hyrcanus
Hirene, *see* Irene
Histria or Istria, N645
Hobbes, Thomas, A19, A50
Holland, *see* Low Countries
Holland, earl of, *see* Baldwin V, ct. of Flanders, *and* William, emp. of Germany
Holland, Philemon, A62
Holstein (Holsatia, Holst, etc.), 83, 117, 241
Holster, Gaspar, 548
Homar, *see* Omar
Homer, 10, 15, 19, 35, 99, 196, 211, 293, 436, 500, 558, N564, 702, 719, 761
Hongres, *see* Huns
Honorius II or Peter Cadalus (Cadol), antipope, 143
Honorius III, pope, 140, N142, N651
Honorius, Flavius, emp. of Rome, 670
Honorius, k. of the Vandals, *see* Huneric
Horapollo (Orus Apollo), 439
Horatia, gens, 391
Horatia, lex, *see* Valeria et Horatia
Horatii, the three, N529, 595
Horatius Barbatus, Marcus, 156, 339
Horatius Cocles, 594

Horatius Flaccus (Horace), Quintus, the poet, A56, N548, N648
Hormisdas, pope, 731
Hortarius(?), k. of the Lombards, 655
Hortensia, gens, 391
Hortensia, lex, 276
Hortensius (Hortentius), Quintus, dictator, 156
Hortensius, Quintus, orator, 398
Hospitalis, *see* L'Hôpital
Hostienses, *see* Hestiaea
Hostilia, gens, 391
Hostilius, Tullus, k. of Rome, 85, 413, N464, 494, N529, 775
Hostilius Mancinus, Aulus, 339
Hotoman or Hotman, François, 304
Howard, Henry, earl of Surrey, A40, N97
Howard, Thomas, 3rd d. of Norfolk, A40, N97
Howard, Thomas, 4th d. of Norfolk, N749
Huascar (Gaca), k. of Peru, 735
Hug (Hugo), Hans, avoyer of Lucerne, 651
Hugh I, d. of Burgundy, N731
Hugh, son of Henry I?, 160
Hugh Capet, k. of France, 209, N217, 229&N, 435, N464, 676, 730, 741
Huguenots, A7–A8
Hull, Henry, fellow of Lincoln, A53
Humbert II, dauphin of Viennois, 41
Humerolles, Nicolas de Livre, sieur de, N453
Hunding (Hundig), son of Syrik, k. of the Saxons, 527
Huneric (Honorius), k. of the Vandals, 738
Hungary, Hungarians (Hongarie, etc.), 118, 121, 126, 140, 148, 167, 209, 288, 413, 435, 448–449, 451–452, 511, 528, 555, 560, 562, 564, 613, 616, 628, 651&N, 694, 725–727, 728&N, 736–738, 746, 748, 750–751. *See also* Huns
Huniades, Joannes Corvinus, 628, 727
Huns (Hongres, Hungarians, Hunnes, etc.), 202, 448, 534, 550&N
Huntington, Henry Hastings, 3rd earl of, N749
Hus, John, 628
Hypatius, 524
Hyperbolus, 588
Hypocrates, *see* Hippocrates
Hyppodamus, *see* Hippodamus
Hyrcanus (Hircanus), John, prince and high priest of the Jews, 682
Hyrcanus (Hircanus) II, k. and high priest of the Jews, 720, 735

Iahia (Iachia), Abu Zakariya, k. of Tunis, 411

Iamblichus, 458
Iapygians (Iapiges), 428
Ibes, in Spain, N738
Ibrahim (Abraham), grand vizier of Turkey, 67, 745
Icetes, *see* Hicetas
Icilia, lex, 296, 349
Idumea, Idumeans, N464, 658
Ihon, *see* John
Ilienses, *see* Trojans
Ilus, 735
Imaus mountains, 562
Imegiagen (Ungiasen), 555
India, Indians, 10, 20, 75, 150, 206, 222, 402, N413, 441, 494, 502, N558, 676, 680, 692, 719, 722
Indian Chinois, *see* China
Indians, in America, 42, 440, 772&N
Indies, 23, 264, 506, 550, 558, 560, 568, 660. *See also* East Indies; West Indies
Ine, k. of Wessex, 116
Inglish(?), Robert, 628
Innocent II, pope, 648&N
Innocent III, pope, 40, 116, 125, 140–141, 687
Innocent IV, pope, 92, 109, 122, 126, 136, 139, 287, 299, 313, 625
Innocent IV, *error for* Honorius III, pope, 142
Innocent V, *error for* Innocent VI, pope, 143
Innocent VI, pope, 368
Interamna, 142&N
Interimists, N567
Ioland, *see* Isabella of Brienne
Ionia, Ionians, 81, 186, 457, N481, 646, 761
Iphicrates, 629
Iphigenia, 35
Ireland, 116–117, 126, 141
Irene (Hirene), empress of Constantinople, 747
Irenicus, Francis Friedlieb, 557
Isaac, the patriarch, 461
Isaak or Abu Bakr Izchia, k. of Tombutto, 555
Isabella, q. of Castile, wife of Ferdinand, k. of Aragon, 199, 746, 748, 751–752
Isabella of Austria, wife of Christian II, k. of Denmark, 749
Isabella or Iolande of Brienne, wife of emp. Frederick II, 747
Isabelle or Elizabeth of France, wife of Edward II, k. of England, 578, 749
Isabelle of Lorraine, wife of René of Anjou, k. of Sicily, 132, 203
Isadas, 599
Isaeus, the orator, 30, 392
Isaiah (Esaias, Esay, Esayas), 463
Isis, 538
Islam, *see* Mahometans
Islip, Adam, A59, A61
Isny (Isne), 131, 725

A189

Index Nominum

Isocrates, 461&N, 547, 641
Israel, Israelites, etc., *see* Jews
Istambul (Stamboll), A51, 410&N
See also Constantinople
Italy, Italians, forms of government in ancient times, 231, 380–381, 443, 561, 719–720, 722, 761; ancient laws and customs, 35, 251, 297, 363, 468; slave revolts, 38, 45; coinage, 697; relations with Rome, 54–55, 79, 164, 481, 608, 610, 612, 620, 628ᵛ, N635, 638, N640, 654, N656, N705; Roman administrative policies, 61, 213, 286, 335, 419; invasions of Pyrrhus and Hannibal, 607, 609, 656, 663, 715; earthquake, 437&N; forms of government in post-classical times, 128, 130–131, 134, 141, 150, 176, 432, 507, 702, 748; magistracies, 293, 330, 344, 368, 479, 482, 485, 763, 778; post-classical laws and customs, 40, 65, 71, 108, 119, N173, 395, 400, 541–542, 559, 628, N629ᵛ, 661, N773, 778; invasions and foreign intervention, 118, 123, 129, 202, 434, 449, N464, 550, 553&N, N567, 608–609, 617, 623, 625, 627ᵛ, 655, 681; Empire and Papacy, 136–139, 142, 144; finance and coinage, 672–675, 691, 693–694, 697; climate and nature of the people, 426, 549, 554&N, 558–559, 562, N564, 565, 613; mentioned, A69–A70, 26, 65–66, N72, 146, 179, 264, 285, 411, 509, 523, N544, 560–561, N612, 613, 619, 621, 648, 738
Ithaca, 10

Jabesh-Gilead (Jabes), 622
Jacob, the patriarch, 29, 203, 461
Jaddua (Jaduε), 534
Jagellon, d. of Lithuania, k. of Poland, 434–435
Jagellon, house of, 728, 749
James I, k. of Aragon, 93, 96, 742
James II, *error for ?*, k. of Aragon, 126
James II, k. of Majorca, 127, 742
James III, k. of Majorca, 176
James III, k. of Scotland, 735
James IV, k. of Scotland, 451&N
James V, k. of Scotland, N451, 677, N748
James VI, k. of Scotland, I of England, N728
James, ct., *see* Piccinino
Jane, daughter of Louis X, k. of France, *see* Jeanne
Janot, *see* Giannotti
Janus, temple of, 463, 530
Jaques de Terranne, *see* Palladino
Jason, tyrant of Pherae, 629
Jason of Maino, 228
Javolenus, Priscus, 178

Jean, *see* John
Jeanne (Joane) of Navarre, wife of Philip IV, k. of France, 748
Jeanne (Jane), q. of Navarre, daughter of Louis X, k. of France, 753
Jeanne d'Albret (Joane, Jone), q. of Navarre, 141, 199, 617
Jeanne, daughter of Raymond, ct. of Toulouse, 408
Jebusites, 410
Jefferson, Thomas, A66
Jehiel (Jeïel) ben Joseph, 18
Jehoiada (Joiada), 147
Jehoiakim (Joachim), k. of Judah, 465–466
Jehoshaphat (Josaphat), k. of Judah, 741
Jehoshaphat (Josophat), recorder of Solomon, 360
Jehu, 224
Jeïel, *see* Jehiel
Jephthah (Jephte), 35, 410
Jeremiah (Hieremy, Jeremie, etc.), 43, 94, 107, 463–465, 541
Jerome (Hierome, etc.), St., 461 &N, 467, 719
Jerome (Jerosme) of Prague, 628
Jerusalem (Hierusalem), 35, 223, 324, 367, 375, 448, 452, 463, 465, 534, 538, 564, 598, 657, 733
Jerusalem (Hierusalem), kingdom of, 126, 140, N631
Jesabel, *see* Jezebel
Jesuits, A53, A62
Jesus Christ, A12, 56, 453, 538
Jethro, 515
Jews, Hebrews, Israelites (Jewes, Hebrewes, Israelits, tribes, people, of Israel, etc.), forms of government among, 94, 153, 196, N205, 206, 224, 340, 363, 410, 413&NN, 416, 500, 666, 719–720, 734–735, 741; magistracies and senate, 56–57, 256, 269, 360, 769; history of, in Old Testament times, 35, 102, 220, 223, 360, 410, 534, 622, 628–628ᵛ, 639, 651; in Roman times, 35, 39, 324, 366–367, 381, 538, 657&N, 682; in post-classical times, 42, 43&N, 46, 381, 383, 427, 537, 575, 628, 745; laws and customs, 9, 18, 22, 32, 43, 293, 364, 399&N, 400–401, 527, 564, 569, N572, 671, 676, 774–776, 781; priesthood among, 392–393, 536, 769; revenues, treasure, coinage, 651, 682, 692, 698, 700; nature of the people, N551, N567, 568; philosophical and religious concepts, A70, 7, N436, 439–440, 444–445, 449–450, 453, 461–462, N519, 560, 562; force of numbers upon, 464&N, 465–466; linguistic references, 9, 16, N50, 362, 634, 723. *See also* Judah; Judaism; Judea; Palestine

Jezebel (Jesabel), 224, 582
Joachim, *see* Jehoiakim
Joane, *see* Jeanne
Joanna I (Joane, Jone), q. of Naples, 30, 122, 150, 747
Joanna II (Joane), q. of Naples, 31
Joannes de Temporibus, 462
Joash (Joas), k. of Judah, 147
John VIII(?), pope, 147
John XXII, pope, 140, 143, 575, 633, 683
John, k. of Bohemia, 134
John, k. of Cyprus, 626ᵛ
John, k. of England, 116, N118, 140, 608, 738
John II, k. of France, 26, 61, 88, 127, 132, 173, 282, 414, 452, 473, 588, 609, 627, 634ᵛ, 667&N, 669, 694, 697, 737, 743
John I, Zápolya, k. of Hungary, 616
John II, Zápolya, k. of Hungary, 121
John of Brienne, k. of Jerusalem, 747
John II, k. of Navarre, 145
John Albert (Albert), k. of Poland, 577
John II, k. of Portugal, 660, 739
John III, k. of Portugal, 660, 739
John III, k. of Sweden, 229, 724, 749, 752
John I, d. of Alençon, 626
John II, d. of Alençon, 229, 513
John III, d. of Alençon, 743
John of Angoulême, *error for ?*, 743&N
John V, ct. of Armagnac, 632
John, d. of Berry, 170, 176
John II, d. of Bourbon, 743
John IV, de Montfort, d. of Brittany, 118, 526, 738–739
John V, de Montfort or the Valiant, d. of Brittany, 117–118, 120, 513
John the Fearless, d. of Burgundy, 95, 230, 452, 526, 606
John of Haderεleben, 209
John of Gaunt, d. of Lancaster, 738, N749
John, lord of Milan, *see* Visconti
John (Ihon) or Ivan II, grand d. of Muscovy, 557
John of Foix (John Vaste), vicomte of Narbonne, 739
John II, ct. of Soissons, 514
John Maria della Rovere, d. of Urbino, *see* Della Rovere
John Digitorum, 147
John of Leyden, 411&N, 544, 558, N567
John of Salisbury, 108
Johnson, Dr. Samuel, A58
Joiada, *see* Jehoiada
Joinville, Jean, sieur de, 667
Jonathan Apphus, the Maccabean, 629
Jonathan ben Uzziel (the Chaldean Interpreter), 57, 439, 720, 759
Jone, *see* Jeanne; Joanna

A190

Index Nominum

Joram or Jehoram, k. of Judah, 735, 741
Jordan (Jordain), river, 440, 568
Jordanes or Jornandes, 451, N558
Josaphat, see Jehoshaphat
Joseph or Yusuf ibn Tashfin, k. of Morocco, 432, 544, 555
Josephus (Joseph), Flavius, 35, 39, 47, 276, 293, 381, 439, 444, N445, 464&N, 465–466, 555, 564, 639, 720, 767
Joshua (Josua), 455, 628, 639
Josophat, see Jehoshaphat
Jovean, see Goveanus
Jovianus (Jovinian), Flavius Claudius, 588
Jovius, Paulus, or Paolo Giovio, A69, 11, 147, 204, 416, N555, 668, 711
Juba I, k. of Numidia, 608
Juba II, k. of Numidia, 205
Judah (Juda), kingdom of, 147, 224, 556, 735, 747. See also Jews
Judaism, A13
Judas Maccabaeus (Machabeus), 464, 719
Judea (Jurie), 325, 463, 538, 676, 735. See also Jews
Judicael I, k. of Brittany, 118
Jugurtha, k. of Numidia, 30, N738
Julia, daughter of Caesar, 30, 499
Julia, daughter of Augustus, 30
Julia, gens, 391
Julia de adulteriis, lex, 17
Julia de bonis cedendis, lex, 67
Julia de civitate, lex, 55
Julia majestatis, lex, 158, 224
Julia et Papia Poppaea, lex, 31, 353, N670
Julia de senatu, lex, N275
Julia vicesimaria, lex, 665
Juliae, leges, 157
Julian de Medici, see Medici
Julian, scribe, 94, 730
Julianus, Didius, emp. of Rome, 159
Julianus (Julian), the Apostate, emp. of Rome, 40, 43, 53, 421, 457, 552, 562, 588, 590
Julianus (Julian), Salvius, jurist, 158
Juliers, 124
Julius (Julio) II, pope, 122, 126, 129–130, 141, 145, 435, 606, 627–627^v, 632
Julius (Julio) III, pope, 141, 595&N, 607, 632^v
Julus, son of Ascanius, 738
Junia, gens, 391
Junia Norbana, lex, N55
Juniae, leges, 55, 281, 339
Junius, Marcus, see Pennus
Juno, 19, 639, N648, 697
Jupiter, 19, 23, 35, 76, 104, 262, 339–340, N436, 500, 512&N, 561, N648, 705, 746. See also Zeus
Jura, mountains, 134, 721
Jurie, see Judea

Justinian, Justinians, see Giustiniani
Justinian, emp. of Rome, 17&N, 19&N, 22, 25–26, 29–31, 34, 41, N114, 159, N202, 208, 281, 286, 294–295, 298, 300, 310, 335, 357&NN, 507, 524, 530, 573–574, 578, 580, 585, N632, 670&N, 766, 782–783
Justinus I, emp. of the East, 29
Justinus III, emp., error for?, 417
Justinus, historian, 9, 17, 39, 463, 554, 735
Juvenal, 548&N, 559

Kalundborg (Calembourg), 229
Kanan, rabbi, see Hananel
Katherine of Valois, wife of Henry V, k. of England, 95
Katherine of Aragon, wife of Henry VIII, k. of England, 617
Kent, A55, A57
Kish (Cis), 734
Knolles, Sir Robert, 165
Koschwitz, E., N633
Kurds (Curdes), 147, 203

La Baume (Baume), house of, 13
Labdac, 568
Labeo, Antistius, jurist, 301, 303, 772
Labienus, Titus, 587, N629^v
Lacedemonia, Lacedemonians (Lacedemon), forms of government, 161, 184, 186–187, 190, 198, N409, 412, 436, 713&N, 761; kingship and succession, 206, 413, 719, 722, 735, 737, 739, 741; aristocracy, 196, 221, 232, 241, 270; senate and magistrates, 85, 207, 224–225, 233, 258, 263, 277, 344, 488, 492, 517, 716; domestic history, 38–39, 566, 714, 716, N738; foreign relations, 79&N, 81, 483, 522–523, 599–600, 620, 627^v, 650; relations with Athens, 101–102, 422, 424, 471, 604, 612, 633^v, 658; laws and customs, 12, 16, 19, 28, 39, 67, 280, 318, 368–369, 399, 496, 551, 569–570, 577&N, 763, 766, 784; nature of the people, 7, 271, 546; mentioned, iv, 8, 51, N292, 428, 443, 454, 494, 525, 584, 591, 596, 606. See also Sparta
Lachares, tyrant of Athens, 433
Lactantius Firmianus, 231, 462, 645
Ladamachus, see Zadamachus
Ladislaus I, k. of Bohemia, 557
Ladislaus (Lancelot), error for Wenceslas VI, k. of Bohemia, 628
Ladislaus I, k. of Hungary, 736
Ladislaus I, error for?, k. of Hungary, 140
Ladislaus II, error for III, k. of Hungary, 140

Ladislaus V, Postumus, k. of Hungary and Bohemia, 726–727
Ladislaus VI, k. of Hungary and Bohemia, 727
Ladislaus I, Lokietek, d. and k. of Poland, 140
Ladislaus II, k. of Poland, see Jagellon
Laertius, see Diogenes
Laetoria, lex, see Plaetoria de praetore urbano, lex
La Forest, Jacques Bochetel, sieur de, 130, 133, N141
La Gasca, Pedro de, 43, 203
La Guette, an embezzler, N685
La Guiche (Guiche), Pierre, seigneur de, 82
Laish (Lays), 622
L'Allemand, see Alamant
La Marche (Marche), 176, 583&N, 731
La Marck (la March), Robert de, lord of Bouillon, 632
Lambert of Hersfeld, 132
Lamech, patriarch, 461
La Molle, Joseph Boniface de, A8
La Mothe-Fénelon, Bertrand de Salignac, seigneur de, N203
Lampridius Aelius, 262
Lancaster, house of, 83, 526, 601
Lancelot, see Ladislaus, k. of Bohemia
Langres, 54, 514&N
Languedoc (Languedocke, Languedouich, etc.), 108, 384, 385&N, 408&N, 479, 552, 562, 564, 566, 583&N, 641&N, 669, 685
Lansac, Louis de St. Gelais, sieur de, 151
Lanuvini, 76
Loadicea (Laodicia), Council of, 724
Laon, A9–A12, A29, N229, 548, 730
La Rochebeaucourt (La Rochegaucourt), Jean de, 122
La Roche-Blanche, 42
La Rochelle (Rochell), 378, 575, 626
Lascaris (Lascare), 554
La Serre (Serre), Jean, sieur de, vi
Laski, Albert, palatine of Sieradz, 672
Laski, Jerome, 672
Laslett, Pete., A64
Latimer, Hugh, bp. of Worcester, A53
Latins (Latines), 9, 13, 16, 54, 55&N, 75–76, 81&N, 164, 181, 217, 219, 231, 255, 265, N271, N283, 310–311, N413, 441, 527, 612, N614, 615, 620, 634^v, 698, 705, 719, 722, 735, 738, 774. See also Rome
La Trémouille (Trimouille), Louis de, vicomte of Thouars, 165
L'Aubespine, Sébastien de, abbé de Bassefontaine, bp. of Limoges, 250

Index Nominum

Laud (Lau), St., 631^v&N
Lauda, merchant of Cambrai, N662
Laude, see Lodi
Lauredan, see Loredan
Laurence de Medicis, see Medici
Laurentum, Laurentini, 634^v
Lausanne (Losanna), 648
La Vacquerie (Lavacrie), Jean de, 315
Laval, house of, 13–14
Lavie, Jean-Charles de, A84–A85
La Vigne, Jean Carcenac, called, 674
Lavinia, 738
Lays, see Laish
Lazar I (Lazarus), prince of Serbia, 523
Lebanon, N565
Le Cirier, Jean, N732, 753
Lectoure or Lactora (Lectore), 42
Leegeois, see Liège
Lefèvre d'Étaples, Jacques, N460
Le Havre (Newhaven, the Port of Grace), 62, 602
Leipzig (Lipsic), 466
Le Juge or de Juge, Claude, A79
Le Maine, see Maine
Le Maistre, Gilles, 177, N345, 664
Lennox, earls of, see Stuart
Lentulus Augur, Cneius Cornelius, 575
Lentulus Clodianus, Cneius Cornelius, 267, 305
Leo IX or Bruno (Brunon), pope, 142
Leo X, pope, 435, 630^v, 734
Leo III, emp. of the East, 137
Leo IV, emp. of the East, 452
Leo V, the Armenian, emp. of the East, 228
Leo VI, emp. of the East, N357
Leo II, k. of Armenia, 613
Leo Africanus, Johannes (Leo of Affrike, etc.), 47, 507, 549, 554–556, N558, 560, 563, N565, 600, 716
Leo of Byzantium, 18
Leo the Hebrew or Judah Abravanel, N450
Leonidas, 207
Leonore, see Eleanor
Leontini (Leonce, Leontium), 420, 481
Leopold (Leupold), son of the d. of Austria, 444
Leosthenes, 610
Leotychides (Leotichides), 737
Leowitz (Leovicius), Cyprian, 439, 449, 453&N
Lepanto, battle of, 452
Lepidus, see Aemilius Lepidus
Leptines, 102
Le Puy (Puy), Antoine II de Chabannes, bp. of, 514
Lesbian rule, 341, N759, 760
L'Escalopier de Nourar, Charles-Armand, A84
Lescun (Lescut), Odet d'Aydie, seigneur de, 631^v

Leucippus, k. of Messene, 186, 198, 742
Leupold, see Leopold
Levi ben Gershom, rabbi, 35
Leviathan, 793
Levinus, see Valerius Laevinus
Levites (Levits), 57, 536, 538, 571–572, 639, 648, 720, 769
Lewes, see Lewis
Lewis I, emp. of Germany, see Lewis I, k. of France
Lewis II, the Young, emp. of the West, k. of Italy, 138
Lewis IV, the Child, emp. of Germany, 729
Lewis V (of Baviere), error for IV, 629^v
Lewis V, of Bavaria, emp. of Germany, 128, 131, 135, 143–144, 241, 725, 727, 733
Lewis, k. of France, see Clovis
Lewis I, the Débonnaire or Pious, k. of France, 39, 118&N, 138, 146, 151, 198, 428, 453, 732, 736, 738
Lewis II, the Stammerer, k. of France, 730, 737
Lewis V, Fainéant, k. of France, N217
Lewis VI, le Gros, k. of France, 160, 608, 730, 732
Lewis VII, the Young, k. of France, 66, 266, 452, 617, 648&N, 664
Lewis VIII, k. of France, 117–118, 652
Lewis IX, k. of France, 120, 122, 127, 134, 139, 173, 177, N205, 268, 331, 377, 408, 425, 482, 489, 514, 524–525, 528, 583&N, 588, 591, 664, 666–667, 674, 676, 689, 742, 748
Lewis X, Hutin, k. of France, 41, 298, 687, 753
Lewis XI, k. of France, accession, 736–737; personal qualities, 253, 255, 516–517; constitutional questions, 167, 284, 288, 293, 315–316, 490, 492; domestic policies, 62, 101, 125, 152, 177, 513, 588–589; taxation, 665, 669, 684; relations with vassals, 110, 176, 180–181, 448, 489, 628^v–629, 631–632, 636, 680, 743; foreign relations, 73, 119, 121, 124, N614, 615, N736; with England, 148, 601, 603, 606, 659; with the Swiss, 58, 75, 622, 706
Lewis XII, k. of France, constitutional questions, 263, 267, 315–317, N354, 371, 484, 684; domestic policies, 64, 112, 173, 180, 573, 577, 652, 666, 743; foreign relations, 126, 145, 165, 170, 629, 631; Italian wars, 110, 128–129, 177, 432, 451, 463, 493, 498, 597, 615, 623–624, 627, 732, 660–661, 712, 725

Lewis the German, k. of Germany, 39, 132, 138–139, 151, 428, 633, 732
Lewis I, the Great, k. of Hungary and Poland, 435, 452, 511, 726, 748–750
Lewis I, k. of Naples, d. of Anjou, 30, 165, 205, 743
Lewis III, error for II, k. of Naples, d. of Anjou, 743
Lewis (error for?), k. of Navarre, ct. of Evreux, 526
Lewis, d. of Anjou, see Lewis, k. of Naples
Lewis II, d. of Bourbon, 134
Lewis of Bourbon, prince of Condé, 171
Lewis II, of Nevers, ct. of Flanders, 739
Lewis III, of Mâle, ct. of Flanders, 376
Lewis of Gonzaga, see Gonzaga
Lewis, d. of Orleans, 83, 128, 133, 230, 635^v, 729
Lewis of Luxemburg, ct. of St. Pol, Constable of France, 628^v, 631–632
Lewis Sforza (Sforce, Sfortia), see Sforza
Lewis of Spain or Luis de la Cerda, 126
L'Hôpital (Hospitalis, etc.), Michel de, Chancellor of France, 91, 169, 346, 485, 789
Libanius, 647
Libitina, Venus, see Venus
Libo, see Scribonius
Libya (Libia), 680
Licinia, gens, 391
Liciniae, leges, 281, 288, 576, 650–651
Licinius, emp. of Rome, 227
Licinius Calvus Stolo, Caius, 302
Licinius Crassus, see Crassus
Licinius Lucullus, see Lucullus
Licinius Macer, Caius (Cassius), 580
Licinus (Lucius Licinius), 260
Licortas, see Lycortas
Licurgus, see Lycurgus
Lidiens, see Lydia
Liège, Liègeois (Leegeois, etc.), 59, 222, 433, 635, 680, 733
Lifland, see Livonia
Ligarius, Quintus, 175, 510
Ligurians, N564
Limagne, valley, N565
Limoges (Limogaea), 250, 399, 565&N, 731
Limousin (Limosin), 554
Linacre, Thomas, 461
Linceus, see Lynceus
Lincoln, John White, bp. of, A54
Lindau (Lindaw), 426, 668, 707, 711
Linus, 446
Lion, Lions, see Lyon
Lipsic, see Leipzig
Lisander, see Lysander

Index Nominum

L'Isle-Jourdain, 583&N
Lisores (Lisoires), Pierre le Jumel, sieur de, 770
Lisieux (Lizieux), Jean III de Dormans, bp. of, 631ᵛ
Lithuania, Lithuanians (Lituania), 44, 66, 136, 381, 435, 548, 555, 728
Littré, Emile, N376
Livia, wife of Augustus, 57, 107, 578
Livia, gens, 391
Livia, lex, 266
Livius, Titus (Livie, Livy), political doctrines of, 73–74, 104, 503, N614, 622, 703; on forms of government at Rome, 205, 411, N706; on powers of the people under the republic, 157, 163–164, 168, 189, 245, N265, 285, 296; on the Senate, 157, 262, 272–274, 660; on magistracies, 274, 290–291, 298, 306, 309, 483, 610; on the Dictatorship, 85, 281, 294, 715–716; on the Consulship, N339, 348, 762; on the Censors, 304, NN638, 643–644, 646; on the Tribuneship, 23, 302–303, 349–351; on Roman laws and customs, 16, 54, 329, 398, 440, N577, 586; on class strife at Rome, 404, 428, NN788; on Roman population and census, 637, 639&N, 640, N642; on Roman religious observances, 14, 391, N604; on foreign history and customs, 58, 81, 187, 201, 261, 268, 478&N, N551, 570, 623–625, 706; on Roman domestic history, 377, 454, 601, 655, N656, 663&N, N670, 774; on relations with Italian peoples, 55, 374–375, 468, 612, 614–615, 620, 633ᵛ–634, 635; on foreign relations beyond Italy, 150, 208, 232, 261–262, 386, 620–621, 627ᵛ&N, 630ᵛ, 635ᵛ, 636&N, N657, 691, 738 &N; on the nature of peoples, 546, 557, 564&N, 565–566; on character of individuals, 211, 499, 558; mentioned, A48, A56, A90
Livius Drusus, Marcus, 188, 301, 303, 349, 642, 697, 705
Livius Salinator, Marcus, 179, 305, 348, 390, 496–497, N586, N638, 665
Livonia (Lifland), 617, 632ᵛ
Livre, Nicolas de, see Humerolles
Lizet, Pierre, 133
Lizieux, see Lisieux
Locarno, 451
Loches, 514
Locke, John, A64–A65
Locri, Locrians (Locris, Locrensians), 470, 761, 781
Lodi (Laude), 729
Lombard, Peter, N107, 504

Lombardy, Lombards (Lombardie, Lumbards), 17, 30, 39, 71, 114&N, 119, 137–138, 143, 155, 202, 449, 463, 527–528, 537, 550, 562, 597, 612, 655, 675, 765
London, A44, A57, A62–A63, 62, 97, N556, 690, 728
Longueville, Léonor d'Orléans, d. of, 68
Lopes, see Sequeira
Loredan (Lauredan, etc.), Pietro, 432, 534
Loredano, Leonardo, doge of Venice, 472
Lorraine (Loraine), 59, 131–132, 138–139, 158, 170, 181, 203, 208, 237, 595, 623, 625ᵛ, 691, 743. See also Charles, d. of Lower Lorraine; Charles of Lorraine
Lorraine, Christina, dowager duchess of, N210
Losanna, see Lausanne
Lot, 634
Lothair I, emp. of the West, 39, 131, 138–139, 428, 453, 732, 736
Lothair II, emp. of Germany, 117
Lothair, k. of the Franks, see Clotaire
Lothair, k. of Italy, error for Lorraine, 138, 648&N
Lothair, jurist, 327, 329, 330&N, 333–334
Louis, see Lewis
Louise of Savoy, mother of Francis I, 172–173
Loup de Ferrières, 590
Low Countries, Netherlanders, (Holland, Netherlands, Dutch), A10, A32–A34, A57, A72, 122, 127, 218, 264, 290, 378, 434, 509, 528, 530, N546, 551, N558, 577, 608, 626ᵛ, N636ᵛ, 661, 662&N, 666, N667, 668, 685, 693&N, 739, 751, N773. See also Flanders
Lübeck (Lubec, Lubech), 84, 100, 131, 194, 238, 241
Lucanus (Lucan), Marcus Annaeus, 54, 198, N548, N713
Lucca, Lucchesi (Luca, Lucque, Luque, Lucenses, Luques, Luquois, etc.), 76, 129, 134, 176, 235–237, 245, 277, 359, 425, 428, 433, 534, 596, 616–617, 625ᵛ, 629ᵛ, 635, 638, 672, 694, 713
Lucceius (Luceius), Lucius, 495, 592
Luccino (Luchin), lord of Milan, see Visconti
Lucerne or Luzern, 76–78, 82, 149, 234&N, 264, 497, 619, 651, 695
Lucianus (Lucian), 198
Lucilius, Caius, 459, 474
Lucius, see Caesar, Lucius
Lucius III, pope, 176
Lucque, see Lucca

Lucretia, 211
Lucretia, gens, 391
Lucrezia (Lucrece), daughter of Alexander VI, see Borgia
Luctatia or Lutatia, gens, 391
Luctatius Catulus, Caius, consul 242 B.C., 164, 347, 585, 631
Luctatius Catulus, Quintus, consul 78 B.C., 281, 497
Luctatius Pinthia, Marcus, 243
Lucullus, Lucius Licinius, consul 74 B.C., 655, 668
Lucullus, Marcus Licinius, consul 73 B.C., 279&N, 295, 298
Lude, Jean de Daillon, sieur du, 606
Ludovicus, see Lewis
Lugano (Lugan), 60, 77
Lugtak (Lugtac), k. of Scotland, 416
Luillier (Lullier), Maximinus (error for Nicolas?), 685
Luis de la Cerda, see Lewis of Spain
Luitprand, k. of the Lombards, 30, 765
Lumbards, see Lombards
Lumes (Lume), 59, 132
Luntuna (Luntune), 147
Luque, Luques, Luquoies, Luquois, see Lucca
Lutatia, Lutatius, see Luctatia, Luctatius
Luther, Martin, 225&N, 453, 461, 466, N567, 628
Luwertz, see Lugano
Luxemburg (Lutzembourg, etc.), Henry of, see Henry VII, emp. of Germany
Luxemburg, Lewis of, see Lewis, ct. of St. Pol
Luzern, see Lucerne
Lycia, Lycians, 20, 81
Lycophron, 392
Lycortas (Licortas), 620
Lycurgus (Licurgus), lawgiver of Sparta, iv, 39, 67, 161, 181, 186–188, 198, 255–256, 280, 363, 397, 399, 409&N, 412, 471–472, 496, 535, N554, N558, 566, 569, 571–572, 576&N, 577, 596, 610, 620, 645, 650, 701, 736, N738, 739, 761, 766, 777, 784
Lycurgus, k. of Sparta, 436, 454
Lycurgus, Athenian orator, 392
Lydia, Lydians (Lidiens, etc.), N413, 457, 646, 666
Lynceus (Linceus), 244
Lyon (Lion, Lions, Lyons), A44, A78, 42, 46, 55, 66, 135, 217, 649, 673, 675, 690
Lyon, Pierre d'Espinac, archbp. of, 371
Lyonnais (Lyonnois), 108
Lysander (Lisander), 186, 206, 235, 241, 263, 494, 569, 591, 600, 625ᵛ, 650, 737
Lysimachus, k. of Thrace, 179, 208, 723

A193

Index Nominum

Lysimachus (Lysimachides), an Athenian, 641

Maas, river, see Meuse
Macedon, Macedonians (Macedonie, Macedons, etc.), 2, 149–150, 162, 206, 292, 386, 413, 417, 422, 451, 464&N, 518, 522, 601, 621, 624–625, N627^v, 628^v, 630^v&N, 633, 655–656, 659, 667, 719, 722–723, 735. See also Antigonus; Demetrius; Perseus; and Philip, k. of Macedon
Machabeus, see Judas Maccabaeus
Machaetas (Machetas), 171
Machiavelli (Machiavel, etc.), Niccolò, A69–A70, 184, 186, 426, 559, 629^v, 702
McIlwain, Charles Howard, A63
Mâcon (Mascon), John, ct. of Poitiers and, 266
Macrinus (Macrin), Marcus Opilius, emp. of Rome, 214, 745
Macrobius, 462
Madianites, see Midianites
Madrid, treaty of, 626^v, 652
Maecenas (Mecenas, Moecenas), 263, 266, 511, 710
Maecia (Metia), gens, 305
Maecianus (Maetian), Volusius, 336
Magdeburg (Maidenburg), 130, 451
Magellan, Fernando, 550
Maggio, Lucio, N453
Magi (Mages), 205, N413
Magnus, Olaus, 547
Magran or Imeghran (Magnan), Mount, 707
Mahomet, see also Mehemet
Mahomet (Mahumet) II, emp. of the Turks, 359, 443, 464, 656
Mahomet (Muhamed), the prophet, 39–40, 147, 203, 448, 537
Mahometans, Mahometan religion (Islam, Musulmans), iii, 42–43, 147, 152, 279, 417, 537, 554–555, N567
Maidenburg, see Magdeburg
Maigret, an embezzler, N685
Maimonides (Maymon), Moses, 15, 18, 720
Maine (Le Maine, Mayne), 13, 116, 316, 482, 579, 583&N
Mainz, 238, 629^v
Majorca (Majorque, Molorque), 127, 139, 176, 687, 693, 742
Malacca (Malache, Malachie), 147, 660
Malancthon, see Melanchthon
Malatesti (Malatestes), 420
Malestroit, Jean Cherruyt, sieur de, A6, 175, 666, 691
Malta, 44, 85, 141, 435
Malta, Knights of, 141, 144, 435, 733–734
Mamercus, tyrant of Catana, 420
Mamercus, see Aemilius Mamercus

Manasseh (Manasses), son of Joseph, 29
Mancinus, Caius Hostilius, 164, 626^v
Manetho, N206
Manfred (Manfroy), k. of Naples, 139, 229, 747
Manfredi family (Manfreds), 420
Manichaeans (Manichies), 199, 459
Manilia, gens, 391
Manilia, lex, 162, 281, 285
Manilius or Manlius, astrologer, 442
Manlius, Lucius, 635^v
Manlius Capitolinus, Marcus, 603
Manlius Capitolinus, Publius, 302
Manlius Capitolinus Imperiosus, Cnaeus, 665
Manlius Capitolinus Imperiosus (called Torquatus in error), Lucius, 23
Manlius Torquatus (error for Capitolinus), Marcus, 219
Manlius Torquatus, Titus, consul 347 B.C., 28, 401, 572, N630
Manlius Torquatus, Titus, consul 235 B.C., 492, 546
Manlius Vulso, Aulus, 477
Manlius Vulso, Cnaeus, 164
Manners, Edward, see Rutland
Mansfeld, Peter Ernst, ct. von, 181
Mansor, see Almansor
Mantes (Mante), 155
Mantinea, Mantineans, 186, 708
Mantua (Mantoue), 114, 129, 154, 158, 181, 417, 432, 625^v, 694, 743
Mantuanus, see Baptista
Manutius, Paulus, 190, 407, 712
Manwood family, A60, A64
Manwood, Sir Peter, A43–A44, A46, A58–A61, A64, iii, N784
Manwood, Sir Roger, A55–A59
Marc, see Mark
Marcel, Claude, 700
Marcelli (Marcelles), 70
Marcellus, Marcus Claudius, consul 222 B.C., 319, 496, 527, 587, 609
Marcellus, Marcus Claudius, consul 51 B.C., 356, 521
Marcellus, Nonius, N567, N614, N631^v
Marcellus, Ulpius, jurist, 704
Marche, see La Marche
Marcia (Martia), concubine of Commodus, 214
Marcia (Martia), gens, 391
Marcia (Martia), lex, 162
Marcianus (Martian), Aelius, 328, N329, 343, 746
Mardocheus, see Mordecai
Margaret (Mary), q. of Denmark, Norway, and Sweden, 31, N210, 748
Margaret, ctss. of Flanders, 746
Maria, gens, 391
Marie, see Mary

Marignano (Marignan), battle of, 452, 588, 597, 616, 625
Marillac, Charles de, archbp. of Vienne, 239
Marillac, Gabriel (?) de, 641
Marini (Marin), Tommaso, 574
Mariscotti family (Marischots), 525
Marius, Caius, 49, 246, 259, 286, 390&N, 429, 481, 497, 530, N629^v, 636, 705&N, 788
Mark (Marc), patriarch or abima of Ethiopia, 558
Maro, see Virgilius Maro
Marocco, Maroch, see Morocco
Marot, Clément, N455
Maroveus, see Meroveus
Mars, 392, 527, 540, 561&N, 705, 738
Marseille (Marseils, etc., Massilia), 3, 17, 58, 144, 232, N277, 578, 625, 671, 690
Marshall, Thomas, fellow of Lincoln, A53
Marsians or Marsi, N564
Martel, Charles, see Charles Martel
Martia, see Marcia
Martialis (Martial), Marcus Valerius, 114, 208, N548
Martian, see Marcianus
Martin V, pope, 31, 127, 299, 574
Martius, see Philippus
Mary, q. of Denmark, Norway, and Sweden, see Margaret
Mary, q. of England, A53, 97, 112, 152, 199, 205, 463, 746, N748, 749&N, 750&N, N752
Mary, q. of Hungary, 746, 748, 750
Mary, q. of Scots, A34–A35, A40, 68, N229, 454, 463, N747, N748, 751&N
Mascon, see Mâcon
Masinissa, k. of Numidia, N558
Massagetae (Massagets), 12
Massilia, see Marseille
Maternianus, Flavius, N214
Maternus, see Firmicus Maternus
Matilda (Maud), q. of England, 748
Matilda (Maud, Mauld), ctss. of Artois, 738&N, 746&N
Matilda (Maud), ctss. of Tuscany, 141, 142&N
Matthias Corvinus (Mathew Corvin), k. of Hungary, 448, 560, 616, 628, 727
Maud, Mauld, see Matilda
Maurice, elector of Saxony, 523, 634^v
Mauritanians, 612
Maxentius, emp. of Rome, 452
Maximilian I, emp. of Germany, 73, 110, 119, 128–129, 238, 606, N614, 629, 727–728
Maximilian II, emp. of Germany, 27, 130, 150, 209, 239, 453
Maximinus I, emp. of Rome, 205, 221, 417, 745

Index Nominum

Maximus, Magnus Clemens, emp. of Rome, 227
Maximus, Valerius, *see* Valerius
Maximus Tyrius (Tirius), 186, 702, 719
Mayer, Charles-Joseph, A85
Mayne, *see* Maine
Meaux, 54, 176, 452
Mecenas, *see* Maecenas
Mecnasa or Meknès (Mecna), 600
Media, Medes, 101–102, 200, 204, 206, 412–413, 417, 443, 464&N, 465, 500, 550, 718, 722, 756
Media, an Athenian, *see* Meidias
Medici (Medices), house of, 422, 424, 431
Medici, Alessandro de', d. of Florence, 216, 220, 416, 418, 424, 630^v
Medici, Cosmo de', grand d. of Tuscany, 64, 129, 150, 205, 216, 220, 418, 424, 426, 433, 523, 604, 668, 721
Medici, Giuliano de', 359
Medici, Giulio de', *see* Clement VII, pope
Medici, Lorenzino (Laurence) de', 418, 424
Medici, Lorenzo de', the Magnificent, 359, 706
Medici, Lorenzo II de', 716
Mediterranean (Mediterannean, etc.), sea, region, 45, 179, 399, 550–551, N579, 613, 690
Megacles, of Mytilene, 417
Megaclides (Megalides), 641
Megal, k. of the Scots, *see* Mogallus
Megalopolis, Megalopolitans, 51, 186
Megara, Megarians (Megarenses, etc.), 101, 162, 423–424, 518, 705
Megasa or Mgassa (Megeza), mount, 563
Megasthenes, 466
Mehemet, *see also* Mahomet
Mehemet or Malik al-Nasir al-din Mahommed, sultan of Egypt, 727
Mehemet, son (*error for* grandson?) of Solyman, emp. of the Turks, 718
Mehemet, pasha, *see* Sokolli
Meidias (Media), 357
Meierus, *see* Meyer
Melanchthon (Malancthon, etc.), Philip, 153, N436, 455, 461
Melaschall, or Malik al-Ashraf Musa?, sultan of Egypt, 727
Melesians, *see* Miletus
Melfi (Melphe), prince of, *see* Caraccioli
Melos, Melians, 186
Melun, 768
Memmius, Gaius, 351, N629^v
Memmius, *see* Mesmes
Memnon, k. of Ethiopia, 558
Ménage, Gilles, N182
Menander, k. of Bactria, 215

Mende, 146
Mendoza, Bernardino de, 557
Mendoza, Diego de, 151
Menenia, gens, 391
Menenius Lanatus, Agrippa, 53, 531, 534, 587, 706, 708
Menenius Lanatus, Titus, 297–298
Merbury, Charles, A62
Mercator, Gerard, 439, 451, 465
Mercury, 363, 561
Meroveus (Merove, Merovee), chief of the Franks, 198, 590
Meroveus (Maroveus), bp. of Poitiers, 638
Merovingians (Merovignes), 729–730
Mesmes (Memmius), Jean-Jacques de, seigneur de Roissi, 773
Mesnard, Pierre, A6, A74, A89
Messahala or Macha-Allah, 449
Messala, *see* Valerius Messala
Messenians, 186, 198, 416, 741
Messin, 621
Messina or Messana, 38, 694
Metellus Macedonicus, Quintus Caecilius, 388
Metellus Nepos, Quintus Caecilius, 654
Metellus Numidicus, Quintus Caecilius, 315, 532, 704
Methuselah (Methusala), 461
Metia, gens, *see* Maecia
Mettius Fuffetius (Metius Suffetius), dictator of Alba, 494, 635, 775
Metz (Mets), A8, 64, 133, 247, 435, 600, 607, 615, 617–618, 621, 741
Meulan (Meullan), 155
Meuse or Maas (Maze), river, 132
Meyer (Meierus), Jacob, 632
Michaloglis, 436, 745
Michell, John, fellow of Lincoln, A53
Micipsa, k. of Numidia, 30
Midianites (Madianites), 410
Milan, Milanese (Millan, Milanois), government, 87, 114, 128, 154, 169, N205, 322, 417, 420, 423, 714, 729, 743–744; laws and customs, 61, 66, 321, 508, 777–779, 784; revenues and coinage, 111, 668, 675, 694; domestic history, 320, 513, 597; external relations, 74, 83, 129–130, 227, 360, 553, 624; with the Empire, 67, 122–123, 144, 172, 239, 376, 625, 627^v; with France, 110, 217, 451, 553, 593, 597, 625^v, 656; mentioned, 82, 119, 155, 629. *See also* Sforza; Visconti
Milan, bp. of, *see* Ambrose
Milan, Council of, 537
Miletus, Milesians (Miletum, Melesians, Mylesians), 17, 186, 393, 429, 546, 570–571, 578, 711
Milo, Titus Annius Papianus, 38
Miltiades, 704, 716

Minden (Minde), 130
Minerva, 584
Minorca (Minorque), 127, 139, 687
Minos, k. of Crete, 500
Minucius (Minutius) Myrtilus, Lucius, 635^v
Minucius (Minutius) Rufus, Marcus, 85, 498
Mirandola (Mirandula), 141, 442, 444, 632–632^v
Mirepoix, 331
Mithridates IV, k. of Pontus, 33, 121
Mithridates VI, k. of Pontus, 162, 281, 285–286, 291, 481, 483, 503, 625, 629, 636
Mitylene, Mitylenaeans (Mitelin, Mytelenians, etc.), 207, 417, 429, 711, 716
Moabites, 523
Modena (Modene), 128–129, 141
Modestinus, Herennius, 52, 346
Modrzewski, Andreas Fricius (Riccee), 773
Moecenas, *see* Maecenas
Mogallus (Megal), k. of the Scots, 416
Moises, *see* Moses
Molins, Charles of, Molinaeus, *see* Du Moulin
Molorque, *see* Majorca
Moluccas (Molucques), 660
Mommorancie, Mompellier, *see* Montmorency, Montpellier
Moncontour (Montcontour), 452
Mondidier, Monluc, Monpellier, *see* Montdidier, Montluc, Montpellier
Monstrelet, Enguerrand de, 588
Monstreuil, *see* Montreuil
Montcornet, 548
Montdidier (Mondidier), 579
Montereau-faut-Yonne, 583&N
Montesquieu, Charles de Secondat, baron de, A84
Montfort, 118, 180, 652. *See also* John de Montfort, d. of Brittany; Simon, ct. of Montfort
Montluc (Monluc), Jean de, bp. of Valence, 152
Montmorency, house of, 13–14
Montmorency (Mommorancie, etc.), Anne, Constable of France, 59, 121, 179, 238, 360, 378, N553, 768
Montmorency (Montmorancie), Matthieu, 514
Montpellier (Mompellier, Monpellier, etc.), 108, 125, 155, 377, 479, 541, 568, 690
Montreuil (Monstreuil), 120
Moore, George Albert, A7, A89, N687
Moors (Moores), 90, 126, 139, 148, 417, 449, 451, 454, 464, 549–550
Moravia, A61
Mordecai (Mardocheus), 680

A195

Index Nominum

More (Moore), Sir Thomas, A27, A40, v, 3, 116, 184, 186, 188, 257, 271, 482, 513&N, 569, 571, 614, 766, 778
Morea, 80, 177
Moreau-Reibel, Jean, N234, N463
Morlet, an embezzler, N685
Morlet du Museau, Antoine, 82, 251
Morocco (Marocco, Maroch), 46, 147, 205, 209, 361, 432–433, 544, 555–556, 563, 600, 660, 682
Morone (Moron), Girolamo, 513 &N, 627ᵛ
Morris, William, fellow of Lincoln, A53
Moschovie, Moscovia, Moscovits, etc., see Muscovy
Moselle, river, 170
Moses (Moises, Moyses), 29, 211, 220, 276, 293, 381, 439–440, 461, 505, 515, 536, N567, 639, 719, 761
Mosse, G. L., A62
Moulin, see Du Moulin
Moulins, Edict of, 178, 300, 696
Moyses, see Moses
Mucamen, k. of Tunis, 411
Mucia (Mutia), gens, 391
Mucius (Mutius), Quintus, eques, 398
Mucius (Mutius), Quintus, jurist, see Scaevola
Muhamed, see Mahomet
Mula (Mule), Marcantonio da, card., 258
Muley Hassan (Muleasses), k. of Tunis, 416, 555&N
Mulhouse or Mühlhausen, 76, 619
Mummius Achaicus, Lucius, 386, 621
Münster, in Westphalia, 12, 130, 380, 411, 544, 558
Munster, Sebastian, 557, 567&N
Musa, Morlet, see Morlet du Museau
Musaeus, 761
Muscovy, Muscovites (Moschovia, Moscovia, Moscovits, etc.), 23, 44, 60, 66, 149, 152, 201, 222, N451, 479, 485, 507, 536, 548, 550, 555, 557, 567, 598, 605, 607, 614, 617, 632ᵛ, 636, 719, 722, 734, 738, 779–780. See also Russia
Mustapha, prince, son of Solyman, emp. of the Turks, 718
Musulmans, etc., see Mahometans
Mutia, Mutius, see Mucia, Mucius
Mylesians, see Miletus
Mytilene, Mytelenians, see Mitylene

Naaman, 539
Nabil, El-Kaïd (Delcaid), 416
Nabis, tyrant of Sparta, 187, 570
Nabonassar, k. of Babylon, 447&N
Naboth, 582

Nabuchodonosor, Nabucodonosor, see Nebuchadnezzar
Naim, see Nay
Naples, Neapolitans, succession to the throne, 31, 139, 205, 425, 594, 738–739, 747&N, 748; government, 87, 128, 169; laws and customs, 61, 63, 65, 228, 529; revenues, coinage, weights, 661, 675, 690, 693; history, 549, 629ᵛ, 630ᵛ, 750; relations with Papacy, 122–123, 125–126, 128, 140, 150, 623, 627ᵛ; foreign relations, 83, 606, 624, 625ᵛ, 631, 656, 674; in classical period, 80, 286, 644; mentioned, N142, 526, 617. See also Alphonsus; Charles; Manfred; and René, k. of Naples
Narbonne (Narbona, Narbone), 42, 55, N408, 554, N565, N773
Narses, 635
Nathan (Natan), 360
Natolia, see Anatolia
Nauck, August, N394
Nautia, gens, 391
Navarra, Pedro, ct. of Navarro, 411, 565
Navarre, 120, 126, 128, 133, 141, 144–145, 155, 199, 218, 411, 513, 516, 526, 565, 583, 602, 617, 622, 625, 631ᵛ, 685, 748
Naxos, Joseph Nasi, d. of, 258
Nay (Naim), 548
Neaera, 49
Neapolitans, see Naples
Nebuchadnezzar (Nabucodonosor, etc.), k. of Babylon, 152, 223, 598
Negropont (Nigropont) or Euboea 206, 723
Nehemiah (Nehemias), 466–467, 573
Nemours, Gaston de Foix, d. of, 609
Nemours, Jacques d'Armagnac, d. of, 632
Nemrod, see Nimrod
Nepos, Cornelius, 59
Neptune, 460
Neratius, see Veratius
Nero, emp. of Rome, 24, 30, 33, 37, 121, 169, 214–215, 221, 226–228, 255, 266, 286, 314, 319, 384, 414, 416–417, 429, 465, 510, 522, 530, 582, 638, 642, 666, 679, 681, 692, N728, 734
Nero, Caius Claudius, 305, 348, 390, 496–497, N586, N638, 665
Nerva, emp. of Rome, 30, 216
Nestorius, 544
Netherlands, see Low Countries
Neuchâtel (Neufchastel), 68
Nevers, 135, 176
Nevers, Jacques II Spifame, bp. of, 353
Nevers (Nivers), John II, ct. of, 743
Nevers (Nivers), Lewis of, see Lewis II, ct. of Flanders
New World, A7, N692

Nicaea (Nice), Council of, 537, 573–574, 647
Nicanor, 723
Niceas, see Nicias
Nicephorus Callistus, 40, 298
Nicholas I, pope, 138, 648
Nicholas IV, pope, 575
Nicholas V, antipope, 143
Nicholas, abbot of Palermo, see Panormitanus
Nicias (Niceas), 421
Nicocles, tyrant of Sicyon, 227, 420
Nicomedes III, k. of Bithynia, 111, 407, 657
Nicopolis, battle of, 452, 716
Nicostratus, 357
Nigaries or Ningaria, in the Canary Islands, 126
Niger, river, N568
Nigropont, see Negropont
Nile (Nilus), river, 62, 683
Nîmes (Nismes, Nysmes), 42, 385
Nimrod (Nemrod, Nimroth), 47, 200, 206, 362, 389&N, 412, 447
Ninus, 412, 463–464
Nithard (Girald, Gitald, Guitard, Guytald, Guytard, Vitald, Vitaldus, Witald, Witard), 118&NN, 132, 138, 633
Nivers, see Nevers
Noack, Ludwig, A12
Noah (Noe), 200, 446, 453
Noailles (Nouaile), Antoine de, 749
Noailles (Nouvaille), François de, bp. of Dax, 151
Noailles (Nouailles, Nouvaille), Gilles de, abbé de l'Isle, bp. of Dax, 152, 548
Nogaret, Guillaume de, 145, 652&N
Nola, Nolani, 40, 76
Norbanus Flaccus, Caius, 367
Norfolk, d. of, see Howard
Normandy, Normans, A8, 26, 116, 118, 139, 171, 173, 194, 222, 284, 313, 331&NN, 384, N385, 447, 482, 527, 550, N567, 574, 577&N, 686, 693, 696, N738, 742, 747, 770, 776
North America, A66, A78
Northamptonshire, A52
Northumberland, John Dudley, d. of, 714&N
Northumberland, Thomas Percy, 7th earl of, 97
Norton, John, A59, A62
Norway, 31, 41, 117, 166, 178, N210, 413, 443–444, 563, N567, 748
Nouaile, Nouailles, Nouvaille, see Noailles
Novara (Novarre), 729
Novum Comum (Novocome), 57, 356
Noyon, 514&N
Nucerians, 286
Numa Pompilius, k. of Rome, 39, 174, 205, 363, 379, 397, 413, 418, 650, 766, 786

Index Nominum

Numantia, Numantines (Numance), 63, 164, 597, 631
Numidia, Numidians, 30, 121, 205, 557, N558, 562, 612, 614, 722, 738&N
Numitor, 735
Nuremberg, 83–84, 131, 166, 235, 240–241, 258, 264, 277, 399, 565, 690, 693, 725
Nysmes, see Nîmes

Ober Ursel, A45
Ochiali (Occhial), pasha, 2
Octacilius Crassus, Titus, 492
Octavianus or Octavius, see Augustus
Octavius, Caius, father of Augustus, N30
Octavius, Marcus, tribune, 244, 301, 350
Odo (Otho), k. of France, see Eudes
Odo, d. of Burgundy, see Eudes
Odoacer (Odocres, Odouacre, etc.), k. of Italy, 202, 464, 655
Oenophyta, N422
Ogodai or Oktai, Tartar khan, 209
Olaus, see Magnus
Oldenburg, N133
Oldradus de Ponte, 90, 108, 136
Olga (Helene), q. and regent of Russia, 635ᵛ
Olorus, k. of Thrace, error for Oroles, k. of the Dacians, 17
Olorus, father of Thucydides, 555
Olybius or Olivier, v
Olympic Games, 440, 586
Omar I (Homar), caliph, 39
Omar es-Sayyaf (Homar Essuein), 555
Onomacles (Onomaches), 584
Onomademus or Demus (Onomadesme), 422
Onophrius, Onuphre, Onuphrius, see Panvinio
Oppia, lex, 16
Oppian of Apamea, A4, 200
Optatus, bp. of Milevi, 536
Oran, N690
Orange (Oreng), 83, 121, 134, 145, 465
Orbais (Orbez), Nicolas de la Croix, abbot of, 77, 619
Orcades, islands, 117, 443, 602
Orestes, Cnaeus Aurelius, 347
Origen, 382
Orites, people of Oreus, see Hestiaea
Orleans (Orleance), 180, 229&N, 626, 632, 732, 741, 743. See also Charles and Lewis, d. of Orleans
Orleans (Orleance), Estates General of, 96, 177&N, 289, 311, 371, 403, 479, 574, 579, 648–649, 681, 684, 783
Ormuz (Ormus), island of, 148, 660
Orosius, Paulus, 611

Orpheus, 446, 538, 761
Orsini family (Ursins), 525
Orsini (Ursin), Giordano, 179
Orsini, Lorenzo, called Renzo de Ceri (Rance), 716
Orsua, 527, 738&N, 739
Orus Apollo, see Horapollo
Osiander, Andreas, N567
Osimo, see Ausimum
Ostrogoths, 202, 448, 550, 567. See also Goths
Oswaldt, Johann, A82
Otho, Marcus Salvius, emp. of Rome, 228, 343, 472, 590, 734
Otho, k. of France, see Eudes
Otto (Otho, Othons), emp. of Germany, 141, 151
Otto (Otho) I, the Great, emp. of Germany, 739
Otto (Otho) II, error for Otto IV, emp. of Germany, 608
Otto (Otho) III, emp. of Germany, 131, 725
Otto (Otho) IV, emp. of Germany, 141, 143
Otto (Otho), d. of Lower Lorraine, 436
Otto or Hatto (Othon), archbp. of Mainz, 629ᵛ
Ottocar (Othocarus) II, k. of Bohemia, 753
Ottoman (Othoman) family, 203, 436, 744–745
Ottoman Empire, see Turkey
Oudenarde, see Audenarde
Ovid, 131, N648
Oxford, A39–A40, A44, A52–A56, A61, 722
Oxylus, k. of Elis, 577
Oye, 116
Ozzasco (Ozasque), Octaviano Cacherano, 133

Pacatus, see Drepanius
Paches, 629ᵛ
Padua (Padoua), 417, 624
Paetilia, lex, see Poetelia
Palaeologi (Palaeologues), 443, 452
Palaepolis, 163
Palatine (Palantine), cts., 13, 134, 145, 239
Palatine, Dorothea, ctss., N210
Palatine, Frederick II, ct., 238
Palermo (Panormo), 398, 694
Palermo (Palerme), the abbot of, see Panormitanus
Palestine, 46, 56–57, 148, 223, 448, 451, 467. See also Jews
Palladino, Jacopo, of Teramo (Jaques de Terranne), 137
Pallas, 36, 262, 392, 746
Panaetius, tyrant of Leontini, 420, 481
Panaetius, philosopher, N436
Pandulphus, see Petrucci
Panormitanus, or Nicolo Tedeschi, archbp. of Palermo (the abbot of Panormo, etc.), 40, N322, N355, 369, 574, 628

Panormo, see Palermo
Panvinio, Onofrio (Onophrius, Augustine Onuphre, etc.), 139, 146–147, 304, N464
Papacy, see Rome, Church of
Pape, Gui, N339
Papia Poppaea, lex, see Julia et Papia Poppaea
Papinianus (Papinian), Aemilius, 46, 160, 161&N, 168, 318–319, 329–330, 332, 334–335, 343, 346, 537, 739, 773
Papiria, gens, 391
Papiria, lex, on canvassing, 592
Papiria, lex, on coinage, 691
Papirius Cursor, Lucius, 85, 172, 290, 341–342, 411, 706
Papirius Mugillanus, Lucius, 638
Papirius (Papyrius) Praetextatus, Lucius, 262
Papius, Caius, 67
Papius Mutilus, Marcus, N670
Pappia Poppeia, lex, see Julia et Papia Poppaea
Paris, history, 83, 135, 377, 530, 571, 598, 741, 753; definition of the city, 52–53; local laws and customs, 14, 46, 50&N, 333, 401, 542, 587; weights and coinage, 688, 690&NN, 693; power of bp. of, 298, 368, 504; Protestants persecuted at, A4, A7; as seat of government, 266, 283, 326, N667, 682, 685–686, 696; Bodin at, A3, A5–A6; mentioned, A9, A37, A55, 18, 111, N234, 436, 444, N565, 675, 736, 783
Paris, Parlement of, constitutional position, 97&N, 170, 180–181, 191, 254, 263, 266–267, 315, 317, 345, 354; organization and procedure, A30, 67, 108, 167, 181, 283, 289, 316–317, 479, 490–492, 514, 765; and Catholicism, A5, A11; decisions of, concerning crown and monarchy, 95, 106–107, 111–113, 145, 159, 177, 288, N590; concerning clergy, 106, 146, 298–300, 353, 369, 526; concerning vassalage, 71, 119, 133, 170, 178; concerning inheritances, 13, 331, 333, N584, 739–740; concerning slavery, 33, 41–42; on miscellaneous cases, N67, 110, 223, N289, 339, 373, 473, 521, 641, 653–654, 777, 783–784; relations with other courts, 171, 352, 356, 513; and foreign issues, 63, 68, 358–359, 625; mentioned, A71
Parkinson, Robert, fellow of Lincoln, A53
Parma, 130, 141, 143, 616, 779
Parmenio, 522, 585
Parsons, Robert, A62
Parthenay, N584
Parthenius, 666

A197

Index Nominum

Parthia, Parthians (Parthies), 9, 39, 152, 204, 447, 466, 485, 550, 557, 592, 599, 625, 629, 631^v, 671, 719, 722, 735, 741

Parysatis, q. of Persia, 737

Passau, treaty of, 634^v

Patagonians (Patagenes), 550

Paterculus, Velleius, *see* Velleius

Patroclus, 35

Paul, St., the apostle, 56&N, 143

Paul (Paulus) III, pope, 123, 625, 694, 768

Paul IV (Theatin), pope, 623

Paulinus, bp. of Nola, 40

Paulus, *see* Aemilius Paulus

Paulus (Paul), Julius, jurist, A71, 25, N278, N333, 335, 348, 388, N629, 783

Paulus Aemilius, *see* Aemilius, Paulus; Aemilius Paulus

Pausanias, k. of Sparta, 187, 221, 443

Pausanias, a Macedonian, 523, 526

Pausanias, author, 207, 640

Pavia (Pavie), 121, 135, 434, 448, 597, 608, 615, 617, 625, 628^v, 729

Pavia (Pavie), Francesco Alidosi, card. bp. of, 498

Payerne, *error for* Arleux in Artois, 135

Pedanius Secundus, 37

Pedius, Quintus, 263

Pedrarias, *see* Arias de Avila

Pellenians, 186

Pelopidas, 58, 420, 483, 523, 609, 706

Peloponnesian War, 101, 186, 424, 426, 430, 454, 541

Pennus, Marcus Junius, praetor 201 B.C., 273

Pennus, Marcus Junius, tribune 126 B.C., 67

Pentapolis, the, in Italy, 138, 142&N, 146

Pepin (Pipin) the Short, k. of France, 137–138, 146–147, 452, 507, 730

Pepin, ruler of Italy, 738

Pepon or Poppo, *see* Damasus II, pope

Pera, 537. *See also* Constantinople

Perche (Perch), 583&N

Perennis (Perennius), 177, 507

Pergamum (Pergame, etc.), 111, 121, 407, 657

Periander, tyrant of Ambracia, 416, 420

Periander, tyrant of Corinth, 210

Pericles, 49, 53, 101–102, 243, 246, 251, 260–261, 413, 430, 432, 454, 497, 517, 531, 534, 544, 600, 610, N631, 640, 653–654, 658, 660, 677–678, 706

Périgord (Perigort), 583&N

Perinthians, A51, 410, 443

Perizzites (Phaerezites), 410

Péronne, 110, 629, 730

Perouza, Perouze, *see* Perugia

Perseus, k. of Macedon, 148–149, 150&N, 178, 262, 285, 292, 422, 451, 454, 597, 603, 607–608, 618, 621, 624, 627^v&N, 628^v–629, 634^v, 735

Persia, Persians, monarchical form of government and succession, 202, 204, 222, 413, 719, 722, 734, 737, 741, 743; administrative policies, 101, 121, 148, 152, 200, 482, 485, 505, 507, 680; history in classical times, 10, 51, 75, 205, N413, 431, 451, 463, 465–467, 561, 597, 600, 627^v, 747; history in post-classical times, 147–148, N537, 544, 550, 628; laws and customs, 22, 29, 211, 256, 527, 555, 557, 578–579, 582, 601, 756, 769, 772, 782; nature of the people, 562, 564, 613; finance, treasure, and coinage, 177, 658–660, 682–683, 692, 697–698; mentioned, 30, 35, 58, 121, 206, 375, 381, 416, 446, N463, 619, 629, 650, 676, 686, 716

Persson, Göran (George Preschon, etc.), 226, 666

Pertinax, Helvius, emp. of Rome, 178, 218, 228, 652

Peru, Peruvians (Peruana, Perusians, Perusines), 35, 46, 126, 203, 551, 557, 563, 631^v, 656, 666–667, 719, 722, 735

Perugia, Perugians (Perouza, Perouze, Perusium, Perusines, etc.), 65, 91, 130, 142&N, 389, 420, 630^v

Pesaro (Pisaurum), 141

Pescara (Pesquiere), Fernando Francesco d'Avalos, marquis of, N513, 526, 627^v

Peter, St., the apostle, 143

Peter II, k. of Aragon, 125

Peter III, k. of Aragon, 125, 527, 742

Peter IV, k. of Aragon, 93, 176, 687

Peter, k. of Castile, 136, 634^v

Peter (*error for* Sweyn?), k. of the Danes, 117, 208

Peter (*error for* John) of Albret, k. of Navarre, 126, 141, 622

Peter II, d. of Bourbon, 743

Peter I, of Dreux, or Mauclerc, d. of Brittany, 117, 118&N, 514, 583

Peter II, d. of Brittany, 120, 577

Peter Aloisius or Louys, d. of Piacenza, *see* Farnese, Pierluigi, d. of Parma

Peter, ct. of Savoy, 754

Peter of Arliac, *see* Ailly, Pierre d'

Peter of Navarre, *see* Navarra, Pedro

Petilia, lex, *see* Poetelia

Petilian, tribune, *see* Poetelius

Petrarch, N461

Petronia, lex, 37

Petronilla (Petronella), q. of Aragon, 748

Petronius, Publius, 324–325

Petrucci, Alfonso (Alphonsus), card., 630^v

Petrucci (Petruce), Raffaello, card. (*error for* Fabio?), tyrant of Siena, 416

Petrucci, Pandolfo (Pandulphus), lord of Siena, 409

Pflug (Pflugius), Julius, bp. of Naumburg, 726

Phaerezites, *see* Perizzites

Phalaris, tyrant of Agrigentum, 214–215, 417, 420, N481

Pharaoh (Pharao), 312, 381, 793

Pharsalia, battle of, 229, 438, 597, 609

Pharsalus, Pharsalians (Pharsalia), 232, 241, 263, 277, 710

Phebe, Francis, *see* Francis Phoebus, k. of Navarre

Phebidas, *see* Phoebidas

Pherae, Pheraeans (Pheree, Phereans, etc.), 213, 417, 420, 423

Phidon, tyrant of Argos, 420, 481

Phidon, lawgiver of Corinth, 571

Philip, emp. of Germany, 143

Philip I, k. of France, 94, 160, 209, 667, 730–732

Philip II, Augustus, k. of France, 43, 116–118, 120, 145, 383, 575, 583, 608, 625, 645, N648

Philip II, *error for* Philip III, k. of France, 107

Philip III, the Bold, k. of France, N107, 452, 588, 664

Philip IV, the Fair, k. of France, A35, 61, 98, 108, 119, 127, 145, 171, 177, 266, 292, 298, 355, 383, 479, 489–490, 528–529, 578, 583, 588, 652, 667&N, 674, 687, 692, 697, 748, 770

Philip V, the Long, k. of France, 61, 124, 171, 177, 266, 383, 491, 514, 633, 665, 746&N, 774

Philip VI, of Valois, k. of France, 26, 81, 107, 120, 124, 134-135, 146, 179, 321, 490, 593, 634^v, 665, 674, 680, 737, 742–743, 753

Philip II, k. of Macedon, N28, 79–80, 171, 177, 246, 523, 526, 627^v, 659, 703

Philip V (the Younger or the Second), k. of Macedon, 80–81, 148, 150&N, 162, N376, 454, 597, 618, 622, 625, 630^v&N, 636&N, N657, 714

Philip I, k. of Spain, archd. of Austria, 170, 618, 631, 728

Philip II, k. of Spain, 96–97, 123, 151, 152&N, 175, 181, 199, 239, 591, 613, 663, 726, 746, 749–750, N752

Philip, archd. of Austria, *see* Philip I, k. of Spain

Philip I, the Bold, d. of Burgundy, 133–134, 513, 528, 743

Index Nominum

Philip II, the Good, d. of Burgundy, 122, 125, 170, 318, 433, 588–589, 606
Philip, landgrave of Hesse, 78, 83, 634ᵛ
Philip Maria, d. of Milan, *see* Visconti
Philip de Dreux, bp. of Beauvais, 514&N
Philippus I, Marcus Julius, emp. of Rome, 745
Philippus (Philip), Lucius Marcius, consul 91 B.C., 188, 301, 349, 575
Philippus, Quintus Marcius, consul 186 B.C., 149, 150&N, 629, 635ᵛ
Philistus (Phyliste), 226, 666
Philo, Quintus Publilius, 156, 285, 390&N, 470
Philo Judaeus (Philon), 47, 211, 366, 381, 414, 444, N445, 446, 458, 462, 465, 719
Philodemius, Eleutherius, A63–A65
Philopoemen (Philopomenes, etc.), 187, 268, 454
Philostratus of Pallene, 584
Philotas, 514, 522–523
Phocaeans (Phocenses), 635ᵛ
Phocas, emp. of the East, 137
Phocians (Phocenses, Phocensians, Phociens), 79, 386, 429, 569, 711
Phocion, 532, 610, 702–704
Phoebidas (Phebidas), 627ᵛ
Phokos (Phox), 360
Phraates, k. of Parthia, 152
Phyliste, *see* Philistus
Phytales, *see* Aphytis
Piacenza, Placentini (Placence), 76, 130, 141, 452, 523, 729
Pibrac, *see* Du Faur
Picardy (Picardie), 606, N738
Piccinino, Jacopo (Cont James), 629
Picquigny (Piqueni), treaty of, 148
Pico (Picus) della Mirandola, Giovanni, 442, 444
Picts, 429, 463, 612, 636ᵛ
Piedmont (Piemont), 133, 218, 528, 553, N565, 593
Pilate (Pilat), Pontius, 56, 538
Pinaria, gens, 391
Pinatel, Jacques, 697–698
Pindarus, 108, 205, 410, 538
Piombino (Plombin), 552
Pipin, k. of France, *see* Pepin
Piqueni, *see* Picquigny
Piraeus (Piree), 432, 545, 563
Pirrhus, *see* Pyrrhus
Pisa, Pisans (Pisani), 76, 129, 143, 376, 625, 726
Pisa, Francesco Salviati, card. archbp. of, 123
Pisander, 422
Pisaurum, *see* Pesaro
Pisistratidae (Pisistratides), N423, 463

Pisistratus, tyrant of Athens, 205, 219&N, 416, 420, 423, 481
Piso, Cnaeus Calpurnius, 342, 635ᵛ
Piso Frugi, Lucius Calpurnius, 348
Piso Licinianus, Lucius Calpurnius, 30, 472
Pistoians, 520
Pithagoras, Pithagorians, *see* Pythagoras, Pythagorians
Pittacus (Pitacus), iv, 206, 210, 723
Pius II or Aeneas Silvius Piccolomini, pope, 461, 736
Pius IV, pope, 78, 150
Pius V, *error for* Pius IV, pope, 123, 141, 617
Pizarro (Pizara, Pizarre, etc.), Francisco, 557, 631ᵛ, 667, 735
Pizarro (Pizarra, Pizzare), Gonzalo, 43, 203
Placence, Placentini, *see* Piacenza
Plaetoria de praetore urbano (Laetoria, Praetoria, etc.), lex, 161&N, 347, 764
Plancus, Cnaeus (*error for* Lucius) Munatius, 274
Plata (Plat, Plate), river, 35, 568
Plato, life and career, 6, 37, N193, 210, 461, 504, 569, 594, 720; on ideal state and forms of government, v, 3, 184&N, 193&N, 702, 710, 719; on the senate, 256, 260, 488; on magistracies, 480, 484–485, 531; on social classes, 69, 389, 394, 610; on filial obligations, 20–21; on communism, 11, 707; on inheritance, 571, N576, N582; on wealth and poverty, 569, 705; on trade and usury, 399–400, 572, 698; other social policies, 338, N554, 565, 579, N637, 646, 736; conception of justice, 754–756, 766, 769, 772, 792; on characteristics of peoples, 7, 518, 563–564; on theory of numbers and changes in states, A22, 193&N, 436, 438, 453, 455–457, 458&N, 459, 460&N, 713; mentioned, A27, A41, A54, A69–A70, 200, 218, 298, 362, N484, 503, 544, 793
Plautia, gens, 391
Plautius Decianus, Caius, 614
Plautius Venno Hypsaeus, Caius, 572
Pliny (Plinie), the Elder, A54, 26, 55&N, 205, 292, 402, 405, 441, 448, 460–462, 549, 551, 554, 558, N565, 650&N, 651, N656, 690–692, 699, 774
Pliny (Plinie), the Younger, 51, 56, 100, 109, 172, 204, 215, 269, 276, 314, 317, 394, 487, 502–503, 582, 638
Plombin, *see* Piombino
Plot, Jean Baptiste de, N66

Plutarch, on forms of government, 10, 47, 187, 206, 232, 250, 424, 702, 706, 711, 719; on tyranny, 205, 210, 213, 418; on senates, 163, N265; on magistracies, 281, 294, 302–304, 312, 494, 643; on military commands, 207, 716; on citizenship, 49, 53, 55, 57; on laws and customs, 18, 35, 200, 610; at Athens, 35, 37, 59, 103, 247, 392; at Sparta, 16, 19, 28, 67, N363, 369, 576–577, 763; at Rome, 17, 33, 36, 70, 174, 478; on characteristics of peoples, 7, 362, 448&N, 545–549, 558, 563, 565, 567; on finance and coinage, 177, 651, 655, 660, 668–669, 678; on history of Athens, 102, 186; of Sparta, 620, 627ᵛ; on astrology, 441–442; on numbers, 460–462; miscellaneous, A48, 149, 415, 440, 503–504, 515, 538, 580, 591, 650, 744
Poeni, 553. *See also* Carthage; Punic Wars
Poetelia (Petilia), lex, on canvassing, 592
Poetelia (Paetilia), lex, on debtors, 67
Poetelius Libo Visolus (Petilian), Caius, 32
Poggio (Poge), Vincenzo di, 629ᵛ
Poggio Bracciolini (Poggius), Giovanni Francesco, 426
Poissy (Possi), Colloquy of, 451
Poitiers, A7, 376, 389, 408, 423, 452, 514, 598, 609, 626, 638, 742
Poitou (Poictou), 120, 575, 632ᵛ, 672
Poland, Poles (Polonia, Polonians), kingship in, A21, 94, 136, 140, 449, 507, 719; elective monarchy, 209, 288, 413, 434–435, 472, 563, 722, 724, 728, 733; succession questions, 258&N, 435, 613, 725&N, 726&N, 727, 742, 748–750; Henry of Anjou and, A8; nobility and its powers, A20, 163, 166, 511, 758; senate, 151–152, 259, 277; magistracies, 168, 258, 293, 479, 485; revenues and coinage, 176, 178, 651–652, 668, 696; laws and customs, 32, 40–42, 64, 158, 381, 576–577, 582, 715, 723, 776, 779–780; climate and characteristics of the people, 548&N, 557, 562, 568, 672; external relations and treaties, 44, 59, 84, 100, 121, 152, 194, N451, 617, 628, 632ᵛ; mentioned, 118, 452, N463
Polemon, k. of Pontus, 407, 657
Polidore, *see* Vergil, Polydore
Politiques, A8–A9, A12
Pollio, Trebellius, *see* Trebellius
Pollio, Vedius, 36
Pollux, Julius, 610, 690, 692
Polyaenus, N631

Index Nominum

Polybius (Polibius), A70, 154, 177, 184, 186–189, 270, 286, 332, 362, 381, 443, 454, 456–457, 469, 536, 547, 552, 555, 564, 586, 603, 612, 628ᵛ, 629ᵛ, 632ᵛ, 635ᵛ, 650, N657, 706, 714
Polycletus (Policletus), 759&N, 760
Polycrates, tyrant of Samos, 420
Polycrates, see John of Salisbury
Polydore, see Vergil, Polydore
Polydorus, k. of Sparta, 187
Pomerania (Pomeran, Pomerland), 31, 118
Pompeia, wife of Julius Caesar, 260, 298
Pompeia, gens, 391
Pompeia, lex, 276
Pompeia de parricidiis, lex, 21, 24, 27
Pompeians, 286
Pompeius, Quintus, consul 141 B.C., 390&N
Pompeius, Trogus, see Trogus
Pompeius Festus, Sextus, see Festus
Pompeius Magnus, Cnaeus (Pompee, Pompey), the triumvir, 30, 51, 61, 86, 90, 98, 199, 229, 281, 285, 291–292, 350, 421, 423, 452, 465, 481, 497, 499, 538, 558, 597, 599, 602, 609, 630, 668, 703, 705–706, 735
Pompeius Magnus, Sextus, son of the triumvir, 39, 419, 743–744
Pompeius Rufus, Quintus, 351
Pompilia, gens, 391
Pomponius, Marcus, tribune 362 B.C., 23
Pomponius, Sextus, jurist, 75, 178, 293, 303
Pont-à-Mousson, 133
Pontano (Pontanus), Giovanni Gioviano, 45
Pontano, Lodovico (Lewis du Pont, called Romain), 628
Ponthieu, 583&N
Ponthieu, Widdo or Gui, ct. of, 731–732
Pontine Marshes (Pontinae), 437
Pontius, Herennius, 432
Pontus, 121, 407, 625, 636, 657
Popilia, lex, see Publilia
Popillius Laenas (Popilius), Caius, 636
Poppaeus Secundus, Quintus, N670
Porcia (Portia), gens, 391
Porcia (Portia), lex, 55–56, 327–328, 331, 580
Porphyry (Porphyree, Porphyrie), 443&N, 450, 460
Port of Grace, see Le Havre
Portugal, Portuguese (Portugall, Portingals, etc.), 39, 43, 126, 136, 147–148, 400, 416, 564, 595, 631ᵛ, 660, 694, 698, 739–740
Poseidonius (Possidonius), N436, 553

Possi, see Poissy
Possevino (Possovinus), Antonio, vi
Posthumia or Postumia, gens, 391
Posthumius, Marcus, 329
Posthumius Albinus, Spurius, 159, 164, 626ᵛ
Potier, Jacques, sieur du Blancmesnil, 487&N
Potitia, gens, 391, 428
Poyet, Guillaume, 344, 513, 640 &N
Praeneste, Praenestini (Preneste, Prenestines), 76, 163, 341, 376
Praetius, see Raecius
Praetoria, lex (Pretorian law), see Plaetoria
Prat, see Du Prat
Preschon or Prescon, George, see Persson
Privernates, 614
Proclerus, see Parthenius
Procles (Proclus, Proculus), k. of Sparta, 198, N738, 741
Proclus, philosopher, 20, 458
Procopius, 30, 738, N740
Prometheus, 513
Pronski (Pruinski), Alexander, 548
Protestants, A7, A9, A11–A13, A57, 60, 77–78, 84, 123, 144, 313, 381, 474–475, 625–625ᵛ
Protogenes, 400
Provence (Province), 108, 134, N181, 384, 549, 641, 669, 742
Pruinski, see Pronski
Prusias II, k. of Bithynia, 121
Prussia, Prussians (Prusse, Prutenian knights), 136, 166, 176
Prynne, William, A63, A65
Ptolemais (Ptolomais), an old woman, 766
Ptolemy (Ptolomee), k. of Cyprus, 286
Ptolemy (Ptolomie, etc.), k. of Cyrene, 111, 407, 657
Ptolemy I, Lagus (Ptolomey, etc.), k. of Egypt, 208, 538, 619, N723, 735, 744
Ptolemy II, Philadelphus (Ptolome, etc.), k. of Egypt, 110, 211, 657, 680
Ptolemy IV, Philopator (Ptolomeus, etc.), k. of Egypt, 211, 454, 632ᵛ
Ptolemy VI, Philometor (Ptolemee), k. of Egypt, 211
Ptolemy VII, Physcon (Ptolomee), k. of Egypt, 735
Ptolemy XI, Auletes (Ptolomie), k. of Egypt, 668
Ptolemy XII (Ptolome, etc.), k. of Egypt, 229, 608
Ptolemy, statue of, at Cyrene, 37
Ptolemy (Ptolomee, etc.), Claudius, astronomer, A54, 144, 444, 447, 455, 557
Publilia (Popilia), lex, 276
Publilius, Volero, 530
Pucci (Puccinus), Orazio de', 418

Puna, island of, 558
Punic (Punicke, Punike, Punique) Wars, 530, 635, 644, 665, 691. See also Carthage; Poeni
Puteoli, 54, 451
Puy, see Le Puy
Pyrenees (Pyrenei, Pyrenean hilles, etc.), 118, 460, 549, 562, N565, 579
Pyrrhus (Pirrhus), k. of Epirus, 422, 504, 508, 587, 603, 607, 609, 613, 627, 735
Pythagoras (Pithagoras), 458
Pythagorians (Pithagorians), 80, 231, 364, 380, 561, 720, 780

Quadratus, Caius Ummidius, 538
Querini family, N711
Quinctia or Quintia, gens, 391
Quinctia (Quintia), lex, 575
Quinctius (Quintius), Titus, 377
Quinctius Cincinnatus Poenus (Quintus), Titus, 163
Quintilia, gens, 391
Quintilius Varus (Quinctilius Varro), Publius, 464
Quirites, 198, 407. See also Rome

Rabirius, Caius, N629ᵛ
Radamanthus, see Rhadamanthus
Radicofani (Rodicofanum), 142 &N
Raecius (Praetius), Lucius, 398
Ragusa, Ragusans (Rhaguse, Rhagusium, Rhagusians, etc.), 10, 60, 148, 152, 235, 237, 242, 245, 258, 264, 268, 277, 280, 420, 428, 433, 488, 554, 605, 628, 713, 757. See also Epidaurians
Rais or Retz (Raiz), 619, 766
Ramus, Peter, A3–A5, A20, A25–A28, A30, A40–A41, A50
Rance, see Orsini
Ranconet, Aimar de, 783–784
Randolph (Randall), Sir Thomas, 591
Raoul, k. of France, see Rudolph
Ratisbon, Diet of (1546), 237
Ravenna (Ravenne), 138, 142&N, 146–147, 609, 624
Raymond VII (Raimond), ct. of Toulouse, 408, 583&N
Raymond Berenger, ct. of Barcelona, 748
Raymond Berenger, ct. of Provence, 134
Reate or Rieti, 142&N
Red Sea, 148
Reggio (Rhegium), in Calabria, 168, 275, 420
Reggio (Rege, Rhegium), in Emilia, 129, 141
Regiomontanus or Johann Müller, 447, 450
Regulus, see Atilius
Rehoboam (Roboam), 668
Reims (Rheims, Rheimes), 54, 94, 112, 514&N, 730, 732
Reims, Gervasius, archbp. of, 731

Index Nominum

Rely (Relli), Jean de, bp. of Angers, 95
Remigius (Rhemigius, Rhimigius), St., 731
Remus, 198
René (Renat, Renate), k. of Naples, d. of Anjou, 31, 132, 134, 181, 203, 513, 691, 743
Rennes, seneschal of, *see* Argentraeus
Reulos, Michel, A79, A89, N50, N225, N233, N360
Reynolds, Beatrice, A89
Rhadamanthus (Radamanthus), 500
Rhaetians, 77
Rhaguse, Rhagusians, etc., *see* Ragusa
Rhegium, *see* Reggio
Rheims, Rheimes, *see* Reims
Rhemigius, Rhimigius, *see* Remigius
Rhine (Rheine, Rhene, Rhin), river, 118, 122, 124, 131–132, 550, 608
Rhinocolura (Rhinocura), 376
Rhoderike, k. of Spain, *see* Roderic
Rhodes, Rhodians (Rhodiots), 58–59, 232, 235, 400, 420, 430, 448, 546, 566, 624–625, 628ᵛ, 634ᵛ, 657&N
Rhodez, *see* Rodez
Rhodia, lex, 135
Rhône, river, 134
Riccee, Andrew, *see* Modrzewski
Richard I, k. of England, ct. of Poitou, 62, 575, 625, 626
Richard II, k. of England, 738&N
Richard III, k. of England, d. of Gloucester, 601
Richmond, earl of, *see* Henry VII, k. of England
Ridley, Nicholas, bp. of London, A53
Riga (Rigie), 632ᵛ
Rimini or Ariminum, 420, 537, 624
Rincon, Antonio, 68, 635ᵛ
Ripuarian Franks (Ripuaires, Ripuaries), 30, 39, 527, 559, 769, 772
Roan, *see* Rouen
Robert, emp. of Germany, 724
Robert II, k. of France, 209, 490, 676, 730, 732, N736
Robert, k. of Naples, 122, 738
Robert II, k. of Naples, *error for?*, 739
Robert III, ct. of Artois, 526, 738&N, 746&N
Robert, *error for* Philip, brother of Maud, ctss. of Artois, 738
Robert de la Marck, lord of Bouillon, *see* La Marck
Robert I, d. of Burgundy, 731&N, 732&N, N736
Robert, ct. of Clermont, *error for* Robert I, ct. of Artois?, 742
Robert III, ct. of Flanders, 514
Robert, d. of France, 730
Robert II, Curthose, d. of Normandy, 229, 742
Robert, son of Henry I?, 160
Roboam, *see* Rehoboam
Rochelle (Rochell), *see* La Rochelle
Roches, *see* Des Roches
Roderic (Roderike, Rhoderike), k. of Spain, 416–417, 451, 464
Rodez (Rhodez), 13
Rodicofanum, *see* Radicofani
Rodolph, Rodolphe, *see* Rudolph
Roe, son of Haldan, k. of the Danes, 527
Romagna (Romandiola), 147
Romain or Romanus, Lewis du Pont, called, *see* Pontano
Romans, town of, 42
Romanus (Romane), St., archbp. of Rouen, 173–174
Rome, Romans, sovereignty and type of state under the republic, A20, 90–91, 99, 154, 156–159, 162–165, 168–169, 172, 176, 178, 184, 188–190, 276, 411, 470, 518, 705–706, 785; under the monarchy, 185, 255, 409, 423; under the Decemviri, 207, 230, 248, 282; under the Empire, A17, 98–100, 196, 213, 221, 412, 727–728, 743–744; procedure in assemblies, 48, 244–247, 269, 294, 372, 480; the Senate, 157, 160, 259–262, 266–267, 270–273, 275, 277, 319, 355, 367, 488, 491–492; magistracies and commissions, 104, 157, 166, 195, 238, 268, 274, 280–281, 284–286, 291–292, 301, 306–308, 315, 327, 339–340, 344–345, 347–351, 355–356, 366, 421, 483–484, 488, 491, 495–499, 592, 717–718; Consuls, 151, 331, 420, 716; Praetors, 161, 332, 335–337, 769; Censors, 304–306, 637–638, 642–644, 646&N, 647, 649; Tribunes, 274–275, 301–303, 371; Dictator, 85–86, 344, 715–716; other magistrates, 295–296, 303–304, 306, 326, 334, 352–353; Roman law, its general nature and influence, 108, N202, 357&NN, 757, 765, 770–771; legal procedure, 103, 308, 317, 471, 487, 515, 580, 704, 765; punishments and fines, 296–298, 307&N, 510, 555, 583–584, 773–775, 778, 780; laws on marriage and divorce, 15–19, 558; on paternal power, 22–25, 27–28; on adoption, 29–30; on citizenship, 54–63, 65–66; on inheritance, 28, 578, 740; on lands, 11, 650–651; on usury, 572; other laws and customs, 440, 478, 586–588, 595, 601, N645, N702; characteristics of the people, 8, 545–547, 550, 551&N, 562, 601, 602&N, 603, 606–608, 613, 625, 626–626ᵛ, N630; social structure, 70, 243, 249, 388–392, 396–400, 404–405, 577, 610, 660, 745, 787–788; class dissension and civil strife, 38, 45, 53, 428, 430, 433, 531, 570, 575–577, 705&N, 762; population, 10, 639&N, 640–641; revenues and taxation, 651, 655–656, 657&N, 658, 661, 663–665, 667–669, 671&N, 678–679, 682–683, 686; coinage, 690–692, N694, 697, 700; religion, 14, 174, 186, 279, 299, 380, 393, 538, N604, 645&N; relations with Italian cities, 51, 75–76, 79, 196–198, 374–375, 433, 468–469, 612, 614–615, 620, 628ᵛ, 633–635, N656; relations with other peoples, 52, 73–74, 80–81, 121, 148–150, 202, 208, 362, 381, 386, 407, 416, N614, 620–621, 628ᵛ, 630, N630ᵛ, 631–631ᵛ, 635–636ᵛ, N656, 657, 726; force of astrology and numbers on Roman history, 441–444, 448, 451, 454, 463&N, 464&NN, 465; Rome in post-classical period, 174, 565, 600, 613, 693–694, 724; miscellaneous and mentions, *passim. See also* Latins; Quirites

Rome, Church of, bp. of, court of, Papacy, Vatican, etc., A41, A82, 40, 64, 82&N, 122–123, 125, 126&N, 129, 136–147, 151, 169, 208, 237–239, 258, 299–300, 314, 354, 359, N366, 443&N, 474, 617, 623, 632–632ᵛ, 683, 691, 723–724, 731–732. *See also* Catholics
Romilius Rocus Vaticanus, Titus, 583
Romulus, founder of Rome, 11, 16–17, 22, 25, 37, 53, 70–71, 198, 245, 255, 260, 390, 392, 397, 407, 409, 418, 442, 463, 515, 527, N639, 650&N, 651
Roscia theatralis, lex, 405
Roscius, Sextus, 396
Roscius Otho, Lucius, 405
Rostock (Rostoc), 84
Rosdrazeroski, *see* Rozdrazewski
Rotelen (Rotelin), Jacqueline de Rohan, marquise de, 68
Rotharis (Rotaris), k. of the Lombards, 528, 537
Rottweil (Rotuille, Rotwill), 76, 619
Rouen (Roan, Rouan), 173&N, 266, 284, 360, 514, 579, 652, 690, 770
Rouergue, 698
Rousseau, Jean-Jacques, N50
Rozdrazewski (Rosdrazeroski), Stanislas, 59, 121
Rubicon, river, 131
Rudolph I (Rodolphe, etc.), emp. of Germany, 129, 142, 452, 724, 727, 753

Index Nominum

Rudolph or Raoul (Rodolph, etc.), k. of France, d. of Burgundy, N463, 730
Rullus, Lucius, *see* Servilius Rullus
Ruscius (Russius), Caepio, 261, 367
Russia, Russians, 118, 410, 528, 635^v, 751. *See also* Muscovy
Rustem (Rustan), pasha, Grand Vizier of Turkey, 674
Rutilius Rufus, Publius, 430, 704
Rutland, Edward Manners, 3rd earl of, N499
Ruzé, Guillaume, bp. of Angers, 371

Sabellicus, Marcantonio Coccio, 190–191
Sabines (Sabins), 54, 198, 260, 297, 363, 407, 568
Saguntum, Saguntines, 598, 631
St. Adrian, Mount, *see* Cantabrian mountains
St. Allyre (S. Allier), 94
St. Amand, A4, A8
St. André, Jacques d'Albon, seigneur de, N553, N584
St. Bernard, Mount, 671
St. Claudius, Mount, *see* Jura
St. Denis (Denys, Dionyse, etc.), N40, 41, N43, 146, 160, 452, 608
St. Gall (Gal), 77, 264, 619
St. James of Compostella, *see* Santiago
St. Jean de Luz, 671
St. John of Jerusalem, Knights of, *see* Malta, Knights of
St. Julian, card., *see* Cesarini
St. Maur les Fossés, 91, 684
St. Omer, 652
Saintonge (Saintonges), 54
St. Pol (S. Paule, etc.), 176. *See also* Lewis of Luxemburg, ct. of St. Pol
St. Quentin, battle of, N553
S. Severine, *see* Sanseverino
St. Vallier (Valier), Jean de Poitiers, seigneur de, 514
St. Veit (Vitus), 89
Saladin, sultan of Egypt and Syria, 452, 612, 744
Salamis (Salamine), battle of, 463&N
Salerno or Salernum (Salerne), 54, 693
Salian Franks (Saliens, etc.), 30, 527, 559, 753&N, 769, 772–773, 780
Salic Law, concerning male succession, A16–A17, 95, N205, 741, 748, 753–754
Salisburg, *see* Salzburg
Sallust, A56, N788
Salmon, J. H. M., A65
Salomon, *see* Solomon
Salonica (Salonick), 85. *See also* Thessalonica
Saluzzo (Salusse, etc.), 119, 513, N553, 583&N, 694, 736

Salvia, 142&N
Salvianus (Salvian), 616
Salzburg (Salisburg), 84
Samarcand, 769
Samaria, 556, 582
Samnites, 63, 163–165, 273, 432, N564, 609, N614, 620, 622, 626^v, 631, 633–633^v, 635&N, 655
Samos, Samians (Samiens), 186, 235, 420, 424, 427, 711
Sampac, *see* Sempach
Sampiero d'Ornano (Sampetre Corse), 27
Samuel, 94, 153, 224, 340, N413, 500, 603, 665–666, 719, 734
Samuel Yarhina'ah, 439
Sancho IV (Sanxius), k. of Castile, 738
Sancho III (Sanctius), the Great, k. of Navarre, 90
Sandaeus, *see* Felinus
Sandwich, A55–A60, A62, iii
Sanseverino (S. Severine), 739
Santiago (Saint James) de Compostella, 516
Saône, river, 134
Saphadin (Sephadin), brother of Saladin, 744
Sapin, an embezzler, N685
Saracens (Sarasins), 181
Sarah (Sara), 29
Sardanapalus, k. of Assyria, 412, 416–417, 464, 683
Sardinia, 125–126, 139–140, 304
Sardis, 537
Saturn (Saturne), 561, 682, 719
Saturninus, Lucius Appuleius, 99, 315, 351, 629^v&N, 705
Saul, k. of Israel, N205, 223–224, 324, 464&N, 556, 734, 786
Savello, Antimo (Anthonie Savelle), 724
Saveuses, Philip, sieur de, 110
Savona (Savonne), 629
Savonarola (Savanarola), Girolamo 185, 544&N
Savoy, (Savoie, Savoye), 41, 75, 108, 114, 133–135, 144, 154, 158, 173, 179, 181, 218, 233, 553, 588, 593, 615, 623, 632^v, 723, 729, 743, 754, 758, 762–763
Saxo Grammaticus, 528&N, 547
Saxony, Saxons (Saxonie), 13, 83, 118, 134, 158, 202, 238, 449, 527, 555, N567, 568, 613, 725, 729, 769, 773. *See also* Anglo-Saxons
Sboroschi, *see* Zborowski
Scaevola, Caius Mucius, 523
Scaevola, Publius Mucius, consul 133 B.C., 63
Scaevola (Scevola), Quintus Cervidius, jurist, 369
Scaevola, Quintus Mucius, consul 95 B.C., 75
Scaliger, Giulio Cesare (Veronensis), 566–567
Scaligers, lords of Verona, *see* Della Scala

Scanderberg or Alexander, prince of Albania, 448
Scandinavia, A20. *See also* Denmark; Norway; Sweden
Scaurus, *see* Aemilius Scaurus
Scevola, jurist, *see* Scaevola
Scevoles, *see* Sevoli
Schaffhausen (Schaffouse, Schaffuse), 76, 78, 234, 264, 497
Schröder, Johann, A83
Schwedt (Suid), 84
Schwyz (Schwits, Swits, etc.), 10, 76–78, 80, 82, 149, 241, 247, 250, 264, N424, 497, 619, N709
Schythians, *see* Scythians
Scipio, Cnaeus, *error for* Cnaeus Servilius Caepio, 286
Scipio, Publius, father of Africanus Major, 164
Scipio Africanus Major, Publius, 31, 38, 164, 189, 215, 273, 285, 292, 377, 404, 430, 454, 468–469, 483, 497, 527, 607–609, 655, 704, 706&N, 738–739, 759, 774
Scipio Africanus, Publius, son of Africanus Major, 30
Scipio Aemilianus Africanus Minor, Publius, grandson of Africanus Major, A70, 30, 52, 188, 422, 443, 603, 612, 635^v
Scipio Asiaticus, Lucius, 350, 430, 497, 608, 655, 704
Scipio Calvus, Cnaeus, uncle of Africanus Major, 164
Scithia, etc., *see* Scythia
Sclavonia, *see* Slavonia
Scoronconcolo lo Sgozzano (Caracciolus), Baccio del Tavolaccino, called, 424
Scotland, Scots (Scottishmen), 33, 59, 60&N, 61, 68, 73, 88, 116–117, 128, 133, 202, 222, N229, 416, 429, 443, 451, 454, 463, 485, 508, 535, N543, 550, 565, N567, 583, 612, 614&N, 619, 634^v, 636^v, 677, 683, 693, 722, N728, 733, 735, N738, N747, 748&N, 751, N784
Scribonius Libo, Lucius, 404
Scylax, 502
Scylla, *see* Sulla
Scythia, Scythians (Scithia, Scythes, Schythians), 23, 35, 44, 118, 202, 206, N413, 550, 551 &N, 552, 554, 557, 558&N, 559, N561, N567, 596, 719
Sea towns, *see* Hanseatic towns
Sebastia, 410
Sebastian I (Sebastien), k. of Portugal, 739
Secundus, *error for* Cratippus?, 438
Sedechia, Sedechias, *see* Zedekiah
Segelmessa or Sijilmassa, 426
Seine (Sequana), river, 62
Sejanus (Seian), Aelius, 226, 343, 507
Selasia or Sellasia, battle of, 600
Selestadius, *see* Carlstadt

Index Nominum

Seleucia, 378, 537
Seleucus I, Nicator, k. of Syria, 208–209, 229
Selii or Silvi family (Selians), 711
Selim I (Selymus), emp. of Turkey, 167, 612
Selim II, emp. of Turkey, 606, 634ᵛ
Selim et-Toumi, prince of Algiers, 612
Selve (Selva), Jean de, 514, 626ᵛ&N
Sem, see Shem
Semeas (Semneas), 414
Semiramis (Semyramis), q. of Assyria, 747
Sempach (Sampac, etc.), 76–77, 251, 422, 706
Sempronia, gens, 391
Sempronia, lex, on governors of provinces, 421
Sempronia agraria (Agraria), lex, 301, 350, 576
Sempronia de capite civium, lex, 55, 328, 580
Sempronia judiciaria, lex, 308
Sempronia militaris, lex, 275
Sempronius Atratinus, Lucius, 638
Sempronius Gracchus, Caius, 275, 304, 576, N656, 705. See also Gracchi
Sempronius Gracchus, Tiberius, consul 177 B.C., 350–351
Sempronius Gracchus, Tiberius, tribune 133 B.C., 244–245, 301, 350, 576, 705. See also Gracchi
Sempronius Sophus, Publius, consul 304 B.C., 301, 350
Sempronius Sophus, Publius, consul 268 B.C., 305
Sempronius Tuditanus, Caius, 347
Semyramis, see Semiramis
Seneca, 20, 22, 24, 32, 35, 37, 104, 110, 221, 319, 342, 419, 427, N436, 459–460, 511–512, 578, 582, 585, 644&N, 645&N, 702, 765, 767, 773–774
Sennacherib, k. of Assyria, N447
Sens, Daimbert, archbp. of, 732
Sephadin, see Saphadin
Septimania, see Languedoc
Sequana, see Seine
Sequeira, Diogo Lopes de (Lopes), 148
Sergia, gens, 54, 391
Serranus, see Atilius Serranus
Serre, see La Serre
Servia, 523
Serviae, leges, 21, 86, 220, 391
Servilia, gens, 391
Servilius Priscus, Publius, consul 495 B.C., 531
Servilius Priscus, Quintus, dictator 435 B.C., 85, 189, 349
Servilius Rullus, Publius (Lucius Rullus), 245
Servius Tullius, k. of Rome, 37, 81, 154, 177, 205, 231, 245–246, 362, 397, 419, 637, 639&N, 643, N671

Sestius Capitolinus, Publius, 297–298
Setinus (Setin), Lucius Annius, 620
Seton-Watson, R. W., A38
Severini, Girolamo (Hierome Severin), 423
Severus, Alexander, emp. of Rome, 25, 218, 262, 306, 343, 414, 484, 508, 538, 590, 592, 595, 677, 685, 745
Severus, Septimius, emp. of Rome, 57, 218, 228, 318, 330, 343, 410, 443, 598, 673
Seville (Sivill, Civill), 568, 656
Sevoli family (Scevoles), 711
Sextia, lex, 281
Sextus, pope, see Sixtus
Sforza family (Sforces), lords of Milan, 110, 128, 228, 320, 420, 463, 597
Sforza, Francesco I, d. of Milan, 553, 729
Sforza, Francesco II, d. of Milan, 625
Sforza, Galeazzo Maria (Galeace Sfortia), d. of Milan, 416
Sforza, Gian Galeazzo (Galeas), d. of Milan, 119
Sforza, Ludovico il Moro (Lewes Sfortia, etc.), d. of Milan, 119, 451, 714
Shakespeare, William, A50
Shem (Sem), 200
Sibarites, see Sybarites
Sicily, Sicilians (Sicilia, Sicile, etc.), 40, 57–58, 65, 83, 90, 104, 122–123, 125–126, 128, 139–140, 142, 150, 181, 203, 205, 226, 254, 275, 384, 411, 415–416, 418, 504, 513, 565, 657, 694, 719, 740, 744, 750
Sicyon, Sicyonians (Sicione, Sicionians, etc.), 186, 206, 213, 227, 413, 420, 719, 762
Siena (Sienna, Sienne), 129–130, 239, 409, 416, 423, 426, 433, 441, 616–617, 625ᵛ, 630ᵛ, 668, 672, 694, 707, 711, 745
Sigebert I (Sigisbert), k. of the Franks, 738&N, 741, 754
Sigebert III, k. of the Franks, 741
Sigebert of Gembloux, chronicler, N118
Sigeth, see Szigeth
Sigismund, emp. of Germany, 13, 82, 132–133, 135–136, 628, 728, 746, 750–751
Sigismund I, k. of Poland, N451, 576, 725, 779
Sigismund Augustus, error for Sigismund I, k. of Poland, 158, 176, 577
Sigismund II, Augustus, k. of Poland, 64, 84, 100&N, 121, 166, 168, 209, 259, 435, N451, 576, 617, 632ᵛ, 725, 728, 749
Sigonio (Sigonius), Carlo, N72, 146–147, 279, 283, 292&N, 304–305, N487

Silanus (Syllanus), error for?, 290
Silanus, Caius Junius, 38
Silanus (Syllanus), Lucius Junius, 396
Silesia, A61, 136
Silla, see Sulla
Silo (Sillon), k. of Asturias, 748
Silvius, k. of Alba, 738
Silvius, Aeneas, see Pius II
Simler, Josias, N234
Simon IV, ct. of Montfort, 744
Simon, ct. of Montfort, error for?, 331
Simon ben Giora, 39
Simplicius, 447
Sinan, pasha, 44, 628ᵛ
Siracusa, Siracusians, see Syracuse
Siria, see Syria
Sirmich (Sirme), Council of, 537
Sitten or Sion (Syon), 82, N565
Sivill, see Seville
Sixtus IV (Sextus), pope, 64, 123
Slavonia (Sclavonia), 71, 148, 208, 636, 658
Sleidan (Sledan), Johann, 12, 225&NN, N567, 606, N627
Smyth, Thomas, fellow of Lincoln, A53
Socina, q. of Castile, v. Adosinda
Socrates, 11, 193&N, 704
Soderini (Soderin), Francesco, card., 534
Soderini, Paolantonio (Antonie Soderine, etc.), 172, 429, 544 &N, 546, 706, 710
Soderini (Soderin), Piero, error for Paolantonio, 185, 277, 706, 710
Soderini, Piero, N544
Sodom (Sodome), 437&N
Soissons, 123, 452, 625–625ᵛ, 730, 741
Soissons, William, ct. of, 731–732
Sokolli, Mohammed (Mehemet), Grand Vizier of the Turks, 258
Soleure or Solothurn (Soleurre, Solure), 76, 77&N, 149, 234, 264, 497, 695
Solinus, Caius Julius, 559
Solomon (Salomon, the maister of wisedome, the wise Hebrew), k. of Israel, 9, 15, 46, 104, 270, 360, 467, 501, 503, 506, 516, 541–542, 597–598, 707–708, 725
Solon, lawgiver of Athens, iv, 21, 23, 47, 58–59, 103, 161, 219&N, 249, 252, 256, 259, 261, 268, 277, 297, 340, 362–363, 372, 383, 394–395, 413, 446, 471, 540–541, 546, 565, 569–570, 572, 576, 595–596, 602, 645&N, 678, 702, 757, 761, 766, 769, 775, 780, 782
Solyman II (Soliman), the Magnificent, emp. of the Turks, 2, 121, 451, 453, 668, 718, 727, 745
Somerset, William, 3rd earl of Worcester, N749
Sophocles, N438, 645

Index Nominum

Soria, see Syria
South Africa, Union of, A18
Spain, Spaniards (Spayne, Spanyards, etc.), form of government, 10, 90, 96, 128, 192, 222, 485, 719, 722, 733, 743; offices and magistracies, 169, 293, 344, 492, 595; councils, 264, 272; estates, 371, 384; laws and customs, 38, 44, N57, 60, 108, N173, 181, 299, 311, 398, 479, 529, 536, 575, 577, 582, 680, N773; nature of the people, N44, 447, 549–554, 557–563, 566, 568; taxation, revenues, and finance, N96, 97, 651, 657&N, 665, 667, 675; coinage, 688–689, N690, 691, 693–694, 697–698, 700; history, in Moorish period, 39, 416–417, 451, 464, 503, 554; in modern period, 229, 379, 383, 579&N, 594, 602; relations with the Romans, 49, 55, 164, 481, 607&N, 626ᵛ; with America and the Indies, A7, 43, 47, 61, 201, 203, 631ᵛ, 656; with the Low Countries, A10, 59, 290, 378, N546, 656, 666; with France, 67–68, 73, 127, 151, 152&N, 162, 175, 434, 448, 516, N553, N614, 615, 622, 626ᵛ–627, 629, 662, 667, 681; with the Papacy, 64, 126&N, 141, 144, 623, 627ᵛ, 630ᵛ; with Italy, 87, 129–130, 227–228, 617, 630ᵛ; with other peoples, 199, 248, 435, 506&N, 565, 612–613, 715, 746, 749–750; as authorities on other peoples, 440, 553, 562, 568; mentioned, A58, 2, 22, 42, 63, 68, 72, N90, 118, 122, 138, 179, 239, 285, 351, 395, 432, 609, 612, 630, 723, 780
Sparta, Spartans, 564, 576, 577&N, 578, 596, 599–600, 620, 650. See also Lacedemonia
Spartacus, 38–39, 45, 630
Spartianus, Aelius, 590
Spendius, 555
Spifame, an embezzler, N685
Spifame, Jacques, see Nevers
Spinola family, 713
Spinola, Antonio, 628ᵛ
Spinoza, Baruch, A19
Spires or Speyer, 241
Spoleto (Spolet), 139
Stagira, 213
Stamboll, see Istanbul
Stampe, Thomas, fellow of Lincoln, A53
Stancari, Francesco, N567
Stanislas, St., bp. of Cracow, 140
Stanz (Stance), 634
Staseas, N461
Stella, Mount, 221
Stephanus, Athenian orator, 357
Stephen IX or Frederick, pope, 142

Stephen, k. of England, ct. of Boulogne, 108, 748
Stephen I, St., k. of Hungary, 140
Stephen Báthory (Bathor), k. of Poland, 258
Stephen, ct. of Boulogne, error for?, 132
Stephen, voivode of Wallachia (error for Moldavia?), 121, 636
Stephen, bp. of Noyon, 514&N
Steuco, Agostino, of Gubbio (Augustin Egubin), 147
Stiria, see Styria
Stobaeus, Joannes, 394&N
Stockholm, 548
Stoics (Stoikes, etc.), 6, N436, 438, 585
Stour, river, A57
Strabo, the geographer, A54, 81, 386, 448, 554, N565, 635&N, 668
Strabo, Seius, 343
Strasbourg (Strausbourg, etc.), 53, 78, 238, 240–241, 247, 426, 622, 690&N, 693, 707, 711
Strasbourg Oaths, N633
Stratocles, 705
Strozzi (Strossie), Leone, prior of Capua (Capoua, Campania), 179, 523, 554
Stuart, Lady Arabella, N728
Stuart, Charles, earl of Lennox, N728
Stuart, Henry, lord Darnley, 68, N751
Stuart, Matthew, earl of Lennox, 68, N751
Sturm or Sturmius, Jacob, 461
Styria (Stiria), 90
Sucro, 377
Suetonius Tranquillus, Caius, 19, 30, 100, 160, 196–197, N212, N278, N283, 330, 346, 352, 367, 414, 506, 516, 590–592, 611, 635ᵛ, N664, 673, 680, 690, 719
Suevi, N548
Suevia, see Sweden
Suevia, League of, see Swabian League
Suffolk, Edmund de la Pole, earl of, 618
Suger (Suggerius, etc.), N40, 41, 608
Suid, see Schwedt
Suidas, 766
Suisserland, Suissers, Suisses, Suisers, see Switzerland
Sulla (Sylla, Silla, Scylla), Lucius Cornelius, 37–38, 49, 86, 195, 211, 219, 246, 259, 286, 328, 376, 408, 420, 481, 497, 517, 583, 598, N635, 668, N705
Sulpicia (Sulpitia), gens, 391
Sulpicia, lex, 162
Sulpicius Galba, emp. of Rome, see Galba
Sulpicius Galba, Servius, consul 144 B.C., 172, 510
Sulpicius Gallus, see Gallus
Sulpicius Longus, Quintus, 559

Sulpicius Rufus, Publius, 49, 246, 286, 705&N
Surenas (Surenus), 557
Susan, heiress of Bourbon, 743
Sutrium, Sutrini, 76, 178, 665
Swabian League (League of Suevia), 84
Sweden, Swedes (Sueden, Suevia, Swedens), 31, 41, 61, 83, 163, 166, 194, 209, N210, 221, 293, 413, 444, 485, 507, 535, 546, 548–549, 563, 567&N, 614, 722, N728, 748, 779. See also Eric; Gustavus; and John, k. of Sweden
Switzerland, the Swiss (Suisserland, Swisserland, Suissers, Suisses, Suisers, Swissers, Swissars), sovereignty in the cantons, A21, 10, 76–77, 81, 149, 237, 407, 611; type of state, 191, 251, 422–423, 518, 705–706, 708–709, 721, 786–787; governmental institutions, 197, 233–235, 248, 250, 264–265, 268, 308, 385, 482, 492; laws and customs, 50, 53, 62, N66, N99, 359, 364, 542, 574, 605, N709; religious questions, A41, 60, 299, 535, N567; nature of the people, 424, 546, 563, 564&N, 604&N; as soldiers, 452, 554, N612; taxes, revenues, and coinage, 651, 668, 690, N693, 695; relations with France, 58, 61, 74–75, 78, 112, 165, 217, 454, 611, N614, 616, 622, 625, N630, 631, 633ᵛ–634, 658–660, 674, 681, 718, N736; with the Empire, 80, 82&NN, 83, 131, 134, 241, 597; with other countries, N51, 64, 227, 360, 430, 619, 634ᵛ. See also Helvetians
Syagrius, N464
Sybarites (Sibarites), 427, N565
Sydney, Algernon, A64
Sylla, see Sulla
Syllanus, see Silanus
Sylvia, error for Silia?, gens, 391
Synesius, bp. of Ptolemais, 36, 357
Syon, see Sitten
Syon, Mount, see Zion
Syracuse, Syracusans (Siracusa, Siracusians, etc.), 70, 104, 162, 210, 398, 410, 415, 418, 420–424, 431, N461, 469, 481, 504, 524, 546, 594, 597, 604, 666, 702, 720, 739, 745
Syria, Syrians (Siria, Soria), 43, 140, 218, 324, 376, 454, 464, 539, 543, 550, 562, 566, 612–613, 622, 628, 629, 635ᵛ, 684, 690, 714, 719, 737
Szigeth (Sigeth), 451&N, 453

Tabriz (Tauris), 769
Tacfarinas (Tacferin), 39, 630
Tacitus, Claudius, emp. of Rome, 687

Index Nominum

Tacitus, Caius Cornelius, the historian, on government, 193, 522, 591, 716; on Roman history, 37, 54, N91, 208, 276, 282, 286, 465, 572, 581; on Roman laws and customs, 16, 396, 635ᵛ, 690; on the Germans, 29, 37, 550–552, 554–555, 557, N558, 559, 565, 567, 576&N, 585, 743, 784; on other peoples, N448, 548&N, 566, 631ᵛ, 725, N748
Tagodast (Togoda), 426
Talmudists, N464
Tamerlane (Tamberlan, Tamarlan, etc.), 221, 410, 600
Tamesna or Temesna (Tenesme), 555
Taprobana, see Ceylon
Tarafa (Tarapha), Francisco, 464
Tarare (Tarrare), 514
Tarentum, Tarentines, 163, N265, 422, 428, 613, 635, 677, 706, 761
Tarius Rufus, Lucius, 24
Tarpeius Capitolinus, Spurius, 297–298
Tarquinii (Tarquins), 463, 600
Tarquinius Priscus, k. of Rome, 196–197, 208, N517
Tarquinius Superbus (Tarquin the Proud, etc.), k. of Rome, 81, 208, 211, 255, 383, 416–417, 423, 463, 475, N671
Tarquitia (Tarquinia), gens, 391
Tarrare, see Tarare
Tarsus (Tarsis, Tharsis), 56, 537
Tartary, Tartars (Tartaria, Tartarians, etc.), government, 89, 222, 485, 563, 719, 722, 728, 769; laws and customs, 23, 46, 60, 66, 121, 507, 555, 596–597, 601, 614, 780; domestic history, 209, 448, N567, 612, 744; external relations, 44, 147–149, 221, 410, 550, 600, 607, 636, 660; mentioned, 10, 136, 150, 202, 562, 676
Tartereau, an embezzler, N685
Tarutius Firmanus (Taruntius Firmianus), see Firmanus
Tatius, Titus, k. of the Sabines, 198, 407
Tauris, see Tabriz
Taurus, Mount, 562, N565
Taxiles (Taxilas), 494
Tebessa (Telesse), 598
Tedeschi, Nicolo, see Panormitanus
Tefza, capital of Tedla, 433
Telesin, Telensin, see Tlemsen
Telesse, see Tebessa
Tempe, N565
Templars (Templers), A35, 383, 575&N
Tenesme, see Tamesna
Tepoliennes, see Tiepolo
Teramo, N559
Terranne, Jaques de, see Palladino
Terentius, Marcus, 297

Terentius Afer, Publius, dramatist, A56
Terentius Arsa, Caius, 244, 762
Terentius Varro, Caius, consul 216 B.C., 166, 464, 468, 716
Terentius Varro, author, see Varro
Termes, see Thermes
Terracina, Francesco Beltramini, bp. of, N77
Tertullian, 17, 41, 56, 273, 382, 540, N645
Teuta (Tuca), q. of Illyria, 636
Thanet, Isle of, A57
Tharsis, see Tarsus
Theagenes (Theagines), tyrant of Megara, 705
Theatin, pope, see Paul IV
Thebe, 213
Thebes, Thebans, 75, 79, 232, 360, 399, 410, 420, 422, 483, 523, 563, 569, 599–600, 604, 622, 627ᵛ, 706, 722
Themistocles, 35, 49, 51, 105, 182, 200, 428, 471, 497, 600, 610, 627ᵛ, 651, 669, 704
Theobald V, the Good, ct. of Blois, 87
Theobald, ct. of Blois (error for Champagne?), 41
Theobald II (Thibaud), ct. of Champagne, IV of Blois, 617
Theobald IV (Thibaut), ct. of Champagne, 583, 738
Theodebert I, k. of the Franks, 666, 730
Theodora, wife of Justinian, 17, 19, 578
Theodore II, Ducas, emp. of Nicaea, 554
Theodoric I, k. of the Franks, 730, 741
Theodoric III(?), k. of the Franks, 666
Theodoric, k. of the Ostrogoths, 30, 100, 168, 259, 321, 503, N538, 539
Theodoric, bastard of France, see Theodoric I, k. of the Franks
Theodosian Code, 357&N
Theodosius I, the Great, emp. of the East, 42, 105, 314, 375, 382, 452, 537, 540, 648&N
Theodosius I, error for II?, emp. of the East, 67
Theodosius II, emp. of the East, 25, 29, 101, 103, 227, 670
Theodosius II, error for Arcadius, emp. of the East, 507
Theodotion, 467
Theon of Alexandria, 458
Theon of Smyrna, 458
Theophilus, emp. of the East, 228
Theophrastus, 17, 226, 401, 461&N, 511, 545, 556, 586, 658
Theopompus, k. of Sparta, 187, 517
Theopompus of Chios, historian, 102, N206
Thera, 249
Theramenes, 471, 541

Thermes (Termes), Paule de la Barthe, seigneur de, 290
Thérouanne or Térouanne (Therouenne), 609
Theseus, 9, 29, 37, 62, 177, 309
Thespis, 645
Thessalonica, 375, 690. See also Salonica
Thessaly, Thessalians (Thessalie, Thessaliens), 71, 186, 207, 232, 314, 344, 423, N565, 631, 709, 716, 789
Thetmarsh, see Ditmarsh
Theucidides, see Thucydides
Thibaud, Thibaut, see Theobald
Tholose, Tholouse, Tholouze, see Toulouse
Thomas, emp. of the East, error for?, 137, 381
Thomas, ct. of Flanders, 514
Thomas à Becket, archbp. of Canterbury, 140
Thomas Aquinas, St., see Aquinas
Thorius Balbus, Spurius, 575–576
Thoul, see Toul
Thoulouse, Thoulouze, see Toulouse
Thrace, Thracians (Thracia), 17, 35, 179, 208, 443, 554–555, 562, 564, N607, 631, 723
Thrasybulus, tyrant of Syracuse, 420
Thrasybulus (Thrasibulus), Athenian statesman, 110, 227, 230, 273, 429
Thrasyllus or Thrasylus, 422, 429
Thuanus or de Thou (Thuan), Christophe, 479
Thucydides (Thucidides, Theucidides), 47, 101, 186–187, NN205, 206, 281, 362, 424, 430, 497, 515, 555, 706, N722
Thunes, Thunis, see Tunis
Thurii, Thurians (Thuriens), 427, 570, N656
Thyane, see Tyana
Thyestes, 198, 736
Tiber, river, 131, N453, 705
Tiberias, 324
Tiberius I (Tyberius), emp. of Rome, 10, 16, 30, 35, 37, 54–56, 91&N, 160, 197, 201, 214, 226, 262, 266, 271, 276, 286, 303, 313, 343, 381, 414, 416, 452, 483–484, 506–507, 509, 538, 581–582, 630, 635ᵛ, 638, 642, 680, 683, 717, 728&N
Tiberius II, emp. of the East, 689
Tiburtines (Tiburtes), 76
Tiepolo, Bajamonte (Tepoliennes, Bajamontaines), 711&N
Tietmarsh, see Ditmarsh
Tifernas, see Città di Castello
Tigellinus (Tigillin), Sophonius, 226
Tili, Tillet, see Du Tillet
Timaeus, historian, 102
Timocrates, k. of Cyrene, error for?, 416

A205

Index Nominum

Timocrates, of Athens, 697
Timoleon, 213, 221
Timondas, 206, 723
Tiridates I, k. of Armenia, 121
Tirol, *see* Tyrol
Tissaphernes, N631
Titius, Sextus, 575
Titus, emp. of Rome, 452, 509, 591, 728
Tlemsen (Telesin, Telensin), 147, 410, 433, 711
Togoda, *see* Tagodast
Toledo, 96, 693
Tombutto or Timbuktu (Tombut), 47, 147, 507, 555
Tonnerre (Tonerre), 632
Torcy (Torci), Jean, seigneur de, 110
Torelli, Lelio, N114
Toresans, Torresans, etc., *see* Della Torre
Torquatus, *see* Manlius Torquatus *and* Manlius Capitolinus
Torquatus, *error for* Decius Junius Silanus Manlianus, son of Titus Manlius Torquatus, consul 165 B.C., 21
Tortona (Derthone), 729
Toryism, A64
Totila, k. of the Ostrogoths, N464
Toul (Thoul), 615, 617
Toulouse (Tholouze, Tholouse, Thoulouse, etc.), A4–A5, A28, A34, A71, 42, 140, N151, 307&N, 317, 401, 408, N445, N565, 583&N, 690
Toulouse (Tholose, Thoulouze, Toulouze, etc.), Parlement of, 22, 42, 133, 145, 266, 288, 317, 359, 369, 385, 446&N, 764
Touraine, 116, 352, 482, 583&N
Tournay (Turnay), 66, 564
Tournon, François de, card., 673
Tours, N43, 66, 95, 97, 118, 208, 403, 588, 665, 684, 689–690
Trajan, emp. of Rome, 30, 43, 51, 56, 99&N, 100, 109, 135, 172, 204, 215, 227, 255, 262, 269, 314, 394, 412, 508, 550, 638, 665, 680, N681, 683, 728, 734, 773, 775
Tranquillus, *see* Suetonius
Transylvania (Transilvania), 555, 607
Trebatius Testa, Caius, 578, 767
Trebellius Pollio, 566
Trent, Council of, 151, N575
Trent, Cristoforo Madruzzo, card. bp. of, 78
Trèves or Trier (Trevers), 124, 666
Trevisan, Domenico, 624
Treviso (Trevisan), 624
Trezenians, *see* Troezenians
Trimouille, *see* La Trémouille
Triphon, *see* Tryphon
Tripoli (Tripolis), 44, 141, 411, 628ᵛ
Trivulzio (Trivultius), Gian Giacomo, 228, 389

Troezenians (Trezenians), 51, 427, 711
Trogus Pompeius, 463
Trojans (Ilienses), 20, 54
Troyes (Troy), 127, 283, 353
Truchsess von Waldburg (Truces), Otto, *error for* Georg, 555
Tryphon (Triphon), Diodotus, 629, 714
Tsadoc, *see* Zadok
Tubero, Aelius, *see* Aelius
Tubulus (Tubullus), Lucius Hostilius, 286
Tuca, q. of Slavonia, *see* Teuta
Tuditanus, *see* Sempronius Tuditanus
Tullia, gens, 391
Tullia de ambitu, lex, 592
Tullius, Tullie, Tully, *see* Cicero
Tullius, Servius, k. of Rome, *see* Servius
Tullus Hostilius, k. of Rome, *see* Hostilius
Tunis (Tunes, Thunes, Thunis), A51, 147–148, 205, 209, 361, 411, 416, 433, 454, 554, 598, 723, 726
Turacans, 436, 745
Turenne (Turene), 146, 176
Turin, N565
Turkey, Turks (Turkie, Turkes, Grand Signior, Ottoman Empire, etc.), form of government, 201, 222, 436, 718–719, 722; governmental institutions, 167, 188, 259, 263, 343, 360, 488; laws and customs, 44–45, 66, 114, 121, 396, 400, 507, 541–542, 604–605, 613; religious policies, 279, 393, 537–538, N567, 769; finance and revenues, 656, 661, 682, 686; expansion and conquest, A58–A59, A61, 147, 221, 242, 428, 443, 451–453, 464, 550, 600, 612, 628ᵛ; revolts against, 448, 454, 523; foreign relations, 59, 67–68, 148, 152, 358–359, 607, 616, 628, 635, 674, 727; mentioned, A51, iii, 2, 10, 141, 149–150, 258, 410, 485, 554, N559, 560, 660, 668, 676, 723
Turnay, *see* Tournay
Turnebus, Adrian, A4
Turnus, k. of the Rutulians, 609
Turpilianus, Caius Petronius, 328
Turqueman or Malik al-Moazzam Turanshah, sultan of Egypt, 727
Tuscany, Tuscans (Tuscane, Tuscanie), 81&N, 122, 139, N142, 147, 196, 562, 602, 724
Tusculans (Tusculani), 54, 76
Tyana (Thyane), 375
Tyberius, *see* Tiberius
Tyre, 463, 537, 600
Tyrol (Tirol), 90

Ulm (Ulme), 131, N240
Ulmo (Ulmeus), Jean de, 773

Ulpianus (Ulpian), Domitius, 16&N, 25, 161, 292, 295, 302, 304–306, 330, 343, 346, 348, 356, 399, N640, 647, 733, 764
Ulysses (Ulisses), 10, N564
Ungiasen, *see* Imegiagen
Unterwalden (Undervald, Undervall, etc.), 76–78, 82, 149, 241, 247, 250, N424, 497, 604, 695
Urban, *error for* Leo I, pope, 534
Urban III, pope, 40
Urban V, *error for* IV, pope, 122, 139
Urban (Urbin) V, pope, 136, 146, 368, 574&N
Urbino (Urbin), 129, 147, 498, 597, 716
Uri (Urie), 76–78, 82, 149, 241, 247, 250, 264, N424, 497, 597, 604
Ursicinus, antipope, 724
Ursin, Ursins, *see* Orsini
Utrecht (Utrech), 616
Uzun Hasan (Usun Cassan), 544

Valachia, *see* Wallachia
Valaisans (Valesians, Vallesians, Valoisians, etc.), 58, 76&N, 77, 619, 631, 634ᵛ
Val d'Aosta (Valdaost), 619
Val d'Or, N565
Valence, in France, N40, 152
Valencia (Valence), in Spain, 126, 554, 562–563, 694&N
Valens, emp. of the East, 40, N382, 567
Valens, Vettius, of Antioch, 443
Valentina (Valentine), wife of Lewis, d. of Orleans, *see* Visconti
Valentinian, emp. of Rome, 56, 306, N382, 452
Valentinois, d. of, *see* Borgia, Cesare
Valeria, gens, 55, 391
Valeria, lex, on Sulla's dictatorship, 86, 219
Valeriae, leges, after expulsion of the kings, 55, 168, 179, 219, 328, 665
Valeria et Horatia (Horatia), lex, 339
Valerianus, emp. of Rome, 638
Valerius Corvus, Marcus, 55
Valerius Falto, Quintus, 347, 585–586
Valerius Flaccus, Lucius, 538
Valerius Laevinus, Marcus, 374
Valerius Maximus, author, 17, 21, 23, 208, 305, 340, 547, 580, N645, 772–773
Valerius Maximus, Manius, dictator 494 B.C., 154, 156
Valerius Messala, Marcus, consul 263 B.C., 305
Valerius Messala, Marcus, consul 53 B.C., 300, 302–303, 304&N, 309, 347, 349
Valerius Messala Corvinus, Marcus, 212&N, 735

A206

Index Nominum

Valerius Potitus, Lucius, consul 483 B.C., 302
Valerius Potitus, Lucius, consul 449 B.C., 55
Valerius Publicola, Publius, 55, 166, 219, 390, 668
Valesians, Vallesians, Valoisians, see Valaisans
Valier, see St. Vallier
Valla, Lorenzo, 147
Valois, A11, 743. See also Philip VI, k. of France, ct. of Valois
Valois, Raoul, ct. of, 731–732
Valori, Francesco, 168, 211, 429
Vandales, see Hanseatic towns
Vandals (Vandales), 40, 550, 738 &N, 740
Varennes, Charles de Mornay, sieur de, 194
Varro, see Quintilius Varus and Terentius Varro, consul 216 B.C.
Varro, Marcus Terentius, author, 4, 6, 19, 35, 50, 157, 294&N, 297&N, 300, 303–304, 309, 336, 441, 464, 512&N, 557, 568, N614, N631^v, 650&N, 671
Vascosanus, Michael, A4
Vashti (Vasthi), wife of Ahasuerus, 747
Vaste, John, see John, vicomte of Narbonne
Vatican, see Rome, Church of
Vatinius, Publius, 274
Vaudémont, 132, 203, 237
Vectius, see Vettius and Veturius
Vegetius, Flavius Renatus, 550, 554
Veii, Veientines (Veios, Veians, Veientes, Vientes), 390, 428, 538, 601, 635
Veliterni (Veliternians), 635
Velleius Paterculus, 642
Venaissin, 667
Venceslaus, see Wenceslaus
Venda or Wanda, q. of Russia (error for Poland), 751
Vendôme (Vendosme), 579&N, 748
Venice, Venetians, form of state and government, 99–100, 128, 158, 172, 184, 188, 190–191, 197, 221, 235, 249, 546&N, 702, 710–713, 719, 785; changes in form of government, N236, 407, 428, 434&N; senate and councils, 165, 169, 232–233, 241, 258, 264–265, 268, 273, 393, 470; the Great Council, 168, 237, 247, 275, 277, 517; offices and magistracies, 166, 182, 240–241, 280, 284, 302, 307, 326, 353, 420, 472, 480, 493, 596, 638, 651, 716; voting procedures, 48, 245, 271&N, 308, 780; laws and customs, 26, 60, 62, 66, 82, 359, 364, 574, 605–606, 630, 776–778, 783; social classes, 46, 64, 69, 389, 398, 432, 534, 577, 678;
census of population, 427, 578, 640; characteristics of the people, 399, 424, 553, 563, 568; finance, trade, and coinage, 660, 673, 690, 693–694; foreign relations, 51, 67–68, 144, 151, 227, 358, 376, 417, 432, 434, 516, 523, 597, 624–625^v, 630^v, 661, 729; with the Turks, 148, 152, 628, 634^v; mentioned, 63, 418, 463, 597, 615, N709
Venus, 557, N561, 566, 639
Veratius (Neratius), Lucius, 775, 778
Vercelli (Versel), 729
Vercingetorix (Vercingentorix), 79
Verdun, 615, 617
Vergil, Polydore (Polidore, Polydore), 97, 101, N645
Vermandois, A8, N95, 120, 322, 370, 617, 700, 730–732
Veronà, 420, 566, 624
Veronensis, see Scaliger
Verres, Caius, 157, 266, 335–336, 348, 398, 580, 704
Versel, see Vercelli
Vertus (Virtus), 118
Verus, Aelius Aurelius, 30, 198, 728
Vespasian (Vespatian, etc.), emp. of Rome, 35, 98, 196, 284, 414, 452, 598, 638, 664&N, 678, 680, 692, 697
Vespucci (Vespucius), Guidantonio, N544, 546
Vestini (Vestines), 163
Vettius (Vectius), augur, 464
Veturia, gens, 391
Veturius (Vectius), Caius, 340
Vicenza (Vincentia), 624
Victor II, pope, 142, 731
Victor, Aurelius, see Aurelius
Vide, see Gui
Vienna, 130, 144, 151, 452, 616
Vienne, 42, 55
Viennois, 134
Vientes, see Veii
Villefranche-de-Rouergue, 698
Villemor, sieur de, 699
Villeneuve-lès-Avignon, 698
Villia, lex, 280
Villiers, sieur de, 740
Vimare, see Wismar
Vincent, Barthélemy, A44, A74
Vincentia, see Vicenza
Virgilius Maro (Maro, Virgil), Publius, A56, 36, 459, 533–534, 552, 609, N648
Virginia, 337
Virginia, gens, 391
Virginius, Lucius, 337
Virginius Tricostus Rutilus, Proculus, 705
Viriathus (Viriatus), 3, 39
Virtus, see Vertus
Viscellia, lex, 772
Visconti family, lords of Milan, N205. See also Anglerie
Visconti, Azzo (Actius), 128
Visconti, Bernabò (Barnabus), 128, 744
Visconti, Galeazzo I (Galeace), 128, 154
Visconti, Galeazzo II (Galeace, John Galeace), 128, 744
Visconti, Giangaleazzo (Galeace III), d. of Milan, 128
Visconti, Giovanni (John), archbp. and ruler of Milan, 144
Visconti, Giovanni Maria, d. of Milan, 417
Visconti, Luccino (Luchin), 144
Visconti, Filippo Maria, d. of Milan, 111, 729
Visconti, Valentina, wife of Lewis, d. of Orleans, 729
Visigoths, 567. See also Goths
Vitald, Vitaldus, see Nithard
Vitelli family, lords of Città di Castello, 420
Vitelli, Vitello, 716
Vitellius, Aulus, emp. of Rome, 228, 414, 417, 734
Vitruvius Pollio, Marcus, 441, 447–448, 550
Vivières (Viviers in Brie), 685
Vlad Dracul, voivode of Wallachia (Dracula, d. of Transilvania), 555
Voconia, lex, 107, 578, 753
Voconius Saxa, Quintus, 578
Volero, see Publilius
Volga, river, 148
Volmar, see Waldemar
Volscians (Volsians, Volsques), 54, 429, 609, 635
Vopiscus, Flavius, 30, 169
Vulcanus, N559

Wade, William, A7
Waldemar (Volmar, Wolmar), dynasty of, 31, N210, 748
Waldenses, N567
Wales, Prince of, see Edward the Black Prince; Edward, son of Henry VI
Wallachia (Valachia, Walachie), 59, 121, 258, 636
Walloons, A57
Warwick (Warwike), Richard Neville, earl of, 585, 601
Washington, A66
Weiss, Nathanael, A7
Wenceslaus (Venceslaus), emp. of Germany, 221, 237, 725, 728
Werdenhagen, Johann Angelius von, A83
West Indies, West Indians (Westerne Islands, etc.), 22, 34, 40&N, 43, 45–47, 61, 126, 555, 557, 560, 563, 568, 656, 735, 780. See also Indies; Indians, in America
Westminster, Statute of, A18
Westmoreland (Westmerland), Charles Neville, 6th earl of, 97
Weston, Hugh, rector of Lincoln, A53

Index Nominum

Westphal, Joachim, N567
Westphalia, 380, 411, 544, 558
West Saxons, *see* Anglo-Saxons
Whigs, A64–A65
William, emp. of Germany, ct. of Holland, N81, 723, 725, 727
William I, the Conqueror, k. of England, 203, 209, 601, 655, 742
William II, Rufus, k. of England, 742
William, k. of Sicily, 40, 750
William I, prince of Orange, 145, 465
William, bp. of Châlons, 514&N
Windsor, 589
Wirciburg, Wirtzburg, *see* Würzburg
Wisedome, the maister of, etc., *see* Solomon
Wismar (Vimare), 84
Witald, Witard, *see* Nithard
Wittemberg, *see* Würtemberg
Wolmar, *see* Waldemar
Wood, Anthony à, A52–A53, A60
Worcester, earl of, *see* Somerset
Worms (Wormes), 143, 237, 240–241, 628, 659
Würtemberg, Ulric VI, d. of, 144
Würtemberg (Wittemberg), Christopher, d. of, 27&N

Würzburg (Wirciburg, Wirtzburg), 84, 693
Wycliffe, John, A52

Xanthians (Xanthiques), 20
Xanthippus, N292
Xenocrates, N632
Xenophon, v, 8, 168, 186–187, 193, 200, 206, 212, 215, 243, 263, 346, 397, 424, 517, 531, 558, 620, 702–704, 719, 756&N, 782
Xerxes I, k. of Persia, 375, 466, 507, 622, 627ᵛ, 737

Yolande (Yoland), daughter of René of Anjou, 132
York, A53
York (Yorke), house of, 526, 601, 632
York, Richard, d. of, 632
Ysunza, Gaspar de Añastro, A82

Zabarella, Francesco, card., 626ᵛ
Zacharias, *see* Zechariah
Zachary (Zacharie), pope, 137, 146
Zadamachus, prince of the Tartars, 448
Zadok (Tsadoc), 360
Zamoyski (Zamosche, Zamoschy), Jan Sarius, 511, 723

Zara (Zarafi), 235
Zárate, Agustín de (Augustus Zarata), 667
Zborowski, Jan (Salomon Sboroschi), castellan of Odolano, 435
Zechariah (Zacharias), 466
Zedekiah (Sedechias, etc.), k. of Judah, 223, 463, 464&N
Zeeland, N558
Zeneta or Zenata (Zenetes), 147
Zeno, emp. of the East, 29, 382
Zeno, philosopher, N436
Zenobia, q. of Palmyra, 727, 747
Zerubbabel (Zerubabel), N464, 466
Zeus, N394. *See also* Jupiter
Ziani (Cian, Cyanee), Sebastiano, doge of Venice, 190, 712
Ziklag (Ziceleg), 651
Zion (Syon), Mount, 536
Zoilus, N548
Zug, 76, 78, 149, 247, 250, 268, 497
Zurich (Zuric, Zurike, Zuricke), 76–78, 82, 149, 233, 234&N, 242, 250–251, 264, 426, 431, 497, 619, 706, 711, 786
Zvonimir Demetrius (Demetrius), k. of Croatia, 208
Zwingli (Zuinglius), Ulrich, 78, N567

INDEX RERUM

For an explanation of the pagination series found in this index, and of the method of indexing the endnotes (pp.A105–A172), see the first paragraph of the introductory note to the Index Nominum, p. A173 above.

Absolute authority, absolute power, *see* Power
Accountability, 477–478, 685
Action, life of, 4–7, 402
Adoption, 29–31
Adultery, 16–17
Aediles, curule, 303
Aerarium, 653
Age, of senators, 255–256; of the world, 444, N445, 446–447. *See also* Longevity
Agrarian laws, *see* Lands
Agriculture, 400–402
Aliens, 48, 60–69, 75, 359, 749–751
Alliances, *see* Treaties
Allies, 69, 73–75, 611–612, 614–615, 633&N, 633^v–634
Alms, *see* Charity
Ambassadors, 67, 151–152, 635^v, 636&N, 656&N
Ambition, 480
Amity, *see* Friendship
Anarchy, A21, A70, N185, 410, 701, 717&N, 723
Apanages, 741–743
Apparel, *see* Dress
Appeals, 168–171, 337–338, 351–353, 356–358, N543
Appetite, 549–550
Arbitrators, 526, 625, 630^v–631, 634
Archons, 86, 197, 354
Areopagites, 261, 268, 277
Aristocracy, A76, 95, 99, 183–188, 190–193, 196, 221, 230–244, 246, 248–249, 265&N, 709–712, 713&N, 721, 785–786. *See also* Oligarchy
Arithmetic justice, *see* Justice
Armies, 549, N551. *See also* Military training; War
Arms, law of, *see* Force; Military discipline
Arms, training in, *see* Military training
Arms, wearing of, 542, 564&N
Artificers, artisans, *see* Handicraftsmen
Artists, 400, 402
Assassination, 228–229, 416–418, 523. *See also* Murder
Assemblies, in democracies, 702–703
Astrology, astronomy, *see* Stars
Atheism, A69, 539, 625^v, 645
Augurs, 351
Authority, *see* Power
Autumn, significance of, 451–452, 453&N

Balance of power, *see* Power
Ballots, N232, 271&N. *See also* Lots; Voting
Banishment, 431, 632^v, 704. *See also* Ostracism
Barbarism, 552&N, 565
Barrenness, of soil, 565&N
Bastards, 29, 741
Bells, 541–542
Benefices, 64
Birth control, 571
Bishops, jurisdiction of, *see* Priests
Blood, N554, 558

Body, human, compared to the state, 387, 493, 531, 669, 708, 717–718, 720, 790–791; compared to the world, 7, 561–562
Bodyguards, 418–420
Borderlands, 59–60, 132–133, 565
Burgess, 50&NN

Capital punishment, *see* Death penalty; Punishment
Cardinals, College of, 435
Castles, *see* Fortifications
Censors, censorship, 70, 299, 301, 304–305, 347, 350, 481, 546, 637, 638&NN, 640&N, 642–643, 644&NN, 645&N, 646&N, 647, 648&NN, 649, N713, 771
Census, 427, 578, 637&N, 639&NN, 640&N, 641&N
Chain of Being, the, A22, 436, 793–794
Chancellor, of France, 354
Change, in worldly things, 406, 408; in states, 406–436, 467–469, 542–543; related to the stars, 437–455; related to numbers, 455–465; in laws, 469–472; inevitability of, 438
Chaos, 386–387, 451
Character, national, A22–A23, 447–448, 456–457, 546–568
Charity, 676
Chastity, 557
Children, 9, 20–21, 23, 557, N558, 571, 670&NN, 714, 718. *See also* Youth
Citadels, *see* Fortifications
Citizens, citizenship, A5, A33, A75, 47–48, 50&N, 53–69, 76, 386–387, 403–404. *See also* Subjects
City, N3, 49–53
Civil strife, A9, v, 433, 476–477, 563, 601–603, 705&N, 706, 711–712, 714–715, 719, 724, 733, 746–747. *See also* Factions; Religious strife
Civility, 552&N, 565, 722
Classes, social, 68–69, 193, 386–405, 570–571, 610, 790. *See also* Estates
Clemency, 229, 375, 379, 509–511, 521–522. *See also* Lenity
Clergy, *see* Priests
Clients, *see* Protection
Climate, theory of, A22–A23, 5, 545–568
Coinage, 175–177, 639, 687&NN, 688–700
Cold, 548, 551&N, 552, 557–558, 563
Colleges, A77, 349, 361&N, 364–386
Colonies, 54–55, 406, 566, 568, 576, 655, 656&N
Combats, 527–529, 559, 627, 738–739, 776
Comedies, *see* Plays
Command, power to, *see* Power
Commissions, commissioners, A77, 85, 207, 278–293, 473, 630^v–631
Commonweal or state, defined, A74, 1, 9–11, 84, 361&N, 637; other definitions, 3, 154; origins and growth, 47, 361–363, 406; types of, A19, 184, 250, 409, 546&N, 547, 700 (*see also* Aristocracy; Democracy; Monarchy); concept of the mixed

A209

Index Rerum

Commonweal or state—continued
state, 154, 184–195, 200, 250, 755; compared to city (*civitas*), N3, 49; compared to man, 531, 561, 790–791; studied from different standpoints, 437; *other references, passim*
Communism, *see* Property, community of
Commutative justice, *see* Justice
Confiscation, 180, 580–584
Conjunctions, planetary, 444, 445&NN, 446–450, 452–454
Conquest, 655–656
Consent, in lawmaking, 159–160
Conspiracies, A8, 380, 522–524, 750&N
Constable, of France, 354
Constancy, 566, 567&NN
Constitutional limitations, *see* Limitations
Consuls, consulship, 99, 188–190, 302, 339&N, 345, 347, 348&NN, 349, 351, 353–354, 788&NN
Contemplation, 4–7, 402, 480, 560–561, N564, 791
Contempt, for kings, 516
Continence, N558
Contracts, *see* Promises
Copper, 688, 691, 693, 696–699
Coronation, 93–95, 100–101, 112, 143–144, 146, 209, 730–732
Corporations, A77, 349, 361&N, 364–365
Councils, privy councils, 158, 190–191, 232–234, 262–265, 267–268, 272. *See also* Senates
Counterfeiting, 687, 690, 697–699
Covenants, *see* Promises
Covenants, matrimonial, 20
Covetousness, 683&N
Creation, 15, 439–440, 444, 459
Creditors, 66–67, 676
Criticism, of *République*, A33–A34, A71–A73
Crowd, the, *see* Populace
Cruelty, 341–342, 368, 375–377, 379&N, 416–417, 511, 522, 555–556, 636
Curriculum, at Oxford, A54–A55; at Manwood's School, A56
Custom, customary law, N92, 95, 98, 160–161, 317, 395, 475, N766
Customs duties, 661&N, 662–663

Death penalty, 159, 773&N, 774, 776–780
Debts, debtors, 66, 471, 569–570, 572, 675, 781
Deceit, 399, 564&N. *See also* Faith; Lying; Promises
Decemviri, 161, 282, 348
Decimation, 374
Decreta, 333
Definition, A74, 183, 279&N, 280, N361
Deformity, 736–737
Degeneration, of men, 550, 551&N
Democracy, A76, 99, 183–188, 191–193, 195–196, 230, 233, 244–251, 265&N, 383, 530, 701–709, 755–756, 759–760, 785–786
Deposition, of kings by popes, 136, 732&N
Deputies, *see* Lieutenants
Destruction, of the world, 449–450, 453
Dictator, dictatorship, 85–86, 188–189, 281, 345, 420, 481, 715–716
Dignity, *see* Gravity
Discipline, civil, *see* Education
Discord, of magistrates, 493–499. *See also* Harmony
Discretion, of magistrates, *see* Equity
Disease, 467–468, 472, 558&N, 562
Distributive justice, *see* Justice
Division, of monarchies among heirs, 741–744
Divorce, 18
Doge, of Venice, 191

Domaine, 130, 650&N, 651&N, 652–655, 664&N, 724–725. *See also* Property
Dominium, N202, N408
Donations, 88, 726
Dowries, 577&N, 578, 579&N, 667–668
Dress, 684, 770–771
Drunkenness, 270, 503, 551&N
Duarchy, 198, 409
Duration, of types of state and government, 204, 719
Duumviri, duumvirate, 198, 295–296
Dux, N292

Earth, motion of the, 454, 455&N
Earthquakes, 437, 451, N453, N455
Eclipses, 439, 449–450, 454
Edicts, 156–157, 159, 336
Education, related to natural forces, 547&N, 565–566; should be public, 645
Election, of kings, 89–90, N95, 206–207, 209–210, 288, 563, 613, 616, 722–730, 732–734, 749&N; of the Emperor, 236, 434, 472; of popes, 138–139, 142–143; of the Venetian Doge, 472; in aristocracies, 230; of magistrates, 308
Election, pays d', N385
Elephantiasis, 558&N
Eloquence, 271, 485, 543–544
Emancipation, of slaves, *see* Manumission
Environment, *see* Climate
Ephors, 187
Equality, 387, 471, 477, 485&N, 569–572, 576–578, 701, 707–708, 756–759, 761–762
Equites, 390, 398, 404–405
Equity, 228, 315–317, 333–335, 341, 760–765, 767–769. *See also* Justice
Errors, in translation, A42–A43, A88; in typography, A43–A44, A88
Estates, or parliaments, meetings of, A9, A16, 90, 95–98, 103, 191–192, 236–239, 370–371, 384–385, 403, 499&N, N654. *See also* Assemblies; Classes
Eternity, of the world, 450
Evil, *see* Vice
Excommunication, 138–140, 143–145, 647, 648&N, 649, N736
Executioner, 307&N, 401
Expediency, *see* Profit
Experience, A71, 485, 719
Exports, 661&N, 662&N, 663
Eyes, color of, 548&N

Factions, 403–404, 493–494, 519–522, 524–527, 530–531, 534–537, 540–541, 545, 571, 707, 711–715, 725, 733. *See also* Civil strife; Religious strife
Fairs, power to grant, 180&N
Faith, keeping and breaking of, 625ᵛ–626ᵛ, 627&NN, 627ᵛ, 628&N, 628ᵛ–629, 629ᵛ&N, 630&NN, 630ᵛ&N, 631–631ᵛ, 635–635ᵛ, 676, 775. *See also* Deceit; Lying; Perfidy; Promises
Family, A74–A75, 8–12, 361, 363, 388, 391, 577, 707&N, 746–747
Fate, 357&N, N436, N457
Fatal number, 463&N
Father, power of the, *see* Power
Fealty, fees, fiefs, homage, lords, vassals, vassalage, 70–71, 114&NN, 115–135, 140–142, 147–150, 152–153, 170–171, 175, 202–203, 239, 355, 395, 632ᵛ&N, 752–753
Fear, 226, 418
Feasts, 364
Federalism, A19, A21
Fees, professional, 783–784

A210

Index Rerum

Female succession, female rule, see Women
Fertility, of men and animals, N558; of soil, 565&N
Fetiales, N614
Feudum, N114
Finance, see Treasure
Fines, 296–298, 769–771, 773, 775–776
Fiscus, 653
Flexibility, 720
Floods, 437, N445, 446, N448, 450–451, 453
Foedus, N614. See also Treaties
Force, 204–205, 219, 221–222, 323, 418, 532, 537, 559. See also Violence
Foreigners, see Aliens
Forests, 284, 682
Forgery, 777&N
Form, 792
Fortifications, fortresses, 596–601, 604–606, 608, 613, 711&NN, 750–751
Fortune, 230, 270–271, 396, 407, 436, N457, 474
Four Monarchies, see Monarchies
Fraternities, 362–364
Free will, see Necessity
Friendship, 363–364, 427, 431–432, 499, N567, 570, 759
Frontiers, see Borderlands
Fugitives, 357, 359–360

Generals, 80–82, 206–207, N292
Geometric justice, see Justice
Gifts, 584–595, 656–658, 679, 680&N, 681&N. See also Rewards
Gilding, 692&NN
Gold, A7, 399, 666–668, 682–683, 688–700
Golden Age, 47, 200
Government or rule, A20, A76, 199, 207, 230, 249–250, 409, 567, 755, 760, 785
Gradualism, 471–475
Gravity, in magistrates, 328, 341
Guards, see Bodyguards
Gymnastics, N554. See also Wrestling

Hair, color of, 548&NN
Handicraftsmen, 386, 397–398, 402
Hangman, see Executioner
Harmonic justice, see Justice
Harmony, 11, 199, 205, 455–456, 498, 760, 786–788, 790–793
Heat, 548, 549&N, 557–558
Heresy, heretics, N487, 628
History, A5, A27
Homage, see Fealty
Honesty, 105, 109
Honor, 585–589; may be separated from power, 240, 307, 353
Horoscopes, of cities, 441–442, 443&N
Hostages, 165, 626ᵛ–627, 629, 635
Houses, valuation of, 441&N
Humanism, A3–A4, A27
Humidity, 548–549
Humors, theory of, 554, 567&N
Husband, power of, over wife, see Power

Idlers, 401, 602–603, 641, 644, 678
Ignominy, 304–305, 646&N, 647&N
Images, 381, N559
Imitation, of princes by subjects, 503–504, 537
Immovables, see Land
Imperator, 292&N
Imperium, 291–292, 304, 327, 329–333, 347, 348&NN, N646. See also Merum imperium; Power

Impiety, 380
Imports, 663
Imposts, see Taxation
Imprisonment, of Bodin, A7
Inalienability, of domaine, A16–A17, 130, 651–652
Inconstancy, 422, 424, 471, 566, 567&NN
Indivisibility, of monarchies, 741–743
Infamy, 304–305, 647&N
Infidels, 628&N
Inflation, see Prices
Informers, 581–582
Inheritance, 13, 25, 28–29, 31, 65–66, 202–203, 475, 571–572, 574&NN, 576–584, 665, 670&N, 739–740, 784&NN; of offices, 482. See also Legacies; Testaments
Injustice, see Justice
Innovation, 469–470, 484, 713–714, 717–718
Insanity, 556&N
Insignia, of royalty, 208–209
Intent, in punishing offenses, 778
Intercourse, sexual, 557, N558
Interest, see Usury
Interpretation, of laws, 161
Interregnum, 723–724
Intervention, by foreign princes, 220&N, 221, 632–632ᵛ; by God in human affairs, see Providence
Intestacy, 574–575
Iron, 699

Jealousy, 557–558, 747, 749
Judges, 333&N, 478–479, 487–488, 500–502, 506–516, 720. See also Magistrates
Jurisdiction, 298–300, 355, 646&N
Jus or right, A75, 108
Jus gentium, see Law
Justice and injustice, A35–A37, A69–A70, A77, 8, 154, 243, 270&N, 311–312, 315–318, 323, 374, N379, 487, 500–502, 506–507, 509, 515, 626, 755–794. See also Equity
Just war, see War

Kings, kingship, see Monarchy
Knights, knighthood, 135, 587–589
Knowledge, 4&N, 5–6, 255, N256, 258, 394, 480&N, 561. See also Wisdom

Laesa majestas, 158. See also Treason
Land, 65–66, 575–577, 650–651, 655&N, 663, 669, 671–672. See also Domaine
Language, 181, 612
Law, human, A46, A75–A76, iii, 27, 91–94, 98–108, 156, 243, 293, 300, 314–318, 325, 333–334, 469–470, 644–645, 717, 760–769; divine and natural, A15–A16, A20, A70–A71, 92, 104, 113, 174, 200, 203–205, 312–315, 323–324, 359, 484, N644, 717, 761; Roman, A4–A6, A46, 108; of nations (jus gentium), A6, 90&N, 113, 313; family, 13–14; universal, Bodin's scheme of, A6, A24–A25, A28, A36–A37; fundamental, in France A17; rule of, 490, 509, 701, 768. See also Custom; Leges imperii; Lex regia
Lawmaking, central to sovereignty, A14–A15, 159–162, 185
Lawsuits, 559–561, 670–671, 766–767
Lawyers, 400, 402
Lead, 699&N
Leadership, in democracies, 706
Leagues, see Treaties
Left side, significance of, 562

Legacies, 366–367, 658. *See also* Inheritance; Testaments
Leges imperii, A16–A19, 95&N, 231
Legis actio, 333&N, 353, 760
Legitimacy, A20–A21
Lenity, 216–218, 341, 377–378, 379&N, 509. *See also* Clemency
Leprosy, 558&N
Lèse-majesté, see *Laesa majestas*
Lettres de justice, 310–311
Lex, A75–A76. *See also* Law
Lex regia, 88, 98, 733
Liberality, 594
Libertini, 388–389, 398
Liberty, natural, 14, 47, 200, 204, 701; principle of, in states, 250–251, 427, 563; for slaves, *see* Manumission
Licensing, of *Six Bookes*, A59
Lie, giving the, 528–529. *See also* Lying
Liege homage, 124–125, 175. *See also* Fealty
Lieutenants or deputies, 88, 134–135, 726
Lightning, 512
Limitations, constitutional, A21, 94–95
Logic, A25–A27
Longevity, 461–462, 558
Lots, casting of, N232, 243, 308, 734, 757, 759–760
Lords, *see* Fealty
Love, of subjects for kings, 505, 512–513
Luxuries, 670&N, 671
Lying, 531. *See also* Deceit; Faith; Promises

Madness, *see* Insanity
Magistrates, magistracies, A5, A77, 85–88, 90, 154–157, 166–168, 224–225, 241–242, 259, 271–272, 274, N277, 278–285, 288–361, 367–368, 402, 420–421, 476–499, 707, 760–765. *See also* Judges; Officers
Magnanimity, 607–608
Majesty or *majestas*, 157–158. *See also* Sovereignty
Majorities, 247, 349–351, 370&N, 371–372, 710, 715
Manufacturing, 663
Manumission, of slaves, 37–43, 46, 388, 665
Marginalia, A41–A42, A48
Marque and reprisal, 180
Marriage, 15, 36, 388, 577, N648, 670, 746, 749&N, 750, 751&N, 752&N, 757–758
Matter, 792
Mayors of the Palace, 741
Mean, concept of the, 485–486, 492–493, 552, 554&N, N567, 709–710
Medicines, 761
Mercenaries, 564, 605–606, 611–612
Merchandise, valuation of, 671&N
Merchants, 399–400, 402, 564. *See also* Trade
Merum imperium, 327, 329–333
Middle class, 432
Migration, 554. *See also* Colonies
Military discipline, 275, 331–332, 342, 677, 716
Military service, nobility and, 389, 402
Military training, 596, 598–599, 601–606, 610–614, 711, N713. *See also* Armies; War
Militia ex casu, N114, N395
Missionaries, Catholic, A53
Mixed state, *see* Commonweal
Mixture, of metals, 687–688, 693, 696
Monarchies, the Four, 465–466
Monarchy, A15, A76, 99–101, 183–186, 188, 190–192, 196–218, 230, 265&N, 402, 410–413, 713–754, 786–787. *See also* Tyranny
Money, *see* Coinage

Moneylending, *see* Usury
Monogamy, *see* Wives
Monopolies, 386
Motion, of the earth, 454, 455&N. *See also* Earthquakes
Mountains, 562–563, 564&NN, 565&N
Mounts of piety, 672
Multitude, the, *see* Populace
Murder, 174, 542, 779–780. *See also* Assassination
Music, 455–457, 556, 564, 565&N, 646, 790–791
Mutiny, 377–378. *See also* Rebellion

Nationalism, Bodin's, A31
Naturalization, 63–64
Nature, 408, 436–438
Nature, law of, *see* Law
Nature, of peoples, *see* Character
Necessity, A23, 408, 436&N, 438, 450, N463, 467, 547&N, 568
Nephew, right of, over uncle, 738–740
Nepotism, 479
Neutrality, 541, 622–625
Nobility, 19–20, 163, 166, 235, 258–259, 388–397, 400, 402, 404, 706–707, 712–713, 758, 772–774. *See also Patricii*; Peers
Nonresistance, *see* Obedience; Resistance
Novelty, *see* Innovation
Novus homo, 390–391, 788&NN
Numbers, force of, 455–458, 459&N, 460&N, 461–463, 464&N, 465; in families, 9, 571; in colleges, 365–366; in senates, 259–265, 267–268; of magistrates, 497–498; illustrating proportions, 760, 787–788, 790

Oaths, *see* Coronation; Promises
Obedience, A70, v; to husbands, 19, 746, 752; to parents, 20, 368–369; to magistrates, 340; to kings, 64, 500; of magistrates to kings, 309, 323–324
Obstinacy, *see* Stubbornness
Ocean, *see* Sea
Occupations, base, 398–403
Officers, offices, A77, 64, 278–285, 288–295, 308, 309&N, 330–333, 345, 390–393, 399, 401, 413, 472–474, 585, 588, 610, 684–686, 696, 705, 789; sale of offices, 259, 482, 484, 591–592, 661. *See also* Magistrates
Oligarchy, 190, 230, 241. *See also* Aristocracy
Omissions, in Knolles's version, A39–A41, A88
Orators, 543–544
Order, A21, A24, 386–387, 450
Origins, of state and society, 47, 293, 361–363, 599
Ornamentation, in Knolles's version, A50–A51
Ostracism, 247, 251, 430–431, 588. *See also* Banishment.

Pactio, N614. *See also* Treaties
Painting, 400
Pardon, 171–175, 376, 378, 510
Parlements, 192, 266, 354, 490–492. *See also* Paris; Rouen; Toulouse, *etc., in Index Nominum*
Parliaments, *see* Estates
Parricide, 21, 24, 26
Paternal power or *patria potestas*, *see* Power
Patricii, 390–391, 404. *See also* Nobility
Patrons, *see* Protection
Peace, 598, 603–604
Peers, 513–514. *See also* Nobility
Penalties, *see* Death penalty; Punishment
Pensions, 148, 251, 258, 616–617, 658–660, 681–682
Peoples, nature of, *see* Character

Index Rerum

Perfection, in states, 411
Perfidy, 567&N. See also Faith
Physicians, 400, 402
Pictures, see Portraits
Pirates, 1–3, 215, 630. See also Robbers
Pity, 510–511
Plague, 562
Planets, see Stars
Plays, 645&NN, 646, 776. See also Theater
Plebiscitum, 156
Polygamy, see Wives
Poor, the, see Poverty
Populace, the, behavior of, 531–533, 702–704
Popular state, see Democracy
Population, 427, 550–551, N558, 571–572, 639&N, 640&N, 767
Portraits, 255, 400, 751
Potestas, see Power
Poverty, the poor, 45, 396, 411, 569–570, 572–574, 576–578, 580, 668–670, 672, 676, 677&N, 678, 775
Power, over wives, 14–17, 19–20, 746, 752; over children, or *patria potestas*, 20, 22–27, 340, 634&N, 644, 746; over slaves and servants, 32–33; over citizens and subjects, or power to command (*potestas* or *imperium*), 14, 272, 278–279, 291–292, 299–300, 304, 306–307, 312, 327, 344–345, 488; not appropriate to senates, 272–274; may be separated from honor, 240, 307, 353; absolute, concept of, A15, 88–90, 109; corrupting influence of, 714, 725; balance of, among states, 624, 625ᵛ. See also Imperium; Obedience; Sovereignty
Praetors, 296, 303, 306, 328–329, 335–337, 339&N, 347, 348&NN, 349, 353–354
Precedence, among states, 149–152
Prescription, 132–133, 142, 178&N, 182, 220, 651–652
Presents, see Gifts
Prices, A6, 667&NN, 668&N, 692
Priests, priesthood, clergy, 258, 279, 295, 298–300, 392–393, 402, 574&N, 575, 647, 648&N, 649. See also Rome, Church of, *in Index Nominum*
Primogeniture, 734–741
Prince, principate, 80, 91, 95, 99&N, 100, 158, 191, 196, 221–222, 419
Privileges, 91, 156, 160, 176, 180&N, 321–322, 762
Privy councils, see Councils
Prodigality, 679
Professors, 402
Profit or utility, 105, N270, 318, 374, 585, 587
Promises, covenants, etc., A16, 92–95, 106–107, 111–113. See also Deceit; Faith; Lying
Pronunciation, 568
Property, public, 11, 637, 752; private, A16, 11–13, 109–110, 200–204, 569–571, 575–583, 641–643, 707&N, 752; of the Church, 575; community of, 11–12, 193, 707. See also Domaine
Protection, 69–72, 80–81, 114–115, 149, N614, 615–621, 632–633
Providence, divine, A11–A12, A70, 325, 410, 436&N, 437–438, 793–794. See also Retribution
Public works, 677–678, 679&N
Punishment, 16–17, 19, 21, 28, 56, 159, N335, 359, 368–369, 373–379, 477, 508–509, 512–513, 542, 543&N, 580–582, 584–585, 593&N, 771–782, 784. See also Death penalty; Fines

Quaestors, 304&N, 352
Quicksilver, 699
Quorum, in Roman senate, 261
Quotations, translation of, A47

Ransoms, 667&N
Ratification, of tyrants and their deeds, 219–220, 227–228; of treaties, 631
Raw materials, 663&N
Realism, A35, A37
Reason, A70, 14, N367, 559, 561, 563
Rebellion, 38–39, 373–379, 632–632ᵛ. See also Mutiny; Resistance
Records, written, 679, 680&N
Refugees, A57
Regents, 86–87
Regia, lex, see *Lex regia*
Registration, of edicts, 267, 280
Religion, A12–A13, A60–A61, A70, 270, 298–300, 325, 380–381, 534–536, 537&NN, 538–540, 559&N, 560&N, 566&N, 567&N
Religious strife, A9, 60, N67, 77–78, 233, 313, 381–382, 535–539, 566&N, 567, 583. See also Civil strife; Factions
Remonstrances, by magistrates, 313–314
Representation, of father, 753&N
Reprisal, see Marque
Reserves, of treasure, 682–683
Resistance, A16, 222–225, 337–339. See also Obedience; Rebellion
Restitution, 782&N
Retrait lignager, 572&N
Retribution, A11–A12, A33, 780–781
Revenues, see *Domaine*; Property
Revocation, of commissions, 286–287
Revolution, see Rebellion
Rewards, 2, 228, 512–513, 584–596. See also Gifts
Riches, the rich, 232, 259, 395–396, 402, 411, 569–570, 574–578, 668–669, 709&N, 775
Right, see *Jus*
Right side, significance of, 562&N
Robbers, robbery, 1–3, 45, 109, 200, 204, 362, 385, 389, 599, 601, 630&N, 641, 778&N. See also Pirates; Theft
Rule, types of, see Government
Rule of law, see Law

Sacrifice, human, 35
Safe-conduct, 27, 629ᵛ–630
Salt, imposts on, 179, 661–662, 665
Sanctuaries, for slaves, 37
Sanhedrim, 720
Science, natural, A12
Sea, the, effects of, N549, 564; rights over, 179
Secrecy, in senates, 253–254, 262, 267
Sedition, civil, see Civil strife; Factions; Religious strife
Senates, A77, 87, 157, 168–169, 188–190, 253–278, 383, 402, 404–405, 646–647, 710, 713. See also Councils
Senatus consultum, 156
Seneschals, 352
September, significance of, see Autumn
Servants, 33
Servility, 204, 507
Severity, 216–218, 228–229, 341, 368, 378, 592–593, 709&N
Shipwreck, 179
Sieges, 600
Silver, 399, 666–668, 683, 688–700
Skin, color of, 568&N
Slaves, slavery, A35, 32–48, 200–201, 387–388, 670&N, 772
Social classes, see Classes
Soldiers, see Military discipline; Military training

A213

Index Rerum

Sorcery, *see* Witchcraft
Soul, the, 7, 36, 214, 226; compared to the state, 561, 790–791
Sovereignty, A5, A13–A21, A27, A33, A45, A63–A64, A75, 9–10, 84–88, 90–91, 98–100, 109–110, 114, 117–121, 128, 131–133, 137, 142, 147, 153–183, 194, 220–225, 249–250, 265&N, 327, 344, 395, 517–518, 618, 715, 741, 745–746, 749, 785. *See also* Aristocracy; Democracy; *Imperium*; Majesty; Monarchy; Power
Speech, manner of, 506, 543–544, 636&N
Sponsio, N614
Stars, planets, influence of, A22, A34, 437–454, 792
State, the, *see* Commonweal
Statu liberi, 388
Statues, 392, N759
Strangers, *see* Aliens
Strength, 550, N554, N567
Style, of the *République*, A25, A27, A30–A31, A72–A73; of the English version, A49–A51
Stubbornness, 257, N567
Subjects, 48, 115, 122, 632. *See also* Citizens
Subtlety, 424, 553&N, 554, 559, 563
Succession, in monarchies, 111–113, 206–209, 210&N, 288, 415, 434–435, 713, 721–723, 728&N, 729–730, 732–748, 749&N, 752–754; in fiefs, etc., *see* Inheritance
Suicide, N307
Summum bonum, 4–7
Sumptuary laws, 646, 671, 770–771
Sword, power of the, *see* Merum imperium

Taxation, A16, A33, 97, 177–179, 385&N, 641, 649, N654, 655, 657&NN, 658, 663–672, 683–684
Temples, 560, 682
Testaments, 65–66, 574&N, 576–578, 658. *See also* Inheritance; Legacies
Tetrarchy, 409
Text, evolution of, A78
Theater, 404–405, 759. *See also* Plays
Theft, 636ᵛ, 778, 780. *See also* Robbery
Thirst, 551
Timariots, 114, 201, 613
Timber, *see* Forests
Tithes, 571
Titles, 158, 180–182, 239–240, 295
Toleration, religious, A13, A57–A58, A61, 381–382, 537–538
Town, concept of, 50&NN, 51–53
Trade, 398–400, 564, 660–661, 662&N, 663
Tragedies, *see* Plays
Translations, into English, A51
Treachery, *see* Faith; Inconstancy; Perfidy
Treason, 37, 158, 222–224, 513&N
Treasure, 649–686
Treaties, 60–61, 72–84, 110, 149, 164–165, 359–360, 553&N, 606–608, 611–612, 614&N, 615–635ᵛ, 658, 662, 714, 718. *See also* Allies
Trepidation, in astronomy, 447, 450
Trial, of tyrants, 219, 221–222
Triangles, 455–456, 458, 792&NN
Triarchy, 409. *See also* Triumvirate
Tribunes or *tribuni plebis*, 85–86, 188–190, 274–276, 282, 301–304, 339, 345, 349–351, 383, 787–788
Tribuni militum, 292
Tribuni militum cum consulari potestate, 302
Tribute, 115&N, 147–149, 152–153, 616, 658
Triplicities, in astronomy, 446–447, 449, 453
Triumphs, 586
Triumvirate, 199, 409, 706
Triumviri capitales, 306
Truce, N614, 635
Twins, N558, 735
Tyranny, tyrants, A20–A21, A33, A69–A70, A76, 153&N, N184, 197, 199–201, 203–204, 210–229, 383–384, 412–418, 475, 486, 519&N, 520, 525, 632, 679, 700, 718&NN, 720–722. *See also* Monarchy

Umpires, *see* Arbitrators
Uncle, right of, over nephew, 738–740
Union, of states, 407–408
University or *universitas*, A77, 52–53, N361, 365
Unjust commands, *see* Justice
Unjust war, *see* War
Usury, N399, 569–570, 572–573, 673–676, 782–783
Utility, *see* Profit

Valleys, 562–563, N565
Vassals, vassalage, *see* Fealty
Venality, of offices, *see* Offices
Venery, 557, N558. *See also* Wantonness
Veto, 301–302, 349–350, 371
Vice, 211, 503–504, 558–559, 603, 644&N, 645&N, 670, 703–704
Violence, 338–339, 408, 427, 437, 475, 636ᵛ. *See also* Force
Virtue, 211, 243, 394, 411–412, 476–477, 494–495, 558–559, 586–589, 603, 643–644
Voting, 48–49, 195, 232&N, 245–247, 271&N

Walls, *see* Fortifications
Wantonness, in rulers, 416. *See also* Venery
War, 75, 162–163, 165, 530, 550–551, 598–599, 601–602; just and unjust, 201, 203&N, 204, 601, N602; and peace, power of, 162–165. *See also* Armies; Civil strife; Military training; Religious strife
Wealth, *see* Riches
Weights, 177, 690&N, 693
Wheat, prices of, N667
Will, 436&N, 437–438, 778
Wills, *see* Testaments
Winds, 564&N, 565&N
Wine, 16–17, 270, N662, 670
Wisdom, 253–254, 489. *See also* Knowledge
Witchcraft, A10, N543, N552, 734
Wives, 9, 14–20, 557, 558&N, 571
Women, 203&N, 405, 577–579, 639&N, 640&N, 776; rule by, A40–A41, N210, 746, 747&NN, 748&N, 749&N, 750–754. *See also* Wives
World, compared to the state, 7, 498, 718, 793–794
Wreckage, on sea coasts, 179
Wrestling, 565. *See also* Gymnastics

Year, beginning of the, 439–440, 450–451
Youth, NN567, 645, N776. *See also* Children

Zones, climatic, 547